CREATIVE CAKES

World-renowned cake designer

Rosalind Chan presents 14 cakes inspired by

her journeys around the globe

ROSALIND CHAN

whitecap

Whitecap Books is known for its expertise in the cookbook market, and has produced some of the most innovative and familiar titles found in kitchens across North America. Visit our website at www.whitecap.ca.

EDITOR Penny Hozy
COVER DESIGN Andrew Bagatella
FOOD PHOTOGRAPHY Mike McColl
PROOFREADERS Lisa Ferdman and Jesse Marchand

Printed in Canada

Library and Archives Canada Cataloguing in Publication

Chan, Rosalind, author

Creative cakes : world-renowned cake designer Rosalind Chan presents 14 cakes inspired by her journeys around the globe / Rosalind Chan.

ISBN 978-1-77050-213-0 (bound)

1. Cake decorating. I. Title.

TX771.2.C43 2014 641.86'539 C2014-903229-3

The publisher acknowledges the financial support of the Government of Canada through the Canada Book Fund (CBF) and the Province of British Columbia through the Book Publishing Tax Credit.

22 21 20 19 18 17 16 15 14 1 2 3 4 5 6 7 8

To my family—my mother, sisters and brothers, and especially to my husband—for their patience, understanding and unconditional support throughout the writing of this book. The long nights would have been difficult without my husband's constant companionship and my son Timson's hot tea.

A special thanks to all my students and friends from around the world, especially Vivian, who have persistently encouraged me to pursue and write my first book.

CONTENTS

INTRODUCTION

When I first sat down to write this book, I knew I wanted to engage my readers' creative sides. While this book teaches you a multitude of techniques it also encourages you to think "outside the box" and create your own wonderful pieces of sugar work. My inspiration for this book comes from my world travels and the privelege I have had to share my decorating skills with many cake enthusiasts. Each of the 14 major projects in this book showcases the culture and national flower of a different country I have had the opportunity to visit.

Before writing the book I explored and created the projects one by one to ensure that each project could be completed in the most efficient manner for both beginners and advanced cake decorators. In part one of this book you will find the basic methods and recipes most suitable to a beginner. If you are new to cake art, try your hand at one of the simple cake recipes and a sugarpaste flower, using the Mexican hat technique (page 32).

If you are a more advanced decorator, part two of *Creative Cakes* utilizes sugarpaste, gumpaste and modelling chocolate to create larger projects sure to impress your friends, family and clients. The introduction of moulds and cutters allows for even greater creativity, especially for beginners. These tools are excellent short cuts for those who are not yet confident in working free-hand.

And of course, the book would not be complete without a recipe for SugarTier's bestselling French Macarons (page 14). Made as part of the Parisian Afternoon project (page 14) these macarons are also great treats to make on their own.

My techniques may not be the only ones available to aspiring cake decorators, but I hope that from the creations in this book you will be further motivated and inspired to create many more awesome projects in the wonderful world of cake decorating.

— ROSALIND CHAN

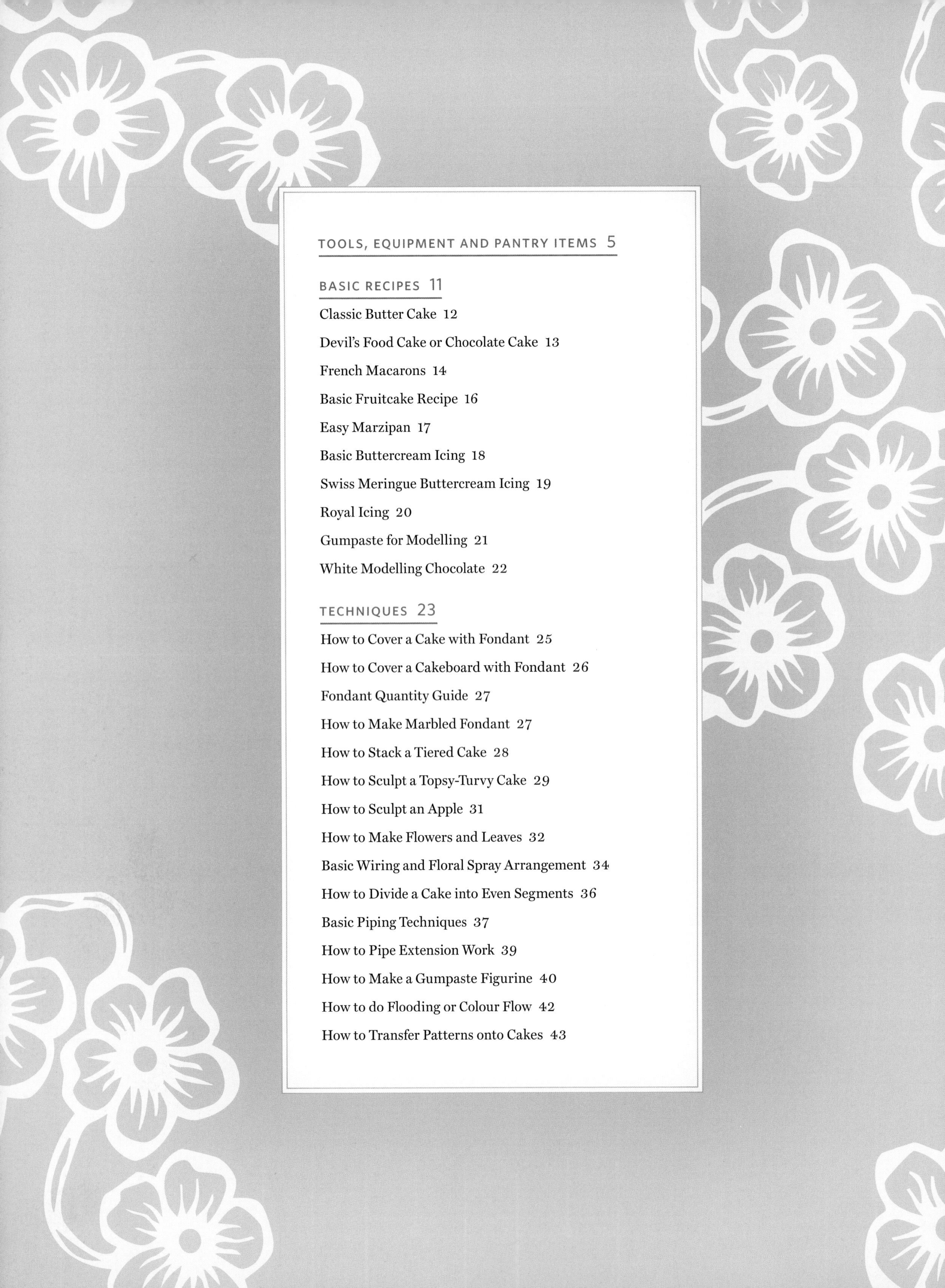

1 THE BASICS

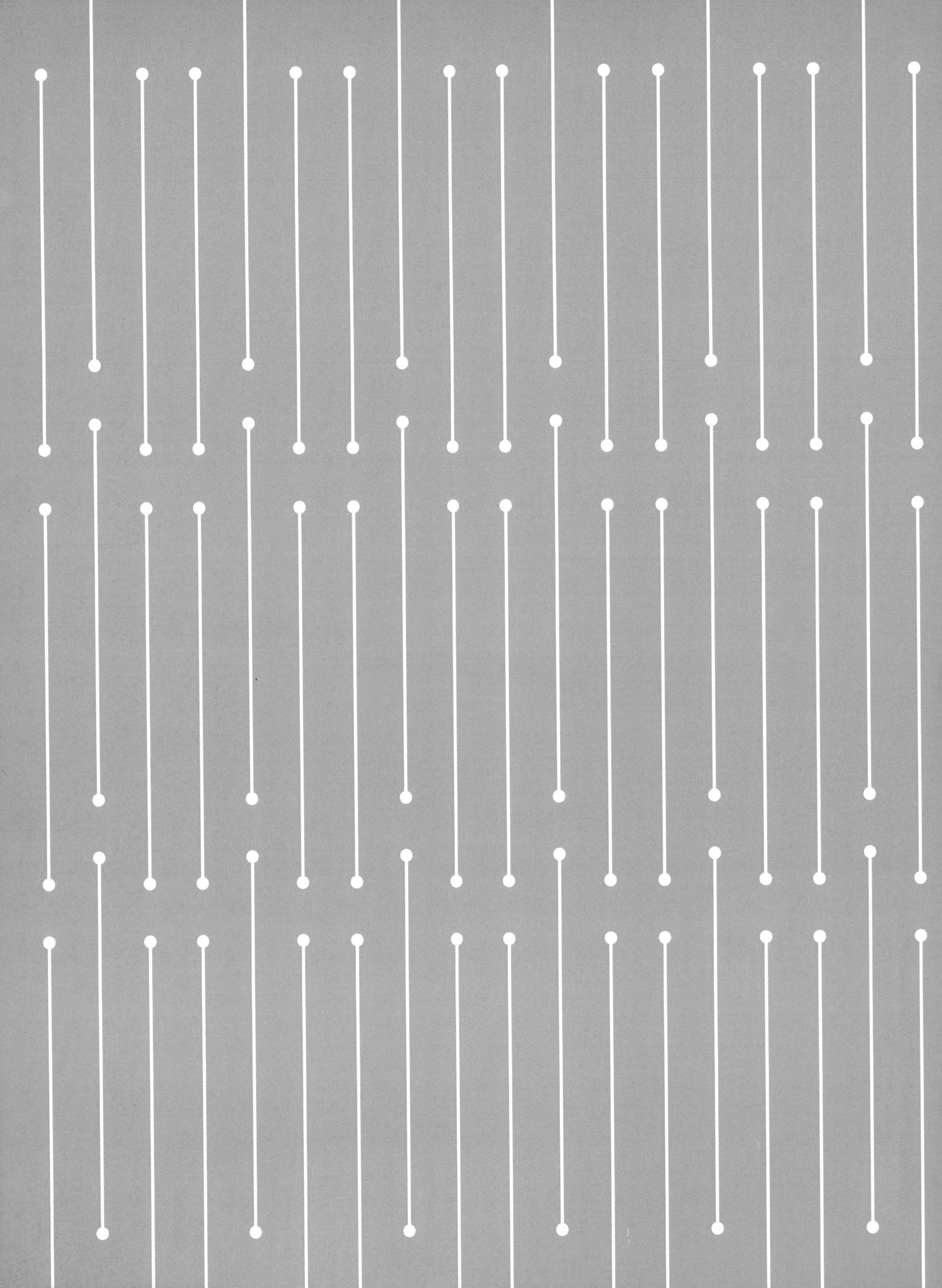

TOOLS, EQUIPMENT AND PANTRY ITEMS

THIS IS A collection of the basic tools and equipment I have used for the projects in this book. Many of the gumpaste tools form the basic kit owned by most cake decorators, while others are more specialized or reflect individual preferences. You may have collected many moulds and tools throughout the years, and I hope you will be able to find some of the things that I have used in this book in your collection.

TOOLS AND EQUIPMENT

The tools and equipment used for cake decorating are commonly found in stores that specialize in cake decorating equipment and in craft or hardware stores. Many of these items are pictured on pages 7 and 9.

1. AIRBRUSH MACHINE AND COLOURS A machine used to spray edible colours onto finished pieces of fondant cakes, sculptures and flowers.
2. ALUMINUM FOIL OR TIN FOIL This is often used to create a base for drying leaves with natural curves.
3. APPLE TRAYS Trays found in supermarkets that are designed to hold apples. Perfect for drying gumpaste flower petals to give them a slight curve instead of drying flat. A cheap alternative to flower formers.
4. BALL TOOL A metal or plastic stick-like tool with a ball on one or both ends. Used for modelling gumpaste.
5. CAKEBOARDS Available in many sizes, shapes and thicknesses, they provide a smooth surface for your cake.
6. CAKE LEVELLER A tool used to level cakes on the top or to cut cakes into equal layers.
7. COTTON THREAD This is used for making stamens in flowers, such as the golden wattle (page 108) in this book. Black thread is often used to make poppy stamens.
8. CUTTERS Made from either metal or plastic and used to cut various shapes, such as flowers, cherry blossoms, butterflies and diamond patchwork shapes.
9. CUTTING WHEEL A tool with a wheel on one side, usually used in sewing. It can come either with jagged edges on one side or smooth. Both can be used to cut fondant or gumpaste. The one with the jagged edges can be used to create a stitching effect on cakes.
10. DOWEL ROD Inserted into a cake to support the bottom tier from collapsing.
11. DRESDEN TOOL A tool with a slightly curved end. Used for ruffling or veining petals.
12. DUSTING PUFFS Cheesecloth or "J" cloths filled with icing sugar or cornstarch, for dusting onto surfaces that are used for rolling. Dusting puffs prevent fondant or gumpaste from sticking to surfaces.
13. EXTRUDER Used to extrude sugarpaste in various shapes and sizes, using different discs. Great for creating edible hair, for example.
14. FLORIST'S TAPES Used to tape floral sprays or flower petals together. Available in many colours.
15. FLORIST'S WIRES Available in white or green, with various gauges for different flowers or petals. The higher the gauge, the finer the wire. These wires are used to support petals when making gumpaste flowers and for extending the length of floral sprays.

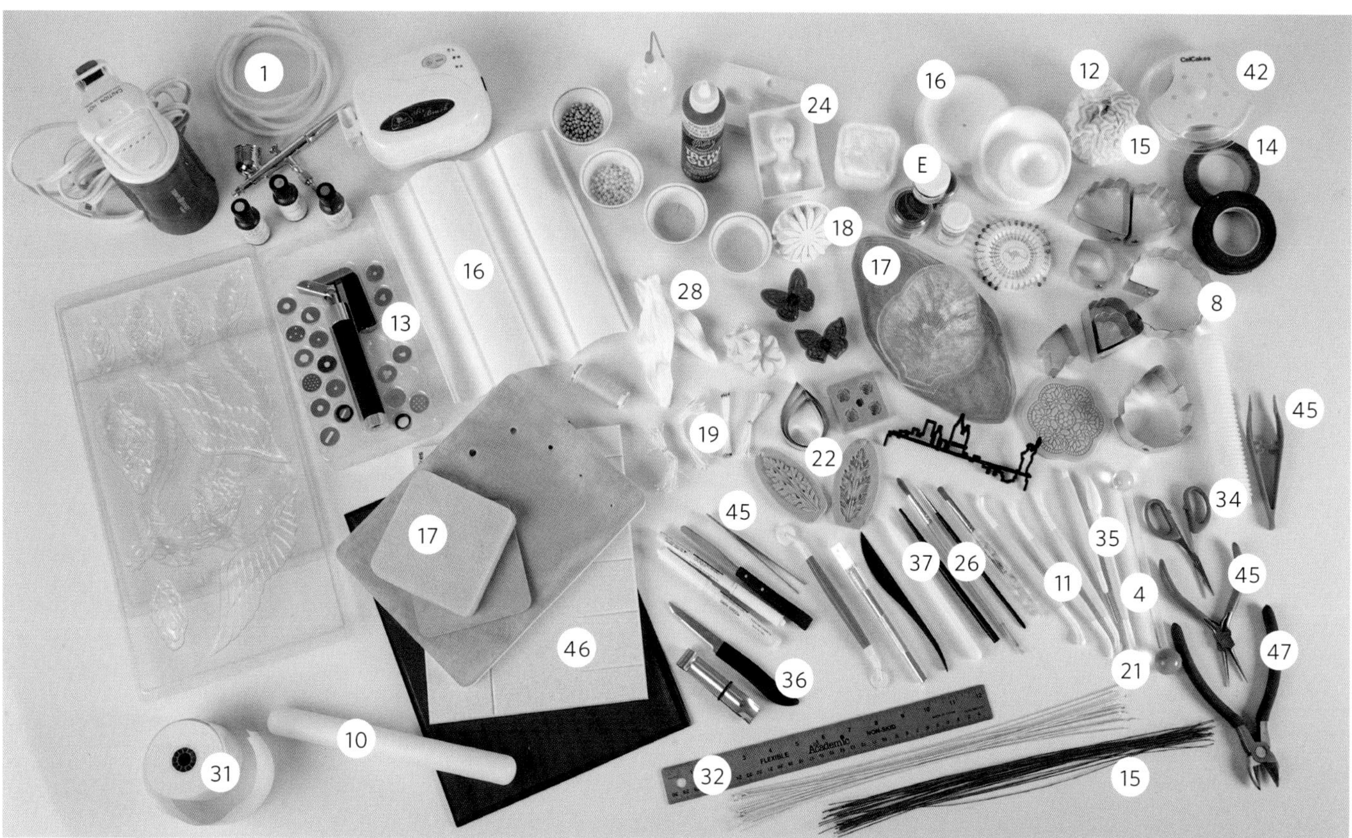

16. FLOWER FORMERS Plastic forms that are usually curved and are used to dry gumpaste flower petals or leaves to obtain a more realistic effect. Apple trays, as described on the previous page, can be used as an alternative.

17. FLOWER PAD A soft foam pad, used to place or to rest gumpaste petals on.

18. FLOWER PLUNGERS Used for cutting flower petals and leaves with a veining effect. Usually made from plastic.

19. FLOWER STAMENS Non-edible stamens, used to create flower centres, that are available in many sizes and colours. Usually sold in bunches, in craft stores.

20. GROOVED ROLLING PIN A rolling pin with deep grooves, used to create smocking lines on fondant or gumpaste.

21. GUMPASTE TOOLS Available in various shapes and sizes, and used for modelling work or for gumpaste flowers. You can also create different textures and effects with some of the gumpaste tools.

22. LEAF VEINER A type of mould that makes the impression of veins on a leaf.

23. MEASURING TOOLS Along with the usual measuring cups used in North American kitchens, a cake decorator should also have a digital scale for weighing exact amounts.

24. MOULDS Come in various shapes and depths, to create shapes and jewels. Mainly used for gumpaste, fondant or sugar work (sugar pieces created from isomalt or sugar). These moulds can be made and used of plastics, resin or silicone.

25. NON-STICK MAT Used to roll fondant, gumpaste or other sticky concoctions, to prevent the paste from sticking to surfaces.

26. PAINTBRUSHES Acrylic brushes found in craft or art supply stores. Used for painting and adding delicate details to cakes, and for applying edible dusting colors.

27. PALETTE KNIFE A necessity. Used for spreading, mixing and lifting.

28. PETAL VEINERS Available in both resin and silicone, and used for creating veins on leaves and flower petals.

29. PIPING BAGS Available in many sizes and materials. Disposable bags are best.

30. PIPING TIPS AND NOZZLES Available in all sizes, and used for piping.

31. RECEIPT PAPER Sometimes referred to as calculator roll paper. Usually comes in white and in a roll that ordinarily is inserted into automatic calculators for the printing of receipts. Used in baking to measure cake circumferences and to divide cakes into even segments.

32. RULER A standard ruler can be used to measure out equal cake sections and to make exact markings on templates.

33. ROLLING PINS Come in all sizes and are used for rolling out fondant, gumpaste and dough. Non-stick ones are best.

34. SCISSORS Ensure that they are sharp. Useful for trimming fondant and gumpaste.

35. SCRIBER A needle-like tool, used to scratch or prick a design onto fondant-covered cakes.

36. SHARP KNIFE A must-have item. Ensure that it is sharp; otherwise, it will tear your fondant. Useful for trimming fondant or gumpaste.

37. SILK VEINING TOOL Available in both ceramic and plastic, and used to create fine lines or texture on gumpaste or fondant.

38. SMALL POINTED SCISSORS Used to cut out finger shapes on gumpaste figurines and the edges of flower calyxes.

39. SMOOTHER To smooth out bumps and lumps on fondant- and marzipan-covered cakes.

40. SPATULA Used to apply icing.

41. STYROFOAM These comes in various sizes and heights, and are used to replace real cakes for display purposes or used as dividers.

42. TAPE CUTTER Available in many sizes, and used to cut florist's tapes into different widths.

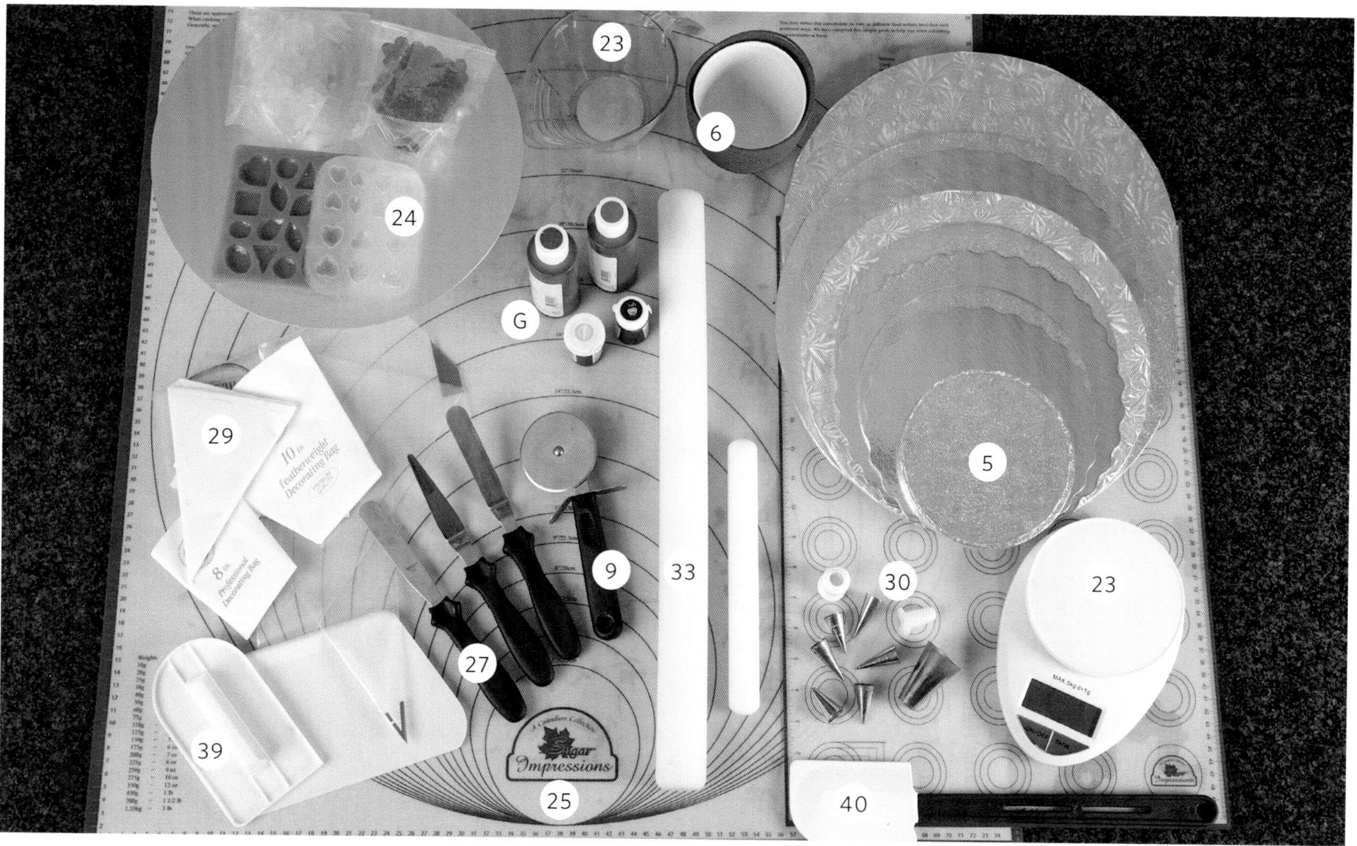

43. TEXTURED ROLLERS Many designs are available for creating texture on fondant-covered cakes and boards.

44. TURNTABLE A must-have for all cake decorators. Tilting ones are best for doing string or extension work.

45. TWEEZERS AND PLIERS Both straight and angled, and used for picking up dragees or delicate pieces of sugar work.

46. VEINING BOARD Used for rolling gumpaste and fondant on one side. If rolled on the other side, it creates a vein on the paste, for easy insertion of wires.

47. WIRE CUTTER Used for cutting florist's wires into different lengths.

48. WOODEN SKEWERS For dipping in gel pastes, as well as for creating a support structure in gumpaste figurines.

THE CAKE DECORATOR'S PANTRY

The raw ingredients or edible things that are used for cake decorating are usually sold in stores that specialize in cake decorating tools, or in baking supply stores. Certain items can also be found in your local supermarket or grocery aisles.

1. CONFECTIONER'S GLAZE Used to coat gumpaste petals or leaves to give them a shine.
2. CORNSTARCH Often used to fill dusting puffs for modelling chocolate work, to prevent the paste from sticking to surfaces and to hands. Very useful for cleaning dusting colours from brushes. Just dip the brushes into cornstarch and rub the dry dust off on a paper towel.
3. DUSTING COLOURS Edible dry food powder colours, used to colour and shade gumpaste flowers.
4. FONDANT A dough-like paste used to cover cakes. Usually made of gelatin, corn syrup and glycerin.
5. GEL PASTES Edible gel food colours, used to colour fondant/sugarpaste, buttercream, Royal Icing and gumpaste.
6. GUM GLUE An edible glue made from gum tragacanth or CMC mixed with hot water, until it is of a tacky consistency. It is useful for attaching gumpaste decorations.
7. GUMPASTE Available in white but can be coloured, and used for making gumpaste flowers and edible figurines. Must be kept sealed in airtight containers when not in use. Always knead some vegetable shortening into the paste before use or when the paste feels a little dry.
8. LEMON EXTRACT Used to dilute gel pastes or dusting colours for painting on cakes.
9. PIPING GEL Edible sticky clear gel-like paste, used for piping and adhering fondant to cakeboards.
10. WHITE VEGETABLE FAT Used for greasing boards or rolling pins or to soften gumpaste when dry.

BASIC RECIPES

I HAVE INCLUDED some basic recipes that can be used for all of the projects in this book. You will note that the projects do not specify the type of cakes to use; most of these recipes can be used for any of the projects shown. For scultping and tiered cakes it is advisable to use a dense cake like butter cake, as it is easily sculptable. If you are doing a project such as the Indian-themed cake (page 93) that needs to stand in an upright position, you will need a denser and heavier cake like the fruitcake.

It is important to follow the recipes exactly; baking requires time and patience. Some measuring tools, such as spoons, may differ slightly in size in different countries so please check them carefully. Flour density may also vary in different countries. I'd advise that you try the recipes before making them in large quantities.

CLASSIC BUTTER CAKE

A BUTTER CAKE is a cake where the main ingredient is butter. It is firm and moist and because of its density it is perfect for scultping work and tiered cake designs. The classic recipe serves as the basis for a wide variety of cake variations through the addition of different flavours or extracts.

MAKES TWO 9-INCH (23 CM) ROUND CAKE LAYERS

- 2¾ cups (685 mL) cake flour
- 2 tsp (10 mL) baking powder
- ¼ tsp (1 mL) salt
- 1 cup (250 mL) unsalted butter at room temperature
- 2 cups (500 mL) granulated sugar
- 4 large eggs at room temperature
- 2 tsp (10 mL) vanilla extract
- 1 cup (250 mL) whole milk at room temperature

1. Preheat the oven to 350°F (175°C).
2. Line two 9-inch (23 cm) round cake pans with parchment paper.
3. In a medium bowl, sift the flour, baking powder and salt. Set aside.
4. In a stand mixer with the paddle attachment, cream the butter and sugar together on medium speed until the mixture is light and airy, about 2 minutes. Add the eggs one at a time, beating for 1 minute after each addition. Scrape the sides of the bowl regularly, using a spatula. After all of the eggs have been added, add the vanilla extract and beat for another minute. Reduce the speed to low, add one-third of the dry ingredients and mix until incorporated. Add half of the milk and mix until incorporated. Continue adding the dry ingredients and the milk, alternating, ending with the dry ingredients.
5. Pour the batter into the prepared cake pans and bake for 30 minutes, or until a skewer inserted into the centre of the cake comes out clean.

DEVIL'S FOOD CAKE OR CHOCOLATE CAKE

THIS CAKE IS lighter than the butter cake. Perfect for chocolate lovers.

MAKES TWO 9-INCH (23 CM) ROUND CAKE LAYERS

- 2¼ cups (560 mL) cake flour
- 1 tsp (5 mL) baking soda
- ¼ tsp (1 mL) salt
- 1 cup (250 mL) unsalted butter at room temperature
- 1 cup (250 mL) firmly packed light brown sugar
- ¾ cup (185 mL) of granulated sugar
- 4 large eggs at room temperature
- 2 tsp (10 mL) vanilla extract
- 4 oz (120 g) unsweetened chocolate, melted
- 1 cup (250 mL) buttermilk, at room temperature

1. Preheat the oven to 350°F (175°C).
2. Line two 9-inch (23 cm) round cake pans with parchment paper.
3. In a medium bowl, sift the flour, baking soda and salt. Set aside.
4. In a stand mixer with the paddle attachment, mix the butter and both sugars on medium speed until the mixture is light and airy and lightens in colour, about 2 minutes. Add the eggs one at a time, beating for 1 minute after each addition. Scrape the sides of the bowl regularly, using a spatula. After all the eggs have been added, add the vanilla extract and beat for 1 minute. Add the melted chocolate and beat until the mixture is uniform in colour. Reduce the speed to low and add the dry ingredients in 3 batches, alternating with the buttermilk in 2 batches and ending with the dry ingredients.
5. Pour the batter into the prepared cake pans and bake for 30 minutes, or until a skewer inserted into the centre of the cake comes out clean.
6. Let cool for 15 minutes before removing from the pan.

TIP Chocolate can easily be melted in two ways:

- In a microwave at 30 second intervals until it is fully melted in a microwavable bowl.
- Using a double boiler where the water in the bottom of the double boiler should not come to boiling or touch the bottom of the bowl where the chocolate is while it is melting.

FRENCH MACARONS

FRENCH MACARONS ARE a signature item at our bakery because we offer over 50 flavours. Our macarons are slightly less sweet than regular macaron recipes. The Swiss Meringue Buttercream Icing (page 19) makes a good filling for these.

MAKES APPROX. 20 SANDWICHED MACARONS

- 1 cup (250 mL) icing sugar
- ¾ cup (185 mL) ground almonds
- 4 egg whites, aged overnight at room temperature
- pinch of salt
- ¼ cup (60 mL) granulated sugar

1. Preheat the oven to 250°F (120°C).
2. Use a non-stick macaron baking mat with pre-drawn circles, or draw macaron-size circles on parchment paper on a baking sheet.
3. In a food processor, add the icing sugar and ground almonds and process until fine.
4. In a large clean, dry bowl whip the egg whites with the salt on medium speed, until foamy. Increase the speed to high and gradually add the sugar. Continue to whip to stiff peaks until the whites are firm and shiny.
5. With a flexible spatula, gently add the icing sugar and ground almond mixture to the egg whites and fold in until completely incorporated. Do not stir. The mixture should be shiny and should fall in ribbons when the batter is lifted up and allowed to fall.
6. Spoon the batter into a piping bag fitted with a ½-inch (1 cm) round tip. Pipe circles of batter onto the macaron baking mat or parchment paper. Tap the tray slightly to remove any air bubbles that might have formed. Let dry at room temperature until a skin forms over the macaron shell, about 45 minutes to an hour. (It may take longer to dry on humid days; if possible, use a dehumidifier in the room.)
7. Bake for 16–20 minutes, until feet form at the bottom of the shell.
8. Remove from the oven and transfer either the non-stick baking mat or parchment paper to a wire rack to cool. When cool, slide a metal offset spatula or paring knife underneath the macaron shell to remove it from the mat. (If baked properly, it should just slide off the mat.)
9. To make a macaron sandwich, pair similarly sized macaron shells. Pipe about ½ tsp (2.5 mL) of filling onto one of the macaron shells and sandwich the macarons together.

TIP You can make macaron shells ahead of time and freeze them for up to six months in an airtight container. Thaw at room temperature before using.

BASIC FRUITCAKE RECIPE

THE USE OF fruitcakes were very common and traditional in the 17th century for celebrations such as weddings and Christmas. Fruitcakes store well for long periods of time due their high alcohol and sugar content, so the first tier can always be kept for the couple's first anniversary or the christening of their first child.

MAKES 1 8-INCH (20 CM) FRUITCAKE

- ½ cup (125 mL) butter
- ½ cup (125 mL) dark brown sugar
- 2 large eggs
- 1 cup (250 mL) all-purpose flour
- Pinch of Salt
- ¼ tsp (1 mL) cinnamon
- 3 Tbsp (45 mL) chopped almonds
- 2 cups (500 mL) mixed fruits (soaked overnight in 2 Tbsp (30 mL) of brandy)
- 3 Tbsp (45 mL) glacé cherries
- 1 tsp (5 mL) black molasses (warmed)
- Finely grated rind of half an orange and half a lemon

1. Preheat the oven to 275°F (140°C).
2. Line an 8-inch (20 cm) baking tin with parchment paper. Set aside.
3. Cream the butter and sugar together with a paddle attachment until light and fluffy.
4. In a separate bowl, beat the eggs. Add a little at a time to the creamed butter and sugar, beating well after each addition.
5. Fold in the flour, salt and cinnamon. Then add in the nuts, cherries, molasses and citrus rinds.
6. Spoon into the prepared baking tin that has been lined with parchment paper. Spread evenly and depress the centre slightly.
7. Bake for approx. 3½ to 4 hours, until a skewer inserted into the centre comes out clean.

EASY MARZIPAN

MARZIPAN IS USED to cover fruitcakes before they are covered in fondant. It acts as a seal to prevent the juices or the alcohol within the fruitcake from seeping out onto the fondant layer. It is also used to cover butter and sponge cakes, especially in petit fours. In the United Kingdom marzipan is often used to cover Victorian sponge cakes.

MAKES APPROX. 4 CUPS (1 L) OF MARZIPAN

- 2 cups (500 mL) white fondant
- 3 cups (375 g) ground almonds
- ⅓ cup (80 mL) corn syrup (approximately)

1. Place the fondant and the sifted ground almonds in a mixing bowl and use the dough hook to mix until it is fully combined and forms into a dough.
2. Gradually add in the corn syrup and mix with dough hook until the dough appears smooth.
3. Wrap with plastic wrap to store. Once mixed, the marzipan can be frozen for up to 6 months.

BASIC BUTTERCREAM ICING

BOTH BUTTERCREAM RECIPES can be used in any of the projects in this book. Basic buttercream is dense and slightly grainy while swiss Meringue is light and fluffy. Using butter will give this icing a richer flavour but the icing will not be pure white.

MAKES APPROX. 3 CUPS (750 ML) OF ICING

- 4 cups (1 L) icing sugar
- 1 cup (250 mL) vegetable shortening or butter
- 2½ Tbsp (37.5 mL) water or milk
- 1 tsp (5 mL) vanilla extract

1. Sift the icing sugar thoroughly.
2. Beat the shortening or butter and icing sugar together until light and fluffy. This may take up to 7 minutes at medium speed.
3. Add in the liquid and vanilla extract and beat until well combined. This should not take more than 10 minutes at medium speed on a mixer.

SWISS MERINGUE BUTTERCREAM ICING

SWISS MERINGUE USES less sugar than buttercream, so it tastes less sweet. This recipe can be used in place of basic buttercream in any projects requiring the use of buttercream.

MAKES APPROX. 6 CUPS (1.5 L) OF ICING

- 10 egg whites
- 3 cups (750 mL) granulated sugar
- 6 cups (1.5 L) unsalted butter, very slightly warmed (moist on the outside; cold on the inside), cut into 2-inch (5 cm) cubes
- 2 Tbsp (30 mL) lemon, almond, orange or vanilla extract

1. In the top of a double boiler, lightly whisk the egg whites and sugar together on top of a double boiler until the mixture is hot, or a candy thermometer reads 140°F (60°C).
2. Pour the mixture while it is still hot into the bowl of a mixer. Using the whisk attachment, mix on medium-high, until it is double in volume and has stiff peaks.
3. Immediately add about half of the butter cubes. Change the whisk attachment to the paddle attachment and beat in the butter slowly, until well combined. Add the remaining butter and then beat the mixture, starting with the lowest speed and slowly increasing the speed, about every 10 seconds, until you reach the medium-high speed.
4. Continue beating until the mixture begins to look light and fluffy. Stop the mixer and scrape the bowl. Reduce the speed to low. Add the extract and continue to beat for 45 seconds. Then increase the speed to medium-high and beat for 45 to 60 seconds.

TIP You can make the buttercream ahead of time and store it in a plastic container with a lid in the freezer for up to 3 months. Before using, defrost completely (which will take several hours) and rewhip.

You can decrease the sugar in this recipe without affecting the consistency, if you find it too sweet.

ROYAL ICING

ROYAL ICING IS made from icing sugar and either fresh egg white or meringue powder. It can also be used as a glue, to adhere sugar flowers and other decorations onto cakes. The gum arabic is only added when you are going to use Royal Icing for extension work (as in the Spanish project on page 127). The added gum will give the icing additional strength.

MAKES APPROX. 3 CUPS (750 ML) OF ICING

- 2 cups (500 mL) icing sugar
- 3 Tbsp (45 mL) of meringue powder
- 5 Tbsp (75 mL) water
- 1 tsp (5 mL) gum arabic (optional)

1. In the bowl of a mixer, combine the icing sugar and meringue powder.
2. Add the water and gum arabic and beat on low speed for 10 minutes, until the mixture is light and fluffy and loses its shine. If the icing is too watery (which may occur on humid days), add a little more icing sugar.
3. Once mixed, the icing should be stored in airtight containers until use.

TIP There are different consistencies for various uses:

Soft peaks Mainly used for writing, dots and icing cakes

Stiff peaks This consistency is used for piping anything that needs to stay upright. Use this consistency to pipe flowers and figurines.

Run-out consistency This is used to coat cakes or for flood work/colour flow (to fill a space within a pipe line). This technique can also be used on cookies or for collar work.

GUMPASTE FOR MODELLING

THIS GUMPASTE DRIES hard and is suitable for making flowers, leaves and figurines. If commercial gumpaste is available in your area, I would recommend buying it rather than making your own.

MAKES APPROX. 1 LB (450 G) OF GUMPASTE

- 2 cups (500 mL) icing sugar
- 3 tsp (15 mL) gum tragacanth or CMC
- 2 tsp (10 mL) powdered gelatin
- 5 tsp (25 mL) cold water
- 2 tsp (10 mL) solid shortening (vegetable fat)
- 2 tsp (10 mL) liquid sugar
- 1 large egg white

1. Sift icing sugar and gum tragacanth together and warm the mixture in a microwave for one minute.
2. Meanwhile, dissolve the gelatin in cold water and leave it to stand until all the grains have melted.
3. Add the shortening and liquid sugar to the gelatin.
4. Dissolve the mixture in a microwave, but do not allow it to boil.
5. Put the icing sugar mixture into a warmed bowl and add the gelatin mixture and egg white.
6. Mix together until white and stretchy.
7. Knead the mixture together on a surface dusted with icing sugar, until it is no longer sticky.
8. Wrap it in two layers of plastic wrap, place in a plastic bag, and leave to rest overnight before using.

TIPS Gumpaste must be sealed in an airtight container when not in use. Always knead some vegetable shortening into the gumpaste before use or whenever the gumpaste feels a little dry.

Gumpaste can be frozen if it needs to be stored longer.

WHITE MODELLING CHOCOLATE

WHITE MODELLING CHOCOLATE tastes much better than gumpaste, but it must be kept in a cool place to avoid melting. People with hot palms may find it difficult to work with this medium.

MAKES 2 LB (900 G) OF MODELLING CHOCOLATE

2 lb (900 g) white compound chocolate

1 cup (250 mL) white corn syrup

1. Melt the chocolate in a microwave on low, white chocolate burns very easily. Melt in minute intervals and stir the chocolate after each interval.
2. Pour the corn syrup into a microwaveable container and warm it up for approximately 1 minute.
3. When chocolate has melted, pour in the warm corn syrup and stir quickly, until mixture thickens and there are no lumps.
4. Line a container with plastic wrap and pour the mixture into it. Leave to rest for 24 hours. After 24 hours, break the chocolate into smaller pieces and knead until the modelling chocolate is no longer crumbly. Knead until smooth and cover with plastic wrap when not using.

TECHNIQUES

CAKE DECORATING INVOLVES more than just baking a very tasty cake. It is about creating a fantastic work of art that takes creativity, patience, and specific skills and techniques. Cake decorating classes teach you the skills needed to create customized celebration cakes, and in this book, I have tried to introduce as many types of techniques as possible that are used in today's cake decorating world.

There are various types of techniques used in cake decorating that may require basic to advanced skills. For each of the cake projects, I have used various techniques and I would recommend that you read through all the steps in each project before starting, so as to get an idea of the skill level involved. I have tried as much as possible to provide and indication at the top of each project of the level of skill required to complete each and every one of the projects in this book.

HOW TO COVER A CAKE WITH FONDANT

THE SECRET TO creating even and smooth cakes when using fondant is to level them before covering. When cakes are baked, they are usually not level on top. All cakes must have level tops before they can be covered with fondant. If the cake has a dome shape on top, use a long serrated kitchen knife or a cake leveller to level the top of the cake.

1. Once levelled, the cake can be layered. Fillings that may be used range from buttercream or ganaches to preserves or fresh fruit.
2. Once the cake has been layered and filled, a thin layer of buttercream should be applied to the top and sides of the cake. This technique can also be referred to as "masking." The cake should then be refrigerated or chilled before covering. As an option, you can also use piping gel or apricot glaze in place of buttercream, to frost or mask the cake.
3. Make sure that you have enough fondant to cover the size of your cake. See the chart on page 27 for required amounts.
4. Roll out the required amount of fondant on a surface lightly dusted with icing sugar or on a non-stick mat. Fondant should be rolled out to a thickness of ⅛-inch (3 mm) for covering cakes.
5. The formula for the size of the rolled fondant needed to cover a certain size cake is as follows: Twice the height plus the diameter of the cake. For example if you need to cover a 6-inch (15 cm) round cake with a 3-inch (8 cm) height, using the formula, you will need a round piece of fondant with a minimum circumference of 12-inch (30 cm) to cover the cake. Lift the rolled fondant with your non-stick rolling pin and transfer it onto the chilled cake.
6. Use the palms of your hands to smooth the fondant onto the sides of the cake. To avoid pleats and to eliminate air bubbles, lift the fondant up slightly before smoothing it down.
7. Trim the excess fondant off using a knife or pizza cutter.
8. Rub the covered cake with a smoother on each side to achieve a flawless finish. A small amount of fondant wrapped in plastic wrap can also be used for polishing the cake sides.

TIP Cake styrofoams are often used as dividers on real or display cakes. They may replace real cakes in situations where the positioning of a particular cake tier is impossible to achieve with a real cake. Styrofoams are light and can be easily covered with fondant. Use the same method for covering real cakes except that, instead of coating the cake with buttercream, water or piping gel is used as a glue to adhere the fondant to the styrofoam. Cake projects in this book that use styrofoams in the place of real cake tiers are Indian Finery (page 93) and A Parisian Afternoon (page 119).

HOW TO COVER A CAKEBOARD WITH FONDANT

CAKEBOARDS ARE AVAILABLE in many different sizes and thicknesses. The type of cake, its weight and its size will determine the thickness and size of the cakeboard. Most celebration and wedding cakes use ¼-inch (6 mm) or ½-inch (1 cm) thick cakeboards.

1. Brush the surface of the cakeboard with piping gel.
2. Knead the required amount of fondant until it is soft (see Fondant Quantity Guide). Roll out the fondant with a rolling pin on a work surface lightly dusted with icing sugar to an approximate thickness of ⅛-inch (3 mm) and slightly larger than the cakeboard to be covered. Fold the fondant over the rolling pin and drop it gently onto the board.
3. Rub a smoother over the entire surface to eliminate air bubbles. If there are air bubbles on your fondant surface, you can use a pin to prick the bubbles.
4. Trim away the excess fondant from the edge of the board, using a sharp paring knife.
5. Cut a piece of satin ribbon that is the same width as the cakeboard to the required length to go around the edge of the cakeboard. Adhere the ribbon to the board with a non-toxic glue or piping gel.

FONDANT QUANTITY GUIDE

SIZE	AMOUNT OF FONDANT NEEDED FOR ROUND CAKES	AMOUNT OF FONDANT NEEDED FOR SQUARE CAKES
6"	18 ounces (510 g)	24 ounces (680 g)
7"	21 ounces (595 g)	30 ounces (850 g)
8"	24 ounces (680 g)	36 ounces (1.02 kg)
9"	30 ounces (850 g)	42 ounces (1.20 kg)
10"	36 ounces (1.02 kg)	48 ounces (1.37 kg)
12"	48 ounces (1.36 kg)	72 ounces (2.04 kg)
14"	72 ounces (2.04 kg)	96 ounces (2.72 kg)
16"	108 ounces (3.06 kg)	120 ounces (3.40 kg)
18"	140 ounces (3.97 kg)	145 ounces (4.11 kg)

HOW TO MAKE MARBLED FONDANT

1. Colour pieces of fondant with gel paste colours.
2. Roll two different colours of fondant into logs or sausages. Twist the two colours together and knead slightly until colours begin to blend, creating marbleized streaks.
3. Roll out to desired shape.

HOW TO STACK A TIERED CAKE

HEAVY CAKES WITH more than one tier or with a heavy topper must be dowelled to prevent collapsing. Whenever a project in this book needs dowelling, it will be noted in the instructions. Dowel rods are available in various lengths and widths and are made from food-safe material or plastic. Each cake tier, apart from the bottom tier, should sit on a thin cakeboard the same size as the tier itself. You can use a thin layer of buttercream to adhere the cakeboard to the cake tiers.

Here are the instructions for dowelling a two-tiered cake, in which the tiered layers sit on top of each other. If your cake has three or more tiers, the steps can be repeated for each tier.

1. Place the bottom tier on the covered cakeboard (see page 26 for covering a cakeboard). Centre a cakeboard that is the same size as the tier to be put on top on the bottom tier. Use a wooden skewer to draw an outline around the edge of the cakeboard onto the bottom tier. Remove the cakeboard.
2. Mark the cake, as in the diagram below, inside the outline on the bottom tier. (The dowels will be inserted into the circled areas.) You may use more dowel rods for heavier and denser cakes, but they must be spaced evenly to hold the weight of the upper tier.
3. Insert the dowels into the circled areas on the bottom tier. With an edible marker, make a mark on the dowel rod at the surface of the cake. Remove the dowels and cut to the marked length. Re-insert the dowels into the same holes in the cake.
4. Apply a thin layer of Royal icing or buttercream to the surface of the bottom tier. Position the top tier on the bottom tier.

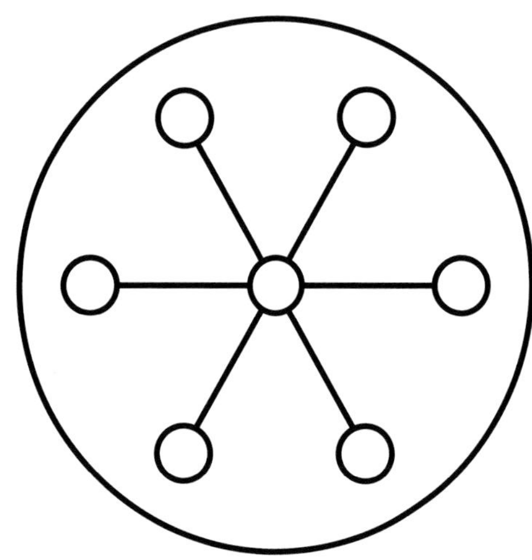

HOW TO SCULPT A TOPSY-TURVY CAKE

FOR SCULPTING CAKES, it is always advisable to use a dense cake base like a Classic Butter Cake (page 12).

1. You will need a 6-inch (15 cm) round cake tier that is 4 to 5-inches (10–13 cm) tall, and a 4-inch (10 cm) round cakeboard. If your cake is not tall enough, bake 2 cakes and sandwich them together with Swiss Meringue Buttercream Icing (page 19).
2. Level the cake evenly with a serrated knife.
3. Freeze the cake for about an hour. Remove from freezer and start sculpting the cake into a topsy-turvy shape.
4. Place the 4-inch (10 cm) round cakeboard on top of the cake and start cutting the cake diagonally as shown, ensuring that you do not cut too much off the sides.
5. Frost the cake with buttercream and re-freeze for another hour before covering with fondant.

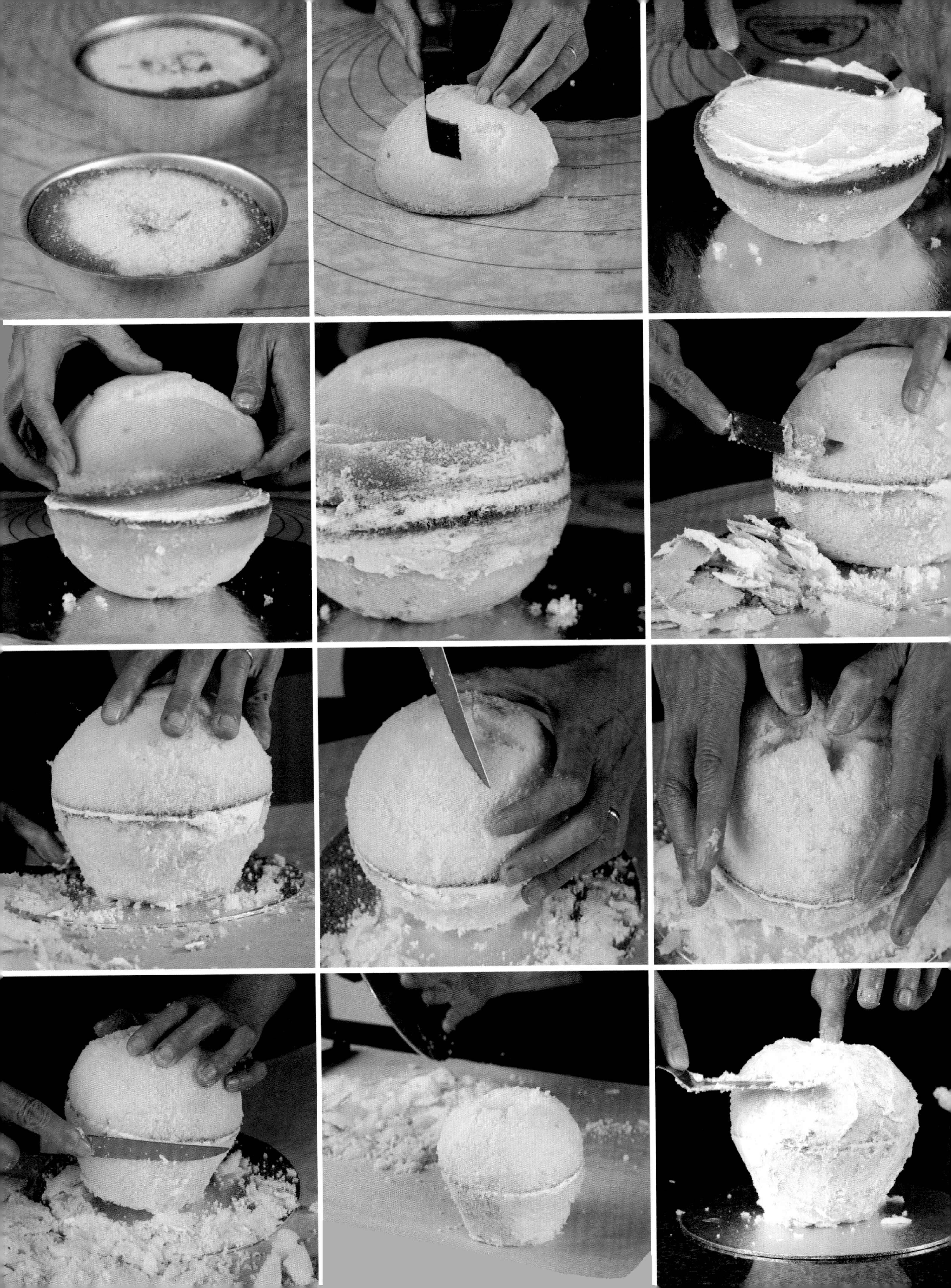

HOW TO SCULPT AN APPLE

FOR SCULPTING CAKES, it is always advisable to use a denser cake base, such as a Classic Butter Cake (page 12). Creating an apple is used in the New York New York project (page 135).

1. Bake 2 half sphere-shaped cakes using a 6-inch (15 cm) ball cake pan. This cake pan is available for purchase from the list of suppliers on page 165.
2. Sandwich the two halves together with Swiss Meringue Buttercream Icing (page 19).
3. Freeze the cake for about an hour. Remove from freezer and start sculpting the cake into the shape of an apple.
4. Frost the sculpted cake with buttercream and put into the freezer for another hour.
5. Remove from the freezer and cover with fondant.

HOW TO MAKE FLOWERS AND LEAVES

THERE ARE SEVERAL ways to make flower petals or leaves. Any of the following methods can be used, and you should try each of them at least once to decide which works best for you. Both leaves and flowers are important elements in cake decorating.

MEXICAN HAT TECHNIQUE

This technique is used to make the basic shape for small flowers and the calyx for larger flowers. It is called the Mexican hat technique because the shape of the cone when the sides are flattened resembles a Mexican sombrero.

1. Shape a small ball of gumpaste into a teardrop or cone.
2. Flatten and pinch out the edges at the base (with the pointed end up), using your thumb and index fingers.
3. Transfer the paste to a non-stick board and, using a small rolling pin, thin the flattened edges from the centre out to the edges.
4. Position the flower-shaped cutter in the centre and cut out the shape.
5. Lift the shape off the board using the narrow end and, with the pointed end of a silk veining tool, make a hole in the centre of the flower or calyx and soften the edges.

SAUSAGE TECHNIQUE

This technique uses florist wire to make flowers.

1. Cut the required gauge florist's wire into 3 sections.
2. Roll a small amount of gumpaste into a ball and then elongate it into the shape of a sausage.
3. Insert a 24-gauge florist's wire into the middle of the paste.
4. Lay the paste onto a greased board or surface. Roll it gently to flatten the paste.
5. The wire will make a raised bump under the paste. Using a small rolling pin, roll the paste thinly away from the centre, leaving a thick ridge where the wire is inserted. Repeat on the other side.
6. Centre a leaf or petal cutter over the paste and cut out the shape. Transfer the cut shape onto a foam flower pad that has been dusted with icing sugar.
7. Soften the edges of the leaf or petal gently, using the ball tool. To do this, place the ball tool half on the foam and half on the paste, and then run the ball tool over the outer edges of the petal.
8. Remove the cut shape from the thin foam and place it in a silicone veiner. You can also vein the flower petals with a silk veining tool by rolling it over the paste. Once veined, you can soften the edges of the cut shape again with the ball tool.
9. The above steps can be repeated to make many petals or leaves.

TWIDDLING TECHNIQUE

Like the Sausage Technique, the Twiddling Technique uses florist wires.

1. Roll a tiny amount of gumpaste onto a florist's wire.
2. Twiddle or roll the paste one-third down the wire, until it is thin. Make as many of these as you can and put them in bags to prevent them from drying out.
3. Roll out another ball of gumpaste very thinly on a board greased with shortening. Cut out the petal or leaf shape you want.
4. Place the leaf or petal on a thin foam and soften the edges with a ball tool. To do this, place the ball tool half on the foam and half on the paste and then run the ball tool over the outer edges of the petal.
5. Apply some gum glue to the middle of the cut shape where the wire is to be placed. Place the florist's wire covered with paste on the shape and press gently. The wire should now adhere to the cut shape.
6. Place the wired shape onto a veiner; vein as required, with the wire on top.

RIDGE TECHNIQUE

The Ridge Technique uses florist wires and a rolling pin.

1. Roll a small amount of gumpaste into a sausage shape.
2. Using a small rolling pin, flatten the sausage and roll away from the centre toward the outer edges of the paste on both sides, leaving a thick ridge in the middle.
3. Insert the florist's wire two-thirds of the way into the thick ridge.
4. Position a leaf or petal cutter over the paste with the raised ridge in the centre and vein as required. The ridge should be the bottom of the petal or leaf.

BASIC WIRING AND FLORAL SPRAY ARRANGEMENT

IT IS IMPORTANT to make all the required flowers and leaves—with spares—for each of the projects before you start assembling them into sprays. If you don't use all the flowers and leaves, you can always save them in airtight containers for another time.

TAPING FLOWERS AND LEAVES INTO SPRAYS

1. Cut the florist's tapes into ½-inch (1 cm) widths, using a florist's tape cutter or a pair of scissors.
2. Sometimes extra lengths are required for a flower when assembling into sprays. This can easily be done by using florist's tape to join a thicker gauge of florist's wire to the existing flower. Stretch the tape to release the glue and place it at the point where the wires join. Holding the tape at an angle, continue to stretch and pull the tape down, to wind it round the two wires.
3. When flowers and leaves are extended to the necessary lengths, they can be taped together into different style sprays, using the same technique with the florist's tape.

POSY SHAPE

This is made by taping the flowers together in a circle with a domed centre. Always start with the focal or largest flower in the centre, and then work your way around the main flower, surrounding it with smaller blooms and leaves. It is a 3-dimensional arrangement that needs height as well as width.

HOGARTH CURVE

This arrangement is bent into an "S" shape and is usually considered a long spray. It starts with a collection of main focal flowers at the top, trailing off with smaller flowers, buds and leaves to create a soft "S" shape.

CRESCENT

This is a teardrop bouquet that is made with a large flower in the centre, trailing off with smaller flowers, leaves and buds at the bottom of the spray. It is narrow at the bottom, widening at the top with the main focal flowers.

RAFIA-COVERED WIRE LOOPS

These can fill gaps or act as fillers in flower sprays. Choose colours that complement the sprays. These wires can be twisted or bent to any shape to act as fillers in the flower sprays used in the Parisian and Southeast Asian projects.

PLACEMENT OF FLOWER SPRAYS ON CAKES

When placing sprays on cakes, take care that the sprays are not inserted directly into them. Food-grade flower spikes or posy holders should be used in cases in which the sprays are to be inserted into the cakes. If the spray is to be arranged on top of a cake, a small piece of fondant should be used as a base to hold the flowers.

HOW TO DIVIDE A CAKE INTO EVEN SEGMENTS

THERE ARE CHARTS on the market that will show you how to divide a cake into segments that you can purchase. You can achieve the same effect by using my receipt roll method.

1. Wrap receipt paper, around the circumference of the cake.
2. Make sure that the 2 ends of the paper meet exactly.
3. Remove the paper and fold it into equal sections. The number of folds will determine the number of segments on the cake. The folds ensure that those segments are evenly spaced. You can cut the buttom of the folded paper into a scalloped look if desired. A scalloped template is used in the ¡Hola! project (page 127).
4. Wrap the paper around the cake again and use a pin or a scriber to mark the folds on top of the cake. Once the marks are made, remove the paper.

BASIC PIPING TECHNIQUES

ANY PIPING BAG can be used for Royal Icing (page 20), but it is advisable to keep separate sets of bags for Royal Icing and for Buttercream Icing (page 18). Any grease will break down the icing making it runny and unsuitable for piping work. Therefore, all equipment used for Royal Icing must be oil- and grease-free. This includes all piping tips. In other respects, the same kinds of piping tips may be used for either technique. Royal Icing should also be kept in airtight containers at all times, as it dries very quickly once exposed to air.

DOTS

1. Any round tip can be used to pipe bead borders. I prefer to use tips 2 or 3, because they provide a more elegant finish.
2. Hold the tip slightly above the surface of your cake and squeeze out the icing to create a dot. If the dot has a point at the end, you can always use a damp brush to flatten it.
3. Gradually lift the tip as the dot gets larger. Stop piping at the desired size, then lift the tip away.

BEAD BORDER

Many of the projects in this book use this technique or border.

1. Follow steps 1 and 2 for dots.
2. When the dot has reached its desired size, stop squeezing and pull the tip of your bag down to create a short, narrow tail, stopping where the next dot should start.
3. To start another dot, repeat the process at the tail end of the previous dot, ensuring that all of the dots are the same size.
4. Continue with this process until the full border is completed.

ZIGZAG BORDER

1. Use tip number 1.5 and hold the bag at a 45-degree angle, with the back of your bag pointing at a 3 o'clock position for right-hand users.
2. Start piping lines in an up-and-down motion as close to each other as possible.

LINES

1. Hold the bag between the thumb and the fingers of your preferred hand. Use the index finger of your other hand to guide the tip as you squeeze and move the bag.
2. Touch the surface of the cake with the tip of your bag where you would like to start the border and slowly squeeze out the icing. Lift the bag slightly as you squeeze and pull the line of icing straight toward you.

3. When you are approaching the end of the border, lighten up the squeezing, gradually bring the bag down, stop squeezing, and drop the line by touching the surface of the cake with the tip where you would like to end the border.

RUB DOWN METHOD

This method is used to break or to eliminate air bubbles in icing.

1. Put a small amount of Royal Icing onto the surface of the table.
2. Using a palette knife, spread the Royal Icing back and forth on the table surface until it is smooth and all the air bubbles have been removed.

STRINGWORK

Stringwork is a term used in cake decorating to describe the process of piping an icing mixture like Royal Icing in dramatic, swag-like patterns that usually hang elegantly from the top rim of a decorated cake. Stringwork can either drop in a single pattern as a loop, or can overlap in a series of dropped stringwork.

BRIDGES

Bridges are layers of fine piped Royal Icing lines that are built up on top of each other in a scalloped fashion on the sides of the cake. The bridges provide support to which the extension work can adhere. However, there are other techniques of extension work that do not require bridges; this is known as bridgeless extension work.

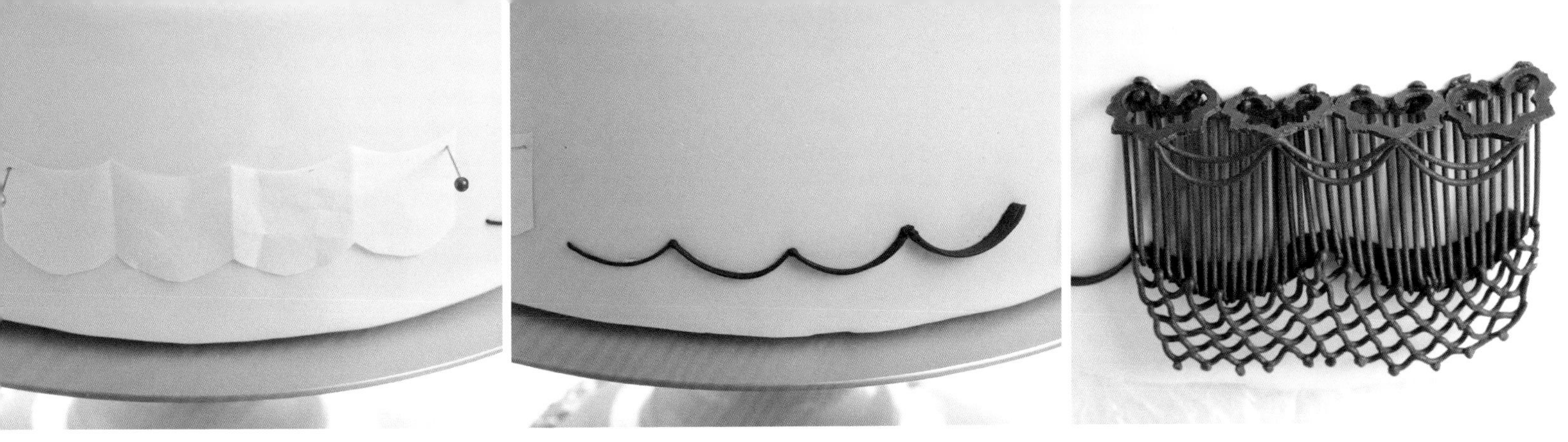

HOW TO PIPE EXTENSION WORK

STRINGWORK THAT IS more delicate and that uses finer tips (like number 1.5, 1, 0, or 00) to pipe on the sides of a cake in curtain-like forms or lace forms is known as extension work. This technique is considered by most cake decorators to be the highest and most difficult form of stringwork, and is usually very fragile.

1. Before you start piping, check that your Royal Icing (page 20) is of stiff peak consistency and that all air bubbles have been eliminated, using the rub-down method (page 38). The icing should flow smoothly through the tip when continuous pressure is applied.
2. If the icing is too soft or runny, the string will either sag or break. If the icing is too stiff, it will be hard to pipe the strings.
3. Place the cake at eye level when piping. It may be necessary to put your cake on top of another styrofoam to bring it to eye level.
4. Do not fill your piping bag too full. Icing should be changed every 20 minutes to ensure that it does not break down.
5. Keep leftover icing covered at all times with a damp cloth and plastic wrap, to prevent crusting. It is essential that leftover Royal Icing be kept in an airtight grease-free container at all times.
6. Attach the paper template (see step 3 in How to Divide a Cake into Even Segments on page 36) on to the cake sides with pins.
7. Using a pin or scriber, mark the edges af the template and remove the template.
8. Pipe the Royal Icing strings onto the marked points on the cake.

HOW TO MAKE A GUMPASTE FIGURINE

THERE ARE VARIOUS sizes and shapes of head moulds on the market, made of different materials. Silicone moulds are the best, but they are more expensive than others. You can also make your own silicone moulds from any number of mediums that are available. For figurines, I usually like to use the double-sided moulds.

UPPER BODY AND HEAD

1. Roll out a piece of gumpaste of approximately 1¼ oz (35 mL) into a 4-inch (10 cm) long sausage that will fit into the mould for the upper body and head.
2. Using your thumb, press the gumpaste into the mould. Ensure that your thumb presses right into the detailed features of the head part of the mould, such as the nose and lips. If you are using a mould other than silicone, you may have to grease it properly first, to ensure that the gumpaste does not stick to it and that it can easily be removed. I like to use vegetable spray to coat my moulds.
3. Roll out another smaller ball of gumpaste to fit into the hollow area that you have created with your thumb while pressing the gumpaste into the mould.
4. Press the 2 sides of the mould together, to create the back of the head and body.
5. Trim off the excess gumpaste with a knife.
6. Insert a wooden skewer right through the gumpaste, from the bottom, halfway up the head. Take extreme care when inserting the stick through the narrow part of the neck. The stick will act as a support for the structure.
7. Remove the head and upper body carefully from the mould. While the gumpaste is still soft, shape the head slightly, if necessary, to resemble a human head. At this point, you can tilt the head to any position you desire. Leave it to dry overnight or longer, until it has completely hardened.
8. For the ears, knead a tiny amount of ivory gumpaste, proportionate to the head size, into a teardrop. Flatten the teardrop and twist it to resemble a "C." The narrower part of the teardrop will be the ear lobe. Attach to the sides of the head with gum glue.
9. Once dried, you can paint on the facial features with edible paste colours, using thin brushes or with edible food pens.

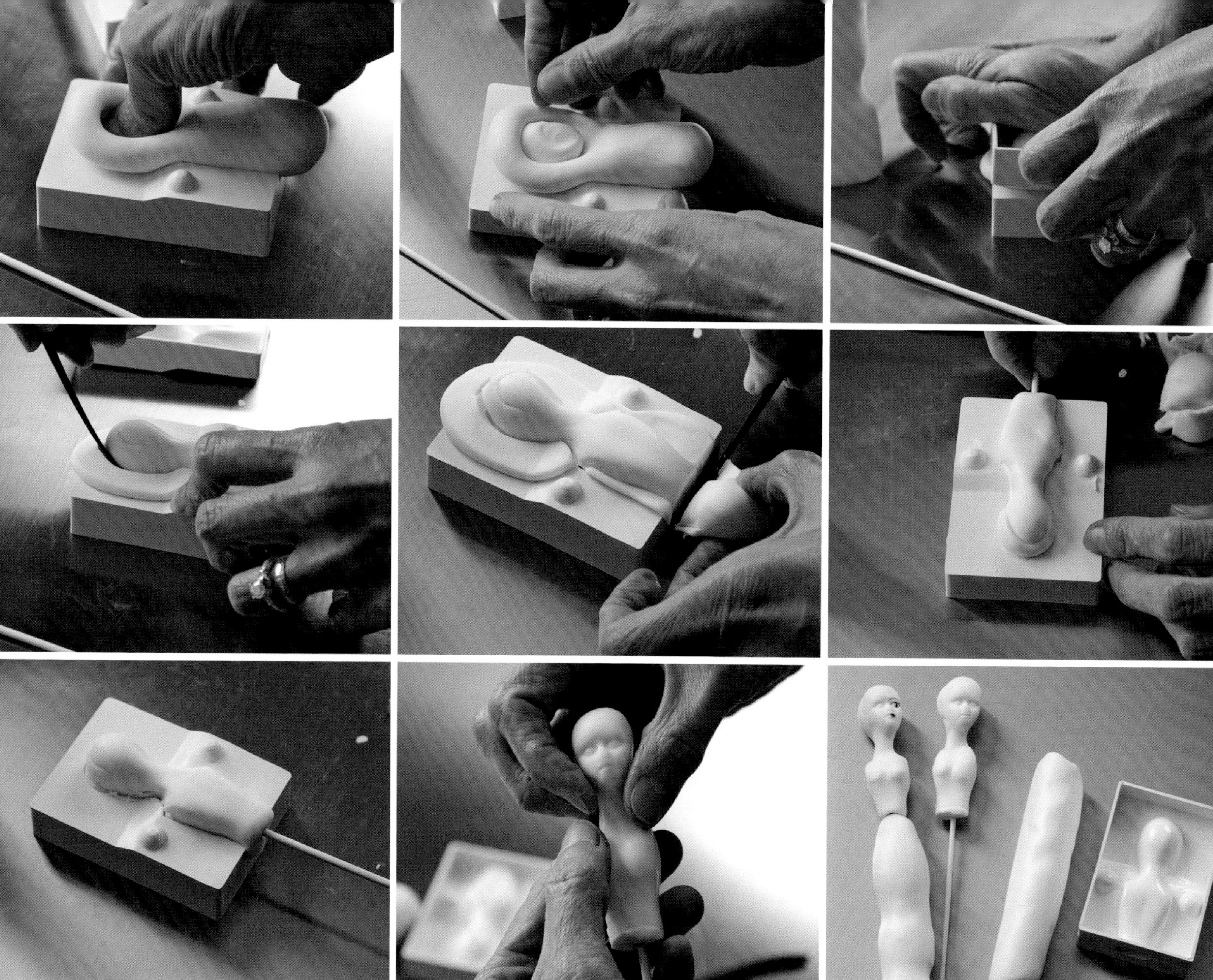

LOWER BODY

1. Take another piece of gumpaste of approximately 4 oz (120 g) and roll it into a ball, then into a cone shape approximately 5-inch (12 cm) in height. Shape the cone slightly to resemble the position required. (The shape will be covered with clothing.) Allow to dry 24 to 48 hours, until fully dry, before using.
2. When both pieces are completely dry, attach the upper torso to the lower body.
3. To attach, insert a skewer into the lower body, leaving a part of the stick protruding at the top. Apply some gum glue around the skewer in the lower body.
4. Attach the upper torso to the skewer protruding from the lower body and allow to dry 24 to 48 hours, until fully dried.

HOW TO DO FLOODING OR COLOUR FLOW

THIS METHOD IS also known as run outs. It is a technique used mostly on cookies and on collars on cakes, and is usually done using Royal Icing (page 20). Both the floating collar used in the Japan project and certain pieces of the template for the Eiffel Tower in the France project use this technique. (See page 49 for a picture.)

1. Transfer the image or design you wish to flood onto a piece of parchment paper.
2. Using tip number 2, outline the design using a stiff consistency Royal Icing, and ensuring that there are no breaks in the line. The piped lines will act as a dam to hold in the runny or soft Royal Icing.
3. Dilute the stiff Royal Icing with water so that when a line is drawn through the icing with a palette knife, the icing line will disappear only at the count of ten.
4. Fill the icing bag with the diluted icing and fill in the space within the piped lines of the design using tip number 3. If there is an air bubble, ensure that you prick it immediately with a pin before the icing hardens.
5. Leave to dry before removing from the paper. It usually takes about 24 hours to 3 days, depending up on the local humidity, to fully dry. The pieces can be put under a bright light (such as a table lamp) to speed up the drying process.
6. Colour flow pieces can be attached directly to a cake using Royal Icing. In the Springtime Japanese-inspired project (page 47) it is attached with piped strings.

HOW TO TRANSFER PATTERNS ONTO CAKES

TO TRANSFER PATTERNS onto cakes, the cakes must be covered in fondant and left to dry overnight.

NON-TOXIC PENCIL METHOD

1. Draw the design onto parchment paper. Patterns transferred using this method will show the reverse image on the cakes.
2. Attach the design template onto the cake with pins. Make sure the pencilled side of the image is facing the cake.
3. Outline the design gently onto the cake with a pencil. Remove the parchment paper. The design should appear on the cake.

SCRIBER OR PIN METHOD (PICTURED ABOVE)

1. Draw the pattern or image on parchment paper.
2. Attach the template of the design, right side up, onto the cake with pins.
3. Using a scriber or a pin, prick holes in the cake, following the outline of the design.
4. Remove the paper. Patterns transferred onto cakes using this method will not be a reverse image.

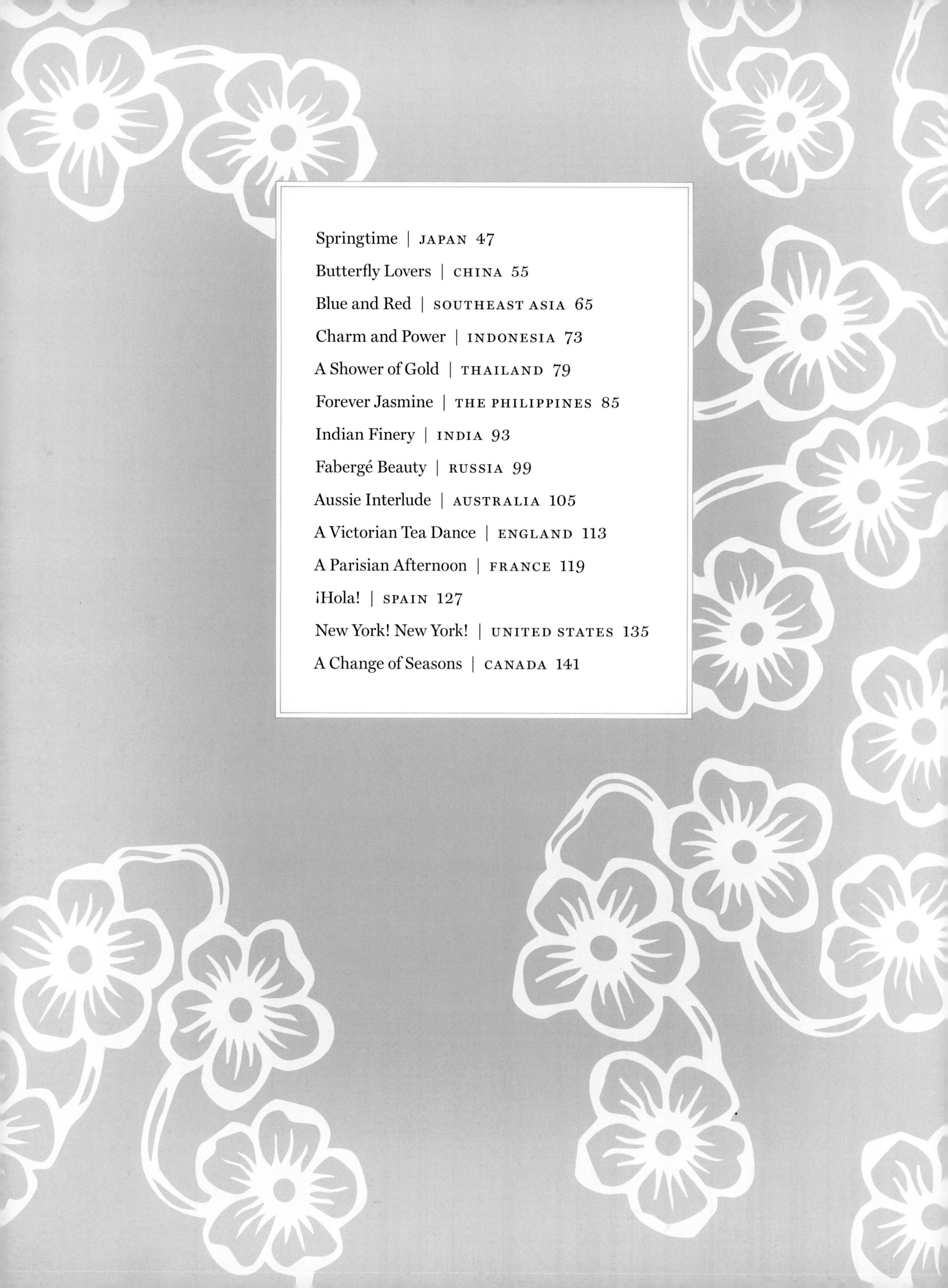

2

THE CAKES

SPRINGTIME

JAPAN

JAPAN DOES NOT formally have a national flower, but for many this is the cherry blossom. The cherry blossom comes in numerous colours and has single petals or double petals, some more frilly than others. The delicate flower blooms for a very short time. For many Japanese, it represents the transience of life. Geisha's are traditional entertainers specializing in dance, song and a variety of instruments, including hard drum, shoulder drum, shamisen or Japanese flute.

LEVEL OF DIFFICULTY moderate skill

TECHNIQUES USED piping skills, figure modelling, flooding, stringwork, gumpaste flowers and leaves

CAKES AND EDIBLES

- about 7 lb (3.15 kg) white fondant
- about 4 oz (120 g) chocolate fondant
- black fondant
- about 5 oz (150 g) red gumpaste
- about 10 oz (300 g) white gumpaste
- about 2 oz (60 g) green gumpaste
- about 5 oz (150 g) grey gumpaste
- Dusting Colours vine, green bean, light and dark pink, yellow and plum
- white Royal Icing (page 20)
- confectioner's glaze
- gum glue
- skin-tone or ivory gel paste
- lemon extract or vodka

TOOLS AND EQUIPMENT

- green florist's tape
- 26 and 24 gauge white florist's wires
- small blossom or cherry blossom cutters
- small rose calyx cutter
- small rose leaf cutter
- cutting wheel
- leaf veiner
- multi-purpose veiner
- fine seed head stamens
- piping bag
- piping tip 2
- metal ball tool
- rolling pin
- Dresden tool
- foam pads
- brushes
- scriber

TEMPLATES

- Floating Collar (page 149)
- Cherry Blossom (page 149)

CAKE PREPARATION

See pages 25–28 for stacking and fondant-covering techniques.

1. Cover a 16-inch (40 cm) wavy oval board with white fondant.
2. Cover a 8-inch (20 cm) round cake with white fondant. You may have to bake two cakes to obtain the 6-inch (15 cm) height.
3. Insert dowels into 8-inch (20 cm) cake.
4. Cover a 6-inch (15 cm) round cake with white fondant. Height must be 5-inch (13 cm).
5. Centre the 6-inch (15 cm) round tier on top of the 8-inch (20 cm) round and attach both tiers together with Royal Icing.

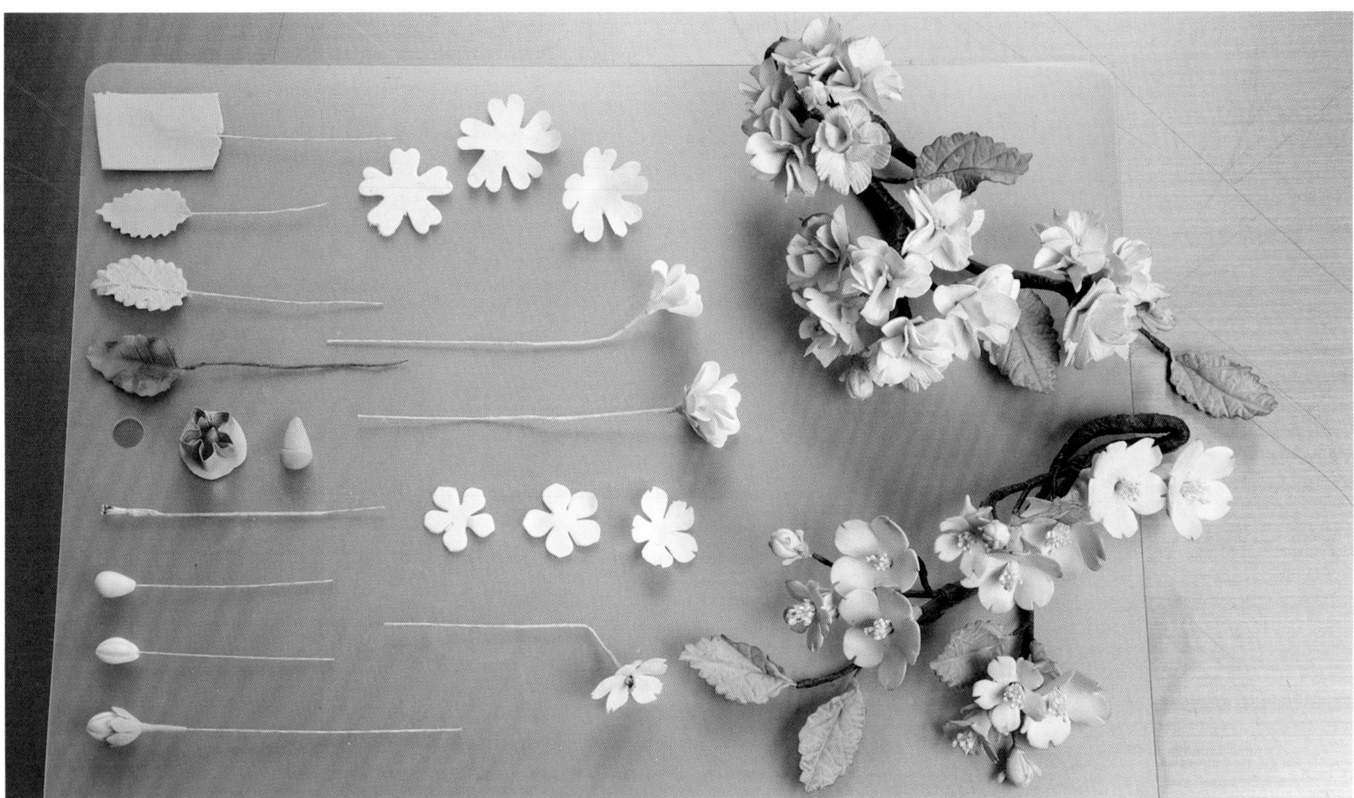

The pieces of the cherry blossom tree

6. All 3 tiers should be positioned in the centre but toward the back of the 16-inch (40 cm) oval board and attached to the board with a small amount of Royal Icing.

CHERRY BLOSSOM TREE

See pages 32–35 for techniques on making flowers and leaves.

Tree

1. Knead and roll some chocolate fondant into a sausage approximately 16-inch (40 cm) long.
2. Flatten the sausage and shape it to resemble a tree trunk and attach to the sides of the 2 tiers with gum glue.
3. Repeat the same technique as above, with the branches extending from the main trunk of the tree.
4. Texturize the bark of the trunk and branches with a veining mat, or use a knife to cut shallow slits in the bark and branches.

Cherry Blossom (Double Petal)

1. Using half-width green florist's tape, attach some fine white head stamens to a white 26-gauge florist's wire that has been cut into 4 sections. You will need to make at least 30 of these stamens.
2. Roll a piece of gumpaste thinly. Cut approximately 120 petals, to allow for breakage, as you will need 2 petals for each flower. Since this flower appears in clusters, you will need to make approximately 60 individual flowers for this project. Ensure you have the cut petals covered at all times to prevent them from hardening and drying.
3. Using a fine pair of scissors, create a small "V" cut at the centre of each of the blossom petals.
4. Transfer the petal to a foam pad and soften the edges of the petal with a ball tool.
5. Vein the petal either with a veining tool or a multipurpose veiner.
6. Apply a little gum glue to the base of the stamens.
7. Push the petals up the stamens and pinch the petals to create pleats or folds around the stamens. Repeat

the same with the second layer of petals, but try to taper the fondant down the stamen slightly.

8. Repeat, to create approximately 55 blossoms.

Cherry Blossom (Single Petal)

1. Using half-width green florist's tape, attach some fine white head stamens to a white 26-gauge florist's wire that has been cut into 4 sections.
2. Using the Mexican hat technique as described on page 32, make approximately 15 petals.
3. Soften the edges with a ball tool, and make a small "V" slit in the centre of each petal.
4. Brush gum glue on the petal and feed it up the wire to meet the base of the stamen. Pinch to secure at the end.
5. Cut the calyx and attach beneath the flower.
6. You can make some smaller blooms using the smaller cutter as well to create a spray.

Buds

1. The buds can easily be made freehand.
2. Form a ball of white gumpaste into a teardrop shape. Insert a green 26-gauge florist's wire into the narrow end.
3. Squeeze and thin the gumpaste putting it down the wire to a narrow end. The tip of the bud should be a little rounded. You can use either a cutting wheel or a small knife to create lines on the bud to reflect unopened petals.
4. Cut a green calyx and insert into the bottom of the bud with gum glue.

Calyx

1. Knead some green gumpaste and roll until thin.
2. Cut the calyx with the small rose calyx cutter.
3. Transfer to a foam pad and soften the edges, stretching the points slightly.
4. Insert the calyx up the blossom and attach with gum glue.
5. Leave to dry for 24 hours or overnight.

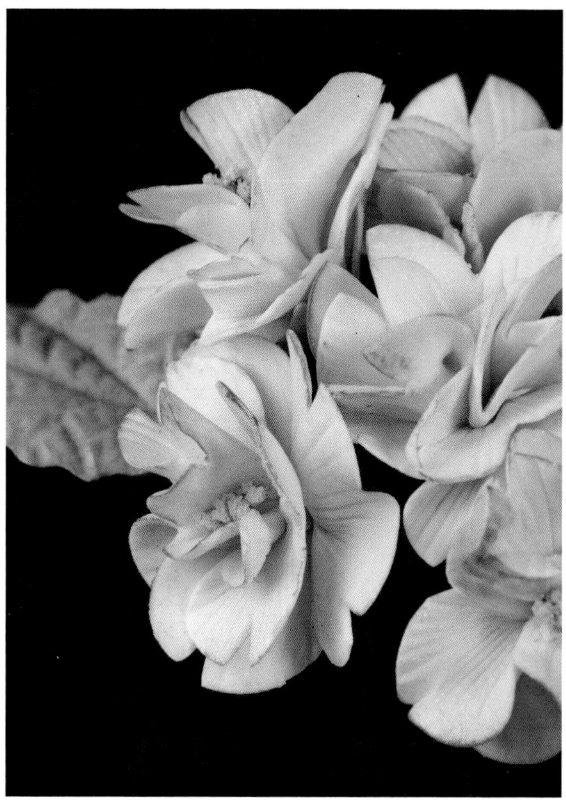

The blossoms for the bottom of the cake

Leaves

1. Using your leaf-making technique of choice, make approximately 12 leaves with a small leaf cutter.
2. Pinch the base of the leaf slightly to accentuate the central vein and leave to dry on foil that has been crumpled to give the leaf shape some movement when dried.

Dusting

1. Use light pink to dust the petals. Dust the centre of the blossom with a darker pink and highlight some of the outer edges of the petal with the same dark pink.
2. Dust the calyx with a mixture of vine-green and green-bean. Dust a bit of plum at the base of each calyx.
3. For the leaves, dust with green-bean and plum, shading from the base to the outer edges of the leaf. When dry, steam or dip in confectioner's glaze, to give it a shine.

The floating collar, shown here in black, tops this cake

Assembly

1. Attach the blossoms to the tree in clusters with Royal Icing. Attach a few leaves to the tree with Royal Icing.
2. For the spray, attach the blossoms in clusters onto a green 24-gauge florist's wire. Tape the leaves in sets of 3 and tape them onto the blossoms. The individual sprays can be arranged in an "S" manner (see Hogarth Curve on page 34). You will need to make a total of 3 sprays with different size clusters of flowers.

FLOATING COLLAR OR RUN OUT

See page 42 for the flooding technique.

1. Pipe the outline of the template provided with stiff Royal Icing.
2. Flood the design with colour flow or flood-work-consistency icing (see photo above).
3. Leave to dry for 24 to 48 hours.
4. Cut 3 pieces of foam 1-inch (2.5 cm) high.
5. Position the dried collar in the centre on top of the 6-inch (15 cm) top tier. Place the 3 foams to support the collar.
6. Use a 1.5 tip to pipe stringwork on the sides of the collar, as shown. Let stringwork dry thoroughly for at least 24 hours before removing the foam supports. Pipe extra stringwork to close the gap.

BUTTERFLIES

1. Roll a small amount of white gumpaste until thin.
2. Using butterfly cutters, cut out 2 butterfly shapes.
3. Leave to dry on folded cardboard as shown in the photo.
4. Use dusting colors diluted with lemon extract or edible food markers to draw designs on the butterfly wings.
5. Paint some edible glue onto the sides of the wings and sprinkle some metallic dusting colors on the edges of the wings as shown in the photo.
6. Cut a 28 gauge florist wire into two sections.
7. Roll three tiny balls of white gumpaste into varying sizes.
8. Elongate the largest ball of gumpaste into a teardrop and narrow the end of the teardrop into a sharp point to form the body of the butterfly as shown. Curl the narrow end of the teardrop slightly upward.
9. Insert the wire into the medium size gumpaste ball.
10. Join the 3 pieces of gumpaste together with edible gum glue as shown in the photo.
11. Stick two white stamens into the smallest ball of gumpaste to resemble the butterfly feelers.
12. Allow all the pieces of gumpaste to dry for 24 hours.
13. Tape the butterfly pieces together with some half-width florist tape.

GEISHA

See How to Make a Gumpaste Figurine on pages 40–41 for more on this technique.

1. Colour some gumpaste with skin-tone or ivory gel paste.
2. Create the upper body and head of the geisha, as shown in the photo on page 52.
3. Create the lower body of the geisha. Ensure that the lower body shape resembles that of a body kneeling down, as shown in the photo on page 52.

Above: The pieces for constructing the butterflies; Below: A completed butterfly

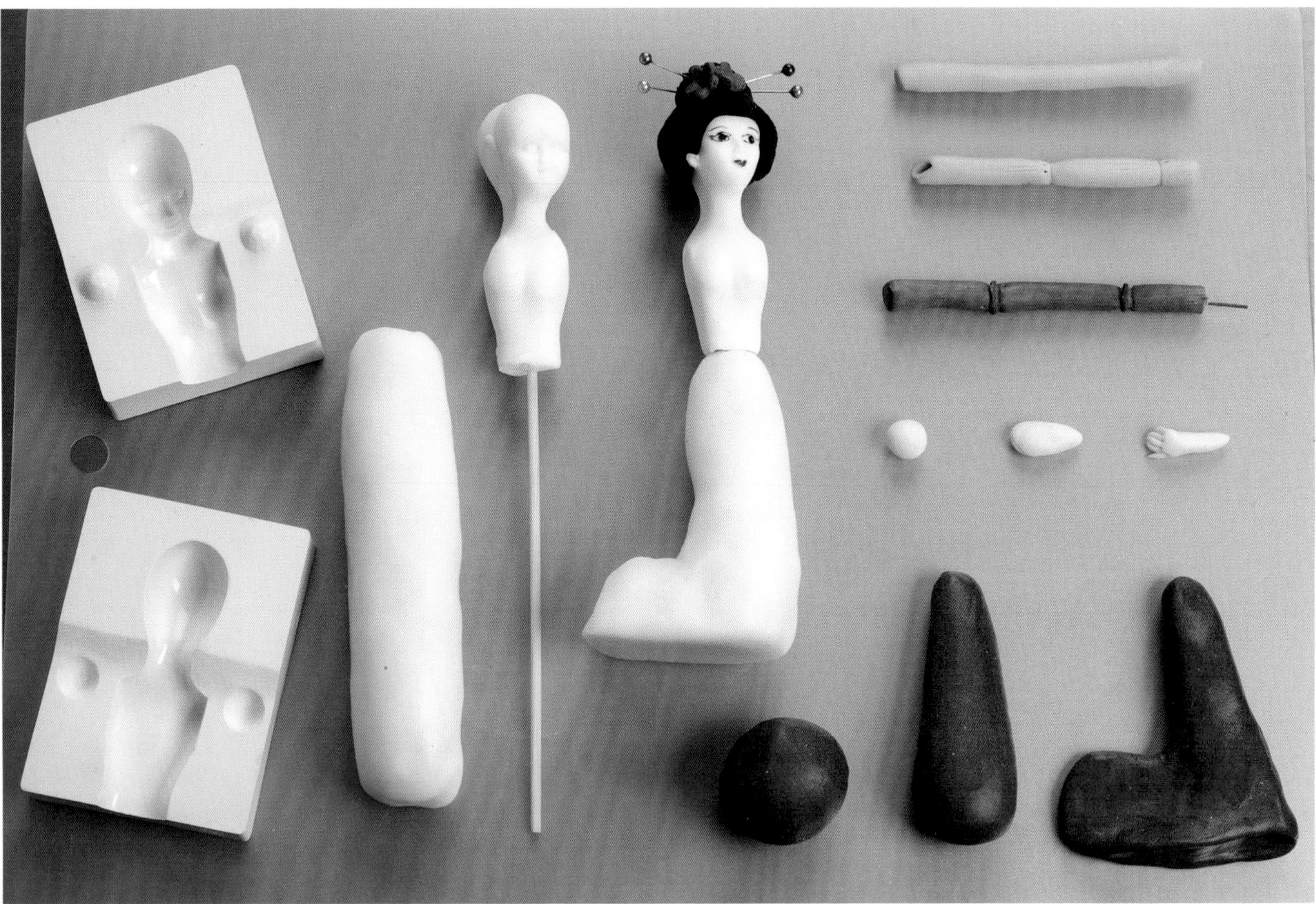

Moulds and pieces for the geisha

Hair

1. For the hair, roll a ball of black fondant. Flatten and attach to the head, using gum glue. Shape the hair as desired and texturize it with the pointed end of the Dresden tool.
2. Accessorize the head as shown in the photo.

Dressing the Figurine

1. Roll some red gumpaste thinly. Apply a small amount of gum glue to the body.
2. Cut a 6-inch (15 cm) square piece of red fondant and wrap it around the torso and skirt area, cutting off the excess.

Arms

1. Roll 2 red pieces of fondant, approximately 1 oz (30 g) each, into sausages measuring approximately 3-inch (8 cm) long or proportionate to the body size.
2. Flatten one end of the sausage, as shown in the photo.
3. Apply some gum glue to the shoulder area where the arm is to be attached.
4. Push the arms into the skewer protruding from the shoulder and attach.
5. On the wider side of the sleeve, indent a hole using your index finger where the hand is to be attached.

Hands

1. Roll a small piece of skin-tone gumpaste almost the size of a pea into a teardrop.
2. Using a small pair of scissors, flatten and cut the fingers.
3. Shape the fingers appropriately as shown in the photo. Insert the hand into the hole of the sleeve with some gum glue.
4. Paint freehand designs on the dress or kimono with dusting colours mixed with a little lemon extract or clear vodka.

BAMBOO AND ROCKS

Bamboo

1. Knead some green gumpaste of different sizes into a sausage. Insert a green 24-gauge florist's wire into the sausage.
2. Indent an opening at the top end of the sausage with the wide end of the Dresden tool.
3. Using fine tweezers, pinch the gumpaste at different intervals, to represent the nodes on the main bamboo stem.
4. Using a scriber, indent some tiny holes above and below the different sections of the nodes.
5. Texturize the bamboo stem either with a sharp knife or a texturizing tool.
6. Repeat the same for different lengths of the bamboo and leave to dry overnight for at least 24 hours.
7. Dust the bamboo with green dusting colour, as shown.

Bamboo Leaves

1. Roll tiny sausages of green gumpaste.
2. Flatten and roll until thin.
3. Using a cutting wheel, cut leaf shapes freehand. Using the twiddling technique from page 33, attach 26-gauge green florist's wires of 1-inch (2.5 cm) length onto the leaves.
4. Leave to dry for an hour and insert the leaves into the nodes of the bamboo stems.

Rocks

1. Roll small balls of gumpaste in different shades of grey into various sizes.
2. Flatten some of them to resemble rocks.

Assembly

1. Take a small mound of green gumpaste the size of a golf ball, flatten, and attach with gum glue to the board.
2. Insert the various lengths of bamboo stems into the green gumpaste. Surround the green mound with the grey rocks.

The completed geisha as shown on the cake

FINAL ASSEMBLY

1. Stack the 2 tiered cakes together on the pre-covered cakeboard with Royal Icing, using the stacked cake technique on page 28.
2. Arrange the geisha next to the mound of bamboos, as shown in the photo of this project.
3. Place the sprays of cherry blossoms next to the geisha on the board.
4. Insert a flower spike into the top cake tier in the centre of the floating collar and place the smallest spray of cherry blossoms in it.
5. Glue a ¼-inch (6 mm) white satin ribbon to the sides of the cakeboard.

BUTTERFLY LOVERS

CHINA

ALTHOUGH CHINA does not have an official national flower, the tree peony is a traditional favourite, symbolizing wealth, honour, nobility, peace and female beauty. A peony, a Chinese dragon (symbolizing auspicious powers) and an Asian carp representing the ability to resist hurdles and to achieve success are features of this golden, three-tiered cake.

To create it, you will need a turntable, or an overturned round cake pan (at least 9-inch [23 cm] in diameter) to serve as a turntable. You will need a mould for the dragon and cutters for the peony, leaves and butterflies as shown in the photo. The carp, stones and waves are shaped by hand.

LEVEL OF DIFFICULTY advanced skills

TECHNIQUES USED stringwork, brush embroidery, pattern transfer, modelling, gumpaste flowers and leaves

CAKES AND EDIBLES

- about 8 lb (3.6 kg) yellow fondant
- Airbrush Colours gold
- Dusting Colours gold
- edible gold dragees
- gum glue
- 1 Tbsp (15 mL) lemon extract
- vegetable spray (for greasing dragon mould)
- 1 lb (450 g) Royal Icing (stiff consistency) (page 20)

TOOLS AND EQUIPMENT

- airbrush machine
- a roll of receipt paper
- pins for marking
- piping bag
- piping tip numbers 1.5, 3 and 5
- tracing paper (about 6 x 6 inches [15 x 15 cm])
- scriber
- a set of Wilton paintbrushes
- dragon mould
- ball tool
- Dresden tool
- scissors
- 28-gauge florist's wire
- 24-gauge florist's wire
- fine needle-nose pliers
- fine tweezers
- ¼-inch (6 mm) green florist's tape
- ½-inch (1 cm) green florist's tape
- 3 bunches of yellow stamens
- set of peony cutters (small, medium and large)
- foam pad
- petal veiner
- veining tool
- confectioner's glaze (optional, to create shine)
- small leaf cutter
- butterfly-shape cutters
- ¼-inch (6 mm) wide gold ribbon

TEMPLATES

- Peony Template (page 150)
- Lotus (page 151)

CAKE PREPARATION

See pages 25–28 for stacking and fondant-covering techniques.

1. Cover an 18-inch (45 cm) oval hexagon cakeboard with marbled chocolate fondant.
2. Cover the 4-inch (10 cm) round, 8-inch (20 cm) and 12-inch (30 cm) oval cakes with yellow fondant.

Finished embroidery and stringwork on the China cake

3. Leave cake tiers to dry for at least 24 hours.
4. Using an airbrush, spray the cakes with gold colour. Allow to dry.

CAKE EMBROIDERY AND STRINGWORK

See pages 38–39 for more on extension and stringwork.

8-inch (20 cm) & 12-inch (30 cm) Oval Tiers

1. To mark a guide on the 2 oval cakes for the Oriental stringwork, first measure the circumference of each of the tiers with a length of receipt paper.
2. Then fold each strip into equal sections of about ½-inch (8 mm) wide for the 8-inch (20 cm) tier; and 1-inch (2.5 cm) wide for the 12-inch (30 cm) tier.
3. Open each strip of paper and wrap it around the corresponding tier, fastening it to the cake with a pin. Each strip of paper should wrap comfortably around each cake.

8-inch (20 cm) Cake

1. Position the strip around the sides of the cake in the centre and hold it in position with a pin.
2. Using a scriber or pin, prick a tiny hole above each of the folded lines on the paper and onto the cake.
3. Remove the paper.

12-inch (30 cm) Cake

1. Repeat the steps as in the 8-inch (20 cm) cake above, with the exception that the strip of paper is now placed closer to the top edge of the cake.

12-inch (30 cm) Cake Oriental stringwork

1. Place the 12-inch (30 cm) cake on the turntable. Fill a piping bag fitted with the 1.5 tip with stiff yellow Royal Icing.
2. Flip the cake upside down onto a smaller stryrofoam on the turntable, allowing room for your fingers and the strings when you turn the cake back to right side up.
3. Pipe a dot on each spot that you marked with a pin around the top edge of the cake. Stick a gold dragee onto each of the piped dots as you pipe and allow the dragee to dry for about 10 minutes.

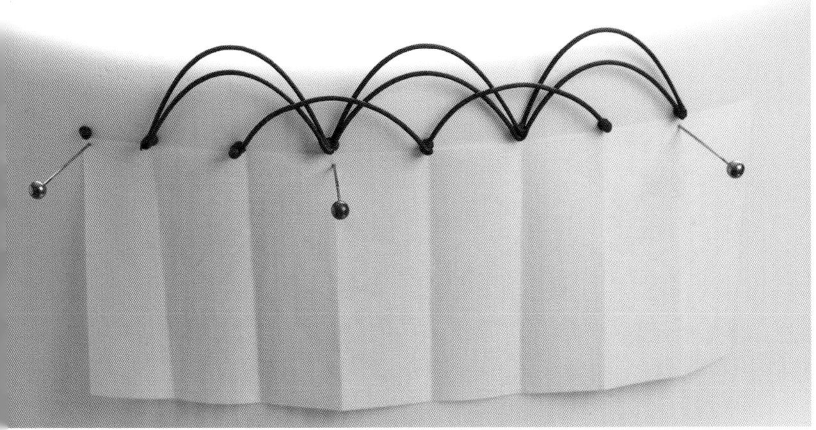

The pin method for creating embroidery and stringwork

4. Pick any 1 dragee as your starting point. Pipe a drop string on every other dot, dropping about 1-inch (2.5 cm) down from the dots around the cake. Continue piping around the cake, and allow to dry for about 10 minutes.
5. Once the first layer of dropped string is dry with another set of dropped strings, overlapping that of the first layer of strings on the missed dots.
6. Pipe another shorter dropped string on the missed dots, creating a double layer effect on the second layer of dropped stringwork. Allow to dry for 10 minutes.
7. Pipe another dot of Royal Icing on top of the existing dots. Attach another dragee on top of each of the dots before they dry. Turn the cake right side up and allow to dry for a further 10 minutes.
8. Repeat steps 4 to 7.
9. Flip the cake upside down, and pipe another shorter layer of dropped stringwork on every other dot.
10. Pipe another layer of dropped stringwork on the missed dots, to create an overlapping effect.
11. Repeat step 7.
12. Repeat steps 9 and 10, ending with step 7.

8-inch (20 cm) Tier Oriental stringwork

1. Repeat steps 1 to 3 as with 12-inch (30 cm) cake above.
2. Pipe a dropped string on every other dot, ensuring that the strings are dropped about ½-inch (1 cm) from the dots. Allow to dry for 10 minutes.
3. Pipe another row of shorter dropped strings on the missed dots, to create an overlapping effect. Leave to dry for 10 minutes.
4. Flip the cake upside down and pipe a dot of Royal Icing on each of the marker dots. Stick a yellow dragee on each of the dots before it dries.
5. Repeat steps 2 and 3.
6. Repeat step 4.
7. Leave to dry for 10 minutes.

Brush Embroidery on 4-inch (10 cm) Cake

1. Trace the peony template (page 150) onto tracing paper. Attach the tracing paper to the side of the 4-inch (10 cm) cake with pins. Using a scriber, prick the lines of the peony design onto the surface of the cake. Make sure that the fondant-covered cake is fully dry before attempting this technique. Remove the tracing paper.
2. Fill a piping bag fitted with a number 3 tip with medium consistency Royal Icing. Working with one petal at a time and starting with the petal furthest

Brush embroidery

Yellow gumpaste is used here in the dragon mould to create the dragon's head

away from you, pipe a thick line of Royal Icing on the outline of the petal.

3. Using a small brush dampened with water, place the tip of the brush on the line of Royal Icing and brush the icing in gently toward the centre of the petal, so that the icing is spread thicker at the outer part of the petal and thinner toward the centre of the petal. (The visible brushstrokes give the peony an embroidered look.)
4. Repeat steps 2 and 3 for the rest of the petals and allow to dry.
5. For the centre of the design or peony, pipe little dots of Royal Icing and then stick a silver edible dragee on each of the dots.

DRAGON, CARP, STONES AND WAVES

Dragon Mould

This mould can be purchased from the list of suppliers on page 165.

1. Spray the inside of the dragon mould with vegetable spray to prevent the gumpaste from sticking to the mould. Wipe off the excess oil with a paper towel.
2. Knead and roll about 2 oz (60 g) of yellow gumpaste until soft and pliable. Press firmly into the upper dragon head mould. Cut and level off the gumpaste on the mould. Carefully remove the gumpaste piece from the mould.

3. Using another piece of gumpaste, repeat step 2 and press into the lower dragon head mould.
4. Using gum glue, join the pieces together to form the 3-dimensional dragon head.
5. Wind two 3-inch (8 cm) long 28-gauge white florist's wires around a small paintbrush, to create a twisted loop effect for the whiskers. Stick these next to the dragon's nostrils and allow to dry overnight or 24 hours.

Dragon Body

1. Repeat the dragon head steps 1 to 4 for making in order to make the dragon body, legs and hands. You will need to make 2 of each of the body parts and to join them together with gum glue to create the 3-dimensional effect.
2. Leave the parts to dry overnight.
3. Using an airbrush, spray all the parts of the dragon, including the head, with gold colour. Allow to dry overnight.

Carp

1. For the body, roll about 2½ oz (75 g) yellow gumpaste into a ball and shape it into a 5-inch (12 cm) long teardrop shape. Flatten the narrower part of the teardrop shape and curl it slightly upward. Leave to dry for about an hour.
2. Roll another small ball of yellow gumpaste, about ½ oz (15 g), into a teardrop. Flatten the teardrop. Press the wider part of the teardrop slightly to shape it into a fan shape, representing the carp's tail.
3. Using the Dresden tool, create lines on the tail and curl it slightly. Leave to dry for about 1 hour.
4. Using gum glue, attach the carp's tail to the body.
5. For the scales, hold the small end of a number 5 tip with your fingers. Starting from the tail end of the body, gently press the edge of the larger end of the tip into the surface of the body, creating a shallow half-circle. Repeat, in rows, all over the surface of the body.
6. For the gills, roll about 1 oz (30 g) of yellow gumpaste into a ball. Flatten, stretch and shape the gumpaste into a figure-8 shape about 2-inch (5 cm) long.

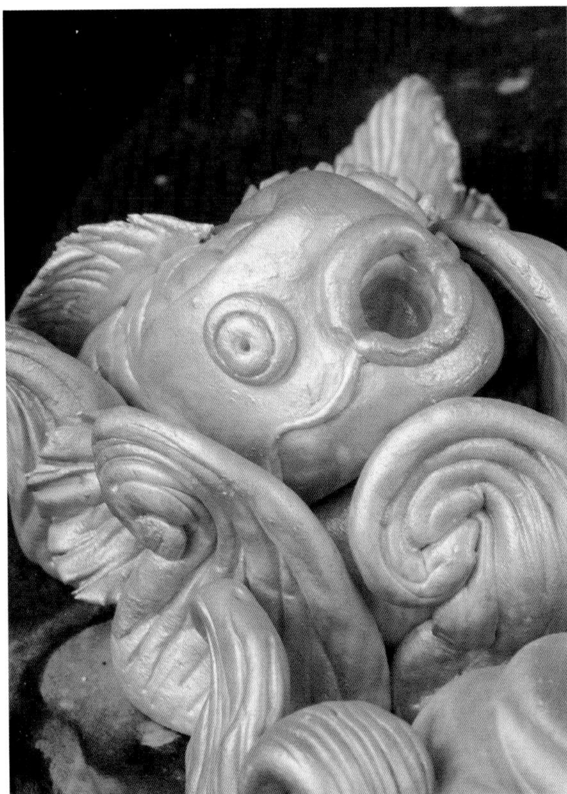

The completed carp

Position the centre of the figure-8 shape on top of the wider part of the carp's body. Attach to the body with gum glue.

7. For the mouth, use the small end of the ball tool to create an indentation. Roll a tiny amount of yellow gumpaste into a thin sausage. Position the sausage shape around the mouth opening, to outline it. Attach with gum glue.
8. For the side fins, roll a pea-size ball of yellow gumpaste into a teardrop shape and then flatten it into a fan shape. Using the pointed end of the Dresden tool, mark fine lines on the surface. Using the tips of a pair of scissors, snip along the end of the fin to create a slightly ragged edge.
9. Repeat step 8 to create an additional fin. Position one fin on each side of the carp body. Attach with gum glue.
10. For the top fin, roll a half-pea-size piece of gumpaste into a teardrop shape and then flatten it. Using the pointed end of the Dresden tool, mark fine lines on the surface. Using the tips of a pair of scissors, snip along the end of the fin, to create a slightly ragged edge.

The pieces for constructing the peony

Position on the top of the body. Attach with gum glue.

11. For the head fin, roll a pea-size ball of yellow gumpaste into a sausage. Flatten half the sausage. Using the pointed end of the Dresden tool, mark fine lines on the sides that have been flattened. Using the tips of a pair of scissors, snip along the end of the fin to create a slightly ragged edge. Attach the fin, with gum glue to the head of the carp.

12. Allow the carp to dry fully for 24 hours. Using an airbrush, spray the carp with gold colour. Allow to dry.

Rocks and Waves

1. For the stones, roll various pieces of yellow gumpaste into irregular ball and oval shapes. Using the Dresden tool, freely mould into rock formations.

2. For the waves, roll pieces of yellow gumpaste into teardrop shapes. Flatten the shapes slightly and roll the thin ends into scroll-like shapes to form wave crests. (See the photo for the pattern.) Using the pointed end of the Dresden tool, draw fine lines on the surface.

3. Allow the stones and waves to dry.

4. Using an airbrush, spray the stones and waves with gold colour. Allow to dry.

Assembly

1. Position the dragon body and head on the sides of the cakeboard. Use Royal Icing to adhere to the cakeboard. See photo for positioning.

2. Use the waves and the stones to camouflage and to hide the joined parts of the dragon and the carp.

TREE PEONY (OVARY, STAMENS, PETALS, CALYX, LEAVES)

Ovary

1. Roll a half-pea-size amount of green gumpaste into a ball. Form the ball into a teardrop shape. Elongate and thin down the narrow side of the teardrop. Curl the thinned end of the teardrop as per photo.

2. Cut a white 28-gauge florist's wire into 3 pieces. Using fine needle-nose pliers, bend one end of each piece into a small hook. Moisten the hook with gum glue and insert it into the wider end of the teardrop, pushing it in deep to give the hook ample support.

3. Using fine tweezers, gently pinch a ridge down one side of the teardrop. Repeat to create a few more ridges on the teardrop. It is not necessary to have a fixed number of ridges.

4. Repeat steps 1 to 3 to create two more ovaries.
5. Using ¼-inch (6 mm) green florist's tape, join the 3 wired teardrops together while the gumpaste is still soft, so that they can sit closely together. See above photo. Allow to dry.
6. Dust the teardrops with vine-green dusting powder, and the curled tips of the teardrops with plum dusting powder.

Stamens

1. Divide each bunch of the yellow stamens into half-bunches.
2. Gather up each bunch neatly, and apply tacky non-toxic glue to the centre to bond them together. Flatten the bunch slightly and allow the glue to dry. Cut each bunch in half crosswise. You will now have 6 bunches. Trim the ends of the bunches so that they are about the same length as the ovary.
3. Apply glue to the end of a bunch. Firmly press the bunch to the outside of the ovary, to attach it. Repeat with the remaining bunches, to surround the ovary completely. Allow to dry.
4. Dust the tip of the stamens with yellow dusting powder.

Petals

1. The set of peony cutters and leaves are available for purchase from the list of suppliers on page 165.
2. Using red gumpaste and the techniques to make petals on pages 32–33, make 7 small peony petals, 7 medium peony petals and 7 large peony petals, either using the templates on page 150 or metal peony cutters.
3. Leave the petals to dry for 24 hours in apple trays, to create a slight curve.
4. Dust the front of the petals with a solid coat of poppy-red dusting powder. To create a light, glittery effect, dust the base of each petal with gold, fading out to the outer edge. Repeat the red and gold dusting on the back of the petals.
5. Starting with the small petals, arrange the petals around the stamen centre and tape them in place with ½-inch (1 cm) width green florist's tape. Repeat with the medium petals, arranging them in between the small petals. Repeat with the large petals, arranging them in between the medium petals. Tape each row of petals together with ½-inch (1 cm) width green florist's tape.

Calyx

1. There are 3 rounded sepals and 2 or 3 long leaf-like sepals that make up the calyx.
2. Knead a pea-size ball of green paste. Insert a green 28-gauge florist's wire into the ball. Taper the sides of the paste down the wire, to create a teardrop. Flatten the paste and pinch the tips together slightly at the top, to create a point.
3. Knead a small ball of green paste. Insert a green 28-gauge florist's wire, into the ball. Roll the paste down the wire to create a slender sausage shape with pointed ends. Flatten the shape with the petal veiner. Soften the edges with a ball tool and pinch the shape together from the base to the top, creating a central vein.
4. Dust each of the sepals with vine-green dusting colour. You may steam the sepals to give them a shine.

Assembly

1. Use half-width florist's tapes to secure the sepals to the base of the peony, alternating the round sepals with the leaf-like sepals.

Leaves

1. Make 3 large and 3 small peony leaves out of green gumpaste, using either the peony leaf template on page 150 or metal peony leaf cutters.
2. Dust the leaves with green-bean dusting colour. Apply an aubergine or plum dusting colour at the base of the leaf, fading out toward the edges of the leaf. If you want to give the leaves a shine, you can steam them or dip them into confectioner's glaze.

Assembly

1. Attach a small leaf next to a large leaf, overlapping slightly, and tape the 2 leaves together with ½-inch (1 cm) florist's tape, creating a double leaf.

2. Repeat with the remaining leaves. Position the 3 double leaves around the tree peony and tape them together with ½-inch (1 cm) florist's tape.

BUTTERFLIES

1. Roll a small amount of white gumpaste until thin.
2. Using butterfly cutters as shown in the photo, cut out 2 butterfly shapes.
3. Leave to dry on folded cardboard, as shown in the photo.
4. Using an airbrush, spray the butterflies with gold colour.
5. Roll half a pea-size amount of yellow gumpaste into a teardrop and elongate slightly.
6. Insert a 28-gauge wire into the teardrop shape.
7. Using gum glue, attach a butterfly to the surface of a teardrop. Repeat with the second butterfly.
8. Leave to dry overnight. When dried, tape the butterflies to the peony, opposite each other with ½-inch (1 cm) green florist's tape.

FINAL ASSEMBLY

1. Being careful not to touch the stringwork, place the 12-inch (30 cm) oval cake on the pre-covered cakeboard. Attach to the cakeboard with a little Royal Icing.
2. Insert dowels into the 12-inch (30 cm) oval cake (see page 28 for How to Stack a Tiered Cake).
3. Centre the 8-inch (20 cm) oval cake on top of the 8-inch (20 cm) oval cake. Attach with Royal Icing.
4. Insert dowels into the 8-inch (20 cm) oval cake.
5. Centre the 4-inch (10 cm) round cake on the 8-inch (20 cm) oval cake. Attach with Royal Icing.
6. Attach a ¼-inch (6 mm) wide gold ribbon on the bottom of each of the oval cakes with gum glue.
7. Using the bead border technique on page 37, pipe a bead border around the base of the 4-inch (10 cm) round cake with yellow Royal Icing.
8. To attach the dragon, carp, rocks and waves, pipe a small amount of Royal Icing on the oval cakeboard where you will set each figure. Carefully set each figure in place as shown in the photo.
9. Place the peony with the butterflies attached on top of the 4-inch (10 cm) round cake.

Above: Folded cardboard for shaping the butterflies;
Below: A finished butterfly

BLUE AND RED

SOUTHEAST ASIA

SOUTHEAST ASIA consists of the countries south of China, east of India, west of New Guinea and north of Australia. In this book, I have chosen to feature Malaysia and Singapore.

*The national flower of Malaysia is the red hibiscus (*bunga raya*). Red colour represents courage, while the five petals symbolize* rukun negara *(Malaysia's Five Principles of Nationhood).*

Singapore's national flower is the orchid known as Vanda, Miss Joaquim. The ability of this flower to bloom throughout the year is believed to symbolize Singapore's continuous quest for progress and prosperity. The flower's natural resilience reflects the determination of Singaporean people to succeed despite tough times.

This is an exquisite 3-tiered cake depicting the flowers of both nations.

LEVEL OF DIFFICULTY moderate skills

TECHNIQUES USED painting on cake, gumpaste flowers and leaves

CAKES AND EDIBLES

- about 8 lb (3.5 kg) marbleized blue fondant (page 27)
- Dusting Colours rose red or poppy, yellow and green bean
- white Royal Icing (page 20)
- gum glue
- yellow gumpaste

TOOLS AND EQUIPMENT

- 26, 24 and 28 gauge florist's wires
- fine yellow head stamens
- hibiscus petal cutter
- hibiscus leaf cutter
- hibiscus petal veiner
- leaf veiner
- vanda orchid cutter set
- rose calyx cutter
- small daisy cutter
- piping bag
- lemon extract
- Gel Paste red, yellow, green, magenta, light and dark purple
- metal ball tool
- foam pads
- gumpaste tools
- brushes
- Dresden tool
- scriber
- silk veining tool

TEMPLATE

- Hibiscus (page 152)
- Hibiscus Leaves (page 153)

CAKE PREPARATION

See pages 25–28 for stacking and fondant-covering techniques.

1. Cover the 14-inch (35 cm) round cakeboard with the marbleized fondant.
2. Cover the 5-inch (12 cm) round cake with the marbleized fondant.
3. Cover a 6-inch (15 cm) round cake with marbleized fondant. You may have to bake 2 cakes to obtain the 6-inch (15 cm) height.
4. Insert dowels into the 6-inch (15 cm) round cake.
5. Cover a 8-inch (20 cm) round cake with marbleized fondant. You may have to bake 2 cakes to obtain the 6-inch (15 cm) height.

Left: The painted hibiscus, as shown on the cake; Right: A completed gumpaste hibiscus

6. Insert dowels into the 8-inch (20 cm) round cakes.
7. Centre the 5-inch (12 cm) round cake on top of the 6-inch (15 cm) round cake and attach both tiers together with Royal Icing.
8. Centre these 2 tiers on top of the 8-inch (20 cm) round cake and attach the cakes together with a small amount of Royal Icing.
9. All 3 tiers should be positioned in the centre but toward the back of the 14-inch (35 cm) round board. Attach the cakes to the board with a small amount of Royal Icing.

PAINTED HIBISCUS

See pages 32–35 for flower-making techniques.

1. Transfer the design of the hibiscus template onto the cakes, using the scriber method as seen on page 43.
2. It is best to transfer the design onto the cakes first before joining them together with Royal Icing.
3. Use lemon extract to dilute the gel paste colours. Alternatively, you can use airbrush colours to paint the template design on the cakes. Squires Kitchen (UK) provides an excellent choice of edible paint colours for painting on cakes.
4. Pipe a bead border, as described on page 37, around the base of each of the cakes, using white Royal Icing.

GUMPASTE HIBISCUS FLOWER AND LEAVES

See pages 32–35 for flower-making techniques. To create the project, you will need to make 3 full hibiscus flowers.

Stamens and Pistil

1. Tape 5 small white stamens to a white 24-gauge florist's wire with half-width florist's tape.
2. Paint the stamens with red petal dust and allow to dry.
3. Knead a small amount of yellow gumpaste and thread it through the wire so that the gumpaste is just below the red stamens.

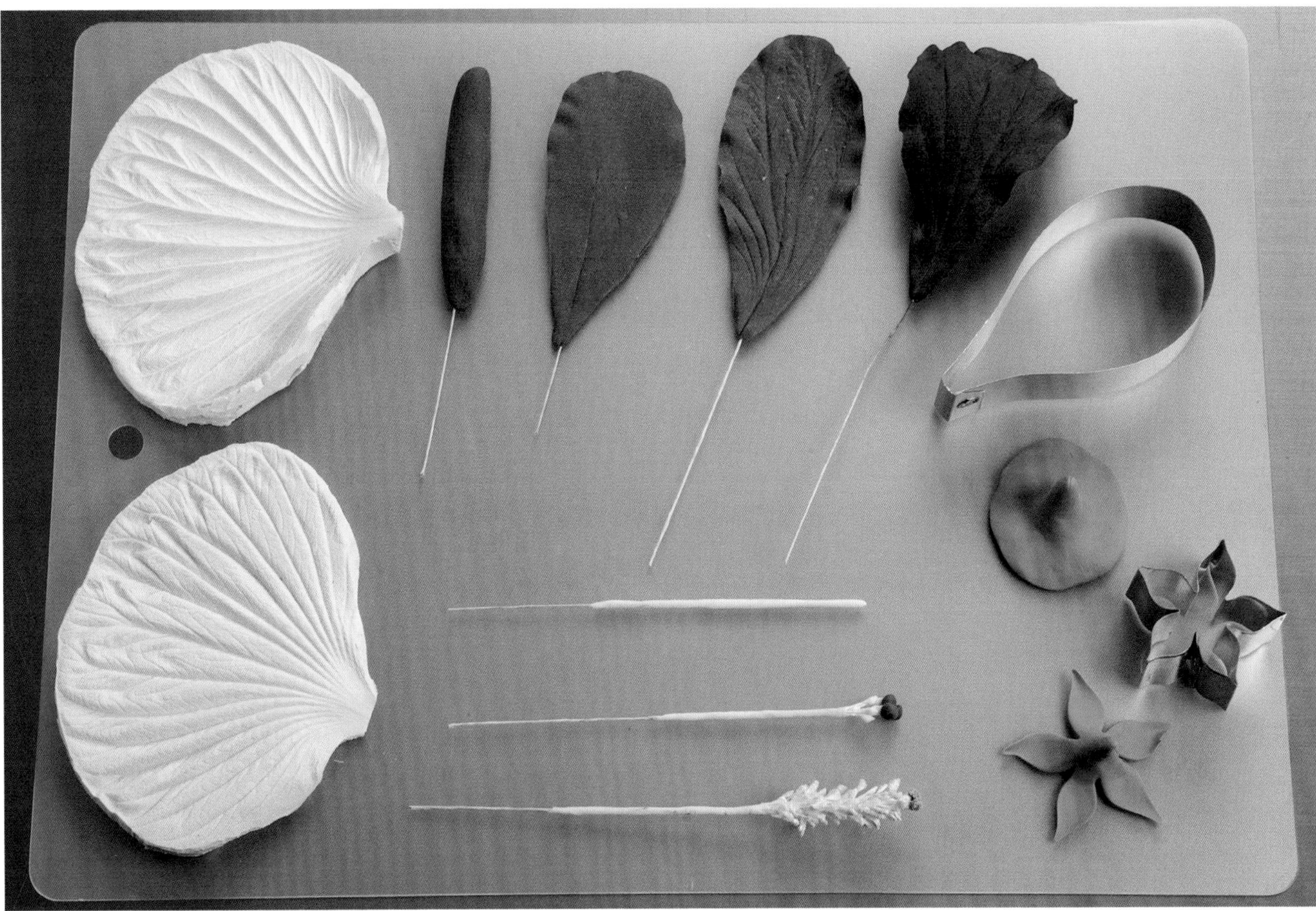

Pieces for creating the hibiscus flowers

4. Work the gumpaste down the wire to form a very slim pistil. The length should measure at least the length of 1 of the main petals, or slightly longer. Bend the wire to a curved shape.
5. Cut some fine yellow stamens very short, and insert these onto the top part of the pistil about ¾-inch (2 cm) down from the red stamens. Then apply a little gum glue to the top of the stamens and dip them into yellow-coloured cornmeal, to resemble the pollen effect.

Petals

1. Knead a small amount of red gumpaste and make 5 petals for each Hibiscus flower. In total, you will need 15 petals for 3 flowers, but always make 1 or 2 extra to allow for breakage.
2. Dry the petals on flower formers, to create a gentle curve.
3. When dry, dust the petals with red dusting colour. Dust a little yellow dusting colour at the base of each petal.
4. Steam the petals, to give them a shiny look.
5. Tape the petals around the stamens with half-width green florist's tape, overlapping them slightly.

Calyx

The hibiscus has a double calyx.

1. Roll out some green gumpaste thinly on a non-stick mat. Cut out the calyx, using a rose calyx cutter. Widen and soften the edges of each sepal with a ball tool, and draw a central vein down each sepal with the pointed end of the Dresden tool.
2. Apply gum glue to the calyx, and thread it up the wire to fit underneath the petals.
3. Cut another calyx, using the small daisy cutter. Soften the edges of each of the sepals with a ball tool. Attach the second calyx underneath the first and curl it back slightly.

4. Dust the calyx with green dusting colour.

Leaves

1. Knead a small amount of green gumpaste and make 15 leaves, using the small and large leaf templates on page 153 or metal leaf cutters.
2. Vein the leaf using the leaf veiner and pinch the leaves slightly to accentuate the central vein.
3. Leave to dry on foil.
4. Dust with green dusting colour when dry. Add a little plum dusting colour to the edges of each of the leaves.
5. Steam the leaf, to give it a shine.

VANDA MISS JOAQUIM ORCHID

Column

This part of the orchid, located just above the throat, contains the flower's reproductive organs.

1. Roll a half-pea-size amount of white gumpaste into a teardrop. The gumpaste teardrop should be no longer than the section of the pointed base of the throat cutter in the orchid cutter, set to the start of the 2 side sections of the petal.
2. Hollow out the underside of the column with the Dresden tool.
3. Pinch a very subtle ridge on the back of the column.
4. Roll a tiny piece of sugarpaste into a ball, and tuck it under the hollow part of the column. Use a knife to create 2 sections on the ball, forming the anther cap of the orchid.
5. Bend a 22-gauge wire into a ski pole shape, as shown in the photo. Dip the wire into gum glue and push it into the other side of the hollow part of the column. Pinch the column from behind, to hold the wire in place. Add a tiny piece of white gumpaste underneath the column.

Throat

The inner portion of a tubular orchid lip, called the "throat," is often quite colourful.

1. Roll out a small amount of white gumpaste thinly, leaving the centre part slightly thicker. Use the throat cutter to cut out the throat.

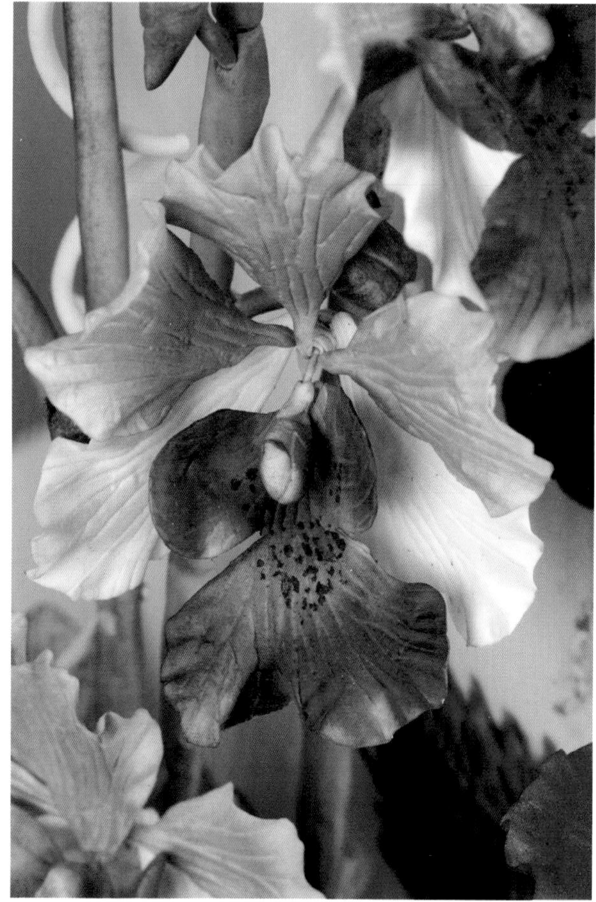

A completed orchid

2. Vein the throat with the hibiscus petal veiner.
3. Using the veining tool, frill the throat slightly, either on the pad or on your finger.
4. Pinch the petal down the centre, to create a subtle ridge. Using tweezers, pinch 2 small ridges at the base of the throat.
5. Place the petal on the pad and slightly cup the 2 small side petals.
6. Apply some gum glue to the base of the throat and position the column at the base, with the pointed end of the column on the end part of the throat.
7. Wrap the base of the throat over the column.
8. Curl back slightly the edges of the 2 side petals of the throat, and leave, to dry.
9. Dust the base of the throat very lightly with a little vine green. Then mix some light purple and yellow together, to dust the inside of the throat. Add depth by dusting some dark purple on the edges of the throat. Dust some yellow on the pointed end of the throat.

Pieces for creating the orchids

10. Add some fine dots of dark purple dust, diluted with lemon extract, to the lip area of the throat. Try to paint a few very fine dark purple lines on the 2 side petals of the throat.

Orchid Petals

This orchid consists of 2 wing petals, 1 dorsal sepal and 2 lateral sepals. These petals are all cut from the petal-shaped cutters pictured above.

Lateral Petals

1. Roll and knead a small amount of white gumpaste into a sausage.
2. Cut a white 28-gauge florist's wire into 3 sections. Dip the end of each wire into gum glue and insert into the sausage.
3. Roll the paste thinly on both sides of the sausage, leaving a thicker ridge at the centre where the wire sits.
4. Cut out the wing petal. Pinch the gumpaste at the base down onto the wire.
5. Place the petal onto a form and soften the edges with a ball tool.
6. Vein the petal, using the hibiscus petal veiner, and frill the petals with the silk veining tool.
7. Repeat the above to make the other petal.
8. Dust the wing petals with light purple and then with dark purple, fading toward the outer edge of the petal.

Dorsal and Lateral Sepals

1. Roll out and cut out the 3 lateral sepal shapes the same way as the wing petals.
2. Allow to dry slightly before taping them behind the wing petals.
3. Dust the dorsal petal with light purple and then with dark purple, fading toward the outer edge of the petal.
4. Dust the lateral sepals with a tiny hint of dark purple toward the base of the petal.

Assembly

1. Tape the 2 wing petals to the throat with half-width florist's tape.
2. Tape the dorsal and the lateral petals with half-width florist's tape.
3. Paint some dots just above the lip of the throat with magenta colour diluted with lemon extract.
4. Attach all the petals together as shown in the photo.
5. Repeat the steps above to make an additional 5 orchids, making a total of 7 orchids for this project.

ORCHID BUDS, STEMS AND ROOTS

Buds

The buds of the orchid are an odd shape.

1. Roll a pea-size ball of green gumpaste into a small teardrop, and insert a 26-gauge florist's wire dipped into gum glue. Taper some green gumpaste down the wire.
2. Pinch out 2 pointed ends on the broad top of each teardrop. Curl in the pointed end of the teardrop slightly.
3. Divide the surface of the bud, as shown, with a cutter wheel or, scalpel, to create 2 curved petal shapes. Repeat to make about 3 to 5 buds of different sizes.
4. Dust with vine green for the small buds. For the larger buds, dust some yellow and magenta onto the edges.

Stems and Roots

1. To make the stems, roll a ball of green gumpaste and insert into a green 26-gauge wire. Work the gumpaste down the wire, to create a thin sausage.
2. Mark some lines at different intervals along the wire.
3. Using a scriber or a hook tool, press an indent into the line, to create a hollow area into which to insert the flowers and buds. Make a few of these stems in various lengths.
4. To create roots, put some white sugarpaste into an extruder with a small round-hole disc. Attach the roots to the main stem with gum glue.

FINAL ASSEMBLY

1. Attach the buds with gum glue to the top of the stems where the indentation has been made.
2. Attach the orchids to the stem with gum glue at various heights where the indentation has been made.
3. Tape 2 of the hibiscus flowers with leaves together at varying heights to form the spray at the top of the cake. Rafia-covered wires are bent into scroll-like shapes and loops, as decorative fillers for the spray.
4. Tape and wire 3 of the orchids together onto an 18-gauge green florist's wire.
5. For the bottom spray, take a golf-ball size amount of green gumpaste, flatten slightly and place it to one side of the cakeboard, next to the bottom cake tier, to create a mound. Attach it to the cakeboard with a small amount of Royal Icing.
6. Insert the orchid stems into the mound with the roots.
7. Arrange 1 of the hibiscus flowers next to the orchid stems. Place the spray of orchids in front of the hibiscus on the board.
8. Camouflage or hide the mound with the hibiscus leaves.

CHARM AND POWER
INDONESIA

INDONESIA'S NATIONAL SYMBOL is the Garuda, a divine creature traditionally portrayed with bird-like and human features. The Garuda symbolizes knowledge, power, bravery, loyalty and discipline. The moth orchid, known as the flower of charm, is one of Indonesia's national flowers.

LEVEL OF DIFFICULTY moderate skills

TECHNIQUES USED modelling chocolate and gumpaste flowers

CAKES AND EDIBLES

- 5½ lb (2.35 kg) chocolate fondant
- 2 lb (900 g) white modelling chocolate
- Airbrush Colours black and white
- Dusting Colours yellow, pearl and magenta
- gum glue
- white Royal Icing (page 20)
- lemon extract

TOOLS AND EQUIPMENT

- 26 and 24 gauge florist's wires
- moth orchid cutter set
- piping bag
- metal ball tool
- Dresden tool
- foam pads
- gumpaste tools
- brushes
- cutting wheel

TEMPLATE

- Moth Orchid Petal (page 54)

CAKE PREPARATION

See pages 25–27 for instructions on how to cover a cake and cakeboard with fondant.

1. Cover a 12-inch (30 cm) board with chocolate fondant. Using the pointed end of a paintbrush, indent lines onto the surface of the cakeboard to create a ridged effect. Repeat the steps around the cakeboard.
2. Cover a 8-inch (20 cm) round cake with marbleized chocolate fondant. You may have to bake 2 cakes to obtain the 6-inch (15 cm) height.

GARUDA

The Garuda figurine is moulded freehand from white modelling chocolate. See all the pieces in the photo on page 74.

Garuda Head

1. Knead about 8 oz (235 g) of modelling chocolate into a ball.
2. Use a ball tool to create an indentation for the eyes. Pinch the nose area and elongate the paste to form the beak.
3. Using your thumb, press and indent an opening in the mouth area and enlarge it to resemble that of the photo. Roll small balls of modelling chocolate into teardrop shapes. Attach them to the upper and lower parts of the mouth, to resemble teeth.

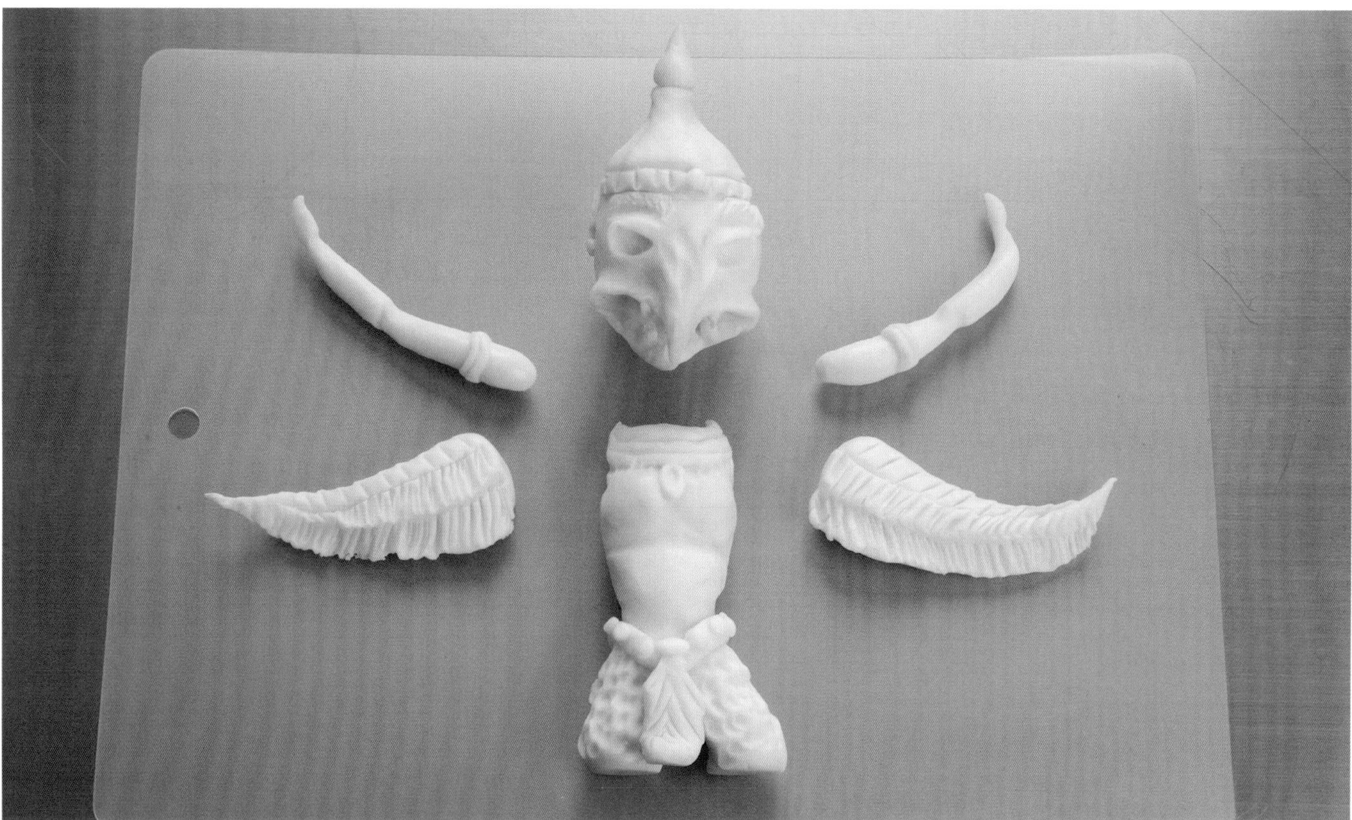

Individual pieces for forming the Garuda

4. Roll 2 half-pea-size balls of modelling chocolate into a teardrop, flatten them and shape them into ears. Indent lines onto the ear with the sharp side of the Dresden tool.
5. For the hat, roll a 2 oz (60 g) piece of modelling chocolate into a teardrop. Elongate the narrow part of the teardrop and shape it as shown in the photo. Using your thumb, slightly hollow out the bottom part of the teardrop so that it resembles a hat.
6. Add a small piece of modelling chocolate to the bottom of the head, to sculpt the neck area.

Garuda Body

7. Knead a 8 oz (235 g) ball of modelling chocolate into a sausage. Flatten the sausage slightly and elongate to about 6-inch (15 cm) long.
8. Indent the stomach area about one-third of the way down the sausage. Build up the chest area with your thumbs by pushing the paste upwards from the stomach area.
9. Indent and narrow the paste where the waist starts, about two-thirds of the way down the paste.
10. Where the legs begin, cut the paste into 2 even sections with a pair of scissors, to resemble legs.
11. Indent the legs with the wide end of the Dresden tool, to create a scale-like effect.
12. Roll a thin strip of paste, flatten it slightly and attach it to the waist area in a V-shape, to resemble the belt. Attach small flat round dots to the belt, as shown.
13. Cut a small leaf-like shape and mark lines on it with the pointed end of the Dresden tool. Attach the leaf to the centre of the belt.
14. Roll narrow strips of modelling chocolate of varying widths to form the necklace in the neck area. Knead a tiny oval shape to attach to the necklace as a medallion.
15. Insert a wooden skewer halfway down the body, with a bit of the skewer protruding from the neck area. Leave to dry for an hour.

Wings

1. Knead 168 g (6 oz) of gumpaste into a sausage.

Pieces for creating the moth orchid

2. Flatten and roll out to about ¼-inch (6 mm) thick.
3. Cut out the wing pattern. If you have a wing or leaf cutter that is the correct size, you can also use that.
4. Indent the design of the wing by pressing down on the gumpaste with the pointed end of the Dresden tool.
5. Repeat steps 1 to 4 for the second wing.

Arms

1. Roll about 3 oz (90 g) of gumpaste into a long sausage, rounding off 1 end for the hand.
2. Press down on the hand to flatten it slightly. Make a cut for the thumb, and 3 shorter cuts across the top to create separate fingers.
3. Smooth the surface gently, to remove ridges and to bend the fingers. Push down the thumb toward the palm, for a more natural look.
4. Bend the hand slightly upwards, as per the photo on the left.
5. Repeat steps 1 to 3 for the other arm.

MOTH ORCHID

For this project, you will need to make a total of 5 flowers: 2 for one spray and 3 for another spray. You will also need to make 4 buds.

Throat and Lip

1. Roll out a small amount of white gumpaste, leaving a thick ridge in the centre for the wire. Cut out the labellum, or lip shape, with the throat cutter. Insert a white 24-gauge florist's wire into the thick ridge of the throat.
2. Use tweezers to pinch some ridges at the back of the throat.
3. Transfer the throat to a foam pad. Soften, elongate, and broaden the 2 rounded side sections. Use a veining tool to vein and to shape the 2 rounded sides, to achieve a more oval shape.
4. Cup the 2 oval shapes.
5. The tip of the throat may be left pointed; or you may cut some slits on both sides. If slits are cut, try to curl them back toward the throat.

6. Roll a small piece of yellow gumpaste into a ball and attach it to the centre of the throat. Use a scalpel to make a cut in the ball, dividing it into 2 sections.
7. Dust the centre of the throat with a little bit of yellow. Dust the 2 oval-shaped petals and the lip with magenta dusting colour.
8. Paint some fine lines on to the oval shapes and dots onto the labellum, using magenta colour diluted with lemon extract.

Column

1. Bend a hook on the end of a white 26-gauge florist's wire. Roll a piece of white gumpaste in to a cone shape and hollow out the bottom. Insert the hooked wire into the back of the column. Curve the column to the required shape.
2. Roll a tiny ball of gumpaste and attach it to the tip of the column on the hollow side.

Petals and Sepals

1. Roll and knead a small amount of white gumpaste. Make 3 sepals and 2 side petals for each orchid, using either the template on page 154 or the metal moth orchid cutters.
2. Place the shape onto a form and soften the edges with a ball tool.
3. Vein the petal with the hibiscus veiner.

Buds

1. Make a hook at the end of a 24-gauge wire. Roll a small piece of white sugarpaste in to a blunt teardrop or a cone.
2. Dip wire into gum glue and insert into the teardrop on the broad side. Pinch 1 end of the bud to a sharp point.
3. Mark the bud with the cutting wheel, to indicate unopened petals.
4. Dust the buds with lime-green and holly-ivy. Some of the buds may be left white.

Orchid Assembly

1. Tape the 2 side wing petals opposite each other with ½-inch (1 cm) width green florist's tape.
2. Tape the throat in the centre, between the 2 side wing petals, with ½-inch (1 cm) width florist's tape.
3. Tape the dorsal and lateral sepals to the back of the wing petals with ½-inch (1 cm) width green florist's tape.
4. Tape the buds and 3 flowers together to form a spray for the top of the cake, as shown in photo.
5. Tape the balancing 2 orchids into a spray with ½-inch (1 cm) width green florist's tape.

FINAL ASSEMBLY

1. Attach the Garuda body to the cake with a small amount of Royal Icing.
2. Attach the Garuda head to the body by pushing it into the wooden skewer that is protrudes from the body.
3. Attach the wings to the Garuda body with a small amount of Royal Icing.
4. Attach the arms on top of the wings.
5. Insert flower spike on top of the cake where the arm of the Garuda is attached.
6. Place the orchid spray with 3 blooms on the flower spike
7. Arrange the orchid spray with 2 blooms next to the legs of the Garuda on the cakeboard.

A SHOWER OF GOLD

THAILAND

THAILAND HAS BEEN culturally influenced by many other countries: India, Laos, Burma, Cambodia and China, to name a few. Thai temples are known as wats. *Usually resplendent with gold, they are easily identified by their ornate, multi-coloured, pointy roofs. The golden shower tree* (cassia fistula) *is the official flower of Thailand, and is locally known as* ratchaphruek. *It symbolizes dignity, with its vibrant yellow petals representing Buddhism, prosperity and national unity.*

LEVEL OF DIFFICULTY advanced skills

TECHNIQUES USED modelling, gumpaste flowers, pattern transfer and piping

CAKES AND EDIBLES

- about 5 lb (2.2 kg) red fondant
- about 3 lb (1.4 kg) yellow fondant
- about 2 lb (900 g) yellow gumpaste
- Dusting Colours gold, yellow and brown
- black Royal Icing (page 20)
- gum glue

TOOLS AND EQUIPMENT

- 26, 28 and 24 gauge florist's wires
- piping bag
- piping tip 1.5
- gold dragees
- large acanthus leaf mould
- medium size rose calyx cutter
- metal ball tool
- Dresden tool
- foam pads
- gumpaste tools
- brushes
- golden shower cutter
- cutting wheel
- scriber
- silk veining tool

TEMPLATES

- Cassia Fistula (page 155)
- Thai Figurine (page 155)

CAKE PREPARATION

See pages 25–27 for instructions on how to cover a cake and cakeboard with fondant.

1. Cover a 14-inch (35 cm) round cakeboard with yellow fondant. Airbrush with gold.
2. Cover an 8-inch (20 cm) round cake with red fondant. You may have to bake 2 cakes to obtain the 6-inch (15 cm) height.
3. Bake a 6-inch (15 cm) hexagon cake in a hexagon cake pan. Cover the cake with yellow fondant. Airbrush with gold.
4. Cover a 5-inch (12 cm) round cake with red fondant. Ensure that the cake is 5-inch (12 cm) high. You may have to bake 2 cakes to obtain the 5-inch (12 cm) height.

ACANTHUS LEAVES

You will need about 150 acanthus leaves altogether for this project. This mould is available for purchase from the list of suppliers on page 165.

1. Grease the acanthus leaf mould with vegetable spray.

Left: Using the mould to make acanthus leaves; Right: The scriber method is used to make the Thai figures

2. Put a small amount of yellow gumpaste into the mould and press the 2 sides of the mould together. Cut the excess gumpaste from the mould.
3. Remove the leaf carefully from the mould.
4. Leave to dry in flower formers to create a curved shape.
5. When the leaves are dry, airbrush with gold. Leave to fully dry for a few hours and then set aside until you are ready to apply the leaves to the cake tiers.

Bottom Tier

You will need about 104 acanthus leaves for this tier.

1. Take a piece of acanthus leaf and pipe a small amount of Royal Icing to attach to the cake. The pointed part of the leaf should bend outwards, as shown in the photo. Start attaching the lower layer of leaves first. The right side of the leaves should face upwards.
2. Attach the second layer of leaves in between the first and second layers using Royal Icing.
3. Continue in the same manner with the third and fourth layers.
4. When the leaves have dried overnight, fill a piping bag with tip 1.5 with yellow Royal Icing.
5. Pipe a dot of yellow Royal Icing at the tip of each leaf and attach a golden dragee on it using a pair of tweezers. Do the same on all the leaves until done.
6. Fill another piping bag with tip 1.5 with black Royal Icing. The Royal Icing should be rubbed down.
7. Pipe a small loop at each end of the leaf tip around the dragee, until all are done.

Middle Tier

You will need about 18 acanthus leaves for this tier.

1. For this tier, you will need to attach 2 leaves for each panel of the cake, with a leaf in between each panel, as shown in the photo.
2. To attach the leaves and dragees, follow steps 1 to 5, as above (for bottom tier).
3. Using tip number 1.5 and black Royal Icing, pipe 2 layers of drop string, connecting the tips of 2 leaves at each panel. Repeat this step for the other panels.

4. For the single leaf in between each panel, use tip number 1.5 to pipe a small loop at the tip of each leaf in between the dragees.

TOP TIER THAI FIGURE AND PAGODA

Thai Figure

1. Trace the Thai figure template (on page 155) onto parchment paper.
2. Attach the parchment paper to the side of the top tier with pins.
3. Using a scriber, prick the outline of the Thai figure onto the surface of the cake. Remove the parchment paper.
4. Fill a piping bag fitted with a number 1.5 tip with black Royal Icing. Pipe the design, following the marks on the cake. Airbrush very lightly with gold.

Pagoda Top

1. Knead and mould about 15 oz (450 g) of yellow gumpaste into a round mound with a 6-inch (15 cm) base and a height of 2 inches (5 cm). Flatten the top slightly.
2. Use about 10 oz (300 g) of yellow gumpaste to mould another round mound with a 4-inch (10 cm) base and a height of 2 inches (5 cm). Fatten the top slightly, as above.
3. Using gum glue, stack both mounds together on top of each other, with the smaller one on top. Blend in the joints slightly with a little bit of water so that they are not too conspicuous.
4. Make a set of 8 rings with yellow gumpaste. Flatten each ring slightly and stack them together with gum glue, with the smallest ring on top, to form a cone shape.
5. Take a pea-size amount of yellow gumpaste and knead it into a ball and then into a teardrop. Elongate the tail of the teardrop slightly and attach with gum glue on top of the smallest ring.
6. Attach the set of rings to the centre of the 2 stacked mounds. Leave to dry overnight.
7. Fill a piping bag with tip 1.5 with yellow Royal Icing. Pipe dots on the outer sides of each of the rings and attach a gold dragee to each dot.

Above: The completed Pagoda top; Below: The completed golden shower flower

8. On each of the mounds, attach the pre-made curved acanthus leaves to the sides of each of the mounds with a small amount of Royal Icing.

The pieces for creating the golden shower flower

9. Pipe yellow Royal Icing dots onto the lower part of each of the acanthus leaves and attach a gold dragee to it.
10. Airbrush with gold and allow to dry for at least 24 hours.

GOLDEN SHOWER FLOWER

Petals

You will need to make a spray of 3 flowers for this project. See pages 32–35 for techniques on making flowers.

1. Make 5 petals with yellow gumpaste. Use the cutter template on page 155 for each flower.
2. Vein the petal with the hibiscus veiner.
3. Dust the petals with yellow dusting colour.

Stamens

You will need 5 short stamens, about 3 inches (8 cm) long, and 4 long curled stamens, about 5 inches (12 cm) long.

1. Cut the 28-gauge wire into 4 sections. Make a hook at the end of the wire. Insert a small ball of yellow gumpaste to the top of the wire and work the paste down to cover the wire.
2. Knead and roll a small piece of yellow gumpaste in to a teardrop shape. Hollow out 1 piece of the teardrop with a silk veining tool.
3. With a cutting wheel, cut a small slit on the other side of the teardrop.
4. Insert the hook end of the wire into the hollow side of the teardrop.
5. Repeat the steps above to make another teardrop for the other end of the wire.
6. Dust with yellow dusting colour, with a hint of brown at the pointed end.
7. Make 5 of these stamens, of various lengths. Fold each of them in half and tape the 5 sets of stamens together with ½-inch (1 cm) width green florist's tape. Make an additional 2 sets of stamens.
8. Repeat steps 1 to 5 to make 3 longer stamens, of about 5 inches (12 cm) in length. Curl these slightly inward.

9. Take another small piece of green gumpaste and insert a 28-gauge wire that has been cut into 3 sections. Work the paste down the wire to create a long, thin sausage, about 6 inches (15 cm) long. Curl this slightly inward as well. Dust with pale green dusting colour.

Calyx

1. Knead and roll a pea-size amount of green gumpaste into a ball. Using the Mexican hat technique on page 32, make the calyx with the medium-size rose calyx cutter.
2. Repeat the steps above to make an additional 2 calyxes. You will need a calyx for each bundle of short stamens.
3. Hollow the calyx slightly with the pointed end of the silk veining tool.
4. Apply some gum glue in the hollow part of the calyx and insert the bundle of short stamens into it.

Assembly

1. Tape together the 3 long curled stamens with the green stamen in the centre, using ½-inch (1 cm) width florist's tape.
2. Tape the long curled stamens underneath the bundle of short stamens with ½-inch (1 cm) width green florist's tape.
3. Tape the 5 yellow petals around the stamens in an orchid formation.
4. Use full-width green florist's tape to create a posy shape 3 with the sets of flowers.

FINAL ASSEMBLY

1. Using the stacked cake technique on page 28, stack the 3 cake tiers on the pre-covered cakeboard with a small amount of Royal Icing. Ensure that each tier is dowelled.
2. Attach the pagoda top to the 5-inch (12 cm) cake tier with Royal Icing.
3. Place the spray of golden shower flowers next to the cake.

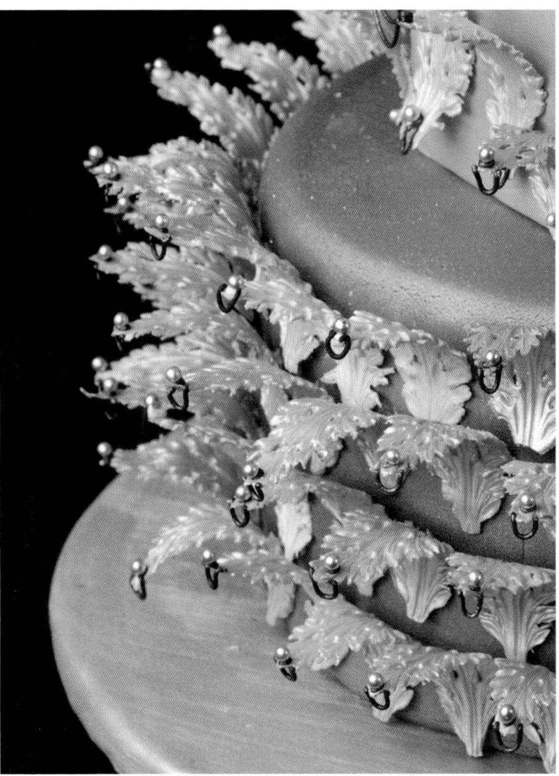

Above: The acanthus leaves, as shown on the bottom tier of the project; Below: The piped Thai figures in place on the finished cake

FOREVER JASMINE

THE PHILIPPINES

(JASMINE) SAMPAGUITA IS the national flower of the Philippines. Used in tea and religious offerings, this flower symbolizes hope. There are several species of jasmine—some with single petals and some with double petals, some more frilly than others.

This cake's intricately patterned tiers reflect the famous Philippine art of smocking, in which tiny pleats are decorated with embroidery.

LEVEL OF DIFFICULTY moderate skills

TECHNIQUES USED gumpaste puffs, gumpaste flowers, gumpaste bow and smocking

CAKES AND EDIBLES

- about 8 lb (3.5 kg) white fondant
- about 2 lb (900 g) pink gumpaste
- about 1 lb (450 g) white gumpaste
- Dusting Colours yellow and green
- white Royal Icing (page 20)
- confectioner's glaze (optional, to create shine)
- gum glue

TOOLS AND EQUIPMENT

- 26 and 24 gauge green florist's wires
- small fine white head stamens
- small rose calyx
- piping bag
- tips 1, 1.5 and 2
- metal ball tool
- Dresden tool
- pearl dragees
- foam pads
- leaf cutter
- leaf veiner
- grooved rolling pin
- plastic tweezers
- gumpaste tools
- brushes
- pizza cutter
- pleated puff mould
- silk veining tool

TEMPLATES

- Jasmine Petal and Calyx (page 156)

CAKE PREPARATION

See pages 25–27 for instructions on how to cover a cake and cakeboard with fondant.

1. Cover a 14-inch (35 cm) cakeboard with white fondant.
2. Cover a 8-inch (20 cm) round cake with red fondant. You may have to bake 2 cakes to obtain the 6-inch (15 cm) height.
3. Cover a 6-inch (15 cm) round (with a height of 5 inches [12 cm]) and a 4-inch (10 cm) round (with a height of 4-inch [10 cm]) cake with white fondant.

BOTTOM TIER

Using the plastic pleated puff mould, which can be purchased from the list of suppliers on page 165, make about 30 large, 30 medium and 40 small pleated puffs.

1. Attach the 8-inch (20 cm) round cake to the pre-covered cakeboard with a small amount of Royal Icing.
2. Dowel the cake. (See How to Stack a Cake on page 28.)

Above: The completed pleated puffs; Right: The smocking for the middle tier shown with black icing

3. Grease the pleated puff mould well with vegetable spray. Wipe off excess oil with a piece of paper towel.
4. Roll a small ball of pink gumpaste and insert into the large puff mould. Use the fingers to ease the gumpaste into the sides of the mould.
5. Cut off any excess gumpaste. Remove the puff from the mould and leave to dry for about an hour. Repeat until all puffs are made.
6. When the puffs are semi-dried, attach the large puff first to the sides of the 8-inch (20 cm) cake. The puffs should start at the cakeboard. Continue all around the cake.
7. Repeat step 6 on top of the first row of puffs, ensuring that the second row of puffs is staggered in relation to the bottom row.
8. Continue building up the sides of the 8-inch (20 cm) tier with 2 rows of large puffs, 2 rows of medium puffs, and 2 rows of small puffs, ending with the smallest row of puffs on top.
9. Roll pea-size amounts of pink fondant into tiny balls and flatten them slightly. Attach these balls in between each row of puffs with a small amount of Royal Icing.
10. Pipe a small dot of Royal Icing in the centre of each of the flattened balls with a tip 1, and attach a pearl dragee to it.
11. Pipe a row of bead border above the smallest row of puffs. (See also page 37.)

MIDDLE TIER

See page 28 for instructions on how to stack a tiered cake.

1. Stack the middle cake tier on the bottom tier and attach with Royal Icing. Remember to dowel the cake tier after stacking.
2. To create a template for the smocking, take a piece of parchment paper about 18 inches (45 cm) long and fold it to a width of 5 inches (12 cm).
3. Wrap the parchment paper around the sides of the 5-inch (12 cm) cake and cut to the exact length. Cut the template into 3 sections, each section longer than the length of the grooved roller.

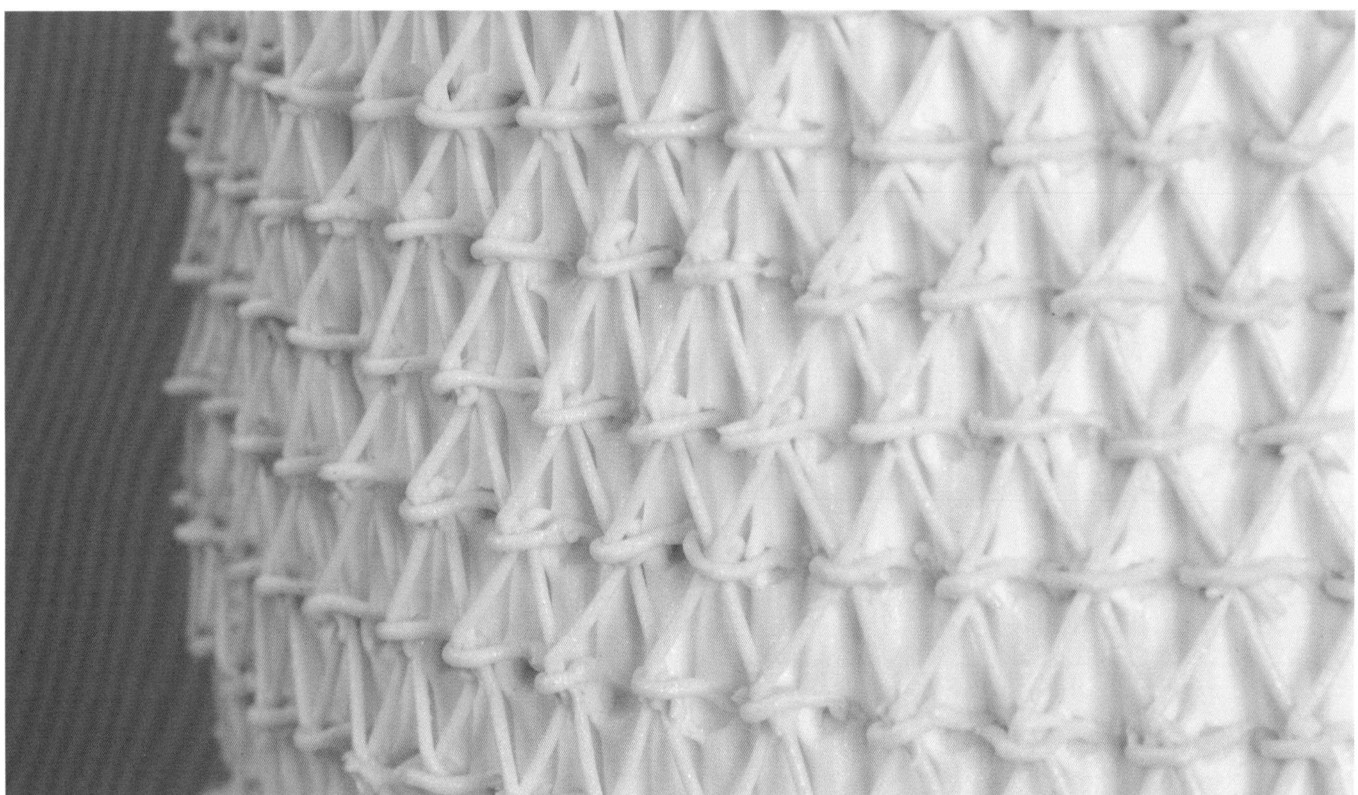

The completed smocking on the middle tier

4. Roll out a piece of white gumpaste to approximately ⅛-inch (3 mm) thick, and larger than a section of the cut template.
5. To create a smocking surface, use the grooved rolling pin to roll over the gumpaste template, as shown in the top right photo on the previous page. Place the parchment template over the rolled surface and cut to exact size with a pizza cutter.
6. Using the plastic tweezers, create the smocking pattern by gently pinching together the pair of ridges or pleats as shown on the previous page.
7. Brush the panel with water and attach to the side of the 5-inch (13 cm) cake. The panel should fit perfectly.
8. Repeat the process until the sides of the cake are covered.
9. Pipe the embroidery stitches with tip 1.5 and pink Royal Icing that has been rubbed down. Pipe lines with tip 1.5, from the centre of each pinched pleat on the first row down to the pinched pleats on the second row. Pipe a second row of short horizontal stitches over the ends of the previous row. Pipe more threads to the next row of pinched pleats. Continue this process until the entire cake is done.
10. Using tip 2, pipe a bead border on top and at the base of the 5-inch (12 cm) cake.

TOP TIER

1. Stack the top tier onto the middle cake tier and attach with Royal Icing (see page 20).
2. Repeat steps 1 to 4 above for Middle Tier, to create a template.
3. Roll a piece of pink gumpaste to about ⅛-inch (3 mm) thick. Use a grooved roller to create the lines on gumpaste.
4. Using the template, cut the gumpaste to exact size.
5. Brush some water on to the gumpaste and attach it to the sides of the cake. Taper the ends toward the front.
6. Pipe a bead border on top of the grooved gumpaste strip.
7. To make butterfly bow, roll a piece of pink sugar-paste and texture it with the grooved rolling pin.

Cut 2 strips measuring 3 inches (8 cm) in height and 4 inches (10 cm) in length.

8. Make a box pleat on 1 side of the strip. A box pleat is a pleat consisting of 2 parallel creases facing opposite directions and forming a raised section in between. When a box pleat is formed on 1 side, the opposite side will tend to fan out. You will need 2 of these to create a box.
9. To make the centre strip for the bow, cut another small piece of pink gumpaste measuring 2 inches (5 cm) wide and 3 inches (8 cm) long. Fold both sides of the width to meet the centre point. Turn over and fold it over to make a loop, and allow to dry. Place the 2 pieces of butterfly bows (back facing up) on top of the cut piece at the centre. Fold both ends of the centre strip over the butterfly bows at the centre, and glue the ends down with gum glue. Turn the bow right side up to dry for 24 hours.
10. Attach the bow to the cake with white Royal Icing.

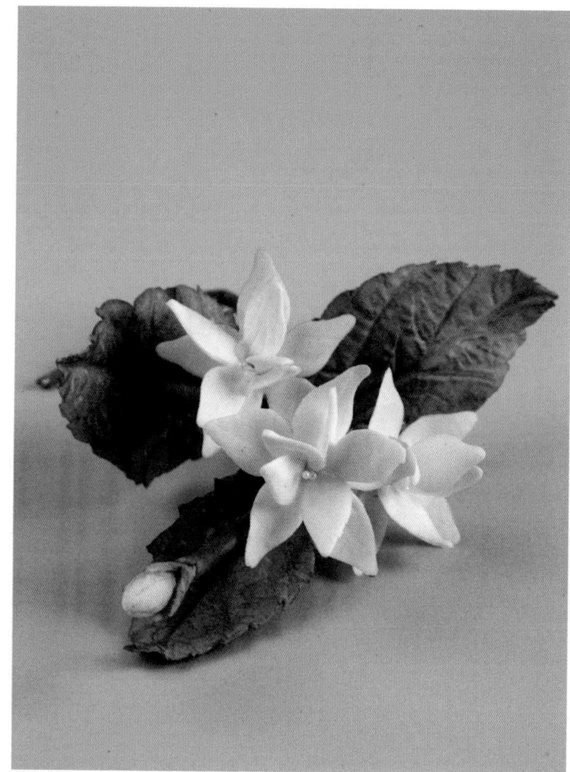

Flower spray for the bottom of the cake

JASMINE

For this project, you will need to make 15 flowers, 10 buds, and 12 leaves. See pages 32–35 for flower-making techniques.

Petal

1. Cut a 24-gauge wire into 3 sections. Using half-width green florist's tape, tape 2 white head stamens to the cut wire. Make 15 of these.
2. Roll a piece of white gumpaste thinly and cut out the shape with the small rose calyx cutter. Cut off the pointed ends of the calyx. Transfer the cut shape to a foam pad and soften the edges with a ball tool.
3. Vein each of the petals with the silk veining tool.
4. Brush the wired stamen lightly with gum glue.
5. Thread the petal up the wired stamen, and pinch the ends of the petal to adhere to the wire.
6. Using the Mexican hat technique on page 32, make another petal with the small rose calyx cutter.
7. Hollow out the centre of the petal with the round end of the silk veining tool. Cut off the pointed ends of the calyx.
8. Soften the petals on a foam pad. With the ball tool, vein each of the petals with the silk veining tool.
9. Insert the wire with the first layer of petals into the centre of the second layer of petals. Pinch the base of the gumpaste to the wire, to adhere.
10. Thinly roll a small amount of green gumpaste thinly. Using the calyx cutter, cut the calyx out and attach it to the base of the flower with some gum glue.
11. Make an additional 14 flowers using the above technique.

Buds

1. Roll a half-pea-size ball of white gumpaste into a teardrop, to form the bud.
2. Cut a 24-gauge green wire into 3 sections. Insert the cut 24-gauge wire into the broad side of the teardrop.
3. Taper the broad base of the teardrop slightly down the wire.
4. Make a few small cuts on the bud with a small paring knife, to represent unopened petals.
5. Dust the buds slightly with green dusting colour at the bottom of the bud and on the calyx.

The pleated puff moulds and the pieces for the Jasmine flower

Leaf

1. Make 12 small rose leaves with green gumpaste. Vein the leaf with the leaf veiner. Pinch the leaves slightly to accentuate the central vein.
2. Repeat the steps above, to make an additional 11 leaves.
3. Dry the leaves on foil so that they dry with natural curves.
4. When dry, dust the leaves with green-bean dusting colour.
5. Steam or dip the leaves into confectioner's glaze, to give them a shine.

Assembly

To create a spray, tape the buds first and then the flowers underneath, as shown in the photo. The leaves may alternate with the flowers on the spray.

FINAL ASSEMBLY

1. Insert a flower spike into the front of the top tier.
2. Insert the flower spray into the flower spike.

IN INDIA, THE lotus (or water lily) is considered a sacred flower and occupies a unique position in art and mythology. The lotus represents honour, longevity and good fortune. It is also a symbol of triumph.

This cake is inspired by Mehndi, also known as henna art. A symbol of good luck, Mehndi is used to paint temporary intricate designs on the skin for participation in weddings and festivals.

Because of the position and layout of the top tier in this project, it is recommended that you use a petal-shape styrofoam instead of a real cake for the top tier.

LEVEL OF DIFFICULTY moderate to advanced skills

TECHNIQUES USED piping and gumpaste flowers

CAKES AND EDIBLES

- about 8 lb (3.5 kg) black fondant
- about 2 lb (900 g) white fondant
- white and green gumpaste
- blue piping gel
- Dusting Colours vine, green bean, plum, red and yellow
- white Royal Icing (page 20)
- gum glue
- confectioner's glaze (optional, to create shine)

TOOLS AND EQUIPMENT

- 26 and 24 gauge white florist's wires
- lotus petal cutter
- lotus leaf cutter
- multi-purpose long leaf veiner
- fine yellow seed head stamens
- piping bag
- piping tips 1.5, 2 and 3
- paisley cutters
- metal ball tool
- rolling pin
- Dresden tool
- foam pads
- brushes
- 9-inch (23 cm) petal shape styrofoam

TEMPLATES

- Lotus (page 157)
- Peacock (page 158)

CAKE PREPARATION

Cakes should be covered a day in advance. See pages 25–27 for details on how to cover a cake with fondant.

1. Cover a 16-inch (40 cm) oval-shaped petal cakeboard with white fondant.
2. Cover a 9-inch (23 cm) petal-shaped styrofoam with black fondant.
3. Cover a 12-inch (30 cm) petal-shaped cake with black sugarpaste. A petal-shaped cake pan is recommended for baking. Petal pans are usually sold in sets of 3 sizes.

BOTTOM-TIER MEHNDI DESIGN

1. Mark along the top edge of the 12-inch (30 cm) cake with the paisley cutter, positioning the centre bottom of the cutter at each of the scallops on the edge of the cake.

Above: Mehndi design as shown on the cake; Below: In this image, the peacock design has been traced onto parchment paper and pinned to a cake styrofoam covered in white fondant. Shown here is the scriber method of transferring the pattern to the cake

2. Fill a piping bag fitted with a 1.5 tip with white Royal Icing. Pipe the decorative lines and dots inside each paisley design on the cake.
3. Pipe a bead border along the top edge of the cake (see technique on page 37).
4. Mark the centre point of each of the petal segments. With a scriber, mark 2 lines of scallop marks on the sides of each of the petal segments, using the centre point as a guide to align them evenly.
5. Using a number 2 tip, pipe a row of beads. on each scallop line. The bottom scallop mark should have 2 rows of bead border.
6. Pipe another row of beads along the bottom edge of the cake.
7. Pipe the design inside each of the scallops with a tip 1.5 and white Royal Icing.
8. Using the same tip, pipe 4 dots, as shown on design, in between each of the scallops.
9. Leave to dry overnight.

TOP-TIER PEACOCK DESIGN

1. Transfer the peacock design template onto the 9-inch (23 cm) pre-covered styrofoam. (See technique on page 43.)
2. Fill a piping bag fitted with a number 1.5 tip with white Royal Icing. Pipe the peacock design.
3. Pipe a bead border with tip 2 and white Royal Icing on the top and bottom edges of the styrofoam.
4. Leave to dry overnight.

LOTUS FLOWER

See pages 32–35 for techniques on how to make flowers.

Ovary

1. Knead and roll a small amount of green sugarpaste, slightly larger than pea-size, into a cone or a teardrop shape.
2. Moisten with gum glue a green 18-gauge florist's wire with a hook, and insert it into the thinner end of the cone. Roll the sugarpaste down the wire, to elongate the cone slightly. Flatten the top side of the

Leaf cutters and pieces for the lotus flower

shape. Using tweezers, pinch around the sides and the top, outer edge to create a ridge. Use the point of the veining tool to create some small indents on the flattened top side of the cone.

3. Roll about 10 tiny balls of green sugarpaste and insert them into the small indents. Use the scriber tool to indent the centre of each of the inserted balls, giving them the natural look of lily pods.
4. Dust the pods with green dusting colour and highlight some spots with plum colour.

Stamens

1. Take about 3 bunches of yellow head stamens. (These stamens are sold in bunches.) Divide the stamens into smaller bunches and line up their tips. Apply some tacky glue to the centre of each bunch, binding the stamens together. Flatten each bunch slightly and allow the glue to dry. Cut the bunches in half and line up their tips.
2. Apply a little tacky glue to each bunch of stamens and attach them firmly around the pod. (Trim the stamens shorter, if necessary, to fit under the pod.) Allow to dry for about an hour.
3. Dust the tips with yellow dusting colour.

Petals

The lotus flower in this cake has 5 small petals, 7 medium petals and 7 large petals. You can vary the number and size of petals according to the kind of lotus flower you want to make.

1. Make the required number of petals.
2. Dry the petals in apple trays, to give them a curve. Leave to dry overnight.
3. When dry, dust two-thirds of the petal with red dusting colour. Dust from the top edge of the petal, fading toward the centre.
4. Steam the petals or dip them into confectioner's glaze, to give them a shine. Leave to dry overnight.

Lotus Leaves

1. Make 5 lotus leaves, either with lotus leaf cutters or the templates on page 157.
2. Repeat the above steps to create leaves of various sizes. Dry the leaves in an apple tray to give them a slight cup-like shape.

The finished lotus, as shown on the cake

3. When dry, dust the leaves with green-bean dusting colour. Dust a little aubergine or plum colour at the base of the leaf, fading out toward the edges of the leaf.
4. Steam each leaf to give it a shine.

Assembly

1. Tape the small petals around the stamens and the pod. Then tape the medium petals underneath and in between the small petals.
2. Lastly, tape the large petals underneath and in between the medium petals.
3. Use full-width brown florist's tape to tape around the stem a few times, creating a thicker stem.

FINAL ASSEMBLY

1. With some Royal Icing, attach the bottom tier of the cake slightly toward the back of the pre-covered cakeboard.
2. Position the top styrofoam tier on its side on top of the bottom tier, with the peacock design toward the front of the cake. Remove it and insert a wooden skewer into the bottom tier where the styrofoam tier will sit. Apply Royal Icing around the skewer.
3. Insert the styrofoam tier gently into the skewer, to attach it to the bottom cake tier.
4. With a piping bag, pipe some blue piping gel onto the board next to the bottom tier in the front, to create the water effect. Cut a small hole at the bottom of the bag to allow the piping gel to come out; you will not require a tip for this purpose.
5. Place the lotus leaves on the piping gel, with the lotus flower in the centre, as shown in the photo. Both the leaves and the lotus will adhere to the very sticky gel.

FABERGÉ BEAUTY

RUSSIA

RUSSIA'S NATIONAL FLOWER is the chamomile. Looking very much like a daisy, the chamomile symbolizes energy. Russia is known for its famous jewelled eggs, made by the House of Fabergé from 1885 to 1917 for the Russian imperial family.

LEVEL OF DIFFICULTY easy to moderate skills

TECHNIQUES USED gumpaste flowers, appliqués, sugarwork and piping

CAKES AND EDIBLES

- about 2 lb (900 g) red fondant
- about 4 lb (1.8 kg) dark blue fondant
- about 2 lb (900 g) black fondant
- about 1 lb (450 g) red fondant
- about 1 lb (450 g) yellow fondant
- about 8 oz (235 g) white gumpaste
- about 8 oz (235 g) green gumpaste
- Dusting Colours gold and yellow
- gold sugar dragees
- black and yellow Royal Icing (page 20)
- red and blue isomalt nibs
- a small amount of vodka or any clear alcohol for colouring
- gum glue

TOOLS AND EQUIPMENT

- diamond patchwork cutters
- 24 and 28 gauge florist's wires
- silicone gem mould
- extruder
- large daisy cutter (optional)
- small daisy cutter (optional)
- silicone daisy centre mould
- metal ball tool
- silicone rose mould
- acanthus leaf mould
- Dresden tool
- foam pad
- brushes
- pizza cutter

TEMPLATES

- Daisy (page 159)
- Design (page 159)

CAKE PREPARATION

See pages 25–27 for techniques on how to cover a cake and cakeboard with fondant.

1. Cover a 16-inch (40 cm) square cakeboard with black fondant.
2. Cover a 10-inch (25 cm) pillow-shaped cake with dark blue fondant. Pillow-shaped cake pans are sold in sets of 3 and are available from the list of suppliers on page 165.
3. Emboss or mark the diamond design on the 10-inch (25 cm) cake with the diamond patchwork cutter immediately after covering the cake.
4. Cover a 6-inch (15 cm) pillow-shaped cake with red fondant.
5. Bake 2 egg-shaped cakes in egg-shaped cake pans. These egg pans are available for purchase from the list of suppliers on page 165.
6. Cover 1 egg-shaped cake with yellow fondant and the other with red fondant. Leave them to dry for at least 24 hours.
7. Airbrush the yellow-covered egg with gold colour and leave it to dry overnight.

Left: Pouring the isomalt into moulds for the heart jewels; Right: Rope trim and tassels with the complete hearts

BOTTOM TIER JEWELS, ROPE TRIM AND LACE POINTS

Jewels

You will need to make approximately 130 isomalt gems for this project. The gem mould can be purchased through the list of suppliers on page 165.

1. To make the jewels, spray the silicone gem moulds with vegetable spray.
2. Put about 5 or 6 isomalt nibs in a silicone cup and microwave for about 20 to 30 seconds. When the isomalt has melted, stir it with a wooden skewer to eliminate the air bubbles. Be careful when working with the melted isomalt, as it is very hot and can cause serious burns.
3. Pour the melted isomalt into the gem moulds and allow to set for about 20 minutes or slightly more, depending upon the local humidity. You may need to melt more isomalt to make the required number of gems.
4. When cooled, attach the gems to the embossed diamond design on the top section of the 10-inch (25 cm) bottom cake tier by holding the isomalt gems with tweezers and dipping them very slightly into the melted isomalt. Be very careful not to touch the isomalt directly.

Rope Trim and Tassels

1. To make the rope: Fit the extruder with the rope disc and fill it with softened yellow fondant. Extrude about 10-inch (25 cm) of rope for each of the 4 sides of the bottom cake tier. Attach the rope border to the edge of each section with some gum glue.
2. Repeat the same steps for the top tier cake, except that you will only need to extrude a length of approximately 7 inches (18 cm) for each of the 4 sides of the cake.
3. To make the tassels: Fit the extruder with the hair or fine holes disc. You will need to make 4 bunches of tassels for each cake, comprising a total of 8 bunches for the bottom and top cake tiers.

4. Attach the tassels to the 4 corners of each of the cake tiers.
5. Paint the rope borders and the tassels gold, by diluting the gold dusting colour with some clear Vodka.

Rose

You will need to make 8 of these small roses from the silicone mould, to be attached to the top part of each of the tassels. The rose mould can be purchased from the list of suppliers on page 165.

1. Knead a pea-size amount of yellow gumpaste into a ball.
2. Insert the ball into the silicone rose mould.
3. Remove from mould.
4. Attach to the top of each tassel with Royal Icing.

Lace Points

1. Pipe the lace points with tip number 1.5 and white Royal Icing. You can pipe them freehand or make your own template for consistency. The shape of the lace points is similar to 4 petals of a flower. You will need about 50 lace points, to allow for breakage.
2. Leave the lace points to dry for an hour before airbrushing.
3. Airbrush the lace points with gold colour and leave to dry overnight, if possible.
4. Position and attach the bottom tier at an angle in the centre of the pre-covered cakeboard with Royal Icing.
5. Attach the lace points with dots of yellow Royal Icing underneath the rope border of the bottom cake tier.

TOP TIER APPLIQUÉ AND FABERGÉ EGGS

Appliqués

1. To make the appliqués, roll a small piece of black gumpaste to about ⅛ inch (3 mm) thick. Cut out the appliqués, using the templates on page 159. You will need 8 pieces of the larger appliqués and 16 of the narrower appliqués.
2. Attach the appliqués to the top tier with gum glue, as shown in the project photo.

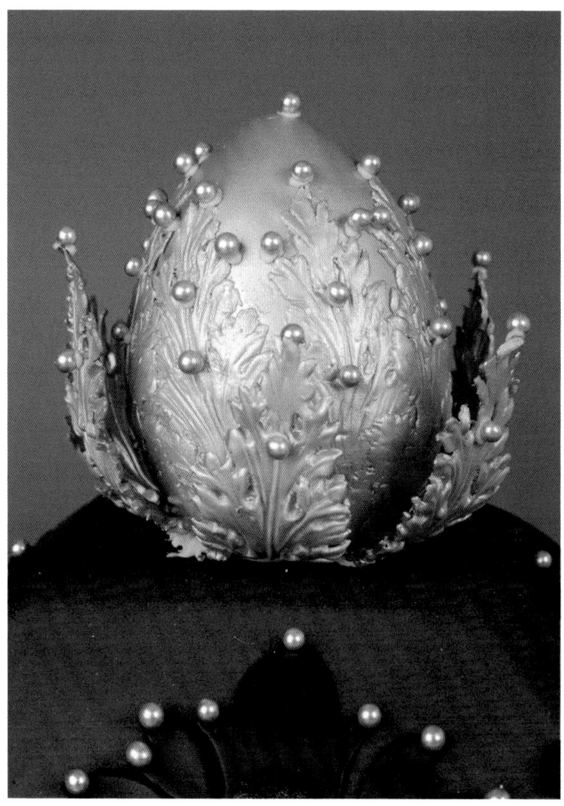

Gold Fabergé egg

3. Attach the gold dragees onto the outline of the larger appliqués, as shown in the project photo, with a dot of black Royal Icing. You will need about 115 gold dragees.

Gold Fabergé Egg

1. Cut the acanthus leaves as per instructions in the A Shower of Gold project on page 79. You will need about 20 yellow acanthus leaves.
2. Attach about 8 acanthus leaves before they harden by applying gum glue to the sides of the yellow egg that has already been covered in fondant.
3. Leave the rest of the acanthus leaves to dry on formers for 24 hours. When dried, attach 6 acanthus leaves to the bottom of the egg with yellow Royal Icing. Leave to dry for a further 24 hours.
4. Airbrush with gold colour and leave to dry for a few hours.
5. Attach the gold dragees to the tips of the acanthus leaves, as shown in the project photo.

Left: Red Fabergé egg; Right: Completed chamomile flowers

Red Fabergé Egg

1. Roll some black gumpaste very thinly. Create the large daisy shape by using the large daisy cutter or the template on page 159.
2. Roll some yellow gumpaste very thinly. Create the small daisy shape by using the small daisy cutter or the template on page 159.
3. Attach the daisy shapes to the sides of the egg with some gum glue, placing the small daisy on top of the large one. You may further paint the petals of the daisy, if you wish, with gold airbrush colour. Pipe a few yellow dots onto the top of the daisy shapes and attach a gold dragee to each of the dots.
4. Attach the 4 dried, curved acanthus leaves to the sides of the egg with yellow Royal Icing. Leave to dry for 24 hours.

CHAMOMILE

You will need to make 6 flowers and 6 leaves. The daisy centre mould can be purchased from the list of suppliers on page 165.

Chamomile Centre

1. Cut a 24-gauge green wire into 3 sections.
2. Make a hook at the end of 1 of the cut 24-gauge wires. Bend the hook down with pliers.
3. Knead a pea-size ball of yellow gumpaste and insert it into the daisy centre mould.
4. Remove the gumpaste from the mould. Insert the moistened hooked wire into the moulded shape from underneath.
5. Leave to dry overnight.

Petals

1. Roll white gumpaste thinly on a non-stick mat.
2. Create the required shape with the daisy cutter. You do not need to make individual petals for this flower.
3. Make a hole in the centre of the cut-out pieces and leave them to dry in apple trays, to give them a curved shape.
4. Repeat the above steps to make an additional 5 petals.

Pieces for creating the chamomile flowers

Leaves and Stem

1. Cut a 28-gauge wire into 4 sections.
2. Tape the wires with half-width green florist's tape. Make a number of these.
3. Cut a 24-gauge wire into 3 sections.
4. Tape the wire with half-width green florist's tape.
5. Tape the short 28-gauge covered wires to the 24-gauge wire, to to lend the leaves a needle-like effect.
6. Cut the shorter wires if necessary to create the leaf shape.
7. Repeat the above steps to make an additional 5 sets of leaves.

Assembly

1. Apply a small amount of Royal Icing to the bottom of the dried chamomile centre. Insert the dried chamomile centre through a hole in the dried petal, from the top.
2. Cut a small piece of aluminum foil and crumple it. Shape it into a small cup and insert the wired flower through the foil, to support the flower while drying. Use a paper clip underneath the foil to support it.
3. When dried, attach 4 of the flowers together, with leaves in between, to form an "S" spray with half-width green florist's tape. (See also Hogarth Curve on page 34.)
4. Attach each of the 2 balancing flowers with leaves with half-width green florist's tape, to create 2 separate small sprays.

FINAL ASSEMBLY

1. Attach the top tier to the bottom cake tier with Royal Icing. (See How to Stack a Tiered Cake on page 28.) Ensure that the bottom cake is dowelled to prevent the top tier from sinking into the bottom cake tier.
2. Attach the dried gold Fabergé egg to the centre of the top tier with yellow Royal Icing.
3. Attach the dried red Fabergé egg to the front of the cake with black Royal Icing.
4. Position the "S" flower spray next to the cake and place one of the smaller sprays next to the red Fabergé egg. The last flower spray may be placed on the opposite side of the cake, as shown in the project photo.

AUSSIE INTERLUDE

AUSTRALIA

AUSTRALIA'S NATIONAL FLOWER, the golden wattle, belongs to the mimosa family and symbolizes unity. In this project, I have not only featured the national flower but also the koala, which is endemic to Australia and recognized around the world. The added feature of this cake is the cobweb stringwork, which is a technique I created to correlate to the wildlife ambience of this cake.

LEVEL OF DIFFICULTY moderate to advanced skills

TECHNIQUES USED piping, stringwork, gumpaste flowers and figure modelling

CAKES AND EDIBLES

- about 1 lb (450 g) light brown fondant
- about 1½ lb (700 g) brown fondant
- about 2½ lb (1.2 kg) dark brown fondant
- about 1½ lb (700 g) marbleized brown fondant (see page 27)
- about 1 lb (450 g) grey modelling chocolate
- about 1 oz (30 g) black modelling chocolate
- about 10 oz (300 g) dark brown modelling chocolate
- Dusting Colours yellow and vine green
- brown Royal Icing (page 20)
- gum glue
- about 1 lb (450 g) yellow gumpaste
- about 8 oz (235 g) green gumpaste
- some yellow-coloured cornmeal

TOOLS AND EQUIPMENT

- half-width green florist's tape
- 26 and 24, 33 gauge florist's wires
- yellow thread
- leaf veiner
- piping bag
- metal ball tool
- Dresden tool
- foam pads
- brushes
- nail file
- sea holly mould

CAKE PREPARATION

Various shades of brown fondant from dark to light can be achieved by mixing different amounts of white fondant. See pages 25–27 for techniques on how to cover a cake and cake-board with fondant.

1. Cover a 14-inch (35 cm) board with marbleized fondant.
2. Cover a 4-inch (10 cm) round cake with light brown fondant. Ensure that the cake has a minimum height of 5 inches (12 cm).
3. Cover a 6-inch (15 cm) round cake with brown fondant.
4. Cover an 8-inch (20 cm) round cake with dark brown fondant. You may have to bake 2 cakes to obtain the 6-inch (15 cm) height

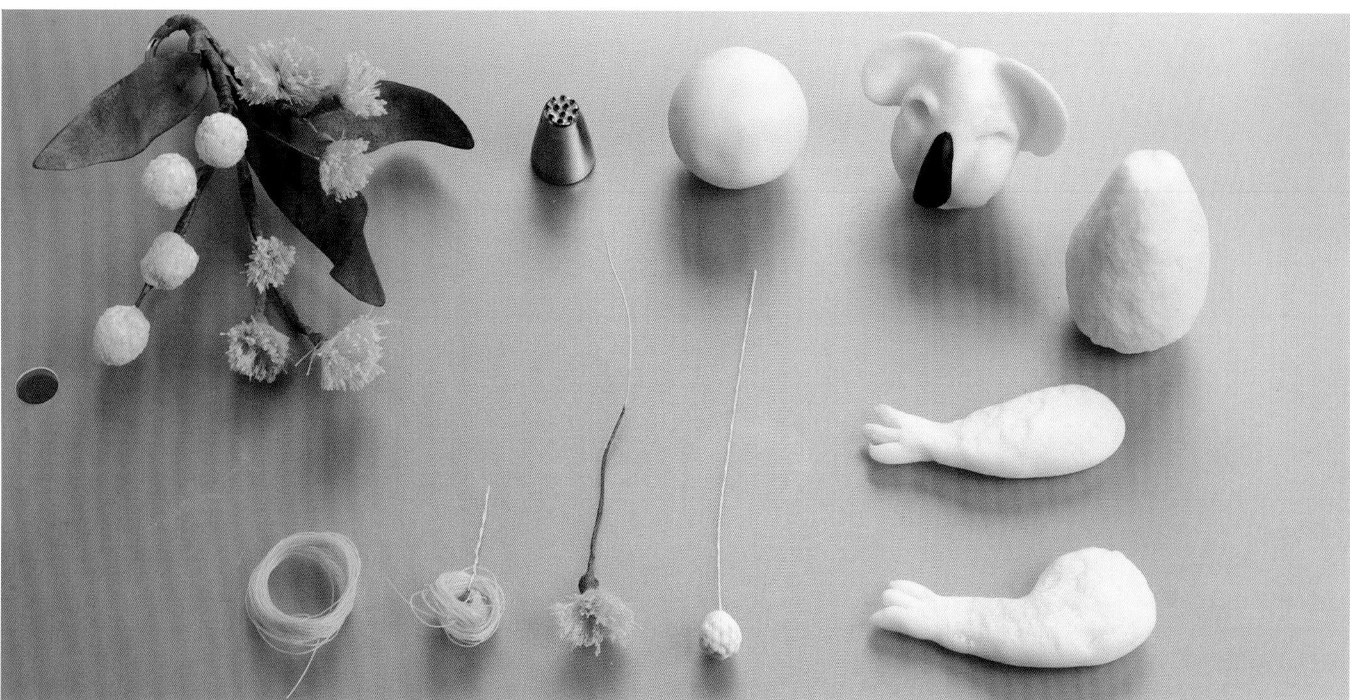

The golden wattle and pieces for the chocolate koala

KOALA AND TREE TRUNK

Koala

1. The koala bear is modelled freehand, using modelling chocolate.
2. Roll about 4 oz (113 g) of modelling chocolate into a ball.
3. Use the wide end of the Dresden tool to indent the eye sockets.
4. Roll a tiny black sausage of modelling chocolate and attach it to the nose area.
5. Attach a small piece of modelling chocolate to the base of the nose, to create the mouth area. Blend in the seams with the Dresden tool.
6. Attach 2 small balls of modelling chocolate to each side of the nose to create cheeks. Blend in the seams with the Dresden tool.
7. For the ears, roll a piece of modelling chocolate into a ball and flatten it. Shape the base of one side slightly into a point.
8. Attach the ears to the head with gum glue, and smooth out the seams.
9. Repeat steps 7 and 8 for the other ear.
10. For the body, roll about 10 oz (300 g) of modelling chocolate to an oval shape about 5 inches (12 cm) long.
11. Indent the broader section of the oval slightly, for the thigh to fit in.
12. For the arms, knead about 1 oz (30 g) of grey modelling chocolate into a long narrow cone and elongate the narrow end to form the hand area. Flatten the hand area. Make 3 small teardrops and attach them with gum glue to the end of the hand, for the paws. Make tiny black teardrops to stick onto the ends of the paws to represent the nails.
13. For the legs, knead about 2 oz (60 g) of grey modelling chocolate into a larger cone, and elongate the narrow end slightly to form the foot. Flatten the wider end of the cone slightly, to create the thigh area. Make tiny black teardrops to stick onto the end of the foot, to represent the nails.
14. Texture the fur on the body and head by pushing tip number 366 against it.
15. Attach the hands and legs to the body with gum glue and leave to dry for 24 hours.

Tree Trunk

1. To make the tree trunk, roll a piece of dark brown

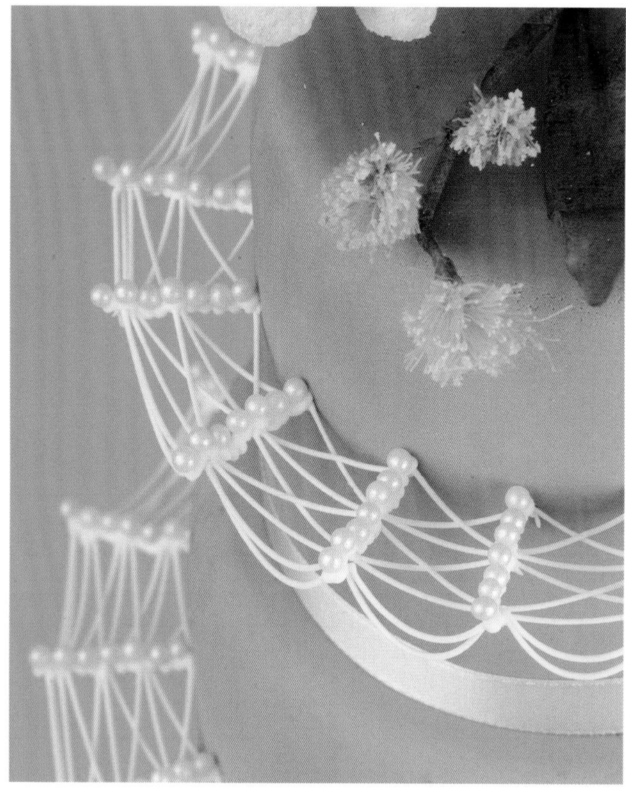

Left: The cobweb stringwork and completed golden wattle; Right: How to make the wattle

modelling chocolate to a wide sausage about 8 inches (20 cm) long.

2. Hollow the top of the trunk slightly with the wide end of the Dresden tool.
3. Texture the trunk with slits, using a small paring knife or a textured mat to create the bark effect on the trunk.
4. You may also indent some holes into the trunk, to create a more natural look.

GOLDEN WATTLE

You will need about 20 to 30 flowers and approximately 10 buds to create 1 spray of golden wattle. You will need 2 sprays for this cake.

Flowers

1. Wind fine yellow thread around 2 fingers about 60 times. Remove the cotton thread from your fingers and twist into a figure-8. Fold the 2 loops together to make a small circle or loop.
2. Thread a 28-gauge wire through the circle and twist it firmly at the base to secure.
3. Cut the loop open at the top, to create many strands of thread. Trim down slightly if threads are too long.
4. Tape the bottoms of the threads with half-width green florist's tape. Trim around the threads with a pair of scissors to create a ball shape.
5. Brush the threads against a nail file to open up the threads.
6. Brush the ends of the thread with some gum glue and dip them into yellow-coloured cornmeal. Allow to dry.
7. Repeat the above steps until you have about 20 flowers.

Buds

1. Roll a pea-size amount of yellow gumpaste into a ball and elongate the ball slightly.
2. Push the ball into the silicone sea holly mould (available from the list of suppliers on page 165). Remove the paste from the mould.
3. Insert a hooked 24-gauge wire into the moulded paste.
4. Brush gum glue on to the moulded paste and dip into the yellow cornmeal. Leave to dry for a few minutes.
5. Repeat the process until you have about 10 buds.

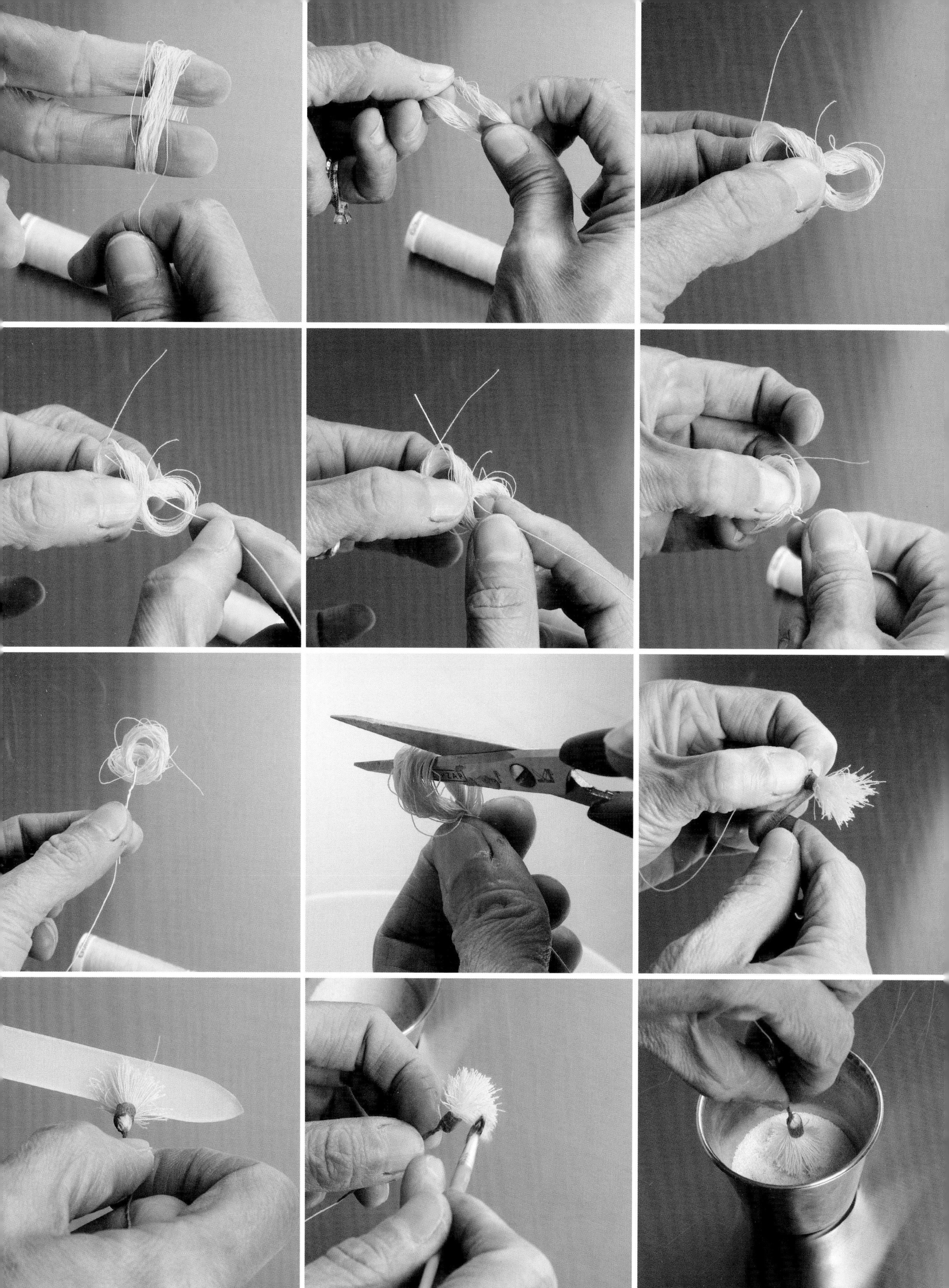

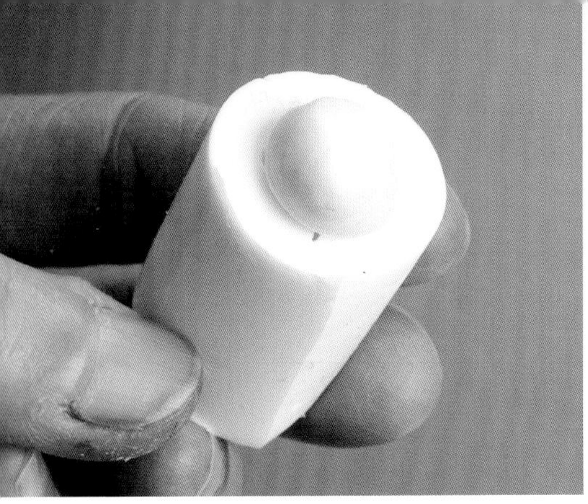

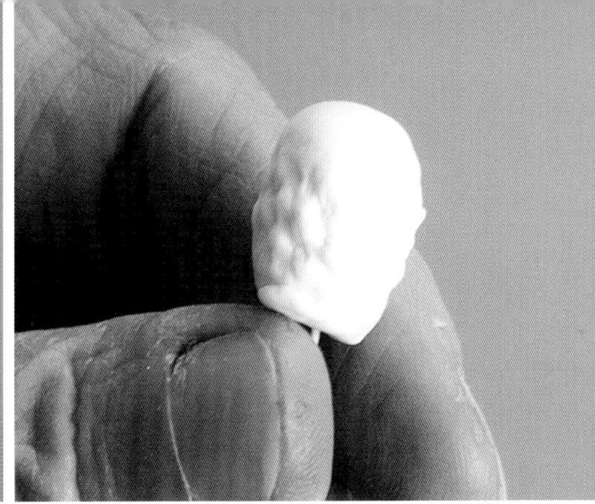

Making the golden wattle buds

Leaves

1. Using the techniques on page 32–35, make about 3 to 5 small leaves and about 12 large leaves.
2. Vein the leaves with the leaf veiner.
3. Dust the leaves with vine-green dusting colour and leave to dry overnight.

Flower Spray Assembly

1. Tape the flowers and buds together in a cluster with half-width green florist's tape.
2. Attach the small leaves below the cluster of flowers and buds with half-width green florist's tape.

COBWEB STRINGWORK

Top Tier

1. Divide and mark the sides of the cake evenly into ½-inch (1 cm) spaces in the centre. (See technique on page 36.)
2. Cut about sixteen to eighteen 1-inch (2.5 cm) lengths of 33-gauge white florist's wires, or enough to go around each of the marked spaces on the tier.
3. Insert the cut 33-gauge white florist's wires into the marked spaces, ensuring that all the lengths protruding from the tier are of the same length.
4. Using a 1.5 tip, pipe white Royal Icing strings onto the wire in an "X" formation.
5. Repeat the process until the end of the wire is reached.
6. Pipe an additional 2 loops of dropped stringwork at the end of the wires.
7. Using the 1.5 tip and white Royal Icing, pipe a small bead border onto the 33-gauge wire. (See technique on page 37.)
8. Using a pair of tweezers, attach the pearl dragees onto the piped bead border.
9. Leave to dry for 24 hours.

Middle Tier

1. Divide and mark the sides of the cake evenly into ½-inch (1 cm) spaces two-thirds of the way down from the top of the cake. (See technique on page 36.)
2. Repeat steps 2 to 9 of the directions for the top tier.

FINAL ASSEMBLY

1. Attach the bottom cake tier to one side of the pre-covered cakeboard with Royal Icing. Ensure that the bottom cake tier is dowelled to support the top tier. (See How to Stack a Tiered Cake on page 28.)
2. Attach a ¼-inch (6 mm) white satin ribbon to the bottom of each of the tiers with some gum glue.
3. Attach the tree trunk to the side of the bottom tier with some Royal Icing.
4. Attach the koala to the cakeboard next to the tree trunk with Royal Icing. While the modelling chocolate is still slightly soft and flexible, move the arms gently to wrap them around the tree trunk.
5. Knead about 2 oz (60 g) of green gumpaste into a long thin rope, to resemble a branch. Attach the branch to the side of the bottom tier with gum glue, in a vine-like manner.
6. Attach the large leaves sporadically along the branch with a small amount of Royal Icing.
7. Attach the middle tier to the bottom tier and the top tier to the middle tier.
8. Place the Golden Wattle spray on the top tier.
9. Glue a ¼-inch (6 mm) brown satin ribbon to the sides of the cakeboard.

A VICTORIAN TEA DANCE

ENGLAND

THE NATIONAL FLOWER of England is the English rose, which is usually red. In this project, I have chosen pink-and-white roses instead as they better express the era of Queen Victoria's reign. Fashions of the time often displayed realistic flower trimmings and lacework, which are depicted in this champagne-coloured cake.

LEVEL OF DIFFICULTY moderate to advanced skills

TECHNIQUES USED figure modelling, piping, stringwork and gumpaste flowers

CAKES AND EDIBLES

- about 7 lb (3.15 kg) ivory fondant
- about 5 lb (2.2 kg) ivory gumpaste
- Dusting Colors pearl dust
- white Royal Icing (page 20)
- gum glue
- confectioner's glaze (optional, to create shine)

TOOLS AND EQUIPMENT

- 18 and 24 gauge florist's wires
- silicone rose petal veiner
- leaf veiner
- lace embossers
- piping bag
- piping tips 1 and 1.5
- pearl dragees
- metal ball tool
- Dresden tool
- foam pads
- brushes
- textured rolling pin
- scriber
- silk veining tool

TEMPLATE

- Calyx (page 160)
- Rose (page 160)

CAKE PREPARATION

See pages 25–27 for techniques on how to cover a cake and cakeboard with fondant.

1. Cover the ¼-inch (6 mm) cakeboard with ivory fondant.
2. Cover a 6-inch (15 cm) cake with a height of 5 inches (12 cm) minimum, and a 8-inch (20 cm) cake with a height of 6 inches (15 cm), with ivory fondant. You may have to bake 2 cakes to obtain the 6-inch (15 cm) height.
3. Using receipt paper, go around the circumference of the bottom of the 6-inch (15 cm) cake. Allow the paper to meet exactly at the 2 ends. (See also page 36 for this technique.)
4. Fold the piece of paper into equal sections. The number of folds will determine the amount of dropped stringwork on the cake. The folds will ensure that the dropped stringwork will be evenly spaced around the cakes. (This technique is pictured on page 39.)
5. Use a pin or a scriber to mark the folds on top of the cake. Once the markings are done, remove the paper.
6. Using the same method as above, divide the bottom part of the 8-inch (20 cm) tier into 3 segments, and mark the folds on the cake with a scriber or pin.

Fabric Roses

You will need to make about 150 fabric roses for this project.

1. Knead about 1 oz (30 g) of ivory gumpaste into a long sausage.
2. Flatten the sausage and roll the paste into a strip about 1⁄16-inch (2 mm) thick.
3. Using a pizza cutter, cut the paste into rectangular strips about 6 inches (15 cm) long and 1 inch (2.5 cm) wide. The longer the strips, the larger the roses will be.
4. Using a damp brush, apply some water to the bottom part of a strip.
5. Roll one end of the strip to resemble a Swiss roll or the centre of a rose bud.
6. Gather, pleat and pinch the bottom of the strip around the bud until you reach the end of the strip.
7. Repeat steps 1 to 6 to make additional fabric roses for the project.

Bottom Tier

1. Attach the bottom tier to the middle of the pre-covered cakeboard with Royal Icing. Ensure that the bottom tier is dowelled to support the top tier. (See How to Stack a Tiered Cake on page 28.)
2. Fill a piping bag fitted with a round number 1 tip with white Royal Icing. Pipe a dot on each of the spots that you marked earlier around the top edge of the cake.
3. Attach a pearl dragee to each of the piped dots and allow to dry for a few minutes.
4. Fill another piping bag, fitted with a tip number 1.5, with white Royal Icing. Pipe a dropped string loop to connect to each of the pearl dragees. Repeat this all around the cake. The dropped string loop should extend down about 2 inches (5 cm) from the top of the cake.
5. Pipe another series of dots with tip number 1 on top of each of the pearl dragees.
6. Attach another pearl dragee on top of each of the second row of dots, as shown in the photo, and allow to dry for a further few minutes.

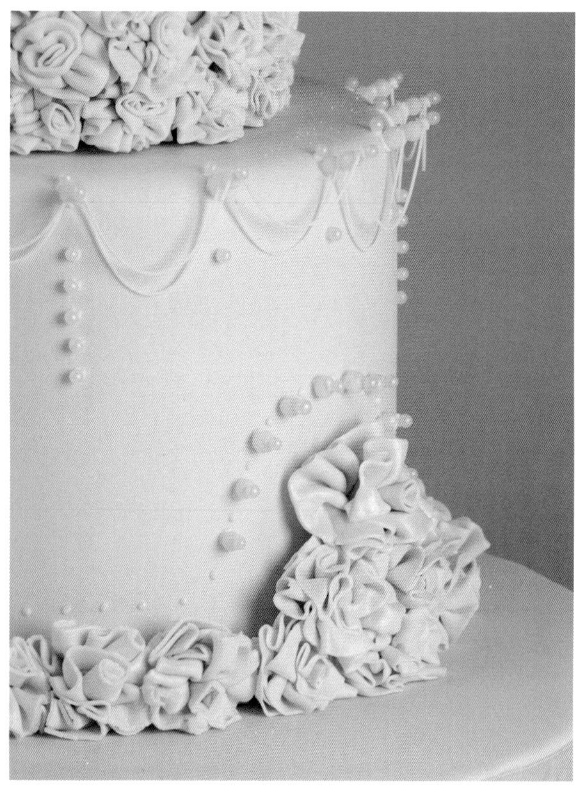

Pearl dragees and fabric roses

7. Change to tip number 1.5 and pipe another series of dropped string loops to connect each of the pearl dragees. This time around, the loop should extend down about 1 inch (2.5 cm) from the top of the cake.
8. Finish off with another series of piped dots, using tip number 1 and attaching a pearl dragee on top of each of the dots.
9. Using tip number 1.5, pipe dots in between the dropped string loops, as shown.
10. For the bottom part of the tier, create a border by attaching a row of pre-made fabric roses all around the bottom section of the cake.
11. Where the 3 points of the cakes are marked, attach an additional cluster of 3 fabric roses creating a half-circle effect as shown in the project photo.
12. Using tip number 1.5, pipe a series of dots above the bottom row of fabric roses. Attach some pearl dragees to the series of dots just above the 3 clusters of roses.

Top Tier

1. Attach the top tier to the bottom dowelled tier with Royal Icing.

2. Pipe a small amount of Royal Icing onto the back of each of the fabric roses, to attach them to the side of the cake. You should start from the bottom of the tier and continue upward. Each row of fabric roses should be staggered with the row below.

BALLROOM DANCER

1. Colour some gumpaste with skin-tone or ivory. Using the How to Make a Gumpaste Figurine directions on page 40, make the head and body of the doll.
2. Insert a cocktail stick across the shoulders, leaving both ends sticking out to support the arms. Allow the figure to dry overnight.
3. For the arms: Roll out 2 slightly-larger-than-pea-size amounts of ivory gumpaste, at an angle, into sausages with one end narrower. Look at the arms next to the body, to ensure that they look proportionate. The length of the arms should reach to just above the knees of the figurine. Divide the sausage into 2 sections. Elongate the narrow section slightly and flatten it with your thumb, to make the hand. Use a small fine pair of scissors to cut a "V" on 1 side for the thumb and make another 3 shorter cuts for the fingers. Elongate and roll each of the fingers as much as possible.
4. Make a small cut where the elbow is and bend the arm slightly, as shown.
5. Repeat the same for the other arm.
6. For the hair: Put some softened brown fondant into the extruder with the multiple hole disc. Extrude the paste and attach the hair to the figurine with gum glue.
7. For the feathers: Roll a small piece of ivory gumpaste thinly. Cut small leaf-like shapes with a wheel cutter or pizza cutter. Using fine scissors, cut fine slits along the edge of the leaf to create a feather effect. Leave to dry for 24 hours and attach to the head of the doll with gum glue.
8. For the dress: Roll and cut out a piece of ivory gumpaste measuring about 4 × 4 inches (10 × 10 cm). Apply some gum glue to the body of the doll and wrap the gumpaste around it. Cut off the excess gumpaste with a pair of scissors. Cut a "V" opening in the front and back, to represent the neckline.

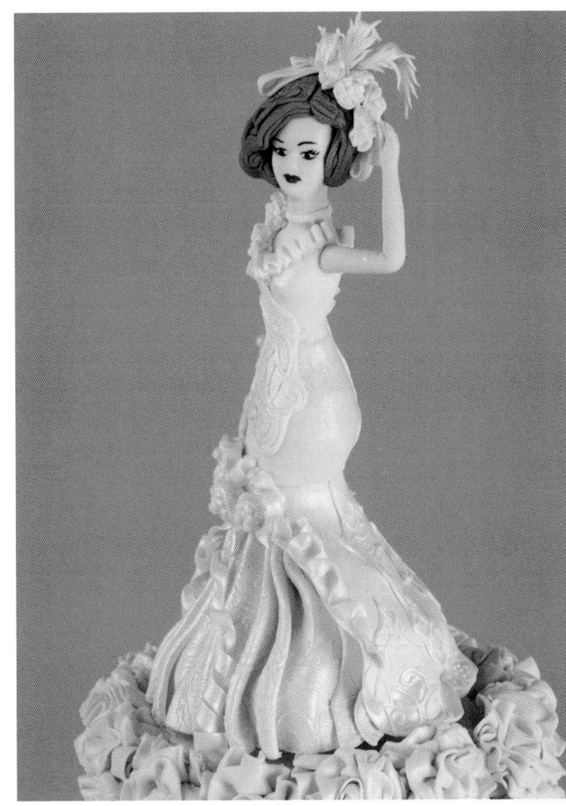

The completed ballroom dancer

9. Roll a piece of ivory gumpaste and then use textured rolling pins to create an embossed fabric effect. Create pleats with wooden skewers, as shown. Once the pleats are formed, remove the skewers and flatten the top to hold the pleats in position. Attach the pleats to the front of the figurine with gum glue as shown, cutting off the excess length. Allow to dry for an hour. Cut another piece of ivory gumpaste and attach it to the back of the body, to create the back portion of the skirt. Use crumpled tissue paper to hold it up while it is drying.
10. Make some lace designs with ivory gumpaste as shown, using the lace embossers (available from the list of suppliers on page 165). Remember to grease the lace embossers with vegetable spray before using. Cut the lace pieces to the desired sizes and attach to the front and back part of the dress with gum glue.
11. The roses on the dress are made the same way as the fabric roses described on the previous page. The strips, however, should be narrower, to create smaller roses.
12. Cut a number of tiny, long, narrow strips of ivory gumpaste and gather them together to create the trim along the neckline and on the skirt. Attach these strips with gum glue.

Individual leaves for the rose construction

13. For the facial features: Once the figurine has dried, you can either paint on the facial features or use edible pens or markers.

ROSES

Large Open Rose

You will need to make 1 large open rose, 1 medium open rose and 1 rose bud with 6 leaves. See pages 32–35 for flower-making techniques.

1. For the centre: Cut a green 18-gauge florist's wire into 2. Make a hook at the end of the wire. Roll a piece of white gumpaste into a narrow cone. Dip the hook into gum glue and insert it into the broad end of the cone. Leave to dry overnight.
2. For the first layer of petals: Roll out white gumpaste thinly on a non-stick mat. Using the small rose petal cutter, cut out 5 petals. Do not wire the petals.
3. Vein the petals with the silicone rose petal veiner. Repeat the same steps with the other 4 petals. Brush gum glue onto the dried cone and wrap the first petal over it. Try to cover the cone entirely, leaving the last end of the petal open. Brush a little gum glue on 1 side of the second petal and tuck the glue side underneath the first petal, to create a spiral effect. Do not glue the end of the second petal to the cone. Continue in the same manner with the third, fourth, and fifth petal, to create the spiral centre of the rose. (Refer to the photo above.)
4. For the second layer of petals: Roll and cut out another 5 petals using the technique above but with the medium-size cutter. Brush a little gum glue onto the base of the petal in a "V" shape and attach it to the spiral petals, overlapping the joints. Repeat the same with the other 4 petals overlapping each other.
5. For the third layer of petals: Roll and cut out another 7 petals with the large-size cutter. Soften the edges of the petals as indicated above. Vein the petals with the petal veiner and turn them over. Curl both sides of the petals with the silk veining tool.
6. Leave the petals to dry a little in the apple tray, with the curled sides underneath.
7. For the fourth layer of petals: Using the wired petal technique, make 5 wired petals with the large-size cutter.

8. Vein the petals and frill them slightly with the broad end of the Dresden tool. Turn over and curl both sides of the petal slightly with a cocktail stick. Leave to dry in an apple tray, with the curled sides underneath.

Medium Open Rose

Repeat steps 1 to 6 of the Large Open Rose.

Rose Assembly

1. To assemble the petals: Attach the semi-dried third layer of petals over the second layer of petals with gum glue. Try to overlap them slightly with the second layer.
2. To make the large open rose: Attach the final wired petal layers, overlapping the third layer with half-width green florist's tape.

Rose Bud

Repeat steps 1 to 4 of the Large Open Rose.

Calyx

1. Roll out some green gumpaste thinly and cut out the calyx shape using the rose calyx cutter. Cut a few fine slits on both sides of each calyx segment. Attach to the rose bottom with some gum glue.
2. Repeat the same for the medium open rose and rosebud.

Leaves

1. Using the wired petal and leaf technique, make 6 leaves with the rose leaf cutter.
2. Dry the leaves on foil, to create natural curves.
3. When dry, dust the leaves with green bean dusting powder. Dust a little aubergine or plum colour at the base of the leaf, fading out toward the edges of the leaf.
4. Steam or dip the leaves in confectioner's glaze to give them a shine. Leave to dry for 24 hours.

Assembly

1. Tape 3 leaves beneath the large open rose with half-width green florist's tape.
2. Tape 2 leaves beneath the medium open rose with half-width green florist's tape.
3. Tape 1 leaf beneath the rosebud with half-width green florist's tape.

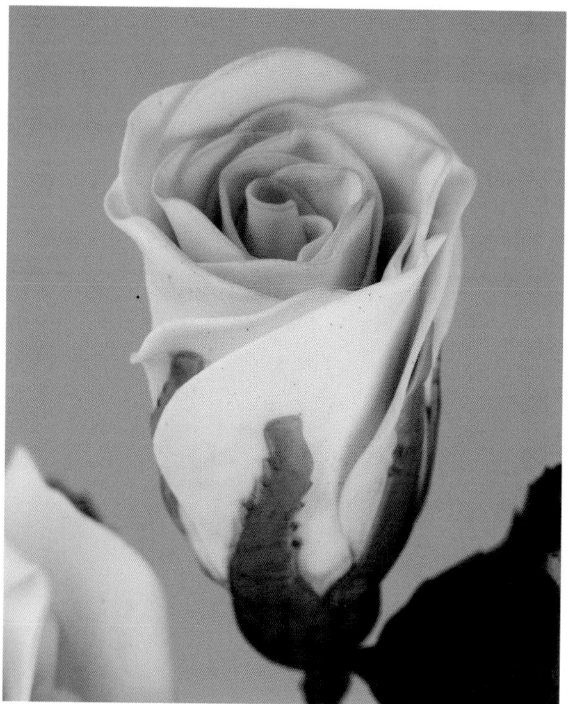

Two types of roses, above

FINAL ASSEMBLY

1. Attach the gumpaste figurine to the top tier of the cake with a small amount of Royal Icing.
2. Arrange the roses in a vase next to the stacked cakes.
3. Glue a ¼-inch (6 mm) white satin ribbon to the sides of the cakeboard.

A PARISIAN AFTERNOON

FRANCE

FRANCE'S NATIONAL FLOWER is the iris. A stylized version of the iris is used in the country's insignia and national emblem. The iris's three main petals represent faith, valour and wisdom. The world-famous Eiffel Tower is the symbol of Paris and the topper for this cake. The Eiffel Tower portion needs to be made at least one week in advance, so give yourself plenty of time when making this cake.

LEVEL OF DIFFICULTY advanced skills

TECHNIQUES USED piping, macarons, modelling chocolate and gumpaste flowers

CAKES AND EDIBLES

- about 4 lb (1.8 kg) dark chocolate fondant
- about 3½ lb (1.65 kg) pink fondant
- about ½ lb (250 g) black fondant
- Dusting Colours violet and white
- white Royal Icing (page 20)
- gum glue
- Swiss Meringue Buttercream Icing (page 19)
- about 3 lb (1.4 kg) dark brown modelling chocolate
- about 1 lb (450 g) purple gumpaste
- small amount of yellow gumpaste
- French macarons (page 14)
- Airbrush Colours pink and pearl
- rainbow sparkles
- confectioner's glaze (optional, to create shine)

TOOLS, EQUIPMENT

- 18, 26 and 24 gauge florist's wires
- iris cutter set
- piping bag
- tip 1.5
- metal ball tool
- Dresden tool
- foam pad
- brushes
- cutting wheel
- wax paper
- round 3-inch (8 cm) styrofoam

TEMPLATES

- Poodle (page 161)
- Eiffel Tower (page 162)

CAKE PREPARATION

See pages 25–27 for techniques on how to cover a cake and cakeboard with fondant.

1. Cover a 14-inch (35 cm) round cakeboard with pink fondant.
2. Texture the cakeboard by pushing or indenting the surface of the fondant with the back end of a paintbrush.
3. Cover an 8-inch (20 cm) cake with dark chocolate fondant. You may have to bake 2 cakes to obtain the 6 inch (15 cm) height.
4. Cover a 6-inch (15 cm) round cake with a minimum height of 5 inches (12 cm) with pink fondant.
5. Cover a 4-inch (10 cm) round cake with a minimum height of 5 inches (12 cm) with dark chocolate fondant.

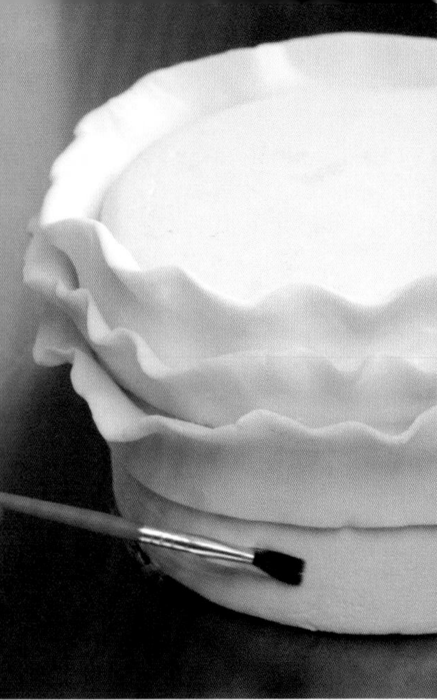

The bottom tier ruffles shown here in white with black dots

6. Cover a round 3-inch (8 cm) styrofoam with a height of ½-inch (1 cm) with dark chocolate fondant.
7. Cover a round 4-inch (10 cm) styrofoam with a height of 1-inch (2.5 cm) with black fondant.

BOTTOM 8-INCH (20 CM) TIER

1. Attach the bottom tier to the centre of the pre-covered texturized cakeboard with Royal Icing. (See How to Stack a Tiered Cake on page 28.)
2. Roll a piece of dark brown modelling chocolate into a sausage measuring about 30 inches (75 cm) long. Flatten and roll the sausage to about ⅛-inch (3 mm) thick. Cut it into 1-inch (2.5 cm) width ribbon strips.
3. Brush some gum glue onto the bottom of the strip and attach it to the top side of the cake. Always start with the top row and work down the sides of the cake. Using your fingers, create waves or frills on top of the strip. (See photo above.)
4. Repeat the same until the entire side is covered with the modelling chocolate strips.
5. Pipe pink Royal Icing dots on the top edge of the frills with tip 1. (See photo above for this technique shown with black icing.)

MIDDLE 6-INCH (15 CM) TIER

1. First measure the circumference of the tier. Cut the length of the receipt paper to the exact length of the tier's circumference. Fold the paper into equal sections of about ½-inch (1 cm) wide.
2. Open and wrap the paper around the tier. Position the strip around the sides of the cake at the top and hold it in position with a pin. The strip of paper should wrap comfortably around the cake.
3. Using a scriber or pin, prick a tiny hole above each of the folded lines on the paper onto the cake, to mark the division. Remove the paper.
4. Using a bag fitted with a number 1.5 tip filled with white Royal Icing, pipe two layers of dropped stringwork connecting the dots. The longer dropped stringwork should extend 1-inch (2.5 cm) from the top and the shorter dropped stringwork should extend about ½-inch (1 cm) from the top.
5. Pipe another layer of overlapping dropped stringwork about ⅔ inch (1.5 cm) from the top over the 2 layers of dropped stringwork.
6. Pipe vertical rows of 3 dots, alternating with vertical rows of 2 dots, with tip 1.5 in the centre under each row of the dropped stringwork.
7. Roll modelling chocolate thinly to about ⅛-inch (3 mm) thick. Cut 5 poodle shapes, using the template provided on page 161.
8. Using the receipt paper technique described in step 1, fold the paper strip into 5 segments. Mark the segments on the cake. Position the 5 poodle shapes at the marked points on the side of the cake, at the bottom.
9. Roll tiny white fondant balls and attach them to the

head, tail and legs of the poodle, as shown. You will need to make about 10 balls for each poodle.

TOP 4-INCH (10 CM) TIER

1. Repeat steps 1 to 5 of the directions for the bottom 8-inch (20 cm) tier (above) to create the frills on the sides of the cakes. The only exception is that the sausages from step 2 should be rolled into lengths of 16-inch (40 cm) for the tier.

EIFFEL TOWER BASE (4-INCH [10 CM] STYROFOAM)

1. Use the same receipt paper technique as above for dividing the 4-inch (10 cm) base into ½-inch (1 cm) sections.
2. Using tip number 1.5 and white Royal Icing, pipe a layer of dropped stringwork around the base at the marked points on the sides. The first row of dropped stringwork should extend down to about ¼-inch (6 mm) from the top of the cake.
3. Using tip number 1.5 but with black Royal Icing, pipe another 3 rows of dropped stringwork underneath the first row of white dropped stringwork, so that the last row of dropped stringwork almost touches the base of the styrofoam.
4. Pipe a dot with the same tip on top of each of the marked areas where the dropped stringwork connects.

IRIS

You will need to make 2 sets of flowers for this project. See pages 32–35 for techniques on how to make flowers and leaves.

Fall Petals

1. Cut and make 3 petals with the large fork-like cutter.
2. Insert into the thick ridge of the petal a 24-gauge green wire that has been cut into 4 sections.
3. Place the petal on a thin foam and indent the central vein with the thin end of the Dresden tool, to create a channel in the centre.
4. Roll a tiny, narrow sausage of yellow gumpaste and elongate 1 end to a point. Attach this with gum glue to the channel in the centre of the petal.

Above: A close up on the completed modelling chocolate strips; Below: The iris, as shown in a vase display method

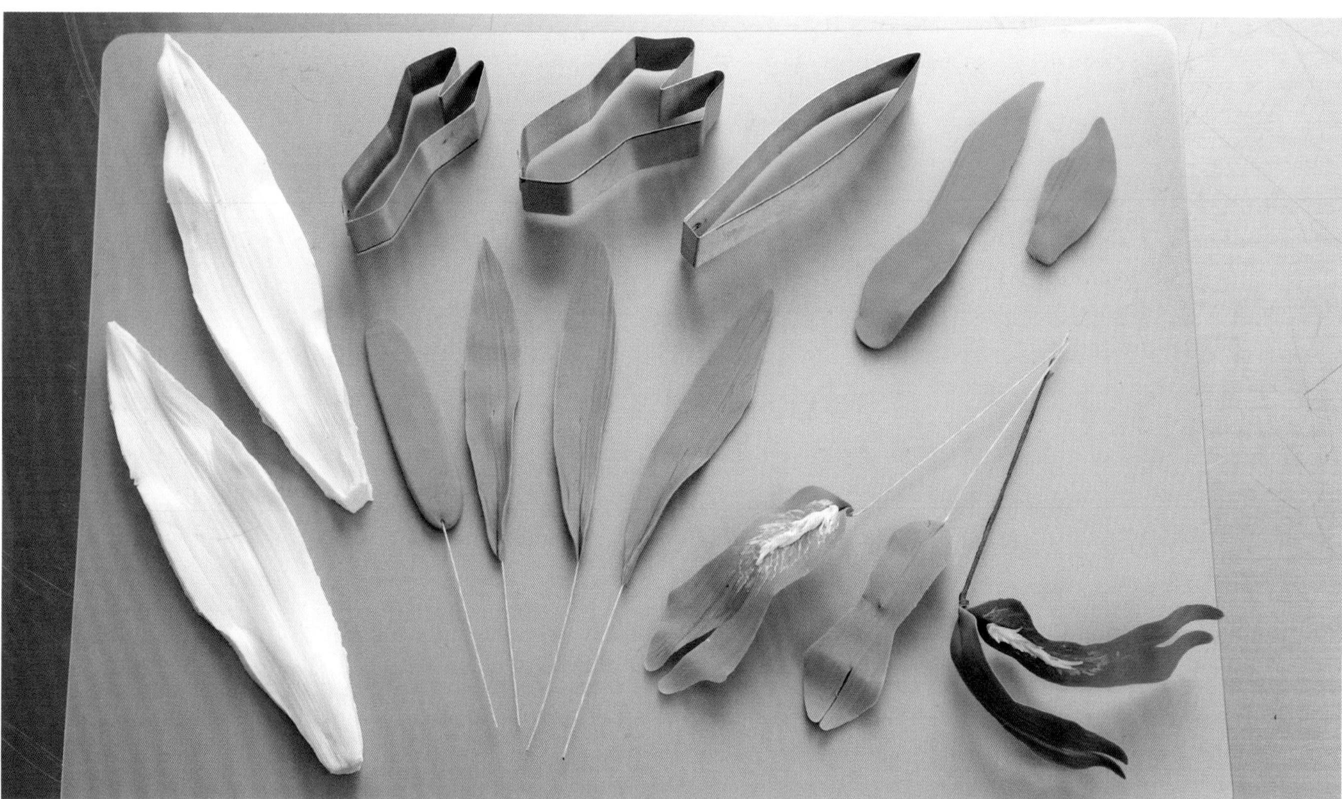

Cutters, moulds and pieces for the iris construction

5. Using a fine pair of scissors, snip the sausage to create feather-like points.
6. Place the petals to semi-dry in a curved position in an apple tray, for about 30 minutes.
7. Dust the edges of the petals with violet dusting colour, fading off toward the centre.
8. Dilute the white dusting powder with some vodka or clear alcohol. Use a fine brush to paint some fine white lines around the yellow sausage.

Crest Petals

1. Repeat steps 1 and 2 for the fall petals, to create 3 petals with the narrow fork-like cutters.
2. Using the fine point of the Dresden tool, indent a central vein in each of the petals. Soften the sides of the petals on a thin foam with the ball tool.
3. Put the ball tool on the fork-like points of the petal and move the ball tool toward the base, with slight pressure on the petal. This movement will cause the tip to curve back slightly. Repeat this process for the other 2 petals.
4. Leave to dry slightly in an apple tray.
5. Dust the petals with violet dusting colour.

Standard Petals

1. Repeat steps 1 and 2 for the crest petals, to create 3 standard petals with the slim petal shape cutter.
2. Place the petal on a thin form and soften the sides with a ball tool. Then use the pointed end of the Dresden tool to make the central vein.
3. Repeat this process for the other 2 petals.
4. Dust the petals with violet dusting colour.
5. Leave to dry slightly.

Assembly

1. Use half-width green florist's tape to tape together the standard upright petals together.
2. Tape the fall and crest petals together with the half-width green florist's tape. Ensure that the fork-like ends of both petals are curved downward. Do the same for the other two sets of petals.
3. Tape the combined fall and crest petals individually between the standard upright petals.

4. Tape an 18-gauge green wire to the stem with half-width green florist's tape for additional support.

Bracts

1. This flower has pointed leaf-like bracts that are attached to the main stem.
2. Roll green gumpaste thinly and use a cutting wheel to cut freehand some long leaf-like shapes, or use the templates provided on page 161.
3. Indent a central vein and texture the bracts lightly with fine lines, using the pointed end of the Dresden tool.
4. Attach the bracts under the flower with gum glue, in a vertical position overlapping the main stem.
5. Repeat to make 1 or 2 additional bracts for each iris stem.
6. Dust the bracts with green dusting colour.
7. Steam the bracts or brush with confectioner's glaze to give them a shine.

EIFFEL TOWER

When piping this structure, make sure to give yourself plenty of time; begin at least a week prior to doing the cake. Drying takes longer on humid days and because the pieces are so fragile and intricate the chances of breakage are extremely high. Leave yourself plenty of time for eye breaks and to repipe any broken pieces. Always pipe additional pieces of the templates, to allow for breakage. (See templates on page 162.) Make sure to use the rub-down method on page 38 for the Royal Icing with which you pipe the templates.

1. Cut a piece of wax paper large enough to fit over the templates.
2. Fill a bag fitted with tip number 1.5 with black Royal Icing and start piping the outlines of the template.
3. Leave the pieces to dry at least for 24 to 48 hours before removing them from the wax paper for assembly.

Assembly

To assemble the pieces you will need to fill a piping bag fitted with tip number 1.5 with black Royal Icing.

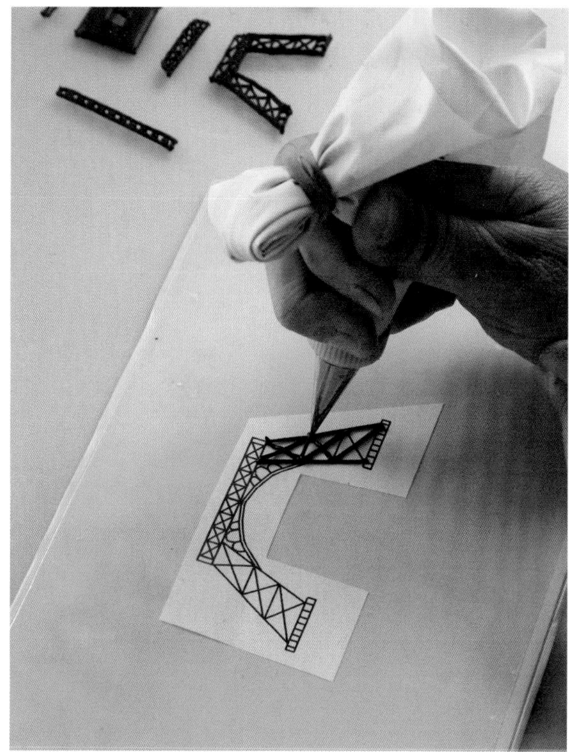

Piping the Eiffel Tower base

Base

1. Remove the pieces very carefully from the wax paper.
2. Cut a piece of foam to the same height as the base pieces and the width of piece #2 on the templates.
3. Join the 4 base pieces together with black Royal Icing, leaning the pieces against them.
4. Pipe a small bead border with black Royal Icing, using tip 1.5 to join the pieces together. Overpipe the seams with a zigzag border to strengthen them.
5. Leave the base to dry for 24 hours.
6. Pipe a line of icing underneath piece #2 on the 4 edges.
7. Place piece #2 on top of the base. Pipe a bead border with tip 1.5 to join the piece to the base. (See technique on page 37.)

Middle Section

1. Follow the steps for joining the base to create the middle section. Change the foam to fit the height of the middle section and the width of piece #5.
2. Leave to dry for 24 hours.
3. When dry, attach the middle section to the base

The completed macarons

section by piping a line of Royal Icing at the corners of piece #2.

4. Place the middle section on top and pipe Royal Icing into any gaps. Allow to dry for a few hours.

Top Section

1. Pipe icing along the bottom of piece #7 and on the corners of piece #5.
2. Place piece #7 onto piece #5 and stick the second piece of #7 in place. Ensure that the pieces are stuck together. Repeat this process with the balancing 2 pieces of #7 and allow to dry for 24 hours.

Finishing the Eiffel Tower

1. When the tower is fully dried, begin attaching the accent pieces with Royal Icing.
2. Overpipe the seams with additional zigzag borders wherever you think they might not be secured or sturdy enough.
3. Finish off the tower with piece #10.

FRENCH MACARONS

You will need to make about 30 mini-size macarons for this project.

1. Make the French macarons by following the recipe on page 14.
2. Use the smallest circle on the non-stick macaron mat (available for purchase from the list of suppliers on page 165) to make the macarons.
3. When baked, sandwich the macarons together with Swiss Meringue Buttercream Icing.
4. Airbrush the macarons with pink and pearl airbrush colours. Sprinkle some edible rainbow sparkles on the macarons.

FINAL ASSEMBLY

1. Use Royal Icing to position the middle 6-inch (15 cm) tier on top, in the centre of the already dowelled bottom 8-inch (20 cm) tier. Dowel the 6-inch (15 cm) tier. (See How to Stack a Tiered Cake on page 28.)
2. Repeat step 1 above for the 4-inch (10 cm) top tier. Ensure that you insert at least 3 dowels of the same height as the cake into the 4-inch (10 cm) cake tier underneath the 3-inch (8 cm) styrofoam, to support the weight of the Eiffel Tower.
3. Attach the 3-inch (8 cm) pre-covered styrofoam to the top of the 4-inch (10 cm) tier with Royal Icing.
4. Attach the 4-inch (10 cm) pre-covered styrofoam to the top of the 3-inch (8 cm) styrofoam with Royal Icing.
5. Attach the mini-macarons at the base of the 8-inch (20 cm) tier on the cakeboard with Royal Icing
6. Pipe a white Royal Icing bead border at the bottom of the 6-inch (15 cm) pink tier and at the bottom of the 4-inch (10 cm) styrofoam with a tip number 1.5.
7. Lastly, very carefully pipe some small dots of black Royal Icing onto the feet of the Eiffel Tower and place it on the 4-inch (10 cm) styrofoam. Allow the Royal Icing to fully dry for a few hours before moving the cake.

¡HOLA! SPAIN

SPAIN'S NATIONAL FLOWER is the red carnation. Associated with Spanish folklore, this flower symbolizes passion, caprice and desire. Biting the stem of a carnation while dancing is a means of expressing those characteristics.

The predominant colours of this cake are red and black, popular choices for flamenco dancers. Spanish lace is also incorporated.

LEVEL OF DIFFICULTY advanced skills

TECHNIQUES USED extension stringwork, piping, gumpaste flowers, figure modelling, lace points and lacework

CAKES AND EDIBLES

- about 9 lb (4 kg) red fondant
- about 3 oz (90 g) black fondant
- about 1 lb (450 g) black gumpaste
- about 1 lb (450 g) red gumpaste
- about 3 oz (90 g) green gumpaste
- Dusting Colours red and green
- black Royal Icing (page 20)
- gum glue
- cornstarch, for dusting

TOOLS AND EQUIPMENT

- 26 and 24 gauge florist's wires
- fine white head flower stamens
- carnation cutter
- rose calyx cutter
- lace embossers
- lace point stencils
- silicone rose mould
- piping bag
- piping tips 1.5, 2, 3 and 101
- metal ball tool
- Dresden tool
- foam pads
- cutting wheel
- silk veining tool
- brushes
- scriber
- round 4-inch (10 cm) styrofoam

TEMPLATES

- Carnation (page 163)

CAKE PREPARATION

Cakes for this project can be baked in petal-shaped cake pans that are available for purchase from the list of suppliers on page 165. It is advisable to cover the cakes a day ahead before starting on the piping work. See pages 25–27 for fondant-covering techniques.

1. Cover a 12-inch (30 cm) petal-shaped cakeboard, ¼-inch (6 mm) high, with red fondant.
2. Cover a 6-inch (15 cm) petal-shaped cake with red fondant.
3. Cover a 8-inch (20 cm) petal-shaped cake with red fondant. You may have to bake 2 cakes and stack them together in order to achieve the 6-inch (15 cm) height for this cake.
4. Cover a round 4-inch (10 cm) styrofoam, 3 inches (8 cm) high, with red fondant. This styrofoam will separate the top tier from the bottom tier.

Lace point stencil with black Royal Icing

5. To mark a guide for the extension work on the two cakes, first measure the circumference of each of the tiers with a length of receipt paper. (See also pages 36–39.) Then fold each strip into equal sections of about 1 inch (2.5 cm) wide for the 8-inch (20 cm) tier, and ½-inch (1 cm) wide for the 6-inch (15 cm) tier.
6. Using a pair of scissors, cut a gentle curve or scallop pattern from 1 side of the paper to the other. The width of the paper will also determine how high each piece of extension work will be. For this project, the width of the paper should be about 2 inches (5 cm) for the 8-inch (20 cm) tier, and 1 inch (2.5 cm) for the 6-inch (15 cm) tier.
7. Open each of the scalloped strips of paper and wrap around the appropriate tier. Position the straight side of the strips about ½ inch (1 cm) from the bottom of each tier, and hold them in position with pins. Each strip of paper should wrap comfortably around each cake. Using a scriber or pin, mark the scalloped lines and the height of the extension work onto the cake. The scalloped outline will be the guidelines for piping the bridges. Remove the paper.
8. Attach the 8-inch (20 cm) cake tier to the centre of the pre-covered cakeboard with some Royal Icing. Use the stacking technique on page 28 and dowel the 8-inch (20 cm) cake tier.
9. Attach the 4-inch (10 cm) pre-covered styrofoam to the top of the 8-inch (20 cm) cake tier, with Royal Icing.
10. Attach the 6-inch (15 cm) cake tier to the top of the 4-inch (10 cm) cake, with Royal Icing.
11. Pipe a bead border with black Royal Icing, using tip number 3, at the bottom of the 8-inch (20 cm) cake tier. (See technique on page 37.)
12. Pipe a bead border with black Royal Icing, using tip number 1.5, at the bottom of the 4-inch (10 cm) styrofoam tier.

DECORATIVE ICING

Bridges

1. Fill a piping bag one-third full with black Royal Icing and fit it with a number 2 tip. Do not overfill the bag.
2. Pipe the outline of the scallops around the sides of the cake for both tiers. Please ensure that each piped line touches the sides of the cake.
3. Repeat the previous step by piping another 4 layers of lines. Each layer of the piped lines must sit next to or against the previous layer. Use a damp brush, if necessary, to push the piped lines together and slightly against each other so that there are no gaps or holes between the layers of piped lines.
4. Leave to dry completely, preferably for a few hours.
5. When the bridge is completely dry, flood the bridge with thin red icing. (See How to Do Flooding on page 42.) This will give the bridge additional strength.

Extension Work

1. Place a number 1.5 tip in a piping bag filled with medium peak rubbed-down black Royal Icing. (See page 38 for the rub-down method.)
2. Starting at the top of the markings and at the centre of the first curve, pipe a straight line down to the bridge, ensuring that the end of the line touches the bridge. Clean off any extra icing or points with a damp brush.

Left: Lace loops as shown on the final cake; Right: Finished lace points

3. The extension line must not break or sag. Maintaining even pressure is essential; if any line breaks, the broken lines must be removed entirely from the bridge with a damp brush or a pin.
4. Pipe the next line close to the first line, ensuring that there is not enough space between these lines to pipe another line, and that all lines are evenly spaced.
5. Repeat steps 1 to 4 until the sides of both cake tiers are done.
6. To give a clean finish to the extension lines, pipe a small bead border, using the same tip, at the top and bottom of the extension lines.

Lace Loops

1. Using the same tip, pipe layers of loops at the bottoms of the bridges. Each loop should touch the lines above it for it to adhere.
2. You will need to pipe about 2 layers of loops underneath the 8-inch (20 cm) cake bridges, and 4 layers of loops underneath the 6-inch (15 cm) cake bridges. Each row of loops should be staggered with the row below it.

Lace Point Stencil

The lace point stencil is available for purchase from the list of suppliers on page 165.

1. Rub down a small amount of black Royal Icing with a palette knife. (See technique on page 38.)
2. Place the lace point stencil on top of some wax paper.
3. Spread the rubbed down Royal Icing on top of the stencil, using a palette knife.
4. Ensure that Royal Icing has been spread over every part of the stencil before gently removing it from the wax paper.
5. Leave the lace points on the wax paper to dry for a few hours. When dried, they should just slide off the paper. You will need to make about 80 pieces of these lace points.
6. Use a fine tweezer to lift the lace point from the paper.
7. Pipe 2 tiny dots of black Royal Icing at the bottom of each lace point and attach it to the top of the bead borders on both cake tiers.

Left: The lace appliqué as applied to white fondant; Right: The completed Flamenco dancer

Lace Appliqués

1. Roll some black gumpaste thinly onto a non-stick board.
2. Grease the lace embosser (available from the list of suppliers on page 165) lightly with vegetable spray.
3. Press the gumpaste into the lace embosser with a thin piece of foam.
4. Remove the lace from the embosser and use an X-Acto or utility knife to cut the round and long appliqués from the lace piece.
5. You will need to cut about 10 pieces of each of the round and long lace appliqués.
6. Attach the round lace appliqués to every other scallop edge of the 6-inch (15 cm) cake tier, with gum glue.
7. Attach the round appliqués to every scallop edge of the 8-inch (20 cm) cake tier. Attach the long lace appliqués in between the round appliqués with gum glue.
8. Overpipe the outline of each of the lace appliqué designs with black Royal Icing, using tip number 1.5.

Assembly

1. Using black Royal Icing and tip number 1.5, pipe lace loops in between the round lace appliqués on the 6-inch (15 cm) cake tiers, to resemble the outline of a shawl. (See the project photo.)
2. Pipe lace loops in between the round and long lace appliqués on the 8-inch (20 cm) cake tier with black Royal Icing, using tip number 1.5. (See the project photo.)

FLAMENCO DANCER

1. Colour some gumpaste with skin tone or ivory. Using the technique described in How to Make a Gumpaste Figurine on page 40, make the head and body of the doll.
2. Insert a cocktail stick across the shoulders, leaving both ends sticking out to support the arms. Allow the figure to dry overnight.
3. For the hair: Put some softened black fondant into the extruder with the multiple hole disc. Extrude the paste and attach the hair to the figurine using gum glue.

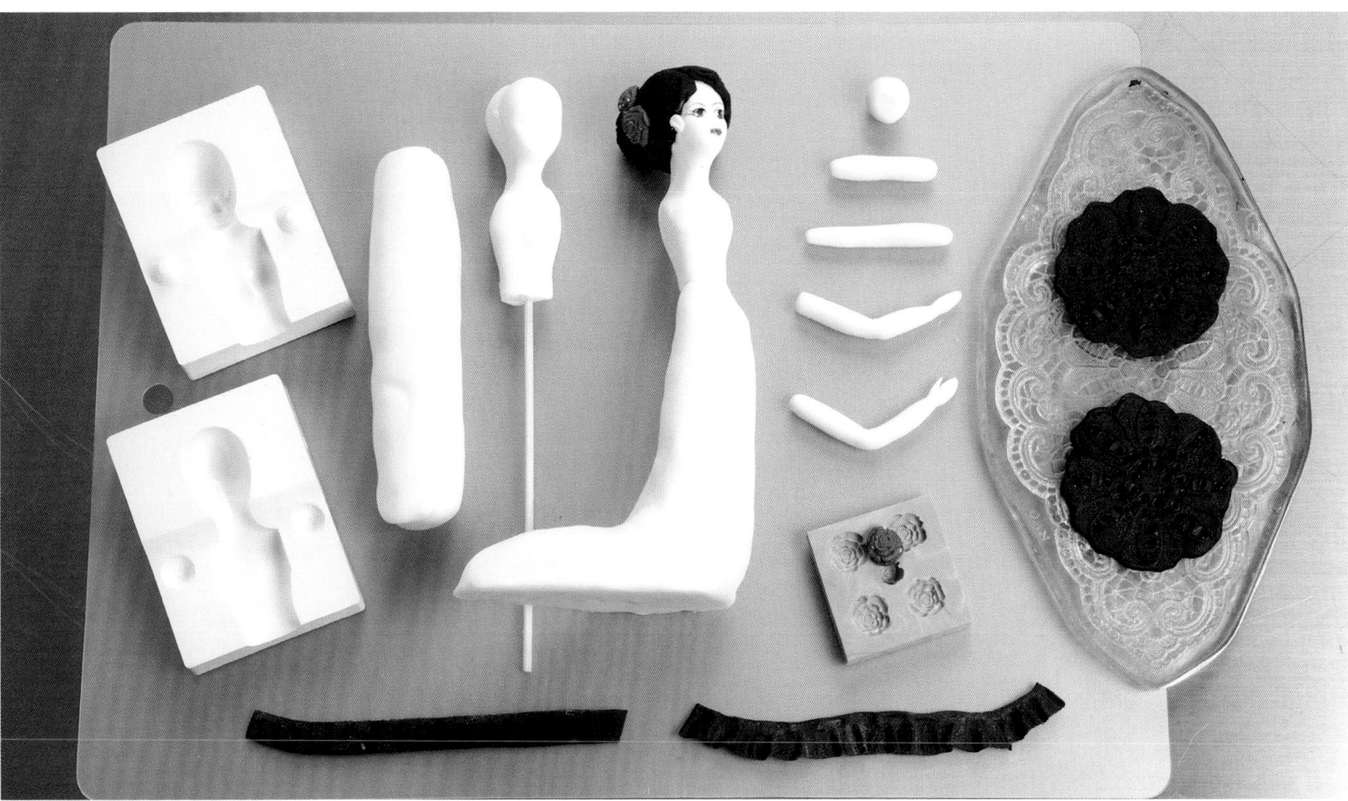

Moulds for creating the lace appliqué and Flamenco dancer

4. For each rose on the dancer's head or neck, knead a pea-size amount of red gumpaste into a ball and insert it into the silicone rose mould (available from the list of suppliers on page 165). Remove the rose from the mould and leave to dry for a few hours before attaching it to the hair and neck with gum glue. You will need to make about 6 of these roses.

Arms and Leg

1. To make the sleeves: Roll a medium piece of red gumpaste into a teardrop shape. Flatten the broad end slightly. Repeat to make a second sleeve.
2. To make the arms: Roll a small piece of ivory gumpaste into a column, with 1 end narrower than the other. Repeat to create a second arm, bending it slightly toward one end to create a bent elbow. (The sleeves and the arms together will make a full arm length.)
3. To make the hands: Roll a tiny piece of ivory gumpaste into a sausage shape, making one end narrower than the other. Flatten this end to resemble a hand. Use small fine-tip scissors to cut the fingers.
4. Using a ball tool, indent a hole into the broad end of the sleeve. Insert a short wooden skewer into the sleeve. Apply some gum glue around the skewer and attach the arm to the sleeve. Leave it to dry for a few hours.
5. Roll a small pea-size amount of ivory gumpaste into a narrow sausage, tapering off on 1 side to a length of about 1½ inches (4 cm).
6. Knead a tiny piece of red gumpaste into a teardrop. Elongate the point and flatten it slightly at the top, to resemble a shoe. Attach the shoe to the leg with gum glue.
7. Attach the leg to the front of the body with gum glue before attaching the frills of the skirt.

The Dress

1. For the dress: Roll and cut out a piece of red gumpaste measuring about 4 × 4 inches (10 × 10 cm). Apply some gum glue to the body of the doll and wrap the gumpaste around it. Cut off the excess gumpaste with a pair of scissors. Cut a "V" opening in the front and back, to resemble the neckline.

Carnation mould and gumpaste pieces

2. Use tip number 1.5 to pipe black Royal Icing dots on the body of her dress.
3. For the frills: Roll a long thin sausage of black gumpaste to about 6-inch (15 cm). Flatten it with a rolling pin and roll thinly. Use a cutting wheel to cut into ½-inch (1 cm) strips.
4. Sprinkle cornstarch onto your working surface and place the strip on top of it. Using your index finger, exert pressure toward the pointed end of the silk veining tool and roll it back and forth on the strip to create the frills. You will need at least 10 of these strips for the skirt.
5. Attach the rows of frills onto the skirt portion, overlapping each other as shown in the project photo. Always attach the bottom row of frills first, then work your way up.

Assembly

1. Apply some gum glue around the cocktail stick that has been inserted across the shoulders, with both ends sticking out to support the arms. Insert the sleeves into it. Allow to dry for a few hours.
2. Attach the figure to the top tier of the cake with a small amount of Royal Icing at the bottom of the figurine.

CARNATIONS

You will need to make 6 carnations for this project.

Stamens

1. Take a fine white head stamen, fold it in 2 and tape it to a white 26-gauge florist's wire that has been cut into 4 sections.
2. Roll a tiny ball of red gumpaste and thread it through the end of the wire, to prevent the stamens from moving.

Petals

1. Roll some red gumpaste very thinly on a no-stick mat.
2. Cut the petals with the carnation cutter.
3. Dust the surface you are working on with cornstarch.
4. With an X-Acto or paring knife, make a series of short cuts into the petal, extending the indentations around the edges.
5. Using the pointed end of the silk veining tool, frill the outside edges by exerting pressure on the veining tool and rolling it in a back-and-forth motion to create the frills.
6. Brush some gum glue in the centre of the petal and thread it up the wire. Fold the petal in half and stick the sides together to create a fan shape.

7. Brush a little gum glue onto the left side of the petal about one-third of the way in from the edge. Fold this section up and back onto itself, so that the bottom edge on the left hand side is now against 1 side of the wire. Turn the flower over and repeat the same process on the other side. Gently squeeze the base of the petals around the centre, to create a base.
8. Cut another petal and soften it as above. Brush gum glue in the centre and thread it up the wire, squeezing the base gently to secure the petal to the first layer.
9. Continue with this process for at least another 3 layers, until the carnation looks full and rounded.
10. Ensure that the centre stamens do not protrude higher than the petals. If they do, cut them to the desired height.

Calyx

1. Roll a thick Mexican hat out of green sugarpaste. Position a rose calyx cutter over the central point and cut out the calyx. Use a small ball tool to hollow and widen out the calyx. Remove the pointed ends of the calyx, leaving it quite rounded. Brush gum glue up the wire to meet the base of the flower. Try to fit the base of the flower in the hollow part of the calyx. Snip 5 small slits at the base of the calyx and push it up against the side of the calyx.

FINAL ASSEMBLY

1. Tape the carnations together with half-width green florist's tape into a posy shape. Place it on the cakeboard next to the bottom cake tier.

The finished carnations, above

NEW YORK! NEW YORK!

UNITED STATES

NICKAMED THE BIG APPLE, New York is one of the world's most populous cities. The rose is New York State's official flower, and symbolizes development and growth.

This project reflects New York's essense, with a sculptured apple cake, exuberant roses and a graffiti-covered building.

LEVEL OF DIFFICULTY easy to moderate skills

TECHNIQUES USED gumpaste flowers and cake sculpting

CAKES AND EDIBLES

- about 3 lb (1.4 kg) grey fondant
- about 2 lb (900 g) black fondant
- about 1½ lb (700 g) red fondant
- about 1 lb (450 g) red gumpaste
- about 3 oz (90 g) black gumpaste
- Dusting Colours red and green
- white Royal Icing (page 20)
- gum glue
- confectioner's glaze (optional, to create shine)

TOOLS AND EQUIPMENT

- 24-gauge florist's wires
- New York skyline patchwork cutters
- rose petal cutters
- rose leaf cutter
- leaf veiner
- metal ball tool
- Dresden tool
- foam pad
- brick wall texture mat
- brushes
- pizza cutter
- petal veiner
- rolling pin
- silk veining tool

TEMPLATES

- Rose (page 160)

CAKE PREPARATION

1. Cover a 14-inch (35 cm) square cakeboard with black fondant.
2. Stack three 6-inch (15 cm) square cakes on top of each other, to reach a height of approximately 9 inches (23 cm). Cover them with grey fondant. (See page 25 for How to Cover a Cake with Fondant.)
3. Using the brick wall texture mat, press the mat firmly against the fondant-covered cake, to imprint or emboss the design onto it. Continue embossing the brick wall effect on 3 sides of the cake.

BUILDING

1. Airbrush the brick with orange airbrush colour, followed by red and brown airbrush colours. You can overlap the colours onto each other to give it a more natural look.
2. Using the airbrush, spray the words "New York" on 1 side of the building to resemble graffiti. This is done freehand.
3. Grease the patchwork cutters well with vegetable spray. Wipe off the excess oil with a piece of paper towel.
4. Roll a piece of black gumpaste thinly on a non-stick mat.

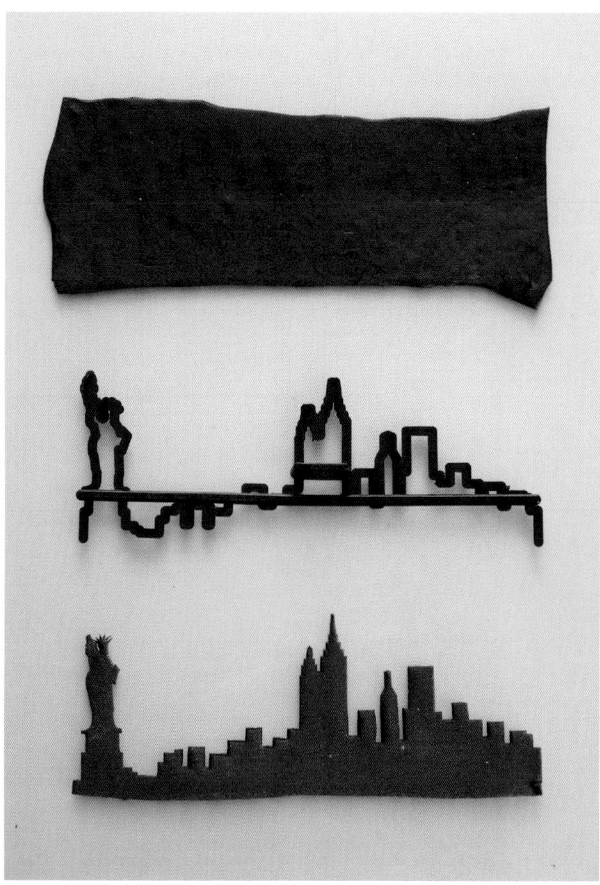

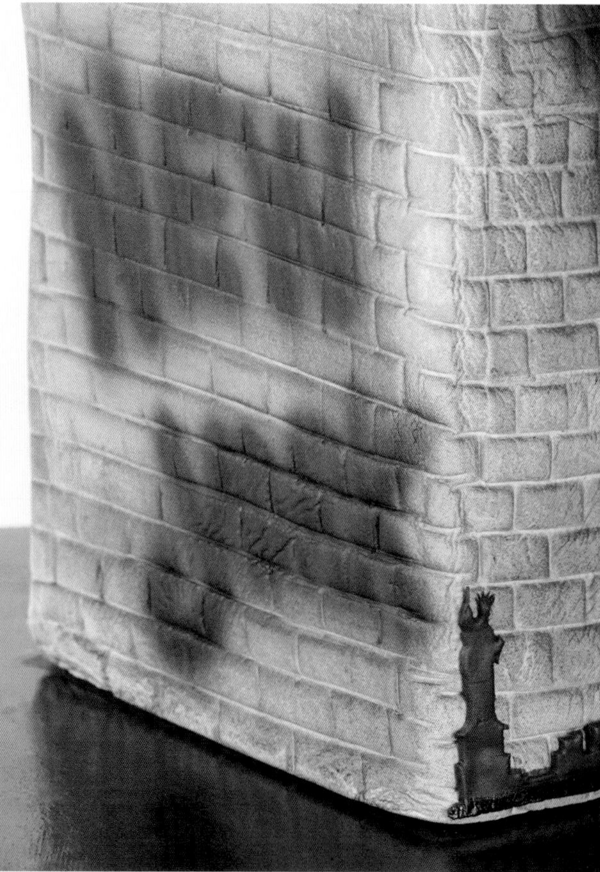

Left: Creating the New York skyline; Right: The completed building with iconic graffiti and New York skyline applied

5. Position the patchwork cutter on the gumpaste. Press hard on the cutter, to create the skyline shape.
6. Leave the cut skyline shape to dry for at least 24 hours.
7. When dried, brush some gum glue onto the back of the skyline shape and attach it to the front side of the brick wall.

APPLE CAKE

1. Refer to the technique on How to sculpt an Apple on page 31.
2. Frost the sculpted cake with buttercream and put it into the freezer for another hour
3. Remove from the freezer. Roll about 1½ lb (700 g) of red fondant to a thickness of ⅛-inch (3 mm).
4. Lift the fondant with a rolling pin and drape it over the cake. Smooth the fondant over the cakes with your hands.
5. Cut off the excess fondant with a pizza cutter.
6. Airbrush the cake with different tones of red, brown and yellow airbrush colours. Leave to dry for a few hours.
7. Roll about 1 oz (30 g) of brown gumpaste into a thin sausage. Flatten the top slightly, to resemble the stalk of an apple.
8. Insert a piece of wooden skewer into the top centre of the sculpted cake. Insert the stalk into the skewer.
9. Using the techniques on pages 32–33 for making petals and leaves create about 5 leaves. Vein the leaves on the leaf veiner.
10. Leave the leaves to dry on foil, so that they will curve slightly.
11. Dust the leaves with green and dip them into confectioner's glaze, to give them a shine.
12. Tape the leaves together into an "S" spray, using half-width green florist's tape.
13. Insert the leaf spray next to the apple stalk.

ROSE

You will need to make 5 medium open roses and 5 leaves for this project.

Centre

1. Cut a green 18-gauge florist's wire into 2. Make a hook at the end of the wire.
2. Roll a piece of red gumpaste into a narrow cone. Dip the hook into gum glue and insert into the broad end of the cone. Leave to dry overnight.
3. Repeat the steps above to make 4 more centres.

Petals

1. For the first layer of petals: Roll out white gumpaste thinly on a non-stick mat. Using the small rose petal cutter, cut out 5 petals. Do not wire the petals.
2. Vein the petals in the silicone rose petal veiner. Repeat the same steps with the other 4 petals. Brush gum glue onto the dried cone and wrap the first petal over it. Try to cover the cone entirely, but leave the last end of the petal open. Brush a little gum glue on 1 side of the second petal and tuck the glue side underneath the first petal, to create a spiral effect. Do not glue the end of the second petal to the cone. Continue in the same manner with the third, fourth and fifth petal to create the spiral centre of the rose.
3. For the second layer of petals: Roll and cut out another 5 petals, using the technique above but with the medium size cutter. Brush a little gum glue on the base of the petal in a "V" shape, and attach it to the spiral petals overlapping the joints. Repeat the same with the other 4 petals, overlapping each other.
4. For the third layer of petals: Roll and cut out another 7 petals, using the large size cutter. Soften the edges of the petals as above. Vein the petals with the petal veiner and turn over. Curl both sides of the petal with the silk veining tool.
5. Leave the petals to dry a little in the apple tray, with the curled sides underneath.
6. Attach the petals to the second layer in an overlapping manner.
7. Crumple some foil and shape it into a cup. Place the rose in the foil cup, to support it while it is drying.

Above: Completed apple with leaves; Below: Rose colour spray

Hold the foil up to the flower by using a paper clip underneath the foil, to prevent the foil cup from sliding down. Leave to dry for 24 hours.

8. Repeat steps 1 to 8 above to make 4 more roses.

Calyx

1. Roll out some green gumpaste thinly and cut out the calyx using the rose calyx cutter. Cut fine slits on both sides of each calyx segment. Attach to the rose bottom with gum glue.

Leaves

1. Using the wired petal and leaf techniques on pages 19–20, make 6 leaves with the rose leaf cutter.
2. Dry the leaves on foil, so that they will curve slightly.
3. When dry, dust the leaves with green-bean dusting powder. Dust a little aubergine or plum colour at the base of the leaf, fading out toward the edges of the leaf.
4. Steam or dip the leaves in confectioner's glaze, to give them a shine. Leave to dry for 24 hours.

Assembly

1. Tape the 4 roses, with different sizes of leaves between them, into an "S" spray. (See also Hogarth Curve on page 34.)
2. Tape 1 leaf beneath the last rose with half-width green florist's tape, to create a single spray.

FINAL ASSEMBLY

1. Use Royal Icing to attach the building cake to the pre-covered cakeboard, at an angle.
2. Dowel the cake with dowel rods, as shown in the stacking technique on page 28.
3. Attach the sculpted apple cake on top of the building cake with Royal Icing.
4. Insert a flower spike into the right top side of the building cake. Insert the "S" rose spray into the spike, to create a cascading effect on the side of the building.
5. Place the single rose spray next to the building on the cakeboard.

A CHANGE OF SEASONS
CANADA

CANADA DOES NOT have a national flower, but the maple leaf—which appears on its flag—symbolizes unity, tolerance and peace. The moose became a Canadian symbol in 1982.

Since Canada is known for its change of seasons, this project depicts three of the four seasons: winter, summer and autumn.

LEVEL OF DIFFICULTY easy to moderate skills

TECHNIQUES USED gumpaste modelling, gumpaste flowers and foliage, piping, stringwork and sugarwork

CAKES AND EDIBLES

- about 1½ lb (700 g) white fondant
- about 1½ lb (700 g) orange fondant
- about 3 lb (1.4 kg) yellow fondant
- about 2½ lb (1.25 kg) green fondant
- about 1 lb (450 g) white gumpaste
- about 1 lb (450 g) brown modelling chocolate
- small amount of blue gumpaste
- small amount of red gumpaste
- White Royal Icing (page 20)
- white isomalt nibs
- rainbow sparkles
- gum glue
- white dragee
- star anise
- Dusting Colours orange, brown, red and yellow
- confectioner's glaze (optional, to create shine)

TOOLS AND EQUIPMENT

- 24 and 26 gauge florist's wires
- brown florist's tape
- silicone snowflake mould
- piping bag
- tip number 1.5, 44 and 12
- maple leaf cutters
- small blossom cutter
- maple leaf veiner
- oak leaf template
- metal ball tool
- Dresden tool
- foam pad
- brushes
- pizza cutter
- textured rolling pin
- silk veining tool

TEMPLATES

- Maple Leaves (page 164)

CAKE PREPARATION

See pages 25–27 for fondant-covering techniques as well as page 29 for constructing a Topsy-Turvy Cake.

1. Cover a 14-inch (35 cm) square cakeboard with green fondant.
2. Cover a 10-inch (25 cm) topsy-turvy cake with yellow fondant.
3. Cover an 8-inch (20 cm) topsy-turvy cake with orange fondant.
4. Cover a 6-inch (15 cm) topsy-turvy cake with white fondant.
5. Attach the 10-inch (25 cm) cake tier to the centre of the cakeboard with some Royal Icing.
6. Stack the 8-inch (20 cm) and 6-inch (15 cm) cake tiers on top of the 10-inch (25 cm) cake, using the stacking technique on page 28. Ensure that each tier is

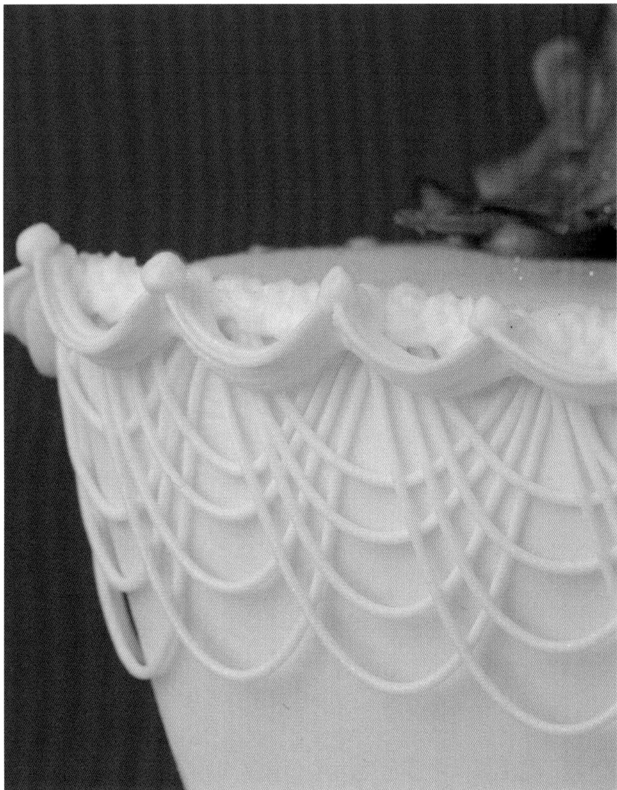

Left: Piped bridges on the bottom tier; Right: Isomalt snowflakes and beaded border on the finished project

dowelled and positioned at the angles shown in the project photo.

BOTTOM 10-INCH (25 CM) TIER

1. Divide the cake into 1-inch (2.5 cm) segments, using the technique on page 36.
2. Pipe dots on the marked segments for the overlapping dropped stringwork.
3. Use a bag fitted with tip number 1.5, with white Royal Icing, to pipe 4 rows of dropped stringwork, with the longest dropped string being 2 inches (5 cm) from the top edge of the cake. Connect alternate dots.
4. Pipe another set of 4 dropped stringwork, connecting the dots that are missed to create an overlapping effect.
5. Repeat steps 3 to 4 all around the cake.
6. Using the same tip, pipe a zigzag border on the top edge of the cake. (See technique on page 37.)
7. Pipe bridges connecting the dots at the top of the overlapping dropped stringwork. Refer to the bridge technique in the ¡Hola! Spain project on page 128.
8. Pipe a bead border at the bottom of the cake, using tip number 44 and white Royal Icing.

MIDDLE 8-INCH (20 CM) TIER

1. Divide the bottom tier evenly into ¼-inch (6 mm) spaces, using the dividing technique on page 36.
2. Pipe dots on the marked segments for the overlapping dropped stringwork
3. Using a 1.5 tip, pipe Royal Icing strings between the spaces, starting with the longest, which should extend down about 1 inch (2.5 cm) from the top edge of the cake.
4. Repeat the process with another 2 layers of dropped strings, making each one shorter than the last, as shown.
5. Repeat the above process with overlapping stringwork, as shown.
6. Using the same tip, pipe a bead border at the top edge of the middle tier. (See technique on page 37.)

TOP 6-INCH (15 CM) TIER

1. Use 1 tsp (5 mL) of water to every 1 cup (250 mL) of stiff Royal Icing in order to make Royal Icing of medium consistency. Then use tip 12 to pipe the Royal Icing onto the sides of the cake in an up-and-down

Pieces for the moose and acorns

motion. Let the Royal Icing run slightly down to the middle tier. This method will create a snow effect on the cake.

2. Attach the isomalt snowflakes (described below) to the top edge of the tier with some white Royal Icing, leaving a gap of about ½-inch (1 cm) between each snowflake.
3. Pipe 2 rows of dropped strings connecting the two lower points of each snowflake with the longest dropped string, extending about 1½ inches (4 cm) from the centre of each snowflake.
4. Attach a white dragee to each of the 2 points of the dropped strings, with a dot of white Royal Icing.

ISOMALT SNOWFLAKES

You will need to make about 12 snowflakes for this project. The silicone snow mould can be purchased from the list of supplies on page 165.

1. To make the snowflakes, spray the silicone snowflake mould with vegetable spray.
2. Put about 5 or 6 isomalt nibs in a silicone cup and microwave for about 20 to 30 seconds. When the isomalt has melted, stir it with a wooden skewer to eliminate the air bubbles. Be careful with melted isomalt, as it is very hot and can cause serious burns.
3. Add rainbow sparkles to create glitter in the snowflakes.
4. Pour the melted isomalt into the snowflake mould and allow it to set for about 20 minutes or slightly more, depending upon local humidity. You may need to melt more isomalt in order to make the required number of snowflakes for this project.

MOOSE

1. To make the head: Using your fingers, shape a small piece of brown modelling chocolate into a teardrop shape. Use the Dresden tool to model the teardrop into a moose head, as shown.
2. To make the body: Using your fingers, roll a large piece of brown modelling chocolate into a large teardrop or cone shape. Use the Dresden tool to model it into a moose body shape, as shown in the photo.
3. To make the legs: Roll 4 medium pieces of brown modelling chocolate into sausage shapes

Above: Completed moose; Below: Completed snowman

proportionate to the size of the moose's body. Using your fingers, mould the sausages into legs, creating bumps for the knees, calves and hooves.

4. To make the antlers: Using your fingers, shape two small pieces of white modelling chocolate into sausage shapes. Use the Dresden tool to model them into antlers.

Assembly

1. Using gum glue, attach the legs to the body, then attach the head to the body, and then attach the antlers to the head. Allow to dry for 24 hours.

SNOWMAN

Body

1. Roll a large piece of white gumpaste into a ball 3 inches (8 cm) in diameter.

Head and Face

1. Roll a smaller ball of white gumpaste to about 2¼ inches (5.6 cm) in diameter. Roll 2 smaller pieces of gumpaste and attach them with gum glue to the sides of the smaller ball, to represent the cheeks. Roll a small piece of white fondant to cover the two small balls. Smooth out the seams with the broad end of the Dresden tool.
2. Use the pointed end of a veining tool to indent 2 holes into the head for eye sockets. Roll 2 tiny pieces of blue gumpaste into balls. Using gum glue, attach the 2 blue balls into the eye sockets. Roll 2 tiny balls of black gumpaste, flatten them, and attach them on top of the blue balls for pupils. With a brush, paint a white dot in the middle of each pupil.
3. Roll a small ball of orange paste into a cone shape for the nose and attach with gum glue.
4. Indent the mouth with the "smile" end of the silk veining tool.
5. Dust the cheeks slightly with pink dust.
6. Attach the body and head together with gum glue. Leave to dry for a few hours.

Arms

1. Roll 2 sausages made of white gumpaste and attach them to the body with gum glue, as arms.

Mittens

1. Roll 2 red teardrops, flatten them slightly and create thumbs with a sharp pair of scissors. Attach these to the arms, using gum glue. Roll a thin sausage to hide the joint between the mittens and the arm.

Buttons

1. Roll out about 4 small balls of yellow gum-paste for the buttons. Attach them to the body of the snowman with gum glue.

Scarf

1. Roll a rectangular piece of blue gumpaste, and texture it with a texturized rolling pin. Cut slits at both ends of the rectangular paste with a pair of scissors.

Hat

1. Roll a red ball of paste large enough to cover the head. Flatten the paste and attach it to the head with gum glue. Roll a piece of yellow gumpaste into a sausage, then flatten and elongate it to go around the head, on top of the red paste, hat band. Texture to form the band with the pointed end of the Dresden tool.
2. Roll a small red ball of gumpaste and cut slits into it with a pair of scissors. Attach this to the back of the hat as a pompom.

MAPLE LEAVES, ACORNS AND OAK LEAVES

Maple Leaves

1. Roll a large piece of white gumpaste thinly onto a non-stick cutting board.
2. Using the 2 different sizes of maple leaf templates on page 164, cut out 15 maple leaves.
3. Leave them to dry for 24 hours on crumpled aluminum foil, so that they curve naturally.
4. When dry, dust the leaves with various shades of orange, brown, red and yellow dusting colours, to create the effect of autumn colours.

The completed acorns and rocks for the bottom tier

Acorns

1. Cut a 26-gauge wire into 3 sections and make a hook at the end of each wire.
2. Roll a pea-size amount of white gumpaste into an egg shape.
3. Moisten the hook with gum glue and insert it into the rounded end of the egg shape.
4. Use tweezers to insert the pointed end of star anise at the pointed end of the egg shape, to resemble the tip of an acorn.
5. Dust with yellow and brown dusting colours. Steam or dip into confectioner's glaze, to give it a shine.
6. Roll another small piece of white gumpaste into a ball. Flatten the top of the ball slightly and make a hole in it with the ball tool, creating a cup-like shape. Then use the ball tool to hollow out and thin down the edges of the cup.
7. Brush the base of the acorn with gum glue and push the gumpaste cup up beneath the acorn, roughly to

resemble the calyx. Taper the gumpaste around and down the bottom of the cup to ensure that it fits neatly onto the wire and does not slide off.

8. Use the pointed end of a wooden skewer to prick and to texture the cup's surface. Leave it to dry for a few hours.
9. When dried, dust the cup with various shades of brown, yellow and green dusting colours. Dust the cup so as to look slightly darker than the acorn.

Oak Leaves

1. Using the techniques to make wired petals and leaves on pages 32–33, make about 12 oak leaves with an oak leaf cutter.
2. Allow the oak leaves to dry on crumpled aluminum foil, so that they will curl slightly.
3. When dried, dust the leaves with shades of brown, orange, yellow, and red dusting colours.
4. Steam or dip into confectioner's glaze, to give them a shine.

Assembly

1. Tape the acorns with half-width brown florist tape, singly, in pairs or in clusters of 3 with leaves around them. Tape the stem down with half-width brown florist's tape.

ROCKS, FORGET-ME-NOTS AND LEAVES

Rocks

1. Mix black, grey, brown and ivory gumpaste together, to create a marbleized effect.
2. Roll the mixed gumpaste into differently sized balls, to represent rocks.

Forget-Me-Nots

1. Roll tiny balls of yellow gumpaste. Cut 26-gauge wires into 2-inch (5 cm) lengths.
2. Insert the wires into the little balls, having dipped them first into gum glue.
3. Roll blue gumpaste thinly. Cut out the flower, using the blossom plunger.
4. Apply gum glue to the flower petal and insert the wire through it.
5. Make about 6 to 12 of these flowers and attach them to a white 24-gauge wire.

Leaves

1. Roll green gumpaste thinly into a sausage. Insert a 26-gauge wire into the sausage.
2. Flatten the sausage until thin. Cut it into long leaf shapes, using a cutting wheel.
3. Allow to dry.
4. When dry, dust with green dusting colour.

FINAL ASSEMBLY

1. Using Royal Icing, attach the maple leaves to the sides of the middle tier in an overlapping fashion.
2. Roll a small piece of white fondant and attach it with Royal Icing to the top of the 6-inch (15 cm) tier, creating a platform for the snowman to sit on. Leave it to dry for an hour.
3. Insert a wooden skewer into the cake, in the centre of the platform. Ensure that the wooden skewer that is protruding from the cake is no higher than the snowman.
4. Insert the base of the snowman into the wooden skewer.
5. Pipe some Royal Icing with tip number 12, to both hide the platform and to act as glue for attaching the snowman.
6. Leave to dry for a few hours.
7. Place the acorn sprays next to the maple leaves on the board, as shown in project photo.
8. Attach the moose to one side of the cakeboard, with some Royal Icing.
9. Position and attach the rocks on the other side of the cakeboard, with Royal Icing.
10. Insert the blue forget-me-not flowers into the rocks.
11. Glue a ¼-inch (6 mm) green satin ribbon to the sides of the cakeboard.

SPRINGTIME: JAPAN

Floating Collar

Cherry Blossom

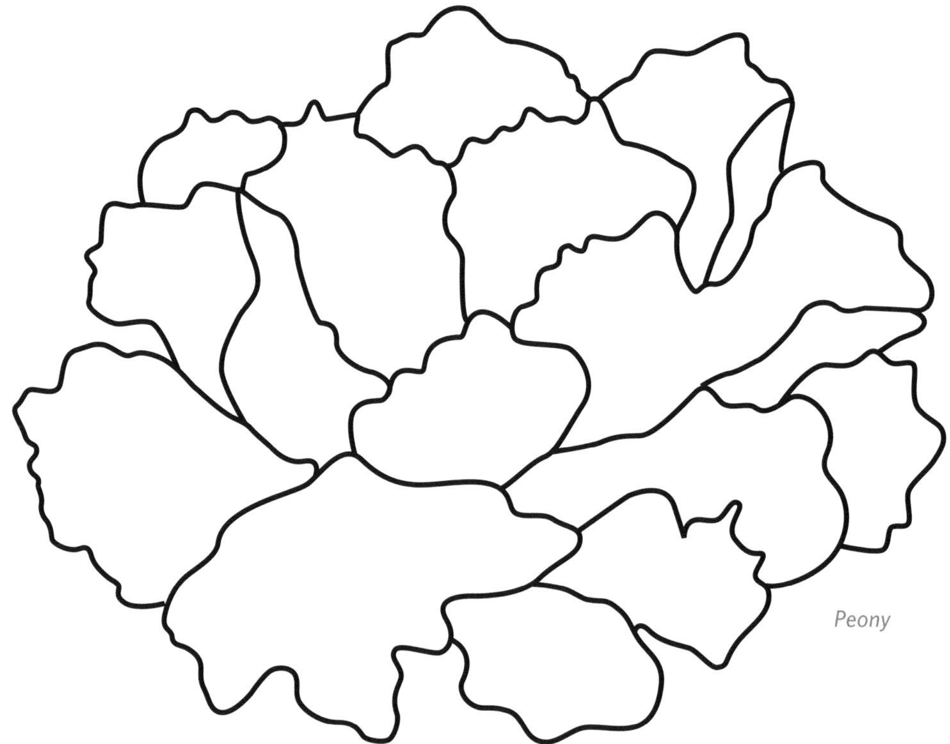

Peony

Peony Petals
Leaves

Hibiscus

Hibiscus Leaves

Moth Orchid Petal

A SHOWER OF GOLD: THAILAND

Cassia Fistula

Thai Figurine

Jasmine Petal and Calyx

Lotus

Lotus Leaves

Peacock

Daisy

Design

Calyx
Rose

A PARISIAN AFTERNOON: FRANCE

Poodle

Iris Petals

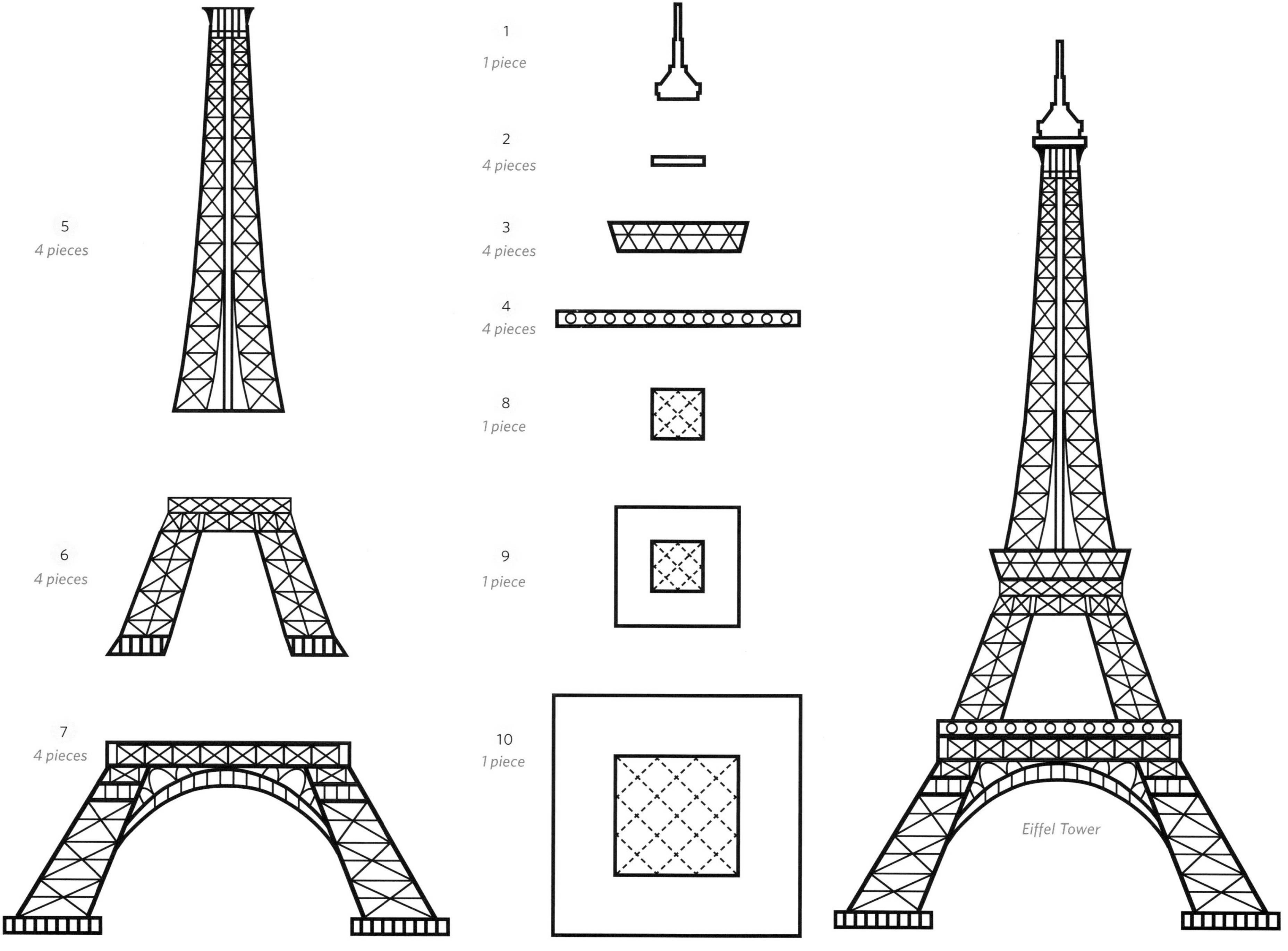
5
4 pieces
6
4 pieces
7
4 pieces
1
1 piece
2
4 pieces
3
4 pieces
4
4 pieces
8
1 piece
9
1 piece
10
1 piece
Eiffel Tower

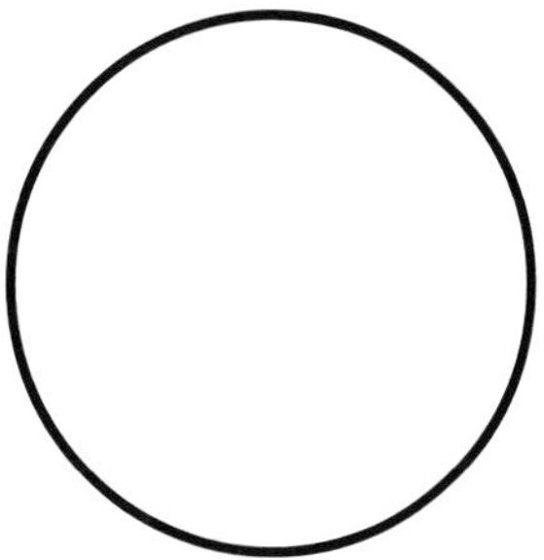

Carnation

Maple Leaves

SUPPLIERS

CANADA

Creative Cutters
561 Edward Avenue, Unit 1,
Richmond Hill, Ontario L4C 9W6 Canada
Telephone: 905 883 5638

SugarTiers Inc.
Unit 4, 735 Markland Street
Markham, Ontario L6C 0G6 Canada
Telephone: 905 888 9880
Website: www.sugartiers.ca

MALAYSIA

International Centre of Cake
Artistry Sdn. Bhd. (ICCA)
Wisma ICCA, 1 Jalan PJU 5/15
Dataran Sunway, Kota Damansara
Petaling Jaya, Selangor 47810 Malaysia
Telephone: 603 6140 8835
Website: www.iccacakedecor.com

Tan See Fong Unique Cake Decorating
No. G65-A/1, Jln. Bukit Melaka 1/5
Tmn Bukit Melaka, Bukit Brung
Melaka 75450 Malaysia
Telephone: 606 2329 268

UNITED KINGDOM

Squires Kitchen UK
3 Waverley Lane
Farnham, Surrey GU9 8BB United Kingdom
Telephone: +44 1252 260 260 (outside the UK) or
0845 61 71 810 (in the UK)

Patchwork Cutters
Unit 12, Arrowe Commerical Park,
Arrowebrook Road,
Upton, Wirral CH49 1AB United Kingdom.
Telephone: 0151 678 5053
Website: www.patchworkcutters.co.uk/

Orchard Products
51 Hallyburton Road,
Hove, East Sussex BN3 7GP United Kingdom
Telephone: 01273 419418
Website: www.orchardproducts.co.uk

Tinkertech Two (TT)
40 Langdon Road,
Parkstone, Poole,
Dorset BH14 9EH United Kingdom.

CelCakes and CelCrafts (CC)
Springfield House
Gate Helmsley, York YO41 INF United Kingdom.
Website: www.celcrafts.com

FMM Sugarcraft
Unit 7, Chancerygate Business Park
Whiteleaf Road
Hemel Hempstead, Herts HP3 9HD United Kingdom
Telephone: +44 01442 292970
Website: www.fmmsugarcraft.com

The Old Bakery
Kingston St. Mary
Taunton TA2 8HW United Kingdom
Telephone: +44 (0)1823 451205
Website: www.oldbakery.co.uk

EUROPE

Flower Veiners
Boetonstraat 8-H
1095 XL Amsterdam, Netherlands
Telephone: +31 20 707 0446
Email: info@flowerveiners.nl

U.S.A.

Wilton USA
7511 Lemont Road
Darien, IL 60561 USA
Telephone: 630 985 6000
Website: www.wilton.com

Cake Play LLC
15770 85th Pl. N.
Maple Grove MN 55311 USA
Telephone: 763 496 1779
Website: www.cakeplay.com

Designer Stencils
2503 Silverside Road
Wilmington, DE 19810 USA
Telephone: 1 302 475 7300
Website: www.designerstencils.com

Satin Fine Foods, Inc.
(Satin Ice Fondant)
32 Leone Lane, Unit 1
Chester, NY 10918 USA
Telephone: 845 469 1034
Website: www.satinice.com

Americolor Corporation
341 C Melrose Street
Placentia, CA 92870 USA
Telephone: 714 996 1820
Website:

ACKNOWLEDGEMENTS

My sincere thanks and appreciation to Whitecap Books for giving me the opportunity to publish my first book on cake decorating.

My sincere thanks to Neil for his belief in my work. As a sugarpaste artist and as someone who loves to teach and to share my skills, I believe that a book is truly the best legacy I can leave to those who love this art.

I would like to thank the many people who have touched my life in this field.

To all my past instructors, the outstanding sugarpaste artists and mentors who have shared their knowledge and skills, my profound thanks and gratitude. My sincere thanks to all my staff at International Centre of Cake Artistry (Malaysia), Sugartiers (Canada) and Evalin for their patience, support and understanding.

A special thanks to my friends at Wilton (USA) who were there at the very beginning of my interest in this art. My sincere appreciation to Sandy Folsom for my first Masters Diploma in cake decorating.

I would also like to express my gratitude and appreciation to all my friends at Squires Kitchen (UK), especially to Beverley and Robert Dutton for their support, belief and confidence in my work.

My heartfelt thanks to Alan Dunn, a great sugarpaste artist, mentor and friend, who gave me excellent tips and instructions for creating the flowers and for writing this book. There are countless other instructors and artists I would like to thank: Geraldine Randlesome (my first instructor in Canada), Rose Wallace, Eddie Spence, Jamie Ho, Debbie Brown, Peggy Porschen, Alex Tan, Paddi Clark, Colette Peters, Nicholas Lodge, Lorraine McKay, and many others who have contributed to my cake decorating journey. These include my tutors at the Ritz Escoffier (Paris), who guided me throughout my Masters in French pastry and during my internship at the Ritz Hotel in Paris. It was a good thing not to know too much French in those days; I discovered that when you made a mistake and got a telling-off in French, it didn't feel so bad if you didn't know what they were saying!

Finally, my thanks to my beloved mum, who was the first mentor and supporter of my cake decorating skills. Without you, Mum, there would not be me or this book.

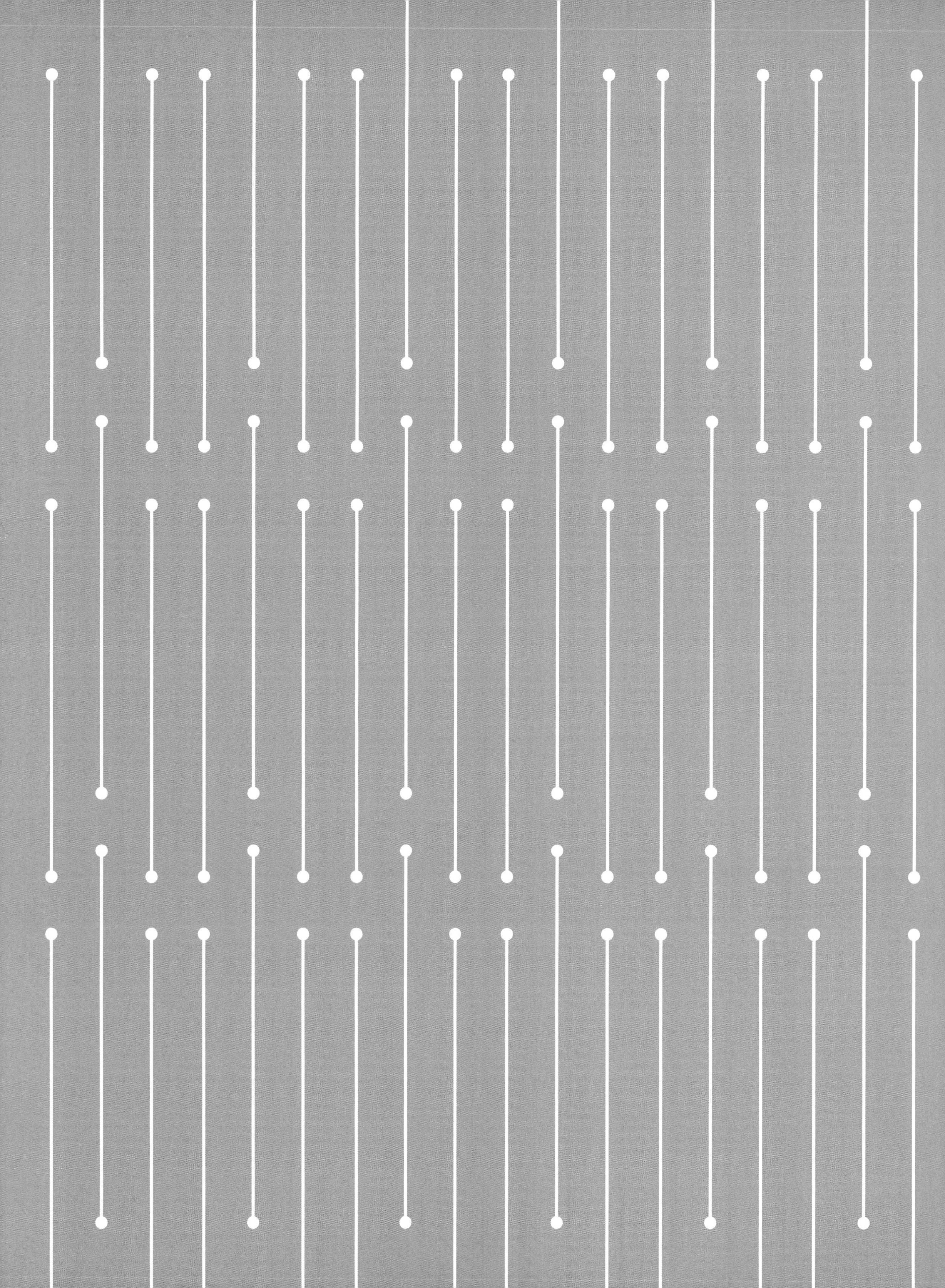

INDEX

s

s

	1B	2B	3A	4A	5A	6A	7A	8A
							1 **H** 1.008	2 **He** 4.003
			5 **B** 10.81	6 **C** 12.01	7 **N** 14.01	8 **O** 16.00	9 **F** 19.00	10 **Ne** 20.18
			13 **Al** 26.98	14 **Si** 28.09	15 **P** 30.97	16 **S** 32.06	17 **Cl** 35.45	18 **Ar** 39.95
8 **Ni** .69	29 **Cu** 63.55	30 **Zn** 65.38	31 **Ga** 69.72	32 **Ge** 72.64	33 **As** 74.92	34 **Se** 78.96	35 **Br** 79.90	36 **Kr** 83.80
6 **d** 6.4	47 **Ag** 107.9	48 **Cd** 112.4	49 **In** 114.8	50 **Sn** 118.7	51 **Sb** 121.8	52 **Te** 127.6	53 **I** 126.9	54 **Xe** 131.3
8 **t** 5.1	79 **Au** 197.0	80 **Hg** 200.6	81 **Tl** 204.4	82 **Pb** 207.2	83 **Bi** 209.0	84 **Po** [209]	85 **At** [210]	86 **Rn** [222]
0 **s** 31]	111 **Rg** [280]	112 **Cn** [285]	113 [283]	114 [289]	115 [288]	116 [293]	117 [294]	118 [294]
3 **u** 2.0	64 **Gd** 157.3	65 **Tb** 158.9	66 **Dy** 162.5	67 **Ho** 164.9	68 **Er** 167.3	69 **Tm** 168.9	70 **Yb** 173.1	71 **Lu** 175.0
5 **m** 43]	96 **Cm** [247]	97 **Bk** [247]	98 **Cf** [251]	99 **Es** [252]	100 **Fm** [257]	101 **Md** [258]	102 **No** [259]	103 **Lr** [262]

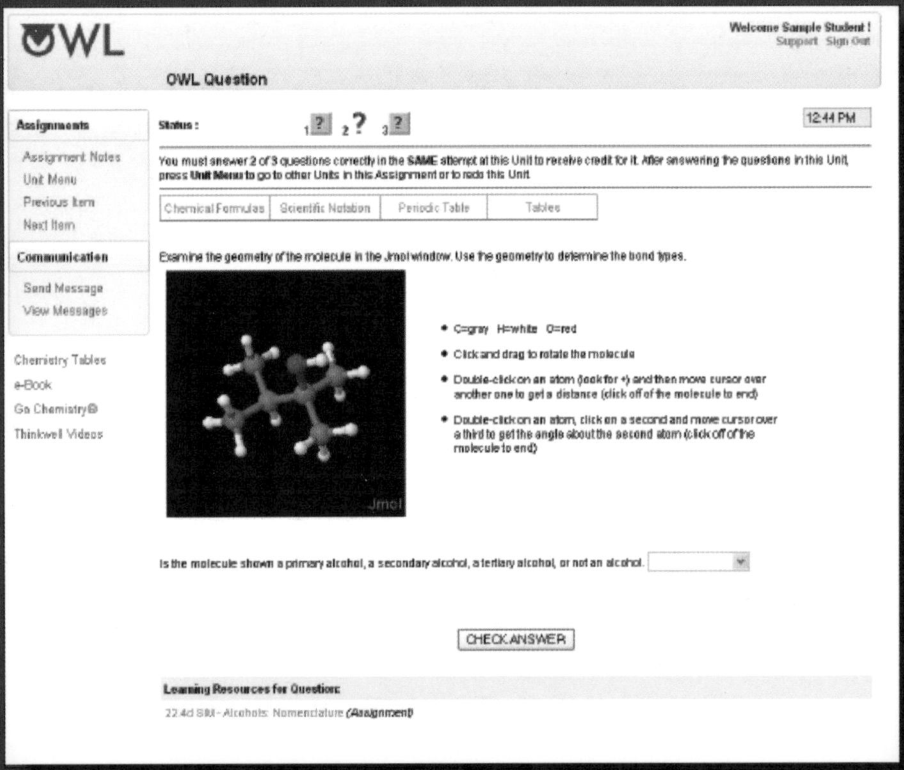

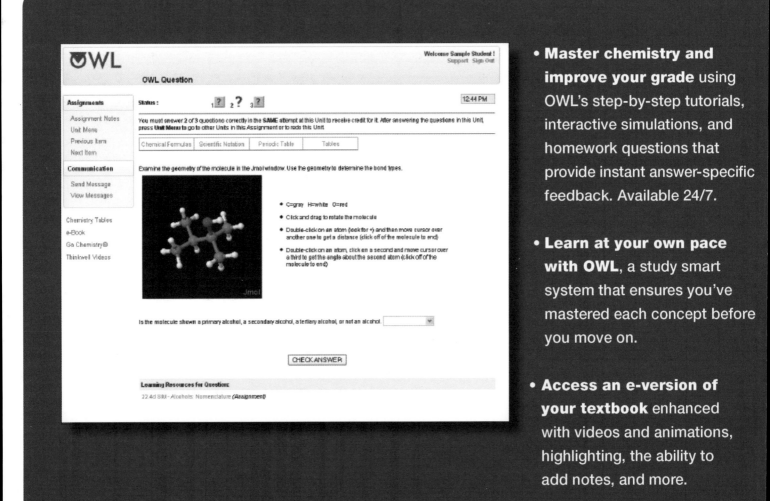

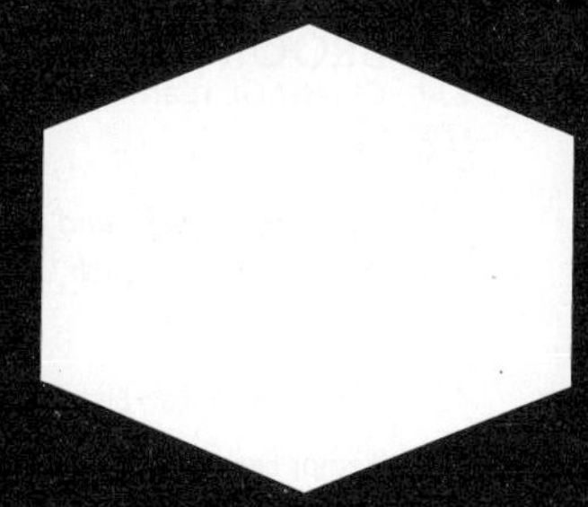

General, Organic, and Biochemistry:

An Applied Approach

James Armstrong
City College of San Francisco

Contributions by
Kellee Hollyman, RN, BSN, MN-Nurse Educator

Australia • Brazil • Japan • Korea • Mexico • Singapore • Spain • United Kingdom • United States

General, Organic, and Biochemistry: An Applied Approach
James Armstrong

Executive Editor: Lisa Lockwood
Senior Development Editor: Sandra Kiselica
Assistant Editor: Elizabeth Woods
Senior Media Editor: Lisa Weber
Media Editor: Stephanie Van Camp
Marketing Director: Nicole Hamm
Marketing Assistant: Kevin Carroll
Marketing Communications Manager: Linda Yip
Content Project Manager: Teresa Trego
Design Director: Rob Hugel
Art Director: John Walker
Print Buyer: Judy Inouye
Rights Acquisitions Specialist/Text: Roberta Broyer
Rights Acquisitions Specialist/Image: Don Schlotman
Production Service: Graphic World, Inc.
Text Designer: Brian Salisbury
Art Editor: Steve McEntee
Photo Researcher: Bill Smith Group
Copy Editor: Graphic World, Inc.
OWL Producers: Stephen Battisti, Cindy Stein, David Hart (Center for Educational Software Development, University of Massachusetts, Amherst)
Illustrators: Steve McEntee, Laura Brown, Graphic World, Inc.
Cover Designer: John Walker
Cover Image: hemoglobin © Kallista Images/Getty Images; spinach (RF photo) © Corbis; exercisers (RF photo) © Master file; blood cells © Micro Discovery/Corbis
Compositor: Graphic World, Inc.

Library of Congress Control Number: 2010935204
ISBN-13: 978-0-534-49349-3
ISBN-10: 0-534-49349-1

Brooks/Cole
20 Davis Drive
Belmont, CA 94002-3098
USA

Cengage Learning is a leading provider of customized learning solutions with office locations around the globe, including Singapore, the United Kingdom, Australia, Mexico, Brazil, and Japan. Locate your local office at **www.cengage.com/global.**

Cengage Learning products are represented in Canada by Nelson Education, Ltd.

To learn more about Brooks/Cole, visit **www.cengage.com/brookscole**
Purchase any of our products at your local college store or at our preferred online store **www.cengagebrain.com.**

Printed in China
2 3 4 5 14 13 12 11

Dedication

To my wife Debbie, for keeping me sane, for being the partner of my dreams, and for making sure that I take time to walk among the flowers and the redwoods.

To my children Becky and Casey, for reminding me every day how miraculous the world is, for being the most wonderful daughters any father could have, and for making sure that I take the time to make music and play Yahtzee.

To my parents, for a lifetime of love and support.

The Author, Jim Armstrong

Jim Armstrong grew up on the East coast and attended Harvard University as an undergraduate student, then moved to the West coast for graduate school. Since earning his Master's degree at the University of California at Berkeley, Jim has taught in the California community college system. He has been on the faculty of City College of San Francisco for the past 20 years, during which time he has taught the full range of lower-division chemistry courses, with particular emphasis on the single-term GOB course. Ten years ago, he collaborated with the CCSF biology and nursing departments on an extensive revision of the GOB curriculum, and the success of the course revision led to the writing of this textbook. Besides teaching and writing, Jim enjoys playing piano and trombone, collecting topographic maps, hiking, birdwatching, and doting on his wonderful twin daughters.

Contributor and Expert Reviewer, Kellee Hollyman

Kellee Hollyman enjoys residing with her family in the Pacific Northwest of the United States. As a nursing professor, she teaches students at all levels and in varying collegiate nursing programs from Associate's Degree to Alternative Entry Master's degree. As a Registered Nurse, she is a dedicated healthcare provider who has practiced in many areas: intensive care, cardiac intensive care, medical-surgical, and clinic management.

She received her Bachelor's degree in Nursing and Master's degree in Nursing Education from Washington State University and her RN degree from Clark College.

While a graduate student, she received the 2008 Student Activist Award, given in recognition of outstanding, forward-looking achievement in nursing care, health promotion, and leadership. She also received the 2008 Washington State University, Vancouver—Excellence in Leadership Award, given in recognition of quality leadership.

Her interest in chemistry heightened in 2005 and continued, as her master project was "Developing an Online Chemistry Course and Laboratory for the Health Science Student: Using Collaboration between Disciplines and Best Online Practices."

CONTENTS

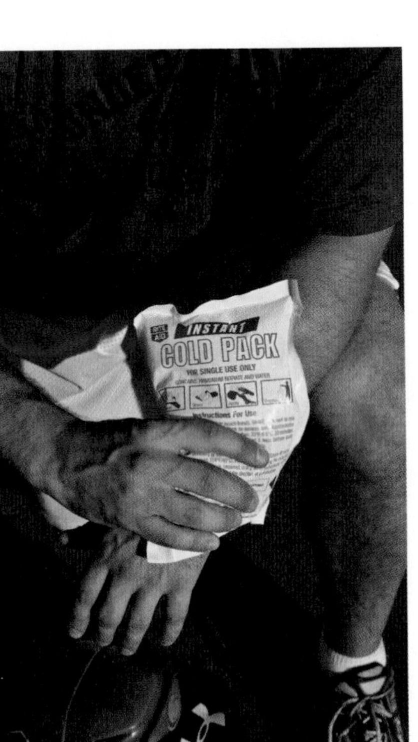

INSTANT
COLD PACK
FOR SINGLE USE ONLY

8 Hydrocarbons: An Introduction to Organic Molecules 304

9 Hydration, Dehydration, and Alcohols 358

10 Carbonyl Compounds and Redox Reactions 398

11 Organic Acids and Bases 440

16 Nuclear Chemistry 682

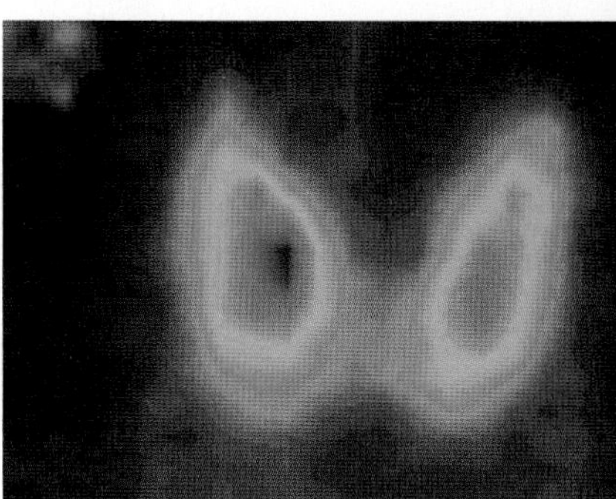

17 Nucleic Acids, Protein Synthesis, and Heredity

This chapter is available online on the Companion Website, which is accessible from **www.cengagebrain.com**

Appendix A
Essential Mathematics for Chemistry A-0

Appendix B
The Quantitative Behavior of Gases A-17

To Students

"Why study chemistry?" There is broad agreement among healthcare professionals that chemistry is essential background for an understanding of the workings of the human body. Although you may not have realized it, you have undoubtedly already encountered some of the ideas that are covered in this book, including:

- measurements such as weight, height, blood pressure, and blood sugar levels
- electrolytes and their importance to human health
- the energy value (Calorie content) of food
- the major nutrient types, including carbohydrates, fats, and proteins
- the role of vitamins and minerals in human health
- DNA, genetic diseases, and heredity in general
- x-rays and other types of diagnostic imaging

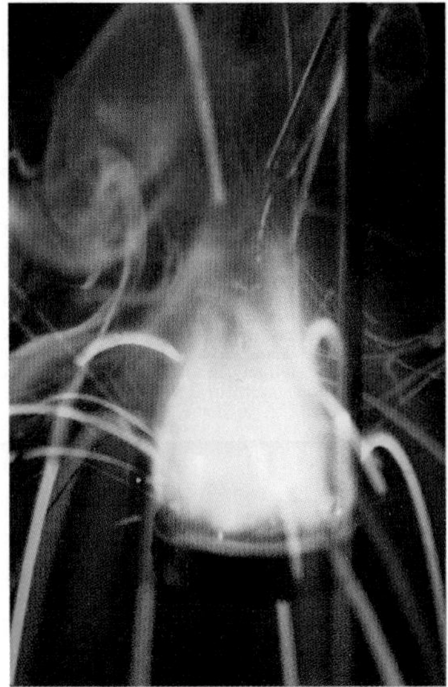

As you will see, every aspect of human biology is grounded in chemistry. In a real sense, chemistry provides the principles we need to understand life itself.

Learning chemistry is like learning a new language. You begin with a set of new words that allow you to express ideas in the language of chemistry, as well as some basic principles that are analogous to the grammatical rules of a language. Later, you learn more sophisticated concepts, allowing you to express more complex (and more interesting) ideas. The first few chapters of this book cover the basic principles and vocabulary of chemistry, without which the rest of the book would not make sense. At times, these early principles may not seem particularly relevant to human health, and you may find yourself wishing that you could hurry on to the "good stuff." Be patient! The time you spend learning the fundamental concepts will allow you to understand and appreciate the chemistry of the human body.

This book is written for students who want to pursue a career in the health sciences, and it assumes no prior knowledge of chemistry. To take full advantage of this text, here are a few tips:

1. *Keep up with the reading assignments.* Read each section either before your instructor covers the material in class or immediately afterward. Many lessons build on the previous ones, making it particularly important not to fall behind.
2. *Pace yourself when reading.* Some of the concepts may be difficult to grasp on first reading, and most of them will require your full attention. Read a little at a time, making sure that you understand the material. If you find your attention wandering, take a break.
3. *Do the sample problems.* This book contains many sample problems, and you should treat these as an integral part of the text. Each sample problem is worked out in detail, and is followed by a second exercise labeled "Try It Yourself." Doing these additional exercises will help you to gauge whether or not you understood the solution to the sample problem.
4. *Do as many problems as you can.* Problem solving is where the actual learning happens. It hones your ability to apply the knowledge you've learned, and it points out the areas where you need more studying. Each section of this book ends with a set of Core Problems and each chapter ends with a set of Concept Problems. Doing these problems will help you to determine your level of understanding.
5. *Use the chapter summaries as study guides.* Each section of this book begins with a learning objective. These objectives are collected at the end of the chapter, along with a thorough summary of the concepts.

Student-Friendly Features

Here are samples that illustrate the features you will find throughout the book.

Mrs. Blackstone has been diagnosed with hypertension, and her doctor prescribes a diuretic called hydrochlorothiazide (HCTZ) to help lower her blood pressure. Because this medication also raises the level of calcium in the blood, the doctor has Mrs. Blackstone's blood calcium level checked regularly. The lab reports that her calcium level is 3.1, and Mrs. Blackstone would like to know whether this is a normal value. However, when she does a little research, she discovers that the normal range is reported in three ways:

8.5 to 10.5 mg/dL or 4.3 to 5.3 mEq/L or 2.2 to 2.7 mmol/L

Which one should she use? She asks her doctor, who tells her that the lab gives the test results in millimoles per liter (mmol/L). Mrs. Blackstone's calcium level is slightly elevated, but is not a concern.

The preceding three units are all ways to show the concentration of a solute. Concentrations of substances such as sodium, glucose, and cholesterol in our blood are important indicators of our health. However, we cannot understand or interpret the results unless we know how they are being reported to us. In this chapter, we will explore the variety of ways in which we can express concentrations of solutions.

5.2 Moles and Formula Weights

OBJECTIVES: *Use the mole concept to express numbers of formula units, and interconvert moles and masses.*

In Section 5.1, we saw that we can safely inject a 5.0% (w/v) solution of glucose into a patient, but we cannot do so for glucose solutions that are significantly stronger or weaker. As we will see in Section 5.4, we must use a 5.0% solution because red blood cells cannot survive in other concentrations; they either burst or shrivel up, depending on the concentration. What happens if we replace the glucose with ordinary table sugar (sucrose)? Red blood cells can survive in a sucrose solution too, but only if the concentration of sucrose in the solution is 9.25% (w/v). Why do we need so much more sucrose? These two solutions have the same effect on red blood cells because *they contain the same number of molecules of solute per liter.* In order to predict the effect of a solution on our cells, then, we must have a way to express the number of solute particles in a solution.

We cannot count the particles (atoms, molecules, or ions) in a solution directly, because there are too many of them in even a tiny amount of solution. Instead, we use an indirect method that is based on the weights of the atoms. Our starting point is hydrogen, the lightest element, which has an atomic weight of 1.008 amu. Individual hydrogen atoms are extremely small and light, but if we put enough of them into a box, we will

Health Applications: Connecting Chemistry to Health and the Human Body

- Each chapter has a short health-related introduction, followed by several numbered sections that begin with the important learning objectives. Key Terms are given in bold face the first time they are used and are collected at the back of the chapter.
- The apple icon points to a health-related application of the concepts.
- Marginal Health Notes show the relevance of chemistry to health and the human body.

We can make hydroxide ions by dissolving an ionic compound such as NaOH or $Ca(OH)_2$ in water. These compounds are strong electrolytes, breaking apart into a metal ion and hydroxide ions.

$$NaOH(s) \rightarrow Na^+(aq) + OH^-(aq)$$

$$Ca(OH)_2(s) \rightarrow Ca^{2+}(aq) + 2\,OH^-(aq)$$

In addition, many compounds can pull H^+ off a water molecule, forming OH^-. Compounds that form hydroxide ions when they dissolve in water are bases. We will look at the chemistry of bases in Section 7.4.

Health Note: NaOH (caustic lye) is an ingredient in some brands of drain and oven cleaners. It can break down and dissolve fats, grease, and proteins. NaOH can cause severe chemical burns, so you should always wear hand and face protection if you use any product that contains it.

Problem-Solving Approach

- Problem-solving strategies are given in the margin of some of the Sample Problems to guide you through the process.
- Each Sample Problem is paired with a closely related *Try It Yourself* question. Do these questions right away, so you can be sure that you have acquired the needed skills. The answers to the Try It Yourself questions are in Appendix D at the back of the book. Most of the Sample Problems list additional Core Problems that you can do to practice your new skills.

Sample Problem 5.4

Calculating the mass of solute from a mass per volume concentration

The concentration of cholesterol in Mr. Lee's blood plasma is 186 mg/dL. How many milligrams of cholesterol are there in a 5.0 mL sample of his blood plasma?

SOLUTION

STEP 1: Identify the original measurement and the final unit.

We are given the volume of the solution (the plasma) and asked to calculate the number of milligrams of cholesterol in this solution.

STEP 2: Write conversion factors that relate the two units.

The concentration of cholesterol tells us that 1 dL of plasma contains 186 mg of cholesterol. The corresponding conversion factors are

$$\frac{186 \text{ mg cholesterol}}{1 \text{ dL}} \quad \text{and} \quad \frac{1 \text{ dL}}{186 \text{ mg cholesterol}}$$

In order to use this relationship, we must first convert our volume from milliliters into deciliters. We can do this using the metric railroad, or we can use an additional conversion factor. The relationship between milliliters and deciliters is 100 mL = 1 dL, so we can write two more conversion factors:

$$\frac{100 \text{ mL}}{1 \text{ dL}} \quad \text{and} \quad \frac{1 \text{ dL}}{100 \text{ mL}}$$

STEP 3: Choose the conversion factors that allow you to cancel units.

Now we can set up our conversion factors, making sure that we can cancel both deciliters and milliliters. Once we have the correct setup, we cancel units and do the arithmetic.

STEP 4: Do the math and round your answer.

$$5.0 \text{ mL} \times \frac{1 \text{ dL}}{100 \text{ mL}} \times \frac{186 \text{ mg cholesterol}}{1 \text{ dL}} = 9.3 \text{ mg cholesterol}$$

TRY IT YOURSELF: *The concentration of iron in Mrs. Lee's blood plasma is 88 μg/dL. If the total volume of her plasma is 2.9 L, how much iron is there in Mrs. Lee's blood plasma?*

For additional practice, try Core Problems 5.9 and 5.10.

Review and Practice

- Paired Core Problems given at the end of each section immediately reinforce the objectives of the section and help gauge your knowledge of the content.
- Key Terms are collected at the end of the chapter and referenced to section numbers where they are discussed.
- Concept Questions encourage you to describe how the ideas in the chapter apply to specific examples.
- End-of-chapter problems can be assigned in OWL, an online homework assessment tool.

CORE PROBLEMS

All Core Problems are paired and the answers to the blue odd-numbered problems appear in the back of the book.

6.1 Which of the following are physical changes, and which are chemical reactions?
a) You bend a piece of steel.
b) A piece of steel rusts.
c) Your body burns fat.
d) You compress the air in a bicycle pump.

6.2 Which of the following are physical changes, and which are chemical reactions?
a) A drop of alcohol evaporates.
b) A drop of alcohol catches fire and burns.
c) You dissolve some salt in water.
d) You digest a piece of pizza.

6.3 Which of the following are physical properties, and which are chemical properties?
a) Hydrogen burns if it is mixed with air.
b) Hydrogen is a gas at room temperature.
c) Hydrogen combines with nitrogen to make ammonia.
d) Hydrogen condenses at −253°C.

6.4 Which of the following are physical properties, and which are chemical properties?
a) The density of HgO is 11.1 g/mL.
b) If you heat HgO, it breaks down into pure elements.
c) HgO is poisonous.
d) HgO is an orange–red solid.

6.5 When you boil water, the water turns to steam. If you boil 5 g of water, how much does the resulting steam weigh?

6.6 If you heat chalk, it breaks down into lime (calcium oxide) and carbon dioxide. If you heat 10 g of chalk, what can you say about the weight of the lime you make? What can you say about the total weight of the lime and the carbon dioxide?

6.7 Does the following sentence describe a typical physical change or a typical chemical change?
"The starting materials and the products have different chemical formulas."

6.8 Does the following sentence describe a typical physical change or a typical chemical change?
"The change is reversible."

Key Terms

activation energy – 6.6
catalyst – 6.6
chemical equation – 6.2
chemical equilibrium – 6.7
chemical property – 6.1
chemical reaction (chemical change) – 6.1
coefficient – 6.2
combustion reaction – 6.5
endothermic reaction – 6.4
energy diagram – 6.6
equilibrium mixture – 6.7
exothermic reaction – 6.4
heat of reaction (ΔH) – 6.4
law of mass conservation – 6.1
Le Châtelier's principle – 6.7
net ionic equation – 6.5
nutritive value – 6.4
physical change – 6.1
physical property – 6.1
precipitation reaction – 6.5
product – 6.2
rate of reaction – 6.6
reactant – 6.2
reversible reaction – 6.7
spectato

SUMMARY OF OBJECTIVES

Now that you have read the chapter, test yourself on your knowledge of the objectives, this summary as a guide.

Section 6.1: **Determine whether a process is a physical change or a chemical reaction.**
- In a physical change, the chemical formulas do not change; in a chemical reaction they do.
- Physical changes can be reversed, but many chemical reactions cannot.
- Physical properties can be measured without changing a chemical formula, while che properties always involve a chemical reaction.
- In any change, the mass of the products equals the mass of the reactants (law of mas conservation).

Section 6.2: **Write a balanced chemical equation to represent a chemical reaction.**
- Any chemical reaction can be expressed as a balanced chemical equation.
- In a balanced equation, each side must have the same number of atoms of each elem
- Balancing a chemical equation involves changing coefficients, never changing a chem formula.

Section 6.3: **Relate the mass of any substance in a chemical reaction to the masses of substances in the reaction.**
- The molar masses of the chemicals in a balanced equation are used to relate the mass chemicals used or formed during the reaction.

Section 6.4: **Relate the amount of heat involved in a reaction to the masses of the che describe the differences between exothermic and endothermic reactions, and use nut values to calculate the energy provided by foodstuffs.**
- Reactions can either produce (exothermic) or absorb (endothermic) heat.
- In an exothermic reaction, the heat can be written into the balanced equation as a pr it can be written separately (ΔH) as a negative number. In an endothermic reaction, t written as a reactant, or it is written separately as a positive number.
- The energy produced or absorbed in a reaction is directly proportional to the amount chemicals used in the reaction.
- Each type of major nutrient produces a characteristic amount of heat when it burns (the value), which is normally given as a number of Calories (kilocalories) per gram. The stan nutritive values are 4 Cal/g for carbohydrates and proteins and 9 Cal/g for fats.

Section 6.5: **Recognize and write chemical equations for combustion and precipitatio reactions.**
- Combustion is the reaction of a compound with O_2, to produce the oxides of each ele the original compound.
- When a compound that contains carbon and hydrogen is burned, the products are H_2O and CO_2.
- Precipitation is the reaction of two soluble compounds to form an insoluble product.
- Precipitation reactions can be represented using net ionic equations, which show onl that combine to form the insoluble compound.

Section 6.6: **Understand and use the relationships between the rate of a reaction and tion energy, temperature, concentration, surface area, and catalysts.**
- The rate of a reaction increases as you increase the concentration of the reactants an contact area between the reactants.

Concept Questions

OWL Online homework for this chapter may be assigned in OWL.
* indicates more challenging problems.

7.91 All aqueous solutions contain H_3O^+ ions and OH^- ions. Where do these ions come from?

7.92 Using Le Châtelier's principle, explain why the concentration of OH^- in water decreases when you add HCl to the water.

7.93 Why are acid–base reactions often called proton transfer reactions?

7.94 A student is asked to calculate the pH of 10^{-3} M NaCl solution. The student answers, "3." Why is this answer incorrect? What is the actual pH of this solution?

7.95 What element must all acids contain, and why?

7.96 Why are bases often referred to as proton acceptors?

7.97 a) What is the difference between a strong acid and a weak acid?
b) What is the difference between a strong base and a weak base?

7.99 Solutions of sodium acetate ($NaC_2H_3O_2$) conduct electricity better than solutions of acetic acid ($HC_2H_3O_2$). Why is this?

7.100 Ethyl acetate and butyric acid are chemical compounds that contain the same atoms. Why is the formula of ethyl acetate written $C_4H_8O_2$, while the chemical formula of butyric acid is written $HC_4H_7O_2$?

7.101 What are the two common types of bases?

7.102 What is a conjugate pair?

7.103 What is an amphiprotic substance?

7.104 a) What do buffers do?
b) Buffers contain two chemicals. How are these chemicals related to each other?

7.105 Explain why solutions of CO_2 in water do not have a pH of 7.00.

Summary and Challenge Problems

7.106 A 0.075 M solution of acetoacetic acid ($HC_4H_5O_3$) has a pH of 2.37.
a) Use the pH to calculate the concentrations of H_3O^+ and OH^- ions in this solution.
b) Is acetoacetic acid a strong acid, or is it a weak acid? (Hint: How does the molarity of H_3O^+ compare to the molarity of the acetoacetic acid?)

7.107 *How many grams of acetoacetic acid ($HC_4H_5O_3$) are needed to prepare 250 mL of a 0.075 M solution?

7.108 Calculate the pH of each of the following solutions:
a) 0.075 M HCl, a strong acid
b) 3.1×10^{-4} M KOH
c) 2.3×10^{-3} M $Ba(OH)_2$

7.109 *a) HBr is a strong acid. What is the pH of a solution that is made by dissolving 450 mg of HBr in enough water to make 100 mL of solution?
*b) What is the pH of a solution that is made by dissolving 525 mg of $Ba(OH)_2$ in enough water to make 75 mL of solution?

7.110 *At 0°C, the ion product of water is 1.1×10^{-15}. If the concentration of H_3O^+ in an aqueous solution is 1.0×10^{-7} M at 0°C, what is the concentration of OH^-? Should this solution be considered acidic, basic, or neutral?

7.111 From each of the following pairs of solutions, tell which solution has the higher pH.

7.112 *Match each solution with its correct pH, using the fact that HNO_3 is stronger than $HCHO_2$, which is stronger than $HC_2H_3O_2$.

0.05 M HNO_3	pH = 3.5
0.05 M $HCHO_2$	pH = 3.0
0.05 M $HC_2H_3O_2$	pH = 2.5
0.005 M $HC_2H_3O_2$	pH = 1.3

7.113 A molecule of malonic acid contains three carbon atoms, four hydrogen atoms, and four oxygen atoms, and the chemical formula of malonic acid is normally written $H_2C_3H_2O_4$. Based on this formula, which of the following ionic compounds probably do not exist?

$NaHC_3H_2O_4$ $Na_2C_3H_2O_4$
$Na_3C_3HO_4$ $Na_4C_3O_4$

7.114 Oxalic acid is a weak acid with the chemical formula $H_2C_2O_4$.
a) Write chemical equations for the two ionizations of oxalic acid.
b) Which of these reactions produces most of the H_3O^+ ions in a solution of oxalic acid?

7.115 Only one of the six hydrogen atoms in lactic acid can be removed by a base. Which one is it?

H–C(H)(H)–C(H)(O–H)–C(=O)–O–H

Lactic acid

Mini Study Guide

- End-of-Chapter material acts like a study guide to help you review for quizzes and tests.
- The Summary and Challenge Problems cover all sections of the chapter and give your instructor an opportunity to assign questions at a wide range of levels. Challenge problems are marked with an asterisk and require a greater depth of understanding; many involve concepts from earlier chapters.

I encourage you to send me feedback about the book. Constructive criticism is always welcomed and will help improve the book for future users. You can reach me by e-mail at jarmstro@ccsf.edu.

Finally, let me welcome you to the study of chemistry. The study of the processes that occur in the human body is difficult, and it can be frustrating—no surprise, given the extraordinary complexity of even the simplest living organism. However, it is also endlessly fascinating and deeply rewarding. I hope that this textbook helps you to gain a deeper insight into the elegance, beauty, and wonder of life.

To Instructors

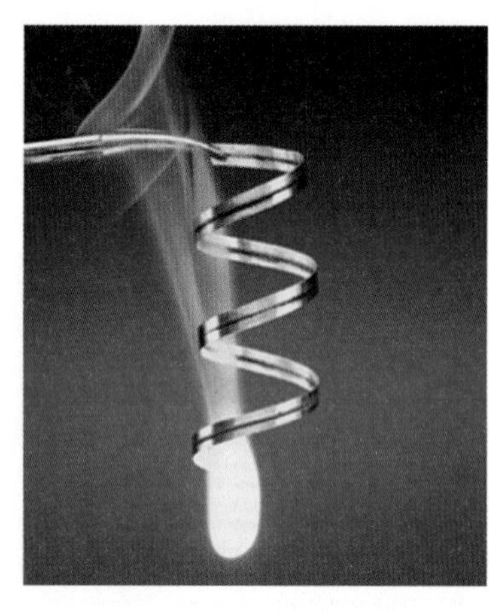

This textbook grew out of my experiences teaching a one-semester survey of chemistry for nursing majors at City College of San Francisco. At that time, virtually all of the available textbooks for the "GOB course" covered far too much material for a single term, and all available books enforced a rigid separation between general chemistry, organic chemistry, and biochemistry topics. In addition, the coverage of many of the core concepts in general chemistry, including the metric system, ionic compound formation, chemical equations, and moles was so terse as to be of little help to the beginning student. It was clear to me that there was a need for a textbook that offered a more integrated approach to health-related chemistry and that could be used in a single-term course with no chemistry prerequisite. With this in mind, my primary goals in writing this textbook were:

- to pitch the text at a level that can be read and understood by students who had no prior exposure to chemistry, but that has sufficient rigor for a college-level course.
- to describe and illustrate the fundamental concepts of chemistry in detail (including worked examples), never sacrificing pedagogy in the interest of space.
- to focus on the needs and interests of allied-health majors, eliminating topics that are of limited relevance to these students.
- to take the most direct path to biomolecules and metabolic processes.
- to minimize the number of asides (boxed essays, marginal notes, and graphics) that were not connected to health fields.

Consistent with this strategy, the topic coverage in this book differs from other texts in many ways.

Key Content Features

- Covalent bonding (in Chapter 3) is covered before ion formation, consistent with the fact that most biologically significant substances are molecular rather than ionic. Coverage of covalent bonding before ions also allows a rational presentation of polyatomic ions.
- Organic structures are incorporated into the presentation of covalent bonding in Chapter 3, and the relationships between physical properties and structures of organic molecules are introduced in Chapter 4.
- The vital role of hydrogen bonding in determining physical properties is introduced in Chapter 4 and emphasized throughout, preparing students for the role of hydrogen bonding in protein and nucleic acid structure.
- Concentration units that are commonly encountered in clinical work are covered in detail.
- The coverage of acid-base chemistry uses the proton transfer (Brønsted-Lowry) model consistently, preparing the student to understand the physiological behavior of acids and bases.

- Biomolecules are integrated into the organic chapters; NAD^+ and FAD are introduced in Chapter 10, amino acids in Chapter 11, and polypeptides, triglycerides, and phosphate esters in Chapter 12.
- Organic chapters emphasize physical behavior and chemical reactivity over nomenclature. Nomenclature is used primarily as an aid in functional group recognition and to help the student understand structural isomerism.
- Sections on organic reactivity focus on reaction types that are prominent in biological systems. For example, the decarboxylation of ketoacids plays a critical role in catabolic pathways and is covered in detail, whereas hydrohalogenation of alkenes is omitted.
- Optical isomerism is introduced early in the organic chapters and is reinforced prior to the formal presentation of biomolecules.
- The role of enzymes in biological processes is introduced immediately after the first organic reaction is covered in Chapter 9, and is reinforced throughout the rest of the text.
- The concept of a metabolic pathway is introduced in Chapter 10, using the key catabolic sequence dehydrogenation—hydration—oxidation as an archetype.
- Hydrolysis reactions and condensation (esterification, amidation, phosphorylation) reactions are introduced in a single chapter (Chapter 12), emphasizing the fundamental similarity between these key reaction types.
- Proteins are covered before carbohydrates and lipids. Proteins are the most versatile biomolecules; virtually all biological structures and processes involve a protein in some fashion. In addition, no other class of biological molecules illustrates so clearly the relationship between structure and function.
- The overview of metabolism in Chapter 15 focuses on ATP production and how it is related to the structures of metabolites.
- The presentation of metabolic pathways in Chapter 15 emphasizes familiar organic transformations, rather than being a catalog of unfamiliar structures and reactions.

Key Pedagogical Features

- Chapter-opening essays show how common clinical chemistry lab tests are related to human health.
- Health notes in the margins, reviewed by Kellee Hollyman, RN, BSN, MN, a nursing educator, point out significant connections between chemistry and human health.
- Key medical topics such as physiological buffers and diagnostic imaging are integrated into the main text.
- Space-filling structures use color to show hydrogen bonding donor/acceptor ability.
- Abundant Sample Problems with paired Try It Yourself exercises encourage students to use new skills immediately.
- Problem-solving strategies in the margins are used to help students solve conversion problems.
- Paired Core Problems at the end of each section allow immediate reinforcement of the concepts and skills learned in that section.
- Key Terms and a Summary of Objectives serve as a mini study guide for students.
- A wide range of end-of-chapter problems including concept questions, problems that summarize the main ideas in the chapter, and problems that require extensive recall of prior material round out each chapter.
- Problems at a variety of levels allow the instructor to make the course expectations clear. Problems marked with an asterisk are more challenging. Problems can also be assigned in OWL for GOB chemistry, an online learning and homework assessment tool.

Although this book is intended for use in a one-term course, it contains more material than can be covered in a single semester. The final three chapters in particular (metabolism, nuclear chemistry, and nucleic acids) can be considered capstone topics, to be covered if time and the student level allows.

Support Package

For Instructors

OWL
Online Web Learning

OWL for General, Organic, and Biochemistry/Allied Health
OWL with eBook 6-Month Instant Access ISBN-13: 978-1-111-37664-2
By Roberta Day, Beatrice Botch, and David Gross of the University of Massachusetts, Amherst; William Vining of the State University of New York at Oneonta; and Susan Young of Hartwick College. **OWL** Online Web Learning offers more assignable, gradable content (including end-of-chapter questions specific to this textbook) and more reliability and flexibility than any other system. OWL's powerful course management tools allow instructors to control due dates, number of attempts, and whether students see answers or receive feedback on how to solve problems. OWL includes the **Cengage YouBook,** a Flash-based eBook that is interactive and customizable. It features a text edit tool that allows instructors to modify the textbook narrative as needed. With Cengage YouBook, instructors can quickly re-order entire sections and chapters or hide any content they don't teach to create an eBook that perfectly matches their syllabus. Instructors can further customize the Cengage YouBook by publishing Web links. It also includes animated figures, video clips, highlighting, notes, and more.

Developed by chemistry instructors for teaching chemistry, OWL is the only system specifically designed to support **mastery learning,** where students work as long as they need to master each chemical concept and skill. OWL has already helped hundreds of thousands of students master chemistry through a wide range of assignment types, including tutorials, interactive simulations, and algorithmically generated homework questions that provide instant, answer-specific feedback.

OWL is continually enhanced with online learning tools to address the various learning styles of today's students such as:

- **Quick Prep** review courses that help students learn essential skills to succeed in General and Organic Chemistry
- **Jmol** molecular visualization program for rotating molecules and measuring bond distances and angles
- **Go Chemistry®** mini video lectures on key concepts that students can play on their computers or download to their video iPods, smart phones, or personal video players

In addition, when you become an OWL user, you can expect service that goes far beyond the ordinary. For more information or to see a demo, please contact your Cengage Learning representative or visit us at www.cengage.com/owl.

Instructor's Manual by Simon Bott of the University of Houston. This manual features complete solutions to all problems in the text as well as chapter outlines to help instructors plan their lectures. ISBN-13: 978-0-534-49351-6

PowerLecture™

PowerLecture with ExamView® Instructor's CD/DVD Package (ISBN-13: 978-0-534-49355-4) This dual-platform, one-stop digital library and presentation tool includes:

- Prepared Microsoft® PowerPoint® Lecture Slides by Melanie Harvey and Krista Thomas of Johnson County Community College that cover all key points from the text in a convenient format you can enhance with your own materials.

- Image Libraries in PowerPoint and in JPEG format that provide electronic files for all text art, most photographs, and all numbered tables in the text. Use these files to print transparencies or to create your own PowerPoint lectures.
- **ExamView** testing software, with all test items that you would expect from a printed Test Bank in electronic format so you can create customized tests in print or online. Software and testing banks are available on the PowerLecture.
- **Instructor's Manual for *Laboratory Experiments*, First Edition** This manual will help instructors in grading the answers to questions and in assessing the range of experimental results obtained by students. The Instructor's Manual also contains important notes for professors to tell students and details on how to handle the disposal of waste chemicals.

Faculty Companion Website Accessible from www.cengagebrain.com, this website provides downloadable files for the Instructor's Manuals for the lab manual as well as WebCT and Blackboard versions of the Test Bank.

For Students

Student Solutions Manual by Lenore Hoyt of the University of Louisville contains worked-out solutions to all odd-numbered problems in the book. This manual will show students how to approach, work, and solve problems using the same step-by-step explanations found in the core text examples. ISBN-13: 978-0-534-49352-3

Lecture Notebook This printed form of the instructor's PowerPoint slides allows the student to always have a copy of the key lecture points while providing room for the student's own additions. ISBN-13: 978-0-8400-6826-2

OWL (Online Web Learning) for General, Organic, and Biochemistry/Allied Health See the description above in the "For the Instructor" section.

OWL

CengageBrain.com App Now students can prepare for class anytime and anywhere using the CengageBrain.com application developed specifically for the Apple iPhone® and iPod touch®, which allows students to access free study materials—book-specific quizzes, flash cards, related Cengage Learning materials and more—so they can study the way they want, when they want to . . . even on the go. For more information about this complimentary application, please visit www.cengagebrain.com.

Basic Laboratory Experiments for General, Organic, and Biochemistry
Joseph M. Landesberg. Fourteen experiments illustrate important concepts and principles in general, organic, and biochemistry. All experiments have new Pre- and Post-lab Questions. ISBN-13: 978-1-111-42661-3

Student Companion Website Accessible from www.cengagebrain.com, this website includes a glossary, flash cards, and an interactive Periodic Table.

Visit CengageBrain.com To access these and additional course materials, please visit www.cengagebrain.com. At the CengageBrain.com home page, search for the ISBN (from the back cover of your book) using the search box at the top of the page. This will take you to the product page where these resources can be found. (Instructors can log in at login.cengage.com.)

Apple, iPhone, iPod touch, and iTunes are trademarks of Apple, Inc., registered in the U.S. and other countries.

Acknowledgments

This book would not exist without the dedication and talents of many people, both inside and outside Cengage, and I would be remiss if I did not acknowledge the key players. Senior development editor Sandi Kiselica gets the honor of first mention; her knowledge of biological chemistry and her ability to spot both stylistic and chemical infelicities made her an indispensable partner in my efforts, and it has been a pleasure and a privilege to have worked with her throughout the long gestation period of this book. Lisa Lockwood, executive editor, was a fount of both good ideas and encouragement, as well as being a tireless advocate for my vision. Teresa Trego ably oversaw the hectic and bewildering production process, as well as putting in some thankless hours readying my manuscript for use as a preliminary edition. Media editors Lisa Weber and Stephanie Van Camp did an outstanding job creating the online projects for my book, while Elizabeth Woods skillfully developed all the print ancillaries. Outside of Cengage, Laura Sullivan took care of the day-to-day shepherding of the book through the production process, keeping track of hundreds of details and somehow not getting an ulcer when I sprang a last-minute vacation on her in the middle of it all. Copy editor Julie Laing had the thankless job of cleaning up my prose and preparing the manuscript for production, and she did both with consistent professionalism and skill. The high quality of the art is due to Steve McEntee, whose ability to read my mind and turn my amateurish sketches into "just what I wanted" amazes me still. Photo researcher Chris Althof likewise managed to play mind-reader, coming up with photos to satisfy my most impractical requests. Many thanks to all of you!

Many people reviewed this manuscript at various stages, and I am very grateful for all their helpful suggestions. Focus groups with professors teaching the course were conducted on both coasts and I applaud the experience and knowledge that participants brought to the table. Many people used this text in a preliminary stage and offered suggestions for improvement along the way. In particular, I am grateful to Lenore Hoyt of the University of Louisville, who gave me many comments about how students use the book. I also want to thank my Spring 2007 Chem 32 students, who used this book in its very first incarnation and who offered a wealth of practical suggestions, as well as over a hundred typo corrections. It was an honor to have Kellee Hollyman, RN, read and check the manuscript for health-related accuracy and ideas. Her contributions, including the marginal health notes, reinforced the need for chemistry in the health sciences. Many thanks, Kellee. Three people served as accuracy reviewers for the text, reading and checking all the page proofs. Many thanks to Krista Thomas and Melanie Harvey of Johnson Community College, and David Shinn who served in this capacity. Double-checking the accuracy of the organic-related chapters and the biochemistry-related chapters was accomplished by Scott Snyder of Columbia University and Shawn Farrell, coauthor of *Biochemistry*, 6e (Cengage Learning).

Reviewers and Focus Group Attendees

Nicholas Alteri, *Community College of Rhode Island*
Pamila Ball, *Northern Kentucky University*
Loyd Bastin, *Widener University*
Dianne Bennett, *Sacramento Community College*
Carol Berg, *Bellevue College*
Martin L. Brock, *Eastern Kentucky University*
Kathy Carrigan, *Portland Community College*
Laura Choudhury, *Broward College*
Jessica Correa, *Miami Dade College*
Jeffrey Cramer, *Stark State University*
Milagros Delgado, *Florida International University*
Nancy Faulk, *Blinn College/Bryan Campus*

Coretta Fernandes, *Lansing Community College*
Karen Frindell, *Santa Rosa Junior College*
Carol Frishberg, *Ramapo College*
Eric Goll, *Brookdale Community College*
Donna Gosnell, *Valdosta State University*
Lenore Hoyt, *University of Louisville*
Melanie Harvey, *Johnson Community College*
Michael A. Hauser, *St. Louis Community College, Meramec*
Kirk Kawagoe, *Fresno City College*
Peter Krieger, *Palm Beach Community College*
Jennifer Lillig, *Sonoma State University*
Angela McChesney, *Ozarks Technical Community College*
Patrick McKay, *Skyline College*
Behnoush Memari, *Broward Community College*
Michael Myers, *California State University, Long Beach*
Felix Ngassa, *Grand Valley State University*
Janice J. O'Donnell, *Henderson State University*
Mark Ott, *Jackson Community College*
Tchao Podona, *Miami Dade College, North Campus*
Laura Precedo, *Broward Community College, Central Campus*
Lesley Putman, *Northern Michigan University*
Lisa Reece, *Ozarks Technical Community College*
Linda Roberts, *Sacramento State University*
Deboleena Roy, *American River College*
Mary E. Rumpho, *University of Maine*
Karen Sanchez, *Florida Community College at Jacksonville*
Sara Selfe, *Edmonds Community College*
Clarissa Sorensen-Unruh, *Central New Mexico Community College*
Daryl Stein, *Stark State Technological College*
Jeffrey A. Taylor, *North Central State College*
Krista Thomas, *Johnson County Community College*
Suzanne Williams, *Northern Michigan University*
Carmen Works, *Sonoma State University*
Pamela Zelmer, *Miami Dade College*

General, Organic, and Biochemistry:

An Applied Approach

1

Measurements in Science and Medicine

George's 40th birthday is next week and he hasn't had a checkup in a while, so he calls the medical office to schedule a physical exam. When he arrives, the nurse has him fill out a questionnaire to see how his health has been recently. She then checks George's height, weight, temperature, pulse rate, breathing rate, and blood pressure. Comparing these to George's last visit three years ago, she sees that he has put on a bit of weight. Since his pulse rate and blood pressure are good, the weight gain is probably a result of the workout program that George started three months ago. At the end of the checkup, George's doctor orders several routine blood tests to help assess George's health. The results of the tests confirm that George is keeping himself in good physical condition.

Much of what we know about our bodies comes from **measurements**, numbers that we can use to describe something. For instance, our weight tells us whether we are eating more or less food than we need to supply our energy requirements, and our body temperature is a sensitive indicator of infection. Other measurements can show us whether we are at risk for health problems later in life; for example, if George's cholesterol level is high, he has a higher-than-normal risk of heart attack or stroke as he ages.

In this chapter, we begin our exploration of chemistry by looking at measurements and how we can use them. This chapter is the foundation for everything that follows, and the concepts you learn here will play a major role in your preparation for a career in health care.

OUTLINE

PATIENT INFORMATION

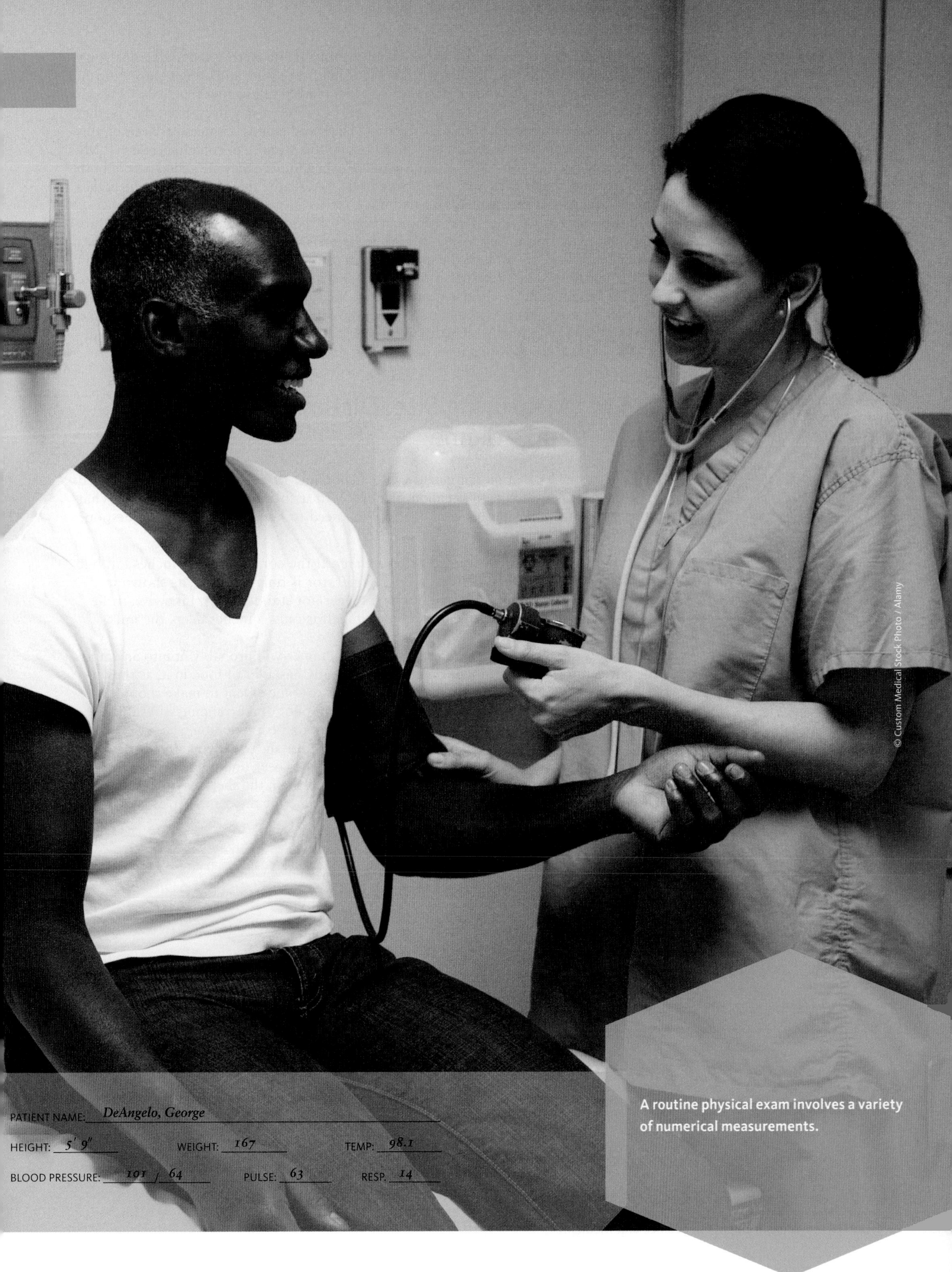

A routine physical exam involves a variety of numerical measurements.

OWL Online homework for this chapter may be assigned in OWL, an online homework assessment tool.

Numerical measurements are a part of our identity. If you were asked to describe yourself, you might say, "I have shoulder-length black hair, olive skin, and brown eyes," but you would probably also say things like, "I'm 31 years old," "I'm five foot four," and "I weigh 129 pounds." Numbers are also an integral part of our everyday lives, from the weather ("It's 61 degrees outside"), to transportation ("The speed limit is 35 miles per hour on this street"), to groceries ("Broccoli is only 89¢ a pound this week"), to communications ("My cell phone service gives me 800 anytime minutes"). In addition, they are a vital part of both chemistry and health care; we use measurements to describe the condition of our bodies and the behavior of the materials around us.

In this chapter, we take a close look at some of the kinds of measurements that are important to medicine. We start by looking at the sorts of properties that can be expressed in numbers. Then we examine the metric system (the standard system of measurement in most countries and in all branches of science) and its relationship to the English system, which is in common use in the United States. We take a detailed look at how we can "translate" measurements from one system to the other, as well as such issues as how and when to round off a number. Finally, we look at compound measurements, which are derived from the basic measurements described in the beginning of the chapter.

OBJECTIVES: *Define distance, mass, and volume, and know how to express each of these properties as a metric measurement.*

1.1 Measuring Size: Distance, Mass, and Volume

Let us start our look at measurements with a container of milk. You have just returned from the grocery store with a gallon of milk. Will it fit into your refrigerator? What properties of the milk and its container do you need to know to answer this question? You need to consider three properties:

1. *The individual dimensions of the container.* If the container is 10 inches tall but the distance between shelves in the refrigerator is only 8 inches, as shown in Figure 1.1, the container will not fit (at least not standing up). Likewise, if the container is 6 inches wide and the door shelf is only 3 inches deep, the milk will not fit in the shelf.
2. *The overall size of the container.* The milk container will probably fit into an empty refrigerator. But what if your refrigerator already has a lot of food in it, as shown in Figure 1.2? You can always rearrange items to some extent to make room for the milk, but if the refrigerator is too full, no amount of rearranging will suffice. You might have room for a quart of milk, but not an entire gallon.
3. *The weight of the container.* A gallon of milk is fairly heavy. If you already have a half gallon of orange juice, a two-liter bottle of root beer, and the leftover watermelon from your picnic last weekend sitting on a shelf, the shelf may break if you add the gallon of milk, even if there is enough room for the container, as shown in Figure 1.3.

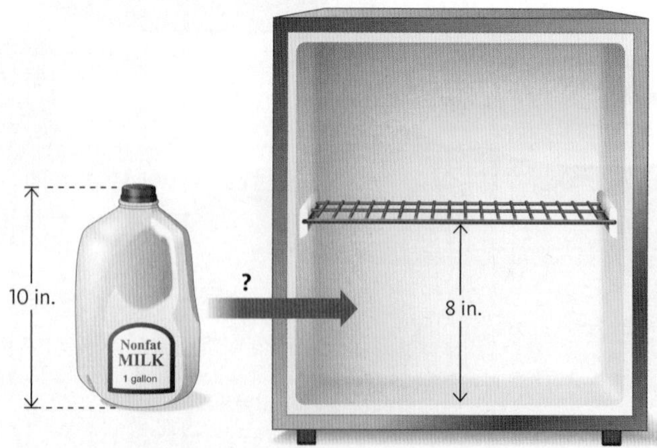

FIGURE 1.1 Using height to describe an object.

When we express a property such as height or weight, we must start with a **unit**. *A unit is a measurement whose size everyone agrees upon, so it can be used as a basis for other measurements.* For example, an inch is a unit that we can use to express any sort of distance (height, width, or length). When we say that our milk container is 10 inches tall, we mean that if we take 10 objects that are 1 inch tall and stack them atop one another, the stack will be the same height as the container, as shown in Figure 1.4.

The vast majority of measurements consist of a number and a unit. The unit tells us what type of property we are measuring (for example, height, weight, or time), and it allows us to understand the size of the measurement. For instance, if someone asked you, "How long are you going to be visiting your Aunt Martha?" and you answered, "Three," you might be staying at Aunt Martha's for three *hours* (a brief social call), three *days* (a long weekend visit), or three *months* (an extended vacation). In chemistry, most of the numbers you see will be measurements, and every measurement will include the appropriate unit (if any). You should get into the habit of including the unit for any number you write as you study chemistry.

Let us now return to our container of milk. If we wanted to describe the container, we could say that it is 10 inches tall, it takes up 1 gallon of space, and it weighs $8^{2}/_{3}$ pounds. Each of these measurements includes a number (10, 1, and $8^{2}/_{3}$) and a unit (inch, gallon, and pound). Table 1.1 summarizes the properties of this container of milk.

FIGURE 1.2 Using overall size to describe an object.

FIGURE 1.3 Using weight to describe an object.

The Metric System Uses Base Units and Derived Units

Each of the measurements in Table 1.1 uses an English unit. The English system of units is used for everyday measurements in the United States, but it is not used in most other countries, and it is not used in science. The primary system of measurement in the world is the **metric system**, which was developed in the late 1700s as a rational alternative to the confusing collection of units that were in use at the time.

In the metric system, each type of measurement has a **base unit**, from which all other units are derived. For example, the base unit of distance (length, width, or height) is a *meter*, which is a little more than three feet. The most common base units that you will encounter in health care are given in Table 1.2. We will explore each of these types of measurements later in this section.

Attaching a prefix to the name of a base unit gives a **derived unit**. For instance, *kilo-* and *centi-* are prefixes that mean 1000 base units and $^{1}/_{100}$ of a base unit, respectively, so a kilometer is 1000 meters and a centimeter is $^{1}/_{100}$ of a meter. Table 1.3 lists the metric prefixes you are most likely to encounter and their meanings. Note that we can express the relationship between a derived unit and the base unit as both a number (such as 1000 or $^{1}/_{1000}$) and a power of ten (10^3 or 10^{-3}). Appendix A.6 describes how we write powers of ten.

The milk container is the same height as a stack of ten 1-inch objects, so it is **10 inches tall.**

FIGURE 1.4 Using the inch as a unit of height.

TABLE 1.1 Some Properties of a Gallon of Milk

Type of Measurement	Unit	Measurement
Height	Inch	10 inches
Overall size	Gallon	1 gallon
Weight	Pound	$8^{2}/_{3}$ pounds

TABLE 1.2 The Most Common Metric Base Units

Unit	Abbreviation*	Type of Measurement
Meter	m	Distance (how long, wide, or tall an object is)
Liter	L	Volume (the amount of space an object occupies)
Gram	g	Mass (how heavy an object is)

*Most abbreviations for metric base units are written using lowercase letters. The abbreviation for liter is an exception, because the lowercase *l* looks too much like the number *1* or an uppercase *I*.

TABLE 1.3 The Most Common Prefixes in the Metric System

Prefix	Abbreviation	Meaning	Example
Kilo-	k	1000 base units (10^3 base units)	**Kilo**meter (km) A kilometer is 1000 meters.
Deci-	d	$^1/_{10}$ of the base unit (10^{-1} base units)	**Deci**meter (dm) A decimeter is $^1/_{10}$ of a meter.
Centi-	c	$^1/_{100}$ of the base unit (10^{-2} base units)	**Centi**meter (cm) A centimeter is $^1/_{100}$ of a meter.
Milli-	m	$^1/_{1000}$ of the base unit (10^{-3} base units)	**Milli**meter (mm) A millimeter is $^1/_{1000}$ of a meter.
Micro-	μ	$^1/_{1,000,000}$ of the base unit (10^{-6} base units)	**Micro**meter (μm) A micrometer is $^1/_{1,000,000}$ of a meter.

Health Note: In clinical work, you may see *mc* used as an abbreviation for *micro* instead of the Greek letter μ.

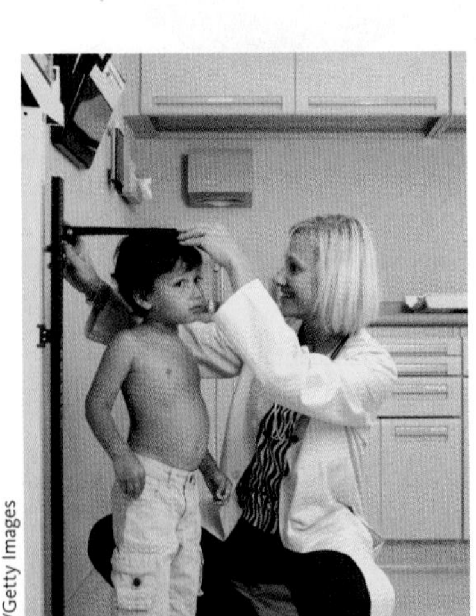

Katrina Wittkamp/Getty Images

Kresimir Juraga

Some representative metric distances. (a) This child is about one meter tall. (b) The width of a dime is about a centimeter.

Every metric unit has a standard abbreviation, as shown in Tables 1.2 and 1.3. The abbreviation for the base unit is the first letter of the unit's name. For derived units, the abbreviation usually contains the first letter of the prefix and the first letter of the base unit. For example, the abbreviation for *centimeter* is *cm*. Be sure to write all of the prefix abbreviations in Table 1.3 as lowercase letters, because the metric system uses uppercase letters for some less common derived units. For example, a capital M stands for the prefix *mega-*, which means 1,000,000 base units. Also, note that the abbreviation for the prefix *micro-* uses the Greek letter μ ("mu"), because *m* is used for *milli-*.

Distance Expresses How Far Apart Two Things Are

When we speak of the height of an object, or its length or width, we are referring to the *distance* between two points. For example, the height of our milk container is the distance between the bottom and the top of the container. Table 1.4 shows the metric units that are usually used to express distances in science and in everyday life, along with their English equivalents. Try to become familiar with the size of each unit so that you can understand metric measurements without having to translate them into English equivalents.

When we use the English system, we normally choose a unit that is a convenient size for our measurement. For instance, we generally express the distance between cities in miles, rather than in inches, to avoid extremely large numbers. (Saying that two cities are 44 miles apart makes more sense than saying that they are 2,800,000 inches apart.) Likewise, in the metric system we express distances between cities in kilometers, rather than meters or centimeters. The kilometer is a large distance, comparable to a mile, while meters and centimeters are much shorter distances.

Sample Problem 1.1

Choosing an appropriate metric unit of distance

Which of the following is a reasonable value for the thickness of a pen?

5 km 5 m 5 cm 5 mm 5 μm

continued

TABLE 1.4 Metric Units of Distance

Unit	Rough Description	Typical Uses	Relationship to English Units
Kilometer (km)	If you walk all the way around a large stadium, you have walked about a kilometer.	Measuring the distance between cities or the length of a marathon	1 mile = 1.609 km
Meter (m)	The distance from the floor to the countertop in a typical kitchen is around a meter.	Measuring the dimensions of a house or the length of a footrace	3.281 feet = 1 m 39.37 inches = 1 m
Centimeter (cm)	The thickness of your little finger is roughly a centimeter.	Measuring the length of a hair or the length of a pencil	1 inch = 2.54 cm
Millimeter (mm)	A millimeter is about the thickness of a dime.	Measuring the width of a fingernail or the length of an ant	1 inch = 25.4 mm
Micrometer or micron (μm)	A micrometer is less than the thickness of a human hair.	Measuring the width of a hair or the size of a bacterium	*(No comparable English unit exists)*

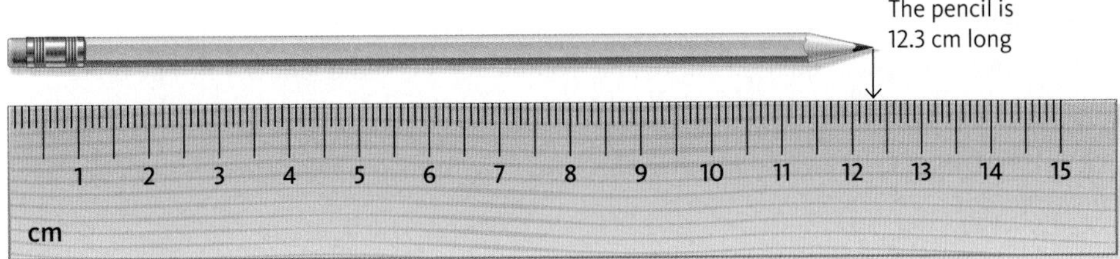

FIGURE 1.5 Measuring a length in metric units.

Health Note: In nursing, heights are often expressed in centimeters, sizes of tumors and lesions are expressed in centimeters or millimeters, and pore sizes of intravenous filters (to filter out bacteria and debris) are expressed in micrometers.

SOLUTION

A pen is likely to be around 5 **mm** thick. A millimeter is around the thickness of a dime, so 5 mm is a reasonable thickness for a pen.

TRY IT YOURSELF: *Which of the preceding measurements is a reasonable value for the width of a room?*

For additional practice, try Core Problems 1.11 (parts c, f, and g) and 1.12 (parts a, c, and d).

A metric ruler is normally marked in centimeters and millimeters. The longer, numbered marks indicate centimeters, and the closely spaced lines between each centimeter mark are millimeters. In Figure 1.5, the pencil extends three small divisions beyond the 12-cm line, so its length is 12 cm + 3 mm. Metric measurements are not normally expressed in mixed units, so the length of the pencil would be written as 12.3 cm or as 123 mm.

Sample Problem **1.2**

Measuring a length in metric units

Express the length of this crayon in centimeters.

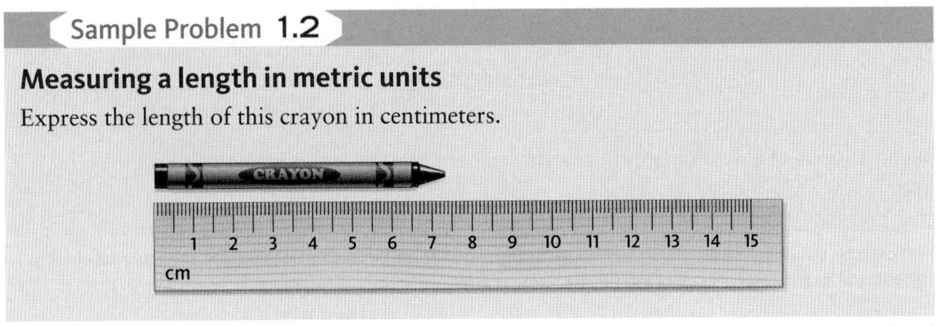

continued

SOLUTION

The crayon extends about three small marks beyond the 7-cm line, so it is **7.3 cm** long.

TRY IT YOURSELF: *Express the length of the crayon in millimeters.*

Volume Is the Amount of Space an Object Takes Up

The amount of space something occupies is its **volume**. The volume of any object is related to the individual dimensions of the object, but we can change the dimensions without changing the volume. For example, you can mold a lump of modeling clay into a variety of shapes, but the lump always has the same volume, as shown in Figure 1.6. The English system uses many familiar volume units, including the gallon, quart, pint, cup, fluid ounce, and teaspoon.

The base unit of volume in the metric system is the *liter,* which is roughly the same size as a quart. The most common derived units are the deciliter, the milliliter, and the microliter. Table 1.5 lists these metric units and their English equivalents.

Kresimir Juraga

Many beverages are sold in one liter containers.

Sample Problem 1.3

Choosing an appropriate metric unit of volume

Which of the following is the volume of a typical cooking pot?
4 L   4 dL   4 mL   4 μL

SOLUTION

Since a liter is around a quart, a reasonable volume for a cooking pot is **4 L**. The other volumes are too small, although a 4 dL pot is plausible (4 dL is around 2 cups).

TRY IT YOURSELF: *Which of the preceding measurements is a reasonable volume for a small spoon?*

For additional practice, try Core Problems 1.11 (parts b and e) and 1.12 (parts e and g).

Health Note: When converting doses of liquid medicines, a useful guideline is one teaspoon equals 5 mL and one tablespoon equals 15 mL.

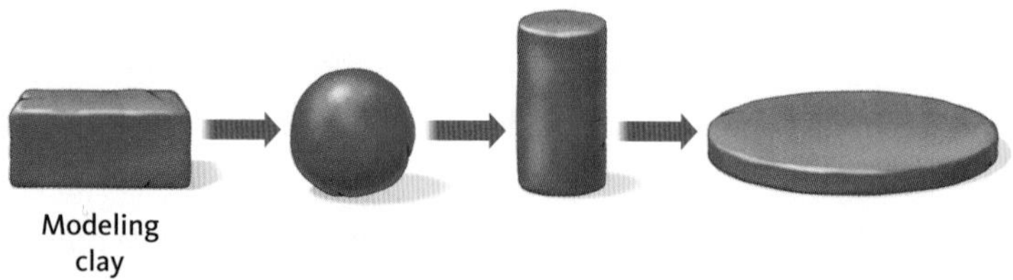

FIGURE 1.6 Changing the shape of an object without changing its volume.

TABLE 1.5 Metric Units of Volume

Unit	Rough Description	Typical Uses	Relationship to English Units
Liter (L)	A liter is roughly the same volume as a quart.	Sizes of large beverage containers and amounts of gasoline	1.057 quarts = 1 L
Deciliter (dL)	A deciliter is around a half of a cup.	Concentrations of substances in body fluids	1 cup = 2.366 dL 3.381 fluid ounces = 1 dL
Milliliter (mL or cc*)	A milliliter is around a fifth of a teaspoon.	Sizes of small beverage containers and doses of liquid medications	1 teaspoon = 4.93 mL 1 fluid ounce = 29.57 mL 1 quart = 946.4 mL
Microliter (μL)	A microliter is roughly the size of a single grain of sand.	Primarily in analytical laboratories	*(No comparable English unit exists)*

**cc* (or *cm³*) stands for *cubic centimeter,* the volume of a 1 cm cube. A milliliter equals a cubic centimeter, so the two units can be used interchangeably. The abbreviation *cc* is often used in clinical work, although it is rarely seen in other branches of science.

Liquids are most commonly measured and dispensed by volume. For example, you might purchase 10 gallons of gasoline, two quarts of milk, a pint of whipping cream, and a 12-fluid ounce can of diet cola. The liter is probably the most familiar metric unit in the United States, since soft drinks are often sold in 1 or 2 L bottles.

If your chemistry course includes a laboratory, you will probably measure liquid volumes using a *graduated cylinder*. Figure 1.7 shows a volume measurement using a typical graduated cylinder. When you view the cylinder at eye level, the liquid forms a curved surface called the **meniscus**. To obtain an accurate reading of liquid volume, you should always compare the scale on the cylinder with the *bottom of the meniscus.*

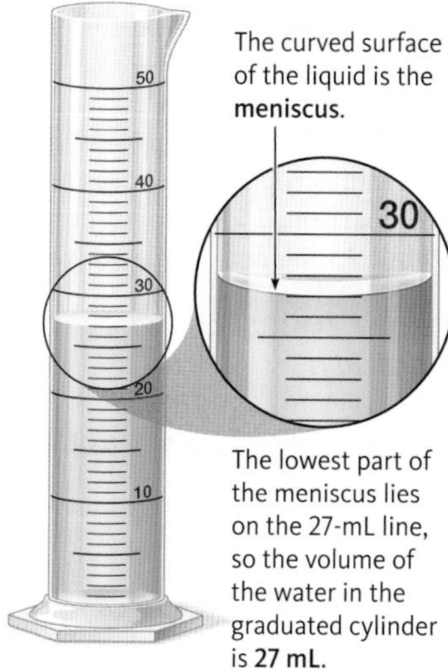

Each line on this cylinder represents 1 mL
The curved surface of the liquid is the **meniscus.**
50
40
30
20
10
30
The lowest part of the meniscus lies on the 27-mL line, so the volume of the water in the graduated cylinder is **27 mL.**

FIGURE 1.7 Measuring a volume with a graduated cylinder.

Health Note: When health care workers fill a syringe, they must compare the bottom of the meniscus with the marks on the syringe. To avoid injecting air into the patient, they then turn the syringe upside down and expel all of the air.

Mass Is Closely Related to Weight

The concept of weight is familiar to everyone. However, there are two ways to answer the question "How heavy is this object?" In the English system we use the object's weight, but in the metric system we use the **mass** of the object. Mass is a measurement of how strongly an object resists being moved when it is pushed, while weight is a measure of how strongly an object is attracted by gravity. A bowling ball that weighs 12 pounds on Earth would weigh 32 pounds on Jupiter and only 2 pounds on the moon, because the force of gravity is different. However, the ball's mass would be the same in all three places, because we must use the same amount of force to start it rolling. Therefore, mass is a more fundamental property than weight.

In health care, weights and masses tend to be used interchangeably, depending on which system of units is being used. The English system has no commonly used mass unit, and weights are rarely used in the metric system. In addition, we use the word *weighing* regardless of whether we are measuring weight or mass. For example, we say that a person who weighs 130 pounds (an English unit of weight) also weighs 59 kilograms (a metric unit of mass).

In the metric system, the base unit of mass is the *gram,* which is roughly the mass of a small paper clip. The most common derived units are the kilogram, the milligram, and the microgram. Table 1.6 lists these units and their English equivalents.

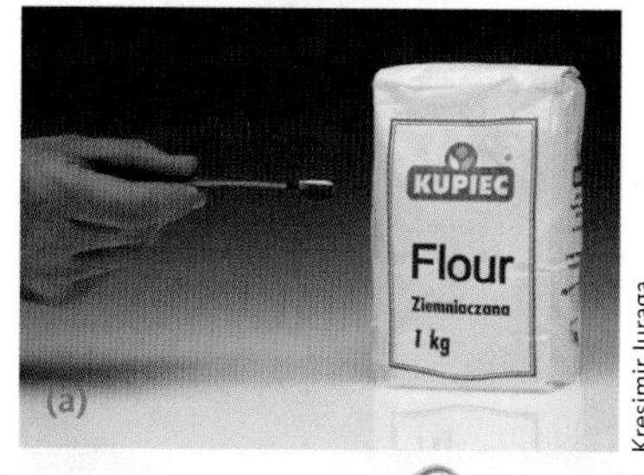

KUPIEC
Flour
Ziemniaczana
1 kg
(a)

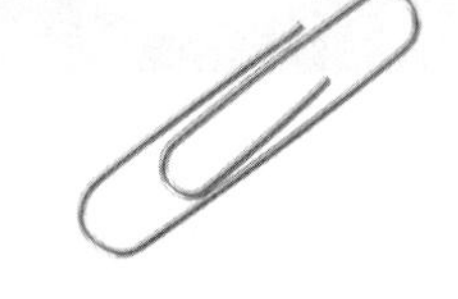

(b)

Some representative metric masses. (a) This package contains a kilogram of flour. (b) A small paperclip weighs around one gram.

TABLE 1.6 Metric Units of Mass

Unit	Rough Description	Typical Uses	Relationship to English Units
Kilogram (kg)	A quart of water weighs about a kilogram.	Masses of people, kitchen appliances, and other sizable items	2.205 pounds = 1 kg
Gram (g)	A small paper clip weighs about a gram.	Food packaging, amounts of proteins, fats, etc., in food	1 ounce = 28.35 g 1 pound = 453.6 g
Milligram (mg)	A large grain of sand weighs around a milligram.	Amounts of most vitamins and minerals in food	*(No comparable English unit exists)*
Microgram (μg)*	The smallest droplet of water that you can see without a microscope weighs around a microgram.	Amounts of some trace nutrients in food, such as cobalt and vitamin B_{12}	*(No comparable English unit exists)*

*The abbreviation *mcg* is often used for micrograms in clinical work to avoid confusing *mg* and μg.

Health Note: All nutritional information uses metric units. For example, a cup of cooked broccoli contains 4 g of protein, 70 mg of calcium, and 80 μg of folic acid.

Sample Problem 1.4

Measuring a mass in metric units

Which of the following is a reasonable mass for a pencil?
15 kg   15 g   15 mg   15 μg

SOLUTION

A gram is roughly the mass of a paper clip, so the most likely mass of a pencil is **15 g.** By comparison, 15 kg would be very heavy (about the mass of a medium-sized television), while 15 mg and 15 μg are very small masses.

TRY IT YOURSELF: *Which of the preceding measurements is a reasonable mass for a small ant?*

For additional practice, try Core Problems 1.11 (parts a and d) and 1.12 (parts b and f).

(a)

Image copyright zcw, 2010. Used under license from Shutterstock.com

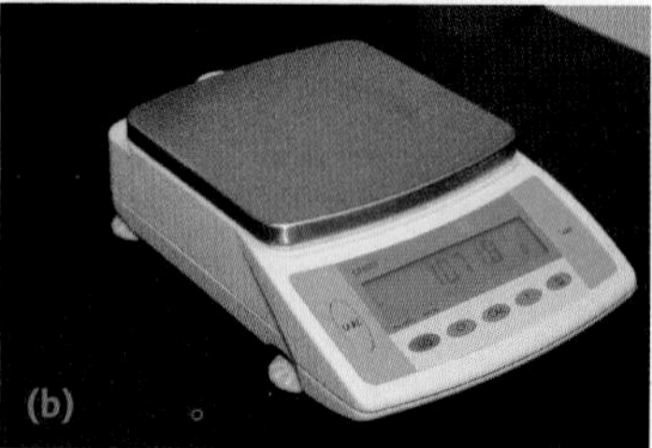

(b)

Image copyright Ron Kloberdanz, 2010. Used under license from Shutterstock.com

(a) An old style balance and (b) a modern electronic balance.

We measure both mass and weight with a balance. A century ago, a balance was two plates suspended from the ends of a metal bar, and weighing was a time-consuming and tedious affair. Today, we weigh objects with a digital electronic balance, which is easy and convenient to use. Ironically, old-style balances measure masses, while modern electronic balances measure weights. All modern balances convert the weight to a mass, but the display is only correct if the balance is used on Earth.

The original metric system has been modified several times since it was first devised. The modern version of the metric system is called the *International System of Units,* universally abbreviated to **SI** (for the French *Système International*). In SI, the base unit for mass is the kilogram rather than the gram, and the base unit for volume is the cubic meter rather than the liter (one cubic meter equals 1000 L). SI was adopted because it simplifies a variety of calculations, primarily involving mass, volume, force, work, and energy. However, the adoption of SI did not affect the names of mass units, which are still based on adding prefixes to the word *gram,* and in practice volumes are normally expressed using units derived from the liter.

CORE PROBLEMS

All Core Problems are paired and the answers to the blue odd-numbered problems appear in the back of the book.

1.1 State whether each of the following is a unit of distance, volume, or mass:
a) kilogram b) deciliter c) centimeter

1.2 State whether each of the following is a unit of distance, volume, or mass:
a) microliter b) kilometer c) milligram

1.3 Give the standard abbreviation for each of the following units:
a) liter b) centimeter c) milligram d) microliter

1.4 Give the standard abbreviation for each of the following units:
a) gram b) milliliter c) kilometer d) centigram

1.5 Write the full name for each of the following metric units:
a) m b) dL c) kg d) μm

1.6 Write the full name for each of the following metric units:
a) L b) cm c) μg d) mL

1.7 The following three measurements describe properties of a television. Which of these is the mass of the television, which is its volume, and which is its height?
a) 50 cm b) 18 kg c) 47 L

1.8 The following three measurements describe properties of a glass of milk. Which of these is the mass of the milk, which is its volume, and which is its depth?
a) 225 mL b) 234 g c) 92 mm

1.9 a) Which is a more appropriate unit to express the mass of a piano: grams or kilograms?
b) Which is a more appropriate unit to express the volume of a drinking cup: microliters or milliliters?
c) Which is a more appropriate unit to express the width of this page: centimeters or meters?

1.10 a) Which is a more appropriate unit to express the width of a pencil: millimeters or kilometers?
b) Which is a more appropriate unit to express the volume of a bucket: milliliters or liters?
c) Which is a more appropriate unit to express the mass of a bee's wing: milligrams or grams?

continued

1.11 From the following list , select all of the statements that cannot possibly be correct based on the size of the measurement:
a) The mass of this pebble is 8.2 g.
b) My kitchen sink has a capacity of 22 μL of water.
c) The distance between Jill's house and her office is 6.3 km.
d) This plastic drinking cup weighs 85 kg.
e) My coffee cup holds 150 mL.
f) The width of Bob's classroom is 8.1 mm.
g) A mouse is 9 cm long.

1.12 From the following list , select all of the statements that cannot possibly be correct based on the size of the measurement:
a) My bookcase is 143 m high.
b) Julia's car weighs 980 kg.
c) Mai runs 3 cm every morning before breakfast.
d) My fingernails are about 12 mm long.
e) It takes 55 μL of gas to fill my car.
f) This computer weighs 18 mg.
g) We will need 8 L of soft drinks for our picnic.

1.2 Measurements in Science: Precision and Accuracy

OBJECTIVES: *Report a measured value to the correct number of digits, interpret the uncertainty in a measurement, and distinguish between precision and accuracy.*

Mr. Jones is concerned about his cholesterol level, so his doctor orders a serum cholesterol test for him. The lab carries out the test twice, using two portions of the same blood sample. The first test result is 174 mg/dL, while the second result is 172 mg/dL. Did some of the cholesterol disappear from Mr. Jones's blood between the two tests? No, the cholesterol level in his blood almost undoubtedly stayed the same. The difference between the two test results is caused by the inherent limitations of the method used to measure cholesterol. A cholesterol test will tell you the *approximate* concentration of cholesterol in your blood, but it cannot tell you the *exact* concentration.

In fact, with the exception of measurements that involve counting entire objects, no measurement can be exact. *Every measurement involves some uncertainty, regardless of the tool or technique used to make the measurement.* As a result, you will normally get slightly different results whenever you repeat a measurement several times.

Health Note: Plasma is the liquid portion of blood that surrounds the cells. Serum is plasma from which the clotting factors have been removed.

Measurements that are not exact are still useful to us, because the uncertainty does not generally affect how we interpret the measurement. For instance, the healthy range for serum cholesterol is considered to be less than 200 mg/dL. Therefore, it makes no difference whether Mr. Jones's actual level is 174 mg/dL or 172 mg/dL, because both values are well within the acceptable range. However, if the lab reports that his cholesterol level is 198 mg/dL, the uncertainty of the testing method will come into play. This value is very close to 200 mg/dL, so the doctor cannot be sure that Mr. Jones's cholesterol level really falls within the healthy range. At the very least, the doctor might recommend that Mr. Jones cut back on the double bacon cheeseburgers that are a staple of his lunchtime diet.

All Measurements Include One Uncertain Digit

In science, it is important to indicate the uncertainty in any measurement. The simplest way to do this is to report one (and only one) uncertain digit, in addition to all of the certain digits. For instance, the lab might report Mr. Jones's cholesterol level as 173 mg/dL (the average of the two measurements). The implication is that the first two digits (the 1 and the 7) are known, but the final digit (the 3) is uncertain.

173 mg/dL

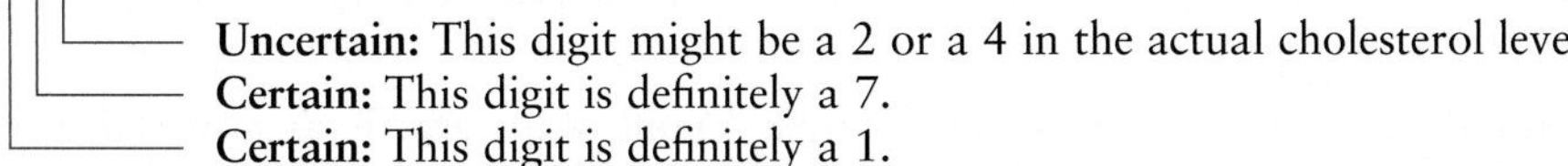

Uncertain: This digit might be a 2 or a 4 in the actual cholesterol level.
Certain: This digit is definitely a 7.
Certain: This digit is definitely a 1.

The rule in science and medicine is that *the final digit in any measured number is assumed to be uncertain.* Here are two other examples of uncertainty in common measurements:

"You weigh 125 pounds."

In this measurement, the 5 (the ones place) is uncertain. Your actual weight could be 124 or 126 pounds, but it is not 142 or 216 pounds.

"Your temperature is 99.7°F."

In this measurement, the 7 (the tenths place) is uncertain. Your actual temperature could be 99.6 or 99.8°F, but it is not 98.6°F. (There is no doubt that you are running a mild fever.)

Sample Problem 1.5

Interpreting the uncertainty of a measurement

The nutritional label on a package of breakfast cereal states that one serving of cereal contains 28 g of carbohydrate. Which digit in this measurement is uncertain?

SOLUTION

In any measured number, the last digit is uncertain. Therefore, **the ones place is uncertain.** A serving of this cereal might actually contain a gram or two more or less than the amount stated on the package.

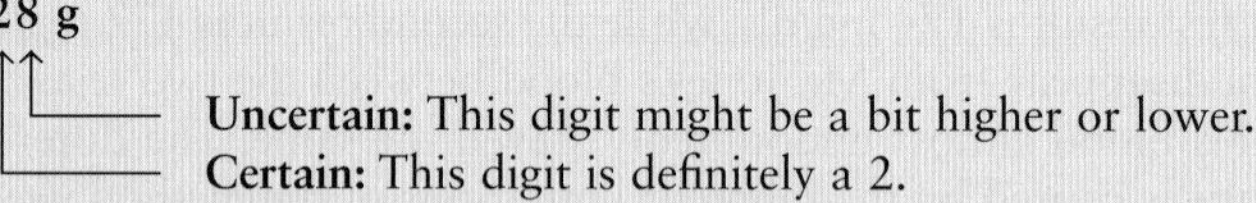
28 g
Uncertain: This digit might be a bit higher or lower.
Certain: This digit is definitely a 2.

TRY IT YOURSELF: *A patient is found to have 0.9 mg/dL of creatinine in his blood. Which digit in this measurement is uncertain?*

For additional practice, try Core Problems 1.13 and 1.14.

When you do measurements in a laboratory, you should always report one (and only one) uncertain digit. The total number of digits you report will depend on the tool you use to make your measurement. In general, two types of tools are in use, digital instruments and graduated instruments.

1. **Digital instruments** display a measurement electronically. All digital instruments show one uncertain digit automatically. For example, let's say that you weigh your calculator on a digital balance, and the balance displays "22.306 g." The final digit (the 6) is uncertain and could be a bit off, so the calculator might weigh anywhere from 22.305 to 22.307 g. The exact uncertainty in a digital measurement depends on the specific instrument and on how carefully it is used.
2. **Graduated instruments** have a series of marks (called *graduations*) that must be matched to the object you are measuring. A ruler is a graduated instrument, as is a graduated cylinder. If you want the best possible results from a graduated instrument, you should estimate one digit beyond the actual graduations. For example, in Figure 1.8, the bottom of the meniscus is between 31 and 32 mL, but it is closer to the higher value. A reasonable guess might be 31.7 mL. However, the 7 is just an estimate; you could have said 31.8 or 31.6 mL. Any of these would be an acceptable value. We can be confident that the first decimal is not a 2, but we cannot be certain that it is a 7.

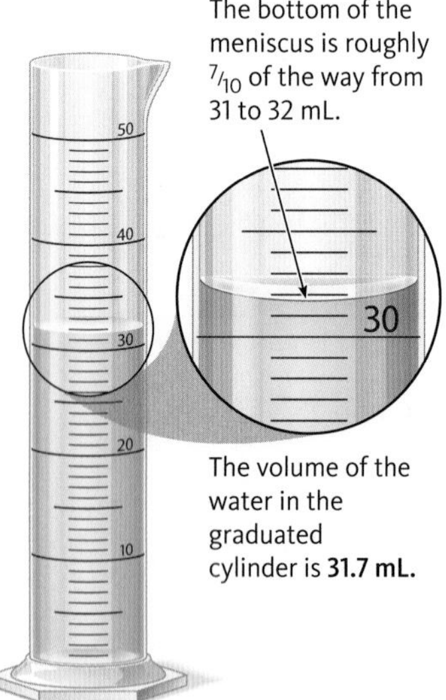
The bottom of the meniscus is roughly 7/10 of the way from 31 to 32 mL.
50
40
30
20
10
30
The volume of the water in the graduated cylinder is **31.7 mL.**

FIGURE 1.8 Estimating a digit in a volume measurement.

What if the bottom of the meniscus lies right on one of the graduations, as it does in Figure 1.7? In this case, our best estimate for the tenths place is a zero. We would report the volume as 27.0 mL. The extra zero tells everyone that the actual volume might be 27.1 or 26.9 mL, but it is certainly not 26 or 28 mL. If we reported the volume as 27 mL, we would mean that the actual volume *could* be 26 or 28 mL; this would be acceptable if we only needed to know an approximate volume and we did not take the time to measure the exact position of the meniscus.

Sample Problem 1.6

Measuring volume using a graduated cylinder

What is the volume of liquid in the graduated cylinder pictured here?

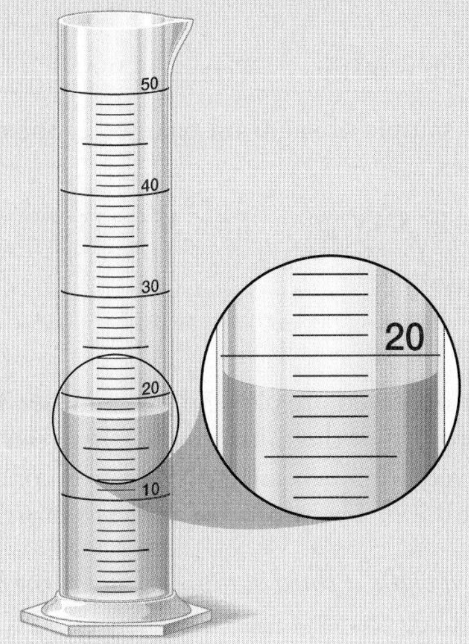

SOLUTION

The bottom of the meniscus is slightly above the 18 mL graduation, so a reasonable value for the volume is **18.2 mL** (18.1 or 18.3 mL would also be reasonable).

TRY IT YOURSELF: *What is the volume of liquid in the graduated cylinder pictured here?*

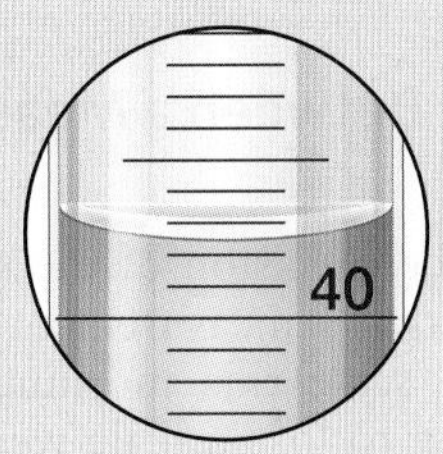

For additional practice, try Core Problems 1.17 and 1.18.

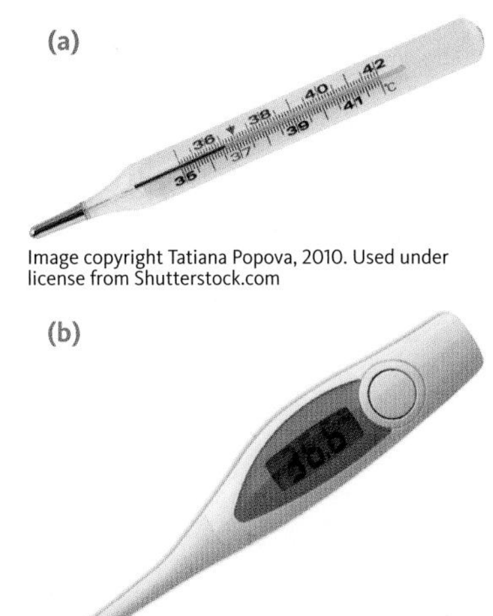

(a)

Image copyright Tatiana Popova, 2010. Used under license from Shutterstock.com

(b)

Image copyright Veniamin Kraskov, 2010. Used under license from Shutterstock.com

(a) An old-style thermometer is an example of a graduated instrument. (b) Modern thermometers are digital instruments.

A similar issue arises when you use a digital instrument. For instance, you might see "15.300 g" on the display of an electronic balance. You should *never* drop the zeros at the end of a digital measurement, because they tell you which digit is uncertain. In this case, the balance tells us that the actual mass could be 15.301 g, but it is not 15.31 or 15.4 g. (The actual mass could be 15.299 g also, but this does not mean that all three decimal places are uncertain. The change in the tenths and hundredths places is a result of counting in base 10.)

Health Note: Modern clinical thermometers have digital displays, but old-style thermometers are graduated. If you have an old thermometer in your home, replace it, but don't throw it in the trash—it contains mercury, which is poisonous.

Precision Is the Agreement Between Repeated Measurements

The uncertainty in a measurement is called **precision**. *A measurement is precise when repeating it many times always produces approximately the same number.* For example, if you weigh the same pencil four times and get the following values, your measurement is quite precise, because the only digit that changes is the thousandths place:

8.29(4) g 8.29(5) g 8.29(4) g 8.29(3) g

On the other hand, if you see the following values, your measurement is not very precise:

8.[288] g 8.[322] g 8.[250] g 8.[423] g

In the first set of measurements, all the digits agreed except the last. (We expect this kind of precision from a digital balance.) In the second set, all three decimal places changed; the only digit that remained constant was the initial 8. The second set of measurements would be unacceptable in laboratory work.

Sample Problem **1.7**

Determining the precision of a tool

Javier weighs a sample of sugar on balance 1. He does a total of three trials and obtains the following masses:

Trial 1: 5.998 g Trial 2: 6.001 g Trial 3: 5.999 g

Mickayla weighs a different sample of sugar on balance 2. She does three trials and obtains the following masses:

Trial 1: 5.236 g Trial 2: 5.437 g Trial 3: 5.335 g

Which balance is more precise?

SOLUTION

The three masses that Javier observed are close to one another. His first trial and his second trial are only 0.003 g apart, and the third trial lies between the other two. The three masses that Mickayla observed are much farther apart from one another; her first and second trials differ by about 0.2 g. **Therefore, balance 1 is more precise.**

TRY IT YOURSELF: *Karina weighs a third sample of sugar on balance 3 and observes the following masses:*

Trial 1: 6.982 g Trial 2: 7.004 g Trial 3: 6.991 g

Which is more precise, balance 2 or balance 3?

For additional practice, try Core Problems 1.19 (part a) and 1.20 (part a).

Accuracy Is the Agreement Between a Measurement and the True Value

Even after we have established the precision of the tool we are using to carry out a measurement, we cannot be sure that a measurement is correct. For instance, perhaps you stepped on your bathroom scale this morning and found that you weighed 136 pounds. You have been trying to lose a little weight, and last week you weighed 141 pounds, so you are pleased. However, later that day your cousin Bert stops by to visit. Bert has weighed 162 pounds for the past 15 years, and he checked his weight just before he left his house, but when he steps on your scale the display reads 157 pounds. Since Bert could not have lost 5 pounds in the few minutes it took him to walk to your house, your scale must be showing weights today that are 5 pounds too low. Unfortunately, you haven't lost any weight this week.

The ability of a measuring tool to give us the correct answer is called **accuracy**. In this case, your bathroom scale is not very accurate, because it does not report the actual weight of the person using it. Accuracy, like precision, affects measurements, but accuracy and precision are not the same thing. *A tool is precise if it gives the same*

Neither precise nor accurate.

Precise but not accurate. The darts aren't on the bull's-eye.

Precise and accurate. The darts are close together and on the bull's-eye.

FIGURE 1.9 Precision and accuracy.

TABLE 1.7 Determining the Accuracy and Precision of a Test Method

Method 1	Method 2	Method 3
Trial 1: 224 mg/dL Trial 2: 225 mg/dL Trial 3: 222 mg/dL Trial 4: 225 mg/dL Average: 224 mg/dL True value: 200 mg/dL *(the standard)* Method 1 is **precise** (the individual trials are close to one another) but **not accurate** (the average is far from the true value).	Trial 1: 199 mg/dL Trial 2: 204 mg/dL Trial 3: 202 mg/dL Trial 4: 203 mg/dL Average: 202 mg/dL True value: 200 mg/dL *(the standard)* Method 2 is **precise** (the individual results are close to one another) and **accurate** (the average is close to the true value).	Trial 1: 182 mg/dL Trial 2: 206 mg/dL Trial 3: 215 mg/dL Trial 4: 193 mg/dL Average: 199 mg/dL True value: 200 mg/dL *(the standard)* Method 3 is **not precise** (the individual trials are far apart), but it appears to be **accurate** (the average is close to the true value—this could be simple coincidence, though).

answer when we repeat a measurement. It is accurate if it gives the right answer. A dart game provides a useful analogy; you are precise if you hit the same spot every time, but you are only accurate if you can hit the bull's-eye, as shown in Figure 1.9.

How can we determine whether a tool is giving accurate measurements? Repeating the measurement will not help, since an inaccurate tool may give the same incorrect result every time. The only way to determine whether a tool is accurate is to measure an object whose properties are already known. For example, you can check the accuracy of your scale by weighing something that is already known to weigh 100 pounds. If your scale also displays 100 pounds, your scale is accurate (at least for weights that are close to 100 pounds). An object that is used to determine the accuracy of a measuring tool is called a **standard**. Table 1.7 shows how a standard can be used to determine the accuracy of three cholesterol testing methods. All three methods are used to test a solution whose cholesterol content is already known to be 200 mg/dL.

Sample Problem **1.8**

Determining the accuracy of a test method

A standard solution is used to test two methods for determining blood sugar levels. The standard solution is known to have a concentration of 90 mg/dL. The results for the two methods are

Method 1:	Trial 1 = 84 mg/dL	Trial 2 = 82 mg/dL	Trial 3 = 83 mg/dL
Method 2:	Trial 1 = 91 mg/dL	Trial 2 = 88 mg/dL	Trial 3 = 94 mg/dL

Which method is more accurate?

SOLUTION

Method 1 consistently gives results that are too low (the average of the three trials is 83 mg/dL), while Method 2 gives results that are close to the correct value (the average is 91 mg/dL). Therefore, **Method 2 is more accurate.** (Method 1 is more precise, since the individual trials are closer to one another, but Method 2 appears more likely to give the "right answer.")

TRY IT YOURSELF: *If the standard solution in this problem had a concentration of 85 mg/dL, which of the two methods would be more accurate?*

For additional practice, try Core Problems 1.19 (part b) and 1.20 (part b).

CORE PROBLEMS

1.13 Which digit (if any) is uncertain in the following measurement?
"One cup of sliced peaches contains 1.19 mg of vitamin E."

1.14 Which digit (if any) is uncertain in the following measurement?
"Only 0.4% of the people in our town have red hair."

1.15 Using the ruler pictured here, measure the length of the nail as precisely as you can. Express your answer in centimeters, to an appropriate number of decimal places.

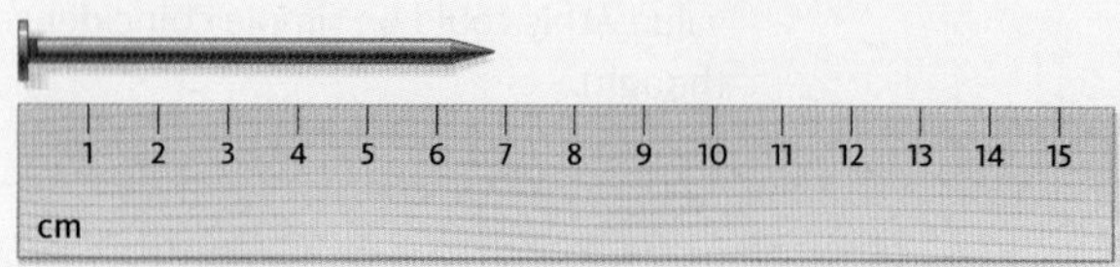

1.16 Using the ruler pictured here, measure the length of the screwdriver as precisely as you can. Express your answer in centimeters, to an appropriate number of decimal places.

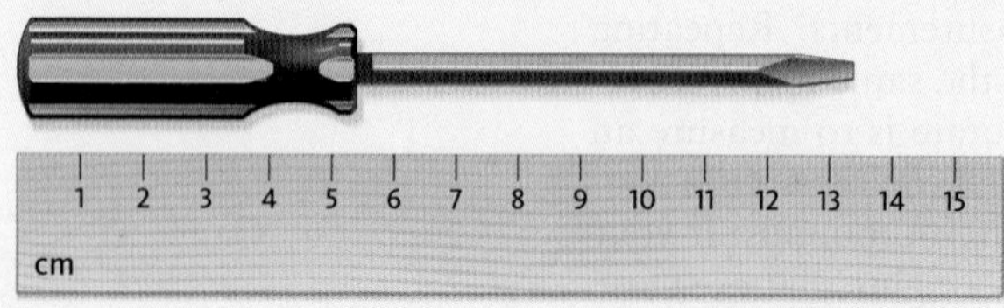

1.17 What is the volume of water in the following graduated cylinder? (Note that each small graduation is 0.5 mL.)

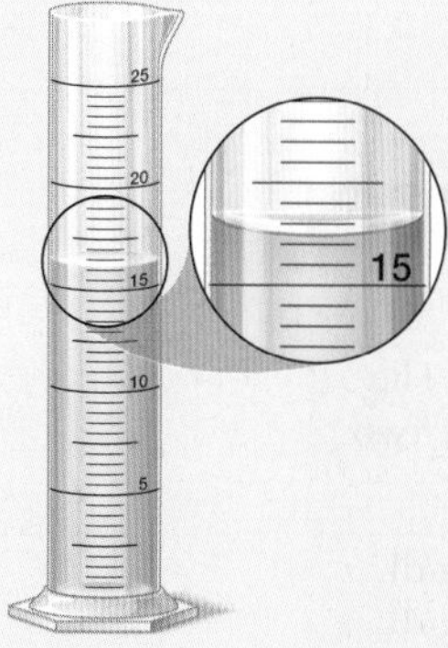

1.18 What is the volume of water in the following graduated cylinder? (Note that each small graduation is 0.2 mL.)

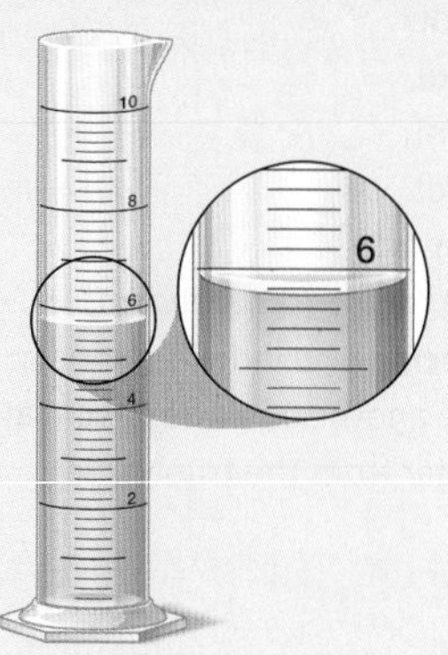

1.19 A piece of metal weighing 26.386 g is used to check two different balances. The piece of metal is weighed three times on each balance, with the following results:

Balance 1: 26.375 g 26.377 g 26.378 g
Balance 2: 26.389 g 26.381 g 26.385 g

a) Which balance is more precise? Explain your reasoning.
b) Which balance is more accurate? Explain your reasoning.

1.20 A metal bar that is exactly 20 cm long is used to check two different measuring tools. Three people measure the length of the bar using each tool, with the following results:

Tool 1: 19.98 cm 19.96 cm 19.99 cm
Tool 2: 20.41 cm 20.37 cm 20.44 cm

a) Which tool is more precise? Explain your reasoning.
b) Which tool is more accurate? Explain your reasoning.

OBJECTIVES: *Convert distance, volume, and mass measurements from one metric unit to another.*

1.3 Metric Units and Their Relationships

One of the great advantages of the metric system over the English system is the simple way in which units are related to one another. For instance, relationships between English units of distance involve numbers that are not connected to one another in any rational way.

1 foot = 12 inches   1 yard = 3 feet   1 mile = 1760 yards = 5280 feet

• Powers of ten are covered in Appendix A.6.

These numbers can be hard to remember, and they make it difficult to express an English measurement using a different unit. By contrast, metric relationships are based on powers of ten:

1 cm = $^1/_{100}$ m (10^{-2} m)   1 km = 1000 m (10^3 m)

Another advantage of the metric system is that it uses the same set of relationships for all types of measurements. For instance, the prefix *milli-* means the same thing regardless of what unit we attach it to, so one meter equals 1000 millimeters, one liter equals 1000 milliliters, and one gram equals 1000 milligrams. These prefixes are so convenient that scientists occasionally use them for nonmetric units. For example, 1000 years is sometimes called a kiloyear.

Sample Problem 1.9

Using the definition of a derived unit

The potential of a battery is measured using a unit called a volt. How is a millivolt related to a volt?

SOLUTION

The prefix *milli-* means $^1/_{1000}$ of the base unit, so a *millivolt* is $^1/_{1000}$ of a volt. We can also express this relationship by saying that 1000 millivolts equals one volt.

TRY IT YOURSELF: *Electrical power is measured using a unit called a watt. How is a kilowatt related to a watt?*

Metric Measurements Can Be Converted from One Unit to Another by Moving the Decimal Point

In both the English system and the metric system, we can express a single measurement in several ways, depending on the units we choose. For example, we can say that the length of a yardstick is 1 yard, 3 feet, or 36 inches. Likewise, we can express metric measurements in a variety of units. For example, suppose we want to measure the length of a pencil. Figure 1.10 shows how we can express the length using three different metric units. We can say that the pencil is 0.5 dm, 5 cm, or 50 mm long. These three expressions represent the same distance, just as 1 foot and 12 inches represent equal distances in the English system.

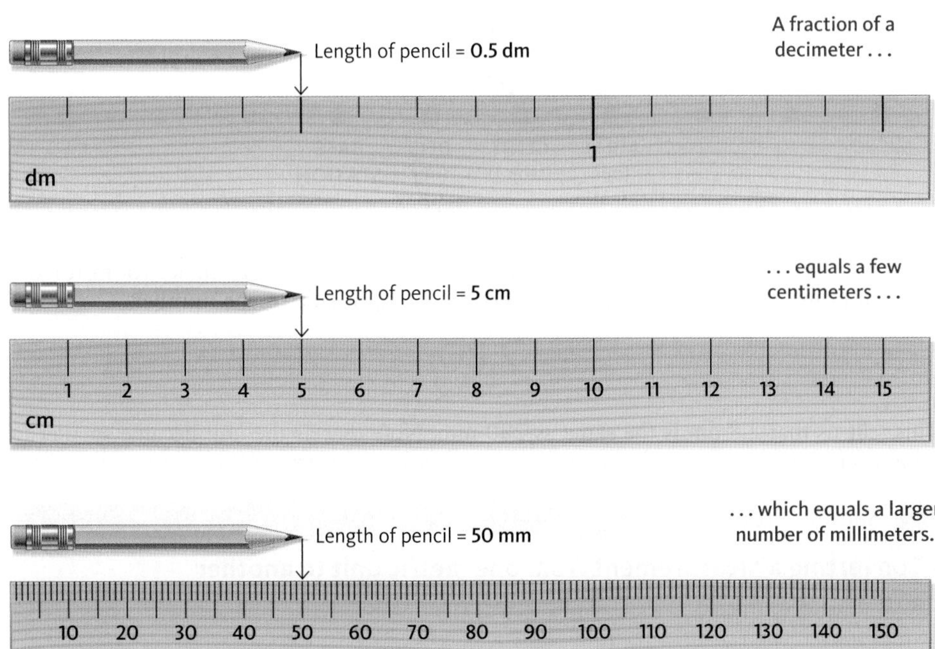

FIGURE 1.10 Measuring a length using three different metric units.

MICRO | this station has no name | this station has no name | MILLI | CENTI | DECI | BASE STATION | this station has no name | this station has no name | KILO

FIGURE 1.11 The metric railroad.

In science and medicine, we frequently need to express a metric measurement using a different unit. To do so, it is helpful to think of the metric prefixes as stations on a railroad, as shown in Figure 1.11. Moving from one station to another corresponds to increasing or decreasing the size of the unit by a factor of 10. For example, if we move from the deci station to the centi station, we decrease the size of the unit by a factor of 10; a centimeter is 10 times smaller than a decimeter.

Some stations do not have names, and others have names that are not in common use. For example, the units that correspond to $^1/_{10,000}$ and $^1/_{100,000}$ of the base unit (between the milli and the micro stations) have no names in the metric system. On the other hand, the units that correspond to 10 and 100 base units (between the base station and the kilo station) do have names; 10 meters is a decameter and 100 meters is a hectometer. The prefixes *deca-* and *hecto-* are occasionally used outside the United States, but they do not appear in health care applications or in any measurements in the United States.

Because all metric units are related to one another by factors of 10, we can translate any metric measurement into a different unit by simply moving the decimal point in the number. To do this conversion correctly, we need two rules:

1. *The number of stations you move equals the number of places you must move the decimal point.* For example, if you want to translate a measurement from decimeters into millimeters, you move two stations on the metric railroad, and you must therefore move the decimal point two places.
2. *If you increase the size of the unit, you decrease the size of the number (and vice versa).* In practice, this means that the "metric train" and the decimal point move in opposite directions.

For example, suppose we know that the height of a textbook is 2.8 dm and we want to express this measurement in millimeters. Looking at the metric railroad, we see that we must move two stations to the left.

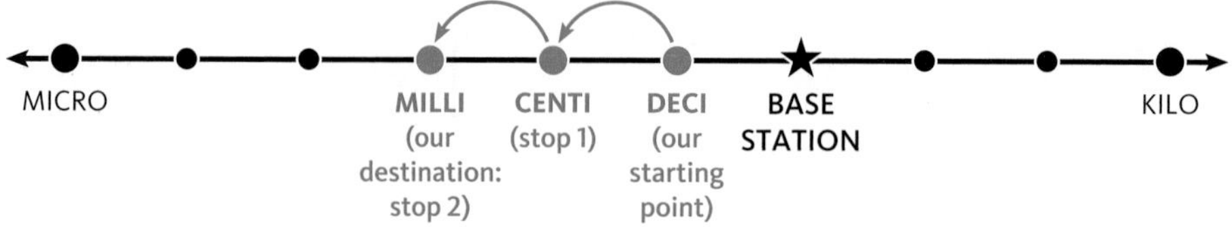

Therefore, we move the decimal point two places to the right. To make room for the decimal point, we must add one extra zero to the right side of the number.

2.80.

This tells us that 2.8 dm is the same as 280 mm. Note that as the unit became smaller (a millimeter is smaller than a decimeter), the number became larger (280 is larger than 2.8).

Sample Problem 1.10

Converting a measurement from one metric unit to another

A tissue sample weighs 450 cg. Express this mass in kilograms.

SOLUTION

Looking at the metric railroad, we see that we must move five stations to the right when we go from the centi station to the kilo station.

continued

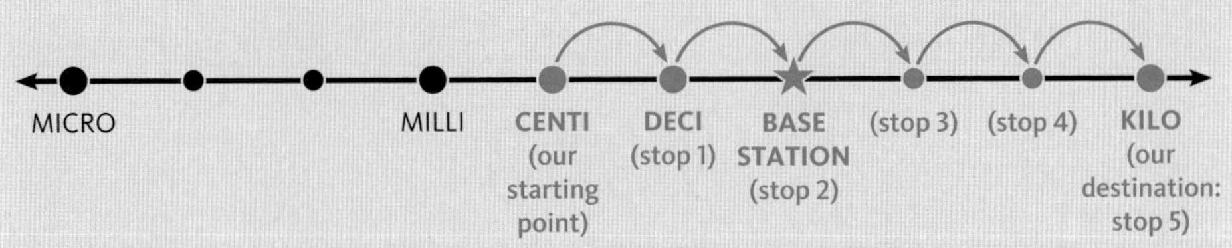

Therefore, we must move the decimal point five places to the left. To do so, we must add three zeroes to the left side of our original number.

0.00450.

Our tissue sample weighs **0.0045 kg.** When writing decimal numbers that are smaller than 1, always include a zero to the left of the decimal point (do not write ".0045 kg").

TRY IT YOURSELF: *A pipet holds 245 μL of water. Express this volume in milliliters.*

For additional practice, try Core Problems 1.23 and 1.24.

In clinical work, you will generally express measurements using a unit that fits the size of the measurement. For example, you would express the mass (or weight) of an adult patient in pounds or in kilograms, rather than in tons or in milligrams. However, the unit and the size of the measurement occasionally do not match well. In such cases, you will need to use a very large or very small number to express the measurement. For example, the speed of light is 1,079,000,000 km per hour and the mass of a single flu virus is around 0.000000000000000005 g. Extremely large or small numbers are normally written using **scientific notation**, which uses powers of ten to make the number easier to read and use. Using scientific notation, the speed of light is 1.079×10^9 km/hr and the mass of the flu virus is 5×10^{-18} g. Appendix A.6 describes how to write and use numbers in scientific notation.

We Can Write a Relationship Between Any Two Metric Units

Using the metric railroad, we can also write relationships between two metric units. To do so, use the following steps:

1. *Start with the larger unit.* For instance, if we want to write a relationship between deciliters and milliliters, we start with 1 dL (because a deciliter is larger than a milliliter).
2. *Use the metric railroad to find the equivalent measurement in the smaller unit.* In this case, traveling from the deci station to the milli station requires moving two stops to the left, so we move the decimal two places to the right.

1.00.

This tells us that one deciliter is the same as 100 milliliters.

Sample Problem 1.11

Writing a relationship between metric units

What is the relationship between kilometers and millimeters?

SOLUTION

The larger unit is the kilometer, so we start with 1 km and use the metric railroad to find the equivalent number of millimeters. We must move six stations to the left when we go from the kilo station to the milli station.

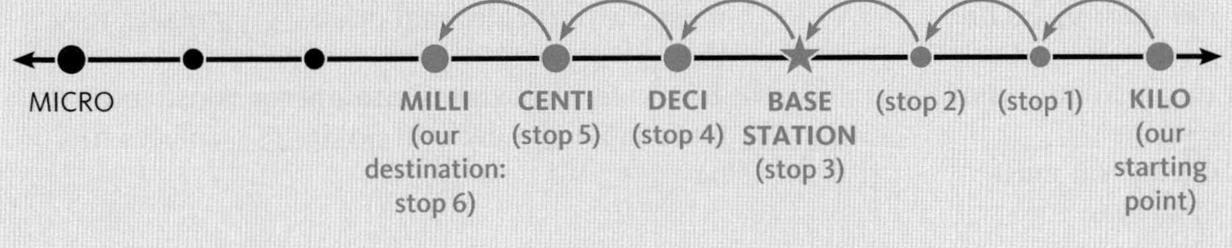

continued

Therefore, we must move the decimal point six places to the right, adding six zeroes as we do so.

1.000000.

Adding a couple of commas to make this number more legible, we see that **1 kilometer equals 1,000,000 millimeters.**

TRY IT YOURSELF: *What is the relationship between micrometers and centimeters?*

For additional practice, try Core Problems 1.25 and 1.26.

Health Note: Water filters for backpackers typically have pores that are between 100 and 300 nm, preventing bacteria and other microorganisms (but not viruses) from passing through the filter.

Other Metric Prefixes Are Used for Specialized Applications

The metric system has many other prefixes that are used to express larger or smaller amounts than the common units we have already seen. For example, the width of a typical cold virus (0.00000002 m) is normally expressed in *nanometers*. A nanometer is a billionth of a meter, so the virus is 20 nm wide. Computer memory capacities are typically expressed in *megabytes* (1,000,000 bytes) or *gigabytes* (1,000,000,000 bytes). Table 1.8 shows other commonly used metric prefixes, and Figure 1.12 shows an extended version of the metric railroad that includes several of these prefixes. Note that beyond *kilo-* and *milli-*, each of the named units is separated from its neighbors by three powers of ten.

TABLE 1.8 Other Metric Prefixes in Common Use

Prefix	Abbreviation	Meaning	Example
Tera-	T	1,000,000,000,000 base units (10^{12} base units)	Terameter (Tm)
Giga-	G	1,000,000,000 base units (10^{9} base units)	Gigameter (Gm)
Mega-	M	1,000,000 base units (10^{6} base units)	Megameter (Mm)
Nano-	n	$^{1}/_{1,000,000,000}$ of a base unit (10^{-9} base units)	Nanometer (nm)
Pico-	p	$^{1}/_{1,000,000,000,000}$ of a base unit (10^{-12} base units)	Picometer (pm)

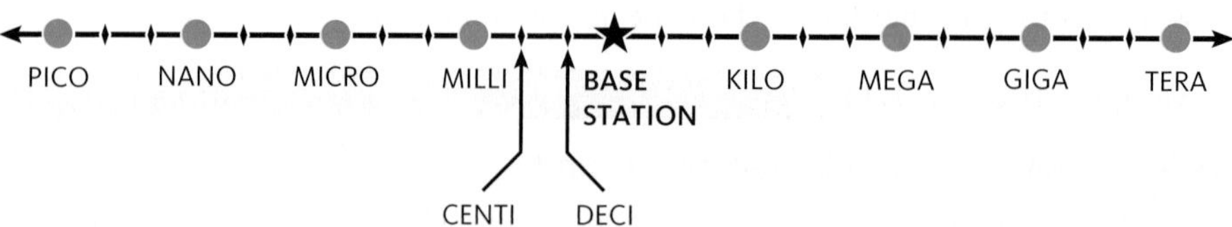

FIGURE 1.12 The extended metric railroad.

CORE PROBLEMS

1.21 Complete the following statements. *Example: To convert meters into centimeters, you must move the decimal point two places to the right.*

a) To convert grams into milligrams, you must move the decimal point _____ places to the _____.

b) To convert milliliters into deciliters, you must move the decimal point _____ places to the _____.

c) To convert centimeters into millimeters, you must move the decimal point _____ places to the _____.

d) To convert kilograms into micrograms, you must move the decimal point _____ places to t he _____.

continued

1.22 Complete the following statements. See Problem 1.21 for an example.
a) To convert grams into kilograms, you must move the decimal point _____ places to the _____.
b) To convert centimeters into micrometers, you must move the decimal point _____ places to the _____.
c) To convert deciliters into kiloliters, you must move the decimal point _____ places to the _____.
d) To convert decigrams into milligrams, you must move the decimal point _____ places to the _____.

1.23 A textbook is 27.2 cm tall. Express this measurement in each of the following units:
a) meters
b) millimeters
c) micrometers (use scientific notation)

1.24 A serving of cereal contains 120 mg of sodium. Express this measurement in each of the following units:
a) grams
b) micrograms
c) kilograms (use scientific notation)

1.25 Write a relationship between each of the following units:
a) liters and deciliters
b) kilometers and meters
c) grams and micrograms
d) millimeters and centimeters

1.26 Write a relationship between each of the following units:
a) grams and centigrams
b) centimeters and kilometers
c) microliters and milliliters
d) decigrams and centigrams

1.4 Unit Conversions and Conversion Factors

OBJECTIVE: *Convert a measurement from one unit to another using a conversion factor*

When the author's twin daughters were born, the extended family was buzzing with excitement. Are they healthy? (Yes.) What sex are they? (Two girls.) How much do they weigh? The hospital staff supplied this information:

Baby A: 3348 g   Baby B: 3774 g

However, these weights did not convey anything meaningful to the family members. "How much do the babies weigh in pounds and ounces?" everyone wanted to know. "Could you translate grams into weights we can understand?"

The conversion of a measurement from one unit to another is a fact of life in science and medicine, made necessary by the existence of two systems of measurement (English and metric) and by the existence of multiple units within each system. Scientists must be able to translate milliliters into liters, inches into centimeters, pounds into kilograms, and so forth. In Section 1.3, we saw how we can relate metric units to each other, but this method does not work for conversions involving English units. Let us now look at a systematic method that we can use for any unit conversion.

Conversion Factors Express a Relationship Between Two Units

The starting point for our general method is a **conversion factor**. *A conversion factor is a fraction that shows how two different units are related to one another.* For example, one foot is the same as 12 inches. If we write these two measurements as a fraction, we have a conversion factor. We can write two different conversion factors, depending on which measurement we put in the numerator and which we put in the denominator.

The **numerator** (the top of the fraction) →
The **denominator** (the bottom of the fraction) →

$$\frac{12 \text{ inches}}{1 \text{ foot}} \quad \text{or} \quad \frac{1 \text{ foot}}{12 \text{ inches}}$$

A fraction is a conversion factor only if the numerator and denominator represent the same measurement. In this case, 12 inches and 1 foot are two ways to express the same length, so each of these fractions is a conversion factor. On the other hand, a fraction such as

$$\frac{1 \text{ inch}}{12 \text{ feet}}$$

is *not* a conversion factor, because 1 inch and 12 feet are different distances.

Sample Problem 1.12

Writing conversion factors

There are 5280 feet in one mile. Write two conversion factors that express this relationship.

SOLUTION

Each conversion factor must contain two measurements: 5280 feet and 1 mile. One conversion factor has 5280 feet in the numerator and 1 mile in the denominator, and the other conversion factor has the two reversed. The two conversion factors are

$$\frac{5280 \text{ feet}}{1 \text{ mile}} \quad \text{and} \quad \frac{1 \text{ mile}}{5280 \text{ feet}}$$

TRY IT YOURSELF: *There are 39.37 inches in one meter. Write two conversion factors that express this relationship.*

For additional practice, try Core Problems 1.27 and 1.28.

The Systematic Approach to Unit Conversions Uses Conversion Factors

You can use conversion factors to translate almost any measurement from one unit to another. To do so, use the following four steps:

1. Identify the original measurement and the unit you need in the final answer.
2. Write conversion factors that express the relationship between the two units in the problem.
3. Multiply the original measurement by the conversion factor that allows you to cancel units.
4. Do the arithmetic and (if necessary) round off your final answer to an appropriate number of digits.

The first two steps help you identify the problem and locate the information you need, and the remaining two steps allow you to solve the problem.

To illustrate this technique, let us convert 4 feet into the corresponding number of inches. If you know that a foot equals 12 inches, you can probably do this conversion without resorting to conversion factors (4 × 12 = 48 inches). However, working this exercise using conversion factors will help prepare you for more complex problems.

1. *Identify the original measurement and the unit needed in the final answer.* We need to convert 4 feet into inches, so our original measurement is 4 feet and our answer must be a number of inches. We can represent the problem with the following sketch:

4 feet **convert to** ? inches

(the measurement we are given) (the unit we need in our answer)

2. *Write conversion factors that express the relationship between the two units in the problem.* Our two units are feet and inches, and we know that one foot is the same as 12 inches. The corresponding conversion factors are

$$\frac{12 \text{ inches}}{1 \text{ foot}} \quad \text{and} \quad \frac{1 \text{ foot}}{12 \text{ inches}}$$

3. *Multiply the original measurement by the conversion factor that allows us to cancel units.* This conversion factor must have the original unit (feet) in the denominator.

$$4 \text{ feet} \times \frac{12 \text{ inches}}{1 \text{ foot}}$$

The original unit (feet) must appear in the **denominator** of the conversion factor.

In effect, we are dividing feet by feet, which allows us to cancel out the *feet* units. (Singular *foot* and plural *feet* represent the same unit.) Doing this step is the key to the unit conversion method, so you should always show how the units cancel out by drawing a line through each label that you are canceling.

$$4 \cancel{\text{feet}} \times \frac{12 \text{ inches}}{1 \cancel{\text{foot}}}$$

4. *Carry out the arithmetic and round off the final answer to the correct number of digits.* In unit conversions, we should always end up with the unit that we need in the final answer after we cancel the other units. In this case, we end up with inches, the unit we need.

$$4 \times \frac{12 \boxed{\text{inches}}}{1}$$

After we cancel "feet," we are left with inches as the unit for our answer.

Now we can attend to the arithmetic. A fraction represents division, so our calculation is

$$4 \times 12 \div 1$$

Appendix A.2 describes in more detail how to do arithmetic that involves fractions.

When we do this arithmetic on a calculator, we get 48. Therefore, the conversion factor method gives us **48 inches,** as it should.

This method is particularly useful when we need to translate an English measurement into a metric unit, or vice versa. Sample Problem 1.13 illustrates how we can use a conversion factor to solve the problem at the beginning of this section, converting an infant's weight from grams to pounds.

Sample Problem 1.13

Using a conversion factor to do a unit conversion

One of the author's daughters weighed 3348 g at birth. Express this as a weight in pounds.

SOLUTION

STEP 1: The problem gives us a weight (really a mass) in grams and asks us to convert this weight into pounds. We can depict the problem as follows:

3348 g → convert to → ? pounds

STEP 1: Identify the original measurement and the final unit.

STEP 2: To do this conversion, we need to find a relationship between grams and pounds. Table 1.6 tells us that there are 453.6 grams in one pound. We can use this relationship to write two conversion factors.

$$\frac{453.6 \text{ g}}{1 \text{ pound}} \quad \text{and} \quad \frac{1 \text{ pound}}{453.6 \text{ g}}$$

STEP 2: Write conversion factors that relate the two units.

STEP 3: Our original measurement is in grams, so we must choose the conversion factor that has grams in the denominator. Doing so allows us to cancel the *g* unit and leaves us with pounds as the unit of our answer.

$$3348 \text{ g} \times \frac{1 \text{ pound}}{453.6 \text{ g}}$$

We can cancel these units.

STEP 3: Choose the conversion factor that allows you to cancel units.

STEP 4: Finally, we do the arithmetic and cancel our units.

$$3348 \cancel{\text{g}} \times \frac{1 \text{ pound}}{453.6 \cancel{\text{g}}} = 7.38095238 \text{ pounds} \quad \text{calculator answer}$$

On a calculator, the arithmetic looks like this:

$$3348 \times 1 \div 453.6 =$$

STEP 4: Do the math and round your answer.

continued

To complete our solution, we should round our answer to a reasonable number of digits, as described in Appendix A.5. Since this calculation involves multiplication and division, we round our answer based on significant figures. Both our original measurement and our conversion factor have four significant figures:

$$\underset{1234}{3348}\text{ g} \times \frac{1\text{ pound}}{\underset{1234}{453.6}\text{ g}}$$

Our answer must be rounded to match the number with the fewest significant figures. In this case, both numbers have four significant figures, so our answer should be rounded to four significant figures as well.

7.38095238 pounds → round off → 7.381 pounds

The answer is 7.381 pounds, or roughly 7 pounds 6 ounces, a healthy birth weight.

TRY IT YOURSELF: *The author's other daughter weighed 3774 g at birth. Express this weight in pounds.*

For additional practice, try Core Problems 1.31 and 1.32.

We can also use the conversion factor method to change a metric measurement into a different metric unit. To do so, we must work out the relationship between the two metric units, using the method you learned in Section 1.3. For example, suppose we need to express 350 mL as a number of deciliters. Milliliters and deciliters are two stops apart on the metric railroad, with deciliters being the larger unit. Therefore, the relationship between these two units is

$$1\text{ dL} = 100\text{ mL}$$

We can use this relationship to write a pair of conversion factors.

$$\frac{100\text{ mL}}{1\text{ dL}} \quad \text{and} \quad \frac{1\text{ dL}}{100\text{ mL}}$$

Which of these do we use? Our original measurement is in milliliters, so we must choose the second conversion factor.

$$350\text{ }\cancel{\text{mL}} \times \frac{1\text{ dL}}{100\text{ }\cancel{\text{mL}}}$$

Doing the arithmetic gives us 3.5 dL as our final answer.

Sample Problem 1.14

Using a conversion factor to do a metric conversion

A micropipet dispenses 25 μL of liquid. Convert this volume to milliliters, using a conversion factor.

SOLUTION

STEP 1: Identify the original measurement and the final unit.

STEP 1: We are given a volume in microliters and asked to convert the volume to milliliters.

25 μL → convert to → ? mL

STEP 2: Write conversion factors that relate the two units.

STEP 2: From the metric railroad, we see that microliters and milliliters are three stations apart, and the milliliter is the larger unit. Therefore, 1 mL is the same as 1000 μL. Our conversion factors are

$$\frac{1000\ \mu\text{L}}{1\text{ mL}} \quad \text{and} \quad \frac{1\text{ mL}}{1000\ \mu\text{L}}$$

continued

STEP 3: Our original measurement is in microliters, so we choose the conversion factor that has microliters in the denominator.

$$25\ \mu L \times \frac{1\ mL}{1000\ \mu L}$$

We can cancel these units.

STEP 3: Choose the conversion factor that allows you to cancel units.

STEP 4: Finally, we do the arithmetic and cancel our units.

$$25\ \cancel{\mu L} \times \frac{1\ mL}{1000\ \cancel{\mu L}} = 0.025\ mL$$

The metric conversion factor is an exact number, so we ignore it when we work out how to round our answer. Since the original measurement (25 μL) had two significant figures, our answer must have two significant figures as well. The calculator result (0.025) already has the correct number of significant figures, so we report our answer as **0.025 mL.**

STEP 4: Do the math and round your answer.

Reminder: You can find a detailed description of the significant figure rules in Appendix A.5.

TRY IT YOURSELF: *A syringe is 11.3 cm long. Convert this length to millimeters, using a conversion factor.*

For additional practice, try using this method to solve Core Problems 1.23 and 1.24 (Section 1.3).

The conversion factor method is powerful and can be applied to a wide range of problems that involve calculations. In the next section, we will use this method to carry out unit conversions that require more than one step.

CORE PROBLEMS

1.27 Express each of the following relationships as a pair of conversion factors:
a) There are 1.609 kilometers in a mile.
b) An object that weighs one kilogram weighs 2.205 pounds.
c) A deciliter equals 100 milliliters.

1.28 Express each of the following relationships as a pair of conversion factors:
a) One cup is the same as 236.6 milliliters.
b) There are 6 teaspoons in a fluid ounce.
c) 1000 meters equals a kilometer.

1.29 What (if anything) is wrong with each of the following conversion factor setups?
a) $5.3\ cm \times \frac{100\ m}{1\ cm} = 5300\ m$
b) $5.3\ cm \times \frac{100\ cm}{1\ m} = 5300\ m$

1.30 What (if anything) is wrong with each of the following conversion factor setups?
a) $82\ m \times \frac{1000\ km}{1\ m} = 82{,}000\ km$
b) $82\ m \times \frac{1000\ m}{1\ km} = 82{,}000\ km$

1.31 Carry out each of the following unit conversions, using only the information given in the problem. Use a conversion factor to solve each problem.
a) There are 32 fluid ounces in a quart. If a beverage container holds 19.7 fluid ounces of juice, how many quarts of juice does it hold?
b) One ounce equals 28.35 g. If a beaker weighs 4.88 ounces, how many grams does it weigh?
c) There are 236.6 mL in one cup. If a flask holds 247 mL of water, how many cups of water does it hold?
d) There are 39.37 inches in one meter. If a woman is 1.52 m tall, what is her height in inches?
e) A typical member of the species *Vibrio cholerae* (the bacterium that causes cholera) is 8.8×10^{-6} m long. How long is this in inches, given that there are 39.37 inches in one meter?

1.32 Carry out each of the following unit conversions, using only the information given in the problem. Use a conversion factor to solve each problem.
a) There are 2000 pounds in a ton. If a refrigerator weighs 245 pounds, how many tons does it weigh?
b) There are 2.54 centimeters in one inch. If a plant is 39.6 cm tall, how many inches tall is it?
c) One quart is the same as 946 mL. If a pitcher holds 2500 mL of liquid, how many quarts does it hold?
d) There are 2.205 pounds in one kilogram. If a dog weighs 41.3 pounds, how many kilograms does it weigh?
e) A $^1/_3$ cup serving of peanuts contains 5.7×10^{-5} ounces of zinc. How many grams is this, given that one ounce equals 28.35 grams?

OBJECTIVE: *Use multiple conversion factors to carry out unit conversions.*

1.5 Using Multiple Conversion Factors

In the last section, you learned a method for converting a measurement from one unit to another. In each of the examples, we were able to find a conversion factor that related the two units. However, in some cases you may not know or be able to find a single conversion factor. These problems require the use of more than one conversion factor. In this section, we will see how to approach such problems.

The most important part of problem solving is to plan a strategy before you start to do the arithmetic. For example, suppose a friend who lives in Japan says she is 163 cm tall and we want to translate her height into feet. Table 1.4 does not list a relationship between centimeters and feet, but it does tell us that one meter is the same as 3.281 feet. If we convert centimeters into meters first, we can then use this relationship to convert meters into feet. We can draw a diagram to summarize our strategy.

163 centimeters → convert to → ? meters → convert to → ? feet

(the measurement we are given) … (the unit we need in our answer)

Once we have planned our strategy, we can carry out the details. First, we convert 163 cm into meters.

$$163\,\text{cm} \times \frac{1\,\text{m}}{100\,\text{cm}} = 1.63\,\text{m}$$

We could also do this step using the metric railroad.

This calculation tells us that 163 cm is the same as 1.63 m. Now we convert 1.63 m into feet.

$$1.63\,\text{m} \times \frac{3.281\,\text{feet}}{1\,\text{m}} = 5.34803\,\text{feet}$$

Our answer, after rounding to three significant figures, is 5.35 feet (about 5 feet 4 inches).

Multiple Conversion Factors Can Be Written As a Single Calculation

Writing out each step individually is the safest way to carry out a multiple-step conversion. However, as you become more familiar with unit conversions, you will find that doing the conversions one at a time becomes cumbersome. A shorter way to set up the calculations is to write the unit conversion factors one after another. First, we write the factor that translates centimeters into meters.

$$163\,\text{cm} \times \frac{1\,\text{m}}{100\,\text{cm}}$$

Then, we multiply this setup by the factor that converts meters into feet. We now can cancel two sets of units, centimeters and meters.

$$163\,\text{cm} \times \frac{1\,\text{m}}{100\,\text{cm}} \times \frac{3.281\,\text{feet}}{1\,\text{m}}$$

The only unit that we have not canceled out is feet, so this setup converts centimeters directly into feet. All that remains is to do the arithmetic, which we enter like this:

$$163 \times 1 \div 100 \times 3.281 \div 1 = 5.34803$$

We get the same numerical answer that we did before, because we have used the same conversion factors. The only difference is that we have carried out the arithmetic in one step, rather than two.

There May Be More Than One Way to Set Up a Multiple-Step Unit Conversion

You will often find that there is more than one way to solve a problem that involves several conversion factors. For instance, in this example we could have converted

163 cm into inches first, using the fact that one inch equals 2.54 cm. Then we can convert the measurement from inches into feet. Our strategy map looks like this:

163 cm **convert to** ? inches **convert to** ? feet

(the measurement we are given) (the unit we need in our answer)

The conversion factor setup for this strategy is

$$163\ \cancel{\text{cm}} \times \frac{1\ \cancel{\text{inch}}}{2.54\ \cancel{\text{cm}}} \times \frac{1\ \text{foot}}{12\ \cancel{\text{inches}}}$$

The first conversion factor translates centimeters into inches, and the second translates inches into feet. When we do the arithmetic, we get a slightly different calculator answer, because the number of feet in one meter is not exactly 3.281. (Most metric-to-English conversion factors that you will see in textbooks and tables are rounded off.)

$163 \times 1 \div 2.54 \times 1 \div 12 = 5.34776903$ Last time, we got 5.34803.

However, when we round the calculator answer to three significant figures, we get the same result, 5.35 feet.

Sample Problem 1.15

Using multiple conversion factors

A recipe calls for 4.5 tablespoons of cooking oil. Convert this volume into milliliters, using the information in Table 1.5 and the fact that one tablespoon equals 3 teaspoons.

SOLUTION

STEP 1: The problem gives us a number of tablespoons of cooking oil and asks us to convert this amount into milliliters. We are also told that one tablespoon equals 3 teaspoons, but this is a relationship between two units, not an actual measurement. We can draw a tentative strategy map.

STEP 1: Identify the original measurement and the final unit.

4.5 tablespoons **convert to** ? mL

STEP 2: We begin by checking Table 1.5 for a relationship between tablespoons and milliliters. Table 1.5 does not give us this information, but it does give us a relationship between teaspoons and milliliters (one teaspoon = 4.93 mL), and the problem tells us that one tablespoon equals 3 teaspoons. To solve this problem, then, we need two steps, which we can represent by an expanded strategy map.

STEP 2: Write conversion factors that relate the two units.

4.5 tablespoons **convert to** ? teaspoons **convert to** ? mL

The conversion factors that relate tablespoons to teaspoons are

$$\frac{3\ \text{teaspoons}}{1\ \text{tablespoon}} \quad \text{and} \quad \frac{1\ \text{tablespoon}}{3\ \text{teaspoons}}$$

The conversion factors that relate teaspoons to milliliters are

$$\frac{4.93\ \text{mL}}{1\ \text{teaspoon}} \quad \text{and} \quad \frac{1\ \text{teaspoon}}{4.93\ \text{mL}}$$

STEP 3: Our original measurement is 4.5 tablespoons, and we must first convert tablespoons into teaspoons. Therefore, we select the conversion factor that has tablespoons in the denominator.

STEP 3: Choose the conversion factors that allow you to cancel units.

$$4.5\ \text{tablespoons} \times \frac{3\ \text{teaspoons}}{1\ \text{tablespoon}}$$

These units cancel each other.

This setup converts tablespoons into teaspoons. (If we did the arithmetic now, we would get 13.5 teaspoons of oil.) Now, we add a second conversion factor that

continued

translates teaspoons into milliliters. In this factor, teaspoons must be in the denominator.

$$4.5 \text{ tablespoons} \times \frac{3 \text{ teaspoons}}{1 \text{ tablespoon}} \times \frac{4.93 \text{ mL}}{1 \text{ teaspoon}}$$

These units cancel each other.

These units cancel each other.

STEP 4: Do the math and round your answer.

STEP 4: Now we do the arithmetic.

$$4.5 \text{ tablespoons} \times \frac{3 \text{ teaspoons}}{1 \text{ tablespoon}} \times \frac{4.93 \text{ mL}}{1 \text{ teaspoon}} = 66.555 \text{ mL} \quad \text{calculator answer}$$

Finally, we round our answer to two significant figures, because 4.5 has only two significant figures and 4.93 has three. The relationship between teaspoons and tablespoons is an exact number, so we ignore it. The recipe calls for **67 mL** of cooking oil.

TRY IT YOURSELF: *A storage tank holds 17,000 L of crude oil. How many barrels of oil does the tank hold? Use the following relationships: one gallon equals 3.785 liters and one barrel equals 42 gallons.*

For additional practice, try Core Problems 1.35 and 1.36.

Some problems require a fair amount of ingenuity to solve. For example, suppose that you find an old bottle of aspirin tablets. The label tells you that each tablet contains 1.5 grains of aspirin. How many milligrams of aspirin are in each tablet? Looking in the dictionary, you find that there are 437.5 grains in one ounce and 16 ounces in one pound. You also find that there are 454 grams in one pound. Using these relationships and the fact that there are 1000 milligrams in one gram, you can construct a four-step strategy map that allows you to solve the problem.

1.5 grains ➡ ? ounces ➡ ? pounds ➡ ? grams ➡ ? milligrams

The conversion factor setup looks like this:

$$1.5 \text{ grains} \times \frac{1 \text{ ounce}}{437.5 \text{ grains}} \times \frac{1 \text{ pound}}{16 \text{ ounces}} \times \frac{454 \text{ g}}{1 \text{ pound}} \times \frac{1000 \text{ mg}}{1 \text{ g}} = 97 \text{ mg}$$

Health Note: Regular-strength aspirin tablets contain 325 mg of aspirin, and low-dose aspirin tablets (to prevent heart attacks) contain 81 mg of aspirin.

For complex problems that involve several conversion factors, you may want to do one conversion at a time. If you do so, do not round off any of your intermediate answers; only round the final answer.

CORE PROBLEMS

1.33 Fred does not know how many ounces are in a ton, but he knows how each of these units is related to a pound. Propose a strategy that Fred could use to convert a weight in ounces into the corresponding weight in tons.

1.34 Lauren does not know how many inches are in a mile, but she knows how each of these units is related to a foot. Propose a strategy that Lauren could use to convert a distance in miles into the equivalent distance in inches.

1.35 Carry out each of the following conversions, using a combination of two conversion factors for each conversion:

a) Convert 0.235 km into feet, using the fact that one km equals 0.621 mile and one mile equals 5280 feet.
b) Convert 0.175 g into grains, using the fact that one ounce equals 28.35 g and one ounce equals 437.5 grains.
c) Convert 25 teaspoons into fluid ounces, using only the relationships in Table 1.5.
d) Convert 5.1×10^7 kg into tons, using the fact that there are 2.205 pounds in one kilogram and 2000 pounds in a ton.

continued

1.36 Carry out each of the following conversions, using a combination of two conversion factors for each conversion:

a) Convert 82 furlongs into kilometers, using the fact that one mile equals 8 furlongs and 1.609 km equals one mile.

b) Convert 313 fluid drams into deciliters, using the fact that one pint equals 128 fluid drams and one deciliter equals 0.211 pints.

c) Convert 1.25 quarts into teaspoons, using only the relationships in Table 1.5.

d) Convert 6.27×10^{11} m into light-years, given that one mile equals 1609 m and a light-year equals 5.88×10^{12} miles.

1.37 A quatern is an English unit of volume. There are eight quaterns in one quart. Using this fact, the information in Table 1.5, and your knowledge of metric units, convert 0.125 L into quaterns.

1.38 There are 42 gallons in one barrel of crude oil, and one gallon equals 4 quarts. Using these facts, the information in Table 1.5, and your knowledge of metric units, convert 16.85 barrels into kiloliters.

1.6 Density, Dosage, and Other Compound Units

OBJECTIVES: *Use compound units to relate different types of measurements, including measurements involving dosages, and calculate and use density and specific gravity.*

If you go to your local grocery store, you are likely to see signs such as these:

Apples: 89¢ per pound
Milk: \$3.19 per gallon

If you drove to the store, you might have noticed a sign that said

Speed limit 35 miles per hour

Perhaps the car you drove was recently bought. On the price sticker, you might have seen

Mileage: 22 miles per gallon

Each of these represents a relationship between two fundamentally different units of measurement. For example, the gas mileage of a car relates a distance (in miles) to a volume of gasoline (in gallons). Distance and volume are entirely different types of measurement and are not normally interchangeable; you would not tell someone that you just put "285 miles of gasoline" into your car, and you would not say, "The distance from Boston to New York is 148 gallons." However, miles and gallons of gasoline are related when you drive a car. In a real sense, 22 miles *does* equal one gallon of gasoline, at least for this particular car. Likewise, 89¢ equals one pound of apples (at your grocery store today) and 35 miles equals one hour (if you drive at exactly the posted speed limit).

Many types of relationships are similar to these, both in everyday life and in technical fields. Each of them can be expressed as a number followed by a **compound unit**. A compound unit is made up of two or more fundamental units. Most commonly, the compound unit takes the form:

unit A **per** unit B
(unit A/unit B)

The meaning of such unit labels is that some number of unit A is equivalent to one unit B. We can write this kind of relationship as an equation, such as 22 miles = 1 gallon, and as a pair of conversion factors. Table 1.9 shows various ways of interpreting the compound units at the beginning of this section.

We see conversion factors in many places in our everyday lives.

TABLE 1.9 Some Compound Units and Their Interpretation

Measurement	Meaning	Written as an Equation	Written as a Conversion factor
89¢ per pound (89¢/lb)	*One pound* of apples costs *89 cents.*	89 cents = 1 pound	$\frac{\text{89 cents}}{\text{1 pound}}$ or $\frac{\text{1 pound}}{\text{89 cents}}$
\$3.19 per gallon (\$3.19/gal)	*One gallon* of milk costs *3.19 dollars.*	3.19 dollars = 1 gallon	$\frac{\text{3.19 dollars}}{\text{1 gallon}}$ or $\frac{\text{1 gallon}}{\text{3.19 dollars}}$
35 miles per hour (35 miles/hr)	In *one hour,* you will travel *35 miles.*	35 miles = 1 hour	$\frac{\text{35 miles}}{\text{1 hour}}$ or $\frac{\text{1 hour}}{\text{35 miles}}$
22 miles per gallon (22 miles/gal)	*One gallon* of gas is enough to drive *22 miles.*	22 miles = 1 gallon	$\frac{\text{22 miles}}{\text{1 gallon}}$ or $\frac{\text{1 gallon}}{\text{22 miles}}$

Sample Problem 1.16

Writing a relationship as a conversion factor

Minimum wage in the United States is \$7.25 per hour. Express this relationship as a pair of conversion factors.

SOLUTION

If you are paid minimum wage, you earn \$7.25 for every hour you work. In effect, one hour of work is equivalent to 7.25 dollars. Here are the two conversion factors that correspond to this relationship:

$$\frac{\text{7.25 dollars}}{\text{1 hour}} \quad \text{or} \quad \frac{\text{1 hour}}{\text{7.25 dollars}}$$

TRY IT YOURSELF: *At rest, a typical adult uses air at a rate of 6 L per minute. Express this relationship as a pair of conversion factors.*

For additional practice, try Core Problems 1.39 and 1.40.

Health Note: Air contains several gases, but your body only uses the oxygen, which constitutes about 20% of normal air.

We can use a compound unit to interconvert measurements, just as we used statements such as "1000 g = 1 kg" to interconvert centimeters and meters in Section 1.4. Here is an example.

Sample Problem 1.17

Using a compound unit as a conversion factor

Mrs. Jamali goes to the store with \$4.00. Apples cost 89¢ per pound today. How many pounds of apples can she buy?

SOLUTION

STEP 1: Identify the original measurement and the final unit.

Our original measurement is \$4.00, the amount of money that Mrs. Jamali has. To be sure that we can keep track of the unit, let us rewrite this as 4.00 dollars. We must work out how many pounds of apples Mrs. Jamali can buy, so our answer must be a number of pounds.

STEP 2: Write conversion factors that relate the two units.

The problem tells us that apples cost 89 cents per pound, which is the same as 0.89 dollars per pound. This compound unit tells us that one pound of apples is equivalent to 0.89 dollars, and we can write this relationship as a pair of conversion factors.

$$\frac{\text{0.89 dollars}}{\text{1 pound}} \quad \text{and} \quad \frac{\text{1 pound}}{\text{0.89 dollars}}$$

continued

Our original measurement is in dollars, so we must use the conversion factor that has dollars in the denominator. Doing so allows us to cancel units.

$$4.00 \text{ dollars} \times \frac{1 \text{ pound}}{0.89 \text{ dollars}}$$

We can cancel these units.

STEP 3: Choose the conversion factors that allow you to cancel units.

Once we have the correct setup, we do the arithmetic.

$$4.00 \cancel{\text{dollars}} \times \frac{1 \text{ pound}}{0.89 \cancel{\text{dollars}}} = 4.49438202 \text{ pounds} \quad \text{calculator answer}$$

STEP 4: Do the math and round your answer.

To complete our solution, we round off to two significant figures and attach the unit. Mrs. Jamali has enough money to buy **4.5 pounds of apples.**

TRY IT YOURSELF: *Gasoline costs $2.08 per gallon today. If you spend $10.00 on gasoline, how many gallons of gasoline will you buy?*

For additional practice, try Core Problems 1.41 through 1.44.

Dosage Calculations Can Be Done Using Conversion Factors

Nurses use compound units extensively in dosage calculations. The label on a package of medicine generally gives the amount of active ingredient in some specific amount of the preparation. For example, penicillin VK (a commonly used antibiotic) can be purchased in several forms, two of which are labeled as follows:

Tablets: 500 mg/tablet
Liquid: 250 mg/5 mL

The first of these labels tells us that each tablet contains 500 mg of penicillin VK, and the second tells us that 5 mL of liquid contains 250 mg of penicillin VK. We can express each of these relationships as a pair of conversion factors, as shown in Table 1.10.

A nurse is often called upon to calculate the number of tablets or the volume of liquid that provides a specific dose of medication. Sample Problem 1.18 gives an example of this type of dosage calculation.

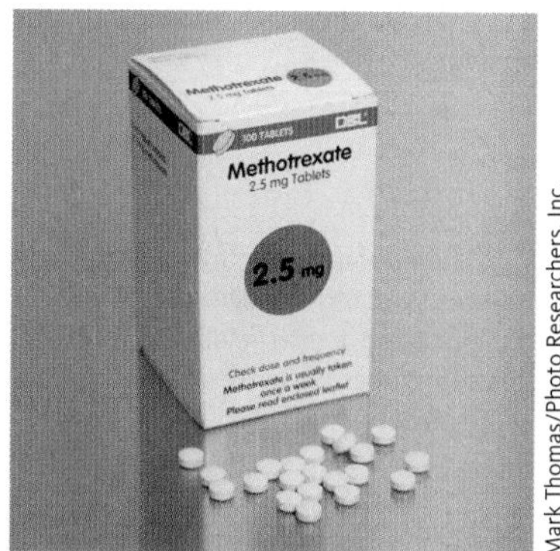

Mark Thomas/Photo Researchers, Inc.

Many medicines use conversion factors to show the amount of active ingredient.

TABLE 1.10 Compound Units in Medicine

Measurement	Meaning	Written as an Equation	Written as a Conversion Factor
500 mg of penicillin per tablet (500 mg/tablet)	**One tablet** contains **500 milligrams** of penicillin.	1 tablet = 500 mg	$\frac{500 \text{ mg}}{1 \text{ tablet}}$ or $\frac{1 \text{ tablet}}{500 \text{ mg}}$
250 mg of penicillin per 5 mL (250 mg/5 mL)	**Five milliliters** of liquid medication contains **250 milligrams** of penicillin.	5 mL = 250 mg	$\frac{250 \text{ mg}}{5 \text{ mL}}$ or $\frac{5 \text{ mL}}{250 \text{ mg}}$

Sample Problem 1.18

Using a conversion factor in a dosage calculation

Mr. Fancelli's doctor has prescribed 125 mg of penicillin to be taken four times daily. If the pharmacy has supplied a solution that contains 250 mg/5 mL, how many milliliters of solution should Mr. Fancelli take in each dose?

SOLUTION

Mr. Fancelli must take 125 mg of penicillin in each dose, so that is the original measurement. We must calculate the corresponding number of milliliters of penicillin solution.

STEP 1: Identify the original measurement and the final unit.

continued

Notice that since the problem asked for the volume of solution in each dose, we do not need to know or use the number of doses per day.

STEP 2: Write conversion factors that relate the two units.

The penicillin solution contains 250 mg of penicillin in each 5 mL of liquid. The two conversion factors that express this relationship are

$$\frac{250 \text{ mg}}{5 \text{ mL}} \quad \text{and} \quad \frac{5 \text{ mL}}{250 \text{ mg}}$$

STEP 3: Choose the conversion factors that allow you to cancel units.

The original measurement is in milligrams, so we need the conversion factor that has milligrams in the denominator:

$$125 \text{ mg} \times \frac{5 \text{ mL}}{250 \text{ mg}}$$

We can cancel these units.

This setup leaves us with the correct unit (milliliters) after we cancel milligrams, so we can now do the arithmetic.

STEP 4: Do the math and round your answer.

$$125 \text{ mg} \times \frac{5 \text{ mL}}{250 \text{ mg}} = 2.5 \text{ mL} \quad \text{calculator answer}$$

Strictly, the final answer should have three significant figures, so we report our result as **2.50 mL of solution.** (In clinical work, zeroes at the end of a decimal number are omitted.)

Health Note: Vistaril relieves symptoms of allergic reactions and acts as a sedative. It is sometimes prescribed for acute anxiety.

TRY IT YOURSELF: *A prescription calls for 10 mg of Vistaril to be taken four times daily. The pharmacy supplies a solution that contains 25 mg of Vistaril per 5 mL of liquid. How many milliliters of solution should be dispensed per dose?*

For additional practice, try Core Problems 1.45 through 1.50.

Pediatric health care providers often must calculate dosages based on a child's body mass. These calculations may require two or more conversion factors, particularly if the medication is in liquid form. Sample Problem 1.19 illustrates a typical dosage calculation of this type.

Sample Problem **1.19**

Using multiple conversion factors to calculate a dosage

Bayliss is being treated for a severe ear infection. His pediatrician prescribes amoxicillin at a daily dose of 40 mg/kg, to be given in three injections 8 hours apart. If the medication is supplied as a solution that contains 125 mg of amoxicillin per 5 mL of liquid, how many milliliters should Bayliss receive in each injection? Bayliss weighs 9.68 kg.

SOLUTION

STEP 1: Identify the original measurement and the final unit.

We should begin by planning a strategy. The problem gives us two relationships, the daily dosage (40 mg per kg) and the amount of medication in the solution (125 mg per 5 mL). We are also given the child's body mass, 9.68 kg. Our final answer must be a number of milliliters. Based on this information, we can construct the following plan. Note that we must start with Bayliss's body mass, because we are not given the actual amount of medication.

9.68 kg → convert to → ? mg of amoxicillin → convert to → ? mL of liquid → divided by 3 → ? mL per injection

STEP 2: Write conversion factors that relate the two units.

We can use the fact that Bayliss should receive 40 mg of amoxicillin for each kilogram of body mass to do the first conversion. The relevant conversion factors are

$$\frac{40 \text{ mg amoxicillin}}{1 \text{ kg}} \quad \text{and} \quad \frac{1 \text{ kg}}{40 \text{ mg amoxicillin}}$$

continued

For the second conversion, we use the fact that there are 125 mg of amoxicillin in 5 mL of the solution, which gives us the following conversion factors:

$$\frac{125 \text{ mg amoxicillin}}{5 \text{ mL liquid}} \quad \text{and} \quad \frac{5 \text{ mL liquid}}{125 \text{ mg amoxicillin}}$$

Arranging the conversion factors to cancel units gives us

STEP 3: Choose the conversion factors that allow you to cancel units.

$$9.68 \text{ kg} \times \frac{40 \text{ mg amoxicillin}}{1 \text{ kg}} \times \frac{5 \text{ mL liquid}}{125 \text{ mg amoxicillin}}$$

These units cancel each other. (kg and kg)

These units cancel each other. (mg amoxicillin and mg amoxicillin)

We can now do the arithmetic and cancel units.

$$9.68 \cancel{\text{kg}} \times \frac{40 \text{ mg } \cancel{\text{amoxicillin}}}{1 \cancel{\text{kg}}} \times \frac{5 \text{ mL liquid}}{125 \text{ mg } \cancel{\text{amoxicillin}}} = 15.488 \text{ mL liquid} \quad \text{calculator answer}$$

STEP 4: Do the math and round your answer.

This is the daily dosage of amoxicillin. To find the amount needed for each injection, we divide this dosage by three.

$$15.488 \text{ mL} \div 3 = 5.16266667 \text{ mL}$$

Bayliss should receive roughly **5.16 mL** of this medication in each injection.

TRY IT YOURSELF: *Claudio is being treated with gentamicin at a dosage of 1.6 mg/kg every eight hours. The gentamicin is supplied as a solution that contains 80 mg in each 2 mL of liquid. If Claudio weighs 62 kg, how many milliliters of the solution should he receive every eight hours?*

For additional practice, try Core Problems 1.51 and 1.52.

Density Is the Relationship Between Mass and Volume

The relationship between the mass and the volume of a particular substance is called the **density** of the substance. To calculate the density, we divide the mass by the volume.

$$\text{density} = \frac{\text{mass}}{\text{volume}}$$

For example, 100 mL of gasoline weighs 74 g, so the density of gasoline is 74 g ÷ 100 mL = 0.74 g/mL. Density is an important property, because it does not change if we take a different amount of the substance. For example, if we double the volume of gasoline (to 200 mL), the mass also doubles (to 148 g), so the density is still 0.74 g/mL, as shown in Figure 1.13.

We can use density to help identify a material, because different materials generally have different densities. Sample Problem 1.20 gives an illustration.

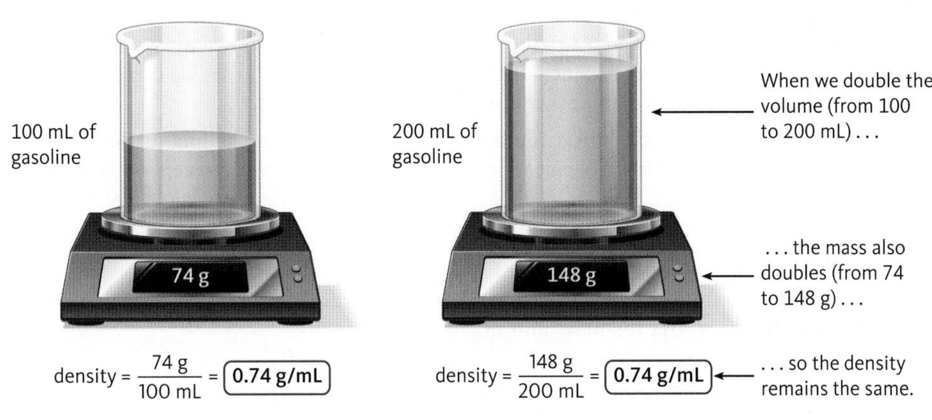
100 mL of gasoline
74 g
density = 74 g / 100 mL = 0.74 g/mL
200 mL of gasoline
148 g
density = 148 g / 200 mL = 0.74 g/mL
When we double the volume (from 100 to 200 mL) . . .
. . . the mass also doubles (from 74 to 148 g) . . .
. . . so the density remains the same.

FIGURE 1.13 The density of a substance does not depend on the amount.

Health Note: Bone density measurements do not actually measure the density of bone tissue. Instead, they measure the mineral content in a cross-section of bone using X-rays. The mineral content decreases as a person ages, putting the person at increased risk for fractures.

Sample Problem 1.20

Calculating a density

A piece of jewelry made of a bright yellow metal weighs 19.48 g and has a volume of 2.3 mL. It is probably made of one of the following three materials. Calculate the density of the piece of jewelry, and identify the metal.

Brass (a mixture of copper and zinc): density = 8.5 g/mL
14-carat gold (a mixture of gold and silver): density = 15.6 g/mL
24-carat gold (pure gold): density = 19.3 g/mL

SOLUTION

To calculate the density, we must divide the mass of the jewelry by its volume.

$$\text{density} = \frac{\text{mass}}{\text{volume}} = \frac{19.48\text{ g}}{2.3\text{ mL}} = 8.5\text{ g/mL}$$

Comparing this density to the values for the metals, we see that (unfortunately) the piece of jewelry is made of **brass.**

TRY IT YOURSELF: *Frances's wedding band weighs 9.38 g and has a volume of 0.6 mL. Calculate the density of her ring, and identify the metal.*

For additional practice, try Core Problems 1.53 and 1.54.

Density, like any compound unit, can be used as a conversion factor, so the density of a substance can be used to convert any mass of an object into the corresponding volume, or vice versa. For example, on page 33 we found that the density of gasoline is 0.74 g/mL. This tells us that one milliliter of gasoline weighs 0.74 grams. We can write two conversion factors that correspond to this relationship.

$$\frac{0.74\text{ g}}{1\text{ mL}} \text{ and } \frac{1\text{ mL}}{0.74\text{ g}}$$

This conversion factor is sometimes called "inverse density."

Sample Problem 1.21 shows how we can use the density to convert the mass of an object into its volume.

Sample Problem 1.21

Using density to relate mass and volume

A piece of brass weighs 57.93 g. What is its volume? The density of brass is 8.5 g/mL.

SOLUTION

STEP 1: Identify the original measurement and the final unit.

Our original measurement is 57.93 g, the mass of the piece of brass. We must calculate the volume of the piece of brass. Since we are not told what unit to use, we can give our answer in milliliters, liters, or any other convenient unit of volume.

STEP 2: Write conversion factors that relate the two units.

The density gives us a direct relationship between mass and volume, telling us that one mL of brass weighs 8.5 grams. We can write this relationship as two conversion factors.

$$\frac{8.5\text{ g}}{1\text{ mL}} \text{ and } \frac{1\text{ mL}}{8.5\text{ g}}$$

STEP 3: Choose the conversion factor that allows you to cancel units.

We must multiply our original measurement by the second of our two conversion factors, since we need to cancel out the mass unit (g).

$$57.93\text{ g} \times \frac{1\text{ mL}}{8.5\text{ g}}$$

continued

Canceling the mass unit leaves us with milliliters, which is a reasonable unit of volume. Now we do the arithmetic and cancel units.

$$57.93\ \cancel{g} \times \frac{1\ \text{mL}}{8.5\ \cancel{g}} = 6.81529412\ \text{mL} \quad \text{calculator answer}$$

STEP 4: Do the math and round your answer.

Rounding to two significant figures gives us a volume of **6.8 mL** for the piece of brass.

TRY IT YOURSELF: *A solid piece of glass has a volume of 23.8 mL. The density of glass is 2.6 g/mL. What is the mass of this piece of glass?*

For additional practice, try Core Problems 1.55 and 1.56.

Specific Gravity Has Several Clinical Applications

The **specific gravity** of a substance is closely related to its density. Specific gravity is defined as follows:

$$\text{specific gravity of a substance} = \frac{\text{density of the substance}}{\text{density of water}}$$

The density of water is very close to 1 g/mL, so the specific gravity of a substance is roughly equal to its density in grams per milliliter. However, the density units in the formula cancel out, so specific gravity is one of the few measurements that have no unit. For example, the density of brass is 8.5 g/mL and the specific gravity of brass is 8.5. Because they have the same numerical value, density and specific gravity tend to be used interchangeably.

Specific gravity has a variety of uses in medicine. For example, the specific gravity of blood is used at blood donation centers in a rapid screening test for anemia (low levels of iron in the blood). The iron-containing protein in blood (hemoglobin) is denser than the other blood components, so blood that does not contain enough iron has a lower specific gravity than blood that contains adequate iron. If the specific gravity of whole blood is significantly below 1.05 g/mL, the iron concentration in the donor's blood is low and the donor will normally be rejected. The specific gravity is usually tested by putting a drop of blood into a liquid that has a specific gravity of 1.05. Blood that has a lower specific gravity floats in the liquid, while blood that has a higher specific gravity sinks, as shown in Figure 1.14.

Urine analysis always includes a measurement of specific gravity. Urine is primarily water, mixed with a variety of waste products that have higher densities than water. Therefore, as the specific gravity of the urine increases, the amount of water present in the urine decreases. The normal range of urine specific gravity is between 1.002 and 1.028. A specific gravity above 1.028 is usually a symptom of dehydration, which can be caused by inadequate water intake, diarrhea, or vomiting. A specific gravity below 1.002 means that the kidneys are producing urine that is almost entirely water; this can be a symptom of kidney failure, or it may simply be the result of drinking too much water over a short period.

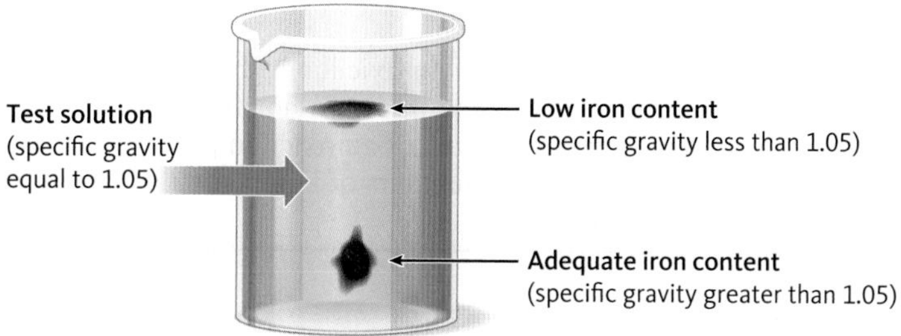

FIGURE 1.14 Using specific gravity to test the iron content of blood.

CORE PROBLEMS

1.39 Write each of the following as a pair of conversion factors:

a) A pound of watermelon costs 22¢.
b) There is 0.8 mg of antihistamine in each teaspoon of cold medicine.
c) The flow rate of an intravenous solution is 65 mL per hour.
d) The density of lead is 11.3 g/mL.

1.40 Write each of the following as a pair of conversion factors:

a) A gallon of milk costs $3.49.
b) One cup of apple juice contains 29 g of sugar.
c) George's blood contains 88 mg of glucose per deciliter of blood.
d) The density of air is around 0.0012 g/mL.

continued

1.41 Orange juice contains 2.10 mg of potassium per milliliter of juice.
a) If you want to get your daily recommended amount of potassium (3500 mg) from orange juice, how many milliliters of juice must you drink?
b) If you drink one cup (236.5 mL) of orange juice, how many milligrams of potassium will you consume?

1.42 Milk contains 1.65 μg of riboflavin per milliliter of milk.
a) If you want to get your daily recommended amount of riboflavin (1300 μg) from milk, how many milliliters of milk must you drink?
b) If you drink one quart (946 mL) of milk, how many micrograms of riboflavin will you consume?

1.43 A car gets 31 miles per gallon of gasoline.
a) How far can you travel on 8.2 gallons of gasoline?
b) How many gallons of gasoline do you need to go 186 miles?

1.44 The grocery store sells sliced ham for $4.29 per pound.
a) How much will it cost you to buy 0.23 pounds of sliced ham?
b) How much sliced ham can you buy for $2.50?

1.45 A doctor prescribes 0.2 g of carbamazepine to be taken three times daily. The pharmacy supplies tablets that contain 100 mg of carbamazepine per tablet. How many tablets should be taken per dose?

1.46 A doctor prescribes 15 mg of Inderal to be taken four times daily. The pharmacy supplies tablets that contain 10 mg of Inderal per tablet. How many tablets should be taken per dose?

1.47 A doctor prescribes 300 mg of Pediazole to be taken every six hours. The pharmacy supplies a solution that contains 200 mg of Pediazole per 5 mL of solution. How many milliliters of solution should be taken per dose?

1.48 A doctor prescribes 100 mg of amoxicillin to be taken every six hours. The pharmacy supplies a liquid suspension that contains 250 mg of amoxicillin per 5 mL of liquid. How many milliliters of liquid should be taken per dose?

1.49 An intravenous solution is infused at a rate of 135 mL per hour. At this rate, how long will it take to infuse 500 mL of solution? (Give your answer to three significant figures.)

1.50 A patient is given intravenous morphine at a rate of 0.35 mg per hour. At this rate, how long will it take to give the patient 1.5 mg of morphine?

1.51 A doctor prescribes chloramphenicol at a dosage of 25 mg/kg every 12 hours for an infant who weighs 3160 g. This medication is available as a solution containing 500 mg in each 5 mL of liquid. How many milliliters of liquid should the infant receive every 12 hours?

1.52 A doctor prescribes cephalexin at a daily dosage of 40 mg/kg, to be given in four doses six hours apart. Cephalexin is supplied as a solution containing 125 mg in each 5 mL of liquid. How many milliliters of this medication should be given every six hours to a child who weighs 38 kg?

1.53 A piece of cork weighs 7.545 g and has a volume of 31.7 mL.
a) Calculate the density of cork.
b) What is the specific gravity of cork, based on your answer to part a?

1.54 A block of lead has a volume of 246 mL and weighs 2790 g.
a) Calculate the density of lead.
b) What is the specific gravity of lead, based on your answer to part a?

1.55 The density of concrete is 2.8 g/mL.
a) If the volume of a piece of concrete is 235 mL, what is its mass?
b) If the mass of a piece of concrete is 1600 g, what is its volume?

1.56 The density of steel is 7.9 g/mL.
a) If the volume of a piece of steel is 2.18 mL, what is its mass?
b) If the mass of a piece of steel is 51.3 g, what is its volume?

OBJECTIVE: *Interconvert temperatures between the Celsius and Fahrenheit scales.*

1.7 Temperature

You are undoubtedly familiar with the general notion of temperature. A hot object has a high temperature, while a cold one has a low temperature. Temperature is an important measurement in medicine, because your body temperature is a very sensitive indicator of your state of health. In this section, we will examine the two commonly used temperature scales, and we will explore how temperatures can be converted from one scale to the other.

The Fahrenheit scale is the most frequently used temperature scale in the United States. In the rest of the world, however, the Celsius (or centigrade) scale is used. In medicine, both scales are used, with the Celsius scale gaining increasing acceptance in the United States. Neither scale is formally part of the metric system, but Celsius temperatures are closely related to (and easily converted to) temperatures in the Kelvin scale, which is the actual metric temperature scale. Therefore, Celsius temperatures are considered to be metric units, and they are used in preference to Fahrenheit in most branches of science.

All temperature scales are based on two fixed points, temperatures at which some easily reproduced phenomenon occurs. For the Celsius and Fahrenheit scales, the two fixed points are the temperatures at which water freezes and boils. On the Celsius scale, the freezing temperature of water is 0 degrees and the boiling temperature is 100 degrees. On the Fahrenheit scale, these two temperatures are 32 degrees and 212 degrees, respectively.

These fixed points are then used to construct a thermometer, which was originally a hollow tube containing a liquid that expands when it is heated. The most common liquids in these traditional thermometers are alcohol and mercury. Both liquids expand when they are heated, so the length of the column of liquid is a measure of the temperature. The thermometer is graduated to allow the user to read the temperature conveniently. Figure 1.15 compares a variety of temperatures in the two scales.

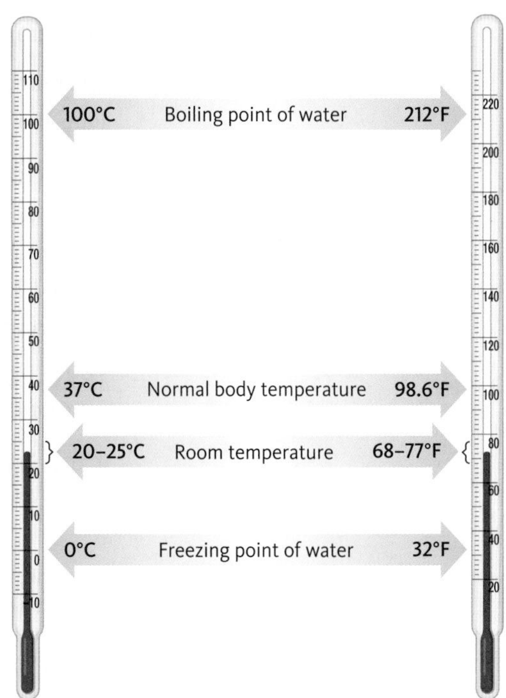

FIGURE 1.15 A comparison of temperatures in the Celsius and Fahrenheit scales.

Temperature Conversions Require a Special Formula

Temperature differs from all other common measurements in that the two temperature scales are *not* directly proportional to each other. The reason for this is that the two temperature scales have different zero points: 0°C is not the same temperature as 0°F. Therefore, *you cannot use the conversion factor method of Section 1.4 to do temperature conversions.* To convert a Fahrenheit temperature into a Celsius temperature, you must first subtract 32 from the Fahrenheit temperature, because 0°C equals 32°F. Then you must divide the answer by 1.8 to get the Celsius temperature. We can write this procedure as the following formula:

$$(°F - 32) \div 1.8 = °C$$

Health Note: 37°C (98.6°F) is the traditional value for body temperature when measured orally, but the average value appears to be closer to 36.8°C (98.2°F). Body temperature also varies through the day, reaching its high point in the afternoon and its low point around 4 a.m.

Sample Problem 1.22

Converting a Fahrenheit temperature into Celsius

Catherine is not feeling well today. She takes her temperature and finds that it is 100.6°F. Convert this temperature into Celsius.

SOLUTION

To convert a Fahrenheit temperature into Celsius, we must do two arithmetic operations:

a) Subtract 32 from the Fahrenheit temperature: $100.6 - 32 = 68.6$

b) Divide the result by 1.8: $68.6 \div 1.8 = 38.11111111$ calculator answer

Celsius and Fahrenheit temperatures are equally precise, so they are reported to the same number of decimal places. Catherine's temperature is **38.1°C.**

TRY IT YOURSELF: *It is 53°F outside today. Convert this temperature into Celsius.*

For additional practice, try Core Problems 1.57 (part a) and 1.58 (part a).

To convert from Celsius to Fahrenheit, the two steps must be inverted (add instead of subtract, multiply instead of divide), and they must be done in the reverse order. Here is a formula for this conversion:

$$(°C \times 1.8) + 32 = °F$$

Sample Problem 1.23

Converting a Celsius temperature into Fahrenheit

Pure grain alcohol boils at 78.5°C. Convert this temperature into Fahrenheit.

SOLUTION

To convert a Celsius temperature into Fahrenheit, we must do two arithmetic operations:

a) Multiply the Celsius temperature by 1.8: $78.5 \times 1.8 = 141.3$

b) Add 32 to the result: $141.3 + 32 = 173.3$°F

Grain alcohol boils at **173.3°F.**

TRY IT YOURSELF: *A recipe calls for baking a cake at 175°C. Convert this temperature into Fahrenheit.*

For additional practice, try Core Problems 1.57 (part b) and 1.58 (part b).

Be sure that you do the arithmetic operations in the correct order. If you are not sure that you are using (or remembering) a formula correctly, try converting the boiling point of water from one scale to the other. Since you already know the answer (100°C = 212°F), you can immediately see whether you have done the conversion correctly.

In some calculations, particularly computations involving gas volumes and pressures, scientists use a different temperature scale called the **Kelvin scale**. To calculate a Kelvin temperature, you simply add 273 to the Celsius temperature. For example, the boiling point of water is 100°C + 273 = 373 K. Note that the abbreviation for Kelvin temperatures does not use the degree sign. The Kelvin scale was devised so that the coldest possible temperature (−273°C, often called *absolute zero*) becomes 0 K. In the Kelvin scale, unlike the Fahrenheit or Celsius scales, it is not possible to have a negative temperature. The Kelvin scale is not used in health care, but it is used extensively in other branches of science.

Temperature is closely connected with the concept of energy, which plays a vital role in biological chemistry. We will explore this connection in Chapter 4.

CORE PROBLEMS

1.57 a) When aspirin is heated, it melts at 275°F. Convert this to a Celsius temperature.
b) Isopropyl alcohol boils when it is heated to 82.5°C. Convert this to a Fahrenheit temperature.
c) Convert the boiling temperature of isopropyl alcohol to a Kelvin temperature.

1.58 a) The highest temperature ever recorded in Australia is 123°F. Convert this to a Celsius temperature.
b) Acetone boils when it is heated to 56°C. Convert this to a Fahrenheit temperature.
c) Convert the boiling temperature of acetone to a Kelvin temperature.

1.59 What is the freezing point of water in Celsius and in Fahrenheit?

1.60 What is the boiling point of water in Celsius and in Fahrenheit?

CONNECTIONS

Why Do We Struggle Against the Metric System?

Most countries use the metric system primarily or exclusively, but the United States is a major exception. Americans cling tenaciously to the antiquated English system, even though the metric system makes more sense and is far easier to learn and use. When we use the English system, we have to deal with a labyrinth of peculiar relationships. How many feet are in a mile, or pounds in a ton? Are there as many ounces in a pound as there are fluid ounces in a pint? With the metric system, relationships between units are straightforward; *kilo* always means 1000, regardless of what it is attached to. Despite this simplicity, few Americans are comfortable with metric units. Why is that?

The main reason for Americans' dislike of anything metric is that there is a disconnect between the types of "book facts" you encountered in this chapter and the "gut level" understanding that comes from growing up with a system of measurement. In most countries, children learn metric measurements by default, because they do not encounter another system. If "the temperature is in the 30s," it is a warm day; if Dad is more than 2 meters tall, he is probably taller than most other adults. Americans, on the other hand, have treated the metric system as an alternative way of expressing measurements, rather like a second language. For example, some road signs give distances in both miles and kilometers, but drivers ignore the kilometers. Worse yet, all too often a measurement is a simple number in an English unit but a peculiar number when expressed in metric. A 12-ounce can of a soft drink contains 355 mL of the beverage; a one-pound package of spaghetti weighs 454 g. Such numbers make metric measurements seem complicated and unnatural.

Almost no one who grew up in the United States is completely comfortable with metric units, but most Americans are familiar with at least one metric unit. For instance, most people are used to the size of a liter, because large soft drink containers now use metric volumes (1 or 2 L). We have grown accustomed to the sizes of these containers, so when someone tells you "I bought a 2 L bottle of ginger ale," you do not need to have this "translated" into an English unit. Competitive runners are familiar with distances in kilometers or meters because they have run 5 km races or 200 m sprints many times. Health care workers measure body temperatures in Celsius degrees and (increasingly) heights and weights in centimeters and kilograms. However, the same nurse who has no difficulty visualizing a 162 cm woman is at a loss about whether a 500 g package of rice would be enough for a family dinner.

A road sign in English and metric units.

Regardless of the measurement system you use, it is important that you understand it well and that you not confuse it with a different system. Confusing English with metric units led to a spectacular mishap in 1999, in which a $125 million spacecraft was lost as it approached Mars. The manufacturer used English units during the spacecraft's construction and programming, but NASA sent final instructions to the craft in metric units, causing it to approach the planet too closely and suffer irreparable damage from the Martian atmosphere. In health care, where measurements are ubiquitous, mistakes in carrying out unit conversions or simply reading unit labels have cost patients their lives. In any branch of health care, you will have a responsibility to understand the units of all measurements you use in your professional life.

Key Terms

accuracy – 1.2
base unit – 1.1
compound unit – 1.6
conversion factor – 1.4
density – 1.6
derived unit – 1.1
digital instrument – 1.2
graduated instrument – 1.2
Kelvin scale – 1.6
mass – 1.1
meniscus – 1.1
metric system – 1.1
precision – 1.2
scientific notation – 1.3
SI system – 1.1
specific gravity – 1.6
standard – 1.2
unit – 1.1
volume – 1.1

SUMMARY OF OBJECTIVES

Now that you have read the chapter, test yourself on your knowledge of the objectives, using this summary as a guide.

Section 1.1: **Define distance, mass, and volume, and know how to express each of these properties as a metric measurement.**

- Any numerical measurement has two parts, a number and a unit.
- Length, width, and height are examples of distances, and they are measured with a ruler.
- Volume is the amount of space an object takes up. Liquid volumes are often measured using a graduated cylinder.
- Mass is the resistance of an object to being set in motion, and it is closely related to the weight of the object. Mass is measured with a balance.
- There are two commonly used systems of units, the English system and the metric system.
- The metric system is built on a set of base units: the meter, the liter, and the gram.
- Derived units are named by adding a prefix to the base unit.

Section 1.2: **Report a measured value to the correct number of digits, interpret uncertainty in a measurement, and distinguish between precision and accuracy.**

- In any measurement, the last reported digit is uncertain.
- When you make a measurement using a digital instrument, report all of the digits.
- When you make a measurement using a graduated tool, estimate one digit beyond the markings on the tool.
- Precision is the ability of a method or tool to produce similar numbers when a measurement is made several times.
- Accuracy is the agreement between a measurement and the true value. It is determined by checking the method or tool with a standard.

Section 1.3: **Convert distance, volume, and mass measurements from one metric unit to another.**

- All derived units in the metric system are related to the base unit by a power of ten.
- Metric units can be interconverted by moving the decimal point in the number.

Section 1.4: **Convert a measurement from one unit to another using a conversion factor.**

- Conversion factors express a relationship between two units.
- A unit conversion involves multiplying the original measurement by a conversion factor that cancels the original unit.

Section 1.5: **Use multiple conversion factors to carry out unit conversions.**

- Some unit conversions require two or more conversion factors.
- Multiple-step conversions can be written as a single calculation.

Section 1.6: **Use compound units to relate different types of measurements, including measurements involving dosages, and calculate and use density and specific gravity.**

- Compound units are used to show relationships between fundamentally different types of measurement, such as money and weight of food.
- A compound unit can be used as a conversion factor.
- Compound units are often used in dosage problems.
- The density of a substance is its mass divided by its volume, and density can be used to interconvert mass and volume.
- The specific gravity of a substance is roughly equal to its density in grams per milliliter, but specific gravity has no unit.
- Density and specific gravity have a variety of practical uses in health care.

Section 1.7: **Interconvert temperatures between the Celsius and Fahrenheit scales.**

- The Celsius and Fahrenheit temperature scales are based on two fixed points, the freezing and boiling points of water.
- Celsius and Fahrenheit temperatures can be interconverted using the following formulas:

$$°C = (°F - 32) \div 1.8 \qquad °F = (°C \times 1.8) + 32$$

- To calculate a Kelvin temperature, add 273 to the Celsius temperature.

Concept Questions

OWL Online homework for this chapter may be assigned in OWL.
* indicates more challenging problems.

1.61 You are getting a new washing machine. Each of the people below asks you, "How large is it?" In each case, tell whether the person is likely to be asking you for a mass, a volume, or a distance (length, width, or height), and explain your answer.

a) the person who is calculating the shipping charge
b) the person who is designing the arrangement of appliances in the laundry room
c) the person who will be using the machine to wash clothing
d) the people who have to carry the washing machine up a flight of stairs

1.62 Describe the difference between mass and volume, using a pillow and a brick to illustrate your answer.

1.63 What is a unit, and why are units important in health care?

1.64 A student asks why it is important to include a unit label with every measurement. He points out that if he asks someone's age, the other person can reply "35" without being misunderstood. If you were a teacher, how would you respond to this?

1.65 The most common mass units in the metric system are the gram, the kilogram, and the milligram. The mass of a calculator could be expressed using any of these units, but in practice it would normally be expressed in grams. Why is this?

1.66 Is it possible for a measuring tool to be precise, but not accurate? What about accurate, but not precise? Explain your answer in each case.

1.67 At her annual checkup on May 2, Katie was 127.2 cm tall. On May 6, Katie went back to her pediatrician and was measured again. This time, she was 127.4 cm tall. Is it safe to conclude that Katie grew between the two visits to the doctor? Why or why not?

1.68 a) Calvin weighs a sample of sugar on an electronic balance. The balance display reads 52.300 g. Should Calvin drop the zeros and record the mass as 52.3 g? Why or why not?

b) Felicia weighs herself on an electronic scale as part of a project in her anatomy class. The display on her scale reads 62.3 kg. Felicia was instructed to record her weight as precisely as possible. Should Felicia add a zero to the displayed weight and record it as 62.30 kg? Why or why not?

1.69 A friend who is not yet familiar with the metric system tells you that 5 L is the same volume as 0.005 mL. How would you explain to your friend that this is incorrect?

1.70 The amount of medication in a tablet is listed as "15 mg (0.23 grains)." Based on this information, which is a larger mass, 1 mg or 1 grain? Explain your answer.

1.71 You have two pieces of aluminum, one larger than the other. Which of the following will be the same for both pieces, and which will be different?

a) mass b) volume
c) density d) specific gravity

1.72 Explain why a small rock sinks when it is dropped into water while a large piece of wood floats, even though the wood is heavier than the rock.

1.73 Mr. Huynh goes out for a long walk on a hot summer day. On the way home, he stops at his doctor's office for a routine urinalysis. The lab finds that the specific gravity of his urine is above the normal range. Suggest a reasonable explanation for this.

1.74 You know that 100°C is the same as 212°F. Why can't you use this relationship as a conversion factor when you convert Celsius temperatures into Fahrenheit temperatures?

1.75 In each of the pictures that follow, an object has been placed into a container of alcohol. The density of alcohol is 0.78 g/mL. Match each picture with one of the following descriptions:

a) The density of the object is 0.89 g/mL.
b) The density of the object is 0.71 g/mL.
c) The density of the object is 0.78 g/mL.

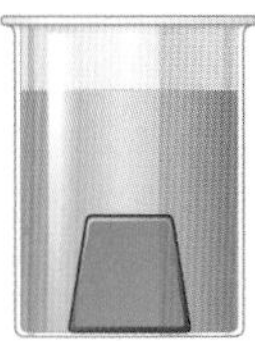

Summary and Challenge Problems

1.76 A company is developing a new type of electronic balance, and has built four different models. Each model is then tested using an object that is known to weigh 100.000 g. The object is weighed four times using each balance, with the following results:

Model 1:	100.058 g	100.060 g	100.060 g	100.059 g
Model 2:	99.998 g	100.001 g	99.997 g	99.999 g
Model 3:	100.031 g	99.924 g	99.976 g	100.067 g
Model 4:	100.085 g	99.996 g	100.062 g	100.011 g

a) Which of these balances appear to be very precise?
b) Which of these balances appear to be very accurate?
c) Which model should the company manufacture?

1.77 A company has built a new device that can monitor blood sugar levels. The company tests the device by measuring the blood sugar level three times using the same blood sample, and obtains the following results:

Test 1: 77.3 mg/dL Test 2: 79.7 mg/dL
Test 3: 78.9 mg/dL

Calculate the average of these three tests, and round your answer to a reasonable number of decimal places. Remember that the answer should have only one uncertain digit.

1.78 Use the information in Tables 1.4 through 1.6 to carry out each of the following unit conversions:

a) If an animal has a mass of 327 g, what is its mass in pounds?
b) A bone is 18 inches long. Convert this to centimeters.
c) A patient excretes 16.2 fluid ounces of urine in an eight-hour period. How many milliliters of urine did the patient produce?
d) A child weighs 96.2 pounds. What is the child's mass in kilograms?
e) Sylvia drives from San Francisco to Los Angeles. According to her car odometer, she travels 423.8 miles. Convert this distance to kilometers.
f) If a pitcher holds 2.75 cups of liquid, how many deciliters does it hold?

1.79 Use the information in Tables 1.4 through 1.6 and your knowledge of metric-to-metric conversions to carry out each of the following unit conversions:

a) A rod is an old English unit of distance. There are 320 rods in one mile. If a road is 618 rods long, how long is it in kilometers?
b) A dram is an old English unit of weight. There are 16 drams in one ounce. If a bottle of medicine weighs 3.26 drams, what is its mass in grams?
c) A troy ounce is a unit of weight, used to measure the weight of gold and other precious metals. One troy ounce equals 1.097 "normal" ounces. Convert 31.5 g into troy ounces. (The "normal" weight units are called avoirdupois weights.)
d) Until recently, large volumes were measured in British gallons in the United Kingdom. One British gallon equals 1.201 "normal" (American) gallons. Convert 26.5 L into British gallons.
e) Using the fact that one teaspoon equals 4.93 milliliters, convert 15 teaspoons into deciliters.
f) Using the fact that one cup equals 2.366 dL, convert 5 cups into liters.

1.80 *A child weighs 26 pounds 9 ounces. Convert this weight into a mass in kilograms. (Hint: Convert the ounces into pounds first, and then convert the total number of pounds into kilograms.)

1.81 The total mass of living organisms on Earth is estimated to be 3.6×10^{14} kg. Convert this mass into tons (1 ton = 907 kg).

1.82 Acetone and chloroform are liquids that can be used to dissolve chemicals that do not dissolve in water. Acetone boils at 133.2°F, while chloroform boils at 61.7°C. Which liquid boils at a lower temperature?

1.83 The store is advertising 3 pounds of oranges for $1.00.

a) If you buy 8.5 pounds of oranges, how much money will you spend?
b) If you spend $2.75 on oranges, how many pounds of oranges will you buy?

1.84 A package contains 4.72 pounds of chicken and costs $11.28.

a) What is the price of chicken per pound?
b) Using your answer to part a, how many pounds of chicken could you buy for $5.00?
c) Using your answer to part a, how much would 2.28 pounds of chicken cost?

1.85 * An intravenous solution is infused at a rate of 0.75 mL per minute. At this rate, how many hours will it take to infuse 100 mL of solution?

1.86 Milk contains 1.25 mg of calcium per milliliter. The recommended daily amount of calcium for an adult is 1000 mg.

a) How much milk would you need to drink to get your recommended daily amount of calcium?
b) How much calcium is in 118 mL (a half of a cup) of milk?

1.87 * Chicken broth contains 6.27 mg of sodium per milliliter. The U.S. government recommends that adults consume no more than 2400 mg of sodium per day. How many cups of chicken broth would you need to eat to consume 2400 mg of sodium? (See Table 1.5 for useful information.)

1.88 * Children's Tylenol contains 32 mg of acetaminophen per milliliter of liquid. The recommended dose of this medicine for a 50-pound child is 2 teaspoons. How many milligrams of acetaminophen are in 2 teaspoons of Children's Tylenol?

1.89 * At the local store, a gallon of milk costs \$3.29, a 0.75 L bottle of wine costs \$9.49, a box containing 12 cans of cola costs \$5.89, and a box containing 24 bottles of drinking water costs \$5.99. (A can of cola contains 12 fluid ounces, and a bottle of water contains 500 mL.) Calculate the cost of one fluid ounce of each beverage, and then rank the beverages in order from lowest cost to highest cost per fluid ounce.

1.90 Susan pours some water into a graduated cylinder. The volume of water in the cylinder is 32.6 mL, and the total mass of the cylinder and water is 94.095 g. Susan then puts a rubber stopper into the cylinder. The water level rises to 39.8 mL, and the total mass is now 102.663 g.

a) What is the mass of the stopper?
b) What is the volume of the stopper?
c) What is the density of the stopper?
d) A different stopper weighs 10.313 g. What is the volume of this stopper, assuming that it is made from the same type of rubber?

1.91 Sharon has inherited a set of tableware. She thinks that it is made of silver (density = 10.5 g/mL), but she knows that it could also be made from aluminum (density = 2.7 g/mL), stainless steel (density = 8.0 g/mL), or nickel (density = 8.9 g/mL). Sharon carries out the following measurements on a fork from the set. From her data, help her identify what metal the tableware is made from.

Mass of fork = 45.718 g Volume of fork = 5.7 mL

1.92 Normal urine has a specific gravity between 1.002 and 1.028. A patient supplies a 50.0 mL urine sample. What range of masses would be considered normal for this sample?

1.93 Potential blood donors are screened for iron deficiency. If the blood density is below 1.05 g/mL, the blood iron level is too low. A 1.50 mL sample of blood from a prospective donor weighs 1.593 g. Would this person be accepted as a blood donor?

1.94 * Mercury is a silver-colored liquid. One quart of mercury weighs 28.4 pounds. Calculate the density of mercury in grams per milliliter.

1.95 * A bottle contains 22.6 fluid drams of alcohol. Calculate the mass of alcohol in the bottle using the following information:

1 fluid ounce = 8 fluid drams

density of alcohol = 0.79 g/mL

1 fluid ounce = 29.57 mL

2

Atoms, Elements, and Compounds

A runner becomes exhausted and confused toward the end of a long race on a warm day. She is taken to the emergency room, where she seems disoriented and complains of nausea and muscle cramps. Because she does not appear to be dehydrated, the doctor suspects that she suffers from water intoxication caused by drinking too much water in a short time. The doctor orders a set of blood tests, one of which measures the concentration of **sodium** in the patient's blood. The test shows that the sodium level is unusually low, a condition called hyponatremia ("low sodium") that is consistent with water intoxication. The runner is given intravenous saline (salt dissolved in water) to correct the condition, and she soon feels better, although she does not recover from the queasiness until the next day.

Sodium is one of the chemical elements that are the basic building blocks of our bodies. We need sodium in our diet (although too much can be harmful), and every type of tissue contains sodium, with the highest concentration being in body fluids. Potassium, calcium, iron, and oxygen are other examples of elements that are essential to human health. Everything in the universe is made from around 90 chemical elements, and it takes only 20 of these elements to build the human body. In this chapter, you will be introduced to these most fundamental of all substances.

OUTLINE

2.1 **Classifying matter: mixtures, compounds, and elements**
2.2 **The chemical elements: an introduction to the periodic table**
2.3 **Atoms**
2.4 **Subatomic particles and atomic structure**
2.5 **Isotopes and atomic weight**
2.6 **Chemical formulas**
2.7 **Electron shells**
2.8 **Chemical behavior, valence electrons, and the periodic law**
2.9 **The organization of the periodic table**

LABORATORY REQUISITION—CHEMISTRY

☑ Sodium	NA	☐ Fructosamine	FRU/ALB
☐ Potassium	K	☐ PSA	PSA
☐ Creatinine	CREAT	☐ Chloride	CL
☐ BUN	BUN	☐ Calcium	CA
☐ Glucose–fasting	GLUCF	☐ Phosphorus	PHOS
☐ Glucose–random	GLUCR	☐ Phenylalanine	PKU
☐ Hemoglobin A1C	HGBA1C	☐ Uric Acid	URIC

For an athlete, having the correct amounts of several elements in the blood is vital for peak performance.

Online homework for this chapter may be assigned in OWL.

"What am I made of?" Looking at yourself in the mirror, you can see that you are not made from just one substance. The color and texture of your lips are different from those of your skin or your hair. Your eyes are made of soft tissue, while your fingernails are hard. Medical science makes it possible to look inside the human body, where we see still more variation. Muscles, brains, bones, and blood look different from one another, and they behave in different ways. Yet underlying this diversity is a fundamental similarity in the building blocks that make up the human body. When we explore the properties and behavior of these building blocks, we enter the world of chemistry.

Health Note: You will see these terms repeatedly in your anatomy and physiology classes.

Figure 2.1 shows the human body in increasing magnification. Our bodies are made up of tissues, such as muscle, bone, nerves, and tendons. Many of these tissues are organized into organs (the brain, the stomach, the heart, the lungs), which in turn are linked to form systems (the circulatory system, the respiratory system, the skeletal system, the nervous system, the digestive system). Using a microscope, we can see that all tissues are made of tiny building blocks called cells, and each kind of tissue is composed of specific types of cells. Cells are the smallest structural units that can grow and reproduce, and they come in a wide range of sizes and shapes. For instance, muscle cells are long and thin, while the red cells in blood are roughly circular. Cells in turn contain a range of internal structures, including a nucleus, mitochondria, lysosomes, and Golgi complexes.

Special techniques allow us to observe still smaller structures within and surrounding the organelles. The largest of these are macromolecules such as proteins, complex carbohydrates, and nucleic acids. Greater magnification allows us to see smaller molecules such as sugars and fats, and still greater magnification reveals even smaller molecules like water and carbon dioxide. Ultimately, we find that all of these molecules are built from atoms. Atoms are the basic building blocks of a human being, as well as everything else in the universe, living and nonliving. Furthermore, the properties of the atoms determine the properties of all types of matter. In this chapter, then, we explore the chemical world by examining the nature of the atom.

OBJECTIVES: *Describe properties as intensive or extensive; classify a sample of matter as a mixture, a compound, or an element; and describe a mixture as homogeneous or heterogeneous.*

2.1 Classifying Matter: Mixtures, Compounds, and Elements

Look around you. Examine the materials that make up the objects you observe. You may see furniture made of wood, metal, or plastic, and fabrics made of cotton, silk, or synthetic materials. If you have food or a beverage in front of you, think of the vast range of products that you can eat and drink. If you are outdoors, you may see buildings made of stone and glass, and streets paved with asphalt or concrete. You may see trees, or flowers, or birds, or a neighbor's cat, reminders of the great diversity of the living world. Blow on your hand, and feel the invisible air that surrounds you. Take a (very brief) glance at the sun, or look longer at the stars.

All of these things—in fact, all things that have mass—are **matter**. Chemistry is the study of matter: how we can describe it, and how it behaves. It is an immensely practical study, and an immensely important one. Chemistry is the foundation of our

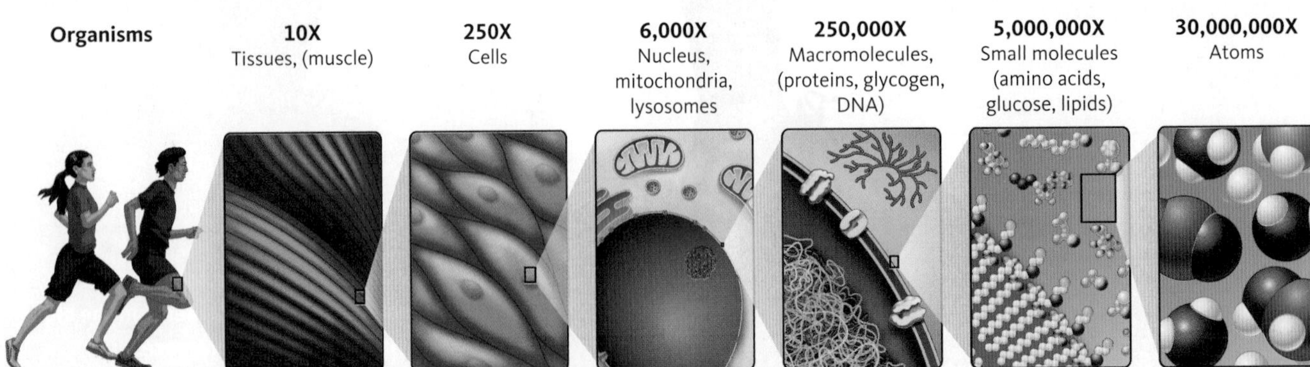

FIGURE 2.1 From organisms to atoms.

understanding of health and nutrition, fuels and energy, the raw materials of our world and the things we can make from them, and the very nature of our bodies.

iStockphoto.com/Jim Mercure

Everything you can see in this picture is made of matter.

We Can Classify Matter Based On Its Properties

Let us begin our study of chemistry by looking at matter and how we can describe it. We can describe a sample of matter in a variety of ways. For example, we can tell what color it is, how much it weighs, and whether it is edible or not. Any description of a sample of matter that is based on observations or measurements is called a **property** of matter. If the property does not depend on the size of the sample we selected, it is an **intensive property**. For example, the statement "salt is white" is true of any sample of salt, regardless of how large or small it is, so the color of salt is an intensive property. By contrast, **extensive properties** such as mass and volume depend on the size of the sample we choose. If we say, "This pile of salt weighs 3.5 g," we are describing a particular sample of salt (not all samples of salt weigh this much).

Health Note: Chemistry is not just about "chemicals"—it is about our food, our health, and our bodies.

Sample Problem 2.1

Recognizing intensive and extensive properties

Which of the following statements describes an intensive property, and which describes an extensive property?

"There is one liter of milk in this bottle."
"The density of milk is 1.04 g/mL."

SOLUTION

The first statement describes an **extensive property,** since it depends on the size of the sample of milk. (Not all bottles of milk hold one liter.) The second statement describes an **intensive property,** since density does not depend on the size of the sample, as we saw in Chapter 1.

TRY IT YOURSELF: *If you say "Glycerin tastes sweet," are you describing an intensive or an extensive property of glycerin?*

For additional practice, try Core Problems 2.5 and 2.6.

When people want to describe a particular type of matter, such as water or salt, they normally do so using intensive properties, because intensive properties apply to all possible samples of that type of matter. Chemists use a great variety of intensive properties to describe and classify matter. Some of these properties involve numbers, like the density or the melting point (the temperature at which the solid form turns into the liquid form). Others can be expressed in words, like color or flavor. Table 2.1 gives some examples of the ways we can describe matter using intensive properties. We will explore some of these properties in more detail later in this book.

Health Note: An aging person with heavy bones (mass, an extensive property) may still have concerns about low bone density (an intensive property).

TABLE 2.1 Some Intensive Properties of Matter by Toxicity

Chemical Name	State	Color	Density	Toxicity	Behavior When Mixed with Water
Oxygen	Gas	Colorless	0.0013 g/mL	Nontoxic (your body needs oxygen to live)	Nothing happens
Chalk (calcium carbonate)	Solid	White	2.8 g/mL	Nontoxic (you can eat chalk)	Gets wet, but does not change otherwise
Blue vitriol (copper sulfate)	Solid	Blue	2.3 g/mL	Moderately poisonous	Dissolves
Quicklime (calcium oxide)	Solid	White	3.3 g/mL	Very poisonous	Gets wet and becomes very hot
Battery acid (sulfuric acid)	Liquid	Colorless	1.8 g/mL	Very poisonous	Dissolves and becomes very hot
Sodium metal	Solid	Silvery	0.97 g/mL	Very poisonous	Fizzes violently and can catch fire or explode

Health Note: In our diet, sodium is combined with other elements to form compounds.

Health Note: All of our body fluids are mixtures. For example, urine is a mixture of water, table salt, urea, creatinine, and many other substances.

Most Types of Matter Can Be Made from Other Types of Matter

We can make almost any kind of matter by mixing other kinds of matter. For instance, we can make salt water by mixing table salt and water. We can likewise make table salt by mixing a soft, silvery solid called sodium with a pale green gas called chlorine. However, there is a fundamental difference between salt water and table salt. We can make salt water by mixing a cup of water with a few grains of salt, a teaspoon of salt, or several tablespoons of salt. All of these mixtures look alike, and each of them fits any reasonable definition of the term *salt water.* By contrast, *table salt always contains a specific proportion of sodium to chlorine.* Any sample of table salt, regardless of where it comes from or how it was made, contains 39.3% sodium and 60.7% chlorine by weight. Matter that can have different proportions of its ingredients, like salt water, is called a **mixture**. Matter that has only one possible composition, like table salt, is called a **chemical substance**.

Figure 2.2 illustrates the difference between mixtures and chemical substances by comparing salt water to salt and water. The composition of the salt water (a mixture)

(a) Salt water is a **mixture**, because it can contain different proportions of water and salt.

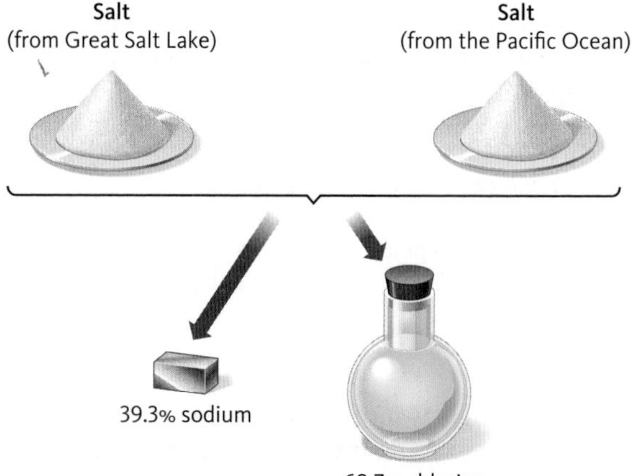

(b) Salt is a **compound**, because all samples of salt have the same proportions of sodium and chlorine.

FIGURE 2.2 Comparing **(a)** a mixture and **(b)** a compound.

depends on the source, but the salt and the water (chemical substances) always contain the same percentages of their components.

Charles D. Winters

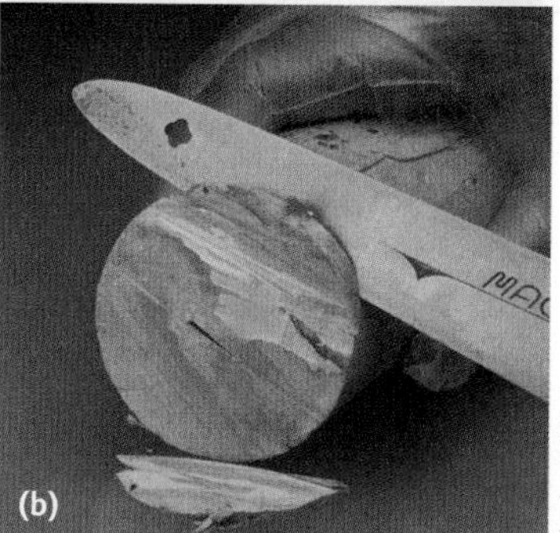
Charles D. Winters

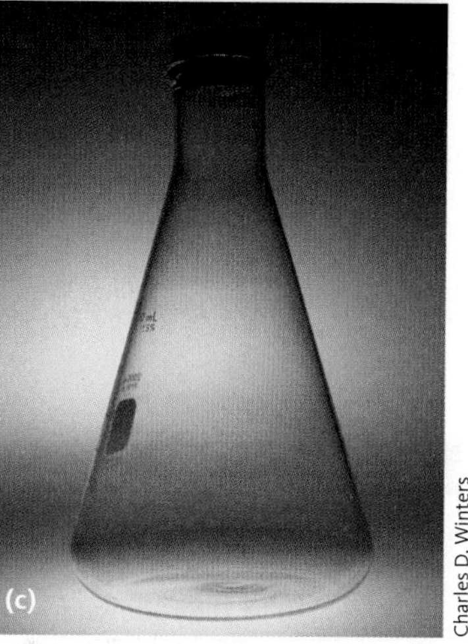
Charles D. Winters

Table salt (a) is a combination of two substances, (b) sodium (a shiny metal) and (c) chlorine (a pale green gas).

Sample Problem 2.2

Classifying matter as a chemical substance or a mixture

Which of the following is a description of a mixture, and which is a description of a chemical substance?

a) Stainless steel is used to make knives and other utensils. Two samples of stainless steel have the following compositions:
Sample 1: 72% iron, 17% chromium, 6% manganese, 4% nickel, 1% silicon
Sample 2: 69% iron, 18% chromium, 2% manganese, 9% nickel, 2% silicon

b) Washing soda is an old-fashioned cleaning agent. All samples of washing soda have the following composition:
16% sodium, 4% carbon, 73% oxygen, 7% hydrogen

SOLUTION

a) Since stainless steel can have different compositions, it is a mixture.

b) Since washing soda has a constant composition, it is a chemical substance.

TRY IT YOURSELF: *Air is made up of several gases, including water vapor. The percentage of water vapor in air can be anywhere from 0.0005% to 4%. Based only on this information, is air a chemical substance, or is it a mixture?*

For additional practice, try Core Problems 2.7 through 2.10.

We can classify mixtures based on whether they appear to be a single substance. If we can see two or more different-looking components in our mixture, we have a **heterogeneous mixture**. For example, pond water is a heterogeneous mixture; under a microscope, we can see bits of dirt and a variety of microorganisms floating in the water. If the mixture looks like a single substance, it is a **homogeneous mixture**. Salt water is a homogeneous mixture, because the salt and water are mixed together so completely that they cannot be discerned as individual substances, even under the most powerful magnification. Some other examples of homogeneous mixtures are brass (a mixture of copper and zinc), coffee (a mixture of water, caffeine, and many other substances), and air (a mixture of nitrogen, oxygen, water vapor, and several other gases).

Elements Are the Fundamental Building Blocks of All Matter

As we saw, salt and water are made from other substances. Any chemical substance that can be made by combining two or more other substances is called a **compound**. The vast majority of chemical substances we encounter are compounds, including nutrients such as carbohydrates, proteins, fats, and vitamins. However, a few substances, called **elements**, cannot be made from or broken down into anything else. Sodium, chlorine, hydrogen, and oxygen are elements, as are such familiar substances as gold, silver, copper, aluminum, helium, tin, and iodine. The elements are the fundamental materials from which our planet and everything on it (including our bodies) is made. There are a total of 90 elements on Earth, and scientists have made an additional 28 elements using nuclear reactions. By comparison, more than 20 million compounds have been discovered and classified, along with countless millions of mixtures.

Health Note: Your blood is a heterogeneous mixture, containing a variety of cells floating in a liquid (the plasma).

Both compounds and mixtures are ultimately built from elements. However, as we have seen, mixtures can have a variety of proportions, while all compounds have a fixed composition. Also, mixtures tend to look and act like their components, while compounds do not. For instance, salt water looks like water and tastes like salt, so it is clearly similar to its components. The white crystals of table salt, by contrast, are unlike both sodium (a soft, silvery metal) and chlorine (a greenish-yellow gas). In addition, mixtures are generally easy to separate into their components, while compounds tend to be much more difficult to break down. Table 2.2 summarizes the differences between the various classes of matter we have examined in this section.

Health Note: Our bodies are built from just 20 elements (although our bodies contain other elements that have no known function).

Martyn F. Chillmaid/Photo Researchers, Inc.

(a) Salt and water form a homogeneous mixture. (b) Chalk dust and water form a heterogeneous mixture.

TABLE 2.2 Classifying Matter

CHEMICAL SUBSTANCES		MIXTURES
Elements	**Compounds**	
Cannot be made from other substances	Are made from other substances (Salt is made from sodium and chlorine.)	Are made from other substances (Salt water is made from water and salt.)
	Have a fixed composition (Salt is always 39.3% sodium and 60.7% chlorine.)	Have a variable composition (Salt water can contain 25% salt, or 2.5% salt, or 0.25% salt . . .)
	Usually look different from their components (Salt does not look like either sodium or chlorine.)	Usually resemble at least one of their components (Salt water looks like water and tastes like salt.)
	Have different physiological effects from their components (Sodium and chlorine are very poisonous, while salt is nontoxic.)	Have similar physiological effects to their components (Salt water is no more toxic than the original salt and water.)
Cannot be separated into other substances	Are usually hard to separate into their components (To separate salt into sodium and chlorine, you must heat it to 800°C and pass an electrical current through it.)	Are usually easy to separate into their components (You can separate salt water into salt and water by letting it stand in an open container: the water will evaporate, but the salt will not.)

CORE PROBLEMS

*All Core Problems are paired and the answers to the **blue** odd-numbered problems appear in the back of the book.*

2.1 Which of the following will make a homogeneous mixture, and which will make a heterogeneous mixture? Assume that the two components are stirred well.
a) a teaspoon of salt and a cup of water
b) a teaspoon of pepper and a cup of water

2.2 Which of the following will make a homogeneous mixture, and which will make a heterogeneous mixture? Assume that the two components are stirred well.
a) a small flake of soap and a cup of water
b) a small flake of candle wax and a cup of water

2.3 Give an example of a substance (other than salt) that could form a homogeneous mixture if it were mixed with water.

2.4 Give an example of a substance (other than chalk) that will form a heterogeneous mixture if it is mixed with water.

2.5 Which of the following statements describe an intensive property, and which describe an extensive property?
a) The glass in my front window is transparent.
b) The glass in my front window weighs 1.2 kg.
c) The glass in my front window is 2 mm thick.
d) The glass in my front window does not dissolve in water.

2.6 Which of the following statements describe an intensive property, and which describe an extensive property?
a) Orange juice tastes sweet.
b) The density of orange juice is 1.01 g/mL.
c) This glass contains 200 mL of orange juice.
d) The orange juice in this container supplies 45% of your daily vitamin C requirement.

2.7 Chalk is a naturally occurring mineral. In ancient times, people discovered that if chalk is heated, it breaks down into a fluffy white powder (called quicklime) and a colorless, odorless gas (called fixed air). A sample of chalk from anywhere on Earth will break down to produce 56% quicklime and 44% fixed air.
a) Based only on this information, is chalk an element, a compound, or a mixture? Or can you tell? Explain your reasoning.
b) Based on this information, is quicklime an element, a compound, or a mixture? Or can you tell? Explain your reasoning.

2.8 Montroydite is a naturally occurring mineral. In ancient times, people discovered that if montroydite is heated, it breaks down into a silver-colored liquid (called quicksilver) and a colorless, odorless gas (once called dephlogisticated air). A sample of montroydite from anywhere on Earth will break

continued

down to produce 92.6% quicksilver and 7.4% dephlogisticated air.

a) Based only on this information, is dephlogisticated air an element, a compound, or a mixture? Or can you tell? Explain your reasoning.

b) Based on this information, is montroydite an element, a compound, or a mixture? Or can you tell? Explain your reasoning.

2.9 Because pure gold is rather soft, gold-colored jewelry is often made out of 14-carat gold, which contains 58% gold and 42% silver. Gold-colored jewelry can also be made from 16-carat gold, which contains 67% gold and 33% silver. Based on this information, do gold and silver form a compound when they are mixed, or do they form a mixture? Explain your reasoning.

2.10 Two bottles are labeled "muriatic acid." Each bottle contains a liquid that looks like water. The composition of each liquid is as follows:

bottle 1: 77.1% oxygen, 12.8% chlorine, 10.1% hydrogen

bottle 2: 82.5% oxygen, 6.9% chlorine, 10.6% hydrogen

Based only on this information, is muriatic acid an element, a compound, or a mixture? Explain your reasoning.

2.11 Sulfur and oxygen are both nontoxic. When these substances are mixed and heated, they can combine to make a poisonous gas. Based on this information, is this combination likely to be a compound, or is it probably a mixture? Explain your reasoning.

2.12 Barium is a silvery solid, and oxygen is an invisible gas. When these substances are mixed and heated, they can combine to make a white, fluffy powder. Based on this information, is this combination likely to be a compound, or is it probably a mixture? Explain your reasoning.

2.2 The Chemical Elements: An Introduction to the Periodic Table

OBJECTIVES: *Know the names and symbols of common elements, the differences between metals, metalloids, and nonmetals, and the organization of the periodic table.*

All substances on Earth are built from the elements. Therefore, it is worth spending time to become acquainted with the elements that occur in nature. We will begin by looking at the three broad categories of chemical elements.

Most of the elements that have been discovered are classified as **metals**. The metallic elements have many characteristics in common. Metals are normally gray or silvery (the exceptions are copper and gold) and can be polished to a mirrorlike sheen. All but one of the metals are solids (mercury is a silvery liquid), all can be bent and shaped freely (most other solids will break or shatter when bent), and all conduct electricity. Most metals can be mixed with one another if they are melted first, and the mixtures look and act like metals.

Health Note: Several metals are required nutrients, including potassium, calcium, magnesium, iron, copper, and zinc.

The **nonmetals** make up the majority of the remaining elements, and they are as diverse as the metals are similar. Indeed, the only general statement that can be made about nonmetals is that they do not share the characteristics of metals. Table 2.3 lists some common nonmetals and illustrates their great diversity.

The remaining eight elements are **metalloids**. The metalloids resemble metallic elements in being gray or silvery solids, but they are more brittle than metals and conduct

TABLE 2.3 Five Common Nonmetallic Elements by Atomic Number

Element	Appearance (at Room Temperature)
Oxygen	Colorless, odorless, invisible gas
Chlorine	Greenish-yellow, acrid-smelling gas
Sulfur	Yellow, brittle solid that melts when heated gently
Bromine	Dark red–brown liquid
Iodine	Dark purple solid that vaporizes to a purple gas when heated gently

Charles D. Winters

Three metallic elements. All of these metals are shiny when polished, conduct electricity well, and can be bent and shaped easily.

The nonmetallic elements bromine (left) and iodine (right).

Charles D. Winters

Silicon is a typical metalloid.

TABLE 2.4 The Three Classes of Elements

Metals	Metalloids	Nonmetals
Most metals are solids at room temperature. (Only mercury is a liquid.)	All metalloids are solids at room temperature.	Eleven nonmetals are gases, five are solids, and one (bromine) is a liquid at room temperature.
Most metals are gray or silvery and look shiny when polished. (Gold and copper are colored.)	All metalloids are gray and look shiny when polished.	Nonmetals have a variety of colors and do not look shiny when polished.
Metals conduct electricity well.	Metalloids conduct electricity poorly.	Most nonmetals do not conduct electricity. (Only the graphite form of carbon can conduct electricity.)
Metals can be bent and shaped.	Metalloids are brittle and break instead of bending.	Solid nonmetals are brittle and break instead of bending.

electricity rather poorly. Metalloids have intermediate properties between metals and nonmetals. Table 2.4 summarizes the differences between the three classes of elements.

The Symbols of the Elements Are Organized in the Periodic Table

Every element has a one- or two-letter symbol to identify it. Most of these symbols are taken from the English names of the elements, such as Ca for calcium and C for carbon. However, several symbols are derived from the names of the elements in other languages, usually Latin. For example, the symbol for sodium is Na (from the Latin word *natrium*), and the symbol for iron is Fe (from the Latin word *ferrum*). These symbols and other information about the elements are presented in a standard form called the **periodic table**. Figure 2.3 shows a simplified version of the periodic table. We will examine the organization of the periodic table in detail later in this chapter. For now, you should learn the following information:

- The metals are on the left side of the periodic table and the nonmetals are on the right side, with the metalloids between them. Most periodic tables use a heavy line to show the location of the metalloids.
- A horizontal row of elements is called a **period**. The periods are numbered from top to bottom. For example, the fourth period contains the elements from K (potassium) through Kr (krypton).
- A vertical column of elements is called a **group**. The groups are labeled 1A through 8A and 1B through 8B. For example, Group 4A contains the elements C (carbon), Si (silicon), Ge (germanium), Sn (tin), and Pb (lead). The group labels are always shown at the top of the periodic table.
- The periodic table in this book lists hydrogen in both Group 1A and Group 7A, for reasons that will be explained in Section 2.9. Some versions of the table show hydrogen only in Group 1A.

Health Note: Our bodies need the alkali metals sodium and potassium, the alkaline earth metals magnesium and calcium, and the halogens chlorine and iodine.

The group labels in Figure 2.3 follow the traditional numbering system used in the United States. However, chemists have proposed several other ways to designate the groups. The system that has gained the greatest acceptance uses the numbers 1 through 18, without a letter. You may encounter these alternate group labels in other periodic tables, but they do not affect the arrangement of elements.

Several groups of elements have traditional names. The elements in Groups 1A and 2A are called the **alkali metals** and the **alkaline earth metals**, respectively. These names

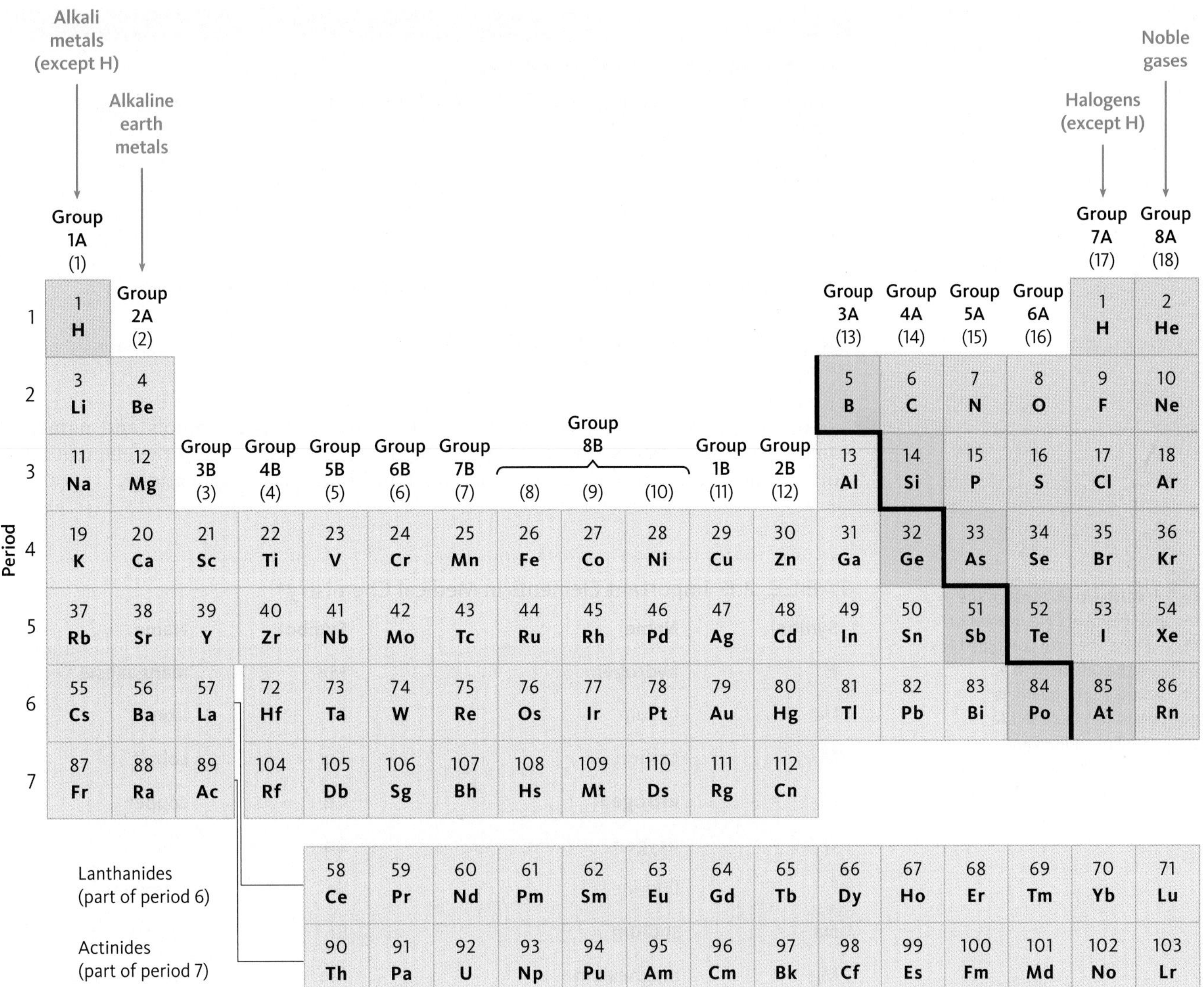

FIGURE 2.3 The periodic table.

come from the tendency of these metals to combine with other elements to form alkaline compounds, substances that neutralize acids. The elements in Group 7A are called the **halogens** ("salt-formers"), because compounds containing these elements generally resemble table salt in many of their properties. Note that hydrogen is not considered to be either an alkali metal or a halogen, because its compounds do not resemble those of the other Group 1A or 7A elements. The Group 8A elements, all of which are gases, are called the **noble gases** because they do not generally combine with other elements to form compounds.

Elements 58 through 71 and 90 through 103 belong in periods 6 and 7, respectively, but including them in the main table would make it too wide to fit easily on one page. Therefore, these elements are placed at the bottom of the table. These two sets of elements, called the lanthanides and actinides, respectively, are rather rare, and most have little use in medicine or health care.

Sample Problem 2.3

Locating an element in the periodic table

What element is in Period 4 and Group 6A? Is this element a metal, a metalloid, or a nonmetal?

SOLUTION

Group 6A contains the elements O, S, Se, Te, and Po. Of these elements, only **Se** (selenium) is in Period 4. Se is a nonmetal.

TRY IT YOURSELF: *Give the symbol of a metalloid that is in the same group as lead.*

For additional practice, try Core Problems 2.17 and 2.18.

To use the language of chemistry, you need to learn the symbols and names of some common elements. Table 2.5 gives the names and symbols of the elements that you are most likely to encounter in medical and biological applications.

Health Note: Most of the required elements are useless or toxic unless they are combined with another element in a compound. Pure sodium is poisonous, but table salt (a compound of sodium and chlorine) is nontoxic. Oxygen and iron are the only pure elements we can use.

TABLE 2.5 Important Elements in Medical Chemistry*

Symbol	Name	Symbol	Name
H	**hydrogen**	**Mn**	**manganese**
He	helium	**Fe**	**iron**
C	**carbon**	**Co**	**cobalt**
N	**nitrogen**	**Cu**	**copper**
O	**oxygen**	**Zn**	**zinc**
F	fluorine	**Se**	**selenium**
Na	**sodium**	Br	bromine
Mg	**magnesium**	**Mo**	**molybdenum**
Al	aluminum	Ag	silver
Si	silicon	Sn	tin
P	**phosphorus**	**I**	**iodine**
S	**sulfur**	Ba	barium
Cl	**chlorine**	Au	gold
K	**potassium**	Hg	mercury
Ca	**calcium**	Pb	lead
Cr	**chromium**		

*Elements that are required in human nutrition are shown in **boldface**.

CORE PROBLEMS

2.13 Write the name of each of the following elements:
a) C b) N c) Cl d) Mg e) Co f) Se

2.14 Write the name of each of the following elements:
a) H b) O c) Ca d) Cr e) I f) Ba

2.15 Each of the following elements has a symbol that does not match its English name. What is the symbol for each of these?
a) iron b) sodium c) silver d) lead

2.16 Each of the following elements has a symbol that does not match its English name. What is the symbol for each of these?
a) potassium b) mercury c) gold d) tin

2.17 Using the periodic table, find elements that match each of the following descriptions:
a) a nonmetal in Group 6A
b) a metal in the same group as carbon
c) a metalloid in the same period as calcium
d) an element that is shiny and conducts electricity
e) a halogen in Period 3
f) an alkaline earth metal

2.18 Using the periodic table, find elements that match each of the following descriptions:
a) a metal in Group 4A
b) a nonmetal in the same group as aluminum
c) a metalloid in the same period as nitrogen
d) an element that does not conduct electricity
e) an alkali metal in Period 4
f) a noble gas

2.19 Columbium is a name that was once used for one of the chemical elements. Columbium is a shiny, silvery solid that conducts electricity well and can bend without shattering. Is columbium a metal, a metalloid, or a nonmetal?

2.20 Brimstone is a name that was once used for one of the chemical elements. Brimstone is a pale yellow solid that does not conduct electricity and breaks when any attempt is made to bend it. Is brimstone a metal, a metalloid, or a nonmetal?

2.3 Atoms

OBJECTIVES: *Understand the significance of atoms in chemistry, and describe the size of an atom.*

Aluminum is a common element, used to make aluminum foil for wrapping and storing food. If you take a piece of aluminum foil and tear it in half, each of the pieces is aluminum. Tear one of these smaller pieces in half, in half again, and in half yet again; the resulting smaller pieces are still aluminum. Is there a limit, a smallest possible amount of aluminum, that cannot be further subdivided? Yes, there is. The smallest possible piece of aluminum, or of any other element, is called an **atom**.

Atoms are the basic building blocks of all matter, and there are as many types of atoms as there are elements. A piece of aluminum foil is a large collection of aluminum atoms, and the helium in a balloon is a large collection of helium atoms. Compounds are made from two or more elements and contain two or more types of atoms. Table salt, for instance, is made from the elements sodium and chlorine, so salt contains sodium atoms and chlorine atoms. Figure 2.4 shows the atoms in aluminum and salt.

It is not easy to describe the size of an atom in a meaningful way, because atoms are far smaller than anything we can observe with our senses. For instance, it would take more than 3 million carbon atoms to span the width of the period at the end of this

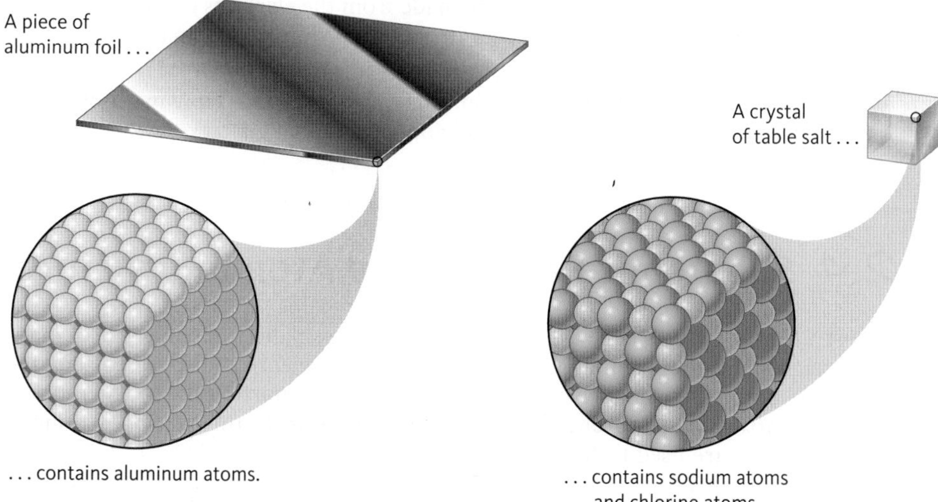
A piece of aluminum foil . . .
A crystal of table salt . . .
. . . contains aluminum atoms.
. . . contains sodium atoms and chlorine atoms.

FIGURE 2.4 The atomic nature of matter.

sentence. Furthermore, it is impossible to describe the appearance of an atom, because atoms are too small to observe using normal microscopes. Indirect evidence tells us that atoms are spheres (round balls). However, most of the descriptive terms that we use when talking about normal-sized objects, such as texture and color, are meaningless when applied to atoms.

Masses of Atoms Are Expressed in Atomic Mass Units

The mass of an atom is an important property. Unfortunately, atoms are so light that our normal units of mass are useless when applied to them. For example, here is the mass of an iron atom:

1 atom of iron weighs 0.000000000000000000000093 grams (9.3×10^{-23} g)

Regardless of whether we use decimal or scientific notation, this number is incomprehensibly small, because the gram is an inappropriate unit for such a small object. Therefore, chemists use a special unit called the **atomic mass unit (amu)** when describing the mass of an atom. An atomic mass unit is roughly the mass of a typical hydrogen atom, the lightest of all atoms. The relationship between atomic mass units and grams can be stated in two ways:

1 g = 602,200,000,000,000,000,000,000 amu (6.022×10^{23} amu)

1 amu = 0.000000000000000000000001661 g (1.661×10^{-24} g)

Health Note: The 3 μg of cobalt our bodies need per day contains as many atoms as there are blades of grass in a field the size of Montana.

Using this scale, a typical atom of iron weighs about 56 amu, a more manageable number than its mass in grams. Masses of atoms of naturally occurring elements range from 1 amu for hydrogen to 238 amu for uranium.

CORE PROBLEMS

2.21 Only one of the following statements could possibly be true. Which one is it?
a) A gold coin contains 0.00000000000000000000252 atoms of gold.
b) A gold coin contains 528 atoms of gold.
c) A gold coin contains 0.25 atoms of gold.
d) A gold coin contains 86,800,000,000,000,000,000,000 atoms of gold.

2.22 Only one of the following statements could possibly be true. Which one is it?
a) One breath of air contains 2,890,000,000,000,000,000,000 oxygen atoms.
b) One breath of air contains 1366 oxygen atoms.
c) One breath of air contains 0.035 oxygen atoms.
d) One breath of air contains 0.0000000000000000000346 oxygen atoms.

2.23 Only one of the following could possibly be a true statement. Which one is it?
a) A penny weighs 0.00000000000000000000000827 amu.
b) A penny weighs 3680 amu.
c) A penny weighs 1,810,000,000,000,000,000,000,000 amu.

2.24 Only one of the following could possibly be a true statement. Which one is it?
a) A drop of water weighs 30,100,000,000,000,000,000,000 amu.
b) A drop of water weighs 844 amu.
c) A drop of water weighs 0.00000000000000000000408 amu.

2.25 Proteins are made from the elements carbon, oxygen, hydrogen, nitrogen, and sulfur. How many types of atoms are in proteins?

2.26 Fats contain three types of atoms. How many elements would you need to make a fat?

OBJECTIVES: *Know the properties of the subatomic particles, and determine the mass and charge of an atom from the number of each type of subatomic particle.*

2.4 Subatomic Particles and Atomic Structure

For almost a century, it was believed that atoms were the smallest possible bits of matter. However, around the beginning of the 20th century, scientists discovered that atoms are made up of even smaller objects, called **subatomic particles**. The three types of subatomic particles are **protons, neutrons**, and **electrons**. In this section, we show how these particles are used to build atoms.

The two important properties of a subatomic particle are its mass and its electrical charge. Electrical charge is the "static electricity" that produces a shock when you walk across a carpet on a cold day and then touch a metal doorknob. There are two kinds of electrical charge, positive and negative. *Any two objects that have the same type of charge repel each other, while objects that have opposite charges attract each other.* Figure 2.5 summarizes the behavior of charged particles. Protons are positively charged and electrons are negatively charged, while neutrons have no charge. Therefore, protons and electrons attract each other.

Table 2.6 summarizes the properties of the subatomic particles. Note that the masses of protons and neutrons are similar, while electrons are much lighter.

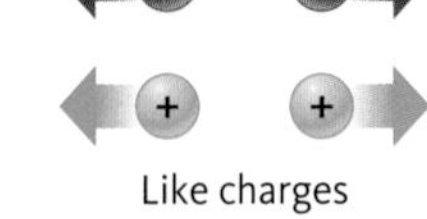

Opposite charges attract each other
Like charges repel each other

FIGURE 2.5 The behavior of charged particles.

The Atom Contains a Nucleus Surrounded by Electrons

All atoms contain at least one proton and at least one electron, and most atoms contain at least one neutron as well. In any atom, the protons and neutrons form a compact ball at the center of the atom, called the **nucleus** of the atom. The nucleus contains virtually all of the mass of the atom, and it contains all of the positive charge. However, the nucleus occupies only a minute fraction of the atom's volume. If an atom were the size of a typical house, its nucleus would look like a tiny speck of dust, barely visible to the eye. Most of an atom is empty space.

The electrons occupy the space around the nucleus. Electrons are sometimes depicted as orbiting the nucleus, much as the moon orbits Earth, but this is not correct. Although we can identify a region in which the electrons can usually be found, it is not possible to describe the path of an electron around the nucleus in any meaningful way.

Figure 2.6 shows the structure of a typical atom.

Health Note: The attraction and repulsion of charged atoms play a key role in nerve impulse transmission.

The Numbers of Protons and Electrons Are Related to the Atomic Number

The number of protons in an atom is called the **atomic number**. All atoms of a particular element have the same number of protons, so the atomic number can be used to identify the element. For instance, the atomic number of carbon is 6, which means that all carbon atoms have six protons. The periodic table lists the atomic number above the symbol for each element, as shown here.

6
C

The **atomic number** tells us that all atoms of carbon contain six protons.

TABLE 2.6 The Subatomic Particles and Their Properties

Subatomic Particle	Mass	Electrical Charge
Proton	**1 amu**	**+1** (protons have a **positive** charge)
Neutron	**1 amu** (neutrons are slightly heavier than protons, but the difference is insignificant)	**No charge**
Electron	$^{1}/_{1800}$ **amu**	**−1** (electrons have a **negative** charge)

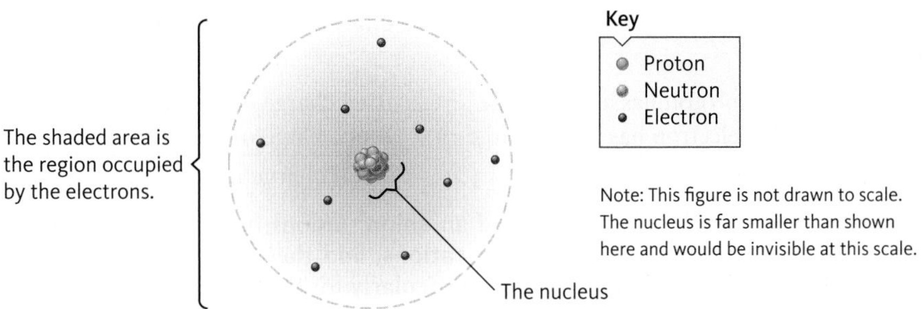

The shaded area is the region occupied by the electrons.
The nucleus
Key
Proton
Neutron
Electron
Note: This figure is not drawn to scale. The nucleus is far smaller than shown here and would be invisible at this scale.

FIGURE 2.6 The structure of an atom.

Sample Problem 2.4

Identifying the number of protons in an element

a) How many protons are in a potassium atom?

b) An atom contains 29 protons. What element is it?

SOLUTION

a) The symbol for potassium is K, and its atomic number (from the periodic table) is 19. Therefore, all potassium atoms have **19 protons.**

b) The number of protons equals the atomic number. The element that has atomic number 29 is **copper** (Cu).

TRY IT YOURSELF: *An atom contains 56 protons. What element is it?*

For additional practice, try Core Problems 2.29 (part a) and 2.30 (part a).

Atoms normally have no electrical charge. Because protons are positively charged, an atom must have enough negatively charged electrons to balance the charge on the protons. Therefore, *atoms normally have equal numbers of protons and electrons.* An atom with equal numbers of protons and electrons is said to be an **electrically neutral atom**.

Sample Problem 2.5

Determining the number of electrons in an electrically neutral atom

How many electrons are in an electrically neutral nitrogen atom?

SOLUTION

The symbol for nitrogen is N, and its atomic number (from the periodic table) is 7. Therefore, a nitrogen atom always has 7 protons. Since an electrically neutral atom must have equal numbers of protons and electrons, this nitrogen atom must have **7 electrons.**

TRY IT YOURSELF: *An electrically neutral atom contains 17 electrons. What element is it?*

For additional practice, try Core Problems 2.31 (part c) and 2.32 (part c).

Atoms do not normally lose or gain protons, but they can lose or gain electrons. The electrons come from or go to other atoms. When an atom gains or loses electrons, the atom becomes electrically charged, because the number of electrons no longer matches the number of protons. Any atom that has an electrical charge, either positive or negative, is called an **ion**. For example, all oxygen atoms have eight protons, but many oxygen atoms on Earth have 10 electrons instead of 8 electrons. Since the numbers of protons and electrons are different, these atoms are ions. We can calculate the electrical charge of an oxygen ion by adding the charges of the protons and the electrons.

8 protons $\rightarrow$	each proton has a $+1$ charge $\rightarrow$	total charge of the protons	$= +8$
10 electrons $\rightarrow$	each electron has a -1 charge $\rightarrow$	total charge of the electrons	$= -10$
		Total charge of this ion	$= -2$

An ion that has a negative charge is called an **anion**. Anions have more electrons than protons. Positively charged ions are called **cations**, and they have more protons than electrons. Ions play a key role in chemistry, particularly for the metallic elements. We will examine how and why atoms form ions in Chapter 3.

Health Note: All of the metallic elements in our bodies are in the form of ions, as is the nonmetal chlorine.

Sample Problem 2.6

Determining the number of electrons in an ion

An atom of magnesium has a +2 charge. Is this a cation or an anion? How many protons and how many electrons does it contain?

SOLUTION

This atom has a positive charge, so it is a **cation.** The periodic table tells us that the atomic number of magnesium is 12, so this atom must have **12 protons.** The charge on this atom is +2, so the charges on the protons and the electrons must add up to +2. We have 12 protons, giving us 12 positive charges. How many negative charges must we add to this atom to produce the +2 overall charge? We need 10 negative charges, so this atom must have **10 electrons.** Here is a picture that may help you to visualize how the positive and negative charges cancel each other out:

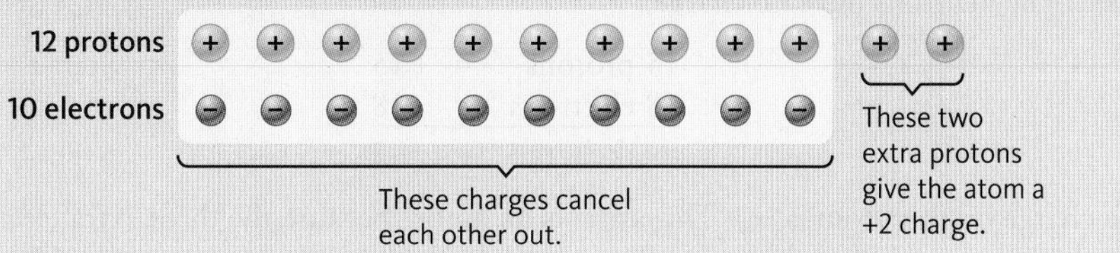

TRY IT YOURSELF: *An atom of fluorine has a −1 charge. Is this a cation or an anion? How many protons and how many electrons does it contain?*

For additional practice, try Core Problems 2.31 (parts a and d) and 2.32 (parts a and d).

The Mass Number of an Atom Is the Sum of the Protons and Neutrons

Because neutrons are electrically neutral, they do not affect the charge of an atom, and they have little impact on the behavior of the atom. However, neutrons do contribute to the mass of an atom. Neutrons and protons each weigh roughly 1 amu, and the mass of the electrons is negligible by comparison, so we can estimate the mass of an atom by simply adding up the numbers of protons and neutrons in the atom. For example, sodium atoms contain 11 protons and 12 neutrons, so the mass of a sodium atom is around 23 amu (11 + 12 = 23). The total number of protons and neutrons in an atom is called the **mass number** of the atom. Table 2.7 shows the relationship between the number of subatomic particles, the mass number, and the mass for atoms of three other elements.

TABLE 2.7 The Relationship Between Mass Number and Subatomic Particles

Element	Atomic Number (Number of Protons)	Number of Neutrons	Mass Number (Protons + Neutrons)	Exact Mass of This Atom
Fluorine	9	10	9 + 10 = **19**	18.9984 amu
Cobalt	27	32	27 + 32 = **59**	58.9332 amu
Iodine	53	74	53 + 74 = **127**	126.9045 amu

Sample Problem 2.7 shows how we can calculate the mass number of an atom if we know how many of each subatomic particle the atom contains.

Sample Problem 2.7

Calculating the mass number and charge of an atom

An atom contains 15 protons, 18 electrons, and 16 neutrons. What element is this? What is the mass number of this atom, and what is this atom's electrical charge?

SOLUTION

The atom contains 15 protons, so its atomic number is 15. From the periodic table, we see that element number 15 is **phosphorus** (P).

To get the mass number of the atom, we add up the numbers of protons and neutrons.

$$15 \text{ protons} + 16 \text{ neutrons} = 31 \text{ particles in the nucleus}$$

The mass number of this atom is **31**.

In the charge calculation, each proton has a charge of +1, and each electron has a charge of −1. The neutrons have no charge.

$$\begin{array}{lcr} 15 \text{ protons} & = & +15 \\ \underline{18 \text{ electrons}} & = & \underline{-18} \\ \text{total charge} & = & -3 \end{array}$$

The charge on this atom is **−3**. This atom is an anion, because the three extra electrons give the atom a negative charge.

TRY IT YOURSELF: *An atom contains 26 protons, 30 neutrons, and 24 electrons. What is the mass number of this atom, and what is this atom's electrical charge?*

For additional practice, try Core Problems 2.29 and 2.30.

Health Note: Fluorine-18 (^{18}F) is radioactive and is used in positron emission tomography, an important diagnostic technique. All naturally occurring fluorine atoms are ^{19}F, so ^{18}F must be made using a particle accelerator.

When we need to refer to the mass number of an atom, we express it in several ways. If we are using the symbol, we can write the mass above and to the left of the symbol, or we can write it after the symbol, using a hyphen to connect them. If we are writing the name of the element, we write the mass immediately after the name. For instance, here are the ways we can represent a fluorine atom that has a mass number of 19:

$$^{19}F \quad \textit{or} \quad \text{F-19} \quad \textit{or} \quad \text{fluorine-19}$$

The exact masses of most atoms are not whole numbers, for two reasons. First, neutrons and protons do not weigh exactly 1 amu (for example, a proton actually weighs 1.0073 amu), and electrons are not weightless. Second, atoms always weigh a bit less than the sum of the masses of their subatomic particles, because some of the mass of the particles is converted into energy when the particles combine to make an atom. For example, if we add the masses of the protons, neutrons, and electrons that make up an atom of ^{19}F, we get 19.157 amu, but a ^{19}F atom actually weighs only 18.998 amu. The energy produced when subatomic particles combine to form atoms is the source of the heat and light produced by the sun and the stars.

Since the mass number of any atom is the sum of the numbers of protons and neutrons, we can work out the number of neutrons in an atom if we know its mass number.

Sample Problem 2.8

Calculating the number of neutrons from the mass number

How many protons and neutrons are in an atom of carbon-13?

SOLUTION

The atomic number of carbon is 6, so this atom must have **6 protons.** The mass number of this atom is 13, so the numbers of protons and neutrons must add up to 13. To get the number of neutrons, we must subtract the protons from the total:

$$13 \text{ (mass number)} - 6 \text{ protons} = \mathbf{7 \text{ neutrons}}$$

Here is a diagram that may help you see how these numbers are related:

We have 13 heavy particles.

Six of them are protons . . .

. . . so the remaining seven are neutrons.

TRY IT YOURSELF: *How many protons and neutrons are in an atom of zinc-66?*

For additional practice, try Core Problems 2.31 (parts a and b) and 2.32 (parts a and b).

CORE PROBLEMS

2.27 Fill in the blanks in the following statements with the names of the appropriate subatomic particles:
a) _____ have a negative charge.
b) _____ and _____ have roughly the same mass.
c) The number of _____ determines which element an atom is.
d) To find the charge on an atom, you must know the numbers of _____ and _____.

2.28 a) _____ are found outside the nucleus of an atom.
b) _____ have no electrical charge.
c) To find the mass number, you must add the numbers of _____ and _____.
d) _____ are the lightest subatomic particles.

2.29 You have an atom that contains 16 protons, 17 neutrons, and 18 electrons.
a) What element is this?
b) What is the mass number of this atom?
c) What is the atomic number of this atom?
d) What is the charge on this atom?
e) What is the approximate mass of this atom in amu?

2.30 You have an atom that contains 20 protons, 22 neutrons, and 18 electrons.
a) What element is this?
b) What is the mass number of this atom?
c) What is the atomic number of this atom?
d) What is the charge on this atom?
e) What is the approximate mass of this atom in amu?

2.31 Many silver atoms have a mass number of 107.
a) How many protons are in an atom of silver-107?
b) How many neutrons are in an atom of silver-107?
c) How many electrons are in an electrically neutral atom of silver-107?
d) Silver commonly has a charge of +1. How many electrons are in a silver-107 atom that has this charge?

2.32 Many copper atoms have a mass number of 63.
a) How many protons are in an atom of copper-63?
b) How many neutrons are in an atom of copper-63?
c) How many electrons are in an electrically neutral atom of copper-63?
d) Copper commonly has a charge of +2. How many electrons are in a copper-63 atom that has this charge?

2.33 What is the significance of the number 16 in the symbol ^{16}O?

2.34 What is the significance of the number 40 in potassium-40?

2.5 Isotopes and Atomic Weight

OBJECTIVES: *Know how isotopes are related to one another, and understand the relationship of atomic weight to the masses of individual atoms.*

As we saw in Section 2.4, all atoms of the same element have the same number of protons and, therefore, the same atomic number. It is possible, however, for two atoms of the same element to have different numbers of neutrons, giving the atoms different masses. Atoms of the same element that have different masses are called **isotopes.**

Most naturally occurring elements have at least two isotopes. For instance, table salt contains two types of chlorine atoms. Table 2.8 lists the properties of these two isotopes of chlorine. Substances that are made from chlorine contain some atoms of each isotope, but they do not contain equal numbers of each. Around three-quarters of the atoms are the lighter isotope, chlorine-35.

The periodic table does not list the isotopes of each element. Instead, it gives the average mass of an atom of the element, based on the distribution of isotopes that

• When chemists measure the atomic weight of an element, they use the exact masses of the isotopes, not the mass numbers.

TABLE 2.8 The Isotopes of Chlorine

Isotope	Number of Protons	Number of Electrons	Number of Neutrons	Mass Number	Exact Mass	Percentage of Atoms
^{35}Cl	17	17	18	35	34.9689 amu	75.8%
^{37}Cl	17	17	20	37	36.9659 amu	24.2%

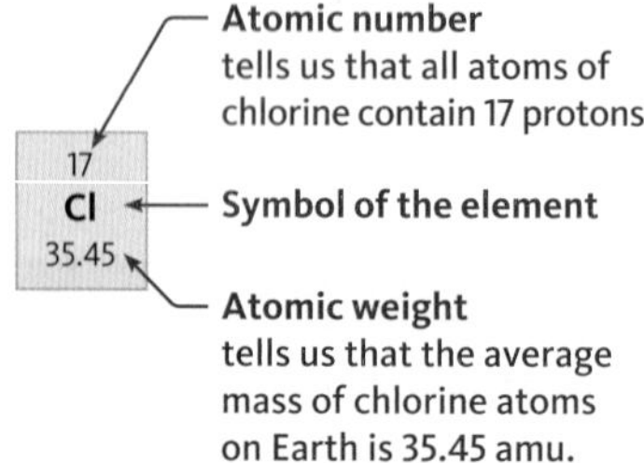
Atomic number
tells us that all atoms of chlorine contain 17 protons.
17
Cl
35.45
Symbol of the element
Atomic weight
tells us that the average mass of chlorine atoms on Earth is 35.45 amu.

FIGURE 2.7 Interpreting the information in the periodic table.

we see on Earth. This average mass is called the **atomic weight** or **atomic mass** of the element (the two terms are used interchangeably). The atomic weight appears below the symbol for the element in the periodic table. Figure 2.7 shows how to interpret the periodic table entry for chlorine. The atomic weight of chlorine is 35.45, which means that the average mass of all of the chlorine atoms on Earth is 35.45 amu. This number is between the masses of the individual isotopes, but it is closer to the lower mass (34.9689 amu) because the majority of chlorine atoms are chlorine-35.

Although the periodic table gives us the average mass of all atoms of an element, it does not tell us the mass of any particular atom, and we cannot use it to calculate the number of neutrons in a typical atom. For instance, the atomic weight of bromine is 79.90 amu, which is close to 80 amu, but there are no bromine-80 atoms on Earth. All bromine on Earth is actually a roughly equal mixture of bromine-79 and bromine-81 atoms.

Isotopes are atoms of the same element, so they behave almost identically. For example, salt that contains ^{35}Cl looks and tastes exactly like salt that contains ^{37}Cl. The primary difference between isotopes is their masses and, by extension, their densities. All isotopes of an element are roughly the same size, because the volume of an atom depends primarily on the numbers of protons and electrons, and isotopes have equal numbers of both. However, isotopes have different masses, so heavier isotopes are denser than lighter ones. For example, salt that contains only ^{37}Cl is noticeably denser than salt that contains only ^{35}Cl.

Health Note: Some isotopes of common elements are radioactive, which means that they produce harmful radiation. However, some of these radioactive isotopes can be used to diagnose and treat certain illnesses.

CORE PROBLEMS

2.35 Which of the following pairs of atoms are isotopes?
a) ^{39}K and ^{40}K
b) an atom with seven protons and eight neutrons, and an atom with eight protons and eight neutrons

2.36 Which of the following pairs of atoms are isotopes?
a) ^{40}K and ^{40}Ca
b) an atom with seven protons and eight neutrons, and an atom with seven protons and seven neutrons

2.37 A beaker is filled with a large number of atoms, all of which have 34 protons and 44 neutrons. Which of the following would look and behave similarly to this collection of atoms?
a) a group of atoms that have 33 protons and 45 neutrons
b) a group of atoms that have 35 protons and 44 neutrons
c) a group of atoms that have 34 protons and 45 neutrons

2.38 A beaker is filled with a large number of atoms, all of which have 20 protons and 20 neutrons. Which of the following would look and behave similarly to this collection of atoms?
a) a group of atoms that have 20 protons and 19 neutrons
b) a group of atoms that have 19 protons and 20 neutrons
c) a group of atoms that have 21 protons and 19 neutrons

2.39 The atomic weight of gold (from the periodic table) is 197.0 amu. Based on this fact, which of the following conclusions can be drawn?
a) All gold atoms weigh 197 amu.
b) Most gold atoms weigh 197 amu.
c) More gold atoms weigh 197 amu than any other mass.
d) We cannot conclude anything about the masses of individual gold atoms.

2.40 The atomic weight of copper (from the periodic table) is 63.55 amu. Based on this fact, which of the following conclusions can be drawn?
a) All copper atoms weigh 63.55 amu.
b) More copper atoms weigh 63.55 amu than any other mass.
c) Copper is a roughly equal mixture of atoms weighing 63 amu and 64 amu.
d) We cannot conclude anything about the masses of individual copper atoms.

2.6 Chemical Formulas

OBJECTIVES: *Write and interpret chemical formulas for compounds.*

Only a few elements can be found in the pure state (uncombined with other elements) on Earth. The most conspicuous of these are the Group 8A elements (He, Ne, Ar, Kr, Xe, and Rn), the atmospheric gases oxygen and nitrogen, and the precious metals silver, gold, and platinum. In general, however, elements tend to combine with other elements to form compounds. In Chapter 3, we will see how and why compounds form, but for now let us take a brief look at how we can use the symbols of the elements to represent a compound.

Water is a familiar compound, and it is formed from the elements hydrogen and oxygen. Atoms of these elements combine in a specific ratio, with each atom of oxygen linked to two atoms of hydrogen. This group of three atoms is called a **formula unit**, and we can represent a formula unit of water by writing a **chemical formula**. Here are the rules for writing a chemical formula:

- Write the symbol of each element in the compound.
- If there is more than one atom of a particular element in the formula unit, write the number of atoms immediately after the symbol for the element.

Using these rules, we write the chemical formula for water as H_2O. By convention, we do not write the number *1* in a chemical formula.

Baking soda (or sodium bicarbonate) is a more complex example. The chemical formula for baking soda is written $NaHCO_3$, and it tells us that a formula unit of baking soda contains one sodium atom, one hydrogen atom, one carbon atom, and three oxygen atoms. Figure 2.8 illustrates the relationship between the chemical formula and the numbers of atoms in water and baking soda.

You may be wondering about the order in which we listed the elements. Why, for instance, didn't we write OH_2 for water, or $CHNaO_3$ (alphabetical order) for baking soda? We will look at the rules for writing chemical formulas in Chapter 3. We will also see why atoms form only certain combinations; why (for example) water is H_2O rather than HO, H_3O, or HO_2.

Health Note: Between 60% and 80% of a healthy human body is water.

Health Note: Baking soda is an old-fashioned home remedy for acid indigestion, but it adds sodium to your diet and can interfere with your body's ability to regulate its pH.

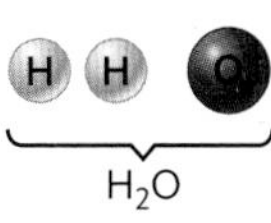

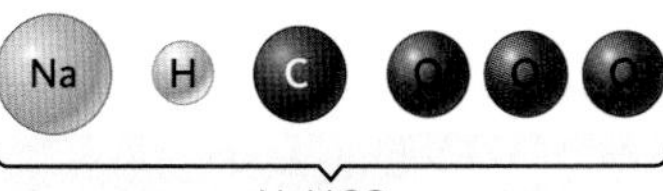

FIGURE 2.8 Writing chemical formulas for water and baking soda.

Health Note: Hydrogen and oxygen also combine to make hydrogen peroxide (H_2O_2). This compound has been used for years to kill bacteria in open wounds and sores, but it damages surrounding tissues and has largely been replaced in clinical work.

Sample Problem 2.9

Writing a chemical formula

Acetaminophen is the active ingredient in Tylenol. One formula unit of acetaminophen contains eight carbon atoms, nine hydrogen atoms, one nitrogen atom, and two oxygen atoms. Write the chemical formula of acetaminophen.

SOLUTION

The formula of this compound is $C_8H_9NO_2$. Remember that we do not write a *1*, so $C_8H_9N_1O_2$ is not correct.

TRY IT YOURSELF: *The vitamin folic acid has the chemical formula $C_{19}H_{19}N_7O_6$. How many atoms of each element are in one formula unit of folic acid?*

For additional practice, try Core Problems 2.43 and 2.44.

CORE PROBLEMS

2.41 A formula unit of table sugar (sucrose) contains 12 carbon atoms, 22 hydrogen atoms, and 11 oxygen atoms. Write the chemical formula of table sugar.

2.42 A formula unit of niacin contains six carbon atoms, five hydrogen atoms, one nitrogen atom, and two oxygen atoms. Write the chemical formula of niacin.

2.43 Monosodium glutamate (MSG) is a commonly used food additive that has the chemical formula $NaC_5H_8NO_4$.

a) How many atoms of each element are in one formula unit of MSG?

b) If you have three formula units of MSG, how many carbon atoms do you have?

2.44 Penicillin V is an antibiotic that has the chemical formula $C_{16}H_{18}N_2O_5S$.

a) How many atoms of each element are in one formula unit of penicillin V?

b) If you have four formula units of penicillin V, how many hydrogen atoms do you have?

OBJECTIVES: *Understand how electrons are arranged in an atom, and write electron arrangements for the first 18 elements.*

2.7 Electron Shells

In Section 2.4, we saw that atoms contain a positively charged nucleus surrounded by electrons. The electrons are in constant motion around the nucleus, but their motion is random and unpredictable. It is a fundamental law of nature that *we can never know exactly where an electron is and where it is going*. However, the electrons in any atom are organized in a specific way, and this organization determines how the atom can join with other atoms to form compounds.

Electrons Are Arranged in Shells

In any atom, the electrons are arranged in definite layers, starting from the nucleus and proceeding outward. These layers are regions within which the electrons move randomly and unpredictably. Although the layers do not actually have definite boundaries, we can treat them as if they do. We can then make some specific statements about these layers and the way the electrons fill them:

- Each layer has a limit to the number of electrons it can hold. The innermost layer (closest to the nucleus) is the smallest and can accommodate the fewest electrons. The farther from the nucleus a layer lies, the larger it is and the more electrons it can hold.
- Electrons prefer to occupy the innermost layers, because they are attracted to the nucleus of the atom. Recall that electrons and protons have opposite charges, so they attract each other.
- The ability of an element to form compounds, and the formulas of those compounds, are determined primarily by the number of electrons in the outermost occupied layer.

Turning on a neon sign pushes the electrons in the neon atoms into higher shells by giving the atoms extra energy. As the electrons drop back into their normal shells, they release the energy in the form of light.

The layers are generally referred to as **electron shells** or **energy levels**. This book will use the term *shell*, but you should not take this word too literally; atoms do not contain anything analogous to the shell of an egg. The term *energy level* refers to the energy required to move electrons from one layer to another. The electrons within any shell are in constant motion, but electrons do not move from one shell to another unless a source of energy (heat, light, or electrical current) is available.

Figure 2.9 illustrates the electron shells for an atom of argon (Ar). Argon has 18 electrons, arranged in three shells. The innermost shell (shell 1) holds two electrons, and the other two shells hold eight electrons each. Note that the electrons do not stay on the surface of the electron shell; they can go anywhere within the shell, and they can even go outside the surface. Because electrons can go anywhere, pictures of electron shells always show the area where the electrons spend most of their time.

Electron shells, in turn, have internal structure. For example, the second shell can accommodate eight electrons, but these electrons divide themselves into four pairs, each of which occupies a different region of the shell, called an **orbital**. Figure 2.10 shows the four orbitals that make up the second electron shell of an argon atom. We will not look at the details of orbital structure, because they do not play a significant role in the formation of compounds. Our primary interest is in determining the num-

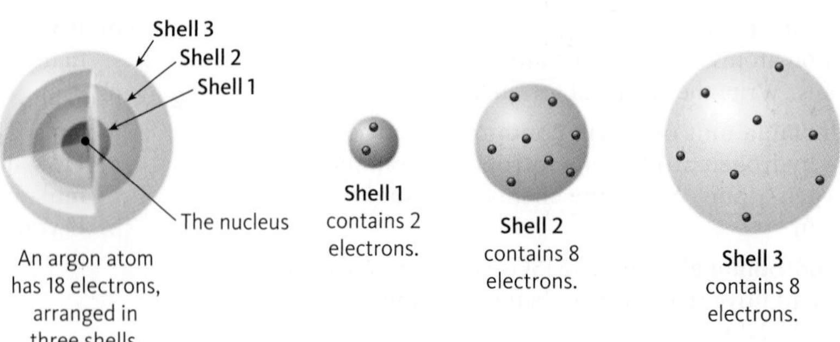

FIGURE 2.9 The electron shells in an argon atom.

ber of electrons in the outermost occupied shell of an atom, because we can use this number to predict the behavior of the atom.

Each shell has a limit to the number of electrons it can hold. The limits for the first four shells are shown in Table 2.9. There are additional shells beyond these four, but no atom fills any of them completely. The largest known atoms have seven occupied shells.

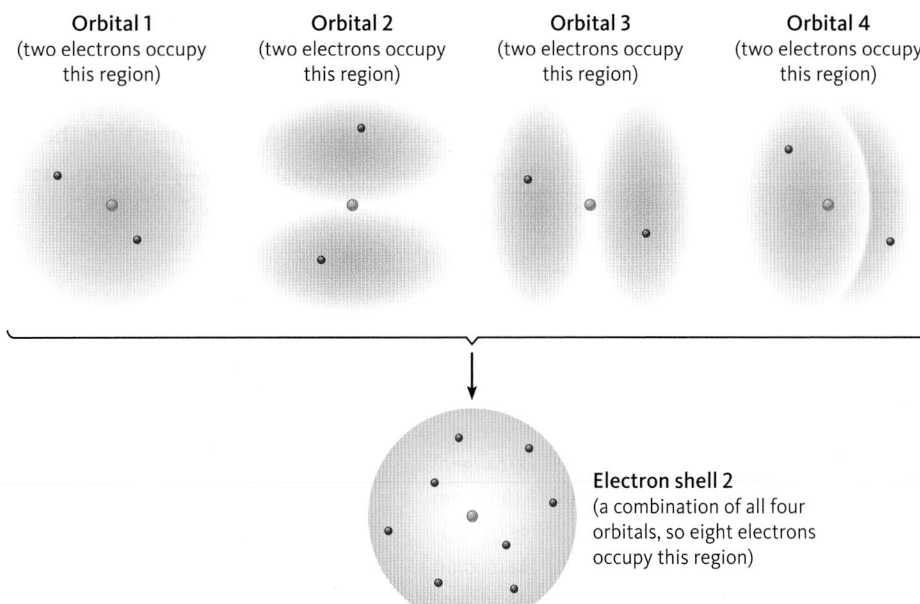

FIGURE 2.10 An electron shell and the orbitals that make it up.

Each Element Has a Specific Arrangement of Electrons in the Shells

Every element has a preferred arrangement of the electrons within its shells. This arrangement is determined by the number of electrons in the atom, the capacity of each shell, the amount of overlap between the larger shells, and the electrons' preference to be close to the nucleus. You should learn the arrangements for the first 18 elements, which occupy the first three rows of the periodic table. These arrangements are straightforward, because *the electrons in the first 18 elements occupy the lowest possible shells.* For example, an electrically neutral magnesium atom has 12 electrons. The electrons prefer to be in shell 1, because it is the closest to the nucleus, but this shell can only hold up to two electrons. Therefore, when we write the electron arrangement of magnesium, we start by putting two electrons into shell 1.

TABLE 2.9 The Capacity of the First Four Electron Shells

Shell Number	Electron Capacity
1	2
2	8
3	18
4	32

shell 1: 2 electrons (12 − 2 = 10 electrons remaining)

Shell 1 is now full. Shell 2 is the best place for the remaining electrons, but it can only hold up to eight electrons, so we put eight of our remaining electrons into shell 2.

shell 1: 2 electrons shell 2: 8 electrons (12 − 10 = 2 electrons remaining)

Shell 2 is now full as well. The remaining two electrons go into shell 3, so the electron arrangement for magnesium is

shell 1: 2 electrons shell 2: 8 electrons shell 3: 2 electrons

Sample Problem 2.10

Writing the electron arrangement for an atom

What is the electron arrangement in a carbon atom?

SOLUTION

The atomic number of carbon is six, so an electrically neutral carbon atom has six electrons. Two of these electrons occupy shell 1. The remaining four electrons occupy shell 2, so the electron arrangement is

shell 1: 2 electrons shell 2: 4 electrons

TRY IT YOURSELF: *What is the electron arrangement in a chlorine atom?*

For additional practice, try Core Problems 2.47 and 2.48.

Table 2.10 gives the electron arrangements for the first 18 elements. The outermost electrons are particularly important, so they are shown in yellow in the table.

TABLE 2.10 Electron Arrangements for the First 18 Elements

Element	Total Electrons	Shell 1	Shell 2	Shell 3
H (hydrogen)	1	1		
He (helium)	2	2		
Li (lithium)	3	2	1	
Be (beryllium)	4	2	2	
B (boron)	5	2	3	
C (carbon)	6	2	4	
N (nitrogen)	7	2	5	
O (oxygen)	8	2	6	
F (fluorine)	9	2	7	
Ne (neon)	10	2	8	
Na (sodium)	11	2	8	1
Mg (magnesium)	12	2	8	2
Al (aluminum)	13	2	8	3
Si (silicon)	14	2	8	4
P (phosphorus)	15	2	8	5
S (sulfur)	16	2	8	6
Cl (chlorine)	17	2	8	7
Ar (argon)	18	2	8	8

CORE PROBLEMS

2.45 Which of the following is a true statement? Refer to Figure 2.9 as you answer this question.
a) Electrons in the first shell must remain inside the region labeled shell 1.
b) Electrons in the first shell must remain on the surface of the shell.
c) Electrons in the first shell can sometimes be outside the region labeled shell 1.

2.46 Which of the following is a true statement? Refer to Figure 2.9 as you answer this question.
a) Electrons in the second shell cannot go into the region labeled shell 1.
b) Electrons in the second shell can go into the region labeled shell 1, but they cannot go outside the region labeled shell 2.
c) Electrons in the second shell can go into the regions labeled shell 1 and shell 3.

2.47 Write the electron arrangement for each of the following elements:
a) nitrogen b) magnesium

2.48 Write the electron arrangement for each of the following elements:
a) fluorine b) phosphorus

2.49 An atom has the following electron arrangement. What element is it?
shell 1: 2 electrons shell 2: 8 electrons
shell 3: 8 electrons

2.50 An atom has the following electron arrangement. What element is it?
shell 1: 2 electrons shell 2: 6 electrons

OBJECTIVES: *Recognize elements that have similar chemical behavior, and understand the relationship between chemical behavior and number of valence electrons.*

2.8 Chemical Behavior, Valence Electrons, and the Periodic Law

Certain elements combine to form compounds with strikingly similar chemical formulas. For example, the metallic elements lithium and sodium (both in Group 1A of the periodic table) combine with oxygen atoms in a 2:1 ratio. The chemical formulas of these compounds are Li_2O and Na_2O, respectively. Elements that form analogous compounds, like lithium and sodium, are said to show similar chemical behavior. They are generally interchangeable in chemical formulas, so if we know the correct formula of a compound that contains one of them, we can substitute the other element and produce another correct chemical formula. Figure 2.11 shows the compounds that are formed when lithium and sodium combine with three other nonmetals.

Not all elements can be exchanged for lithium or sodium in this fashion. For instance, magnesium (a Group 2A element) combines with oxygen in a 1:1 ratio (to form MgO), which is different from the 2:1 ratio we see for lithium and sodium. However, all Group 1A elements below sodium in the periodic table (K, Rb, Cs, and Fr) show similar chemical behavior to lithium and sodium. This similarity applies to the other groups as well; elements from the same group show similar chemical behavior.

Health Note: Although lithium and sodium show similar behavior, they are not interchangeable in our bodies. Lithium compounds are used to treat conditions such as bipolar disorder, but the corresponding sodium compounds have no effect on this condition.

Health Note: Rubidium (Rb) is so similar to the essential element potassium (K) that the body will sometimes substitute a Rb atom for a K atom with no apparent ill effect. As a result, our bodies always contain a small amount of rubidium.

Elements That Behave Similarly Have the Same Number of Outer-Shell Electrons

The similarities in the behavior of elements are related to the electron arrangements of the elements. We have seen that lithium and sodium show similar chemical behavior. The electron arrangements of these two elements are different, since lithium has three elec-

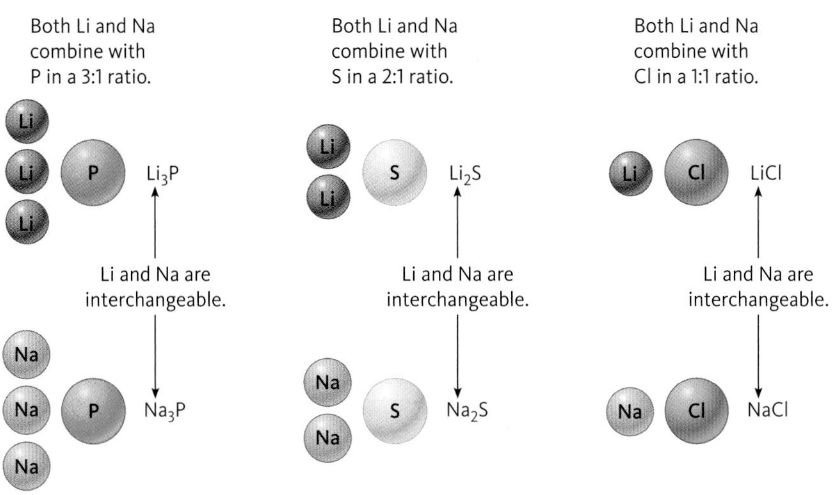

Both Li and Na combine with P in a 3:1 ratio.
Both Li and Na combine with S in a 2:1 ratio.
Both Li and Na combine with Cl in a 1:1 ratio.
Li
Li
Li
P
Li3P
Li
Li
S
Li2S
Li
Cl
LiCl
Li and Na are interchangeable.
Li and Na are interchangeable.
Li and Na are interchangeable.
Na
Na
Na
P
Na3P
Na
Na
S
Na2S
Na
Cl
NaCl

FIGURE 2.11 Lithium and sodium show similar chemical behavior.

(a)
Charles D. Winters
(b)
Charles D. Winters

An example of similar chemical behavior. The alkali metals (a) sodium and (b) potassium both react violently with water.

Sample Problem 2.11

Writing chemical formulas for compounds formed by similar elements

Aluminum and oxygen combine to form Al_2O_3. Boron is similar to aluminum in its chemical behavior. Write the formula of the compound that is formed when boron combines with oxygen.

SOLUTION

When two elements show similar chemical behavior, you can exchange one for the other in chemical formulas. Replacing aluminum by boron gives us the formula of the boron compound: B_2O_3.

TRY IT YOURSELF: *Aluminum and oxygen combine to form Al_2O_3. Sulfur is similar to oxygen in its chemical behavior. Write the formula of the compound that is formed when aluminum combines with sulfur.*

For additional practice, try Core Problems 2.51 and 2.52.

trons and sodium has 11, but each of them has one electron in the outermost occupied shell. The four other elements that behave like lithium and sodium (K, Rb, Cs, and Fr) also contain one electron in their outermost shells. The electron arrangements of these six elements are shown in Table 2.11.

Health Note: Carbon tetrachloride (CCl_4) is an inexpensive liquid and dissolves oils and grease. It was once used to dry-clean clothing. However, it is toxic and a possible carcinogen, so it has been replaced by other chemicals.

When we investigate other elements whose chemical behavior is similar to one another, we find that in all cases, these elements have the same number of electrons in their outermost shells. For example, fluorine, chlorine, bromine, and iodine form similar compounds. When these elements combine with carbon, for instance, they form CF_4, CCl_4, CBr_4, and CI_4, all of which have a 1:4 atom ratio. Each of these four elements has seven electrons in its outermost shell. In general, *elements that show similar chemical behavior have the same number of outer-shell electrons.*

The electrons in the outermost shell of an atom are called the **valence electrons**, and the outermost shell is the valence shell of the atom. As we will see, we can predict much of the chemical behavior of an element simply by knowing the number of valence electrons in an atom of that element. In Chapter 3, we will explore the relationship between the number of valence electrons and the chemical compounds that an element can form.

TABLE 2.11 Electron Arrangements of Some Elements That Have Similar Chemical Behavior

Element	Shell 1	Shell 2	Shell 3	Shell 4	Shell 5	Shell 6	Shell 7
Li	2	1					
Na	2	8	1				
K	2	8	8	1			
Rb	2	8	18	8	1		
Cs	2	8	18	18	8	1	
Fr	2	8	18	32	18	8	1

Sample Problem 2.12

Relating chemical behavior to electron arrangements

Tin and iodine are representative elements and have the following electron arrangements:

	Shell 1	Shell 2	Shell 3	Shell 4	Shell 5
Tin:	2 electrons	8 electrons	18 electrons	18 electrons	4 electrons
Iodine:	2 electrons	8 electrons	18 electrons	18 electrons	7 electrons

Would you expect these two elements to show similar chemical behavior? Why or why not?

SOLUTION

For the representative elements, the number of valence electrons controls the chemical behavior. Tin has four valence electrons and iodine has seven, so these elements should show different chemical behavior.

TRY IT YOURSELF: *Silicon has the following electron arrangement:*

shell 1: 2 electrons *shell 2: 8 electrons* *shell 3: 4 electrons*

Would you expect silicon to show similar chemical behavior to tin? Why or why not?

For additional practice, try Core Problems 2.57 and 2.58.

Lewis Structures Show the Number of Valence Electrons in an Atom

Chemists have devised a way to represent the number of valence electrons in a simple form, called a **Lewis structure** or **dot structure**. The first name honors the work of G. N. Lewis, who laid much of the foundation for chemists' understanding of how electrons participate in chemical bonding. As we will see in Chapter 3, Lewis structures are ideally suited for showing how atoms combine to form compounds, because they allow us to keep track of valence electrons while ignoring all other electron shells.

To draw the Lewis structure of an atom, we write the symbol for the element, and then we draw dots around the symbol to represent the valence electrons. It is customary to draw the dots occupying the four sides of an imaginary square around the symbol. If there are four or fewer valence electrons, chemists normally draw each dot on a separate side of the square. For five or more valence electrons, we add a second dot to each side of the square. Here are the Lewis structures of elements 3 through 10 (Li through Ne):

Li· Ḃe· ·Ḃ· ·Ċ· ·N̈· :Ö· :F̈· :N̈e:

When you have fewer than four dots, or a combination of single and paired dots, you can place the dots in a variety of ways. Here are three other acceptable ways to draw the Lewis structure of oxygen:

·Ö· :Ȯ: ·Ö:

Sample Problem 2.13

Drawing the Lewis structure of an atom

Draw the Lewis structure of a phosphorus atom.

SOLUTION

Before we draw a Lewis structure, we must find the number of valence electrons. Phosphorus has 15 electrons, arranged as follows:

shell 1: 2 electrons   shell 2: 8 electrons   shell 3: 5 electrons

The third shell is the outermost (valence) shell, so phosphorus has five valence electrons. Therefore, the Lewis structure of a phosphorus atom has five dots arranged around the symbol. Normally we draw one pair of dots and three single dots. Here are two acceptable ways to draw the Lewis structure of phosphorus:

·P̈· :Ṗ·

TRY IT YOURSELF: *Draw the Lewis structure of a silicon atom.*

For additional practice, try Core Problems 2.55 and 2.56.

CORE PROBLEMS

2.51 Beryllium combines with nitrogen to form the compound Be_3N_2.
a) Magnesium and beryllium show similar chemical behavior. Write the chemical formula for the compound that is formed by magnesium and nitrogen.
b) Phosphorus and nitrogen show similar chemical behavior. Write the chemical formula for the compound that is formed by beryllium and phosphorus.

2.52 Carbon combines with sulfur to form the compound CS_2.
a) Oxygen and sulfur show similar chemical behavior. Write the chemical formula for the compound that is formed by carbon and oxygen.
b) Silicon (Si) and carbon show similar chemical behavior. Write the chemical formula for the compound that is formed by silicon and oxygen.

2.53 The electron arrangement of selenium (Se) is
shell 1: 2 electrons   shell 2: 8 electrons
shell 3: 18 electrons   shell 4: 6 electrons
a) How many valence electrons does an atom of selenium contain?
b) Draw the Lewis structure of a selenium atom.

2.54 The electron arrangement of iodine (I) is
shell 1: 2 electrons   shell 2: 8 electrons
shell 3: 18 electrons   shell 4: 18 electrons
shell 5: 7 electrons
a) How many valence electrons does an atom of iodine contain?
b) Draw the Lewis structure of an iodine atom.

2.55 Draw the Lewis structure of a carbon atom.

2.56 Draw the Lewis structure of a magnesium atom.

continued

2.57 Lead (Pb) has four valence electrons. What element from Period 2 (Li through Ne) should show similar chemical behavior to lead, based on its number of valence electrons?

2.58 Indium (In) has three valence electrons. What element from Period 3 (Na through Ar) should show similar chemical behavior to indium, based on its number of valence electrons?

OBJECTIVES: *Locate the representative elements in the periodic table, and predict the number of valence electrons in a representative element by its position in the periodic table.*

2.9 The Organization of the Periodic Table

In Section 2.2, you were introduced to the periodic table. The table is designed to allow us to recognize sets of elements that have similar chemical properties. Figure 2.12 shows a simplified version of the table. The key features of the periodic table are:

- *All elements with the same number of valence electrons are found in the same group.* These elements show similar chemical behavior. For example, the elements F, Cl, Br, I, and At have seven valence electrons and form analogous compounds, as we saw in the previous section. The table lists these elements in a single group, Group 7A.
- Elements 3 through 10 (lithium through neon) and all of the elements below them are the **representative elements**, and their groups are designated with an *A*. Hydrogen and helium are also classified as representative elements. *The chemical behavior of the representative elements depends entirely on the number of valence electrons.*
- *The group numbers of the representative elements equal the number of valence electrons.* This allows us to determine the number of valence electrons at a glance. For instance, Ca is in Group 2A, so we know that calcium atoms have two valence electrons.
- Elements 21 through 30 (scandium through zinc) and all of the elements below them are the **transition elements**, and their groups are labeled with a *B*. Unlike the representative elements, *the group numbers of the transition elements do not equal the number of valence electrons.* In addition, the chemical behavior of the transition

Health Note: The transition elements iron, zinc, copper, chromium, cobalt, and molybdenum are essential nutrients.

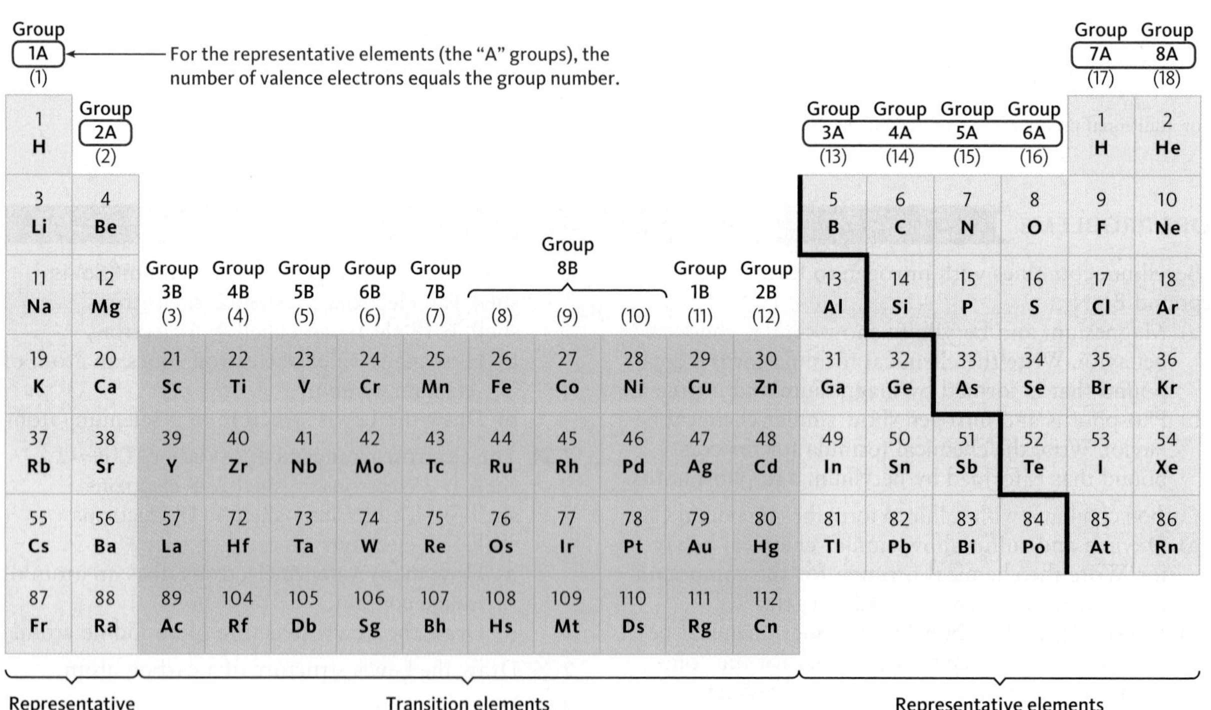

FIGURE 2.12 Predicting the number of valence electrons using the periodic table.

elements depends on the number of electrons in the outermost two shells. For example, the behavior of iron (Fe) depends on the number of electrons in both the fourth shell (the valence shell) and the third shell.

- For all of the elements, *the period number equals the number of the valence shell.* For example, Ca is in Period 4, so its outermost electrons are in shell 4.

Sample Problem 2.14

Determining the number of valence electrons from the position in the periodic table

How many valence electrons are in an atom of tin (Sn, atomic number 50)? Which shell are they in?

SOLUTION

Sn is in Group 4A. Since the group number equals the number of valence electrons, an atom of tin has **four valence electrons.** Tin is in the fifth period (the fifth row), so the valence electrons are in **shell 5.**

TRY IT YOURSELF: *How many valence electrons are in an atom of iodine? Which shell are they in?*

For additional practice, try Core Problems 2.59 and 2.60.

Sample Problem 2.15

Identifying elements from the number of valence electrons

List the symbols of the elements that have six valence electrons.

SOLUTION

The number of valence electrons equals the group number for the representative elements. Therefore, the elements in Group 6A have six valence electrons: **O, S, Se, Te, and Po.**

TRY IT YOURSELF: *List the symbols of the representative elements that have two valence electrons.*

For additional practice, try Core Problems 2.65 (part a) and 2.66 (part a).

Sample Problem 2.16

Identifying an element from the electron arrangement

An electrically neutral atom has the following electron arrangement:

shell 1: 2 electrons	shell 2: 8 electrons	shell 3: 18 electrons
shell 4: 18 electrons	shell 5: 3 electrons	

How many valence electrons does this element have? Which group should it be placed in? What element is this?

SOLUTION

Level 5 is the outermost occupied shell in this atom, so this element has **three** valence electrons. It should therefore be placed in **Group 3A** in the periodic table.

One way to determine the element is to add up all of the electrons.

$$2 + 8 + 18 + 18 + 3 = 49 \text{ electrons}$$

Since the atom is electrically neutral, it must also have 49 protons, which means that it is atomic number 49. This is an atom of **indium (In)**. You can also work out the element by realizing that it must be in Period 5 (since shell 5 is the valence shell). The Group 3A element that is in Period 5 is indium.

continued

TRY IT YOURSELF: *An electrically neutral atom of a representative element has the following electron arrangement:*

shell 1: 2 electrons *shell 2: 8 electrons* *shell 3: 18 electrons*
shell 4: 18 electrons *shell 5: 8 electrons* *shell 6: 1 electron*

How many valence electrons does this element have? Which group should it be placed in? What element is this?

For additional practice, try Core Problems 2.61 and 2.62.

Hydrogen and Helium Are Grouped with Elements That Show Similar Chemical Behavior

The placement of the common elements helium and hydrogen in the periodic table deserves special attention. Helium has two valence electrons, but it behaves like the Group 8A elements and is always placed in that group. Helium, unlike the Group 2A elements, has no empty spaces in its valence shell. The filled valence shell makes helium behave like neon, the next element in Group 8A. Figure 2.13 compares the electron structures of helium, beryllium, and neon.

Health Note: Nearly two-thirds of the atoms in your body are hydrogen atoms, and most of these hydrogen atoms are bonded to oxygen atoms to form water.

The placement of hydrogen poses more of a problem than that of helium. Hydrogen atoms have one valence electron like the Group 1A elements, and many hydrogen compounds have counterparts in the Group 1A elements. However, hydrogen bears at least as strong a similarity to the Group 7A elements as it does to Group 1A. We can understand this similarity by recognizing that the valence shells of both hydrogen and Group 7A elements have a single empty space. Figure 2.14 compares the electronic structure of hydrogen to the structures of lithium and fluorine.

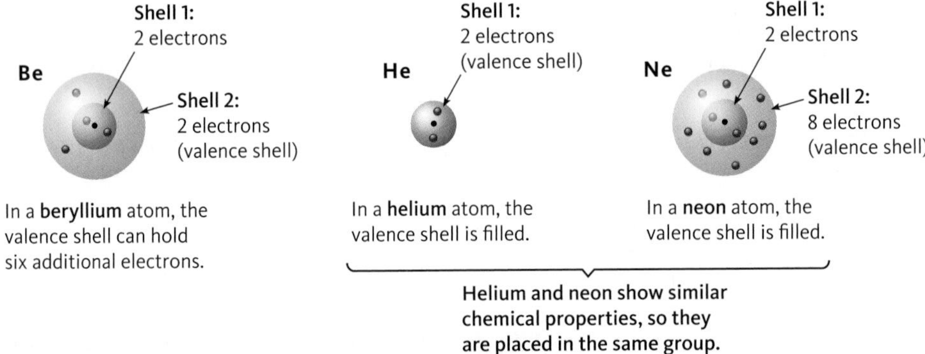

FIGURE 2.13 The relationship of helium to beryllium (a Group 2A element) and neon (a Group 8A element).

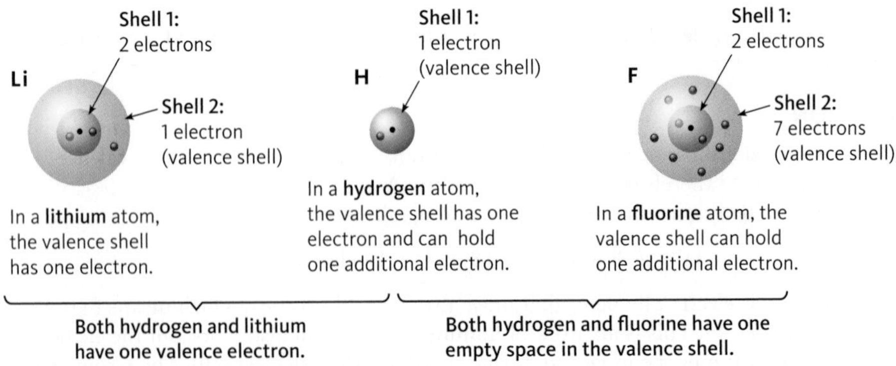

FIGURE 2.14 The relationship of hydrogen to lithium (a Group 1A element) and fluorine (a Group 7A element).

It is best to think of hydrogen in a group of its own, having some similarities with both Groups 1A and 7A but being essentially unique. The periodic table in this book reflects this behavior by placing hydrogen at the head of both groups.

CORE PROBLEMS

2.59 Based on its position in the periodic table, how many valence electrons does an atom of selenium (Se) contain? Which shell do they occupy?

2.60 Based on its position in the periodic table, how many valence electrons does an atom of strontium (Sr) contain? Which shell do they occupy?

2.61 A representative element has the following electron arrangement:

shell 1: 2 electrons shell 2: 8 electrons
shell 3: 18 electrons shell 4: 8 electrons
shell 5: 1 electron

Without looking at the periodic table, answer the following questions:

a) How many valence electrons does this element have?
b) What is the group number for this element?
c) Which period is this element in?

2.62 A representative element has the following electron arrangement:

shell 1: 2 electrons shell 2: 8 electrons
shell 3: 18 electrons shell 4: 32 electrons
shell 5: 18 electrons shell 6: 8 electrons
shell 7: 2 electrons

Without looking at the periodic table, answer the following questions:

a) How many valence electrons does this element have?
b) What is the group number for this element?
c) Which period is this element in?

2.63 Draw Lewis structures for each of the following atoms. You may use the periodic table.

a) K b) Pb c) Br

2.64 Draw Lewis structures for each of the following atoms. You may use the periodic table.

a) Al b) Ba c) Sb

2.65 Using the periodic table, give an example of each of the following:

a) a metal that has five valence electrons
b) a representative element that has its valence electrons in the sixth shell
c) a transition element that is in the fourth period
d) an element that should show similar chemical behavior to oxygen

2.66 Using the periodic table, give an example of each of the following:

a) a nonmetal that has four valence electrons
b) a representative element that has its valence electrons in the fifth shell
c) a transition element that is in the sixth period
d) an element that should show similar chemical behavior to magnesium

CONNECTIONS

The Elements of Life

About 90 elements occur naturally on Earth. It takes only 20 elements to build a human body, although several other elements are present without having any apparent function. Of these 20 essential elements, four of them (carbon, oxygen, hydrogen, and nitrogen) make up 96% of the mass and 99% of the atoms. In coming chapters, you will encounter familiar substances such as carbohydrates, proteins, fats, vitamins, and nucleic acids (DNA). These compounds are largely made up of these four elements.

Figure 2.15 illustrates the elements that make up the human body. We can divide these elements into three rough categories, based on their functions. The seven most common elements (oxygen, carbon, hydrogen, nitrogen, calcium, phosphorus, and sulfur) are *structural elements.* These elements combine with one another to form the framework of virtually every chemical compound in our bodies. The next three elements (potassium, sodium, and chlorine) are *electrolytes,* elements that form ions and that are always dissolved in water, giving our body fluids their correct properties. The remaining elements are *trace elements* and fulfill more specialized roles, some of which we will examine in later chapters. For example, iron is the element that allows our blood to carry oxygen throughout our bodies. Be aware that these categories are not mutually exclusive; for instance, potassium and sodium have other functions beyond serving as simple electrolytes.

Most of the oxygen and hydrogen in our bodies is combined in the form of water. As we will see in coming chapters, water has a variety of properties that make it uniquely suited to support life. It is a liquid at normal temperatures, dissolves a wide range of other chemical substances, and can absorb a great deal of energy without becoming too hot. Water is stable and does not burn or explode, but it can contribute its atoms to other chemical substances under the correct conditions. All living organisms contain a great deal of water, and most scientists believe that if we find life elsewhere in the universe, it will also be based on water.

If water is the key compound that makes life possible, carbon is the key element. When we remove the water from a human body, we find that about two-thirds of the remaining mass is carbon. This is no

continued

accident: the overwhelming majority of the compounds that make up our bodies are built on a framework of carbon atoms. Carbon atoms can link to one another to build a long chain, and they can form strong bonds to all of the nonmetals except the noble gases. As a result, carbon forms the backbone of an immense array of compounds in our bodies, many of them extremely large and complex.

Curiously, Earth's crust contains a different mixture of elements from a human body. For example, silicon makes up almost 26% of Earth's crust and is a major component in many rocks and minerals, but there is very little silicon in most organisms, and silicon has no known function in the human body. However, silicon lies directly below carbon in the periodic table, so it has many chemical similarities to carbon. This fact has led science fiction writers to fantasize about silicon-based life forms. Unfortunately for the science fiction devotees, chains of silicon atoms are rather fragile, so silicon cannot form the great variety of complex compounds that carbon can, making it unlikely that silicon-based organisms could exist.

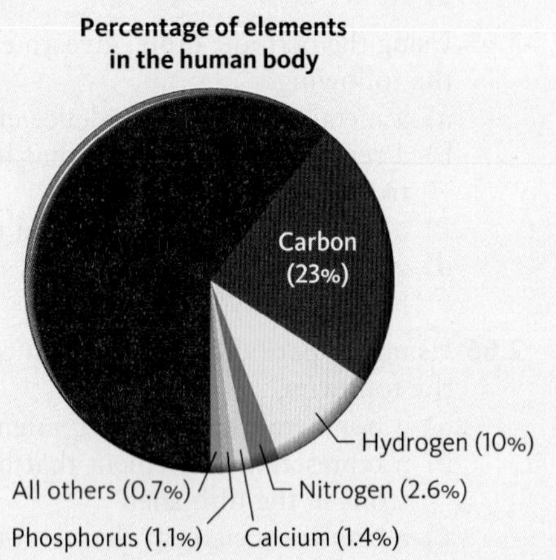

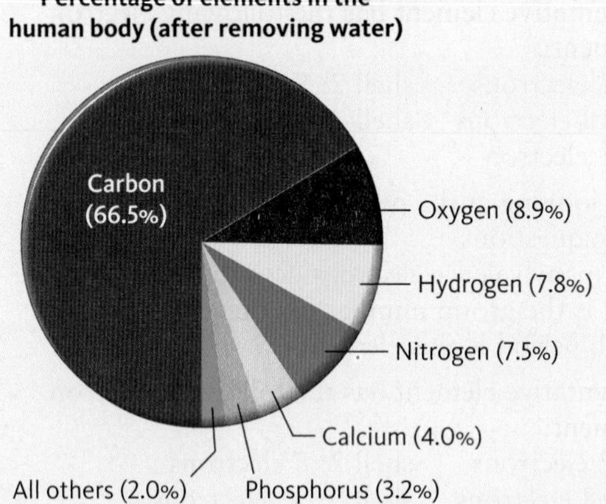

Other elements:

Sulfur 0.2%	Iron 0.006%	Molybdenum 0.00001%
Potassium 0.2%	Zinc 0.0033%	Selenium 0.000005%
Sodium 0.14%	Copper 0.0001%	Chromium 0.000003%
Chlorine 0.12%	Manganese 0.00002%	Cobalt 0.000002%
Magnesium 0.027%	Iodine 0.00002%	

FIGURE 2.15 The composition of the human body.

Key Terms

alkali metal – 2.2
alkaline earth metal – 2.2
anion – 2.4
atom – 2.3
atomic mass unit (amu) – 2.3
atomic number – 2.4
atomic weight (atomic mass) – 2.5
cation – 2.4
chemical formula – 2.6
chemical substance – 2.1
compound – 2.1
electrically neutral atom – 2.4
electron – 2.4
electron shell – 2.7
element – 2.1
energy level – 2.7
extensive property – 2.1
formula unit – 2.6
group – 2.2
halogen – 2.2
heterogeneous mixture – 2.1
homogeneous mixture – 2.1
intensive property – 2.1
ion – 2.4
isotope – 2.5
Lewis structure (dot structure) – 2.8
mass number – 2.4
matter – 2.1
metal – 2.2
metalloid – 2.2
mixture – 2.1
neutron – 2.4
noble gas – 2.2
nonmetal – 2.2
nucleus – 2.4
orbital – 2.7
period – 2.2
periodic table – 2.2
property – 2.1
proton – 2.4
representative element – 2.9
subatomic particle – 2.4
transition element – 2.9
valence electron – 2.8

SUMMARY OF OBJECTIVES

Now that you have read the chapter, test yourself on your knowledge of the objectives, using this summary as a guide.

Section 2.1: Describe properties as intensive or extensive; classify a sample of matter as a mixture, a compound, or an element; and describe a mixture as homogeneous or heterogeneous.

- Extensive properties depend on the amount of substance, whereas intensive properties do not.
- Mixtures contain two or more pure substances in variable proportions, and they generally look and behave like their components.
- Homogeneous mixtures appear to be a single substance, while heterogeneous mixtures have areas of differing appearance.
- Compounds are made from two or more different elements in a fixed proportion, and they look and behave differently from the elements that make them up.
- Elements are the fundamental building blocks of all matter, and they cannot be made from or broken down into other substances.

Section 2.2: Know the names and symbols of common elements, the differences between metals, metalloids, and nonmetals, and the organization of the periodic table.

- The three broad classes of elements are metals, metalloids, and nonmetals.
- Metals are rather similar to one another, while nonmetals are diverse.
- Each element has a chemical symbol, which is listed in the periodic table.
- The periodic table organizes elements by columns (groups) and rows (periods).

Section 2.3: Understand the significance of atoms in chemistry, and describe the size of an atom.

- The smallest possible amount of any element is an atom.
- The mass of an atom is expressed in atomic mass units (amu).

Section 2.4: Know the properties of the subatomic particles, and determine the mass and charge of an atom from the numbers of subatomic particles.

- Atoms are made from subatomic particles: protons, neutrons, and electrons.
- Each subatomic particle has a specific mass and electrical charge.
- The protons and neutrons form a nucleus in the center of an atom, with the electrons surrounding them.
- The mass number of an atom is the sum of the numbers of protons and neutrons.
- The number of protons in an atom determines the identity of the element.
- The number of electrons in an electrically neutral atom equals the number of protons.

Section 2.5: Know how isotopes are related to one another, and understand the relationship of atomic weight to the masses of individual atoms.

- Atoms of the same element that have different numbers of neutrons are called isotopes.
- Most elements have more than one isotope.
- The atomic weight of an element is the average mass of all atoms of that element on Earth.

Section 2.6: Write and interpret chemical formulas for compounds.

- Chemical formulas show the number of atoms of each element in one formula unit of a compound.
- In a chemical formula, the number of atoms of each element is written after the symbol of the element.

Section 2.7: Understand how electrons are arranged in an atom, and write electron arrangements for the first 18 elements.

- Electrons in an atom are arranged in shells (energy levels) numbered outward from the nucleus. Each shell has a specific capacity for electrons.
- Every element has its own electron arrangement.
- For the first 18 elements, each shell fills before electrons enter the next shell.

Section 2.8: Recognize elements that have similar chemical behavior, and understand the relationship between chemical behavior and number of valence electrons.

- Some elements show similar chemical behavior, forming sets of compounds in which one of the elements is exchanged for the other.
- Elements that show similar chemical behavior have the same number of valence electrons.
- Lewis structures show the number of valence electrons in an atom.

Section 2.9: Locate the representative elements in the periodic table, and predict the number of valence electrons in a representative element by its position in the periodic table.

- The periodic table arranges the elements by their numbers of valence electrons.
- The elements in a group have similar chemical properties.
- There are two broad classes of elements: representative elements (for which the valence electrons completely determine the chemical behavior) and transition elements (for which inner-shell electrons also play a role).
- Hydrogen and helium are grouped with the elements to which they are most similar.

Concept Questions

OWL Online homework for this chapter may be assigned in OWL.

* indicates more challenging problems.

2.67 a) What is the fundamental difference between a mixture and a compound?
b) What is the fundamental difference between an element and a compound?

2.68 You can make a homogeneous mixture of salt and water by adding a spoonful of salt to a cup of water and stirring. Is it possible to make a heterogeneous mixture of salt and water? If so, how?

2.69 Physiological saline is a mixture of salt and water that can be used in intravenous injections. It always contains 0.9% salt and 99.1% water. Is physiological saline a compound? Explain your answer.

2.70 If you started dividing a piece of copper into smaller and smaller pieces, is there a limit to the number of times you could do this? Or could you keep dividing the copper forever? Explain your answer.

2.71 A student says, "A carbon atom is not the smallest possible amount of carbon, because atoms are built from smaller particles." How would you respond to this student?

2.72 Electrons are not attached to the nucleus of an atom. Why don't they fly away from the nucleus and leave the atom?

2.73 Why do chemists express the masses of atoms using atomic mass units, rather than a normal metric unit such as grams or milligrams?

2.74 Zinc has five naturally occurring isotopes: ^{64}Zn, ^{66}Zn, ^{67}Zn, ^{68}Zn, and ^{70}Zn.
a) How are atoms of these five isotopes similar to one another?
b) How are atoms of these five isotopes different from one another?
c) ^{64}Zn can combine with chlorine to make $ZnCl_2$. Would you expect the other four isotopes to combine with chlorine? If so, what will be the chemical formulas of the compounds that the other isotopes make?
d) The density of ^{64}Zn is around 7.0 g/mL. Would you expect the density of ^{70}Zn to be higher than, lower than, or roughly the same as this? Explain your answer.

2.75 The atomic weight of selenium is approximately 79 (the actual value is 78.96), and the atomic number of selenium is 34. Based on this, is it reasonable to conclude that a typical selenium atom has 34 protons and 45 neutrons? Justify your answer.

2.76 a) What is an electron shell?
b) What is an orbital, and what is the relationship between an orbital and a shell?

2.77 Using electron arrangements, explain why nitrogen and phosphorus show similar chemical behavior.

2.78 a) Which Group 8A element does not have eight valence electrons?
b) How many valence electrons does this element have?
c) Why is this element placed in Group 8A?

2.79 The following drawing represents the arrangement of the atoms in acetaminophen. Write the chemical formula for acetaminophen.

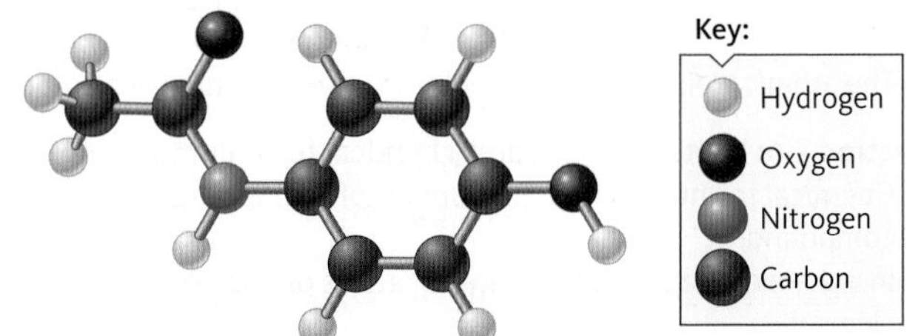

Summary and Challenge Problems

2.80 Which of the following are true statements?
a) Compounds generally look different from any of the elements they are made from.
b) Elements are made from atoms, but compounds are not.
c) You can always tell whether a substance is a compound or a mixture by looking at it.
d) Wood is a heterogeneous mixture.
e) You cannot make an element by combining two other substances.

2.81 Which of the following are true statements?
a) Elements that are in the same group generally show similar chemical behavior.
b) Elements that are in the same period generally show similar chemical behavior.
c) The nonmetals are on the left side of the periodic table.
d) The elements in Group 7A are called halogens.
e) The elements in Group 6A are representative elements.

2.82 An atom contains 29 protons, 36 neutrons, and 27 electrons.

a) What is the atomic number of this atom?
b) What is the mass number of this atom?
c) What is the approximate mass of this atom?
d) What is the electrical charge on this atom?
e) What element is this?
f) What group is this element in?
g) What period is this element in?

2.83 *One amu is the same as 1.661×10^{-24} g.

a) A Mg-24 atom weighs 23.985 amu. How many grams does it weigh? How many micrograms?
b) If an atom weighs 1.395×10^{-22} g, how many atomic mass units does it weigh?
c) What would be the total mass of 10,000 atoms of ^{24}Mg? Give your answer in kilograms.

2.84 Iodine-131 is used to diagnose and treat thyroid conditions.

a) How many protons, neutrons, and electrons are in an electrically neutral atom of iodine-131?
b) How many protons, neutrons, and electrons are in an ion of iodine-131 that has a charge of -1?

2.85 An ion has a charge of $+2$. This ion has a mass number of 42 and contains 22 neutrons.

a) What element is this?
b) How many electrons are in this atom?

2.86 a) Atom X and atom Y have the same mass number, but they have different atomic numbers. Are they isotopes? Explain your answer.
b) Atom Q and atom Z have the same atomic number, but they have different mass numbers. Are they isotopes? Explain your answer.

2.87 One formula unit of morphine contains 17 carbon atoms, 19 hydrogen atoms, 1 nitrogen atom, and 3 oxygen atoms. Write the chemical formula of morphine.

2.88 *Lipitor (atorvastatin calcium) is a chemical compound that decreases the concentration of low-density lipoprotein (so-called "bad cholesterol") in the blood. It has the chemical formula $CaC_{66}H_{70}F_2N_4O_{10}$.

a) How many hydrogen atoms are in one formula unit of Lipitor?
b) If you have 20 formula units of Lipitor, how many fluorine atoms do you have?
c) A sample of Lipitor contains a total of 200 nitrogen atoms. How many formula units of Lipitor are in this sample?
d) A sample of Lipitor contains 2100 hydrogen atoms. How many oxygen atoms does it contain?

2.89 a) Explain why it is not possible to have a sample of morphine that contains five carbon atoms. (See Problem 2.87.)
b) Is it possible to have a sample of morphine that contains five nitrogen atoms? Explain why or why not.

2.90 How many electrons are in shell 2 of each of the following?

a) a calcium atom
b) a carbon atom
c) a helium atom
d) a fluorine ion that has a -1 charge
e) a lithium atom that has a $+1$ charge

2.91 Give one example of each of the following:

a) an element that has five valence electrons
b) an element that has two electrons in shell 4 (Hint: It can have electrons in other shells.)
c) an element that has eight electrons in shell 2 (See the hint to part b.)
d) an element that has a total of eight electrons

2.92 An element has the following electron arrangement:

shell 1: 2 electrons shell 2: 8 electrons
shell 3: 13 electrons shell 4: 2 electrons

What element is this? Explain how you can tell.

2.93 *Lead has the following electron arrangement:

shell 1: 2 electrons shell 2: 8 electrons
shell 3: 18 electrons shell 4: 32 electrons
shell 5: ?? electrons shell 6: ?? electrons

Use the atomic number of lead and its position in the periodic table to figure out the number of electrons in shells 5 and 6.

3

Chemical Bonds

Mr. Ramirez has not been feeling well for the past month. He hasn't had much appetite, he has tended to feel tired a lot, and lately he has noticed that his eyes look puffy and his ankles and wrists seem a bit swollen. Finally, he goes to his doctor, who orders a variety of lab tests, including a blood urea nitrogen (BUN) test. Our bodies make urea whenever we break down protein, and our blood carries the urea to our kidneys, which excrete it. Because our bodies have no other way to get rid of urea, the urea concentration in the blood is a good indicator of kidney function. In this case, Mr. Ramirez's lab results show that he has an unusually high level of urea in his blood. Along with other tests, the elevated BUN level shows that Mr. Ramirez is suffering from chronic kidney disease.

Urea is a chemical compound, built from the elements carbon, hydrogen, nitrogen, and oxygen. Like all compounds, urea has a specific ratio of these atoms, which we can write as a chemical formula: CH_4N_2O. The atoms in urea are held together by chemical bonds, formed by the electrons in the outer shell of each atom. In this chapter, we begin our exploration of chemical compounds by looking at how atoms bond to one another.

```
   H  :O:  H
   |   ||  |
H—N̤—C—N̤—H
```

Urea

OUTLINE

LABORATORY REQUISITION—CHEMISTRY

☐ Sodium	NA	☐ Fructosamine	FRU/ALB
☐ Potassium	K	☐ PSA	PSA
☐ Creatinine	CREAT	☐ Chloride	CL
☑ BUN	BUN	☐ Calcium	CA
☐ Glucose-fasting	GLUCF	☐ Phosphorus	PHOS
☐ Glucose-random	GLUCR	☐ Phenylalanine	PKU
☐ Hemoglobin A1C	HGBA1C	☐ Uric Acid	URIC

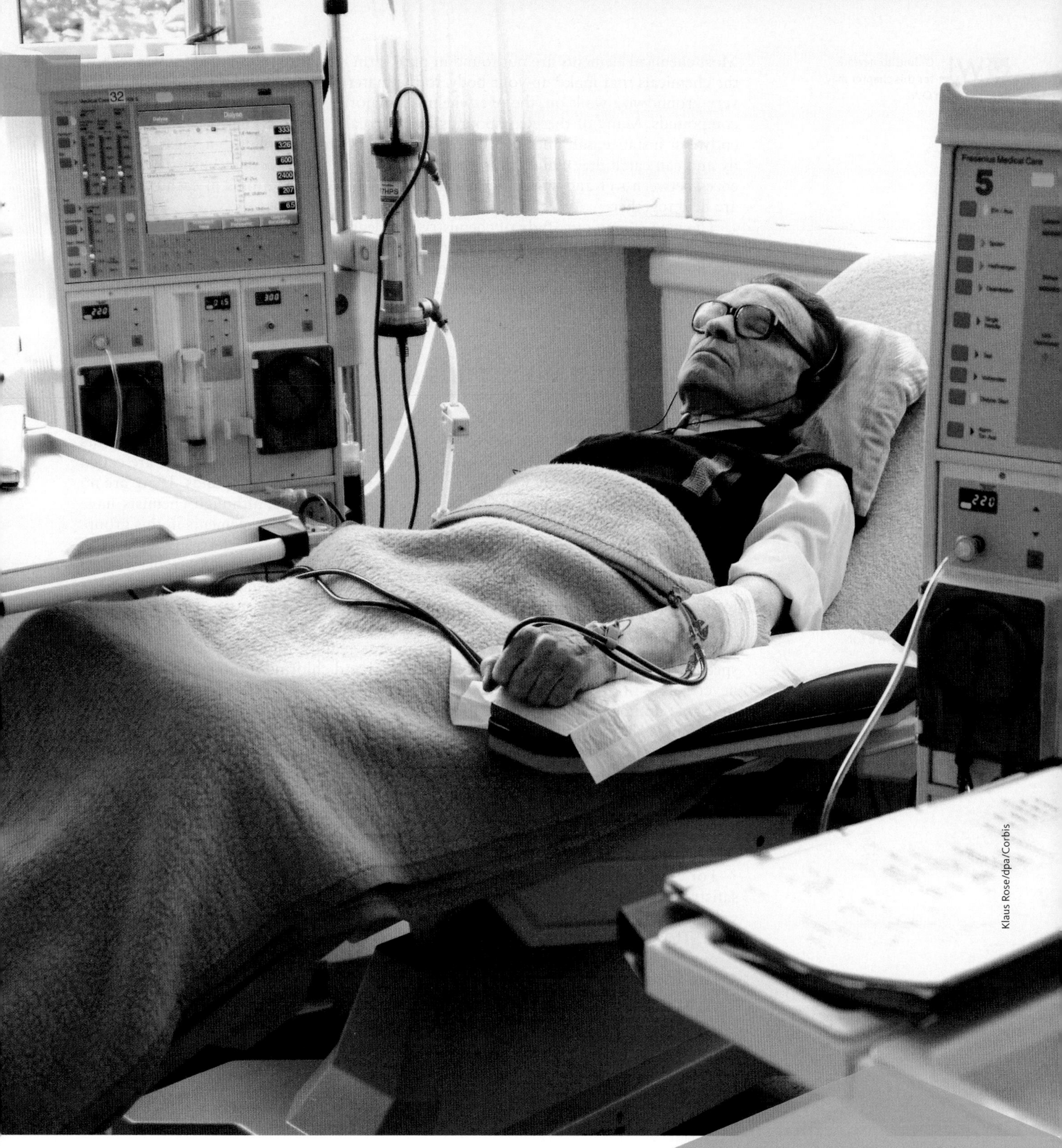

☐ Total Bilirubin	BILIT	☐ TSH	TSH	☐ Amylase	AMYL
☐ Neonate T. Bilirubin	BILITN	☐ Alk Phos	ALKP	☐ Cholesterol	CHOL
☐ Serum Protein Elect.	PEP	☐ SGOT (AST)	AST	☐ HDL	HDL
☐ Ferritin	FERR	☐ Albumin	ALB	☐ LDL–fasting	LDL
☐ Iron/TIBC	IRON/TIBC	☐ SGPT (ALT)	ALT	☐ Triglycerides–fasting	TRIG
☐ Hgb Electrophoresis	HGB EP	☐ CPK (CK)	CK		
☐ T4/FTI	T4S	☐ CKMB	CKMB		

Kidney function is essential to life, so people with advanced kidney failure must rely on hemodialysis to remove wastes from the blood.

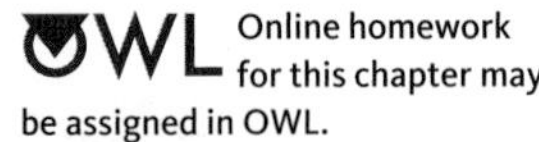 Online homework for this chapter may be assigned in OWL.

Most chemical elements are not found in pure form in nature. From the food you eat, to the chemicals that make up your body, to the materials in the clothing you wear, to the very ground you walk on, the overwhelming majority of substances you encounter are compounds. Many of these compounds look virtually identical, but behave very differently. For instance, salt and sugar are both white, crystalline solids, but sugar melts easily and can catch fire, while salt is very difficult to melt and will not burn. These differences between salt and sugar are determined by the way the atoms in each compound are held together.

The next step in our study of chemistry is to learn how and why elements form compounds. We will explore how atoms of different elements bond to one another in a compound and how the different types of bonds lead to different properties. We will also discover why atoms can only form certain combinations—why, for instance, hydrogen and oxygen can form H_2O but not HO_2 or HO.

OBJECTIVES: *Understand how covalent bonds are formed, use the octet rule to predict the number of covalent bonds an atom can form, and draw Lewis structures for molecules that contain single bonds.*

3.1 Covalent Bonds and the Octet Rule

As we saw in Chapter 2, elements can combine to form compounds, in which atoms of two or more elements are linked to one another. However, the Group 8A elements He, Ne, Ar, Kr, Xe, and Rn are a conspicuous exception. These six elements are called the noble gases because they do *not* normally form chemical compounds. There are no naturally occurring compounds that contain these elements, although chemists have succeeded in making a few compounds that contain the heavier elements in this group. All of the Group 8A elements except helium have eight valence electrons, so we can conclude that *elements that have eight valence electrons are unusually stable and do not generally form chemical compounds.* Helium is included in this group because it too does not form compounds; its two electrons fill its valence shell, as we saw in Chapter 2.

Health Note: Xenon (Xe) is a general anesthetic and is an environmentally friendly alternative to nitrous oxide and halogenated compounds, but it is currently too expensive for widespread use.

Most of the other elements form compounds readily, and these compounds have specific chemical formulas. For example, sodium and chlorine combine to make NaCl, never $NaCl_2$ or any other formula. In Chapter 2, you learned that elements that have the same number of valence electrons tend to behave the same way when they form compounds. For the representative elements, chemical behavior is governed by the **octet rule**: *The representative elements tend to form compounds in which each atom has the electron arrangement of a Group 8A element.* All of the Group 8A elements except helium have eight valence electrons, so we can also state the octet rule as follows: *Representative elements normally form compounds in which each atom has eight electrons in its outermost shell.* The word *octet* refers to the eight valence electrons in atoms that satisfy the octet rule.

For example, fluorine has seven valence electrons, so a single fluorine atom does not satisfy the octet rule. As a result, fluorine atoms are never found alone; a fluorine atom will always combine with another atom to bring the number of valence electrons up to eight. The same is true of the other Group 7A elements. This is in direct contrast to the Group 8A elements, which have eight valence electrons and do not combine with other atoms. We can use Lewis structures to show this difference.

Fluorine has seven valence electrons, so it does not satisfy the octet rule. Fluorine atoms combine with other atoms to form compounds.

Neon has eight valence electrons, so it satisfies the octet rule. Neon atoms do not combine with other atoms to form compounds.

Atoms Can Satisfy the Octet Rule by Forming a Covalent Bond

Let us compare the behavior of neon (Ne) and fluorine (F) atoms when we put them in a box. Neon satisfies the octet rule while fluorine does not, and therefore the two elements behave quite differently. The neon atoms remain independent of one another, but the fluorine atoms form pairs, as shown in Figure 3.1. Clearly, the fluorine atoms are attracted to one another. Whenever any two atoms are attracted to each other strongly enough to keep them in contact, we say that the atoms have formed a **chemical bond.**

When two fluorine atoms form a chemical bond, they move together until their valence shells overlap, as shown in Figure 3.2. Each atom contributes one electron to the region where the shells overlap. Therefore, the two fluorine atoms share a pair of electrons. Since these electrons lie within the valence shells of both atoms, *each fluorine atom now has eight electrons in its valence shell,* satisfying the octet rule.

Whenever two atoms share a pair of electrons, the shared electrons are called a **bonding electron pair.** This pair of electrons forms a powerful bond between the two atoms, called a **covalent bond.**

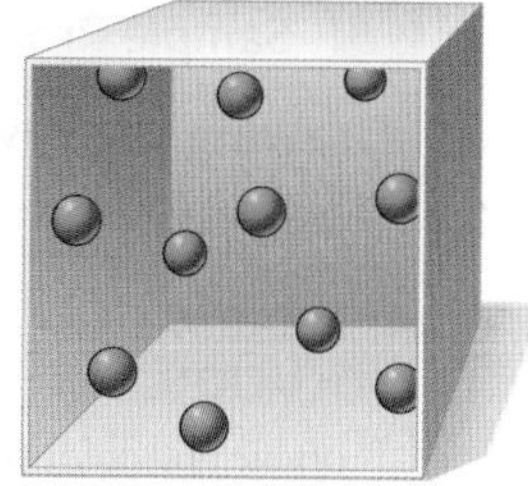

Neon atoms are independent of one another.
(a)

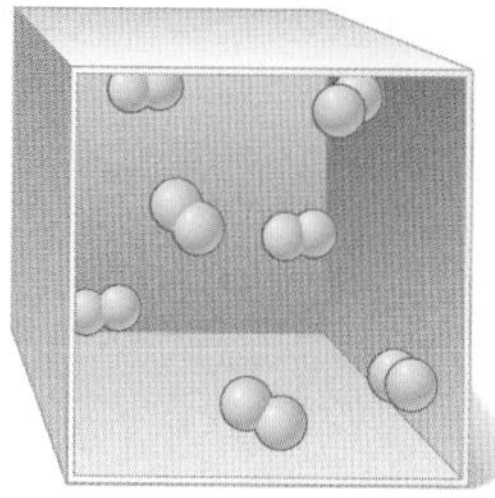

Fluorine atoms form chemical bonds with one another.
(b)

FIGURE 3.1 The differing behavior of (a) neon atoms and (b) fluorine atoms.

Covalent Bonds Can Be Represented by Lewis Structures

We can use Lewis structures to represent the formation of a covalent bond. Lewis structures allow us to keep track of the valence electrons around each atom. For a covalent bond, the two electrons in the bonding pair are drawn side by side:

:F· ·F: ⟶ :F:F:

The bonding pair

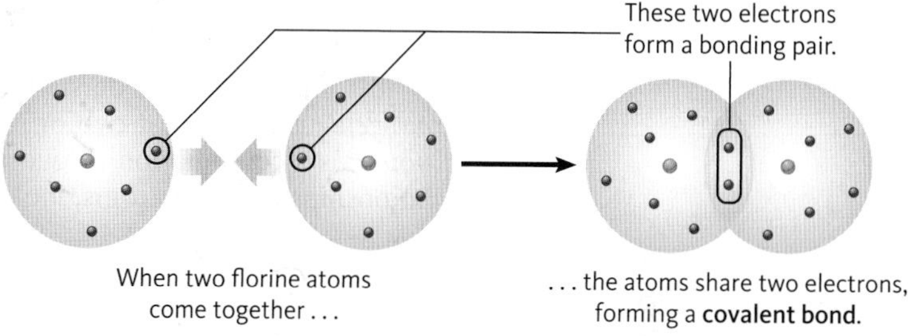
These two electrons form a bonding pair.
When two florine atoms come together . . .
. . . the atoms share two electrons, forming a **covalent bond.**

FIGURE 3.2 The formation of a covalent bond between two fluorine atoms.

In the Lewis structure that follows, the shading shows the valence shell of each fluorine atom. Again, note that each atom has eight electrons in its valence shell, satisfying the octet rule.

:F:F:

When two or more atoms are linked by covalent bonds, the group of atoms is called a **molecule.** The pair of fluorine atoms we made earlier is an example of a molecule. When atoms form a molecule, the chemical formula must show how many atoms the molecule contains, so we write the formula of fluorine as F_2. We can distinguish the behavior of neon and fluorine in Figure 3.1 by saying that one box contains Ne atoms and the other box contains F_2 molecules.

The other Group 7A elements also form molecules that contain two atoms. This should not be surprising, because elements in the same group have the same number of valence electrons. For example, here is the structure of the molecule that is formed by two chlorine atoms. The chemical formula of this molecule is Cl_2.

:Cl:Cl:

The Lewis structure of Cl_2

:Cl:Cl:

In this structure, the shading shows the valence shell of each atom.

Health Note: Cl_2 kills bacteria, so it is used to disinfect drinking water and swimming pools. The odor of bleach is actually chlorine.

The Group 7A elements can also form covalent bonds with one another. For example, a chlorine atom can combine with a fluorine atom to make a molecule that contains two different atoms. This molecule is called chlorine monofluoride, and its chemical formula is written ClF. Because it contains atoms of two different elements, chlorine monofluoride is a compound, whereas Cl_2 and F_2 are the normal forms of the elements chlorine and fluorine.

:Cl· ·F: ⟶ :Cl:F:

Two different atoms come together . . .

. . . to form a molecule of ClF.

Sample Problem 3.1

Drawing the Lewis structure of a molecule that contains two atoms

Draw the Lewis structure of a molecule that contains one bromine atom and one chlorine atom.

SOLUTION

Bromine and chlorine are both in Group 7A, so they have seven valence electrons and one empty space in their valence shells. Each atom contributes one valence electron to a bonding pair.

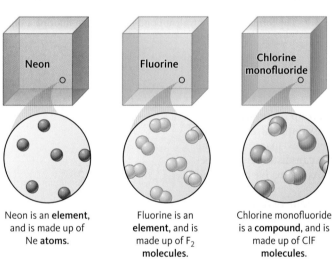

:Br· ·Cl: ⟶ :Br:Cl:

The individual atoms combine . . . . . . to form a BrCl molecule.

TRY IT YOURSELF: *Draw the Lewis structure of a molecule that contains one chlorine atom and one iodine atom.*

It is important to understand the distinction between a molecule and a compound. A *molecule* is a group of two or more atoms, which may be identical or different. A *compound* is a combination of two or more different elements. Figure 3.3 illustrates the relationships between atoms, molecules, elements, and compounds.

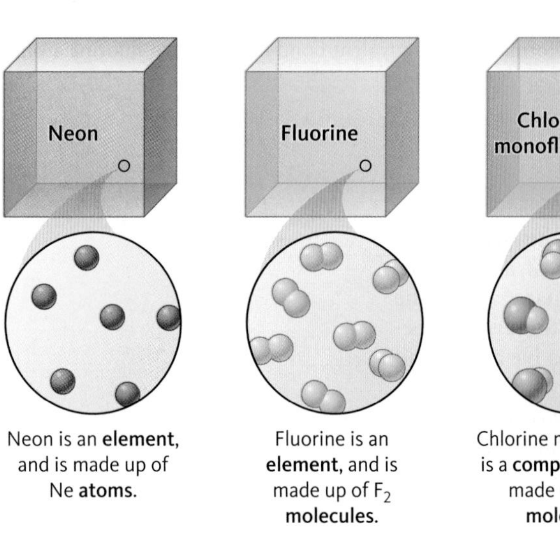

Neon is an **element**, and is made up of Ne **atoms**.

Fluorine is an **element**, and is made up of F_2 **molecules**.

Chlorine monofluoride is a **compound**, and is made up of ClF **molecules**.

FIGURE 3.3 The relationships between elements, compounds, atoms, and molecules.

Hydrogen Forms a Covalent Bond to Achieve the Electron Arrangement of Helium

Recall from Chapter 2 that helium is placed in Group 8A because it does not form compounds. The two electrons in a helium atom fill its valence shell, making the atom very stable. The stability of helium in turn dictates the chemical behavior of hydrogen. Hydrogen atoms usually form bonds so that they can achieve the electron arrangement of helium. Since hydrogen needs only one more electron, it behaves like the Group 7A elements when it forms covalent bonds. Hydrogen atoms can pair up to form H_2, and they can combine with other Group 7A elements to form molecules such as HF.

H· ·H ⟶ H:H

Two hydrogen atoms can pair up to make a molecule of H_2.

In these molecules, each hydrogen atom has two valence electrons (the same as helium).

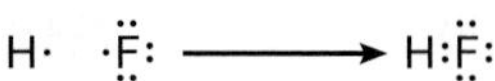

H:F:

A hydrogen atom and a fluorine atom can make a molecule of HF.

Because the valence shell of hydrogen is the first shell, hydrogen atoms *never* have eight valence electrons and the octet rule does not apply to hydrogen.

Sample Problem 3.2

Drawing the Lewis structure of a molecule that contains hydrogen

Draw the Lewis structure of a molecule of HI.

SOLUTION

Iodine has seven valence electrons and one empty space in its valence shell. Hydrogen has one valence electron, but its valence shell can only accommodate two electrons, so hydrogen too has one empty space in the valence shell. Each atom contributes one valence electron to a bonding pair.

H· ·Ï: ⟶ H:Ï:

The individual atoms combine . . . . . . to form an HI molecule.

TRY IT YOURSELF: *Draw the Lewis structure of a molecule of HCl.*

Atoms That Need More Than One Electron Form Several Covalent Bonds

Let us now turn to oxygen, which has six valence electrons. An oxygen atom needs two additional electrons to satisfy the octet rule. Hydrogen atoms can supply electrons to fill the holes in the valence shell of oxygen. However, an oxygen atom must share electrons with two hydrogen atoms, because each hydrogen atom can only contribute one electron to the valence shell of oxygen.

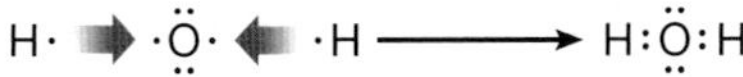

⟶ H:Ö:H H:Ö:H

Oxygen has two empty spaces in its valence shell, so it must combine with two hydrogen atoms.

The Lewis structure of H_2O

Each hydrogen atom has two valence electrons, and the oxygen atom has eight valence electrons.

This is the structure of water, the most familiar and common chemical compound on Earth. We can now understand why water is H_2O, rather than H_3O, HO, HO_2, or some other formula. *The chemical formula of water is a direct result of the two empty spaces in the valence shell of oxygen, and of hydrogen's ability to fill only one of those spaces.*

Sample Problem 3.3

Predicting the formula and structure of a molecule from the number of valence electrons

What is the simplest molecule that could be formed by sulfur atoms and chlorine atoms? Draw its Lewis structure.

SOLUTION

Sulfur is in Group 6A, so it has six valence electrons. A sulfur atom needs two more electrons to complete its octet, so it needs to form bonds with two other atoms. Chlorine, on the other hand, needs only one more valence electron to complete its octet, so it only forms one bond. The simplest possible compound of sulfur and chlorine has two chlorine atoms bonded to one sulfur atom.

:C̤̈l· ·S̤̈· ·C̤̈l: ⟶ :C̤̈l:S̤̈:C̤̈l:

The individual atoms combine . . . . . . to form a SCl_2 molecule.

TRY IT YOURSELF: *What is the simplest molecule that could be formed by fluorine and selenium atoms? Draw its Lewis structure.*

For additional practice, try Core Problems 3.3 and 3.4.

Many molecules contain valence electrons that are not involved in covalent bonding. These electrons are called **nonbonding electron pairs** or **lone pairs**, while the shared electrons are called bonding electron pairs, as explained earlier. For example, a water molecule contains four nonbonding electrons (two lone pairs) and four bonding electrons (two bonding pairs). In the following structure, the bonding electrons are shown in red and the nonbonding electrons in green:

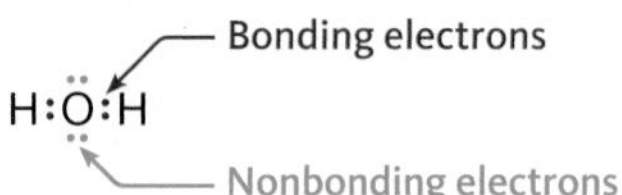

The reasoning we used to construct a water molecule can be extended to elements that have three or four empty spaces in their valence shells. For example, nitrogen has five valence electrons, leaving it with three empty spaces. Therefore, a nitrogen atom needs to share electrons with three other atoms, forming three covalent bonds. If the other element is hydrogen, we form a molecule of ammonia (NH_3), a common cleaning agent and an important compound in biochemistry.

Health Note: Ammonia is responsible for the acrid smell of old urine. Our bodies produce ammonia as we break down proteins to get energy, but we immediately convert the ammonia into a much less toxic compound called urea.

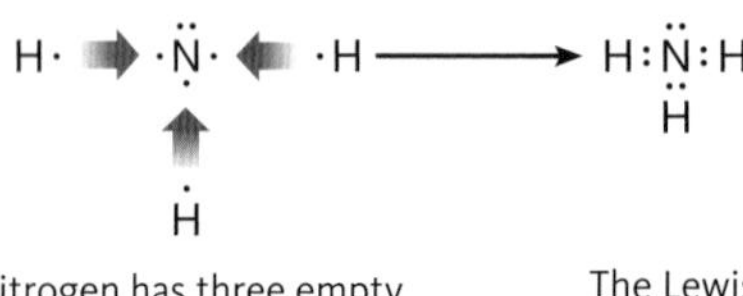

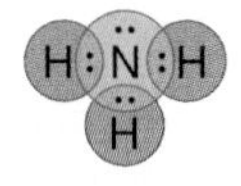

Nitrogen has three empty spaces in its valence shell, so it must combine with three hydrogen atoms.

The Lewis structure of NH_3

Each hydrogen atom has two valence electrons, and the nitrogen atom has eight valence electrons.

Carbon has four valence electrons, leaving it with four empty spaces in its valence shell. Carbon needs to form covalent bonds with four other atoms to fill these empty spaces. If the other atoms are hydrogen, we form a molecule of methane (CH_4), a fundamental compound of organic chemistry.

Health Note: About one third of all people produce methane when they "pass gas"—the rest produce hydrogen. These gases form when bacteria in the large intestine break down undigested carbohydrates. Both methane and hydrogen are odorless—if your gas smells bad, it contains sulfur compounds such as H_2S.

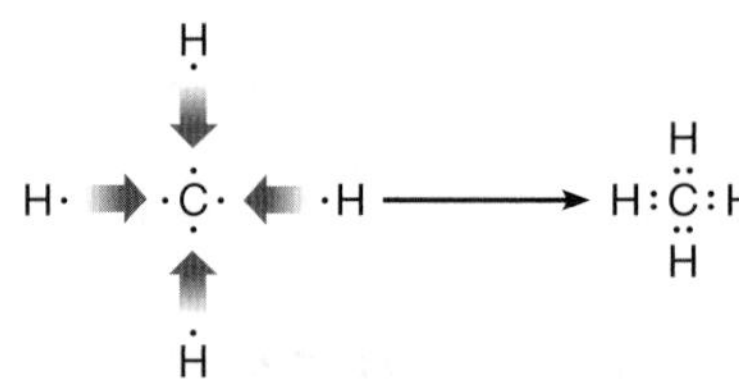

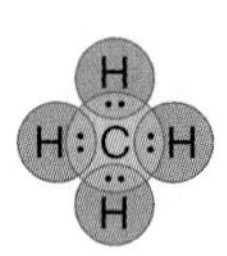

Carbon has four empty spaces in its valence shell, so it must combine with four hydrogen atoms.

The Lewis structure of CH_4

Each hydrogen atom has two valence electrons, and the carbon atom has eight valence electrons.

Sample Problem 3.4

Drawing the Lewis structure of a molecule

Carbon tetrachloride has the formula CCl_4. It was used for many years in the dry-cleaning industry, but it is now known to be toxic to the liver and carcinogenic. Draw the Lewis structure of CCl_4.

SOLUTION

Carbon has four empty spaces in its valence shell, so it forms four covalent bonds. Each chlorine atom makes one covalent bond, so the carbon atom shares electrons with each of the chlorine atoms.

:Cl:
:Cl· ·C· ·Cl: ⟶ :Cl:C:Cl:
:Cl:

The Lewis structure of CCl_4

TRY IT YOURSELF: *Draw the Lewis structure of PF_3.*

For additional practice, try Core Problems 3.7 and 3.8.

What about elements that have five or more empty spaces in their valence shells? With one notable exception (boron), these elements do not normally form covalent bonds, because they do not have enough electrons of their own to satisfy the octet rule, even if they use all of their electrons to form covalent bonds. For example, aluminum has three valence electrons. If an aluminum atom combines with hydrogen atoms, the aluminum can only form three covalent bonds, leaving it with just six valence electrons.

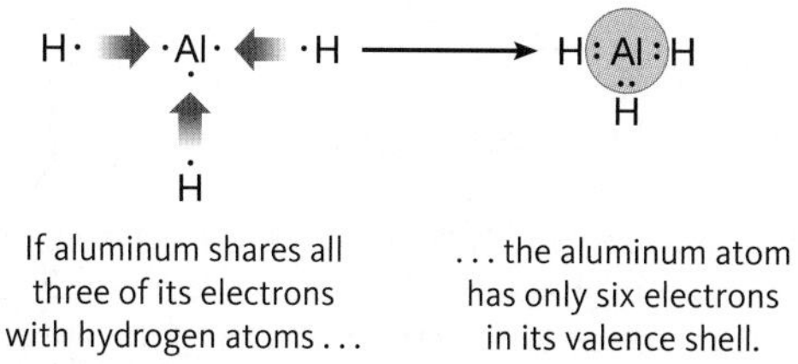

H· → ·Al· ← ·H ⟶ H:Al:H
H (below Al, arrow up) ⟶ H (below Al)

If aluminum shares all three of its electrons with hydrogen atoms . . .

. . . the aluminum atom has only six electrons in its valence shell.

However, elements with three or fewer valence electrons *can* satisfy the octet rule by forming ionic compounds. We will look at ions and ionic compounds later in this chapter.

Let us summarize the key concepts we have encountered about covalent bonds:

- Elements in Groups 4A through 7A can satisfy the octet rule by sharing electrons with one another.
- The number of covalent bonds an atom makes equals the number of empty spaces in the valence shell of the atom. (See Table 3.1.)

A common problem in drawing Lewis structures is deciding which atoms are attached to one another. For instance, how should we arrange the atoms in a molecule of HClO (hypochlorous acid)? This molecule has only three atoms, but we could put any one of those atoms in the middle. Doing so gives us the following three arrangements:

H:Cl:O	H:O:Cl	Cl:H:O
(Cl in the center)	(O in the center)	(H in the center)

Here is a useful guideline: *the atom that forms the most bonds is normally at the center of the molecule*. In this case, oxygen can form two covalent bonds, because it has two spaces in its valence shell. Hydrogen and chlorine, though, have only one space in their valence shells and can form only one bond. Therefore, our best guess is that the oxygen atom is in the middle. This guess turns out to be correct; the Lewis structure of hypochlorous acid is as follows:

H:Ö:C̤l̈:

TABLE 3.1 Covalent Bond Formation in Groups 4A Through 8A

	Group 4A	Group 5A	Group 6A	Group 7A	Group 8A
Number of Valence Electrons	4	5	6	7	8
Number of Empty Spaces in the Valence Shell	4	3	2	1	0
Number of Covalent Bonds Formed	4	3	2	1	0
Example of a Typical Molecule	H H:C:H H **Methane**	H:N:H H **Ammonia**	H:O:H **Water**	H:F: **Hydrogen fluoride**	:Ne: **Neon**

Health Note: Methyl bromide is toxic and contributes to ozone depletion, so its use is being phased out. The United States has reduced its use of methyl bromide to control agricultural pests by over 90% as of 2011.

Many water treatment plants use chloramine to kill bacteria and viruses in tap water. Chloramine remains active longer than chlorine and does not have the unpleasant smell of chlorine. In addition, chloramine has less of a tendency than does chlorine to react with organic compounds to form carcinogenic products.

Sample Problem 3.5

Determining the central atom in a Lewis structure

Strawberry farmers often use methyl bromide to sterilize the soil before planting their crop. Methyl bromide has the chemical formula CH_3Br. Identify the central atom in this molecule, and draw the Lewis structure of methyl bromide.

SOLUTION

Here are the atoms that make up CH_3Br:

·Ċ̣· H· ·B̤̈r:

Carbon has four valence electrons, so it needs four more electrons to satisfy the octet rule. Therefore, the carbon atom should form four covalent bonds. Hydrogen and bromine need only one electron apiece, so they should form only one covalent bond. Since carbon forms the most bonds, **carbon is the central atom.** The other four atoms form covalent bonds to the carbon atom, as follows:

```
       H                          H
       ·                          ¨  ..
  H·  ·C·  ·Br:    ——————>      H:C:Br:
       ·    ..                    ¨  ..
       H                          H
```

TRY IT YOURSELF: *Chloramine has the chemical formula NH_2Cl. This compound is used to kill bacteria in drinking water. Identify the central atom in this molecule, and draw the Lewis structure of chloramine.*

For additional practice, try Core Problems 3.9 and 3.10.

CORE PROBLEMS

All Core Problems are paired and the answers to the blue odd-numbered problems appear in the back of the book.

3.1 Which of the following elements satisfies the octet rule?
a) Br b) Kr c) Ni

3.2 Which of the following elements satisfies the octet rule?
a) Ar b) Fe c) K

3.3 How many covalent bonds does a phosphorus atom normally form, based on the number of valence electrons in the atom?

3.4 How many covalent bonds does a sulfur atom normally form, based on the number of valence electrons in the atom?

3.5 Give an example of an element that normally forms two covalent bonds.

3.6 Give an example of an element that normally forms only one covalent bond.

3.7 Draw Lewis structures for each of the following molecules:
a) HBr b) $SiCl_4$ c) PH_3 d) H_2S

3.8 Draw Lewis structures for each of the following molecules:
a) BrCl b) CI_4 c) SBr_2 d) NCl_3

3.9 In the compound SiH_2BrI, which element is at the center of the molecule? Explain your answer, and draw the Lewis structure of this molecule.

3.10 In the compound HPBrCl, which element is at the center of the molecule? Explain your answer, and draw the Lewis structure of this molecule.

3.2 Double and Triple Bonds

OBJECTIVES: Draw Lewis structures for molecules that contain double or triple bonds, and use lines to represent bonding electrons.

In all of the covalent bonds we have seen so far, two atoms share one pair of electrons. These bonds are called **single bonds**. In some molecules, however, a single bond is not sufficient to satisfy the octet rule. For example, oxygen and nitrogen behave like fluorine in that their atoms pair up to form molecules of O_2 and N_2, respectively. However, both oxygen and nitrogen have more than one empty space in their valence shell, so a singly bonded structure for O_2 or N_2 cannot satisfy the octet rule. For instance, forming a single bond between two oxygen atoms leaves each atom with one empty space in its valence shell.

·Ö· ➡ ⬅ ·Ö· ⟶ ·Ö:Ö·

Each oxygen starts with six valence electrons . . .   . . . and ends up with seven.

Image copyright Kenneth William Caleno, 2010. Used under license from Shutterstock.com

Normal air contains enough oxygen (in the form of O_2) for our needs, but people with breathing difficulties may require supplemental oxygen.

To satisfy the octet rule, the two oxygen atoms share a second pair of electrons. As a result, the two atoms in an O_2 molecule share a total of four electrons, two from each atom. The resulting bond is called a **double bond**. Figure 3.4 shows how we might represent this kind of bonding.

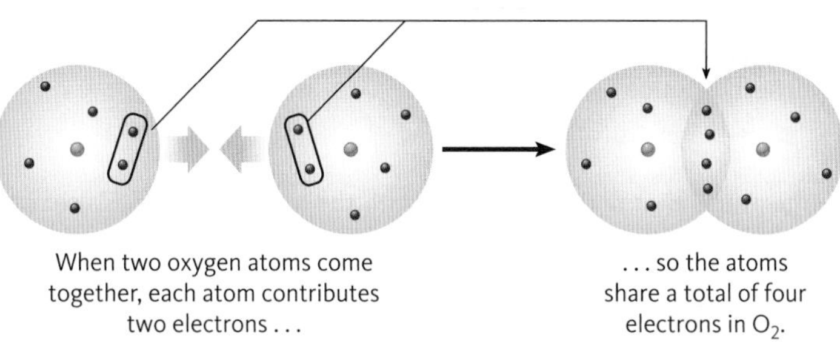

When two oxygen atoms come together, each atom contributes two electrons . . .
. . . so the atoms share a total of four electrons in O2.

FIGURE 3.4 The formation of the double bond in O_2.

In a Lewis structure, the double bond in O_2 is represented using two pairs of dots, as follows. All four of the electrons between the two atoms are shared, so each atom has a total of eight electrons in its valence shell.

Ö::Ö

The Lewis structure of O_2

(This structure uses shading to show the valence shell of each atom.)

Health Note: O_2 is the normal form of oxygen in the atmosphere. Oxygen atoms can also form O_3, called ozone, which can irritate the lungs and accelerate the formation of plaque in arteries. Ozone is toxic, but some cells in our immune system make ozone to help destroy invading microorganisms.

Oxygen atoms normally share two pairs of electrons with other atoms, forming either two single bonds (as in H_2O) or one double bond (as in O_2). It may help you to think of a double bond as two single bonds that connect the same two atoms.

In the N_2 molecule, the nitrogen atoms share six electrons, forming a **triple bond**. In Lewis structures, triple bonds are represented by three pairs of dots between the atoms. Here is the Lewis structure of N_2:

:N:::N:

The Lewis structure of N_2

(This structure uses shading to show the valence shell of each atom.)

We saw earlier that nitrogen (a Group 5A element) normally forms three covalent bonds. In N_2, all three bonding electron pairs are incorporated into the triple bond. We can summarize the three types of covalent bonds as follows:

A *single* bond is the sharing of *two* electrons between a pair of atoms.

A *double* bond is the sharing of *four* electrons between a pair of atoms.

A *triple* bond is the sharing of *six* electrons between a pair of atoms.

In principle, any atom that can form at least two bonds can form a double bond, and any atom that can form at least three bonds can form a triple bond. Double bonds are common in biological molecules, but triple bonds are quite rare. Sample Problem 3.6 shows some examples of molecules that contain double and triple bonds. When you are working out the structures of such molecules, the key is to remember the number of bonds each atom prefers to make.

Health Note: Formaldehyde (H_2CO) is a toxic gas with a pungent aroma. Plywood and particleboard contain adhesives that can release formaldehyde into the air. After the disastrous hurricanes of 2006, the U.S. government supplied mobile homes for displaced residents of the Gulf Coast, but the materials used to build the mobile homes released unhealthy levels of formaldehyde, leading to a variety of health problems.

Sample Problem 3.6

Drawing Lewis structures of molecules that contain double and triple bonds

Draw Lewis structures for the following molecules:

a) H_2CO, formaldehyde
b) HCN, hydrogen cyanide

SOLUTION

a) Here are the atoms that make up H_2CO, with the numbers of bonds that each atom must form:

H· H·

Hydrogen atoms:
Each atom needs one valence electron
Each atom will form one bond

·C· (with dots above and below)

Carbon atom:
Needs four valence electrons
Will form four bonds

·O: (with dots above and below)

Oxygen atom:
Needs two valence electrons
Will form two bonds

The carbon atom forms the largest number of bonds, so we put it at the center of the molecule. However, we only have three other atoms, and carbon must form four bonds. The solution is to draw a double bond between the carbon and oxygen atoms; doing so satisfies the bonding requirements of both elements.

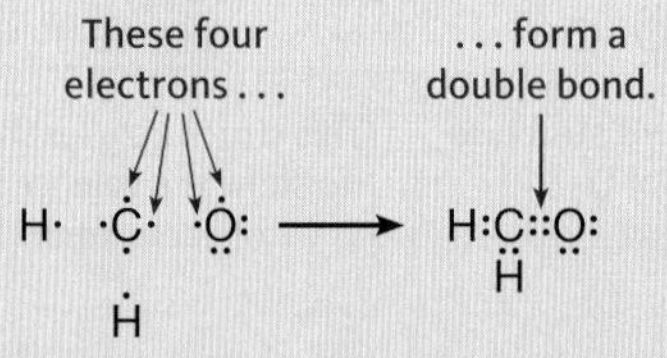

These four electrons . . .

. . . form a double bond.

H· ·C· ·O: → H:C::O:
H (below C)

b) Here are the atoms that make up HCN, with the numbers of bonds that each atom must form:

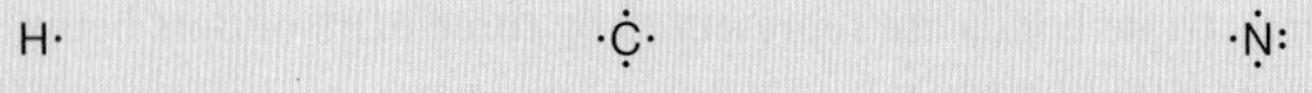

H·

Hydrogen atom:
Needs one valence electron
Forms one bond

·C·

Carbon atom:
Needs four valence electrons
Forms four bonds

·N:

Nitrogen atom:
Needs three valence electrons
Forms three bonds

Again, we expect the carbon atom to be at the center of the molecule, but we do not have four other atoms to attach to carbon. In this case, the solution is to have carbon form a

continued

triple bond to nitrogen. Since nitrogen must form three bonds, the triple bond satisfies the bonding requirements of both nitrogen and carbon.

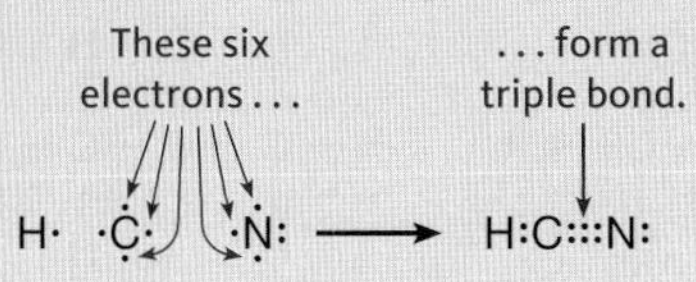

These six electrons . . . ... form a triple bond.

H· ·C: :N: ⟶ H:C:::N:

TRY IT YOURSELF: *Draw the Lewis structure of $CSCl_2$.*

For additional practice, try Core Problems 3.13 through 3.16.

When we draw Lewis structures for large molecules, drawing the dots becomes tedious, and the sheer number of dots makes the structures hard to read. For example, the following molecule, called hexachloroethane, has 50 valence electrons. It is not easy to tell which atoms are bonded to which in this structure. Can you tell?

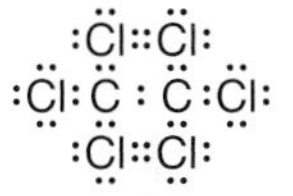

:Cl::Cl:
:Cl:C : C:Cl:
:Cl::Cl:

Hexachloroethane, C_2Cl_6

To make such structures clearer, chemists commonly use lines instead of dots to represent bonding electron pairs. Each bonding electron pair is represented as a line. For example, here are the Lewis structures of F_2, H_2O, O_2, and N_2, using lines to represent the bonding pairs. The dot structures we drew earlier are shown underneath for comparison.

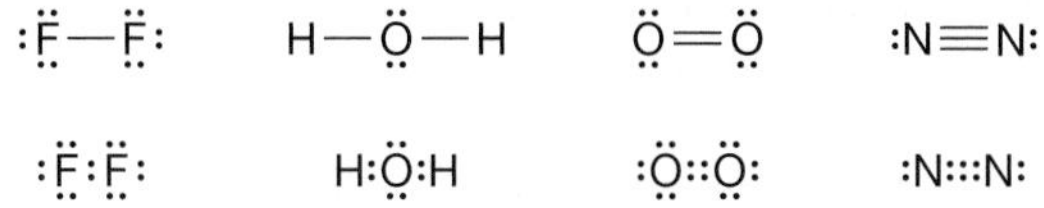

:F—F: H—O—H O=O :N≡N:

:F:F: H:O:H :O::O: :N:::N:

Here is the Lewis structure of hexachloroethane, drawn using lines to represent bonding electron pairs:

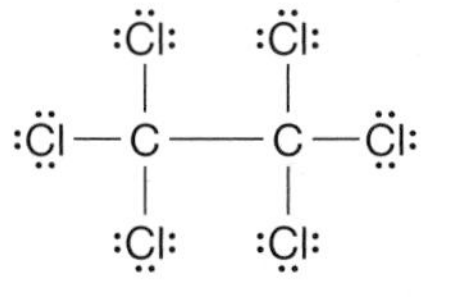

:Cl: :Cl:
:Cl—C——C—Cl:
:Cl: :Cl:

Hexachloroethane, C_2Cl_6

Regardless of how you draw a Lewis structure, be sure to include the nonbonding electron pairs. Lewis structures must clearly show how each atom satisfies the octet rule.

Sample Problem 3.7

Using lines to represent bonding electrons in Lewis structures

Redraw each of the following Lewis structures using lines to represent bonding electron pairs:

H
H:C:Cl:
:Cl:

H :O: H
H:C : C : C:H
H H

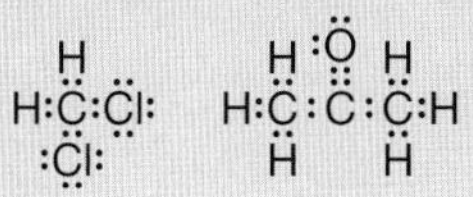

continued

SOLUTION

Replace each of the bonding electron pairs (the dots between atoms) with a line:

```
      H                H  :Ö  H
      |                |  ||  |
  H—C—C̤l:          H—C—C—C—H
      |                |      |
     :C̤l:              H      H
```

TRY IT YOURSELF: *Redraw the following Lewis structure using lines to represent bonding electron pairs:*

```
          Ö:
  H:C:::C:C̈:H
```

For additional practice, try Core Problems 3.17 through 3.20.

Structures with lines are easier to read and interpret for complicated molecules. However, since these structures do not show every electron as a dot, we must check our electron counts in a different way. When we count electrons, a line represents two electrons in the valence shell of each atom that it connects. Here is how we would count the electrons in a simple molecule, ClNO:

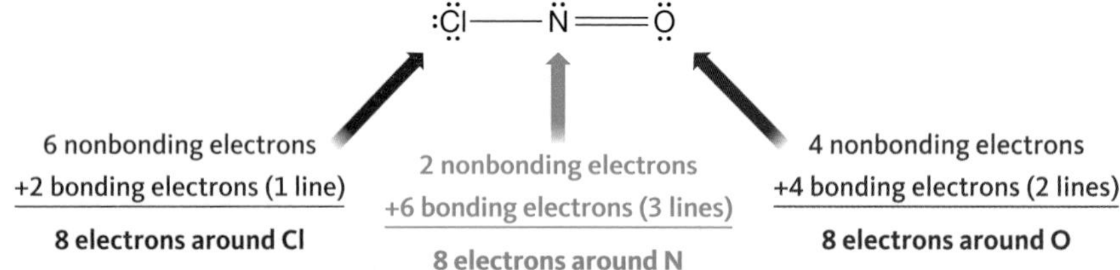

In Section 3.1, we saw that the number of single bonds a nonmetal normally forms is related to the number of electrons in its valence shell. We can extend this reasoning to double and triple bonds by remembering that a double bond is equivalent to two single bonds and a triple bond is equivalent to three single bonds. Table 3.2 shows the most common covalent bonding patterns for electrically neutral atoms.

TABLE 3.2 Bonding Patterns for Electrically Neutral Atoms

Group Number	Normal Number of Covalent Bonds	Possible Bonding Patterns	Examples
4A	4	—X— with single bonds above and below (four single bonds)	CH_4: H—C—H with H above and below
		=X— with single bond below	Ö=C—H with H below
		≡X—	:N≡C—H
5A	3	—Ẍ— with single bond below	H—N̈—H with H below
		=Ẍ—	Ö=N̈—H
		≡X:	:N≡N:
6A	2	—Ẍ— (two lone pairs)	H—Ö—H
		=Ẍ (two lone pairs)	Ö=Ö
7A	1	—Ẍ: (three lone pairs)	:F̤—F̤:

The guidelines we have developed so far are very useful for predicting structures of molecules. However, they are not infallible. A significant number of compounds contain atoms that do not make the expected numbers of bonds. An example is nitric acid (HNO_3), a very corrosive chemical that is used extensively in chemical manufacturing. In this molecule, the nitrogen atom makes four bonds rather than its normal three, and one of the oxygen atoms makes one bond rather than two. However, all of the atoms in this molecule satisfy the octet rule.

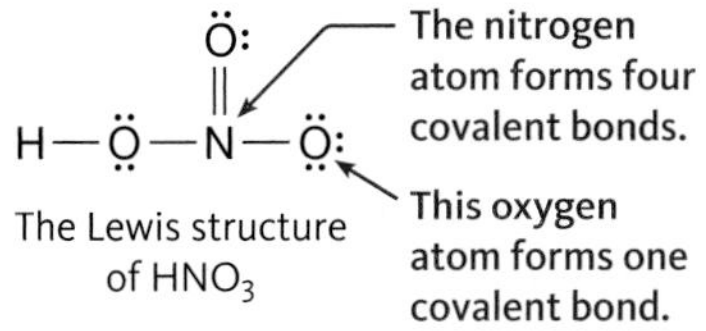

```
        Ö:
        ‖
H—Ö—N—Ö:
```

The nitrogen atom forms four covalent bonds.

This oxygen atom forms one covalent bond.

The Lewis structure of HNO_3

Nonmetals in the third period and beyond can make compounds that violate the octet rule. A particularly important example is phosphoric acid (H_3PO_4), an ingredient in many soft drinks and an important material for fertilizer manufacturers. The phosphorus atom in this molecule has ten electrons (five bonding pairs) in its valence shell. Many vital compounds in the human body contain portions that are similar to phosphoric acid.

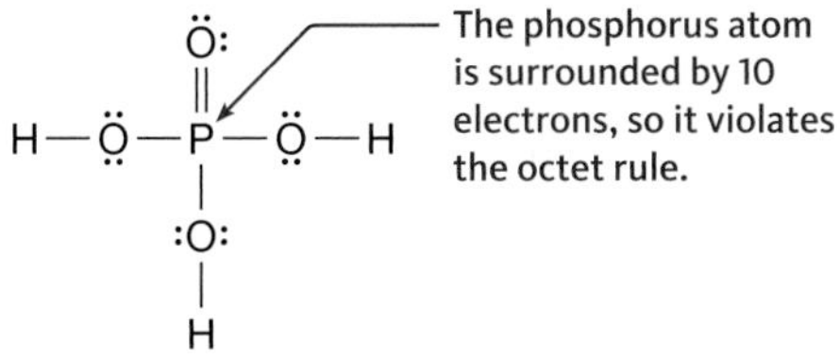

```
        Ö:
        ‖
H—Ö—P—Ö—H
        |
       :O:
        |
        H
```

The phosphorus atom is surrounded by 10 electrons, so it violates the octet rule.

Health Note: Phosphorus is a required nutrient, but pure phosphorus is poisonous. All of the phosphorus in our diet comes from compounds closely related to phosphoric acid.

In this textbook, you will not be asked to draw structures of molecules that violate the octet rule, but you should be aware that such molecules exist.

CORE PROBLEMS

3.11 Which of the following elements cannot form double bonds? Explain your reasoning.
a) C b) N c) O d) F

3.12 Which of the following elements cannot form triple bonds? Explain your reasoning.
a) C b) N c) O d) F

3.13 Nitrosyl bromide contains one bromine atom, one oxygen atom, and one nitrogen atom, linked by covalent bonds. Which of the following arrangements would you expect for these three atoms? Explain your reasoning.
a) Br–O–N b) N–Br–O c) O–N–Br

3.14 Cyanogen bromide contains one bromine atom, one carbon atom, and one nitrogen atom, linked by covalent bonds. Which of the following arrangement would you expect for these three atoms? Explain your reasoning.
a) Br–C–N b) Br–N–C c) C–Br–N

3.15 Draw Lewis structures for each of the following molecules. Each molecule contains one double or triple bond.
a) $ClNO$
b) CF_2O
c) C_2H_2 (The two carbon atoms are bonded to each other, and each carbon atom is bonded to one hydrogen atom.)

3.16 Draw Lewis structures for each of the following molecules. Each molecule contains one double or triple bond.
a) $ClCN$
b) N_2H_2 (The two nitrogen atoms are bonded to each other, and each nitrogen atom is bonded to one hydrogen atom.)
c) $CSCl_2$

3.17 Redraw each of the following structures, using lines to represent bonding electron pairs:

```
      :C̈l:              H H
a) :C̈l:P̈:C̈l:     b) H:C̈:C̈::Ö
                         H
```

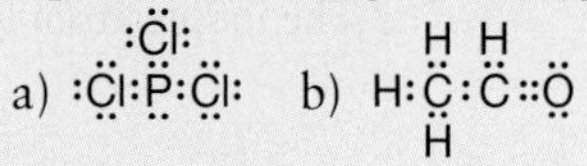

3.18 Redraw each of the following structures, using lines to represent bonding electron pairs:

```
         H                  H
a) :B̈r:C̈:H     b) :N:::C:C̈:H
         H                  H
```

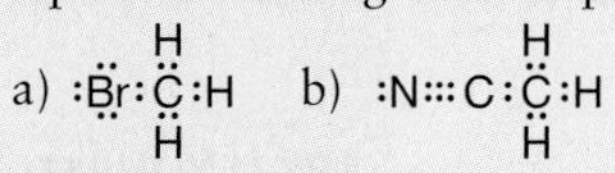

3.19 Draw the structures of each of the following molecules, using lines to represent bonding electron pairs:
a) NH_3 b) SiF_4 c) CH_2O

3.20 Draw the structures of each of the following molecules, using lines to represent bonding electron pairs:
a) CH_4 b) PCl_3 c) HCN

OBJECTIVES: *Use electronegativities to predict whether a covalent bond is polar or nonpolar, and determine the type of charge on each bonding atom.*

3.3 Electronegativity and Polar Bonds

When chemists examine the properties of molecules that contain two different atoms, they find that, in most cases, the atoms are electrically charged. For example, in a molecule of HF, the hydrogen atom is positively charged and the fluorine atom is negatively charged. Since the original H and F atoms were electrically neutral, these charges must be connected to the formation of the covalent bond. Let us examine how atoms become charged in covalently bonded molecules.

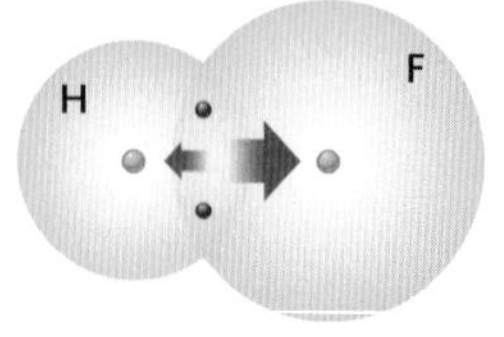

When hydrogen and fluorine share electrons, fluorine attracts the bonding pair more strongly than hydrogen does . . .

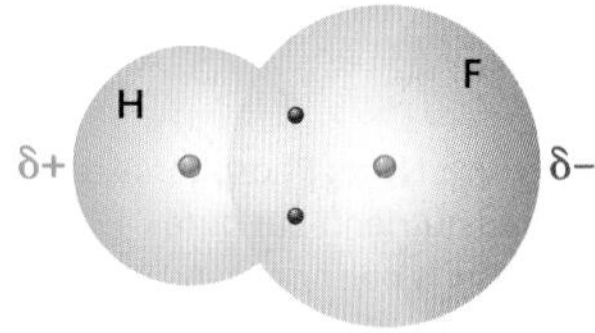

. . . so the bonding pair moves toward the fluorine atom, making F slightly negative and H slightly positive. HF has a **polar covalent bond.**

FIGURE 3.5 Formation of a polar covalent bond.

Atoms of Different Elements Form a Polar Covalent Bond

Atoms of different elements vary in their ability to attract electrons. For example, fluorine atoms have a very powerful attraction for electrons. They hold their own electrons very tightly, and they have a strong tendency to pull electrons away from other atoms. Hydrogen, by contrast, has a much weaker attraction for electrons. When a hydrogen atom and a fluorine atom share a pair of electrons, this unequal attraction for electrons produces an unequal sharing of the electron pair. The two bonding electrons are pulled closer to the fluorine nucleus and away from the hydrogen nucleus, giving the fluorine atom a negative charge. The hydrogen atom, left without its equal share of the bonding electrons, becomes positively charged. A covalent bond in which the bonding electrons are not shared equally is called a **polar covalent bond.** Chemists use the symbol δ (the Greek letter *delta*) to represent the small electrical charges in a polar covalent bond, as shown in Figure 3.5.

Two Identical Atoms Form a Nonpolar Covalent Bond

What happens when two atoms that have an equal attraction for electrons form a covalent bond? In this case, the bonding electrons effectively remain centered between the atoms. The result is a **nonpolar covalent bond,** in which neither atom has an electrical charge. For example, in an F_2 molecule, the two fluorine atoms are identical, so they pull equally strongly on the bonding electron pair. Figure 3.6 shows the nonpolar covalent bond in F_2.

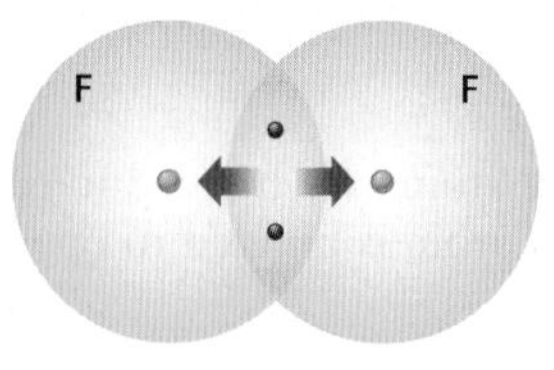

In F_2, each atom attracts the electrons equally, so neither atom is charged. F_2 has a **nonpolar covalent bond.**

FIGURE 3.6 Formation of a nonpolar covalent bond.

Sample Problem 3.8

Relating charge to an element's attraction for electrons

Chlorine has a stronger attraction for electrons than does iodine. What are the electrical charges on each atom in a molecule that has chlorine bonded to iodine?

SOLUTION

The chlorine atom pulls the bonding electrons toward itself and away from the iodine. Since electrons are negatively charged, the chlorine atom becomes negatively charged. The iodine atom loses electrons and becomes positively charged.

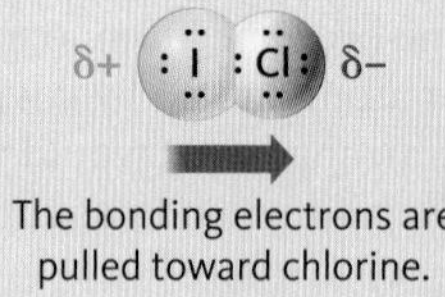

The bonding electrons are pulled toward chlorine.

TRY IT YOURSELF: *In BrCl, the bromine atom is positively charged and the chlorine atom is negatively charged. Which of the two elements in this compound has the stronger attraction for electrons?*

Electronegativity Measures the Attraction of an Element for Electrons

To tell whether a covalent bond between two atoms is polar or nonpolar, we need to know how strongly each atom attracts electrons. The attraction of an element for electrons is called the **electronegativity** of the element. A high electronegativity means that

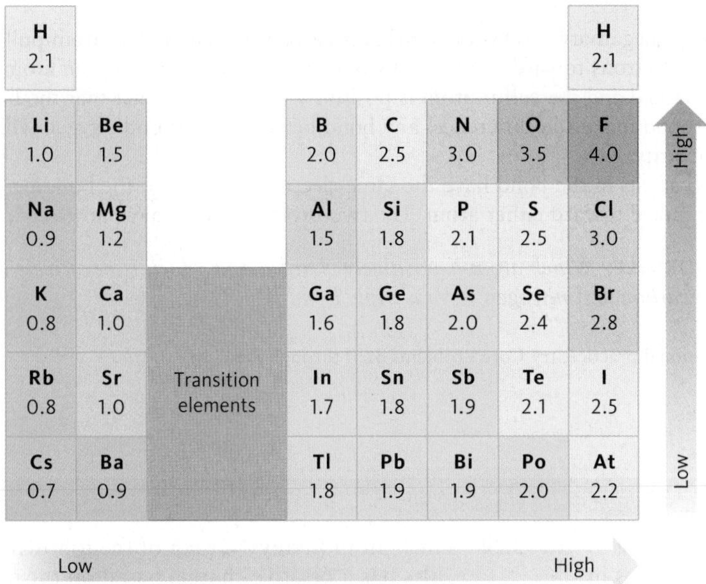

H 2.1							H 2.1
Li 1.0	Be 1.5		B 2.0	C 2.5	N 3.0	O 3.5	F 4.0
Na 0.9	Mg 1.2		Al 1.5	Si 1.8	P 2.1	S 2.5	Cl 3.0
K 0.8	Ca 1.0	Transition elements	Ga 1.6	Ge 1.8	As 2.0	Se 2.4	Br 2.8
Rb 0.8	Sr 1.0		In 1.7	Sn 1.8	Sb 1.9	Te 2.1	I 2.5
Cs 0.7	Ba 0.9		Tl 1.8	Pb 1.9	Bi 1.9	Po 2.0	At 2.2

FIGURE 3.7 Electronegativity values for some elements.

the element has a strong attraction for electrons, while a low electronegativity corresponds to a weak attraction. Figure 3.7 shows the electronegativities of the representative elements. The Group 8A elements are omitted because they form very few compounds and are normally found only as elements.

If we examine the table, we can see two trends:

1. *Electronegativities increase from left to right.* The Group 1A elements have the weakest attraction for electrons, and the Group 7A elements have the strongest.
2. *Electronegativities increase from bottom to top.* For instance, in Group 7A the electronegativities increase from 2.2 for astatine (At) to 4.0 for fluorine (F).

Note that the electronegativity of hydrogen lies in the middle of the range, further reinforcing our notion that hydrogen does not fit comfortably into either Group 1A or Group 7A.

When two atoms form a covalent bond, *the atom with the higher electronegativity is negatively charged, and the atom with the lower electronegativity is positively charged.* For example, the electronegativity of fluorine is 4.0, while that of hydrogen is 2.1. These numbers tell us that fluorine attracts electrons more strongly than hydrogen does. We can conclude that the covalent bond in HF is polar, with a negatively charged fluorine atom and a positively charged hydrogen atom, as we saw earlier.

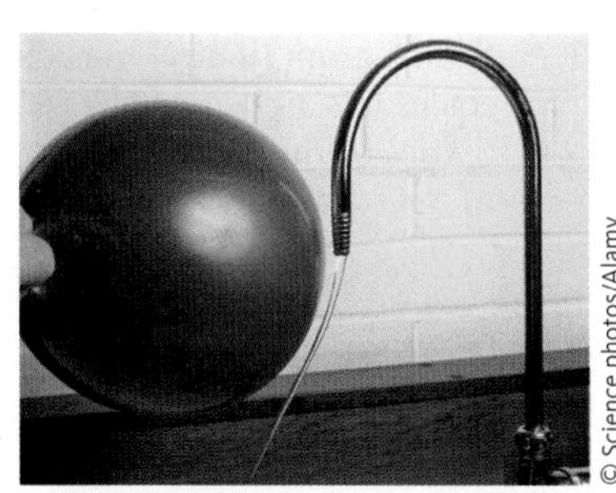

The balloon in this photo has been given an electrical charge. Water is polar and is attracted to the balloon.

Sample Problem **3.9**

Using electronegativity to predict charges in a polar covalent bond

Which atom will be positively charged and which will be negatively charged (if any) in each of the following bonds?

a) C−Cl
b) S=O
c) Br−Br

SOLUTION

a) The electronegativity of Cl is higher than that of C, so the chlorine atom pulls the bonding electrons toward itself and away from the carbon. The chlorine atom is negatively charged and the carbon atom is positively charged.

continued

b) The electronegativity of O is higher than that of S, so the oxygen atom pulls the bonding electrons toward itself and away from the sulfur. The oxygen atom is negatively charged and the sulfur atom is positively charged. The fact that the bond is a double bond makes no difference; any bond between sulfur and oxygen will have the same polarity.

c) The two atoms in the bond have the same electronegativity, so the bonding electrons are not pulled toward either atom. The two bromine atoms have no electrical charge.

TRY IT YOURSELF: *Which atom is positively charged and which is negatively charged (if any) when carbon and nitrogen form a triple bond (C≡N)?*

For additional practice, try Core Problems 3.23 through 3.26.

CORE PROBLEMS

3.21 Which of the Group 5A elements has the strongest attraction for electrons? Use the electronegativities in Figure 3.7 to answer this question.

3.22 Which of the Group 7A elements has the weakest attraction for electrons? Use the electronegativities in Figure 3.7 to answer this question.

3.23 Which atom (if any) in each of the following molecules has a positive charge, based on the electronegativities of the elements?
a) NO b) HCl c) N_2

3.24 Which atom (if any) in each of the following molecules has a positive charge, based on the electronegativities of the elements?
a) IBr b) Cl_2 c) HF

3.25 In each of the following chemical bonds, identify the positively charged atom:
a) Br—C b) N═O c) H—H

3.26 In each of the following chemical bonds, identify the negatively charged atom:
a) N═C b) C≡C c) S—F

OBJECTIVES: *Write names for binary covalent compounds.*

3.4 Naming Covalent Compounds

There are millions of known compounds, and more are being discovered all the time. The majority of these compounds have an effect on humans. Sometimes the effect is beneficial, in which case the compound may have value as a nutrient or a medication. In other cases, the effect is harmful. Either way, information about these compounds must be readily available to health care professionals. It is essential that every substance have a name that is universally agreed upon, so that the compound can be located in appropriate reference sources. In this section, we will examine how covalent compounds are named.

Covalent Compounds Are Named Using Systematic Rules

The rules for naming chemical compounds were developed by the International Union of Pure and Applied Chemistry (IUPAC), and are usually called the IUPAC rules. The IUPAC rules allow chemists to name any compound that contains atoms linked by covalent bonds, but we will confine ourselves to the names of **binary compounds**, compounds that contain two elements:

1. *Write the name of the element that has the lower electronegativity first.* (This will be the first element in the chemical formula, so you do not need to look up electronegativities if you know the formula.)
2. *Write the name of the other element, using modified names that end with the suffix -ide.* Table 3.3 lists the modified names for the most common nonmetals.
3. *Add prefixes to tell how many atoms of each element are present.* Table 3.4 lists the standard prefixes for one through six atoms.

TABLE 3.3 Modified Names for Nonmetals in Covalent Compounds

Symbol	Name	Modified Name
N	Nitrogen	Nitride
O	Oxygen	Oxide
F	Fluorine	Fluoride
S	Sulfur	Sulfide
Cl	Chlorine	Chloride
Br	Bromine	Bromide
I	Iodine	Iodide

TABLE 3.4 Prefixes for Numbers of Atoms in a Covalent Compound

Number of Atoms	Prefix	Example
One	Mono (only used for the second element, and shortened to *mon* before oxide)	Iodine **mono**bromide (IBr) Carbon **mon**oxide (CO)
Two	Di	Carbon **di**sulfide (CS_2)
Three	Tri	Sulfur **tri**oxide (SO_3)
Four	Tetra (shortened to *tetr* before oxide)	Silicon **tetra**iodide (SiI_4)
Five	Penta (shortened to *pent* before oxide)	Phosphorus **penta**chloride (PCl_5)
Six	Hexa (shortened to *hex* before oxide)	Sulfur **hexa**fluoride (SF_6)

Sample Problem 3.10

Using the IUPAC rules to name covalent compounds

Name the following compounds, using the IUPAC rules:
a) SO_3
b) N_2O_5

SOLUTION

a) sulfur trioxide
b) dinitrogen pentoxide

TRY IT YOURSELF: *Name the following compounds, using the IUPAC rules:*
a) PF_5 *b)* S_2Cl_2

For additional practice, try Core Problems 3.27 and 3.28.

• IUPAC is often pronounced *eye-you-pack.*

Sample Problem 3.11

Writing the formula of a covalent compound

Chlorine dioxide is used to remove the brown tint from paper. What is its chemical formula?

SOLUTION

The name tells us that this compound contains one atom of chlorine and two atoms of oxygen, so its formula is ClO_2.

TRY IT YOURSELF: *Sulfur hexafluoride is used as an insulator in electrical transformers. What is its chemical formula?*

For additional practice, try Core Problems 3.29 and 3.30.

Many Covalent Compounds Have Special Names

In practice, the IUPAC rules for naming binary covalent compounds are rarely used in biological and medical applications. Some of the most common covalent compounds have traditional names that are used instead of the systematic IUPAC names. For example, H_2O is commonly called water, not dihydrogen monoxide. (Imagine what would happen if you went into a restaurant and asked for a glass of dihydrogen monoxide!) Table 3.5 lists the traditional names for four common compounds.

Health Note: Most binary covalent compounds are toxic. The obvious exception is water, the most abundant compound in living organisms.

TABLE 3.5 Special Names for Common Covalent Compounds

Compound	Common Name	Comments
H_2O	Water	No other name is accepted for this compound.
NH_3	Ammonia	No other name is accepted for this compound.
N_2O	Nitrous oxide	*Dinitrogen oxide* and *dinitrogen monoxide* are allowed, but these names are not generally used.
NO	Nitric oxide	*Nitrogen oxide* and *nitrogen monoxide* are allowed, but these names are not generally used.

In general, compounds containing hydrogen and one other element are not named using these rules. Some hydrogen compounds are named as if they were made from ions, using the rules for ionic compounds that you will learn in Section 3.7. Other hydrogen-containing compounds are acids and have special names that you will learn in Chapter 7.

Most of the covalent compounds you will encounter in medical applications contain carbon and are classified as organic molecules. IUPAC uses an entirely different set of naming rules for organic compounds. For example, C_2H_6 is called ethane, obeying the IUPAC rules for organic compounds, rather than dicarbon hexahydride. You will learn how to name organic molecules in Chapters 8 through 11.

CORE PROBLEMS

3.27 Name the following compounds, using the IUPAC rules:
a) ClF_3 b) N_2F_4 c) CO

3.28 Name the following compounds, using the IUPAC rules:
a) PBr_3 b) SF_6 c) CCl_4

3.29 Write chemical formulas for the following compounds:
a) carbon tetrafluoride b) sulfur dioxide

3.30 Write chemical formulas for the following compounds:
a) sulfur trioxide b) dichlorine monoxide

3.31 Give the common names for the following compounds:
a) H_2O b) NO

3.32 Give the common names for the following compounds:
a) NH_3 b) N_2O

OBJECTIVES: *Predict ion charges for representative elements, and use Lewis structures to show how atoms gain and lose electrons to form an ionic compound.*

3.5 Ions and Ionic Compounds

For compounds that contain a metallic element, it is not possible to draw a structure that satisfies the octet rule. Perhaps the most familiar compound of this type is table salt, which has the chemical formula NaCl. Let us try to draw a Lewis structure for this compound. Sodium is in Group 1A and chlorine is in Group 7A, so they have one and seven valence electrons, respectively. If we draw a structure that has a covalent bond between sodium and chlorine, the chlorine atom satisfies the octet rule but the sodium atom does not.

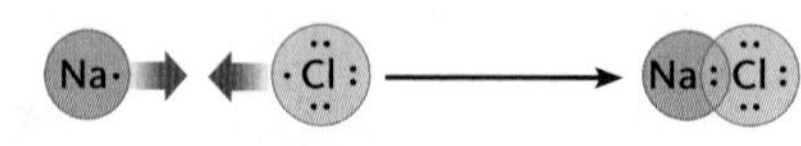

If sodium and chlorine form a covalent bond . . .

. . . the sodium atom has only two electrons in its valence shell.

Health Note: NaCl is our main dietary source of the essential elements sodium and chlorine. Sea salt (salt that is made by evaporating ocean water) also contains magnesium, calcium, and potassium. Standard table salt comes from salt mines and is refined to be almost pure NaCl.

In general, elements that have fewer than four valence electrons cannot satisfy the octet rule by forming covalent bonds, because they need too many electrons. Instead, *atoms with fewer than four valence electrons satisfy the octet rule by losing electrons to form ions.* These electrons are absorbed by other atoms that have empty spaces in their valence shells, allowing all of the atoms to reach eight valence electrons.

Atoms Can Satisfy the Octet Rule by Losing or Gaining an Electron

To see how sodium can satisfy the octet rule, let us look at the complete electron arrangement of sodium. Sodium is atomic number 11, so it has a total of 11 electrons. These electrons are distributed as follows.

shell 1: 2 electrons shell 2: 8 electrons shell 3: 1 electron

If we remove the single electron from shell 3, we produce the following arrangement.

shell 1: 2 electrons shell 2: 8 electrons

The third shell is now unoccupied, so shell 2 becomes the outermost occupied shell. Since this shell contains eight electrons, the sodium atom now satisfies the octet rule. Note that the octet rule does not specify which level the electrons must be in; it simply says that the outermost occupied shell must have eight electrons. Figure 3.8 illustrates how sodium can lose an electron to satisfy the octet rule.

As we saw in Chapter 2, atoms normally have equal numbers of protons and electrons. When we remove electrons from an atom, the atom becomes a cation (a positively charged ion), because the atom now has fewer electrons than protons. In this case, removing one electron from a sodium atom gives the atom a +1 charge, as shown here. The sodium atom becomes a sodium ion.

$$Na\cdot \xrightarrow{\text{Remove the valence electron}} Na^+$$

A sodium **atom**: Na	A sodium **ion**: Na^+
11 protons: charge = +11	11 protons: charge = +11 ← The number of protons always matches the atomic number, even when the atom becomes an ion.
11 electrons: charge = −11	10 electrons: charge = −10
Total charge = 0	Total charge = +1

Health Note: All of the sodium you consume is in the form of sodium ions. Pure sodium (which contains sodium atoms) reacts violently with water, forming caustic NaOH.

The electron that is removed from sodium must move to some other atom, because electrons cannot simply disappear. When sodium combines with chlorine, the electron moves from sodium to chlorine. Chlorine has seven valence electrons, so this additional electron fills the single empty space in the valence shell of chlorine, as shown in Figure 3.9.

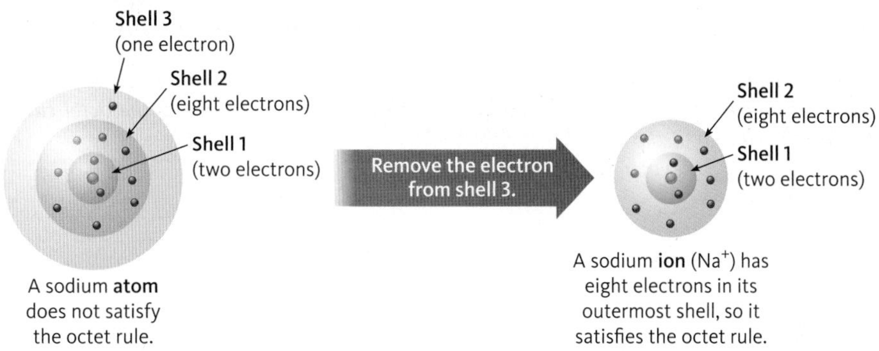

FIGURE 3.8 Sodium can satisfy the octet rule by losing an electron.

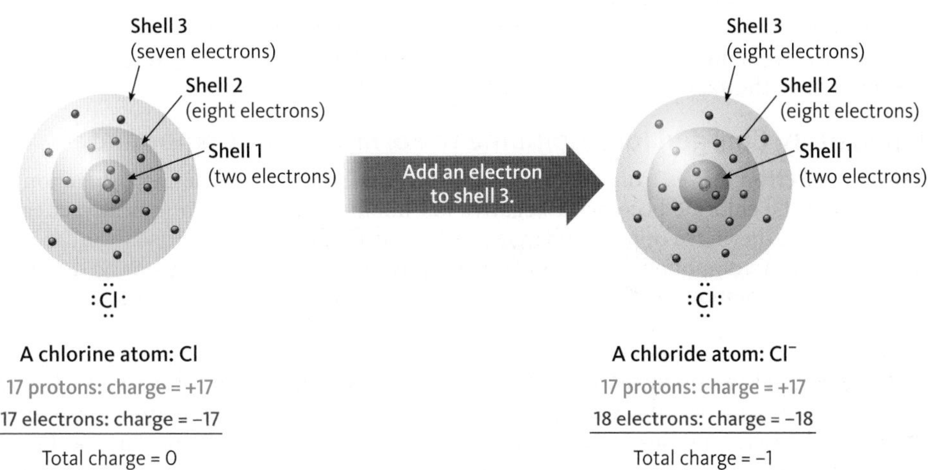

FIGURE 3.9 Chlorine can satisfy the octet rule by gaining an electron.

Health Note: Cl (the electrically neutral element) is poisonous to all living organisms, while chloride, Cl^- (the ionized form of chlorine) is an essential nutrient for all forms of life.

When we add electrons to an atom, we make an anion (a negatively charged ion). We have added one electron to the chlorine atom, so we have made an ion with a −1 charge. Anions are named by changing the ending of the element name to *ide*, so the ion is called a *chloride ion*.

Atoms can lose or gain more than one electron. In general, when an atom forms an ion, it loses or gains enough electrons to satisfy the octet rule. A helpful guideline is that *atoms with one, two, or three valence electrons can satisfy the octet rule by losing all of their valence electrons*, because these atoms always have eight electrons in the next shell below the valence shell.

Sample Problem **3.12**

Using Lewis structures to show the formation of an ion

The electron arrangement of calcium is shown here. Use the electron arrangement to show how calcium can form an ion that satisfies the octet rule, and write the ion charge.

shell 1: 2 electrons   shell 2: 8 electrons   shell 3: 8 electrons
shell 4: 2 electrons

SOLUTION

Calcium has two electrons in its valence shell, so we expect it to lose these electrons. When the calcium atom loses the electrons in shell 4, it is left with the following electron arrangement.

shell 1: 2 electrons   shell 2: 8 electrons   shell 3: 8 electrons

The outermost shell is now shell 3. Because this shell has eight electrons in it, the calcium atom now satisfies the octet rule.

To determine the ion charge, we can compare the numbers of protons and electrons in the ion. The atomic number of calcium is 20, so the calcium atom has 20 protons. However, it has lost two electrons, leaving it with 18 electrons. Protons are positively charged, so the two extra protons give the atom a +2 charge. We write the symbol for this ion Ca^{2+}.

TRY IT YOURSELF: *The electron arrangement of selenium (Se) is shown here. Use the electron arrangement to show how selenium can form an ion that satisfies the octet rule, and write the charge of the ion.*

shell 1: 2 electrons   shell 2: 8 electrons   shell 3: 18 electrons
shell 4: 6 electrons

For additional practice, try Core Problems 3.33 and 3.34.

When we write the symbol for an ion, we must include the ion charge. For an ion that has a +1 or −1 charge, we simply write the sign, so the symbols for sodium and chloride ions are written Na^+ and Cl^-, respectively. For ions with higher charges, we must specify the number. We write the number before the sign, so the ions formed by magnesium and selenium have the symbols Mg^{2+} and Se^{2-}, respectively.

Oppositely Charged Ions Combine to Form an Ionic Compound

When an electron moves from sodium to chlorine, the sodium becomes a positive ion (a cation) and the chlorine becomes a negative ion (an anion). These two ions attract each other, because they have opposite charges, and the attraction binds the ions together into a compound. A compound that is made from positively and negatively charged ions is called an **ionic compound**. When we write the formula of an ionic compound, we list the cation first, followed by the anion, so the formula of table salt is written NaCl. The formula of an ionic compound does not include the charges on the individual ions.

We can represent the formation of NaCl using Lewis structures, as shown in Figure 3.10. First, an electron moves from sodium to chlorine, converting the atoms into ions, and then the two ions then come together to form a compound. Note that the Lewis structure of the sodium ion is written with no dots (instead of eight) to show that the atom has lost its original valence electron.

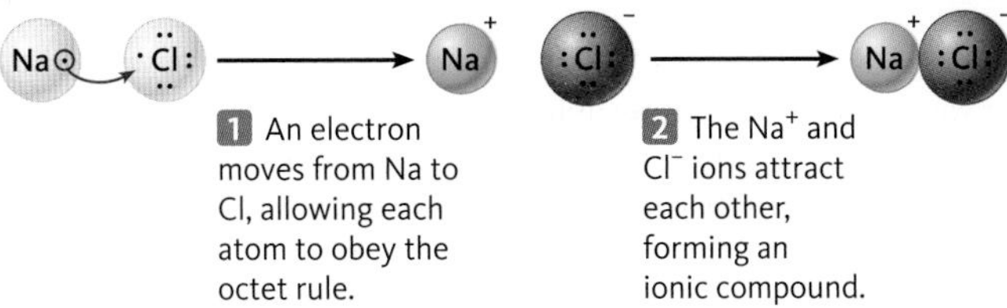

Na
Cl
Na
Cl
Na
Cl
1 An electron moves from Na to Cl, allowing each atom to obey the octet rule.
2 The Na⁺ and Cl⁻ ions attract each other, forming an ionic compound.

FIGURE 3.10 The formation of NaCl.

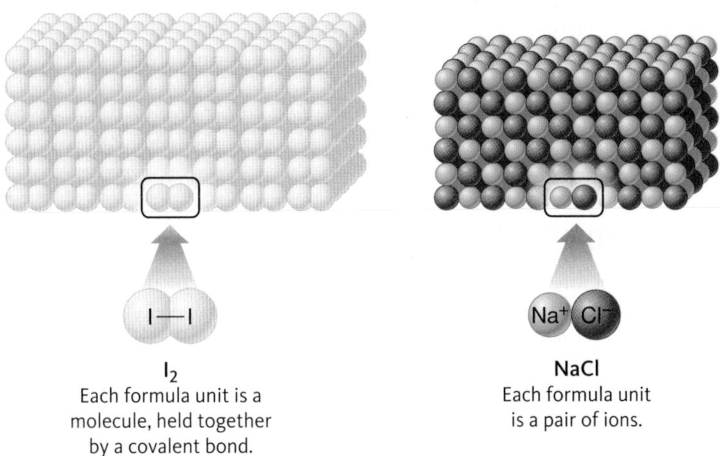

Each formula unit is a pair of ions.

FIGURE 3.11 The difference between a molecular substance and an ionic substance.

The attraction between the Na^+ and the Cl^- (or any other pair of oppositely charged ions) is often called an **ionic bond**, but this "bond" is fundamentally different from the covalent bonds that we encountered in the first part of this chapter. It is important to recognize that *no electrons are shared in NaCl,* so there is no true chemical bond between Na and Cl. In addition, the NaCl unit is not a molecule, because it is not held together by a covalent bond. Figure 3.11 shows the difference between I_2 (a covalently bonded molecule) and NaCl.

Magnesium can combine with oxygen to form an ionic compound. As was the case with NaCl, the two elements lose or gain just enough electrons to form ions that satisfy the octet rule. The magnesium atom has two valence electrons, and it can satisfy the octet rule if it loses both of these electrons to form a cation with a +2 charge. The oxygen atom has six valence electrons, so it can satisfy the octet rule if it gains two more electrons, forming an anion with a −2 charge. As a result, the two valence electrons in the magnesium atom move to the oxygen atom, forming Mg^{2+} and O^{2-} ions.

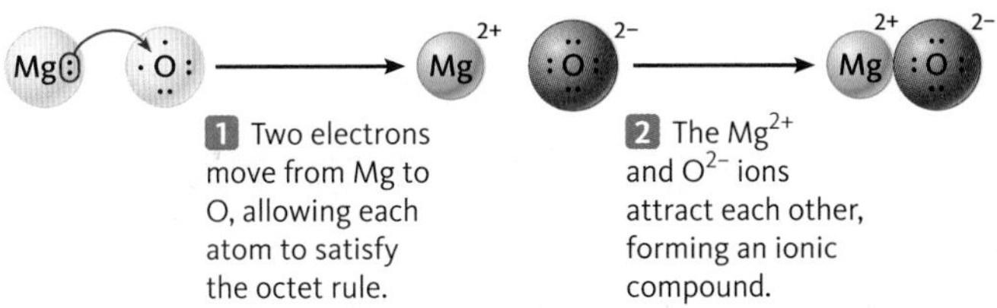

Mg
O
Mg
O
Mg
O
1 Two electrons move from Mg to O, allowing each atom to satisfy the octet rule.
2 The Mg²⁺ and O²⁻ ions attract each other, forming an ionic compound.

The two ions then come together to form an ionic compound with the chemical formula MgO. Remember that we always list the positive ion first, and we do not include the ion charges in the chemical formula of the compound.

Charles D. Winters

Charles D. Winters

(a) Iodine is a molecular substance. (b) Sodium chloride is an ionic substance.

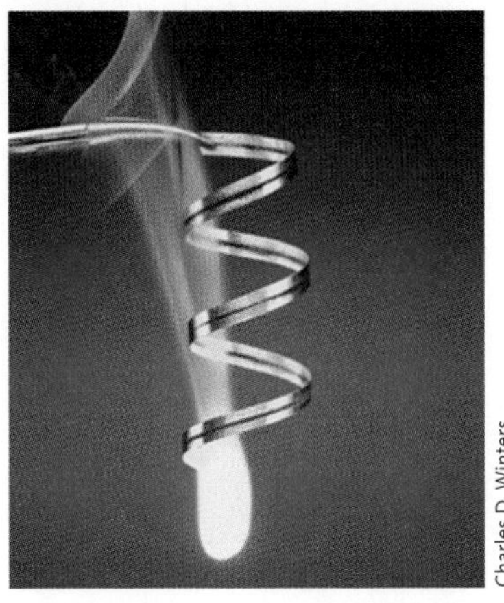

Charles D. Winters

Magnesium combines with oxygen to form a compound, MgO. The reaction produces a brilliant white glow and is sometimes used in fireworks and flares.

Sample Problem 3.13

Using Lewis structures to show the formation of an ionic compound

Show how a nitrogen atom and an aluminum atom can satisfy the octet rule by forming an ionic compound.

continued

SOLUTION

Aluminum has three valence electrons, while nitrogen has five. Aluminum can satisfy the octet rule by losing its three outermost electrons, and nitrogen can satisfy the octet rule by gaining three electrons. Therefore, three electrons move from aluminum to nitrogen.

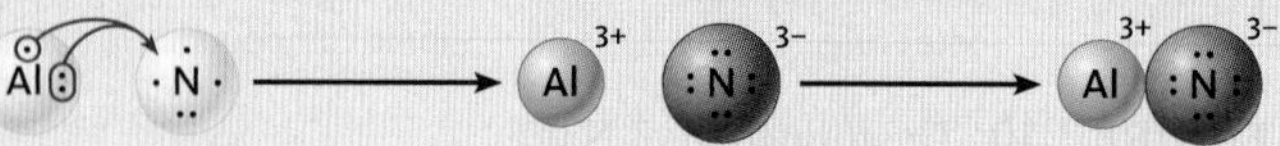

Nitrogen has gained three electrons, so the nitrogen atom becomes an anion, N^{3-}. Aluminum has lost three electrons, so it becomes a cation, Al^{3+}. Once these two ions form, they attract each other and form a compound, which has the formula AlN.

TRY IT YOURSELF: *Show how a calcium atom and a sulfur atom can satisfy the octet rule by forming an ionic compound.*

Ion Charges Can Be Predicted Using the Periodic Table

Elements form ions for the same reason that they form covalent bonds: to satisfy the octet rule. We can predict the ion charges of most of the representative elements by their positions in the periodic table. Elements with one, two, or three valence electrons lose these electrons, since there are always eight electrons in the next lower shell. Elements with five, six, or seven valence electrons gain electrons to reach an octet. Table 3.6 summarizes this behavior.

TABLE 3.6 Normal Ion Charges for the Representative Elements

Group number	1A	2A	3A	4A	5A	6A	7A
Number of valence electrons	1	2	3	4	5	6	7
How the elements form ions	Lose 1 electron	Lose 2 electrons	Lose 3 electrons	*(Only Sn and Pb form ions: Group 4A elements prefer to form covalent bonds)*	Gain 3 electrons	Gain 2 electrons	Gain 1 electron
Normal ion charge	+1	+2	+3		−3	−2	−1
Example	Na^+ (sodium ion)	Mg^{2+} (magnesium ion)	Al^{3+} (aluminum ion)		N^{3-} (nitride ion)	O^{2-} (oxide ion)	F^- (fluoride ion)

Sample Problem 3.14

Predicting the charge on an ion

Rubidium (Rb) can form an ion. What is the charge on a rubidium ion? What is the symbol for this ion?

SOLUTION

Rb is in Group 1A, so it has one valence electron. The rubidium atom loses this electron to form an ion with a +1 charge. The symbol for this ion is Rb^+.

TRY IT YOURSELF: *Selenium (Se) can form an ion. What is the charge on this ion? What is the symbol for this ion?*

For additional practice, try Core Problems 3.37 through 3.42.

The Ion Charge Does Not Depend on the Other Element in a Compound

When two elements form an ionic compound, the number of electrons gained or lost by each element does not depend on the number of electrons that the other element loses or gains. For instance, let us examine what happens when magnesium and chlorine form a compound. Magnesium has two valence electrons, which it must lose to satisfy the octet rule. However, chlorine has seven valence electrons, so a chlorine atom has room for only one electron in its valence shell. A second chlorine atom must absorb the other electron from magnesium. As a result, when Mg and Cl form a compound, *each magnesium atom must combine with two chlorine atoms*. The magnesium atom loses two electrons and becomes a Mg^{2+} ion.

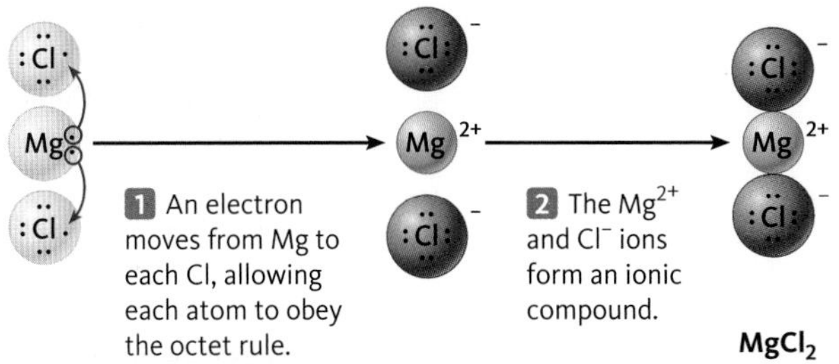
:Cl·
Mg
:Cl·
1 An electron moves from Mg to each Cl, allowing each atom to obey the octet rule.
:Cl: -
Mg 2+
:Cl: -
2 The Mg2+ and Cl⁻ ions form an ionic compound.
MgCl2

FIGURE 3.12 The formation of $MgCl_2$.

	A magnesium atom	Remove two electrons →	A magnesium ion
Remember that the number of protons always equals the atomic number. →	12 protons: charge = +12		12 protons: charge = +12
	12 electrons: charge = −12		10 electrons: charge = −10
	Total charge = 0		Total charge = +2

Each chlorine atom gains an electron and becomes a Cl^- ion.

A chlorine atom	Add one electron →	A chloride ion
17 protons: charge = +17		17 protons: charge = +17
17 electrons: charge = −17		18 electrons: charge = −18
Total charge = 0		Total charge = −1

The magnesium ion combines with the two chloride ions to form a compound, which has the chemical formula $MgCl_2$. Remember that we write the cation before the anion when we put together the formula of an ionic compound. Also, remember that the formula must tell us how many atoms of each element we have. Figure 3.12 illustrates how $MgCl_2$ is formed from magnesium and chlorine atoms.

Health Note: Our bodies require the ionized form of all of the metallic elements we need in our diet with the exception of iron, because the acid in our stomach can convert the Fe atoms into Fe^{2+} ions. However, our bodies do not absorb this form of iron very well. This form of dietary iron is called *reduced iron* on ingredient labels.

Sample Problem 3.15

Forming an ionic compound that contains ions with unequal charges

Using Lewis structures, show how potassium and oxygen atoms can combine to form an ionic compound, and write the formula of the ionic compound.

SOLUTION

Potassium (K) has one valence electron, while oxygen has six. The oxygen atom must gain two electrons to achieve an octet. Since a potassium atom can only supply one electron, the oxygen atom must combine with *two* potassium atoms.

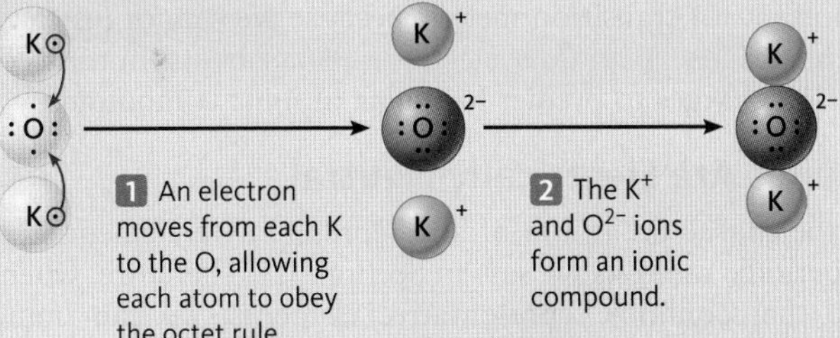
K
:O:
K
1 An electron moves from each K to the O, allowing each atom to obey the octet rule.
K +
:O: 2−
K +
2 The K+ and O2− ions form an ionic compound.

Each potassium atom loses one electron, leaving it with one more proton than it has electrons. The extra proton gives the potassium atom a +1 charge. The oxygen atom gains two electrons, leaving it with two more electrons than protons and giving it a −2 charge. The resulting ionic compound contains two K^+ ions and one O^{2-} ion. When we write the chemical formula of the compound, we write the cation first, so the formula is K_2O.

continued

Remember that the formula must show the number of atoms of each element, and the ion charges do not appear in the formula of the compound.

TRY IT YOURSELF: *Using Lewis structures, show how lithium and nitrogen atoms can combine to form an ionic compound, and write the formula of the ionic compound.*

For additional practice, try Core Problems 3.43 and 3.44.

CORE PROBLEMS

3.33 Use the electron arrangement of aluminum to show that aluminum satisfies the octet rule if it loses three electrons.

3.34 Use the electron arrangement of magnesium to show that magnesium satisfies the octet rule if it loses three electrons.

3.35 Use Lewis structures to show how each of the following atoms can form an ion that satisfies the octet rule.
a) chlorine b) magnesium

3.36 Use Lewis structures to show how each of the following atoms can form an ion that satisfies the octet rule.
a) nitrogen b) sodium

3.37 Each of the following elements can form a stable ion. What is the charge on each ion?
a) Mg b) Br c) Se d) Cs

3.38 Each of the following elements can form a stable ion. What is the charge on each ion?
a) Li b) S c) Ba d) Ga

3.39 The Group 7A elements can all form ions. What is the charge on these ions?

3.40 All of the Group 3A elements except boron can form ions. What is the charge on these ions?

3.41 Give an example of a representative element that can form an ion with a +2 charge.

3.42 Give an example of a representative element that can form an ion with a −2 charge.

3.43 Potassium and sulfur can combine to form an ionic compound.
a) Which element loses electrons, and how many electrons does each atom lose?
b) Which element gains electrons, and how many electrons does each atom gain?
c) What is the charge on each atom in the ionic compound?
d) Write the formula of the ionic compound.

3.44 Calcium and bromine can combine to form an ionic compound.
a) Which element loses electrons, and how many electrons does each atom lose?
b) Which element gains electrons, and how many electrons does each atom gain?
c) What is the charge on each atom in the ionic compound?
d) Write the formula of the ionic compound.

OBJECTIVES: *Predict the formulas of ionic compounds using the ion charges, and learn the names and charges of common transition metal ions.*

3.6 Writing Formulas for Ionic Compounds

In Section 3.5, we worked out the formulas of some ionic compounds using the number of electrons in the valence shell of each atom. You now need to learn how to predict ionic formulas without going back to the electron arrangements of the original atoms. This is particularly important for transition metals, because we cannot predict how many electrons transition metals lose from their electron arrangements. In this section, we will see how we can use ion charges to predict formulas of ionic compounds.

Ionic Compounds Are Electrically Neutral

We can predict the charge on an ion of any representative element from that element's position on the periodic table, as we saw in Section 3.5. Therefore, whenever we have an ionic compound that contains representative elements, we can immediately tell the charges on the ions that make up the compound. For example, if an ionic compound contains calcium (a Group 2A element) and oxygen (a Group 6A element), it must actually be made from Ca^{2+} and O^{2-} ions, because all Group 2A elements have a +2 charge and all Group 6A elements have a −2 charge when they form ions.

Once we know the charges on the ions, we can write the formula of the compound that contains them by recognizing that ionic compounds are always electrically neutral. That is, all ionic compounds obey the **rule of charge balance:** *in any ionic compound,* *the total amount of positive charge equals the total amount of negative charge.* The charges on the ions always add up to zero.

Let us apply the rule of charge balance to some compounds. The simplest examples are compounds made from ions that have the same amount of charge. For example, when Ca^{2+} combines with O^{2-}, the ion charges are the same size (2 charge units). To satisfy the rule of charge balance, we simply combine one calcium ion with one oxide ion, because +2 and −2 add up to zero. Therefore, the correct formula of this compound is CaO. Likewise, when Na^+ combines with Br^-, the ion charges are the same size (1 charge unit), so the resulting compound contains one of each ion and has the formula NaBr.

What happens if we combine calcium ions with bromide ions? A calcium ion carries two positive charges, while bromide carries one negative charge. We need *two* Br^- ions to balance the Ca^{2+}, as shown in Figure 3.13. The chemical formula of this compound is $CaBr_2$.

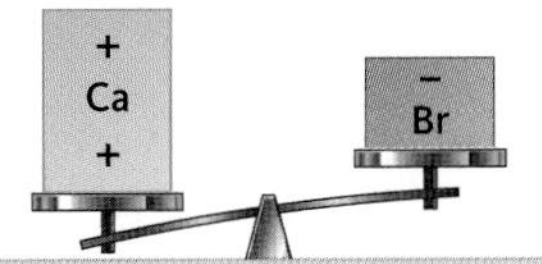

Ion charges are not balanced: CaBr is **not correct.**

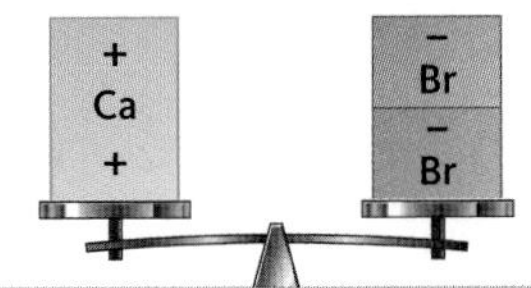

Ion charges are balanced: the correct formula is $\mathbf{CaBr_2}$.

FIGURE 3.13 Balancing the charges of calcium and bromide ions.

Sample Problem 3.16

Writing the formula of an ionic compound from the ion charges

Write the chemical formula of the ionic compound that is formed when Al^{3+} combines with Cl^-.

SOLUTION

Aluminum has a higher charge than does chlorine, so we need extra Cl^- ions to balance the charge on Al^{3+}. We can achieve charge balance by grouping one Al^{3+} ion with three Cl^- ions, so the chemical formula is $AlCl_3$.

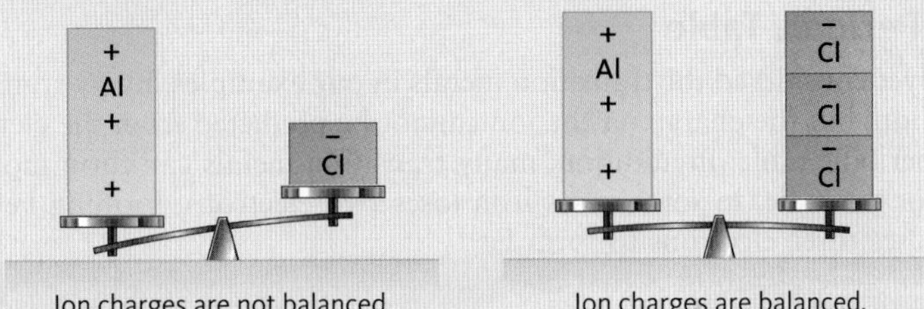

TRY IT YOURSELF: *Write the chemical formula of the ionic compound that is formed when Na^+ combines with S^{2-}.*

For additional practice, try Core Problems 3.47 and 3.48.

If you have difficulty making the charges balance, here is a useful trick: *if the number of each ion equals the charge on the other ion, the compound will be electrically neutral.* Sample Problem 3.17 shows how we can use this trick to write a chemical formula.

Sample Problem 3.17

Using the ion charges to write the formula of an ionic compound

Write the chemical formula of the ionic compound that is formed from Al^{3+} ions and O^{2-} ions.

SOLUTION

We can achieve charge balance by setting the number of each ion equal to the charge on the other ion.

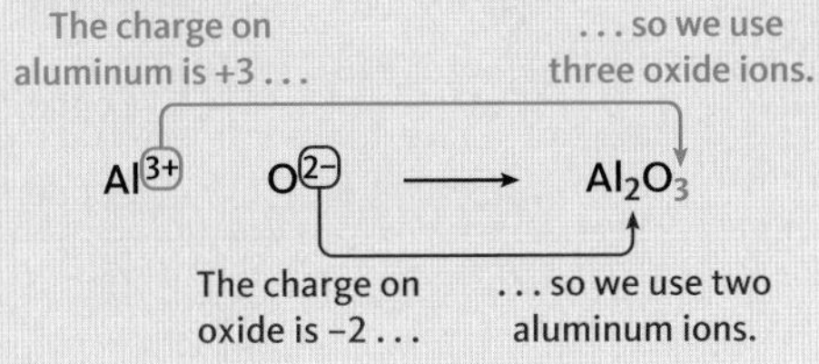

continued

The chemical formula is Al_2O_3. This formula contains two Al^{3+} ions, giving a total positive charge of +6, and three O^{2-} ions, giving a total negative charge of −6.

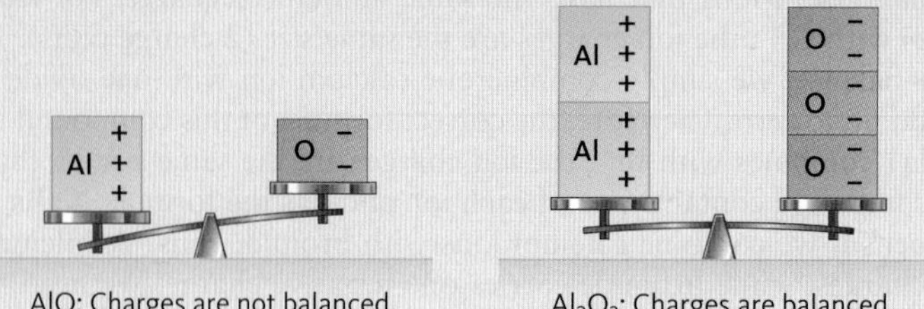

TRY IT YOURSELF: *Write the chemical formula of the ionic compound that is formed from Mg^{2+} ions and N^{3-} ions.*

You should always write the simplest possible formula for an ionic compound. If we use the method in Sample Problem 3.17 to get the formula of a compound that contains Ca^{2+} and O^2, we would write Ca_2O_2, which is not the simplest possible formula. We need only one of each ion to make an electrically neutral compound, not two, so the correct formula is CaO.

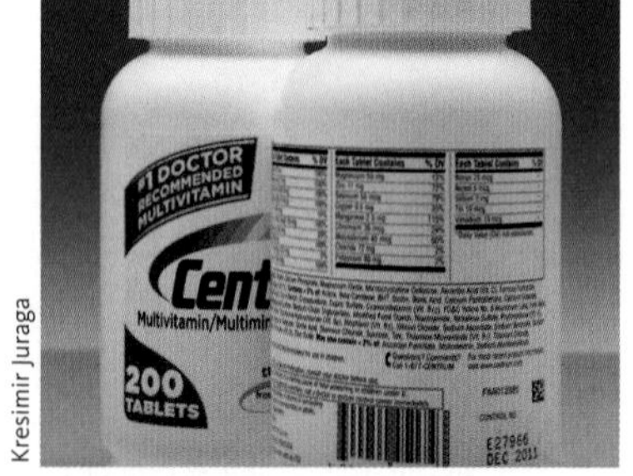

Kresimir Juraga

Multivitamin supplements often contain several essential transition metals.

Health Note: Five of the elements in Table 3.7 can form two different ions, but all of them except iron have a strong preference for one of the two possible ions. Iron's ability to gain or lose an electron easily while remaining ionized gives it more roles in our bodies than any other transition metal.

The Charges of Transition Metal Ions Cannot Be Predicted Using the Periodic Table

We have not yet considered the transition metals in our examples. Every transition metal can form an ion, but the charge on the ion cannot be predicted from the element's position on the periodic table. In addition, many transition metals can form more than one stable ion. For example, in some cases iron loses two electrons, forming Fe^{2+}, while in others iron loses three electrons to form Fe^{3+}.

One helpful generalization is that *all of the biologically significant transition metals form ions with a +2 charge.* Beyond that, the ion charges must be learned case by case. Table 3.7 lists the transition metals that occur in humans and their stable ions.

TABLE 3.7 Biologically Important Transition Metals and Their Ions*

Element	Symbol	Stable Ions	Names of Ions
Chromium	Cr	Cr^{2+}	Chromium(II) or chromous
		Cr^{3+}	Chromium(III) or chromic
Manganese	Mn	Mn^{2+}	Manganese(II) or manganous
		Mn^{3+}	Manganese(III) or manganic
Iron	Fe	Fe^{2+}	Iron(II) or ferrous
		Fe^{3+}	Iron(III) or ferric
Cobalt	Co	Co^{2+}	Cobalt(II) or cobaltous
		Co^{3+}	Cobalt(III) or cobaltic
Nickel	Ni	Ni^{2+}	Nickel
Copper	Cu	Cu^{+}	Copper(I) or cuprous
		Cu^{2+}	Copper(II) or cupric
Zinc	Zn	Zn^{2+}	Zinc

*Molybdenum also occurs in humans, but not in the form of a simple ion; its chemistry is beyond the level of this text.

When a transition metal can form two different ions, the names of the ions must tell us the ionic charges. In the traditional naming system for transition metals, we add the suffix *ous* for the ion with the smaller charge, and we add the suffix *ic* for the ion with the larger charge. In this system, the ion names use the same root as the chemical symbols, so the names for the ions of iron and copper are derived from the Latin words *ferrum* and *cuprum*. For instance, the traditional names for Fe^{2+} and Fe^{3+} are *ferrous* and *ferric*, respectively. In the IUPAC naming system, the charge on the ion is written as a Roman numeral after the name of the element, so the two ions of iron are called *iron(II)* and *iron(III)* (read "iron two" and "iron three"). Both systems are in common use.

Transition metal ions form compounds in the same way that representative ions do. The existence of two ions for some transition metals means that two possible compounds can be made from the same pair of elements. For instance, copper and chlorine can form CuCl and $CuCl_2$, because copper can form either a Cu^+ or a Cu^{2+} ion when it combines with chlorine.

Health Note: Ferrous sulfate and ferrous fumarate are the most common sources of iron in vitamin supplements. Both of these contain Fe^{2+}, which is more readily absorbed by our bodies than Fe^{3+}.

Sample Problem 3.18

Writing the formulas of compounds that contain transition metal ions

Iron and fluorine can form two different ionic compounds. Write their chemical formulas.

SOLUTION

Iron forms two stable ions, Fe^{2+} and Fe^{3+}. When Fe^{2+} combines with F^-, charge balance gives us the formula FeF_2. When Fe^{3+} combines with F^-, we get the formula FeF_3.

TRY IT YOURSELF: *Copper and sulfur can form two different ionic compounds. Write their chemical formulas.*

For additional practice, try Core Problems 3.49 (part d) and 3.50 (part d).

CORE PROBLEMS

3.45 Using the rule of charge balance, explain why sodium and oxygen cannot combine to make a compound that has the formula NaO.

3.46 Using the rule of charge balance, explain why magnesium and fluorine cannot combine to make a compound that has the formula MgF.

3.47 Write the chemical formula of the ionic compound that is formed by each of the following pairs of ions:
a) Fe^{2+} and O^{2-} b) Na^+ and Se^{2-}
c) F^- and Sr^{2+} d) Cr^{3+} and I^-
e) N^{3-} and Mg^{2+}

3.48 Write the chemical formula of the ionic compound that is formed by each of the following pairs of ions:
a) Cr^{3+} and N^{3-} b) S^{2-} and Ag^+
c) Ba^{2+} and Br^- d) F^- and Fe^{3+}
e) Ga^{3+} and O^{2-}

3.49 Using the normal ion charges for the elements, give the chemical formula of the ionic compound that is formed by each of the following pairs of elements:
a) potassium and bromine
b) zinc and chlorine
c) aluminum and sulfur
d) cobalt and chlorine (There are two possible compounds; give both of them.)

3.50 Using the normal ion charges for the elements, give the chemical formula of the ionic compound that is formed by each of the following pairs of elements:
a) magnesium and oxygen
b) sodium and sulfur
c) calcium and nitrogen
d) iron and oxygen (There are two possible compounds; give both of them.)

3.7 Naming Ionic Compounds

OBJECTIVES: *Write the names and formulas of ionic compounds that contain two elements.*

Ionic compounds are named using a different set of rules from covalent compounds. To name an ionic compound, we simply list the names of the two ions, without telling how many of each ion the compound contains. For example, NaCl is called sodium chloride, and $CaBr_2$ is called calcium bromide. We write the positive ion before the negative ion, so the name and the formula of an ionic compound are written in the

Health Note: In some medications that contain ions, the positive ion is named after the negative ion. For example, the chemical name of the cholesterol-lowering medication Lipitor is generally written *atorvastatin calcium*, although the calcium is a +2 ion.

TABLE 3.8 Modified Names for Nonmetals in Ionic Compounds

Element	Ion	Name of Ion	Compound Formed When This Ion Combines with Na^+
Nitrogen	N^{3-}	Nitride	Na_3N sodium nitride
Oxygen	O^{2-}	Oxide	Na_2O sodium oxide
Fluorine	F^-	Fluoride	NaF sodium fluoride
Sulfur	S^{2-}	Sulfide	Na_2S sodium sulfide
Chlorine	Cl^-	Chloride	NaCl sodium chloride
Bromine	Br^-	Bromide	NaBr sodium bromide
Iodine	I^-	Iodide	NaI sodium iodide

same order. For the negative ion, we use the same modified names that you learned in Section 3.4. Table 3.8 lists these modified names and an example of a compound that contains each ion.

Sample Problem 3.19

Naming ionic compounds

$MgCl_2$ is an ionic compound. What is its name?

SOLUTION

$MgCl_2$ contains one Mg^{2+} ion and two Cl^- ions. To name the compound, we write the names of the two ions. Metal ions have the same name as the element, while nonmetals use the modified names in Table 3.8, so this compound is called magnesium chloride. Note that we do not use the prefixes *mono, di, tri,* and so forth, when we name ionic compounds.

TRY IT YOURSELF: *Na_2O is an ionic compound. What is its name?*

For additional practice, try Core Problems 3.51 (parts a through c) and 3.52 (parts a through c).

You may also need to write the chemical formula when you are given the name. Because the name does not tell you how many of each element is present, you must work this out from the charges on the individual ions. You do this in exactly the same way that we put together ionic formulas in Section 3.5. For example, suppose we wanted to write the chemical formula of aluminum chloride. We must start by working out the charges on each ion from the positions of the elements on the periodic table. Aluminum is in Group 3A and makes an ion with a +3 charge, and chlorine is in Group 7A and makes an ion with a −1 charge. Once we know these charges, we can use the rule of charge balance to get the formula of the compound. We need three chloride ions to balance the charge on one aluminum ion, so the chemical formula of aluminum chloride is $AlCl_3$.

Sample Problem 3.20

Writing the formulas of ionic compounds

Write the chemical formulas of the following ionic compounds:

a) calcium fluoride
b) sodium iodide

continued

SOLUTION

a) We must start with the correct charges on the ions. Calcium is in Group 2A, so it forms a +2 ion (Ca^{2+}). Fluorine is in Group 7A, so it forms a −1 ion (F^-). Now we can use charge balance to determine the formula. We need two F^- ions to balance the charge on one Ca^{2+} ion, so the correct formula is CaF_2.

b) Again, we start with the charges on the ions. Sodium ion is Na^+ and iodide ion is I^-. Since the charges are the same size, the chemical formula is NaI.

TRY IT YOURSELF: *Write the chemical formulas of potassium oxide and aluminum sulfide.*

For additional practice, try Core Problems 3.53 (parts a and b) and 3.54 (parts a and b).

For those transition elements that form more than one ion, the name must specify which ion is present. The formula does not tell you the charge on the transition element directly, so you must start with the charge on the nonmetal and use the fact that the total positive and negative charge must be equal.

Sample Problem 3.21

Naming a compound that contains a transition metal ion

Name the following ionic compound: Fe_2O_3.

SOLUTION

Iron can be either Fe^{2+} or Fe^{3+}, so we must determine which of these is present in Fe_2O_3. The key is to start with the oxide ions, because the charge on oxide is always −2. The formula tells us that we have three O^{2-} ions, so the total negative charge is −6.

Next, we use the rule of charge balance. Since the total amounts of positive and negative charge must be equal, the total positive charge must be +6.

Finally, we divide up this positive charge among all of the iron atoms. The formula has only two iron atoms, so each iron gets half of the positive charge. Therefore, the charge on the iron atom is +3. The name of the Fe^{3+} ion is iron(III), so the name of this compound is iron(III) oxide. We can also call this compound ferric oxide, using the traditional name for Fe^{3+}.

TRY IT YOURSELF: *$CrCl_2$ is an ionic compound. What is its name?*

For additional practice, try Core Problems 3.51 (parts d through f) and 3.52 (parts d through f).

Sample Problem 3.22

Writing the formula of a transition metal compound from its name

Write the chemical formula of copper(I) oxide.

SOLUTION

Copper(I) is Cu^+, and oxide is O^{2-}. Charge balance requires that we have two Cu^+ ions and one O^{2-} ion, so the chemical formula is Cu_2O.

TRY IT YOURSELF: *Write the chemical formula of cobalt(III) fluoride.*

For additional practice, try Core Problems 3.53 (parts c through e) and 3.54 (parts c through e).

Charles D. Winters

Samples of copper(I) oxide (red) and copper(II) oxide (black). The color of a transition metal compound depends on the charge on the metal ion.

TABLE 3.9 Naming Ions in an Ionic Compound

Type of Element	How Ion Is Named	Examples
Metals that can form only one ion (Groups 1A and 2A, some of the transition metals, Al)	The name of the ion is the same as the name of the element.	Na^+ sodium Ca^{2+} calcium Zn^{2+} zinc
Metals that can form more than one ion (most transition metals)	Write the name of the element, and then write the charge as a Roman numeral.	Fe^{2+} iron(II) Cr^{3+} chromium(III) Cu^+ copper(I)
Nonmetals	Change the ending of the element name to *ide*.	Cl^- chloride O^{2-} oxide S^{2-} sulfide

Table 3.9 summarizes the naming rules for ions in ionic compounds.

CORE PROBLEMS

3.51 Name the following ionic compounds:
a) K_2O b) MgS c) $AlCl_3$ d) $CuCl_2$
e) Cr_2O_3 f) MnS

3.52 Name the following ionic compounds:
a) CaI_2 b) KBr c) Na_3N d) $FeCl_3$
e) CoO f) ZnF_2

3.53 Write the chemical formulas of the following ionic compounds:
a) sodium fluoride
b) calcium iodide
c) chromium(II) sulfide
d) ferric chloride
e) zinc oxide

3.54 Write the chemical formulas of the following ionic compounds:
a) magnesium sulfide
b) potassium oxide
c) nickel chloride
d) iron(II) oxide
e) chromous bromide

3.55 The correct name for $CaCl_2$ is calcium chloride, but $CuCl_2$ is not called "copper chloride." Explain this difference, and give the correct name for $CuCl_2$.

3.56 The correct name for AlF_3 is aluminum fluoride, but FeF_3 is not called "iron fluoride." Explain this difference, and give the correct name for FeF_3.

OBJECTIVES: *Learn the names and formulas of common polyatomic ions, and write the names and formulas of compounds that contain polyatomic ions.*

Health Note: NaOH destroys many of the vital molecules that make up our bodies, making it very toxic. Cleaning products that contain this compound should always be used with care.

3.8 Polyatomic Ions

A number of cleaning products (notably drain and oven cleaners) contain *caustic lye,* a compound that has the chemical formula NaOH. Here are the Lewis structures of the three atoms that make up NaOH:

Na·	·Ö·	·H
Sodium A Group 1A element One valence electron	**Oxygen** A Group 6A element Six valence electrons	**Hydrogen** One valence electron

How do these atoms form a compound? Oxygen needs two additional electrons to satisfy the octet rule. Each of the other two atoms can supply one electron, but the atoms do so in different fashions. Hydrogen *shares* its electron with oxygen, forming a covalent bond. Sodium, by contrast, *loses* its valence electron altogether. This electron becomes part of the valence shell of the oxygen, completing the electron octet. Both oxygen and sodium satisfy the octet rule, and hydrogen has the electron configuration of helium, so all three atoms are stable. Figure 3.14 shows the bonding in NaOH.

NaOH contains two oppositely charged ions, so it is an ionic compound. The positive ion is Na^+, a typical **monatomic ion**. Monatomic ions are made from a single atom, and they include all of the ions you have seen in earlier sections. By contrast, the negative ion in NaOH contains a pair of atoms held together by a covalent bond. Any ion that contains two or more atoms is called a **polyatomic ion**. The formula of this polyatomic ion is OH^- (note the charge), and it is called the hydroxide ion.

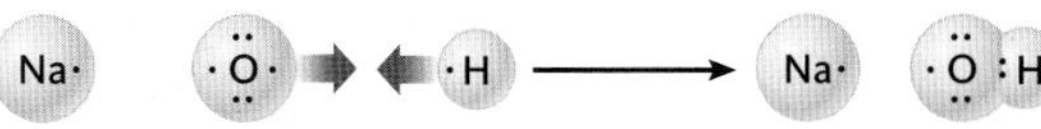

First, hydrogen and oxygen share electrons . . .

. . . to form a covalent bond.

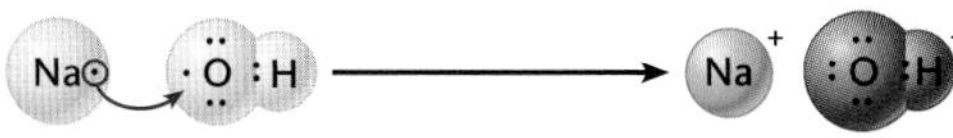

Then sodium gives up an electron to the OH group . . .

. . . to form a pair of ions.

FIGURE 3.14 The formation of NaOH.

The Ammonium Ion Is a Common Positively Charged Polyatomic Ion

The ammonium ion (NH_4^+) is a positively charged polyatomic ion. The ammonium ion is related to the covalent compound NH_3 (ammonia), but it contains a nitrogen atom and *four* hydrogen atoms. One electron has been removed to produce the +1 charge. Figure 3.15 shows how we can envision the formation of NH_4^+.

Once they are formed, ammonium ions can form ionic compounds by combining with any negative ion. For example, NH_4^+ can combine with Cl^- to form a compound that has the formula NH_4Cl. Polyatomic ions such as hydroxide and ammonium are common in chemistry, and these ions are very stable, because the covalent bonds that hold them together are very strong.

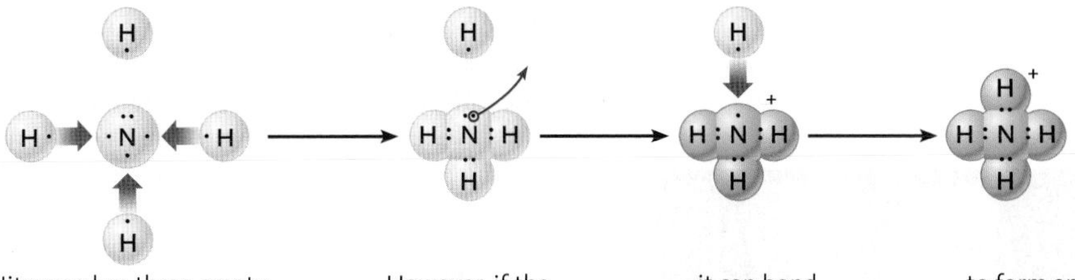

Nitrogen has three empty spaces in its valence shell, so it normally bonds to only three hydrogen atoms, to form ammonia (NH_3).

However, if the nitrogen atom in NH_3 loses an electron and forms a cation . . .

. . . it can bond to a fourth hydrogen atom . . .

. . . to form an **ammonium ion** (NH_4^+).

FIGURE 3.15 The formation of the ammonium ion.

Polyatomic Ions Form Ionic Compounds in the Same Manner as Monatomic Ions

Like monatomic ions, polyatomic ions can combine with other ions to form ionic compounds. The rule of charge balance applies to these compounds as well. Figure 3.16 shows how Ca^{2+} and OH^- ions can combine to form a compound. To satisfy the rule of charge balance, the compound must contain two OH^- ions and one Ca^{2+} ion. When a compound contains more than one of a particular polyatomic ion, we enclose the formula of the ion in parentheses, and we write the number of polyatomic ions after the right parenthesis. Therefore, the chemical formula of this compound is written $Ca(OH)_2$. You should compare Figure 3.16 to the formation of $CaBr_2$ in Figure 3.13.

Health Note: Some dentists use $Ca(OH)_2$ to kill bacteria inside infected teeth during endodontic treatment, but its use is controversial.

Sample Problem 3.23

Writing the formula of a compound that contains a polyatomic ion

Write the chemical formula of the compound that contains NH_4^+ ions and S^{2-} ions.

SOLUTION

The ammonium ion has a +1 charge, but sulfide has a −2 charge, so NH_4S does not give balanced charges. We need two NH_4^+ ions and one S^{2-} ion, so the chemical formula is $(NH_4)_2S$.

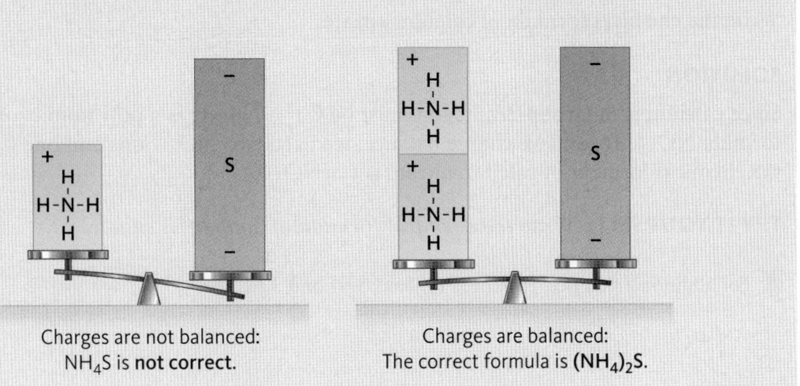

Charges are not balanced: NH_4S is **not correct.**

Charges are balanced: The correct formula is $\mathbf{(NH_4)_2S}$.

continued

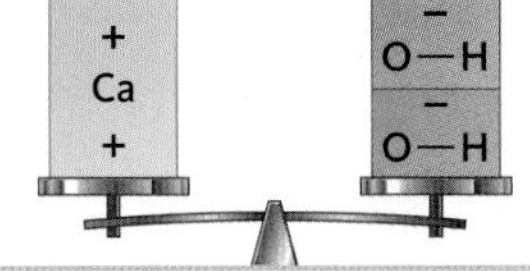

Ion charges are **not** balanced: CaOH is **not correct.**

Ion charges are balanced: the correct formula is $\mathbf{Ca(OH)_2}$.

FIGURE 3.16 Balancing the charges of calcium and hydroxide ions.

Note that since we have two of the polyatomic ions, we need to write parentheses around the NH_4 group.

TRY IT YOURSELF: *Write the chemical formula of the compound that contains Fe^{3+} ions and OH^- ions.*

For additional practice, try Core Problems 3.59 and 3.60.

Several Polyatomic Ions Are Important in Medical Chemistry

Many polyatomic ions occur in biological systems. Table 3.10 lists some polyatomic ions that are particularly important in medicine and biology. You should learn the formulas and the charges of these ions, so that you can write formulas of compounds that contain the ions. Note that polyatomic ions whose names end in *ate* always contain several oxygen atoms and have a negative charge.

When we name a compound that contains a polyatomic ion, we name the positive ion first, followed by the negative ion, just as we do for compounds of monatomic ions. For example, $Al(OH)_3$ is an ionic compound that is made from aluminum ions (Al^{3+}) and hydroxide ions (OH^-), so it is called aluminum hydroxide. This compound is used in some antacid tablets.

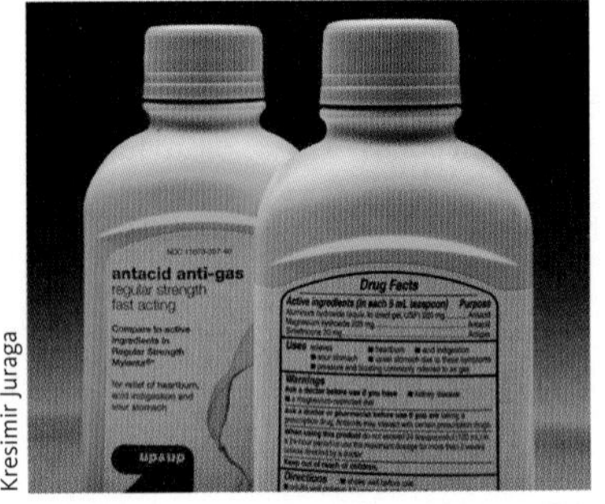

Kresimir Juraga

Aluminum hydroxide neutralizes stomach acid, so it is an ingredient in some antacids.

TABLE 3.10 Formulas and Names of Common Polyatomic Ions

Formula	Name	Example of a Compound That Contains This Ion
NH_4^+	Ammonium	NH_4Cl (ammonium chloride: sal ammoniac)
OH^-	Hydroxide	$Mg(OH)_2$ (magnesium hydroxide: milk of magnesia)
NO_3^-	Nitrate	KNO_3 (potassium nitrate: saltpeter)
CO_3^{2-}	Carbonate	$CaCO_3$ (calcium carbonate: chalk)
SO_4^{2-}	Sulfate	$MgSO_4$ (magnesium sulfate: Epsom salt)
PO_4^{3-}	Phosphate	$Fe_3(PO_4)_2$ (iron(II) phosphate: ferrous phosphate)
HCO_3^-	Hydrogen carbonate (or bicarbonate)	$NaHCO_3$ (sodium hydrogen carbonate: sodium bicarbonate, baking soda)

Sample Problem **3.24**

Writing the formula of a compound that contains a polyatomic ion from its name

Write the chemical formula of calcium nitrate.

SOLUTION

Since calcium is in Group 2A, its ion must be Ca^{2+}. Nitrate is a polyatomic ion with the formula NO_3^-. To achieve charge balance, we need two NO_3^- ions and one Ca^{2+} ion, so the chemical formula of calcium nitrate is $Ca(NO_3)_2$.

TRY IT YOURSELF: *Write the chemical formula of copper(II) sulfate.*

For additional practice, try Core Problems 3.61 and 3.62.

TABLE 3.11 A Comparison of Ionic Compounds Containing Monatomic and Polyatomic Ions

CATION	COMPOUNDS FORMED WITH −1 IONS (Cl^- and NO_3^-)		COMPOUNDS FORMED WITH −2 IONS (S^{2-} and CO_3^{2-})	
Na^+	NaCl (sodium chloride)	$NaNO_3$ (sodium nitrate)	Na_2S (sodium sulfide)	Na_2CO_3 (sodium carbonate)
Mg^{2+}	$MgCl_2$ (magnesium chloride)	$Mg(NO_3)_2$ (magnesium nitrate)	MgS (magnesium sulfide)	$MgCO_3$ (magnesium carbonate)
Al^{3+}	$AlCl_3$ (aluminum chloride)	$Al(NO_3)_3$ (aluminum nitrate)	Al_2S_3 (aluminum sulfide)	$Al_2(CO_3)_3$ (aluminum carbonate)

Sample Problem **3.25**

Naming a compound that contains a polyatomic ion

Name the following compound: Na_2CO_3.

SOLUTION

The key is to recognize that the CO_3 group is actually the carbonate ion, which has a −2 charge. This compound is made from two Na^+ ions and one CO_3^{2-} ion. To name the compound, we need only name the two ions, so this compound is called sodium carbonate.

TRY IT YOURSELF: *$Mg_3(PO_4)_2$ is an ionic compound. What is its name?*

For additional practice, try Core Problems 3.63 and 3.64.

It can be helpful to think of a polyatomic ion as a single unit that can be substituted for a monatomic ion of the same charge. For example, OH^-, NO_3^-, and HCO_3^- can all be substituted for the Cl^- in NaCl, giving us NaOH, $NaNO_3$, and $NaHCO_3$. Table 3.11 shows how two polyatomic ions (NO_3^- and CO_3^{2-}) can be exchanged for monatomic ions of the same charge (Cl^- and S^{2-}).

CORE PROBLEMS

3.57 Complete each of the following statements by writing either a name or a formula:
a) The chemical formula of nitrate ion is _____.
b) The chemical formula of _____ ion is NH_4^+.
c) The chemical formula of hydrogen carbonate ion is _____.
d) The chemical formula of _____ ion is PO_4^{3-}.

3.58 Complete each of the following statements by writing either a name or a formula:
a) The chemical formula of bicarbonate ion is _____.
b) The chemical formula of _____ ion is OH^-.
c) The chemical formula of sulfate ion is _____.
d) The chemical formula of _____ ion is CO_3^{2-}.

3.59 Write the chemical formulas of the ionic compounds that are formed by each of the following pairs of ions:
a) Zn^{2+} and OH^- b) SO_4^{2-} and Ag^+
c) K^+ and PO_4^{3-} d) Br^- and NH_4^+

3.60 Write the chemical formulas of the ionic compounds that are formed by each of the following pairs of ions:
a) Fe^{3+} and NO_3^- b) SO_4^{2-} and Ca^{2+}
c) NH_4^+ and CO_3^{2-} d) PO_4^{3-} and Mg^{2+}

3.61 Write the chemical formulas of the following compounds:
a) calcium carbonate
b) magnesium phosphate
c) chromium(III) hydroxide
d) cobalt(II) nitrate

3.62 Write the chemical formulas of the following compounds:
a) potassium sulfate
b) sodium bicarbonate
c) ammonium fluoride
d) iron(II) hydroxide

3.63 Name the following compounds:
a) $KHCO_3$ b) $Cu_3(PO_4)_2$ c) $(NH_4)_2SO_4$

3.64 Name the following compounds:
a) $FePO_4$ b) $Ca(NO_3)_2$ c) Na_2CO_3

OBJECTIVES: *Distinguish ionic and covalent compounds based on their chemical formulas.*

3.9 Recognizing Ionic and Molecular Compounds

Chemists generally divide compounds into two categories based on whether or not they contain ions. Any compound that contains ions is classified as an ionic compound, including substances that contain polyatomic ions. Compounds that contain only covalent bonds, such as H_2O and CO_2, are classified as **molecular compounds** or **covalent compounds**. This classification is based on the properties of the compounds. For example, Li_2CO_3 (which contains both ionic and covalent bonding) is quite similar to Li_2O (which is entirely ionic) and very different from CO_2 (which contains only covalent bonds and is classified as molecular). Table 3.12 shows the structures and behavior of these three compounds.

It is important to be able to identify a compound as ionic or molecular, based on its formula. Here are three guidelines that will help you classify compounds based on their formulas:

1. Compounds that contain a metallic element are usually ionic.
   Examples: CaO, $Fe(NO_3)_3$, $NaC_2H_3O_2$
2. Compounds that contain only nonmetals are usually molecular.
   Examples: CO_2, H_2SO_4, CH_3OH, $C_3H_5(NO_3)_3$
3. Compounds that contain the NH_4 group are ionic. (This is the important exception to guideline 2).
   Examples: NH_4Cl, $(NH_4)_3PO_4$

TABLE 3.12 Comparing Ionic and Molecular Compounds

Compound	Lewis Structure	Behavior	Classification
Li_2O	Li^+ $[:\ddot{O}:]^{2-}$ Li^+	White solid, must be heated above 500°C to melt	Ionic (contains monatomic ions)
Li_2CO_3	Li^+ $[CO_3]^{2-}$ Li^+	White solid, must be heated above 500°C to melt	Ionic (contains two monatomic ions and one polyatomic ion)
CO_2	$\ddot{O}::C::\ddot{O}$	Colorless gas at room temperature	Molecular (no ions: held together by covalent bonds)

Sample Problem 3.26

Recognizing ionic and molecular compounds from the chemical formulas

Predict whether each of the following compounds is ionic or molecular, based on its formula:

a) SnF_2 c) $(CH_3)_2SO_4$
b) SeF_2 d) NH_4NO_3

SOLUTION

a) Sn is a metal, so SnF_2 is an ionic compound.
b) Both Se and F are nonmetals, so SeF_2 is a molecular compound.
c) All of the elements in this compound are nonmetals, so $(CH_3)_2SO_4$ is a molecular compound. The SO_4 group in the formula is reminiscent of the sulfate ion (SO_4^{2-}),

continued

but an ionic compound must also have a positive ion, which will be either a metal or an ammonium ion.

d) The formula contains the NH_4 group, which is always a polyatomic ion (NH_4^+). Therefore, NH_4NO_3 is an ionic compound.

TRY IT YOURSELF: *Predict whether each of the following compounds is ionic or molecular, based on its formula:*
a) $HgCl_2$ *b)* HNO_3

For additional practice, try Core Problems 3.67 and 3.68.

Hydrogen is a nonmetal, and it forms molecular compounds with other nonmetals. Compounds such as HCl and H_2SO_4 are molecular substances, containing covalent bonds. Hydrogen is often placed in Group 1A on the periodic table, but do not let that mislead you; compounds like HCl and H_2SO_4 are very different from true ionic substances like NaCl and Na_2SO_4.

When you name a chemical compound, you must first determine whether the compound is ionic or molecular, because the two types are named differently. Remember that names of ionic compounds do not tell you how many of each element is present, while names of molecular compounds do. Table 3.13 summarizes the differences between ionic and molecular compounds.

TABLE 3.13 Guidelines for Classifying and Naming Compounds

	Ionic Compound	Molecular Compound
Type of bond	Ionic bonds (attraction between oppositely charged ions). *(Polyatomic ions are held together by covalent bonds.)*	Covalent bonds (shared electrons).
How to recognize	The formula starts with a metal or with NH_4.	The formula contains only nonmetals and does not contain the NH_4 group.
How to name	Name the cation and then the anion. Do not include *di, tri,* etc. *(Name polyatomic ions as a single unit.)*	Name the elements in the order they appear in the formula. Use *di, tri,* etc., to tell how many atoms of each element are present.

Sample Problem **3.27**

Using the correct rules to name ionic and molecular compounds

$AlCl_3$ and PCl_3 have identical atom ratios. What are their names?

SOLUTION

Al is a metal, so $AlCl_3$ is an *ionic* compound, containing Al^{3+} and three Cl^- ions. The correct name is **aluminum chloride.** Both P and Cl are nonmetals, so PCl_3 is a *molecular* compound, held together by covalent bonds. Names of molecular compounds must show the number of atoms, so this compound is called **phosphorus trichloride.**

TRY IT YOURSELF: Fe_2O_3 *and* N_2O_3 *have identical atom ratios. What are their names?*

For additional practice, try Core Problems 3.69 and 3.70.

CORE PROBLEMS

3.65 Draw Lewis structures that clearly show the difference between the bonds in IBr (a molecular compound) and those in NaBr (an ionic compound).

3.66 Draw Lewis structures that clearly show the difference between the bonds in $MgCl_2$ (an ionic compound) and those in SCl_2 (a molecular compound).

3.67 Tell whether each of the following compounds is ionic or molecular:
a) KCl b) HCl c) $CuSO_4$
d) $SOCl_2$ e) $Al(OH)_3$ f) $C_6H_4(OH)_2$

3.68 Tell whether each of the following compounds is ionic or molecular:
a) CaO b) CO c) NH_4Br
d) NH_2Br e) HNO_3 f) $Mn(NO_3)_2$

3.69 Name the following compounds, using the correct naming system for each:
a) SCl_2 b) $MgCl_2$

3.70 Name the following compounds, using the correct naming system for each:
a) $AlCl_3$ b) NCl_3

CONNECTIONS

Nitrogen and Oxygen: A Remarkable Partnership

Nitrogen and oxygen can combine to form a surprising number of different compounds. The three simplest of these are nitric oxide (NO), nitrous oxide (N_2O), and nitrogen dioxide (NO_2). The Lewis structures of these compounds are shown here. NO and NO_2 are among the very few stable molecules that have an odd number of electrons and therefore cannot obey the octet rule. Each of these compounds plays a significant role in medicine and human health, but each does so for different reasons.

$\cdot\ddot{N}=\ddot{O}:$	$:\ddot{O}-\dot{N}=\ddot{O}:$	$:N\equiv N-\ddot{O}:$
Nitric oxide (NO)	**Nitrogen dioxide (NO_2)**	**Nitrous oxide (N_2O)**

The red-brown color of the smoggy air over this city is due to NO_2.

Nitrogen dioxide (NO_2) is a red-brown, acrid-smelling, poisonous gas that is a major component of the smog that forms over urban areas in the summer. NO_2 is formed during the decomposition of organic matter by bacteria. However, the major sources of this gas are the engines of automobiles and other transportation vehicles, as well as power plants that use coal and natural gas to produce electricity.

NO_2 is highly irritating to the lungs and can trigger asthma attacks. In addition, NO_2 dissolves in rainwater and forms nitric acid, HNO_3, a strong and very corrosive acid. Acidic rainwater is toxic to most aquatic animals and plants and can even dissolve some types of rock, including the limestone and marble that are used to make many buildings and statues.

The second common compound of nitrogen and oxygen is nitrous oxide (N_2O), a colorless gas with a characteristic sweet odor. N_2O is most familiar as the propellant gas in canned whipped cream, but it has been used for more than 150 years as an anesthetic for minor surgical procedures and is still widely used in dentistry. The compound is often called "laughing gas," because it produces a sensation of exhilaration when inhaled in small amounts. In higher concentrations, N_2O is a strong analgesic (it suppresses the sensation of pain), and in still higher concentrations, the gas becomes an anesthetic (it induces unconsciousness). Like any general anesthetic, N_2O must be used with considerable care, because excessive concentrations can cause death by depressing the breathing reflex.

The third common compound of nitrogen and oxygen is nitric oxide (NO), a colorless, poisonous gas with a remarkable history. This compound is actually the first product formed when nitrogen and oxygen combine at high temperatures, but it reacts almost instantly with oxygen to form NO_2, so the actual concentration of NO in the atmosphere is negligible. Because of its toxicity, NO was long believed to have no role in living organisms. However, in 1986 it was identified as the primary chemical responsible for relaxation of arteries (vasodilation) in humans. This led to an intense burst of research into the biochemical effects of NO and to the identification of a remarkable range of roles. In addition to its effect on arteries, NO helps regulate muscle contractions in the digestive tract (peristalsis), relaxes the muscles that line the respiratory passages, assists in transmitting nerve impulses, and kills bacteria, tumor cells, and cells that have been infected by viruses. NO is also believed to trigger apoptosis, the "programmed suicide" that aged and damaged cells undergo when they are no longer needed by the body.

NO, NO_2, and N_2O are not the only examples of multiple compounds that can be formed by a single pair of elements, but they are perhaps the most dramatic illustration that a chemical compound is truly "more than the sum of its parts."

Key Terms

binary compound – 3.4
bonding electron pair – 3.1
chemical bond – 3.1
covalent bond – 3.1
double bond – 3.2
electronegativity – 3.3
ionic bond – 3.5
ionic compound – 3.5
molecular compound (covalent compound) – 3.9
molecule – 3.1
monatomic ion – 3.8
nonbonding electron pair (lone pair) – 3.1
nonpolar covalent bond – 3.3
octet rule – 3.1
polar covalent bond – 3.3
polyatomic ion – 3.8
rule of charge balance – 3.6
single bond – 3.2
triple bond – 3.2

SUMMARY OF OBJECTIVES

Now that you have read the chapter, test yourself on your knowledge of the objectives, using this summary as a guide.

Section 3.1: Use the octet rule to predict the number of covalent bonds an atom can form, and draw Lewis structures for molecules that contain single bonds.

- The Group 8A elements are unusually stable and do not normally form compounds.
- Atoms of representative elements from other groups interact with one another to achieve the electron arrangement of a Group 8A element (the octet rule).
- Atoms having four or more valence electrons can satisfy the octet rule by sharing electrons, forming covalent bonds.
- The number of covalent bonds formed by an atom equals the number of empty spaces in the valence shell.
- In simple molecules, the atom that can form the most covalent bonds is normally the central atom.

Section 3.2: Draw Lewis structures for molecules that contain double or triple bonds, and use lines to represent bonding electrons.

- Two atoms can share four or six electrons with each other, forming double or triple bonds.
- A double bond is equivalent to two single bonds, and a triple bond is equivalent to three single bonds.
- Lewis structures can be drawn using lines in place of dots to represent bonding electron pairs. These structures are easier to interpret for complex molecules.
- Some molecules contain atoms that do not form the normal numbers of bonds or that violate the octet rule.

Section 3.3: Use electronegativities to predict whether a covalent bond is polar or nonpolar, and to determine the charge on each bonding atom.

- Covalent bonds between atoms of different elements are usually polar.
- In a polar covalent bond, the atom with the greatest attraction for electrons is negatively charged, and the other atom is positively charged.
- Electronegativity is a measure of an element's attraction for electrons, and it can be used to predict the polarity of a covalent bond.
- Atoms with equal electronegativities form nonpolar covalent bonds.

Section 3.4: Write names for binary covalent compounds.

- Compounds containing two nonmetals are named using the IUPAC rules. These names list the elements in the compound and tell how many atoms of each element are present.
- Many medically important covalent compounds are named using other systems; some covalent compounds have traditional names.

Section 3.5: Predict ion charges for representative elements, and use Lewis structures to show how atoms gain and lose electrons to form an ionic compound.

- Metallic elements in Groups 1A, 2A, or 3A satisfy the octet rule by losing 1, 2, or 3 electrons to form positively charged ions.
- Nonmetallic elements in Groups 5A, 6A, or 7A can satisfy the octet rule by gaining 1, 2, or 3 electrons to form negatively charged ions.
- Oppositely charged ions combine to form ionic compounds.
- The ion charge for a representative element can be predicted from the position of the element on the periodic table.

continued

Section 3.6: Predict the formulas of ionic compounds using the ion charges, and learn the names and charges of common transition metal ions.

- In any ionic compound, the amount of positive charge must equal the amount of negative charge (rule of charge balance).
- The simplest possible formula that obeys the rule of charge balance is the correct formula for an ionic compound.
- Transition metals form ions whose charges cannot be predicted using the periodic table.
- Whenever a transition metal can form two different ions, the name of each ion must tell the charge on that ion.

Section 3.7: Write the names and formulas of ionic compounds that contain two elements.

- To name an ionic compound, write the name of the positive ion followed by the name of the negative ion.
- Positive ions have the same names as the original elements, while names of negative ions are modified to end in *ide*.
- Names of ionic compounds do not tell how many of each ion is present.

Section 3.8: Learn the names and formulas of common polyatomic ions, and write the names and formulas of compounds that contain polyatomic ions.

- Polyatomic ions contain two or more atoms, linked by covalent bonds.
- Polyatomic ions form compounds that are analogous to those formed by monatomic ions and that obey the rule of charge balance.
- The names of compounds containing polyatomic ions use the same system as the names of simpler ionic compounds.

Section 3.9: Distinguish ionic and covalent compounds based on their chemical formulas.

- Any compound that is made from ions is classified as an ionic compound, while compounds that contain only covalently bonded atoms are classified as molecular.
- Compounds that contain one or more metals are normally ionic, and compounds that contain only nonmetals are normally molecular.
- Compounds that contain the NH_4 group are ionic, even if they do not contain a metallic element.

Concept Questions

OWL **Online homework for this chapter may be assigned in OWL.**

* indicates more challenging problems.

3.71 What is the octet rule?

3.72 Explain why phosphorus and hydrogen can combine to form PH_3 but not PH_4.

3.73 Use Lewis structures to show that potassium and oxygen cannot both satisfy the octet rule if they form a covalently bonded K_2O molecule.

3.74 In the compound BrCFHI, one of the five atoms is at the center of the molecule, with the other four atoms bonded to it. Which atom is at the center of the molecule, and why?

3.75 The following are possible Lewis structures for H_2 and Li_2. One of these two molecules is very stable, while the other is not. Which one is which? Explain your answer.

H:H   Li:Li

3.76 Carbon and oxygen can combine to form a molecule that contains one carbon atom and one oxygen atom. Why is this compound called *carbon monoxide* instead of "oxygen monocarbide"?

3.77 Using electron arrangements, explain why removing one electron from a sodium atom makes an ion that satisfies the octet rule.

3.78 Lithium has the following electron arrangement.
shell 1: 2 electrons   shell 2: 1 electron

When a lithium atom loses one electron, it forms a Li^+ ion that has the following electron arrangement.
shell 1: 2 electrons

Explain why this ion is very stable, even though it does not have eight electrons in its outermost shell.

3.79 A student says, "N_2O_3 is an ionic compound, made from N^{3-} and O^{2-} ions." Explain why this cannot be true.

3.80 Both polar covalent bonds and ionic bonds involve charged atoms. How do these two types of bonds differ from each other? Use H_2O and K_2O to illustrate your answer.

3.81 a) Which of the following drawings represent molecules, and which represent individual atoms?
b) Which of the following drawings represent compounds, and which represent elements?
c) Write a chemical formula for each of these substances.

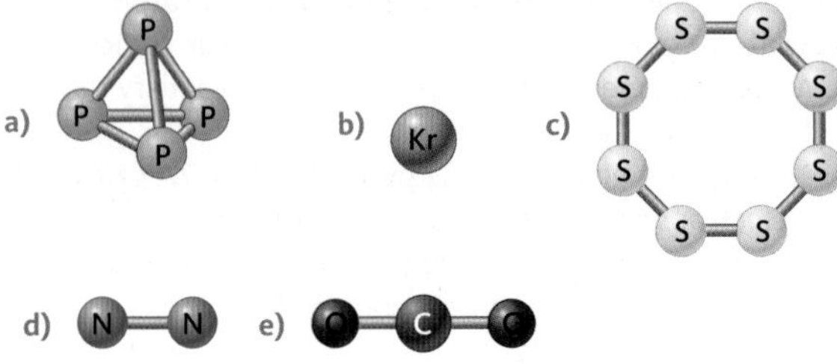

Summary and Challenge Problems

3.82 Draw Lewis structures for each of the following molecules. Use lines to represent bonding electron pairs. (You may want to draw dot structures first.)

a) H_2S
b) SI_2
c) AsF_3
d) CF_2I_2
e) CH_2S
f) C_2Br_2
g) HNO_2 (Hint: The atoms are arranged H–O–N–O.)
h) $SiOCl_2$
i) ClCN
j) BrNO

3.83 *Aspartic acid is a vital component of most proteins. It has the basic structure shown here. Complete this structure by adding bonds, nonbonding electron pairs, or both so that all atoms obey the octet rule and satisfy their normal bonding requirements.

```
                O   H
                |   |
 H   O   H      C — O
 |   |   |      |
 O — C — C —    C — H
         |      |
         H      N — H
                |
                H
```

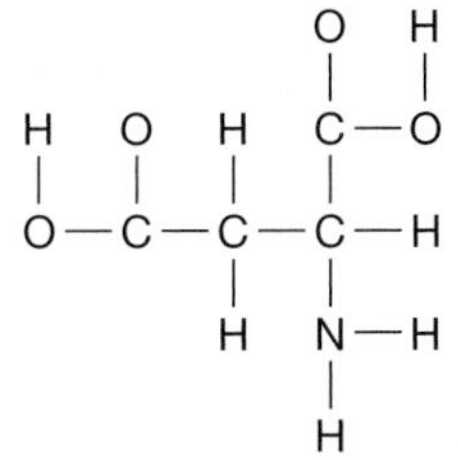

3.84 a) Acetonitrile is a colorless liquid that is used to dissolve compounds that do not dissolve in water. It has the chemical formula C_2H_3N. Which of the following is a reasonable structure for acetonitrile, based on the normal bonding requirements of the atoms?

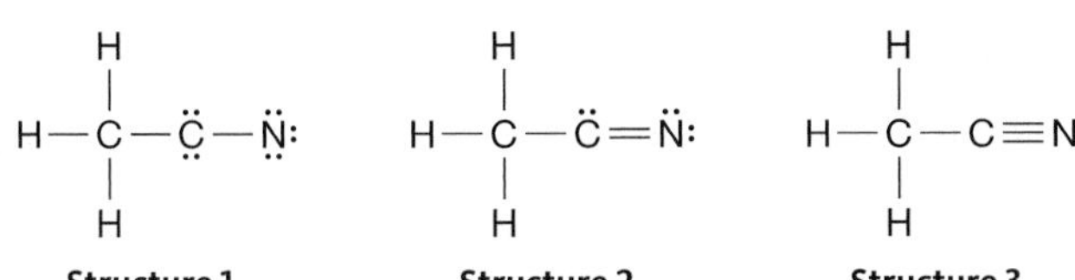

b) *There is another way to assemble two carbon atoms, three hydrogen atoms, and a nitrogen atom into a molecule that satisfies the octet rule and the normal bonding requirements of these three elements. Draw the structure of this second molecule.

3.85 *X and Z are elements in Period 3. They form the compound ZX_2, which has the Lewis structure shown here. Identify elements X and Z.

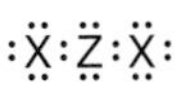

:Ẍ:Z̈:Ẍ:

3.86 Nitrous oxide (also called "laughing gas") has the chemical formula N_2O and the structure shown here. This compound is used as a sedative in dental work.

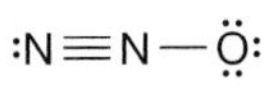

:N≡N—Ö:

a) Do any of the atoms in this molecule violate the octet rule? If so, which atoms?
b) Do all of the atoms in this molecule form the normal number of bonds? If not, which atoms form unusual numbers of bonds?

3.87 Refer to the following molecule:

```
     H   H   Ö:
     |   |   ||
 H — C — C — C — H
     |   |
     H   H
```

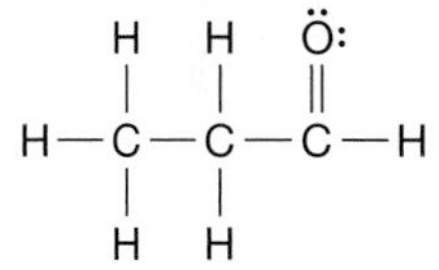

a) Find one nonpolar bond in this molecule, and draw an "X" through it.
b) Find one polar bond in this molecule, and draw a circle around it.
c) One atom in this molecule is strongly negatively charged. Draw an arrow that points toward this atom.
d) Are there any positively charged atoms in this molecule? If so, which ones are they?

3.88 *The compound $Mg(ClO_3)_2$ is called magnesium chlorate. It contains a magnesium ion and two polyatomic ions (the two ClO_3 groups). What is the charge on each of the polyatomic ions? (Hint: Use the rule of charge balance.)

3.89 *The element titanium can combine with oxygen to form the ionic compounds listed here. What is the charge on each titanium atom in each compound?

a) TiO b) TiO_2 c) Ti_2O_3

3.90 Write the chemical formulas of each of the following compounds:

a) zinc bromide
b) sulfur tetrafluoride
c) sodium nitride
d) dinitrogen pentoxide
e) silver phosphate
f) potassium sulfide
g) nickel hydroxide
h) nitrogen triiodide
i) chromium(III) nitrate
j) cuprous oxide
k) ammonium bromide
l) carbon disulfide
m) nitrous oxide
n) potassium hydrogen carbonate

3.91 Tell whether each of the compounds in Problem 3.90 is ionic or molecular. (You should not need to draw structures of the compounds.)

3.92 Name each of the following compounds, using the appropriate naming system:

a) MgS
b) CO
c) NH_3
d) $AlBr_3$
e) Co_2O_3
f) $CaSO_4$
g) K_3PO_4
h) SO_3
i) CCl_4
j) ZnF_2
k) $Fe(NO_3)_3$
l) $Cu(OH)_2$
m) $(NH_4)_2S$

3.93 Each of the following names is incorrect. Explain why, and give the correct name for each compound.

a) $CaCl_2$ "calcium dichloride"
b) FeO "iron oxide"
c) $NaNO_3$ "sodium nitrogen trioxide"
d) ICl "iodine chloride"

3.94 *The nitrate ion (NO_3^-) has three oxygen atoms bonded to the nitrogen atom. Draw a Lewis structure for this ion. (Hint: The ion has one extra electron. Put the extra electron on one of the oxygen atoms, and then form bonds that satisfy the octet rule.)

4

Energy and Physical Properties

In the middle of the night, Mr. Nilsson is awakened by agonizing pain at the base of his big toe. He turns on the light and sees that the joint is swollen and red. After a miserable, sleepless night, he goes to the emergency room, where the physician tells him that he is suffering from an attack of gout. A lab test shows that Mr. Nilsson has a high level of uric acid in his blood, putting him at increased risk of more attacks of gout in the future.

Our bodies constantly make uric acid as we break down proteins and nucleic acids. However, the amount of uric acid that can dissolve in body fluids, called the solubility, is rather low. If our bodies produce too much uric acid or our kidneys do not excrete it rapidly enough, some of the uric acid forms solid crystals, usually in a joint. The crystals irritate the joint, producing the swelling and pain of gout. To treat Mr. Nilsson's pain and swelling, the doctor prescribes medications that decrease the inflammation and inhibit the formation of uric acid crystals. The doctor also recommends that Mr. Nilsson decrease the amount of meat in his diet and drink plenty of water during the day to keep the concentration of uric acid low.

Solubility is one of the physical properties we can use to describe a chemical substance. Like many physical properties, the solubility depends on the chemical structure of the substance. In this chapter, we will explore the physical behavior of chemical substances and how it is related to structure.

Uric acid

OUTLINE

4.1 **Heat and energy**
4.2 **The three states of matter**
4.3 **The properties of gases**
4.4 **Changes of state**
4.5 **Attractive forces and the physical properties of matter**
4.6 **Solutions and the dissolving process**
4.7 **Electrolytes and dissociation**
4.8 **Solubility**
4.9 **The relationship between solubility and molecular structure**

LABORATORY REQUISITION—CHEMISTRY

☐ Sodium	NA	☐ Fructosamine	FRU/ALB
☐ Potassium	K	☐ PSA	PSA
☐ Creatinine	CREAT	☐ Chloride	CL
☐ BUN	BUN	☐ Calcium	CA
☐ Glucose–fasting	GLUCF	☐ Phosphorus	PHOS
☐ Glucose–random	GLUCR	☐ Phenylalanine	PKU
☐ Hemoglobin A1C	HGBA1C	☑ Uric Acid	URIC

Food rich in complex carbohydrates, such as whole grains, fruits, and vegetables, can help prevent a variety of health problems.

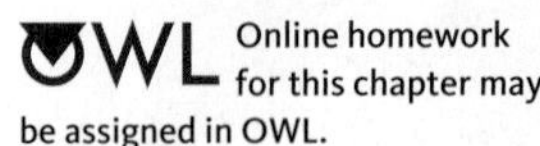
Online homework for this chapter may be assigned in OWL.

Pour yourself a glass of water and put a couple of ice cubes in it. Over the next few minutes, the outside of the glass will become moist and the ice cubes will shrink. A couple of hours later, the ice will have vanished and the outside of the glass will be dry again. If you let the glass sit undisturbed for a month, the water in it will gradually disappear, leaving the glass empty. Now pour yourself a second glass of water, add a sugar cube, and stir. In a minute or two, the sugar will disappear, just as the ice did. If you let this mixture sit undisturbed for a month, the water will vanish but the sugar will reappear.

All of the events just described are examples of physical changes, in which the chemical formulas of the substances involved remain the same. For instance, when ice turns into water, its chemical formula does not change; both ice and water have the formula H_2O. The melted ice, along with the rest of the water in the glass, eventually changes into invisible water vapor, the gaseous form of H_2O. Likewise, when the sugar dissolves in the water, it remains sugar and keeps its chemical formula, $C_{12}H_{22}O_{11}$.

In this chapter, we will take a deeper look at physical changes such as melting, boiling, and dissolving. We will explore why sugar and salt are solids while water and alcohol are liquids, and we will examine why ice melts on your kitchen counter but not in your freezer. We will also investigate why sugar and salt dissolve in water but chalk and butter do not. We can explain much of the behavior of matter by looking at two concepts: the energy that the molecules, atoms, and ions that make up the substance have, and the strength of the attraction between these individual particles. Our starting point is the concept of energy.

OBJECTIVES: *Understand kinetic energy and potential energy and the relationship between thermal energy and temperature, and calculate the heat needed to change the temperature of a substance.*

4.1 Heat and Energy

When we say that we don't have much energy today, or if we note that a country needs to develop new energy sources, what do we mean? To a chemist, **energy** has a specific meaning: *energy is the ability to do work*. Any object that can do work has energy. In science, the term *work* means any movement of matter against a resistance. We do work whenever we lift a cup off the table or push a dresser across the floor. Table 4.1 lists some other familiar forms of work.

What kinds of things have energy? Any object that is in motion can do work if it collides with another object. For example, a rolling bowling ball can knock over the pins, while a stationary ball cannot. This energy of motion is called **kinetic energy**. Any moving object has kinetic energy, and the amount of kinetic energy the object has depends on its mass and on how fast it is moving, as shown in Figure 4.1. This should seem reasonable: a heavy bowling ball can knock over more pins than a light one, and a fast-moving ball can knock over more pins than a slow-moving one.

TABLE 4.1 Examples of Work

Type of Work	Why Is This Work?
Climbing a flight of stairs	The person is moving upward against the force of gravity.
Playing music on an electronic device	Electrons are being pushed through the circuits in the device.
Driving a car	The car is moving against air resistance.

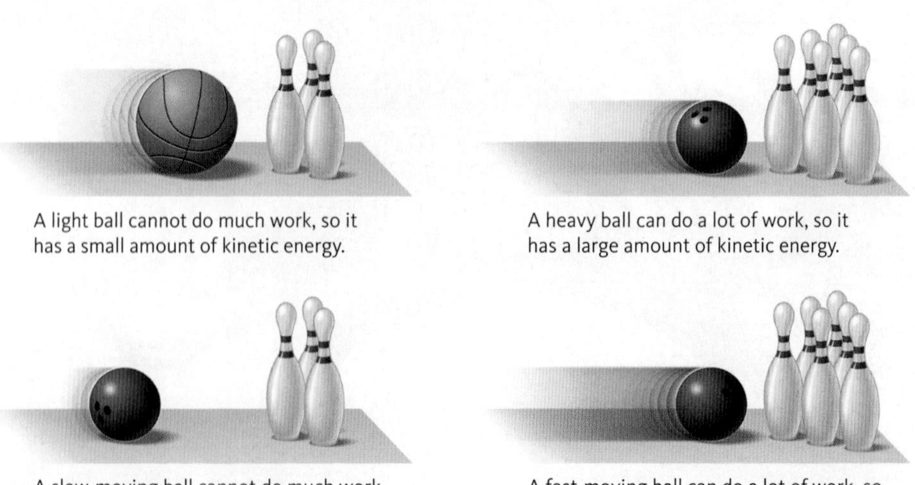
A light ball cannot do much work, so it has a small amount of kinetic energy.

A heavy ball can do a lot of work, so it has a large amount of kinetic energy.

A slow-moving ball cannot do much work, so it has a small amount of kinetic energy.

A fast-moving ball can do a lot of work, so it has a large amount of kinetic energy.

FIGURE 4.1 The kinetic energy of an object depends on its mass and its speed.

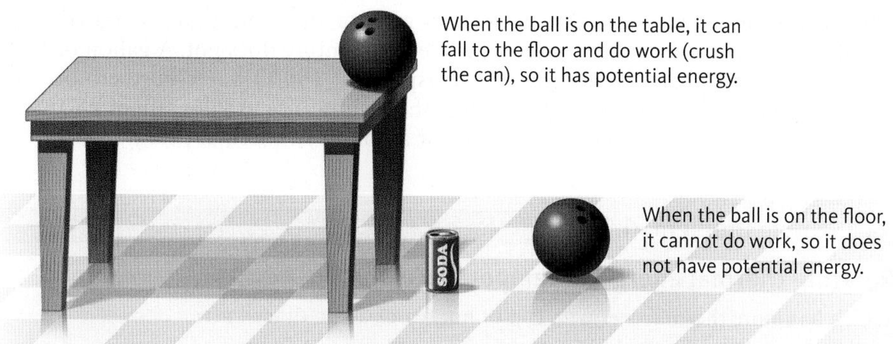

When the ball is on the table, it can fall to the floor and do work (crush the can), so it has potential energy.
When the ball is on the floor, it cannot do work, so it does not have potential energy.
SODA

FIGURE 4.2 The potential energy of an object depends on its position.

Health Note: Your body is constantly changing potential energy (the energy in the food you eat) into kinetic energy (the energy of muscle contractions).

Any object that is not in its most stable position also has energy. For example, imagine a bowling ball that is sitting on the edge of a high shelf. If the bowling ball falls off the shelf, it will fall to the floor (its most stable position), and it can do a considerable amount of work when it lands, as illustrated in Figure 4.2. The energy an object has that is due to its position is called **potential energy**. Other examples are the energy in a tightly wound spring, the energy in a battery, and the energy in a slice of pizza. The energy in the battery and the pizza are examples of chemical energy, which we will explore in Chapter 6.

We can change potential energy into kinetic energy. For instance, if we hold a bowling ball in the air and let go of it, it will fall. The ball loses potential energy (it gets closer and closer to the ground), but it gains kinetic energy (it speeds up). We can also change kinetic energy into potential energy. Figure 4.3 shows another way that we can exchange these two forms of energy.

As we will see in Chapter 16, nuclear reactions can change matter into energy. In general, however, *energy cannot be created or destroyed*. We can change energy from one form into another, but we cannot create energy from nothing. This principle is called the **law of conservation of energy.**

The individual atoms in any substance have kinetic energy, because *atoms are always in motion*. The atoms move in random directions and at a variety of speeds. This random kinetic energy of atoms is called **thermal energy**. When the atoms are moving very rapidly, the substance feels hot to the touch, and when the atoms are moving more slowly, the substance feels cooler. This random, ceaseless motion of atoms can be harnessed to do work. For example, engines use chemical reactions to produce hot gases, and they harness this thermal energy to move objects such as cars and airplanes.

Thermal energy is closely related to temperature. As temperature rises, an object's thermal energy increases and its atoms move faster, as shown in Figure 4.4. When you heat a pot of water on the stove, you are increasing both its temperature and its thermal energy. Likewise, when you put your leftover dinner in the refrigerator, you are decreasing both its temperature and its thermal energy.

Charles D. Winter

Image copyright Photo storm, 2010. Used under license from Shutterstock.com reresearched for lower cost and more up-to-date options

New batteries (a) and a drawn bow (b) contain potential energy.

Health Note: If your body does not have enough thermal energy to maintain your body temperature, you suffer from hypothermia.

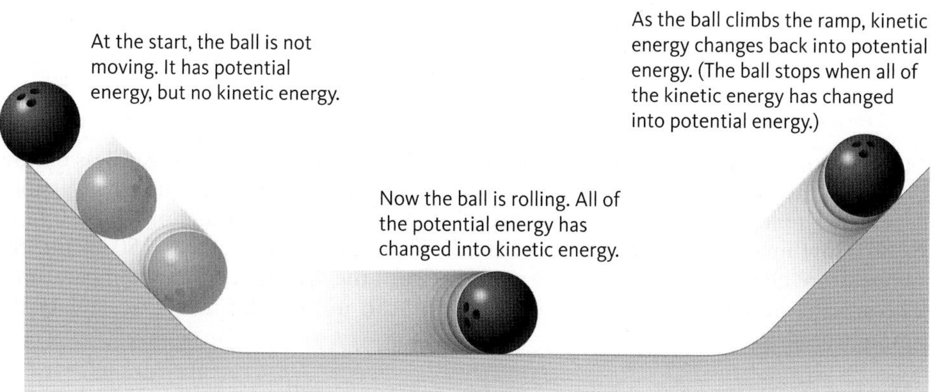

At the start, the ball is not moving. It has potential energy, but no kinetic energy.
As the ball climbs the ramp, kinetic energy changes back into potential energy. (The ball stops when all of the kinetic energy has changed into potential energy.)
Now the ball is rolling. All of the potential energy has changed into kinetic energy.

FIGURE 4.3 Converting one form of energy into another.

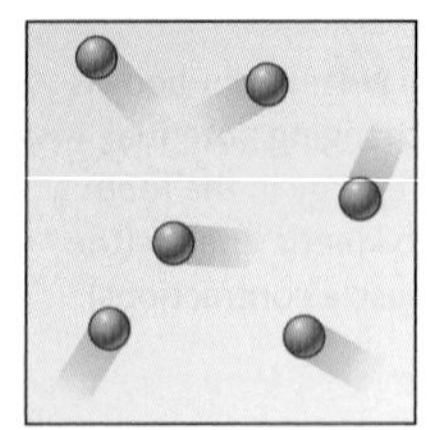

At low temperatures, atoms move slowly, so they have low thermal energies.

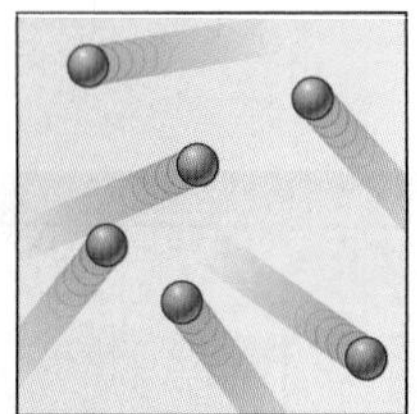

At high temperatures, atoms move rapidly, so they have high thermal energies.

FIGURE 4.4 The relationship between temperature and thermal energy.

However, temperature and thermal energy are not the same thing. Thermal energy depends on the amount of the substance, while temperature does not. A gallon of 100°C water has far more thermal energy than a teaspoon of 100°C water. Furthermore, thermal energy depends on the chemical makeup of the substance. A kilogram of 25°C water and a kilogram of 25°C alcohol have different amounts of thermal energy.

Sample Problem 4.1

Relating thermal energy to temperature

Which has more thermal energy: a cup of hot tea or a cup of iced tea?

SOLUTION

Thermal energy is directly related to temperature: as a substance grows hotter, its thermal energy increases. Therefore, hot tea has more thermal energy than iced tea. (Remember that this reasoning is only valid when you are comparing equal amounts of the same substance.)

TRY IT YOURSELF: *In which cup of tea, hot or iced, are the molecules moving faster?*

For additional practice, try Core Problems 4.9 and 4.10.

Energy Is Measured in Calories

It is impossible to measure the thermal energy of a substance directly, but we can use other properties to calculate changes in thermal energy. Thermal energy that is added to or removed from a substance is called **heat**, and heat normally produces a change in the temperature of the substance. The relationship between heat and temperature changes is

$$\text{heat} = \text{mass} \times \text{temperature change} \times \text{specific heat}$$

Using symbols, the formula looks like this:

$$\text{heat} = m \times \Delta T \times C_p$$

Health Note: "Calories" on nutritional labels are actually kilocalories (1 kcal = 1000 cal), because a calorie is a very small amount of energy.

In this formula, ΔT ("delta T") stands for the temperature change, which is the difference between the starting and final temperatures and which must be in Celsius degrees. Units for heat vary widely, but in medicine and nutrition, heat (and energy in general) is usually measured in *calories (cal)*. The **specific heat**, C_p, is the conversion factor that allows us to translate temperature changes into the corresponding energy. The formula for heat also includes the mass, because we need more energy to raise the temperature of a large mass than we do to raise the temperature of a small mass. The mass must be expressed in grams.

Health Note: Our bodies usually generate enough heat to maintain our body temperature by carrying out normal cellular activities, but muscles can produce additional heat by shivering, and some fat deposits (called brown adipose tissue) are specifically adapted to produce heat.

A calorie is the amount of heat needed to raise the temperature of 1 g of water by 1°C. Therefore, the specific heat of water is one calorie per gram of water, per degree Celsius of temperature change. We can write the specific heat of water as a conversion factor that has two units in the denominator:

$$\text{specific heat of water} = \frac{1.00\ \text{cal}}{1\ \text{g}\cdot°\text{C}}$$

but it is more common to write the units in a single line: 1.00 cal/g·°C. Regardless of how you write the units, be sure that they cancel out, just as they do in any unit conversion.

For example, suppose we want to heat 250 g of water (about a cup) from 20°C to 50°C. How much heat (energy) do we need? The mass of the water is 250 g, and the temperature change is 30°C, the difference between the starting and final temperatures. The specific heat of water is 1.00 cal/g·°C. We can use our formula to calculate the amount of heat:

$$\begin{aligned}\text{heat} &= 250\ \cancel{\text{g}} \times 30\cancel{°\text{C}} \times 1.00\ \frac{\text{cal}}{\cancel{\text{g}}\cdot\cancel{°\text{C}}} \\ &= 7500\ \text{cal}\end{aligned}$$

It takes 7500 cal of heat to warm the water to 50°C. Note that we can cancel out the units of mass and temperature in this calculation, leaving us with calories as our unit of energy.

Every substance has its own specific heat. For most substances, the specific heat is less than 1 cal/g·°C, which means that it takes more energy to change the temperature of water than it does to change the temperature of most other substances. For example, the specific heat of ethyl alcohol (grain alcohol) is 0.58 cal/g·°C, only about half the value for water. Table 4.2 lists some specific heats for common substances. When you calculate the amount of energy needed in a temperature change, be sure to use the correct specific heat.

TABLE 4.2 Specific Heats of Common Liquids and Solids

Substance	Specific Heat
Water	1.00 cal/g·°C
Ethyl alcohol	0.58 cal/g·°C
Gasoline	0.40 cal/g·°C
Aluminum	0.22 cal/g·°C
Sand	0.19 cal/g·°C
Glass	0.18 cal/g·°C
Steel	0.11 cal/g·°C

Sample Problem 4.2

Calculating the heat required for a temperature change

How much heat do you need to raise the temperature of a 500 g steel pan from 20°C to 100°C? Use the information in Table 4.2 to solve this problem.

SOLUTION

We can use the heat formula to do this problem, but we must use the specific heat of steel, which is 0.11 cal/g·°C. The mass of the pan is 500 g, and the temperature change is 100°C − 20°C = 80°C.

$$\text{heat} = 500\ \cancel{\text{g}} \times 80\cancel{^\circ\text{C}} \times 0.11\ \frac{\text{cal}}{\cancel{\text{g}}\cdot\cancel{^\circ\text{C}}}$$
$$= 4400\ \text{cal}$$

TRY IT YOURSELF: *A pile of sand sits in the sun on a summer day, and it warms up from 15°C to 36°C. If the sand weighs 250 g, how much heat does the sand absorb? Use the information in Table 4.2.*

For additional practice, try Core Problems 4.11 (part a) and 4.12 (part a).

Health Note: The average specific heat of a human body is around 0.7 cal/g·°C. The specific heat of body fat is only 0.5 cal/g·°C, so a person with a high percentage of body fat has a lower average specific heat than a person with a lower fat percentage.

If we cool a substance, we must remove heat from it. We can use the same formula to calculate the amount of heat we must remove. For example, in Sample Problem 4.2 we found that we need 4400 calories to heat a 500 g pan from 20°C to 100°C. If we want to cool the pan from 100°C to 20°C, we must remove 4400 calories of heat. The mass of the pan is still 500 g, the temperature difference is still 100°C − 20°C = 80°C, and the specific heat of the pan is still 0.11 cal/g·°C:

$$\text{heat} = 500\ \cancel{\text{g}} \times 80\cancel{^\circ\text{C}} \times 0.11\ \frac{\text{cal}}{\cancel{\text{g}}\cdot\cancel{^\circ\text{C}}}$$
$$= 4400\ \text{cal}$$

Many processes produce or absorb large amounts of heat, and we can use the *kilocalorie (kcal)* to express these large numbers. From its prefix, we know that 1 kcal equals 1000 cal, so the amount of energy we needed to heat the pan in Sample Problem 4.2 is only 4.4 kcal. In addition, many branches of science express energy in *joules (J)* or *kilojoules (kJ)*. The joule is the standard metric unit of energy, but it is not commonly used in medicine or nutrition. Table 4.3 lists the relationships between these units.

TABLE 4.3 Energy Units

Energy Unit	Relationship to the calorie
Kilocalorie (kcal)	1 kcal = 1000 cal
Joule (J)	1 cal = 4.184 J
Kilojoule (kJ)	1 kJ = 239 cal (1 kcal = 4.184 kJ)

Sample Problem 4.3

Converting energy units

It takes 303,000 cal of heat to raise the temperature of a gallon of water from 20°C to 100°C. Convert this amount of heat into (a) kilocalories, (b) joules, and (c) kilojoules.

SOLUTION

We can do each of these unit conversions using the techniques you learned in Chapter 1.

a) To convert the heat from calories into kilocalories, we simply move the decimal point three places to the left (remember the metric railroad).

$$303{,}000.\ \text{cal} = 303\ \text{kcal}$$

continued

If you prefer, you can also use a conversion factor to do this problem.

STEP 1: Identify the original measurement and the final unit.

b) To do this conversion, we must use the four-step method from Chapter 1, because calories and joules are not related by a power of ten. Our original heat measurement was 303,000 cal, and we must convert the heat to joules. We can use the fact that 1 cal equals 4.184 J to write a pair of conversion factors.

STEP 2: Write conversion factors that relate the two units.

$$\frac{4.184\ \text{J}}{1\ \text{cal}} \quad \text{and} \quad \frac{1\ \text{cal}}{4.184\ \text{J}}$$

The second of these factors allows us to cancel units correctly.

STEP 3: Choose the conversion factor that allows you to cancel units.

$$303{,}000\ \text{cal} \times \frac{4.184\ \text{J}}{1\ \text{cal}}$$

← We cancel these units

Next, we do the arithmetic and cancel our units.

STEP 4: Do the math and round your answer.

$$303{,}000\ \cancel{\text{cal}} \times \frac{4.184\ \text{J}}{1\ \cancel{\text{cal}}} = 1{,}267{,}752\ \text{J} \quad \text{calculator answer}$$

Finally, we round our answer to three significant figures: 1,270,000 J (or 1.27×10^6 J).

c) To convert joules into kilojoules, we again move the decimal point three places to the left.

$$1{,}270{,}000. = \mathbf{1270\ kJ}\ (\text{or } 1.27 \times 10^3\ \text{kJ})$$

TRY IT YOURSELF: *It takes 83.5 kJ of heat to raise the temperature of one gallon of gasoline from 20°C to 40°C. Convert this amount of heat into joules, calories, and kilocalories.*

For additional practice, try Core Problems 4.11 (part b) and 4.12 (part b).

CORE PROBLEMS

*All Core Problems are paired and the answers to the **blue** odd-numbered problems appear in the back of the book.*

4.1 A baseball player hits a ball straight up. As the ball rises, does its potential energy increase, decrease, or remain the same? What about its kinetic energy?

4.2 A rock falls off a cliff. As the rock falls, does its potential energy increase, decrease, or remain the same? What about its kinetic energy?

4.3 Which of the following are examples of kinetic energy, and which are examples of potential energy?
a) the energy in a gallon of gasoline
b) the energy in a cup of boiling water
c) the energy in a spinning top

4.4 Which of the following are examples of kinetic energy, and which are examples of potential energy?
a) the energy in a rolling ball
b) the energy in a handful of crackers
c) the energy in a hot piece of metal

4.5 For each of the following pairs of objects, tell which one has more kinetic energy:
a) a car moving at 30 mph (miles per hour) or the same car moving at 40 mph
b) a car moving at 15 mph or a bicycle moving at 15 mph
c) the atoms in a cup of 80°C water or the atoms in a cup of 70°C water
d) a new battery or a used battery

4.6 For each of the following pairs of objects, tell which one has more kinetic energy:
a) a soccer ball moving at 20 m/sec or a soccer ball moving at 10 m/sec
b) a soccer ball lying on the ground or a soccer ball lying on the roof of a building
c) an ice cube at 0°C or an ice cube at −20°C
d) a soccer ball moving at 10 m/sec or a ping-pong ball moving at 10 m/sec

4.7 For each of the following pairs of objects, tell which one has more potential energy:
a) an airplane at 30,000 feet or an airplane at 20,000 feet
b) a new battery or a used battery
c) a warm piece of bread or a cool piece of bread
d) a small stone on top of a building or a large stone on top of the same building

4.8 For each of the following pairs of objects, tell which one has more potential energy:
a) a mixture of gasoline and air or the exhaust gases after the gasoline burns
b) a bird perched on the roof of your house or the same bird flying close to the ground
c) a set mousetrap or the same mousetrap after it has been sprung
d) an ice cube at 0°C or an ice cube at −20°C

continued

4.9 Misti puts a bottle of water in the refrigerator.
a) As the water cools, do the water molecules speed up, slow down, or continue to move at the same speeds?
b) Does the amount of thermal energy in the water increase, decrease, or remain the same?

4.10 Yelena heats a cup of coffee in the microwave.
a) As the coffee warms up, do the water molecules speed up, slow down, or continue to move at the same speeds?
b) Does the amount of thermal energy in the coffee increase, decrease, or remain the same?

4.11 a) How many calories of heat do you need if you want to raise the temperature of 350 g of gasoline from 18.0°C to 22.0°C?
b) Express your answer in joules and in kilocalories.

4.12 a) How many calories of heat must you remove if you want to lower the temperature of 350 g of steel from 18.0°C to 12.0°C?
b) Express your answer in joules and in kilocalories.

4.2 The Three States of Matter

OBJECTIVES: *Distinguish the bulk properties of the three states of matter, and relate these properties to the behavior of the particles that make up the substance.*

As we saw at the start of this chapter, the chemical substance H_2O can exist in three forms: as a **solid** (ice), a **liquid** (normal water), or a **gas** (water vapor or steam). These three forms are called the three **states of matter**. The state we observe depends on the temperature; we see ice in the freezer, liquid water in the refrigerator, and steam coming from the teakettle. Most other chemical substances can also exist in solid, liquid, or gaseous states, and their state likewise depends on the temperature. In this section, we will examine the properties of the three states of matter and the relationship between the state of a substance and its temperature.

To begin, let us ask how we can tell what state a particular substance is in. Two key questions allow us to determine the state of a substance:

1. *Does the substance keep a fixed shape when moved from one container to another?* If it does, it is a solid. Liquids and gases flow freely and take the shape of their containers.
2. *Does the substance keep a fixed volume when moved from one container to another?* Solids and liquids do not change volume when they are moved to a different container, but gases always expand to fill the entire container. Therefore, if the substance does not keep a fixed volume, it is a gas.

Gases also have far lower densities than solids or liquids. Both ice and liquid water are more than a thousand times more dense than steam; the density of water is around 1.00 g/mL, but the density of the steam from a boiling teakettle is only 0.0006 g/mL. Table 4.4 summarizes the behavior of the three states of matter.

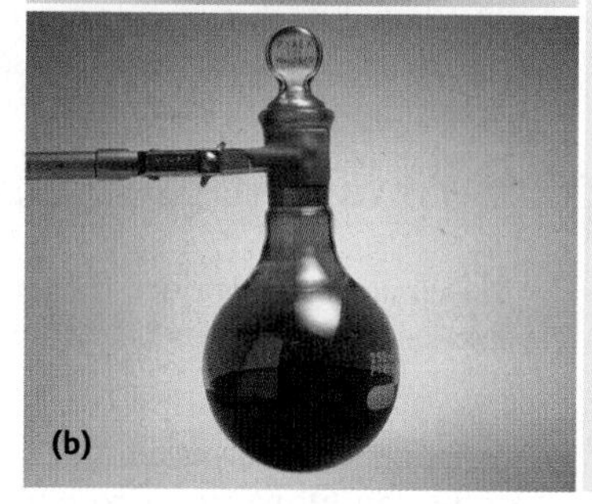

Charles D. Winters

The behavior of the three states of bromine. (a) The shape of a solid does not depend on the shape of the container. (b) Liquids take the shape of their containers, but they maintain the same volume. (c) Gases take up all of the space available to them.

TABLE 4.4 The Three States of Matter

	Solid	Liquid	Gas
Shape	Fixed	Variable (liquids can be poured)	Variable (gases can be poured)
Volume	Fixed	Fixed	Variable (gases can expand and contract dramatically)
Typical density	Moderate to high (0.5 to 10 g/mL)	Moderate to high (0.5 to 10 g/mL)	Very low (0.0005 to 0.005 g/mL at room temperature)

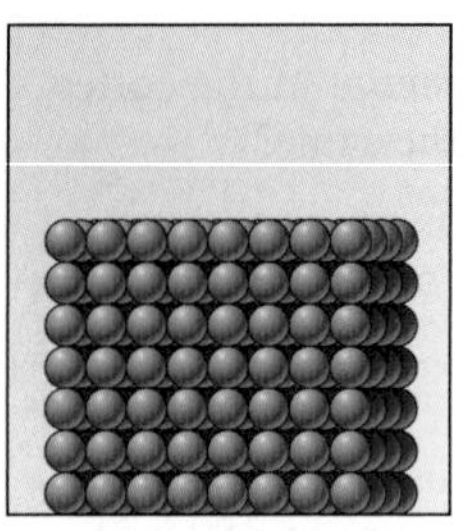
Solid: The particles remain in fixed positions.

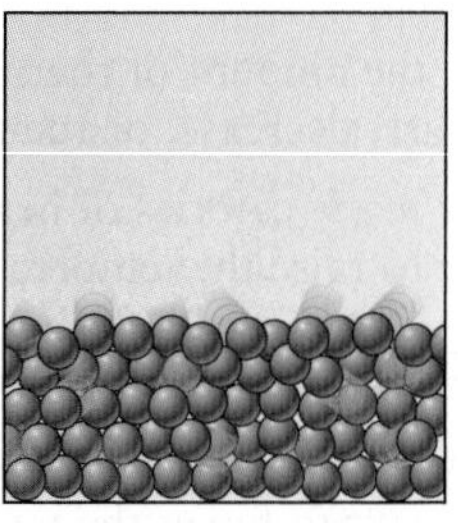
Liquid: The particles move about but remain in contact with one another.

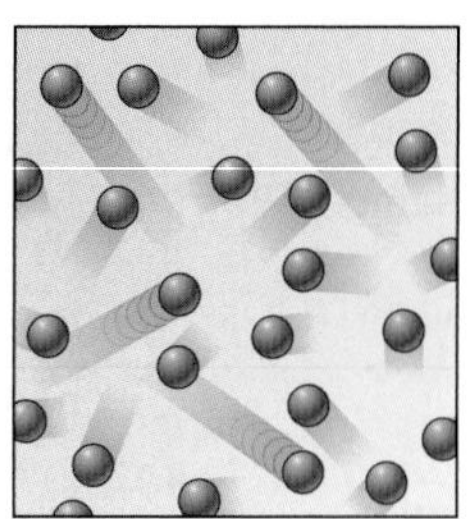
Gas: The particles are free to move throughout the container.

FIGURE 4.5 The molecular behavior of the three states of matter.

Some common substances do not seem to fit these categories at first glance. For example, sand is a solid, but it can be poured from one container to another. However, when we look closely, we see that the individual grains of sand do not change their shape when the sand is poured. Only the air between the grains (a gas) changes shape.

The Properties of Each State Are Related to the Behavior of the Particles

The properties of the three states that we can observe can be related directly to the behavior of the individual particles (atoms, molecules, or ions) in a substance, as shown in Figure 4.5. In a solid, the particles are packed tightly together, and they cannot move around, although they vibrate about a fixed position. Liquids also contain closely packed particles, but in a liquid the particles are free to move around within the sample. In a gas, the particles are not in contact with one another and can move throughout the entire volume of the container.

Sample Problem **4.4**

Describing the behavior of molecules

Describe the behavior of a water molecule in a glass of water.

SOLUTION

In a liquid, each molecule moves around randomly. A particular water molecule will wander throughout the entire sample of water if we watch it long enough. However, the water molecule is in contact with other molecules at all times.

TRY IT YOURSELF: *Describe the behavior of a water molecule in a piece of ice.*

For additional practice, try Core Problems 4.17 and 4.18.

Atoms themselves cannot expand or contract, so a substance can only contract if its atoms can move closer to one another. In solids and liquids, there is little empty space between the particles, so solids and liquids have a very limited ability to expand and contract. Gases, on the other hand, are mostly empty space. They can contract because the particles can readily move closer together, and they can expand because the particles do not need to remain in contact with one another, as shown in Figure 4.6. In addition, gases have very low densities because a given volume of a gas contains far fewer particles (and consequently much less mass) than the same volume of a liquid or a solid.

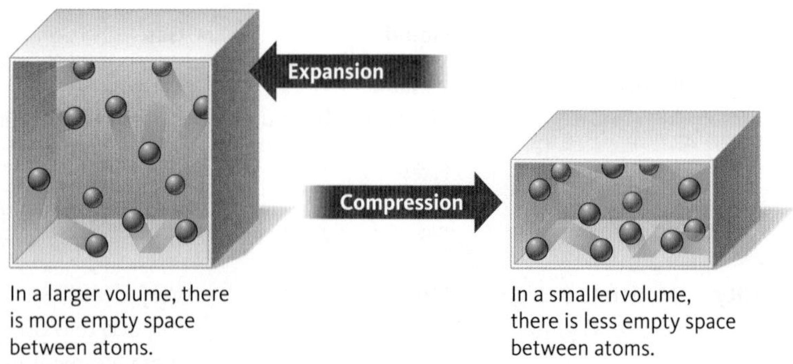

In a larger volume, there is more empty space between atoms.

In a smaller volume, there is less empty space between atoms.

FIGURE 4.6 The expansion and compression of a gas.

TABLE 4.5 The Relationship Between State and Energy

	Solid	Liquid	Gas
Temperature	Lowest	Intermediate	Highest
Thermal energy	Lowest	Intermediate	Highest
Speed of atoms	Lowest	Intermediate	Highest

The State of a Substance Is Related to Its Temperature

Based on our experience with water, we can relate the various states of matter to temperature. We must cool water to change it into ice, and we heat it to change it to water vapor. If we look at a range of chemical substances, we see that they always become solids when they are extremely cold and gases when they are extremely hot.

• Many compounds break down into elements or simpler compounds when heated, and these simpler substances become gases at high temperatures.

We have seen that temperature is directly related to the thermal energy of a substance, which in turn is related to the motion of the atoms. Therefore, we can relate the state of a substance to thermal energy and to atomic motion. To change a substance into a gas, we must increase its thermal energy, and in doing so we increase the speeds of the atoms. In contrast, to change a substance into a solid, we must decrease its thermal energy, which decreases the speeds of the atoms. Table 4.5 summarizes these relationships.

The state of a substance is related to its temperature, but the temperature cannot be the only factor that determines the state. If it were, salt, water, and air would all be in the same state at room temperature. We will explore the other factors that determine the state of a substance in Section 4.5.

CORE PROBLEMS

4.13 For each of the following statements, tell whether it describes a solid, a liquid, a gas, or more than one of these:
a) Sulfur dioxide has an extremely low density.
b) Carbon disulfide can be poured from one container to another, but it does not change its volume.
c) A piece of calcium chloride does not change its shape when it is put into a different container.

4.14 For each of the following statements, tell whether it describes a solid, a liquid, a gas, or more than one of these:
a) Bromine changes its shape when it is placed into a new container, and it has a rather high density.
b) Chlorine can expand and contract easily.
c) Iodine forms rigid crystals.

4.15 If you remove thermal energy from a glass of water, which of the following will happen to the water? (List all of the correct answers.)
a) The temperature of the water will go down.
b) The temperature of the water will go up.
c) The water will freeze.
d) The water will boil.

4.16 If you add thermal energy to a glass of water, which of the following will happen to the water? (List all of the correct answers.)
a) The temperature of the water will go down.
b) The temperature of the water will go up.
c) The water will freeze.
d) The water will boil.

4.17 Describe the behavior of a helium atom inside a balloon that is filled with helium.

4.18 Describe the behavior of a copper atom inside a copper penny.

4.19 Carbon dioxide is a gas at room temperature. At which of the following temperatures is it most likely to be a solid?
−100°C 0°C 100°C

4.20 Palmitic acid is a solid at room temperature. At which of the following temperatures is it most likely to be a liquid?
−100°C 0°C 100°C

4.21 Explain why 1 g of gaseous nitrogen takes up far more space than 1 g of liquid nitrogen.

4.22 Explain why 1 g of solid butter takes up roughly the same amount of space as 1 g of melted butter.

OBJECTIVES: *Understand and apply the relationships between pressure, volume, and temperature for a gas.*

4.3 The Properties of Gases

As we saw in Section 4.2, gases differ strikingly from liquids and solids. In fact, solids and liquids are classified as **condensed states** to emphasize their dissimilarity to gases. Solids and liquids have similar densities to each other, do not expand or contract significantly when they are heated, and remain at the bottom of any container they are placed into. By contrast, gases have far lower densities, expand and contract dramatically in response to temperature, and escape rapidly from any open container.

One of the most conspicuous differences between gases and condensed states is the ability of gases to expand and contract. The volume of a sample of a solid or liquid material does not greatly depend on the conditions it is exposed to. For example, if you put 500 mL of 0°C water into a container and then heat the water to 70°C, the volume of the water expands to 511 mL, an observable change but certainly not a dramatic one. On the other hand, the volume of a balloon filled with 500 mL of air (or any other gas) will increase to 628 mL under the same conditions. Since gases like oxygen and carbon dioxide play an important role in the chemistry of living organisms, let us look more closely at their properties and behavior.

Gases are difficult and inconvenient to weigh, because they have low densities and they can escape from open containers. Therefore, gases are usually described by measuring their temperature, volume, and pressure. You are already familiar with temperature and volume, and if you have ever ridden an elevator to the top of a tall building, taken a ride in an airplane, or dived to the bottom of a swimming pool, you have a general sense of what pressure is. The uncomfortable sensation in your ears is produced by changes in the pressure that the air (or water) around you exerts on your body. **Pressure** is defined as *the force applied on a surface, divided by the area of the surface.* We can write this definition as a mathematical formula:

$$\text{pressure} = \frac{\text{force}}{\text{area}}$$

In the English system, force is measured in pounds, and area is measured in square inches. Figure 4.7 illustrates how force and area are related to pressure.

To understand the difference between force and pressure, compare the effect of pushing a thumbtack against a bulletin board to that of pushing your thumb against the bulletin board. The thumbtack will be driven into the board, but your thumb will not dent the board significantly. The force is roughly the same in both cases, but the pressure is much higher when you use a thumbtack, because the point of the thumbtack has a tiny surface area. The higher pressure drives the thumbtack into the bulletin board.

All gases exert pressure on the walls of their containers. The gas molecules are in constant motion, bouncing off one another and off the walls. Every impact on the wall of the container gives a little push, and the pressure on the wall is the result of a continuous succession of these impacts. The air around you also exerts pressure on everything it touches, including your body. At sea level, atmospheric pressure averages 14.7 *pounds per square inch (psi)*. This means that the atmosphere is pressing on every square inch of your body with a force of 14.7 pounds. The total force on your body is around 20 tons (40,000 pounds)!

Atmospheric pressure depends on your elevation above sea level. For example, the air pressure at the top of a 500-foot skyscraper is around 14.45 psi, as compared with 14.7 psi at the base of the building (if the base is at sea level). If you have ever ridden an elevator to the top of a tall building, you know that your ears can easily detect the pressure change between the bottom and the top of the building. For higher elevations, the pressure difference becomes much larger. Figure 4.8 shows how atmospheric pressure varies with elevation.

There are a number of pressure units in common use. In health care, blood pressures and blood gas measurements are normally measured in *torrs*. A pressure

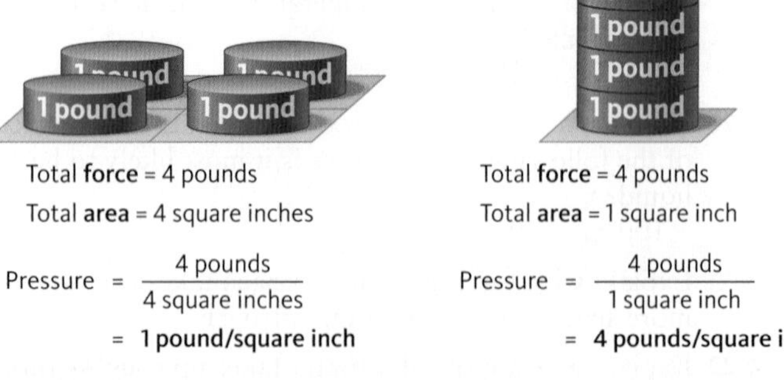

FIGURE 4.7 The relationship of pressure to force and area.

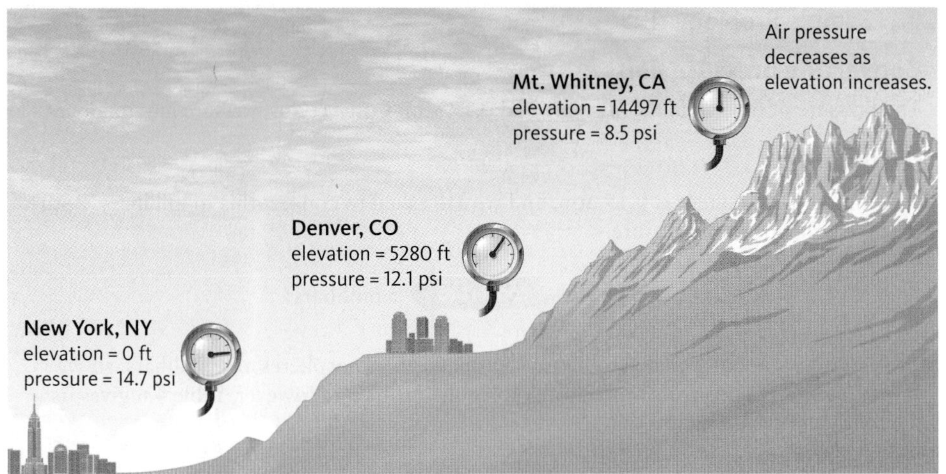

FIGURE 4.8 The relationship between atmospheric pressure and elevation.

Health Note: Hikers who ascend to a high altitude may get altitude sickness because of the low air pressure. The exact cause is not understood, but the symptoms are well known, with headache, dizziness, and nausea being the most typical. Severe altitude sickness can cause potentially fatal fluid buildup in the lungs or brain.

of 110 torr, which is a typical blood pressure at the moment the heart beats, corresponds to a bit more than 2.1 psi. Other pressure units you may encounter are the *atmosphere (atm)* and the *bar.* These are large pressure units and are quite similar to each other, so they are often used to express very high pressures, such as the pressure in a tank of compressed air. Meteorologists frequently use the *millibar,* which is 1/1000 of a bar, to express atmospheric pressures. The standard metric unit of pressure is the *pascal (Pa),* but this unit is rarely used in practice, because a pascal is so small that we must use very large numbers to express common pressures. For example, if your blood pressure is 110 over 60 torr, it is 14,700 over 8000 Pa. Table 4.6 summarizes these pressure units and gives some conversion factors.

Health Note: Blood pressure is the pressure that the blood exerts on the walls of the arteries. The first value (systolic pressure) is the pressure during a heart contraction, and the second value (diastolic pressure) is the pressure while the heart is at rest.

TABLE 4.6 Pressure Units in Common Use

Unit	Relationship to Torr	Comment
Pound per square inch (psi)	1 psi = 51.7 torr	Pounds per square inch is the most commonly used pressure unit in the United States.
Atmosphere (atm)	1 atm = 760 torr	The average air pressure at sea level is 1 atm. This unit is used to express very high pressures.
Torr		This unit is used in medicine to express blood pressures and blood gas measurements. It is also called a *millimeter of mercury (mm Hg).*
Bar	1 bar = 750 torr	A bar equals 100,000 Pa. The bar is used as an alternate to the atmosphere, because they are similar in size.
Millibar	1 millibar = 0.75 torr	A millibar is 1/1000 of a bar, or 100 Pa. The millibar is commonly used to express air pressures in meteorology.
Pascal (Pa)	1 torr = 133 Pa	The pascal is the standard metric unit, but it is rarely used in medicine because it is very small.

Sample Problem 4.5

Converting pressure units

The pressure of oxygen in the air is around 0.19 atm. Convert this pressure into millibars.

SOLUTION

Our initial measurement is 0.19 atm, and we are asked to convert this to millibars. Both of these units measure pressure.

STEP 1: Identify the original measurement and the final unit.

0.19 atm —convert to→ ? millibars

Table 4.6 does not give a direct relationship between atmospheres and millibars, so we cannot use a single conversion factor to solve the problem. However, Table 4.6 gives us the following relationships:

STEP 2: Write conversion factors that relate the two units.

$$1 \text{ atm} = 760 \text{ torr}$$
$$1 \text{ millibar} = 0.75 \text{ torr}$$

Based on these relationships, we can construct the following two-step pathway:

0.19 atm —convert to→ ? torr —convert to→ ? millibars

The relevant conversion factors for each step are

$$\frac{760 \text{ torr}}{1 \text{ atm}} \quad \text{and} \quad \frac{1 \text{ atm}}{760 \text{ torr}}$$

$$\frac{0.75 \text{ torr}}{1 \text{ millibar}} \quad \text{and} \quad \frac{1 \text{ millibar}}{0.75 \text{ torr}}$$

Now we can select the conversion factors that allow us to cancel units. The correct setup is:

STEP 3: Choose the conversion factors that allow you to cancel units.

$$0.19 \text{ atm} \times \frac{760 \text{ torr}}{1 \text{ atm}} \times \frac{1 \text{ millibar}}{0.75 \text{ torr}}$$

These units cancel each other out. (torr)

These units cancel each other out. (atm)

Finally we can cancel units and do the arithmetic.

STEP 4: Do the math and round your answer.

$$0.19 \cancel{\text{atm}} \times \frac{760 \cancel{\text{torr}}}{1 \cancel{\text{atm}}} \times \frac{1 \text{ millibar}}{0.75 \cancel{\text{torr}}} = 192.5333333 \text{ millibars} \quad \text{calculator answer}$$

Rounding the calculator answer to two significant figures gives us **190 millibars.**

TRY IT YOURSELF: *The pressure of neon in the air is around 1.8 Pa. Convert this pressure to millibars.*

For additional practice, try Core Problems 4.29 and 4.30.

Health Note: When you inhale, your diaphragm pulls the bottom of your lungs downward, increasing their volume. As a result, the air pressure inside your lungs becomes lower than the pressure of the atmosphere. Air then moves into your lungs, restoring the pressure balance between the lungs and the surrounding air.

Gas Pressure Depends on Volume, Temperature, and Number of Molecules

The pressure of a gas in any container is a result of molecules bouncing off the walls of the container. Therefore, the pressure that a gas exerts depends on the number of molecules that collide with each square inch of the wall and on the speed of the molecules. We can change the number of collisions per square inch by either changing the number of molecules in the container or changing the volume of the container. We can change the speed of the molecules by changing the temperature. Therefore, the pressure of any

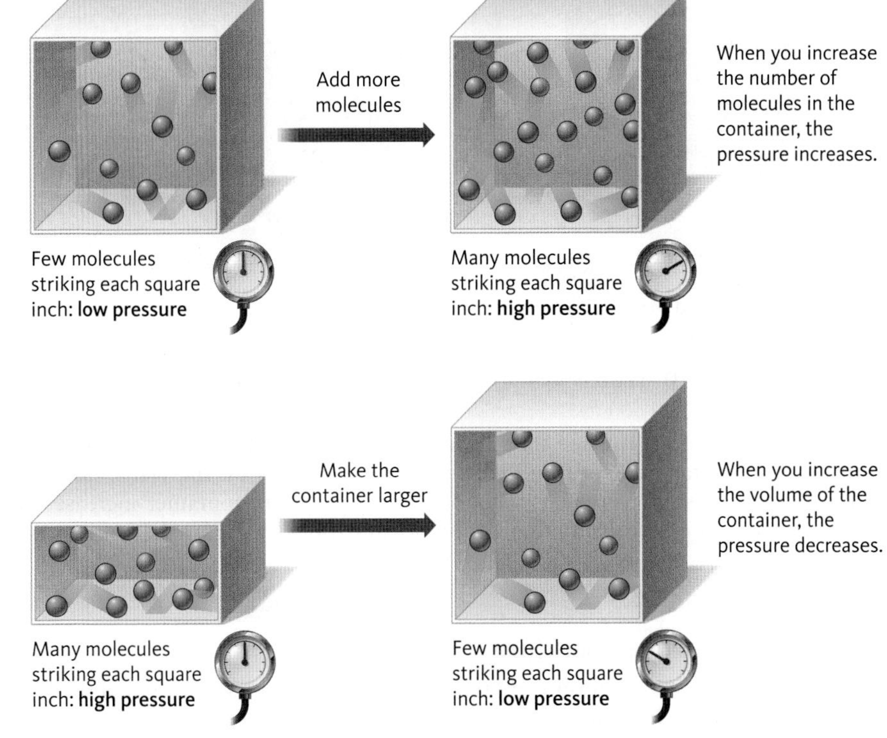

FIGURE 4.9 The pressure of a gas is related to the number of molecules and the volume.

gas depends on all three of these factors (number of molecules, volume, and temperature). The specific relationships are:

- As the number of molecules *increases,* the pressure of the gas *increases.*
- As the volume of the container *increases,* the pressure of the gas *decreases.*
- As the temperature *increases,* the pressure of the gas *increases.*

Figure 4.9 illustrates the first two relationships. If we add more molecules to a container, the number of molecules that collide with the walls of the container will increase, so the pressure will go up. If we make the container larger, though, we will spread out the molecules, so fewer molecules will hit each square inch of the container wall. Therefore, making the container larger decreases the pressure. Conversely, if we make the container smaller, the pressure of the gas in the container will increase.

Sample Problem **4.6**

Relating pressure to volume and number of molecules

Which exerts more pressure: 5 g of oxygen gas in a 10-L container, or 10 g of oxygen gas in a 10-L container?

SOLUTION

We can see that 10 g of oxygen contains twice as many molecules as 5 g of oxygen. When we put more molecules into a container, the molecules hit the walls of the container more often, so 10 g of oxygen exerts more pressure than 5 g of oxygen.

TRY IT YOURSELF: *Which exerts more pressure: 5 g of oxygen gas in a 10-L container, or 5 g of oxygen gas in a 20-L container?*

For additional practice, try Core Problems 4.23 (parts a and c) and 4.24 (parts a and b).

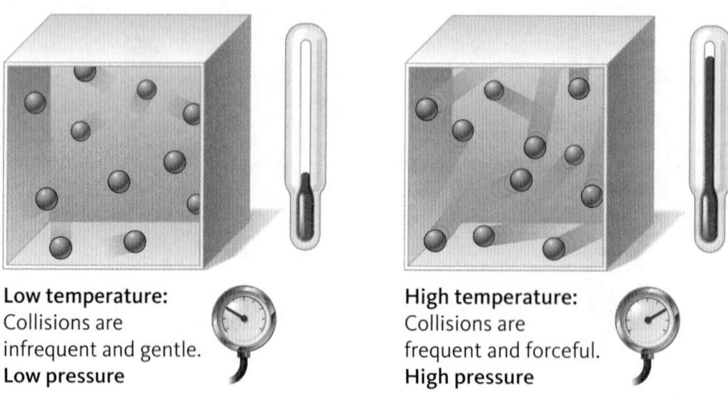

Low temperature:
Collisions are
infrequent and gentle.
Low pressure
High temperature:
Collisions are
frequent and forceful.
High pressure

FIGURE 4.10 The relationship between pressure and temperature.

As we saw in Section 4.1, when the temperature of a substance rises, the molecules of the substance move faster. As a result, the molecules of a gas hit the walls more often and more forcefully, so the pressure that the gas exerts on its container increases. The relationship between pressure and temperature is illustrated in Figure 4.10.

Sample Problem **4.7**

Relating pressure to temperature

A bicyclist fills her tires to a pressure of 60 psi. She then starts riding on a paved road on a hot, sunny day. What happens to the pressure in her tires?

SOLUTION

The air pressure in the tire goes up. As the bicyclist rides on the hot pavement, the tires and the air inside them become warmer. When a gas becomes warmer, it exerts more pressure, because its molecules move more rapidly and hit the walls of the tire more often.

TRY IT YOURSELF: *At noon, Mr. Smith fills his car tires with enough air to exert a pressure of 32 psi. He then leaves the car in his driveway. If he measures the pressure in the tires at midnight, what will he see?*

For additional practice, try Core Problems 4.23 (part b) and 4.24 (part c).

If a gas is in a container that can expand or contract, the volume of the gas changes when its temperature changes. Gases tend to expand when they are heated and contract when they are cooled. We can rationalize this behavior by thinking about pressure. When we heat a gas, its pressure increases, as we just saw. If the gas is in a flexible container, such as a balloon, the increasing pressure forces the container to expand. The relationship between temperature and volume is illustrated in Figure 4.11.

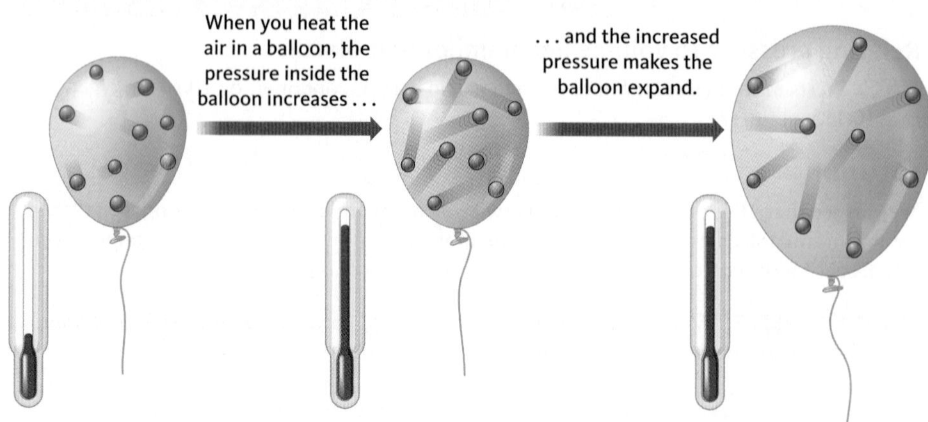

When you heat the
air in a balloon, the
pressure inside the
balloon increases . . .
. . . and the increased
pressure makes the
balloon expand.

FIGURE 4.11 The relationship between temperature and volume.

TABLE 4.7 Partial Pressures of Gases in Air at Sea Level

Gas	Partial Pressure in Normal Air	Partial Pressure in Exhaled Air
Nitrogen (N_2)	587 torr	562 torr
Oxygen (O_2)	157 torr	116 torr
Water vapor (H_2O)	9 torr	47 torr
Argon (Ar)	7 torr	7 torr
Carbon dioxide (CO_2)	0 torr*	28 torr
Total pressure	760 torr	760 torr

*All values are rounded to the nearest whole number. The partial pressure of CO_2 in normal air is 0.25 torr.

Air is a mixture of several gases, primarily nitrogen, oxygen, water vapor, argon, and carbon dioxide. Each gas contributes to the overall pressure that the air exerts. Furthermore, the pressure each gas contributes is directly related to the number of molecules of that gas. For example, roughly 80% of the molecules in normal air are nitrogen (N_2), so nitrogen is responsible for about 80% of the pressure. In a gas mixture, the pressure that each gas exerts is called the **partial pressure** of that gas. Partial pressures behave the same way that the total pressure does; the partial pressure of every gas in a mixture increases if we raise the temperature and decreases if we increase the volume of the container. Furthermore, the partial pressures of the gases in any mixture add up to the total pressure of the gas mixture. This relationship between partial pressures and total pressure is called **Dalton's law of partial pressures.** Table 4.7 shows typical partial pressures of the gases in the air we breathe.

CORE PROBLEMS

4.23 Oxygen for medical use is sold in steel cylinders, because the container must be strong enough to withstand the high pressure when the cylinder is filled with a large amount of oxygen.
a) As the oxygen is drained from the cylinder, what happens to the pressure inside the cylinder?
b) If the temperature of the cylinder is lowered to 0°C, what happens to the pressure inside the cylinder?
c) If the cylinder is dented, the volume of the oxygen inside the cylinder decreases. What happens to the pressure inside the cylinder?

4.24 Tires are filled with air. The rubber must be strong enough to withstand the pressure of the air inside the tire and any bumps in the road.
a) If you add air to the tire, what happens to the pressure inside the tire?
b) If the tire is getting old, it may bulge outward. What happens to the pressure inside the tire when this happens?
c) If the temperature of the tire rises from 20°C to 30°C, what happens to the pressure inside the tire?

4.25 Many household products are packaged in aerosol cans, which contain a high-pressure propellant gas. These cans always carry a warning against heating the can. Why is this?

4.26 Yvonne buys a can of spray paint and leaves it outdoors for a few hours on a cold day. When she then tries to paint a chair with the spray paint, she is surprised to see that a weak stream of paint comes from the can. Explain why this happened.

4.27 A hiker drinks half of the water in her water bottle at the top of a mountain. When she gets to the bottom of the mountain, she notices that the water bottle has partially collapsed. Why is this?

4.28 A pilot blows up a balloon and brings it with him in his airplane. As his plane climbs, the balloon swells, and eventually it pops. Why did this happen?

4.29 The air pressure inside a bicycle tire is 80 psi. Convert this into the following units:
a) torrs b) bars

4.30 The weather map shows that the atmospheric pressure in Boston today is 100.9 millibars. Convert this into the following units:
a) torrs b) atmospheres

4.31 A scuba-diving tank contains a mixture of oxygen and helium at a total pressure of 6.25 atm. If the partial pressure of the oxygen is 0.61 atm, what is the partial pressure of the helium?

4.32 In Denver, Colorado, the total atmospheric pressure is 626 torr. If the partial pressure of nitrogen in Denver is 494 torr and the partial pressure of argon is 6 torr, what is the partial pressure of oxygen? You may assume that no other gases exert significant pressures.

OBJECTIVES: *Describe the significance of melting and boiling points, calculate the energy needed to melt or boil a substance from the heats of fusion and vaporization, and interpret a typical heating curve.*

4.4 Changes of State

You have undoubtedly observed substances changing state in your everyday life. Ice turns to water in your drink, water turns to ice in your freezer, water turns to steam during cooking, and so forth. We can change any state of water into any other state. However, all of these changes of state require either a particular temperature or a particular range of temperatures. In this section, we will examine changes of state: how we describe them and how they are related to temperature and energy.

To begin, it is important to be familiar with the terms we use to describe changes of state. Many of these are familiar words, but a few may not be. Figure 4.12 illustrates the words we use for changes of state. Note that there is no generally accepted term for a gas turning directly into a solid.

Melting, freezing, evaporation, and boiling are familiar processes. **Condensation** may not be so familiar, but if you have ever seen your breath turn to mist on a cold day, or water droplets forming on the outside of a cold glass of beverage, you have seen condensation. We do not normally observe **sublimation**, but only because most solids sublime extremely slowly. However, if you leave an ice cube in your freezer for several months, it will shrink as the ice turns directly to invisible water vapor. The reverse process (water vapor turning to ice) is responsible for the formation of snowflakes and frost.

Kresimir Juraga

Some changes of state. (a) The ice is turning into liquid water (melting). (b) The water is turning into steam (boiling). (c) Water vapor is turning into droplets of liquid water (condensing).

If you heat an ice cube, its temperature rises until it reaches 0°C. At this temperature, the ice melts, and the temperature remains at 0°C until the ice has turned to water. Most other solids behave similarly when they are heated; they become warmer until they reach a specific temperature, and then they melt without getting any warmer. The temperature at which a solid melts is called its **melting point**, and it is an important property of most chemical substances. The melting point is also the temperature at which the liquid form freezes, so it also called the **freezing point**. The melting point (or freezing point) of a substance is the only temperature at which we can have both the solid and the liquid forms of that substance.

In contrast, solids can sublime at any temperature below their melting point, and this process is generally invisible. If we heat most solids, they do not reach a point where they sublime visibly; instead, they melt. However, some solids do not melt under ordinary conditions. Instead, they simply sublime more rapidly as the temperature rises. Carbon dioxide is the most familiar example; solid CO_2 cannot melt unless it is put under substantial pressure, so it simply turns

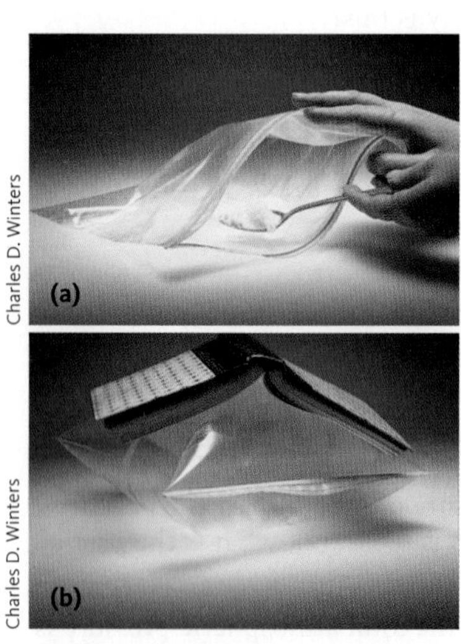

Charles D. Winters

Solid carbon dioxide (dry ice) sublimes instead of melting as it warms up. (a) Dry ice being added to a plastic bag. (b) The bag after the dry ice has sublimed.

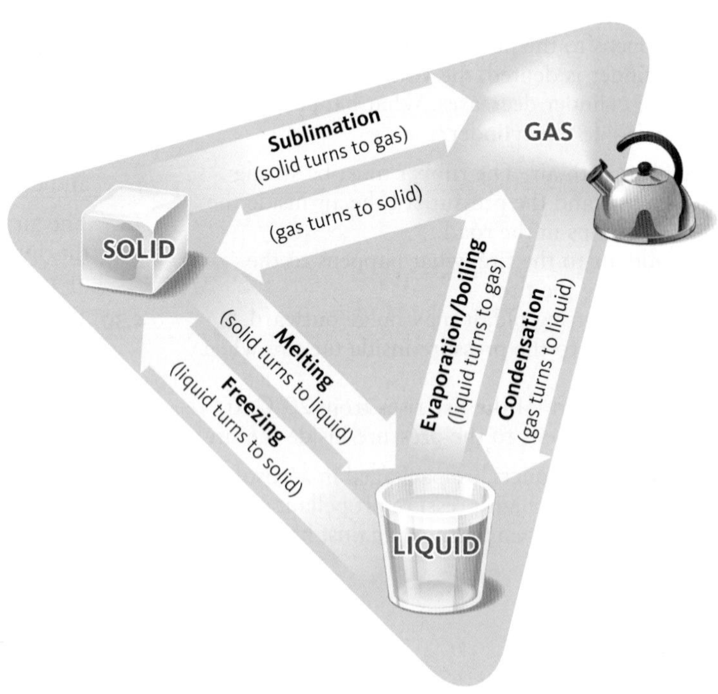

FIGURE 4.12 Terms for changes of state.

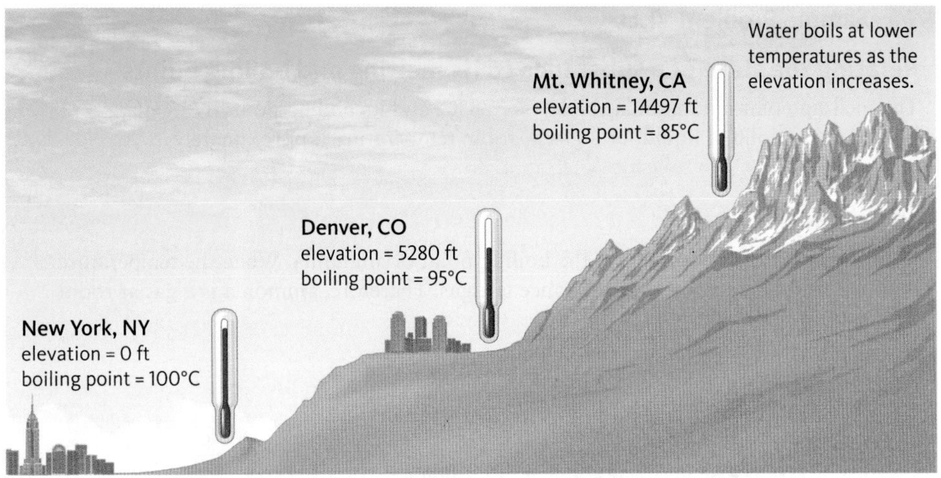

FIGURE 4.13 The relationship between elevation and the boiling point of water.

directly into gaseous CO_2. As a result, solid carbon dioxide is familiarly called dry ice, because it looks like ice but does not melt.

Liquids can turn into gases at any temperature above the melting point. If you spill some water on your kitchen counter and leave it overnight, the water will be gone in the morning, regardless of the temperature. Most of the time, this process (called evaporation) is invisible. However, if you heat the liquid enough, it begins to boil, forming bubbles of vapor that rise to the surface and pop. Once the liquid starts to boil, the temperature does not climb any higher until the liquid is completely gone. The temperature at which a liquid boils is called its **boiling point**, and it is also the highest temperature at which we can see the vapor condense back to a liquid.

The boiling points of all substances depend on the atmospheric pressure. If the atmospheric pressure increases, the boiling point of any liquid goes up. The boiling point also depends on elevation above sea level, because atmospheric pressure drops as the elevation increases. As a result, the boiling points of liquids decrease as the elevation increases. Figure 4.13 illustrates the relationship between the boiling point of water and elevation.

The melting and boiling points are important properties of a substance, because they determine whether the substance is a solid, a liquid, or a gas at any particular temperature. If the temperature is above the boiling point, the substance must be a gas. When the temperature is between the melting point and the boiling point, the substance is normally a liquid. However, there will also be some vapor because of evaporation, and it is possible to have only vapor in this temperature range. Below the melting point, the substance is normally a solid, but even at low temperatures a very small amount of vapor is present. Figure 4.14 summarizes the relationship between temperature and state.

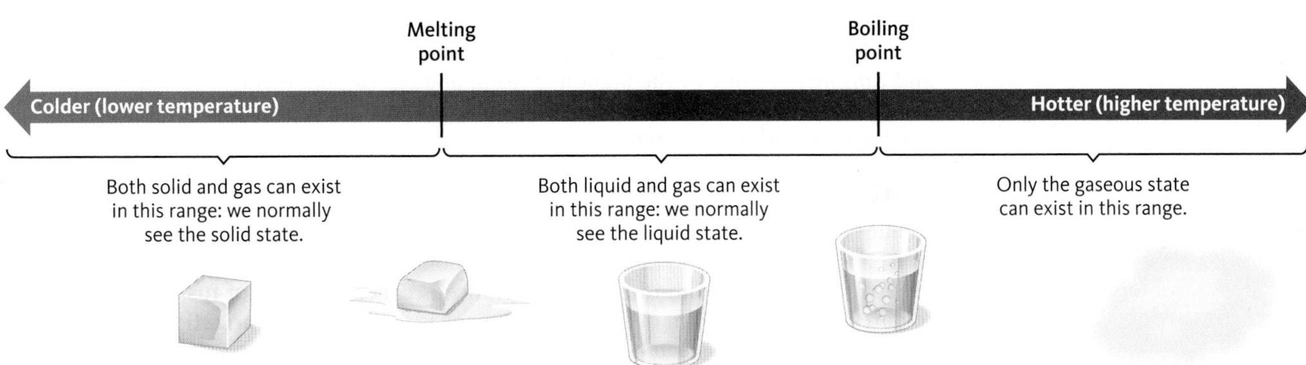

FIGURE 4.14 The relationship between temperature and state.

Sample Problem 4.8

Relating the state of a substance to its melting and boiling points

The melting point of ammonia (NH_3) is −78°C, and its boiling point is −33°C. Is ammonia a solid, a liquid, or a gas at room temperature (approximately 25°C)?

SOLUTION

Room temperature is well above the boiling point of ammonia. When the temperature is above the boiling point, the substance is a gas. Therefore, ammonia is a gas at room temperature.

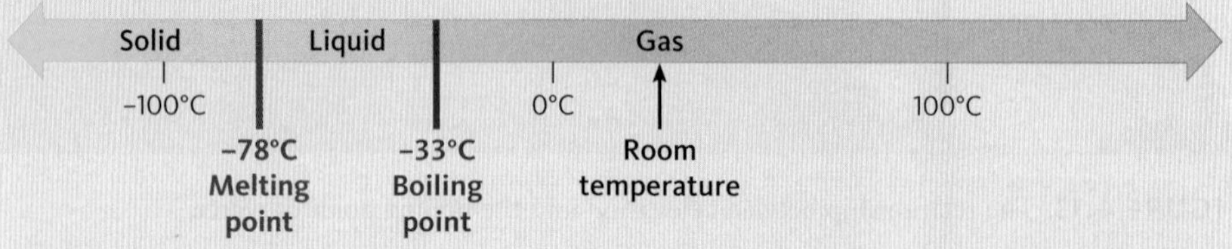

TRY IT YOURSELF: *The melting point of acetic acid is 17°C, and its boiling point is 118°C. Is acetic acid a solid, a liquid, or a gas at room temperature?*

For additional practice, try Core Problems 4.35 and 4.36.

TABLE 4.8 Melting and Boiling Points for Some Elements

Element	Melting Point	Boiling Point	State at Room Temperature (25°C)
Hydrogen	−259°C	−253°C	Gas
Chlorine	−101°C	−34°C	Gas
Mercury	−39°C	357°C	Liquid
Sulfur	119°C	445°C	Solid
Copper	1083°C	2595°C	Solid
Tungsten	3410°C	5660°C	Solid

Table 4.8 lists the melting and boiling points of several chemical elements, showing the wide range of melting and boiling points that can be observed. Hydrogen has the second-lowest melting and boiling points of all known substances (only helium is lower), and tungsten has one of the highest melting and boiling points known. The filaments in ordinary lightbulbs are made from tungsten, because this element can be heated to incandescence without melting.

Melting and Boiling Points Are Related to Attractive Forces

Changes of state require energy. For instance, we need 80 calories of heat to melt a gram of ice, and it takes 540 calories of heat to boil a gram of water. The amount of heat needed to melt one gram of a solid substance is called the **heat of fusion**, and the heat required to boil one gram of a liquid substance is the **heat of vaporization**. Sample Problem 4.9 shows how we can use the heat of fusion to calculate the total amount of energy needed to melt a sample of ice.

Sample Problem 4.9

Calculating the energy needed for a change of state

How much heat is needed to melt 15 g of ice? The heat of fusion of ice is 80 cal/g.

SOLUTION

The question asks for an amount of heat, so our answer should be in calories. The problem gives us two numbers, but one of them (the heat of fusion) is a relationship between two types of measurements, heat and mass. The other (15 g of ice) is our original measurement.

STEP 1: Identify the original measurement and the final unit.

15 g —convert to→ ? cal

STEP 2: Write conversion factors that relate the two units.

The heat of fusion tells us that we need 80 cal of heat to melt 1 g of ice. We can write this relationship as two different conversion factors:

$$\frac{80 \text{ cal}}{1 \text{ g}} \quad \text{and} \quad \frac{1 \text{ g}}{80 \text{ cal}}$$

STEP 3: Choose the conversion factor that allows you to cancel units.

To cancel our original unit, we must use the first of these conversion factors.

$$15 \text{ g} \times \frac{80 \text{ cal}}{1 \text{ g}}$$

We can cancel these units.

STEP 4: Do the math and round your answer.

Now we can cancel units and do the arithmetic:

$$15 \text{ g} \times \frac{80 \text{ cal}}{1 \text{ g}} = 1200 \text{ cal}$$

It takes 1200 cal of heat (or 1.2 kcal) to melt 15 g of ice.

TRY IT YOURSELF: *How much heat will be needed to boil 6.00 g of water? The heat of vaporization of water is 540 cal/g.*

For additional practice, try Core Problems 4.43 and 4.44.

Health Note: When you perspire, the water in your perspiration absorbs heat from your body as it evaporates. One teaspoon of perspiration (about 5 mL) can remove about 2700 cal of heat—as long as you don't wipe it off first.

The effect of the heats of fusion and vaporization becomes apparent if we heat a solid and monitor the temperature until the solid has changed into a gas. A graph of temperature against heating time is called a **heating curve**. Figure 4.15 shows the general shape of a heating curve and the heating curve we observe when we use water. In each case, the heating curve has five sections. At the beginning, we have the solid form of the

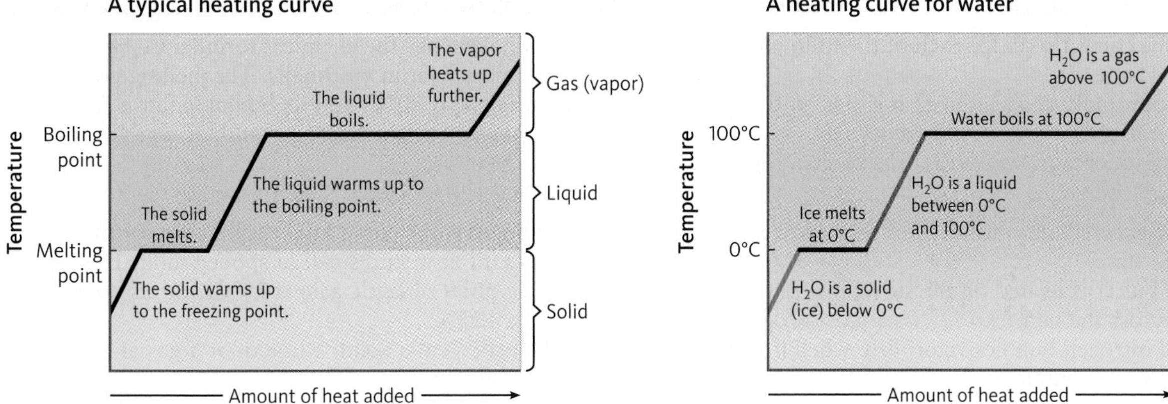

A typical heating curve
Temperature
Boiling point
Melting point
The vapor heats up further.
The liquid boils.
The liquid warms up to the boiling point.
The solid melts.
The solid warms up to the freezing point.
Gas (vapor)
Liquid
Solid
Amount of heat added
A heating curve for water
Temperature
100°C
0°C
H₂O is a gas above 100°C
Water boils at 100°C
H₂O is a liquid between 0°C and 100°C
Ice melts at 0°C
H₂O is a solid (ice) below 0°C
Amount of heat added

FIGURE 4.15 Interpreting heating curves.

substance, and as we heat it, its temperature rises. Next, the temperature stops rising and remains level. During this time, the solid melts, and the temperature in this level region is the melting point of the substance. Once the solid has changed into a liquid, the temperature rises again. Then the temperature levels off once more. During this time, the liquid boils, and the temperature remains at the boiling point of the substance. Finally, after the substance has been completely converted into a gas, the temperature can rise once again.

Sample Problem 4.10

Interpreting a heating curve

Using the following heating curve, estimate the melting point of mercury (Hg). This heating curve starts with solid mercury at −100°C.

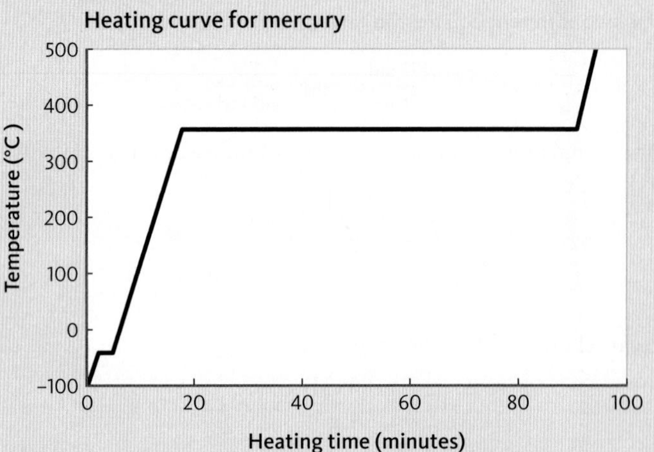

SOLUTION

The graph slopes upward at first while the solid mercury warms up. Then the graph levels off as the solid melts and the temperature remains constant. The temperature during this period is around −40°C, so the melting point of mercury should be close to this temperature. (The actual melting point of mercury is −39°C.)

TRY IT YOURSELF: *Using the heating curve of mercury, estimate the boiling point of mercury.*

For additional practice, try Core Problems 4.47 and 4.48.

CORE PROBLEMS

4.33 What is the correct term for each of the following changes of state?
a) Alcohol rapidly vanishes after it is put on the skin.
b) Water turns to ice on a cold winter day.
c) If air that contains water vapor is cooled, fog forms.

4.34 What is the correct term for each of the following changes of state?
a) When butter is heated on the stove, it begins to flow across the pan.
b) Liquid nitrogen bubbles vigorously when it is put into a warm container.
c) Solid iodine turns into purple vapor when it is warmed.

4.35 Naphthalene has the chemical formula $C_{10}H_8$. It is the active ingredient in mothballs. The melting point of naphthalene is 80°C, and its boiling point is 218°C.
a) Is naphthalene a solid, a liquid, or a gas at room temperature?
b) What is the normal state of naphthalene at 100°C?

4.36 Lactic acid is the compound responsible for the unpleasant taste and smell of spoiled milk. The melting point of lactic acid is 18°C, and its boiling point is 122°C.
a) Is lactic acid a solid, a liquid, or a gas at room temperature?
b) What is the normal state of lactic acid at 0°C?

continued

4.37 Sodium chloride (NaCl) melts at 801°C. If you have some liquid NaCl at 1000°C and you cool it down, at what temperature will it freeze?

4.38 Acetone is an organic liquid that is used to dissolve substances that do not mix with water. The boiling point of acetone is 56°C. If you have some gaseous acetone at 100°C and you cool it down, at what temperature will it start to condense?

4.39 Methane (CH_4) is a gas at 25°C. Is the boiling point of methane higher than 25°C, or is it lower than 25°C? How can you tell?

4.40 Aluminum chloride ($AlCl_3$) is a solid at 25°C. Is the melting point of aluminum chloride higher than 25°C, or is it lower than 25°C? How can you tell?

4.41 The sentence that follows is not entirely correct. How could you make it into a true statement?
"At 20°C, water is a liquid."

4.42 The sentence that follows is not entirely correct. How could you make it into a true statement?
"At −10°C, water is a solid."

4.43 Isopropyl alcohol can be used to cool the skin, because it evaporates easily and absorbs a large amount of heat as it does so. The heat of vaporization of isopropyl alcohol is 159 cal/g. How much heat is needed to evaporate 25 g of isopropyl alcohol?

4.44 The heat of fusion of butter is around 19 cal/g. How much heat is needed to melt 25 g of butter?

4.45 Isopropyl alcohol is a liquid at room temperature. If you cool isopropyl alcohol, its temperature will drop to −89°C. However, the temperature then remains at −89°C for a few minutes before dropping further. Explain.

4.46 If you heat isopropyl alcohol, its temperature will rise to 82°C. However, the temperature then remains at 82°C for a long time before rising further. Explain.

4.47 Use the following heating curve to answer the following questions:

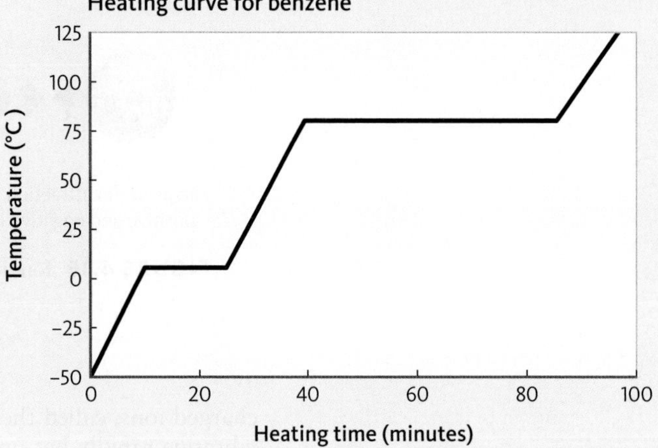

a) What is the melting point of benzene?
b) Is benzene a solid, a liquid, or a gas at 100°C?
c) If you cool benzene from 25°C to −25°C, what will you observe?

4.48 Use the heating curve in Problem 4.47 to answer the following questions:
a) What is the boiling point of benzene?
b) Is benzene a solid, a liquid, or a gas at 25°C?
c) If you cool benzene from 100°C to 50°C, what will you observe?

4.5 Attractive Forces and the Physical Properties of Matter

OBJECTIVES: *Describe the attractive forces between molecules or ions, and relate the strength of these forces to physical properties.*

Why is salt a solid at room temperature, while water is a liquid and oxygen is a gas? What factors determine the melting and boiling points of a substance? The answer lies in the forces that attract molecules and ions to one another. Recall that all particles (atoms, molecules, and ions) are in constant motion, giving them kinetic energy. This type of kinetic energy is called thermal energy, and it depends on the temperature: as the temperature rises, the amount of thermal energy the particles have increases. Because of their thermal energy, particles of any substance tend to move away from one another, turning the substance into a gas. The substance can only be a liquid or a solid if the particles are attracted to one another strongly enough to overcome their thermal energy. *The state of a substance at any temperature is a balance between the attraction of particles to one another and the thermal energy of the particles.*

Ion–Ion Attraction Determines the Physical Properties of Ionic Compounds

We start by examining ionic compounds, which are solids at room temperature and generally melt and boil at very high temperatures. A good example is sodium chloride (table salt), which is made up of Na^+ and Cl^- ions. The attraction between oppositely

The powerful attraction between positive and negative ions . . .

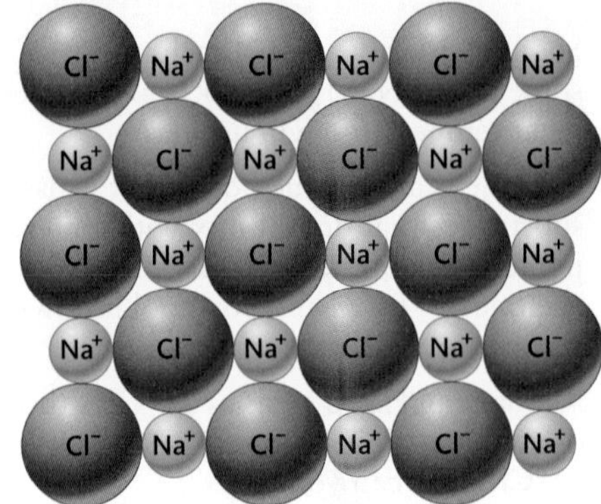

. . . overcomes their thermal energy and produces an organized array of ions.

FIGURE 4.16 Ion–ion attraction in an ionic substance.

charged ions, called the **ion–ion attraction**, is so strong that the ions are held in place, vibrating rapidly but unable to move any significant distance from their fixed positions. As shown in Figure 4.16, the sodium and chloride ions in NaCl form an array of alternating positive and negative ions, with each ion held in place by its attraction to its neighbors.

As a result of the strong attraction between positive and negative ions, *all ionic compounds are solids at room temperature.* If we want to melt an ionic compound like NaCl, we must raise the temperature until the thermal energy of the ions is high enough to disrupt the organized array of ions. Boiling an ionic compound requires a still higher temperature, because the thermal energy must be high enough to pull ions entirely away from one another. For example, the melting point of NaCl is 801°C and the boiling point is 1413°C.

Attraction Between Molecules Determines the Physical Properties of Molecular Substances

The attraction between molecules is weaker than the attraction between oppositely charged ions. As a result, molecular substances melt and boil at much lower temperatures than ionic compounds. For example, HCl is a typical molecular compound, containing atoms held together by a covalent bond. The bond between hydrogen and chlorine is strong, but individual HCl molecules are only weakly attracted to one another, as shown in Figure 4.17. The attraction between HCl molecules is so feeble that even at room temperature the thermal energy of the HCl molecules can overcome it. Therefore, the molecules remain independent of one another, and HCl is a gas at 25°C. HCl can become a liquid, or even a solid, but it must be cooled until the thermal energy is too low to overcome the attractive forces between molecules. We must cool HCl to −85°C to condense it to a liquid, and liquid HCl freezes at −114°C. (For comparison, the coldest temperature ever recorded on Earth is −89°C in Antarctica.)

Not all molecular substances are gases at room temperature, and in fact it is difficult to predict the state of a molecular substance. The one general statement that we can make is that *the attraction between molecules is always weaker than the attraction between ions.* As a result, molecular substances have lower melting and boiling points than ionic compounds. Table 4.9 summarizes the behavior of the two types of substances.

H–Cl H–Cl

The weak attraction between HCl molecules . . .

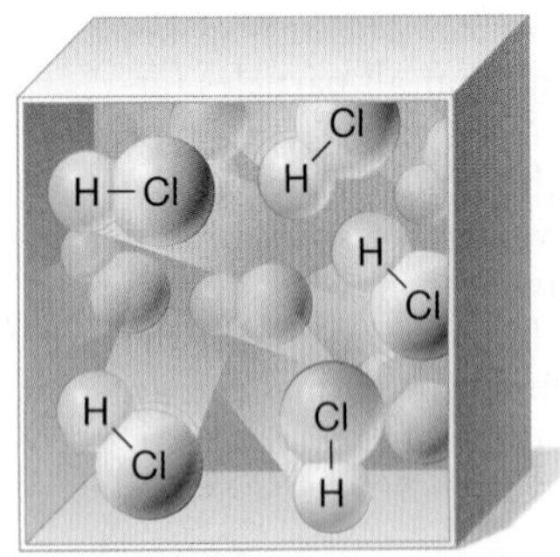

. . . cannot overcome their thermal energy. (HCl is a gas at room temperature.)

FIGURE 4.17 The balance between attractive forces and thermal energy in a molecular substance.

TABLE 4.9 Physical Properties of Ionic and Molecular Substances

Type of Compound	Typical Melting Point	Typical Boiling Point	Examples
Ionic	500°C to 2500°C	1000°C to 3000°C (Many break down into simpler substances instead of boiling.)	Table salt (NaCl) melts at 801°C and boils at 1413°C. Quicklime (CaO) melts at 2614°C and boils at 2850°C.
Molecular	−200°C to 200°C	−150°C to 400°C (Many break down into simpler substances instead of boiling.)	Ethyl alcohol (C_2H_6O) melts at −117°C and boils at 78°C. Cholesterol ($C_{27}H_{46}O$) melts at 148°C and boils at 360°C.

(a)

Charles D. Winters

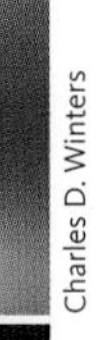

(b)

Charles D. Winters

(c)

Charles D. Winters

Containers of (a) chlorine, (b) bromine, and (c) iodine at room temperature. The melting and boiling points of these elements depend on the sizes of the atoms.

Sample Problem 4.11

Relating physical properties to the type of compound

MgO and NO both have 1 : 1 atom ratios. However, MgO melts at 2800°C, while NO melts at −164°C. Why do these compounds have such different melting points?

SOLUTION

MgO contains a metal and a nonmetal, so it is an ionic compound. We would expect it to have a high melting point because of the strong attraction between the Mg^{2+} and O^{2-} ions. On the other hand, both nitrogen and oxygen are nonmetals, so NO is a molecular compound. The NO molecules are very weakly attracted to one another, so solid NO is easy to melt. The covalent bond between nitrogen and oxygen is very strong, but this bond does not need to be broken to melt (or boil) NO.

TRY IT YOURSELF: *HF and LiF both have 1 : 1 atom ratios. However, one of these compounds boils at 20°C, while the other boils at 1681°C. Match each compound with its boiling point, and explain your answer.*

For additional practice, try Core Problems 4.49 and 4.50.

The Attraction Between Molecules Depends on Molecular Size

The physical properties of molecular substances are related to the size of the molecules. All molecules, regardless of their structures, are attracted to one another, because the electrons of each molecule are attracted to the protons of nearby molecules. This attraction is called the **dispersion force**. In general, large molecules (both in numbers of atoms and in the sizes of the atoms) exert a stronger dispersion force on one another than small molecules do. As a result, *larger molecules tend to have higher melting and boiling points than smaller molecules.* Tables 4.10 and 4.11 illustrate these trends. Table 4.10 compares the physical properties of the Group 7A elements chlorine, bromine, and iodine, all three of which form diatomic molecules. Chlorine has the smallest atoms and therefore the weakest attraction between molecules. As a result, chlorine requires the least energy to melt and boil, giving it the lowest melting and boiling points of these three elements. Iodine, with the largest atoms, has the highest melting and boiling points.

TABLE 4.10 The Effect of Atomic Size on Physical Properties

	Substance	Strength of Dispersion Force	Melting Point	Boiling Point	State At 25°C
Increasing atomic size ↓	Chlorine (Cl_2) formula weight = 70.9 amu	Weakest	Lowest (−101°C)	Lowest (−34°C)	Gas
	Bromine (Br_2) formula weight = 159.8 amu	Intermediate	Intermediate (−7°C)	Intermediate (59°C)	Liquid
	Iodine (I_2) formula weight = 253.8 amu	Strongest	Highest (114°C)	Highest (185°C)	Solid

TABLE 4.11 The Effect of Molecular Size on Physical Properties

	Substance	Strength of Dispersion Force	Melting Point	Boiling Point	State At 25°C
Increasing numbers of atoms ↓	CH_4	Weakest	Lowest (−183°C)	Lowest (−161°C)	Gas
	$C_{10}H_{22}$	Intermediate	Intermediate (−30°C)	Intermediate (174°C)	Liquid
	$C_{20}H_{42}$	Strongest	Highest (37°C)	Highest (343°C)	Solid

Table 4.11 compares three compounds that are built from the same two elements, carbon and hydrogen. In this case, the molecule that contains the greatest number of atoms ($C_{20}H_{42}$) has the strongest dispersion force and the highest melting and boiling points.

Sample Problem 4.12

Relating boiling point to molecular size

Which would you expect to have the higher boiling point: SiH_4 or Si_2H_6? Explain your answer.

SOLUTION

Both SiH_4 and Si_2H_6 are molecular compounds, since silicon and hydrogen are nonmetals. Si_2H_6 contains more atoms than SiH_4, so molecules of Si_2H_6 should be more strongly attracted to one another than molecules of SiH_4 are attracted to one another. Molecules with stronger attractive forces require more energy to pull them away from one another, so Si_2H_6 should have the higher boiling point.

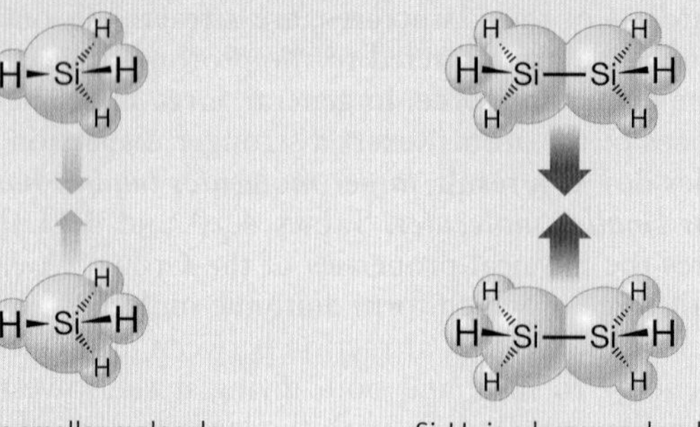

SiH_4 is a smaller molecule, so the attraction between two SiH_4 molecules is weaker.

Si_2H_6 is a larger molecule, so the attraction between two Si_2H_6 molecules is stronger.

continued

TRY IT YOURSELF: *Carbon combines with the Group 7A elements fluorine, chlorine, and bromine to form CF_4, CCl_4, and CBr_4. One of these compounds is a solid at room temperature, one is a liquid, and one is a gas. Match each compound with its state at room temperature, and explain your answer.*

For additional practice, try Core Problems 4.51 and 4.52.

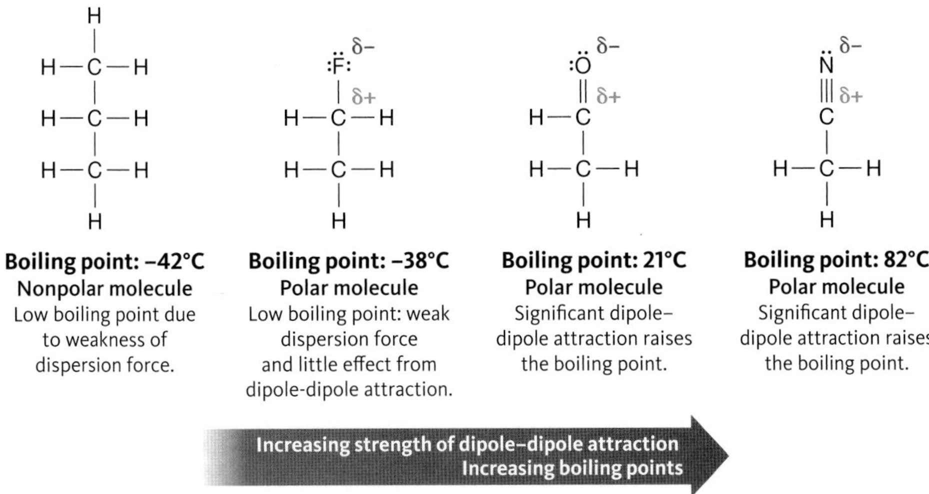

FIGURE 4.18 The effect of the dipole–dipole attraction on boiling points.

Dipole–Dipole Attraction Raises the Boiling Points of Molecular Compounds

As we saw in Section 3.4, many molecules contain polar bonds. Recall that in a polar bond, the bonding electrons are unequally shared, giving one atom a slight positive charge and the other a slight negative charge. Molecules that contain polar bonds tend to attract one another more strongly than molecules that are nonpolar, because the positively charged atoms in one molecule attract the negatively charged atoms in the neighboring molecules. This attraction, called the **dipole–dipole attraction**, is generally rather weak, but it has an observable impact on the boiling points of many substances. The dipole–dipole attraction has little effect on the properties of compounds that contain halogens (Group 7A elements), but it is important for compounds that contain oxygen or nitrogen atoms, as shown in Figure 4.18.

Hydrogen Bonding is a Particularly Strong Type of Dipole–Dipole Attraction

Polar molecules attract one another unusually strongly whenever the positive atom is hydrogen and the negative atom is oxygen or nitrogen. This attraction plays a key role in biological chemistry, affecting the properties of all compounds that contain O–H or N–H bonds.

Water provides an excellent illustration of this attraction on the properties of a molecular compound. H_2O molecules are very small. Most molecular substances that are made up of such small molecules are gases at room temperature, because the dispersion force between the molecules is extremely weak. However, water is a liquid at room temperature. To understand why, let us look more closely at the structure of water. Figure 4.19 shows the actual shape of a water molecule. Note that each of the covalent bonds between hydrogen and oxygen is polar, so the hydrogen atoms are positively charged and the oxygen atom is negatively charged.

The positively charged hydrogen atoms in a water molecule are attracted to the negatively charged oxygen atoms in other water molecules. This attraction is called a **hydrogen bond.** Figure 4.20 illustrates a hydrogen bond between two water molecules.

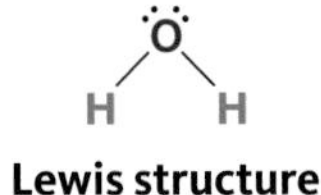

Lewis structure

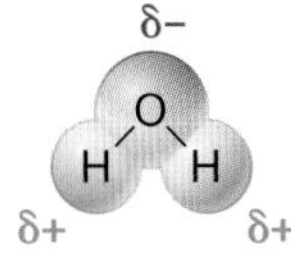

Molecular shape

This is a space-filling model which shows the actual shape of the molecule. The round balls represent the regions around the nuclei where the electrons are most likely to be found.

FIGURE 4.19 The structure of a water molecule.

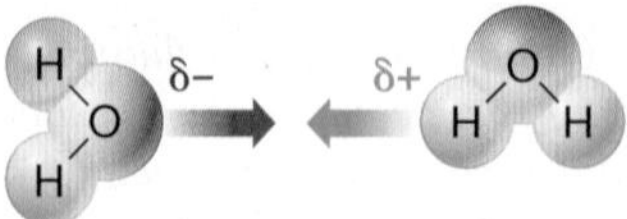

The attraction between the positively charged hydrogen and the negatively charged oxygen is called a **hydrogen bond**.

In the rest of this chapter, hydrogen atoms that can participate in hydrogen bonds are colored green. Negatively charged oxygen and nitrogen atoms that can participate in hydrogen bonds are colored red.

FIGURE 4.20 The formation of a hydrogen bond between two water molecules.

Hydrogen bonds are related to the attraction between ions in an ionic compound such as NaCl, but they are much weaker. The hydrogen bonds in a sample of water are strong enough to keep the water molecules near one another at room temperature, but they are not quite strong enough to lock them into fixed positions. As a result, water is a liquid at room temperature.

• Molecules of hydrogen fluoride (HF) can also form hydrogen bonds, but this is the only fluorine-containing compound that can do so.

Any molecule in which a hydrogen atom is covalently bonded to oxygen can participate in hydrogen bonds. In addition, molecules that contain a hydrogen atom covalently bonded to nitrogen can also participate in hydrogen bonds, because the bond between hydrogen and nitrogen is also polar. Here are three more examples of molecules that can form hydrogen bonds. In each structure, the atoms that can participate in hydrogen bonds are shown in color.

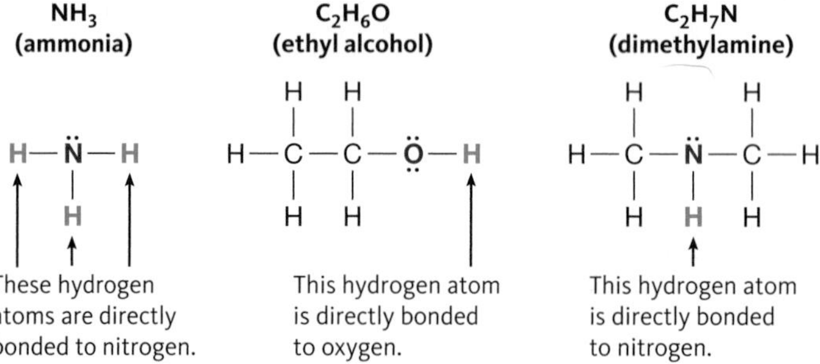

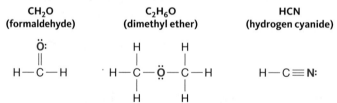

To form a hydrogen bond, a hydrogen atom must be directly attached to oxygen or nitrogen. Here are some examples of compounds in which the molecules cannot form hydrogen bonds with one another. Each of these molecules contains at least one hydrogen atom, but none of the hydrogen atoms are covalently bonded to nitrogen or oxygen.

CH_2O (formaldehyde) — **C_2H_6O (dimethyl ether)** — **HCN (hydrogen cyanide)**

H—C—H (with =Ö: above the C)   H—C—Ö—C—H (each C bearing two further H)   H—C≡N:

The hydrogen atoms in these molecules are not bonded to oxygen or nitrogen, so they cannot participate in hydrogen bonds.

Figure 4.21 illustrates the hydrogen bonding that occurs among molecules of ammonia and among molecules of ethanol. Ammonia (NH_3) is formed as a by-product whenever your body breaks down proteins to obtain energy. This compound is a gas at room temperature, but it can be converted to a liquid by cooling it to −33°C, an unusually high temperature for such a light molecule. Ammonia contains three N–H bonds. These bonds are polar, so each of the hydrogen atoms is positively charged and is attracted to the negatively charged nitrogen atom on a different ammonia molecule.

Ethanol (C_2H_6O), also called ethyl alcohol or grain alcohol, is the "alcohol" in beverages such as beer and wine. Like water, this compound is a liquid at room temperature because the hydrogen bonds among ethanol molecules are strong enough to overcome the thermal energy of the molecules. In this case, only one of the six hydrogen atoms can participate in a hydrogen bond. To participate in a hydrogen bond, a hydrogen atom must be *strongly positively charged*, which only happens when the hydrogen is covalently bonded to *oxygen* or to *nitrogen*.

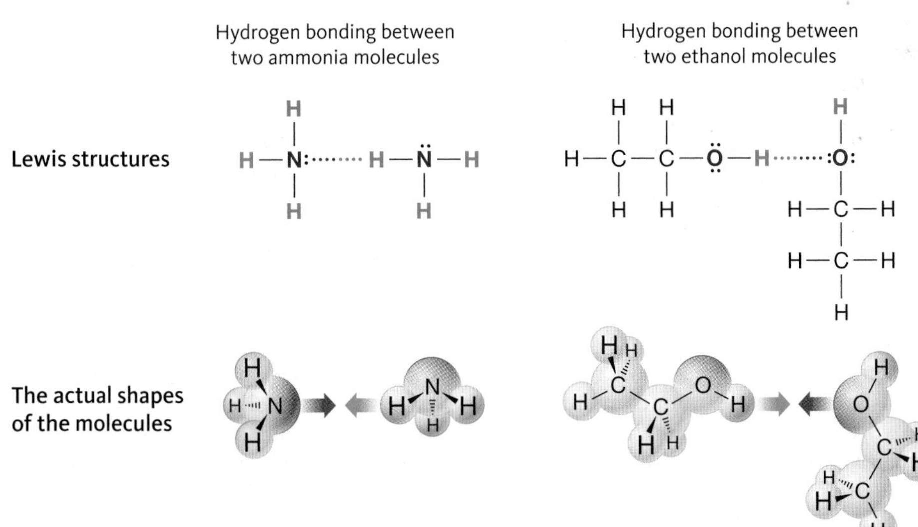

FIGURE 4.21 Hydrogen bonding in ammonia and ethanol.

Sample Problem 4.13

The effect of hydrogen bonds on boiling point

The structure of hydrogen sulfide (H_2S) is similar to that of water (H_2O), and sulfur is a larger atom than oxygen. However, the boiling point of H_2S is $-60°C$, much lower than that of water. Why is this?

SOLUTION

This is an excellent example of the effect of hydrogen bonds. Covalent bonds between hydrogen and sulfur are not very polar, so the hydrogen atoms in H_2S cannot participate in hydrogen bonds. We have already seen that water molecules form hydrogen bonds, so the attraction between H_2O molecules is substantially stronger than the attraction between H_2S molecules. Therefore, it takes a good deal less energy to pull H_2S molecules away from one another, allowing us to boil H_2S at a much lower temperature than H_2O.

H_2O molecules form hydrogen bonds, so they are attracted to each other fairly strongly.

H_2S molecules cannot form hydrogen bonds, so the attraction between molecules is weak.

TRY IT YOURSELF: *The structure of phosphine (PH_3) is similar to that of ammonia (NH_3), and phosphorus is a larger atom than nitrogen. However, the boiling point of PH_3 ($-88°C$) is much lower than the boiling point of NH_3 ($-33°C$). Why is this?*

For additional practice, try Core Problems 4.57 through 4.60.

Some Polar Molecules Cannot Form Hydrogen Bonds

How significant is the impact of hydrogen bonds on the physical properties of a molecular compound? The compound in Figure 4.22, called dimethyl ether, gives us a direct illustration of the effect of hydrogen bonds. This compound contains the same set of atoms that were used to make ethanol (both have the molecular formula C_2H_6O), but the atoms are arranged so there is no O—H bond. The oxygen atom is negatively charged, but C—H bonds are very weakly polar, so none of the hydrogen atoms bears a significant positive charge. Molecules of dimethyl ether are attracted to one another by

• Molecules with the same formula but different arrangements of atoms are called isomers.

This molecule has no positively charged hydrogen atoms, so it cannot form hydrogen bonds to itself.

```
     H       H
     |       |
 H — C — Ö — C — H
     |   ··  |
     H       H
```

Lewis structure

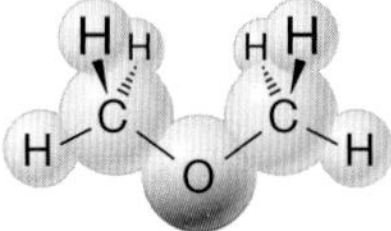

Molecular shape

FIGURE 4.22 The structure of dimethyl ether.

the dispersion force and dipole–dipole attraction, but both of these are very weak, so this compound boils at −24°C and is a gas at room temperature, whereas ethanol is a liquid and boils at 78°C.

Hydrogen bonding plays a critical role in determining the properties of many compounds, including proteins and sugars, and the inability to form hydrogen bonds affects many of the properties of fats. Hydrogen bonding is also important in determining whether a molecular compound can dissolve in water. Therefore, you should learn to recognize molecules that can form hydrogen bonds. In general, *any molecule that contains O—H or N—H covalent bonds will form hydrogen bonds.* In addition, molecules that do not contain O—H or N—H bonds but that do contain oxygen or nitrogen can usually participate in hydrogen bonds with water. We will explore the dissolving process in the next section.

You should also recognize that the term *hydrogen bond* is misleading. Hydrogen bonds are not covalent bonds and do not involve the sharing of electrons between atoms. A hydrogen bond is simply an attraction between atoms that have opposite charges. Furthermore, hydrogen bonds are much weaker than either covalent or ionic bonds. Figure 4.23 illustrates the three types of interactions that we call bonds.

A covalent bond:
Two atoms share valence electrons.

A **nonpolar covalent bond** between two atoms that have the same electronegativity

A **polar covalent bond** between two atoms that have different electronegativities

An ionic bond (ion–ion attraction):
A positive ion and a negative ion attract each other.

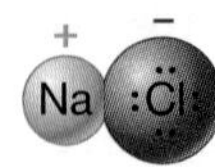

A hydrogen bond (not a true chemical bond):
A positive hydrogen and a negative oxygen or nitrogen attract each other.

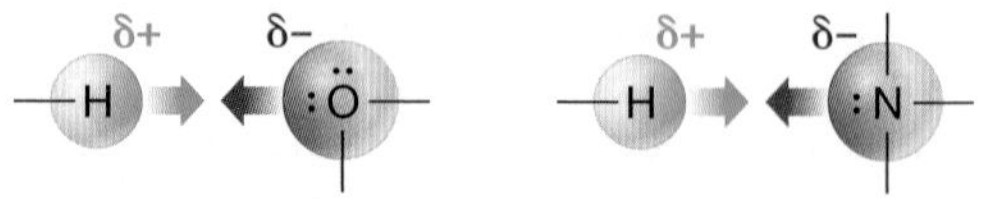

FIGURE 4.23 A comparison of three types of bonds.

Sample Problem 4.14

Identifying hydrogen bonding atoms in a structure

Compounds 1 and 2 have the same chemical formula (C_3H_9N). Explain why compound 1 has a substantially higher boiling point than compound 2.

```
     H   H       H              H       H
     |   |       |              |       |
 H — C — C — N — C — H      H — C — N — C — H
     |   |   |   |              |   |   |
     H   H   H   H              H   |   H
                                    |
                                H — C — H
                                    |
                                    H
```

Compound 1: Boiling point 37°C **Compound 2: Boiling point 4°C**

SOLUTION

Compound 1 contains an N—H bond, so this molecule can form hydrogen bonds. In compound 2, by contrast, all of the hydrogen atoms are bonded to carbon atoms, so compound 2 cannot form hydrogen bonds. Since compound 1 can form hydrogen bonds, its molecules are more strongly attracted to one another than molecules of compound 2

continued

are attracted to one another. Therefore, compound 1 requires more energy to boil, and it has the higher boiling point.

```
   H  H      H              H          H
   |  |      |              |          |
H—C—C—N̈—C—H         H—C—N̈—C—H
   |  |  |   |              |    |     |
   H  H  H   H              H    |     H
         ↑                   H—C—H
                                 |
                                 H
```

This hydrogen atom is directly attached to nitrogen, so it is positively charged and can participate in hydrogen bonds.

None of the hydrogen atoms in this molecule are attached to nitrogen, so this compound cannot participate in hydrogen bonds.

TRY IT YOURSELF: *Would you expect the boiling point of compound 3 to be closer to that of compound 1 or compound 2? (Compound 3 also has the formula C_3H_9N.)*

```
   H  H  H
   |  |  |
H—C—C—C—N̈—H
   |  |  |  |
   H  H  H  H
```

Compound 3

For additional practice, try Core Problems 4.61 and 4.62.

Table 4.12 summarizes the types of attractive forces that we have examined in this section.

TABLE 4.12 Attractive Forces That Have an Impact on Boiling and Melting Points

Type of Force	Types of Compounds That Exhibit This Force	Strength of This Force
Dispersion force	All molecular compounds	Weak, increases as the size of the molecule increases
Dipole–dipole attraction	Molecular compounds that contain polar bonds	Weak, primarily significant for molecules that contain N or O
Hydrogen bond	Molecular compounds that contain O—H or N—H groups	Weak, but always raises the melting and boiling point significantly
Ion–ion attraction	All ionic compounds	Very strong (ionic compounds have very high melting and boiling points)

CORE PROBLEMS

4.49 Explain why NF_3 is a gas at room temperature, while CrF_3 is a solid that must be heated to 1100°C to melt it.

4.50 Explain why H_2O is a liquid at room temperature, while Li_2O is a solid that must be heated to 1500°C to melt it.

4.51 a) Which of the following compounds has the strongest dispersion force between individual molecules? How can you tell?

b) Which of the following compounds has the highest boiling point? How can you tell?

c) Which of the following compounds is the most likely to be a gas at room temperature? How can you tell?

```
   H            H            H
   |            |            |
H—C—C̈l:     H—C—B̈r:     H—C—Ï:
   |            |            |
   H            H            H
```

Methyl chloride **Methyl bromide** **Methyl iodide**

continued

4.52 a) Which of the following compounds has the strongest dispersion force between individual molecules? How can you tell?
b) Which of the following compounds has the lowest boiling point? How can you tell?
c) Which of the following compounds is *least* likely to be a gas at room temperature? How can you tell?

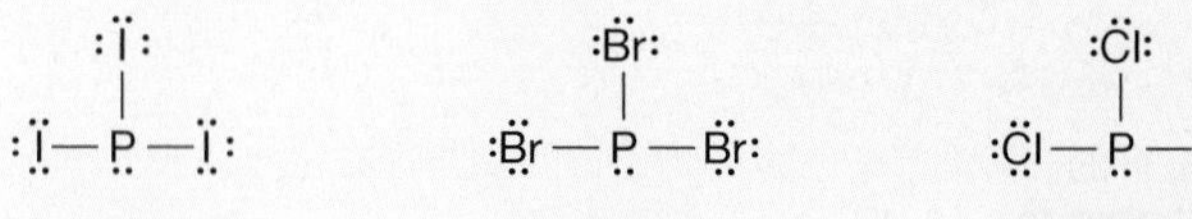

Phosphorus triiodide | **Phosphorus tribromide** | **Phosphorus trichloride**

4.53 Each of the following compounds contains a covalent bond that is strongly polar.

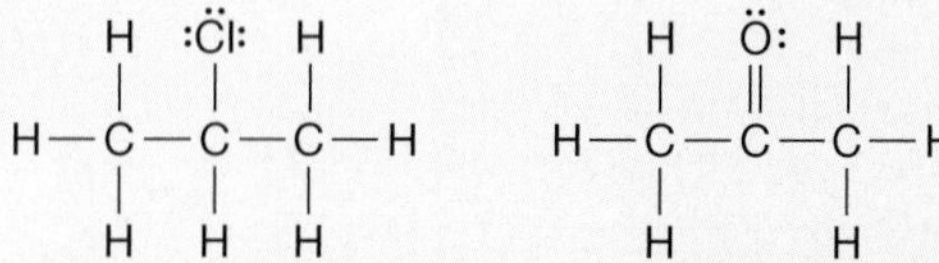

Isopropyl chloride | **Acetone**

a) Identify the polar bond in each molecule.
b) For which of these compounds should dipole–dipole attraction have a significant effect on the boiling point?
c) Which compound should have the higher boiling point?

4.54 Each of the following compounds contains a covalent bond that is strongly polar.

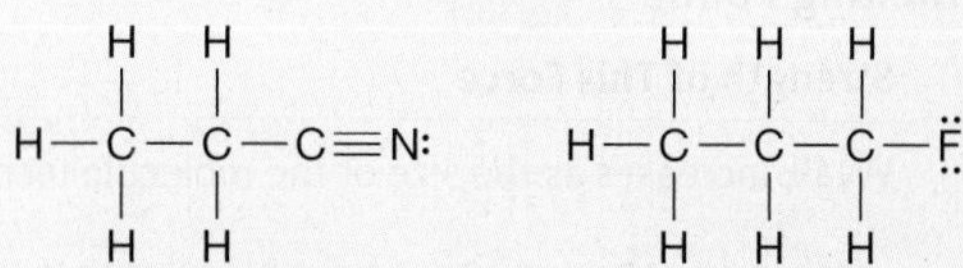

Propionitrile | **Propyl fluoride**

a) Identify the polar bond in each molecule.
b) For which of these compounds should dipole–dipole attraction have a significant effect on the boiling point?
c) Which compound should have the higher boiling point?

4.55 Draw structures to show how two molecules of the following compound can form a hydrogen bond.

4.56 Draw structures to show how two molecules of the following compound can form a hydrogen bond.

4.57 The following compounds have the same formula (C_3H_6O), but one of them boils at 95°C while the other boils at 49°C. Match each compound with its boiling point, and explain your answer.

Compound 1 | **Compound 2**

4.58 The following compounds have the same formula ($C_4H_{10}O$), but one of them boils at 39°C while the other boils at 117°C. Match each compound with its boiling point, and explain your answer.

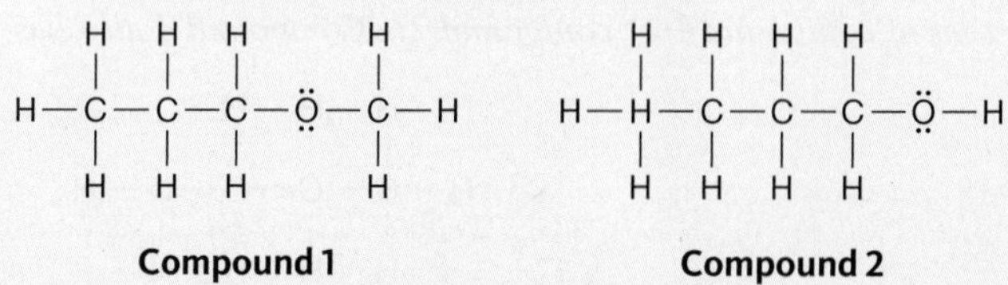

Compound 1 | **Compound 2**

4.59 The molecules that follow are roughly the same size, but they have very different boiling points. Explain the differences in their boiling points.

Butane
Boiling point –1°C

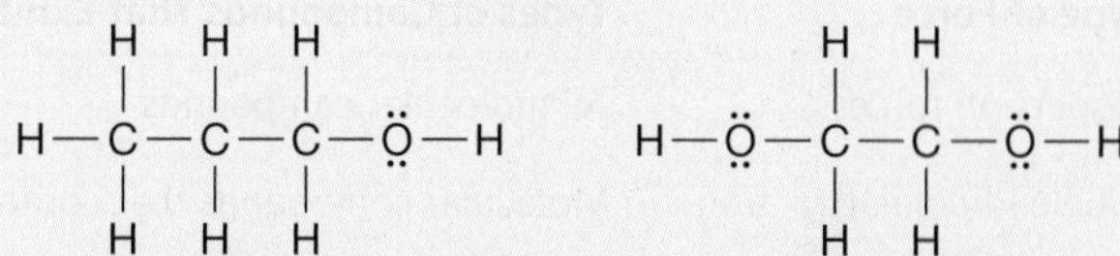

1-propanol
Boiling point 97°C

Ethylene glycol
Boiling point 198°C

4.60 The molecules that follow are roughly the same size, but they have very different boiling points. Explain the differences in their boiling points.

Butane
Boiling point –1°C

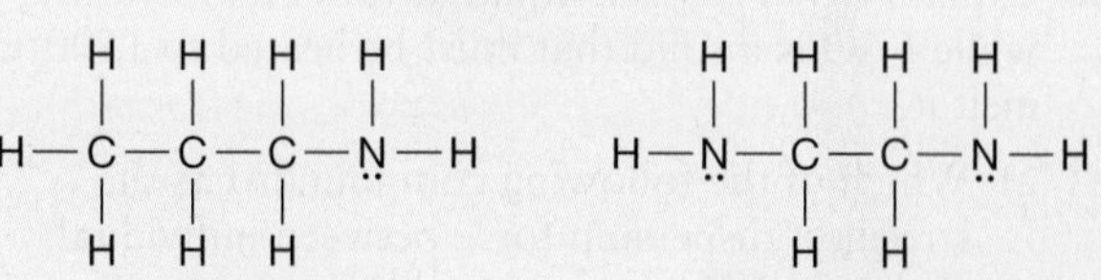

Propylamine
Boiling point 48°C

Ethylenediamine
Boiling point 116°C

continued

4.61 Asparagine is one of the building blocks of proteins. Identify all of the hydrogen atoms that can participate in hydrogen bonds in this compound by drawing a circle around each atom.

```
        H   Ö:  H
        |   ||  |
    H — C — C — N — H
        |       ..
H — N — C — C — Ö — H
    |   |   ||  ..
    H   H   O:
            ..
```

4.62 Cytosine is one of the building blocks of DNA, and its ability to form hydrogen bonds is essential to the function of DNA. Identify all of the hydrogen atoms that can participate in hydrogen bonds in this compound by drawing a circle around each atom.

```
          H
          |
   H      N      Ö:
    \   / ..\  //
     C        C
     ||       |
     C        N.
    / \     //
   H    C
        |
       :N — H
        |
        H
```

For Problems 4.63 and 4.64, select from the following types of attractive forces: covalent bonds, ionic bonds, hydrogen bonds, and dispersion forces.

4.63 a) What types of attractive forces keep the hydrogen atoms attached to the oxygen atom in a water molecule?

b) What types of attractive forces exist between two separate water molecules?

c) Which of these forces (if any) must be overcome to boil water?

4.64 a) What types of attractive forces keep the hydrogen atoms attached to the nitrogen atom in a molecule of ammonia?

b) What types of attractive forces exist between two separate ammonia molecules?

c) Which of these forces (if any) must be overcome to boil ammonia?

4.6 Solutions and the Dissolving Process

OBJECTIVES: *Describe what happens when a molecular compound dissolves in water, and understand the role of hydrogen bonding in water solubility.*

Pour yourself a glass of water, add a teaspoon of sugar, and stir the mixture. After a few seconds, the sugar will vanish, although you can still detect it by taste. You have made a type of homogeneous mixture called a **solution**. The solution looks like water, but the sugar is still present and retains many of its familiar properties, including its sweet flavor and its nutritive value. We can recover the sugar by simply letting the water evaporate; the sugar will be left behind as colorless crystals.

Much of the chemistry that occurs in the human body, and in any living organism, involves solutions. All of the fluids that our bodies make are solutions, including blood plasma, lymph, urine, saliva, and perspiration. In addition, the cells in our bodies are filled with a variety of solutions. In all of these solutions, the principal ingredient is water, making water vital to life as we know it. In the remainder of this chapter, we will look at solutions and at the factors that determine whether a substance can mix with water.

Charles D. Winters

When solid nickel nitrate is added to water, it forms a solution.

TABLE 4.13 Common Solutions

Solution	Solute	State of Solute at Room Temperature	Solvent
Ammonia cleaning solution	Ammonia (NH_3)	Gas	Water
Vinegar	Acetic acid ($HC_2H_3O_2$)	Liquid	Water
Household bleach	Sodium hypochlorite (NaOCl)	Solid	Water

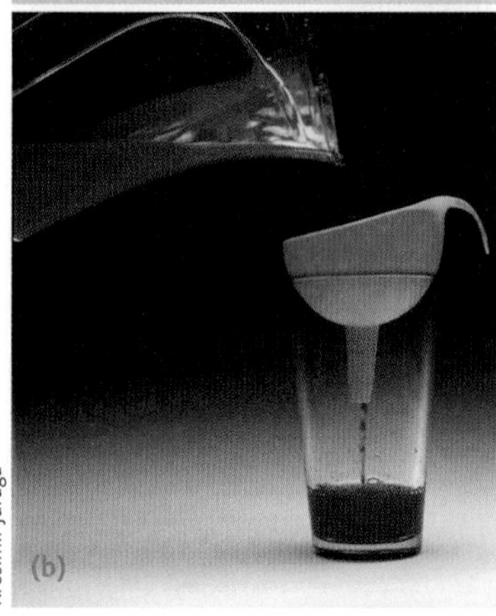

Kresimir Juraga

(a) Muddy water is a suspension and can be separated by filtering it. (b) Water with food coloring is a true solution and cannot be separated by filtration.

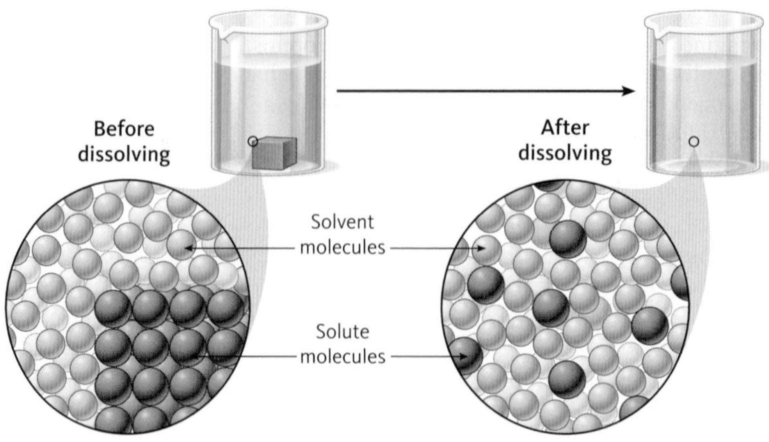

FIGURE 4.24 The dissolving of a molecular substance.

Strictly speaking, a solution is simply a homogeneous mixture of two or more substances. In practice, though, only mixtures that are liquids are called solutions. For instance, sugar water is always called a solution, but air (a homogeneous mixture of several gases) usually is not. Normally, at least one of the substances that make up a solution is a liquid. If a solution contains only one liquid, that liquid is called the **solvent**, and all of the other substances that are mixed with the liquid are called **solutes**. When a solution is made from two or more liquids, the liquid that is present in the greatest amount is the solvent, and the others are solutes. Water is the most common and important solvent, and a solution that contains water as the solvent is called an **aqueous solution**.

Solutes can be solids, liquids, or gases, and solutions can contain more than one type of solute. For example, a sparkling wine contains sugar (a solid), grain alcohol (a liquid), and carbon dioxide (a gas), all dissolved in water. Table 4.13 gives some other examples of solutions that you might encounter.

When a solute dissolves in a solvent, the molecules of the solute become evenly dispersed among the solvent molecules, as shown in Figure 4.24. Since the solution is a liquid, the solute and solvent molecules are constantly moving about.

Not all substances form homogeneous mixtures when they are added to water. If we add a solid to water and the solid remains visible, we call the mixture a **suspension**. For instance, if we add a spoonful of sand to a glass of water, the sand will remain visible, no matter how long we stir, so this mixture is a suspension. In addition, the sand will settle to the bottom of the glass once we stop stirring, and we can remove the sand from this suspension by filtering it.

Some substances appear to dissolve in water, but they do not form a true solution. We can detect their presence by shining a bright light through the solution; the beam of light is visible as it passes through the liquid. Such a mixture is called a **colloid**. Colloids contain solutes that are very large molecules or large clusters of ions that are not completely dissociated. However, a colloid is a homogeneous mixture, and in most ways it behaves like a true solution. The solute particles in both colloids and solutions do not settle out if the mixture is allowed to stand, and we cannot separate the solute from the solvent by filtering (passing it through a piece of paper).

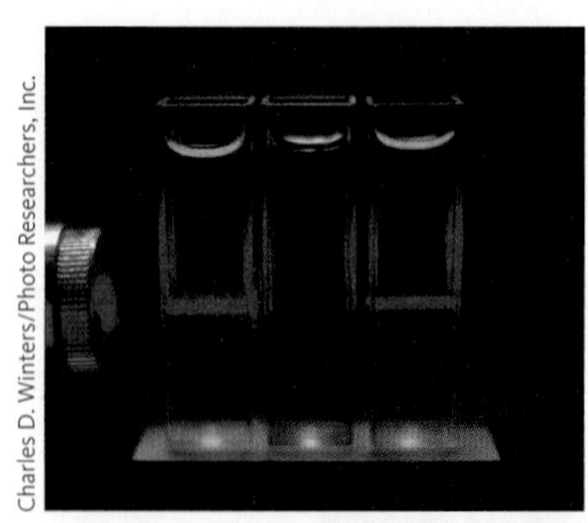

Charles D. Winters/Photo Researchers, Inc.

Solutions and colloids. The liquid in the middle is a true solution. The other two liquids are colloids, so the beam of light is visible as it passes through them.

Compounds That Form Hydrogen Bonds Dissolve in Water

Water molecules are attracted to one another by hydrogen bonds. When a molecular solute dissolves in water, some of the water molecules must move away from one another to make room for solute molecules. In the process, the hydrogen bonds between the water molecules must be disrupted, and this only occurs if water can form hydrogen bonds with the solute molecules. As long as the attraction between water and the solute is comparable to the attraction between water molecules, the solute molecules can mix with water, as illustrated in Figure 4.25.

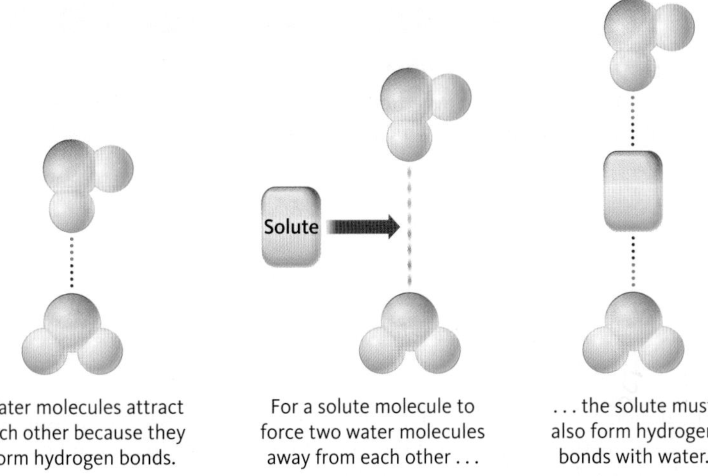
Solute
Water molecules attract each other because they form hydrogen bonds.
For a solute molecule to force two water molecules away from each other . . .
. . . the solute must also form hydrogen bonds with water.

FIGURE 4.25 The role of hydrogen bonding in making an aqueous solution.

For example, ethanol (grain alcohol) is a molecular compound that dissolves in water. Here is the Lewis structure of ethanol:

```
    H   H
    |   |
H — C — C — Ö — H
    |   |   ¨
    H   H
```

The Lewis structure of ethanol

We saw in Section 4.5 that ethanol molecules can form hydrogen bonds with one another. However, an ethanol molecule can also form two types of hydrogen bonds with water molecules, as shown in Figure 4.26. In each type of hydrogen bond, the molecule that supplies the hydrogen atom is called the **hydrogen bond donor**, because it is "donating" its hydrogen to the bond, while the molecule that contributes the negatively charged atom (nitrogen or oxygen) is the **hydrogen bond acceptor**. In one of the two types of hydrogen bonds, ethanol is the donor and water is the acceptor; in the other type, water is the donor and ethanol is the acceptor.

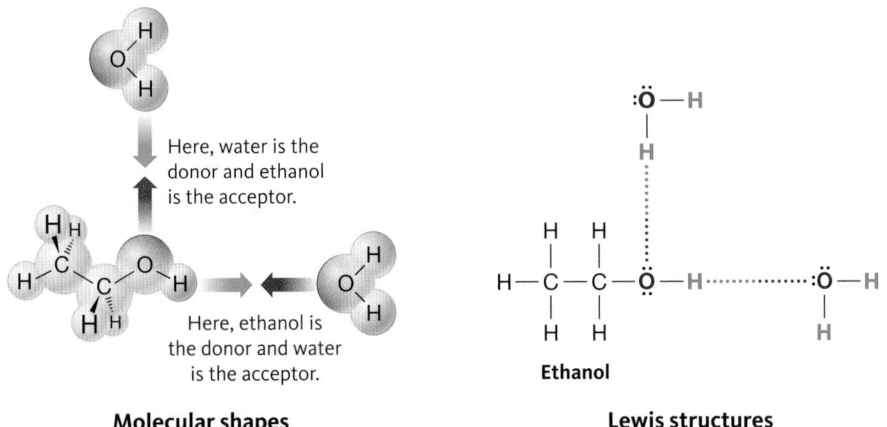
Here, water is the donor and ethanol is the acceptor.
Here, ethanol is the donor and water is the acceptor.
Ethanol
Molecular shapes
Lewis structures

FIGURE 4.26 Hydrogen bonding between water and ethanol.

Health Note: Don't wear a cotton T-shirt if you exercise on a cool day. Cotton is mainly cellulose, which forms hydrogen bonds readily and tends to attract water. Cotton fabrics become soaked with perspiration and take a long time to dry, leaving you with wet fabric against your skin. Many synthetic fabrics do not form hydrogen bonds readily and do not retain water.

Sample Problem 4.15

Recognizing hydrogen bonds between water and a solute

Methylamine dissolves in water. Show how a molecule of methylamine and a molecule of water can form a hydrogen bond in which water is the donor.

```
    H
    |   ..
H — C — N — H
    |   |
    H   H
```

Methylamine

SOLUTION

Water is the donor, so the hydrogen bond involves one of the hydrogen atoms in the water molecule. The methylamine molecule is the acceptor, so the hydrogen bond involves the negatively charged nitrogen atom in methylamine.

```
               ..
              :O — H            Water
               |
               H
               :
               :
    H   H      :
    |   |      ..
H — C — C — N — H               Methylamine
    |   |   |
    H   H   H
```

TRY IT YOURSELF: *Show how water and methylamine can form a hydrogen bond in which methylamine is the donor.*

For additional practice, try Core Problems 4.73 and 4.74.

Health Note: Acetone is one of the ketone bodies, compounds that form when the body obtains most of its energy by burning fats rather than carbohydrates, as is the case in severe diabetes. Acetone cannot be broken down by the body and evaporates easily from the lungs, giving breath a sweet aroma.

Some compounds dissolve in water even though their molecules cannot form hydrogen bonds to one another. A good example of this type of molecule is acetone, a common ingredient in paint thinners and nail polish removers. Acetone has the following Lewis structure:

```
    H   Ö:  H
    |   ||  |
H — C — C — C — H
    |       |
    H       H
```

Acetone

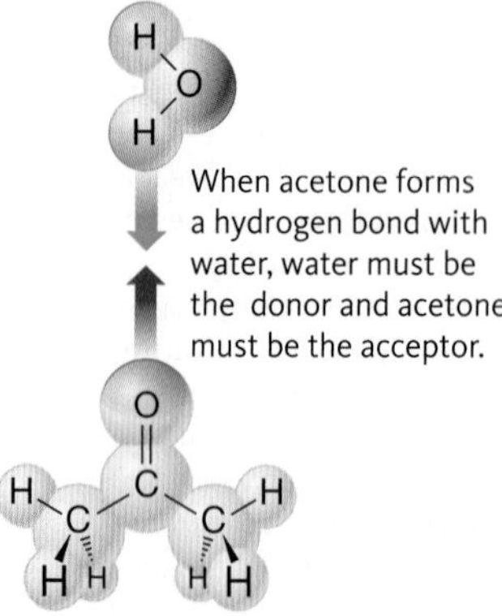

H
O
H
When acetone forms a hydrogen bond with water, water must be the donor and acetone must be the acceptor.
O
C
H
C
C
H
H H
H H

Molecular shapes

```
        ..
    H — O:
        |
        H
        :
        :
    H   Ö:  H
    |   ||  |
H — C — C — C — H
    |       |
    H       H
```

Lewis structures

FIGURE 4.27 Hydrogen bonding between acetone and water.

None of the hydrogen atoms in acetone are bonded to the oxygen atom, so these hydrogen atoms are not strongly charged and cannot participate in hydrogen bonds. However, the oxygen atom is negatively charged and can be a hydrogen bond acceptor. When acetone is mixed with water, the hydrogen atoms from water are attracted to the oxygen atom in acetone, as shown in Figure 4.27. As a result, acetone can dissolve in water.

The compound that follows, called trimethylamine, is another example of a molecule that dissolves in water because it can be a hydrogen bond acceptor. Trimethylamine does not have a hydrogen atom bonded to the nitrogen, so it cannot be a hydrogen bond donor. However, the nitrogen atom in this molecule is negatively charged and is attracted to the hydrogen atoms in water.

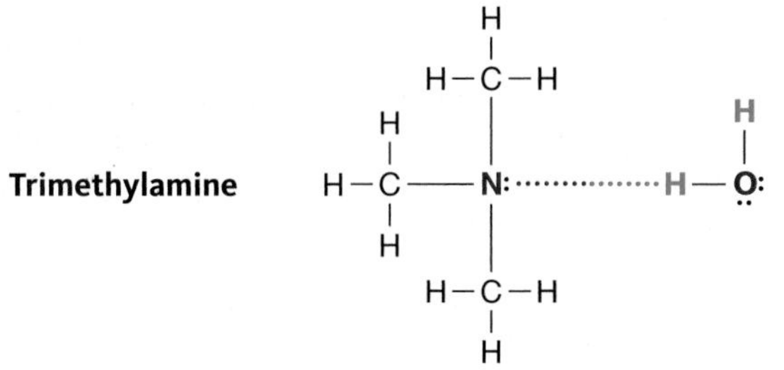

Trimethylamine (structural formula: $N(CH_3)_3$ with the nitrogen lone pair N: hydrogen-bonded ··· to H—O of water)

In practice, most molecular compounds that contain oxygen or nitrogen atoms can dissolve in water to some extent, because they can accept hydrogen bonds from water. The exceptions are molecules that contain a very large region that cannot participate in hydrogen bonds, as we will see in Section 4.9.

Sample Problem 4.16

Recognizing hydrogen bond acceptors

Acetonitrile cannot be a hydrogen bond donor, but it dissolves in water. Explain why this compound dissolves in water.

$$\mathrm{H_3C{-}C{\equiv}N{:}}$$

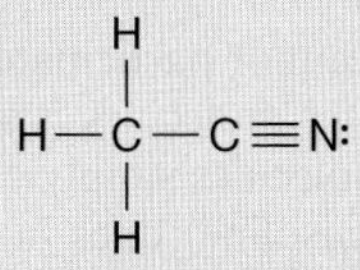

Acetonitrile

SOLUTION

The nitrogen atom in acetonitrile is bonded to a carbon atom. Nitrogen has a higher electronegativity than carbon, so the nitrogen atom is negatively charged and can act as a hydrogen bond acceptor. The hydrogen atoms in water are attracted to the nitrogen atom in acetonitrile, allowing the acetonitrile molecules to mix with the water molecules.

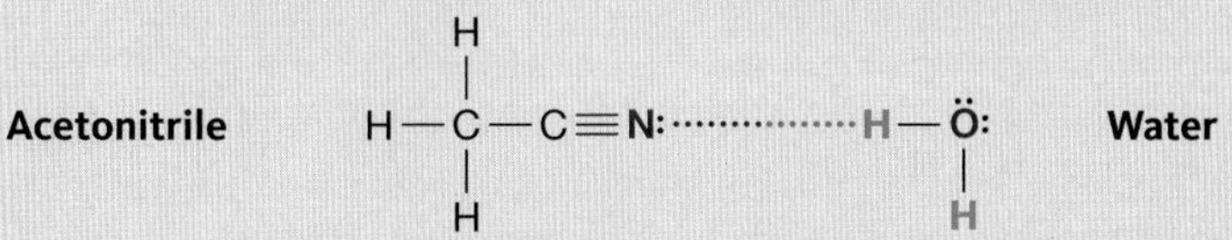

Acetonitrile $\mathrm{H_3C{-}C{\equiv}N{:}\cdots H{-}\ddot{O}{:}{-}H}$ **Water**

TRY IT YOURSELF: *Tetrahydrofuran cannot be a hydrogen bond donor, but it dissolves in water. Explain why this compound dissolves in water.*

(Structure: five-membered ring of one O and four C atoms, each carbon bearing two H atoms)

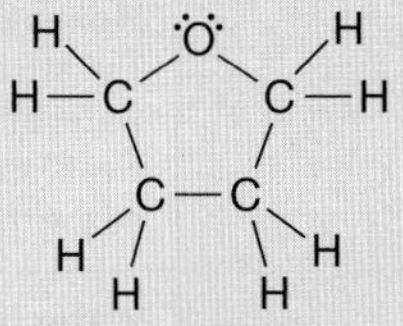

Tetrahydrofuran

For additional practice, try Core Problems 4.75 and 4.76.

Sample Problem 4.17

Recognizing water-soluble compounds

Which of the following compounds should be reasonably soluble in water, based on ability to form hydrogen bonds?

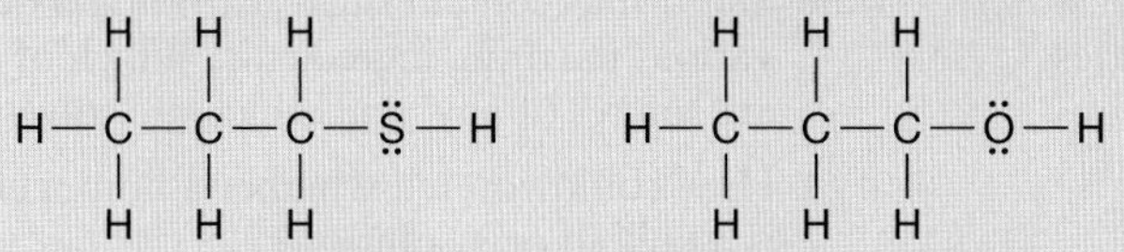

$$\mathrm{CH_3{-}CH_2{-}CH_2{-}\ddot{S}{-}H} \qquad \mathrm{CH_3{-}CH_2{-}CH_2{-}\ddot{O}{-}H}$$

1-propanethiol **1-propanol**

continued

SOLUTION

1-Propanol contains an oxygen atom, making it a hydrogen bond acceptor. It also contains a hydrogen atom that is directly attached to oxygen, making it a hydrogen bond donor. Therefore, 1-propanol should be soluble in water. In contrast, 1-propanethiol does not contain any atoms that can be hydrogen bond donors or acceptors.

TRY IT YOURSELF: *Which of the following compounds should be reasonably soluble in water, based on ability to form hydrogen bonds?*

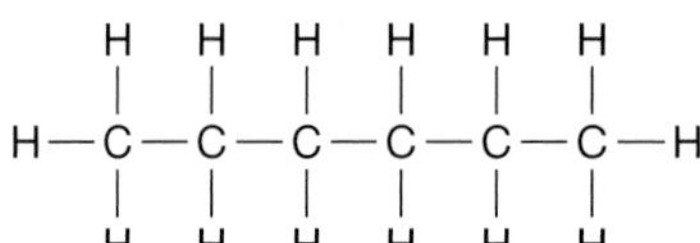

Ethylmethylamine

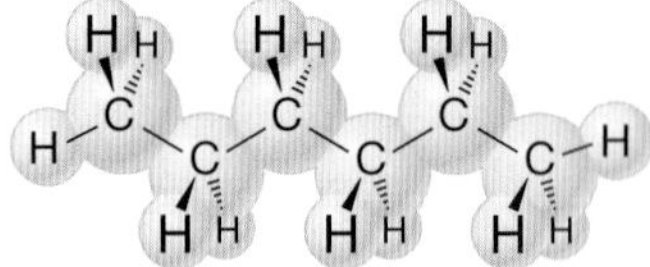

Ethyl methyl phosphine

For additional practice, try Core Problems 4.71 and 4.72.

Most molecular substances that cannot participate in hydrogen bonds do not dissolve in water. The attraction between water molecules is stronger than the attraction between water and the solute, so the water molecules simply cluster together. For example, hexane (C_6H_{14}, one of the components of gasoline) does not dissolve in water, because hexane molecules cannot participate in hydrogen bonds. A mixture of hexane and water separates into two layers, with the denser water molecules grouping together at the bottom of the mixture and the hexane molecules forming a separate layer on top of the water. Figure 4.28 shows the structure of hexane and the behavior of a mixture of hexane and water.

The Lewis structure of hexane

The molecular shape of hexane

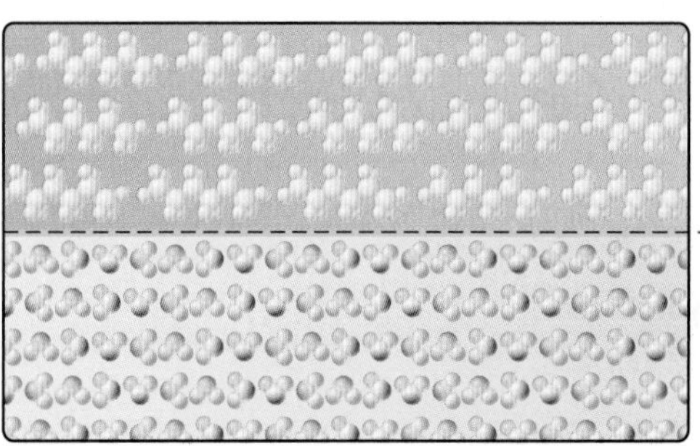

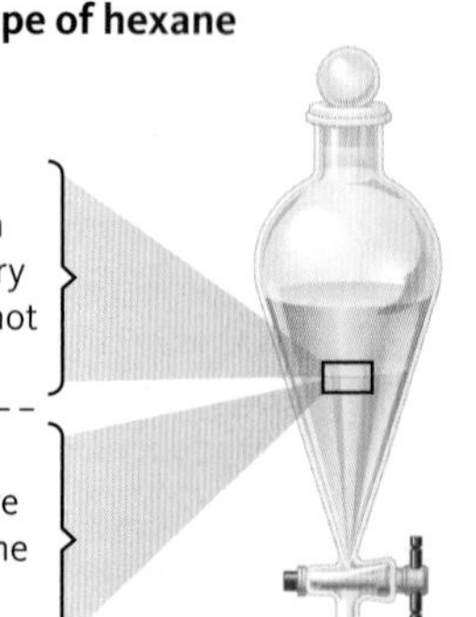

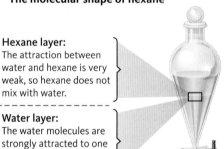

Hexane layer:
The attraction between water and hexane is very weak, so hexane does not mix with water.

Water layer:
The water molecules are strongly attracted to one another.

FIGURE 4.28 Hexane and water do not mix.

CORE PROBLEMS

4.65 When 10 g of NaOH (a white solid) and 10 g of water are mixed, the resulting mixture is a clear, colorless liquid. Is this mixture a solution? If so, which substance is the solute and which is the solvent in this mixture?

4.66 Soft drinks contain sugar, carbon dioxide, water, and various flavoring ingredients. Which of these substances are solutes (if any) and which are solvents (if any)?

4.67 How could you tell whether a homogeneous mixture is a colloid or a solution?

4.68 How do colloids differ from suspensions?

continued

4.69 If you put a little flour into a glass of water and stir vigorously, will you produce a solution or will you produce a suspension? Explain your answer briefly.

4.70 If you put a little salt into a glass of water and stir vigorously, will you produce a solution or will you produce a suspension? Explain your answer briefly.

4.71 Which of the following compounds should dissolve reasonably well in water, based on their ability to form hydrogen bonds?

```
  H  H  H          :Ö:           H  H
  |  |  |          ||            |  |
H—C—C—C—H        H—C—H         H—C—N—H
  |  |  |                        |
  H  H  H                        H
     a)             b)              c)
```

4.72 Which of the following compounds should dissolve reasonably well in water, based on their ability to form hydrogen bonds?

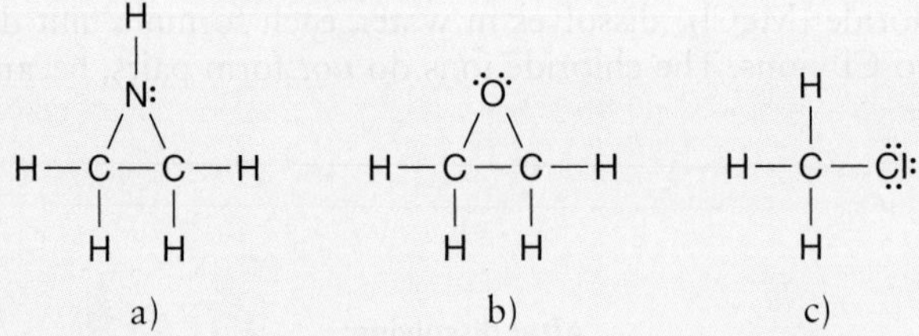

4.73 The following compound can form two types of hydrogen bonds with a water molecule:

```
  H  H
  |  |
H—N—N—H
  ¨  ¨
```

a) Draw structures that show these two types of hydrogen bonds.
b) For each type of hydrogen bond, tell which molecule is the donor and which is the acceptor.

4.74 The following compound can form two types of hydrogen bonds with a water molecule:

```
  H  H
  |  |
H—C—C=N̈—H
  |
  H
```

a) Draw structures that show these two types of hydrogen bonds.
b) For each type of hydrogen bond, tell which molecule is the donor and which is the acceptor.

4.75 Which of the following molecules can function as both a hydrogen bond donor and a hydrogen bond acceptor, and which can only function as a hydrogen bond acceptor?

```
  H       H  H
  |       |  |
H—C—N̈=C—C—H
  |          |
  H          H
   Compound 1

  H  H  H              H     H
  |  |  |              |     |
H—C—C—C=Ö:          H—C—N—C—H
  |  |                 |  ¨  |
  H  H                 H     H
 Compound 2           Compound 3
```

4.76 Which of the following molecules can function as both a hydrogen bond donor and a hydrogen bond acceptor, and which can only function as a hydrogen bond acceptor?

Compound 1

Compound 2

Compound 3

4.7 Electrolytes and Dissociation

OBJECTIVES: *Describe what happens when an ionic compound dissolves in water, and recognize ions that generally produce water-soluble compounds.*

Advertisements for sports beverages often point out that the beverages supply a variety of **electrolytes**. An electrolyte is a chemical compound that conducts electricity when it dissolves in water. A solution of an electrolyte behaves like a metal wire, allowing electrical current to pass through it, as shown in Figure 4.29. Electrolytes are our dietary sources for many essential elements, including potassium, sodium, and magnesium. In this section, we will look at electrolytes: what they are, and how they behave in solution.

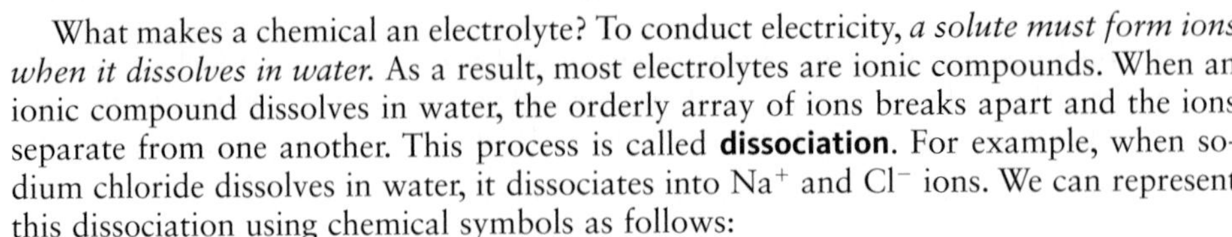

What makes a chemical an electrolyte? To conduct electricity, *a solute must form ions when it dissolves in water.* As a result, most electrolytes are ionic compounds. When an ionic compound dissolves in water, the orderly array of ions breaks apart and the ions separate from one another. This process is called **dissociation**. For example, when sodium chloride dissolves in water, it dissociates into Na^+ and Cl^- ions. We can represent this dissociation using chemical symbols as follows:

$$NaCl(s) \rightarrow Na^+(aq) + Cl^-(aq)$$

This is an example of a *chemical equation,* and it means that solid sodium chloride turns into separate sodium and chloride ions, which are dissolved in water. The ions are entirely independent of one another. Figure 4.30 illustrates the dissociation of sodium chloride.

Water plays an active role in the dissociation of ionic compounds. When an ionic compound dissolves in water, water molecules surround the ions and pull them away from one another, a process called **solvation**. Water can do this because the hydrogen and oxygen atoms in water are electrically charged. The positively charged hydrogen atoms in H_2O are attracted to negative ions, and the negatively charged oxygen atom in H_2O is attracted to positive ions. Figure 4.31 shows how sodium and chloride ions are solvated when NaCl dissolves in water.

The formulas of many ionic compounds contain two or more of a particular ion. When these compounds dissolve in water, all of the ions separate from one another. For example, when magnesium chloride ($MgCl_2$) dissolves in water, each formula unit dissociates into one Mg^{2+} and two Cl^- ions. The chloride ions do *not* form pairs, because

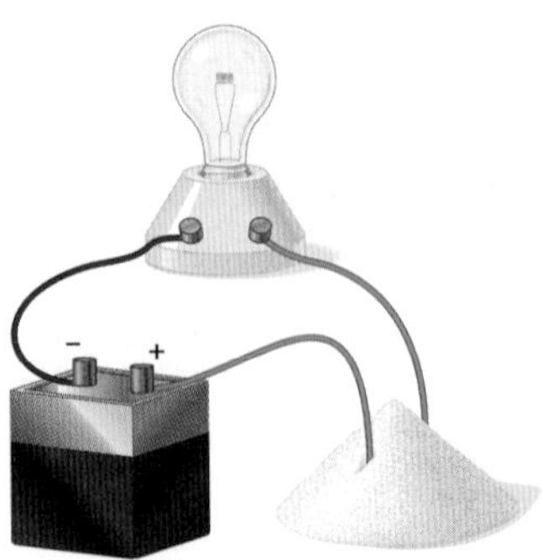

Salt does not conduct electricity.

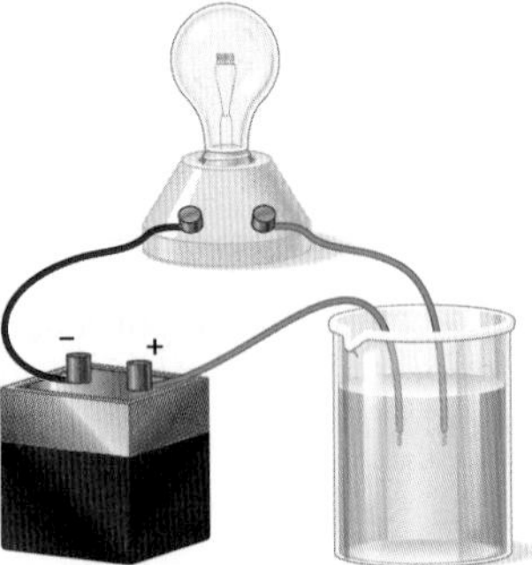

Water does not conduct electricity.

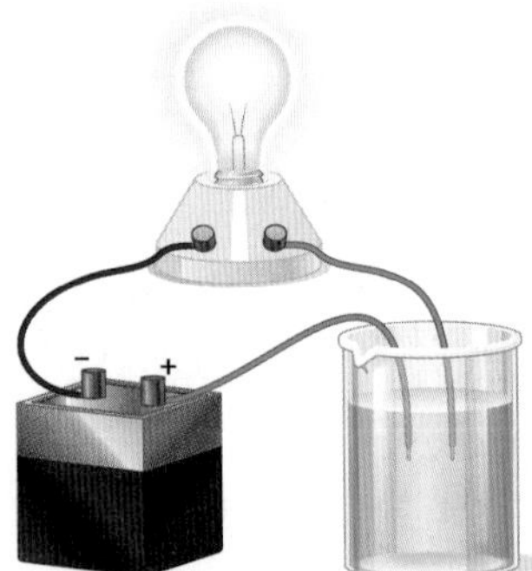

Salt water conducts electricity, so salt is an electrolyte.

FIGURE 4.29 Electrolytes conduct electricity when they dissolve in water.

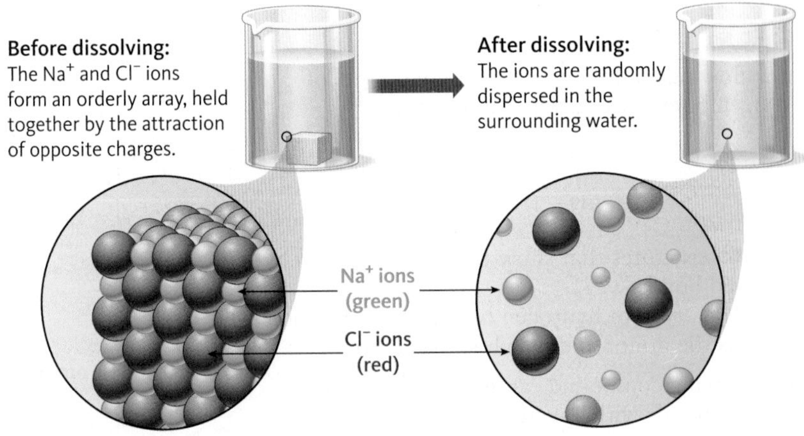

FIGURE 4.30 The dissociation of sodium chloride in water.

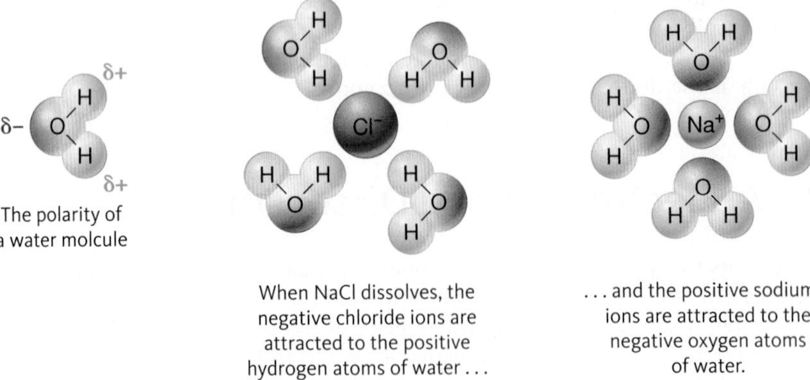

FIGURE 4.31 The solvation of sodium and chloride ions.

they are negatively charged and repel one another. We can represent this behavior using another chemical equation:

$$MgCl_2(s) \longrightarrow Mg^{2+}(aq) + \boxed{2}Cl^-(aq)$$

The "2" tells us that we get two chloride ions when one formula unit of $MgCl_2$ dissolves.

Many ionic compounds contain polyatomic ions. When these compounds dissolve, the polyatomic ions separate from the other ions, but they do not fall apart. For example, when potassium phosphate (K_3PO_4) dissolves in water, it dissociates into three K^+ ions and one PO_4^{3-} ion. The phosphate ion does *not* break down into phosphorus and oxygen atoms, because water cannot break the covalent bonds that hold the phosphate ion together. The chemical equation for dissolving potassium phosphate is

$$K_3PO_4(s) \longrightarrow \boxed{3}K^+(aq) + PO_4^{3-}(aq)$$

The "3" tells us that we get three potassium ions when one formula unit of K_3PO_4 dissolves.

Health Note: Electrolyte balance is a key concept in physiology. Our bodies have an elaborate mechanism to ensure that body fluids maintain the correct concentrations of ions, particularly Na^+, K^+, Cl^-, HCO_3^-, and Ca^{2+}.

Sample Problem 4.18

Describing the dissociation of an ionic compound

What happens to sodium carbonate when it dissolves in water?

SOLUTION

Sodium carbonate is an ionic compound with the chemical formula Na_2CO_3. When this compound dissolves in water, it dissociates into sodium ions (Na^+) and carbonate ions (CO_3^{2-}). These ions are independent of one another and are free to move throughout the solution. We can represent the dissociation with a chemical equation:

$$Na_2CO_3(s) \rightarrow 2\ Na^+(aq) + CO_3^{2-}(aq)$$

Each ion is solvated by water molecules. The oxygen atoms of the surrounding water molecules face the sodium ions, and the hydrogen atoms of the water molecules face the carbonate ions:

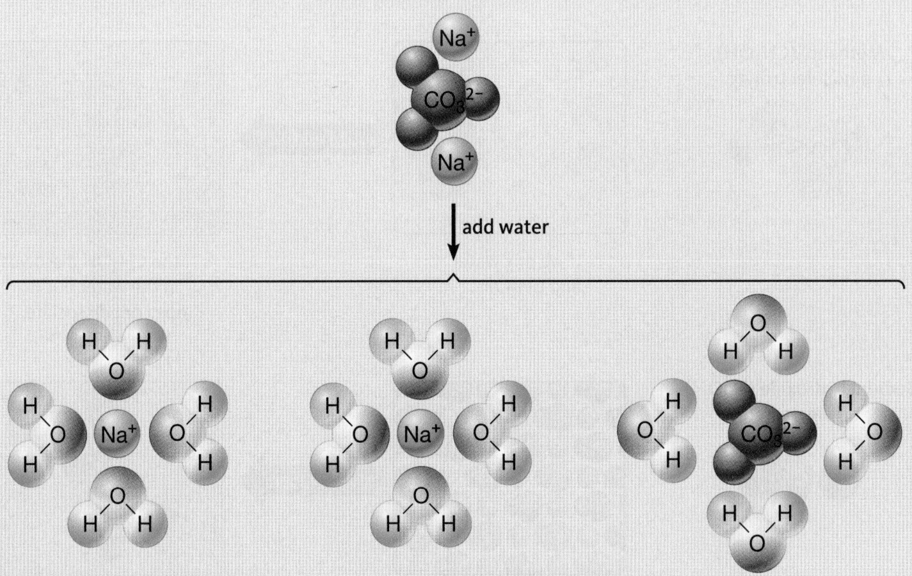

TRY IT YOURSELF: *What happens to calcium nitrate when it dissolves in water?*

For additional practice, try Core Problems 4.79 through 4.84.

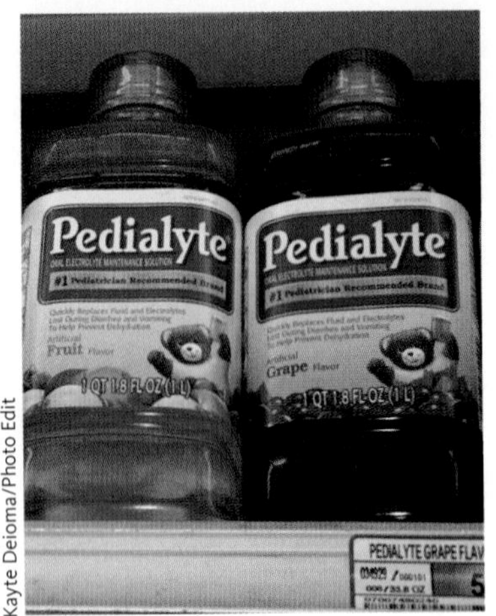

Kayte Deioma/Photo Edit

Oral rehydration solutions replace essential electrolytes that are lost when a child has severe diarrhea.

It is important to recognize the difference between molecular and ionic compounds when they dissolve in water. In general, when a molecular compound dissolves, the molecules move away from one another, but they do not break apart into ions. Therefore, most molecular solutes are **nonelectrolytes,** substances that do not conduct electricity when they dissolve in water. In general, you should assume that any molecular compound is a nonelectrolyte and any ionic compound is an electrolyte. Remember also that ionic compounds contain either a metallic element or the NH_4 group (actually the ammonium ion, NH_4^+) at the start of their chemical formulas, while molecular compounds are made entirely of nonmetals and do not contain ammonium ions. Table 4.14 lists some common electrolytes and nonelectrolytes, and Figure 4.32 illustrates the difference between electrolytes and nonelectrolytes.

TABLE 4.14 Common Electrolytes and Nonelectrolytes

Electrolytes (contain a metallic element or the NH_4 group)	Nonelectrolytes (do not contain a metal or NH_4)
NaCl (table salt: a major source of sodium and chloride ions)	$C_{12}H_{22}O_{11}$ (table sugar)
KI (potassium iodide: added to table salt as a source of iodide ions)	C_2H_5OH (ethanol, also called ethyl alcohol or grain alcohol)
$(NH_4)_2CO_3$ (ammonium carbonate: an ingredient in smelling salts and some leavening agents)	C_3H_6O (acetone: an ingredient in many paint thinners and in nail polish remover)
KH_2PO_4 (monobasic potassium phosphate: used in sports beverages as a source of potassium)	C_2H_6SO (dimethyl sulfoxide: used to reduce inflammation and transport medications through the skin; also called DMSO)*
$Ca(C_3H_5O_3)_2$ (calcium lactate: used in sports beverages as a source of calcium)	$C_{10}H_{19}PS_2O_6$ (malathion: an insecticide)

*DMSO is not approved for most medical uses in the United States.

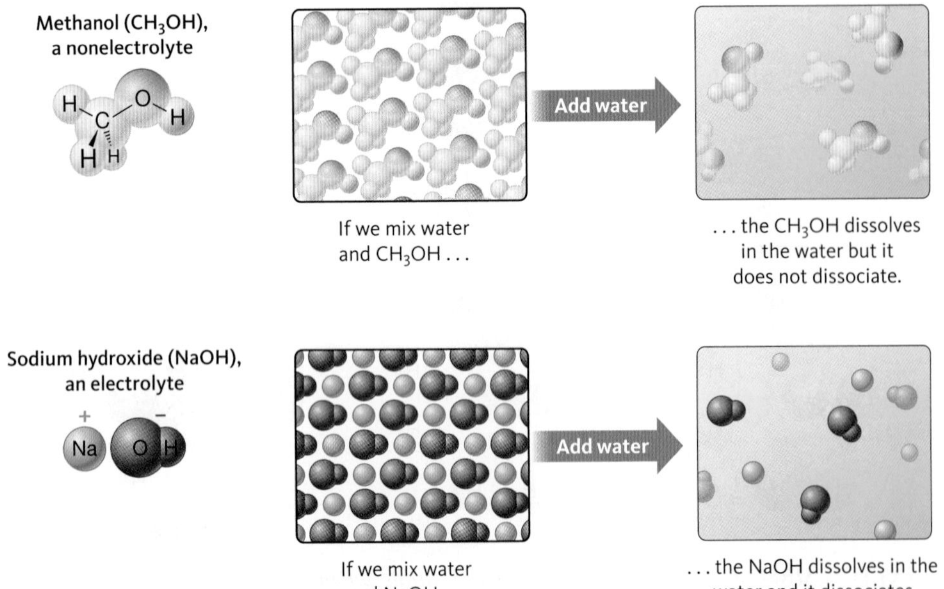

FIGURE 4.32 An electrolyte and a nonelectrolyte dissolving in water.

Not all molecular compounds are nonelectrolytes. Some molecular compounds form ions when they dissolve in water. The vast majority of these compounds convert water into an ion by either adding or removing a hydrogen ion. Chemicals that can transfer H^+ ions to or from water are called acids and bases, and we will look at their chemistry in Chapter 7.

NaCl dissolves in water because the attraction between the ions and H_2O is as strong as the attraction between Na^+ and Cl^-.

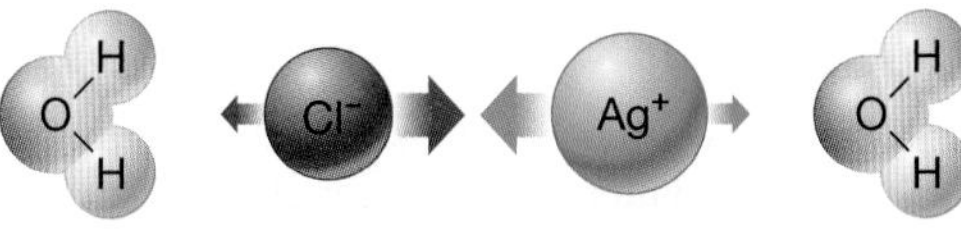

AgCl does not dissolve in water because the attraction between the ions and H_2O is weaker than the attraction between Ag^+ and Cl^-.

FIGURE 4.33 Comparing a soluble ionic compound to an insoluble ionic compound.

The Ability of an Ionic Compound to Dissolve in Water Is Important in Health Care and Nutrition

The ability of ionic compounds to dissolve in water is the result of a delicate balance between two very strong attractive forces. Whenever the ions that make up a compound are as strongly attracted to water molecules as they are to each other, the compound dissolves in water. However, in a number of ionic compounds, the attraction between the ions is significantly stronger than the ions' attraction to water. As a result, these compounds do not dissolve in water. $CaCO_3$ (chalk), $Mg(OH)_2$ (milk of magnesia), and $Fe(OH)_3$ (rust) are examples of ionic compounds that are insoluble in water. Figure 4.33 illustrates the role that these attractive forces play in the dissolving of ionic compounds.

Ionic compounds that contain sodium or potassium play an important role in health care and nutrition, because *all ionic compounds that contain Na^+ or K^+ dissolve in water.* In addition, these compounds are generally readily available and inexpensive, and sodium and potassium are relatively nontoxic. As a result, sodium and potassium compounds are useful sources of negative ions. For example, salt manufacturers add KI to supply the essential nutrient I^-, and toothpaste manufacturers add NaF as a source of F^- to prevent tooth decay. These compounds dissolve easily in water and dissociate as they dissolve, making the iodide and fluoride ions available to our bodies. Similarly, compounds that contain chloride ions are useful sources of positive ions such as magnesium and calcium, because most ionic compounds that contain Cl^- dissolve in water, and these compounds are also inexpensive and readily available.

Sample Problem **4.19**

Identifying a water-soluble ionic compound

If you need to prepare a solution that contains phosphate ions, what chemical compound might you use as a solute?

SOLUTION

It is not possible to prepare a solution that contains only one type of ion (positive or negative), because all ionic compounds contain both positive and negative ions. Therefore, we need to find an ionic compound that contains phosphate ions (PO_4^{3-}) and that is soluble in water. All sodium and potassium compounds are water soluble, so the best choices are either sodium phosphate (Na_3PO_4) or potassium phosphate (K_3PO_4).

TRY IT YOURSELF: *If you need to prepare a solution that contains carbonate ions, what chemical compound might you use as a solute?*

For additional practice, try Core Problems 4.85 and 4.86.

The ability of water to dissolve a variety of ionic compounds, in addition to a range of molecular substances, sets it apart from all other common liquids. Very few liquids are polar enough to overcome the ion–ion attraction in an ionic compound, and of these, only water retains the capacity to dissolve molecular substances. The solvent power of water is vitally important in your body, because water (in your blood) must transport a wide range of nutrients, both ionic (potassium ions, calcium ions, and bicarbonate ions) and molecular (sugars, amino acids, and so forth). However, water is a poor solvent for molecular substances that are unable to participate in hydrogen bonds and for large molecules that form few hydrogen bonds. Such substances include fats, cholesterol, and elemental oxygen (O_2), all of which require special handling by our bodies. We will examine how our bodies transport such substances in later chapters.

CORE PROBLEMS

4.77 All of the following compounds dissolve in water. Which of them are electrolytes? (You should not need to draw Lewis structures.)
a) $CaCl_2$ b) $HCONH_2$ c) $KC_2H_3O_2$

4.78 All of the following compounds dissolve in water. Which of them are electrolytes? (You should not need to draw Lewis structures.)
a) C_3H_6O b) BaO c) $C_2H_4(OH)_2$

4.79 Describe what happens to the individual molecules and ions when magnesium chloride dissolves in water.

4.80 Describe what happens to the individual molecules and ions when sodium sulfate dissolves in water.

4.81 The following ionic compounds dissolve in water. What ions are formed when they dissolve?
a) K_2S b) $FeSO_4$ c) $(NH_4)_2CO_3$

4.82 The following ionic compounds dissolve in water. What ions are formed when they dissolve?
a) $CuBr_2$ b) NH_4Cl c) $Cr(NO_3)_3$

4.83 Draw a picture to show how calcium ions are solvated by water molecules.

4.84 Draw a picture to show how fluoride ions are solvated by water molecules.

4.85 Molybdenum is a required nutrient. It occurs primarily in the molybdate ion, a polyatomic ion with the formula MoO_4^{2-}. Suggest a water-soluble compound that contains this ion and could be used in foods.

4.86 Compounds containing the dichromate ion ($Cr_2O_7^{2-}$) are used to prevent rusting in certain types of steel. Suggest a water-soluble compound that contains this ion. (All compounds that contain dichromate are poisonous.)

OBJECTIVES: *Describe and interpret the solubility of a compound, and predict the effects of temperature and pressure on solubility.*

4.8 Solubility

If we put a liter of water in a container and add a little table salt (NaCl), the salt dissolves easily. If we continue to add salt, though, we must stir the mixture longer and longer before the salt disappears. Once we have added about 360 grams of salt, we cannot dissolve any more, no matter how hard we stir. Any additional salt that we add simply sinks to the bottom of the container.

For almost all substances, there is an upper limit to the mass that we can dissolve in a liter of water. This limit is called the **solubility** of the substance. For instance, the solubility of sodium chloride in water is 360 grams per liter (360 g/L), which means that we can dissolve up to 360 grams of NaCl in a liter of water, but no more. If we use less than this amount of solute, we make an **unsaturated solution**, and we can continue to dissolve more solute. Once we reach the solubility limit, though, we have a **saturated solution**.

Often, we only need a general idea of the solubility, rather than a specific number. Chemists normally say that a compound is **insoluble** when the solubility is less than 1 g/L, because the amount that dissolves in water is so small that we do not notice it. If the solubility is significantly higher than this, generally at least 10 g/L, the compound is **soluble**. *Soluble* and *insoluble* are rough terms, and they correspond to a wide range of solubilities, as shown in Table 4.15. Note that "insoluble" compounds do dissolve in water, but they only do so to a small extent.

A compound with a high solubility: 85 g of sodium acetate can dissolve in 50 mL of water.

TABLE 4.15 Solubilities of Some Substances in Water at 25°C

SOLUBLE COMPOUNDS		INSOLUBLE COMPOUNDS	
Compound	Solubility	Compound	Solubility
$C_{12}H_{22}O_{11}$ (table sugar)	2000 g/L	C_6H_6 (benzene)	0.6 g/L
NaCl (table salt)	360 g/L	$C_{27}H_{46}O$ (cholesterol)	0.002 g/L
C_6H_6O (phenol)	65 g/L	AgI (silver iodide)	0.00003 g/L
$Ca(OH)_2$ (slaked lime)	2 g/L (usually described as slightly soluble)	SiO_2 (quartz)	Too low to measure

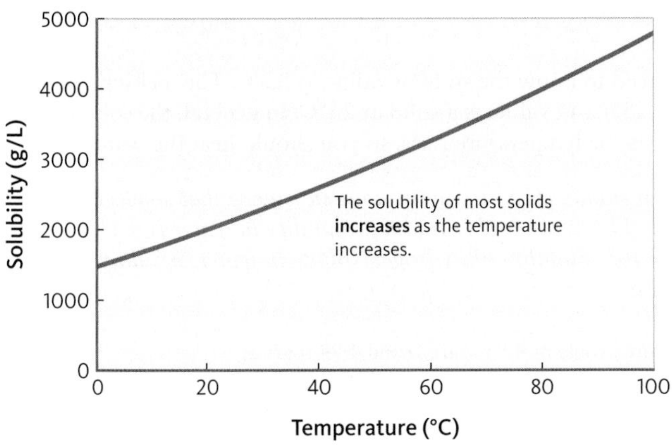

FIGURE 4.34 The effect of temperature on the solubility of sugar in water.

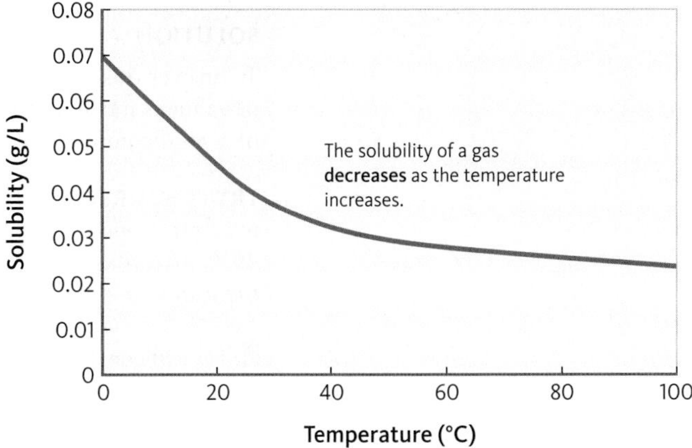

FIGURE 4.35 The effect of temperature on the solubility of oxygen in water.

The solubility of a compound is an important property and can be found in a variety of reference sources. Unfortunately, these sources list solubilities in a variety of units, so it can be difficult to compare them directly. In this text, all solubilities are expressed in grams per liter.

Sample Problem 4.20

Classifying a compound as soluble or insoluble

Up to 14 mg of calcium carbonate ($CaCO_3$) can be dissolved in 1 L of water. Should calcium carbonate be described as a soluble compound or an insoluble compound?

SOLUTION

We know that 14 mg equals 0.014 g, so the solubility is only 0.014 g/L. Compounds with such low solubilities are considered to be insoluble in water.

TRY IT YOURSELF: *Up to 0.09 kg of sodium bicarbonate ($NaHCO_3$) can be dissolved in 1 L of water. Should sodium bicarbonate be described as a soluble compound or an insoluble compound?*

For additional practice, try Core Problems 4.87 and 4.88.

Solubility Depends on Temperature and Pressure

The solubility of many compounds depends on the temperature. For instance, if you have ever made rock candy, you already know that sugar dissolves better in hot water than in cold water. In general, *the solubility of a solid in water increases as you raise the temperature.* Figure 4.34 shows how the solubility of table sugar (sucrose) depends on the temperature.

For gases, the situation is reversed: *gases dissolve better in cold water than in hot water.* For example, the solubility of oxygen is higher in cold water than in warm water. Many fish cannot survive in water that is too warm, because warm water does not contain enough dissolved oxygen to meet the fish's needs. Figure 4.35 shows how the solubility of oxygen in water depends on temperature.

Sample Problem 4.21

The effect of temperature on solubility

Valine ($C_5H_{11}NO_2$) is one of the building blocks of proteins. The melting point of valine is 315°C, and the solubility of valine in water is 88 g/L at 25°C. If you want to increase the solubility of valine in water, should you heat the water, or should you cool it?

continued

SOLUTION

To answer this question, we need to know the state of valine at 25°C. The melting point of valine is much higher than 25°C, so valine is a solid at 25°C. In general, the solubility of a solid compound goes up as the temperature rises, so you should heat the water.

TRY IT YOURSELF: *Hydrogen sulfide (H_2S) is a poisonous substance that smells like rotten eggs. It melts at −85°C and boils at −60°C, and its solubility in water is 4.1 g/L at 20°C. If you want to increase the solubility of hydrogen sulfide in water, should you heat the water, or should you cool it?*

For additional practice, try Core Problems 4.93 (part a) and 4.94 (part a).

• The relationship between pressure and solubility of gases is called Henry's law.

The solubility of solids and liquids does not depend on the pressure. However, *the solubility of any gas increases as you increase the pressure of the gas.* For example, the solubility of oxygen in water goes up as we increase the oxygen pressure, as shown in Figure 4.36. A patient with respiratory difficulties is often given pure oxygen to breathe, because the oxygen pressure is 760 torr in pure oxygen, compared to 150 torr in normal air. The higher pressure of oxygen allows more of the gas to dissolve in the patient's blood.

Charles D. Winters

Releasing the pressure on a bottle of carbonated water decreases the solubility of CO_2, allowing bubbles of gaseous CO_2 to form.

Sample Problem **4.22**

The effect of pressure on solubility

At 25°C, which of the compounds that follow should be more soluble at high pressures than at low pressures?

carbon monoxide: melting point = −205°C, boiling point = −191°C
carbon disulfide: melting point = −112°C, boiling point = 46°C

SOLUTION

Changing the pressure only affects the solubility of a gas, so we start by determining which of these two substances is a gas at 25°C. Because 25°C is far above the boiling point of carbon monoxide, this compound is a gas at 25°C and is more soluble at high pressures. By contrast, 25°C is between the melting and boiling points of carbon disulfide, so this compound is a liquid at room temperature and its solubility is not affected by pressure.

TRY IT YOURSELF: *How will the pressure affect the solubility of carbon disulfide in water at 75°C?*

For additional practice, try Core Problems 4.93 (part b) and 4.94 (part b).

Health Note: Deep-water scuba divers use air that contains little nitrogen, because the high pressure under water increases the solubility of nitrogen in blood. The blood nitrogen causes symptoms similar to the effect of drinking too much alcohol. These symptoms, called nitrogen narcosis, become significant when the diver is more than 100 feet (30 m) below the surface, and they can be fatal or lead to a fatal decision.

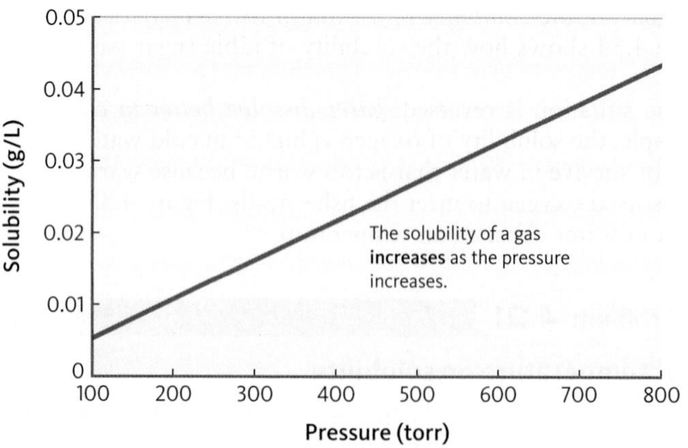

FIGURE 4.36 The effect of pressure on the solubility of oxygen in water.

CORE PROBLEMS

4.87 Vitamin A is always described as insoluble in water. Does this mean that you cannot dissolve vitamin A in water? If not, what does it mean?

4.88 Thiamine (a B vitamin) is always described as soluble in water. Does this mean that you can dissolve any amount (even a very large amount) of thiamine in water? If not, what does it mean?

4.89 The solubility of aspirin in water is around 3 g/L at 25°C. If you mix 2.5 grams of aspirin with a liter of water at 25°C, will all of the aspirin dissolve? Will you make a saturated solution or an unsaturated solution?

4.90 The solubility of calcium sulfate in water is around 2 g/L at 25°C. If you mix 2.5 grams of calcium sulfate with a liter of water at 25°C, will all of the calcium sulfate dissolve? Will you make a saturated solution or an unsaturated solution?

4.91 a) Use Figure 4.34 to determine the temperature at which the solubility of sugar is 3000 g/L.
b) Use Figure 4.35 to determine the solubility of oxygen when the temperature is 20°C.

4.92 a) Use Figure 4.36 to determine the pressure at which the solubility of oxygen is 0.02 g/L.
b) Use Figure 4.34 to determine the solubility of sugar when the temperature is 80°C.

4.93 Calcium sulfate is a solid at room temperature.
a) Will the solubility of calcium sulfate in water increase, remain the same, or decrease as you increase the temperature?
b) Will the solubility of calcium sulfate in water increase, remain the same, or decrease as you increase the pressure?

4.94 Carbon dioxide is a gas at room temperature.
a) Will the solubility of carbon dioxide in water increase, remain the same, or decrease as you increase the temperature?
b) Will the solubility of carbon dioxide in water increase, remain the same, or decrease as you increase the pressure?

4.9 The Relationship between Solubility and Molecular Structure

OBJECTIVES: *Recognize hydrophilic and hydrophobic regions in a molecular compound, and rank the solubilities of structurally related compounds.*

In Section 4.6, we saw that molecular compounds that can form hydrogen bonds are more soluble in water than compounds that cannot. However, many molecules can form hydrogen bonds yet do not dissolve well in water. The ability to dissolve in water depends on the structure of the entire molecule.

For instance, many insoluble compounds that are important in health care contain a long chain of carbon and hydrogen atoms. A good example is lauric acid, one of the building blocks of fats and vegetable oils. The structure of lauric acid is shown in Figure 4.37.

In lauric acid, the two oxygen atoms and the neighboring hydrogen atom can participate in hydrogen bonds. This portion of the molecule is attracted to water and is called **hydrophilic** ("water-loving"). However, the rest of this rather large molecule cannot form hydrogen bonds and has little attraction for water, so it is said to be **hydrophobic** ("water-fearing"). When a molecule of lauric acid is surrounded by water, most of the water molecules around the lauric acid are unable to form hydrogen bonds with the solute. The lauric acid is forced out of solution, as if it were entirely unable to form hydrogen bonds. Lauric acid is therefore insoluble in water.

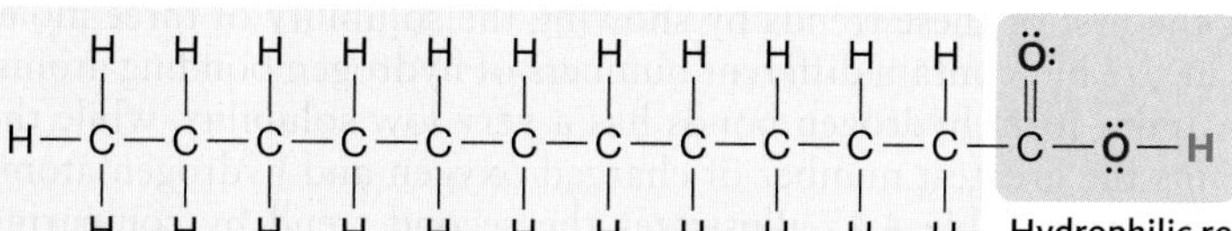

FIGURE 4.37 The structure of lauric acid.

Sample Problem 4.23

Identifying hydrophilic and hydrophobic regions in a molecule

Octylamine can form hydrogen bonds, but it is insoluble in water. Identify the hydrophilic and hydrophobic regions in this molecule.

```
     H   H   H   H   H   H   H   H   H
     |   |   |   |   |   |   |   |   |
 H — C — C — C — C — C — C — C — C — N — H
     |   |   |   |   |   |   |   |   ··
     H   H   H   H   H   H   H   H
```

Octylamine

SOLUTION

The nitrogen atom is negatively charged and can act as a hydrogen bond acceptor. The two hydrogen atoms that are bonded to the nitrogen are positively charged and can act as hydrogen bond donors. These atoms constitute the hydrophilic region of the molecule. The rest of the molecule cannot participate in hydrogen bonds and is hydrophobic.

```
     H   H   H   H   H   H   H   H   H
     |   |   |   |   |   |   |   |   |
 H — C — C — C — C — C — C — C — C — N — H
     |   |   |   |   |   |   |   |   ··
     H   H   H   H   H   H   H   H     Hydrophilic
                                       region
 Hydrophobic region
```

TRY IT YOURSELF: *4-Heptanol can form hydrogen bonds, but it is insoluble in water. Identify the hydrophilic and hydrophobic regions in this molecule.*

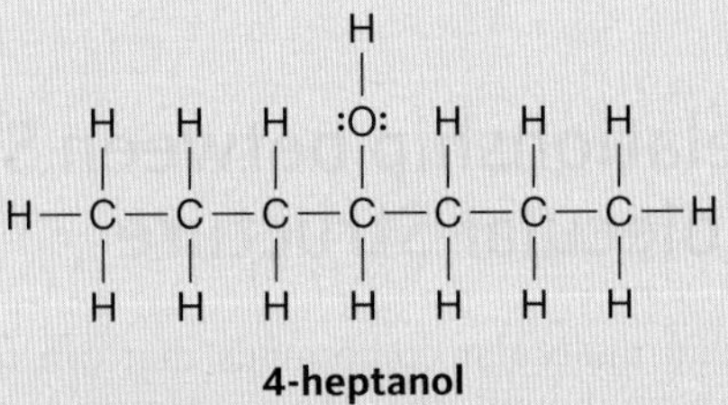

4-heptanol

For additional practice, try Core Problems 4.95 and 4.96.

Charles D. Winters

Oil contains compounds made primarily from carbon and hydrogen, so it is hydrophobic and does not mix with water. Oil is less dense than water, so it floats atop the water layer.

A vast number of compounds in our bodies are built from the elements carbon, hydrogen, oxygen, and nitrogen. The solubility of these compounds is an important property, because it determines how our bodies can store and transport them. Although it is impossible to predict the exact solubility of any compound, we can make two general statements about solubility trends for molecular compounds:

- The more *hydrogen bonds* a molecule can form, the *higher* its solubility.
- The more *carbon and hydrogen atoms* a molecule contains, the *lower* its solubility.

Table 4.16 illustrates the first of these trends by showing the solubility of three molecules that are similar in size but contain different numbers of hydrogen bonding atoms. The compound that cannot form hydrogen bonds has a very low solubility, while the compound that contains the greatest number of charged oxygen and hydrogen atoms dissolves fairly well in water. Table 4.17 illustrates the second trend by comparing molecules that have the same hydrophilic region but different hydrophobic regions. The compound with the fewest carbon and hydrogen atoms dissolves well in water, while the compound that contains a lengthy chain of carbon and hydrogen atoms is essentially insoluble.

TABLE 4.16 The Effect of Adding Hydrogen-Bonding Atoms on Water Solubility

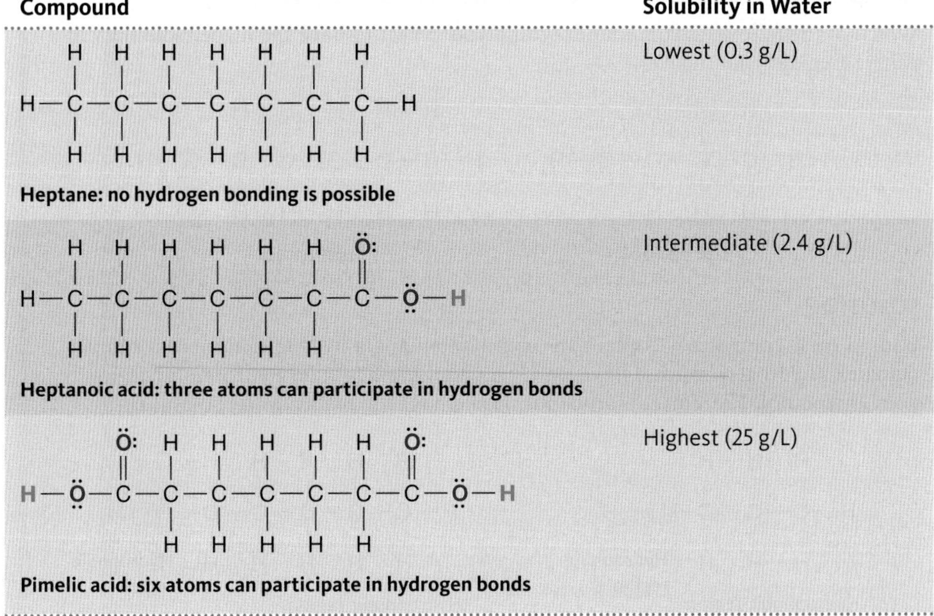

Compound	Solubility in Water
Heptane: no hydrogen bonding is possible	Lowest (0.3 g/L)
Heptanoic acid: three atoms can participate in hydrogen bonds	Intermediate (2.4 g/L)
Pimelic acid: six atoms can participate in hydrogen bonds	Highest (25 g/L)

TABLE 4.17 The Effect of Increasing Hydrophobic Character on Water Solubility

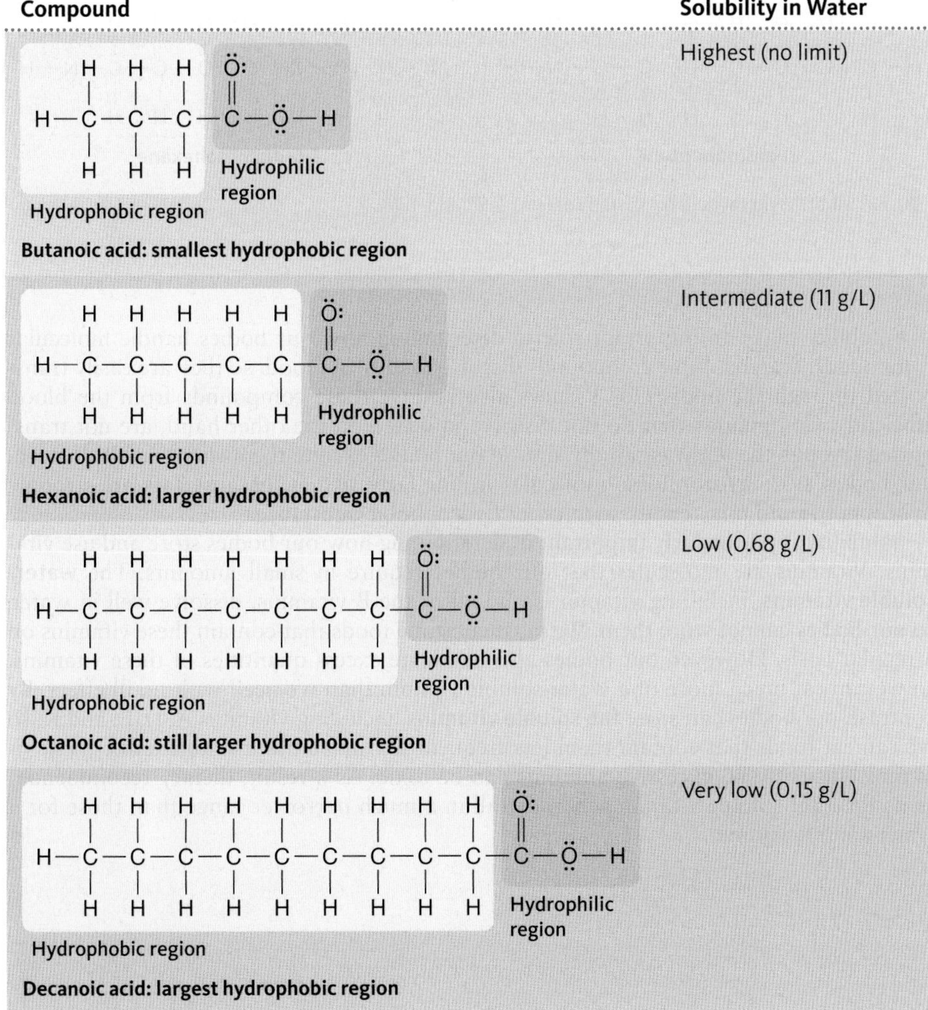

Compound	Solubility in Water
Butanoic acid: smallest hydrophobic region	Highest (no limit)
Hexanoic acid: larger hydrophobic region	Intermediate (11 g/L)
Octanoic acid: still larger hydrophobic region	Low (0.68 g/L)
Decanoic acid: largest hydrophobic region	Very low (0.15 g/L)

Sample Problem 4.24

Comparing solubilities based on molecular structure

Which of the following compounds would you expect to have the higher solubility in water? Explain your answer.

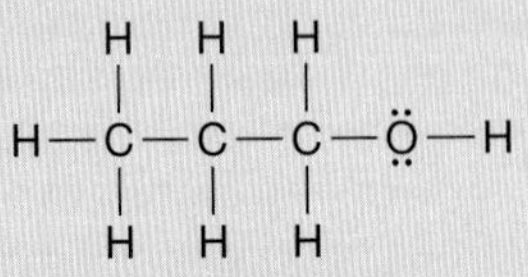

1-propanol 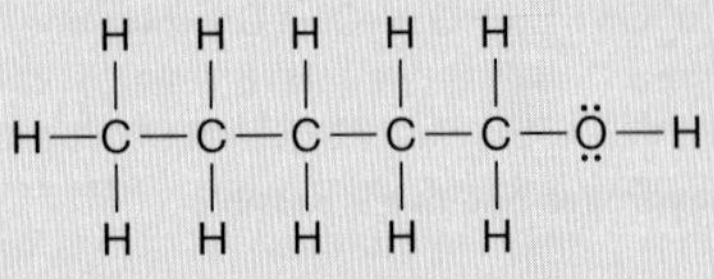 **1-pentanol**

SOLUTION

Both of these compounds contain an oxygen atom and a hydrogen atom that can participate in hydrogen bonds. However, 1-propanol has a smaller hydrophobic region than does 1-pentanol. Therefore, 1-propanol should have the higher water solubility.

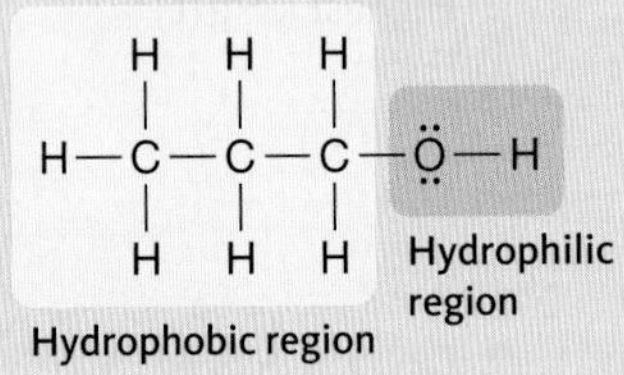

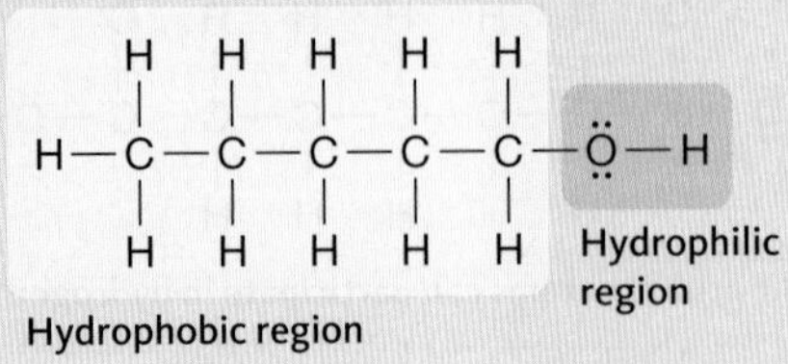

Hydrophilic region
Hydrophobic region
Hydrophilic region
Hydrophobic region

TRY IT YOURSELF: *Which of the following compounds would you expect to have the higher solubility in water? Explain your answer.*

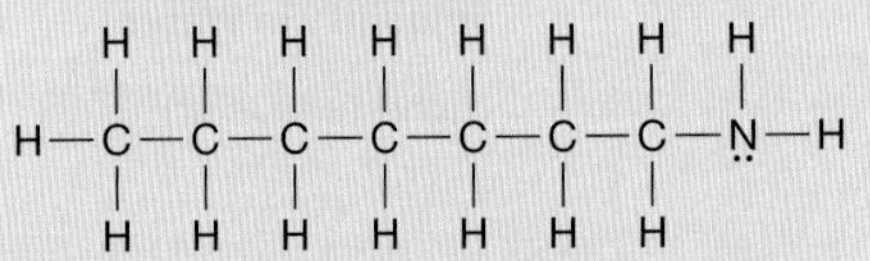

1-aminoheptane 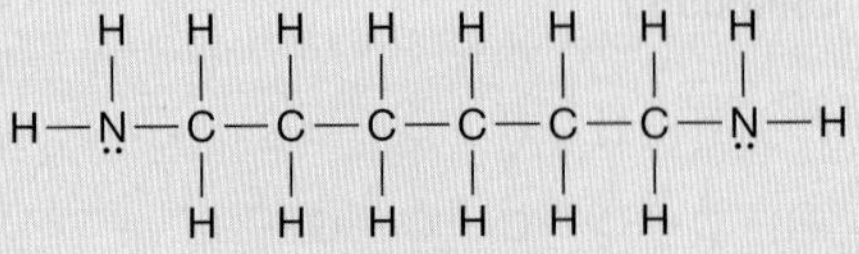 **1,6-diaminohexane**

For additional practice, try Core Problems 4.97 and 4.98.

Solubility plays an important role in determining how our bodies handle molecular compounds. Water-soluble compounds dissolve readily in blood, so they are easily transported through the body. Our kidneys also remove these compounds from the blood efficiently. Compounds that do not dissolve in water, on the other hand, are not transported through the body as rapidly, nor do our bodies excrete them very quickly. Instead, our bodies store hydrophobic molecules in our fatty tissues, because fats are strongly hydrophobic and mix readily with other hydrophobic substances.

Solubility is particularly important in determining how our bodies store and use vitamins. Vitamins are molecules that our bodies require in small amounts. The **water-soluble vitamins**, including vitamin C and all of the B vitamins, dissolve well in water, so our bodies cannot store them. We must consume foods that contain these vitamins on a regular basis. However, our bodies also eliminate excess quantities of these vitamins, so we can eat much more of a water-soluble vitamin than we need with no ill effect. By contrast, our bodies can store **fat-soluble vitamins**, including vitamins A, D, E, and K, so we can eat foods that contain them less frequently. Our bodies do not excrete these vitamins efficiently, so excessive amounts can be toxic. As a result, dietary recommendations for a fat-soluble vitamin generally fall in a much narrower range than those for a water-soluble vitamin.

CORE PROBLEMS

4.95 Identify the hydrophilic regions and hydrophobic regions in niacinamide.

```
   H    N    H
    \ // \ /
     C     C
     ||    |
     C     C
    / \  // \
   H   C      C—N—H
       |      ||  |
       H     :O   H
```

Niacinamide (one of the B vitamins)

4.96 Identify the hydrophilic regions and hydrophobic regions in valine.

```
           H
           |
         H—C—H
           |
         H  H  O:
         |  |  ||
     H—C—C—C—C—O—H
         |  |
         H  H :N—H
               |
               N
```

Valine (an amino acid)

4.97 From each of the following pairs of compounds, select the compound that will have the higher solubility in water:

```
      H  H  H  H  H :O                   H  H  H :O
      |  |  |  |  |  ||                  |  |  |  ||
a) H—C—C—C—C—C—C—H          or       H—C—C—C—C—H
      |  |  |  |  |                      |  |
      H  H  H  H  H                      H  H

      H     H  H  H                      H     H     H
      |     |  |  |                      |     |     |
b) H—C—O—C—C—C—H            or       H—C—O—C—O—C—H
      |     |  |  |                      |     |     |
      H     H  H  H                      H     H     H

      H  H  H                     H  H  H  H
      |  |  |                     |  |  |  |
c) H—C—C—C—H        or        H—C—C—C—C—O—H
      |  |  |                     |  |  |  |
      H  H  H                     H  H  N  H
```

4.98 From each of the following pairs of compounds, select the compound that will have the higher solubility in water:

```
         H        H
         |        |
       H—C—H    H—C—H
         |        |
      H  |   H    |  H                    H  H  H  H  H
      |  |   |    |  |                    |  |  |  |  |
a) H—C—C——C——C—N—H           or       H—C—C—C—C—N—H
      |  |   |    |                       |  |  |  |
      H  H   H    H                       H  H  H  H

         H                                   H
         |                                   |
      H :O: H  H  H  H  H                 H :O: H  H     H
      |  |  |  |  |  |  |                 |  |  |  |     |
b) H—C—C—C—C—C—C—C—H          or       H—C—C—C—C—C—O—C—H
      |  |  |  |  |  |  |                 |  |  |  |     |
      H  H  H  H  H  H  H                 H  H  H  H     H

      H  H  H                        H  H  H
      |  |  |                        |  |  |
c) H—C—C—C—O—H          or       H—C—C—C—Cl:
      |  |  |                        |  |  |
      H  H  H                        H  H  H
```

CONNECTIONS

Temperature, Pressure, and Volume in Everyday Life

The states of matter, physical changes, and effects of temperature, pressure, and volume are part of our everyday lives, both in obvious and in not-so-obvious ways. Let's look at a few examples.

Why does it take so long to heat water to boiling on your stove? Water has an unusually high specific heat, which means that you must use a great deal of energy to change the temperature of water. While this may be annoying when you are trying to get your spaghetti dinner on the table quickly, it is vital to life on Earth. Oceans, lakes, and rivers can absorb an enormous amount of energy from the sun without changing temperature too much, so the temperature on Earth does not vary too much from day to night. This is particularly true near the ocean; the temperature in San Francisco (surrounded on three sides by water) changes little with the seasons, while the temperature in Sacramento, just 75 miles inland, soars to more than 100°F on a typical summer day and drops to near freezing in the winter.

If you read the label on many foods, especially those designed for backpacking, the instructions tell you to increase the cooking time at high altitude. The water you are using to cook the food (and the water in the food) cannot get hotter than its boiling point. The boiling point of water depends, in turn, on the atmospheric pressure, so water boils at a lower temperature at higher altitudes. If you boil an egg in New York City, you are cooking the egg at 100°C, but if you boil your egg in Denver, your cooking temperature is 95°C. Even this small temperature difference has a significant effect on cooking time.

Anyone who drives a car or rides a bicycle needs to deal with gas pressures. With automobiles, tire pressure is important to the way the car handles and to the life expectancy of the tires. Poorly inflated tires tend to overheat and wear out more quickly because too much of the tire's surface rubs the road. Overinflated tires are less common and less problematic, but they give a rougher ride on bumpy roads. Ideally, you could simply inflate your tires to the recommended pressure and then ignore them, but tire pressure requires regular attention. Most tires and valves begin to leak sooner or later, so you have to add air periodically. In addition, temperature changes affect the tire pressure. A tire that is correctly filled in the fall will probably be underinflated in the winter and overinflated in the summer.

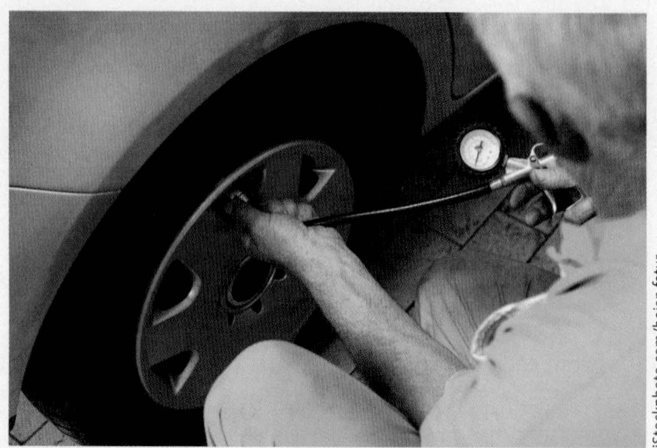

iStockphoto.com/bojan fatur

Your safety in a car depends on the pressure of the air inside your tires.

Airplane tires, which must support much heavier loads than automobile tires and may be extremely cold upon landing, must be inflated with nitrogen rather than air. Air, particularly humid air, contains a significant amount of water vapor. When the plane is aloft, the tire may cool to −50°C, a temperature at which all of the water vapor changes to ice. As a result, the air pressure in the tire can become too low to support the weight of the airplane. The nitrogen used to inflate airplane tires contains no water vapor, so the amount of gas in the tires remains constant. The pressure inside the tires decreases as the temperature drops, but not as much as if there were water vapor present, so the pressure remains at a safe level.

Key Terms

aqueous solution - 4.6
boiling point - 4.4
colloid - 4.6
condensation - 4.4
condensed state - 4.3
conservation of energy, law of - 4.3
Dalton's law of partial pressures - 4.3
dipole–dipole attraction - 4.5
dispersion force - 4.5
dissociation - 4.7
electrolyte - 4.7
energy - 4.1
fat-soluble vitamin - 4.6
gas - 4.2
heat - 4.1
heat of fusion - 4.4
heat of vaporization - 4.4
heating curve - 4.4
hydrogen bond - 4.5
hydrogen bond acceptor - 4.6
hydrogen bond donor - 4.6
hydrophilic - 4.9
hydrophobic - 4.9
insoluble - 4.8
ion–ion attraction - 4.5
kinetic energy - 4.1
liquid - 4.2
melting point (freezing point) - 4.4
nonelectrolyte - 4.7
partial pressure - 4.3
potential energy - 4.1
pressure - 4.3
saturated solution - 4.8
solid - 4.2
solubility - 4.8
soluble - 4.8
solute - 4.6
solution - 4.6
solvation - 4.7
solvent - 4.6
specific heat - 4.1
state of matter - 4.2
sublimation - 4.4
suspension - 4.6
thermal energy - 4.1
unsaturated solution - 4.8
water-soluble vitamin - 4.6

SUMMARY OF OBJECTIVES

Now that you have read the chapter, test yourself on your knowledge of the objectives, using this summary as a guide.

Section 4.1: Understand kinetic energy and potential energy and the relationship between thermal energy and temperature, and calculate the heat needed to change the temperature of a substance.

- Energy is the ability to do work.
- An object has kinetic energy if it is in motion, and the kinetic energy depends on the mass and speed of the object.
- An object has potential energy if it is not in its most stable position.
- Thermal energy is due to random motions of atoms in a substance, and it is directly related to temperature.
- Thermal energy that is transferred from one object to another is called heat.
- For any temperature change, heat = mass × temperature change × specific heat.

Section 4.2: Distinguish the bulk properties of the three states of matter, and relate these properties to the behavior of the particles that make up the substance.

- The three states of matter differ in density, ability to keep a constant shape, and ability to keep a constant volume.
- The bulk properties of each state of matter are the result of the behavior of molecules, atoms, or ions in that state.
- Substances become gases when heated and solids when cooled.

Section 4.3: Understand and apply the relationships between pressure, volume, and temperature for a gas.

- Gases are described by giving their pressure, volume, and temperature.
- The pressure of a gas increases when the temperature or the number of molecules increases, and it decreases when the volume increases.
- In a flexible container, the volume of a gas increases when its temperature increases.

Section 4.4: Describe the significance of melting and boiling points, calculate the energy needed to melt or boil a substance from the heats of fusion and vaporization, and interpret a typical heating curve.

- The melting point is the temperature at which the solid and liquid forms can be interconverted.
- The boiling point is the temperature above which only the gaseous form can exist.
- Melting and boiling require energy. The heat of fusion is the energy required to melt 1 g of a substance, and the heat of vaporization is the energy required to boil 1 g of a substance.
- A heating curve shows the state of a substance at any temperature, as well as the energy needed to melt and boil that substance.

Section 4.5: Describe the attractive forces between molecules or ions, and relate the strength of these forces to physical properties.

- Ionic compounds are high-melting solids because of the strong ion–ion attraction.
- The attractive forces between molecules are much weaker than those between ions, so many molecular compounds are liquids or gases at room temperature.
- All molecules are attracted to one another by the dispersion force, which depends on the sizes and numbers of the atoms in each molecule.
- Molecules containing O–H or N–H bonds are attracted to one another by hydrogen bonds.
- Compounds that form hydrogen bonds have higher melting and boiling points than compounds of similar size that cannot form hydrogen bonds.

Section 4.6: Describe what happens when a molecular compound dissolves in water, and understand the role of hydrogen bonding in water solubility.

- Solutions contain one or more solutes dissolved in a solvent, and they normally look like the solvent.
- When a molecular substance dissolves in water, its molecules become evenly dispersed among the water molecules.
- Molecular substances that can form hydrogen bonds generally dissolve better in water than those that cannot.
- Substances that cannot form hydrogen bonds can dissolve in water if they contain a nitrogen or oxygen atom that can serve as a hydrogen bond acceptor.

Section 4.7: Describe what happens when an ionic compound dissolves in water, and recognize ions that generally produce water-soluble compounds.

- Ionic compounds dissociate into independent ions when they dissolve in water. Each ion is solvated by several water molecules.
- Solutions of ionic compounds conduct electricity, because the ions are free to move throughout the solution.
- Ionic compounds dissolve whenever the ions are as strongly attracted to water molecules as they are to one another.
- All compounds that contain Na^+ or K^+ dissolve in water, as do most compounds that contain Cl^-.

Section 4.8: Describe and interpret the solubility of a compound, and predict the effect of temperature and pressure on solubility.

- The solubility of a substance is the maximum amount of the substance that can dissolve in a fixed amount of water.
- Compounds whose solubilities are less than 1 g/L are generally described as insoluble.
- Most solids dissolve better in warm water than in cold, while gases dissolve better in cold water than in warm.
- The solubility of a gas increases when the gas pressure increases.

Section 4.9: Recognize hydrophilic and hydrophobic regions in a molecular compound, and rank the solubilities of structurally related compounds.

- A hydrophilic region is a part of a molecule that contains atoms that can form hydrogen bonds. Hydrophilic regions are attracted to water.
- A hydrophobic region is a part of a molecule that cannot participate in hydrogen bonding.
- Larger hydrophobic regions give a molecule lower solubility.
- More hydrogen bonds give a molecule higher solubility.

Concept Questions

OWL Online homework for this chapter may be assigned in OWL.

* indicates more challenging problems.

4.99 A piece of pizza can supply your body with a good deal of energy. Explain why the amount of energy your body gets from the pizza does not change if you heat the pizza.

4.100 A battery is lying on a table. Which of the following will change the kinetic energy of the battery, which will change its potential energy, and which will change both?

a) pushing the battery so that it starts to roll across the table
b) putting the battery on the floor
c) pushing the battery off the edge of the table so that it starts to fall
d) heating the battery
e) charging the battery

4.101 Describe the motions and behavior of molecules of each of the following substances at room temperature:

a) sugar
b) gasoline

4.102 If you squeeze a soft plastic container that is filled with air, you can make a sizeable dent in the container. However, if you squeeze a plastic container that is filled with water or ice, you will not be able to make a dent. Explain this difference using the behavior of the atoms and molecules in each container.

4.103 A student concludes that sand is a liquid, because he can pour the sand from one container to another and the sand takes the shape of its container. Is this a reasonable conclusion? Why or why not?

4.104 Why do liquids turn into gases when they are heated?

4.105 You have a bicycle tire that has been filled with air. List three ways to make the pressure inside the tire increase.

4.106 If you have ever pumped up a bicycle tire, you have probably noticed that it becomes increasingly difficult to push the pump handle as you put air into the tire. Why is this?

4.107 Why do ionic compounds have much higher melting points and boiling points than molecular compounds do?

4.108 Define each of the following terms:

a) specific heat
b) heat of fusion
c) heat of vaporization

4.109 When you boil a molecular substance, you must add enough energy to overcome some attractive forces. Which of the following must be overcome? (Select all of the correct answers.)

a) covalent bonds
b) dispersion forces
c) hydrogen bonds
d) ion–ion attractions

4.110 If you open a bottle of a carbonated beverage (which contains carbon dioxide dissolved in water), you will see bubbles appear and rise to the surface. If you heat a pot of water for a while, you will also see bubbles appear and rise to the surface. How are these processes similar? How are they different?

4.111 Which of the following is the most accurate description of the structure of water?

a) Water is an ionic compound, containing H^+ and O^{2-} ions.
b) Water is an ionic compound, containing H^+ and OH^- ions.
c) Water is a covalent compound, with a small positive charge on each H and a small negative charge on the O.
d) Water is a covalent compound, with a small negative charge on each H and a small positive charge on the O.
e) Water is a covalent compound, and all three atoms in a water molecule have no charge.

4.112 Molecular compounds do not generally dissolve in water unless they contain one (or both) of two specific elements. Identify these two key elements.

4.113 Carbon tetrachloride (CCl_4) does not dissolve in water. Which of the following statements is a reasonable explanation?

a) CCl_4 molecules and H_2O molecules repel each other.
b) CCl_4 molecules are strongly attracted to one another and only weakly attracted to H_2O molecules.
c) H_2O molecules are strongly attracted to one another and only weakly attracted to CCl_4 molecules.
d) CCl_4 molecules are heavier than H_2O molecules.

4.114 FeS does not dissolve in water. Which of the following is a reasonable explanation?

a) FeS molecules are repelled by H_2O molecules.
b) H_2O molecules are attracted to one another more strongly than they are to FeS molecules.
c) Fe^{2+} and S^{2-} ions are attracted to one another more strongly than they are attracted to H_2O molecules.
d) H_2O molecules are attracted to one another more strongly than they are attracted to Fe^{2+} and S^{2-} ions.

4.115 What is the difference between dissolving and dissociating?

4.116 Which of the following will change the solubility of a gas in water? (Select all of the correct answers.)

a) pressure
b) temperature
c) amount of water
d) amount of the gas

4.117 What is a hydrophobic region, and how is the size of a hydrophobic region related to solubility?

4.118 Each of the following drawings represents the behavior of acetone (C_3H_6O) at some temperature. Match each drawing with the correct temperature from the following list, given that the melting point of acetone is −94°C and the boiling point is 56°C:

a) −25°C
b) 75°C
c) −94°C
d) −120°C

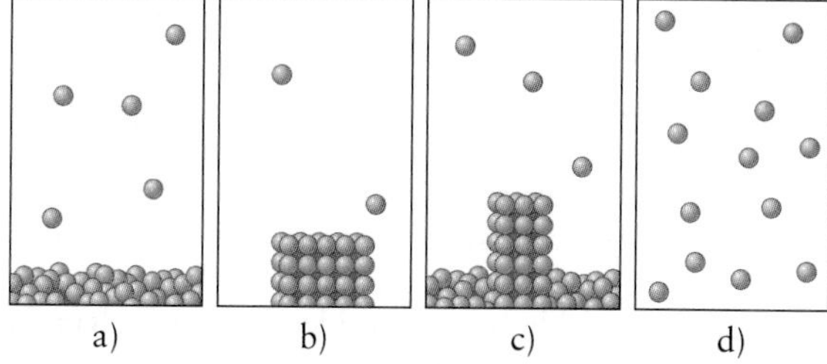

4.119 Each of the following pictures represents the results of mixing a compound with water. Match each of the following descriptions with the correct picture:

a) an insoluble ionic compound
b) an insoluble molecular compound
c) a soluble ionic compound
d) a soluble molecular compound

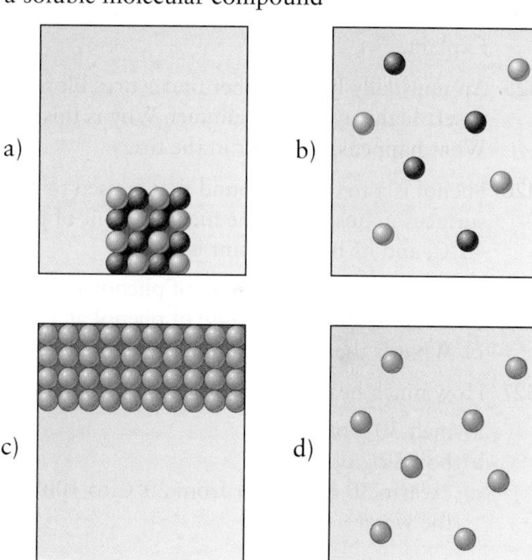

Summary and Challenge Problems

4.120 Which has more thermal energy, a liter of water at 20°C or a liter of water at 10°C? In which one are the water molecules moving faster?

4.121 *The specific heat of ethanol is 0.58 cal/g·°C, and the density of ethanol is 0.79 g/mL.

a) How much heat is needed to raise the temperature of 2.5 kg of ethanol from 20°C to 30°C?
b) How much heat must you remove from 25 pounds of ethanol to cool it from 70°F to 40°F?
c) How much heat must you add to 150 mL of ethanol to increase its temperature from 0°C to 50°C?

4.122 A chef puts 100 g of vegetable oil in one pot and 100 g of water in another pot. She then puts them on the stove and heats them for two minutes. The two pots are exactly the same size and made of the same material, and the stove burners are the same temperature, but the vegetable oil becomes considerably hotter than the water. Which liquid has the higher specific heat? Explain your answer.

4.123 At room temperature, you can have 100 mL of water in a 1000-mL container, but you can't have 100 mL of oxygen in a 1000-mL container. Why not?

4.124 If you fill a balloon with air in San Francisco (at sea level) and then take the balloon to Denver (1600 m above sea level), the volume of the balloon increases. Explain.

4.125 An unusually high number of car tires blow out on desert highways in the summer. Why is this? (Hint: What happens to the air in the tire?)

4.126 Phenol is a toxic compound that is used to disinfect surfaces in hospitals. The melting point of phenol is 43°C, and its boiling point is 182°C.

a) What is the normal state of phenol at 25°C?
b) What is the normal state of phenol at 100°C?
c) What is the normal state of phenol at 200°C?

4.127 How much heat would you need to do the following?

a) melt 30 g of ice
b) boil 30 g of water
c) *warm 30 g of water from 20°C to 100°C and boil the water

4.128 *If you add 300 cal of heat to 100 g of sand at 20°C, what will be the final temperature of the sand? The specific heat of sand is 0.19 cal/g·°C.

4.129 What types of bonds or attractive forces are responsible for each of the following?

a) Calcium and chlorine atoms remain essentially in fixed positions in a crystal of $CaCl_2$.
b) Hydrogen atoms are attached to oxygen atoms in a water molecule.
c) Water molecules tend to stay close to one another at room temperature.

4.130 Explain each of the following observations:

a) The boiling point of C_2H_2 (acetylene) is much lower than the boiling point of C_6H_6 (benzene).
b) H_2SO_4 is a liquid at room temperature, while Na_2SO_4 is a solid.
c) The boiling point of H_2O is much higher than the boiling point of H_2S.
d) The boiling point of CH_2O is much higher than the boiling point of C_2H_4. (See the structures that follow.)

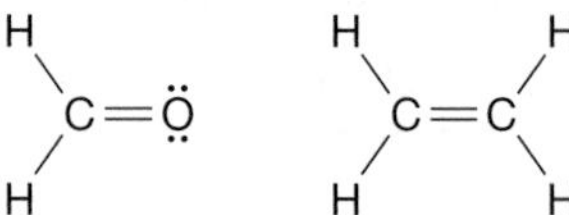

4.131 A student is asked to compare the melting points of H_2O and NaOH. He draws the following Lewis structures:

H—Ö—H   Na—Ö—H

He then states that H_2O should have the higher melting point, because it has two hydrogen atoms that can participate in hydrogen bonds, while NaOH has only one. Would you agree with this reasoning? Explain.

4.132 The structures of ethylene glycol and hexane are shown here. Ethylene glycol does not dissolve in hexane. Which of the following statements is a reasonable explanation?

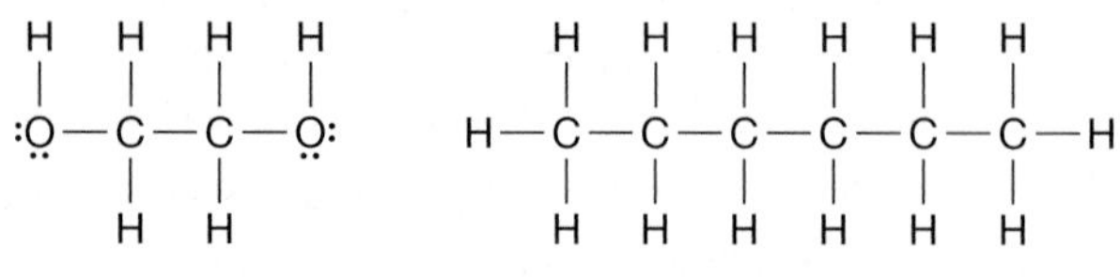

Ethylene glycol   **Hexane**

a) Hexane molecules and ethylene glycol molecules repel each other.
b) Hexane molecules are strongly attracted to one another, but they are only weakly attracted to ethylene glycol molecules.
c) Ethylene glycol molecules are strongly attracted to one another, but they are only weakly attracted to hexane molecules.
d) Hexane molecules are larger than ethylene glycol molecules.

4.133 Methanol (wood alcohol) is a liquid that can dissolve some ionic compounds, including NaCl. Show how sodium ions and chloride ions can be solvated by methanol molecules.

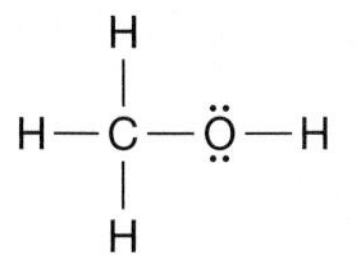

```
      H
      |
  H—C—Ö—H
      |  ..
      H
```

Methanol

4.134 *Niacin is one of the B vitamins. The maximum amount of niacin that can dissolve in 1 mL of water is 0.017 g. Would you describe niacin as soluble or insoluble in water? Explain.

4.135 A solution that contains 3 g of aspirin in 1 L of water is a saturated solution at 25°C, but it is an unsaturated solution at 35°C. Explain how this is possible.

4.136 The following graph shows the solubility of citric acid between 10°C and 50°C. Use this graph to answer part a through part e.

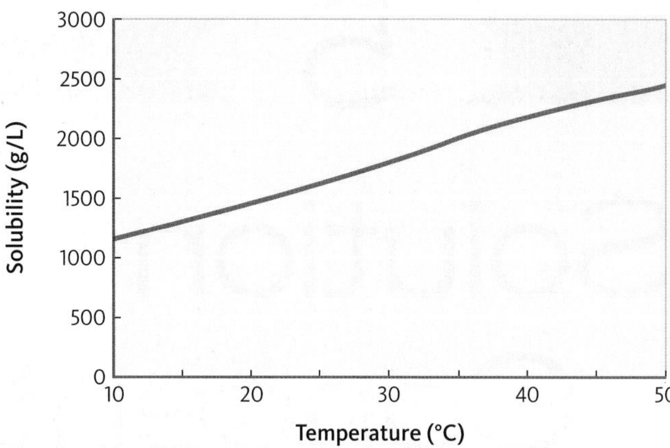

a) Would you expect citric acid to be a solid, a liquid, or a gas in the temperature range shown on the graph?
b) Based on your answer to part a, what effect will pressure have on the solubility of citric acid in this temperature range?
c) What is the solubility of citric acid at 25°C?
d) If you need to dissolve 2000 g of citric acid in 1 L of water, what is the lowest temperature you can use?
e) Can citric acid form hydrogen bonds with water? Give your reasoning. (Citric acid is a molecular compound.)

4.137 *a) Some intravenous solutions contain magnesium ions. Magnesium chloride can be used to supply the magnesium ions in these solutions, but magnesium carbonate cannot. What is the most likely reason for this?
b) Many intravenous solutions contain chloride ions. $HgCl_2$ dissolves in water, but it is never used as a source for the chloride ions in intravenous solutions. Can you think of a possible reason?

5

Solution Concentration

Mrs. Blackstone has been diagnosed with hypertension, and her doctor prescribes a diuretic called hydrochlorothiazide (HCTZ) to help lower her blood pressure. Because this medication also raises the level of calcium in the blood, the doctor has Mrs. Blackstone's blood calcium level checked regularly. The lab reports that her calcium level is 3.1, and Mrs. Blackstone would like to know whether this is a normal value. However, when she does a little research, she discovers that the normal range is reported in three ways:

8.5 to 10.5 mg/dL or 4.3 to 5.3 mEq/L or 2.2 to 2.7 mmol/L

Which one should she use? She asks her doctor, who tells her that the lab gives the test results in millimoles per liter (mmol/L). Mrs. Blackstone's calcium level is slightly elevated, but is not a concern.

The preceding three units are all ways to show the concentration of a solute. Concentrations of substances such as sodium, glucose, and cholesterol in our blood are important indicators of our health. However, we cannot understand or interpret the results unless we know how they are being reported to us. In this chapter, we will explore the variety of ways in which we can express concentrations of solutions.

OUTLINE

LABORATORY REQUISITION—CHEMISTRY

☐ Sodium	NA	☐ Fructosamine	FRU/ALB
☐ Potassium	K	☐ PSA	PSA
☐ Creatinine	CREAT	☐ Chloride	CL
☐ BUN	BUN	☑ Calcium	CA
☐ Glucose-fasting	GLUCF	☐ Phosphorus	PHOS
☐ Glucose-random	GLUCR	☐ Phenylalanine	PKU
☐ Hemoglobin A1C	HGBA1C	☐ Uric Acid	URIC

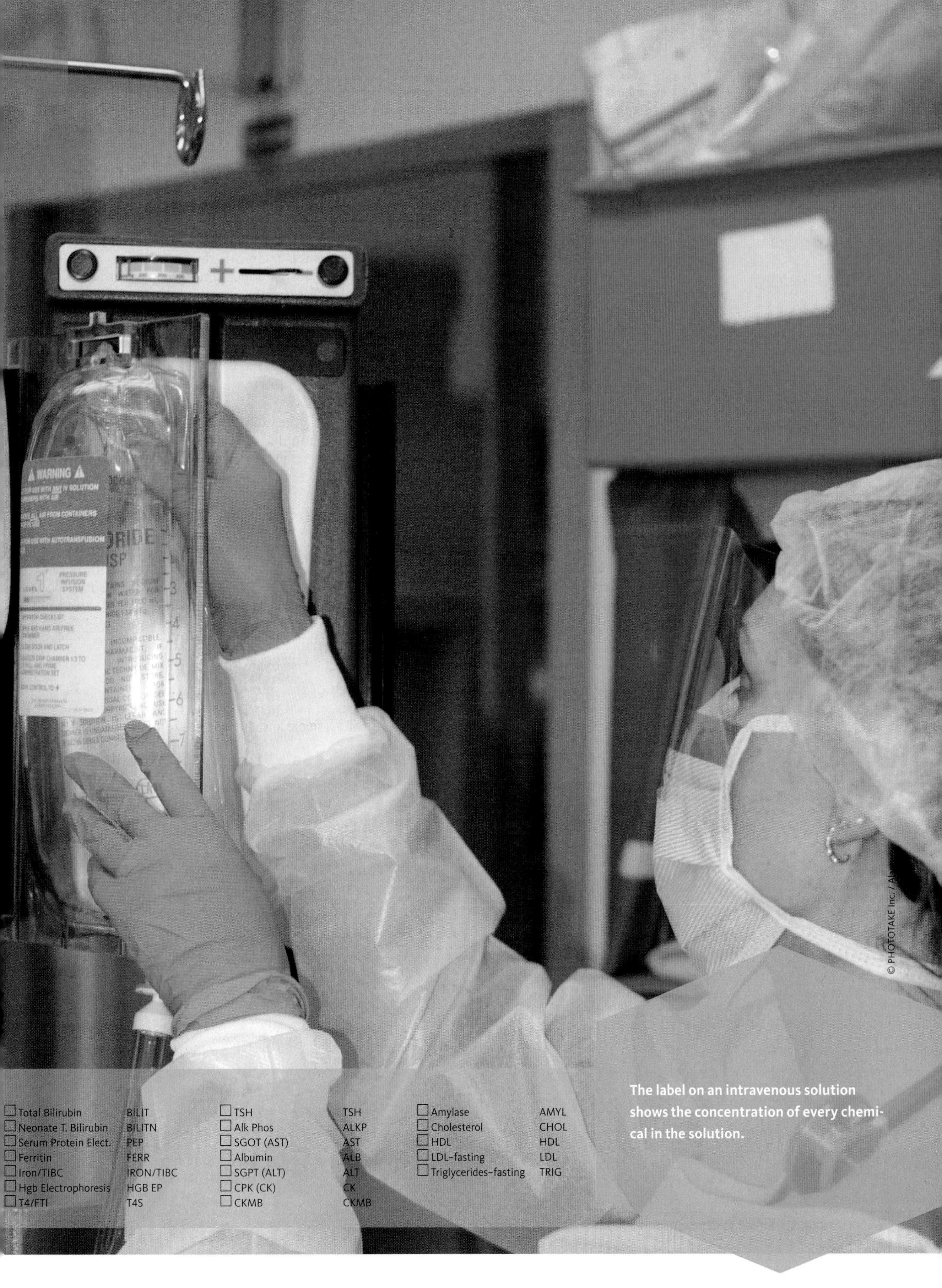

The label on an intravenous solution shows the concentration of every chemical in the solution.

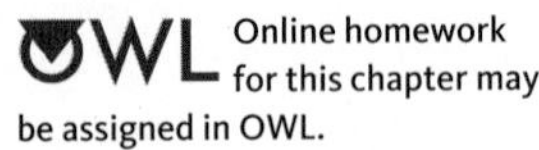
Online homework for this chapter may be assigned in OWL.

A runner collapses on a hot summer day and is rushed to the hospital, suffering from severe dehydration. Because she is unconscious, she is connected to an intravenous line and rehydrated with a solution containing salt (NaCl) and water. This solution must contain 9 g of salt in each liter of liquid; using a different amount of salt or injecting pure water could do more harm than good. This ratio, 9 g of salt per liter of solution, describes the **concentration** of the solution.

Concentration is what we generally mean when we refer to the strength of a solution. For example, strong coffee contains higher concentrations of various solutes (including caffeine), while weak coffee contains lower concentrations of the same solutes. Our body fluids contain a wide range of solutes, and good health requires that our bodies be able to maintain many of these at very specific concentrations. As a result, in health care the concentration of a solution can be as important as the chemicals that make it up.

In this chapter, we will look at some ways in which concentration is measured in medicine. We will also examine why the concentration of solutes in our bodies is so important to our health.

OBJECTIVES: *Calculate and use percent concentrations, and interpret other common concentration units involving masses of solute.*

5.1 Concentration

To illustrate what concentration is, let us start with an example. Suppose you dissolve a teaspoon of sugar in a cup of water, while your friend dissolves 4 teaspoons of sugar in 4 cups (one quart) of water, as illustrated in Figure 5.1. These two solutions contain different amounts of sugar, but they contain the same ratio of sugar to water (1 teaspoon per cup). The two solutions therefore have the same concentration. Because their concentrations are equal, the solutions have identical intensive properties; for example, they taste equally sweet.

The concentration of a solution is a measurement, so we can express it using numbers, just as we do weights or volumes. To do so, though, we need a more precise definition of concentration. The concentration of any solution is *the amount of solute divided by the amount of solution.* We can write this definition as a mathematical formula:

$$\text{concentration} = \frac{\text{amount of solute}}{\text{amount of solution}}$$

For instance, the concentration of sugar in each of the solutions in Figure 5.1 is 1 teaspoon/cup. The amount of solute can be expressed as a mass, a volume, or even a number of molecules, while the amount of solution is usually expressed as a volume.

Percent Concentration Is the Amount of Solute in 100 mL of Solution

In medicine, concentrations of solutions are often expressed as **percent concentrations.** *The percent concentration is the amount of solute in 100 mL of solution.* The amount of solute can be expressed in either grams or milliliters. If the solute is a solid, its amount

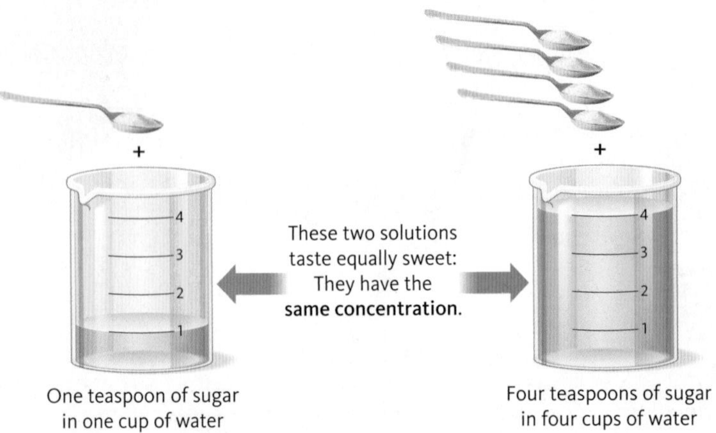
+
+
4
3
2
1
4
3
2
1
These two solutions
taste equally sweet:
They have the
same concentration.
One teaspoon of sugar
in one cup of water
Four teaspoons of sugar
in four cups of water

FIGURE 5.1 Solutions that have the same proportions have the same properties.

A 5% (w/v) solution contains 5 **grams** of solute in each 100 mL of solution.

A 5% (v/v) solution contains 5 **milliliters** of solute in each 100 mL of solution.

FIGURE 5.2 Comparing w/v and v/v percentages.

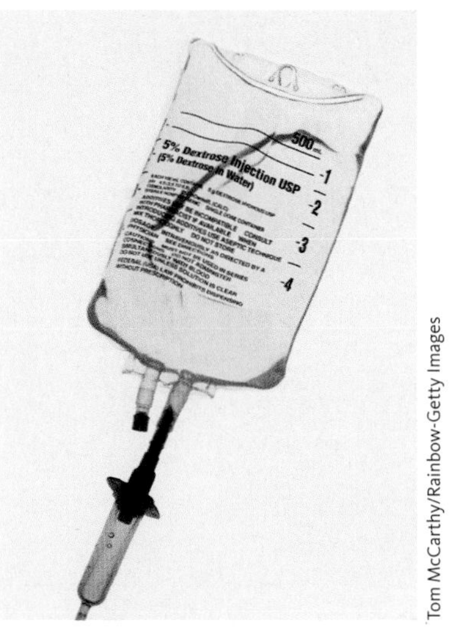

Tom McCarthy/Rainbow-Getty Images

A 5% (w/v) solution of glucose is called physiological dextrose and is abbreviated D_5W in clinical work. It is an important intravenous solution, because it can be injected into the blood without harming blood cells.

is given in grams and the percentage is called a **weight per volume (w/v)** percentage. For example, physiological dextrose is a solution of glucose in water, and it is widely used in intravenous medications because it does not harm blood cells. The concentration of this solution is 5.0% (w/v), which means that every 100 mL of solution contains 5.0 g of glucose. We can express this proportion as a conversion factor:

$$5.0\%\ (\text{w/v})\ \text{glucose means}\ \frac{5.0\ \text{g glucose}}{100\ \text{mL solution}}$$

If the solute is a liquid, it is more convenient to express its amount in milliliters. Doing so gives us a **volume (v/v) percentage**. For instance, medications that do not dissolve in water are sometimes dispensed in a mixture of water and alcohol. If the concentration of alcohol is 5% (v/v), then every 100 mL of solution contains 5 mL of alcohol. This proportion can also be expressed as a conversion factor:

$$5.0\%\ (\text{v/v})\ \text{alcohol means}\ \frac{5.0\ \text{mL alcohol}}{100\ \text{mL solution}}$$

Figure 5.2 illustrates the difference between w/v and v/v percentages.

If we use a glucose solution in an intravenous line, the concentration of the solution must be 5.0% (w/v). Any other concentration is potentially hazardous. What if we prepare an aqueous solution that contains 37 g of glucose in 740 mL of liquid; can we use this solution in an intravenous line? To answer this question, we must be able to calculate the percent concentration of the solution. We can do so by using the following relationship:

$$\text{percent concentration} = \frac{\text{amount of solute}}{\text{volume of solution (in milliliters)}} \times 100$$

The amount of solute can be expressed in grams or milliliters. If we use grams, we get a w/v percentage, and if we use milliliters we get a v/v percentage. We multiply by 100 because percentage is the amount of solute in 100 mL of solution. Here is the calculation for our glucose solution:

$$\text{percent concentration (w/v)} = \frac{37\ \text{g glucose}}{740\ \text{mL solution}} \times 100$$

$$= 0.050\ \text{g/mL} \times 100$$

$$= 5.0\%\ (\text{w/v})$$

This solution has the correct concentration, so we can use it for intravenous injection. Note that when we calculate a w/v percent concentration, we must supply the correct unit, because mass and volume units do not cancel out.

We will look at a range of ways to express concentration in this chapter, and you will need to be able to calculate concentrations using a variety of units. To calculate concen-

Health Note: When you or your doctor measures blood sugar, you are measuring the concentration of glucose in the blood. *Dextrose* is an alternate name for glucose.

Health Note: Medical suppliers make intravenous glucose solutions with higher concentrations, but these must be mixed with water before use. Only 5% (w/v) glucose solutions are safe for intravenous use.

tration, you must divide the amount of solute by the amount of solution, but each type of concentration uses its own specific units for these amounts. The general procedure for calculating concentrations is as follows:

1. Determine the *type of concentration* you must calculate and the *units* you must use for the solute and the solution.
2. If needed, convert the amount of solute and the amount of the solution into the *correct units*.
3. *Divide* the amount of solute by the amount of solution.
4. If the concentration is a percentage, *multiply* your answer by 100.

Sample Problem **5.1**

Calculating a percent concentration

A solution contains 75 mL of glycerin and has a total volume of 2.5 L. What is the percent concentration of this solution? What type of percentage is this?

SOLUTION

STEP 1: Determine the units you must use.

For all types of concentrations, we must start by working out the correct units for the amount of solute and the amount of solution. In both w/v and v/v percentages, the amount of solution must be in milliliters. However, the amount of solute can be in either grams or milliliters, depending on which type of percentage we calculate. We are given the volume of solute (75 mL) but not the mass, so we must calculate the v/v percentage.

STEP 2: Convert the amounts into the correct units.

Our solute volume is already in milliliters, but our solution volume is given in liters. To convert liters into milliliters, we move the decimal point three places to the right (review Section 1.3 if you need a refresher on metric unit conversions):

$$2.500 \text{ L} = \mathbf{2500 \text{ mL}}$$

STEP 3: Divide the solute by the solvent.

Now we can do the calculation. We divide the amount of solute (the glycerin) by the amount of solution.

$$\frac{75 \text{ mL glycerine}}{2500 \text{ mL solution}} = 0.03$$

In this example, the units cancel.

STEP 4: For a percentage, multiply by 100.

Finally, we multiply our answer by 100, because we are calculating a percentage. We also attach the appropriate unit for this type of percentage.

$$0.03 \times 100 = 3\% \text{ (v/v)}$$

Our answer should have two significant figures, so we add a zero after the decimal point. The concentration of this solution is 3.0% (v/v).

TRY IT YOURSELF: *A solution contains 15 g of NaCl and has a total volume of 360 mL. What is the percent concentration of this solution? What type of percentage is this?*

For additional practice, try Core Problems 5.3 and 5.4.

In general, health care professionals do not need to prepare solutions. However, in an emergency you may be called upon to make a solution that has a specific percent concentration. In such a situation, you will generally know the concentration of the solution and the volume you need, and you will have to calculate the amount of solute. For this type of problem, it is helpful to think of the percent concentration as a conversion factor, as shown here:

$$5\% \text{ (w/v) NaCl} \quad \text{means} \quad \frac{5 \text{ g NaCl}}{100 \text{ mL solution}} \quad \text{or} \quad \frac{100 \text{ mL solution}}{5 \text{ g NaCl}}$$

$$5\% \text{ (v/v) alcohol} \quad \text{means} \quad \frac{5 \text{ mL alcohol}}{100 \text{ mL solution}} \quad \text{or} \quad \frac{100 \text{ mL solution}}{5 \text{ mL alcohol}}$$

Sample Problem 5.2 shows how we can use this kind of conversion factor to calculate the mass of solute we need to make a solution.

Sample Problem 5.2

Calculating the mass of solute in a solution from the percent concentration

Normal saline is a 0.90% (w/v) solution of NaCl in water. If you need to prepare 250 mL of this solution, how much NaCl will you need?

SOLUTION

STEP 1: Identify the original measurement and the final unit.

Here is an opportunity to apply the conversion factor method you learned in Chapter 1. In this problem, our original measurement is the volume of the solution (250 mL), and we need to calculate an amount of NaCl. The concentration will serve as our conversion factor. The problem does not specify the unit for our answer, so we can use any reasonable unit of mass or volume.

250 mL of solution **convert to** ? amount of NaCl (mass or volume)

STEP 2: Write conversion factors that relate the two units.

The concentration is given as a w/v percentage, and it tells us that every 100 mL of solution contains 0.90 g of NaCl. In essence, 100 mL of solution is equivalent to 0.90 g of NaCl. We can use this relationship to write two conversion factors that relate the volume of solution to the mass of NaCl.

$$\frac{0.90 \text{ g NaCl}}{100 \text{ mL solution}} \quad \text{or} \quad \frac{100 \text{ mL solution}}{0.90 \text{ g NaCl}}$$

These conversion factors allow us to relate any number of milliliters of solution to the corresponding number of grams of NaCl, so it is easiest to express our final answer in grams.

STEP 3: Choose the conversion factor that allows you to cancel units.

To convert our original volume (250 mL) into the corresponding mass of NaCl, we must use the first conversion factor, so the volume unit cancels out.

$$250 \text{ mL solution} \times \frac{0.90 \text{ g NaCl}}{100 \text{ mL solution}}$$

We can cancel these units.

STEP 4: Do the math and round your answer.

Now we cancel units and do the arithmetic.

$$250 \cancel{\text{mL solution}} \times \frac{0.90 \text{ g NaCl}}{100 \cancel{\text{mL solution}}} = 2.25 \text{ g NaCl}$$

Rounding our answer to two significant figures gives us 2.2 g of NaCl needed to make this solution. Is this reasonable? We know that each 100-mL portion of the solution requires 0.9 g of NaCl. To make 200 mL of solution, we need twice this mass (1.8 g of NaCl). Making another 50 mL requires an additional 0.45 g of NaCl, making our total 2.25 g.

TRY IT YOURSELF: *A bottle of liquid is labeled "5% (w/v) urea." The total volume of the solution in the bottle is 600 mL. What is the mass of the urea in the bottle?*

For additional practice, try Core Problems 5.5 and 5.6.

Concentrations Are Expressed in Many Other Ways in Clinical Work

The concentrations of many solutes in body fluids are very low and are inconvenient to express as percentages. For example, the concentration of estradiol (a female sex hormone) in the plasma of postmenopausal women is around 0.000000002% (w/v). A variety of units are used in medicine to express very low concentrations, but most of these are closely related to mass percentages. We can group these units into two categories:

1. *Mass per volume.* The concentration of a solute can be expressed as the mass of the solute in any chosen amount of solution. In practice, the most common unit in clinical use is the *mass per deciliter.* A deciliter equals 100 mL, so a concentration

TABLE 5.1 Some Common Concentration Units in Clinical Chemistry

Mass Unit	Concentration Unit	Relationship to Percentage (w/v)	Example
Milligrams ($1\ mg = \frac{1}{1000}\ g$)	mg/dL	1 mg/dL = 0.001%	Typical blood glucose concentration = 90 mg/dL
Micrograms ($1\ \mu g = \frac{1}{1,000,000}\ g$)*	μg/dL	1 μg/dL = 0.000001%	Typical iron concentration in plasma = 100 μg/dL
Nanograms ($1\ ng = \frac{1}{1,000,000,000}\ g$)	ng/dL	1 ng/dL = 0.000000001%	Typical free thyroxine concentration in plasma = 1.1 ng/dL

*Micrograms are often abbreviated *mcg* in clinical work.

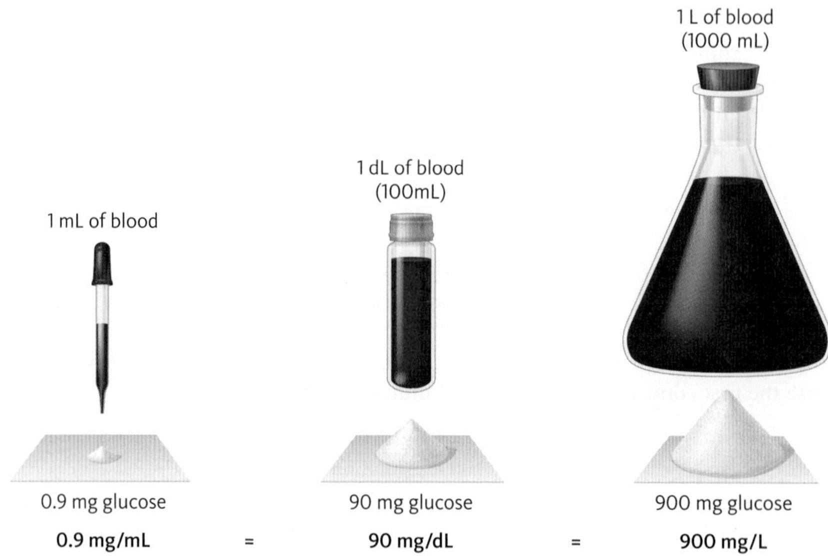

FIGURE 5.3 Three ways to express the same blood glucose concentration.

of 1 g/dL is the same as 1% (w/v). However, the mass of solute is usually expressed in milligrams, micrograms, or nanograms. Concentrations of this type are commonly used to express concentrations of solutes in blood. Table 5.1 shows the three common concentration units in this category.

Less commonly, concentrations are expressed as the mass of solute per milliliter or per liter. Figure 5.3 shows three ways to express the concentration of glucose in blood. This concentration is often called the blood sugar level, and it is usually expressed in milligrams per deciliter (mg/dL).

2. *Parts per million and related units.* Concentrations of chemicals in the environment are often expressed in *parts per million* (ppm) or *parts per billion* (ppb). A concentration of 1 ppm means that there is $\frac{1}{1,000,000}$ g (1 μg) of solute in 1 mL of solution, while 1 ppb means that there is $\frac{1}{1,000,000,000}$ g (1 ng) of solute in 1 mL of solution.

parts per million = number of micrograms of solute in 1 mL of solution (μg/mL)
parts per billion = number of nanograms of solute in 1 mL of solution (ng/mL)

Health Note: Drinking water in several countries has been found to contain dangerous concentrations of dissolved arsenic, including parts of Taiwan, Argentina, and Bangladesh. Several regions of the United States also have groundwater that contains more than 10 ppb of arsenic.

These units are extremely small, so they are best suited for expressing tiny concentrations of solutes. For example, arsenic is an extremely toxic element that is found in trace amounts in drinking water. The current limit for arsenic in tap water in the United States is 10 ppb. We can use this concentration as a conversion factor to calculate the amount of arsenic in a typical volume of tap water. For example, suppose you drink two liters of water (about a half gallon) per day. If the concentration of arsenic in the water is 10 ppb, the mass of arsenic is

$$2\text{ L} \times \frac{1000\text{ mL}}{1\text{ L}} \times \frac{10\text{ ng arsenic}}{1\text{ mL}} = 20{,}000\text{ ng of arsenic}$$

This conversion factor changes liters into milliliters.

Here, we use the concentration as a conversion factor to relate milliliters of water to nanograms of arsenic.

This is equal to 20 μg of arsenic, or roughly the mass of a speck of dust.

To calculate a concentration in any unit that involves a mass of solute, we divide the mass of solute by the volume of solution, just as we did for a percent concentration. The only difference is that we must use the appropriate mass and volume units.

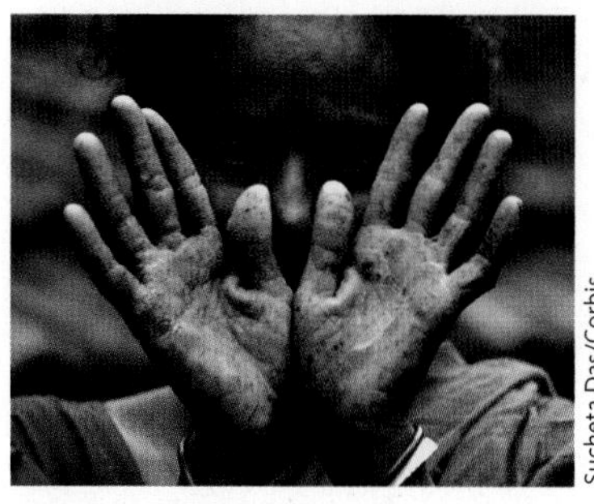
Sucheta Das/Corbis

Arsenic is toxic and carcinogenic. This Bangladeshi woman is suffering from arsenic poisoning caused by contaminated drinking water.

Sample Problem **5.3**

Calculating concentrations involving mass and volume

A solution contains 20 mg of iron dissolved in a total volume of 2.0 L. Calculate the concentration of this solution in milligrams per deciliter and in parts per million.

SOLUTION

Let us begin by calculating the concentration in milligrams per deciliter. The concentration unit tells us that the amount of solute must be expressed in milligrams and the volume of the solution must be expressed in deciliters.

STEP 1: Determine the units you must use.

The problem gives us the number of milligrams of the solute (iron), but it gives the solution volume in liters. To convert liters to deciliters, we move the decimal point one place to the right, giving us 20 dL.

STEP 2: Convert the amounts into the correct units.

$$2.0\text{ L} = 20\text{ dL}$$

Next, we divide the number of milligrams of iron by the number of deciliters of solution:

STEP 3: Divide the solute by the solvent.

$$\frac{20\text{ mg iron}}{20\text{ dL solution}} = 1\text{ mg/dL}$$

Now let us calculate the concentration in parts per million. To begin, we must recognize that the number of parts per million is the same as the number of micrograms of solute per milliliter of solution. Therefore, we must express the mass of iron in micrograms and the volume of solution in milliliters.

• We use the same three-step procedure to calculate the concentration in ppm.

To convert the mass of iron from milligrams to micrograms, we must move the decimal point three places to the right, giving us 20,000 μg of iron. To convert the volume of solution from liters to milliliters, we must also move the decimal point three places to the right, giving us 2000 mL of solution.

$$20.000\text{ mg} = 20{,}000\ \mu\text{g} \qquad 2.000\text{ L} = 2000\text{ mL}$$

Now we divide the mass of iron by the volume of solution.

$$\frac{20{,}000\ \mu\text{g iron}}{2000\text{ mL solution}} = 10\ \mu\text{g/mL}$$

Micrograms per milliliter is the same as parts per million, so our concentration is 10 ppm.

TRY IT YOURSELF: *A solution contains 250 μg of niacin in a total volume of 500 mL. Calculate the concentration of this solution in milligrams per deciliter and in parts per million.*

For additional practice, try Core Problems 5.7 and 5.8.

Any concentration unit can be interpreted as a conversion factor. For instance, we used the concentration of arsenic as a conversion factor when we found the amount of arsenic in drinking water.

Sample Problem 5.4

Calculating the mass of solute from a mass per volume concentration

The concentration of cholesterol in Mr. Lee's blood plasma is 186 mg/dL. How many milligrams of cholesterol are there in a 5.0 mL sample of his blood plasma?

SOLUTION

STEP 1: Identify the original measurement and the final unit.

STEP 2: Write conversion factors that relate the two units.

We are given the volume of the solution (the plasma) and asked to calculate the number of milligrams of cholesterol in this solution.

The concentration of cholesterol tells us that 1 dL of plasma contains 186 mg of cholesterol. The corresponding conversion factors are

$$\frac{186 \text{ mg cholesterol}}{1 \text{ dL}} \quad \text{and} \quad \frac{1 \text{ dL}}{186 \text{ mg cholesterol}}$$

In order to use this relationship, we must first convert our volume from milliliters into deciliters. We can do this using the metric railroad, or we can use an additional conversion factor. The relationship between milliliters and deciliters is 100 mL = 1 dL, so we can write two more conversion factors:

$$\frac{100 \text{ mL}}{1 \text{ dL}} \quad \text{and} \quad \frac{1 \text{ dL}}{100 \text{ mL}}$$

STEP 3: Choose the conversion factors that allow you to cancel units.

STEP 4: Do the math and round your answer.

Now we can set up our conversion factors, making sure that we can cancel both deciliters and milliliters. Once we have the correct setup, we cancel units and do the arithmetic.

$$5.0 \cancel{\text{mL}} \times \frac{1 \cancel{\text{dL}}}{100 \cancel{\text{mL}}} \times \frac{186 \text{ mg cholesterol}}{1 \cancel{\text{dL}}} = 9.3 \text{ mg cholesterol}$$

TRY IT YOURSELF: *The concentration of iron in Mrs. Lee's blood plasma is 88 μg/dL. If the total volume of her plasma is 2.9 L, how much iron is there in Mrs. Lee's blood plasma?*

For additional practice, try Core Problems 5.9 and 5.10.

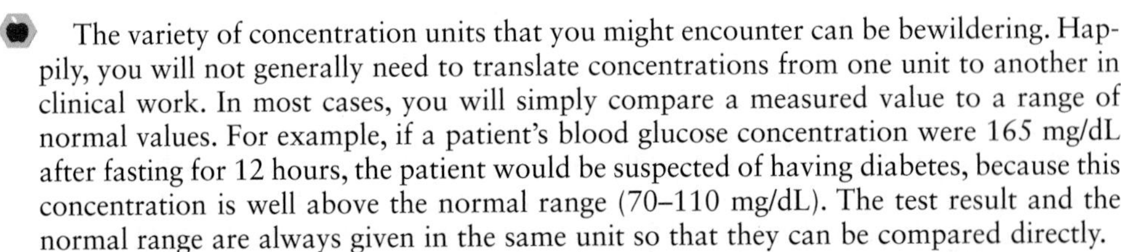

The variety of concentration units that you might encounter can be bewildering. Happily, you will not generally need to translate concentrations from one unit to another in clinical work. In most cases, you will simply compare a measured value to a range of normal values. For example, if a patient's blood glucose concentration were 165 mg/dL after fasting for 12 hours, the patient would be suspected of having diabetes, because this concentration is well above the normal range (70–110 mg/dL). The test result and the normal range are always given in the same unit so that they can be compared directly.

CORE PROBLEMS

All Core Problems are paired and the answers to the blue odd-numbered problems appear in the back of the book.

5.1 Write conversion factors that correspond to the following concentrations:
a) 0.15% (v/v) acetic acid
b) 50 ppm Br^-
c) 3 mg/dL fructose
d) 6.5% (w/v) $MgSO_4$
e) 20 ppb Pb^{2+}

5.2 Write conversion factors that correspond to the following concentrations:
a) 46 mg/dL HDL
b) 30% (v/v) acetone
c) 5 ppb arsenic
d) 3 ppm NO_3^-
e) 2.47% (w/v) urea

5.3 Calculate the percent concentration of each of the following solutions:
a) 2.31 g of sucrose dissolved in enough water to make 25.0 mL of solution
b) 177 mL of isopropyl alcohol dissolved in enough water to make 243 mL of solution
c) 275 g of $MgSO_4$ dissolved in enough water to make 3.25 L of solution

continued

5.4 Calculation the percent concentration of each of the following solutions:
a) 2.78 g of $NaHCO_3$ dissolved in enough water to make 200.0 mL of solution
b) 3.25 mL of H_2SO_4 dissolved in enough water to make 68.0 mL of solution
c) 125 mg of valine dissolved in enough water to make 5.00 mL of solution

5.5 Calculate the mass or volume of solute that would be needed to make each of the following solutions:
a) 500.0 mL of 0.75% (w/v) $CaCl_2$
b) 625 mL of 15.0% (v/v) ethylene glycol
c) 2.50 L of 0.125% (w/v) vitamin C

5.6 Calculate the mass or volume of solute that would be needed to make each of the following solutions:
a) 30.0 mL of 4.0% (v/v) ethanol
b) 750.0 mL of 0.15% (w/v) sodium lactate
c) 5.00 L of 2.4% (w/v) $CuSO_4$

5.7 A solution contains 57.3 mg of niacin in a total volume of 125 mL. Calculate the concentration of this solution in each of the following units:
a) mg/dL b) μg/dL c) ppm d) ppb

5.8 A blood sample contains 205 μg of calcium in a total volume of 2.0 mL. Calculate the concentration of this solution in each of the following units:
a) mg/dL b) μg/dL c) ppm d) ppb

5.9 Calculate the mass of solute in 25.0 mL of each of the following solutions:
a) water that contains 2.5 ppm of fluoride ions
b) blood plasma that contains 92 mg/dL of glucose
c) water that contains 31 ppb of lead ions

5.10 Calculate the mass of solute in 500.0 mL of each of the following solutions:
a) blood plasma that contains 85 μg/dL of free iron
b) water that contains 25 ppm of nitrate ions
c) water that contains 1.3 ppb of arsenic

5.2 Moles and Formula Weights

OBJECTIVES: *Use the mole concept to express numbers of formula units, and interconvert moles and masses.*

In Section 5.1, we saw that we can safely inject a 5.0% (w/v) solution of glucose into a patient, but we cannot do so for glucose solutions that are significantly stronger or weaker. As we will see in Section 5.4, we must use a 5.0% solution because red blood cells cannot survive in other concentrations; they either burst or shrivel up, depending on the concentration. What happens if we replace the glucose with ordinary table sugar (sucrose)? Red blood cells can survive in a sucrose solution too, but only if the concentration of sucrose in the solution is 9.25% (w/v). Why do we need so much more sucrose? These two solutions have the same effect on red blood cells because *they contain the same number of molecules of solute per liter.* In order to predict the effect of a solution on our cells, then, we must have a way to express the number of solute particles in a solution.

We cannot count the particles (atoms, molecules, or ions) in a solution directly, because there are too many of them in even a tiny amount of solution. Instead, we use an indirect method that is based on the weights of the atoms. Our starting point is hydrogen, the lightest element, which has an atomic weight of 1.008 amu. Individual hydrogen atoms are extremely small and light, but if we put enough of them into a box, we will

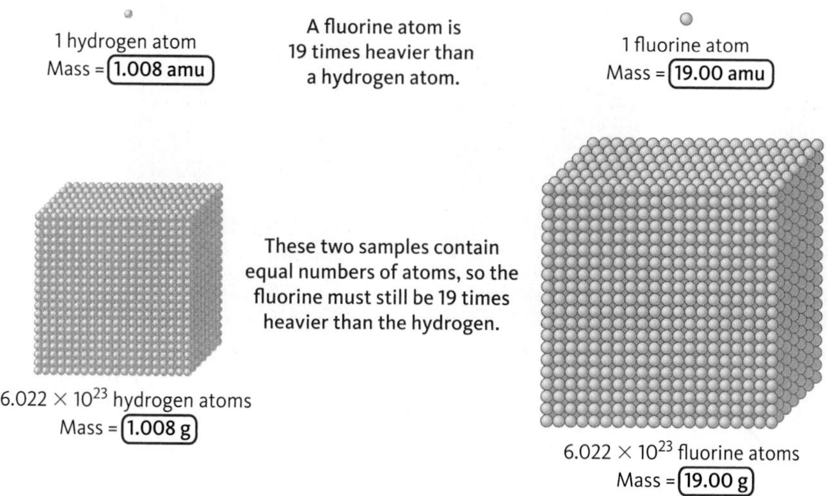

FIGURE 5.4 The mass relationship between hydrogen and fluorine.

have a sample that we can weigh. Let us put hydrogen atoms into our box until the mass of the hydrogen is 1.008 g. A gram is vastly larger than an atomic mass unit, so our box must contain an enormous number of atoms. The actual number is 6.022×10^{23} and is called **Avogadro's number.** To appreciate the size of this number, it helps to write it out in normal form:

1.008 g hydrogen contains 602,200,000,000,000,000,000,000 atoms   Avogadro's number

Now let us take a second box and put the same number of fluorine atoms into the box. How much does the fluorine weigh? Each fluorine atom weighs about 19 times as much as a hydrogen atom, so our box of fluorine atoms should weigh about 19 times as much as our box of hydrogen atoms. In fact, the fluorine weighs 19.00 g, matching the atomic weight of fluorine (19.00 amu). Figure 5.4 illustrates this relationship.

We can extend our reasoning to all of the other elements, using their atomic weights. For example, the atomic weight of lead is 207.2 amu, so a sample that contains 6.022×10^{23} atoms of lead must weigh 207.2 g. When we measure out a sample of an element whose mass (in grams) equals the atomic weight of the element, we are in effect counting out 6.022×10^{23} atoms of that element. This amount, whether expressed as a mass or as a number of atoms, is called a **mole** and abbreviated mol. *A mole is the atomic weight of an element expressed in grams, and contains 6.022×10^{23} atoms of that element.* Figure 5.5 illustrates the relationships between moles, masses, and numbers of atoms.

Sample Problem 5.5

Using the relationships between moles, mass, and number of atoms

What is the mass of one mole of magnesium, and how many magnesium atoms are there in one mole of magnesium?

SOLUTION

The atomic weight of magnesium (Mg) is 24.31 amu, so one mole of Mg must weigh **24.31 grams.** One mole of Mg contains $\mathbf{6.022 \times 10^{23}}$ Mg atoms, because one mole of any element contains this number of atoms.

TRY IT YOURSELF: *If a sample of nitrogen contains 6.022×10^{23} nitrogen atoms, how much does the sample weigh?*

For additional practice, try Core Problems 5.11 (parts a and b) and 5.12 (parts a and b).

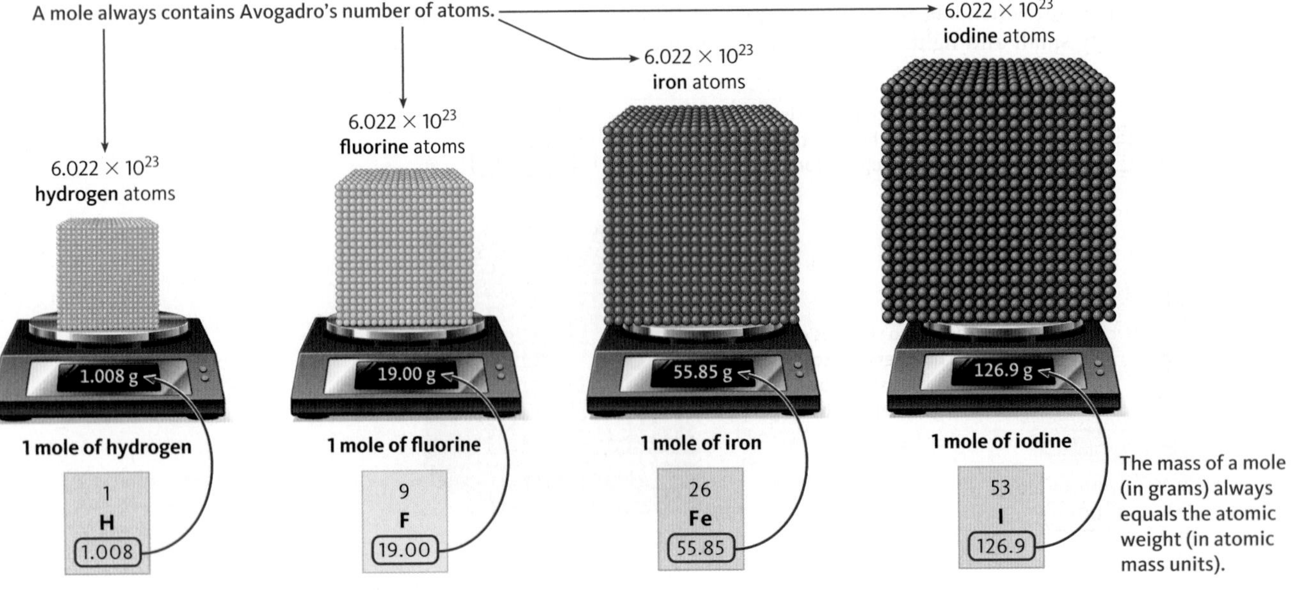

FIGURE 5.5 Comparing a mole of four elements.

1 mole of H
(**atomic** weight = 1.008 amu)
6.022×10^{23} H atoms

1 mole of F
(**atomic** weight = 19.00 amu)
6.022×10^{23} F atoms

1 mole of HF
(**formula** weight = 20.008 amu)
6.022×10^{23} HF molecules

FIGURE 5.6 The relationship between a mole of a compound and a mole of an element.

It is easy to confuse the mass of a mole with the mass of an atom, because they use the same number. Here is a good example of the importance of paying attention to units: The mass of a single atom is extremely small, and it is measured in atomic mass units. A mole of an element, by contrast, weighs a significant amount and is expressed in grams. A mole of fluorine weighs 19 *grams*. A single fluorine atom weighs 19 *atomic mass units*, which equals 0.00000000000000000000003155 grams.

The Mole Concept Also Applies to Compounds

We can extend the concept of a mole to include chemical compounds such as HF. To do so, we must first determine the weight of a single molecule of the compound, called the **formula weight** or **molecular weight**. We calculate the formula weight by adding the weights of the individual atoms in the molecule. For HF, this gives us:

$$\begin{array}{r l} & 1.008 \text{ amu (mass of one H atom)} \\ + & 19.00 \text{ amu (mass of one F atom)} \\ \hline & 20.008 \text{ amu (mass of one HF molecule)} \end{array}$$

Since one molecule of HF weighs 20.008 amu, *1 mole of HF weighs 20.008 grams*. The mass of a mole of a substance is called the **molar mass** of the substance. The molar mass is closely related to the formula weight, but formula weights are expressed in atomic mass units while molar masses are given in grams per mole. For instance, the formula weight of HF is 20.008 amu, whereas the molar mass of HF is 20.008 g/mol.

We can also describe a mole of a compound using Avogadro's number. A mole of HF contains 6.022×10^{23} individual units, just as a mole of hydrogen or fluorine does. However, the smallest units of HF are molecules rather than atoms, so 1 mol of HF contains 6.022×10^{23} molecules of HF. Figure 5.6 compares a mole of HF molecules to a mole of hydrogen and fluorine atoms.

Charles D. Winters

Charles D. Winters

Each of these samples contains one mole of a chemical. (a) Six elements. Top row: A mole of copper, aluminum, and lead. Bottom row: A mole of sulfur, chromium, and magnesium. (b) Four compounds. A mole of water (H_2O), aspirin ($C_9H_8O_4$), table salt (NaCl), and hydrated nickel chloride ($NiCl_2{\cdot}6\ H_2O$).

Sample Problem 5.6

Calculating the molar mass of a compound

Copper (II) nitrate has the chemical formula $Cu(NO_3)_2$. What is the molar mass of this compound?

SOLUTION

Since copper(II) nitrate is a compound, we must start by calculating its formula weight. To get the formula weight, we add up the weights of all of the atoms in the chemical formula. A single formula unit of $Cu(NO_3)_2$ contains one copper atom, two nitrogen atoms, and six oxygen atoms. Adding the weights of these atoms gives:

$$\begin{array}{r l l l} \text{1 Cu:} & 1 \times 63.55 & = & 63.55 \text{ amu} \\ \text{2 N:} & 2 \times 14.01 & = & 28.02 \text{ amu} \\ \text{6 O:} & 6 \times 16.00 & = & 96.00 \text{ amu} \\ \hline \text{total:} & & & 187.57 \text{ amu} \end{array}$$

The formula weight of copper(II) nitrate is 187.57 *amu*, so 1 mol of copper(II) nitrate weighs 187.57 *grams*. The molar mass of this compound is 187.57 g/mol.

continued

TRY IT YOURSELF: *Ammonium sulfate has the chemical formula $(NH_4)_2SO_4$. Calculate the molar mass of this compound.*

For additional practice, try Core Problems 5.11 (parts c through f) and 5.12 (parts c through f).

We can convert any number of grams of a substance into the corresponding number of moles or vice versa, using the molar mass as a conversion factor. Sample Problems 5.7 and 5.8 illustrate these types of conversions. We will use moles extensively in the rest of this chapter, so be sure to practice these conversions until you are comfortable with them.

Sample Problem **5.7**

Converting a number of moles into a mass

A beaker contains 0.350 mol of $CaCl_2$. What is the mass of the $CaCl_2$?

SOLUTION

STEP 1: Identify the original measurement and the final unit.

This question gives us a number of moles of a compound and asks us for the corresponding mass. The problem does not specific the mass unit, but it is easiest to relate moles to grams, so our answer will probably be in grams.

0.350 mol of $CaCl_2$ → convert to → ? g $CaCl_2$

Whenever we need to relate a number of moles to a mass, we must first calculate the formula weight of the chemical, because the formula weight gives us the molar mass.

$$\begin{array}{lrl} \text{1 Ca:} & 1 \times 40.08 = & 40.08 \text{ amu} \\ \text{2 Cl:} & 2 \times 35.45 = & 70.90 \text{ amu} \\ \hline \text{total:} & & 110.98 \text{ amu} \end{array}$$

STEP 2: Write conversion factors that relate the two units.

One formula unit of $CaCl_2$ weighs 110.98 amu, so 1 mol of $CaCl_2$ weighs 110.98 g. Using the molar mass, we can write two conversion factors that express the relationship between mass and moles.

$$\frac{110.98 \text{ g}}{1 \text{ mol}} \quad \text{and} \quad \frac{1 \text{ mol}}{110.98 \text{ g}}$$

STEP 3: Choose the conversion factor that allows you to cancel units.

We are given the number of moles (0.350 mol), so we must use the first of our conversion factors. The mol unit cancels out, so our answer will be in grams.

$$0.350 \text{ mol} \times \frac{110.98 \text{ g}}{1 \text{ mol}}$$

We can cancel these units.

STEP 4: Do the math and round your answer.

Now we cancel units and do the arithmetic.

$$0.350 \cancel{\text{mol}} \times \frac{110.98 \text{ g}}{1 \cancel{\text{mol}}} = 38.843 \text{ g} \quad \text{calculator answer}$$

Rounding our answer to three significant figures gives us 38.8 g. Is this a reasonable answer? An entire mole of this compound weighs 110.98 g. Because 0.350 mol is substantially less than 1 mol, the mass should be less than 110.98 g. Therefore, 38.8 g seems plausible.

TRY IT YOURSELF: *Calculate the mass of 0.0275 mol of Na_2SO_4.*

For additional practice, try Core Problems 5.13 and 5.14.

Sample Problem 5.8

Converting a mass into a number of moles

If we have 2.65 g of $CaCl_2$, how many moles of this compound do we have?

SOLUTION

In this problem, we must convert a mass into a number of moles.

STEP 1: Identify the original measurement and the final unit.

$$2.65\text{ g }CaCl_2 \xrightarrow{\text{convert to}} ?\text{ mol }CaCl_2$$

As we saw in Sample Problem 5.7, the conversion factors that relate grams of $CaCl_2$ to moles are:

STEP 2: Write conversion factors that relate the two units.

$$\frac{110.98\text{ g}}{1\text{ mol}} \quad \text{and} \quad \frac{1\text{ mol}}{110.98\text{ g}}$$

In this problem, though, we must cancel grams, so we use the second conversion factor.

STEP 3: Choose the conversion factor that allows you to cancel units.

$$2.65\text{ g} \times \frac{1\text{ mol}}{110.98\text{ g}}$$

We can cancel these units.

Now we cancel units and do the arithmetic.

STEP 4: Do the math and round your answer.

$$2.65\text{ g} \times \frac{1\text{ mol}}{110.98\text{ g}} = 0.02387818\text{ mol} \quad \text{calculator answer}$$

Rounding our answer to three significant figures and attaching the unit gives us 0.0239 mol of $CaCl_2$. Is this reasonable? An entire mole of $CaCl_2$ weighs about 111 g, so 2.65 g should be much less than 1 mol. Our answer (0.0239 mol) is indeed much less than 1 mol, so it seems reasonable.

TRY IT YOURSELF: *A beaker contains 58.4 g of sodium sulfate (Na_2SO_4). How many moles is this?*

For additional practice, try Core Problems 5.15 and 5.16.

We are now ready to see why a 5.0% glucose solution and a 9.25% sucrose solution have the same effect on red blood cells. The glucose solution contains 5.0 g of solute in 100 mL of solution, while the sucrose solution contains 9.25 g of solute in 100 mL. Let us convert the mass of each solute into moles. (See if you can do this conversion on your own.)

Glucose Solution

Mass of glucose in 100 mL of solution: 5.0 g
Chemical formula of glucose: $C_6H_{12}O_6$
Formula weight of glucose: 180.156 amu
Mass of 1 mol of glucose: 180.156 g
5.0 g of glucose = **0.028 mol**

Sucrose Solution

Mass of sucrose in 100 mL of solution: 9.25 g
Chemical formula of sucrose: $C_{12}H_{22}O_{11}$
Formula weight of sucrose: 342.296 amu
Mass of 1 mol of sucrose: 342.296 g
9.25 g of sucrose = **0.027 mol**

Health Note: Sucrose solutions are not used in intravenous lines, because cells cannot absorb sucrose.

These two solutions contain roughly the same number of moles of solute. Since 1 mol is always 6.022×10^{23} molecules, the two solutions also contain the same number of molecules of solute. The behavior of a red blood cell depends on the concentration of molecules in a solution. In the next section, we explain how to express this concentration using the mole unit.

CORE PROBLEMS

5.11 How much does each of the following weigh? Be sure to use the appropriate unit for each answer.
a) one atom of sulfur
b) one mole of sulfur
c) one molecule of N_2O
d) one mole of N_2O
e) one formula unit of $(NH_4)_3PO_4$
f) one mole of $(NH_4)_3PO_4$

5.12 How much does each of the following weigh? Be sure to use the appropriate unit for each answer.
a) one atom of sodium
b) one mole of sodium
c) one molecule of H_2S
d) one mole of H_2S
e) one formula unit of $Ca_3(PO_4)_2$
f) one mole of $Ca_3(PO_4)_2$

5.13 a) If you have 25 moles of iron, how many grams of iron do you have?
b) If you have 0.0615 moles of sodium lactate ($NaC_3H_5O_3$), how many grams of sodium lactate do you have?

5.14 a) If you have 0.0275 moles of lead, how many grams of lead do you have?
b) If you have 2.28 moles of saccharin ($C_7H_5NO_3S$), how many grams of saccharin do you have?

5.15 Convert each of the following masses into moles:
a) 6.75 g of aluminum
b) 12.99 g of leucine ($C_6H_{13}NO_2$)
c) 1.35 kg of $Cu(NO_3)_2$

5.16 Convert each of the following masses into moles:
a) 21.5 g of helium
b) 8.18 g of citric acid ($C_6H_8O_7$)
c) 7.6 kg of $Al_2(SO_4)_3$

OBJECTIVES: *Calculate and use molarities.*

5.3 Molarity

As we saw in the last section, the effect of a solution on a living cell depends on the concentration of molecules in the solution. Because the number of molecules in even a small volume of solution is inconveniently large, chemists express the concentration by calculating the number of moles of solute in one liter of solution. The ratio of moles of solute to liters of solution is called the **molarity** (or **molar concentration**) of the solution.

• When you see "M," say "molar," so "1 M" solution is read as "one molar."

$$\text{molarity} = \frac{\text{moles of solute}}{\text{liters of solution}}$$

The unit of molarity is moles per liter, which is usually abbreviated by writing a capital M. For example, both "1 mol/L glucose" and "1 M glucose" describe a solution that contains 1 mol of glucose in each liter of liquid. Figure 5.7 shows the relationship between 1 mol of glucose ($C_6H_{12}O_6$) and a 1 M solution of glucose.

To calculate the molarity of a solution, we must first know (or calculate) how many *liters* of solution we have and how many *moles* of solute are dissolved in it. We then divide the moles by the liters to get the molarity.

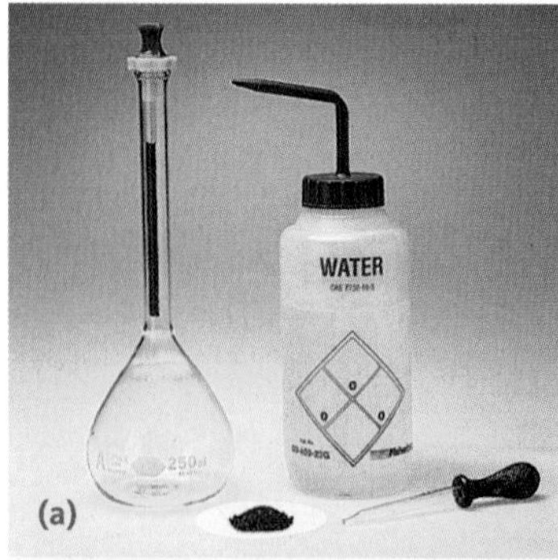

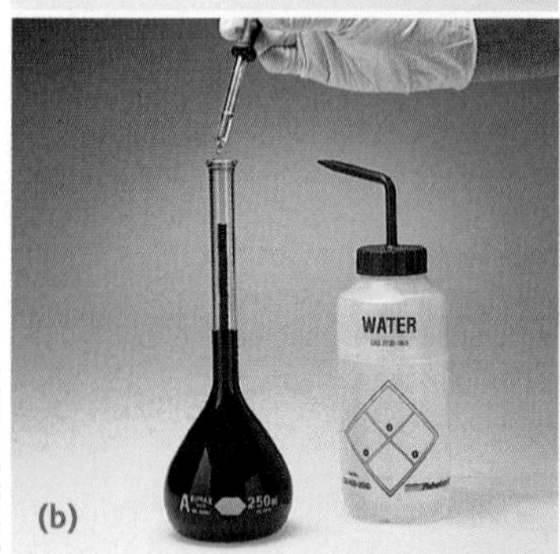

Making a 0.01 M solution of $KMnO_4$. (a) Weigh out 0.0025 mol (0.395 g) of $KMnO_4$. (b) Dissolve the $KMnO_4$ in enough water to give a total volume of 0.25 L.

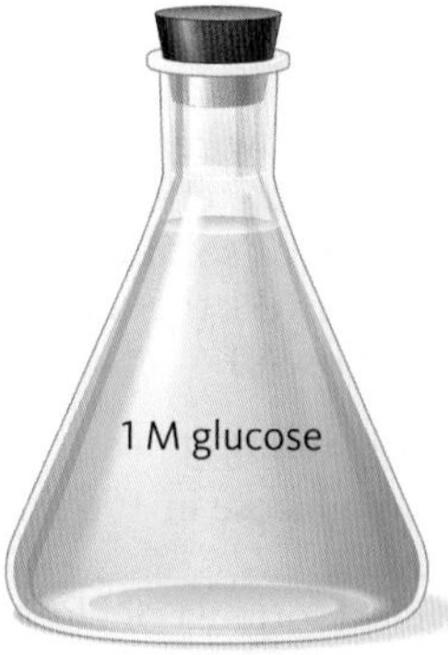

1 mole of glucose
means
180.16 g of glucose

1 M glucose
or
1 molar glucose
or
1 mol/L glucose
all mean
1 mole of glucose per liter
which means
this solution contains 180.16 g of glucose in each liter of liquid

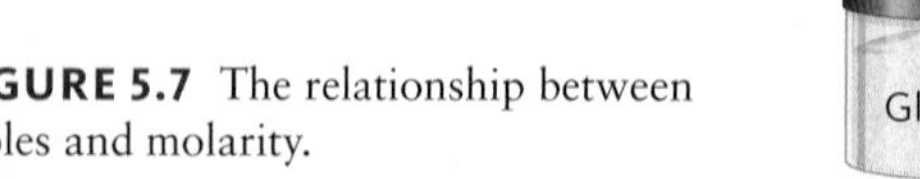

FIGURE 5.7 The relationship between moles and molarity.

Sample Problem 5.9

Calculating the molarity of a solution

A solution contains 3.00 g of vitamin C ($C_6H_8O_6$) dissolved in enough water to make 200 mL of solution. Calculate the molarity of this solution.

SOLUTION

STEP 1: Determine the units you must use.

To calculate the molarity of a solution, we must divide the number of moles of solute (vitamin C) by the number of liters of solution. We are not given either of these values, but we can calculate them from the information we do have. Our strategy for solving this problem is:

3.00 g of vitamin C → convert to → ? mol of vitamin C

200 mL of solution → convert to → ? L of solution

? mol of vitamin C and ? L of solution → divide → ? molarity

STEP 2: Convert the amounts into the correct units.

First, let us convert the number of grams of vitamin C into a number of moles. As we saw in the previous section, we need the formula weight of the compound to do this conversion. Adding the masses of the atoms in $C_6H_8O_6$ gives us 176.124 amu, so 1 mol of vitamin C weighs 176.124 g. Using this relationship, we can convert 3.00 g of vitamin C into moles.

$$3.00\ \cancel{g} \times \frac{1\ \text{mol}}{176.124\ \cancel{g}} = 0.017033454\ \text{mol vitamin C}$$

Since this is not our final answer, we won't round off yet.

Next, we need to convert the volume of the solution from milliliters to liters. To do this conversion, we move the decimal point three places to the left.

$$200.\ \text{mL} = \mathbf{0.200\ L}$$

In whole-number volumes such as 50 mL or 200 mL, assume that all digits are significant.

STEP 3: Divide the solute by the solvent.

Finally, we calculate the molarity by dividing the number of moles by the number of liters.

$$\frac{0.017033454\ \text{mol}}{0.200\ \text{L}} = 0.08516727\ \text{mol/L}$$

We should round this to three significant figures, so the molarity of this solution is **0.0852 mol/L.** We can also express our answer as **0.0852 M,** using the standard abbreviation for molarity.

TRY IT YOURSELF: *A solution contains 6.82 g of glycine ($C_2H_5NO_2$) dissolved in enough water to make 75 mL of solution. Calculate the molarity of this solution.*

For additional practice, try Core Problems 5.17 and 5.20.

What if we are asked to make a solution that has a specific molarity? In that case, we have to calculate the number of grams of solute that we will use to prepare the solution.

Sample Problem 5.10

Using molarity to calculate the mass of solute

Chemical laboratories often have a bottle of 0.20 M acetic acid. If we needed to prepare 150 mL of this solution, what mass of acetic acid must we use? The chemical formula of acetic acid is $C_2H_4O_2$, and its molar mass is 60.052 g/mol.

continued

SOLUTION

This problem is an exercise in conversion factors, and it requires the use of two key concepts. The molarity (0.20 M) tells us that one liter of solution contains 0.20 moles of acetic acid, so it allows us to translate the volume of solution into the number of moles of acetic acid. Once we know the number of moles, we can use the molar mass of acetic acid to convert moles into grams. Our volume is given in milliliters, so we must convert the volume into liters before we do anything else. Our strategy is

150 mL of solution → convert to → ? L of solution → convert to → ? mol of acetic acid → convert to → ? g of acetic acid

We begin by converting 150 mL into liters. To do so, we move the decimal point three places to the left.

$$150.\text{ mL} = \mathbf{0.150\text{ L}}$$

• Here we use our four-step unit conversion method to translate liters into moles.

Next, we use the molarity to convert liters of solution into moles of acetic acid. The molarity tells us that 1 L of solution contains 0.20 mol of acetic acid. We can use this relationship to write a pair of conversion factors.

$$\frac{0.20\text{ mol acetic acid}}{1\text{ L}} \quad \text{and} \quad \frac{1\text{ L}}{0.20\text{ mol acetic acid}}$$

When we multiply the volume of solution (0.15 L) by the first of these conversion factors, the volume unit cancels out.

$$0.150\text{ }\cancel{\text{L}} \times \frac{0.20\text{ mol acetic acid}}{1\text{ }\cancel{\text{L}}} = 0.030\text{ mol acetic acid}$$

• Now we use our unit conversion method to translate moles into grams.

We now know that we need 0.030 mol of acetic acid to make the solution. Our final task is to convert the number of moles into a mass. The molar mass tells us that one mole of acetic acid weighs 60.052 g, so we can write two more conversion factors.

$$\frac{60.052\text{ g}}{1\text{ mol}} \quad \text{and} \quad \frac{1\text{ mol}}{60.052\text{ g}}$$

We use the first of these conversion factors, so we can cancel moles.

$$0.030\text{ }\cancel{\text{mol}} \times \frac{60.052\text{ g}}{1\text{ }\cancel{\text{mol}}} = 1.80156\text{ g} \quad \text{calculator answer}$$

This answer should be rounded to two significant figures. We must use 1.8 g of acetic acid in order to make 150 mL of 0.20 M acetic acid solution.

TRY IT YOURSELF: *0.050 M $AgNO_3$ is a common laboratory solution. If you needed to prepare 500 mL of this solution, what mass of $AgNO_3$ would you need?*

For additional practice, try Core Problems 5.21 and 5.22.

We have seen that red blood cells survive in solutions of glucose or sucrose when the concentration of the solution is around 0.28 M. What about other solutes? In general, *a solution whose total solute concentration is around 0.28 M will not damage red blood cells.* For example, a solution that contains 0.14 M glucose and 0.14 M sucrose will not harm red blood cells, because the concentrations of the two solutes add up to 0.28 M. By contrast, red blood cells will shrivel up and die in a solution that contains 0.28 M glucose and 0.28 M sucrose, because the total solute concentration is 0.56 M. In the next section, we will explore the reasons for this behavior. We will also look at the effect of ionic solutes on blood cells.

CORE PROBLEMS

5.17 Calculate the molarity of each of the following solutions:

a) 0.350 mol of acetic acid ($HC_2H_3O_2$) in a total volume of 0.250 L

b) 0.0624 mol of thiamine hydrochloride ($C_{12}H_{18}N_4OSCl_2$) in a total volume of 85.5 mL

c) 6.1×10^{-4} mol of nitric acid (HNO_3) in a total volume of 7.5 mL

5.18 Calculate the molarity of each of the following solutions:

a) 0.185 mol of sodium chloride (NaCl) in a total volume of 1.45 L

b) 0.0410 mol of potassium dichromate ($K_2Cr_2O_7$) in a total volume of 329 mL

c) 8.6×10^{-5} mol of aspirin ($C_9H_8O_4$) in a total volume of 31 mL

5.19 Calculate the molarity of each of the following solutions:

a) 62.4 g of $MgSO_4$ in a total volume of 2.50 L

b) 3.37 g of tryptophan ($C_{11}H_{12}N_2O_2$) in a total volume of 453 mL

c) 45.5 mg of vitamin C ($C_6H_8O_6$) in a total volume of 2.75 mL

5.20 Calculate the molarity of each of the following solutions:

a) 3.51 g of NaH_2PO_4 in a total volume of 0.500 L

b) 27.9 g of citric acid ($C_6H_8O_5$) in a total volume of 193 mL

c) 135 mg of lidocaine hydrochloride ($C_{14}H_{23}N_2OCl$) in a total volume of 5.00 mL

5.21 a) How many grams of NaOH would you need to prepare 2.50 L of 0.100 M NaOH?

b) How many grams of $Cu(NO_3)_2$ would you need to prepare 100.0 mL of 0.255 M $Cu(NO_3)_2$?

c) How many grams of glucosamine ($C_6H_{13}NO_5$) would you need to prepare 550 mL of 1.4 M glucosamine?

5.22 a) How many grams of $FeSO_4$ would you need to prepare 2.50 L of 0.050 M $FeSO_4$?

b) How many grams of $(NH_4)_2SO_4$ would you need to prepare 500.0 mL of 0.162 M $(NH_4)_2SO_4$?

c) How many grams of glycine ($C_2H_5NO_2$) would you need to prepare 60.0 mL of 0.00855 M glycine?

5.4 Osmosis, Dialysis, and Tonicity

OBJECTIVES: *Determine the direction of osmosis and dialysis, and predict the effect of a solution on red blood cells using the overall molarity of the solution.*

If a red blood cell is placed into a 0.28 M solution of glucose, the cell will show no evident ill effects. However, if the cell is placed into pure water, it will swell and burst; and if the cell is placed into 0.5 M glucose, the cell will shrivel up, as shown in Figure 5.8. To understand this behavior, we must first look at how molecules behave when two substances are mixed.

In any solution, the solute particles (molecules or ions) are in constant, random motion. This motion tends to distribute the particles evenly throughout the solution. For example, if we put a drop of food coloring into a glass of pure water and then let the mixture stand for a while, the food coloring will become evenly distributed throughout the liquid. Although we only see the solute molecules (the dye) move about, the water

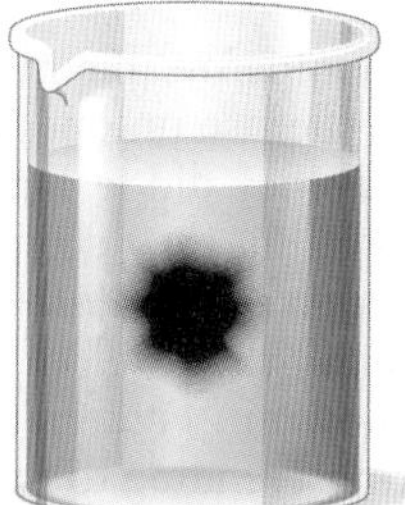

Red blood cell in **pure water:** The cell swells and bursts.

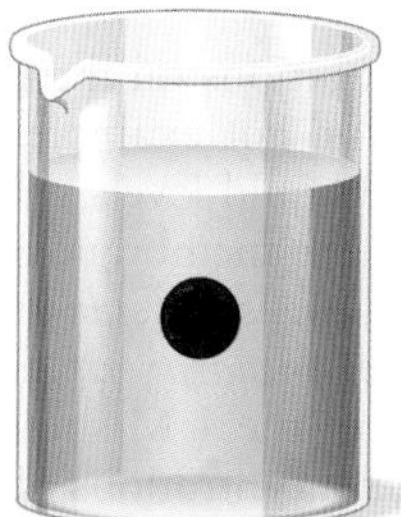

Red blood cell in **0.28 M sucrose:** No effect on the cell.

Red blood cell in **0.5 M sucrose:** The cell shrivels up.

FIGURE 5.8 The effect of different solutions on red blood cells.

Solute
Solvent
When you add a drop of coloring to water . . .
. . . the solute and solvent molecules move about . . .
. . . until they are evenly distributed.

FIGURE 5.9 Diffusion mixes a solute evenly throughout a solvent.

molecules are in motion as well, moving into the spaces that are vacated by the solute. The tendency of the particles in a mixture to become uniformly distributed is called **diffusion**, and is illustrated in Figure 5.9.

Diffusion will mix any two aqueous solutions as long as the solute and solvent can move freely from one solution to the other. However, some types of materials allow only certain types of particles to pass through them. Any barrier that permits diffusion of some particles, but not all, is called a **semipermeable membrane**. Most commonly, a semipermeable membrane allows water and other small molecules to pass through (it is *permeable* to these molecules), but it does not allow passage of large molecules.

Osmosis Is the Movement of Solvent Through a Membrane

Let us look at what happens when we put pure water and 1 M sucrose solution on opposite sides of a semipermeable membrane, as illustrated in Figure 5.10. Water molecules can pass through the membrane, but sucrose molecules are too large to fit through the membrane pores. On the side with pure water, many water molecules hit the membrane pores and pass through to the other side. On the side with 1 M sucrose, fewer water molecules hit and pass through the pores, because some of the molecules that hit the membrane are sucrose. As a result, the volume of the pure water decreases and the volume of the sucrose solution increases. Although water passes through the membrane in both directions, we observe a net flow of water into the sucrose solution. This net movement of water through a semipermeable membrane is called **osmosis**.

Whenever the molarities of the solutions on the two sides of a semipermeable membrane are different, osmosis can occur. For example, if we use 1 M sucrose on one side and 0.5 M sucrose on the other, the liquid levels will change, just as they did in Figure 5.10. Water molecules pass through the membrane in both directions, but they do so in unequal numbers. As a result, *water leaves the side with the lower molarity of solute and moves into the side with the higher molarity of solute.* In this case, the level of the 0.5 M solution drops and the level of the 1 M solution rises, as shown in Figure 5.11. The flow of water also changes the concentrations of the two solutions, tending to make them equal.

When a solution contains two or more solutes, we must add up the molarities of all of the solutes to predict the direction of osmosis. For instance, if a solution contains 0.1 moles of glucose and 0.1 moles of fructose per liter, the total molarity of the solution is 0.2 M. Sample Problem 5.11 illustrates how we can use the total molarity to determine the direction of osmosis.

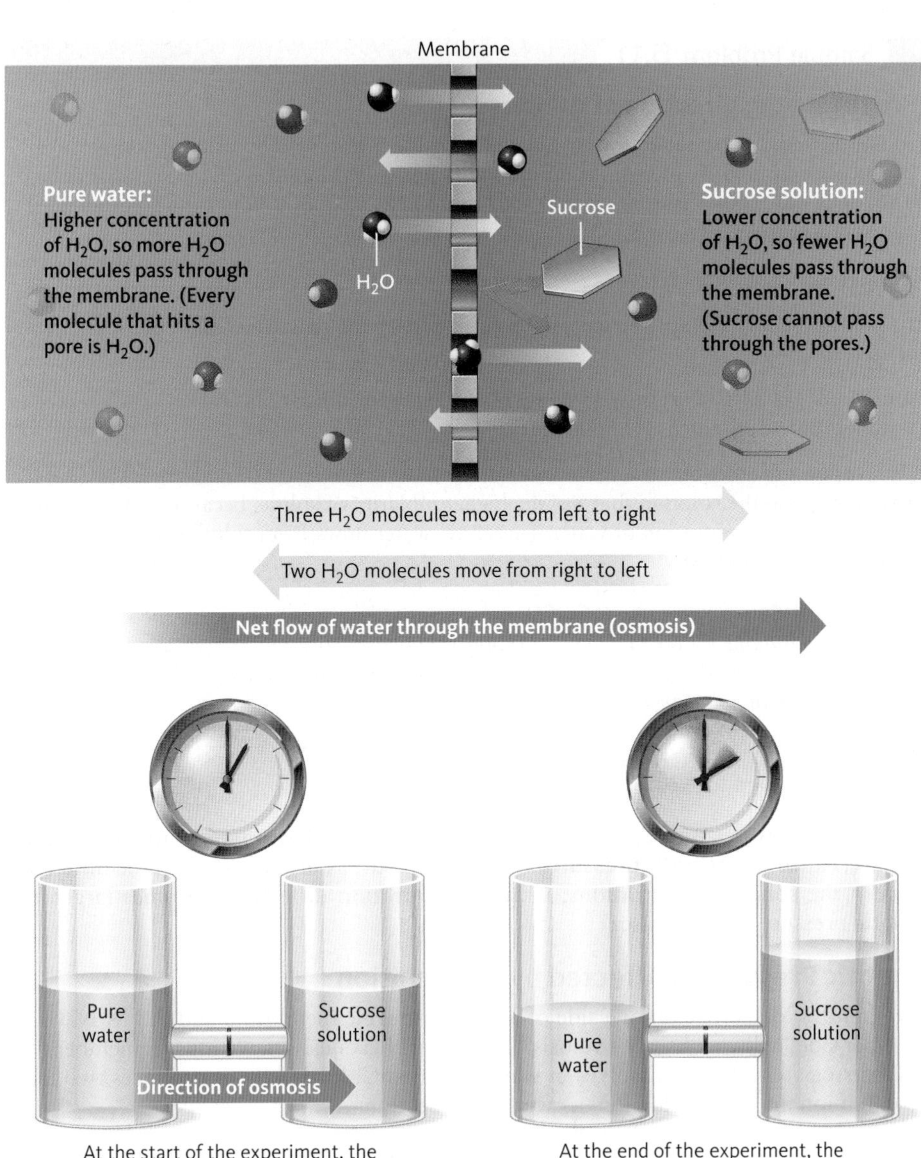
Membrane
Pure water:
Higher concentration of H_2O, so more H_2O molecules pass through the membrane. (Every molecule that hits a pore is H_2O.)
H_2O
Sucrose
Sucrose solution:
Lower concentration of H_2O, so fewer H_2O molecules pass through the membrane. (Sucrose cannot pass through the pores.)
Three H_2O molecules move from left to right
Two H_2O molecules move from right to left
Net flow of water through the membrane (osmosis)
Pure water
Sucrose solution
Direction of osmosis
Pure water
Sucrose solution
At the start of the experiment, the two liquid levels are equal.
At the end of the experiment, the level of the sucrose solution is higher.

FIGURE 5.10 Osmosis is the unbalanced flow of water through a membrane.

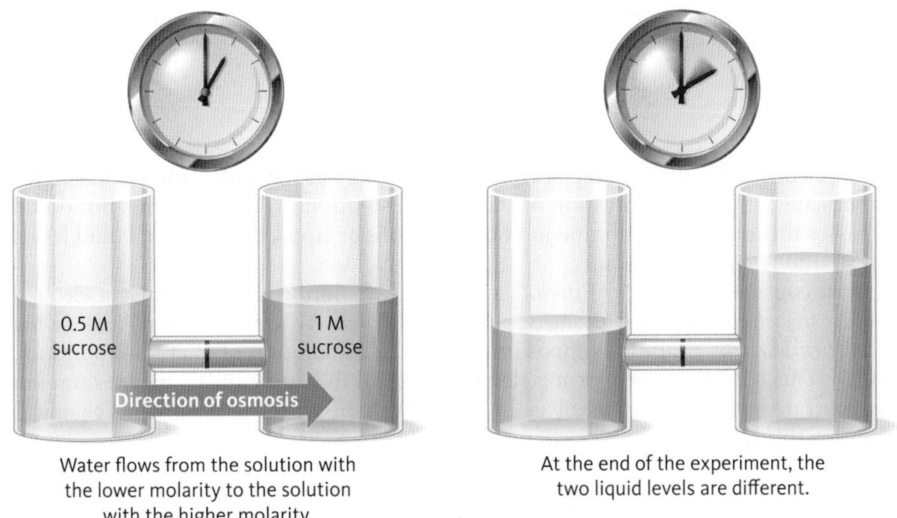
0.5 M sucrose
1 M sucrose
Direction of osmosis
Water flows from the solution with the lower molarity to the solution with the higher molarity.
At the end of the experiment, the two liquid levels are different.

FIGURE 5.11 Osmosis occurs when two solutions have unequal concentrations.

Sample Problem 5.11

Predicting the direction of osmosis

Solutions A and B are separated by a semipermeable membrane. Solution A contains 0.1 M glucose and 0.05 M sucrose. Solution B contains 0.12 M glucose. Does osmosis occur? If so, does water flow from solution A into solution B, or does it flow from solution B into solution A?

SOLUTION

To predict the direction of osmosis, we need to add up the molarities of all of the solutes in each solution.

Solution A: 0.1 M glucose + 0.05 M sucrose = 0.15 M (total molarity)
Solution B: 0.12 M glucose (total molarity)

Osmosis occurs here, because the two solutions have different total molarities. Water always flows into the solution that has the higher molarity of solute, because that solution has the lower concentration of water. Therefore, water flows **from solution B (0.12 M) into solution A (0.15 M).**

TRY IT YOURSELF: *Solutions C and D are separated by a semipermeable membrane. Solution C contains 0.005 M urea and 0.004 M glucose. Solution D contains 0.011 M fructose. Does osmosis occur? If so, does water flow from solution C into solution D, or does it flow from solution D into solution C?*

For additional practice, try Core Problems 5.23 and 5.24.

The flow of water into the solution with the higher molarity builds up a substantial pressure, called the **osmotic pressure.** Osmotic pressure is proportional to the difference between the solute concentrations; if the concentration difference becomes larger, the osmotic pressure will increase.

Osmotic Pressure Is Affected by Dissociation

If we put 0.2 M sucrose on one side of a semipermeable membrane and 0.1 M NaCl on the other side, will we observe osmosis? To answer this question, we must remember that NaCl dissociates when it dissolves in water. Each NaCl formula unit produces two ions, a sodium ion and a chloride ion, as we saw in Section 4.7.

$$NaCl(s) \rightarrow Na^+(aq) + Cl^-(aq)$$

The *s* means "solid," and the *aq* means "aqueous" (dissolved in water).

Therefore, when a *mole* of NaCl dissolves, the solution contains two *moles* of ions: one mole of Na^+ ions and one mole of Cl^- ions, as shown in Figure 5.12. Each liter of our 0.1 M NaCl solution contains 0.1 mol of NaCl, but the concentration of individual ions is twice as large:

$$0.1\ \cancel{\text{mol NaCl}} \times \frac{2\ \text{mol ions}}{1\ \cancel{\text{mol NaCl}}} = 0.2\ \text{mol ions}$$

The total concentration of independent solute particles in the NaCl solution is 0.2 M. This is the same as the concentration of the sucrose solution, so osmosis does not occur. Water passes through the membrane in both directions at equal rates, so the liquid levels of both solutions remain constant.

Health Note: The total molarity of a solution is called its *osmolarity* and is sometimes printed on intravenous solution labels.

We must consider the effect of dissociation for any solution that contains an electrolyte. To do so, *we multiply the molarity of the electrolyte by the number of ions in the chemical formula.* For example, suppose we had a 0.2 M solution of magnesium nitrate, $Mg(NO_3)_2$. This compound is a strong electrolyte, breaking down into a magnesium ion and two nitrate ions when it dissolves in water. We can write the following chemical equation for this dissociation:

$$Mg(NO_3)_2(s) \rightarrow Mg^{2+}(aq) + 2\ NO_3^-(aq)$$

Magnesium nitrate breaks down into a total of three ions, so the total molarity of our solution is 0.2 M × 3 = 0.6 M.

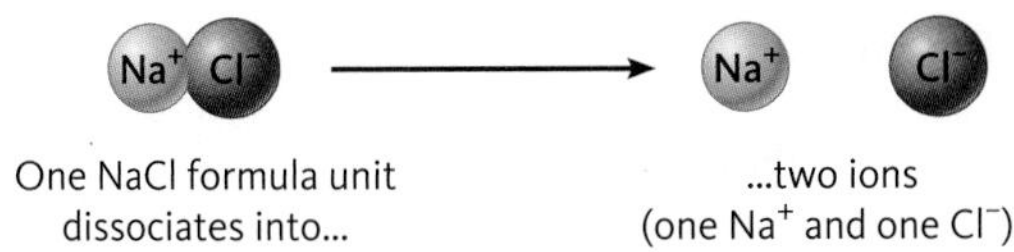
Na+ Cl−
Na+
Cl−
One NaCl formula unit dissociates into...
...two ions (one Na+ and one Cl−).

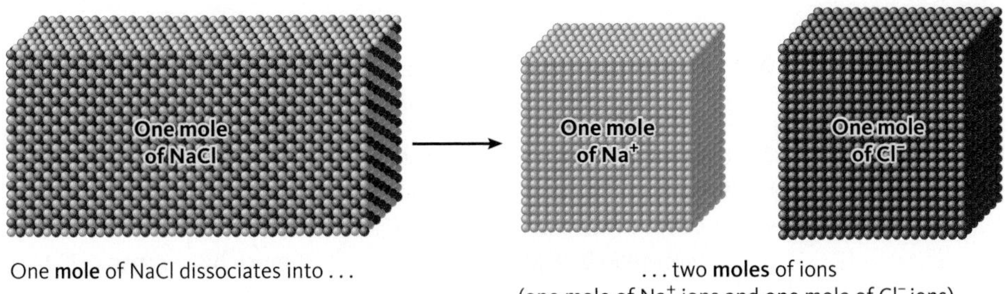
One mole of NaCl
One mole of Na+
One mole of Cl−
One mole of NaCl dissociates into . . .
. . . two moles of ions (one mole of Na+ ions and one mole of Cl− ions).

FIGURE 5.12 The mole relationship between an electrolyte and its ions.

Sample Problem **5.12**

Calculating the total molarity of a solution

A solution contains 0.050 M $FeSO_4$ and 0.19 M glucose. What is the total molarity of solute particles in this solution? (Glucose is a nonelectrolyte.)

SOLUTION

Each $FeSO_4$ formula unit breaks down into two ions, Fe^{2+} and SO_4^{2-}. (Remember that SO_4^{2-} is a polyatomic ion and does not break apart into sulfur and oxygen.) Therefore, the molarity of ions in this solution is

$$0.050 \text{ M} \times 2 = 0.10 \text{ M} \quad \text{total concentration of ions}$$

The $FeSO_4$ contributes 0.10 moles of solute particles per liter. We must also consider the glucose. Glucose is a nonelectrolyte, so it contributes 0.19 moles of solute per liter. The total concentration of solute particles is therefore 0.10 M + 0.19 M = 0.29 M.

TRY IT YOURSELF: *A solution contains 0.07 M glucose and 0.07 M Na_2CO_3. What is the total molarity of solute particles in this solution? (Glucose is a nonelectrolyte.)*

For additional practice, try Core Problems 5.25 and 5.26.

The Behavior of Cells Depends on the Tonicity of Their Surroundings

Let us return to the question of why red blood cells are affected by the surrounding solution. Red blood cells, like all other cells in our bodies, are surrounded by a semipermeable membrane, which allows water to pass through but is impermeable to most solutes. Inside the membrane is a liquid called the cytosol, which contains a variety of solutes. The overall concentration of solutes in the cytosol is roughly 0.28 M. If the concentration of solutes outside the red blood cell is also 0.28 M, osmosis will not occur, because water flows into and out of the cell at the same rate. However, when the concentration outside the cell is higher than 0.28 M, water flows out of the cell, and the cell volume shrinks. If the cell loses too much water, it shrivels up and dies, a process called *crenation.* If the solute concentration outside the cell is lower than 0.28 M, water flows into the cell, and the cell swells. The cell will burst if it absorbs too much water, a process called *hemolysis.*

In medicine, solutions that are intended for intravenous injection are classified based on their **tonicity**, which is the relationship between the overall concentration of the solution and the normal solute concentration in blood cells. Any solution that contains 0.28 mol/L of solute is called an **isotonic** solution (*iso* means "equal"). Solutions that have higher solute concentrations are **hypertonic** (*hyper* = "above"), while solutions that have lower solute concentrations are **hypotonic** (*hypo* = "below"). Table 5.2 summarizes the effects of these three types of solutions on red blood cells.

Health Note: The isotonic concentration depends to a small extent on the solute, with large molecules having somewhat lower isotonic concentrations.

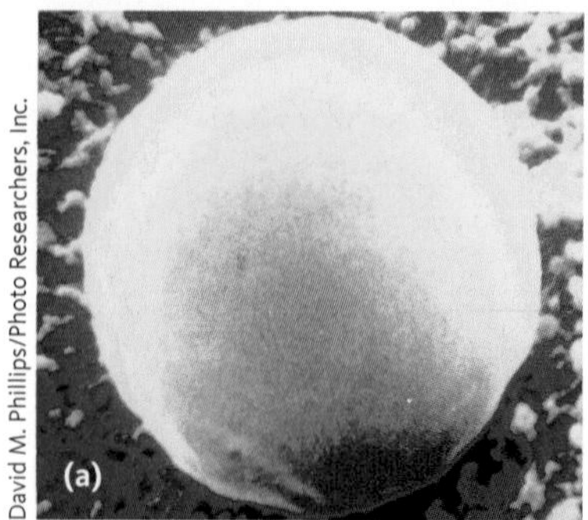

David M. Phillips/Photo Researchers, Inc.

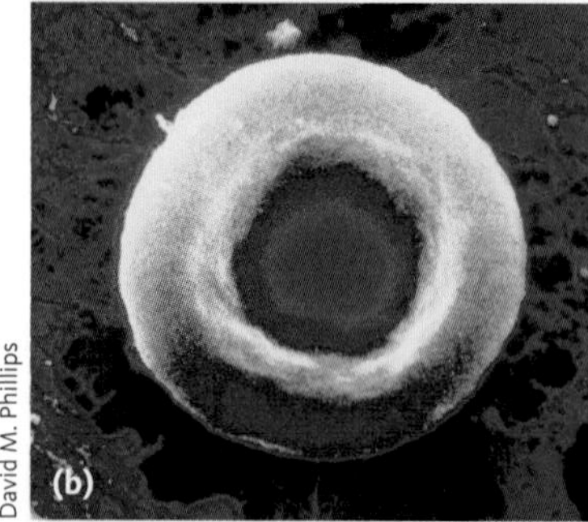

David M. Phillips

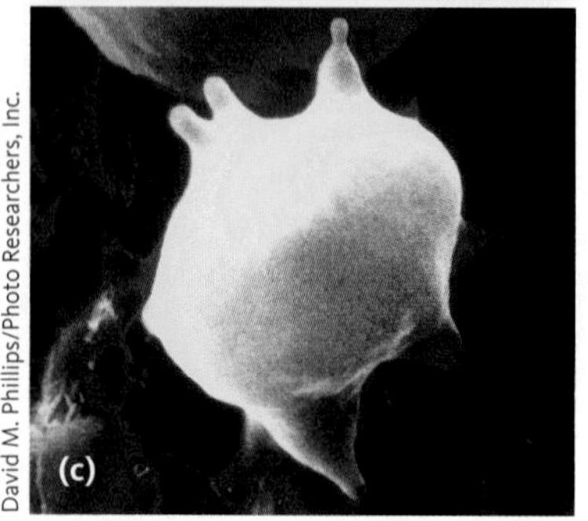

David M. Phillips/Photo Researchers, Inc.

Red blood cells in (a) a hypotonic solution, (b) an isotonic solution, and (c) a hypertonic solution.

TABLE 5.2 The Effect of Tonicity on Red Blood Cells

Tonicity of the solution	Hypotonic	Isotonic	Hypertonic
Total solute concentration	Less than 0.28 M	0.28 M	Greater than 0.28 M
Direction of osmosis	Water flows into the cell.	No osmosis occurs.	Water flows out of the cell.
Effect on a red blood cell	The cell swells, and it will burst *(hemolyze)* if the solute concentration is much lower than 0.28 M.	The cell is unaffected.	The cell shrinks, and it will shrivel up *(crenate)* if the solute concentration is much higher than 0.28 M.

TABLE 5.3 Typical Molarities of Solutions Inside and Outside a Cell

BLOOD PLASMA (OUTSIDE THE CELL)		TYPICAL CYTOSOL (INSIDE THE CELL)	
Solute	**Molarity**	**Solute**	**Molarity**
Na^+	0.12 M	K^+	0.12 M
Cl^-	0.10 M	Proteins	0.07 M
HCO_3^-	0.02 M	HPO_4^{2-}	0.04 M
Proteins	0.02 M	$H_2PO_4^-$	0.03 M
Other solutes	0.02 M	Other solutes	0.02 M
Total	0.28 M	Total	0.28 M

In our bodies, blood cells are suspended in an aqueous solution called the plasma. The total concentration of solutes in the plasma is roughly 0.28 M, so plasma is isotonic. However, the actual solutes in plasma are different from those in the cytosol. Table 5.3 lists the principal solutes in blood plasma and in the cytosol of a typical cell.

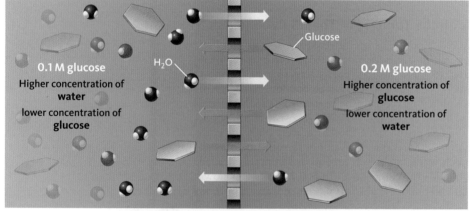

FIGURE 5.13 Osmosis and dialysis move in opposite directions.

Dialysis Is the Movement of Solute Through a Membrane

Some solutes can pass through semipermeable membranes. *Any solute that can cross a membrane will move toward the solution that has the lowest concentration of that solute.* Once again, we see diffusion in action, as solute particles spread out until they reach a uniform concentration on both sides of the membrane. The movement of solute through a membrane is called **dialysis.** For example, suppose we use a semipermeable membrane to separate two glucose solutions that have different concentrations. If the membrane does not allow glucose to pass through, only osmosis will occur, but if the membrane is permeable to glucose, we will see dialysis and osmosis simultaneously. As shown in Figure 5.13, glucose and water flow in opposite directions, with each substance moving toward the side that has the lower concentration of that substance.

Sample Problem 5.13

Predicting the direction of osmosis and dialysis

Two solutions are separated by a semipermeable membrane. Solution A contains 0.1 M glucose and 0.05 M sucrose. Solution B contains 0.05 M glucose and 0.05 M sucrose. The membrane allows both glucose and sucrose to pass through.

a) Predict the direction of dialysis for each solute.

b) Will osmosis occur? If so, which way will water flow?

SOLUTION

a) Glucose moves from solution A to solution B, because solution A has the higher concentration of glucose. Sucrose does not dialyze, because the concentrations of sucrose in the two solutions are equal.

b) The total solute concentration in solution A is 0.15 M, and it is 0.1 M in solution B. These two concentrations are not equal, so osmosis will occur. Water flows from solution B to solution A, because water always moves into the solution that has the higher total solute concentration. (Remember that this solution must have the lower concentration of water.)

TRY IT YOURSELF: *Two solutions are separated by a semipermeable membrane. Solution A contains 0.1 M glucose and 0.05 M sucrose. Solution B contains 0.05 M glucose and 0.1 M sucrose. The membrane allows both glucose and sucrose to pass through.*

a) Predict the direction of dialysis for each solute.

b) Will osmosis occur? If so, which way will water flow?

For additional practice, try Core Problems 5.35 and 5.36.

Dialysis is used to remove waste solutes such as urea from the blood of people whose kidneys do not function adequately. In this process, called *hemodialysis,* the person's blood is passed through a tube made from a membrane that is permeable to water and small molecules. The tube is submerged in an isotonic solution that contains an appropriate mixture of solutes for normal blood plasma. Since the plasma and the external solution (the *dialysate*) have approximately the same tonicity, very little osmosis occurs, but solutes cross the membrane until the concentrations of key solutes reach reasonable values. Figure 5.14 shows how hemodialysis removes urea (a waste product that is formed when our bodies break down proteins) from blood.

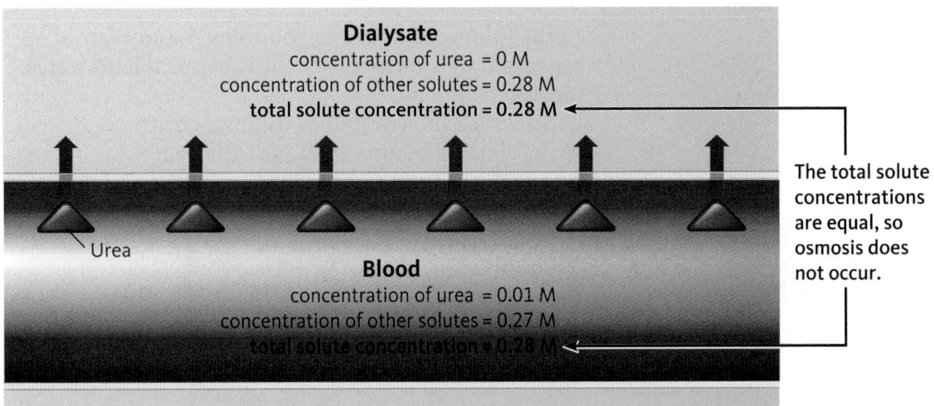

FIGURE 5.14 Removing urea from blood by hemodialysis.

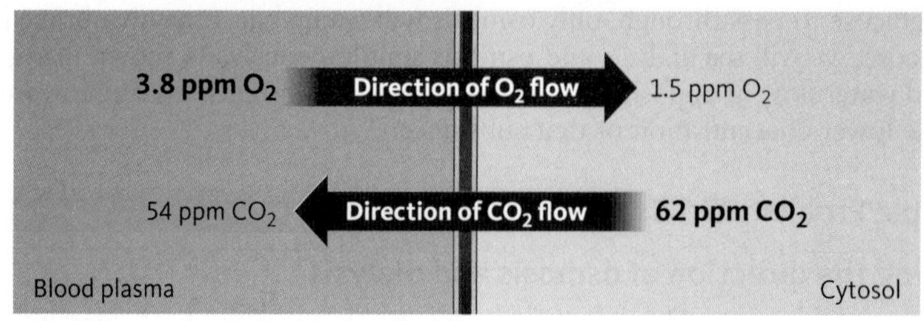

FIGURE 5.15 Exchange of oxygen and carbon dioxide across cell membranes.

In our bodies, dialysis plays an important role in the movement of oxygen and carbon dioxide into and out of cells. Cells require a constant supply of oxygen, which is supplied by the blood. The concentration of oxygen in the blood is higher than that in the cells, so oxygen moves from the blood into the cells. By contrast, cells produce carbon dioxide as a waste product, so the concentration of carbon dioxide in the cells is higher than the concentration in the blood. Figure 5.15 shows the concentrations of oxygen and carbon dioxide in arterial blood (blood that is arriving from the heart) and in the cytosol. We will examine how our bodies transport carbon dioxide in more detail in Chapter 7.

CORE PROBLEMS

5.23 Two solutions are separated by a membrane. Solution A contains 0.05 M sucrose, while solution B contains 0.07 M sucrose. If the membrane is permeable to water but not to sucrose, in which direction will osmosis occur?

5.24 Two solutions are separated by a membrane. Solution C contains 0.2% (w/v) albumin, while solution D contains 0.15% (w/v) albumin. If the membrane is permeable to water but not to albumin, in which direction will osmosis occur?

5.25 Calculate the total molarity of each of the following solutions:
a) 0.125 M NaCl
b) 0.22 M Na_2CO_3
c) a solution that contains 0.12 M glucose (a non-electrolyte) and 0.21 M KBr

5.26 Calculate the total molarity of each of the following solutions:
a) 0.075 M $MgBr_2$
b) 0.31 M KNO_3
c) a solution that contains 0.15 M sucrose (a non-electrolyte) and 0.05 M $MgSO_4$

5.27 Label each of the following solutions as isotonic, hypotonic, or hypertonic. Be sure to account for the dissociation of electrolytes.
a) 0.14 M lactose ($C_{12}H_{22}O_{11}$)
b) 0.14 M KCl
c) 0.14 M $MgCl_2$

5.28 Label each of the following solutions as isotonic, hypotonic, or hypertonic. Be sure to account for the dissociation of electrolytes.
a) 0.14 M $CaCl_2$
b) 0.14 M urea (N_2H_4CO)
c) 0.14 M NaBr

5.29 What will happen to a red blood cell if it is placed into each of the solutions in Problem 5.27?

5.30 What will happen to a red blood cell if it is placed into each of the solutions in Problem 5.28?

5.31 You need to make 500 mL of an isotonic solution of urea (N_2H_4CO). How many grams of urea do you need? Urea is a nonelectrolyte.

5.32 You need to make 3.50 L of an isotonic solution of lactose ($C_{12}H_{22}O_{11}$). How many grams of lactose do you need? Lactose is a nonelectrolyte.

5.33 A solution contains 0.04 M $MgSO_4$, 0.05 M NaCl, and 0.15 M sucrose. (Sucrose is a nonelectrolyte.)
a) Calculate the total molarity of solute particles in this solution.
b) Is this solution isotonic, hypotonic, or hypertonic?

5.34 A solution contains 0.03 M Na_2CO_3, 0.06 M KCl, and 0.07 M glucose. (Glucose is a nonelectrolyte.)
a) Calculate the total molarity of solute particles in this solution.
b) Is this solution isotonic, hypotonic, or hypertonic?

5.35 In the following diagram, solutions A and B are separated by a membrane that is permeable to water, glucose, and ions.
a) In which direction does osmosis occur?
b) In which direction does Na^+ dialyze?
c) In which direction does glucose dialyze?

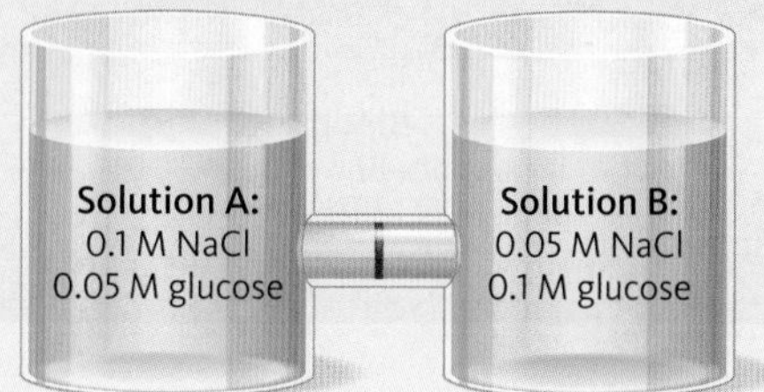

continued

5.36 In this diagram, solutions C and D are separated by a membrane that is permeable to water, glucose, and ions.
a) In which direction does osmosis occur?
b) In which direction does Cl^- dialyze?
c) In which direction does glucose dialyze?

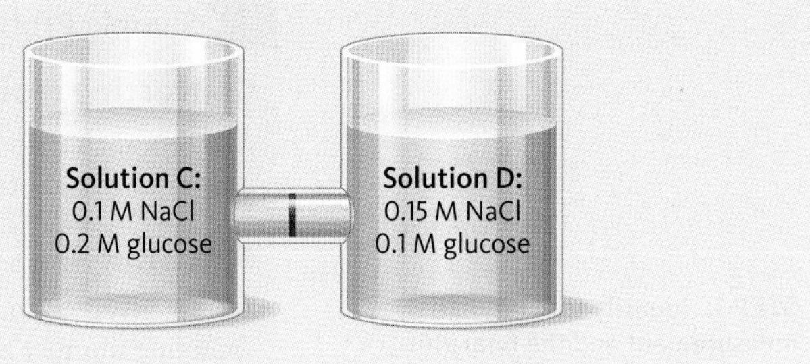

5.5 Equivalents

OBJECTIVES: *Interconvert moles and equivalents for ionic solutes, and use equivalents to describe the concentration of an ion in a solution.*

All body fluids, both inside and outside cells, contain dissolved ions. The rule of charge balance applies to these solutions, just as it does to ionic compounds, so the solutions must contain equal amounts of positive and negative charge. However, the solutions do not contain equal numbers of cations and anions, because the ions do not all have the same charge. For example, if a solution contains Mg^{2+} as the cation and Cl^- as the anion, it must contain twice as many chloride ions as it does magnesium ions.

In clinical work, concentrations of ions are often expressed in terms of equivalents (Eq) or milliequivalents (mEq) per liter. For example, the concentration of sodium ions in blood plasma is most commonly given as 140 milliequivalents per liter (mEq/L). An **equivalent** is defined as the amount of any ion that has the same total charge as a mole of hydrogen ions (H^+). In practice, this definition means that *the number of equivalents equals the number of moles times the charge.* For example, one mole of Mg^{2+} has the same total charge as two moles of H^+, because each magnesium ion has twice as much electrical charge as a hydrogen ion. Therefore, if we have one mole of Mg^{2+}, we also have two equivalents of Mg^{2+}, as illustrated in Figure 5.16.

For negative ions, we ignore the sign, so 1 mol of S^{2-} equals 2 Eq of S^{2-}. We can express amounts of polyatomic ions in terms of equivalents similarly; for instance, 1 mol of sulfate ions ($SO_4{}^{2-}$) equals 2 Eq of sulfate ions. Here are some other examples that illustrate the relationship between moles and equivalents:

Ions with Charges of +1 or −1
(1 mol = 1 Eq)
1 mol of K^+ = 1 Eq of K^+
1 mol of $NH_4{}^+$ = 1 Eq of $NH_4{}^+$
1 mol of Cl^- = 1 Eq of Cl^-
1 mol of OH^- = 1 Eq of OH^-

Ions with Charges of +2 or −2
(1 mol = 2 Eq)
1 mol of Ca^{2+} = 2 Eq of Ca^{2+}
1 mol of S^{2-} = 2 Eq of S^{2-}
1 mol of $CO_3{}^{2-}$ = 2 Eq of $CO_3{}^{2-}$

Ions with Charges of +3 or −3
(1 mol = 3 Eq)
1 mol of Fe^{3+} = 3 Eq of Fe^{3+}
1 mol of $PO_4{}^{3-}$ = 3 Eq of $PO_4{}^{3-}$

We can use these relationships to convert any number of moles of an ion into the corresponding number of equivalents, as illustrated in Sample Problem 5.14.

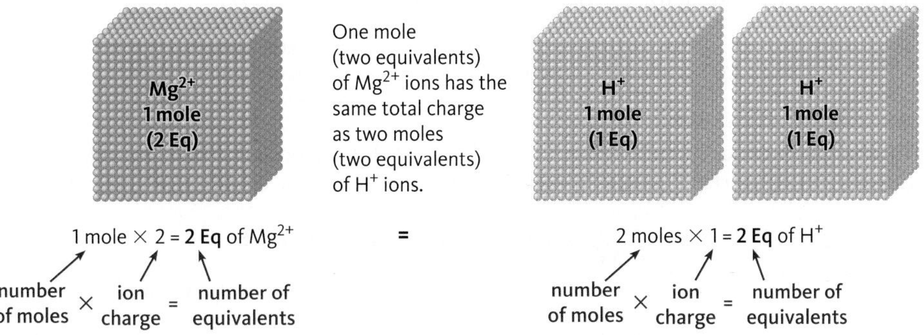

FIGURE 5.16 The relationship between moles and equivalents for an ion.

STEP 1: Identify the original measurement and the final unit.

STEP 2: Write conversion factors that relate the two units.

STEP 3: Choose the conversion factor that allows you to cancel units.

STEP 4: Do the math and round your answer.

Sample Problem **5.14**

Converting moles into equivalents

A solution contains 0.31 mol of phosphate ions. How many equivalents of phosphate ions does the solution contain?

SOLUTION

We are given a number of moles of an ion, and we are asked to convert to the corresponding number of equivalents.

The formula of phosphate ion is PO_4^{3-}, so 1 mol of phosphate equals 3 Eq. Expressing this relationship as a pair of conversion factors gives us:

$$\frac{3 \text{ Eq}}{1 \text{ mol}} \quad \text{and} \quad \frac{1 \text{ mol}}{3 \text{ Eq}}$$

Our initial measurement is a number of moles, so we must use the first of these conversion factors. Now we can cancel units and do the arithmetic.

$$0.31 \cancel{\text{mol}} \times \frac{3 \text{ Eq}}{1 \cancel{\text{mol}}} = 0.93 \text{ Eq}$$

The solution contains 0.93 Eq of phosphate ions.

TRY IT YOURSELF: *A solution contains 0.075 Eq of carbonate ions. How many moles of carbonate ions does the solution contain?*

For additional practice, try Core Problems 5.37 and 5.38.

As we saw in Section 5.2, we can relate any number of moles of a chemical to the corresponding mass, using the formula weight of the chemical. We now have a relationship between moles and equivalents, so we can convert any one of these ways of measuring amounts of ions into the other two, as shown here:

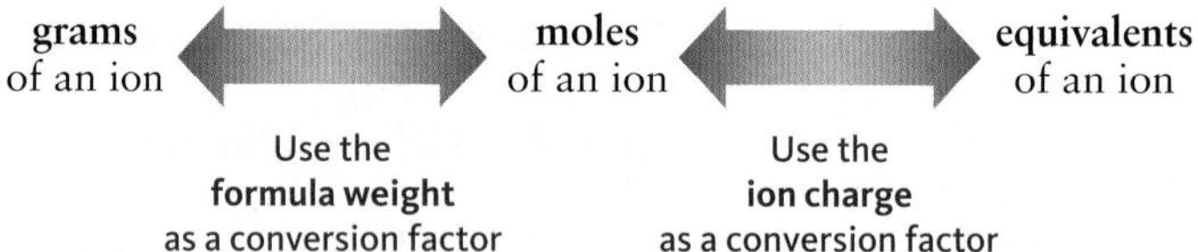

For example, suppose we have a solution that contains 2.00 g of carbonate ions (CO_3^{2-}). How many equivalents do we have? We cannot convert a mass directly into equivalents, but we can convert the mass into moles. To do so, we need the formula weight of CO_3^{2-}:

$$\begin{array}{lrl} 1 \text{ C:} & 1 \times 12.01 = & 12.01 \text{ amu} \\ 3 \text{ O:} & 3 \times 16.00 = & 48.00 \text{ amu} \\ \hline \text{total:} & & 60.01 \text{ amu} \end{array}$$

The formula weight tells us that 1 mol of CO_3^{2-} equals 60.01 g. We use this relationship as a conversion factor to convert 2.00 g into moles.

$$2.00 \cancel{\text{g}} \times \frac{1 \text{ mol}}{60.01 \cancel{\text{g}}} = 0.03332778 \text{ mol}$$ calculator answer, but don't round off yet

The charge on the carbonate ion is −2, so 1 mol of this ion equals 2 Eq. This relationship allows us to convert 0.03332778 mol into the corresponding number of equivalents:

$$0.03332778 \cancel{\text{mol}} \times \frac{2 \text{ Eq}}{1 \cancel{\text{mol}}} = 0.06665556 \text{ Eq}$$ calculator answer

$$= 0.0667 \text{ Eq}$$ rounded to three significant figures

Our solution contains 0.0667 Eq of carbonate ions. This small number would normally be expressed in milliequivalents. Remember that the metric prefix *milli-* means $^1/_{1000}$ of the base unit, so a milliequivalent is 1/1000 of an equivalent. Converting equivalents into milliequivalents is just like converting grams into milligrams: we must move the decimal point three places to the right. Our solution therefore contains 66.7 mEq of carbonate ions.

Sample Problem 5.15 illustrates the reverse conversion, translating a number of milliequivalents into the corresponding number of grams.

Sample Problem 5.15

Converting equivalents into mass

A solution contains 25 mEq of citrate ions ($C_6H_5O_7^{3-}$). How many grams of citrate does the solution contain?

SOLUTION

STEP 1: Identify the original measurement and the final unit.

The problem gives us a number of milliequivalents and asks us to calculate a number of grams. However, we cannot convert milliequivalents directly to grams, so we need to plan a multiple-step strategy. Our first step will be to convert milliequivalents into equivalents. Once we know the number of equivalents, we can convert that into the number of moles, because the ion charge tells us that 1 mol of this ion equals 3 Eq. Finally, we can convert moles into grams using the formula weight of citrate ion. Our strategy is

25 mEq → convert to → ? Eq → convert to → ? mol → convert to → ? g

STEP 2: Write conversion factors that relate the two units.

We can write conversion factors for each of these unit conversions. The two conversion factors that relate milliequivalents to equivalents are

$$\frac{1000 \text{ mEq}}{1 \text{ Eq}} \quad \text{and} \quad \frac{1 \text{ Eq}}{1000 \text{ mEq}}$$

We can also convert milliequivalents into equivalents using the metric railroad.

The charge on citrate ion is −3, so 1 mol of citrate equals 3 Eq.

$$\frac{3 \text{ Eq}}{1 \text{ mol}} \quad \text{and} \quad \frac{1 \text{ mol}}{3 \text{ Eq}}$$

The formula weight of $C_6H_5O_7^{3-}$ is 189.10 amu, so 1 mol of this ion weighs 189.10 g.

$$\frac{189.10 \text{ g}}{1 \text{ mol}} \quad \text{and} \quad \frac{1 \text{ mol}}{189.10 \text{ g}}$$

STEP 3: Choose the conversion factors that allow you to cancel units.

Now we can set up our conversion factors so that the units cancel out.

$$25 \text{ mEq} \times \frac{1 \text{ Eq}}{1000 \text{ mEq}} \times \frac{1 \text{ mol}}{3 \text{ Eq}} \times \frac{189.10 \text{ g}}{1 \text{ mol}}$$

Milliequivalents cancel here.
Equivalents cancel here.
Moles cancel here.

STEP 4: Do the math and round your answer.

Finally, we cancel units and do the arithmetic.

$$25 \cancel{\text{mEq}} \times \frac{1 \cancel{\text{Eq}}}{1000 \cancel{\text{mEq}}} \times \frac{1 \cancel{\text{mol}}}{3 \cancel{\text{Eq}}} \times \frac{189.10 \text{ g}}{1 \cancel{\text{mol}}} = 1.57583333 \text{ g}$$ calculator answer

$$= 1.6 \text{ g}$$ rounding to two significant figures

The solution contains 1.6 g of citrate ions. Note that we could also have solved this problem by doing one conversion at a time; we would find that the solution contains 0.025 Eq of citrate, which equals 0.0083333333 mol, which equals 1.6 g.

TRY IT YOURSELF: *A solution contains 0.166 Eq of NH_4^+ ions. How many grams is this?*

For additional practice, try Core Problems 5.39 and 5.44.

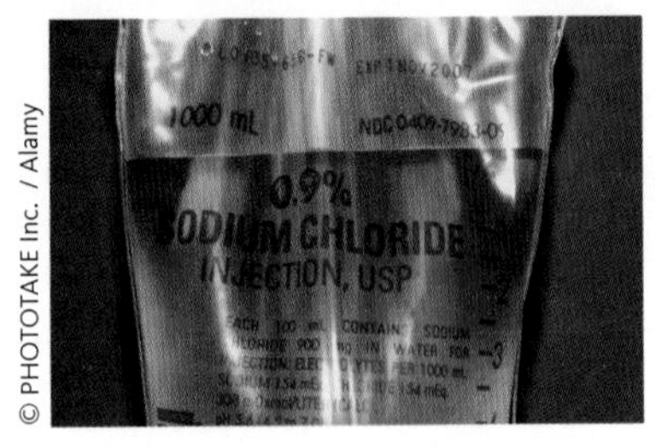

In this IV solution, the amounts of sodium and chloride ions are given in mEq.

Concentrations of Ions Can Be Expressed Using Equivalents

Concentrations of ions in body fluids and in electrolyte solutions are often expressed in milliequivalents per liter. We can calculate such a concentration by dividing the number of equivalents of solute by the volume of the solution. For instance, if we have 5.0 L of a solution that contains 225 mEq of Cl^-, the concentration of chloride ions in the solution is 45 mEq/L.

$$\frac{225 \text{ mEq}}{5.0 \text{ L}} = 45 \text{ mEq/L}$$

Sample Problem 5.16 shows how we can calculate the concentration of an ion in milliequivalents per liter starting from the mass of the ion and the solution volume.

Sample Problem 5.16

Calculating a concentration in milliequivalents per liter

A solution contains 2.50 g of sulfate ions, dissolved in enough water to give a total volume of 100.0 mL. Calculate the concentration of sulfate in this solution in milliequivalents per liter.

SOLUTION

STEP 1: Determine the units you must use.

As in any problem where we must calculate a concentration, we start by working out the units we must use to express the amounts of solute and solution. The problem asks for a concentration in milliequivalents per liter, so the amount of solute (sulfate ions) must be in milliequivalents and the amount of solution must be in liters. We are given the mass of sulfate ions, so we must convert from grams to milliequivalents. As in Sample Problem 5.15, we must do this conversion in three steps. We must also convert the solution volume from milliliters into liters. Here is our strategy:

2.50 g of SO_4^{2-} → convert to → ? mol of SO_4^{2-} → convert to → ? Eq of SO_4^{2-} → convert to → ? mEq of SO_4^{2-}

100.0 mL of solution → convert to → ? L of solution

divide → ? mEq/L

STEP 2: Convert the amounts into the correct units.

The chemical formula of sulfate is SO_4^{2-} and its formula weight is 96.06 amu. Using the formula and the charge, we can write the two relationships we need.

$$1 \text{ mol } SO_4^{2-} = 96.06 \text{ g } SO_4^{2-}$$
$$1 \text{ mol } SO_4^{2-} = 2 \text{ Eq } SO_4^{2-}$$

Next, we use these relationships as conversion factors to translate the number of grams into a number of milliequivalents. Here is the conversion written as a single step:

$$2.50 \text{ g} \times \frac{1 \text{ mol}}{96.06 \text{ g}} \times \frac{2 \text{ Eq}}{1 \text{ mol}} \times \frac{1000 \text{ mEq}}{1 \text{ Eq}} = 52.050802 \text{ mEq}$$

Our solution contains 52.050802 mEq of sulfate ions.

Next, we must convert the volume from milliliters to liters, moving the decimal point three places to the left.

$$100.0 \text{ L} = \mathbf{0.1000 \text{ mL}}$$

STEP 3: Divide the solute by the solvent.

We now have all of our amounts in the correct units. To calculate the concentration, we divide the amount of sulfate by the volume of the solution.

$$\frac{52.0508 \text{ mEq}}{0.1000 \text{ L}} = 520.508 \text{ mEq/L} \quad \text{calculator answer}$$

Finally, we round our answer to three significant figures. The concentration of sulfate ions in our solution is 521 mEq/L.

continued

TRY IT YOURSELF: *A solution contains 3.75 g of iron(III) ions, dissolved in enough water to give a total volume of 250 mL. Calculate the concentration of iron(III) in this solution in milliequivalents per liter.*

For additional practice, try Core Problems 5.47 and 5.48.

Body fluids contain a variety of electrolytes. Our bodies regulate the concentrations of ions in body fluids, but a variety of illnesses can cause ion concentrations to go outside their normal ranges. In such cases, health care workers use solutions of electrolytes to bring the ion concentrations back to normal. Some solutions are given by mouth, but most are administered directly into the bloodstream. Table 5.4 lists the electrolyte composition of blood plasma and some solutions that are commonly used in medicine. Note that *the total concentrations of cations and anions are equal when we express them in milliequivalents per liter.* This is another consequence of the rule of charge balance: any electrolyte that we dissolve in water must contain equal amounts of positive and negative charge.

What if we know the volume of a solution and its concentration in milliequivalents per liter, and we want to know the mass of the solute? It is normally best to begin by working out the number of milliequivalents of the solute, using the concentration as a conversion factor. For example, suppose we have 2.5 L of a solution that contains 50 mEq/L of calcium ions. The concentration tells us that each liter of solution contains

TABLE 5.4 Concentrations of Ions In Plasma and Three Clinically Important Solutions

BLOOD PLASMA*		LACTATED RINGER'S SOLUTION (GIVEN INTRAVENOUSLY TO TREAT SHOCK)		INTRAVENOUS MAINTENANCE SOLUTION (SUPPLIES ELECTROLYTES TO PATIENTS WHO CANNOT TAKE FOOD BY MOUTH)		ORAL REHYDRATION SOLUTION (REPLACES FLUIDS LOST IN SEVERE VOMITING AND DIARRHEA)	
Cations		**Cations**		**Cations**		**Cations**	
Na^+	140 mEq/L	Na^+	130 mEq/L	Na^+	40 mEq/L	Na^+	90 mEq/L
K^+	4 mEq/L	K^+	4 mEq/L	K^+	13 mEq/L	K^+	20 mEq/L
Ca^{2+}	5 mEq/L	Ca^{2+}	3 mEq/L	Mg^{2+}	3 mEq/L		
Mg^{2+}	2 mEq/L						
Total:	151 mEq/L	Total:	137 mEq/L	Total:	56 mEq/L	Total:	110 mEq/L
Anions		**Anions**		**Anions**		**Anions**	
Cl^-	103 mEq/L	Cl^-	109 mEq/L	Cl^-	40 mEq/L	Cl^-	80 mEq/L
HCO_3^-	26 mEq/L	$Lactate^-$	28 mEq/L	$Acetate^-$	16 mEq/L	$Citrate^{3-}$	30 mEq/L
Proteins	15 mEq/L						
$H_2PO_4^-$	1 mEq/L						
HPO_4^{2-}	2 mEq/L						
Other	4 mEq/L						
Total:	151 mEq/L	Total:	137 mEq/L	Total:	56 mEq/L	Total:	110 mEq/L

*The composition of blood plasma is variable. The values here are within the normal range. There are many different proteins in plasma, which have a range of ionic charges.

50 mEq of calcium. We can use this relationship as a conversion factor to calculate the number of milliequivalents of calcium ions in the entire 2.5 L.

$$2.5\,\cancel{L} \times \frac{50\text{ mEq}}{1\,\cancel{L}} = 125\text{ mEq}$$

Once we know the number of milliequivalents of calcium in the solution, we can convert to moles or to grams as necessary.

Sample Problem 5.17

Using a concentration in milliequivalents per liter to calculate the mass of solute

The concentration of sodium ions in an intravenous solution is 130 mEq/L. Calculate the mass of sodium in 250 mL of this solution.

SOLUTION

Let's plan a strategy for solving this problem. The concentration allows us to relate liters of solution to milliequivalents of Na^+. However, we are given the volume in milliliters, and we must find the mass of Na^+ (probably in grams). Here is a possible pathway that will lead to an answer:

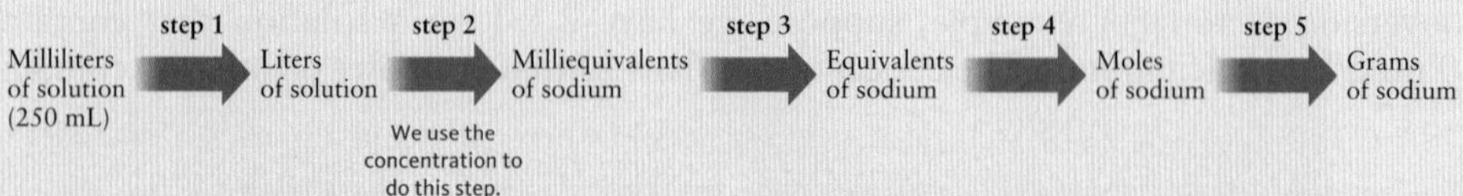

STEP 1: We must start by converting our volume of solution from milliliters to liters, so we can use the concentration. To convert milliliters into liters, we move the decimal point three places to the left.

$$0250.\text{ mL} = \mathbf{0.25\text{ L}}$$

• Steps 2, 4, and 5 use the unit conversion method of problem 1.

STEP 2: The concentration of Na^+ in this solution is 130 mEq/L, which means that one liter of solution contains 130 mEq of Na^+ ions. We can write this relationship as a pair of conversion factors.

$$\frac{130\text{ mEq Na}^+}{1\text{ L}} \quad \text{and} \quad \frac{1\text{ L}}{130\text{ mEq Na}^+}$$

We actually have 0.25 L of solution, so we must use one of these conversion factors to translate liters of solution into milliequivalents of sodium ions. To cancel our units correctly, we use the first of these conversion factors.

$$0.25\,\cancel{L} \times \frac{130\text{ mEq Na}^+}{1\,\cancel{L}} = 32.5\text{ mEq Na}^+$$

We now know that our solution contains 32.5 mEq of sodium. The remaining steps change this into a number of grams.

STEP 3: Now we convert milliequivalents into equivalents. Moving our decimal point three places to the left, we find that we have 0.0325 Eq of Na^+ in our solution.

$$0032.5\text{ mEq} = \mathbf{0.0325\text{ Eq}}$$

STEP 4: Next, we convert equivalents into moles. The charge on a sodium ion is +1, so one equivalent of Na^+ equals one mole. Using this relationship as a conversion factor, we get

$$0.0325\,\cancel{\text{Eq}} \times \frac{1\text{ mol}}{1\,\cancel{\text{Eq}}} = 0.0325\text{ mol}$$

continued

STEP 5: Our final conversion step is to translate 0.0325 mol of Na^+ into grams. The formula weight of Na^+ is 22.99 amu, so one mole of sodium ions weighs 22.99 g. Using this relationship as a conversion factor gives us

$$0.0325 \text{ mol} \times \frac{22.99 \text{ g}}{1 \text{ mol}} = 0.747175 \text{ g} \quad \text{calculator answer}$$

Finally, we round the answer to three significant figures. The solution contains 0.747 g of Na^+ (747 mg).

TRY IT YOURSELF: *The concentration of calcium ions in an intravenous solution is 5.0 mEq/L. How many grams of calcium are there in 25 L of this solution?*

For additional practice, try Core Problems 5.49 and 5.50.

Our discussion of equivalents has left one loose end. If we wanted to prepare a solution that contained, say, 5 mEq/L of Ca^{2+}, how could we do it? A calculation tells us that we need 0.1 g of Ca^{2+} for each liter of solution (try this yourself). However, *we cannot simply weigh out 0.1 g of calcium ions.* Ions can only occur in ionic compounds, and ionic compounds must obey the rule of charge balance. We must therefore use an ionic compound such as $CaCl_2$ to prepare our solution. This creates a new problem: how much $CaCl_2$ will we need in order to get 0.1 g of Ca^{2+}? You will learn how to answer this question when we explore the relationships between masses of chemical substances in the next chapter.

You have seen several ways of expressing concentration in this chapter. Table 5.5 lists some of the most common concentration units. For illustration, it also shows the plasma concentration of two solutes: urea (N_2H_4CO, a product of the breakdown of amino acids) and sodium chloride.

TABLE 5.5 The Relationships between Common Concentration Units

Unit	Definition	Plasma Concentration of NaCl*	Plasma Concentration of Urea
Percentage (w/v)	Grams of solute in 100 mL of solution	0.60% (w/v)	0.025% (w/v)
Milligrams per deciliter (mg/dL)	Milligrams of solute in 1 dL (100 mL) of solution	600 mg/dL	25 mg/dL
Parts per million (ppm)	Micrograms of solute in 1 mL of solution	6000 ppm	250 ppm
Parts per billion (ppb)	Nanograms of solute in 1 mL of solution	6,000,000 ppb	250,000 ppb
Molarity (M)	Moles of solute in 1 L of solution	0.103 M	0.0042 M
Milliequivalents per liter (mEq/L)	Milliequivalents of solute in 1 L of solution	103 mEq/L of Na^+ 103 mEq/L of Cl^-	*Not used for nonelectrolytes*

*The total concentration of Na^+ in plasma is 140 mEq/L. The table gives the concentration of sodium that is associated with Cl^-.

CORE PROBLEMS

5.37 If a solution contains 0.2 mol of CO_3^{2-}, how many equivalents does it contain?

5.38 If a solution contains 0.1 mol of PO_4^{3-}, how many equivalents does it contain?

5.39 A solution contains 0.15 Eq of Mg^{2+} ions.
a) How many moles of Mg^{2+} does this solution contain?
b) How many grams of Mg^{2+} does this solution contain?

5.40 A solution contains 0.020 Eq of SO_4^{2-} ions.
a) How many moles of SO_4^{2-} does this solution contain?
b) How many grams of SO_4^{2-} does this solution contain?

5.41 a) Convert 6.25 g of Ca^{2+} into equivalents and into milliequivalents.
b) Convert 27.3 g of $C_4H_4O_4^{2-}$ (succinate ions) into equivalents and into milliequivalents.

continued

5.42 a) Convert 3.50 g of Fe^{3+} into equivalents and into milliequivalents.
b) Convert 8.50 g of PO_4^{3-} into equivalents and into milliequivalents.

5.43 a) A solution contains 127 mEq of Cu^{2+}. How many grams is this? How many milligrams?
b) A solution contains 34 mEq of CO_3^{2-}. How many grams is this? How many milligrams?

5.44 a) A solution contains 65 mEq of Mn^{2+}. How many grams is this? How many milligrams?
b) A solution contains 336 mEq of $C_3H_2O_4^{2-}$ (malonate ions). How many grams is this? How many milligrams?

5.45 You have a 0.25 M solution of $CaCl_2$. Calculate the concentrations of Ca^{2+} and Cl^- in this solution, in milliequivalents per liter.

5.46 You have a 0.037 M solution of K_2SO_4. Calculate the concentrations of K^+ and SO_4^{2-} ion this solution, in milliequivalents per liter.

5.47 A solution contains 2.88 g of sulfate ions in a total volume of 3.38 L. Calculate the concentration of sulfate ions in each of the following units:
a) Eq/L b) mEq/L

5.48 A solution contains 6.33 g of calcium ions in a total volume of 850 mL. Calculate the concentration of calcium ions in each of the following units:
a) Eq/L b) mEq/L

5.49 You have 750 mL of a solution that contains 4.2 mEq/L of SO_4^{2-} ions. Calculate the mass of the sulfate ions in this solution.

5.50 You have 4500 mL of a solution that contains 2.5 mEq/L of $C_6H_5O_7^{3-}$ ions (citrate ions). Calculate the mass of the citrate ions in this solution.

OBJECTIVES: *Calculate the final volume or concentration of a solution after a dilution, and calculate the volumes of a concentrated solution and water needed to carry out a dilution.*

5.6 Dilution

Products ranging from orange juice to soup to household floor cleaner are sold in a form that requires adding water before use. For instance, the directions on a can of frozen orange juice instruct you to add three cans of water to each can of concentrate. The manufacturer evaporated some of the water from the juice to reduce its volume, so the resulting product has a much higher solute concentration than normal orange juice. When you add water, you lower the concentration of the juice to the correct value. Adding solvent to reduce the concentration of a solution is called **dilution**. Dilution is a common way of preparing solutions, and it is often more convenient and safer than preparing a solution from the pure solute and solvent.

Health Note: Many hospitals and clinics use concentrated potassium chloride solutions for immediate treatment of low blood potassium levels. However, an overdose of KCl can be lethal, because it interferes with heart action. Therefore, nurses only use diluted KCl solutions to maintain potassium levels once the patient is stabilized.

When we add water to an aqueous solution, the concentration of the solution always decreases, because the volume of the solution increases while the amount of solute remains unchanged. For instance, if we add 100 mL of water to 100 mL of 2% NaCl solution, the concentration of NaCl in the mixture is only 1%, as shown in Figure 5.17.

Dilution Obeys an Inverse Proportion

The relationship between the volume of a solution and its concentration is an **inverse proportion**, which means that increasing one value decreases the other. This relationship can be expressed by a mathematical rule, which we can write in words or in symbols:

initial concentration × initial volume = final concentration × final volume

$$C_1 \times V_1 = C_2 \times V_2$$

In the formula, C stands for concentration and V stands for volume. The subscript 1 tells us that we need to use the values before adding water (the initial values), and subscript 2 tells us that we must use the values after adding water (the final values). We can use any units of concentration and volume in this formula, as long as we use the same units on both sides.

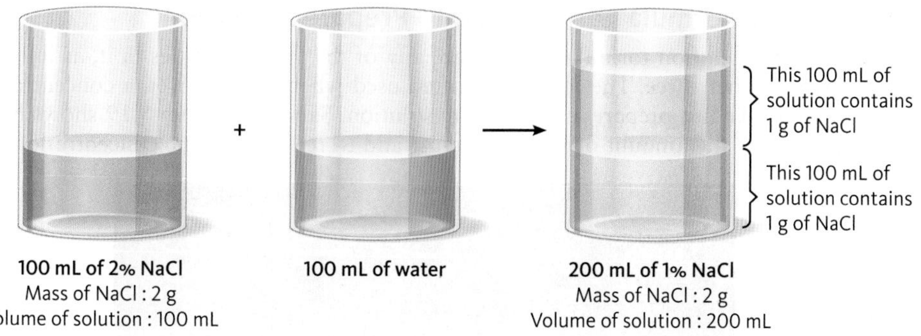

FIGURE 5.17 Diluting a sodium chloride solution.

Sample Problem **5.18**

Using the dilution formula to calculate a final concentration

If we add 50 mL of water to 25 mL of 0.9% (w/v) NaCl, what will be the concentration of the diluted solution?

SOLUTION

Our original solution has a concentration of 0.9%, and we have 25 mL of this solution. If we add 50 mL of water, we end up with 25 mL + 50 mL = 75 mL of solution as our final volume. We therefore know three of the four numbers in the dilution formula:

$C_1 = 0.9\%$ $\quad C_2 = ?$
$V_1 = 25\text{ mL}$ $\quad V_2 = 75\text{ mL}$

Our next step is to put these numbers into the formula.

$$0.9\% \times 25\text{ mL} = C_2 \times 75\text{ mL}$$

C_2 must be a percentage, since the two concentrations must have the same units. The most efficient way to find the correct value of C_2 is to divide both sides of this equation by 75 mL.

$$\frac{(0.9\% \times 25\text{ mL})}{75\text{ mL}} = \frac{(C_2 \times 75_2\text{ mL})}{75\text{ mL}}$$

The number 75 cancels out in the right-hand fraction, and we can cancel milliliters from both sides. Doing so leaves us with C_2 on the right side of our equation.

On this side of the equation, we are canceling the **unit** (mL).

$$\frac{(0.9\% \times 25\text{ }\cancel{\text{mL}})}{75\text{ }\cancel{\text{mL}}} = \frac{(C_2 \times \cancel{75\text{ mL}})}{\cancel{75\text{ mL}}}$$

On this side of the equation, we are canceling the **entire measurement** (75 mL).

$$\frac{(0.9\% \times 25)}{75} = C_2$$

The only unit that remains on the left side is the percent sign, so our answer will be a percentage, as it should be. We finish our solution by doing the arithmetic on the left side; multiply 0.9 by 25, and then divide the answer by 75.

$$\frac{(0.9\% \times 25)}{75} = \frac{22.5}{75}\% = C_2$$

$$0.3\% = C_2$$

Finally, we attach the (w/v) label. The concentration of the diluted solution is 0.3% (w/v).

TRY IT YOURSELF: *If you add 100 mL of water to 20 mL of 5.0% (v/v) alcohol, what will be the final concentration of the solution?*

For additional practice, try Core Problems 5.51 and 5.54.

The Dilution Formula Can Be Used to Prepare a Solution

We can use the dilution formula to calculate any of the four quantities in it, as long as we know the other three. The formula is often used when we are given a concentrated solution and asked to prepare a more dilute solution. Sample Problem 5.19 shows how we can calculate the amount of water we must add to reach a specific concentration.

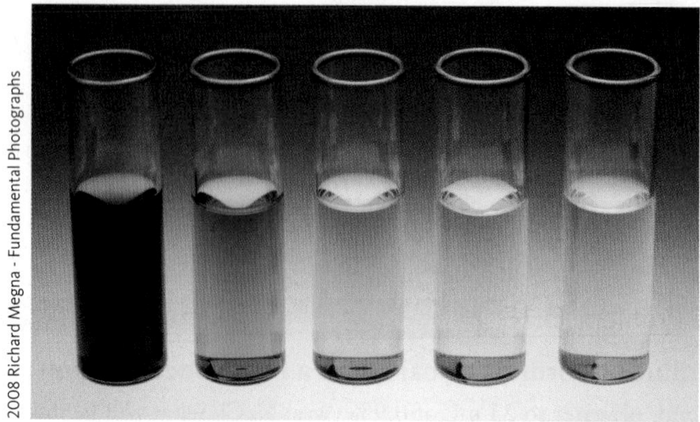

2008 Richard Megna - Fundamental Photographs

Dilution of copper (II) nitrate. Each solution is 10 times more dilute than the previous one.

Sample Problem **5.19**

Using the dilution formula to calculate the amount of added solvent

We have 30 mL of a solution that contains 100 ppm of iron. How much water must we add if we want to dilute this solution to a final concentration of 20 ppm?

SOLUTION

The dilution formula cannot give us the amount of water that we must add, but we can use it to calculate the *total* volume of our diluted solution. To start, we need to list the values we know.

$C_1 = 100$ ppm $C_2 = 20$ ppm
$V_1 = 30$ mL $V_2 = ?$

Now we substitute these into the dilution formula.

$$100 \text{ ppm} \times 30 \text{ mL} = 20 \text{ ppm} \times V_2$$

To calculate V_2, we divide both sides by 20 ppm, cancel units, and do the arithmetic.

$$\frac{(100 \cancel{\text{ppm}} \times 30 \text{ mL})}{20 \cancel{\text{ppm}}} = \frac{(\cancel{20 \text{ ppm}} \times V_2)}{\cancel{20 \text{ ppm}}}$$

$$\frac{(100 \times 30 \text{ mL})}{20} = V_2$$

$$\frac{3000 \text{ mL}}{20} = V_2$$

$$150 \text{ mL} = V_2$$

The final volume of this solution must be 150 mL. This is not our final answer, though, because the problem asked for the amount of water that we must add. We started with 30 mL of the concentrated solution, and we must end up with 150 mL, so we must add 150 mL − 30 mL = 120 mL of water. (See Figure 5.18.)

TRY IT YOURSELF: *You have 100 mL of a 10% (w/v) solution of sulfuric acid. How much water must you add if you want to dilute this solution to a final concentration of 2.5%?*

For additional practice, try Core Problems 5.55 and 5.56.

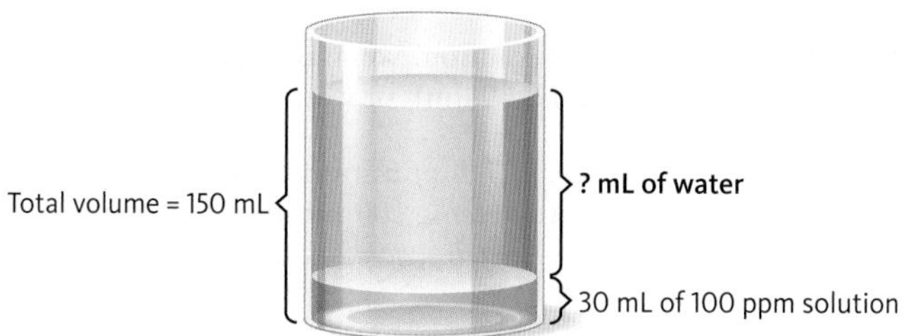

FIGURE 5.18 Calculating the amount of water to add in a dilution.

Health Note: Intravenous solutions of antibiotics and other medications are often diluted with isotonic NaCl or dextrose as they are administered; this reduces the concentration of the active medication to a safe level.

In Sample Problem 5.20, we are given the volume and concentration of the solution we want to make, and we must work out the volume of the concentrated solution that we need.

Sample Problem 5.20

Using the dilution formula to calculate the initial volume

We have a bottle of 2.0 M NaI, and we must use this solution to prepare 100 mL of 0.12 M NaI. How much of the 2.0 M NaI solution must we use, and how much water should we add?

SOLUTION

Figure 5.19 may help you visualize this problem. We must end up with 100 mL of diluted solution, and we don't know how much of the concentrated (2.0 M) solution to use.

FIGURE 5.19 Calculating the initial volume in a dilution.

Again, we start by listing the values that we know.

$C_1 = 2.0\text{ M}$ $\quad C_2 = 0.12\text{ M}$
$V_1 = ?$ $\quad V_2 = 100\text{ mL}$

Next, we substitute into the dilution formula.

$$2.0\text{ M} \times V_1 = 0.12\text{ M} \times 100\text{ mL}$$

To solve this, we divide both sides of the equation by 2.0 M. We always want to eliminate the number that is *next to our unknown* (V_1 in this case), regardless of which side of the equation our unknown lies on.

$$\frac{(\cancel{2.0\text{ M}} \times V_1)}{\cancel{2.0\text{ M}}} = \frac{(0.12\ \cancel{\text{M}} \times 100\text{ mL})}{2.0\ \cancel{\text{M}}}$$

$$V_1 = \frac{(0.12 \times 100\text{ mL})}{2.0}$$

$$V_1 = \frac{12\text{ mL}}{2.0}$$

$$V_1 = 6.0\text{ mL}$$

continued

We will need **6.0 mL** of the 2.0 M NaI solution. We must then add enough water to reach a total volume of 100 mL, so we will add **94 mL of water.**

• If the original solution is very concentrated, the volume of the original solution plus the volume of water may not add up to the final volume. This is rarely a concern in medical applications.

TRY IT YOURSELF: *You need to prepare 1 L of a solution that contains 3 mEq/L of magnesium by diluting a solution that contains 100 mEq/L of magnesium. How much of this solution must you use, and how much water must you add to it?*

For additional practice, try Core Problems 5.57 and 5.58.

CORE PROBLEMS

5.51 a) You have 100 mL of 0.50 M sodium lactate solution. If you add water until the total volume reaches 750 mL, what will be the molarity of sodium lactate in the resulting solution?

b) You have 33.5 mL of 2.50% (w/v) NaCl solution. If you add water until the total volume reaches 150.0 mL, what will be the percent concentration of NaCl in the resulting solution?

5.52 a) You have 5.00 mL of 1.60 M potassium bromide solution. If you add water until the total volume reaches 500.0 mL, what will be the molarity of potassium bromide in the resulting solution?

b) You have 32.5 μL of 0.300% (w/v) fructose solution. If you add water until the total volume reaches 250 μL, what will be the percent concentration of fructose in the resulting solution?

5.53 a) If you mix 50 mL of water with 10 mL of 1.14% (w/v) H_2SO_4, what will be the percent concentration of H_2SO_4 in the resulting solution?

b) If you mix 1.50 L of water with 250 mL of 0.60 M KI, what will be the molarity of KI in the resulting solution?

5.54 a) If you mix 100 mL of water with 25 mL of 4.45% (w/v) glucose ($C_6H_{12}O_6$), what will be the percent concentration of glucose in the resulting solution?

b) If you mix 500 mL of water with 1.25 L of 0.00600 M $HgCl_2$, what will be the molarity of $HgCl_2$ in the resulting solution?

5.55 Intravenous sodium lactate solutions contain 1.72% (w/v) sodium lactate in water. If you have 100 mL of 5.00% (w/v) sodium lactate, and you need to dilute it to 1.72%, what must the final volume be? How much water will you add?

5.56 You have 100 mL of solution that contains 1.25% (w/v) sodium citrate in water. You need to dilute this solution to a final concentration of 0.15% (w/v). What must the total volume of the solution be after adding water? How much water will you add?

5.57 You need to make 100 mL of 0.90% (w/v) sodium chloride solution. You have a bottle of 5.0% (w/v) sodium chloride solution, which you must dilute to the correct concentration. What volume of the 5.0% solution should you use, and how much water must you add to it?

5.58 You need to make 400 mL of 4.0% (w/v) NaOH solution. You have a bottle of 10.0% (w/v) NaOH solution, which you must dilute to the correct concentration. What volume of the 10.0% solution should you use, and how much water must you add to it?

CONNECTIONS

Physiological Dehydration

Water is truly the "elixir of life" on this planet, and all living things depend on it in more ways than we can count. In this chapter, you learned about the importance of having the right balance of water and dissolved solutes in your blood and cells. Your body takes in water whenever you eat or drink, and it loses water in urine, feces, perspiration, and exhaled air. Normally, these processes are in balance. If they are not, you either become dehydrated (too little water) or overhydrated (too much water). Your kidneys normally remove excess water rapidly—think of how quickly you need to urinate after you drink a large beverage—so overhydration is rarely a concern. However, your body can never completely stop the loss of water, so drinking enough water is always important to prevent dehydration.

Dehydration is a result of taking in less water than the body loses. Although it is possible to become dehydrated by simply failing to drink enough water, significant dehydration is generally a result of unusually rapid loss of water. A common cause of dehydration is sweating due to high temperatures or prolonged exercise. Some chemical compounds in food, such as ethanol (grain alcohol) and caffeine, stimulate the kidneys to produce excess urine and can cause dehydration. Diseases that affect the kidneys can produce dehydration if the kidney removes too much water or too little solute from the blood. Finally, a variety of gastrointestinal disorders can cause excessive loss of water through diarrhea or vomiting. Dehydration from severe diarrhea kills more than 4 million children every year, mostly in regions where access to health care is limited. Most of these deaths could be prevented with a simple, inexpensive oral rehydration mixture, a powder that contains electrolytes and sugar. The powder is mixed with water and given to the child as needed to counteract the loss of water.

The body's first response to excess water loss is the sensation of thirst. However, humans (unlike other animals) do not always respond to thirst, and the thirst sensation is not sufficient to counteract severe, rapid water loss. The kidneys also respond by moving less water from the blood into the urine, so the urine becomes more concentrated. People who are mildly to moderately dehydrated produce little urine, and the urine is deep amber colored rather than pale yellow. If dehydration becomes severe, the person becomes dizzy, stops sweating, gets muscle cramps, and (ironically) starts vomiting, which makes the situation worse. Dehydration that reaches this stage is a medical emergency and is fatal if not treated immediately.

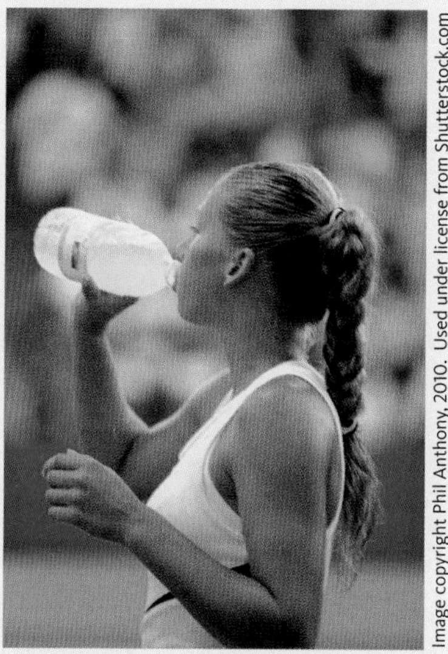

Athletes rely on sports beverages to replace water, fuel (carbohydrate), and electrolytes during strenuous exercise.

Water is crucial to anyone engaged in athletics or strenuous exercise. A water loss amounting to just 1% of an athlete's body weight has an adverse effect on the athlete's performance. For a 70-kg (154-pound) athlete, this means losing 700 g (about 3 cups) of water during an event, and in warm weather the athlete may lose this much water in as little as half an hour. People engaged in strenuous exercise should drink small amounts of water often, not waiting until they feel thirsty. In addition, because perspiration contains several electrolytes, beverages that contain electrolytes such as sodium, potassium, and chloride maintain the body's water balance more effectively than pure water during long periods of exercise. However, when you look at the displays of sports beverages, remember that the most important ingredient by far is the one that comes from your tap.

Key Terms

Avogadro's number – 5.2
concentration – 5.1
dialysis – 5.4
diffusion – 5.4
dilution – 5.6
equivalent (Eq) – 5.5
formula weight (molecular weight) – 5.2
hypertonic – 5.4
hypotonic – 5.4
inverse proportion – 5.6
isotonic – 5.4
molar mass – 5.2
molarity (molar concentration) – 5.3
mole (mol) – 5.2
osmosis – 5.4
osmotic pressure – 5.4
percent concentration – 5.1
semipermeable membrane – 5.4
tonicity – 5.4
volume (v/v) percentage – 5.1
weight per volume (w/v) percentage – 5.1

SUMMARY OF OBJECTIVES

Now that you have read the chapter, test yourself on your knowledge of the objectives using this summary as a guide.

Section 5.1: Calculate and use percent concentrations, and interpret other common concentration units involving masses of solute.

- The concentration of a solution is the amount of solute that is dissolved in a fixed amount of solution.
- Percent concentration is the mass or volume of solute that is dissolved in 100 mL of solution.
- Clinical concentrations are often expressed as a mass of solute per deciliter of solution.
- Very low concentrations can be expressed in parts per million (milligrams of solute per liter of solution) or parts per billion (micrograms of solute per liter of solution).

Section 5.2: Use the mole concept to express numbers of formula units, and interconvert moles and masses.

- One mole of any substance equals the formula weight of that substance expressed in grams.
- One mole of any substance contains 6.022×10^{23} formula units (Avogadro's number).
- The molar mass can be used to interconvert grams and moles of a substance.

Section 5.3: Calculate and use molarities.

- The molarity of a solution (abbreviated mol/L or M) is the number of moles of solute divided by the number of liters of solution.

Section 5.4: Determine the direction of osmosis and dialysis, and predict the effect of a solution on red blood cells using the overall molarity of the solution.

- When two substances are mixed, they diffuse until the solute is evenly distributed throughout the solution.
- Osmosis is the net flow of water across a semipermeable membrane, and it occurs when the solutions on either side of a membrane have different molarities.
- Osmosis depends on the overall molarity of solute particles after all electrolytes have dissociated.
- Isotonic solutions have an overall molarity around 0.28 M, and they do not affect red blood cells.
- Red blood cells hemolyze in hypotonic solutions (molarities below 0.28 M) and crenate in hypertonic solutions (molarities above 0.28 M).
- Dialysis is the flow of solute across a membrane, and it occurs when the concentrations of the solute on each side of the membrane are not equal.

Section 5.5: Interconvert moles and equivalents for ionic solutes, and use equivalents to describe the concentration of an ion in a solution.

- An equivalent is the amount of an ion that has the same charge as 1 mol of Na^+ or Cl^-.
- The mass of 1 Eq is the formula weight (expressed in grams) divided by the ion charge.
- Physiological concentrations of ions are expressed in equivalents or milliequivalents per liter.
- The rule of charge balance requires that any solution contain equal numbers of equivalents of positive and negative ions.

Section 5.6: Calculate the final volume or concentration of a solution in a dilution, and calculate the volumes of a concentrated solution and water needed to carry out a dilution.

- When water is added to an existing solution, the concentration of the solution decreases. This process is called dilution.
- Dilution always obeys the relationship $C_1 \times V_1 = C_2 \times V_2$. This formula can be used to calculate any one of the four quantities as long as the other three are known.
- The volume of water that must be added is the difference between the final volume (V_2) and the initial volume (V_1).

Concept Questions

OWL Online homework for this chapter may be assigned in OWL.
* indicates more challenging problems.

5.59 Define each of the following concentration units:

a) percentage (w/v) b) percentage (v/v)
c) molarity d) ppm
e) mg/dL f) ppb
g) mEq/L

5.60 The concentration of lead in drinking water is typically expressed in parts per billion. Why isn't this concentration expressed as a percentage?

5.61 Charlene needs to prepare a 30% (v/v) solution of ethanol in water. She mixes 30 mL of ethanol with 100 mL of water.

a) Why doesn't this produce a 30% (v/v) solution?
b) How could Charlene have made the solution correctly?

5.62 You have a piece of aluminum and a piece of iron. The two pieces have the same mass. Which contains more atoms? Explain your answer.

5.63 The chemical formula of calcium oxide is CaO. Does this mean that calcium oxide contains equal weights of calcium and oxygen? Explain your answer.

5.64 You have two boxes. Box A contains 1 mol of C_2Cl_4, and box B contains 1 mol of C_2Cl_6. Answer the following questions about the two boxes, and explain each of your answers:

a) Which box contains more molecules?
b) Which box contains more atoms?
c) Which box contains more carbon atoms?
d) Which box contains more chlorine atoms?
e) Which box contains more grams of matter?

5.65 Samson sees a bottle labeled "2 M HCl" in his laboratory. He tells Pierre that this bottle contains two moles of HCl. Is this correct? If not, what can you say about the number of moles of HCl in the bottle?

5.66 If you open a chocolate bar in a crowded room, everyone in the room will smell the chocolate within a few minutes. Explain how this is an illustration of diffusion.

5.67 You can make a pickle by putting a cucumber into an aqueous solution that contains salt, vinegar, and some flavoring ingredients.

a) Why does the cucumber shrink as it sits in this solution?
b) Why does the cucumber taste like vinegar after a while?
c) Why doesn't the cucumber become salty?

5.68 Why is it dangerous to inject pure water directly into a person's bloodstream, even if the person is dehydrated?

5.69 A red blood cell is placed into a 1.0% (w/v) solution of sodium lactate. The cell rapidly swells and bursts.

a) Why did the cell do this?
b) What does this observation tell you about the percent concentration of isotonic sodium lactate solutions?

5.70 Ching-Mei says, "Isotonic solutions have the same concentration as blood plasma." Tyrone then asks how this can be true, since isotonic NaCl is 0.9% (w/v) but isotonic glucose is 5% (w/v). How should Ching-Mei respond?

5.71 Javier says, "Isotonic solutions always have a concentration around 0.28 M." LaShawndra then asks why the concentration of isotonic NaCl is only 0.14 M. How should Javier respond?

5.72 Ionic compounds that dissociate into three ions, such as Na_2CO_3 and $CaCl_2$, have isotonic concentrations around 0.09 M. Why is this?

5.73 What is the difference between osmosis and dialysis?

5.74 In the following diagram, solutions E and F are separated by a membrane that is permeable to water and to glucose, but is not permeable to starch.

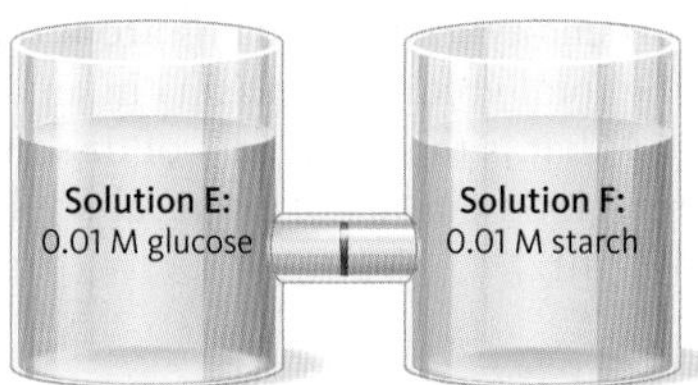

a) When the solutions are first put into their containers, does osmosis occur? If so, in which direction does it occur?
b) Which solute dialyzes, and in which direction does it move?
c) After a few minutes, does osmosis occur? If so, in which direction does it occur?

5.75 Why do electrolyte solutions always contain the same numbers of equivalents of cations and anions?

5.76 Complete the following statements by inserting the correct number:

a) One mole of Ca^{2+} ions is the same as _____ Eq of Ca^{2+} ions.
b) One mole of Ca^{2+} ions is the same as _____ g of Ca^{2+} ions.

5.77 If you add water to a 1% (w/v) solution of sugar, will the concentration of the solution increase, decrease, or remain the same? Explain your answer.

Summary and Challenge Problems

5.78 One cup (236 mL) of freshly squeezed orange juice contains around 120 mg of vitamin C. What is the concentration of vitamin C in orange juice when expressed in the following units?

a) percent
b) milligrams per deciliter
c) parts per million
d) molarity (the chemical formula of vitamin C is $C_6H_8O_6$)

5.79 You have a solution that contains 175 mEq/L of citrate ($C_6H_5O_7^{3-}$) ions. Calculate the concentration of citrate ions in this solution in each of the following units:

a) Eq/L b) M

5.80 *Calculate the concentration of citrate ions in the solution in Problem 5.79, using each of the following units:

a) % (w/v) b) ppm c) mg/dL

5.81 *Folic acid is an essential vitamin and is linked to the prevention of neural tube defects in developing embryos. One cup (236 mL) of fresh orange juice contains around 75 μg of folic acid. Calculate the concentration of folic acid in orange juice in each of the following units:

a) mg/dL b) μg/dL c) ppm d) ppb

5.82 *Blood plasma typically contains around 25 ppm of Mg^{2+}. The total volume of plasma in an adult is around 5.9 pints. What is the total mass of dissolved magnesium ions in the blood plasma of a typical adult? (One pint equals 473 mL.)

5.83 *Concentrations of nitrate above 45 ppm are considered hazardous to infants, because they interfere with the ability of the blood to carry oxygen. If you drink 8.0 fluid ounces of water that contains 45 ppm of nitrate, what mass of nitrate ions are you consuming?

5.84 a) If you have 50.0 g of calcium nitrate, how many moles of calcium nitrate do you have?
b) If you have 0.0875 mol of potassium phosphate, how many grams of potassium phosphate do you have?

5.85 A millimole (mmol) equals $^1/_{1000}$ of a mole. Convert 38 mmol of NaCl into the following units:

a) moles b) grams c) milligrams

5.86 *Which contains more atoms, 25.0 g of magnesium or 50.0 g of iron? Back up your answer with appropriate calculations.

5.87 *A solution is prepared by dissolving 2.5 ounces of $AgNO_3$ in enough water to make 32 fluid ounces of solution. Calculate the molarity of this solution. You may use the information in Tables 1.5 and 1.6.

5.88 You need to make a 0.28 M solution of glucose ($C_6H_{12}O_6$). You have 100 g of glucose available. If you use all of the glucose to make the solution, what will be the total volume of the solution?

5.89 *Boric acid (H_3BO_3) has been used to treat eye infections. Calculate the percent concentration of a 0.28 M solution of boric acid.

5.90 *What is the approximate molarity of an isotonic solution of $MgBr_2$?

5.91 *An isotonic solution contains glucose and KCl. The concentration of KCl is 0.08 M. What is the approximate molarity of glucose in this solution?

5.92 *A chemist intends to prepare 250 mL of an isotonic solution containing glucose ($C_6H_{12}O_6$) and KCl. If the chemist uses 1.25 g of KCl to prepare this solution, what mass of glucose must be used?

5.93 A solution contains 480 mg of SO_4^{2-}. Convert this into the following units:

a) g b) mol c) Eq d) mEq

5.94 A solution contains 80 mEq of Zn^{2+}. Convert this into the following units:

a) Eq b) mol c) g d) mg

5.95 A solution contains 2.0 mEq/L of $C_4H_4O_5^{2-}$ (malate ions).

a) How many milligrams of $C_4H_4O_5^{2-}$ are there in 350 mL of this solution?

b) The entire bottle of solution contains 0.52 g of $C_4H_4O_5^{2-}$ ions. What is the total volume of the solution in the bottle?

5.96 Lactated Ringer's solution contains 109 mEq/L of Cl^-. How many grams of chloride are there in 175 mL of this solution?

5.97 A solution contains 250 mg of Ca^{2+} in a total volume of 500 mL. Calculate the concentration of calcium in this solution in each of the following units:

a) M b) mEq/L c) mg/dL d) ppm

5.98 A bottle was filled with 80 mL of a solution that contained 62 ppb of lead. LaShawndra accidentally poured some water into the bottle. She measured the volume of the resulting solution and found it to be 98 mL. What is the concentration of lead in the diluted solution?

5.99 Frozen orange juice concentrate contains 166 mg/dL of vitamin C. If you mix one can of the concentrate with three cans of water, what will be the concentration of vitamin C in the resulting juice?

5.100 *Table salt is "manufactured" by evaporating ocean water: the water evaporates and the salt is left behind. Ocean water contains 2.7% (w/v) NaCl. If 10,000 gallons of ocean water is allowed to stand until its volume is reduced to 900 gallons, what will be the concentration of NaCl? (Hint: The dilution formula also works for evaporation of solvent from a solution.)

5.101 *You have 100 mL of 1.0 M NaCl. You need to add enough water to make this into an isotonic solution. How much water must you add?

6

Chemical Reactions

The day after Shanna was born, her parents noticed that the whites of her eyes had turned pale yellow. The next day, the palms of Shanna's hands began to turn yellowish as well. Shanna's pediatrician diagnosed her with physiological neonatal jaundice, a common and usually harmless condition in newborns, and ordered blood tests to monitor the concentration of bilirubin in her blood. Bilirubin is a deep yellow compound that is formed when the spleen breaks down the hemoglobin in aging red blood cells. The liver converts bilirubin into other compounds and secretes these compounds into the small intestine. Newborns must break down a lot of hemoglobin during their first days of life as they adjust to life outside the womb. In many newborns, the liver cannot process all of the bilirubin, so it builds up in the blood, discoloring the skin.

Making and breaking down bilirubin are examples of **chemical reactions**, in which the atoms in chemical compounds change the way that they are bonded to one another. All living organisms are constantly carrying out a host of chemical reactions throughout our lives, building and breaking down thousands of different compounds. Throughout the rest of this book, we look at different types of chemical reactions, many of which play a key role in our bodies.

When Shanna's bilirubin level continued to rise over the next couple of days, the pediatrician ordered that she be treated using phototherapy. In phototherapy, the infant's skin is exposed to a bright light for part of each day. The light disrupts some of the bonds in bilirubin, changing it into other compounds that the infant can excrete. After a week of phototherapy, Shanna's bilirubin level dropped significantly and the yellow color of her skin started to fade, and two weeks later her bilirubin level was in the normal range. Shanna suffered no ill effects from her jaundice.

OUTLINE

LABORATORY REQUISITION—CHEMISTRY

Test	Code	Test	Code
☐ Sodium	NA	☐ Fructosamine	FRU/ALB
☐ Potassium	K	☐ PSA	PSA
☐ Creatinine	CREAT	☐ Chloride	CL
☐ BUN	BUN	☐ Calcium	CA
☐ Glucose-fasting	GLUCF	☐ Phosphorus	PHOS
☐ Glucose-random	GLUCR	☐ Phenylalanine	PKU
☐ Hemoglobin A1C	HGBA1C	☐ Uric Acid	URIC

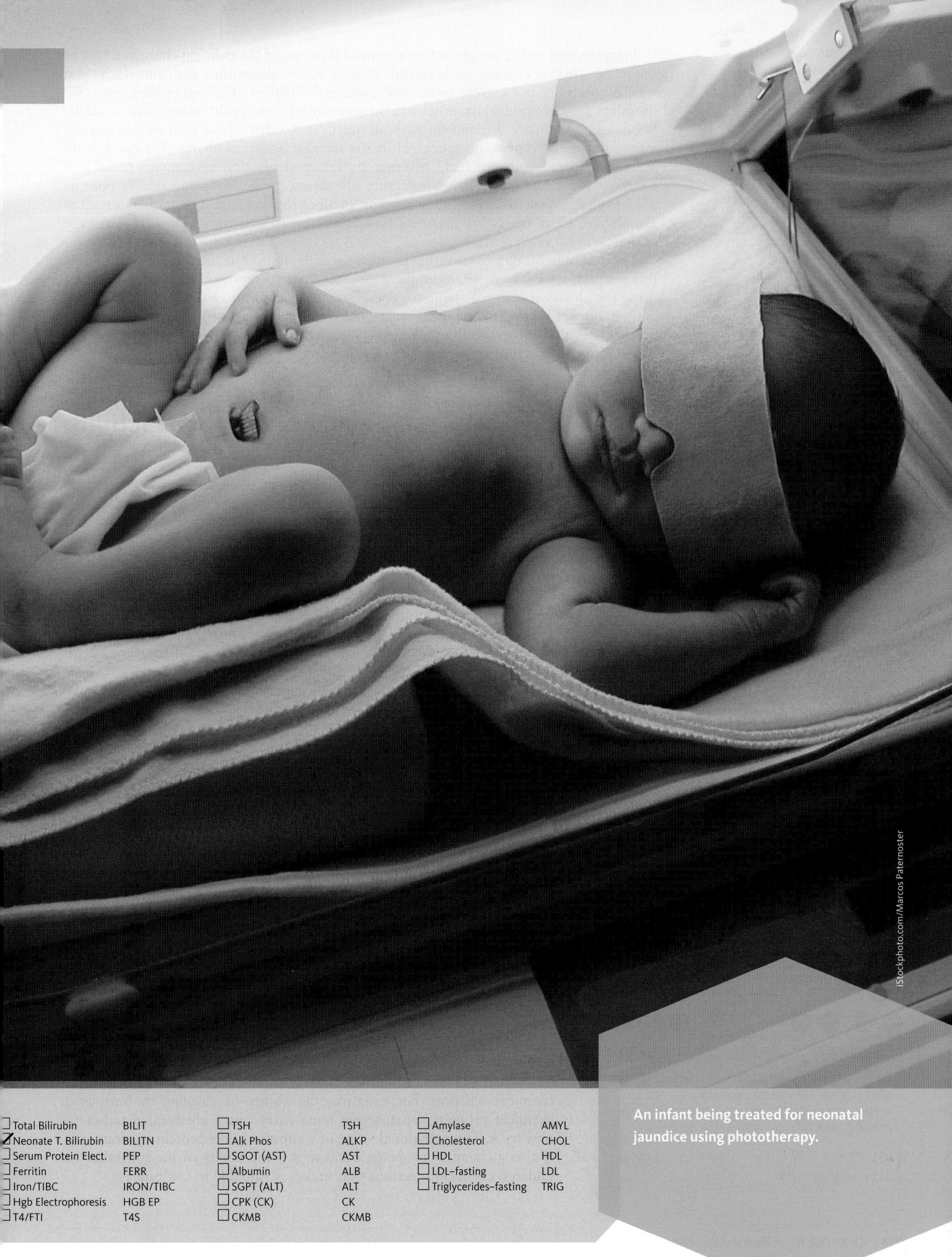

iStockphoto.com/Marcos Paternoster

An infant being treated for neonatal jaundice using phototherapy.

OWL Online homework for this chapter may be assigned in OWL.

From ancient times, people have recognized that one of the defining characteristics of the living world is change. Seeds sprout, flowers bloom and wither, and fruit ripens and rots. Animals are born, grow to maturity, and give birth to offspring of their own. We ourselves are changing constantly from the moment of conception, as we grow to adulthood, age, and finally die; and throughout our lives we change the food we eat and the air we breathe into new substances. Humans are also agents of change, for good or ill. We convert crude oil into fuel, solvents, asphalt, and plastics; we convert rocks into concrete, glass, and steel; we manufacture life-saving medications and deadly poisons alike from the substances we find around us. In all of these changes, chemical substances are altered, as atoms switch partners and bonds break and form. These changes are called chemical reactions.

Chemistry is fundamentally the attempt to understand chemical reactions, and in this chapter, we begin to examine them. We see how to represent chemical reactions using the chemical formulas we have encountered in previous chapters and how mass and energy are related to chemical reactions. We also look at why some reactions are much faster than others and at reactions that can be reversed. This chapter lays the foundation for much of the remainder of this book.

OBJECTIVE: *Determine whether a process is a physical change or a chemical change.*

6.1 Physical Changes and Chemical Reactions

Let us start by comparing two familiar processes: the boiling of water and the burning of a candle. Both of these processes require a high temperature, and in both cases, the original substance (water or candle wax) disappears. However, if we look more closely, we see a fundamental difference between the two. When we boil water, we convert liquid water into gaseous water. Both water and steam have the chemical formula H_2O, so boiling water does not affect the chemical bonds between the atoms that make up a water molecule. Burning a candle, on the other hand, changes the original candle wax into something quite different. Candle wax is a mixture of chemical compounds called paraffins, all of which are made from the elements carbon and hydrogen (a typical example is $C_{20}H_{42}$). When the wax burns, the end result is two new compounds, carbon dioxide and water. The original paraffins are no longer present.

Boiling and burning are examples of the two types of change that we observe on Earth. Processes that do not alter the chemical formulas of the starting materials, such as the boiling of water, are called **physical changes.** By contrast, the burning of a candle is a **chemical change**, in which the chemical formulas of the starting materials and final products differ. In a chemical change, more commonly referred to as a **chemical reaction**, atoms change the ways in which they are bonded to one another. Figure 6.1 illustrates the difference between a physical change (the boiling of water) and a chemical change (the burning of methane, the main compound in natural gas).

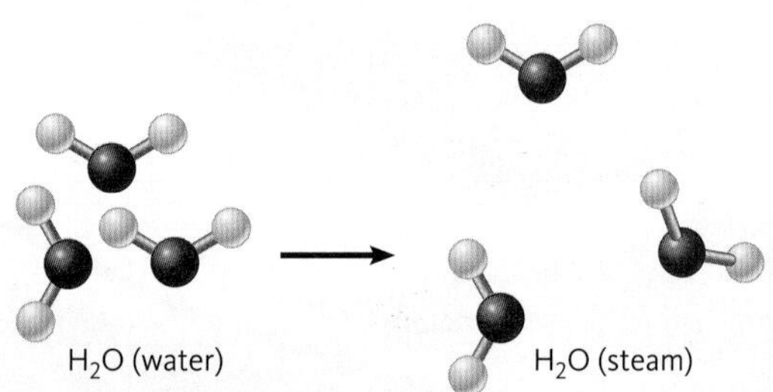

(a) Boiling water is a **physical change:** the chemical bonds do not change, so water and steam have the same chemical formula.

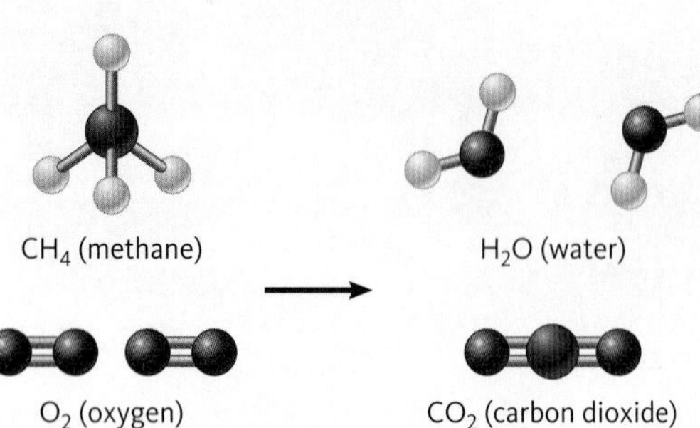

(b) Burning methane is a **chemical change:** the atoms change the way they are bonded to one another, so the starting materials and the final products have different chemical formulas.

FIGURE 6.1 The difference between (a) physical and (b) chemical changes.

Physical changes and chemical changes also differ in that we can readily reverse most physical changes, but we cannot undo most chemical changes. For instance, boiling is reversible, since we can easily change steam back into water by cooling it. By contrast, we cannot change carbon dioxide and water back into candle wax. Table 6.1 summarizes the differences between physical and chemical changes.

As we have seen, we can describe matter in a variety of ways. The properties that we have examined so far, such as color, mass, density, boiling point, and solubility, are called **physical properties.** A physical property is any attribute of a substance that can be measured or described without changing the chemical formula of the substance. On the other hand, some properties, called **chemical properties**, involve a chemical reaction. For example, the ability of gasoline to burn is a chemical property, because we must carry out a chemical reaction to observe it. The nutritional value of a substance like protein or vitamin C is also a chemical property, because it is the ability of the substance to undergo chemical reactions that makes it valuable to our bodies.

TABLE 6.1 Comparing Physical Changes and Chemical Reactions

Physical Change	Chemical Reaction
The starting material and the final product have the same chemical formula.	The starting materials and the final products have different chemical formulas.
The change can be reversed.	The change often cannot be reversed.
Examples: The boiling of water The melting of ice The dissolving of sugar in water The expansion of a gas when it is heated	Examples: The rusting of steel The digestion of food The burning of a candle

Charles D. Winters

Boiling water is a physical change because water and steam have the same chemical formula (H_2O).

Sample Problem **6.1**

Identifying physical and chemical changes

Which of the following is a physical change, and which is a chemical reaction?

a) Water evaporating from a glass

b) Gasoline burning in an engine

SOLUTION

a) The evaporation of water is a **physical change.** Liquid water turns into water vapor when it evaporates, but it does not change its chemical formula: both liquid and gaseous water are H_2O.

b) The burning of gasoline is a **chemical reaction.** The gasoline reacts with oxygen, producing products that have different chemical formulas from the original materials. (In fact, the products are carbon dioxide and water.)

TRY IT YOURSELF: *Which of the following is a physical change, and which is a chemical reaction?*

a) Starch being digested in your intestine

b) Alcohol dissolving in water

For additional practice, try Core Problems 6.1 and 6.2.

All of the changes we have looked at in Chapters 4 and 5 are physical changes, including heating and cooling, changes of state, expansion and contraction of gases, and dissolution of a solute in water. In each of these, a change in state or in some physical property such as volume or temperature occurs, but there is no change in the chemical formula or chemical properties of the substance. In this chapter, we explore chemical reactions, which change both the physical and the chemical properties of the starting materials. For example, candle wax can burn, but neither carbon dioxide nor water can do so. Most of the changes that occur in a living organism are chemical reactions; indeed, the growth and development of even the smallest bacterium involves a vast number of chemical changes.

All changes, both physical and chemical, are governed by two fundamental principles. The first of these, called the **law of mass conservation**, states that *in any change, the mass of the final products equals the mass of the starting materials.* The second principle states that *in any change, the number of atoms of each element remains constant.* The first of these principles was discovered by the French chemist Antoine Lavoisier in the late 1700s, and the second was a cornerstone of the atomic theory proposed by John Dalton in the early 1800s. Together, they form the foundation of chemistry.

CORE PROBLEMS

All Core Problems are paired and the answers to the blue odd-numbered problems appear in the back of the book.

6.1 Which of the following are physical changes, and which are chemical reactions?
a) You bend a piece of steel.
b) A piece of steel rusts.
c) Your body burns fat.
d) You compress the air in a bicycle pump.

6.2 Which of the following are physical changes, and which are chemical reactions?
a) A drop of alcohol evaporates.
b) A drop of alcohol catches fire and burns.
c) You dissolve some salt in water.
d) You digest a piece of pizza.

6.3 Which of the following are physical properties, and which are chemical properties?
a) Hydrogen burns if it is mixed with air.
b) Hydrogen is a gas at room temperature.
c) Hydrogen combines with nitrogen to make ammonia.
d) Hydrogen condenses at −253°C.

6.4 Which of the following are physical properties, and which are chemical properties?
a) The density of HgO is 11.1 g/mL.
b) If you heat HgO, it breaks down into pure elements.
c) HgO is poisonous.
d) HgO is an orange–red solid.

6.5 When you boil water, the water turns to steam. If you boil 5 g of water, how much does the resulting steam weigh?

6.6 If you heat chalk, it breaks down into lime (calcium oxide) and carbon dioxide. If you heat 10 g of chalk, what can you say about the weight of the lime you make? What can you say about the total weight of the lime and the carbon dioxide?

6.7 Does the following sentence describe a typical physical change or a typical chemical change?
"The starting materials and the products have different chemical formulas."

6.8 Does the following sentence describe a typical physical change or a typical chemical change?
"The change is reversible."

OBJECTIVE: *Write a balanced chemical equation to represent a chemical reaction.*

6.2 Chemical Equations

When chemists describe a chemical reaction, they write a symbolic representation called a **chemical equation**. Chemical equations allow us to keep track of which atoms are bonded to each other before and after the reaction, and they account for the number of atoms of each element. For example, let us look at the change that occurs when calcium and sulfur combine with each other to form a compound. Calcium, like most metals, is a shiny, silver-colored solid, and sulfur is a brittle, bright yellow solid. If we mix these two elements and heat the mixture gently, the elements turn into a white powder that has the chemical formula CaS. The chemical equation that corresponds to this reaction is

$$Ca + S \rightarrow CaS$$

The arrow in the equation means *become* or *turn into*. The chemical formulas to the left of the arrow represent the **reactants**, the substances that are present before the reaction occurs. The chemical formula to the right of the arrow represents the **product**. The plus sign tells us that the two reactants are independent substances (not bonded to each other) before the reaction. The entire chemical equation can be read as follows:

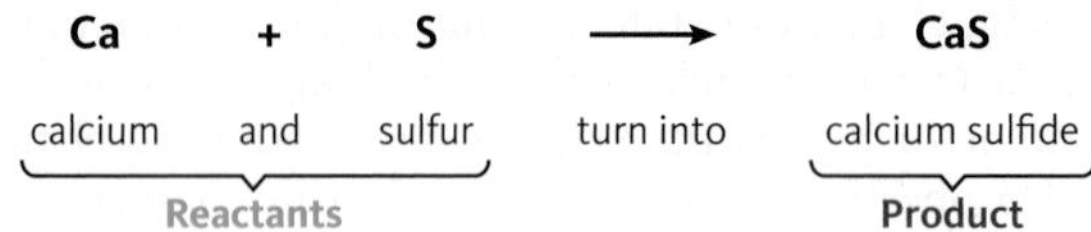

Each symbol represents a single atom of that element, so the chemical equation shows what happens to each atom.

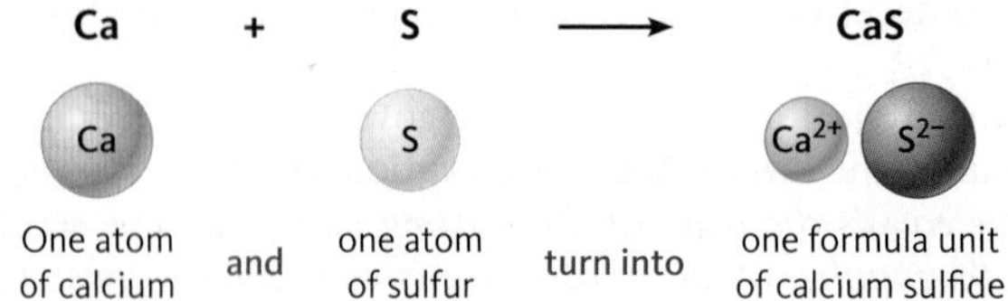

Note that although the charges on the atoms change, the number of each kind of atom does not. We start with one calcium atom and one sulfur atom, and we end with one calcium atom and one sulfur atom.

Coefficients Show the Number of Formula Units of Each Substance in a Reaction

Chemical equations also tell us how many formula units of each substance are used and formed in a reaction. For example, sodium reacts with sulfur to form a compound that has the formula Na_2S. This compound, called sodium sulfide, contains two atoms of sodium for each atom of sulfur. Therefore, to make one formula unit of sodium sulfide, we need to start with two sodium atoms. We show this by writing a 2 before the symbol for sodium.

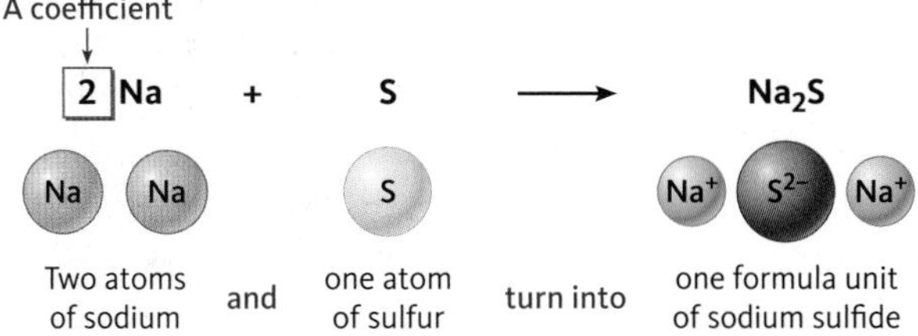

This number, which shows how many atoms of sodium we need, is called a **coefficient**.

You may be wondering why we did not write Na_2 to represent the two sodium atoms on the left side of the equation. Writing Na_2 means that there is a chemical bond between the two sodium atoms, which is not the case. By writing 2 Na on the left side, we show that we start with two *independent* sodium atoms.

Compare this with the reaction of hydrogen and sulfur. Here, too, one atom of sulfur reacts with two atoms of another element to form a compound having a 2:1 atom ratio. However, as we saw in Chapter 3, hydrogen atoms pair up to form covalently bonded molecules. The two hydrogen atoms are not independent, and we show this in our equation by writing H_2 instead of 2 H.

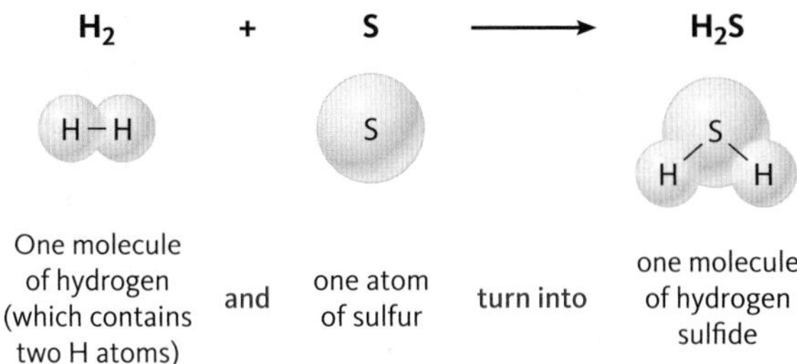

Health Note: Hydrogen sulfide (H_2S) is a gas that is responsible for the smell of rotten eggs and (to a lesser extent) intestinal gas. Many bacteria produce H_2S when they break down sulfur-containing nutrients, including proteins. H_2S is extremely toxic, so workers where the gas is generated wear gas detectors that sound a warning when the concentration in the air reaches 5 ppm.

Sample Problem 6.2

Distinguishing coefficients from chemical formulas

The elements magnesium and chlorine react to form magnesium chloride. Which of the following is a correct representation of this reaction?

$$Mg + 2\,Cl \rightarrow MgCl_2$$

$$Mg + Cl_2 \rightarrow MgCl_2$$

SOLUTION

The only difference between these two equations is the way that the two chlorine atoms are represented. In the first equation, 2 Cl means that there is no chemical bond between the atoms. However, this is not correct, because chlorine atoms form molecules that contain two atoms held together by a covalent bond. The chemical formula must be written Cl_2 to show the bond between the two atoms. Therefore, the second equation is correct.

TRY IT YOURSELF: *The elements sodium and phosphorus react to form sodium phosphide. Which of the following is a correct representation of this reaction?*

$$3\,Na + P \rightarrow Na_3P$$

$$Na_3 + P \rightarrow Na_3P$$

In each of the chemical equations we have written so far, all of the atoms in our reactants are accounted for in the products. This must be true of any chemical equation. Chemists often speak of a *balanced chemical equation*, to emphasize the idea that the products and reactants contain equal numbers of atoms of each element. A chemical equation such as

$$Na + S \rightarrow Na_2S$$

is *not* correct, because the atoms are not balanced. This equation implies that we have converted one sodium atom into two, which is not possible.

We can also use coefficients to show the number of formula units of a compound. For instance, the chemical equation that follows represents the elements hydrogen and oxygen combining to make water. Note that hydrogen and oxygen both form molecules that contain two atoms, as we saw in Chapter 3.

$$2\,H_2 + O_2 \rightarrow 2\,H_2O$$

In this equation, we have two coefficients. The 2 in front of H_2 tells us that we use two molecules of H_2. Each molecule contains two hydrogen atoms, so we use a total of four hydrogen atoms. The 2 in front of H_2O tells us that we make two molecules of H_2O. Each molecule contains two hydrogen atoms and one oxygen atom, so the water molecules contain a total of four hydrogen atoms and two oxygen atoms, as shown in Figure 6.2. We have the same number of atoms of each element on each side of the arrow, so this is a balanced chemical equation.

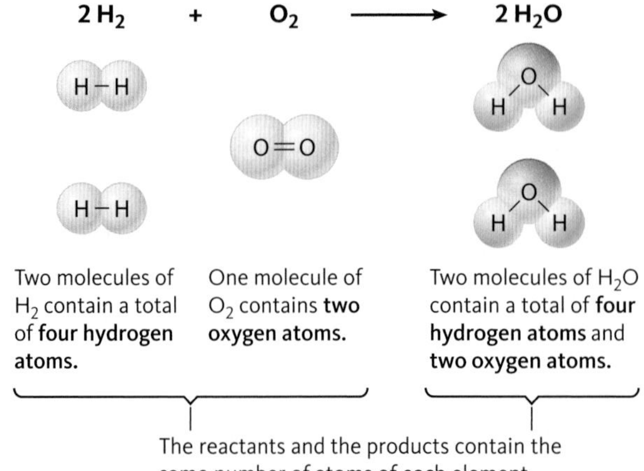

FIGURE 6.2 Counting atoms in a chemical equation.

Sample Problem 6.3

Counting atoms when there is a coefficient

A chemical equation contains the expression 2 $FeCl_3$. How many atoms of each element does this expression represent?

SOLUTION

The 2 tells us that we have two formula units of $FeCl_3$. Each formula unit contains one iron atom and three chlorine atoms. Therefore, we have a total of two atoms of iron and six atoms of chlorine.

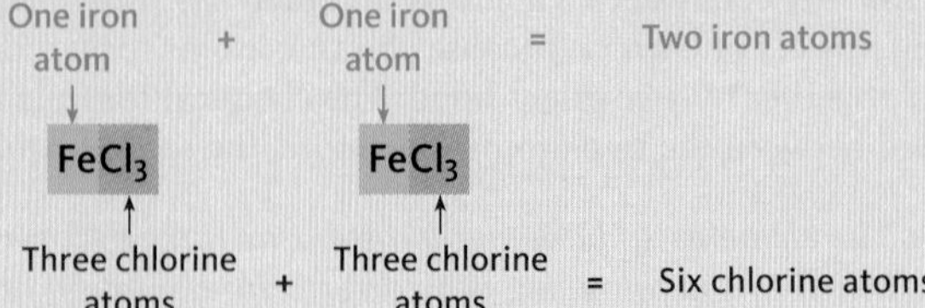

TRY IT YOURSELF: *A chemical equation contains the expression 3 Cu_2O. How many atoms of each element does this expression represent?*

If you can count the number of atoms in a compound correctly, accounting for any coefficients, you can identify a balanced chemical equation.

Sample Problem 6.4

Recognizing a balanced chemical equation

Is the following chemical equation balanced? If not, explain.

$$2\,CO + O_2 \rightarrow 2\,CO_2$$

SOLUTION

We have two reactants, one of which has a coefficient. Let us count the atoms in each substance first and then work out the total number of atoms of each element in the reactants.

2 CO: This represents two molecules of CO. Each molecule contains one carbon atom and one oxygen atom, so we have a total of two carbon atoms and two oxygen atoms.

O_2: This represents a molecule that contains two oxygen atoms.

Now we can add up the atoms on the left side of the arrow. We have a total of two carbon atoms and four oxygen atoms in our reactants.

2 CO_2: This represents two molecules of CO_2. Each molecule contains one carbon atom and two oxygen atoms, so we have a total of two carbon atoms and four oxygen atoms in our product.

Finally, we compare the reactants to the products. Both the reactants and the products contain two carbon atoms and four oxygen atoms, so this is a balanced equation.

TRY IT YOURSELF: *Is the following chemical equation balanced? If not, explain.*

$$2\,FeO + O_2 \rightarrow Fe_2O_3$$

For additional practice, try Core Problems 6.13 and 6.14.

Health Note: Carbon monoxide (CO) is a toxic, odorless gas that is produced when fuels burn in a limited air supply. When sufficient air is available, carbon monoxide reacts with oxygen to make carbon dioxide (CO_2), which is relatively harmless. Because of the danger of carbon monoxide poisoning, you should never use a charcoal barbecue or heater indoors.

Balancing an Equation Gives the Coefficients of Every Substance in a Reaction

In many cases, we know the chemical formulas of the products and reactants in a reaction, but we must work out the number of formula units of each substance that we need to produce a valid chemical equation. This process is called balancing an equation. For example, let us consider the reaction of magnesium with oxygen to produce magnesium oxide. The reactants are magnesium (Mg) and oxygen (which we must write as O_2 because oxygen atoms form covalently bonded molecules), and the product is magnesium oxide (MgO). Our starting point is to write the reactants on the left side and the products of the right side of an arrow.

$$Mg + O_2 \rightarrow MgO$$

Is this a balanced equation? Let us do a bit of bookkeeping. On the left side of the arrow, we have one magnesium atom and two oxygen atoms. On the right side, we have one atom of each element.

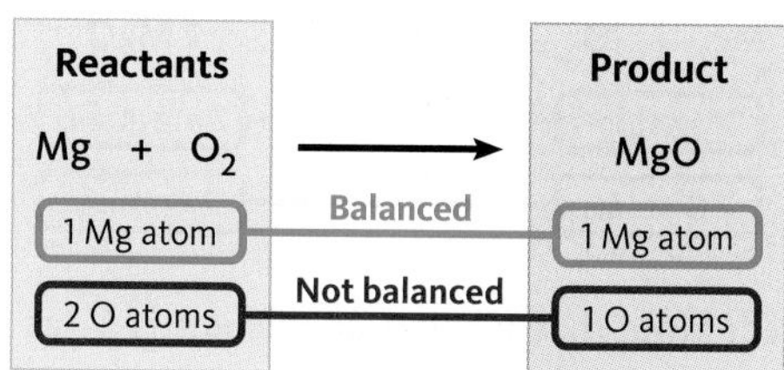

Because we have unequal numbers of oxygen atoms on the two sides of the reaction, *this is not a balanced equation.*

To balance this equation, we must write a coefficient in front of one or more of the chemical formulas. When we find the correct set of coefficients, the numbers of oxygen and magnesium atoms on each side of the arrow will be equal. During this process, *we*

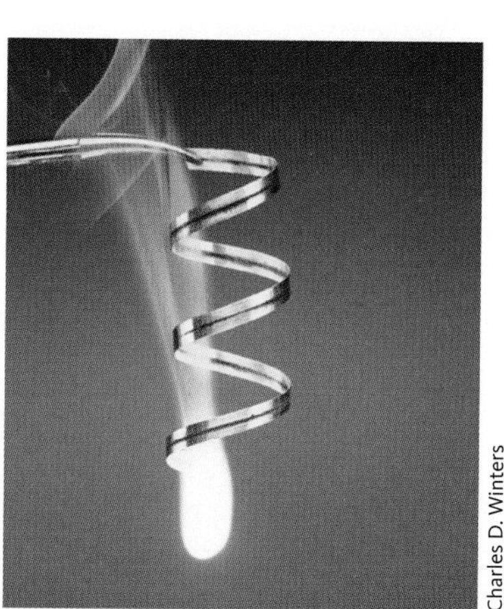
Charles D. Winters

The reaction of magnesium and oxygen is a dramatic example of a chemical change.

cannot change the subscript numbers in the chemical formulas. These numbers reflect the chemical bonds that the atoms form, which are determined by the valence electrons. Since we can only write coefficients, we can think of balancing an equation as "filling in the blanks."

$$\boxed{?}\,Mg + \boxed{?}\,O_2 \longrightarrow \boxed{?}\,MgO$$

Finding the correct coefficients involves trial and error, but here are some helpful guidelines:

1. Focus on one element at a time. Do not try to balance everything at a glance.
2. Save those elements that appear as individual (unbonded) atoms for last.
3. Once you have decided on a coefficient, do not decrease it—you will just start going in circles.

Let us start by trying the simplest possible solution, with one formula unit of each substance.

$$\boxed{1}\,Mg + \boxed{1}\,O_2 \longrightarrow \boxed{1}\,MgO$$

This is not the correct answer, since it leaves us with two oxygen atoms on the reactant side and only one on the product side. Our next step is to change one of the coefficients to balance the oxygen atoms. (Remember that we cannot change the chemical formulas.) The only way to balance oxygen atoms is to put a 2 in front of MgO. This gives us two oxygen atoms on the product side.

$$\boxed{1}\,Mg + \boxed{1}\,O_2 \longrightarrow \boxed{2}\,MgO$$

Every time we change any of the coefficients, we need to revise our atom counts. Be sure that you do this bookkeeping.

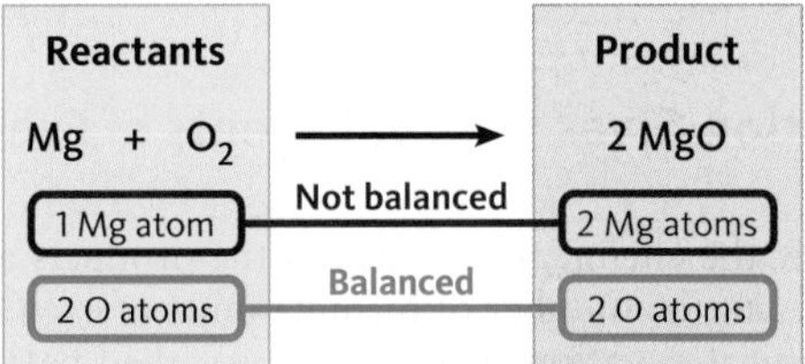

We have balanced the oxygen atoms, but we have simultaneously unbalanced the magnesium atoms. Don't worry: this is typical of equation balancing. Now we turn to magnesium and try to balance it. We could do so by changing the MgO coefficient back to 1, but we would be going in circles. The alternative is to change the Mg coefficient to 2.

$$\boxed{2}\,Mg + \boxed{1}\,O_2 \longrightarrow \boxed{2}\,MgO$$

Once again, we check the atom counts.

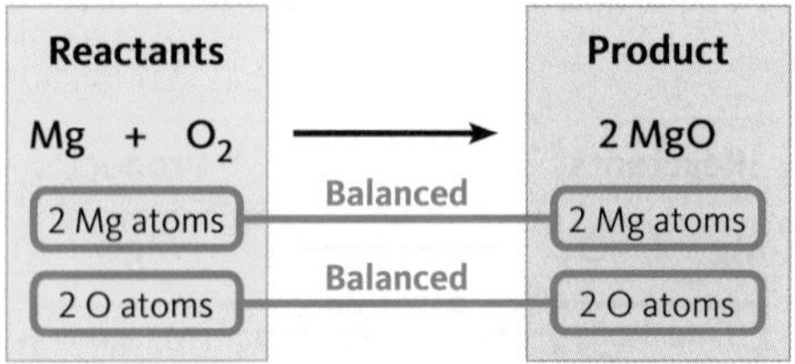

The equation is balanced. Note that when a coefficient is 1 (as is the case for O_2), we omit it from the balanced equation.

Chemical equations can involve many compounds and complicated formulas, but the basic process for balancing such equations is no different from the preceding example. Be patient, count atoms carefully (miscounting even one element can be disastrous), and do not undo your work. Sample Problem 6.5 gives a more complex example of equation balancing.

Sample Problem 6.5

Balancing a chemical equation

Balance the following equation:

$$Al_2O_3 + HCl \rightarrow AlCl_3 + H_2O$$

SOLUTION

We must decide how many formula units of each chemical we need to balance the equation. To begin, we take one formula unit of each substance and then count the number of atoms of each element before and after the reaction.

$$\boxed{1}Al_2O_3 + \boxed{1}HCl \longrightarrow \boxed{1}AlCl_3 + \boxed{1}H_2O$$

Reactants		Products
2 Al atoms	← Unbalanced →	1 Al atom
3 O atoms	← Unbalanced →	1 O atom
1 H atom	← Unbalanced →	2 H atoms
1 Cl atom	← Unbalanced →	3 Cl atoms

All four elements are unbalanced, so we can choose any one as our starting point. Let us choose aluminum. To balance aluminum, we need to put a 2 in front of $AlCl_3$ and check our atom counts again.

$$\boxed{1}Al_2O_3 + \boxed{1}HCl \longrightarrow \boxed{2}AlCl_3 + \boxed{1}H_2O$$

Reactants		Products
2 Al atoms	← Balanced →	2 Al atoms
3 O atoms	← Unbalanced →	1 O atom
1 H atom	← Unbalanced →	2 H atoms
1 Cl atom	← Unbalanced →	6 Cl atoms

Note that we changed the atom counts for both aluminum and chlorine on the product side, although we only balanced the aluminum. Next, let us turn to oxygen. To balance oxygen, we need to put a *3* in front of H_2O. Be sure to recheck the numbers of atoms.

$$\boxed{1}Al_2O_3 + \boxed{1}HCl \longrightarrow \boxed{2}AlCl_3 + \boxed{3}H_2O$$

Reactants		Products
2 Al atoms	← Balanced →	2 Al atoms
3 O atoms	← Balanced →	3 O atoms
1 H atom	← Unbalanced →	6 H atoms
1 Cl atom	← Unbalanced →	6 Cl atoms

Now let us work on hydrogen. Balancing hydrogen requires that we put a *6* in front of HCl. Once again, we need to check the numbers of atoms of each element after we make this change.

$$\boxed{1}Al_2O_3 + \boxed{6}HCl \longrightarrow \boxed{2}AlCl_3 + \boxed{3}H_2O$$

Reactants		Products
2 Al atoms	← Balanced →	2 Al atoms
3 O atoms	← Balanced →	3 O atoms
6 H atoms	← Balanced →	6 H atoms
6 Cl atoms	← Balanced →	6 Cl atoms

Not only did we balance hydrogen in this step, but we balanced chlorine as well. All of the elements are now balanced, so the correct answer is

$$Al_2O_3 + 6\ HCl \rightarrow 2\ AlCl_3 + 3\ H_2O$$

If we had chosen a different starting element (say hydrogen), the balancing process would have taken more steps, because we would have had to rebalance hydrogen after we balanced oxygen. However, the end result would have been the same.

continued

TABLE 6.2 Standard Abbreviations for States of Matter

Abbreviation	State
(*s*)	Solid
(*l*)	Liquid
(*g*)	Gas
(*aq*)	Aqueous (dissolved in water)

Health Note: In medication orders, *aq* means water and stands for the Latin word *aqua*.

TRY IT YOURSELF: *Balance the following equation:*

$$Al + HCl \rightarrow AlCl_3 + H_2$$

For additional practice, try Core Problems 6.15 through 6.18.

When we write a chemical equation, we can list the reactants and the products in any order we choose. However, we cannot move a chemical to the other side of the arrow, and we cannot change any coefficients. For example, the following equations all represent the same reaction, and any one of them is an acceptable chemical equation:

$$2\ NaOH + H_2S \rightarrow Na_2S + 2\ H_2O$$

$$H_2S + 2\ NaOH \rightarrow Na_2S + 2\ H_2O$$

$$H_2S + 2\ NaOH \rightarrow 2\ H_2O + Na_2S$$

Abbreviations Show the State of Each Substance in a Reaction

In some cases, we need to show the physical states of the reactants and products in a balanced equation. We can do this by writing an abbreviation for the state after each chemical formula. The standard abbreviations are listed in Table 6.2.

For example, we produced the following balanced equation for the reaction of Al_2O_3 with HCl:

$$Al_2O_3 + 6\ HCl \rightarrow 2\ AlCl_3 + 3\ H_2O$$

At room temperature, Al_2O_3 is a solid and water is a liquid. The HCl is normally supplied as an aqueous solution, and the product $AlCl_3$ dissolves in water as it forms. Therefore, we can write this equation as

$$Al_2O_3(s) + 6\ HCl(aq) \rightarrow 2\ AlCl_3(aq) + 3\ H_2O(l)$$

Sample Problem 6.6

Using abbreviations to represent states

Write a chemical equation that corresponds to the following statement. Be sure to include a symbol for the state of each substance.

"One molecule of gaseous SO_3 reacts with one formula unit of aqueous $Ca(OH)_2$ to form one formula unit of solid $CaSO_4$ and one molecule of liquid H_2O."

SOLUTION

$$SO_3(g) + Ca(OH)_2(aq) \rightarrow CaSO_4(s) + H_2O(l)$$

TRY IT YOURSELF: *Write a chemical equation that corresponds to the following statement. Be sure to include a symbol for the state of each substance.*

"One atom of solid magnesium reacts with two molecules of aqueous HCl, producing one formula unit of aqueous $MgCl_2$ and one molecule of gaseous H_2."

For additional practice, try Core Problems 6.11 and 6.12.

CORE PROBLEMS

6.9 A student is asked to balance the following equation: $Fe + Cl_2 \rightarrow FeCl_3$. The student gives the following answer: $Fe + Cl_2 \rightarrow FeCl_2$. Is this a reasonable answer? Explain why or why not.

6.10 A student is asked to balance the following equation: $N_2 + O_2 \rightarrow NO_2$. The student gives the following answer: $N + O_2 \rightarrow NO_2$. Is this a reasonable answer? Explain why or why not.

6.11 Write a chemical equation that represents the following reaction: "One molecule of solid PCl_3 reacts with three molecules of liquid water, forming one molecule of aqueous H_3PO_3 and three molecules of aqueous HCl."

6.12 Write a chemical equation that represents the following reaction: "One formula unit of solid CaH_2 reacts with two molecules of liquid water, forming one formula unit of aqueous $Ca(OH)_2$ and two molecules of gaseous H_2."

continued

6.13 Tell whether each of the following is a balanced equation. If it is not balanced, explain why not.
a) $2\ Ca + Cl_2 \rightarrow 2\ CaCl_2$
b) $Mg(OH)_2 + 2\ HF \rightarrow MgF_2 + 2\ H_2O$
c) $C_5H_{12}O + 8\ O_2 \rightarrow 5\ CO_2 + 6\ H_2O$

6.14 Tell whether each of the following is a balanced equation. If it is not balanced, explain why not.
a) $CaO + H_2O \rightarrow Ca(OH)_2$
b) $Cr_2O_3 \rightarrow 2\ CrO_3$
c) $C_4H_9OH + 6\ O_2 \rightarrow 4\ CO_2 + 5\ H_2O$

Problems 6.15 through 6.22 are equation-balancing questions. They are ordered from easiest to hardest.

6.15 Balance the following equations:
a) $S + Cl_2 \rightarrow SCl_4$
b) $Ag + S \rightarrow Ag_2S$
c) $K + Cl_2 \rightarrow KCl$

6.16 Balance the following equations:
a) $Al + S \rightarrow Al_2S_3$
b) $Mn + O_2 \rightarrow MnO$
c) $N_2 + O_2 \rightarrow NO$

6.17 Balance the following equations:
a) $CaO + HCl \rightarrow CaCl_2 + H_2O$
b) $Fe + O_2 \rightarrow Fe_2O_3$
c) $CH_4 + O_2 \rightarrow CO_2 + H_2O$

6.18 Balance the following equations:
a) $AgCl + H_2S \rightarrow Ag_2S + HCl$
b) $Al + Br_2 \rightarrow AlBr_3$
c) $SiH_4 + F_2 \rightarrow SiF_4 + HF$

6.19 Balance the following equations:
a) $C_4H_{10} + O_2 \rightarrow CO_2 + H_2O$
b) $AlCl_3 + H_2O \rightarrow Al_2O_3 + HCl$
c) $AgNO_3 + MgI_2 \rightarrow AgI + Mg(NO_3)_2$

6.20 Balance the following equations:
a) $PH_3 + Cl_2 \rightarrow PCl_3 + HCl$
b) $Ca(NO_3)_2 + Na_2SO_4 \rightarrow CaSO_4 + NaNO_3$
c) $Cr_2O_3 + HF \rightarrow CrF_3 + H_2O$

6.21 Balance the following equations:
a) $Al(OH)_3 + H_2SO_4 \rightarrow Al_2(SO_4)_3 + H_2O$
b) $C_5H_{11}NO_2 + O_2 \rightarrow CO_2 + H_2O + N_2$

6.22 Balance the following equations:
a) $H_3PO_4 + Mg(OH)_2 \rightarrow Mg_3(PO_4)_2 + H_2O$
b) $NH_3 + O_2 \rightarrow N_2 + H_2O$

6.3 Mass Relationships in a Chemical Reaction

OBJECTIVE: *Relate the mass of one substance in a chemical reaction to the mass of any other substance in the reaction.*

When you eat some table sugar (sucrose), your body uses the sugar as fuel. In effect, your body burns the sugar, just as a car burns gasoline or a fireplace burns wood. The overall chemical reaction that your body carries out is

$$C_{12}H_{22}O_{11} + 12\ O_2 \rightarrow 12\ CO_2 + 11\ H_2O$$

This equation shows that your body produces 11 molecules of water for every molecule of sucrose you consume. Does this mean that if you eat 1 g of sugar, your body will produce (and excrete) 11 g of water? No, it does not. In fact, your body only produces about half of a gram of water for every gram of sucrose that it burns. The coefficients in a balanced equation do not give us the relationship between the masses of the products and those of the reactants. However, we can combine a balanced equation with the atomic weights of the elements to calculate the mass of each product formed in a chemical reaction. Let us explore how to calculate the mass of water that your body makes when you burn sugar.

Health Note: Your body produces water and carbon dioxide whenever you obtain energy from food. If you are at rest, you produce about 250 g of water and 700 g of carbon dioxide per day from burning nutrients in food, and you use around 550 g of oxygen.

Formula Weights Give the Relationship Between Masses of Chemicals in a Reaction

Because the equation for the burning of sucrose involves a large number of atoms, we will begin our investigation with a simpler reaction, the formation of sodium sulfide from sodium and sulfur. As we saw in Section 6.2, the balanced equation for this reaction is

$$2\ Na + S \rightarrow Na_2S$$

This equation tells us that two atoms of sodium react with one atom of sulfur to form one formula unit of Na_2S. Two sodium atoms weigh 45.98 amu (2×22.99 amu), and one sulfur atom weighs 32.06 amu. We can therefore say that 45.98 amu of sodium reacts with 32.06 amu of sulfur. We have changed a relationship based on *numbers of atoms* into a relationship based on *masses*.

Two sodium atoms
2×22.99 amu
45.98 amu

One sulfur atom
32.06 amu

If we want to use a larger number of sodium atoms, we must preserve the 2:1 atom ratio. For example, if we use 200 sodium atoms, we need 100 sulfur atoms. We also preserve the mass ratio of these substances: sodium and sulfur always react in a mass ratio of 45.98 to 32.06. In particular, if we use 45.98 *grams* of sodium, we need 32.06 *grams* of sulfur. We can also express this relationship in terms of moles: two *moles* of sodium reacts with one *mole* of sulfur. Figure 6.3 shows the relationships between the masses and the numbers of moles of sodium and sulfur in this reaction.

Sample Problem **6.7**

Describing a mass relationship in a chemical reaction

Sodium reacts with bromine according to the following equation:

$$2\ Na + Br_2 \rightarrow 2\ NaBr$$

Express the mass relationship between sodium and bromine in this reaction in both atomic mass units and grams.

SOLUTION

The reaction tells us that two atoms of Na react with one molecule of Br_2. To get the mass relationship, we use the atomic weights from the periodic table.

2 Na: Each atom of sodium weighs 22.99 amu, so two atoms weigh 2×22.99 amu = 45.98 amu.

Br_2: Each atom of bromine weighs 79.90 amu, so two atoms weigh 2×79.90 amu = 159.80 amu.

We can therefore say that **45.98 amu of Na reacts with 159.80 amu of Br_2.** When we express this relationship in grams, we use the same numbers, so **45.98 g of Na reacts with 159.80 g of Br_2.**

TRY IT YOURSELF: *Aluminum reacts with chlorine according to the following equation:*

$$2\ Al + 3\ Cl_2 \rightarrow 2\ AlCl_3$$

Express the mass relationship between aluminum and chlorine in this reaction in both atomic mass units and grams.

For additional practice, try Core Problems 6.23 and 6.24.

We can use the mass ratio from Figure 6.3 as a conversion factor to translate any mass of one reactant (sodium or sulfur) into the corresponding mass of the other reactant. For example, suppose that a chemist has 2.25 g of sodium available and wants to know how much sulfur she will need to make sodium sulfide. Let us use the stepwise

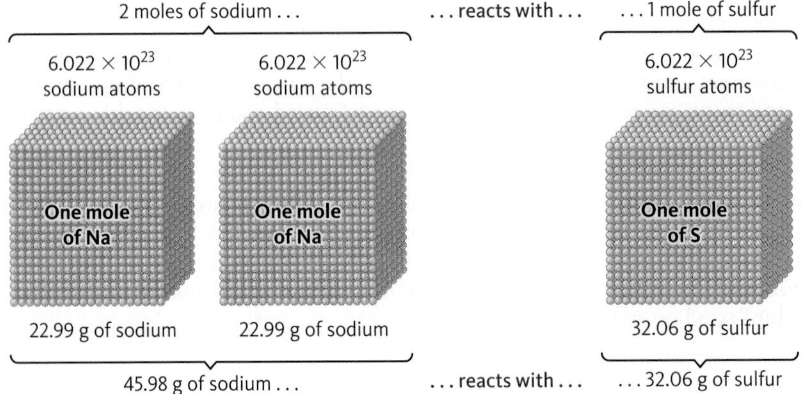

FIGURE 6.3 The mass relationship between sodium and sulfur in the reaction $2\ Na + S \rightarrow Na_2S$.

approach that you learned in Chapter 1. In effect, we want to know how many grams of sulfur corresponds to 2.25 g of sodium.

2.25 g Na **convert** → ? g S

STEP 1: Identify the original measurement and the final unit.

In Figure 6.3, we found that 45.98 g of sodium reacts with 32.06 g of sulfur. We can use these masses to write a pair of conversion factors that express the relationship between the masses of Na and S in this reaction.

$$\frac{45.98 \text{ g Na}}{32.06 \text{ g S}} \quad \text{and} \quad \frac{32.06 \text{ g S}}{45.98 \text{ g Na}}$$

STEP 2: Write conversion factors that relate the two units.

To convert 2.25 g of sodium into the corresponding mass of sulfur, we need to multiply by the second conversion factor so that the mass of sodium cancels. Then we can do the arithmetic.

$$2.25 \cancel{\text{ g Na}} \times \frac{32.06 \text{ g S}}{45.98 \cancel{\text{ g Na}}} = 1.56883428 \text{ g S} \quad \text{calculator answer}$$

STEPS 3 and 4: Choose the correct conversion factor, and then do the math and round the answer.

Finally, we round our answer to three significant figures. The chemist needs 1.57 g of sulfur to react with the 2.25 g of sodium. If she uses more than 1.57 g of sulfur, the extra sulfur will not react. If she uses less than 1.57 g, there will not be enough sulfur to combine with all of the sodium.

We can use the conversion factor method to relate a mass of any chemical in a reaction to the mass of any other chemical in the reaction. Sample Problem 6.8 shows how we can use this technique to solve the problem at the beginning of this section.

Sample Problem 6.8

Using mass relationships in a chemical reaction

When your body reacts 1.00 g of sucrose with oxygen, how many grams of water do you produce? The chemical equation for the burning of sucrose is

$$C_{12}H_{22}O_{11} + 12\ O_2 \rightarrow 12\ CO_2 + 11\ H_2O$$

SOLUTION

The problem mentions three chemicals, but we only need to consider two of them. We are given the mass of sucrose (1.00 g), and we are asked to calculate the number of grams of water. The reaction also requires oxygen, but we do not need to calculate the amount.

STEP 1: Identify the original measurement and the final unit.

1.00 g of sucrose **convert** → ? g of water

To relate these two masses, we need to find a mass relationship between sucrose and water, using the balanced equation. We start by finding the formula weights of the two compounds.

STEP 2: Write conversion factors that relate the two units.

Sucrose: 12 C:	12 × 12.01 amu =	144.12 amu
22 H:	22 × 1.008 amu =	22.176 amu
11 O:	11 × 16.00 amu =	176.00 amu
	Total (formula weight):	342.296 amu

Water: 2 H:	2 × 1.008 amu =	2.016 amu
1 O:	1 × 16.00 amu =	16.00 amu
	Total (formula weight):	18.016 amu

continued

According to the balanced equation, 1 molecule of sucrose produces 11 molecules of water, so we must multiply the formula weight of water by 11.

1 molecule of sucrose: 1×342.296 amu = 342.296 amu

11 molecules of water: 11×18.016 amu = 198.176 amu

We now have a mass ratio. This ratio applies to masses in grams as well as masses in atomic mass units, so we can say that burning 342.296 g of $C_{12}H_{22}O_{11}$ produces 198.176 g of H_2O. Let us write this relationship as a pair of conversion factors.

$$\frac{342.296 \text{ g } C_{12}H_{22}O_{11}}{198.176 \text{ g } H_2O} \quad \text{and} \quad \frac{198.176 \text{ g } H_2O}{342.296 \text{ g } C_{12}H_{22}O_{11}}$$

STEP 3: Choose the conversion factor that allows you to cancel units.

The original question asked us to relate 1.00 g of sucrose to a mass of water. To do so, we need to multiply this mass of sucrose by the second conversion factor so that the mass of sucrose cancels.

Step 4: Do the math and round your answer.

$$1.00 \text{ g } \cancel{C_{12}H_{22}O_{11}} \times \frac{198.176 \text{ g } H_2O}{342.296 \text{ g } \cancel{C_{12}H_{22}O_{11}}} = 0.578960899 \text{ g } H_2O \qquad \text{calculator answer}$$

Finally, we round this answer to three significant figures. When your body burns 1.00 g of sucrose, you produce **0.579 g of water.**

TRY IT YOURSELF: *When your body burns 1.00 g of sucrose, how many grams of oxygen does it use? The balanced equation for this reaction is given at the beginning of the sample problem.*

For additional practice, try Core Problems 6.25 and 6.26.

Figure 6.4 summarizes the relationships between the masses of the compounds involved in the burning of sucrose.

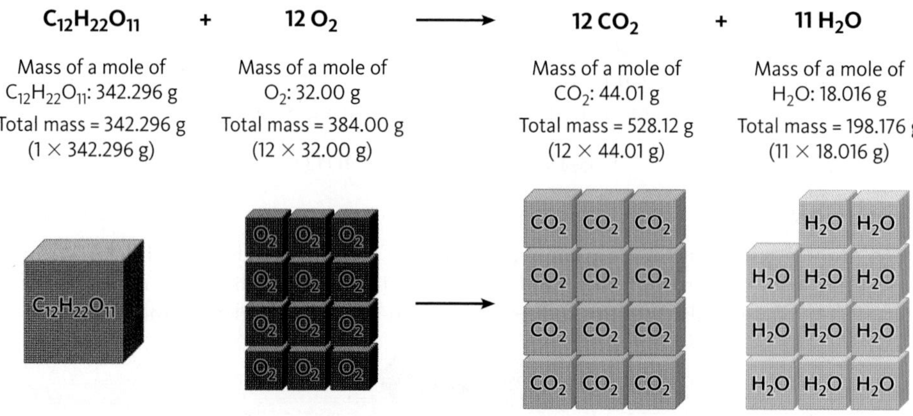

FIGURE 6.4 Mass relationships in the burning of sucrose.

CORE PROBLEMS

6.23 Methane has the chemical formula CH_4 and is the principal constituent of natural gas. When methane burns, it reacts with oxygen according to the following balanced equation:

$$CH_4 + 2\ O_2 \rightarrow CO_2 + 2\ H_2O$$

What is the mass relationship between methane and water in this reaction?

6.24 Glycine ($C_2H_5NO_2$) is one of the amino acid building blocks of proteins. When our bodies burn proteins to obtain energy, we convert the glycine into urea (N_2H_4CO), according to the following balanced equation:

$$2\ C_2H_5NO_2 + 3\ O_2 \rightarrow 3\ CO_2 + 3\ H_2O + N_2H_4CO$$

What is the mass relationship between glycine and urea in this reaction?

continued

6.25 Aluminum hydroxide is an ingredient in some antacids. It reacts with hydrochloric acid (the acid in your stomach) according to the following equation:

$$Al(OH)_3(s) + 3\ HCl(aq) \rightarrow AlCl_3(aq) + 3\ H_2O(l)$$

a) How many grams of HCl react with 2.50 g of $Al(OH)_3$?
b When 2.50 g of $Al(OH)_3$ reacts with HCl, what mass of water is formed?
c) If you want to make 2.50 g of $AlCl_3$ using this reaction, how many grams of HCl do you need?

6.26 Trilaurin is a fat that is often found in animal tissues. It has the chemical formula $C_{39}H_{74}O_6$, and it burns according to the following equation:

$$2\ C_{39}H_{74}O_6 + 109\ O_2 \rightarrow 78\ CO_2 + 74\ H_2O$$

a) If you burn 12.5 g of trilaurin, what mass of oxygen do you need?
b) When 12.5 g of trilaurin reacts with oxygen, how many grams of carbon dioxide are formed?
c) If your body burns enough trilaurin to make 12.5 g of water, how many grams of trilaurin did you burn?

6.4 Heats of Reaction

OBJECTIVES: *Relate the amount of heat involved in a reaction to the masses of the chemicals, describe the differences between exothermic and endothermic reactions, and use nutritive values to calculate the energy provided by foodstuffs.*

All living organisms need a source of energy. For instance, humans need energy to move muscles, transmit nerve impulses, maintain body temperature, move ions and molecules into and out of cells, and construct large molecules out of smaller ones. We, and all other animals, use chemical reactions to supply the energy we need. In this section, we explore the relationship between chemical reactions and energy.

Let us start with the burning of sucrose (table sugar), a reaction we examined in Section 6.3. The chemical equation for this reaction is

$$C_{12}H_{22}O_{11} + 12\ O_2 \rightarrow 12\ CO_2 + 11\ H_2O$$

This reaction produces a large amount of energy. If we include this energy, we can write the equation as

$$C_{12}H_{22}O_{11} + 12\ O_2 \rightarrow 12\ CO_2 + 11\ H_2O + \text{energy}$$

Where does this energy come from? Sucrose and oxygen have a great deal of potential energy. Recall from Chapter 4 that potential energy is the energy that an object has when it is not in its most stable position. In this case, sucrose and oxygen have potential energy because the arrangement of atoms in these substances is not very stable. The potential energy that results from the arrangement of atoms is called chemical energy.

When sucrose reacts with oxygen, the atoms move into a more stable arrangement, making carbon dioxide and water. In the process, most of the chemical energy of the reactants changes into thermal energy, which we feel as heat.

$$\underbrace{C_{12}H_{22}O_{11} + O_2}_{\text{(High chemical energy)}} \longrightarrow \underbrace{CO_2 + H_2O}_{\text{(Low chemical energy)}} + \textbf{Thermal energy}$$

The Amount of Heat Is Proportional to the Amount of Each Substance in a Reaction

How much heat do we produce when we burn table sugar? We saw in Figure 6.3 that the mass ratio of the reactants in this equation is 342.296 g of $C_{12}H_{22}O_{11}$ to 384.00 g of O_2. If we allow these amounts of sucrose and oxygen to react, we get 1342 kcal of heat (see Chapter 4). This energy is called the **heat of reaction**, and we can write it into the balanced equation.

$$C_{12}H_{22}O_{11} + 12\ O_2 \rightarrow 12\ CO_2 + 11\ H_2O + 1342\ \text{kcal}$$

All reactions involve energy, so every reaction has a heat of reaction. Heats of reaction must be measured in a laboratory, because they cannot be calculated from the balanced equation.

The amount of heat that any reaction produces is directly related to the masses of the chemicals in the reaction. Figure 6.5 illustrates the relationship between heat and masses of the chemicals for a simpler reaction, the formation of Na_2S from sodium and sulfur. The balanced equation for this reaction, including the heat, is

$$2\ Na + S \rightarrow Na_2S + 87\ \text{kcal}$$

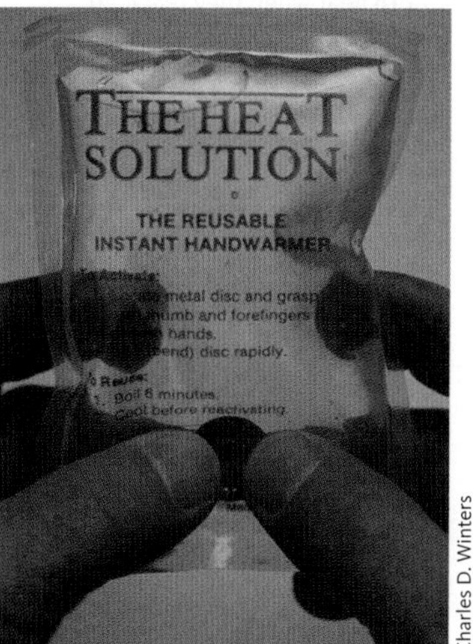

A hot pack contains chemicals that produce heat when they react, an example of an exothermic reaction.

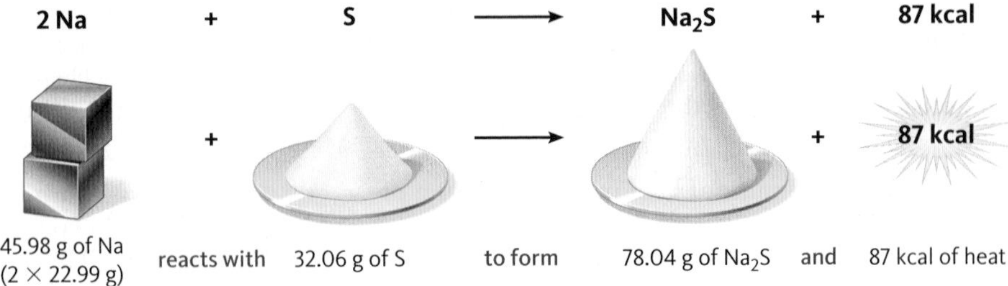

FIGURE 6.5 The relationship between mass and heat for a chemical reaction.

• The atomic weight of Na is 22.99, and the reaction calls for two sodium atoms, so we must use 45.98 g of Na (2 × 22.99 g) to get our 87 kcal of heat.

This equation tells us that we get 87 kcal of heat if we allow 45.98 g of Na to react with 32.06 g of S. We calculate the masses of reactants (and products) just as we did in Section 6.3.

Reactions Can Either Produce or Absorb Heat

Burning sugar and making sodium sulfide are examples of **exothermic reactions**, reactions that produce heat. Exothermic reactions are generally easy to recognize, because they raise the temperature of their surroundings. Most common reactions are exothermic, including the burning of all types of fuels, the rusting of metals, and the reactions that occur in batteries. However, a few reactions, called **endothermic reactions**, absorb heat energy from their surroundings. When we write the equation for an endothermic reaction, we include the heat as a reactant. An example is the reaction of sodium bicarbonate with hydrochloric acid, HCl.

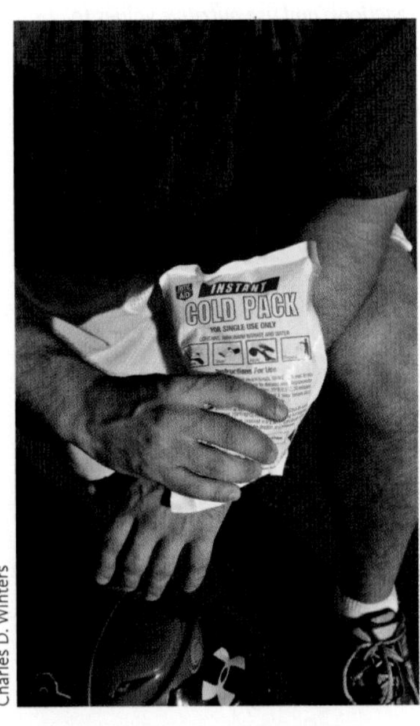

Charles D. Winters

A cold pack contains chemicals that absorb heat when they react, an example of an endothermic reaction.

$$NaHCO_3 + HCl + 2.8\ kcal \rightarrow NaCl + CO_2 + H_2O$$

In an endothermic reaction, thermal energy seems to vanish, so both the chemicals and their surroundings become colder as the reaction proceeds. The products have more chemical energy than the reactants, but we cannot feel or detect this chemical energy.

$NaHCO_3$ + HCl + Thermal energy ⟶ NaCl + CO_2 + H_2O
(Low chemical energy) (High chemical energy)

The formula weights of $NaHCO_3$ and HCl are 84.008 and 36.458 amu, respectively. Therefore, the chemical equation tells us that when 84.008 g of $NaHCO_3$ reacts with 36.458 g of HCl, the chemicals absorb 2.8 kcal of thermal energy and convert it into chemical energy. Figure 6.6 illustrates this relationship.

As an alternative to including the heat in the balanced equation, chemists often write the amount of heat separately, using the symbol ΔH (read "delta H") to represent the heat of reaction. If the reaction is exothermic (heat is a product), the heat of reaction is written as a negative number; if the reaction is endothermic (heat is a reactant), the heat of reaction is positive. Here are the three reactions we have looked at in this section, written in this form:

$$C_{12}H_{22}O_{11} + 12\ O_2 \rightarrow 12\ CO_2 + 11\ H_2O \qquad \Delta H = -1342\ kcal$$
$$2\ Na + S \rightarrow Na_2S \qquad \Delta H = -87\ kcal$$
(ΔH is *negative: heat is a product*)

$$NaHCO_3 + HCl \rightarrow NaCl + CO_2 + H_2O \qquad \Delta H = 2.8\ kcal$$
(ΔH is *positive: heat is a reactant*)

$NaHCO_3$ + HCl + 2.8 kcal ⟶ NaCl + CO_2 + H_2O

+ + 2.8 kcal ⟶ + +

84.008 g of $NaHCO_3$ reacts with 36.458 g of HCl and 2.8 kcal of heat to form 58.44 g of NaCl and 44.01 g of CO_2 and 18.016 g of H_2O

FIGURE 6.6 The relationship between mass and energy for an endothermic reaction.

TABLE 6.3 A Comparison of Exothermic and Endothermic Reactions

	Exothermic Reaction	Endothermic Reaction
Type of energy conversion	Converts chemical energy into thermal energy	Converts thermal energy into chemical energy
Effect of the reaction	Makes its surroundings warmer	Makes its surroundings cooler
Location of the heat in the balanced equation	Heat is on the right side: reactants → products + heat	Heat is on the left side: reactants + heat → products
Sign of ΔH	Negative	Positive

Health Note: In any pharmacy, you can buy a cold pack, a plastic packet that becomes cold when you mix its contents. Cold packs usually contain water and ammonium nitrate. Dissolving ammonium nitrate in water is an endothermic change, so the entire pack becomes ice-cold. Hot packs use exothermic reactions to produce heat and warm up the pack.

Table 6.3 summarizes the differences between exothermic and endothermic reactions.

Sample Problem **6.9**

Describing the relationship between mass and energy in a chemical reaction

The fuel in cigarette lighters is butane (C_4H_{10}), which burns according to the following equation:

$$2\ C_4H_{10} + 13\ O_2 \rightarrow 8\ CO_2 + 10\ H_2O + 1376\ \text{kcal}$$

What is the relationship between the mass of butane and the heat in this reaction? When this reaction occurs, do the surroundings become warmer or do they become cooler? What is the sign of ΔH?

SOLUTION

The formula weight of C_4H_{10} is 58.12 amu. The balanced equation calls for two molecules of C_4H_{10}, so we must multiply the formula weight by two: 2 × 58.12 amu = 116.24 amu. However, when we relate the mass of a chemical to the heat of reaction, we express the formula weight in grams. Therefore, we can state the relationship as follows:

"When 116.24 g of C_4H_{10} burns, the reaction produces 1376 kcal of heat."

In the balanced equation, the heat is written on the right side, so this reaction produces heat (it is an exothermic reaction). Therefore, the surroundings become warmer. In an exothermic reaction, we write ΔH as a negative number, so ΔH = −1376 kcal.

TRY IT YOURSELF: *When a nickel–cadmium battery is recharged, the following reaction occurs:*

$$Cd(OH)_2 + 2\ Ni(OH)_2 + 252\ \text{kcal} \rightarrow Cd + 2\ Ni(OH)_3$$

What is the relationship between the mass of $Ni(OH)_3$ and the heat in this reaction? What is the sign of ΔH for the reaction?

For additional practice, try Core Problems 6.27 and 6.28.

The Heat of Reaction Can Be Used as a Conversion Factor

We can use the relationship between heat and mass to find the amount of heat that will be produced when we use any mass of reactant. For instance, suppose we want to know the amount of heat that our bodies produce when we burn 1.00 g of sucrose. On page 231, we saw that we get 1342 kcal of heat when we burn 342.296 g of sucrose. We can write this relationship as a pair of conversion factors.

$$\frac{1342\ \text{kcal}}{342.296\ \text{g}\ C_{12}H_{22}O_{11}} \quad \text{and} \quad \frac{342.296\ \text{g}\ C_{12}H_{22}O_{11}}{1342\ \text{kcal}}$$

We actually burn 1.00 g of sucrose. To convert this mass into an amount of heat, we must multiply it by the first of these conversion factors so that the mass unit cancels.

$$1.00 \text{ g } \cancel{C_{12}H_{22}O_{11}} \times \frac{1342 \text{ kcal}}{342.296 \text{ g } \cancel{C_{12}H_{22}O_{11}}} = 3.92058335 \text{ kcal} \quad \text{calculator answer}$$

This answer is valid to three significant figures, so our bodies produce 3.92 kcal of heat when we burn 1.00 g of table sugar.

The relationship between heat energy and mass can also be used to translate an amount of heat into the corresponding mass of reactant or product.

Sample Problem 6.10

Using the relationship between mass and heat in a chemical reaction

It takes 151 kcal of heat to raise the temperature of two quarts of water from 20°C to 100°C. How much methane (CH_4) must you burn to obtain this much heat? The balanced equation for the burning of methane is

$$CH_4 + 2\,O_2 \rightarrow CO_2 + 2\,H_2O + 213 \text{ kcal}$$

SOLUTION

The question asks us for an amount of methane, and the balanced equation gives us a way to relate the mass of methane to the amount of heat produced by the reaction. Therefore, we do not need to use the volume of water or the temperatures. Our initial measurement is 151 kcal, and we must convert that into the corresponding mass of methane. As in all calculations of this type, our answer is in grams.

STEP 1: Identify the original measurement and the final unit.

151 kcal of heat → convert → ? g of methane

Let us begin by using the balanced equation to find a relationship between heat and mass of CH_4. The formula weight of CH_4 is

1 C:	1 × 12.010 amu =	12.010 amu
4 H:	4 × 1.008 amu =	4.032 amu
	Total (formula weight):	16.042 amu

No coefficient precedes the CH_4 in the balanced equation, so we know that we need just one mole (16.042 g) of CH_4 to produce 213 kcal of heat. We can write this relationship as a pair of conversion factors.

STEP 2: Write conversion factors that relate the two units.

$$\frac{16.042 \text{ g } CH_4}{213 \text{ kcal}} \quad \text{and} \quad \frac{213 \text{ kcal}}{16.042 \text{ g } CH_4}$$

To convert 151 kcal of heat into the corresponding mass of CH_4, we must multiply by the first conversion factor so that we can cancel kilocalories.

STEP 3: Choose the conversion factor that allows you to cancel units.

$$151 \cancel{\text{kcal}} \times \frac{16.042 \text{ g } CH_4}{213 \cancel{\text{kcal}}} = 11.37249765 \text{ g } CH_4 \quad \text{calculator answer}$$

STEP 4: Do the math and round your answer.

Finally, we round our answer to three significant figures. We must burn 11.4 g of methane to obtain 151 kcal of heat.

TRY IT YOURSELF: *Hydrogen can be used as a fuel, since it produces a substantial amount of heat when it burns.*

$$2\,H_2 + O_2 \rightarrow 2\,H_2O + 137 \text{ kcal}$$

If you want to obtain 151 kcal of heat from this reaction, how many grams of hydrogen must you burn?

For additional practice, try Core Problems 6.31 through 6.34.

The Nutritive Value of a Food Is the Amount of Energy It Produces When It Is Burned

Most of the chemical compounds that we eat or drink can be burned to produce energy. However, our bodies obtain the energy they need by burning three main classes of nutrients: carbohydrates, fats, and proteins. You have probably heard of these substances already, and you will learn about their structures and chemical behavior in Chapters 13 and 14.

As we saw on page 234, our bodies obtain around 4 kcal of heat when we burn 1 g of sucrose (table sugar). Sucrose is a typical carbohydrate, as are fructose (fruit sugar), lactose (milk sugar), and starch. The structures of these compounds are quite similar to one another, and this structural similarity is reflected in the energy we get from them. One gram of any carbohydrate, regardless of its structure, supplies roughly 4 kcal of energy to our bodies. This energy is called the **nutritive value** of carbohydrates.

Our bodies also burn proteins and fats, and each of these has a nutritive value. One gram of any protein provides us with roughly 4 kcal of energy, and one gram of any fat (both animal fats and vegetable oils) supplies roughly 9 kcal of energy.

When nutritionists list nutritive values of foods, they use the word *Calorie* (written with a capital C and abbreviated *Cal*) in place of the word *kilocalorie*. For example, Figure 6.7 shows part of the nutritional label on a typical snack bar. The label shows the masses of carbohydrate, fat, and protein, which are used to calculate the energy that a person would obtain from eating the bar. When we use the nutritive values to calculate the energy content of the snack bar, we get 134 kcal. The nutritional label gives the energy content as 130 Cal. Note that since the nutritive values are approximate numbers, the energy content is rounded to the nearest 10 Cal.

Some sources of nutritional energy. (a) These foods contain sugars and starches, examples of carbohydrates. (b) Both vegetable oils and animal fats are sources of fat.

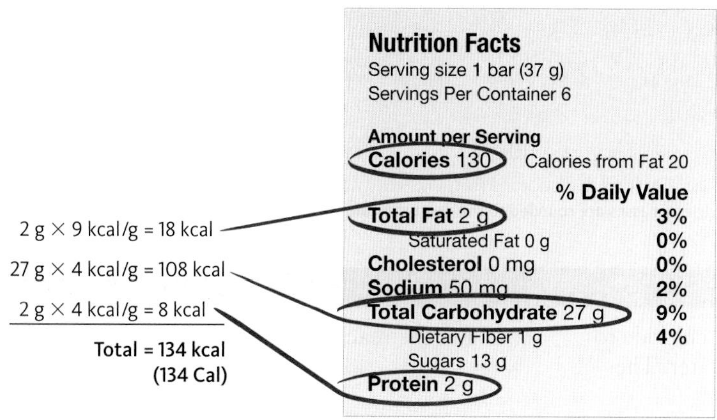

FIGURE 6.7 The relationship between masses of nutrients and Calories.

Sample Problem 6.11

Using nutritive values to estimate the Calorie content of food

One cup of low-fat vanilla yogurt contains the following nutrients: 32 g of carbohydrate, 3.5 g of fat, and 9 g of protein. Estimate the energy content of the yogurt in Calories and in kilocalories.

SOLUTION

To calculate the Calorie content of a food, we multiply the mass of each type of nutrient by the nutritive value of that nutrient.

mass of nutrient	×	nutritive value	=	Calories
32 g carbohydrate	×	4 Cal/g	=	128 Cal
3.5 g fat	×	9 Cal/g	=	31.5 Cal
9 g protein	×	4 Cal/g	=	36 Cal
		TOTAL	=	195.5 Cal

Rounding this value to the nearest 10 Cal gives 200 Cal. The energy content can also be expressed as 200 kcal.

• The nutritive values are conversion factors and can be written in the form $\frac{4\ \text{Cal}}{1\ \text{g}}$

continued

TRY IT YOURSELF: *Two tablespoons of peanut butter (32 g) contain the following nutrients: 7 g of carbohydrate, 16 g of fat, and 8 g of protein. Estimate the energy content of the peanut butter in Calories and in kilocalories.*

For additional practice, try Core Problems 6.35 through 6.38.

Table 6.4 shows the energy content of some foods. To simplify comparisons, the table shows the composition of 100 g of each food.

TABLE 6.4 Energy Content of Various Foods*

Food item	Amount	Carbohydrate	Fat	Protein	Calories (kcal)
Apple	100 g (half of a large apple)	15 g	0 g	0 g	60
Broccoli	100 g ($^1/_2$ cup of chopped broccoli)	5 g	0 g	3 g	30
Kidney beans	100 g ($^2/_5$ cup)	16 g	0 g	5 g	80
White rice	100 g ($^2/_3$ cup of cooked rice)	28 g	0 g	2 g	120
Ground beef (lean)	100 g (one patty, cooked)	0 g	18 g	28 g	270
Chicken (breast meat)	100 g (one portion, roasted)	0 g	3 g	31 g	150
Egg	100 g (two eggs)	2 g	10 g	12 g	150
Whole milk	100 g ($^2/_5$ cup)	5 g	3 g	3 g	60
Orange juice	100 g ($^2/_5$ cup)	10 g	0 g	1 g	40

*Energy content is rounded to the nearest 10 Cal (10 kcal), and nutrient masses are rounded to the nearest gram.

CORE PROBLEMS

6.27 Barium hydroxide reacts with ammonium chloride to produce barium chloride, ammonia and water. The balanced equation for this reaction is

$$Ba(OH)_2(s) + 2\ NH_4Cl(s) + 5.5\text{ kcal} \rightarrow BaCl_2(s) + 2\ NH_3(g) + 2\ H_2O(l)$$

a) When this reaction occurs, do the surroundings become cooler, or do they become warmer?
b) Is this reaction exothermic, or is it endothermic?
c) What is the correct sign (positive or negative) of ΔH for this reaction?
d) What is the relationship between the mass of NH_4Cl and the heat for this reaction?

6.28 Sulfur dioxide reacts with sodium hydroxide to produce sodium sulfite and water. The balanced equation for this reaction is

$$SO_2(g) + 2\ NaOH(aq) \rightarrow Na_2SO_3(aq) + H_2O(l) + 39.3\text{ kcal}$$

a) Is this reaction exothermic, or is it endothermic?
b) When this reaction occurs, do the surroundings become cooler, or do they become warmer?
c) Is the sign of ΔH positive or negative for this reaction?
d) What is the relationship between the mass of NaOH and the heat for this reaction?

6.29 For the reaction that follows, ΔH is −287 kcal:

$$2\ Mg(s) + O_2(g) \rightarrow 2\ MgO(s)$$

a) During this reaction, do the surroundings become hotter, or do they become cooler?
b) Is heat a product in this reaction, or is it a reactant?
c) Rewrite the chemical equation so that it includes the heat.

6.30 For the reaction that follows, ΔH is +7.3 kcal:

$$NH_4Cl(aq) + NaOH(aq) \rightarrow NaCl(aq) + NH_3(g) + H_2O(l)$$

a) When this reaction occurs, do the surroundings become hotter, or do they become cooler?
b) Is heat a product in this reaction, or is it a reactant?
c) Rewrite the chemical equation so that it includes the heat.

6.31 Benzene is a chemical compound in gasoline. When gasoline burns, the benzene reacts with oxygen.

$$2\ C_6H_6 + 15\ O_2 \rightarrow 12\ CO_2 + 6\ H_2O + 1562\text{ kcal}$$

How much heat is given off when 4.32 g (one teaspoon) of benzene reacts with oxygen?

continued

6.32 If you want to obtain 125 kcal of heat by reacting benzene with oxygen, how many grams of benzene must you use? Use the information in Problem 6.31.

6.33 Your body breaks down glucose (blood sugar) into lactic acid when it needs an immediate source of energy. The chemical equation for this reaction (called a fermentation reaction) is

$$C_6H_{12}O_6 \rightarrow 2\ C_3H_6O_3 + 16.3\ \text{kcal}$$

a) Calculate the amount of heat that is formed when your body makes 1.00 g of lactic acid ($C_3H_6O_3$) using this reaction.
b) How many grams of glucose must your body break down in this fashion to produce 5.00 kcal of heat?

6.34 In winemaking, microorganisms break down the sugar in grapes into ethanol (grain alcohol) and carbon dioxide. The balanced equation for this reaction is

$$C_6H_{12}O_6 \rightarrow 2\ C_2H_6O + 2\ CO_2 + 16.6\ \text{kcal}$$

a) Given that 100 mL of wine contains 9.5 g of ethanol (C_2H_6O), how much heat was produced as this ethanol was being formed?
b) How many grams of sugar must be broken down to produce 10.0 kcal of heat?

6.35 One cup of cottage cheese contains 6 g of carbohydrate, 28 g of protein, and 10 g of fat. How many Calories are there in a cup of cottage cheese?

6.36 One cup of soft-serve ice cream contains 38 g of carbohydrate, 7 g of protein, and 22 g of fat. How many Calories are there in a cup of soft-serve ice cream?

6.37 A Mega-Sweet snack cake contains 160 Cal. The manufacturer wants to remove enough sugar to lower the Calorie value to 140 Cal. How many grams of sugar must the manufacturer remove? (Sugar is a carbohydrate.)

6.38 Greesy-Snax potato chips contain 180 Cal per serving. The manufacturer wants to remove enough vegetable oil to lower the Calorie value to 130 Cal. How many grams of vegetable oil must the manufacturer remove? (Vegetable oil is a fat.)

6.5 Combustion and Precipitation Reactions

OBJECTIVE: *Recognize and write chemical equations for combustion and precipitation reactions.*

Chemical substances react with one another in many ways, so you will see many kinds of reactions during your study of chemistry. In this section, we examine two common types of chemical reactions: combustion and precipitation.

Combustion Is the Reaction of a Substance with Oxygen

You have undoubtedly seen that some substances catch fire and burn when they are heated. The chemical process that we call burning is a **combustion reaction**. Combustion is the reaction of a chemical compound with oxygen (in the form of O_2), and it normally converts the compound into small oxygen-containing molecules such as CO_2, H_2O, and SO_2. In particular, compounds made from the elements carbon, hydrogen, and oxygen react with O_2, producing carbon dioxide and water. Combustion reactions are important because they produce a great deal of heat, so we use them to supply the majority of the energy we need for heating our homes, powering our motor vehicles, generating electricity, and other activities.

Let us examine a specific combustion reaction. Xylene (C_8H_{10}) is added to gasoline because it burns smoothly and improves the octane rating of the fuel. Since xylene contains only carbon and hydrogen, it forms carbon dioxide and water when it burns. To write the equation for the combustion of xylene, we start by listing the reactants and products.

$$C_8H_{10} + O_2 \rightarrow CO_2 + H_2O$$

None of the three elements in this equation is balanced, so we must decide which element to attend to first. In general, it is easiest to balance carbon, hydrogen, and then oxygen.

1. We balance carbon by writing a coefficient in front of CO_2. We need eight molecules of CO_2, which gives us

$$C_8H_{10} + O_2 \rightarrow 8\ CO_2 + H_2O$$

Combustion reactions produce a great deal of energy and are among the most conspicuous and dramatic reactions we observe.

2. Next, we balance hydrogen by writing a coefficient in front of H_2O. We need five molecules of H_2O.

$$C_8H_{10} + O_2 \rightarrow 8\ CO_2 + 5\ H_2O$$

3. Finally, we balance oxygen. We have a total of 21 oxygen atoms on the product side of the equation, so we cannot write a whole number in front of O_2. *If you are faced with an odd number of oxygen atoms, you must multiply all of the coefficients by 2 before you balance oxygen.* Therefore, we need to double the coefficients of C_8H_{10}, CO_2 and H_2O.

$$2\ C_8H_{10} + O_2 \rightarrow 16\ CO_2 + 10\ H_2O$$

Doubling the coefficients always produces an even number of oxygen atoms, allowing us to balance oxygen using O_2. In this case, we now have 42 oxygen atoms on the product side (32 from the CO_2 and 10 from the H_2O). We need 21 molecules of O_2.

$$2\ C_8H_{10} + 21\ O_2 \rightarrow 16\ CO_2 + 10\ H_2O$$

Sample Problem **6.12**

Writing a balanced equation for a combustion reaction

Stearic acid has the chemical formula $C_{18}H_{36}O_2$. It is a component of fat and can be burned to produce energy. Write the balanced equation for the combustion of stearic acid.

SOLUTION

To begin, we need to identify the reactants and the products. One of the reactants is stearic acid, and in any combustion reaction, the other reactant is O_2. Since stearic acid contains only carbon, hydrogen, and oxygen, the products of combustion are carbon dioxide and water. Our initial reaction is

$$C_{18}H_{36}O_2 + O_2 \rightarrow CO_2 + H_2O$$

Now we must balance the equation. Stearic acid contains 18 carbon atoms, so we must make 18 molecules of carbon dioxide.

$$C_{18}H_{36}O_2 + O_2 \rightarrow 18\ CO_2 + H_2O$$

Next, we balance hydrogen. Stearic acid contains 36 hydrogen atoms, so we need to make enough water to give us 36 hydrogen atoms. Each water molecule contains 2 hydrogen atoms, so we need 18 water molecules.

$$C_{18}H_{36}O_2 + O_2 \rightarrow 18\ CO_2 + 18\ H_2O$$

Finally, we balance oxygen. Our products contain a total of 54 oxygen atoms (36 from the carbon dioxide and 18 from the water), so the reactants must also contain 54 oxygen atoms. The stearic acid has 2 oxygen atoms, so the other 52 oxygen atoms must come from O_2. We need 26 O_2 molecules.

$$C_{18}H_{36}O_2 + 26\ O_2 \rightarrow 18\ CO_2 + 18\ H_2O$$

TRY IT YOURSELF: *Diethyl ether has the chemical formula $C_4H_{10}O$. It was used for many years as a general anesthetic, but it is no longer used because it is a severe fire hazard. Write the balanced equation for the combustion reaction for diethyl ether.*

For additional practice, try Core Problems 6.39 and 6.40.

Combustion reactions are the primary source of energy for animals, fungi, and many microorganisms. In addition, green plants use the energy of sunlight to build large molecules from carbon dioxide and water; they then burn these molecules to supply the energy for all other tasks. The combustion of coal, petroleum, and natural gas has been the principal source of energy for human society for many years. It is no exaggeration to say that the world as we know it is fueled by combustion.

Precipitation Is the Formation of an Insoluble Compound

The magnificent stone formations in Mammoth Caves in Kentucky or Carlsbad Caverns in New Mexico are made from calcium carbonate ($CaCO_3$), which is formed by reactions such as the following:

$$CaCl_2(aq) + Na_2CO_3(aq) \rightarrow CaCO_3(s) + 2\ NaCl(aq)$$

This reaction is an example of a **precipitation reaction**, in which two soluble reactants produce an insoluble product. In this case, the reaction occurs because calcium carbonate is insoluble in water. The calcium and carbonate ions are so strongly attracted to each other that water molecules cannot hold them apart. As a result, when any two solutions containing calcium ions and carbonate ions are mixed, calcium carbonate forms. In general, a precipitation reaction occurs when solutions that contain ions are mixed and one of the possible combinations of ions does not dissolve in water.

These beautiful cave formations are the result of precipitation reactions.

Sample Problem 6.13

Recognizing precipitation reactions

Which of the following are precipitation reactions?

$$2\ HCl(aq) + Ba(OH)_2(aq) \rightarrow BaCl_2(aq) + 2\ H_2O(l)$$

$$2\ HCl(aq) + Pb(NO_3)_2(aq) \rightarrow PbCl_2(s) + 2\ HNO_3(aq)$$

$$2\ HCl(aq) + Pb(OH)_2(s) \rightarrow PbCl_2(s) + 2\ H_2O(l)$$

SOLUTION

Only the second reaction is a precipitation reaction. In a precipitation reaction, one of the products must be a solid and all of the reactants must be dissolved in water. In the first equation, none of the products is a solid, and in the third reaction, one of the reactants is a solid.

TRY IT YOURSELF: *Which of the following is a precipitation reaction?*

$$CaSO_4(s) + Na_2CO_3(aq) \rightarrow CaCO_3(s) + Na_2SO_4(aq)$$

$$MgSO_4(aq) + Na_2CO_3(aq) \rightarrow MgCO_3(s) + Na_2SO_4(aq)$$

For additional practice, try Core Problems 6.41 and 6.42.

A precipitation reaction. When solutions of NaI and $Pb(NO_3)_2$ are mixed, yellow PbI_2 forms.

Figure 6.8 shows what happens when solutions of $CaCl_2$ and Na_2CO_3 are mixed. Note that only the calcium and carbonate ions actually become bonded to each other. The Na^+ and Cl^- ions are unaffected by this reaction. In general, precipitation reactions

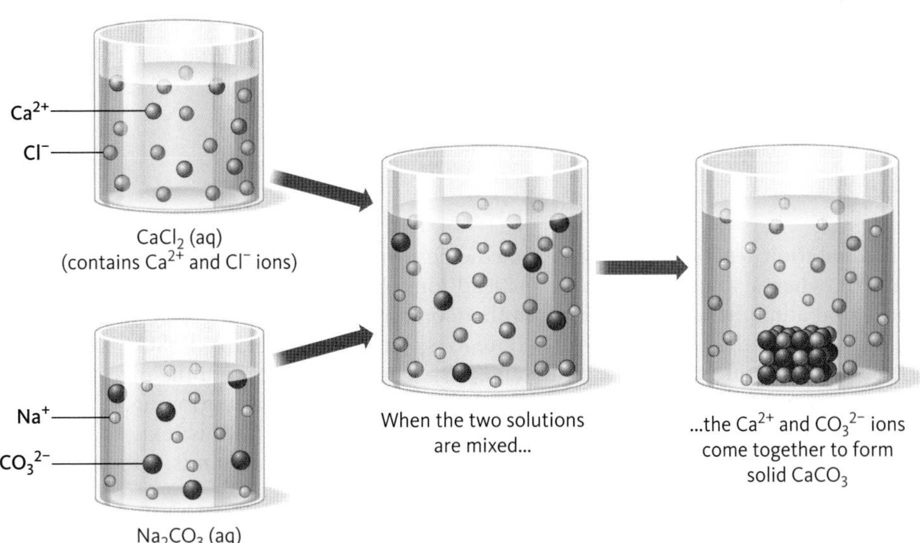

FIGURE 6.8 The precipitation of calcium carbonate.

Health Note: Many elderly people suffer from calcium pyrophosphate dihydrate deposition disease, a condition in which calcium pyrophosphate ($Ca_2P_2O_7$) precipitates as tiny crystals in the joints. The crystals irritate the joints, producing swelling and severe pain. The precipitation reaction is $2\ Ca^{2+}(aq) + P_2O_7^{4-}(aq) \rightarrow Ca_2P_2O_7(s)$.

only involve two of the four ions in the reaction mixture. Because of this, chemists often write a precipitation reaction in a simplified form called a **net ionic equation**. Net ionic equations show only the substances that change during a reaction. In a precipitation reaction, the net ionic equation shows the two ions that combine to form the insoluble compound. The net ionic equation for this reaction is

$$Ca^{2+}(aq) + CO_3^{2-}(aq) \rightarrow CaCO_3(s)$$

The Na^+ and Cl^- ions are called **spectator ions** because they are present in the reaction mixture but do not form a bond or change into some other chemical during the reaction. Spectator ions do not appear in a net ionic equation.

If you have ever seen the white deposit that forms on the sides of a bathtub after a long, soapy bath (a "bathtub ring"), you have seen the product of a precipitation reaction. The white material is produced when soap reacts with the minerals in your tap water. Soap is a mixture of several closely related ionic compounds that contain sodium plus a large polyatomic ion. Sodium laurate ($NaC_{12}H_{21}O_2$) is a typical soap and is made up of Na^+ and $C_{12}H_{21}O_2^-$ ions. Tap water contains various calcium and magnesium compounds such as $CaCl_2$ and $MgCl_2$. Soap reacts with the calcium and magnesium ions in these compounds to produce insoluble substances. When sodium laurate reacts with calcium chloride, the precipitation reaction is

$$2\ NaC_{12}H_{23}O_2(aq) + CaCl_2(aq) \rightarrow Ca(C_{12}H_{23}O_2)_2(s) + 2\ NaCl(aq)$$

The net ionic equation for this reaction makes it clear that the reaction only involves the calcium and laurate ions.

$$Ca^{2+}(aq) + 2\ C_{12}H_{23}O_2^-(aq) \rightarrow Ca(C_{12}H_{23}O_2)_2(s)$$

Sample Problem **6.14**

Writing a net ionic equation for a precipitation reaction

When a solution of $AgNO_3$ is mixed with a solution of Na_3PO_4, solid Ag_3PO_4 forms. Write the net ionic equation for this precipitation reaction.

SOLUTION

The product is Ag_3PO_4, which contains Ag^+ and PO_4^{3-} ions. Therefore, the net ionic equation must be the reaction of Ag^+ and PO_4^{3-} to form Ag_3PO_4.

$$Ag^+(aq) + PO_4^{3-}(aq) \rightarrow Ag_3PO_4(s)$$

Be sure to balance the equation. It takes three Ag^+ ions and one PO_4^{3-} ion to make Ag_3PO_4, so the balanced equation is

$$3\ Ag^+(aq) + PO_4^{3-}(aq) \rightarrow Ag_3PO_4(s)$$

TRY IT YOURSELF: *When a solution of $FeSO_4$ is mixed with a solution of KOH, solid $Fe(OH)_2$ forms. Write the net ionic equation for this precipitation reaction.*

For additional practice, try Core Problems 6.43 and 6.44.

Precipitation reactions are used in medicine to treat certain types of poisoning. For example, when a solution that contains lead ions (Pb^{2+}) is consumed, the treatment includes oral administration of a solution that contains sulfate ions (SO_4^{2-}). Lead ions are highly toxic, but they combine with sulfate ions to produce insoluble $PbSO_4$, which cannot be absorbed into the bloodstream and passes harmlessly through the digestive tract. Table 6.5 lists some precipitation reactions that are used to treat poisoning.

You will not be expected to predict precipitation reactions in this text, because doing so requires knowing the solubilities of many ionic compounds. However, you should be able to recognize a precipitation reaction when you see it written as a balanced equation, and you should know that a precipitation reaction normally occurs whenever a pair of aqueous ions can combine to form an insoluble compound. You should also be able to write the net ionic equation for a precipitation reaction if you know the product of the reaction.

TABLE 6.5 Precipitation Reactions in the Treatment of Poisoning

Poison	Treatment	Active Substance	Precipitation Reaction
Pb^{2+} (lead: found in old paint and leaded gasoline)	Na_2SO_4 $MgSO_4$ $Al_2(SO_4)_3$	SO_4^{2-}	$Pb^{2+}(aq) + SO_4^{2-}(aq) \rightarrow PbSO_4(s)$
Ba^{2+} (barium: used in some chemical analyses)	Na_2SO_4 $MgSO_4$ $Al_2(SO_4)_3$	SO_4^{2-}	$Ba^{2+}(aq) + SO_4^{2-}(aq) \rightarrow BaSO_4(s)$
Ag^+ (silver: used in photographic film)	NaCl	Cl^-	$Ag^+(aq) + Cl^-(aq) \rightarrow AgCl(s)$
F^- (fluoride: used in toothpaste)	$CaCl_2$	Ca^{2+}	$Ca^{2+}(aq) + 2\,F^-(aq) \rightarrow CaF_2(s)$
$C_2O_4^{2-}$ (oxalate ion: found in some vegetables)	$CaCl_2$	Ca^{2+}	$Ca^{2+}(aq) + C_2O_4^{2-}(aq) \rightarrow CaC_2O_4(s)$

CORE PROBLEMS

6.39 Write a chemical equation that represents the combustion reaction of each of the following:
a) C_7H_8 (toluene, a compound that increases the octane rating of gasoline)
b) C_4H_{10} (butane, the fuel in cigarette lighters)
c) $C_4H_{10}O$ (*t*-butyl alcohol, a compound that increases the octane rating of gasoline)

6.40 Write a chemical equation that represents the combustion reaction of each of the following:
a) C_7H_{16} (heptane, a component of gasoline)
b) $C_{14}H_{10}$ (anthracene, a compound found in wood smoke)
c) $C_{12}H_{24}O_2$ (lauric acid, a component of fats)

6.41 Which of the following equations represent combustion reactions, which represent precipitation reactions, and which represent neither of these types?
a) $C_2H_6O + 3\,O_2 \rightarrow 2\,CO_2 + 3\,H_2O$
b) $NaOH(aq) + HBr(aq) \rightarrow NaBr(aq) + H_2O(l)$
c) $2\,PbBr_2 + O_2 \rightarrow 2\,PbO + 2\,Br_2$
d) $AlCl_3(aq) + 3\,NaOH(aq) \rightarrow Al(OH)_3(s) + 3\,NaCl(aq)$

6.42 Which of the following equations represent combustion reactions, which represent precipitation reactions, and which represent neither of these types?
a) $C_2H_6O + O_2 \rightarrow C_2H_4O_2 + H_2O$
b) $AgNO_3(aq) + HBr(aq) \rightarrow AgBr(s) + HNO_3(aq)$
c) $CuO(s) + 2\,HCl(aq) \rightarrow CuCl_2(aq) + H_2O(l)$
d) $4\,NH_3(g) + 3\,O_2(g) \rightarrow 2\,N_2(g) + 6\,H_2O(l)$

6.43 Write a net ionic equation for each of the following precipitation reactions:
a) $AgNO_3(aq) + KBr(aq) \rightarrow AgBr(s) + KNO_3(aq)$
b) $3\,MgCl_2(aq) + 2\,Na_3PO_4(aq) \rightarrow Mg_3(PO_4)_2(s) + 6\,NaCl(aq)$
c) $Pb(NO_3)_2(aq) + CaI_2(aq) \rightarrow Ca(NO_3)_2(aq) + PbI_2(s)$

6.44 Write a net ionic equation for each of the following precipitation reactions:
a) $BaCl_2(aq) + K_2SO_4(aq) \rightarrow BaSO_4(s) + 2\,KCl(aq)$
b) $AlCl_3(aq) + 3\,NaOH(aq) \rightarrow Al(OH)_3(s) + 3\,NaCl(aq)$
c) $Pb(NO_3)_2(aq) + MgBr_2(aq) \rightarrow Mg(NO_3)_2(aq) + PbBr_2(s)$

6.6 Reaction Rate and Activation Energy

OBJECTIVES: *Understand and use the relationships between the rate of a reaction and activation energy, temperature, concentration, surface area, and catalysts.*

Many winter sports enthusiasts use heat packs designed to combat frostbite and keep their hands and feet warm. When the outer plastic wrapper is opened, the packet gradually becomes warm and then remains warm for several hours. The packets contain powdered iron, which reacts with oxygen from the air, producing iron(III) oxide and a great deal of heat.

$$4\,Fe(s) + 3\,O_2(g) \rightarrow 2\,Fe_2O_3(s) + 393\text{ kcal}$$

Another exothermic reaction that is commonly used in the United States is the combustion of natural gas. This reaction is the heat source in gas furnaces, water heaters, and even clothes dryers. Natural gas is primarily methane, which burns as follows:

$$CH_4(g) + 2\,O_2(g) \rightarrow CO_2(g) + 2\,H_2O(l) + 213\text{ kcal}$$

In principle, the reaction of iron and oxygen could be used to heat a home, while the reaction of methane and oxygen could be used to warm a skier's cold hands. In practice, however, this is never the case. The usefulness of a reaction does not depend solely on the products of the reaction or on the amount of energy that the reaction produces; it also depends on how rapidly the starting materials react with each other. Iron and oxygen react at room temperature, and the reaction is slow, making it ideal for a sustained, gradual production of heat. Methane and oxygen, on the other hand, react only at high temperatures, and the reaction is rapid and violent. This reaction is acceptable in a furnace but not in a skier's mitten.

The Rate of a Reaction Is Determined by Several Factors

Health Note: The amount of any medicine that you can take depends on the rate at which your body can break down and eliminate the medicine. For example, your body requires at least four hours to break down most of a typical dose of ibuprofen, so you should not take the next dose of ibuprofen less than four hours after the previous one.

The speed of a reaction is called its **rate**. A reaction that consumes its reactants quickly (a fast reaction) is said to have a high reaction rate, while one that consumes its reactants slowly has a low reaction rate. The rate of a reaction is influenced by the concentration of each reactant, the contact area between the reactants, the temperature, the availability of a catalyst, and the nature of the reaction. Let us examine each of these factors in turn.

1. *The concentration of each reactant.* The higher the concentration of reactant, the faster the reaction proceeds, as shown in Figure 6.9. Atoms and molecules can only react if they collide with one another. At high concentrations, the reactant molecules are crowded together, so they collide and react often. At low concentrations, the reactants collide less frequently.
2. *The contact area between the reactants.* When a reactant is a solid, only its surface is exposed to the other reactants. A larger surface area results in a faster reaction. Breaking a large block of solid into smaller pieces increases its surface area, so chemists often grind a solid reactant into powder to speed up a reaction. Likewise, if two liquids do not mix, stirring them speeds up their reaction by producing small droplets, thereby increasing the contact area between the liquids, as shown in Figure 6.10.
3. *The temperature.* All reactions speed up when the temperature is increased. As we saw in Chapter 4, when the temperature goes up, atoms and molecules move more rapidly and collide more often. In addition, the collisions are more violent, making it more likely that the necessary bond breaking can occur. We will examine this in more detail in a moment.

   If you have ever seen the sluggish movements of a lizard or an insect on a cold day, you have already seen the effect of temperature on chemical reactions. Lizards and insects are cold blooded, so their body temperatures are the same as that of the surrounding atmosphere. When these organisms are cold, all of the chemical reactions inside their bodies slow down.
4. *The presence of a catalyst.* A **catalyst** is a chemical that speeds up a reaction but is not consumed by the reaction. For example, the exhaust system of every car built in the United States includes a catalytic converter, which contains a small amount of platinum metal. The platinum speeds up the breakdown of nitric oxide into nitrogen and oxygen.

   $$2\ NO(g) \rightarrow N_2(g) + O_2(g)$$

   Nitric oxide is a toxic by-product of automobile and truck engines and is a major source of air pollution in urban areas. It breaks down into the nontoxic gases nitrogen and oxygen, but this reaction is normally slow. Platinum speeds up the reaction by weakening the bond between nitrogen and oxygen, decreasing the amount of nitric oxide that is released into the atmosphere. The platinum is a catalyst, since it is not a reactant and is

Charles D. Winters
(a)

Charles D. Winters
(b)

Two reactions that have different rates. (a) The reaction that occurs when you put an Alka-Seltzer tablet into water is fast. (b) Rusting is a slow reaction.

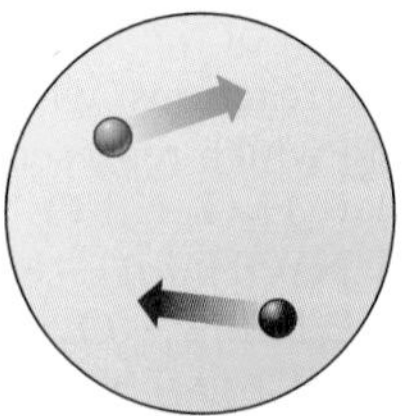
When the reactant concentrations are low, the reaction is slow because the molecules do not collide often.

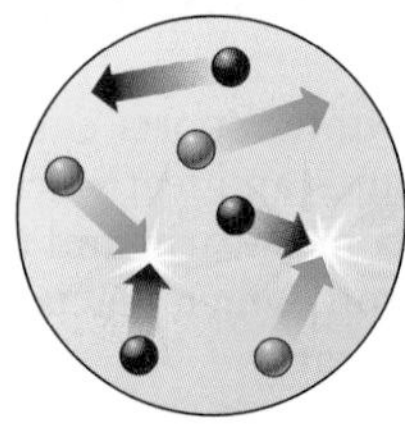
When the reactant concentrations are high, the reaction is fast because the molecules collide frequently.

FIGURE 6.9 The effect of concentration on the rate of reaction.

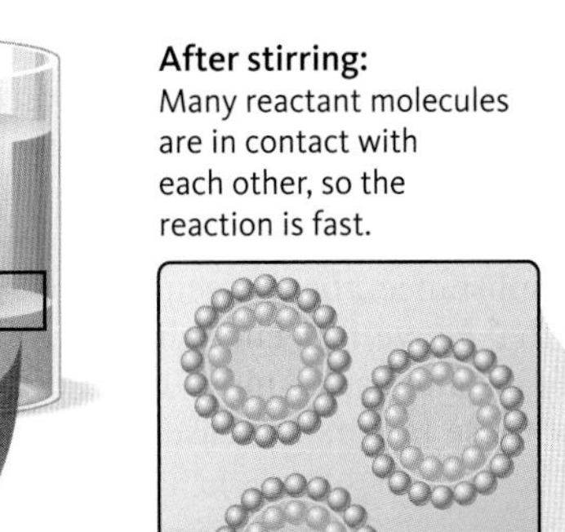

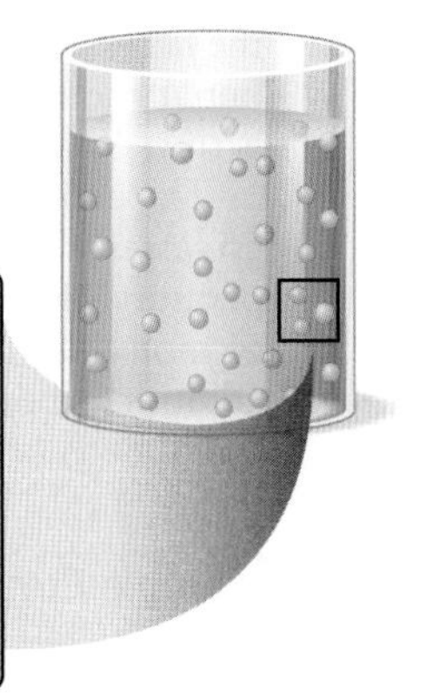

Before stirring:
Few reactant molecules are in contact with each other, so the reaction is slow.
After stirring:
Many reactant molecules are in contact with each other, so the reaction is fast.

FIGURE 6.10 The effect of stirring on the surface area of a heterogeneous mixture.

Health Note: In hypothermia, the body temperature drops significantly below 35°C. Hypothermia decreases the rate of all reactions in the body, leading to impaired consciousness, irregular or weak heartbeat, and other symptoms. A body temperature below 32°C is likely to be fatal unless treated immediately.

TABLE 6.6 Some Digestive Reactions That Require Catalysts

Reaction	Catalyst
Sucrose (table sugar) → glucose + fructose	Sucrase
Lactose → glucose + galactose	Lactase
Fats → glycerol + fatty acids	Lipase
Proteins → amino acids	Pepsin, trypsin, and other enzymes
Starch → glucose	Amylase and other enzymes

not used up during the reaction. Chemists sometimes write the formula of the catalyst above the arrow in a balanced equation:

$$2\ NO(g) \xrightarrow{Pt} N_2(g) + O_2(g)$$

Catalysts are extremely important in biology, because reactions must occur rapidly to be of use to a living organism. As a result, most reactions that occur in a living organism involve a catalyst. For example, when you digest food, your digestive tract breaks down a variety of large molecules into smaller pieces that can be absorbed into your bloodstream. Your body makes a catalyst (called an enzyme) for each of these reactions. Some examples of digestive reactions are listed in Table 6.6.

5. *The nature of the reaction.* Some reactions are inherently faster than others. For instance, the reaction of vinegar (acetic acid) with baking soda (sodium bicarbonate) is almost instantaneous, while the rusting of iron can take years to complete.

To explain why some reactions are faster than others, we need to look at energy again. For two (or more) molecules to react, they must collide with sufficient energy to break any chemical bonds that must be disrupted during the reaction. In essence, if the molecules are moving too slowly, they will not react, even if they collide. The minimum energy that the molecules need to react is called the **activation energy** of the reaction. You may find it helpful to think of the activation energy as an energy investment that you must put into the reactants to make the products.

For example, hydrogen and iodine can react to form hydrogen iodide.

$$H_2(g) + I_2(g) \rightarrow 2\ HI(g)$$

However, for this reaction to occur, some of the covalent bonds in the reactants must break before hydrogen and iodine atoms can combine to form hydrogen iodide. Only a violent collision between the reactant molecules can supply enough energy to break a covalent bond. The activation energy of this reaction is 41 kcal, which means that we must put in 41 kcal of energy to accelerate the molecules to the necessary speed. The molecules in a mixture of H_2 and I_2 have a range of speeds, but at room temperature the number of molecules that have enough energy to react is tiny. As a result, this reaction is extremely slow at room temperature.

The concept of activation energy allows us to explain more fully why reactions go faster when the reactants are heated. Remember that when we increase the temperature of a substance, the molecules move more rapidly. As a result, the number of molecules that move fast enough to react increases as the temperature rises. In addition, since the molecules move more rapidly, they collide with each other more often. Both of these factors increase the reaction rate.

Sample Problem **6.15**

Relating activation energy to reaction rate

If the following two reactions occur at the same temperature and reactant concentration, which reaction is faster?

$$CH_4 + Br_2 \rightarrow CH_3Br + HBr \text{ (activation energy = 20 kcal)}$$

$$CH_4 + Cl_2 \rightarrow CH_3Cl + HCl \text{ (activation energy = 4 kcal)}$$

SOLUTION

The reaction with the smaller activation energy is faster. When the activation energy is small, many reactant molecules have enough energy to react when they collide, so the reaction is rapid. Therefore, the second reaction is faster than the first.

TRY IT YOURSELF: *If the following two reactions occur at the same temperature and reactant concentration, which reaction is faster?*

$$CH_3I + NaCl \rightarrow CH_3Cl + NaI \text{ (activation energy = 16.9 kcal)}$$

$$CH_3I + NaBr \rightarrow CH_3Br + NaI \text{ (activation energy = 17.3 kcal)}$$

For additional practice, try Core Problems 6.49 and 6.50.

An Energy Diagram Shows How Energy Changes During a Reaction

We can summarize how energy is involved in a chemical reaction with an **energy diagram**, which shows how the energy of the atoms changes as they are converted from reactants to products. The energy diagram for the formation of hydrogen iodide is shown in Figure 6.11.

We must put in 41 kcal of energy (the activation energy) to push the molecules to the top of the energy hill. Once the molecules are moving fast enough, they react, and the reaction produces energy. In this reaction, we get back our 41 kcal, and the reaction produces an additional 2 kcal. The 2 kcal is the heat of reaction, which we can write into the balanced equation.

$$H_2(g) + I_2(g) \rightarrow 2\,HI(g) + 2 \text{ kcal}$$

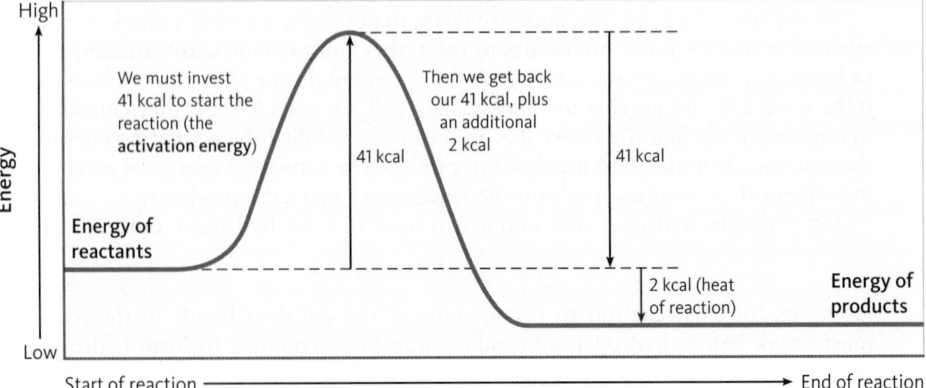

FIGURE 6.11 The energy diagram for the reaction of hydrogen and iodine.

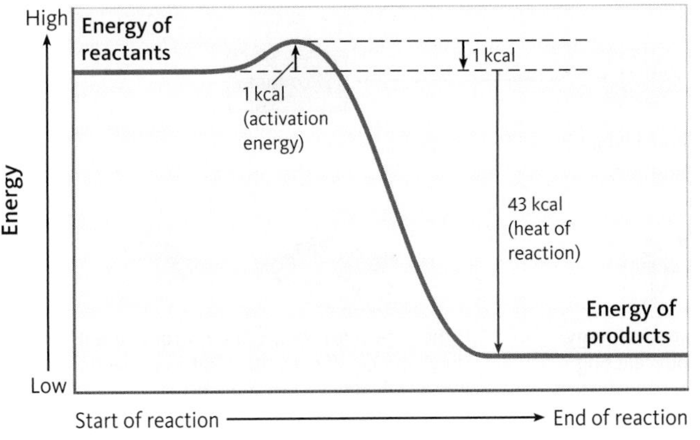

FIGURE 6.12 The energy diagram for the reaction of hydrogen iodide and ammonia.

High
Low
Energy
We must invest 99 kcal to start the reaction (the **activation energy**)
We only get back 60 kcal out of our original 99 kcal
60 kcal
Energy of products
99 kcal
39 kcal (heat of reaction)
Energy of reactants
Start of reaction
End of reaction

FIGURE 6.13 The energy diagram for the formation of nitrous oxide.

Since this reaction produces heat, it is an exothermic reaction. Note that the product energy is lower than the reactant energy. This is why we write ΔH for an exothermic reaction as a negative number.

By contrast, let us examine the reaction of hydrogen iodide with ammonia (NH_3).

$$HI(g) + NH_3(g) \rightarrow NH_4I(s) + 43\text{ kcal}$$

Figure 6.12 shows the energy diagram for this reaction. The activation energy of this reaction is less than 1 kcal, which means that the reactant molecules do not have to be moving at high speeds to form the product. At room temperature, the vast majority of reactant molecules are moving rapidly enough to react when they collide, so this reaction is almost instantaneous. In general, *the lower the activation energy, the faster the reaction proceeds.*

Figure 6.13 shows the energy diagram for the formation of nitrous oxide (N_2O).

$$2\,N_2(g) + O_2(g) + 39\text{ kcal} \rightarrow 2\,N_2O(g)$$

The activation energy of this reaction is 99 kcal, so this is the amount of energy that we must invest to break some of the chemical bonds. However, in this case, the reaction only returns 60 kcal of energy to us. The net effect is that we must put in 39 kcal of energy to convert nitrogen and oxygen into nitrous oxide. Since this reaction absorbs energy (in the form of heat), it is an endothermic reaction. It is also an extremely slow reaction, because the activation energy is large. Table 6.7 summarizes the relationship between the heat of reaction and the activation energy.

TABLE 6.7 Energy Relationships in Chemical Reactions

	Exothermic Reaction	Endothermic Reaction
Sign of ΔH	Negative	Positive
Effect of the reaction	Makes the surroundings **warmer** (it gives off heat)	Makes the surroundings **cooler** (it absorbs heat)
Relative energy of reactants and products	Energy of reactants is **higher** than energy of products	Energy of reactants is **lower** than energy of products
How much of the activation energy is returned?	All of the activation energy, plus some extra energy	Some of the activation energy
Typical energy diagram		

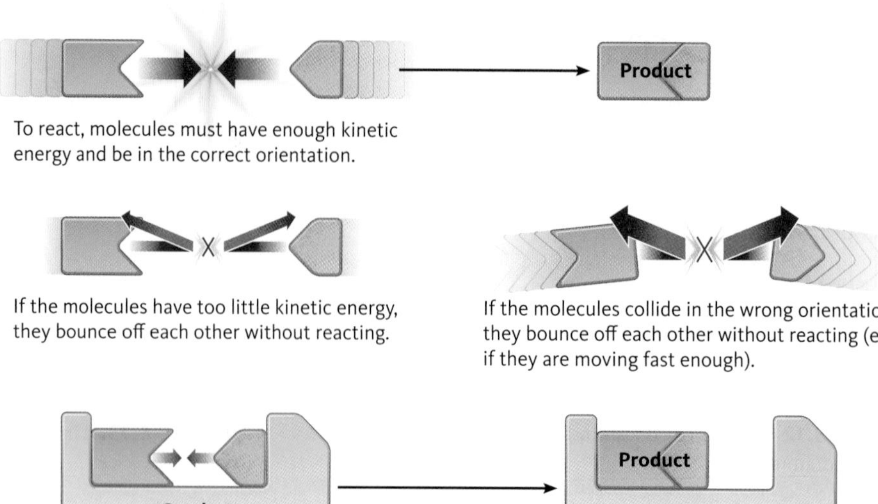

Product
To react, molecules must have enough kinetic energy and be in the correct orientation.
If the molecules have too little kinetic energy, they bounce off each other without reacting.
If the molecules collide in the wrong orientation, they bounce off each other without reacting (even if they are moving fast enough).
Catalyst
Product
A catalyst positions the molecules in the correct orientation and allows them to react with less energy (lower kinetic energies).

FIGURE 6.14 How a catalyst increases the rate of a reaction.

Catalysts Decrease the Activation Energy of a Reaction

Recall that a catalyst is a chemical that speeds up a reaction without being consumed in the reaction. Catalysts accomplish this in two ways. Many catalysts are able to position the reactant molecules so that they can react more easily, by holding the reactants close to each other and in the correct orientation. However, *the primary role of a catalyst is to lower the activation energy of a reaction.* If you think of the activation energy as a hill that the reactants must climb, a catalyst provides a tunnel through the hill. Figure 6.14 illustrates how a catalyst speeds up a reaction.

Health Note: Hydrogen peroxide destroys the pigments in hair, so it is used in hair-coloring products. Also, as we age, the cells that produce hair lose some of their ability to destroy naturally occurring hydrogen peroxide, and the increasing concentration of hydrogen peroxide damages the enzymes that produce hair pigments, giving us the gray hair of advancing age.

For example, let us look at the breakdown of hydrogen peroxide (H_2O_2) into water and oxygen.

$$2\ H_2O_2(aq) \rightarrow 2\ H_2O(l) + O_2(g) + 57\ \text{kcal}$$

This is an important reaction in our bodies, because we form hydrogen peroxide constantly as we burn nutrients to obtain energy. Hydrogen peroxide is poisonous, because it reacts with many of the complex and vital molecules in living cells, so it must be destroyed immediately. Cells that use oxygen make a catalyst that speeds up the breakdown of hydrogen peroxide. This compound, a protein called catalase, is such an effective catalyst that

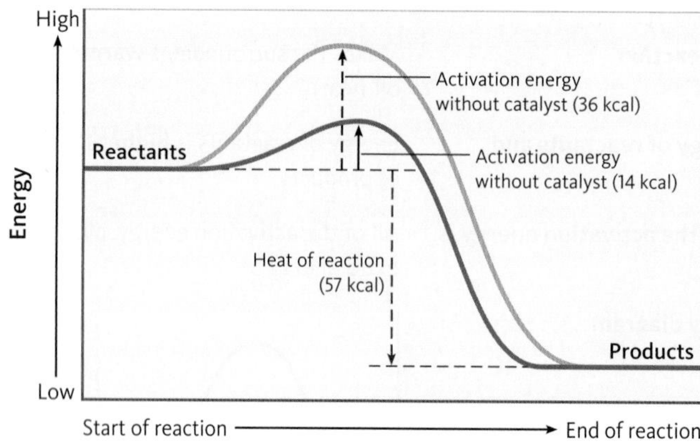

FIGURE 6.15 The effect of a catalyst on the activation energy of a reaction.

this reaction occurs a hundred million times faster with it than without it. Catalase accomplishes this remarkable feat by decreasing the activation energy of the reaction from 36 to 14 kcal. Figure 6.15 shows the energy diagram for this reaction.

Note that catalase makes the activation energy of the reaction smaller but does not change the heat of reaction. The breakdown of hydrogen peroxide gives off 57 kcal of heat whether or not a catalyst is used. Catalysts decrease the activation energy of a reaction, but *they do not change the heat of reaction.*

Sample Problem **6.16**

Drawing an energy diagram for a reaction

When our bodies use proteins as an energy source, they make the compound urea. In turn, urea can break down into carbon dioxide and ammonia.

$$N_2H_4CO + H_2O + 7\text{ kcal} \rightarrow CO_2 + 2\ NH_3$$

The activation energy of this reaction is 28 kcal. Draw an energy diagram for this reaction, and label the activation energy and the heat of reaction on your diagram.

SOLUTION

The activation energy is 28 kcal, so the energy must initially increase by 28 kcal. The reaction is endothermic (the balanced equation has the heat on the reactant side), so the energy of the products must be 7 kcal higher than that of the reactants. Putting this together gives us the following diagram:

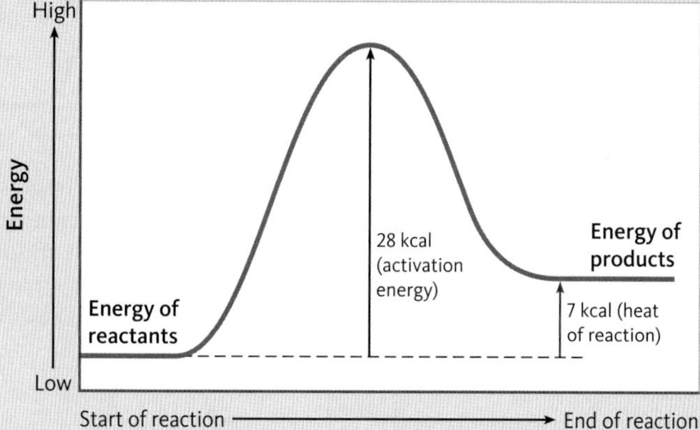

TRY IT YOURSELF: *Many organisms make a catalyst (a protein called urease) that speeds up the breakdown of urea. The catalyst reduces the activation energy to 8 kcal. Draw an energy diagram for the breakdown of urea using urease as a catalyst.*

For additional practice, try Core Problems 6.51 through 6.54.

CORE PROBLEMS

6.45 Iron reacts with sulfuric acid (H_2SO_4) according to the following equation:

$$Fe(s) + H_2SO_4(aq) \rightarrow FeSO_4(aq) + H_2(g)$$

Will the rate of this reaction increase, decrease, or remain the same if

a) the concentration of sulfuric acid is increased?
b) the temperature is decreased?
c) the iron is ground into powder?
d) a catalyst is added?

6.46 Vitamin C has the chemical formula $C_6H_8O_6$. It reacts with oxygen according to the following equation:

$$2\ C_6H_8O_6(aq) + O_2(g) \rightarrow 2\ C_6H_6O_6(aq) + 2\ H_2O(l)$$

Will the rate of this reaction increase, decrease, or remain the same if

a) the concentration of vitamin C is decreased?
b) the pressure of oxygen is increased?
c) the temperature is increased?
d) the mixture is shaken vigorously?

continued

6.47 Food spoils when it is left at room temperature, because bacteria convert some of the nutrients in the food into unpleasant (and occasionally toxic) products. Explain why refrigerating the food slows down the spoiling process.

6.48 Paper reacts with oxygen to form carbon dioxide, water, and ash. (If you have ever seen a piece of paper burn, you have seen this reaction.) Explain why all of your books and papers have not caught fire and burned to ash.

6.49 Both carbon and sodium can react with oxygen, but sodium reacts more rapidly than carbon does.

$$C(s) + O_2(g) \rightarrow CO_2(g)$$

$$4\ Na(s) + O_2(g) \rightarrow 2\ Na_2O(s)$$

Which of these reactions has the larger activation energy?

6.50 When a solution that contains $CrCl_2$ and HCl is exposed to oxygen, the oxygen is consumed within seconds.

$$4\ CrCl_2(aq) + 4\ HCl(aq) + O_2(g) \rightarrow 4\ CrCl_3(aq) + 2\ H_2O(l)$$

A solution that contains $FeCl_2$ and HCl also absorbs oxygen, but the reaction takes several minutes.

$$4\ FeCl_2(aq) + 4\ HCl(aq) + O_2(g) \rightarrow 4\ FeCl_3(aq) + 2\ H_2O(l)$$

Which of these reactions has the larger activation energy?

6.51 Carbonic acid breaks down into water and carbon dioxide according to the following equation:

$$H_2CO_3(aq) + 1\ \text{kcal} \rightarrow CO_2(aq) + H_2O(l)$$

The activation energy of this reaction is 21 kcal, but a catalyst in human blood reduces the activation energy to 12 kcal. Draw an energy diagram for this reaction, showing both the uncatalyzed and the catalyzed reaction.

6.52 The superoxide ion (O_2^-) is a toxic by-product of reactions that involve oxygen. This ion breaks down into oxygen and hydrogen peroxide according to the following equation:

$$2\ O_2^- + 2\ H^+ \rightarrow O_2 + H_2O_2 + 7\ \text{kcal}$$

The activation energy of this reaction is 5.5 kcal, but a catalyst inside most cells reduces the activation energy to 0.5 kcal. Draw an energy diagram for this reaction, showing both the uncatalyzed and the catalyzed reaction.

6.53 Using the energy diagram that follows, estimate the activation energy and the heat of reaction. Also, tell whether this is an exothermic or an endothermic reaction.

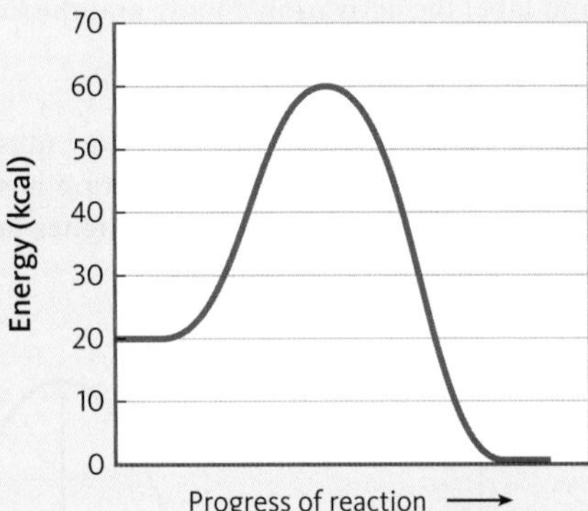

6.54 Using the energy diagram that follows, estimate the activation energy and the heat of reaction. Also, tell whether this is an exothermic or an endothermic reaction.

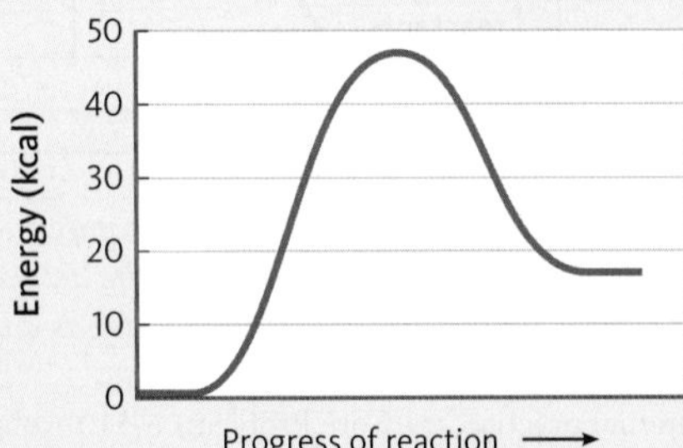

OBJECTIVES: *Understand the concept of chemical equilibrium, and use Le Châtelier's principle to predict the effect of a disturbance on an equilibrium mixture.*

6.7 Chemical Equilibrium

A number of important reactions in our bodies occur rapidly at first but slow down and stop before all of the reactants have been consumed. For instance, most cells in your body produce carbon dioxide, which your blood carries to your lungs for disposal. In your blood, the carbon dioxide reacts with water to form carbonic acid (H_2CO_3).

$$CO_2 + H_2O \rightarrow H_2CO_3$$

However, when carbon dioxide reacts with water, a small fraction of the carbon dioxide always remains unchanged. As a result, your blood always contains a mixture of reactants and products.

The reaction of carbon dioxide with water is an example of a **reversible reaction.** Reversible reactions can occur in either direction and normally proceed in both directions simultaneously. Carbon dioxide combines with water to make carbonic acid, and carbonic acid breaks back down into water and carbon dioxide.

$$CO_2 + H_2O \rightarrow H_2CO_3$$
$$H_2CO_3 \rightarrow CO_2 + H_2O$$

The second reaction is the reverse of the first. The reverse reaction makes carbon dioxide and water, so the carbon dioxide is never consumed completely. Chemists often write the equation for a reversible reaction with a double arrow to show that the reaction can occur in both directions.

$$CO_2 + H_2O \rightleftharpoons H_2CO_3$$

At the start, the mixture contains only reactants, so the reaction can only go forward.

After a while, the mixture contains both reactants and products, but the forward reaction is still faster than the reverse reaction.

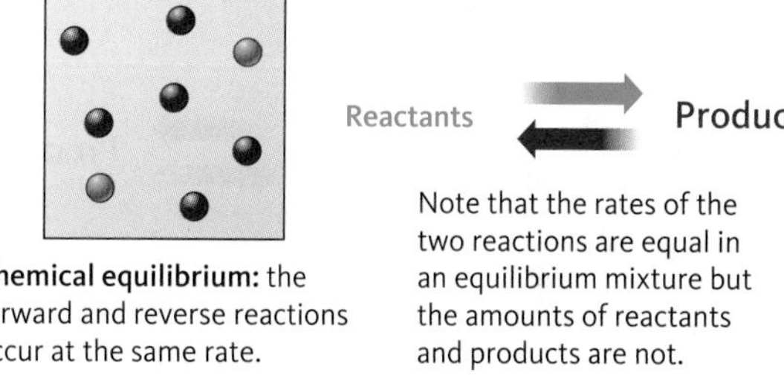

Chemical equilibrium: the forward and reverse reactions occur at the same rate.

Note that the rates of the two reactions are equal in an equilibrium mixture but the amounts of reactants and products are not.

FIGURE 6.16 The formation of an equilibrium mixture.

Reversible Reactions Form an Equilibrium Mixture

Any reversible reaction eventually produces a stable, unchanging mixture of reactants and products called an **equilibrium mixture.** In the equilibrium mixture, *the forward and reverse reactions occur at the same rate.* The forward reaction produces products exactly as fast as the reverse reaction converts them back into reactants, so the number of molecules of each substance in the reaction remains constant. When the concentrations of products and reactants no longer change, we say that the reaction has reached **chemical equilibrium.**

Figure 6.16 illustrates how a reaction reaches chemical equilibrium. Initially, only the forward reaction can occur, because no product molecules are available. Over time, the forward reaction slows down, because the concentrations of the reactants decrease. At the same time, the backward reaction speeds up, because the concentrations of the products increase. Eventually, the forward and backward reactions occur at the same rate, and the overall reaction reaches chemical equilibrium.

An equilibrium mixture does not normally contain equal amounts of reactants and products. The actual concentrations in an equilibrium mixture depend on the reaction and on the starting concentrations of the reactants. For example, when the reaction that follows reaches equilibrium, the equilibrium mixture contains 95% products and only 5% reactants. This reaction plays an important role in blood chemistry, allowing our bodies to neutralize lactic acid that is formed by our muscles.

$HC_3H_5O_3$	+	HCO_3^-	$\rightleftharpoons$	$C_3H_5O_3^-$	+	H_2CO_3
lactic acid		**bicarbonate ion**		**lactate ion**		**carbonic acid**

It is important to realize that the terms *forward* and *reverse* do not mean that the reaction has a preferred direction. They simply correspond to the two possible ways of reading the balanced equation: forward means left to right, and backward means right to left. For example, if we prepare a mixture of the products of the preceding reaction, lactate ion and carbonic acid, the reaction goes in the "reverse" direction until it reaches equilibrium. If we choose, we can turn the chemical equation around to better represent what we actually observe.

$$C_3H_5O_3^- + H_2CO_3 \rightleftharpoons HC_3H_5O_3 + HCO_3^-$$

You cannot tell whether a reaction is reversible from the chemical equation. The only way to determine whether a reaction is reversible is to mix the reactants and see whether they are completely converted into products. You also cannot tell what the concentrations of the reactants and products in the equilibrium mixture will be. Some reversible reactions convert only a small fraction of the reactants into products, while others convert almost all of the reactant molecules into products.

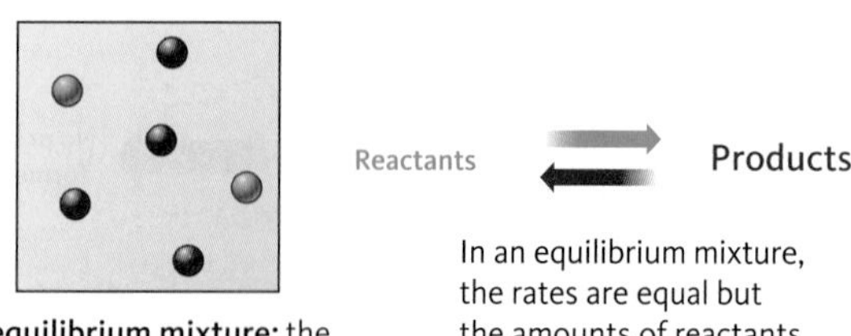
Reactants
Products
In an equilibrium mixture, the rates are equal but the amounts of reactants and products are not.

An equilibrium mixture: the forward and reverse reactions occur at the same rate.

Reactants
Products

If we add some reactant molecules, the forward reaction becomes faster than the backward reaction. The reaction "goes forward" to remove the excess reactant molecules.

Reactants
Products

After a while, the reaction returns to equilibrium, but the equilibrium mixture is now different from before.

FIGURE 6.17 Le Châtelier's principle.

Le Châtelier's Principle Allows Us to Predict the Behavior of an Equilibrium Mixture

Suppose we take an equilibrium mixture and add a little of one of the reactants. What will happen? When we add the reactant, we upset the balance between the forward and reverse reactions. As a result, the mixture is no longer at equilibrium. Likewise, if we add one of the products, the mixture will not be at equilibrium. We can predict how a reaction will respond when we disturb an equilibrium using a rule called **Le Châtelier's principle**. Le Châtelier's principle says that *when we disturb an equilibrium, the reaction will go in the direction that counteracts the disturbance.* A simple way to interpret this rule is "Whatever you do, the reaction will undo."

For instance, suppose we have an equilibrium mixture of the products and reactants in the reaction between lactic acid and bicarbonate ion.

$$HC_3H_5O_3 + HCO_3^- \rightleftharpoons C_3H_5O_3^- + H_2CO_3$$

What happens if we add a few drops of a concentrated solution of lactic acid to our mixture? When we add this solution, we increase the number of lactic acid molecules in our mixture. Le Châtelier's principle tells us that the reaction will go in the direction that *decreases* the number of lactic acid molecules, counteracting the disturbance. Therefore, the reaction will go forward, consuming lactic acid molecules (and bicarbonate ions) until the forward and backward rates are equal again, as shown in Figure 6.17.

In Figure 6.17, we added more reactant molecules to our equilibrium mixture, and the reaction responded by going forward. If instead we add more product molecules to an equilibrium mixture, the reaction will go backward. By Le Châtelier's principle, the reaction must go in the direction that removes the product molecules. When the reaction goes backward, it converts products into reactants, decreasing the number of product molecules in our mixture.

Sample Problem 6.17

Predicting the effect of an added chemical on an equilibrium mixture

The following reaction is at equilibrium:

$$HC_3H_5O_3 + HCO_3^- \rightleftharpoons C_3H_5O_3^- + H_2CO_3$$

If you add a solution that contains lactate ions ($C_3H_5O_3^-$) to the preceding equilibrium mixture, which way will the reaction proceed?

SOLUTION

When we add lactate ions, we increase their concentration in our mixture. By Le Châtelier's principle, the reaction will counteract this disturbance by decreasing the number of lactate ions in the mixture. Lactate ion is a product, so the reaction will go backward, consuming lactate ions (and carbonic acid). We can represent this by writing the equation with a backward arrow:

$$HC_3H_5O_3 + HCO_3^- \leftarrow C_3H_5O_3^- + H_2CO_3$$

Alternatively, we can simply reverse the direction of the equation:

$$C_3H_5O_3^- + H_2CO_3 \rightarrow HC_3H_5O_3 + HCO_3^-$$

TRY IT YOURSELF: *If you add a solution that contains bicarbonate ions to this equilibrium mixture, which way will the reaction proceed?*

For additional practice, try Core Problems 6.61 (parts a and b) and 6.62 (parts a and b).

The reaction

$N_2 + 3\,H_2 \rightleftharpoons 2\,NH_3$

is at equilibrium.

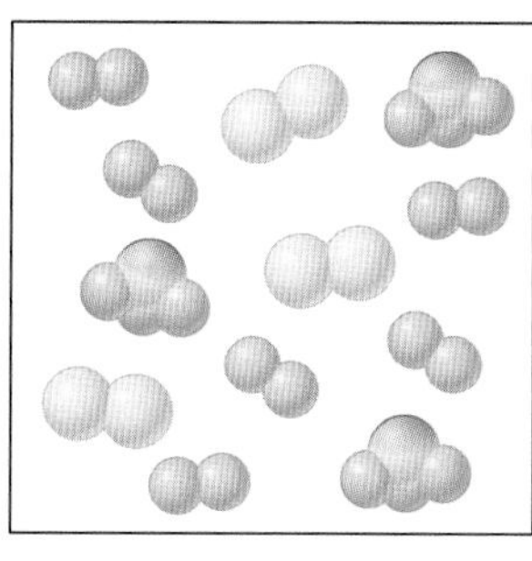

When the reaction mixture is exposed to water, the NH_3 dissolves in the water and is removed from the mixture.

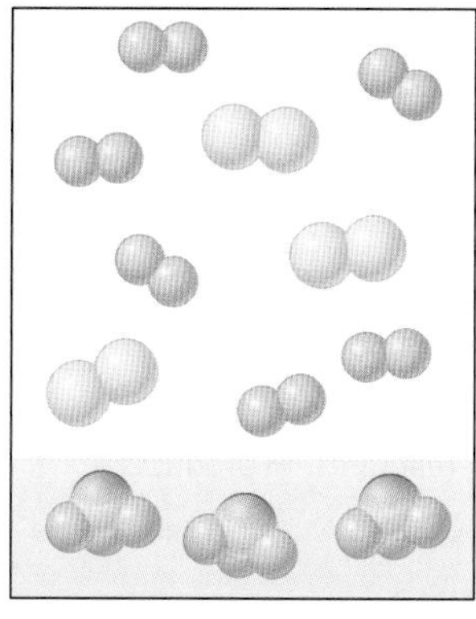

By Le Châtelier's principle, the reaction goes forward to replace the NH_3 that was removed:

$N_2 + 3\,H_2 \longrightarrow 2\,NH_3$

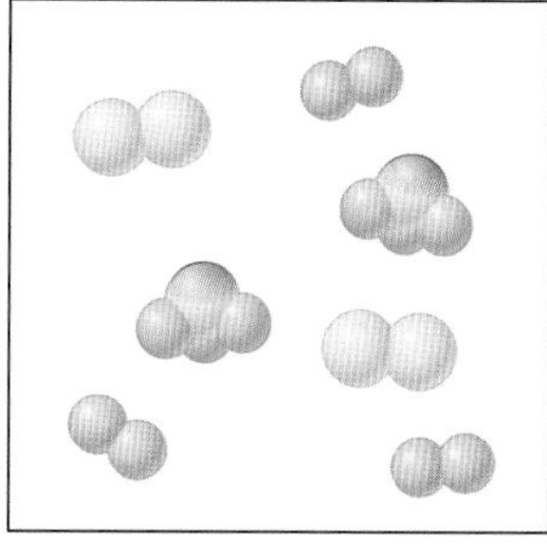

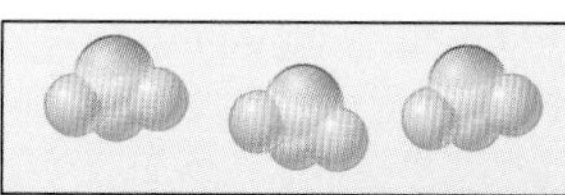

FIGURE 6.18 Removing a component from an equilibrium mixture.

We can also disturb an equilibrium by removing one of the chemicals from the equilibrium mixture. For example, the equilibrium reaction that follows is used to make ammonia, which is an important ingredient in many fertilizers:

$$N_2(g) + 3\,H_2(g) \rightleftharpoons 2\,NH_3(g)$$

To increase the amount of ammonia that we make, we can expose the reaction mixture to water, as illustrated in Figure 6.18. Ammonia dissolves in water while nitrogen and hydrogen do not, so the water removes ammonia from the equilibrium mixture. The reaction responds by making more ammonia, returning the mixture to equilibrium.

Sample Problem **6.18**

Removing a component from an equilibrium mixture

The reaction that follows is at equilibrium. If you remove bicarbonate ions (HCO_3^-) from the equilibrium mixture, which way will the reaction proceed?

$$HC_3H_5O_3 + HCO_3^- \rightleftharpoons C_3H_5O_3^- + H_2CO_3$$

SOLUTION

By Le Châtelier's principle, the reaction will go in the direction that counteracts the disturbance to the equilibrium mixture. We removed bicarbonate ions, so the reaction will go in the direction that makes bicarbonate ions. Therefore, the reaction will go backward.

TRY IT YOURSELF: *If you remove H_2CO_3 (carbonic acid) from the equilibrium mixture, which way will the reaction proceed?*

For additional practice, try Core Problems 6.61 through 6.64.

Table 6.8 summarizes the results of the various ways of disturbing an equilibrium that we have discussed in this section.

Le Châtelier's principle plays an important role in our bodies. In many cases, our cells use a reversible reaction both to build and to break down a compound. When a cell contains too much of the compound, the reaction breaks it down, and when the cell contains too little of the compound, the same reaction makes more of it. In this way, our cells ensure that they have the correct amount of the compound at all times.

Health Note: Our bodies make the amino acids glycine and alanine (two of the building blocks of all proteins) using reversible reactions. When our diet contains more of these amino acids than we need, we use the same reactions to obtain energy by breaking down the extra molecules.

TABLE 6.8 Summary of Le Châtelier's Principle

Disturbance to Equilibrium	Result
Adding a reactant	The reaction goes forward (to remove the excess reactant). reactants $\rightarrow$ products
Adding a product	The reaction goes backward (to remove the excess product). reactants $\leftarrow$ products
Removing a reactant	The reaction goes backward (to replace the missing reactant). reactants $\leftarrow$ products
Removing a product	The reaction goes forward (to replace the missing product). reactants $\rightarrow$ products

CORE PROBLEMS

6.55 What is an equilibrium mixture?

6.56 Why do reversible reactions produce equilibrium mixtures?

6.57 Which of the following statements are true about *all* equilibrium mixtures?
a) The concentration of products equals the concentration of reactants.
b) The mass of products equals the mass of reactants.
c) The rate of the forward reaction equals the rate of the reverse reaction.
d) The forward and reverse reactions stop.

6.58 When chlorine dissolves in water, some of it reacts with the water as follows:

$$Cl_2(aq) + H_2O(l) \rightleftharpoons HCl(aq) + HClO(aq)$$

These chemicals eventually form an equilibrium mixture. Which of the following statements are true about this equilibrium mixture?
a) The concentration of Cl_2 equals the concentration of HCl.
b) The number of Cl_2 molecules consumed in one minute equals the number made in one minute.
c) Water molecules are being made and broken down simultaneously.
d) The total mass of Cl_2 plus H_2O equals the total mass of HCl plus HClO.

6.59 Grain alcohol (ethanol) that is not intended for human consumption is often made by the following reaction:

$$C_2H_4(g) + H_2O(g) \rightleftharpoons C_2H_6O(g)$$

If you mix some C_2H_4 and some H_2O and heat them to 100°C, you end up with a mixture of C_2H_4, H_2O, and C_2H_6O.
a) Explain why neither of the reactants runs out.
b) If you heat some C_2H_6O to 100°C, what will happen?

6.60 Wood alcohol (methanol) is an important industrial solvent, although it is quite poisonous. It can be made by reacting carbon monoxide with hydrogen.

$$CO(g) + 2\ H_2(g) \rightleftharpoons CH_4O(g)$$

If you mix some CO and some H_2 and heat them to 200°C, you end up with a mixture of CO, H_2, and CH_4O.
a) Explain why neither of the reactants runs out.
b) If you heat some CH_4O to 200°C, what will happen?

6.61 One way to make hydrogen gas is to heat a mixture of steam and carbon monoxide. (This reaction also makes carbon dioxide, which can easily be separated from the hydrogen.)

$$H_2O(g) + CO(g) \rightleftharpoons H_2(g) + CO_2(g)$$

Suppose that you have an equilibrium mixture of these four substances. Which way will the reaction proceed (forward or backward) if you
a) add some carbon monoxide to the mixture?
b) add some carbon dioxide to the mixture?
c) remove some hydrogen from the mixture?

6.62 Nitrogen dioxide is a poisonous gas that is responsible for the red–brown color of polluted air in cities. Nitrogen dioxide molecules can combine to make dinitrogen tetroxide.

$$2\ NO_2(g) \rightleftharpoons N_2O_4(g)$$

Suppose that you have an equilibrium mixture of these two substances. Which way will the reaction proceed (forward or backward) if you
a) add some nitrogen dioxide to the mixture?
b) add some dinitrogen tetroxide to the mixture?
c) remove some nitrogen dioxide from the mixture?

continued

6.63 In the equilibrium in Problem 6.61, which of the following would increase the amount of hydrogen gas in the equilibrium mixture?
a) adding some carbon monoxide to the mixture
b) removing some carbon monoxide from the mixture
c) adding some carbon dioxide to the mixture
d) removing some carbon dioxide from the mixture

6.64 In the equilibrium in Problem 6.61, which of the following would increase the amount of carbon monoxide in the equilibrium mixture?
a) adding some hydrogen gas to the mixture
b) removing some hydrogen gas from the mixture
c) adding some steam to the mixture
d) removing some steam from the mixture

CONNECTIONS

Energy from Food

How much food do I need? The answer to this question depends on many factors. Our bodies use food to provide water, electrolytes, vitamins, amino acids to build proteins, and a variety of other essential nutrients. However, we use most of the food we eat to supply our bodies with energy. Our nutritional requirements are determined primarily by the amount of energy our bodies use. An active person uses more energy and needs more food than a sedentary person.

We obtain all of our energy from burning chemical compounds built primarily from carbon, hydrogen, and oxygen. The two main sources of energy for our bodies are carbohydrates and fats. For example, here is the chemical reaction that occurs when our bodies obtain energy from sucrose (table sugar), a typical carbohydrate:

$$C_{12}H_{22}O_{11} \text{ (sucrose)} + 12\ O_2 \rightarrow 12\ CO_2 + 11\ H_2O + 1342 \text{ kcal}$$

1342 kcal is a great deal of energy, but getting this much energy requires one mole (342 g, or about 3/4 of a pound) of sugar. One gram of table sugar supplies your body with around 4 kcal of energy, which is typical for a carbohydrate.

Image copyright auremar, 2010. Used under license from Shutterstock.com

When you are physically active, you must eat more food to supply your energy needs.

Everyone's body has a basal metabolic requirement (BMR), which is the minimum amount of energy needed to keep that person alive. Your BMR depends on your proportions, your body composition, and your age. For instance, if you are a 30-year-old, 5-foot-4-inch woman who weighs 130 pounds, your BMR is around 1400 kcal per day. However, you also need energy for physical activities, even if you are a couch potato; simply sitting upright or digesting a meal requires energy that is not included in the BMR. If you are moderately active, your daily energy requirement might be around 2100 kcal per day. Remember that a nutritional Calorie is actually a kilocalorie, so you would need to eat enough food to supply 2100 Cal every day. You could get this energy by eating 535 g of sugar (ugh) or any other combination of carbohydrates, fats, and proteins that totals 2100 Cal.

What happens if you eat more or less food than your body needs? If you are healthy, you body absorbs virtually all of the useable nutrients in your food, so any excess does not simply leave with your feces. Instead, your body burns some of the extra food and uses the energy to convert the rest into fat. Fat is our long-term energy storage system, allowing us to survive extended periods when food is scarce. Body fat is as vital to our well-being as muscle and bone, but too much body fat puts a strain on many of our bodies' systems and can lead to a variety of long-term health problems. If you eat too little food, your body must break down its own molecules to supply its energy needs. Your body starts by burning all of the available carbohydrate, then turns to fat (along with a little protein), and finally burns proteins, primarily from muscle tissues. At the same time, you become lethargic as your body attempts to conserve energy by limiting your physical activity. You may be able to survive for a couple of months without eating, but eventually you must eat to live.

Key Terms

activation energy – 6.6
catalyst – 6.6
chemical equation – 6.2
chemical equilibrium – 6.7
chemical property – 6.1
chemical reaction (chemical change) – 6.1
coefficient – 6.2
combustion reaction – 6.5
endothermic reaction – 6.4
energy diagram – 6.6
equilibrium mixture – 6.7
exothermic reaction – 6.4
heat of reaction (ΔH) – 6.4
law of mass conservation – 6.1
Le Châtelier's principle – 6.7
net ionic equation – 6.5
nutritive value – 6.4
physical change – 6.1
physical property – 6.1
precipitation reaction – 6.5
product – 6.2
rate of reaction – 6.6
reactant – 6.2
reversible reaction – 6.7
spectator ion – 6.5

SUMMARY OF OBJECTIVES

Now that you have read the chapter, test yourself on your knowledge of the objectives, using this summary as a guide.

Section 6.1: **Determine whether a process is a physical change or a chemical reaction.**

- In a physical change, the chemical formulas do not change; in a chemical reaction, they do.
- Physical changes can be reversed, but many chemical reactions cannot.
- Physical properties can be measured without changing a chemical formula, while chemical properties always involve a chemical reaction.
- In any change, the mass of the products equals the mass of the reactants (law of mass conservation).

Section 6.2: **Write a balanced chemical equation to represent a chemical reaction.**

- Any chemical reaction can be expressed as a balanced chemical equation.
- In a balanced equation, each side must have the same number of atoms of each element.
- Balancing a chemical equation involves changing coefficients, never changing a chemical formula.

Section 6.3: **Relate the mass of any substance in a chemical reaction to the masses of all other substances in the reaction.**

- The molar masses of the chemicals in a balanced equation are used to relate the masses of chemicals used or formed during the reaction.

Section 6.4: **Relate the amount of heat involved in a reaction to the masses of the chemicals, describe the differences between exothermic and endothermic reactions, and use nutritive values to calculate the energy provided by foodstuffs.**

- Reactions can either produce (exothermic) or absorb (endothermic) heat.
- In an exothermic reaction, the heat can be written into the balanced equation as a product, or it can be written separately (ΔH) as a negative number. In an endothermic reaction, the heat is written as a reactant, or it is written separately as a positive number.
- The energy produced or absorbed in a reaction is directly proportional to the amounts of chemicals used in the reaction.
- Each type of major nutrient produces a characteristic amount of heat when it burns (the nutritive value), which is normally given as a number of Calories (kilocalories) per gram. The standard nutritive values are 4 Cal/g for carbohydrates and proteins and 9 Cal/g for fats.

Section 6.5: **Recognize and write chemical equations for combustion and precipitation reactions.**

- Combustion is the reaction of a compound with O_2, to produce the oxides of each element in the original compound.
- When a compound that contains carbon and hydrogen is burned, the products are H_2O and CO_2.
- Precipitation is the reaction of two soluble compounds to form an insoluble product.
- Precipitation reactions can be represented using net ionic equations, which show only the ions that combine to form the insoluble compound.

Section 6.6: **Understand and use the relationships between the rate of a reaction and activation energy, temperature, concentration, surface area, and catalysts.**

- The rate of a reaction increases as you increase the concentration of the reactants and the contact area between the reactants.
- All reactions have an activation energy, which is the amount of energy that must be added to the reactants for them to collide violently enough to react. The smaller the activation energy, the faster the reaction.
- Reaction rates increase when you increase the temperature, because the molecules are moving faster (giving more of them the needed activation energy) and are colliding more often.
- A catalyst is a substance that increases the rate of a reaction without being consumed in the reaction. Catalysts function primarily by lowering the activation energy of a reaction.
- The activation energy and the heat of reaction can be shown using an energy diagram.

continued

Section 6.7: Understand the concept of chemical equilibrium, and use Le Châtelier's principle to predict the effect of a disturbance on an equilibrium mixture.

- Some reactions are reversible: they can occur in either direction.
- Any reversible reaction will reach chemical equilibrium, at which point the reaction appears to stop, leaving a mixture of both reactants and products.
- At equilibrium, a reversible reaction occurs in both directions simultaneously. The forward and reverse rates are equal.
- When an equilibrium mixture is disturbed, the reaction goes in the direction that counteracts the disturbance (Le Châtelier's principle).

Concept Questions

OWL Online homework for this chapter may be assigned in OWL.

* indicates more challenging problems.

6.65 a) What is the primary difference between a physical change and a chemical reaction?
b) Which is more likely to be reversible?

6.66 When a log burns in a fireplace, it turns into ash. The ash weighs much less than the original log. Explain why this does not violate the law of mass conservation. Where did the rest of the log's mass go?

6.67 What is the difference between writing 2 *N* and writing N_2 in a chemical equation?

6.68 How can you tell if a chemical equation is balanced?

6.69 Jackie is asked to balance the equation $Na + Cl_2 \rightarrow NaCl$. She writes the following answer: $Na + Cl_2 \rightarrow NaCl_2$.

a) Is this answer a balanced equation? If not, explain why not.
b) Is this answer correct? If not, explain why not.

6.70 When sodium hydroxide reacts with HCl, the mixture becomes hot.

a) Is this an exothermic reaction, or is it an endothermic reaction?
b) In the chemical equation, should the heat appear as a reactant or as a product?
c) Is ΔH for this reaction positive, or is it negative?

6.71 What is the nutritive value of a food?

6.72 Most fuels are mixtures of hydrocarbons, compounds that contain the elements carbon and hydrogen.

a) When a hydrocarbon burns, what are the products of the combustion?
b) What other chemical is required in the combustion of a hydrocarbon?

6.73 What is a precipitation reaction?

6.74 When solutions of Na_2CO_3 and $CaCl_2$ are mixed, a white solid forms. This reaction can be written as follows:

$$CaCl_2(aq) + Na_2CO_3(aq) \rightarrow CaCO_3(s) + 2\ NaCl(aq)$$

The reaction can also be written as

$$Ca^{2+}(aq) + CO_3^{2-}(aq) \rightarrow CaCO_3(s)$$

What is the advantage of writing this reaction in the second way?

6.75 Explain why each of the following increases the rate of a reaction:

a) increasing the temperature
b) stirring the mixture (if it is heterogeneous)
c) breaking up a solid reactant into smaller pieces
d) increasing the concentration of an aqueous reactant

6.76 Catalysts speed up reactions in two ways. What are they? Which one has a greater impact on the reaction rate?

6.77 Stefan says, "When you increase the temperature, the activation energy increases."

a) Explain why this is not correct.
b) Explain why increasing the temperature speeds up reactions, using the concept of activation energy in your answer.

6.78 What types of reactions form an equilibrium mixture, and why do they do so?

6.79 When you eat table sugar (sucrose), your body breaks down the sucrose into two other sugars, glucose and fructose, using a reversible reaction.

$$\text{sucrose} + H_2O \rightleftharpoons \text{glucose} + \text{fructose}$$

Suppose you have an equilibrium mixture of these four substances. If you add some glucose to this mixture and then wait a few minutes, what will happen to the concentration of fructose in the mixture?

Summary and Challenge Problems

6.80 Which of the following equations represent physical changes, and which represent chemical changes?

a) $H_2O(s) \rightarrow H_2O(l)$
b) $2\ HgO(s) \rightarrow 2\ Hg(l) + O_2(g)$
c) $C_2H_5OH(l) \rightarrow C_2H_5OH(aq)$

6.81 Balance each of the following equations:

a) $Mg + Cl_2 \rightarrow MgCl_2$
b) $Al + S \rightarrow Al_2S_3$
c) $P_4 + Cl_2 \rightarrow PCl_3$
d) $MgI_2 + O_2 \rightarrow MgO + I_2$
e) $Na_2S + AgF \rightarrow NaF + Ag_2S$

6.82 *The element phosphorus is usually represented as P in chemical equations, but it often forms molecules containing four phosphorus atoms.

a) Write the chemical formula for one of these molecules.
b) Using the formula you wrote in part a, write a chemical equation for the reaction of phosphorus and chlorine to form PCl_3. (Remember that chlorine forms Cl_2 molecules when it is not combined with another element.)

6.83 Aluminum reacts with HCl to form aluminum chloride and hydrogen gas (H_2).

a) Write a balanced chemical equation for this reaction.
b) If 10.0 g of aluminum reacts with HCl , how many grams of hydrogen are formed?

6.84 Alanine and asparagine are amino acids. Both of them can be burned by mammals according to the following equations:

Alanine: $2\ C_3H_7NO_2 + 6\ O_2 \rightarrow 5\ CO_2 + 5\ H_2O + N_2H_4CO$

Asparagine: $C_4H_8N_2O_3 + 3\ O_2 \rightarrow 3\ CO_2 + 2\ H_2O + N_2H_4CO$

Which produces a larger mass of N_2H_4CO (urea) when it is burned: 10.0 g of alanine or 10.0 g of asparagine?

6.85 *Vitamin C ($C_6H_8O_6$) reacts with oxygen as follows:

$$2\ C_6H_8O_6 + O_2 \rightarrow 2\ C_6H_6O_6 + 2\ H_2O$$

a) How many grams of oxygen will react with 500 mg of vitamin C (the mass in a typical vitamin C supplement)?
b) The density of oxygen is roughly 1.3 g/L under typical atmospheric conditions. Using this fact and your answer to part a, calculate the number of milliliters of oxygen that will react with 500 mg of vitamin C.

6.86 *Calcium carbonate is used in some antacids. It reacts with HCl (the acid in your stomach) as follows:

$$CaCO_3 + 2\ HCl \rightarrow CaCl_2 + CO_2 + H_2O$$

a) How many grams of HCl will react with 1.00 g of calcium carbonate?
b) How many moles of HCl will react with 1.00 g of calcium carbonate?
c) The concentration of HCl in your stomach is around 0.01 M. How many milliliters of 0.01 M HCl are consumed when you eat 1.00 g of calcium carbonate?

6.87 *Silver nitrate solution reacts with sodium hydroxide solution as follows:

$$2\ AgNO_3(aq) + 2\ NaOH(aq) \rightarrow Ag_2O(s) + H_2O(l) + 2\ NaNO_3(aq)$$

a) If you mix 50.0 mL of 0.150 M $AgNO_3$ with a large amount of 0.100 M NaOH, how many grams of Ag_2O do you form?
b) How many mL of the 0.100 M NaOH do you need to consume all of the $AgNO_3$?

6.88 Write a balanced chemical equation that represents each of the following reactions:

a) The reaction of potassium with oxygen to form potassium oxide
b) The combustion of octane, C_8H_{18}
c) A precipitation reaction that forms Ag_3PO_4 (write a net ionic equation)

6.89 *Acetylene (C_2H_2) is used in welding torches, because it produces an extremely hot flame when it burns. How many grams of carbon dioxide are formed in the combustion of 5.00 g of acetylene?

6.90 *When 1.00 g of propane (C_3H_8) burns, 12.0 kcal of heat is produced. Use this information to calculate the heat of reaction for the combustion of propane.

$$C_3H_8 + 5\ O_2 \rightarrow 3\ CO_2 + 4\ H_2O + ?\ \text{kcal}$$

6.91 Mammals can "burn" amino acids (the building blocks of proteins) to obtain energy. An example is the burning of the amino acid alanine ($C_3H_7NO_2$).

$$2\ C_3H_7NO_2 + 6\ O_2 \rightarrow N_2H_4CO + 5\ CO_2 + 5\ H_2O + 624\ \text{kcal}$$

a) If a mammal burns 1.00 g of alanine, how much heat is produced?
b) How does your answer to part a compare with the Calorie value for proteins (4 Cal/g)? Remember that a Calorie (a nutritional calorie) is actually a kilocalorie.

6.92 *When the amino acid glycine burns in a normal combustion reaction, the chemical equation is

$$4\ C_2H_5NO_2 + 9\ O_2 \rightarrow 2\ N_2 + 8\ CO_2 + 10\ H_2O + 936\ \text{kcal}$$

When this amino acid is burned by your body to obtain energy, the chemical equation is

$$2\ C_2H_5NO_2 + 3\ O_2 \rightarrow N_2H_4CO + 3\ CO_2 + 3\ H_2O + 316\ \text{kcal}$$

a) Calculate the amount of heat produced when 1.00 g of glycine is burned in each reaction.
b) What percentage of the heat of combustion is lost when your body uses glycine to obtain energy?

6.93 Fred wants to know how much of each nutrient is in the Twinkie he is about to eat. He sees that the Twinkie contains 1 g of protein, 27 g of carbohydrate, and 160 Cal. However, the nutritional label has been damaged, so he cannot read the amount of fat. How many grams of fat are there in Fred's Twinkie?

6.94 *Ethanol (grain alcohol) can be burned by your body to obtain energy. The chemical reaction is

$$C_2H_6O + 3\ O_2 \rightarrow 2\ CO_2 + 3\ H_2O + 327\ \text{kcal}$$

Use this information to calculate the Calorie value for ethanol (i.e., the amount of energy your body obtains by burning 1.00 g of ethanol). How does this compare with the Calorie value for carbohydrates (4 Cal/g)?

6.95 *When your body produces excess heat, you perspire. The perspiration (which is mostly water) evaporates, removing the excess heat.

a) If 10.0 g of water evaporates from your skin, how much heat does it remove from your body? (The heat of vaporization of water is 540 cal/g.)
b) How many grams of fat must your body burn to supply the heat that was removed from your body in part a?

6.96 The U.S. government recommends that no more than 30% of the Calories in your diet come from fats, and no more than 10% should come from saturated fats. If your daily diet includes 2000 Cal, what is the maximum number of grams of fat and saturated fat that you should eat?

6.97 Sucrose (table sugar) breaks down in your digestive tract, producing two other types of sugar, glucose (blood sugar) and fructose (fruit sugar). In your stomach, this reaction is catalyzed by HCl, and the activation energy is 26 kcal. In your intestine, the reaction is catalyzed by an enzyme called sucrase, and the activation energy is 9 kcal. In which part of your digestive system is sucrose broken down more rapidly?

6.98 Proteins can react with water, breaking down into their amino acid building blocks.

$$\text{protein} + \text{water} \rightarrow \text{amino acids}$$

This reaction is extremely slow unless a catalyst is added. When the catalyst is HCl, the reaction requires several days to complete, but when the catalyst is a digestive enzyme, the reaction is complete within an hour.

a) Which has the larger activation energy, the HCl–catalyzed reaction or the enzyme-catalyzed reaction?
b) Sketch an energy diagram for this reaction. Your diagram should show the pathway with no catalyst, the HCl–catalyzed pathway, and the enzyme-catalyzed pathway. (The reaction is exothermic.)

6.99 A chemist puts 2.00 g of N_2O_4 into a container. Some of the N_2O_4 breaks down into NO_2, forming an equilibrium mixture.

$$N_2O_4(g) \rightarrow 2\ NO_2(g)$$

If the chemist then puts 2.00 g of NO_2 into an identical container, which of the following statements will be true?

a) Some of the NO_2 will turn into N_2O_4.
b) All of the NO_2 will turn into N_2O_4.
c) None of the NO_2 will turn into N_2O_4.

6.100 When you exercise vigorously, your body breaks down glucose (blood sugar) into lactic acid using a sequence of several reactions. The last reaction in this sequence is

$$\text{pyruvic acid} + \text{NADH} + H^+ \rightarrow \text{lactic acid} + \text{NAD}^+$$

This reaction forms an equilibrium mixture. Tell whether each of the following will change the concentration of lactic acid in this mixture, and if so, whether the concentration of lactic acid will increase or decrease:

a) Your body makes more NADH.
b) Your body makes more NAD^+.
c) Your body uses some of the pyruvic acid to make alanine (an amino acid).
d) Some of the H^+ ions react with HCO_3^- ions to form H_2CO_3.

7

Acids and Bases

Eunice has smoked for more than 40 years, and lately she has been feeling short of breath most of the time. After one particularly difficult morning, when she became exhausted after simply climbing the stairs in her house, she goes to the doctor. To help diagnose the cause of Eunice's symptoms, the doctor orders a test called arterial blood gases. This test shows how effectively Eunice's breathing is able to keep the pH of her blood within an acceptable range. pH is a measure of the balance between acids and bases (alkalis) in a solution, and in the blood, the pH reflects the balance between carbon dioxide and bicarbonate ions. Our health depends on keeping these two substances in the correct proportion, and we rely on our breathing to maintain the correct concentration of carbon dioxide.

The test shows that although Eunice's blood has roughly the correct ratio of carbon dioxide to bicarbonate ions, the concentrations of both are substantially higher than normal. Eunice's damaged lungs cannot expel carbon dioxide rapidly enough to keep up with her body's production of it, and her kidneys have compensated by raising the concentration of bicarbonate ions. Because the kidneys cannot respond to rapid changes in carbon dioxide levels, though, Eunice's blood tends to become more acidic than normal, a condition called respiratory acidosis. Together with measurements of Eunice's breathing capacity, these results confirm that Eunice is suffering from emphysema, a gradual destruction of the lining of the lung sacs that reduces the ability of the lungs to move air in and out. Eunice's doctor urges her to quit smoking to slow the progression of her disease, and he prescribes medications to ease her breathing.

$$CO_2 + H_2O \rightleftharpoons \underset{\text{carbonic acid}}{H_2CO_3} \rightleftharpoons H^+ + \underset{\text{bicarbonate ion}}{HCO_3^-}$$

OUTLINE

7.1 **The self-ionization of water**
7.2 **The pH scale**
7.3 **Properties of acids**
7.4 **Properties of bases**
7.5 **Acid–base reactions**
7.6 **Amphiprotic molecules and ions**
7.7 **Buffers**
7.8 **The role of buffers in human physiology**

LABORATORY REQUISITION—CHEMISTRY

BLOOD GASES
Includes pH, pCO$_2$, pO$_2$, HCO$_3$, BE, O$_2$Sat

Temp °F ___95___

FIO$_2$% ________ ☑ Room Air
☑ Arterial ABG
☐ Mixed Venous VBG
☐ Capillary CBG

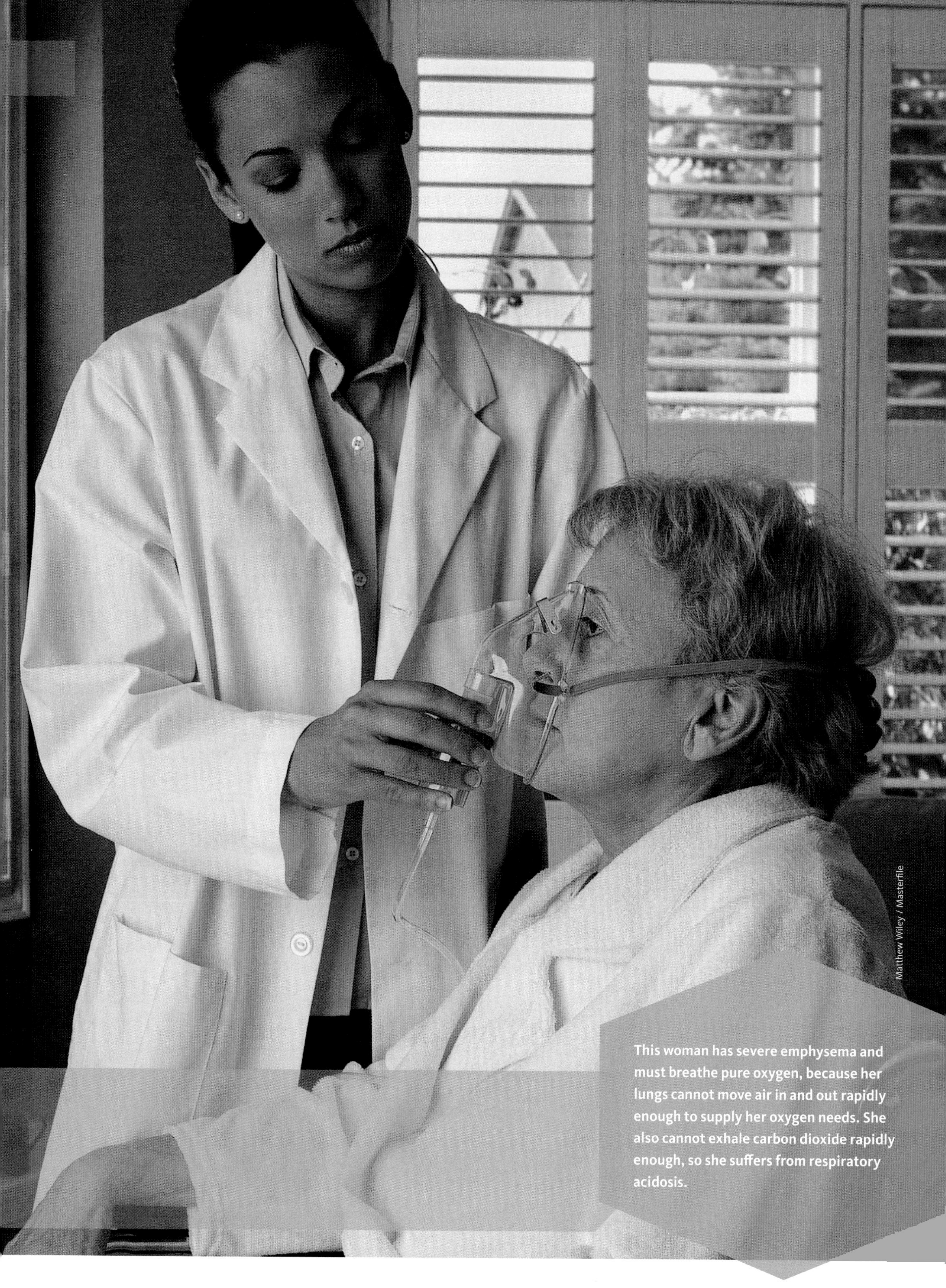

Matthew Wiley / Masterfile

This woman has severe emphysema and must breathe pure oxygen, because her lungs cannot move air in and out rapidly enough to supply her oxygen needs. She also cannot exhale carbon dioxide rapidly enough, so she suffers from respiratory acidosis.

Online homework for this chapter may be assigned in OWL.

Since ancient times, people have been aware that some natural substances have sharp, sour flavors and pungent aromas. These substances have the ability to dissolve certain minerals (notably limestone, which bubbles when one of these substances is poured on it), and they can change the color of many vegetable pigments. Eventually, these substances became known as acids, based on the Latin word for "sour," *acidus*. Over time, more and more acids were discovered, the names of which often reflect their original sources. Table 7.1 lists some naturally occurring acids and the sources of their names.

Eventually, acids were found to play key roles in virtually all of the chemical processes that occur in living organisms. Paradoxically, acids are also toxic, because they can react with and destroy many of the chemical compounds that are vital to living organisms. Your body's ability to handle the acids that it constantly produces is a key indicator of your health.

In this chapter, we will examine the structure and chemical behavior of acids. We will also look at bases, which are chemicals that react with and neutralize acids. Water plays a fundamental role in the chemistry of both acids and bases, so we begin by taking a closer look at the chemical behavior of water.

OBJECTIVES: *Write the self-ionization reaction for water, and use the concentration of either hydronium or hydroxide ion to calculate the concentration of the other ion.*

7.1 The Self-Ionization of Water

In Chapter 4, we saw that water is a polar compound, because of the shape of the molecule and the large electronegativity difference between hydrogen and oxygen. As a result, water is an excellent solvent for ionic compounds. Water molecules are attracted to ions so strongly that they can pull the ions away from one another, overcoming the powerful attraction between opposite charges. Solutions of ionic compounds conduct electricity because these ions are free to move throughout the solution.

Water itself is not an ionic substance. However, careful measurements show that pure water conducts electricity slightly, so pure water must contain some ions. These ions come from the **self-ionization of water**. When two water molecules collide, one of the molecules occasionally pulls a hydrogen ion away from the other molecule. The products of the reaction are a hydronium ion (H_3O^+) and a hydroxide ion (OH^-), and the chemical equation for this reaction is

$$H_2O + H_2O \rightleftharpoons H_3O^+ + OH^-$$

or

$$2\,H_2O \rightleftharpoons H_3O^+ + OH^-$$

We write this equation with a double arrow to show that only a fraction of the water molecules self-ionize. In practice, there is only 1 ion for every 280 million molecules in a sample of pure water.

TABLE 7.1 Sources of Some Common Acids

Name	Biological Role	Origin of the Name
Formic acid	Produces the painful sensation of some insect bites	Latin *formica* = "ant"
Acetic acid	Forms when grain alcohol reacts with oxygen; gives vinegar its taste and aroma	Latin *acetum* = "vinegar"
Citric acid	Forms when the body obtains energy from sugars, fats, and proteins; gives citrus fruits their tart flavor	Latin *citrus* = "citron fruit" (a type of citrus fruit)
Lactic acid	Forms when certain bacteria digest lactose (milk sugar); gives sour milk its unpleasant flavor and aroma	Latin *lac* = "milk"
Oleic acid	Found in most fats and vegetable oils	Latin *oleum* = "oil" (especially olive oil)

Figure 7.1 shows the Lewis structures of the reactants and products in the self-ionization of water. In this reaction, the two electrons that originally formed the bond between hydrogen and oxygen remain behind, becoming a nonbonding electron pair in the OH^- ion. At the same time, a nonbonding pair of electrons in the other water molecule becomes a bonding electron pair in the H_3O^+ ion.

H⁺ moves from one water molecule to the other.
In these Lewis structures, a nonbonding electron pair (colored blue) becomes a bonding pair, and a bonding pair (colored red) becomes a nonbonding pair.

FIGURE 7.1 The self-ionization of water.

A hydrogen atom contains one proton and one electron, so a hydrogen ion (H^+) is simply a proton. As a result, the terms *proton* and *hydrogen* ion are used interchangeably in chemistry. Chemists often refer to reactions like the self-ionization of water as **proton transfer reactions.** In a proton transfer reaction, H^+ moves from one molecule or ion to another. We will encounter many other proton transfer reactions in this chapter.

Many Solutes Form H_3O^+ or OH^- When They Dissolve in Water

H_3O^+ and OH^- can be formed in other reactions. For example, we form H_3O^+ ions when we dissolve hydrochloric acid (HCl) or nitric acid (HNO_3) in water. These compounds can transfer a proton (H^+) to a water molecule.

$$HCl(aq) + H_2O(l) \rightarrow H_3O^+(aq) + Cl^-(aq)$$

$$HNO_3(aq) + H_2O(l) \rightarrow H_3O^+(aq) + NO_3^-(aq)$$

Substances that can donate H^+ to water are called acids. We will take a closer look at the behavior of acids in Section 7.3.

We can make hydroxide ions by dissolving an ionic compound such as NaOH or $Ca(OH)_2$ in water. These compounds are strong electrolytes, breaking apart into a metal ion and hydroxide ions.

Health Note: NaOH (caustic lye) is an ingredient in some brands of drain and oven cleaners. It can break down and dissolve fats, grease, and proteins. NaOH can cause severe chemical burns, so you should always wear hand and face protection if you use any product that contains it.

$$NaOH(s) \rightarrow Na^+(aq) + OH^-(aq)$$

$$Ca(OH)_2(s) \rightarrow Ca^{2+}(aq) + 2\ OH^-(aq)$$

In addition, many compounds can pull H^+ off a water molecule, forming OH^-. Compounds that form hydroxide ions when they dissolve in water are bases. We will look at the chemistry of bases in Section 7.4.

The Ion Product of Water Relates the Concentrations of H_3O^+ and OH^- Ions

Any reaction that forms H_3O^+ or OH^- ions has an effect on the ionization of water. We just saw that water forms an equilibrium mixture with hydronium and hydroxide ions.

$$2\ H_2O(l) \rightleftharpoons H_3O^+(aq) + OH^-(aq)$$

If we add some other source of H_3O^+ or OH^-, we disturb this equilibrium. According to Le Châtelier's principle, the reaction goes backward to counteract the disturbance. As a result, whenever we add an acid or a base to water, the number of water molecules that self-ionize decreases. The practical result of this is that the concentrations of H_3O^+ and OH^- are inversely proportional. Whenever the concentration of one of these ions increases, the concentration of the other ion decreases.

The molar concentrations of hydronium and hydroxide ions in any aqueous solution are mathematically related to each other. At room temperature, the relationship is

$$\text{molarity of } H_3O^+ \times \text{molarity of } OH^- = 1.0 \times 10^{-14}$$

Recall from Chapter 5 that the molarity of a solution is the number of moles of solute per liter of solution. Chemists abbreviate molarity by writing the formula of the solute in square brackets, so we can write our relationship in abbreviated form as

$$[H_3O^+] \times [OH^-] = 1.0 \times 10^{-14}$$

This relationship is called the **ion product of water**.

Health Note: HCl solutions destroy living tissues, so your stomach produces a thick layer of mucus to protect the wall of the stomach from the digestive fluids. Infection by the bacterium *Helicobacter pylori* can reduce the stomach's ability to produce mucus, leaving the stomach wall vulnerable to the HCl solution. The result is an ulcer, in which part of the stomach lining is damaged and becomes sensitive to the acidic surroundings.

We can use the ion product of water to calculate the concentration of either H_3O^+ or OH^-, as long as we know the concentration of the other ion. However, you need to be able to use numbers such as 1.0×10^{-14} in calculations. If you are unfamiliar with scientific notation, you should review the information in Appendix A.6 before attempting the calculations in this section.

Let us explore how we can use the ion product of water. Your stomach secretes digestive fluids that contain hydronium ions, which are a product of the reaction of HCl with water:

$$HCl(aq) + H_2O(l) \rightarrow H_3O^+(aq) + Cl^-(aq)$$

The digestive fluid typically contains 0.020 mol of H_3O^+ in each liter of solution, so the molarity of H_3O^+ in your stomach is 0.020 mol/L (0.020 M).

Digestive fluids, like all body fluids, are primarily water, so they must contain OH^- ions in addition to H_3O^+ ions. The OH^- ions are formed by the self-ionization of water. We can calculate the concentration of OH^- using the ion product of water, since we know that the concentration of H_3O^+ is 0.020 M. When we use the ion product equation, we do not include units.

This is the concentration of H_3O^+ ions in the digestive fluids.

$$0.020 \times [OH^-] = 1.0 \times 10^{-14}$$

To calculate the concentration of OH^-, we divide both sides of this equation by 0.020. Doing so allows us to cancel the number 0.020 from the left side of the equation.

$$\frac{\cancel{0.020} \times [OH^-]}{\cancel{0.020}} = \frac{1.0 \times 10^{-14}}{0.020}$$

$$[OH^-] = (1.0 \times 10^{-14}) \div 0.020$$
$$= 5.0 \times 10^{-13}\ M$$

The concentration of hydroxide ions in stomach acid is 5.0×10^{-13} M, which is extremely small (written as a decimal number, it is 0.00000000000050 M). Note that we must supply the correct unit for the hydroxide concentration, because the ion product equation does not include units.

How does this answer compare with the concentration of hydroxide ions in pure water? In pure water, the only source of both H_3O^+ and OH^- is the self-ionization of water.

$$2\,H_2O(l) \rightleftharpoons H_3O^+(aq) + OH^-(aq)$$

This reaction produces equal numbers of hydronium and hydroxide ions, so the molar concentrations of H_3O^+ and OH^- must be equal. The only number that satisfies both the ion product equation and the requirement that the two concentrations be equal is 1.0×10^{-7}. Therefore, *in pure water, the concentrations of* H_3O^+ *and* OH^- *are both* 1.0×10^{-7} *M*. The concentration of OH^- in stomach acid (5.0×10^{-13} M) is therefore much lower than the OH^- concentration in pure water. It may be easier to see this if we write both numbers out as decimals.

In pure water: $[OH^-] = 0.00000010$ M

In stomach acid: $[OH^-] = 0.00000000000050$ M

By contrast, the concentration of hydronium ions in stomach acid is much higher than that in pure water.

In pure water: $[H_3O^+] = 0.00000010$ M

In stomach acid: $[H_3O^+] = 0.020$ M

Sample Problem 7.1

Using the ion product of water

Milk of magnesia is a suspension of $Mg(OH)_2$ in water, and it is used to treat acid indigestion. $Mg(OH)_2$ is an electrolyte, but its solubility in water is very low, so the OH^- concentration in milk of magnesia is only 3.2×10^{-4} M. Calculate the concentration of H_3O^+ in this solution.

continued

SOLUTION

We can use the ion product of water to calculate the concentration of H_3O^+ ions.

$$[H_3O^+] \times [OH^-] = 1.0 \times 10^{-14}$$

First, we insert the actual concentration of OH^- ions into the formula.

$$[H_3O^+] \times (3.2 \times 10^{-4}) = 1.0 \times 10^{-14}$$

To find the concentration of H_3O^+, we need to divide both sides by 3.2×10^{-4}, and then we cancel this number from the left side of our equation.

$$\frac{[H_3O^+] \times \cancel{(3.2 \times 10^{-4})}}{\cancel{(3.2 \times 10^{-4})}} = \frac{(1.0 \times 10^{-4})}{(3.2 \times 10^{-4})}$$

Now we can do the arithmetic.

$$(1.0 \times 10^{-14}) \div (3.2 \times 10^{-4}) = 3.125 \times 10^{-11} \text{ M}$$

Our answer is only precise to two significant figures, so we round it to 3.1×10^{-11} M. Note that in ion product calculations you must supply the correct unit, because the ion product does not include units.

TRY IT YOURSELF: *What is the molar concentration of OH^- in a solution that contains 3.5×10^{-3} M H_3O^+?*

For additional practice, try Core Problems 7.5 through 7.8.

For many years, chemists believed that water formed ions by simply breaking apart into H^+ and OH^-.

$$H_2O(l) \rightleftharpoons H^+(aq) + OH^-(aq)$$

They also believed that acids like HCl were ionic compounds and simply dissociated in water.

$$HCl(aq) \rightarrow H^+(aq) + Cl^-(aq)$$

It is now known that these simple dissociation reactions are not correct. Hydrogen ions cannot exist as independent ions in an aqueous solution. However, the term *hydrogen ion* and the symbol *$H^+(aq)$* are still commonly used to represent $H_3O^+(aq)$. You should recognize that both H^+ and H_3O^+ represent hydrogen ions that are dissolved in and *covalently bonded to* water molecules.

CORE PROBLEMS

All Core Problems are paired and the answers to the blue odd-numbered problems appear in the back of the book.

7.1 Write the chemical equation for the self-ionization of water.

7.2 Why is the self-ionization of water referred to as a proton transfer reaction?

7.3 Why is the chemical equation that follows *not* an accurate representation of the self-ionization of water?

$$H_2O(l) \rightleftharpoons H^+(aq) + OH^-(aq)$$

7.4 Why is the chemical equation that follows *not* an accurate representation of the ionization of HNO_3?

$$HNO_3(aq) \rightarrow H^+(aq) + NO_3^-(aq)$$

7.5 Calculate the molar concentrations of the following ions. Give your answer as a power of ten.
a) OH^- in a solution that contains 10^{-11} M H_3O^+
b) H_3O^+ in a solution that contains 10^{-5} M OH^-
c) OH^- in a solution that contains 0.001 M H_3O^+

7.6 Calculate the molar concentrations of the following ions. Give your answer as a power of ten.
a) OH^- in a solution that contains 10^{-2} M H_3O^+
b) H_3O^+ in a solution that contains 10^{-9} M OH^-
c) H_3O^+ in a solution that contains 0.00001 M OH^-

7.7 Calculate the molar concentration of H_3O^+ in each of the following solutions:
a) a solution that contains 4.1×10^{-13} M OH^-
b) a solution that contains 0.0075 M OH^-

7.8 Calculate the molar concentration of OH^- in each of the following solutions:
a) a solution that contains 8.7×10^{-8} M H_3O^+
b) a solution that contains 0.022 M H_3O^+

7.9 Explain why the concentration of H_3O^+ increases when you add HCl to water.

7.10 Explain why the concentration of OH^- increases when you add NaOH to water.

OBJECTIVES: *Relate the pH of a solution to the hydronium ion concentration, and use pH to determine the acidity or basicity of a solution.*

7.2 The pH Scale

The concentration of H_3O^+ in body fluids such as blood and urine is a key indicator of human health. In addition, the molarity of H_3O^+ is a concern in a range of fields that deal with aqueous solutions, including the making of beer and wine, swimming pool maintenance, gardening and agriculture, and environmental monitoring. In most cases, the concentration of hydronium ions in fluids is very small and can be cumbersome to write. Therefore, the H_3O^+ concentration is usually expressed in an abbreviated notation called **pH**. To illustrate how pH works, let us look at the following three common liquids:

Charles D. Winters

A pH meter measuring the pH of a carbonated beverage.

Coca-Cola	Pure water	Ammonia cleaner
$[H_3O^+] = 10^{-3}$ M	$[H_3O^+] = 10^{-7}$ M	$[H_3O^+] = 10^{-11}$ M
pH = 3	pH = 7	pH = 11

Compare the molar concentration of hydronium ions in each solution with the pH of the solution. The pH is simply the exponent (the power of 10), without the minus sign. A good way to remember this is to think of pH as meaning the *power* of *hydronium*.

The pH is the power (the exponent) in the concentration of hydronium ions, without the minus sign.

$$[H_3O^+] = 10^{\boxed{-3}}\text{ M} \qquad \text{pH} = \boxed{3}$$

Sample Problem 7.2

Calculating the pH of a solution

A solution contains 0.0001 M H_3O^+. What is the pH of this solution?

SOLUTION

We can express 0.0001 as a power of 10: $0.0001 = 10^{-4}$. The pH of this solution is the exponent, without the minus sign, so the pH is 4.

TRY IT YOURSELF: *A solution contains 0.01 M H_3O^+. What is the pH of this solution?*

For additional practice, try Core Problems 7.15 and 7.16.

The pH Scale Is a Convenient Way to Express the Acidity or Basicity of a Solution

Since all aqueous solutions contain H_3O^+ ions, all aqueous solutions have a pH value. Most pH values lie between 0 and 14, although very concentrated solutions of compounds like HCl or NaOH can have pH values outside this range. The pH of a solution can be used to classify the solution as acidic, basic, or neutral, and it can be used to describe how acidic or basic a solution is, as shown in Figure 7.2.

Health Note: The pH of blood and the fluid inside most cells is around 7.4. The pH of digestive fluids varies from 1 to 2 (in the stomach) to 8 (pancreatic secretions and bile). The pH of urine can vary from 4.5 to 8, depending on whether the body needs to eliminate acids or bases from the blood.

- If the pH of a solution is below 7, the solution is **acidic**. Acidic solutions have a higher H_3O^+ concentration than that of pure water, and they have a lower OH^- concentration. They usually taste sour, and they turn various vegetable pigments red or pink.
- If the pH of a solution is exactly 7, the solution is **neutral**. The concentrations of H_3O^+ and OH^- in a neutral solution match those in pure water (10^{-7} M).
- If the pH of a solution is above 7, the solution is called **basic** or **alkaline**. Basic solutions have a higher OH^- concentration than that of pure water, and they have a lower H_3O^+ concentration. They usually taste bitter, and they turn various vegetable pigments blue, green, or yellow. Basic solutions also feel slippery, like soapy water.

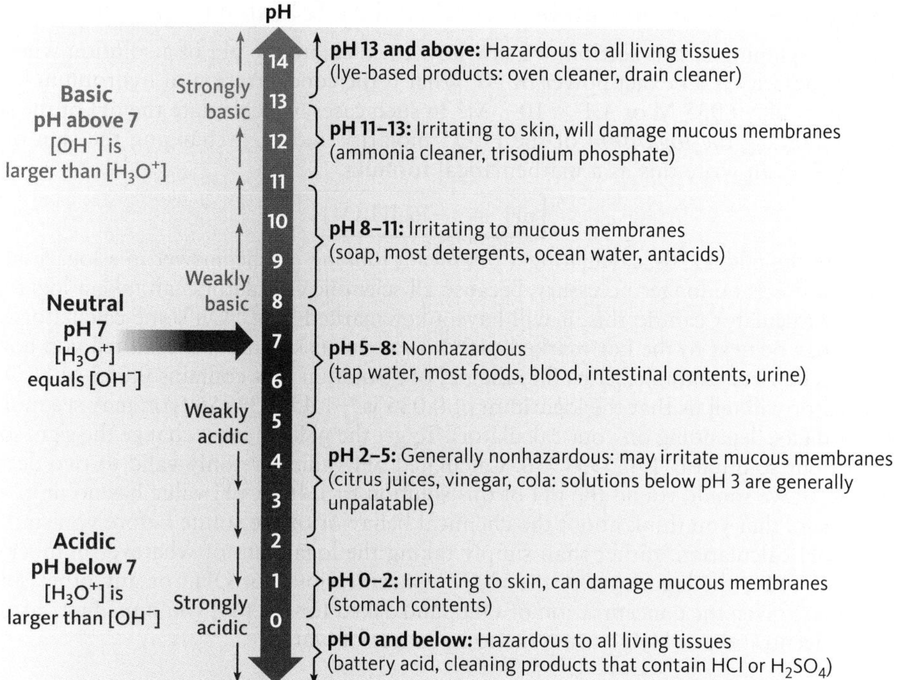

FIGURE 7.2 The pH scale and pH values for common solutions.

- As the pH moves further from 7, the solution becomes more acidic or basic. For example, black coffee has a pH of around 5, while the pH of apple juice is around 4. Both solutions are acidic, but apple juice is more acidic than coffee, because its pH is further from 7.

Sample Problem 7.3

Relating pH to acidity and basicity

A hospital laboratory receives three urine specimens and determines the pH of each to be as follows:

Specimen 1: pH = 5.9 Specimen 2: pH = 7.4 Specimen 3: pH = 6.6

Which of these solutions are acidic, and which are basic? Rank the solutions from most acidic to most basic.

SOLUTION

Specimens 1 and 3 have pH values below 7, so they are acidic. Specimen 2 has a pH above 7, so it is basic. The pH of specimen 1 is lower than that of specimen 3, so specimen 1 is more acidic than specimen 3. The correct ranking is as follows:

Specimen 1 (most acidic) → **Specimen 3** → **Specimen 2** (most basic)

TRY IT YOURSELF: *A high school science class measures the pH of three liquid cleaning products and gets the following results:*

Product 1: pH = 10.5 Product 2: pH = 8.7 Product 3: pH = 3.2

Which of these cleaning solutions are acidic, and which are basic? Rank the solutions from most acidic to most basic.

For additional practice, try Core Problems 7.11 through 7.14.

The pH of a Solution Can Be Calculated by Taking a Logarithm

At the beginning of this section, we saw how to calculate the pH of a solution when the H_3O^+ molarity is an exact power of 10. What if the concentration of hydronium ions is a number like 0.035 M or 4.1×10^{-9} M? In such cases, we calculate the pH of the solution by taking the *logarithm* of the H_3O^+ molarity and then changing the sign of the result. We can write this as a mathematical formula.

• This formula is often written $pH = -\log[H^+]$. Remember that H^+ is an alternate way to represent H_3O^+.

$$\boxed{pH = -\log[H_3O^+]}$$

Until the mid-1970s, calculating a pH meant looking up the answer in a logarithm table, but this is no longer necessary, because all scientific calculators can take a logarithm. If your calculator can do this, it will have a key marked "log." On some calculators, this label may be next to the key marked "10^x." Your owner's manual should tell you how to use this key. For example, let us find the pH of a solution that contains 0.035 M H_3O^+. A calculator will tell us that the logarithm of 0.035 is −1.455931956 (you may see more or fewer digits, depending on your calculator). To get the pH, we must change the sign, so the pH of our solution is 1.455931956. Calculated pH values are only valid to two decimal places, so we should round the pH of this solution to 1.46. A pH value has no unit.

Be sure that you think about the chemical behavior of the solute before you start doing a pH calculation, rather than simply taking the logarithm of whatever number you see. The pH is the logarithm of the H_3O^+ concentration, not OH^- or any other solute. If you are given the concentration of OH^- and asked for the pH, you must first calculate the concentration of H_3O^+ using the ion product of water.

Sample Problem **7.4**

Using logarithms to calculate pH

The concentration of OH^- in ocean water is 2.5×10^{-6} M. Calculate the pH of ocean water.

SOLUTION

Think about the chemistry before you pull out your calculator. To calculate a pH, we need the concentration of H_3O^+ ions, but we are not given this information. Instead, we are given the concentration of OH^-. However, we can use the ion product of water to calculate the concentration of H_3O^+.

$$[H_3O^+] \times [OH^-] = 1.0 \times 10^{-14}$$

Substitute the concentration of OH^- ions into this equation:

$$[H_3O^+] \times (2.5 \times 10^{-6}) = 1.0 \times 10^{-14}$$

To find the concentration of H_3O^+, we divide both sides by 2.5×10^{-6}:

$$\frac{[H_3O^+] \times \cancel{(2.5 \times 10^{-6})}}{\cancel{(2.5 \times 10^{-6})}} = \frac{(1.0 \times 10^{-14})}{(2.5 \times 10^{-6})}$$

$$[H_3O^+] = 4.0 \times 10^{-9} \text{ M}$$

Now we can calculate the pH. The logarithm of 4.0×10^{-9} is −8.397940009. To get the pH, we change the sign and round off to two decimal places, so the pH of ocean water is 8.40.

TRY IT YOURSELF: *The concentration of hydroxide ions in household bleach is 8.5×10^{-3} M. Calculate the pH of household bleach.*

For additional practice, try Core Problems 7.17 and 7.18.

Taking the Antilogarithm of the pH Gives the Hydronium Concentration

At the beginning of this section, we saw that when the molarity of H_3O^+ is an exact power of 10, the pH is simply the exponent without the minus sign. For example, if the H_3O^+ concentration is 10^{-5} M, the pH is 5. How are the pH values that we calculate using logarithms related to this? A logarithm is actually an exponent. When we say that the logarithm

TABLE 7.2 The Relationship Between Hydronium Concentration and pH

$[H_3O^+]$ (as a decimal)	$[H_3O^+]$ (as a power of 10)	pH ($-\log[H_3O^+]$)
0.001 M	10^{-3} M	3
0.035 M	$10^{-1.46}$ M	1.46
0.0000000041 M (4.1×10^{-9} M)	$10^{-8.39}$ M	8.39

of 0.035 is −1.46, we mean that an alternate way of writing the number 0.035 is $10^{-1.46}$. Table 7.2 shows the relationship between hydronium ion concentration and pH.

If we know the pH of a solution, we can therefore calculate the molarity of H_3O^+ by "putting the exponent back." This is often called *taking an antilogarithm.*

$$[H_3O^+] = 10^{-pH}$$

For example, if the pH of a solution is 6.25, the concentration of H_3O^+ is $10^{-6.25}$ M. However, this is not an acceptable form; we must convert this expression into either a decimal number or a value in scientific notation. Any calculator that can take a logarithm can also take an antilogarithm, and it has a key (usually labeled "10^x") for this purpose. The calculator tells us that $10^{-6.25}$ equals 0.000000562.

When the calculator result is a very small number, we should write it in scientific notation. We should also round the result to two significant figures (not two decimal places), because concentrations that are calculated from pH values are only valid to two significant figures. Therefore, we report the concentration of H_3O^+ as 5.6×10^{-7} M.

Sample Problem 7.5

Using pH to calculate hydronium and hydroxide ion concentrations

The pH of orange juice is 3.54. Calculate the concentrations of H_3O^+ and OH^- in orange juice.

SOLUTION

To calculate the concentration of H_3O^+ from the pH, we raise 10 to the −3.54 power. The calculator tells us that $10^{-3.54}$ equals 0.000288403. This answer is only valid to two significant figures, so the concentration of H_3O^+ is 0.00029 M. Since this is a small number, it is best written as $\mathbf{2.9 \times 10^{-4}}$ **M.**

Now that we know the concentration of H_3O^+, we can calculate the concentration of OH^- using the ion product of water. The ion product of water is

$$[H_3O^+] \times [OH^-] = 1.0 \times 10^{-14}$$

We can substitute the concentration of H_3O^+ ions into this equation. Remember that when you do a problem that requires several calculation steps, you must always use unrounded numbers in each step beyond the first.

$$0.000288403 \times [OH^-] = 1.0 \times 10^{-14}$$

To find the concentration of OH^-, we divide both sides by 0.000288403:

$$\frac{0.000288403 \times [OH^-]}{(0.000288403)} = \frac{(1.0 \times 10^{-14})}{(0.000288403)}$$

$$[OH^-] = 3.46737 \times 10^{-11} \text{ M} \qquad \text{calculator answer}$$

This concentration must also be rounded to two significant figures, so the concentration of OH^- in orange juice is $\mathbf{3.5 \times 10^{-11}}$ **M.**

TRY IT YOURSELF: *The pH of a urine specimen is 5.89. Calculate the concentrations of H_3O^+ and OH^- in this specimen.*

For additional practice, try Core Problems 7.19 and 7.20.

CORE PROBLEMS

7.11 Which of the following solutions are acidic, which are neutral, and which are basic?
a) a solution of NH_4Cl in water (pH = 3.86)
b) a solution of Na_2CO_3 in water (pH = 10.95)
c) a solution of NaCl in water (pH = 7.00)

7.12 Which of the following solutions are acidic, which are neutral, and which are basic?
a) bile (pH = 7.00)
b) intestinal contents (pH = 8.01)
c) stomach contents (pH = 1.94)

7.13 Which of the following solutions is the most acidic, and which is the least acidic?
0.1 M NH_4Cl (pH = 5.12)
0.1 M $NaHSO_3$ (pH = 4.00)
0.1 M $NaHSO_4$ (pH = 1.54)

7.14 Which of the following solutions is the most basic, and which is the least basic?
0.1 M Na_2CO_3 (pH = 11.62)
0.1 M $NaNO_2$ (pH = 8.17)
0.1 M Na_2HPO_4 (pH = 9.94)

7.15 Calculate the pH of each of the following solutions. Give your answers as whole numbers.
a) a solution that contains 10^{-5} M H_3O^+
b) a solution that contains 10^{-3} M OH^-
c) a solution that contains 0.0001 M H_3O^+
d) a solution that contains 0.00001 M OH^-

7.16 Calculate the pH of each of the following solutions. Give your answers as whole numbers.
a) a solution that contains 10^{-8} M H_3O^+
b) a solution that contains 10^{-10} M OH^-
c) a solution that contains 0.1 M H_3O^+
d) a solution that contains 1 M OH^-

7.17 The concentration of H_3O^+ in a solution of soapy water is 3.1×10^{-9} M.
a) What is the concentration of OH^- in the soapy water?
b) What is the pH of the soapy water?

7.18 The concentration of OH^- in a solution of dishwasher detergent is 0.0052 M.
a) What is the concentration of H_3O^+ in the detergent?
b) What is the pH of the detergent?

7.19 The pH of a cup of coffee is 5.13. Calculate the concentration of H_3O^+ and OH^- in the coffee.

7.20 The pH of a urine sample is 7.24. Calculate the concentration of H_3O^+ and OH^- in the urine.

OBJECTIVES: *Write the equation for the ionization of an acid in water, relate the strength of the acid and its molarity to pH, and recognize common structural features in acidic compounds.*

7.3 Properties of Acids

It is time to take a detailed look at the class of compounds we call **acids.** *An acid is a compound that can lose H^+.* The hydrogen ion must be transferred to another molecule or ion, because H^+ is a bare proton and cannot exist as an independent ion, as we saw in Section 7.1. Therefore, we can say that acids are compounds that donate hydrogen ions to some other molecule. Since a hydrogen ion is just a proton, acids are often called *proton donors.*

HCl is a typical acid. When HCl dissolves in water, it donates a proton to a water molecule. Because the products are ions, this reaction is called an **ionization reaction.** The chemical equation for this ionization of HCl is

$$HCl + H_2O \rightarrow H_3O^+ + Cl^-$$

Figure 7.3 shows the structures of the reactants and products in the ionization of HCl. You should compare this reaction with the self-ionization of water in Figure 7.1.

H^+ moves from HCl to H_2O.

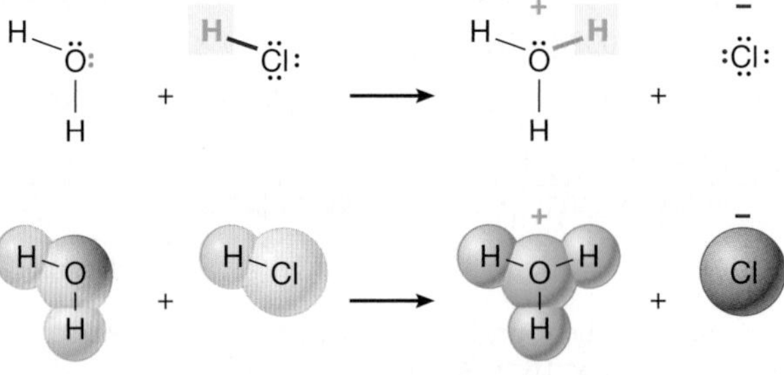

In this figure, the reaction is written
$H_2O + HCl \longrightarrow H_3O^+ + Cl^-$
Remember that you can write the reactants (and the products) in a chemical equation in any order you choose.

FIGURE 7.3 The ionization of HCl in water.

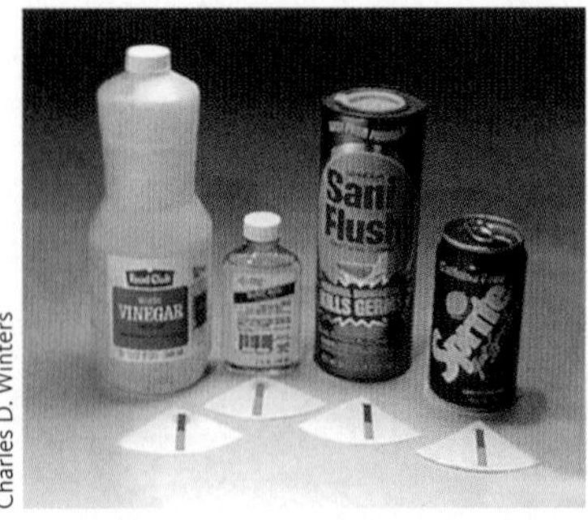

Charles D. Winters

Each of these common household products contains an acid. The indicator paper strips contain a dye that turns red or orange in the presence of acids.

TABLE 7.3 Some Common Acids and Their Ionization Reactions

Formula	Name	Ionization Reaction
HCl	Hydrochloric acid	$HCl(aq) + H_2O(l) \rightarrow H_3O^+(aq) + Cl^-(aq)$
HNO_3	Nitric acid	$HNO_3(aq) + H_2O(l) \rightarrow H_3O^+(aq) + NO_3^-(aq)$
H_2SO_4	Sulfuric acid	$H_2SO_4(aq) + H_2O(l) \rightarrow H_3O^+(aq) + HSO_4^-(aq)$
H_3PO_4	Phosphoric acid	$H_3PO_4(aq) + H_2O(l) \rightarrow H_3O^+(aq) + H_2PO_4^-(aq)$
H_2CO_3	Carbonic acid	$H_2CO_3(aq) + H_2O(l) \rightarrow H_3O^+(aq) + HCO_3^-(aq)$
$HC_2H_3O_2$	Acetic acid	$HC_2H_3O_2(aq) + H_2O(l) \rightarrow H_3O^+(aq) + C_2H_3O_2^-(aq)$

Many acids are important compounds in medicine, industry, or daily life. All common acids are molecular compounds, made up of nonmetallic atoms that are covalently bonded to one another. Table 7.3 lists the names and chemical formulas of some common acids, along with their ionization reactions.

Hydrochloric, nitric, sulfuric, and phosphoric acids are called *mineral acids,* because they are made from mineral sources (air, water, salt, sulfur deposits, and phosphate-containing minerals). These acids are manufactured in huge amounts, and they are used to make a host of other chemicals. Acetic acid is an example of an *organic acid.* Organic acids contain carbon and are generally derived from living organisms. We will look at the structures and properties of organic acids in detail in Chapter 11.

Acids Can Be Strong or Weak Electrolytes

All acids are electrolytes, because they form ions when they dissolve in water. However, acids vary in their ability to give up a proton. Some acids donate H^+ so easily that every molecule of the acid breaks down when the acid dissolves in water. For example, when HCl dissolves in water, every molecule of HCl loses H^+. The concentration of ions in a solution of HCl is high, so the solution conducts electricity well. Therefore, HCl is called a **strong electrolyte.** Any compound that ionizes completely in water is a strong electrolyte, including virtually all water-soluble ionic compounds. For example, both HCl and NaCl are strong electrolytes because they break down completely into ions when they dissolve, although the chemical reactions look somewhat different.

$NaCl(s) \rightarrow Na^+(aq) + Cl^-(aq)$ Every NaCl formula unit breaks down into Na^+ and Cl^-.

$HCl(aq) + H_2O(l) \rightarrow H_3O^+(aq) + Cl^-(aq)$ Every HCl molecule reacts with water to make H_3O^+ and Cl^-.

In most acids, the bond between H^+ and the rest of the molecule is not as easily broken as the bond in HCl. As a result, only a fraction of the molecules of the acid donate a proton to a water molecule. A good example is acetic acid, the compound that gives vinegar its characteristic flavor and aroma. Acetic acid ionizes when we dissolve it in water, but we end up with a mixture of products and reactants.

$HC_2H_3O_2(aq) + H_2O(l) \rightleftharpoons H_3O^+(aq) + C_2H_3O_2^-(aq)$ The double arrow means that we form an equilibrium mixture of products and reactants.

In a typical solution of acetic acid, less than 5% of the molecules donate H^+ to a water molecule. As a result, solutions of acetic acid contain few ions and do not conduct electricity well. Substances that ionize to a limited extent when they dissolve in water are called **weak electrolytes.** Acetic acid is a weak electrolyte, as are most other acids.

Chemists often use the terms *strong acid* and *weak acid* to refer to acids that are strong electrolytes and weak electrolytes, respectively. All strong acids behave the same way, ionizing completely when they dissolve in water. Weak acids do not ionize completely, but they vary quite a bit in their ability to ionize. In a 0.1 M solution of acetic acid, roughly 1% of the molecules are ionized. By contrast, in a 0.1 M solution of phenol (also called carbolic acid), only 0.004% of the molecules are ionized. We will look more closely at the ability of weak acids to ionize in a moment.

Figure 7.4 illustrates the differing behaviors of strong and weak acids in aqueous solution.

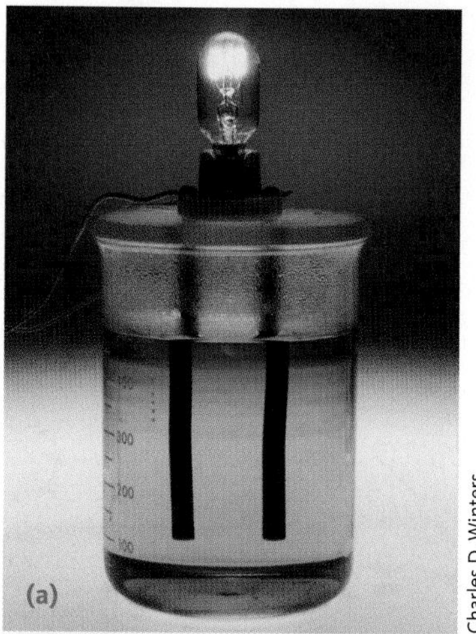
(a) Charles D. Winters

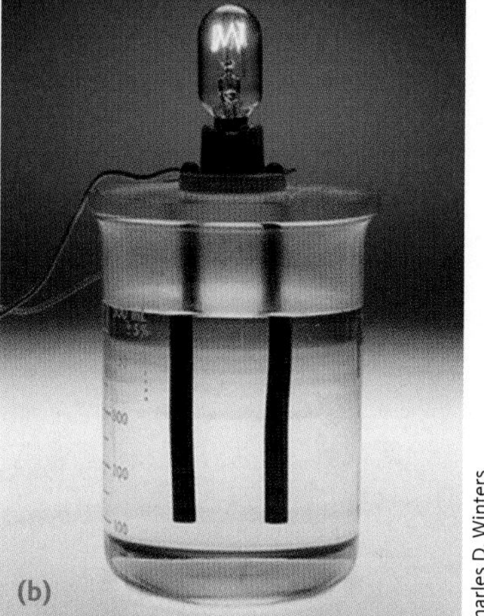
(b) Charles D. Winters

(c) Charles D. Winters

Testing solutions for electrical conductivity. (a) Copper(II) sulfate ($CuSO_4$) solutions conduct electricity well, so $CuSO_4$ is a strong electrolyte. (b) Vitamin C solutions conduct electricity poorly, making Vitamin C a weak electrolyte. (c) A solution of table sugar does not conduct electricity, so table sugar is a nonelectrolyte.

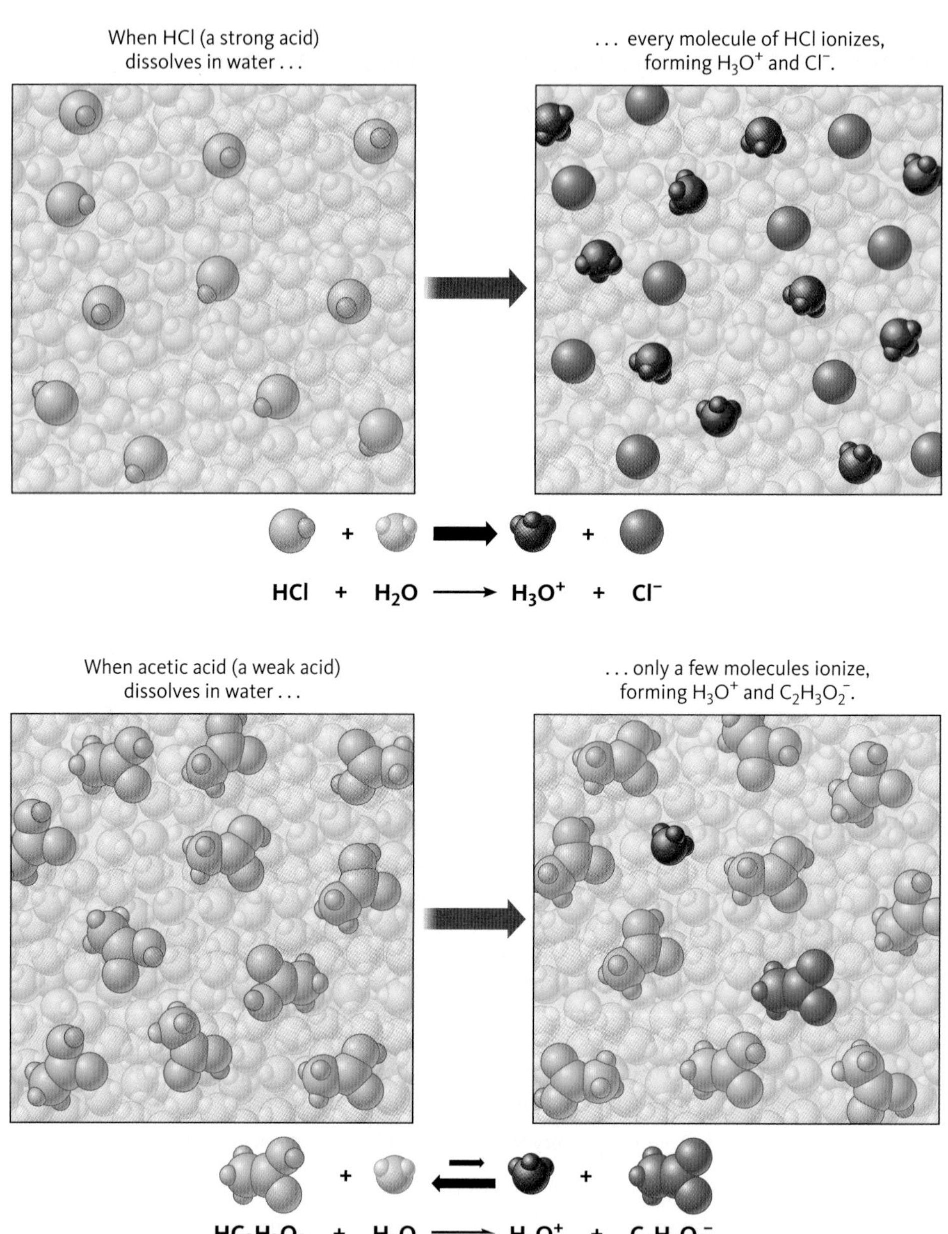
When HCl (a strong acid) dissolves in water . . .
. . . every molecule of HCl ionizes, forming H_3O^+ and Cl^-.
$HCl + H_2O \longrightarrow H_3O^+ + Cl^-$
When acetic acid (a weak acid) dissolves in water . . .
. . . only a few molecules ionize, forming H_3O^+ and $C_2H_3O_2^-$.
$HC_2H_3O_2 + H_2O \rightleftharpoons H_3O^+ + C_2H_3O_2^-$

FIGURE 7.4 Ionization of a strong and a weak acid.

Sample Problem 7.6

Writing a chemical equation for the ionization of an acid

$HClO_4$ is a strong acid, called perchloric acid. Write the chemical equation for the ionization of perchloric acid in aqueous solution.

SOLUTION

Acids ionize by donating a proton (a hydrogen ion) to a water molecule. The $HClO_4$ molecule loses H^+, becoming ClO_4^-. The water molecule gains the H^+, becoming H_3O^+. The balanced equation is

$$HClO_4 + H_2O \rightarrow H_3O^+ + ClO_4^-$$

Since $HClO_4$ is a strong acid, we write a single arrow to show that every molecule of $HClO_4$ ionizes.

continued

TRY IT YOURSELF: *The unpleasant odor and flavor of spoiled milk is caused by lactic acid, which is a weak acid with the chemical formula $HC_3H_5O_3$. Write the chemical equation for the ionization of lactic acid in aqueous solution.*

For additional practice, try Core Problems 7.21 and 7.22.

TABLE 7.4 The Relationship Between Molarity of an Acid and pH

Molarity (M) of Acetic Acid ($HC_2H_3O_2$)	pH	
1 M	2.37	Most acidic solution
0.1 M	2.88	
0.01 M	3.38	↓
0.001 M	3.90	
0.0001 M	4.46	Least acidic solution

The pH of an Acid Solution Depends on the Molarity and the Strength of the Acid

When we dissolve an acid in water, the pH of the solution depends on the concentration of the acid. A solution that has a high concentration of an acid contains more H_3O^+ ions than a solution that has a low concentration of the same acid. As a result, *as the concentration of an acid increases, the pH of the solution goes down* (see Figure 7.2). Table 7.4 shows how the pH of an acetic acid solution depends on the molarity of the acid.

Sample Problem 7.7

Using molarity to compare pH

Lactic acid ($HC_3H_5O_3$) is a weak acid that is responsible for the tart flavor of yogurt and some cheeses. Which has a higher pH, 0.1 M lactic acid or 0.03 M lactic acid?

SOLUTION

The 0.1 M solution has the higher concentration, so it contains a higher concentration of H_3O^+ ions. However, a higher concentration of H_3O^+ corresponds to a lower pH, so the 0.03 M solution has the higher pH.

TRY IT YOURSELF: *Sorbic acid ($HC_6H_7O_2$) is a weak acid that is used to prevent mold formation on cheese. Which has a higher pH, 2×10^{-4} M sorbic acid or 2×10^{-5} M sorbic acid?*

For additional practice, try Core Problems 7.23 and 7.24.

For weak acids, the pH of the solution also depends on the ability of the acid to donate H^+ to water. The ability to donate a proton is called the **strength of an acid**. Stronger acids release H^+ more readily, so solutions of stronger acids contain more H_3O^+ than solutions of weaker acids. As a result, *a solution of a stronger acid has a lower pH than a solution of a weaker acid.* Bear in mind that this comparison is only valid if the molarities of the two solutions are equal. Table 7.5 lists the pH values of 0.1 M solutions of various acids.

Health Note: Foods contain a variety of acids, including citric acid (in citrus fruits), lactic acid (in sour cream), acetic acid (in vinegar), malic acid (in apples), and tartaric acid (in grapes). All of these are weak acids, so they do not pose any danger to our bodies.

TABLE 7.5 The Relationship Between Acid Strength and pH

	Acid Solution	pH	Percentage of Ionized Molecules	Type of Acid
Strongest acid	0.1 M HCl (hydrochloric acid)	1.00	100%	Strong
	0.1 M H_3PO_4 (phosphoric acid)	1.62	24%	Weak
	0.1 M $HC_2H_3O_2$ (acetic acid)	2.88	1.3%	Weak
	0.1 M H_2CO_3 (carbonic acid)	3.68	0.21%	Weak
Weakest acid	0.1 M HC_6H_5O (phenol, or carbolic acid)	5.40	0.004%	Weak

Of the acids in Table 7.5, only HCl is classified as a strong acid, because it is the only one that ionizes completely. The other four acids are weak, but they vary tremendously in their ability to ionize. For this reason, chemists often make statements such as "phosphoric acid is stronger than acetic acid." Be aware that such a statement does not mean that phosphoric acid is *strong* (100% ionized); it only means that a *larger percentage* of phosphoric acid molecules ionize.

Sample Problem 7.8

Using acid strength to compare pH

Citric acid is stronger than carbonic acid. Which has a higher pH, 0.01 M citric acid or 0.01 M carbonic acid?

SOLUTION

Citric acid is the stronger acid, so it ionizes to a greater extent, producing a higher concentration of H_3O^+ ions. Therefore, the citric acid solution should be more acidic than the carbonic acid solution. A more acidic solution has a lower pH, so the carbonic acid solution has the higher pH.

TRY IT YOURSELF: *Hydrochloric acid is stronger than hydrofluoric acid. Which has a higher pH, 0.25 M hydrochloric acid or 0.25 M hydrofluoric acid?*

For additional practice, try Core Problems 7.29 and 7.30.

Sample Problem 7.9

Using pH to compare acid strength

The pH of 0.1 M lactic acid is 2.44, and the pH of 0.1 M acetic acid is 2.88. Based on this information, which is the stronger acid?

SOLUTION

We must remember that a lower pH indicates a more acidic solution. In this case, the pH of the lactic acid solution is lower than the pH of the acetic acid solution, so the lactic acid solution contains a higher concentration of H_3O^+ ions. Therefore, lactic acid ionizes to a greater extent than acetic acid, so lactic acid is the stronger acid.

TRY IT YOURSELF: *The pH of 0.1 M $H_2C_6H_6O_6$ (ascorbic acid) is 2.56 and the pH of 0.1 M H_2S is 4.00. Based on this information, which is the stronger acid?*

For additional practice, try Core Problems 7.27 and 7.28.

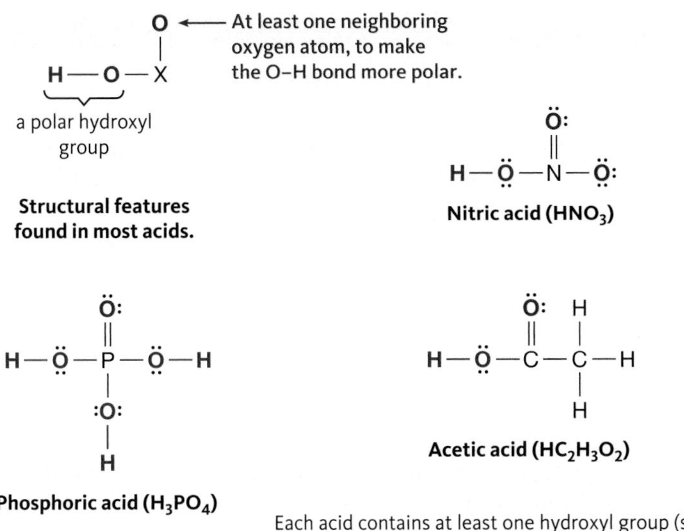
At least one neighboring oxygen atom, to make the O-H bond more polar.
a polar hydroxyl group
Structural features found in most acids.
Nitric acid (HNO_3)
Phosphoric acid (H_3PO_4)
Acetic acid ($HC_2H_3O_2$)
Each acid contains at least one hydroxyl group (shown in red). The hydrogen atoms in the hydroxyl groups are acidic and can be transferred to H_2O.
Oxygen atoms (shown in **purple**) also help to make these compounds acidic.

FIGURE 7.5 Structural features of common acids.

Many Acids Share Certain Structural Features

What makes a compound acidic? This question does not have a simple answer. However, we can recognize two structural features that are found in most acids. First, acids normally contain at least one *hydroxyl group*. A hydroxyl group is made up of an oxygen atom and a hydrogen atom that are covalently bonded to each other, as shown here. The bond between oxygen and hydrogen is polar, just as it is in water, so the hydrogen atom is positively charged.

$$\overset{\delta^-}{\mathbf{O}}-\overset{\delta^+}{\mathbf{H}} \quad \text{a hydroxyl group}$$

Second, the atom that is attached to the hydroxyl group is normally bonded to at least one other oxygen atom. These oxygen atoms pull electrons away from the hydroxyl group, making the O—H bond even more polar. As a result, the hydrogen atom has an unusually strong positive charge, allowing it to be pulled off by other molecules. Figure 7.5 illustrates the two structural features that we find in most acids, along with three common acids that contain these structural features.

Of the acids in Figure 7.5, acetic acid is noteworthy in that it contains four hydrogen atoms, but only one of these hydrogen atoms is acidic. The three hydrogen atoms that are bonded to carbon cannot be transferred to water or to any other molecule. The following molecule, called formic acid, is another example of a compound in which not all of the hydrogen atoms are acidic:

This hydrogen atom is acidic and can be transferred to H_2O. ⟶ H—Ö—C(=Ö:)—H ⟵ This hydrogen atom is not acidic.

When chemists write the chemical formula of an acid, they list the hydrogen atoms first. As a result, *the chemical formulas of acids start with H, and the chemical formulas of compounds that are not acids start with some other element.* The only exception to this rule is water, which is written H_2O but is not generally considered to be an acid. For example, HF and H_2S are acidic, whereas NH_3 and CH_4 are not. If a molecule contains both acidic and nonacidic hydrogen atoms, chemists normally put all of the acidic hydrogen atoms at the start of the formula and write nonacidic hydrogen atoms later. For example, the formula of formic acid is usually written $HCHO_2$ to show that only one of the two hydrogen atoms can be removed as H^+.

Sample Problem 7.10

Using a Lewis structure to identify acidic hydrogen atoms

Phosphorous acid has the chemical formula H_3PO_3 and the following structure. Only two of the three hydrogen atoms in a molecule of phosphorous acid can be removed. Is this reasonable, based on the structure? Which two hydrogen atoms can be removed?

```
        Ö:
        ‖
H—Ö—P—Ö—H
        |
        H
```

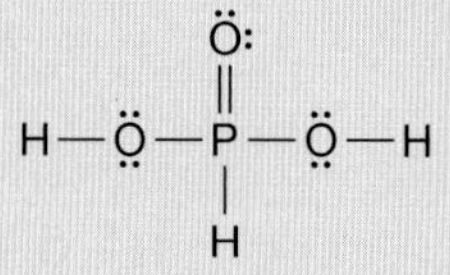

SOLUTION

Only two of the three hydrogen atoms are bonded to oxygen, while the third is bonded to phosphorus. Therefore, it is not surprising that this compound can only lose two hydrogen atoms. The two hydrogen atoms that are bonded to oxygen are acidic, but the hydrogen that is bonded to phosphorus is not.

TRY IT YOURSELF: *Malonic acid has the following structure. Only two of the four hydrogen atoms in a molecule of malonic acid can be removed. Is this reasonable, based on the structure? Which two hydrogen atoms can be removed?*

```
     :Ö   H   Ö:
      ‖   |   ‖
H—Ö—C—C—C—Ö—H
          |
          H
```

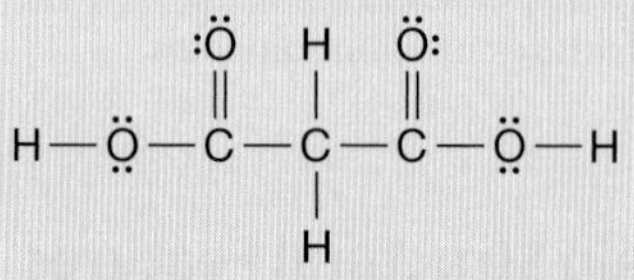

For additional practice, try Core Problems 7.33 and 7.34.

Some Acids Can Lose More Than One Hydrogen

HCl, HNO_3, and $HC_2H_3O_2$ are examples of **monoprotic acids**. A monoprotic acid is only able to transfer one hydrogen ion to water. However, some acids, called **polyprotic acids**, are capable of losing more than one hydrogen ion. For example, H_2SO_4 can lose both of its hydrogen atoms (in the form of H^+), and H_3PO_4 can lose all three. Some polyprotic acids also contain nonacidic hydrogen atoms, and these are written separately, just as they are for monoprotic acids. For example, citric acid (which gives citrus fruits their tart flavors) has eight hydrogen atoms, but it can only lose three of them, so the chemical formula of citric acid is written $H_3C_6H_5O_7$.

In most polyprotic acids, the second hydrogen is much more difficult to remove than the first, and the third (if there is a third) is more difficult still. As a result, the second and third ionizations of most polyprotic acids are insignificant when the acids are dissolved in water. For example, here are the percentages for the three ionization steps in a 1 M solution of H_3PO_4:

Health Note: Phosphoric acid is used to make colas and other soft drinks taste tart; it is also used to adjust the pH of some cosmetics and skin-care products. The old story that a tooth will dissolve overnight in a glass of cola because of the acid is not true, though, as you can easily verify if you have a young child with a loose tooth.

$H_3PO_4 + H_2O \rightleftharpoons H_2PO_4^- \quad H_3O^+$ **8% of H_3PO_4 molecules lose a proton in a 1 M solution**

$H_2PO_4^- + H_2O \rightleftharpoons HPO_4^{2-} + H_3O^+$ **0.000006% of the molecules lose a second proton**

$HPO_4^{2-} + H_2O \rightleftharpoons PO_4^{3-} + H_3O^+$ **0.00000000000001% of the molecules lose a third proton**

However, the second and third hydrogen ions can be removed by substances that have a strong attraction to H^+. In particular, the HPO_4^{2-} ion (formed when two protons are removed from phosphoric acid) plays an important role in maintaining the pH of body fluids, as we will see in Section 7.8.

CORE PROBLEMS

7.21 Write the chemical equations for the ionization of the following acids in water:
a) HNO_3 (nitric acid, a strong acid that is used in the manufacture of fertilizers)
b) $HC_3H_5O_3$ (lactic acid, a weak acid that is found in sour milk)
c) $H_2C_4H_4O_4$ (succinic acid, a weak acid that is formed when sugars are burned by your body)

7.22 Write the chemical equations for the ionization of the following acids in water:
a) HBr (hydrobromic acid, a strong acid that is used in chemical manufacturing)
b) $HC_7H_5O_5$ (gallic acid, a weak acid that is used in photo developing)
c) $H_3C_6H_5O_7$ (citric acid, a weak acid that gives citrus fruits their tart flavors)

7.23 Which solution has the higher pH: 0.1 M formic acid or 0.01 M formic acid?

7.24 Which solution has the lower pH: 1.0×10^{-3} M acetic acid or 2.0×10^{-4} M acetic acid?

7.25 If you dissolve 0.1 mol of formic acid in 1 L of water, the resulting solution contains 0.004 mol of H_3O^+. Based on this information, is formic acid a strong acid, or is it a weak acid?

7.26 If you dissolve 0.025 mol of HBr in 1 L of water, the resulting solution contains 0.025 mol of H_3O^+. Based on this information, is HBr a strong acid, or is it a weak acid?

7.27 The pH of 0.01 M benzoic acid is 3.12, and the pH of 0.01 M cyanoacetic acid is 2.33. Based on this information, which is the stronger acid, benzoic acid or cyanoacetic acid?

7.28 The pH of 0.01 M ascorbic acid is 3.10, and the pH of 0.01 M succinic acid is 3.21. Based on this information, which is the stronger acid, ascorbic acid or succinic acid?

7.29 Nitric acid (HNO_3) is stronger than nitrous acid (HNO_2). Based on this information, answer the following questions:
a) Which contains a higher concentration of H_3O^+ ions, 0.01 M nitric acid or 0.01 M nitrous acid?
b) Which solution has the higher pH?
c) Which solution contains a higher concentration of OH^- ions?

7.30 Hydrochloric acid (HCl) is stronger than hydrofluoric acid (HF). Based on this information, answer the following questions:
a) Which contains a higher concentration of H_3O^+ ions, 0.01 M HF or 0.01 M HCl?
b) Which solution has the higher pH?
c) Which solution contains a higher concentration of OH^- ions?

7.31 Both formic acid and carbonic acid contain two hydrogen atoms. Why is the chemical formula of formic acid written $HCHO_2$ (with the two hydrogen atoms listed separately), while the chemical formula of carbonic acid is written H_2CO_3 (with the two hydrogen atoms written together)?

7.32 Both acetaldehyde and acetic acid contain four hydrogen atoms. Why is the chemical formula of acetaldehyde written C_2H_4O (with all four hydrogen atoms listed together), while the chemical formula of acetic acid is written $HC_2H_3O_2$ (with one hydrogen atom listed separately from the others)?

7.33 Methylphosphoric acid has the chemical formula CH_5PO_4.

```
    H       Ö:
    |       ||
H—C—Ö—P—Ö—H
    |       |
    H      :Ö—H
```

a) Based on the structure of this compound, how many hydrogen ions can be removed from a molecule of methylphosphoric acid?
b) Write the chemical formula of methylphosphoric acid in a way that clearly shows the number of ionizable hydrogen atoms.

7.34 Malic acid has the chemical formula $C_4H_6O_5$.

```
              H
              |
      :O:  :O:  H  :O:
      ||    |   |   ||
H—Ö—C—C—C—C—Ö—H
            |   |
            H   H
```

a) Based on the structure of this compound, how many hydrogen ions can be removed from a molecule of malic acid?
b) Write the chemical formula of malic acid in a way that clearly shows the number of ionizable hydrogen atoms.

7.35 Carbonic acid (H_2CO_3) is a polyprotic acid. When carbonic acid dissolves in water, which is higher, the concentration of HCO_3^- ions or the concentration of CO_3^{2-} ions?

7.36 Citric acid ($H_3C_6H_5O_7$) is a polyprotic acid. When citric acid dissolves in water, which is higher, the concentration of $H_2C_6H_5O_7^-$ ions or the concentration of $HC_6H_5O_7^{2-}$ ions?

OBJECTIVES: *Write the equation for the ionization of a base in water, recognize the two common types of bases, identify conjugate pairs, and relate the strength of a base to the pH of a basic solution.*

Health Note: The most common active ingredients in over-the-counter antacids are aluminum hydroxide, magnesium hydroxide, and calcium carbonate.

Health Note: Human urine contains a compound called urea, which is rapidly broken down into ammonia and carbon dioxide by bacteria. The ammonia is a base and changes the pH of the urine, so the pH of urine specimens should be tested immediately after collection.

7.4 Properties of Bases

People have known for centuries that certain chemicals, called **bases**, are able to counteract acids. Some common examples of bases are NaOH, $CaCO_3$, and NH_3. Adding any of these bases to an acidic solution makes the solution less acidic, and if we add enough of the base we can bring the pH up to 7 (neutral). Chemists describe this behavior by saying that bases *neutralize* acids. If you have ever taken an antacid to soothe an upset stomach, you have exploited this ability of bases.

We now know that a base neutralizes an acid by forming a bond to the hydrogen ion from the acid. Therefore, chemists define a base as *any compound that can bond to H^+*. Since a hydrogen ion is a proton, bases are also called *proton acceptors*. Recall from Section 7.3 that an acid is a proton donor, so acids and bases complement each other. These definitions of acids and bases were proposed by Johannes Bronsted and Thomas Lowry in 1923, and they are called the **Bronsted-Lowry concept** of acids and bases.

We begin our study of bases by looking at how a base behaves when it dissolves in water. When we mix a base with water, *the base pulls a hydrogen ion away from a water molecule*. For example, the base ammonia reacts with water as follows:

$$NH_3(aq) + H_2O(l) \rightarrow NH_4^+(aq) + OH^-(aq)$$

In this reaction, a proton moves from the water molecule to the ammonia molecule. The proton becomes bonded to the nitrogen atom of ammonia, using the nonbonding electron pair to supply the electrons. This reaction is very similar to the self-ionization of water, as shown in Figure 7.6.

Any substance that can remove a hydrogen ion from a water molecule is a base. As a result, *bases always produce hydroxide ions when they dissolve in water*. The hydroxide ions raise the pH of the solution, so solutions of bases always have pH values above 7.

Bases are more difficult to recognize than acids. However, most common bases fall into one of two categories:

1. *Most anions are bases.* This should seem reasonable, because opposite charges attract each other. Anions are negatively charged ions, so they are attracted to H^+. Some examples of anion bases are S^{2-}, OH^-, CO_3^{2-}, and PO_4^{3-}.
2. *Most molecules that contain nitrogen covalently bonded to carbon, hydrogen, or both are bases.* The nitrogen atom can bond to a hydrogen ion, converting its nonbonding electron pair to a fourth bonding pair. The reaction of ammonia with water in Figure 7.6 illustrates how nitrogen-containing compounds can bond to H^+. Here are some examples of bases that contain nitrogen:

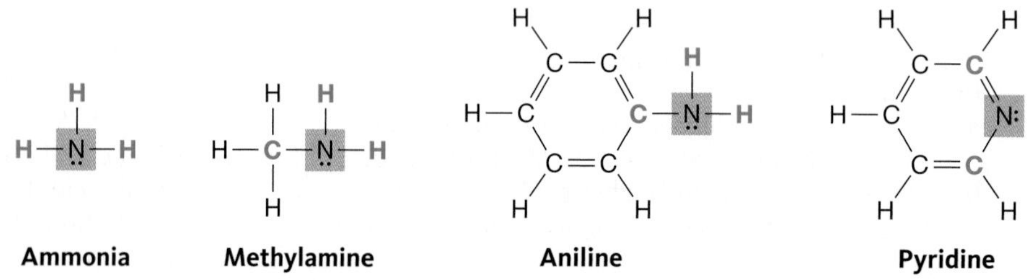

Each of these bases contains nitrogen bonded to carbon or hydrogen.

When we want to prepare a solution of an ionic base such as OH^- or CO_3^{2-}, we cannot simply drop the ions into water. We must use an ionic compound that contains the anion and that dissolves easily in water. The best choices in general are compounds that contain Na^+ or K^+, because all sodium and potassium compounds dissolve in water and dissociate completely when they dissolve. In addition, Na^+ and K^+ are relatively nontoxic, making them a good choice for medical uses. Therefore, if we need to prepare a solution that contains OH^- ions, we can make the solution by dissolving NaOH or KOH in water.

H^+ moves from H_2O to NH_3.

$$H_3N{:} + H{-}\ddot{O}{:}{-}H \longrightarrow [H_3N{-}H]^+ + [{:}\ddot{O}{-}H]^-$$

Reaction of ammonia with water

H^+ moves from H_2O to H_2O.

$$H{-}\ddot{O}{:}{-}H + H{-}\ddot{O}{:}{-}H \longrightarrow [H{-}\ddot{O}(H){-}H]^+ + [{:}\ddot{O}{-}H]^-$$

Self-ionization of water

FIGURE 7.6 The basic behavior of ammonia.

Charles D. Winters

Each of these common household products contains a base. The indicator paper turns blue or purple in the presence of bases.

Sample Problem **7.11**

Identifying a source of an ionic base

Carbonate ion (CO_3^{2-}) is a base. If we needed to prepare a solution that contains carbonate ions, what compound could we use as the solute?

SOLUTION

The best choices are the compounds that contain carbonate and either sodium or potassium. The rule of charge balance tells us that we need two Na^+ or K^+ ions to match the charge on a CO_3^{2-} ion, so the correct chemical formulas of these compounds are Na_2CO_3 and K_2CO_3.

TRY IT YOURSELF: *Phosphate ion (PO_4^{3-}) is a base. If you needed to prepare a solution that contains phosphate ions, what compound could you use as the solute?*

Bases Are Classified As Strong or Weak Based on Their Ability to Produce OH^-

In the last section, we classified acids as strong or weak based on how effective they were at donating H^+ to water. Likewise, we classify bases as strong or weak based on how effective they are at removing hydrogen ions from water molecules. If every molecule of a substance removes a proton from a water molecule, the substance is classified as a *strong base.* When we dissolve a strong base in water, every molecule of the base reacts with a water molecule to produce a hydroxide ion. The hydroxide ion itself is a strong base and is an important substance in chemistry; but beyond this, strong bases are not common. The sulfide ion is an example.

$$S^{2-}(aq) + H_2O(l) \rightarrow HS^-(aq) + OH^-(aq)$$

We write the balanced equation for this reaction with a single arrow, which tells us that every sulfide ion is converted to HS^-.

Other than OH^-, all of the bases that play a significant role in medicine are *weak bases.* Weak bases react with water to produce hydroxide ions, but they only do so to a limited extent. For example, ammonia is a weak base. When ammonia dissolves in water, a few ammonia molecules remove a proton from a water molecule, but most of the ammonia molecules remain unchanged. To show this, we write the equation with a double arrow.

$$NH_3(aq) + H_2O(l) \rightleftharpoons NH_4^+(aq) + OH^-(aq)$$

TABLE 7.6 Some Weak Bases and Their Reactions with Water

Formula	Name	Reaction with Water
C_5H_5N	Pyridine	$C_5H_5N(aq) + H_2O(l) \rightleftharpoons HC_5H_5N^+(aq) + OH^-(aq)$
N_2H_4	Hydrazine	$N_2H_4(aq) + H_2O(l) \rightleftharpoons N_2H_5^+(aq) + OH^-(aq)$
C_2H_7NO	Ethanolamine	$C_2H_7NO(aq) + H_2O(l) \rightleftharpoons HC_2H_7NO^+(aq) + OH^-(aq)$
$C_2H_3O_2^-$	Acetate ion	$C_2H_3O_2^-(aq) + H_2O(l) \rightleftharpoons HC_2H_3O_2(aq) + OH^-(aq)$
CO_3^{2-}	Carbonate ion	$CO_3^{2-}(aq) + H_2O(l) \rightleftharpoons HCO_3^-(aq) + OH^-(aq)$
PO_4^{3-}	Phosphate ion	$PO_4^{3-}(aq) + H_2O(l) \rightleftharpoons HPO_4^{2-}(aq) + OH^-(aq)$

Table 7.6 lists some other weak bases and their reactions with water. In each case, the base removes H^+ from the water molecule, forming hydroxide ion.

Acids and Bases Become Their Conjugates When They React with Water

When an acid or a base reacts with water, the reactant and the product bear a special relationship to each other. When a base reacts with water, the base gains H^+, and when an acid reacts with water, the acid loses H^+. In both cases, the formulas of the reactant and the product differ by one hydrogen ion, Two substances whose formulas differ by one H^+ are called a **conjugate pair**. The substance that contains H^+ is called the **conjugate acid**, and the substance that is missing the H^+ is called the **conjugate base.** For instance, HF and F^- differ by one hydrogen ion, so they are a conjugate pair. In this pair, HF is the conjugate acid and F^- is the conjugate base. NH_3 and NH_4^+ also make up a conjugate pair, with NH_4^+ as the conjugate acid and NH_3 as the conjugate base.

The reaction of an acid with water always produces the conjugate base, so we need to be able to write the chemical formulas of conjugate bases. To do so, we remove one hydrogen atom from the chemical formula of the original acid. We must also subtract one from the charge, because the hydrogen atom we remove has a charge of +1. For example, when we write the formula of the conjugate base of HSO_4^-, we get SO_4^{2-}. The ionization reaction of HSO_4^- is

$$\underset{\text{acid}}{HSO_4^-} + H_2O \rightleftharpoons \underset{\text{conjugate base}}{SO_4^{2-}} + H_3O^+$$

The reaction of a base with water always produces the conjugate acid, so we must also be able to write formulas for conjugate acids. To do so, we add one hydrogen atom to the formula of the original base, and we add one to the charge. For example, the conjugate acid of HPO_4^{2-} is $H_2PO_4^-$. If our base is a neutral molecule, such as aniline (C_6H_7N), we normally add the hydrogen atom at the beginning of the formula ($HC_6H_7N^+$). The chemical equations for the reactions of these bases with water are

$$\underset{\text{base}}{HPO_4^{2-}} + H_2O \rightleftharpoons \underset{\text{conjugate acid}}{H_2PO_4^-} + OH^-$$

$$\underset{\text{base}}{C_6H_7N} + H_2O \rightleftharpoons \underset{\text{conjugate acid}}{HC_6H_7N^+} + OH^-$$

Sample Problem **7.12**

Writing the formulas of conjugates

Write chemical formulas for each of the following:

a) the conjugate acid of the bicarbonate ion (HCO_3^-)

b) the conjugate base of the dihydrogen phosphate ion ($H_2PO_4^-$)

continued

SOLUTION

a) To write the formula of a conjugate acid, we add one hydrogen atom and add one to the charge, giving us H_2CO_3.

b) To write the formula of a conjugate base, we remove one hydrogen atom and subtract one from the charge, giving us HPO_4^{2-}. Note that subtracting 1 from the original charge (−1) gives us −2.

TRY IT YOURSELF: *Write the chemical formulas of each of the following:*

a) the conjugate base of sulfuric acid (H_2SO_4)

b) the conjugate acid of serine ($C_3H_7NO_2$), an amino acid

For additional practice, try Core Problems 7.39 and 7.40.

Sample Problem **7.13**

Writing the equation for the reaction of a base with water

Citrate ion ($C_6H_5O_7^{3-}$) is a weak base that is used to adjust the pH of fruit juices. Write the chemical equation for the reaction of citrate ion with water.

SOLUTION

When a base reacts with water, a hydrogen ion moves from the water molecule to the base. The products are OH^- and the conjugate acid of our original base. To write the formula of the conjugate acid, we add a hydrogen atom to the formula of citrate, and we add one to the charge, giving us $HC_6H_5O_7^{2-}$. The chemical equation is

$$C_6H_5O_7^{3-} + H_2O \rightleftharpoons HC_6H_5O_7^{2-} + OH^-$$

TRY IT YOURSELF: *Lactate ion ($C_3H_5O_3^-$) is a weak base that is used in many intravenous solutions. Write the chemical equation for the reaction of lactate ion with water.*

For additional practice, try Core Problems 7.41 and 7.42.

The pH of a Basic Solution Depends on the Strength of the Base

As was the case with weak acids, weak bases vary in their ability to remove protons from other molecules. The ability of a base to remove H^+ from water is called the **strength of the base**. A stronger base reacts more with water and forms more hydroxide ions than a weaker base. As a result, *a solution of a stronger base has a higher pH than a solution of a weaker base.* Remember that a high pH tells us that the solution is very basic and contains a high concentration of OH^- ions. Table 7.7 shows the pH of 0.1 M solutions of several bases.

Health Note: Sodium hypochlorite (NaClO) is the active ingredient in chlorine bleach and is a potent disinfectant. Many hospitals use solutions of sodium hypochlorite to disinfect hard surfaces in areas where patients are treated. It is also used in root canal treatments to kill bacteria and dissolve dead tissue before the canal is filled.

TABLE 7.7 **The Relationship Between Base Strength and pH**

	Solution	Base	pH	Percentage of the Base That Reacts with Water	Type of Base
Strongest base	0.1 M Na_2S	S^{2-} (sulfide ion)	13.00	100%	Strong
	0.1 M Na_2CO_3	CO_3^{2-} (carbonate ion)	11.62	4.1%	Weak
	0.1 M NH_3	NH_3 (ammonia)	11.12	1.3%	Weak
	0.1 M NaClO	ClO^- (hypochlorite ion)	10.23	0.17%	Weak
	0.1 M C_6H_7N	C_6H_7N (aniline)	8.85	0.0071%	Weak
Weakest base	0.1 M Na_2SO_4	SO_4^{2-} (sulfate ion)	7.46	0.00029%	Weak

Sample Problem 7.14

Using pH to compare base strength

The pH of 0.1 M hydrazine (N_2H_4) is 10.74, and the pH of 0.1 M ammonia is 11.12. Based on this information, which compound is the stronger base?

SOLUTION

A higher pH indicates a more basic solution. The ammonia solution has the higher pH, so it contains a larger concentration of OH^- ions. Therefore, ammonia reacts with water to a greater extent than does hydrazine, so ammonia is the stronger base.

TRY IT YOURSELF: *The pH of 0.1 M NaCN is 11.10, and the pH of 0.1 M $NaNO_2$ is 8.20. Based on this information, which is a stronger base, CN^- or NO_2^-?*

For additional practice, try Core Problems 7.45 and 7.46.

Sample Problem 7.15

Comparing the pH of basic solutions

Phosphate ion is a stronger base than carbonate ion. Use this information to determine which of the following has a higher pH:

a) 0.1 M Na_3PO_4 or 0.1 M Na_2CO_3

b) 0.1 M Na_3PO_4 or 0.01 M Na_3PO_4

SOLUTION

a) To do this problem, we must understand how the two solutes behave when they dissolve in water. Na_3PO_4 is an ionic compound, so it dissociates completely into Na^+ ions and PO_4^{3-} ions. Likewise, Na_2CO_3 dissociates completely into Na^+ ions and CO_3^{2-} ions. The two solutions contain the same concentration of solute (0.1 mol/L), and each formula unit of solute makes one anion when it dissociates. Therefore, 0.1 M Na_3PO_4 contains 0.1 mol/L of phosphate ions, and 0.1 M Na_2CO_3 contains 0.1 mol/L of carbonate ions.

$$Na_3PO_4 \rightarrow 3\,Na^+ + PO_4^{3-}$$

Each mole of Na_3PO_4 . . . . . . produces one mole of PO_4^{3-} ions.

$$Na_2CO_3 \rightarrow 2\,Na^+ + CO_3^{2-}$$

Each mole of Na_2CO_3 . . . . . . produces one mole of CO_3^{2-} ions.

These two solutions contain the same *concentration* of base, so we can focus on the *strength* of each base. Phosphate ion is a stronger base than carbonate ion, so phosphate reacts with water to a greater extent, producing a higher concentration of OH^- ions. Therefore, the Na_3PO_4 solution is more basic than the Na_2CO_3 solution and thus has a higher pH.

b) In this problem, both solutions contain the same base, phosphate ion. However, the 0.1 M solution has the higher concentration of phosphate. Therefore, the 0.1 M solution must also contain a higher concentration of OH^- ions, giving it the higher pH.

TRY IT YOURSELF: *Fluoride ion is a weaker base than ammonia. Which has a higher pH, 0.25 M NaF or 0.25 M NH_3?*

For additional practice, try Core Problems 7.47 and 7.48.

There is one final point that should be clarified before we leave bases. Compounds that contain hydroxide ions (such as NaOH and KOH) are often referred to as strong bases, but this is not quite correct. NaOH itself does not form a bond to H^+. However, when NaOH dissolves in water, it dissociates to produce OH^-, which does bond to hydrogen. It is more accurate to say that NaOH *contains* a strong base. Nonetheless, the description of NaOH and KOH as "strong bases" has a long tradition in chemistry, and it should not confuse you as long as you remember that the "active ingredient" in NaOH and KOH is the hydroxide ion.

CORE PROBLEMS

7.37 Methylamine is a base because it can form a bond to H^+. Draw Lewis structures to show how methylamine reacts with water to form a hydroxide ion (see Figure 7.6).

```
    H   H
    |   |
H — C — N̈ — H
    |
    H
```

7.38 Methoxide ion is a base, because it can form a bond to H^+. Draw Lewis structures to show how methoxide ion reacts with water to form a hydroxide ion (see Figure 7.6).

```
    H
    |      −
H — C — Ö:
    |   ¨
    H
```

7.39 Write the chemical formula for each of the following:
a) the conjugate acid of amide ion, NH_2^-
b) the conjugate base of nitric acid, HNO_3
c) the conjugate acid of nicotine, $C_{10}H_{14}N_2$
d) the conjugate base of sulfurous acid, H_2SO_3
e) the conjugate acid of dihydrogen citrate ion, $H_2C_6H_5O_7^-$
f) the conjugate base of dihydrogen citrate ion, $H_2C_6H_5O_7^-$

7.40 Write the chemical formula for each of the following:
a) the conjugate acid of hypochlorite ion, ClO^-
b) the conjugate base of benzoic acid, $HC_7H_5O_2$
c) the conjugate acid of tryptophan, $C_{11}H_{12}N_2O_2$
d) the conjugate base of citric acid, $H_3C_6H_5O_7$
e) the conjugate acid of bisulfite ion, HSO_3^-
f) the conjugate base of bisulfite ion, HSO_3^-

7.41 Write chemical equations that show how the following bases react with water to produce hydroxide ions:
a) methoxide ion (OCH_3^-), a strong base
b) hypochlorite ion (ClO^-), a weak base
c) imidazole ($C_3H_4N_2$), a weak base
d) sulfite ion (SO_3^{2-}), a weak base

7.42 Write chemical equations that show how the following bases react with water to produce hydroxide ions:
a) acetylide ion (HC_2^-), a strong base
b) nitrite ion (NO_2^-), a weak base
c) arginine ($C_6H_{14}N_4O_2$), a weak base
d) citrate ion ($C_6H_5O_7^{3-}$), a weak base

7.43 Explain why you get a basic solution when you dissolve NaF in water.

7.44 Explain why you get a basic solution when you dissolve Na_3PO_4 in water.

7.45 The pH of 0.01 M NaF is 7.57, and the pH of 0.01 M NaCN is 10.60. Based on this information, which is the stronger base, F^- or CN^-? Explain your answer.

7.46 The pH of 0.01 M Na_2CO_3 is 11.10, and the pH of 0.01 M Na_2SO_3 is 9.50. Based on this information, which is the stronger base, CO_3^{2-} or SO_3^{2-}? Explain your answer.

7.47 Piperidine ($C_5H_{11}N$) is a stronger base than piperazine ($C_4H_{10}N_2$). Use this information to answer the following questions:
a) Which solution has a higher pH, 0.01 M piperidine or 0.01 M piperazine?
b) Which solution contains a higher concentration of OH^- ions?
c) Which solution contains a higher concentration of H_3O^+ ions?

7.48 Quinine ($C_{20}H_{24}N_2O_2$) is a stronger base than quinoline (C_9H_7N). Use this information to answer the following questions:
a) Which solution has a higher pH, 10^{-4} M quinine or 10^{-4} M quinoline?
b) Which solution contains a higher concentration of OH^- ions?
c) Which solution contains a higher concentration of H_3O^+ ions?

7.5 Acid–Base Reactions

OBJECTIVES: *Write net ionic equations for acid–base reactions, recognize the role of conjugate pairs in an acid–base reaction, and use the strength of the acid and the base to describe the properties of the product mixture.*

In the last two sections, we looked at what happens when an acid or a base dissolves in water. It is time to examine the reactions that occur when acids are mixed with bases. Remember that an acid can give up a proton (H^+) and a base can bond to a proton. In an **acid–base reaction,** *a proton moves from the acid to the base.* All acid–base reactions are proton transfers.

Our starting point is the reaction of HCN with NH_3. HCN is an acid because it can lose H^+. NH_3 cannot lose H^+, but it can bond to H^+ (as we saw in Section 7.4), so NH_3 is a base. When these two compounds are mixed, a proton moves from HCN to NH_3, forming NH_4^+ and CN^- ions.

$$HCN + NH_3 \rightarrow CN^- + NH_4^+$$

In this reaction, the nucleus of the hydrogen atom (a single proton) moves from HCN to NH_3. The two electrons that bonded the hydrogen to the carbon remain on the carbon atom, while the two nonbonding electrons on the nitrogen atom become a bonding pair. We can represent the changes in the reaction using Lewis structures.

$$H{-}C{\equiv}N\!: \; + \; H{-}\overset{\displaystyle H}{\underset{\displaystyle H}{N}}\!: \; \longrightarrow \; {}^{-}\!:C{\equiv}N\!: \; + \; H{-}\overset{\displaystyle H}{\underset{\displaystyle H}{N^+}}{-}H$$

H^+ moves from HCN to NH_3.

The reaction of HCN with NH_3 is reversible and illustrates an important principle of acid–base reactions. Let us turn the chemical equation around.

$$NH_4^+ + CN^- \rightarrow NH_3 + HCN$$

Here are the Lewis structures of the substances in this reaction:

$$H{-}\overset{\displaystyle H}{\underset{\displaystyle H}{N^+}}{-}H \; + \; {}^{-}\!:C{\equiv}N\!: \; \longrightarrow \; H{-}\overset{\displaystyle H}{\underset{\displaystyle H}{N}}\!: \; + \; H{-}C{\equiv}N\!:$$

H^+ moves from NH_4^+ to CN^-.

In this reaction, a proton moves from NH_4^+ to CN^-. Because NH_4^+ loses H^+, it is an acid; because CN^- bonds to H^+, it is a base. Both the forward and the reverse reactions are acid–base reactions. *Any acid–base reaction is still an acid–base reaction when it is reversed.*

Acid–Base Reactions Involve Two Conjugate Pairs

Let us write the reaction of NH_3 with HCN as an equilibrium, listing the function of each substance beneath its formula.

	HCN	+	NH_3	$\rightleftharpoons$	CN^-	+	NH_4^+	
Forward direction	acid	+	base	$\longrightarrow$				
				$\longleftarrow$	base	+	acid	Reverse direction

In the forward direction, the reaction converts the acid HCN into the base CN^-. These two substances form a conjugate pair, with HCN as the conjugate acid and CN^- as the conjugate base. NH_3 and NH_4^+ form another conjugate pair, but in this case the forward reaction converts the conjugate base into the conjugate acid.

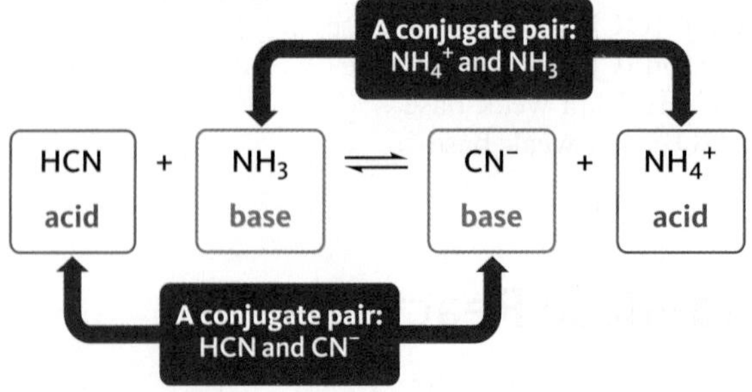

Let us now look at the acid–base reaction that occurs when solutions of $NaNO_2$ and HF are mixed. HF is an acid and can lose H^+. $NaNO_2$ is not a base, but it ionizes completely in water to form Na^+ and NO_2^-. The NO_2^- ion (like most negative ions) can bond to H^+, so NO_2^- is a base. Here is the balanced equation for this reaction, which is reversible:

$$HF(aq) + NO_2^-(aq) \rightleftharpoons HNO_2(aq) + F^-(aq)$$

In the forward direction, HF loses H^+ (it is the acid), and NO_2^- gains H^+ (it is the base). In the backward direction, HNO_2 loses H^+, and F^- gains H^+. Again, this reaction involves two conjugate pairs.

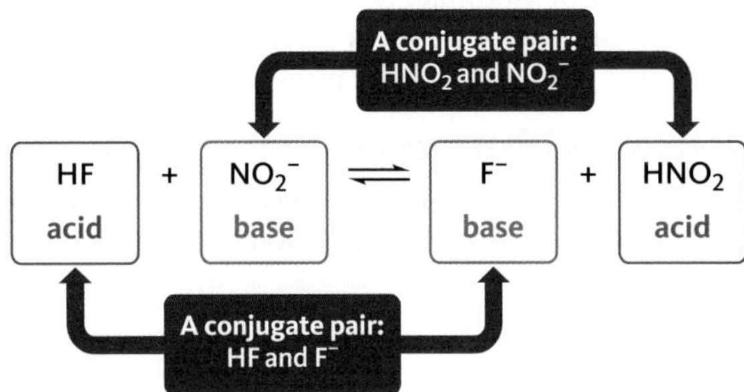

All equations for acid–base reactions contain two conjugate pairs. One member of each pair is a reactant, and the other member is a product.

Health Note: Sodium nitrite ($NaNO_2$) is added to processed meats to prevent the growth of bacteria, particularly the organism that causes botulism. However, when meat that contains sodium nitrite is cooked, the nitrite ion reacts with proteins to form carcinogenic compounds called nitrosamines. Meat packagers in the United States are required to add an antioxidant such as sodium erythorbate or vitamin C to decrease the formation of nitrosamines.

Sample Problem **7.16**

Writing the equation for an acid–base reaction

When solutions of acetic acid ($HC_2H_3O_2$) and sodium carbonate (Na_2CO_3) are mixed, an acid–base reaction occurs between the acetic acid and the carbonate ion. Write the chemical equation for this acid–base reaction, and identify the two conjugate pairs in the equation.

SOLUTION

We can begin by recognizing that Na_2CO_3 is an ionic compound. All ionic compounds dissociate when they dissolve in water, so the sodium carbonate solution really contains Na^+ ions and CO_3^{2-} ions.

Identify the acid and the base: We know that acetic acid is acidic, because the name contains the word *acid* (don't ignore this kind of clue). In addition, neither the Na^+ nor the CO_3^{2-} in the sodium carbonate solution contains hydrogen, so these two substances cannot be acids. Therefore, the acid in this reaction is $HC_2H_3O_2$. The problem tells us that the acid–base reaction involves acetic acid and carbonate ion, so the base must be CO_3^{2-}. The sodium ions are spectator ions and do not participate in the chemical reaction.

Write our chemical equation: The acid must lose H^+, turning into its conjugate base. To write the formula of the conjugate base, we remove the hydrogen atom and subtract one from the charge, giving us $C_2H_3O_2^-$. The base must gain H^+, turning into its conjugate acid. To write the formula of the conjugate acid, we add a hydrogen atom and add one to the charge, giving us HCO_3^-. Our chemical equation is

$$HC_2H_3O_2(aq) + CO_3^{2-}(aq) \rightarrow HCO_3^-(aq) + C_2H_3O_2^-(aq)$$

$HC_2H_3O_2$ and $C_2H_3O_2^-$ make up one conjugate pair, and HCO_3^- and CO_3^{2-} form the other conjugate pair.

TRY IT YOURSELF: *When solutions of ammonium chloride (NH_4Cl) and potassium fluoride (KF) are mixed, an acid–base reaction occurs between ammonium ion and fluoride ion. Write the chemical equation for this acid–base reaction, and identify the two conjugate pairs in the equation.*

For additional practice, try Core Problems 7.51 through 7.54.

Acid–base reactions are often called **neutralization reactions**, but this term is potentially misleading. An acid–base reaction only produces a neutral solution if the acid and base are equally strong. This happens most commonly when a strong acid reacts with hydroxide ions. For example, when HNO_3 (a strong acid) reacts with NaOH, the product mixture has a pH of 7.0. Reactions of weak acids and bases produce a neutral solution if the acid and the base have equal strengths. Otherwise, the pH of the product solution depends on the relative strengths of the reactants. If the acid is stronger than the base, the final solution will be acidic, and if the base is stronger than the acid, the final solution will be basic. For example, if we mix equal amounts of HCN and NH_3 solutions, the product mixture will be basic, because the base NH_3 is substantially stronger than the acid HCN. The actual pH of the product mixture is around 9.2.

Polyprotic Acids React with Bases in Several Steps

When a polyprotic acid reacts with a base, the base removes one hydrogen atom at a time. For example, if we add hydroxide ions to a solution of phosphoric acid, the initial reaction is

$$H_3PO_4 + OH^- \rightarrow H_2PO_4^- + H_2O$$

If we continue to add hydroxide ions, they will remove the second hydrogen from phosphoric acid.

$$H_2PO_4^- + OH^- \rightarrow HPO_4^{2-} + H_2O$$

If we add still more hydroxide ions, they will remove the third hydrogen from phosphoric acid.

$$HPO_4^{2-} + OH^- \rightarrow PO_4^{3-} + H_2O$$

The actual products we observe will depend on the amounts of phosphoric acid and hydroxide we use.

Sample Problem 7.17

Writing the equations for the reaction of a polyprotic acid

If we add a solution of NaOH to a solution of succinic acid ($H_2C_4H_4O_4$), two chemical reactions will occur. Write the chemical equations for these reactions.

SOLUTION

We must begin by recalling that the NaOH solution actually contains OH^- ions and Na^+ ions. Hydroxide ion is a strong base, so it will react with succinic acid. Sodium ion has no acid–base properties, so it is a spectator ion.

The formula of succinic acid shows us that this compound contains two acidic hydrogen atoms. When succinic acid reacts with OH^-, it will do so in two steps. In the first step, one hydrogen ion moves from succinic acid to hydroxide ion. The succinic acid is converted into its conjugate base, $HC_4H_4O_4^-$.

$$H_2C_4H_4O_4 + OH^- \rightarrow HC_4H_4O_4^- + H_2O$$

$HC_4H_4O_4^-$ still contains an acidic hydrogen atom, so it can react with hydroxide ion. In this second reaction, $HC_4H_4O_4^-$ is converted into its conjugate base, $C_4H_4O_4^{2-}$.

$$HC_4H_4O_4^- + OH^- \rightarrow C_4H_4O_4^{2-} + H_2O$$

TRY IT YOURSELF: *If you add a solution of NaOH to a solution of sulfurous acid (H_2SO_3), two chemical reactions will occur. Write the chemical equations for these reactions.*

For additional practice, try Core Problems 7.57 and 7.58.

We Can Represent Acid–Base Reactions with a Molecular Equation

We have been representing acid–base reactions with net ionic equations, which show the actual chemical process that occurs when the acid and the base are mixed. Acid–base reactions are sometimes written in a form that ignores the ionization of strong electrolytes. For example, when solutions of $HC_2H_3O_2$ and NaOH are mixed, the actual reaction is

$$HC_2H_3O_2(aq) + OH^-(aq) \rightarrow C_2H_3O_2^-(aq) + H_2O(l)$$

but the reaction is often represented by the equation

$$HC_2H_3O_2(aq) + NaOH(aq) \rightarrow NaC_2H_3O_2(aq) + H_2O(l)$$

This type of equation is called a **molecular equation.** Molecular equations include spectator ions such as Na^+ (which are not actually involved in the breaking and forming of bonds), and they do not make a distinction between weak electrolytes such as $HC_2H_3O_2$ and strong electrolytes such as NaOH or $NaC_2H_3O_2$.

The reaction between solutions of HCl and NaOH can also be represented by a molecular equation. Because HCl is a strong acid (ionized into H_3O^+ and Cl^-), the actual reaction that occurs is

$$H_3O^+(aq) + OH^-(aq) \rightarrow 2\,H_2O(l)$$

The molecular equation for this reaction is

$$HCl(aq) + NaOH(aq) \rightarrow NaCl(aq) + H_2O(l)$$

Although the sodium and chloride ions do not actually combine to form NaCl molecules, the product mixture is identical to the solution we would get by dissolving solid NaCl in water. If we evaporate the water, we will be left with solid NaCl. Almost any ionic compound can be made by an acid–base reaction of this type. Ionic compounds that do not contain H^+ or OH^- are often called **salts.** The word *salt* here is a general term that includes the familiar table salt (NaCl) and compounds such as KNO_3, $MgSO_4$, and $CaBr_2$.

CORE PROBLEMS

7.49 Draw Lewis structures to show how H^+ is transferred when HNO_2 and NH_3 react with each other. The Lewis structure of HNO_2 is

H—Ö—N̈=Ö

7.50 Draw Lewis structures to show how H^+ is transferred when OH^- reacts with HCO_3^-. The Lewis structure of HCO_3^- is

:Ö:⁻ (bonded to C)
H—Ö—C=Ö

7.51 Write chemical equations for the acid–base reactions that occur when solutions of the following substances are mixed:

a) HNO_2 (nitrous acid) and C_2H_7NO (ethanolamine, a base)
b) H_3O^+ and F^-
c) OH^- and $H_2PO_4^-$
d) C_5H_5N (pyridine, a base) and $HC_2H_3O_2$ (acetic acid)

7.52 Write chemical equations for the acid–base reactions that occur when solutions of the following substances are mixed:

a) HClO (hypochlorous acid) and OH^-
b) H_3O^+ and NH_3O (hydroxylamine, a base)
c) $C_6H_{14}N_2O_2$ (lysine, a base) and $HC_3H_5O_3$ (lactic acid)
d) HF and CHO_2^-

7.53 Write chemical equations for the acid–base reactions that occur when

a) solutions of $HC_2H_3O_2$ (acetic acid) and KOH are mixed.
b) solutions of HCN (hydrocyanic acid) and Na_2CO_3 are mixed.

7.54 Write chemical equations for the acid–base reactions that occur when

a) solutions of $HC_3H_5O_3$ (lactic acid) and NaOH are mixed.
b) solutions of $HC_2H_4NO_2$ (glycine, a weak acid) and KF are mixed.

7.55 Identify the conjugate pairs in the following acid–base reaction:

$$H_2CO_3(aq) + C_5H_5N(aq) \rightarrow HCO_3^-(aq) + HC_5H_5N^+(aq)$$

7.56 Identify the conjugate pairs in the following acid–base reaction:

$$HSO_3^-(aq) + HSO_4^-(aq) \rightarrow H_2SO_3(aq) + SO_4^{2-}(aq)$$

7.57 If you add a solution of NaOH to a solution of H_2CO_3, two reactions occur, one after the other. Write the chemical equations for these two reactions. (Hint: NaOH dissociates into Na^+ and OH^-, and the hydroxide ion is the actual base.)

7.58 If you add a solution of KOH to a solution of tartaric acid ($H_2C_4H_4O_6$), two reactions occur, one after the other. Write the chemical equations for these two reactions. (See the hint in Problem 7.57.)

OBJECTIVES: *Define and identify amphiprotic substances, and determine whether a solution of an amphiprotic substance is acidic or basic.*

7.6 Amphiprotic Molecules and Ions

Let us return once more to the self-ionization of water. When water ionizes, one water molecule functions as an acid and the other functions as a base.

H moves from one H_2O molecule to the other.

$$H_2O + H_2O \longrightarrow H_3O^+ + OH^-$$

base (gains H^+) acid (loses H^+)

In this reaction, one water molecule gains a hydrogen ion, while the other loses a hydrogen ion. The clear implication of this reaction is that water is both an acid and a base—but how is this possible? For that matter, how can water be either an acid or a base? After all, water is the prototypical neutral substance: pure water has a pH of exactly 7.

The answer lies in our use of the terms *acid* and *base*. Strictly, these terms tell us how a substance behaves *in a particular chemical reaction.* When we mix water with a substance that can lose H^+ easily (an acid), water gains H^+, functioning as a base. For example, water acts as a base when it is mixed with acetic acid.

$$HC_2H_3O_2(aq) + H_2O(l) \rightleftharpoons H_3O^+(aq) + C_2H_3O_2^-(aq)$$

acid (loses H^+) base (gains H^+)

When water is mixed with a substance that can gain H^+ easily (a base), water behaves as an acid. For example, water acts as an acid when it is mixed with ammonia.

$$NH_3(aq) + H_2O(l) \rightleftharpoons NH_4^+(aq) + OH^-(aq)$$

base (gains H^+) acid (loses H^+)

A single water molecule never loses and gains H^+ simultaneously, so a water molecule cannot be an acid *and* a base at the same time. However, a water molecule can be an acid *or* a base, depending on what else we mix with the water. Substances that can either gain or lose H^+ are called **amphiprotic**. Water is an amphiprotic molecule, since it can gain H^+ (to form H_3O^+) or lose H^+ (to form OH^-).

Most Negative Ions That Can Lose H^+ Are Amphiprotic

The most common amphiprotic substances are negative ions that contain an ionizable H^+, such as HCO_3^-, $H_2PO_4^-$, and HPO_4^{2-}. These ions are formed by removing some of the hydrogen ions from a polyprotic acid such as H_2CO_3 or H_3PO_4. For example, the bicarbonate ion (HCO_3^-) is an important amphiprotic substance. Bicarbonate can bond to H^+, so it can function as a base. Bicarbonate can also lose H^+, so it can function as an acid. Here are reactions that illustrate each type of behavior.

The reaction of bicarbonate ion with HF:

$$HF(aq) + HCO_3^-(aq) \longrightarrow H_2CO_3(aq) + F^-(aq)$$

acid loses H^+ | base gains H^+

The reaction of bicarbonate ion with NH_3:

$$HCO_3^-(aq) + NH_3(aq) \longrightarrow NH_4^+(aq) + CO_3^{2-}(aq)$$

acid loses H^+ | base gains H^+

© Peter Arnold, Inc. / Alamy

Baking soda can react with both acids and bases because it contains bicarbonate, an amphiprotic ion.

As was the case with water, HCO_3^- can be either the acidic or the basic member of a conjugate pair. In the first reaction, H_2CO_3 and HCO_3^- are conjugates, with HCO_3^-

being the conjugate base. In the second reaction, HCO_3^- and CO_3^{2-} are conjugates, with HCO_3^- being the conjugate acid.

Sample Problem 7.18

Writing chemical equations for reactions involving amphiprotic ions

$H_2PO_4^-$ is an amphiprotic ion. Write the chemical equations for the reactions that occur when $H_2PO_4^-$ reacts with each of the following compounds:

a) HF

b) NH_3

SOLUTION

a) $H_2PO_4^-$ is amphiprotic, so it can be either an acid or a base. The behavior of $H_2PO_4^-$ is determined by the other chemical in the mixture. HF is an acid, so when $H_2PO_4^-$ reacts with HF, $H_2PO_4^-$ must behave as a base: the HF molecule loses H^+, and the $H_2PO_4^-$ ion gains H^+. The chemical equation is

$$HF(aq) + H_2PO_4^-(aq) \rightarrow H_3PO_4(aq) + F^-(aq)$$

b) To write the chemical equation, we must determine whether NH_3 is an acid or a base. Although NH_3 contains hydrogen atoms, it never behaves as an acid; this is why the chemical formula does not start with hydrogen. However, as we have seen, NH_3 can behave as a base. Therefore, when $H_2PO_4^-$ reacts with NH_3, $H_2PO_4^-$ must behave as an acid. The $H_2PO_4^-$ ion loses H^+, and the NH_3 molecule gains H^+. The chemical equation is

$$H_2PO_4^-(aq) + NH_3(aq) \rightarrow HPO_4^{2-}(aq) + NH_4^+(aq)$$

TRY IT YOURSELF: *HPO_4^{2-} is an amphiprotic ion. Write the chemical equations for the reactions that occur when HPO_4^{2-} reacts with each of the following compounds:*

a) HF b) NH_3

For additional practice, try Core Problems 7.59 and 7.60.

If HCO_3^- can be either an acid or a base, what happens when HCO_3^- dissolves in water? Aqueous solutions of $NaHCO_3$ are slightly basic, because HCO_3^- is a stronger base than it is an acid. This means that HCO_3^- has a stronger tendency to produce OH^- ions than it does to produce H_3O^+ ions.

Health Note: The digestive fluids that are secreted by your pancreas contain HCO_3^- ions, so they are slightly basic, with a pH of 8. The bicarbonate ions neutralize the HCl that is produced by your stomach, so it does not harm the intestinal lining.

Some Molecular Compounds Are Amphiprotic

A molecular compound is amphiprotic if it contains an acidic hydrogen atom and an atom that can bond to H^+. The most common and important amphiprotic compounds are the amino acids, which are the building blocks of proteins. We will examine the chemistry of amino acids and proteins in Chapter 13. Figure 7.7 shows the structures of two amphiprotic compounds that play an important role in human health.

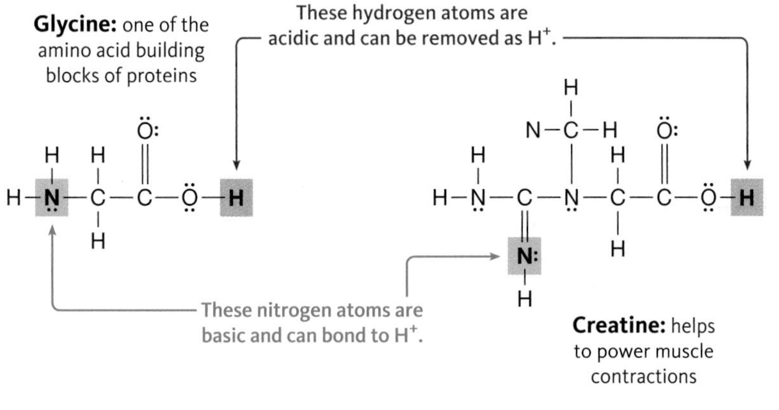

FIGURE 7.7 The structures of two amphiprotic compounds.

Health Note: Creatine is required by all muscle cells to supply immediate energy for brief, intense muscular contractions. It is a popular dietary supplement for bodybuilders to increase body strength, but creatine is not a necessary nutrient, as the body can make it from protein. The ability of creatine to increase muscle mass is reasonably well established, but most of the other claims for creatine have not been verified experimentally.

CORE PROBLEMS

7.59 Sodium bisulfite is an ionic compound that is used as a mild bleaching agent and a food preservative. It contains the bisulfite ion, an amphiprotic ion with the chemical formula HSO_3^-.

a) Write the chemical equation for the reaction of HSO_3^- with OH^-. Is the bisulfite ion functioning as an acid in this reaction, or is it functioning as a base?

b) Write the chemical equation for the reaction of HSO_3^- with H_3O^+. Is the bisulfite ion functioning as an acid in this reaction, or is it functioning as a base?

7.60 Potassium bitartrate is one of the ingredients in baking powder. It contains the bitartrate ion, an amphiprotic ion with the chemical formula $HC_4H_4O_6^-$.

a) Write the chemical equation for the reaction of bitartrate ion with OH^-. Is the bitartrate ion functioning as an acid in this reaction, or is it functioning as a base?

b) Write the chemical equation for the reaction of bitartrate ion with H_3O^+. Is the bitartrate ion functioning as an acid in this reaction, or is it functioning as a base?

7.61 Alanine ($HC_3H_6NO_2$) is an amino acid, one of the building blocks of proteins. Like all amino acids, it is an amphiprotic molecule.

a) Write the chemical equation for the reaction of alanine with OH^-.

b) Write the chemical equation for the reaction of alanine with H_3O^+.

7.62 Asparagine ($HC_4H_7N_2O_3$) is an amino acid, one of the building blocks of proteins. Like all amino acids, it is an amphiprotic molecule.

a) Write the chemical equation for the reaction of asparagine with OH^-.

b) Write the chemical equation for the reaction of asparagine with H_3O^+.

7.63 Taurine is an amphiprotic compound that your body uses to make bile salts.

```
        H   H   H   Ö:
        |   |   |   ||
    H—N̤—C—C—S—Ö—H
            |   |   ||
            H   H   Ö:
```

Taurine

a) Which hydrogen atom in this compound is acidic (i.e., which one can be removed by a base)?

b) When taurine functions as a base, where does H^+ bond?

7.64 Phosphoethanolamine is an amphiprotic compound that your body uses to make cell membranes.

```
          :Ö        H   H   H
           ||       |   |   |
    H—Ö—P—Ö—C—C—N—H
           |        |   |
        H—Ö:        H   H
```

Phosphoethanolamine

a) Which two hydrogen atoms in this compound are acidic (i.e., which can be removed by a base)?

b) When phosphoethanolamine functions as a base, where does H^+ bond?

OBJECTIVES: *Recognize buffer solutions, describe how buffers resist pH changes, and estimate the pH of a buffer from the pK_a of the acid and the concentrations of the buffer components.*

7.7 Buffers

Chemical reactions that occur in your body generally require a specific pH. The catalysts that allow these reactions to occur at a reasonable rate are very sensitive to the pH of their surroundings, and they are damaged or destroyed if the pH goes outside a narrow range. Paradoxically, many of these reactions produce acidic or basic products that can change the pH enough to destroy the molecules that catalyze them. For example, when you engage in strenuous exercise, your body breaks glucose (blood sugar) down into lactic acid to produce energy.

$$\underset{\text{glucose}}{C_6H_{12}O_6(aq)} \rightarrow \underset{\text{lactic acid}}{2\ HC_3H_5O_3(aq)} + \text{energy}$$

Even small amounts of lactic acid can have a dramatic impact on pH. If your body breaks down just 1 g of glucose, it will produce enough lactic acid to lower the pH of 3 L of water (the approximate volume of blood plasma in an adult) from 7.0 to 3.2. Such a large pH change would be lethal. The pH of your blood plasma is normally maintained in the range 7.35 to 7.45, and a plasma pH below 6.8 causes death within seconds. However, your plasma pH stays virtually constant during strenuous exercise. In this section, we will examine the chemical means by which the pH of a solution can be controlled, and we will look at some specific substances that control the pH in your body.

The pH of most aqueous solutions in your body is kept at a constant level by a **buffer**. A buffer is any solution that resists pH changes when an acid or a base is added to it. To be a buffer, a solution must contain a substance that can neutralize acids and a substance that can neutralize bases. In practice, *most buffers are solutions that contain a conjugate*

TABLE 7.8 Some Buffers and Their pH Values

Buffer Components	Source of the Conjugate Acid	Source of the Conjugate Base	Buffer pH (When the Molarities Are Equal)
$HC_2H_3O_2$ and $C_2H_3O_2^-$	$HC_2H_3O_2$ (acetic acid)	$NaC_2H_3O_2$ (sodium acetate)	4.74
H_3PO_4 and $H_2PO_4^-$	H_3PO_4 (phosphoric acid)	NaH_2PO_4 (sodium dihydrogen phosphate)	2.12
$H_2PO_4^-$ and HPO_4^{2-}	NaH_2PO_4 (sodium dihydrogen phosphate)	Na_2HPO_4 (sodium mono-hydrogen phosphate)	7.21
HPO_4^{2-} and PO_4^{3-}	Na_2HPO_4 (sodium mono-hydrogen phosphate)	Na_3PO_4 (sodium phosphate)	12.32
NH_4^+ and NH_3	NH_4Cl (ammonium chloride)	NH_3 (ammonia)	9.25

acid–base pair, and in this book we will confine ourselves to this type of buffer. Table 7.8 gives some examples of buffers, along with the pH we observe if the buffer contains equal concentrations of the acid and base. Note that we can make three different buffers based on phosphoric acid, each of which has its own pH.

Sample Problem **7.19**

Determining the components of a buffer solution

Succinic acid is a weak acid with the chemical formula $H_2C_4H_4O_4$. If a buffer solution contains succinic acid, what other substance must be present in the solution? What chemical could we use as a source of this substance?

SOLUTION

Buffers contain a conjugate acid–base pair. Since succinic acid is an acid, the other component of the buffer must be the conjugate base, which has the chemical formula $\mathbf{HC_4H_4O_4^-}$. To identify a compound that supplies this ion, we combine the ion with Na^+ to get $\mathbf{NaHC_4H_4O_4}$. The potassium compound $KHC_4H_4O_4$ is also a reasonable answer.

TRY IT YOURSELF: *Formate ion is a weak base with the chemical formula CHO_2^-. If a buffer solution contains formate ion, what other substance must be present in the solution?*

For additional practice, try Core Problems 7.65 through 7.68.

Buffers Resist pH Changes When Acids and Bases are Added to Them

What does a buffer do? Let us use the buffer that contains acetic acid ($HC_2H_3O_2$) and sodium acetate ($NaC_2H_3O_2$) as an example. This solution has a pH around 4.7. If we add a small amount of HCl (a strong acid) to our buffer, the pH goes down a bit, but the change is very small. If we instead add a small amount of NaOH (a strong base) to our buffer, the pH goes up a bit, but again the change is minimal. This solution is able to maintain a pH very close to 4.7. (See Figure 7.8.) Compare this to the results we see when we add a little 1 M HCl or NaOH to an unbuffered solution that has a pH of 4.7. Adding 1 mL of HCl to 100 mL of this solution brings the pH down to 2.0, and adding 1 mL of NaOH raises the pH to 12.0.

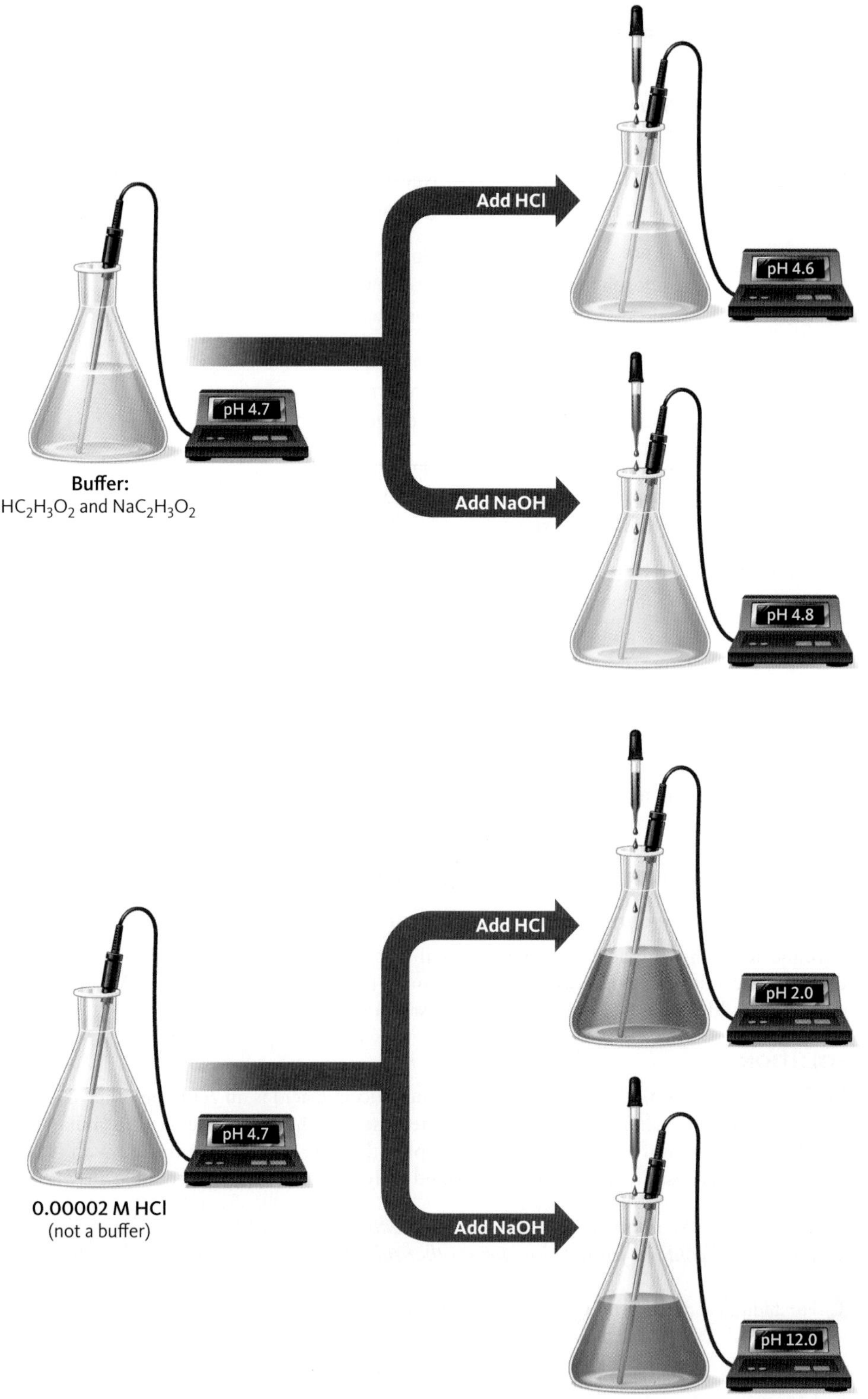

FIGURE 7.8 The behavior of a buffer solution.

The pH of a Buffer Is Close to the pK_a of the Conjugate Acid

The pH of a buffer depends primarily on the strength of the acid we use to make it. To describe the strength of the acid, chemists use a number called the **pK_a**. *The* pK_a *of an acid is the pH of a buffer that contains equal molar concentrations of the acid and its conjugate base.* For example, the pK_a of citric acid ($H_3C_6H_5O_7$) is 3.08, so a buffer that contains equal molarities of $H_3C_6H_5O_7$ and $H_2C_6H_5O_7^-$ has a pH of 3.08. Table 7.9 lists a number of weak acids and their pK_a values.

Health Note: Oxalic acid is a toxic compound found in many plants. It forms bonds to calcium and magnesium ions, preventing the body from using these essential minerals. Most plant foods do not contain enough oxalic acid to pose a health risk. However, rhubarb leaves contain high concentrations of oxalic acid, so you should only eat the stems.

TABLE 7.9 pK_a Values for Selected Weak Acids

Acid	Name	pK_a
$H_2C_2O_4$	Oxalic acid	1.19
H_3PO_4	Phosphoric acid	2.12
$H_3C_6H_5O_7$	Citric acid	3.08
$HCHO_2$	Formic acid	3.76
$HC_3H_5O_3$	Lactic acid	3.86
$H_2C_6H_6O_6$	Ascorbic acid (vitamin C)	4.10
$HC_2H_3O_2$	Acetic acid	4.74
H_2CO_3	Carbonic acid	6.37
$H_2PO_4^-$	Dihydrogen phosphate ion	7.21
H_3BO_3	Boric acid	9.24
NH_4^+	Ammonium ion	9.25
HCO_3^-	Bicarbonate ion	10.25
HC_6H_5O	Phenol (carbolic acid)	10.80
HPO_4^{2-}	Hydrogen phosphate ion	12.32

We can compare the strengths of acids by comparing their pK_a values. A lower pK_a indicates a stronger acid. For instance, the pK_a of phosphoric acid is 2.12, which is lower than the pK_a of citric acid. Therefore, phosphoric acid is stronger than citric acid.

Sample Problem 7.20

Determining the pH of a buffer

What is the pH of a solution that contains equal molar concentrations of ammonia and ammonium chloride? Use the information in Table 7.9.

SOLUTION

The chemical formulas of ammonia and ammonium chloride are NH_3 and NH_4Cl, respectively. Ammonium chloride is an ionic compound and is completely dissociated in solution. Therefore, this solution contains NH_4^+ and Cl^- ions, in addition to the NH_3. Ammonia and ammonium ion differ by one H^+ ion, so they are a conjugate pair. As a result, this solution is a buffer solution.

The molarities of the ammonium ion and ammonia are equal, so the pH of this buffer must equal the pK_a of the acid, NH_4^+. The pH of the solution is 9.25.

TRY IT YOURSELF: *What is the pH of a solution that contains equal molar concentrations of formic acid and sodium formate ($NaCHO_2$)? Use the information in Table 7.9.*

For additional practice, try Core Problems 7.71 (part a) and 7.72 (part a).

We can fine-tune the pH of a buffer by changing the proportions of acid and base in the solution. If we use a higher concentration of the conjugate acid, the pH will be a little lower than the pK_a. If we use a higher concentration of the conjugate base, the pH will be a little higher than the pK_a. For example, a buffer that contains equal concentrations of acetic acid and its conjugate base has a pH of 4.74, equaling the pK_a of acetic acid. If we prepare a buffer that contains twice as much acetic acid as its conjugate, the pH of this buffer will be 4.44. By choosing the correct chemicals and adjusting the proportions of conjugate acid and conjugate base, chemists can prepare a buffer that maintains virtually any pH value.

Buffers Contain Substances That Can Neutralize Both Acids and Bases

How does a buffer work? Buffers maintain a stable pH because they contain both a substance that can neutralize bases and a substance that can neutralize acids. In our acetic acid–acetate buffer, the acetic acid neutralizes any bases that we add. Here is the reaction that occurs when we add a source of OH^- ions, such as NaOH or KOH, to our buffer:

$$\underset{\text{acetic acid}}{HC_2H_3O_2(aq)} + OH^-(aq) \rightarrow \underset{\text{acetate ion}}{C_2H_3O_2^-(aq)} + H_2O(l)$$

The acetate ions in our buffer can neutralize any acids that we add. Here is the reaction that occurs when we add a source of H_3O^+, such as HCl or H_2SO_4, to our buffer:

$$\underset{\text{acetate ion}}{C_2H_3O_2^-(aq)} + H_3O^+(aq) \rightarrow \underset{\text{acetic acid}}{HC_2H_3O_2(aq)} + H_2O(l)$$

In each reaction, we produce water and the other component of our buffer. Adding OH^- converts acetic acid (the conjugate acid in our buffer) into acetate ion (the conjugate base), while adding H_3O^+ converts acetate (the conjugate base in our buffer) into acetic acid (the conjugate acid). In either case, the solutes in the buffer remain the same: acetic acid and acetate ion. Only the relative amounts of the two solutes change. Since we change the proportion of acetic acid to acetate, the pH of the buffer changes, but the change is small. Figure 7.9 shows how our acetic acid–acetate buffer can neutralize strong acids and bases.

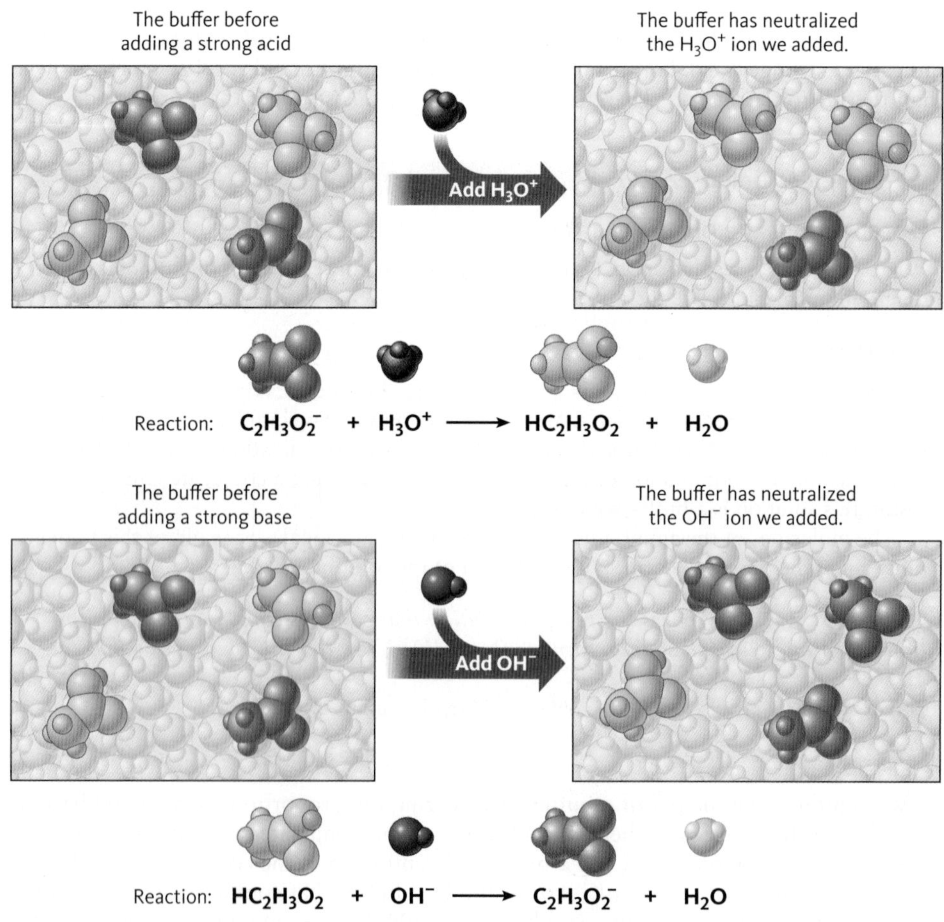

FIGURE 7.9 The neutralization of acids and bases by a buffer.

Sample Problem 7.21

Writing acid–base reactions for a buffer solution

A buffer solution contains HC_6H_5O (phenol, a weak acid) and NaC_6H_5O. Write balanced equations to show how this buffer neutralizes a strong acid (H_3O^+) and a strong base (OH^-).

SOLUTION

The active ingredients in this buffer are the conjugate pair HC_6H_5O and $C_6H_5O^-$. The first of these substances is the conjugate acid, so its role is to neutralize bases. The chemical reaction is

$$\underset{\text{(the conjugate acid)}}{HC_6H_5O(aq)} + \underset{\text{(a strong base)}}{OH^-(aq)} \rightarrow C_6H_5O^-(aq) + H_2O(l)$$

The conjugate base in our buffer is $C_6H_5O^-$. This ion can react with acids, because it can form a bond to H^+. The chemical reaction is

$$\underset{\text{(the conjugate base)}}{C_6H_5O^-(aq)} + \underset{\text{(a strong acid)}}{H_3O^+(aq)} \rightarrow HC_6H_5O(aq) + H_2O(l)$$

Note that only one of the two components in a buffer is a reactant in any neutralization reaction. The other component is formed during the reaction.

TRY IT YOURSELF: *A solution that contains both NH_3 and NH_4^+ is a buffer. Write balanced equations to show how this buffer neutralizes a strong acid (H_3O^+) and a strong base (OH^-).*

For additional practice, try Core Problems 7.71 (parts b and c) and 7.72 (parts b and c).

Summary of Buffer Chemistry

- A buffer is a solution that *resists pH changes* when acids and bases are added to it.
- Any solution that contains a *conjugate acid–base pair* will be a buffer.
- The pH of any buffer is *close to the pK_a of the acid* (a little higher if the buffer contains more base than acid, a little lower if the buffer contains more acid than base).
- The conjugate acid in the buffer neutralizes any bases that are added to the buffer.
- The conjugate base in the buffer neutralizes any acids that are added to the buffer.

CORE PROBLEMS

7.65 The following table lists five buffer solutions. In each case, one of the two ingredients in the buffer is missing. Supply the missing chemical.

	Acidic Component	Basic Component
Buffer 1	$HCHO_2$	
Buffer 2		$C_3H_5O_3^-$
Buffer 3	$HC_2O_4^-$	
Buffer 4		$HC_2O_4^-$
Buffer 5	H_2SO_3	

7.66 The following table lists five buffer solutions. In each case, one of the two ingredients in the buffer is missing. Supply the missing chemical.

	Acidic Component	Basic Component
Buffer 1	HCN	
Buffer 2		$C_3H_6NO_2^-$
Buffer 3	$HC_6H_5O_7^{2-}$	
Buffer 4		$HC_6H_5O_7^{2-}$
Buffer 5	$H_2C_4H_4O_4$	

7.67 You need to make a buffer that contains $C_4H_4O_4^{2-}$ ions. What chemical compound could you use to supply this ion?

7.68 You need to make a buffer that contains $C_6H_5O_7^{3-}$ ions. What chemical compound could you use to supply this ion?

7.69 Which of the following pairs of chemicals produce a buffer solution when dissolved in water? (List all of the correct answers.)

a) HCN and NaCN
b) HCl and NaOH
c) $H_3C_6H_5O_7$ (citric acid) and $NaH_2C_6H_5O_7$
d) $H_2C_2O_4$ (oxalic acid) and $Na_2C_2O_4$

continued

7.70 Which of the following pairs of chemicals produce a buffer solution when dissolved in water? (List all of the correct answers.)
a) H_2SO_4 and KOH
b) HNO_2 and KNO_2
c) $H_2C_4H_2O_4$ (fumaric acid) and $KHC_4H_2O_4$
d) NH_3 and NH_4Cl

7.71 The pK_a of mandelic acid ($HC_8H_7O_3$) is 3.8.
a) What is the pH of a buffer that contains equal concentrations of $HC_8H_7O_3$ and $NaC_8H_7O_3$?
b) If you make a buffer that contains 0.1 M $HC_8H_7O_3$ and 0.2 M $NaC_8H_7O_3$, what is the approximate pH of the solution? (You can give a pH range.)
c) What substance in this buffer neutralizes acids? Write a balanced equation for the reaction between this substance and H_3O^+.
d) What substance in this buffer neutralizes bases? Write a balanced equation for the reaction between this substance and OH^-.

7.72 The pK_a of bicarbonate ion (HCO_3^-) is 10.25.
a) What is the pH of a buffer that contains equal concentrations of $NaHCO_3$ and Na_2CO_3?
b) If you make a buffer that contains 0.2 M $NaHCO_3$ and 0.1 M Na_2CO_3, what will be the approximate pH of the solution? (You can give a pH range.)
c) What substance in this buffer neutralizes acids? Write a balanced equation for the reaction between this substance and H_3O^+.
d) What substance in this buffer neutralizes bases? Write a balanced equation for the reaction between this substance and OH^-.

7.73 You need to prepare a buffer that has a pH of 6.9, using $H_2PO_4^-$ (pK_a = 7.21) and HPO_4^{2-}.
a) Should you use equal concentrations of the two substances in the buffer? If not, which one should be present in higher concentration, and why?
b) Which of the two substances in this buffer neutralizes acids?
c) Write the chemical equation that shows how this buffer would react with OH^- ions.

7.74 You need to prepare a buffer that has a pH of 4.5, using $HC_2O_4^-$ (pK_a = 4.20) and $C_2O_4^{2-}$.
a) Should you use equal concentrations of the two substances in the buffer? If not, which one should be present in higher concentration, and why?
b) Which of the two substances in this buffer neutralizes bases?
c) Write the chemical equation that shows how this buffer would react with H_3O^+ ions.

7.75 A buffer has a pH of 8.3. If a little NaOH is added to this buffer, which of the following is the most likely pH value for the mixture?
a) 4.1 b) 7.0 c) 8.1 d) 8.3
e) 8.5 f) 11.5

7.76 A buffer has a pH of 6.1. If a little HCl is added to this buffer, which of the following is the most likely pH value for the mixture?
a) 2.7 b) 5.9 c) 6.1 d) 6.3
e) 7.0 f) 10.2

OBJECTIVES: *Identify the three important physiological buffers, describe the role of CO_2 in the carbonic acid buffer, and describe the role of the lungs and the kidneys in controlling plasma pH.*

7.8 The Role of Buffers in Human Physiology

The human body normally maintains the pH of blood between 7.35 and 7.45, and it cannot tolerate pH values that are significantly beyond this range. As a result, the pH of blood is a key indicator of health. If your blood pH drops below 7.35 because of excess acid or insufficient base, you have **acidosis**. If your blood pH rises above 7.45, you have **alkalosis**. Either of these can be life threatening, so your body has an elaborate mechanism for maintaining the proper pH. Likewise, the pH of the fluid inside cells must be maintained within a narrow range (normally close to 7), and your body has a separate chemical system for maintaining intracellular pH. Both of these systems rely on buffers.

There are three important buffers in the human body, as illustrated in Figure 7.10: the protein buffer, the phosphate buffer, and the carbonic acid buffer. These buffers work together to maintain a pH near 7 in body fluids. We will examine each of these, with a particular emphasis on the carbonic acid system, which brings together a range of topics that you have seen so far.

1. *The protein buffer system.* Proteins are enormous molecules, constructed from smaller compounds called amino acids. One of these amino acids, called histidine, is a weak base and is readily converted into its conjugate acid. The conjugate acid of histidine has a pK_a of 6.0, but when histidine is incorporated into a protein, its pK_a can be as high as 7.0. Thus, proteins that contain histidine can be effective buffers around a pH of 7. A range of proteins can act as buffers. Protein buffers are particularly important inside cells, maintaining the intracellular fluid at a constant pH.
2. *The phosphate buffer system.* The pK_a of phosphoric acid (H_3PO_4) is 2.1, which is too low to serve as an effective buffer around a pH of 7. However, removing one proton from phosphoric acid produces $H_2PO_4^-$, which has a pK_a of 7.2. Therefore, a buffer that contains $H_2PO_4^-$ and HPO_4^{2-} has a pH close to 7.2, and the pH can

be adjusted as needed by changing the relative concentrations of these two ions. This system works with the protein buffer to maintain the pH of intracellular fluid at an appropriate level.

3. *The carbonic acid buffer system.* Carbonic acid (H_2CO_3) and bicarbonate ion (HCO_3^-) are the primary buffering agents in blood plasma, which must be maintained at a pH of 7.4. However, the pK_a of carbonic acid at body temperature (37°C) is only 6.1, so a buffer that contains equal concentrations of H_2CO_3 and HCO_3^- has a pH of 6.1, significantly below the plasma pH. Raising the buffer pH to 7.4 requires that the concentration of HCO_3^- be 20 times larger than that of H_2CO_3. Since a very high concentration of HCO_3^- would disrupt the osmotic balance between the plasma and the intracellular fluids, the only expedient is to maintain the concentration of H_2CO_3 at a very low level. The normal concentrations of carbonic acid and bicarbonate in plasma are 0.0012 M and 0.024 M, respectively. The low concentration of carbonic acid has several important consequences, which we will examine in a moment.

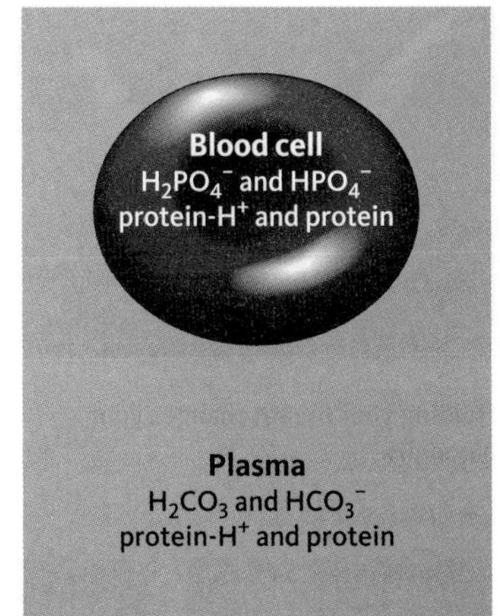

FIGURE 7.10 Buffers in human blood.

Carbon Dioxide Plays a Key Role in the Carbonic Acid Buffer

The ultimate source of the carbonic acid in your blood is the burning of carbohydrates, fats, and proteins by the cells in your body. Recall that one of the products of burning (combustion) is carbon dioxide. As you saw in Chapter 6, carbon dioxide can combine with water to form carbonic acid.

$$CO_2(aq) + H_2O(l) \rightleftharpoons H_2CO_3(aq)$$

This reaction is rather fast under any circumstances, but all organisms that burn their fuels produce a catalyst called *carbonic anhydrase,* which makes this reaction occur almost instantaneously. CO_2 and H_2CO_3 reach equilibrium so quickly that *under physiological conditions, CO_2 behaves as if it were H_2CO_3.* The pK_a of carbonic acid takes this into account, giving us the acid strength of the combined $CO_2 + H_2CO_3$ pool in a solution. Likewise, the concentration of "carbonic acid" in the plasma (0.0012 M) is actually the total concentration of CO_2 plus H_2CO_3. The principal result of this chemistry is that the concentration of carbon dioxide in the blood is directly connected to plasma pH:

When $[CO_2]$ increases, the plasma pH goes down (the blood becomes more acidic).

When $[CO_2]$ decreases, the plasma pH goes up (the blood becomes more basic).

Most cells in your body produce carbon dioxide, which is released into the bloodstream. This CO_2 makes your blood more acidic if it is allowed to build up, so it must be eliminated. Elimination of carbon dioxide is one of the principal functions of the lungs. Your lungs contain vast number of tiny air sacs, called *alveoli.* Your blood circulates through your lungs, passing through a network of tiny vessels called *capillaries,* which surround the alveoli. Carbon dioxide can easily diffuse through the walls of the capillaries and the alveoli. Since the pressure of CO_2 in blood is higher than that in the air in your lungs, CO_2 diffuses from your blood into your lungs. The CO_2 is then expelled into the atmosphere when you exhale. Under normal conditions, your lungs remove CO_2 from your body as fast as it is formed, so the concentration of CO_2 (and hence the pH) in your blood remains constant. Figure 7.11 illustrates carbon dioxide transport from the cells to the lungs.

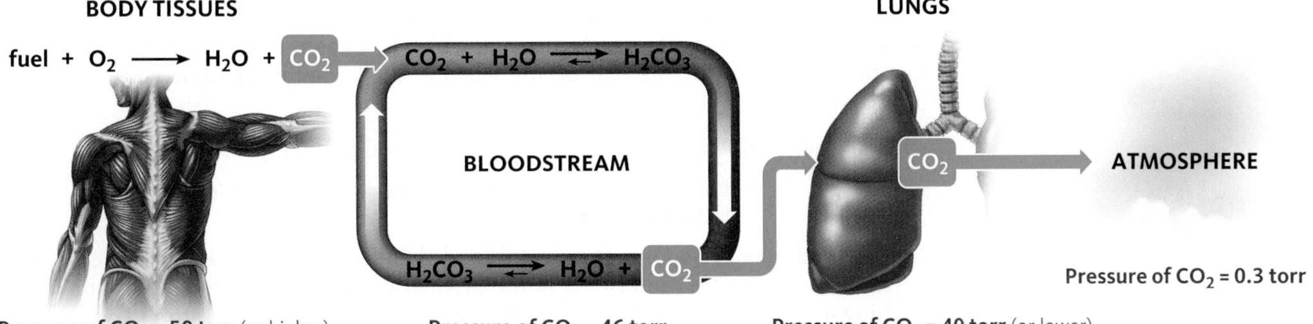

FIGURE 7.11 Carbon dioxide transport in the human body.

iStockphoto.com/Phil Date

Holding your breath changes your blood pH.

Plasma pH Can Be Changed by Changing the Breathing Rate

Your ability to breathe efficiently is intimately connected with your ability to maintain a constant plasma pH. Any sort of respiratory disorder has an impact on your blood's buffering ability. For example, patients with severe emphysema typically have plasma pH values below normal, because carbon dioxide cannot escape from their damaged lungs as quickly as it is produced. You can simulate this effect by holding your breath for a few seconds. When you hold your breath, CO_2 cannot escape from your lungs. Your blood continues to carry CO_2 to your lungs, so the partial pressure of gaseous CO_2 goes up. When this happens, some of the gaseous CO_2 redissolves in your blood, producing the following equilibrium:

$$CO_2(aq) \rightleftharpoons CO_2(g)$$

In effect, holding your breath causes carbon dioxide to "back up" into your bloodstream. The extra CO_2 behaves as if it were carbonic acid, because of the extremely fast interconversion of CO_2 and H_2CO_3.

$$CO_2(aq) + H_2O(l) \rightleftharpoons H_2CO_3(aq)$$

The added carbon dioxide and carbonic acid upsets the 20 : 1 ratio of HCO_3^- to H_2CO_3 in your blood buffer, lowering the pH of your blood. In practice, you can only produce a very small change in your blood pH by holding your breath, because for most people the breathing reflex (the "need to take a breath") becomes overwhelming. You will start breathing again, regardless of how hard you try not to do so. In any case, you would pass out long before your plasma pH drops to dangerous levels, and once you pass out, your breathing rate and plasma pH return to normal.

You can also alter your blood pH by breathing rapidly (hyperventilating) when you are not exercising. When you do so, the partial pressure of CO_2 in your lungs drops, as you expel CO_2 from your lungs faster than it is brought to your lungs by your blood. This in turn allows more CO_2 to pass from your bloodstream to your lungs, lowering the concentrations of both CO_2 and H_2CO_3 in your blood. Your blood becomes more basic, because you do not have a high enough concentration of the acidic component of your plasma buffer. Humans have no instinct to slow their breathing rate when they hyperventilate, but if you continue to breathe rapidly, you will become dizzy and pass out before your blood pH rises to dangerous levels. Again, your breathing and plasma pH return to normal once you lose consciousness. Figure 7.12 shows the relationship between breathing rate and plasma pH.

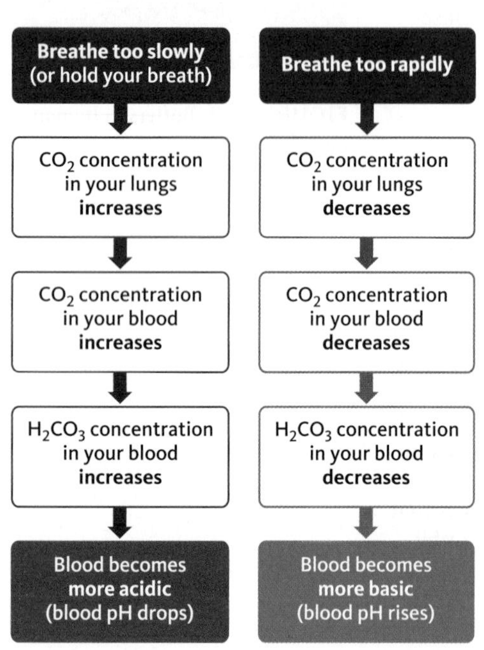

FIGURE 7.12 The effect of breathing rate on plasma pH.

Changes In the Breathing Rate Can Correct a Plasma pH Imbalance

Carbon dioxide is not the only acidic substance that is produced by your body. Whenever you break down nutrients in your food to obtain energy, you make acids such as lactic acid, sulfuric acid, and a variety of fatty acids. In addition, your body produces ammonia (a base) when it obtains energy from proteins. All of these substances make their way into your blood, where they must be neutralized. Your blood buffer carries out these neutralizations, but in the process the 20 : 1 ratio of HCO_3^- to H_2CO_3 and CO_2 is disturbed. The resulting changes in plasma pH are small, but they must be corrected before they become significant. Your body's ability to adjust plasma pH by changing its breathing rate plays an important role in restoring the correct blood pH.

For example, a burst of heavy exercise triggers rapid breathing, because your muscles break down carbohydrates into lactic acid, which is released into your blood. Let us follow the sequence of events that occurs when a small amount of lactic acid is released into your blood:

1. The lactic acid reacts with HCO_3^- in your blood plasma, producing H_2CO_3.

$$\underset{\text{lactic acid}}{HC_3H_5O_3(aq)} + HCO_3^-(aq) \rightarrow C_3H_5O_3^-(aq) + H_2CO_3(aq)$$

   The additional H_2CO_3 makes your blood slightly more acidic, because it changes the ratio of HCO_3^- to H_2CO_3 in the plasma buffer. (Much of the H_2CO_3 breaks down into CO_2 and H_2O, but the CO_2 remains in equilibrium with H_2CO_3.)
2. When your plasma pH drops, your body responds by breathing more rapidly. As a result, you expel CO_2 from your lungs more rapidly, and the concentration of CO_2

in the alveoli drops. This allows more CO_2 to diffuse from your blood into your lungs. Since CO_2 and H_2CO_3 are in equilibrium, removing CO_2 is equivalent to removing H_2CO_3.

$$H_2CO_3(aq) \rightarrow CO_2(aq) + H_2O(l)$$

3. Eventually, all of the excess H_2CO_3 is exhaled (in the form of CO_2), and your blood pH returns to normal.

Sample Problem **7.22**

The effect of breathing rate on plasma pH

People who take large doses of sodium bicarbonate to treat acid indigestion occasionally make their blood too alkaline. How can the breathing rate change to help restore normal plasma pH?

SOLUTION

When blood plasma is too basic, the body needs to increase the concentration of H_2CO_3 (the conjugate acid in the plasma buffer). It can do so by slowing the breathing rate, which decreases the rate at which CO_2 is removed from the blood. As CO_2 is produced by the cells faster than it is eliminated from the lungs, the concentration of CO_2 increases. Since CO_2 is always in equilibrium with H_2CO_3, when the concentration of CO_2 increases, so does the concentration of H_2CO_3.

TRY IT YOURSELF: *Mr. Smith takes an overdose of aspirin. A few minutes later, he starts to breathe more rapidly than normal, as the aspirin overdose affects his body. Based on this observation, and assuming that Mr. Smith's body is trying to maintain the correct plasma pH, did the aspirin overdose make Mr. Smith's blood more acidic, or did his blood become more basic?*

For additional practice, try Core Problems 7.85 and 7.86.

The Kidneys Help Regulate Blood pH

The carbon dioxide–carbonic acid cycle is one of the two principal mechanisms by which your body eliminates excess acids. Your kidneys also play an important role in maintaining acid–base balance. While your lungs can only eliminate carbonic acid (in the form of CO_2), your kidneys can eliminate both acids and bases. Table 7.10 lists the substances that your kidneys can excrete to maintain or restore acid–base balance in your blood.

TABLE 7.10 **Acid–Base Regulation by the Kidneys**

Substance Eliminated	Type of Substance	Result of Excretion	Comments
H_3O^+	Strong acid	Plasma pH *rises*	The kidneys make H_3O^+ by removing H^+ from H_2CO_3; the HCO_3^- is retained in the blood. This is the body's primary way to make HCO_3^- ions.
NH_4^+	Weak acid	Plasma pH *rises*	The kidneys make NH_4^+ by breaking down amino acids, so the body eliminates NH_4^+ only if the diet contains excess protein.
$H_2PO_4^-$	Weak acid*	Plasma pH *rises*	$H_2PO_4^-$ is only available if excess phosphate is present in the diet.
HCO_3^-	Weak base*	Plasma pH *drops*	This is the body's primary means of eliminating excess base.

* $H_2PO_4^-$ and HCO_3^- are amphiprotic ions, but $H_2PO_4^-$ functions as an acid and HCO_3^- functions as a base under physiological conditions.

The excretion of H_3O^+ is particularly important, because this ion is made by the following reaction:

$$H_2CO_3(aq) + H_2O(l) \rightarrow H_3O^+(aq) + HCO_3^-(aq)$$

Carbonic acid is very weak, so this reaction normally produces only a tiny trace of products. However, your kidneys are able to expel the H_3O^+ into your urine while retaining the HCO_3^-. This is your body's primary mechanism for making HCO_3^-, the conjugate base in your plasma buffer. Your kidneys are also able to excrete HCO_3^- when necessary, so they can regulate the bicarbonate concentration in blood plasma.

Both your lungs and your kidneys play important roles in maintaining blood pH, and both have their limitations. Your lungs can only excrete H_2CO_3, while your kidneys can eliminate a wider range of substances. Furthermore, only your kidneys can make and eliminate bicarbonate ions. However, your lungs can respond rapidly to pH changes in your blood, while your kidneys require several hours to correct blood pH. The lungs and the kidneys thus complement each other.

CORE PROBLEMS

7.77 What are the two primary buffers in intracellular fluid?

7.78 What are the two primary buffers in blood plasma?

7.79 One of the important buffer systems in living cells is the phosphate buffer.
a) What two substances make up this buffer?
b) Which of these substances neutralizes acids?
c) Which of these substances neutralizes bases?

7.80 The carbonic acid buffer plays an important role in blood chemistry.
a) What two substances make up this buffer?
b) Which of these substances neutralizes acids?
c) Which of these substances neutralizes bases?

7.81 Explain why proteins that contain histidine can help maintain the pH of body fluids around 7.

7.82 Proteins contain an amino acid called tyrosine, which is a weak acid with a pK_a of 10.1. Is this amino acid likely to contribute to the ability of a protein to maintain a pH of around 7? Why or why not?

7.83 Carbonated beverages contain CO_2 dissolved in water. As CO_2 dissolves in water, the pH of the water changes. Does the pH go up, or does it go down? Explain your answer.

7.84 When you open a carbonated beverage, the beverage "goes flat" as CO_2 escapes from solution, and the pH of the beverage changes. Does the pH go up, or does it go down? Explain your answer.

7.85 Explain why the pH of your blood plasma goes up when you breathe too fast.

7.86 Explain why the pH of your blood plasma goes down when you hold your breath.

7.87 If the concentration of HCO_3^- ions in your blood becomes too high, how does your body get rid of the excess bicarbonate ions?

7.88 If the concentration of HCO_3^- ions in your blood becomes too low, your kidneys can make more bicarbonate ions. How do they do this?

7.89 People with severe kidney failure excrete excessive amounts of HCO_3^- in their urine. The HCO_3^- comes from blood plasma. How does this affect the pH of the blood plasma?

7.90 Our bodies require phosphorus, which we obtain in the form of phosphate ions. If we consume too much phosphorus, though, our kidneys excrete the excess phosphorus in the form of $H_2PO_4^-$ ions. How does this affect the pH of the blood plasma?

CONNECTIONS

Consequences of Blood pH Changes

As we have seen, your body has an elaborate mechanism for maintaining the blood pH very close to 7.4. However, a variety of conditions can push the pH outside this range. Let us look at some of the causes of blood pH imbalance.

In acidosis, the blood's pH drops significantly below 7.35. There are two broad categories of acidosis. The first type, called *respiratory acidosis,* occurs when you cannot breathe effectively, a condition called hypoventilation. Respiratory acidosis can be caused by an obstructed windpipe, emphysema, pneumonia, asthma, or pulmonary edema (excess fluid in the lungs), all of which reduce the lungs' ability to exchange gases effectively. Respiratory acidosis also occurs in overdoses of drugs that depress the breathing reflex, such as morphine, barbiturates, and general anesthetics. Regardless of the cause, the end result is the same; your body cannot rid itself of CO_2 fast enough, and some of the excess CO_2 combines with water in your blood to form carbonic acid, H_2CO_3.

Working muscles produce lactic acid, which makes your blood acidic and limits your ability to do strenuous exercise. If you are physically fit, your heart and lungs can move more oxygen and carbon dioxide, increasing the level at which you can exercise without becoming exhausted.

Oddly, hypoventilation does not necessarily make the blood overly acidic. The kidneys can compensate for inadequate breathing by making more bicarbonate ions (HCO_3^-), restoring the balance between bicarbonate and carbonic acid. People with breathing disorders often have *compensated respiratory acidosis,* in which their blood contains unusually high concentrations of both H_2CO_3 and HCO_3^- but the blood pH is near normal.

Any kind of acidosis that is not a result of breathing abnormalities is called *metabolic acidosis.* Vigorous exercise can produce metabolic acidosis, but this is temporary and rapidly corrected by the body. More serious causes of metabolic acidosis include long-term fasting, uncontrolled diabetes, and hyperthyroidism (an overactive thyroid gland). In these conditions, the body must break down fatty acids to supply most of its energy needs, producing acids called *ketone bodies* which lower your blood pH. Severe diarrhea can also produce metabolic acidosis, because the intestinal fluids contain bicarbonate ions, which are supplied by the blood. The bicarbonate is normally absorbed by the large intestine and returned to the blood, but in severe diarrhea, this cannot occur, so the concentration of bicarbonate in the blood drops, making the blood more acidic.

Alkalosis can also be caused by either abnormal breathing or a metabolic disorder. In *respiratory alkalosis,* your body breathes more rapidly than necessary. As a result, you exhale CO_2 more rapidly than you make it, lowering the concentration of carbonic acid in your blood. The most common cause of respiratory alkalosis is extreme anxiety, which triggers hyperventilation (overly rapid breathing). People who are hyperventilating become dizzy and get a tingly sensation in their fingers and toes. The best treatment for hyperventilation is breathing into a bag, because it forces your body to reabsorb some of the CO_2 that you exhale. *Metabolic alkalosis,* in which the blood pH rises without a change in breathing rate, is most often a result of stomach illness. Your stomach contents are very acidic, so if you vomit, your body must transfer acid from your blood to your stomach to replace the lost acid. The same is true if you take large amounts of antacid to relieve an upset stomach or the symptoms of an ulcer, although modest amounts of antacid have no ill effects.

Acidosis and alkalosis can be serious conditions, regardless of their cause. However, our bodies are remarkably adept at keeping our pH within the correct range. Our ability to maintain a constant pH is one of the best examples of the many ways that the human body adapts to its surroundings and its needs. So enjoy that vigorous workout; your body can handle it!

Key Terms

acid – 7.3
acid–base reaction – 7.5
acidosis – 7.8
acidic – 7.2
alkalosis – 7.8
amino acids – 7.6
amphiprotic – 7.6
base – 7.4
basic (alkaline) – 7.2
Bronsted-Lowry concept – 7.4
buffer – 7.7
conjugate acid – 7.4
conjugate base – 7.4
conjugate pair – 7.4
ion product of water – 7.1
ionization reaction – 7.3
molecular equation – 7.5
neutralization reaction – 7.5
neutral – 7.2
monoprotic acid – 7.3
pH – 7.2
pK_a – 7.7
polyprotic acid – 7.3
proton transfer reaction – 7.1
salt – 7.5
self-ionization of water – 7.1
strength of an acid – 7.3
strength of a base – 7.4
strong electrolyte – 7.3
weak electrolyte – 7.3

SUMMARY OF OBJECTIVES

Now that you have read the chapter, test yourself on your knowledge of the objectives using this summary as a guide.

Section 7.1: Write the self-ionization reaction for water, and use the concentration of either hydronium or hydroxide ion to calculate the concentration of the other ion.

- Water self-ionizes according to the following equation:

$$2\ H_2O(l) \rightleftharpoons H_3O^+(aq) + OH^-(aq)$$

- The ion product of water relates the concentrations of hydronium and hydroxide ions.

$$[H_3O^+] \times [OH^-] = 1.0 \times 10^{-14} \text{ (at room temperature)}$$

- Hydrogen ions (protons) are always covalently bonded to some other substance and cannot exist in solution as independent ions.

Section 7.2: Relate the pH of a solution to the hydronium ion concentration, and use pH to determine the acidity or basicity of a solution.

- The pH of a solution is a shorthand way of expressing the H_3O^+ concentration.

$$\text{pH} = -\log[H_3O^+]$$

- Converting pH back into a hydronium ion concentration requires taking an antilogarithm.

$$[H_3O^+] = 10^{-\text{pH}}$$

- Neutral solutions (including pure water) have a pH of 7.00.
- Acidic solutions have pH values below 7, while basic solutions have pH values above 7.
- As pH moves further from 7, the solution becomes more acidic or basic.

Section 7.3: Write the equation for the ionization of an acid in water, relate the strength of the acid and its molarity to pH, and recognize common structural features in acidic compounds.

- An acid (or proton donor) is a substance that can lose H^+.
- Acids ionize by transferring H^+ to a water molecule, forming H_3O^+.
- Acids may be strong or weak electrolytes. Strong electrolytes ionize completely, while weak electrolytes ionize to a limited extent.
- The pH of a solution of an acid depends on the strength and the molar concentration of the acid.
- In most acids, the acidic hydrogen is bonded to oxygen, and there are other oxygen atoms adjacent to this O—H group.
- Polyprotic acids can lose more than one proton. Each successive proton is more difficult to remove than the one before, so polyprotic acids react with bases in a stepwise fashion.

Section 7.4: Write the equation for the ionization of a base in water, recognize the two common types of bases, identify conjugate pairs, and relate the strength of a base to the pH of a basic solution.

- A base (or proton acceptor) is a substance that can bond to H^+.
- Bases accept a proton from water molecules, forming OH^-.
- Most negative ions are bases, and most compounds in which nitrogen forms bonds to carbon and hydrogen exclusively are bases.
- The strength of a base is determined by its ability to produce OH^- ions when it is dissolved in water.
- A conjugate pair is an acid and a base that differ by one H^+.

Section 7.5: Write net ionic equations for acid–base reactions, recognize the role of conjugate pairs in an acid–base reaction, and use the strengths of the acid and the base to describe the properties of the product mixture.

- In an acid–base reaction, H^+ moves from the acid to the base. These reactions always produce an acid and a base.
- Acid–base reactions always involve two conjugate pairs, with one member of each pair on the reactant side and the other member on the product side.
- In an acid–base reaction, the pH of the product mixture is determined by the relative strengths of the two reactants.

Section 7.6: Define and identify amphiprotic substances, and determine whether a solution of an amphiprotic substance is acidic or basic.

- Amphiprotic substances can either lose or gain H^+, so they can function as either acids or bases.
- The pH of a solution of an amphiprotic substance is determined by the relative strengths of the substance as an acid and as a base.

Section 7.7: Recognize buffer solutions, describe how buffers resist pH changes, and estimate the pH of a buffer from the pK_a of the acid and the concentrations of the buffer components.

- Buffer solutions resist pH changes when acids or bases are added to them.
- Buffers normally contain a conjugate pair.
- The pH of any buffer is close to the pK_a of the conjugate acid in the buffer.
- The exact pH of a buffer depends on the relative concentrations of the acid and base. If the two concentrations are equal, the pH equals the pK_a of the acid. If more acid is present, the pH is lower than the pK_a; if more base is present, the pH is higher than the pK_a.
- The conjugate acid in a buffer neutralizes bases, and the conjugate base neutralizes acids.

Section 7.8: Identify the three important physiological buffers, describe the role of CO_2 in the carbonic acid buffer, and describe the role of the lungs and the kidneys in controlling plasma pH.

- Proteins are an important buffer inside and outside cells.
- The phosphate buffer is the other important intracellular buffer system.
- Blood plasma is buffered by the carbonic acid buffer.
- Most cells in the body produce CO_2, which is eliminated by the lungs. In plasma, CO_2 is equivalent to H_2CO_3 and serves as additional acid in the buffer, because of the equilibrium reaction $H_2O(l) + CO_2(aq) \rightleftharpoons H_2CO_3(aq)$.
- The concentration of CO_2 in blood plasma has a direct effect on pH: as the CO_2 concentration increases, the pH decreases.
- The CO_2 concentration in plasma is regulated by changing the breathing rate. This allows the body to compensate for plasma pH changes from other sources.
- The kidneys play a versatile role in regulating blood pH, because they can excrete a range of acidic and basic ions.

Concept Questions

OWL Online homework for this chapter may be assigned in OWL.
* indicates more challenging problems.

7.91 All aqueous solutions contain H_3O^+ ions and OH^- ions. Where do these ions come from?

7.92 Using Le Châtelier's principle, explain why the concentration of OH^- in water decreases when you add HCl to the water.

7.93 Why are acid–base reactions often called proton transfer reactions?

7.94 A student is asked to calculate the pH of 10^{-3} M NaCl solution. The student answers, "3." Why is this answer incorrect? What is the actual pH of this solution?

7.95 What element must all acids contain, and why?

7.96 Why are bases often referred to as proton acceptors?

7.97 a) What is the difference between a strong acid and a weak acid?
b) What is the difference between a strong base and a weak base?

7.98 a) What two factors determine the pH of a solution that contains an acid?
b) What two factors determine the pH of a solution that contains a base?

7.99 Solutions of sodium acetate ($NaC_2H_3O_2$) conduct electricity better than solutions of acetic acid ($HC_2H_3O_2$). Why is this?

7.100 Ethyl acetate and butyric acid are chemical compounds that contain the same atoms. Why is the formula of ethyl acetate written $C_4H_8O_2$, while the chemical formula of butyric acid is written $HC_4H_7O_2$?

7.101 What are the two common types of bases?

7.102 What is a conjugate pair?

7.103 What is an amphiprotic substance?

7.104 a) What do buffers do?
b) Buffers contain two chemicals. How are these chemicals related to each other?

7.105 Explain why solutions of CO_2 in water do not have a pH of 7.00.

Summary and Challenge Problems

7.106 A 0.075 M solution of acetoacetic acid ($HC_4H_5O_3$) has a pH of 2.37.

a) Use the pH to calculate the concentrations of H_3O^+ and OH^- ions in this solution.
b) Is acetoacetic acid a strong acid, or is it a weak acid? (Hint: How does the molarity of H_3O^+ compare to the molarity of the acetoacetic acid?)

7.107 *How many grams of acetoacetic acid ($HC_4H_5O_3$) are needed to prepare 250 mL of a 0.075 M solution?

7.108 Calculate the pH of each of the following solutions:

a) 0.075 M HCl, a strong acid
b) 3.1×10^{-4} M KOH
c) 2.3×10^{-3} M $Ba(OH)_2$

7.109 *a) HBr is a strong acid. What is the pH of a solution that is made by dissolving 450 mg of HBr in enough water to make 100 mL of solution?
*b) What is the pH of a solution that is made by dissolving 525 mg of $Ba(OH)_2$ in enough water to make 75 mL of solution?

7.110 *At 0°C, the ion product of water is 1.1×10^{-15}. If the concentration of H_3O^+ in an aqueous solution is 1.0×10^{-7} M at 0°C, what is the concentration of OH^-? Should this solution be considered acidic, basic, or neutral?

7.111 From each of the following pairs of solutions, tell which solution has the higher pH.

a) a solution of NaOH or a solution of HCl
b) a 1.0 M solution of HCl or a 0.1 M solution of HCl
c) a 1.0 M solution of NaOH or a 0.1 M solution of NaOH
d) a solution that contains 6.0×10^{-4} M H_3O^+ or a solution that contains 5.0×10^{-3} M H_3O^+
e) a solution that contains 0.0025 M OH^- or a solution that contains 3.1×10^{-4} M OH^-
f) a 0.1 M solution of a strong acid or a 0.1 M solution of a weak acid

7.112 *Match each solution with its correct pH, using the fact that HNO_3 is stronger than $HCHO_2$, which is stronger than $HC_2H_3O_2$.

0.05 M HNO_3	pH = 3.5
0.05 M $HCHO_2$	pH = 3.0
0.05 M $HC_2H_3O_2$	pH = 2.5
0.005 M $HC_2H_3O_2$	pH = 1.3

7.113 A molecule of malonic acid contains three carbon atoms, four hydrogen atoms, and four oxygen atoms, and the chemical formula of malonic acid is normally written $H_2C_3H_2O_4$. Based on this formula, which of the following ionic compounds probably do not exist?

$NaHC_3H_2O_4$ $Na_2C_3H_2O_4$
$Na_3C_3HO_4$ $Na_4C_3O_4$

7.114 Oxalic acid is a weak acid with the chemical formula $H_2C_2O_4$.

a) Write chemical equations for the two ionizations of oxalic acid.
b) Which of these reactions produces most of the H_3O^+ ions in a solution of oxalic acid?

7.115 Only one of the six hydrogen atoms in lactic acid can be removed by a base. Which one is it?

```
     H  :Ö—H
     |   |
  H—C—C—C—Ö—H
     |   |  ‖
     H   H  O:
```

Lactic acid

7.116 HCN and KCN have similar chemical formulas. However, 0.1 M HCN has a pH of 5.2, while 0.1 M KCN has a pH of 11.2. Why do these two compounds behave so differently when they dissolve in water?

7.117 *When acetic acid dissolves in water, it reacts with the water as follows:

$$HC_2H_3O_2(aq) + H_2O(l) \rightleftharpoons C_2H_3O_2^-(aq) + H_3O^+(aq)$$

Use Le Châtelier's principle to explain why adding some $NaC_2H_3O_2$ to this solution makes its pH go up.

7.118 a) Write a balanced chemical equation for the acid–base reaction that occurs when solutions of $HC_2H_3O_2$ and NH_3 are mixed.

*b) How many grams of $HC_2H_3O_2$ are needed to completely neutralize 5.00 g of NH_3?

7.119 When solutions of HCN and C_2H_7N are mixed, the following acid–base reaction occurs:

$$HCN(aq) + C_2H_7N(aq) \rightarrow CN^-(aq) + HC_2H_7N^+(aq)$$

a) Which reactant is the acid, and which is the base?

b) If you mix equal volumes of 0.1 M HCN and 0.1 M C_2H_7N, the product mixture will have a pH of 10.00. Based on this information, what can you say about the relative strengths of HCN and C_2H_7N?

7.120 Many brands of sunscreen contain PABA, an amphiprotic compound that has the following structure:

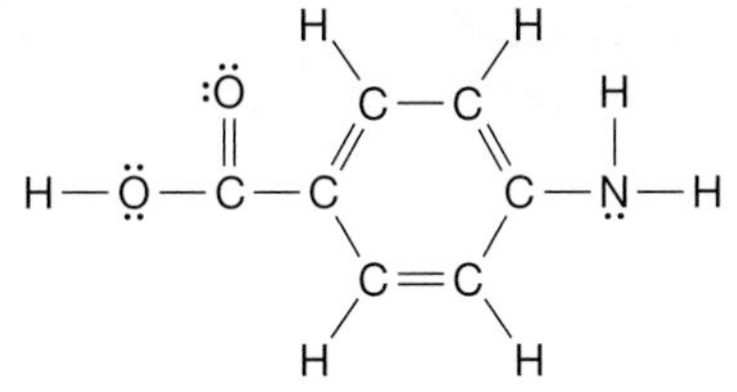

```
               H         H
                \       /
      :Ö         C — C         H
      ||        //     \\      |
 H — Ö — C — C           C — N — H
                \       /
                 C = C
                /       \
               H         H
```

PABA

a) Draw the structure of the ion that is formed when PABA loses H^+.

b) Draw the structure of the ion that is formed when PABA gains H^+.

c) When a small amount of PABA is dissolved in water, the pH of the resulting solution is 5.13. Based on this information, is PABA a stronger acid, or is it a stronger base?

7.121 For each of the following solutions, give the formula of a chemical that you could add to the solution to make a buffer:

a) 0.1 M $HC_7H_5O_2$ (benzoic acid)

b) 0.1 M $NaCHO_2$ (sodium formate)

c) 0.1 M C_3H_9N (trimethylamine, a weak base)

d) 0.1 M K_2HPO_4

7.122 *Use the pK_a values in Table 7.9 (page 291) to answer the following questions:

a) Which of the acids in the table would be the best choice if you needed to prepare a buffer that had a pH of 3.0?

b) What is the conjugate base of the acid you selected from the table?

c) Which of these two substances (the acid or the conjugate base) would need to be present in higher concentration in this buffer? Explain your answer.

7.123 *A buffer that contains 0.10 M NaH_2PO_4 and 0.10 M Na_2HPO_4 has a pH of 7.21. If you need to prepare 3.0 L of this buffer, how many grams of NaH_2PO_4 and how many grams of Na_2HPO_4 will you need?

7.124 If you blow through a straw into a basic solution, you can neutralize the base. (You can also do this by bubbling a stream of room air into the solution, but it takes a very long time.) Explain why your breath can neutralize bases.

7.125 *A patient who is suffering a bout of severe vomiting loses a substantial amount of acid, because the stomach contents are very acidic. His body moves H_3O^+ from his blood plasma into his stomach to replace the lost acid, but this makes the pH of his blood plasma go up. As a result, the patient's breathing rate changes, returning the plasma pH to the correct value. Does the patient's breathing rate increase, or does it decrease? Explain your answer.

7.126 *Mr. Schlossberg is suffering from severe diabetes, and he does not follow his doctor's recommendations for treating the disease. One of the consequences is that his body breaks down large quantities of fat into acidic compounds such as acetoacetic acid ($HC_4H_5O_3$), which are released into his blood, making the plasma pH drop. As a result, Mr. Schlossberg's breathing rate changes, as his body attempts to return his plasma pH to the correct value. Does his breathing rate increase, or does it decrease? Explain your answer.

8

Hydrocarbons: An Introduction to Organic Molecules

Eduardo has just turned 40 and decides to get a physical exam after not visiting the doctor for several years. As part of the exam, Eduardo's doctor orders several blood tests. When the results come back from the lab, the doctor calls Eduardo to tell him that his cholesterol level is higher than the doctor would like, and his high-density lipoprotein (HDL) level is a little low. The doctor explains that these levels put Eduardo at increased risk of a heart attack, because some of the excess cholesterol tends to be deposited in the tiny arteries that supply Eduardo's heart with blood. If these deposits become too thick, one of the arteries can be blocked altogether, triggering a heart attack. HDL helps protect against heart disease by carrying excess cholesterol to the liver, where it can be broken down.

Cholesterol is an example of an organic compound, a molecule built upon a framework of carbon atoms. The human body contains tens of thousands of organic substances, including proteins, fats, carbohydrates, vitamins, and DNA. Although organic compounds can contain many elements, cholesterol is built almost entirely from just two elements, carbon and hydrogen. These two elements are the building blocks of the hydrocarbons, the simplest organic compounds. Although hydrocarbons are rare in living organisms, they are the ideal entry to the fascinating world of organic molecules.

OUTLINE

LABORATORY REQUISITION—CHEMISTRY

Test	Code	Test	Code
☐ Sodium	NA	☐ Fructosamine	FRU/ALB
☐ Potassium	K	☐ PSA	PSA
☐ Creatinine	CREAT	☐ Chloride	CL
☐ BUN	BUN	☐ Calcium	CA
☐ Glucose-fasting	GLUCF	☐ Phosphorus	PHOS
☐ Glucose-random	GLUCR	☐ Phenylalanine	PKU
☐ Hemoglobin A1C	HGBA1C	☐ Uric Acid	URIC

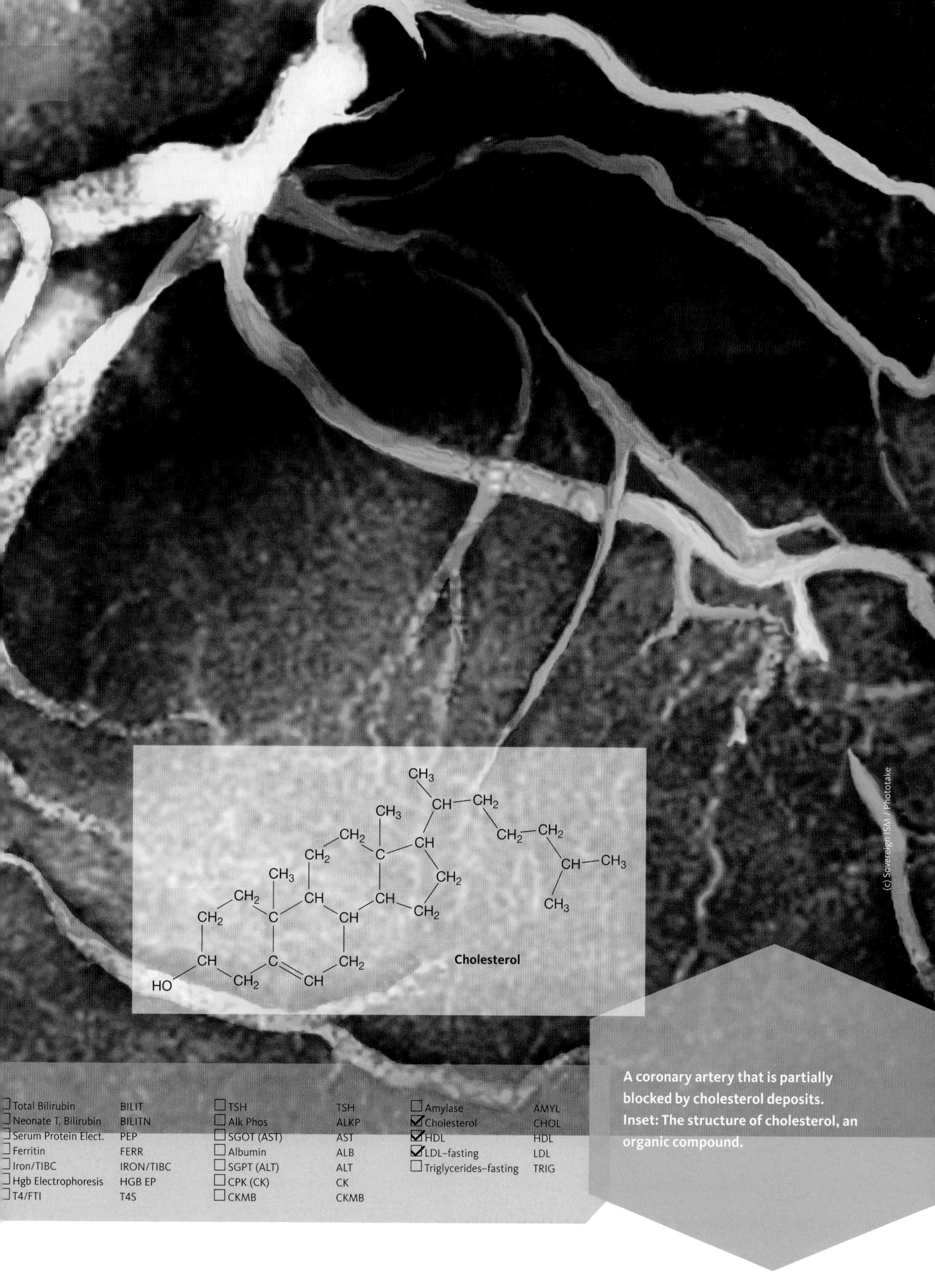

A coronary artery that is partially blocked by cholesterol deposits. Inset: The structure of cholesterol, an organic compound.

Online homework for this chapter may be assigned in OWL.

A human body is made up of a vast number of different chemical compounds. The same is true of any living organism, even the simplest. While some compounds are small molecules like water and carbon dioxide, or ions such as Na^+ and Cl^-, most substances in a living organism are large, complex molecules. If we examine these molecules, we find that every one of them contains carbon and hydrogen. Virtually all of these compounds also contain oxygen, and many other nonmetals can be found as well. Table 8.1 lists some typical examples.

Early chemists believed that these substances could only be formed by living organisms, so these compounds became known as *organic compounds*. Only in 1828 was this belief proved incorrect, when the German chemist Friedrich Wöhler found a way to make an organic compound (urea) from substances that are found in the mineral world.

Health Note: The meaning of the word *organic* in "organic chemistry" should not be confused with its meaning in such phrases as "organic produce." These phrases refer to agricultural techniques that limit the types and amounts of fertilizers, pesticides, hormones, antibiotics, and other chemicals that can be used.

We now know that the fundamental similarity among all of these diverse substances is that they are built upon a framework of carbon atoms. Carbon is the basic structural element of the molecules of life, and it is unique in its ability to serve in this role. In a real sense, the chemistry of life is the chemistry of carbon. However, since 1828, chemists have made millions of carbon-containing compounds that are closely related to naturally occurring substances but that do not occur in any living organism. In modern usage, then, any covalent compound that contains carbon as its primary structural element is called an *organic compound*, and the study of these compounds is called *organic chemistry*.

In this chapter, we will look at the ways in which carbon atoms bond to one another, as we explore the range of molecules that can be formed from just two elements, carbon and hydrogen. In Chapters 9 through 11, we will expand our horizon by adding other nonmetallic elements to this basic framework, producing the full range of organic compounds that dominate the chemistry of all life on Earth.

8.1 The Special Properties of Carbon

OBJECTIVES: *Explain why carbon is uniquely suited to be the main structural element of organic chemistry, and describe the ways in which carbon atoms form covalent bonds.*

Why is carbon found in so many different compounds? There are two properties of carbon that, taken together, make this element unique. First, carbon atoms can form strong, stable chains, linked by covalent bonds. We can build large, complex structures by linking carbon atoms together. Second, carbon atoms can form four covalent bonds, more than needed to make a chain. This allows each carbon atom in a chain to form bonds to additional atoms that are not part of the chain. We can attach almost any nonmetal to a carbon chain, producing molecules with a vast range of chemical properties. No other element shows the versatility of carbon.

TABLE 8.1 Some Compounds in the Human Body

Compound	Chemical Formula	Function
Ascorbic acid (vitamin C)	$C_6H_8O_6$	Required in the formation of connective tissue
Lactose (milk sugar)	$C_{12}H_{22}O_{11}$	The main energy source in milk
Tristearin	$C_{57}H_{110}O_6$	A typical fat that serves as an energy source and provides insulation
Thyroxine	$C_{15}H_{11}I_4NO_4$	A hormone that regulates the overall metabolic rate
Insulin	$C_{257}H_{383}N_{65}O_{77}S_6$	A hormone that helps regulate how rapidly sugars are burned to obtain energy
Transfer RNA	$C_{726}H_{931}N_{282}O_{543}P_{76}$ *(one of many types of transfer RNA)*	Important in building proteins

TABLE 8.2 Bonding Patterns for a Carbon Atom

Bonds Formed	Lewis Structure	Example
Four single bonds	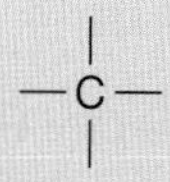 —C— (four single bonds)	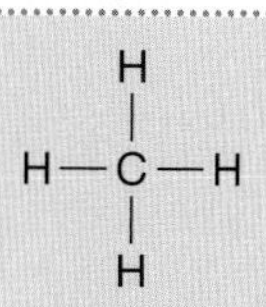 H—C—H with H above and below; CH_4, methane
One double bond Two single bonds	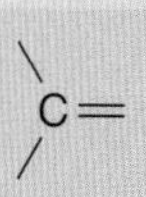 \C= /	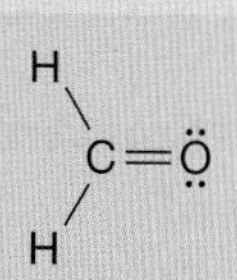 H\C=Ö /H; CH_2O, formaldehyde
Two double bonds	=C=	Ö=C=Ö; CO_2, carbon dioxide
One triple bond One single bond	—C≡	H—C≡N:; HCN, hydrogen cyanide

Carbon Atoms Always Share Four Electron Pairs

Let us take a moment to review the behavior of a carbon atom. Carbon has four valence electrons and four empty spaces in its valence shell. As a result, carbon shares its four electrons with other atoms, and it uses four electrons from the other atoms to fill its valence shell. Carbon atoms are capable of forming single, double, and triple bonds. The possible bonding options for a carbon atom are shown in Table 8.2.

You will see (and draw) the structures of many carbon-containing compounds throughout the rest of this book. Try to get into the habit of checking your structures to be sure that each carbon atom is sharing four electron pairs. *Every carbon atom should be surrounded by four lines.*

Sample Problem 8.1

Identifying carbon atoms that form the correct number of bonds

Which of the carbon atoms in the following molecule (if any) do not form the correct number of bonds?

```
     H   H   H   H
     |   |   |   |
  H—C—C=C—C≡C—H
     |1  2   3   4   5
     H
```

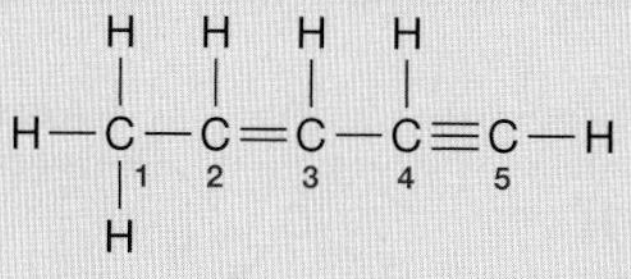

SOLUTION

Carbon 4 is surrounded by five lines, which means that it has five pairs of electrons in its valence shell. Since carbon atoms must be surrounded by four electron pairs, carbon 4 forms an impossible number of bonds. The other four carbon atoms have four lines (four electron pairs) around them and obey the rules of valence.

continued

TRY IT YOURSELF: *Which of the carbon atoms in the following molecule (if any) do not form the correct number of bonds? Draw a circle around each atom.*

```
    H   H   H   H   H
    |   |   |   |   |
H — C = C — C — C = C — H
                    |
                    H
```

For additional practice, try Core Problems 8.7 through 8.10.

The Four Atoms Around a Carbon Atom Form a Tetrahedral Arrangement

When we draw the Lewis structure of a molecule like CH_4 (methane), we normally draw the four bonds at right angles to one another.

```
    H
    |
H — C — H
    |
    H
```

The Lewis structure of methane (CH_4)

Health Note: Some people have bacteria in their large intestines that produce methane as they break down nutrients in the intestines. The intestinal gas produced by these people contains methane. Most people, though, have different bacteria and produce hydrogen (H_2) instead of methane. Both gases are nontoxic and odorless; the unpleasant aroma of intestinal gas is due to other compounds.

However, when carbon forms four single bonds, the four electron pairs around the carbon atom (and the atoms to which they are bonded) *do not actually lie at right angles*. We can predict the orientation of the bonds using a model called the **valence shell electron pair repulsion model**, or the **VSEPR model**, which states that the electron pairs around any atom will always be as far from one another as possible. For any carbon atom that is surrounded by four single bonds, the best arrangement of the electrons is a three-sided pyramid called a tetrahedron, as shown in Figure 8.1. The resulting arrangement of atoms is called a **tetrahedral arrangement**.

In most cases, it is acceptable to draw a Lewis structure that shows bonds at right angles to one another. When chemists want to show the actual positions of the atoms in a molecule like CH_4, they most commonly use a system of wedges and dashed lines to show perspective. The wedge–dash structure of CH_4 is shown in Figure 8.2. Because two-dimensional images of molecules can be hard to interpret, the best way to visualize the tetrahedral arrangement is by building a three-dimensional molecular model, and you should do this if possible. Most college bookstores sell model kits that are designed to represent organic molecules.

Hydrogen Atoms Always Form One Covalent Bond

Virtually all organic molecules also contain hydrogen atoms. A hydrogen atom has one valence electron and one empty space in its valence shell, so it forms only one covalent bond. Hydrogen atoms can share electrons with all of the nonmetals except the inert gases. Note that because hydrogen only forms one bond, *hydrogen is never found between two other atoms.* Figure 8.3 shows two real molecules that contain hydrogen and an impossible structure in which a hydrogen atom forms two bonds.

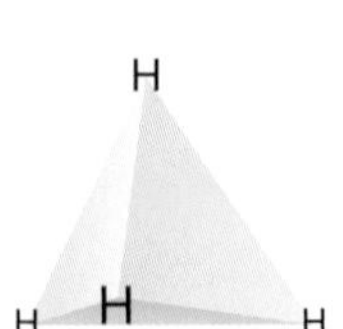
H
H
H
H

The four hydrogen atoms form the corners of a three-sided pyramid . . .

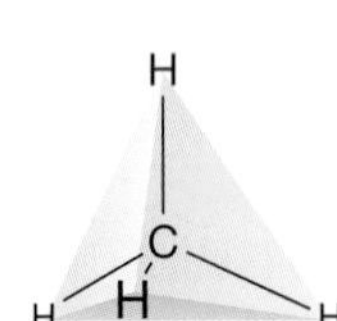
H
C
H
H
H

. . . with the carbon atom at the center of the pyramid.

FIGURE 8.1 The tetrahedral structure of methane.

```
    H
    |
H — C — H
    |
    H
```

A Lewis structure: does not show the actual position of the atoms.

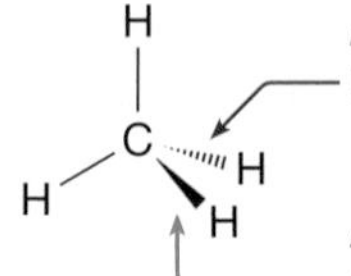
H
C
H
H
H
A dashed wedge represents a bond that is going away from you (into the paper).
A solid wedge represents a bond that is coming toward you (out of the paper).

A wedge–dash structure: shows the actual positions of the atoms.

FIGURE 8.2 Comparing Lewis and wedge–dash structures of methane.

```
    H          H   H
    |          |   |
H—C—H      H—C—C—H
    |          |   |
    H          H   H
```

These are real compounds.
Each hydrogen atom forms one bond.

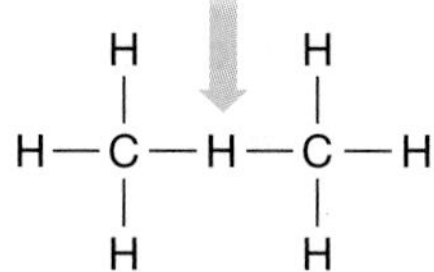

```
    H       H
    |       |
H—C—H—C—H
    |       |
    H       H
```

This is an impossible molecule.
The central hydrogen forms two bonds.

FIGURE 8.3 The bonding requirements of hydrogen.

CORE PROBLEMS

All Core Problems are paired and the answers to the blue odd-numbered problems appear in the back of the book.

8.1 Why do carbon atoms always share four electron pairs in chemical compounds?

8.2 Why do hydrogen atoms always share one pair of electrons in chemical compounds?

8.3 What is a tetrahedral arrangement? Give an example of a compound that has this arrangement of atoms.

8.4 Name one element other than carbon that can form a tetrahedral arrangement when it bonds to other elements.

8.5 Which of the following molecules contain at least one tetrahedral arrangement of atoms?

```
    H            H
    |            |
H—C—H        H—C=Ö
    |              ..
    H

    H  H
    |  |
H—C—C—H      H—C≡C—H
    |  |
    H  H
```

8.6 Which of the following molecules contain at least one tetrahedral arrangement of atoms?

```
H—C≡N:       H—C=C—H
                 |  |
                 H  H

H  H  H  H  H          H
|  |  |  |  |          |
C=C—C—C=C          :F̤—C—F̤:
|     |     |          |
H     H     H          H
```

8.7 Using your knowledge of valence electrons and the octet rule, explain why the following compound is unlikely to exist:

```
    H
    |
H—C—H
```

8.8 Using your knowledge of valence electrons and the octet rule, explain why the following compound is unlikely to exist:

```
    H       H
    |       |
H—C—H—C—H
    |       |
    H       H
```

8.9 In each of the following molecules, find the atom or atoms (if any) that do not form the correct number of covalent bonds, and draw a circle around each atom.

```
  H  H  H  H  H              H
  |  |  |  |  |              |
H—C=C—C—C=C—H          H—C—C≡C—H
                             |
                             H

     H  H  H                 H
     |  |  |                 |
   H—C=C—C—H             H—C—H—H
     |  |  |                 |
     H  H  H                 H
```

8.10 In each of the following molecules, find the atom or atoms (if any) that do not form the correct number of covalent bonds, and draw a circle around each atom.

```
  H  H  H  H  H            H  H  H
  |  |  |  |  |            |  |  |
H—C—C≡C—C—C—H          H—C—C=C—H
  |  |  |  |  |
  H  H  H  H  H

      H   H
       \ /
     H  C  H               H  H
     |  ‖  |               |  |
   H—C—C—C—H             H—C—C=H
     |     |               |
     H     H               H
```

8.2 Linear Alkanes: The Foundation of Organic Chemistry

OBJECTIVES: *Learn the names of the first 10 linear alkanes, and use common conventions to draw their structural formulas.*

It is time to begin our exploration of the world of organic molecules. In this chapter, we focus on **hydrocarbons**, compounds that contain only carbon and hydrogen atoms. Because they contain only two elements, hydrocarbons are the simplest of all organic compounds.

Chemists classify hydrocarbons based on the types of carbon–carbon bonds they contain. If a hydrocarbon contains only single bonds between carbon atoms, it is an

TABLE 8.3 Classes of Hydrocarbons

Class	Description	Example
Alkane	Alkanes do not contain double or triple bonds	Propane
Alkene	Alkenes contain at least one carbon–carbon double bond.	Propene
Alkyne	Alkynes contain at least one carbon–carbon triple bond.	Propyne
Aromatic compound (Arene)	Aromatic compounds contain a six-membered ring of carbon atoms, linked by alternating single and double bonds.	Benzene

alkane. Compounds with at least one double or one triple bond between carbon atoms are called **alkenes** and **alkynes**, respectively. In addition, some hydrocarbons contain a six-membered ring of atoms that has alternating single and double bonds. These compounds have quite different chemical properties from alkenes, so they are a separate class of molecules called **aromatic compounds** or **arenes**. Table 8.3 shows an example of each class of hydrocarbons.

In this section, we begin our study of hydrocarbons by looking at **linear alkanes**. These molecules contain a single continuous chain of carbon atoms, connected to one another by single bonds. We will examine more complex alkanes in Section 8.3, and we will explore the other classes of hydrocarbons in Sections 8.6 through 8.8.

Linear Alkanes Contain a Chain of Carbon Atoms Surrounded by Hydrogen Atoms

The smallest linear alkane is *methane,* which contains only one carbon atom. Carbon must form four bonds, so the carbon atom in methane is bonded to four hydrogen atoms. Methane has the molecular formula CH_4, and its Lewis structure is

Methane

The next member of the linear alkanes contains two carbon atoms, which are linked to each other by a single bond.

```
C—C
```

In this skeleton structure, each carbon atom forms only one bond (the bond that links it to the other carbon atom). However, carbon atoms must form four bonds. Let us add lines to represent the remaining three bonds on each carbon atom.

```
      |       |
      1       1
 —2·C·3—2·C·3—
      4       4
      |       |
```

Alkanes contain only carbon and hydrogen, so all of the bonds we just added must link carbon to hydrogen. Adding the hydrogen atoms gives us the structure of the complete molecule, which is named *ethane* and which has the molecular formula C_2H_6.

```
    H   H
    |   |
H—C—C—H
    |   |
    H   H
```

Ethane

We can continue this process by extending our carbon chain. Here is how we can construct *propane,* the linear alkane that contains three carbon atoms:

```
C—C—C
```

Start with a three-carbon chain.

```
      |       |       |
      1       1       1
 —2·C·3—2·C·3—2·C·3—
      4       4       4
      |       |       |
```

Add bonds until each carbon atom is surrounded by four bonds.

```
    H   H   H
    |   |   |
H—C—C—C—H
    |   |   |
    H   H   H
```

Add hydrogen atoms to complete the structure of propane.

iStockphoto.com/Don Nichols

Propane is flammable and is used as a fuel. It is a gas at room temperature, but it can be turned into a liquid if it is put under high pressure.

Propane has the molecular formula C_3H_8. Notice that in this molecule the left-hand and right-hand carbon atoms are attached to three hydrogen atoms, but the central carbon atom is only bonded to two hydrogen atoms. The central carbon is linked to two carbon atoms in our original chain, so it only needs two more bonds to satisfy the octet rule.

Sample Problem **8.2**

Drawing the structure of a linear alkane

The linear alkane that contains four carbon atoms is called butane. Draw the structure of butane.

SOLUTION

Start by drawing a skeleton structure that contains four carbon atoms.

```
C—C—C—C
```

Then add enough bonds so that each carbon atom forms a total of four bonds, and add hydrogen atoms to complete the structure.

```
    H   H   H   H
    |   |   |   |
H—C—C—C—C—H
    |   |   |   |
    H   H   H   H
```

TRY IT YOURSELF: *The linear alkane that contains six carbon atoms is called hexane. Draw the structure of hexane.*

Organic chemists refer to the structures we have drawn so far as **full structural formulas.** A full structural formula shows every atom and bond in a molecule, but it does not show any nonbonding electrons. For example, here is the Lewis structure and the full structural formula of water:

H—Ö—H (with a lone pair below O)

A Lewis structure shows the nonbonding electrons.

H—O—H

A full structural formula does not show nonbonding electrons.

Full structural formulas of large molecules take up a great deal of space and are tedious to draw, so they are often written in an abbreviated fashion called a **condensed structural formula.** In a condensed structural formula, the carbon atoms are listed individually, but all of the hydrogen atoms that are bonded to a carbon atom are written immediately after that carbon atom. For example, a carbon atom that is bonded to two hydrogen atoms is written $—CH_2—$. Figure 8.4 shows the full and condensed structural formulas of propane.

Full structural formula

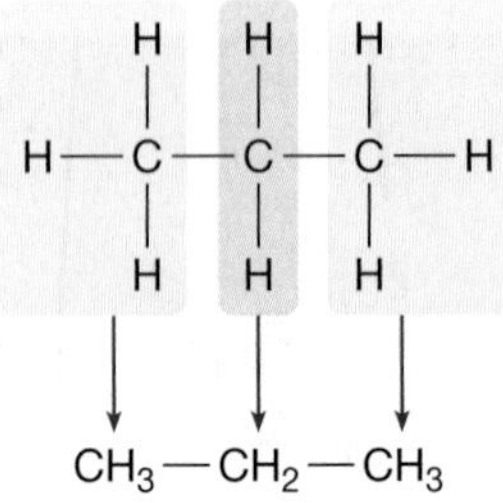

$CH_3—CH_2—CH_3$

Condensed structural formula

FIGURE 8.4 Drawing the condensed structure of propane.

Sample Problem **8.3**

Drawing a condensed structural formula

The full structural formula of butane is shown in Sample Problem 8.2. Draw the condensed structural formula of butane.

SOLUTION

List each carbon atom in the molecule, and then add the hydrogen atoms that are bonded to each carbon.

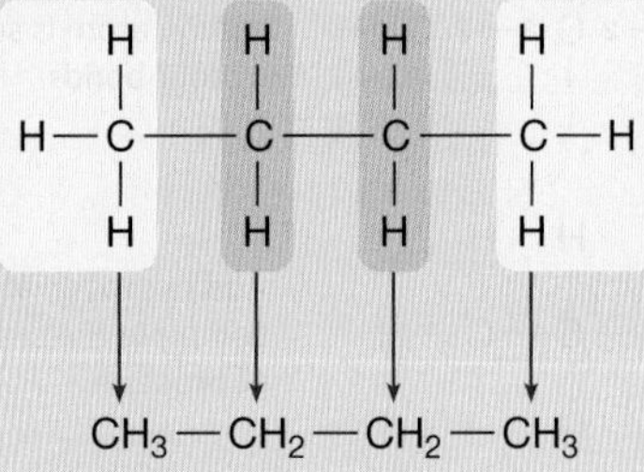

$CH_3—CH_2—CH_2—CH_3$

Condensed structural formula

TRY IT YOURSELF: *In the Try It Yourself section of Sample Problem 8.2, you drew the full structural formula of hexane. Now draw the condensed structural formula of hexane.*

For additional practice, try Core Problems 8.13 and 8.14.

The names and structural formulas of the first 10 linear alkanes are shown in Table 8.4. We will use this information when we name more complex organic molecules, so you should begin by learning these names and structures.

Each Carbon Atom in an Alkane Forms a Tetrahedral Arrangement

As was the case with methane (CH_4), the actual arrangements of atoms in the linear alkanes do not look like the structural formulas we draw. Whenever a carbon atom forms four single bonds, the four bonds (and the four neighboring atoms) form a tetrahedral arrangement. For example, the following structures show the actual shape of an ethane molecule. Each half of the molecule rotates freely, so these are just two of the many possible ways in which ethane can appear.

TABLE 8.4 The Names and Structures of the Linear Alkanes

Name and Molecular Formula	Full Structural Formula	Condensed Structural Formula
Methane (CH_4)	H | H—C—H | H	CH_4
Ethane (C_2H_6)	H H | | H—C—C—H | | H H	$CH_3—CH_3$
Propane (C_3H_8)	H H H | | | H—C—C—C—H | | | H H H	$CH_3—CH_2—CH_3$
Butane (C_4H_{10})	H H H H | | | | H—C—C—C—C—H | | | | H H H H	$CH_3—CH_2—CH_2—CH_3$ *or* $CH_3—(CH_2)_2—CH_3$
Pentane (C_5H_{12})	H H H H H | | | | | H—C—C—C—C—C—H | | | | | H H H H H	$CH_3—CH_2—CH_2—CH_2—CH_3$ *or* $CH_3—(CH_2)_3—CH_3$
Hexane (C_6H_{14})	H H H H H H | | | | | | H—C—C—C—C—C—C—H | | | | | | H H H H H H	$CH_3—CH_2—CH_2—CH_2—CH_2—CH_3$ *or* $CH_3—(CH_2)_4—CH_3$
Heptane (C_7H_{16})	H H H H H H H | | | | | | | H—C—C—C—C—C—C—C—H | | | | | | | H H H H H H H	$CH_3—CH_2—CH_2—CH_2—CH_2—CH_2—CH_3$ *or* $CH_3—(CH_2)_5—CH_3$
Octane (C_8H_{18})	H H H H H H H H | | | | | | | | H—C—C—C—C—C—C—C—C—H | | | | | | | | H H H H H H H H	$CH_3—CH_2—CH_2—CH_2—CH_2—CH_2—CH_2—CH_3$ *or* $CH_3—(CH_2)_6—CH_3$
Nonane (C_9H_{20})	H H H H H H H H H | | | | | | | | | H—C—C—C—C—C—C—C—C—C—H | | | | | | | | | H H H H H H H H H	$CH_3—CH_2—CH_2—CH_2—CH_2—CH_2—CH_2—CH_2—CH_3$ *or* $CH_3—(CH_2)_7—CH_3$
Decane ($C_{10}H_{22}$)	H H H H H H H H H H | | | | | | | | | | H—C—C—C—C—C—C—C—C—C—C—H | | | | | | | | | | H H H H H H H H H H	$CH_3—CH_2—CH_2—CH_2—CH_2—CH_2—CH_2—CH_2—CH_2—CH_3$ *or* $CH_3—(CH_2)_8—CH_3$

Each of the carbon atoms is at the center of a tetrahedral arrangement, as shown in Figure 8.5.

In larger alkanes, the tetrahedral arrangement forces the carbon chain into a zigzag shape. The term *linear alkane* is misleading, because the carbon atoms in an alkane cannot really form a straight line. Figure 8.6 shows the actual structure of hexane, the linear alkane that contains six carbon atoms. In this figure, the tetrahedral arrangement around one of the carbon atoms is shown by shading.

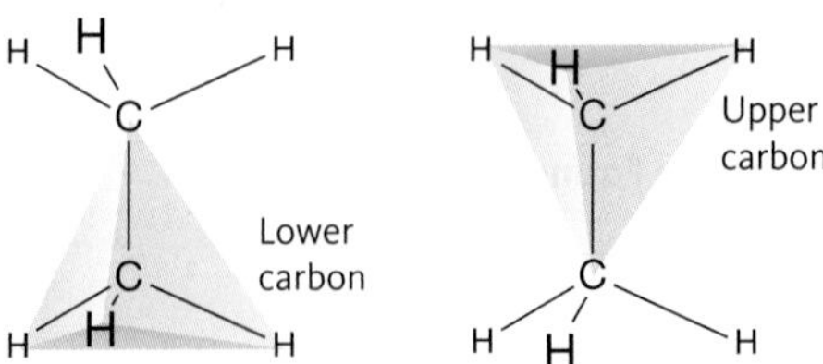

FIGURE 8.5 The tetrahedral arrangements in a molecule of ethane.

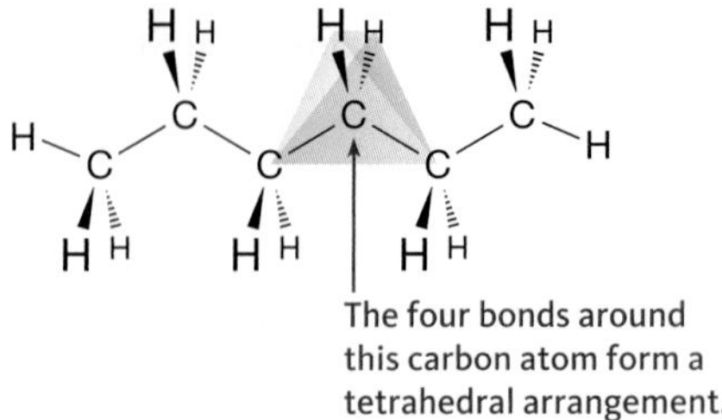

The four bonds around this carbon atom form a tetrahedral arrangement.

FIGURE 8.6 The tetrahedral arrangement in a molecule of hexane.

There Are Many Ways to Represent an Organic Molecule

Chemists have devised many ways to depict an organic molecule. Each of these strikes a different balance between showing the exact structure of a molecule (including the positions of all of the atoms) and keeping the structure simple and compact. The most detailed type of structure is the wedge–dash structure, which shows the position of each atom and bond in the molecule. Full and condensed structural formulas show each atom, but they do not give information about the shape of the molecule.

An even simpler way to show an alkane is with a **line structure.** Line structures show the shape of the carbon chain, but they do not label the carbon atoms, and they omit the hydrogen atoms altogether. Here are the line structure and the condensed structural formula of butane:

$$= \quad CH_3-CH_2-CH_2-CH_3$$

Line structure of butane — Condensed structural formula of butane

To draw a line structure, simply draw a zigzag line that has enough corners to represent all of the carbon atoms. To interpret a line structure, put a carbon atom at each end of the structure and at each corner. Then add enough hydrogen atoms to satisfy the bonding requirement of each carbon atom.

Sample Problem 8.4

Drawing a line structure

Draw the line structure of pentane. The condensed structural formula of pentane is

$$CH_3-CH_2-CH_2-CH_2-CH_3$$

SOLUTION

Pentane contains five carbon atoms. In a line structure, the two ends of the line represent the two end carbon atoms, so we must draw a zigzag line that has three corners.

$$CH_3-CH_2-CH_2-CH_2-CH_3$$

The line structure of pentane

TRY IT YOURSELF: *Draw the line structure of hexane. The condensed structural formula of hexane is*

$$CH_3-CH_2-CH_2-CH_2-CH_2-CH_3$$

For additional practice, try Core Problems 8.15 and 8.16.

The simplest way to depict an organic molecule is by writing its molecular formula. For example, the molecular formula of butane is C_4H_{10}. A molecular formula tells us how many atoms of each element are present, but it tells us nothing about how the atoms are bonded to one another. For this reason, chemists usually use molecular formulas only when they are writing a balanced chemical equation and do not need to show any structural information.

Table 8.5 summarizes the ways in which we can depict an organic molecule.

TABLE 8.5 Common Ways to Represent Hexane, an Organic Molecule

Structure	Type of Structure and Uses of This Type
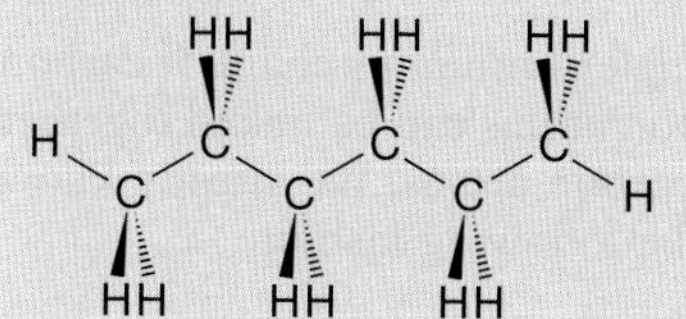	**Wedge–dash structure** Shows the actual positions of atoms and bonds in the molecule.
H H H H H H H—C—C—C—C—C—C—H H H H H H H	**Full structural formula** Shows all of the bonds and atoms in the molecule.
$CH_3—CH_2—CH_2—CH_2—CH_2—CH_3$ or $CH_3(CH_2)_4CH_3$	**Condensed structural formula** Shows all of the atoms in a compact format.
	Line structure Shows the carbon framework in a simple, easy-to-draw format.
C_6H_{14}	**Molecular formula** Useful for writing balanced equations.

CORE PROBLEMS

8.11 Which of the following molecules (if any) are alkanes?

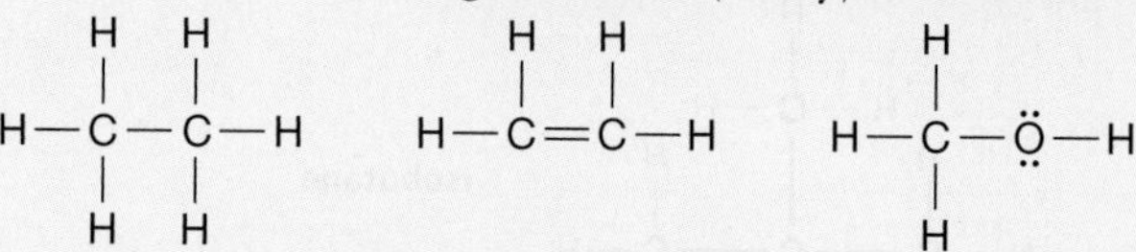

8.12 Which of the following molecules (if any) are alkanes?

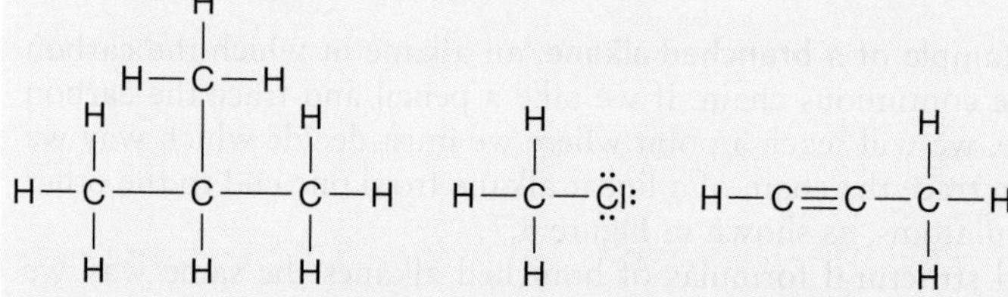

8.13 a) Draw the condensed structural formula that corresponds to the following full structural formula:

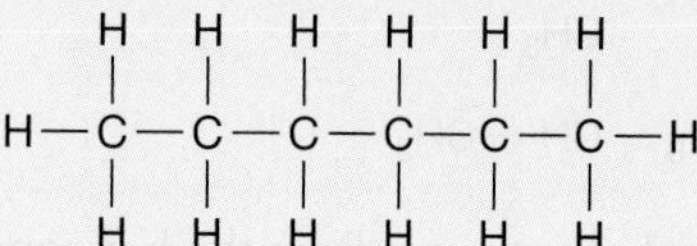

b) Draw the full structural formula that corresponds to the following condensed structural formula:

$CH_3—CH_2—CH_2—CH_3$

8.14 a) Draw the condensed structural formula that corresponds to the following full structural formula:

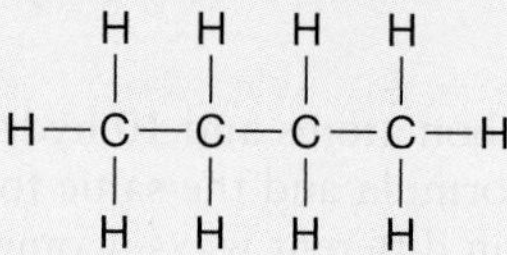

b) Draw the full structural formula that corresponds to the following condensed structural formula:

$CH_3—CH_2—CH_2—CH_2—CH_2—CH_2—CH_2—CH_3$

8.15 Draw the line structures of the molecules in Problem 8.13.

8.16 Draw the line structures of the molecules in Problem 8.14.

8.17 Draw the full and condensed structural formulas of each of the following molecules:
a) octane b) propane

8.18 Draw the full and condensed structural formulas of each of the following molecules:
a) ethane b) heptane

8.19 a) Draw the full and condensed structural formulas of the compound that has the following line structure:

b) Write the molecular formula of this molecule.
c) Name this molecule.

8.20 a) Draw the full and condensed structural formulas of the compound that has the following line structure:

b) Write the molecular formula of this molecule.
c) Name this molecule.

OBJECTIVES: *Distinguish linear and branched alkanes and cycloalkanes, and recognize and draw isomers of simple alkanes.*

8.3 Branched Alkanes, Cycloalkanes, and Isomers

Many aerosol products use isobutane as a propellant, sometimes mixed with butane and propane. These gases are flammable, so aerosol products should not be used around open flames or sparks.

In Section 8.2, we looked at molecules that contain a single continuous chain of carbon atoms. Let us now explore the other ways in which carbon atoms can be linked together using single bonds. Our starting point is a set of four carbon atoms. We already know that we can link four carbon atoms to one another in the following fashion:

$$C-C-C-C$$

When we add enough hydrogen atoms so that each carbon atom makes four bonds, we produce the structure of butane.

```
    H   H   H   H
    |   |   |   |
H — C — C — C — C — H      Butane
    |   |   |   |
    H   H   H   H
```

There is a second way to build a molecule using four carbon atoms. If we build a three-carbon chain, and then we attach the fourth carbon atom to the middle of our chain, we produce a different skeleton structure:

```
    C
    |
C — C — C
```

We can convert this skeleton structure to an alkane by adding enough hydrogen atoms so that each carbon makes four bonds. The central carbon atom already has three bonds, so it needs just one additional bond. The other carbon atoms need three bonds apiece. Adding the hydrogen atoms gives us the structure of a new alkane, called *isobutane*.

```
            H
            |
        H — C — H
    H       |       H
    |       |       |          Isobutane
H — C ————— C ————— C — H
    |       |       |
    H       H       H
```

Isobutane is our first example of a **branched alkane**, an alkane in which the carbon atoms do not form a single continuous chain. If we take a pencil and trace the carbon chain of a branched alkane, we will reach a point where we must decide which way we will go. By contrast, we can trace the chain of a linear alkane from one end to the other without missing any carbon atoms, as shown in Figure 8.7.

We draw the condensed structural formulas of branched alkanes the same way we draw them for linear alkanes. For example, the condensed structural formula of isobutane is

```
          CH3
          |
CH3 — CH — CH3
```

To draw the line structure of a branched alkane, we draw the horizontal carbon chain as a zigzag line, and then we add extra lines pointing upward or downward. Figure 8.8 shows four examples of branched alkanes drawn as condensed structural formulas and as line structures.

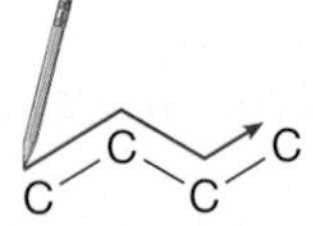

Butane (a linear alkane): We can trace the carbon chain from start to finish.

Isobutane (a branched alkane): When we reach the central carbon, we have a choice of direction.

FIGURE 8.7 The carbon chains of linear and branched alkanes.

Isomers Have the Same Molecular Formula, But They Have Different Structures

Both butane and isobutane contain four carbon atoms and 10 hydrogen atoms, so these two compounds have the same molecular formula and the same formula weight. However, the atoms are bonded to one another in different ways. Compounds that have the

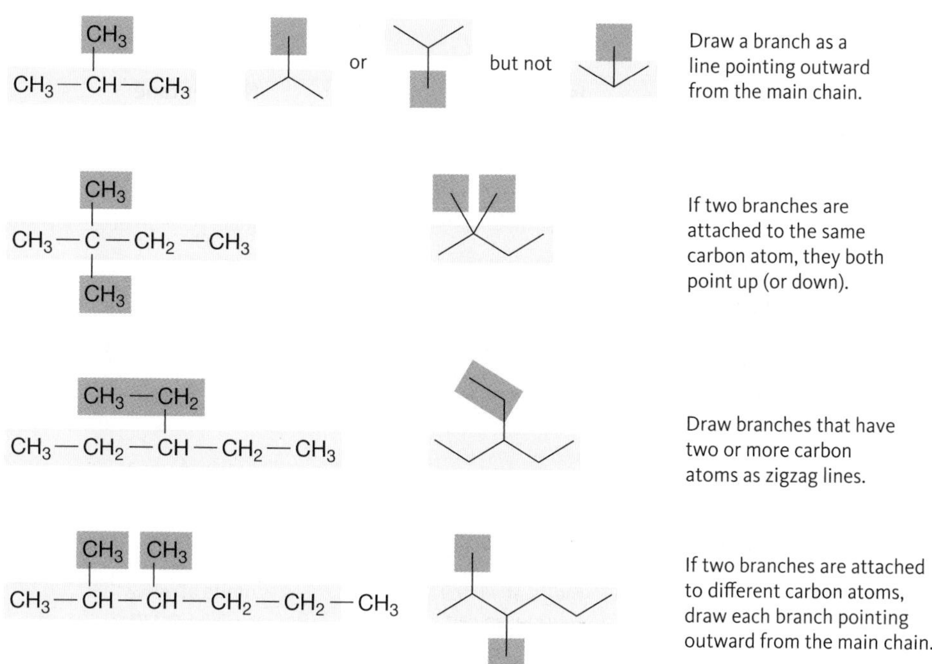

CH_3
CH_3—CH—CH_3
or
but not
Draw a branch as a line pointing outward from the main chain.
CH_3
CH_3—C—CH_2—CH_3
CH_3
If two branches are attached to the same carbon atom, they both point up (or down).
CH_3—CH_2
CH_3—CH_2—CH—CH_2—CH_3
Draw branches that have two or more carbon atoms as zigzag lines.
CH_3 CH_3
CH_3—CH—CH—CH_2—CH_2—CH_3
If two branches are attached to different carbon atoms, draw each branch pointing outward from the main chain.

FIGURE 8.8 Representing branched alkanes using line structures.

same molecular formula but different structures are called **isomers**. Isomers play an important role in organic chemistry and biochemistry; often a different arrangement of atoms will produce a molecule with dramatically different physiological effects.

• The prefix *iso-* means "similar to" and appears in many other names of organic molecules.

There are several types of isomers in organic chemistry. In this section, we will explore **constitutional isomers**, which have their atoms connected to one another in a different order. Constitutional isomers have different shapes, which in turn give them different physical and chemical properties. For instance, butane and isobutane are constitutional isomers, because the four carbon atoms are attached to one another differently. Table 8.6 lists some of the properties of these two compounds. In Section 8.7, we will see an example of *stereoisomers*, isomers that differ in the arrangement of the bonds around a particular atom.

TABLE 8.6 The Properties of Two Constitutional Isomers

	Butane	**Isobutane**
Molecular formula	C_4H_{10}	C_4H_{10}
Condensed structural formula	CH_3—CH_2—CH_2—CH_3	CH_3—CH(CH_3)—CH_3
Line structure		
Appearance at room temp.	colorless, odorless gas	colorless, odorless gas
Boiling point	-0.5°C	-11.7°C
Freezing point	-138.3°C	-159.4°C
Density of liquid at −20°C	0.620 g/mL	0.605 g/mL
Amount of energy obtained from burning one gram of this compound	10.92 kcal	10.89 kcal

TABLE 8.7 Pentane and Its Isomers

	Pentane	Isopentane	Neopentane
Skeleton structure	C—C—C—C—C	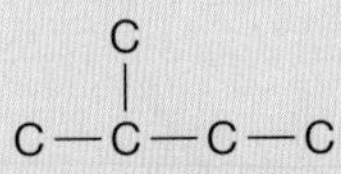 C | C—C—C—C	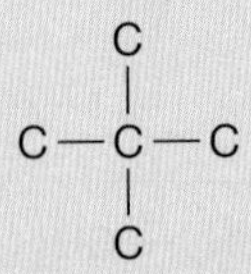 C | C—C—C | C
Condensed structural formula	$CH_3-CH_2-CH_2-CH_2-CH_3$	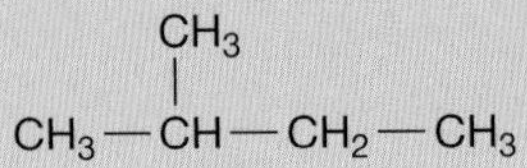 CH_3 | $CH_3-CH-CH_2-CH_3$	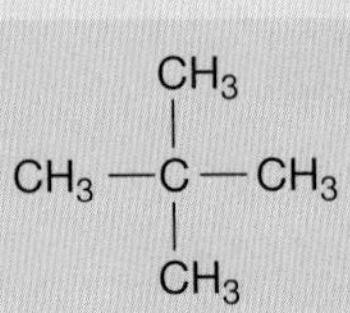 CH_3 | CH_3-C-CH_3 | CH_3
Line structure		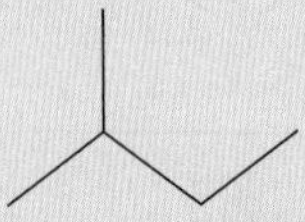	
Physical properties	melts at –129.8°C boils at 36.1°C density: 0.56 g/mL	melts at –159.9°C boils at 29.9°C density: 0.62 g/mL	melts at –16.8°C boils at 9.4°C density: 0.59 g/mL

Butane and isobutane are the only compounds that have the formula C_4H_{10}. However, if we increase the number of carbon atoms, the number of different molecules that we can make increases as well. For example, three different alkanes contain five carbon atoms. One of these compounds is a linear alkane, while the other two are branched. As was the case for butane and isobutane, all three five-carbon alkanes have the same molecular formula (C_5H_{12}) but different properties. The linear alkane is pentane, and the branched alkanes are called isopentane and neopentane. The structures of these compounds are shown in Table 8.7.

• The prefix *neo-* means "new," and it denotes that neopentane was the last of the pentane isomers to be discovered.

Sample Problem **8.5**

Drawing isomers of a linear alkane

Which of the following molecules (if any) are isomers of hexane?

a) $CH_3-CH_2-CH_2-CH_2-CH_2-CH_3$

b) 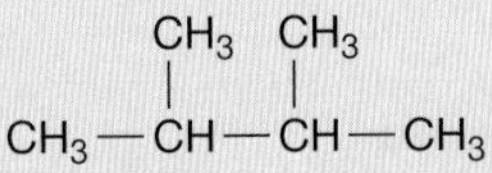 $CH_3-\underset{|}{\overset{CH_3}{CH}}-\overset{CH_3}{CH}-CH_3$

c) 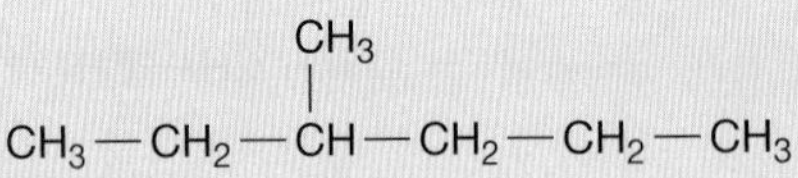 $CH_3-CH_2-\overset{CH_3}{CH}-CH_2-CH_2-CH_3$

SOLUTION

a) To be an isomer of hexane, the molecule must have a different structure from hexane. This molecule is hexane, so it is not an isomer of hexane.

b) The molecular formula of hexane (see part a) is C_6H_{14}. The molecule here also contains six carbon atoms and 14 hydrogen atoms. However, hexane is unbranched and this molecule is branched, so this compound is not hexane. Since this compound has the same molecular formula as hexane but a different structure, it is an isomer of hexane.

c) This molecule contains seven carbon atoms and 16 hydrogen atoms. Its molecular formula is different from that of hexane, so this compound is not an isomer of hexane.

continued

TRY IT YOURSELF: *Which of the following molecules (if any) are isomers of hexane?*

a) $CH_3—CH_2—CH_2—CH_2—CH_3$

b)
```
                CH3
                |
CH3—CH2—CH—CH2—CH3
```

For additional practice, try Core Problems 8.31 and 8.32.

Recognizing isomers is complicated by the variety of ways in which we can draw a given organic molecule. For instance, here are some ways to represent the structure of the linear alkane pentane. These structures do *not* represent different molecules, and they are *not* isomers. They are simply different ways to draw a five-carbon alkane that has no branches.

```
                            CH3          CH3         CH2—CH2
                            |            |           |    |
CH3—CH2—CH2—CH2—CH3         CH2—CH2—CH2        CH3—CH2   CH3
```

Likewise, there are many ways to draw the structures of most branched alkanes. Here are three ways to draw the structure of isopentane:

```
     CH3                       CH3            CH2—CH—CH3
     |                         |              |    |
CH3—CH—CH2—CH3       CH3—CH2—CH—CH3        CH3  CH3
```

Again, all of these structural formulas represent the same compound. In each case, we have a chain of four carbon atoms, with a one-carbon branch bonded to the chain. In this text, the structures of branched alkanes are drawn in a way that matches how these compounds are named. We will look at the systematic names for branched alkanes in the next section.

Cycloalkanes Contain a Ring of Carbon Atoms

If we have at least three carbon atoms, we can arrange them in a ring. For instance, here are the rings we can make from three, four, five, and six carbon atoms, respectively:

```
  C       C—C       C           C
 / \      |  |    /   \      /     \
C—C      C—C     C     C    C       C
                  \   /     |       |
                  C—C       C       C
                             \     /
                                C
```

Adding enough hydrogen atoms to satisfy the bonding requirements of carbon gives us a **cycloalkane**. A cycloalkane is a special type of alkane in which the carbon atoms are arranged in a ring. We name cycloalkanes by adding the prefix *cyclo-* to the names of the corresponding linear alkanes. Chemists often use line structures for cycloalkanes, so you should become familiar with this type of structure and be able to convert it into a structural formula. Table 8.8 shows the names and structures of the first four cycloalkanes.

Sample Problem 8.6

Naming cycloalkanes

Name the following cycloalkane:

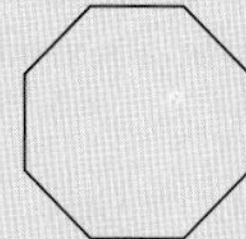

SOLUTION

This compound contains eight carbon atoms, so we name it by adding the prefix *cyclo-* to the name of the eight-carbon linear alkane *(octane)*. The name of this compound is cyclooctane.

TRY IT YOURSELF: *What is the name of the cycloalkane that contains seven carbon atoms?*

TABLE 8.8 The Structures and Names of Some Cycloalkanes

Name	Full Structural Formula	Condensed Structural Formula	Line Structure
cyclopropane			
cyclobutane			
cyclopentane			
cyclohexane			

Health Note: Cyclopropane is an odorless gas that was once used as a general anesthetic. Because it is extremely flammable, cyclopropane was replaced by safer compounds by the mid-20th century.

Cycloalkanes and alkanes are closely related, but they are not isomers. The carbon skeleton of a cycloalkane, unlike that of an alkane, has no ends, so cycloalkanes have two fewer hydrogen atoms than the corresponding alkanes. For example, the molecular formula of propane is C_3H_8, while that of cyclopropane is C_3H_6.

Cycloalkanes can be linked to chains of carbon atoms. The following compound is an example of a molecule that contains both a six-membered ring and a two-carbon open chain:

Ethylcyclohexane

Molecules like ethylcyclohexane are often drawn as line structures, or they are shown as mixed structures in which the ring is drawn as a line structure and the branch is drawn

The chair conformation of the carbon ring in cyclohexane.

The full structure of cyclohexane (The tetrahedral arrangement around the leftmost carbon is shown by shading.)

FIGURE 8.9 The shape of the carbon ring in cyclohexane.

as a condensed structural formula. Here is how the structure of ethylcyclohexane appears as a line structure and as a mixed structure:

$CH_2—CH_3$

Line structure **Mixed structure**

In cycloalkanes, as in open-chain alkanes, the bonds around each carbon atom form a tetrahedral arrangement. As a result, the carbon rings of most cycloalkanes are not flat. For instance, the carbon ring in cyclohexane usually adopts the arrangement in Figure 8.9, called the *chair conformation.*

Alkanes and cycloalkanes are called **saturated hydrocarbons**. Saturated hydrocarbons contain no double or triple bonds. These molecules contain more hydrogen atoms than hydrocarbons that contain double or triple bonds within the same carbon framework, so they are *saturated* with hydrogen.

CORE PROBLEMS

8.21 Identify each of the following molecules as a linear alkane, a branched alkane, or a cycloalkane:

a) $CH_3—CH_2—CH_3$

b) $CH_3—CH(CH_3)—CH_2—CH_3$

c) $CH_2(CH_3)—CH_2—CH_2—CH_3$

d) $CH_2—CH_2$ / $CH_2—CH_2$ (ring)

8.22 Identify each of the following molecules as a linear alkane, a branched alkane, or a cycloalkane:

a) $CH_3—CH_2—CH(CH_3)—CH_3$

b) $CH_3—CH_2—CH_2—CH_2—CH_3$

c) CH_2, CH_2, CH_2, CH_2, CH_2 (ring)

d) $CH_3—CH(CH_2—CH_3)—CH_3$

8.23 a) Draw the condensed structural formula that corresponds to the following full structural formula:

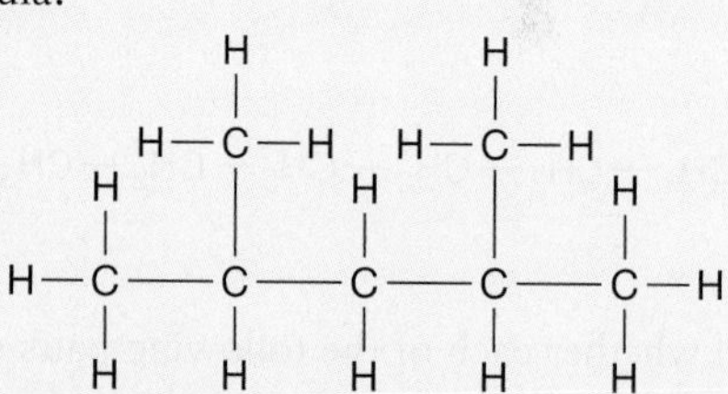

b) Draw the full structural formula that corresponds to the following condensed structural formula:

$CH_3—CH_2—CH(CH_2—CH_3)—CH_2—CH_3$

continued

8.24 a) Draw the condensed structural formula that corresponds to the following full structural formula:

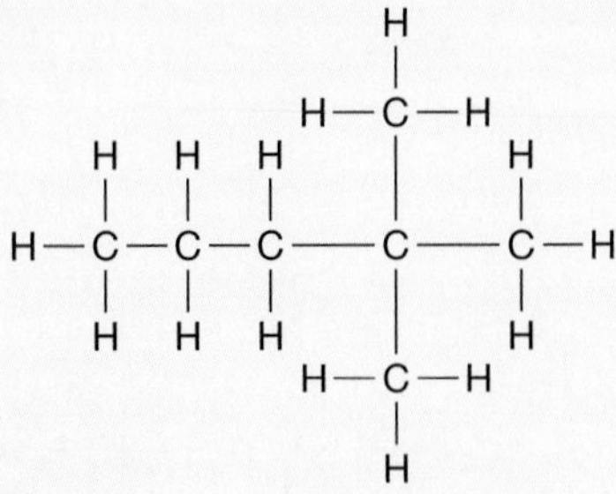

b) Draw the full structural formula that corresponds to the following condensed structural formula:

$$\begin{array}{c} \quad\quad\quad CH_3 \\ \quad\quad\quad | \\ CH_3-CH_2-CH-CH-CH_2-CH_3 \\ \quad\quad\quad\quad\quad | \\ \quad\quad\quad\quad\quad CH_3 \end{array}$$

8.25 Draw the line structures of the molecules in Problem 8.23.

8.26 Draw the line structures of the molecules in Problem 8.24.

8.27 Draw the condensed structural formulas that correspond to the following line structures:

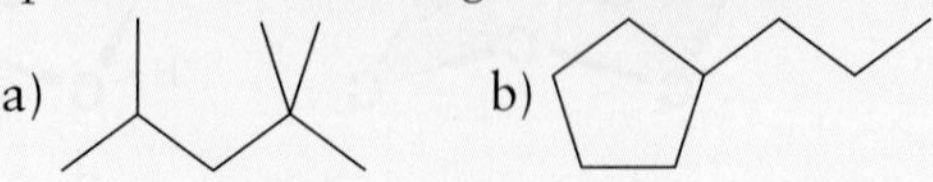

8.28 Draw the condensed structural formulas that correspond to the following line structures:

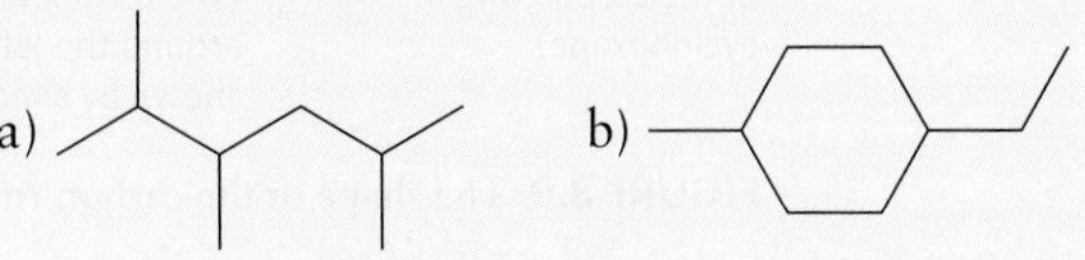

8.29 What, if anything, is wrong with the following condensed structural formula?

$$\begin{array}{c} \quad CH_3 \\ \quad | \\ CH_3-CH_2-CH-CH_2-CH_2-CH_3 \end{array}$$

8.30 What, if anything, is wrong with the following condensed structural formula?

$$\begin{array}{c} CH_3-CH-CH_2-CH_3 \\ | \\ CH_3-CH_2-CH_2 \end{array}$$

8.31 Tell whether each of the following pairs of molecules are isomers. If they are not, explain why not.

a) $CH_3-CH_2-CH_2-CH_2-CH_2-CH_3$ and $\begin{array}{c} CH_3 \quad CH_3 \\ | \quad\quad | \\ CH_3-CH-CH-CH_3 \end{array}$

b) $\begin{array}{l} CH_3 \\ | \\ CH_2-CH_2-CH_2-CH_3 \end{array}$ and $CH_3-CH_2-CH_2-CH_2-CH_3$

c) $CH_3-CH_2-CH_2-CH_2-CH_2-CH_3$ and $\begin{array}{c} CH_2\text{-}CH_2 \\ / \quad\quad \backslash \\ CH_2 \quad\quad CH_2 \\ \backslash \quad\quad / \\ CH_2\text{-}CH_2 \end{array}$

8.32 Tell whether each of the following pairs of molecules are isomers. If they are not, explain why not.

a) $CH_3-CH_2-CH_2-CH_2-CH_3$ and $\begin{array}{l} CH_3 \\ | \\ CH_2-CH_2-CH_2-CH_2-CH_3 \end{array}$

b) $\begin{array}{c} CH_3 \\ | \\ CH_3-CH_2-CH-CH_2-CH_3 \end{array}$ and $\begin{array}{c} CH_3 \\ | \\ CH_3-CH-CH_2-CH_2-CH_3 \end{array}$

c) $\begin{array}{c} CH_2 \\ / \quad \backslash \\ CH_3-CH \quad\quad CH-CH_3 \\ \backslash \quad\quad / \\ CH_2\text{-}CH_2 \end{array}$ and $\begin{array}{c} CH_2 \\ / \quad \backslash \\ CH_2 \quad\quad CH-CH_2-CH_3 \\ \backslash \quad\quad / \\ CH_2\text{-}CH_2 \end{array}$

8.4 Naming Branched Alkanes: The IUPAC System

OBJECTIVES: *Name branched alkanes and cycloalkanes.*

Methane, ethane, and propane are the only alkanes that contain one, two, and three carbon atoms, respectively. However, as we saw in Section 8.3, two alkanes contain four carbon atoms and three contain five carbon atoms. If we continue to increase the number of carbon atoms, the number of isomers also increases. All of the additional isomers are branched alkanes, because there is only one possible linear alkane that corresponds to a given number of carbon atoms. Chemists were able to name the two isomers of butane and the three isomers of pentane using prefixes (pentane, isopentane, and neopentane). However, inventing a new prefix for each isomer clearly becomes impractical as the number of isomers increases. To name larger alkanes, we use a system that was devised by the International Union of Pure and Applied Chemistry and is commonly known as the IUPAC rules.

To name a branched alkane, we start by identifying the longest continuous carbon chain in the molecule. This chain is called the *principal carbon chain.* Then we identify the branches that are attached to the principal chain. These branches are called **alkyl groups.** An alkyl group is an alkane that is lacking one hydrogen atom, allowing it to be attached to a larger molecule, as shown in Figure 8.10.

We name alkyl groups by replacing the *-ane* ending of the corresponding alkane with *-yl,* so a one-carbon alkyl group is called a *methyl* group (pronounced "METH-ull"), a two-carbon alkyl group is an *ethyl* group ("ETH-ull"), and so forth. For chains that contain three or more carbon atoms, there is more than one possible alkyl group, depending on where we remove the hydrogen atom. The names *propyl, butyl,* and so forth, are reserved for the alkyl groups that are missing a hydrogen from the end of the chain. Other alkyl groups have more complex names, which we will not explore. The one exception is the *isopropyl* group, which has a hydrogen atom missing from the middle carbon of propane. The names and structures of the most common alkyl groups are listed in Table 8.9.

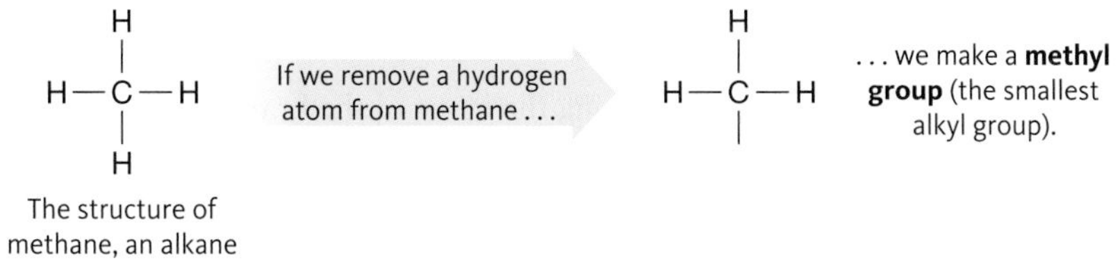

H
|
H—C—H
|
H

The structure of methane, an alkane

If we remove a hydrogen atom from methane . . .

H
|
H—C—H
|

. . . we make a **methyl group** (the smallest alkyl group).

FIGURE 8.10 The relationship between an alkane and an alkyl group.

TABLE 8.9 The Structures of Common Alkyl Groups

Number of Carbon Atoms	Structure	Name
1	CH_3 (bond from C)	methyl
2	CH_2-CH_3 (bond from first C)	ethyl
3	$CH_2-CH_2-CH_3$ (bond from first C)	propyl
3	$CH_3-CH-CH_3$ (bond from middle C)	isopropyl
4	$CH_2-CH_2-CH_2-CH_3$ (bond from first C)	butyl

Let us begin with the IUPAC rules for naming an alkane that has only one branch. We can use isopentane as a typical example. When we name any alkane, we focus on the carbon chain and ignore the hydrogen atoms, so we start with the skeleton structure of isopentane.

```
      CH3                              C
      |                                |
CH3—CH—CH2—CH3                    C—C—C—C
```

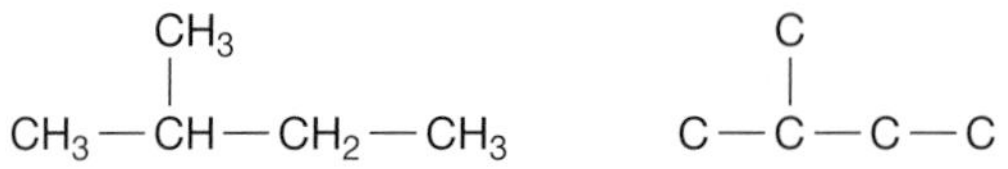

Isopentane | **The skeleton structure of isopentane**

1. Identify and name the principal carbon chain and the alkyl group. The longest continuous chain of carbon atoms in isopentane contains four atoms, as shown here. This is our principal chain, and we name it *butane*. The name of the principal chain does not use the *-yl* ending.

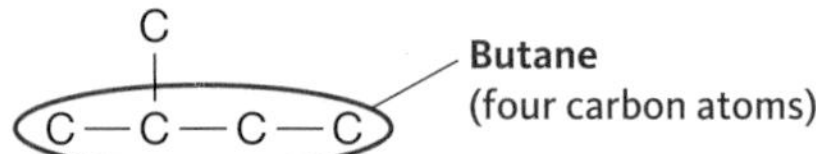

The remaining carbon atom is our branch. This branch is a one-carbon alkyl group, so it is called a *methyl* group.

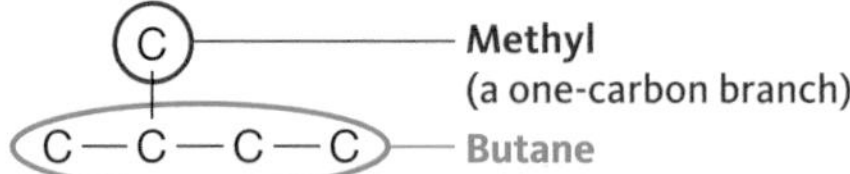

2. Number the carbon atoms in the principal chain, starting from the end that is closest to the alkyl group, and use these numbers to tell where the alkyl group is attached to the principal chain. In isobutane, we number the principal chain from left to right, because the methyl group is closer to the left end of the chain. When we do this, we see that the methyl group is attached to carbon 2 of the principal chain. Therefore, we add a 2 to the name of the alkyl group, giving us *2-methyl.*

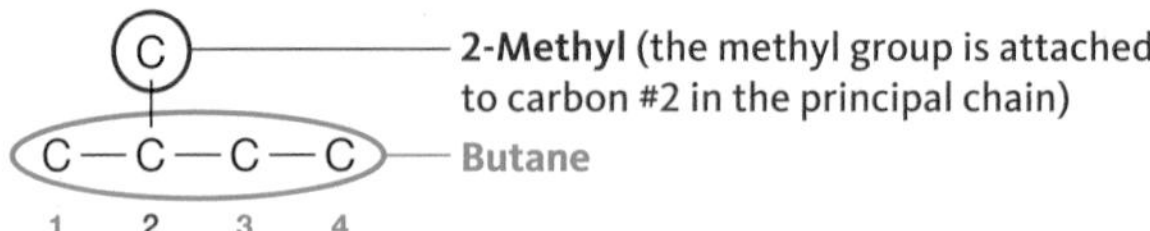

3. Assemble the complete name by writing the name of the branch in front of the name of the principal chain. The IUPAC name for isopentane is *2-methylbutane.* Note that the entire name is written as one word.

The IUPAC rules are designed to give every organic molecule a unique name that does not depend on how we draw the structure of the molecule. For instance, here is another way to draw the carbon skeleton of isopentane:

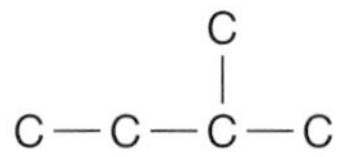

```
        C
        |
  C—C—C—C
```

When we name this structure using the IUPAC rules, we number the principal chain from right to left, because in this drawing the methyl group is closest to the right end of the principal chain. As a result, the name of the molecule is still 2-methylbutane, as shown here. Numbering the chain from left to right would give us two names for the same molecule, which is not allowed in the IUPAC system.

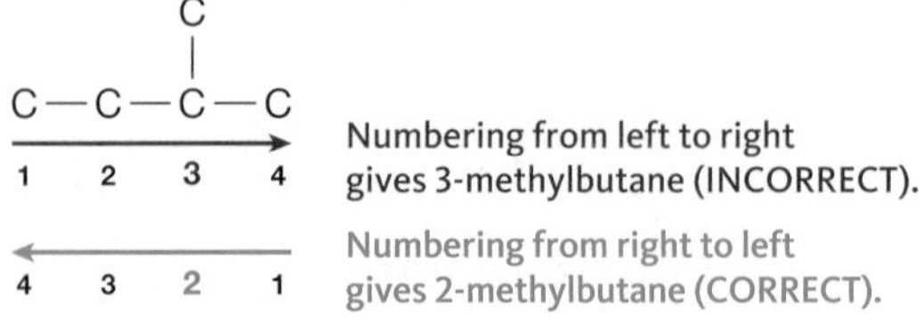

The IUPAC system can help us work out whether two structural formulas represent the same compound or isomers. *If two structural formulas have the same IUPAC name, they represent the same chemical compound.* If the two structural formulas have different IUPAC names but the same chemical formula, they must be isomers.

Sample Problem 8.7

Naming a branched alkane

Name the compound that has the following structure:

$$\begin{array}{c} \qquad\qquad\qquad CH_2-CH_3 \\ \qquad\qquad\qquad | \\ CH_3-CH_2-CH_2-CH-CH_2-CH_3 \end{array}$$

SOLUTION

We can start by drawing the skeleton structure of this molecule, to focus our attention on the carbon atoms.

$$\begin{array}{c} \qquad\quad C-C \\ \qquad\quad | \\ C-C-C-C-C-C \end{array}$$

The principal carbon chain in this structure contains six carbon atoms and is called hexane. The branch is an ethyl group (a two-carbon alkyl group).

$$\begin{array}{c} \qquad\quad C-C \text{ — Ethyl} \\ \qquad\quad | \\ C-C-C-C-C-C \text{ — Hexane} \end{array}$$

Our name must specify where the ethyl group is attached to the principal chain, so we number the principal chain, starting from the end closest to the ethyl group. The ethyl group is bonded to the third carbon atom, so the name of our branch is 3-ethyl.

$$\begin{array}{c} \qquad\quad C-C \text{ — 3-Ethyl} \\ \qquad\quad | \\ C-C-C-C-C-C \text{ — Hexane} \\ 6 \quad 5 \quad 4 \quad 3 \quad 2 \quad 1 \end{array}$$

Finally, we assemble the name. The branch is written before the principal chain, so our molecule is called 3-ethylhexane.

TRY IT YOURSELF: *Name the compound that has the following structure:*

$$\begin{array}{c} \qquad\qquad\qquad CH_2-CH_2-CH_3 \\ \qquad | \\ CH_3-CH_2-CH_2-CH_2-CH-CH_2-CH_2-CH_3 \end{array}$$

For additional practice, try Core Problems 8.35 (parts a and b) and 8.36 (parts a and b).

The rules for naming a cycloalkane that is attached to an alkyl group are similar, except that we do not write a number to show the location of the alkyl group. For example, the following compound is called *methylcyclobutane:*

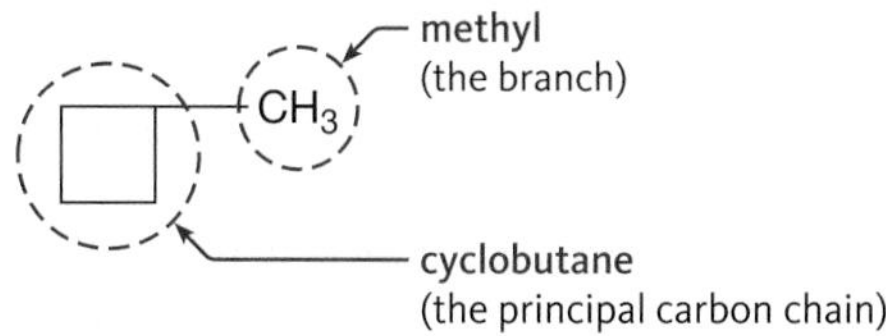

CH_3
methyl
(the branch)
cyclobutane
(the principal carbon chain)

We do not use a number to show where the methyl group is attached because there is only one possible molecule that we can make by connecting a single alkyl group to a ring. For example, all of the structures that follow represent methylcyclobutane. We can produce any of these structures by simply rotating the first one, so these are not isomers.

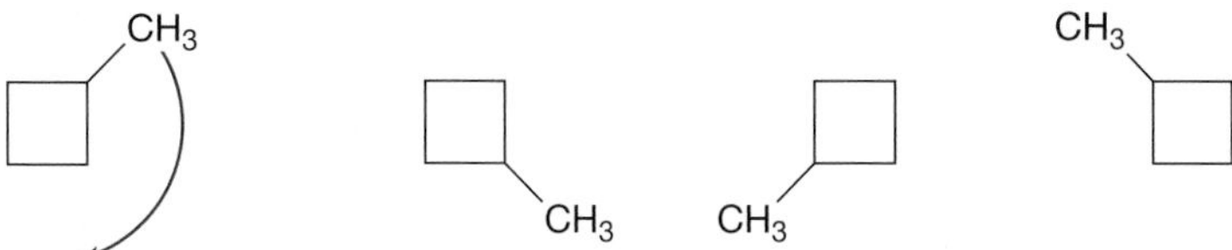

CH_3
CH_3
CH_3
CH_3
We can produce any of the other structures by rotating this one.
These are just different ways of drawing the first structure.

If an alkane has more than one branch, the naming rules become more complex. We will not look at all of the possibilities, but here are the most common situations you might encounter:

1. *The alkane has two or more identical branches.* When an alkane has two or more identical branches, we use the prefixes *di-*, *tri-*, *tetra-*, and so forth, to show the number of identical alkyl groups. Each alkyl group gets a number, and we separate the numbers with commas. If two alkyl groups are attached to the same carbon atom of the principal chain, we write the number twice. For example, here are the two possible molecules we can make by adding two methyl groups to a butane chain:

$CH_3-C(CH_3)_2-CH_2-CH_3$ (carbons numbered 1, 2, 3, 4)

2,2-Dimethylbutane
(Both methyl groups are attached to carbon #2 in the principal chain.)

$CH_3-CH(CH_3)-CH(CH_3)-CH_3$ (carbons numbered 1, 2, 3, 4)

2,3-Dimethylbutane
(One methyl group is attached to carbon #2 and one is attached to carbon #3.)

Regardless of the number of branches, we number the principal chain from the side that is closest to a branch. For example, the following compound is called *2,5,6-trimethyloctane,* not 3,4,7-trimethyloctane:

$CH_3-CH_2-CH(CH_3)-CH(CH_3)-CH_2-CH_2-CH(CH_3)-CH_3$

Numbering from right to left (8 7 6 5 4 3 2 1): CORRECT
2,5,6-trimethyloctane

Numbering from left to right (1 2 3 4 5 6 7 8): INCORRECT

2. *The molecule contains two or more different branches.* In molecules that have alkyl groups that are different sizes, we list the alkyl groups alphabetically. For example, the following molecule contains a propyl group bonded to carbon 4 and a methyl group bonded to carbon 5. This compound is called *5-methyl-4-propylnonane.* Note that we number the principal chain of this molecule from the left side, since the left end is closest to a branch.

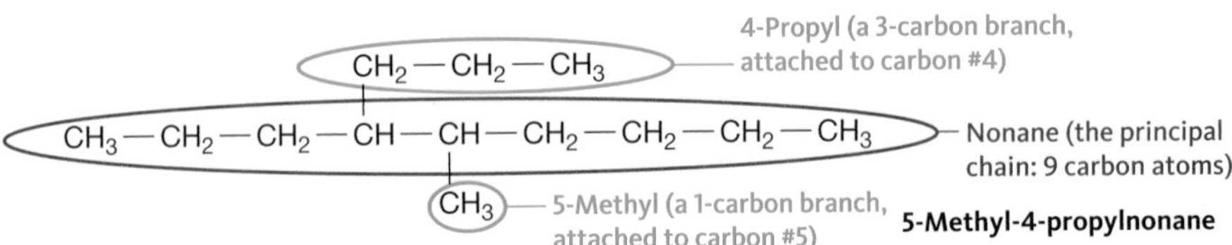

3. *The molecule contains both identical and different branches.* If we have two or more identical branches, we ignore the prefix (*di-*, *tri-*, *tetra-*, and so on) when we alphabetize the names. For example, the molecule that follows is called *4-ethyl-2,3-dimethylhexane.* When we alphabetize the alkyl groups, we ignore the *di-*, so we list *ethyl* before *methyl.*

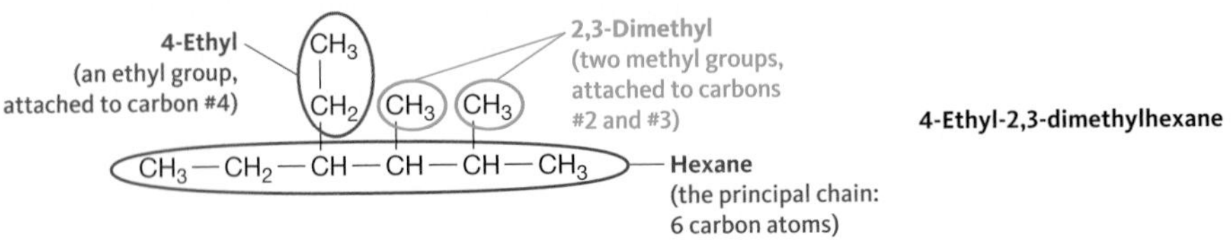

4. *Both ends of the principal chain are the same distance from a branch.* If this happens, we simply proceed to the next branch. For example, in the following molecule, we have a methyl group at position 2 regardless of which way we

number the principal chain. However, we reach a second alkyl group earlier when we number the chain from right to left, so the molecule is called *2,3,5-trimethylhexane.*

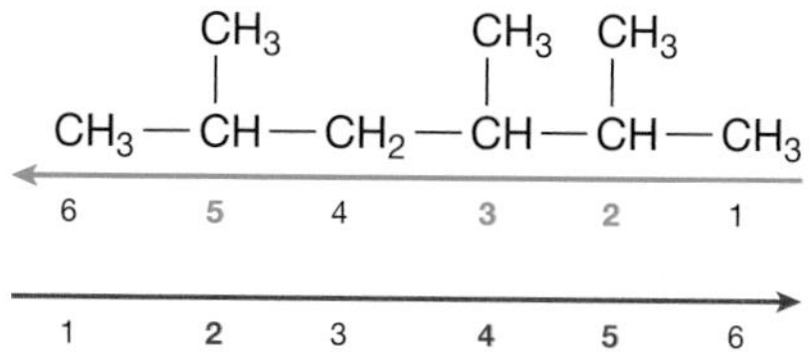

```
CH3            CH3   CH3
 |              |     |
CH3—CH—CH2—CH—CH—CH3
<-------------------------
6    5    4    3    2    1

------------------------->
1    2    3    4    5    6
```

2,3,5-Trimethylhexane

Numbering from right to left: CORRECT
(The second branch is at position 3.)

Numbering from left to right: INCORRECT
(The second branch is at position 4.)

Sample Problem 8.8

Naming an alkane with more than one branch

Name the following alkane, using the IUPAC system:

```
     CH3            CH3   CH3
      |              |     |
CH3—CH—CH2—CH—CH—CH—CH2—CH3
                |
               CH2—CH2—CH3
```

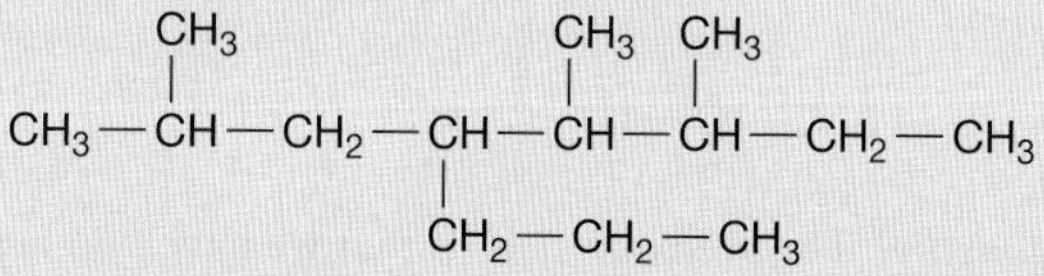

SOLUTION

We begin by identifying the principal chain and the branches. The principal chain contains eight carbon atoms, so we call it octane. There are four alkyl groups attached to the principal chain. Three of these are methyl groups, and one is a propyl group (a three-carbon alkyl group).

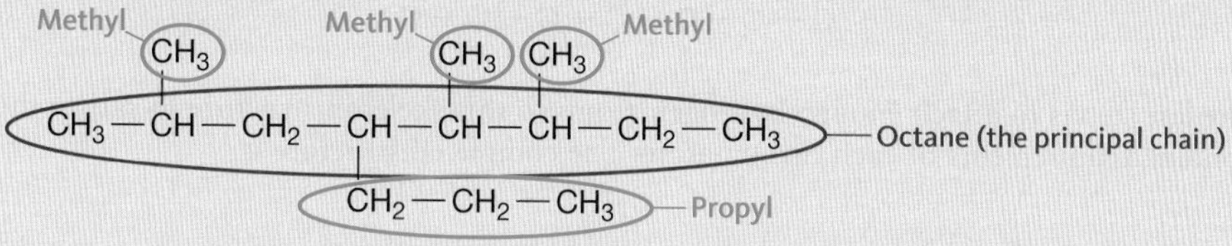

```
Methyl          Methyl       Methyl
 (CH3)           (CH3) (CH3)
   |               |     |
(CH3—CH—CH2—CH—CH—CH—CH2—CH3)—Octane (the principal chain)
              |
          (CH2—CH2—CH3)—Propyl
```

Next, we number the principal chain, being sure to start from the side that is closest to an alkyl group. In this case, the left end of the chain is closest to an alkyl group, so we number from left to right.

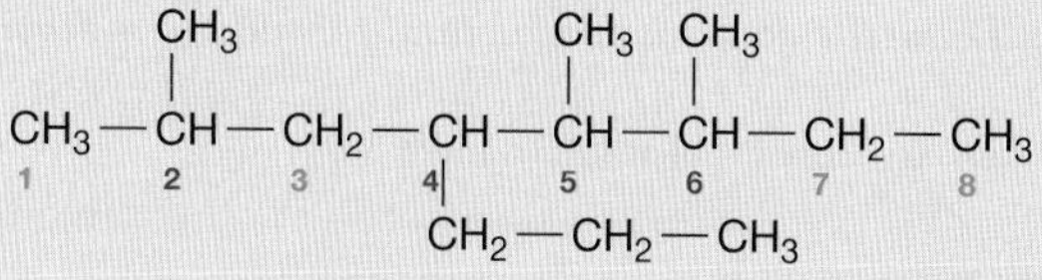

```
     CH3            CH3   CH3
      |              |     |
CH3—CH—CH2—CH—CH—CH—CH2—CH3
 1    2    3   4|  5   6   7    8
               CH2—CH2—CH3
```

Finally, we assemble the name. We write the three methyl groups together, giving each one a number: *2,5,6-trimethyl.* The propyl group is listed separately: *4-propyl.* We then list these groups in alphabetical order, ignoring the prefix *tri-*. The complete IUPAC name of this molecule is 2,5,6-trimethyl-4-propyloctane.

TRY IT YOURSELF: *Name the following alkane, using the IUPAC system:*

```
            CH3—CH2   CH3
                  |     |
CH3—CH2—CH2—C——CH—CH2—CH3
                  |
            CH3—CH2
```

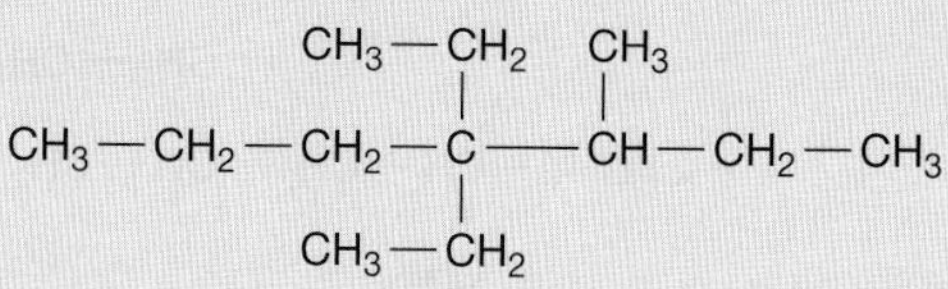

For additional practice, try Core Problems 8.35 (parts c through f) and 8.36 (parts c through f).

When we need to draw the structure of an organic compound from the IUPAC name, we start from the end of the name and work forward, because the principal chain is named last in the IUPAC system. Sample Problem 8.9 illustrates how we can draw the structure of an alkane from its IUPAC name.

Sample Problem 8.9

Drawing the structure of a branched alkane

Draw the condensed structural formula of 2,5-dimethyl-4-ethylheptane.

SOLUTION

The last part of the name is *heptane,* so we know that the principal chain contains seven carbon atoms:

```
C—C—C—C—C—C—C
```

Working our way forward, we come to *4-ethyl.* This tells us that we have a two-carbon alkyl group attached to carbon 4 of the principal chain.

• When you draw a structure, you can number the chain in either direction as long as you keep the same direction from start to finish.

```
            C
            |
            C
            |
C—C—C—C—C—C—C
1  2  3  4  5  6  7
```

Next, we come to *dimethyl.* The prefix *di-* tells us that we have two branches, and the *methyl* tells us that each branch is a single carbon atom. The *2,5* combination at the start of the name tells us that the methyl groups are attached to the second and fifth carbon atoms in our principal chain.

```
            C
            |
     C      C  C
     |      |  |
C—C—C—C—C—C—C
1  2  3  4  5  6  7
```

The last step is to attach enough hydrogen atoms to this skeleton structure to satisfy the bonding requirements of each carbon atom. The completed structure is

• The complete IUPAC rules cover all conceivable structures, but we will not cover more complex alkanes in this text.

```
                        CH3
                        |
         CH3            CH2  CH3
         |              |    |
CH3 — CH — CH2 — CH — CH — CH2 — CH3
```

TRY IT YOURSELF: *Draw the condensed structural formula of 4-ethyl-3-methyloctane.*

For additional practice, try Core Problems 8.37 and 8.38.

CORE PROBLEMS

8.33 What is the name of the following alkyl group?

$CH_3—CH_2—CH_2—$

8.34 What is the name of the following alkyl group?

$CH_3—CH_2—CH_2—CH_2—$

8.35 Name the following compounds using the IUPAC system:

```
              CH3
              |
a) CH3—CH2—CH—CH2—CH3
```

```
                         CH3—CH—CH3
                              |
b) CH3—CH2—CH2—CH2—CH—CH2—CH2—CH3
```

```
                  CH2—CH3
                  |
c) CH3—CH—CH2—CH—CH2—CH2—CH3
       |
       CH3
```

continued

```
   CH3  CH3
    |    |
d) CH3—CH—CH—CH2—CH2—CH3
```

```
      CH3   CH3
       |     |
e) CH3—C—————CH—CH2—CH3
       |
      CH3
```

```
              CH2—CH3      CH3
               |            |
f) CH3—CH2—C—CH2—CH2—CH—CH3
               |
              CH2—CH3
```

g) (cyclohexane ring)   h) (cyclopentane ring with CH3)

8.36 Name the following compounds using the IUPAC system:

```
                     CH3
                      |
                     CH2
                      |
a) CH3—CH2—CH2—CH—CH2—CH2—CH3
```

```
                                   CH3
                                    |
b) CH3—CH2—CH2—CH2—CH2—CH2—CH—CH3
```

```
                  CH3  CH2—CH2—CH3
                   |    |
c) CH3—CH2—CH2—CH—CH—CH2—CH2—CH2—CH3
```

```
              CH2—CH3
               |
d) CH3—CH2—C—CH2—CH3
               |
              CH2—CH3
```

```
             CH3  CH3  CH3
              |    |    |
e) CH3—CH—CH—C—CH3
                        |
                       CH3
```

```
                CH3—CH—CH3
                     |
f) CH3—CH—C—CH2—CH2—CH3
            |   |
           CH3 CH3
```

g) (cyclobutane ring)

h) (cyclohexane ring)—CH2—CH2—CH2—CH3

8.37 Draw condensed structural formulas for each of the following compounds:
a) 4-propylheptane
b) 2,2-dimethylpentane
c) 3-ethyl-4-propylnonane
d) 5-butyl-2,3,4-trimethyldecane
e) cyclopentane
f) isopropylcyclobutane

8.38 Draw condensed structural formulas for each of the following compounds:
a) 5-butylnonane
b) 4-isopropyl-2-methylheptane
c) 2,3,3,4-tetramethylhexane
d) 3,3-diethyl-6,6-dimethyloctane
e) cyclobutane
f) ethylcyclohexane

8.39 Are 3-ethylpentane and 2-methylhexane isomers? Explain why or why not.

8.40 Are 2-methylpentane and 2,2-dimethylbutane isomers? Explain why or why not.

8.5 Functional Groups

OBJECTIVES: *Understand how and why chemists use functional groups to classify organic molecules.*

Saturated hydrocarbons are considered to be the foundation of organic chemistry, because they contain only two elements linked by only one type of bond. In addition, saturated hydrocarbons are very stable and do not react with most other chemicals. For instance, alkanes and cycloalkanes do not react with either strong acids or strong bases, while virtually all other organic compounds react with one or both of these.

Chemists classify all other organic compounds based on how they differ from saturated hydrocarbons. For example, compounds that contain carbon, hydrogen, and chlorine atoms linked by single bonds are classified as *chloroalkanes,* because the chlorine atoms distinguish them from alkanes. Chloroalkanes can react with a range of substances that do not affect alkanes. For example, chloroalkanes react with the strong base NaOH, exchanging the chlorine atom for an O—H group as shown in Figure 8.11. Note that the reaction in Figure 8.11 leaves the hydrocarbon portion of the molecule unchanged. In general, reactions of chloroalkanes only involve the chlorine atom and its immediate neighbors.

Health Note: Ethyl chloride, $CH_3—CH_2—Cl$, is used to numb the skin and relieve pain. When it is sprayed on the skin, it evaporates almost instantly, absorbing heat as it does. The resulting temperature drop numbs the nerve endings in the skin.

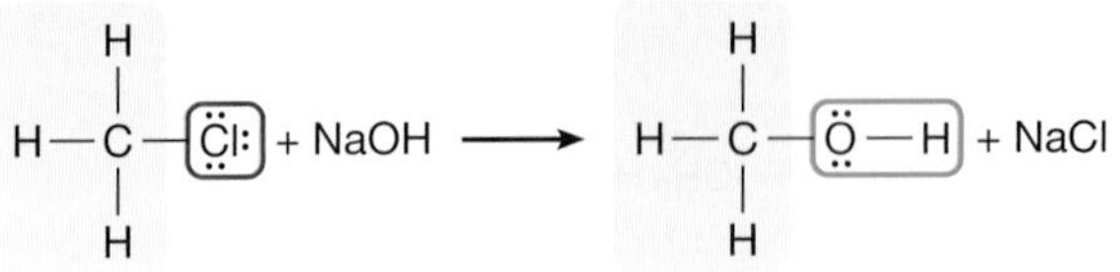

$$H{-}\underset{H}{\overset{H}{C}}{-}\boxed{\ddot{\underset{..}{Cl}}:} + NaOH \longrightarrow H{-}\underset{H}{\overset{H}{C}}{-}\boxed{\ddot{\underset{..}{O}}{-}H} + NaCl$$

FIGURE 8.11 The reaction of a chloroalkane with NaOH.

Organic Compounds Are Classified by Their Functional Groups

Chemists describe and classify organic molecules in terms of **functional groups.** *A functional group is a structural feature that is not found in saturated hydrocarbons.* The structural feature can contain atoms such as oxygen, nitrogen, or chlorine, or it can be a double or triple bond between carbon atoms. For example, compounds that contain a carbon–carbon double bond are called alkenes, and the double bond is called an alkene functional group. Table 8.10 shows several important functional groups.

TABLE 8.10 Some Representative Functional Groups in Organic Chemistry

Functional Group	Name	An Example of a Compound That Contains This Group:
$\rangle C{=}C\langle$	alkene	$CH_3{-}CH{=}CH_2$ propene
$-C{\equiv}C-$	alkyne	$CH_3{-}C{\equiv}CH$ propyne
$-\overset{\mid}{\underset{\mid}{C}}-\ddot{\underset{..}{Cl}}:$	chloroalkane	$CH_3{-}CH_2{-}CH_2{-}Cl$ 1-chloropropane
$-\overset{\mid}{\underset{\mid}{C}}-\ddot{\underset{..}{O}}-H$	alcohol	$CH_3{-}CH_2{-}CH_2{-}OH$ 1-propanol
$-\overset{\mid}{\underset{\mid}{C}}-\overset{\mid}{\underset{..}{N}}-$	amine	$CH_3{-}CH_2{-}CH_2{-}NH_2$ propylamine
$-\overset{\ddot{O}:}{\overset{\Vert}{C}}-H$	aldehyde	$CH_3{-}CH_2{-}\overset{O}{\overset{\Vert}{C}}{-}H$ propanal
$-\overset{\ddot{O}:}{\overset{\Vert}{C}}-\ddot{\underset{..}{O}}-H$	carboxylic acid	$CH_3{-}CH_2{-}\overset{O}{\overset{\Vert}{C}}{-}OH$ propanoic acid

In the rest of this chapter, we will look at the remaining classes of hydrocarbons: alkenes, alkynes, and aromatic compounds. Each of these contains at least one multiple bond (double or triple) between a pair of carbon atoms. In Chapters 9 through 12, we examine some of the properties and reactions of the other important functional groups.

Sample Problem 8.10

Identifying compounds that contain the same functional group

Ethanol has the following condensed structural formula:

$$CH_3{-}CH_2{-}OH$$

continued

Which of the following molecules should show similar chemical behavior to ethanol, based on their functional groups?

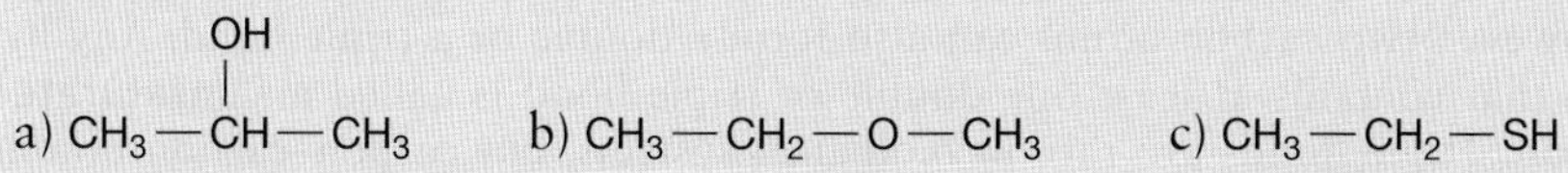

a) $CH_3-\underset{}{\overset{OH}{\overset{|}{C}H}}-CH_3$ **2-Propanol**

b) $CH_3-CH_2-O-CH_3$ **Ethyl methyl ether**

c) CH_3-CH_2-SH **Ethanethiol**

SOLUTION

Ethanol contains an alcohol functional group, in which a carbon atom is bonded to an OH group. Of the three molecules in the problem, only 2-propanol contains this functional group, so 2-propanol should show similar chemical behavior to ethanol.

TRY IT YOURSELF: *Acetic acid has the following condensed structural formula:*

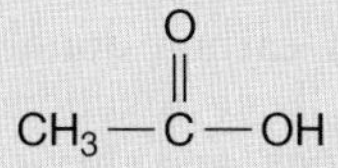

$$CH_3-\overset{O}{\overset{\|}{C}}-OH$$

Which of the following molecules should show similar chemical behavior to acetic acid, based on their functional groups?

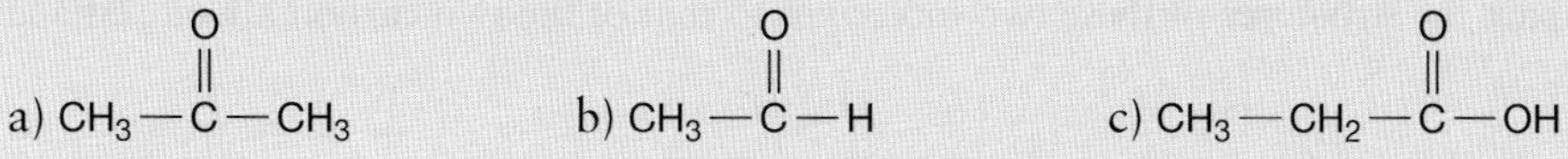

a) $CH_3-\overset{O}{\overset{\|}{C}}-CH_3$ **Acetone**

b) $CH_3-\overset{O}{\overset{\|}{C}}-H$ **Acetaldehyde**

c) $CH_3-CH_2-\overset{O}{\overset{\|}{C}}-OH$ **Propanoic acid**

For additional practice, try Core Problems 8.43 and 8.44.

CORE PROBLEMS

8.41 Which of the following molecules contain a functional group? Circle the functional group (if any) in each molecule.

$CH_3-\overset{CH_3}{\overset{|}{C}H}-CH_3$ $\quad$ $CH_3-\overset{OH}{\overset{|}{C}H}-CH_3$

$CH_3-\overset{CH_2}{\overset{\|}{C}}-CH_3$ $\quad$ cyclopentane: CH_2 ring (CH_2 / CH_2 CH_2 / CH_2-CH_2)

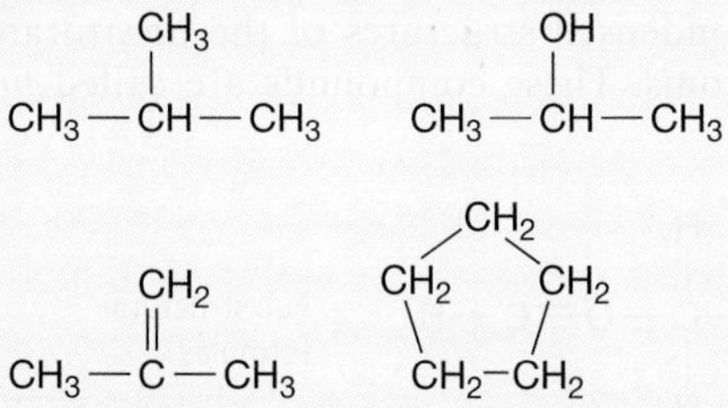

8.42 Which of the following molecules contain a functional group? Circle the functional group (if any) in each molecule.

$HC\equiv C-CH_3$ $\quad$ $\overset{CH_3}{\overset{|}{CH_3-CH_2}}$ $\quad$ $CH_3-\overset{O}{\overset{\|}{CH}}$

$CH_3-\overset{Br}{\overset{|}{CH_2}}$ $\quad$ cyclobutane ring: $CH_2-CH-CH_3$ / CH_2-CH_2 (four-membered ring with CH_3 substituent)

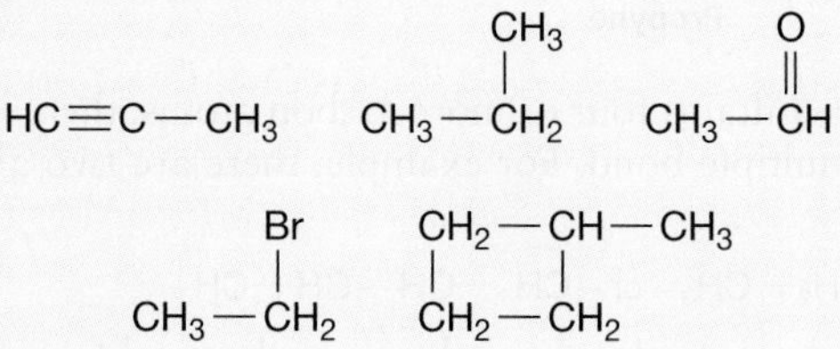

8.43 The following molecule is called 1-butene:

$$CH_2=CH-CH_2-CH_3$$

Which of the following compounds should show similar chemical behavior to 1-butene, based on their functional groups?

a) $O=CH-CH_2-CH_3$
b) $NH=CH-CH_2-CH_3$
c) $CH_3-CH=CH-CH_2-CH_3$
d) $CH_2=CH-CH_3$

8.44 The following molecule is called 1-propyne:

$$CH_3-C\equiv CH$$

Which of the following compounds should show similar chemical behavior to 1-propyne, based on their functional groups?

a) $CH_3-C\equiv N$

b) $CH_3-\overset{CH_3}{\overset{|}{C}H}-\overset{CH_3}{\overset{|}{C}H}-C\equiv CH$

c) $CH_3-C\equiv C-CH_3$

d) $CH_3-CH=CH_2$

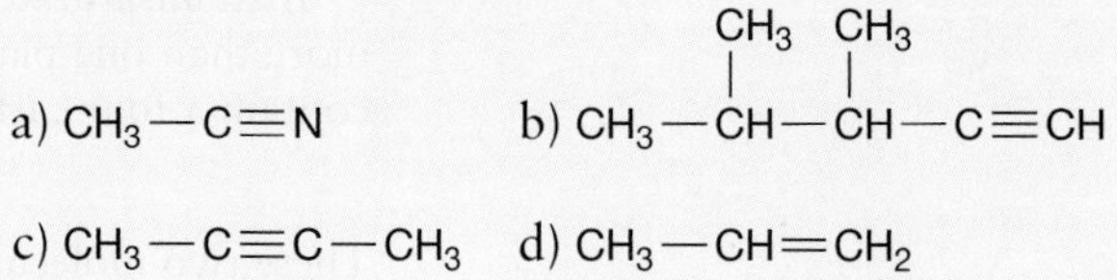

OBJECTIVES: *Name and draw the structures of linear alkenes and alkynes, and describe how the atoms are arranged around a double or triple bond.*

Health Note: Limonene is toxic to insects and is the active ingredient in termite treatments that use orange oil. It is not hazardous to humans or pets, but it does not reach all parts of a building and it breaks down within a week, so it can only be used for limited infestations.

The smell of oranges is due primarily to limonene, an alkene.

8.6 Alkenes and Alkynes

In a saturated hydrocarbon, all of the carbon atoms are linked to one another by single bonds. However, two carbon atoms can also form a double or a triple bond. Any hydrocarbon that contains at least one double or triple bond is called an **unsaturated hydrocarbon.** Triple bonds are rare in biological systems, but carbon–carbon double bonds are fairly common. For example, the compound that is responsible for the characteristic aroma of oranges is limonene, a hydrocarbon that contains two double bonds.

CH_3—(ring)—$C(CH_3){=}CH_2$

Limonene

Molecules that contain a carbon–carbon double bond are called **alkenes**, and the double bond is referred to as the alkene functional group. Molecules that contain a carbon–carbon triple bond are **alkynes**, and they contain the alkyne functional group. Alkenes and alkynes are similar in many of their physical and chemical properties, and they are named in similar ways, so we will consider them together.

The simplest alkene and alkyne are called *ethylene* and *acetylene*, respectively. Let us compare the structures of these two molecules to that of the two-carbon alkane, ethane.

$H_3C{-}CH_3$ $H_2C{=}CH_2$ $H{-}C{\equiv}C{-}H$

Ethane (C_2H_6) An alkane   **Ethylene (C_2H_4)** An alkene   **Acetylene (C_2H_2)** An alkyne

Note that ethylene and acetylene contain fewer hydrogen atoms than ethane, because the double and triple bonds account for two or three of the four bonds around the carbon atoms. Alkanes always contain more hydrogen atoms than unsaturated hydrocarbons with the same carbon skeleton.

Larger alkenes and alkynes contain single bonds in addition to the double or triple bond. Here are the full and condensed structures of the unsaturated hydrocarbons that contain three carbon atoms. These compounds are called *propylene* and *propyne*.

Full structural formulas: $H_3C{-}CH{=}CH_2$ $H_3C{-}C{\equiv}C{-}H$

Condensed structural formulas: $CH_3{-}CH{=}CH_2$ $CH_3{-}C{\equiv}CH$

Propylene   **Propyne**

If an unsaturated hydrocarbon contains four or more carbon atoms, there is generally more than one place to put the multiple bond. For example, there are two alkenes that contain a four-carbon chain:

$$CH_2{=}CH{-}CH_2{-}CH_3 \quad \text{or} \quad CH_3{-}CH{=}CH{-}CH_3$$

These two molecules are isomers, because they have the same chemical formula but different structures. We can also draw a third isomer that contains a branched chain.

$$CH_2{=}C(CH_3){-}CH_3$$

Trigonal planar arrangement of bonds around a carbon atom

H H / C=C / H H

The actual structure of ethylene: each carbon atom forms a trigonal planar arrangement.

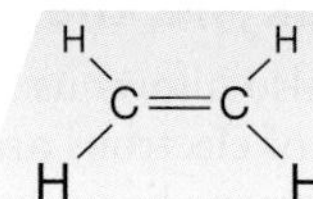

Side view of ethylene (all six atoms can be placed on a flat surface)

FIGURE 8.12 The trigonal planar arrangement.

For most compounds that contain a functional group, we can generate isomers either by moving the functional group to a different location or by rearranging the carbon skeleton. As a result, compounds with functional groups generally have more isomers than do the corresponding alkanes. For instance, there are three five-carbon alkanes, but we can make six five-carbon alkenes.

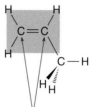

These two carbon atoms form the double bond and adopt the trigonal planar arrangement.

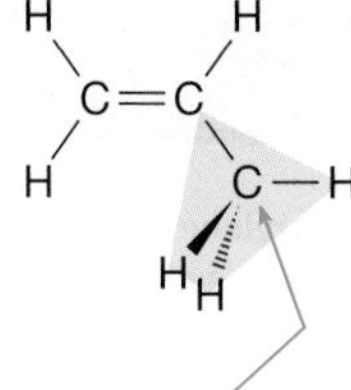

This carbon atom forms four single bonds and adopts the tetrahedral arrangement.

FIGURE 8.13 The structure of propylene.

Alkenes Contain a Trigonal Planar Arrangement of Atoms

The actual structures of alkenes, like those of alkanes, do not look like the structural formulas as we normally draw them. Using the VSEPR model, we can predict that when a carbon atom forms a double bond, the other two bonds to the carbon atom arrange themselves so that the three sets of electrons are as far apart as possible, as shown in Figure 8.12. This is called the **trigonal planar arrangement.**

Only the two carbon atoms that form the double bond adopt the trigonal planar arrangement. In propylene, for example, one carbon atom forms four single bonds. These bonds arrange themselves in a tetrahedron, just as they do in alkanes. Figure 8.13 shows the actual shape of the propylene molecule.

Sample Problem 8.11

Drawing the trigonal planar arrangement

Vinyl chloride is used to make polyvinyl chloride (PVC), and it has the condensed structure shown here. Draw a full structural formula that shows the actual shape of this molecule.

$$CH_2{=}CH{-}Cl$$

SOLUTION

First, we can sketch the arrangement of bonds around the carbon–carbon double bond.

C=C

The left-hand carbon atom is bonded to two hydrogen atoms, while the right-hand carbon atom is bonded to hydrogen and to chlorine. Adding these atoms gives our structure.

H Cl / C=C / H H

The chlorine atom has three additional pairs of electrons around it, but structural formulas normally omit these nonbonding electrons.

TRY IT YOURSELF: *Tetrafluoroethylene is used to make Teflon, and it has the condensed structure shown here. Draw a full structural formula that shows the actual shape of this molecule.*

$$CF_2{=}CF_2$$

For additional practice, try Core Problem 8.49.

PVC is durable and does not rust, so PVC pipes are widely used in plumbing.

In an Alkyne, the Triple Bond and the Neighboring Bonds Line Up

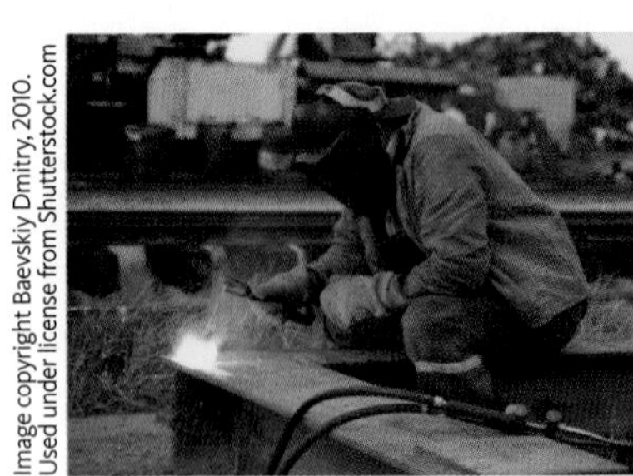

Acetylene produces an extremely hot flame when it burns, so it is the fuel of choice for welding.

VSEPR also allows us to predict the arrangement of atoms in an alkyne. There are only two sets of electrons around each carbon atom (the single bond and the triple bond), so these electrons lie on opposite sides of the carbon atom. As a result, the triple bond and the two adjacent single bonds form a straight line. In acetylene, all four atoms line up.

These two bonds lie on opposite sides of the left-hand carbon atom, as far apart as possible.

$$H-C\equiv C-H$$

These two bonds lie on opposite sides of the right-hand carbon atom, as far apart as possible.

In propyne, four of the atoms form a straight line, as shown here. The hydrogen atoms attached to the left-hand carbon atom adopt the tetrahedral arrangement.

$$H_3C-C\equiv C-H$$

Alkenes and Alkynes Can Be Named Using the IUPAC Rules

The naming of alkenes and alkynes by the IUPAC system provides a good introduction to how we name organic compounds that contain a functional group. In general, the name must describe the hydrocarbon framework of the molecule, identify the functional group, and tell where the functional group is located. Here are the IUPAC rules for naming unbranched alkenes and alkynes:

1. Name the compound as if it were an alkane, ignoring the functional group.
2. Change the *-ane* ending of the alkane name to *-ene* (for an alkene) or *-yne* (for an alkyne). The ending of an IUPAC name identifies the functional group.
3. Number the carbon–carbon bonds starting from the end closest to the functional group, and use these numbers to identify the position of the multiple bond.
4. Assemble the name by writing the number (from step 3) followed by the name. Use a hyphen to separate numbers from words.

Let us apply the IUPAC rules to the two compounds that follow. Both of these compounds contain a four-carbon unbranched chain, so we start with the name *butane*. Since the compounds contain a double bond, we change the ending from *-ane* to *-ene*, giving us *butene*. Finally, we number the carbon–carbon bonds so that we can show the position of the double bond. In the left-hand compound, the double bond is the first carbon–carbon bond, so this compound is *1-butene*. The second compound has the double bond at the second position, making it *2-butene*.

$$CH_2\overset{1}{=}CH\overset{2}{-}CH_2\overset{3}{-}CH_3 \qquad CH_3\overset{1}{-}CH\overset{2}{=}CH\overset{3}{-}CH_3$$

1-Butene   **2-Butene**

Sample Problem 8.12

Naming alkenes and alkynes

Name the compound whose condensed structure is

$$CH_3-CH_2-CH_2-C\equiv C-CH_3$$

SOLUTION

Let's start by drawing the skeleton structure of this molecule, being sure to keep the triple bond.

$$C-C-C-C\equiv C-C$$

continued

This is a six-carbon chain, which would be called *hexane* if it were an alkane. However, there is a triple bond in the chain, so we must change the ending of the name to *-yne*, giving us *hexyne*.

Our name is not yet complete, because we need to tell where the functional group is. To do so, we number the bonds in our chain, starting from the right side because it is closer to the triple bond.

$$C \overset{5}{-} C \overset{4}{-} C \overset{3}{-} C \overset{2}{\equiv} C \overset{1}{-} C$$

The second bond is the triple bond, so the complete name of our molecule is 2-hexyne.

TRY IT YOURSELF: *Name the compound whose condensed structure is*

$$CH_3-CH=CH-CH_2-CH_2-CH_2-CH_3$$

For additional practice, try Core Problems 8.51 (omit part b) and 8.52 (omit part c).

Sample Problem 8.13

Drawing the structures of alkenes and alkynes

Draw the full and condensed structural formulas of 1-pentene.

SOLUTION

The name *pentene* tells us that we have a five-carbon chain *(pent-)* that contains a double bond *(-ene)*. Let's start by drawing the carbon chain, using single bonds for now.

$$C-C-C-C-C$$

Next, we need to add the double bond. The *1* at the beginning of the name tells us that the first carbon–carbon bond is the double bond.

$$C \overset{1}{=} C \overset{2}{-} C \overset{3}{-} C \overset{4}{-} C$$

This is our skeleton structure. To complete the structure, we must add the correct number of hydrogen atoms to each carbon atom. Remember that the double bond counts as two bonds.

```
 H   H   H   H   H
 |   |   |   |   |
H—C═C—C—C—C—H
         |   |   |
         H   H   H
```

Full structural formula of 1-pentene

$$CH_2=CH-CH_2-CH_2-CH_3$$

Condensed structural formula of 1-pentene

We can also draw line structures of alkenes. Here is the line structure of 1-pentene:

TRY IT YOURSELF: *Draw the full and condensed structural formulas of 3-hexyne.*

For additional practice, try Core Problems 8.53 (omit part a) and 8.54 (omit part c).

For the alkenes and alkynes that contain two or three carbon atoms, there is only one possible position for the multiple bond. When there is only one possible location for a functional group, the IUPAC name does not include a number. For example, the IUPAC name for acetylene is *ethyne* (not 1-ethyne) and the IUPAC name for propylene is *propene* (not 1-propene). However, we can make at least two alkenes or alkynes from any carbon chain that contains four or more carbon atoms, so we must use numbers to show the position of the double bond in all larger alkenes and alkynes.

Cycloalkenes Contain a Double Bond within a Ring of Carbon Atoms

A ring of carbon atoms cannot contain a triple bond unless it is very large, but any ring can contain a double bond. When a hydrocarbon contains an alkene group within a ring of carbon atoms, it is called a **cycloalkene**. To name a cycloalkene, we need only change the ending of the corresponding cycloalkane from *-ane* to *-ene*. We do not need to add a number to show the position of the double bond. The structures of the three smallest cycloalkenes are shown in Table 8.11.

TABLE 8.11 The Structures and Names of Some Cycloalkenes

Name	Condensed Structural Formula	Line Structure
cyclopropene	CH_2 (ring) / $CH{=}CH$	△
cyclobutene	$CH_2{-}CH_2$ / $CH{=}CH$	□
cyclopentene	CH_2 / CH_2 CH_2 / $CH{=}CH$	⬠

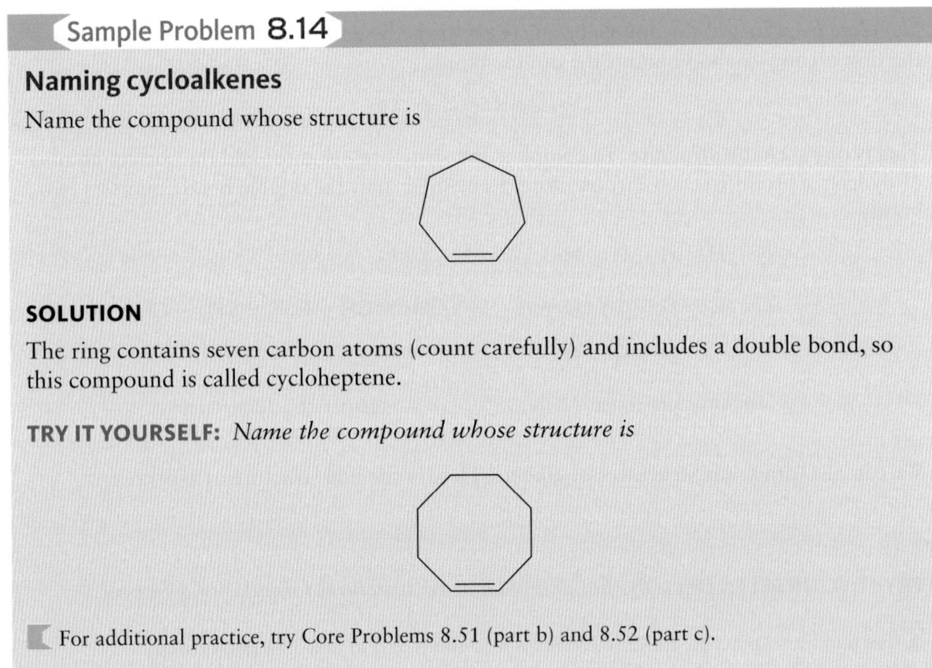

Sample Problem 8.14

Naming cycloalkenes

Name the compound whose structure is

SOLUTION

The ring contains seven carbon atoms (count carefully) and includes a double bond, so this compound is called cycloheptene.

TRY IT YOURSELF: *Name the compound whose structure is*

For additional practice, try Core Problems 8.51 (part b) and 8.52 (part c).

In a Branched Alkene or Alkyne, the Functional Group Determines the Principal Chain

Alkenes and alkynes can contain branches. To name a branched alkene or alkyne using the IUPAC system, we need two additional rules:

1. *The principal chain is the longest chain that includes the functional group.* This may not be the longest carbon chain in the molecule.
2. *The principal chain is numbered from the side closest to the functional group, regardless of the positions of the branches.*

For instance, let us name the following molecule using the IUPAC rules:

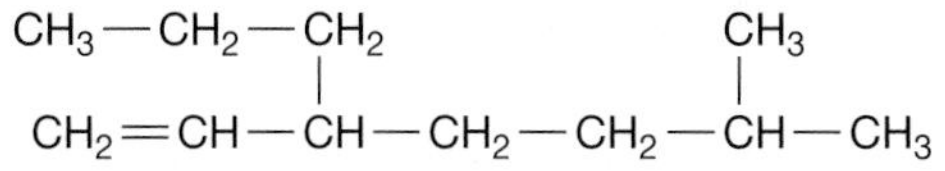

$$\begin{array}{l} CH_3-CH_2-CH_2 \qquad\qquad\qquad CH_3 \\ \qquad\qquad\qquad\;\; | \qquad\qquad\qquad\qquad\;\; | \\ CH_2{=}CH-CH-CH_2-CH_2-CH-CH_3 \end{array}$$

The longest chain in the molecule contains eight carbon atoms, but this chain does not contain the functional group. The longest chain that includes the alkene group contains seven carbon atoms.

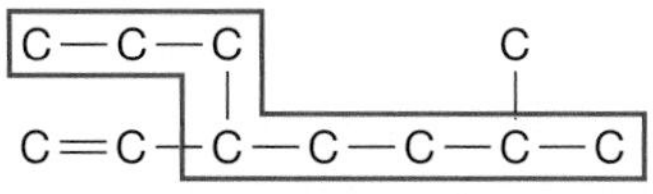

Incorrect principal chain—8 carbon atoms (does not contain the alkene group)

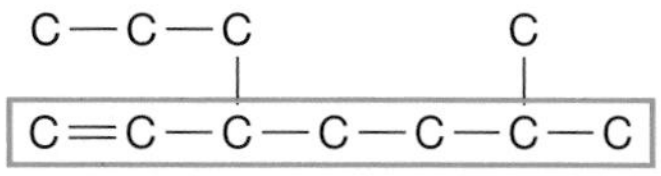

Correct principal chain—7 carbon atoms (contains the alkene group)

Now we number the principal chain. We must start from the side *closest to the alkene group,* so we number the chain from left to right. The double bond is the first carbon–carbon bond, so our principal chain is called 1-heptene.

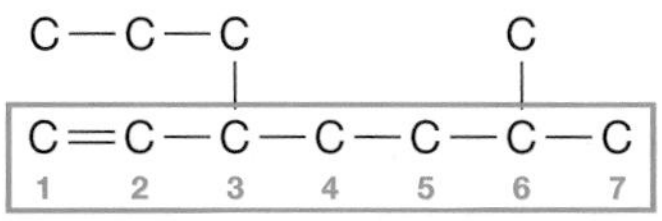

1-Heptene

Finally, we list the alkyl groups. We have a propyl group (three carbon atoms) attached to carbon 3, and we have a methyl group attached to carbon 6.

3-Propyl 6-Methyl 1-Heptene

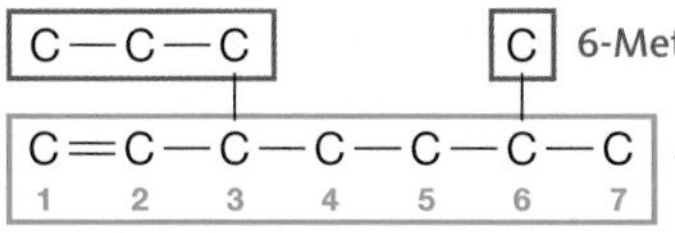

When we assemble the name, we alphabetize the alkyl groups, so the IUPAC name for this molecule is *6-methyl-3-propyl-1-heptene.*

Many Organic Compounds Have Trivial Names

The names ethylene, propylene, and acetylene are commonly used, but they are not part of the IUPAC system. They are examples of **trivial names**, names that were given to compounds that were discovered before the IUPAC system came into widespread use. Many common organic compounds have trivial names. Sometimes the trivial name is used almost exclusively. For example, the two-carbon alkyne is virtually always called *acetylene* rather than ethyne. Trivial names are particularly common when the IUPAC name for a compound is cumbersome. Imagine the confusion that would result if we used the IUPAC name 8,13-dimethyl-14-(1,5-dimethylhexyl)tetracyclo[8.7.0.$0^{3,8}$.$0^{13,17}$]heptadec-2-en-5-ol for the common compound we know as cholesterol!

In some cases, both the IUPAC name and the trivial name are in common use. For example, the molecule that follows is called both *isopropyl alcohol* (a trivial name) and *2-propanol* (an IUPAC name). This compound is the main constituent of most rubbing alcohols.

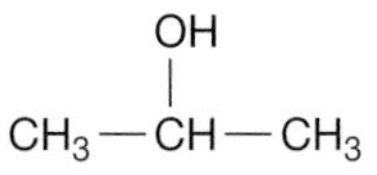

$$\begin{array}{c} OH \\ | \\ CH_3-CH-CH_3 \end{array}$$

2-Propanol (IUPAC name)

Isopropyl alcohol (trivial name)

This text uses trivial names whenever they are most familiar to users of common organic compounds, with the IUPAC names given as alternatives when they are also in widespread use.

CORE PROBLEMS

8.45 What structural feature is present in an alkene?

8.46 What structural feature is present in an alkyne?

8.47 Classify each of the following molecules as an alkane, an alkene, or an alkyne:

a)
$$\begin{array}{c} \quad\; CH_3 \\ \quad\;| \\ CH_3-CH-CH_3 \end{array}$$

b) $CH_3-C\equiv C-CH_3$

c)
$$\begin{array}{l} \quad\;\;\; CH_3 \\ \quad\;\;\;| \\ CH_3-CH-CH=CH_2 \end{array}$$

8.48 Classify each of the following molecules as an alkane, an alkene, or an alkyne:

a)
$$\begin{array}{l} \qquad\quad CH_3 \\ \qquad\quad | \\ HC\equiv C-CH-CH_3 \end{array}$$

b)
$$\begin{array}{l} \qquad\qquad\quad CH_3 \\ \qquad\qquad\quad | \\ CH_3-CH_2-CH-CH_3 \end{array}$$

c)
$$\begin{array}{l} \qquad\; CH_3 \\ \qquad\; | \\ CH_2=C-CH_2-CH_3 \end{array}$$

8.49 Draw a full structure of perchloroethylene that shows the actual arrangement of the atoms.

$$\begin{array}{l} \quad\; Cl \;\; Cl \\ \quad\; | \quad\; | \\ Cl-C=C-Cl \end{array}$$

Perchloroethylene

8.50 Draw a full structure of dichloroacetylene that shows the actual arrangement of the atoms.

$$\begin{array}{l} Cl \;\; Cl \\ | \quad\; | \\ C\equiv C \end{array}$$

Dichloroacetylene

8.51 Name the following compounds, using the IUPAC system:

a) $CH_2=CH-CH_2-CH_2-CH_2-CH_3$

b) 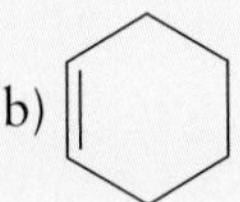

c) $CH_3-CH_2-CH_2-CH_2-C\equiv C-CH_3$

d) $HC\equiv C-CH_3$

e)
$$\begin{array}{l} \qquad\; CH_3 \\ \qquad\; | \\ CH_3-CH-CH_2-CH=CH-CH_2-CH_3 \end{array}$$

f)
$$\begin{array}{l} \qquad\qquad CH_3-CH_2 \;\; CH_3 \\ \qquad\qquad\qquad\quad | \qquad\;\; | \\ CH_3-CH_2-C=C-CH_3 \end{array}$$

8.52 Name the following compounds, using the IUPAC system:

a) $CH_3-CH_2-CH_2-CH=CH-CH_2-CH_3$

b) $HC\equiv C-CH_2-CH_3$

c) [cyclopentene ring]

d) $CH_2=CH_2$

e)
$$\begin{array}{l} \qquad\qquad\qquad\qquad\quad CH_2-CH_3 \\ \qquad\qquad\qquad\qquad\quad | \\ CH_3-CH_2-CH_2-CH-CH=CH_2 \end{array}$$

f)
$$\begin{array}{l} \qquad\qquad\qquad\qquad\quad CH_3 \;\; CH_3 \\ \qquad\qquad\qquad\qquad\quad | \qquad | \\ CH_3-CH_2-C\equiv C-CH-CH-CH_3 \end{array}$$

8.53 Draw condensed structural formulas for the following molecules:

a) cyclobutene
b) 3-octene
c) 1-hexyne
d) acetylene
e) 3-ethyl-1-hexene
f) 2,2-dimethyl-3-octyne

8.54 Draw condensed structural formulas for the following molecules:

a) propene
b) 2-heptyne
c) cyclohexene
d) ethylene
e) 3-methyl-3-hexene
f) 4-ethyl-3-methyl-1-hexyne

8.55 Draw the line structure of 4-methyl-1-pentene.

8.56 Draw the line structure of 2-methyl-3-hexene.

8.57 Draw the condensed structural formula that corresponds to the following line structure:

[line structure]

8.58 Draw the condensed structural formula that corresponds to the following line structure:

[line structure]

8.59 What (if anything) is wrong with the following condensed structural formula?

$$\begin{array}{l} \qquad\; CH_3 \\ \qquad\; | \\ CH_3-CH=CH-CH_3 \end{array}$$

8.60 What (if anything) is wrong with the following condensed structural formula?

$CH_2\equiv CH-CH_3$

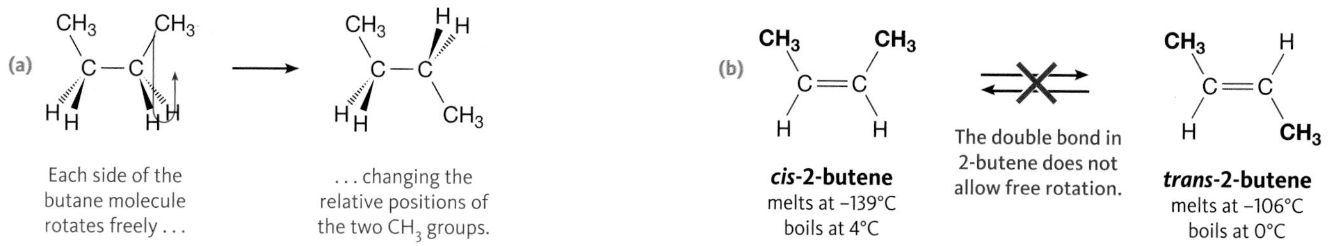

(a)

Each side of the butane molecule rotates freely . . .

. . . changing the relative positions of the two CH_3 groups.

(b)

cis-2-butene
melts at −139°C
boils at 4°C

The double bond in 2-butene does not allow free rotation.

trans-2-butene
melts at −106°C
boils at 0°C

FIGURE 8.14 The structures and behaviors of (a) butane and (b) 2-butene.

8.7 *Cis* and *Trans* Isomers of Alkenes

OBJECTIVES: *Name and draw the* cis *and* trans *forms of an alkene, and distinguish constitutional isomers and stereoisomers.*

In an alkane such as ethane, the single bond permits free rotation of the two carbon atoms that it joins. As a result, each end of the ethane molecule can rotate like a little propeller.

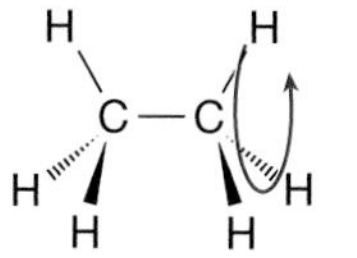

This rotation has a significant impact on the shapes of larger alkanes. In butane, rotation around the central carbon–carbon bond moves the CH_3 groups on the ends of the molecule alternately closer together and farther apart, as shown in Figure 8.14a. As a result, alkanes are flexible molecules, able to adopt a range of shapes while retaining the tetrahedral arrangement around each carbon atom.

By contrast, *carbon–carbon double bonds do not permit free rotation.* Let us look at the structure of 2-butene, focusing our attention on the atoms surrounding the double bond. The condensed structural formula of 2-butene is

$$CH_3{-}CH{=}CH{-}CH_3$$

If we draw the double bond in a way that shows the actual locations of the neighboring atoms, we find that we can produce two possible structures for 2-butene. One structure has the two CH_3 groups closer together than the other does, as shown in Figure 8.14b. The double bond does not allow rotation, so the two CH_3 groups are locked into their relative positions, either closer together or farther apart. As a result, there are two forms of 2-butene. The molecule that has the two CH_3 groups on the same face of the double bond is called *cis*-2-butene, and the other form is called *trans*-2-butene.

Many other alkenes have *cis* and *trans* forms. If a linear alkene has the double bond in the first position (such as 1-butene or 1-hexene), it has only one form, but *all other linear alkenes have* cis *and* trans *isomeric forms.* The easy way to tell whether a linear alkene has cis and trans forms is to look at the number at the beginning of the name. If this number is 2 or larger, the alkene can be either *cis* or *trans.*

Sample Problem 8.15

Identifying alkenes that have *cis* and *trans* forms

Does 1-heptene have *cis* and *trans* isomeric forms?

SOLUTION

1-heptene has the double bond in the first position, so it cannot have *cis* and *trans* forms. There is only one possible form of 1-heptene.

TRY IT YOURSELF: *Does 2-heptene have* cis *and* trans *isomeric forms?*

For additional practice, try Core Problems 8.61 (parts b and c) and 8.62 (parts b and c).

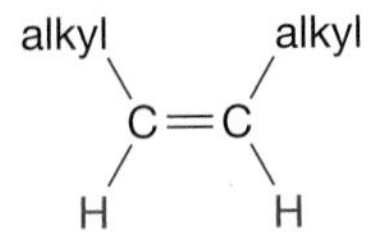

alkyl alkyl
C=C
H H

Cis isomer: The two hydrogen atoms are on the same side of the double bond.

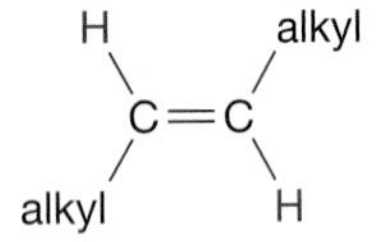

H alkyl
C=C
alkyl H

Trans isomer: The two hydrogen atoms are on opposite sides of the double bond.

FIGURE 8.15 *Cis* and *trans* isomers of alkenes.

At times, we need to draw the structure of a *cis* or *trans* alkene so that we can clearly see which isomer we have. The key is to be able to draw the atoms in the immediate vicinity of the double bond in their correct orientations. In both types of alkene, each of the doubly bonded carbon atoms is linked to a hydrogen atom and an alkyl group. In a *cis* alkene, the two hydrogen atoms are on the same side (both are up or both are down). In a *trans* alkene, the hydrogen atoms are opposite each other (one up and one down). The relationship between the two forms of an alkene is shown in Figure 8.15.

Sample Problem 8.16

Naming *cis* and *trans* isomers

Name the following alkene:

$CH_3—CH_2$ H
C=C
H $CH_2—CH_2—CH_3$

Health Note: Fats and vegetable oils contain alkene groups, and these groups are virtually always in the *cis* form. However, partially hydrogenated vegetable oils contain *trans* alkene groups and are called trans fats. Diets that contain trans fats increase the risk of heart attacks.

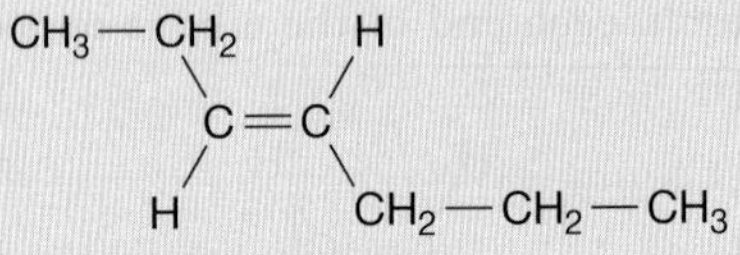

SOLUTION

We begin by naming the molecule without identifying the specific form. This compound contains an unbranched chain of seven carbon atoms, as shown here. The double bond is the third carbon–carbon bond in the chain, so this molecule is a form of 3-heptene.

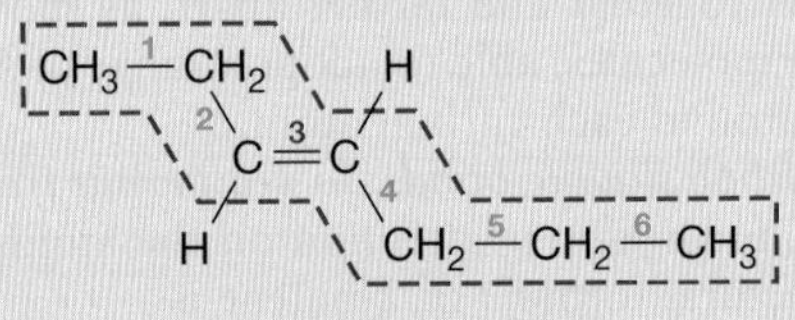

CH_3 —1— CH_2 H
2 C =3= C 4
H CH_2 —5— CH_2 —6— CH_3

Now we identify the specific form. The two hydrogen atoms that are attached to the alkene group are on opposite sides of the double bond, so this compound is *trans*-3-heptene.

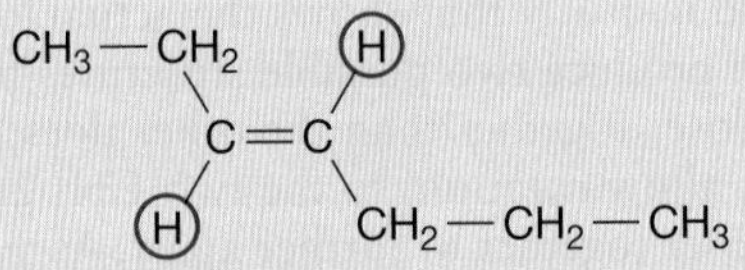

$CH_3—CH_2$ (H)
C=C
(H) $CH_2—CH_2—CH_3$

TRY IT YOURSELF: *Name the following alkene:*

CH_3 $CH_2—CH_2—CH_2—CH_2—CH_2—CH_3$
C=C
H H

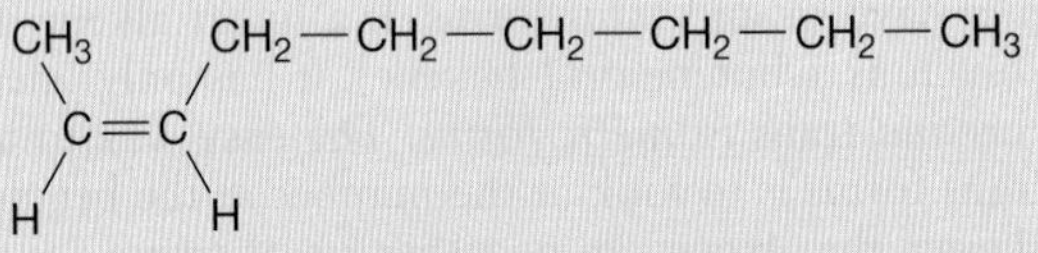

For additional practice, try Core Problems 8.63 and 8.64.

Sample Problem 8.17

Drawing the *cis–trans* geometry in an alkene

Draw the structure of *trans*-2-pentene, showing the correct arrangement of atoms around the double bond.

SOLUTION

It is easiest to begin by drawing a carbon–carbon double bond with the surrounding bonds in the correct orientations.

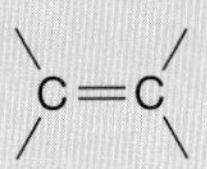

C=C

continued

The compound we need to draw is a *trans* alkene, so we attach two hydrogen atoms to our double bond, putting them in the *trans* orientation. There are two ways to draw the *trans* orientation, and we can choose either one.

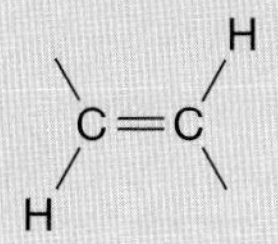

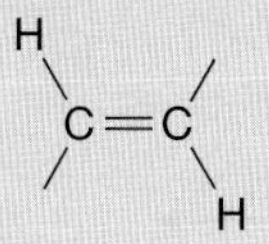

This arrangement is also correct.

Our next task is to add the rest of the carbon atoms. To do so, we need to draw the skeleton structure of 2-pentene (ignoring the *cis–trans* geometry).

C—C=C—C—C

We have one carbon atom to the left and two carbon atoms to the right of the double bond. These are our alkyl groups, and we can add them to the *trans* double bond we drew before.

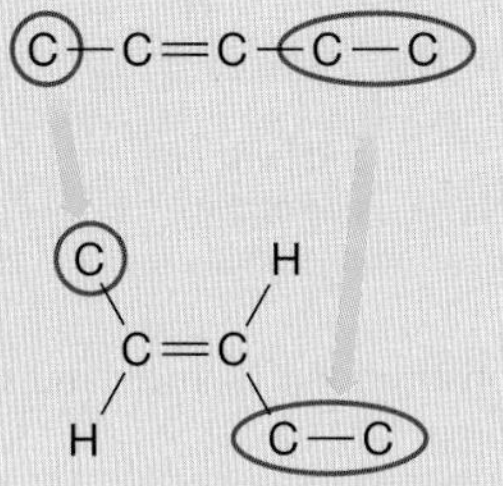

Finally, we must add the correct number of hydrogen atoms to the three carbon atoms that we just drew.

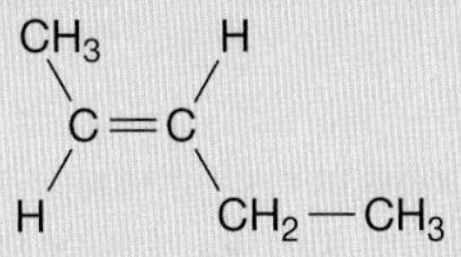

The structure of *trans*-2-pentene

TRY IT YOURSELF: *Draw the structure of* cis-3-heptene, *showing the correct arrangement of atoms around the double bond.*

For additional practice, try Core Problems 8.65 and 8.66.

The *cis* and *trans* forms of alkenes are our first example of **stereoisomers**. Stereoisomers are two compounds that differ only in the arrangement of the bonds around one or more atoms. As a result, we can (in principle) change one stereoisomer into another without breaking any chemical bonds, although in practice most stereoisomers are very difficult to interconvert and require special reaction conditions. For example, rotating one side of the molecule would convert *cis*-2-butene into *trans*-2-butene, so the *cis* and *trans* forms of 2-butene are stereoisomers, as shown in Figure 8.16. By contrast, the atoms in constitutional isomers are connected to one another in a different sequence, so we cannot convert one constitutional isomer into another without breaking chemical bonds. For instance, 2-methylpentane and 3-methylpentane are constitutional isomers, as are 1-butene and *cis*-2-butene. Note that the reactions illustrated in Figure 8.16 do not normally occur; most isomers are stable and require special conditions to be interconverted.

1-Butene and *cis*-2-butene are *constitutional isomers*, because we must break covalent bonds to change one into the other.

Start with 1-butene . . .

. . . break the bonds to CH_3 and H . . .

. . . and exchange their positions to make *cis*-2-butene.

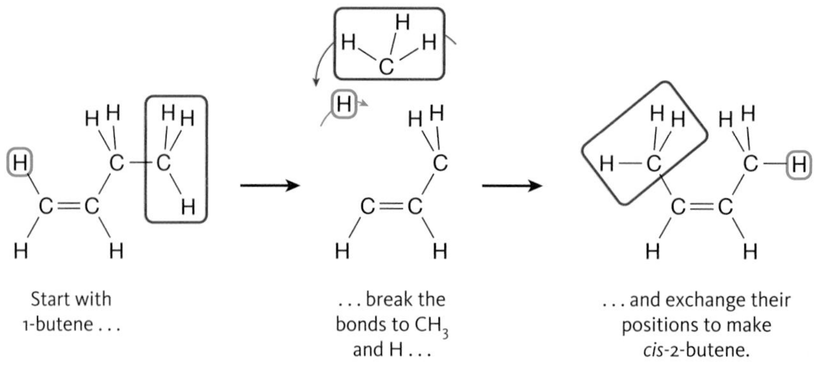

Cis-2-butene and *trans*-2-butene are *stereoisomers*, because we can change one into the other without breaking a covalent bond.

Start with *cis*-2-butene . . .

. . . and twist one side of the double bond . . .

. . . to make *trans*-2-butene.

• The reactions in this figure do not normally occur.

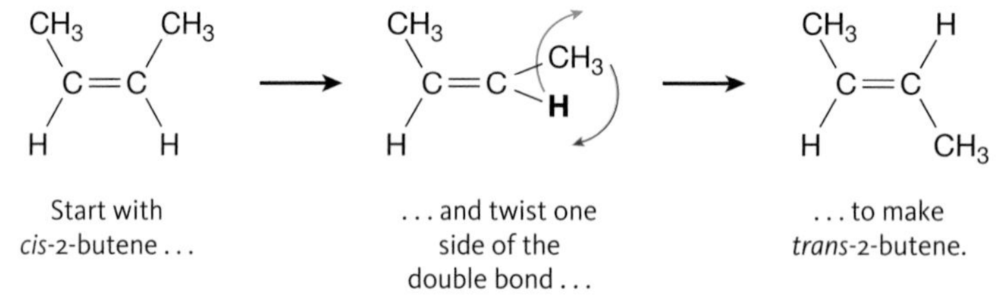

FIGURE 8.16 Comparing constitutional isomers and stereoisomers.

Sample Problem **8.18**

Identifying constitutional isomers and stereoisomers

Are cyclopropane and propene constitutional isomers, or are they stereoisomers?

SOLUTION

We can imagine several ways of rearranging the atoms in cyclopropane, but all of them involve breaking at least one carbon–carbon bond and moving at least one hydrogen atom. Since we must break covalent bonds to change cyclopropane into propene, the two molecules are constitutional isomers.

Cyclopropane **Propene**

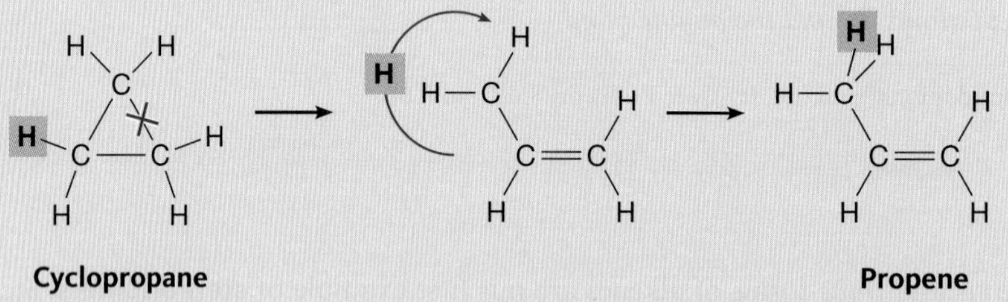

TRY IT YOURSELF: *Are* cis*-2-hexene and* trans*-3-hexene constitutional isomers, or are they stereoisomers?*

For additional practice, try Core Problems 8.67 and 8.68.

Unlike alkenes, alkanes and alkynes do not have *cis* and *trans* forms. In an alkane, the carbon–carbon bonds are all single bonds. These bonds allow free rotation, so the neighboring groups are not in fixed positions. In an alkyne, there are only two groups adjacent to the triple bond, and these groups form a straight line, so twisting the triple bond does not change their positions.

Twisting one end of the triple bond . . .

alkyl—C≡C—alkyl

. . . does not change the position of this alkyl group.

These fruits and vegetables are sources of carotene, which our bodies can convert to *cis*-retinal.

Cis–trans isomerism plays a critical role in the chemistry of vision. The key chemical step in seeing is the conversion of *cis*-retinal to *trans*-retinal, as shown in Figure 8.17. In this reaction, one of the five carbon–carbon double bonds in the retinal molecule rotates from the *cis* configuration to the *trans*. This reaction requires energy, which is supplied by the light that enters the eye. When *trans*-retinal returns to the *cis* form, it releases the energy, which is passed to the optic nerve and the visual center of the brain.

energy (from light)

***Cis*-retinal** → ***Trans*-retinal**

FIGURE 8.17 The interconversion of the *cis* and *trans* forms of retinal.

CORE PROBLEMS

8.61 Which of the following have *cis* and *trans* isomeric forms?
a) hexane b) 1-hexene c) 3-hexene
d) 1-hexyne e) 3-hexyne

8.62 Which of the following have *cis* and *trans* isomeric forms?
a) octane b) 2-octene c) 4-octene
d) 2-octyne e) 4-octyne

8.63 Name the following compounds, using the IUPAC system. Be sure to specify whether each molecule is the *cis* or the *trans* form.

a) $CH_3—CH_2$ and H on one carbon, C=C, H and $CH_2—CH_2—CH_3$ on the other

b) $CH_3—CH_2—CH_2$ and H on one carbon, C=C, $CH_2—CH_2—CH_3$ and H on the other

8.64 Name the following compounds, using the IUPAC system. Be sure to specify whether each molecule is the *cis* or the *trans* form.

a) CH_3 and H on one carbon, C=C, $CH_2—CH_2—CH_2—CH_2—CH_3$ and H on the other

b) $CH_3—CH_2—CH_2—CH_2—CH_2$ and H on one carbon, C=C, H and $CH_2—CH_3$ on the other

8.65 Draw condensed structural formulas for the following molecules. Be sure to show the *cis–trans* geometry clearly in your structures.
a) *cis*-2-heptene b) *trans*-3-hexene

8.66 Draw condensed structural formulas for the following molecules. Be sure to show the *cis–trans* geometry clearly in your structures.
a) *trans*-4-decene b) *cis*-2-pentene

continued

8.67 Which of the following pairs of molecules are constitutional isomers, which are stereoisomers, and which are not isomers?
a) *cis*-3-hexene and *trans*-3-hexene
b) *cis*-3-hexene and *trans*-2-hexene
c) *cis*-3-hexene and 1-hexene
d) *cis*-3-hexene and cyclohexene

8.68 Which of the following pairs of molecules are constitutional isomers, which are stereoisomers, and which are not isomers?
a) *trans*-2-heptene and *cis*-3-heptene
b) *trans*-2-heptene and *cis*-2-heptene
c) *trans*-2-heptene and *trans*-2-hexene
d) *trans*-2-heptene and 1-heptene

OBJECTIVES: *Draw the structure of benzene, and recognize the benzene structure in aromatic compounds.*

8.8 Benzene and Aromatic Compounds

The prototype of the final class of hydrocarbons is a compound called *benzene,* which has the molecular formula C_6H_6. The six carbon atoms are arranged in a ring, with one hydrogen atom bonded to each carbon. Originally, chemists thought that the ring in benzene contained alternating single and double bonds.

Health Note: Long-term exposure to benzene vapor damages the bone marrow, leading to insufficient production of red blood cells (the cells that carry oxygen in the blood). Exposure to benzene vapors also increases the risk of leukeumia.

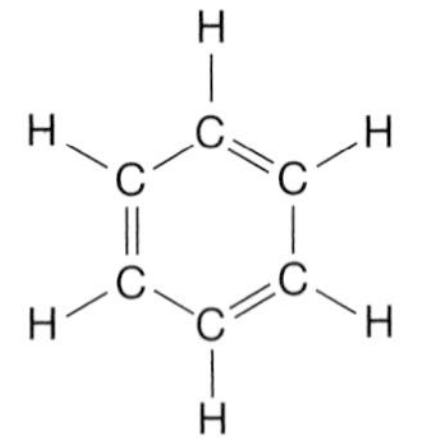

Benzene

However, benzene does not behave like an alkene. Alkenes react with a range of chemicals, including water and strong acids, and these reactions usually convert the double bond into a single bond. Benzene does not react with water or with acids, and the chemicals that do react with benzene do not normally affect the carbon ring.

Chemists now know that benzene does not contain alternating single and double bonds. Instead, the three extra electron pairs move freely around the ring. To show this, chemists often draw benzene as a circle inside a hexagon, as shown in Figure 8.18. However, this type of structure does not allow us to account for all of the electrons, so we use the alternating bond structure to represent the benzene ring in this text. You should recognize, though, that *compounds that contain the benzene ring structure are fundamentally different from alkenes in their chemical properties.* In the rest of this section, we will examine some of the properties of this important class of hydrocarbons.

Aromatic Compounds Contain the Benzene Ring

Compounds that contain the benzene ring are called aromatic compounds This name *aromatic* reflects the fact that many of these hydrocarbons have pleasant, fruity aromas.

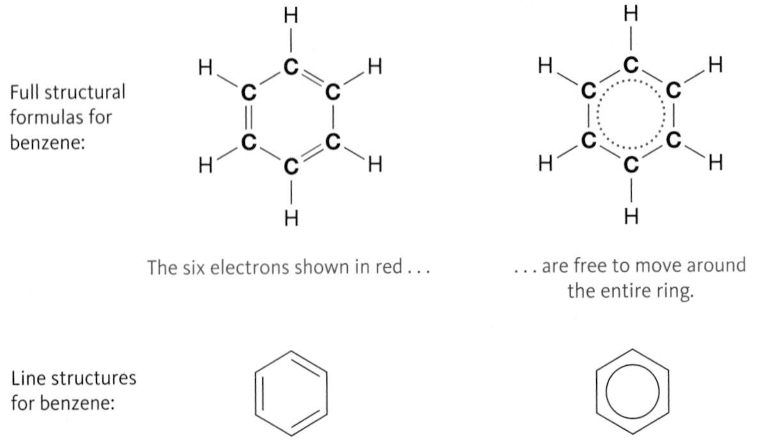

Full structural formulas for benzene:

The six electrons shown in red . . .

. . . are free to move around the entire ring.

Line structures for benzene:

FIGURE 8.18 Alternative ways to represent the benzene ring.

Unfortunately, aromatic hydrocarbons are toxic and many are potent carcinogens, so the pleasant odors of these compounds have no practical use.

Alkyl groups can be bonded to the benzene ring. Adding one or two methyl groups to benzene produces *toluene* and *xylene,* which are used as gasoline additives and nonpolar solvents. There are three isomers of xylene, but their physical properties are so similar that solvent-grade xylene is normally a mixture of the three.

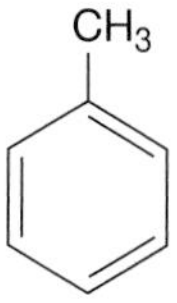

CH_3 CH_3 CH_3 CH_3 CH_3 CH_3 CH_3

Toluene 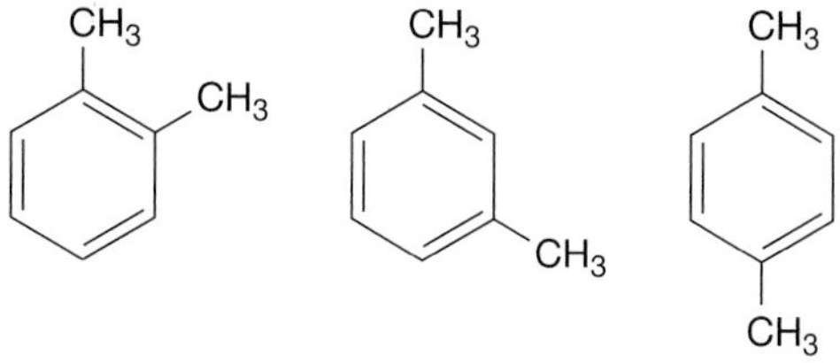 **The three isomers of xylene**

Toluene and xylene are trivial names that were incorporated into the IUPAC system as acceptable alternate names. When a larger alkyl group is attached to benzene, the compound is named using the same system that was used for cycloalkanes.

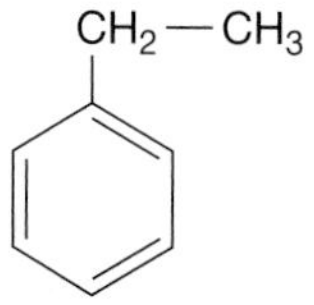

$CH_2—CH_3$ $CH_2—CH_2—CH_2—CH_2—CH_3$

Ethylbenzene 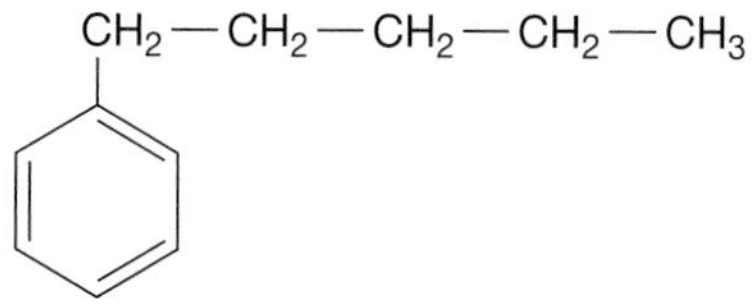 **Pentylbenzene**

The benzene ring is found in an enormous range of chemical compounds, many of which you will encounter in the coming chapters. Styrene and naphthalene are examples of important hydrocarbons that contain benzene rings; styrene is used to make the plastic polystyrene (the solid ingredient in Styrofoam), and naphthalene is the active ingredient in some types of mothballs. Note that naphthalene contains two benzene rings that share a side.

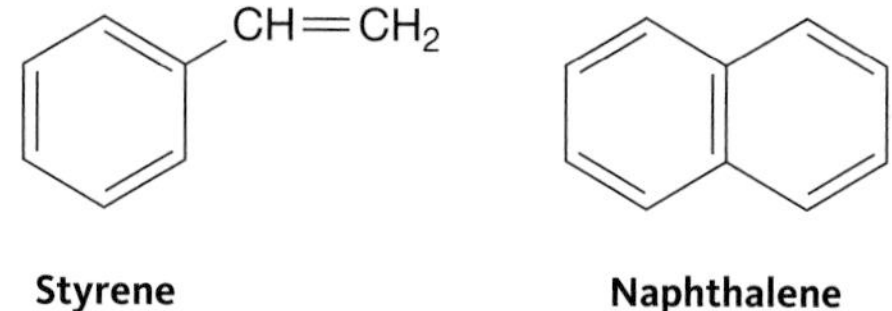

Styrene **Naphthalene**

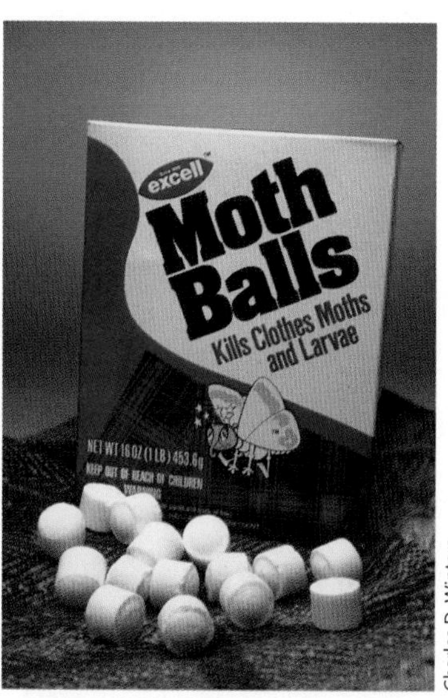

Charles D. Winters

Naphthalene is the active ingredient in some brands of mothballs. It sublimes at room temperature, and its vapors are poisonous to insects and their larvae.

Sample Problem **8.19**

Identifying aromatic compounds

Which of the following molecules contains an aromatic ring?

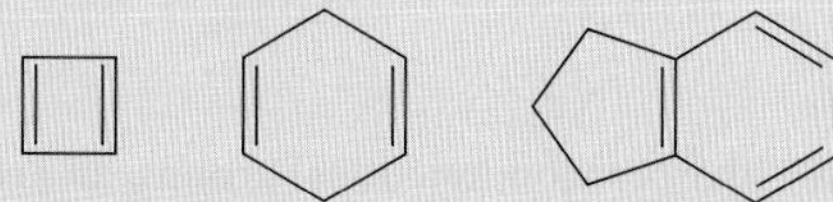

SOLUTION

Only the third molecule contains a six-membered ring with alternating double and single bonds, so the third molecule contains an aromatic ring. The first molecule does not contain a six-membered ring, while the second molecule does not contain the correct number of double bonds in the ring.

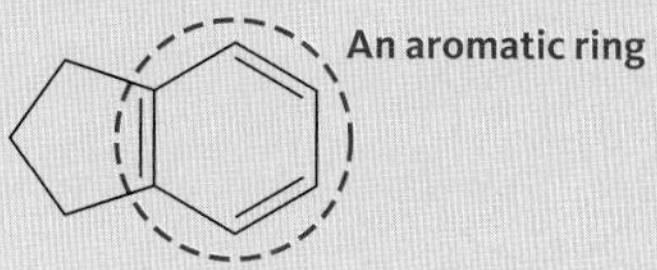

continued

TRY IT YOURSELF: *Which of the following molecules contains an aromatic ring?*

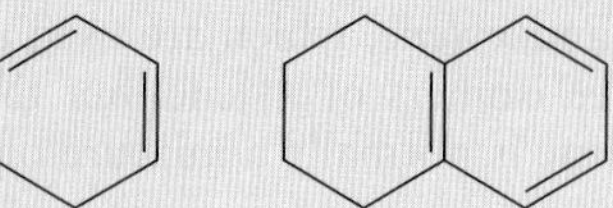

For additional practice, try Core Problems 8.69 and 8.70.

Most Organic Compounds Contain Several Functional Groups

Molecules in living organisms often contain several functional groups, and these functional groups determine how the molecules react. You should learn to recognize the functional groups you have learned when they appear in complex molecules. For example, the antibiotic ciprofloxacin contains both an aromatic ring and an alkene group, as shown here. This molecule also contains several other functional groups that we will encounter in coming chapters.

Health Note: Ciprofloxacin kills the bacteria that cause anthrax and was used to treat people who were potentially exposed to anthrax spores during the 2001 U.S. anthrax attacks. This antibiotic kills a wide range of other bacteria, but it can have significant side effects, including weakening of major tendons, so it (like all antibiotics) should only be taken as prescribed.

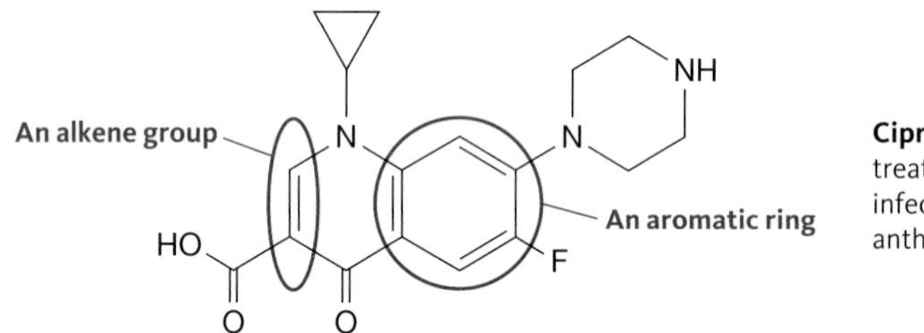

Ciprofloxacin—used to treat a variety of bacterial infections, including anthrax

Sample Problem 8.20

Identifying functional groups in a complex molecule

The following compound acts as an estrogen (the primary female sex hormone) and has been used in oral contraceptives. Identify any alkene, alkyne, and aromatic functional groups in this molecule.

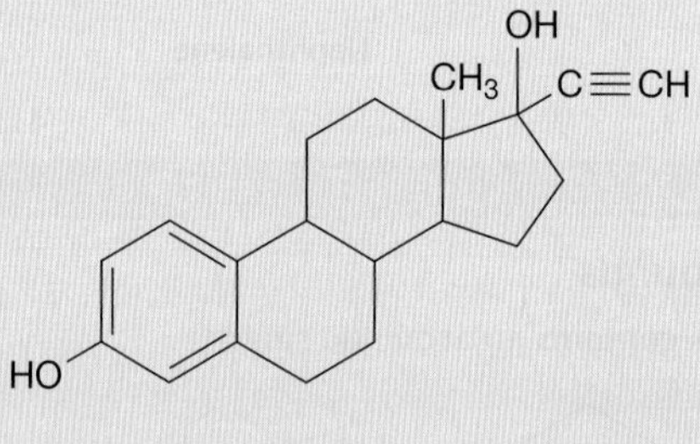

OH, CH_3, C≡CH, HO

Ethynylestradiol

SOLUTION

This molecule contains two hydrocarbon functional groups: an **aromatic ring** (like benzene) and an **alkyne group** (a carbon–carbon triple bond). It contains two other functional groups (the OH groups), which you will learn about in the next chapter.

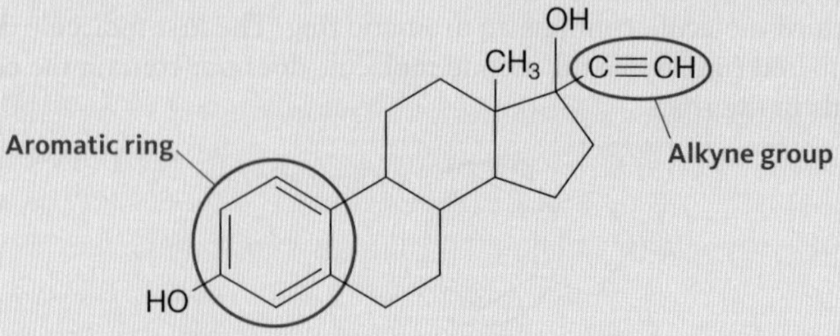

OH, CH_3, C≡CH, HO

Aromatic ring — **Alkyne group**

continued

TRY IT YOURSELF: *The following compound acts as a progestin (a hormone that regulates the menstrual cycle) and has been used in oral contraceptives. Identify any alkene, alkyne, and aromatic functional groups in this molecule.*

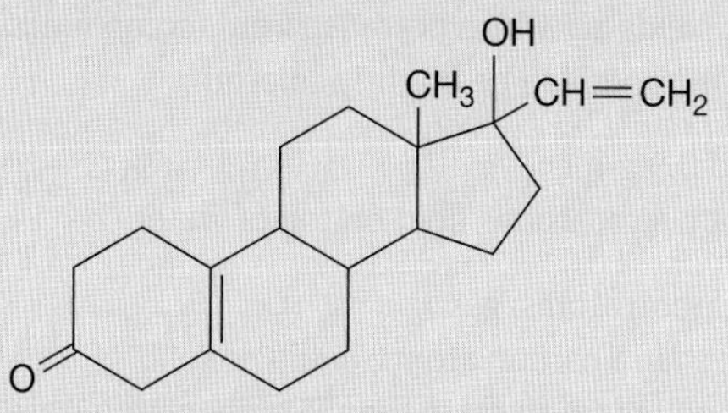

OH, CH_3, $CH{=}CH_2$

Norgesterone

For additional practice, try Core Problems 8.75 and 8.76.

CORE PROBLEMS

8.69 Which of the following compounds (if any) contain an aromatic ring?

CH_2-CH_3 CH_3 $CH_2-CH_2-CH_3$

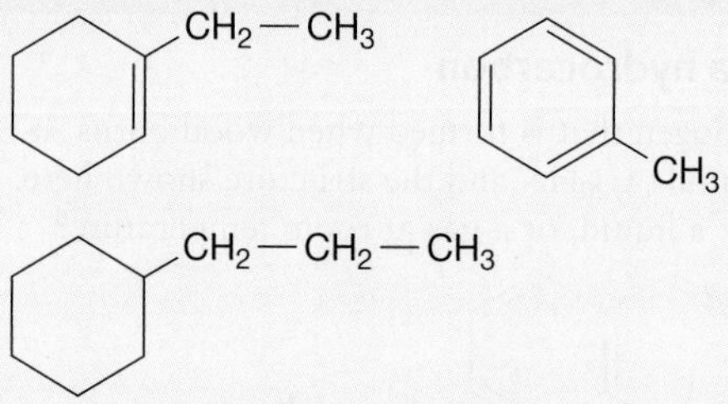

8.70 Which of the following compounds (if any) contain an aromatic ring?

CH_3 CH_3 CH_3 CH_3 CH_3 CH_3

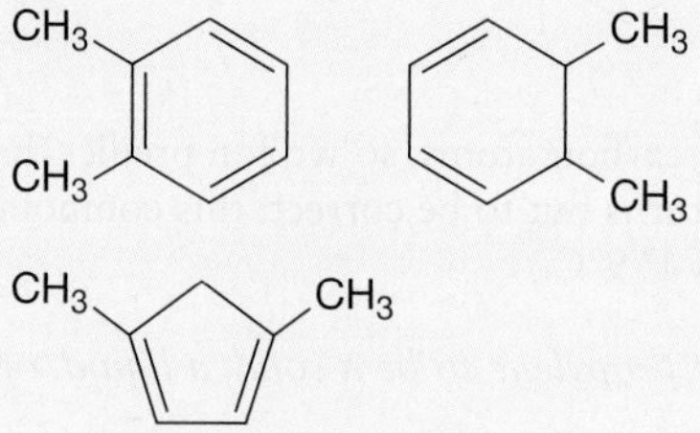

8.71 Draw the structures of the following molecules:
a) toluene b) propylbenzene

8.72 Draw the structures of the following molecules:
a) xylene (draw one isomer) b) butylbenzene

8.73 Name the following molecule, using the IUPAC system:

CH_2-CH_3

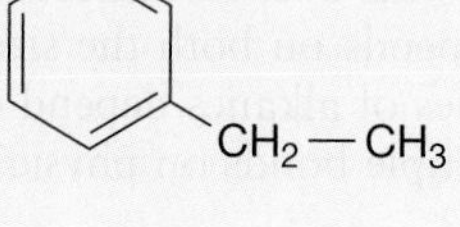

8.74 Name the following molecule, using the IUPAC system:

$CH_2-CH_2-CH_2-CH_2-CH_3$

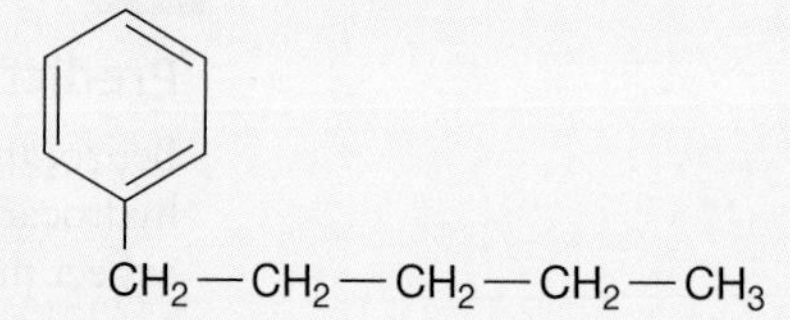

8.75 The following molecule contains several of the functional groups you have studied in this chapter. Identify each functional group in this molecule, and tell whether it is an alkene, alkyne, or aromatic group.

$CH{=}CH-C{\equiv}CH$

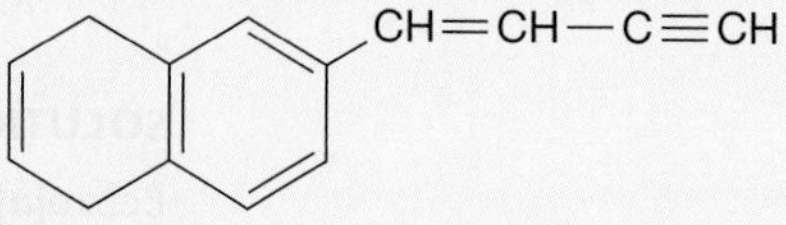

8.76 The following molecule contains several of the functional groups you have studied in this chapter. Identify each functional group in this molecule, and tell whether it is an alkene, alkyne, or aromatic group.

$CH_2{=}CH-$ $-C{\equiv}C-$ CH_3

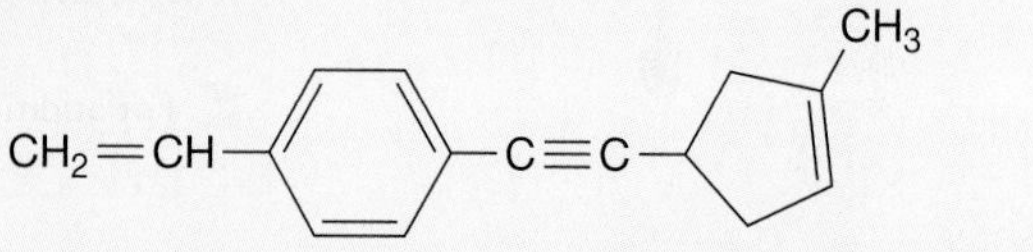

8.9 Properties of Hydrocarbons

OBJECTIVES: *Describe how the physical properties of hydrocarbons are related to their structures, and write the chemical equation for the combustion reaction of a hydrocarbon.*

All of the hydrocarbons are built from just two elements, carbon and hydrogen. All carbon–carbon bonds are nonpolar, because the two carbon atoms that form the bond have the same electronegativity. In addition, carbon and hydrogen have similar electronegativities, so carbon–hydrogen bonds are essentially nonpolar. As a result, hydrocarbon molecules do not contain atoms with significant electrical charges. As we saw in Section 4.5, nonpolar molecules have little attraction for one another, so hydrocarbons are generally easy to melt and to boil. Many hydrocarbons are liquids at room temperature, and the lightest ones are gases. Table 8.12 summarizes the typical physical properties of hydrocarbons.

Charles D. Winters

A mixture of hydrocarbons and water. Hydrocarbons are hydrophobic and most are less dense than water, so they form a separate layer on top of the water layer.

TABLE 8.12 The Physical Properties of Hydrocarbons

Typical appearance	Liquids and gases are clear and colorless. Most solids are white or transparent (compounds with many double bonds can be brightly colored).
Typical density (liquids and solids)	0.6 to 0.9 g/mL (Most hydrocarbons float on top of water.)
State at room temperature	1–4 carbon atoms: gas More than 5 carbon atoms: liquid or solid (Compounds with more than 15 carbon atoms are usually solids, but the cutoff is quite variable; the shape of the molecule plays an important role in determining the melting point.)
Solubility in water	Very low: hydrocarbons are considered to be insoluble in water.

Sample Problem 8.21

Predicting the properties of a hydrocarbon

Benzo[*a*]pyrene is a powerful carcinogen that is formed when wood burns. It is a hydrocarbon with the chemical formula $C_{20}H_{12}$ and the structure shown here. Would you expect this compound to be a solid, a liquid, or a gas at room temperature?

Benzo[a]pyrene

SOLUTION

Benzo[*a*]pyrene contains more than 15 carbon atoms, so we can predict that it is a solid at room temperature. (Our prediction turns out to be correct: this compound is a pale yellow solid and has a melting point of 179°C.)

TRY IT YOURSELF: *Would you expect propylene to be a solid, a liquid, or a gas at room temperature?*

For additional practice, try Core Problems 8.77 and 8.78.

The melting and boiling points of hydrocarbons are closely related to their size. As we saw in Section 4.5, larger molecules have higher melting and boiling points than smaller molecules. The presence of double or triple bonds does not affect the boiling point much, but it can affect the melting point, which depends on both the size and the shape of the molecule. Table 8.13 shows how the properties of alkanes depend on the size of the molecule, and Table 8.14 shows the effect of multiple bonds on physical properties.

Health Note: Petroleum jelly is a soft, semisolid mixture of hydrocarbons, primarily alkanes with 25 or more carbon atoms. It is nontoxic and insoluble in water, so it is used to protect damaged skin from bacteria and water loss while the skin heals.

TABLE 8.13 The Effect of Size on the Physical Properties of Alkanes

Compound	Attraction Between Molecules	Melting Point	Boiling Point	State at Room Temperature
Ethane (C_2H_6)	weakest	−183°C	−89°C	Gas
Butane (C_4H_{10})		−138°C	−1°C	Gas
Hexane (C_6H_{14})		−95°C	69°C	Liquid
Octane (C_8H_{18})	strongest	−57°C	126°C	Liquid

TABLE 8.14 The Effect of Multiple Bonds on Physical Properties

Compound	Type of Compound	Melting Point	Boiling Point
Hexane	Alkane	−95°C	69°C
1-Hexene	Alkene	−140°C	63°C
1-Hexyne	Alkyne	−132°C	71°C

Sample Problem 8.22

Comparing the physical properties of hydrocarbons

Which should have the higher boiling point, propane or octane?

SOLUTION

In general, when we are comparing hydrocarbons, the larger compound boils at a higher temperature, because the attraction between large molecules is stronger than the attraction between small molecules. Propane contains three carbon atoms and has the formula C_3H_8, while octane contains eight carbon atoms and has the formula C_8H_{18}. Therefore, we expect octane to have the higher boiling point. (The actual boiling points of propane and octane are −42°C and 126°C, respectively.)

TRY IT YOURSELF: *Which should have the higher boiling point, cyclopentane or cyclohexane?*

For additional practice, try Core Problems 8.85 and 8.86.

Recall from Chapter 4 that molecular compounds dissolve in water only if they can participate in hydrogen bonds. Hydrocarbons do not contain oxygen or nitrogen, so they cannot form hydrogen bonds or accept them from water molecules. As a result, the solubilities of hydrocarbons in water are extremely low. Hydrocarbons are normally described as insoluble in water. However, you should remember that "insoluble" compounds dissolve to a small degree, and under certain circumstances this can be a significant concern. The solubility of benzene in water, for instance, is roughly 0.6 g/L, which is high enough to pose a health hazard in drinking water. Drinking water supplies are routinely monitored for the presence of hydrocarbons.

The four classes of hydrocarbons differ from one another in their chemical behavior. Alkanes are the least reactive and are virtually inert at room temperature. Alkenes and alkynes are the most reactive hydrocarbons, while aromatic compounds are intermediate. Hydrocarbons play a limited role in biological systems, because of their extremely low solubility in water. However, carbon–carbon double bonds are found in many biologically significant molecules that contain other functional groups. We will examine some of the chemical reactions of alkenes in Chapters 9 and 10.

Health Note: All liquid hydrocarbons can cause severe lung damage if they are inhaled. Therefore, if a person accidentally swallows a liquid such as gasoline or paint thinner that contains hydrocarbons, the person should not be induced to vomit, because there is a risk that the hydrocarbons will be breathed into the lungs.

Combustion Is an Important Reaction of Hydrocarbons

The most important role of hydrocarbons in human society is as fuels. Natural gas, gasoline, kerosene, diesel fuel, aviation gasoline, heating oil, and even candle wax are mixtures of hydrocarbons. All hydrocarbons react with oxygen when they are heated, producing carbon dioxide, water, and a great deal of energy. These are combustion reactions, which you encountered in Section 6.5. Here are two typical examples:

The combustion of methane (the primary ingredient in natural gas):

$$CH_4(g) + 2\,O_2(g) \rightarrow CO_2(g) + 2\,H_2O(l) + 213\text{ kcal}$$

The combustion of isooctane (a component of gasoline):

$$2\,C_8H_{18}(l) + 25\,O_2(g) \rightarrow 16\,CO_2(g) + 18\,H_2O(l) + 2608\text{ kcal}$$

Sample Problem 8.23

Writing the equation for the combustion reaction of a hydrocarbon

Write the balanced chemical equation for the combustion of benzene.

SOLUTION

Before we can write an equation, we need to know the molecular formula of benzene. The full structural formula of benzene is

Counting the atoms gives us the molecular formula C_6H_6.

In any combustion reaction, the hydrocarbon reacts with oxygen (O_2), forming carbon dioxide and water.

$$C_6H_6 + O_2 \rightarrow CO_2 + H_2O$$

To balance this equation, we must write coefficients in front of the chemical formulas to show how many molecules of each compound are being used or formed. You have already seen how to balance combustion reactions in Chapter 6. The correct answer is

$$2\ C_6H_6 + 15\ O_2 \rightarrow 12\ CO_2 + 6\ H_2O$$

TRY IT YOURSELF: *Write the balanced chemical equation for the combustion of cyclopropane.*

For additional practice, try Core Problems 8.81 and 8.82.

The hydrocarbons that we use as fuels are produced when plant matter is covered by water and sediment before it can decay. As this organic material becomes buried under successively deeper layers of sediment, it is compressed and heated to the point where chemical bonds are broken and rearranged. During this process, the oxygen and nitrogen are driven out of the organic compounds, leaving complex mixtures of hydrocarbons. Under some conditions, these hydrocarbons collect in pockets underground in the form of a heavy, dark liquid called petroleum (or crude oil). The lightest hydrocarbons in this mixture are gases and rise to the surface of the petroleum pocket as natural gas. In many cases, though, most of the hydrogen is also driven out of the organic matter as it is compressed and heated, producing coal, a solid that is primarily carbon. Coal, petroleum, and natural gas are the *fossil fuels,* the remnants of living organisms from hundreds of millions of years ago.

CORE PROBLEMS

8.77 One of the following compounds is a liquid at room temperature, while the other is a solid. Which is which? Explain your reasoning.

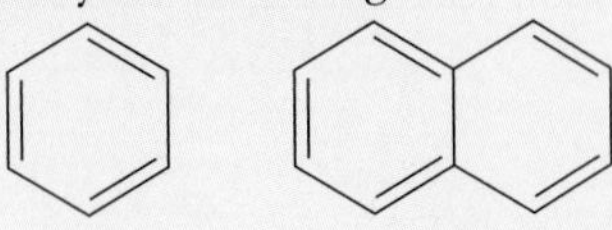

Benzene **Naphthalene**

8.78 One of the following compounds is a liquid at room temperature, while the other is a gas. Which is which? Explain your reasoning.

$CH_3-CH(CH_3)-CH_3$

2-Methylpropane

$CH_3-CH_2-CH_2-CH_2-CH(CH_3)-CH_3$

2-Methylhexane

continued

8.79 Explain why pentane is insoluble in water.

8.80 Would you expect cyclohexane to be soluble in water? Explain your answer.

8.81 Write the balanced chemical equation for the combustion of acetylene, C_2H_2.

8.82 Write the balanced chemical equation for the combustion of cyclopentane, C_5H_{10}.

8.83 Would you expect butane and 1-butene to have similar boiling points, or would you expect their boiling points to be quite different? Explain your answer.

8.84 Would you expect butane and 1-butene to have similar melting points, or would you expect their melting points to be quite different? Explain your answer.

8.85 Arrange the following compounds from lowest boiling point to highest boiling point. If two compounds should have roughly the same boiling point, list them together.

butane 2-methylbutane
2,2-dimethylbutane pentane

8.86 Arrange the following compounds from lowest boiling point to highest boiling point. If two compounds should have roughly the same boiling point, list them together.

cyclohexane methylcyclohexane
methylcyclopentane cyclopentane

8.87 What is the significance of combustion reactions in modern society?

8.88 Can you name some practical sources of energy for modern societies that do not involve combustion?

CONNECTIONS

High-Octane Hydrocarbons

Petroleum is a complex mixture of hydrocarbons we learned about in this chapter—alkanes, cycloalkanes, alkenes, and aromatic compounds. There are thousands of hydrocarbon compounds in the crude oil that is pumped out of the ground. To meet our needs for liquid fuels such as gasoline, kerosene, diesel, and lubricating oils, the crude oil must be refined. Refining crude oil means separating out components by a process called fractional distillation, which takes advantage of the different boiling points of the hydrocarbons. The crude oil is heated to 400°C to produce a mixed vapor of all the hydrocarbons. The vapor is then sent up a fractional distillation tower. As the vapor climbs, the temperature decreases, and the component hydrocarbons condense at different temperatures at different heights in the tower. In this way, different fractions of crude oil can be separated and collected. These fractions are then further treated to produce modern fuels.

A higher octane rating means the gasoline burns more smoothly—and costs more.

The most familiar petroleum-based fuel is gasoline, which is composed of hydrocarbons containing primarily between 5 and 10 carbon atoms. This range reflects the engine's requirement for a fuel that is a liquid at room temperature but evaporates rapidly in the hot engine chamber. Hydrocarbons with fewer carbon atoms are gases at room temperature and would not be suitable for a liquid fuel, although gasoline normally contains a small amount of butane to increase its evaporation rate. Hydrocarbons with many carbon atoms do not evaporate rapidly enough to burn smoothly in the engine. However, heavier hydrocarbons can be used in diesel engines, which run at higher temperatures. Diesel fuel typically contains hydrocarbons having between 10 and 15 carbon atoms.

The octane number on a gasoline pump is a measure of the ability of the gasoline to burn efficiently in a car's engine. In the engine, gasoline should ignite only when the spark plug fires and should not burn too rapidly, so it pushes the piston at the correct moment in the engine cycle. In general, branched and aromatic hydrocarbons burn more smoothly than unbranched alkanes, so gasoline with a higher octane rating contains a higher proportion of unbranched alkanes and aromatic compounds. To determine the octane rating, chemists compare the gasoline's performance to various mixtures of heptane and 2,2,4-trimethylpentane (called isooctane). The octane rating is the percentage of isooctane in the heptane–isooctane mixture that duplicates the performance of the gasoline. For instance, 87-octane gasoline behaves like a mixture of 87% isooctane and 13% heptane.

It is difficult and expensive to make gasoline that has a high enough octane rating from petroleum alone, so most gasoline also contains octane enhancers. Currently, the main octane enhancers are toluene and small alcohols like methanol and ethanol, but before 1975 the main enhancer was tetraethyllead, $Pb(C_2H_5)_4$, and gasoline containing that compound was referred to as leaded gasoline. However, as a result of the Clean Air Act of 1970, all cars sold in the United States starting in 1975 required unleaded gasoline, and leaded gasoline effectively vanished from gas stations

continued

over the next two decades. The result was a dramatic drop in blood lead levels due to exposure to lead in exhaust gases, particularly among young children.

Between concerns about the environment and the impending scarcity of crude oil, scientists have developed engines that run on a variety of alternative fuels. There are now motor vehicles that use hydrogen, natural gas (primarily methane), propane, ethanol, and biodiesel (diesel fuel made from vegetable oil and animal fat). There are also vehicles that run on batteries, replacing refueling with recharging. Many of these are likely to become increasingly familiar on roadways as petroleum becomes scarcer. Expect the fueling station of the future to look very different from today's "regular or premium" pumps.

Key Terms

alkane – 8.2
alkene – 8.6
alkyl group – 8.4
alkyne – 8.6
aromatic compound (arene) – 8.8
branched alkane – 8.3
condensed structural formula – 8.3
constitutional isomer – 8.7
cycloalkane – 8.3
cycloalkene – 8.6
full structural formula – 8.2
functional group – 8.5
hydrocarbon – 8.2
isomer – 8.3
line structure – 8.3
linear alkane – 8.2
saturated hydrocarbon – 8.3
stereoisomers – 8.7
tetrahedral arrangement – 8.1
trigonal planar arrangement – 8.6
trivial name – 8.6
unsaturated hydrocarbon – 8.6
valence-shell electron pair repulsion model (VSEPR model) – 8.1

Classes of Organic Compounds

Class	Functional group	IUPAC suffix	Example
Alkane	None	-ane	$CH_3—CH_2—CH_2—CH_2—CH_3$ pentane
Alkene	$\rangle C=C \langle$	-ene	$CH_2=CH—CH_2—CH_2—CH_3$ 1-pentene
Alkyne	$—C≡C—$	-yne	$CH≡C—CH_2—CH_2—CH_3$ 1-pentyne
Aromatic compound	(benzene ring)	-ene	(benzene ring)$—CH_2—CH_3$ ethylbenzene

SUMMARY OF OBJECTIVES

Now that you have read the chapter, test yourself on your knowledge of the objectives using this summary as a guide.

Section 8.1: Explain why carbon is uniquely suited to be the main structural element of organic chemistry, and describe the ways in which carbon atoms form covalent bonds.

- Carbon atoms normally share four pairs of electrons when they form compounds.
- Carbon can form single, double, and triple bonds.
- When a carbon atom forms four single bonds, the bonds form a tetrahedral arrangement.
- Hydrogen atoms normally share one pair of electrons when they form compounds.

Section 8.2: Learn the names of the first 10 linear alkanes, and use common conventions to draw their structural formulas.

- Alkanes are hydrocarbons that contain only single bonds, and linear alkanes contain a single, continuous chain of carbon atoms.

- Linear alkanes (and all organic compounds) can be represented using Lewis dot structures, full structural formulas, condensed structural formulas, line structures, or wedge–dash structures.

Section 8.3: Distinguish linear and branched alkanes and cycloalkanes, and recognize and draw isomers of simple alkanes.

- Isomers are molecules that have the same molecular formula but different structures, and they normally have different physical and chemical properties.
- Constitutional isomers differ in the order in which atoms are connected to one another.
- Branched alkanes contain a branched chain of carbon atoms.
- Cycloalkanes contain a ring of carbon atoms.

Section 8.4: Name branched alkanes and cycloalkanes.

- The IUPAC system provides a systematic way to name branched alkanes, by identifying the principal carbon chain, the individual branches (alkyl groups), and the locations of the branches on the principal chain.
- The IUPAC rules can be used to name branched cycloalkanes.

Section 8.5: Understand how and why chemists use functional groups to classify organic molecules.

- A functional group is any bond or atom that is not found in a saturated hydrocarbon.
- A functional group includes all of the atoms and bonds that give a molecule its characteristic chemical properties.
- Compounds that contain the same functional group typically undergo the same types of reactions.
- Organic reactions normally affect the functional group without changing the carbon skeleton of a molecule.

Section 8.6: Name and draw the structures of linear alkenes and alkynes, and describe how the atoms are arranged around a double or triple bond.

- Alkenes and alkynes are hydrocarbons that contain a double or triple bond, respectively.
- The bonds around the two carbon atoms that make up an alkene group form a trigonal planar arrangement.
- The bonds around the two carbon atoms that make up an alkyne group are arranged in a straight line.
- The IUPAC system names alkenes and alkynes by identifying the corresponding alkane, changing the ending of the alkane name to a suffix that identifies the functional group, and adding a number to show the location of the double bond.
- Cycloalkenes contain a carbon–carbon double bond within a ring of carbon atoms.

Section 8.7: Name and draw the *cis* and *trans* forms of an alkene, and distinguish constitutional isomers and stereoisomers.

- Molecules that have the same molecular formula but differ in the arrangement of bonds around a carbon atom are called stereoisomers.
- Alkenes that have an internal double bond can occur in *cis* and *trans* forms, which are examples of stereoisomers.

Section 8.8: Draw the structure of benzene, and recognize the benzene structure in aromatic compounds.

- Benzene is a six-membered ring of carbon atoms with alternating single and double bonds. Two of the electrons that make up each double bond are free to move around the entire ring.
- Aromatic compounds contain one or more benzene rings.
- Aromatic hydrocarbons are less reactive than alkenes.

Section 8.9: Describe how the physical properties of hydrocarbons are related to their structures, and write the chemical equation for the combustion reaction of a hydrocarbon.

- Hydrocarbons are typically easy to melt and boil, are less dense than water, and have very low solubilities in water.
- The melting and boiling points of hydrocarbons depend on the number of carbon atoms. Melting points also depend on the shape of the carbon skeleton, but the presence of double and triple bonds usually has a limited impact on physical properties.
- Hydrocarbons react with oxygen to form carbon dioxide and water (the combustion reaction).
- Combustion reactions produce large amounts of energy, and they are the primary energy source for modern society.

Concept Questions

OWL Online homework for this chapter may be assigned in OWL.

* indicates more challenging problems.

8.89 Sulfur atoms are similar to carbon atoms in that they can form long chains, linked by covalent bonds. Explain why sulfur would not be likely to be the fundamental element for living organisms on some other planet.

8.90 Explain why carbon atoms normally share four pairs of electrons when they form chemical compounds.

8.91 Chloroform has the molecular formula $CHCl_3$. Which of the following could be the correct structural formula for chloroform, based on the bonding properties of carbon, hydrogen, and chlorine?

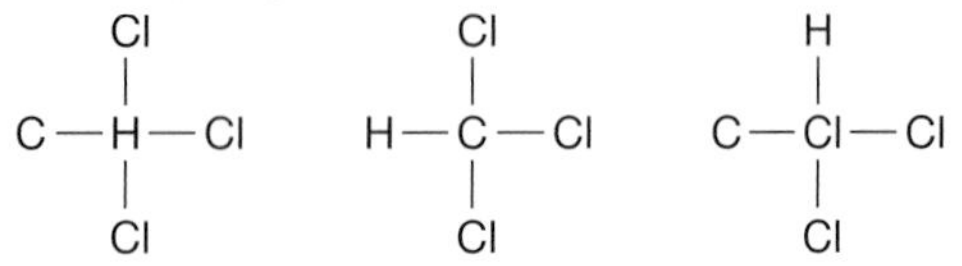

```
     Cl              Cl              H
     |               |               |
  C—H—Cl          H—C—Cl          C—Cl—Cl
     |               |               |
     Cl              Cl              Cl
```

8.92 In the following molecule, circle a carbon atom that forms a tetrahedral arrangement of bonds, and draw a box around a carbon atom that forms a trigonal planar arrangement of bonds:

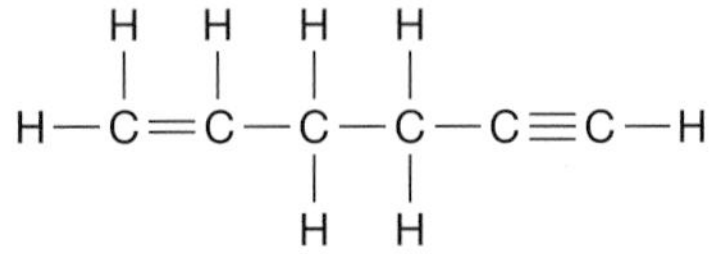

```
    H   H   H   H
    |   |   |   |
H—C=C—C—C—C≡C—H
            |   |
            H   H
```

8.93 Define each of the following terms:

a) alkane b) alkene c) alkyne
d) branched alkane e) aromatic compound

8.94 A student says that the following molecule is a branched alkane, called 1-ethylbutane. Is this correct? If not, give the correct name, and explain why the student was incorrect.

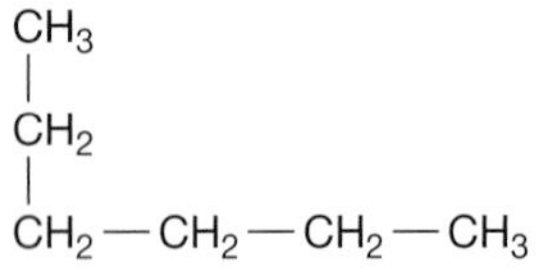

```
CH3
|
CH2
|
CH2—CH2—CH2—CH3
```

8.95 The IUPAC rules allow us to write "methylpropane" instead of 2-methylpropane, but they do not allow us to write "methylhexane" instead of 2-methylhexane. Why is this?

8.96 Which of the following structures are ways to represent hexane, and which represent some other molecule?

a) $CH_3—CH_2—CH_2—CH_2—CH_2—CH_3$

```
      CH3
      |
b) CH3—CH—CH2—CH2—CH3
```

```
                                CH3
                                |
c) CH3—CH2—CH2—CH2—CH2—CH2
```

```
                CH2—CH2—CH3
                |
d) CH3—CH2—CH2
```

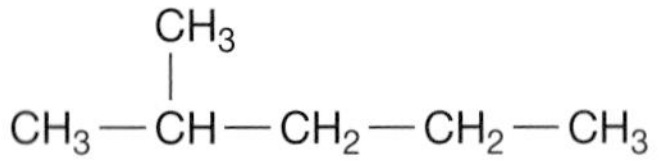

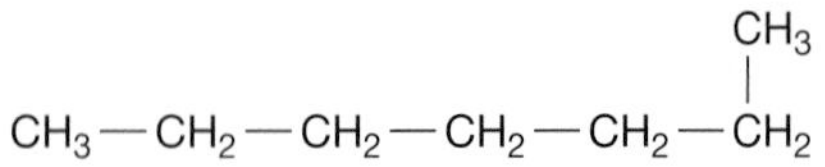

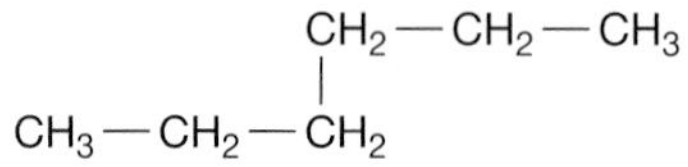

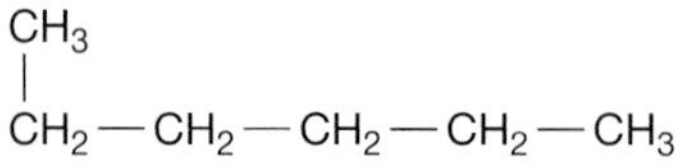

```
   CH3
   |
e) CH2—CH2—CH2—CH2—CH3
```

```
          CH3
          |
f) CH3—CH—CH2—CH2—CH2—CH3
```

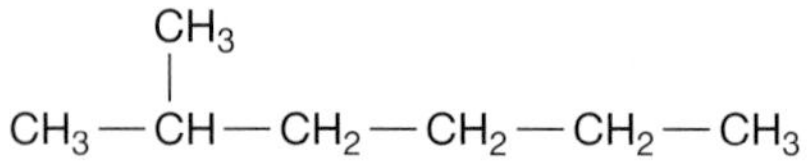

8.97 Beside each of the following molecules is an incorrect name. Explain why each name is wrong, and give the correct name.

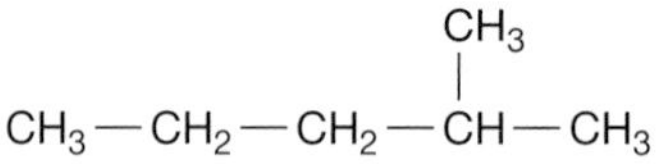

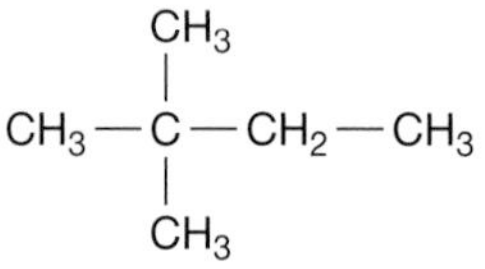

```
                     CH3
                     |
a) CH3—CH2—CH2—CH—CH3      4-Methylpentane
```

```
         CH3
         |
b) CH3—C—CH2—CH3      2-Dimethylbutane
         |
         CH3
```

d) 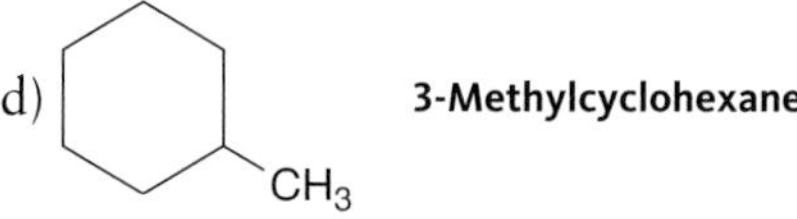

3-Methylcyclohexane

8.98 The smallest alkane has one carbon atom, but the smallest alkene has two carbon atoms. Why isn't there a one-carbon alkene?

8.99 Why isn't it necessary to use a number to show the position of the double bond in cyclopentene (i.e., why don't we write "1-cyclopentene," "2-cyclopentene," etc.)?

8.100 Alkenes like 2-butene have *cis* and *trans* forms, but alkynes like 2-butyne do not. Why is this?

8.101 There are *cis* and *trans* forms of 2-butene, but there is only one form of 1-butene. Why is this?

8.102 Explain why *cis*-2-hexene and *trans*-3-hexene are constitutional isomers rather than stereoisomers.

8.103 a) In the combustion reaction of a hydrocarbon, what additional reactant is necessary?
b) What are the products of the combustion reaction?

8.104 Why is the boiling point of hexane higher than the boiling point of butane?

Summary and Challenge Problems

8.105 Draw condensed structural formulas for each of the following hydrocarbons. You may draw line structures for any rings.

a) pentane
b) 2-methylhexane
c) 3,3-diethylheptane
d) 4-ethyl-2-methyloctane
e) cyclopropane
f) propylcyclopentane
g) 2-heptyne
h) *trans*-2-hexene
i) ethylene
j) cyclopentene
k) 2-propyl-1-pentene
l) benzene
m) 4,4-dimethyl-2-hexyne
n) 4-methyl-*cis*-2-hexene
o) propylbenzene

8.106 Draw line structures for each of the following hydrocarbons:

a) pentane
b) 2-methylhexane
c) 3,3-diethylheptane
d) 4-ethyl-2-methyloctane
e) propylcyclopentane
f) 2-heptyne
g) 2-methyl-1-pentene
h) 2,3-dimethyl-2-butene
i) butylbenzene

8.107 Name the following compounds, using the IUPAC rules. Be sure to indicate the *cis* or *trans* isomer where appropriate.

a) $CH_3-CH_2-CH_2-CH_2-CH_3$

b) 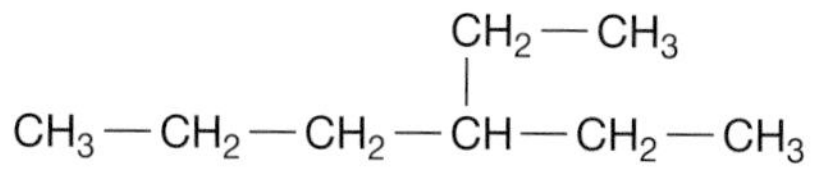
$$\begin{array}{c} \qquad\qquad\qquad\quad CH_2-CH_3 \\ \qquad\qquad\quad | \\ CH_3-CH_2-CH_2-CH-CH_2-CH_3 \end{array}$$

c)
$$\begin{array}{c} CH_3 \qquad\qquad\qquad\qquad\qquad\qquad CH_3 \\ | \qquad\qquad\qquad\qquad\qquad\qquad\quad | \\ CH_3-C-CH_2-CH_2-CH_2-CH_2-CH-CH_3 \\ | \\ CH_3 \end{array}$$

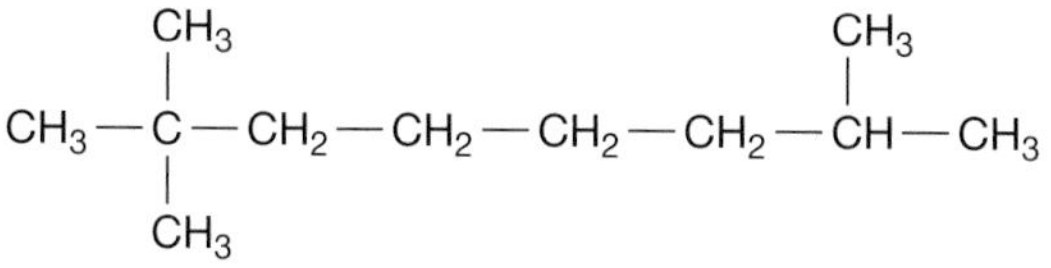

d) 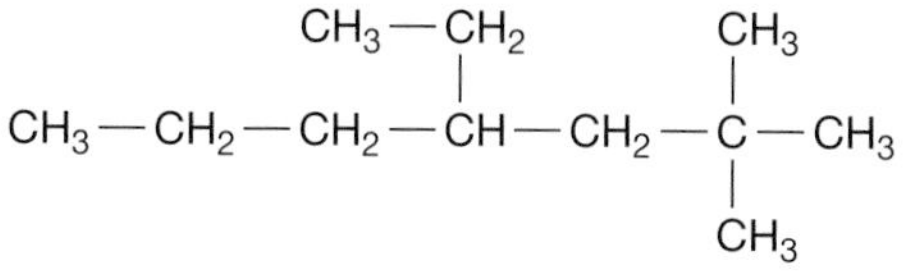
$$\begin{array}{c} CH_3-CH_2 \qquad\quad CH_3 \\ | \qquad\qquad\quad | \\ CH_3-CH_2-CH_2-CH-CH_2-C-CH_3 \\ | \\ CH_3 \end{array}$$

e) 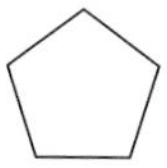 [cyclopentane ring]

f) 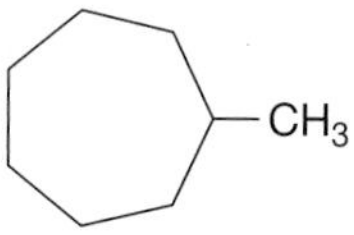 [cycloheptane ring]$-CH_3$

g) $CH_3-CH_2-C\equiv C-CH_3$

h) 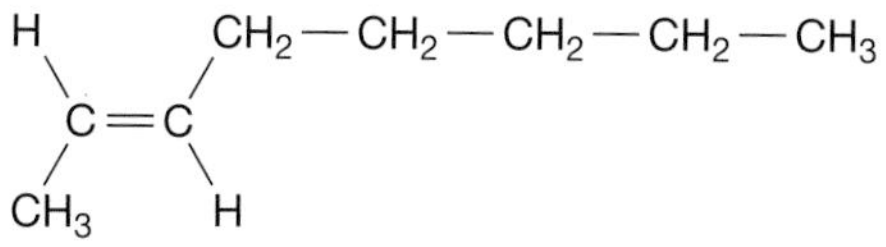
$$\begin{array}{c} H \qquad\quad CH_2-CH_2-CH_2-CH_2-CH_3 \\ \backslash \quad / \\ C=C \\ / \quad \backslash \\ CH_3 \qquad H \end{array}$$

i) 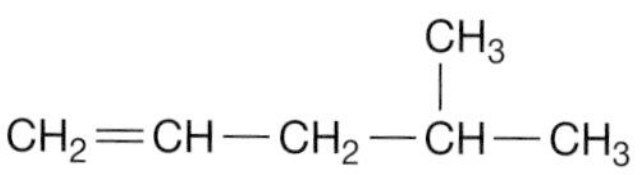
$$\begin{array}{c} \qquad\qquad\qquad CH_3 \\ \qquad\qquad\qquad | \\ CH_2=CH-CH_2-CH-CH_3 \end{array}$$

j) 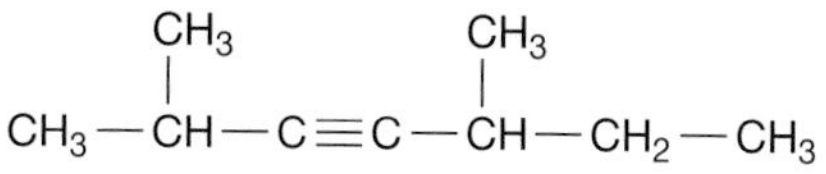
$$\begin{array}{c} CH_3 \qquad\qquad\qquad CH_3 \\ | \qquad\qquad\qquad\quad | \\ CH_3-CH-C\equiv C-CH-CH_2-CH_3 \end{array}$$

k) 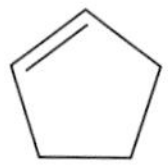 [cyclopentene ring]

l) 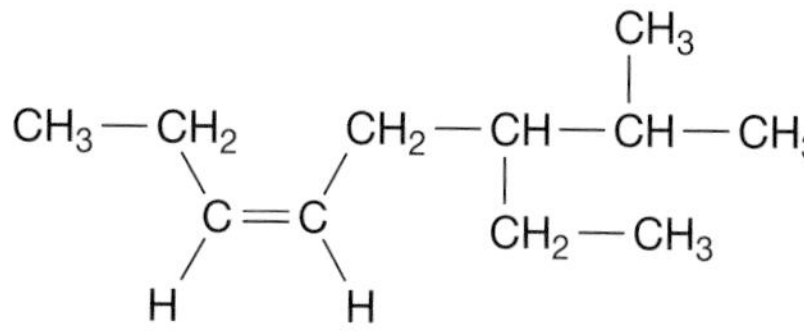
$$\begin{array}{c} \qquad\qquad\qquad\qquad\qquad\qquad CH_3 \\ \qquad\qquad\qquad\qquad\qquad\qquad | \\ CH_3-CH_2 \qquad CH_2-CH-CH-CH_3 \\ \backslash \qquad / \qquad | \\ C=C \qquad CH_2-CH_3 \\ / \quad \backslash \\ H \qquad H \end{array}$$

m) 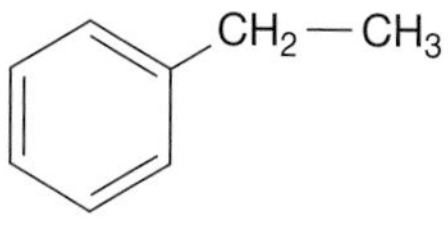 [benzene ring]$-CH_2-CH_3$

n)  [line structure]

o) 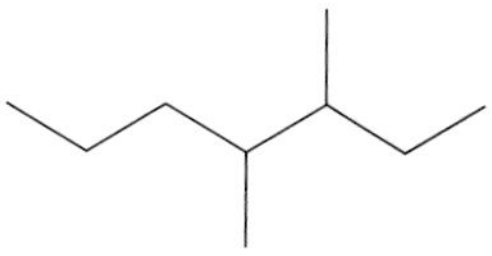 [line structure]

p) 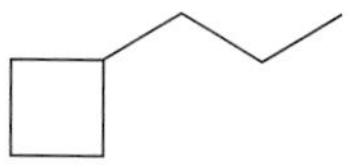 [cyclobutane ring with line-structure chain]

8.108 Draw a condensed structural formula that corresponds to the following skeleton structure:

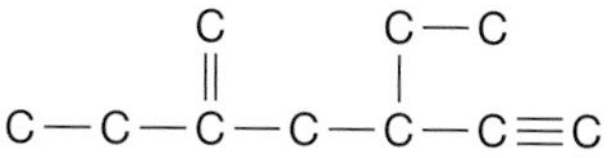

$$\begin{array}{c} \qquad C \qquad\quad C-C \\ \qquad \| \qquad\quad | \\ C-C-C-C-C-C\equiv C \end{array}$$

8.109 What is the molecular formula of the cycloalkane that has the following line structure?

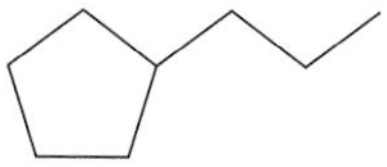

8.110 Which of the following pairs of compounds are isomers?

a) hexane and 2-methylpentane
b) pentane and 2-methylpentane
c) 1-hexene and cyclohexene
d) 1-hexene and cyclohexane
e) *cis*-3-heptene and *trans*-2-heptene
f) 2-methylhexane and 2,3-dimethylpentane

8.111 *Draw the structure of a compound that fits each of the following descriptions.

a) a branched alkane that is an isomer of 2-methylhexane
b) a linear alkane that is an isomer of 2-methylhexane
c) an alkene that is a stereoisomer of *trans*-3-octene
d) an unbranched alkene that is a constitutional isomer of *trans*-3-octene
e) a branched alkene that is a constitutional isomer of *trans*-3-octene

8.112 *Which of the following compounds are isomers of 2-pentyne?

a) $HC{\equiv}C{-}CH_2{-}CH_2{-}CH_3$

b) $CH_3{-}CH_2{-}C{\equiv}C{-}CH_3$

c) 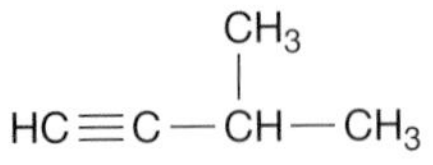 $HC{\equiv}C{-}CH(CH_3){-}CH_3$

d) 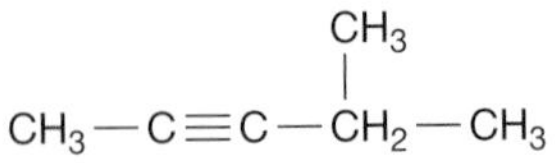 $CH_3{-}C{\equiv}C{-}C(CH_3){-}CH_2{-}CH_3$

e) 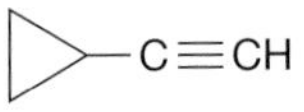 (cyclopropyl)$-C{\equiv}CH$

f) $CH_2{=}CH{-}CH{=}CH{-}CH_3$

g) 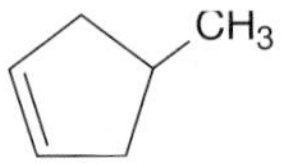 (cyclopentene ring) CH_3

8.113 *There are six compounds that have the molecular formula C_4H_8. Four of them contain one C=C bond, and the other two contain only single bonds. Draw their structures.

8.114 Which of the following compounds (if any) contains an aromatic ring?

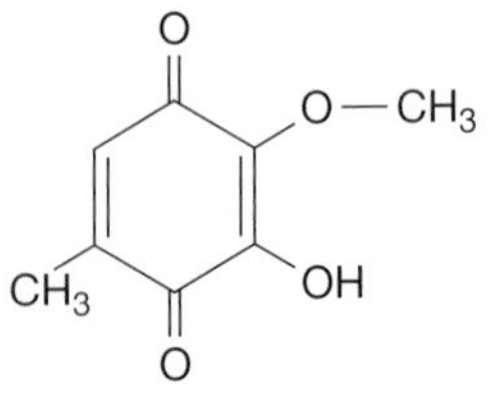

O, O—CH_3, CH_3, OH, O

Fumigatin
(a toxin found in some fungi)

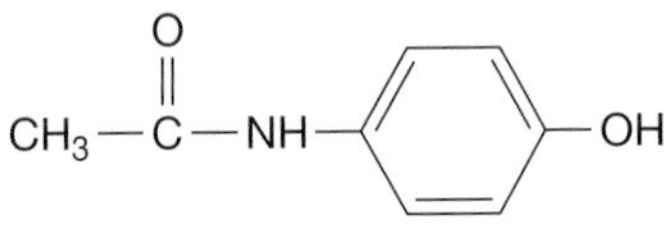

$CH_3{-}C(=O){-}NH{-}$(ring)$-OH$

Acetaminophen
(a pain medication, the active ingredient in Tylenol)

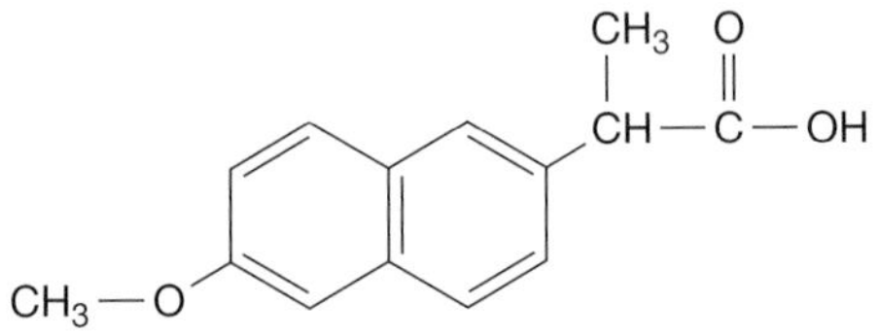

$CH_3{-}O{-}$(naphthalene ring)$-CH(CH_3){-}C(=O){-}OH$

Naproxen
(a pain medication, the active ingredient in Aleve)

8.115 Each of the following molecules contains one or more of the hydrocarbon functional groups you have studied in this chapter (alkene, alkyne, and aromatic ring). Circle each hydrocarbon functional group, and tell what type of functional group it is.

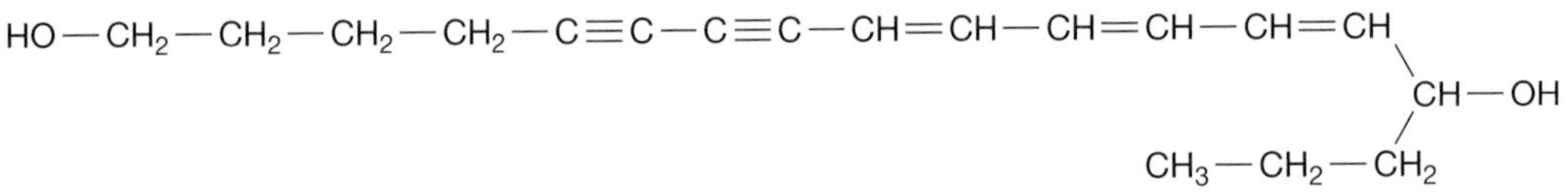

$HO{-}CH_2{-}CH_2{-}CH_2{-}CH_2{-}C{\equiv}C{-}C{\equiv}C{-}CH{=}CH{-}CH{=}CH{-}CH{=}CH{-}CH(OH){-}CH_2{-}CH_2{-}CH_3$

Cicutoxin
(a toxic compound found in water hemlock)

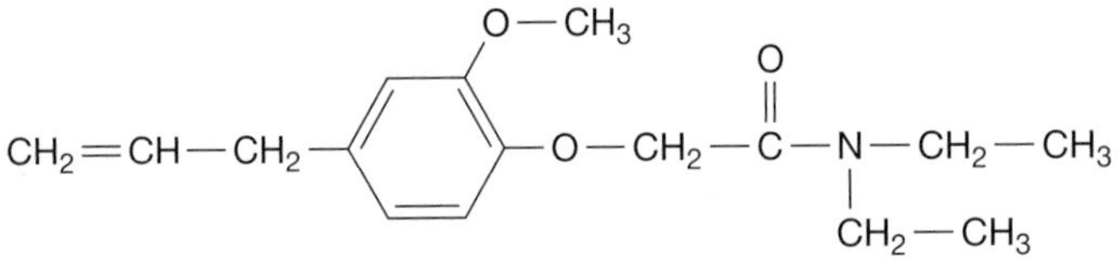

$CH_2{=}CH{-}CH_2{-}$(ring with $O{-}CH_3$)$-O{-}CH_2{-}C(=O){-}N(CH_2{-}CH_3){-}CH_2{-}CH_3$

Estil
(an anesthetic)

8.116 *The chemical equations for the combustion reactions of methane and propane are:

$$CH_4 + 2\ O_2 \rightarrow CO_2 + 2\ H_2O + 213\ \text{kcal}$$

$$C_3H_8 + 5\ O_2 \rightarrow 3\ CO_2 + 4\ H_2O + 531\ \text{kcal}$$

a) Based on these equations, which produces more heat when it burns: 1.00 g of methane or 1.00 g of propane?
b) Based on these equations, which produces more carbon dioxide when it burns: 1.00 g of methane or 1.00 g of propane?

8.117 *If you have 2.50 g of pentane, how many moles do you have?

8.118 *A sample of toluene has a volume of 75.0 mL and weighs 65.0 g.

a) Calculate the density and the specific gravity of toluene.
b) What is the mass of 3.22 L of toluene?
c) If some toluene is poured into a container of water, will the toluene float or sink?

8.119 *The U.S. government has set the maximum level of xylene in drinking water at 10 ppm. Is this level greater than or less than the solubility of xylene in water (0.17 g/L)? Based on this comparison, could xylene in drinking water be a significant health concern?

8.120 *A heating curve for 2,2-dimethylpropane is shown here. Based on this diagram, answer the following questions:

a) What is the boiling point of 2,2-dimethylpropane?
b) What state is 2,2-dimethylpropane in at 0°C?
c) If you want to make a mixture of solid and liquid 2,2-dimethylpropane, what temperature must you use?

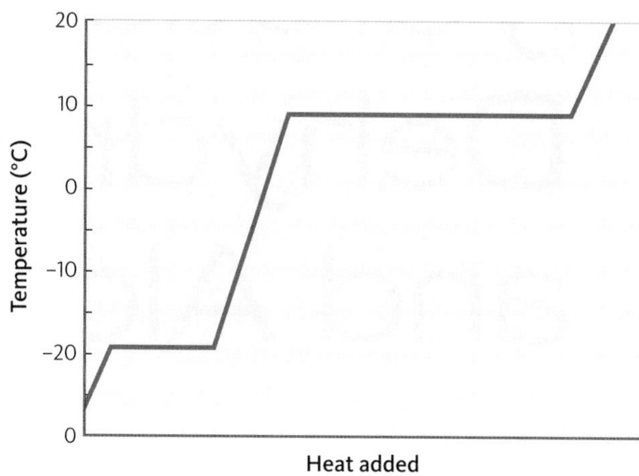

9

Hydration, Dehydration, and Alcohols

At her routine checkup, Sandra mentions that she has been feeling more tired than usual, probably due to a stressful couple of months at work. After some hesitation, Sandra adds that she has been drinking quite a bit of wine during and after dinner to help her unwind after her workday, to the point where she frequently feels hung over the next morning. Her doctor decides to order a set of blood tests to evaluate Sandra's liver function. These tests check the levels of several enzymes that occur in liver cells, where they assist in the processing of amino acids and other nutrients. Conditions that damage the liver kill large numbers of liver cells, and the enzymes that were in the cells end up in the bloodstream.

Sandra's blood shows higher-than-normal levels of two enzymes, alanine aminotransferase and aspartate aminotransferase, with the increase in the latter level being particularly conspicuous. The level of another enzyme, alkaline phosphatase, is within the normal range. Based on these and other results, Sandra's doctor tells her that she has mild alcoholic hepatitis, an inflammation of the liver that is a result of her increased drinking. The alcohol in wine (called ethanol) is metabolized by the liver, but it can also damage liver tissue, and excessive drinking can have serious long-term effects. However, Sandra's liver function returns to normal when she cuts back on her alcohol consumption, and she suffers no lasting ill effects.

$CH_3—CH_2—OH$ ethanol
(grain alcohol, ethyl alcohol)

OUTLINE

LABORATORY REQUISITION—CHEMISTRY

☐ Sodium	NA	☐ Fructosamine	FRU/ALB
☐ Potassium	K	☐ PSA	PSA
☐ Creatinine	CREAT	☐ Chloride	CL
☐ BUN	BUN	☐ Calcium	CA
☐ Glucose-fasting	GLUCF	☐ Phosphorus	PHOS
☐ Glucose-random	GLUCR	☐ Phenylalanine	PKU
☐ Hemoglobin A1C	HGBA1C	☐ Uric Acid	URIC

Drinking alcohol in moderation is generally not harmful, but heavy drinking has a variety of adverse health consequences.

OWL Online homework for this chapter may be assigned in OWL.

Oxygen is a key element in the chemistry of living organisms. Virtually every organic compound in the human body contains oxygen atoms, and these atoms play an important role in giving the organic molecules their characteristic physical and chemical properties. It is not surprising, then, that many of the reactions that occur in the human body involve adding or removing oxygen atoms. In most cases, our bodies use water to add oxygen atoms to organic molecules, in a reaction called a hydration. Hydration reactions produce a class of organic compounds called alcohols, which provide the link between hydrocarbons and the rest of organic chemistry.

In this chapter, we examine the hydration reaction, and we look at some of the properties of alcohols. We also examine the dehydration reaction, the main way that our bodies remove oxygen atoms from organic molecules

OBJECTIVE: *Predict the products that are formed when water reacts with an alkene.*

9.1 The Hydration Reaction

In Chapter 8, you learned to recognize and name alkenes, compounds that contain a carbon–carbon double bond. The double bond in an alkene can react with a range of substances. In most reactions involving an alkene, two or more atoms become bonded to the original alkene and the double bond becomes a single bond. Figure 9.1 shows the general scheme for this type of reaction. In this figure, A–B represents a covalent molecule. Note that the reaction changes the positions of two bonding electron pairs (shown in red).

• There is a summary of important organic reaction types at the end of this chapter.

The most important type of reaction that alkenes undergo in biological chemistry is the **hydration reaction.** In this reaction, the A–B of Figure 9.1 is a water molecule (H—OH). The product of a hydration reaction contains an OH group (called a *hydroxyl group*) bonded to a carbon atom. Figure 9.2 shows a general scheme for the hydration of alkenes.

The product of the hydration reaction is called an **alcohol.** Alcohols contain a hydroxyl group bonded directly to a hydrocarbon chain. Alcohols play a key role in a wide range of biological reactions, and you will encounter many examples of this class of compounds as you continue your study of organic molecules.

Many Alkenes Produce Two Hydration Products

Most alkenes can produce two isomeric alcohols when they are hydrated, because the hydroxyl group can become bonded to either side of the original alkene group. For ex-

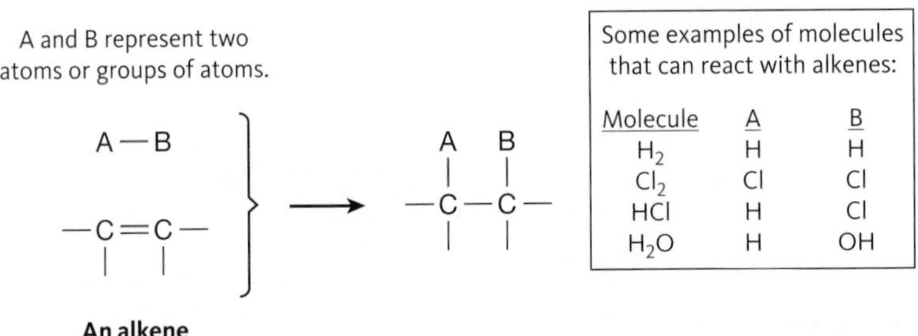

FIGURE 9.1 The general scheme for alkene reactions.

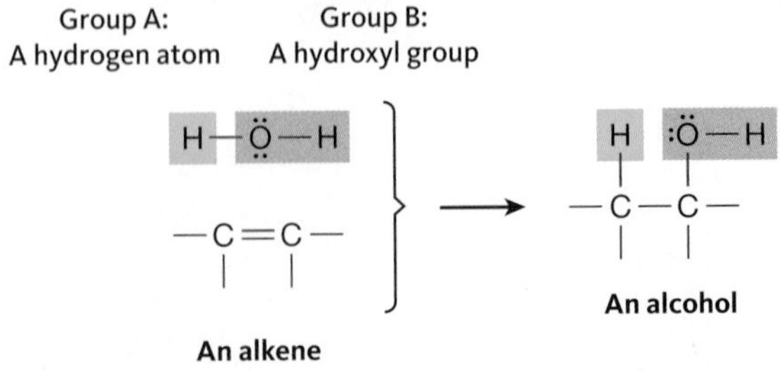

Health Note: *Hydration* is a general term that means adding water to something. When you hydrate yourself by drinking water, though, you are not carrying out a hydration reaction. You are simply replacing water that your body has lost due to breathing, perspiration, and urination.

Group A: A hydrogen atom

Group B: A hydroxyl group

H—Ö—H + —C=C— (An alkene) → H and :Ö—H on —C—C— (An alcohol)

FIGURE 9.2 The hydration reaction of alkenes.

ample, if we react water with 2-pentene (either the *cis* or the *trans* isomer), we make a mixture of two alcohols, as shown here:

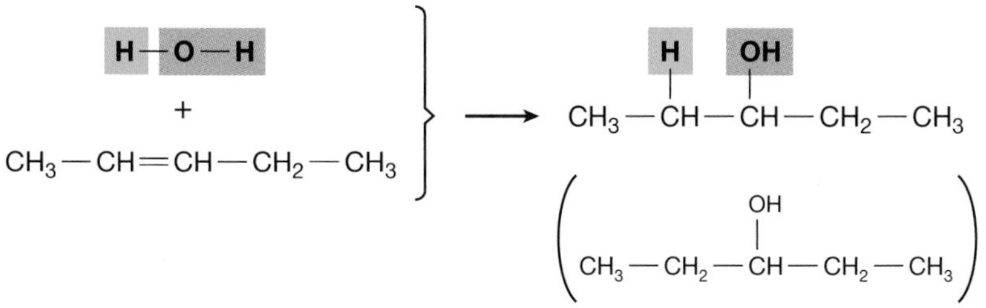

$$\left.\begin{array}{c} \text{H—O—H} \\ + \\ CH_3-CH=CH-CH_2-CH_3 \end{array}\right\} \longrightarrow \underset{\text{H}}{CH_3-CH}-\underset{\text{OH}}{CH}-CH_2-CH_3 \quad \text{Product 1}$$

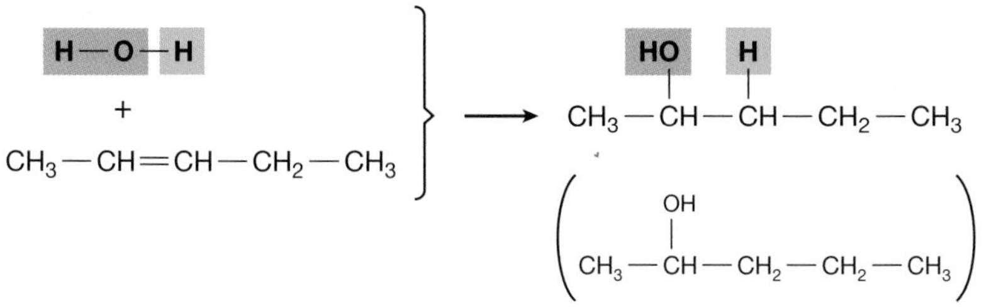

$$\left(CH_3-CH_2-\overset{\text{OH}}{\overset{|}{CH}}-CH_2-CH_3\right)$$

$$\left.\begin{array}{c} \text{H—O—H} \\ + \\ CH_3-CH=CH-CH_2-CH_3 \end{array}\right\} \longrightarrow CH_3-\overset{\text{HO}}{\overset{|}{CH}}-\overset{\text{H}}{\overset{|}{CH}}-CH_2-CH_3 \quad \text{Product 2}$$

$$\left(CH_3-\overset{\text{OH}}{\overset{|}{CH}}-CH_2-CH_2-CH_3\right)$$

Sample Problem 9.1

Drawing the products of a hydration reaction

Draw the structures of the two products that are formed when water reacts with the following alkene:

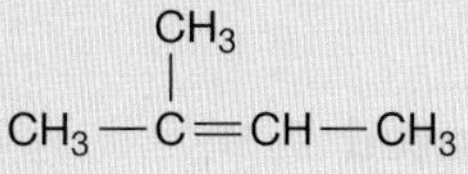

$$CH_3-\overset{CH_3}{\overset{|}{C}}=CH-CH_3$$

SOLUTION

In a hydration reaction, H and OH bond to the two carbon atoms that form the alkene group. One product has H on the left and OH on the right, while the other has these reversed. It is easiest to draw the H and OH below the carbon chain, because the branch is drawn above the chain.

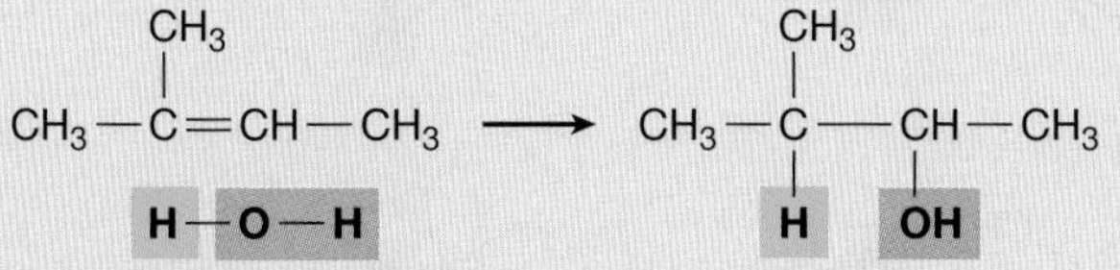

$$\underset{\text{H—O—H}}{CH_3-\overset{CH_3}{\overset{|}{C}}=CH-CH_3} \longrightarrow CH_3-\underset{\text{H}}{\underset{|}{\overset{CH_3}{\overset{|}{C}}}}-\underset{\text{OH}}{\underset{|}{CH}}-CH_3 \quad \text{Product 1}$$

$$\underset{\text{H—O—H}}{CH_3-\overset{CH_3}{\overset{|}{C}}=CH-CH_3} \longrightarrow CH_3-\underset{\text{OH}}{\underset{|}{\overset{CH_3}{\overset{|}{C}}}}-\underset{\text{H}}{\underset{|}{CH}}-CH_3 \quad \text{Product 2}$$

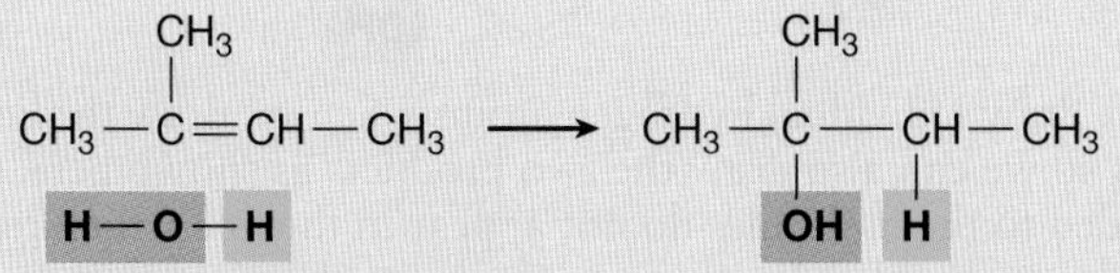

When we draw condensed structural formulas, we normally do not show individual hydrogen atoms, so we can also draw the structures of the products as

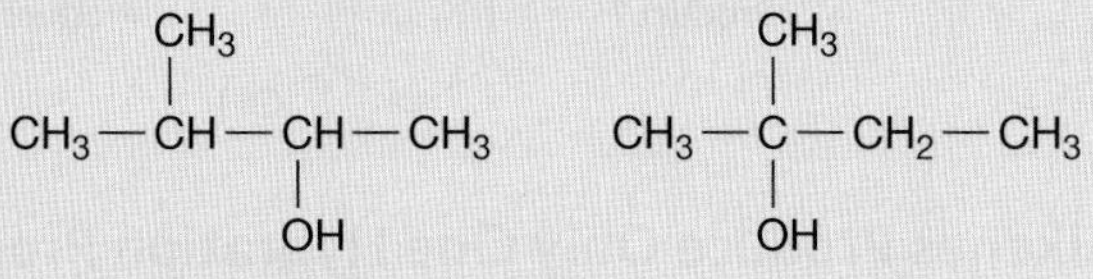

$$CH_3-\overset{CH_3}{\overset{|}{CH}}-\underset{\text{OH}}{\underset{|}{CH}}-CH_3 \qquad CH_3-\underset{\text{OH}}{\underset{|}{\overset{CH_3}{\overset{|}{C}}}}-CH_2-CH_3$$

Product 1   Product 2

continued

TRY IT YOURSELF: *Draw the structures of the two products that are formed when water reacts with the following alkene:*

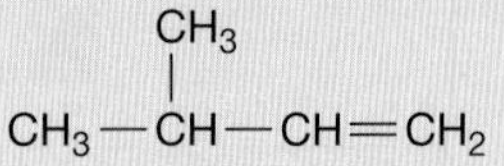

$$CH_3-\underset{|}{\overset{CH_3}{CH}}-CH{=}CH_2$$

For additional practice, try Core Problems 9.1 (parts a and b) and 9.2 (parts a and c).

If we react an alkene with water in a laboratory, we do not normally make equal amounts of the two possible products. In general, the hydrogen atom of water prefers to become attached to the alkene carbon that is bonded to more hydrogen atoms. This tendency is called *Markovnikov's rule.* For example, when 1-pentene reacts with water, the product mixture contains only a miniscule amount of one of the two possible products. The hydrogen from water attaches to carbon 1 of 1-pentene, because carbon 1 is bonded to two hydrogen atoms, while carbon 2 is bonded to only one hydrogen atom.

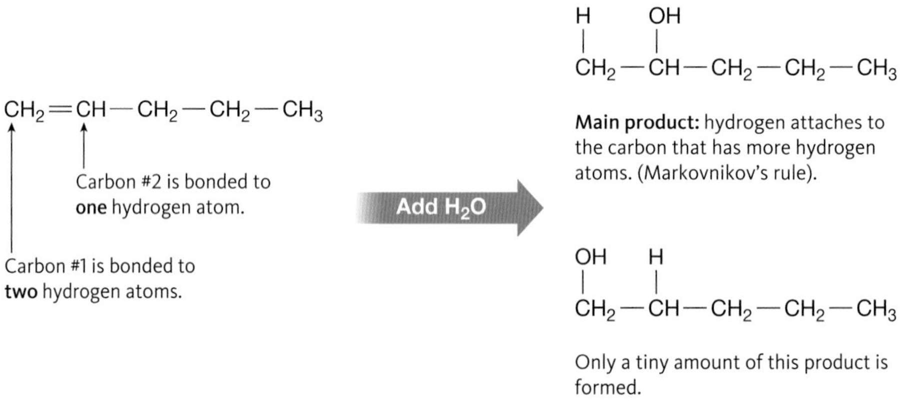

$CH_2{=}CH-CH_2-CH_2-CH_3$

Carbon #2 is bonded to **one** hydrogen atom.

Carbon #1 is bonded to **two** hydrogen atoms.

Add H_2O

H (on C1), OH (on C2): $CH_2-CH-CH_2-CH_2-CH_3$

Main product: hydrogen attaches to the carbon that has more hydrogen atoms. (Markovnikov's rule).

OH (on C1), H (on C2): $CH_2-CH-CH_2-CH_2-CH_3$

Only a tiny amount of this product is formed.

Cycloalkenes Can Be Hydrated

Cycloalkenes can also react with water to form alcohols. The double bond in the cycloalkene becomes a single bond, and H and OH become attached to the ring. Here is a typical example:

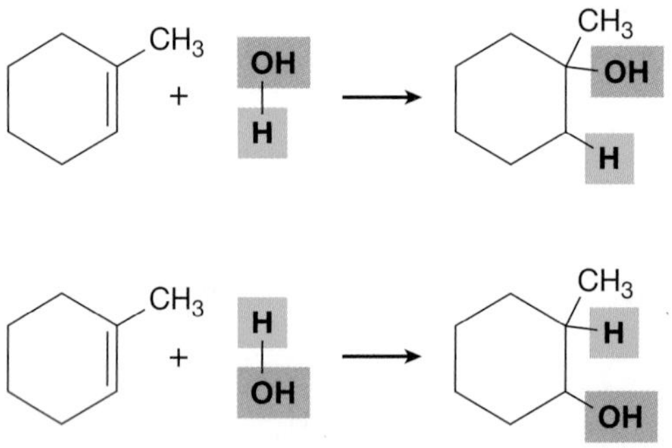

CH3 + OH–H ⟶ CH3, OH, H — Product 1

CH3 + H–OH ⟶ CH3, H, OH — Product 2

We do not normally draw individual hydrogen atoms when we draw the line structure of a cyclic compound, so we can also draw the two products as shown here. The hydrogen atoms that we added to the molecules do not appear in the line structures, although they are present in the actual molecules.

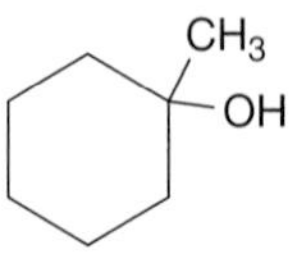

CH3, OH — Product 1

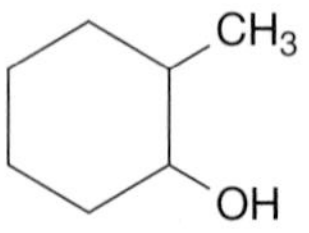

CH3, OH — Product 2

Symmetrical Alkenes Produce Only One Hydration Product

Some alkenes produce only one product when they react with water. If the two sides of the alkene are identical, we obtain the same alcohol regardless of which carbon atom bonds to the hydroxyl group. For example, when water reacts with 2-butene, the two products are actually the same compound.

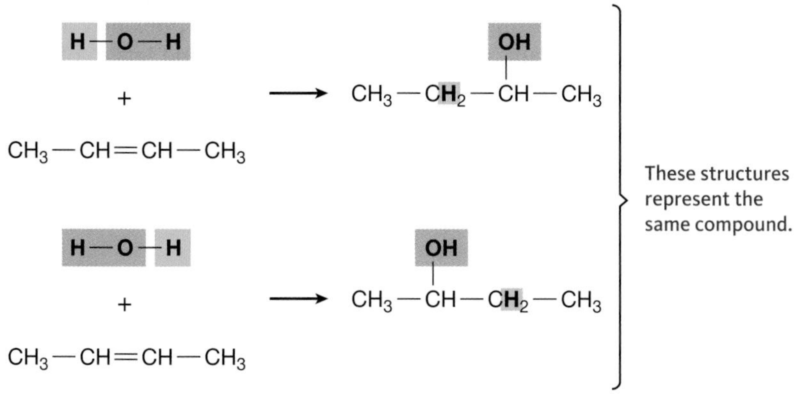

$$H{-}O{-}H + CH_3{-}CH{=}CH{-}CH_3 \longrightarrow CH_3{-}CH_2{-}\underset{}{\overset{OH}{\overset{|}{C}H}}{-}CH_3$$

$$H{-}O{-}H + CH_3{-}CH{=}CH{-}CH_3 \longrightarrow CH_3{-}\overset{OH}{\overset{|}{C}H}{-}CH_2{-}CH_3$$

These structures represent the same compound.

Sample Problem 9.2

Determining the number of possible hydration products

Tell whether each of the following alkenes forms one product or two products when it reacts with water.

a) propene b) cyclopentene

SOLUTION

a) When we divide the propene molecule at the double bond, we get two different pieces.

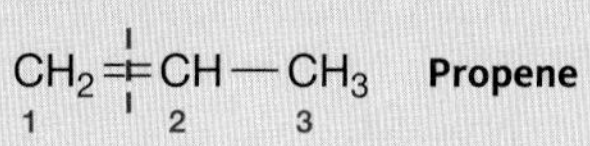

$$\underset{1}{CH_2}\,{=}\!\!\mid\!\!{=}\,\underset{2}{CH}{-}\underset{3}{CH_3} \quad \textbf{Propene}$$

Since the left and right sides of this alkene are dissimilar, we form two different hydration products.

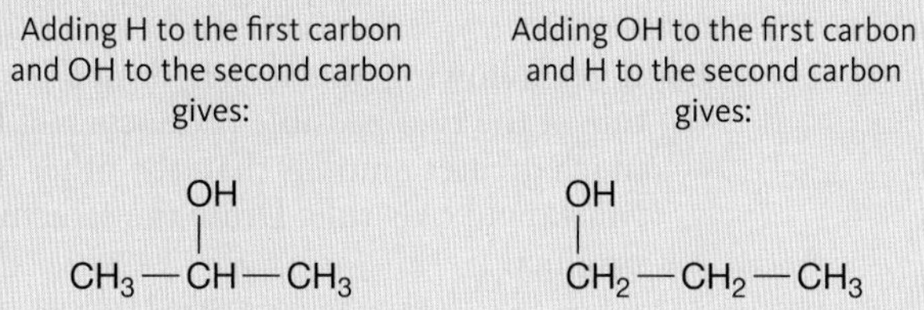

Adding H to the first carbon and OH to the second carbon gives:

$$CH_3{-}\overset{OH}{\overset{|}{C}H}{-}CH_3$$

Adding OH to the first carbon and H to the second carbon gives:

$$\overset{OH}{\overset{|}{C}H_2}{-}CH_2{-}CH_3$$

b) There is only one hydration product for cyclopentene. If we draw a line through the double bond, the line divides the cyclopentene molecule into two identical parts.

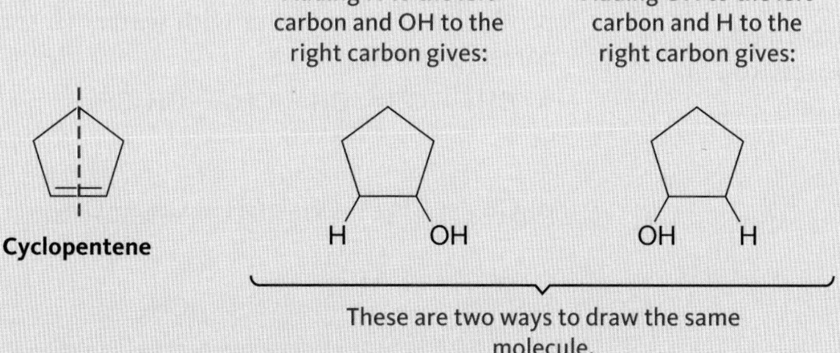
Adding H to the left carbon and OH to the right carbon gives:
Adding OH to the left carbon and H to the right carbon gives:
Cyclopentene
H
OH
OH
H
These are two ways to draw the same molecule.

TRY IT YOURSELF: *Tell whether each of the following alkenes forms one product or two products when it reacts with water.*

a) ethylene

b) cis*-2-hexene*

For additional practice, try Core Problems 9.5 and 9.6.

The hydration reaction is important in biological chemistry because it introduces a hydrogen-bonding functional group into a molecule. As we will see in Section 9.4, alcohols are more soluble in water than hydrocarbons, making them easier for our bodies to transport through our bloodstream. In addition, hydration reactions play an important role when our bodies burn organic compounds such as sugars and fats to obtain energy, as we will see in coming chapters.

CORE PROBLEMS

All Core Problems are paired and the answers to the **blue** *odd-numbered problems appear in the back of the book.*

9.1 Draw the structures of the products that are formed when the following alkenes are hydrated. Be sure to tell whether the reaction forms two products or only one.

a) $CH_2{=}CH{-}CH_2{-}CH_2{-}CH_3$

b) 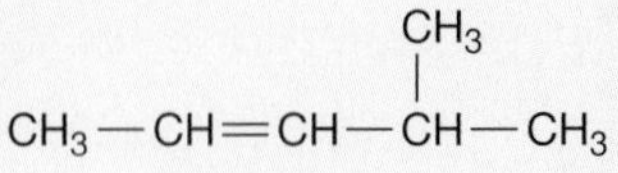 $CH_3{-}CH{=}CH{-}CH(CH_3){-}CH_3$

c) 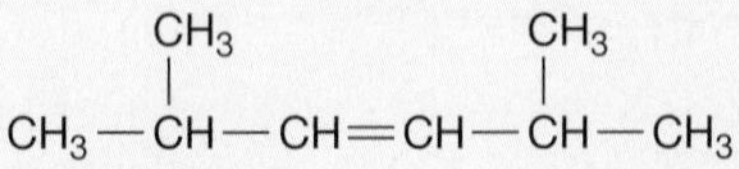 $CH_3{-}CH(CH_3){-}CH{=}CH{-}CH(CH_3){-}CH_3$

d) 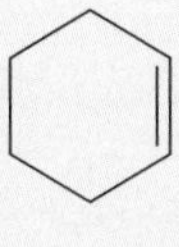 (cyclohexene)

e) 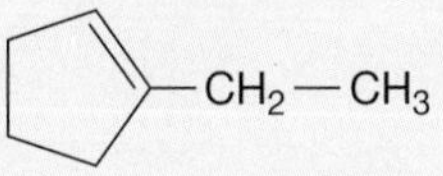 (cyclopentene ring)$-CH_2{-}CH_3$

f) 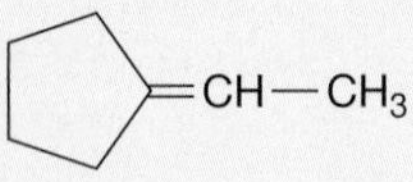 (cyclopentane ring)$=CH{-}CH_3$

g) 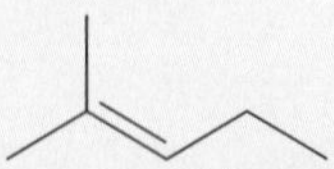 (skeletal structure)

9.2 Draw the structures of the products that are formed when the following alkenes are hydrated. Be sure to tell whether the reaction forms two products or only one.

a) $CH_3{-}CH{=}CH{-}CH_2{-}CH_2{-}CH_3$

b) 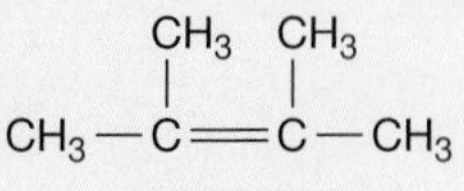 $CH_3{-}C(CH_3){=}C(CH_3){-}CH_3$

c) $CH_3{-}CH_2{-}C(CH_3){=}CH_2$

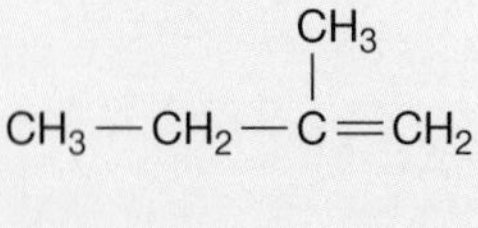

d) 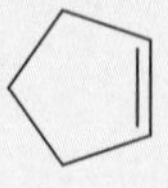 (cyclopentene)

e) 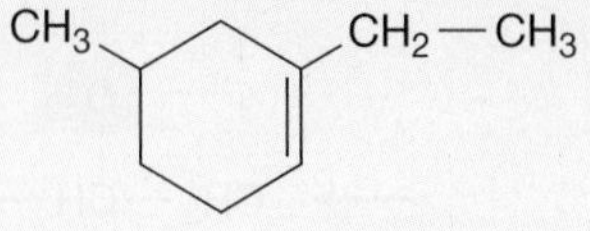 CH_3 (cyclohexene ring) $CH_2{-}CH_3$

f) 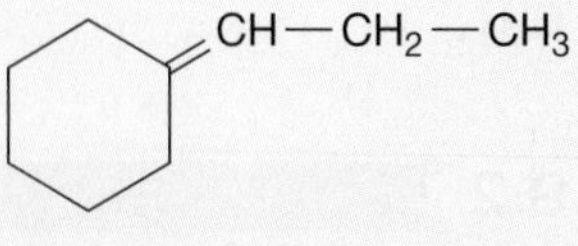 (cyclohexane ring)$=CH{-}CH_2{-}CH_3$

g) 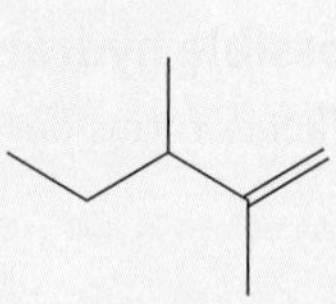 (skeletal structure)

9.3 If the following alkene is hydrated in a laboratory, one of the two possible products will be formed in much greater amount than the other, based on Markovnikov's rule. Draw the structure of this product.

$CH_3{-}CH(CH_3){-}CH{=}CH_2$

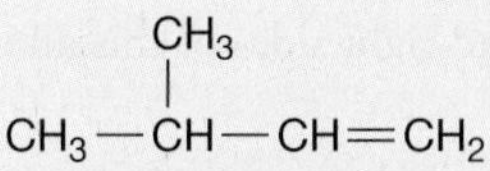

9.4 If the following alkene is hydrated in a laboratory, one of the two possible products will be formed in much greater amount than the other, based on Markovnikov's rule. Draw the structure of this product.

$CH_2{=}C(CH_3){-}CH_2{-}CH_3$

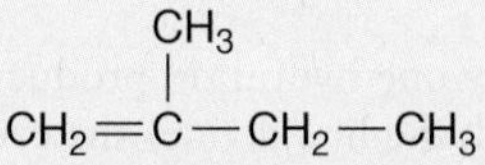

9.5 Which of the following alkenes can form only one product when they react with water? (List all of the correct answers.)

a) $CH_3{-}CH{=}CH{-}CH_2{-}CH_2CH_3$

b) $CH_3{-}CH_2{-}CH{=}CH{-}CH_2{-}CH_3$

c) 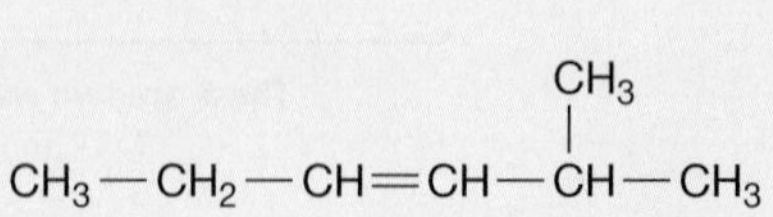 $CH_3{-}CH_2{-}CH{=}CH{-}CH(CH_3){-}CH_3$

d) 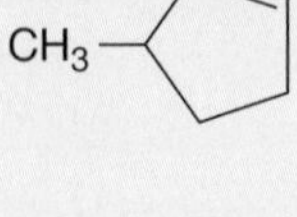 CH_3-(cyclopentene ring)

e) 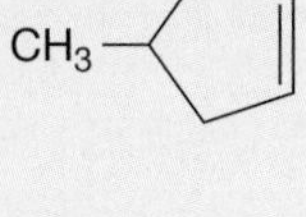 CH_3-(cyclopentene ring)

continued

9.6 Which of the following alkenes can form only one product when they react with water? (List all of the correct answers.)

a) $CH_3-CH_2-C(CH_3)=C(CH_3)-CH_2-CH_3$

b) $CH_3-CH=C(CH_3)-CH(CH_3)-CH_2-CH_3$

c) $CH_3-CH_2-C(=CH_2)-CH_2-CH_3$

d) 1,2-dimethylcyclohex-3-ene (CH_3, CH_3 on ring)

e) (CH_3, CH_3 on ring, double bond on opposite side)

9.2 Controlling the Product: An Introduction to Enzymes

OBJECTIVE: *Describe the role of enzymes in determining which of several possible products is formed in a biochemical reaction.*

Living organisms carry out many reactions. As we will see in coming chapters, these reactions occur in specific sequences, in which each product becomes the starting material for the next reaction. Figure 9.3 illustrates a general sequence of reactions.

Many reaction sequences involve one or more hydration reactions. As we saw in the previous section, the hydration of an alkene produces a mixture of two alcohols whenever the two sides of the alkene are different. This creates a potential problem in living organisms, because they normally can only use one of the two possible alcohols. The other product is of no use to the organism, and it may be quite toxic.

For example, our bodies carry out several lengthy sequences of reactions whenever we obtain energy from proteins. These reactions break down the proteins into their building blocks (called amino acids), and then they break down each amino acid into inorganic waste materials. The two steps shown here are part of one of these reaction sequences. (The second step is an example of an oxidation, a type of reaction that we will explore in Chapter 10.)

$$CH_2=C(CH_3)-C(=O)-OH + H_2O \xrightarrow[\text{hydration}]{\text{Step 1:}} CH_2(OH)-CH(CH_3)-C(=O)-OH \xrightarrow[\text{oxidation (removal of two H atoms)}]{\text{Step 2:}} CH(=O)-CH(CH_3)-C(=O)-OH$$

The first step in this sequence is a hydration reaction and adds water to the alkene group of the starting material. Because the alkene is not symmetrical, there are two possible products of this reaction. However, our bodies can only use this particular

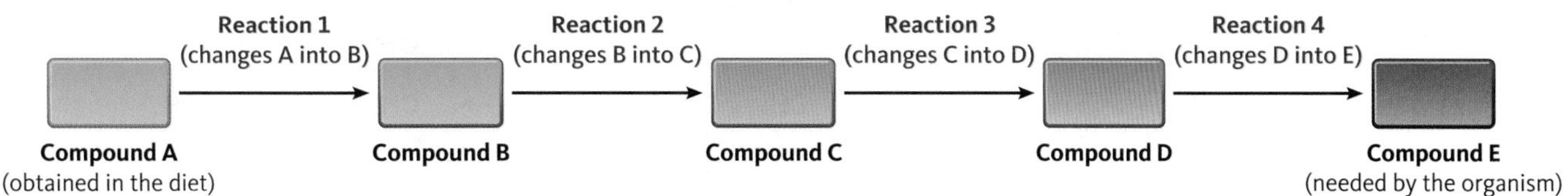

FIGURE 9.3 A sequence of reactions in a living organism.

alcohol as the starting material for the second step. The other possible product cannot be oxidized:

$$CH_2{=}C(CH_3){-}C({=}O){-}OH + H_2O \longrightarrow CH_3{-}C(OH)(CH_3){-}C({=}O){-}OH$$

Alternate product: cannot be used by the body

Hydration is not the only class of reaction that can form two or more products. Most reaction sequences in living organisms contain several reactions that could potentially make unwanted products. Organisms cannot afford to waste their nutritional resources, so they must be able to control each reaction so that it makes only the desired product.

Enzymes Are Biological Catalysts That Produce a Single Product

Health Note: If you have ever taken Beano to reduce gas, you are already familiar with the benefits of enzymes. Beano contains an enzyme called *alpha-galactosidase,* which breaks down certain carbohydrates that humans cannot normally digest. Without this enzyme, the carbohydrates pass unchanged into the large intestine, where they serve as food for bacteria that produce intestinal gas.

Living organisms solve the problem of multiple products by using **enzymes** to catalyze virtually every reaction that occurs in them. Enzymes are a class of proteins, and they are complex molecules that control every aspect of a reaction. The primary role of an enzyme is as a catalyst, a molecule that speeds up a reaction, but enzymes also ensure that the correct product is formed whenever two or more products are possible. For example, the preceding hydration reaction requires an enzyme in order to occur reasonably rapidly. The enzyme that catalyzes this reaction also ensures that the H and OH groups are placed in the correct orientation. Figure 9.4 illustrates the ability of the enzyme to select the correct product. (Note that the enzyme does not follow Markovnikov's rule; this rule only applies to laboratory hydration reactions.)

In some cases, the enzyme does not need to select a particular product, because only one product is possible. For instance, the following hydration reaction has only one possible product, because the two sides of the alkene group are identical. However, this reaction still requires an enzyme to speed it up.

$$HO{-}C({=}O){-}CH{=}CH{-}C({=}O){-}OH + H_2O \longrightarrow HO{-}C({=}O){-}CH_2{-}CH(OH){-}C({=}O){-}OH$$

Fumaric acid (the two sides of the molecule are identical)

Malic acid (the only possible product)

Kresimir Juraga

Some cleaning products use enzymes to break down and remove organic materials.

Enzymes are also selective about the reactants that they can use. For example, the enzyme that catalyzes the hydration reaction in Figure 9.4 does not add water to other compounds that contain the alkene functional group, because they do not fit into the enzyme correctly. Our bodies make many compounds that contain carbon–carbon double bonds, so it is important for the enzyme to leave these molecules alone.

Enzymes are remarkable molecules and play a fundamental role in all organisms, from the simplest to the most complex. We will return to the subject of enzymes from time to time throughout the remainder of this book.

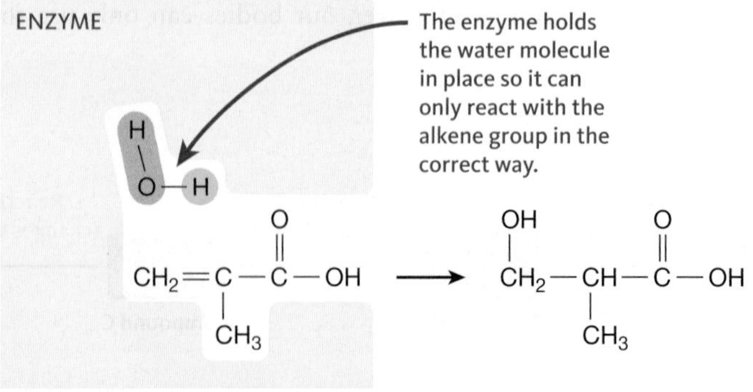

FIGURE 9.4 Enzyme selectivity in a hydration reaction.

CORE PROBLEMS

9.7 What is an enzyme?

9.8 List two ways in which enzymes affect reactions in our bodies.

9.9 The following reaction occurs when your body breaks down carbohydrates, fats, and proteins to obtain energy. The reaction is catalyzed by an enzyme. Must this enzyme select one of the possible products in this reaction? If so, what is the other possible product?

$$\text{HO—C(=O)—CH=C(—C(=O)—OH)—CH}_2\text{—C(=O)—OH} + \text{H}_2\text{O} \longrightarrow \text{HO—C(=O)—CH(OH)—CH(—C(=O)—OH)—CH}_2\text{—C(=O)—OH}$$

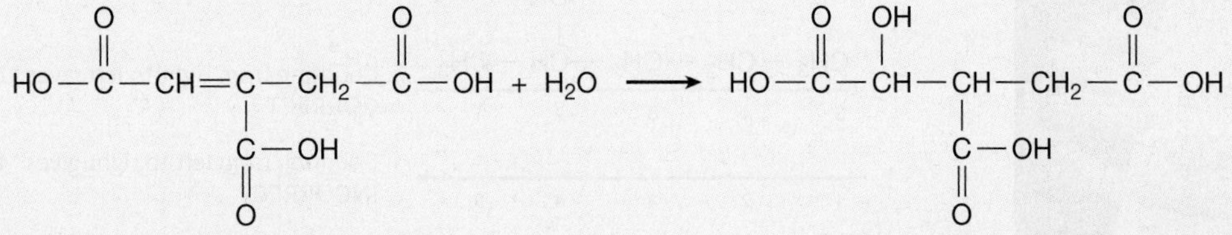

Aconitic acid → **Isocitric acid**

9.10 The following reaction occurs when your body breaks down fats to obtain energy. The reaction is catalyzed by an enzyme. Must this enzyme select one of the possible products in this reaction? If so, what is the other possible product?

$$\text{CH}_3\text{—CH=CH—C(=O)—rest of molecule} + \text{H}_2\text{O} \longrightarrow \text{CH}_3\text{—CH(OH)—CH}_2\text{—C(=O)—rest of molecule}$$

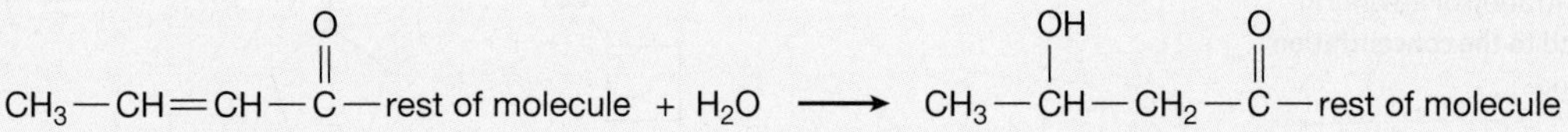

9.3 Naming Alcohols

OBJECTIVES: *Name simple alcohols using the IUPAC system, and learn the trivial names for common alcohols.*

In Section 9.1, we saw how we can add water to an alkene to form an alcohol, and in Section 9.4 we explore the properties of these important compounds. Let us now look at how alcohols are named.

The naming of alcohols by the IUPAC system follows the rules you learned for alkenes and alkynes in Chapter 8:

1. Name the hydrocarbon framework.
2. Identify the functional group by modifying the ending of the alkane name.
3. Add a number to tell where the functional group is located.

You have already learned how to name hydrocarbons, so we will focus on steps 2 and 3. To identify the alcohol group, we replace the *-e* at the end of the alkane name with *-ol.* The two simplest alcohols are called *methanol* and *ethanol.*

CH_4	CH_3—**OH**	CH_3—CH_3	CH_3—CH_2—**OH**
Methane (no functional group)	**Methanol** (an alcohol)	**Ethane** (no functional group)	**Ethanol** (an alcohol)

Health Note: Methanol (methyl alcohol or wood alcohol) is toxic and damaging to vision, with even small amounts causing partial or complete blindness. If methanol is confused with ethanol (the "alcohol" in alcoholic beverages), tragic results occur. *Denatured alcohol* is ethanol that is mixed with up to 10% methanol or another liquid to make the ethanol poisonous; it is used as an industrial solvent and as a fuel for lightweight camping stoves.

Once we reach three carbon atoms, we have more than one possible location for our alcohol group. For instance, two alcohols contain a hydroxyl group bonded to propane. To tell them apart, we add a number that tells us which carbon atom is bonded to the functional group. As was the case with alkenes, we write the number before the rest of the name, and we separate the number from the name with a hyphen.

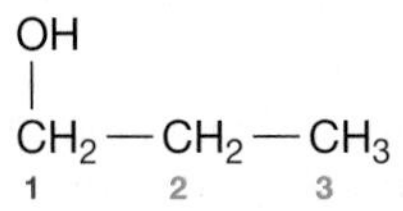

$CH_2(OH)$—CH_2—CH_3 (carbons 1, 2, 3)	CH_3—$CH(OH)$—CH_3 (carbons 1, 2, 3)
1-Propanol (The hydroxyl group is bonded to carbon 1.)	**2-Propanol** (The hydroxyl group is bonded to carbon 2.)

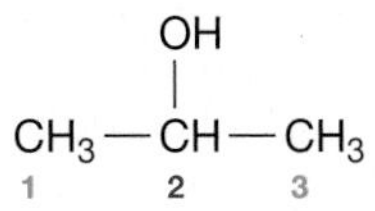

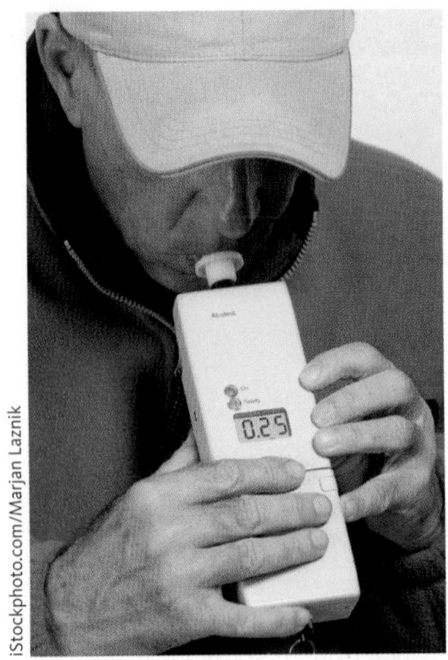

The Breathalyzer test uses a chemical reaction to detect ethanol in a person's breath. The concentration of ethanol in the breath is related to the concentration in the person's blood.

These two compounds are constitutional isomers, because they have the same molecular formula (C_3H_8O), but their atoms are connected to one another in a different order. 1-Propanol and 2-propanol, like all constitutional isomers, have different physical and chemical properties.

As we saw when we named alkenes and alkynes, the IUPAC rules require us to number the carbon chain from the end that is closest to the functional group to prevent us from giving two different names to the same molecule. For instance, the compound shown here is called 2-pentanol, not 4-pentanol:

$$CH_3-CH_2-CH_2-\underset{\displaystyle |}{\overset{OH}{CH}}-CH_3$$

5 4 3 2 1 ← Counting from right to left gives "2-pentanol." CORRECT

1 2 3 4 5 → Counting from left to right gives "4-pentanol." INCORRECT

If we attach a hydroxyl group to a ring of carbon atoms, we make a cyclic alcohol. We name cyclic alcohols by changing the end of the name of the corresponding hydrocarbon from *-e* to *-ol,* just as we do for open-chain alcohols. For example, here are the structures of the cyclic alcohols cyclobutanol and cyclopentanol:

OH OH

Cyclobutanol **Cyclopentanol**

As was the case with cycloalkanes that contain an alkyl substituent, we do not use a number to show the location of the functional group in a cyclic alcohol. Regardless of which carbon atom we attach to the hydroxyl group, we make the same molecule, as shown here:

OH OH OH HO HO

We can produce any of the other structures by rotating this one.

These are different ways of drawing the first structure.

Sample Problem 9.3

Naming alcohols using the IUPAC rules

Name the following alcohols:

a) $CH_3-CH_2-CH_2-CH_2-\overset{OH}{\overset{|}{CH}}-CH_2-CH_3$ b) (cyclopropane ring)—OH

SOLUTION

a) This alcohol contains a seven-carbon chain, so the corresponding alkane is heptane. To show the alcohol functional group, we change the ending to *-ol,* giving us heptanol. The hydroxyl group is bonded to the third carbon in the chain (counting from the right side, which is closest to the functional group), so this is 3-heptanol.

b) The alkane that corresponds to this alcohol is cyclopropane. Changing the ending to show the presence of the hydroxyl group gives us cyclopropanol. Since this is a cyclic

continued

alcohol, we do not need to show where the hydroxyl group is located, so the correct name is cyclopropanol.

TRY IT YOURSELF: *Name the following alcohol:*

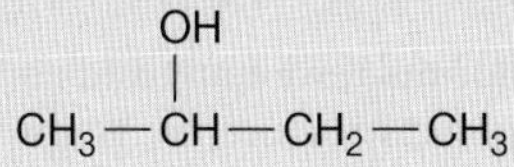

$$CH_3-\underset{}{\overset{\displaystyle OH}{\overset{|}{C}H}}-CH_2-CH_3$$

For additional practice, try Core Problems 9.11 and 9.12.

To draw the structure of an alcohol, we start with the hydrocarbon chain and then add the functional group. For example, let us draw the structure of 2-heptanol. This name is derived from *heptane,* the name of the seven-carbon linear alkane. Therefore, we start by drawing a chain that contains seven carbon atoms.

$$C-C-C-C-C-C-C$$

The *-ol* ending tells us that our molecule contains a hydroxyl group, and the 2 tells us that this group is attached to the second carbon in the chain. When we draw a structure, we can number the principal chain from either end.

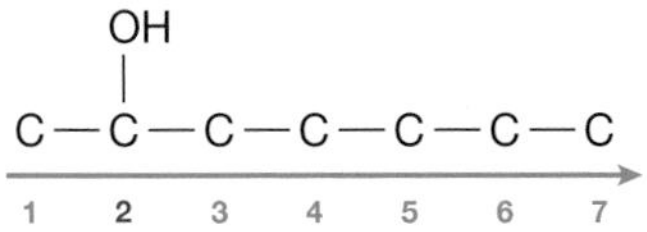

$$\underset{1}{C}-\underset{2}{\overset{\displaystyle OH}{\overset{|}{C}}}-\underset{3}{C}-\underset{4}{C}-\underset{5}{C}-\underset{6}{C}-\underset{7}{C} \quad \text{or} \quad \underset{7}{C}-\underset{6}{C}-\underset{5}{C}-\underset{4}{C}-\underset{3}{C}-\underset{2}{\overset{\displaystyle OH}{\overset{|}{C}}}-\underset{1}{C}$$

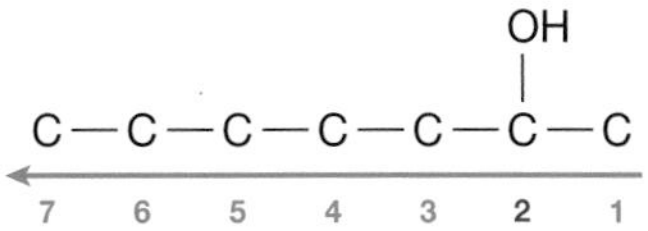

We complete the structure by adding enough hydrogen atoms to give each carbon atom four bonds.

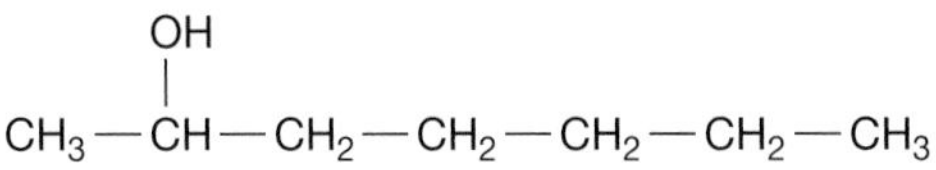

$$CH_3-\overset{\displaystyle OH}{\overset{|}{C}H}-CH_2-CH_2-CH_2-CH_2-CH_3$$

or

$$CH_3-CH_2-CH_2-CH_2-CH_2-\overset{\displaystyle OH}{\overset{|}{C}H}-CH_3$$

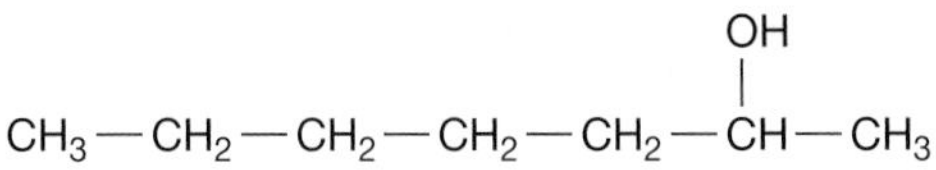

To draw a line structure, we again start by drawing the hydrocarbon chain, this time as a zigzag line. Be sure that the line has the correct number of corners.

(zigzag chain numbered 1–7)

We complete the structure by adding the functional group. Again, we can number the chain from either end.

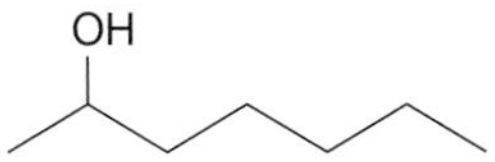

(line structures of 2-heptanol with OH on carbon 2, drawn from either end) or

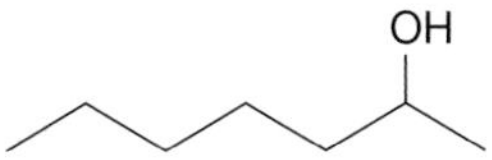

Sample Problem 9.4

Drawing the structure of an alcohol

Draw the condensed structural formula and the line structure of 1-hexanol.

SOLUTION

The name *1-hexanol* is derived from the alkane name *hexane,* so we start with a six-carbon chain.

$$C-C-C-C-C-C$$

continued

Next, we add the hydroxyl group to carbon 1.

$$\overset{\text{OH}}{\overset{|}{\text{C}}}-\text{C}-\text{C}-\text{C}-\text{C}-\text{C} \quad \left(\text{or} \quad \text{C}-\text{C}-\text{C}-\text{C}-\text{C}-\overset{\text{OH}}{\overset{|}{\text{C}}}\right)$$

To draw a condensed structural formula, we must add enough hydrogen atoms to give each carbon its four bonds. For a line structure, we simply redraw the carbon chain as a zigzag line.

$$\overset{\text{OH}}{\overset{|}{CH_2}}-CH_2-CH_2-CH_2-CH_2-CH_3$$ or [line structure]

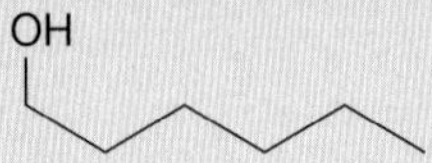

TRY IT YOURSELF: *Draw the condensed structural formula and the line structure of 3-nonanol.*

For additional practice, try Core Problems 9.13 and 9.14.

Some Alcohols Have Commonly Used Trivial Names

Health Note: Rubbing alcohol is usually a mixture of 70% isopropyl alcohol and 30% water, although some formulations contain denatured ethanol instead of isopropyl alcohol. Rubbing alcohol produces a pleasant soothing, cooling sensation on the skin, and it is commonly used to kill bacteria on skin before hypodermic injections.

A number of alcohols have alternate names that are in common use. These names usually contain the name of an alkyl group followed by the word *alcohol*. Here are the trivial names for three common alcohols, along with their IUPAC names:

CH_3-OH	CH_3-CH_2-OH	$CH_3-\overset{\text{OH}}{\overset{|}{CH}}-CH_3$
Methyl alcohol (methanol)	**Ethyl alcohol** (ethanol)	**Isopropyl alcohol** (2-propanol)

The name *isopropyl alcohol* is used for 2-propanol because *propyl alcohol* is reserved for 1-propanol.

CORE PROBLEMS

9.11 Write the IUPAC names for each of the following alcohols:

a) $CH_3-CH_2-CH_2-CH_2-OH$

b) 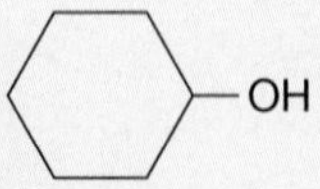 [cyclohexane ring]—OH

c) $CH_3-CH_2-CH_2-\overset{\text{OH}}{\overset{|}{CH}}-CH_2-CH_2-CH_2-CH_3$

d) 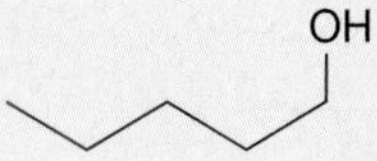 [line structure with OH]

9.12 Write the IUPAC names for each of the following alcohols:

a) CH_3-CH_2-OH

b) $CH_3-CH_2-CH_2-CH_2-CH_2-\overset{\text{OH}}{\overset{|}{CH}}-CH_3$

c) 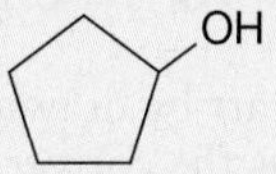 [cyclopentane ring]—OH

d) 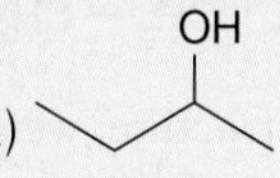 [line structure with OH]

9.13 Draw the condensed structural formula and the line structure of each of the following alcohols:
a) 3-pentanol b) 2-nonanol c) cyclobutanol

9.14 Draw the condensed structural formula and the line structure of each of the following alcohols:
a) cyclopropanol b) 4-heptanol c) 1-pentanol

9.15 Draw the structure of methyl alcohol, and give its IUPAC name.

9.16 Draw the structure of isopropyl alcohol, and give its IUPAC name.

9.17 Which of the following names are incorrect, according to the IUPAC rules? Explain your answer.
a) pentanol b) 1-pentanol
c) 2-pentanol d) 4-pentanol

9.18 Which of the following names are incorrect, according to the IUPAC rules?
a) ethanol b) propanol
c) 3-butanol d) 3-pentanol

9.4 The Physical Properties of Alcohols

OBJECTIVE: *Relate the physical properties of alcohols to their structures.*

The two covalent bonds in the alcohol functional group are strongly polar. Oxygen has a higher electronegativity than either carbon or hydrogen, so the oxygen atom is negatively charged, and the hydrogen and carbon atoms are positively charged. In addition, the two bonds to oxygen lie at an angle to each other, just as they do in a water molecule.

δ− H O H δ+ δ+ — The arrangement of atoms in **water**

δ− C O H δ+ — The arrangement of atoms in an **alcohol**

The polar O—H bond allows alcohols to form hydrogen bonds. The hydrogen atom from one alcohol group is attracted to the oxygen atom of a second alcohol group, as shown here:

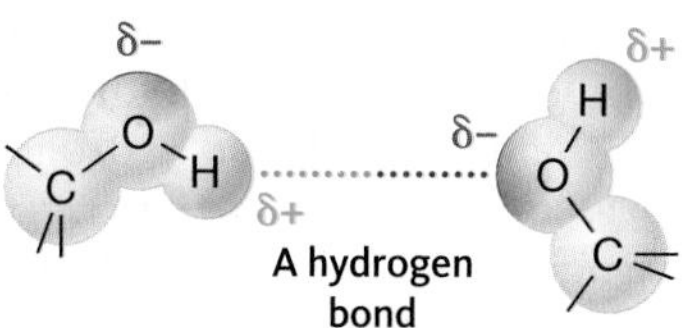

The ability to form hydrogen bonds gives alcohols quite different physical properties from those of hydrocarbons. For example, alcohols have much higher boiling points than alkanes that have the same carbon skeleton. Remember that when we boil a liquid, we must supply enough energy to overcome the attraction between molecules. The molecules of an alcohol attract one another more strongly than the molecules of an alkane do, because the alcohol forms hydrogen bonds. As a result, we must heat the alcohol to a higher temperature in order to boil it. Table 9.1 compares the boiling points of some alcohols to those of the corresponding alkanes.

TABLE 9.1 The Physical Properties of Some Alkanes and Alcohols

Alkane	Boiling Point	State at Room Temperature	Alcohol	Boiling Point	State at Room Temperature
Methane	−161°C	Gas	Methanol	65°C	Liquid
Ethane	−88°C	Gas	Ethanol	78°C	Liquid
Propane	−26°C	Gas	1-Propanol	82°C	Liquid
Pentane	36°C	Liquid	1-Pentanol	137°C	Liquid
Octane	126°C	Liquid	1-Octanol	194°C	Liquid

Sample Problem 9.5

Comparing the physical properties of alcohols and alkanes

Arrange the following compounds in order from lowest to highest boiling point:

2-butanol   2-pentanol   butane

SOLUTION

First, we must draw the structures of these three molecules.

$CH_3—CH(OH)—CH_2—CH_3$ — **2-butanol**

$CH_3—CH(OH)—CH_2—CH_2—CH_3$ — **2-pentanol**

$CH_3—CH_2—CH_2—CH_3$ — **butane**

continued

Butane is an alkane and cannot form hydrogen bonds, so it has the lowest boiling point. 2-Butanol and 2-pentanol are both alcohols, but 2-butanol is a smaller molecule than 2-pentanol, so 2-butanol should have a lower boiling point than 2-pentanol. The correct order is

butane 2-butanol 2-pentanol

TRY IT YOURSELF: *Which should have the higher boiling point, cyclohexanol or cyclohexene?*

For additional practice, try Core Problems 9.21 and 9.22.

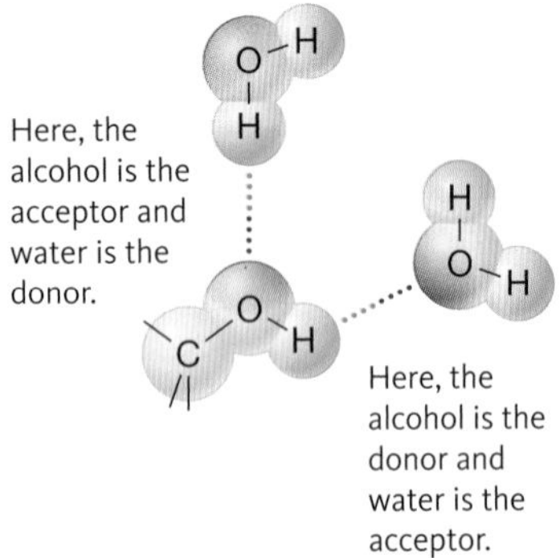
Here, the alcohol is the acceptor and water is the donor.
Here, the alcohol is the donor and water is the acceptor.

FIGURE 9.5 Hydrogen bonding between water and an alcohol.

Alcohols are also more soluble in water than hydrocarbons. Recall from Section 8.9 that hydrocarbons are essentially insoluble in water, because they cannot participate in hydrogen bonds. As a result, hydrocarbons are strongly hydrophobic. By contrast, the hydroxyl group of an alcohol is hydrophilic, because it can form hydrogen bonds with water. Both the oxygen and the hydrogen atom can participate in hydrogen bonding, as shown in Figure 9.5. These hydrogen bonds allow alcohols to mix with water. In general, *organic compounds that can form hydrogen bonds are more soluble in water than organic compounds that cannot.* We will see many other examples of the role of hydrogen bonding in water solubility as we continue our survey of organic chemistry.

The Solubility of an Alcohol Depends on the Size of Its Carbon Chain

When we look at the ability of alcohols to dissolve in water, we find a striking relationship between the size of a molecule and its solubility: as the carbon skeleton gets larger, the solubility decreases. The smallest alcohols can mix with water in any proportion, while alcohols with long carbon chains are scarcely more soluble than alkanes. Table 9.2 lists the solubilities of some alcohols.

The relationship between solubility and size of the carbon skeleton applies to all classes of organic compounds that can participate in hydrogen bonding. As we saw in Section 4.9, the solubility of a molecular compound depends on the relative sizes of the hydrophilic and hydrophobic regions in the molecule. In an alcohol, the hydroxyl group is hydrophilic and the hydrocarbon portion of the molecule is hydrophobic. If the hydrophobic region of the molecule is small, the ability of the hydroxyl group to form hydrogen bonds dominates, and the compound mixes with water in all proportions, as illustrated in Figure 9.6. If the hydrophobic region is large, its properties dominate, and the compound behaves more like an alkane. Any alcohol is more soluble than the corresponding alkane, but the difference becomes progressively smaller as the number of carbon atoms increases.

TABLE 9.2 The Solubilities of Some Alcohols

Compound	Carbon Atoms	Solubility in 100 g of Water
Methanol	One	No limit (any amount of these alcohols will mix with water)
Ethanol	Two	
1-Propanol	Three	
1-Butanol	Four	7.4 g
1-Pentanol	Five	2.7 g
1-Hexanol	Six	0.7 g
1-Heptanol	Seven	0.1 g

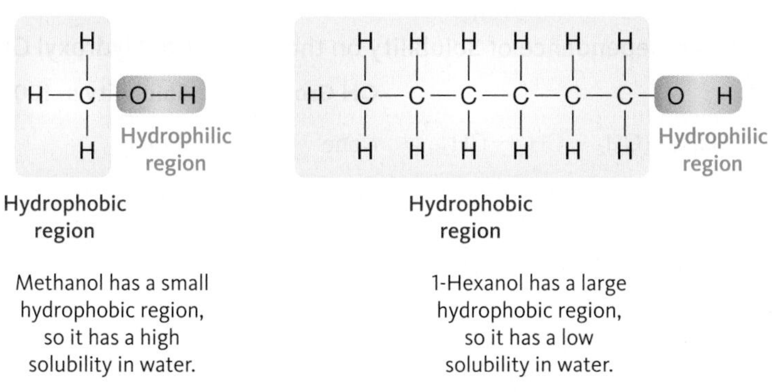

H—C—O—H
Hydrophilic region
Hydrophobic region
Methanol has a small hydrophobic region, so it has a high solubility in water.
H—C—C—C—C—C—C—O H
Hydrophilic region
Hydrophobic region
1-Hexanol has a large hydrophobic region, so it has a low solubility in water.

FIGURE 9.6 The effect of the hydrophobic region on the solubility of alcohols.

120
100
80
60
40
20

Chartes D. Winters

Like other small alcohols, ethanol mixes with water in any proportion.

Sample Problem 9.6

Predicting relative solubilities of organic compounds

From each of the following pairs of compounds, predict which compound is more soluble in water:

a) 2-butanol and butane
b) cyclooctanol and cyclopentanol

SOLUTION

a) 2-Butanol contains a hydroxyl group, which is hydrophilic and can form hydrogen bonds with water. Butane cannot form hydrogen bonds, so it is entirely hydrophobic. Therefore, 2-butanol should be more soluble in water than butane.

$$CH_3-\underset{}{\overset{OH}{\overset{|}{C}H}}-CH_2-CH_3 \qquad CH_3-CH_2-CH_2-CH_3$$

2-Butanol **Butane**

b) Both cyclooctanol and cyclopentanol contain a hydrophilic alcohol group. However, cyclopentanol has a smaller hydrophobic region (the hydrocarbon ring) than cyclooctanol. Therefore, cyclopentanol should be more soluble in water than cyclooctanol.

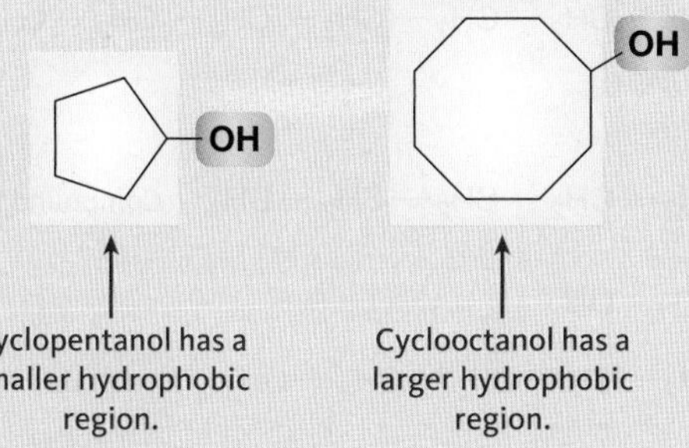

OH
OH
Cyclopentanol has a smaller hydrophobic region.
Cyclooctanol has a larger hydrophobic region.

TRY IT YOURSELF: *Which is more soluble in water, 3-pentanol or propane?*

For additional practice, try Core Problems 9.23 and 9.24.

Adding Hydroxyl Groups Increases the Solubility of an Alcohol

Many organic compounds contain more than one hydroxyl group. In general, water solubility increases as we add hydrophilic groups to a carbon framework. Table 9.3 shows a series of compounds that illustrates this trend.

TABLE 9.3 The Dependence of Solubility on the Number of Hydroxyl Groups

Compound	OH Groups	Solubility in 100 g of H_2O
$CH_3-CH_2-CH_2-CH_2-CH_2-CH_3$	None	0.04 g
$CH_2(OH)-CH_2-CH_2-CH_2-CH_2-CH_3$	One	0.7 g
$CH_2(OH)-CH_2-CH_2-CH_2-CH_2-CH_2(OH)$	Two	6 g
$CH_2(OH)-CH_2-CH(OH)-CH_2-CH_2-CH_2(OH)$	Three	No limit

The actual solubility of any organic compound in water depends on the number of hydrophilic groups, the locations of those groups, and the structure and size of the carbon skeleton. It is not possible to predict the exact solubility of a specific alcohol from its structure, but we can make some general statements about solubility trends.

Health Note: Menthol is a sparingly soluble alcohol and is one of the compounds responsible for the flavor of mint. It stimulates the nerve receptors that respond to coldness, so it produces a cooling sensation on the skin and in the mouth without actually lowering their temperature. It also is an analgesic, a compound that relieves pain. As a result, menthol is used in products that relieve muscle and joint pain.

HO, CH_3, CH_3, $CH-CH_3$

Menthol

- Compounds with a hydrogen-bonding group (a hydrophilic group) dissolve better than compounds that cannot form hydrogen bonds, regardless of the sizes of the molecules.
- If two compounds have the same hydrophilic group, the molecule with the *smaller carbon framework* is the more soluble.
- If two compounds have the same carbon framework, the molecule with *more hydrophilic groups* is the more soluble.

Sample Problem 9.7

Ranking the solubilities of alcohols

Rank the following four compounds in order of their solubility in water, starting with the least soluble:

$CH_3-CH(OH)-CH_2-CH_2-CH_2-CH_2-CH_2-CH_3$ **Compound A: 2-octanol**

$CH_3-CH(OH)-CH_2-CH_2-CH_2-CH_2-CH_3$ **Compound B: 2-heptanol**

$CH_3-CH(OH)-CH_2-CH(OH)-CH_2-CH_2-CH_3$ **Compound C: 2,4-heptanediol**

$CH_3-CH_2-CH_2-CH_2-CH_2-CH_2-CH_3$ **Compound D: heptane**

SOLUTION

Compound C has two hydroxyl groups and therefore has the highest solubility in water, since each hydroxyl group can form hydrogen bonds with water molecules. Compound D has no hydroxyl groups, so it has the lowest solubility. Compounds A and B have one hydroxyl group each, but their carbon chains are different lengths. Compound B has the shorter chain, so it is more soluble than compound A. This reasoning gives us the following ranking:

Compound D	Compound A	Compound B	Compound C
Least soluble	→	→	Most soluble

continued

TRY IT YOURSELF: *Rank the following three compounds in order of their solubility in water, starting with the least soluble:*

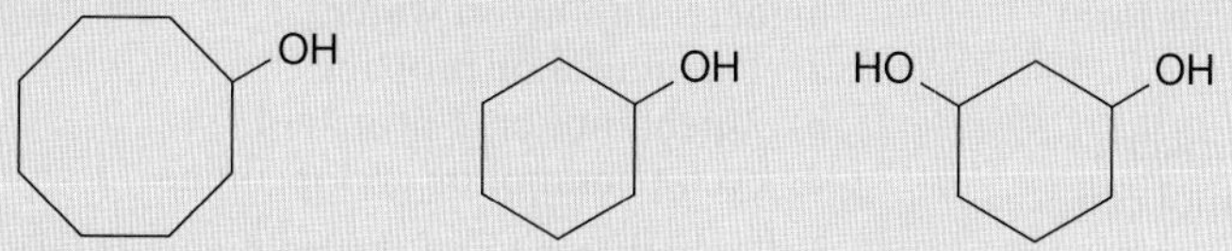

Compound X   Compound Y   Compound Z

Most Organic Compounds Mix Readily with One Another

Of course, water is not the only solvent. Water is of particular interest to us, because it is the primary solvent in living organisms, but other solvents are often used in laboratory settings. There is a wide range of common organic solvents, and there is no simple way to work out which compounds dissolve in which solvents. However, as a general guideline, *most organic compounds dissolve reasonably well in organic solvents.* For instance, all of the common alcohols mix with one another, and all of them dissolve in hydrocarbons such as hexane or benzene. Only compounds that approach water in their ability to form hydrogen bonds do not dissolve in hydrocarbons. A good example is glycerol (also called glycerin), which has this structure:

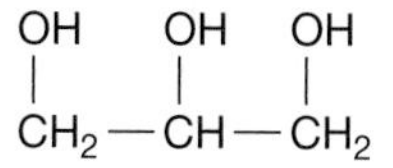

$$\begin{array}{ccccc} OH & & OH & & OH \\ | & & | & & | \\ CH_2 & - & CH & - & CH_2 \end{array}$$

Glycerol

Because of the three hydroxyl groups and the small carbon chain, glycerol has such a high tendency to form hydrogen bonds that it does not mix with hydrocarbons such as hexane and benzene. As you might expect, though, glycerol dissolves extremely well in water and in alcohols such as methanol and ethanol.

The Hydroxyl Group in Alcohols Is Not Acidic or Basic

When an alcohol dissolves in water, the solution is not appreciably acidic or basic. This may surprise you, because in Chapter 7 you learned to associate hydroxide ions (OH^-) with basic solutions. However, *alcohols do not contain hydroxide ions.* The hydroxyl group is covalently bonded to a carbon atom in an alcohol, and it does not dissociate from the rest of the molecule when the alcohol dissolves in water. For example, sodium hydroxide forms ions when it dissolves in water, while methanol does not. Note that carbon and oxygen share two electrons in methanol, while sodium and oxygen do not share electrons in NaOH.

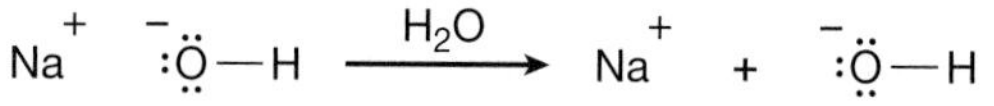

$$Na^+ \ {}^-:\ddot{\underset{..}{O}}-H \xrightarrow{H_2O} Na^+ + {}^-:\ddot{\underset{..}{O}}-H$$

NaOH is an ionic compound . . .   . . . and forms ions when it dissolves in water.

$$H-\overset{H}{\underset{H}{\overset{|}{\underset{|}{C}}}}-\ddot{\underset{..}{O}}-H \xrightarrow{H_2O} H-\overset{H}{\underset{H}{\overset{|}{\underset{|}{C}}}}-\ddot{\underset{..}{O}}-H$$

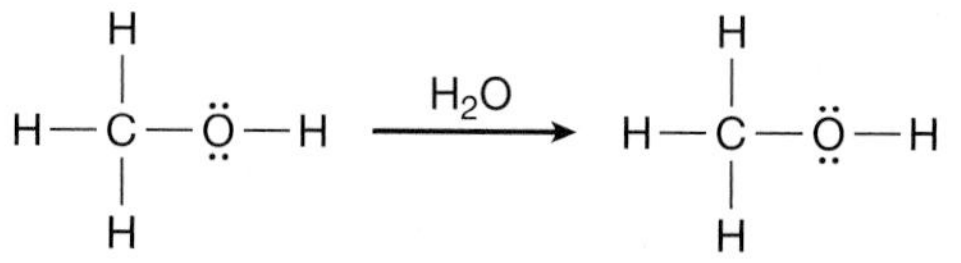

Methanol is a covalent compound . . .   . . . and remains intact when it dissolves in water.

Health Note: Consuming methanol can lead to a dangerous lowering of blood pH, but not because methanol is acidic. When your body metabolizes methanol, it converts the molecule into a formic acid. Your body can only eliminate formic acid rather slowly, so it builds up in the blood and can produce a fatal acidosis.

How can we recognize a true hydroxide ion in the formula of a compound? Compounds that contain hydroxide ions also contain a metallic element, which forms a positively charged ion. For example, KOH, $Ca(OH)_2$, and $Al(OH)_3$ contain the metallic elements potassium, calcium, and aluminum, respectively, so we can confidently say that the OH groups in these compounds are actually hydroxide ions, OH^-. On the other hand, compounds like CH_3OH and CH_3CH_2OH do not contain a metal, so the OH group in these molecules is a covalently bonded hydroxyl group.

CORE PROBLEMS

9.19 Draw a picture that shows the two ways in which a water molecule and a molecule of methanol can form hydrogen bonds with each other.

9.20 Draw a picture that shows the two ways in which a molecule of methanol and a molecule of ethanol can form hydrogen bonds with each other.

9.21 From each pair of compounds, select the one with the higher boiling point.
a) 3-pentanol or pentane
b) 2-butanol or 2-heptanol
c) $CH_3-CH_2-CH(OH)-CH_2-CH_3$

or

$CH_2(OH)-CH_2-CH(OH)-CH_2-CH_3$

9.22 From each pair of compounds, select the one with the higher boiling point.
a) 1-propanol or 2-pentanol
b) ethane or 2-butanol
c) $HO-CH_2-CH_2-CH_2-OH$ or $CH_3-CH_2-CH_2-CH_2-OH$

9.23 From each pair of compounds, select the one with the higher solubility in water.
a) 2-butanol or 2-hexanol
b) 2-butanol or hexane
c) ethanol or ethyne

9.24 From each pair of compounds, select the one with the higher solubility in water.
a) 1-pentanol or propane
b) 2-pentanol or 2-propanol
c) cyclopentanol or cyclopentene

9.25 Tell whether each of the following solutions is acidic, neutral, or basic:
a) 0.01 M KOH b) 0.01 M CH_3OH

9.26 Tell whether each of the following solutions is acidic, neutral, or basic:
a) 0.01 M CH_3-CH_2-OH b) 0.01 M NaOH

9.27 One of the following compounds does not dissolve in benzene. Which one?
a) $CH_3-CH_2-CH_2-CH_3$
b) $CH_3-CH_2-CH_2-OH$
c) $HO-CH_2-CH_2-OH$

9.28 One of the following compounds does not dissolve in cyclohexane. Which one?
a) $CH_2(OH)-CH_2(OH)$
b) $CH_2(OH)-CH(OH)-CH_3$
c) $CH_2(OH)-CH(OH)-CH_2-CH_3$

OBJECTIVES: *Recognize chiral objects, and identify chiral carbon atoms in a molecule.*

These two figurines are mirror images of each other but are not superimposible, so they are chiral.

9.5 Chirality in Organic Molecules

Hold your right hand up to a mirror and look at its reflection. Your mirror image will be holding up its left hand. If you compare your left hand with the reflection of your right hand, they will probably look virtually identical. However, your hands are not interchangeable; your right hand does not fit into a left glove. The same is true of your feet; your right and left feet are mirror images of each other, but they do not fit into each other's shoes.

Hands and feet are examples of **chiral** objects (pronounced "KYE-rull"). *A chiral object is an object that cannot be superimposed on its mirror image.* As Figure 9.7 shows, if you hold your hands with the palms facing you, the thumbs will be on opposite sides. Your left and right hands are mirror images of each other, and they cannot be superimposed on each other. By contrast, your nose can be superimposed on its mirror image, so it is not chiral (the technical term is **achiral**).

Many other everyday objects are chiral, including scissors, shoes, golf clubs, and baseball gloves. Any chiral object can exist in two mirror-image forms, and each form fits one hand (or foot) better than the other form does. For example, most scissors are designed to cut most efficiently when held with the right hand, to the annoyance of generations of left-handed children. This is an example of an important principle: *chiral objects can distinguish the two forms of other chiral objects.*

Some other examples of achiral objects are pens, hammers, tennis rackets, and baseball bats. All of these can be used equally well with either hand, because an achiral object fits the two forms of a chiral object equally well.

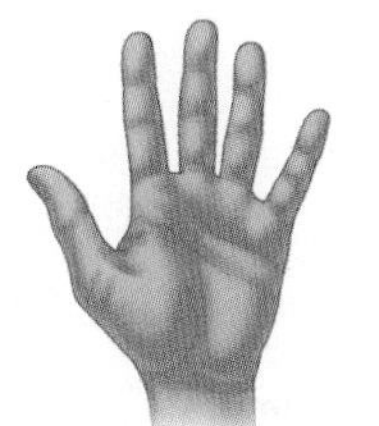

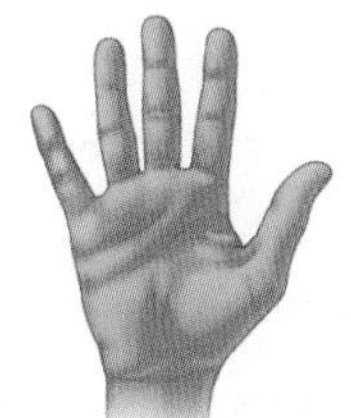

A left hand is chiral, because it cannot be superimposed on its mirror image (a right hand).

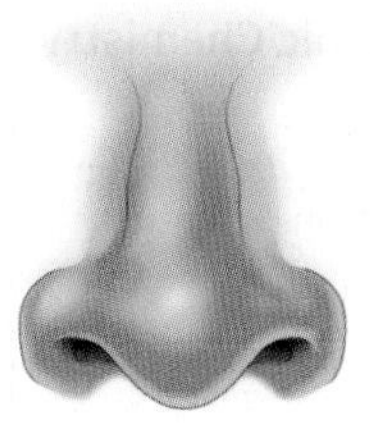

A nose is achiral, because it is identical to its mirror image.

FIGURE 9.7 Comparing chiral and achiral objects.

One form of 2-butanol looks like this:

HO H C CH_3 CH_2 CH_3

H OH C CH_3 CH_2 CH_3

The other form of 2-butanol is the mirror image of the first form.

FIGURE 9.8 The two enantiomers of 2-butanol, a chiral compound.

Molecules can also be chiral. Many of the alcohols in this chapter have two possible forms that are mirror images of each other. For instance, 2-butanol is chiral, because it has two possible mirror-image forms that cannot be superimposed. The two mirror-image forms of a chiral molecule are called **enantiomers**. The two enantiomers of 2-butanol are shown in Figure 9.8.

Note that in Figure 9.8, the mirror-image form of 2-butanol has the hydrogen and hydroxyl groups on carbon 2 exchanged. One enantiomer has the hydroxyl group on the left side and the hydrogen atom on the right, and the other has the two groups reversed. Because these two groups are in different positions, the two forms of 2-butanol cannot be superimposed, making 2-butanol a chiral molecule.

Not all alcohols are chiral. For example, methanol is identical to its mirror image, as shown in Figure 9.9. As a result, methanol is achiral; there is only one form of this molecule, not two.

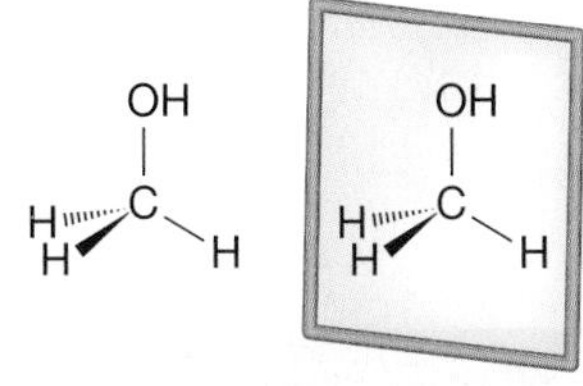

Methanol is identical to its mirror image.

FIGURE 9.9 The mirror image of methanol, an achiral compound.

Enantiomers are a type of stereoisomers, like the *cis* and *trans* forms of alkenes. Recall from Section 8.7 that stereoisomers have different arrangements of bonds around a particular atom. However, enantiomers are unlike any other kind of isomers. All of the other types of isomers we have seen have different chemical and physical properties. For instance, the constitutional isomers 1-butanol and 2-butanol have different melting points and boiling points, and they react somewhat differently with many chemicals. The same is true of *cis–trans* stereoisomers such as *cis*-2-butene and *trans*-2-butene. By contrast, enantiomers are equally stable and have identical physical properties, and most of their chemical properties are identical as well. Both forms of 2-butanol freeze at −115°C and boil at 98°C, and the two forms produce identical mixtures of 1-butene and 2-butene if we dehydrate them in the laboratory. Table 9.4 summarizes these types of isomers.

Many important substances in medicine and biochemistry are chiral, including all proteins, most fats, all common carbohydrates, cholesterol, and a range of medications, including ibuprofen (Advil), fluoxetine (Prozac), penicillin, cortisone, and procaine (novocaine). Each of these substances occurs in two mirror-image forms. However, *our bodies can normally use only one of the two forms of a chiral compound.* The other form has little or no activity, and it may even be harmful. For example, ascorbic acid (Vitamin C) is a chiral molecule and is a required nutrient for

TABLE 9.4 Common Types of Isomers in Organic Chemistry

	Constitutional Isomers	Stereoisomers	
	The atoms are connected to one another in different sequence.	The atoms are connected in the same sequence, but they differ in their orientation.	
		***Cis–trans* Isomers**	**Enantiomers***
		The groups around a double bond are oriented differently.	The groups around a single carbon atom are oriented differently, making the two molecules mirror images of each other.
Examples	**cyclopropane** and $CH_2{=}CH{-}CH_3$ **propene** $CH_2(OH){-}CH_2{-}CH_3$ **1-propanol** and $CH_3{-}CH(OH){-}CH_3$ **2-propanol**	**_cis_-2-butene** and **_trans_-2-butene**	$CH_3{-}C(HO)(H){-}CH_2{-}CH_3$ and $CH_3{-}C(H)(OH){-}CH_2{-}CH_3$ The two enantiomers of 2-butanol

*The naming rules for enantiomers are not covered in this book.

humans. Our bodies can only use one of the two enantiomers of ascorbic acid; the other has no effect.

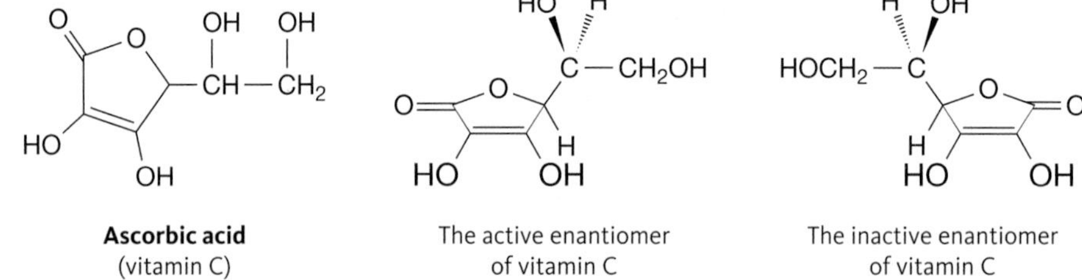

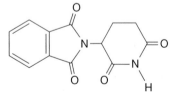

Ascorbic acid (vitamin C)

The active enantiomer of vitamin C

The inactive enantiomer of vitamin C

In at least one case, the inactive enantiomer had a devastating side effect. In the 1960s, many European women took a chiral compound called thalidomide to alleviate the nausea of early pregnancy. Only one of the enantiomers of thalidomide is active. Tragically, the medication contained both enantiomers of this compound, and the inactive form proved to cause severe birth defects. An estimated 10,000 children were born with a variety of birth defects before thalidomide was withdrawn, and half of these children died before reaching adulthood.

PA Photos /Landov

The severe birth defects in this child are due to one of the enantiomers of thalidomide.

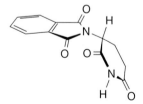

Thalidomide

This enantiomer of thalidomide is an effective medication.

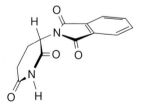

This enantiomer of thalidomide causes birth defects.

How can we recognize chiral molecules? In general, if a molecule contains a carbon atom that is bonded to four different groups of atoms, the molecule is chiral. Such a carbon atom is called a *chiral carbon atom.* For example, in 2-butanol, the second carbon atom is attached to a hydroxyl group, a hydrogen atom, a methyl group, and an ethyl group, as shown here. Since no two of these are the same, the second carbon atom is chiral, making 2-butanol a chiral molecule.

This carbon atom is attached to four different groups of atoms, so 2-butanol is chiral.

$$CH_3-\underset{\displaystyle H}{\overset{\displaystyle OH}{\underset{|}{\overset{|}{C}}}}-CH_2-CH_3$$

On the other hand, 2-propanol is not chiral. Regardless of which carbon atom we check, we always find at least two identical groups attached to that carbon, as shown here. 2-Propanol contains no chiral carbon atoms, so it is not a chiral molecule.

The first carbon is not chiral, because the three groups shaded in red are identical.

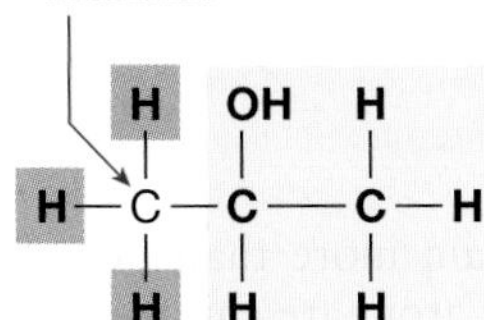

The second carbon is not chiral, because the two groups shaded in red are identical.

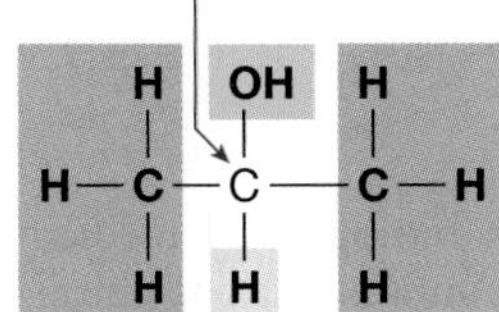

The third carbon is not chiral, because the three groups shaded in red are identical.

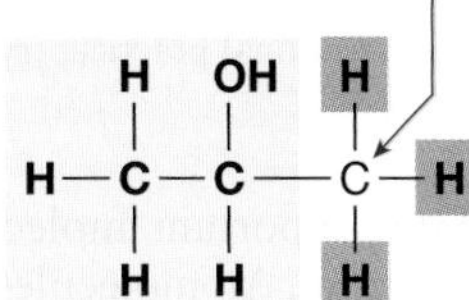

To be chiral, a carbon atom must be attached to *four* different groups. For example, the carbon atom in the following molecule is not chiral, because it is only bonded to three groups, not four:

This carbon atom is not chiral, because it is only attached to three groups.

$$H-\overset{\displaystyle O}{\overset{\|}{C}}-Cl$$

Sample Problem 9.8

Identifying chiral carbon atoms

When our bodies break down glucose to obtain energy, they produce a small amount of glyceraldehyde. Identify the chiral carbon atoms in glyceraldehyde.

$$\overset{\displaystyle OH}{\overset{|}{CH_2}}-\overset{\displaystyle OH}{\overset{|}{CH}}-\overset{\displaystyle O}{\overset{\|}{C}}-H$$ **Glyceraldehyde**

SOLUTION

To identify chiral carbon atoms, we must look at each carbon atom and determine whether the atom is attached to four different groups. Let us start with the left-hand carbon atom. This atom is attached to two hydrogen atoms, a hydroxyl group, and a large piece that contains several atoms. Because two of the groups are identical (the two hydrogen atoms), this carbon atom is not chiral.

The left-hand carbon is not chiral, because two of the four attached groups are identical.

$$H-\underset{\displaystyle H}{\overset{\displaystyle OH}{\underset{|}{\overset{|}{C}}}}-\underset{\displaystyle H}{\overset{\displaystyle OH}{\underset{|}{\overset{|}{C}}}}-\overset{\displaystyle O}{\overset{\|}{C}}-H$$

continued

To complete the problem, we check each of the other two carbon atoms. The central carbon atom is attached to four different groups, so it is chiral. The left-hand carbon is only attached to three groups, so it is not chiral.

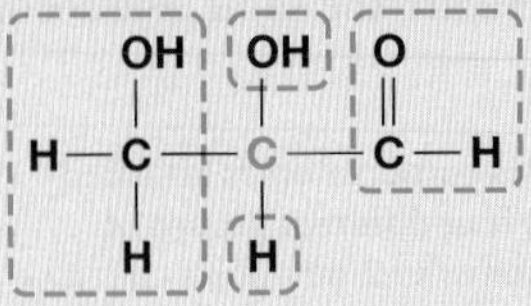

The central carbon is chiral because it is bonded to four different groups of atoms.

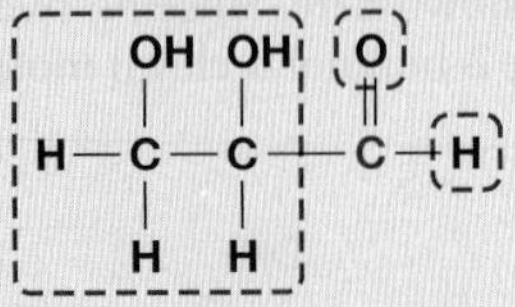

The right-hand carbon is not chiral because it is bonded to only three groups of atoms.

TRY IT YOURSELF: *Glycerol is one of the building blocks of fats. Is glycerol a chiral compound?*

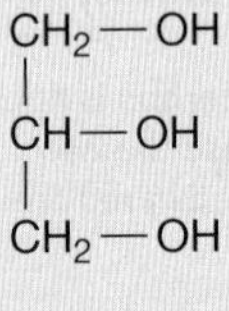

$$\begin{array}{l} CH_2-OH \\ | \\ CH-OH \\ | \\ CH_2-OH \end{array}$$ **Glycerol**

For additional practice, try Core Problems 9.31 through 9.34.

Many important molecules in biology and medicine contain more than one chiral carbon atom. All molecules that contain just one chiral carbon atom are chiral, but molecules that have two or more chiral carbon atoms are not necessarily chiral. For example, 2,3-dimethylhexane contains two chiral carbon atoms, but it is an achiral molecule, because it is identical to its mirror image.

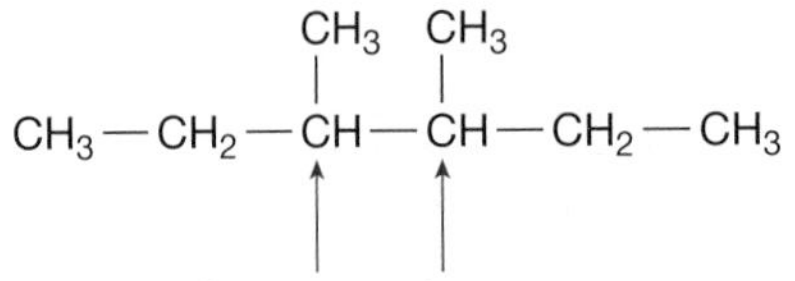

$$CH_3-CH_2-\underset{}{\overset{CH_3}{\overset{|}{CH}}}-\overset{CH_3}{\overset{|}{CH}}-CH_2-CH_3$$

These two carbon atoms are chiral.

2,3-Dimethylhexane is an achiral molecule that contains two chiral carbon atoms.

Determining whether such molecules are chiral is beyond the scope of this textbook. However, the vast majority of biomolecules that contain two or more chiral carbon atoms are chiral.

All enzymes are chiral molecules, so they can distinguish between the two forms of other chiral molecules. As we will see in Chapter 13, enzymes have a pocket or cavity that fits around the reactant. If the reactant is chiral, only one of the two enantiomers can fit inside the pocket. In addition, if the product is chiral, the enzyme makes only one of the two possible enantiomers. For example, the enzyme that catalyzes the following reaction selects one of the two forms of the product. This reaction occurs when our bodies break down the amino acid valine.

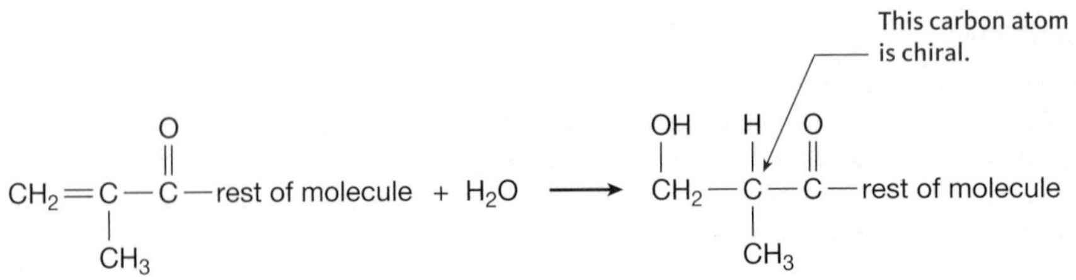

$$CH_2=\underset{CH_3}{\underset{|}{C}}-\overset{O}{\overset{||}{C}}-\text{rest of molecule} + H_2O \longrightarrow \overset{OH}{\overset{|}{CH_2}}-\underset{CH_3}{\underset{|}{\overset{H}{\overset{|}{C}}}}-\overset{O}{\overset{||}{C}}-\text{rest of molecule}$$

This carbon atom is chiral.

The reaction makes only one of the two enantiomers of this molecule.

Again, we have an example of the remarkable ability of enzymes to control chemical reactions.

CORE PROBLEMS

9.29 Tell whether each of the following objects is chiral or achiral:

a) shoe b) sock c) spoon d) coffee cup

9.30 Tell whether each of the following objects is chiral or achiral:

a) fork b) screw c) car d) hammer

9.31 Find and circle each of the chiral carbon atoms in the following molecules:

```
                                          CH3
                                          |
                                     HO—CH    O
                                          |    ||
a) HO—CH2—CH2—NH2           b) NH2—CH—C—OH
```

Ethanolamine, a component of cell membrane lipids

Threonine, an amino acid

```
                       O
                       ||
           O          C—OH     O
           ||          |          ||
c) HO—C—CH2—CH—CH—C—OH
                                 |
                                OH
```

Isocitric acid, a product of the oxidation of carbohydrates, fats, and proteins

9.32 Find and circle each of the chiral carbon atoms in the following molecules:

```
                                                   CH3
                                                   |
                 O                          CH3—CH    O
                 ||                                |    ||
a) HO—CH2—C—CH2—OH          b) NH2—CH—C—OH
```

Dihydroxyacetone, a simple carbohydrate

Alanine, an amino acid

```
              CH3   OH   O                         O
               |      |     ||                         ||
c) HO—CH2—C—CH—C—N—CH2—CH2—C—OH
               |                 |
              CH3               H
```

Pantothenic acid, a B vitamin

9.33 One of the following molecules is chiral, but the other two are not. Tell which molecule is chiral, and explain your answer.

a) 2-methylheptane
b) 3-methylheptane
c) 4-methylheptane

9.34 Two of the following molecules are chiral, but the other one is not. Tell which molecules are chiral, and explain your answer.

a) 1-hexanol b) 2-hexanol c) 3-hexanol

9.35 Why is it important that enzymes are chiral molecules?

9.36 Most amino acids are chiral, and our bodies can only use one of the two enantiomers. Would you expect enzymes that break down amino acids to be able to break down both enantiomers? Why or why not?

9.6 The Dehydration Reaction

OBJECTIVE: *Predict the products that are formed when an alcohol is dehydrated.*

In Section 9.1, you learned how our bodies can add a hydroxyl group to an organic compound using a hydration reaction. This reaction can be reversed, and the reverse reaction (called a **dehydration reaction**) is the primary means by which our bodies remove oxygen atoms from organic compounds. Dehydration reactions are common in living organisms, particularly in sequences of reactions that make fats and other compounds that are insoluble in water.

Health Note: In your body, dehydration occurs when you lose more water (by sweating, vomiting, or diarrhea) than you take in. This type of dehydration is not connected to the dehydration reaction.

Figure 9.10 shows the general scheme for the dehydration reaction. In this reaction, a hydrogen atom and a hydroxyl group are removed from an alcohol. The hydrogen and the hydroxyl combine to make water, and the alcohol becomes an alkene. Note that this reaction is the opposite of the hydration reaction in Figure 9.2.

In a dehydration reaction, the hydrogen atom and the hydroxyl group must be attached to neighboring carbon atoms. Removing these allows the two carbon atoms to form an additional bond. For example, when we dehydrate 1-propanol, we remove the OH group from carbon 1, so we must remove the H from carbon 2, as shown in Figure 9.11.

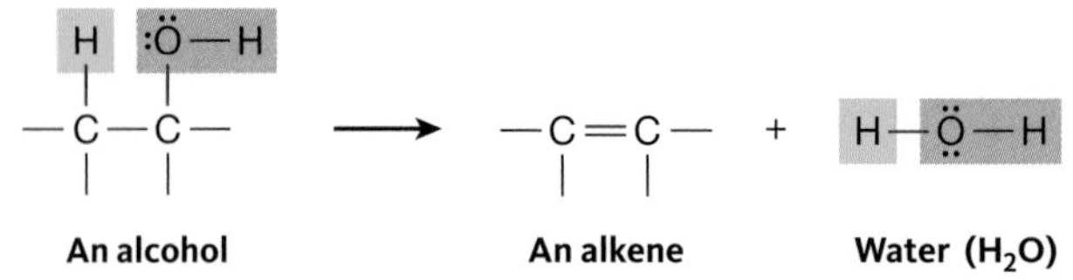

An alcohol → An alkene + Water (H_2O)

FIGURE 9.10 The dehydration reaction of alcohols.

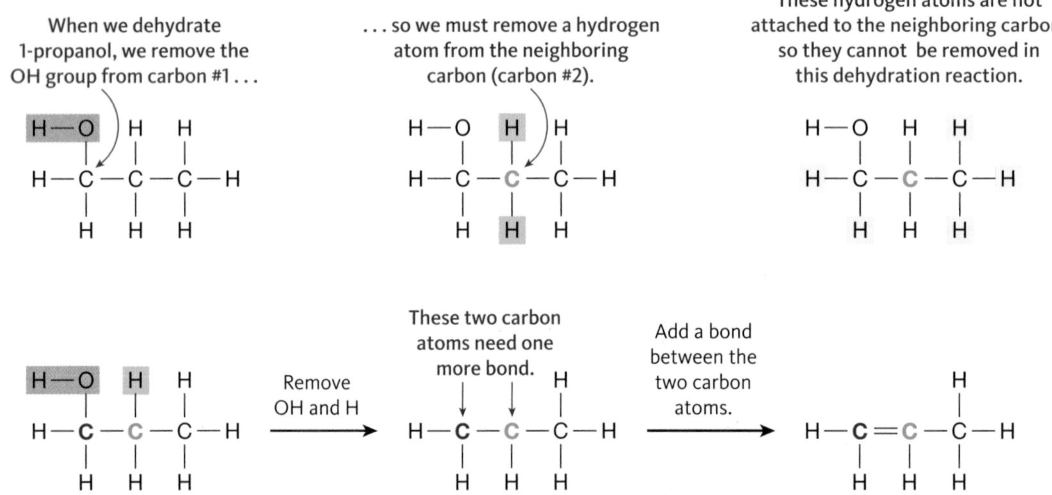
When we dehydrate 1-propanol, we remove the OH group from carbon #1...
...so we must remove a hydrogen atom from the neighboring carbon (carbon #2).
These hydrogen atoms are not attached to the neighboring carbon, so they cannot be removed in this dehydration reaction.
Remove OH and H
These two carbon atoms need one more bond.
Add a bond between the two carbon atoms.

FIGURE 9.11 The dehydration of 1-propanol.

Sample Problem 9.9

Drawing the products of a dehydration reaction

Draw the structure of the alkene that is formed when the following alcohol is dehydrated:

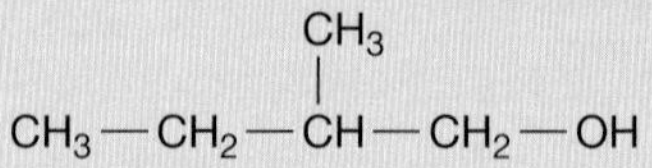

$$CH_3-CH_2-\underset{}{\overset{CH_3}{\overset{|}{CH}}}-CH_2-OH$$

SOLUTION

A dehydration reaction removes OH and H from adjacent carbon atoms. First, we must locate the hydroxyl group in our molecule and the carbon to which it is bonded.

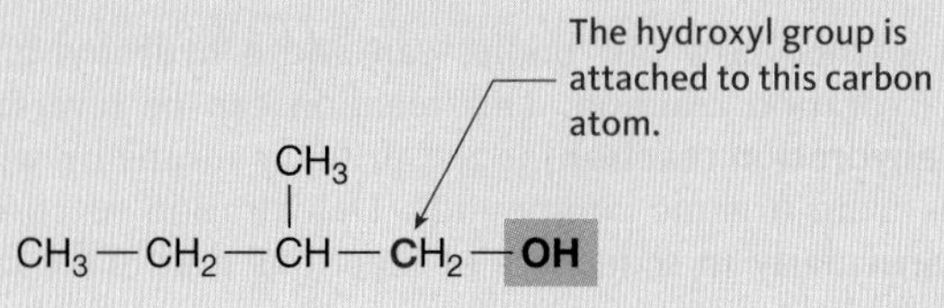

The hydroxyl group is attached to this carbon atom.

$$CH_3-CH_2-\overset{CH_3}{\overset{|}{CH}}-\mathbf{CH_2}-\mathbf{OH}$$

continued

To find the adjacent carbon atom, we simply move to the next carbon atom in the chain. We must remove the hydrogen from this carbon atom. It can be helpful to draw out this portion of the molecule as a full structural formula.

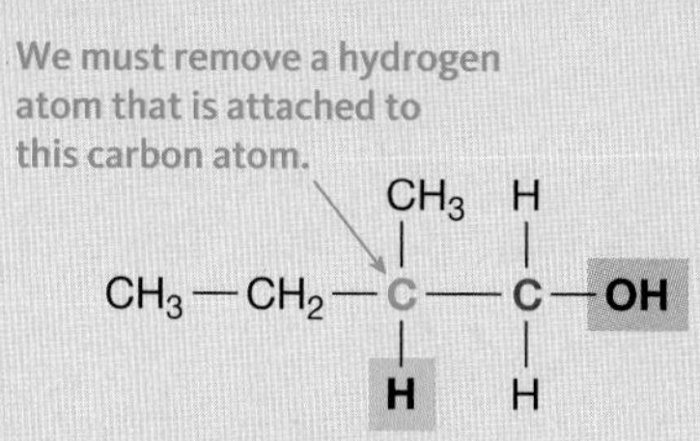

We must remove a hydrogen atom that is attached to this carbon atom.

$$\begin{array}{ccccccc} & & & CH_3 & & H & \\ & & & | & & | & \\ CH_3 & - & CH_2 - & C & - & C & - OH \\ & & & | & & | & \\ & & & H & & H & \end{array}$$

Now we are ready to remove the H and OH groups.

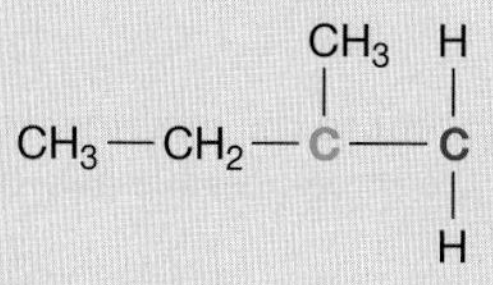

$$\begin{array}{ccccc} & & CH_3 & & H \\ & & | & & | \\ CH_3 - CH_2 & - & C & - & C \\ & & & & | \\ & & & & H \end{array}$$

Finally, we complete the structure of the product by drawing a second bond between the two carbon atoms that have only three bonds.

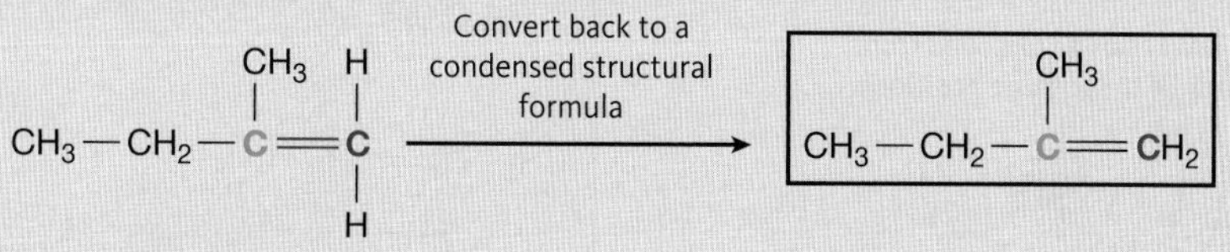

$$\begin{array}{ccccc} & & CH_3 & & H \\ & & | & & | \\ CH_3 - CH_2 & - & C & = & C \\ & & & & | \\ & & & & H \end{array} \xrightarrow{\text{Convert back to a condensed structural formula}} \boxed{\begin{array}{ccc} & CH_3 & \\ & | & \\ CH_3 - CH_2 - & C & = CH_2 \end{array}}$$

TRY IT YOURSELF: *Draw the structure of the product that will be formed when the following alcohol is dehydrated:*

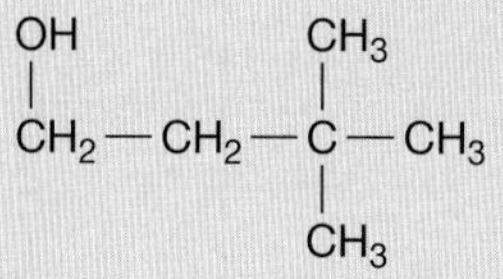

$$\begin{array}{ccccc} OH & & & CH_3 & \\ | & & & | & \\ CH_2 & - CH_2 - & & C & - CH_3 \\ & & & | & \\ & & & CH_3 & \end{array}$$

For additional practice, try Core Problems 9.37 (part a) and 9.38 (part a).

Many Dehydration Reactions Produce More Than One Product

If an alcohol has more than one carbon atom next to the functional group, it can usually form more than one dehydration product. For instance, the dehydration of 2-butanol can produce two alkenes, 1-butene and 2-butene. The hydroxyl group is attached to the second carbon atom, so both the first and the third carbons are adjacent and can lose the hydrogen atom, as shown in Figure 9.12.

If the alcohol has three carbon atoms adjacent to the functional group, it can give three products when it is dehydrated.

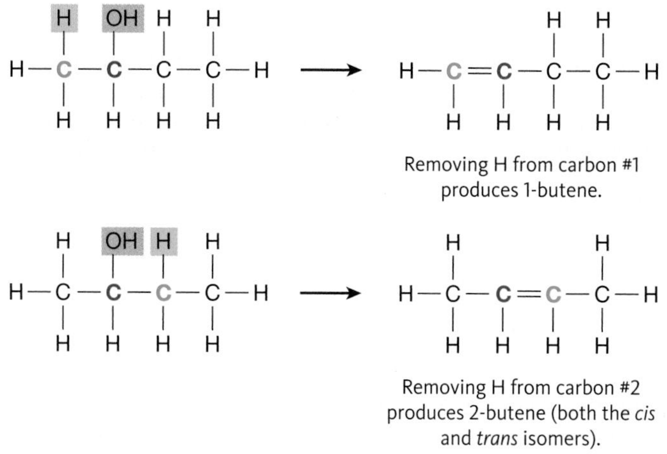

$$\begin{array}{c} H\ \ OH\ \ H\ \ H \\ H-C-C-C-C-H \\ H\ \ \ H\ \ \ H\ \ \ H \end{array} \longrightarrow \begin{array}{c} \quad\ \ H\ \ \ H \\ H-C=C-C-C-H \\ H\ \ \ H\ \ \ H\ \ \ H \end{array}$$

Removing H from carbon #1 produces 1-butene.

$$\begin{array}{c} H\ \ OH\ \ H\ \ H \\ H-C-C-C-C-H \\ H\ \ \ H\ \ \ H\ \ \ H \end{array} \longrightarrow \begin{array}{c} H\ \ \ \ \ \ \ \ \ \ \ \ H \\ H-C-C=C-C-H \\ H\ \ \ H\ \ \ H\ \ \ H \end{array}$$

Removing H from carbon #2 produces 2-butene (both the *cis* and *trans* isomers).

FIGURE 9.12 The dehydration of 2-butanol.

Sample Problem 9.10

Drawing multiple dehydration products

Draw the structures of all of the products that can be formed when the following alcohol is dehydrated:

OH
|
$CH_3—C—CH_2—CH_3$
|
CH_2
|
CH_2—(cyclopentyl)

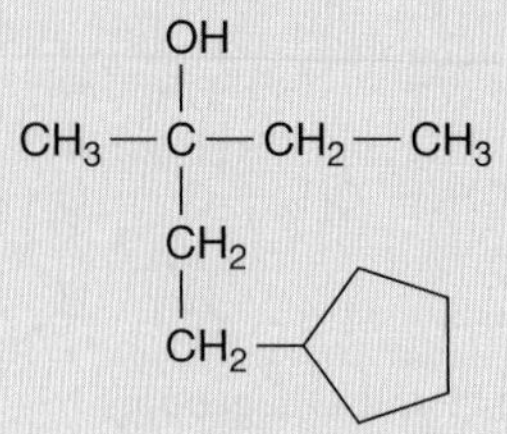

SOLUTION

There are three carbon atoms adjacent to the functional group, each of which can lose a hydrogen atom. Therefore, there are three possible dehydration products:

The H can be removed from any of these three positions.

OH
|
$CH_3—C—CH_2—CH_3$ ⟶
|
CH_2
|
CH_2—(cyclopentyl)

$CH_2{=}C—CH_2—CH_3$
|
CH_2
|
CH_2—(cyclopentyl)

Product #1

$CH_3—C{=}CH—CH_3$
|
CH_2
|
CH_2—(cyclopentyl)

Product #2

$CH_3—C—CH_2—CH_3$
‖
CH
|
CH_2—(cyclopentyl)

Product #3

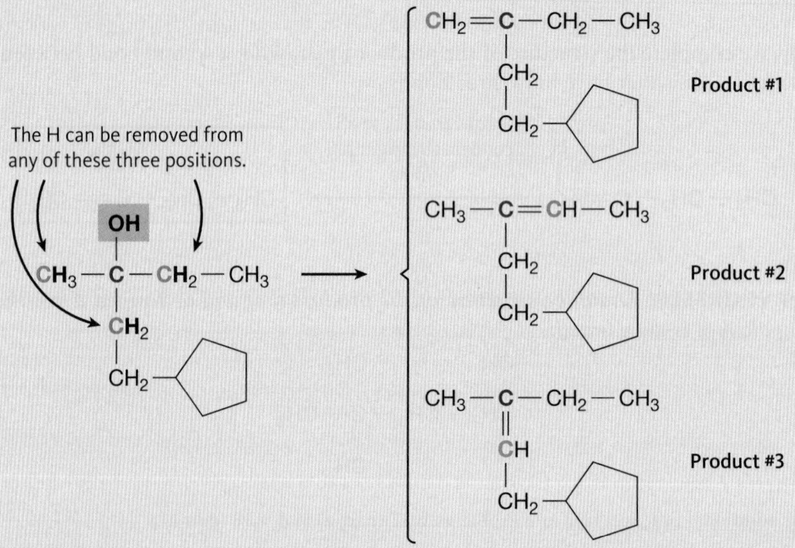

TRY IT YOURSELF: *Draw the structures of all of the products that can be formed when the following alcohol is dehydrated:*

CH_3 OH
| |
$CH_3—CH_2—CH—CH—CH_3$

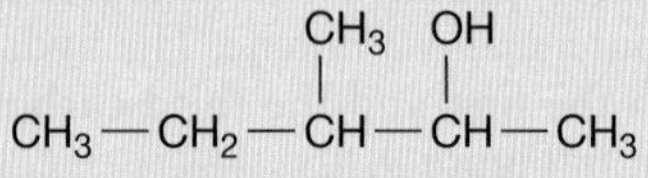

For additional practice, try Core Problems 9.37 (parts b through e) and 9.38 (parts b through e).

Cyclic alcohols can also be dehydrated. The carbon ring in a cyclic alcohol is usually drawn as a line structure, so the hydrogen atoms may not appear in the structure. Remember that each ring carbon is attached to enough hydrogen atoms to give the carbon four bonds. For example, suppose we want to dehydrate the following molecule:

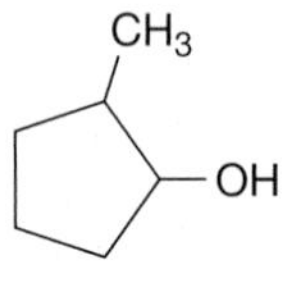

CH_3
(cyclopentane ring)—OH

As always, we start by locating the carbon atom that is attached to the hydroxyl group. Then we locate the adjacent carbon atoms, to see where the hydrogen atom will come from. In this compound, there are two adjacent carbon atoms, both of which are attached to at least one hydrogen atom.

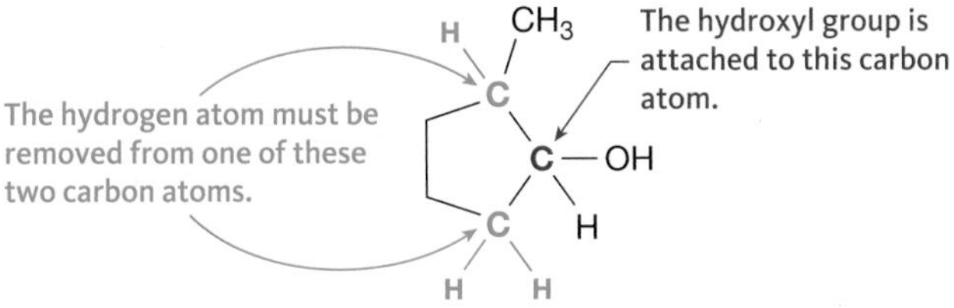

The hydrogen atom must be removed from one of these two carbon atoms.

The hydroxyl group is attached to this carbon atom.

Since there are two ways to remove the hydrogen atom, there are two possible products of this reaction.

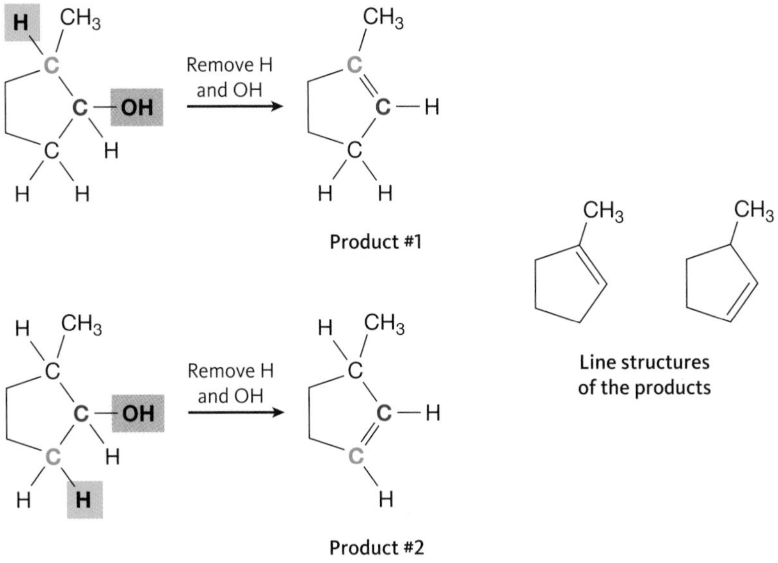

Remove H and OH

Product #1

Remove H and OH

Product #2

Line structures of the products

Some alcohols do not have any hydrogen atoms attached to the adjacent carbon. These alcohols cannot be dehydrated. The following molecule is a good example:

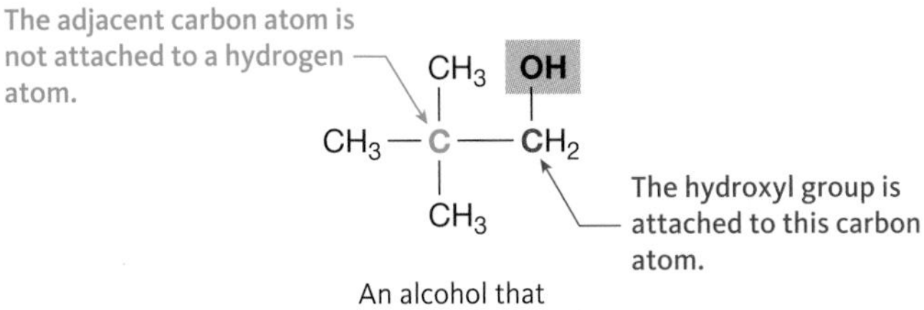

The adjacent carbon atom is not attached to a hydrogen atom.

The hydroxyl group is attached to this carbon atom.

An alcohol that cannot be dehydrated

In our bodies, enzymes catalyze dehydration reactions. As was the case with hydration reactions, these enzymes are specific about the products they form, so our bodies make only one alkene when they dehydrate an alcohol. For example, the following dehydration is part of the sequence of reactions that our bodies use to make fats from other nutrients. In this reaction, there are two possible dehydration products, but the enzyme that catalyzes this reaction only makes one of them. This is important because the enzyme that carries out the next step in the sequence cannot use the other alkene.

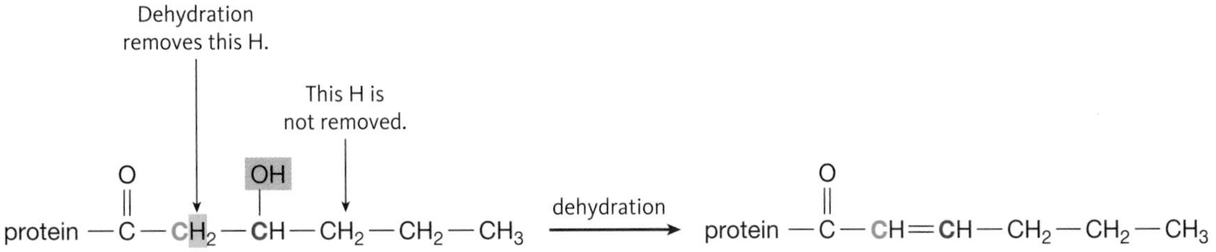

Dehydration removes this H.

This H is not removed.

protein—C(=O)—CH_2—CH(OH)—CH_2—CH_2—CH_3 —dehydration→ protein—C(=O)—CH=CH—CH_2—CH_2—CH_3

CORE PROBLEMS

9.37 Draw the structures of the products that are formed when the following alcohols are dehydrated. Be sure to draw all of the possible products for each reaction.

a) CH_3-CH_2-OH

b) 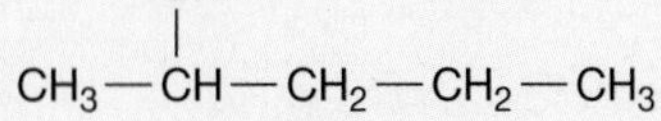 $CH_3-CH(OH)-CH_2-CH_2-CH_3$

c) 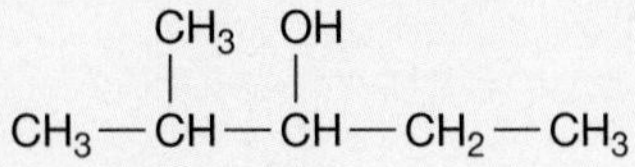 $CH_3-CH(CH_3)-CH(OH)-CH_2-CH_3$

d) 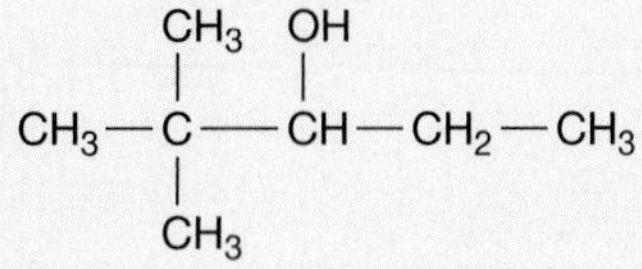 $CH_3-C(CH_3)_2-CH(OH)-CH_2-CH_3$

e) 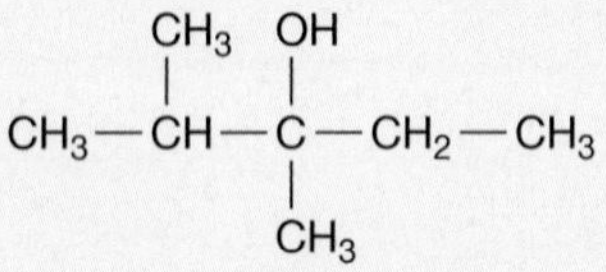 $CH_3-CH(CH_3)-C(OH)(CH_3)-CH_2-CH_3$

f) 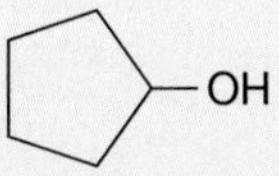 cyclopentane ring with OH

9.38 Draw the structures of the products that are formed when the following alcohols are dehydrated. Be sure to draw all of the possible products for each reaction.

a) $CH_3-CH_2-CH_2-CH_2-OH$

b) 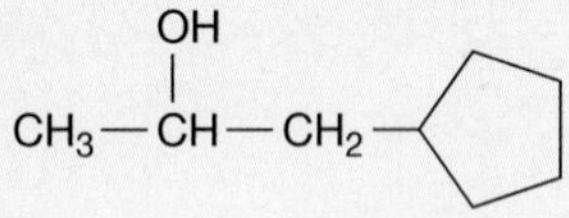 $CH_3-CH(OH)-CH_2-$cyclopentyl

c) 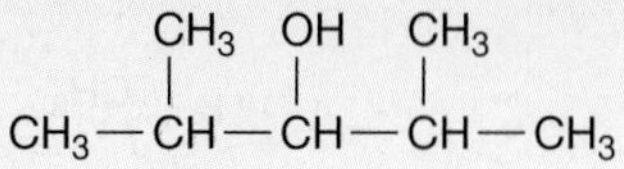 $CH_3-CH(CH_3)-CH(OH)-CH(CH_3)-CH_3$

d) 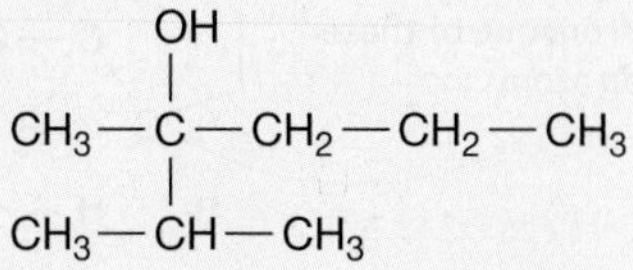 $CH_3-C(OH)(CH(CH_3)-CH_3)-CH_2-CH_2-CH_3$

e) 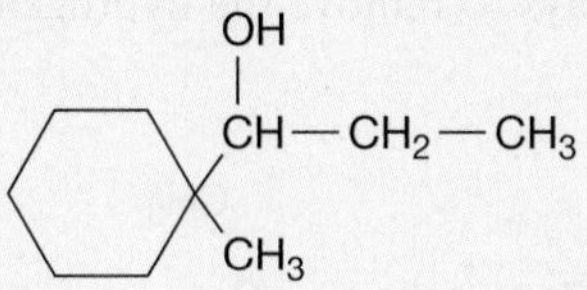 cyclohexane ring bearing CH_3 and $CH(OH)-CH_2-CH_3$ on the same carbon

f) 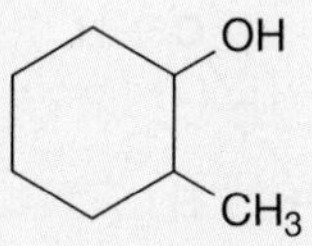 cyclohexane ring with OH and CH_3 on adjacent carbons

9.39 The following alcohol cannot be dehydrated. Explain.

benzene ring$-CH_2-OH$

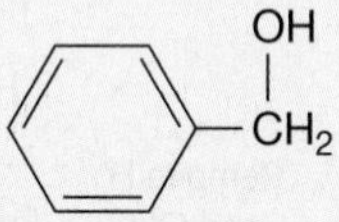

9.40 The following alcohol cannot be dehydrated. Explain.

cyclopentane ring bearing CH_3 and CH_2-OH on the same carbon

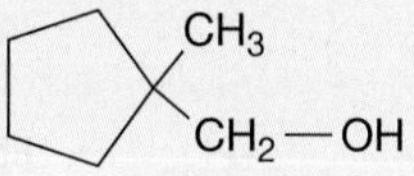

OBJECTIVES: *Identify the phenol and thiol functional groups in organic compounds, and relate the physical properties of phenols and thiols to those of alcohols and alkanes.*

9.7 Phenols and Thiols

Two classes of organic compounds are closely related to alcohols and occur regularly in biochemistry. The first is based on a compound called **phenol**, which contains a hydroxyl group bonded to a benzene ring.

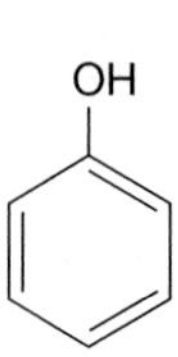

OH
benzene ring
Phenol

This grouping can also occur in more complex molecules, and such molecules are referred to as phenols. Here are two examples of compounds that contain the phenol functional group:

The phenol group

Thymol: Responsible for the aroma of thyme, used to treat topical fungal infections.

Salicylic acid: Used to treat acne and other skin disorders.

Thymol is one of the chemicals responsible for the flavor and aroma of thyme.

Sample Problem 9.11

Identifying the phenol functional group

Which of the following compounds contains a phenol group?

a) b)

SOLUTION

The second compound contains a phenol group, since it contains a hydroxyl group directly attached to a benzene ring. In the first compound, the ring contains only one double bond, so it is not aromatic.

TRY IT YOURSELF: *Does the following compound contain a phenol group?*

Health Note: Phenol (also called carbolic acid) is used to disinfect hard surfaces in hospitals and industrial settings, and it is added to many mouthwashes, throat sprays, and lozenges. It kills bacteria and relieves pain in low concentrations. However, it is toxic if swallowed in significant amounts, and high concentrations of phenol produce painful chemical burns when applied to skin.

You have already seen that benzene has unusual properties and does not behave at all like an alkene. The benzene ring also tends to modify the chemical properties of functional groups that are directly attached to it, and phenols are an excellent example of this. Here are some differences between phenols and alcohols:

- Most alcohols can be dehydrated, but phenols cannot.
- Most alcohols can be made by adding water to an alkene, but phenols cannot.
- Alcohols are neither acidic nor basic, but phenols are weak acids.

On the other hand, the hydroxyl groups in both alcohols and phenols can form hydrogen bonds. As a result, the physical properties of phenols resemble those of similar-sized alcohols. Phenols dissolve fairly well in water, and they have higher boiling points than the corresponding hydrocarbons. Table 9.5 compares the properties of phenol with those of cyclohexanol (a typical alcohol) and benzene.

Health Note: Poison ivy and its relatives contain *urushiols,* compounds that have a phenol group bonded to a long hydrocarbon chain. Urushiols cause an intense allergic reaction in most people, producing itchy, oozing rashes that generally last a week or more before subsiding.

A urushiol

Thiols Are the Sulfur Analogues of Alcohols

The other class of compounds that are related to alcohols is the **thiols**, in which the oxygen atom of the hydroxyl group is replaced by sulfur. Sulfur and oxygen are in the

TABLE 9.5 The Properties of a Phenol, an Alcohol, and a Hydrocarbon

	Phenol	Cyclohexanol	Benzene
Structure	(benzene ring)—OH	(cyclohexane ring)—OH	(benzene ring)
Boiling point	182°C	161°C	80°C
Solubility in water	65 g/L	36 g/L	0.6 g/L
pH of 1% solution	5.5 (weakly acidic)	7.0 (neutral)	We cannot make a 1% solution.

TABLE 9.6 The Properties of an Alcohol, a Thiol, and an Alkane

	Ethanol	Ethanethiol	Propane
Structure	$CH_3—CH_2—OH$	$CH_3—CH_2—SH$	$CH_3—CH_2—CH_3$
Boiling point	78°C	35°C	−42°C
Solubility in water	No limit	7 g/L	0.1 g/L

same group in the periodic table, so they have the same bonding requirements. The elements require two additional electrons to form an octet, so they normally form two covalent bonds. Here are the structures of methanol and the corresponding thiol:

```
      H                    H
      |                    |
  H—C—Ö—H              H—C—S̈—H
      |    ··              |    ··
      H                    H
```

Methanol
An alcohol

Methanethiol
A thiol

Although thiols are structurally similar to alcohols, the two classes of compounds are quite different in most other ways. The thiol group cannot form hydrogen bonds, so thiols have lower boiling points and evaporate more readily than do alcohols, and they are substantially less soluble in water. However, thiols are more soluble in water than similar-sized alkanes, because the thiol group is weakly polar and is attracted to water molecules. Table 9.6 compares the properties of a typical thiol to those of a similar-sized alcohol and alkane.

The chemical properties of thiols are also different from those of alcohols. For instance, thiols cannot normally be converted to alkenes by removing H_2S, and only a few alkenes can be converted to thiols by combining with H_2S.

Sample Problem 9.12

The effect of the thiol group on water solubility

Rank the following three compounds in order of their solubility in water, starting with the least soluble:

```
      SH                        OH                        CH3
      |                         |                         |
CH3—CH—CH2—CH3           CH3—CH—CH2—CH3           CH3—CH—CH2—CH3
```

Compound A Compound B Compound C

SOLUTION

Compound B has the highest solubility, because it is the only one that contains a group that can form hydrogen bonds. Neither compound A nor compound C should dissolve

continued

very well, but compound A is more soluble than compound C, because the thiol group is weakly polar. The order is

Compound C → Compound A → Compound B
Least soluble → Most soluble

TRY IT YOURSELF: *Rank the following three compounds in order of their solubility in water, starting with the least soluble:*

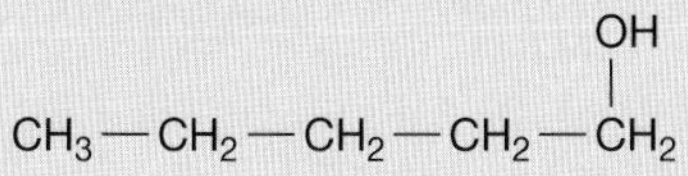

$CH_3-CH_2-CH_2-CH_2-CH_2-OH$
Compound X

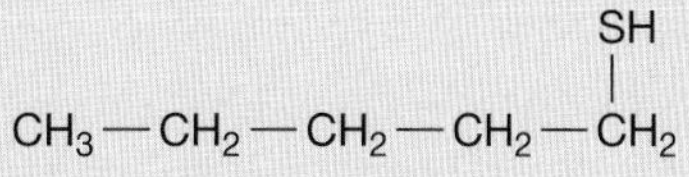

$CH_3-CH_2-CH_2-CH_2-CH_2-SH$
Compound Y

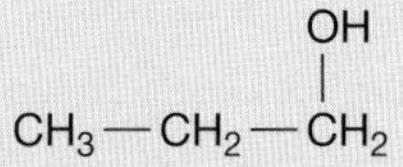

$CH_3-CH_2-CH_2-OH$
Compound Z

For additional practice, try Core Problems 9.43 and 9.44.

The most conspicuous property of thiols is their odors. Low-molecular-weight thiols have some of the most offensive aromas in all of chemistry. The odor of skunk is a good example, as is the scent of freshly cut onions. Natural gas suppliers add a tiny amount of a thiol to natural gas, which is primarily methane and has no odor. The thiol gives the gas its characteristic unpleasant smell, allowing people to recognize when potentially dangerous amounts of natural gas are escaping into the air. However, not all thiols smell bad; the pleasant aroma of grapefruit is also due in large part to a thiol. The structures of some thiols are shown here:

$CH_3-CH{=}CH-CH_2-SH$
2-Butene-1-thiol, a component of skunk spray

$CH_2{=}CH-CH_2-SH$
2-Propene-1-thiol, responsible for the irritating odor of onions

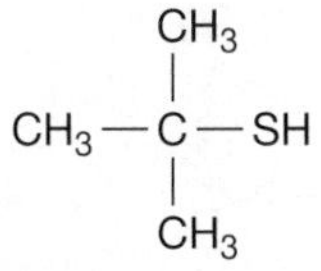

$(CH_3)_3C-SH$
1,1-Dimethylethanethiol, added to natural gas

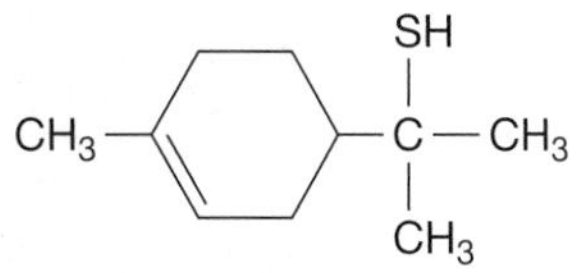

CH_3–(cyclohexene ring)–$C(SH)(CH_3)-CH_3$
Thioterpineol, responsible for the aroma of grapefruit

Charles D. Winters

These foods contain thiols that contribute to their characteristic flavors and aromas.

CORE PROBLEMS

9.41 Classify each of the following molecules as an alcohol, a phenol, or a thiol:

(cyclohexane–SH) (cyclohexane–OH) (benzene ring with OH and CH_3) (cycloheptatriene–OH)

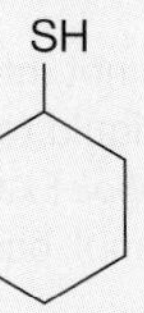

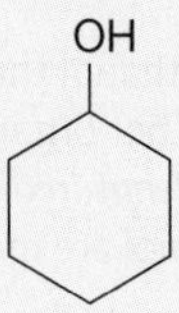

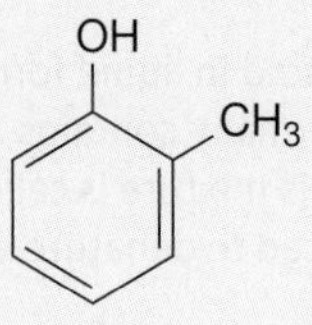

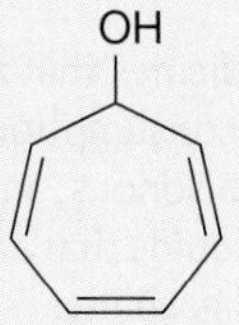

9.42 Classify each of the following molecules as an alcohol, a phenol, or a thiol:

(benzene ring)$-CH_2-OH$

CH_3–(benzene ring)–SH

CH_3–(benzene ring)–OH

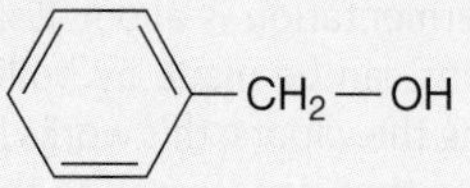

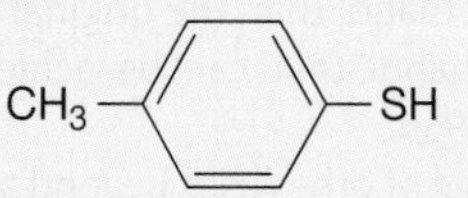

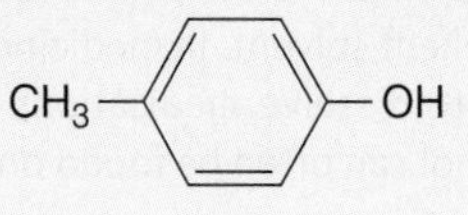

continued

9.43 From each of the following pairs of molecules, select the compound that has the higher solubility in water.
a) phenol or benzene
b) $CH_3—CH_2—CH_2—SH$ or $CH_3—CH_2—CH_2—OH$

9.44 From each of the following pairs of molecules, select the compound that has the higher solubility in water.

a) —OH or —CH_3

a) —OH or —SH

9.45 Which of the following compounds should have the higher boiling point?

$CH_3—CH_2—CH_2—SH$ or $CH_3—CH_2—CH_2—OH$

9.46 Which of the following compounds should have the higher boiling point?

$CH_3—CH_2—CH_2—SH$ or $CH_3—CH_2—CH_2—CH_3$

CONNECTIONS

Alcohols for Drinking—Or Not

To a chemist, the word *alcohol* refers to any compound that contains the alcohol functional group. However, when most people speak of "alcohol," they are referring specifically to ethanol, the chemical compound that is responsible for the effects of beverages such as wine, beer, and vodka. Alcoholic beverages have been made by people since prehistoric times, and beer and wine routinely rank among the most popular beverages in the world.

Virtually all alcoholic beverages are made by a process called *alcoholic fermentation,* in which organisms called yeasts break down sugar into ethanol and carbon dioxide. The carbon dioxide can be allowed to escape, as is done with most wines, or it can be kept in solution to produce a carbonated beverage, such as beer or sparkling wine. The overall reaction can be represented as

$$C_6H_{12}O_6 \rightarrow 2\ CO_2 + 2\ CH_3CH_2OH$$

In this equation, $C_6H_{12}O_6$ is the molecular formula for the most common simple sugars, including glucose (dextrose) and fructose. Yeasts can also use table sugar ($C_{12}H_{22}O_{11}$), breaking it down into glucose and fructose before fermenting it.

Almost any solution of sugar in water can be fermented if it is not too concentrated. Mixtures of starch and water can also be fermented if an additional enzyme is added to break down the starch into sugar, which is then fermented by the yeast. Fermentation, however, is limited by the fact that high concentrations of ethanol are toxic to yeast. In practice, the highest concentration that can be achieved by direct fermentation is about 15% ethanol (v/v). More concentrated solutions can be made by boiling the fermentation product and collecting the vapors: this works because ethanol boils at a lower temperature than does water, so the vapors have a higher concentration of ethanol than the original solution. The highest concentration of ethanol that can be achieved by this method (called *distillation*) is 95%.

Ethanol has a range of other uses beyond alcoholic beverages. It is added to gasoline to improve the octane rating and reduce pollution, and it is an excellent solvent. In medicine, mixtures of ethanol and water are used to dissolve medications that are insoluble in water alone, so ethanol can often be found on the ingredient list of

iStockphoto.com/YinYang

There are about 20 million acres of grape vineyards in the world. The grapes from this vineyard will be used to make wine.

medicines that are sold in liquid form. Ethanol that is not intended for consumption normally contains another organic liquid to make it poisonous, and this mixture is called *denatured alcohol.* Examples of liquids that are used to denature ethanol are methanol, benzene, and gasoline.

In contrast to ethanol, methanol is quite poisonous, being particularly notorious for its ability to cause blindness. It does, however, find wide use in industry as a solvent and as a starting material for manufacturing certain types of rigid plastics. Isopropyl alcohol (2-propanol), often called rubbing alcohol, finds some use in medicine as an antiseptic and a soothing agent for the skin. It is

continued

also used as a solvent for some types of cosmetic products. Isopropyl alcohol is occasionally consumed by people who mistake it for ethanol, but it too is substantially more toxic than ethanol; a lethal dose is approximately 100 mL.

Ethylene glycol and glycerol are compounds with multiple hydroxyl groups. Both are viscous, sweet-tasting liquids that are extremely soluble in water, but they are strikingly different in their physiological behavior. Ethylene glycol is poisonous, being particularly damaging to the kidneys. Its main use is as an engine coolant and antifreeze; mixtures of ethylene glycol and water have a substantially higher boiling point and a lower freezing point than water alone. Unfortunately, the sweet taste of ethylene glycol is attractive to animals; many dogs and cats die after drinking antifreeze that has been spilled by a careless user. Glycerol, by contrast, is nontoxic: it is almost as sweet as cane sugar and finds some use as a nutritive sweetener, as well as being used as a lubricant. Glycerol is also one of the building blocks of fats, making it an important compound in biochemistry.

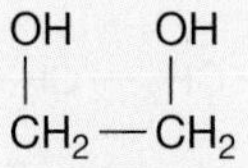

$$HO{-}CH_2{-}CH_2{-}OH$$

Ethylene glycol
(1,2-ethanediol)

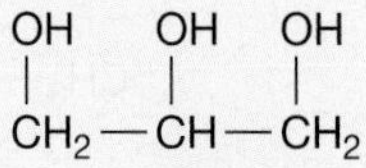

$$HO{-}CH_2{-}CH(OH){-}CH_2{-}OH$$

Glycerol
(1,2,3-propanetriol)

Key Terms

achiral - 9.5
alcohol - 9.1
chiral - 9.5
dehydration reaction - 9.6
enantiomer - 9.5
enzyme - 9.2
hydration reaction - 9.1
phenol - 9.7
thiol - 9.7

Classes of Organic Compounds

Class	Functional group	IUPAC suffix	Example
Alcohol	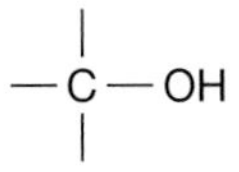 $-\overset{\vert}{\underset{\vert}{C}}-OH$	*-ol*	$CH_3{-}CH_2{-}CH_2{-}CH_2{-}OH$ *1-butanol*
Thiol	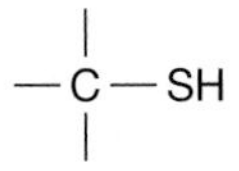 $-\overset{\vert}{\underset{\vert}{C}}-SH$	*-thiol**	$CH_3{-}CH_2{-}CH_2{-}CH_2{-}SH$ *1-butanethiol**
Phenol	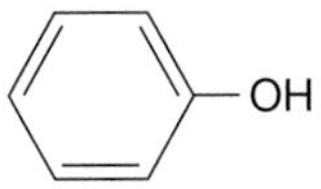 $C_6H_5{-}OH$ (benzene ring–OH)	*-ol**	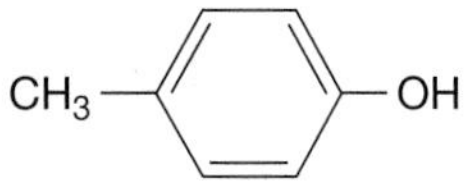 $CH_3{-}C_6H_4{-}OH$ *4-methylphenol**

*The IUPAC names for thiols and phenols are not covered in this text.

Summary of Organic Reactions

1) Hydration of alkenes

$$\textit{alkene} + H_2O \longrightarrow \textit{alcohol}$$

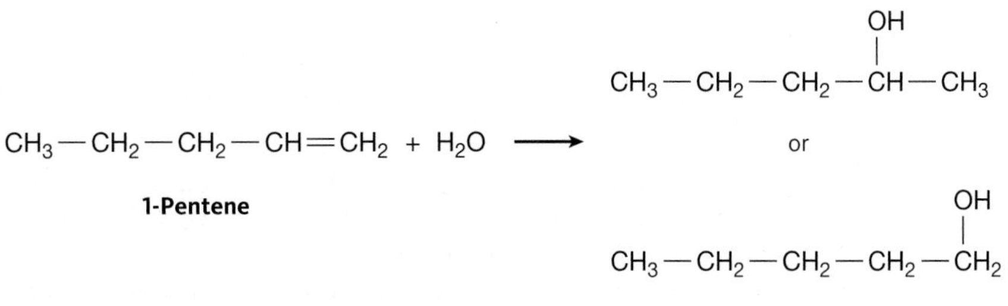

$$CH_3{-}CH_2{-}CH_2{-}CH{=}CH_2 + H_2O \longrightarrow$$

1-Pentene

2-Pentanol

$$CH_3{-}CH_2{-}CH_2{-}CH(OH){-}CH_3$$

or

$$CH_3{-}CH_2{-}CH_2{-}CH_2{-}CH_2{-}OH$$

1-Pentanol

continued

2) Dehydration of alcohols

$$\text{alcohol} \longrightarrow \text{alkene} + H_2O$$

$$\underset{\textbf{2-Pentanol}}{CH_3-CH_2-CH_2-\overset{\displaystyle OH}{\overset{|}{C}H}-CH_3} \longrightarrow H_2O + \begin{cases} \textbf{1-Pentene} \\ CH_3-CH_2-CH_2-CH=CH_2 \\ \text{or} \\ CH_3-CH_2-CH=CH-CH_3 \\ \textbf{2-Pentene} \end{cases}$$

SUMMARY OF OBJECTIVES

Now that you have read the chapter, test yourself on your knowledge of the objectives, using this summary as a guide.

Section 9.1: **Predict the products that are formed when water reacts with an alkene.**

- In a hydration reaction, the double bond of an alkene becomes a single bond, and hydrogen and hydroxyl groups become bonded to the two carbons that formed the double bond.
- Any alkene that is not symmetrical can form two different alcohols when it reacts with water, corresponding to the two ways of adding H and OH to the alkene carbon atoms.

Section 9.2: **Describe the role of enzymes in determining which of several possible products is formed in a biochemical reaction.**

- Enzymes are proteins that speed up reactions, making them useable in biological systems.
- In living organisms, reactions that can form more than one product must be controlled so that only the desired product is obtained. Enzymes determine the product of such reactions.
- Enzymes will only interact with specific reactants.

Section 9.3: **Name simple alcohols using the IUPAC system, and learn the trivial names for common alcohols.**

- In the IUPAC system, alcohols are identified by changing the *-e* at the end of the corresponding alkane name to *-ol*.
- When showing the location of an alcohol group, the hydrocarbon chain must be numbered from the end closest to the hydroxyl group.
- Several alcohols have trivial names that are in common use.

Section 9.4: **Relate the physical properties of alcohols to their structures.**

- The hydroxyl group is polar an can participate in hydrogen bonding.
- Hydrogen bonding gives alcohols higher boiling points and solubilities than alkanes of similar size.
- The water solubility of alcohols decreases as the size of the carbon framework increases, and it increases as the number of hydroxyl groups increases.
- Alcohols do not dissociate to produce hydroxide ions when they are dissolved in water.
- Most alcohols dissolve in other organic liquids, including alkanes.

Section 9.5: **Recognize chiral objects, and identify chiral carbon atoms in a molecule.**

- Any object or molecule whose mirror image is not superimposable on the original object is chiral.
- Chiral molecules have two mirror-image forms, called enantiomers.
- To be chiral, a molecule must contain at least one carbon atom that is bonded to four different groups of atoms (a chiral carbon atom).

Section 9.6: **Predict the products that are formed when an alcohol is dehydrated.**

- In a dehydration reaction, alcohols break down into an alkene and water. This reaction is the exact reverse of the hydration reaction.
- Many alcohols produce more than one alkene when they are dehydrated.

Section 9.7: Identify the phenol and thiol function groups in organic compounds, and relate the physical properties of phenols and thiols to those of alcohols and alkanes.

- Phenols contain a hydroxyl group directly bonded to a benzene ring.
- Phenols differ from alcohols in that they cannot be dehydrated and they are weakly acidic.
- Thiols are analogues of alcohols, in which the oxygen atom is replaced by a sulfur atom. The solubilities and boiling points of thiols are between those of alcohols and those of alkanes.
- Thiols cannot be made by reacting alkenes with H_2S, nor do they break down into alkenes and H_2S.

Concept Questions

OWL Online homework for this chapter may be assigned in OWL.

* indicates more challenging problems.

9.47 a) When water reacts with an alkene, what type of compound is formed?

b) When an alcohol is dehydrated, what type of organic compound is formed?

9.48 Give an example of an alkene that would react with water to make only one possible alcohol. Why can't your alkene make two different alcohols?

9.49 Most reactions in our bodies require an enzyme, even if they have only one possible product. Why is this?

9.50 Why must enzymes be able to select a particular product when more than one product is possible?

9.51 Both of the following compounds are polar, but only one of them dissolves well in water. Which one is the water-soluble compound? Explain your reasoning.

$$\underset{\text{F}}{\text{CH}_2}-\underset{\text{F}}{\text{CH}_2} \qquad \underset{\text{OH}}{\text{CH}_2}-\underset{\text{OH}}{\text{CH}_2}$$

Ethylene difluoride **Ethylene glycol**

9.52 Ethanol is an acceptable name according to the IUPAC rules, but propanol is not. Why is this?

9.53 Why is ethanol more soluble in water than ethane is?

9.54 Ethanol and dimethyl ether (shown here) are isomers, because they have the same numbers of atoms of carbon, hydrogen, and oxygen. Yet they have very different boiling points, as shown below their structures; in fact, dimethyl ether is similar to propane in its properties. Explain why the boiling point of dimethyl ether is closer to that of propane than it is to that of ethanol.

CH_3-CH_2-OH	CH_3-O-CH_3	$CH_3-CH_2-CH_3$
Ethanol: boiling point = 78°C a liquid at room temp.	**Dimethyl ether:** boiling point = −24°C a gas at room temp.	**Propane:** boiling point = −42°C a gas at room temp.

9.55 How can you identify a chiral carbon atom in a molecule?

9.56 If a carbon atom forms a double bond, can that carbon atom be chiral? Explain why or why not.

9.57 What is the maximum number of alkenes that could be formed by dehydrating an alcohol? Explain your answer.

9.58 Methanol cannot be dehydrated. Why is this?

9.59 What is the difference between an alcohol and a phenol?

9.60 Why are thiols less soluble in water than similarly sized alcohols?

Summary and Challenge Problems

9.61 Draw structures of molecules that fit each of the following descriptions:

a) a cyclic alcohol
b) a thiol that contains three carbon atoms
c) an alcohol that contains a branched carbon chain
d) a constitutional isomer of 1-pentanol
e) a phenol that contains more than six carbon atoms

9.62 Draw the structures of the products of each of the following reactions. If a reaction can produce more than one organic product, draw all of the possible products, but do not draw the same molecule twice.

a) the hydration of ethene
b) the dehydration of 1-propanol
c) the dehydration of 2-propanol
d) the hydration of $-CH_2-CH=CH_2$
e) the dehydration of $CH_3-CH(OH)-CH(CH_3)-CH_3$
f) the dehydration of $CH_3-CH(OH)-C(CH_3)_2-CH_3$
g) the dehydration of $CH_2(OH)-C(CH_3)_2-CH_3$
h) the hydration of 3-hexene *(cis* or *trans)*
i) the dehydration of cyclohexanol
j) the hydration of $-CH_3$
k) the dehydration of $-C(OH)(CH_3)-CH_2-CH_2-CH_2-CH_3$

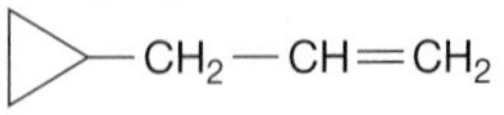

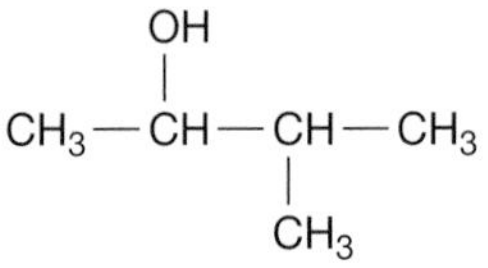

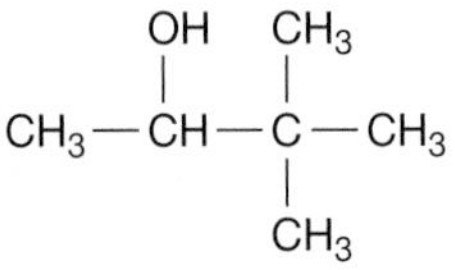

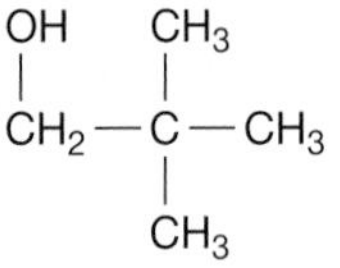

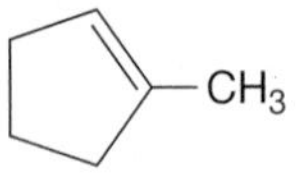

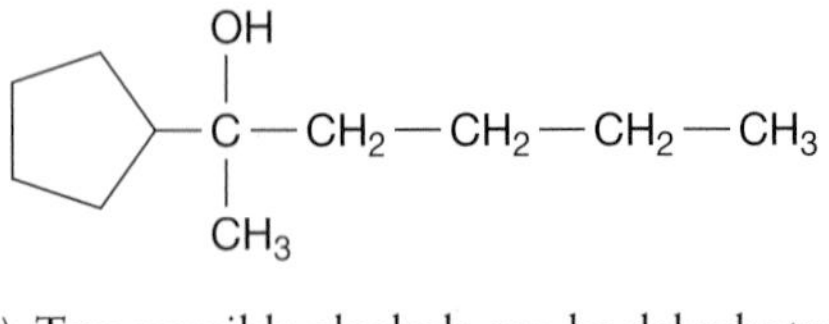

9.63 *a) Two possible alcohols can be dehydrated to form the alkene shown here. Draw the structures of these two alcohols.

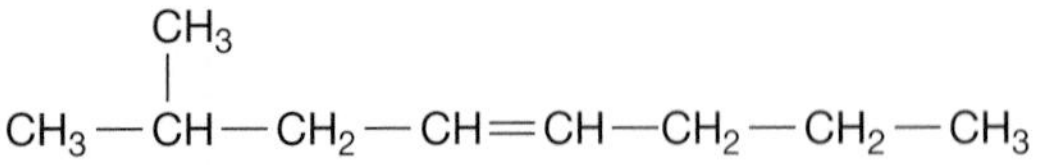

$$CH_3-CH(CH_3)-CH_2-CH=CH-CH_2-CH_2-CH_3$$

*b) Each of the alcohols you drew in part a can make a second alkene. Draw the structures of the other alkenes that you could make by dehydrating these alcohols.

9.64 In Problem 9.62 parts d and j, which of the two possible products will be the main product, based on Markovnikov's rule?

9.65 Name the following compounds:

a) CH_3-OH
b) 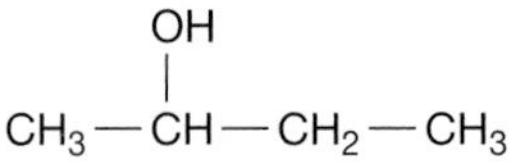 $CH_3-CH(OH)-CH_2-CH_3$
c) 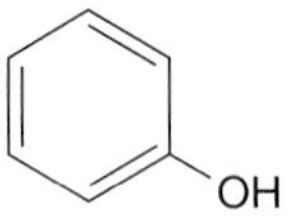 OH
d) 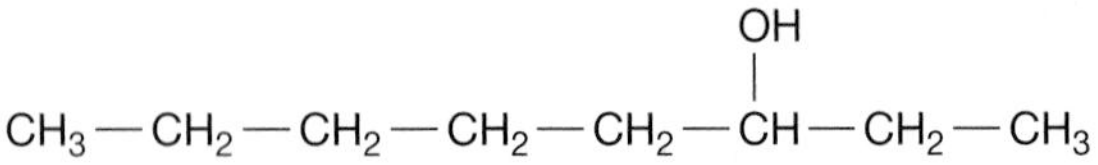 $CH_3-CH_2-CH_2-CH_2-CH_2-CH(OH)-CH_2-CH_3$
e) 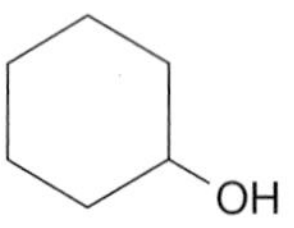 OH

9.66 Draw the structure of each of the following compounds:

a) ethyl alcohol
b) 2-pentanol
c) cyclobutanol
d) isopropyl alcohol
e) 1-hexanol

9.67 Write the molecular formula of each of the following molecules:

a) 2-propanol
b) cyclopropanol

9.68 From each of the following pairs of molecules, select the compound that is more soluble in water:

a) $CH_3-CH_2-CH_2-OH$ or $CH_3-CH_2-CH_3$
b) $CH_3-CH_2-CH_2-OH$ or $CH_3-CH_2-CH_2-SH$
c) 1-pentene or 1-pentanol
d) 2-pentanol or 2-heptanol
e) $CH_3-CH_2-CH_3$ or $CH_3-CH_2-CH_2-CH_2-CH_2-CH_2-CH_2-CH_2(OH)$
f) 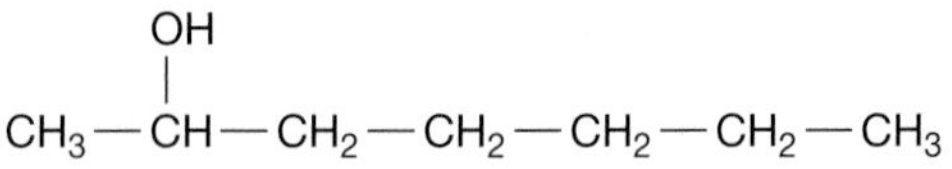 $CH_3-CH(OH)-CH_2-CH_2-CH_2-CH_2-CH_3$ or $CH_3-CH(OH)-CH_2-CH_2-CH_2-CH(OH)-CH_3$

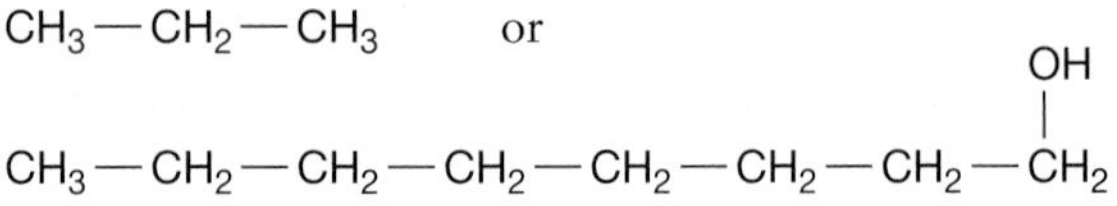

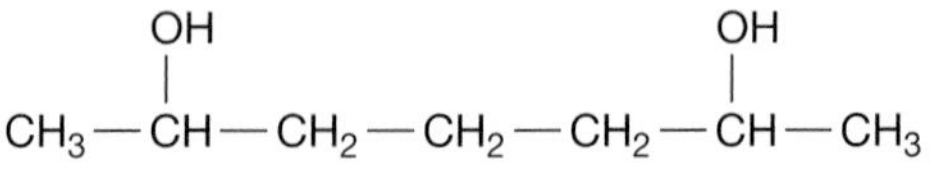

9.69 Answer the following questions by selecting compounds from the following list:

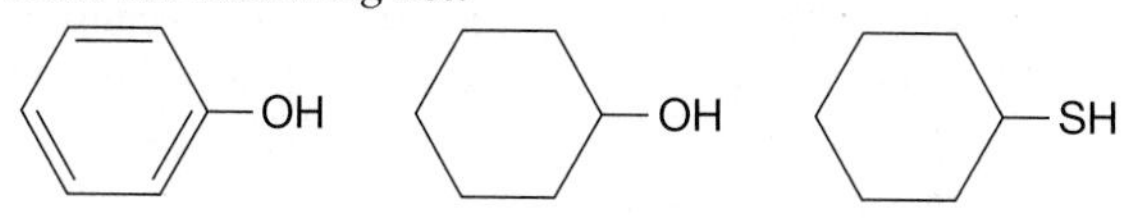

—OH　　—OH　　—SH

Compound A　　Compound B　　Compound C

a) Which compound has the lowest solubility in water?
b) Which compounds can be dehydrated?
c) Which compounds can form hydrogen bonds?

9.70 The boiling point of dimethyl ether (see Problem 9.54) is similar to that of propane, but dimethyl ether is far more soluble in water than propane is. You can dissolve about 70 g of dimethyl ether in 1 L of water, whereas you can only dissolve about 0.1 g of propane in 1 L of water. Explain why dimethyl ether is so much more soluble in water than propane is.

9.71 Examine the following pairs of structures. In each case, are the two molecules constitutional isomers of each other? If not, explain why not.

a)  $CH_2(OH)-CH_2-CH_2-CH_3$ and $CH_3-CH(OH)-CH_2-CH_3$

b)  $CH_3-CH(OH)-CH_2-CH_3$ and $CH_3-CH_2-CH(OH)-CH_3$

c) 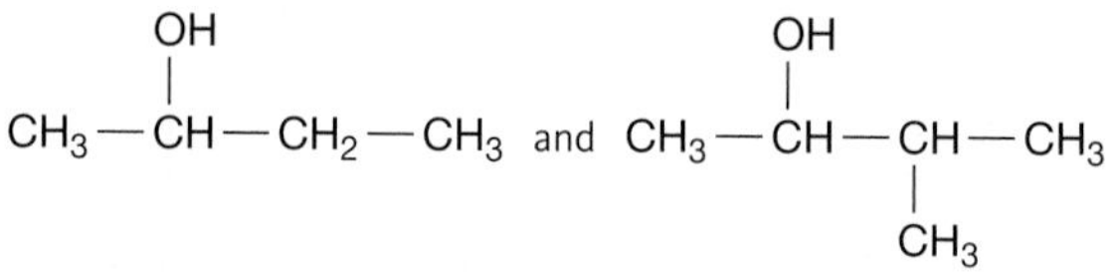 $CH_3-CH(OH)-CH_2-CH_3$ and $CH_3-CH(OH)-CH(CH_3)-CH_3$

d) 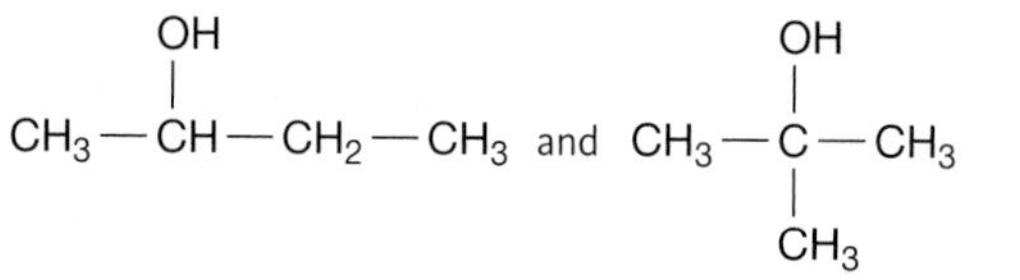 $CH_3-CH(OH)-CH_2-CH_3$ and $CH_3-C(OH)(CH_3)-CH_3$

e) 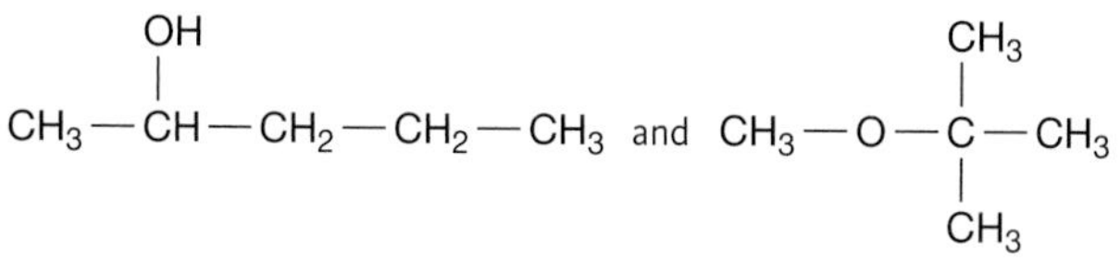 $CH_3-CH(OH)-CH_2-CH_2-CH_3$ and $CH_3-O-C(CH_3)_2-CH_3$

f) 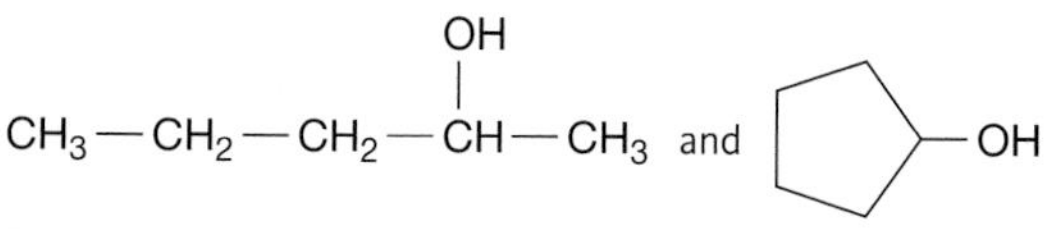 $CH_3-CH_2-CH_2-CH(OH)-CH_3$ and —OH

g) 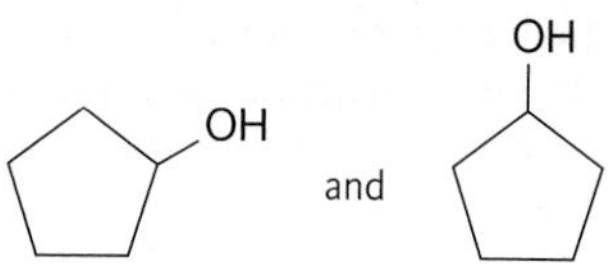 OH and OH

h) 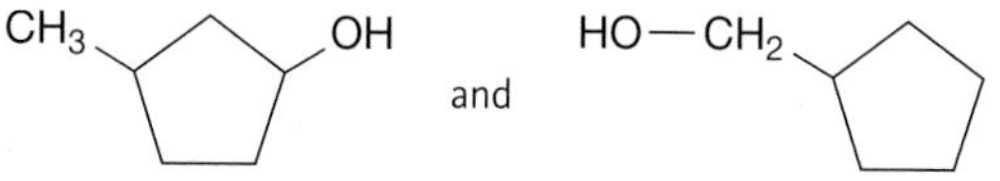 CH_3 OH and $HO-CH_2$

i) 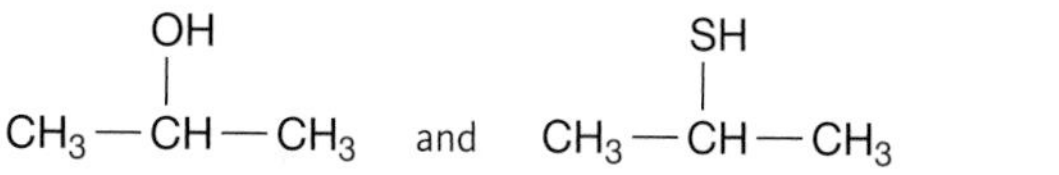 $CH_3-CH(OH)-CH_3$ and $CH_3-CH(SH)-CH_3$

j) 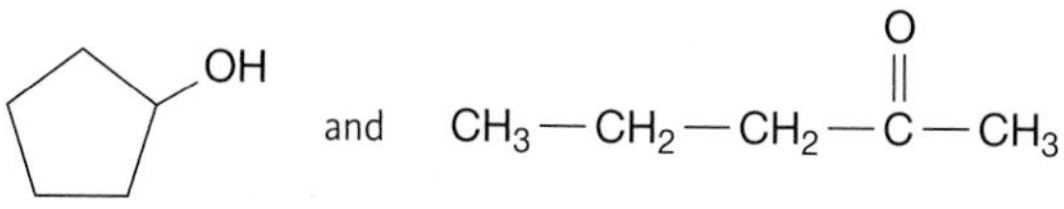 OH and $CH_3-CH_2-CH_2-C(=O)-CH_3$

k) 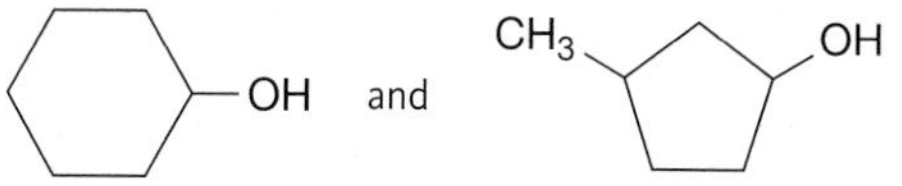 —OH and CH_3 OH

9.72 Find and circle all of the chiral carbon atoms in the following molecules:

a) $CH_3-CH_2-CH_2-CH_3$

b) 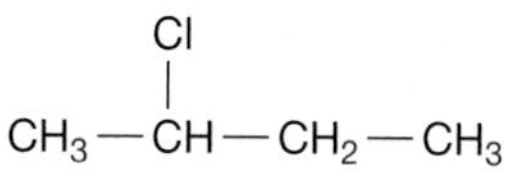 $CH_3-CH(Cl)-CH_2-CH_3$

c) 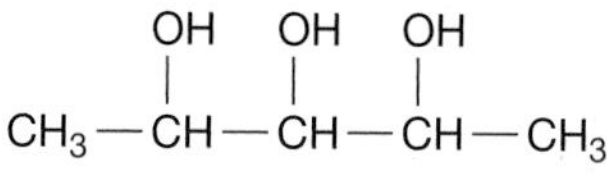 $CH_3-CH(OH)-CH(OH)-CH(OH)-CH_3$

d) 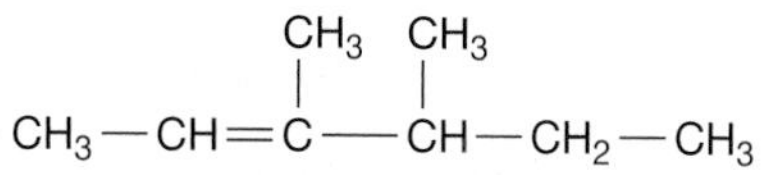 $CH_3-CH=C(CH_3)-CH(CH_3)-CH_2-CH_3$

9.73 *a) How many different alcohols can you make by replacing one hydrogen atom in hexane with a hydroxyl group? Draw the structures and give names for these compounds.
*b) Which of the compounds you drew in part a are chiral?

9.74 The following dehydration reactions occur in most living organisms. In which reaction must the enzyme select among more than one possible product?

$$CH_2(OH)-CH(O-PO_3^{2-})-C(=O)-OH \longrightarrow CH_2{=}C(O-PO_3^{2-})-C(=O)-OH + H_2O$$

Reaction 1: occurs during the breakdown of carbohydrates

$$CH_3-CH(OH)-CH_2-C(=O)-OH \longrightarrow CH_3-CH{=}CH-C(=O)-OH + H_2O$$

Reaction 2: occurs during the formation of fatty acids

9.75 In one of the reactions in Problem 9.74, the enzyme selected one of the two possible products. Draw the structure of the product that is *not* formed in this reaction.

9.76 *The following molecule can react with two molecules of water. Draw the structures of all of the possible products of this double hydration.

$$CH_3-CH{=}CH-CH_2-CH{=}CH_2$$

9.77 *The following molecule can lose two molecules of water. Draw the structures of all of the possible products of this double dehydration. (You may ignore *cis–trans* isomerism.)

$$CH_3-CH(OH)-CH_2-CH_2-CH(OH)-CH_3$$

9.78 *a) Two possible alkenes can be hydrated to form 3-hexanol. Draw their structures, and give their names. (Ignore *cis–trans* isomers.)

*b) If you wanted to make 3-hexanol in a laboratory, and you did not want to waste any of your starting alkene, which of the two alkenes would be the better choice? Explain your reasoning.

9.79 *Joshua says, "When you dehydrate 2-pentanol, you make two alkenes, 1-pentene and 2-pentene." Rayelle answers, "No, there are more than two, because you've forgotten about *cis–trans* isomers." Is Rayelle correct? If so, how many alkenes can you make, and what are their names and structures?

9.80 *Draw the structure of an alcohol that gives the following when it is dehydrated:

a) only one product
b) two products
c) three products
d) no products (the alcohol cannot be dehydrated)

9.81 Answer the following questions by selecting compounds from the following list:

OH

Compound A

OH
CH_2

Compound B

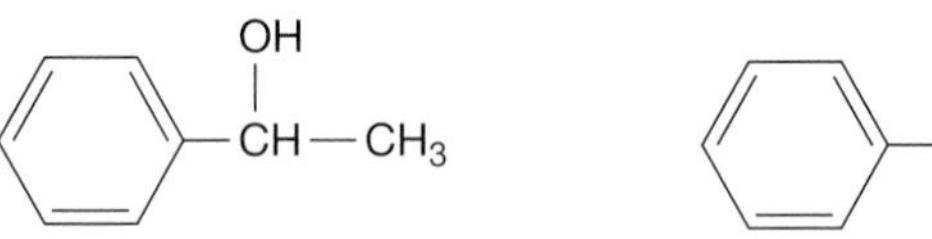

Compound C   Compound D

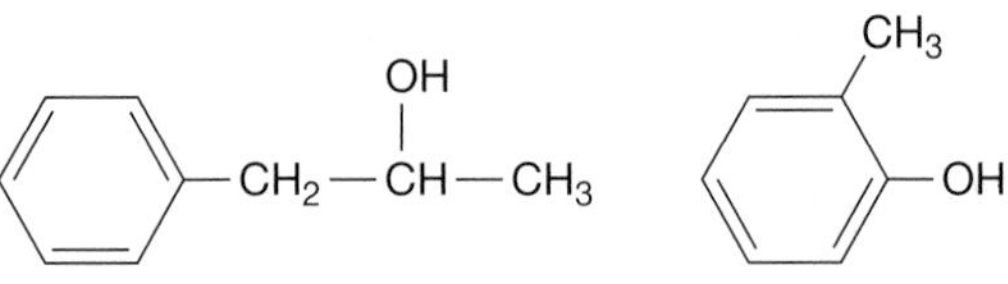

Compound E   Compound F

a) Which of these compounds are phenols?
b) Which of these compounds cannot be dehydrated?
c) Which of these compounds form only one product when dehydrated?
d) Which of these compounds form two different products when dehydrated?

9.82 Ethynylestradiol is a synthetic estrogen and is used in a variety of birth control formulations. Identify the functional groups in this compound.

9.83 Would you expect ethynylestradiol (see Problem 9.82) to be soluble in water? Explain your answer.

9.84 The following compound (called dimercaprol) is used to counteract mercury poisoning. It works by forming strong bonds to mercury atoms, preventing mercury from reacting with other substances in the body. Identify the functional groups in this molecule.

$$CH_2(OH)-CH(SH)-CH_2(SH)$$

9.85 *a) How much would 2.50 mol of 2-butanol weigh?
*b) 2-Butanol is a liquid with a density of 0.802 g/mL. What would be the volume of 2.00 mol of 2-butanol?

9.86 *If you have 50.0 mL of cyclopentanol, how many moles of cyclopentanol do you have? The density of cyclopentanol is 0.95 g/mL.

9.87 *How many grams of isopropyl alcohol would you need if you wanted to make the following?

a) 150 mL of a 2.00% (w/v) solution of isopropyl alcohol in water
b) 150 mL of a 0.200 M solution of isopropyl alcohol in water

9.88 *A solution contains 2.5 g of ethanol in enough water to give a total volume of 75.0 mL. Express the concentration of this solution as:

a) a percent concentration (w/v)
b) a molarity

9.89 *If you dissolve 4.0 g of glycerol in enough water to make 100 mL of solution, will this solution be isotonic, hypertonic, or hypotonic? Show your reasoning.

9.90 *If 8.5 g of ethene reacts with water, how many grams of ethanol will be formed?

9.91 *Alcohols can burn, just as hydrocarbons can. The combustion of alcohols follows the same general scheme as that of hydrocarbons:

$$\text{alcohol} + O_2 \rightarrow CO_2 + H_2O$$

Using this information, write the balanced equation for the combustion of ethanol.

9.92 *Sodium chloride (NaCl) can dissolve in methanol. When it dissolves, it dissociates, just as it does in water, and the individual ions are solvated by methanol molescules. Draw a picture that shows how sodium and chloride ions are solvated by methanol.

9.93 *Ethanol is used in some rubbing alcohol formulas, because it evaporates readily and cools the skin. The specific heat of ethanol is 0.58 cal/g·°C, and the heat of vaporization is 201 cal/g.

a) How much heat is needed to raise the temperature of 25.0 g of ethanol from 20°C to 37°C (body temperature)?
b) How much heat is needed to evaporate 25.0 g of ethanol?

10

Carbonyl Compounds and Redox Reactions

Celeste has been trying to lose weight for the past five years without much success. A friend tells her about a special diet plan that restricts carbohydrates but lets the dieter eat unlimited amounts of fat and protein. Celeste decides to try this diet, so she stops eating carbohydrate-rich foods such as pasta, bread, rice, and potatoes. She also avoids sweet foods and beverages, including most fruits. Instead, she starts eating a lot of meat and fatty foods to supply her calorie needs. Celeste loses quite a bit of weight, but she notices that she has less energy and tends to be more irritable than usual. After a few weeks, she also notices that her breath has an odd, sweet smell to it. Concerned about this aroma, Celeste goes to her doctor, who requests a urinalysis. The lab reports that Celeste's urine has a high concentration of ketone bodies, compounds that are formed when the body obtains most of its energy from fats. The sweet smell of Celeste's breath is due to acetone, a volatile ketone that cannot be metabolized by the body and that escapes from the blood via the lungs.

Celeste's doctor explains that when Celeste's body uses fats as its primary energy source, her liver converts the fatty acids into ketone bodies rather than burning them completely. Her brain then uses two of the ketone bodies to supply most of its energy needs. Mildly elevated concentrations of ketone levels in the blood (a condition called ketosis) are not harmful, but long-term consumption of a high-fat diet poses a variety of health risks. As a result, Celeste decides to abandon this diet, and within a few days the ketone bodies vanish from her urine.

OUTLINE

LABORATORY REQUISITION—CHEMISTRY

iStockphoto.com/Kin Shing chan

These food items are marketed to dieters as being low in carbohydrates.

OWL Online homework for this chapter may be assigned in OWL.

One of the primary activities of any living organism is obtaining energy. Humans and all other animals use the organic compounds in the food they eat as their energy source. We burn the carbohydrates, fats, and proteins in our food to get energy, and we use this energy to carry out all of the activities we do. The overall reaction is a combustion, in which the nutrients combine with oxygen to form inorganic compounds. For example, when we burn table sugar (sucrose), our bodies produce carbon dioxide and water, along with a great deal of energy.

$$C_{12}H_{22}O_{11} + 12\,O_2 \rightarrow 12\,CO_2 + 11\,H_2O + \text{energy}$$

However, if we simply allow sugar to catch fire and burn, the energy is released so rapidly that it cannot be harnessed. Therefore, our bodies actually burn sugar and all other nutrients using a lengthy series of small steps. By doing so, we produce the energy in small increments.

As our bodies break down any sort of organic nutrient to obtain energy, we must remove the hydrogen atoms from the organic molecule, because the final products do not contain bonds between carbon and hydrogen. The reactions that remove hydrogen atoms from an organic molecule are called oxidations, and they play a key role in the production of energy. Living organisms have evolved an elaborate mechanism for removing hydrogen atoms from organic compounds, requiring several specialized molecules that bind to hydrogen and move it from one molecule to another. Eventually, these hydrogen atoms become bonded to oxygen from air, forming water and releasing energy.

In this chapter, we will explore oxidations. We will also look at reductions, which add hydrogen to organic compounds and occur when we build organic molecules from simpler precursors. Finally, we will examine how oxidation can be combined with the hydration reaction you learned in Chapter 9. This combination of reactions is the basis for most metabolic pathways, sequences of reactions that convert one compound in a living organism into another.

OBJECTIVES: *Understand the relationship between oxidation and reduction, and recognize oxidation and reduction reactions that involve hydrocarbons.*

10.1 Hydrogenation and Dehydrogenation

In Chapter 9, you learned that alcohols can lose water to form alkenes (the dehydration reaction). It is also possible to convert an alkane into an alkene. In this reaction, called a **dehydrogenation reaction**, the alkane loses two hydrogen atoms to make room for the additional carbon–carbon bond.

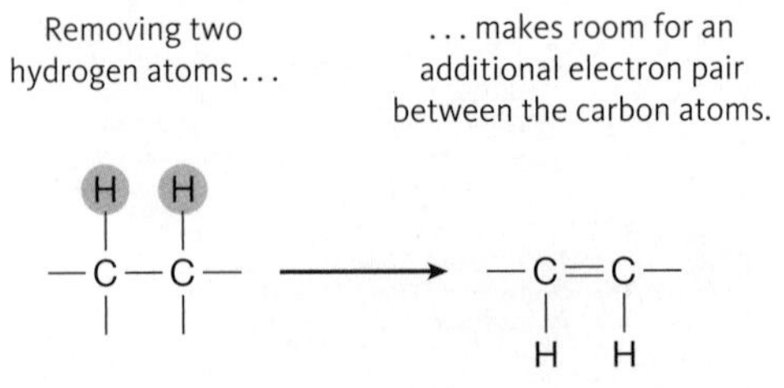

Removing two hydrogen atoms . . .

. . . makes room for an additional electron pair between the carbon atoms.

$$\text{—}\underset{|}{\overset{\text{H}}{\overset{|}{\text{C}}}}\text{—}\underset{|}{\overset{\text{H}}{\overset{|}{\text{C}}}}\text{—} \longrightarrow \text{—}\underset{\text{H}}{\underset{|}{\text{C}}}\text{=}\underset{\text{H}}{\underset{|}{\text{C}}}\text{—}$$

Alkane **Alkene**

For example, propylene can be made by removing two hydrogen atoms from propane, as shown here. The two hydrogen atoms combine to make H_2. This is an important reaction in industry, because propylene is the starting material for polypropylene plastics.

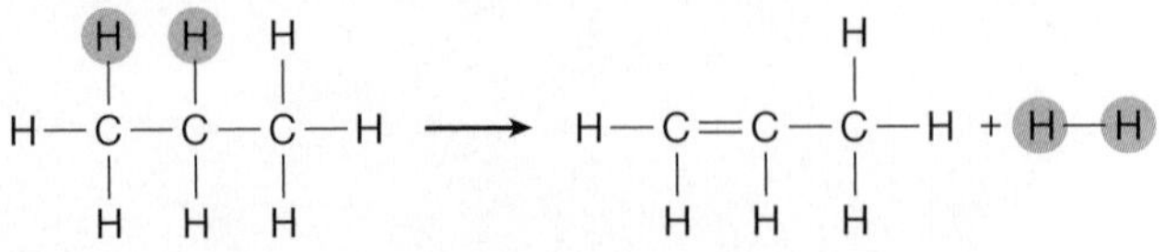

$$\text{H—}\underset{\text{H}}{\underset{|}{\overset{\text{H}}{\overset{|}{\text{C}}}}}\text{—}\underset{\text{H}}{\underset{|}{\overset{\text{H}}{\overset{|}{\text{C}}}}}\text{—}\underset{\text{H}}{\underset{|}{\overset{\text{H}}{\overset{|}{\text{C}}}}}\text{—H} \longrightarrow \text{H—}\underset{\text{H}}{\underset{|}{\text{C}}}\text{=}\underset{\text{H}}{\underset{|}{\text{C}}}\text{—}\underset{\text{H}}{\underset{|}{\overset{\text{H}}{\overset{|}{\text{C}}}}}\text{—H} + \text{H—H}$$

$$CH_3\text{—}CH_2\text{—}CH_3 \longrightarrow CH_2\text{=}CH\text{—}CH_3 + H_2$$

Propane **Propylene**

Normally, it is very difficult to remove hydrogen atoms from alkanes. Removing hydrogen atoms from an alkane requires special catalysts and high temperatures. However, the dehydrogenation reaction becomes easier if a molecule contains a functional group close to the new alkene double bond. For instance, the following reaction is one of the steps our bodies carry out when we burn any type of nutrient to obtain energy. In this dehydrogenation, the reactant contains a functional group (the carboxylic acid group) next to each of the carbon atoms that loses hydrogen.

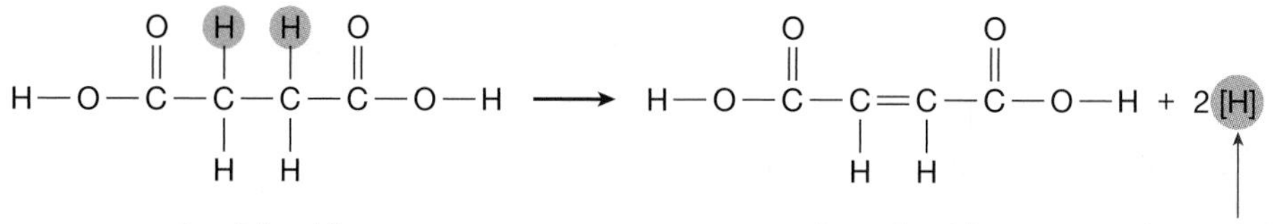

$$\mathrm{H{-}O{-}\overset{\overset{\Large O}{\|}}{C}{-}\underset{H}{\overset{H}{C}}{-}\underset{H}{\overset{H}{C}}{-}\overset{\overset{\Large O}{\|}}{C}{-}O{-}H \longrightarrow H{-}O{-}\overset{\overset{\Large O}{\|}}{C}{-}\underset{H}{C}{=}\underset{H}{C}{-}\overset{\overset{\Large O}{\|}}{C}{-}O{-}H + 2\,[H]}$$

Succinic acid — Fumaric acid — This symbol is explained below.

Health Note: Fumaric acid is used to give a tart flavor to candies, beverages, and some baked goods. When it is mixed with sodium bicarbonate (baking soda), it forms carbon dioxide gas, so it is also used to make baked goods rise.

In this dehydrogenation, the two hydrogen atoms do not combine to make a molecule of H_2. Instead, they are transferred to a different organic molecule. *Our bodies always transfer hydrogen atoms to some other molecule when we carry out a dehydrogenation.* Rather than including this other compound in the chemical equation, we simply use the symbol [H] to represent a hydrogen atom that is attached to an organic molecule. We can therefore represent any dehydrogenation reaction as

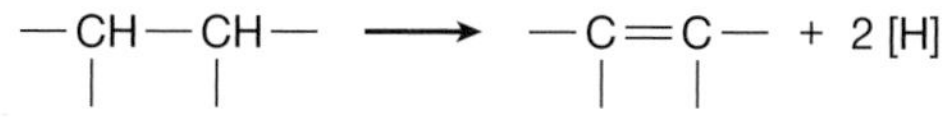

$$\mathrm{{-}\underset{|}{C}H{-}\underset{|}{C}H{-} \longrightarrow {-}\underset{|}{C}{=}\underset{|}{C}{-} + 2\,[H]}$$

Note that in a dehydrogenation, the organic molecule loses hydrogen *atoms,* not hydrogen *ions.* Alkanes are not acids and cannot lose H^+ ions. In the dehydrogenation reaction, the hydrogen atoms have no ionic charge.

Sample Problem 10.1

Drawing the product of a dehydrogenation reaction

The following molecule is dehydrogenated during the breakdown of leucine (one of the amino acid building blocks of proteins). The part of the molecule that is dehydrogenated is circled. Draw the structure of the product of this reaction.

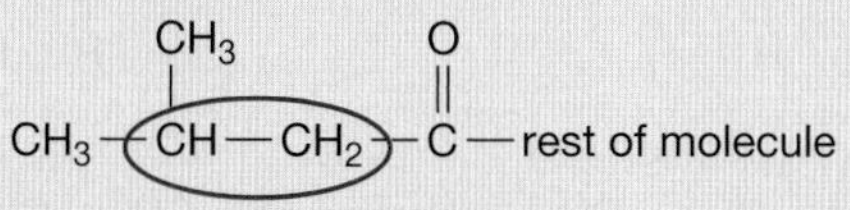

$$\mathrm{CH_3{-}\overset{\overset{\Large CH_3}{|}}{C}H{-}CH_2{-}\overset{\overset{\Large O}{\|}}{C}{-}rest\ of\ molecule}$$

SOLUTION

To draw the product of a dehydrogenation reaction, we must first remove one hydrogen atom from each of the carbon atoms that are involved in the reaction. (The carbon atoms are adjacent to each other.)

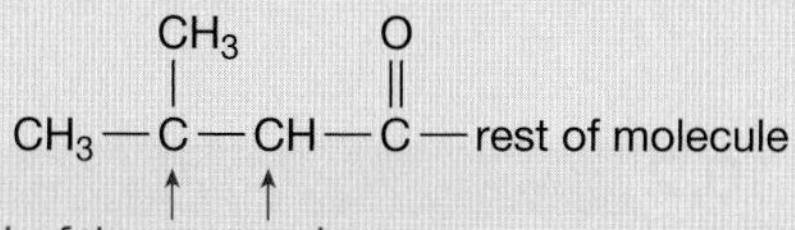

$$\mathrm{CH_3{-}\overset{\overset{\Large CH_3}{|}}{C}{-}CH{-}\overset{\overset{\Large O}{\|}}{C}{-}rest\ of\ molecule}$$

Each of these two carbon atoms has lost a hydrogen atom.

To complete the structure, we add a bonding electron pair between the two carbon atoms, turning the single bond into a double bond. The structure of the product is

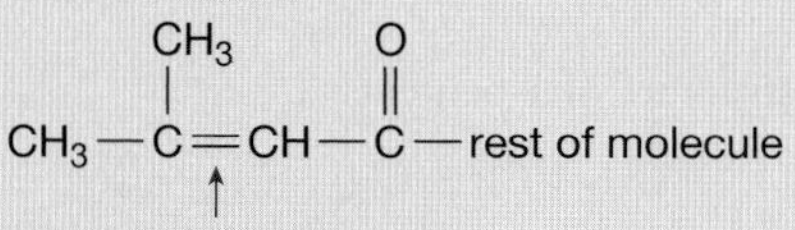

$$\mathrm{CH_3{-}\overset{\overset{\Large CH_3}{|}}{C}{=}CH{-}\overset{\overset{\Large O}{\|}}{C}{-}rest\ of\ molecule}$$

The single bond in the reactant becomes a double bond.

continued

TRY IT YOURSELF: *Stearic acid is a component of animal fats. It can be dehydrogenated in the body; the part of the molecule that reacts is circled here. Draw the structure of the product of this reaction.*

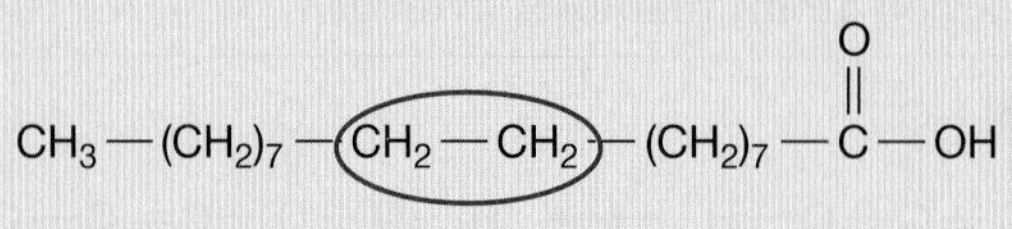

$$CH_3-(CH_2)_7-\boxed{CH_2-CH_2}-(CH_2)_7-\overset{O}{\overset{\|}{C}}-OH$$

For additional practice, try Core Problems 10.1 and 10.2.

The dehydrogenation reaction is our first example of an **oxidation reaction.** *Any reaction that removes two hydrogen atoms from an organic compound is an oxidation.* You will see several other examples of oxidation reactions in this chapter.

Alkenes Can Gain Hydrogen Atoms

Removing hydrogen atoms from an alkane is very difficult, but adding hydrogen atoms to an alkene is not. Any alkene can be converted into an alkane by adding hydrogen to it, along with an appropriate catalyst. This reaction is called the **hydrogenation reaction,** and it is the reverse of the dehydrogenation reaction.

$$H-H + -\underset{H}{\underset{|}{C}}=\underset{H}{\underset{|}{C}}- \longrightarrow -\overset{H}{\overset{|}{\underset{H}{\underset{|}{C}}}}-\overset{H}{\overset{|}{\underset{H}{\underset{|}{C}}}}-$$

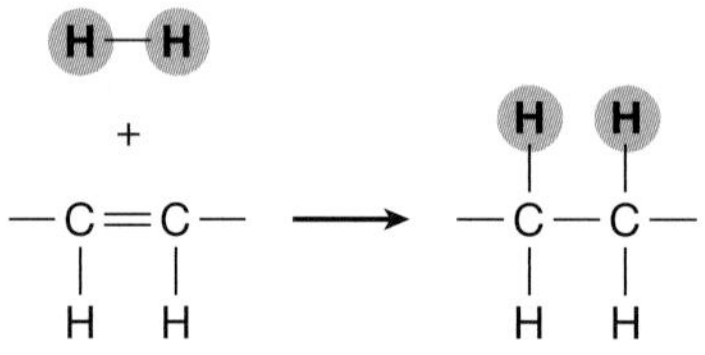

An alkene reacts with hydrogen . . . . . . to produce an alkane.

For example, 1-butene reacts with hydrogen to form butane.

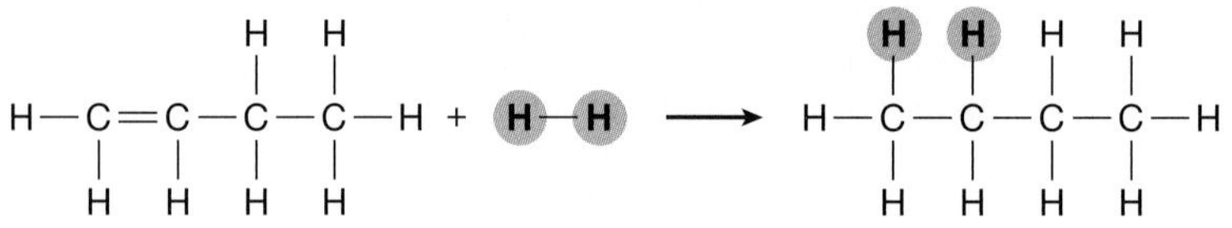

$$H-\underset{H}{\underset{|}{C}}=\underset{H}{\underset{|}{C}}-\overset{H}{\overset{|}{\underset{H}{\underset{|}{C}}}}-\overset{H}{\overset{|}{\underset{H}{\underset{|}{C}}}}-H + H-H \longrightarrow H-\overset{H}{\overset{|}{\underset{H}{\underset{|}{C}}}}-\overset{H}{\overset{|}{\underset{H}{\underset{|}{C}}}}-\overset{H}{\overset{|}{\underset{H}{\underset{|}{C}}}}-\overset{H}{\overset{|}{\underset{H}{\underset{|}{C}}}}-H$$

$$CH_2=CH-CH_2-CH_3 + H_2 \longrightarrow CH_3-CH_2-CH_2-CH_3$$

1-Butene **Butane**

Be careful not to confuse the *hydrogenation* reaction with the *hydration* reaction that you learned in Section 9.1. Both of these reaction types involve alkenes, but a hydrogenation reaction adds two hydrogen atoms, whereas a hydration reaction adds H and OH.

Sample Problem **10.2**

Drawing the product of a hydrogenation reaction

Draw the structure and give the name of the product that is produced when 1-pentene is hydrogenated.

SOLUTION

We must first draw the structure of 1-pentene.

$$CH_2=CH-CH_2-CH_2-CH_3$$

continued

To draw the product of this hydrogenation reaction, we change the double bond to a single bond, and we add a hydrogen atom to each of the carbon atoms that formed the double bond.

$$\underset{\text{H}}{\overset{}{\text{CH}_2}}-\underset{\text{H}}{\text{CH}}-\text{CH}_2-\text{CH}_2-\text{CH}_3 \xrightarrow{\text{Redraw the product as a condensed structure.}} \text{CH}_3-\text{CH}_2-\text{CH}_2-\text{CH}_2-\text{CH}_3$$

The product of the reaction: **pentane.**

TRY IT YOURSELF: *Draw the structure and give the name of the product that is formed when the following alkene is hydrogenated:*

$$\text{CH}_3-\overset{\text{CH}_3}{\overset{|}{\text{C}}}=\text{CH}-\text{CH}_2-\text{CH}_2-\text{CH}_3$$

For additional practice, try Core Problems 10.3 and 10.4.

ROBERT SULLIVAN/AFP/Getty Images

Some foods that contain partially hydrogenated vegetable oils.

Alkynes and aromatic compounds can also be hydrogenated, but these reactions do not play a significant role in biological chemistry. Alkynes are rare in living organisms, and aromatic rings are so stable that they do not undergo this type of reaction under physiological conditions.

The hydrogenation reaction is widely used in food manufacturing. Vegetable shortening, margarine, and many fried foods (including an enormous array of snack foods) contain "hydrogenated vegetable oil." Vegetable oils (and animal fats) are mixtures of organic compounds called triglycerides, which you will learn about in Chapter 14. The melting points of triglycerides depend on the number of alkene groups they contain: triglycerides with several double bonds are liquids at room temperature, while triglycerides with few or none are solids. Hydrogenation converts liquid vegetable oils (which contain several alkene groups) into solids, so they can be used as a substitute for animal fats such as butter. Here is a typical hydrogenation reaction:

$$\begin{array}{l} \text{CH}_3-(\text{CH}_2)_7-\text{CH}=\text{CH}-(\text{CH}_2)_7-\overset{\text{O}}{\overset{\|}{\text{C}}}-\text{O}-\text{CH}_2 \\ \text{CH}_3-(\text{CH}_2)_7-\text{CH}=\text{CH}-(\text{CH}_2)_7-\overset{\text{O}}{\overset{\|}{\text{C}}}-\text{O}-\text{CH} \\ \text{CH}_3-(\text{CH}_2)_7-\text{CH}=\text{CH}-(\text{CH}_2)_7-\overset{\text{O}}{\overset{\|}{\text{C}}}-\text{O}-\text{CH}_2 \end{array} + 3\,\text{H}_2 \longrightarrow \begin{array}{l} \text{CH}_3-(\text{CH}_2)_7-\text{CH}_2-\text{CH}_2-(\text{CH}_2)_7-\overset{\text{O}}{\overset{\|}{\text{C}}}-\text{O}-\text{CH}_2 \\ \text{CH}_3-(\text{CH}_2)_7-\text{CH}_2-\text{CH}_2-(\text{CH}_2)_7-\overset{\text{O}}{\overset{\|}{\text{C}}}-\text{O}-\text{CH} \\ \text{CH}_3-(\text{CH}_2)_7-\text{CH}_2-\text{CH}_2-(\text{CH}_2)_7-\overset{\text{O}}{\overset{\|}{\text{C}}}-\text{O}-\text{CH}_2 \end{array}$$

Triolein
An unsaturated fat:
liquid at room temperature

Tristearin
A saturated fat:
solid at room temperature

Our bodies carry out many hydrogenation reactions, but we do not use H_2 as the source of the hydrogen atoms. Instead, we use large organic molecules that can donate hydrogen atoms. These hydrogen donors are closely related to the compounds that accept hydrogen atoms in biological oxidations. Rather than including these molecules when we write a balanced equation, we can represent a biological hydrogenation reaction as

$$-\underset{|}{\text{C}}=\underset{|}{\text{C}}- + 2\,[\text{H}] \longrightarrow -\underset{|}{\text{CH}}-\underset{|}{\text{CH}}-$$

Hydrogenation is an example of a **reduction reaction**. *Any reaction in which hydrogen atoms are added to an organic molecule is called a reduction.* Reduction and oxidation reactions are opposites, and they occur together in living organisms. Whenever one compound is oxidized, another must be reduced, because the oxidation supplies the hydrogen atoms for the reduction. Here is a summary of oxidation and reduction reactions:

- Oxidation reactions remove hydrogen atoms from an organic molecule.
- Reduction reactions add hydrogen atoms to an organic molecule.
- Whenever one compound is oxidized, another must be reduced.

CORE PROBLEMS

All Core Problems are paired and the answers to the blue odd-numbered problems appear in the back of the book.

10.1 The following compound is dehydrogenated during the breakdown of lysine (one of the components of proteins). The portion of the molecule that is dehydrogenated is circled. Draw the structure of the product of this reaction.

HO—C(=O)—CH_2—(CH_2—CH_2)—C(=O)—rest of molecule

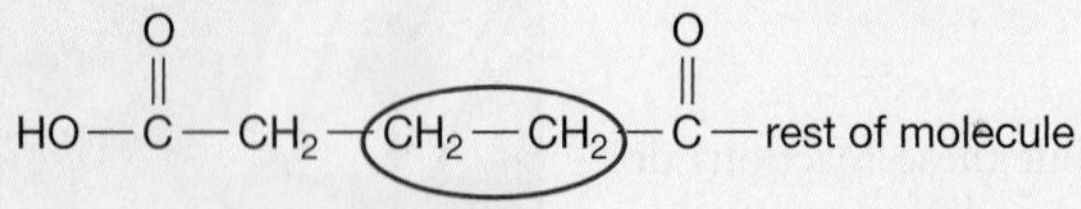

10.2 The following compound is dehydrogenated during the breakdown of isoleucine (one of the components of proteins). The portion of the molecule that is dehydrogenated is circled. Draw the structure of the product of this reaction.

CH_3—(CH_2—CH(CH_3))—C(=O)—rest of molecule

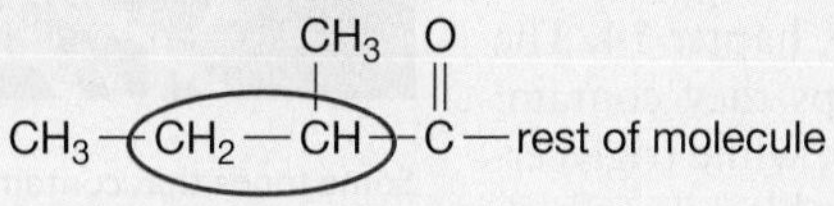

10.3 Draw the structures of the products that are formed when each of the following alkenes is hydrogenated:

a) 1-pentene b) 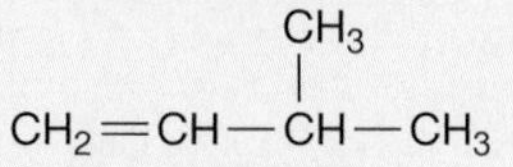 CH_2=CH—CH(CH_3)—CH_3

10.4 Draw the structures of the products that are formed when each of the following alkenes is hydrogenated:

a) *cis*-2-hexene b) 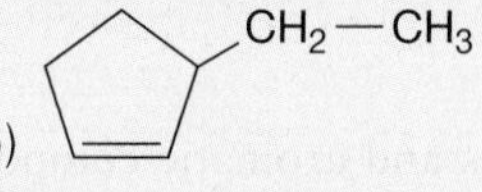 (cyclopentene ring bearing CH_2—CH_3)

10.5 Is the following reaction an oxidation, or is it a reduction? Explain your answer.

(cyclohexadiene → benzene ring)

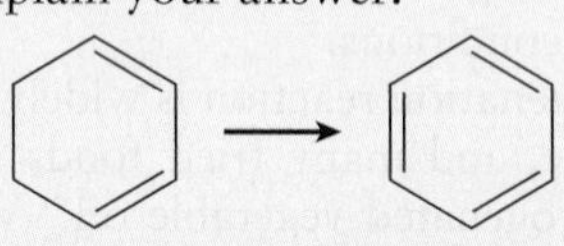

10.6 Is the following reaction an oxidation, or is it a reduction? Explain your answer.

(cyclohexadiene → cyclohexene)

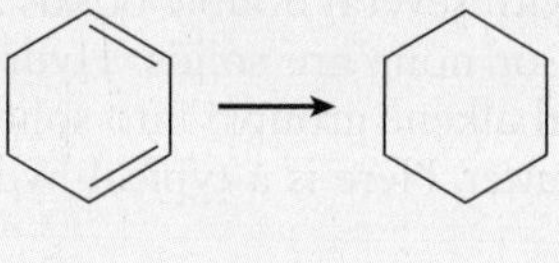

OBJECTIVES: *Predict the products of the oxidation of an alcohol or the reduction of an aldehyde or ketone, and classify alcohols as primary, secondary, or tertiary.*

10.2 Oxidation and Reduction Reactions and the Carbonyl Group

In Chapter 9, you learned about the alcohol functional group and how it can be made by adding water to an alkene. In this section, we explore the oxidation–reduction chemistry of the alcohol group.

The oxidation of an alcohol is an important reaction in biological chemistry. This reaction is analogous to the oxidation of an alkane. In both reactions, we remove two hydrogen atoms from the organic compound, and we convert a single bond to a double bond. The C=O group in the product is called a **carbonyl group** (pronounced "carba-NEEL").

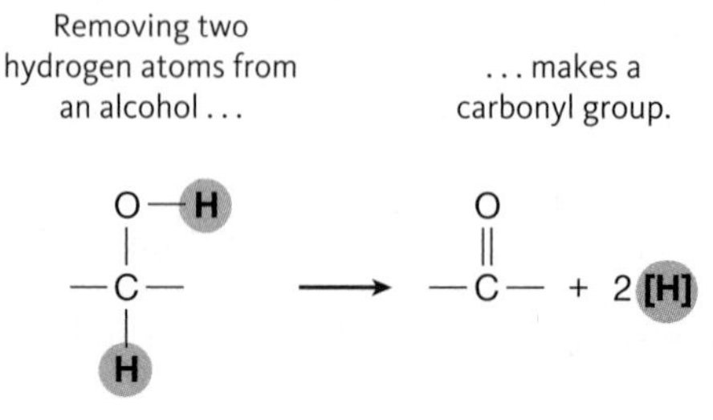

Removing two hydrogen atoms from an alcohol . . .

. . . makes a carbonyl group.

—C(—O—H)(—H)— ⟶ —C(=O)— + 2 [H]

For instance, if you consume any sort of alcoholic beverage, your body oxidizes the ethanol as shown here:

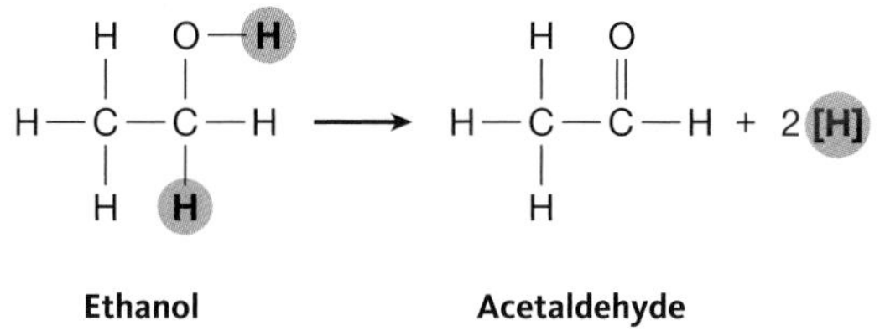

$$\text{H}_3\text{C}{-}\text{CH}_2{-}\text{OH} \longrightarrow \text{H}_3\text{C}{-}\text{CHO} + 2[\text{H}]$$

Ethanol **Acetaldehyde**

Health Note: Acetaldehyde is toxic and is normally converted to acetic acid by the liver. However, if you consume too much ethanol in alcoholic beverages, your liver cannot oxidize the acetaldehyde as quickly as it is formed. The excess acetaldehyde helps produce the unpleasant sensations of a hangover.

Sample Problem 10.3

Drawing the product of the oxidation of an alcohol

When your body burns nutrients to obtain energy, it produces malic acid. Your body then oxidizes the alcohol group in malic acid (circled below). Draw the structure of the product of this oxidation.

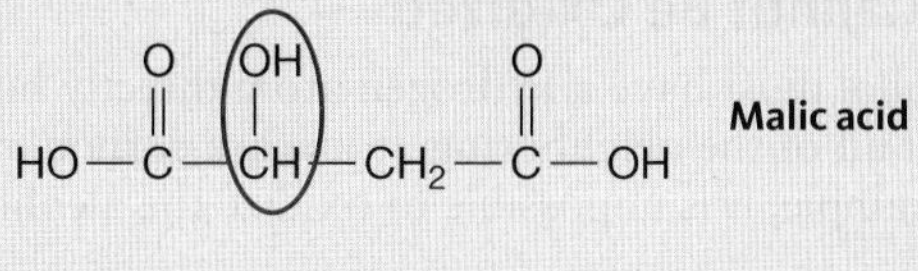

$$\text{HO}{-}\text{C}({=}\text{O}){-}\text{CH}(\text{OH}){-}\text{CH}_2{-}\text{C}({=}\text{O}){-}\text{OH}$$

Malic acid

SOLUTION

To draw the product of the oxidation, we remove two hydrogen atoms from the functional group. One of these comes from the hydroxyl group, and the other comes from the carbon atom that is bonded to the hydroxyl group. We then change the single bond between carbon and oxygen into a double bond.

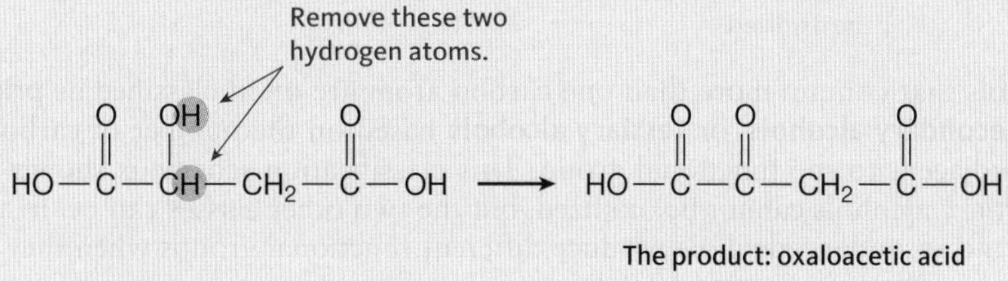

Remove these two hydrogen atoms.

$$\text{HO}{-}\text{C}({=}\text{O}){-}\text{CH}(\text{OH}){-}\text{CH}_2{-}\text{C}({=}\text{O}){-}\text{OH} \longrightarrow \text{HO}{-}\text{C}({=}\text{O}){-}\text{C}({=}\text{O}){-}\text{CH}_2{-}\text{C}({=}\text{O}){-}\text{OH}$$

The product: oxaloacetic acid

TRY IT YOURSELF: *Draw the structure of the product that is formed when the alcohol group in the following molecule is oxidized:*

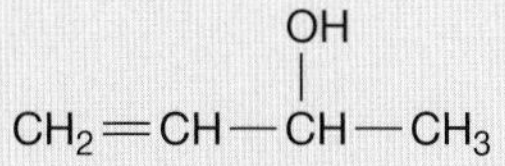

$$\text{CH}_2{=}\text{CH}{-}\text{CH}(\text{OH}){-}\text{CH}_3$$

For additional practice, try Core Problems 10.7 and 10.8.

The oxidation of an alcohol is closely related to the dehydrogenation reaction you learned in Section 10.1. In fact, dehydrogenation is a special class of oxidation. If we draw the alcohol functional group in a different orientation, the relationship between the oxidation of alcohols and that of alkanes becomes clearer.

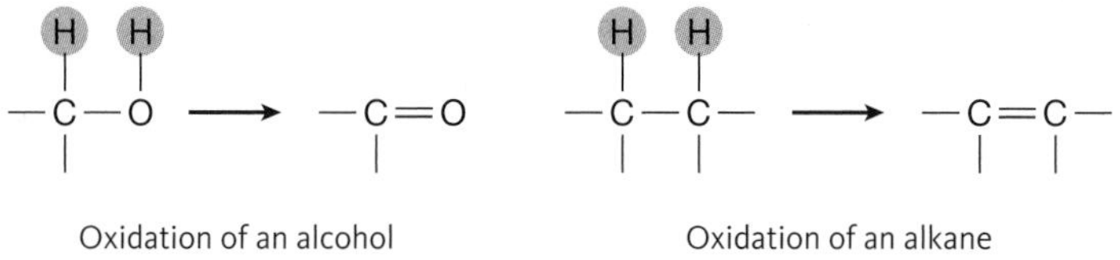

$$-\text{C}(\text{H}){-}\text{O}(\text{H}) \longrightarrow -\text{C}{=}\text{O} \qquad -\text{C}(\text{H}){-}\text{C}(\text{H})- \longrightarrow -\text{C}{=}\text{C}-$$

Oxidation of an alcohol — Oxidation of an alkane

The primary difference between these two reactions is that alcohols are far easier to oxidize than alkanes are. As a result, when an alcohol is oxidized, the product almost always contains a carbon–oxygen double bond rather than a carbon–carbon double bond. For example, when we oxidize 2-propanol, we do not form an alkene. Instead, the product contains a carbonyl group.

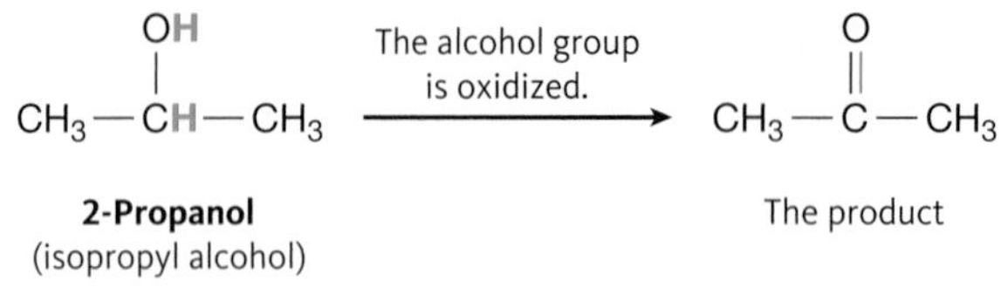

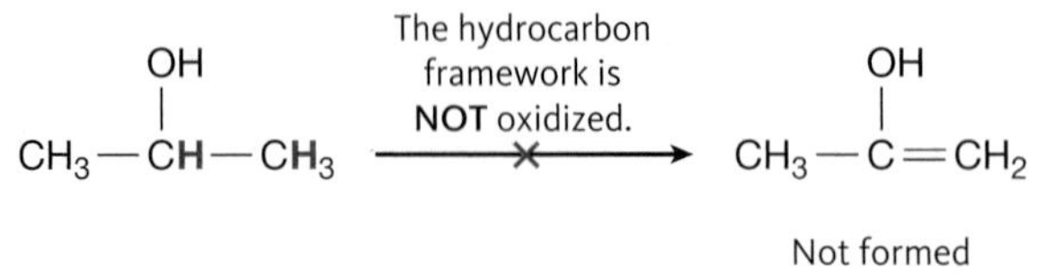

$$\underset{\text{2-Propanol (isopropyl alcohol)}}{CH_3-\underset{|}{\overset{OH}{CH}}-CH_3} \xrightarrow[\text{is oxidized.}]{\text{The alcohol group}} \underset{\text{The product}}{CH_3-\overset{O}{\overset{\|}{C}}-CH_3}$$

$$CH_3-\overset{OH}{\overset{|}{CH}}-CH_3 \xrightarrow[\text{NOT oxidized.}]{\text{The hydrocarbon framework is}} \underset{\text{Not formed}}{CH_3-\overset{OH}{\overset{|}{C}}=CH_2}$$

Tertiary Alcohols Cannot Be Oxidized

To be oxidized, an alcohol must have a hydrogen atom directly bonded to the carbon of the functional group. If all of the neighboring atoms are carbon atoms, the alcohol cannot be oxidized. For example, it is impossible to oxidize the alcohol group in the following compound:

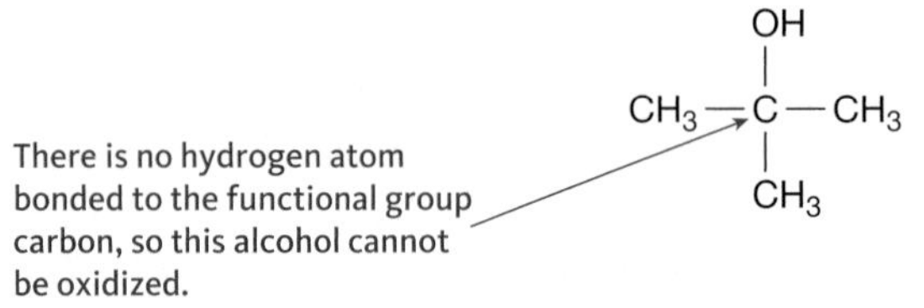

$$CH_3-\underset{\underset{CH_3}{|}}{\overset{OH}{\overset{|}{C}}}-CH_3$$

There is no hydrogen atom bonded to the functional group carbon, so this alcohol cannot be oxidized.

Alcohols that contain more than one carbon atom are often classified as **primary alcohols**, **secondary alcohols**, or **tertiary alcohols** based on the number of carbon atoms that are adjacent to the functional group. This classification scheme is shown in Table 10.1. Tertiary alcohols cannot be oxidized, but the two other classes can be. In addition, primary and secondary alcohols produce different functional groups when they are oxidized, as we will see in Section 10.3.

TABLE 10.1 Classification of Alcohols

	Methanol	Primary	Secondary	Tertiary
Carbon atoms adjacent to the functional group	None	One	Two	Three
General structure (adjacent carbon atoms are shown in red)	$H-\underset{\underset{H}{\vert}}{\overset{OH}{\overset{\vert}{C}}}-H$	$C-\underset{\underset{H}{\vert}}{\overset{OH}{\overset{\vert}{C}}}-H$	$C-\underset{\underset{H}{\vert}}{\overset{OH}{\overset{\vert}{C}}}-C$	$C-\underset{\underset{C}{\vert}}{\overset{OH}{\overset{\vert}{C}}}-C$
Example	$\overset{OH}{\overset{\vert}{CH_3}}$ (methanol is the only member of this class)	$CH_3-CH_2-CH_2-\overset{OH}{\overset{\vert}{CH_2}}$	$CH_3-CH_2-\overset{OH}{\overset{\vert}{CH}}-CH_3$	$CH_3-CH_2-\underset{\underset{CH_3}{\vert}}{\overset{OH}{\overset{\vert}{C}}}-CH_3$

Sample Problem 10.4

Classifying alcohols

Classify each of the following alcohols as primary, secondary, or tertiary:

a) 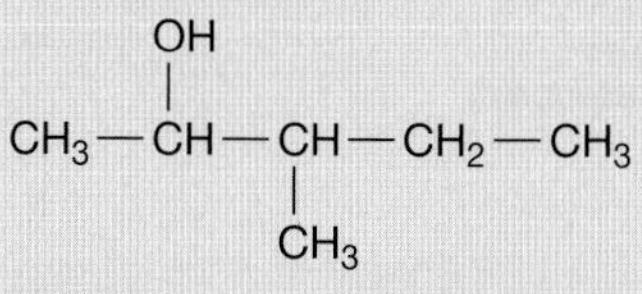 $CH_3-CH(OH)-CH(CH_3)-CH_2-CH_3$ b) 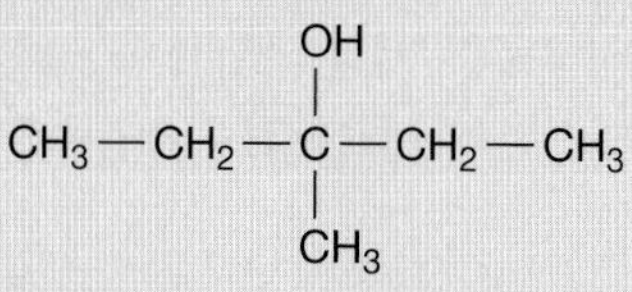 $CH_3-CH_2-C(OH)(CH_3)-CH_2-CH_3$

SOLUTION

a) The molecule has two carbon atoms adjacent to the functional group carbon, so this compound is a secondary alcohol.

b) The molecule has three carbon atoms adjacent to the functional group carbon, making it a tertiary alcohol.

In the following structures, the functional group carbon is green, and the carbon atoms that are bonded to it are red:

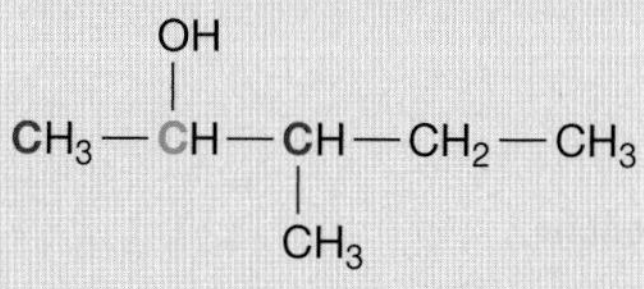

a) $CH_3-CH(OH)-CH(CH_3)-CH_2-CH_3$ A secondary alcohol

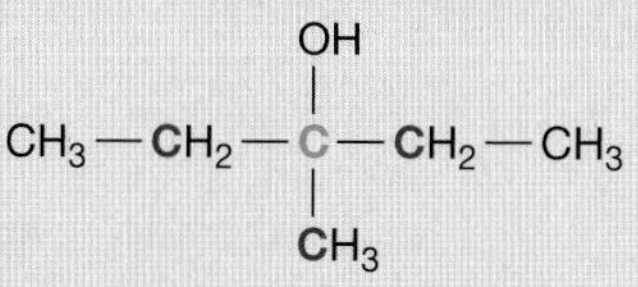

b) $CH_3-CH_2-C(OH)(CH_3)-CH_2-CH_3$ A tertiary alcohol

TRY IT YOURSELF: *Classify each of the following alcohols as primary, secondary, or tertiary:*

a) 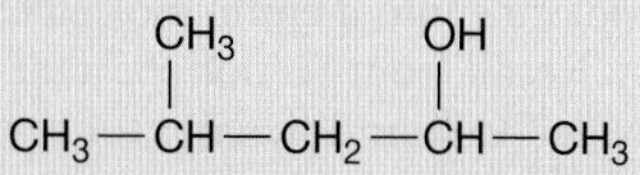 $CH_3-CH(CH_3)-CH_2-CH(OH)-CH_3$ b) 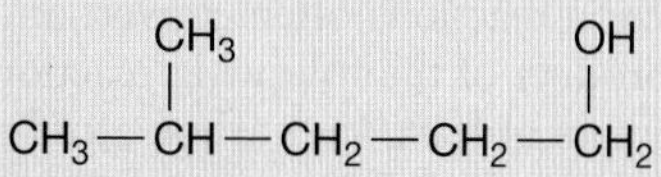 $CH_3-CH(CH_3)-CH_2-CH_2-CH_2(OH)$

For additional practice, try Core Problems 10.9 and 10.10.

Carbonyl Groups Can Be Reduced to Alcohols

When we oxidize an alcohol, we produce a carbonyl group. Compounds that contain carbonyl groups can be reduced, just like compounds that contain carbon–carbon double bonds (alkene groups). In this reaction, the double bond becomes a single bond, and the carbon and oxygen of the original carbonyl group each gain a hydrogen atom. The carbonyl group becomes a hydroxyl group, so the product of the reaction is an alcohol. This reaction is the exact reverse of the oxidation reaction we saw on page 404. Here is the general scheme for the reduction of a carbonyl group:

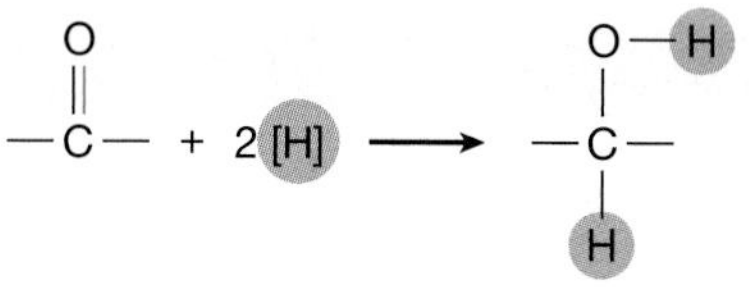

$$-C(=O)- \; + \; 2\,[H] \longrightarrow -C(O-H)(H)-$$

Carbonyl group → Alcohol group

We are primarily interested in reductions that occur in living organisms. In these reactions, the hydrogen atoms are supplied by organic molecules, often the same ones that accept the hydrogen atoms in oxidations. As before, we can write these hydrogen atoms using the symbol [H]. Here is a specific example of a reduction:

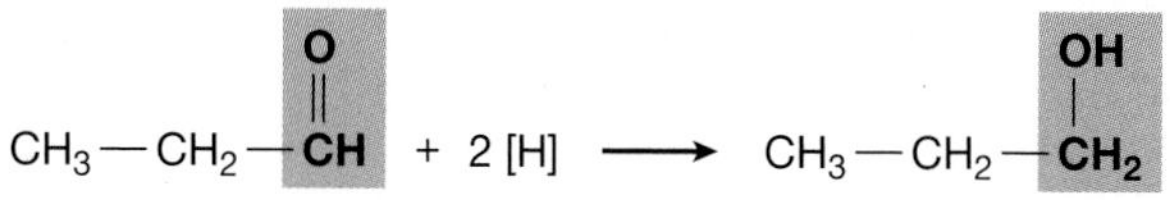

$$CH_3-CH_2-CH(=O) \; + \; 2\,[H] \longrightarrow CH_3-CH_2-CH_2(OH)$$

Sample Problem 10.5

Drawing the product of a reduction reaction

Draw the structure of the product that is formed when the following compound is reduced:

$$CH_3-\overset{\overset{\large O}{\|}}{C}-CH_2-CH_3$$

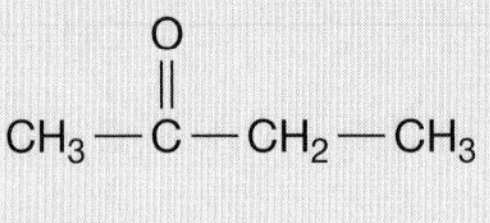

2-Butanone

SOLUTION

To draw the product of the reduction reaction, we must convert the double bond to a single bond and we must add two hydrogen atoms to our molecule. One becomes bonded to the oxygen atom, and the other becomes bonded to the neighboring carbon atom.

The double bond has been converted to a single bond. →

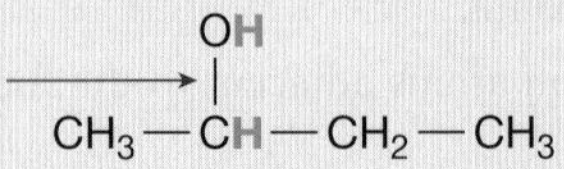

$$CH_3-\overset{\overset{\large OH}{|}}{CH}-CH_2-CH_3$$

The product of the reaction: **2-butanol**

TRY IT YOURSELF: *Draw the structure of the product that is formed when the following compound is reduced:*

$$C_6H_5-\overset{\overset{\large O}{\|}}{C}-CH_3$$

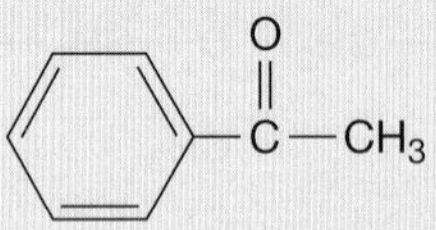

Acetophenone

For additional practice, try Core Problems 10.11 and 10.12.

Reduction reactions often convert an achiral molecule into a chiral molecule. For example, the product of the following reaction is chiral. Recall from Section 9.5 that chiral molecules contain at least one carbon atom that is bonded to four different groups of atoms.

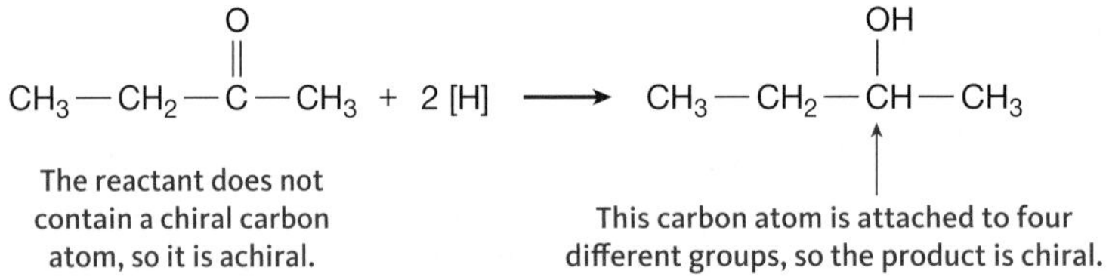

$$CH_3-CH_2-\overset{\overset{\large O}{\|}}{C}-CH_3 + 2\,[H] \longrightarrow CH_3-CH_2-\overset{\overset{\large OH}{|}}{CH}-CH_3$$

The reactant does not contain a chiral carbon atom, so it is achiral.

This carbon atom is attached to four different groups, so the product is chiral.

When chemists make a chiral alcohol by reducing a carbonyl compound in the laboratory, they normally make a 50:50 mixture of the two possible forms of the product. However, in our bodies, the enzymes that catalyze reductions make only one of the two enantiomers.

CORE PROBLEMS

10.7 Draw the structures of the carbonyl compounds that are formed when the following alcohols are oxidized. If the alcohol cannot be oxidized, write "no reaction."

a) 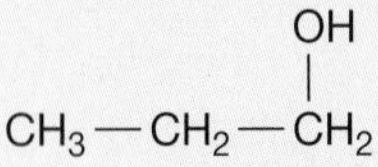 $CH_3-CH_2-\overset{\overset{\large OH}{|}}{CH_2}$

b) 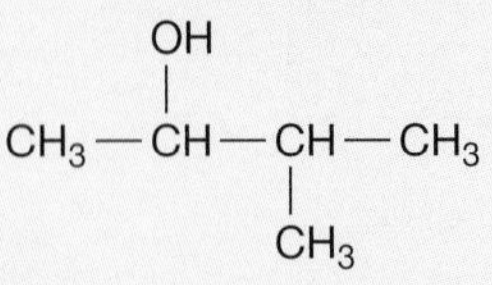 $CH_3-\overset{\overset{\large OH}{|}}{CH}-\underset{\underset{\large CH_3}{|}}{CH}-CH_3$

c) 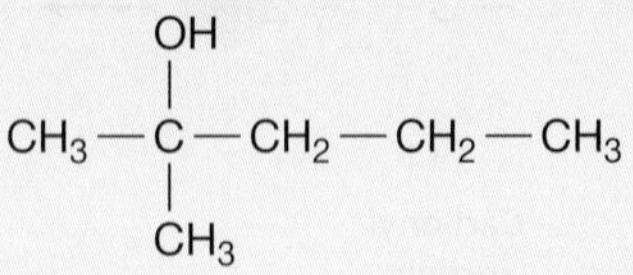 $CH_3-\overset{\overset{\large OH}{|}}{\underset{\underset{\large CH_3}{|}}{C}}-CH_2-CH_2-CH_3$

d) 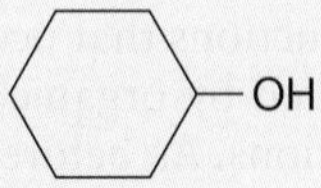 cyclohexane$-OH$

continued

10.8 Draw the structures of the carbonyl compounds that are formed when the following alcohols are oxidized. If the alcohol cannot be oxidized, write "no reaction."

a) 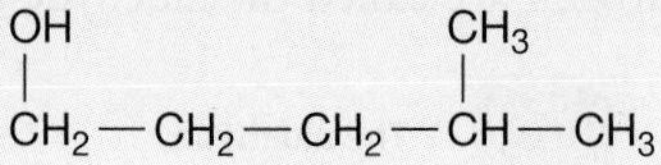 $CH_2(OH)-CH_2-CH_2-CH(CH_3)-CH_3$

b) 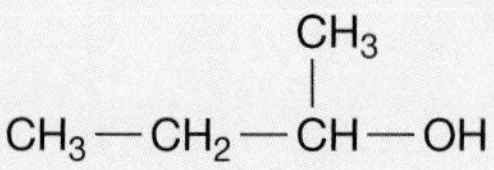 $CH_3-CH_2-CH(CH_3)-OH$

c) 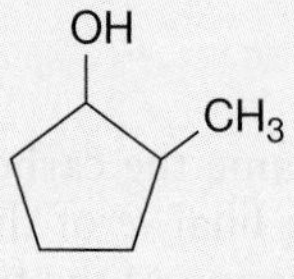 OH, CH_3

d) 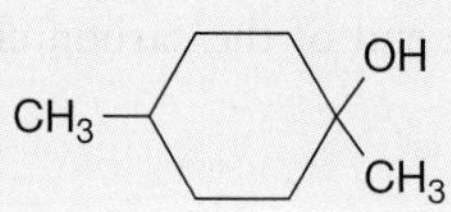 CH_3, OH, CH_3

10.9 Classify each of the alcohols in Problem 10.7 as a primary, secondary, or tertiary alcohol.

10.10 Classify each of the alcohols in Problem 10.8 as a primary, secondary, or tertiary alcohol.

10.11 Draw the structures of the alcohols that are formed when the following carbonyl compounds are reduced:

a) 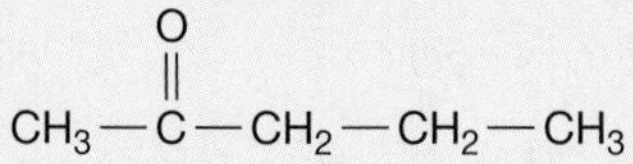 $CH_3-C(=O)-CH_2-CH_2-CH_3$

b) $CH_3-C(=O)-CH_2-CH(CH_3)-CH_3$

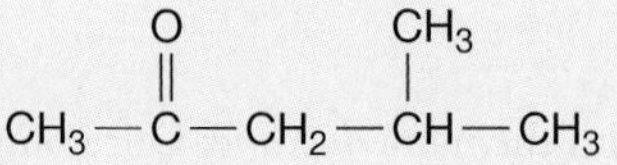

c) =O

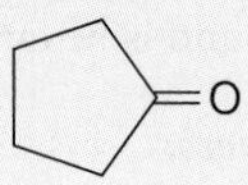

d) 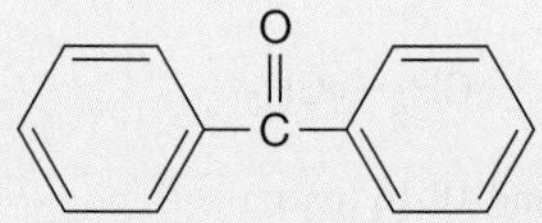 O, C

10.12 Draw the structures of the alcohols that are formed when the following carbonyl compounds are reduced:

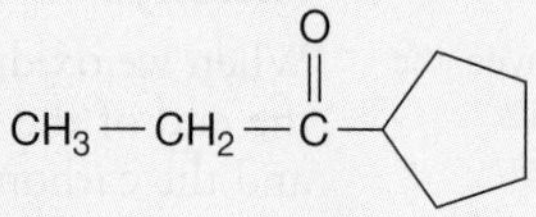

a) 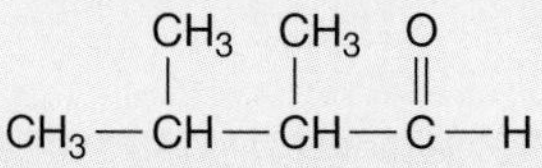 $CH_3-CH(CH_3)-CH(CH_3)-C(=O)-H$

b) $CH_3-CH_2-C(=O)-$

c) CH_3, O

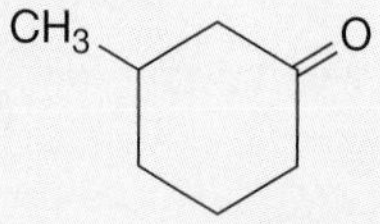

d) 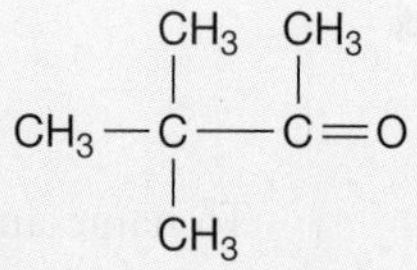 $CH_3-C(CH_3)_2-C(CH_3)=O$

10.13 Both of the following compounds can be reduced, but one produces a chiral alcohol while the other does not. Which is which? Explain your answer.

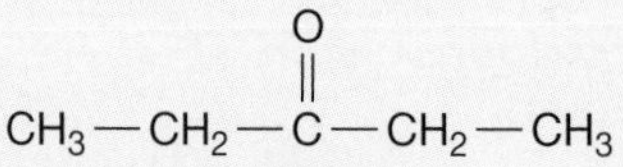

$CH_3-CH_2-C(=O)-CH_2-CH_3$

3-Pentanone

$CH_3-C(=O)-CH_2-CH_2-CH_3$

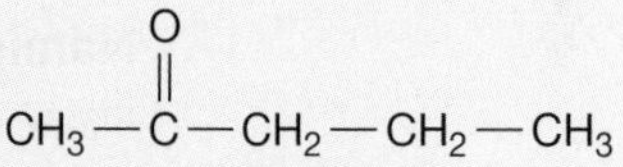

2-Pentanone

10.14 Both of the following compounds can be reduced, but one produces a chiral alcohol while the other does not. Which is which? Explain your answer.

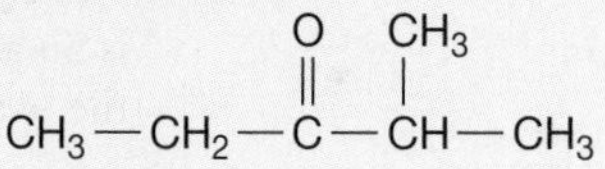

$CH_3-CH_2-C(=O)-CH(CH_3)-CH_3$

2-Methyl-3-pentanone

$CH_3-CH(CH_3)-C(=O)-CH(CH_3)-CH_3$

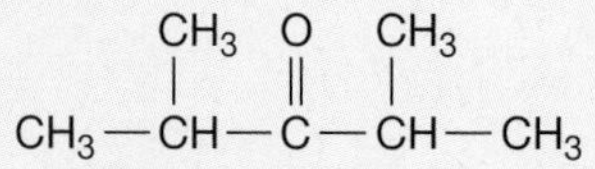

2,4-Dimethyl-3-pentanone

10.3 The Naming and Properties of Aldehydes and Ketones

OBJECTIVES: *Identify and name aldehydes and ketones, and relate the physical properties of aldehydes and ketones to their structures.*

In Section 10.2, we saw that we make a carbonyl group when we oxidize an alcohol. Compounds that contain carbonyl groups are common in biological chemistry, and they play an important role in metabolism. Let us now look at how these compounds are classified and named, and then examine some of their properties.

Health Note: Cinnamaldehyde, the compound that gives cinnamon its characteristic taste and aroma, is relatively nontoxic to humans, but it kills the larvae of the mosquito species that transmits yellow fever, so it could replace more toxic insecticides in reducing mosquito-borne disease.

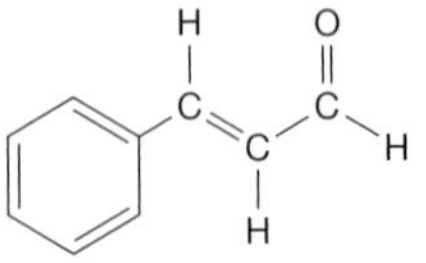

Cinnamaldehyde

Aldehydes Contain a Carbonyl Group on the End Carbon

When we oxidize a primary alcohol (or methanol), the product has a carbonyl group on the end of the carbon chain. Compounds that have this structure are called **aldehydes**, and the carbonyl group plus its neighboring hydrogen are called the aldehyde group.

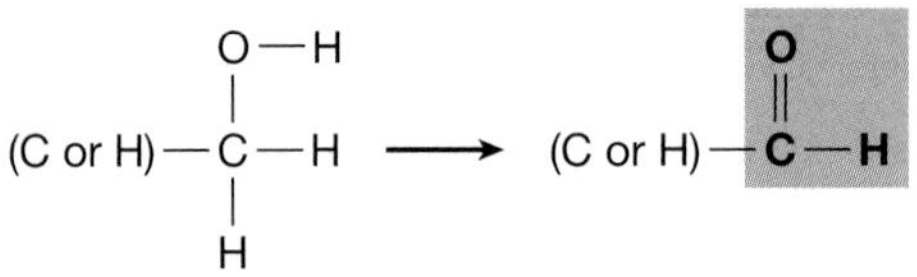

$$\text{(C or H)}-\underset{\displaystyle H}{\overset{\displaystyle O-H}{\underset{|}{\overset{|}{C}}}}-H \longrightarrow \text{(C or H)}-\overset{\displaystyle O}{\overset{\|}{C}}-H$$

The aldehyde functional group

Oxidation of a primary alcohol or methanol . . . . . . produces an **aldehyde.**

To name an aldehyde using the IUPAC rules, we must first name the carbon chain, being sure to include the aldehyde carbon. Then, we replace the final *-e* of the alkane name with *-al*. We do not need to write a number to show the location of the functional group, because the aldehyde group must always be at the end of the carbon chain. For instance, the following compound is called *butanal:*

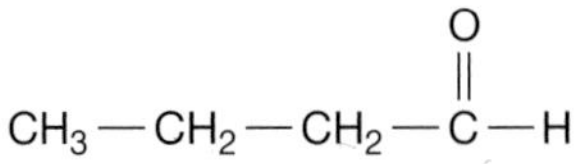

$$CH_3-CH_2-CH_2-\overset{\displaystyle O}{\overset{\|}{C}}-H$$

Butanal

Sample Problem 10.6

Naming aldehydes

Name the compound whose structure is shown here:

$$CH_3-CH_2-CH_2-CH_2-CH_2-\overset{\displaystyle O}{\overset{\|}{C}}-H$$

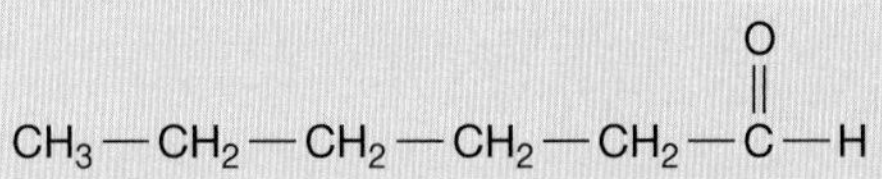

SOLUTION

The carbon chain contains six atoms, so we start with the name *hexane*. Our compound is an aldehyde, because it contains a carbonyl group at the end of the chain, so we replace the *-e* at the end of the alkane name with *-al*. The name of this compound is hexanal.

TRY IT YOURSELF: *Name the compound whose structure is shown here:*

$$H-\overset{\displaystyle O}{\overset{\|}{C}}-CH_2-CH_2-CH_2-CH_2-CH_2-CH_3$$

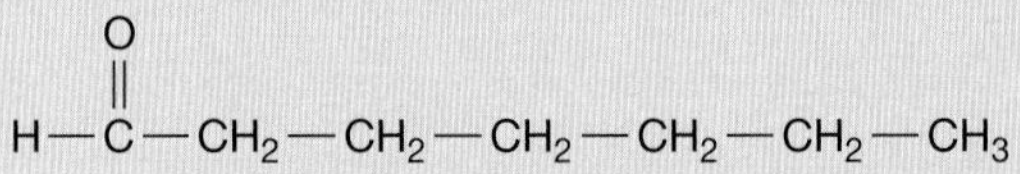

For additional practice, try Core Problems 10.15 (part b) and 10.16 (part a)

Sample Problem 10.7

Drawing the structure of an aldehyde

Draw the condensed structural formula of pentanal.

SOLUTION

The name tells us that the carbon chain contains five atoms *(pentan-)* and that the compound contains an aldehyde group *(-al)*. As always when drawing structures, it is best to start with the carbon skeleton.

$$C-C-C-C-C$$

continued

Next, we add the oxygen atom of the aldehyde group. The oxygen is bonded to the end of the carbon chain, and we can put it on either end of the chain. The aldehyde carbon is part of the main chain, so we don't add another carbon atom.

$$C-C-C-C-\overset{\overset{\displaystyle O}{\|}}{C}$$

Finally, we add enough hydrogen atoms so that each carbon shares four electron pairs.

$$CH_3-CH_2-CH_2-CH_2-\overset{\overset{\displaystyle O}{\|}}{C}-H$$

TRY IT YOURSELF: *Draw the condensed structural formula of octanal.*

For additional practice, try Core Problems 10.19 (part b) and 10.20 (part a).

Many aldehydes have trivial names, and some of these are used in preference to the IUPAC names. For example, the aldehydes with one and two carbon atoms are called *formaldehyde* and *acetaldehyde*. Their IUPAC names *methanal* and *ethanal* are rarely used.

$$H-\overset{\overset{\displaystyle O}{\|}}{C}-H \qquad CH_3-\overset{\overset{\displaystyle O}{\|}}{C}-H$$

Formaldehyde (methanal) — **Acetaldehyde** (ethanal)

Health Note: Formaldehyde is a pungent-smelling gas that is irritating to mucous membranes and toxic if taken internally. In 2005 and 2007, food manufacturers in Indonesia and Vietnam were found to have added formaldehyde to noodles, tofu, chicken, and other foods to improve shelf life, despite the adverse health effects.

When chemists draw the structure of an aldehyde, they often abbreviate the aldehyde group to —CHO. For example, here are two ways to draw the condensed structural formula of acetaldehyde (ethanal):

$$CH_3-\overset{\overset{\displaystyle O}{\|}}{C}-H \quad \text{or} \quad CH_3-CHO$$

You should learn to recognize this way of representing an aldehyde functional group. Do not confuse this with an alcohol group, which is occasionally written as HO—C— when it appears on the left side of a condensed structural formula.

Formaldehyde solutions are used to preserve biological specimens.

Ketones Contain a Carbonyl Group in the Interior of the Carbon Chain

When we oxidize a secondary alcohol, the product has a carbonyl group in the interior of the carbon chain. Compounds that have this structure are called **ketones**, and the functional group is called a ketone group.

$$C-\underset{\underset{\displaystyle H}{|}}{\overset{\overset{\displaystyle O-H}{|}}{C}}-C \longrightarrow C-\overset{\overset{\displaystyle O}{\|}}{C}-C$$

Oxidation of a secondary alcohol . . . . . . produces a **ketone.** (The ketone functional group)

To name a ketone using the IUPAC rules, we again start with the name of the carbon chain, and then we replace the final *-e* with *-one*. Since the oxygen atom can be bonded to any of the internal carbon atoms in a ketone, we must also include a number to show the location of our functional group, just as we did for alcohols. For example, the following compound is called *3-hexanone:*

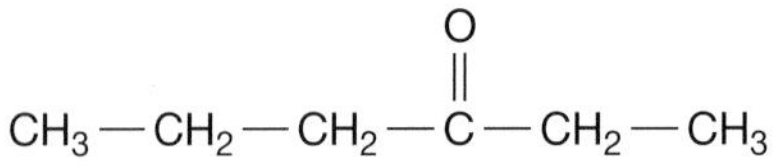

$$CH_3-CH_2-CH_2-\overset{\overset{\displaystyle O}{\|}}{C}-CH_2-CH_3$$

3-Hexanone

Remember to number the chain from the side that is closest to the functional group.

Sample Problem 10.8

Naming a ketone

Name the compound whose structure is shown here:

$$CH_3-CH_2-\overset{\overset{\displaystyle O}{\|}}{C}-CH_2-CH_3$$

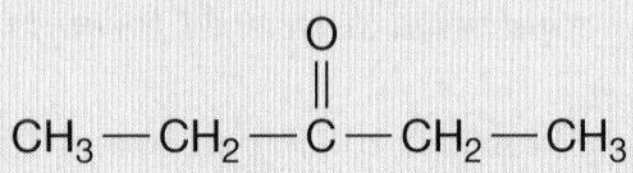

SOLUTION

This molecule contains five carbon atoms, so we start with the name of the five-carbon alkane: *pentane*. The compound contains an oxygen atom that is doubly bonded to an internal carbon atom in our chain, so this molecule is a ketone. To name a ketone, we replace the *-e* in *pentane* with the suffix *-one,* giving us the name *pentanone*. Finally, we add a number to tell the location of the functional group. The oxygen atom is attached to the third carbon atom in the chain, so this molecule is 3-pentanone.

TRY IT YOURSELF: *Name the compound whose structure is shown here:*

$$CH_3-\overset{\overset{\displaystyle O}{\|}}{C}-CH_2-CH_2-CH_2-CH_3$$

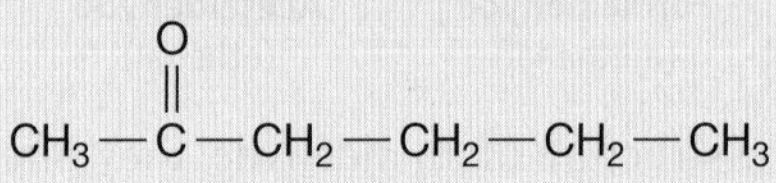

For additional practice, try Core Problems 10.15 (parts a and e) and 10.16 (parts b and e).

The ketone group can also be incorporated into a ring of carbon atoms. When we name a cyclic ketone, we do not need to include a number, just as was the case with cyclic alcohols and alkenes. Here are three ways to draw the structure of the five-carbon cyclic ketone *cyclopentanone:*

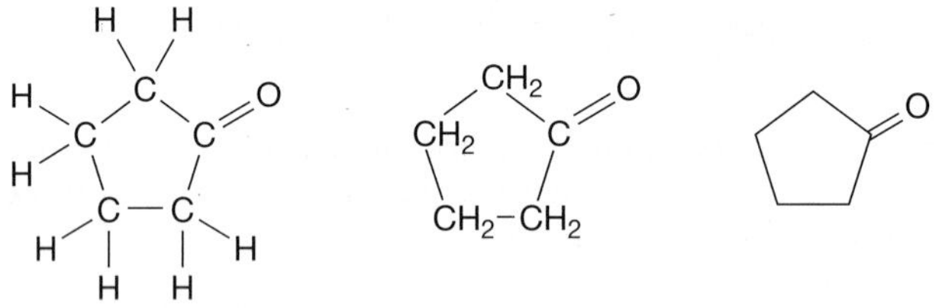

Full structural formula

Condensed structural formula

Line structure

Health Note: One of the symptoms of uncontrolled diabetes is the smell of acetone on the breath. The acetone is a by-product of rapid breakdown of fats, and it is formed because in diabetes the body must obtain most of its energy by burning fats and proteins instead of carbohydrates.

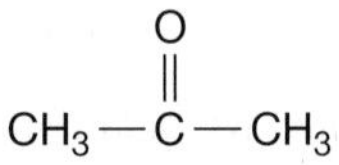

The only trivial ketone name that is in common use in medicine is *acetone,* the alternate name for 2-propanone. Acetone is an excellent solvent for molecular compounds that do not dissolve in water, so it is used in a variety of degreasing products and as the active ingredient in nail polish remover.

$$CH_3-\overset{\overset{\displaystyle O}{\|}}{C}-CH_3$$

Acetone

To draw the line structure of an aldehyde or a ketone, we draw the carbon chain as a zigzag line, and then we add the oxygen atom with its double bond. For aldehydes, it

TABLE 10.2 A Comparison of the Properties of an Alkane, a Ketone, and an Alcohol

	Isobutane (2-Methylpropane)	Acetone (2-Propanone)	Isopropyl Alcohol (2-Propanol)
Structure	$CH_3-CH(CH_3)-CH_3$	$CH_3-C(=O)-CH_3$	$CH_3-CH(OH)-CH_3$
Functional group	None	Ketone	Alcohol
Attraction between molecules	Weakest	Intermediate (the polar carbonyl groups attract each other)	Strongest (the alcohol groups form hydrogen bonds with each other)
Boiling point	−12°C (lowest)	56°C	82°C (highest)
State at room temperature	Gas	Liquid	Liquid

Charles D. Winters

Acetone is a common ingredient in nail polish remover.

is customary to include the functional group hydrogen. Here are the line structures of butanal and 2-butanone:

Butanal **2-Butanone**

Aldehydes and Ketones Have Similar Physical Properties

The physical properties of ketones and aldehydes are similar. The carbon–oxygen bond is quite polar, so molecules containing a carbonyl group are more strongly attracted to one another than are hydrocarbons of the same size. On the other hand, alcohols can form hydrogen bonds to one another, while aldehydes and ketones cannot. Compounds with stronger attractive forces between molecules have higher boiling points, so aldehydes and ketones have boiling points that are higher than those of hydrocarbons but lower than those of alcohols. All common aldehydes and ketones are liquids at 20°C except formaldehyde, which is a gas. Table 10.2 compares the boiling point of acetone to those of a comparable alkane and alcohol.

Sample Problem 10.9

The effect of the carbonyl group on boiling point

Rank the following compounds from lowest to highest boiling point:

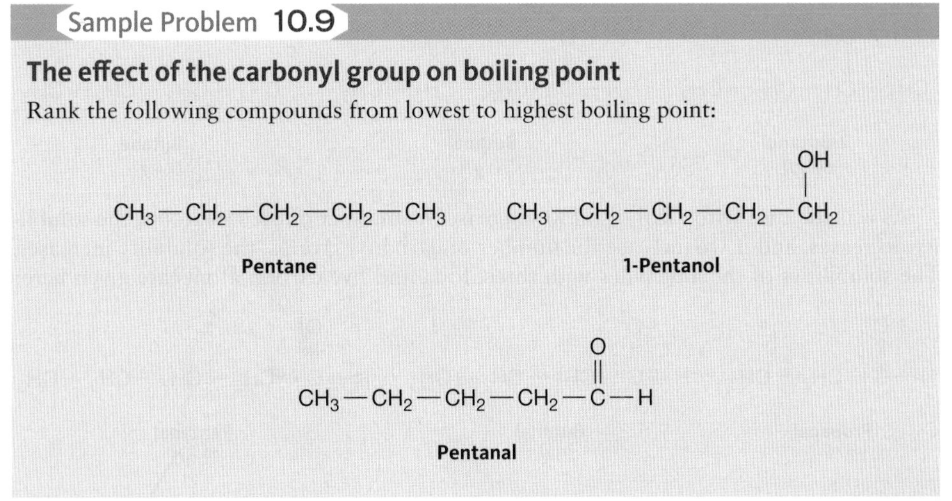

continued

SOLUTION

Pentane is an alkane and is entirely nonpolar, so pentane molecules have little attraction for one another. The other two molecules contain polar functional groups, so pentane has the lowest boiling point of the three.

1-Pentanol is an alcohol. The alcohol group can form hydrogen bonds, so molecules of 1-pentanol are strongly attracted to one another. As a result, 1-pentanol has the highest boiling point. A large amount of energy is required to convert 1-pentanol into a gas.

Pentanal is an aldehyde. The aldehyde group is polar, so molecules of pentanal have a stronger attraction to one another than do molecules of pentane. However, no hydrogen bonding is possible between two aldehyde molecules, because none of the hydrogen atoms are directly bonded to the oxygen. Therefore, the boiling point of pentanal lies between those of the other two compounds.

The correct order is

Pentane **Pentanal** **1-Pentanol**

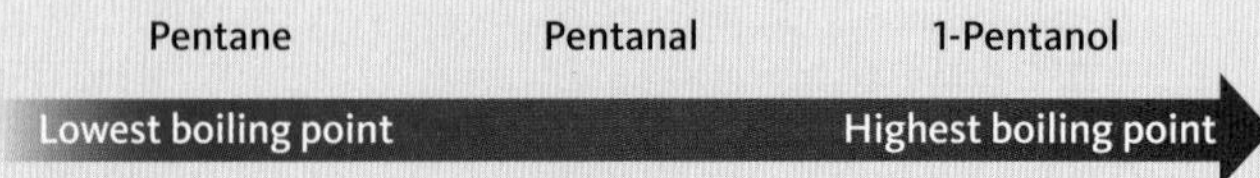

TRY IT YOURSELF: *Rank the following compounds from lowest to highest boiling point:*

Cyclohexanone **Cyclohexanol** **Cyclohexane**

For additional practice, try Core Problems 10.21 and 10.22.

Aldehydes and ketones tend to dissolve well in water, because the oxygen atom is a hydrogen bond acceptor. The positively charged hydrogen atom in a water molecule is attracted to the negatively charged oxygen atom in the organic compound.

$$\text{C}{=}\overset{\delta^-}{\text{O}}\text{- - - - - - - -}\overset{\delta^+}{\text{H}}{-}\text{O}{-}\text{H}$$

Because the carbonyl group can form hydrogen bonds with water, the solubilities of aldehydes and ketones in water are similar to those of alcohols, and they are far higher than those of hydrocarbons. Here are the solubilities of the four-carbon compounds 2-butanol, butanal, and butane:

$$CH_3-CH(OH)-CH_2-CH_3 \qquad H-C(=O)-CH_2-CH_2-CH_3 \qquad CH_3-CH_2-CH_2-CH_3$$

2-Butanol 80 g/L **Butanal** 70 g/L **Butane** 0.4 g/L

As was the case with alcohols, if we increase the number of carbon atoms, the solubility decreases, and if we increase the number of carbonyl groups, the solubility increases. The solubilities of the aldehydes with three, four, and five carbon atoms are given here:

$$H-C(=O)-CH_2-CH_3 \qquad H-C(=O)-CH_2-CH_2-CH_3 \qquad H-C(=O)-CH_2-CH_2-CH_2-CH_3$$

Propanal no limit **Butanal** 70 g/L **Pentanal** 12 g/L

Sample Problem 10.10

The effect of the carbonyl group on water solubility

Rank the following compounds from lowest to highest solubility in water:

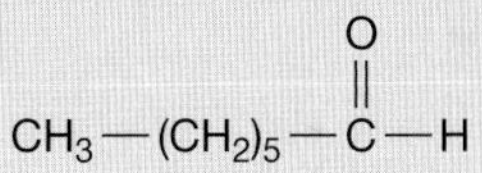

$CH_3-(CH_2)_5-C(=O)-H$ **Heptanal**

$H-C(=O)-(CH_2)_5-C(=O)-H$ **Heptanedial**

$CH_3-(CH_2)_5-CH_3$ **Heptane**

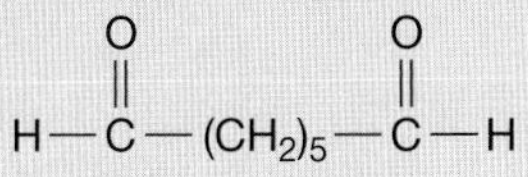

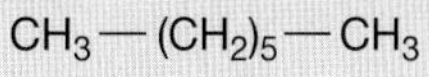

SOLUTION

Heptane has no oxygen or nitrogen atoms, so it cannot be a hydrogen bond donor or acceptor. Therefore, heptane is essentially insoluble in water. The other two compounds contain aldehyde groups, which are hydrogen bond acceptors, so they are attracted to water. Heptanedial contains two aldehyde groups, so it is more strongly attracted to water than heptanal is, giving it a higher solubility. The correct order is

Heptane **Heptanal** **Heptanedial**

Lowest solubility → Highest solubility

TRY IT YOURSELF: *Rank the following compounds from lowest to highest solubility in water:*

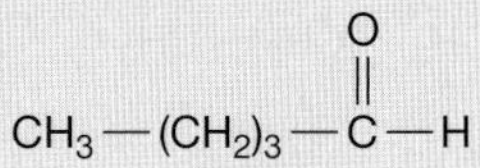

$CH_3-(CH_2)_3-C(=O)-H$ **Pentanal**

$CH_3-(CH_2)_5-C(=O)-H$ **Heptanal**

$CH_3-(CH_2)_7-C(=O)-H$ **Nonanal**

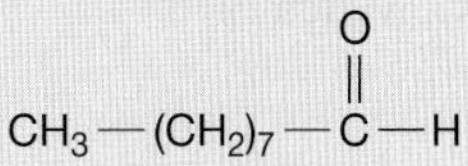

For additional practice, try Core Problems 10.23 and 10.24.

CORE PROBLEMS

10.15 Name the following compounds, using the IUPAC rules:

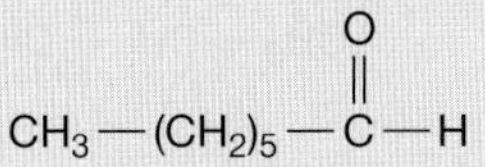

a) 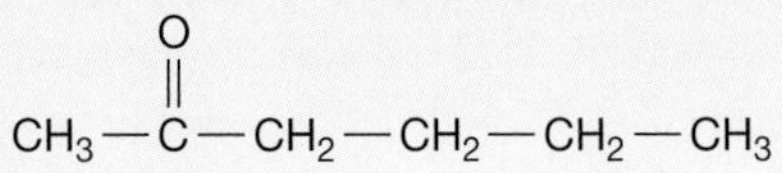 $CH_3-C(=O)-CH_2-CH_2-CH_2-CH_3$

b) 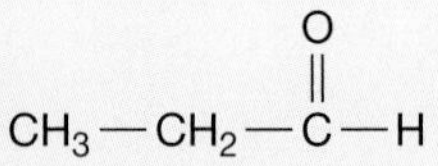 $CH_3-CH_2-C(=O)-H$

c) $CH_3-CH_2-CH_2-CH_2-CHO$

d) 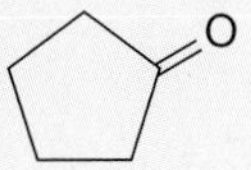 (cyclopentanone ring structure)

e) 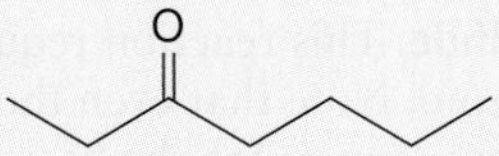 (skeletal structure: ketone with C=O on a chain)

10.16 Name the following compounds, using the IUPAC rules:

a) 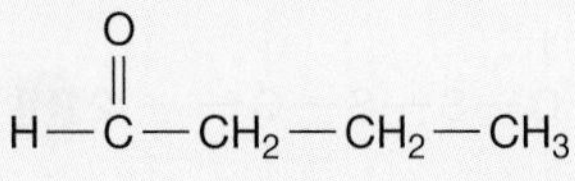 $H-C(=O)-CH_2-CH_2-CH_3$

b) 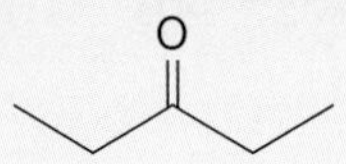 (skeletal structure: ketone with C=O on a chain)

c) CH_3-CH_2-CHO

d) 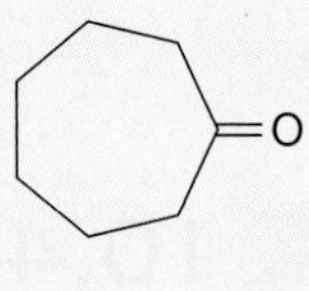 (cycloheptanone ring structure, $=O$)

e) 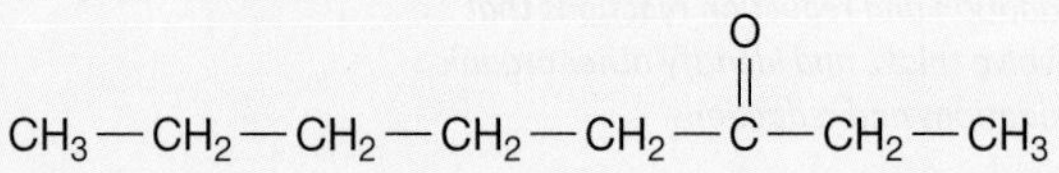 $CH_3-CH_2-CH_2-CH_2-CH_2-C(=O)-CH_2-CH_3$

10.17 Give the trivial name of the following compound:

$CH_3-C(=O)-CH_3$

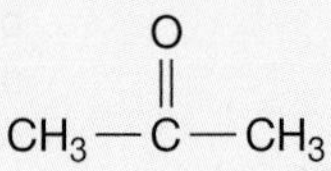

10.18 Give the trivial name of the following compound:

$H-C(=O)-H$

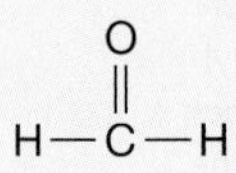

continued

10.19 Draw the structure of each of the following compounds:
a) 3-pentanone b) octanal
c) formaldehyde d) cyclobutanone

10.20 Draw the structure of each of the following compounds:
a) propanal b) 2-hexanone
c) acetaldehyde d) cyclopentanone

10.21 One of the following compounds boils at 36°C, one boils at 75°C, and one boils at 99°C. Match each compound with its boiling point.

$CH_3-CH_2-CH_2-CH=O$
Butanal

$CH_3-CH_2-CH_2-CH_2-OH$
1-Butanol

$CH_3-CH_2-CH_2-CH_2-CH_3$
Pentane

10.22 One of the following compounds boils at 119°C, one boils at 102°C, and one boils at 60°C. Match each compound with its boiling point.

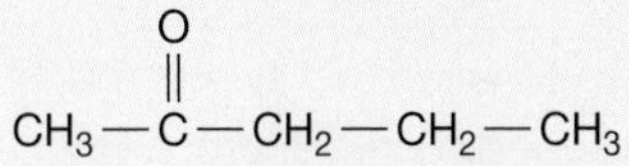

$CH_3-C(=O)-CH_2-CH_2-CH_3$
2-Pentanone

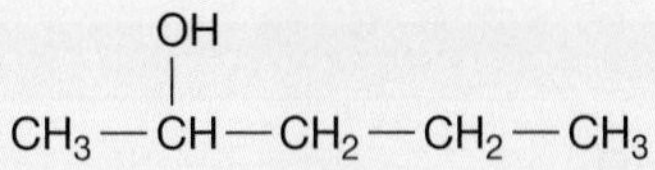

$CH_3-CH(OH)-CH_2-CH_2-CH_3$
2-Pentanol

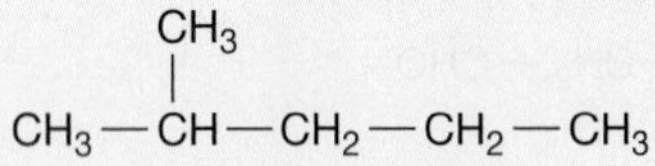

$CH_3-CH(CH_3)-CH_2-CH_2-CH_3$
2-Methylpentane

10.23 The solubilities of the following three compounds are 12 g/L, 1.2 g/L, and 0.1 g/L. Match each compound with its solubility.

$CH_3CH_2CH_2CH_2CH_3$
Pentane

$CH_3CH_2CH_2CH_2CHO$
Pentanal

$CH_3CH_2CH_2CH_2CH_2CH_2CHO$
Heptanal

10.24 The solubilities of the following three compounds are 40 g/L, 4.6 g/L, and 0.14 g/L. Match each compound with its solubility.

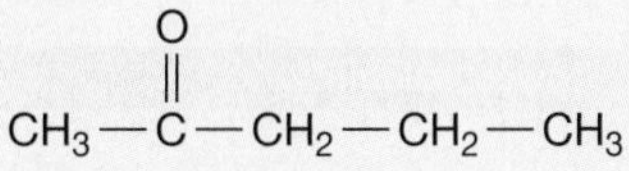

$CH_3-C(=O)-CH_2-CH_2-CH_3$
2-Pentanone

$CH_3-CH_2-CH_2-CH_2-CH_2-CH_3$
Hexane

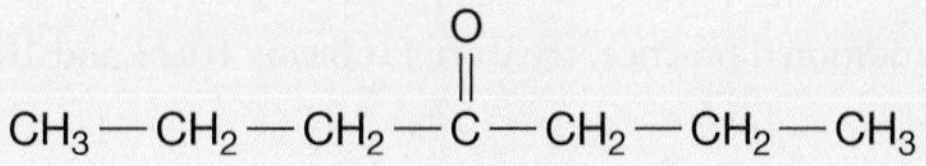

$CH_3-CH_2-CH_2-C(=O)-CH_2-CH_2-CH_3$
4-Heptanone

OBJECTIVES: *Predict the products of oxidation and reduction reactions that involve thiols, and identify other organic oxidations and reductions.*

10.4 Other Oxidation and Reduction Reactions

Thiols are the sulfur analogues of alcohols, and like alcohols, they can be oxidized. However, the oxidation of a thiol does not produce a carbon–sulfur double bond. In biological systems, the product of this reaction is a **disulfide**. This reaction requires two molecules of the thiol, each of which loses a hydrogen atom. Note that even though this reaction looks quite different from the oxidations you have seen so far, the basic features are the same. Two hydrogen atoms are removed, and a new covalent bond is formed between the atoms that lost hydrogen atoms.

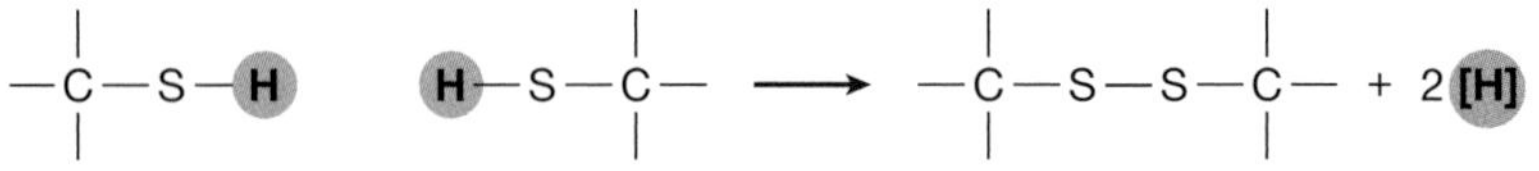

$$-C-S-H \quad H-S-C- \longrightarrow -C-S-S-C- + 2[H]$$

Each thiol group loses its hydrogen atom . . .

. . . and a new bond forms between the two sulfur atoms, giving a **disulfide**.

Health Note: Like thiols, disulfides have strong, offensive odors. For example, when you eat garlic, your body converts sulfur-containing molecules into diallyl disulfide. This compound escapes from the lungs when you breathe, giving your breath an unpleasant "garlicky" aroma.

For example, let us look at the oxidation of the following thiol:

$$CH_3-CH_2-SH$$

The oxidation reaction requires two molecules of the thiol. We must draw the second molecule so that its thiol group faces the thiol group of the first molecule.

$$CH_3-CH_2-SH \qquad HS-CH_2-CH_3$$

To draw the product of the reaction, we begin by removing the hydrogen atom from each of the thiol groups.

$$CH_3-CH_2-S \qquad S-CH_2-CH_3$$

Then we draw a bond between the two sulfur atoms to make the disulfide.

$$CH_3-CH_2-S-S-CH_2-CH_3$$

Sample Problem **10.11**

Drawing the product of the oxidation of a thiol

Draw the structure of the product that is formed when the following thiol is oxidized:

$$CH_3-CH_2-\underset{}{\overset{\displaystyle CH_3}{\overset{|}{C}H}}-CH_2-SH$$

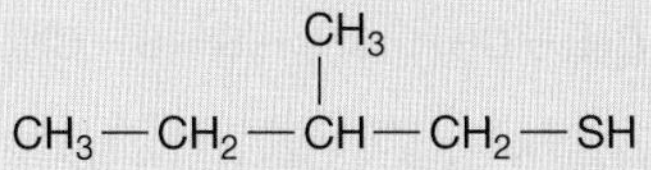

SOLUTION

The oxidation reaction requires two molecules of the thiol. We must draw one of the molecules reversed so that the two thiol functional groups face each other.

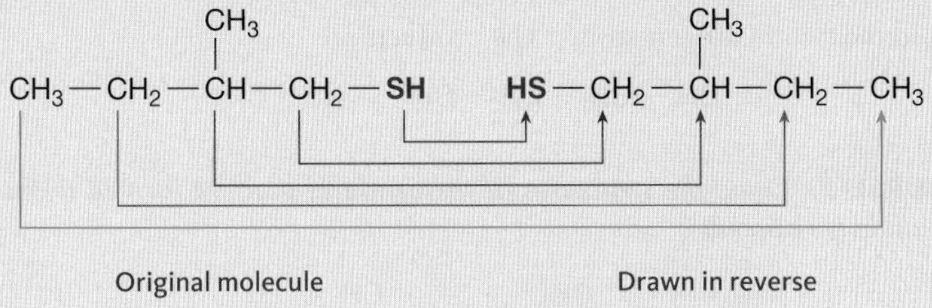

$$CH_3-CH_2-\overset{\displaystyle CH_3}{\overset{|}{C}H}-CH_2-\mathbf{SH} \qquad \mathbf{HS}-CH_2-\overset{\displaystyle CH_3}{\overset{|}{C}H}-CH_2-CH_3$$

Original molecule | Drawn in reverse

Next, we remove the hydrogen atom from each of the thiol groups.

$$CH_3-CH_2-\overset{\displaystyle CH_3}{\overset{|}{C}H}-CH_2-\mathbf{S} \qquad \mathbf{S}-CH_2-\overset{\displaystyle CH_3}{\overset{|}{C}H}-CH_2-CH_3$$

Each of these two sulfur atoms has lost a hydrogen atom.

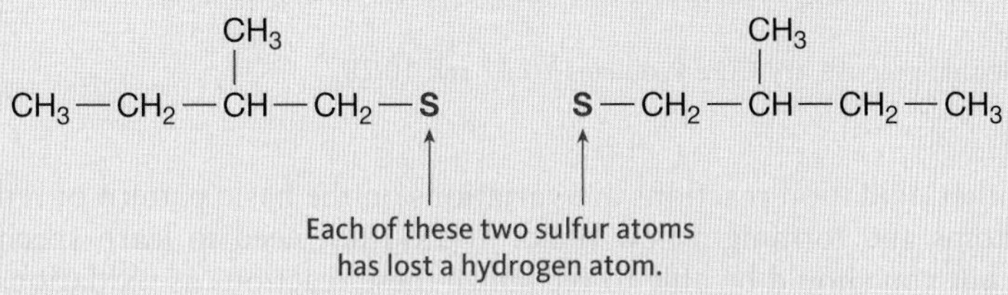

Finally, we add a bonding electron pair between the two sulfur atoms, creating the disulfide link.

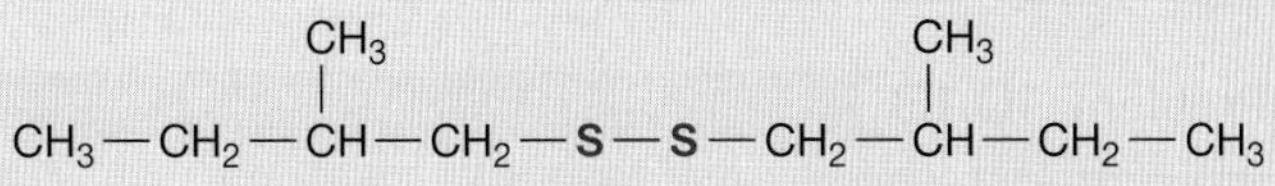

$$CH_3-CH_2-\overset{\displaystyle CH_3}{\overset{|}{C}H}-CH_2-\mathbf{S}-\mathbf{S}-CH_2-\overset{\displaystyle CH_3}{\overset{|}{C}H}-CH_2-CH_3$$

TRY IT YOURSELF: *Draw the structure of the product that will be formed when the following thiol is oxidized:*

(cyclohexane ring)$-CH_2-SH$

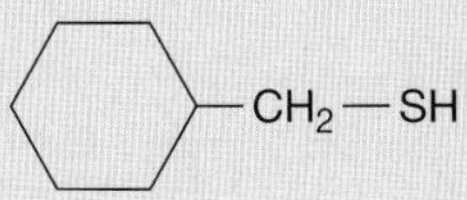

For additional practice, try Core Problems 10.25 and 10.26.

It is also possible to combine two different thiols using an oxidation reaction. Here is an example:

$$CH_3{-}SH + HS{-}CH_2{-}CH_2{-}CH_3 \rightarrow CH_3{-}S{-}S{-}CH_2{-}CH_2{-}CH_3 \quad +2\,[H]$$

We can reduce a disulfide back to two thiols. This reaction is the exact reverse of the oxidation of a thiol. Here are two examples of the reduction reaction of a disulfide. (Note that in the first reaction, the two thiols are the same compound, so we can write the products as separate molecules or as a single structure with a 2 in front of it.)

$$CH_3{-}CH_2{-}S{-}S{-}CH_2{-}CH_3 + 2\,[H] \rightarrow CH_3{-}CH_2{-}SH + HS{-}CH_2{-}CH_3$$
$$(\text{or } 2\ CH_3{-}CH_2{-}SH)$$

$$CH_3{-}CH_2{-}S{-}S{-}CH_3 + 2\,[H] \rightarrow CH_3{-}CH_2{-}SH + HS{-}CH_3$$

The formation and breaking of disulfide groups plays a significant role in protein chemistry, making it possible to form or destroy a link between two parts of a protein molecule or between two separate molecules.

Sample Problem 10.12

Drawing the product of the reduction of a disulfide

Draw the structures of the products that are formed when the following disulfide is reduced:

$$CH_3{-}CH_2{-}CH_2{-}S{-}S{-}CH_3$$

SOLUTION

We must break the bond between the two sulfur atoms, and we must add a hydrogen atom to each sulfur atom. First, let us break the sulfur–sulfur bond.

$$CH_3{-}CH_2{-}CH_2{-}S \qquad S{-}CH_3$$

Then we add the two hydrogen atoms. The products are

$$CH_3{-}CH_2{-}CH_2{-}\mathbf{SH} + \mathbf{HS}{-}CH_3$$

TRY IT YOURSELF: *Draw the structures of the products that are formed when the following disulfide is reduced:*

$$CH_3{-}CH_2{-}\underset{}{\overset{\displaystyle CH_3}{\overset{|}{CH}}}{-}S{-}S{-}\overset{\displaystyle CH_3}{\overset{|}{CH}}{-}CH_2{-}CH_3$$

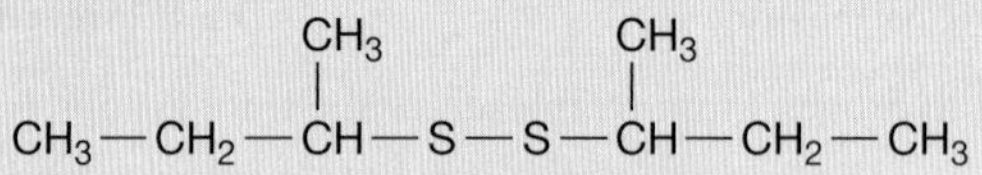

For additional practice, try Core Problems 10.27 and 10.28.

Health Note: Antioxidants are compounds that can be oxidized easily, so they protect other molecules from oxidation. The body uses antioxidants to prevent substances derived from atmospheric oxygen (such as the superoxide ion, O_2^-, and hydrogen peroxide, H_2O_2) from reacting with and damaging critical molecules inside cells. Vitamins C and E are important antioxidants.

Several other oxidation reactions are variations on the basic pattern of removing two hydrogen atoms and forming a new bond. You do not need to learn specific types of oxidations, but you should be able to recognize these reactions as oxidations when you encounter them. Remember that *any reaction that involves the removal of two hydrogen atoms from a molecule (or from two molecules) is an oxidation, and any reaction that adds two hydrogen atoms to a molecule is a reduction.*

Sample Problem 10.13

Identifying organic oxidations and reductions

The following reaction is used in developing photographic film after it has been exposed. Is this reaction an oxidation, or is it a reduction?

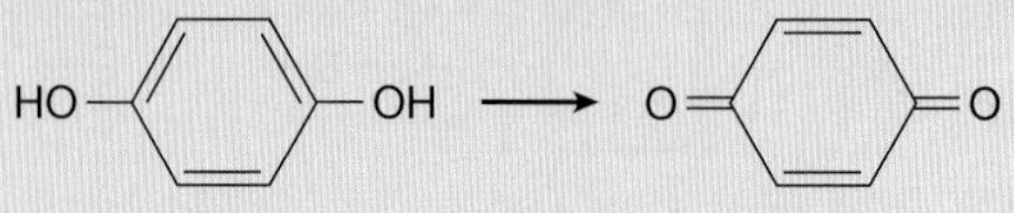

HO–(benzene ring)–OH ⟶ O=(ring)=O

Hydroquinone **Quinone**

continued

SOLUTION

In this reaction, hydroquinone loses two hydrogen atoms, and the product contains one additional double bond. Since the reactant loses two hydrogen atoms, the reaction is an oxidation. Notice that the hydrogen atoms are removed from opposite sides of the molecule in this oxidation reaction.

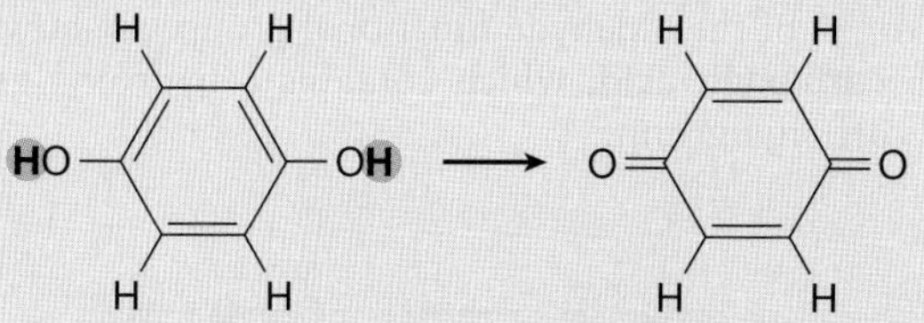

TRY IT YOURSELF: *The following reaction occurs during the formation of proline (one of the components of proteins). Is this an oxidation, or is it a reduction?*

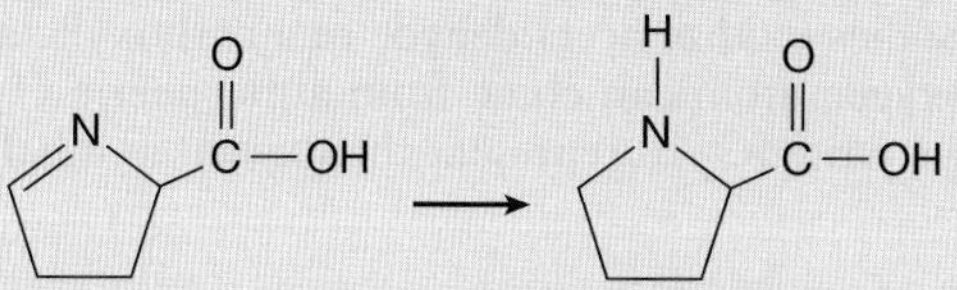

For additional practice, try Core Problems 10.29 and 10.30.

CORE PROBLEMS

10.25 Draw the structure of the compound that is formed when the following thiol is oxidized. (Hint: You need two molecules of the thiol.)

$CH_3-CH_2-CH_2-CH(CH_3)-SH$

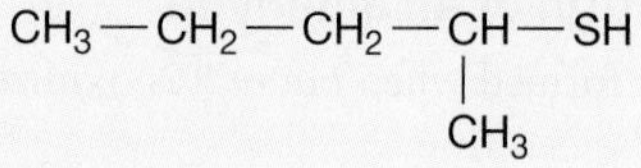

10.26 Draw the structure of the compound that is formed when the following thiol is oxidized. (Hint: You need two molecules of the thiol.)

$CH_3-C(CH_3)_2-CH_2-SH$

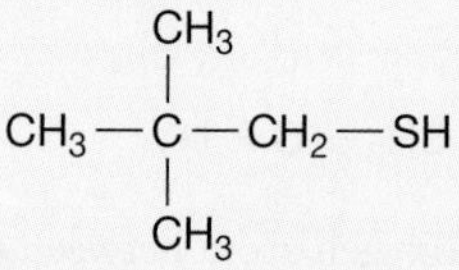

10.27 Draw the structures of the products that are formed when the following disulfide is reduced:

$CH_3-CH_2-S-S-CH_2-CH_3$

10.28 Draw the structures of the products that are formed when the following disulfide is reduced:

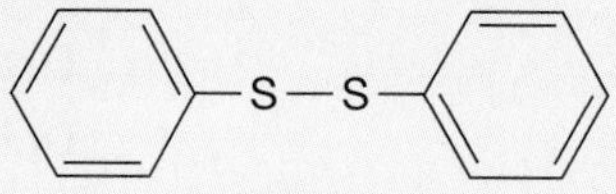

10.29 Ascorbic acid (vitamin C) reacts with many substances. In these reactions, the ascorbic acid is converted into dehydroascorbic acid, as shown here. Is this reaction an oxidation, or is it a reduction? Explain your answer.

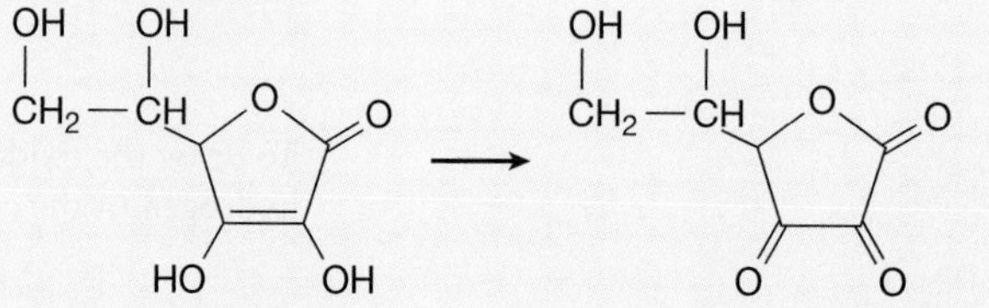

Ascorbic acid → Dehydroascorbic acid

10.30 The following reaction is an essential step in the breakdown of the amino acid phenylalanine. Is this reaction an oxidation, or is it a reduction? Explain your answer.

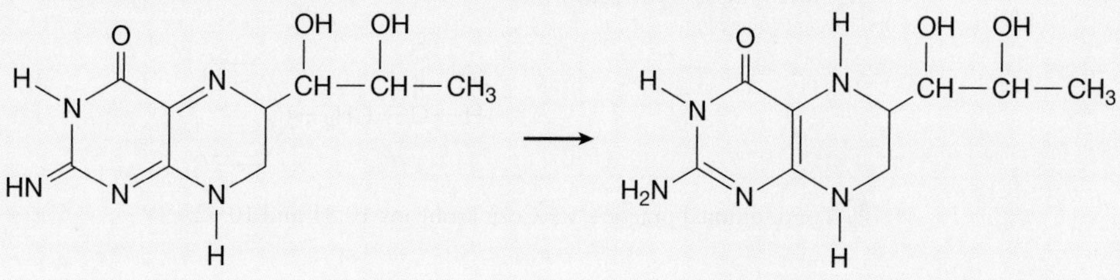

OBJECTIVES: *Predict the product of the oxidation of an aldehyde, identify and name carboxylic acids, and relate the physical properties of carboxylic acids to their structures.*

10.5 Carboxylic Acids

So far, all of the oxidation reactions we have considered involve removing hydrogen atoms from a molecule. There is, however, another important class of oxidation reactions: the addition of an oxygen atom to a compound. The most important example is the oxidation of an aldehyde. In this reaction, an oxygen atom is inserted between the carbon and the hydrogen of the aldehyde functional group, as shown here. The product of this reaction is a **carboxylic acid**, which contains a hydroxyl group bonded to the carbon atom of the carbonyl group.

$$-\overset{\overset{\displaystyle O}{\|}}{C}-H \longrightarrow -\overset{\overset{\displaystyle O}{\|}}{C}-\mathbf{O}-H$$

When an aldehyde is oxidized, it gains an oxygen atom . . . . . . to form a **carboxylic acid.**

For example, our bodies oxidize acetaldehyde to a carboxylic acid called acetic acid, as shown here. The oxygen atom can come from atmospheric O_2 or from a variety of other substances, so we write [O] to represent the oxygen in a balanced equation.

$$CH_3-\overset{\overset{\displaystyle O}{\|}}{C}-H + [O] \longrightarrow CH_3-\overset{\overset{\displaystyle O}{\|}}{C}-\mathbf{OH}$$

Acetaldehyde **Acetic acid**

As we saw on page 405, we make acetaldehyde when our bodies oxidize the ethanol in wine and other alcoholic beverages. Acetaldehyde is toxic, so we rapidly convert it to acetic acid using the preceding reaction.

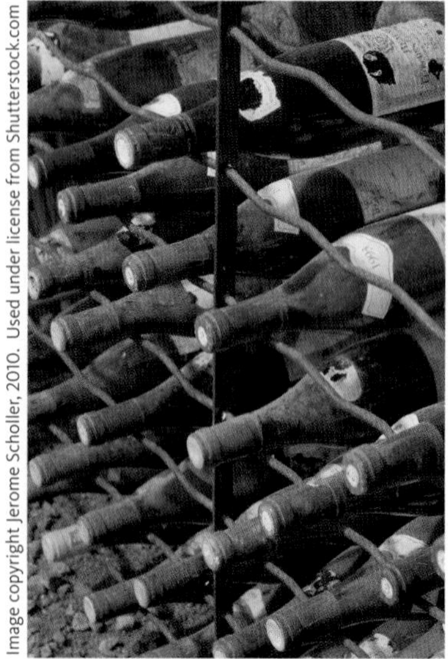

Oxygen will convert the ethanol in wine to acetic acid, so wine must be protected from air exposure.

Sample Problem 10.14

Drawing the product of the oxidation of an aldehyde

Draw the structure of the product that is formed when butanal is oxidized.

SOLUTION

First, we must draw the structure of butanal. Butanal is a four-carbon aldehyde (the *-al* ending tells us that this is an aldehyde), so its structure is

$$CH_3-CH_2-CH_2-\overset{\overset{\displaystyle O}{\|}}{C}-H$$

To draw the oxidation product, we insert an oxygen atom between the carbon and the hydrogen of the carbonyl group.

$$CH_3-CH_2-CH_2-\overset{\overset{\displaystyle O}{\|}}{C}-\mathbf{O}-H \quad \text{or} \quad CH_3-CH_2-CH_2-\overset{\overset{\displaystyle O}{\|}}{C}-OH$$

TRY IT YOURSELF: *Draw the structure of the product that is formed when the following aldehyde is oxidized:*

$$H-\overset{\overset{\displaystyle O}{\|}}{C}-CH_2-C_6H_5$$

For additional practice, try Core Problems 10.31 and 10.32.

To name a carboxylic acid using the IUPAC system, we first name the carbon chain. We then replace the *-e* at the end of the alkane name with *-oic acid*. As was the case with aldehydes, we do not need to tell where the functional group is located, because it must be at the end of the carbon chain. For example, the four-carbon carboxylic acid that follows is called *butanoic acid*. Note that the functional group carbon counts as part of the principal chain.

Butanoic acid

$$CH_3-CH_2-CH_2-\overset{\overset{\displaystyle O}{\|}}{C}-OH$$

The carboxylic acid functional group

Carboxylic acids were among the first organic compounds to be discovered, so most carboxylic acids have trivial names that were given before the IUPAC system was devised. Many of these trivial names are still used in preference to the IUPAC names. For example, the carboxylic acids with one and two carbon atoms are almost always called *formic acid* and *acetic acid*, respectively.

$$H-\overset{\overset{\displaystyle O}{\|}}{C}-OH \qquad CH_3-\overset{\overset{\displaystyle O}{\|}}{C}-OH$$

Formic acid
Methanoic acid

Acetic acid
Ethanoic acid

Health Note: Ant and bee venoms contain formic acid, but the pain and swelling of ant and bee stings are due to several proteins, not to the formic acid.

The carboxylic acid functional group is often abbreviated as $-COOH$ or $-CO_2H$. Be sure that you do not confuse these with the condensed form of the aldehyde group ($-CHO$). Here are three ways to draw the condensed structural formula of acetic acid:

$$CH_3-\overset{\overset{\displaystyle O}{\|}}{C}-OH \quad \text{or} \quad CH_3-COOH \quad \text{or} \quad CH_3-CO_2H$$

The Physical Properties of Carboxylic Acids Are Similar to Those of Alcohols

The carboxylic acid group can function as both a donor and an acceptor of hydrogen bonds, so carboxylic acids have melting and boiling points that are much higher than those of similarly sized hydrocarbons. In fact, carboxylic acids generally have higher melting and boiling points than compounds with any of the functional groups we have encountered so far. Here are the melting and boiling points of five compounds that contain three carbon atoms:

$$CH_3-CH_2-CH_3$$

Propane
m.p. = −188°C
b.p. = −42°C

$$CH_3-CH_2-\overset{\overset{\displaystyle OH}{|}}{CH_2}$$

1-Propanol
m.p. = −127°C
b.p. = 97°C

$$CH_3-CH_2-\overset{\overset{\displaystyle O}{\|}}{C}-H$$

Propanal
m.p. = −81°C
b.p. = 49°C

$$CH_3-\overset{\overset{\displaystyle O}{\|}}{C}-CH_3$$

2-Propanone
m.p. = −94°C
b.p. = 56°C

$$CH_3-CH_2-\overset{\overset{\displaystyle O}{\|}}{C}-OH$$

Propanoic acid
m.p. = −21°C
b.p. = 141°C

Aldehydes and carboxylic acids are responsible for the odors our bodies produce when we exercise.

Carboxylic acids with up to nine carbon atoms are colorless liquids at room temperature, while acids with 10 or more carbon atoms are white solids.

The carboxylic acid group can also form hydrogen bonds with water molecules, so carboxylic acids with few carbon atoms are very soluble in water. As was the case with alcohols, aldehydes, and ketones, the solubility decreases as the carbon skeleton becomes larger, so carboxylic acids with long carbon chains have similar solubilities to alkanes. For instance, butanoic acid can be mixed with water in any proportion, but the solubility of octanoic acid is only 0.7 g/L.

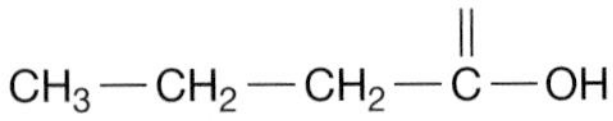

$$CH_3-CH_2-CH_2-\overset{\displaystyle O}{\overset{\|}{C}}-OH$$

Butanoic acid
Unlimited solubility

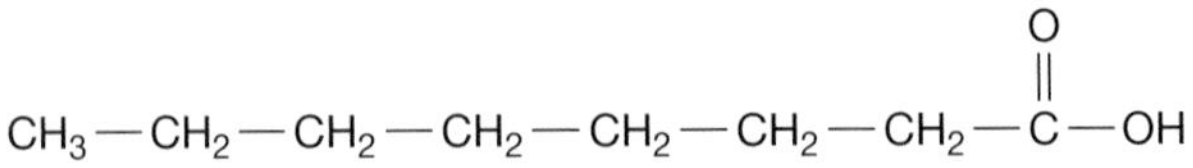

$$CH_3-CH_2-CH_2-CH_2-CH_2-CH_2-CH_2-\overset{\displaystyle O}{\overset{\|}{C}}-OH$$

Octanoic acid
Solubility = 0.7 g/L

Carboxylic acids containing 10 or more carbon atoms are called *fatty acids,* because they are the building blocks of fats. We will look at the role of fatty acids in our bodies in Chapter 14.

Sample Problem 10.15

Comparing boiling points of carboxylic acids

Which of the acids shown here would you expect to have the following?

a) highest boiling point
b) highest solubility in water

$$CH_3-(CH_2)_2-\overset{\displaystyle O}{\overset{\|}{C}}-OH \qquad CH_3-(CH_2)_4-\overset{\displaystyle O}{\overset{\|}{C}}-OH \qquad CH_3-(CH_2)_6-\overset{\displaystyle O}{\overset{\|}{C}}-OH$$

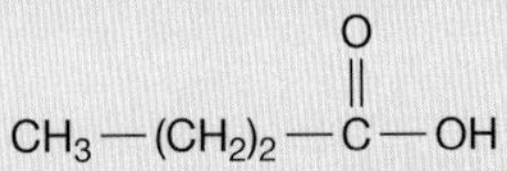

Butanoic acid 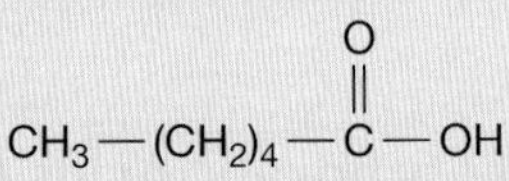 **Hexanoic acid** 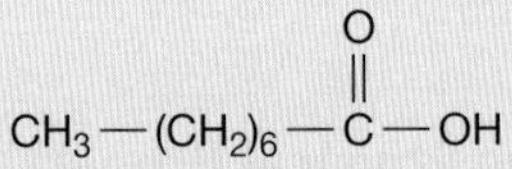 **Octanoic acid**

SOLUTION

a) All three molecules contain the same functional group, so the compound with the largest carbon skeleton will have the highest boiling point: octanoic acid.
b) The compound with the smallest carbon skeleton has the highest solubility in water, because hydrocarbon chains are not attracted to water and tend to decrease the solubility of an organic molecule. Therefore, butanoic acid has the highest solubility in water.

TRY IT YOURSELF: *Which of the compounds shown here would you expect to have the following?*

a) highest boiling point
b) highest solubility in water

$$CH_3-(CH_2)_4-CH_3 \qquad CH_3-(CH_2)_4-\overset{\displaystyle O}{\overset{\|}{C}}-OH \qquad HO-\overset{\displaystyle O}{\overset{\|}{C}}-(CH_2)_4-\overset{\displaystyle O}{\overset{\|}{C}}-OH$$

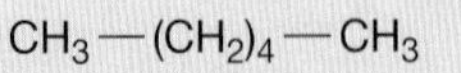

Hexane 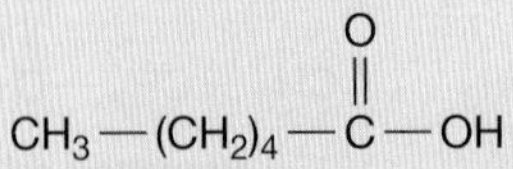 **Hexanoic acid** 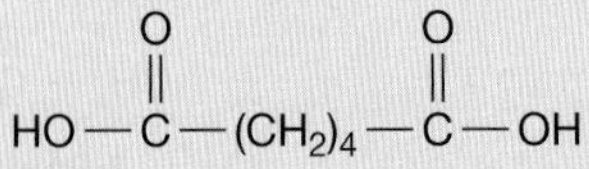 **Adipic acid**

For additional practice, try Core Problems 10.37 through 10.40.

CORE PROBLEMS

10.31 Draw the structures of the products that are formed when the following aldehydes are oxidized:

a) 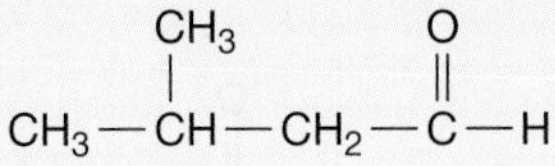 $CH_3-CH(CH_3)-CH_2-C(=O)-H$

b) 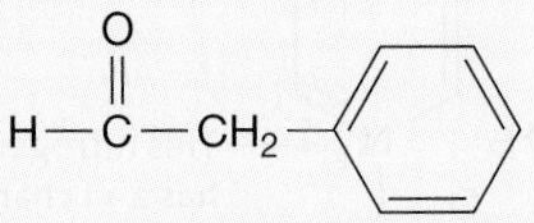 $H-C(=O)-CH_2-C_6H_5$

10.32 Draw the structures of the products that are formed when the following aldehydes are oxidized:

a) 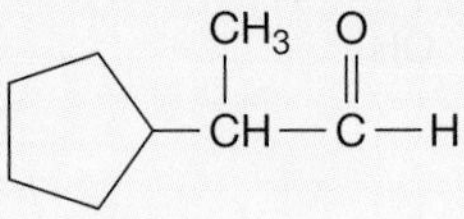 cyclopentyl$-CH(CH_3)-C(=O)-H$

b) 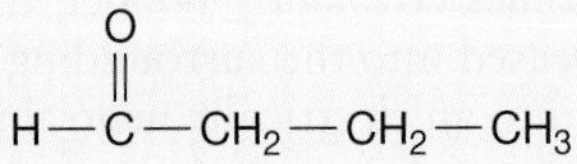 $H-C(=O)-CH_2-CH_2-CH_3$

10.33 Name the following compounds, using the IUPAC rules:

a) 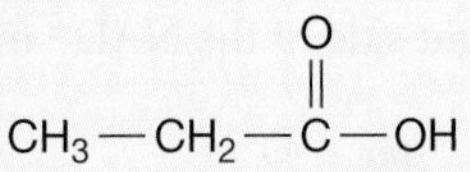 $CH_3-CH_2-C(=O)-OH$

b) $CH_3-CH_2-CH_2-CH_2-CH_2-CH_2-COOH$

c) 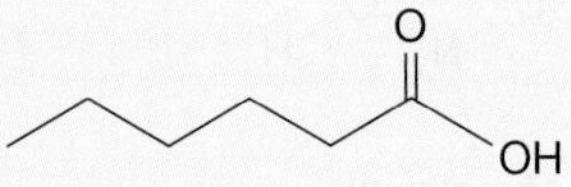 (skeletal structure: six-carbon chain ending in C(=O)OH)

10.34 Name the following compounds, using the IUPAC rules:

a) CH_3-COOH

b) 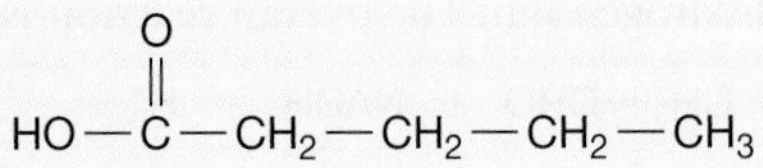 $HO-C(=O)-CH_2-CH_2-CH_2-CH_3$

c) (skeletal structure: four-carbon chain ending in C(=O)OH)

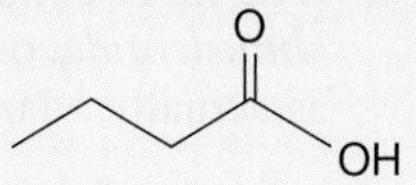

10.35 Draw the structures of the following compounds:
a) pentanoic acid b) formic acid

10.36 Draw the structures of the following compounds:
a) nonanoic acid b) acetic acid

10.37 One of the following compounds is more soluble in water than the other one. Which compound has the higher solubility?

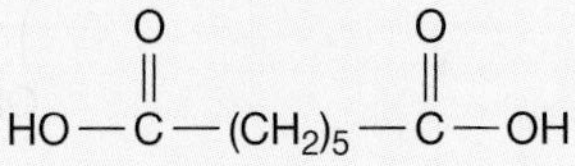

$HO-C(=O)-(CH_2)_5-C(=O)-OH$ — **Pimelic acid**

$HO-C(=O)-(CH_2)_5-CH_3$ — **Heptanoic acid**

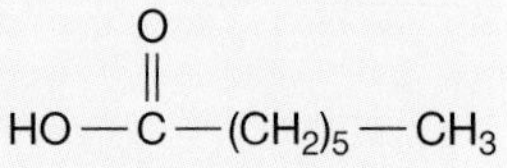

10.38 One of the following compounds is more soluble in water than the other one. Which compound has the higher solubility?

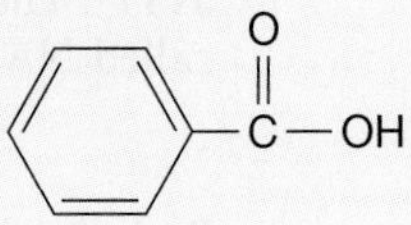

$C_6H_5-C(=O)-OH$ — **Benzoic acid**

$C_6H_5-CH_3$ — **Toluene**

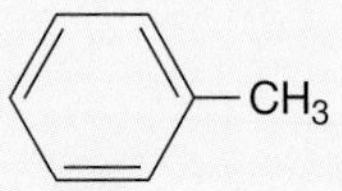

10.39 One of the compounds in Problem 10.37 is a solid at room temperature, and one is a liquid. Which is which? Explain your answer.

10.40 One of the compounds in Problem 10.38 is a solid at room temperature, and one is a liquid. Which is which? Explain your answer.

10.6 Biological Oxidations and Reductions: The Redox Coenzymes

OBJECTIVE: *Describe the role of the common redox coenzymes in biological oxidation and reduction reactions.*

In this chapter, we have examined a number of reactions that add hydrogen atoms to or remove them from organic compounds. In our bodies, hydrogen atoms are usually donated and removed by a set of organic compounds called the **redox coenzymes**. The term *redox* (pronounced "REE-docks") is an abbreviation for *reduction/oxidation*, and a *coenzyme* is an organic compound that helps an enzyme carry out its catalytic function. There are three important redox coenzymes, each of which has its own function.

• We will examine coenzymes in more detail when we look at the chemistry of proteins in Chapter 13.

NAD^+ Is the Hydrogen Acceptor in Most Oxidations

The most common redox coenzyme in biochemical reactions is *nicotinamide adenine dinucleotide*, or *NAD^+*. This molecule contains a positively charged nitrogen atom, so it is actually a large polyatomic ion with a +1 charge.

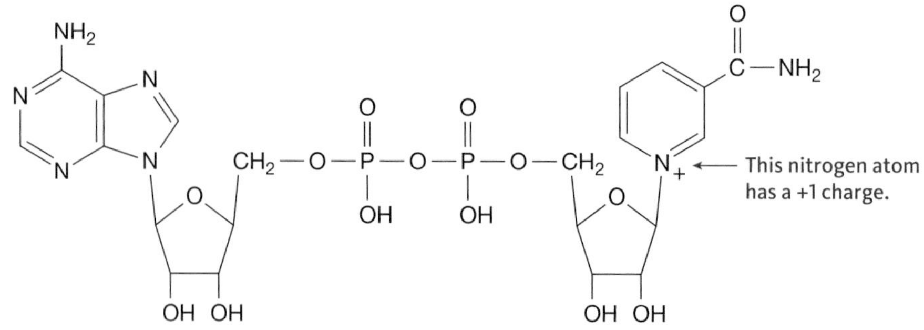

This nitrogen atom has a +1 charge.

The structure of NAD^+, a redox coenzyme

When NAD^+ reacts with another organic molecule, it removes two hydrogen atoms from the molecule. One of the hydrogen atoms becomes covalently bonded to NAD^+. The other hydrogen atom loses its electron and is released into the surrounding solution as H^+. The electron is added to NAD^+, converting it into an electrically neutral molecule called NADH. We can write this reaction as follows:

$$NAD^+ + 2\,[H] \rightarrow NADH + H^+$$

Both the electron and the hydrogen atom are added to the right side of the NAD^+ molecule.

rest of molecule

NAD^+

rest of molecule

NADH

Health Note: Our bodies use the vitamin niacin to make the active portion of NAD^+. Niacin deficiency produces *pellagra,* a disease whose symptoms include diarrhea, skin lesions, and neurological disorders. Our bodies can make niacin from the amino acid tryptophan, so pellagra only occurs in people whose diets are deficient in both protein and niacin.

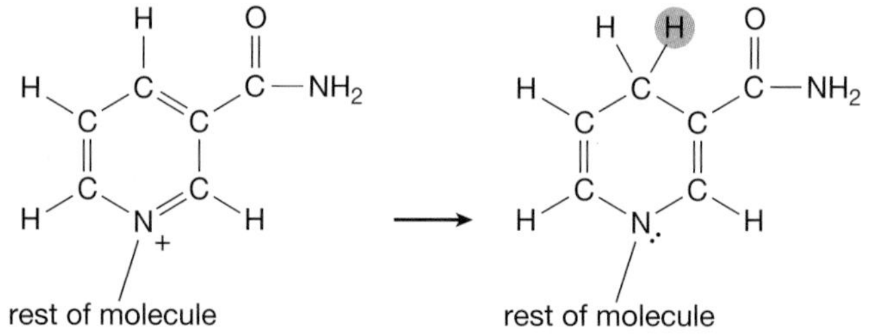

Let us look at some reactions that involve NAD^+. When our bodies oxidize ethanol to acetaldehyde, we remove two hydrogen atoms from ethanol. One of these atoms becomes bonded to NAD^+, and the other becomes a hydrogen ion. The overall reaction is

$$CH_3{-}CH_2{-}OH + NAD^+ \rightarrow CH_3{-}CHO + NADH + H^+$$

Ethanol **Acetaldehyde**

Drawing out the structures of ethanol and acetaldehyde allows us to see where the hydrogen atoms go.

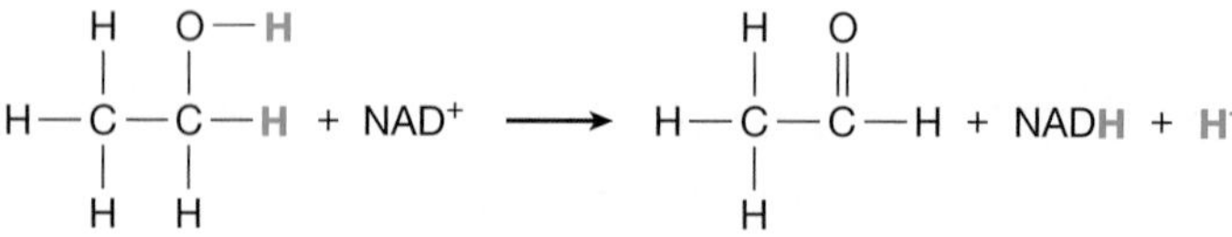

Another example is the oxidation of a thiol to form a disulfide. This reaction is important in protein chemistry, as we will see in Chapter 13.

$$\text{protein}{-}CH_2{-}S{-}H + H{-}S{-}CH_2{-}\text{protein} + NAD^+ \longrightarrow$$

$$\text{protein}{-}CH_2{-}S{-}S{-}CH_2{-}\text{protein} + NADH + H^+$$

NAD$^+$ is also involved in the oxidation of aldehydes. Recall that aldehydes gain an oxygen atom rather than losing hydrogen atoms when they are oxidized. In our bodies, the oxygen atom comes from a water molecule, and NAD$^+$ removes the two hydrogen atoms from water. The balanced equation for this reaction is

$$CH_3{-}CHO + H_2O + NAD^+ \rightarrow CH_3{-}COOH + NADH + H^+$$

Acetaldehyde **Acetic acid**

Again, drawing out the structures allows us to see where the atoms go.

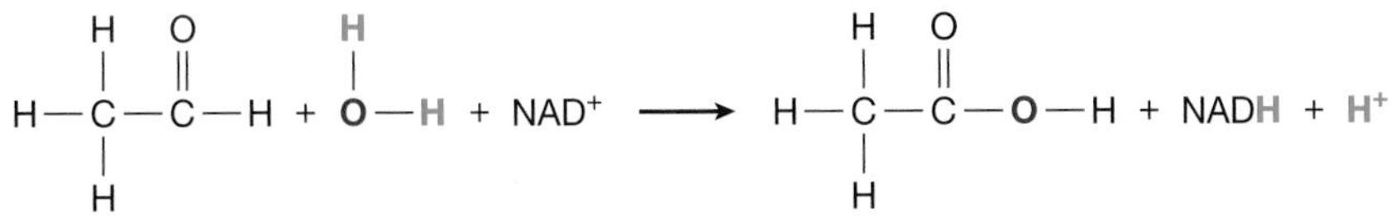

$$H{-}\underset{\underset{H}{|}}{\overset{\overset{H}{|}}{C}}{-}\overset{\overset{O}{\|}}{C}{-}H + O{-}H\ (\text{with } H \text{ above } O) + NAD^+ \longrightarrow H{-}\underset{\underset{H}{|}}{\overset{\overset{H}{|}}{C}}{-}\overset{\overset{O}{\|}}{C}{-}O{-}H + NADH + H^+$$

Sample Problem 10.16

Writing a chemical equation involving NAD$^+$

When our bodies break down proteins to obtain energy, one of the reactions they carry out is the oxidation of a compound called glutamic acid semialdehyde. Both NAD$^+$ and H_2O are involved in this oxidation. Write a balanced equation for this reaction.

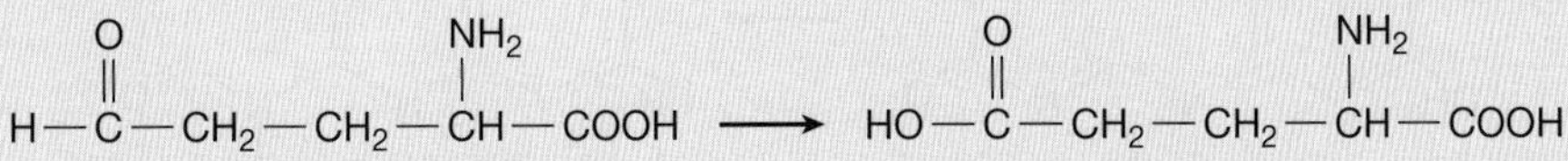

$$H{-}\overset{\overset{O}{\|}}{C}{-}CH_2{-}CH_2{-}\overset{\overset{NH_2}{|}}{CH}{-}COOH \longrightarrow HO{-}\overset{\overset{O}{\|}}{C}{-}CH_2{-}CH_2{-}\overset{\overset{NH_2}{|}}{CH}{-}COOH$$

Glutamic acid semialdehyde **Glutamic acid**

SOLUTION

In this reaction, the aldehyde group on the left side of the reactant is oxidized to a carboxylic acid. To write the balanced equation for the oxidation of an aldehyde, we must add NAD$^+$ and H_2O on the reactant side, and we must add NADH and H$^+$ on the product side. (Remember that the H_2O supplies the oxygen atom for the oxidation, and the NAD$^+$ removes the hydrogen atoms from the water molecule.) The overall reaction is

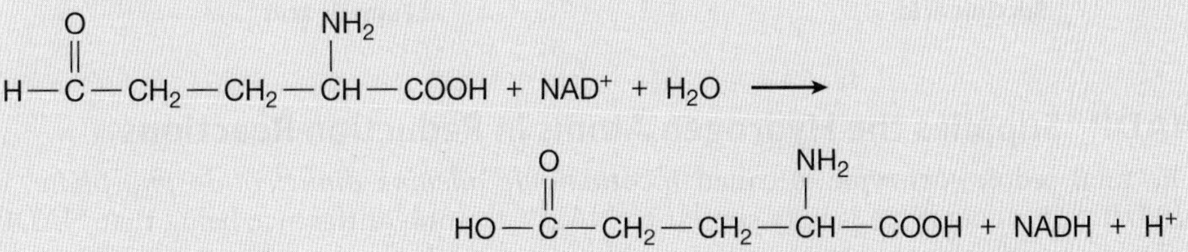

$$H{-}\overset{\overset{O}{\|}}{C}{-}CH_2{-}CH_2{-}\overset{\overset{NH_2}{|}}{CH}{-}COOH + NAD^+ + H_2O \longrightarrow$$

$$HO{-}\overset{\overset{O}{\|}}{C}{-}CH_2{-}CH_2{-}\overset{\overset{NH_2}{|}}{CH}{-}COOH + NADH + H^+$$

TRY IT YOURSELF: *The tart flavor of apples is due in part to a compound called malic acid. Your body oxidizes malic acid as shown here, using NAD$^+$ to remove the hydrogen atoms. Write a balanced equation for this reaction.*

$$HO{-}\overset{\overset{O}{\|}}{C}{-}\overset{\overset{OH}{|}}{CH}{-}CH_2{-}\overset{\overset{O}{\|}}{C}{-}OH \longrightarrow HO{-}\overset{\overset{O}{\|}}{C}{-}\overset{\overset{O}{\|}}{C}{-}CH_2{-}\overset{\overset{O}{\|}}{C}{-}OH$$

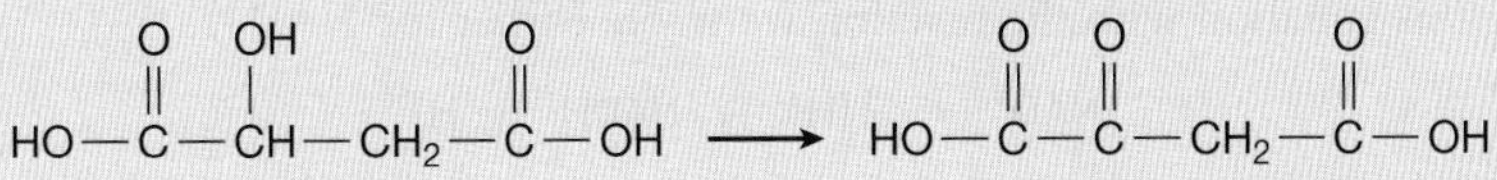

Malic acid **Oxaloacetic acid**

FAD Accepts Hydrogen Atoms When a Hydrocarbon Is Oxidized

The second redox coenzyme that is involved in oxidation reactions is *flavin adenine dinucleotide*, or *FAD*.

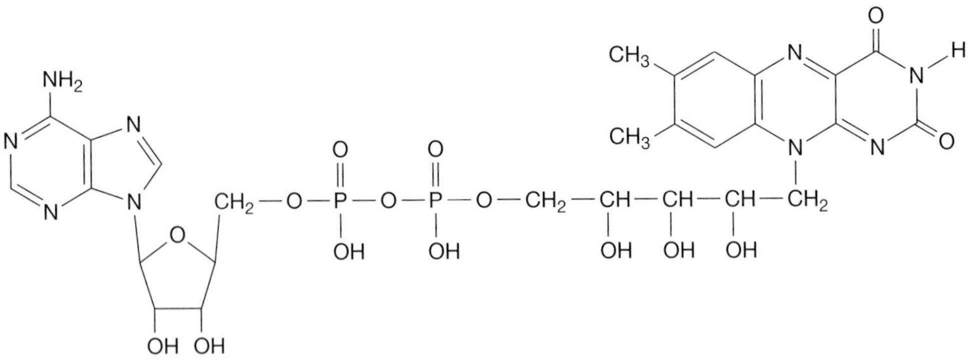

The structure of FAD, a redox coenzyme

When FAD reacts with an organic molecule, it removes two hydrogen atoms. Both hydrogen atoms become covalently bonded to FAD, forming a compound called $FADH_2$.

Health Note: Our bodies use the vitamin riboflavin to make the active portion of FAD. Riboflavin occurs in a wide range of foods, so riboflavin deficiency is very rare and is generally accompanied by the symptoms of other dietary deficiencies.

$$FAD + 2\,[H] \longrightarrow FADH_2$$

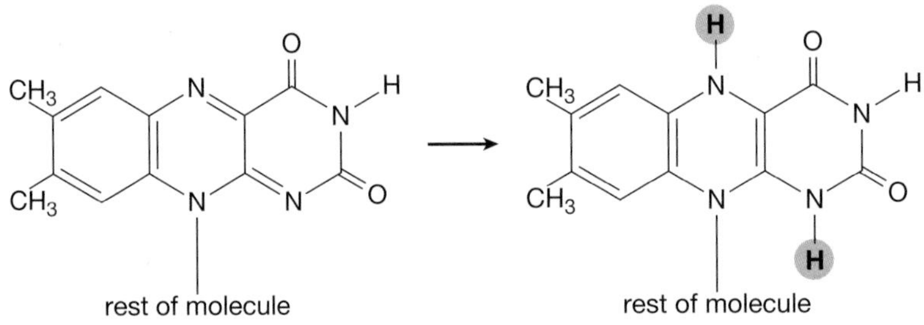

FAD → **$FADH_2$**

FAD is primarily involved in dehydrogenation reactions that form an alkene group. For example, FAD removes the hydrogen atoms when succinic acid is dehydrogenated. We encountered this reaction in Section 10.1.

$$HOOC-CH_2-CH_2-COOH + FAD \longrightarrow HOOC-CH{=}CH-COOH + FADH_2$$

Succinic acid — **Fumaric acid**

$NADP^+$ Supplies the Hydrogen Atoms in Reduction Reactions

The final redox coenzyme is called *nicotinamide adenine dinucleotide phosphate*, or *$NADP^+$*. This coenzyme is very similar to NAD^+, the only difference being that $NADP^+$ contains an additional phosphate group. However, our bodies usually use this coenzyme in reduction reactions, whereas we use NAD^+ in oxidations. As a result, the reactant is actually NADPH rather than $NADP^+$, and the reaction forms $NADP^+$ as a product. We can write a balanced equation for this reaction.

$$NADPH + H^+ \rightarrow NADP^+ + 2\,[H]$$

Compare this equation with the reaction we wrote earlier for NAD^+.

$$NAD^+ + 2\,[H] \rightarrow NADH + H^+$$

These two reactions are essentially opposites. NADPH donates hydrogen atoms to another compound, while NAD^+ removes hydrogen atoms from another compound.

For example, when our bodies make fatty acids, we must reduce the ketone group in a molecule called acetoacetyl-ACP. Here is the equation for this reaction:

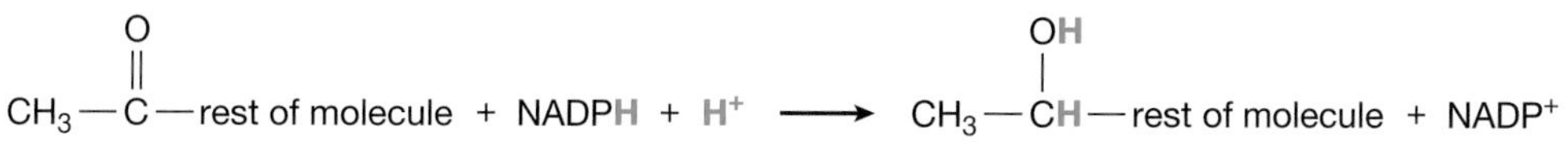

$$\underset{\textbf{Acetoacetyl-ACP}}{CH_3-\overset{\overset{\displaystyle O}{\|}}{C}-\text{rest of molecule}} + \text{NADPH} + H^+ \longrightarrow \underset{\textbf{β-Hydroxybutyryl-ACP}}{CH_3-\overset{\overset{\displaystyle OH}{|}}{CH}-\text{rest of molecule}} + \text{NADP}^+$$

Table 10.3 summarizes the roles of the three redox coenzymes.

TABLE 10.3 The Roles of the Redox Coenzymes

Coenzyme	Role	Reaction*
NAD^+	NAD^+ accepts the hydrogen atoms that are removed in most types of oxidation reactions.	$NAD^+ + 2\,[H] \rightarrow NADH + H^+$
FAD	FAD accepts the hydrogen atoms that are removed during dehydrogenation reactions ($-CH-CH- \rightarrow -C{=}C-$).	$FAD + 2\,[H] \rightarrow FADH_2$
NADPH	NADPH supplies the hydrogen atoms that are added during reduction reactions.	$NADPH + H^+ \rightarrow NADP^+ + 2\,[H]$

*In the reactions in this table, [H] represents a hydrogen atom that is part of an organic molecule.

Sample Problem 10.17

Identifying the redox coenzyme in a biochemical reaction

The following reaction occurs during the formation of proline (one of the amino acid building blocks of proteins). Which redox coenzyme is most likely to be involved in this reaction?

[Structure: five-membered ring with C=N double bond bearing C(=O)–OH] $\longrightarrow$ [Structure: pyrrolidine ring with N–H bearing C(=O)–OH]

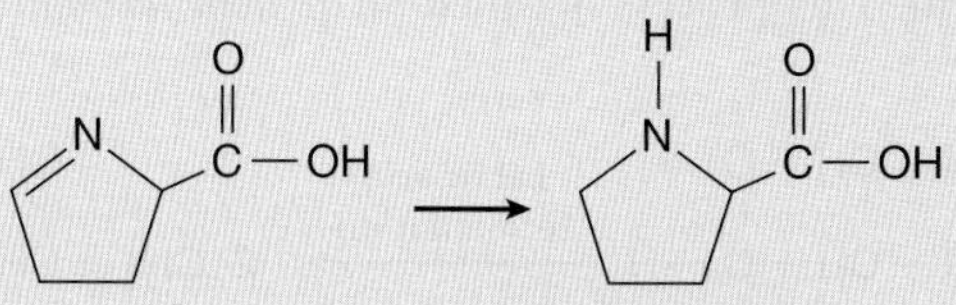

SOLUTION

Before we can answer this question, we need to know what type of reaction this is. In this reaction, two hydrogen atoms are added to the reactant. One hydrogen atom becomes attached to the nitrogen atom, and one becomes attached to the adjacent carbon atom. This is a reduction reaction, and the coenzyme that supplies the two hydrogen atoms in most biochemical reductions is NADPH.

TRY IT YOURSELF: *The following reaction occurs during the breakdown of the amino acid valine. Which redox coenzyme is most likely to be involved in this reaction?*

$$CH_3-\overset{\overset{\displaystyle CH_3}{|}}{CH}-\overset{\overset{\displaystyle O}{\|}}{C}-\text{rest of molecule} \longrightarrow CH_2{=}\overset{\overset{\displaystyle CH_3}{|}}{C}-\overset{\overset{\displaystyle O}{\|}}{C}-\text{rest of molecule}$$

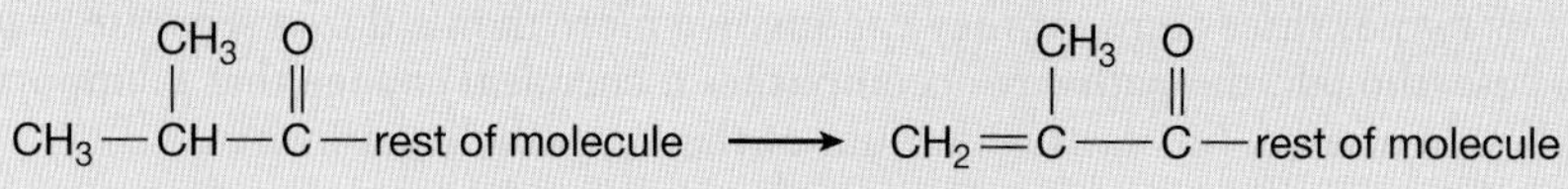

For additional practice, try Core Problems 10.43 and 10.44.

CORE PROBLEMS

10.41 Which of the redox coenzymes is normally used to supply the hydrogen atoms for biological reduction reactions?

10.42 Which two redox coenzymes are normally used to remove hydrogen atoms in biological oxidation reactions?

10.43 The following reaction occurs in many kinds of plants:

$$\underset{\text{Glycolic acid}}{\overset{\text{OH}}{\text{CH}_2}-\overset{\text{O}}{\overset{\|}{\text{C}}}-\text{OH}} + ? \longrightarrow \underset{\text{Glyoxylic acid}}{\text{H}-\overset{\text{O}}{\overset{\|}{\text{C}}}-\overset{\text{O}}{\overset{\|}{\text{C}}}-\text{OH}} + ?$$

a) Which of the redox coenzymes is most likely to be involved in this reaction?

b) Complete the preceding reaction by writing the correct form of the redox coenzyme on each side of the equation.

10.44 Plants and bacteria can make the amino acid lysine from other nutrients, using a sequence of several reactions. One of these reactions is shown here:

HOOC–(ring with N, double bond)–COOH + ? ⟶ HOOC–(ring with N)–COOH + ?

a) Which of the redox coenzymes is most likely to be involved in this reaction?

b) Complete the preceding reaction by writing the correct form of the redox coenzyme on each side of the equation.

10.45 When an organic molecule is oxidized by NAD^+, the molecule loses two hydrogen atoms. However, NAD^+ only gains one hydrogen atom (to form NADH) in this type of reaction. What happens to the other hydrogen atom?

10.46 When an organic molecule is reduced by NADPH, the organic molecule gains two hydrogen atoms. Only one of these comes from NADPH. Where does the other hydrogen atom come from?

OBJECTIVES: *Understand the significance of metabolic pathways, and describe the sequence of reactions that converts a CH_2 group into a carbonyl group.*

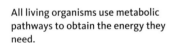

10.7 Introduction to Metabolic Pathways

Our bodies must make and break down many different chemical compounds every day. We digest the food we eat, burn a variety of nutrients to obtain energy, convert compounds that we do not need into other compounds that we do need, and build larger molecules from smaller pieces. In virtually every case, we carry out these processes in several steps, each of which changes some small part of a molecule. For example, when our bodies need a sudden burst of energy, we break down glucose (blood sugar) into two molecules of lactic acid. This process is called *lactic acid fermentation,* and the overall reaction is

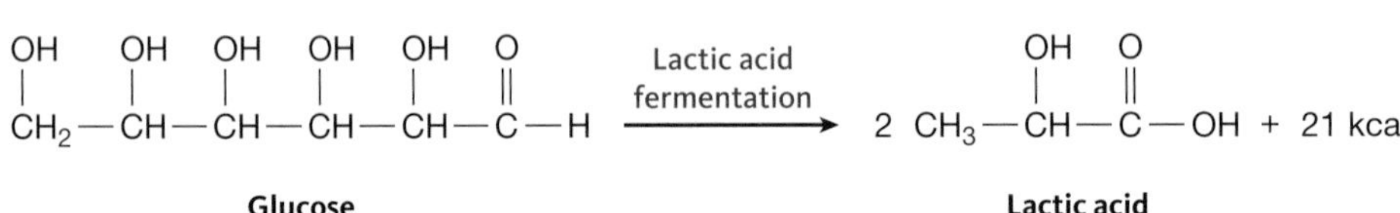

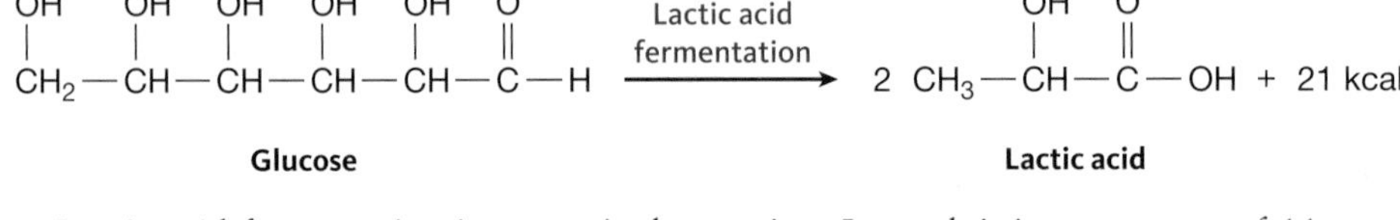

$$\underset{\text{Glucose}}{\overset{\text{OH}}{\text{CH}_2}-\overset{\text{OH}}{\text{CH}}-\overset{\text{OH}}{\text{CH}}-\overset{\text{OH}}{\text{CH}}-\overset{\text{OH}}{\text{CH}}-\overset{\text{O}}{\overset{\|}{\text{C}}}-\text{H}} \xrightarrow{\text{Lactic acid fermentation}} 2\ \underset{\text{Lactic acid}}{\text{CH}_3-\overset{\text{OH}}{\text{CH}}-\overset{\text{O}}{\overset{\|}{\text{C}}}-\text{OH}} + 21\text{ kcal}$$

All living organisms use metabolic pathways to obtain the energy they need.

Lactic acid fermentation is not a single reaction. Instead, it is a sequence of 11 reactions, as illustrated in Figure 10.1. The first reaction converts glucose into a molecule called glucose-6-phosphate, the second reaction converts glucose-6-phosphate into a different compound, and so forth. Each reaction uses the product of the preceding reaction as its reactant. A sequence of reactions that changes one important biological molecule into another is called a **metabolic pathway.**

Our bodies carry out a vast array of metabolic pathways throughout our lives, because we must make and break down many different molecules. These pathways can be as short as two or three steps, or they can involve more than a dozen separate reactions. In each case, though, the pathway accomplishes a chemical change that is important to our bodies. In a sense, life itself is the sum of these metabolic pathways.

Many Oxidation Pathways Use the Same Three-Reaction Sequence

Many of the metabolic pathways our bodies carry out are involved in energy production. Almost all of these energy-producing pathways involve oxidation reactions, because the oxidation of an organic functional group normally produces a significant amount of energy.

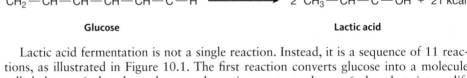

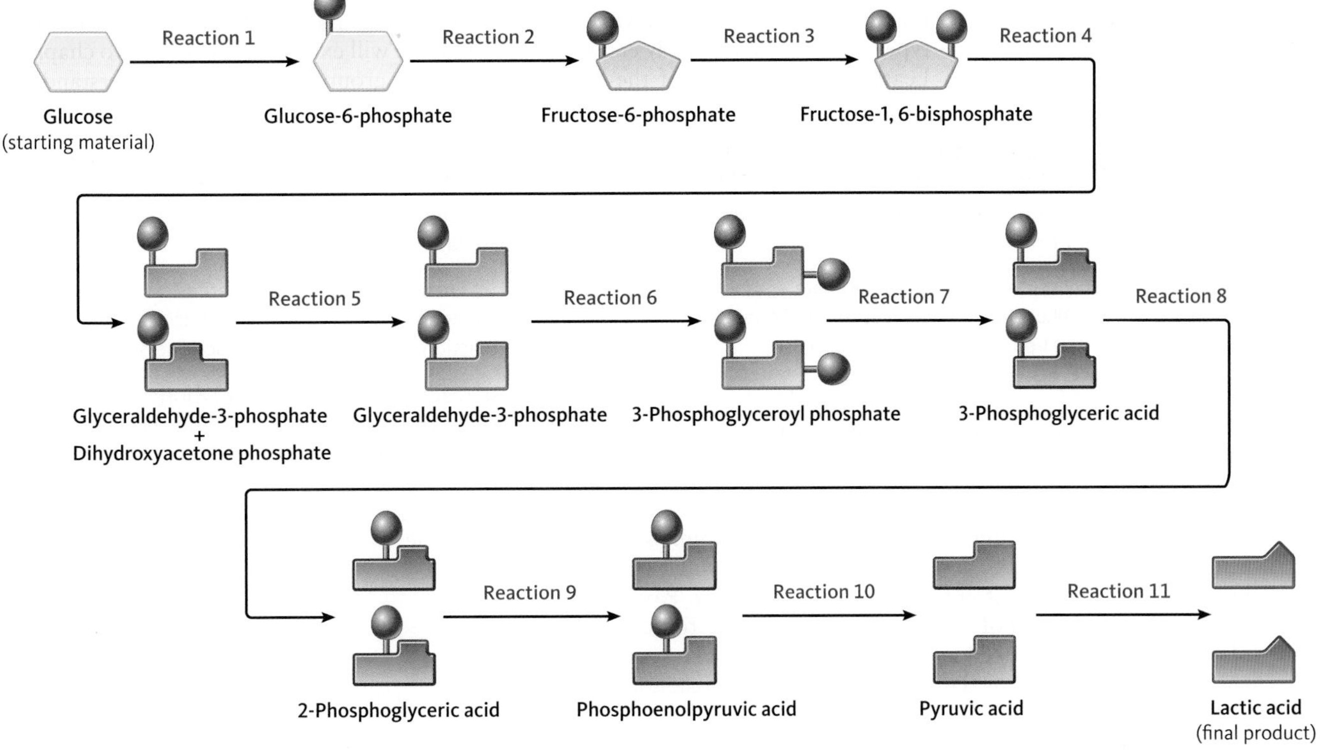

FIGURE 10.1 Lactic acid fermentation, a metabolic pathway.

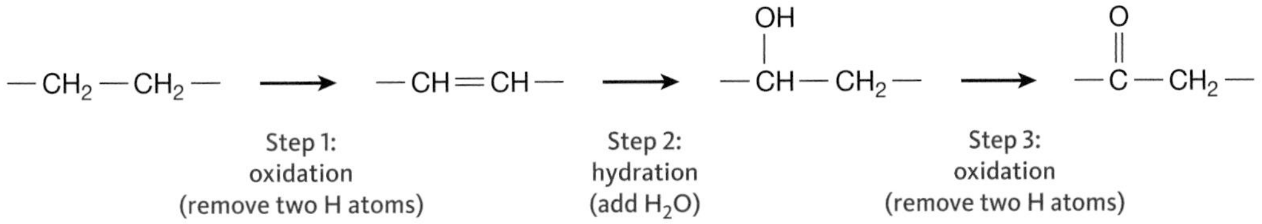

$$-CH_2-CH_2- \xrightarrow[\text{(remove two H atoms)}]{\text{Step 1: oxidation}} -CH{=}CH- \xrightarrow[\text{(add } H_2O)]{\text{Step 2: hydration}} -\underset{}{\overset{OH}{\overset{|}{C}H}}-CH_2- \xrightarrow[\text{(remove two H atoms)}]{\text{Step 3: oxidation}} -\overset{O}{\overset{\|}{C}}-CH_2-$$

FIGURE 10.2 An energy-producing pathway.

For example, many energy-producing pathways convert $-CH_2-$ groups into carbonyl groups, using a sequence of three reactions that we have already encountered. The first and third reactions are oxidations, and the second is a hydration, as shown in Figure 10.2.

Each of the oxidation steps in this pathway produces two hydrogen atoms. As we saw in Section 10.6, these hydrogen atoms become bonded to redox coenzymes. Step 1 is a dehydrogenation reaction and produces an alkene group, so FAD is the hydrogen atom acceptor in this step. Step 3 uses NAD^+, the normal hydrogen acceptor for most oxidations. We can therefore write our pathway as a series of balanced equations as follows:

Step 1: $$-CH_2-CH_2- + FAD \longrightarrow -CH{=}CH- + FADH_2$$

Step 2: $$-CH{=}CH- + H_2O \longrightarrow -\overset{OH}{\overset{|}{C}H}-CH_2-$$

Step 3: $$-\overset{OH}{\overset{|}{C}H}-CH_2- + NAD^+ \longrightarrow -\overset{O}{\overset{\|}{C}}-CH_2- + NADH + H^+$$

In Chapter 15, we will look at several of the key metabolic pathways in our bodies. Many of the organic compounds involved in these pathways are complex and contain several functional groups, but the reactions in each pathway generally change only one functional group at a time. Most of these functional group transformations are reaction types that you have already encountered or that we will explore in the next two chapters. Learning the reactions of the common functional groups allows us to understand the chemistry of life.

CORE PROBLEMS

10.47 The following reactions occur in plants. (These are not balanced equations.)

reaction 1: glucose → glucose-6-phosphate
reaction 2: glucose-6-phosphate → glucose-1-phosphate
reaction 3: glucose-1-phosphate → ADP-glucose
reaction 4: ADP-glucose → starch

Do these reactions make up a metabolic pathway? If so, what are the starting material and the final product of this pathway?

10.48 The following reactions occur in our bodies. (These are not balanced equations.)

reaction 1: glycine → serine
reaction 2: serine → pyruvic acid
reaction 3: pyruvic acid → lactic acid

Do these reactions make up a metabolic pathway? If so, what are the starting material and the final product of this pathway?

10.49 One of the most important metabolic pathways in animals and plants is the citric acid cycle (or Krebs cycle), a series of eight reactions that is involved in the breakdown of all types of nutrients to produce energy. Part of this pathway involves the conversion of succinic acid into oxaloacetic acid, using the sequence of three reactions described in this section. Draw the structures of each of the compounds that are formed during this sequence of reactions.

$$HO-\overset{O}{\overset{\|}{C}}-CH_2-CH_2-\overset{O}{\overset{\|}{C}}-OH \longrightarrow \longrightarrow \longrightarrow HO-\overset{O}{\overset{\|}{C}}-\overset{O}{\overset{\|}{C}}-CH_2-\overset{O}{\overset{\|}{C}}-OH$$

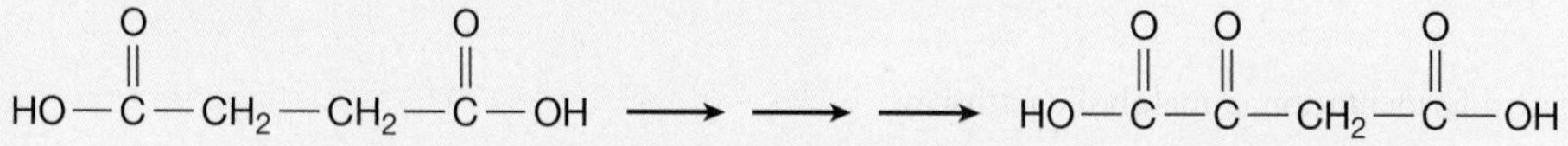

Succinic acid — **Oxaloacetic acid**

10.50 Our bodies break down fatty acids to obtain energy using a series of reactions. Part of this metabolic pathway involves the three-step sequence of reactions illustrated here. Draw the structures of each of the compounds that are formed during this sequence of reactions. (Hint: The reactions involve only the circled portion of the starting compound.)

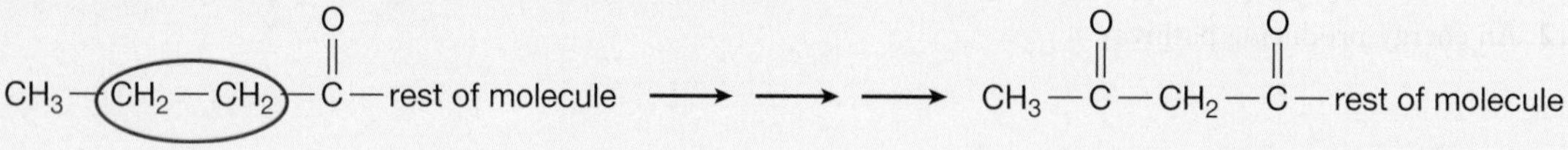

$$CH_3-\boxed{CH_2-CH_2}-\overset{O}{\overset{\|}{C}}-\text{rest of molecule} \longrightarrow \longrightarrow \longrightarrow CH_3-\overset{O}{\overset{\|}{C}}-CH_2-\overset{O}{\overset{\|}{C}}-\text{rest of molecule}$$

CONNECTIONS

Fragrances and Flavors

Think of your favorite food. Chances are that it has a characteristic aroma and that you enjoy that aroma. People (and many animals) are attracted to the aromas of fruits and other edible material. But what produces the aroma of a particular food item?

The aroma of any food is your body's response to volatile chemicals in the food, molecules that evaporate easily and diffuse through the air to your nose. In your nose, the chemicals bind to receptors, proteins that contain pockets into which the chemicals fit. When an odor-producing molecule attaches to a receptor, the receptor triggers a nerve impulse that your brain interprets as "this smells good" (or "this smells bad"). An extraordinary variety of chemicals have a detectible smell, because our noses have many different receptors, each of which triggers a different reaction in our brains. These receptors are an evolutionary adaptation that helps us find food and avoid toxic substances.

In order to have a smell, a chemical must be able to evaporate. Table salt and sugar have no aroma because they do not become gases at room temperature. The salty "smell" of the ocean is actually due to tiny droplets of salt water that form when waves crash onto land; in effect, we are tasting the salt rather than smelling it. In addition, our noses only respond to chemicals that are not part of the atmosphere. We do not smell oxygen, carbon dioxide, or water vapor because our bodies do not have receptors that fit these molecules. We have no need to detect these gases, because they are always present in the air and they are not connected with food or danger.

continued

Many of the most unpleasant-smelling compounds we encounter are either toxic themselves or signs of something we should avoid. For example, the nauseating aroma of rotten eggs is due to hydrogen sulfide (H_2S), an extremely poisonous gas that is produced when bacteria break down proteins in the absence of air. Hydrogen sulfide is also produced by volcanoes and volcanic hot springs, sometimes in dangerous concentrations, and our noses' reaction to the gas is an adaptation that keeps us away from danger. The aroma of decaying flesh (particularly decaying fish) is due to two nitrogen-containing molecules called putrescine and cadaverine. These names are a testament to early chemists' opinion of their aromas!

$$NH_2-CH_2-CH_2-CH_2-CH_2-NH_2$$

Putrescine

$$NH_2-CH_2-CH_2-CH_2-CH_2-CH_2-NH_2$$

Cadaverine

Image copyright kavram, 2010. Used under license from Shutterstock.com

This hot pool has a rotten-egg smell due to hydrogen sulfide, a gas that is produced when molten rock rises to the Earth's surface.

The attractive aromas of many foods are due to organic compounds that contain oxygen. Some of these compounds contain functional groups you have already learned. For example, the aromas of cinnamon and vanilla are largely produced by compounds that contain an aldehyde group, and the pleasant smell of melted butter is produced by a ketone.

Benzaldehyde: aroma of bitter almond

Vanillin: aroma of vanilla

Cinnamaldehyde: aroma of cinnamon

$$CH_3-\overset{\overset{\large O}{\|}}{C}-\overset{\overset{\large O}{\|}}{C}-CH_3$$

Biacetyl: aroma of melted butter

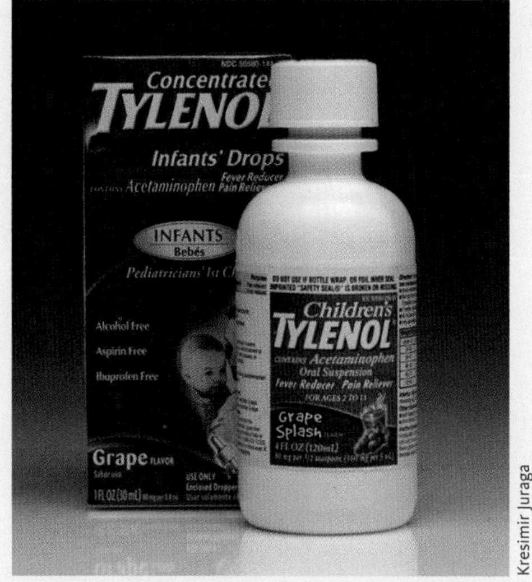

Kresimir Juraga

Manufacturers add grape flavoring and sweeteners to medicines to make them palatable to children.

The most common functional group in fruit-scented compounds is the ester group, which you will encounter in Chapter 12. The structures of some fruity esters are shown here, along with their characteristic smells. These compounds can be made relatively easily in a laboratory, so manufacturers often add them to otherwise odorless foods and other products. For instance, you can find methyl anthranilate (grape flavoring) in products ranging from Popsicles and chewing gum to medicines and children's shampoo.

$$-\overset{\overset{\large O}{\|}}{C}-O-\overset{|}{\underset{|}{C}}-$$ The ester functional group

Methyl anthranilate: aroma of grapes

Methyl salicylate: aroma of mint (wintergreen)

$$CH_3-\overset{\overset{\large CH_3}{|}}{CH}-CH_2-CH_2-O-\overset{\overset{\large O}{\|}}{C}-CH_3$$

Isoamyl acetate: aroma of bananas

Natural aromas are usually produced by mixtures of several compounds, and no single compound can duplicate the exact smell (or flavor) of a specific fruit. Some aromas are complicated mixtures indeed. The smell of a fresh rose is the total of dozens of dif-

continued

ferent molecules, three of which are shown here. A rose by any other name would smell as sweet . . . .

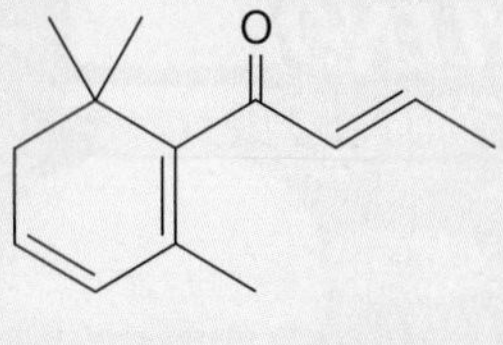

β-damascenone

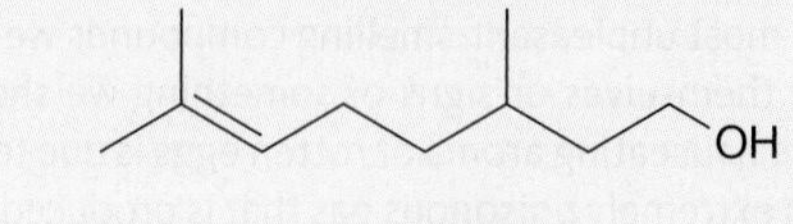

Citronellol

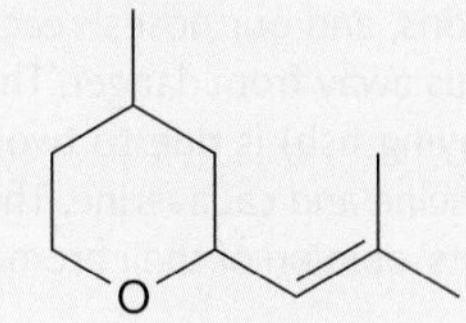

Rose oxide

Key Terms

aldehyde – 10.3
carbonyl group – 10.2
carboxylic acid – 10.5
dehydrogenation reaction – 10.1
disulfide – 10.4
hydrogenation reaction – 10.1
ketone – 10.3
metabolic pathway – 10.7
oxidation reaction – 10.1
primary alcohol – 10.2
redox coenzyme – 10.6
reduction reaction – 10.1
secondary alcohol – 10.2
tertiary alcohol – 10.2

Classes of Organic Compounds

Class	Functional group	IUPAC suffix	Example
Aldehyde	$-\overset{O}{\overset{\|}{C}}-H$	*-al*	$CH_3-CH_2-CH_2-\overset{O}{\overset{\|}{C}}-H$ **Butanal**
Ketone	$C-\overset{O}{\overset{\|}{C}}-C$	*-one*	$CH_3-CH_2-\overset{O}{\overset{\|}{C}}-CH_3$ **2-Butanone**
Carboxylic acid	$-\overset{O}{\overset{\|}{C}}-OH$	*-oic acid*	$CH_3-CH_2-CH_2-\overset{O}{\overset{\|}{C}}-OH$ **Butanoic acid**
Disulfide	$C-S-S-C$	*disulfide**	$CH_3-S-S-CH_3$ **Dimethyl disulfide***

*The IUPAC names for disulfides are not covered in this text.

Summary of Organic Reactions

1) **reduction reactions**

a) hydrogenation of an alkene

alkene + 2 [H] → alkane

$$CH_2{=}CH{-}CH_2{-}CH_2{-}CH_3 + 2\,[H] \longrightarrow CH_3{-}CH_2{-}CH_2{-}CH_2{-}CH_3$$

1-Pentene → **Pentane**

b) reduction of a carbonyl group (aldehyde or ketone)

aldehyde + 2 [H] → primary alcohol
ketone + 2 [H] → secondary alcohol

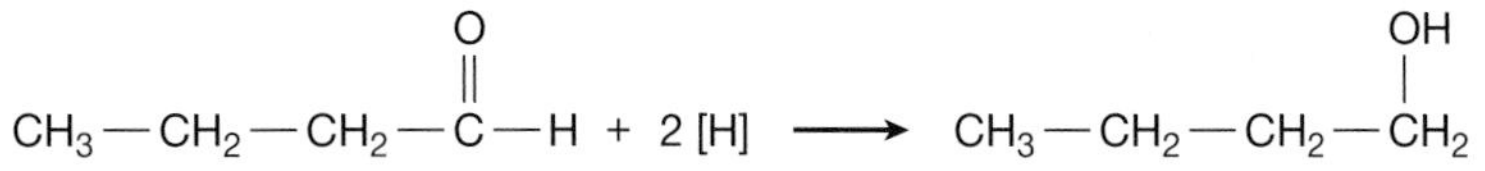

$$CH_3{-}CH_2{-}CH_2{-}\overset{\overset{\large O}{\|}}{C}{-}H + 2\,[H] \longrightarrow CH_3{-}CH_2{-}CH_2{-}\overset{\overset{\large OH}{|}}{CH_2}$$

Butanal → **1-Butanol**

$$CH_3{-}CH_2{-}\overset{\overset{\large O}{\|}}{C}{-}CH_3 + 2\,[H] \longrightarrow CH_3{-}CH_2{-}\overset{\overset{\large OH}{|}}{CH}{-}CH_3$$

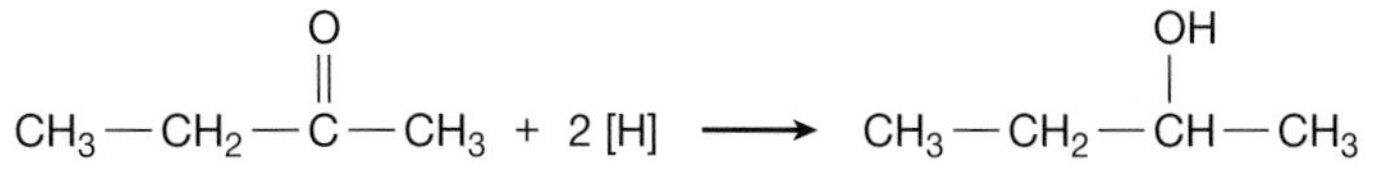

2-Butanone → **2-Butanol**

c) reduction of a disulfide

disulfide + 2 [H] → 2 thiols

$$CH_3{-}S{-}S{-}CH_3 + 2[H] \longrightarrow CH_3{-}SH + HS{-}CH_3$$

dimethyl disulfide → **methanethiol (2 molecules)**

2) **oxidation reactions**

a) dehydrogenation of an alkane

alkane → alkene + 2 [H]

$$CH_3{-}CH_2{-}CH_3 \longrightarrow CH_2{=}CH{-}CH_3 + 2[H]$$

propane → **propene**

b) oxidation of an alcohol

primary alcohol → aldehyde + 2 [H]
secondary alcohol → ketone + 2 [H]

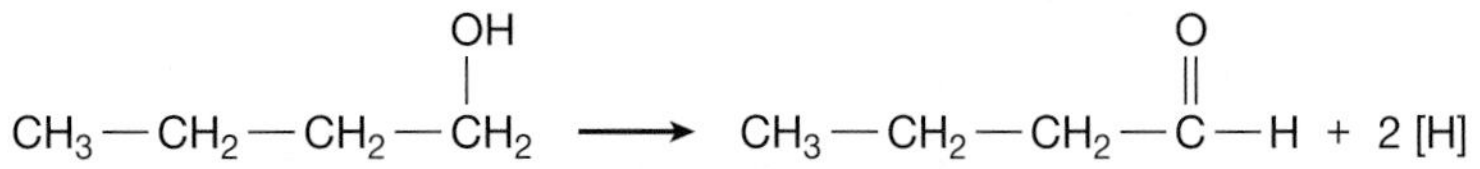

$$CH_3{-}CH_2{-}CH_2{-}\overset{\overset{\large OH}{|}}{CH_2} \longrightarrow CH_3{-}CH_2{-}CH_2{-}\overset{\overset{\large O}{\|}}{C}{-}H + 2\,[H]$$

1-Butanol → **Butanal**

$$CH_3{-}CH_2{-}\overset{\overset{\large OH}{|}}{CH}{-}CH_3 \longrightarrow CH_3{-}CH_2{-}\overset{\overset{\large O}{\|}}{C}{-}CH_3 + 2\,[H]$$

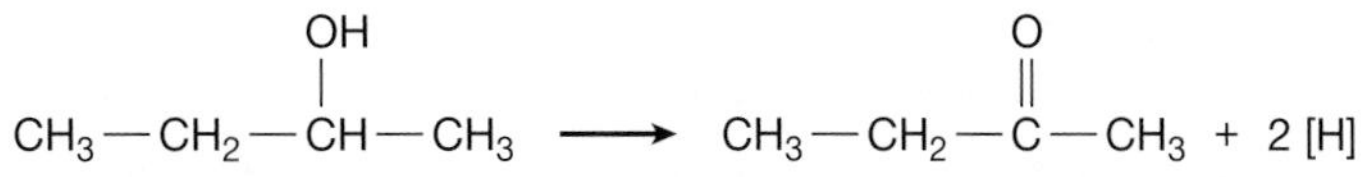

2-Butanol → **2-Butanone**

continued

c) oxidation of an aldehyde

aldehyde + [O] → carboxylic acid

$$CH_3-CH_2-CH_2-\overset{\overset{\displaystyle O}{\|}}{C}-H + [O] \longrightarrow CH_3-CH_2-CH_2-\overset{\overset{\displaystyle O}{\|}}{C}-OH$$

Butanal **Butanoic acid**

d) oxidation of a thiol

2 thiols → disulfide + 2 [H]

$$CH_3-SH + HS-CH_3 \longrightarrow CH_3-S-S-CH_3 + 2[H]$$

methanethiol (2 molecules) **dimethyl disulfide**

SUMMARY OF OBJECTIVES

Now that you have read the chapter, test yourself on your knowledge of the objectives, using this summary as a guide.

Section 10.1: **Understand the relationship between oxidation and reduction, and recognize oxidation and reduction reactions that involve hydrocarbons.**

- The dehydrogenation reaction converts a $-CH_2-CH_2-$ group in a molecule into a $-CH{=}CH-$ group.
- Any reaction (such as a dehydrogenation) that removes two hydrogen atoms from an organic compound is an oxidation.
- The hydrogenation reaction converts an alkene into an alkane.
- Any reaction (such as a hydrogenation) that adds two hydrogen atoms to an organic compound is a reduction.
- Dehydrogenations are limited to certain specific molecules that contain other functional groups, whereas any alkene can be hydrogenated.

Section 10.2: **Predict the products of the oxidation of an alcohol or the reduction of an aldehyde or ketone, and classify alcohols as primary, secondary, or tertiary.**

- The oxidation of an alcohol produces a carbonyl group.
- Alcohols are classified as primary, secondary, or tertiary based on the number of carbon atoms bonded to the functional group carbon.
- Tertiary alcohols cannot be oxidized.
- The carbonyl group can be reduced to an alcohol group.

Section 10.3: **Identify and name aldehydes and ketones, and relate the physical properties of aldehydes and ketones to their structures.**

- The oxidation of primary and secondary alcohols produces aldehydes and ketones, respectively.
- Aldehydes and ketones can be named using the IUPAC endings *-al* and *-one.*
- Aldehydes and ketones have boiling points between those of similarly sized hydrocarbons and alcohols.
- Aldehydes and ketones have similar solubilities in water to those of alcohols.

Section 10.4: **Predict the products of oxidation and reduction reactions that involve thiols, and identify other organic oxidations and reductions.**

- The oxidation of two molecules of a thiol produces a disulfide, which can be reduced back to the thiol.
- Any reaction that removes two hydrogen atoms from an organic compound is an oxidation, and any reaction that adds two hydrogen atoms to an organic compound is a reduction.

Section 10.5: **Predict the product of the oxidation of an aldehyde, identify and name carboxylic acids, and relate the physical properties of carboxylic acids to their structures.**

- When an aldehyde is oxidized, it gains an oxygen atom to become a carboxylic acid.
- Carboxylic acids are named using the IUPAC ending *-oic acid.*

- Carboxylic acids have higher melting and boiling points than similarly sized organic molecules, and their water solubilities are similar to those of alcohols.

Section 10.6: Describe the role of the common redox coenzymes in biological oxidation and reduction reactions.

- In biological oxidation and reduction reactions, hydrogen atoms are passed to or taken from redox coenzymes.
- NAD^+ accepts hydrogen atoms that are removed from organic compounds in most biological oxidations.
- FAD accepts hydrogen atoms during biological dehydrogenations.
- NADPH supplies the hydrogen atoms in biological reductions.

Section 10.7: Understand the significance of metabolic pathways, and describe the sequence of reactions that converts a CH_2 group into a carbonyl group.

- A metabolic pathway is a sequence of reactions that converts one biologically important molecule into another.
- Most energy-producing pathways involve one or more oxidation steps.
- The oxidation of a CH_2 group into a C=O group is accomplished in three reactions that appear in many metabolic pathways.

Concept Questions

OWL Online homework for this chapter may be assigned in OWL.
* indicates more challenging problems.

10.51 What do most biological oxidation reactions have in common with one another?

10.52 What is the general term for reactions that add two hydrogen atoms to an organic molecule?

10.53 In a carbonyl group, both the carbon atom and the oxygen atom are electrically charged.

a) Which atom is positively charged, and which is negatively charged?
b) Using electronegativities, explain your answer to part a.

10.54 What type of functional group (if any) is formed when each of the following is oxidized?

a) primary alcohol
b) secondary alcohol
c) tertiary alcohol
d) aldehyde
e) ketone

10.55 Each of the following names violates the IUPAC rules, but each does so for a different reason. Explain why each name is incorrect.

a) 1-pentanal
b) 2-pentanal

10.56 a) Explain why aldehydes and ketones tend to be more soluble in water than hydrocarbons are.
b) Under what circumstances would the solubility of an aldehyde or ketone be similar to that of a hydrocarbon?

10.57 Explain why the boiling points of aldehydes and ketones are substantially lower than the boiling points of similarly sized alcohols.

10.58 What kind of compound is formed when a thiol is oxidized?

10.59 What are the three common redox coenzymes, and what do our bodies use each of them for?

10.60 What is a metabolic pathway?

10.61 The following reactions occur in some types of yeast. Put the reactions in order so that they form a metabolic pathway.

pyruvic acid → acetaldehyde + CO_2
phosphoenolpyruvic acid → pyruvic acid
acetaldehyde → ethanol

10.62 What three reactions do our bodies use to convert a $-CH_2-$ group into a carbonyl group, and in what order do they occur?

Summary and Challenge Problems

10.63 Name the following compounds using the IUPAC rules:

a) 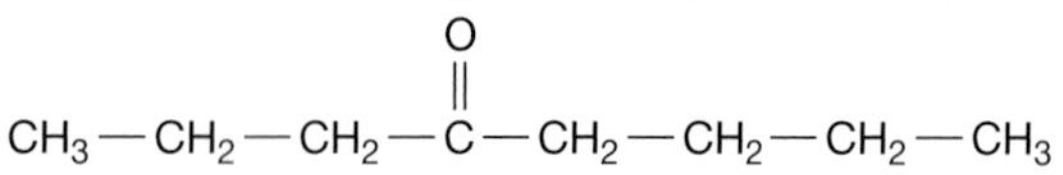 $CH_3—CH_2—CH_2—\overset{\overset{\large O}{\|}}{C}—CH_2—CH_2—CH_2—CH_3$

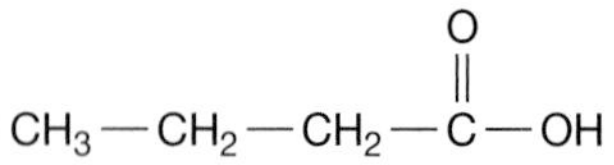

b) $CH_3—CH_2—CH_2—\overset{\overset{\large O}{\|}}{C}—OH$

c) $CH_3—CH_2—CH_2—CH_2—CH_2—\overset{\overset{\large O}{\|}}{C}—H$

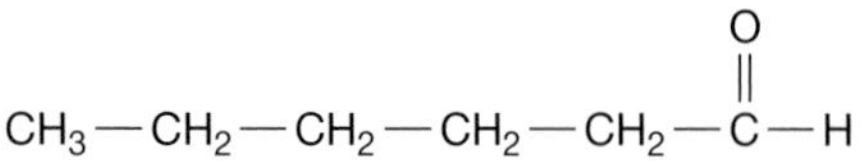

d) 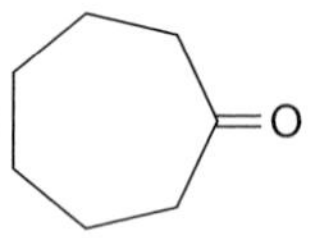 =O

e) 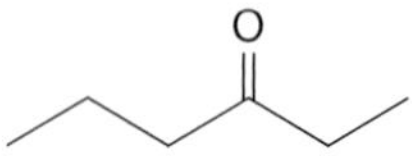 O

f) 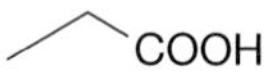 COOH

g)  CHO

10.64 Give the trivial names for each of the following compounds:

a) 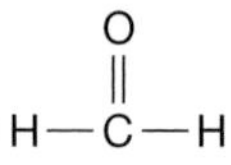 $H—\overset{\overset{\large O}{\|}}{C}—H$

b) 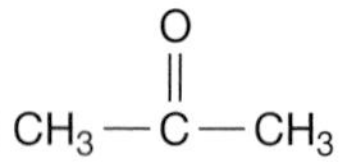 $CH_3—\overset{\overset{\large O}{\|}}{C}—CH_3$

c) $CH_3—COOH$

10.65 Draw condensed structural formulas for each of the following compounds:

a) 2-hexanone b) pentanal
c) heptanoic acid d) cyclobutanone
e) acetaldehyde f) formic acid

10.66 Draw line structures for each of the following compounds:

a) 3-pentanone b) hexanal
c) cyclohexanone d) butanoic acid

10.67 *Draw the structure of a molecule that fits each of the following descriptions:

a) an isomer of 1-butanol
b) an isomer of butanal
c) a ketone that has the same carbon skeleton as 2-methylpentane
d) a carboxylic acid that contains a cyclohexane ring
e) an isomer of cyclopentanol

10.68 Draw the structure of the product that is formed when each of the following compounds is oxidized. If the compound cannot be oxidized, write "no reaction."

a) 3-pentanol
b) acetaldehyde
c) $HO—CH_2—CH_2—CH_2—CH_3$

d) $CH_3—CH_2—SH$

e) 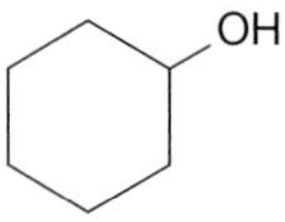 OH

f) 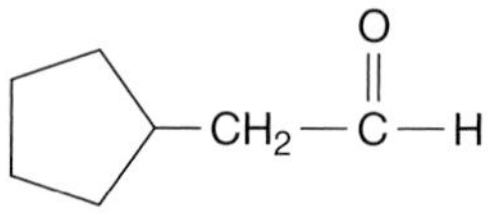 $—CH_2—\overset{\overset{\large O}{\|}}{C}—H$

g) $CH_3—CH_2—CH_2—\underset{\underset{\large CH_3}{|}}{\overset{\overset{\large CH_3}{|}}{C}}—OH$

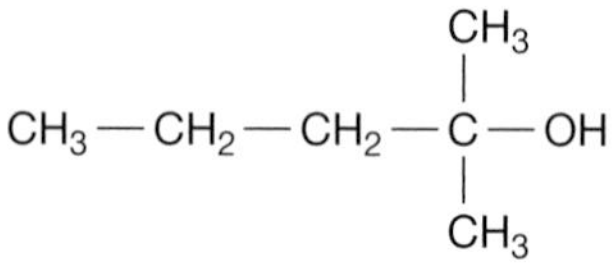

h) $CH_3—\overset{\overset{\large O}{\|}}{C}—CH_3$

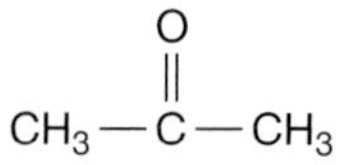

10.69 Draw the structure of the product that is formed when each of the following molecules is hydrogenated:

a) $CH_3—CH{=}CH—CH_2—CH_3$

b) 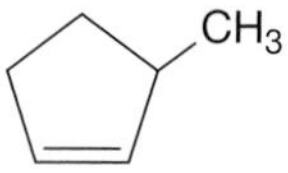 CH_3

10.70 Draw the structure of the product that is formed when each of the following compounds is reduced:

a) pentanal b) acetone

c) 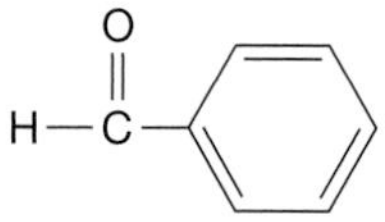 $H—\overset{\overset{\large O}{\|}}{C}—$ d) 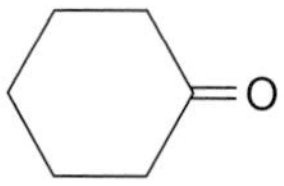 =O

e) $CH_3—S—S—CH_3$

10.71 The burning of fats to produce energy involves many reactions, one of which is the dehydrogenation of the following compound. The portion of the molecule that reacts is circled. Draw the product of this reaction.

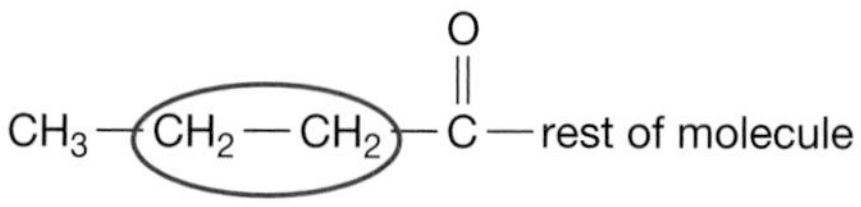

$CH_3—(CH_2—CH_2)—\overset{\overset{\large O}{\|}}{C}—$rest of molecule

10.72 Classify each of the following alcohols as primary, secondary, or tertiary:

a) 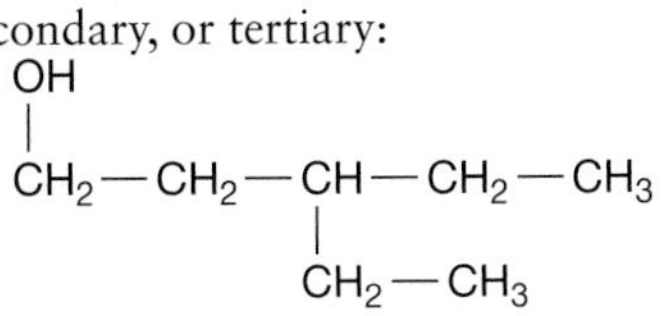 $CH_2(OH)—CH_2—CH(CH_2—CH_3)—CH_2—CH_3$

b) 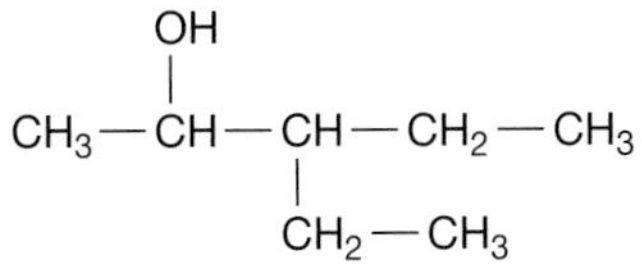 $CH_3—CH(OH)—CH(CH_2—CH_3)—CH_2—CH_3$

c) 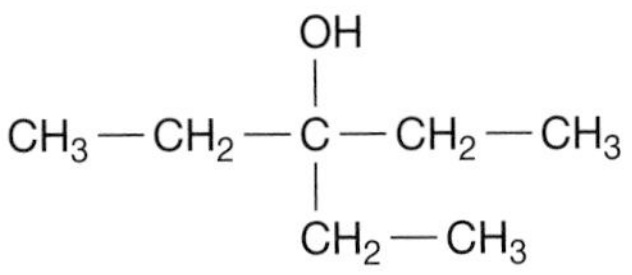 $CH_3—CH_2—C(OH)(CH_2—CH_3)—CH_2—CH_3$

d) 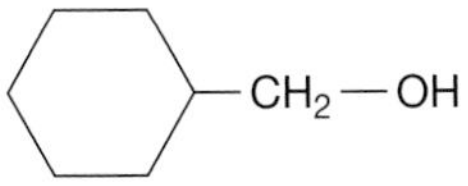 (cyclohexane ring)$—CH_2—OH$

e) 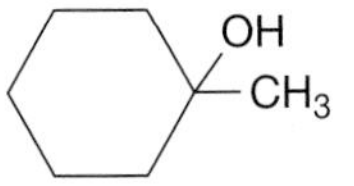 (cyclohexane ring bearing OH and CH_3 on the same carbon)

f) 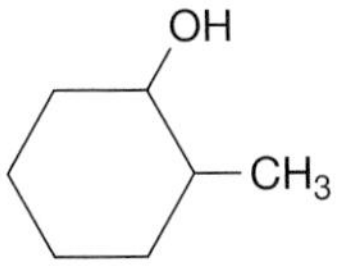 (cyclohexane ring bearing OH and, on the adjacent carbon, CH_3)

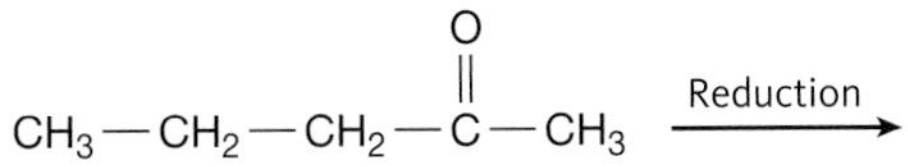

10.73 Which of the alcohols in Problem 10.72 can be oxidized?

10.74 *Tell whether the product of each of the following reactions is a chiral compound:

a) 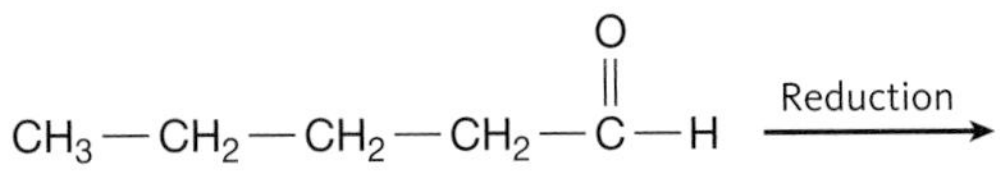 $CH_3—CH_2—CH_2—CH_2—C(=O)—H \xrightarrow{\text{Reduction}}$

b) $CH_3—CH_2—CH_2—C(=O)—CH_3 \xrightarrow{\text{Reduction}}$

c) $CH_3—CH_2—C(=O)—CH_2—CH_3 \xrightarrow{\text{Reduction}}$

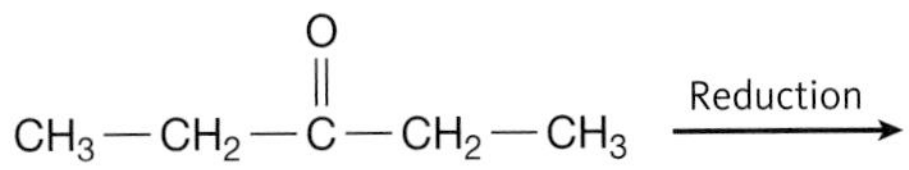

d) 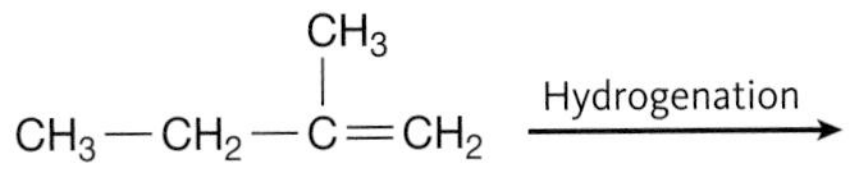 $CH_3—CH_2—C(CH_3)=CH_2 \xrightarrow{\text{Hydrogenation}}$

e) 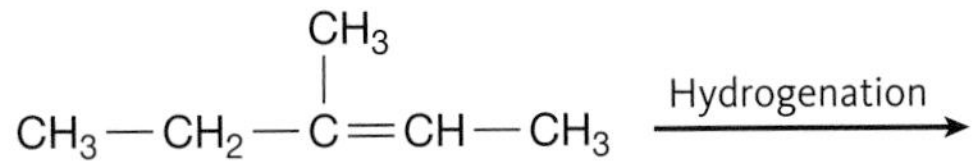 $CH_3—CH_2—C(CH_3)=CH—CH_3 \xrightarrow{\text{Hydrogenation}}$

f) 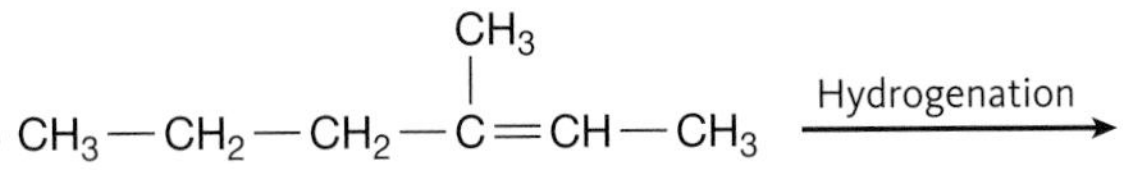 $CH_3—CH_2—CH_2—C(CH_3)=CH—CH_3 \xrightarrow{\text{Hydrogenation}}$

10.75 Which of the following pairs of compounds are constitutional isomers?

a) 2-pentanone and 3-pentanone
b) 2-pentanone and pentanal
c) 2-pentanone and 2-pentanol
d) 2-pentanone and cyclopentanol

10.76 A student says, "There are five possible ketones that have an unbranched chain containing five carbon atoms: 1-pentanone, 2-pentanone, 3-pentanone, 4-pentanone, and 5-pentanone." Is this student correct? If not, how many ketones are there?

10.77 From each of the following pairs of compounds, select the compound that should have the higher boiling point:

a) propane or propanal
b) 2-butanol or 2-butanone
c) acetic acid or pentanoic acid

10.78 From each of the following pairs of compounds, select the compound that should have the higher solubility in water:

a) 2-butanone or 2-hexanone
b) pentane or pentanal
c) 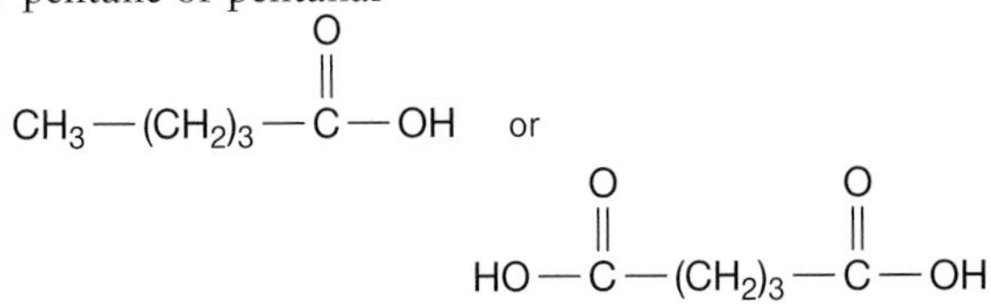 $CH_3—(CH_2)_3—C(=O)—OH$ or $HO—C(=O)—(CH_2)_3—C(=O)—OH$

10.79 *Phenylalanine is a component of proteins. It is made by bacteria, using a sequence of reactions that includes the reduction of the following compound. Only the ketone group of this molecule is reduced. Draw the structure of the product of this reduction.

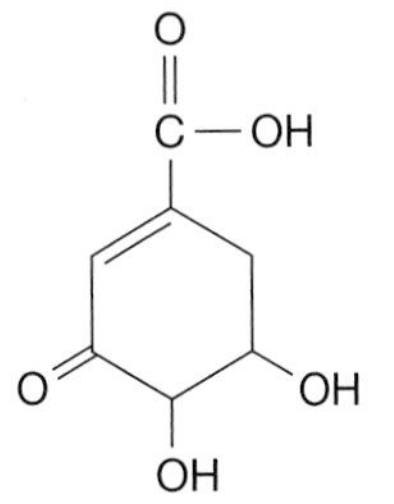

3-Dehydroshikimic acid

10.80 Glucuronic acid is formed in the liver, where it is used to detoxify certain types of compounds.

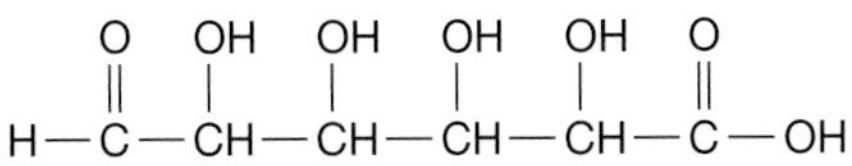

$H—C(=O)—CH(OH)—CH(OH)—CH(OH)—CH(OH)—C(=O)—OH$

Glucuronic acid

a) Circle and name each of the functional groups in glucuronic acid. (The possible options are alcohol, aldehyde, ketone, carboxylic acid, alkene, alkyne, and aromatic ring.)
b) Which of these functional groups can be oxidized?
c) Which of these functional groups can be reduced?

10.81 When 1-butanol is oxidized, it is converted into compound A. Compound A can also be oxidized, and the product of this second oxidation is compound B. Draw the structures of compounds A and B.

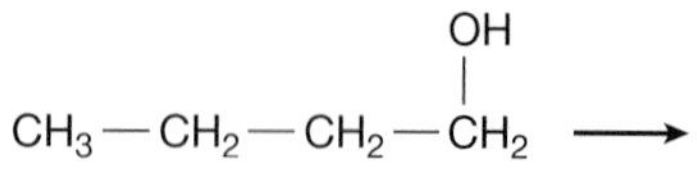

$$CH_3-CH_2-CH_2-CH_2(OH) \longrightarrow$$

Compound A ⟶ Compound B

10.82 *When the following ketone is reduced, it is converted into compound E. Compound E can be dehydrated, and the product of this reaction is compound F. Compound F can be hydrogenated, giving compound G. Draw the structures of compounds E, F, and G. (Hint: The benzene ring is not affected during these reactions.)

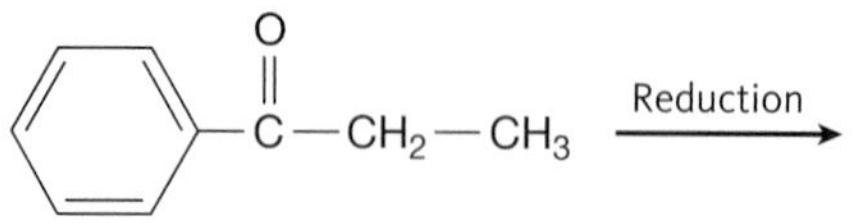

$$C_6H_5-C(=O)-CH_2-CH_3 \xrightarrow{\text{Reduction}}$$

$$\text{Compound E} \xrightarrow{\text{Dehydration}} \text{Compound F}$$

$$\xrightarrow{\text{Hydrogenation}} \text{Compound G}$$

10.83 Identify each of the following biochemical reactions as an oxidation or a reduction:

a) [dihydroorotic acid ring: HN, C=O, N–H, COOH] ⟶ [orotic acid ring: HN, C=O, N–H, C=C, COOH]

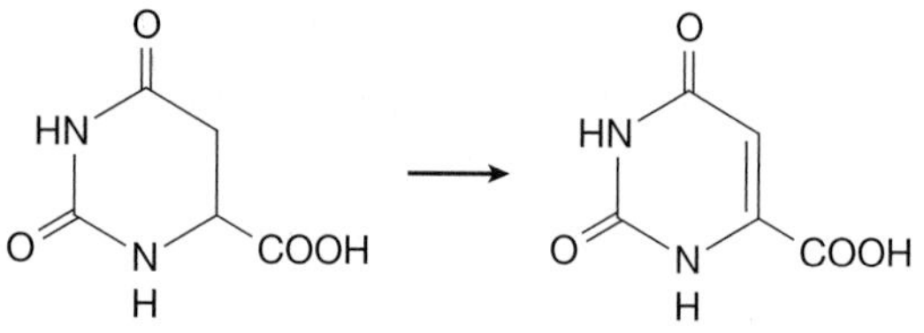

b) [ring with N=C–COOH] ⟶ [saturated ring with N, COOH]

c) [imidazole ring: N=, NH]–CH_2–$CH(NH_2)$–CH_2–OH ⟶ [imidazole ring: N=, NH]–CH_2–$CH(NH_2)$–C(=O)–H

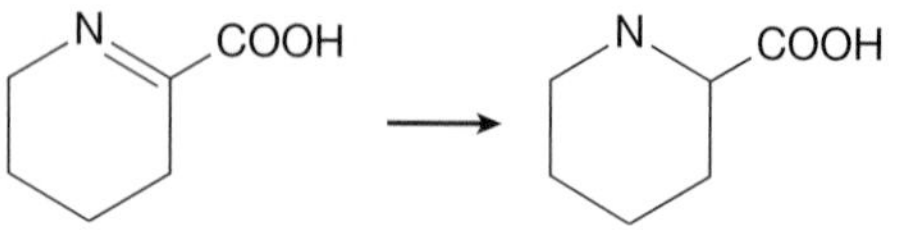

$$H_2N-CH-CH_2-OH \longrightarrow H_2N-CH-C(=O)-H$$

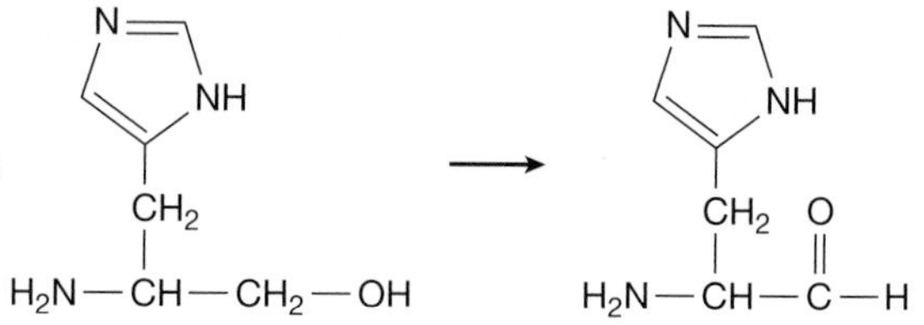

d) [imidazole ring: N=, NH]–CH_2–$CH(NH_2)$–C(=O)–H ⟶ [imidazole ring: N=, NH]–CH_2–$CH(NH_2)$–C(=O)–OH

$$H_2N-CH-C(=O)-H \longrightarrow H_2N-CH-C(=O)-OH$$

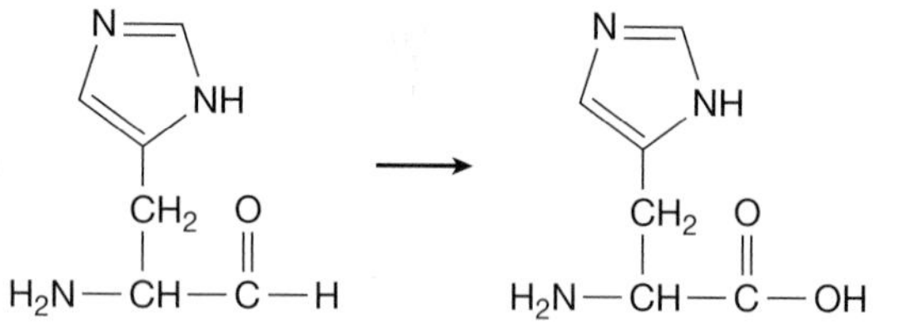

e) $$HO-C(=O)-CH_2-C(=O)-C(=O)-OH \longrightarrow HO-C(=O)-CH_2-CH(OH)-C(=O)-OH$$

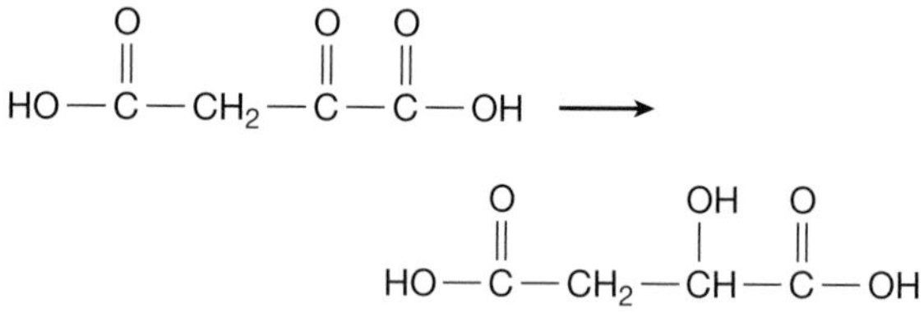

10.84 Which of the redox coenzymes is most likely to be involved in each of the reactions in Problem 10.83?

10.85 *The following molecule contains three functional groups, but only two of the functional groups can be oxidized:

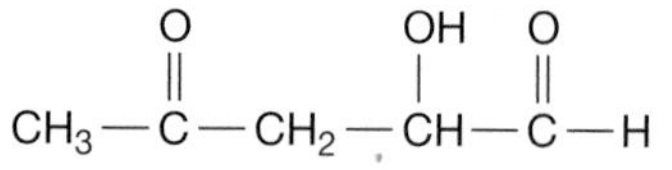

$$CH_3-C(=O)-CH_2-CH(OH)-C(=O)-H$$

a) Draw the structure of the product that will be formed if the alcohol group is oxidized.
b) Draw the structure of the product that will be formed if the aldehyde group is oxidized.
c) Draw the structure of the product that will be formed if both groups are oxidized.

10.86 *The molecule in Problem 10.85 contains two functional groups that can be reduced.

a) Draw the structure of the product that will be formed if the ketone group is reduced.
b) Draw the structure of the product that will be formed if the aldehyde group is reduced.
c) Draw the structure of the product that will be formed if both groups are reduced.

10.87 Which of the redox coenzymes is most likely to be involved in each of the following types of reactions?

a) the conversion of an alcohol into a ketone
b) the conversion of an alkene into an alkane
c) the conversion of a thiol into a disulfide
d) the conversion of an aldehyde into a carboxylic acid

10.88 *Butanal can react with oxygen to form butanoic acid. The (unbalanced) reaction is

$$\text{butanal} + O_2 \rightarrow \text{butanoic acid}$$

a) Draw the structures of the two organic compounds in this reaction.
b) Write the molecular formulas of these two compounds.
c) Using the molecular formulas you wrote in part b, write a balanced chemical equation for this reaction.
d) If you oxidize 10.0 g of butanal, how many grams of butanoic acid will you form?

10.89 *If you have 13.5 g of cyclopentanol, how many moles do you have?

10.90 *If you need to make 75 mL of a 0.50 M solution of acetic acid, how many grams of acetic acid will you need?

10.91 A student is asked to draw the structure of the product that is formed when ethanol is oxidized. The student writes the reaction shown here. Explain why this answer is not reasonable, and draw the actual product of this oxidation.

$$CH_3{-}CH_2{-}OH \rightarrow CH_2{=}CH{-}OH$$

Ethanol **Oxidation product?**

10.92 A student is asked to write the structure of the product that is formed when benzaldehyde is reduced. The student writes the reaction shown here. Explain why this answer is not reasonable, and draw the actual product of this reduction.

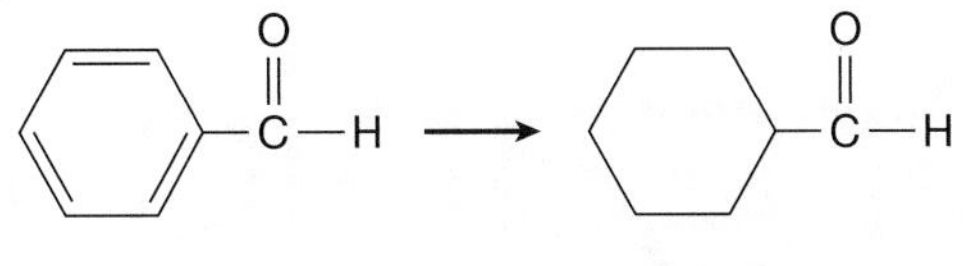

$$C_6H_5{-}\overset{\overset{\displaystyle O}{\|}}{C}{-}H \longrightarrow C_6H_{11}{-}\overset{\overset{\displaystyle O}{\|}}{C}{-}H$$

Benzaldehyde **Reduction product?**

10.93 *Isoleucine is one of the components of proteins. It can be burned to obtain energy by a metabolic pathway that involves a sequence of nine reactions. Part of this pathway involves the conversion shown here, using the sequence of three reactions described in Section 10.7. Draw the structures of each of the compounds that are formed during this sequence of reactions.

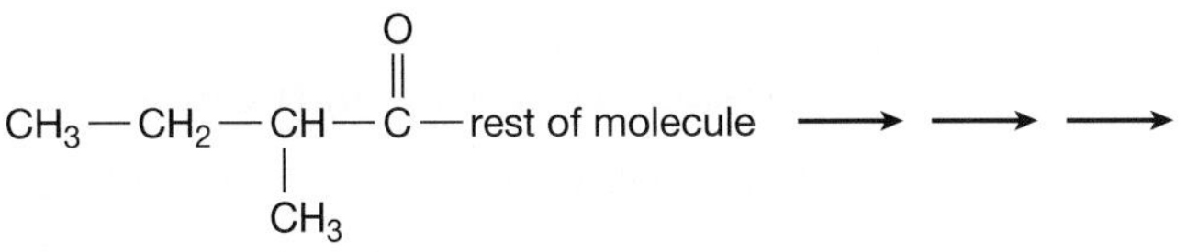

$$CH_3{-}CH_2{-}\underset{\underset{\displaystyle CH_3}{|}}{CH}{-}\overset{\overset{\displaystyle O}{\|}}{C}{-}\text{rest of molecule} \longrightarrow \longrightarrow \longrightarrow$$

α-Methylbutyryl-coenzyme A

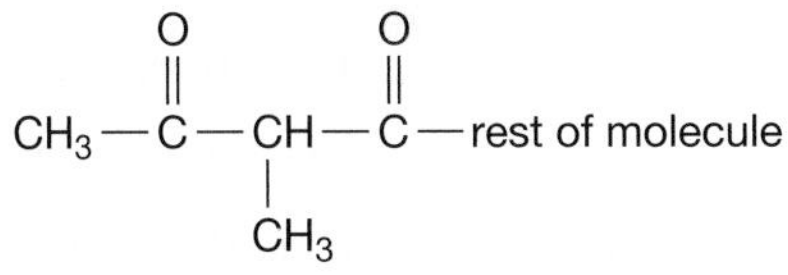

$$CH_3{-}\overset{\overset{\displaystyle O}{\|}}{C}{-}\underset{\underset{\displaystyle CH_3}{|}}{CH}{-}\overset{\overset{\displaystyle O}{\|}}{C}{-}\text{rest of molecule}$$

α-Methylacetoacetyl-coenzyme A

10.94 Two of the reactions in Problem 10.93 involve redox coenzymes. Which two reactions are they, and which redox coenzyme is involved in each reaction?

11

Organic Acids and Bases

Joshua has had high blood pressure for a number of years. At Joshua's last checkup, his doctor orders tests to measure the amount of creatinine in Joshua's blood and urine. Creatinine is a compound that forms whenever muscles break down creatine, a chemical that helps supply energy for muscle contractions. Muscles release creatinine into the blood, and the kidneys eliminate it by transferring it to the urine. Healthy kidneys remove creatinine rapidly, so the relative concentrations of creatinine in blood and urine are a good indicator of kidney health.

Creatinine, like many molecules that contain nitrogen, is a base, while creatine contains both acidic and basic functional groups. Whenever our bodies break down nutrients, we make a variety of acidic and basic products, including lactic acid, citric acid, and ammonia. As we have seen, our blood, lungs, and kidneys work together to neutralize these compounds and maintain our blood pH at a normal level.

The lab results show that Joshua's blood contains an elevated concentration of creatinine, while the concentration of creatinine in his urine is slightly lower than normal. Based on these results and on other tests, the doctor tells Joshua that his high blood pressure is starting to damage his kidneys. Joshua is surprised and notes that he has not noticed any problems urinating or any discomfort, but the doctor tells him that chronic kidney damage often does not produce any symptoms until it becomes a life-threatening condition. Joshua decides to make a serious commitment to lower his blood pressure by changing his diet and exercising, reducing the stress on his kidneys and the other negative effects of high blood pressure.

OUTLINE

LABORATORY REQUISITION—CHEMISTRY

☐ Sodium	NA	☐ Fructosamine	FRU/ALB
☐ Potassium	K	☐ PSA	PSA
☑ Creatinine	CREAT	☐ Chloride	CL
☐ BUN	BUN	☐ Calcium	CA
☐ Glucose–fasting	GLUCF	☐ Phosphorus	PHOS
☐ Glucose–random	GLUCR	☐ Phenylalanine	PKU
☐ Hemoglobin A1C	HGBA1C	☐ Uric Acid	URIC

☐ Total Bilirubin	BILIT	☐ TSH	TSH	☐ Amylase	AMYL
☐ Neonate T. Bilirubin	BILITN	☐ Alk Phos	ALKP	☐ Cholesterol	CHOL
☐ Serum Protein Elect.	PEP	☐ SGOT (AST)	AST	☐ HDL	HDL
☐ Ferritin	FERR	☐ Albumin	ALB	☐ LDL–fasting	LDL
☐ Iron/TIBC	IRON/TIBC	☐ SGPT (ALT)	ALT	☐ Triglycerides–fasting	TRIG
☐ Hgb Electrophoresis	HGB EP	☐ CPK (CK)	CK		
☐ T4/FTI	T4S	☐ CKMB	CKMB		

Blood pressure is an important indicator of health. Many medications affect blood pressure, so patients taking these medications must monitor their blood pressure regularly.

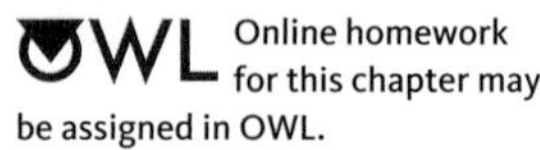
Online homework for this chapter may be assigned in OWL.

Humans and other living organisms are exposed to a range of organic acids and bases. Much of the food we eat is mildly acidic, containing organic compounds such as citric acid, lactic acid, and acetic acid. In addition, whenever our bodies burn nutrients to obtain energy, we produce organic acids. We also produce organic bases when we burn proteins, and organic bases such as dopamine and serotonin have profound effects on our bodies.

In this chapter, we will explore the world of organic acids and bases. Much of the behavior of these compounds is simply a specific application of the general principles of acid–base chemistry that we encountered in Chapter 7, but we will also encounter some new reactions and we will examine the role of nitrogen in organic molecules. As you study this chapter, you will find it useful to review the material in Chapter 7.

OBJECTIVES: *Write chemical equations for the reactions of organic acids with water and with bases, and relate the physical properties of the acids to those of their salts.*

11.1 Reactions of Organic Acids

In Chapter 10, you learned that aldehydes can be oxidized to form carboxylic acids. Carboxylic acids are the most common and important organic acids. In this section, we will look at the behavior of carboxylic acids. We will also examine two other classes of organic acids, phenols and thiols.

Carboxylic Acids Ionize When They Dissolve in Water

Recall from Chapter 7 that acids can donate a hydrogen ion to bases. In a carboxylic acid, the hydrogen that is bonded to oxygen can be transferred to a base. When a carboxylic acid dissolves in water, this hydrogen can move from the acid to a water molecule. This reaction is generally called the ionization (or dissociation) of an acid. The ionization of acetic acid is a typical example.

H^+ moves from CH_3CO_2H to H_2O.

$$CH_3{-}CO_2H + H_2O \rightleftharpoons CH_3{-}CO_2^- + H_3O^+$$

Acetic acid **Acetate ion**

The products of this reaction are a hydronium ion (H_3O^+) and the conjugate base of acetic acid ($CH_3{-}CO_2^-$), which is called the *acetate* ion. We use a double arrow when we write this ionization reaction, because carboxylic acids are weak acids. For instance, only about 1% of the molecules are ionized in a 1% solution of acetic acid.

Carboxylic Acids React with Bases

When acetic acid reacts with water, the water molecule functions as a base, accepting the hydrogen ion from acetic acid. Acetic acid can react with other bases as well. The reaction of acetic acid with hydroxide ion is shown here. Hydroxide ion is a strong base, so we write this equation with a single arrow to show that the reaction proceeds until one of the reactants runs out.

$$CH_3{-}CO_2H + OH^- \longrightarrow CH_3{-}CO_2^- + H_2O$$

Sample Problem 11.1

Writing equations for acid–base reactions of carboxylic acids

Using structural formulas, write a balanced equation for the reaction of propanoic acid with hydroxide ion.

SOLUTION

Propanoic acid is a three-carbon carboxylic acid and has the following structure:

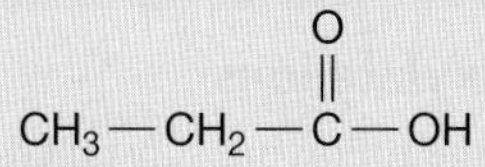

$$CH_3-CH_2-\overset{\displaystyle O}{\overset{\|}{C}}-OH$$

When a carboxylic acid reacts with a base, a hydrogen ion moves from the acid functional group to the base.

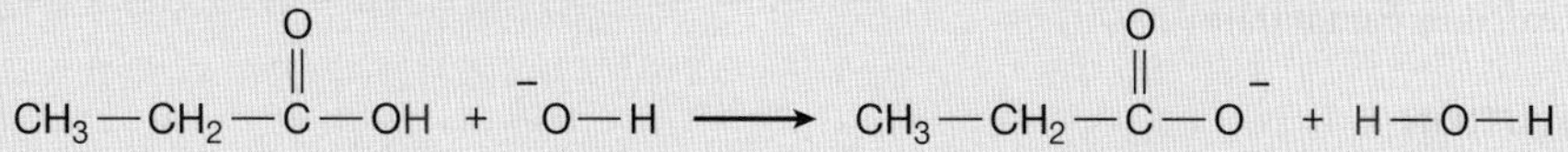

$$CH_3-CH_2-\overset{\displaystyle O}{\overset{\|}{C}}-OH + {}^{-}O-H \longrightarrow CH_3-CH_2-\overset{\displaystyle O}{\overset{\|}{C}}-O^{-} + H-O-H$$

TRY IT YOURSELF: *Using structural formulas, write the balanced equation for the ionization of butanoic acid in water.*

For additional practice, try Core Problems 11.1 and 11.2.

TABLE 11.1 The Structures of Some Carboxylic Acids and Their Conjugate Bases

Acid	Name of Acid	Conjugate Base	Name of Conjugate Base
$H-\overset{\displaystyle O}{\overset{\|}{C}}-OH$	Formic acid (methanoic acid)	$H-\overset{\displaystyle O}{\overset{\|}{C}}-O^{-}$	Form*ate* ion (methano*ate* ion)
$CH_3-\overset{\displaystyle O}{\overset{\|}{C}}-OH$	Acetic acid (ethanoic acid)	$CH_3-\overset{\displaystyle O}{\overset{\|}{C}}-O^{-}$	Acet*ate* ion (ethano*ate* ion)
$CH_3-CH_2-CH_2-\overset{\displaystyle O}{\overset{\|}{C}}-OH$	Butanoic acid	$CH_3-CH_2-CH_2-\overset{\displaystyle O}{\overset{\|}{C}}-O^{-}$	Butano*ate* ion
$CH_3-(CH_2)_6-\overset{\displaystyle O}{\overset{\|}{C}}-OH$	Octanoic acid	$CH_3-(CH_2)_6-\overset{\displaystyle O}{\overset{\|}{C}}-O^{-}$	Octano*ate* ion

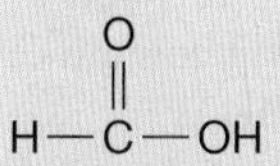

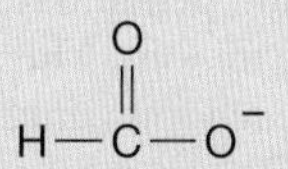

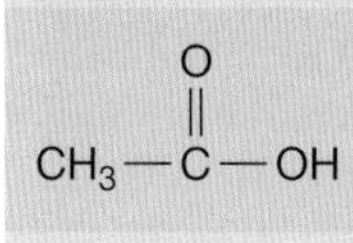

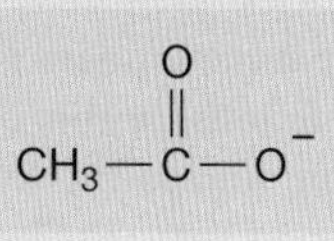

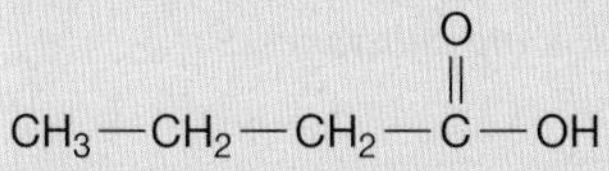

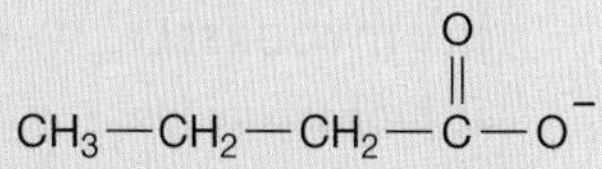

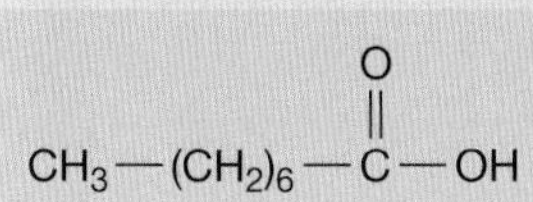

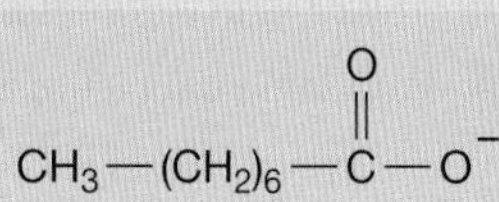

Carboxylate Ions Can Form Ionic Compounds

Whenever a carboxylic acid reacts with a base, one of the products is the conjugate base of the original acid, which is called a **carboxylate ion**. The names of carboxylate ions are derived from the names of the original acids. To name a carboxylate ion, we remove *-ic acid* from the name of the acid and add the suffix *-ate*. This system is used for both trivial and IUPAC names. Table 11.1 lists some common examples.

Like any negative ion, carboxylate ions can pair up with positive ions to form ionic compounds called *carboxylate salts*. The rule of charge balance controls the chemical formulas of these salts, as it does for all other ionic compounds. For example, calcium ions and acetate ions can form an ionic compound. Since the charge on a calcium ion is +2, we need two acetate ions to satisfy the rule of charge balance, so the chemical for-

• The term *salt* is commonly used for any ionic compound that does not contain OH^- ion.

mula of this compound is $Ca(CH_3CO_2)_2$. The organic ions in such salts are often written as if they were molecular formulas, listing the numbers of carbon, hydrogen, and oxygen atoms without any structural information, so the formula of calcium acetate can be written as $Ca(C_2H_3O_2)_2$ and the formula of sodium butanoate can be written as $NaC_4H_7O_2$ (rather than $NaCH_3CH_2CH_2CO_2$).

Sample Problem 11.2

Writing structures of carboxylate ions

Write the molecular formulas of the following substances:

a) pentanoate ion

b) potassium pentanoate

c) calcium pentanoate

SOLUTION

a) Pentanoate ion is the conjugate base of pentanoic acid. We can draw the structure of pentanoate ion by removing H^+ from the functional group of pentanoic acid.

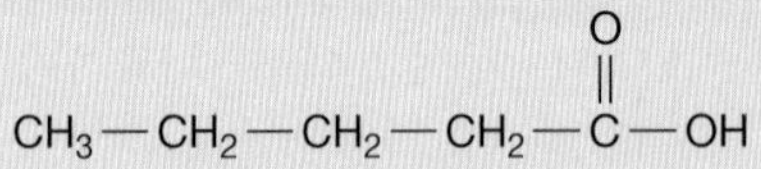

$$CH_3-CH_2-CH_2-CH_2-\overset{\overset{\displaystyle O}{\|}}{C}-OH \qquad CH_3-CH_2-CH_2-CH_2-\overset{\overset{\displaystyle O}{\|}}{C}-O^-$$

Pentanoic acid 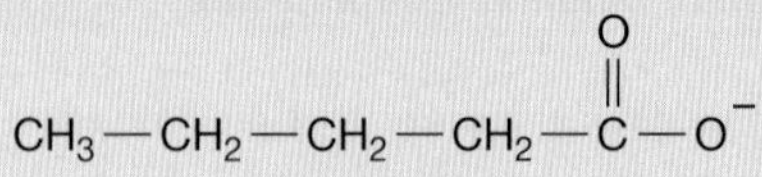 **Pentanoate ion**

To write the molecular formula, we need to count the atoms in pentanoate ion. There are five carbon atoms, nine hydrogen atoms, and two oxygen atoms, so the molecular formula of pentanoate ion is $C_5H_9O_2^-$. (Don't forget the charge.)

b) Potassium pentanoate is an ionic compound that contains potassium ions (K^+) and pentanoate ions. The rule of charge balance tells us that the compound will contain one of each ion (since the total charge must add up to zero), so the formula is $KC_5H_9O_2$.

c) Calcium pentanoate is an ionic compound that contains calcium ions (Ca^{2+}) and pentanoate ions. In this case, we need two pentanoate ions to balance the charge on one calcium ion, so the formula is $Ca(C_5H_9O_2)_2$.

TRY IT YOURSELF: *Write the molecular formulas of the following substances:*

a) propanoate ion

b) magnesium propanoate

For additional practice, try Core Problems 11.3 through 11.6.

Health Note: Sodium benzoate and potassium benzoate are widely used preservatives in soft drinks, salad dressings, fruit juices, and other products that are mildly acidic.

The carboxylate functional group is an ion, so it is attracted to water. As a result, many carboxylate salts dissolve well in water. However, the solubility depends strongly on the positive ion. In this book, we focus on sodium and potassium salts, because they have high solubilities in water. Most sodium and potassium salts are more soluble than the corresponding acids. For example, the solubility of sodium benzoate is more than 100 times larger than the solubility of the corresponding acid, benzoic acid.

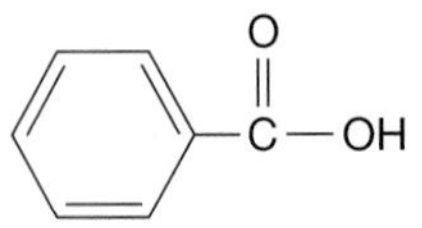

$$C_6H_5-\overset{\overset{\displaystyle O}{\|}}{C}-OH \qquad C_6H_5-\overset{\overset{\displaystyle O}{\|}}{C}-O^-\ Na^+$$

Benzoic acid (a carboxylic acid)
Solubility in water = 3.4 g/L

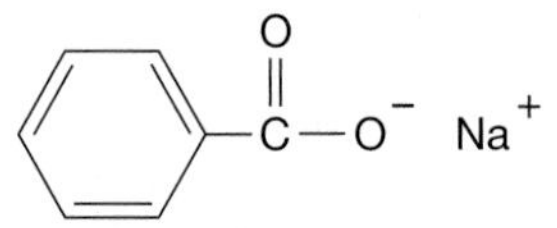

Sodium benzoate (a carboxylate salt)
Solubility in water = 550 g/L

For sodium and potassium salts, the size of the hydrocarbon chain does not have a dramatic effect on the solubility. Even sodium and potassium salts of very large carboxylic acids dissolve reasonably well in water. However, most other salts of long-chain carboxylic acids are insoluble in water.

Sample Problem 11.3

Predicting solubilities of carboxylate salts

Lauric acid has the following structure:

$$CH_3-CH_2-CH_2-CH_2-CH_2-CH_2-CH_2-CH_2-CH_2-CH_2-CH_2-\overset{\overset{\displaystyle O}{\|}}{C}-OH$$

Which of the following would you expect to be soluble and which would likely be insoluble in water?

a) lauric acid
b) potassium laurate
c) magnesium laurate

SOLUTION

a) Lauric acid is insoluble in water. Carboxylic acids with large hydrophobic regions do not dissolve to any significant extent in water.
b) Potassium laurate is soluble in water. This compound is a salt made from potassium ion and laurate ion (the conjugate base of lauric acid). Potassium salts of long-chain carboxylic acids dissolve well in water.
c) Magnesium laurate is insoluble in water. Salts containing a large carboxylate ion and a metal ion other than Na^+ or K^+ do not dissolve in water.

TRY IT YOURSELF: *Which of the following would you expect to be soluble and which would likely be insoluble in water?*

a) calcium laurate
b) sodium laurate

For additional practice, try Core Problems 11.9 and 11.10.

Phenols and Thiols Are Acidic

Carboxylic acids are by far the most important class of organic acids, but phenols and thiols are also acidic. In both phenols and thiols, only the hydrogen atom that is part of the functional group can be removed by a base. Both types of compounds are much weaker than carboxylic acids. Figure 11.1 shows the reactions of phenols and thiols with water and with hydroxide ion.

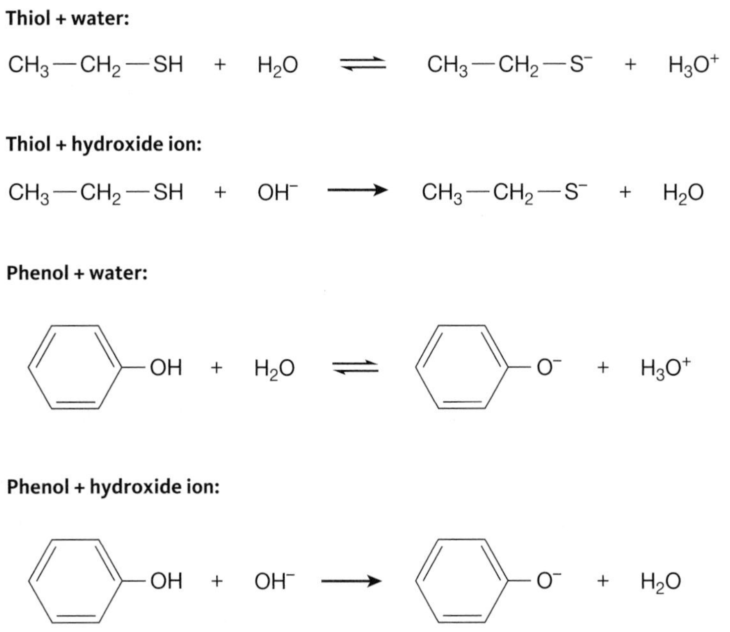

Thiol + water:

$$CH_3-CH_2-SH + H_2O \rightleftharpoons CH_3-CH_2-S^- + H_3O^+$$

Thiol + hydroxide ion:

$$CH_3-CH_2-SH + OH^- \longrightarrow CH_3-CH_2-S^- + H_2O$$

Phenol + water:

$$C_6H_5-OH + H_2O \rightleftharpoons C_6H_5-O^- + H_3O^+$$

Phenol + hydroxide ion:

$$C_6H_5-OH + OH^- \longrightarrow C_6H_5-O^- + H_2O$$

FIGURE 11.1 Reactions of thiols and phenols.

Sample Problem 11.4

Writing equations for acid–base reactions of phenols and thiols

Using condensed structural formulas, write a balanced equation for the ionization of *ortho*-cresol in water.

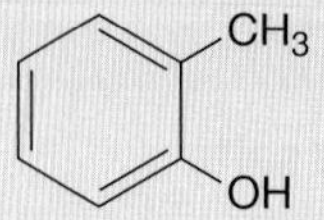

CH$_3$ / OH — ***Ortho*-cresol**

SOLUTION

This compound is a phenol, so the hydrogen in the hydroxyl group is acidic and can be transferred to a water molecule. Since phenols are weak acids, we write a double arrow.

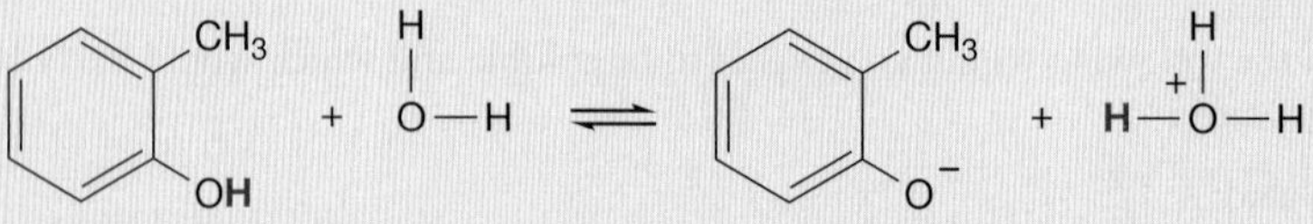

$$\text{(ortho-cresol, OH)} + H{-}O{-}H \rightleftharpoons \text{(ortho-cresolate, } O^-) + H{-}\overset{+}{O}(H){-}H$$

TRY IT YOURSELF: *Methanethiol has the structural formula $CH_3{-}SH$. Using condensed structural formulas, write the balanced equation for the reaction of methanethiol with hydroxide ions.*

For additional practice, try Core Problems 11.11 and 11.12.

Sample Problem 11.5

Ranking solutions of organic acids by pH

Rank the following solutions from lowest pH to highest pH:
0.02 M phenol   0.02 M acetic acid   0.02 M ethanol

SOLUTION

Ethanol is not an acid (alcohols are not acidic), so the 0.02 M ethanol is a neutral solution and has a pH of 7. Phenol and acetic acid are acidic, so their solutions have pH values below 7. Acetic acid is a carboxylic acid, so it is a stronger acid than phenol. Stronger acids have a lower pH than weaker ones (if the concentrations are equal), so the acetic acid solution has the lowest pH. The correct order is

0.02 M acetic acid   0.02 M phenol   0.02 Methanol

(lowest pH = strongest acid) ⟶ *(highest pH = weakest acid)*

TRY IT YOURSELF: *You have 0.01 M solutions of the following compounds. Rank them from lowest pH to highest pH.*

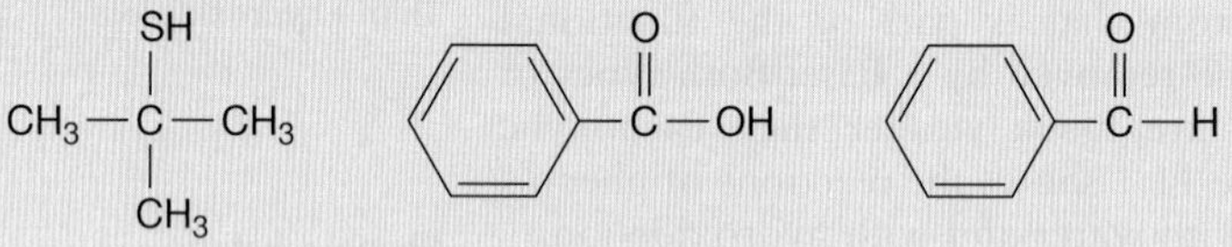

A: $CH_3{-}C(SH)(CH_3){-}CH_3$

B: $C_6H_5{-}C(=O){-}OH$

C: $C_6H_5{-}C(=O){-}H$

CORE PROBLEMS

All Core Problems are paired and the answers to the blue odd-numbered problems appear in the back of the book.

11.1 Using structural formulas, write chemical equations for the following reactions:
a) the ionization reaction of pentanoic acid in water
b) the reaction of pentanoic acid with hydroxide ion

11.2 Using structural formulas, write chemical equations for the following reactions:
a) the ionization reaction of propanoic acid in water
b) the reaction of propanoic acid with hydroxide ion

11.3 Draw structural formulas for the following:
a) butanoate ion   b) potassium butanoate

continued

11.4 Draw structural formulas for the following:
a) hexanoate ion b) sodium hexanoate

11.5 Write the molecular formula of calcium butanoate.

11.6 Write the molecular formula of magnesium heptanoate.

11.7 Name the following substances:

a) $CH_3-C(=O)-O^-$

b) $Mg^{2+}\left(CH_3-C(=O)-O^-\right)_2$

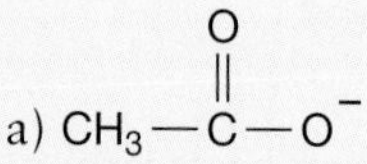

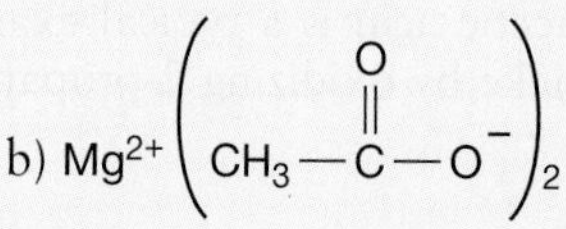

11.8 Name the following substances:

a) $CH_3-CH_2-CH_2-CH_2-CH_2-CH_2-CH_2-C(=O)-O^-$

b) $Al^{3+}\left(CH_3-CH_2-CH_2-CH_2-CH_2-CH_2-CH_2-C(=O)-O^-\right)_3$

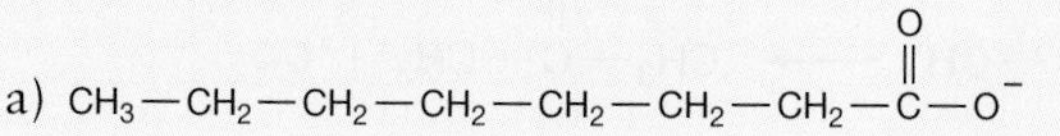

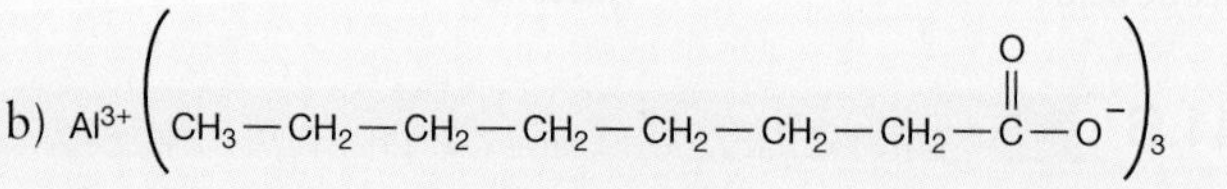

11.9 Which of the following compounds should have the higher solubility in water? Explain your reasoning.

$CH_3-(CH_2)_4-C(=O)-OH$ $CH_3-(CH_2)_4-C(=O)-O^-\ Na^+$

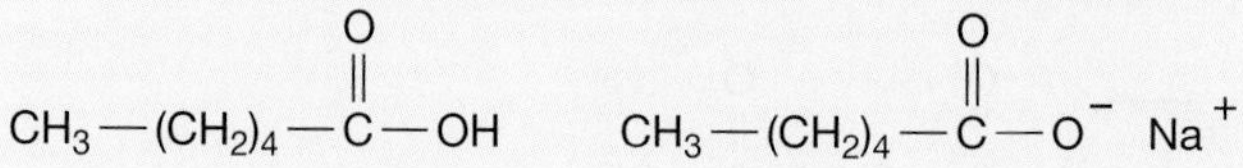

Hexanoic acid **Sodium hexanoate**

11.10 Which of the following compounds should have the higher solubility in water? Explain your reasoning.

$CH_3-(CH_2)_6-C(=O)-O^-\ K^+$ $CH_3-(CH_2)_6-C(=O)-OH$

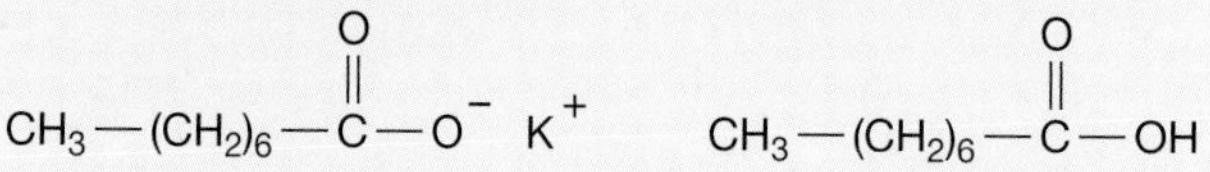

Potassium octanoate **Octanoic acid**

11.11 Using structural formulas, write chemical equations for the following reactions:
a) the ionization reaction of $CH_3–CH_2–CH_2–SH$ in water:
b) the reaction of the following compound with hydroxide ion:

$CH_3-C_6H_4-OH$ (para-substituted benzene ring)

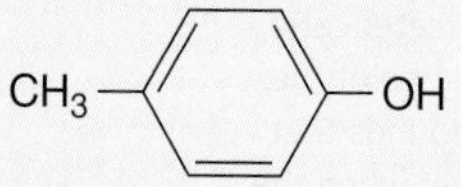

11.12 Using structural formulas, write chemical equations for the following reactions:
a) the ionization reaction of the following compound in water:

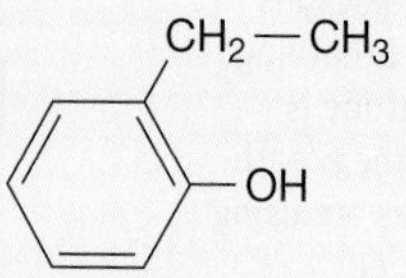

(benzene ring bearing CH_2-CH_3 and, on the adjacent carbon, OH)

b) the reaction of the following compound with hydroxide ion:

(cyclopentane ring bearing SH)

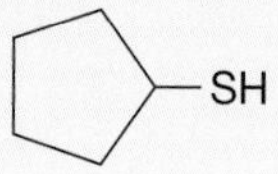

11.2 Decarboxylation Reactions

OBJECTIVES: *Draw the products of decarboxylation reactions, and identify coenzymes that are required in decarboxylation reactions.*

When our bodies burn nutrients to obtain energy, the final products are carbon dioxide and water. As you have seen, though, our bodies carry out this combustion in a series of steps, each one making a small change to the organic molecule. If we examine many of these metabolic pathways in detail, we find that carboxylic acids play a prominent role in all of them. Any nutrient that we burn will be converted to a carboxylic acid sometime during the sequence of reactions that makes up the entire metabolic pathway. For example, the last five compounds formed during lactic acid fermentation (Figure 10.1) contain a carboxylic acid group. In this section, we will explore the reasons for the prominence of carboxylic acids in metabolic pathways, and we will look at the fate of these acids.

Carboxylic Acids Can Lose Carbon Dioxide

The carboxylic acid functional group cannot normally be oxidized or reduced by living organisms. However, many carboxylic acids can undergo a **decarboxylation reaction**, in which the acid breaks apart into a molecule of CO_2 and a smaller organic molecule that no longer contains the carboxylic acid group.

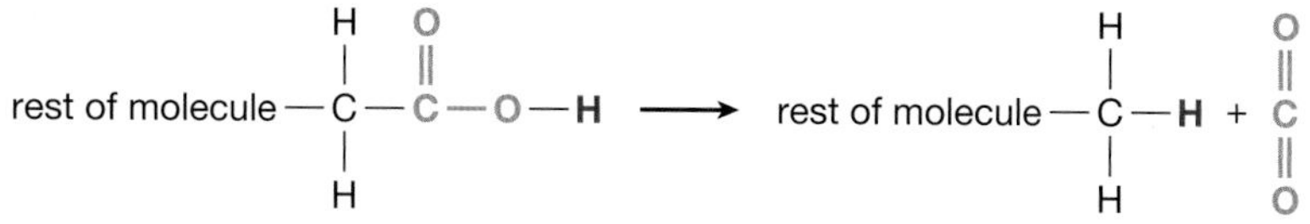

$$\text{rest of molecule}-CH_2-C(=O)-O-\mathbf{H} \longrightarrow \text{rest of molecule}-CH_2-\mathbf{H} + O=C=O$$

• Alpha and beta are the first two letters of the Greek alphabet, equivalent to the letters *a* and *b* in the English alphabet.

In practice, a decarboxylation reaction will only occur if there is another functional group (usually a carbonyl group) on one of the two carbons closest to the acid group. These nearby carbon atoms are called the *alpha* (α) and *beta* (β) carbon atoms.

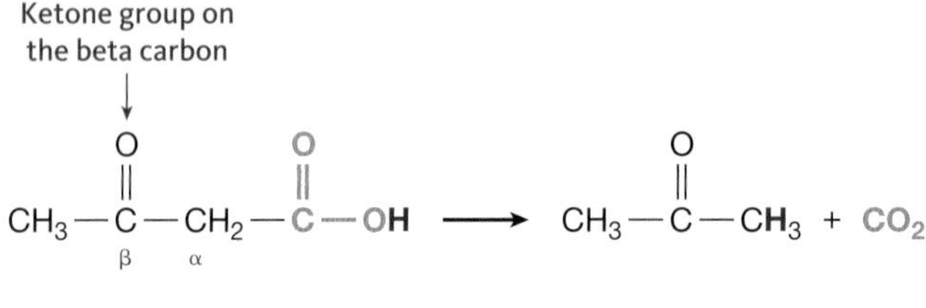

Carboxylic acids that contain a ketone group on the β-carbon can be decarboxylated by simply heating them. The decarboxylation of acetoacetic acid is a typical example. The product is acetone, a compound that we can also make by oxidizing 2-propanol.

Health Note: Acetoacetic acid and acetone are two of the ketone bodies, compounds that are formed by the liver when the body must rely primarily on fats and proteins for energy. Many tissues can burn acetoacetic acid to obtain energy, but most of the acetone is excreted or escapes from the lungs during breathing. The fruity smell of acetone is readily detectable on the breath of people whose bodies are using fats as their primary fuel, including uncontrolled diabetics.

Ketone group on the beta carbon

$$CH_3-\overset{\overset{O}{\|}}{\underset{\beta}{C}}-\underset{\alpha}{CH_2}-\overset{\overset{O}{\|}}{C}-OH \longrightarrow CH_3-\overset{\overset{O}{\|}}{C}-CH_3 + CO_2$$

Acetoacetic acid **Acetone**

Sample Problem 11.6

Drawing the product of a decarboxylation reaction

Draw the structure of the organic product that will be formed when the following compound is decarboxylated:

$$C_6H_5-\overset{\overset{O}{\|}}{C}-CH_2-\overset{\overset{O}{\|}}{C}-OH$$

SOLUTION

First, we must find the carboxylic acid group in our molecule:

$$C_6H_5-\overset{\overset{O}{\|}}{C}-CH_2-\boxed{\overset{\overset{O}{\|}}{C}-OH}$$

The carboxylic acid group

To draw the product of the reaction, we remove this group. The carbon atom and the two oxygen atoms form CO_2. The hydrogen becomes bonded to the end carbon of the organic molecule, so the $-CH_2$ group becomes $-CH_3$. The structure of our organic product is

$$C_6H_5-\overset{\overset{O}{\|}}{C}-CH_3$$

The reaction also produces a molecule of CO_2. If we wanted to write a balanced equation for the reaction, we would need to include the carbon dioxide in our equation.

TRY IT YOURSELF: *Draw the structure of the organic product that will be formed when the following compound is decarboxylated:*

$$CH_3-\overset{\overset{O}{\|}}{C}-\underset{\underset{CH_3}{|}}{CH}-\overset{\overset{O}{\|}}{C}-OH$$

For additional practice, try Core Problems 11.17 and 11.18.

Decarboxylation Is Often Combined with Oxidation in Biological Reactions

Most decarboxylation reactions that occur in our bodies are more complex than the ones we have seen so far. Our bodies usually combine decarboxylation with an oxidation in a reaction called **oxidative decarboxylation.** In this reaction, one of the reactants is a carboxylic acid that also has a carbonyl group on the α-carbon atom.

$$\text{rest of molecule}-\overset{\overset{\large O}{\|}}{C}-\overset{\overset{\large O}{\|}}{C}-OH$$

An alpha-keto carboxylic acid

The other reactants are a thiol and a molecule of NAD^+. The products of the reaction are carbon dioxide, NADH, H^+, and an organic compound called a **thioester** (pronounced "THIGH-oh-ES-ter"). The general scheme for the oxidative decarboxylation reaction is shown here:

$$\text{α-Keto carboxylic acid} + \text{HS-R (Thiol)} + NAD^+ \xrightarrow{\text{Oxidative decarboxylation}} R-\overset{\overset{\large O}{\|}}{C}-S-R' + CO_2 + NADH + H^+$$

α-Keto carboxylic acid **Thiol**

A thioester

For example, when our bodies break down sugars to obtain energy, we form a compound called pyruvic acid. Pyruvic acid then reacts with a thiol called *coenzyme A* in an oxidative decarboxylation. Coenzyme A is a rather complex molecule and is usually abbreviated HS–CoA to emphasize the thiol group. The chemical equation for this reaction is

$$CH_3-\overset{\overset{\large O}{\|}}{C}-\overset{\overset{\large O}{\|}}{C}-OH + HS-CoA + NAD^+ \longrightarrow CH_3-\overset{\overset{\large O}{\|}}{C}-S-CoA + CO_2 + NADH + H^+$$

Pyruvic acid **Coenzyme A**

Acetyl-coenzyme A (a thioester)

It can be helpful to think of an oxidative decarboxylation as occurring in two steps, a decarboxylation followed by an oxidation. In the decarboxylation step, the acid loses its carboxylic acid group and becomes an aldehyde. For pyruvic acid, the products of this step are CO_2 and acetaldehyde.

$$CH_3-\overset{\overset{\large O}{\|}}{C}-\overset{\overset{\large O}{\|}}{C}-OH \longrightarrow CH_3-\overset{\overset{\large O}{\|}}{C}-H + CO_2$$

Pyruvic acid **Acetaldehyde**

In the second step, the aldehyde combines with the thiol to form a thioester. Each of the reactants loses a hydrogen atom, so this step is an oxidation. As in most biological oxidations, the hydrogen atoms are transferred to NAD^+.

$$CH_3-\overset{\overset{\large O}{\|}}{C}-H + H-S-CoA + NAD^+ \longrightarrow CH_3-\overset{\overset{\large O}{\|}}{C}-S-CoA + NADH + H^+$$

Acetaldehyde **Coenzyme A** **Acetyl-coenzyme A** (a thioester)

Table 11.2 summarizes the differences between a simple decarboxylation and an oxidative decarboxylation.

TABLE 11.2 A Comparison of the Two Types of Decarboxylation Reactions

Decarboxylation	Oxidative Decarboxylation
The reaction is not an oxidation (no NAD^+ is required).	The reaction requires NAD^+ to remove hydrogen atoms.
No thiol is required.	The reaction requires a thiol (usually coenzyme A).
The carboxylic acid usually has a ketone group on the β-carbon.	The carboxylic acid has a ketone group on the α-carbon.
The product is a ketone.	The product is a thioester.

Sample Problem 11.7

Drawing the product of an oxidative decarboxylation

α-Ketoglutaric acid forms when our bodies burn nutrients to obtain energy. This compound undergoes oxidative decarboxylation, using coenzyme A as the thiol. Draw the structure of the thioester that is formed in this reaction.

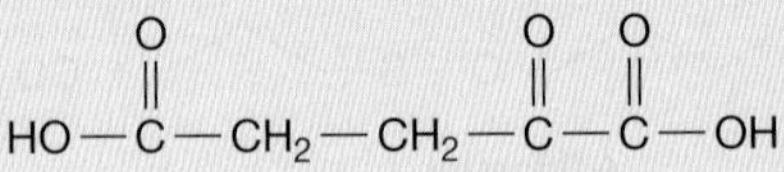

$$HO-\overset{\overset{O}{\|}}{C}-CH_2-CH_2-\overset{\overset{O}{\|}}{C}-\overset{\overset{O}{\|}}{C}-OH$$

α-Ketoglutaric acid

SOLUTION

We can work out the product of this reaction in two steps. The first step is the decarboxylation, in which the molecule loses a carboxylic acid group in the form of CO_2. This compound has two carboxylic acid groups (one at each end), so we must decide which of these will come off. Since oxidative decarboxylation requires a ketone group on the α-carbon atom, only the group on the right will be removed in the reaction.

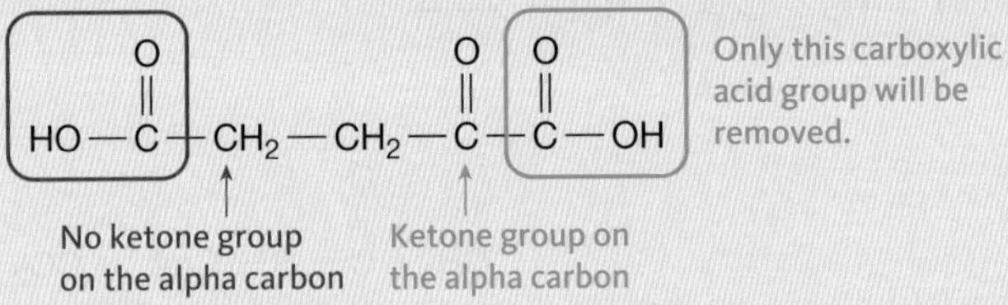

$$HO-\overset{\overset{O}{\|}}{C}-CH_2-CH_2-\overset{\overset{O}{\|}}{C}-\overset{\overset{O}{\|}}{C}-OH$$

Only this carboxylic acid group will be removed.

No ketone group on the alpha carbon

Ketone group on the alpha carbon

In the decarboxylation, we remove CO_2 and move the remaining hydrogen atom over to the next carbon, to form an aldehyde.

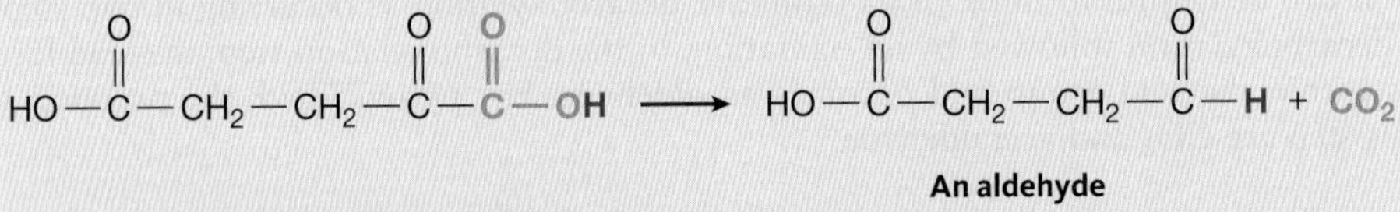

$$HO-\overset{\overset{O}{\|}}{C}-CH_2-CH_2-\overset{\overset{O}{\|}}{C}-\overset{\overset{O}{\|}}{C}-OH \longrightarrow HO-\overset{\overset{O}{\|}}{C}-CH_2-CH_2-\overset{\overset{O}{\|}}{C}-H + CO_2$$

An aldehyde

The second step is the oxidation. In this step, the aldehyde reacts with coenzyme A to form a thioester. We need to remove two hydrogen atoms and connect the remaining fragments to form the thioester.

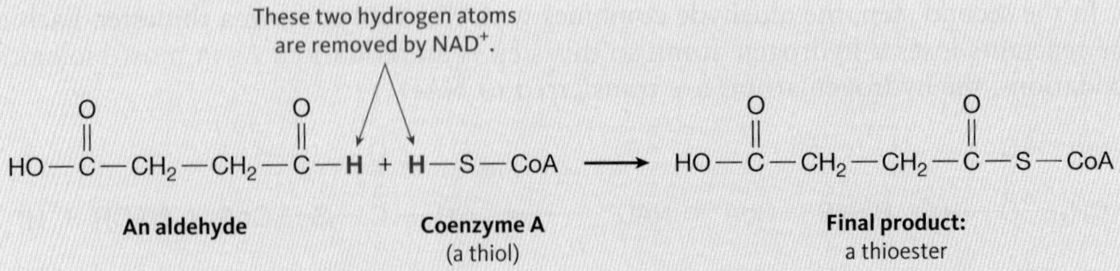

These two hydrogen atoms are removed by NAD^+.

$$HO-\overset{\overset{O}{\|}}{C}-CH_2-CH_2-\overset{\overset{O}{\|}}{C}-H + H-S-CoA \longrightarrow HO-\overset{\overset{O}{\|}}{C}-CH_2-CH_2-\overset{\overset{O}{\|}}{C}-S-CoA$$

An aldehyde — **Coenzyme A** (a thiol) — **Final product:** a thioester

TRY IT YOURSELF: *The following compound is formed when proteins are burned to produce energy. Draw the structure of the thioester that will be formed when*

continued

this compound undergoes oxidative decarboxylation, using coenzyme A as the thiol.

$CH_3-CH(CH_3)-CH_2-C(=O)-C(=O)-OH$ **α-Ketoisocaproic acid**

For additional practice, try Core Problems 11.19 and 11.20.

When our bodies burn nutrients to obtain energy, the final products are carbon dioxide and water. The vast majority of the CO_2 is formed by the two types of decarboxylation reactions we have explored in this section. Together with oxidation and hydration, decarboxylation plays a key role in allowing us, and all other higher organisms, to obtain energy from the organic compounds in our food.

CORE PROBLEMS

11.13 What small molecule is formed in all decarboxylation reactions?

11.14 In any decarboxylation reaction, the reactant must have a specific functional group. What is that functional group?

11.15 a) Identify the α- and β-carbon atoms in the following carboxylic acid:

(cyclohexane ring)$-C(=O)-OH$

b) Can this compound be decarboxylated? Explain how you can tell.

11.16 a) Identify the α- and β-carbon atoms in the following carboxylic acid:

$CH_3-CH_2-C(=O)-CH(CH_3)-C(=O)-OH$

b) Can this compound be decarboxylated? Explain how you can tell.

11.17 Draw the structures of the organic compounds that will be formed when each of the following molecules is decarboxylated:

a) $CH_3-CH_2-C(=O)-CH_2-C(=O)-OH$

b) (cyclopentanone ring with $-C(=O)-OH$ on the carbon adjacent to the ring C=O)

11.18 Draw the structures of the organic compounds that will be formed when each of the following molecules is decarboxylated:

a) $H-C(=O)-CH(CH_3)-C(=O)-OH$

b) $HO-C(=O)-$(cyclohexane ring)$-CH_2-CH_3$

11.19 Each of the following organic acids is formed during the breakdown of an amino acid. The next step in each of these metabolic pathways is an oxidative decarboxylation, using coenzyme A as the thiol. Draw the structures of the organic products of these reactions.

a) $CH_3-CH_2-CH(CH_3)-C(=O)-C(=O)-OH$

Formed when isoleucine is broken down

b) $HO-C(=O)-CH_2-CH_2-CH_2-C(=O)-C(=O)-OH$

Formed when lysine is broken down

11.20 Each of the following organic acids is formed during the breakdown of an amino acid. The next step in each of these metabolic pathways is an oxidative decarboxylation, using coenzyme A as the thiol. Draw the structures of the organic products of these reactions.

a) $CH_3-CH(CH_3)-C(=O)-C(=O)-OH$

Formed when valine is broken down

b) $CH_3-CH(CH_3)-CH_2-C(=O)-C(=O)-OH$

Formed when leucine is broken down

OBJECTIVES: Name and draw the structures of simple amines, and relate the structures of amines to their physical properties.

11.3 Amines

Our bodies contain a range of substances that can function as bases, including carboxylate ions and inorganic ions such as bicarbonate. However, the most important bases in biological chemistry are compounds that contain nitrogen. Nitrogen plays a key role in biological chemistry, being found in proteins, nucleic acids, and several vitamins. In this section, we will explore the chemistry of a class of compounds called amines, which are the simplest organic compounds that contain nitrogen.

Nitrogen Forms Three Covalent Bonds

Nitrogen is in Group 5A in the periodic table, so a nitrogen atom has five valence electrons. To satisfy the octet rule, nitrogen must gain three more electrons, and it normally does so by forming three covalent bonds. For example, if we attach a nitrogen atom to three hydrogen atoms, we make a molecule of ammonia.

Nitrogen can bond to three hydrogen atoms . . . → . . . to form a molecule of **ammonia**.

H· ·N̈· ·H + ·H (below) ⟶ H—N̈—H with H bonded below

Nitrogen can also form four covalent bonds. All substances in which nitrogen makes four bonds are positively charged ions, because the nitrogen atom must lose an electron to accommodate the extra bond. A familiar example is the ammonium ion, NH_4^+.

H—N⁺—H with H above and H below: **Ammonium ion**

If we replace one or more of the hydrogen atoms in ammonia with alkyl groups, we make an organic compound called an **amine**. Amines contain nitrogen directly bonded to at least one carbon atom. Chemists classify amines as primary, secondary, or tertiary based on the number of carbon atoms that are bonded to the nitrogen, as shown in Table 11.3.

TABLE 11.3 The Classes of Amines

Class	Atoms Bonded to Nitrogen	General Structure	Example
Ammonia (not an organic compound)	3 hydrogen atoms	H—N̈—H, with H on N	H—N—H, with H on N
Primary amine	**1 carbon atom** + 2 hydrogen atoms	C—N̈—H, with H on N	CH_2—CH_2—N—H, with H on N
Secondary amine	**2 carbon atoms** + 1 hydrogen atom	C—N̈—C, with H on N	CH_3—CH_2—N—CH_3, with H on N
Tertiary amine	**3 carbon atoms**	C—N̈—C, with C on N	CH_3—CH_2—N—CH_3, with CH_2—CH_3 on N

Sample Problem 11.8

Classifying amines

Classify each of the following amines as primary, secondary, or tertiary:

```
              NH2
               |
a) CH3 — C — CH2 — CH3        b) CH3 — N — CH2 — CH3
               |                        |
              CH3                      CH3
```

SOLUTION

a) In this molecule, the nitrogen atom is bonded to two hydrogen atoms and one carbon atom, making it a primary amine. Drawing a full structural formula can be helpful when classifying amines.

```
         (H)— N —(H)
     H        |       H   H
     |        |       |   |
 H — C ————— (C) ———— C — C — H
     |        |       |   |
     H        |       H   H
          H — C — H
              |
              H
```

b) In this molecule, the nitrogen atom is bonded to three carbon atoms, so this is a tertiary amine.

```
     H                H   H
     |                |   |
 H —(C)————— N ————— (C)— C — H
     |       |        |   |
     H       |        H   H
         H —(C)— H
             |
             H
```

TRY IT YOURSELF: *Classify each of the following amines as primary, secondary, or tertiary:*

```
a) CH3 — CH — NH — CH3        b) CH3 — CH — CH2 — CH3
          |                            |
         CH3                          NH2
```

For additional practice, try Core Problems 11.21 and 11.22.

Simple Amines Are Named Using a Traditional System

The IUPAC names for amines are somewhat cumbersome and are rarely used in health care. Instead, simple amines are generally named using an older system. In this system, we list each alkyl group that is bonded to the nitrogen, and then we add the suffix *-amine*. The alkyl groups are listed alphabetically. If we have two or three identical alkyl groups, we use the prefixes *di-* and *tri-*, rather than writing the name of the alkyl group several times. The entire name is written as one word. Here are some examples of amine names:

```
[CH3 — CH2 — CH2] — N — H      [CH3] — N — [CH2 — CH3]      [CH3] — N — [CH3]
                    |                  |                            |
                    H                  H                          [CH3]
```

Propylamine **Ethylmethylamine** **Trimethylamine**

Health Note: Bacteria in our digestive tract produce trimethylamine as they break down some nitrogen-containing compounds in our food, particularly choline. Most people oxidize the trimethylamine, but people with a genetic disorder called *trimethylaminuria* lack the ability to oxidize this amine. As trimethylamine leaves the body in the breath and sweat, it gives the unfortunate person a pungent odor reminiscent of decaying fish.

Sample Problem 11.9

Naming and drawing amines

a) Name the following amine:

$$CH_3-CH_2-CH_2-CH_2-CH_2-CH_2-CH_2-NH-CH_3$$

b) Draw the structure of ethyldipropylamine.

SOLUTION

a) The nitrogen atom is bonded to two alkyl groups and one hydrogen atom. One of the alkyl groups is a heptyl group (remember that the seven-carbon alkane is heptane), and the other alkyl group is a methyl group. To name the compound, we list the alkyl groups in alphabetical order, followed by *-amine*. This compound is named heptylmethylamine.

$$CH_3-CH_2-CH_2-CH_2-CH_2-CH_2-CH_2-NH-CH_3$$

Heptylmethylamine

b) The name *ethyldipropylamine* has three parts: *ethyl* (a two-carbon alkyl group), *dipropyl* (two separate three-carbon groups), and *amine* (a nitrogen atom). The ethyl group and the two propyl groups must be bonded to the nitrogen atom. The completed structure is

$$CH_3-CH_2-N(-CH_2-CH_2-CH_3)-CH_2-CH_2-CH_3$$

Note: you can arrange the three alkyl groups around the nitrogen in any way you like.

TRY IT YOURSELF: *Draw the structure of ethylpentylamine.*

For additional practice, try Core Problems 11.25 and 11.26.

When a nitrogen atom is bonded to a cycloalkane, we use the same naming system. The following compound is called *cyclohexylamine:*

(cyclohexane ring)$-NH_2$ **Cyclohexylamine**

The NH_2 group appears in many compounds in our bodies, including all of the amino acid building blocks of proteins. This group is called an *amino group.*

Cyclic Amines Contain Nitrogen Atoms within a Ring

Nitrogen atoms can also be incorporated into a ring, to form a *cyclic amine.* These compounds are common in biological chemistry, and each ring has its own special name. Figure 11.2 gives some examples of cyclic amines, which will allow you to familiarize yourself with the ways in which nitrogen can form part of a cyclic molecule.

Amines Are Polar Molecules and Form Hydrogen Bonds

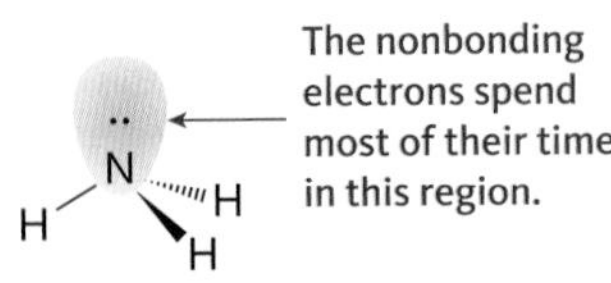
N
H
H
H
The nonbonding electrons spend most of their time in this region.

The pyramidal structure of ammonia and the position of the nonbonding electron pair.

When a nitrogen atom forms three single bonds, these bonds do not lie at right angles to one another. Recall that according to the VSEPR theory, valence electron pairs prefer to be as far apart as possible. As a result, ammonia takes the shape of a flattened pyramid with the nitrogen atom at the top, and the shapes of amines are similar. This arrangement allows the four electron pairs surrounding the nitrogen atom to be as far apart as possible. The nonbonding electron pair on nitrogen is exposed to the surrounding molecules, and it plays an important role in the behavior of amines.

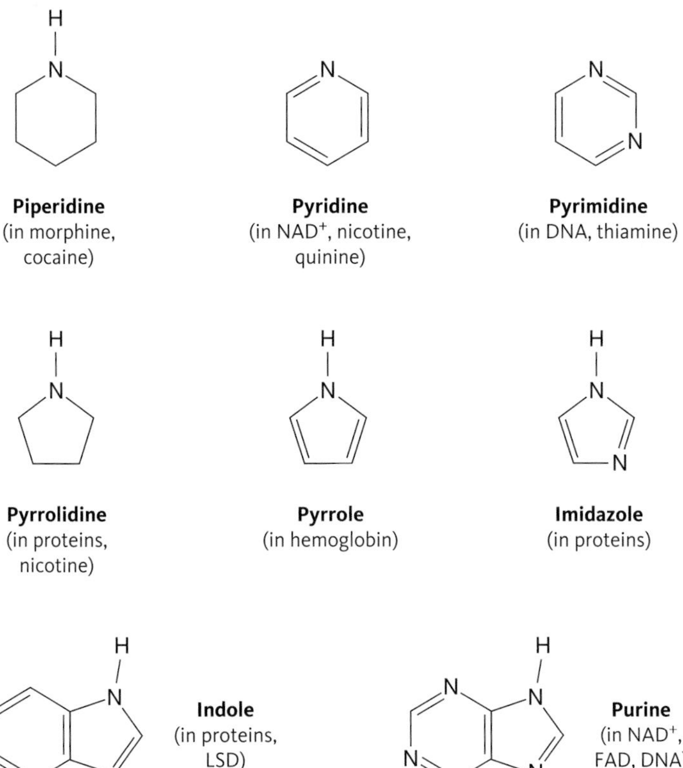

FIGURE 11.2 Some cyclic amines and molecules that contain them.

Health Note: People with gout are advised to limit their consumption of food that is rich in compounds that contain the purine system. The liver converts the purine in these compounds into uric acid, which crystallizes in the joints, causing the pain and swelling of gout.

Covalent bonds between nitrogen and either carbon or hydrogen are polar, because nitrogen has a higher electronegativity than carbon or hydrogen. The nitrogen atom in an amine is negatively charged, and the three neighboring atoms are positively charged. As a result, the nitrogen atom can participate in hydrogen bonds, acting as a hydrogen bond acceptor. In addition, any hydrogen atoms that are bonded to nitrogen are hydrogen bond donors. Therefore, primary and secondary amines (and ammonia) form hydrogen bonds to each other, with the negative nitrogen in one molecule attracted to the positive hydrogen in another molecule.

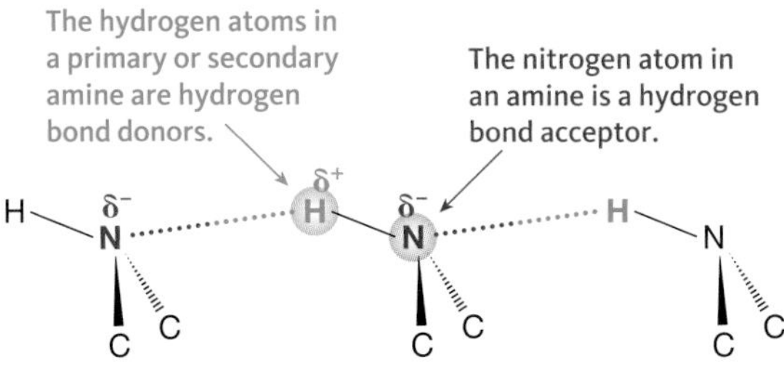

Low-molecular-weight amines tend to have unpleasant aromas and are responsible for the repulsive smell of decaying fish.

By contrast, tertiary amines do not have a hydrogen atom bonded to the nitrogen, so they cannot be hydrogen bond donors. As a result, the attraction between molecules of a tertiary amine is weaker than the attraction between molecules of other amines. This difference is reflected in their boiling points. Tertiary amines cannot form hydrogen bonds to each other, so their boiling points are close to those of similarly sized alkanes. Both primary and secondary amines can form hydrogen bonds, providing additional attraction between molecules and raising the boiling points. Table 11.4 compares the boiling points of three amines and an alkane. Note that the boiling points of the primary and secondary amines are substantially higher than that of a similarly sized alkane, while the boiling point of the tertiary amine is similar to that of the alkane.

TABLE 11.4 The effect of hydrogen bonding on the boiling point of an amine

Compound	Structure	Boiling Point
Propylamine (a primary amine: hydrogen bonding occurs between molecules)	$CH_3—CH_2—CH_2—N(H)—H$	48°C
Ethylmethylamine (a secondary amine: hydrogen bonding occurs between molecules)	$CH_2—CH_2—N(H)—CH_3$	37°C
Trimethylamine (a tertiary amine: no hydrogen bonding is possible)	$CH_3—N(CH_3)—CH_3$	3°C
Butane (an alkane: no hydrogen bonding is possible)	$CH_3—CH_2—CH_2—CH_3$	−1°C

Sample Problem 11.10

Relating the boiling points of amines to their structure

The following compounds are constitutional isomers. Which of them would you expect to have the higher boiling point?

$CH_3—CH_2—N(CH_3)—CH_2—CH_3$ **Diethylmethylamine**

$CH_3—CH_2—CH_2—CH_2—CH_2—NH_2$ **Pentylamine**

SOLUTION

Pentylamine is a primary amine, so molecules of pentylamine can form hydrogen bonds to one another. Diethylmethylamine is a tertiary amine and cannot form hydrogen bonds in this fashion. Therefore, molecules of pentylamine are more strongly attracted to one another than are molecules of diethylmethylamine. We predict that **pentylamine** has the higher boiling point. (The actual boiling points are 104°C and 66°C, respectively.)

TRY IT YOURSELF: *The following compounds are constitutional isomers. Which of them would you expect to have the higher boiling point?*

[cyclopentane ring]—NH_2 **Cyclopentylamine**

[pyrrolidine ring] N—CH_3 **N-methylpyrrolidine**

For additional practice, try Core Problems 11.31 and 11.32.

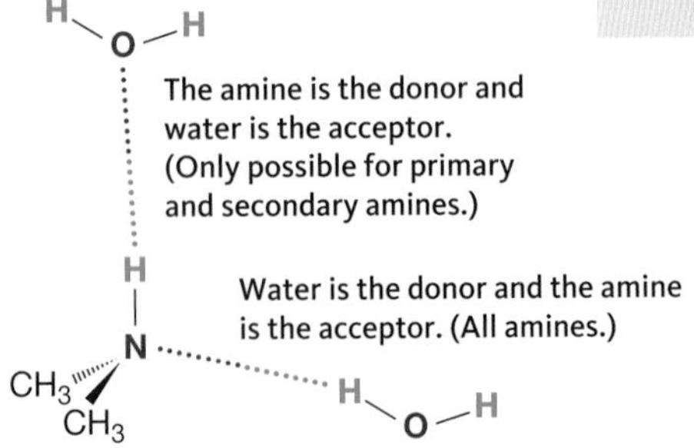
H
O
H
The amine is the donor and water is the acceptor. (Only possible for primary and secondary amines.)
H
N
Water is the donor and the amine is the acceptor. (All amines.)
CH3
CH3
H
O
H

FIGURE 11.3 Hydrogen bonding between dimethylamine and water.

Many Amines Dissolve Well in Water

Since nitrogen can form hydrogen bonds, amines are attracted to water. Figure 11.3 shows the hydrogen bonding between an amine and water. Primary and secondary amines can form two types of hydrogen bonds with water molecules, while tertiary amines can only form one, but this difference does not have a significant effect on amine solubility. The solubilities of amines in general are similar to those of the oxygen-containing compounds you studied in Chapters 9 and 10. Amines that contain few carbon atoms dissolve well in water, because the nitrogen atom is attracted to the hydrogen atoms in water. Amines that contain many carbon atoms have lower solubilities, because the hydrophobic character of the molecule becomes dominant.

Sample Problem 11.11

Drawing hydrogen bonds between amines and water

Draw structures to show how a molecule of methylamine can form hydrogen bonds with a molecule of water.

SOLUTION

Methylamine is a primary amine, so it can function as both a donor and an acceptor of hydrogen bonds. When methylamine is the donor, water is the acceptor:

$$CH_3-\underset{|\atop H}{N}-H \cdots\cdots \underset{|\atop H}{O}-H$$

When water is the donor, methylamine is the acceptor:

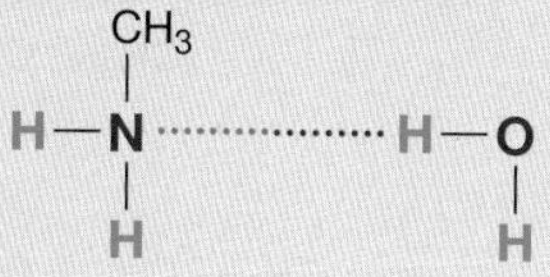

$$H-\overset{CH_3\atop |}{\underset{|\atop H}{N}} \cdots\cdots H-\underset{|\atop H}{O}$$

Both types of hydrogen bonds occur in a mixture of methylamine and water.

TRY IT YOURSELF: *Draw structures to show how a molecule of trimethylamine can form hydrogen bonds with a molecule of water.*

For additional practice, try Core Problems 11.29 and 11.30.

CORE PROBLEMS

11.21 Classify each of the following compounds as a primary, secondary, or tertiary amine:

a) 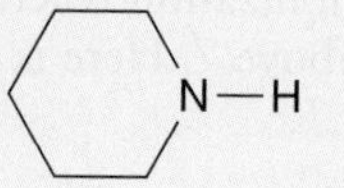 [six-membered ring containing N—H]

b) 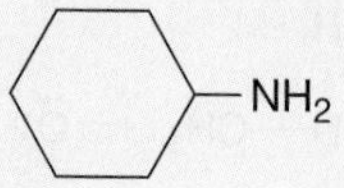 [cyclohexane ring]—NH_2

c) 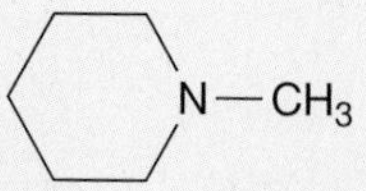 [six-membered ring containing N—CH_3]

11.22 Classify each of the following compounds as a primary, secondary, or tertiary amine:

a) 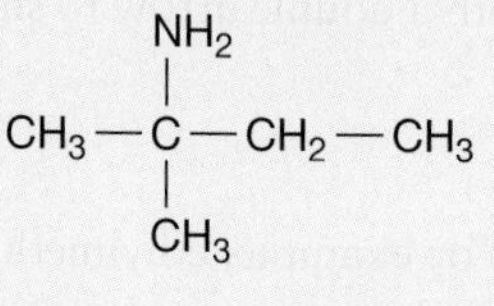 $CH_3-\overset{NH_2\atop |}{\underset{|\atop CH_3}{C}}-CH_2-CH_3$

b) $CH_3-\underset{|\atop CH_3}{CH}-\overset{NH_2\atop |}{CH}-CH_3$

c) $CH_3-\underset{|\atop CH_3}{CH}-NH-CH_3$

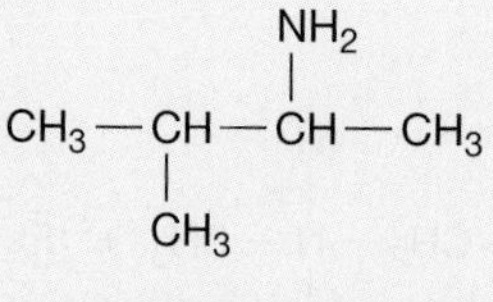

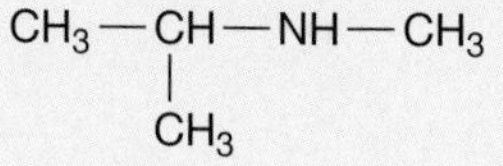

11.23 One of the compounds in Problem 11.21 contains an amino group. Which compound is it?

11.24 Two of the compounds in Problem 11.22 contain an amino group. Which compounds are they?

11.25 Draw the structures of the following amines:
a) pentylamine
b) dipropylamine
c) cyclohexylmethylamine

11.26 Draw the structures of the following amines:
a) triethylamine
b) cyclopropylethylamine
c) hexylamine

11.27 Name the following amines:

a) 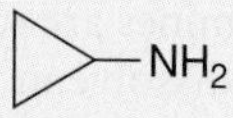 [cyclopropane ring]—NH_2

b) $CH_3-CH_2-NH-CH_2-CH_2-CH_2-CH_3$

c) 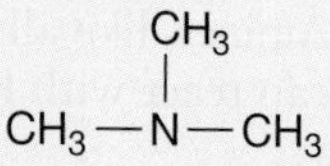 $CH_3-\overset{CH_3\atop |}{N}-CH_3$

11.28 Name the following amines:

a) 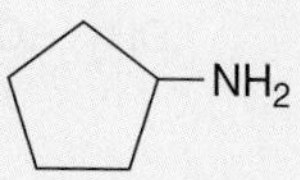 [cyclopentane ring]—NH_2

b) 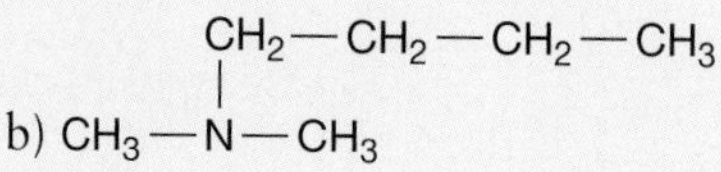 $CH_3-\overset{CH_2-CH_2-CH_2-CH_3\atop |}{N}-CH_3$

c) $CH_3-CH_2-NH-CH_2-CH_2-CH_3$

continued

11.29 Using structural formulas, show how hydrogen bonding can occur between the following:
a) two molecules of ethylamine
b) a molecule of ethylamine and a molecule of water

11.30 Using structural formulas, show how hydrogen bonding can occur between the following:
a) two molecules of dimethylamine
b) a molecule of dimethylamine and a molecule of water

11.31 The following two compounds are constitutional isomers. One boils at 145°C, while the other boils at 185°C. Match each structure with its boiling point, and explain your answer.

$CH_3-C_5H_4N$ (4-Methylpyridine) $\quad$ $NH_2-C_6H_5$ (Aniline)

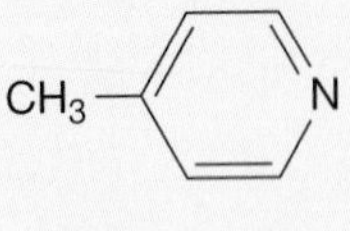

4-Methylpyridine 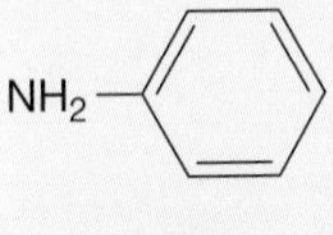 **Aniline**

11.32 The two following compounds are constitutional isomers. One boils at 3°C, while the other boils at 33°C. Match each structure with its boiling point, and explain your answer.

$$NH_2-\underset{\substack{|\\CH_3}}{CH}-CH_3 \qquad CH_3-\overset{\substack{CH_3\\|}}{N}-CH_3$$

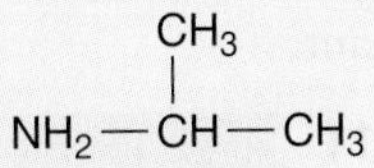

Isopropylamine 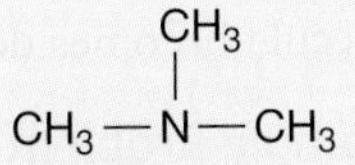 **Trimethylamine**

11.33 Which of the following compounds should have the higher solubility in water? Explain your answer.

$$CH_3-CH_2-NH_2$$

Ethylamine

$$CH_3-CH_2-CH_2-CH_2-CH_2-CH_2-NH_2$$

Hexylamine

11.34 Which of the following compounds should have the higher solubility in water? Explain your answer.

$$CH_3-CH_2-CH_2-CH_3$$

Butane

$$CH_3-CH_2-CH_2-CH_2-CH_2-NH_2$$

Pentylamine

OBJECTIVES: *Write chemical equations for the reactions of amines with water and with acids, and draw the zwitterion form of molecules that contain both acid and amine groups.*

11.4 Acid–Base Reactions of Amines

In Section 7.4, you saw that ammonia is a base because the nitrogen atom can bond to a hydrogen ion. Because most amines can also accept a hydrogen ion, *most amines are bases.* As we saw in Chapter 7, when an amine dissolves in water, the nitrogen atom in the amine pulls a hydrogen ion away from water. Because this ionization reaction produces OH^-, solutions of amines are basic and have pH values above 7. Here is the ionization reaction of ethylmethylamine:

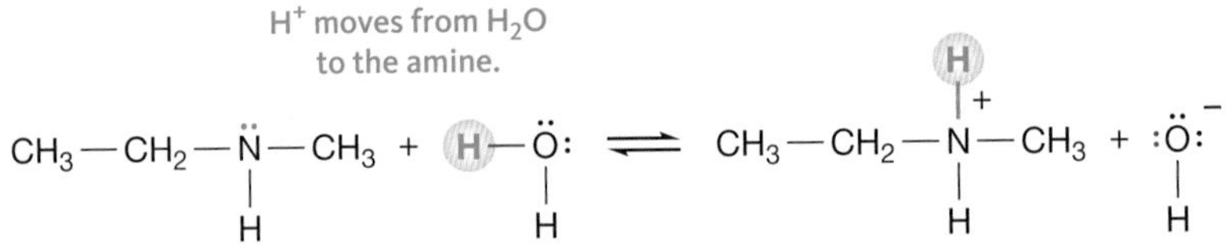

H^+ moves from H_2O to the amine.

$$CH_3-CH_2-\underset{\substack{|\\H}}{\ddot{N}}-CH_3 + H-\underset{\substack{|\\H}}{\ddot{O}}: \rightleftharpoons CH_3-CH_2-\underset{\substack{|\\H}}{\overset{\substack{H\\|}}{N^+}}-CH_3 + :\underset{\substack{|\\H}}{\ddot{O}}:^-$$

$$C_2H_5-NH-CH_3 \quad + \quad H_2O \quad \rightleftharpoons \quad C_2H_5-\overset{+}{N}H_2-CH_3 \quad + OH^-$$

Amines are weak bases, producing only a small concentration of hydroxide ions when they dissolve in water. We write the ionization reaction with a double arrow to show that only a few molecules of the amine become bonded to H^+.

Amines React with All Types of Acids

Amines, like all bases, can react with any source of H^+. For example, ethylmethylamine can react with HF, a typical inorganic acid.

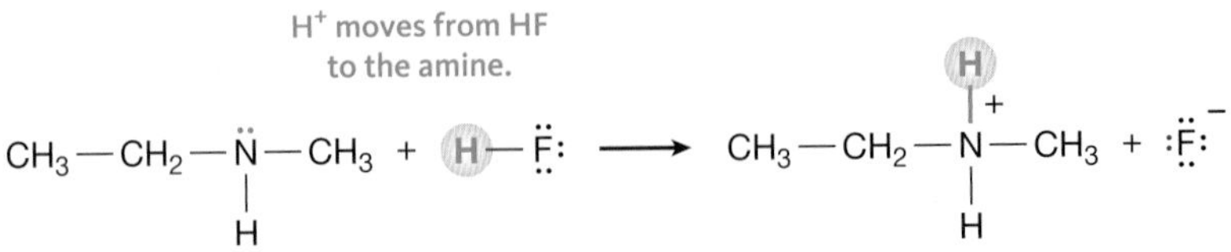

H^+ moves from HF to the amine.

$$CH_3-CH_2-\underset{\substack{|\\H}}{\ddot{N}}-CH_3 + H-\ddot{\underset{..}{F}}: \longrightarrow CH_3-CH_2-\underset{\substack{|\\H}}{\overset{\substack{H\\|}}{N^+}}-CH_3 + :\ddot{\underset{..}{F}}:^-$$

$$C_2H_5-NH-CH_3 \quad + \quad HF \quad \longrightarrow \quad C_2H_5-\overset{+}{N}H_2-CH_3 \quad + F^-$$

This amine also reacts with organic acids such as acetic acid.

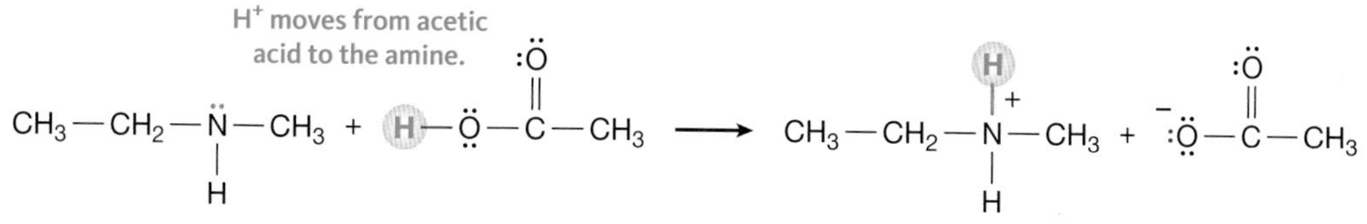

H^+ moves from acetic acid to the amine.

$$CH_3-CH_2-\ddot{N}(H)-CH_3 + H-\ddot{O}-C(=\ddot{O})-CH_3 \longrightarrow CH_3-CH_2-\overset{+}{N}(H)(H)-CH_3 + {}^{-}:\ddot{O}-C(=\ddot{O})-CH_3$$

$$C_2H_5-NH-CH_3 \quad + \quad HOOC-CH_3 \longrightarrow C_2H_5-\overset{+}{N}H_2-CH_3 \quad + \quad {}^{-}OOC-CH_3$$

Sample Problem 11.12

Writing acid–base reactions involving organic acids and bases

Using structural formulas, write a chemical equation for the acid–base reaction that occurs when methylamine and propanoic acid are mixed.

SOLUTION

Methylamine is a base, so it can accept H^+ from propanoic acid. The hydrogen ion bonds to the nitrogen atom of methylamine.

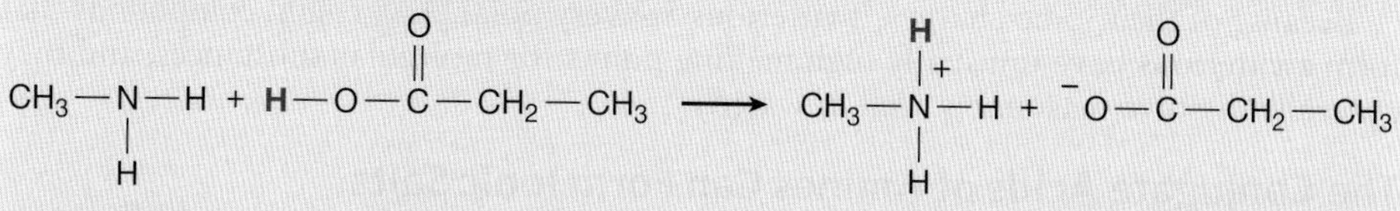

$$CH_3-N(H)-H + H-O-C(=O)-CH_2-CH_3 \longrightarrow CH_3-\overset{+}{N}(H)(H)-H + {}^{-}O-C(=O)-CH_2-CH_3$$

Methylamine **Propanoic acid**

We can write these structures in condensed form as follows:

$$CH_3-NH_2 + CH_3-CH_2-CO_2H \rightarrow CH_3-NH_3^+ + CH_3-CH_2-CO_2^-$$

TRY IT YOURSELF: *Using structural formulas, write a chemical equation for the acid–base reaction that will occur when piperidine reacts with formic acid. The structure of piperidine is shown in Figure 11.2.*

For additional practice, try Core Problems 11.35 and 11.36.

As we saw in Chapter 7, some compounds contain an amino group and a carboxylic acid group within the same molecule. These substances, called *amino acids,* are the building blocks of proteins, as we will see in Chapter 13. The structures of two common amino acids are shown here:

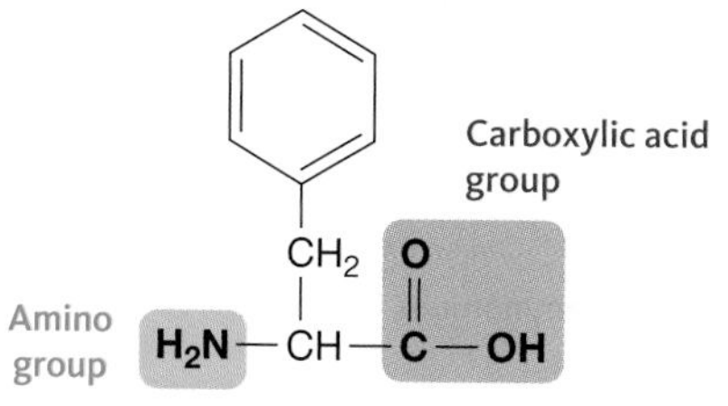

$$\underset{\text{Amino group}}{H_2N}-CH(CH_2-C_6H_5)-\underset{\text{Carboxylic acid group}}{C(=O)-OH}$$

Phenylalanine

$$\underset{\text{Amino group}}{H_2N}-CH(CH_2-OH)-\underset{\text{Carboxylic acid group}}{C(=O)-OH}$$

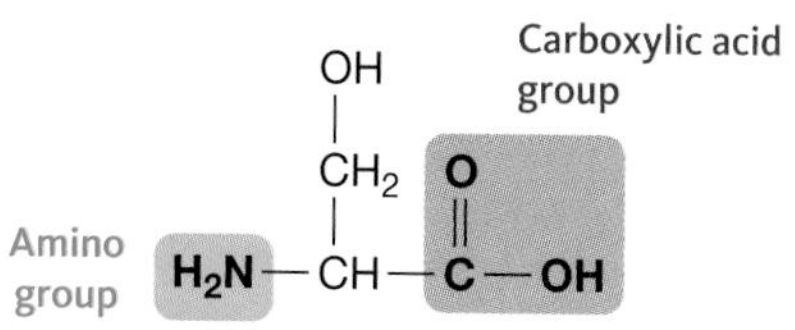

Serine

In an amino acid, the carboxylic acid group reacts directly with the amino group, as shown here. The product is a molecule with a positive and a negative ionic charge, called a **zwitterion.** The zwitterion form of an amino acid is so much more stable than the union-

© Chuck Franklin / Alamy

PABA absorbs ultraviolet light, making it a useful ingredient in sunscreens.

ized form that only about 1 out of every 10,000,000 molecules of any amino acid remains in the unionized form. Here are the two forms of glycine, a typical amino acid:

Glycine (an amino acid) unionized form

$$H_2N\text{—}CH_2\text{—}C(=O)\text{—}O\text{—}H \rightleftharpoons H_3N^+\text{—}CH_2\text{—}C(=O)\text{—}O^-$$

Zwitterion form of glycine

H^+ moves from the carboxylic acid group to the amino group.

Any molecule that contains both an acidic and a basic functional group can form a zwitterion. For example, the sunscreen ingredient PABA contains a carboxylic acid and an amino group, so it forms a zwitterion.

$$H_2N\text{—}C_6H_4\text{—}C(=O)\text{—}OH \qquad {}^+H_3N\text{—}C_6H_4\text{—}C(=O)\text{—}O^-$$

PABA Unionized form — **PABA** Zwitterion form

Because of their ionic charges, zwitterions are very polar. As a result, compounds that form zwitterions have unusually high melting points for molecular substances, and they generally dissolve reasonably well in water.

The Conjugate Acids of Amines Can Form Ionic Salts

The conjugate acids of amines are called **alkylammonium ions.** For example, the conjugate acids of methylamine and diethylamine are named methylammonium ion and diethylammonium ion, respectively.

$$CH_3\text{—}NH_2 \qquad CH_3\text{—}NH_3^+$$

Methylamine — **Methylammonium ion**

$$CH_3\text{—}CH_2\text{—}NH\text{—}CH_2\text{—}CH_3 \qquad CH_3\text{—}CH_2\text{—}NH_2^+\text{—}CH_2\text{—}CH_3$$

Diethylamine — **Diethylammonium ion**

Alkylammonium ions can combine with anions to form salts. For instance, methylammonium ions can combine with chloride ions to form methylammonium chloride. As with all ionic compounds, we name the cation first, followed by the anion. Molecular formulas for such salts are potentially confusing, so it is generally best to draw a structural formula.

$$CH_3\text{—}NH_3^+ \quad Cl^-$$

Methylammonium chloride

Salts that contain alkylammonium ions generally dissolve well in water, and they ionize completely when they dissolve. For example, an aqueous solution of methylammonium chloride contains independent methylammonium and chloride ions, just as a solution of sodium chloride contains independent Na^+ and Cl^- ions.

Health Note: PABA, like other active ingredients in sunscreens, absorbs ultraviolet (UV) radiation, reducing the amount of skin damage when the skin is exposed to sunlight. PABA is particularly effective at absorbing UVB, the higher-energy UV radiation that causes the redness and pain of sunburns.

Health Note: Quaternary ammonium salts contain four alkyl groups attached to nitrogen. The alkylammonium ion in these salts is toxic to most bacteria and some viruses. These salts are also excellent detergents, so they are used to clean and disinfect hospital surfaces, and they are added to hand sanitizers and moist wipes.

$$C_6H_5\text{—}CH_2\text{—}N^+(CH_3)_2\text{—}(CH_2)_{17}\text{—}CH_3 \quad Cl^-$$

Sample Problem 11.13

Drawing the structure of an ammonium salt

Draw the structure of trimethylammonium acetate.

SOLUTION

This compound is a salt that contains trimethylammonium ion and acetate ion. Trimethylammonium ion is the conjugate acid of trimethylamine, so we can draw its structure by adding H^+ to the nitrogen atom of trimethylamine. Acetate ion is the conjugate base of acetic acid. We can draw its structure by removing H^+ from the functional group of acetic acid. To draw the structure of the salt, we simply draw the two ions beside each other. We do not draw a line between them, because there is no covalent bond connecting the two ions.

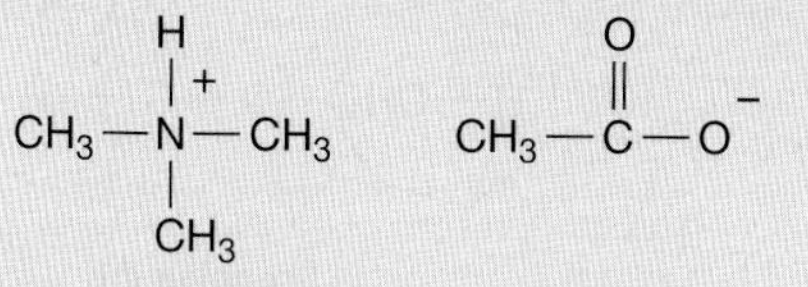

```
        H                  O
        | +                ‖      –
  CH3 — N — CH3     CH3 — C — O        Trimethylammonium acetate
        |
       CH3

 Trimethylammonium ion   Acetate ion
```

TRY IT YOURSELF: *Draw the structure of ethylmethylammonium fluoride.*

For additional practice, try Core Problems 11.39 and 11.40.

CORE PROBLEMS

11.35 Using condensed structures, write a chemical equation for each of the following reactions:
a) the ionization of ethylmethylamine in water
b) the reaction of ethylmethylamine with H_3O^+
c) the reaction of ethylmethylamine with acetic acid

11.36 Using condensed structures, write a chemical equation for each of the following reactions:
a) the ionization of trimethylamine in water
b) the reaction of trimethylamine with H_3O^+
c) the reaction of trimethylamine with propanoic acid

11.37 The following amino acid forms a zwitterion. Draw the structure of the zwitterion.

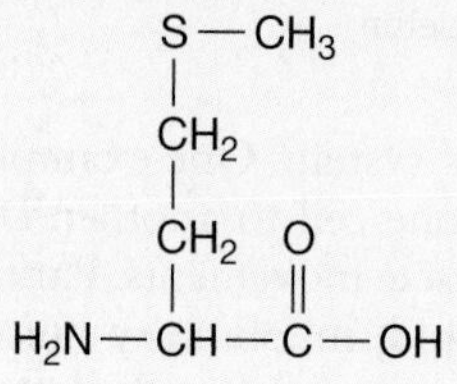

```
         S — CH3
         |
         CH2
         |                  Methionine
         CH2  O             An amino acid
         |    ‖
   H2N — CH — C — OH
```

11.38 The following amino acid forms a zwitterion. Draw the structure of the zwitterion.

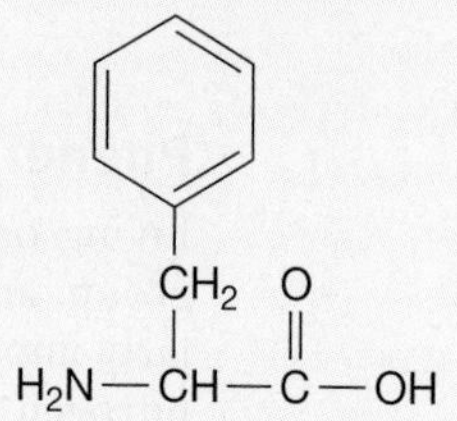

```
         (benzene ring)
         |                  Phenylalanine
         CH2  O             An amino acid
         |    ‖
   H2N — CH — C — OH
```

11.39 Draw the structures of the following:
a) the conjugate acid of propylamine
b) butylammonium bromide
c) hexylmethylammonium formate

11.40 Draw the structures of the following:
a) the conjugate acid of cyclopentylamine
b) ethyldimethylammonium fluoride
c) tripropylammonium propanoate

11.5 Amines in Biology and Medicine

OBJECTIVES: *Recognize the phenethylamine and tryptamine structures in physiologically active amines, identify alkaloids, and explain the use of amine salts as medications.*

Amines that do not contain other functional groups tend to be quite toxic and have little use in medicine. However, a range of medications contain the amine functional group, along with one or more other groups. Some of these compounds are made by other organisms, while others are manufactured. Figure 11.4 shows some examples of compounds that contain the amine functional group.

Lidocaine
(a topical anesthetic)

Glucosamine
(claimed to improve arthritis symptoms)

Nicotinic acid
(niacin, a B vitamin)

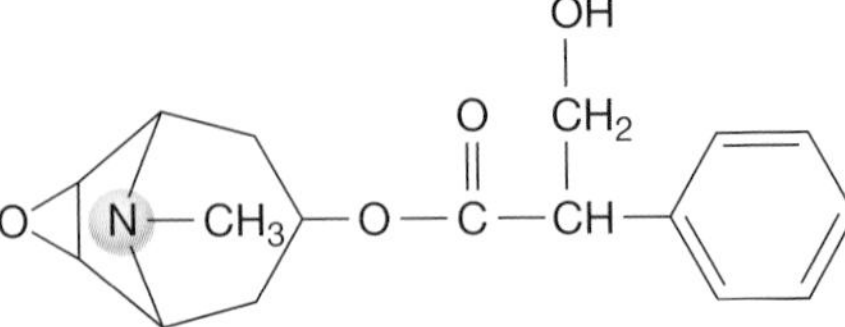

Scopolamine
(used to treat motion sickness)

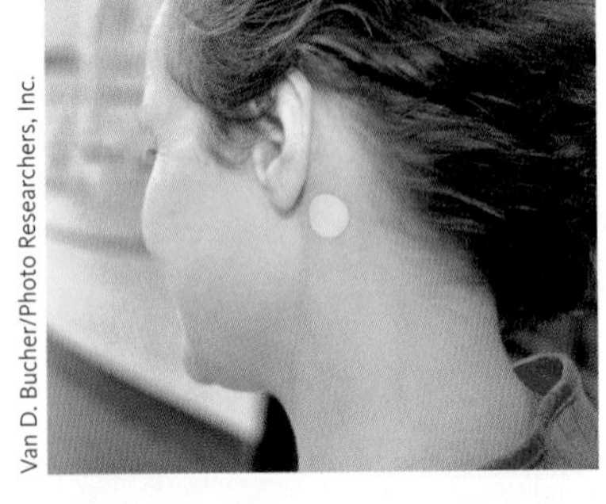

This skin patch contains scopolamine and helps to prevent seasickness.

Note: the nitrogen atoms that are not shaded are part of the amide functional group, which you will learn about in Chapter 12.

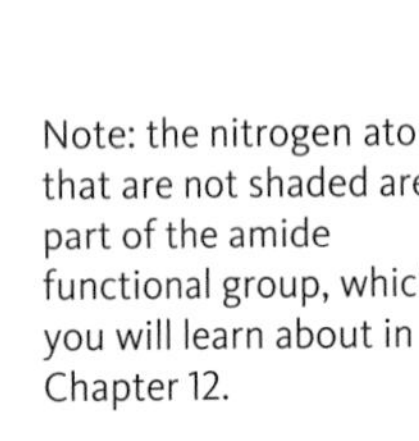

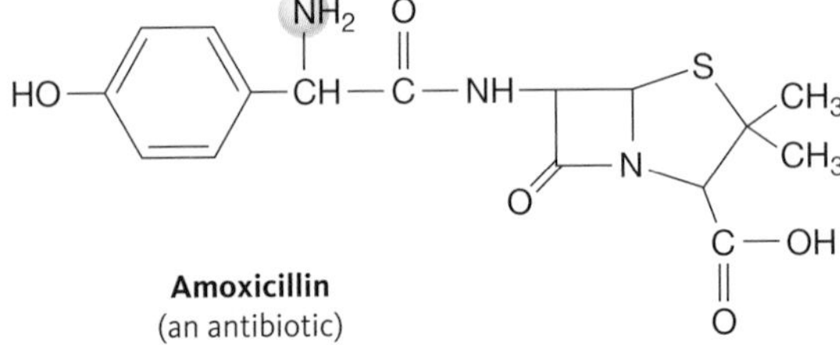

Amoxicillin
(an antibiotic)

FIGURE 11.4 Some amines in medicine and nutrition.

Phenethylamines Have Potent Physiological Effects

Living organisms produce a variety of compounds that contain the amine functional group, and many of these have impressive physiological effects on humans. A particularly important class of active amines is the *phenethylamines,* compounds that contain a nitrogen atom and a benzene ring separated by two carbon atoms. The phenethylamine framework is shown here:

The phenethylamine skeleton

Many phenethylamines affect the central nervous system. One example is *dopamine,* which our bodies use to pass nerve impulses from one cell to another. Dopamine plays a critical role in the control of gradual, sustained muscle movements. Parkinson's disease, a debilitating condition that is characterized by rapid, involuntary muscle movements and the loss of muscle control, is caused by the destruction of cells that produce dopamine. Dopamine is also known to help regulate the release of milk in lactating women, and it is believed to influence emotional behavior. Here is the structure of dopamine, with the phenethylamine framework outlined in red:

Dopamine

Another important phenethylamine in our bodies is *epinephrine* (also called *adrenaline*), a hormone that is produced by the adrenal glands in response to sudden stress.

Epinephrine has a range of effects on the human body, all of which make the body more able to defend itself or flee from danger (the "fight or flight" syndrome).

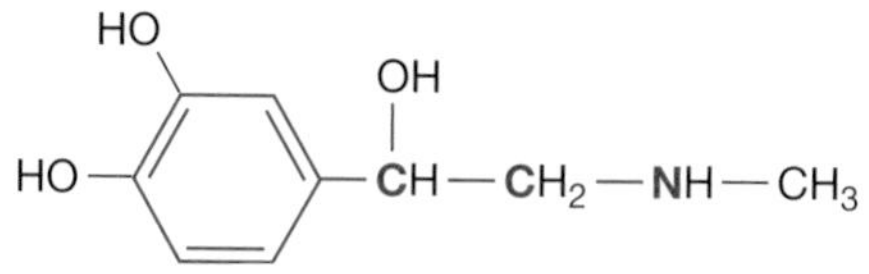

Epinephrine
The phenethylamine framework is outlined in red.

The following list summarizes some of the more significant effects of epinephrine:

- Increases heart rate and efficiency
- Constricts most blood vessels while dilating vessels in muscles, to allow blood to reach muscles more rapidly
- Dilates respiratory airways, to increase the efficiency of breathing
- Reduces digestive activity
- Reduces kidney activity and inhibits urination
- Stimulates the liver to release glucose (a sugar) into the bloodstream, for use as fuel
- Increases the breakdown of stored fats, for use as fuel
- Stimulates the production of sweat, to remove excess heat from the body
- Stimulates the central nervous system, to enhance the ability to make rapid decisions

Tryptamines Have a Range of Physiological Effects

A second important category of physiologically active amines, called *tryptamines*, contains indole in place of the benzene ring of the phenethylamines. The most important example of the tryptamines is *serotonin*, a molecule that (like dopamine) is involved in the transmission of nerve impulses.

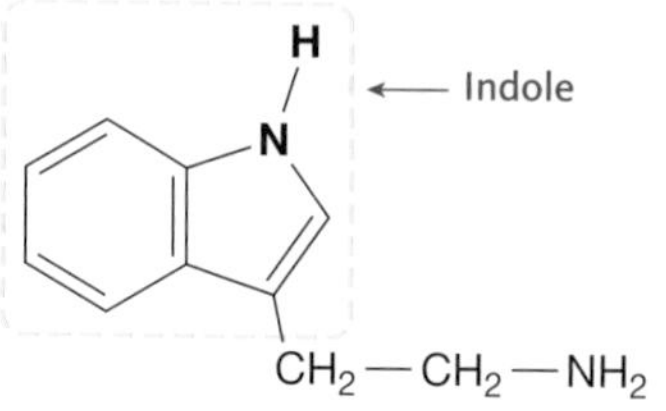

Tryptamine

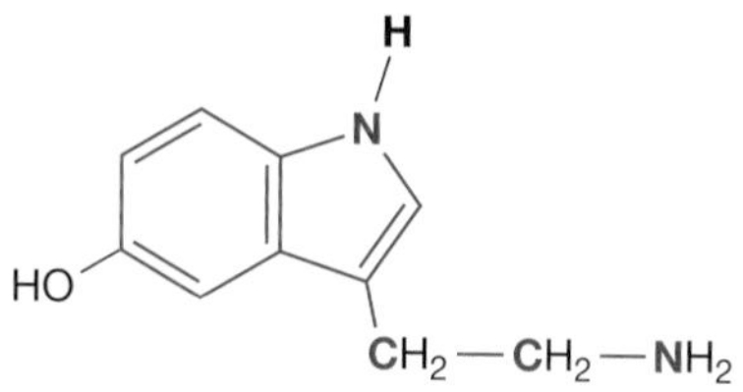

Serotonin
The tryptamine framework is outlined in red.

Serotonin has a remarkable range of effects, some of which are given in the following list:

- Influences emotions, mood, judgment, and behavior
- Influences the ability to learn and remember information
- Helps regulate digestion and appetite
- Helps regulate body temperature
- Helps regulate the sleep cycle
- Controls the sensation of pain

The inability to make enough serotonin has been implicated in clinical depression, a condition that can have devastating effects on its sufferers. Many of the currently available medications to treat depression increase serotonin levels in the brain, generally by slowing the rate at which this compound is absorbed by cells in the nervous system.

A number of widely used (and abused) drugs contain the phenethylamine or tryptamine framework and mimic one or more of the effects of dopamine or serotonin. Figure 11.5 shows the structures of three of these. Methamphetamine and mescaline are related to dopamine, while LSD is related to serotonin.

Health Note: The body controls the levels of phenethylamines and tryptamines in nerve tissues using enzymes called *monoamine oxidases,* which remove the amino group from these organic molecules. Some antidepressant medications, called *monoamine oxidase inhibitors (MAOIs)* interfere with the breakdown of serotonin, increasing the concentration of serotonin in nerve tissues. MAOIs have potentially serious interactions with many other medications, so they are generally prescribed only in severe cases and when other antidepressants have proven ineffective.

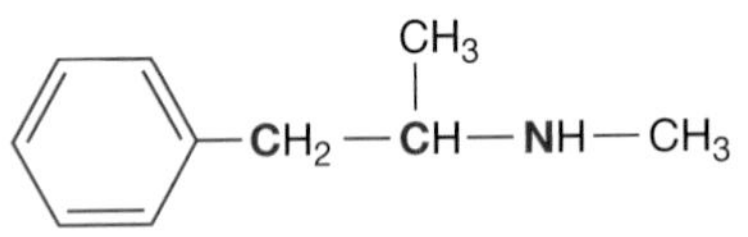

Methamphetamine ("speed") a phenethylamine

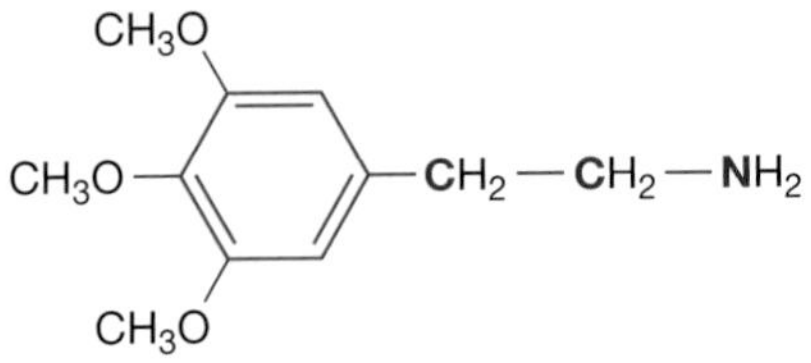

Mescaline (active chemical in peyote) a phenethylamine

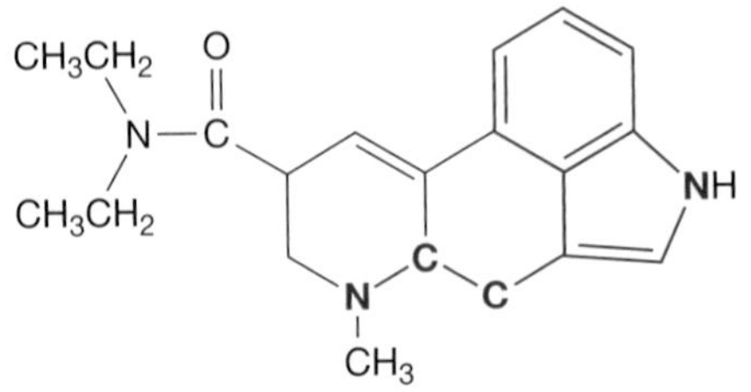

LSD (lysergic acid diethylamide) a tryptamine

FIGURE 11.5 The structures of some relatives of dopamine and serotonin.

Sample Problem 11.14

Identifying phenethylamines and tryptamines

The following compound is used to treat migraine headaches. Is this compound a phenethylamine, a tryptamine, or neither?

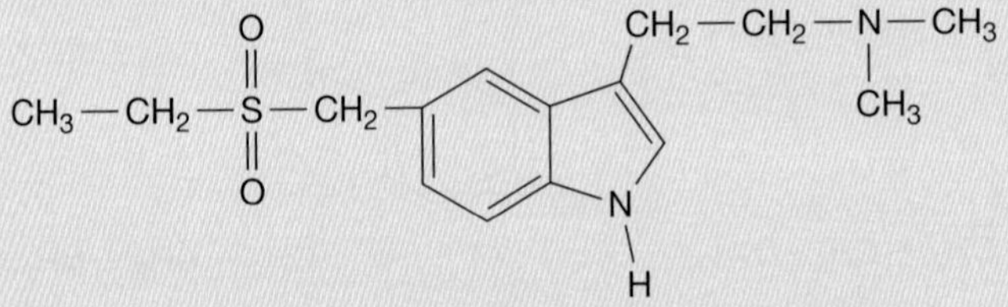

Sumatriptan

SOLUTION

This molecule contains the two-ring indole framework linked to a chain containing two carbon atoms and a nitrogen atom, as shown here. Therefore, sumatriptan is a tryptamine.

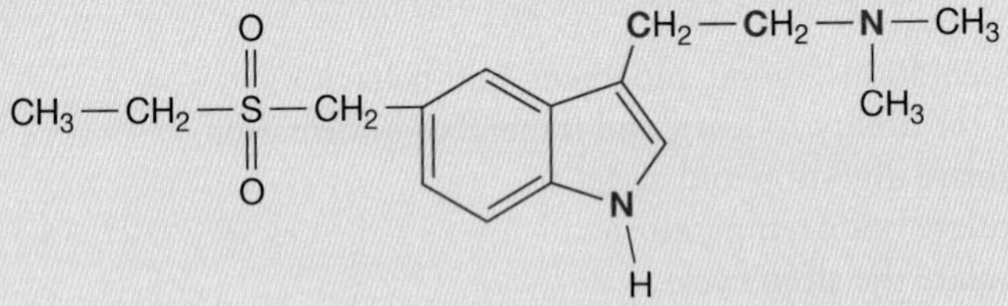

TRY IT YOURSELF: *The following compound is used as an antidepressant. Is this compound a phenethylamine, a tryptamine, or neither?*

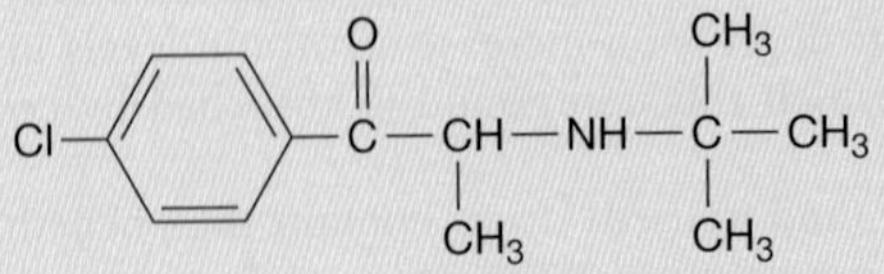

Bupropion

For additional practice, try Core Problems 11.41 and 11.42.

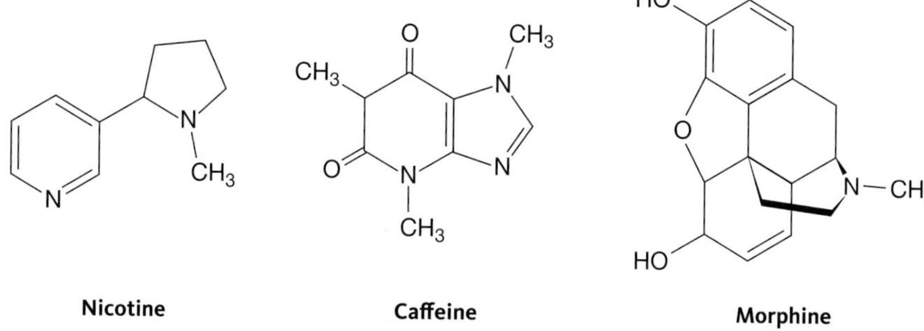

FIGURE 11.6 The structures of some important alkaloids.

Alkaloids Are Physiologically Active Amines That Are Made by Plants

The popularity of these beverages is due in part to the caffeine they contain.

The **alkaloids** are an important class of amines in medicine. Alkaloids are organic bases that are produced by plants or fungi and that have some sort of physiological activity. For example, mescaline (see Figure 11.5) is an alkaloid made by a cactus that is native to arid regions of North and Central America. Mescaline produces hallucinations when ingested, and its effects have been known since prehistoric times. Other alkaloids with which you may be familiar are nicotine (the addictive compound in tobacco smoke), morphine (a potent pain reliever that is found in the opium poppy), and caffeine (the mild stimulant in coffee). The structures of these alkaloids are shown in Figure 11.6.

Alkaloids that have similar structures generally have similar physiological effects. Beyond this, though, it is not normally possible to predict the effect of an alkaloid from its structure.

Alkaloids are bases, so they can react with acids to produce salts. The salts are more soluble in water and have higher melting points than the original amines. For example, morphine can react with sulfuric acid to form a salt called morphine sulfate. The solubility of this salt is around 60 g/L, while the solubility of the original base is only 0.2 g/L. Solutions of morphine are widely used to relieve severe pain, and the morphine is always in the form of its soluble salt.

Sample Problem 11.15

Drawing the salt of a physiologically active amine

Nicotine reacts with hydrochloric acid to form a water-soluble salt called nicotine hydrochloride. In this salt, the hydrogen ion is bonded to the nitrogen atom in the five-membered ring. Draw the structure of this salt. (See Figure 11.6 for the structure of nicotine.)

SOLUTION

Attaching the hydrogen ion from HCl to the correct nitrogen atom in nicotine gives us the conjugate acid of nicotine. The salt contains this conjugate acid and a chloride ion, as shown here:

+ HCl ⟶ { Cl^- }

The structure of nicotine hydrochloride

continued

TRY IT YOURSELF: *The cold medication Sudafed contains pseudoephedrine hydrochloride, a salt that is formed when pseudoephedrine reacts with hydrochloric acid. The structure of pseudoephedrine is shown here. Draw the structure of pseudoephedrine hydrochloride.*

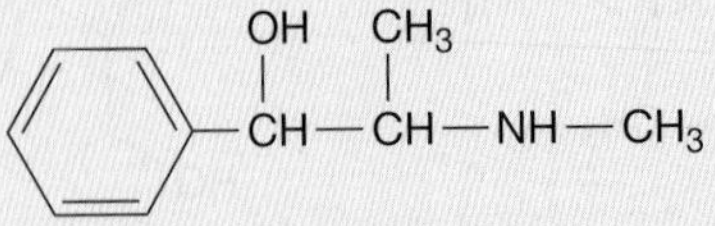

OH CH3

CH—CH—NH—CH3 **Pseudoephedrine**

For additional practice, try Core Problems 11.43 and 11.44.

CORE PROBLEMS

11.41 Which of the following substances are structurally related to phenethylamine, and which are structurally related to tryptamine?

OH CH3

CH—CH—NH—CH3

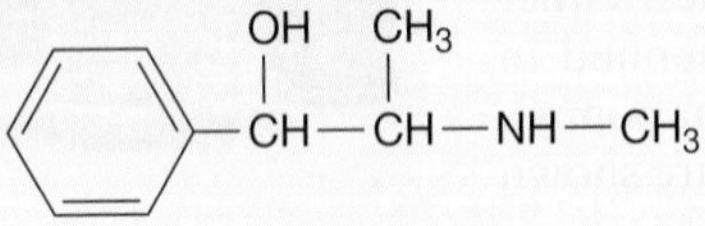

Pseudoephedrine: a nasal decongestant found in many cold remedies

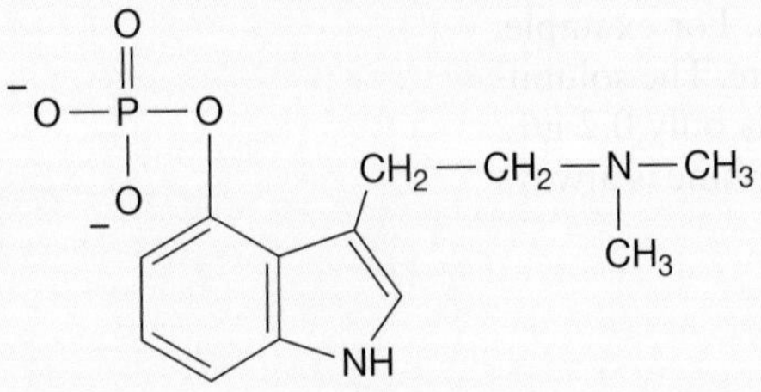

O

⁻O—P—O

O⁻

CH2—CH2—N—CH3

CH3

NH

Psilocybin: a hallucinogen found in certain species of mushrooms

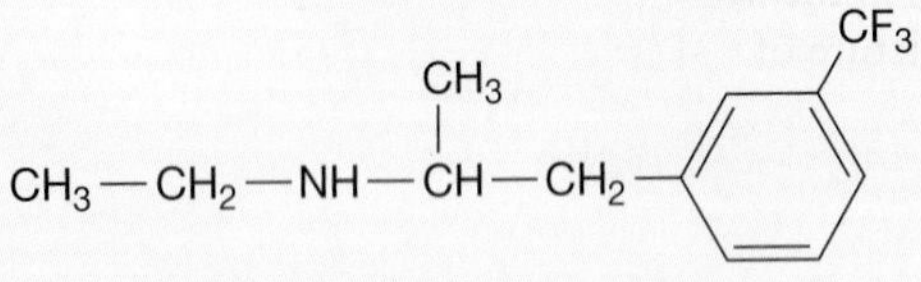

CF3

CH3

CH3—CH2—NH—CH—CH2—

Fenfluramine: an appetite suppressant

11.42 Which of the following substances are structurally related to phenethylamine, and which are structurally related to tryptamine?

NH2

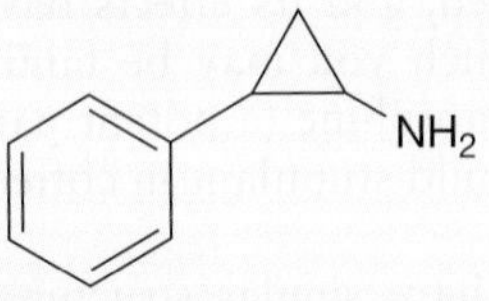

Tranylcypromine: an antidepressant medication

CH3

NH2—C—CH2—

CH3

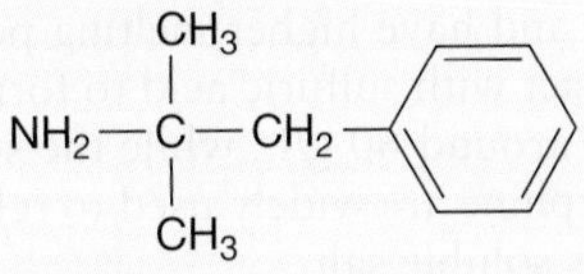

Phentermine: an appetite suppressant

NH

O

CH3—O

CH2—CH2—NH—C—CH3

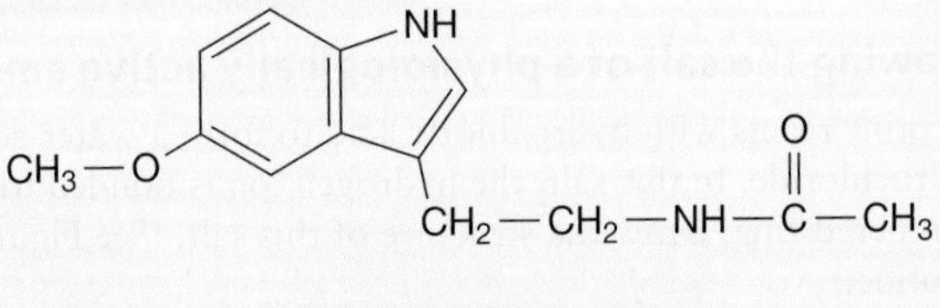

Melatonin: regulates the sleep/wake cycle in humans

11.43 The active ingredient in the antidepressant medication Zoloft is sertraline hydrochloride, which is formed when sertraline reacts with HCl. The structure of sertraline is shown here:

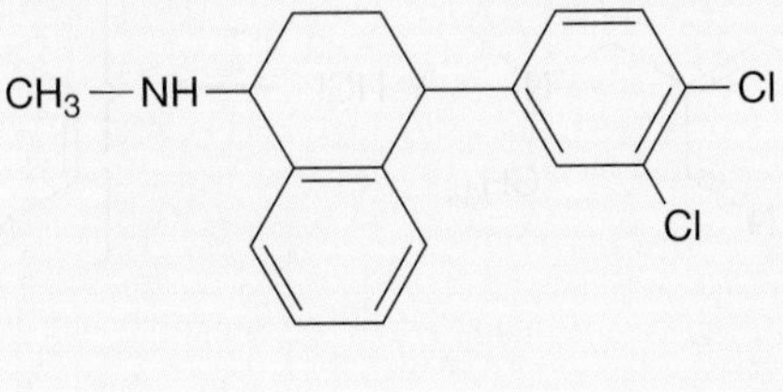

CH3—NH— Cl

Cl **Sertraline**

continued

a) Draw the structure of sertraline hydrochloride.
b) Why do you think that the manufacturers of Zoloft use this salt, rather than sertraline itself?

11.44 Fenfluramine hydrochloride is the active ingredient in many appetite suppressants. This compound is formed when fenfluramine reacts with HCl.
a) Draw the structure of fenfluramine hydrochloride. (The structure of fenfluramine is given in Problem 11.41.)
b) Why do you think that the manufacturers of appetite suppressants use this salt, rather than fenfluramine itself?

11.45 Tetrahydrocannabinol (THC) is the physiologically active compound in marijuana, which is made from the dried seed pods of the hemp plant *(Cannabis sativa)*. The structure of THC is shown here. Is THC an alkaloid? Why or why not?

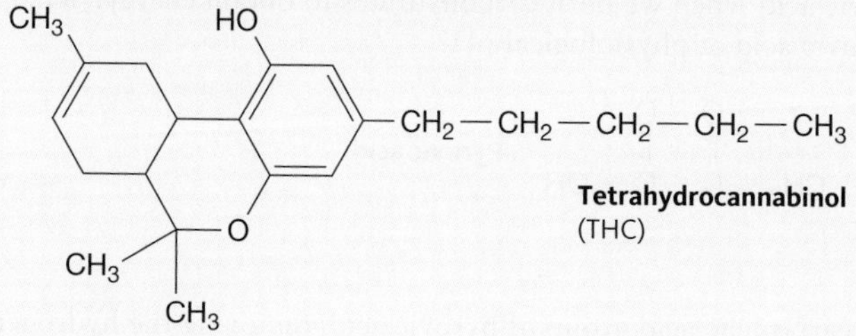

CH_3, HO, $-CH_2-CH_2-CH_2-CH_2-CH_3$, O, CH_3, CH_3

Tetrahydrocannabinol (THC)

11.46 Cocaine is a widely abused drug that is found in the leaves of the coca plant *(Erythroxylon coca)*. The structure of cocaine is shown here. Is cocaine an alkaloid? Why or why not?

O, $C-O-CH_2-CH_3$, $N-CH_3$, $O-C$(=O)

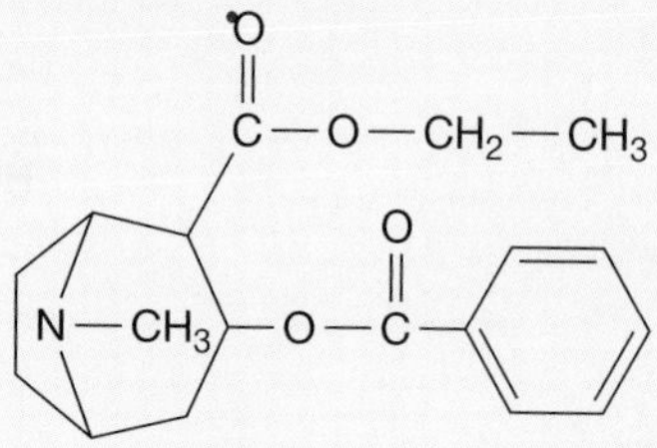

Cocaine

11.6 The Physiological Behavior of Organic Acids and Bases

OBJECTIVE: *Draw the structures of organic acids and bases as they exist under physiological conditions.*

In your body, the pH is maintained close to 7 by a variety of buffer systems, as we saw in Section 7.8. These buffers neutralize most of the organic acids and bases that are produced by your body, removing or adding hydrogen ions as needed to maintain the proper pH. In this section, we will see how organic acids and bases are affected by the buffers in body fluids.

Carboxylic Acids Are Converted to Their Conjugates at pH 7

Carboxylic acids are the most common acidic compounds in our bodies. When a carboxylic acid dissolves in water, the resulting solution is acidic, so our bodies must neutralize carboxylic acids by removing the H^+ from them. This is one of the functions of the buffers in our body fluids. For example, working muscles produce lactic acid and release it into the blood. The HCO_3^- ions in blood plasma neutralize the lactic acid instantly, converting the acid into harmless lactate ions. The chemical equation for this reaction is

$$HC_3H_5O_3 + HCO_3^- \rightleftharpoons C_3H_5O_3^- + H_2CO_3$$

Lactic acid — **Lactate ion**

A small percentage of the lactic acid remains after this reaction, but more than 99% of the lactic acid molecules are neutralized.

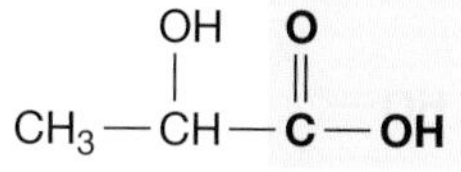

$CH_3-CH(OH)-C(=O)-OH$

Lactic acid
Present only in low concentration in body fluids

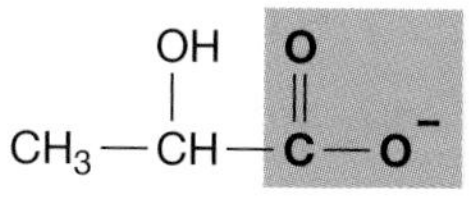

$CH_3-CH(OH)-C(=O)-O^-$

Lactate ion
The dominant form at physiological pH

Health Note: When the body produces so many molecules of carboxylic acid that the body's buffering systems cannot maintain the correct pH, the result is *metabolic acidosis.* Metabolic acidosis can also occur during severe diarrhea, when large amounts of HCO_3^- ions in the digestive fluids are lost before they can be reabsorbed, and in kidney failure, when the kidneys lose the ability to remove and excrete H^+ ions from H_2CO_3.

Many of the organic acids that are important in biochemistry contain two or more carboxylic acid functional groups. In our bodies, all of these groups are converted to the corresponding carboxylate ions. A good example is succinic acid, which is produced when our bodies break down carbohydrates, fats, and proteins to obtain energy. Succinic acid is one of the products of the citric acid cycle, which we will examine in Chapter 15.

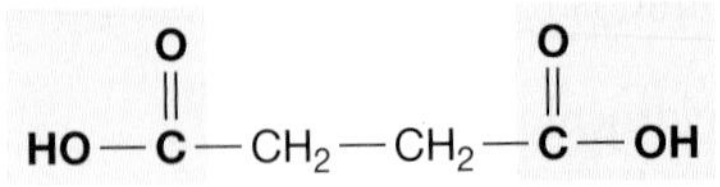

$$HO{-}\overset{\overset{\displaystyle O}{\|}}{C}{-}CH_2{-}CH_2{-}\overset{\overset{\displaystyle O}{\|}}{C}{-}OH$$

Succinic acid

$$^{-}O{-}\overset{\overset{\displaystyle O}{\|}}{C}{-}CH_2{-}CH_2{-}\overset{\overset{\displaystyle O}{\|}}{C}{-}O^{-}$$

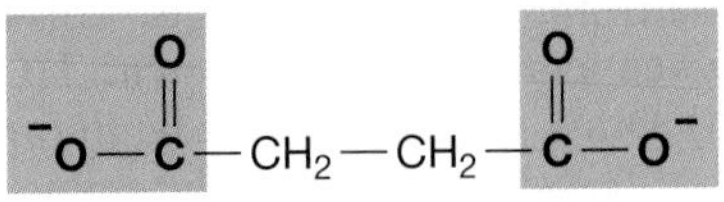

Succinate ion
The dominant form at physiological pH

Sample Problem **11.16**

Identifying the dominant form of an organic acid at pH 7

Our bodies produce pyruvic acid when we burn carbohydrates to obtain energy. What is the dominant form of pyruvic acid at physiological pH?

$$CH_3{-}\overset{\overset{\displaystyle O}{\|}}{C}{-}\overset{\overset{\displaystyle O}{\|}}{C}{-}OH$$

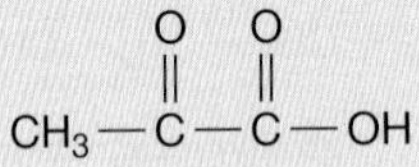

Pyruvic acid

SOLUTION

Our bodies neutralize the carboxylic acid group of pyruvic acid, removing the hydrogen ion and converting the acid into its conjugate base. The dominant form of this acid is the pyruvate ion.

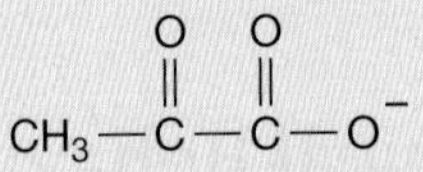

$$CH_3{-}\overset{\overset{\displaystyle O}{\|}}{C}{-}\overset{\overset{\displaystyle O}{\|}}{C}{-}O^{-}$$

Pyruvate ion

TRY IT YOURSELF: *Our bodies produce oxaloacetic acid when we burn any kind of nutrient to obtain energy. What is the dominant form of oxaloacetic acid at physiological pH?*

$$HO{-}\overset{\overset{\displaystyle O}{\|}}{C}{-}\overset{\overset{\displaystyle O}{\|}}{C}{-}CH_2{-}\overset{\overset{\displaystyle O}{\|}}{C}{-}OH$$

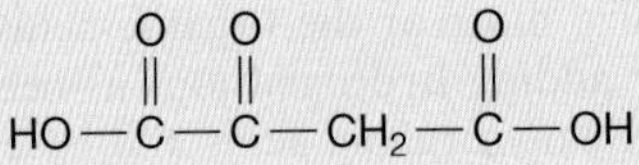

Oxaloacetic acid

For additional practice, try Core Problems 11.47 (parts a and d) and 11.48 (parts b and d).

Phenols and thiols are also acidic, but our bodies do not neutralize these functional groups. Phenols and thiols are much weaker than carboxylic acids, so they have little effect on the pH of body fluids and they do not react to any significant extent with the buffer chemicals in our bodies. For example, when our bodies break down the amino acid tyrosine, they form the compound shown here. At physiological pH, the carboxylic acid group in this compound is converted to its conjugate, but the phenol group is not.

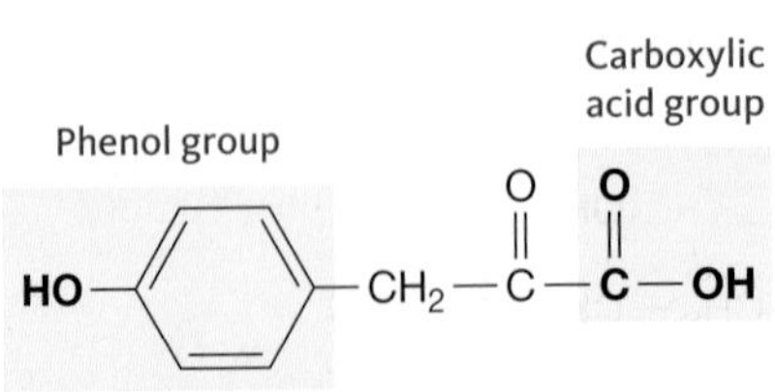

Phenol group

Carboxylic acid group

$$HO{-}C_6H_4{-}CH_2{-}\overset{\overset{\displaystyle O}{\|}}{C}{-}\overset{\overset{\displaystyle O}{\|}}{C}{-}OH$$

4-Hydroxyphenylpyruvic acid

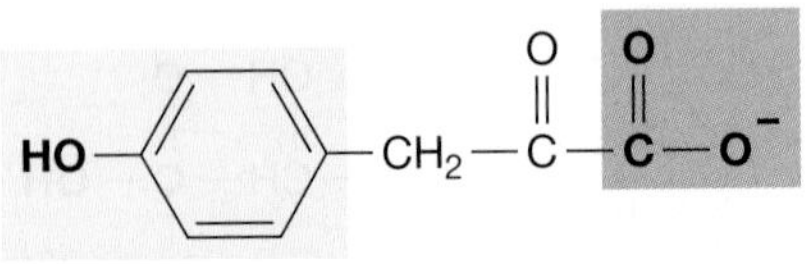

Carboxylate ion

$$HO{-}C_6H_4{-}CH_2{-}\overset{\overset{\displaystyle O}{\|}}{C}{-}\overset{\overset{\displaystyle O}{\|}}{C}{-}O^{-}$$

4-Hydroxyphenylpyruvate ion
(the dominant form at physiological pH)

Many Amines Are Converted to Their Conjugates at pH 7

Amines are bases, and many amines are strong enough to have a significant impact on the pH of their solutions. Our bodies neutralize these amines, using the same buffer systems that neutralize acids. However, neutralizing a base means *adding* H^+, which converts the base into its conjugate acid. For example, our bodies produce an amine called dopamine that affects many aspects of our nervous system. The amine group in dopamine is neutralized by carbonic acid in body fluids, as shown here:

$$(HO)_2C_6H_3-CH_2-CH_2-\mathbf{NH_2} + H_2CO_3 \longrightarrow (HO)_2C_6H_3-CH_2-CH_2-\mathbf{NH_3^+} + HCO_3^-$$

Dopamine
Present only in low concentration in body fluids

Dopammonium ion
The dominant form at physiological pH

Unlike carboxylic acids, amines have a range of strengths. If the nitrogen atom is attached to alkyl groups, the amine is a strong enough base to require neutralization in our bodies. However, amines in which the nitrogen atom is attached to an aromatic ring, or is part of an aromatic ring, are much weaker and do not react with the buffers to a significant extent. For example, nicotine contains two nitrogen atoms, but only one of them bonds to H^+ at physiological pH, as shown here. The nitrogen atom that is part of the aromatic ring is so weakly basic that it does not react with the buffers in our bodies.

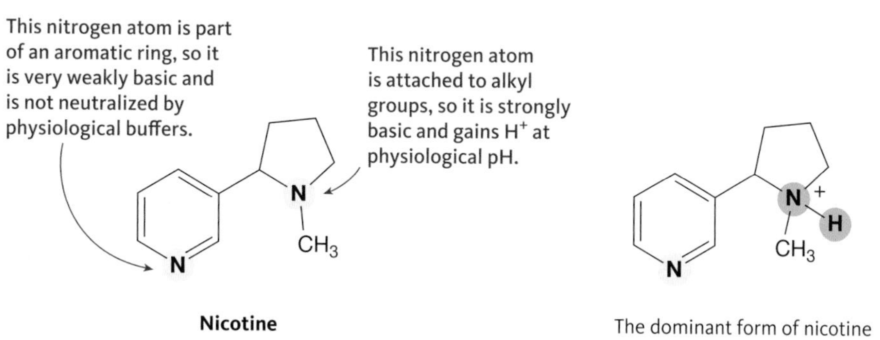

This nitrogen atom is part of an aromatic ring, so it is very weakly basic and is not neutralized by physiological buffers.
This nitrogen atom is attached to alkyl groups, so it is strongly basic and gains H⁺ at physiological pH.
N
CH3
N
N
H
CH3
N

Nicotine

The dominant form of nicotine at physiological pH

Health Note: Nicotine is a poisonous alkaloid found in tobacco. Pure nicotine has a variety of physiological effects, but it is not significantly addictive and it does not cause cancer. However, tobacco also contains MAOIs (see Health Note on page 463), and this combination produces the dependency that is characteristic of tobacco addiction.

The nitrogen atom in the five-membered ring of tryptamines also does not react with the buffers in body fluids.

If a compound contains two nitrogen atoms that are attached to alkyl groups or hydrogen atoms, both nitrogen atoms become bonded to H^+ at physiological pH. A good example of a molecule that contains two amino groups is putrescine, one of the compounds responsible for the unpleasant smell of decaying fish.

$$NH_2-CH_2-CH_2-CH_2-CH_2-NH_2 \qquad {}^+NH_3-CH_2-CH_2-CH_2-CH_2-NH_3^+$$

Putrescine
Present only in low concentration at pH 7

Putrescinium ion
The dominant form at physiological pH

Sample Problem 11.17

Identifying the dominant form of an amine at pH 7

What is the dominant form of the following amine at physiological pH?

$$H-N(C_5H_9)-CH_2-NH-CH_3$$

continued

SOLUTION

This molecule contains two nitrogen atoms, neither of which is part of an aromatic ring or bonded to an aromatic ring. Therefore, both nitrogen atoms are fairly strong bases and will be bonded to H^+ at physiological pH. The dominant form of this molecule is

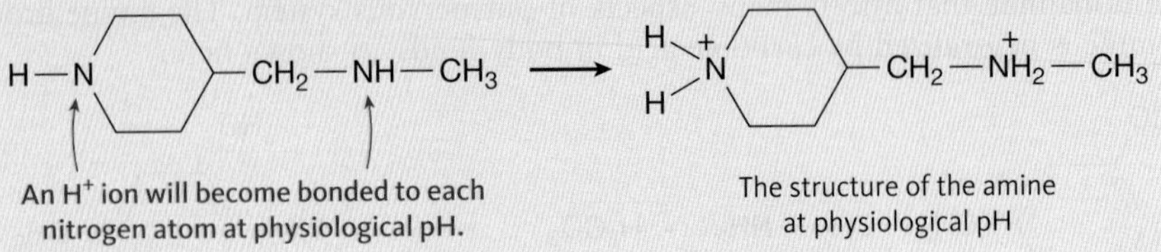

H—N(ring)—CH_2—NH—CH_3 → H_2N^+(ring)—CH_2—$\overset{+}{N}H_2$—CH_3

An H^+ ion will become bonded to each nitrogen atom at physiological pH.

The structure of the amine at physiological pH

TRY IT YOURSELF: *What is the dominant form of the following amine at physiological pH?*

(pyridine ring)—CH_2—CH_2—NH_2

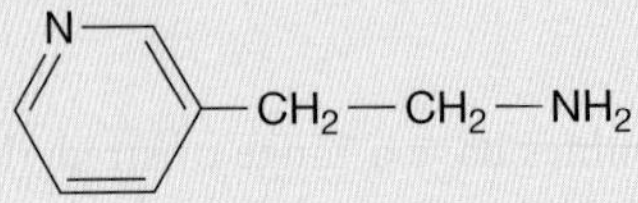

For additional practice, try Core Problems 11.47 (parts b and f) and 11.48 (parts a and f).

Organic Phosphates Form Buffers at pH 7

Phosphate ions play an important role in allowing us to obtain energy from food. The structure of the phosphate ion is shown here. Note that in this ion, the phosphorus atom does not satisfy the octet rule.

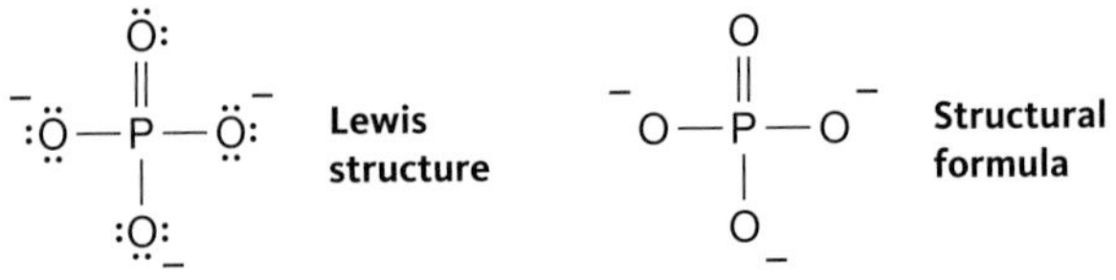

Lewis structure

Structural formula

Phosphate is a strong base, so it bonds to H^+ at physiological pH. As we saw in Chapter 7, at pH 7 phosphate forms a buffer that contains a mixture of $H_2PO_4^-$ and HPO_4^{2-} ions. The phosphate ions do not bond to three hydrogen ions, because H_3PO_4 is a rather strong acid.

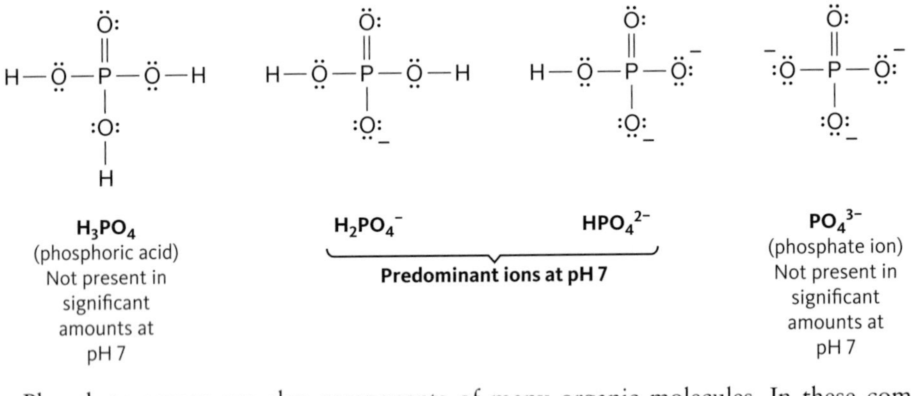

H_3PO_4 (phosphoric acid) Not present in significant amounts at pH 7

$H_2PO_4^-$ **HPO_4^{2-}** Predominant ions at pH 7

PO_4^{3-} (phosphate ion) Not present in significant amounts at pH 7

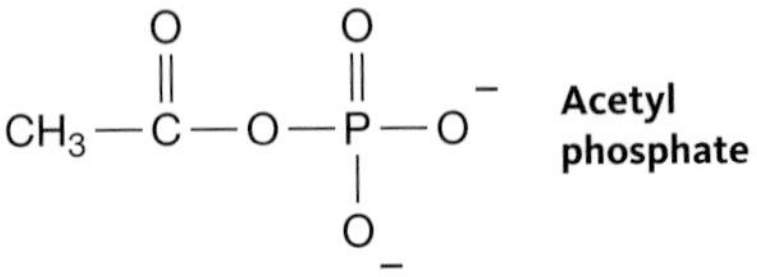

Health Note: Our bodies must make a range of molecules that contain phosphate, so phosphorus is an essential element. However, the phosphorus must come from phosphate ions or organic molecules that contain them; pure phosphorus and other phosphorus-containing compounds are useless to us, and many of them are highly poisonous.

Phosphate groups are also components of many organic molecules. In these compounds, the phosphate group is directly attached to a carbon atom. An example is acetyl phosphate, a compound that is made by some species of bacteria.

$CH_3—C(=O)—O—P(=O)(O^-)—O^-$ **Acetyl phosphate**

Like the phosphate ion itself, organic phosphates form buffer solutions that contain a mixture of two ions. In one of the ions, the phosphate group is bonded to a hydrogen atom, while in the other the hydrogen atom is absent.

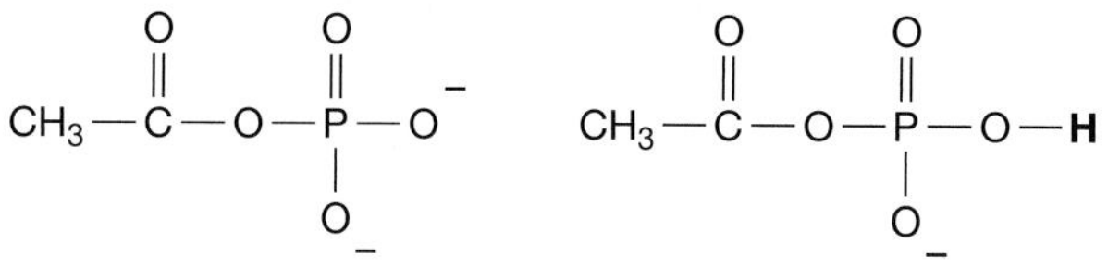

$$CH_3{-}C(=O){-}O{-}P(=O)(O^-){-}O^- \qquad CH_3{-}C(=O){-}O{-}P(=O)(O^-){-}O{-}\mathbf{H}$$

The two forms of acetyl phosphate in a physiological solution

The behavior of acetyl phosphate is typical of organic phosphates, and this behavior presents a problem when we want to draw an accurate structure of these substances. In practice, organic phosphates are generally drawn in the form that contains no hydrogen atoms bonded to phosphate. You should be aware, though, that both forms are present at pH 7 and that organic phosphates function as buffers at physiological pH.

Sample Problem 11.18

Drawing the structure of an organic phosphate at pH 7

When your body burns fats to produce energy, one of the compounds that it forms during this process is glycerol-1-phosphate. How will this molecule actually appear at pH 7?

$$CH_2(OH){-}CH(OH){-}CH_2{-}O{-}P(=O)(O^-){-}O^-$$

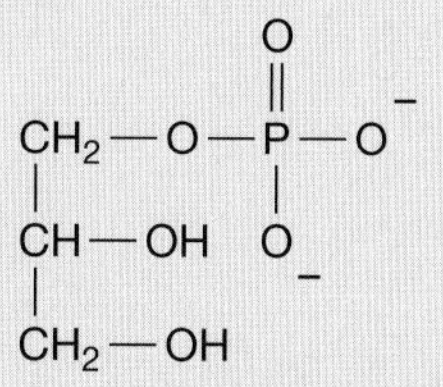

Glycerol-1-phosphate

SOLUTION

Organic phosphates appear in a mixture of two forms at pH 7. One form has no hydrogen atoms bonded to the oxygen atoms of the phosphate group, as shown earlier. The other form has one hydrogen atom bonded to the phosphate. We can draw the hydrogen atom attached to either of the two singly bonded oxygen atoms in the phosphate group.

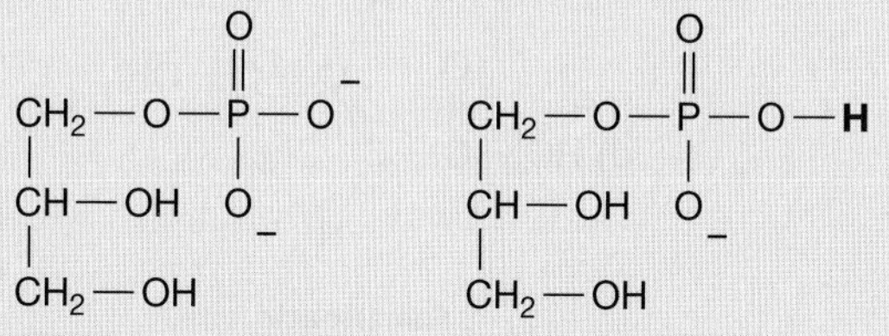

$$CH_2(OH){-}CH(OH){-}CH_2{-}O{-}P(=O)(O^-){-}O^- \qquad CH_2(OH){-}CH(OH){-}CH_2{-}O{-}P(=O)(O^-){-}O{-}\mathbf{H}$$

TRY IT YOURSELF: *When your body burns carbohydrates to produce energy, one of the compounds that it forms during this process is dihydroxyacetone phosphate. How will this molecule actually appear at pH 7?*

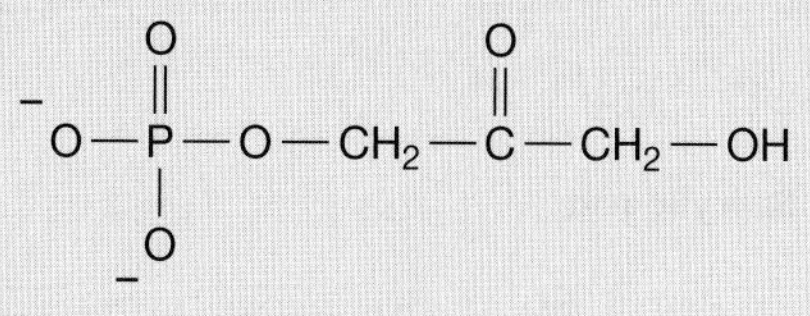

$$^-O{-}P(=O)(O^-){-}O{-}CH_2{-}C(=O){-}CH_2{-}OH$$

Dihydroxyacetone phosphate

For additional practice, try Core Problems 11.49 and 11.50.

Table 11.5 summarizes the behavior of the organic acids and bases that you have encountered in this chapter.

TABLE 11.5 Summary of Organic Acids and Bases under Physiological Conditions

Functional Group	Structure of Functional Group	Structure at Physiological pH (around 7)
Carboxylic acid	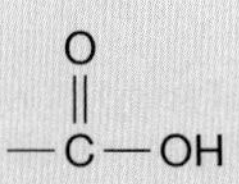 $-C(=O)-OH$	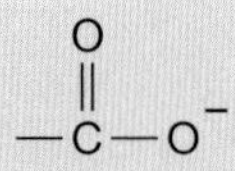 $-C(=O)-O^-$
Phenol	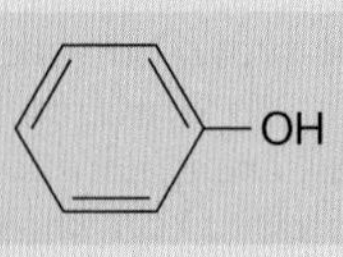 C_6H_5-OH	Same as original phenol
Thiol	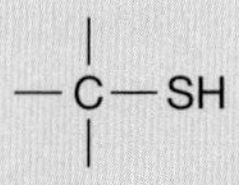 $-C-SH$	Same as original thiol
Amine (if the nitrogen atom is not attached to or part of an aromatic ring)	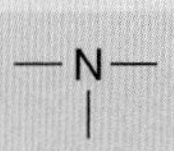 $-N-$	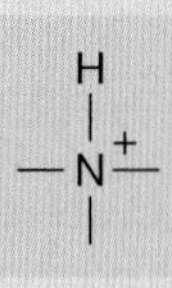 $-N^+H-$
Organic phosphate	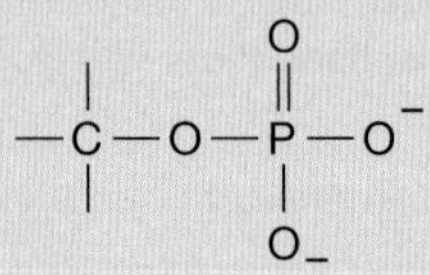 $-C-O-P(=O)(O^-)-O^-$	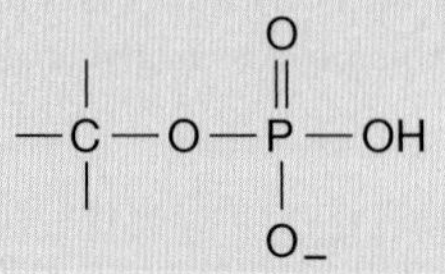 $-C-O-P(=O)(O^-)-OH$ and $-C-O-P(=O)(O^-)-O^-$ 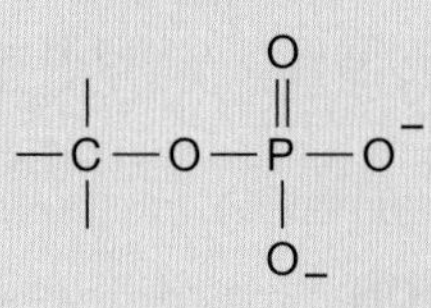

CORE PROBLEMS

11.47 What is the dominant form of each of the following compounds at physiological pH?

a) 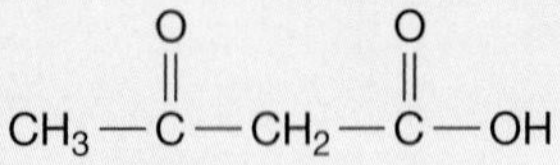 $CH_3-C(=O)-CH_2-C(=O)-OH$

Acetoacetic acid

b) 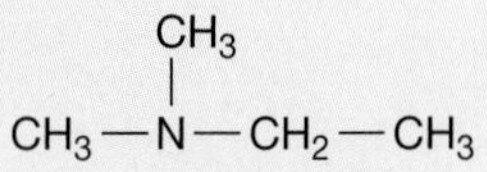 $CH_3-N(CH_3)-CH_2-CH_3$

Ethyldimethylamine

c) 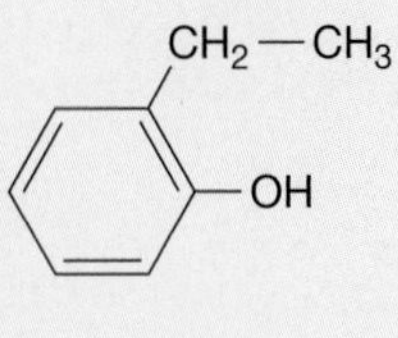 Benzene ring bearing CH_2-CH_3 and, on the adjacent carbon, OH

Phlorol

d) 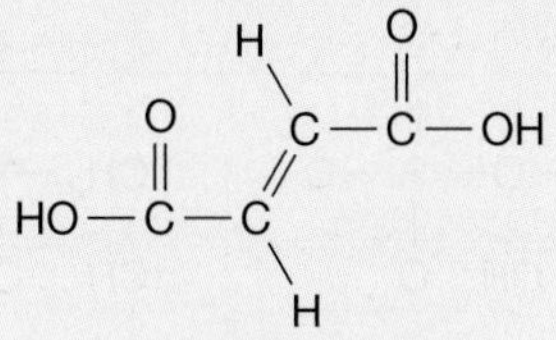 $HO-C(=O)-CH=CH-C(=O)-OH$ (H atoms on opposite sides of the C=C)

Fumaric acid

e) 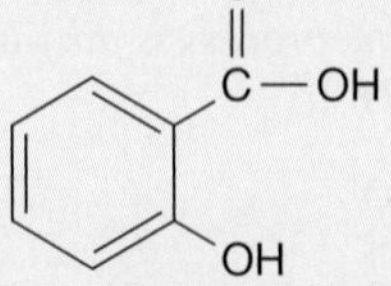 Benzene ring bearing $C(=O)-OH$ and, on the adjacent carbon, OH

Salicylic acid

f) $NH_2-CH_2-CH_2-CH_2-CH_2-CH_2-NH_2$

Cadaverine

continued

11.48 What is the dominant form of each of the following compounds at physiological pH?

a) 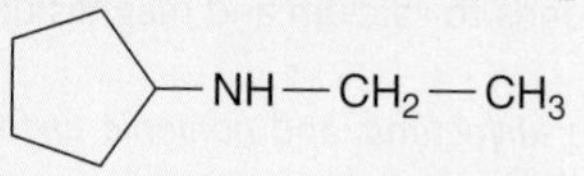 Cyclopentyl—$NH-CH_2-CH_3$

Cyclopentylethylamine

b) 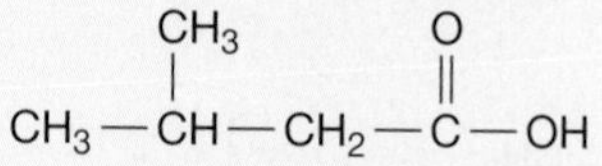 $CH_3-CH(CH_3)-CH_2-C(=O)-OH$

Isovaleric acid

c) 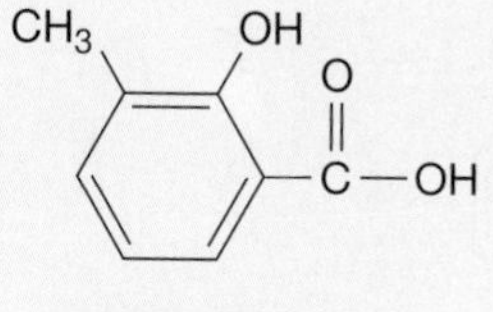 Benzene ring with CH_3, OH, and $C(=O)-OH$ substituents

***Ortho*-cresotic acid**

d) 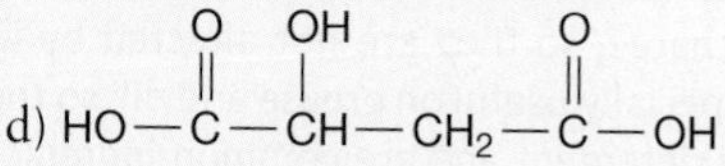 $HO-C(=O)-CH(OH)-CH_2-C(=O)-OH$

Malic acid

e) 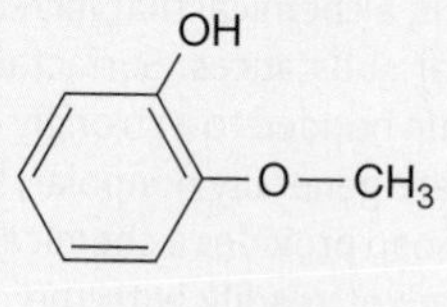 Benzene ring with OH and $O-CH_3$ substituents

Guaiacol

f) $NH_2-CH_2-CH_2-CH_2-NH_2$

Propylenediamine

11.49 Glyceraldehyde-3-phosphate is formed in the metabolic pathway that breaks down sugars to produce energy. How will this molecule actually appear at physiological pH?

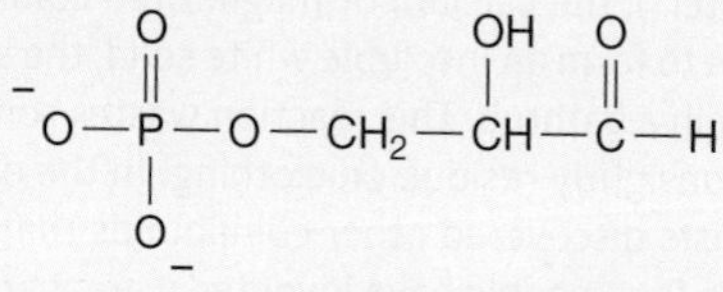

$^{-}O-P(=O)(O^{-})-O-CH_2-CH(OH)-C(=O)-H$

Glyceraldehyde-3-phosphate

11.50 Another compound that is formed when our bodies break down sugars is 3-phosphoglyceric acid. How will this molecule actually appear at physiological pH?

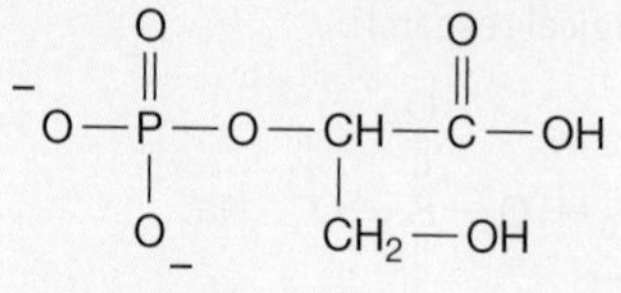

$^{-}O-P(=O)(O^{-})-O-CH(CH_2-OH)-C(=O)-OH$ **3-Phosphoglyceric acid**

CONNECTIONS

Soaps and Detergents

We have seen that carboxylic acids react with strong bases, like KOH and NaOH, to form carboxylate salts. However, a much older way of making long-chain carboxylate salts is heating animal fats with a strong base. You will learn more about this reaction in Chapter 12, but here is a typical example:

$$C_{39}H_{74}O_6 + 3\ NaOH \rightarrow C_3H_8O_3 + 3\ NaC_{12}H_{23}O_2$$

a fat **glycerol** **a carboxylate salt**

The carboxylate salt that is formed in this reaction is soap, and this is an example of a *saponification* reaction ("making soap"). People have known how to make soap for at least 4000 years, although for most of that time they used potassium carbonate (K_2CO_3) instead of sodium hydroxide. The potassium carbonate was made by simply rinsing wood ashes with water, so making soap only required water, wood, and fat. However, potassium-containing soaps are liquids while sodium-based soaps are solids, so once NaOH became commercially available in the 1800s, sodium soaps became the dominant form.

Jonathan Ross/Getty Images

Hand washing helps to prevent the spread of infections, making it a critical component of health care.

continued

Soap is an example of a *surfactant*, a chemical that increases the ability of water to moisten nonpolar substances. Surfactants contain a hydrophobic hydrocarbon chain bonded to a strongly charged hydrophilic region. Dirt and grease are generally nonpolar, so water cannot wet them or rinse them off. Soap provides a chemical bridge; the hydrophobic part of the soap mixes readily with the dirt, and the hydrophilic carboxylate group allows the soap to be carried away by rinse water.

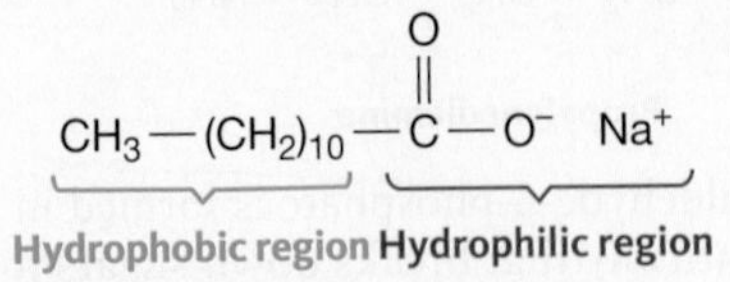

$$\underbrace{CH_3-(CH_2)_{10}}_{\text{Hydrophobic region}}-\underbrace{\overset{\overset{\displaystyle O}{\|}}{C}-O^- \quad Na^+}_{\text{Hydrophilic region}}$$

Soap is an excellent cleaning agent, but it has some drawbacks. If soap is dissolved in water that contains calcium or magnesium ions ("hard water"), the calcium or magnesium combines with the carboxylate ion to form an insoluble white solid, the soap scum you may have seen in a bathtub. This reaction wastes some of the soap and leaves an unsightly residue on clothing. In the early twentieth century, chemists discovered other compounds that act as surfactants, and since then people have invented a great array of alternatives to soap. These compounds, called *detergents*, range from mild hand cleansers to harsh cleaners for dishes and laundry, but they all contain a large hydrocarbon portion bonded to a strongly hydrophilic portion.

You can find examples of detergents in most household cleaning products. A common example is sodium dodecyl sulfate (SDS, also called sodium lauryl sulfate), an ingredient in many shampoos and a useful chemical in biological research.

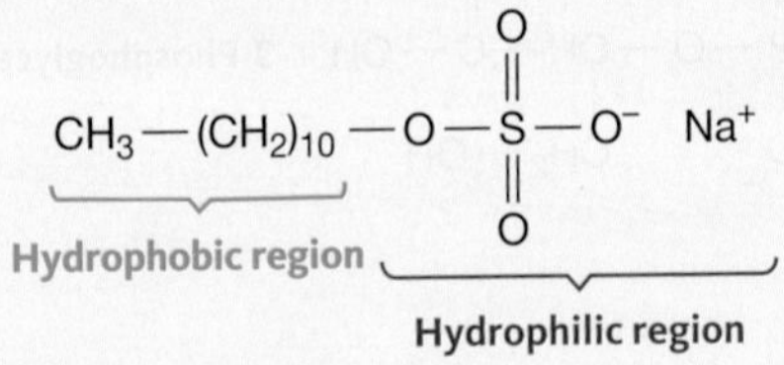

$$\underbrace{CH_3-(CH_2)_{10}}_{\text{Hydrophobic region}}-\underbrace{O-\overset{\overset{\displaystyle O}{\|}}{\underset{\underset{\displaystyle O}{\|}}{S}}-O^- \quad Na^+}_{\text{Hydrophilic region}}$$

Soap and SDS are called *anionic surfactants*, because the organic part of these compounds is negatively charged. Anionic surfactants are particularly effective at loosening and removing dirt particles from fabrics and skin. However, all anionic surfactants are attracted to the cations in hard water, reducing their effectiveness. Adding an ionic compound such as washing soda (sodium carbonate, Na_2CO_3) or borax ($Na_4B_4O_5(OH)_4$) decreases the amount of laundry detergent you need by forming tight bonds to calcium and magnesium ions in hard water.

You can also find *cationic surfactants* and *nonionic surfactants* in household products. Cationic surfactants such as benzalkonium chloride (shown here) have a positive charge on their organic portion. Many of them kill bacteria, so they are used in antibacterial cleaning products.

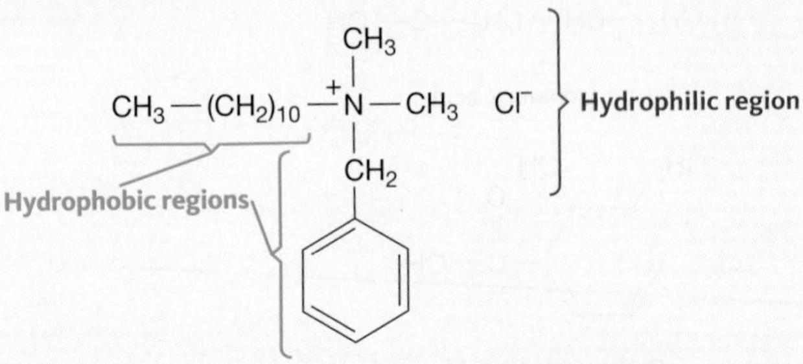

$$CH_3-(CH_2)_{10}-\overset{+}{N}(CH_3)_2(CH_2C_6H_5) \quad Cl^-$$

Hydrophobic regions: the $CH_3-(CH_2)_{10}$ chain and the benzene ring. Hydrophilic region: the $\overset{+}{N}$ with its CH_3 groups and Cl^-.

Nonionic surfactants like cocamide DEA (cocamide diethanolamine) have no ionic charge, so they are not affected by ions in hard water. They are especially useful on grease and oil, so they are often added to laundry detergent and are common ingredients in shampoos.

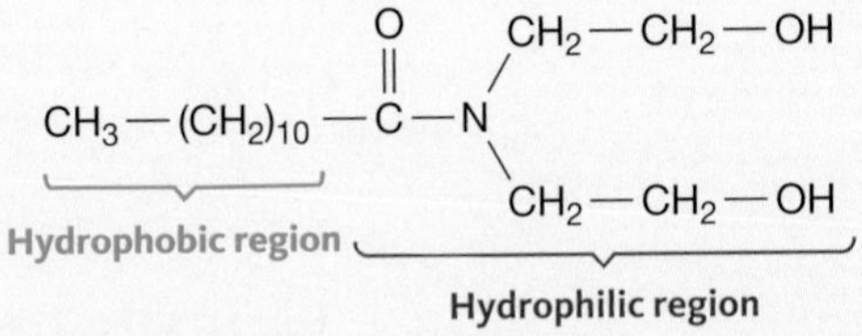

$$\underbrace{CH_3-(CH_2)_{10}}_{\text{Hydrophobic region}}-\underbrace{\overset{\overset{\displaystyle O}{\|}}{C}-N(CH_2-CH_2-OH)_2}_{\text{Hydrophilic region}}$$

Cleaning products contain many other substances that are not surfactants. For examples, hand cleaners may contain glycerol to soften the skin, pumice to increase abrasion, titanium dioxide (TiO_2) to make the product opaque, preservatives, dyes, and perfumes. Most of these are added to increase sales of the products rather than to make them more effective. The ingredient list on a typical cleaning product can look formidable, but in the end these products are just fancy variations on the same chemistry that your great-great-grandparents used to clean their clothes and their bodies.

Key Terms

alkaloid – 11.5
alkylammonium ion – 11.4
amine – 11.3
carboxylate ion – 11.1
decarboxylation reaction – 11.2
oxidative decarboxylation – 11.2
thioester – 11.2
zwitterion – 11.4

Classes of Organic Compounds

Class	Functional group	IUPAC suffix	Example
Carboxylate ion	$-\overset{\overset{\large O}{\|\|}}{C}-O^-$	*-oate*	$CH_3-CH_2-CH_2-\overset{\overset{\large O}{\|\|}}{C}-O^-$ **Butanoate ion**
Amine	$C-\underset{\|}{N}-$	*-amine**	$CH_3-CH_2-\underset{\underset{\large H}{\|}}{N}-CH_3$ **Ethylmethylamine** (trivial name)
Alkylammonium ion	$C-\overset{\overset{\large H}{\|}}{\underset{\|}{N}}{}^{+}-$	*-ammonium**	$CH_3-CH_2-\overset{\overset{\large H}{\|}}{\underset{\underset{\large H}{\|}}{N}}{}^{+}-CH_3$ **Ethylmethylammonium ion** (trivial name)

*Not an IUPAC suffix; the IUPAC names for amines and alkylammonium ions are not covered in this text.

Summary of Organic Reactions

1) ionization of a carboxylic acid

carboxylic acid + H_2O $\rightleftharpoons$ *carboxylate ion* + H_3O^+

$$CH_3-CH_2-\overset{\overset{\large O}{\|\|}}{C}-OH + H_2O \rightleftharpoons CH_3-CH_2-\overset{\overset{\large O}{\|\|}}{C}-O^- + H_3O^+$$

2) neutralization of a carboxylic acid

carboxylic acid + OH^- $\longrightarrow$ *carboxylate ion* + H_2O

$$CH_3-CH_2-\overset{\overset{\large O}{\|\|}}{C}-OH + OH^- \longrightarrow CH_3-CH_2-\overset{\overset{\large O}{\|\|}}{C}-O^- + H_2O$$

3) ionization of other organic acids

$$CH_3-CH_2-SH + H_2O \rightleftharpoons CH_3-CH_2-S^- + H_3O^+$$

A thiol

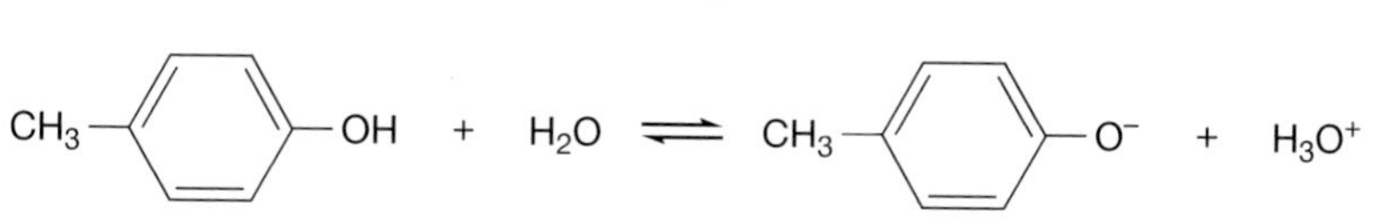

$$CH_3-C_6H_4-OH + H_2O \rightleftharpoons CH_3-C_6H_4-O^- + H_3O^+$$

A phenol

continued

4) neutralization of other organic acids

$$CH_3{-}CH_2{-}SH \;+\; OH^- \longrightarrow CH_3{-}CH_2{-}S^- \;+\; H_2O$$

A thiol

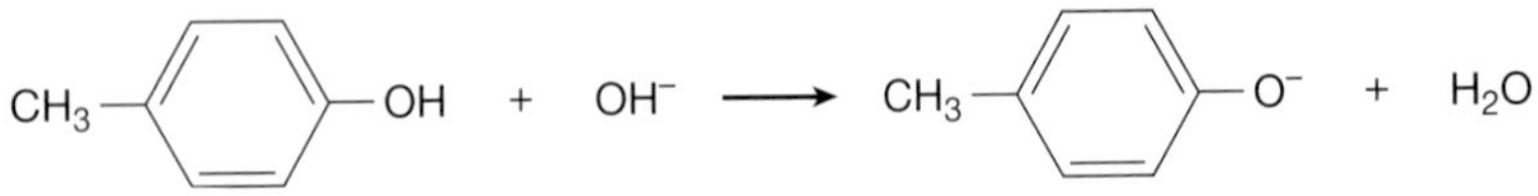

$$CH_3{-}C_6H_4{-}OH \;+\; OH^- \longrightarrow CH_3{-}C_6H_4{-}O^- \;+\; H_2O$$

A phenol

5) decarboxylation reaction

carboxylic acid ⟶ *organic molecule* + CO_2

$$CH_3{-}\overset{O}{\overset{\|}{C}}{-}CH_2{-}\overset{O}{\overset{\|}{C}}{-}OH \longrightarrow CH_3{-}\overset{O}{\overset{\|}{C}}{-}CH_3 \;+\; CO_2$$

6) oxidative decarboxylation

carboxylic acid + *thiol* ⟶ *thioester* + *2 [H]* + CO_2

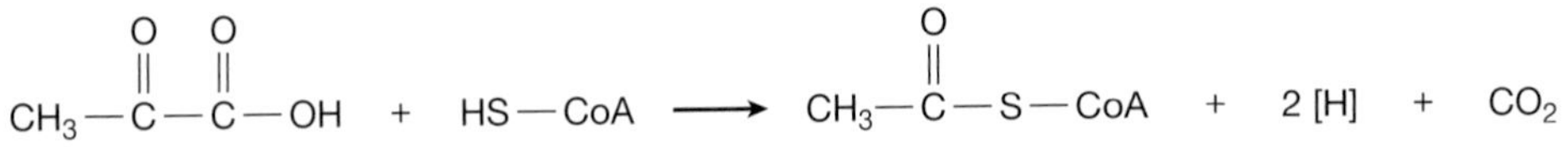

$$CH_3{-}\overset{O}{\overset{\|}{C}}{-}\overset{O}{\overset{\|}{C}}{-}OH \;+\; HS{-}CoA \longrightarrow CH_3{-}\overset{O}{\overset{\|}{C}}{-}S{-}CoA \;+\; 2\,[H] \;+\; CO_2$$

7) ionization of an amine

amine + H_2O ⇌ *alkylammonium ion* + OH^-

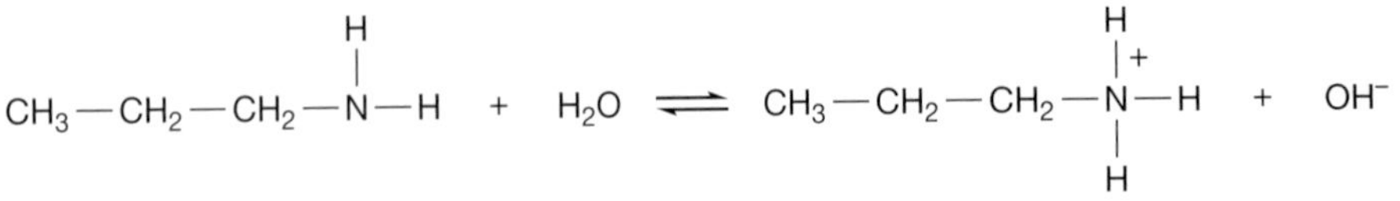

$$CH_3{-}CH_2{-}CH_2{-}\underset{}{\overset{H}{\overset{|}{N}}}{-}H \;+\; H_2O \rightleftharpoons CH_3{-}CH_2{-}CH_2{-}\underset{\underset{H}{|}}{\overset{H}{\overset{|}{N^+}}}{-}H \;+\; OH^-$$

8) neutralization of an amine

amine + *HX* ⟶ *alkylammonium ion* + X^-

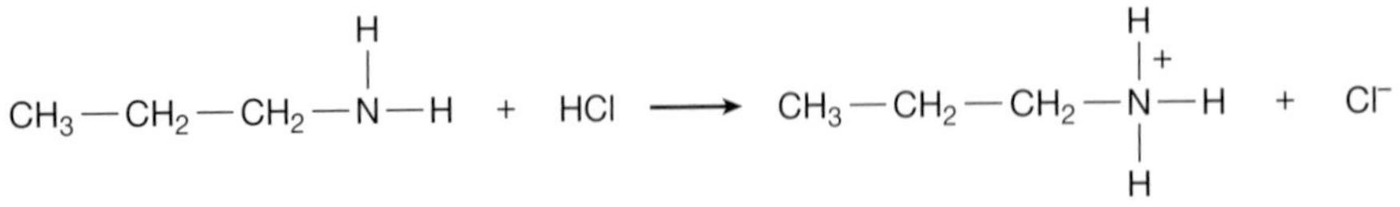

$$CH_3{-}CH_2{-}CH_2{-}\overset{H}{\overset{|}{N}}{-}H \;+\; HCl \longrightarrow CH_3{-}CH_2{-}CH_2{-}\underset{\underset{H}{|}}{\overset{H}{\overset{|}{N^+}}}{-}H \;+\; Cl^-$$

SUMMARY OF OBJECTIVES

Now that you have read the chapter, test yourself on your knowledge of the objectives, using this summary as a guide.

Section 11.1: **Write chemical equations for the reactions of organic acids with water and with bases, and relate the physical properties of the acids to those of their salts.**

- Carboxylic acids, phenols, and thiols are weak acids, with carboxylic acids being the strongest of the three types.
- Carboxylic acids ionize when they dissolve in water, producing H_3O^+ and a carboxylate ion.
- Carboxylic acids react with bases, transferring H^+ to the base.
- Carboxylate ions combine with cations to form salts.
- For most carboxylic acids, the solubility of the sodium or potassium salt is higher than that of the original acid.
- Phenols and thiols also ionize in water and react with bases.

Section 11.2: **Draw the products of decarboxylation reactions, and identify coenzymes that are required in decarboxylation reactions.**

- Carboxylic acids can lose CO_2 in a decarboxylation reaction.
- Simple decarboxylations normally require a carbonyl group on the β-carbon atom.
- In an oxidative decarboxylation, the acid loses CO_2 and becomes bonded to coenzyme A.
- Oxidative decarboxylations normally require a carbonyl group on the α-carbon atom of the carboxylic acid, and they use NAD^+ to remove the hydrogen atoms.

Section 11.3: **Name and draw the structures of simple amines, and relate the structures of amines to their physical properties.**

- Nitrogen forms three covalent bonds in organic compounds.
- Amines contain nitrogen bonded to carbon, and they are classified as primary, secondary, or tertiary based on the number of carbon atoms bonded to the nitrogen atom.
- Amines are named by listing the alkyl groups that are bonded to the nitrogen and adding the suffix *-amine.*
- Cyclic amines have special names that do not follow any system.
- Amines are polar molecules and can participate in hydrogen bonds, making them soluble in water and giving them higher boiling points than hydrocarbons.

Section 11.4: **Write chemical equations for the reactions of amines with water and with acids, and draw the zwitterion form of molecules that contain both acid and amine groups.**

- Amines ionize when they dissolve in water, producing OH^- and an alkylammonium ion.
- Amines react with acids, accepting a hydrogen ion from the acid.
- Compounds that contain an amine group and a carboxylic acid group form zwitterions.
- Alkylammonium ions combine with negative ions to form salts.

Section 11.5: **Recognize the phenethylamine and tryptamine structures in physiologically active amines, identify alkaloids, and explain the use of amine salts as medications.**

- A number of physiologically active amines have structures based on phenethylamine or tryptamine.
- Alkaloids are physiologically active amines that are found in plants.
- Medicines that contain amine functional groups are often given as their salts, because the salts are more soluble than the original amines.

Section 11.6: **Draw the structures of organic acids and bases as they exist under physiological conditions.**

- Carboxylic acids are converted into carboxylate ions by the buffers in body fluids.
- Thiols and phenols do not lose H^+ at physiological pH.
- Nonaromatic amines are converted into alkylammonium ions by the buffers in body fluids, but weaker amines do not ionize to a significant extent.
- Organic phosphates exist as a mixture of conjugate ions at pH 7.

Concept Questions

OWL Online homework for this chapter may be assigned in OWL.

* indicates more challenging problems.

11.51 What three types of organic compounds produce an acidic solution when they dissolve in water?

11.52 When we write an ionization reaction for an organic acid, why do we use a double arrow?

11.53 When we write the equation for the reaction of an organic acid with hydroxide ion, why do we use a single arrow?

11.54 One of the products of any decarboxylation reaction is a small molecule. What is that molecule?

11.55 All oxidative decarboxylation reactions require NAD^+. What is the function of the NAD^+?

11.56 The solubility of octanoic acid in water is 0.7 g/L. Would you expect the solubility of potassium octanoate to be around 0.7 g/L, greater than this number, or less than this number? Explain your answer.

11.57 How many bonds does a nitrogen atom usually form in an organic compound? Explain your answer.

11.58 When a nitrogen atom and a hydrogen atom form a covalent N–H bond, which atom is positively charged (if any)? Explain your answer.

11.59 Why do tertiary amines have lower boiling points than primary and secondary amines that contain the same numbers of atoms?

11.60 Why are the solubilities of amines higher than the solubilities of hydrocarbons?

11.61 When an amine dissolves in water, the resulting solution has a pH above 7. Why is this?

11.62 What is a zwitterion, and what kinds of organic compounds typically form zwitterions?

11.63 Many metabolic pathways produce carboxylic acids. Under normal physiological conditions, these acids immediately lose H^+. Where do these hydrogen ions go? Give a specific example of a substance that is present in body fluids and can accept a hydrogen ion.

11.64 Some metabolic pathways produce amines, which are basic. Under normal physiological conditions, the amines immediately become bonded to H^+. Where do these hydrogen ions come from? Give a specific example of a substance that is present in body fluids and can donate a hydrogen ion.

11.65 What are the two main forms of phosphate ion at physiological pH? Draw their structures, and write their chemical formulas.

Summary and Challenge Problems

11.66 Which of the following organic compounds are acids?

a) 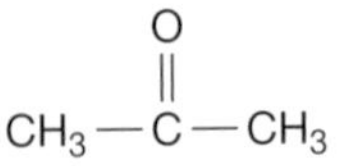 $CH_3-C(=O)-CH_3$

b) $CH_3-C(=O)-OH$

c) $CH_3-C(=O)-H$

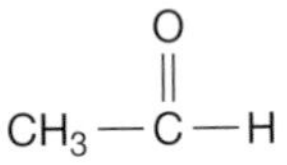

d) CH_3-CH_2-OH

e) 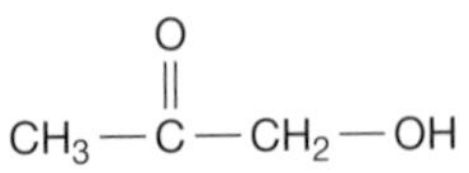 $CH_3-C(=O)-CH_2-OH$

f) 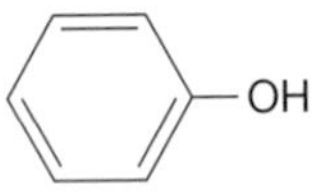 C_6H_5-OH (benzene ring bonded to OH)

g) 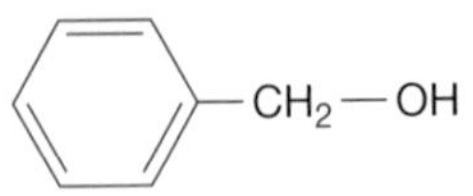 $C_6H_5-CH_2-OH$ (benzene ring bonded to CH_2-OH)

11.67 Complete the following chemical equations. Use condensed structures or line structures for organic compounds.

a) 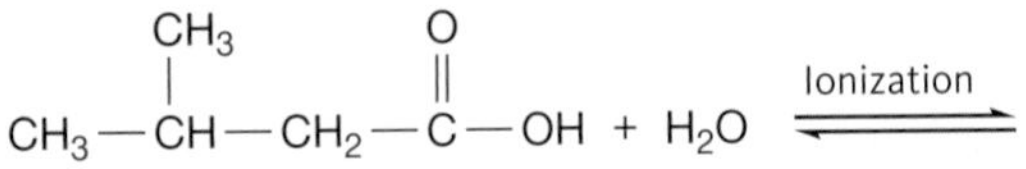 $CH_3-CH(CH_3)-CH_2-C(=O)-OH + H_2O \xrightleftharpoons{\text{Ionization}}$

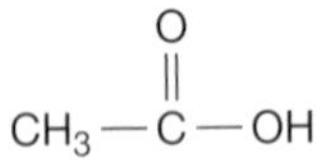

b) 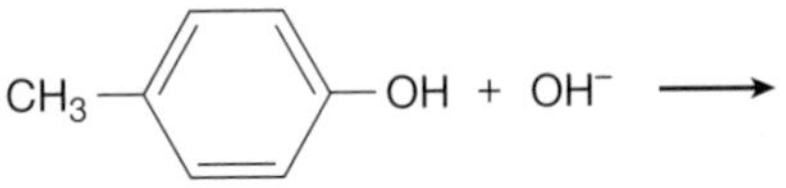 $CH_3-C_6H_4-OH + OH^- \longrightarrow$ (para-substituted benzene ring)

c) $CH_3-CH_2-CH(SH)-CH_3 + OH^- \longrightarrow$

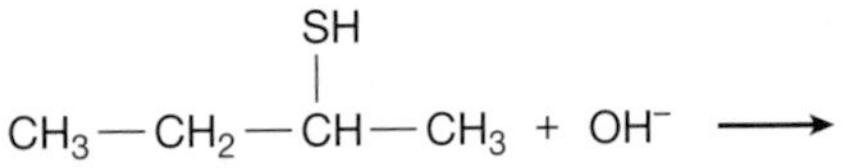

d) 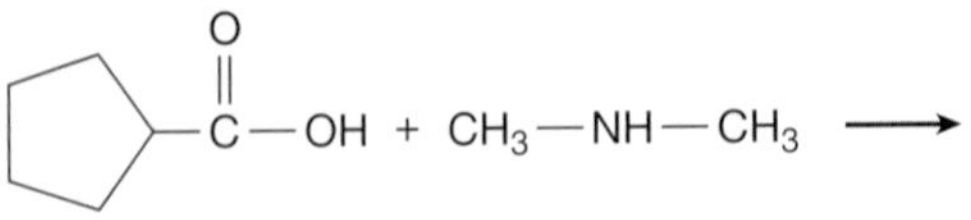 $C_5H_9-C(=O)-OH + CH_3-NH-CH_3 \longrightarrow$ (cyclopentane ring bonded to C(=O)–OH)

e) 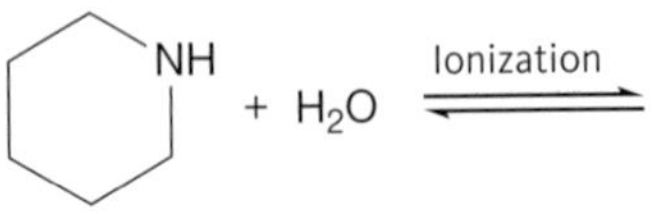 (piperidine ring, NH) $+ H_2O \xrightleftharpoons{\text{Ionization}}$

f) 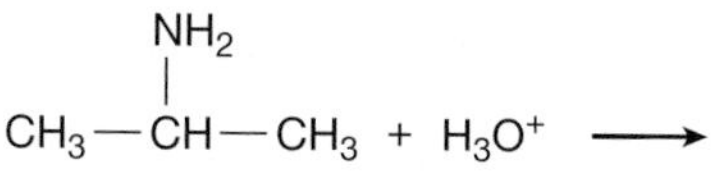 $CH_3-CH(NH_2)-CH_3 + H_3O^+ \longrightarrow$

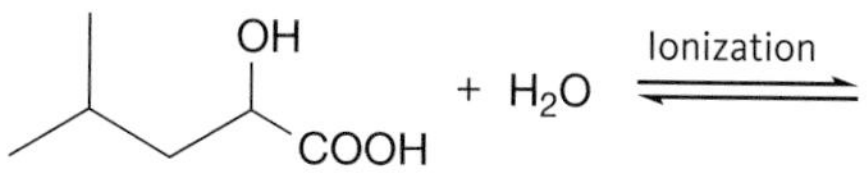

g) (skeletal structure: 3-hydroxy-4-methylpentanoic acid, with OH and COOH labels) $+ H_2O \xrightleftharpoons{\text{Ionization}}$

h) $C_6H_5-CH_2-\overset{O}{\overset{\|}{C}}-CH_2-\overset{O}{\overset{\|}{C}}-OH \xrightarrow{\text{Decarboxylation}}$

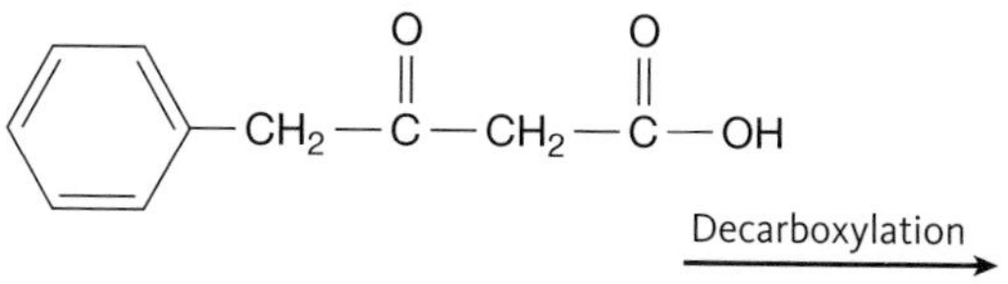

i) 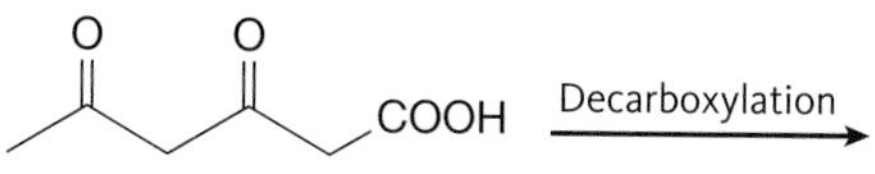 (skeletal structure with two C=O groups and COOH) $\xrightarrow{\text{Decarboxylation}}$

j) 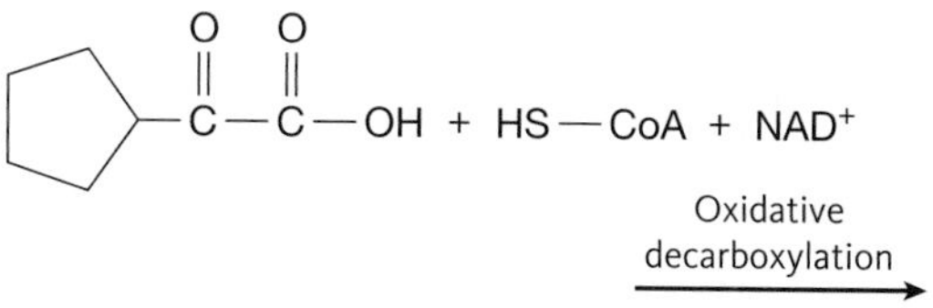 (cyclopentyl)$-\overset{O}{\overset{\|}{C}}-\overset{O}{\overset{\|}{C}}-OH + HS-CoA + NAD^+ \xrightarrow{\text{Oxidative decarboxylation}}$

k) 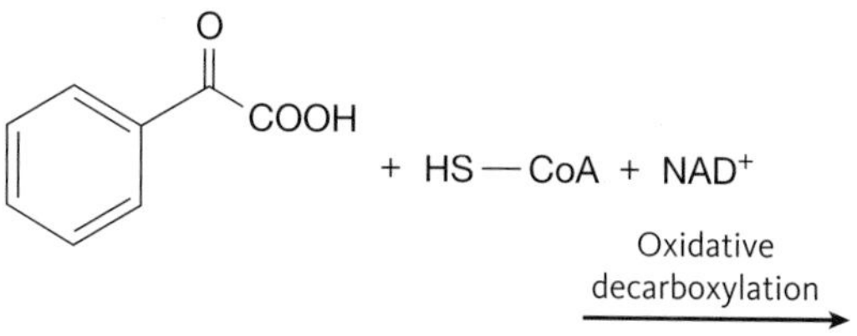 (phenyl)$-\overset{O}{\overset{\|}{C}}-COOH + HS-CoA + NAD^+ \xrightarrow{\text{Oxidative decarboxylation}}$

11.68 The structure of lactic acid is shown here. Using structural formulas, write chemical equations for the following reactions:

a) the ionization reaction of lactic acid in water
b) the reaction of lactic acid with hydroxide ion
c) the reaction of lactic acid with methylamine

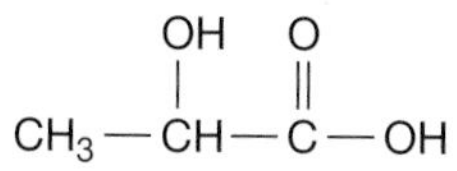

$CH_3-\overset{OH}{\overset{|}{CH}}-\overset{O}{\overset{\|}{C}}-OH$ **Lactic acid**

11.69 Succinic acid can react with two hydroxide ions. Using structural formulas, write a chemical equation for this reaction.

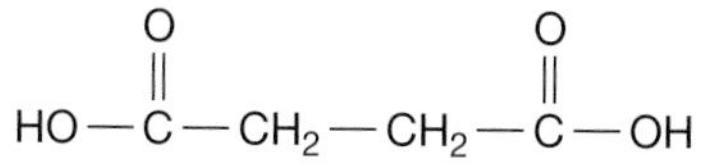

$HO-\overset{O}{\overset{\|}{C}}-CH_2-CH_2-\overset{O}{\overset{\|}{C}}-OH$ **Succinic acid**

11.70 *One of the following compounds reacts with two hydroxide ions, while the other reacts with only one hydroxide ion. Tell which compound is which, and explain your answer.

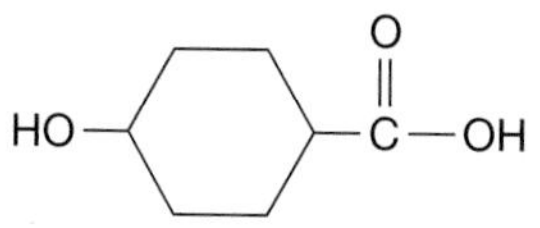

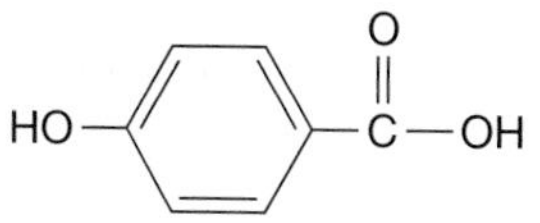

HO–(cyclohexane ring)$-\overset{O}{\overset{\|}{C}}-OH$

HO–(benzene ring)$-\overset{O}{\overset{\|}{C}}-OH$

11.71 The following compound can react with two H_3O^+ ions. Using structures for the organic molecules, write a balanced equation for this reaction.

HN NH

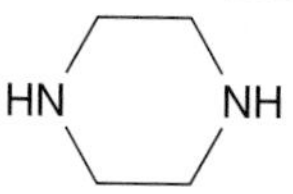

11.72 Draw the structures of the following substances:

a) propanoate ion
b) potassium butanoate
c) calcium formate
d) ethylpentylamine
e) dipropylammonium ion
f) cyclohexylammonium chloride
g) trimethylammonium pentanoate

11.73 Name the following compounds and ions:

a) 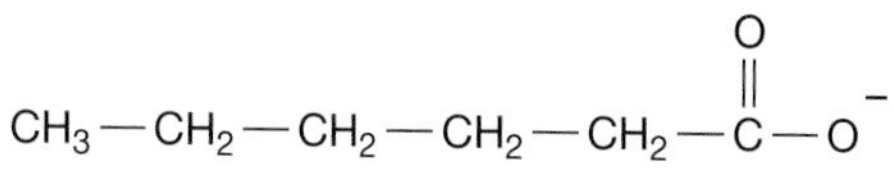 $CH_3-CH_2-CH_2-CH_2-CH_2-\overset{O}{\overset{\|}{C}}-O^-$

b) (skeletal chain)$-\overset{O}{\overset{\|}{C}}-O^-\ Na^+$

c) $CH_3-CH_2-CH_2-CH_2-NH_2$

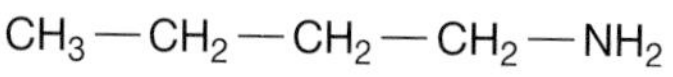

d) 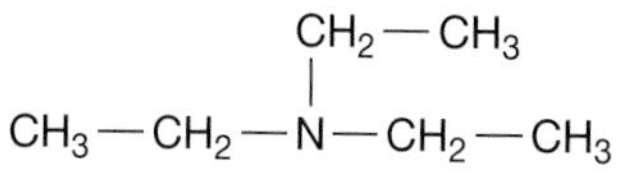 $CH_3-CH_2-\underset{}{\overset{CH_2-CH_3}{\overset{|}{N}}}-CH_2-CH_3$

e) 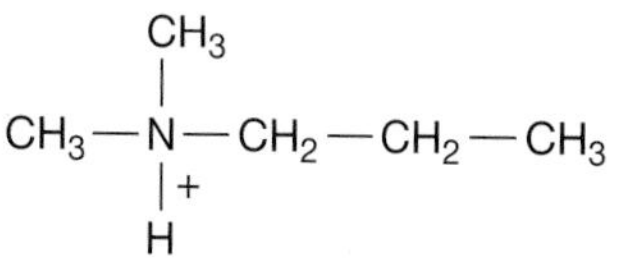 $CH_3-\overset{CH_3}{\overset{|}{\underset{H}{\underset{|+}{N}}}}-CH_2-CH_2-CH_3$

f) 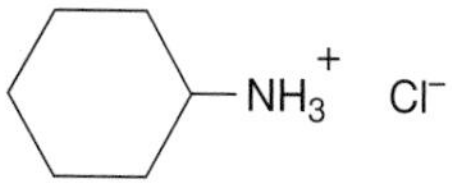 (cyclohexyl)$-\overset{+}{N}H_3\ Cl^-$

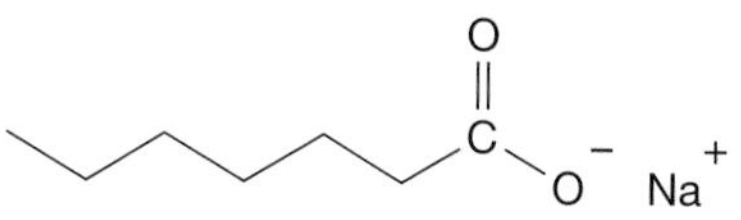

11.74 a) Name the ion whose structure is shown here:

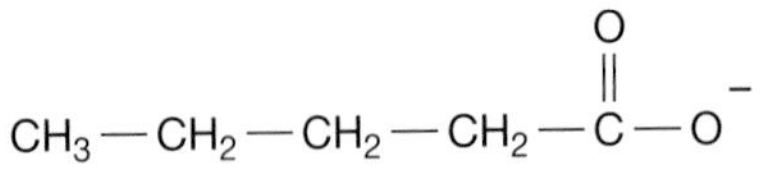

$$CH_3-CH_2-CH_2-CH_2-C(=O)-O^-$$

b) This ion can combine with Mg^{2+} to form a salt. Name the salt.

c) Write the chemical formula of the salt you named in part b. You may use $C_5H_9O_2^-$ to represent the formula of the organic ion.

11.75 The citrate ion has the chemical formula $C_6H_5O_7^{3-}$ and the structure shown here. Write the chemical formula of potassium citrate.

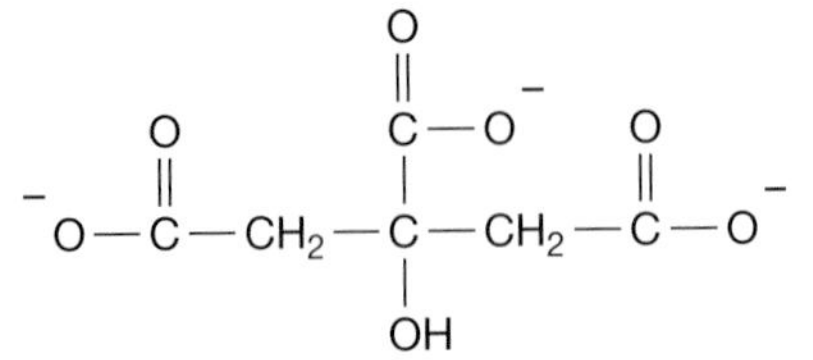

$$^-O-C(=O)-CH_2-C(OH)(C(=O)-O^-)-CH_2-C(=O)-O^-$$

11.76 The two compounds shown here are weak acids. Using structural formulas, write chemical equations for the following reactions:

a) the ionization of methanethiol in water

b) the ionization of *meta*-chlorophenol in water

c) the reaction of methanethiol with hydroxide ion

d) the reaction of *meta*-chlorophenol with hydroxide ion

e) the reaction of methanethiol with ethylamine

f) the reaction of *meta*-chlorophenol with cyclopentylamine

CH_3-SH **Methanethiol**

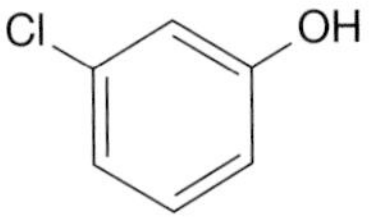

Meta-chlorophenol (benzene ring with Cl and OH)

11.77 The amino acid lysine is a component of all proteins. Our bodies can burn lysine to obtain energy. During this metabolic pathway, the following compound is decarboxylated. Draw the structure of the organic product of this reaction. (Only the circled carboxyl group is involved in this decarboxylation.)

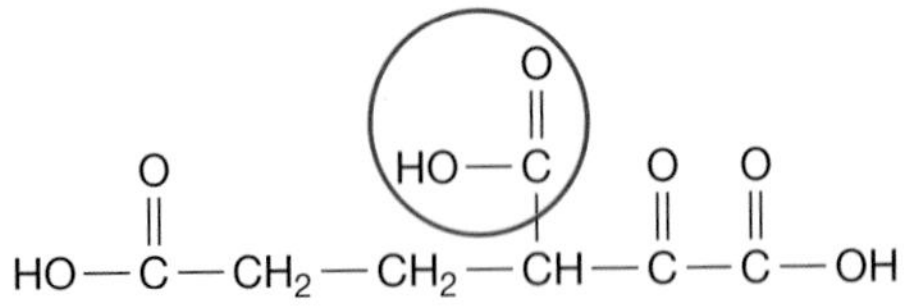

$$HO-C(=O)-CH_2-CH_2-CH(C(=O)-OH)-C(=O)-C(=O)-OH$$

11.78 *The human body makes serotonin from the amino acid tryptophan. The last step in this metabolic pathway is the decarboxylation of 5-hydroxytryptophan. Draw the structure of the product of this decarboxylation reaction.

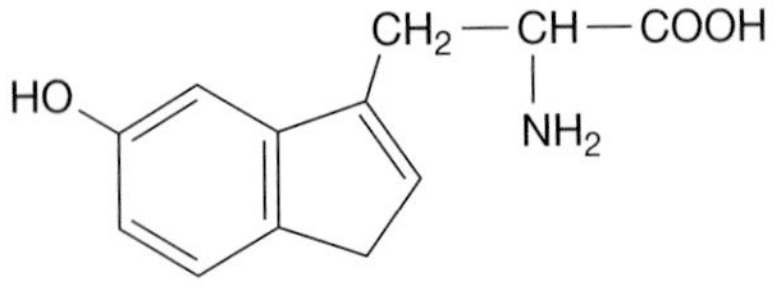

(HO on the fused ring system; side chain $CH_2-CH(NH_2)-COOH$)

5-Hydroxytryptophan

11.79 Classify each of the following compounds as a primary, secondary, or tertiary amine:

a) 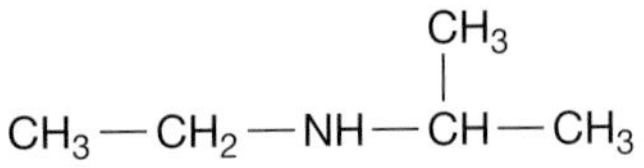 $CH_3-CH_2-NH-CH(CH_3)-CH_3$

b) 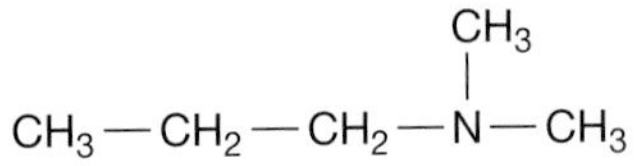 $CH_3-CH_2-CH_2-N(CH_3)-CH_3$

c) 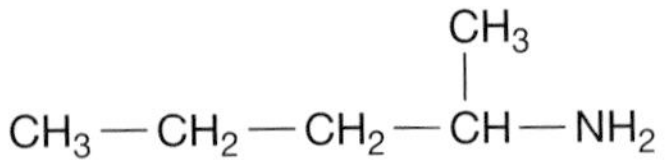 $CH_3-CH_2-CH_2-CH(CH_3)-NH_2$

11.80 Using structural formulas, show each of the following:

a) a hydrogen bond between two molecules of methylamine

b) a hydrogen bond in which methylamine is the donor and water is the acceptor

c) a hydrogen bond in which water is the donor and methylamine is the acceptor

11.81 The following two compounds are constitutional isomers. One of them boils at 36°C, while the other boils at 69°C. Match each compound with its boiling point, and explain your reasoning.

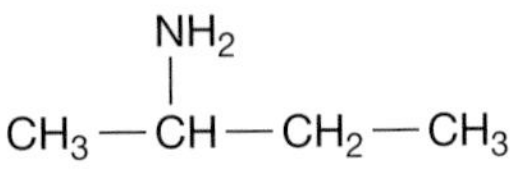

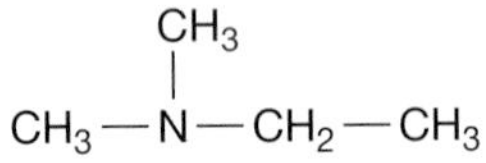

$CH_3-CH(NH_2)-CH_2-CH_3$ $\qquad$ $CH_3-N(CH_3)-CH_2-CH_3$

11.82 Rank the following compounds in order of solubility in water. Start with the most soluble compound.

$CH_3-(CH_2)_7-CH_3$

$NH_2-(CH_2)_7-NH_2$

$CH_3-(CH_2)_7-NH_2$

11.83 Rank the following compounds in order of solubility in water. Start with the most soluble compound.

$CH_3-(CH_2)_{11}-NH_2$

$CH_3-(CH_2)_7-NH_2$

$CH_3-(CH_2)_3-NH_2$

11.84 Threonine is an amino acid. The structure of the unionized form of threonine is shown here:

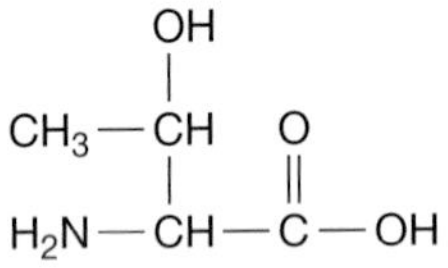

$$CH_3-CH(OH)-CH(NH_2)-C(=O)-OH$$

Threonine

a) Draw the structure of the zwitterion form of threonine.

b) Which is more stable, the zwitterion or the unionized form of threonine?

11.85 Each of the following compounds is soluble in water. If they are dissolved in water, which of the resulting solutions will be acidic, which will be basic, and which will be neutral?

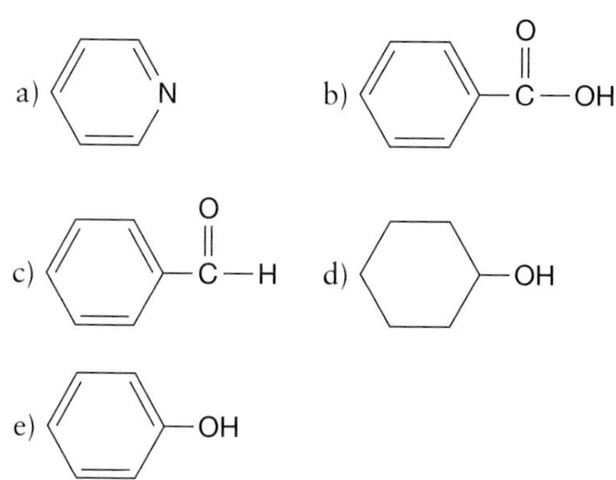

11.86 Coniine is a poisonous alkaloid that is responsible for the toxicity of poison hemlock. Coniine reacts with HBr to form a salt that has been used as an antispasmodic.

a) Draw the structure of this salt.

b) Would you expect the salt to be more or less soluble in water than the original alkaloid?

H—N, $CH_2—CH_2—CH_3$

Coniine

11.87 Is each of the following amines related to phenethylamine, to tryptamine, or to neither?

$HO—CH_2$, HO, OH, $CH—CH_2—NH—CH(CH_3)_2$

Albuterol
(dilates the respiratory passages; also used to prevent pre-term labor)

H—N, $CH_2—CH_2—N$, NH—C(=O)

Indoramin
(used to treat hypertension)

11.88 What is the dominant form of each of the following compounds at physiological pH?

a) $CH_3—CH_2—SH$

b) $Cl—CH_2—C(=O)—OH$

c) OH, OH

d) $HO—C(=O)—C(=O)—OH$

e) $CH_2—NH_2$

11.89 *When your body breaks down carbohydrates to obtain energy, one of the compounds that it forms during the metabolic pathway is phosphoenolpyruvic acid. However, at physiological pH, this compound exists as a mixture of two ions. One ion has a −2 charge, and the other has a −3 charge. Draw the structures of these two ions.

$HO—C(=O)—C(=CH_2)—O—P(=O)(OH)—OH$ **Phosphoenolpyruvic acid**

11.90 *The following amino acids are components of virtually all proteins. The structures show the unionized forms of these amino acids. Draw the structure of each amino acid as it exists at physiological pH.

$HO—C(=O)—CH_2—CH(NH_2)—C(=O)—OH$ **Aspartic acid**

$NH_2—CH_2—CH_2—CH_2—CH_2—CH(NH_2)—C(=O)—OH$ **Lysine**

11.91 *The following sequence of reactions occurs whenever your body breaks down any kind of nutrient to obtain energy. Identify each of these reactions as an oxidation, a reduction, a hydration, a dehydration, an acid–base reaction, a decarboxylation, or an oxidative decarboxylation. Only the organic reactants and products are shown here. (Each molecule is drawn as it appears at physiological pH.)

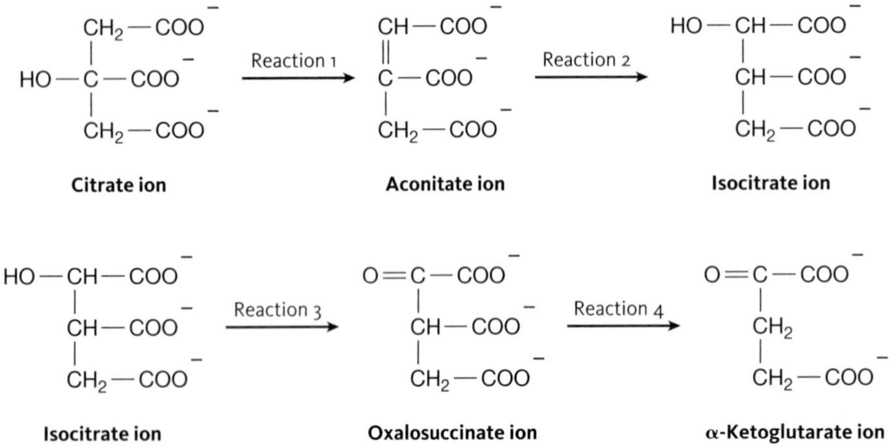

$$\underset{\textbf{Citrate ion}}{^{-}OOC-CH_2-C(OH)(COO^-)-CH_2-COO^-} \xrightarrow{\text{Reaction 1}} \underset{\textbf{Aconitate ion}}{^{-}OOC-CH=C(COO^-)-CH_2-COO^-} \xrightarrow{\text{Reaction 2}} \underset{\textbf{Isocitrate ion}}{^{-}OOC-CH(OH)-CH(COO^-)-CH_2-COO^-}$$

$$\underset{\textbf{Isocitrate ion}}{^{-}OOC-CH(OH)-CH(COO^-)-CH_2-COO^-} \xrightarrow{\text{Reaction 3}} \underset{\textbf{Oxalosuccinate ion}}{^{-}OOC-C(=O)-CH(COO^-)-CH_2-COO^-} \xrightarrow{\text{Reaction 4}} \underset{\boldsymbol{\alpha}\textbf{-Ketoglutarate ion}}{^{-}OOC-C(=O)-CH_2-CH_2-COO^-}$$

11.92 *Which of the reactions in Problem 11.91 requires a coenzyme, and which coenzyme is involved in each of these reactions? (The coenzymes you have seen are coenzyme A, NAD^+, $NADP^+$, and FAD.)

11.93 *Draw the structures of compounds A through E in the sequence of reactions shown here:

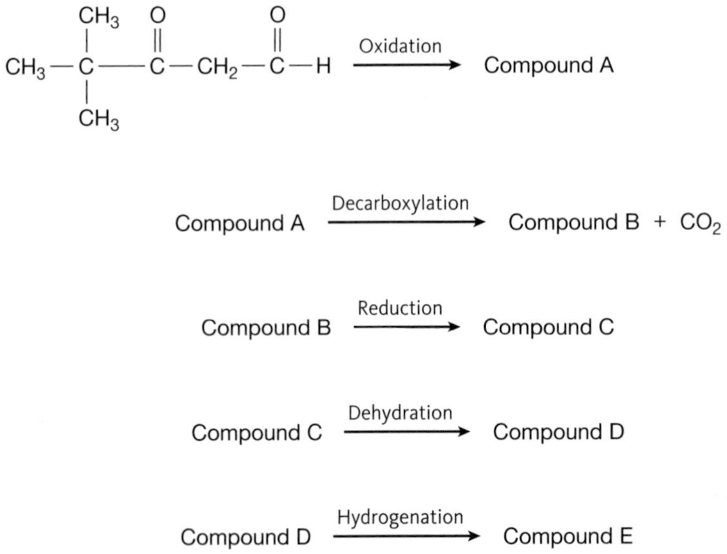

$$(CH_3)_3C-C(=O)-CH_2-C(=O)-H \xrightarrow{\text{Oxidation}} \text{Compound A}$$

$$\text{Compound A} \xrightarrow{\text{Decarboxylation}} \text{Compound B} + CO_2$$

$$\text{Compound B} \xrightarrow{\text{Reduction}} \text{Compound C}$$

$$\text{Compound C} \xrightarrow{\text{Dehydration}} \text{Compound D}$$

$$\text{Compound D} \xrightarrow{\text{Hydrogenation}} \text{Compound E}$$

11.94 *The ion shown here is amphiprotic. Using structural formulas for organic substances, write chemical equations for the following reactions:

a) the reaction of this ion with OH^-
b) the reaction of this ion with H_3O^+

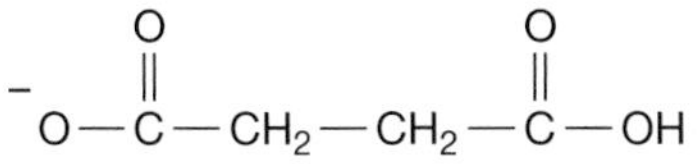

$$^-O-\overset{\overset{\Large O}{\|}}{C}-CH_2-CH_2-\overset{\overset{\Large O}{\|}}{C}-OH$$

11.95 *Draw the structures of organic compounds that match each of the following descriptions:

a) a carboxylic acid that is a constitutional isomer of butanoic acid
b) a primary amine that is a constitutional isomer of methylpropylamine
c) a compound that is a constitutional isomer of butanoic acid and that does not contain a carboxylic acid group

11.96 *A chemist prepares a solution by dissolving 2.30 g of potassium acetate in enough water to make 500.0 mL of solution.

a) What is the percent concentration of this solution?
b) What is the molar concentration of this solution?
c) What is the concentration of acetate ions in this solution, in mEq/L?
d) What is the total molarity of ions in this solution?

11.97 *You need to make 10.0 mL of a 0.50 M solution of triethylamine. How many grams of triethylamine must you use?

11.98 *Sodium lactate is an ionic compound that is widely used in preparing intravenous solutions. The molecular formula of sodium lactate is $NaC_3H_5O_3$.

a) Approximately how many grams of sodium lactate would you need to make 1.00 L of an isotonic solution? Remember that the total concentration of independent solute particles in an isotonic solution is roughly 0.28 M.
b) You have 1.00 L of a solution that contains 0.10 mol/L of glucose. Approximately how many grams of sodium lactate would you need to add to this solution in order to make it isotonic? (Glucose is a nonelectrolyte.)

11.99 *a) If you add 30.0 mL of water to 15.0 mL of 1.50% (w/v) sodium acetate, what will be the concentration of sodium acetate in the resulting solution?
b) How much water must you add to 15.0 mL of 1.50% (w/v) sodium acetate to dilute the solution to 0.30% (w/v)?

11.100 *Butylamine reacts with acetic acid in an acid–base reaction. How many grams of butylamine can react with 4.75 g of acetic acid?

11.101 *How many grams of NaOH can react with 6.22 g of succinic acid? The structure of succinic acid is shown here:

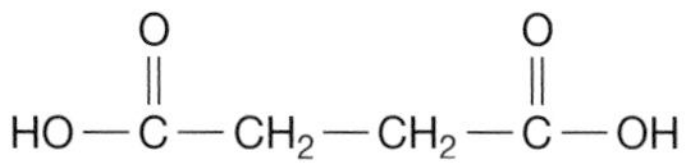

$$HO-\overset{\overset{\Large O}{\|}}{C}-CH_2-CH_2-\overset{\overset{\Large O}{\|}}{C}-OH$$

Succinic acid

12

Condensation and Hydrolysis Reactions

At her aerobics class, Rachelle notices a dull pain in her lower leg. When the pain does not go away after a couple of days, Rachelle decides to have her doctor check her leg. The doctor orders an X-ray, but the X-ray image shows no evidence of injury to the bone. To help him diagnose the cause of Rachelle's pain, the doctor orders a blood test to determine Rachelle's level of alkaline phosphatase, an enzyme that is common in bone tissue. This enzyme removes phosphate groups from a variety of molecules, using a hydrolysis reaction. Because the mineral structure of bone requires phosphate, growing bones produce more alkaline phosphatase than usual, and some of the enzyme is released into the bloodstream.

The lab reports that Rachelle's blood concentration of alkaline phosphatase is significantly higher than normal, suggesting that she has a stress fracture of the bone in her lower leg. The doctor fits Rachelle with a leg brace and tells her that stress fractures often do not show up on X-rays. He advises Rachelle to rest her leg, being particularly careful not to engage in any sort of exercise that puts stress on the bone. After a few weeks, another X-ray shows clear signs of new bone formation, confirming the doctor's diagnosis.

$$\text{organic molecule}-O-\overset{\overset{\displaystyle O}{\|}}{\underset{\underset{\displaystyle O^-}{|}}{P}}-O^- + H_2O \xrightarrow[\text{phosphatase}]{\text{Catalyzed by alkaline}} \text{organic molecule}-OH + HO-\overset{\overset{\displaystyle O}{\|}}{\underset{\underset{\displaystyle O^-}{|}}{P}}-O^-$$

OUTLINE

12.1 **An introduction to condensation reactions: ethers**

12.2 **Esterification, amidation, and phosphorylation**

12.3 **Condensation polymers**

12.4 **Hydrolysis**

12.5 **The effect of pH on the products of hydrolysis**

LABORATORY REQUISITION—CHEMISTRY

☐ Sodium	NA	☐ Fructosamine	FRU/ALB
☐ Potassium	K	☐ PSA	PSA
☐ Creatinine	CREAT	☐ Chloride	CL
☐ BUN	BUN	☐ Calcium	CA
☐ Glucose-fasting	GLUCF	☐ Phosphorus	PHOS
☐ Glucose-random	GLUCR	☐ Phenylalanine	PKU
☐ Hemoglobin A1C	HGBA1C	☐ Uric Acid	URIC

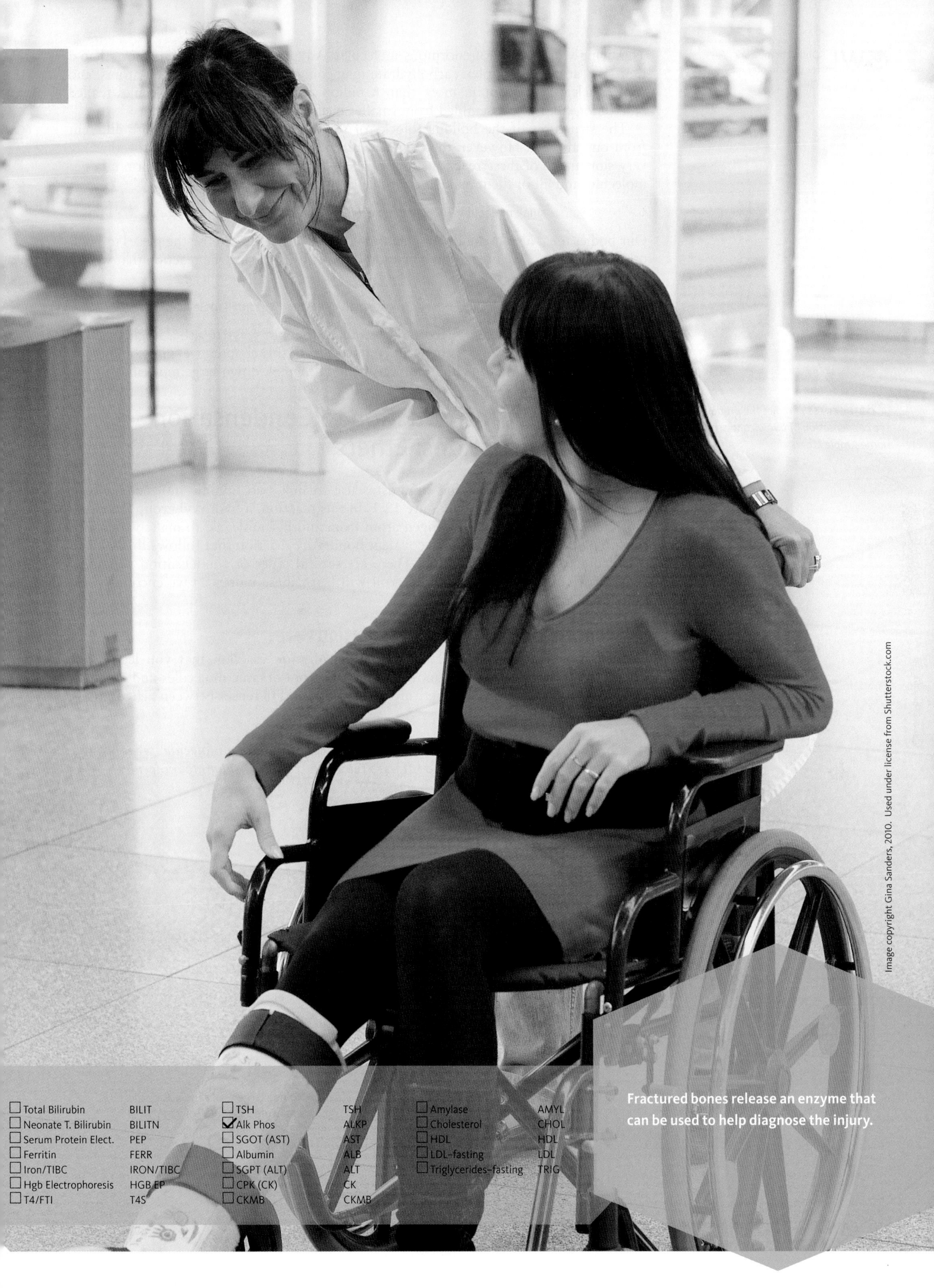

Fractured bones release an enzyme that can be used to help diagnose the injury.

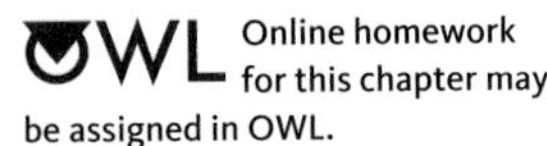

OWL
Online homework for this chapter may be assigned in OWL.

The living world is full of enormous molecules. A typical protein contains more than a thousand atoms, a complex carbohydrate may contain more than a million atoms, and some nucleic acids contain more than a billion atoms. These huge molecules (called *macromolecules*) are assembled from smaller pieces, as shown in Table 12.1.

The structures of the building blocks of these large molecules look quite different from one another. However, the chemical reactions that link these pieces together are very similar. All of these reactions link two smaller molecules together to form a larger molecule, and all of them make a molecule of water.

small molecule + small molecule → **large molecule** + H_2O

Our bodies must also break down macromolecules so that we can use the pieces to build other compounds. We break down macromolecules by reversing the reaction that we use to make them.

large molecule + H_2O → **small molecule** + small molecule

Living organisms have evolved a remarkable variety of ways to use a single reaction type to construct an array of chemical compounds. In this chapter, we will examine the family of reactions that our bodies use to build and break down large molecules.

OBJECTIVES: *Predict the products of the condensation of two alcohols, and name simple ethers.*

12.1 An Introduction to Condensation Reactions: Ethers

The prototypical reaction that organisms use to link two organic molecules into a single compound is shown in Figure 12.1. In this reaction, a hydroxyl group from one molecule combines with a hydrogen atom from another molecule to make water. The remaining fragments form a new covalent bond. Any reaction that follows this scheme is called a **condensation reaction**. There are several types of condensation reactions, some of which have specific names. You will learn these names as we encounter the individual reactions.

Condensations Differ from Dehydrations

Condensation reactions are related to the dehydration reaction that you learned in Chapter 9. In both cases, we remove H and OH from organic molecules and combine them to form water. However, there are two important differences between dehydrations and condensations:

- In a dehydration reaction H and OH come from the *same molecule*, whereas in a condensation reaction H and OH are removed from *two separate molecules*.

TABLE 12.1 Some Biological Macromolecules

Type of Molecule	Example	Pieces
Protein	Muscle protein	Amino acids
Complex carbohydrate	Starch	Simple sugars
Nucleic acid	DNA	Nucleotides

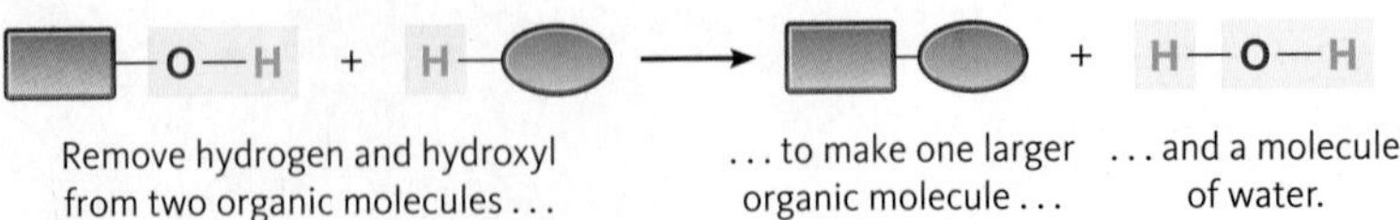

FIGURE 12.1 The general scheme for a condensation reaction.

- In a dehydration reaction H is removed from *carbon*, whereas in a condensation reaction H is removed from *oxygen or nitrogen.*

Ethanol can undergo both types of reactions, so it provides us with a good comparison. When ethanol is dehydrated, the product is an alkene, ethylene.

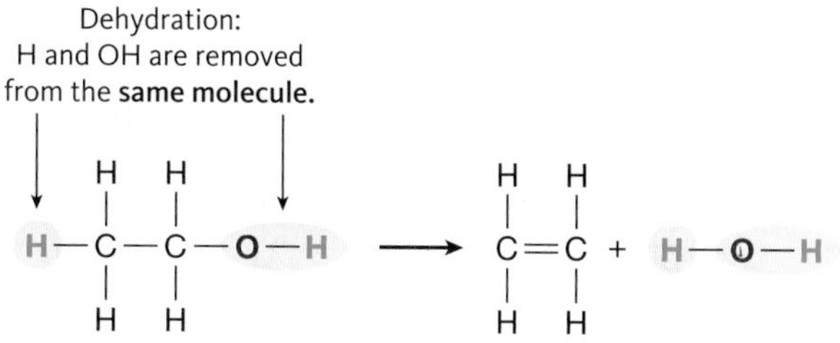

Dehydration:
H and OH are removed
from the **same molecule.**

$$H-\underset{H}{\overset{H}{C}}-\underset{H}{\overset{H}{C}}-O-H \longrightarrow \underset{H}{\overset{H}{C}}=\underset{H}{\overset{H}{C}} + H-O-H$$

Ethylene

In a condensation reaction, one molecule of ethanol loses OH, and a second ethanol molecule loses H. The product of this reaction is called diethyl ether.

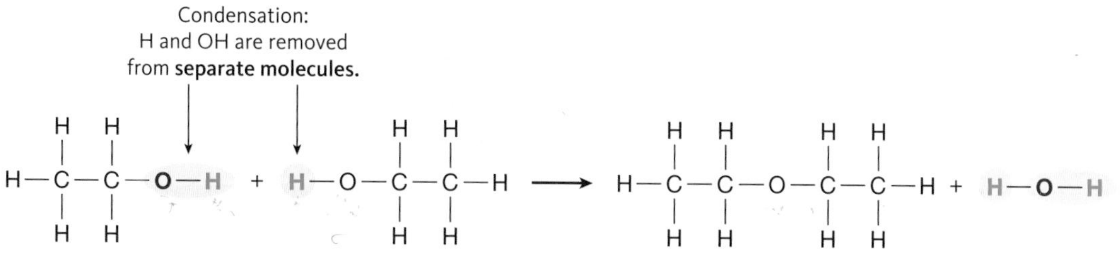

Condensation:
H and OH are removed
from **separate molecules.**

$$H-\underset{H}{\overset{H}{C}}-\underset{H}{\overset{H}{C}}-O-H + H-O-\underset{H}{\overset{H}{C}}-\underset{H}{\overset{H}{C}}-H \longrightarrow H-\underset{H}{\overset{H}{C}}-\underset{H}{\overset{H}{C}}-O-\underset{H}{\overset{H}{C}}-\underset{H}{\overset{H}{C}}-H + H-O-H$$

Diethyl ether

Condensation Reactions Can Be Divided into Two Steps

We can think of a condensation reaction as a two-step process. In the first step, we remove H from one molecule and OH from the other, leaving two organic fragments.

$$CH_3-CH_2-O-H + H-O-CH_2-CH_3 \longrightarrow CH_3-CH_2- + -O-CH_2-CH_3 + H_2O$$

In step 2, we link the two fragments to form a larger organic molecule.

$$CH_3-CH_2- + -O-CH_2-CH_3 \longrightarrow CH_3-CH_2-O-CH_2-CH_3$$

- In this chapter, red and green shading are used to highlight the organic fragments that become bonded together in a condensation reaction.

If you examine the condensation reaction closely, two questions might occur to you. The first is, "Could the other ethanol molecule supply the OH group?" Yes, it can. When two alcohols condense, either molecule can be the source of OH and the other molecule becomes the source of H. Regardless of which molecule supplies the hydroxyl group, we form the same product.

$$CH_3-CH_2-O-H + H-O-CH_2-CH_3 \longrightarrow CH_3-CH_2-O-CH_2-CH_3 + H_2O$$

When the right-hand molecule supplies the OH . . .

. . . we still form diethyl ether.

The second question is, "Can we use any of the other hydrogen atoms in ethanol to make the water molecule?" No, we cannot. *In a condensation reaction, the hydrogen atom always comes from an O—H or N—H group.* Hydrogen atoms that are bonded to carbon cannot be removed in condensation reactions. Therefore, when we write a condensation reaction, we should draw the two reactant molecules with their functional groups facing each other. For instance, if we draw one of our two ethanol molecules in the opposite orientation, we might think that we will make an alcohol. However, the condensation of ethanol never forms 1-butanol.

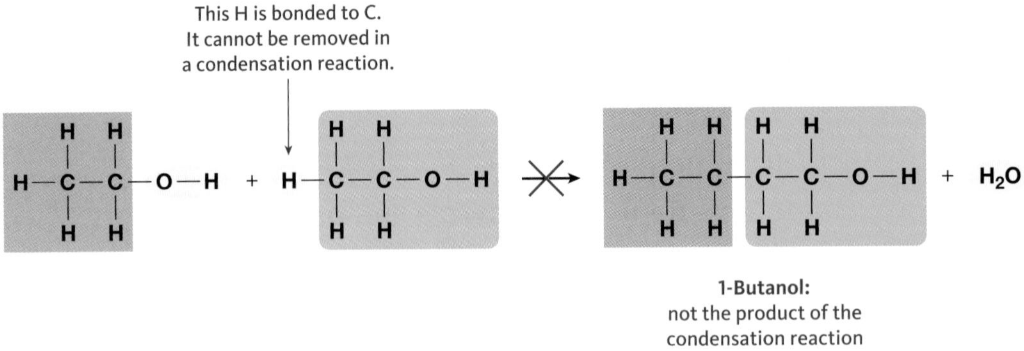

This H is bonded to C.
It cannot be removed in
a condensation reaction.

$$H_3C{-}CH_2{-}O{-}H + H{-}CH_2{-}CH_2{-}O{-}H \not\longrightarrow H_3C{-}CH_2{-}CH_2{-}CH_2{-}O{-}H + H_2O$$

1-Butanol:
not the product of the
condensation reaction

Think about two people who are meeting for the first time. If they want to shake hands, they must face each other and then extend their hands toward each other. Likewise, when two organic molecules react, they must "shake hands." In this case, the "hands" are the functional groups.

Sample Problem 12.1

Drawing the product of the condensation of two alcohols

Draw the structure of the organic product that is formed when a molecule of methanol condenses with a molecule of 2-propanol.

SOLUTION

First, we need to draw the structures of the two reactants.

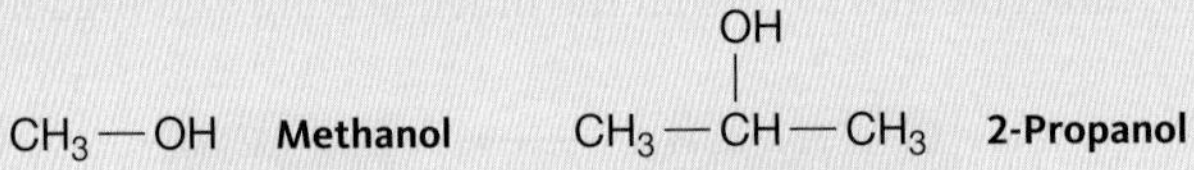

$CH_3{-}OH$ **Methanol** $\quad CH_3{-}CH(OH){-}CH_3$ **2-Propanol**

When we work out the products of a condensation reaction, we need to draw the molecules so that their functional groups can "shake hands." In this case, there are several possible ways to place the molecules so that the hydroxyl groups face each other. One option is to rotate the 2-propanol structure so that the hydroxyl group points to the left.

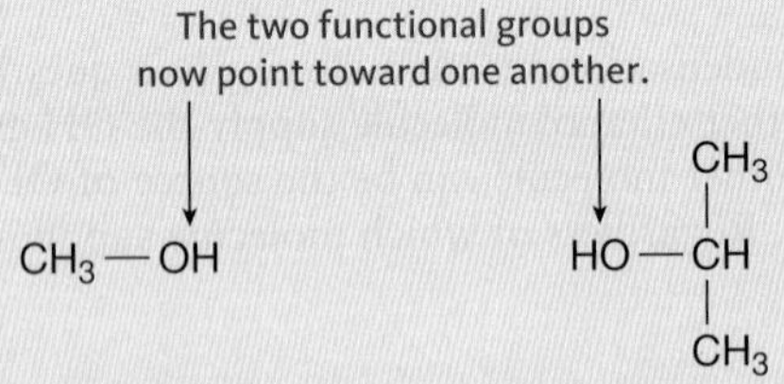

The two functional groups
now point toward one another.

$CH_3{-}OH \qquad HO{-}CH(CH_3)_2$

We draw the reaction in two steps. First, we remove OH from one of the reactants and H from the other. The hydroxyl group will combine with the hydrogen atom to form water.

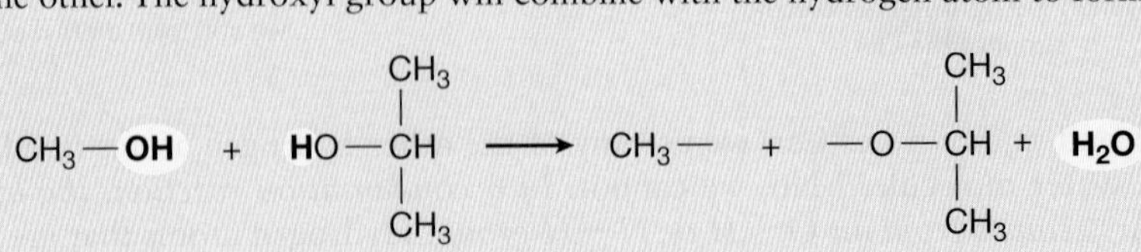

$$CH_3{-}\mathbf{OH} + \mathbf{H}O{-}CH(CH_3)_2 \longrightarrow CH_3{-} \; + \; {-}O{-}CH(CH_3)_2 + \mathbf{H_2O}$$

continued

Finally, we combine the two organic fragments to form the product.

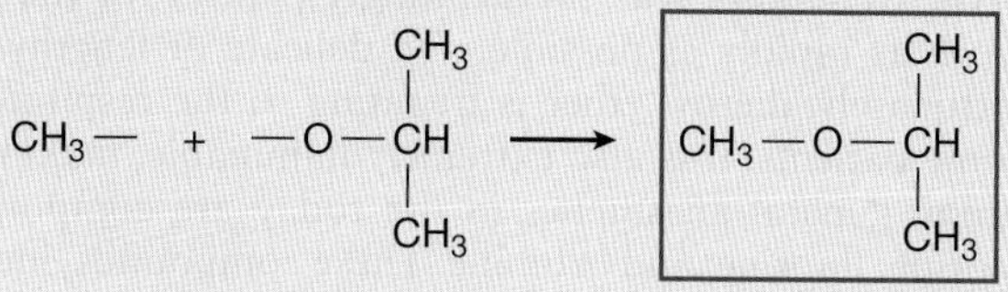

$$CH_3- \; + \; -O-CH(CH_3)_2 \longrightarrow \boxed{CH_3-O-CH(CH_3)_2}$$

The organic product of the condensation reaction.

TRY IT YOURSELF: *Draw the structure of the organic product that is formed when two molecules of 1-propanol condense.*

For additional practice, try Core Problems 12.1 and 12.2.

Alcohols Condense to Form an Ether

The products of the condensation reactions we have seen in this section are called **ethers**. An ether contains an oxygen atom between two alkyl groups. The most commonly used system for naming ethers is analogous to the one we used for amines. To name an ether, we list the two alkyl groups in alphabetical order, and then we write the word *ether.* If the two alkyl groups are identical, we use the prefix *di-* before the name of the alkyl group. Each part of the name is written as a separate word.

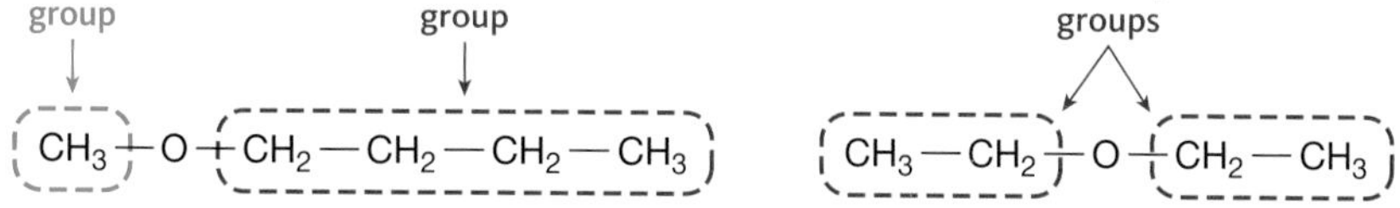

A methyl group → CH_3; A butyl group → $CH_2-CH_2-CH_2-CH_3$

$$CH_3-O-CH_2-CH_2-CH_2-CH_3$$

Butyl methyl ether

Two ethyl groups

$$CH_3-CH_2-O-CH_2-CH_3$$

Diethyl ether

Sample Problem 12.2

Naming and drawing ethers

Draw the structure of cyclopentyl ethyl ether.

SOLUTION

This compound contains a cyclopentyl group and an ethyl group, connected by an oxygen atom. The cyclopentyl group is a five-membered ring, and the ethyl group is a chain of two carbon atoms.

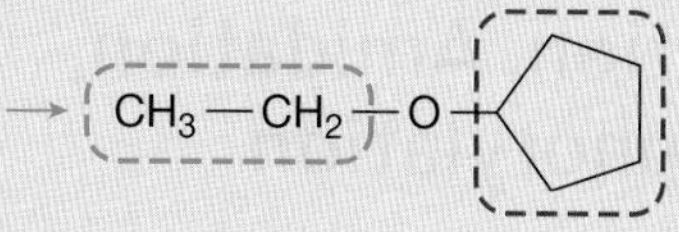

An ethyl group (2 carbon atoms) → CH_3-CH_2-O-(cyclopentyl ring) ← A cyclopentyl group (a ring of 5 carbon atoms)

TRY IT YOURSELF: *Draw the structure of dibutyl ether.*

For additional practice, try Core Problems 12.3 and 12.4.

Health Note: Starting in 1979 in the United States, methyl tertiary butyl ether (MTBE) was added to gasoline to reduce pollution and improve the octane rating. However, MTBE is slightly soluble in water and becomes a groundwater pollutant when it leaks from underground tanks, so gasoline manufacturers in the United States now use ethanol or other additives in place of MTBE.

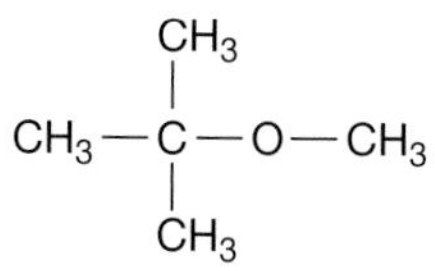

$$CH_3-C(CH_3)_2-O-CH_3$$

MTBE

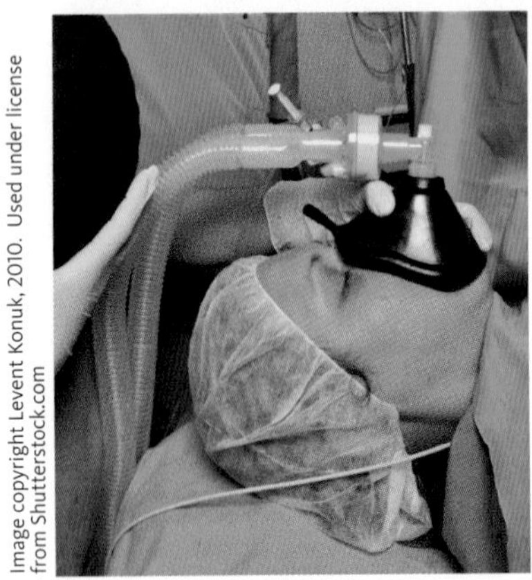

A patient receiving a general anesthetic before surgery.

The discovery that diethyl ether produces general anesthesia led to a revolution in medicine in the nineteenth century, because it made pain-free surgery possible. Before this discovery, any type of surgery was excruciatingly painful for the patient; surgeons were expected to work as rapidly as possible, and delicate or lengthy procedures were impracticable. Unfortunately, diethyl ether is irritating to the respiratory passages and induces nausea in some patients. It is also extremely flammable, making it hazardous to use. The most common general anesthetics in use today are compounds that contain halogens such as chlorine, fluorine, and bromine. These compounds, including halothane (first used in 1956) and sevoflurane (first used in 1990), are much safer to use than diethyl ether, and they are more comfortable for the patient.

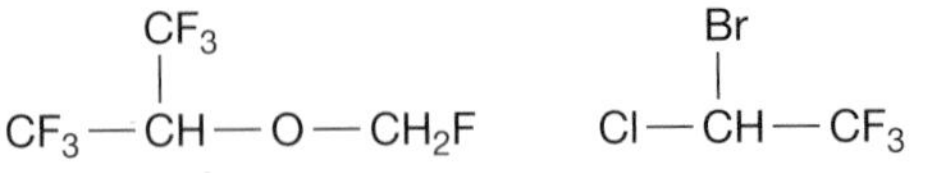

$CF_3-CH(CF_3)-O-CH_2F$

Sevoflurane

$Cl-CH(Br)-CF_3$

Halothane

CORE PROBLEMS

All Core Problems are paired and the answers to the blue odd-numbered problems appear in the back of the book.

12.1 Draw the structures of the products of the following condensation reactions:

a) $CH_3-CH_2-OH + HO-CH_2-CH_2-CH_2-CH_3 \longrightarrow$

b) $CH_3-CH_2-CH_2-OH + CH_3-CH_2-CH_2-OH \longrightarrow$

c) 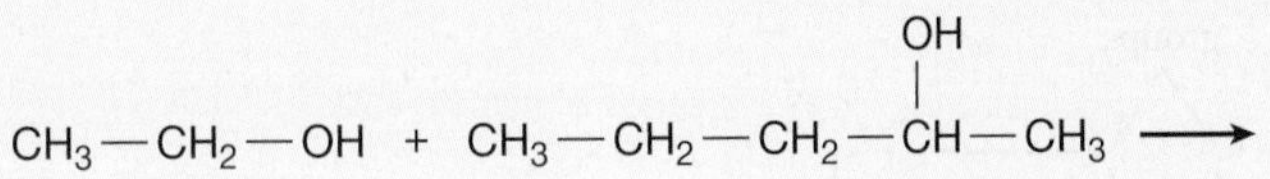 $CH_3-CH_2-OH + CH_3-CH_2-CH_2-CH(OH)-CH_3 \longrightarrow$

12.2 Draw the structures of the products of the following condensation reactions:

a) 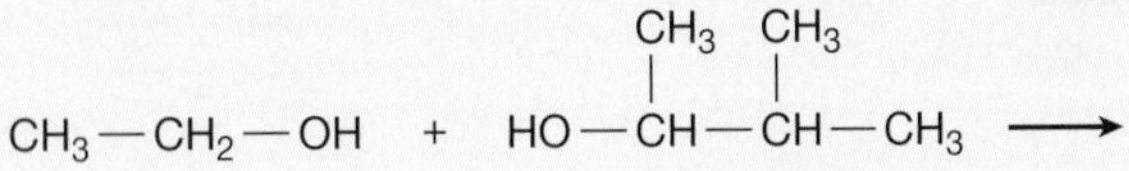 $CH_3-CH_2-OH + HO-CH(CH_3)-CH(CH_3)-CH_3 \longrightarrow$

b) 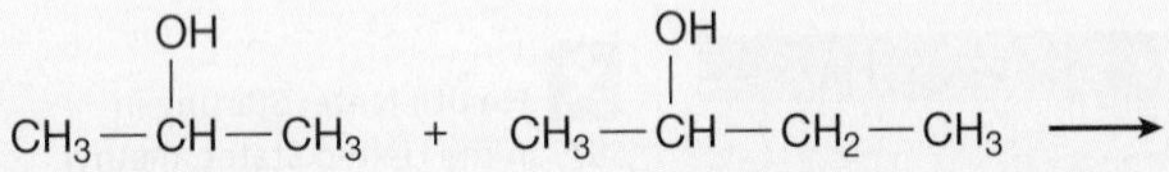 $CH_3-CH(OH)-CH_3 + CH_3-CH(OH)-CH_2-CH_3 \longrightarrow$

c) 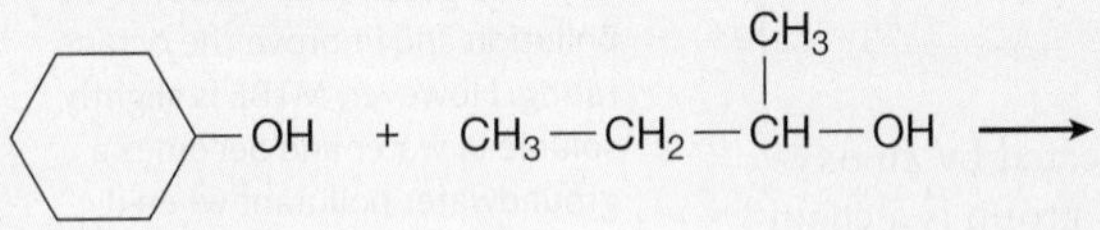 (cyclohexane ring)$-OH + CH_3-CH_2-CH(CH_3)-OH \longrightarrow$

12.3 Name the following ethers:

a) $CH_3-CH_2-CH_2-CH_2-CH_2-O-CH_2-CH_3$

b) CH_3-O-CH_3

12.4 Name the following ethers:

a) $CH_3-CH_2-CH_2-O-CH_2-CH_2-CH_2-CH_3$

b) 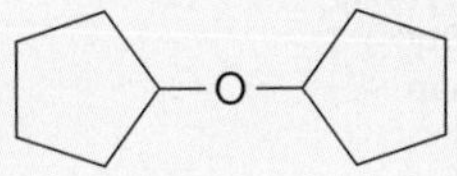 (cyclopentane ring)$-O-$(cyclopentane ring)

OBJECTIVE: *Predict the products of condensation reactions that form esters, amides, and phosphoesters.*

12.2 Esterification, Amidation, and Phosphorylation

In Section 12.1, we saw how we can make ethers by condensing two alcohols. Let us now look at three other ways in which we can use condensation reactions to build large organic molecules from smaller ones. These condensation reactions are summarized in Table 12.2, along with the condensation of two alcohols that you learned in the last section.

TABLE 12.2 Four Common Condensation Reactions

Type of Reaction	Reactants	Products
Ether formation	Alcohol + alcohol	Ether + water
Esterification	Carboxylic acid + alcohol	Ester + water
Amidation	Carboxylic acid + amine	Amide + water
Phosphorylation	Phosphoric acid + alcohol	Phosphoester + water

As we explore a variety of condensations, you should always keep the basic reaction pattern of Figure 12.1 in mind. In any condensation, we remove H from one molecule and OH from another, and then we connect the pieces to make a larger organic compound.

Carboxylic Acids and Alcohols Combine to Form Esters

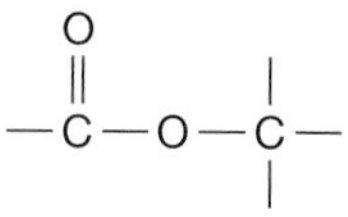

The first type of condensation we will examine is called an **esterification reaction.** In this reaction, a carboxylic acid reacts with an alcohol to form an **ester**. Figure 12.2 shows the basic scheme for this reaction.

$$-\overset{\overset{\large O}{\|}}{C}-O-\overset{|}{\underset{|}{C}}-$$

The ester functional group

The reaction of acetic acid with ethanol is a typical esterification. We can break this reaction into two steps, just as we did with the condensation of ethanol in Section 12.1. In the first step, we remove H from the alcohol and OH from the acid.

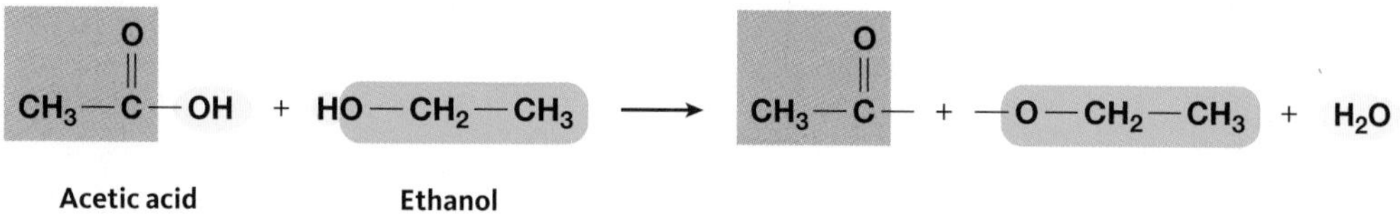

$$CH_3-\overset{\overset{O}{\|}}{C}-OH + HO-CH_2-CH_3 \longrightarrow CH_3-\overset{\overset{O}{\|}}{C}- + -O-CH_2-CH_3 + H_2O$$

Acetic acid Ethanol

In the second step, we connect the remaining organic fragments.

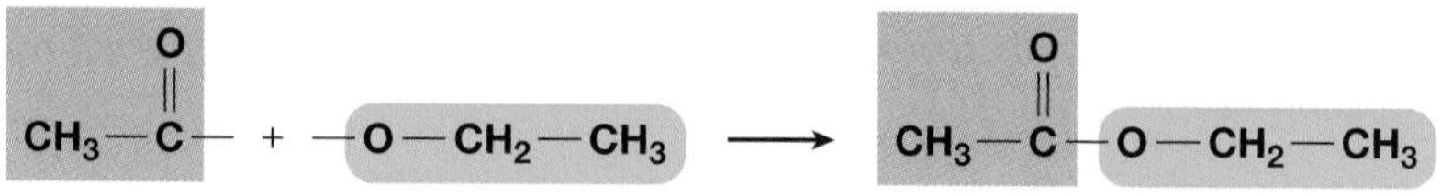

$$CH_3-\overset{\overset{O}{\|}}{C}- + -O-CH_2-CH_3 \longrightarrow CH_3-\overset{\overset{O}{\|}}{C}-O-CH_2-CH_3$$

Ethyl acetate
(an ester)

The overall reaction is

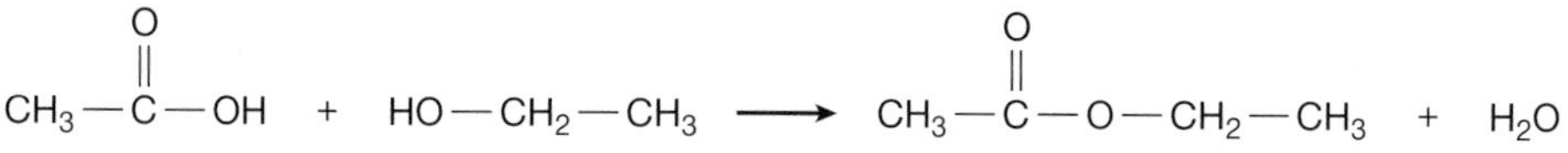

$$CH_3-\overset{\overset{O}{\|}}{C}-OH + HO-CH_2-CH_3 \longrightarrow CH_3-\overset{\overset{O}{\|}}{C}-O-CH_2-CH_3 + H_2O$$

We can, if we wish, remove H from the acid and OH from the alcohol when we work out the product of an esterification. As was the case with the condensation of two alcohols, we get the same product regardless of which reactant supplies the hydroxyl group.

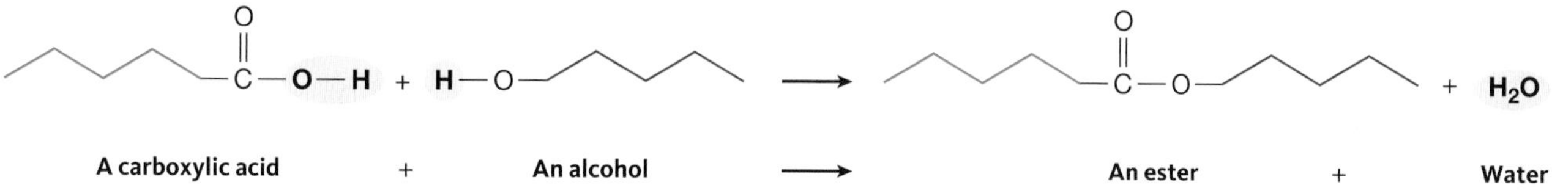

$$\text{R}-\overset{\overset{O}{\|}}{C}-O-H + H-O-\text{R}' \longrightarrow \text{R}-\overset{\overset{O}{\|}}{C}-O-\text{R}' + H_2O$$

A carboxylic acid + An alcohol ⟶ An ester + Water

FIGURE 12.2 The general scheme for an esterification reaction.

Sample Problem 12.3

Drawing the product of an esterification

Draw the structure of the ester that is formed when formic acid reacts with 2-butanol.

SOLUTION

First, we must draw the structures of the reactants so that their functional groups face each other. We can do this by drawing the 2-butanol molecule with its alcohol group next to the hydroxyl group of formic acid.

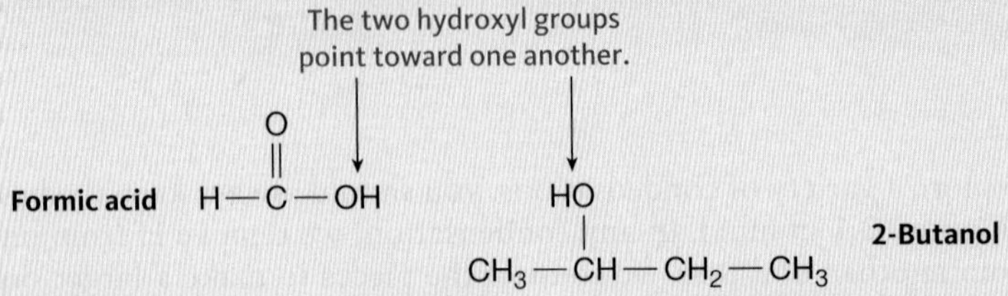

The two hydroxyl groups point toward one another.

Formic acid H—C(=O)—OH   HO—CH(CH_3)—CH_2—CH_3 **2-Butanol**

Now we can carry out the reaction. In step 1, we remove OH from the acid and H from the alcohol. In step 2, we join the two fragments we produced in step 1.

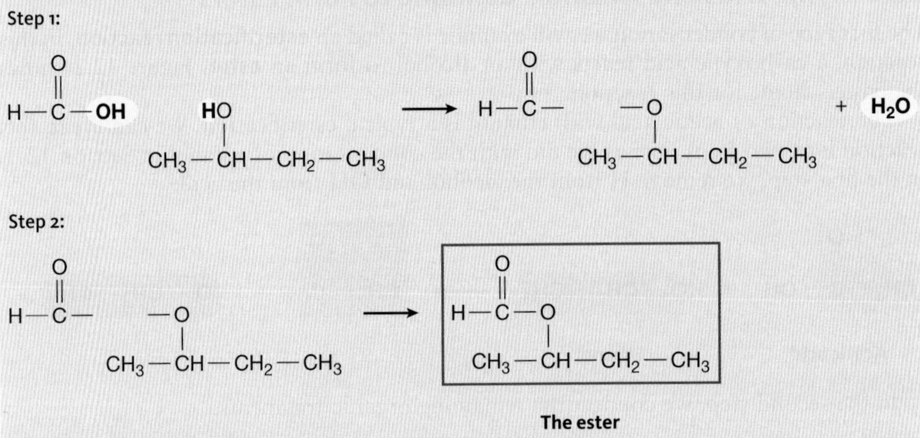

Step 1:

H—C(=O)—**OH**   **H**O—CH(CH_3)—CH_2—CH_3 ⟶ H—C(=O)—   —O—CH(CH_3)—CH_2—CH_3 + **H_2O**

Step 2:

H—C(=O)—   —O—CH(CH_3)—CH_2—CH_3 ⟶ H—C(=O)—O—CH(CH_3)—CH_2—CH_3

The ester

TRY IT YOURSELF: *Draw the structure of the ester that is formed when phenol reacts with propanoic acid.*

For additional practice, try Core Problems 12.5 and 12.6.

Esters are not very reactive compounds. They cannot be oxidized, and they are difficult to reduce. Fats and vegetable oils are esters, made from glycerol (the alcohol) and fatty acids (long-chain carboxylic acids), and they are important sources of energy for many organisms. Other examples of compounds that contain ester groups are waxes, aspirin, and many of the compounds that give fruits their characteristic flavors and aromas. In the structures that follow, the ester functional group is circled:

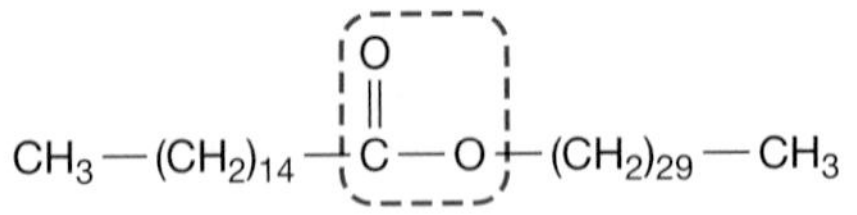

CH_3—$(CH_2)_{14}$—C(=O)—O—$(CH_2)_{29}$—CH_3

Myricyl palmitate
(a component of beeswax)

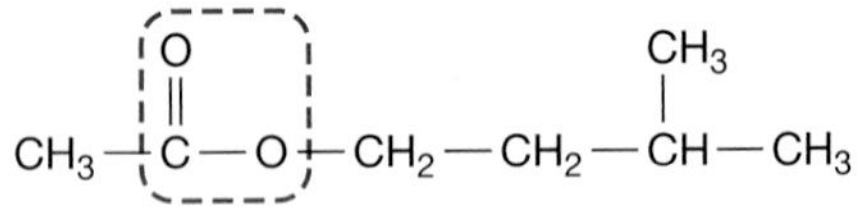

CH_3—C(=O)—O—CH_2—CH_2—CH(CH_3)—CH_3

Isoamyl acetate
(banana flavor)

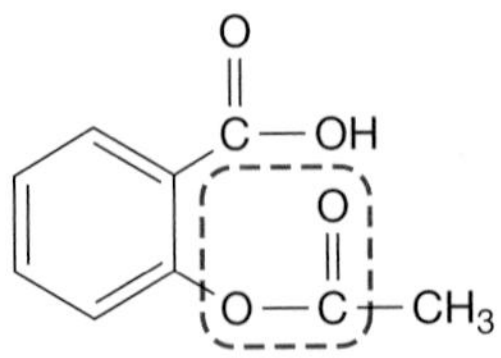

C(=O)—OH on benzene ring, ortho O—C(=O)—CH_3

Aspirin

O=(lactone ring O)—$(CH_2)_5$—CH_3

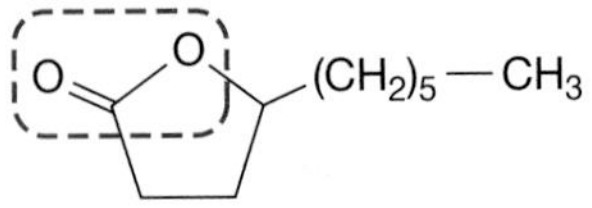

Gamma-decalactone
(peach flavor)

Health Note: Aspirin has been used to relieve pain and inflammation and to reduce fever since 1900, and low doses of aspirin reduce the risk of heart attacks and strokes in people with cardiovascular disease. However, children who take aspirin for a viral infection have a significantly increased risk of Reye's syndrome, a potentially fatal inflammation of the brain and liver, so aspirin should not be given to anyone under the age of 18.

Carboxylic Acids and Amines Combine to Form Amides

The second type of condensation is the **amidation reaction.** In this reaction, a carboxylic acid reacts with an amine to form an **amide**, as shown in Figure 12.3. The amine nitrogen must be bonded to at least one hydrogen atom, so this reaction can only occur with primary and secondary amines (and ammonia).

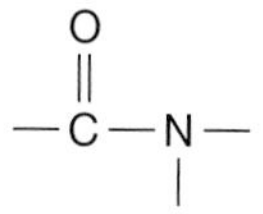

O
‖
—C—N—
|

The amide functional group

For example, propanoic acid reacts with methylamine to form an amide. Again, we can break this reaction into two steps. In the first step, the acid loses OH and the amine loses H.

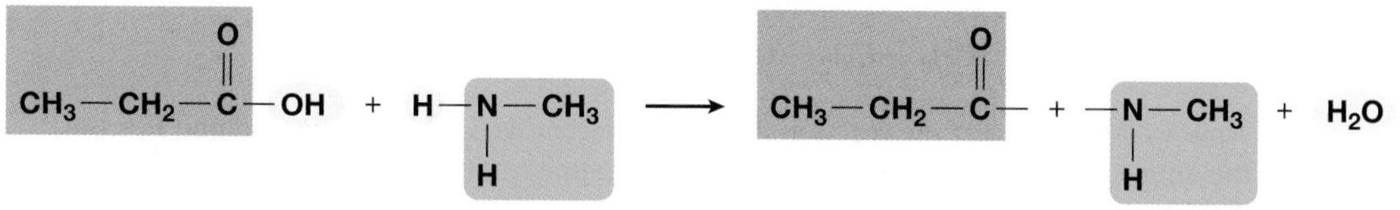

$$CH_3-CH_2-\overset{\displaystyle O}{\overset{\|}{C}}-OH \; + \; H-\underset{\displaystyle H}{\underset{|}{N}}-CH_3 \longrightarrow CH_3-CH_2-\overset{\displaystyle O}{\overset{\|}{C}}- \; + \; -\underset{\displaystyle H}{\underset{|}{N}}-CH_3 \; + \; H_2O$$

Propanoic acid **Methylamine**

In the second step, we connect the remaining organic fragments to make our amide.

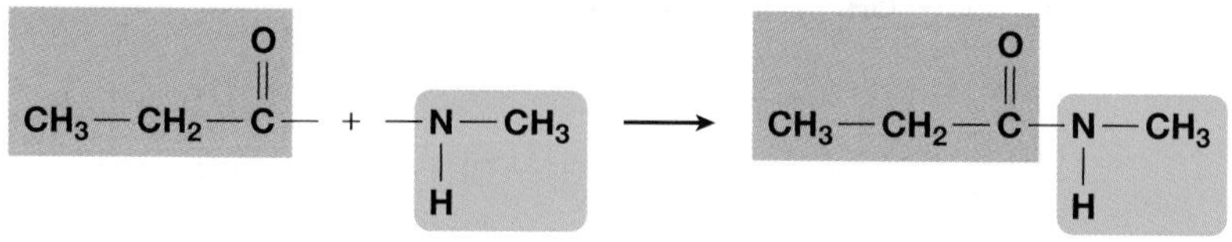

$$CH_3-CH_2-\overset{\displaystyle O}{\overset{\|}{C}}- \; + \; -\underset{\displaystyle H}{\underset{|}{N}}-CH_3 \longrightarrow CH_3-CH_2-\overset{\displaystyle O}{\overset{\|}{C}}-\underset{\displaystyle H}{\underset{|}{N}}-CH_3$$

N-methylpropanamide
(an amide)

The overall reaction is

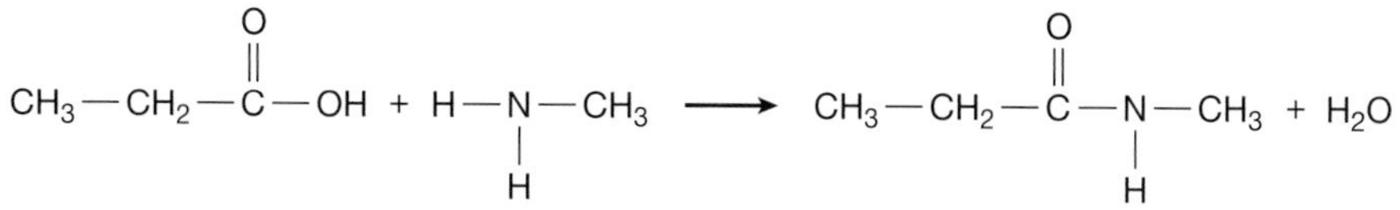

$$CH_3-CH_2-\overset{\displaystyle O}{\overset{\|}{C}}-OH + H-\underset{\displaystyle H}{\underset{|}{N}}-CH_3 \longrightarrow CH_3-CH_2-\overset{\displaystyle O}{\overset{\|}{C}}-\underset{\displaystyle H}{\underset{|}{N}}-CH_3 + H_2O$$

In this text, the naming systems for esters and amides will not be covered. You will occasionally see the name of an ester or an amide, but you will not need to learn the naming rules for these compounds.

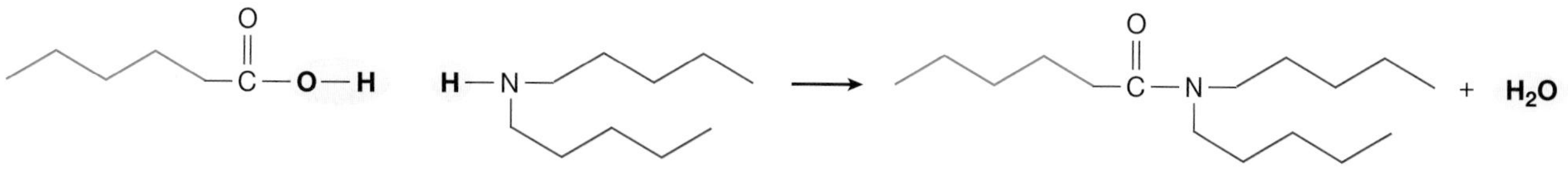

O
‖
—C—O—H   H—N—   ⟶   O ‖ —C—N—   + H_2O

A carboxylic acid + **An amine** ⟶ **An amide** + **Water**

FIGURE 12.3 The general scheme for an amidation reaction.

Sample Problem 12.4

Drawing the product of an amidation

Draw the structure of the amide that is formed when butanoic acid reacts with methylamine.

SOLUTION

First, we draw the structures of the reactants.

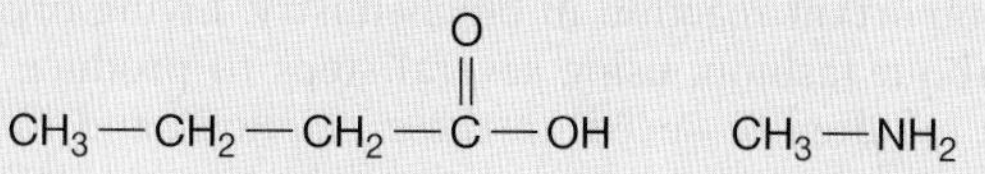

$$CH_3-CH_2-CH_2-\overset{\displaystyle O}{\overset{\|}{C}}-OH \qquad CH_3-NH_2$$

Butanoic acid **Methylamine**

continued

The amidation reaction involves the hydroxyl group and the amino group, so we need to draw the reactants in a way that puts these groups close to each other. Drawing the hydrogen atoms in the amine can also be helpful. The easiest way to put the two functional groups in the right orientation is to reverse the order of the methylamine molecule.

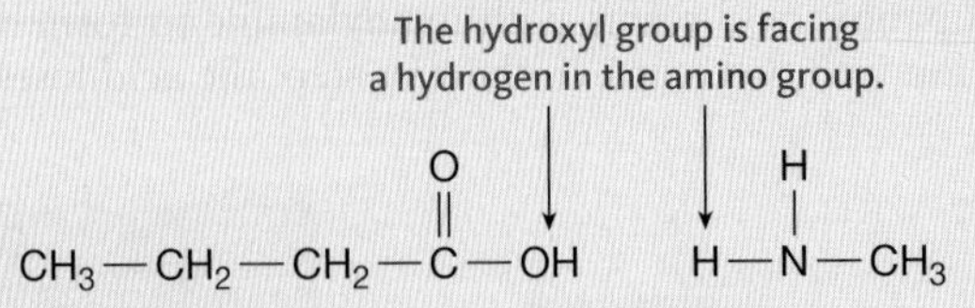

The hydroxyl group is facing a hydrogen in the amino group.

$$CH_3-CH_2-CH_2-\overset{\displaystyle O}{\overset{\|}{C}}-OH \qquad H-\overset{\displaystyle H}{\overset{|}{N}}-CH_3$$

Now we are ready for the reaction. In step 1 we remove OH from the acid and H from the amine, and in step 2 we connect the two organic fragments.

Step 1:

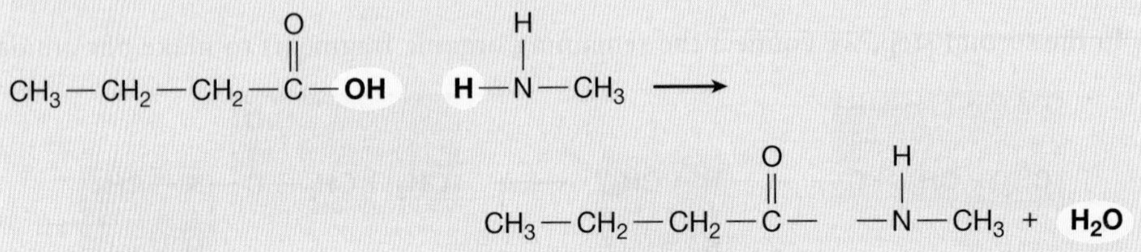

$$CH_3-CH_2-CH_2-\overset{\displaystyle O}{\overset{\|}{C}}-\mathbf{OH} \qquad \mathbf{H}-\overset{\displaystyle H}{\overset{|}{N}}-CH_3 \longrightarrow CH_3-CH_2-CH_2-\overset{\displaystyle O}{\overset{\|}{C}}- \quad -\overset{\displaystyle H}{\overset{|}{N}}-CH_3 + \mathbf{H_2O}$$

Step 2:

$$CH_3-CH_2-CH_2-\overset{\displaystyle O}{\overset{\|}{C}}- \quad -\overset{\displaystyle H}{\overset{|}{N}}-CH_3 \longrightarrow \boxed{CH_3-CH_2-CH_2-\overset{\displaystyle O}{\overset{\|}{C}}-\overset{\displaystyle H}{\overset{|}{N}}-CH_3}$$

The amide

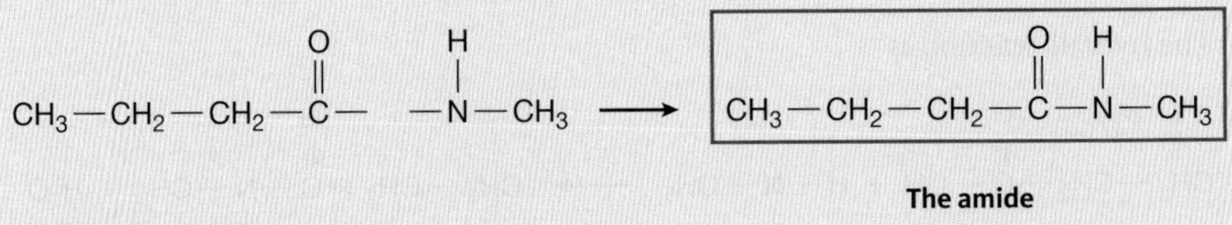

TRY IT YOURSELF: *Draw the structure of the amide that is formed when ammonia reacts with pentanoic acid.*

For additional practice, try Core Problems 12.7 and 12.8.

We do not normally make an amide if we simply mix a carboxylic acid with an amine in the laboratory, because amidation reactions require very high temperatures. Instead, we see an acid–base reaction, in which a hydrogen ion moves from the acid to the amine. For example, if we mix propanoic acid with methylamine at room temperature, we form propanoate ion and methylammonium ion, as shown here. To make an amide from these two compounds, we must heat them above 100°C.

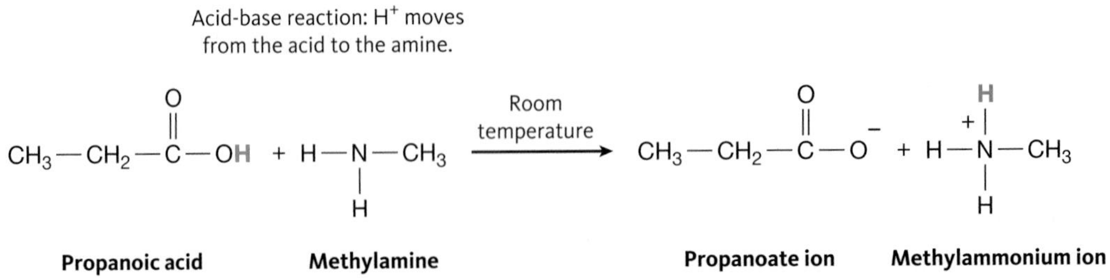

Acid-base reaction: H^+ moves from the acid to the amine.

$$\underset{\textbf{Propanoic acid}}{CH_3-CH_2-\overset{\displaystyle O}{\overset{\|}{C}}-OH} + \underset{\textbf{Methylamine}}{H-\underset{\displaystyle H}{\underset{|}{N}}-CH_3} \xrightarrow{\text{Room temperature}} \underset{\textbf{Propanoate ion}}{CH_3-CH_2-\overset{\displaystyle O}{\overset{\|}{C}}-O^-} + \underset{\textbf{Methylammonium ion}}{H-\overset{\displaystyle H}{\overset{+|}{\underset{\displaystyle H}{\underset{|}{N}}}}-CH_3}$$

• The role of enzymes in biological reactions was introduced in Section 9.2.

Amidation is an important reaction in biochemistry. Living organisms carry out this reaction in a roundabout fashion, using several steps to produce the final product. As always, enzymes are required to speed up these reactions and to ensure that only the correct product is formed.

It is important to recognize the difference between amides and amines. In an amide, the nitrogen atom is attached directly to a carbonyl group. The most conspicuous difference between these two classes of compounds is that amines are bases and can bond to H^+, but *amides are not bases.* Of the following two compounds, only the first one is basic:

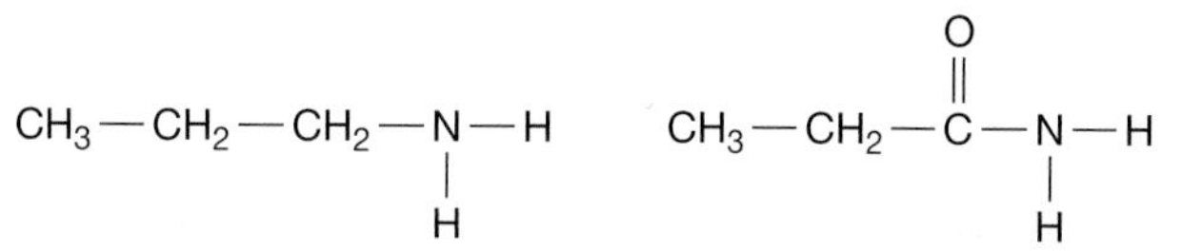

$$CH_3-CH_2-CH_2-NH_2 \qquad CH_3-CH_2-C(=O)-NH_2$$

Propylamine – an amine (a base: can bond to H^+)

Propanamide – an amide (not a base: cannot bond to H^+)

Proteins are the most common and important amides in biochemistry and medicine. We will look at how proteins are formed in Section 12.3. Many common medications also contain the amide functional group, including acetaminophen (Tylenol), barbiturates such as secobarbital (Seconal), and penicillin. The artificial sweeteners saccharin and aspartame also contain amide groups. The structures of some of these amides are shown in Figure 12.4.

Kresimir Juraga

These artificial sweeteners contain the amide group.

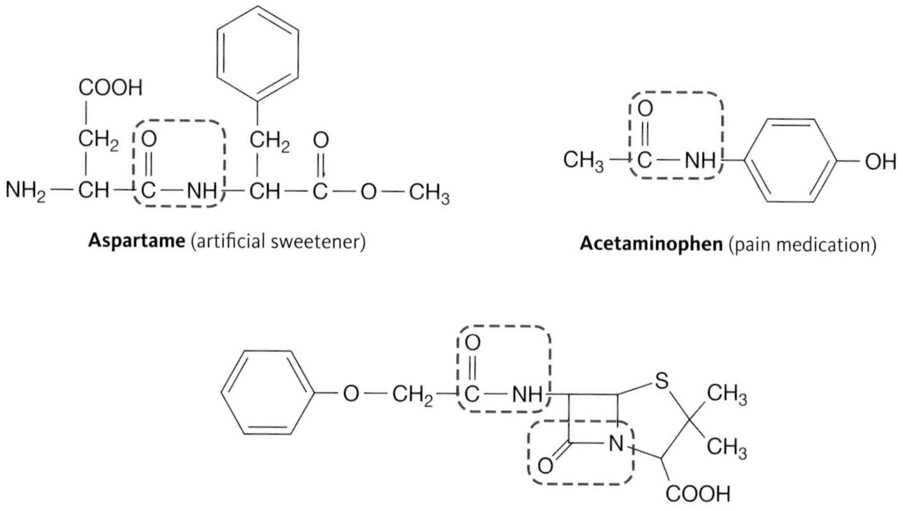

Aspartame (artificial sweetener)

Acetaminophen (pain medication)

Penicillin V (antibiotic)

FIGURE 12.4 Some important amides in nutrition and medicine.

Health Note: Acetaminophen has replaced aspirin in hospitals, clinics, and many households, because it does not irritate the stomach and it is safe for children. However, high doses (more than 10 times the maximum recommended dose) can cause severe liver damage, particularly in people who drink alcoholic beverages.

Alcohols Combine with Phosphate Ion to Form Phosphoesters

The third type of condensation is the **phosphorylation reaction**. In this reaction, an organic molecule becomes bonded to a phosphate group to form a **phosphoester**. The general scheme for a phosphorylation reaction is shown in Figure 12.5. Note that in this reaction, the phosphate ion must be bonded to at least one hydrogen ion.

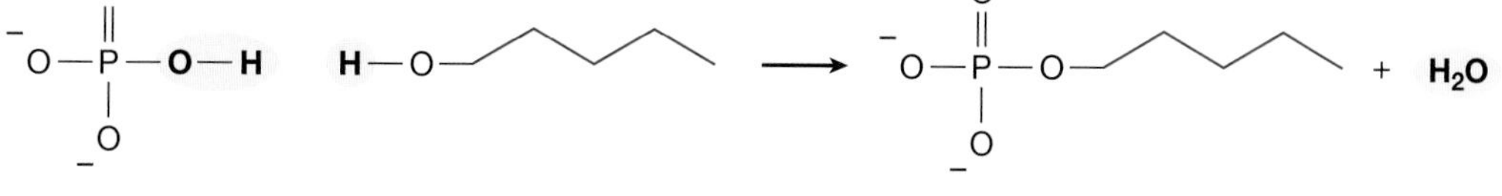

$$^-O-P(=O)(O^-)-\mathbf{O-H} + H-O-R \longrightarrow {}^-O-P(=O)(O^-)-O-R + \mathbf{H_2O}$$

A phosphate ion (in one of its stable forms at pH 7) + **An alcohol** ⟶ **A phosphoester** + **Water**

FIGURE 12.5 The general scheme for a phosphorylation reaction.

The reaction of 1-butanol with phosphate is a typical phosphorylation. As with all condensations, we can break up a phosphorylation reaction into two steps. In the first step, we remove OH from the phosphate ion and H from the alcohol.

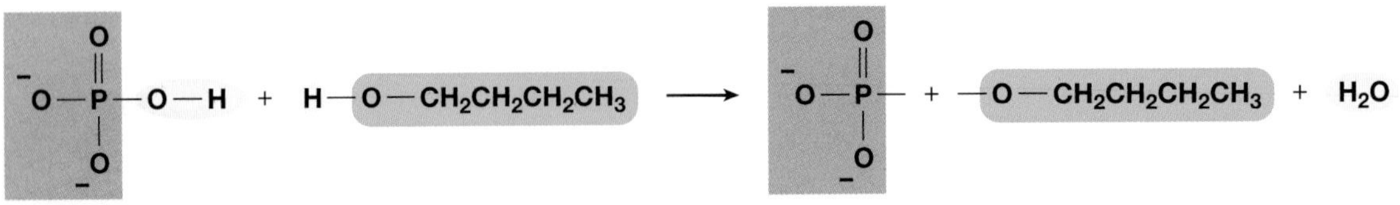

$$^{-}O-P(=O)(O^{-})-O-H + H-O-CH_2CH_2CH_2CH_3 \longrightarrow {}^{-}O-P(=O)(O^{-})- + -O-CH_2CH_2CH_2CH_3 + H_2O$$

Phosphate **1-Butanol**

In step 2, we combine the remaining fragments to make the final product, butyl phosphate.

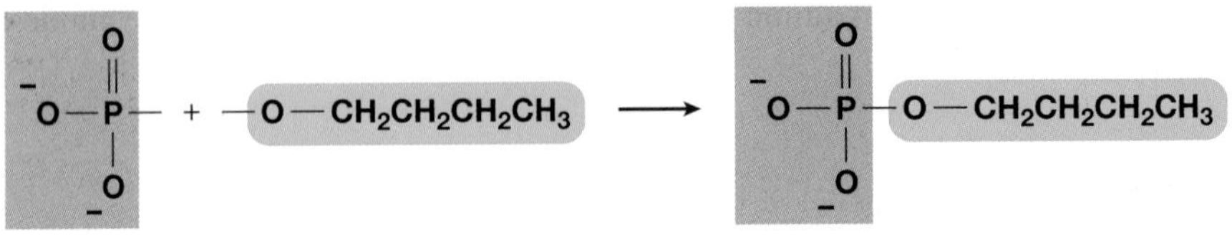

$$^{-}O-P(=O)(O^{-})- + -O-CH_2CH_2CH_2CH_3 \longrightarrow {}^{-}O-P(=O)(O^{-})-O-CH_2CH_2CH_2CH_3$$

Butyl phosphate

The overall reaction is

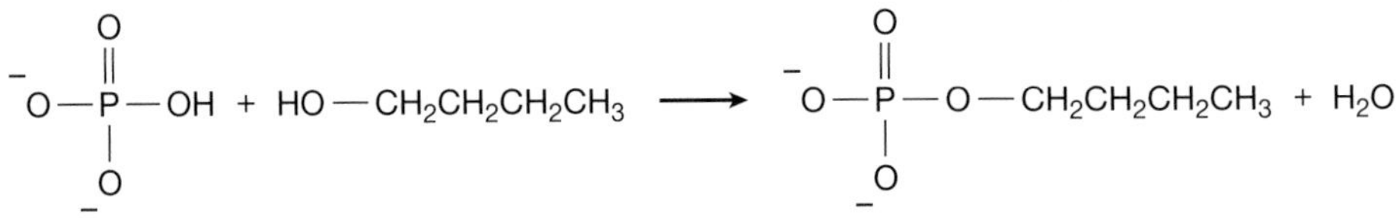

$$^{-}O-P(=O)(O^{-})-OH + HO-CH_2CH_2CH_2CH_3 \longrightarrow {}^{-}O-P(=O)(O^{-})-O-CH_2CH_2CH_2CH_3 + H_2O$$

Sample Problem 12.5

Drawing the product of a phosphorylation

Draw the structure of the phosphoester that is formed when 2-propanol condenses with phosphate.

SOLUTION

We need to draw the reactants so that the hydroxyl group of 2-propanol faces the hydroxyl group in the phosphate ion. (Remember that phosphate ions are bonded to one or two hydrogen ions at pH 7.) Here is one way to draw the structures so that their functional groups face each other:

Phosphate ion (in one of its stable forms at pH 7): $^{-}O-P(=O)(O^{-})-OH$

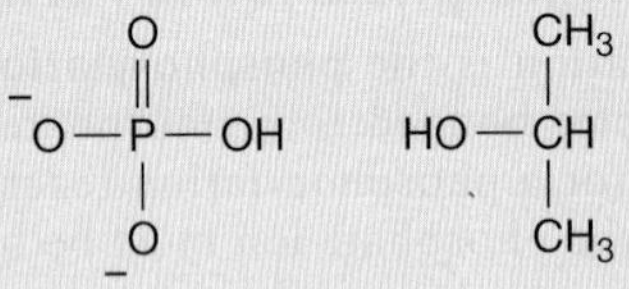

2-Propanol (drawn with a vertical carbon chain): $HO-CH(CH_3)_2$

As always, we divide the condensation reaction into two steps. In the first step, we remove OH from the phosphate and H from the 2-propanol. In the second step, we connect the remaining fragments.

Step 1:

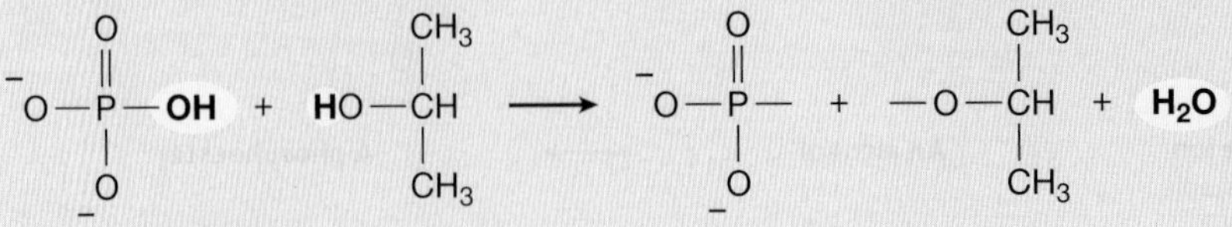

$$^{-}O-P(=O)(O^{-})-\mathbf{OH} + HO-CH(CH_3)_2 \longrightarrow {}^{-}O-P(=O)(O^{-})- + -O-CH(CH_3)_2 + \mathbf{H_2O}$$

continued

Step 2:

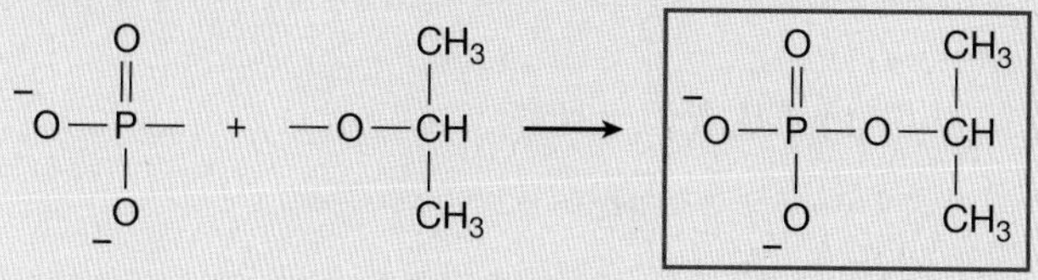

$^{-}O{-}P(=O)(O^{-}){-}$ + ${-}O{-}CH(CH_3)_2$ ⟶ $^{-}O{-}P(=O)(O^{-}){-}O{-}CH(CH_3)_2$

The phosphoester

TRY IT YOURSELF: *Draw the structure of the phosphoester that is formed when methanol condenses with phosphate.*

For additional practice, try Core Problems 12.11 and 12.12.

Phosphoesters are common in biochemistry. For example, when our bodies burn sugars to obtain energy, the organism first combines the sugar molecule with phosphate to form a phosphoester. In addition, a number of important molecules are *phosphodiesters,* in which the phosphate group is attached to two organic fragments, as shown here. The nucleic acids DNA and RNA are built from molecules called nucleotides that are linked together by phosphodiester groups, and the redox coenzymes NAD^{+} and FAD also contain phosphodiester groups.

$R{-}O{-}P(=O)(O^{-}){-}O{-}R'$

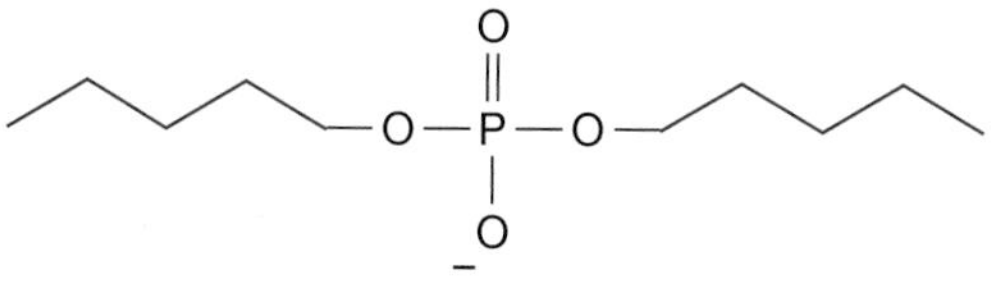

The general structure of a phosphodiester

Condensation reactions are not limited to the three types discussed in this chapter. In principle, any two molecules can undergo a condensation reaction if one of them contains a hydroxyl group and the other contains an N–H or O–H group. In practice, most condensations require special conditions, and some must be carried out in a roundabout fashion involving two or more reactions. Our bodies have evolved a range of strategies to enable them to carry out the kinds of condensation reactions you have learned.

CORE PROBLEMS

12.5 Draw the structures of the products of the following esterification reactions:

a) 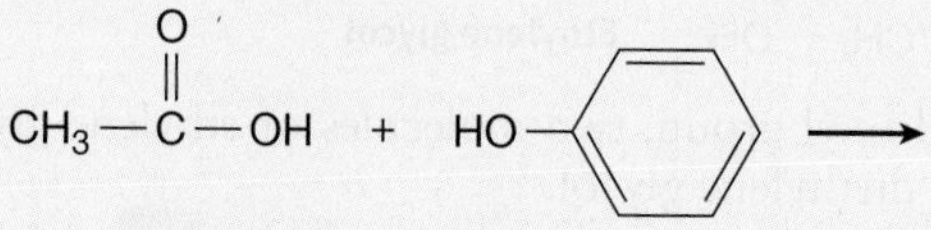 $CH_3{-}C(=O){-}OH$ + $HO{-}C_6H_5$ ⟶

b) 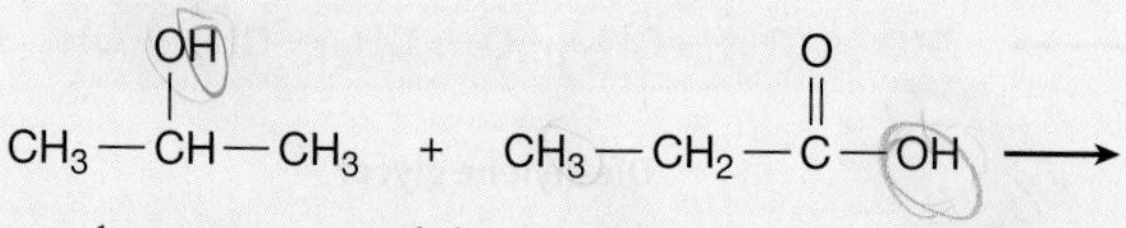 $CH_3{-}CH(OH){-}CH_3$ + $CH_3{-}CH_2{-}C(=O){-}OH$ ⟶

12.6 Draw the structures of the products of the following esterification reactions:

a) 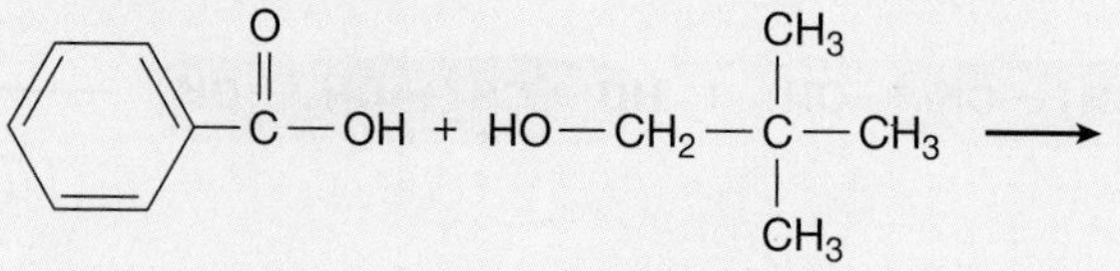 $C_6H_5{-}C(=O){-}OH$ + $HO{-}CH_2{-}C(CH_3)_2{-}CH_3$ ⟶

b) 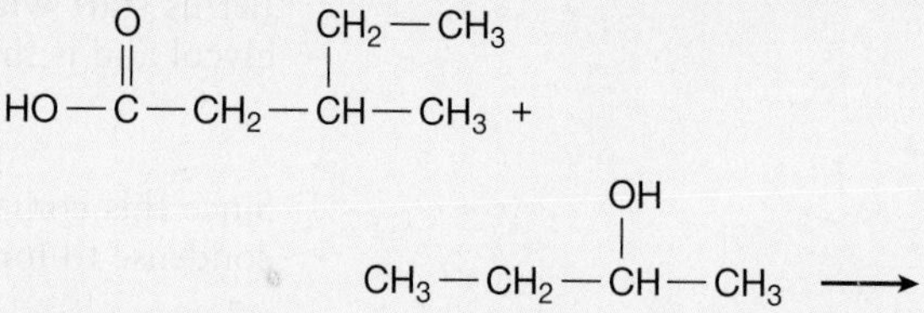 $HO{-}C(=O){-}CH_2{-}CH(CH_2{-}CH_3){-}CH_3$ + $CH_3{-}CH_2{-}CH(OH){-}CH_3$ ⟶

12.7 Draw the structures of the products of the following amidation reactions:

a) 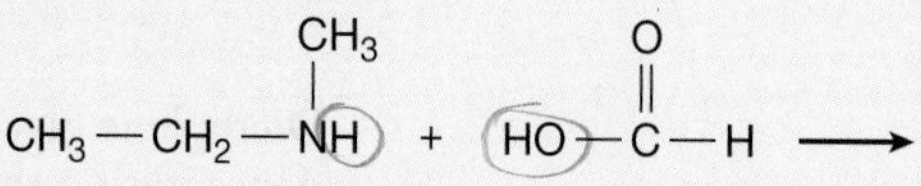 $CH_3{-}CH_2{-}NH(CH_3)$ + $HO{-}C(=O){-}H$ ⟶

b) 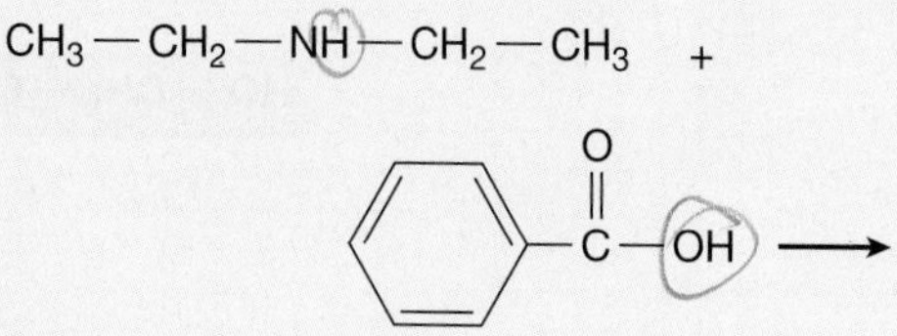 $CH_3{-}CH_2{-}NH{-}CH_2{-}CH_3$ + $C_6H_5{-}C(=O){-}OH$ ⟶

continued

12.8 Draw the structures of the products of the following amidation reactions:

a) 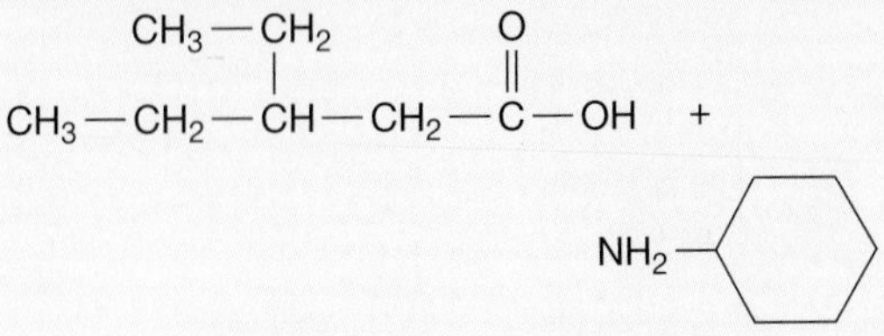 $CH_3-CH_2-CH(CH_2-CH_3)-CH_2-C(=O)-OH$ + NH_2-(cyclohexyl)

b) 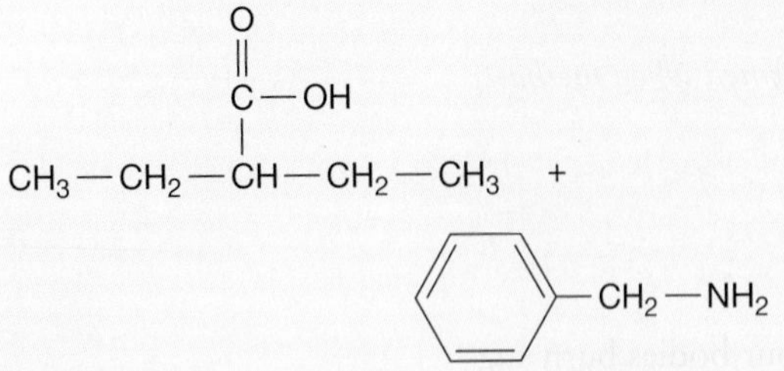 $CH_3-CH_2-CH(C(=O)-OH)-CH_2-CH_3$ + (benzene ring)$-CH_2-NH_2$

12.9 Which of the following molecules will give a pH higher than 7 when it dissolves in water?

a) $CH_3-CH_2-NH-CH_2-CH_3$

b) 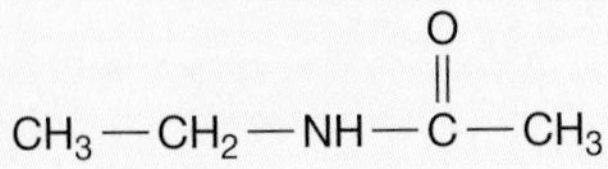 $CH_3-CH_2-NH-C(=O)-CH_3$

12.10 Which of the following molecules will give a pH higher than 7 when it dissolves in water?

a) 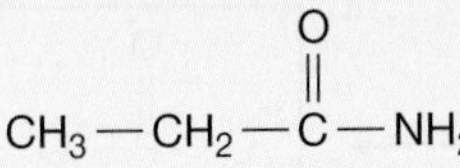 $CH_3-CH_2-C(=O)-NH_2$

b) 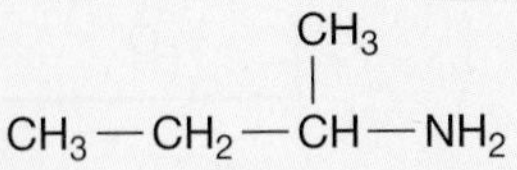 $CH_3-CH_2-CH(CH_3)-NH_2$

12.11 Draw the structures of the phosphoesters that are formed when each of the following compounds reacts with a phosphate ion:

a) $CH_3-CH_2-CH_2-CH_2-OH$

b) 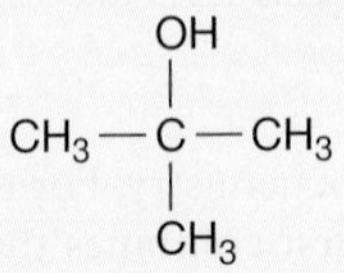 $CH_3-C(OH)(CH_3)-CH_3$

12.12 Draw the structures of the phosphoesters that are formed when each of the following compounds reacts with a phosphate ion:

a) 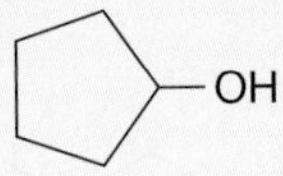 (cyclopentyl)$-OH$

b) 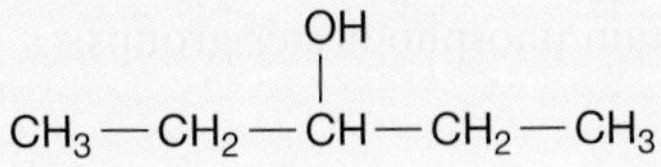 $CH_3-CH_2-CH(OH)-CH_2-CH_3$

OBJECTIVE: *Predict the structures of polymers that are formed by condensation reactions.*

12.3 Condensation Polymers

Condensation reactions combine two molecules into a single, larger compound. However, substances such as proteins and complex carbohydrates are made from many small molecules linked into a long chain. In this section, we will examine how condensation reactions can be used to form such large molecules.

Ethylene Glycol Can Condense to Form a Polymer

Let us start with a nonbiological example. The following compound is called ethylene glycol and is the principal ingredient in automobile coolant:

$HO-CH_2-CH_2-OH$ **Ethylene glycol**

Since this compound contains a hydroxyl group, two molecules of ethylene glycol can condense to form a larger molecule, diethylene glycol.

$$HO-CH_2-CH_2-OH + HO-CH_2-CH_2-OH \longrightarrow HO-CH_2-CH_2-O-CH_2-CH_2-OH + H_2O$$

Diethylene glycol

Diethylene glycol still contains a hydroxyl group (in fact, it contains two), so it can condense with a third molecule of ethylene glycol to form triethylene glycol.

$$HO-CH_2-CH_2-O-CH_2-CH_2-OH + HO-CH_2-CH_2-OH \longrightarrow$$

$$HO-CH_2-CH_2-O-CH_2-CH_2-O-CH_2-CH_2-OH + H_2O$$

Triethylene glycol

Triethylene glycol can condense with yet another molecule of ethylene glycol. We can continue this process indefinitely, making successively larger molecules, each of which has a hydroxyl group on each end.

A large molecule that is made by linking many small units is called a **polymer**. Polymers are often named by adding the prefix *poly-* to the name of the molecule from which it was made. For example, the polymer that we make by linking many molecules of ethylene glycol is called *polyethylene glycol*. It is easy to recognize the structure of a polymer, because it has a set of atoms that repeats over and over. The structure of polyethylene glycol is shown here:

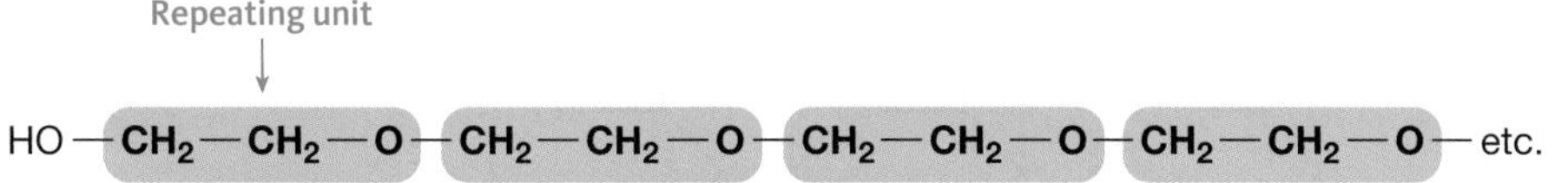

Polyethylene glycol

Kresimir Juraga

All of these household products contain PEG.

Polyethylene glycols of various sizes are used in a wide range of pharmaceutical and cosmetic products, and they usually appear on the ingredients list as PEG.

Health Note: Ethylene glycol has a sweet taste, but it is toxic and is a common cause of poisoning in children and pets. The body oxidizes ethylene glycol to glycolic acid and oxalic acid, which lower the blood pH to dangerous levels. Ethanol slows down the oxidation of ethylene glycol, so it is often used to treat ethylene glycol poisoning.

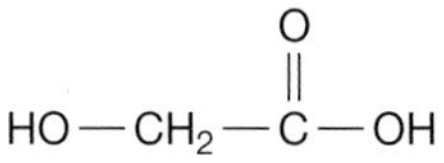

$$HO—CH_2—C(=O)—OH$$

Glycolic acid

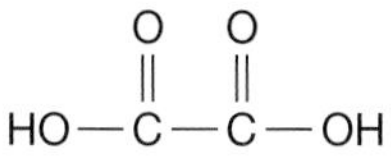

$$HO—C(=O)—C(=O)—OH$$

Oxalic acid

Sample Problem 12.6

Drawing a condensation polymer

Draw the structure of the product that is formed when four molecules of propylene glycol condense to form a single molecule.

$$HO—CH(CH_3)—CH_2—OH$$

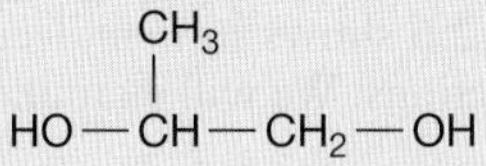

Propylene glycol

SOLUTION

To draw the structure of the product, we begin by lining up the four molecules so that their hydroxyl groups face each other.

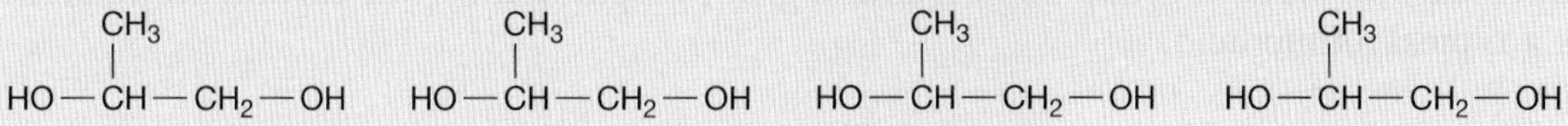

$$HO—CH(CH_3)—CH_2—OH \quad HO—CH(CH_3)—CH_2—OH \quad HO—CH(CH_3)—CH_2—OH \quad HO—CH(CH_3)—CH_2—OH$$

Next, we remove OH and H from each pair of hydroxyl groups.

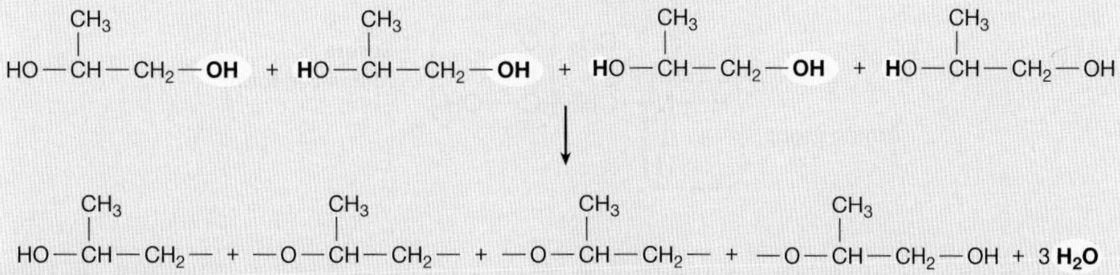

$$HO—CH(CH_3)—CH_2—\mathbf{OH} + \mathbf{H}O—CH(CH_3)—CH_2—\mathbf{OH} + \mathbf{H}O—CH(CH_3)—CH_2—\mathbf{OH} + \mathbf{H}O—CH(CH_3)—CH_2—OH$$

$$\downarrow$$

$$HO—CH(CH_3)—CH_2— + —O—CH(CH_3)—CH_2— + —O—CH(CH_3)—CH_2— + —O—CH(CH_3)—CH_2—OH + 3\ \mathbf{H_2O}$$

Finally, we join the remaining organic pieces to form a single molecule. The structure of the product is

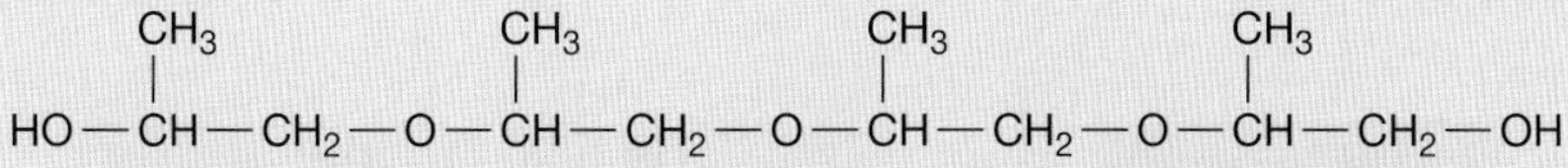

$$HO—CH(CH_3)—CH_2—O—CH(CH_3)—CH_2—O—CH(CH_3)—CH_2—O—CH(CH_3)—CH_2—OH$$

TRY IT YOURSELF: *Draw the structure of the organic product that is formed when three molecules of trimethylene glycol condense to form a single molecule.*

$$HO—CH_2—CH_2—CH_2—OH$$

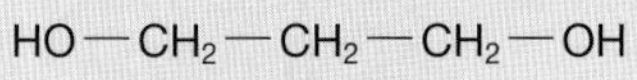

Trimethylene glycol

For additional practice, try Core Problems 12.13 and 12.14.

Health Note: In high concentrations, PEG is a powerful laxative. Patients who will have a colon exam (sigmoidoscopy or colonoscopy) often prepare for the exam by drinking a large volume of a dilute solution containing PEG and electrolytes. This mixture flushes all solid material from the colon, but it does not cause water or electrolytes to pass through the intestinal wall, so it does not cause dehydration or an electrolyte imbalance.

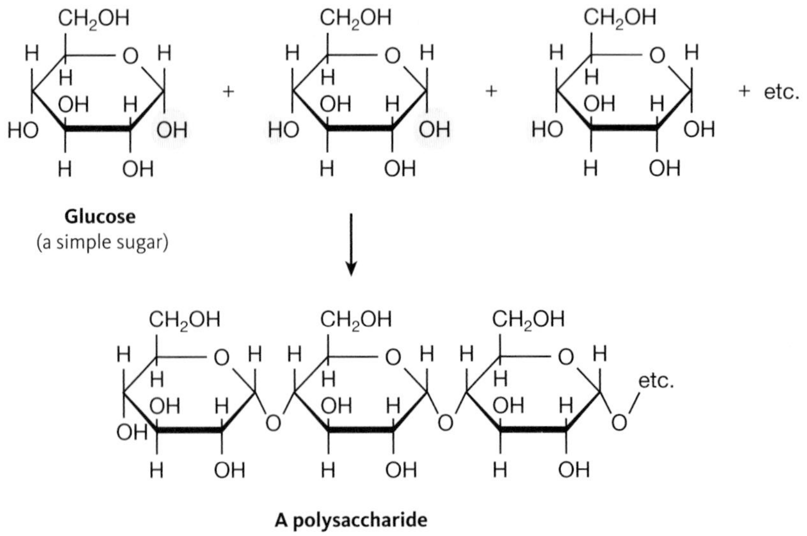

FIGURE 12.6 The formation of a polysaccharide from simple sugars.

Complex carbohydrates such as starch and cellulose are made by a similar reaction. These compounds are composed of molecules called simple sugars, which are linked together into a long chain. Simple sugars contain many hydroxyl groups, so they are ideally suited to form polymers. Figure 12.6 shows how molecules of glucose (a simple sugar) can be linked by condensation reactions. We will examine the chemistry of sugars in detail in Chapter 14.

Amino Acids Condense to Form Proteins

Let us now examine how proteins are formed. A protein is a large molecule that is made from smaller molecules called amino acids. As we saw in Section 11.4, amino acids contain a carboxylic acid group and an amino group, separated by one carbon atom. Serine is a typical amino acid.

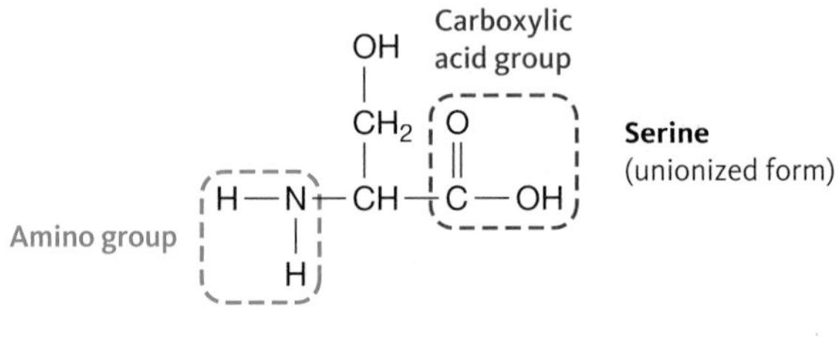

Carboxylic acid group

Amino group

Serine (unionized form)

Two molecules of serine can condense to form a larger molecule, which still contains an amino group and a carboxylic acid group. In this amidation reaction, the amino group from one molecule of serine reacts with the carboxylic acid group from the other molecule.

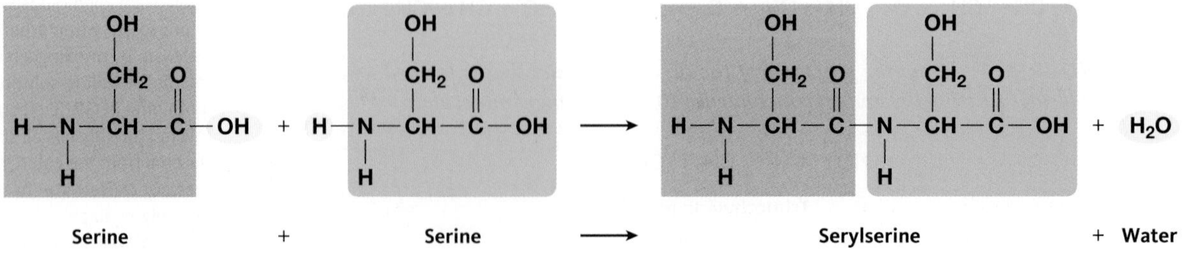

Serine + **Serine** ⟶ **Serylserine** + **Water**

The product of this reaction can react with additional molecules of serine, forming a polymer called *polyserine*.

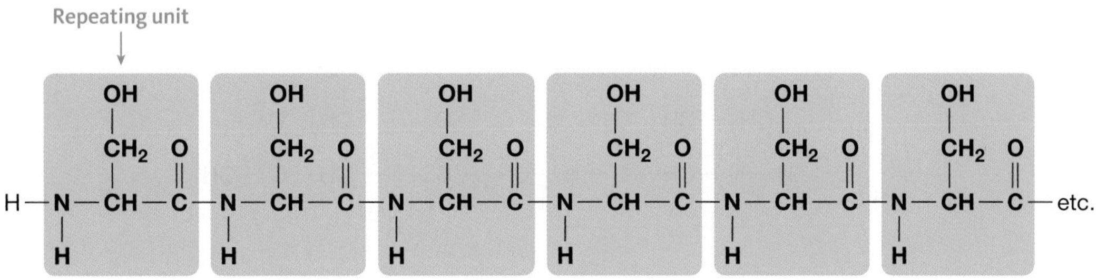

Repeating unit

Polyserine

Proteins are not made from a single amino acid that is repeated over and over. They are made from several different amino acids that are linked together in a specific order. Each amino acid contains a carboxylic acid group and an amino group, so any amino acid can be incorporated into a chain using condensation reactions. Sample Problem 12.7 shows how we can link three different amino acids into a single molecule.

Sample Problem 12.7

Drawing the product of the condensation of amino acids

The structures of three naturally occurring amino acids are shown here. Draw the structure of the organic compound that is formed when these three amino acids condense to form a single molecule:

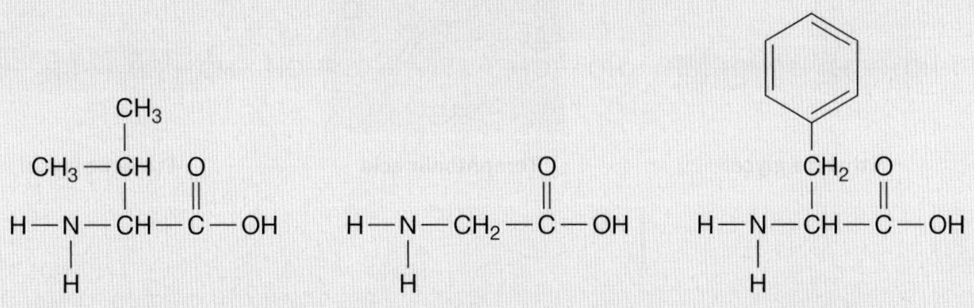

Valine

Glycine

Phenylalanine

SOLUTION

We start by removing the OH group from valine and glycine, and we remove an H atom from the amino groups of glycine and phenylalanine.

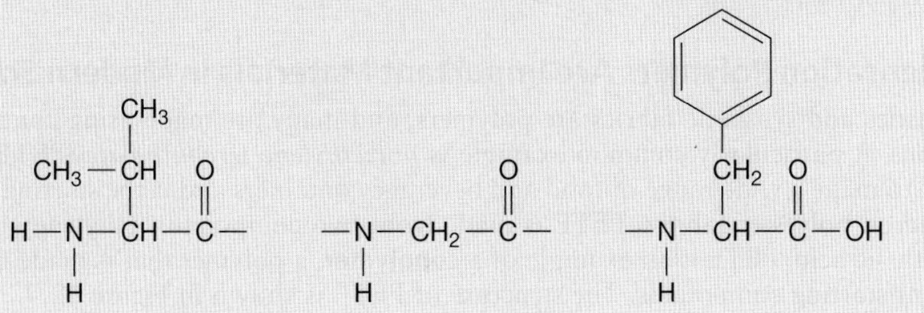

continued

Connecting the fragments gives us the organic product of this condensation.

```
                                            (benzene ring)
                                                  |
         CH3                                      |
          |                                       |
   CH3 — CH    O              O              CH2  O
          |    ||             ||              |   ||
H — N — CH — C — N — CH2 — C — N — CH — C — OH
    |               |               |
    H               H               H
```

The reaction also forms two molecules of water.

TRY IT YOURSELF: *Draw the structure of the product that is formed when the following three amino acids condense to form a single molecule:*

```
                                   O
                                   ||
                            NH2 — C                          NH2
                                   |                          |
       CH3  O                     CH2  O                   (CH2)4   O
        |   ||                     |   ||                     |     ||
H — N — CH — C — OH     H — N — CH — C — OH     H — N — CH ——— C — OH
    |                       |                       |
    H                       H                       H

      Alanine                 Asparagine                 Lysine
```

For additional practice, try Core Problems 12.17 and 12.18.

```
      O            O                                           O            O
      ||           ||                                          ||           ||
HO — C —(benzene)— C — OH   HO — CH2 — CH2 — OH   HO — C —(benzene)— C — OH   HO — CH2 — CH2 — OH

    Terephthalic acid        Ethylene glycol          Terephthalic acid        Ethylene glycol

                                      ↓

      O            O                              O            O
      ||           ||                             ||           ||
HO — C —(benzene)— C — O — CH2 — CH2 — O — C —(benzene)— C — O — CH2 — CH2 — O — etc.
```

PETE (polyethylene terephthalate) – a copolymer

FIGURE 12.7 The formation of a copolymer.

Kresimir Juraga

Much of the clothing we wear is made from condensation polymers.

Condensation Polymers Are Important Materials in Modern Society

All plastics and synthetic fabrics are polymers, and many are made using condensation reactions. A particularly common example is *polyethylene terephthalate* (PETE), which is used to make a wide range of food and beverage containers and is the starting material for Dacron polyester fabrics. PETE is made from two compounds, ethylene glycol and terephthalic acid. PETE is an example of a **copolymer**, a polymer that is made from two different starting compounds. The structure of PETE is shown in Figure 12.7.

In any copolymer, the two starting materials alternate, just as they do in PETE. Sample Problem 12.8 gives another example of a copolymer that is important in modern society.

Sample Problem 12.8

Drawing the structure of a copolymer

Nylon 66 is a copolymer that can be made from adipic acid and hexamethylenediamine. Draw a structure that shows how two molecules of each compound can combine to form the beginning of a nylon molecule.

$$HO{-}\overset{O}{\overset{\|}{C}}{-}(CH_2)_4{-}\overset{O}{\overset{\|}{C}}{-}OH \qquad NH_2{-}(CH_2)_6{-}NH_2$$

Adipic acid **Hexamethylenediamine**

SOLUTION

To make this copolymer, we need to alternate molecules of each reactant. We can start with either compound, but let us begin the chain with a molecule of adipic acid.

$$HO{-}\overset{O}{\overset{\|}{C}}{-}(CH_2)_4{-}\overset{O}{\overset{\|}{C}}{-}OH \qquad H{-}\overset{H}{\overset{|}{N}}{-}(CH_2)_6{-}\overset{H}{\overset{|}{N}}{-}H$$

$$HO{-}\overset{O}{\overset{\|}{C}}{-}(CH_2)_4{-}\overset{O}{\overset{\|}{C}}{-}OH \qquad H{-}\overset{H}{\overset{|}{N}}{-}(CH_2)_6{-}\overset{H}{\overset{|}{N}}{-}H$$

Now we remove OH from the acid groups and H from the amine groups, and we connect the resulting fragments.

$$\text{---}(CH_2)_4{-}\overset{O}{\overset{\|}{C}}{-}\mathbf{OH} + \mathbf{H}{-}\overset{H}{\overset{|}{N}}{-}(CH_2)_6{-}\overset{H}{\overset{|}{N}}{-}\mathbf{H} + \mathbf{HO}{-}\overset{O}{\overset{\|}{C}}{-}(CH_2)_4{-}\overset{O}{\overset{\|}{C}}{-}\mathbf{OH} + \mathbf{H}{-}\overset{H}{\overset{|}{N}}{-}(CH_2)_6\text{---}$$

Remove OH and H.

$$HO{-}\overset{O}{\overset{\|}{C}}{-}(CH_2)_4{-}\overset{O}{\overset{\|}{C}}{-} + {-}\overset{H}{\overset{|}{N}}{-}(CH_2)_6{-}\overset{H}{\overset{|}{N}}{-} + {-}\overset{O}{\overset{\|}{C}}{-}(CH_2)_4{-}\overset{O}{\overset{\|}{C}}{-} + {-}\overset{H}{\overset{|}{N}}{-}(CH_2)_6{-}\overset{H}{\overset{|}{N}}{-}H$$

Connect the fragments.

$$\boxed{HO{-}\overset{O}{\overset{\|}{C}}{-}(CH_2)_4{-}\overset{O}{\overset{\|}{C}}{-}\overset{H}{\overset{|}{N}}{-}(CH_2)_6{-}\overset{H}{\overset{|}{N}}{-}\overset{O}{\overset{\|}{C}}{-}(CH_2)_4{-}\overset{O}{\overset{\|}{C}}{-}\overset{H}{\overset{|}{N}}{-}(CH_2)_6{-}\overset{H}{\overset{|}{N}}{-}H}$$

The reaction also makes three molecules of water.

TRY IT YOURSELF: *Lexan is a hard, clear plastic that is used to make cookware. It is a copolymer that can (in principle) be made from the following compounds. Draw a structure that shows how two molecules of each compound can condense to form the beginning of a Lexan molecule.*

$$HO{-}C_6H_4{-}\underset{CH_3}{\underset{|}{\overset{CH_3}{\overset{|}{C}}}}{-}C_6H_4{-}OH \qquad HO{-}\overset{O}{\overset{\|}{C}}{-}OH$$

For additional practice, try Core Problems 12.19 and 12.20.

The bonds in a polymer are strong covalent bonds, so polymer molecules themselves are strong. Because these molecules can also be very long, they are particularly suited for fibrous materials such as fabrics. In addition, the long chains tend to attract one another rather strongly, so polymers can be used to make a variety of durable materials. These materials are called *plastics,* and they are used to make products such as trash bags, food containers, and automobile bodies.

CORE PROBLEMS

12.13 Draw the structure of the organic product that is formed when three molecules of the following compound condense to form a single molecule:

HO–C_6H_4–OH

12.14 Draw the structure of the organic product that is formed when three molecules of the following compound condense to form a single molecule:

$HO-CH_2-C(CH_3)_2-CH_2-OH$

12.15 Lactic acid is responsible for the unpleasant taste and aroma of spoiled milk. Draw the structure of the product that is formed when three molecules of lactic acid condense to form a single molecule.

$HO-CH(CH_3)-C(=O)-OH$ **Lactic acid**

12.16 Mandelic acid is a weak acid that is used in adult acne medications and other skin care treatments. Draw the structure of the product that is formed when three molecules of mandelic acid condense to form a single molecule.

$HO-CH(C_6H_5)-C(=O)-OH$ **Mandelic acid**

12.17 Isoleucine is one of the naturally occurring amino acids, and it is a required nutrient in our diet. Draw the structure of the organic product that is formed when three molecules of isoleucine condense.

$NH_2-CH(CH(CH_3)-CH_2-CH_3)-C(=O)-OH$ **Isoleucine**

12.18 Phenylalanine is one of the naturally occurring amino acids, and it is a required nutrient in our diet. Draw the structure of the organic product that is formed when three molecules of phenylalanine condense.

$NH_2-CH(CH_2-C_6H_5)-C(=O)-OH$ **Phenylalanine**

12.19 Ethylenediamine and oxalic acid can form a copolymer. Show how two molecules of each compound can condense to form the beginning of a copolymer.

$NH_2-CH_2-CH_2-NH_2$ **Ethylenediamine**

$HO-C(=O)-C(=O)-OH$ **Oxalic acid**

12.20 Hydroquinone and malonic acid can form a copolymer. Show how two molecules of each compound can condense to form the beginning of a copolymer.

HO–C_6H_4–OH **Hydroquinone**

$HO-C(=O)-CH_2-C(=O)-OH$ **Malonic acid**

OBJECTIVE: *Predict the products of hydrolysis reactions of ethers, esters, amides, and phosphoesters.*

12.4 Hydrolysis

The food we eat contains three principal types of nutrients: complex carbohydrates, fats, and proteins. Our digestive tract must break down each of these into smaller molecules, because large molecules cannot pass through the intestinal wall into our bloodstream. We break proteins down into amino acids, fats into glycerol and fatty acids, and complex carbohydrates into simple sugars. Each of these chemical processes is a **hydrolysis reaction**. In a hydrolysis, a large molecule reacts with water, breaking down into two smaller

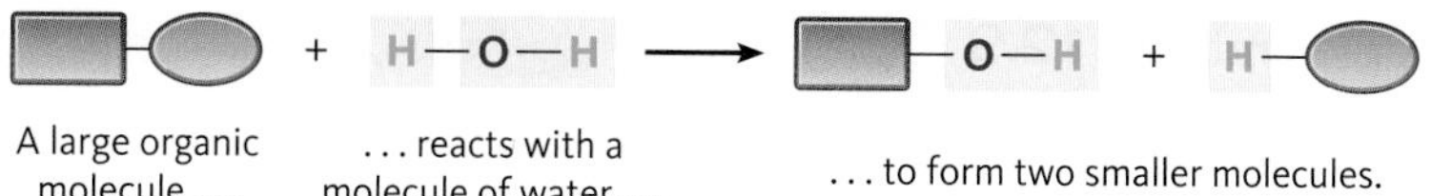
H—O—H
O—H
H
A large organic molecule . . .
. . . reacts with a molecule of water . . .
. . . to form two smaller molecules.

FIGURE 12.8 The general scheme for a hydrolysis reaction.

molecules. Thus, *hydrolysis is the opposite of condensation.* The general scheme for this reaction type is shown in Figure 12.8.

Ethers Can Be Hydrolyzed to Form Alcohols

Let us look at a typical hydrolysis reaction. In Section 12.1, we saw how two molecules of ethanol can condense to form a molecule of diethyl ether and a molecule of water.

$$CH_3{-}CH_2{-}OH + HO{-}CH_2{-}CH_3 \longrightarrow CH_3{-}CH_2{-}O{-}CH_2{-}CH_3 + H{-}O{-}H$$

Two molecules of ethanol → **Diethyl ether** + **Water**

This reaction is reversible, so diethyl ether can react with water to form two molecules of ethanol. The reverse reaction is called the hydrolysis of diethyl ether.

$$CH_3{-}CH_2{-}O{-}CH_2{-}CH_3 + H{-}O{-}H \longrightarrow CH_3{-}CH_2{-}OH + HO{-}CH_2{-}CH_3$$

Diethyl ether + **Water** → **Two molecules of ethanol**

We can divide the hydrolysis reaction into two steps, just as we did with condensation reactions. In the first step, we break the bond between the oxygen atom and the neighboring carbon atom.

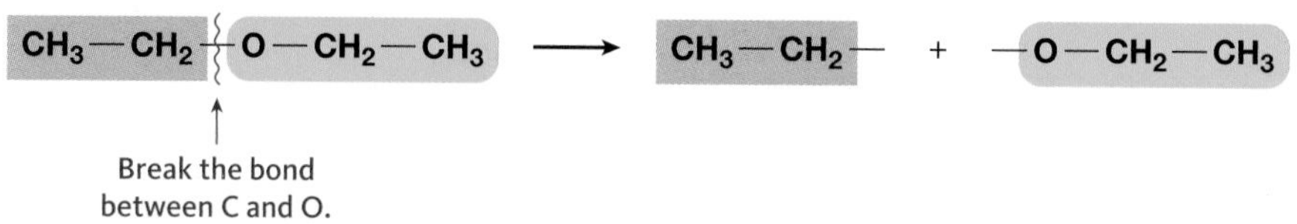

$$CH_3{-}CH_2 \wr O{-}CH_2{-}CH_3 \longrightarrow CH_3{-}CH_2{-} + {-}O{-}CH_2{-}CH_3$$

Break the bond between C and O.

In the second step, we add OH to one of the organic fragments and H to the other.

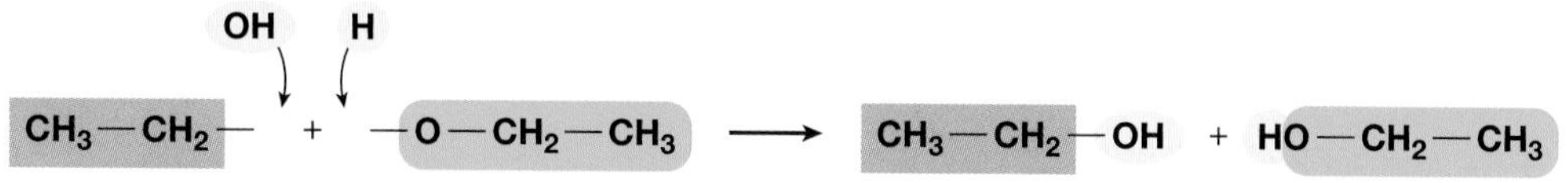

$$\overset{OH}{\downarrow}\ \ \overset{H}{\downarrow}$$

$$CH_3{-}CH_2{-} + {-}O{-}CH_2{-}CH_3 \longrightarrow CH_3{-}CH_2{-}OH + HO{-}CH_2{-}CH_3$$

In step 2, how do we know which fragment becomes bonded to OH and which becomes bonded to H? *The hydroxyl group always bonds to carbon, never to oxygen or nitrogen.* Oxygen–oxygen and nitrogen–oxygen bonds are not very stable, so they do not form in hydrolysis reactions, as shown in Figure 12.9.

You might be wondering how to tell which bond breaks in step 1. You can break either carbon–oxygen bond in this case, because you produce the same products (two molecules of ethanol) regardless of which C–O bond you break. Be sure that you break a carbon–oxygen bond, though: *carbon–carbon bonds never break in a hydrolysis reaction.*

Correct orientation

OH H

$$CH_3{-}CH_2{-} + {-}O{-}CH_2{-}CH_3 \longrightarrow CH_3{-}CH_2{-}OH + H{-}O{-}CH_2{-}CH_3$$

We form a C—O bond and an O—H bond

Incorrect orientation

H HO

???

$$CH_3{-}CH_2{-} + {-}O{-}CH_2{-}CH_3 \not\longrightarrow CH_3{-}CH_3 + HO{-}O{-}CH_2{-}CH_3$$

O—O bond: never formed in a hydrolysis reaction

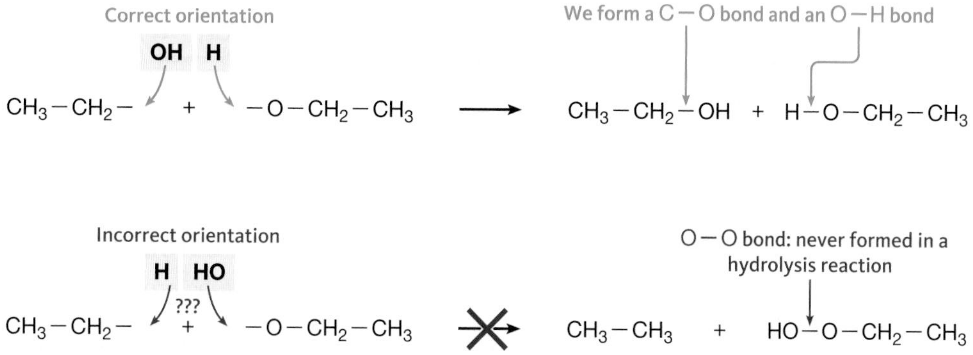

FIGURE 12.9 Determining which way to add H and OH in a hydrolysis reaction.

Sample Problem 12.9

Drawing the products of the hydrolysis of an ether

Draw the structures of the products that are formed when methyl propyl ether is hydrolyzed.

SOLUTION

First, we must draw the structure of methyl propyl ether.

$$CH_3-O-CH_2-CH_2-CH_3$$

Now we can carry out the hydrolysis reaction. The first step is to break one of the carbon–oxygen bonds in our ether. It does not matter which bond we choose.

$$CH_3 \mid O-CH_2-CH_2-CH_3 \longrightarrow CH_3- \quad + \quad -O-CH_2-CH_2-CH_3$$

The second step, we add OH and H to the fragments. We must add the hydroxyl group to the CH_3 fragment, because we cannot form an oxygen–oxygen bond.

$$\overset{OH}{\downarrow}CH_3- \quad + \quad \overset{H}{\downarrow}-O-CH_2-CH_2-CH_3 \longrightarrow \boxed{CH_3-OH + HO-CH_2-CH_2-CH_3}$$

The products are a molecule of methanol and a molecule of 1-propanol.

TRY IT YOURSELF: *Draw the structures of the products that are formed when the following ether is hydrolyzed:*

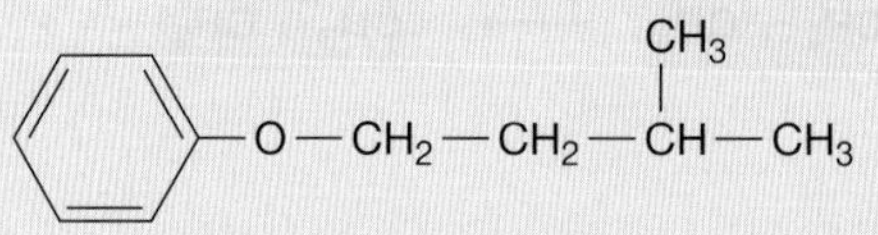

$$C_6H_5-O-CH_2-CH_2-\underset{}{\overset{CH_3}{\overset{|}{CH}}}-CH_3$$

For additional practice, try Core Problems 12.21 and 12.22.

The hydrolysis of ethers is not a useful reaction in general, because ethers are very stable. Breaking down an ether into two alcohols, if it can be done at all, requires harsh conditions and produces an equilibrium mixture of the products and the reactants. However, most other organic compounds that contain the C–O–C group can be hydrolyzed. In particular, our bodies are constantly hydrolyzing complex carbohydrates, which contain a closely related group called an acetal. We will examine this reaction more closely in Chapter 14.

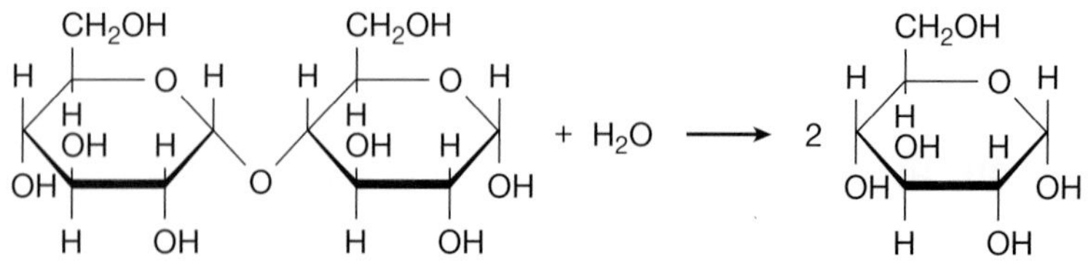

$$\text{Maltose} + H_2O \longrightarrow 2\ \text{Glucose}$$

Maltose – a disaccharide

Glucose – a simple sugar

The Hydrolysis of an Ester Produces an Alcohol and a Carboxylic Acid

Any compound that can be formed by a condensation reaction can be broken down by a hydrolysis reaction. For example, in Section 12.2 we saw that we can make an ester by condensing a carboxylic acid and an alcohol. If we hydrolyze the ester, we get our carboxylic acid and our alcohol back, as shown in Figure 12.10.

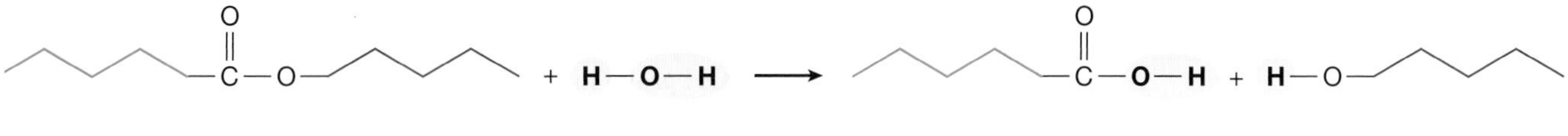

$$\text{CH}_3\text{CH}_2\text{CH}_2\text{CH}_2\text{CH}_2\text{—C(=O)—O—CH}_2\text{CH}_2\text{CH}_2\text{CH}_2\text{CH}_3 + \text{H—O—H} \longrightarrow \text{CH}_3\text{CH}_2\text{CH}_2\text{CH}_2\text{CH}_2\text{—C(=O)—O—H} + \text{H—O—CH}_2\text{CH}_2\text{CH}_2\text{CH}_2\text{CH}_3$$

An ester + **Water** ⟶ **A carboxylic acid** + **An alcohol**

FIGURE 12.10 The general scheme for the hydrolysis of an ester.

Let us look at the hydrolysis of methyl propanoate, a typical ester. We can break this reaction into two steps, just as we did for the hydrolysis of diethyl ether. In the first step, we break a C–O bond.

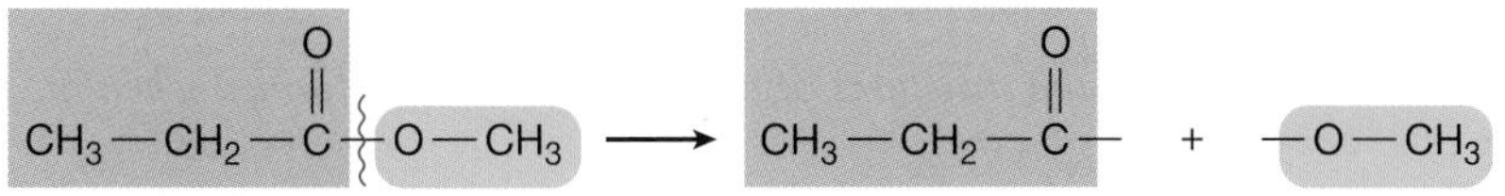

$$\text{CH}_3\text{—CH}_2\text{—C(=O)}\wr\text{O—CH}_3 \longrightarrow \text{CH}_3\text{—CH}_2\text{—C(=O)—} + \text{—O—CH}_3$$

Methyl propanoate

In the second step, we add H and OH to the two organic fragments, forming propanoic acid and methanol.

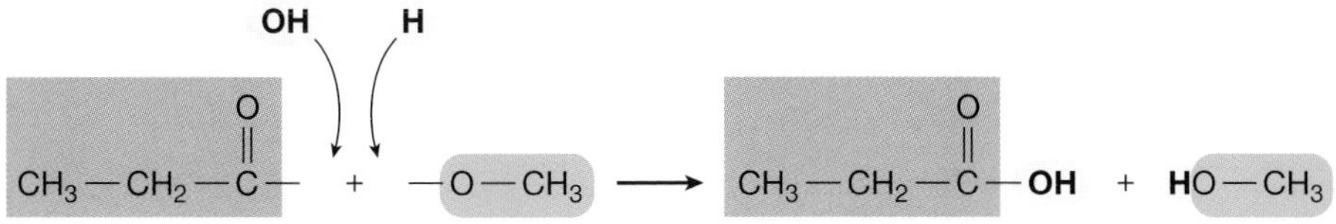

$$\text{CH}_3\text{—CH}_2\text{—C(=O)—} \;(\leftarrow \text{OH}) + (\text{H} \rightarrow)\; \text{—O—CH}_3 \longrightarrow \text{CH}_3\text{—CH}_2\text{—C(=O)—OH} + \text{HO—CH}_3$$

Propanoic acid **Methanol**

Here is the overall reaction for the hydrolysis of methyl propanoate:

$$\text{CH}_3\text{—CH}_2\text{—C(=O)—O—CH}_3 + \text{H—O—H} \longrightarrow \text{CH}_3\text{—CH}_2\text{—C(=O)—OH} + \text{HO—CH}_3$$

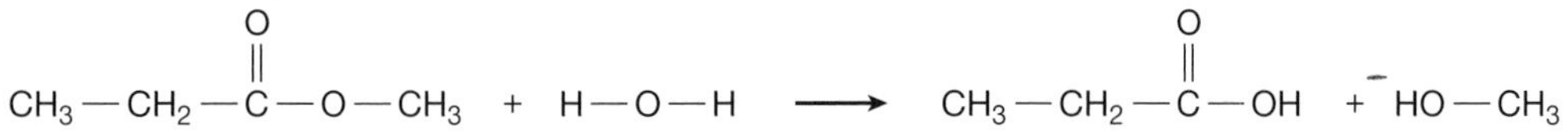

Again, it does not matter which C–O bond we break in step 1. We make the same two products regardless of which C–O bond is broken, as long as we remember that the OH group must bond to carbon. However, in practice the bond that breaks is the one closest to the carbonyl group, and this will become important when we look at the hydrolysis of amides.

Health Note: Aspirin (page 492) is an ester and hydrolyzes when it is mixed with water. It absorbs water from the atmosphere, so aspirin bottles must be kept tightly closed. One of the products of aspirin hydrolysis is acetic acid, which has the odor of vinegar, so aspirin that smells strongly of vinegar should be discarded.

Sample Problem 12.10

Drawing the products of the hydrolysis of an ester

Draw the structures of the products that are formed when ethyl benzoate is hydrolyzed.

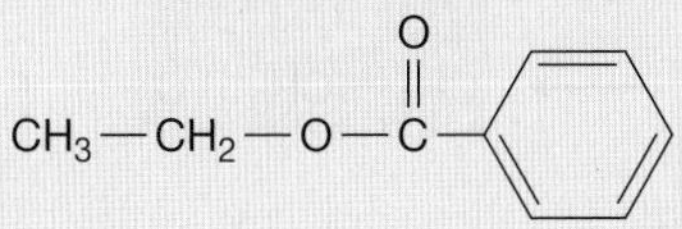

$$\text{CH}_3\text{—CH}_2\text{—O—C(=O)—C}_6\text{H}_5 \quad \textbf{Ethyl benzoate}$$

SOLUTION

First, we need to break one of the carbon–oxygen bonds. We can break either C–O bond, but to be consistent with the hydrolysis of amides, let us break the C–O bond that is closest to the carbonyl group.

$$\text{CH}_3\text{—CH}_2\text{—O}\wr\text{C(=O)—C}_6\text{H}_5 \longrightarrow \text{CH}_3\text{—CH}_2\text{—O—} + \text{—C(=O)—C}_6\text{H}_5$$

Break the C–O bond closest to the carbonyl group.

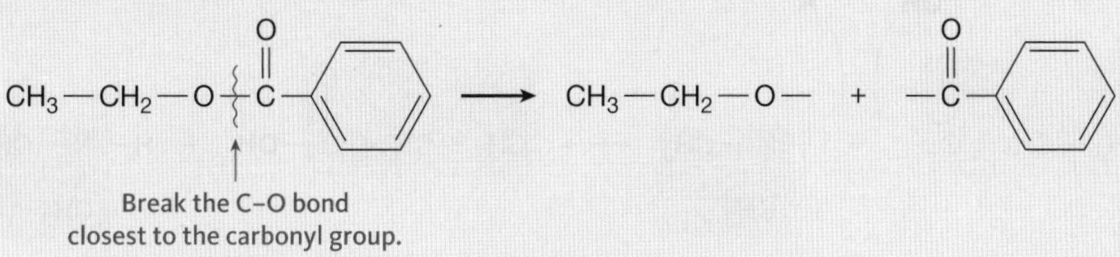

continued

To draw the structures of the final products, we add OH and H to the fragments we just produced. Remember that the OH group must be attached to carbon, never to oxygen.

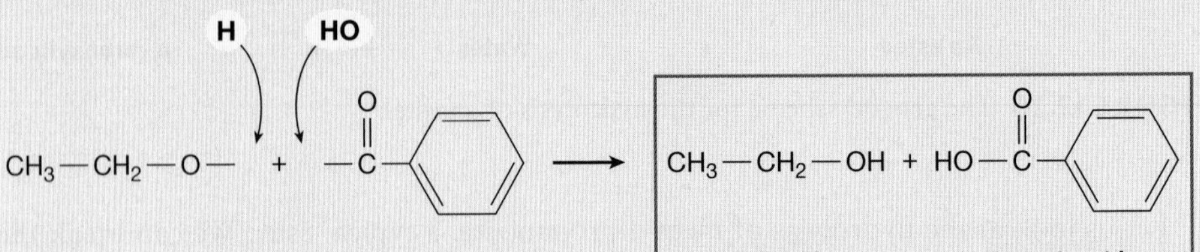

$$CH_3-CH_2-O- \;+\; -\overset{\displaystyle O}{\overset{\|}{C}}-C_6H_5 \;\longrightarrow\; CH_3-CH_2-OH \;+\; HO-\overset{\displaystyle O}{\overset{\|}{C}}-C_6H_5$$

H HO

Ethanol Benzoic acid

The products are ethanol and benzoic acid.

TRY IT YOURSELF: *Draw the structures of the products that are formed when the following ester is hydrolyzed:*

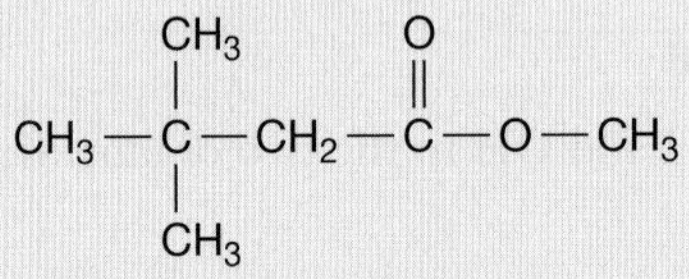

$$CH_3-C(CH_3)_2-CH_2-\overset{\displaystyle O}{\overset{\|}{C}}-O-CH_3$$

For additional practice, try Core Problems 12.23 and 12.24.

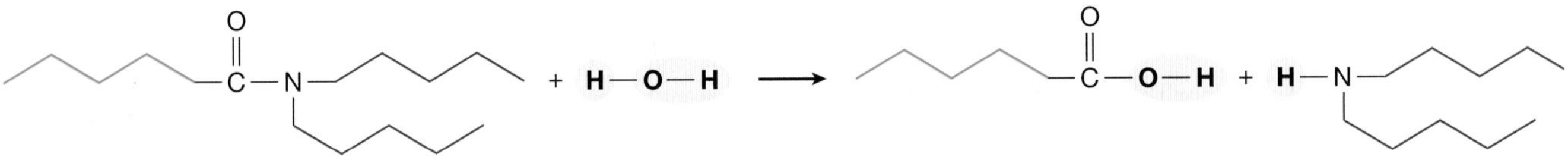

$$\text{R}-\overset{\displaystyle O}{\overset{\|}{C}}-N(\text{R}')(\text{R}'') \;+\; H-O-H \;\longrightarrow\; \text{R}-\overset{\displaystyle O}{\overset{\|}{C}}-O-H \;+\; H-N(\text{R}')(\text{R}'')$$

An amide + Water ⟶ A carboxylic acid + An amine

FIGURE 12.11 The general scheme for the hydrolysis of an amide.

The Hydrolysis of an Amide Produces a Carboxylic Acid and an Amine

We can also hydrolyze an amide. The products are a carboxylic acid and an amine, as shown in Figure 12.11.

Let us look at the hydrolysis of a typical amide. Again, we can break this hydrolysis into two steps. In step 1, we break the C–N bond that is closest to the carbonyl group.

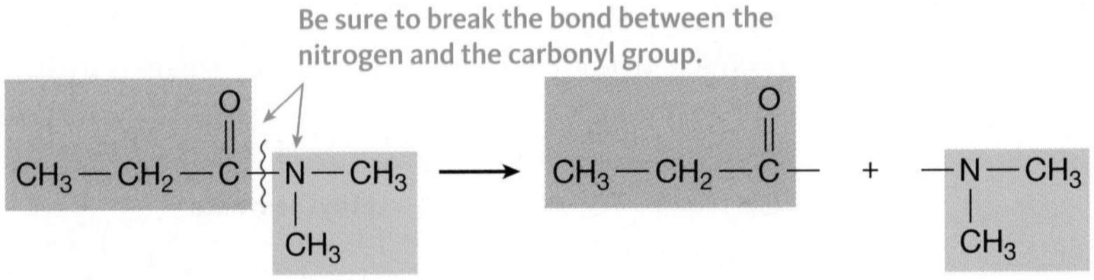

Be sure to break the bond between the nitrogen and the carbonyl group.

$$CH_3-CH_2-\overset{\displaystyle O}{\overset{\|}{C}}-N(CH_3)-CH_3 \;\longrightarrow\; CH_3-CH_2-\overset{\displaystyle O}{\overset{\|}{C}}- \;+\; -N(CH_3)-CH_3$$

N,N-dimethylpropanoate (an amide)

In step 2, we add H and OH to the two fragments. Be sure to attach the OH group to carbon, not to nitrogen. The products of this hydrolysis reaction are propanoic acid and dimethylamine.

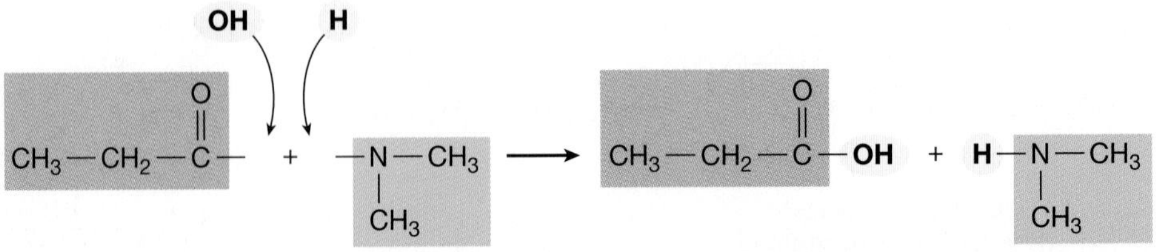

OH H

$$CH_3-CH_2-\overset{\displaystyle O}{\overset{\|}{C}}- \;+\; -N(CH_3)-CH_3 \;\longrightarrow\; CH_3-CH_2-\overset{\displaystyle O}{\overset{\|}{C}}-OH \;+\; H-N(CH_3)-CH_3$$

Propanoic acid Dimethylamine

Here is the overall reaction for this hydrolysis:

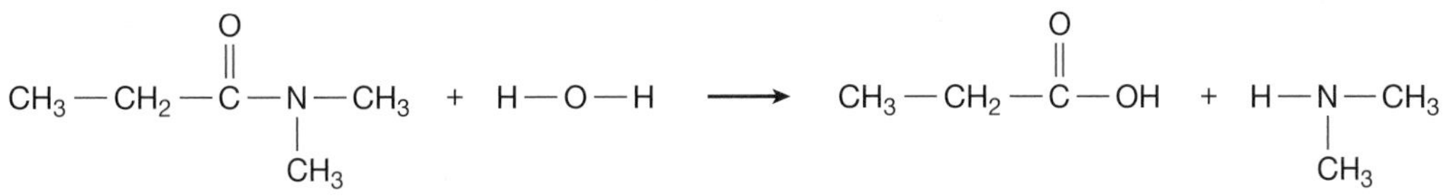

$$CH_3-CH_2-\overset{\overset{\large O}{\|}}{C}-\underset{\underset{\large CH_3}{|}}{N}-CH_3 + H-O-H \longrightarrow CH_3-CH_2-\overset{\overset{\large O}{\|}}{C}-OH + H-\underset{\underset{\large CH_3}{|}}{N}-CH_3$$

Sample Problem 12.11

Drawing the products of the hydrolysis of an amide

Draw the structures of the products that are formed when the following amide is hydrolyzed:

$$CH_3-CH_2-CH_2-\overset{\overset{\large O}{\|}}{C}-N\bigcirc$$

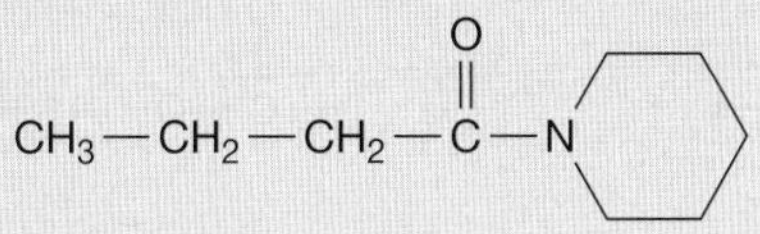

SOLUTION

We start by breaking the carbon–nitrogen bond that is next to the carbonyl group. (Don't break any other C–N bond.)

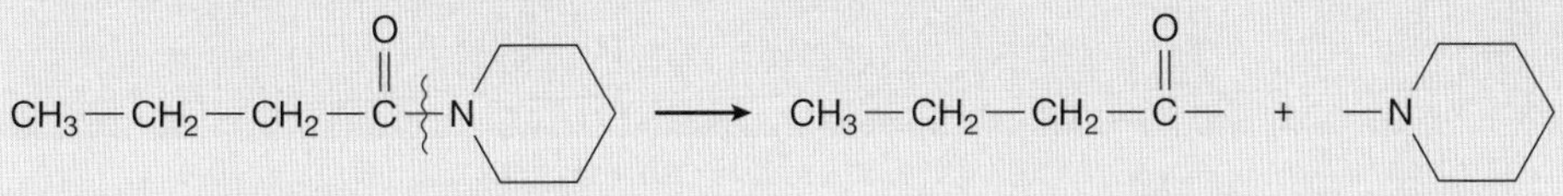

$$CH_3-CH_2-CH_2-\overset{\overset{\large O}{\|}}{C}\wr N\bigcirc \longrightarrow CH_3-CH_2-CH_2-\overset{\overset{\large O}{\|}}{C}- \quad + \quad -N\bigcirc$$

Then we add OH and H to the fragments to make our final products. OH must be bonded to carbon, never to nitrogen.

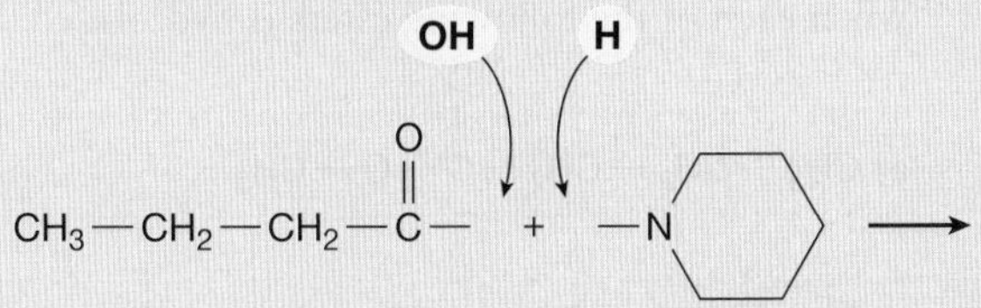

OH **H**

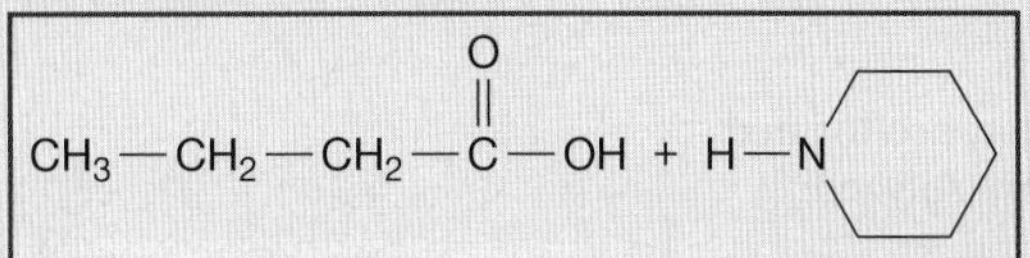

$$CH_3-CH_2-CH_2-\overset{\overset{\large O}{\|}}{C}- \quad + \quad -N\bigcirc \longrightarrow$$

$$CH_3-CH_2-CH_2-\overset{\overset{\large O}{\|}}{C}-OH + H-N\bigcirc$$

Butanoic acid **Piperidine**

The products of this reaction are butanoic acid and piperidine. (Since piperidine is a base, these two compounds will neutralize each other: we will look at the acid–base aspects of this reaction in Section 12.5.)

TRY IT YOURSELF: *Draw the structures of the products that are formed when the following amide is hydrolyzed:*

$$NH_2-\overset{\overset{\large O}{\|}}{C}-CH_2-CH_2-CH_2-CH_3$$

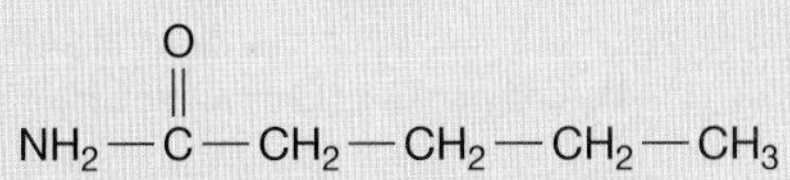

For additional practice, try Core Problems 12.25 and 12.26.

Hydrolysis reactions are very common in living organisms. Table 12.3 lists some other hydrolysis reactions that are important in biological chemistry. The last three reactions in Table 12.3 produce a sizable amount of energy and play key roles in harnessing the energy we obtain from food.

TABLE 12.3 Other Important Hydrolysis Reactions in Biochemistry

Functional Group	Hydrolysis Reaction
Phosphoester	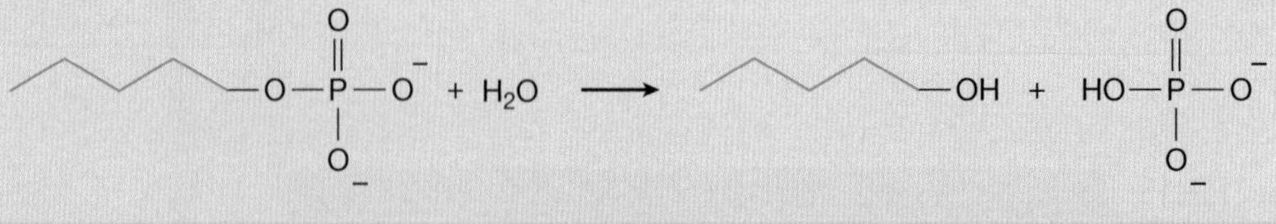 $R{-}O{-}PO_3^{2-} + H_2O \longrightarrow R{-}OH + HO{-}PO_3^{2-}$
Thioester	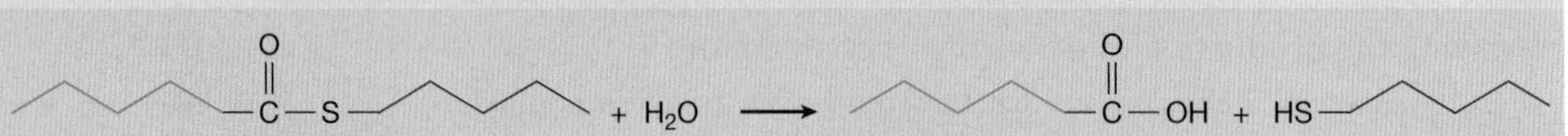 $R{-}C(=O){-}S{-}R' + H_2O \longrightarrow R{-}C(=O){-}OH + HS{-}R'$
Phosphoric anhydride	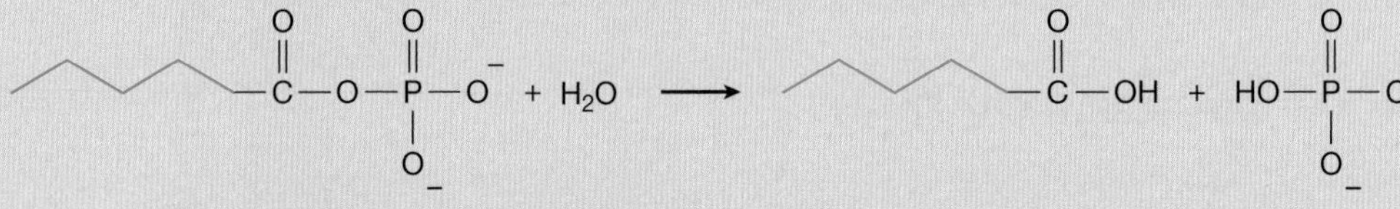 $R{-}C(=O){-}O{-}PO_3^{2-} + H_2O \longrightarrow R{-}C(=O){-}OH + HO{-}PO_3^{2-}$
Diphosphate	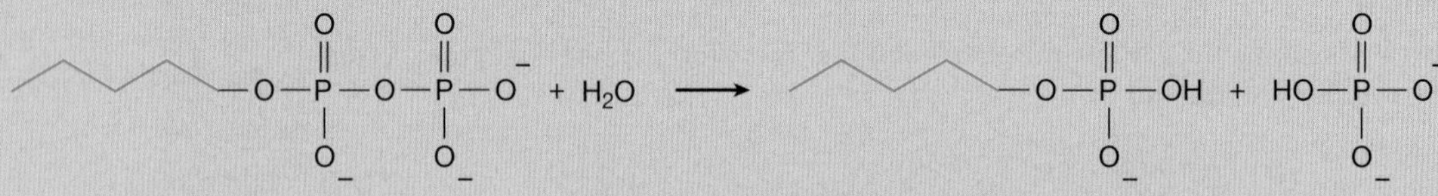 $R{-}O{-}PO_2^{-}{-}O{-}PO_3^{2-} + H_2O \longrightarrow R{-}O{-}PO_2^{-}{-}OH + HO{-}PO_3^{2-}$

CORE PROBLEMS

12.21 Draw the structures of the products that are formed when each of the following ethers is hydrolyzed:

a) 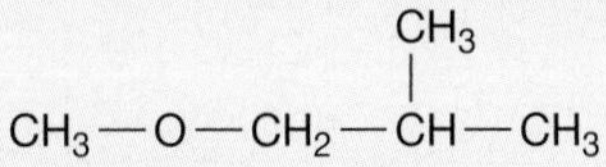 $CH_3{-}O{-}CH_2{-}CH(CH_3){-}CH_3$

b) 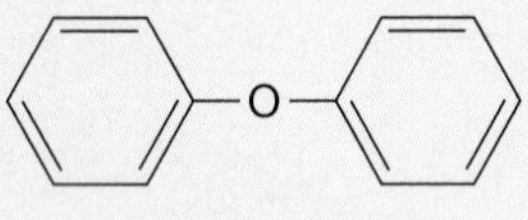 $C_6H_5{-}O{-}C_6H_5$

12.22 Draw the structures of the products that are formed when each of the following ethers is hydrolyzed:

a) 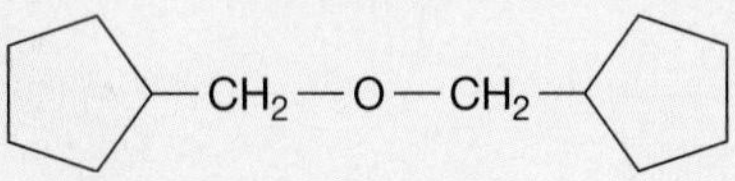 $C_5H_9{-}CH_2{-}O{-}CH_2{-}C_5H_9$ (cyclopentyl groups)

b) 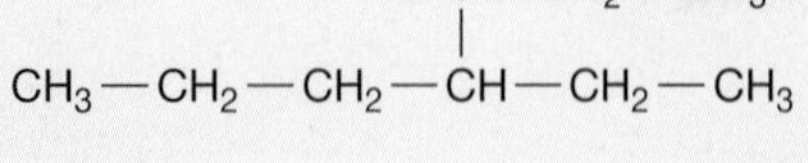 $CH_3{-}CH_2{-}CH_2{-}CH(O{-}CH_2{-}CH_3){-}CH_2{-}CH_3$

12.23 Draw the structures of the products that are formed when each of the following esters is hydrolyzed:

a) 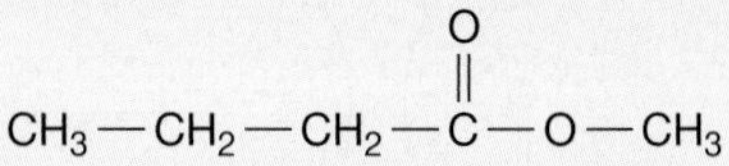 $CH_3{-}CH_2{-}CH_2{-}C(=O){-}O{-}CH_3$

b) $C_5H_9{-}O{-}C(=O){-}H$ (cyclopentyl)

c) $CH_3CH_2{-}C(=O){-}O{-}CH(CH_3)_2$

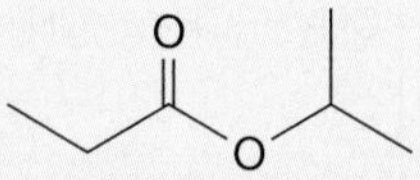

12.24 Draw the structures of the products that are formed when each of the following esters is hydrolyzed:

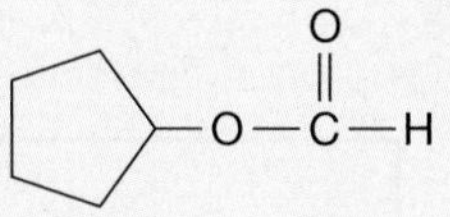

a) 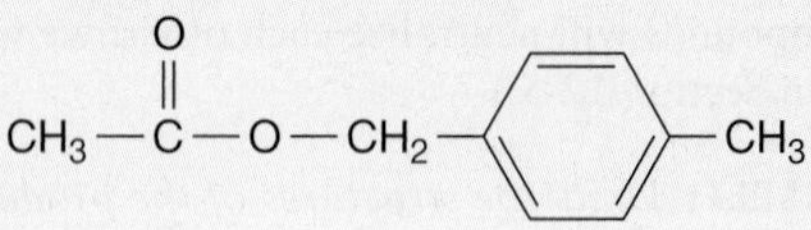 $CH_3{-}C(=O){-}O{-}CH_2{-}C_6H_4{-}CH_3$

b) $CH_3{-}C(CH_3)_2{-}O{-}C(=O){-}CH_2{-}CH_3$

c) $C_6H_{11}{-}C(=O){-}O{-}CH_2CH_2CH_2CH_3$ (cyclohexyl)

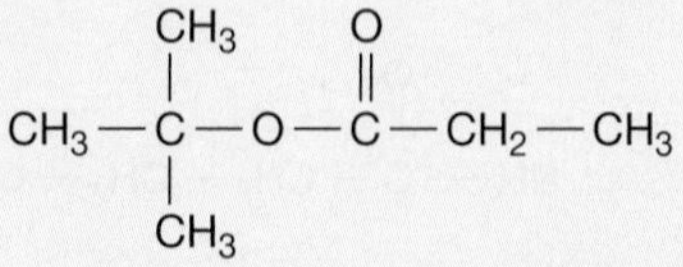

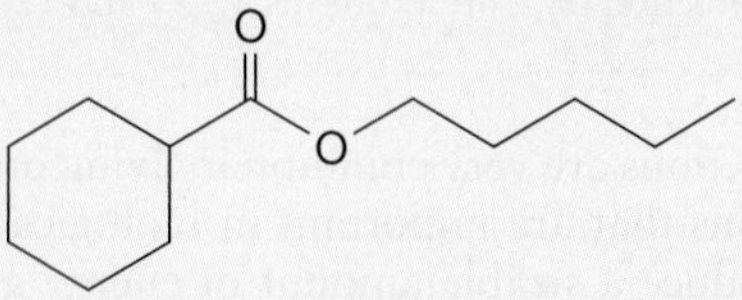

continued

12.25 Draw the structures of the products that are formed when each of the following amides is hydrolyzed:

a) 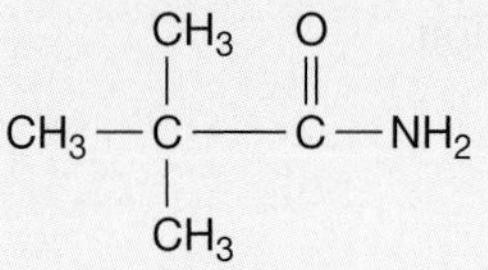 $CH_3-C(CH_3)_2-C(=O)-NH_2$

b) $CH_3-N(CH_3)-C(=O)-CH_2-CH_2-CH_2-CH_2-CH_3$

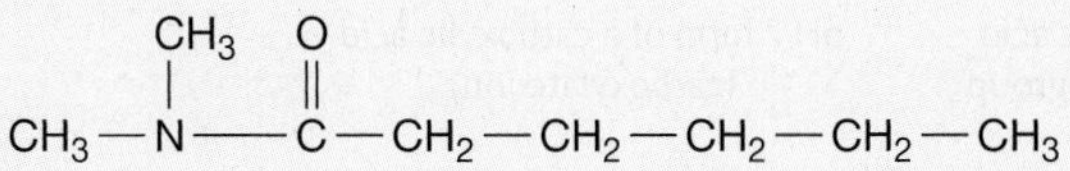

c) N, O

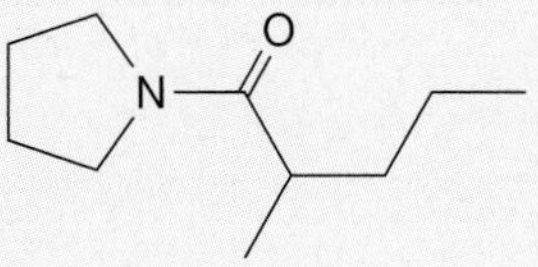

12.26 Draw the structures of the products that are formed when each of the following amides is hydrolyzed:

a) 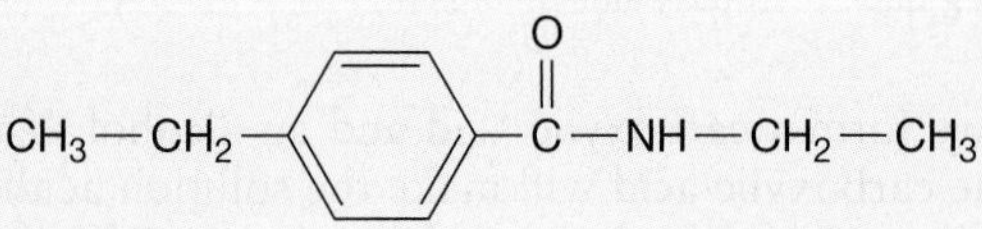 $CH_3-CH_2-C_6H_4-C(=O)-NH-CH_2-CH_3$

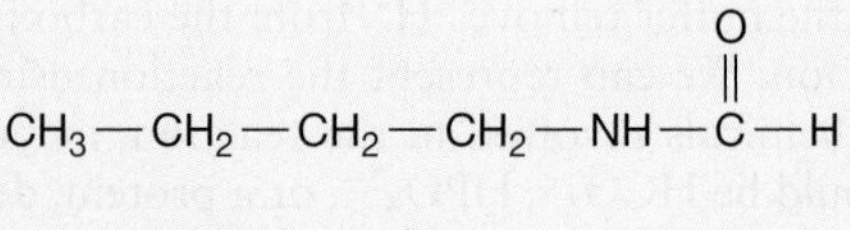

b) $CH_3-CH_2-CH_2-CH_2-NH-C(=O)-H$

c) O, NH

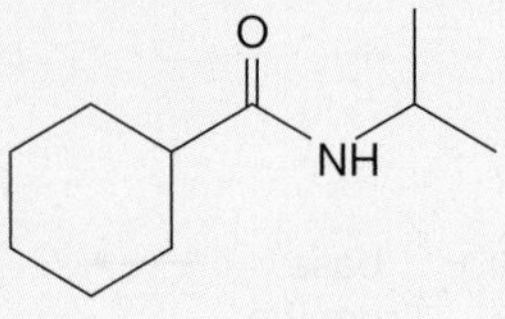

12.27 Draw the structures of the products that are formed when each of the following compounds is hydrolyzed:

a) 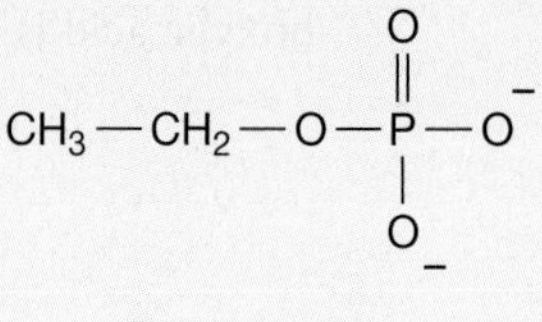 $CH_3-CH_2-O-P(=O)(O^-)-O^-$

b) 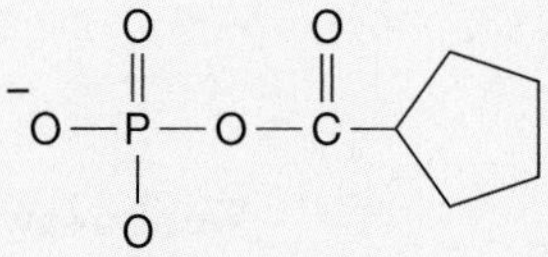 $^-O-P(=O)(O^-)-O-C(=O)-C_5H_9$

c) $CH_3-C(=O)-S-CH_2-CH_3$

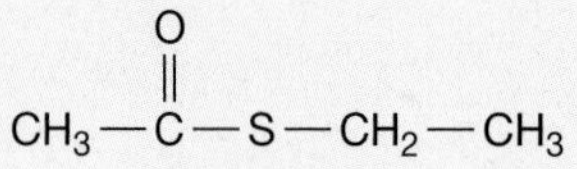

d) 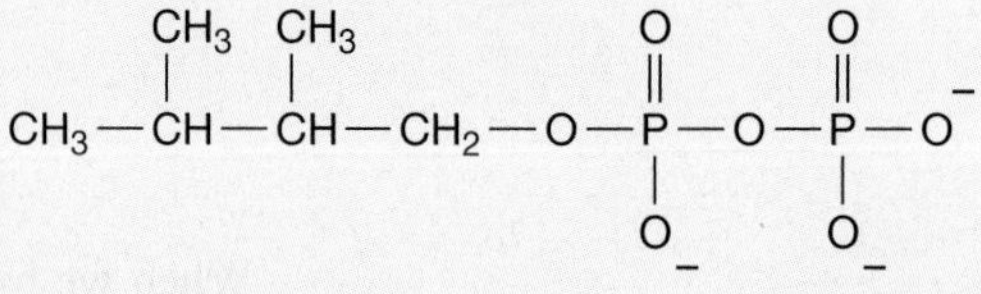 $CH_3-CH(CH_3)-CH(CH_3)-CH_2-O-P(=O)(O^-)-O-P(=O)(O^-)-O^-$

12.28 Draw the structures of the compounds that are formed when each of the following compounds is hydrolyzed:

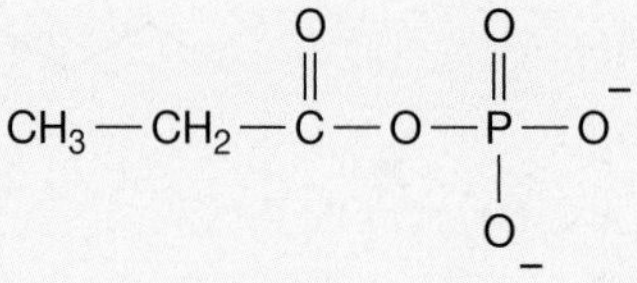

a) 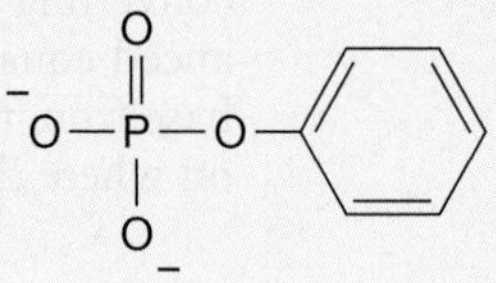 $^-O-P(=O)(O^-)-O-C_6H_5$

b) $CH_3-CH_2-C(=O)-O-P(=O)(O^-)-O^-$

c) $CH_3-CH(CH_3)-S-C(=O)-CH_2-CH_3$

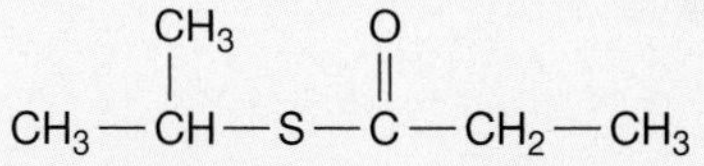

d) 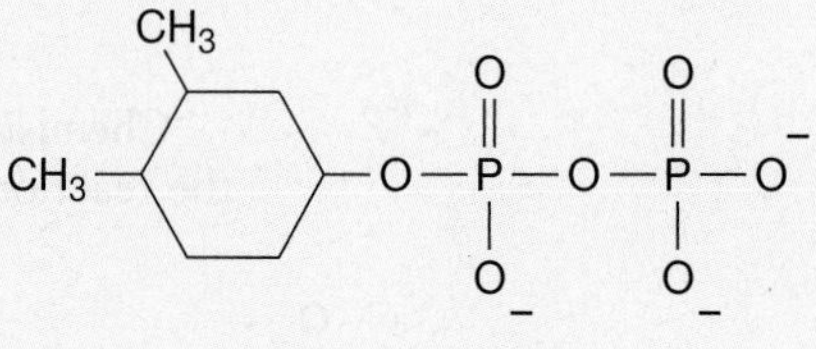 $CH_3-C_6H_{10}(CH_3)-O-P(=O)(O^-)-O-P(=O)(O^-)-O^-$

OBJECTIVES: *Understand the effect of physiological buffers on the structures of the products of a hydrolysis reaction, and predict the products of a saponification reaction.*

12.5 The Effect of pH on the Products of Hydrolysis

Most of the hydrolysis reactions we examined in Section 12.4 produce either an acid or an amine, and the hydrolysis of an amide forms both types of compounds. As we saw in Chapter 11, acids and amines lose or gain hydrogen ions at physiological pH. In this section, we will examine the effect of pH on the products of hydrolysis reactions.

Carboxylic Acids and Some Amines Are Ionized at Physiological pH

In Section 11.6, we saw that carboxylic acids lose H^+ when they are dissolved in a solution that is buffered around pH 7. As a result, under physiological conditions, any carboxylic acid is converted into its conjugate, a carboxylate ion.

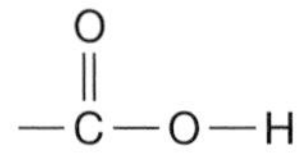

Carboxylic acid functional group

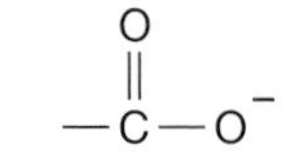

pH 7 form of a carboxylic acid (carboxylate ion)

We also saw that most amines gain H^+ around pH 7, so an amine is usually converted into its conjugate acid, an alkylammonium ion.

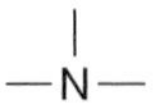

Amine functional group

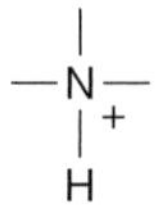

pH 7 form of an amine (alkylammonium ion)

When we hydrolyze an ester, we form a carboxylic acid and an alcohol. If we carry out this reaction in a test tube, the carboxylic acid will make the solution acidic. Under physiological conditions, though, the pH of the solution is kept close to 7 by the buffers in body fluids. The basic component of the buffer removes H^+ from the carboxylic acid, converting the acid into a carboxylate ion. We can represent the reaction using a balanced equation that shows all of the chemicals involved in the reaction, including the base from the buffer. The actual base could be HCO_3^-, HPO_4^{2-}, or a protein, depending on where the reaction takes place in our bodies.

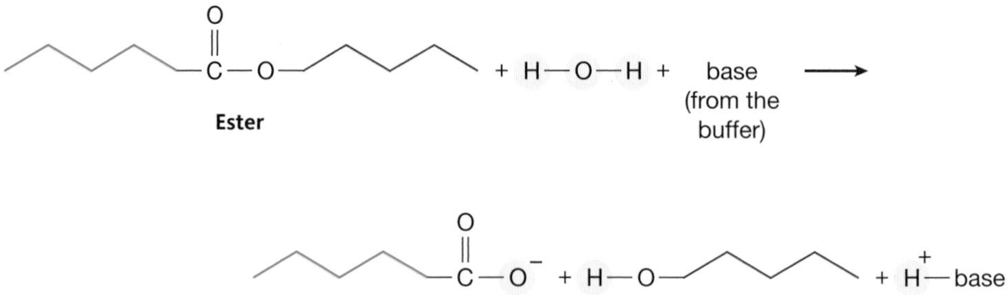

Ester + H—O—H + base (from the buffer) ⟶

Carboxylate ion + H—O— Alcohol + $\overset{+}{H}$—base

Chemists often write a simplified version that shows only the organic substances in the reaction.

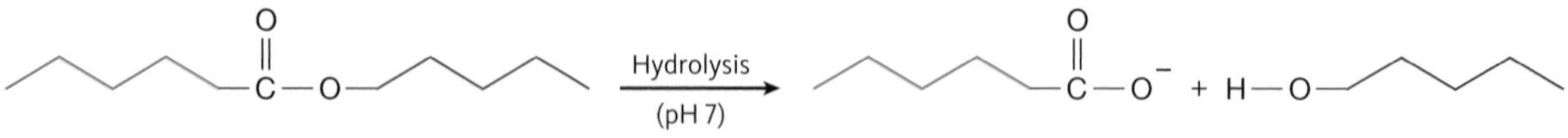

Ester —Hydrolysis (pH 7)→ Carboxylate ion + Alcohol

This version of the reaction is not a balanced equation, but it shows all of the organic reactants and products in their actual form under physiological conditions.

To draw the products of a hydrolysis at physiological pH, it is generally easiest to start by working out the products as we did in Section 12.4, drawing each product in its unionized form. Then, we remove H^+ from the carboxylic acid to form the carboxylate ion. We do not remove H^+ from the alcohol, because alcohols are not acidic and do not react with bases.

Sample Problem 12.12

Drawing the structures of an ester hydrolysis at pH 7

Draw the structures of the products that are formed when ethyl benzoate is hydrolyzed in a solution that is buffered at pH 7.

$$CH_3-CH_2-O-\overset{\overset{\displaystyle O}{\|}}{C}-C_6H_5$$

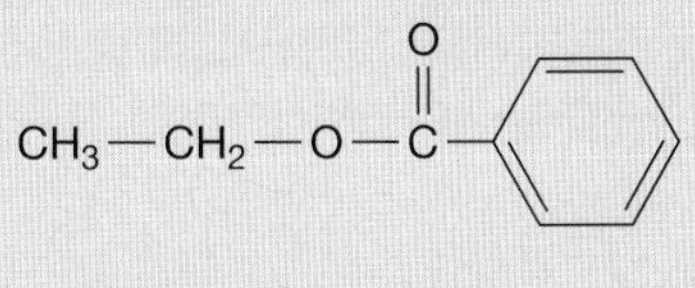

Ethyl benzoate

SOLUTION

In Sample Problem 12.10, we worked out the products of this hydrolysis, but we did not concern ourselves with the pH. The products were ethanol and benzoic acid:

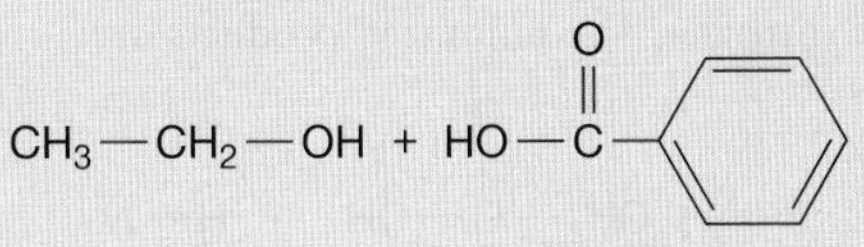

$$CH_3-CH_2-OH + HO-\overset{\overset{\displaystyle O}{\|}}{C}-C_6H_5$$

Ethanol **Benzoic acid**

Benzoic acid is a carboxylic acid, so it is converted into its conjugate base at pH 7. The actual products at this pH are ethanol and benzoate ion.

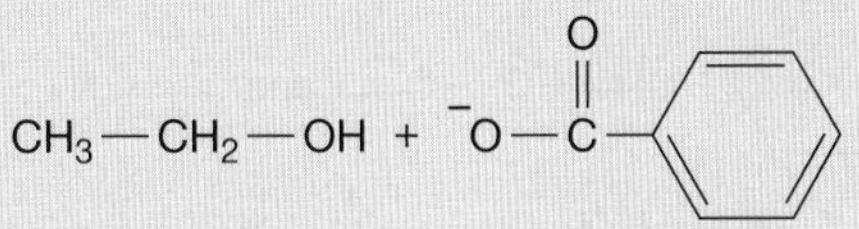

$$CH_3-CH_2-OH + {}^{-}O-\overset{\overset{\displaystyle O}{\|}}{C}-C_6H_5$$

Ethanol **Benzoate ion**

TRY IT YOURSELF: *Draw the structures of the products that are formed when the following ester is hydrolyzed in a solution that is buffered at pH 7:*

$$CH_3-\underset{\underset{\displaystyle CH_3}{|}}{\overset{\overset{\displaystyle CH_3}{|}}{C}}-CH_2-\overset{\overset{\displaystyle O}{\|}}{C}-O-CH_3$$

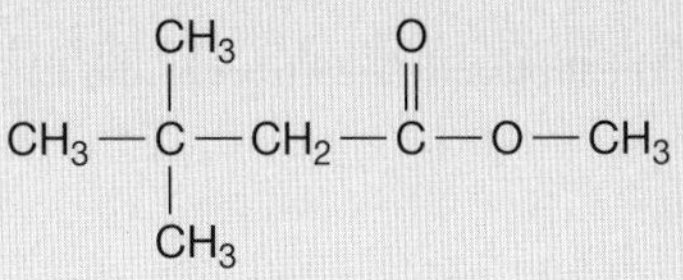

For additional practice, try Core Problems 12.29 (part a) and 12.30 (part a).

When we hydrolyze an amide, we form a carboxylic acid and an amine. Both of these functional groups are ionized at pH 7. Since the acid loses H^+ and the amine gains H^+, we do not need to include the buffer in the balanced equation.

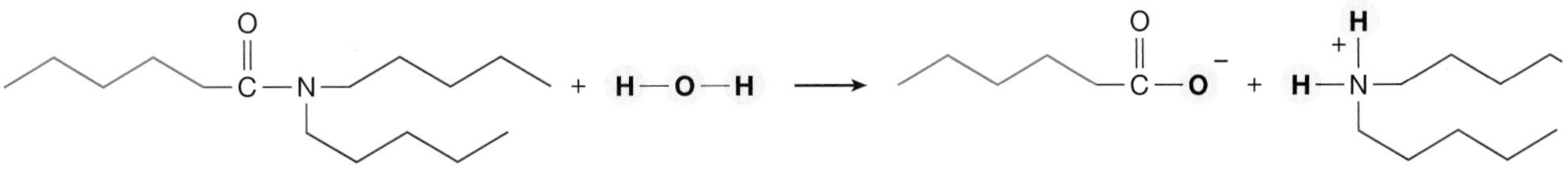

$$\text{Amide} + H-O-H \longrightarrow \text{Carboxylate ion} + \text{Ammonium ion}$$

Amide **Carboxylate ion** **Ammonium ion**

We can represent the hydrolysis of an amide by a simplified reaction that shows only the organic substances, just as we did for esters.

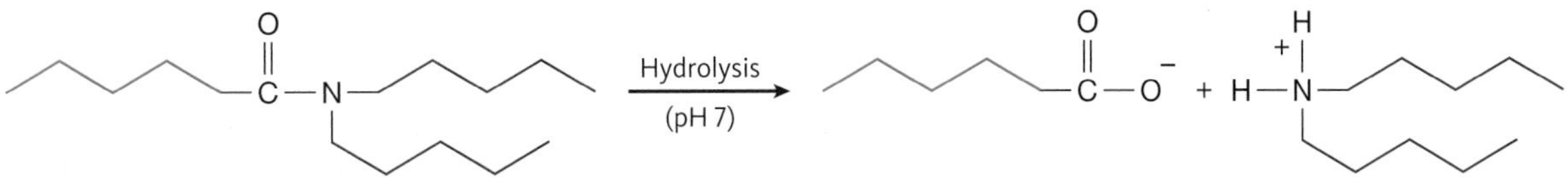

$$\text{Amide} \xrightarrow[\text{(pH 7)}]{\text{Hydrolysis}} \text{Carboxylate ion} + \text{Ammonium ion}$$

Health Note: Penicillin and cephalosporin antibiotics contain an amide group within a four-membered ring (called a *beta-lactam*). The antibiotic reacts with an enzyme that assembles the rigid cell wall in bacteria, preventing the bacterium from maintaining its cell wall and eventually leading to the death of the organism. Antibiotic-resistant bacteria make an enzyme called *beta-lactamase* that hydrolyzes the amide group, breaking the ring and making the antibiotic inactive.

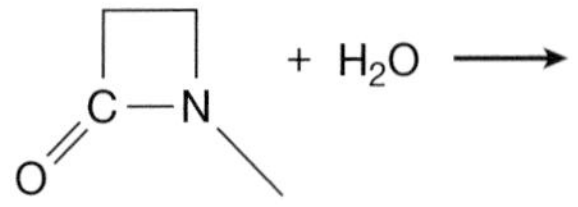

C—N + H_2O →

Beta-lactam group in active antibiotic

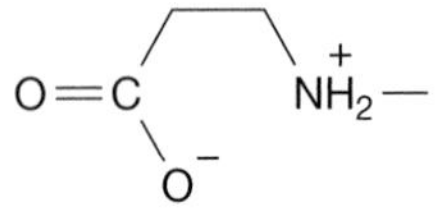

$O{=}C(O^-)$ ... $\overset{+}{N}H_2$—

Hydrolyzed amide group (no antibiotic activity)

Sample Problem 12.13

Drawing the products of an amide hydrolysis at pH 7

Draw the structures of the products that are formed when the following amide is hydrolyzed in a solution that is buffered at pH 7:

$$C_6H_5{-}CH_2{-}\overset{O}{\overset{\|}{C}}{-}N(\text{pyrrolidine ring})$$

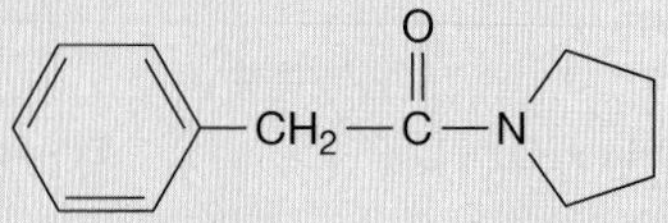

SOLUTION

We begin by working out the products of the hydrolysis without worrying about ionization. First, we break the bond between the carbonyl group and the nitrogen atom, and then we add H and OH to the fragments. Remember to add the OH group to the carbonyl carbon, not to the nitrogen. The unionized products are:

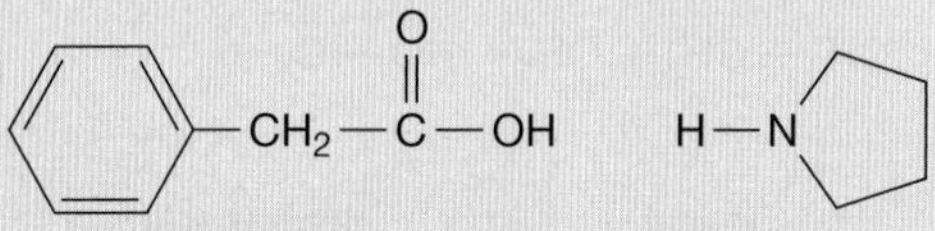

$$C_6H_5{-}CH_2{-}\overset{O}{\overset{\|}{C}}{-}OH \qquad H{-}N(\text{pyrrolidine ring})$$

Now we can account for the pH. At pH 7, the carboxylic acid group loses H^+ and the amine group gains H^+, so the final products of the reaction are

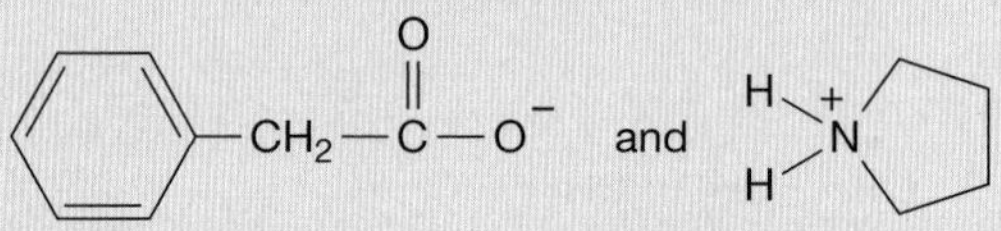

$$C_6H_5{-}CH_2{-}\overset{O}{\overset{\|}{C}}{-}O^- \quad \text{and} \quad H_2\overset{+}{N}(\text{pyrrolidine ring})$$

TRY IT YOURSELF: *Draw the structures of the products that are formed when the following amide is hydrolyzed in a solution that is buffered at pH 7:*

$$CH_3{-}CH_2{-}NH{-}\overset{O}{\overset{\|}{C}}{-}CH_3$$

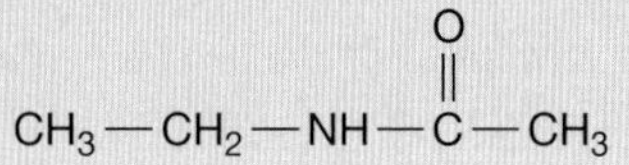

For additional practice, try Core Problems 12.29 (part b) and 12.30 (part b).

Esters Can Be Hydrolyzed Using Strong Bases

Most hydrolysis reactions are extremely slow, so our bodies use enzymes to speed them up. If we want to carry out a hydrolysis reaction in the laboratory, though, we normally use a strong acid or a strong base as a catalyst. A particularly important example is the hydrolysis of an ester using NaOH or KOH as a catalyst. These strong bases both speed up the hydrolysis reaction and remove H^+ from the carboxylic acid that is formed in the reaction. The products are an alcohol and a carboxylate salt. For example, here is the chemical equation for the hydrolysis of ethyl acetate using KOH:

In structural formulas of carboxylate salts, we draw the metal ion beside the carboxylate group.

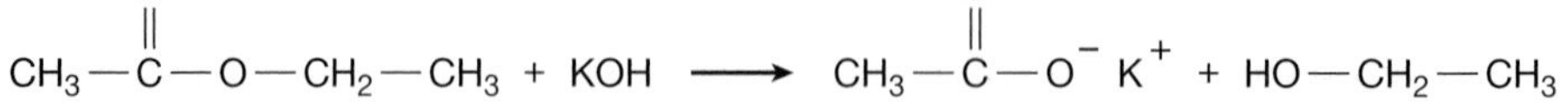

$$CH_3{-}\overset{O}{\overset{\|}{C}}{-}O{-}CH_2{-}CH_3 + KOH \longrightarrow CH_3{-}\overset{O}{\overset{\|}{C}}{-}O^-\ K^+ + HO{-}CH_2{-}CH_3$$

Ethyl acetate (an ester)	**Potassium hydroxide** (a strong base)	**Potassium acetate** (a carboxylate salt)	**Ethanol** (an alcohol)

If the carboxylic acid contains a long hydrocarbon chain, the hydrolysis produces a **soap**. Soaps are salts that contain a sodium or potassium ion and a long-chain carboxylate ion. For instance, the base-catalyzed hydrolysis of ethyl laurate produces ethanol and a soap called sodium laurate. The reaction of an ester with a strong base is often called a **saponification reaction** ("soap-forming" reaction).

$$CH_3-CH_2-CH_2-CH_2-CH_2-CH_2-CH_2-CH_2-CH_2-CH_2-CH_2-\overset{\displaystyle O}{\overset{\|}{C}}-O-CH_2-CH_3 \;+\; NaOH \longrightarrow$$

Ethyl laurate

$$CH_3-CH_2-CH_2-CH_2-CH_2-CH_2-CH_2-CH_2-CH_2-CH_2-CH_2-\overset{\displaystyle O}{\overset{\|}{C}}-O^- \; Na^+ \;+\; HO-CH_2-CH_3$$

Sodium laurate
(a soap)

Hand soap is generally made by hydrolyzing compounds called *triglycerides*, which include animal fats and vegetable oils, and it contains a mixture of compounds with chain lengths ranging from 12 to 18 carbon atoms. Bar soap contains primarily sodium salts, because potassium salts are very soft and do not solidify completely at room temperature.

• You will learn about triglycerides in Chapter 14.

Sample Problem 12.14

Drawing the products of a saponification reaction

Draw the structures of the organic products that are formed when the following ester is saponified using NaOH:

$$CH_3-O-\overset{\displaystyle O}{\overset{\|}{C}}-C_6H_4-CH_3$$

SOLUTION

As before, it is easiest to work out the unionized products and then remove H^+ from the carboxylic acid. To draw the unionized products, we break the bond between the carbonyl group and the neighboring oxygen atom and add H and OH to the resulting fragments.

$$CH_3-O \wr \overset{\displaystyle O}{\overset{\|}{C}}-C_6H_4-CH_3 + H_2O \longrightarrow CH_3-OH + HO-\overset{\displaystyle O}{\overset{\|}{C}}-C_6H_4-CH_3$$

Then we attend to the acid–base chemistry. The strong base NaOH reacts with the carboxylic acid, removing H^+ and converting the acid into a carboxylate salt.

$$HO-\overset{\displaystyle O}{\overset{\|}{C}}-C_6H_4-CH_3 + NaOH \longrightarrow Na^+ \; {}^-O-\overset{\displaystyle O}{\overset{\|}{C}}-C_6H_4-CH_3 + H_2O$$

Therefore, the organic products of this reaction are

$$CH_3-OH \quad \text{and} \quad Na^+ \; {}^-O-\overset{\displaystyle O}{\overset{\|}{C}}-C_6H_4-CH_3$$

TRY IT YOURSELF: *Draw the structures of the organic products that are formed when the following ester is saponified using KOH:*

$$CH_3-\overset{\displaystyle O}{\overset{\|}{C}}-O-C_6H_{10}-CH_3$$

For additional practice, try Core Problems 12.31 and 12.32.

Health Note: Antibacterial soaps usually contain triclosan, and this compound is also added to a range of personal care products such as toothpastes and deodorants. Triclosan kills many types of bacteria, but evidence is lacking that antibacterial soap is more effective than traditional soap at preventing transmission of disease. Triclosan does not break down during wastewater treatment, so it accumulates gradually in waterways and sediments.

Triclosan

iStockphoto.com/Gabor Izso

These soaps are made by reacting vegetable oils and animal fats with a strong base.

CORE PROBLEMS

12.29 Draw the structures of the organic products that are formed when the following compounds are hydrolyzed under physiological conditions:

a) 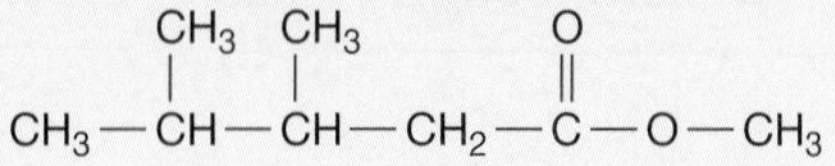 $CH_3-CH(CH_3)-CH(CH_3)-CH_2-C(=O)-O-CH_3$

b) 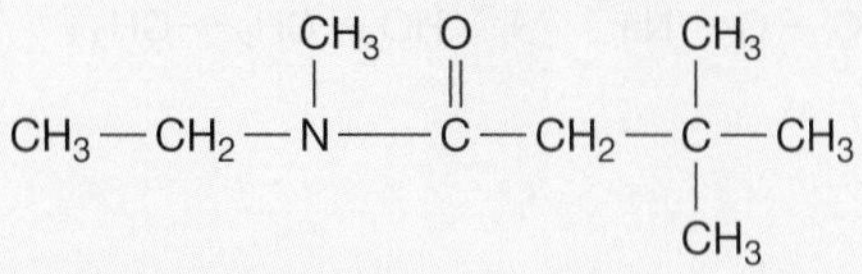 $CH_3-CH_2-N(CH_3)-C(=O)-CH_2-C(CH_3)_2-CH_3$

12.30 Draw the structures of the organic products that are formed when the following compounds are hydrolyzed under physiological conditions:

a) 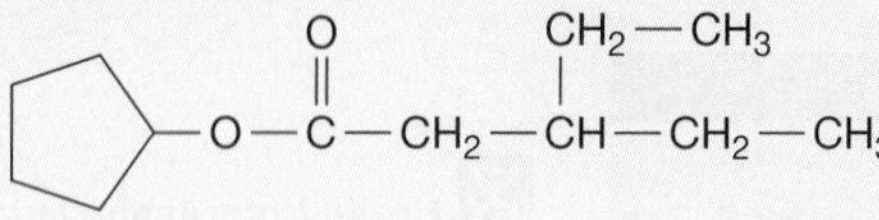 $\text{cyclopentyl}-O-C(=O)-CH_2-CH(CH_2-CH_3)-CH_2-CH_3$

b) 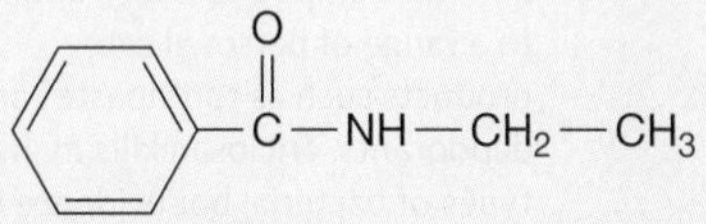 $C_6H_5-C(=O)-NH-CH_2-CH_3$

12.31 Draw the structures of the products that are formed when the following esters are saponified using NaOH:

a) 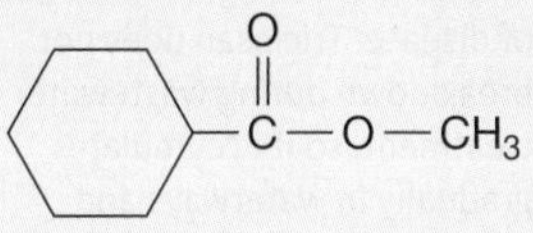 $\text{cyclohexyl}-C(=O)-O-CH_3$

b) 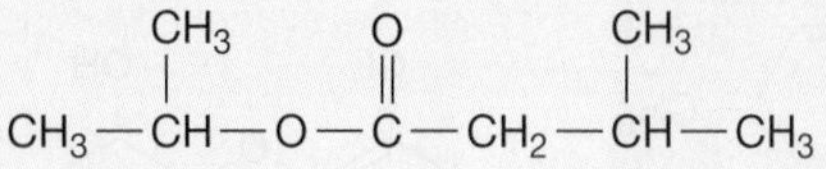 $CH_3-CH(CH_3)-O-C(=O)-CH_2-CH(CH_3)-CH_3$

12.32 Draw the structures of the products that are formed when the following esters are saponified using KOH:

a) 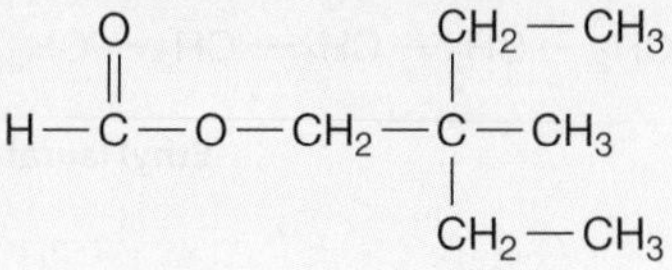 $H-C(=O)-O-CH_2-C(CH_2-CH_3)_2-CH_3$

b) 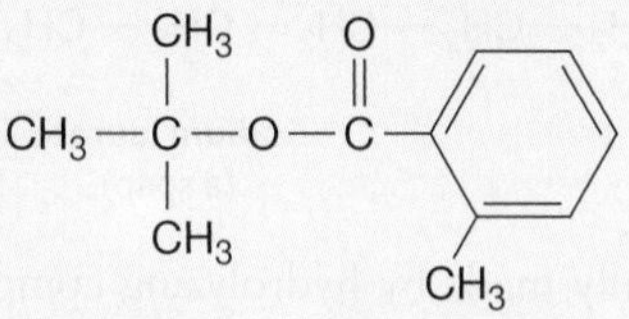 $CH_3-C(CH_3)_2-O-C(=O)-\text{(3-methylphenyl)}$

12.33 The structure of oleic acid (a typical fatty acid) is shown here. Draw the structure of the corresponding soap, using potassium as the positive ion.

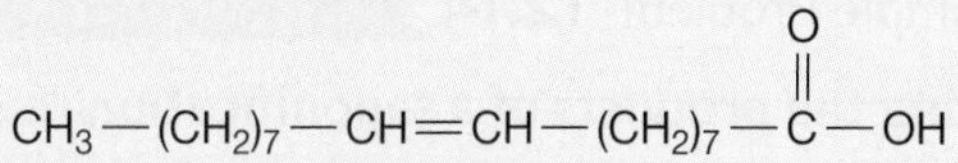

$$CH_3-(CH_2)_7-CH=CH-(CH_2)_7-C(=O)-OH$$

12.34 The structure of stearic acid (a typical fatty acid) is shown here. Draw the structure of the corresponding soap, using sodium as the positive ion.

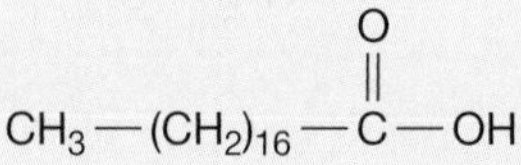

$$CH_3-(CH_2)_{16}-C(=O)-OH$$

CONNECTIONS

Common Pain Relievers

Since prehistoric times, people have searched for substances that could relieve pain. One such substance, which has been known for more than two millennia, is the inner bark of willow trees. In the early 1800s, chemists discovered that the active chemical in willow bark is salicylic acid. Salicylic acid relieves pain and reduces fever, but it is highly irritating to the stomach and can be toxic even in moderate doses. Around 1900, researchers at Bayer Corporation discovered that an ester made from salicylic acid was an equally effective pain remedy but was much less irritating to the stomach. This ester, called acetylsalicylic acid (see page 492), was given the name *aspirin* and rapidly became one of the most widely used medications in the world.

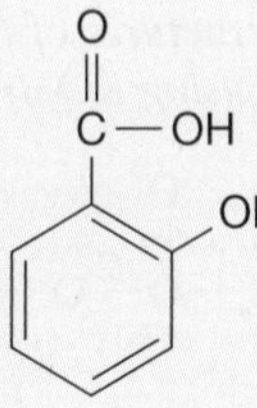

$$C_6H_4(OH)-C(=O)-OH$$

Salicylic acid

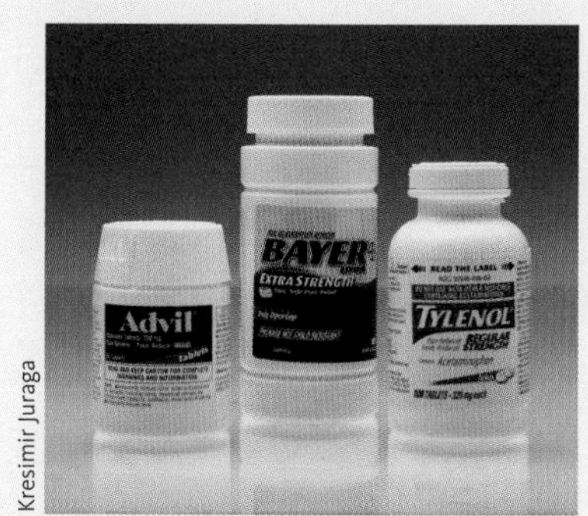

Some common pain relievers.

Aspirin is remarkably effective at relieving pain, reducing inflammation, and lowering body temperature in fever. It also reduces the ability of the blood to clot, lowering the risk of heart attack in patients with coronary artery disease. However, aspirin can produce or worsen stomach bleeding, and it has been linked to a rare but serious illness called Reye's syndrome in children and adolescents. As a result, in the second half of the twentieth century aspirin's status as the main over-the-counter pain remedy was challenged by two newer compounds, acetaminophen (the active ingredient in Tylenol) and ibuprofen (the active ingredient in Advil and Motrin).

Acetaminophen

Ibuprofen

Both of these compounds are less irritating to the stomach than aspirin, and neither causes Reye's syndrome. However, acetaminophen has no effect on inflammation, and it is very toxic to the liver if an overdose is taken. Ibuprofen is similar to aspirin in its effects while being milder on the stomach, but it (like all medications) can have unpleasant side effects in certain people.

Aspirin and ibuprofen are members of a class called *nonsteroidal anti-inflammatory drugs*, or NSAIDs. Their action as pain relievers is due to their ability to inhibit the body's production of *prostaglandins*. Acetaminophen is not an anti-inflammatory, but it too inhibits prostaglandin formation. Prostaglandins, so named because they were initially thought to be made by the prostate gland, are a class of molecules that are made from arachidonic acid (a 20-carbon fatty acid) and that have a wide range of effects, including transmission of the pain sensation, raising the body temperature in response to infection, and dilation of blood vessels in damaged tissues. NSAIDs block the action of enzymes called *cyclooxygenases* (COX) in the pathway that converts arachidonic acid into prostaglandins.

Prostaglandin E_2

There are two main classes of cyclooxygenases in the body, called COX-1 and COX-2. COX-2 is the enzyme responsible for producing prostaglandins that cause inflammation and the associated pain, but the traditional NSAIDs block both COX types. In 1999, new NSAIDs that only block COX-2, called *COX-2 inhibitors*, became available. These drugs, including Vioxx and Celebrex, eliminated most of the unpleasant side effects of the older medications and rapidly became established as treatment for arthritis and other chronic inflammations. However, evidence began to accumulate that COX-2 inhibitors increase the risk of heart attacks, and this led to Merck & Co. withdrawing Vioxx from the market in 2004. Celebrex is still available, but it has strict guidelines for its use.

Vioxx
(rofecoxib)

Key Terms

amidation reaction – 12.2
amide – 12.2
condensation reaction – 12.1
copolymer – 12.3
ester – 12.2
esterification reaction – 12.2
ether – 12.1
hydrolysis reaction – 12.4
phosphoester – 12.2
phosphorylation reaction – 12.2
polymer – 12.3
saponification reaction – 12.5
soap – 12.5

Classes of Organic Compounds

Class	Functional group	Example
Ether	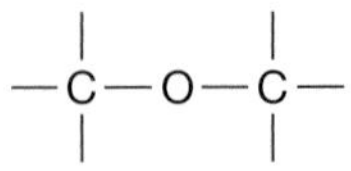 $-\overset{\vert}{\underset{\vert}{C}}-O-\overset{\vert}{\underset{\vert}{C}}-$	$CH_3-CH_2-O-CH_2-CH_3$ *diethyl ether* (trivial name)
Ester	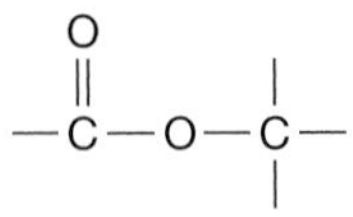 $-\overset{O}{\overset{\Vert}{C}}-O-\overset{\vert}{\underset{\vert}{C}}-$	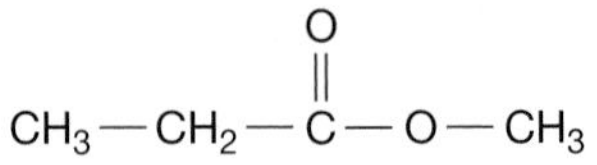 $CH_3-CH_2-\overset{O}{\overset{\Vert}{C}}-O-CH_3$ *methyl propanoate**
Amide	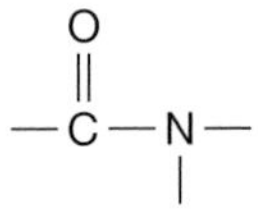 $-\overset{O}{\overset{\Vert}{C}}-\underset{\vert}{N}-$	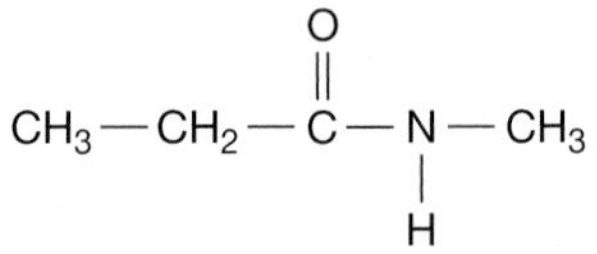 $CH_3-CH_2-\overset{O}{\overset{\Vert}{C}}-\underset{\underset{H}{\vert}}{N}-CH_3$ *N-methylpropanamide**
Phosphoester	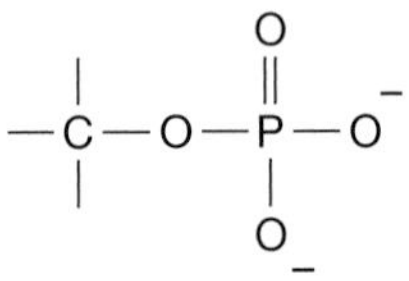 $-\overset{\vert}{\underset{\vert}{C}}-O-\overset{O}{\overset{\Vert}{\underset{\underset{O^-}{\vert}}{P}}}-O^-$	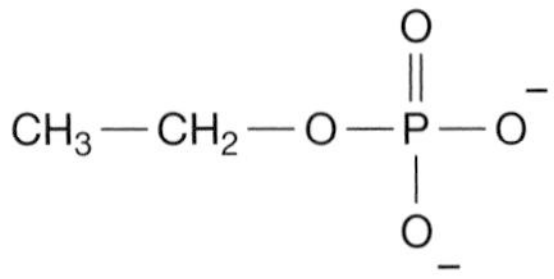 $CH_3-CH_2-O-\overset{O}{\overset{\Vert}{\underset{\underset{O^-}{\vert}}{P}}}-O^-$ *ethyl phosphate**
Phosphodiester	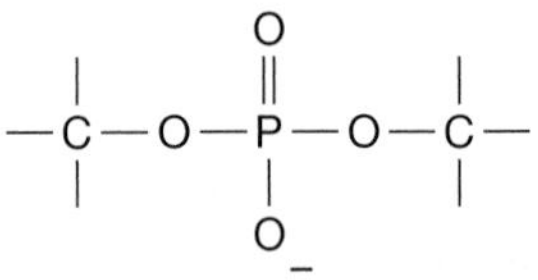 $-\overset{\vert}{\underset{\vert}{C}}-O-\overset{O}{\overset{\Vert}{\underset{\underset{O^-}{\vert}}{P}}}-O-\overset{\vert}{\underset{\vert}{C}}-$	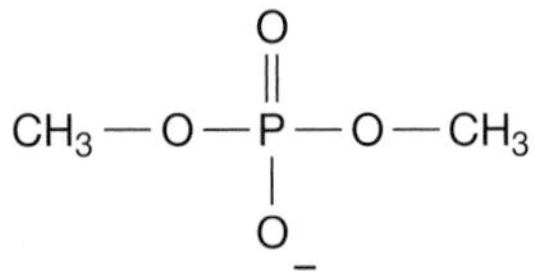 $CH_3-O-\overset{O}{\overset{\Vert}{\underset{\underset{O^-}{\vert}}{P}}}-O-CH_3$ *dimethyl phosphate**

*Names of esters, amides, and organic phosphates are not covered in this text.

Summary of Organic Reactions

1) condensation reactions

a) ether formation

$$\text{2 alcohols} \longrightarrow \text{ether} + H_2O$$

$$CH_3-CH_2-OH + HO-CH_3 \longrightarrow CH_3-CH_2-O-CH_3 + H_2O$$

Ethanol **Methanol** **Ethyl methyl ether**

b) esterification

carboxylic acid + alcohol ⟶ *ester + H_2O*

$$CH_3-CH_2-CH_2-\overset{\overset{\displaystyle O}{\|}}{C}-OH + HO-CH_3 \longrightarrow CH_3-CH_2-CH_2-\overset{\overset{\displaystyle O}{\|}}{C}-O-CH_3 + H_2O$$

Butanoic acid **Methanol** **Methyl butanoate**

c) amidation

carboxylic acid + amine ⟶ *amide + H_2O*

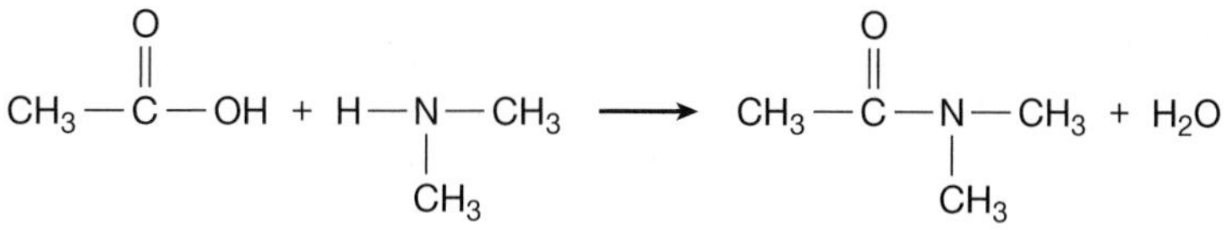

$$CH_3-\overset{\overset{\displaystyle O}{\|}}{C}-OH + H-\underset{\underset{\displaystyle CH_3}{|}}{N}-CH_3 \longrightarrow CH_3-\overset{\overset{\displaystyle O}{\|}}{C}-\underset{\underset{\displaystyle CH_3}{|}}{N}-CH_3 + H_2O$$

Acetic acid **Dimethylamine** **N,N-Dimethylacetamide**

d) phosphorylation

alcohol + phosphate ⟶ *phosphoester + H_2O*

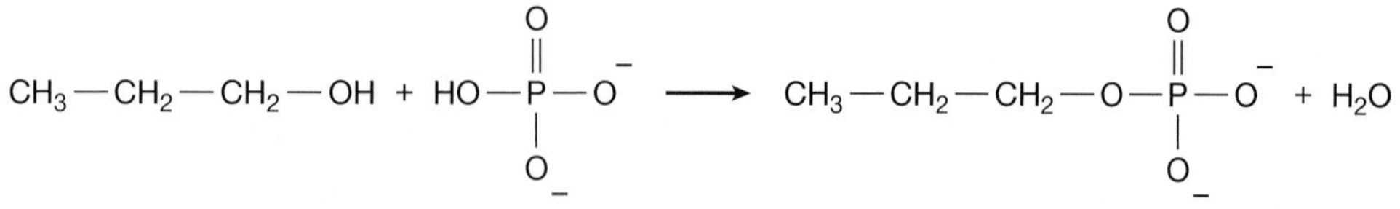

$$CH_3-CH_2-CH_2-OH + HO-\overset{\overset{\displaystyle O}{\|}}{\underset{\underset{\displaystyle O^-}{|}}{P}}-O^- \longrightarrow CH_3-CH_2-CH_2-O-\overset{\overset{\displaystyle O}{\|}}{\underset{\underset{\displaystyle O^-}{|}}{P}}-O^- + H_2O$$

1-Propanol **Propyl phosphate**

2) **hydrolysis reactions**

a) ether hydrolysis

ether + H_2O ⟶ *2 alcohols*

$$CH_3-CH_2-O-CH_3 + H_2O \longrightarrow CH_3-CH_2-OH + HO-CH_3$$

Ethyl methyl ether **Ethanol** **Methanol**

b) ester hydrolysis

ester + H_2O ⟶ *carboxylic acid* + *alcohol*

ester $\xrightarrow[\text{Physiological pH}]{\text{Hydrolysis}}$ *carboxylate ion* + *alcohol*

$$CH_3-CH_2-CH_2-\overset{\overset{\displaystyle O}{\|}}{C}-O-CH_3 + H_2O \longrightarrow CH_3-CH_2-CH_2-\overset{\overset{\displaystyle O}{\|}}{C}-OH + HO-CH_3$$

Methyl butanoate **Butanoic acid** **Methanol**

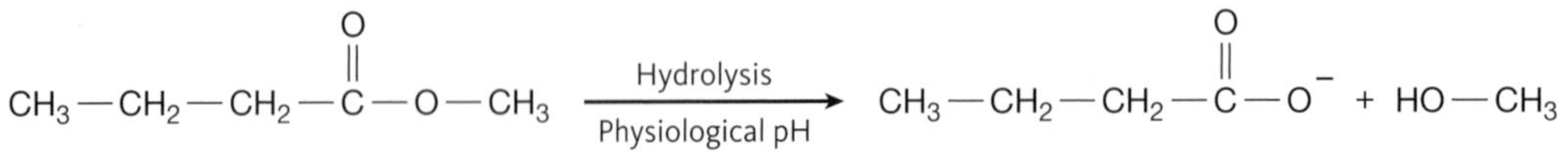

$$CH_3-CH_2-CH_2-\overset{\overset{\displaystyle O}{\|}}{C}-O-CH_3 \xrightarrow[\text{Physiological pH}]{\text{Hydrolysis}} CH_3-CH_2-CH_2-\overset{\overset{\displaystyle O}{\|}}{C}-O^- + HO-CH_3$$

Butanoate ion **Methanol**

c) amide hydrolysis

amide + H_2O ⟶ *carboxylic acid* + *amine*

amide $\xrightarrow[\text{Physiological pH}]{\text{Hydrolysis}}$ *carboxylate ion* + *alkylammonium ion*

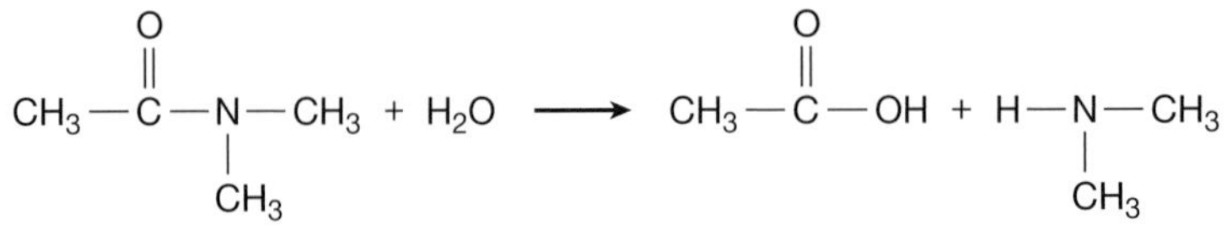

$$CH_3-\overset{\overset{\displaystyle O}{\|}}{C}-\underset{\underset{\displaystyle CH_3}{|}}{N}-CH_3 + H_2O \longrightarrow CH_3-\overset{\overset{\displaystyle O}{\|}}{C}-OH + H-\underset{\underset{\displaystyle CH_3}{|}}{N}-CH_3$$

N,N-dimethylacetamide **Acetic acid** **Dimethylamine**

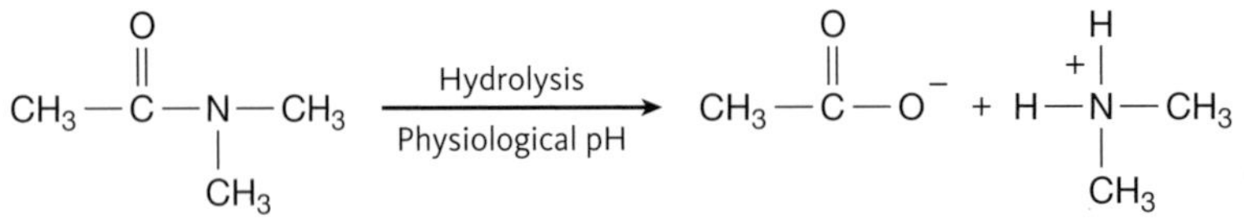

$$CH_3-\overset{\overset{\displaystyle O}{\|}}{C}-\underset{\underset{\displaystyle CH_3}{|}}{N}-CH_3 \xrightarrow[\text{Physiological pH}]{\text{Hydrolysis}} CH_3-\overset{\overset{\displaystyle O}{\|}}{C}-O^- + H-\overset{\overset{\displaystyle H}{+|}}{\underset{\underset{\displaystyle CH_3}{|}}{N}}-CH_3$$

Acetate ion **Dimethylammonium ion**

d) phosphoester hydrolysis

phosphoester + H_2O ⟶ *alcohol* + *phosphate*

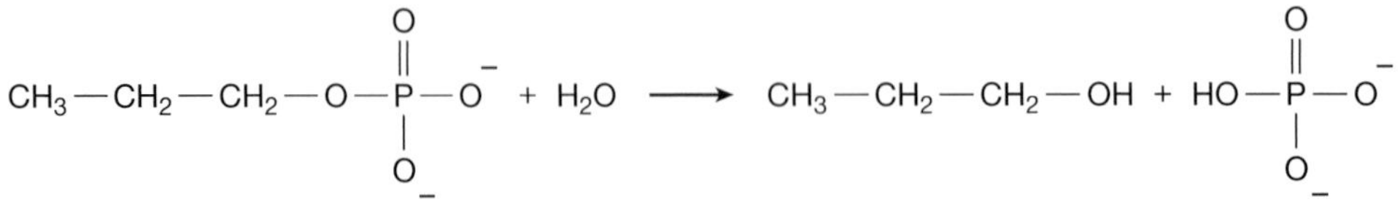

$$CH_3-CH_2-CH_2-O-\overset{\overset{\displaystyle O}{\|}}{\underset{\underset{\displaystyle O^-}{|}}{P}}-O^- + H_2O \longrightarrow CH_3-CH_2-CH_2-OH + HO-\overset{\overset{\displaystyle O}{\|}}{\underset{\underset{\displaystyle O^-}{|}}{P}}-O^-$$

Propyl phosphate **1-Propanol**

SUMMARY OF OBJECTIVES

Now that you have read the chapter, test yourself on your knowledge of the objectives, using this summary as a guide.

Section 12.1: Predict the products of the condensation of two alcohols, and name simple ethers.

- In a condensation reaction, H and OH are removed from two organic molecules, and the remaining fragments become linked together. The hydrogen and hydroxyl groups combine to make water.
- In any condensation, the hydrogen must be removed from oxygen or nitrogen, never from carbon.
- Alcohols can condense to form an ether.
- Simple ethers are named by listing the alkyl groups followed by the word *ether*.

Section 12.2: Predict the products of condensation reactions that form esters, amides, and phosphoesters.

- Alcohols can condense with carboxylic acids to form esters.
- Amines can condense with carboxylic acids to form amides, which are neither acidic nor basic.
- Amines also undergo acid–base reactions with carboxylic acids, and this reaction is faster than amidation. Amidation requires a catalyst or a high temperature.
- Alcohols can condense with phosphate ion to form phosphoesters.

Section 12.3: Predict the structures of polymers that are formed by condensation reactions.

- Compounds that contain two alcohol groups can condense to form a large molecule, called a polymer.
- Polymers contain repeating groups of atoms.
- Amino acids can condense to form a polymer called a protein.
- Molecules that contain an alcohol group and a carboxylic acid group can condense to form a polyester.
- Copolymers are made from alternating molecules of two different compounds.
- Many synthetic fabrics and plastics are polymers and are made using condensation reactions.

Section 12.4: Predict the products of hydrolysis reactions of ethers, esters, amides, and phosphoesters.

- Any condensation reaction can be reversed. This reverse reaction is called a hydrolysis.
- In any hydrolysis, the hydroxyl group always bonds to carbon. Oxygen–oxygen and oxygen–nitrogen bonds do not form in hydrolysis reactions.
- The hydrolysis of an ether produces two alcohols.
- The hydrolysis of an ester produces an alcohol and a carboxylic acid.
- The hydrolysis of an amide produces an amine and a carboxylic acid.
- A number of other functional groups can be hydrolyzed, including organic phosphates, thioesters, and diphosphates.

Section 12.5: Understand the effect of physiological buffers on the structures of the products of a hydrolysis reaction, and predict the products of a saponification reaction.

- Hydrolysis of an ester or an amide at pH 7 produces the ionized forms of carboxylic acids and amines.
- Esters can be hydrolyzed using NaOH or KOH to form an alcohol and a carboxylate salt (the saponification reaction).
- Soaps are sodium or potassium salts of long-chain carboxylic acids.

Concept Questions

■ **Online homework for this chapter may be assigned in OWL.**

* indicates more challenging problems.

12.35 Both the dehydration reaction and the condensation reaction remove water from organic molecules. How do these two reactions differ from each other?

12.36 Both the hydration reaction and the hydrolysis reaction add water to an organic molecule. How do these two reactions differ from each other?

12.37 What functional group is formed when the following compounds condense?

a) two alcohols
b) an alcohol and a carboxylic acid
c) a carboxylic acid and an amine

12.38 What types of organic compounds are formed when the following are hydrolyzed?

a) an ester
b) an amide
c) an ether
d) a thioester

12.39 One of the reactants in any hydrolysis reaction is an inorganic compound. What is this compound, and what happens to it during the reaction?

12.40 Methanol can undergo a condensation reaction, but it cannot undergo a dehydration reaction. Why is this?

12.41 When an ester is hydrolyzed, the pH of the solution changes. Does the pH go up, or does it go down? Explain your answer.

12.42 What type of organic compound can condense with phosphate ion to form a phosphoester?

12.43 Explain why trimethylamine cannot condense with carboxylic acids.

12.44 The products that are formed when esters and amides are hydrolyzed at physiological pH are different from the products that are formed when the reactions are not buffered. How do they differ, and why?

12.45 What is a saponification reaction?

12.46 What is a soap?

Summary and Challenge Problems

12.47 Using structures, write chemical equations for the following reactions:

a) the dehydration of 2-propanol
b) the condensation of two molecules of 2-propanol

12.48 Draw the structures of the products of the following condensation reactions:

a) 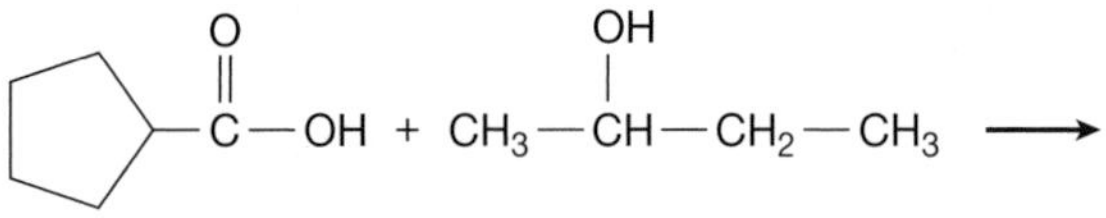 $\text{C}_5\text{H}_9\text{—C(=O)—OH} + \text{CH}_3\text{—CH(OH)—CH}_2\text{—CH}_3 \longrightarrow$ (cyclopentyl ring)

b) $\text{CH}_3\text{—CH}_2\text{—CH}_2\text{—C(=O)—OH} + \text{NH}_3 \longrightarrow$

c) $\text{CH}_3\text{—CH}_2\text{—CH(OH)—CH}_3 + \text{CH}_3\text{—CH(OH)—CH(CH}_3\text{)—CH}_3 \longrightarrow$

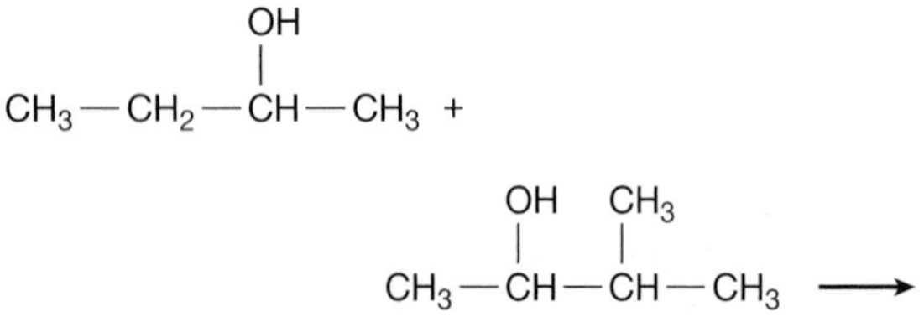

d) 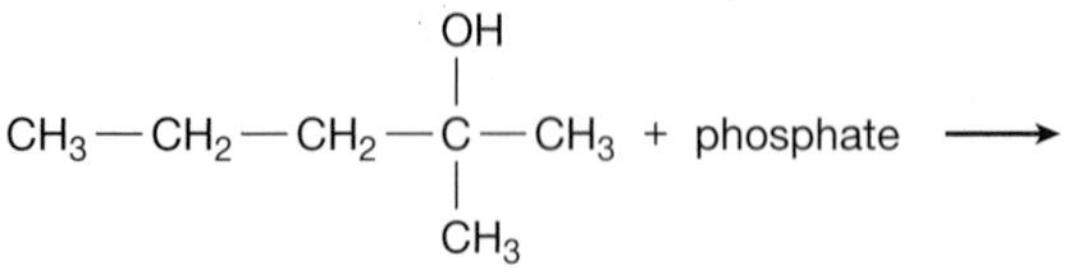 $\text{CH}_3\text{—CH}_2\text{—CH}_2\text{—C(OH)(CH}_3\text{)—CH}_3 + \text{phosphate} \longrightarrow$

e) 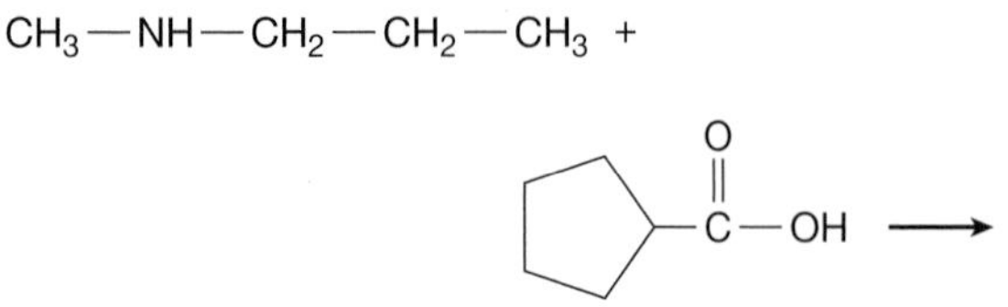 $\text{CH}_3\text{—NH—CH}_2\text{—CH}_2\text{—CH}_3 + \text{C}_5\text{H}_9\text{—C(=O)—OH} \longrightarrow$ (cyclopentyl ring)

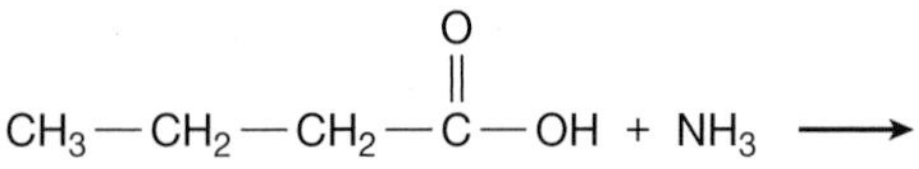

f) 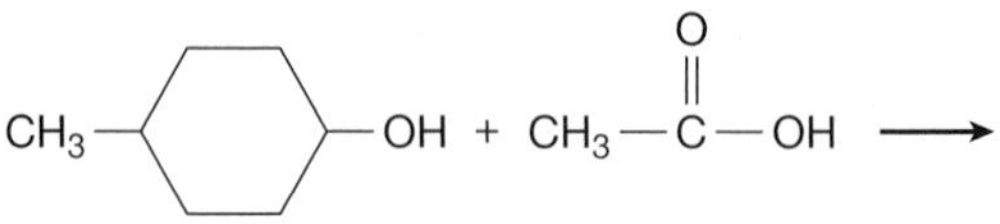 $\text{CH}_3\text{—C}_6\text{H}_{10}\text{—OH} + \text{CH}_3\text{—C(=O)—OH} \longrightarrow$ (cyclohexane ring)

g) hexanoic acid + 2-propanol →
h) butanoic acid + ethylpropylamine →
i) ethanol + 3-pentanol →
j) 3-pentanol + phosphate →

12.49 Malonic acid contains two carboxylic acid groups, so it can condense with two molecules of 1-propanol. Draw the structure of the organic product that will be formed in this reaction.

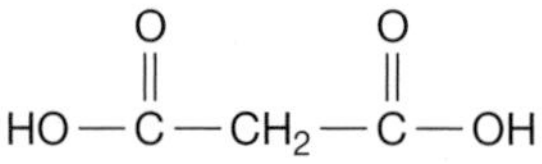

$\text{HO—C(=O)—CH}_2\text{—C(=O)—OH}$ **Malonic acid**

12.50 Malonic acid can condense with two molecules of methylamine. Draw the structure of the organic product of this reaction. (The structure of malonic acid is given in Problem 12.49.)

12.51 *a) Aspirin can be made by condensing salicylic acid with acetic acid to form an ester. Using this information, draw the structure of aspirin.

*b) Oil of wintergreen can be made by condensing salicylic acid with methanol to form an ester. Using this information, draw the structure of oil of wintergreen.

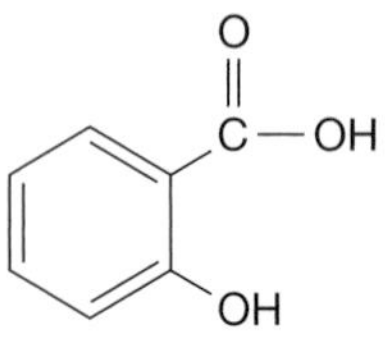

$\text{C}_6\text{H}_4\text{(OH)—C(=O)—OH}$ (benzene ring with ortho OH) **Salicylic acid**

12.52 *A fat is a compound made from glycerol and three long-chain carboxylic acids. These four molecules are linked together by condensation reactions; each of the acids reacts with one of the hydroxyl groups in glycerol to form an ester. Draw the structure of the fat that is formed when glycerol reacts with three molecules of palmitic acid.

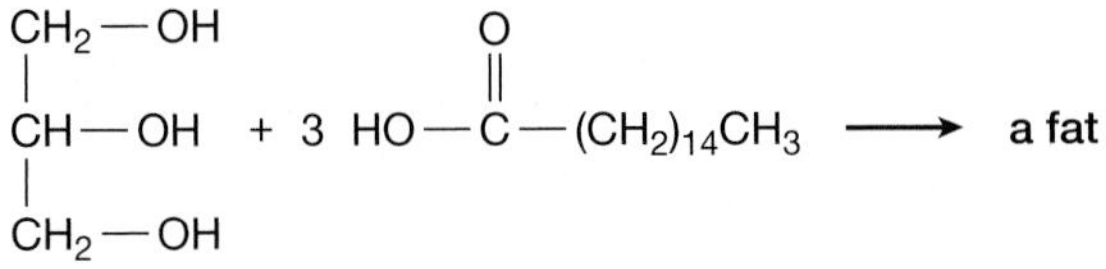

$CH_2(OH)-CH(OH)-CH_2(OH) + 3\ HO-C(=O)-(CH_2)_{14}CH_3 \longrightarrow$ a fat

Glycerol **Palmitic acid**

12.53 The following alcohol can condense with two phosphate ions. Draw the structure of the organic product of this reaction.

$HO-CH_2-CH_2-CH_2-OH$

12.54 *Phosphate can condense with two molecules of ethanol to form a phosphodiester. Draw the structure of this compound. Hint: Start with the phosphate ion in the form shown here:

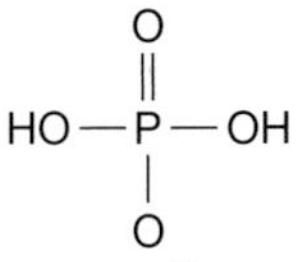

$HO-P(=O)(-O^-)-OH$

12.55 Draw the structure of the organic product that is formed when three molecules of the following compound condense to form a single molecule:

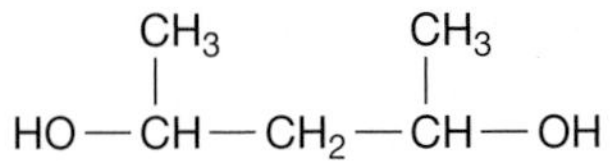

$HO-CH(CH_3)-CH_2-CH(CH_3)-OH$

12.56 The following compound can be used to make a polymer. Draw the structure of the product that will be formed when four molecules of this compound condense.

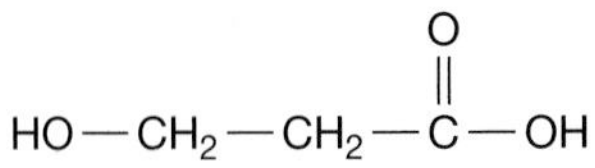

$HO-CH_2-CH_2-C(=O)-OH$

12.57 Asparagine is one of the naturally occurring amino acids. It can be used to make a polymer. Draw the structure of the compound that is formed when three molecules of asparagine condense. (Hint: The amide group in asparagine does not react.)

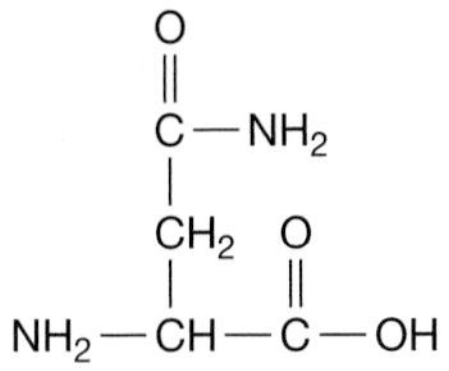

$NH_2-CH(CH_2-C(=O)-NH_2)-C(=O)-OH$ **Asparagine**

12.58 The two compounds that follow can be used to make a copolymer. Show how two molecules of each compound can condense to form the beginning of a copolymer.

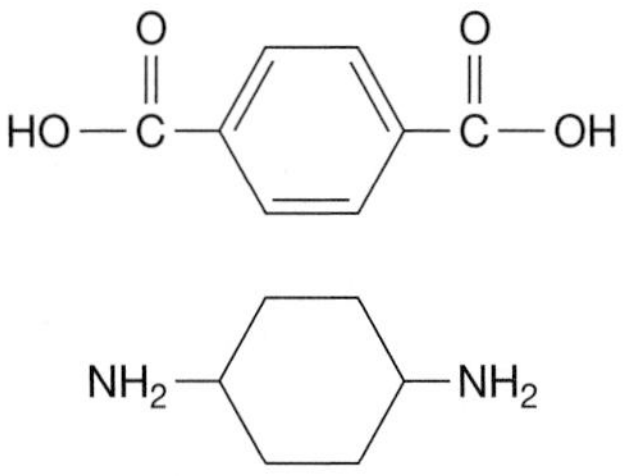

$HO-C(=O)-C_6H_4-C(=O)-OH$ (benzene ring, para)

$NH_2-C_6H_{10}-NH_2$ (cyclohexane ring, 1,4)

12.59 *The structures of the amino acids glycine and valine are shown here. You can make three different molecules by condensing two molecules of glycine with one molecule of valine. Draw the structures of these three compounds.

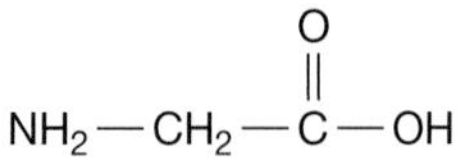

$NH_2-CH_2-C(=O)-OH$ **Glycine**

$NH_2-CH(CH(CH_3)-CH_3)-C(=O)-OH$ **Valine**

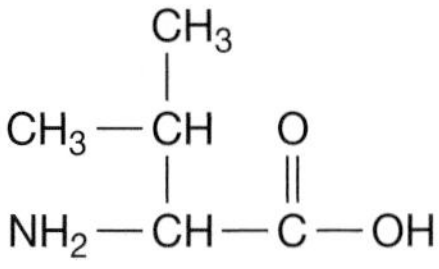

12.60 Using structures, write the chemical equations for the hydrolysis reactions of each of the following compounds. Draw the organic products in their unionized forms.

a) $CH_3-CH_2-O-CH_2-CH_2-CH_3$

b) 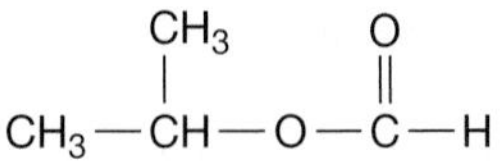 $CH_3-CH(CH_3)-O-C(=O)-H$

c) $CH_3-CH(CH_3)-CH_2-CH(CH_3)-C(=O)-O-CH_3$

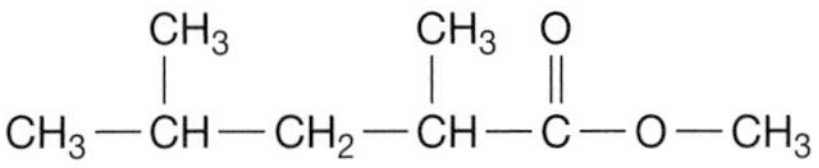

d) 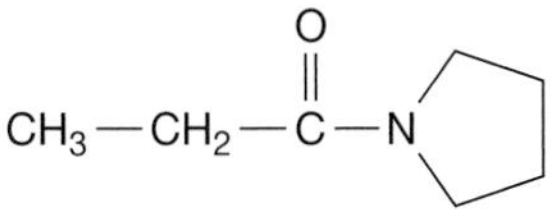 $CH_3-CH_2-C(=O)-N$ (pyrrolidine ring)

e) 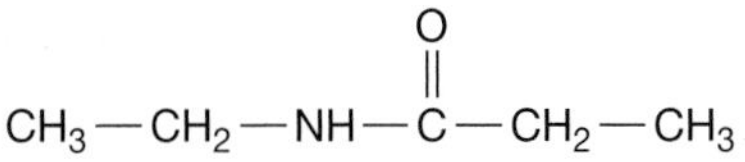 $CH_3-CH_2-NH-C(=O)-CH_2-CH_3$

f) 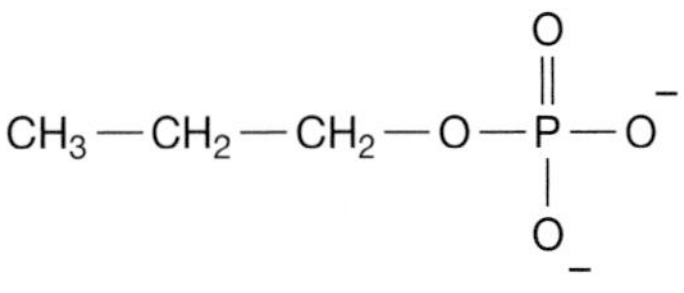 $CH_3-CH_2-CH_2-O-P(=O)(-O^-)-O^-$

12.61 *Two carboxylic acids can condense to form a compound called an anhydride. Using structures, show the condensation reaction of two molecules of acetic acid.

12.62 *The following polymer can be made from a compound that contains two alcohol groups. Draw the structure of this compound.

$$HO-CH_2-CH(O-CH_3)-CH_2-O-CH_2-CH(O-CH_3)-CH_2-O-CH_2-CH(O-CH_3)-CH_2-O-CH_2-CH(O-CH_3)-CH_2-O-\text{etc.}$$

12.63 Draw the structures of the products of the reactions in parts a through e of Problem 12.60 as they will actually appear at physiological pH.

12.64 The hydrolysis of the amide group in asparagine (see Problem 12.57) is an important reaction in biochemistry. Draw the structures of the products that will be formed when asparagine is hydrolyzed. You may ignore any ionization reactions.

12.65 Using structures, write the chemical equations for the hydrolysis reactions of each of the following compounds. Draw the organic products in their unionized forms.

a) $CH_3-C(=O)-S-CH_2-CH_3$

b) $C_6H_5-C(=O)-O-P(=O)(O^-)-O^-$

12.66 a) Using structures, write the chemical equation for the hydrolysis reaction of the following compound. Draw the products in their unionized forms. Hint: This hydrolysis reaction produces more than two molecules.

$$CH_3-O-C(=O)-CH_2-C(=O)-O-CH_3$$

b) Draw the structures of the products in part a as they appear at physiological pH.

12.67 a) When the following compound is hydrolyzed, the products are three amino acids. Draw the structures of these amino acids in their unionized forms.

$$NH_2-CH(CH_3)-C(=O)-NH-CH(CH_2-C(=O)-OH)-C(=O)-NH-CH(CH_2-CH(CH_3)-CH_3)-C(=O)-OH$$

b) Draw the structures of the products in part a as they appear at physiological pH.

12.68 *There are two ways to hydrolyze the following compound. Draw the structures of the products that will be formed when this compound is hydrolyzed in each of the following ways:

a) The bond between the two phosphate groups is hydrolyzed.

b) The bond between the organic fragment and the diphosphate is hydrolyzed.

$$CH_3-CH_2-O-P(=O)(O^-)-O-P(=O)(O^-)-O^-$$

12.69 *Compounds that contain an ester group within a ring of atoms are called lactones. Lactones can be hydrolyzed, but only one product is formed, rather than two. Draw the structure of the product that will be formed when the following lactone is hydrolyzed. You may draw the unionized form of the product.

O O

12.70 *Compounds that contain an amide group within a ring of atoms are called lactams. Lactams can be hydrolyzed, but only one product is formed, rather than two. Draw the structure of the product that will be formed when the following lactam is hydrolyzed. You may draw the unionized form of the product.

O NH

12.71 From each of the following pairs of compounds, select the compound that has the higher solubility in water:

a) $CH_3—CH_2—O—CH_2—CH_3$ or

$CH_3—CH_2—CH_2—CH_2—CH_3$

b) $CH_3—(CH_2)_3—O—(CH_2)_3—CH_3$ or

$CH_3—CH_2—O—CH_2—CH_3$

c) $CH_3—CH_2—CH_2—O—CH_2—CH_2—CH_3$ or

$CH_3—CH_2—O—CH_2—O—CH_2—CH_3$

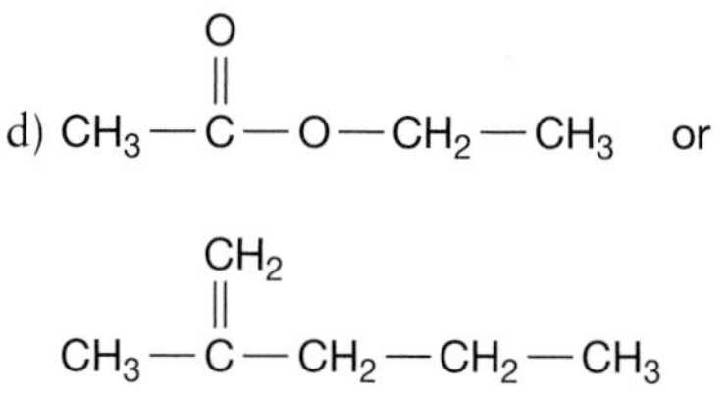

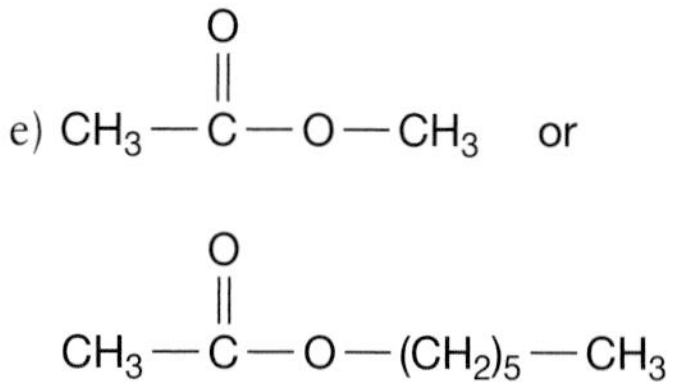

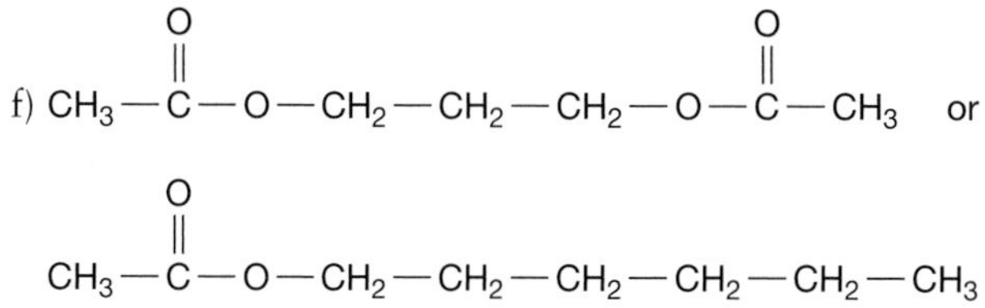

d) $CH_3—C(=O)—O—CH_2—CH_3$ or

$CH_3—C(=CH_2)—CH_2—CH_2—CH_3$

e) $CH_3—C(=O)—O—CH_3$ or

$CH_3—C(=O)—O—(CH_2)_5—CH_3$

f) $CH_3—C(=O)—O—CH_2—CH_2—CH_2—O—C(=O)—CH_3$ or

$CH_3—C(=O)—O—CH_2—CH_2—CH_2—CH_2—CH_2—CH_3$

12.72 Circle and name all of the functional groups in each of the following molecules:

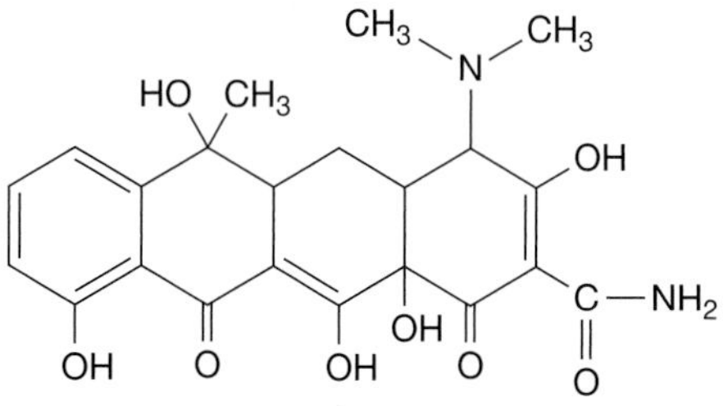

CH_3 CH_3 N; HO CH_3; OH; C—NH_2; OH O OH OH O O

Tetracycline – an antibiotic

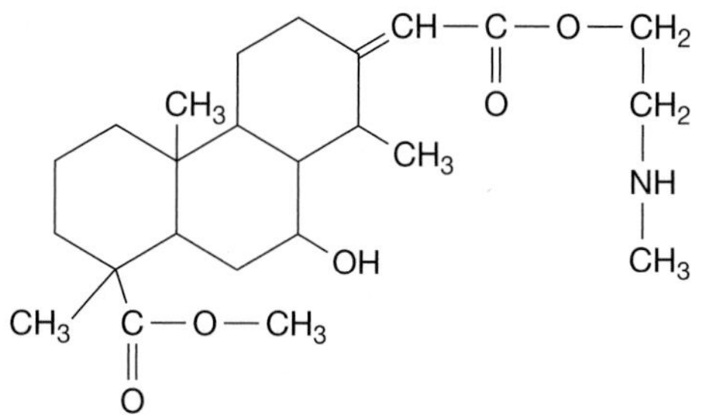

CH—C(=O)—O—CH_2—CH_2—NH—CH_3; CH_3; CH_3; OH; CH_3 C(=O)—O—CH_3

Erythrophleine – a stimulant of heart muscle

12.73 *All of the following compounds are soluble in water. Which of these will produce an acidic solution, which will produce a basic solution, and which will produce a neutral solution?

a) $CH_3—CH_2—CH_2—NH_2$

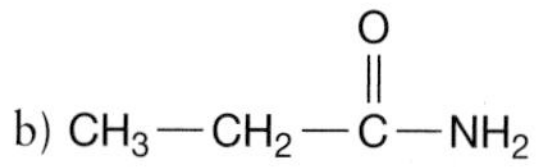

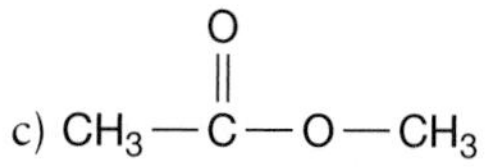

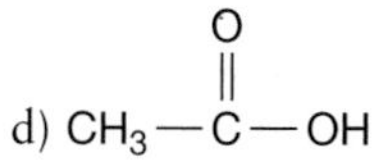

b) $CH_3—CH_2—C(=O)—NH_2$

c) $CH_3—C(=O)—O—CH_3$

d) $CH_3—C(=O)—OH$

e) $CH_3—CH_2—OH$

f) $CH_3—C(=O)—H$

g) (pyridine ring) N

h) (benzene ring)—OH

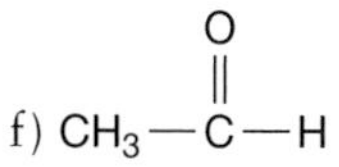

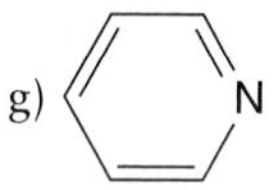

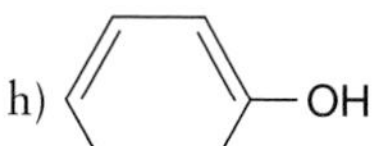

12.74 *Ammonia can be made by either of the following hydrolysis reactions. If you want to make 10.0 g of ammonia, how many grams of the organic reactant must you use in each case?

Reaction #1:

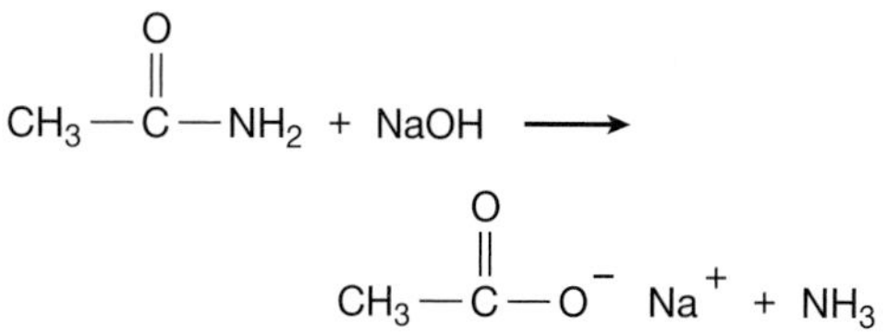

$$CH_3—C(=O)—NH_2 + NaOH \longrightarrow CH_3—C(=O)—O^- \ Na^+ + NH_3$$

Reaction #2:

$$NH_2—C(=O)—NH_2 + 2\ NaOH \longrightarrow Na_2CO_3 + 2\ NH_3$$

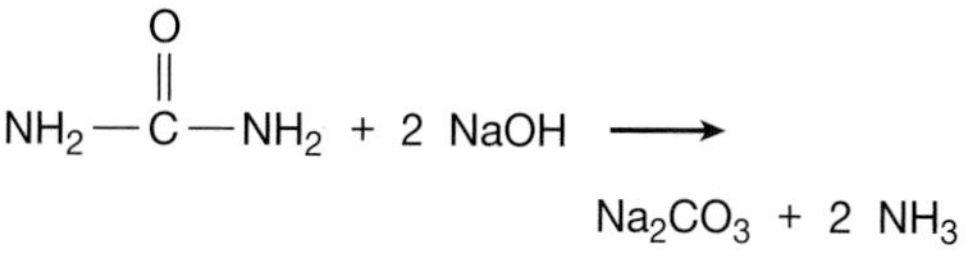

12.75 *Complete the following sequence of reactions by drawing the structures of compounds A through D. Hint: Compound D has the molecular formula $C_4H_8O_2$.

$$CH_2{=}CH_2 + H_2O \longrightarrow \textbf{Compound A}$$

$$\textbf{Compound A} \xrightarrow{\text{Oxidation}} \textbf{Compound B}$$

$$\textbf{Compound B} \xrightarrow{\text{Oxidation}} \textbf{Compound C}$$

$$\textbf{Compound A} + \textbf{Compound C} \xrightarrow{\text{Condensation}} \textbf{Compound D} + H_2O$$

12.76 *Complete the following sequence of reactions by drawing the structures of compounds A through D. Hint: Compound D has the molecular formula $C_5H_8O_4$.

$$HO{-}CH_2{-}CH_2{-}\overset{\overset{\displaystyle O}{\|}}{C}{-}NH_2 \xrightarrow[\text{(pH 1)}]{\text{Hydrolysis}} \textbf{Compound A} + NH_4^+$$

$$\textbf{Compound A} \xrightarrow{\text{Oxidation}} \textbf{Compound B}$$

$$\textbf{Compound B} \xrightarrow{\text{Oxidation}} \textbf{Compound C}$$

$$\textbf{Compound C} + 2\ CH_3{-}OH \xrightarrow{\text{Condensation}} \textbf{Compound D} + 2\ H_2O$$

12.77 *The following condensation reaction forms an equilibrium mixture:

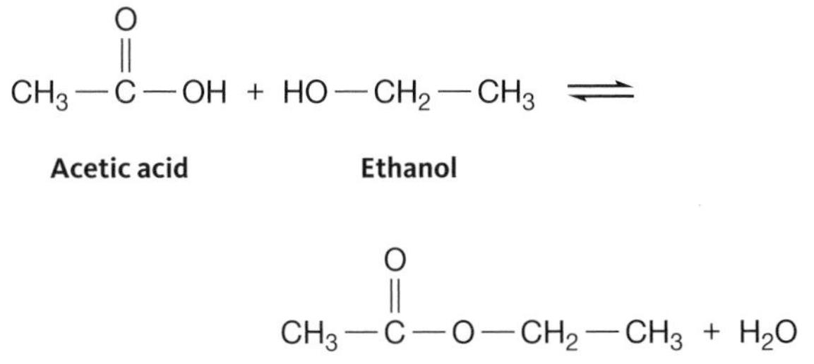

$$CH_3-\overset{\overset{\displaystyle O}{\|}}{C}-OH + HO-CH_2-CH_3 \rightleftharpoons$$

Acetic acid **Ethanol**

$$CH_3-\overset{\overset{\displaystyle O}{\|}}{C}-O-CH_2-CH_3 + H_2O$$

Ethyl acetate

a) If some acetic acid is added to an equilibrium mixture, will the amount of ethyl acetate in the mixture increase, decrease, or remain constant?
b) If some ethanol is added to an equilibrium mixture, will the amount of acetic acid in the mixture increase, decrease, or remain constant?
c) If you remove some acetic acid from an equilibrium mixture, will the amount of ethyl acetate in the mixture increase, decrease, or remain constant?

12.78 *Acetoin is one of the compounds that gives butter its characteristic taste.

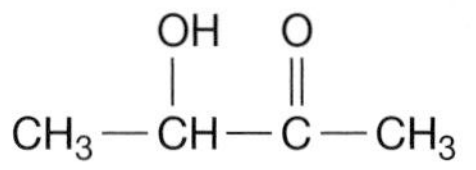

$$CH_3-\overset{\overset{\displaystyle OH}{|}}{CH}-\overset{\overset{\displaystyle O}{\|}}{C}-CH_3$$

Acetoin

a) What two functional groups are present in this compound?
b) Draw an isomer of acetoin that contains a carboxylic acid group as its only functional group.
c) Draw an isomer of acetoin that contains an ester group as its only functional group.
d) Draw an isomer of acetoin that contains an aldehyde group. (The aldehyde group will not be the only functional group in the molecule.)

13

Proteins

A month after Micah's fourth birthday, his mother notices that Micah's eyes seem puffy and his ankles look swollen. Over the next couple of weeks, Micah's feet and ankles continue to swell and he seems to be short on energy, so his mother takes him to the local clinic. The nurse practitioner orders several lab tests, including a measurement of the concentration of albumin in Micah's blood and urine. Albumin is a protein that plays a variety of vital roles in blood, including maintaining the correct osmotic pressure of the blood plasma. The lab reports that Micah's blood albumin level is substantially lower than normal, but he has a significant amount of albumin in his urine. The low concentration of albumin has made Micah's plasma hypotonic, so water is leaving his plasma and entering the surrounding tissues, causing them to swell. The presence of albumin in Micah's urine, along with his other symptoms, strongly suggests that he suffers from minimal change syndrome, a condition in which the membranes in the kidneys are damaged by the immune system, allowing proteins to leak from the bloodstream into the urine.

After further tests, the nurse practitioner determines that Micah's disease is a result of an allergy to tree nuts, and he tells Micah's parents to remove products that contain nuts from their son's diet. He also prescribes medication to reduce the stress on Micah's kidneys. After a few weeks, Micah looks and feels normal again, and his plasma albumin level returns to normal.

OUTLINE

LABORATORY REQUISITION—CHEMISTRY

Test	Code	Test	Code
☐ Sodium	NA	☐ Fructosamine	FRU/ALB
☐ Potassium	K	☐ PSA	PSA
☐ Creatinine	CREAT	☐ Chloride	CL
☐ BUN	BUN	☐ Calcium	CA
☐ Glucose-fasting	GLUCF	☐ Phosphorus	PHOS
☐ Glucose-random	GLUCR	☐ Phenylalanine	PKU
☐ Hemoglobin A1C	HGBA1C	☐ Uric Acid	URIC

Peanuts are a common allergen and can produce a life-threatening reaction in some people.

OWL Online homework for this chapter may be assigned in OWL.

Our bodies contain a remarkable variety of organic molecules. Virtually all of these compounds are *biomolecules*, chemical compounds that are made exclusively by living organisms. Many biomolecules are astoundingly complex, built from thousands or millions of atoms. Yet these intricate chemical structures are built from just a few elements, and their properties and reactions differ little from the behavior of simple organic compounds that we have seen in the last few chapters. In the coming chapters, we will look at some of the main classes of biomolecules.

We begin our study of biomolecules by examining the structure and behavior of **proteins**. Proteins are the most versatile biomolecules, carrying out an enormous range of functions. They are also the most abundant class of biomolecules; the human body can make more than 30,000 different proteins, and scientists have yet to discover the function of thousands of them. In our bodies, proteins catalyze reactions, regulate our metabolism, protect us from disease, carry nutrients throughout our bodies, move our muscles, and give us shape and structure. Proteins are involved in every facet of our lives, as well as the lives of all other living creatures.

OBJECTIVES: *Draw the structure of a typical amino acid as it exists under physiological conditions, and classify amino acids based on the structures of their side chains.*

13.1 Amino Acids

All proteins are large molecules, made from smaller compounds called **amino acids**. You encountered some of the reactions of amino acids in Chapters 11 and 12. Although any compound that contains an amine group and a carboxylic acid group is an amino acid, this term is generally taken to refer to substances in which the two functional groups are separated by one carbon atom, which is called the **alpha (α) carbon**. Figure 13.1 illustrates the structural features that are found in all amino acids.

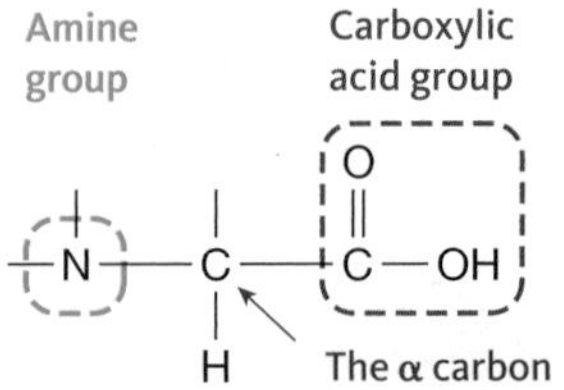

FIGURE 13.1 The structural features of amino acids.

The molecule that follows is a common amino acid called alanine. Alanine, like most amino acids, is a primary amine (it contains an amino group).

The amino group

The carboxylic acid group

The alpha carbon

The structure of alanine, a primary amino acid

As we saw in Chapter 11, whenever a compound contains an amine group and an acid group, the acid neutralizes the amine. A hydrogen ion moves from the acid to the amine nitrogen, forming a zwitterion. This reaction is reversible, but the equilibrium mixture contains only a trace of the unionized form. Therefore, chemists normally draw the structures of amino acids in the zwitterion form, and so will we.

$$-N-CH-C(=O)-O-\mathbf{H} \rightleftharpoons -\overset{+}{N}(\mathbf{H})-CH-C(=O)-O^-$$

Unionized form **Zwitterion form**

Most proteins are built from 20 amino acids. These fundamental building blocks are found in all living organisms, from the simplest to the most complex. All of these amino acids have the basic structure shown in Figure 13.1, but each one has a different group of atoms attached to the α-carbon. This group of atoms is called the **side chain** of the amino acid, and is often denoted with an *R*. In one amino acid (proline), the side chain loops around to attach to the amine nitrogen. In the other 19 amino acids, the side chain is attached only to the α-carbon.

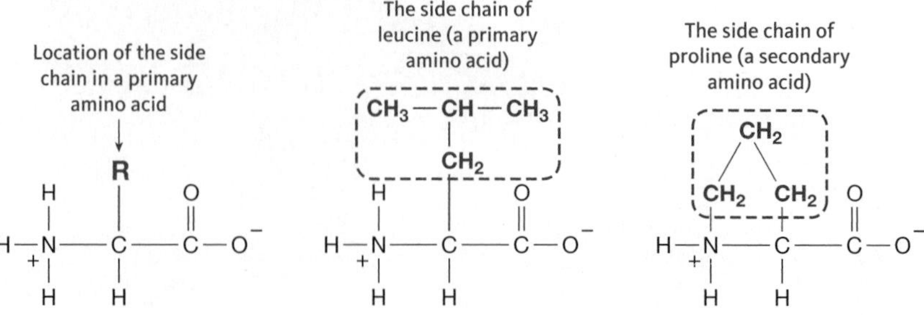

Sample Problem 13.1

Drawing the zwitterion structure of an amino acid

Homocysteine is an uncommon amino acid that is formed when our bodies break down the amino acid methionine. Identify the side chain in homocysteine, and draw the structure of this amino acid in its zwitterion form.

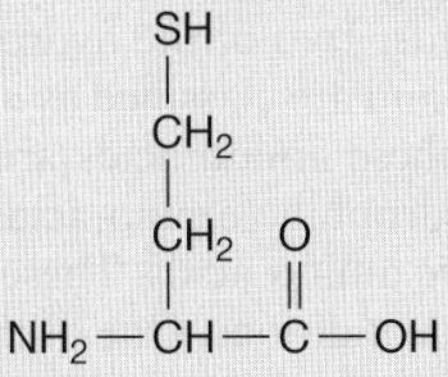

```
        SH
        |
        CH2
        |
        CH2  O
        |    ||
  NH2 — CH — C — OH
```

Homocysteine

SOLUTION

First, we identify the amine and acid groups, and then we locate the α-carbon atom. The side chain is bonded to the α-carbon, as shown here:

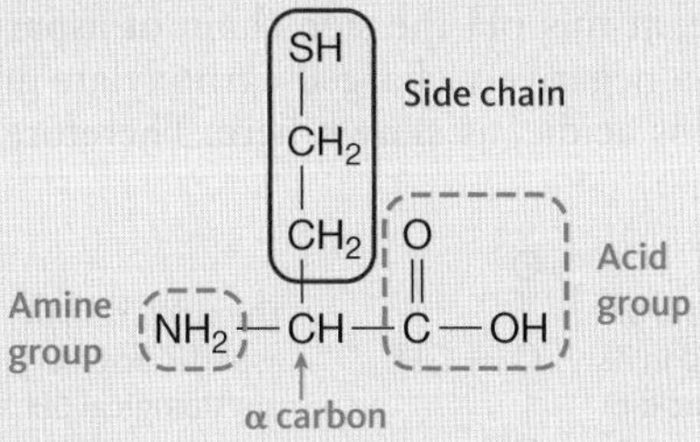

```
        SH
        |        Side chain
        CH2
        |
        CH2  O
        |    ||          Acid
Amine  NH2 — CH — C — OH   group
group        ↑
          α carbon
```

To draw the structure of the zwitterion, we move H^+ from the acid group to the amine group.

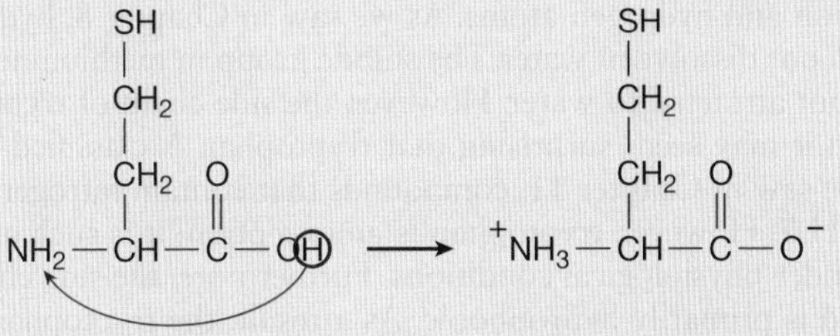

```
        SH                          SH
        |                           |
        CH2                         CH2
        |                           |
        CH2  O                      CH2  O
        |    ||                     |    ||
  NH2 — CH — C — OH   ⟶   +NH3 — CH — C — O−

   Unionized form              Zwitterion form
```

TRY IT YOURSELF: *Norleucine is an amino acid that is not found in proteins. Identify the side chain in this compound, and draw the structure of norleucine in its zwitterion form.*

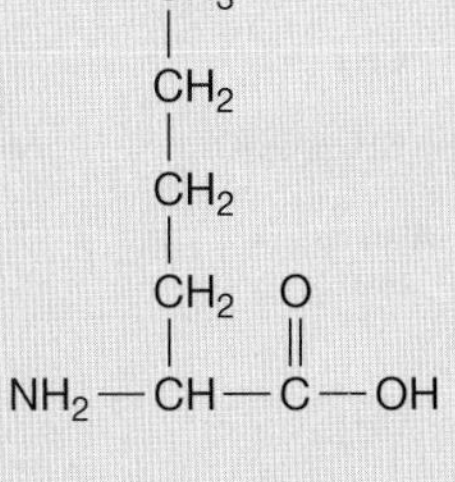

```
        CH3
        |
        CH2
        |
        CH2
        |
        CH2  O
        |    ||
  NH2 — CH — C — OH
```

Norleucine

For additional practice, try Core Problems 13.3 (parts a and b) and 13.4 (parts a and b).

Amino Acids Are Classified Based on Their Side Chains

The structures and abbreviations of the 20 common amino acids are shown in Table 13.1. Chemists divide these amino acids into classes based on the chemical properties of their side chains. The 11 *hydrophilic* (or *polar*) amino acids contain side chains that have polar functional groups and are attracted to water. The other 9 amino acids have side chains that are not attracted to water to any significant extent, so they are classified as *hydrophobic* (or *nonpolar*). Because the amino and acid groups of all amino acids are attracted to water, even the hydrophobic amino acids are reasonably soluble in water. However, when these amino acids are incorporated into a protein, the hydrophobic side chains generally avoid water, as we will see in Section 13.3.

Chemists also classify the hydrophilic amino acids based on their acid–base properties. Six of these amino acids contain functional groups that do not ionize at pH 7, so they are called *neutral* (or *polar neutral*) amino acids. Two of the hydrophilic amino acids contain carboxylic acid groups in their side chains and are classified as *acidic* amino acids. The acid group loses a hydrogen ion at pH 7, so these amino acids are negatively charged under physiological conditions. Three of the hydrophilic amino acids contain amine groups in their side chains and are classified as *basic* amino acids. These amino acids gain H^+ and are positively charged under physiological conditions. One of the basic amino acids (histidine) is too weak to ionize completely, so it forms a conjugate pair at pH 7. The other acidic and basic amino acids are fully ionized at physiological pH. Table 13.1 shows all of the acidic and basic amino acids as they actually appear under physiological conditions.

It is important to recognize that acidic and basic amino acids are classified based on their unionized forms, even though these forms are not present in significant concentration at pH 7. For instance, at this pH the side chain of aspartic acid is actually weakly basic, because it contains a negatively charged carboxylate group. However, the unionized form of aspartic acid is acidic, as shown here. Therefore, aspartic acid is classified as an acidic amino acid.

The side chain of aspartic acid in its unionized (acidic) form: $-CH_2-C(=O)-OH$

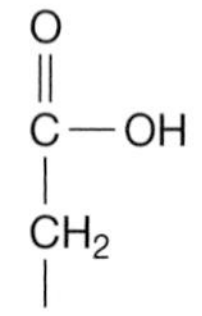

The side chain of aspartic acid at physiological pH: $-CH_2-C(=O)-O^-$

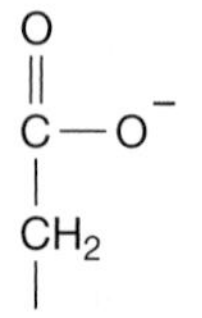

Most of the hydrophobic amino acids are easy to recognize, because their side chains contain only carbon and hydrogen atoms. As we saw in Chapter 8, hydrocarbons are hydrophobic and do not dissolve in water. The sulfide group in methionine is also essentially nonpolar and is not attracted to water. However, the side chain of tryptophan contains a nitrogen atom, so it may seem surprising that tryptophan is classified as a hydrophobic amino acid. As we saw in Chapter 11, compounds that contain nitrogen are usually bases and gain H^+ at pH 7. However, tryptophan is an exception; it is such a weak base that it does not ionize under physiological conditions. Furthermore, the side chain of tryptophan is rather large and is primarily hydrophobic. As a result, the tryptophan side chain tends to avoid water, so we group tryptophan with the hydrophobic amino acids.

Health Note: The body uses tryptophan to make the tryptamine hormones serotonin and melatonin, which promote relaxation and sleepiness in the brain. As a result, tryptophan is claimed to be an effective sleep aid, although clinical research is inconclusive. Tryptophan is also prescribed as a medication to increase the effect of antidepressant drugs.

TABLE 13.1 The 20 Common Amino Acids as They Appear at Physiological pH

Hydrophobic (nonpolar) amino acids

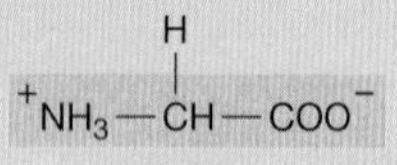

Structure	Name
$^{+}NH_3-CH(H)-COO^-$	**Glycine** (Gly)
$^{+}NH_3-CH(CH_3)-COO^-$	**Alanine** (Ala)
$^{+}NH_3-CH(CH(CH_3)-CH_3)-COO^-$	**Valine** (Val)
$^{+}NH_3-CH(CH_2-CH(CH_3)-CH_3)-COO^-$	**Leucine** (Leu)
$^{+}NH_3-CH(CH(CH_3)-CH_2-CH_3)-COO^-$	**Isoleucine** (Ile)
$^{+}H_2N-CH-COO^-$ (ring: CH_2, CH_2, CH_2)	**Proline** (Pro) (proline is the only secondary amino acid)

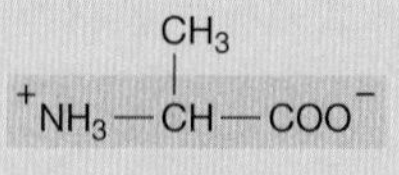

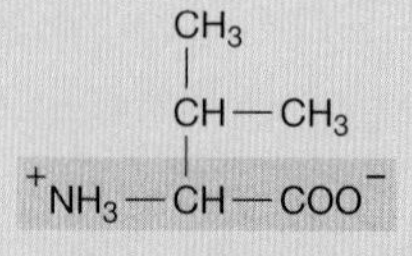

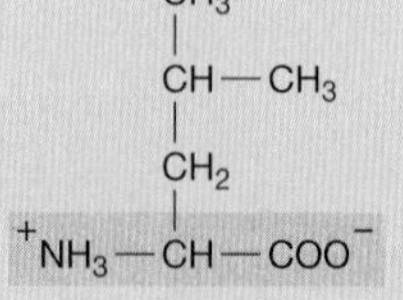

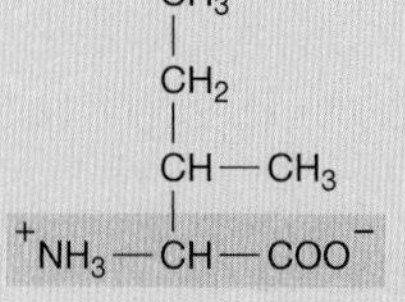

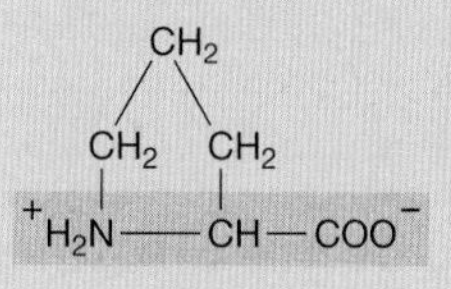

continued

TABLE 13.1 The 20 Common Amino Acids as They Appear at Physiological pH—cont'd

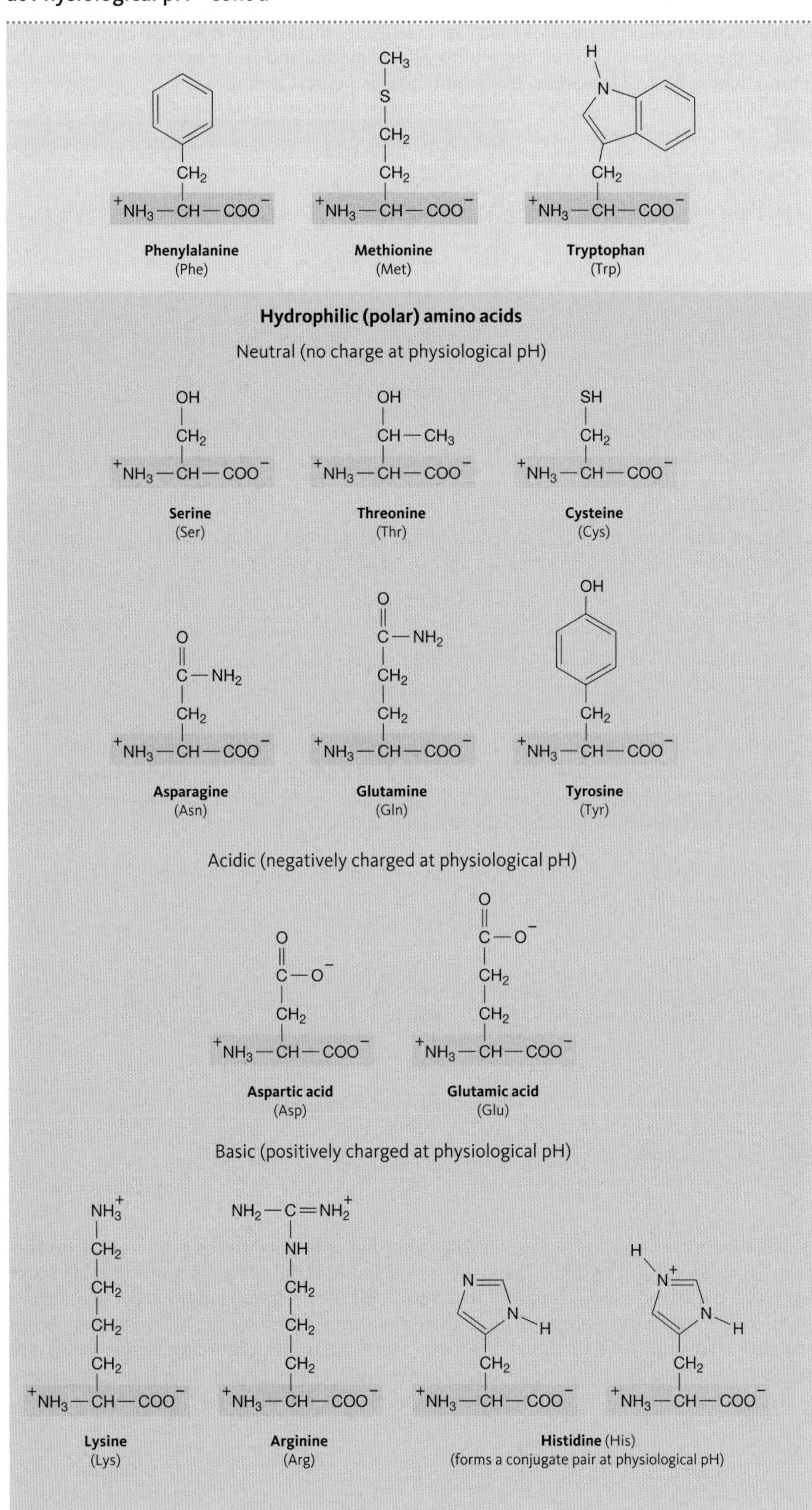

Health Note: Many body-builders take supplements containing mixtures of amino acids. However, there is no evidence that additional amino acids help build muscle tissue in people who consume a normal diet. Muscle proteins are broken down into amino acids during heavy weight training, but the body recycles the amino acids to build new muscle protein. The human body cannot store amino acids, so the extra amino acids in supplements are broken down and excreted—providing energy, but having no other benefit.

Our bodies contain a variety of amino acids that are not in Table 13.1, and we classify these amino acids just as we do the 20 common ones. To classify an amino acid, we must locate the side chain, and then we need to check whether the side chain contains a hydrophilic functional group. If it does, we must tell whether the functional group is ionized. If the group is an anion, the amino acid is acidic, and if the group is a cation, the amino acid is basic. Otherwise, the amino acid is neutral polar.

Sample Problem 13.2

Classifying an amino acid

Ornithine is an uncommon amino acid that is formed when our bodies break down arginine.

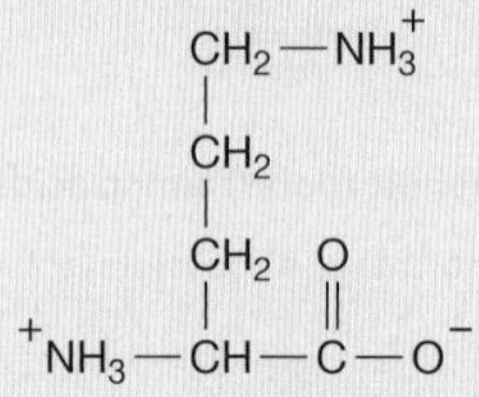

$$\begin{array}{l} \qquad\quad CH_2-NH_3^+ \\ \qquad\quad | \\ \qquad\quad CH_2 \\ \qquad\quad | \\ \qquad\quad CH_2 \quad O \\ \qquad\quad | \qquad \| \\ {}^+NH_3-CH-C-O^- \end{array}$$

Is ornithine a hydrophobic or a hydrophilic amino acid? If it is hydrophilic, is it acidic, basic, or neutral?

SOLUTION

First, we must locate the side chain of ornithine. The side chain of this amino acid is shown here:

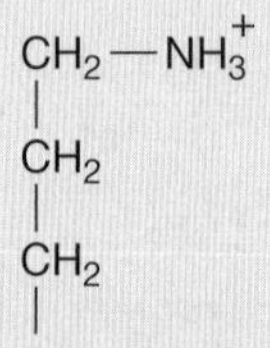

$$\begin{array}{l} CH_2-NH_3^+ \\ | \\ CH_2 \\ | \\ CH_2 \\ | \end{array}$$

This side chain contains an alkylammonium ion, which is strongly attracted to water. Therefore, ornithine is a **hydrophilic** amino acid. The alkylammonium ion is a cation (a positive ion), so ornithine is a **basic** amino acid. (The unionized form of ornithine contains an amino group in its side chain, making it a base.)

TRY IT YOURSELF: *Is the following amino acid hydrophobic or hydrophilic? If it is hydrophilic, is it acidic, basic, or neutral?*

$$\begin{array}{l} \qquad\qquad\quad O \\ \qquad\qquad\quad \| \\ \qquad\quad CH_2-C-O^- \\ \qquad\quad | \\ \qquad\quad CH_2 \\ \qquad\quad | \\ \qquad\quad CH_2 \quad O \\ \qquad\quad | \qquad \| \\ {}^+NH_3-CH-C-O^- \end{array}$$

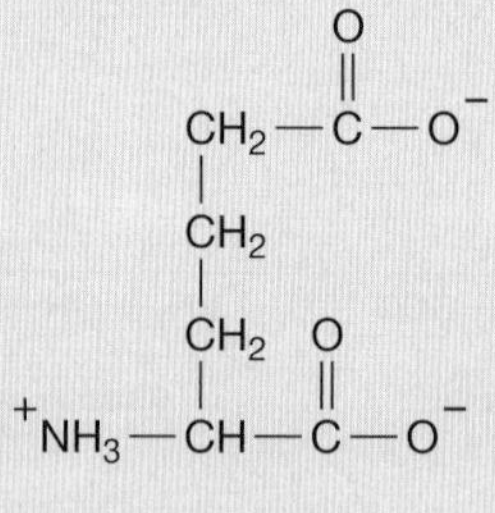

For additional practice, try Core Problems 13.3 (part c) and 13.4 (part c).

Recall from Section 9.5 that a carbon atom that is bonded to four different groups is chiral and can exist in two mirror-image forms. In all of the common amino acids except glycine, the α-carbon atom is chiral. As a result, all of the amino acids except glycine are chiral and have two possible forms, called enantiomers. However, all organisms build proteins from only one of the two forms. These naturally occurring amino acids are called L-amino acids. Their enantiomers, which are not normally found in nature, are called D-amino acids. The two enantiomers of alanine are illustrated here:

L-alanine (used to build proteins): CH_3, H on C; ${}^+H_3N-C-COO^-$

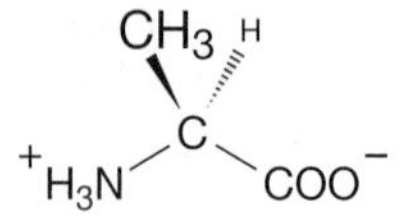

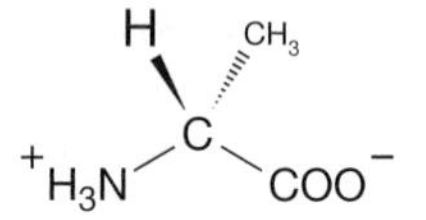

D-alanine (not found in proteins): H, CH_3 on C; ${}^+H_3N-C-COO^-$

CORE PROBLEMS

All Core Problems are paired and the answers to the ***blue*** *odd-numbered problems appear in the back of the book.*

13.1 The unionized form of the amino acid valine is shown here. Identify each of the following pieces of the molecule:

a) amino group b) acid group
c) α-carbon atom d) side chain

```
          CH3
          |
    CH3 — CH    O
          |     ||
    NH2 — CH — C — OH
```

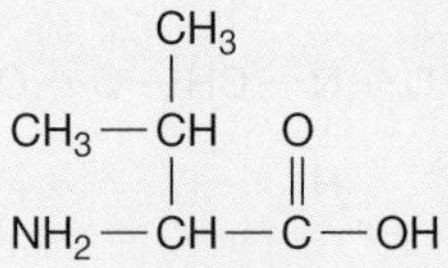

Valine
(unionized form)

13.2 The unionized form of the amino acid asparagine is shown here. Identify each of the following pieces of the molecule:

a) amino group b) acid group
c) α-carbon atom d) side chain

```
          O
          ||
          C — NH2
          |
          CH2   O
          |     ||
    NH2 — CH — C — OH
```

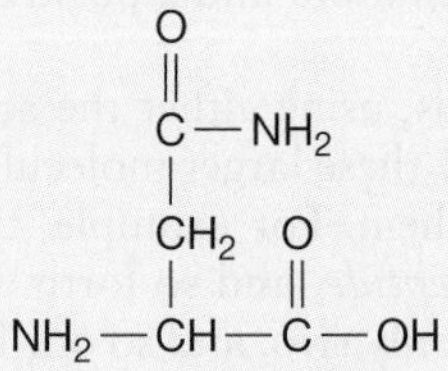

Asparagine
(unionized form)

13.3 Homoserine is an amino acid that is not used to build proteins, but it is produced when some of the normal amino acids are broken down.

a) Identify the side chain in homoserine.
b) Draw the structure of homoserine in the zwitterion form.
c) Is homoserine a hydrophilic or a hydrophobic amino acid? If it is hydrophilic, is it acidic, basic, or neutral?

```
          CH2 — OH
          |
          CH2   O
          |     ||
    NH2 — CH — C — OH
```

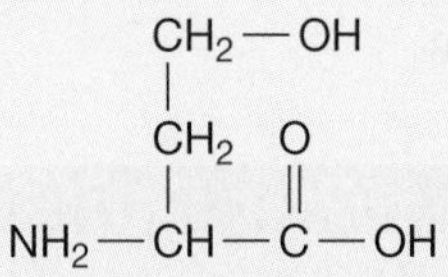

Homoserine

13.4 N-acetyllysine is a rare amino acid that is found in a number of plants.

a) Identify the side chain in N-acetyllysine.
b) Draw the structure of N-acetyllysine in the zwitterion form.
c) Is N-acetyllysine a hydrophilic or a hydrophobic amino acid? If it is hydrophilic, is it acidic, basic, or neutral?

```
                                         O
                                         ||
          CH2 — CH2 — CH2 — NH — C — CH3
          |
          CH2   O
          |     ||
    NH2 — CH — C — OH
```

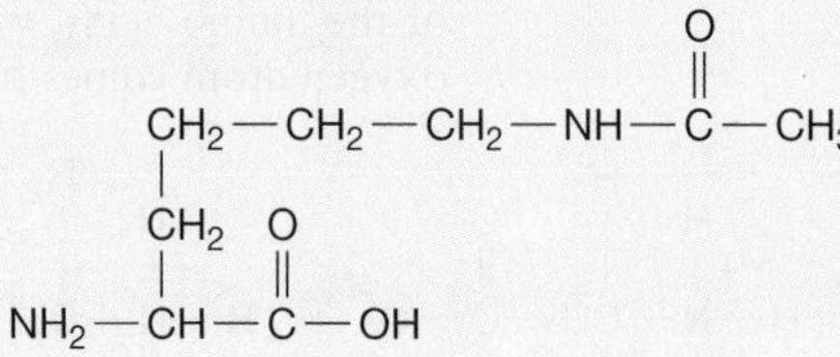

N-acetyllysine

13.5 The amino acid citrulline contains the side chain shown here. Draw the complete structure of this amino acid in its zwitterion form.

```
                      O
                      ||
    CH2 — NH — C — NH2
    |
    CH2
    |
    CH2
    |
```

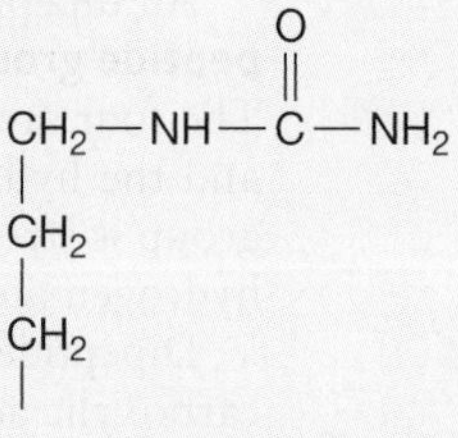

The side chain of citrulline (as it appears at pH 7)

13.6 The amino acid N-methyllysine contains the side chain shown here. Draw the complete structure of this amino acid in its zwitterion form.

```
                  +
    CH2 — CH2 — NH2 — CH3
    |
    CH2
    |
    CH2
    |
```

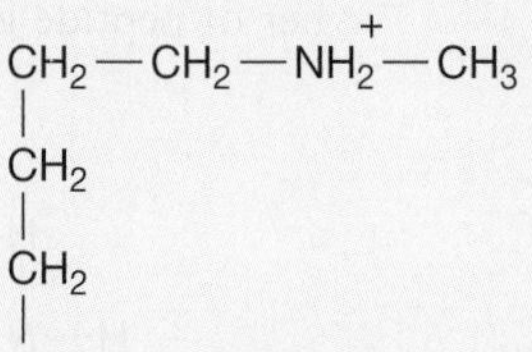

The side chain of N-methyllysine (as it appears at pH 7)

13.7 Lysine is a weak acid under physiological conditions. Explain why lysine is classified as a basic amino acid. (The structure of lysine is shown in Table 13.1.)

13.8 Aspartic acid is a weak base under physiological conditions. Explain why aspartic acid is classified as an acidic amino acid. (The structure of aspartic acid is shown in Table 13.1.)

13.9 Threonine (see Table 13.1) contains two chiral carbon atoms. Draw the structure of threonine, and circle the two chiral carbon atoms in this amino acid.

13.10 Isoleucine (see Table 13.1) contains two chiral carbon atoms. Draw the structure of isoleucine, and circle the two chiral carbon atoms in this amino acid.

13.2 Peptide Bonds and the Secondary Structure of a Protein

OBJECTIVES: *Draw the structure of a polypeptide, and show how peptide groups interact to form the typical secondary structures of a protein.*

In Section 13.1, we examined the structures and behavior of the amino acid building blocks of proteins. Let us now look at how amino acids are linked to form a protein and how the bond between amino acids helps determine the shape of a protein chain.

Amino Acids Condense with Each Other to Form Peptide Groups

Any two amino acids can react with each other to form a single larger molecule. As we saw in Section 12.3, the amino group from one molecule and the acid group from the other molecule undergo a condensation reaction. The organic product is a *dipeptide,* which contains the two amino acids bonded together. When we use the zwitterion forms of the amino acids, we remove both hydrogen atoms from the amino group. Only the oxygen atom comes from the acid group.

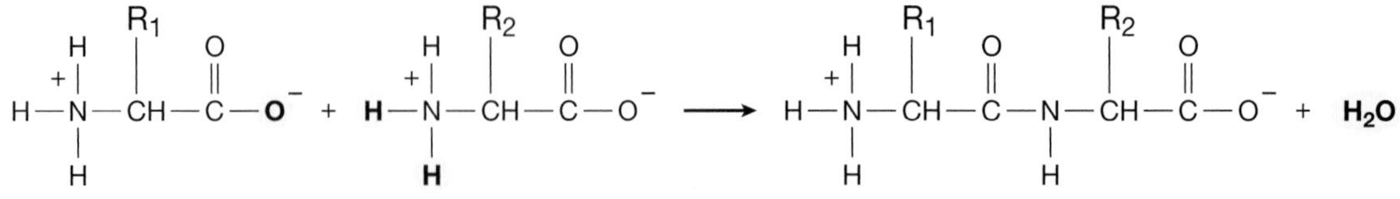

Amino acid #1 + Amino acid #2 → **A dipeptide** + $\mathbf{H_2O}$

All dipeptides contain an amide functional group, which is generally referred to as a **peptide group**. The new bond between carbon and nitrogen is called a **peptide bond.** The four atoms in the peptide group lie in a specific orientation, with the oxygen atom and the hydrogen atom pointing in opposite directions, as shown in Figure 13.2. This group is strongly polar, with a negatively charged oxygen atom and a positively charged hydrogen atom.

Dipeptides can condense with additional amino acids, using either the amino or the carboxylic acid group of the dipeptide. Chemists classify these larger molecules based on the number of amino acids that were used to make them. For example, three amino acids form a *tripeptide,* four amino acids form a *tetrapeptide,* and so forth. Note that a dipeptide contains only one peptide group, a tripeptide only two, and so on. The prefixes *di-* and *tri-* refer to the number of amino acids, which is always one more than the number of peptide groups.

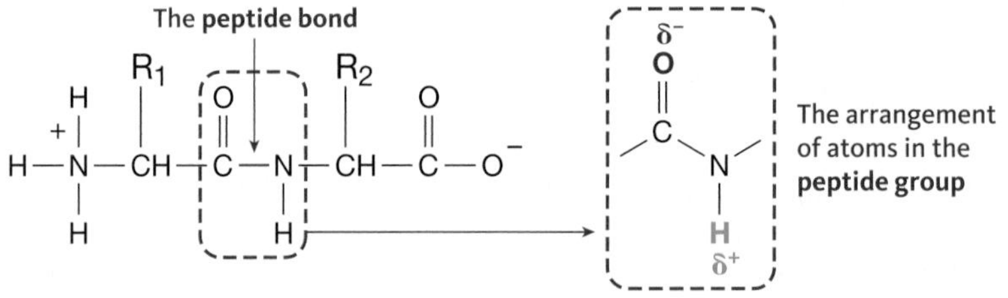

Health Note: The endorphins are pentapeptides that the body produces in response to prolonged, painful stimuli. They bind to nerve cells, reducing the sensation of pain and producing a sense of well-being. Opiates such as morphine and codeine have similar shapes to endorphins, making them highly effective for the relief of pain. However, excessive use of opiates leads the body to produce less endorphins, leading to chemical dependency.

The peptide bond

The arrangement of atoms in the **peptide group**

FIGURE 13.2 The structure of the peptide group.

Sample Problem 13.3

Drawing the structure of a tripeptide

Draw the structure of the tripeptide that contains the amino acids glycine, phenylalanine, and threonine in that order.

SOLUTION

First, we need to draw the structures of the three amino acids side by side, with the amino group of each beside the acid group of the next one.

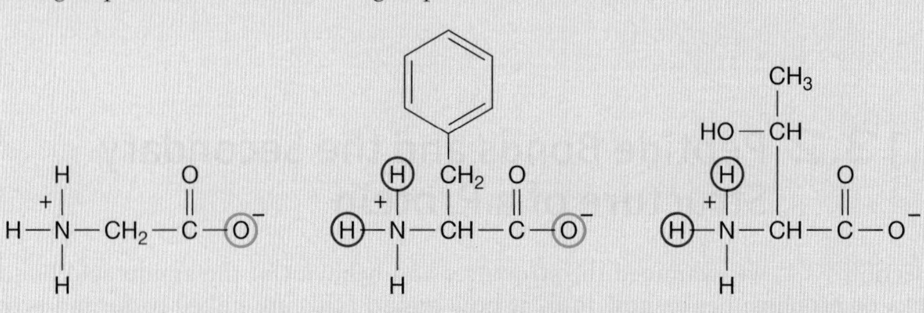

Glycine **Phenylalanine** **Threonine**

continued

Next, we form the peptide bonds, using two condensation reactions. In each condensation, the oxygen atom from an acid group combines with two hydrogen atoms from an amine group to form water. These atoms are circled on the structures of the amino acids. When we remove these atoms and link the remaining pieces, we form the tripeptide.

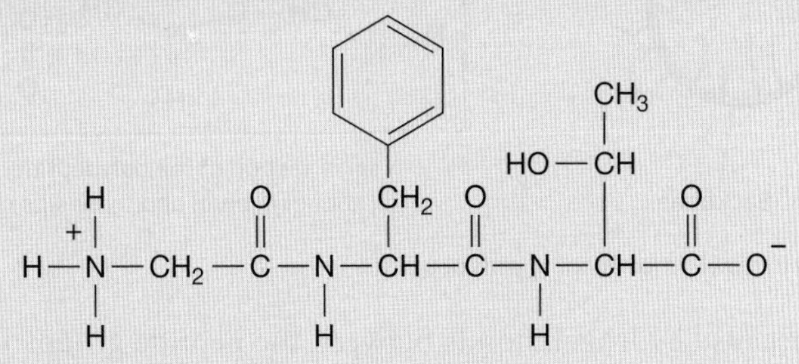

```
                          (C6H5)                  CH3
                            |                      |
                            |                  HO—CH
     H             O       CH2   O                 |      O
    +|             ‖        |    ‖                 |      ‖
  H—N—CH2—C—N—CH—C—N—CH—C—O⁻
     |                 |              |
     H                 H              H
```

TRY IT YOURSELF: *Draw the structure of the tripeptide that contains the amino acids lysine, alanine, and isoleucine in that order.*

For additional practice, try Core Problems 13.11 and 13.12.

(N-terminal) Gly–***Asp***-Val-***Glu***–***Lys***–Gly–***Lys***–***Lys***–Ile–Phe–Ile–Met–***Lys***–*Cys*–*Ser*–*Gln*–*Cys*–***His***–*Thr*–Val–
Glu–***Lys***–Gly–Gly–***Lys***–***His***–***Lys***–*Thr*–Gly–Pro–*Asn*–Leu–***His***–Gly–Leu–Phe–Gly–***Arg***–***Lys***–*Thr*–Gly–*Gln*–
Ala–Pro–Gly–*Tyr*–*Ser*–*Tyr*–*Thr*–Ala–Ala–*Asn*–***Lys***–*Asn*–***Lys***–Gly–Ile–Ile–Trp–Gly–***Glu***–***Asp***–*Thr*–Leu–Met–
Gln–*Tyr*–Leu–***Glu***–*Asn*–Pro–***Lys***–***Lys***–*Tyr*–Pro–Pro–Gly–*Thr*–***Lys***–Met–Ile–Phe–Val–Gly–Ile–***Lys***–***Lys***–***Lys***–
Glu–***Glu***–***Arg***–Ala–***Asp***–Leu–Ile–Ala–*Tyr*–Leu–***Lys***–***Lys***–Ala–*Thr*–*Asn*–***Glu*** (C-terminal)

Key:

Total nonpolar (hydrophobic) amino acids:	47
Total polar neutral amino acids:	*24*
Total acidic and basic (ionized) amino acids:	***33***
Total amino acids in cytochrome C:	104

FIGURE 13.3 The primary structure of human cytochrome C.

The Primary Structure of a Protein Is the Sequence of Amino Acids

If we link a large number of amino acids using peptide bonds, we produce a **polypeptide**. Proteins are polypeptides, typically containing 100 to 500 amino acids, although some proteins are much larger and some are significantly smaller. Every protein contains a specific mixture of amino acids linked in a specific order, and each of the tens of thousands of different proteins in a human has its own unique sequence of amino acids. The order of the amino acids in a protein is called the **primary structure** of the protein.

Chemists write the primary structure of a protein by listing the three-letter abbreviations for the amino acids, starting from the end that has the free amino group. For instance, the primary structure of the tripeptide in Sample Problem 13.3 is written Gly–Phe–Thr. The first amino acid is called the **N-terminal amino acid**. The last amino acid in the chain, which has a free carboxylate group, is called the **C-terminal amino acid**.

Figure 13.3 gives the amino acid composition and the primary structure of cytochrome C, a protein that plays a vital role in our ability to burn nutrients to obtain energy. This protein is found in all multicellular organisms (including animals, plants, and fungi) and in many single-celled organisms. In cytochrome C, nearly a third of the amino acids have acidic or basic side chains and are ionized at pH 7. These side chains are attracted to water, so cytochrome C is a water-soluble protein.

• The primary structure of cytochrome C varies from one species to another, and is a rough measure of the evolutionary relationship between species.

As illustrated in Figure 13.4, every polypeptide contains a backbone, formed by the peptide groups and the α-carbon atoms. The side chains of the amino acids project outward from the backbone. However, most proteins fold up into a rather com-

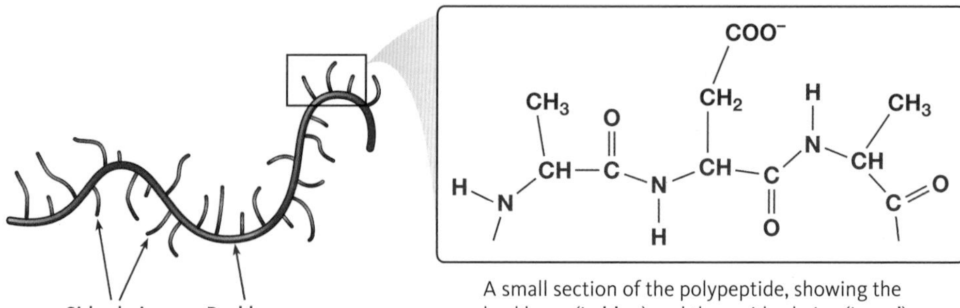

A small section of the polypeptide, showing the backbone (in **blue**) and three side chains (in **red**).

FIGURE 13.4 Structural features of a polypeptide.

pact structure, because hydrogen bonds between the peptide groups in the backbone force the backbone to fold into a specific three-dimensional arrangement. In the remainder of this section, we will look at how the peptide groups affect the structure of a protein.

Sample Problem 13.4

Determining the primary structure of a polypeptide

a) Circle the backbone in the polypeptide whose structure is shown here.

b) Identify the amino acids and write the primary structure of this polypeptide.

$$H_3\overset{+}{N}-CH(CH_3)-C(=O)-NH-CH(CH_2-C_3H_3N_2)-C(=O)-NH-CH(CH_2-COO^-)-C(=O)-NH-CH_2-C(=O)-NH-CH(CH_2-CH(CH_3)-CH_3)-C(=O)-O^-$$

SOLUTION

a) The backbone contains the peptide groups and the α-carbon atoms. The hydrogen atoms that are bonded to the α-carbon atoms are included.

$$H_3\overset{+}{N}-CH(CH_3)-C(=O)-NH-CH(CH_2-C_3H_3N_2)-C(=O)-NH-CH(CH_2-COO^-)-C(=O)-NH-CH_2-C(=O)-NH-CH(CH_2-CH(CH_3)-CH_3)-C(=O)-O^-$$

b) The remaining four groups of atoms are the side chains. By looking at Table 13.1, we can identify these four side chains as belonging to alanine, histidine, aspartic acid, and leucine. In addition, there is one α-carbon that is not attached to a side chain (the CH_2 group marked with the arrow). This carbon atom belongs to the amino acid glycine. Using the standard abbreviations for the amino acids, we write the primary structure of the polypeptide as Ala–His–Asp–Gly–Leu.

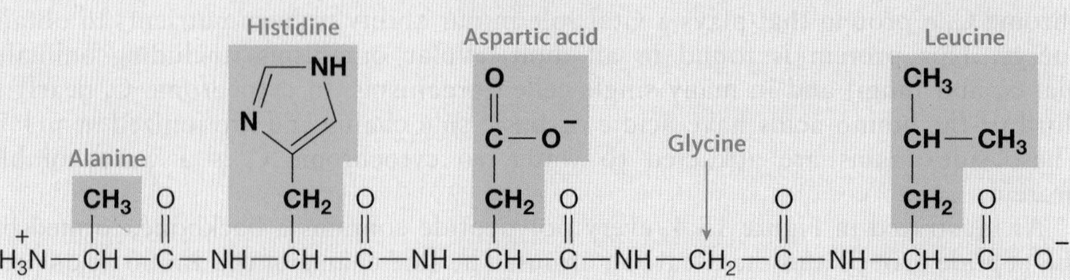

TRY IT YOURSELF: *Circle the backbone in the polypeptide whose structure is shown here, and write the primary structure of this polypeptide.*

HN (indole ring), OH, CH_3, SH

CH_2 O CH_2 O CH_3—CH O CH_2 O

$H_2\overset{+}{N}$—CH—C(=O)—NH—CH(CH_2)—C(=O)—NH—CH(CH_2OH)—C(=O)—NH—CH—C(=O)—NH—CH(CH_2SH)—C(=O)—O^-

For additional practice, try Core Problems 13.13 and 13.14.

The Alpha Helix and the Beta Sheet Are Common Secondary Structures

Chemists have determined the exact shapes of many proteins. At first glance, these structures seem to have no evident organization, but if we look more closely at the backbones of a variety of proteins, we can see two common features. The first of these is a spiral arrangement, called an **alpha (α) helix**. In the α-helix, the backbone forms a tight coil, with the side chains projecting outward. In the second arrangement, called the **beta (β) sheet**, the sections of the backbone line up beside one another in parallel rows, with the side chains projecting upward and downward. These two arrangements are called **secondary structures**, and they are illustrated in Figure 13.5.

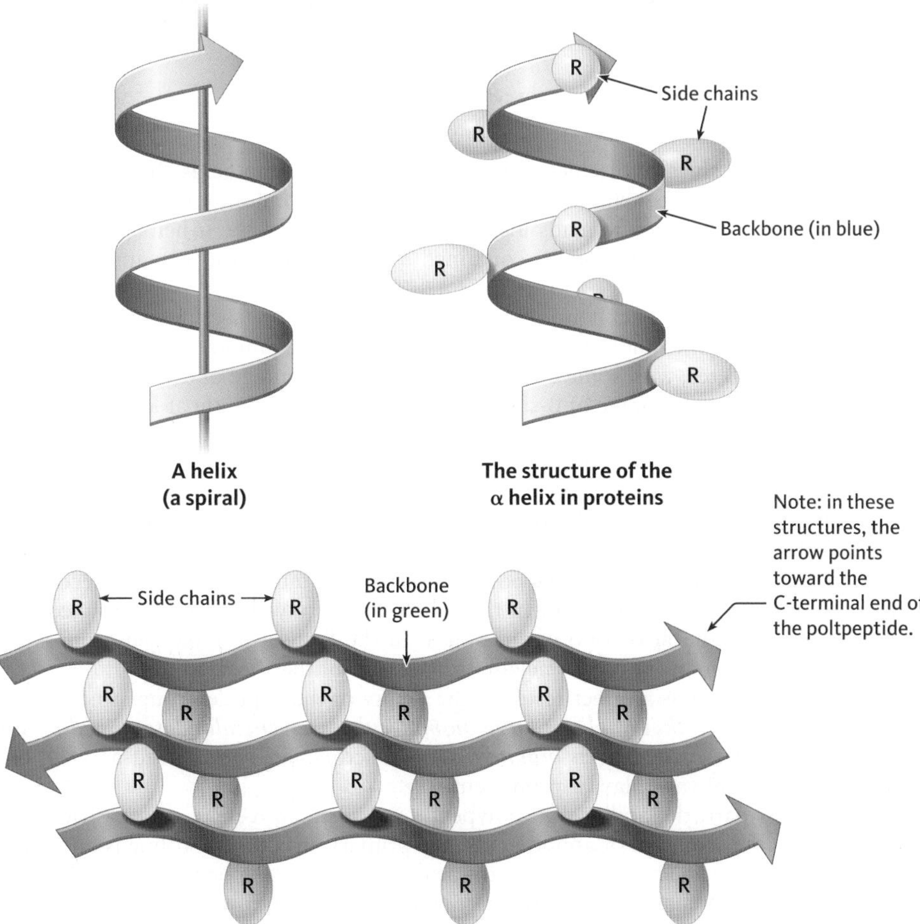

FIGURE 13.5 The structures of the α-helix and the β-sheet.

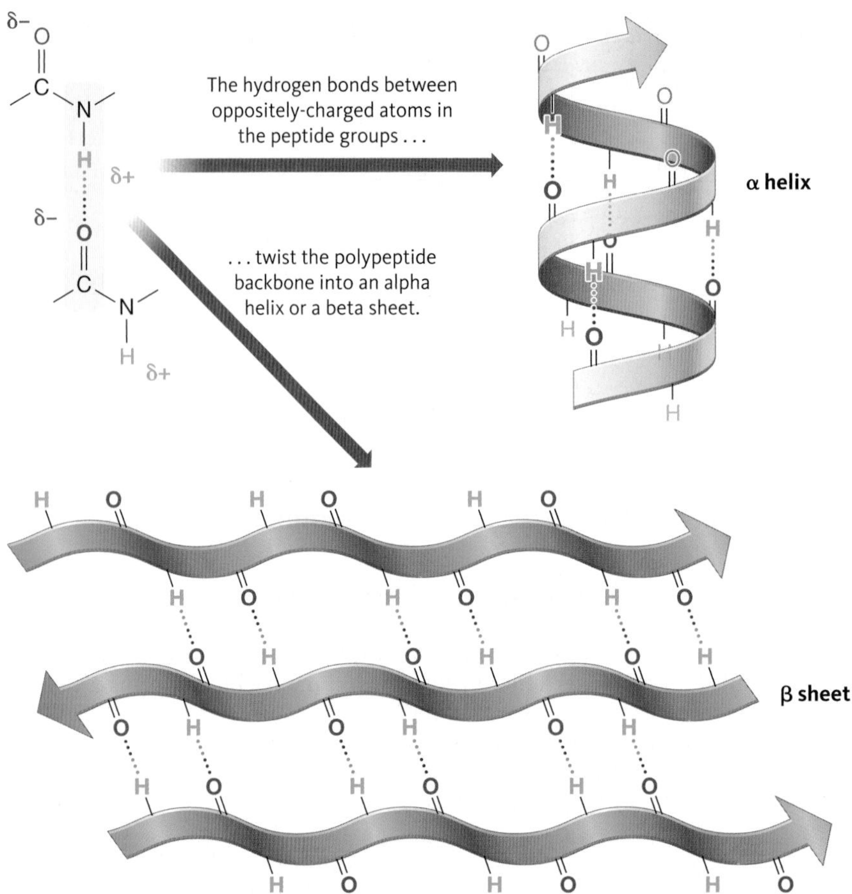

FIGURE 13.6 Hydrogen bonding between peptide groups.

All proteins are chiral molecules, because most of the amino acids from which they are built are chiral. The α-helix is a good illustration of the chirality of proteins. If proteins were built from D-amino acids instead of L-amino acids, the α-helix would spiral in the opposite direction. If proteins contained a mixture of D and L enantiomers, the α-helix could not form.

When we look at the backbone of a typical protein, we see sections of α-helix and β-sheet interspersed with more random arrangements of the amino acid chain. Proteins vary in their structures, with some containing a greater percentage of α-helices and some containing a greater percentage of β-sheets, but most proteins contain at least one region of α-helix or β-sheet.

What makes these features so common? *Proteins fold into α-helices and β-sheets because these structures allow peptide groups to form hydrogen bonds to each other*. There is a strong attraction between the oxygen atoms in peptide groups and the hydrogen atoms in other peptide groups. As these atoms pull toward each other to form hydrogen bonds, they force the backbone of the polypeptide to bend into one of the two secondary structures, as shown in Figure 13.6. In the α-helix, each oxygen atom is attracted to a hydrogen atom on the next loop of the spiral. In the β-sheet, the oxygen atom is attracted to a hydrogen atom on the neighboring strand of the sheet.

Secondary structure is a direct result of the ability of the peptide groups to form hydrogen bonds. In fact, *the shapes of large biomolecules are generally determined by the presence or absence of hydrogen bonding*. Other factors can be involved as well, but hydrogen bonding always plays a prominent role.

For the most part, the ability of a polypeptide to form an α-helix or a β-sheet does not depend on the sequence of amino acids (the primary structure). Proline is an exception, because the five-membered ring in proline does not allow the backbone to twist into the correct arrangement, and because there is no hydrogen atom bonded to nitrogen once proline is incorporated into the polypeptide, as shown in Figure 13.7. Proline tends to produce an abrupt bend or kink in an otherwise regular secondary structure. For

Proline incorporated into a β sheet

Two sections of backbone within a β sheet

Proline (zwitterion form)

A β-turn

FIGURE 13.7 The structure of proline and its role in the β-sheet structure.

example, β-sheets often contain proline at the point where the chain doubles back on itself, but they do not contain proline within the parallel strands inside the sheet. This abrupt turn is called a *β-turn*.

Collagen Forms a Triple Helix

In addition to its function in β-turns, proline plays a critical role in collagen, the protein that gives tissues such as ligaments, tendons, cartilage, bone, and skin their strength. Collagen contains a special type of structure called a **triple helix**. In the triple helix, three separate polypeptide chains wind around one another, held together by hydrogen bonds between peptide groups of adjacent chains. Roughly a third of the amino acids in collagen are glycine, which has a hydrogen atom as its side chain. The compact structure of glycine allows the three chains to pack together tightly. Nearly half of the remaining amino acids are proline or a slightly modified version of proline called hydroxyproline. These two amino acids prevent the collagen chains from forming an α-helix or β-sheet. The result is a long, strong fiber that is ideal for giving strength and flexibility to connective tissues. The structure of collagen is shown in Figure 13.8.

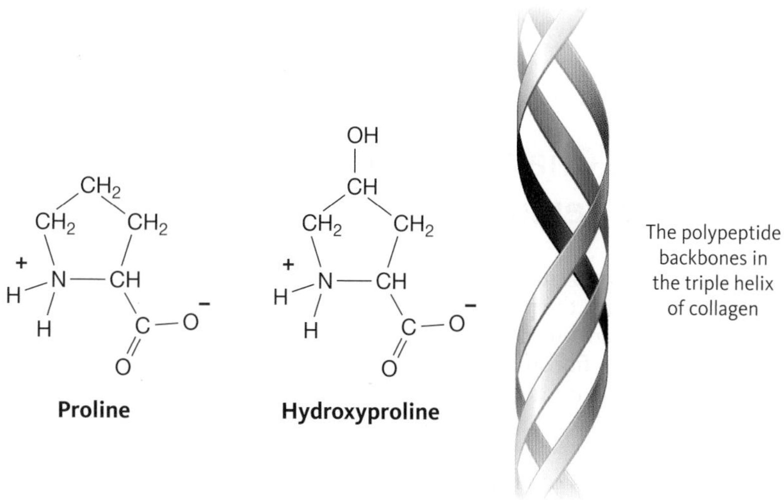

FIGURE 13.8 Proline, hydroxyproline, and the structure of collagen.

When our bodies make collagen, they do not use hydroxyproline directly. Instead, the protein is made using proline, and an enzyme then converts some of the proline in the polypeptide into hydroxyproline. This enzyme requires vitamin C in order to function. Most mammals can make vitamin C from other nutrients, but humans and a few other

Collagen gives skin its elasticity. Once we reach adulthood, our bodies start breaking down collagen, eventually giving us the characteristic wrinkles of advancing age.

Health Note: Roughly 80% of the dry weight of skin (after removing water) is collagen, which gives the skin its strength. As we age, the collagen in skin gradually breaks down and is replaced by other proteins, particularly in areas that are exposed to sunlight, such as the face and hands. The result is skin wrinkles that are associated with aging.

mammals cannot. If we do not get enough vitamin C from our diet, we cannot make adequate amounts of collagen. Some of the typical symptoms of severe vitamin C deficiency (called *scurvy*) are joint pain, bleeding from the gums and other mucous membranes, and loosened teeth. All of these are a direct result of the inability to make enough collagen to maintain healthy connective tissue.

CORE PROBLEMS

13.11 Draw the structures of the following molecules as they appear at pH 7:
a) the dipeptide that contains two molecules of methionine
b) the tripeptide Ala–Arg–Gly

13.12 Draw the structures of the following molecules as they appear at pH 7:
a) the dipeptide that contains two molecules of tyrosine
b) the tripeptide Ser–Glu–Cys

13.13 The structure of a tripeptide is shown here.
a) Circle the backbone of this tripeptide.
b) Which amino acids were used to make this tripeptide?
c) What is the N-terminal amino acid in this tripeptide?

```
  (benzene ring)
        |                      CH3
        |                       |
        |           SH         CH2
        |            |          |
       CH2  O       CH2  O  CH3—CH   O
 +      |   ||       |   ||     |    ||
H3N—CH—C—NH—CH—C—NH—CH—C—O⁻
```

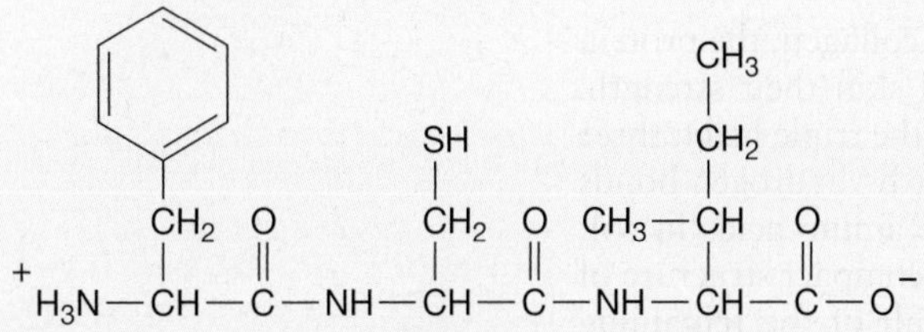

13.14 The structure of a tripeptide is shown here.
a) Circle the backbone of this tripeptide.
b) Which amino acids were used to make this tripeptide?
c) What is the C-terminal amino acid in this tripeptide?

```
        O
        ||
        C—NH2                       O
        |                           ||
       CH2           CH3            C—O⁻
        |             |             |
       CH2  O  CH3—CH   O          CH2  O
 +      |   ||       |   ||         |   ||
H3N—CH—C—NH—CH—C—NH—CH—C—O⁻
```

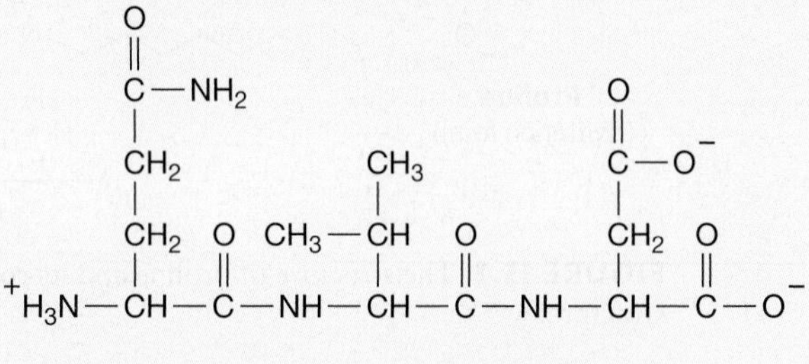

13.15 What is the primary structure of a protein?

13.16 When you write the primary structure of a protein, which is listed first, the C-terminal or the N-terminal amino acid?

13.17 Describe the shape of the polypeptide backbone and the locations of the side chains in an α-helix.

13.18 Describe the shape of the polypeptide backbone and the locations of the side chains in a β-sheet.

13.19 In a peptide group, which two atoms form hydrogen bonds with other peptide groups?

13.20 What are the charges on the atoms you gave in Problem 13.19?

13.21 What is a β-turn, and why is proline often found in a β-turn?

13.22 Why can't proline form an α-helix, and why is this important to the structure of collagen?

OBJECTIVE: *Describe the side chain interactions that produce the tertiary structure of a protein.*

13.3 Side Chain Interactions and Tertiary Structure

Proteins can be divided into three broad classes, based on their shape and their environment. In **globular proteins**, the polypeptide chain is folded into a compact shape, similar to a tangled ball of string. Most water-soluble proteins are globular, including enzymes and transport proteins. In **fibrous proteins**, the polypeptide adopts a long, narrow shape. Fibrous proteins generally do not dissolve in water. The proteins that make up tendons, ligaments, hair, and silk are fibrous proteins. **Membrane proteins** are anchored in the membranes that surround cells and organelles, and they adopt a variety of irregular structures. The three classes of proteins are illustrated in Figure 13.9.

Most fibrous proteins fold into one of the basic types of structures we saw in Section 13.2. However, globular and membrane proteins fold into a bewildering variety of shapes. The structure of a globular or membrane protein usually contains some regions of α-helix and β-sheet, but it also contains regions that do not adopt either of these secondary structures. Globular proteins and membrane proteins fold in a variety of ways because their amino acid side chains interact with one another and with the surroundings. The final shape of a protein, which is the result of all of the interactions involving side chains, is called the **tertiary structure** of the protein.

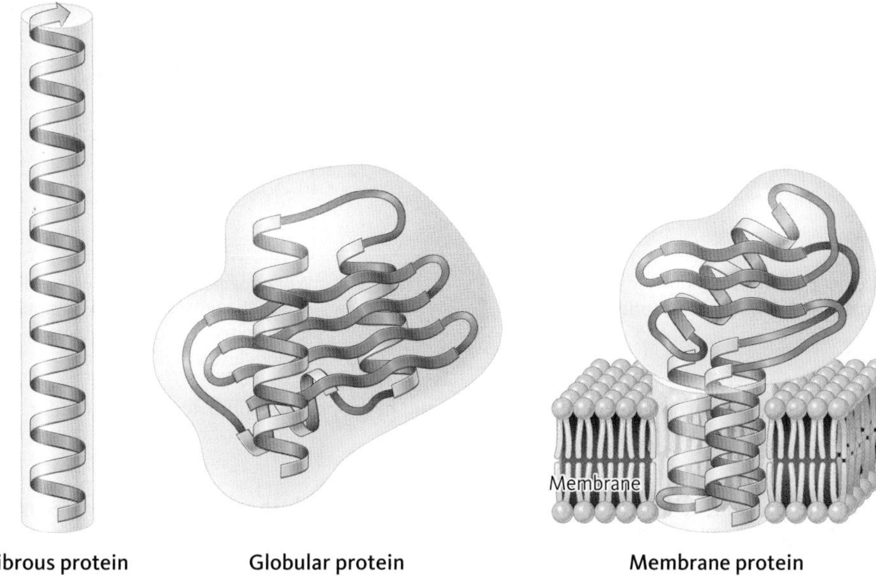
Membrane
Fibrous protein
Globular protein
Membrane protein

FIGURE 13.9 The three classes of proteins.

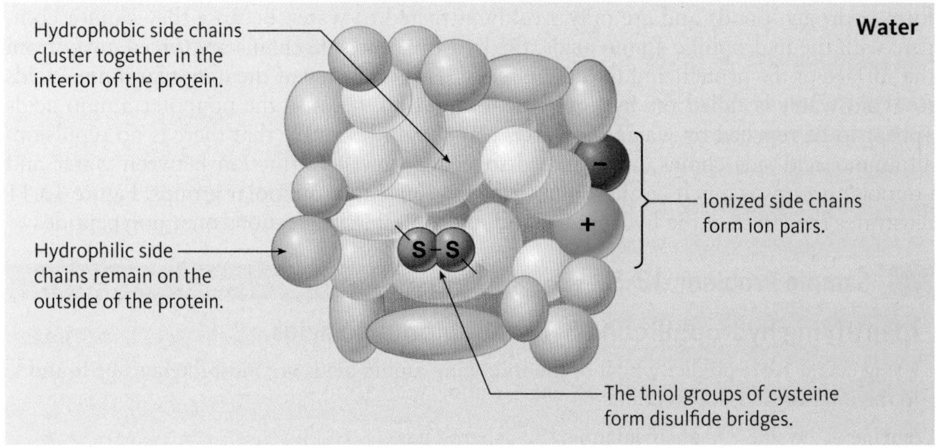
Hydrophobic side chains cluster together in the interior of the protein.
Water
Ionized side chains form ion pairs.
Hydrophilic side chains remain on the outside of the protein.
S–S
The thiol groups of cysteine form disulfide bridges.

FIGURE 13.10 Tertiary structural features in a globular protein.

Hair, silkworm cocoons (used to make silk clothing), and spider webs are examples of fibrous proteins.

We will focus our attention on globular proteins, most of which are soluble in water. When chemists examine the structures of a wide range of globular proteins, they see several consistent tendencies:

- Most of the hydrophobic amino acids are clustered together in the interior of the folded protein.
- Most of the amino acids on the surface of the protein are hydrophilic, and many are ionized at pH 7.
- Ionized amino acids often occur in pairs, with an acidic side chain (which is negatively charged at pH 7) close to a basic side chain (which is positively charged at pH 7).
- Many of the cysteine side chains are bonded together to form disulfide groups.

Figure 13.10 illustrates these structural features of globular proteins.

Side Chains Cluster Together Based on Their Ability to Hydrogen Bond to Water

The tendency of hydrophobic side chains to cluster in the interior of a protein is a dramatic illustration of the importance of hydrogen bonding. When a protein is dissolved in water, the hydrophilic side chains are attracted to water and pulled toward the exte-

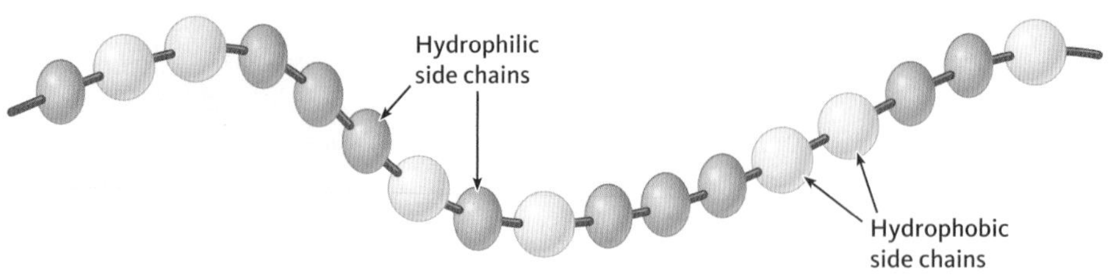

Polar (hydrophilic) and nonpolar (hydrophobic) amino acids are arranged randomly in a polypeptide.

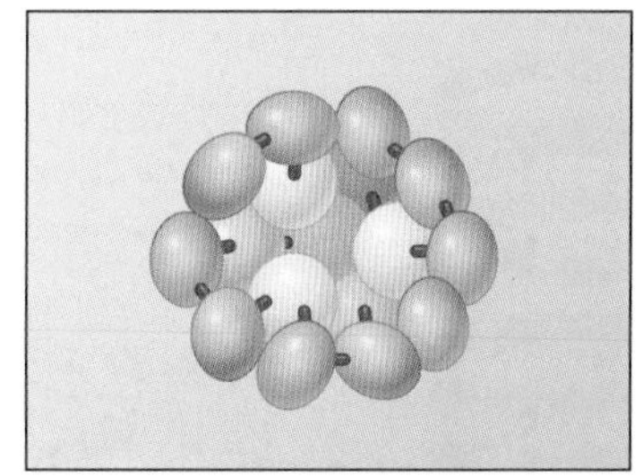
When the polypeptide is surrounded by water, the polar side chains are pulled to the exterior and the nonpolar side chains cluster in the interior.

FIGURE 13.11 The arrangement of hydrophilic and hydrophobic amino acids in a globular protein.

rior of the protein, where they form hydrogen bonds with the surrounding water molecules. The attraction of the polar side chains to water is called the **hydrophilic interaction**. This attraction is particularly strong when the side chain is ionized, so the acidic and basic amino acids (which are ionized at pH 7) are almost always found on the outside of the protein.

The nonpolar side chains of the hydrophobic amino acids, on the other hand, cannot form hydrogen bonds and are only weakly attracted to water. Because they cannot compete with the hydrophilic amino acids, the hydrophobic side chains are forced away from the surface of the protein and into the interior. This tendency of the nonpolar amino acids to avoid water is called the **hydrophobic interaction**, because the nonpolar amino acids appear to be repelled by water. However, you should be aware that there is no repulsion: all amino acid side chains are attracted to water, but the attraction between water and nonpolar groups is much weaker than that between water and polar groups. Figure 13.11 illustrates the effect of the hydrophilic and hydrophobic interactions on a polypeptide.

Sample Problem **13.5**

Identifying hydrophilic and hydrophobic amino acids

Using Table 13.1, predict which of the following amino acids are most likely to be found in the interior of a polypeptide:

leucine   lysine   phenylalanine   asparagine

SOLUTION

The amino acids with hydrophobic side chains are the most likely to be found in the interior of the protein. From Table 13.1, we see that leucine and phenylalanine have hydrophobic side chains, so they will probably be in the interior of the polypeptide. Asparagine and lysine have hydrophilic side chains, so they are attracted to the surrounding water molecules and are less likely to remain in the interior.

TRY IT YOURSELF: *Which of the following amino acids are most likely to be found on the surface of a polypeptide?*

methionine   aspartic acid   tryptophan   arginine

For additional practice, try Core Problems 13.25 and 13.26.

Side Chains Interact with One Another in Several Ways

Side chains also interact with one another, and these interactions contribute to the tertiary structure of a protein, as illustrated in Figure 13.12. First, some of the hydrophilic side chains form hydrogen bonds with each other, rather than with the surrounding water. This attraction between hydrophilic groups is called *side-chain hydrogen bonding*. As a result, the interior of many proteins contains clusters of hydrophilic amino acids that are separate from the hydrophobic chains. Second, the ionized side chains of acids and bases attract each other. Remember that acidic side chains form anions at pH 7,

Lysine and aspartic acid form an ion pair **(ion-ion attraction).**
Two serine side chains form a hydrogen bond **(side chain hydrogen bonding).**
Two cysteine side chains form a **disulfide bridge.**

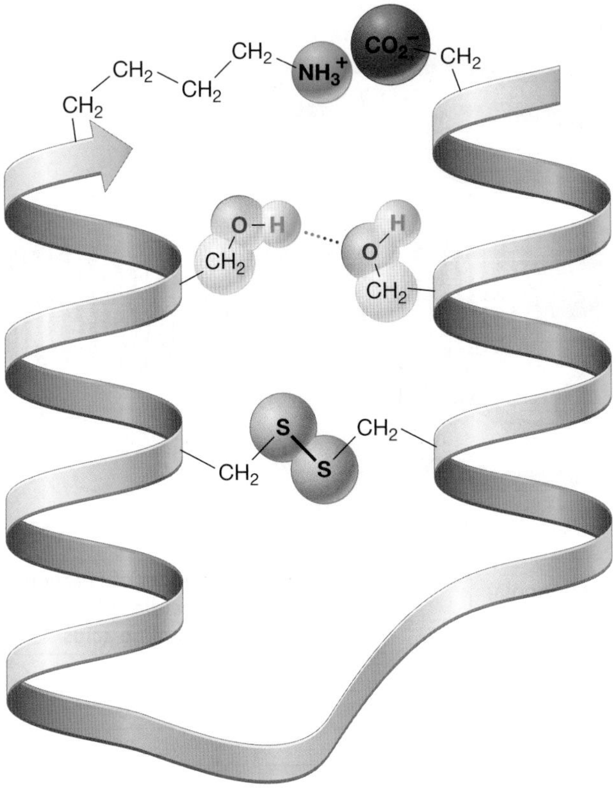

FIGURE 13.12 Side chain interactions in the tertiary structure of a protein.

while basic side chains form cations. These oppositely charged ions attract each other, just as they do in an ionic compound such as NaCl. The formation of ion pairs between acidic and basic amino acids is called the *ion–ion attraction.*

The third type of side chain interaction is the reaction of two cysteine side chains to form a *disulfide bridge.* As we saw in Chapter 10, two thiol groups can react to form a disulfide. This is an oxidation reaction, so it requires either O_2 or a redox coenzyme (normally NAD^+) to remove the hydrogen atoms from the thiol groups. Disulfide bridges can link amino acids within a single polypeptide, or amino acids from two different polypeptides.

Health Note: Hair and fingernails are built almost entirely from a protein called keratin. The skin also contains a layer of keratin, which thickens in response to abrasion, forming calluses on skin that is exposed to unusual wear and tear. Keratin is a fibrous protein that contains many disulfide bridges, which help make it strong and water insoluble. Humans and other animals cannot digest keratin, but certain fungi can feed on this protein, causing fungal infections such as athlete's foot.

Sample Problem 13.6

Identifying interactions between side chains

Which interactions occur between the following?

a) the side chains of arginine and glutamic acid

b) water and the side chain of tyrosine

c) the side chains of isoleucine and leucine

SOLUTION

a) Arginine is a basic amino acid, while glutamic acid is acidic. At pH 7, their side chains are oppositely charged and form an ion pair.

b) Tyrosine contains a hydrophilic side chain, so it can form hydrogen bonds with water (the hydrophilic interaction).

c) Isoleucine and leucine contain nonpolar side chains, so they tend to cluster together in the interior of the protein (the hydrophobic interaction).

TRY IT YOURSELF: *Which interactions occur between the following?*

a) two cysteine side chains

b) the side chains of threonine and asparagine

For additional practice, try Core Problems 13.33 and 13.34.

Exterior of the cell

Extracellular region

Cell membrane

Trans-membrane region

Intracellular region

Interior of the cell

Region	Number of nonpolar amino acids	Number of polar amino acids	Number of charged (acidic or basic) amino acids
Intracellular	16	12	11
Trans-membrane	17	2	0
Extracellular	21	27	22

FIGURE 13.13 The structure and composition of glycophorin.

Health Note: Glycophorin and other membrane proteins bond to the carbohydrates that determine a person's blood group. Type A blood has one carbohydrate bonded to the membrane proteins, while type B has a slightly different carbohydrate. Type AB blood contains both of these carbohydrates, and type O blood contains a smaller carbohydrate that does not produce an immune response.

Membrane Proteins Contain Large Numbers of Nonpolar Amino Acids

Not all proteins are in contact with water. Many proteins are embedded in membranes, the flexible outer layers of cells and organelles. These proteins are in a hydrophobic environment because membranes are composed of molecules that have large nonpolar regions. As a result, the part of the protein that is embedded in the membrane has a high proportion of hydrophobic amino acids on its surface. A good example of a membrane protein is *glycophorin,* which carries some of the chemical compounds that determine blood group. The primary structure of glycophorin contains a region in which 17 out of 19 amino acids are nonpolar. This section of the protein forms an α-helix that is embedded in the outer membrane of red blood cells. The portions of the protein on either side of this hydrophobic region are in contact with water, and they contain a mixture of hydrophobic and hydrophilic amino acids. The structure and composition of glycophorin are shown in Figure 13.13.

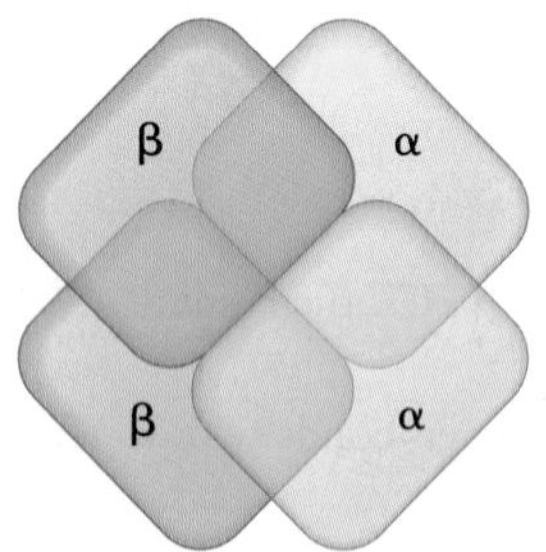

A molecule of hemoglobin contains two α chains and two β chains.

FIGURE 13.14 The quaternary structure of hemoglobin.

Some Proteins Have a Quaternary Structure

Many proteins contain two or more polypeptide chains. These chains are attracted to one another by the same types of interactions we have already encountered: hydrogen bonds, hydrophobic interactions, ion–ion attraction, and disulfide bridges. **Quaternary structure** is the way in which two or more polypeptides join to form an active protein. For example, the quaternary structure of hemoglobin (the protein that carries oxygen in blood) consists of four separate polypeptides, called the α and β chains. Each of the two α chains contains 141 amino acids, while each of the two β chains contains 146 amino acids. The four polypeptide chains of hemoglobin bind tightly to one another, as shown in Figure 13.14.

Health Note: In people who suffer from sickle cell disease, the beta chain of hemoglobin contains valine instead of glutamic acid at the sixth position. This change allows hemoglobin molecules to clump together when the concentration of oxygen in the blood drops, forcing the red blood cells into a long, narrow shape (the sickle shape). The spleen destroys the damaged cells faster than they can be replaced, so people with sickle cell disease also suffer from anemia (low oxygen-carrying capacity).

The same types of forces that create the tertiary structure also hold the quaternary structure of a protein together. Hydrophobic interactions are particularly important; the surfaces of the individual polypeptides generally contain many nonpolar side chains, and the quaternary structure allows these side chains to avoid contact with water.

Table 13.2 summarizes the types of protein structure that we have encountered, and Figure 13.15 illustrates each type of structure. The actual shape of a protein is the result of all of its types of structure.

TABLE 13.2 The Types of Structure in a Protein

Type of Structure	Description	Interactions That Produce This Structure	Potential Participating Amino Acids
Primary	Sequence of amino acids	Covalent bonds (the peptide bonds between amino acids)	All
Secondary	Folding and coiling of specific regions of a polypeptide (α-helix and β-sheet)	Hydrogen bonds between oxygen and hydrogen atoms in peptide groups	All
Tertiary	Long-range folding of the entire polypeptide due to side chain interactions	Hydrophilic interaction (hydrogen bonds between side chains and water)	All hydrophilic
		Hydrophobic interaction (tendency of nonpolar side chains to avoid water)	All hydrophobic
		Hydrogen bonds between side chains	All hydrophilic
		Ion–ion attraction	Acidic and basic
		Disulfide bridge (covalent bond between two sulfur atoms)	Cysteine only
Quaternary	Clustering of two or more separate polypeptide chains	Similar to tertiary structure (the hydrophobic interaction is particularly important)	Similar to tertiary structure

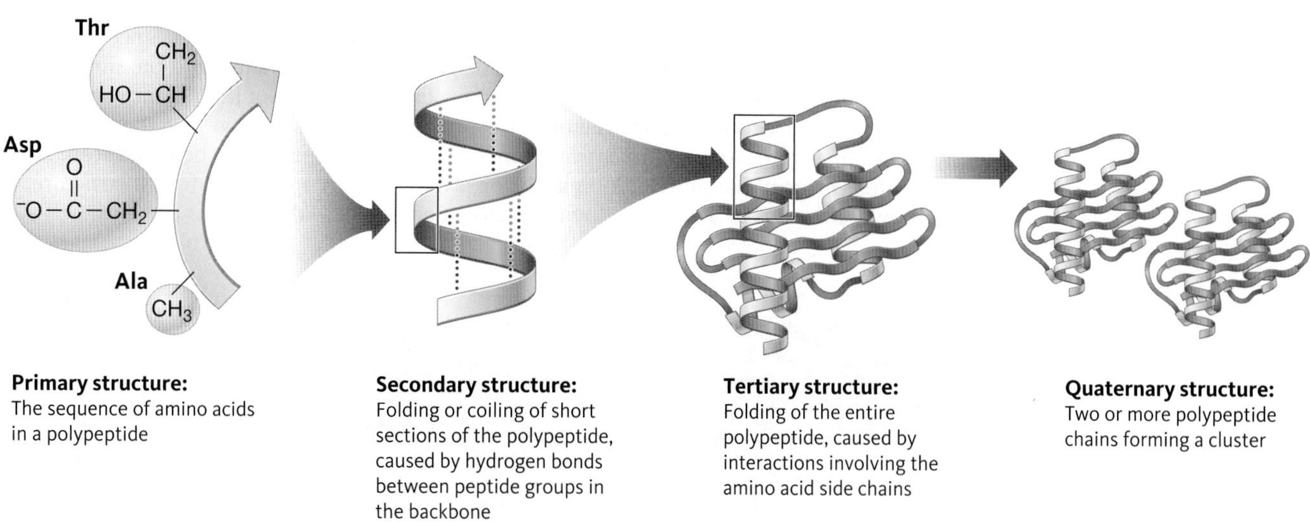

Primary structure: The sequence of amino acids in a polypeptide

Secondary structure: Folding or coiling of short sections of the polypeptide, caused by hydrogen bonds between peptide groups in the backbone

Tertiary structure: Folding of the entire polypeptide, caused by interactions involving the amino acid side chains

Quaternary structure: Two or more polypeptide chains forming a cluster

FIGURE 13.15 The types of protein structure.

CORE PROBLEMS

13.23 Describe the shape of a globular protein.

13.24 Describe the shape of a fibrous protein.

13.25 Which of the following amino acids is the most likely to be found in the interior of a protein? Explain your answer.
a) glycine b) phenylalanine
c) glutamic acid d) serine

13.26 Which of the following amino acids is the most likely to be found on the exterior of a protein? Explain your answer.
a) methionine b) glutamine
c) arginine d) valine

13.27 Draw structures to show the two ways that the side chain of tyrosine can form a hydrogen bond with water.

13.28 Draw structures to show the two ways that the side chain of threonine can form a hydrogen bond with water.

13.29 Draw structures showing two ways to form hydrogen bonds between the side chains of serine and asparagine.

13.30 Draw structures showing two ways to form hydrogen bonds between the side chains of tyrosine and threonine.

13.31 Which of the following amino acids can form an ion pair with lysine at pH 7?
a) arginine b) alanine c) aspartic acid

13.32 Which of the following amino acids can form an ion pair with glutamic acid at pH 7?
a) glutamine b) glycine c) arginine

13.33 What interactions occur between the following?
a) the side chains of asparagine and threonine
b) the side chains of two molecules of methionine
c) a water molecule and the side chain of threonine

13.34 What interactions occur between the following?
a) the side chains of tryptophan and alanine
b) the side chains of lysine and glutamic acid
c) the side chains of serine and glutamine

13.35 For each of the following statements, tell whether it describes the primary, secondary, tertiary, or quaternary structure of a protein:
a) Isocitrate dehydrogenase is made from eight identical polypeptides.
b) Bovine ribonuclease contains five molecules of aspartic acid, all of which are on the exterior of the protein.
c) Bovine ribonuclease contains three sections of α-helix.
d) The interior of citrate synthase contains a cluster made up of the hydrophobic amino acids methionine, phenylalanine, leucine, and alanine.

13.36 For each of the following statements, tell whether it describes the primary, secondary, tertiary, or quaternary structure of the protein:
a) The polypeptide chain of bovine ribonuclease contains four disulfide bridges.
b) In chymotrypsin, a serine side chain forms a hydrogen bond to a histidine side chain.
c) The first five amino acids in myoglobin are glycine, leucine, serine, aspartic acid, and glycine, in that order.
d) Glutathione reductase contains a large region of β-sheet.

OBJECTIVE: *Describe the factors that cause protein denaturation.*

13.4 Protein Denaturation

As we have seen, the structure of a protein is the result of a delicate balance of a large number of interactions involving the peptide groups, the side chains, and the surrounding environment. Any change in the protein's environment can disrupt this balance and change the protein structure. If the structure of a protein changes so much that the protein becomes unable to carry out its normal function, the protein is said to be **denatured.** A denatured protein may unfold completely, or it may shift to a different folded structure, as shown in Figure 13.16. The following factors denature a wide range of proteins.

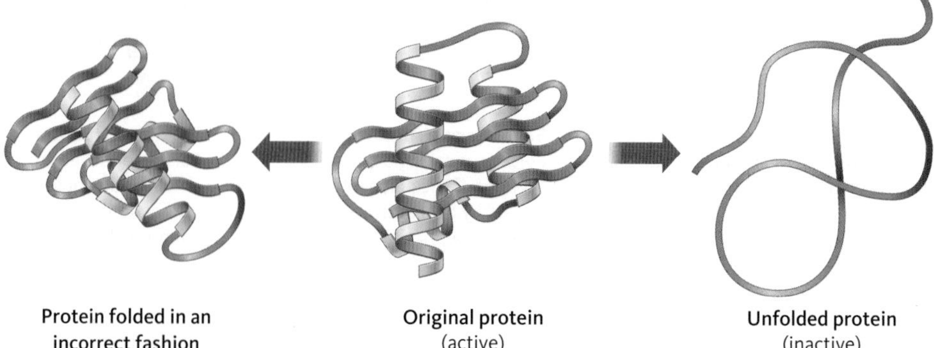

FIGURE 13.16 The denaturing of a protein.

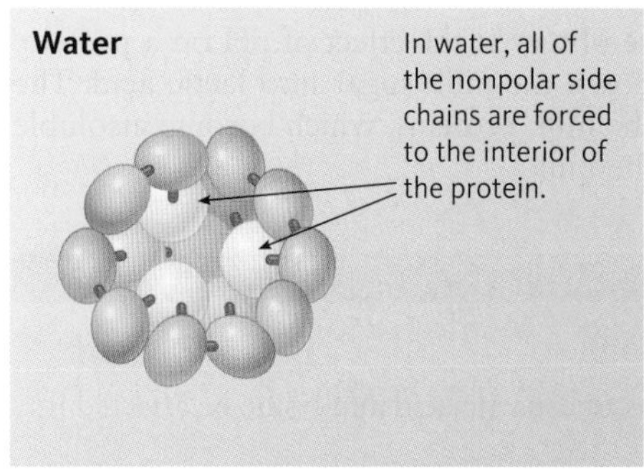

Water
In water, all of the nonpolar side chains are forced to the interior of the protein.

Protein dissolved in water (active form)

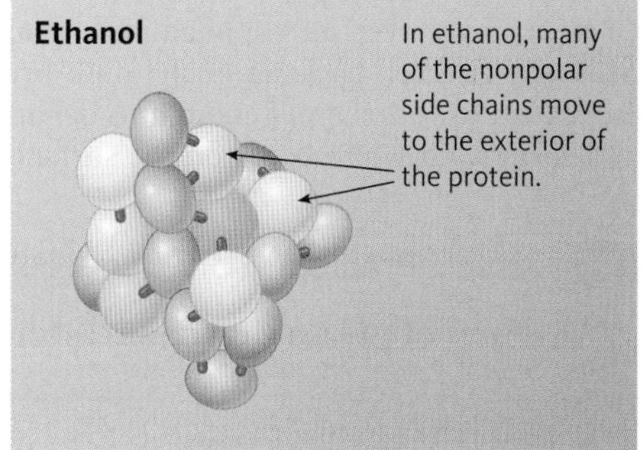

Ethanol
In ethanol, many of the nonpolar side chains move to the exterior of the protein.

Protein dissolved in ethanol (denatured)

FIGURE 13.17 Denaturing a protein by changing the solvent.

1. *Changing the solvent.* If we dissolve a protein in an organic solvent, we disrupt the balance of hydrophilic and hydrophobic interactions, because organic solvents do not form hydrogen bonds as strongly as water does. For example, if we dissolve a protein in ethanol instead of water, the polar side chains are less strongly attracted to the ethanol than they are to water. Since the polar side chains also attract one another, they begin to cluster together. At the same time, the nonpolar side chains are no longer forced to the interior of the protein. In an extreme case, the entire structure can turn inside out, with the polar amino acids moving to the center and the nonpolar amino acids moving to the exterior. This is illustrated in Figure 13.17.
2. *Changing the pH.* If a protein contains acidic or basic side chains and we change the pH of its surroundings, we disrupt the ion–ion interactions. For example, at pH 7, the side chains of the acidic amino acids are negatively charged ions. If we add enough acid to lower the pH of the solution to 2, these side chains gain H^+ and become electrically neutral. As a result, we replace the strong ion–ion attraction between acidic and basic side chains with a weak hydrogen bond, as shown in Figure 13.18. Furthermore, acidic side chains repel each other at pH 7 because they have the same charge, but they do not repel each other at pH 2.

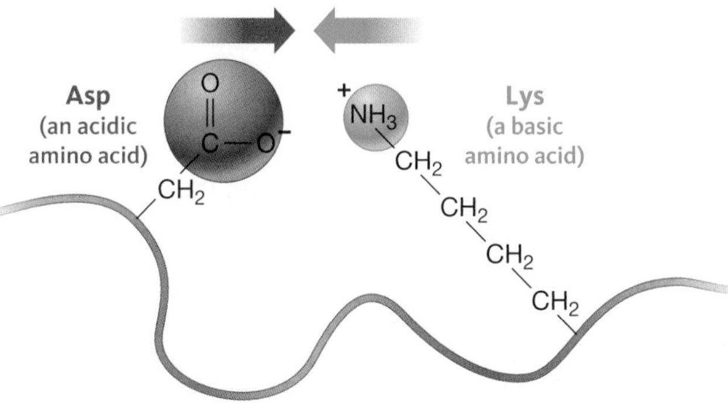

At pH 7, aspartic acid and lysine have opposite charges and form an ion pair.

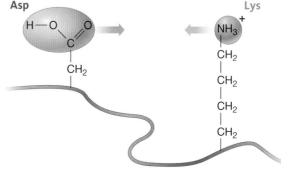

Asp
H—O
O
C
CH2
Lys
+
NH3
CH2
CH2
CH2
CH2

At pH 2, aspartic acid and lysine attract one another, but they cannot form an ion pair.

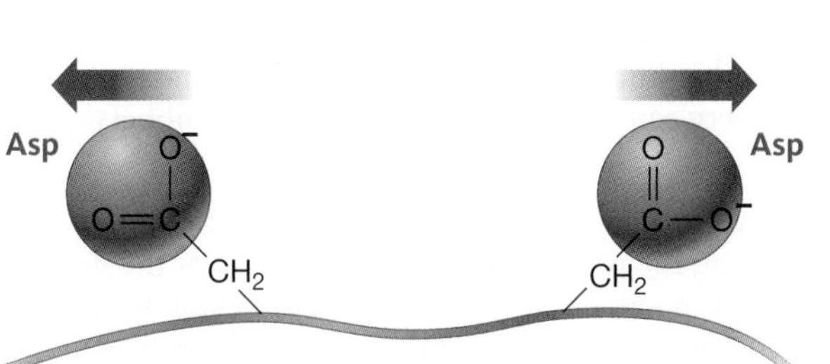

At pH 7, aspartic acid side chains have the same charge, so they repel one another.

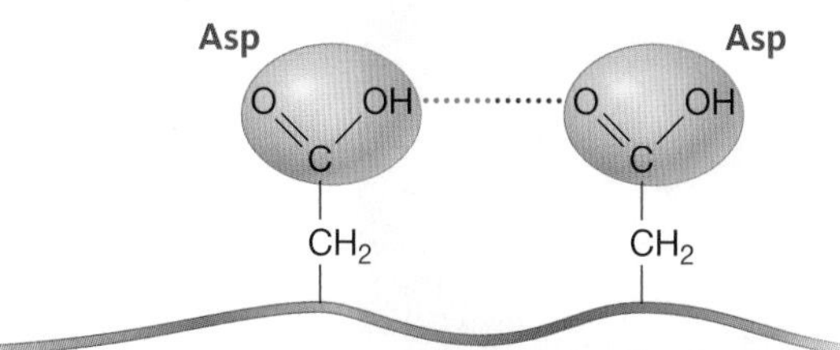

At pH 2, aspartic acid has no net charge, so the side chains can form a hydrogen bond.

FIGURE 13.18 The effect of pH on ion–ion interactions in a protein.

If you have ever seen spoiled milk, you have observed the effect of pH on a protein. Milk spoils when bacteria in the milk break down the milk sugar into lactic acid. The lactic acid lowers the pH enough to denature the milk proteins, which become insoluble and form solid white curds on the surface of the milk.

Sample Problem 13.7

The effect of pH on side chain interactions

How will the interaction between the side chains of aspartic acid and lysine be affected if the pH is raised from 7 to 12?

SOLUTION

At pH 7, aspartic acid and lysine attract each other strongly, because aspartic acid has a negatively charged side chain and lysine has a positively charged side chain. Raising the pH to 12 makes the solution strongly basic. In a basic solution, the side chain of lysine loses its extra H^+ and becomes uncharged. As a result, we no longer have the ion–ion attraction between the two side chains, so the attraction becomes much weaker.

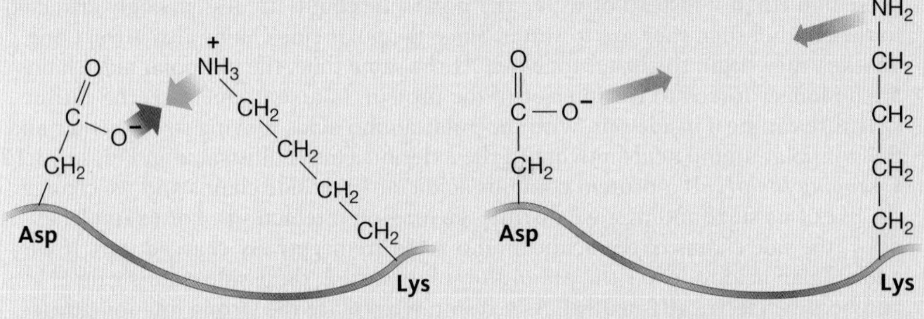

At pH 7 there is a strong ion-ion attraction. At pH 12 the attraction is much weaker.

TRY IT YOURSELF: *How will the interaction between two lysine side chains be affected if the pH is raised from 7 to 12?*

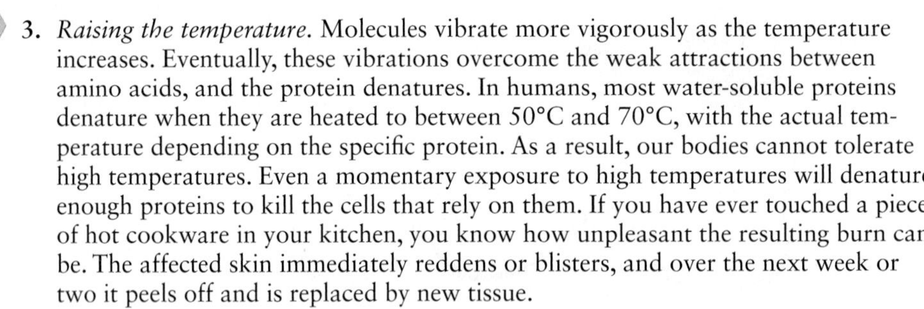

3. *Raising the temperature.* Molecules vibrate more vigorously as the temperature increases. Eventually, these vibrations overcome the weak attractions between amino acids, and the protein denatures. In humans, most water-soluble proteins denature when they are heated to between 50°C and 70°C, with the actual temperature depending on the specific protein. As a result, our bodies cannot tolerate high temperatures. Even a momentary exposure to high temperatures will denature enough proteins to kill the cells that rely on them. If you have ever touched a piece of hot cookware in your kitchen, you know how unpleasant the resulting burn can be. The affected skin immediately reddens or blisters, and over the next week or two it peels off and is replaced by new tissue.

Another familiar example is the change in the white of an egg when it is cooked. Egg white is a very concentrated solution of protein (albumin) in water. The normal, folded form of egg albumin is water soluble, but when the albumin is heated, it denatures. The resulting open chains attract one another and form an insoluble tangled mass of protein. The water is trapped in the spaces between chains, producing the soft, rubbery texture of cooked egg.

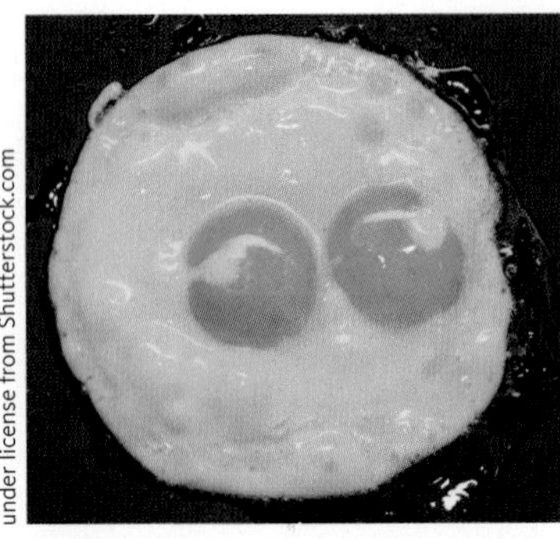

Eggs solidify when they are cooked because the protein in the egg white denatures, making it insoluble in water.

4. *Violent agitation.* The effect of vigorously stirring or beating a solution of a protein is similar to that of heating the protein. The agitation disrupts the delicate balance of attractions between amino acids, allowing the protein chain to unfold. If you have ever made whipped cream, you have seen this effect. The whipping converts the protein in milk from a soluble to an insoluble form, trapping the remaining liquid and producing the semisolid consistency of whipped cream.
5. *Adding ionic substances.* High concentrations of ions interfere with the ion–ion attraction between acidic and basic side chains of proteins. For instance, we can

denature many proteins by simply dissolving them in concentrated salt water. Soaps (which we encountered in Chapter 12) and detergents are particularly effective, because they contain both ionic regions and nonpolar regions, allowing them to interfere with the hydrophilic and hydrophobic interactions as well as the ion–ion attractions in a protein.

Sodium laurate
(a soap)

Sodium lauryl sulfate
(a detergent)

In addition, ions of heavy metals such as lead and mercury are strongly attracted to sulfur. These ions can break the disulfide bridges between cysteine side chains, causing the polypeptide to unfold. As a result, compounds containing lead and mercury denature a range of essential proteins, making them very toxic to most organisms. Interestingly, foods with a high content of soluble protein (such as egg white and milk) are effective initial treatments for mercury poisoning, because the protein binds tightly to the mercury, preventing it from being absorbed into the bloodstream.

Because proteins are so sensitive to their surroundings, all organisms must be able to control the concentrations of ions and the pH inside their cells. We have already seen that our bodies contain a number of chemicals that act as buffers, maintaining the pH in the correct range for the proteins. Likewise, all organisms must be able to prevent their temperature from rising too high. Humans and other warm-blooded animals cool themselves by breathing rapidly or perspiring, both of which allow water to evaporate rapidly, removing excess heat from the body. In addition, most animals avoid places that are subject to extreme temperatures. Plants and many microorganisms cannot move, so they can only live in locations where the temperature does not rise too high.

In health care, we exploit the sensitivity of proteins in a variety of ways. Autoclaves use high temperatures to sterilize dental and surgical instruments. Alcohol kills most microorganisms on skin, and it is used to prepare the skin for injections. Antibacterial soaps contain detergents that both disrupt membranes and denature proteins. Mercury-containing compounds such as thimerosal are used to prevent bacterial growth in vaccines, although concerns about the toxicity of mercury have led to the removal of thimerosal from most vaccines given to children. In all of these cases, we take advantage of the inability of denatured proteins to carry out their normal functions.

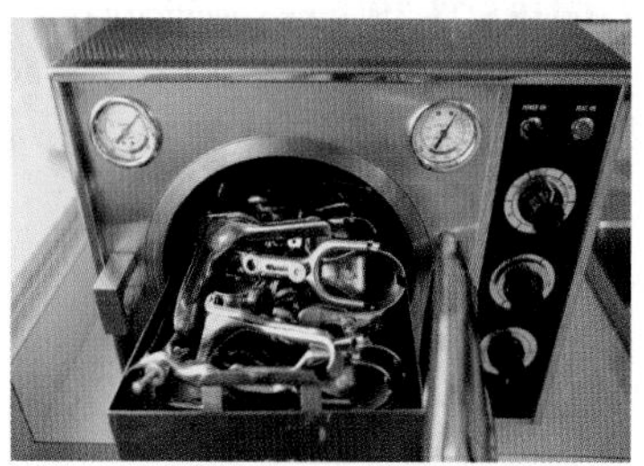

Autoclaves use high temperature steam to kill microorganisms by denaturing their proteins.

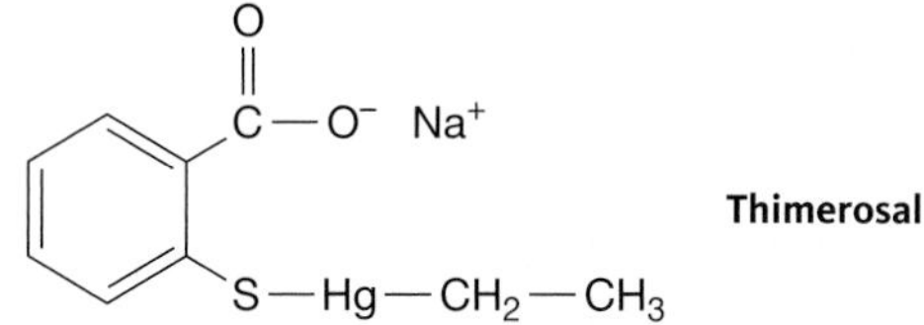

CORE PROBLEMS

13.37 What happens to a protein when it is denatured?

13.38 Which of the following are disrupted when a protein is denatured?
a) primary structure b) secondary structure
c) tertiary structure d) quaternary structure

13.39 Why does each of the following conditions denature proteins?
a) adding a solution of HCl
b) adding a solution that contains Hg^{2+} ions
c) agitating the protein solution

13.40 Why does each of the following conditions denature proteins?
a) adding ethanol
b) adding a concentrated solution of NaCl
c) heating the protein to 70°C

OBJECTIVE: *Describe how an enzyme catalyzes a reaction, the factors that affect enzyme activity, and how a cell regulates the activity of its enzymes.*

13.5 Enzyme Structure and Function

The range of functions of proteins in a human is remarkable for its diversity. Proteins allow us to move, give us shape and structure, catalyze the reactions that occur in our bodies, protect us from pathogens, move water-insoluble nutrients through our bodies, carry signals from one part of our bodies to another, and on and on. In this section, we examine the most pervasive and diverse class of proteins, the enzymes.

You have seen enzymes a number of times as you learned about organic reactions in Chapters 9 through 12. Enzymes are catalysts, molecules that speed up a reaction without being consumed in the reaction. In addition, enzymes often force a reaction to produce just one of several possible products. For example, Figure 13.19 shows an important reaction in the metabolism of fatty acids, long-chain carboxylic acids that our bodies use to build fats and other lipids. In this reaction, an enzyme called *stearoyl-CoA desaturase* removes two hydrogen atoms from a thioester made from stearic acid. This reaction could create a double bond at any of sixteen possible locations in the long hydrocarbon chain, but the enzyme only forms one of the sixteen potential products.

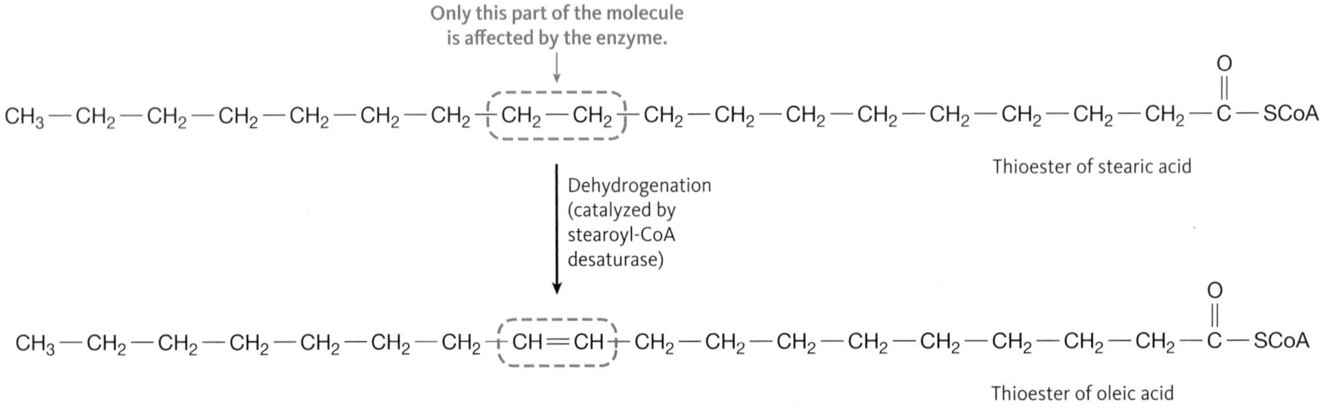

Only this part of the molecule is affected by the enzyme.

$$CH_3-CH_2-CH_2-CH_2-CH_2-CH_2-CH_2-\boxed{CH_2-CH_2}-CH_2-CH_2-CH_2-CH_2-CH_2-CH_2-CH_2-CH_2-\overset{O}{\overset{\|}{C}}-SCoA$$

Thioester of stearic acid

Dehydrogenation (catalyzed by stearoyl-CoA desaturase)

$$CH_3-CH_2-CH_2-CH_2-CH_2-CH_2-CH_2-\boxed{CH=CH}-CH_2-CH_2-CH_2-CH_2-CH_2-CH_2-CH_2-CH_2-\overset{O}{\overset{\|}{C}}-SCoA$$

Thioester of oleic acid

FIGURE 13.19 The specificity of stearoyl-CoA desaturase, an enzyme.

Sample Problem 13.8

Enzyme specificity

Our bodies make glutamine by condensing glutamic acid with an ammonium ion, as shown here. This reaction is catalyzed by an enzyme called glutamine synthetase. Must this enzyme select one particular product in this reaction? Explain your answer.

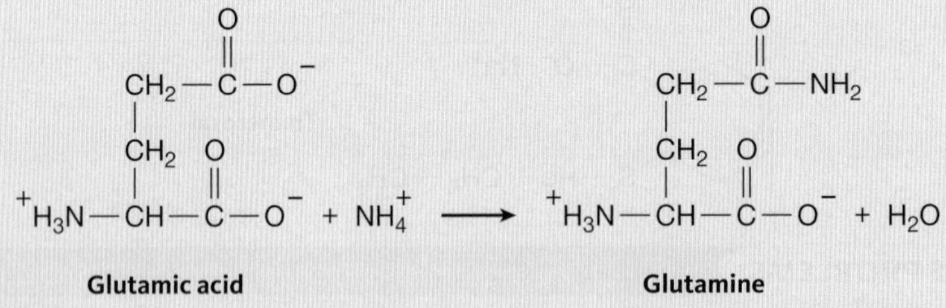

$$\underset{\text{Glutamic acid}}{{}^{+}H_3N-\underset{\underset{\underset{\displaystyle CH_2-\overset{O}{\overset{\|}{C}}-O^-}{|}}{\displaystyle CH_2}}{\overset{}{CH}}-\overset{O}{\overset{\|}{C}}-O^-} + NH_4^+ \longrightarrow \underset{\text{Glutamine}}{{}^{+}H_3N-\underset{\underset{\underset{\displaystyle CH_2-\overset{O}{\overset{\|}{C}}-NH_2}{|}}{\displaystyle CH_2}}{CH}-\overset{O}{\overset{\|}{C}}-O^-} + H_2O$$

SOLUTION

Glutamic acid contains two carboxylate groups, and the ammonium ion could react with either one of them. Therefore, glutamine synthetase must select the correct product from the two possibilities. The structure of the other product is

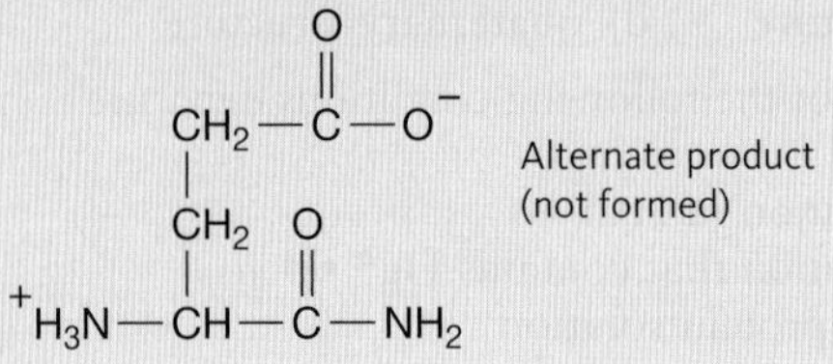

$${}^{+}H_3N-\underset{\underset{\underset{\displaystyle CH_2-\overset{O}{\overset{\|}{C}}-O^-}{|}}{\displaystyle CH_2}}{CH}-\overset{O}{\overset{\|}{C}}-NH_2$$

Alternate product (not formed)

continued

TRY IT YOURSELF: *Your body makes threonine from aspartic acid, using a sequence of five reactions. In the first reaction, an enzyme called aspartate kinase combines aspartic acid with a phosphate group to make a compound called aspartyl phosphate. Must aspartate kinase select one particular product in this reaction? Explain your answer.*

$$^{+}H_3N{-}CH(CH_2{-}COO^-){-}COO^- \xrightarrow{\text{Add phosphate}} {}^{+}H_3N{-}CH(CH_2{-}CO{-}O{-}PO(OH){-}O^-){-}COO^-$$

Aspartic acid → **Aspartyl phosphate**

Although some biological catalysts are nucleic acids (which we will encounter in Chapter 17), the vast majority of catalysts in living organisms are proteins, and the term *enzyme* specifically refers to protein catalysts. Virtually every reaction that occurs in a living cell involves an enzyme, and most biological reactions are extremely slow or will not occur if the enzyme is not present. In a real sense, enzymes make life possible.

Before we look at how enzymes work, you need to learn some terms that are commonly used in biochemistry. Every enzyme is associated with a chemical reaction, which converts one or more chemicals (the reactants) into a new set of chemicals (the products). In biochemistry, the reactants are called the **substrates**. For example, in Chapter 7 we saw that carbonic acid in the bloodstream breaks down into carbon dioxide and water when it reaches the lungs.

Kresimir Juraga

Plant and animal tissues contain catalase, an enzyme that breaks down hydrogen peroxide (H_2O_2) into water and oxygen. Here, hydrogen peroxide is breaking down on the surface of a potato.

$$H_2CO_3(aq) \rightarrow CO_2(g) + H_2O(l)$$

This reaction is fairly rapid, but it is not fast enough to meet our needs, so our bodies make an enzyme called *carbonic anhydrase* that speeds up the reaction. Carbonic acid is the substrate in this reaction, and carbon dioxide and water are the products. Chemists often write the name of the enzyme above the arrow in the balanced equation, as shown here.

$$\underset{\text{The substrate}}{H_2CO_3} \xrightarrow[\text{}]{\text{Carbonic anhydrase (The enzyme)}} \underset{\text{The products}}{CO_2 + H_2O}$$

Enzyme Catalysis Involves Three Steps

How does an enzyme speed up a reaction? There are three fundamental steps in this process:

1. The enzyme binds to the substrate or substrates.
2. The enzyme converts the substrates into the products by helping bonds break and form.
3. The enzyme releases the product or products.

This sequence of steps is illustrated in Figure 13.20.

In the first step of an enzyme reaction, the substrates fit into a cavity in the enzyme, called the **active site.** In many cases, the substrate molecules simply bump into the correct part of the enzyme and drop into the active site. However, some enzymes have amino acids around the active site that attract a substrate. For example, if one of the substrates is a phosphate ion, the enzyme may have several basic amino acids close to the active site. The basic side chains are positively charged and phosphate is negatively charged at pH 7, so the phosphate ion is attracted to the active site.

As the substrates enter the active site, they become attached to the enzyme, forming a cluster called the **enzyme–substrate complex.** In the enzyme–substrate complex, the

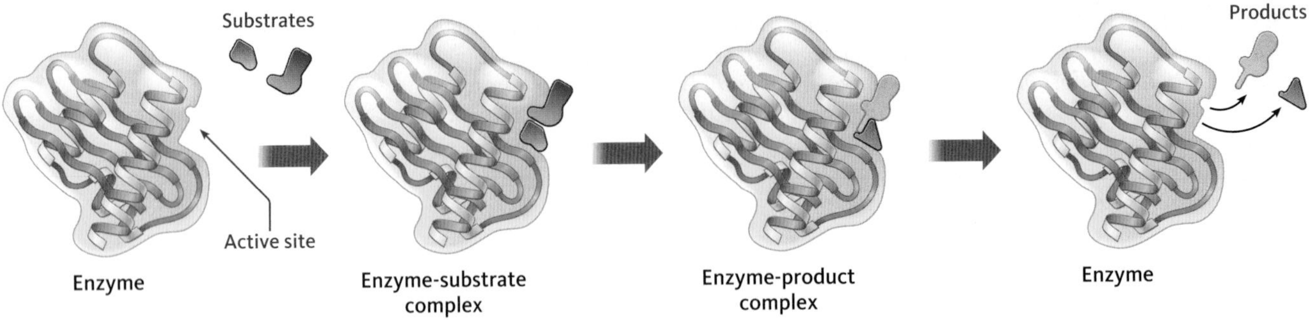

FIGURE 13.20 The steps in an enzyme-catalyzed reaction.

amino acid side chains that form the active site of the enzyme attract the substrates, so the substrates are held in the correct orientations for the reaction to occur. In addition, if the reaction could produce more than one possible set of products, the enzyme places the substrates so that they can only form the correct products. Figure 13.21 shows an example of how the active site of a specific enzyme fits its substrate. The enzyme in this figure is chymotrypsin, a digestive enzyme that hydrolyzes peptide bonds in proteins that we eat. Two hydrogen atoms and one oxygen atom in the active site of chymotrypsin bind to a carbonyl group in the peptide group of the substrate, holding it in place. In addition, the active site contains a nonpolar pocket that can accommodate an aromatic side chain, but does not fit other amino acids. As a result, chymotrypsin can only hydrolyze a protein at a peptide group that is next to an aromatic side chain.

When an enzyme binds to its substrates, the shapes of both the active site and the substrates usually change. These changes allow the enzyme to bind tightly to the substrate molecules. In addition, the binding of the substrates to the enzyme often weakens one or more key bonds in the substrate molecules, making the substrate more susceptible to reaction.

Most enzymes can only bind to a limited number of possible substrates. Other compounds do not bind to the active site for a variety of reasons. Some molecules are too large to fit into the active site, or they have charged groups that are repelled by ionized amino acids in the active site. Other molecules are too small to bind tightly, so they leave the active site immediately. The shape and structure of the active site play critical roles in determining the ability of an enzyme to catalyze a specific reaction.

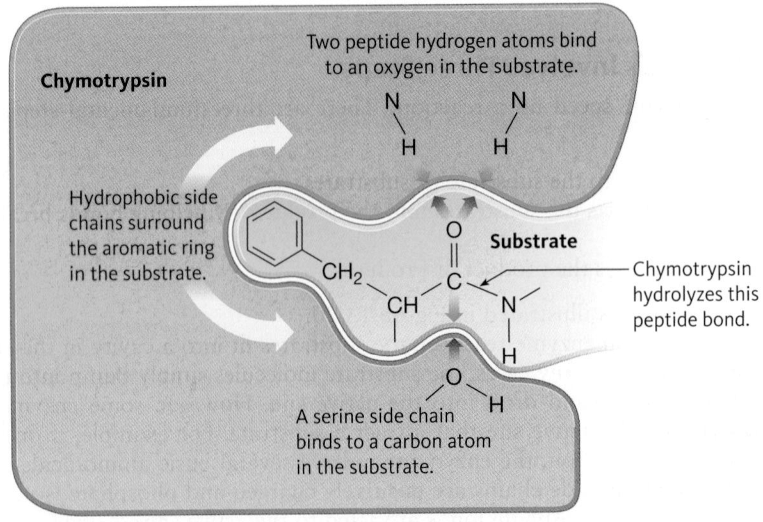

FIGURE 13.21 The active site of chymotrypsin.

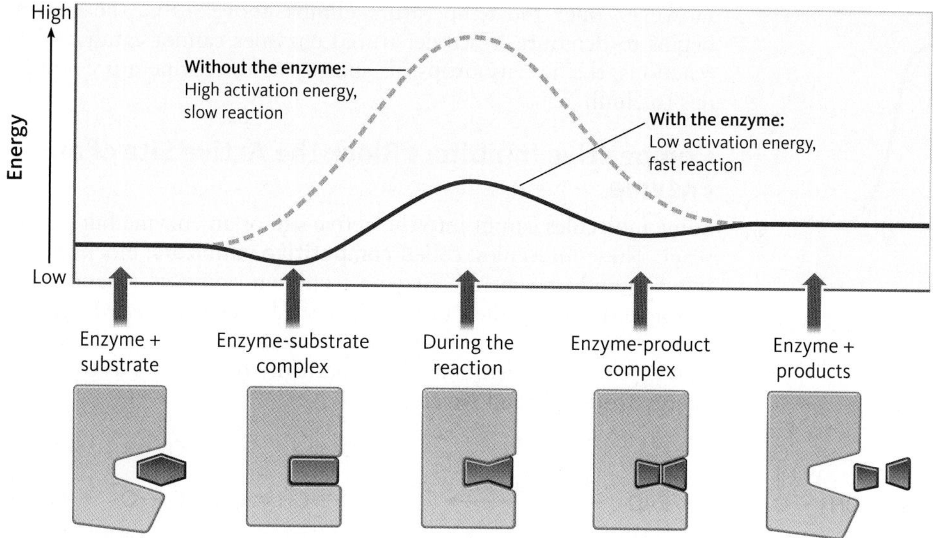

FIGURE 13.22 Enzymes decrease the activation energy of a reaction.

Once the enzyme is bound to the substrates, the reaction can occur. The entire reaction occurs within the active site, producing an **enzyme–product complex**, which contains the products bound to the active site of the enzyme. If the reaction is reversible, the enzyme–product complex can react to form the enzyme–substrate complex. Eventually, though, the products of the reaction leave the active site, freeing the enzyme to bind to other molecules of the substrates. As a result, one molecule of enzyme can convert many reactant molecules into products.

Health Note: People who suffer from ulcers often take medicines such as Prilosec or Nexium to reduce the concentration of acid in the stomach, allowing the ulcer to heal. However, the activity of pepsin decreases as the stomach pH rises, so these medications interfere with protein digestion in the stomach. The body produces other enzymes that assist in protein digestion, so the lower activity of pepsin does not lead to any significant health effects.

Enzymes Lower the Activation Energy of a Reaction

Enzymes, like all catalysts, increase the rate of a reaction. As we saw in Section 6.6, catalysts speed up reactions by decreasing the activation energy of the reaction, the amount of energy that the reactants must have when they collide. Figure 13.22 follows the progress of a reaction with and without an enzyme present. Note that the energy of the enzyme–substrate complex is lower than the energy of the separated enzyme and substrate, so the complex is more stable than the separated components. The same is true of the enzyme–product complex.

The Activity of an Enzyme Depends on Its Surroundings

The **activity** of an enzyme is the number of reaction cycles that the enzyme can catalyze in one second. The fastest known enzymes can carry out their reactions more than 1 million times in one second, while the slowest take more than a second to carry out a single catalytic cycle. However, most enzymes that are involved in normal metabolic reactions have activities between 10 and 1000 reaction cycles per second.

The activity of an enzyme is strongly influenced by its environment. This should not be surprising, since we have seen that proteins in general are sensitive to their surroundings. For example, most enzymes are active in a fairly narrow pH range. Figure 13.23 shows how the activity of two digestive enzymes depends on pH. Note how each enzyme is suited for its environment. Pepsin, which is produced by the stomach, is most active around pH 2, matching the typical pH of stomach contents. Trypsin, which is produced by the pancreas and secreted into the small intestine, is most active at the slightly basic pH that is typical of intestinal contents.

Enzyme activity is also affected by temperature, as shown in Figure 13.24. The shape of the curve is the result of two opposing influences. As we saw in Chapter 6, reactions speed up when the temperature rises, because the molecules collide more often and a larger percentage of molecules have enough energy to react. As a result, the activity increases from 0°C to roughly 50°C.

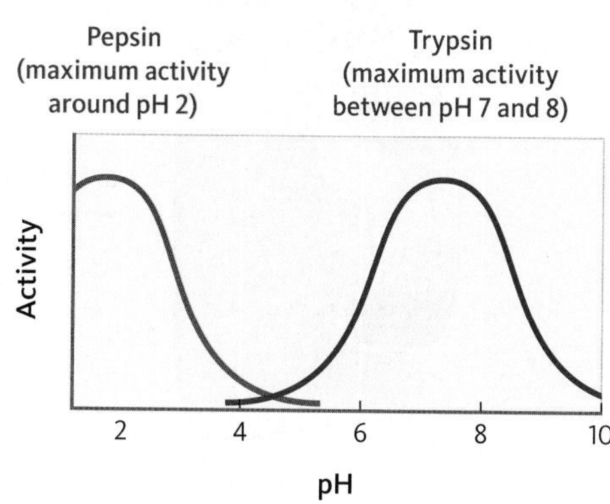

FIGURE 13.23 The effect of pH on the activity of two enzymes.

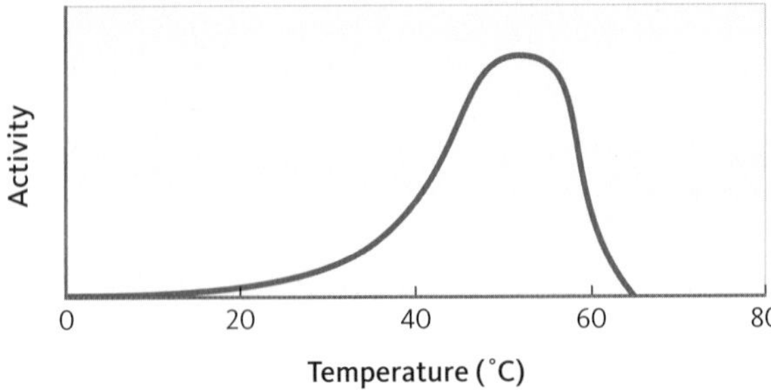

FIGURE 13.24 The effect of temperature on the activity of a typical enzyme.

However, once the temperature climbs above 50°C, the enzyme begins to denature. Since denatured enzymes cannot catalyze their reactions, the activity drops off sharply as the temperature continues to climb.

Competitive Inhibitors Block the Active Site of an Enzyme

Some molecules can fit into the active site of an enzyme but cannot react. These molecules, called **competitive inhibitors**, block the active site and prevent the enzyme from catalyzing its reaction. For example, in our bodies an enzyme called *succinate dehydrogenase* converts succinate ion into fumarate ion, as shown here. This reaction is part of the main metabolic pathway that allows us to obtain energy from the food we eat.

$$^{-}O-\overset{\overset{\displaystyle O}{\|}}{C}-CH_2-CH_2-\overset{\overset{\displaystyle O}{\|}}{C}-O^{-} + FAD \xrightarrow[\text{dehydrogenase}]{\text{Succinate}} {}^{-}O-\overset{\overset{\displaystyle O}{\|}}{C}-CH{=}CH-\overset{\overset{\displaystyle O}{\|}}{C}-O^{-} + FADH_2$$

Succinate ion **Fumarate ion**

Health Note: Many medicines used to treat HIV infections are *protease inhibitors.* These drugs have structures resembling a section of a polypeptide that is produced by infected cells and that will become part of the outer coating of new HIV viruses. The cells also produce an enzyme called a *protease* that hydrolyzes a peptide bond, converting the original polypeptide into its final, active form. Protease inhibitors fit into the active site of the protease, preventing formation of new viruses.

Malonate ion is a competitive inhibitor of this reaction. The structure of malonate is similar to that of succinate, so malonate can fit into the active site of the enzyme. However, malonate cannot be dehydrogenated, because it has only one carbon atom between the two carboxylate groups. Therefore, the malonate ion simply sits in the active site until the enzyme releases it unchanged. During this time, the enzyme cannot bind to succinate, so the overall activity of succinate dehydrogenase is lower when malonate ions are present. Figure 13.25 illustrates the competitive inhibition of succinate dehydrogenase by malonate ion.

$$^{-}O-\overset{\overset{\displaystyle O}{\|}}{C}-CH_2-\overset{\overset{\displaystyle O}{\|}}{C}-O^{-}$$

Malonate ion
(a competitive inhibitor of succinate dehydrogenase)

Effectors Change the Shape of the Active Site

Many enzymes have one or more cavities on their surface in addition to the active site. These cavities can bind to specific molecules called **effectors**. An effector is a molecule that is not directly involved in the chemical reaction, but that binds to the enzyme and changes the shape of the active site. If the molecule is a *positive* effector, the ability of

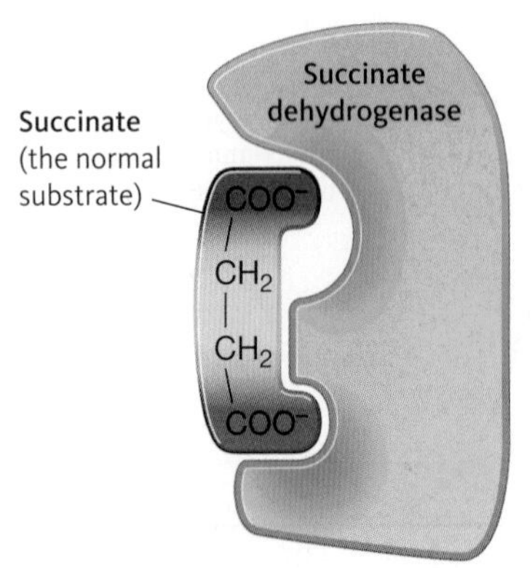

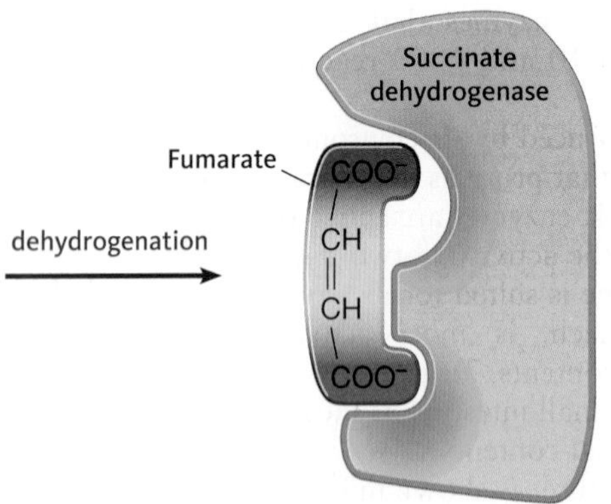

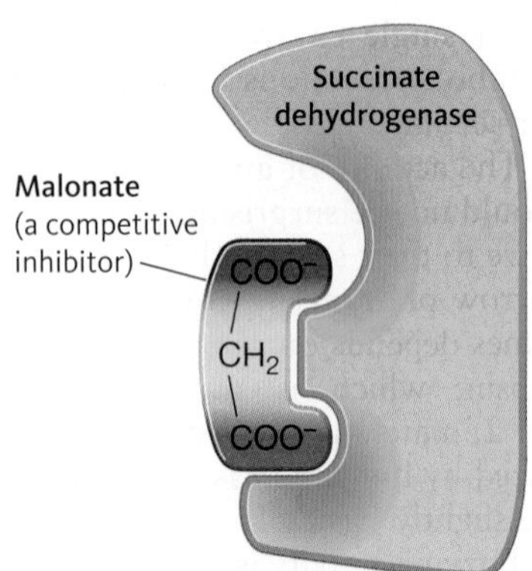

FIGURE 13.25 The behavior of malonate ion, a competitive inhibitor.

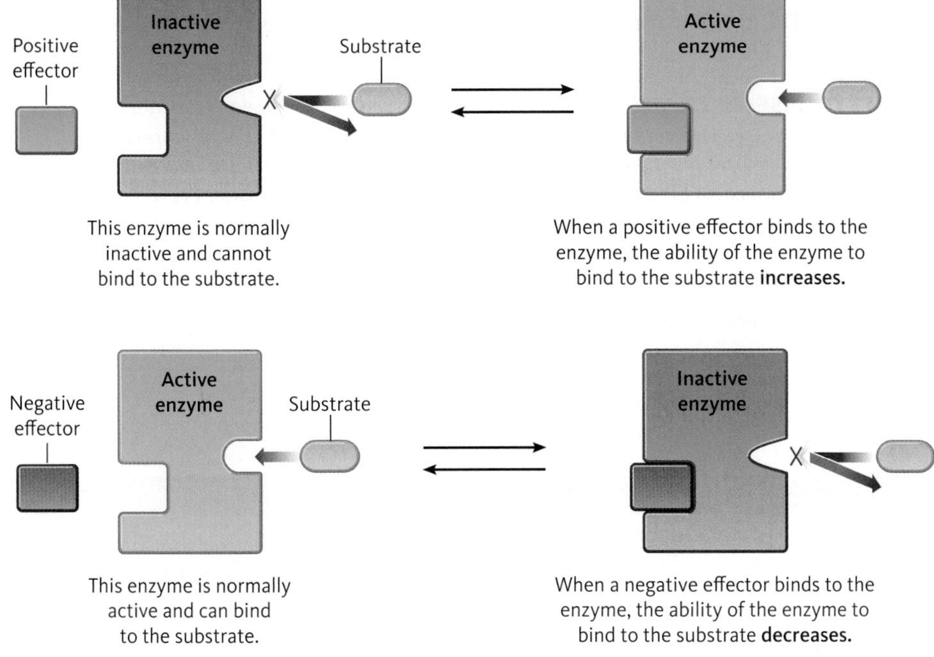
Positive effector
Inactive enzyme
Substrate
X
Active enzyme
This enzyme is normally inactive and cannot bind to the substrate.
When a positive effector binds to the enzyme, the ability of the enzyme to bind to the substrate **increases.**
Negative effector
Active enzyme
Substrate
Inactive enzyme
X
This enzyme is normally active and can bind to the substrate.
When a negative effector binds to the enzyme, the ability of the enzyme to bind to the substrate **decreases.**

FIGURE 13.26 Positive and negative effectors.

the active site to bind to the substrate increases, so the enzyme becomes more active. *Negative* effectors (also called *noncompetitive inhibitors*) make the active site less able to bind to the substrate, decreasing the activity of the enzyme. Figure 13.26 compares these two types of effectors. Our bodies use effectors to regulate the activity of key enzymes, allowing us to control the rates of metabolic pathways.

An effector binds weakly and reversibly to its enzyme, so the cell contains an equilibrium mixture of active and inactive forms of the enzyme. As the concentration of the effector rises, the number of enzyme molecules that are bonded to effector molecules increases. However, even when the concentration of a negative effector is high, there are still a few active enzyme molecules present. A negative effector can slow down a reaction dramatically, but no effector can stop a reaction altogether.

Effectors allow a cell to control the activity of an enzyme. Most metabolic pathways include at least one reaction that is influenced by an effector. The effector allows the cell to control the rate of a key step in the pathway. If a cell needs the end product of the pathway, the cell makes more molecules of a positive effector or breaks down molecules of a negative effector. The result is that the pathway speeds up. If the cell does not need the end product, it breaks down a positive effector or makes a negative effector, slowing the pathway and conserving the starting materials for other purposes.

Sample Problem 13.9

Classifying enzyme inhibitors and effectors

The following reaction is catalyzed by an enzyme called amino acid acyltransferase. The activity of this enzyme decreases dramatically when arginine is added to the reaction mixture, and the activity increases when the arginine is removed. Arginine cannot bind to the active site of the enzyme. Is arginine a competitive inhibitor, a positive effector, or a negative effector?

$$\text{glutamic acid} + \text{acetyl-CoA} \rightarrow \text{N-acetylglutamic acid} + \text{CoA}$$

SOLUTION

There is a good deal of information in this problem, but we can answer the question using two key pieces of information. First, the problem says that arginine does not bind to the active site, so arginine cannot be a competitive inhibitor. Therefore, arginine must be

continued

an effector. The problem also tells us that arginine decreases the activity of the enzyme, so it is a negative effector.

TRY IT YOURSELF: *The following reaction is catalyzed by an enzyme called aspartate transcarbamoylase. The activity of this enzyme increases when ATP (a compound involved in energy use) is added to the reaction mixture, but the activity decreases when the ATP is removed. ATP cannot bind to the active site of the enzyme. Is ATP a competitive inhibitor, a positive effector, or a negative effector?*

carbamoyl phosphate + aspartic acid → N-carbamoyl aspartate + phosphate

For additional practice, try Core Problems 13.57 and 13.58.

CORE PROBLEMS

13.41 What is an enzyme?

13.42 What are the two functions of the enzyme in a typical chemical reaction in our bodies?

13.43 Sucrase is a protein that is produced by your intestinal tract. It catalyzes the hydrolysis of sucrose (table sugar), breaking it down into two simple sugars.

sucrose + H_2O → glucose + fructose

Identify the substrates, the products, and the enzyme in this reaction.

13.44 Lipase is a protein that is produced by your pancreas and secreted into your intestinal tract. It catalyzes the hydrolysis of fats, breaking them down into glycerol and fatty acids.

fat + 3 H_2O → glycerol + 3 fatty acids

Identify the substrates, the products, and the enzyme in this reaction.

13.45 Define the following terms:
a) active site b) enzyme–substrate complex

13.46 Define the following terms:
a) substrate b) enzyme–product complex

13.47 Many enzymes catalyze reactions that involve phosphate ions. Several of these enzymes contain a magnesium ion at the active site. Explain why the magnesium ion helps the enzyme bind to phosphate.

13.48 Glutamine synthetase is an enzyme that converts glutamic acid into glutamine.

glutamic acid + NH_4^+ → glutamine + H_2O

The active site of the enzyme contains an aspartic acid side chain. Explain why the aspartic acid side chain helps the enzyme bind to ammonium ion.

13.49 How does the presence of an enzyme affect the activation energy of a reaction?

13.50 At what point during a reaction is the energy of the reacting molecules highest?

13.51 The following graph shows the relationship between activity and pH for two enzymes, papain and catalase. At what pH does each enzyme show the highest activity?

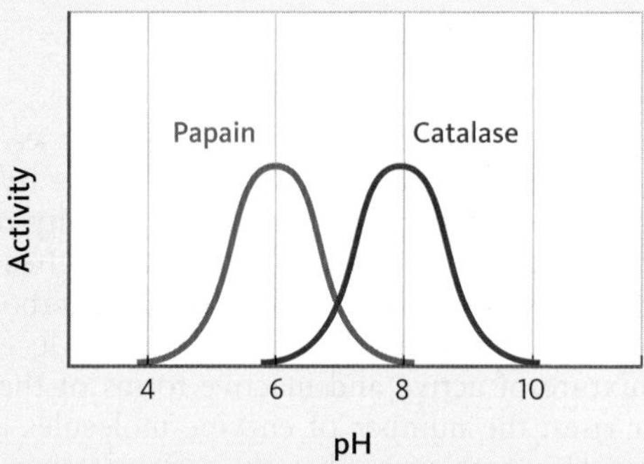

13.52 The following graph shows the relationship between activity and pH for two enzymes, fumarase and arginase. Which enzyme would you expect to show a higher activity at pH 7?

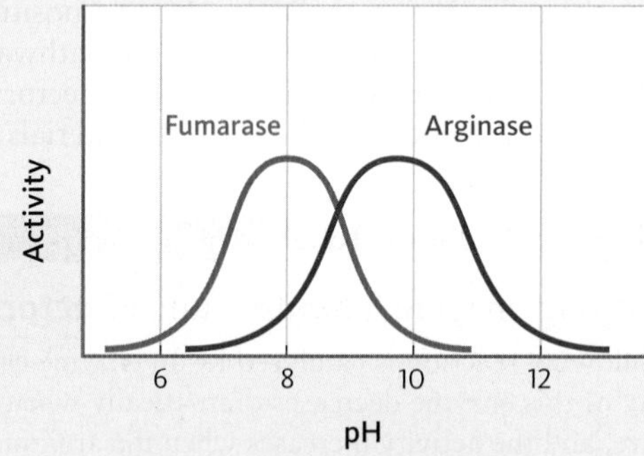

13.53 Does the activity of a typical enzyme decrease, increase, or remain the same as the temperature rises from 10°C to 30°C? Why is this?

13.54 Does the activity of a typical enzyme decrease, increase, or remain the same as the temperature rises from 50°C to 70°C? Why is this?

continued

13.55 Complete the following sentences with the correct terms:

a) A molecule that is similar to the substrate and that blocks the active site of an enzyme is called a/an ________.

b) A molecule that binds to an enzyme outside the active site and that makes the enzyme more active is called a/an ________.

13.56 Complete the following sentences with the correct terms:

a) A molecule that changes the shape of an enzyme's active site so the enzyme cannot bind to the substrate is called a/an ________.

b) The number of substrate molecules that an enzyme can convert into products in one second is called the ________ of the enzyme.

13.57 The following reaction is catalyzed by an enzyme called citrate synthase:

oxaloacetate + acetyl-CoA → citrate + CoA

Citrate synthase becomes less active when the concentration of NADH in the cell increases. Is NADH a positive or a negative effector?

13.58 The following reaction is catalyzed by an enzyme called isocitrate dehydrogenase:

isocitrate + NAD^+ → α-ketoglutarate + CO2 + NADH

Isocitrate dehydrogenase becomes more active when the concentration of a compound called ADP increases. Is ADP a positive or a negative effector?

13.6 Cofactors

OBJECTIVE: *Describe the functions and chemical nature of the two main types of cofactors.*

All enzymes contain at least one chain of amino acids. However, in many cases, the polypeptide alone cannot catalyze the reaction. To be active, the polypeptide must combine with another substance that is not an amino acid. For example, in the previous section we encountered carbonic anhydrase, the enzyme that breaks down carbonic acid into water and carbon dioxide. Like all enzymes, carbonic anhydrase contains a chain of amino acids, but the enzyme also contains a zinc ion. The zinc ion is an essential part of the enzyme; the polypeptide chain alone is completely inactive. The behavior of carbonic anhydrase is illustrated in Figure 13.27.

Any molecule or ion that is required by an enzyme but is not an amino acid is called a **cofactor**. There are two broad categories of cofactors. The first category comprises a number of metal ions, and it includes most of the metals that are required in human nutrition. Some examples of metallic cofactors are iron (either Fe^{2+} or Fe^{3+}), magnesium (Mg^{2+}), zinc (Zn^{2+}), and copper (Cu^{2+}). The second category of cofactors is a set of organic compounds called **coenzymes**. You have encountered a few of these coenzymes in previous chapters, notably coenzyme A and the redox coenzymes NAD^+ and FAD.

Some cofactors, including most of the metallic cofactors, are covalently bonded to the polypeptide chain of the enzyme. This type of cofactor is part of the enzyme and cannot be removed from it without making the enzyme inactive. The zinc ion in carbonic anhydrase is a good example; the Zn^{2+} shares electrons with nitrogen atoms from three different histidine side chains in the polypeptide. Likewise, the FAD that is required in some oxidation reactions is permanently bonded to the polypeptide chains of the enzymes that require it.

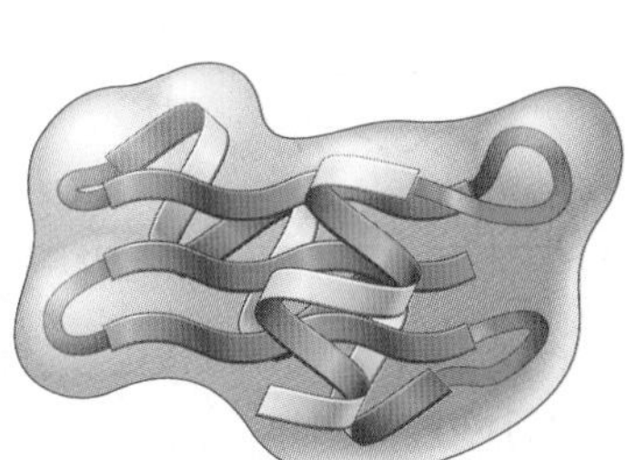

The active form of carbonic anhydrase contains a polypeptide chain and a zinc ion (the cofactor).

The polypeptide chain of carbonic anhydrase has no activity.

FIGURE 13.27 Carbonic anhydrase, an enzyme that contains a cofactor.

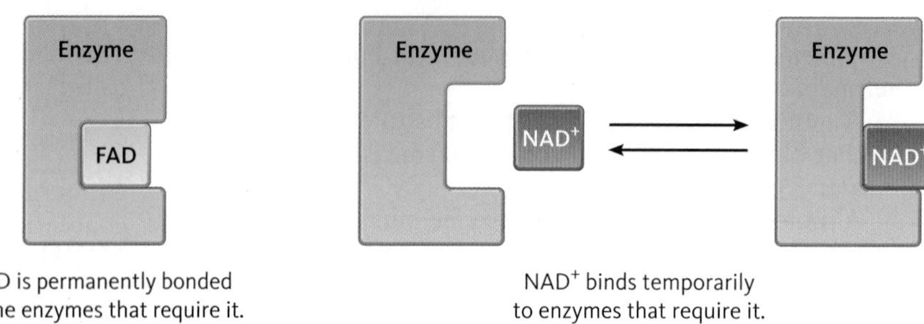
Enzyme
FAD
Enzyme
NAD+
Enzyme
NAD+
FAD is permanently bonded to the enzymes that require it.
NAD+ binds temporarily to enzymes that require it.

FIGURE 13.28 The two types of cofactor behavior.

Other cofactors are not attached to the polypeptide chain. For example, many enzymes require NAD^+ as a cofactor, but none of them bond directly to NAD^+. Enzymes that require this cofactor must collide with a molecule of NAD^+ and bind it long enough for the reaction to occur. This type of coenzyme is actually just another substrate in the reaction. Figure 13.28 compares the differing behavior of the two redox coenzymes.

We Obtain Most Cofactors from Our Diet

In Section 13.7, we will look at how we obtain the amino acids we need to build proteins. Here, we take a brief look at the sources of the cofactors. All metallic cofactors must be part of our diet. If we do not consume foods that contain adequate amounts of these metals, the enzymes that require them will not function properly. Happily, our bodies need so little of most of these elements that virtually any reasonable diet will meet our needs. However, iron deficiencies are common, because iron is required in an unusually wide range of enzymes (as well as in the oxygen-carrying protein hemoglobin), and most foods do not contain much iron. Zinc deficiency is also known, although it is less common. Several enzymes require calcium as a cofactor, but calcium deficiency does not generally affect enzyme activity, because our bones serve as a reservoir of calcium. When our diet does not contain enough calcium, our bodies remove calcium from our bones, supplying the needs of our enzymes at the expense of bone strength.

Coenzymes are complex organic molecules, which our bodies build from smaller pieces. In general, our bodies can make most of these pieces from other nutrients, but one of them must be present in our diet. For example, the redox coenzyme FAD is made from phosphate ions and three organic components: adenine, ribose, and riboflavin. Our bodies can make adenine and ribose from proteins and carbohydrates, but we cannot make riboflavin, so we need a dietary source of this compound. The structure of FAD is shown in Figure 13.29.

• *Vitamin* is a general term for any organic compound that must be present in small amounts in our diet.

The organic compounds that our bodies use to form coenzymes are the *B vitamins*. Table 13.3 lists the B vitamins and the coenzymes that contain them.

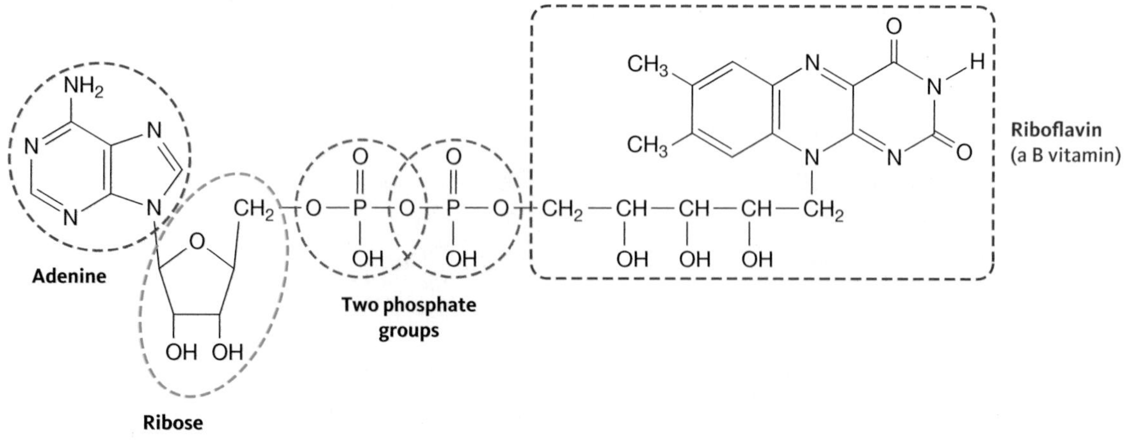

Adenine
Ribose
Two phosphate groups
Riboflavin (a B vitamin)

FIGURE 13.29 The building blocks of FAD.

TABLE 13.3 The B Vitamins and Their Corresponding Coenzymes

Vitamin	Corresponding Coenzymes	Coenzyme Behavior	Coenzyme Function
Niacin	NAD^+ and $NADP^+$	Free	Redox coenzyme
Riboflavin (vitamin B_2)	FAD and flavin mononucleotide (FMN)	Bound to enzyme	Redox coenzyme
Thiamine (vitamin B_1)	Thiamine pyrophosphate (TPP)	Free	Decarboxylations and other reactions that form or break carbon–carbon bonds
Folic acid	Tetrahydrofolate (THF)	Free	Transfer of one-carbon fragments from one molecule to another
Pyridoxine (vitamin B_6)	Pyridoxal-5-phosphate (PLP)	Free	Assistant in a variety of reactions involving amino acids
Pantothenic acid	Coenzyme A	Free	Carrier of organic fragments in metabolic pathways
Cyanocobalamin (vitamin B_{12})	Deoxyadenosylcobalamin	Free	Rearrangements of carbon skeletons
Biotin	Biotin	Bound to enzyme	Carboxylations (reactions that add CO_2 to an organic molecule)

Of the vitamins in Table 13.3, only niacin can be made by the human body, and our ability to do so is rather limited. Mammals, birds, and other vertebrates are likewise incapable of making these compounds. Therefore, all vertebrates rely on other organisms, primarily plants and microorganisms, to make these compounds. For example, while no animals can make thiamine or riboflavin, all plants can do so. Humans can obtain these vitamins by eating either plant or animal foods, but the ultimate sources of these compounds are plants. By contrast, only certain bacteria are capable of making vitamin B_{12}. Many animals harbor colonies of these bacteria in their digestive tracts, providing them with a permanent source of vitamin B_{12}.

Vitamin supplements supply essential vitamins and metallic cofactors, but they are not a substitute for a sound diet.

CORE PROBLEMS

13.59 What is the difference between a cofactor and a coenzyme?

13.60 What is the function of a cofactor?

13.61 FAD is a coenzyme. Is it also a cofactor? Explain.

13.62 Mg^{2+} is a cofactor for many enzymes. Is it also a coenzyme? Explain.

13.63 How do our bodies obtain metallic cofactors?

13.64 All animals need riboflavin to make FAD, but no animals are capable of making this compound. Where does the riboflavin come from?

13.65 What vitamin does the body need to make NAD^+?

13.66 What vitamin does the body need to make coenzyme A?

OBJECTIVES: *Describe the sources of amino acids in humans and other organisms, and identify the factors that cause protein deficiency in humans.*

13.7 Sources of Amino Acids

Our bodies contain a vast number of different proteins. Some of these, such as hormones and digestive enzymes, are broken down within minutes or hours of the time that they are made. Others, such as the collagen in our bones, may last for many years. Virtually every functional protein in our bodies, though, is eventually broken down into amino acids. We can use this pool of amino acids to build other proteins, but we cannot store the amino acids for later use. Our bodies break down any amino acids that we do not need immediately. As a result, the food we eat must provide us with a

Martyn F. Chillmaid/Photo Researchers, Inc.

All of these foods are good sources of protein.

supply of these vital building blocks. In this section, we will examine our dietary requirement for amino acids, and we will look at the ultimate sources of these essential nutrients.

Because our diet does not normally contain free amino acids, we obtain the amino acids we need from proteins. All plant and animal food sources contain protein, since proteins are present in all living organisms. In our digestive tract, enzymes break the protein down into amino acids and small polypeptides, which are absorbed through the intestinal wall into our bloodstream. As a result, none of the proteins we eat retain their original biological activity once we have digested them. For instance, people suffering from diabetes must inject insulin into their bodies, rather than taking some sort of a pill, because insulin is a protein and is broken down by our digestive system.

Health Note: The antibodies found in breast milk are not broken down by an infant's digestive enzymes. Antibodies are proteins that bind to bacteria and other foreign substances, preventing them from causing illness. The antibodies in breast milk help prevent bacterial and viral infections in infants.

Essential Amino Acids Cannot Be Made by the Human Body

Of the 20 amino acids that we use to build proteins, 8 are requirements in our diet, because our bodies have no way to make them from other nutrients. These are called the **essential amino acids**, and they are listed in Table 13.4. Most of these are present in abundance in all common proteins. However, three of them (lysine, tryptophan, and methionine) are present in inadequate amounts in the proteins of many edible plants. For instance, grains such as wheat and rice lack lysine, while legumes such as peas and beans lack methionine. These proteins are called incomplete proteins, while the proteins in animal products (meat, eggs, and dairy) contain all of the essential amino acids and are called complete proteins. In regions where meat and other animal products are in limited supply, traditional diets generally include both a grain and a legume. These diets were established long before the importance of protein was understood, so they are undoubtedly the result of trial and error. They supply adequate amounts of all of the essential amino acids, and they are a model for modern vegetarian diets.

TABLE 13.4 Essential and Nonessential Amino Acids

Essential Amino Acids (Must Be Present in the Human Diet)	Nonessential Amino Acids (Can Be Made from Other Nutrients)	
Isoleucine	Alanine	Glutamine
Leucine	Arginine*	Glycine
Lysine	Asparagine	Histidine*
Methionine	Aspartic acid	Proline
Phenylalanine	Cysteine	Serine
Threonine	Glutamic acid	Tyrosine
Tryptophan		
Valine		

*Humans can make arginine and histidine from other nutrients, but children and some adults cannot make enough of them and need a dietary source.

Our bodies are able to make the other 12 amino acids. Therefore, these are called **nonessential amino acids**, because they do not need to be present in the protein we eat. The division between essential and nonessential amino acids is controversial, though, because children (and some adults) cannot make enough arginine and histidine to meet their needs. As a result, these two amino acids are often classified as essential. In practice, dietary deficiencies of these two amino acids are rare and are normally seen only in individuals who have a general protein insufficiency.

Todd Warnock/Getty Images

Neither rice nor beans contains all of the essential amino acids. However, each supplies the amino acid that the other lacks, so this meal is a complete protein source.

Amino Acids Supply the Nitrogen for Other Amino Acids

Although the human body can make all of the nonessential amino acids from other nutrients, *the nitrogen atoms in these amino acids can only be supplied by other amino acids*. If our diet supplies only the minimum requirement of the 8 essential amino acids, it will be protein deficient, because we will not have the nitrogen we need to make the other 12 amino acids. As a result, our dietary requirement for protein has two parts:

1. *Total protein.* We need to eat enough protein to supply the nitrogen for the nonessential amino acids. The protein we eat must also supply the nitrogen atoms for several other classes of compounds.
2. *Essential amino acids.* Our diet must meet our minimum requirement for the eight essential amino acids, plus any needed arginine and histidine.

Our bodies may not need to make the nonessential amino acids. If our diet contains enough of a nonessential amino acid, our bodies can use the dietary source to make protein. However, we always have the ability to make a nonessential amino acid if our diet does not supply enough of it.

Our overall nutritional state also affects our dietary protein requirement. Humans (and all other organisms) require fuel to supply the energy they need. If we do not consume enough carbohydrate and fat to supply our basic energy needs, our bodies make up the deficit by burning amino acids, either from our diet or from the breakdown of our body proteins. As a result, people who do not consume enough carbohydrate and fat to supply their energy needs can suffer a protein deficiency, even if they consume a seemingly adequate amount of protein.

Sample Problem **13.10**

Identifying causes of protein deficiency

A child exhibits symptoms of protein deficiency. The child's diet consists primarily of rice, and the child eats enough to supply both her Calorie and her protein requirements. Suggest a reason for her protein deficiency.

SOLUTION

Rice does not contain all of the essential amino acids, so the child's diet probably does not contain enough of one or more essential amino acids. Her body cannot make the proteins it needs without an adequate supply of each of the essential amino acids.

TRY IT YOURSELF: *Susan is on a "crash diet" in an attempt to lose weight quickly. She knows the importance of protein in her diet, so she eats 70 g of protein per day, substantially more than the normal requirement. Nonetheless, after two months Susan shows signs of mild protein deficiency. Why?*

For additional practice, try Core Problems 13.73 and 13.74.

Plants and Bacteria Make Amino Acids Using Inorganic Nitrogen Sources

Since we rely on our diet to supply the eight essential amino acids, we are dependent on other organisms to make these compounds. The ultimate sources of the amino acids in our diet are plants. Plants can make all 20 of the amino acids, using ions such as NH_4^+ and NO_3^- as the source of nitrogen and using CO_2 as the source of carbon. In Chapter 14, we will look at how plants use carbon dioxide to build organic compounds. Let us now examine how nitrogen is incorporated into the organic world.

The primary source of nitrogen on Earth is the atmosphere. Nitrogen makes up about 80% of the air around us. This nitrogen is in the form of N_2 molecules, which are extremely stable and cannot be used by most organisms. The only organisms that can utilize atmospheric nitrogen are certain bacteria. These bacteria can convert N_2 into ammonium ions (NH_4^+), much of which they release into their surroundings. This process is called **nitrogen fixation**, and its importance to life on Earth cannot be overemphasized.

Plants can absorb and use NH_4^+ to build amino acids. However, *nitrifying bacteria* in the soil oxidize most of the ammonium ions to nitrite and nitrate ions (NO_2^- and NO_3^-). Plants and some microorganisms absorb these ions and convert them back into ammonium ions, using NADH as a source of hydrogen atoms. The plants then incorporate ammonium ions into amino acids and other nitrogen-containing compounds. At the same time, *denitrifying bacteria* convert some of the nitrate and nitrite back into useless N_2. These reactions are the basis of the **nitrogen cycle**, which is depicted in Figure 13.30.

These bean plants can carry out nitrogen fixation, making them an important source of nitrogen-containing compounds for other plants and animals.

Although all organisms need amino acids to build proteins, many animals (including humans) also burn these compounds to obtain energy. Many other organisms can also break down excess amino acids. Some of the nitrogen is recycled and incorporated into new amino acids, while the rest is excreted. Aquatic animals such as fish and young amphibians produce ammonium ions as a waste product, and they excrete the ammonium ions directly into the surrounding water. However, animals that live on land cannot excrete their wastes continuously, so they must store the nitrogen. Since ammonium ions are poisonous, terrestrial animals store nitrogen in a less toxic form. Mammals and adult amphibians incorporate the nitrogen into *urea*, while birds and most reptiles produce and excrete *uric acid*. Bacteria rapidly break down both of these organic compounds, releasing the nitrogen in the form of ammonium ions. Therefore, living organisms continuously cycle nitrogen between inorganic and organic forms.

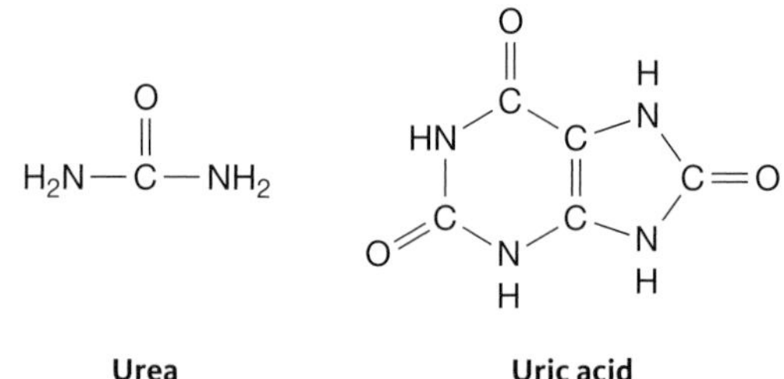

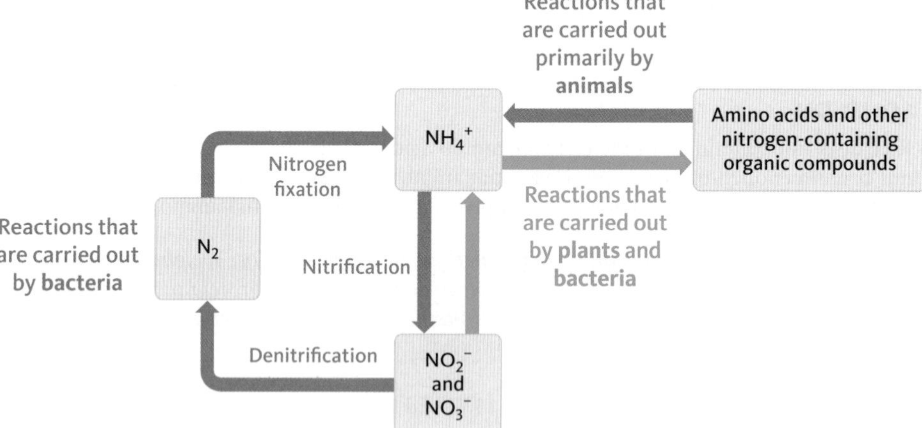

FIGURE 13.30 The nitrogen cycle.

CORE PROBLEMS

13.67 Some people cannot make an enzyme called phenylalanine 4-monooxygenase, which catalyzes the first step in the sequence of reactions that breaks down the amino acid phenylalanine. This disorder is called phenylketonuria (PKU), and it is treated by restricting the amount of phenylalanine in the diet. Explain why PKU cannot be treated with a pill that contains the needed enzyme.

continued

13.68 When a person is bitten by an animal that is suspected to have rabies, the person is given injections of proteins called antibodies that bind to the rabies virus. These injections are quite painful. Why can't the antibodies be given in the form of a pill that can be swallowed?

13.69 We need all 20 amino acids to make proteins. Why are only some of the amino acids classified as "essential"?

13.70 Humans have the ability to make the amino acid arginine from other nutrients. Why is arginine often classified as an essential amino acid?

13.71 Describe the two parts of the nutritional protein requirement.

13.72 What is a complete protein?

13.73 Explain why a person who is undernourished can consume adequate amounts of both essential and nonessential amino acids, yet still exhibit symptoms of protein deficiency.

13.74 Explain why a person who is on a vegetarian diet can consume adequate amounts of both Calories and protein-containing food, yet still exhibit symptoms of protein deficiency.

13.75 What kinds of organisms can make amino acids using inorganic sources of nitrogen such as ammonium ions and nitrate ions?

13.76 What kinds of organisms can make amino acids using atmospheric nitrogen (N_2) as their only source of nitrogen?

13.77 What is nitrogen fixation, and why is it important to life on Earth?

13.78 What are nitrification and denitrification, and what types of organisms are capable of carrying out these reactions?

13.79 What chemical compound do our bodies excrete when we need to get rid of excess nitrogen?

13.80 When our bodies break down amino acids, we convert the amino groups into ammonium ions. Why don't we simply excrete the ammonium ions?

CONNECTIONS

Enzyme Assays in Medicine

An enzyme assay is a measurement of the amount of an enzyme that is present in a given tissue or sample. Students and scientists often assay enzymes as part of a scientific experiment. Given the critical importance of enzymes to every reaction that takes place in our bodies, it would be almost impossible for a person to study any biology-based science without also studying enzymes.

In medicine, doctors exploit changes in enzyme levels to diagnose the diseases their patients have. For instance, an enzyme called *lactate dehydrogenase (LDH)* can be used to help diagnose heart attacks. Our bodies make five forms of LDH, labeled LDH_1 through LDH_5. Each type of tissue makes a different mixture of the five forms (called *isoenzymes* or *isozymes*), with heart muscle being particularly rich in LDH_1. When a cell dies, the enzymes in it (including LDH) are released into the bloodstream. As a result, when unusual numbers of cells die due to disease or injury, the concentration of LDH in the blood increases temporarily. The increase in LDH level is an indicator of tissue damage, and the relative amounts of the five isozymes can help diagnose the type of tissue. If the blood contains a higher-than-normal concentration of LDH_1, a heart attack would be suspected. Increased concentrations of LDH_5, on the other hand, indicate either muscle or liver damage, because these tissues contain more of this isozyme.

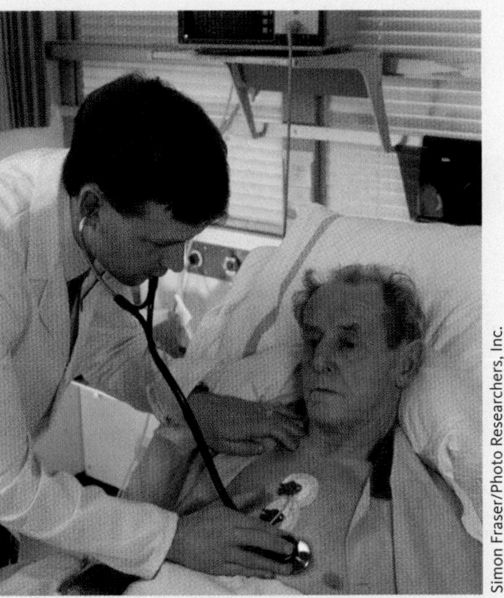
Simon Fraser/Photo Researchers, Inc.

Enzyme assays help health providers diagnose and treat heart attacks.

Because LDH_5 also occurs in kidney tissue, it cannot be used by itself to diagnose heart damage. Typically, hospitals monitor the levels of three enzymes that are associated with heart attacks: LDH, creatine phosphokinase (abbreviated CPK or CK), and aspartate aminotransferase (AST), and the levels of these three enzymes show a characteristic pattern of rising and falling after a heart attack, as shown in Figure 13.31. There is only one form of AST, but there are three isozymes of CPK: the MM form (found primarily in

continued

skeletal muscle), the MB form (found in heart muscle) and the BB form (found in brain tissue). Unusually high concentrations of the MB isozyme signal heart damage and suggest a recent heart attack, while high concentrations of the BB form suggest a stroke or other brain injury.

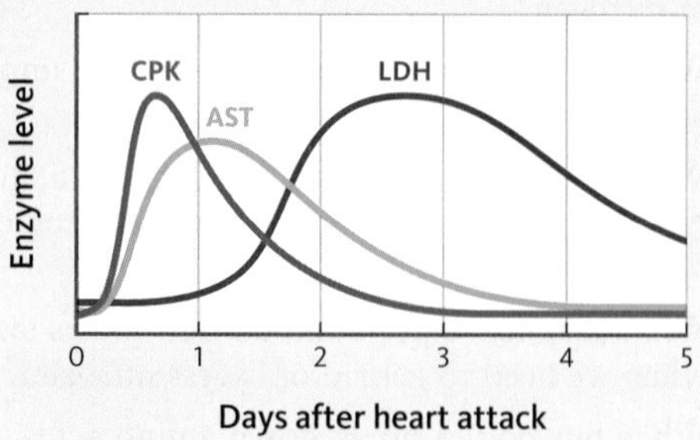

FIGURE 13.31 Levels of key enzymes after a heart attack.

Medical laboratories do not measure the amount of an enzyme directly. Instead, they measure the speed of the reaction that the enzyme catalyzes. For example, the concentration of LDH in blood can be measured by adding pyruvic acid to the blood sample and measuring how quickly the pyruvic acid is converted to lactic acid. However, this type of test cannot distinguish between isozymes. Different forms of the same enzyme must be separated using *electrophoresis*, a technique that separates mixtures of compounds based on their size and electrical charge. The H and M subunits of LDH have different charges, so the different isozymes of LDH can be separated by electrophoresis. An enzyme assay can then determine the concentration of each isozyme.

The field of enzyme measurement is constantly changing as new enzymes are discovered and their usefulness is recognized. For example, many hospitals now prefer to measure the level of troponin T when they suspect heart damage, because this enzyme is made almost exclusively by heart muscle. Enzyme levels in blood can be used to detect liver disease, prostate cancer, stroke, bone disease, and a variety of other disorders. These indispensable catalysts have provided us with greater ability to see inside ourselves.

Key Terms

active site – 13.5
activity – 13.5
alpha (α) carbon – 13.1
alpha (α) helix – 13.2
amino acid – 13.1
beta (β) sheet – 13.2
coenzyme – 13.6
cofactor – 13.6
competitive inhibitor – 13.5
C-terminal amino acid – 13.2
denature – 13.4
effector – 13.5
enzyme–product complex – 13.5
enzyme–substrate complex – 13.5
essential amino acid – 13.7
fibrous protein – 13.3
globular protein – 13.3
hydrophilic interaction – 13.3
hydrophobic interaction – 13.3
membrane protein – 13.3
nitrogen cycle – 13.7
nitrogen fixation – 13.7
nonessential amino acid – 13.7
N-terminal amino acid – 13.2
peptide bond – 13.2
peptide group – 13.2
polypeptide – 13.2
primary structure – 13.2
protein – 13.1
quaternary structure – 13.3
secondary structure – 13.2
side chain – 13.1
substrate – 13.5
tertiary structure – 13.3
triple helix – 13.2

SUMMARY OF OBJECTIVES

Now that you have read the chapter, test yourself on your knowledge of the objectives, using this summary as a guide.

Section 13.1: Draw the structure of a typical amino acid as it exists under physiological conditions, and classify amino acids based on the structures of their side chains.

- All proteins are made from amino acids.
- Amino acids contain an amine group and a carboxylic acid group linked by the α-carbon atom, and they have a side chain that is bonded to the α-carbon atom.
- Amino acids normally occur in the zwitterion form.
- Amino acids are classified as hydrophobic or hydrophilic based on the structures of their side chains, and hydrophilic amino acids are classified as neutral, acidic, or basic.
- Acidic side chains are negatively charged and basic side chains are positively charged at physiological pH.
- Most amino acids are chiral, and only one of the two enantiomeric forms of a chiral amino acid is used to build proteins.

Section 13.2: Draw the structure of a polypeptide, and show how peptide groups interact to form the typical secondary structures of a protein.

- Every protein has a specific sequence of amino acids, called the primary structure of the protein.

continued

- Amino acids are linked to each other by a condensation reaction between the amino group of one molecule and the acid group of another, forming a peptide group.
- Peptide groups are polar and form hydrogen bonds with each other, producing the secondary structure of a protein.
- The two common secondary structural types are the α-helix and the β-sheet.
- Collagen forms a triple helix.

Section 13.3: Describe the side chain interactions that produce the tertiary structure of a protein.
- The side chains of a protein interact with one another to produce the tertiary structure of a protein.
- Hydrophobic amino acids cluster in the interior of a globular protein, while hydrophilic amino acids tend to be on the surface of the protein.
- Hydrophilic side chains can form hydrogen bonds with one another, and acidic and basic amino acids form ion pairs.
- The thiol groups in cysteine can form disulfide bridges.
- Proteins that are imbedded in a membrane contain unusually large numbers of hydrophobic amino acids.
- Some proteins contain two or more chains of amino acids. The arrangement of these chains is the quaternary structure of a protein.

Section 13.4: Describe the factors that cause protein denaturation.
- A protein is denatured when its structure changes enough that the protein cannot carry out its normal function.
- Proteins can be denatured by organic solvents, high temperatures, agitation, acids and bases, heavy metal ions, and high concentrations of ionic compounds.

Section 13.5: Describe how an enzyme catalyzes a reaction, the factors that affect enzyme activity, and how a cell regulates the activity of its enzymes.
- Enzymes are proteins that speed up a reaction and force it to produce a specific product.
- The three steps of an enzyme-catalyzed reaction are the binding of the substrate to the enzyme, the conversion of substrate to product, and the releasing of the product from the active site.
- Both the enzyme and the substrate normally change their shape as they bind to each other.
- Enzymes speed up reactions by decreasing the activation energy for the reaction.
- Enzymes are usually most active at a specific temperature and pH, with the activity decreasing as the temperature and pH move away from these optimum conditions.
- Competitive inhibitors fit into the active site and prevent the enzyme from binding to its normal substrate.
- Effectors control the activity of an enzyme by changing the shape of the active site.

Section 13.6: Describe the functions and chemical nature of the two main types of cofactors.
- A cofactor is any substance that is required by an enzyme but that is not made from amino acids.
- The two categories of cofactors are metal ions and coenzymes (organic cofactors).
- Some cofactors are permanently bonded to the polypeptide chain, while others bind only during the reaction.
- Many coenzymes contain a B vitamin, which must be part of the diet.

Section 13.7: Describe the sources of amino acids in humans and other organisms, and identify the factors that can cause protein deficiency in humans.
- Amino acids that cannot be made by the human body are called essential amino acids, and these must be present in the diet.
- Nonessential amino acids can be made from other nutrients, but the nitrogen must be supplied by other amino acids.
- Protein deficiency can be caused by insufficient total protein, by inadequate amounts of the essential amino acids, and by inadequate amounts of energy-producing nutrients.
- The nitrogen cycle allows atmospheric N_2 to be converted to NH_4^+ and NO_3^-. Plants use these ions as a source of nitrogen to make all of the amino acids.

Concept Questions

OWL Online homework for this chapter may be assigned in OWL.
* indicates more challenging problems.

13.81 What is an amino acid, and why are amino acids important to all organisms?

13.82 Sketch the general structure of an amino acid in its zwitterion form, and label the following:

a) the amino group
b) the acid group
c) the α-carbon atom

13.83 Valine is a polar molecule, because it contains two strongly hydrophilic functional groups (the amino group and the acid group). Why is valine always classified as a hydrophobic amino acid?

$$\begin{array}{c} CH_2 \\ | \\ CH_3-CH \quad O \\ | \quad\quad \| \\ {}^+NH_3-CH-C-O^- \end{array}$$

Valine

13.84 Explain why glycine is the only amino acid that is not a chiral molecule. (The structure of glycine is shown in Table 13.1.)

13.85 Draw the structure of a peptide group, and show which two atoms participate in hydrogen bonds.

13.86 Draw a sketch showing how two peptide groups can form a hydrogen bond.

13.87 What are the two common secondary structures in proteins, and how do they differ from each other?

13.88 What is a triple helix, and why do triple helices contain an unusually large amount of glycine?

13.89 Why do amino acids that have hydrocarbon side chains generally appear in the interior of a globular protein?

13.90 Why do acidic and basic amino acids generally appear on the surface of a globular protein?

13.91 Explain why membrane proteins contain an unusually high proportion of hydrophobic amino acids.

13.92 Both cysteine and methionine contain sulfur, but only cysteine can form a disulfide bridge. Explain why methionine cannot form a disulfide bridge.

13.93 What is the difference between the secondary structure and the tertiary structure of a protein?

13.94 All proteins have primary, secondary, and tertiary structures. However, not all proteins have quaternary structures. Why is this?

13.95 Your saliva contains an enzyme that breaks down starch. If you mix your saliva with a little ethanol, the enzyme becomes inactive. Explain.

13.96 Enzymes affect a chemical reaction in two ways. What are they?

13.97 Describe the three steps that happen when an enzyme catalyzes a reaction.

13.98 a) What effect does an enzyme have on the activation energy of the reaction that it catalyzes?
b) Why does this change in the activation energy make the reaction go faster?

13.99 What is the activity of an enzyme, and what is the typical range of enzyme activities?

13.100 Why does the activity of an enzyme depend on the pH of its surroundings?

13.101 Two samples of an enzyme are dissolved in water. Sample 1 is heated to 100°C, and sample 2 is cooled to 0°C. At these temperatures, the enzyme has no detectable activity. Next, both samples are brought to 37°C. At this temperature, sample 2 is active, but sample 1 is not. Explain this difference.

13.102 What is the difference between an effector and a substrate?

13.103 What is the difference between a competitive inhibitor and a negative effector? Which of these usually has a chemical structure that resembles the substrate?

13.104 What role do cofactors play in enzyme activity?

13.105 What is the difference between an essential amino acid and a nonessential amino acid?

13.106 Describe three ways in which diet could produce a protein deficiency.

13.107 Humans can use the nitrogen atom in leucine to make the amino group in serine, but we cannot use the nitrogen atom in serine to make leucine. Why is this?

13.108 What is the ultimate source of the nitrogen atoms in all living organisms, and how are these nitrogen atoms converted into compounds that can be used by plants and animals?

Summary and Challenge Problems

13.109 Gamma-carboxyglutamic acid is used to build certain proteins that play a role in blood clotting.

a) Identify the side chain in this amino acid, and classify the amino acid as hydrophobic or hydrophilic. If it is hydrophilic, classify it as acidic, basic, or neutral.
b) Draw the structure of this amino acid as it will appear at pH 7.
c) Are there any chiral carbon atoms in this molecule? If so, which ones are they?

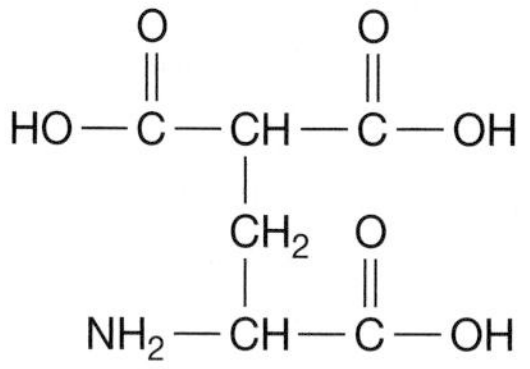

```
       O         O
       ||        ||
HO — C — CH — C — OH
              |
             CH2   O
              |    ||
   NH2 — CH — C — OH
```

Gamma-Carboxyglutamic acid

13.110 Draw the structure of the tetrapeptide Ala–Gly–Glu–Trp as it appears at pH 7.

13.111 *List all of the possible tripeptides that can be made using arginine, isoleucine, and valine (one molecule of each). (One possible tripeptide is Arg–Ile–Val.)

13.112 *The amino acid composition of histone H3 (a protein that binds to DNA) is shown in the following table.

Amino Acid	Number	Amino Acid	Number
Alanine	18	Leucine	12
Arginine	18	Lysine	13
Asparagine	1	Methionine	2
Aspartic acid	4	Phenylalanine	4
Cysteine	2	Proline	6
Glutamic acid	7	Serine	5
Glutamine	8	Threonine	10
Glycine	7	Tryptophan	0
Histidine	2	Tyrosine	3
Isoleucine	7	Valine	6

a) How many hydrophilic amino acids are there in histone H3? How many hydrophobic amino acids?
b) How many polar neutral amino acids are there in histone H3? How many acidic amino acids? How many basic amino acids?
c) Is histone H3 positively charged, negatively charged, or uncharged at pH 7?
d) Histone H3 binds tightly to DNA. Based on this and on your earlier answers, predict whether DNA is positively charged, negatively charged, or uncharged at pH 7.

13.113 When the molecule at the bottom of the page is hydrolyzed, the products are four amino acids. Three of the four are common amino acids, but the other is not.

a) Circle the peptide groups in this molecule. How many peptide groups are there?
b) Draw the structures of the four amino acids that are formed when this compound is hydrolyzed. (Draw the structures as they appear at pH 7.)
c) Identify the three common amino acids, using the information in Table 13.1.
d) Classify the fourth amino acid as hydrophobic or hydrophilic. If it is hydrophilic, classify it as acidic, basic, or neutral.
e) What is the C-terminal amino acid in this molecule?
f) What is the N-terminal amino acid in this molecule?

13.114 Select your answers to each part of this problem from the following list of amino acids:

lysine leucine phenylalanine
threonine glutamic acid

a) For which of these amino acids will the hydrophobic interaction be important?
b) For which of these amino acids will the hydrophilic interaction be important?
c) Which of these amino acids can participate in an ion pair at pH 7?
d) Which of these amino acids are most likely to be found in the interior of a protein?

13.115 *The rare amino acid that follows, called selenocysteine, is found in a few microorganisms. Two molecules of this amino acid can combine to form a diselenide bridge, analogous to the disulfide bridge that is formed by cysteine. Draw the structure of the diselenide bridge that is formed by two selenocysteine molecules.

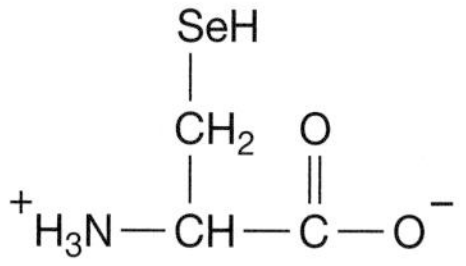

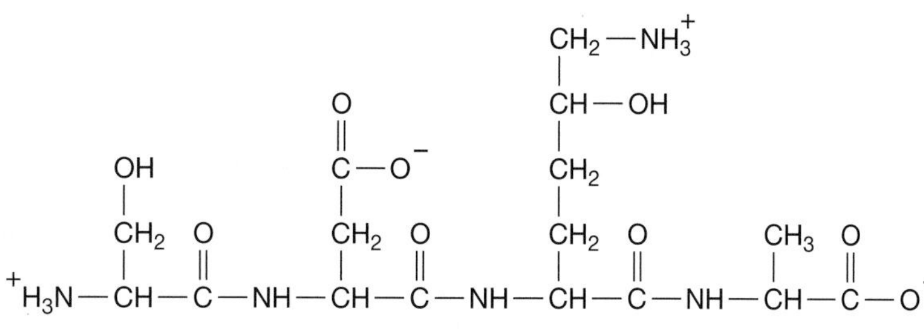

```
           SeH
            |
           CH2   O
            |    ||
+H3N — CH — C — O−
```

```
                                            CH2 — NH3+
                                             |
                          O                  CH — OH
                          ||                 |
         OH               C — O−             CH2
         |                |                  |
         CH2   O          CH2   O            CH2   O          CH3   O
         |     ||         |     ||           |     ||         |     ||
+H3N — CH — C — NH — CH — C — NH — CH — C — NH — CH — C — O−
```

Structure for problem 13.113

13.116 Tell whether each of the following sentences describes the primary, secondary, tertiary or quaternary structure of a protein:

a) Succinate dehydrogenase contains two separate polypeptide chains, one of which is roughly twice as large as the other.
b) In pyruvate kinase, amino acids 124 through 139 form an α-helix.
c) In chymotrypsin, the last five amino acids are Thr–Leu–Ala–Ala–Asn.
d) In the structure of insulin, arginine and glutamic acid form an ion pair.

13.117 The following sequence of amino acids occurs in a globular protein, and it forms an α-helix. Would you expect this section of the polypeptide to be located in the interior or on the exterior of the protein?

Leu–Ser–Phe–Ala–Ala–Ala–Met–Asn–Gly–Leu–Ala

13.118 A solution contains an enzyme dissolved in water. Which of the following will probably denature the enzyme?

a) cooling the solution to 5°C
b) heating the solution to 75°C
c) adding water to the solution
d) adding acetone to the solution
e) adding 1 M HCl to the solution
f) stirring the solution gently

13.119 Draw an energy diagram that compares the activation energy of a reaction with and without an enzyme.

13.120 a) Give three examples of metal ions that are used as cofactors.
b) Give three examples of vitamins that are used to make cofactors.

13.121 The enzyme propionyl-CoA carboxylase contains a molecule of lysine covalently bonded to a molecule of biotin. The structure of biotin is shown here, and the structure of lysine is shown in Table 13.1.

a) Is lysine a cofactor for this enzyme? Is it a coenzyme?
b) Is biotin a cofactor for this enzyme? Is it a coenzyme?

$CH_2-CH_2-CH_2-CH_2-COOH$ (attached to a fused ring system: a cyclic urea, O=C with two HN groups, fused to a ring containing S)

Biotin

13.122 *In the following reaction, must the enzyme select among more than one product? If so, what is the other possible product?

$$HO-\overset{O}{\overset{\|}{C}}-CH_2-CH_2-CH_2-\overset{O}{\overset{\|}{C}}-S-CoA \xrightarrow{\text{Enzyme}} HO-\overset{O}{\overset{\|}{C}}-CH_2-CH{=}CH-\overset{O}{\overset{\|}{C}}-S-CoA$$

13.123 The activity of chymotrypsin reaches a peak at a pH of around 7 to 8. Based on this, would you expect chymotrypsin to play an important role in the digestion of protein in your stomach? Explain your answer.

13.124 If enzyme A requires 1 second to convert 100 molecules of substrate into product, while enzyme B requires 10 seconds to convert 100 molecules of substrate into product, which enzyme has the higher activity?

13.125 *The active site of chymotrypsin is shown in Figure 13.21. Explain why chymotrypsin does not normally hydrolyze peptide bonds between arginine and another amino acid. (The structure of arginine is shown in Table 13.1.)

13.126 Many of the enzymes that function inside a typical cell have pH–activity curves similar to that of trypsin, while very few have curves similar to that of pepsin. (See Figure 13.23.) What does this tell you about the typical pH inside a cell?

13.127 *Lysozyme is an enzyme that destroys the outer walls of some types of bacteria. It is found in egg white (and many other biological fluids). The pH–activity curve of lysozyme peaks around pH 5, but the pH of egg white is normally between 8 and 9. What does this suggest about the effect of bacterial contamination on the pH of egg white?

13.128 **Thermus thermophilus* is a microorganism that lives only in certain natural springs. The relationship between the activity of the enzymes in this organism and the temperature is shown here. What does this imply about the conditions in the habitat of this microorganism?

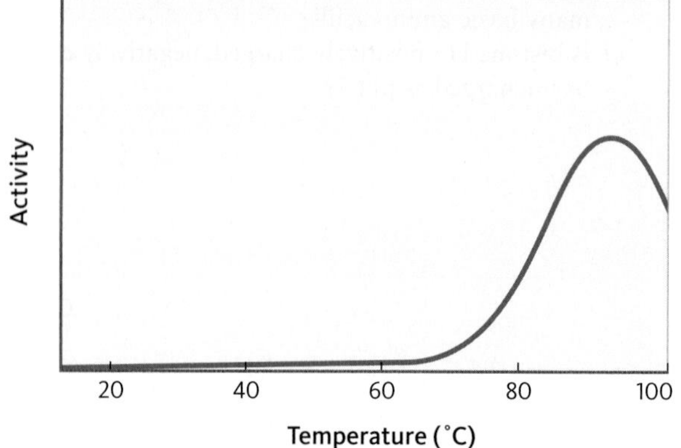

13.129 Atorvastatin (Lipitor) is widely used to lower cholesterol levels. This medication is a competitive inhibitor of HMG-CoA reductase, one of the enzymes that your body uses to build cholesterol. Would you expect the structure of atorvastatin to resemble the structure of the substrate in the reaction that is catalyzed by HMG-CoA reductase?

13.130 *The enzyme dihydropteroate synthetase catalyzes the following reaction in bacteria:

para-aminobenzoate + dihydropteroate diphosphate → dihydropteroate + $H_2P_2O_7^{2-}$

Dihydropteroate synthetase becomes much less active when a small amount of sulfanilamide is added to the reaction mixture, making sulfanilamide toxic to bacteria. Would you expect sulfanilamide to be a competitive inhibitor or a negative effector of dihydropteroate synthetase, given the structures of para-aminobenzoate and sulfanilamide?

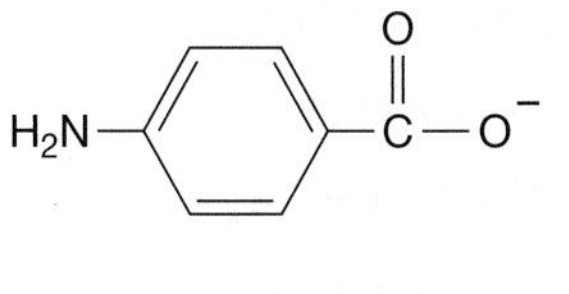

Para-**aminobenzoate**

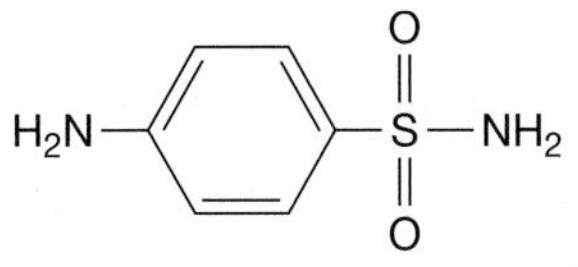

Sulfanilamide

13.131 NAD^+ and FAD are both coenzymes. Intracellular fluid contains a significant concentration of NAD^+, but it has no FAD. Based on this information, which of these coenzymes is permanently bonded to its enzyme?

13.132 A typical person's body might require 25 g of essential amino acids and 25 g of nonessential amino acids to make all of the necessary proteins. Which of the following diets would probably be able to meet this person's amino acid needs, assuming that the person's Calorie needs are also being met? Explain your answer in each case.

a) a diet containing 30 g of essential amino acids and no nonessential amino acids
b) a diet containing 30 g of essential amino acids and 30 g of nonessential amino acids
c) a diet containing 60 g of essential amino acids and no nonessential amino acids

13.133 All amino acids contain the elements hydrogen, carbon, nitrogen, and oxygen. In human nutrition, which of these elements can only be supplied by other amino acids?

13.134 *In addition to being the building blocks of proteins, amino acids are used to make other important molecules. Often, this involves removing NH_3 or CO_2 from the amino acid. Using Table 13.1, tell which amino acid could be used to make each of the following compounds:

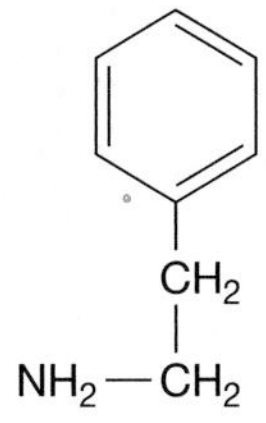

a) **Phenethylamine**

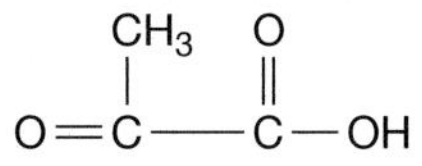

b) **Pyruvic acid**

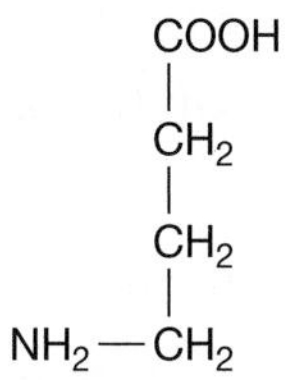

c) **γ-Aminobutyric acid**

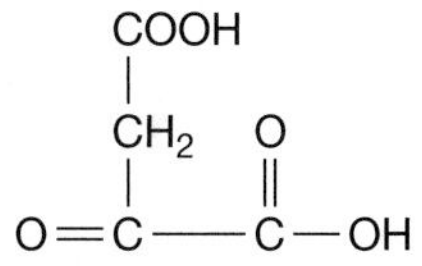

d) **Oxaloacetic acid**

13.135 What is a complete protein? What types of foods supply complete proteins?

13.136 Will a diet that contains pinto beans and rice as the primary protein sources supply all of the necessary amino acids?

14 Carbohydrates and Lipids

Phuong decides to get a physical exam before she starts training for a long bicycle race, and her doctor orders several routine blood tests as part of the physical exam. Two of these tests will check the concentration of glucose and triglycerides in Phuong's blood. These substances are the primary fuels for most cells in our bodies; the cells oxidize these compounds to carbon dioxide and water, obtaining energy from these reactions. However, glucose and triglycerides play different roles, and their concentrations are generally independent of each other. Glucose, a simple sugar (or monosaccharide), is the primary fuel for the cells of the nervous system and is an important energy source for all body tissues. A high concentration of glucose in the blood is most commonly an indicator of diabetes mellitus, a disease in which the cells in the body cannot absorb glucose from the bloodstream efficiently. Triglycerides (fats) are the main fuel for the heart and resting muscles, and they can be used as an energy source by most other tissues. A high concentration of triglycerides in the blood increases the risk of heart disease.

Phuong's lab results show that her glucose level is 87 mg/dL and her triglyceride level is 93 mg/dL. Phuong's doctor tells her that both of these values are well within the normal range, putting her at low risk for diabetes and heart disease.

OUTLINE

LABORATORY REQUISITION—CHEMISTRY

☐ Sodium	NA	☐ Fructosamine	FRU/ALB
☐ Potassium	K	☐ PSA	PSA
☐ Creatinine	CREAT	☐ Chloride	CL
☐ BUN	BUN	☐ Calcium	CA
☑ Glucose–fasting	GLUCF	☐ Phosphorus	PHOS
☐ Glucose–random	GLUCR	☐ Phenylalanine	PKU
☐ Hemoglobin A1C	HGBA1C	☐ Uric Acid	URIC

Total Bilirubin BILIT
Neonate T. Bilirubin BILITN
Serum Protein Elect. PEP
Ferritin FERR
Iron/TIBC IRON/TIBC
Hgb Electrophoresis HGB EP
T4/FTI T4S
TSH TSH
Alk Phos ALKP
SGOT (AST) AST
Albumin ALB
SGPT (ALT) ALT
CPK (CK) CK
CKMB CKMB
Amylase AMYL
Cholesterol CHOL
HDL HDL
LDL–fasting LDL
Triglycerides–fasting TRIG
Combustion of carbohydrates and triglycerides provides most of the energy our bodies use.
Corbis Super RF / Alamy

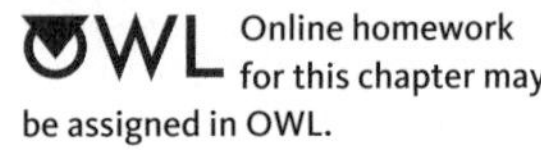
Online homework for this chapter may be assigned in OWL.

The chemical processes of life require a great deal of energy. An adult human consumes between 1200 and 2400 kcal of energy every day just to keep alive. Any physical activity, including eating, adds to this total. Although our bodies burn some protein to supply energy, we humans, and most other organisms, obtain the bulk of the energy we need by burning carbohydrates and fats.

Both carbohydrates and fats are essential components of our diet. In particular, fats supply certain compounds that our bodies require and cannot make from anything else. However, fats have acquired a bad reputation over the past few decades. Researchers have linked fat consumption to obesity, to certain cancers, and to heart disease. With such a reputation, it is little wonder that "fat-free" has become the catchphrase of choice among many people. More recently, carbohydrates have also come under scrutiny, with various diets advocating decreased consumption of both sugars and complex carbohydrates. However, it is the overconsumption of fats or carbohydrates that is unhealthy, not the nutrients themselves.

In this chapter, we will examine the structures and properties of carbohydrates and fats. We will also look at the sources of these compounds, and we will explore how our bodies use them. Let us begin with the carbohydrates.

OBJECTIVE: *Know the structural features and typical physical properties of monosaccharides.*

14.1 Monosaccharides

A tiring runner gulps down a few mouthfuls of a sports drink. A backpacker munches a granola bar on the trail. An overworked student wolfs down a chocolate bar to keep her going through a late-night study session. Within a few minutes, all of these people feel less weary (not to mention less hungry). All of them have taken advantage of the **carbohydrates** in the food or drink they have consumed.

Carbohydrates are, quite literally, the fuel of life. Humans and most other organisms use carbohydrates such as sugar and starch as their primary source of energy. In addition, carbohydrates are components of a wide range of vital chemical compounds in living cells. From the structural fibers of a tree to the cell wall of a bacterium, from the molecules that determine our blood type to the molecules that determine our genetic heritage, carbohydrates are ubiquitous in the living world.

Kresimir Juraga

All of these foods are rich in carbohydrates.

The simplest carbohydrates, and the building blocks of all other carbohydrates, are the **monosaccharides**, or **simple sugars**. Monosaccharides contain carbon, hydrogen, and oxygen in a fixed ratio of 1 to 2 to 1. This ratio led early chemists to think that sugars are made from carbon and water, and it is the origin of the word carbohydrate *(hydrated carbon)*. Although carbohydrates do not actually contain water molecules, they break down into carbon and water if they are heated. The water evaporates, but the carbon remains as a black residue. If you have ever burned a sugary food on your stove or in your oven, you have seen this aspect of carbohydrate chemistry.

Chemists classify monosaccharides based on the number of carbon atoms in the molecule. For example, any simple sugar that contains six carbon atoms is called a *hexose*. The suffix *-ose* identifies the molecule as a carbohydrate, and the prefix *hex-* gives us the number of carbon atoms. Table 14.1 lists the main classes of monosaccharides and gives some examples of each class.

Health Note: Low-calorie foods often contain a sugar alcohol such as sorbitol, mannitol, or xylitol. Sugar alcohols are sweet-tasting compounds that are closely related to monosaccharides but contain two additional hydrogen atoms. They contain fewer Calories than sugars do, and they do not promote tooth decay because bacteria in the mouth do not break them down.

TABLE 14.1 Formulas of Common Monosaccharides

Type of Monosaccharide	Number of Carbon Atoms	Molecular Formula	Examples
Triose	3	$C_3H_6O_3$	Glyceraldehyde
Tetrose	4	$C_4H_8O_4$	Erythrose
Pentose	5	$C_5H_{10}O_5$	Ribose, arabinose, xylose
Hexose	6	$C_6H_{12}O_6$	Glucose, fructose, galactose, mannose

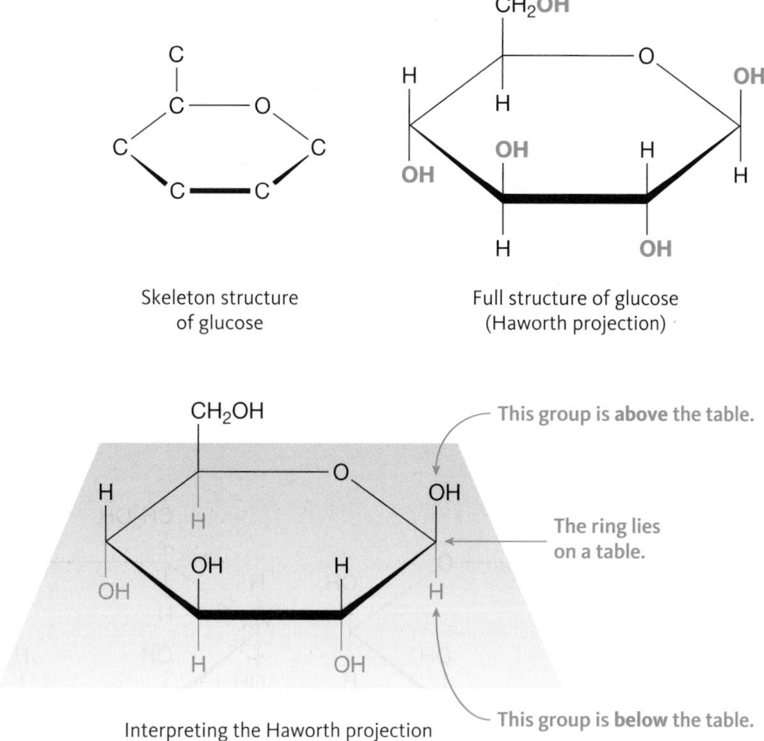

Skeleton structure of glucose
Full structure of glucose (Haworth projection)
This group is above the table.
The ring lies on a table.
This group is below the table.
Interpreting the Haworth projection

FIGURE 14.1 The structure of glucose, a hexose.

All Monosaccharides Have Several Structural Features in Common

Most of the simple sugars that occur in our bodies are pentoses and hexoses. These monosaccharides have the following structural features:

- They contain a five- or six-membered ring of atoms.
- One of the atoms in the ring is oxygen, and the rest are carbon.
- Any carbon atoms that are not part of the ring are attached to the ring carbons nearest to the oxygen.
- All but one of the carbon atoms are bonded to hydroxyl groups.

Figure 14.1 shows the structure of glucose, the most common monosaccharide. Glucose contains six carbon atoms, making it a hexose. Five of the six carbon atoms are incorporated into the ring, along with an oxygen atom. The remaining carbon atom is attached to the carbon immediately to the left of the oxygen atom. When chemists draw the structures of simple sugars, they generally use a *Haworth projection,* in which the ring is drawn as if it is lying on a table and we are viewing it from the side. The groups that are attached to the ring project upward and downward.

Haworth projections do not show the actual shape of a carbohydrate. Remember that when any carbon atom forms four single bonds, the bonds arrange themselves in a tetrahedron, as we saw in Section 8.1. As a result, the bonds that project from the ring do not point straight up and down. Furthermore, the ring does not lie flat; the six-membered ring in glucose adopts the chair configuration, just as it is in cyclohexane. However, drawing the real shape of a carbohydrate is difficult, so Haworth projections provide a convenient alternative. Figure 14.2 compares the Haworth projection with the actual shape of the glucose molecule.

Figure 14.3 shows the structures of the most common pentoses and hexoses. Of the common hexoses, glucose, mannose, and galactose have similar structures, while fructose contains a five-membered ring with two branching carbon atoms. The most common pentose is ribose. Both ribose and fructose contain a five-membered ring, but ribose has only one additional carbon atom while fructose has two.

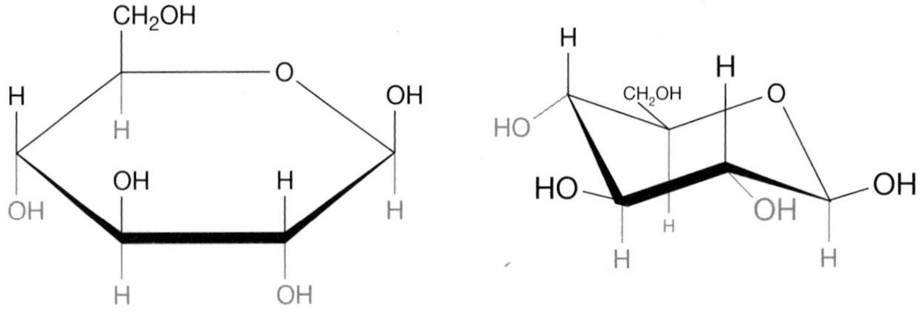

Glucose: Haworth projection

Glucose: actual shape of molecule

FIGURE 14.2 The Haworth projection and the actual shape of glucose.

Galactose (a hexose)

Mannose (a hexose)

Glucose (a hexose)

Fructose (a hexose)

Ribose (a pentose)

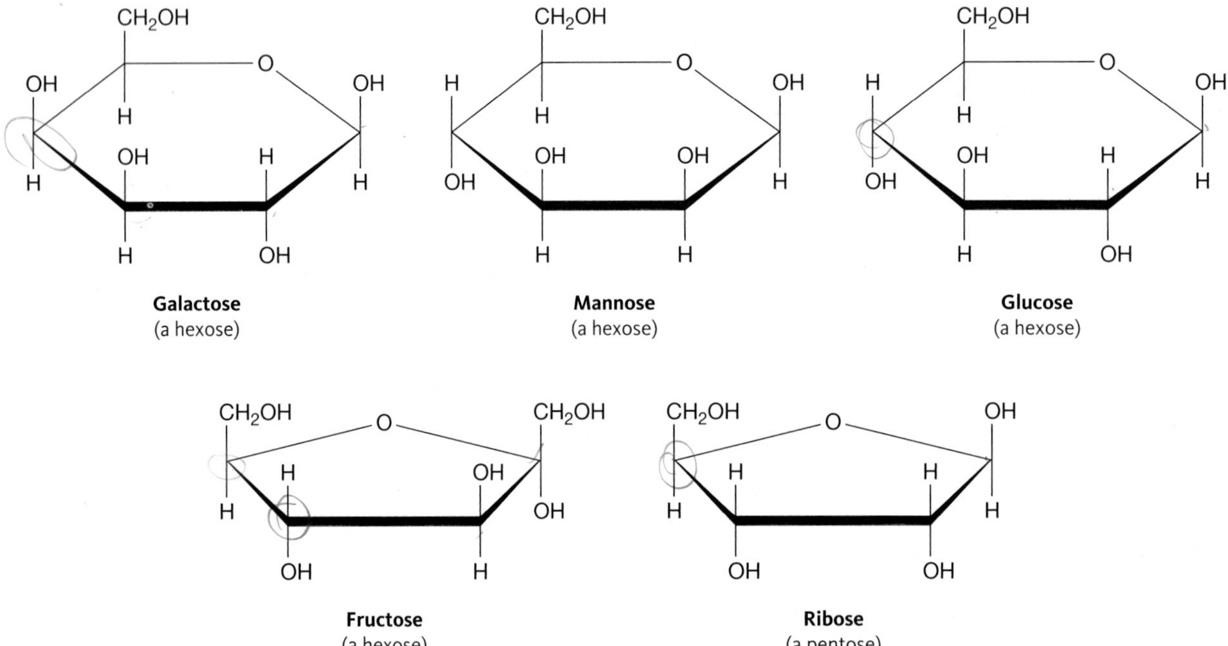

FIGURE 14.3 The structures of the common monosaccharides.

Health Note: In clinical work, isotonic glucose solutions are abbreviated D5W, which stands for a 5% (w/v) solution of *dextrose* in *water*.

The names of most monosaccharides end in *-ose,* but otherwise they are not very informative. It is not possible to work out the structure of a monosaccharide from its name. To make matters worse, two monosaccharides have alternate names that are widely used: glucose is also called *dextrose,* and fructose is called *levulose.* You will probably encounter these names if you pursue a career in health care. You may also see the term *invert sugar,* which is used for a 50:50 mixture of glucose and fructose.

We Identify the Carbon Atoms in a Monosaccharide by Numbering Them

Monosaccharides often form bonds to one another and to other types of compounds. These bonds link specific carbon atoms in the monosaccharides. To identify a particular carbon atom in a simple sugar, chemists number the carbon atoms in the molecule. The numbering begins at the right side of the molecule, starting with the carbon atom that is not part of the ring (if any) or with the rightmost carbon in the ring. Figure 14.4 shows the numbering system for three important monosaccharides.

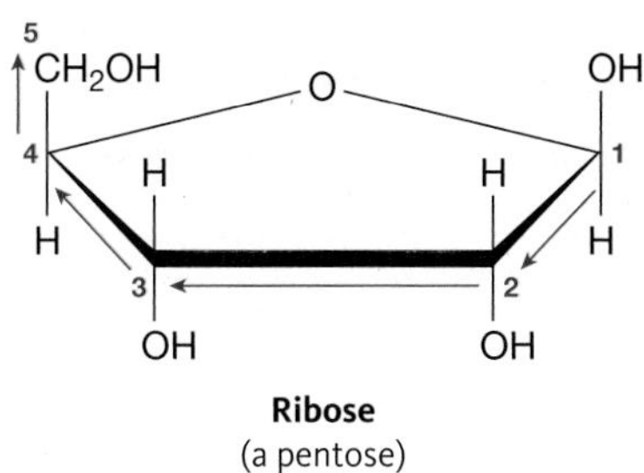

Ribose
(a pentose)

Glucose
(a hexose)

Fructose
(a hexose)

FIGURE 14.4 Numbering the carbon atoms in a monosaccharide.

Sample Problem 14.1

Identifying carbon atoms and classifying a sugar

Identify carbon 3 in lyxose, and classify lyxose as a pentose or a hexose.

Lyxose

SOLUTION

Lyxose contains five carbon atoms, so it is a **pentose.** To identify carbon 3, we number the carbon atoms starting from the right side of the ring, as shown here:

TRY IT YOURSELF: *Identify carbon 2 in tagatose, and classify tagatose as a pentose or a hexose.*

Tagatose

For additional practice, try Core Problems 14.3 through 14.6.

TABLE 14.2 The Properties of Three Hexoses

	Glucose	Galactose	Mannose
Melting point	150°C	167°C	133°C
Solubility in water	900 g/L	2000 g/L	2500 g/L
Heat of combustion	3.72 kcal/g	3.70 kcal/g	3.73 kcal/g

Health Note: Glucose is a common ingredient in intravenous solutions because it is an immediate energy source for all body tissues. It is particularly important to the brain, which cannot burn fats or proteins to obtain energy. In contrast, only the liver can metabolize galactose or mannose, and our bodies excrete most of the mannose that we consume.

The identity of a monosaccharide depends on the exact positions of the hydroxyl groups attached to the ring. In general, if we exchange the positions of the hydrogen and hydroxyl groups on one of the ring carbons, we make a different sugar. For example, in Figure 14.3 we see that glucose differs from galactose in the arrangements of the bonds around carbon 4, and it differs from mannose in the arrangement around carbon 2. These differences give the three compounds different chemical and physical properties, as shown in Table 14.2. Glucose, galactose, and mannose are stereoisomers, because they have different arrangements of bonds around one or more carbon atoms. However, they are not enantiomers of one another, because they are not mirror images.

Our bodies can obtain energy from any of the hexoses in Table 14.2. However, we use glucose in preference to any other fuel, and every cell in our bodies can use glucose as an energy source. Our taste response to each of these sugars is also different. All three compounds taste sweet, but glucose tastes much sweeter than galactose or mannose.

The Physical Properties of Monosaccharides Reflect Their Structures

Monosaccharides tend to have similar physical properties, regardless of their structures. All of the pentoses and hexoses are white crystalline solids, with fairly high melting points (typically above 100°C) and such high boiling points that they break down into carbon and water when they are heated, rather than boiling. Recall that the boiling point of a compound depends on the strength of the attraction between molecules. The hydroxyl groups in simple sugars can form hydrogen bonds, so the attraction between neighboring molecules is fairly strong. As a result, it takes more energy to pull two molecules away from each other than it does to rearrange the covalent bonds that hold each molecule together.

Monosaccharides are very soluble in water, because the hydroxyl groups in any monosaccharide are able to form hydrogen bonds with water molecules. However, monosaccharides do not generally dissolve well in organic solvents. For instance, the solubility of glucose in methanol is only 8 g/L, and glucose is insoluble in hexane.

Monosaccharides Are Used to Build Larger Molecules

Most monosaccharides occur in nature only as components of larger molecules. In the human body, for example, galactose and mannose are used to build several compounds in cell membranes, but there is virtually no free galactose or mannose to be found. Ribose is a component of nucleic acids and several coenzymes (including NAD^+, FAD, and coenzyme A), but it too is essentially undetectable as a free sugar in the human body. However, fructose is a common compound in plants, occurring in most fruit juices, and glucose is present in all higher organisms. Every cell in your body contains glucose, and most body fluids contain some glucose as well. For example, your blood typically contains around 4 g of dissolved glucose, distributed roughly equally between the plasma and the intracellular fluid. Glucose is also the primary building block for the complex carbohydrates starch and cellulose, which we will encounter in Section 14.4.

CORE PROBLEMS

All Core Problems are paired and the answers to the blue odd-numbered problems appear in the back of the book.

14.1 Tagatose is a monosaccharide that has been proposed as a "low-calorie sweetener." One molecule of tagatose contains six carbon atoms. What is the molecular formula of tagatose?

14.2 Ribulose is a monosaccharide that contains five carbon atoms. What is the molecular formula of ribulose?

continued

14.3 Classify each of the following monosaccharides as a triose, a tetrose, a pentose, or a hexose:

a)

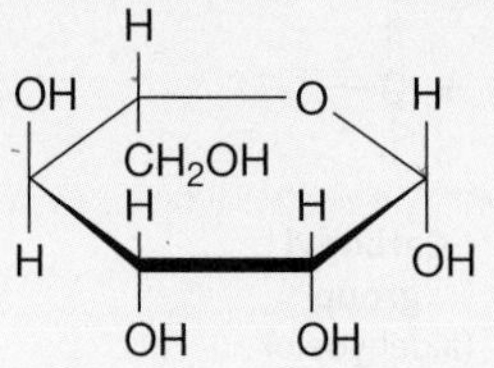

b)

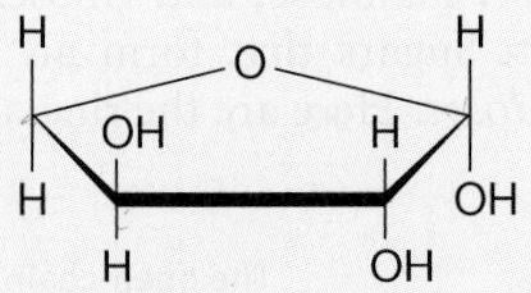

14.4 Classify each of the following monosaccharides as a triose, a tetrose, a pentose, or a hexose:

a)

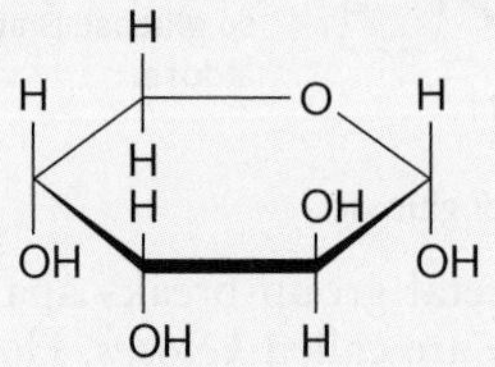

b)

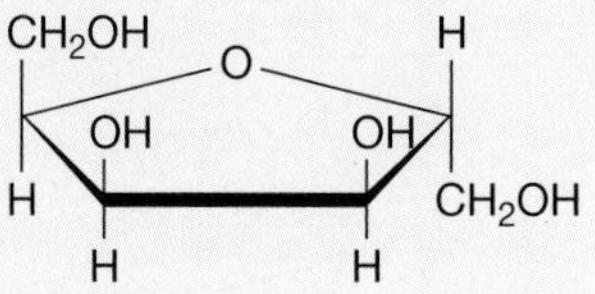

14.5 Find and circle carbon 4 in each of the monosaccharides in Problem 14.3.

14.6 Find and circle carbon 5 in each of the monosaccharides in Problem 14.4.

14.7 Which of the five common monosaccharides contain a six-membered ring?

14.8 Which of the five common monosaccharides contain a five-membered ring?

14.9 Cyclohexane and glucose both contain a six-membered ring. Which compound should have the higher solubility in water, and why?

14.10 Cyclopentanol and ribose both contain a five-membered ring. Which compound should have the higher melting point, and why?

14.2 Isomeric Forms of Monosaccharides: Anomers and Enantiomers

OBJECTIVES: *Understand how anomers are related and how they are interconverted, identify reducing sugars, and understand why living organisms only use one of the two enantiomers of any monosaccharide.*

All monosaccharides can exist in a variety of forms. For example, a solution of naturally occurring glucose contains a mixture of three compounds, all of them in equilibrium with one another. In addition, there are three other forms of glucose that are not found in natural sources. In this section, we will examine some of the forms of monosaccharides.

The Hemiacetal Group in Monosaccharides Can Open

Monosaccharides can exist in several forms because they contain a **hemiacetal** group. A hemiacetal group is similar to an ether group, but one of the two carbon atoms is also bonded to a hydroxyl group. The following structures illustrate the hemiacetal functional group and its location in glucose.

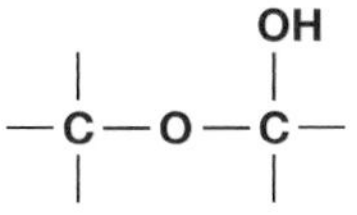

The hemiacetal functional group

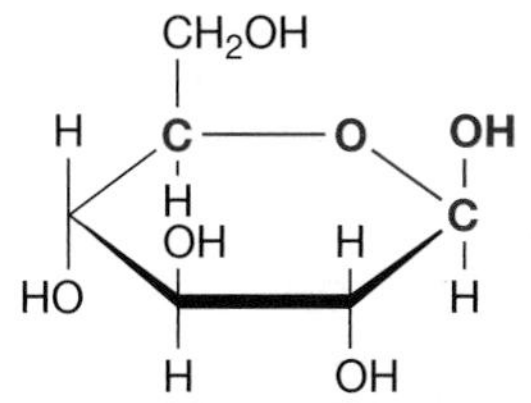

The location of the hemiacetal group in glucose

In any hemiacetal, one of the C–O bonds can break rather easily. In the process, the neighboring atoms rearrange to produce a carbonyl group (an aldehyde or a ketone) and an alcohol group, as shown here. Because the hemiacetal group is part of the ring, this reaction also changes the ring into an open-chain structure.

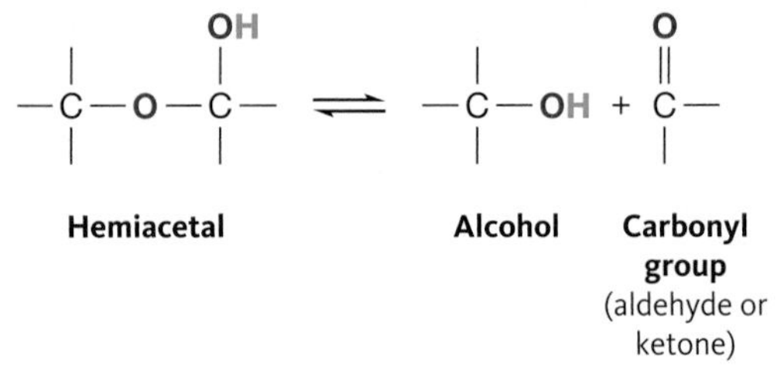

Hemiacetal ⇌ Alcohol + Carbonyl group (aldehyde or ketone)

Most monosaccharides, including glucose, galactose, mannose, and ribose, become aldehydes when their hemiacetal groups break apart. Sugars that form an aldehyde group when their hemiacetal groups open are called *aldoses*. Here are the ring and open-chain forms of glucose, a typical aldose.

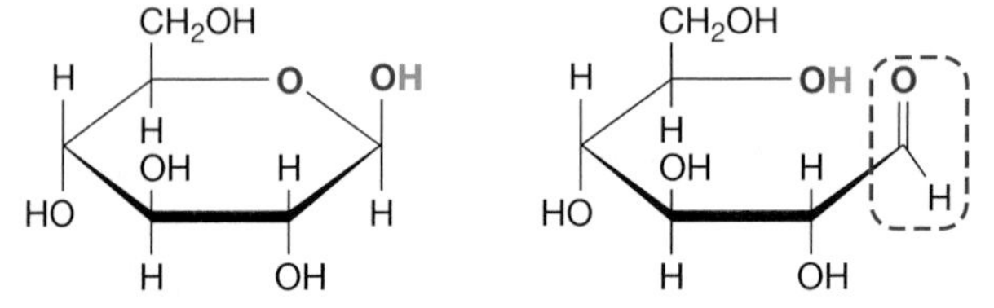

The open-chain form of glucose contains an aldehyde group, so glucose is an aldose.

The ring form of glucose   The open-chain form of glucose

However, fructose forms a ketone when its hemiacetal group breaks apart. Sugars that form a ketone when their hemiacetal groups open are called *ketoses*. Here are the ring and open-chain forms of fructose.

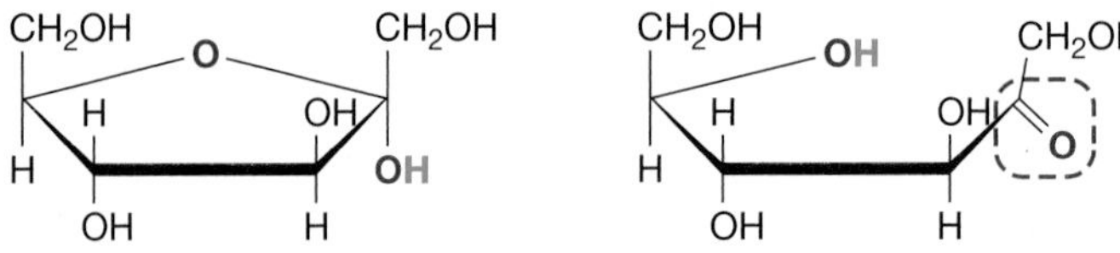

The open-chain form of fructose contains a ketone group, so fructose is a ketose.

The ring form of fructose   The open-chain form of fructose

In general, if the right-hand carbon in the ring is attached to a hydrogen atom (in addition to the hydroxyl group), the sugar is an aldose, as shown in Figure 14.5. If this carbon atom is attached to a carbon atom, the sugar is a ketose.

Whenever a monosaccharide dissolves in water, the solution contains an equilibrium mixture of the ring (hemiacetal) form and the open-chain (aldehyde or ketone) form. The aldehyde group in the open-chain form of an aldose is easy to oxidize. For example, the aldehyde group can be oxidized to a carboxylate group by a solution that contains Cu^{2+} and OH^- ions, called Benedict's reagent. During this reaction, the Cu^{2+} ions gain an electron to become Cu^+, which appears in the form of solid Cu_2O. The original Cu^{2+} ions are bright blue, whereas Cu_2O is brick red, so there is an obvious color change whenever a solution that contains an aldose is mixed with Benedict's reagent. This reaction is called Benedict's test, and carbohydrates that undergo this reaction are called **reducing sugars.** The balanced equation for this reaction (using glucose as the sugar) is

• The sugar "reduces" the charge on the copper ion from +2 to +1.

$$\underbrace{C_6H_{12}O_6(aq)}_{\text{glucose}} + \underbrace{2\ Cu^{2+}(aq) + 5\ OH^-(aq)}_{\text{Benedict's solution}} \rightarrow \underbrace{C_6H_{11}O_7^-(aq)}_{\text{gluconate}} + Cu_2O(s) + 3\ H_2O(l)$$

The structures of glucose and gluconate ion are shown here:

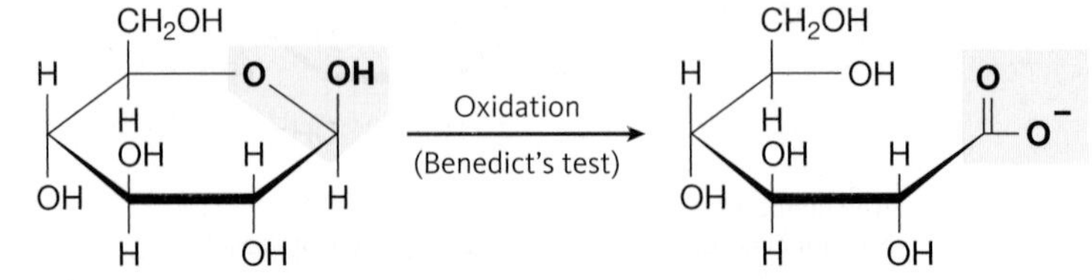

Oxidation (Benedict's test)

Glucose: contains a hemiacetal group   **Gluconate ion:** contains a carboxylate group

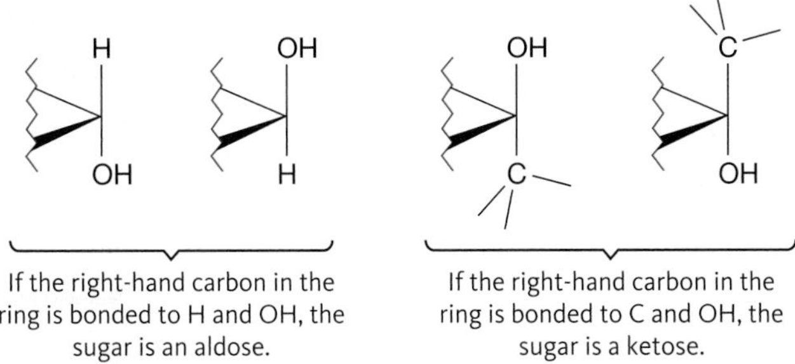
H
OH
OH
H
OH
C
C
OH
If the right-hand carbon in the ring is bonded to H and OH, the sugar is an aldose.
If the right-hand carbon in the ring is bonded to C and OH, the sugar is a ketose.

FIGURE 14.5 Determining whether a monosaccharide is an aldose or a ketose.

All aldoses react with Benedict's reagent and are reducing sugars. Fructose is also a reducing sugar, even though the ketone group in the open-chain form of fructose cannot be oxidized, because fructose reacts with the OH^- ions in Benedict's reagent to become glucose, which can then react with the Cu^{2+} ions.

In uncontrolled diabetes, the cells of a person's body cannot absorb glucose from the blood. As a result, the concentration of glucose in the blood rises to the point where the kidneys allow it to diffuse into the urine. For many years, Benedict's test was used to test urine samples of suspected diabetics for the presence of glucose. However, this test has now been replaced by a more sensitive method that uses an enzyme called *glucose oxidase* to oxidize the glucose.

Monosaccharides Exist in Two Anomeric Forms

Naturally occurring glucose, called D-glucose, is a mixture of two closely related structures called α-D-glucose and β-D-glucose, as shown in Figure 14.6. These two forms are a special type of stereoisomers called **anomers**. Anomers are sugars that differ only in the position of the OH in the hemiacetal group. The α form has the OH group below the ring, while the β form has the OH group above the ring.

Anomers are unusual in that we can interchange them by simply dissolving them in water. If we dissolve a sample of one anomer of glucose in water, some of the molecules gradually turn into the other form. Eventually, regardless of which anomer we start with, we form an equilibrium mixture that contains 64% β-D-glucose and 36% α-D-glucose. Since all of the glucose in a living organism is dissolved in water, all naturally occurring glucose is a mixture of the two anomeric forms.

No other functional groups in a monosaccharide can change positions in this way. For example, the OH and H that are bonded to carbon 4 of glucose do not interchange in solution, so glucose does not change into galactose.

The α and β forms of glucose can interconvert because both forms contain a hemiacetal group. Remember that the hemiacetal can break apart in solution, producing an open-chain molecule. The molecule remains in the open-chain form for only an instant before it returns to the ring form. However, during this time, the aldehyde group rotates freely, moving the oxygen rapidly from one side of the carbon skeleton to the other, as shown in Figure 14.7. When the ring closes, the aldehyde group becomes a hydroxyl

Health Note: The two anomers of glucose have the same nutritional value, but most people find that α-D-glucose tastes a little sweeter than β-D-glucose.

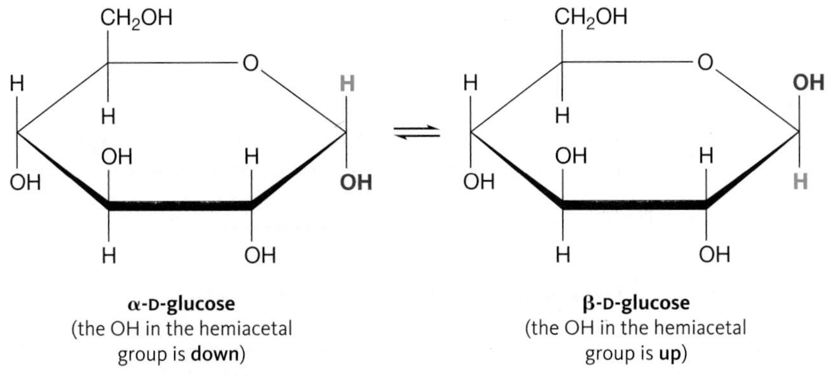

α-D-glucose
(the OH in the hemiacetal group is **down**)

β-D-glucose
(the OH in the hemiacetal group is **up**)

FIGURE 14.6 The structures of the two anomers of D-glucose.

α-D-glucose

β-D-glucose

The ring opens . . .

. . . and the ring closes.

. . . the aldehyde group rotates . . .

FIGURE 14.7 The mutarotation of D-glucose.

group again, locked into whichever position the aldehyde oxygen occupies at the instant the new bond forms. This reaction is called **mutarotation.** All of the steps in this sequence are reversible, so the β anomer can also revert to the α form.

All commonly occurring monosaccharides can form α and β anomers. In each case, the hydroxyl group that shifts position is attached to the rightmost carbon atom in the ring, called the *anomeric carbon.* The α form has the hydroxyl group below the ring, and the β form has it above the ring. The two anomers of D-ribulose are shown here:

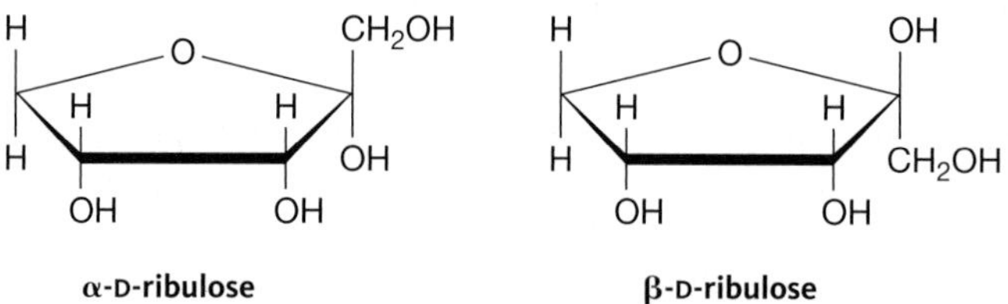

Sample Problem 14.2

Identifying anomers of a monosaccharide

The following structure is one of the two anomers of D-fructose. Is this the α or the β anomer?

SOLUTION

The anomeric carbon atom is carbon 2, at the rightmost corner of the ring. The hydroxyl group on this carbon is **below** the ring, so this is the **α anomer** of D-fructose (α-D-fructose).

The anomeric carbon atom

The hydroxyl group that is bonded to the anomeric carbon is **below** the ring.

continued

TRY IT YOURSELF: *The following structure is one of the two anomers of* D*-ribose. Is this the* α *or the* β *anomer?*

For additional practice, try Core Problems 14.15 and 14.16.

If we hold α-D-glucose up to a mirror, the reflection we see will be α-L-glucose.

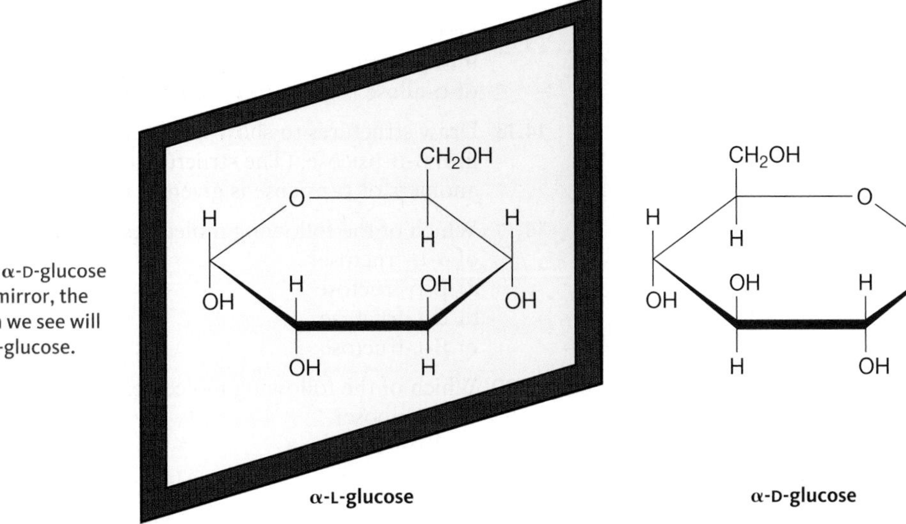

FIGURE 14.8 The structures of the D and L forms of glucose.

Health Note: L-glucose tastes almost as sweet as D-glucose, but it has no nutritive value. As a result, it has been proposed as a sweetener for low-calorie foods. However, L-glucose is more expensive than other low-calorie sweeteners, because it does not occur naturally and must be manufactured. Therefore, no diet foods currently contain L-glucose.

Carbohydrates Have Mirror Image Forms

All of the forms of D-glucose contain several chiral carbon atoms, so each form is chiral and has a non-superimposable mirror image. These mirror-image forms are called *L-glucose*. For instance, α-D-glucose has a mirror image, called α-L-glucose. These two molecules are enantiomers. Likewise, β-D-glucose and β-L-glucose are enantiomers. Figure 14.8 shows the relationship between α-D-glucose and α-L-glucose.

All common monosaccharides contain chiral carbon atoms, so all of them are chiral and have D and L forms. The D and L forms of a monosaccharide, like any pair of enantiomers, are equally stable and have virtually identical chemical and physical properties. However, our bodies have a strong preference for the D form of all carbohydrates. Recall that chiral objects can distinguish the two forms of another chiral object. The enzymes in our bodies that react with carbohydrates are chiral molecules, and they generally can only bind to the D form of a monosaccharide, as shown in Figure 14.9. As a result, our bodies can neither make nor use most L-monosaccharides. Since L-monosaccharides are rare, we will consider only the D forms in the rest of this text.

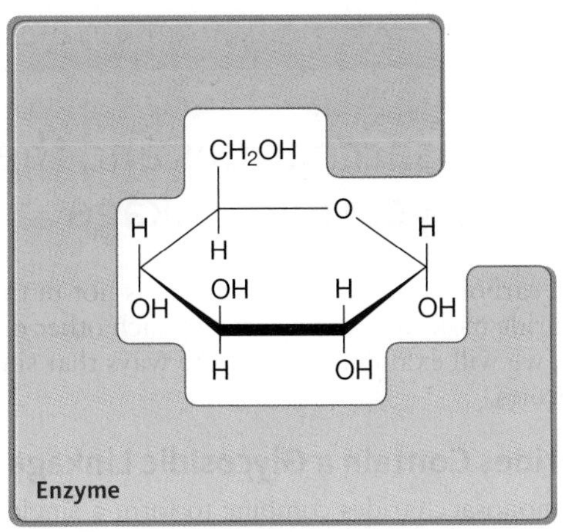

α-D-glucose fits into the active site of the enzyme.

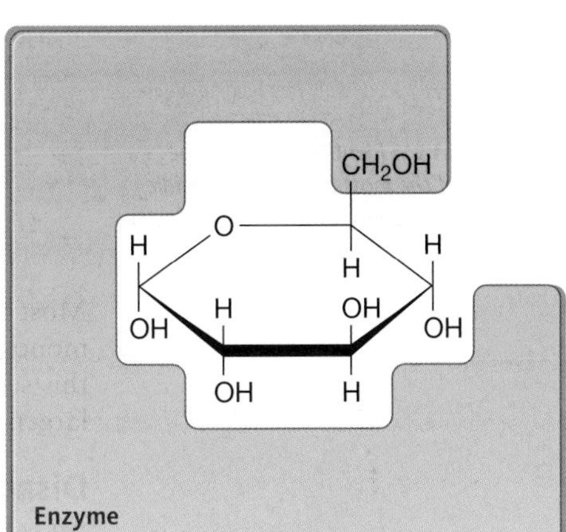

α-L-glucose does not fit into the active site.

FIGURE 14.9 Enzymes can distinguish between enantiomers.

CORE PROBLEMS

14.11 Draw structures to show that when the ring in ribose opens during mutarotation, the open-chain product contains an aldehyde group.

14.12 Draw structures to show that when the ring in fructose opens during mutarotation, the open-chain product contains a ketone group.

14.13 The following monosaccharide is called β-D-ribulose:

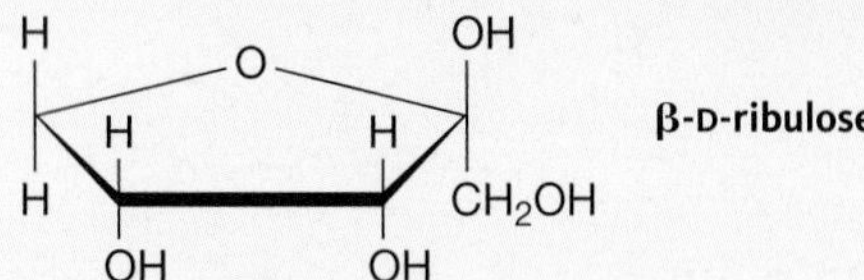

β-D-ribulose

a) Is β-D-ribulose a reducing sugar? Explain why or why not.
b) Is β-D-ribulose an aldose, or is it a ketose?

14.14 The following monosaccharide is called α-D-xylose:

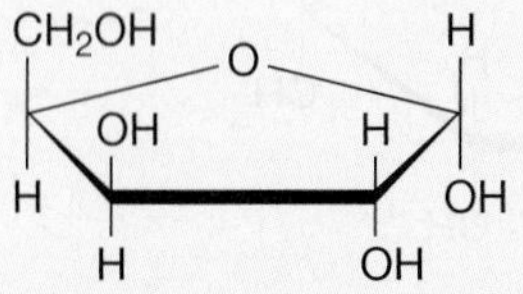

α-D-xylose

a) Is α-D-xylose a reducing sugar? Explain why or why not.
b) Is α-D-xylose an aldose, or is it a ketose?

14.15 The structure of one of the anomers of D-allose is shown here:

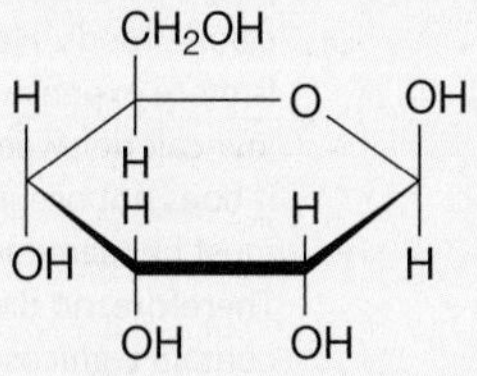

D-allose

a) Which carbon atom is the anomeric carbon?
b) Is this the structure of α-D-allose or β-D-allose?

14.16 The structure of one of the anomers of D-psicose is shown here:

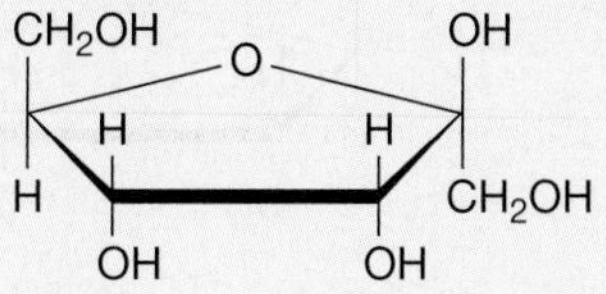

D-psicose

a) Which carbon atom is the anomeric carbon?
b) Is this the structure of α-D-psicose or β-D-psicose?

14.17 Draw structures to show how α-D-allose can change into β-D-allose. (The structure of one of the anomers of D-allose is given in Problem 14.15.)

14.18 Draw structures to show how α-D-psicose can change into β-D-psicose. (The structure of one of the anomers of D-psicose is given in Problem 14.16.)

14.19 Which of the following molecules is the enantiomer of α-D-fructose?
a) β-D-fructose
b) α-L-fructose
c) β-L-fructose

14.20 Which of the following molecules is the enantiomer of β-L-ribose?
a) β-D-ribose
b) α-L-ribose
c) α-D-ribose

OBJECTIVES: *Identify and draw the structures of the most common glycosidic linkages in disaccharides.*

14.3 Disaccharides and the Glycosidic Linkage

Most of the carbohydrate in any organism is not in the form of simple sugars. Instead, monosaccharide molecules are bonded to each other or to other types of compounds. In this section, we will examine some of the ways that simple sugars can combine to make larger molecules.

Disaccharides Contain a Glycosidic Linkage

When two monosaccharides combine to form a single organic molecule, the product is called a **disaccharide**. The reaction to make a disaccharide is a condensation involving hydroxyl groups from each of the two monosaccharides, as shown in Figure 14.10. The product contains two monosaccharide units linked by an oxygen atom. The bridging oxygen and the adjacent bonds are called a **glycosidic linkage**, and this linkage is analogous to the peptide bond that links amino acids in a protein.

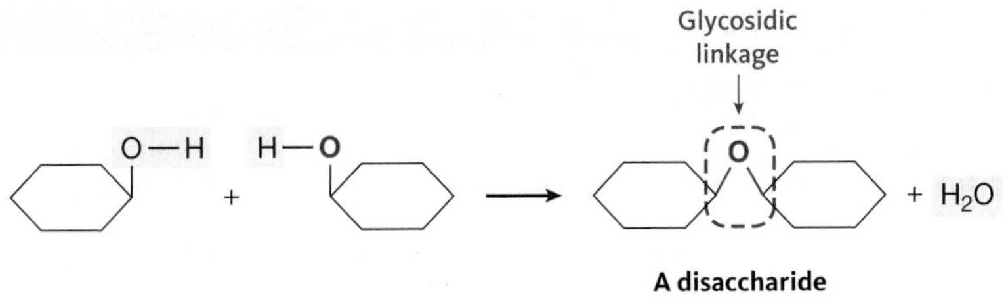

FIGURE 14.10 The formation of a glycosidic linkage.

In principle, there are many ways to link two monosaccharides, because each one contains several hydroxyl groups. In practice, though, some types of glycosidic linkages are particularly common in nature. The most common linkage connects carbon 1 of one sugar with carbon 4 of another. For example, if we connect two molecules of α-D-glucose in this fashion, we form maltose, as shown in Figure 14.11.

The link between the two glucose units in maltose is called an α(1→4) glycosidic linkage. The numbers tell us which two carbon atoms are linked by the bridging oxygen. The α tells us that the original OH on carbon 1 (the anomeric carbon) was in the α position. The oxygen remains below the ring when the glycosidic bond forms, so the α also tells us that the glycosidic bond points *downward* from the anomeric carbon of the left-hand glucose molecule.

If we use the β anomer of glucose instead of the α anomer, the product is cellobiose, as shown in Figure 14.12. Cellobiose contains a β(1→4) glycosidic linkage. The β tells us that the glycosidic bond points *upward* from the left-hand glucose molecule. Note that the bond between the bridging oxygen and the right-hand glucose points downward from the ring in both maltose and cellobiose, because the OH group on carbon 4 of glucose is always below the ring. Remember that only the OH attached to the anomeric carbon can change its position.

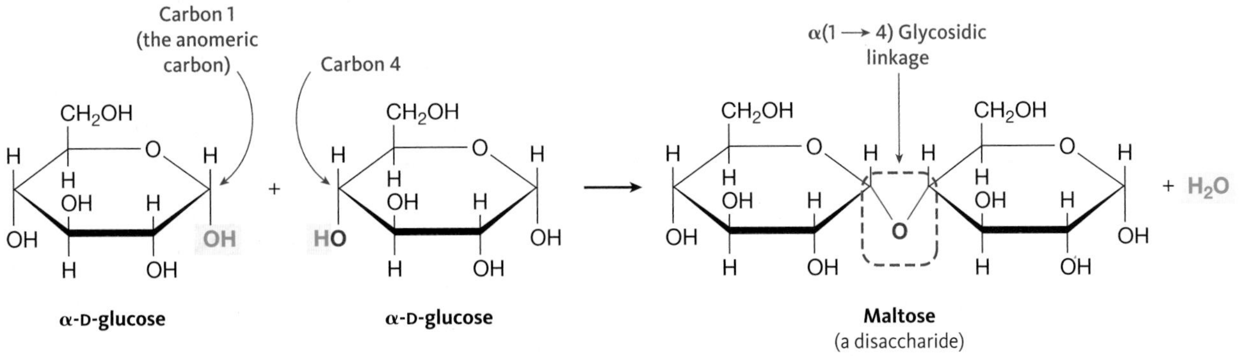

FIGURE 14.11 The formation of an α(1→4) glycosidic linkage.

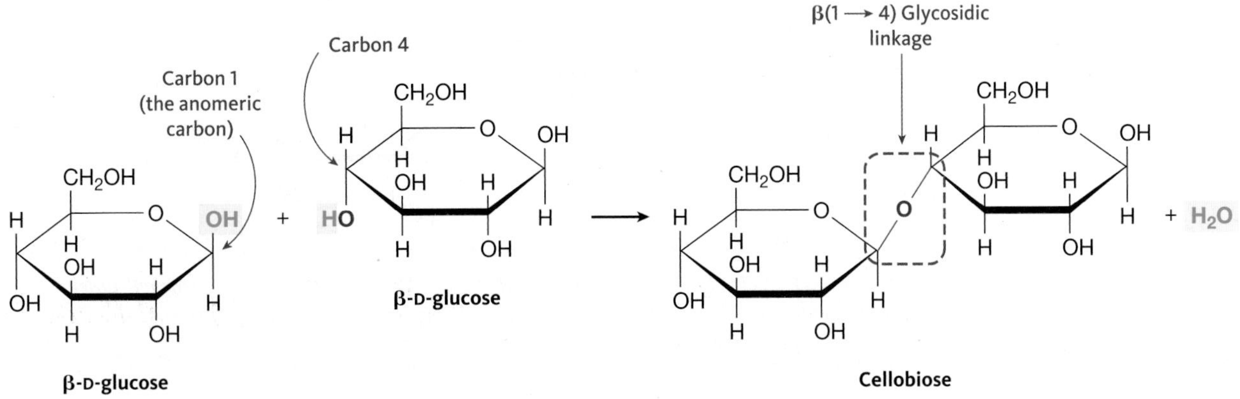

FIGURE 14.12 The formation of a β(1→4) glycosidic linkage.

Sample Problem 14.3

Drawing a glycosidic linkage

Draw the structure of the disaccharide that is formed when two molecules of α-D-galactose form an α(1→4) glycosidic linkage.

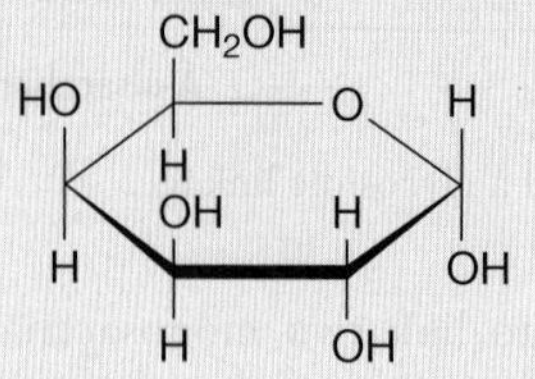

α-D-galactose

SOLUTION

To make the α(1→4) linkage, we start by drawing two molecules of galactose. We need to position our structures so the OH on carbon 1 of one molecule is beside the OH on carbon 4 of the other molecule. We can accomplish this by drawing the right-hand molecule lower than the left-hand molecule.

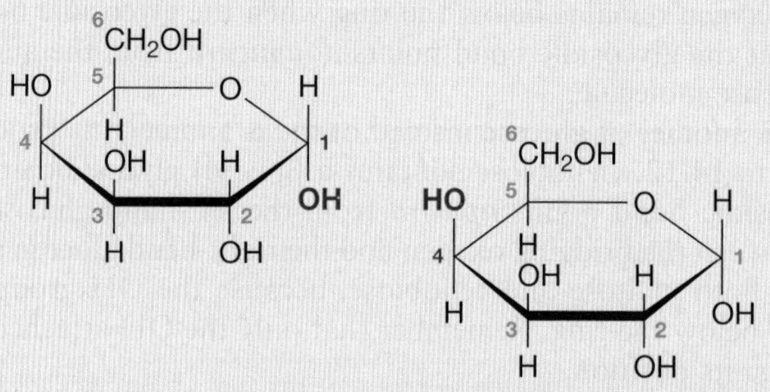

Now we carry out the condensation. We remove one of the circled OH groups (it doesn't matter which), and we remove H from the other OH group. Finally, we draw a bond from the remaining oxygen atom to the sugar that lost its OH group.

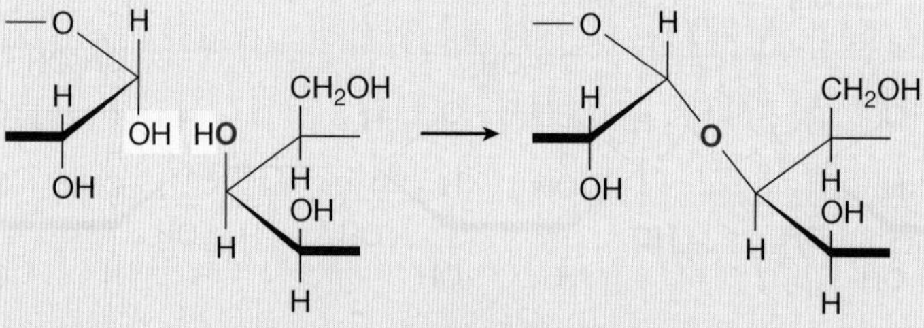

The complete structure of the disaccharide is

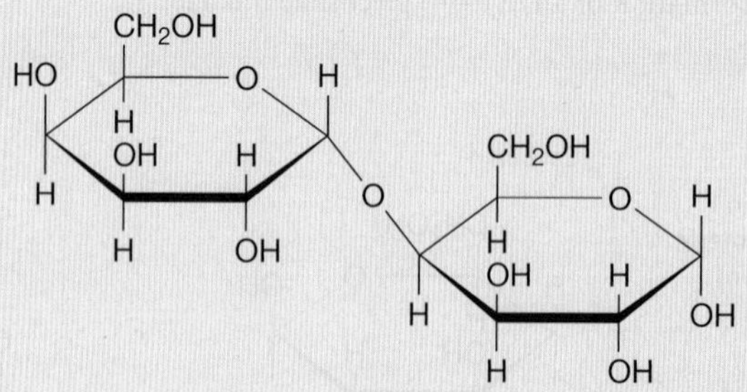

TRY IT YOURSELF: *Draw the structure of the disaccharide that will be formed when two molecules of β-D-galactose form a β(1→4) glycosidic linkage. (Hint: First draw the structure of β-D-galactose.)*

For additional practice, try Core Problems 14.23 and 14.24.

The nutritive value of a carbohydrate depends on the type of glycosidic linkages it contains, because digestive enzymes can only hydrolyze one type of linkage. For example, the human digestive tract makes an enzyme that hydrolyzes α(1→4) linkages between glucose molecules, so we can break down maltose into glucose. However, this enzyme does not hydrolyze β(1→4) linkages, so it cannot break down cellobiose. As a result, we can use maltose as an energy source, but most adults cannot use cellobiose as a significant source of energy. In the next section, we will look at carbohydrates that are built from simple sugars, and we will see how their nutritional roles depend on the types of glycosidic bonds they contain.

CORE PROBLEMS

14.21 Tell whether the glycosidic linkage in the following molecule is α(1→4) or β(1→4), and explain how you can tell:

CH_2OH H O H H H OH H CH_2OH H O OH H OH H HO O H H OH H OH

14.22 Tell whether the glycosidic linkage in the following molecule is α(2→4) or β(2→4), and explain how you can tell:

CH_2OH H O H H H H OH CH_2OH O O H H H CH_2OH OH OH OH OH

14.23 Draw the structure of a disaccharide that contains two molecules of D-galactose connected by an α(1→4) linkage. The structure of galactose is shown in Figure 14.3. (There are two possible answers.)

14.24 Draw the structure of a disaccharide that contains two molecules of D-mannose joined by a β(1→4) linkage. The structure of mannose is shown in Figure 14.3. (There are two possible answers.)

14.4 Common Disaccharides and Polysaccharides

OBJECTIVE: *Describe the building blocks, linkages, and biological functions of the common disaccharides and polysaccharides.*

In Section 14.3, we saw how two glucose molecules can be linked to form the disaccharides maltose and cellobiose. Our bodies produce some maltose when we digest food that contains starch, but otherwise these two disaccharides have little nutritional significance. The most abundant disaccharides, and the most important in human nutrition, are sucrose (table sugar) and lactose (milk sugar). The structures of these two compounds are shown in Figure 14.13.

Sucrose is made from α-D-glucose and β-D-fructose. The glycosidic bond in sucrose connects the anomeric carbon atoms of both monosaccharides, so its name shows the position of the oxygen atom relative to both rings. The oxygen is above the fructose molecule (the β position), but it is below the glucose molecule (the α position), so the bond in sucrose is called an α(1→2)β glycosidic linkage. Lactose is made from β-D-glucose and β-D-galactose. In lactose, the glycosidic bond is β(1→4), connecting carbon 1 of galactose to carbon 4 of glucose.

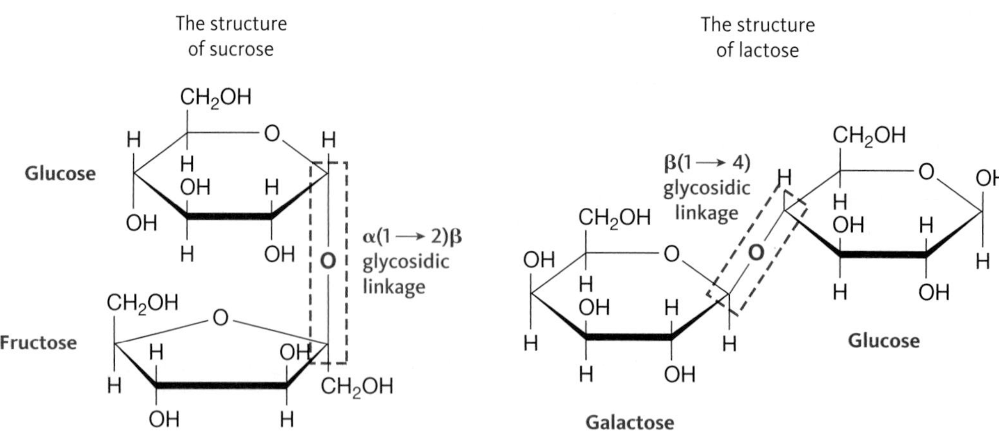

FIGURE 14.13 The structures of sucrose and lactose.

Health Note: Invert sugar is a 50:50 mixture of glucose and fructose that is formed when sucrose is hydrolyzed using either a weak acid or an enzyme as a catalyst. Invert sugar is sweeter than sucrose and does not tend to crystallize from concentrated solutions, so it is used in candy manufacturing to make sweet, syrupy fillings.

Lactose contains a hemiacetal group, so it can be oxidized in Benedict's test. As a result, lactose, like the monosaccharides, is a reducing sugar. In addition, the right-hand ring in lactose can undergo mutarotation, so there are α and β anomers of lactose.

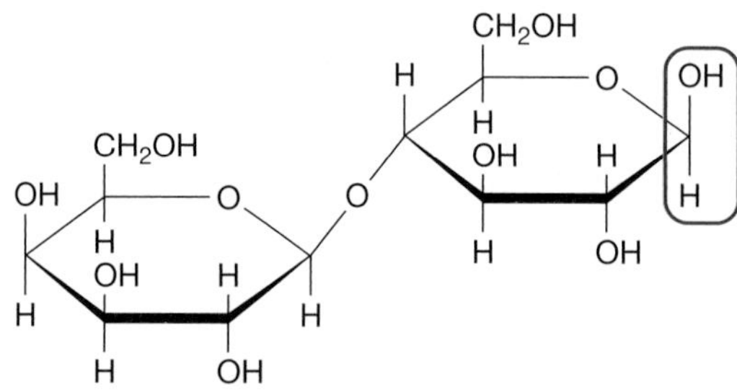

β-Lactose

α-Lactose

However, in sucrose there is no hemiacetal group, because the glycosidic linkage involves the anomeric carbon of both rings. Therefore, sucrose is not a reducing sugar, and there is only one form of sucrose.

Sucrose is the primary sugar in plants, occurring in fruits, nectar, and sap. Enormous quantities of this disaccharide are extracted from sugar cane and sugar beets, refined, and sold to consumers or added to an array of food products. The human body cannot make sucrose, but virtually everyone can digest it, thanks to an enzyme called *sucrase* that hydrolyzes sucrose into glucose and fructose. Normally, the human digestive tract makes abundant amounts of sucrase throughout a person's life.

Lactose is the sole carbohydrate in milk, so it is the only source of carbohydrate for mammals until they are weaned. The digestive tract of normal infants makes an enzyme called *lactase* that can hydrolyze the β(1→4) glycosidic bond in lactose. However, between the ages of 1 and 2 years, humans (and most other mammals) start to lose the ability to make this enzyme. Mammals do not drink milk beyond infancy, and for adult mammals, making lactase constitutes a waste of amino acids. By adulthood,

Soy milk does not contain lactose, making it a useful dairy substitute for people who are lactose intolerant.

most people make little or no lactase, so they are unable to digest milk sugar efficiently. If they consume food that contains a high concentration of lactose, some of the lactose is not broken down and passes unchanged into the large intestine. There, it is broken down into carbon dioxide and various organic acids by the bacteria that are resident in the lower digestive tract. The resulting mixture of gaseous CO_2, acids, and undigested lactose irritates the bowel, producing cramps and diarrhea—the symptoms of *lactose intolerance*.

A few groups of humans have acquired a genetic mutation that prevents their bodies from shutting down lactase production. These people (primarily northern Europeans and certain groups of Africans) can consume dairy products throughout their lives with no ill effects. Many other people retain the ability to make small amounts of lactase, so they can eat dairy products in small amounts. However, people with extremely low levels of lactase must take lactase supplements or consume dairy products from which the lactose has been removed, such as hard cheese or lactose-free milk.

Polysaccharides Are Long Chains of Simple Sugars

The sugars tend to be the most conspicuous members of the carbohydrate family because of their appealing flavor. However, the most abundant carbohydrates by far in the living world are the **polysaccharides**, or **complex carbohydrates.** These compounds contain large numbers of monosaccharide units linked together to form a long chain. The common polysaccharides are all derived from glucose, making glucose the most abundant building block in the biological world.

The two main classes of polysaccharides are the **storage polysaccharides** and the **structural polysaccharides.** Storage polysaccharides are an energy source for animals and plants, while structural polysaccharides are used to build structural components such as plant fibers and the shells of many animals. The principal storage polysaccharides are starch and glycogen, while the most common structural polysaccharides are cellulose and chitin. Let us now examine each of these compounds individually.

Starch Is the Storage Polysaccharide in Plants

As we will see in Section 14.9, plants can make glucose from inorganic substances. Many plants make more glucose than they need, and they store the excess in the form of *starch*. There are two types of starch, called *amylose* and *amylopectin,* and most plants produce a mixture of both types, with amylopectin making up between 70% and 90% of the total weight. Both amylose and amylopectin are long chains of glucose molecules, linked by $\alpha(1\rightarrow4)$ glycosidic bonds. They differ in that amylose is an unbranched chain, while amylopectin is branched. Each branch in amylopectin is connected to the main chain by an $\alpha(1\rightarrow6)$ glycosidic linkage. The structures of these two polymers are shown in Figure 14.14.

Both amylose and amylopectin are huge molecules. The largest molecules contain thousands of glucose units, with amylopectin averaging substantially larger than amylose. Amylose tends to form a helix when it is surrounded by water molecules. Amylopectin, by contrast, cannot adopt an orderly structure in water, presumably because of the numerous branches. The branches in amylopectin occur at irregular intervals, roughly every 25 to 30 glucose units apart, and these branches may themselves have branches. The structures of amylose and amylopectin are shown in Figure 14.15.

Both forms of starch are white, powdery solids, with such high melting points that they simply break down into carbon and water when they are heated. Neither form of starch is soluble in water, but both tend to absorb a great deal of water, much as a sponge can absorb water without dissolving. Amylose can also mix with hot water to make a colloid.

Many plant tissues contain high concentrations of starch, including the grains of rice, wheat, and other grasses, the fleshy roots of potatoes and yams, the fruit of the banana tree, and the seeds of soybeans and other legumes. In many of these, some or all of the water that is normally bound to starch is removed, producing a hard, granular form. This dried starch is ideal for long-term fuel storage (from the plant's point of view), but it is difficult for us to digest, because our digestive enzymes cannot bind to the dried starch granules. Cooking the plant material restores the water, producing a softened form that we can readily digest.

Charles D. Winters

These foods are good sources of starch, a complex carbohydrate.

Amylose

An $\alpha(1 \rightarrow 4)$ glycosidic linkage

Branch

An $\alpha(1 \rightarrow 6)$ glycosidic linkage

Main chain

Amylopectin

FIGURE 14.14 The structures of amylose and amylopectin.

When we digest starch, enzymes called *amylases* hydrolyze the $\alpha(1\rightarrow4)$ glycosidic linkages. Our bodies produce two amylases, one in our saliva and the other in our intestine. Both of these enzymes attack the long chains randomly, chopping them into shorter fragments called *dextrins*. In our intestine, another enzyme called a *debranching enzyme* hydrolyzes the $\alpha(1\rightarrow6)$ linkages in amylopectin. These enzymes eventually break down starch into a mixture of glucose and maltose. The remaining maltose is then broken down to glucose by maltase.

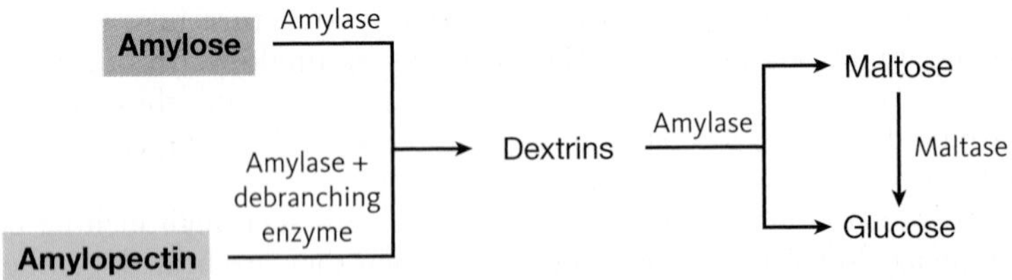

Animals Store Carbohydrate in the Form of Glycogen

Animals also store glucose in the form of a polysaccharide called *glycogen* or animal starch. Glycogen has essentially the same structure as amylopectin, but glycogen molecules are much larger (containing tens of thousands of glucose units) and their branches are typically separated by only 8 to 12 glucose units, rather than the 25 to 30 units typical of amylopectin. When we eat meat, we digest the glycogen in the same way we digest starch, breaking it down into dextrins, then maltose, and finally glucose.

The human body makes and stores glycogen in the liver and in muscles. Muscle glycogen can only be burned by the muscle that formed it, but the liver uses its glycogen to

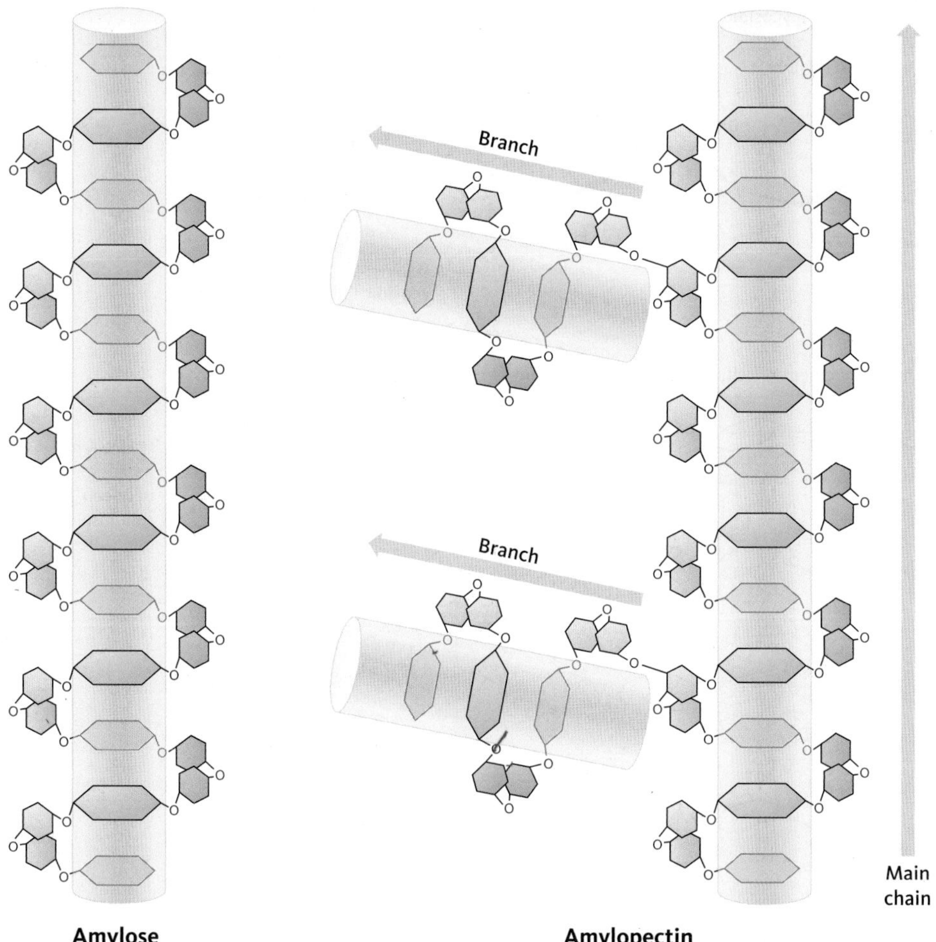

FIGURE 14.15 The arrangements of the chains in amylose and amylopectin.

maintain a constant concentration of glucose in the blood and to supply glucose to other tissues. After a meal, a great deal of glucose passes from the small intestine into the bloodstream. The liver rapidly absorbs the excess glucose, converting it into glycogen for later use. Between meals, the liver gradually breaks down the glycogen and releases the glucose into the blood. As a result, the concentration of glucose in the blood of a normal individual remains close to 80 mg/dL at all times. This ability of the human body to maintain a relatively constant internal environment is called *homeostasis*. You will encounter many other examples of homeostasis if you study human physiology.

Structural Polysaccharides Give Strength and Rigidity to Many Organisms

The second prominent class of polysaccharides is the *structural polysaccharides*. Although these substances are closely related to the storage polysaccharides, they are not used as fuel. Instead, they give shape and strength to the organisms that make them. The two most common structural polysaccharides are *cellulose* and *chitin*.

Cellulose is the primary structural material in plants. It makes up the majority of the fibrous material in plants, from the soft fibers of cotton (which is virtually pure cellulose) to the tough structure of wood, and it is the most abundant organic compound in the living world. Cellulose, like amylose, is an unbranched chain of glucose molecules, but the glycosidic linkages in cellulose are β(1→4). This seemingly minor difference has a great impact on the behavior of cellulose. Cellulose chains have a strong tendency to lie side by side, rather than forming a helix, and the parallel chains form a huge number of hydrogen bonds with each other. As a result, cellulose forms long, strong fibers, as shown in Figure 14.16.

None of the enzymes that digest starch are able to hydrolyze the β(1→4) linkages in cellulose. In fact, neither humans nor any other animal or plant can break down cellulose

Cellulose forms the fibers that give these trees their strength.

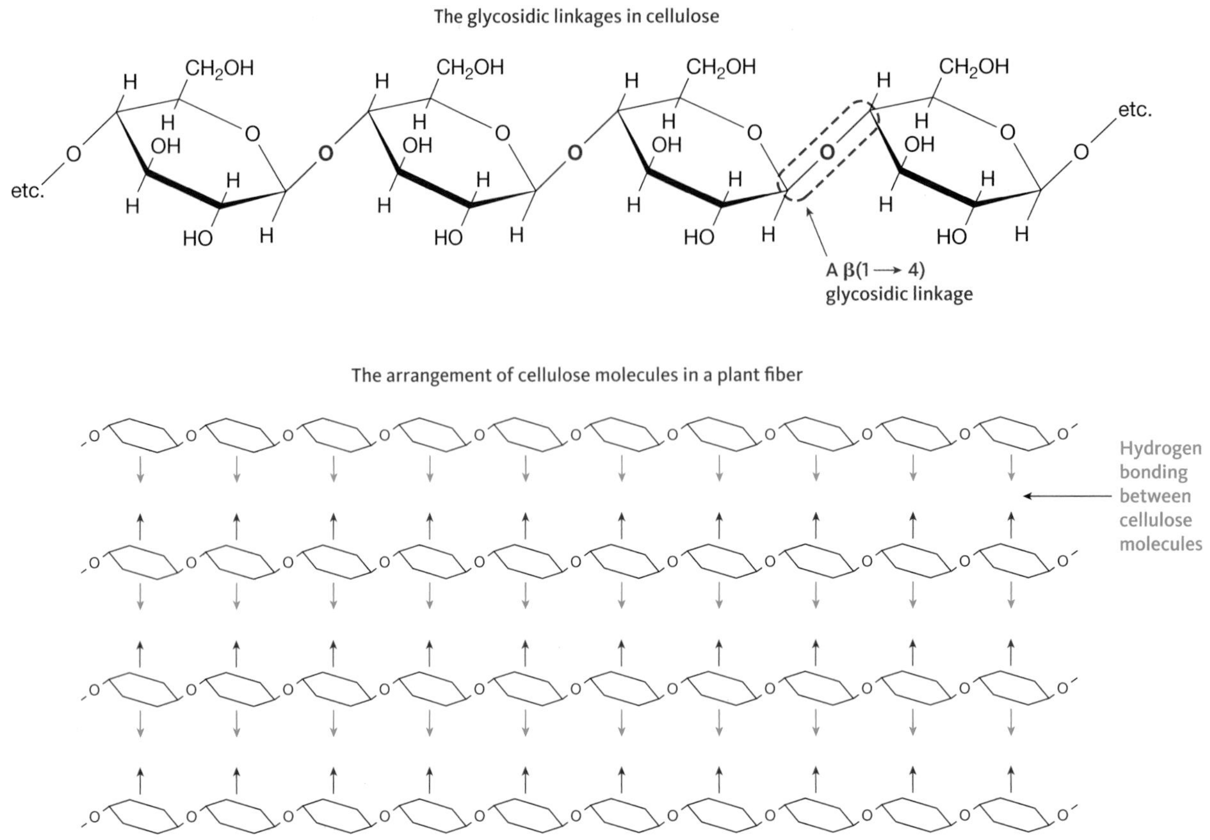

The glycosidic linkages in cellulose

A β(1 → 4) glycosidic linkage

The arrangement of cellulose molecules in a plant fiber

Hydrogen bonding between cellulose molecules

FIGURE 14.16 The structure of cellulose.

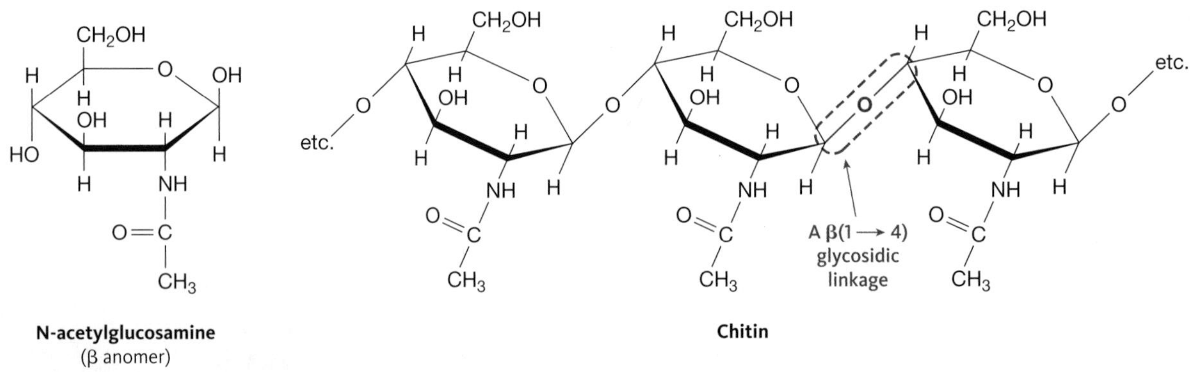

N-acetylglucosamine (β anomer)

Chitin

A β(1 → 4) glycosidic linkage

FIGURE 14.17 The structures of N-acetylglucosamine and chitin.

into glucose. The only organisms that can break down cellulose are certain specialized bacteria and fungi, which produce the enzyme *cellulase*. These organisms have the critical ecological role of breaking down the cellulose in dead plants so other organisms can use the carbohydrate. Some species of bacteria that can break down cellulose find a home in the digestive tract of the ruminants, animals such as cows, goats, and deer that can obtain nutritive value from the fibrous parts of plants. These animals are no more able to digest cellulose than we are, but the bacteria in their digestive tracts can hydrolyze the cellulose. The bacteria use only part of the resulting glucose for their own energy needs, leaving the rest for the animal. Termites also harbor these bacteria in their digestive tracts, giving them the ability to eat wood (and to damage untold numbers of houses every year).

Health Note: Cellulose is one of the principal components of dietary fiber, the indigestible organic material in vegetables and fruits. Cellulose helps prevent constipation and other digestive disorders, and soluble fiber lowers the concentration of LDL cholesterol ("bad cholesterol") in the blood.

The shells of animals such as insects, crustaceans (crabs, shrimp, and lobsters), and spiders contain large amounts of another structural polysaccharide called chitin (pronounced "KY-tin"). Chitin is similar to cellulose in that it contains β(1→4) linkages and it forms strong fibers. However, chitin chains are built from a modified sugar called N-acetylglucosamine. The structures of N-acetylglucosamine and chitin are shown in Figure 14.17.

Table 14.4 summarizes the important disaccharides and polysaccharides that you have encountered in this section.

TABLE 14.4 The Common Disaccharides and Polysaccharides

Compound	Made from	Types of Glycosidic Linkages	Function	Digestible by Humans
Lactose	Galactose + glucose	β(1→4)	Primary carbohydrate in milk	Yes, but many people lose the ability as adults (requires **lactase**)
Sucrose	Glucose + fructose	α(1→2)β	Primary sugar in plants (fruits, nectar, etc.)	Yes (requires **sucrase**)
Amylose	Glucose	α(1→4)	Fuel storage in plants (one of the forms of starch)	Yes (requires **amylase**)
Amylopectin	Glucose	α(1→4) α(1→6) at branch points	Fuel storage in plants (one of the forms of starch)	Yes (requires **amylase** and a **debranching enzyme**)
Glycogen	Glucose	α(1→4) α(1→6) at branch points	Fuel storage in animals (sometimes called "animal starch")	Yes (requires **amylase** and a **debranching enzyme**)
Cellulose	Glucose	β(1→4)	Structural material in plants	No (requires **cellulase**)
Chitin	N-acetylglucosamine	β(1→4)	Structural material in insects, crabs, etc.	No (requires several enzymes)

CORE PROBLEMS

14.25 The structure of one of the two anomers of maltose is shown here.

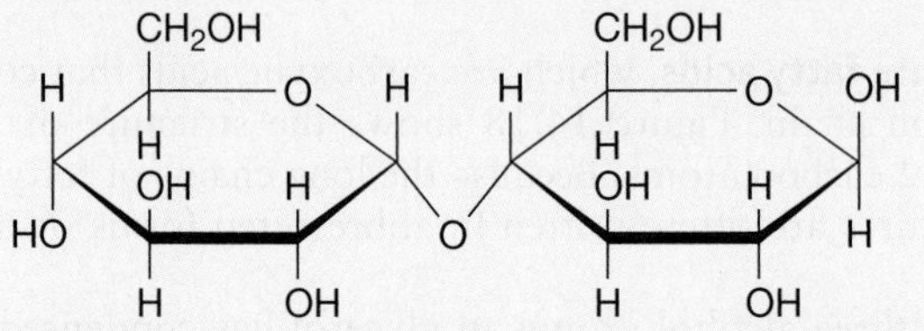

a) Is this the structure of α-maltose or β-maltose?
b) Is this form of maltose a reducing sugar? Explain how you can tell.

14.26 The structure of one of the two anomers of cellobiose is shown here.

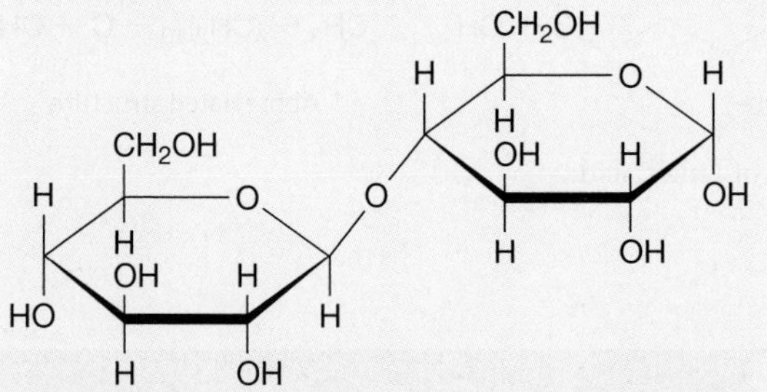

a) Is this the structure of α-cellobiose or β-cellobiose?
b) Is this form of cellobiose a reducing sugar? Explain how you can tell.

14.27 What monosaccharides are formed when sucrose is hydrolyzed?

14.28 What monosaccharides are formed when lactose is hydrolyzed?

14.29 a) Does sucrose have two anomeric forms? Explain.
b) Is sucrose a reducing sugar? Explain

14.30 a) Does lactose have two anomeric forms? Explain.
b) Is lactose a reducing sugar? Explain.

14.31 Virtually all children can digest lactose, but many adults cannot. Why is this?

14.32 Sucrose intolerance (the inability to digest sucrose) is extremely rare. Why is this?

14.33 What types of organisms make each of the following polysaccharides, and what is the biological role of each polysaccharide?
a) chitin b) amylose

14.34 What types of organisms make each of the following polysaccharides, and what is the biological role of each polysaccharide?
a) glycogen b) cellulose

14.35 What monosaccharide is used to build starch and cellulose?

14.36 What monosaccharide is used to build chitin?

continued

14.37 What types of glycosidic bonds are present in each of the polysaccharides in Problem 14.33?

14.38 What types of glycosidic bonds are present in each of the polysaccharides in Problem 14.34?

14.39 What enzymes are required to completely hydrolyze starch? Does the human digestive system make these enzymes?

14.40 What enzymes are required to completely hydrolyze cellulose? Does the human digestive system make these enzymes?

OBJECTIVES: *Classify fatty acids based on their structures, draw structures of triglycerides that contain specific fatty acids, and relate the physical properties of fatty acids and triglycerides to their structures.*

14.5 Fatty Acids and Triglycerides

Carbohydrates are the primary source of energy for our bodies, supplying roughly half of our basal energy requirement. However, the chemical components of fats and oils are also an important energy source. Our bodies use these compounds to supply most of the resting energy needs of our muscles, and they also provide energy for our liver and kidneys.

The chemical compounds in animal fats and vegetable oils are examples of **lipids**. Lipids are organic compounds that are made and used by living organisms and that are not soluble in water. In this section and the next, we will examine the properties and chemical reactions of the triglycerides, the most abundant type of lipids in our bodies, and in Sections 14.7 and 14.8 we will look at some other classes of lipids.

All animal fats and all vegetable oils are members of a family of compounds called **triglycerides**, or **triacylglycerols**. Triglycerides are made from four components. One of these is a compound called *glycerol* (often referred to by the older name *glycerin*).

Health Note: Glycerol is a syrupy, sweet, nontoxic liquid. It absorbs water from the atmosphere, so it is used as a moisturizer in a variety of cosmetics, hair care products, and soaps. Glycerol is also used to thicken and sweeten liquid medicines, mouthwashes, and toothpastes.

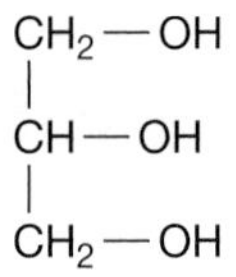

$$\begin{array}{l} CH_2-OH \\ | \\ CH-OH \\ | \\ CH_2-OH \end{array}$$

Glycerol (glycerin)

The other three components are **fatty acids**, which are carboxylic acids that contain a long, unbranched hydrocarbon chain. Figure 14.18 shows the structure of lauric acid, a fatty acid that contains 12 carbon atoms. Because the long chains of fatty acids are tedious to draw, their structures are often written in abbreviated forms or drawn as line structures.

In a triglyceride, each of the three alcohol groups in glycerol has condensed with one molecule of fatty acid. As a result, triglycerides contain three ester functional groups. Sample Problem 14.4 shows how a triglyceride is formed from its components.

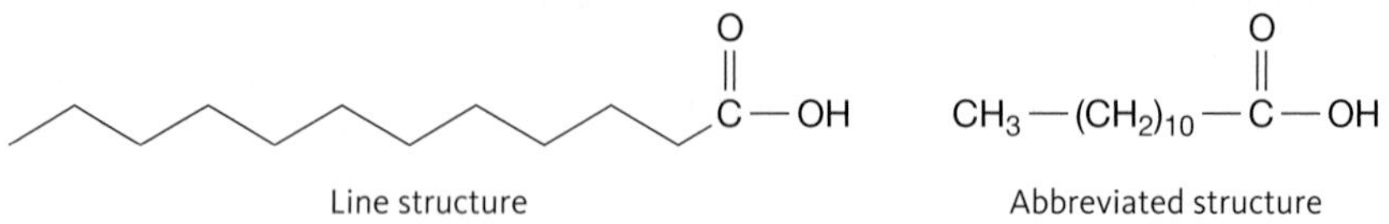

Line structure

$$CH_3-(CH_2)_{10}-\overset{\overset{\displaystyle O}{\|}}{C}-OH$$

Abbreviated structure

FIGURE 14.18 The structure of lauric acid.

Sample Problem 14.4

Drawing the structure of a triglyceride

Draw the structure of the triglyceride that is formed from glycerol and three molecules of lauric acid.

continued

SOLUTION

First, we draw the three fatty acids, one above the other. Then we draw glycerol beside the fatty acids, making sure that the hydroxyl groups of glycerol face toward the carboxylic acid groups of the fatty acids.

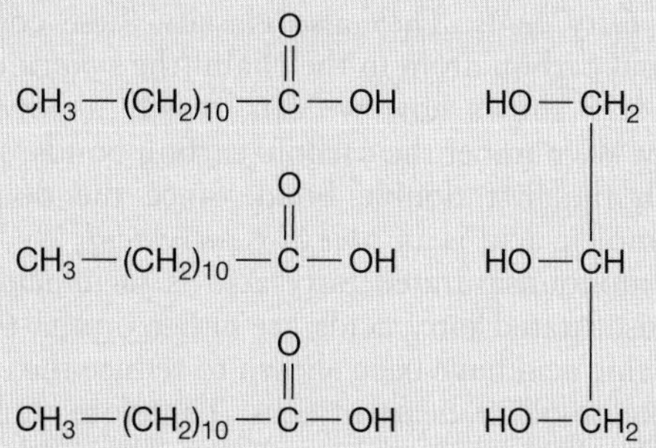

$$\begin{array}{ll} CH_3-(CH_2)_{10}-\overset{O}{\overset{\|}{C}}-OH & HO-CH_2 \\ & \quad\ \ | \\ CH_3-(CH_2)_{10}-\overset{O}{\overset{\|}{C}}-OH & HO-CH \\ & \quad\ \ | \\ CH_3-(CH_2)_{10}-\overset{O}{\overset{\|}{C}}-OH & HO-CH_2 \end{array}$$

To make the triglyceride, we remove OH from each acid and H from each of the three alcohol groups of glycerol. Then we link the organic fragments together.

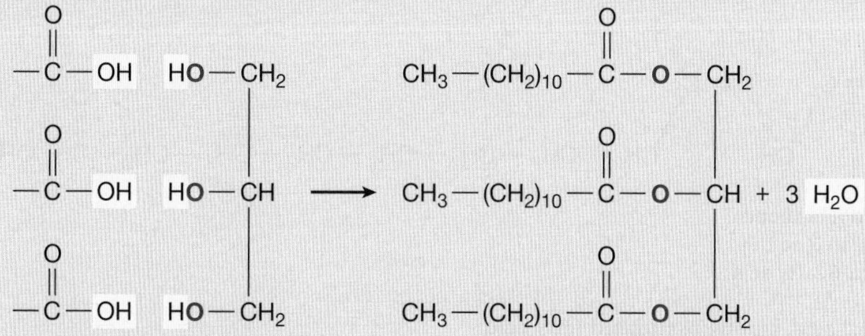

$$\begin{array}{ll} -\overset{O}{\overset{\|}{C}}-OH & HO-CH_2 \\ & \quad\ \ | \\ -\overset{O}{\overset{\|}{C}}-OH & HO-CH \\ & \quad\ \ | \\ -\overset{O}{\overset{\|}{C}}-OH & HO-CH_2 \end{array} \longrightarrow \begin{array}{l} CH_3-(CH_2)_{10}-\overset{O}{\overset{\|}{C}}-O-CH_2 \\ \qquad\qquad\qquad\qquad\qquad\ \ | \\ CH_3-(CH_2)_{10}-\overset{O}{\overset{\|}{C}}-O-CH \\ \qquad\qquad\qquad\qquad\qquad\ \ | \\ CH_3-(CH_2)_{10}-\overset{O}{\overset{\|}{C}}-O-CH_2 \end{array} + 3\ H_2O$$

The triglyceride

TRY IT YOURSELF: *Draw the structure of the triglyceride that contains glycerol and three molecules of oleic acid.*

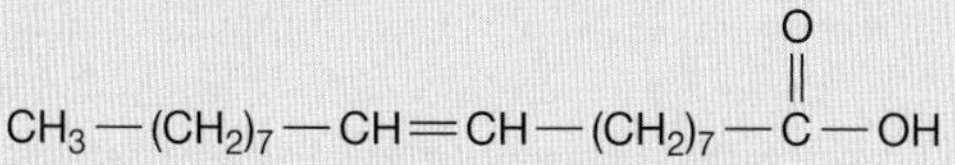

$$CH_3-(CH_2)_7-CH=CH-(CH_2)_7-\overset{O}{\overset{\|}{C}}-OH$$

Oleic acid

For additional practice, try Core Problems 14.47 and 14.48.

Charles D. Winters

The fats and oils in these foods are composed of triglycerides.

Fats from natural sources contain a range of fatty acids. The fatty acids are divided into two main classes based on whether the hydrocarbon chain contains any carbon–carbon double bonds. Fatty acids that do not contain any alkene groups are called *saturated fatty acids,* while fatty acids that contain at least one alkene group are called *unsaturated fatty acids*. For example, in Sample Problem 14.4, lauric acid is a saturated fatty acid, while oleic acid is unsaturated. All commonly occurring unsaturated fatty acids contain *cis* alkene groups, with the two alkene hydrogen atoms on the same side of the double bond. The structures of unsaturated fatty acids are sometimes drawn to make the *cis* geometry evident, as shown here for oleic acid:

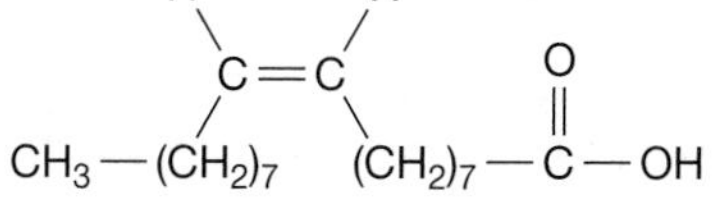

$$\begin{array}{c} H \qquad\quad H \\ \ \backslash \qquad\ / \\ C=C \\ \ / \qquad\ \backslash \\ CH_3-(CH_2)_7 \qquad (CH_2)_7-\overset{O}{\overset{\|}{C}}-OH \end{array}$$

Abbreviated structure of oleic acid, showing the *cis* geometry

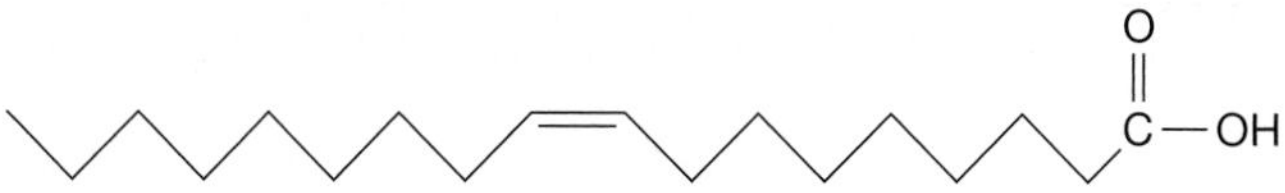

Line structure of oleic acid

Fatty Acids Are Classified by the Number and Position of Alkene Groups

Chemists and nutritionists classify unsaturated fatty acids based on the number of alkene groups in the hydrocarbon chain. Fatty acids with only one alkene group are called *monounsaturated fatty acids,* while compounds with two or more alkene groups are called *polyunsaturated fatty acids.* They also classify these compounds based on the distance between the final carbon atom in the chain (the *omega* carbon) and the nearest double bond. Figure 14.19 shows how we can classify a polyunsaturated fatty acid, linoleic acid, in this way. We number the carbon–carbon bonds, starting from the omega carbon, until we reach the first double bond. Since the double bond is the sixth carbon–carbon bond, linoleic acid is an *omega-6 fatty acid.*

The most common monounsaturated fatty acid is oleic acid, which is an omega-9 fatty acid. Most polyunsaturated fatty acids are either omega-6 or omega-3. Omega-3 fatty acids such as linolenic acid have been shown to reduce the clotting ability of blood, which decreases the likelihood of heart attacks. Therefore, some nutritionists recommend regularly eating foods that are rich in these compounds. Table 14.5 shows the structures of a number of common fatty acids.

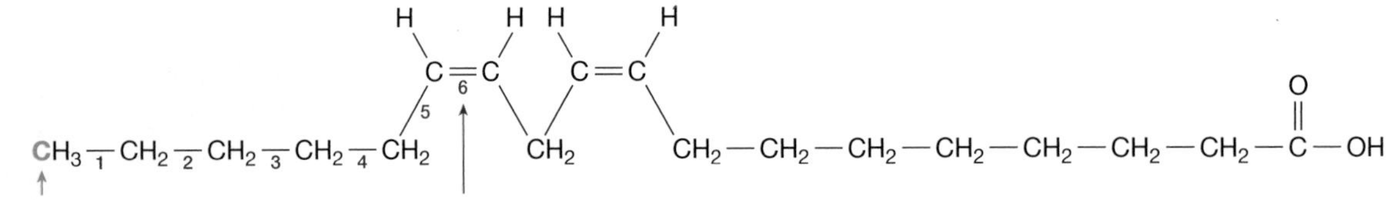

$$CH_3 \overset{1}{-} CH_2 \overset{2}{-} CH_2 \overset{3}{-} CH_2 \overset{4}{-} CH_2 \overset{5}{-} CH{=}CH - CH_2 - CH{=}CH - CH_2 - CH_2 - CH_2 - CH_2 - CH_2 - CH_2 - CH_2 - \overset{O}{\overset{\|}{C}} - OH$$

The omega carbon

The first double bond is at position 6, so this is an **omega-6** fatty acid.

FIGURE 14.19 The structure of linoleic acid, a polyunsaturated fatty acid.

TABLE 14.5 The Structures of Common Fatty Acids

Name (Melting Point)	Structure
Lauric acid (44°C)	$CH_3-(CH_2)_{10}-COOH$
Myristic acid (55°C)	$CH_3-(CH_2)_{12}-COOH$
Palmitic acid (63°C)	$CH_3-(CH_2)_{14}-COOH$
Stearic acid (69°C)	$CH_3-(CH_2)_{16}-COOH$
Palmitoleic acid (0°C)	$CH_3-(CH_2)_5-CH{=}CH-(CH_2)_7-COOH$
Oleic acid (14°C)	$CH_3-(CH_2)_7-CH{=}CH-(CH_2)_7-COOH$
Linoleic acid (−5°C)	$CH_3-(CH_2)_4-CH{=}CH-CH_2-CH{=}CH-(CH_2)_7-COOH$
Linolenic acid (−11°C)	$CH_3-CH_2-CH{=}CH-CH_2-CH{=}CH-CH_2-CH{=}CH-(CH_2)_7-COOH$

Sample Problem 14.5

Classifying a fatty acid

Our bodies use arachidonic acid to make prostaglandins, which play a role in a variety of cellular processes. Classify arachidonic acid using the omega system.

$$CH_3-(CH_2)_4-CH{=}CH-CH_2-CH{=}CH-CH_2-CH{=}CH-CH_2-CH{=}CH-(CH_2)_3-\overset{\overset{\displaystyle O}{\|}}{C}-OH$$

Arachidonic acid

SOLUTION

The abbreviated structure does not show all of the carbon–carbon bonds. To find the position of the first double bond, we need to draw out the structure of the molecule, starting from the carbon atom that is farthest from the carboxylic acid group (the omega carbon). Then we number the carbon–carbon bonds, starting with the omega carbon.

$$CH_3 \underset{1}{-} \overbrace{CH_2 \underset{2}{-} CH_2 \underset{3}{-} CH_2 \underset{4}{-} CH_2}^{(CH_2)_4} \underset{5}{-} CH \underset{6}{=} CH-CH_2-CH{=}CH-\text{etc.}-\overset{\overset{\displaystyle O}{\|}}{C}-OH$$

Since the first double bond we see is carbon–carbon bond 6, arachidonic acid is an omega-6 fatty acid.

TRY IT YOURSELF: *Classify palmitoleic acid using the omega system.*

$$CH_3-(CH_2)_5-CH{=}CH-(CH_2)_7-COOH$$

Palmitoleic acid

For additional practice, try Core Problems 14.45 and 14.46.

Fatty Acids and Triglycerides Have Similar Physical Properties

Both fatty acids and triglycerides are insoluble in water, because their long hydrocarbon chains cannot form hydrogen bonds with water. However, triglycerides and fatty acids have high solubilities in most organic solvents, including ethanol, acetone, diethyl ether, and hydrocarbons such as hexane and benzene. Chemists use hydrocarbon solvents to remove triglycerides (fats and oils) from tissue samples, because the other major components of tissues (water, carbohydrate, protein, and minerals) do not dissolve in hydrocarbons.

The melting points of most common fatty acids and triglycerides range from −20°C to 70°C, and they depend primarily on the number of alkene groups in the fatty acids. Saturated fatty acids melt above body temperature (37°C), so they are solids at room temperature and remain solid under physiological conditions. Triglycerides that contain three saturated fatty acids behave similarly. For example, here are the melting points of palmitic acid (a saturated fatty acid) and tripalmitin (the triglyceride that contains three molecules of palmitic acid):

Palmitic acid: m.p. = 63°C   Tripalmitin: m.p. = 66°C

By contrast, unsaturated fatty acids melt below 15°C, so they are liquids at room temperature, as are triglycerides that contain them. Here are the melting points of oleic acid (a monounsaturated fatty acid) and triolein (a triglyceride that contains three molecules of oleiç acid):

Oleic acid: m.p. = 14°C   Triolein: m.p. = −4°C

These melting points are an excellent example of the relationship between melting point and molecular shape. The hydrocarbon chains of saturated fatty acids can align themselves side by side, with a large amount of contact area between neighboring molecules. By contrast, unsaturated fatty acids cannot align themselves so neatly, because each double bond produces an irregular kink in the hydrocarbon chain. The attraction between hydrocarbon chains depends on the amount of contact area, so saturated fatty acids attract one another more strongly than do unsaturated fatty acids. When we melt a solid, we must add enough energy to overcome these attractive forces. As a result, it takes a higher temperature to melt a saturated fatty acid.

Kresimir Juraga

Butter contains primarily saturated fatty acids, while vegetable oil contains mainly unsaturated fatty acids. Soft margarine uses a mixture of both to produce a desirable texture.

Although triglycerides can contain three identical fatty acids, most naturally occurring triglycerides are made from three different fatty acids and are called mixed triglycerides. The melting points of mixed triglycerides depend on the fatty acids they contain. Triglycerides that contain two or three saturated fatty acids are normally solids at room temperature. Triglycerides that contain fewer than two saturated fatty acids are generally liquids. For example, in butter (which is almost entirely made up of triglycerides), roughly two thirds of the fatty acids are saturated. As a result, butter is a solid at room temperature. By contrast, corn oil contains only a small percentage of saturated fatty acids, so it is a liquid.

Sample Problem **14.6**

Relating the melting points of triglycerides to their structures

Which of the following triglycerides should have the higher melting point?

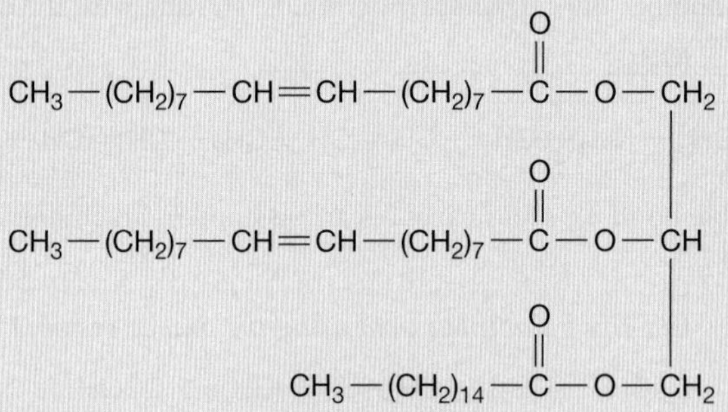

$$CH_3-(CH_2)_7-CH=CH-(CH_2)_7-\overset{O}{\overset{\|}{C}}-O-CH_2$$
$$CH_3-(CH_2)_7-CH=CH-(CH_2)_7-\overset{O}{\overset{\|}{C}}-O-CH$$
$$CH_3-(CH_2)_{14}-\overset{O}{\overset{\|}{C}}-O-CH_2$$

Triglyceride 1

$$CH_3-(CH_2)_7-CH=CH-(CH_2)_7-\overset{O}{\overset{\|}{C}}-O-CH_2$$
$$CH_3-(CH_2)_{14}-\overset{O}{\overset{\|}{C}}-O-CH$$
$$CH_3-(CH_2)_{14}-\overset{O}{\overset{\|}{C}}-O-CH_2$$

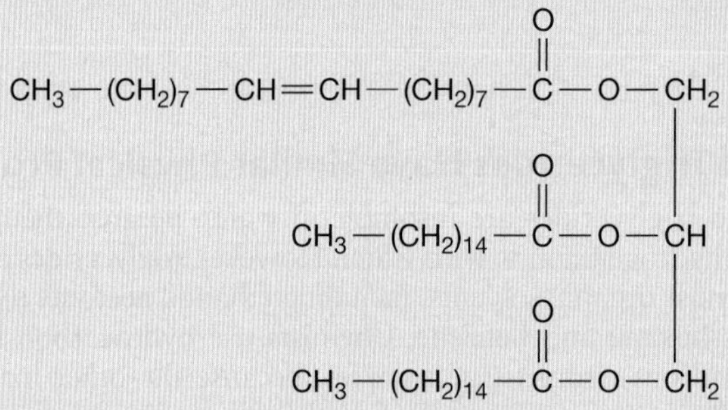

Triglyceride 2

SOLUTION

Triglyceride 1 contains one saturated fatty acid, while triglyceride 2 contains two. In general, triglycerides containing more saturated fatty acids have higher melting points, so we predict that triglyceride 2 has the higher melting point.

TRY IT YOURSELF: *How does the melting point of the following triglyceride compare to the melting points of triglycerides 1 and 2?*

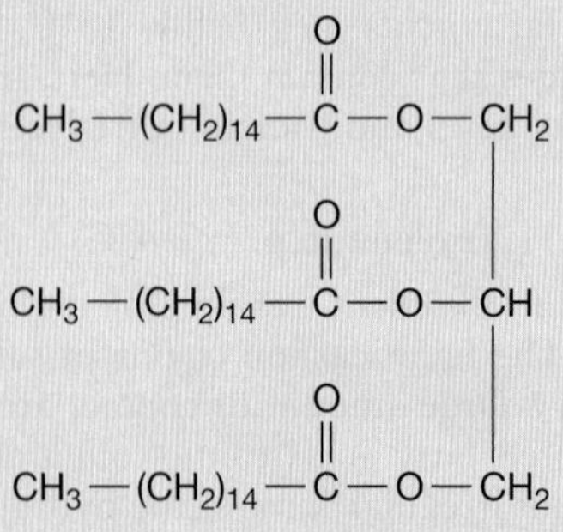

$$CH_3-(CH_2)_{14}-\overset{O}{\overset{\|}{C}}-O-CH_2$$
$$CH_3-(CH_2)_{14}-\overset{O}{\overset{\|}{C}}-O-CH$$
$$CH_3-(CH_2)_{14}-\overset{O}{\overset{\|}{C}}-O-CH_2$$

Triglyceride 3

For additional practice, try Core Problems 14.49 and 14.50.

Naturally occurring mixtures of triglycerides are called fats or oils, depending on their source. The triglyceride mixtures in animal tissues are generally called fats if they are solids, but they are referred to as oils if they are liquids. Plant triglycerides are always called oils, regardless of their state. Table 14.6 shows the composition of some natural fats and oils.

TABLE 14.6 The Physical Properties and Fatty Acid Composition of Some Fats and Oils

Fat or Oil	Melting Point	State at Room Temperature	Saturated Fatty Acids	Monounsaturated Fatty Acids	Polyunsaturated Fatty Acids
Lard (pork fat)	34°C	Solid	41%	47%	12%
Butterfat	32°C	Solid	68%	28%	4%
Coconut oil	25°C	Solid	92%	8%	0%
Cod liver oil	−5°C	Liquid	20%	62%	18%
Olive oil	−6°C	Liquid	15%	75%	10%
Corn oil	−20°C	Liquid	13%	29%	58%

CORE PROBLEMS

14.41 Classify each of the following fatty acids as saturated, monounsaturated, or polyunsaturated:

a) $CH_3-(CH_2)_{12}-C(=O)-OH$

b) $CH_3-(CH_2)_4-CH{=}CH-CH_2-CH{=}CH-(CH_2)_7-C(=O)-OH$

14.42 Classify each of the following fatty acids as saturated, monounsaturated, or polyunsaturated:

a) $CH_3-(CH_2)_5-CH{=}CH-(CH_2)_7-C(=O)-OH$

b) $CH_3-(CH_2)_{14}-C(=O)-OH$

14.43 a) Predict whether the melting points of each of the fatty acids in Problem 14.41 will be higher or lower than room temperature.
b) Predict whether each of these fatty acids will be a solid or a liquid at room temperature.

14.44 a) Predict whether the melting points of each of the fatty acids in Problem 14.42 will be higher or lower than room temperature.
b) Predict whether each of these fatty acids will be a solid or a liquid at room temperature.

14.45 Draw the structures of the triglycerides that contain the following fatty acids:
a) three molecules of myristic acid
b) two molecules of lauric acid and one molecule of linolenic acid (there is more than one possible answer)

14.46 Draw the structures of the triglycerides that contain the following fatty acids:
a) three molecules of oleic acid
b) two molecules of linoleic acid and one molecule of stearic acid (there is more than one possible answer)

14.47 Rank the following triglycerides from highest to lowest melting point:
Triglyceride 1: contains three molecules of stearic acid
Triglyceride 2: contains three molecules of oleic acid
Triglyceride 3: contains two molecules of oleic acid and one molecule of stearic acid

14.48 Rank the following triglycerides from highest to lowest melting point:
Triglyceride 1: contains two molecules of linolenic acid and one molecule of linoleic acid
Triglyceride 2: contains two molecules of lauric acid and one molecule of stearic acid
Triglyceride 3: contains two molecules of oleic acid and one molecule of myristic acid

continued

14.49 The essential fatty acid linolenic acid is sometimes called alpha-linolenic acid. Certain plant oils contain an isomer of this compound, called gamma-linolenic acid. The structure of gamma-linolenic acid is shown here. Classify this fatty acid using the omega system.

$$CH_3-(CH_2)_4-CH{=}CH-CH_2-CH{=}CH-CH_2-CH{=}CH-(CH_2)_4-\overset{\displaystyle O}{\overset{\|}{C}}-OH$$

14.50 Your body contains a small amount of a fatty acid called adrenic acid, whose structure is shown here. Classify this fatty acid using the omega system.

$$CH_3-(CH_2)_4-CH{=}CH-CH_2-CH{=}CH-CH_2-CH{=}CH-CH_2-CH{=}CH-(CH_2)_5-\overset{\displaystyle O}{\overset{\|}{C}}-OH$$

OBJECTIVES: *Predict the products of the hydrogenation and hydrolysis reactions of triglycerides, and understand how fats are digested and absorbed.*

14.6 Chemical Reactions of Triglycerides

The most important reactions of triglycerides are hydrogenation and hydrolysis. You have encountered both of these reaction types already, so this section provides a good opportunity for review.

Unsaturated Triglycerides Can Be Hydrogenated

Recall from Chapter 10 that alkenes can be hydrogenated to form alkanes. Any fatty acid or triglyceride that contains an alkene group can react with hydrogen. This reaction does not occur in our bodies, but it is important in food manufacturing. For example, hydrogenation converts oleic acid (a monounsaturated fatty acid) into stearic acid (a saturated fatty acid), as shown here:

$$CH_3-(CH_2)_7-CH{=}CH-(CH_2)_7-\overset{\displaystyle O}{\overset{\|}{C}}-OH + H_2 \longrightarrow CH_3-(CH_2)_7-CH_2-CH_2-(CH_2)_7-\overset{\displaystyle O}{\overset{\|}{C}}-OH$$

Oleic acid (an unsaturated fatty acid) → **Stearic acid** (a saturated fatty acid)

Sample Problem 14.7

Drawing the product of a hydrogenation reaction

Draw the structure of the product that is formed when the following triglyceride is completely hydrogenated:

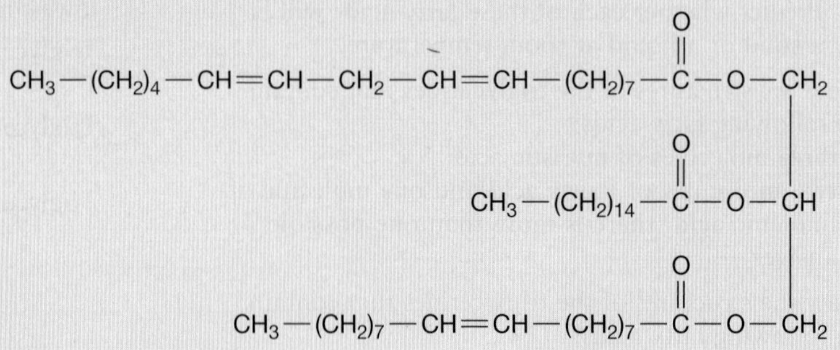

$$\begin{array}{r} CH_3-(CH_2)_4-CH{=}CH-CH_2-CH{=}CH-(CH_2)_7-\overset{\displaystyle O}{\overset{\|}{C}}-O-CH_2 \\ CH_3-(CH_2)_{14}-\overset{\displaystyle O}{\overset{\|}{C}}-O-CH\ \ \\ CH_3-(CH_2)_7-CH{=}CH-(CH_2)_7-\overset{\displaystyle O}{\overset{\|}{C}}-O-CH_2 \end{array}$$

SOLUTION

We need to add a hydrogen atom to each of the alkene carbon atoms, and we need to convert the alkene double bonds into single bonds. (Hydrogenation doesn't affect the

continued

ester C=O.) Here is the structure of the product, with the locations of the original double bonds circled.

$$\begin{array}{l} CH_3-(CH_2)_4-\boxed{CH_2-CH_2}-CH_2-\boxed{CH_2-CH_2}-(CH_2)_7-\overset{\displaystyle O}{\overset{\|}{C}}-O-CH_2 \\ \qquad\qquad\qquad\qquad\qquad\qquad CH_3-(CH_2)_{14}-\overset{\displaystyle O}{\overset{\|}{C}}-O-CH \\ \qquad\qquad CH_3-(CH_2)_7-\boxed{CH_2-CH_2}-(CH_2)_7-\overset{\displaystyle O}{\overset{\|}{C}}-O-CH_2 \end{array}$$

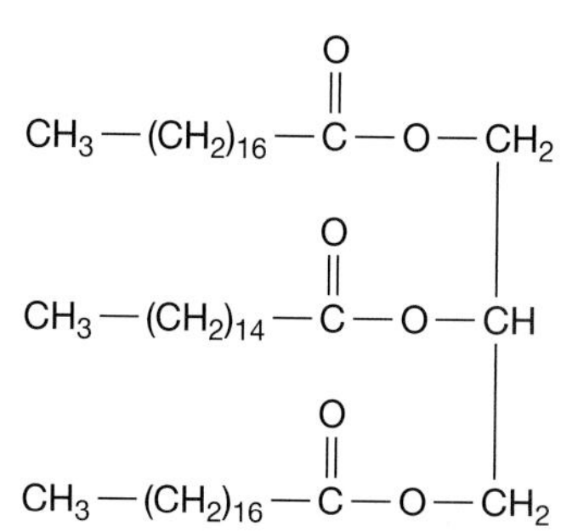

• This structure can also be drawn in the more compact form shown here.

TRY IT YOURSELF: *Draw the structure of the product that is formed when the following triglyceride is completely hydrogenated:*

$$\begin{array}{l} \qquad\qquad\qquad\qquad CH_3-(CH_2)_{10}-\overset{\displaystyle O}{\overset{\|}{C}}-O-CH_2 \\ CH_3-(CH_2)_7-CH=CH-(CH_2)_7-\overset{\displaystyle O}{\overset{\|}{C}}-O-CH \\ CH_3-(CH_2)_5-CH=CH-(CH_2)_7-\overset{\displaystyle O}{\overset{\|}{C}}-O-CH_2 \end{array}$$

For additional practice, try Core Problems 14.51 (part a) and 14.52 (part a).

Adding hydrogen to vegetable oils increases the percentage of saturated fatty acids in the triglycerides. If vegetable oil is completely hydrogenated, the product is a firm solid with the consistency of chilled butter. However, in most cases only some of the double bonds are hydrogenated, producing a partially hydrogenated oil. You can see the difference if you compare soft and hard margarine. Both of these are partially hydrogenated vegetable oils, but the hard margarine contains a higher percentage of saturated fatty acids than does the soft margarine, resulting in a higher melting point and a firmer texture.

Hydrogenation also helps prevent products made from vegetable oils from spoiling. Unsaturated fatty acids react slowly with oxygen from the atmosphere, producing smaller molecules that have strong, unpleasant flavors and aromas. If you have ever had a stick of butter or a bottle of vegetable oil become rancid, you have encountered this type of reaction. However, when an unsaturated fatty acid is converted to a saturated fatty acid, it can no longer react with oxygen. In addition, when unsaturated fatty acids are put in contact with the catalyst that is used in hydrogenation reactions, the *cis* double bonds rapidly convert into *trans* double bonds, as shown here:

$$\underset{\text{(a \textit{cis} fatty acid)}}{\underset{\textbf{Oleic acid}}{\begin{array}{c} H \qquad H \\ C=C \\ CH_3-(CH_2)_7 \qquad (CH_2)_7-\overset{O}{\overset{\|}{C}}-OH \end{array}}} \xrightarrow{\text{Catalyst}} \underset{\text{(a \textit{trans} fatty acid)}}{\underset{\textbf{Elaidic acid}}{\begin{array}{c} CH_3-(CH_2)_7 \qquad H \\ C=C \\ H \qquad (CH_2)_7-\overset{O}{\overset{\|}{C}}-OH \end{array}}}$$

Trans fatty acids become rancid more slowly than their *cis* isomers, so they have a longer shelf life and do not need refrigeration. Because they are so resistant to spoiling, partially hydrogenated oils are used in many food products, including snack chips, baked goods, and many fried items on fast-food restaurant menus. These foods contain significant amounts of *trans* fatty acids. Unfortunately, both *trans* fats (triglycerides that contain *trans* fatty acids) and saturated fats have been linked to an increased incidence of heart disease. *Trans* fats in particular produce a dramatic increase in the risk of heart

© Jeff Greenberg / Alamy

This food product is marketed to consumers who want to eliminate *trans* fats from their diet.

attacks, so nutritionists recommend that people reduce their consumption of partially hydrogenated oils as much as possible. In response, many food manufacturers and restaurant chains are replacing foods that contain hydrogenated oils with oils that do not contain *trans* fats.

Triglycerides Can Be Hydrolyzed

Triglycerides are esters, so they can be hydrolyzed. This reaction requires a catalyst, which can be either a strong acid or a strong base. If we use an acid such as H_2SO_4, the products are glycerol and the original fatty acids. If we use the strong base NaOH, we make glycerol and the sodium salts of the fatty acids. As we saw in Chapter 12, sodium salts of fatty acids are soaps; they are the main constituents of the bar soap that we use to wash our hands.

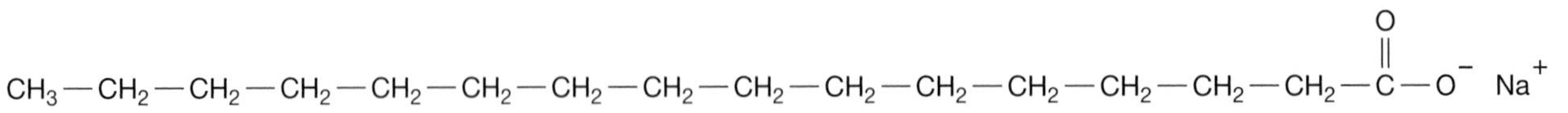

$$CH_3-CH_2-CH_2-CH_2-CH_2-CH_2-CH_2-CH_2-CH_2-CH_2-CH_2-CH_2-CH_2-CH_2-CH_2-\overset{\overset{\displaystyle O}{\|}}{C}-O^-\ Na^+$$

Sodium palmitate
(the sodium salt of palmitic acid)
a soap

Sample Problem 14.8

Drawing the product of the hydrolysis of a triglyceride

Draw the structures of the products that are formed when the triglyceride shown here is hydrolyzed using each of the following solutions:

a) aqueous H_2SO_4

b) aqueous NaOH

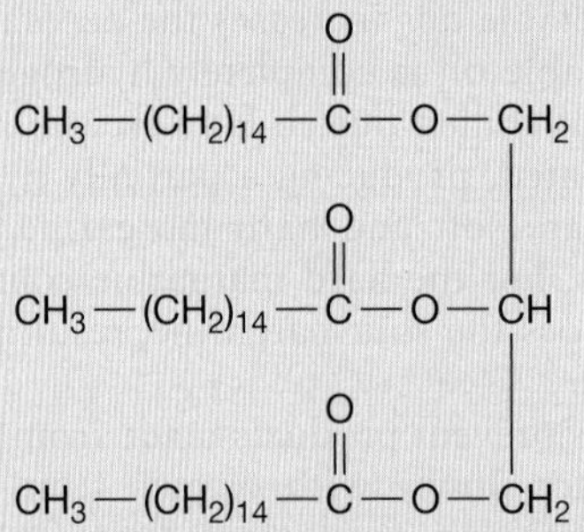

$$\begin{array}{l} CH_3-(CH_2)_{14}-\overset{\overset{\displaystyle O}{\|}}{C}-O-CH_2 \\ CH_3-(CH_2)_{14}-\overset{\overset{\displaystyle O}{\|}}{C}-O-CH \\ CH_3-(CH_2)_{14}-\overset{\overset{\displaystyle O}{\|}}{C}-O-CH_2 \end{array}$$

SOLUTION

When we hydrolyze a triglyceride in a strong acid, we form glycerol and fatty acids. Remember that in a hydrolysis reaction, we break the C–O bond, and then we add H and OH to complete the structures of the products.

$$\begin{array}{l} CH_3-(CH_2)_{14}-\overset{\overset{\displaystyle O}{\|}}{C}\wr O-CH_2 \\ CH_3-(CH_2)_{14}-\overset{\overset{\displaystyle O}{\|}}{C}\wr O-CH \\ CH_3-(CH_2)_{14}-\overset{\overset{\displaystyle O}{\|}}{C}\wr O-CH_2 \end{array} \longrightarrow \begin{array}{l} CH_3-(CH_2)_{14}-\overset{\overset{\displaystyle O}{\|}}{C}-\mathbf{OH} \\ CH_3-(CH_2)_{14}-\overset{\overset{\displaystyle O}{\|}}{C}-\mathbf{OH} \\ CH_3-(CH_2)_{14}-\overset{\overset{\displaystyle O}{\|}}{C}-\mathbf{OH} \end{array} + \begin{array}{l} \mathbf{HO}-CH_2 \\ \mathbf{HO}-CH \\ \mathbf{HO}-CH_2 \end{array}$$

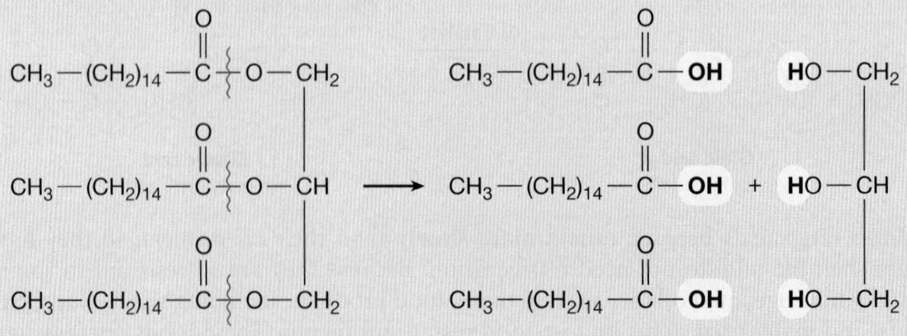

Break the C—O bonds . . .

. . . and add H and OH to the resulting fragments.

continued

When we use NaOH, which is a strong base, we make glycerol and the sodium salts of the fatty acids. In effect, the NaOH neutralizes the fatty acids as they are formed.

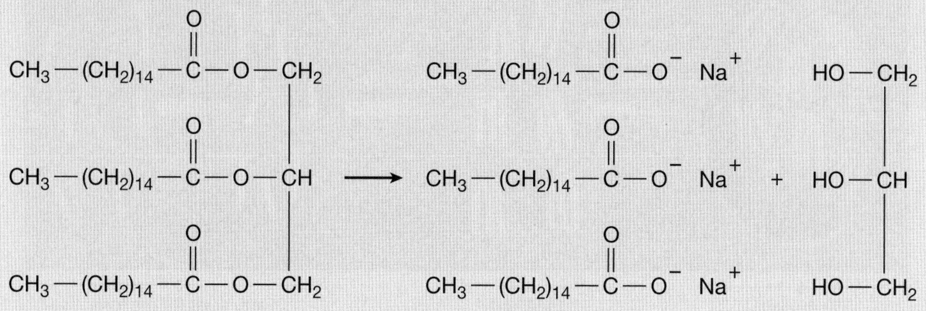

$$CH_3-(CH_2)_{14}-\overset{O}{\overset{\|}{C}}-O-CH_2 \qquad CH_3-(CH_2)_{14}-\overset{O}{\overset{\|}{C}}-O^- \; Na^+ \qquad HO-CH_2$$

$$CH_3-(CH_2)_{14}-\overset{O}{\overset{\|}{C}}-O-CH \longrightarrow CH_3-(CH_2)_{14}-\overset{O}{\overset{\|}{C}}-O^- \; Na^+ \; + \; HO-CH$$

$$CH_3-(CH_2)_{14}-\overset{O}{\overset{\|}{C}}-O-CH_2 \qquad CH_3-(CH_2)_{14}-\overset{O}{\overset{\|}{C}}-O^- \; Na^+ \qquad HO-CH_2$$

Sodium salts of the three fatty acids

TRY IT YOURSELF: *Draw the structures of the products that are formed when the triglyceride shown here is hydrolyzed using each of the following solutions:*

a) aqueous KOH *b) aqueous* H_2SO_4

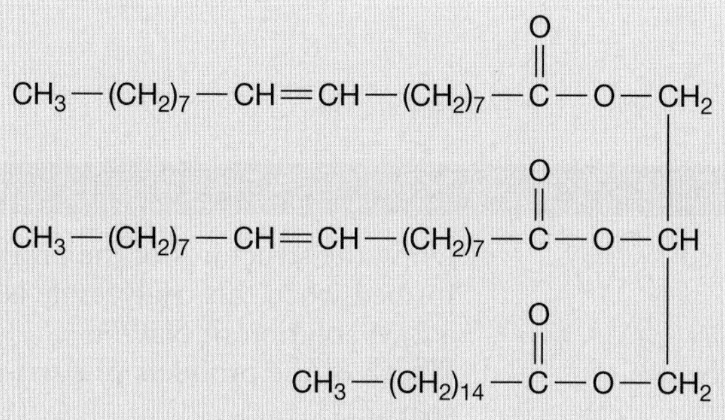

$$CH_3-(CH_2)_7-CH=CH-(CH_2)_7-\overset{O}{\overset{\|}{C}}-O-CH_2$$

$$CH_3-(CH_2)_7-CH=CH-(CH_2)_7-\overset{O}{\overset{\|}{C}}-O-CH$$

$$CH_3-(CH_2)_{14}-\overset{O}{\overset{\|}{C}}-O-CH_2$$

For additional practice, try Core Problems 14.51 (parts b and c) and 14.52 (parts b and c).

Fat Digestion Requires an Enzyme and Bile Salts

Our bodies must hydrolyze the triglycerides in our food, because triglycerides cannot pass through the walls of the digestive tract. In our digestive systems, enzymes called *lipases* are the catalysts that hydrolyze the ester groups in triglycerides. In addition, our bodies make *bile salts* whenever we eat a meal that is rich in triglycerides. Bile salts are powerful detergents, similar in behavior to the detergents we use to clean our clothes and dishes. Triglycerides are insoluble in water and tend to form large droplets when they are mixed with digestive juices. The bile salts break up these droplets, allowing the triglycerides to mix with water. The bile salts thus permit our digestive enzymes to hydrolyze the triglycerides at a reasonable rate.

Normally, lipases remove only two of the three fatty acids from the triglyceride, leaving a combination of glycerol and one fatty acid called a **monoglyceride**. Our digestive juices promptly neutralize the fatty acids, so the final products of fat digestion are a monoglyceride and the conjugate bases of two fatty acids. Figure 14.20 illustrates the digestion of triglycerides.

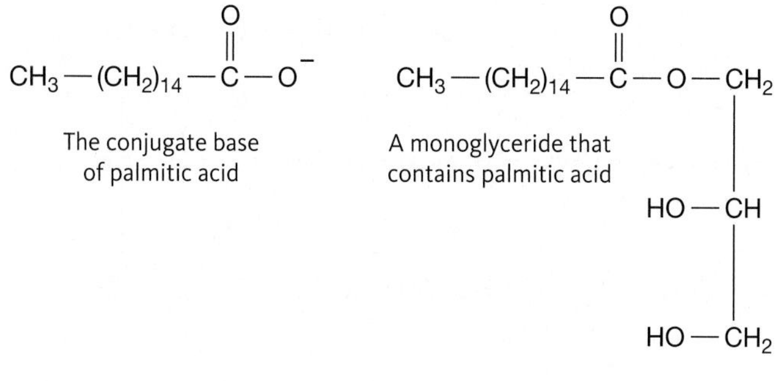

$$CH_3-(CH_2)_{14}-\overset{O}{\overset{\|}{C}}-O^-$$

The conjugate base of palmitic acid

$$CH_3-(CH_2)_{14}-\overset{O}{\overset{\|}{C}}-O-CH_2$$
$$HO-CH$$
$$HO-CH_2$$

A monoglyceride that contains palmitic acid

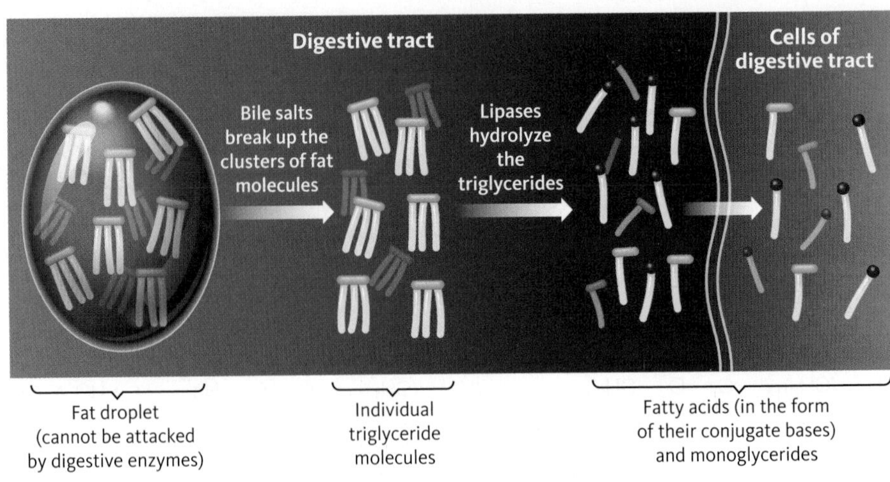

FIGURE 14.20 The digestion of a triglyceride.

CORE PROBLEMS

14.51 a) Draw the structure of the product that is formed when the following triglyceride is completely hydrogenated.
b) Draw the structures of the products that will be formed when this is hydrolyzed using a 2 M solution of H_2SO_4.
c) Draw the structures of the products that will be formed when this triglyceride is hydrolyzed using a 2 M solution of NaOH.
d) Which of the products of parts a through c are soaps?

$$CH_3-(CH_2)_7-CH=CH-(CH_2)_7-\overset{O}{\overset{\|}{C}}-O-CH_2$$
$$CH_3-(CH_2)_4-CH=CH-CH_2-CH=CH-(CH_2)_7-\overset{O}{\overset{\|}{C}}-O-CH$$
$$CH_3-(CH_2)_{14}-\overset{O}{\overset{\|}{C}}-O-CH_2$$

14.52 a) Draw the structure of the product that is formed when the following triglyceride is completely hydrogenated.
b) Draw the structures of the products that will be formed when this triglyceride is hydrolyzed using a 2 M solution of H_2SO_4.
c) Draw the structures of the products that will be formed when this triglyceride is hydrolyzed using a 2 M solution of KOH.
d) Which of the products of parts a through c are soaps?

$$CH_3-(CH_2)_{10}-\overset{O}{\overset{\|}{C}}-O-CH_2$$
$$CH_3-CH_2-CH=CH-CH_2-CH=CH-CH_2-CH=CH-(CH_2)_7-\overset{O}{\overset{\|}{C}}-O-CH$$
$$CH_3-(CH_2)_5-CH=CH-(CH_2)_7-\overset{O}{\overset{\|}{C}}-O-CH_2$$

continued

14.53 Identify the fatty acids that are formed in Problem 14.51, part b, using the information in Table 14.5.

14.54 Identify the fatty acids that are formed in Problem 14.52, part b, using the information in Table 14.5.

14.55 What is a *trans* fatty acid, and under what circumstances are *trans* fatty acids formed?

14.56 A label states that a particular snack food contains "no trans fat." What does this mean?

14.57 What products are formed when a triglyceride is hydrolyzed in the digestive tract?

14.58 If you hydrolyze a monoglyceride, what will you make?

14.59 What is the function of bile salts in fat digestion?

14.60 What is the function of lipases in fat digestion?

14.7 Glycerophospholipids and Cell Membranes

OBJECTIVES: *Draw the structure of a typical glycerophospholipid, relate the structures of glycerophospholipids to the structure and properties of a lipid bilayer, and describe the role of proteins in membrane transport.*

Every cell in our bodies has a *cell membrane,* a thin, flexible outer layer that keeps the contents of the cell from escaping. Inside most cells are a variety of smaller structures, which are likewise surrounded by membranes. The key compounds that make up these membranes are lipids. Since these lipids contain fatty acids and glycerol, they are closely related to triglycerides. In this section, we will look at some of the molecules that our bodies use to build cell membranes.

Glycerophospholipids Contain Ionized and Hydrophobic Groups

The majority of the lipids in most membranes are *phospholipids*. Phospholipids contain one or more long hydrocarbon chains and a phosphate group, and most phospholipids contain one or more additional polar molecules. There are a bewildering number of types of phospholipids, so we will examine just one class, the **glycerophospholipids**. Glycerophospholipids are made from glycerol, two fatty acids, a phosphate group, and one additional polar molecule. The general structure of a glycerophospholipid is related to that of a triglyceride, as shown in Figure 14.21.

In the majority of glycerophospholipids, the polar molecule is an amino alcohol, which contains an amino group and a hydroxyl group separated by two carbon atoms. The three common amino alcohols in glycerophospholipids are shown here. In each compound, the amino group is positively charged at pH 7. Note that serine is actually an amino acid, one of the 20 common amino acid building blocks of proteins.

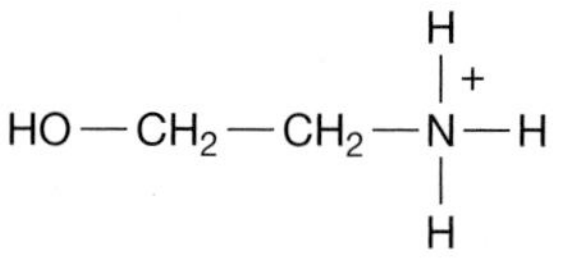

$HO-CH_2-CH_2-NH_3^+$

Ethanolamine

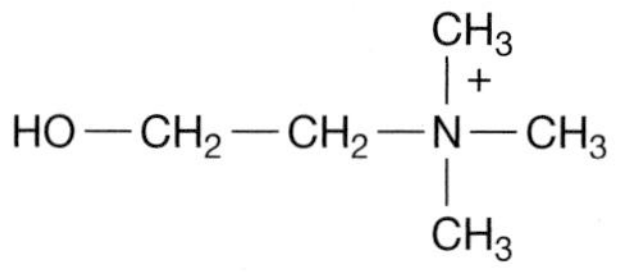

$HO-CH_2-CH_2-N^+(CH_3)_3$

Choline

$HO-CH_2-CH(COO^-)-NH_3^+$

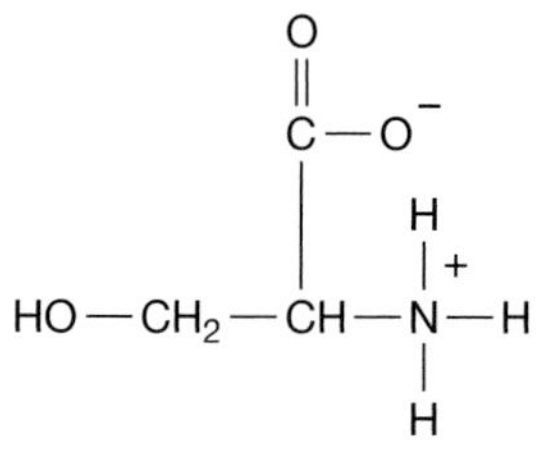

Serine

Health Note: Choline is used to build phospholipids and the nerve transmitter acetylcholine. The recommended daily dosage of choline in adults is around 500 mg. Many foods contain choline, and food manufacturers frequently add lecithins (phospholipids that contain choline) to processed foods, so people who consume a nutritionally balanced diet are not at risk of choline deficiency.

Glycerophospholipids can also contain a second molecule of glycerol or a molecule of inositol, a cyclic alcohol that is related to glucose.

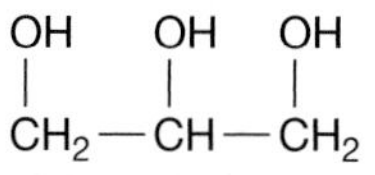

$CH_2(OH)-CH(OH)-CH_2(OH)$

Glycerol

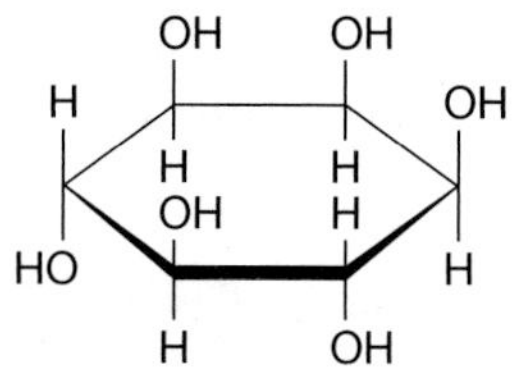

Inositol

Figure 14.22 shows how we can build a glycerophospholipid using myristic acid as the fatty acid and choline as the additional polar molecule. It takes four separate con-

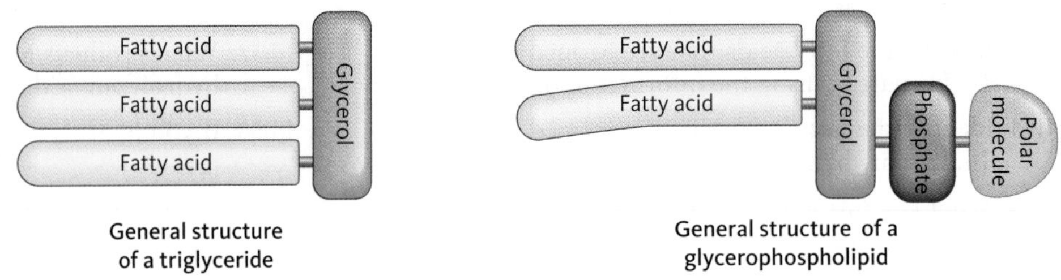

General structure of a triglyceride

General structure of a glycerophospholipid

FIGURE 14.21 The general structures of a triglyceride and a glycerophospholipid.

Glycerol

2 molecules of myristic acid

Phosphate

Choline

Lecithin (a glycerophospholipid)

$+ \; 4 \; H_2O$

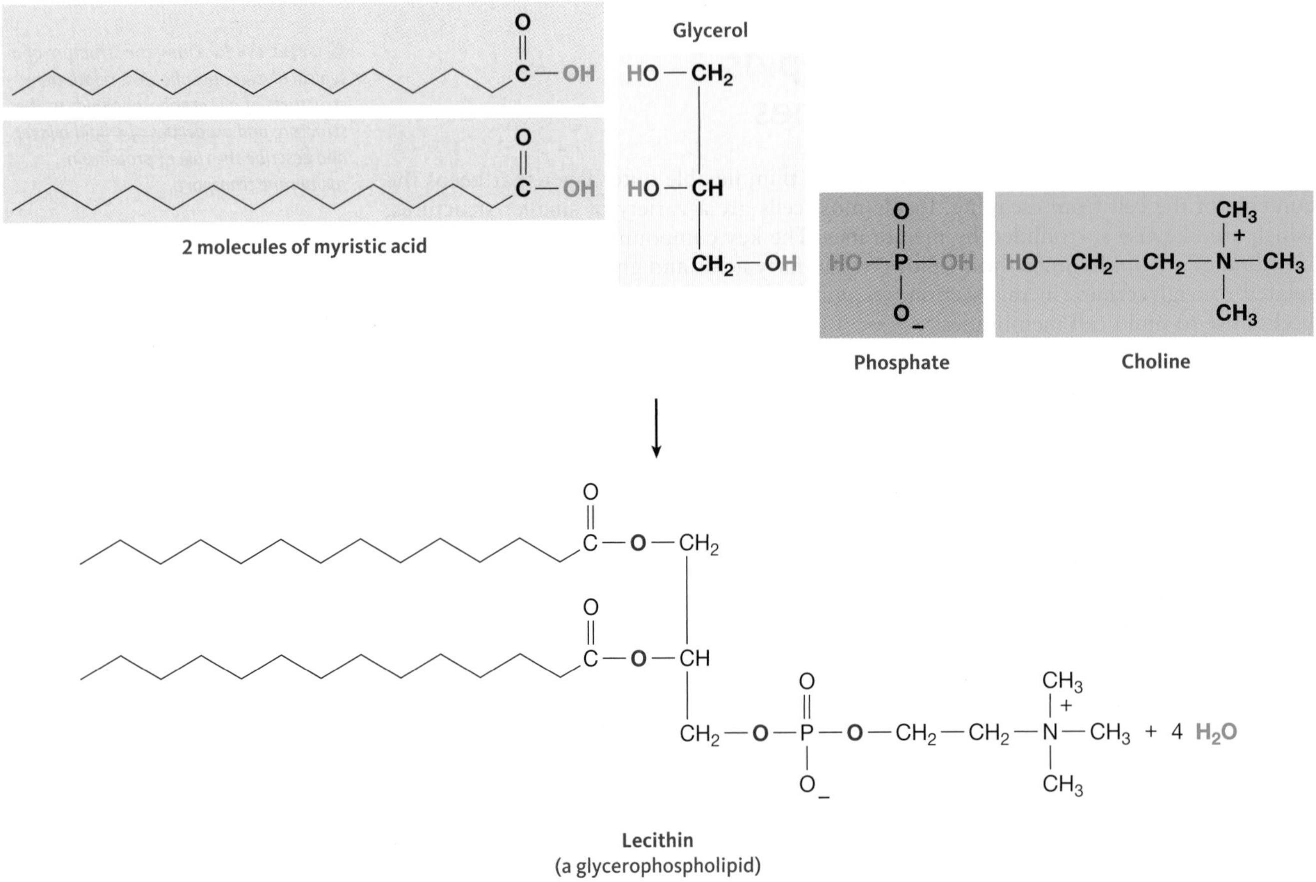

FIGURE 14.22 The formation of a glycerophospholipid.

densation reactions to build this complex molecule. Note that we draw one of the hydroxyl groups in glycerol on the opposite side from the other two, so that we can form the bond between glycerol and phosphate.

The phosphate group and the polar molecule that is attached to it are strongly attracted to water. However, the long hydrocarbon chains of the fatty acids are hydrophobic and do not mix with water. It is the presence of strongly hydrophobic and strongly hydrophilic regions in the same molecule that makes glycerophospholipids suitable building blocks for cell membranes.

Sample Problem 14.9

Drawing the structure of a glycerophospholipid

Draw the structure of the glycerophospholipid that contains two molecules of oleic acid and a molecule of ethanolamine.

continued

SOLUTION

A glycerophospholipid is made from two fatty acids, glycerol, a phosphate group, and an amino alcohol. From the information in the problem, we know that both fatty acids are oleic acid, and we know that the amino alcohol is ethanolamine. Now we can draw the building blocks of our glycerophospholipid, being sure to put them in the correct order and orientation. In the following picture, the circles show the atoms that will be removed when we condense our starting materials.

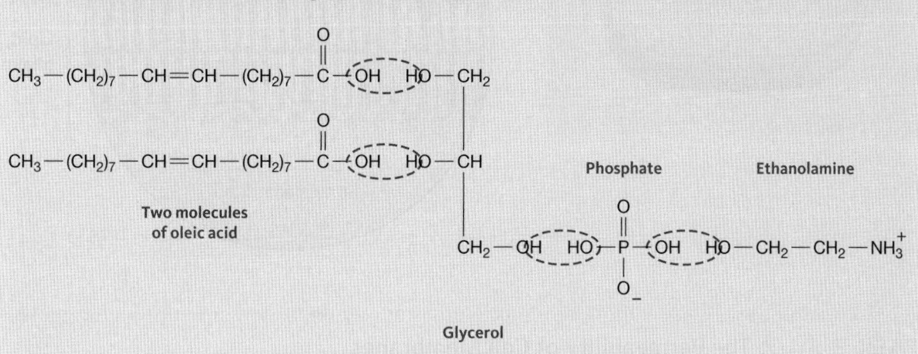

$CH_3-(CH_2)_7-CH=CH-(CH_2)_7-\overset{O}{\overset{\|}{C}}-OH \quad HO-CH_2$

$CH_3-(CH_2)_7-CH=CH-(CH_2)_7-\overset{O}{\overset{\|}{C}}-OH \quad HO-CH$

$CH_2-OH \quad HO-\overset{O}{\overset{\|}{P}}(-O^-)-OH \quad HO-CH_2-CH_2-NH_3^+$

Two molecules of oleic acid

Glycerol

Phosphate

Ethanolamine

Finally, we remove the circled atoms (which will become four water molecules), and we connect the remaining fragments to make our glycerophospholipid.

$CH_3-(CH_2)_7-CH=CH-(CH_2)_7-\overset{O}{\overset{\|}{C}}-O-CH_2$

$CH_3-(CH_2)_7-CH=CH-(CH_2)_7-\overset{O}{\overset{\|}{C}}-O-CH$

$CH_2-O-\overset{O}{\overset{\|}{P}}(-O^-)-O-CH_2-CH_2-NH_3^+$

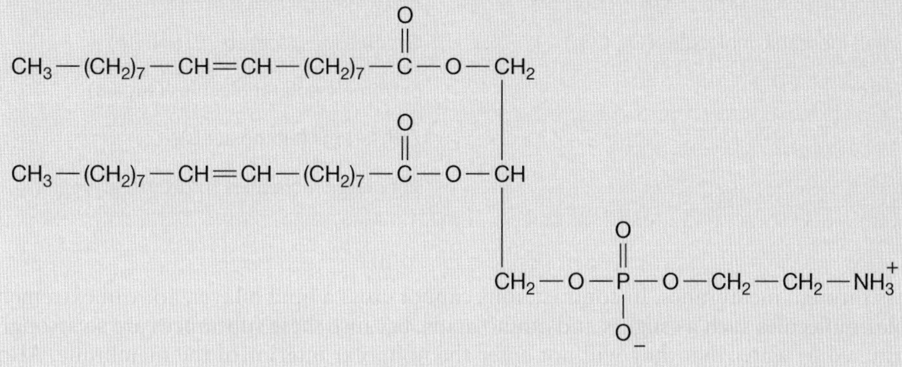

TRY IT YOURSELF: *Draw the structure of the glycerophospholipid that contains one molecule of stearic acid, one molecule of linoleic acid, and a molecule of serine. (The structures of stearic acid and linoleic acid are in Table 14.5.)*

For additional practice, try Core Problems 14.63 and 14.64.

The Lipid Bilayer Is the Basic Structure of All Membranes

The basic structure of membranes is the **lipid bilayer**, the structure of which is shown in Figure 14.23. A bilayer consists of two sheets of glycerophospholipid molecules, each of which completely encloses the cell. The molecules that make up the outer surface of the membrane are arranged so that their hydrophilic groups are in contact with the water that surrounds the cell. The molecules that constitute the inner surface of the membrane have their hydrophilic groups in contact with the intracellular fluid. The nonpolar tails of the two layers face each other and are not in contact with water. The result is a strong, flexible coating for the cell.

The most important function of a membrane is to prevent free exchange of molecules and ions between the inside and the outside of a cell. Lipid bilayers are almost ideally suited for this role, because they do not allow most solutes to pass through them. In general, only molecules that can mix with nonpolar substances can cross a lipid bilayer, because they can dissolve in the nonpolar interior of the bilayer. Most small organic molecules, even rather polar compounds such as ethanol and acetone, are soluble in nonpolar substances and can cross a lipid bilayer. Inorganic molecules can also cross the bilayer if they are nonpolar or weakly polar, so substances like O_2 and CO_2 can freely

FIGURE 14.23 The structure of a lipid bilayer.

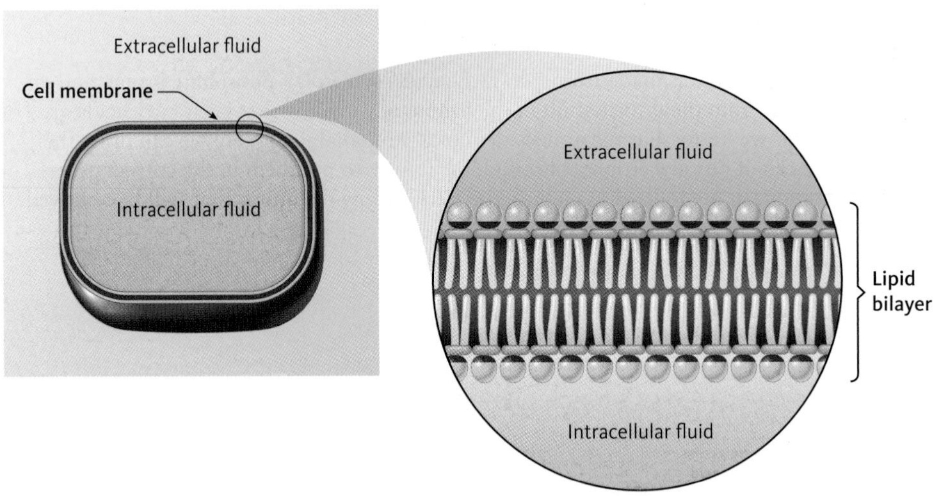

TABLE 14.7 **The Permeability of Cell Membranes**

Will Pass Through the Membrane	Will Not Pass Through the Membrane
Small organic molecules (ethanol, acetone)	Inorganic ions (Na^+, HCO_3^-)
Small inorganic molecules (O_2, CO_2)	Organic ions (acetate, $CH_3NH_3^+$)
Water	Extremely polar molecules (sugars)
	Zwitterions (amino acids)
	Very large molecules (proteins, glycogen)

pass through membranes. In contrast, ions cannot cross a lipid bilayer, nor can extremely polar molecules such as sugars and amino acids, because these substances are so strongly attracted to water that they will not enter the nonpolar interior of the membrane. Also, very large molecules like proteins and starch do not pass through membranes. Curiously, although water cannot pass through a lipid bilayer, it moves freely through most membranes, because proteins that are incorporated into the membrane contain pores that allow passage of water molecules. Table 14.7 summarizes the permeability of cell membranes to various solutes.

Specialized lipids allow this runner's nervous system to signal her muscles to contract at the sound of the starting gun.

Membranes Contain Many Other Compounds

Membranes contain a number of lipids in addition to the glycerophospholipids. These lipids vary from one tissue type to another, giving a cell membrane properties that complement the function of the cell it surrounds. For instance, the membranes surrounding cells in the central nervous system contain large amounts of two classes of lipids that have similar structures to the glycerophospholipids. These molecules, called cerebrosides and sphingomyelins, presumably contribute to the special ability of nerve cells to transmit electrical impulses over large distances. Many of the lipids that make up the outer surface of the cell membrane are bonded to one or more simple sugar molecules. These carbohydrate portions protrude from the outside of the cell and allow our immune system to recognize our own cells and tell them apart from foreign invaders. Cell membranes in animals also contain cholesterol, which allows the membranes to remain flexible over a wide temperature range. Cholesterol is an example of a steroid, a special class of lipids that we will explore in Section 14.8.

All membranes contain a variety of proteins. These proteins play a number of roles in the cell, some of which are listed in Table 14.8. Some proteins are embedded in the lipid bilayer, while others are bound to the surface of the membrane, as we saw in Section 13.3. Both the proteins and the various lipids are free to move around within the membrane. However, the proteins are always oriented in a specific way, so one surface of the protein always faces the interior of the cell and the other always faces the exterior.

TABLE 14.8 Some Functions of Membrane Proteins

Type of Protein	Function
Transport protein	Moves ions and polar molecules through the membrane
Receptor protein	Binds to hormones that affect the cell's activity
Enzyme	Catalyzes reactions (many reactions occur on the surface of a membrane)
Photosystem	Converts light energy into chemical energy during photosynthesis
Cytochrome	Transfers electrons in metabolic pathways

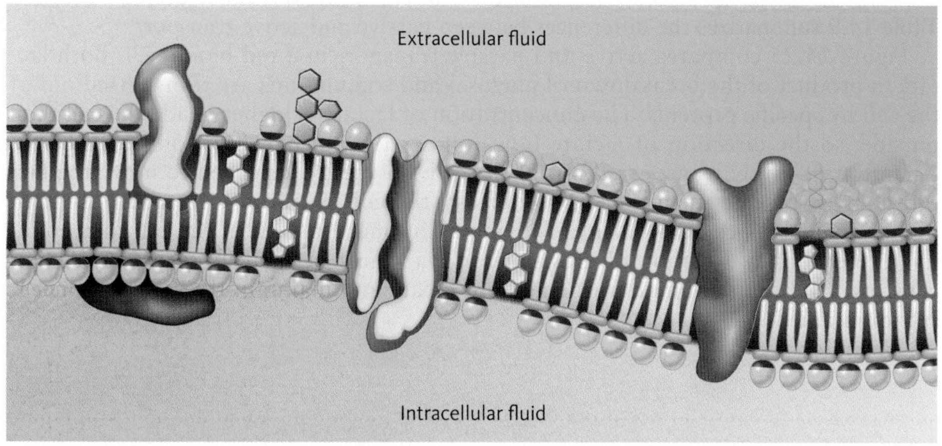

Key to types of molecules in the membrane:

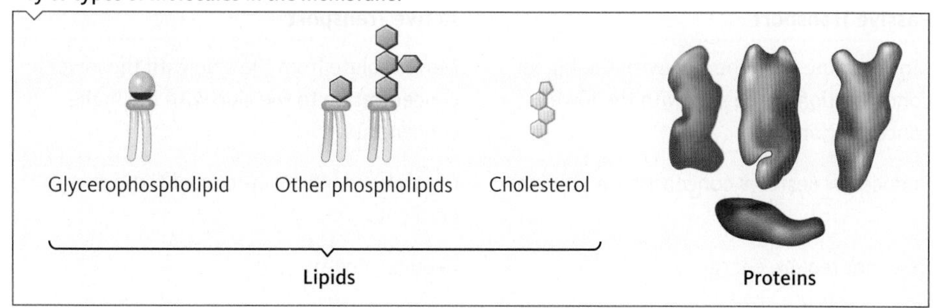

FIGURE 14.24 The structure of a cell membrane.

In addition, the inside and outside faces of the membrane contain different mixtures of lipids. Figure 14.24 shows a simplified picture of a typical cell membrane.

A particularly important function of membrane proteins is to allow polar molecules and ions to pass through the membrane. **Transport proteins** provide passageways through the hydrophobic region of the lipid bilayer. Some transport proteins are simply tunnels and will permit any molecule or ion to pass through as long as it is not too large. However, most transport proteins are as specific as any enzyme, binding to a very limited number of molecules or ions. For example, the membranes of nerve cells contain a protein that binds to glucose and moves it through the cell membrane. This protein will also transport galactose into the cell, because the structure of galactose is almost identical to that of glucose. However, it will not bind to fructose, which has the same chemical formula as glucose but a significantly different structure (see Figure 14.3).

Health Note: The activity of the glucose transporters in muscle and fat cells increases when the concentration of insulin in the blood goes up, so muscle and fat tissues help keep the concentration of glucose in the blood relatively stable. In diabetes mellitus Type 2 (sometimes called adult-onset diabetes), these cells become less responsive to insulin levels in the blood, allowing the concentration of glucose in the blood to increase to potentially damaging levels.

Transport through a Membrane Can Be Active or Passive

A wide range of molecules and ions must be moved into and out of a typical cell, because cells require many different nutrients and produce several waste products. How does the cell control which way the molecules pass through the membrane? In many cases, the direction is determined by the tendency of solutes to diffuse from higher concentration to lower concentration, as we saw in Section 5.4. For example, the concentration of glucose in blood plasma is usually higher than the concentration of glucose inside red blood cells, so glucose tends to diffuse into the cell rather than out of it. This type of transport is called **passive transport**, and the transport protein simply serves as a passageway for the solute molecules.

However, some substances must be moved across a membrane against the normal direction of diffusion. For example, all of the cells in the body actively expel sodium ions, moving them from the intracellular fluid to the extracellular fluid. As a result, the concentration of Na^+ is much higher outside the cells than it is inside. These differing concentrations on either side of the membrane are called a **concentration gradient**. Diffusion cannot produce a concentration gradient—in fact, diffusion always works to eliminate concentration gradients. *A cell can only produce a concentration gradient by expending energy.* Transport proteins use part of the energy that a cell obtains from burning fuels to push sodium ions out of the cell. This process is called **active transport**. Table 14.9 summarizes the differences between passive and active transport.

Figure 14.25 compares active and passive transport in a red blood cell. Both lactate (a product of the breakdown of glucose) and sodium ions are transported out of the cell by specific proteins. The concentration of lactate is higher inside the cell than outside, so the direction of lactate flow follows the normal direction of diffusion. Lactate is passively transported out of the cell: no energy is needed to move the lactate ions across the membrane. By contrast, the concentration of sodium is much higher outside the cell than inside. Moving additional Na^+ out of the cell runs counter to the normal direction of diffusion, so Na^+ must be actively transported. Our cells use a substantial amount of energy to create and maintain the sodium concentration gradient.

TABLE 14.9 A Comparison of Passive and Active Transport

Passive Transport	Active Transport
Moves solute from the side with the higher concentration to the side with the lower concentration	Moves solute from the side with the lower concentration to the side with the higher concentration
Reduces or destroys concentration gradients	Creates and maintains concentration gradients
Does not require energy	Requires energy

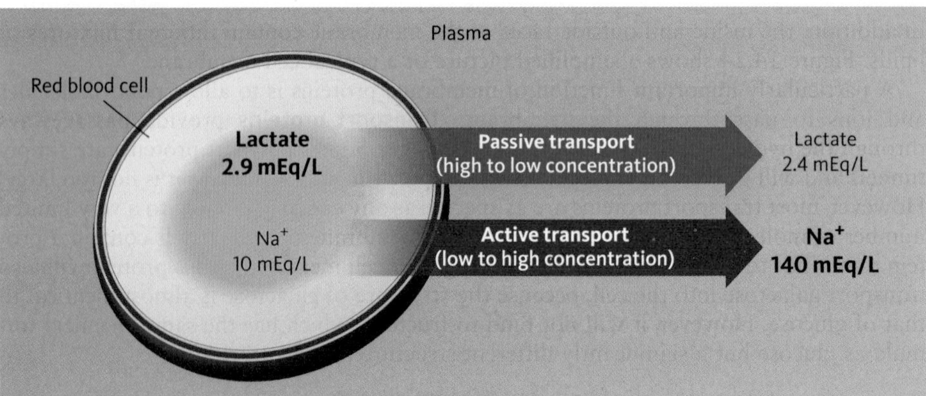

FIGURE 14.25 Active and passive transport in a red blood cell.

Sample Problem 14.10

Identifying active and passive transport

The concentration of potassium ions is 150 mEq/L inside a cell and 5 mEq/L outside the cell.

a) If potassium diffuses passively through the membrane, which way will it flow?

b) A protein moves potassium ions from the outside of the cell to the inside. Is this an example of active or passive transport?

SOLUTION

a) Solutes always diffuse from the side with the higher concentration to the side with the lower concentration. Therefore, if potassium diffuses passively through the membrane, it will flow from the inside of the cell to the outside.

b) The protein is moving potassium ions against the normal direction of diffusion. This is an example of active transport.

TRY IT YOURSELF: *The concentration of calcium outside a muscle cell is around 1.2 mEq/L, while the concentration inside the cell is less than 0.0001 mEq/L. When a muscle contracts, calcium ions flow from the surrounding fluid into the muscle cells through a specific transport protein. Is this an example of active or passive transport?*

For additional practice, try Core Problems 14.71 and 14.72.

Concentration Gradients Can Be Used to Do Cellular Work

Active transport of sodium and potassium ions plays a vital role in physiology, because the resulting concentration gradients have a great deal of potential energy. The cell harnesses this potential energy to do other types of work. For instance, many cells use the sodium concentration gradient to supply the energy to transport glucose through their cell membranes. Nerve cells use the energy of concentration gradients to create and transmit nerve impulses. In Chapter 15, we will see how specialized structures within the cell use active transport to create a hydrogen ion gradient. The cell then uses the energy of this concentration gradient to make ATP, the chemical compound that provides the critical link between energy-producing and energy-consuming pathways in the cell.

Health Note: A nerve impulse is created when a brief burst of sodium ions flows into the cell, followed by a brief burst of potassium ions flowing out of the cell. Both of these depend on concentration gradients: the sodium concentration is higher outside the nerve cell, while the potassium concentration is higher inside the cell.

CORE PROBLEMS

14.61 Which of the building blocks of a glycerophospholipid are strongly hydrophilic?

14.62 Which of the building blocks of a glycerophospholipid are strongly hydrophobic?

14.63 Draw the structure of the glycerophospholipid that contains two molecules of stearic acid and a molecule of serine.

$CH_3-(CH_2)_{16}-COOH$

Stearic acid

$HO-CH_2-CH(COO^-)-NH_3^+$

Serine

14.64 Draw the structure of the glycerophospholipid that contains two molecules of oleic acid and a molecule of choline.

$CH_3-(CH_2)_7-CH=CH-(CH_2)_7-COOH$

Oleic acid

$HO-CH_2-CH_2-N^+(CH_3)_3$

Choline

14.65 Which parts of a glycerophospholipid are on the exterior of a lipid bilayer, and why?

continued

14.66 Which parts of a glycerophospholipid are in the interior of a lipid bilayer, and why?

14.67 CO_2 can cross a lipid bilayer, but HCO_3^- cannot. Why is this?

14.68 $CH_3–Cl$ can cross a lipid bilayer, but NaCl cannot. Why is this?

14.69 What is the function of transport proteins, and why do cells need transport proteins?

14.70 The amino acid tyrosine cannot pass through a lipid bilayer, but it can cross cell membranes. Describe how this happens.

14.71 Cells can absorb the amino acid valine from the surrounding fluid when the concentration of valine is higher inside the cell than outside.
a) Is this an example of active or passive transport?
b) Does this type of transport require energy?
c) Does this type of transport produce a concentration gradient?

14.72 Liver cells produce urea as a waste product. The urea passes through the cell membrane into the surrounding fluid, but it does so only when the concentration of urea is higher inside the cell than outside.
a) Is this an example of active or passive transport?
b) Does this type of transport require energy?
c) Does this type of transport produce a concentration gradient?

14.73 Why are concentration gradients important in living organisms?

14.74 Give an example of a situation in which a cell uses the energy of a concentration gradient to do work.

OBJECTIVES: *Recognize the steroid nucleus, know the functions of physiologically important steroids, and describe the mechanism by which steroids and triglycerides are transported in the body.*

14.8 Steroids and Lipoproteins

All of the lipids you have studied so far contain one or more fatty acids, and all of them can be hydrolyzed in acidic or basic solutions. However, there are several other classes of lipids, the most prominent of which are the **steroids**. Steroids contain a backbone of four linked rings of carbon atoms, called the steroid nucleus.

The steroid nucleus

By far the most abundant steroid in animals is cholesterol. As we saw in Section 14.7, cholesterol is an essential component of cell membranes, allowing them to remain flexible over a broad temperature range. Cholesterol contains an extensive hydrocarbon backbone (with a total of 27 carbon atoms) and only one hydrophilic functional group, so it is insoluble in water.

Health Note: A high concentration of cholesterol in the blood increases the risk of cardiovascular disease, including heart attacks and strokes. Many people with high cholesterol levels take drugs called *statins* to reduce their blood cholesterol levels. These drugs block the formation of cholesterol from other substances in the body, but it is unclear whether they reduce the risk of cardiovascular disease.

CH_3 CH_3
CH—CH_2—CH_2—CH_2—CH—CH_3
CH_3
CH_3
HO

Cholesterol

Many Hormones Contain the Steroid Nucleus

Our bodies use cholesterol as the starting material for making all other steroids. For example, cholesterol is the precursor of the bile salts, the detergent compounds that break up fat droplets in our digestive tracts. We also use cholesterol to make several compounds that serve as chemical messengers within our bodies. These compounds, called **steroid hormones**, are produced by specialized glands and have a profound impact on a broad range of tissues and organs. Table 14.10 shows the five main classes of

TABLE 14.10 The Steroid Hormones in Humans

Hormone Class and Function	Name and Structure of the Primary Human Hormone in This Class
Estrogen Estrogens regulate maturation of the reproductive system and development of secondary sexual characteristics in females, stimulate growth of the uterus and breasts during pregnancy, and trigger ovulation.	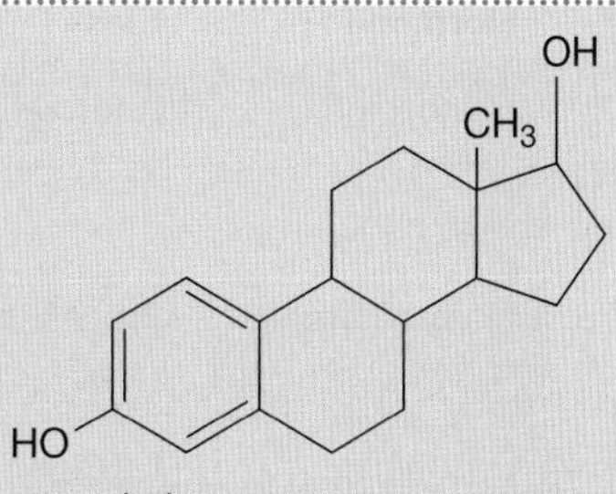 estradiol
Progestin Progestins prepare the uterus for pregnancy, suppress uterine contractions during pregnancy, and prepare the breasts for lactation.	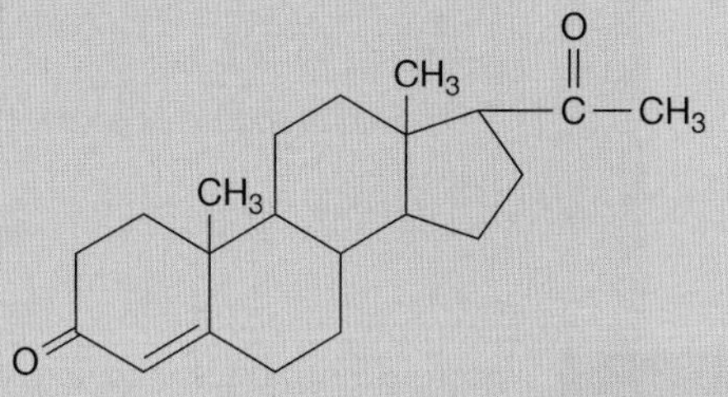 progesterone
Androgen Androgens regulate the development and maturation of the reproductive system and the development of secondary sexual characteristics in males, and they promote protein synthesis and muscle growth.	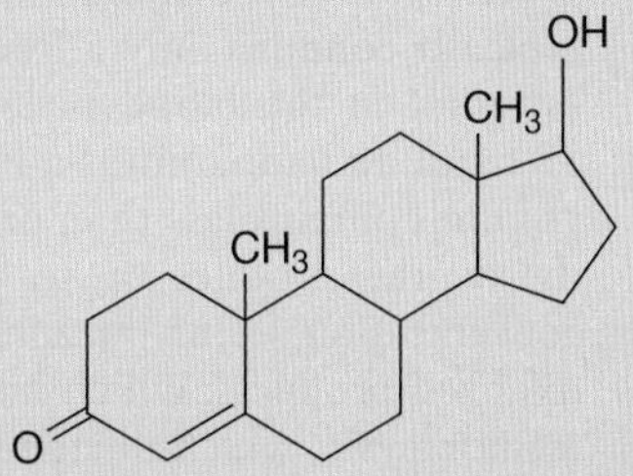 testosterone
Mineralocorticoid Mineralocorticoids regulate Na^+ and K^+ concentration in blood plasma, and they indirectly influence plasma concentrations of water and other ions.	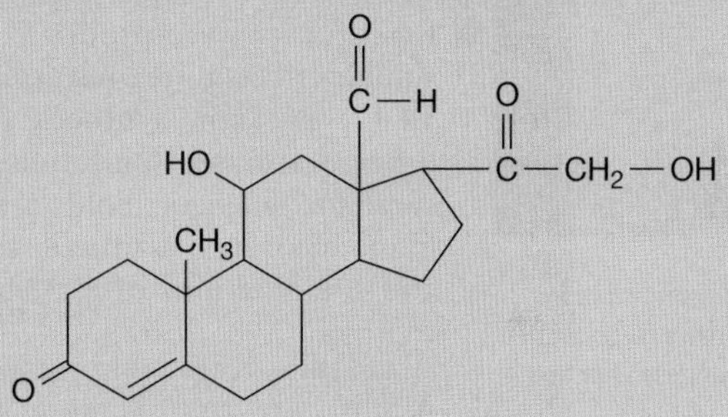 aldosterone
Glucocorticoid Glucocorticoids regulate the blood levels of glucose, amino acids, and fatty acids for use as fuels, and they are involved in the physiological responses to stress.	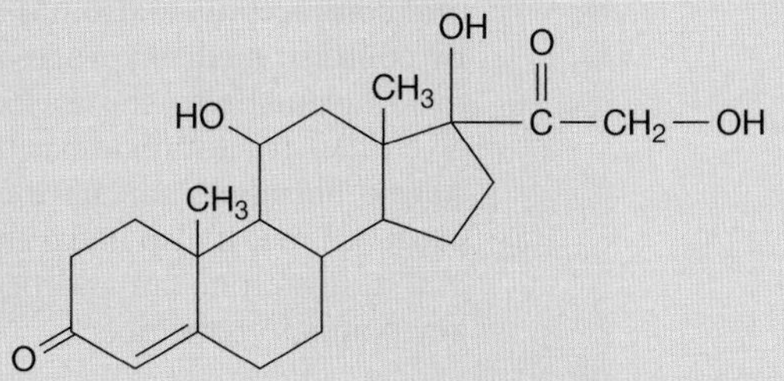 cortisol

TABLE 14.11 Some Synthetic Steroid Hormones

Synthetic Hormone	Class	Use
Stanozolol	Androgen	Treatment of hereditary angioedema, promotion of weight gain after illness (used illegally to increase muscle mass)
Norethindrone	Progestin	Treatment of menstrual irregularity and as a component of some oral contraceptives
Estropipate	Estrogen	Treatment of menopause symptoms and certain types of cancer
Fludrocortisone	Mineralocorticoid	Treatment of adrenal insufficiency
Dexamethasone	Glucocorticoid	Treatment of chronic inflammation due to arthritis, asthma, and other disorders

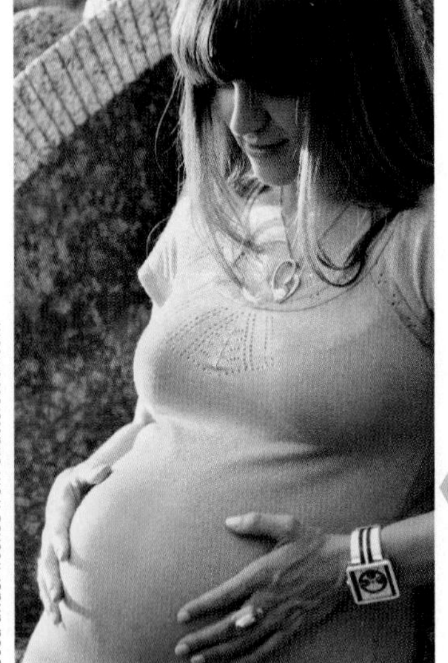

Steroid hormones are responsible for the maturing of a woman's reproductive system and for the changes in her body during pregnancy.

steroid hormones, and it gives the structures and functions of the steroid hormones in the human body.

The steroid hormones have remarkably high biological activities, and our blood typically contains only a trace of any given hormone. For example, the concentration of estradiol in the blood plasma of an adult, premenopausal woman ranges from 3 to 37 ng/dL (a nanogram is a billionth of a gram). This means that a woman's entire blood volume contains less than one microgram (a millionth of a gram) of this hormone. Since the ovaries produce up to 400,000 micrograms of estradiol per day, the low plasma concentration seems puzzling at first. However, the liver rapidly converts estradiol into oxidized products, which are excreted in the urine. This allows the body to control estradiol levels, which fluctuate through a wide range during a woman's menstrual cycle.

Synthetic Steroid Hormones Have a Range of Medical Uses

Researchers have produced many synthetic steroid hormones, compounds that have similar effects to the naturally occurring compounds but are not found in nature. Table 14.11 lists some synthetic steroid hormones that are used in medicine. Synthetic androgens are used (and abused) to increase muscle mass and to increase male potency, synthetic glucocorticoids are used to reduce inflammation and to treat certain autoimmune disorders, synthetic estrogens are used to reduce the symptoms of menopause, and combinations of estrogens and progestins are used as oral and injectable contraceptives.

Synthetic steroid hormones generally have somewhat different physiological effects than the natural versions, and they often combine the properties of two or more classes of steroid hormones. For example, norethindrone, a synthetic progestin that is used in many oral contraceptives, also has some of the physiological effects of androgens and estrogens. By contrast, medroxyprogesterone acetate (MPA, the active progestin in some contraceptive implants) also shows some of the effects of a glucocorticoid. This is not surprising, given the structural similarity of the various steroid hormones. Indeed, even the natural steroid hormones can have overlapping effects. For instance, progesterone is the natural progestin, but it also behaves as a glucocorticoid, and it counteracts some of the effects of both testosterone (an androgen) and aldosterone (a mineralocorticoid). The following are key points to remember:

- Hormones have multiple effects, which overlap one another.
- A small structural change in a hormone can produce a profound change in its physiological effects.

Lipids Are Transported with the Help of Proteins

Most lipids have extremely low solubilities in body fluids, which are primarily water. As a result, our bodies use specialized proteins to transport lipids through the bloodstream.

TABLE 14.12 Typical Approximate Composition of Plasma Lipoproteins

Class of Lipoprotein	Density Range	Percentage of Triglycerides and Phospholipids	Percentage of Cholesterol	Percentage of Protein
Chylomicron	Less than 0.95 g/mL	90%	10%	Very low
Very-low-density lipoprotein (VLDL)	0.95–1.006 g/mL	70%	20%	10%
Intermediate-density lipoprotein (IDL)	1.006–1.019 g/mL	50%	30%	20%
Low-density lipoprotein (LDL)	1.019–1.063 g/mL	25%	50%	25%
High-density lipoprotein (HDL)	1.063–1.21 g/mL	40%	30%	30%

All percentages are rounded off. Chylomicrons typically contain 1%–2% protein.

TABLE 14.13 Cholesterol Levels in Adults

Test	Recommended Level
Total cholesterol	Less than 200 mg/dL
LDL cholesterol	Less than 160 mg/dL (Less than 130 mg/dL for people who are otherwise at risk for heart disease)
HDL cholesterol	More than 40 mg/dL

The two main classes of proteins involved in lipid transport are the lipoproteins and the binding proteins. Lipoproteins carry lipids that the body requires in large amounts, such as cholesterol and the triglycerides, while the binding proteins carry steroid hormones, which are present in far lower concentrations.

Lipoproteins are clusters of cholesterol, triglycerides, and other lipids, surrounded by a hydrophilic protein coating. The lipoproteins are classified by their density, as shown in Table 14.12. The density of a lipoprotein is directly related to the percentage of protein: the higher the percentage of protein, the higher the density. The chylomicrons are the most abundant lipoproteins in blood and are the primary transport mechanisms for triglycerides. The low- and high-density lipoproteins are the main cholesterol transport system, while very-low- and intermediate-density lipoproteins carry both types of lipids.

LDL and HDL both carry cholesterol, but their roles in our body differ. LDL normally moves cholesterol from the liver to other tissues, where it can be used to build cell membranes. HDL carries cholesterol back to the liver, where it can be converted to water-soluble bile salts and excreted through the digestive tract. When the concentration of LDL in the blood is high, body tissues cannot absorb the excess cholesterol. Much of this cholesterol is deposited in the arteries, irritating the arterial wall and leading to a dangerous narrowing of the arteries called atherosclerosis, a primary cause of heart attacks and strokes. As a result, LDL is sometimes called "bad cholesterol." HDL, which helps remove cholesterol from the body and prevent cholesterol deposits in the arteries, is also called "good cholesterol." Table 14.13 shows recommended cholesterol and lipoprotein levels in the blood plasma of healthy adults. The HDL and LDL tests actually measure the amount of cholesterol that is carried by each lipoprotein.

Despite their low plasma concentrations, the steroid hormones also require proteins to transport them through the bloodstream. The bulk of the estradiol and testosterone is carried by a protein called *sex hormone–binding globulin* (SHBG). Most of the cortisol, aldosterone, and progesterone is carried by *corticosteroid-binding globulin* (CBG). In addition, the steroid hormones bind to albumin, the main protein in blood plasma. Only a small fraction of the molecules of these hormones is not bound to a plasma protein at any given time.

CORE PROBLEMS

14.75 What is the function of cholesterol in the human body?

14.76 What is the function of bile salts in the human body?

14.77 Which type of steroid hormone has the following function?
a) regulation of the concentration of sodium ions in the blood
b) regulation of the development of the female reproductive system

14.78 Which type of steroid hormone has the following function?
a) regulation of the development of the male reproductive system
b) regulation of the concentration of glucose and other fuels in the blood

14.79 A chemist carries out a reaction that makes a small change to the structure of a steroid hormone. Is this change likely to have a significant impact on the physiological effect of the hormone, or will it probably have only a minor effect? Explain.

14.80 Is it reasonable to say that every synthetic steroid hormone fits easily into one of the five classes shown in Table 14.10? Explain.

14.81 Why do steroids require specialized molecules to carry them throughout the body?

14.82 Which of the three main types of biomolecules (carbohydrates, proteins, and fats) do our bodies use to transport steroids?

14.83 Which two types of lipoproteins are the primary carriers of cholesterol in the blood? How do their roles differ?

14.84 What type of lipoprotein is the primary carrier of triglycerides in the blood?

OBJECTIVES: *Describe the sources of carbohydrates and fats in human nutrition, and describe the role of the carbon cycle in making organic nutrients available to living organisms.*

14.9 Sources of Carbohydrates and Fats

Carbohydrates and fats supply the bulk of our energy needs. In addition, fats provide us with several fatty acids that our bodies require. As a result, carbohydrates and fats are important components of our diet. In this section, we will look at the dietary sources of these two classes of nutrients.

Humans Have Several Dietary Sources of Carbohydrates

Until the twentieth century, the complex carbohydrates starch and glycogen provided the majority of the metabolic fuel for most people. This is still the case in many regions of the world, but the typical American diet has changed significantly over the past century. The most striking changes are an increasing replacement of carbohydrate by fat and protein as an energy source and a shift from complex carbohydrates to sugars. Table 14.14 shows the energy sources in a typical American diet in comparison with the most recent dietary recommendations.

Sugars are often said to be unhealthy, but there is no firm evidence that sugars are less appropriate than starches as a source of dietary carbohydrate for healthy people. However, there is some concern that the sugars that are added to foods during processing result in overeating and contribute to obesity. Highly sweetened foods such as candies and soft drinks also tend to be low in nutrients such as protein and vitamins, so people who eat large amounts of sugary foods are at risk for dietary deficiencies of these nutrients.

These foods are high in sugars but low in other essential nutrients, so they should be eaten in moderation.

TABLE 14.14 Calorie Sources in the American Diet

Type of Nutrient	Typical American Diet	Dietary Recommendations (U.S. National Academy of Sciences)
Complex carbohydrates (starch, glycogen)	35%	45% to 65% (all carbohydrates)
Sugars (sucrose, fructose, lactose)	12%	
Fats (animal fat, vegetable oil, butter, etc.)	34%	20% to 35%
Proteins	17%	10% to 35%

Our bodies need small amounts of monosaccharides to build a variety of important molecules, but we burn most of our dietary carbohydrate to obtain energy. Humans can make monosaccharides from other nutrients, including most of the amino acids, citric acid (the compound responsible for the tart flavor of many fruits), and glycerol. However, none of these are significant sources of carbohydrate for a well-nourished individual. Humans, along with all other animals, all fungi, and most microorganisms, normally obtain all of the carbohydrate we need directly from our diet.

People Obtain Essential Fatty Acids from Dietary Fat

As is the case with carbohydrates, we use most of the triglycerides in our diet as an energy source. However, we also use the fatty acids in triglycerides to build the membrane lipids, and we use linoleic acid to build the prostaglandins, compounds that play a vital role in the control of the inflammatory response. Our bodies can make saturated and monounsaturated fatty acids from carbohydrates or amino acids, but we cannot make polyunsaturated fatty acids. As a result, linoleic acid and linolenic acid, which contain two and three alkene groups, respectively, are dietary requirements for all humans (and all other mammals) and are called **essential fatty acids**. The structures of these fatty acids are shown in Table 14.5.

In recent years, two other polyunsaturated fatty acids, called *eicosapentaenoic acid (EPA)* and *docosahexaenoic acid (DHA)*, have been shown to play significant roles in human health.

$$CH_3-CH_2-CH=CH-CH_2-CH=CH-CH_2-CH=CH-CH_2-CH=CH-CH_2-CH=CH-(CH_2)_3-COOH$$

EPA

$$CH_3-CH_2-CH=CH-CH_2-CH=CH-CH_2-CH=CH-CH_2-CH=CH-CH_2-CH=CH-CH_2-CH=CH-(CH_2)_2-COOH$$

DHA

EPA and DHA are omega-3 fatty acids. Our bodies can make both of them from linoleic acid, but there is some evidence that eating foods that contain these fatty acids can reduce the risk of cardiovascular disease. EPA and DHA are especially abundant in the fatty tissues of certain fish, but these fish also absorb mercury from the surrounding water and concentrate it in their bodies. As a result, all dietary recommendations involving EPA and DHA are coupled to warnings about the possibility of low-level mercury poisoning, particularly in children and pregnant women.

Plants Make Glucose from Carbon Dioxide and Water

The human body can make both carbohydrates and fats from amino acids, and we can convert carbohydrates into fats. However, we cannot make any of these nutrients from inorganic materials. As a result, we rely on other organisms to make these organic compounds. The same is true of all other animals, as well as fungi (mushrooms, molds, and so forth) and most microorganisms. Ultimately, *all of these organisms rely on green plants to convert the raw materials of the nonliving world into organic compounds.*

The ability of plants to make organic compounds from carbon dioxide and water makes them the foundation of life on Earth.

All green plants can carry out a process called **photosynthesis**, which converts carbon dioxide and water into glucose and gaseous oxygen. Photosynthesis also requires energy, which is provided by sunlight. The overall reaction of photosynthesis is

$$6\ CO_2 + 6\ H_2O + \text{energy} \rightarrow \underset{\textbf{(glucose)}}{C_6H_{12}O_6} + 6\ O_2$$

Photosynthesis can be considered the foundation of life on Earth, because it harnesses the energy of the sun to supply the energy requirements of living organisms. Indeed, the enzyme that binds CO_2 into an organic molecule during photosynthesis (called ribulose-1,5-bisphosphate carboxylase/oxygenase, or *rubisco*) is generally believed to be the most abundant protein on Earth.

The glucose that plants make in photosynthesis is the starting material for a huge array of chemical reactions that connects virtually every part of the living world. The plants themselves burn glucose to supply energy for other metabolic activities, use it to build cellulose and starch, and convert it into amino acids, fats, and other compounds. Animals then eat the plants, obtaining carbohydrates and other nutrients for their own needs. These animals are in turn eaten by other animals, and the remains of dead plants and animals are a food source for microorganisms and fungi.

Eventually, all organic compounds in living organisms are broken down, and most are burned to obtain energy. The burning of any organic compound by a living organism is called **respiration** and is essentially a combustion reaction, which requires oxygen and converts the organic molecule into carbon dioxide and water. As a result, photosynthesis and respiration undo each other. These two processes form the **carbon cycle**, which interconverts inorganic and organic compounds. Figure 14.26 illustrates the carbon cycle.

Photosynthesis fulfills two roles in the living world. First, it is the ultimate source of the organic compounds that are the building blocks of life. Second, photosynthesis stores the energy of the sun in the form of a mixture of glucose and O_2. The combination of glucose and oxygen contains a great deal of potential energy, because oxygen atoms are more strongly attracted to carbon and hydrogen than they are to one another. Most other mixtures of an organic compound with oxygen also contain a lot of potential energy, for the same reason. Animals and plants use this energy to drive all of the activities of life.

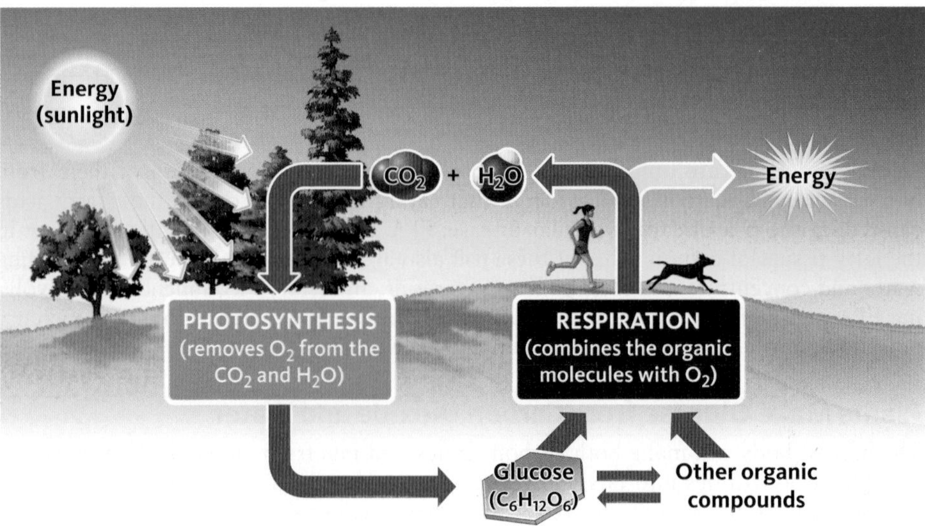

FIGURE 14.26 The carbon cycle.

CORE PROBLEMS

14.85 Many complex molecules in our bodies require glucose as a building block. List two ways in which our bodies can obtain the glucose they need to build these molecules.

14.86 Give two examples of substances other than carbohydrates that our bodies can use to build glucose.

14.87 a) What types of fatty acids are classified as essential, and why?
b) How do our bodies obtain these essential fatty acids?

14.88 Our bodies require saturated fatty acids to build membrane lipids. However, saturated fatty acids are not classified as essential. Explain.

14.89 a) What are the starting materials in photosynthesis, and what are the products?
b) What is the source of the energy that is needed in photosynthesis?

14.90 a) What are the starting materials in respiration, and what are the products?
b) How does respiration differ from photosynthesis?

CONNECTIONS

The Importance of Blood Glucose

Our bodies can burn carbohydrates, fats, and proteins to obtain energy. Not all types of cells can burn all of these, but all types of cells can get energy from glucose, making glucose the most useful and versatile fuel for our bodies. Let us explore how our bodies use glucose.

The most direct source of glucose for most cells is the blood. In healthy people, the concentration of glucose in the blood is fairly constant and is tightly controlled by the liver. The liver absorbs the glucose and most of the other nutrients from the food people eat. Some of the glucose is simply passed into the general circulation, but much of it is converted to glycogen. The liver then breaks down glycogen as needed to keep the blood glucose level constant. The liver can also convert excess amino acids and lactic acid into glucose, giving the body additional flexibility in fuel use.

Many tissues can use more than one type of nutrient to supply energy. For example, muscles can burn both glucose and fatty acids. Resting muscles rely primarily on fatty acids, but as a muscle is exercised more intensely, it increasingly relies on glucose. In moderate exercise, muscles burn most of the glucose, but if the exercise rate exceeds the ability of the blood to supply oxygen, the muscles resort to *lactic acid fermentation,* a series of reactions that break down the glucose into lactic acid. This pathway is extremely rapid, but the quick energy comes at a cost: only a small fraction of the chemical energy of glucose is released during lactic acid fermentation, and the lactic acid must eventually be eliminated. The liver can absorb lactic acid and either burn it or convert it back into glucose, but if muscles produce lactic acid faster than the liver can deal with it, a person becomes exhausted and must stop exercising.

In contrast to muscles, brain cells normally use glucose exclusively as an energy source. The brain cannot tolerate glucose levels below about 70 mg/dL, so the typical blood glucose concentration is between 80 and 110 mg/dL. If someone does not eat a meal for an extended period, the liver first breaks down its glycogen to supply glucose to the blood, and then it begins to break down body proteins and convert their amino acids into glucose. After a week or so, the brain acquires the ability to burn byproducts of fat breakdown called ketone bodies, but the liver continues to break down proteins at a slower rate to maintain the necessary blood glucose level.

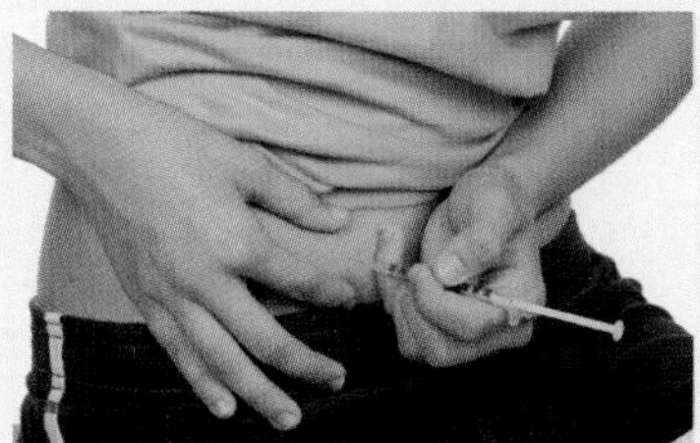

This woman has diabetes and must take regular doses of insulin to regulate her blood glucose level.

The body produces two hormones that work together to control blood glucose. Glucagon prompts the liver to release glucose into the blood, and insulin stimulates muscles and fatty tissues to absorb glucose. Low blood sugar, or *hypoglycemia,* generally occurs in people who are fasting or in diabetics who have taken an overdose of insulin; it is rarely a concern in most individuals. However, high blood sugar *(hyperglycemia)* is a growing medical concern in many countries. Hyperglycemia is usually caused by one of the two forms of *diabetes mellitus,* a disease in which the body cannot use insulin to control its blood glucose level.

In Type 1 diabetes (insulin-dependent diabetes), the pancreas does not make enough insulin, usually because the immune system attacks and destroys the cells that make the hormone. People with this form of the disease have to take regular insulin injections to control their blood sugar levels. In Type 2 diabetes (often called adult-onset diabetes), the more common form, the pancreas makes insulin but the cells do not respond correctly to it. Type 2 diabetes is often associated with obesity and is best treated by a low-carbohydrate (particularly low-sugar) diet and exercise.

Key Terms

active transport – 14.7
anomers – 14.2
carbohydrate – 14.1
carbon cycle – 14.9
concentration gradient – 14.7
disaccharide – 14.3
essential fatty acid – 14.9
fatty acid – 14.5
glycerophospholipid – 14.7
glycosidic linkage – 14.3
hemiacetal – 14.1
lipid –14.7
lipid bilayer – 14.7
lipoprotein – 14.8
monoglyceride – 14.6
monosaccharide (simple sugar) – 14.1
mutarotation – 14.2
passive transport – 14.7
photosynthesis – 14.9
polysaccharide (complex carbohydrate) – 14.4
reducing sugar – 14.1
respiration – 14.9
steroid – 14.8
steroid hormone – 14.8
storage polysaccharide – 14.4
structural polysaccharide – 14.4
transport protein – 14.7
triglyceride (triacylglycerol) – 14.5

SUMMARY OF OBJECTIVES

Now that you have read the chapter, test yourself on your knowledge of the objectives, using this summary as a guide.

Section 14.1: **Know the structural features and typical physical properties of monosaccharides.**

- Monosaccharides contain carbon, hydrogen, and oxygen in a 1:2:1 ratio.
- Typical monosaccharides have a five- or six-membered ring containing one oxygen atom, and they have hydroxyl groups bonded to all but one of the carbon atoms.
- Monosaccharides can be drawn using a Haworth projection, in which the ring is shown as if it lies on a flat surface and the other groups project above and below the surface.
- The carbon atoms in a monosaccharide are identified using a specific numbering system.
- The physical properties of monosaccharides reflect their ability to form several hydrogen bonds.

Section 14.2: **Understand how anomers are related and how they are interconverted, identify reducing sugars, and understand why living organisms only use one of the two enantiomers of any monosaccharide.**

- The ring in a monosaccharide can open up to produce an open-chain form, which contains an aldehyde or a ketone group.
- Benedict's test detects sugars by oxidizing the aldehyde group of the open-chain form.
- Monosaccharides can occur in α and β forms (anomers), differing in the position of the groups bonded to the anomeric carbon.
- The anomers of a monosaccharide can interconvert (mutarotation) by way of the open-chain form.
- All monosaccharides can exist in mirror-image forms (D and L), of which only the D forms normally occur in nature.

Section 14.3: **Identify and draw the structures of the most common glycosidic linkages in disaccharides.**

- Disaccharides contain two monosaccharides joined by a glycosidic linkage.
- The names of glycosidic linkages identify the carbon atoms that form the linkage, and they show which anomer was used to make the linkage.
- Humans can digest a disaccharide only if they make an enzyme that can hydrolyze the glycosidic bond.

Section 14.4: **Describe the building blocks, linkages, and biological functions of the common disaccharides and polysaccharides.**

- Lactose and sucrose are the primary disaccharides in foods. Lactose is made from glucose and galactose, while sucrose is made from glucose and fructose.
- Lactose is a reducing sugar and has α and β anomers, while sucrose is not a reducing sugar and exists in only one form.
- Storage polysaccharides are used as an energy source, while structural polysaccharides provide strength and rigidity to an organism.
- Starch and glycogen are the common storage polysaccharides, and they are built from glucose molecules connected by $\alpha(1\rightarrow4)$ and $\alpha(1\rightarrow6)$ glycosidic linkages.
- Cellulose and chitin are the common structural polysaccharides, and they are built from glucose or N-acetylglucosamine molecules connected by $\beta(1\rightarrow4)$ glycosidic linkages.
- Humans can digest starch and glycogen, but they cannot digest structural polysaccharides.

Section 14.5: **Classify fatty acids based on their structures, draw the structures of triglycerides that contain specific fatty acids, and relate the physical properties of fatty acids and triglycerides to their structures.**

- Triglycerides are formed from glycerol and three fatty acids.

- Fatty acids are long-chain carboxylic acids, and they are classified based on the number of alkene groups and the position of the last alkene group.
- Fatty acids and triglycerides are insoluble in water, but they are soluble in many organic solvents.
- The melting points of fatty acids and triglycerides depend on the number of alkene groups, with saturated fatty acids being solids at room temperature and unsaturated fatty acids being liquids.

Section 14.6: **Predict the products of the hydrogenation and hydrolysis reactions of triglycerides, and understand how fats are digested and absorbed.**

- Unsaturated fatty acids and triglycerides can be hydrogenated. Partial hydrogenation produces *trans* fatty acids in addition to saturated fatty acids.
- Triglycerides can be hydrolyzed using strong acids or bases. The products are glycerol and the fatty acids or their salts.
- Digestion of fats requires an enzyme (lipase) and bile salts. The bile salts break up clusters of fat molecules.
- The products of fat digestion are fatty acids and monoglycerides.

Section 14.7: **Draw the structure of a typical glycerophospholipid, relate the structures of glycerophospholipids to the structure and properties of a lipid bilayer, and describe the role of proteins in membrane transport.**

- Glycerophospholipids are made from glycerol, fatty acids, phosphate, and one additional polar or ionized molecule, and they are ionized at physiological pH.
- The lipid bilayer is the fundamental structural unit of all membranes.
- Ions and large polar molecules cannot cross a lipid bilayer.
- Membranes contain a range of lipids and proteins.
- Transport proteins move ionized and polar solutes across membranes.
- Membrane transport can be active or passive, depending on whether the direction agrees with the normal direction of diffusion.
- Active transport requires energy and creates concentration gradients, which are an energy source and can be harnessed to do cellular work.

Section 14.8: **Recognize the steroid nucleus, know the functions of physiologically important steroids, and describe the mechanism by which steroids and triglycerides are transported in the body.**

- Steroids contain a backbone of four linked rings of carbon atoms (the steroid nucleus).
- Cholesterol is the most common steroid and the starting material for all other steroids.
- Steroid hormones regulate a range of metabolic processes and control human sexual development.
- In the bloodstream, steroids and triglycerides are transported in the form of lipoproteins, whose functions are related to their densities.

Section 14.9: **Describe the sources of carbohydrates and fats in human nutrition, and describe the role of the carbon cycle in making organic nutrients available to living organisms.**

- Carbohydrates are the primary energy source in the human diet.
- The human body can make saturated and monounsaturated fatty acids from other nutrients, but it cannot make polyunsaturated fatty acids.
- In photosynthesis, plants convert carbon dioxide and water into glucose and oxygen, using energy from sunlight.
- The glucose that is made in photosynthesis is the starting material for building organic compounds in nature, and it is the primary energy source for all higher organisms.
- Carbon is cycled between organic and inorganic forms via the carbon cycle.

Concept Questions

Online homework for this chapter may be assigned in OWL.

* indicates more challenging problems.

14.91 Your body uses α-D-glucose to build glycogen. Which of the following could your body use as a source of the α-D-glucose? Explain your answers.

a) β-D-glucose
b) α-L-glucose
c) lactose

14.92 Why do all monosaccharides and disaccharides have extremely high solubilities in water?

14.93 Rank the following solvents based on how well glucose should dissolve in them. Start with the best solvent.

acetone   water   3-pentanone

14.94 Monosaccharides have a 1:2:1 ratio of carbon, hydrogen, and oxygen atoms. However, disaccharides and polysaccharides do not have this atom ratio. Why is this?

14.95 Why can't your body use the L forms of carbohydrates?

14.96 Why does your body require two enzymes to break down glycogen?

14.97 Lactase (the enzyme that breaks down lactose) can also hydrolyze the glycosidic bond in cellobiose. However, lactase cannot break down maltose or sucrose. Based on the structures of these disaccharides, explain why this is reasonable.

14.98 Compare the biological functions of cellulose and chitin.

14.99 If you form a glycosidic bond that links carbon 1 of a glucose molecule to carbon 1 of a second glucose molecule, will the product be a reducing sugar? Why or why not?

14.100 Describe the role of liver glycogen in maintaining a constant glucose level in the blood.

14.101 The nutritional value of carbohydrates is around 4 kcal/g, because all carbohydrates produce this much energy when they burn. However, when nutritionists calculate the Calorie content of the carbohydrates in food, they generally ignore the cellulose. Why is this?

14.102 Fatty acids do not dissolve in water, but they dissolve in ethanol. Explain.

14.103 Why are the sodium salts of fatty acids more soluble than the original fatty acids?

14.104 A food label states that a particular vegetable oil is "high in polyunsaturates." What does this mean?

14.105 a) Why is the melting point of a saturated fatty acid higher than the melting point of an unsaturated fatty acid that contains the same number of carbon atoms?

b) The melting points of *trans* fatty acids are considerably higher than the melting points of *cis* fatty acids that contain the same number of carbon atoms. Why is this?

14.106 Margarine is made from partially hydrogenated corn oil, so it contains significant amounts of *trans* fatty acids and saturated fatty acids, both of which have been implicated in heart disease. Why isn't margarine made from corn oil that has not been hydrogenated?

14.107 Glycerophospholipids form lipid bilayers when they are mixed with water, but they do not do so when they are mixed with ethanol. Why is this?

14.108 Triglycerides do not form lipid bilayers when they are mixed with water, whereas glycerophospholipids do. Explain this difference.

14.109 Why can't ions cross a lipid bilayer?

14.110 What is the difference between passive and active transport? Which one requires an energy source?

14.111 Cells can only move glucose across the cell membrane when there is a much higher concentration of sodium ions outside the cell than there is inside the cell. Explain how these are connected.

14.112 Describe the function of each of the following compounds in a membrane.

a) glycerophospholipids
b) transport proteins
c) cholesterol

14.113 All of the steroid hormones contain hydrophilic functional groups, yet they have very low solubilities in water. Why is this?

14.114 Describe the importance of photosynthesis to the survival of animals (including humans).

14.115 What is the carbon cycle, and what does it accomplish?

Summary and Challenge Problems

14.116 The following monosaccharide is called D-ribulose:

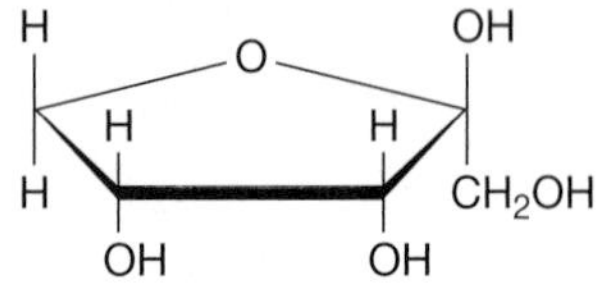

D-Ribulose

a) Classify D-ribulose as a triose, a tetrose, a pentose, or a hexose.
b) Number the carbon atoms in this sugar.
c) Is this the α anomer of D-ribulose, or is it the β anomer?
d) Draw the structure of the other anomer of D-ribulose.
e) Is D-ribulose an aldose, or is it a ketose?
f) Draw the structure of L-ribulose.

14.117 The following two compounds are made from glucose. Which of these compounds (if any) can be oxidized by Benedict's reagent? Explain your answer.

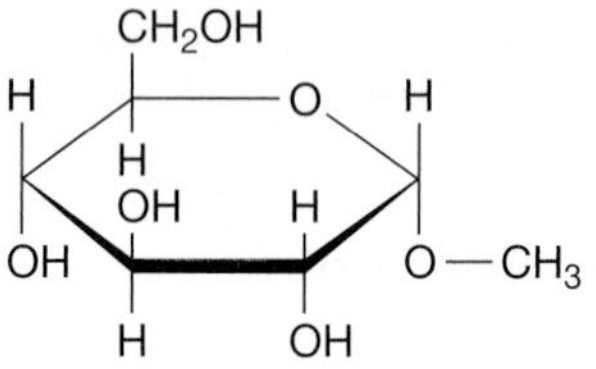

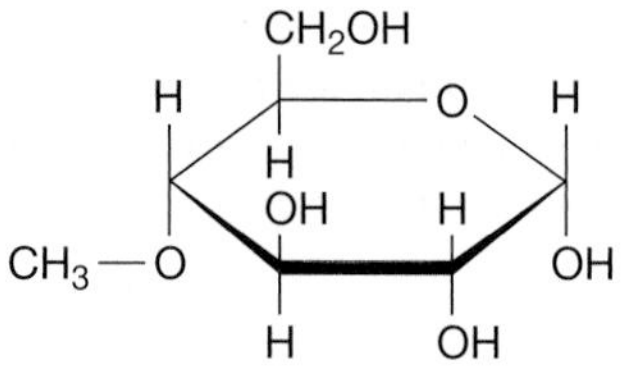

14.118 a) Draw the structure of the open-chain form of ribose. The structure of ribose is shown in Figure 14.3.
b) Draw the structure of the product that is formed when ribose reacts with Benedict's reagent.

14.119 The following monosaccharide is called D-talose. The hydrogen and hydroxyl groups on the anomeric carbon atom have been omitted.

a) Draw the structure of α-D-talose by adding H and OH to this structure.
b) Draw the structure of the disaccharide that is formed when two molecules of α-D-talose form an α(1→4) glycosidic linkage.

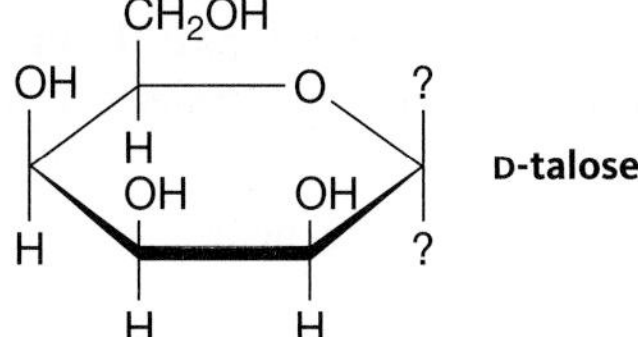

14.120 The enzyme that breaks down the glycosidic linkage in maltose cannot hydrolyze the glycosidic linkage in the disaccharide you drew in Problem 14.119, even though both linkages are α(1→4). Why is this?

14.121 Draw the structure of the molecule that will be formed when three molecules of β-D-glucose are bonded together by β(1→4) glycosidic linkages.

14.122 Stachyose is a tetrasaccharide (a compound made from four simple sugars) that is found in many legumes and grains. Humans cannot digest stachyose, so it passes into the large intestine, where it is broken down by various bacteria. (The bacteria produce substantial amounts of gaseous waste products as they digest stachyose, to the distress of the person who ate the food.)

a) Find the three glycosidic linkages in stachyose.
b) Identify the four simple sugars that make up stachyose. (All of them are common monosaccharides that are shown in Figure 14.3.)

Stachyose

14.123 *Glucose has the molecular formula $C_6H_{12}O_6$. What is the molecular formula of the compound that contains four molecules of glucose connected to one another by α(1→4) glycosidic linkages?

14.124 Give one example of each of the following:

a) a branched polysaccharide
b) a storage polysaccharide that is found in animal tissues
c) a polysaccharide that contains only α(1→4) glycosidic linkages
d) a polysaccharide that humans cannot digest
e) a polysaccharide that is made from N-acetylglucosamine
f) a polysaccharide that contains both α(1→4) and α(1→6) glycosidic linkages

14.125 How does the structure of chitin differ from that of cellulose, and how are their structures similar to each other?

14.126 Immediately after you eat a meal, the mass of glycogen in your liver increases. Why is this?

14.127 *If a food item contains 3 g of sucrose, 1 g of fructose, 3 g of amylose, 8 g of amylopectin, and 2 g of cellulose, how many Calories will you get from it? (Hint: Refer to Problem 14.101.)

14.128 What types of organisms can make carbohydrates from inorganic compounds? What is this process called?

14.129 *Most soft drinks in the United States are sweetened with "high-fructose corn syrup," which contains a mixture of the simple sugars fructose and glucose. A typical 12-ounce can of soft drink (355 mL) contains a total of 44 g of fructose and glucose.

a) What is the percent concentration (w/v) of monosaccharides in a typical soft drink?
b) What is the molar concentration of monosaccharides in a typical soft drink? (The chemical formulas of glucose and fructose are both $C_6H_{12}O_6$, so they can be treated as if they were the same compound.)
c) Is a soft drink isotonic, hypertonic, or hypotonic? (Recall that the isotonic concentration is around 0.28 M.)

14.130 Using the following descriptions, draw the structures of capric acid and myristoleic acid:

a) Capric acid is a 10-carbon saturated fatty acid.
b) Myristoleic acid is a monounsaturated fatty acid. It contains 14 carbon atoms, and it is classified as an omega-5 fatty acid.

14.131 A student draws the following line structure for palmitoleic acid:

Why is this structure potentially misleading? (Hint: What does this structure imply about the double bond?) Draw it in a fashion that would not be misleading.

14.132 A mixture of triglycerides contains 8% saturated fatty acids, 57% monounsaturated fatty acids, and 35% polyunsaturated fatty acids.

a) Is this mixture a solid or a liquid at room temperature? How can you tell?
b) Should this mixture be classified as a fat or as an oil? Why?

14.133 When a sample of the following fatty acid is partially hydrogenated, two products are formed. Draw the structures of these products. (Hint: One contains an alkene group and the other does not.)

$$\mathrm{CH_3{-}(CH_2)_5{-}\overset{H}{C}{=}\overset{H}{C}{-}(CH_2)_7{-}\overset{\overset{\displaystyle O}{\|}}{C}{-}OH}$$

14.134 Using the information in Table 14.5, identify the fatty acids that were used to make the triglyceride below.

$$\mathrm{CH_3{-}(CH_2)_4{-}CH{=}CH{-}CH_2{-}CH{=}CH{-}(CH_2)_7{-}\overset{\overset{\displaystyle O}{\|}}{C}{-}O{-}CH_2}$$
$$\mathrm{CH_3{-}(CH_2)_5{-}CH{=}CH{-}(CH_2)_7{-}\overset{\overset{\displaystyle O}{\|}}{C}{-}O{-}CH}$$
$$\mathrm{CH_3{-}(CH_2)_{10}{-}\overset{\overset{\displaystyle O}{\|}}{C}{-}O{-}CH_2}$$

14.135 Draw the structures of the products that are formed when the triglyceride in Problem 14.134 is hydrolyzed using each of the following solutions:

a) 2 M H_2SO_4
b) 2 M NaOH
c) 2 M KOH

14.136 Which of the products you drew in Problem 14.135 are soaps?

14.137 A sample of triglycerides from the liver of a fish contains 23% saturated fatty acids, 55% monounsaturated fatty acids, and 22% polyunsaturated fatty acids. The sample melts at 4°C.

a) Is this mixture a solid or a liquid at room temperature? How can you tell?
b) Is this a fat or an oil? Explain your answer.

14.138 a) Draw the structure of the compound that will be formed if the triglyceride in Problem 14.134 is completely hydrogenated.
b) Is this compound still a triglyceride? Explain your answer.
c) If this compound is hydrolyzed, what fatty acids will be formed?

14.139 If linoleic acid is completely hydrogenated, what fatty acid will be formed? Draw the structure and give the name of the product.

14.140 *Why are fatty acids more soluble in a solution that is buffered at pH 7 than they are in a solution that is buffered at pH 3?

14.141 Draw the structure of the monoglyceride that contains one molecule of stearic acid.

14.142 What type of functional group forms the link between the fatty acids and glycerol in a glycerophospholipid?

14.143 Tell whether each of the following components of a glycerophospholipid is hydrophilic or hydrophobic. If it is hydrophilic, tell whether it is ionized at pH 7, and give its charge.

a) fatty acids
b) glycerol
c) amino alcohol
d) phosphate

14.144 Some membrane lipids contain carbohydrate portions. What is one known function of these lipids?

14.145 Which of the following can pass through a lipid bilayer (without the assistance of a transport protein)?

a) $H_2PO_4^-$
b) asparagine (an amino acid)
c) acetaldehyde
d) CO_2
e) $CH_3\text{–}NH_3^+$
f) sucrose

14.146 *The kidneys produce urine with a pH of around 6 by moving H^+ from the blood into the urine. The pH of blood is around 7.4.

a) Is this an example of active or passive transport?
b) Does this type of transport require energy?
c) The kidneys always burn glucose while they are transporting hydrogen ions. Why is this?

14.147 *Which would you expect to have the higher solubility in water, aldosterone or testosterone? Explain your answer. (The structures of these steroids are given in Table 14.10.)

14.148 What type of steroid carries out each of the following functions in the human body?

a) assisting the digestion of fats and oils
b) regulating the menstrual cycle in women (two types)
c) helping regulate the concentration of glucose in blood plasma
d) regulating development of male sexual characteristics

14.149 *Androstenedione ("andro") has been used by athletes to increase muscle mass. In the body, it is converted into testosterone. What type of reaction is this? (Hint: Look at the structure of testosterone in Table 14.10.)

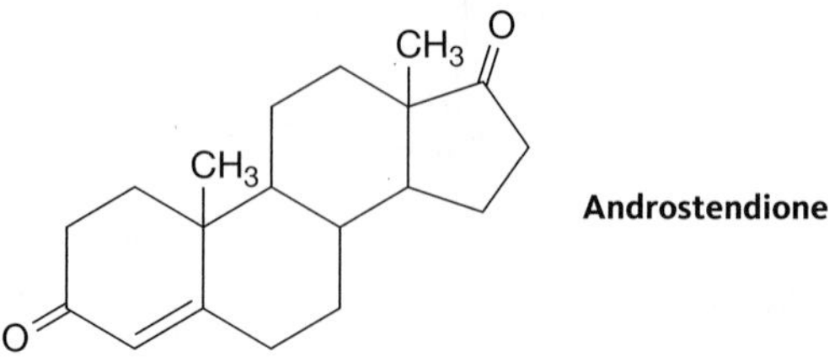

14.150 *Estradiol valerate has been used to treat the symptoms of menopause. In the body, it is broken down into estradiol and pentanoic acid. What type of reaction is this? (Hint: Look at the structure of estradiol in Table 14.10.)

Estradiol valerate

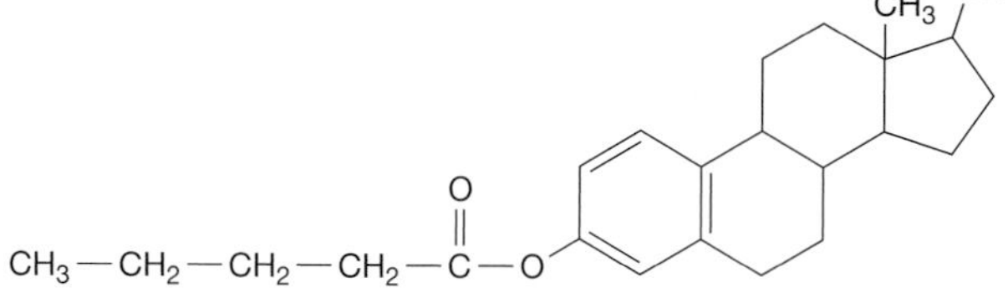

14.151 What types of proteins transport each of the following types of lipids in the blood?

a) triglycerides
b) cholesterol
c) steroid hormones

14.152 *Low-carbohydrate diets such as the Atkins diet have become popular in recent years as a method to lose weight and to maintain the decreased body weight. A typical maintenance program on a low-carbohydrate diet might contain 135 g of protein, 110 g of carbohydrate, and 110 g of fat per day.

a) How many Calories would this diet provide per day?
b) What percentage of the Calories is supplied by carbohydrate?
c) How does this compare with the National Academy of Sciences recommendations for dietary carbohydrate (see Table 14.14)?

14.153 a) Classify DHA using the omega system. (The structure of DHA is shown on page 617.)
b) What is the molecular formula of DHA?
c) Write a balanced chemical equation for the hydrogenation of DHA, using H_2 as the source of hydrogen.

14.154 *Your body converts stearic acid ($C_{18}H_{36}O_2$) into oleic acid ($C_{18}H_{34}O_2$) acid using the following reaction:

$$C_{18}H_{36}O_2 + O_2 + NADPH + H^+ \rightarrow C_{18}H_{34}O_2 + 2\,H_2O + NADP^+$$

a) If your body converts 10.0 g of stearic acid into oleic acid, how many grams of oleic acid do you make?
b) How many grams of oxygen does your body need to convert 10.0 g of stearic acid into oleic acid?
c) The density of gaseous oxygen at room temperature and normal atmospheric pressure is 0.00132 g/mL. How many milliliters of oxygen does your body need to convert 10.0 g of stearic acid into oleic acid?

14.155 * A triglyceride contains only stearic acid. If you react 10.0 g of this triglyceride with enough NaOH to completely saponify the triglyceride, what mass of soap will you form?

14.156 It is possible to make soap by reacting a fatty acid with NaOH. Write a chemical equation that shows this reaction, using palmitic acid as the fatty acid.

14.157 *Fatty acids react with $Ca(OH)_2$ to form an insoluble white solid that is one of the components of "soap scum." Write a chemical equation that shows this reaction, using myristic acid as the fatty acid.

14.158 Norethisterone enanthate is a component of some injectable contraceptives. Find and circle the steroid nucleus in this molecule.

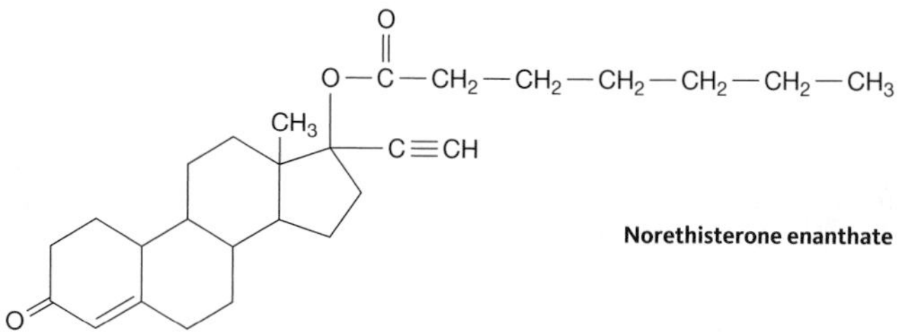

Norethisterone enanthate

14.159 *The structure of aldosterone is shown in Table 14.10.

a) Circle and name all of the functional groups in aldosterone.
b) Which of these functional groups can be oxidized?
c) Which of these functional groups can be reduced?
d) Which of these functional groups can react with acetic acid to form an ester?
e) Which of these functional groups can react with water in a hydration reaction?

14.160 *A solution is prepared by dissolving 1.25 g of cholesterol in enough ethanol to make 250 mL of solution.

a) What is the percent concentration of this solution?
b) What is the molar concentration of this solution?

14.161 *If you dissolve 0.725 g of estradiol in enough acetone to make 350 mL of solution, what will be the molar concentration of the resulting solution?

14.162 *When your body uses carbohydrates and fats as a source of energy, you burn them to form carbon dioxide and water. Write a balanced chemical equation for the combustion of each of the following fuels:

a) glucose
b) oleic acid

14.163 *Glycoproteins contain a carbohydrate bonded to a protein. In some glycoproteins, the side chain of the amino acid serine condenses with the hydroxyl group on carbon 1 of mannose. Draw the structure of the product of this condensation.

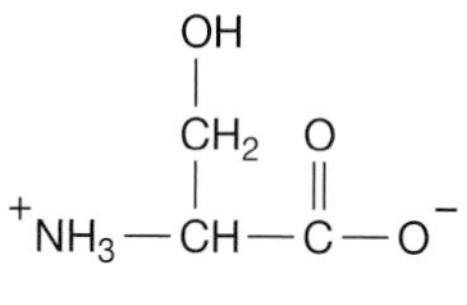

Serine

14.164 *Some enzymes can oxidize the alcohol group on carbon 6 of glucose. The product of this oxidation contains a carboxylic acid group. Draw the structure of the product of this oxidation.

14.165 *When your cells absorb a molecule of glucose, they condense the glucose with a phosphate ion to form glucose-6-phosphate. The condensation reaction involves the alcohol group on carbon 6 of glucose. Draw the structure of the product of this condensation.

14.166 *The amide group in N-acetylglucosamine can be hydrolyzed. Draw the products of this hydrolysis reaction as they would appear at physiological pH. (The structure of N-acetylglucosamine is shown in Figure 14.17.)

15

Metabolism: The Chemical Web of Life

Miriam has always been very active, but as she approaches retirement she has been feeling increasingly tired and depressed. Lately, she has also noticed that she seems to feel cold a lot and has had problems with constipation. She has assumed that she is "just getting old," but she mentions these symptoms to her doctor. The doctor suspects that Miriam's thyroid gland is not working correctly, so she orders blood tests to determine the concentration of two hormones: thyroid-stimulating hormone (TSH) and thyroxine (T4). TSH is a polypeptide produced by the pituitary gland that controls the activity of the thyroid gland. In response to TSH, the thyroid gland produces T4, which in turn controls Miriam's metabolic rate, the speed at which her body carries out its chemical reactions. If the thyroid produces too little T4, the body's energy-producing reactions slow down, leading to an overall lack of energy and making it difficult to keep the body temperature up.

The lab results indicate that Miriam's T4 level is lower than normal, showing that her thyroid is producing too little thyroxine. Her TSH level is elevated, because her pituitary gland detects the low T4 level and is trying to speed up her thyroid. Miriam's doctor prescribes thyroid hormone pills, and within a couple of months Miriam feels like her old self.

OUTLINE

LABORATORY REQUISITION—CHEMISTRY

Test	Code	Test	Code
☐ Sodium	NA	☐ Fructosamine	FRU/ALB
☐ Potassium	K	☐ PSA	PSA
☐ Creatinine	CREAT	☐ Chloride	CL
☐ BUN	BUN	☐ Calcium	CA
☐ Glucose–fasting	GLUCF	☐ Phosphorus	PHOS
☐ Glucose–random	GLUCR	☐ Phenylalanine	PKU
☐ Hemoglobin A1C	HGBA1C	☐ Uric Acid	URIC

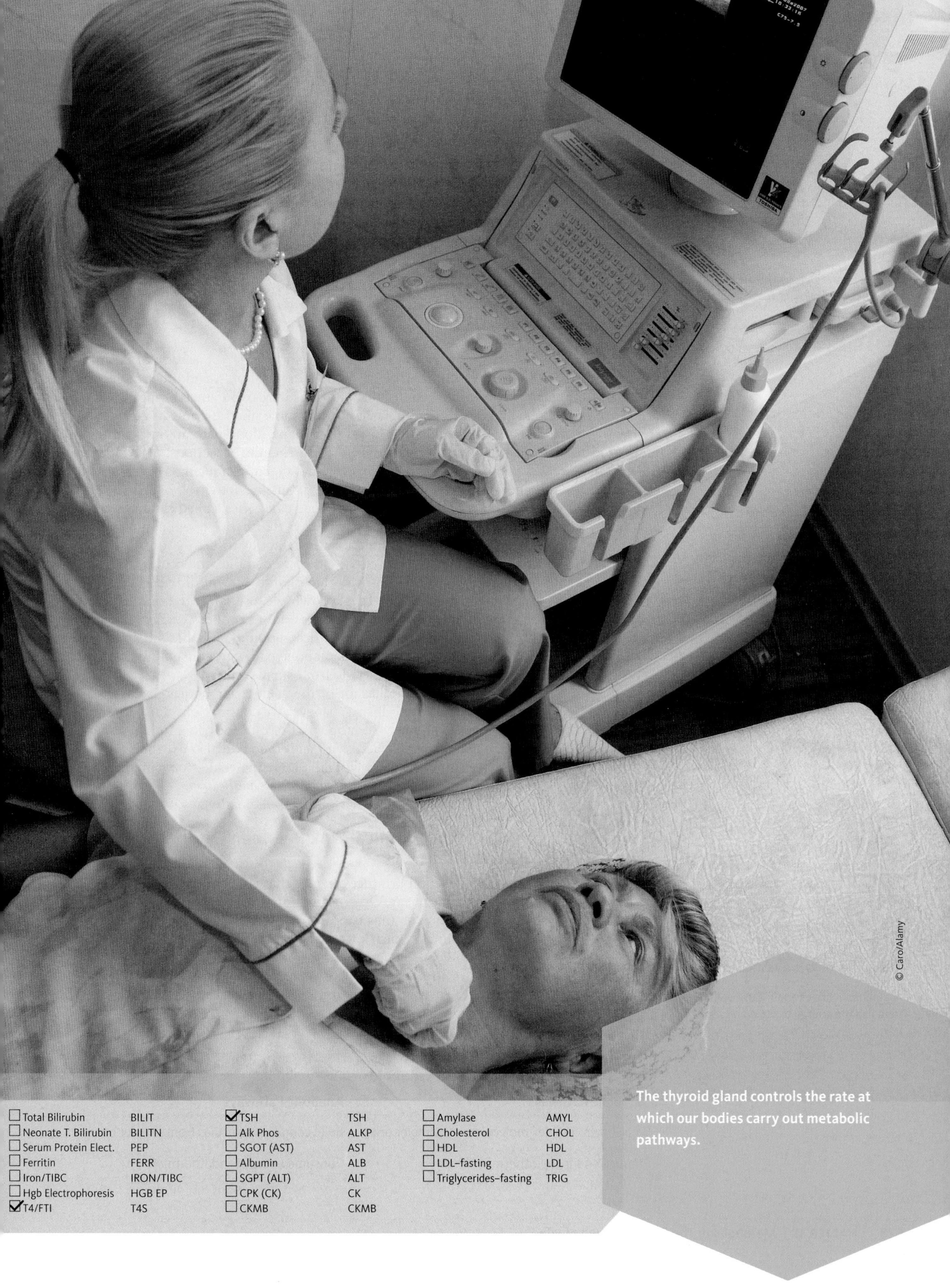

The thyroid gland controls the rate at which our bodies carry out metabolic pathways.

OWL Online homework for this chapter may be assigned in OWL.

In your body, every moment that you are alive, an immense number of chemical reactions are occurring simultaneously. Your body is constantly building and breaking down carbohydrates, proteins, fats, coenzymes, and a host of other molecules. The reactions that accomplish these tasks form an intricate web of activity, all of which must be controlled constantly to ensure that your body has an adequate supply of all of the compounds that it needs.

The sum total of all of the chemical processes that occurs in a living organism is called **metabolism**. In this chapter, we will take a brief tour of human metabolism. A single chapter can only scratch the surface of this vast (and sometimes bewildering) subject, but hopefully you will gain an appreciation of the complexity and elegance of the chemistry that goes on in your body throughout your life.

OBJECTIVE: *Describe how the ATP cycle links catabolic and anabolic pathways.*

15.1 Catabolism, Anabolism, and the ATP Cycle

Humans and all other living organisms must be able to harness the energy of chemical substances. We need energy to build proteins, carbohydrates, lipids, and other molecules. We also need energy to transport molecules and ions across our membranes, and we need it to enable our muscles to contract. Plants and some microorganisms can get the energy they need directly from sunlight. However, humans, along with all other animals, fungi, and most microorganisms, obtain energy from chemical reactions. The food we eat contains organic compounds that can react with oxygen, producing a great deal of energy. We use this energy to drive all of our energy-requiring activities.

Health Note: Testosterone and other androgens are sometimes called *anabolic steroids,* because they increase the rate of reactions that build muscle proteins in the body.

Chemists divide metabolic pathways into two broad categories, called catabolism and anabolism. **Catabolism** is the set of metabolic pathways that break down complex molecules into simpler ones. The primary function of catabolism is to produce energy. **Anabolism** is the set of pathways that use energy to build complex molecules from simpler ones. For instance, our bodies break down glucose into carbon dioxide and water. The sequence of reactions that we use to break down glucose is a catabolic pathway, because it converts a large molecule into smaller ones and it produces energy. Our bodies can also build glucose from two molecules of a compound called lactic acid. This sequence of reactions is an anabolic pathway, consuming energy to construct a larger molecule from smaller ones.

Catabolism supplies all of the energy our bodies need. We use the energy of catabolism whenever we contract our muscles, transmit a nerve impulse from one part of our body to another, or carry out active transport across a membrane. We also use the energy of catabolism whenever we build a large molecule from smaller ones: *catabolism supplies the energy to drive anabolism.* Table 15.1 summarizes the two categories of metabolic pathways.

AP Photo/Charlie Niebergall

Catabolism drives anabolism: our bodies burn the food we eat and use the energy to build and repair tissues.

ATP Is the Chemical Link Between Catabolism and Anabolism

When a reaction produces energy, that energy is normally given off in the form of heat. Organisms cannot use heat to drive their anabolic reactions, so they capture and store the energy from catabolic reactions in the form of chemical potential energy, by making a compound called *adenosine triphosphate (ATP).* The energy stored in ATP is then available for anabolic reactions, muscle contractions, active transport across a membrane, or any other energy-requiring process.

TABLE 15.1 A Comparison of Catabolism and Anabolism

Catabolic Pathways	Anabolic Pathways
Break down complex molecules into simpler ones	Build complex molecules from simpler ones
Produce energy (exothermic)	Consume energy (endothermic)

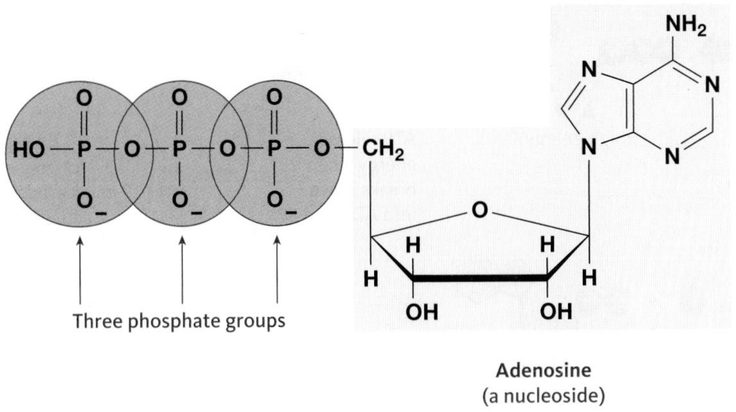

FIGURE 15.1 The structure of ATP.

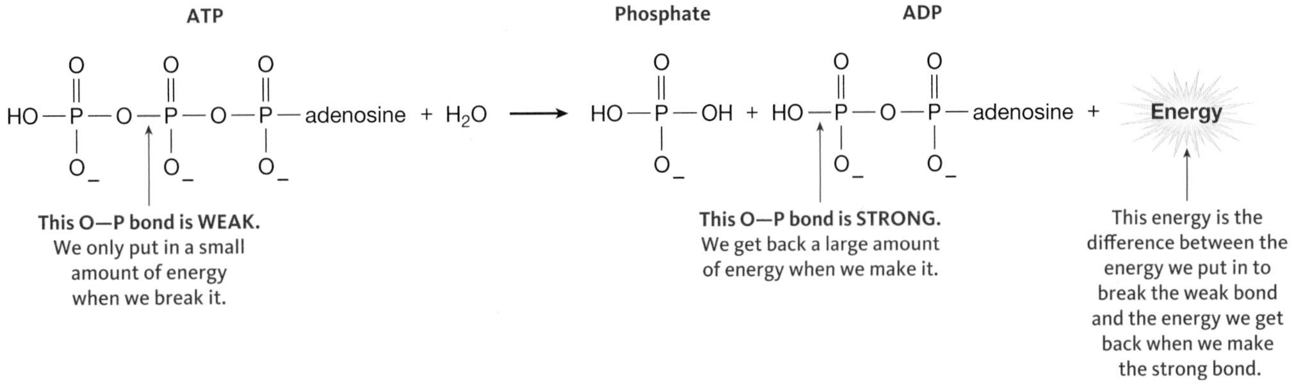

FIGURE 15.2 How breaking down ATP produces energy.

The structure of ATP is shown in Figure 15.1. ATP contains a chain of three phosphate groups bonded to a molecule called adenosine, and it is an example of a *nucleotide,* a type of molecule we will explore more closely in Chapter 16. As we will see, nucleotides are the building blocks of nucleic acids, the molecules that determine our genetic traits, as well as components of the redox coenzymes NAD^+ and FAD.

The key to ATP's ability to store energy is the three linked phosphate groups. Each phosphate group is negatively charged, so these groups repel one another. As a result, the oxygen-to-phosphorus bond that links phosphate ions in ATP is rather weak. Breaking this link, like breaking any chemical bond, requires energy. However, the hydrolysis reaction that breaks the bond in ATP also forms an oxygen-to-phosphorus bond, as shown in Figure 15.2. The bond we form when we hydrolyze ATP is stronger than the one we break, so forming this new bond produces more energy than we consume in breaking the original bond. As a result, *hydrolyzing the bond between any two phosphate groups in ATP produces energy.* By contrast, if we link two phosphate groups, we must break a strong bond, and we make a weak bond to replace it. We put in more energy than we get back, so *forming the bond between any two phosphate groups in ATP consumes energy.*

In general, when a cell needs to carry out a process that requires energy, such as a muscle contraction, the cell breaks the bond that links the third phosphate to the rest of the ATP molecule, as shown in Figure 15.2. The products of this reaction are phosphate ion and *adenosine diphosphate (ADP),* which contains only two phosphate groups bonded to adenosine. We can write this reaction in a simplified form, using P_i as an abbreviation for a phosphate ion.

• The i in P_i stands for "inorganic."

$$\text{ATP} + H_2O \longrightarrow \text{ADP} + P_i + 7.3\ \text{kcal}$$

This is an exothermic reaction. One mole of ATP weighs 504 g, so the balanced equation tells us that we get 7.3 kcal of energy when we break down 504 g of ATP.

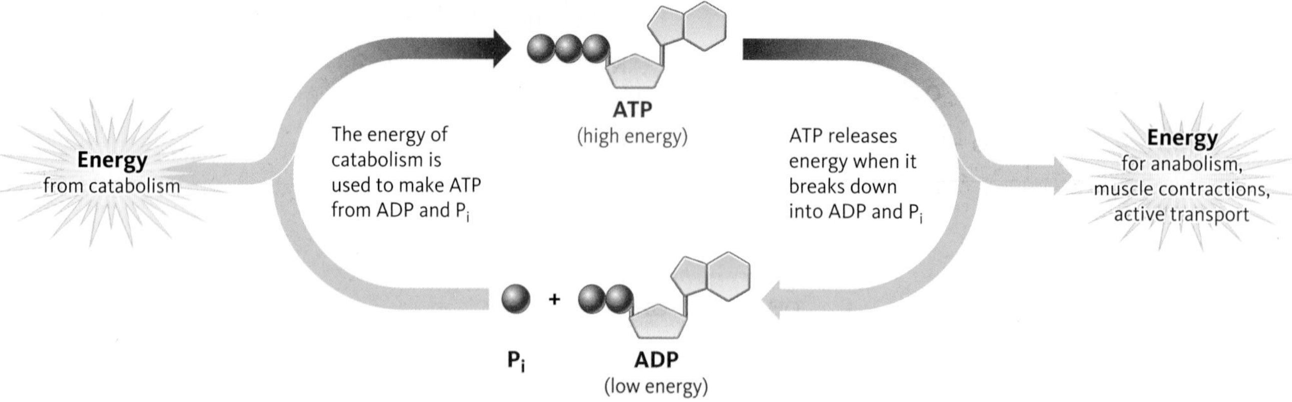

FIGURE 15.3 The ATP cycle.

The cell uses this energy to power the muscle contraction, or for any other energy-requiring process.

Eventually, the cell must build more ATP. To do so, the cell carries out a catabolic pathway, breaking down carbohydrate, fat, or protein to produce energy. The cell then uses some of the energy to connect phosphate ions to ADP, making ATP. It takes the same amount of energy to make ATP that we get from breaking it down, so we need 7.3 kcal of energy to make one mole of ATP.

$$ADP + P_i + 7.3\text{ kcal} \longrightarrow ATP + H_2O$$

In every living cell on Earth, from our own cells to the smallest microorganisms, ATP is constantly being made and broken down. We use the energy of catabolism to make ATP, and we break down ATP to make this energy available for anabolism and other energy-consuming processes. This formation and breakdown of ATP is called the **ATP cycle**, and it is depicted in Figure 15.3.

The ATP Cycle Is Linked to Other Reactions

• Phosphoenolpyruvate is pronounced "foss-foe-ee-nawl-PIE-roo-vate."

Our bodies can make ATP by using the energy that is produced by other reactions. However, the other reaction must produce at least 7.3 kcal of energy per mole of the reactant. For example, when we break down glucose to obtain energy, one of the reactions we carry out is the hydrolysis of phosphoenolpyruvate ion, as shown here. Breaking down one mole of this ion produces 14.9 kcal, more than enough to make ATP. We use 7.3 kcal of this energy to make a mole of ATP, and we give off the rest in the form of heat.

$$CH_2{=}C(O{-}PO_2(OH)^-){-}C({=}O){-}O^- + H_2O \longrightarrow CH_3{-}C({=}O){-}C({=}O){-}O^- + {}^-O{-}P({=}O)(OH){-}OH + 14.9\text{ kcal}$$

Phosphoenolpyruvate ion (formed during the breakdown of glucose) — **Pyruvate ion** — **Phosphate ion** — (7.3 kcal of this energy is used to make ATP.)

The energy stored in ATP can in turn be used to drive any reaction that consumes energy. For example, when our bodies burn glucose to obtain energy, we must first condense the glucose with a phosphate ion. Adding phosphate to one mole of glucose requires 3.3 kcal of energy, which we obtain by breaking down one mole of ATP. The ATP supplies more energy than we need, so the rest of the energy is released as heat.

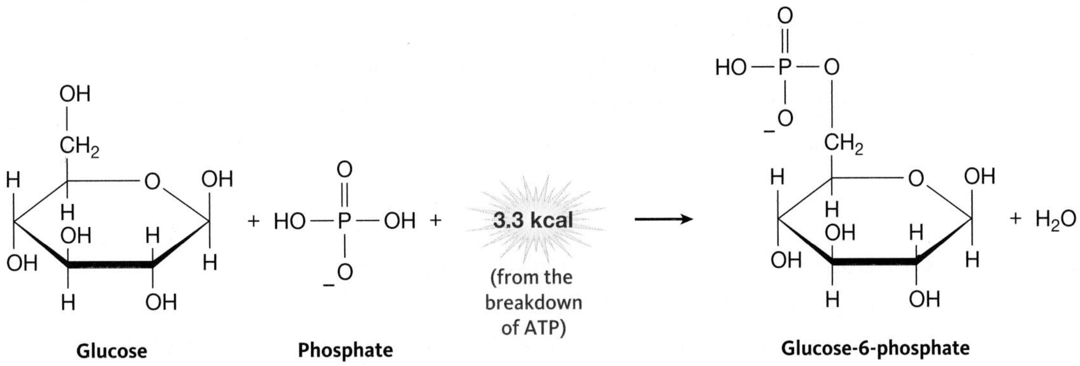

Glucose + Phosphate + 3.3 kcal (from the breakdown of ATP) → Glucose-6-phosphate + H_2O

In general, our bodies can only harness an exothermic reaction to make ATP if the reaction produces at least 7.3 kcal of energy, because making ATP from ADP and phosphate requires 7.3 kcal of energy. We can represent this energy balance by writing a pair of chemical equations.

$$\text{Reactants} \longrightarrow \text{Products} + \text{Energy (more than 7.3 kcal)}$$

$$\text{ADP} + \text{P}_i + \text{7.3 kcal} \longrightarrow \text{ATP} + H_2O$$

Interestingly, our bodies can use the breakdown of ATP to supply the energy for endothermic reactions that require more than 7.3 kcal. However, if the endothermic reaction consumes more than 7.3 kcal, it does not go to completion; instead, it forms an equilibrium mixture that contains more reactant molecules than product molecules.

$$\text{ATP} + H_2O \longrightarrow \text{ADP} + \text{P}_i + \text{7.3 kcal}$$

$$\text{Reactants} + \text{Energy (more than 7.3 kcal)} \rightleftharpoons \text{Products}$$

← This reaction forms an equilibrium mixture

On the other hand, if the endothermic reaction consumes less than 7.3 kcal, it can go to completion, converting virtually all of the reactants into products.

$$\text{ATP} + H_2O \longrightarrow \text{ADP} + \text{P}_i + \text{7.3 kcal}$$

$$\text{Reactants} + \text{Energy (less than 7.3 kcal)} \longrightarrow \text{Products}$$

← This reaction goes to completion

Sample Problem 15.1

Identifying reactions that make and use ATP

Which of the following reactions can our bodies use to make ATP?

phosphocreatine + H_2O → creatine + phosphate + 10.9 kcal

glycerol-1-phosphate + H_2O → glycerol + phosphate + 2.2 kcal

SOLUTION

Only the first reaction gives off enough energy to make ATP. A reaction must produce at least 7.3 kcal of energy to make ATP.

continued

TRY IT YOURSELF: *The following two reactions obtain their energy from the breakdown of ATP. Which one goes to completion, and which forms an equilibrium mixture of products and reactants?*

$$\text{acetate} + \text{phosphate} + 10.3\text{ kcal} \rightarrow \text{acetyl phosphate} + H_2O$$

$$\text{adenosine} + \text{methionine} + 6.1\text{ kcal} \rightarrow \text{S-adenosylmethionine} + H_2O$$

For additional practice, try Core Problems 15.7 through 15.10.

Our Bodies Combine the Formation and Breakdown of ATP with Other Reactions

Health Note: Adding high-energy substances like ATP to our diet does not give us additional energy, because these compounds are hydrolyzed in the digestive tract. Our bodies use high-energy molecules to store the energy that they get from burning carbohydrates, fats, and proteins momentarily, until the energy is used to build another molecule or to do work.

Compounds like ATP and phosphoenolpyruvate are called **high-energy molecules**. A high-energy molecule is a compound that can be made by condensing two other molecules and that requires a significant amount of energy to form. We get this energy back by hydrolyzing the molecule. Many metabolic reactions involve breaking down one high-energy compound and using the energy to build another. These two parts are linked so tightly that they are essentially a single reaction, and chemists usually write a single equation to show the entire process. For example, we can write the following two chemical equations to describe how phosphoenolpyruvate supplies the energy to make ATP. In these equations, the high-energy molecules are shown in blue.

$$\text{phosphoenolpyruvate} + H_2O \longrightarrow \text{pyruvate} + P_i + \text{Energy}$$

$$\text{ADP} + P_i + \text{Energy} \longrightarrow \text{ATP} + H_2O$$

However, it is more accurate to write these as a single chemical equation. In this reaction, a phosphate group moves from phosphoenolpyruvate to ADP, so phosphate and water do not appear in the balanced equation:

$$\text{phosphoenolpyruvate} + \text{ADP} \rightarrow \text{pyruvate} + \text{ATP}$$

Similarly, we can write two equations to show how ATP supplies the energy to combine glucose and phosphate.

$$\text{ATP} + H_2O \longrightarrow \text{ADP} + P_i + \text{Energy}$$

$$\text{glucose} + P_i + \text{Energy} \longrightarrow \text{glucose-6-phosphate} + H_2O$$

However, combining these into a single equation gives us a more accurate picture.

$$\text{ATP} + \text{glucose} \rightarrow \text{ADP} + \text{glucose-6-phosphate}$$

The last equation is an example of an **activation reaction.** Activation reactions use energy from ATP to make a high-energy molecule, usually an organic phosphate or a thioester. We will encounter several other examples of activation reactions in this chapter.

Sample Problem 15.2

Writing a combined equation

Muscle cells hydrolyze a high-energy molecule called phosphocreatine and use the energy of this hydrolysis reaction to make ATP. The chemical equations for these reactions are

$$\text{phosphocreatine} + H_2O \rightarrow \text{creatine} + P_i + \text{energy}$$

$$\text{ADP} + P_i + \text{energy} \rightarrow \text{ATP} + H_2O$$

continued

Write a single chemical equation that combines these two reactions, and tell whether this equation is an activation reaction.

SOLUTION

The first reaction consumes a molecule of water, but the second reaction makes a water molecule, so the combined equation does not include H_2O. Likewise, the first reaction makes a phosphate ion and the second reaction consumes a phosphate ion, so phosphate does not appear in the combined equation. As a result, the reactants are phosphocreatine and ADP, and the products are creatine and ATP. The balanced equation is

$$\text{phosphocreatine} + \text{ADP} \rightarrow \text{creatine} + \text{ATP}$$

This reaction breaks down a high-energy molecule to build ATP, so it is not an activation reaction.

TRY IT YOURSELF: *Our bodies can obtain energy from glycerol. In the first step of this pathway, we condense glycerol with a phosphate ion. This reaction requires energy, which we obtain by hydrolyzing ATP.*

$$\textit{glycerol} + P_i + \textit{energy} \rightarrow \textit{glycerol-3-phosphate} + H_2O$$

$$\textit{ATP} + H_2O \rightarrow \textit{ADP} + P_i + \textit{energy}$$

Write a single chemical equation that combines these two reactions, and tell whether this equation is an activation reaction.

For additional practice, try Core Problems 15.11 and 15.12.

The number of molecules of ATP that our bodies make in a catabolic pathway is a direct measure of that pathway's ability to supply useful energy. For example, the human body has two ways to obtain energy from glucose. The first, called lactic acid fermentation, produces only two molecules of ATP per molecule of glucose.

$$\underset{\text{glucose}}{C_6H_{12}O_6} \longrightarrow \underset{\text{lactic acid}}{2\ C_3H_6O_3} \quad \text{(produces 2 ATP molecules)}$$

The second pathway is the complete oxidation of glucose and produces up to 32 molecules of ATP per molecule of glucose.

$$C_6H_{12}O_6 + 6\ O_2 \longrightarrow 6\ CO_2 + 6\ H_2O \quad \text{(produces up to 32 ATP molecules)}$$

The complete oxidation of glucose produces far more ATP than does fermentation, so it supplies our bodies with more usable energy.

CORE PROBLEMS

All Core Problems are paired and the answers to the blue odd-numbered problems appear in the back of the book.

15.1 What are the chemical building blocks of ATP?

15.2 How does the structure of ATP differ from the structure of ADP?

15.3 Write a chemical equation for the reaction that occurs when your body stores energy in the form of ATP. (You may use abbreviations such as ATP and ADP.)

15.4 Write a chemical equation for the reaction that occurs when your body breaks down ATP to obtain energy.

15.5 Your body is constantly building proteins from amino acids. This process requires energy, which is supplied by ATP. Is this an anabolic process, or is it a catabolic process?

15.6 Your body can break down glycerol to obtain energy, which is stored in the form of ATP. Is this an anabolic process, or is it a catabolic process?

15.7 Both of the following reactions are exothermic. Our bodies use one of them to supply the energy to make a molecule of ATP. Which one? Explain your answer.

$$\text{phosphoarginine} + H_2O \rightarrow \text{arginine} + P_i + 7.7\ \text{kcal}$$

$$\text{glucose-1-phosphate} + H_2O \rightarrow \text{glucose} + P_i + 5.0\ \text{kcal}$$

continued

15.8 Both of the following reactions are endothermic. Our bodies can carry out one of them, using the energy from a molecule of ATP. Which one? Explain your answer.

adenosine + P_i + 12.0 kcal → cyclic AMP + 2 H_2O

fructose + P_i + 3.8 kcal → fructose-1-phosphate + H_2O

15.9 Both of the following reactions require energy, which is supplied by ATP. However, one of these reactions only produces a low concentration of product, while the other goes nearly to completion. Which is which? Explain your answer.

glucose + P_i + 5.0 kcal → glucose-1-phosphate + H_2O

creatine + P_i + 10.3 kcal → creatine phosphate + H_2O

15.10 Both of the following reactions require energy, which is supplied by ATP. However, one of these reactions only produces a low concentration of product, while the other goes nearly to completion. Which is which? Explain your answer.

3-phosphoglycerate + P_i + 11.8 kcal → 1,3-bisphosphoglycerate + H_2O

fructose-6-phosphate + P_i + 4.0 kcal → fructose-1,6-bisphosphate + H_2O

15.11 Our bodies can use fructose as an energy source. The first step of this pathway is the condensation of fructose with phosphate ion.

fructose + P_i + energy → fructose-1-phosphate + H_2O

ATP and ADP are also involved in this reaction.

a) Do our bodies break down ATP when we make fructose-1-phosphate, or do we make ATP? How can you tell?
b) Write a chemical equation for the formation of fructose-1-phosphate that includes ATP and ADP.
c) Is the reaction you wrote in part b an activation reaction? Why or why not?

15.12 A later step in the breakdown of fructose is the reaction of glyceraldehyde with phosphate ion.

glyceraldehyde + P_i + energy → glyceraldehyde-3-phosphate + H_2O

ATP and ADP are also involved in this reaction.

a) Do our bodies break down ATP when we make glyceraldehyde-3-phosphate, or do we make ATP? How can you tell?
b) Write a chemical equation for the formation of glyceraldehyde-3-phosphate that includes ATP and ADP.
c) Is the reaction you wrote in part b an activation reaction? Why or why not?

OBJECTIVES: *Describe the general strategy our bodies use to obtain energy from organic compounds, and write a chemical equation to summarize the breakdown of a typical nutrient.*

15.2 An Overview of Catabolism

In humans, all catabolic pathways involve breaking down an organic compound and harnessing the energy that is produced to make ATP. In this section we will examine the general strategy that cells use to carry out catabolism, and in the next few sections we will look at the various pathways in more detail.

Our bodies use a three-part sequence to extract energy from organic compounds, as shown in Figure 15.4. In the first part, we break down the carbon skeleton of a sugar, fatty acid, or amino acid into CO_2 and other small molecules. During this process, all of the hydrogen atoms from the organic molecule are removed in oxidation reactions. As we saw in Chapter 10, our bodies use the redox coenzymes NAD^+ and FAD to remove hydrogen atoms from organic compounds, and the coenzymes are converted into NADH and $FADH_2$.

$$2\,[H] + NAD^+ \rightarrow NADH + H^+$$
$$2\,[H] + FAD \rightarrow FADH_2$$

In these equations, [H] means a hydrogen atom that is part of an organic molecule.

In the second part, we transfer the hydrogen atoms from NADH and $FADH_2$ to oxygen (O_2), forming H_2O and regenerating the original redox coenzymes. This part produces a great deal of energy, which is used to create a concentration gradient across a membrane inside the cell. In the third part, we use the energy of this concentration gradient to make ATP.

The first part of catabolism is by far the most complex, because each type of nutrient requires its own set of reactions. The remainder of this section gives a general overview of the first part, focusing on the fate of the hydrogen atoms in the original organic molecule. In Section 15.3, we will examine the remaining two parts of catabolism, and in Sections 15.4 through 15.7, we will return to part 1 and examine the specific reactions by which our bodies break down organic molecules.

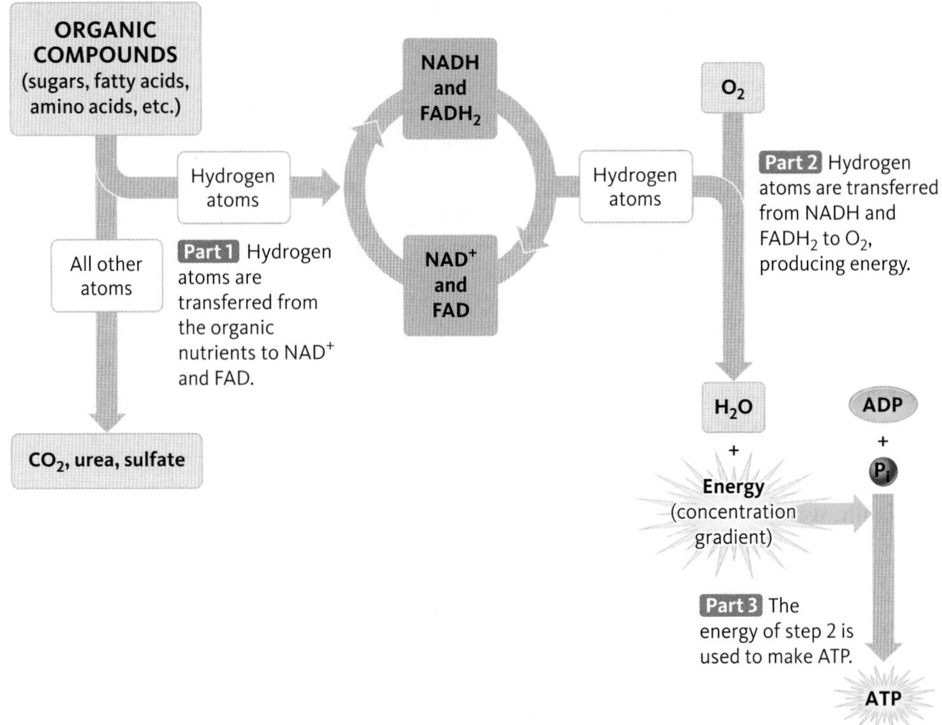

FIGURE 15.4 An overview of catabolism and ATP formation.

We Can Represent the Oxidation of an Organic Compound by a Simplified Chemical Equation

As shown in Figure 15.4, the first part of any catabolic pathway is the breakdown of an organic molecule into carbon dioxide and hydrogen atoms. To keep things simple, we focus on carbohydrates and fats, because they are made entirely of carbon, hydrogen, and oxygen. Proteins also contain nitrogen and a little sulfur, but we will ignore these elements for now. Our bodies employ a consistent strategy when we break down compounds that contain C, H, and O:

- *Break the carbon–carbon bonds.* The only carbon-containing product when most nutrients are broken down is CO_2, so all of the carbon–carbon bonds in the organic compound must be broken. Each carbon atom in the molecule is incorporated into a molecule of CO_2. Usually, our bodies use decarboxylation reactions to break the carbon–carbon bonds.
- *Add oxygen atoms, using water as the source of the oxygen.* When we convert an organic compound into CO_2, we must add a sizable number of oxygen atoms. Most of these oxygen atoms come from water molecules. Our bodies use hydration reactions to add water to the organic molecule.
- *Remove all of the hydrogen atoms.* Since CO_2 contains no hydrogen, we must remove both the hydrogen atoms in the original nutrient and the hydrogen atoms in the water molecules we added. Our bodies use NAD^+ and FAD to remove hydrogen atoms two at a time, using the oxidation reactions you learned in Chapter 10.

We can write a single chemical equation that summarizes how our bodies break down a molecule that is composed of carbon, hydrogen, and oxygen. The reactants are the nutrient molecule and water, which supplies the additional oxygen atoms we need. The products are CO_2 and hydrogen atoms. The chemical equation has this general form, using [H] to represent the hydrogen atoms:

$$\text{organic compound} + ?\ H_2O \rightarrow ?\ CO_2 + ?\ [H]$$

The question marks represent the coefficients, which we must work out as we balance the equation. It is easiest to balance this equation using the following sequence of steps:

1. Balance the carbon atoms by writing the coefficient for CO_2.
2. Balance the oxygen atoms by writing the coefficient for H_2O.
3. Balance the hydrogen atoms by writing the coefficient for [H].

For example, let us write an overall equation that shows how our bodies break down a molecule of glucose into carbon dioxide. We start by balancing carbon atoms. Since glucose contains six carbon atoms, we must make six molecules of carbon dioxide.

$$C_6H_{12}O_6 \rightarrow 6\ CO_2$$

Next, we turn to oxygen. The carbon dioxide that we made contains twelve oxygen atoms, while glucose contains only six. Therefore, we need six more oxygen atoms on the reactant side of our equation. Each oxygen atom comes from a water molecule, so we need six molecules of water.

$$C_6H_{12}O_6 + 6\ H_2O \rightarrow 6\ CO_2$$

Finally, we account for hydrogen. The reactants contain a total of 24 hydrogen atoms, so we need 24 hydrogen atoms on the product side. Our completed chemical equation is

$$C_6H_{12}O_6 + 6\ H_2O \rightarrow 6\ CO_2 + 24\ [H]$$

This balanced equation tells us that when our bodies break down a molecule of glucose into carbon dioxide, we must also break down six molecules of water. The water supplies the extra oxygen we need to make CO_2. In addition, we use NAD^+ and FAD to remove a total of 24 hydrogen atoms from glucose and from water. Our bodies use these hydrogen atoms to produce energy in the later stages of catabolism, as we will see in the next section.

Sample Problem **15.3**

Writing an equation for a catabolic reaction

Write a balanced chemical equation that shows how glycerol is broken down to carbon dioxide and hydrogen atoms. The molecular formula of glycerol is $C_3H_8O_3$.

SOLUTION

We always begin with the carbon atoms. Since glycerol contains three carbon atoms, we must make three molecules of CO_2.

$$C_3H_8O_3 \rightarrow 3\ CO_2$$

The next step is to add enough water molecules to balance the oxygen atoms. Glycerol contains three oxygen atoms, while the three CO_2 molecules contain six oxygen atoms. Therefore, we need three oxygen atoms on the right side of the arrow. These are supplied by water, so we add three water molecules.

$$C_3H_8O_3 + 3\ H_2O \rightarrow 3\ CO_2$$

Finally, we deal with hydrogen. We have a total of 14 hydrogen atoms on the reactant side, so we add 14 hydrogen atoms on the product side. The balanced equation is:

$$C_3H_8O_3 + 3\ H_2O \rightarrow 3\ CO_2 + 14\ [H]$$

TRY IT YOURSELF: *Write a balanced chemical equation that shows how ethanol is broken down to carbon dioxide and hydrogen atoms. The molecular formula of ethanol is* C_2H_6O.

For additional practice, try Core Problems 15.17 and 15.18.

Health Note: Remember that the human body uses the vitamins niacin and riboflavin to build NAD^+ and FAD. The body cannot obtain energy from food without the redox coenzymes, so niacin and riboflavin are essential nutrients.

The Equation Can Be Expanded to Include the Redox Coenzymes

The equation we have just written does not tell us the actual fate of the hydrogen atoms. If we want to show where the hydrogen atoms end up, we need to know how many hydrogen atoms are removed by NAD^+ and how many are removed by FAD. There is no way to tell this from the equation we just wrote, but the numbers of FAD and NAD^+

molecules are known for all important metabolic pathways. In the case of glucose, four of the hydrogen atoms become bonded to FAD. Since one molecule of FAD can only bond to two hydrogen atoms, we need two molecules of FAD to carry these four hydrogen atoms, and we make two molecules of $FADH_2$.

$$4\ [H] + 2\ FAD \rightarrow 2\ FADH_2$$

The remaining 20 hydrogen atoms react with NAD^+. Remember that a molecule of NAD^+ removes two hydrogen atoms from an organic molecule, but it only bonds to one of them. The proton from the second atom is released into solution as H^+.

$$2\ [H] + NAD^+ \rightarrow NADH + H^+$$

Since we must remove 20 hydrogen atoms using NAD^+, we need 10 molecules of NAD^+, so we need to multiply all of the coefficients by 10.

$$20\ [H] + 10\ NAD^+ \rightarrow 10\ NADH + 10\ H^+$$

Including all of the redox coenzymes gives us the following equation:

$$C_6H_{12}O_6 + 6\ H_2O + \underbrace{2\ FAD + 10\ NAD^+}_{\text{We need these redox coenzymes to react with the hydrogen atoms.}} \longrightarrow 6\ CO_2 + \underbrace{2\ FADH_2 + 10\ NADH + 10\ H^+}_{\text{Here are the 24 hydrogen atoms we removed.}}$$

This equation shows us the overall results of the first part of glucose catabolism. In Figure 15.4, when glucose is the organic reactant, part 1 of catabolism produces 6 molecules of CO_2, 2 molecules of $FADH_2$ and 10 molecules of NADH.

Sample Problem 15.4

Writing a catabolic reaction that includes the redox coenzymes

When our bodies burn glycerol to obtain energy, we transfer two hydrogen atoms to FAD. The other hydrogen atoms are removed by NAD^+. Write a balanced equation for the breakdown of glycerol that includes all of the redox coenzymes, using this information and the answer to Sample Problem 15.3.

SOLUTION

In Sample Problem 15.3, we produced 14 hydrogen atoms for each molecule of glycerol that we burn.

$$C_3H_8O_3 + 3\ H_2O \rightarrow 3\ CO_2 + 14\ [H]$$

Only 2 hydrogen atoms become bonded to FAD, forming 1 molecule of $FADH_2$, so we must add one molecule of FAD to the reactant side and 1 molecule of $FADH_2$ to the product side. The remaining 12 hydrogen atoms combine with 6 molecules of NAD^+, forming 6 molecules of NADH and six H^+ ions. The overall reaction is

$$C_3H_8O_3 + 3\ H_2O + FAD + 6\ NAD^+ \rightarrow 3\ CO_2 + FADH_2 + 6\ NADH + 6\ H^+$$

TRY IT YOURSELF: *When our bodies burn ethanol to obtain energy, we transfer two hydrogen atoms to FAD and the rest to NAD^+. Write a balanced equation for the breakdown of ethanol that includes all of the redox coenzymes, using this information and the following chemical equation for the oxidation of ethanol:*

$$C_2H_5OH + 3\ H_2O \rightarrow 2\ CO_2 + 12\ [H]$$

For additional practice, try Core Problems 15.19 and 15.20.

Our bodies eventually oxidize all of the $FADH_2$ and NADH we make in the first part of catabolism, and we use the energy of these reactions to make ATP. In the next section, we will look at the remaining two parts of catabolism.

CORE PROBLEMS

15.13 What two compounds do our bodies use to remove hydrogen atoms from organic molecules when we burn these molecules to obtain energy?

15.14 When your body burns nutrients to obtain energy, all of the carbon atoms in the organic molecules end up in one simple compound. What is this compound?

15.15 Ethanol (C_2H_6O) contains 6 hydrogen atoms. However, when our bodies burn ethanol to obtain energy, we form 12 hydrogen atoms for each ethanol molecule we break down. Where did the other hydrogen atoms come from?

15.16 When we burn a molecule of glycerol to obtain energy, we make three molecules of CO_2, which contain a total of six oxygen atoms. However, glycerol itself only contains three oxygen atoms. Where do the other three oxygen atoms come from?

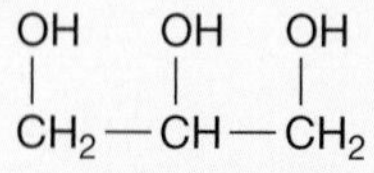

$$CH_2(OH)-CH(OH)-CH_2(OH)$$

Glycerol

15.17 Brain cells normally burn glucose as their only fuel. However, during a prolonged fast, brain cells can also burn 3-hydroxybutyric acid. Write a chemical equation showing how this compound is broken down to CO_2 and hydrogen atoms. Use [H] to represent hydrogen atoms that are removed by the redox coenzymes.

$$CH_3-CH(OH)-CH_2-C(=O)-OH$$

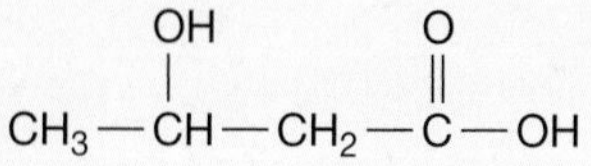

3-Hydroxybutyric acid

15.18 Heart muscle can burn a variety of fuels, including lactic acid. Write a chemical equation showing how lactic acid is broken down into CO_2 and hydrogen atoms. Use [H] to represent hydrogen atoms that are removed by the redox coenzymes.

$$CH_3-CH(OH)-C(=O)-OH$$

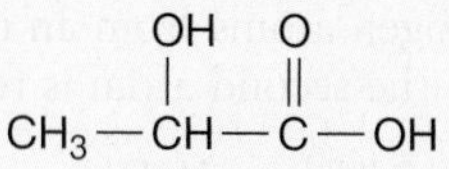

Lactic acid

15.19 When a brain cell burns a molecule of 3-hydroxybutyric acid to obtain energy, it transfers four hydrogen atoms to FAD. The rest of the hydrogen atoms are removed by NAD^+. Using this information and your answer to Problem 15.17, write a balanced chemical equation for the breakdown of 3-hydroxybutyric acid that includes all of the redox coenzymes.

15.20 When a heart muscle cell burns a molecule of lactic acid to obtain energy, it transfers two hydrogen atoms to FAD. The rest of the hydrogen atoms are removed by NAD^+. Using this information and your answer to Problem 15.18, write a balanced chemical equation for the breakdown of lactic acid that includes all of the redox coenzymes.

OBJECTIVE: *Describe the mechanism by which the mitochondria harness the oxidation of NADH and $FADH_2$ to make ATP.*

15.3 ATP Production and the Mitochondria

In the last section, we saw how our bodies break down nutrients such as carbohydrates and fatty acids, using NAD^+ and FAD to remove the hydrogen atoms. Let us now turn to parts 2 and 3 in Figure 15.4, in which our bodies use NADH and $FADH_2$ to produce ATP. In these parts, we transfer the hydrogen atoms from the coenzymes to O_2, forming water. These reactions regenerate FAD and NAD^+, and they produce a great deal of energy. We can represent the reactions as follows:

$$2\,FADH_2 + O_2 \longrightarrow 2\,FAD + 2\,H_2O + 75\text{ kcal}$$

$$2\,NADH + 2\,H^+ + O_2 \longrightarrow 2\,NAD^+ + 2\,H_2O + 105\text{ kcal}$$

Our bodies use the energy from these reactions to make ATP. For many years, the chemical process that links the oxidation of NADH and $FADH_2$ to the formation of ATP was a mystery. However, we now know that the critical link is a concentration gradient. In this section, we will look at how the gradient is created and how a cell can use it to build ATP from ADP and phosphate. First, though, we must take a closer look at the structure of a cell.

The Mitochondria Make Most of the ATP in Eukaryotic Cells

The simplest organisms on Earth are the *prokaryotes,* which include bacteria and some other single-celled microorganisms. Prokaryotic cells have no distinct internal structure; all

TABLE 15.2 Organelles in Eukaryotic Cells

Structure	Function
Endoplasmic reticulum	Builds proteins and lipids
Golgi complex	Processes and sorts proteins after they are synthesized
Lysosome	Hydrolyzes worn-out and damaged cell components
Peroxisome	Oxidizes waste products and foreign material
Mitochondrion	Carries out most catabolic pathways, and produces ATP for the cell
Chloroplast (plants only)	Carries out photosynthesis

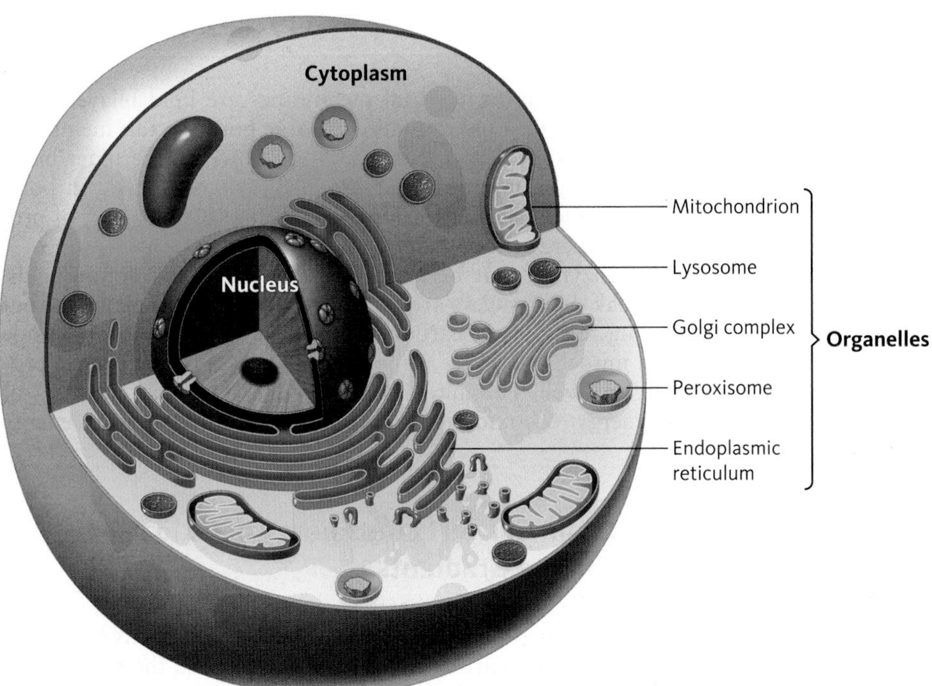

FIGURE 15.5 The structure of a typical cell.

of the chemical components of the cell appear to be mixed together randomly. However, the cells in our bodies and in all other multicelled organisms contain a variety of internal structures. Organisms that are built from such cells are called *eukaryotes*. Eukaryotic cells contain two main compartments: the nucleus, which contains the genetic material of the cell, and the cytoplasm. The cytoplasm in turn contains a variety of small structures called organelles, suspended in a liquid called the cytosol. Figure 15.5 illustrates a typical cell in humans, and Table 15.2 lists some of the organelles in eukaryotic cells.

Most of the ATP that a cell needs is made by the mitochondria. Cells contain hundreds or thousands of mitochondria, scattered randomly throughout the cell. Each mitochondrion consists of a central compartment (the matrix) surrounded by two membranes. The outer membrane is smooth and serves primarily as a cover. The inner membrane is deeply folded and contains a variety of proteins that function in energy production. The space between the membranes is called the intermembrane space. Figure 15.6 shows a diagram of a mitochondrion.

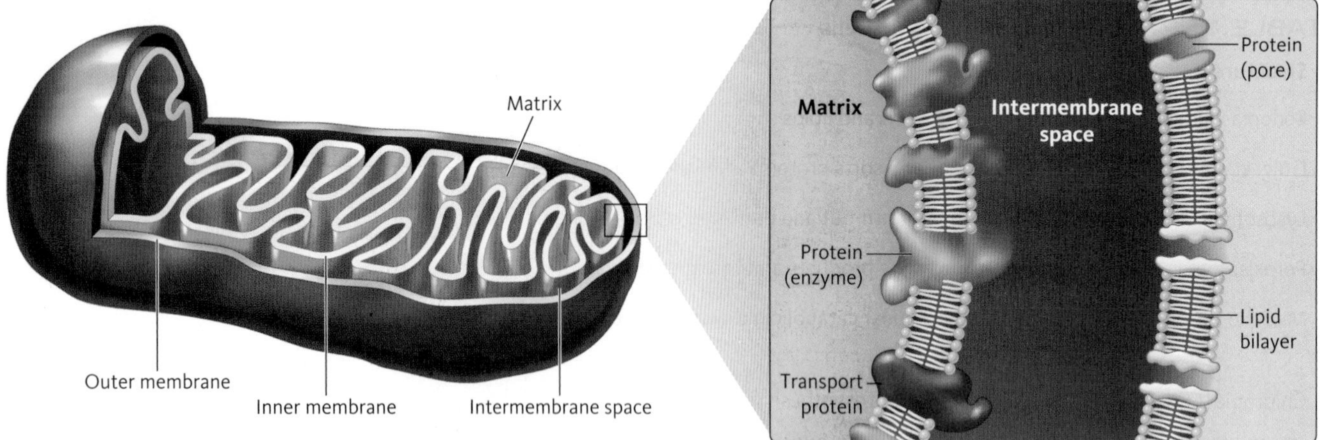

FIGURE 15.6 The structure of a mitochondrion.

Like all membranes, both of the mitochondrial membranes are lipid bilayers. The outer membrane contains a number of proteins that form large pores, so this membrane is permeable to ions and small- to medium-sized molecules. However, the inner mitochondrial membrane contains only a few transport proteins, so most ionic and polar solutes cannot cross this membrane. Instead, the inner membrane contains a set of proteins that play a critical role in energy production.

The matrix contains the enzymes that break down fatty acids and amino acids. Some of the enzymes that break down sugars are located outside the mitochondria, but most of the energy-producing reactions in carbohydrate catabolism also occur inside the matrix. As a result, the mitochondria are responsible for most of the energy production from carbohydrates as well. The mitochondria are the "energy factories" of the cell, converting the energy of oxidation reactions into the chemical energy of ATP.

A mitochondrion. Note how the inner membrane is deeply folded, increasing its surface area.

• Refer to Figure 15.4 for an overview of catabolism.

The Electron Transport Chain Converts the Energy of Oxidation into Concentration and Charge Gradients

In the last section, we examined the first part of catabolism, in which carbohydrates, fats, and proteins are oxidized, producing CO_2 and the reduced coenzymes NADH and $FADH_2$. Let us now look at the second part of catabolism. In this part, the reduced coenzymes react with a set of four enzymes called the **electron transport chain**. These enzymes are embedded in the inner membrane of the mitochondrion, and they contain a variety of cofactors, in addition to several large amino acid chains. The enzymes of the electron transport chain have three functions:

1. The electron transport chain removes two electrons from the reduced coenzyme (either NADH or $FADH_2$). Removing these electrons converts NADH and $FADH_2$ into NAD^+ and FAD. Thus, this step recycles the redox coenzymes so that they can be used in other oxidation reactions. The reactions that occur in this step are:

$$\text{NADH} \rightarrow \text{NAD}^+ + \text{H}^+ + 2 \text{ electrons}$$
$$\text{FADH}_2 \rightarrow \text{FAD} + 2\,\text{H}^+ + 2 \text{ electrons}$$

   Note that the hydrogen atoms from NADH and $FADH_2$ are converted into hydrogen ions, which are released into the matrix. The electrons are absorbed by the electron transport chain.

2. One of the enzymes of the electron transport chain binds to oxygen (O_2), breaks the bond between the two oxygen atoms, and uses the electrons from step 1 to form chemical bonds between the oxygen atoms and hydrogen

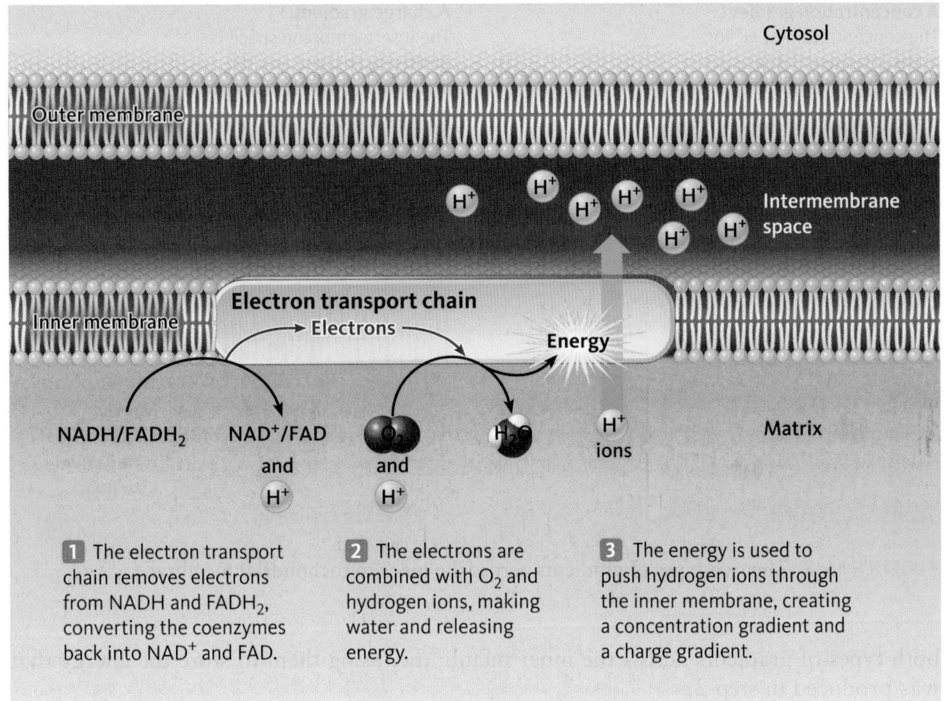
Cytosol
Outer membrane
Intermembrane space
Inner membrane
Electron transport chain
Electrons
Energy
NADH/FADH2
NAD+/FAD
and
H+
O2
and
H+
H2O
H+
ions
Matrix
1 The electron transport chain removes electrons from NADH and FADH2, converting the coenzymes back into NAD+ and FAD.
2 The electrons are combined with O2 and hydrogen ions, making water and releasing energy.
3 The energy is used to push hydrogen ions through the inner membrane, creating a concentration gradient and a charge gradient.

FIGURE 15.7 Part 2 of catabolism: the electron transport chain.

Health Note: Compounds containing the cyanide ion, CN^-, have been known to be poisonous for centuries. Cyanide ions bind to the last enzyme in the electron transport chain, preventing it from transferring the electrons to oxygen. As a result, the cell cannot use oxygen, so it effectively suffocates. Sodium azide (NaN_3), the active chemical in many automobile air bags, has a similar effect, so unused airbags pose a significant safety and disposal hazard.

ions from the matrix. This step produces a great deal of energy. The overall reaction is

$$O_2 + 4\text{ electrons} + 4\,H^+ \longrightarrow 2\,H_2O + \text{Energy}$$

The oxygen in this step is supplied by our bloodstream, which carries oxygen from our lungs to every cell in our bodies.

3. The electron transport chain pushes hydrogen ions through the inner membrane, moving them from the matrix to the intermembrane space. This is an example of active transport, because it creates a concentration gradient. As we saw in Section 14.7, active transport requires energy, which is supplied by step 2.

Figure 15.7 illustrates how the electron transport chain carries out these three steps.

As the electron transport chain moves hydrogen ions from the matrix into the intermembrane space, the concentration of H^+ in the intermembrane space becomes larger than the concentration of H^+ in the matrix, as illustrated in Figure 15.8. This is an example of a concentration gradient, in which two solutions with unequal concentrations of a solute are separated by a membrane. Concentration gradients contain potential energy, because the solute has a natural tendency to flow from the side with the higher concentration to the side with the lower, and this flow of solute particles can be harnessed to do work.

• Concentration gradients are covered in Section 14.7.

The movement of hydrogen ions also produces a second type of gradient, called a **charge gradient**, in which the solutions on either side of the membrane have different electrical charges. This type of gradient is also illustrated in Figure 15.8. Normally, solutions contain equal amounts of positive and negative charge, obeying the rule of charge balance. However, as the electron transport chain forces positively charged hydrogen ions into the intermembrane space, the solution in the intermembrane space becomes positively charged. The matrix loses positive ions, but it does not lose any negative ions, so the matrix becomes negatively charged. Like concentration gradients, charge gradients contain potential energy, because the ions have a strong tendency to pass through the membrane in order to restore charge balance. The electron transport chain produces

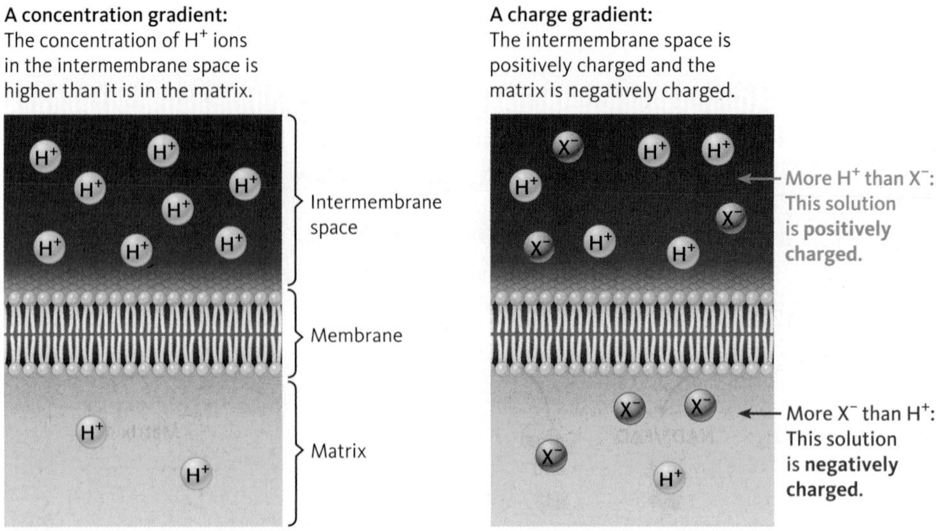

A concentration gradient:
The concentration of H^+ ions in the intermembrane space is higher than it is in the matrix.

A charge gradient:
The intermembrane space is positively charged and the matrix is negatively charged.

Intermembrane space

Membrane

Matrix

More H^+ than X^-: This solution is **positively charged.**

More X^- than H^+: This solution is **negatively charged.**

FIGURE 15.8 The two types of gradients across the inner mitochondrial membrane.

both types of gradients across the inner membrane, using them to store the energy that was produced in step 2.

Sample Problem 15.5

Identifying gradients across a membrane

A membrane separates solution A from solution B. Solution A contains 0.1 M Na^+ and 0.1 M Cl^- ions, and solution B contains 0.2 M Na^+ and 0.2 M Cl^- ions. Is this an example of a concentration gradient, a charge gradient, both, or neither? Explain your answer.

SOLUTION

The total concentration of ions is 0.2 M in solution A and 0.4 M in solution B, so there is a concentration gradient across the membrane. However, both solutions are electrically neutral (each solution contains equal amounts of positively and negatively charged ions), so there is no charge gradient across the membrane.

TRY IT YOURSELF: *A membrane separates solution X from solution Y. Solution X contains 0.100 M Na^+ and 0.101 M Cl^-, and solution Y contains 0.101 M Na^+ and 0.100 M Cl^-. Is this an example of a concentration gradient, a charge gradient, both, or neither? Explain your answer.*

For additional practice, try Core Problems 15.29 and 15.30.

The electron transport chain uses different enzymes to remove electrons from NADH and $FADH_2$, and it obtains different amounts of energy from each reaction. As a result, the number of hydrogen ions that can be pushed through the inner membrane depends on the specific coenzyme that is used to supply electrons. The electron transport chain pushes 10 H^+ ions through the membrane when it oxidizes NADH, but it only moves 6 H^+ ions through the membrane when it oxidizes $FADH_2$.

ATP Synthase Uses the Concentration and Charge Gradients to Make ATP

As we have seen, the electron transport chain stores energy in the form of concentration and charge gradients. In the third part of catabolism, an enzyme called *ATP synthase*

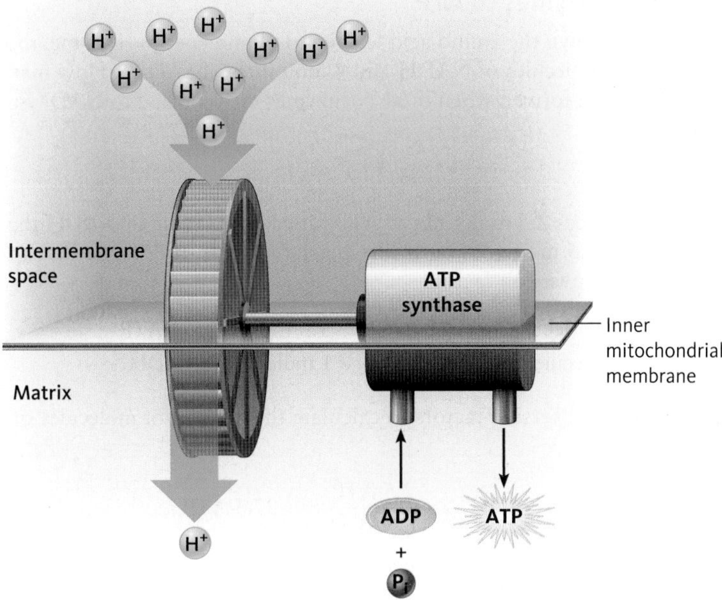

FIGURE 15.9 Part 3 of catabolism: the formation of ATP by ATP synthase.

harnesses the potential energy of the concentration and charge gradients by allowing hydrogen ions to move back through the inner membrane into the matrix. This movement of hydrogen ions releases the energy of the gradients, and ATP synthase uses this energy to convert ADP and phosphate into ATP. You can think of ATP synthase as a machine that uses the movement of hydrogen ions to supply the energy to make ATP, as shown in Figure 15.9.

In order to make a molecule of ATP, ATP synthase must allow three hydrogen ions to move back into the matrix. In addition, the ATP must be moved out of the matrix before the cell can use it. A transport protein embedded in the inner membrane moves ATP through the inner membrane and carries ADP and phosphate into the matrix. In the process, the transport protein also moves one hydrogen ion from the intermembrane space into the matrix. Therefore, *making a molecule of ATP available to the cell consumes four hydrogen ions, three to make the ATP and one to move it out of the matrix.*

We can now relate the number of molecules of reduced coenzymes (NADH and $FADH_2$) formed during the oxidation of organic compounds to the number of molecules of ATP formed. As we saw earlier, when the electron transport oxidizes 1 molecule of NADH, it pushes 10 H^+ ions through the inner membrane. Since 4 H^+ ions are required to make 1 molecule of ATP and release it to the cytosol, the mitochondrion makes 2.5 molecules of ATP ($10 \div 4 = 2.5$) for each molecule of NADH that it oxidizes. Similarly, the oxidation of 1 molecule of $FADH_2$ causes 6 H^+ ions to be pushed through the inner membrane, so the mitochondrion makes 1.5 molecules of ATP ($6 \div 4 = 1.5$) for each molecule of $FADH_2$ that it oxidizes. We can state these relationships simply as follows:

1 NADH is equivalent to 2.5 ATP

1 $FADH_2$ is equivalent to 1.5 ATP

The mitochondrion cannot actually make one half of a molecule of ATP. These numbers are really mole ratios: a cell can produce 2.5 *moles* of ATP when it oxidizes 1 *mole* of NADH. A mitochondrion oxidizes an enormous number of molecules of NADH and $FADH_2$ every second, and it makes an enormous number of molecules of ATP.

Sample Problem 15.6

Relating redox coenzymes to ATP

Our bodies can break down the amino acid leucine to obtain energy. This metabolic pathway produces 11 molecules of NADH and 4 molecules of $FADH_2$. How many molecules of ATP can be formed when these coenzymes are oxidized to NAD^+ and FAD by a mitochondrion?

SOLUTION

A mitochondrion produces 2.5 molecules of ATP for each molecule of NADH that it oxidizes, and it makes 1.5 molecules of ATP for each molecule of $FADH_2$. We can write these relationships as conversion factors:

$$\frac{2.5 \text{ molecules of ATP}}{1 \text{ molecule of NADH}} \quad \text{and} \quad \frac{1.5 \text{ molecules of ATP}}{1 \text{ molecule of FADH}_2}$$

Now we can use these conversion factors to calculate the number of molecules of ATP formed in this pathway:

$$11 \text{ NADH} \times \frac{2.5 \text{ ATP}}{1 \text{ NADH}} = 27.5 \text{ ATP}$$

$$4 \text{ FADH}_2 \times \frac{1.5 \text{ ATP}}{1 \text{ FADH}_2} = 6 \text{ ATP}$$

The mitochondrion produces 27.5 molecules of ATP as it oxidizes the NADH and 6 molecules of ATP as it oxidizes the $FADH_2$. Adding these up, we get a total of 33.5 molecules of ATP.

TRY IT YOURSELF: *When our bodies break down the amino acid phenylalanine to obtain energy, we form 12 molecules of NADH and 3 molecules of $FADH_2$. How many molecules of ATP can be formed when these coenzymes are oxidized to NAD^+ and FAD by a mitochondrion?*

For additional practice, try Core Problems 15.33 and 15.34.

The sequence of reactions from the oxidation of NADH and $FADH_2$ to the formation of ATP is called **oxidative phosphorylation**. Although cells can make ATP in other ways, some of which we will examine in the rest of this chapter, oxidative phosphorylation supplies the majority of the ATP for most organisms on Earth.

Figure 15.10 illustrates the three parts of catabolism. Compare this figure with Figure 15.4, which summarizes the same process but in less detail.

The ATP yield from oxidative phosphorylation has been the subject of controversy for many years. For decades, researchers believed that mitochondria formed three molecules of ATP per molecule of NADH and two molecules of ATP per molecule of $FADH_2$. These numbers were based on measurements made before the actual mechanism of oxidative phosphorylation was understood. The ratios in this book are based on current understanding of how oxidative phosphorylation works. Since some of the details of this process are still unknown and others remain controversial, *you should treat all calculations of ATP yields as estimates rather than exact numbers.* Nonetheless, ATP yield calculations are a useful way to compare the energy production from various metabolic pathways.

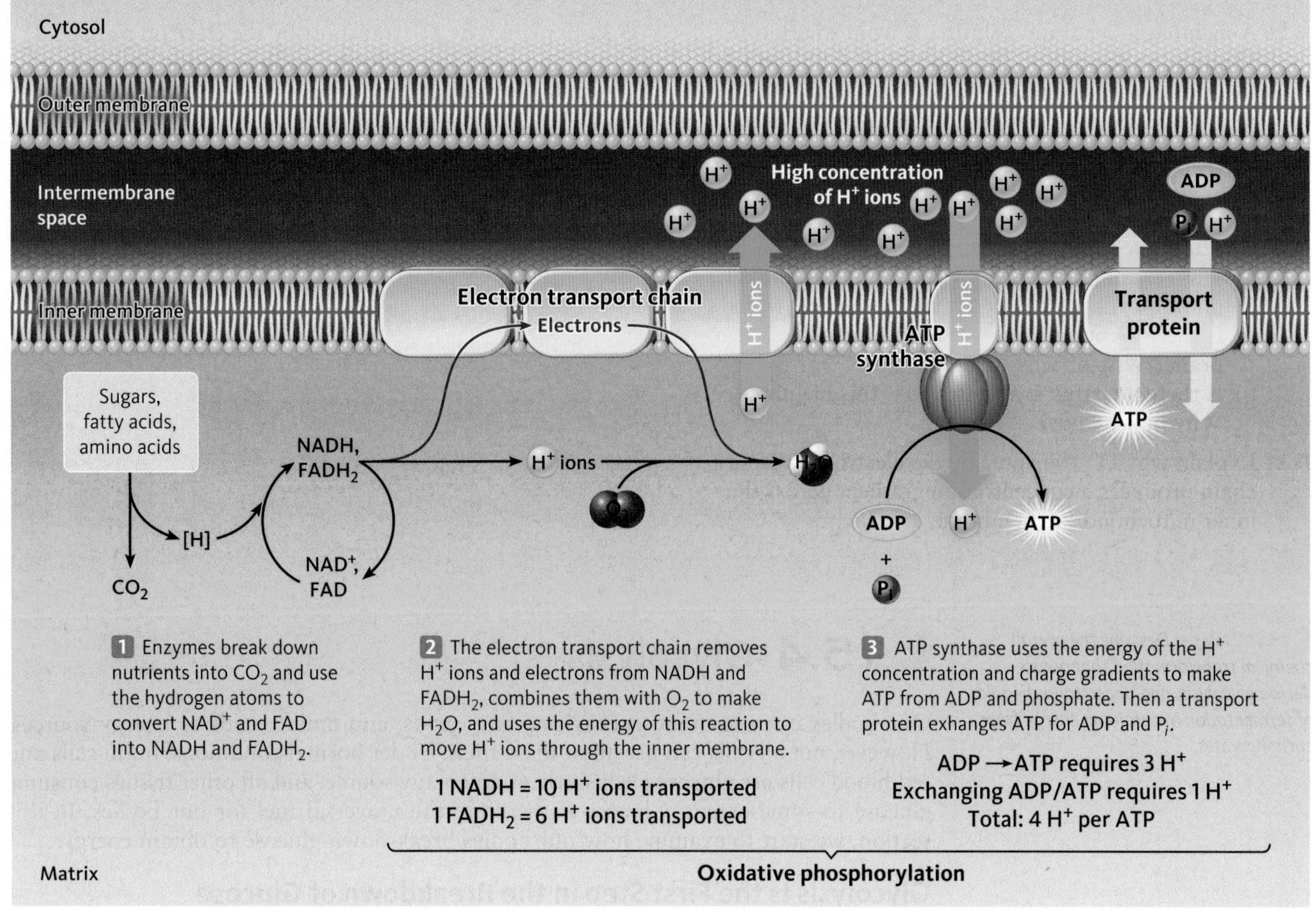

FIGURE 15.10 An overview of catabolism.

CORE PROBLEMS

15.21 Describe the function of the mitochondria in a cell.

15.22 Do mitochondria produce ATP, or do they break ATP down into ADP and phosphate?

15.23 What is the function of the electron transport chain?

15.24 What is the function of ATP synthase?

15.25 Describe how the mitochondrion makes an H^+ concentration gradient.

15.26 Describe how the mitochondrion uses an H^+ concentration gradient to make ATP.

15.27 a) When the electron transport chain oxidizes a molecule of NADH, what does it form?
b) How many hydrogen ions are transferred through the inner membrane as a molecule of NADH is oxidized?
c) How many molecules of ATP (on average) can the mitochondrion make using the energy from the oxidation of one molecule of NADH?
d) If a mitochondrion oxidizes 20 molecules of NADH, how many molecules of ATP can it make?

15.28 a) When the electron transport chain oxidizes a molecule of $FADH_2$, what does it form?
b) How many hydrogen ions are transferred through the inner membrane as a molecule of $FADH_2$ is oxidized?
c) How many molecules of ATP (on average) can the mitochondrion make using the energy from the oxidation of one molecule of $FADH_2$?
d) If a mitochondrion oxidizes 30 molecules of $FADH_2$, how many molecules of ATP can it make?

continued

15.29 A membrane separates solution A from solution B. Solution A contains 0.100 M Na^+ and 0.099 M Cl^-. Solution B contains 0.200 M Na^+ and 0.201 M Cl^-.
a) Is there a concentration gradient across this membrane? Why or why not?
b) Is there a charge gradient across this membrane? Why or why not?

15.30 A membrane separates solution A from solution B. Solution A contains 0.050 M Na^+ and 0.049 M Cl^-. Solution B contains 0.049 M Na^+ and 0.050 M Cl^-.
a) Is there a concentration gradient across this membrane? Why or why not?
b) Is there a charge gradient across this membrane? Why or why not?

15.31 Explain why H^+ transport by the electron transport chain produces a concentration gradient across the inner mitochondrial membrane.

15.32 Explain why H^+ transport by the electron transport chain produces a charge gradient across the inner mitochondrial membrane.

15.33 If a mitochondrion oxidizes two molecules of NADH and two molecules of $FADH_2$, what is the total number of molecules of ATP that the mitochondrion will make available to the cell?

15.34 If a mitochondrion oxidizes five molecules of NADH and one molecule of $FADH_2$, what is the total number of molecules of ATP that the mitochondrion will make available to the cell?

OBJECTIVES: *Describe the overall chemical transformation that occurs during glycolysis, and understand the role of fermentation in obtaining energy from carbohydrates.*

15.4 Glycolysis

Our bodies can use monosaccharides, fatty acids, and amino acids as energy sources. However, not all cells can use all of these fuels. Under normal conditions, brain cells and red blood cells use glucose exclusively as an energy source, and all other tissues consume glucose to some extent. Glucose is therefore the universal fuel for our bodies. In this section, we start to examine how our bodies break down glucose to obtain energy.

Glycolysis Is the First Step in the Breakdown of Glucose

The breakdown of glucose begins with a metabolic pathway called **glycolysis**. Glycolysis is a sequence of 10 reactions that convert the six-carbon sugar glucose into two three-carbon pyruvate ions. The reactions also make two hydrogen ions, which are absorbed by the buffers in body fluids.

Glucose —Glycolysis (10 reactions)→ $2\ CH_3-C(=O)-C(=O)-O^-$ $(+\ 2\ H^+)$

Glucose   Pyruvate ion

$$C_6H_{12}O_6 \longrightarrow 2\ C_3H_3O_3^-\ (+\ 2\ H^+)$$

The original glucose molecule contains 12 hydrogen atoms, but the products contain only 8 hydrogen atoms. The other 4 hydrogen atoms are removed by NAD^+ in a pair of oxidation reactions, so glycolysis also forms two molecules of NADH (and two additional H^+ ions). We can write a more accurate equation for glycolysis as follows:

$$C_6H_{12}O_6 + 2\ NAD^+ \longrightarrow 2\ C_3H_3O_3^- + 2\ NADH + 4\ H^+$$

The mitochondria can use NADH (and $FADH_2$) as a source of energy to make ATP, as we saw in the previous section. As a result, *NADH and $FADH_2$ are classified as high-energy molecules*, and glycolysis is a source of useful energy for our bodies.

Glycolysis also includes four reactions that make or break down ATP directly. Two of these are activation reactions, in which the cell uses energy from ATP to make a different high-energy molecule. For instance, the first reaction of glycolysis converts glucose into glucose-6-phosphate, using the energy (and a phosphate group) from ATP. The overall equation for this reaction is

$$\text{glucose} + \text{ATP} \longrightarrow \text{glucose-6-phosphate} + \text{ADP}$$

As we saw in Section 15.2, this equation is a combination of two other reactions. One reaction breaks down ATP into ADP and phosphate, releasing energy.

$$\text{ATP} + H_2O \longrightarrow \text{ADP} + P_i + 7.3\text{ kcal}$$

The other reaction condenses the phosphate group with glucose. This reaction requires energy, which is supplied by the breakdown of ATP.

$$\text{glucose} + P_i + 3.3\text{ kcal} \longrightarrow \text{glucose-6-phosphate} + H_2O$$

Glycolysis also involves two reactions that transfer a phosphate group from an organic compound to ADP, making a molecule of ATP. One of these reactions is

A phosphate group moves from 1,3-bisphosphoglycerate to ADP.

$$^-O{-}P(=O)(OH){-}O{-}CH_2{-}CH(OH){-}C(=O){-}O{-}P(=O)(OH){-}O^- + \text{ADP} \longrightarrow {}^-O{-}P(=O)(OH){-}O{-}CH_2{-}CH(OH){-}C(=O){-}O^- + \text{ATP}$$

1,3-Bisphosphoglycerate **3-Phosphoglycerate**

This reaction, like the preceding activation reaction, is also a combination of two other equations. The exothermic reaction is the hydrolysis of 1,3-bisphosphoglycerate.

$$\text{1,3-bisphosphoglycerate} + H_2O \longrightarrow \text{3-phosphoglycerate} + P_i + 11.8\text{ kcal}$$

The endothermic reaction is the formation of ATP. This reaction consumes part of the energy that was produced in the first reaction.

$$\text{ADP} + P_i + 7.3\text{ kcal} \longrightarrow \text{ATP} + H_2O$$

The second reaction that makes ATP is the reaction of phosphoenolpyruvate with ADP shown on page 632. Here, too, our bodies make ATP using the energy from the hydrolysis of another high-energy molecule. Reactions that make ATP by hydrolyzing a different high-energy molecule are called **substrate-level phosphorylations**. We will see one other example of a substrate-level phosphorylation in Section 15.5, but you should realize that such reactions are uncommon in metabolism. Our bodies make most of their ATP by oxidizing NADH and $FADH_2$, as we saw in Section 15.3.

There are two separate substrate-level phosphorylation reactions in glycolysis, and each of these reactions occurs twice during the breakdown of a glucose molecule. Therefore, these two reactions make a total of four molecules of ATP.

Glycolysis Produces the High-Energy Molecules ATP and NADH

Let us now look at the overall results of glycolysis. This pathway converts glucose into two pyruvate ions, forming two molecules of NADH in the process. Glycolysis also makes four molecules of ATP using substrate-level phosphorylations. However, each of

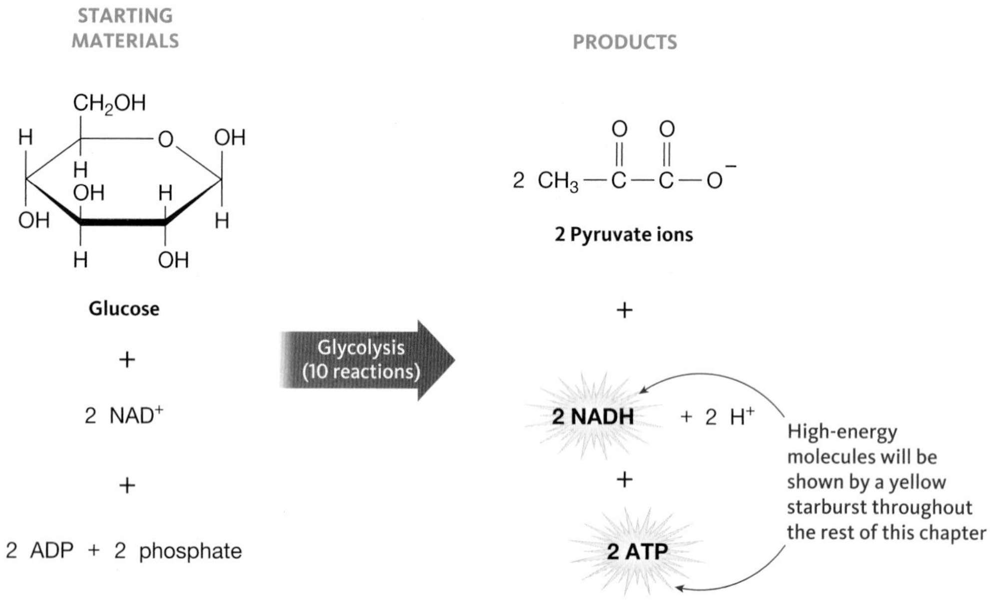

STARTING MATERIALS

PRODUCTS

$$\text{Glucose} + 2\ \text{NAD}^+ + 2\ \text{ADP} + 2\ \text{phosphate} \xrightarrow{\text{Glycolysis (10 reactions)}} 2\ CH_3-\overset{\displaystyle O}{\overset{\|}{C}}-\overset{\displaystyle O}{\overset{\|}{C}}-O^- + \mathbf{2\ NADH} + 2\ H^+ + \mathbf{2\ ATP}$$

Glucose

2 Pyruvate ions

High-energy molecules will be shown by a yellow starburst throughout the rest of this chapter

FIGURE 15.11 An overview of glycolysis.

the two activation reactions of glycolysis breaks down a molecule of ATP, so we gain only two molecules of ATP from glycolysis. The net result is that *our bodies obtain two molecules of ATP and two molecules of NADH for every molecule of glucose that we break down.* Figure 15.11 summarizes the reactants and products of glycolysis.

Health Note: Muscles that are working strenuously get most of their energy from glycolysis, so they produce enough hydrogen ions to overwhelm the cells' buffers and decrease the pH significantly. This drop in pH was believed to cause the sensation of muscle fatigue, but recent research shows that pH plays a minor role in muscle fatigue.

Figure 15.11 is not a balanced equation, because it does not include the hydrogen ions that are formed together with the pyruvate ions. H^+ tends to be an invisible participant in metabolic reactions, because hydrogen ions are supplied and absorbed by the buffers in the surrounding fluids. Rather than trying to account for all of the hydrogen ions that are consumed by buffers in metabolic pathways, we will simply ignore these hydrogen ions throughout the remainder of this chapter. The only hydrogen ions that you will see are those that are involved in oxidations and reductions that involve NAD^+ or NADH, to remind you that NAD^+ removes two hydrogen atoms from organic molecules, not just one.

Lactic Acid Fermentation Converts Glucose into Lactate

Our bodies use the pyruvate that we make during glycolysis in several ways. We can obtain more energy by breaking down pyruvate into CO_2 by a sequence of reactions called the citric acid cycle, which we will examine in the next section. We can also use pyruvate to build triglycerides and some amino acids. However, much of the pyruvate is simply converted into lactate (the ionized form of lactic acid). In this reaction, the ketone group in the pyruvate ion is reduced to an alcohol group, using NADH to supply the hydrogen atoms.

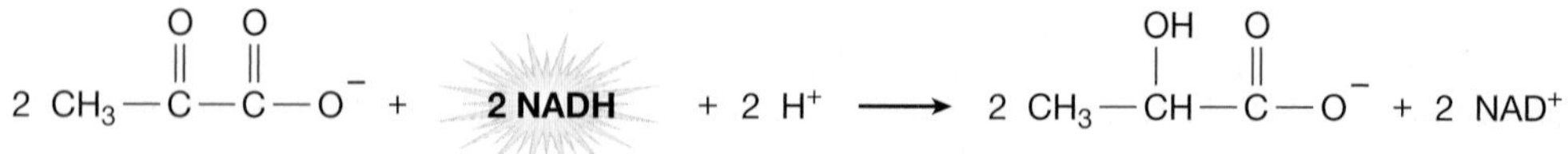

$$2\ CH_3-\overset{\displaystyle O}{\overset{\|}{C}}-\overset{\displaystyle O}{\overset{\|}{C}}-O^- + \mathbf{2\ NADH} + 2\ H^+ \longrightarrow 2\ CH_3-\overset{\displaystyle OH}{\overset{|}{CH}}-\overset{\displaystyle O}{\overset{\|}{C}}-O^- + 2\ NAD^+$$

Pyruvate — Lactate

If we add the conversion of pyruvate into lactate to the rest of the reactions in glycolysis, we have an example of a **fermentation**. Fermentation is a general term for any catabolic pathway that breaks down carbohydrates using all or most of the reactions of glycolysis, but that does not involve any net oxidation. Fermentations are **anaerobic pathways**, meaning that they do not require oxygen, either directly or indirectly.

The sequence of 11 reactions that breaks down glucose into lactate is called **lactic acid fermentation**. Active muscles obtain the majority of their energy from this pathway. The bacteria that are responsible for spoiled milk are also lactic acid fermenters, but they produce lactic acid rather than lactate ions. The lactic acid denatures the milk protein

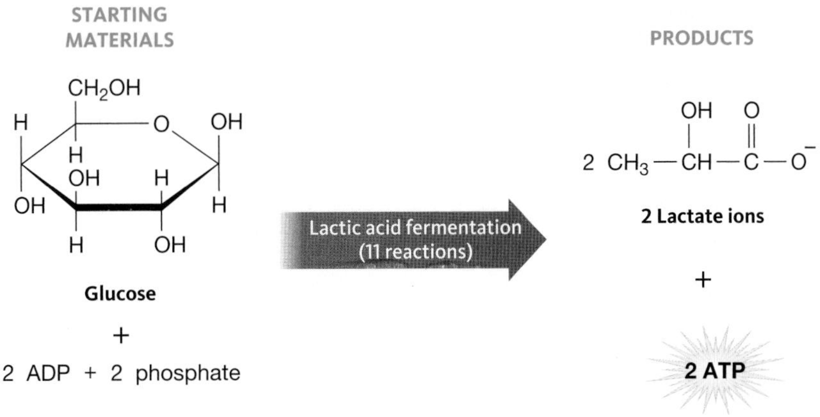

STARTING MATERIALS

Glucose + 2 ADP + 2 phosphate → Lactic acid fermentation (11 reactions) → **PRODUCTS**

$$2\ CH_3-CH(OH)-C(=O)-O^-$$

2 Lactate ions + **2 ATP**

FIGURE 15.12 An overview of lactic acid fermentation.

$$CH_3-CH_2-OH$$
Ethanol

$$H-C(=O)-OH$$
Formic acid

$$CH_3-C(=O)-OH$$
Acetic acid

$$CH_3-CH(OH)-C(=O)-OH$$
Lactic acid

$$HO-C(=O)-CH_2-CH_2-C(=O)-OH$$
Succinic acid

$$CH_3-CH(OH)-CH(OH)-CH_3$$
2,3-Butanediol

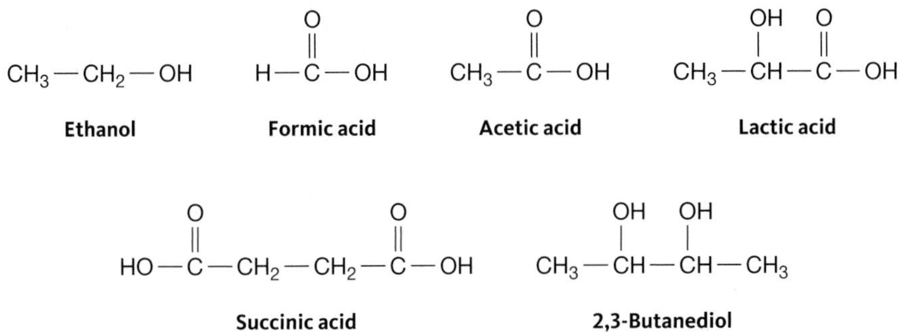

FIGURE 15.13 Typical products of bacterial fermentations.

(producing the characteristic curds) and gives the milk its unpleasant flavor and aroma. Lactic acid fermentation, like glycolysis, makes two molecules of ATP, so it is an energy-producing pathway. However, it does not produce as much energy as glycolysis, because it does not produce NADH. Lactic acid fermentation is summarized in Figure 15.12.

Many microorganisms can use fermentations as their primary energy-producing pathways. These organisms can convert carbohydrates into a variety of organic and inorganic substances, including lactic acid, ethanol, acetic acid, formic acid, succinic acid, 2,3-butanediol, carbon dioxide, and even hydrogen. Figure 15.13 shows the structures of the organic products that can be formed in fermentations.

Alcoholic Fermentation Produces Ethanol and CO_2 from Glucose

A particularly important type of fermentation is **alcoholic fermentation**, which occurs in certain types of yeast and some bacteria. These microorganisms break down pyruvic acid into CO_2 and acetaldehyde, which they then reduce to ethanol. These two reactions are shown here.

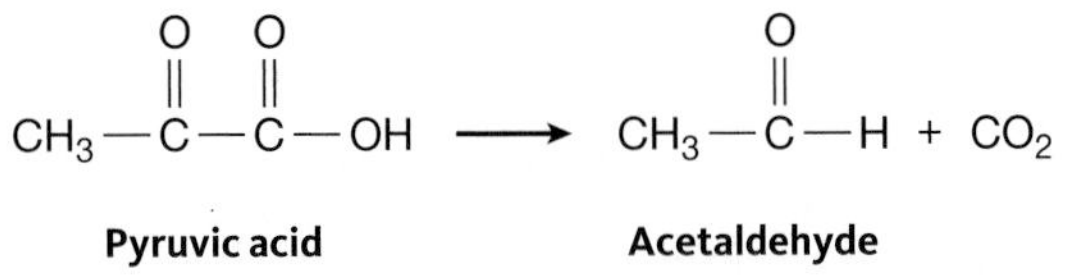

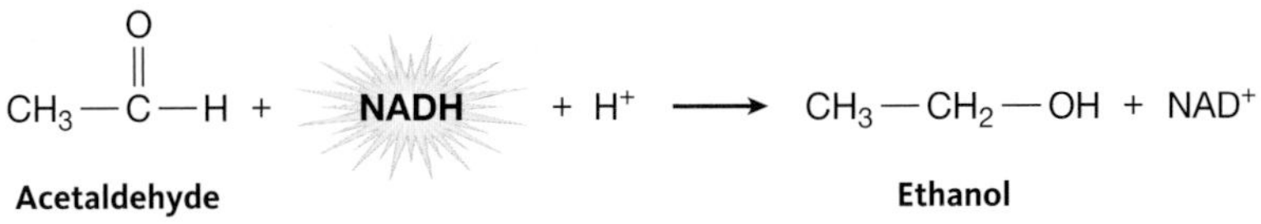

$$\underset{\text{Pyruvic acid}}{CH_3-C(=O)-C(=O)-OH} \longrightarrow \underset{\text{Acetaldehyde}}{CH_3-C(=O)-H} + CO_2$$

$$\underset{\text{Acetaldehyde}}{CH_3-C(=O)-H} + \text{NADH} + H^+ \longrightarrow \underset{\text{Ethanol}}{CH_3-CH_2-OH} + NAD^+$$

Jackson Vereen/Getty Images

Cheese and yogurt makers rely on bacteria that carry out lactic acid fermentation to give their products the correct flavor and consistency.

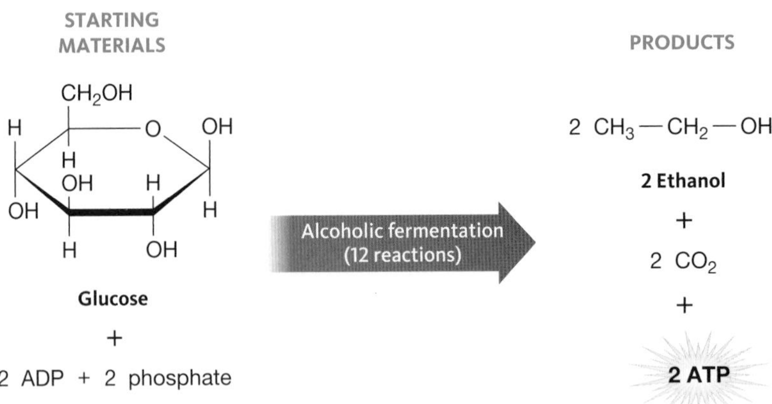

FIGURE 15.14 An overview of alcoholic fermentation.

Alcoholic fermentation is responsible for the familiar properties of bread, beer, and wine.

Note that the second reaction consumes the NADH that was produced during glycolysis. Because all of the NADH that is produced during glycolysis is consumed when acetaldehyde is reduced to ethanol, the only high-energy product of alcoholic fermentation is ATP. Figure 15.14 gives a summary of alcoholic fermentation.

People have exploited alcoholic fermentation since ancient times, both to make alcoholic beverages and to make bread and other baked goods. Beer and sparkling wine are made by fermenting mixtures of water and carbohydrate-containing vegetable matter (grains or grapes) in sealed containers. The ethanol gives the beverages their alcoholic content, and the carbon dioxide gives them their "sparkle." Other wines are made by allowing the carbon dioxide to escape during the fermenting. Bread is made by adding yeast (an alcoholic fermenter) to a mixture of grain and water and then heating the mixture in an oven. The CO_2 makes the bread rise, forming bubbles of gas within the dough, while the ethanol evaporates away.

Glycolysis occupies a special place in catabolism. In its anaerobic form (lactic acid fermentation), glycolysis is the only energy-producing pathway in humans that does not require oxygen, either directly or indirectly. Because its rate is not limited by the availability of oxygen, glycolysis is the fastest energy-producing pathway available to the cells in our bodies, making it particularly suited for brief, intense bursts of muscular effort. Since all of the enzymes of glycolysis are in the cytosol of the cell, glycolysis is also the only catabolic pathway that does not involve the mitochondria. A great deal of evidence supports the theory that glycolysis evolved long before Earth's atmosphere contained oxygen, making glycolysis the most ancient metabolic pathway that remains important in higher animals.

Glycolysis remains an important energy source for most organisms. However, since this pathway does not completely oxidize glucose, it extracts only a small fraction of the energy that we can get from burning carbohydrates. In the next section, we will see how our bodies complete the oxidation of glucose, and we will link the catabolism of glucose to the electron transport chain.

CORE PROBLEMS

15.35 What is an activation reaction, and how is ATP involved in this type of reaction?

15.36 What is a substrate-level phosphorylation reaction, and how is ATP involved in this type of reaction?

15.37 What organic compound is broken down during glycolysis, and what product is formed when this molecule is broken down?

15.38 What high-energy compounds are produced during glycolysis, and how many molecules of each compound are formed?

15.39 Explain why lactic acid fermentation is an anaerobic pathway.

15.40 Explain why alcoholic fermentation is an anaerobic pathway.

15.41 The last reaction in lactic acid fermentation is

$$\text{pyruvate} + \text{NADH} + \text{H}^+ \rightarrow \text{lactate} + \text{NAD}^+$$

What is the source of the NADH for this reaction?

15.42 The last reaction in alcoholic fermentation is

$$\text{acetaldehyde} + \text{NADH} + \text{H}^+ \rightarrow \text{ethanol} + \text{NAD}^+$$

What is the source of the NADH for this reaction?

15.5 The Citric Acid Cycle

OBJECTIVES: *Describe the overall chemical transformation that occurs in the citric acid cycle, and calculate the ATP yield for a typical carbohydrate.*

Pyruvate ion, the product of glycolysis, is a key intermediate in biochemistry. As we will see in Section 15.8, our liver can use pyruvate to build glucose, using a sequence of reactions that essentially reverses the reactions of glycolysis. Pyruvate can also be converted into some of the nonessential amino acids for protein synthesis. However, the most important role of pyruvate is as an energy source. Our bodies can oxidize pyruvate, forming CO_2 and generating ATP. In this section, we will explore the reactions that our bodies use to oxidize pyruvate. All of these reactions occur in the mitochondria.

Pyruvate Is Converted into Acetyl–Coenzyme A

The first step in the oxidation of pyruvate is an oxidative decarboxylation, a reaction we encountered in Section 11.2. In an oxidative decarboxylation, the acid loses its carboxyl group in the form of CO_2, and the rest of the acid combines with a thiol to form a thioester. The thiol is coenzyme A, and the thioester is called acetyl–coenzyme A (abbreviated acetyl-CoA). This reaction also produces a molecule of NADH. The overall reaction is

An acetyl group

$$\underset{\text{Pyruvate}}{CH_3{-}\overset{\overset{O}{\parallel}}{C}{-}\overset{\overset{O}{\parallel}}{C}{-}O^-} + HS{-}CoA + NAD^+ \longrightarrow \underset{\text{Acetyl-CoA}}{CH_3{-}\overset{\overset{O}{\parallel}}{C}{-}S{-}CoA} + CO_2 + NADH + H^+$$

Acetyl-CoA, like pyruvate, is a molecule that plays a variety of roles in metabolism. As we will see in the next section, our bodies make acetyl-CoA when we break down fatty acids to obtain energy. In addition, we break down most of the amino acids into acetyl-CoA. As a result, *most of the energy-producing pathways for carbohydrates, fats, and proteins converge to a single pathway that oxidizes acetyl-CoA.* Using one set of enzymes to break down several types of nutrients is more efficient than using separate pathways, each with its own set of enzymes, because building an enzyme from its amino acids requires a great deal of energy.

The Citric Acid Cycle Completes the Oxidation of Carbohydrates

Our bodies oxidize the acetyl group of acetyl-CoA using a sequence of eight reactions called the **citric acid cycle** (also referred to as the **Krebs cycle** or the tricarboxylic acid cycle). The acetyl group is converted into CO_2, and the coenzyme A is recycled. We can write an overall equation for this reaction, just as we did for glucose in Section 15.2.

$$CH_3\text{–}CO\text{–}S\text{–}CoA + 3\ H_2O \rightarrow 2\ CO_2 + HS\text{–}CoA + 8\ [H]$$

The eight hydrogen atoms are removed by three molecules of NAD^+ and one molecule of FAD, converting these coenzymes into NADH and $FADH_2$, respectively. In addition, one of the reactions in the citric acid cycle is a substrate-level phosphorylation, hydrolyzing a thioester to supply the energy to make a molecule of ATP from ADP and phosphate. We can now account for all of the products and reactants in the citric acid cycle, as shown in Figure 15.15.

Although the citric acid cycle starts with an acetyl group and produces two molecules of CO_2, it does not simply break down the acetyl group. Instead, the acetyl group combines with an organic ion called oxaloacetate. The product of this reaction is citrate ion, which is the completely ionized

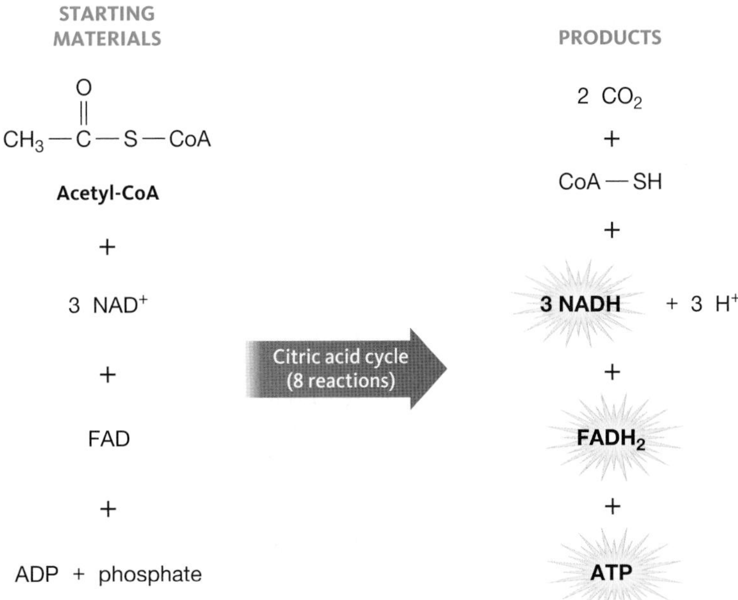

FIGURE 15.15 An overview of the citric acid cycle.

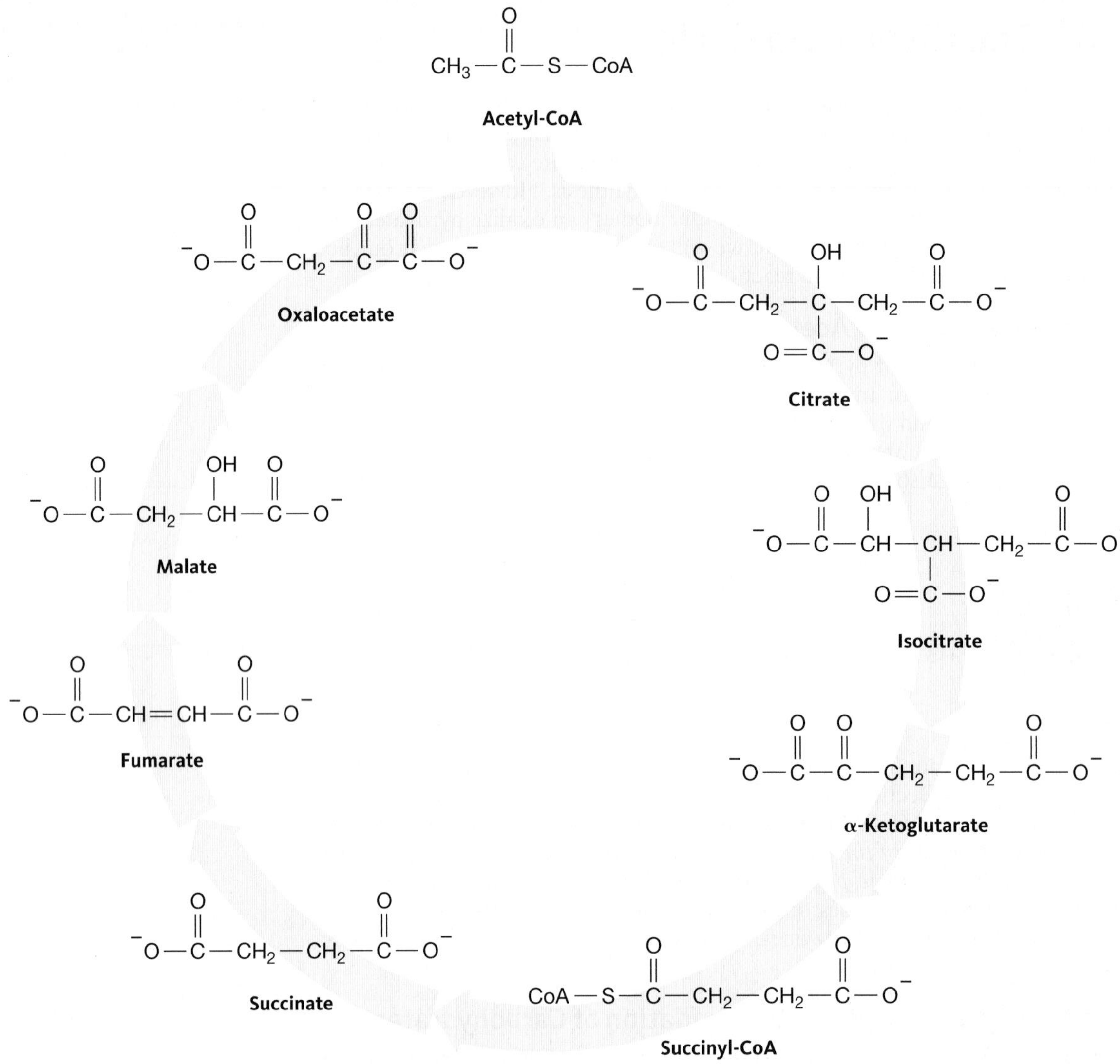

Acetyl-CoA

Oxaloacetate

Citrate

Malate

Isocitrate

Fumarate

α-Ketoglutarate

Succinate

Succinyl-CoA

FIGURE 15.16 The reactions of the citric acid cycle.

form of citric acid, the compound responsible for the tart taste of citrus fruits. Citrate then undergoes seven more reactions that remove two carbon atoms from the citrate skeleton (as CO_2) and produce all of the high-energy molecules in Figure 15.15. The final product is oxaloacetate, which can combine with another acetyl group to start the cycle again. Figure 15.16 summarizes the eight reactions of the citric acid cycle.

Each Step in the Citric Acid Cycle Has a Specific Function

Let us examine the reactions of the citric acid cycle in detail. The first reaction in the citric acid cycle is a type that we do not cover in this book, but each of the other seven reactions involves organic transformations you have seen in Chapters 9 through 12. As you read the descriptions of the reactions, bear in mind that oxidizing the acetyl group involves adding three water molecules, removing eight hydrogen atoms, and producing two molecules of CO_2.

The reactions of the citric acid cycle *Reaction 1* hydrolyzes the thioester group in acetyl-CoA, and it uses the energy of this reaction to combine the acetyl group with oxaloacetate to form citrate. The green shading shows the location of the acetyl group in the product. This reaction consumes the first of the three water molecules in the citric acid cycle.

$$\underset{\textbf{Acetyl-CoA}}{CH_3-\overset{O}{\overset{\|}{C}}-S-CoA} + \underset{\textbf{Oxaloacetate}}{{}^{-}O-\overset{O}{\overset{\|}{C}}-CH_2-\overset{O}{\overset{\|}{C}}-\overset{O}{\overset{\|}{C}}-O^{-}} + H_2O \longrightarrow \underset{\textbf{Citrate}}{{}^{-}O-\overset{O}{\overset{\|}{C}}-CH_2-\underset{O=C-O^{-}}{\overset{OH}{C}}-CH_2-\overset{O}{\overset{\|}{C}}-O^{-}} + HS-CoA$$

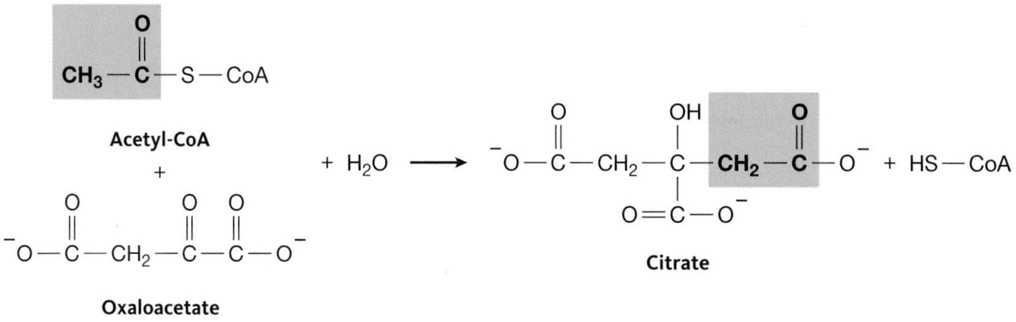

Reaction 2 converts citrate into an isomer called isocitrate, using a dehydration step followed by a hydration step. This reaction is necessary because the next reaction involves the oxidation of the alcohol group. The tertiary alcohol group in citrate cannot be oxidized, but the secondary alcohol group in isocitrate can be.

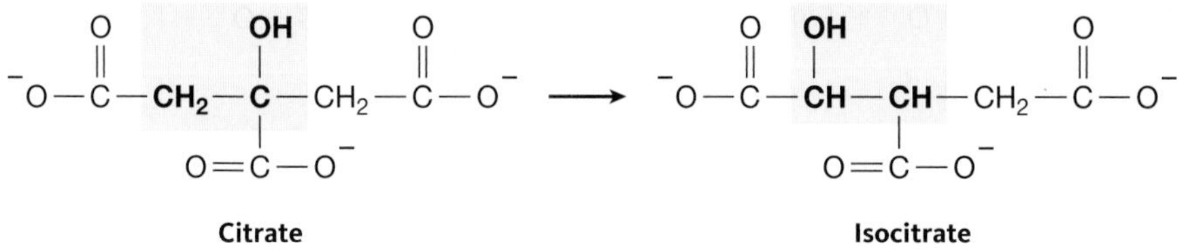

$$\underset{\textbf{Citrate}}{{}^{-}O-\overset{O}{\overset{\|}{C}}-CH_2-\underset{O=C-O^{-}}{\overset{OH}{C}}-CH_2-\overset{O}{\overset{\|}{C}}-O^{-}} \longrightarrow \underset{\textbf{Isocitrate}}{{}^{-}O-\overset{O}{\overset{\|}{C}}-\overset{OH}{CH}-\underset{O=C-O^{-}}{CH}-CH_2-\overset{O}{\overset{\|}{C}}-O^{-}}$$

Reaction 3 is actually two reactions in one, an oxidation and a decarboxylation. The alcohol group in isocitrate is oxidized, and one carboxyl group is removed. Since the oxidation makes NADH, this is the first energy-producing step in the citric acid cycle. The oxidation is shown in green, and the decarboxylation is shown in red.

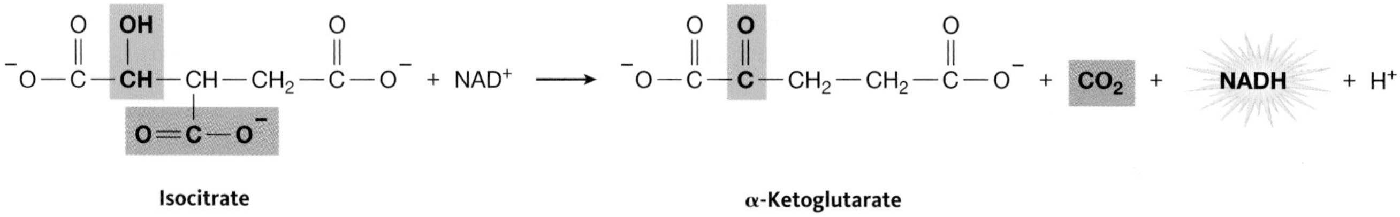

$$\underset{\textbf{Isocitrate}}{{}^{-}O-\overset{O}{\overset{\|}{C}}-\overset{OH}{CH}-\underset{O=C-O^{-}}{CH}-CH_2-\overset{O}{\overset{\|}{C}}-O^{-}} + NAD^{+} \longrightarrow \underset{\alpha\textbf{-Ketoglutarate}}{{}^{-}O-\overset{O}{\overset{\|}{C}}-\overset{O}{\overset{\|}{C}}-CH_2-CH_2-\overset{O}{\overset{\|}{C}}-O^{-}} + CO_2 + NADH + H^{+}$$

Reaction 4 is an oxidative decarboxylation, and it is the second energy-producing step in the citric acid cycle. This reaction produces CO_2 and a thioester, which is a high-energy molecule. The cycle has now produced two molecules of CO_2, corresponding to the two carbon atoms in the acetyl group of acetyl-CoA.

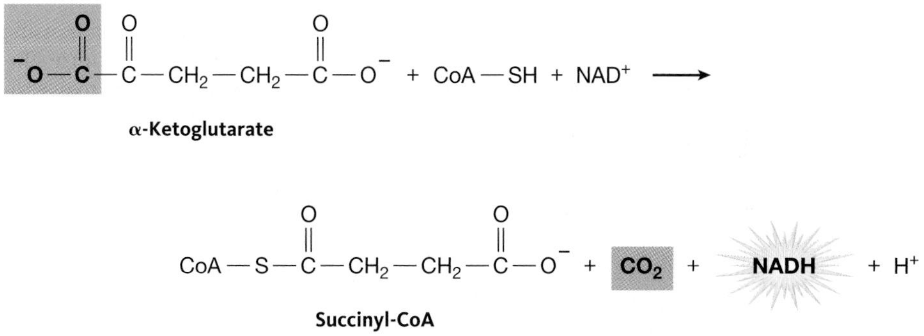

$$\underset{\alpha\textbf{-Ketoglutarate}}{{}^{-}O-\overset{O}{\overset{\|}{C}}-\overset{O}{\overset{\|}{C}}-CH_2-CH_2-\overset{O}{\overset{\|}{C}}-O^{-}} + CoA-SH + NAD^{+} \longrightarrow$$

$$\underset{\textbf{Succinyl-CoA}}{CoA-S-\overset{O}{\overset{\|}{C}}-CH_2-CH_2-\overset{O}{\overset{\|}{C}}-O^{-}} + CO_2 + NADH + H^{+}$$

Reaction 5 is the hydrolysis of the high-energy thioester, succinyl-CoA. The hydrolysis produces energy, which is used to make a molecule of guanosine triphosphate (GTP), a compound that is closely related to ATP and is equivalent to ATP in terms of energy.

Therefore, this is the third energy-producing step in the cycle. (To simplify the "energy bookkeeping," the reaction is written with ATP rather than GTP.)

$$\underset{\textbf{Succinyl-CoA}}{\text{CoA}-\text{S}-\overset{\overset{\displaystyle O}{\|}}{C}-\text{CH}_2-\text{CH}_2-\overset{\overset{\displaystyle O}{\|}}{C}-\text{O}^-} + \text{H}_2\text{O} + \text{ADP} + \text{phosphate} \longrightarrow$$

$$\underset{\textbf{Succinate}}{{}^-\text{O}-\overset{\overset{\displaystyle O}{\|}}{C}-\text{CH}_2-\text{CH}_2-\overset{\overset{\displaystyle O}{\|}}{C}-\text{O}^-} + \text{CoA}-\text{SH} + \textbf{ATP}$$

Reaction 6 is a dehydrogenation reaction. Since dehydrogenation reactions are oxidations, this reaction is the fourth energy-producing step in the cycle.

$$\underset{\textbf{Succinate}}{{}^-\text{O}-\overset{\overset{\displaystyle O}{\|}}{C}-\mathbf{CH_2}-\mathbf{CH_2}-\overset{\overset{\displaystyle O}{\|}}{C}-\text{O}^-} + \text{FAD} \longrightarrow \underset{\textbf{Fumarate}}{{}^-\text{O}-\overset{\overset{\displaystyle O}{\|}}{C}-\mathbf{CH}=\mathbf{CH}-\overset{\overset{\displaystyle O}{\|}}{C}-\text{O}^-} + \mathbf{FADH_2}$$

Reaction 7 is a hydration reaction. The citric acid cycle has now consumed three water molecules, one each in steps 1, 5, and 7.

$$\underset{\textbf{Fumarate}}{{}^-\text{O}-\overset{\overset{\displaystyle O}{\|}}{C}-\mathbf{CH}=\mathbf{CH}-\overset{\overset{\displaystyle O}{\|}}{C}-\text{O}^-} + \text{H}_2\text{O} \longrightarrow \underset{\textbf{Malate}}{{}^-\text{O}-\overset{\overset{\displaystyle O}{\|}}{C}-\mathbf{CH_2}-\overset{\overset{\displaystyle \mathbf{OH}}{|}}{\mathbf{CH}}-\overset{\overset{\displaystyle O}{\|}}{C}-\text{O}^-}$$

Reaction 8 is the oxidation of malate, and it is the fifth and final energy-producing step in the citric acid cycle. The product of this step is oxaloacetate, the starting material for the cycle.

$$\underset{\textbf{Malate}}{{}^-\text{O}-\overset{\overset{\displaystyle O}{\|}}{C}-\text{CH}_2-\overset{\overset{\displaystyle \mathbf{OH}}{|}}{\mathbf{CH}}-\overset{\overset{\displaystyle O}{\|}}{C}-\text{O}^-} + \text{NAD}^+ \longrightarrow \underset{\textbf{Oxaloacetate}}{{}^-\text{O}-\overset{\overset{\displaystyle O}{\|}}{C}-\text{CH}_2-\overset{\overset{\displaystyle \mathbf{O}}{\|}}{\mathbf{C}}-\overset{\overset{\displaystyle O}{\|}}{C}-\text{O}^-} + \textbf{NADH} + \text{H}^+$$

Table 15.3 summarizes the functions of the reactions of the citric acid cycle.

The Complete Oxidation of Glucose Produces 32 Molecules of ATP

We can now calculate the number of molecules of ATP that our bodies can make using the energy from the complete oxidation of a molecule of glucose. When we oxidize glucose, we carry out three sets of reactions: glycolysis, the conversion of pyruvate to acetyl-CoA, and the citric acid cycle. These reactions break down the glucose molecule into CO_2, forming some ATP and converting several molecules of NAD^+ and FAD into NADH and $FADH_2$. The mitochondria then oxidize the NADH and $FADH_2$, using the energy to make additional ATP. Table 15.4 shows the number of high-energy molecules formed in each step.

All of the NADH and $FADH_2$ that is formed during the oxidation of glucose is used to make ATP. As we saw in Section 15.3, the mitochondria can make 2.5 molecules of ATP for each molecule of NADH, and they can make 1.5 molecules of ATP for each molecule of $FADH_2$. We can use these ratios to calculate the number of molecules of ATP that are formed by oxidative phosphorylation.

$$10\ \text{NADH} \times 2.5\ \text{ATP per NADH} = 25\ \text{ATP}$$
$$2\ \text{FADH}_2 \times 1.5\ \text{ATP per FADH}_2 = 3\ \text{ATP}$$

TABLE 15.3 The Reactions of the Citric Acid Cycle

Reaction Number	Reaction Type	Function in the Cycle
1	Special reaction	Starts the cycle by combining the acetyl group with oxaloacetate ion
2	Dehydration, followed by hydration	Moves the hydroxyl group of citrate to a location where it can be oxidized
3	Oxidation and decarboxylation	Produces a high-energy molecule (NADH) and removes a carbon atom (in the form of CO_2)
4	Oxidative decarboxylation	Produces a high-energy molecule (NADH), removes a carbon atom (in the form of CO_2), and makes a thioester, which is a high-energy molecule
5	Hydrolysis of thioester	Produces a high-energy molecule (ATP)
6	Dehydrogenation (oxidation)	Produces a high-energy molecule ($FADH_2$)
7	Hydration	Adds an oxygen atom to allow further oxidation
8	Oxidation	Produces a high-energy molecule (NADH) and regenerates the oxaloacetate ion

The total number of molecules of ATP we form when we oxidize a molecule of glucose (called the *ATP yield*) is

4 ATP	(made during glycolysis and the citric acid cycle)
25 ATP	(from the oxidation of NADH)
+ 3 ATP	(from the oxidation of $FADH_2$)
32 ATP	(overall yield from one molecule of glucose)

When we did this calculation, we ignored the fact that 2 of our 10 molecules of NADH were produced during glycolysis, which does not occur in the mitochondria. Since NADH cannot cross the mitochondrial inner membrane, the energy of these NADH molecules must be harnessed indirectly. Cells have two ways to do this, both of

TABLE 15.4 The Complete Oxidation of Glucose

Pathway	Function	High-Energy Molecules Formed	Number of Occurrences When Glucose Is Oxidized	Total High-Energy Molecules Formed
Glycolysis (Section 15.4)	Breaks glucose down into two pyruvate ions	2 ATP 2 NADH	1	2 ATP 2 NADH
Oxidative decarboxylation (Section 15.5)	Converts pyruvate into acetyl-CoA	1 NADH	2	2 NADH
Citric acid cycle (Section 15.5)	Oxidizes the acetyl group of acetyl-CoA into CO_2	1 ATP 3 NADH 1 $FADH_2$	2	2 ATP 6 NADH 2 $FADH_2$
Overall oxidation of glucose	**Oxidizes glucose into CO_2**			**4 ATP** **10 NADH** **2 $FADH_2$**

which involve transferring the hydrogen atoms from NADH to a molecule that can cross the membrane. However, only one of these methods returns the hydrogen atoms to NAD^+ inside the mitochondrion. The other transfers the hydrogen atoms to FAD, which produces one fewer ATP molecule in oxidative phosphorylation. Because glycolysis makes two molecules of NADH, some cells can only produce $32 - 2 = 30$ molecules of ATP per molecule of glucose. The actual yield depends on the type of cell.

How efficient are our bodies at storing the energy from the oxidation of glucose? The complete oxidation of one mole (180 g) of glucose produces 686 kcal of energy. We use this energy to make 32 moles of ATP. A mole of ATP stores 7.3 kcal of energy, so the total amount of energy we store in the form of ATP is

$$32 \times 7.3 \text{ kcal} = 234 \text{ kcal of energy}$$

This is only around 34% of the total energy from burning glucose. However, the concentration of ATP in our bodies is much higher than the concentrations of ADP and phosphate, and we must use additional energy from glucose oxidation to maintain this ratio. This additional energy is not wasted; we get it back when we break down ATP. As a result, we actually store between 50% and 60% of the energy we get from glucose in the form of ATP. The rest of the energy is released in the form of heat.

CORE PROBLEMS

15.43 In the oxidative decarboxylation of pyruvate, what happens to the three carbon atoms in the pyruvate ion?

15.44 What coenzymes are required in the oxidative decarboxylation of pyruvate, and what happens to them?

15.45 The citric acid cycle oxidizes an organic molecule, breaking part of it down into carbon dioxide. What is this organic molecule?

15.46 What high-energy compounds are formed in one citric acid cycle, and how many molecules of each are formed?

15.47 How many decarboxylation reactions are there in the citric acid cycle? Is this reasonable, given that the citric acid cycle breaks down the acetyl group of acetyl-CoA?

15.48 How many of the reactions of the citric acid cycle involve an oxidation? Is this reasonable, based on the following overall reaction?

$$CH_3\text{-CO-S-CoA} + 3\,H_2O \rightarrow 2\,CO_2 + \text{HS-CoA} + 8\,[H]$$

15.49 What is the purpose of converting citrate into isocitrate during the second step of the citric acid cycle?

15.50 Converting fumarate to malate (the seventh step of the citric acid cycle) does not produce any high-energy molecules. What is the purpose of this reaction?

15.51 What is the total ATP yield when one molecule of acetyl-CoA is broken down to CO_2? Include the ATP that is formed by oxidative phosphorylation.

15.52 What is the total ATP yield when one pyruvate ion is broken down to CO_2? How many of these ATP molecules are formed by oxidative phosphorylation?

15.53 In some cells, the oxidation of glucose produces 32 molecules of ATP. How many of these are made by the electron transport chain?

15.54 In some cells, the oxidation of glucose produces 30 molecules of ATP. How many of these are made by the electron transport chain?

OBJECTIVES: *Write the reactions that occur during the oxidation of a fatty acid, calculate the ATP yield for a fatty acid, and convert ATP yields to a gram basis for comparison.*

15.6 Beta Oxidation: Obtaining Energy from Fatty Acids

Triglycerides are our bodies' most efficient energy source. We obtain 9 kcal for each gram of fat that we burn, as compared with 4 kcal for carbohydrate or protein. Our bodies can burn both glycerol and fatty acids, but we get the vast majority of the energy from the fatty acids. In this section, we will examine the chemical reactions that allow our bodies to break down fatty acids, and we will compare the ATP yield to that from glucose.

Our bodies oxidize fatty acids to CO_2, removing the hydrogen atoms and transferring them to NAD^+ and FAD. If we take lauric acid (the shortest commonly occurring saturated fatty acid) as an example, we can work out the overall reaction just as we did for glucose in Section 15.2. Lauric acid has the molecular formula $C_{12}H_{24}O_2$. Since this compound contains 12 carbon atoms, we must make 12 molecules of CO_2 when we oxidize 1 molecule of lauric acid.

$$\underset{\text{lauric acid}}{C_{12}H_{24}O_2} \rightarrow 12\,CO_2$$

The 12 CO_2 molecules contain a total of 24 oxygen atoms. Lauric acid has only two oxygen atoms, so our bodies need an additional 22 oxygen atoms. As we saw in Section 15.2, these added oxygen atoms are supplied by water molecules, so we must add 22 water molecules to our reaction.

$$C_{12}H_{24}O_2 \quad + \quad 22\ H_2O \quad \rightarrow \quad 12\ CO_2$$

Finally, we account for the hydrogen atoms. Lauric acid contains 24 hydrogen atoms, and the water contains an additional 44 hydrogen atoms (22 × 2), for a total of 68 hydrogen atoms. All of these will be transferred to NAD^+ or FAD, but we can write them as [H] for now.

$$C_{12}H_{24}O_2 \quad + \quad 22\ H_2O \quad \rightarrow \quad 12\ CO_2 \quad + \quad 68\ [H]$$

This equation helps us understand why fatty acids are such a good source of energy. Remember that most of the energy in any catabolic pathway comes from oxidative phosphorylation, which uses the hydrogen atoms in NADH and $FADH_2$. *The more hydrogen atoms a pathway produces, the more energy it can generate.* Lauric acid produces 68 hydrogen atoms while glucose only produces 24, so we expect lauric acid to be a better energy source.

Fatty Acids Must Be Activated Before They Can Be Broken Down

Let us now turn to the specific reactions that break down a fatty acid. The first reaction combines the fatty acid (in its ionized form) with coenzyme A to form a thioester called a *fatty acyl–CoA*. This is an activation reaction, and the thioester is a high-energy molecule. Like all activations, this reaction requires energy, which is supplied by breaking down two molecules of ATP. Here is the activation step for lauric acid:

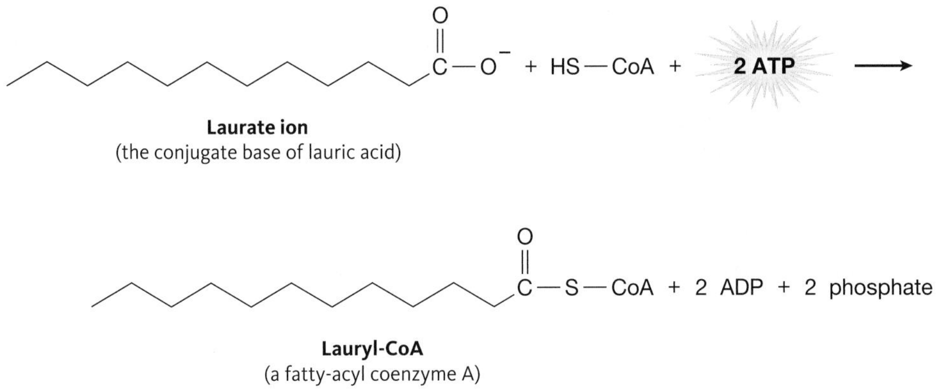

C(=O)—O⁻ + HS—CoA + **2 ATP** ⟶

Laurate ion
(the conjugate base of lauric acid)

C(=O)—S—CoA + 2 ADP + 2 phosphate

Lauryl-CoA
(a fatty-acyl coenzyme A)

Beta Oxidation Removes a Two-Carbon Fragment from the Fatty Acid

The fatty acyl–CoA now undergoes a sequence of four reactions called **beta oxidation**. These reactions remove two carbon atoms from the molecule in the form of acetyl-CoA, leaving a fatty acyl–CoA that is two carbons shorter. The overall conversion for lauryl-CoA is

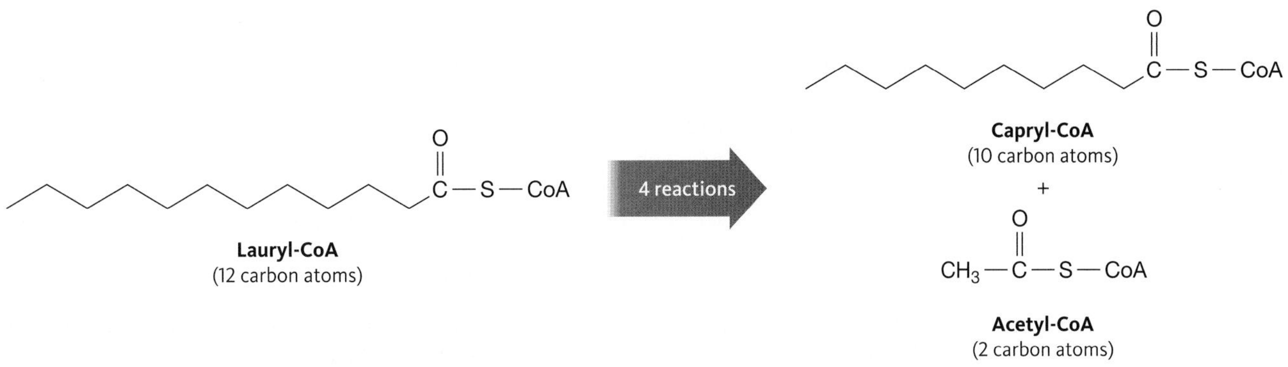

C(=O)—S—CoA

Lauryl-CoA
(12 carbon atoms)

4 reactions

C(=O)—S—CoA

Capryl-CoA
(10 carbon atoms)

+

CH_3—C(=O)—S—CoA

Acetyl-CoA
(2 carbon atoms)

The reactions of beta oxidation illustrate several of the functional group transformations we have seen in earlier chapters, and they are an excellent example of the three-step strategy we saw in Section 10.7. Let us examine these reactions in detail, using lauryl-CoA as an example.

The reactions of beta oxidation *Reaction 1* is a dehydrogenation. An enzyme removes hydrogen atoms from the two carbon atoms nearest to the carbonyl group in lauryl-CoA, creating a carbon–carbon double bond. Since the two hydrogen atoms are transferred to FAD, this is an energy-producing reaction.

$$CH_3-(CH_2)_8-\mathbf{CH_2}-\mathbf{CH_2}-\overset{O}{\overset{\|}{C}}-S-CoA + FAD \longrightarrow$$

Lauryl-CoA

$$CH_3-(CH_2)_8-\mathbf{CH}=\mathbf{CH}-\overset{O}{\overset{\|}{C}}-S-CoA + \mathbf{FADH_2}$$

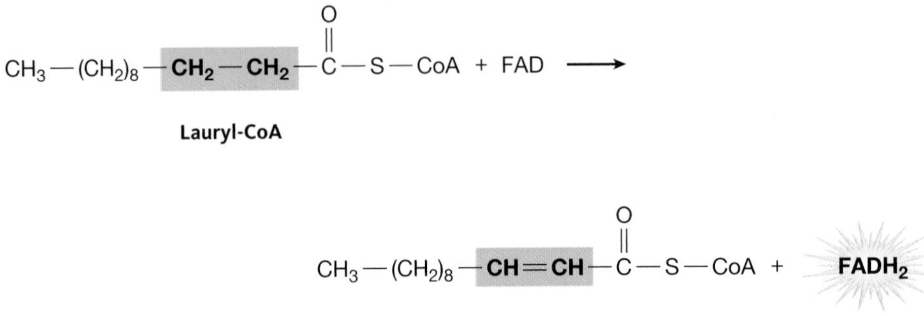

Reaction 2 is a hydration. The hydroxyl group is added to the carbon that is farther from the carbonyl group (the β-carbon). The purpose of this reaction is to add oxygen to the molecule and to allow further oxidation.

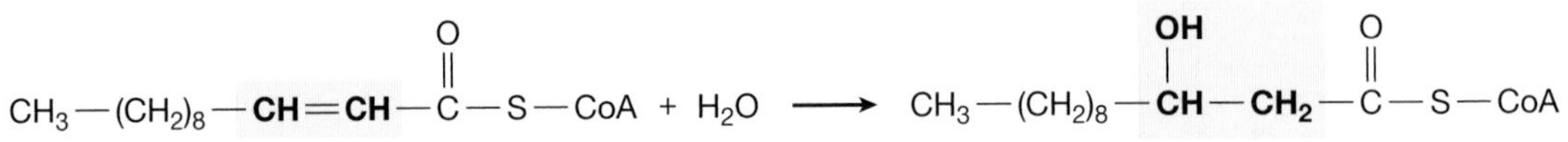

$$CH_3-(CH_2)_8-\mathbf{CH}=\mathbf{CH}-\overset{O}{\overset{\|}{C}}-S-CoA + H_2O \longrightarrow CH_3-(CH_2)_8-\overset{\mathbf{OH}}{\overset{|}{\mathbf{CH}}}-\mathbf{CH_2}-\overset{O}{\overset{\|}{C}}-S-CoA$$

Reaction 3 is the oxidation of the alcohol group. The two hydrogen atoms are transferred to NAD^+, so this is another energy-producing reaction.

$$CH_3-(CH_2)_8-\overset{\mathbf{OH}}{\overset{|}{\mathbf{CH}}}-CH_2-\overset{O}{\overset{\|}{C}}-S-CoA + NAD^+ \longrightarrow$$

$$CH_3-(CH_2)_8-\overset{\mathbf{O}}{\overset{\|}{\mathbf{C}}}-CH_2-\overset{O}{\overset{\|}{C}}-S-CoA + \mathbf{NADH} + H^+$$

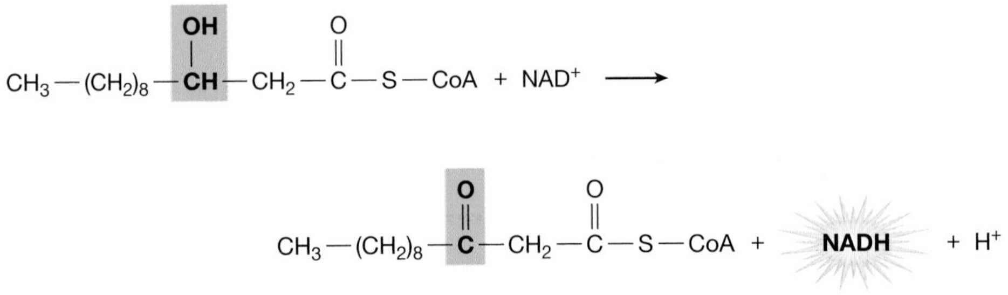

Reaction 4 breaks the carbon–carbon bond to the right of the ketone group, and it adds coenzyme A. This reaction completes a cycle of beta oxidation, producing acetyl-CoA and a new fatty acyl–CoA.

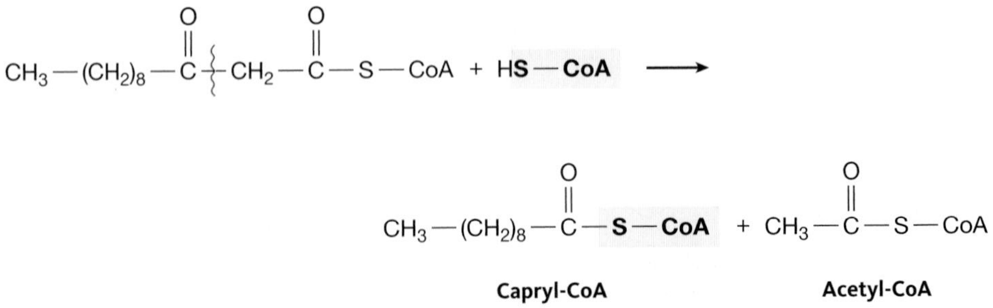

$$CH_3-(CH_2)_8-\overset{O}{\overset{\|}{C}}\wr CH_2-\overset{O}{\overset{\|}{C}}-S-CoA + H\mathbf{S}-\mathbf{CoA} \longrightarrow$$

$$CH_3-(CH_2)_8-\overset{O}{\overset{\|}{C}}-\mathbf{S}-\mathbf{CoA} + CH_3-\overset{O}{\overset{\|}{C}}-S-CoA$$

Capryl-CoA **Acetyl-CoA**

The results of one cycle of beta oxidation are a molecule of NADH, a molecule of $FADH_2$, a molecule of acetyl-CoA, and a new (shorter) fatty acyl–CoA, as shown in Figure 15.17.

Beta oxidation removes two carbon atoms from the original fatty acyl–CoA, leaving us with a shorter fatty acyl–CoA and a molecule of acetyl-CoA. The key to beta

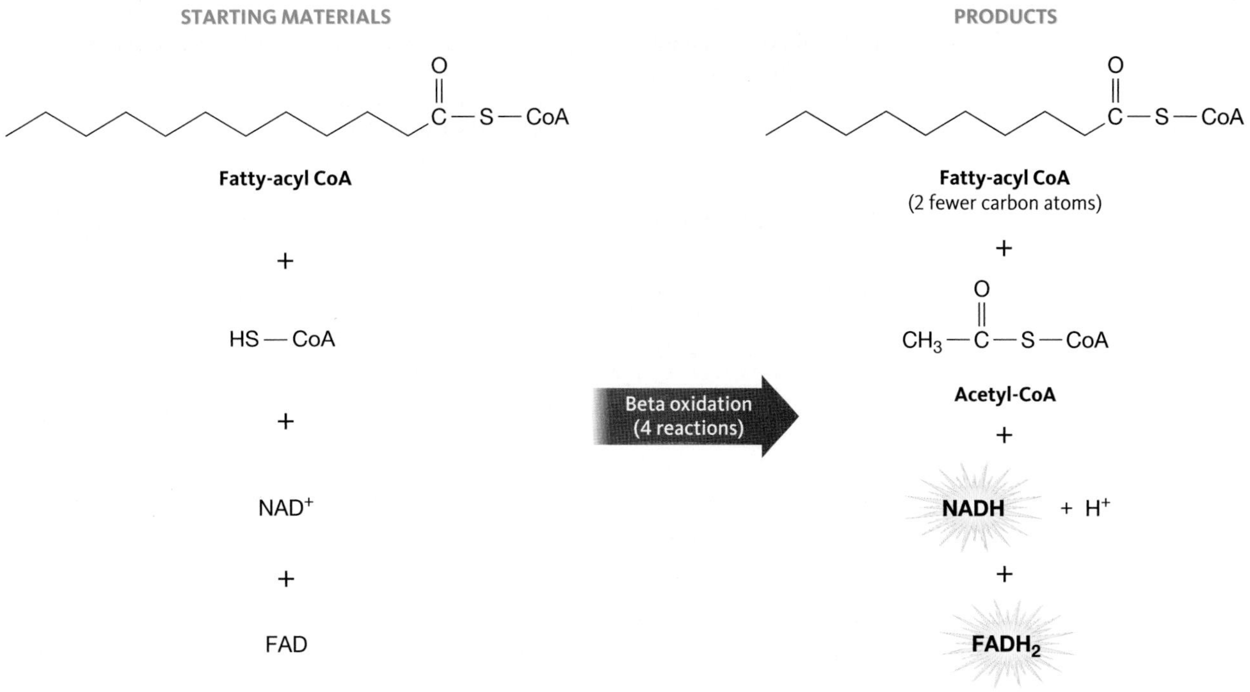

STARTING MATERIALS

Fatty-acyl CoA

+

HS — CoA

+

NAD⁺

+

FAD

Beta oxidation (4 reactions)

PRODUCTS

Fatty-acyl CoA
(2 fewer carbon atoms)

+

Acetyl-CoA

+

NADH + H^+

+

$FADH_2$

FIGURE 15.17 An overview of beta oxidation.

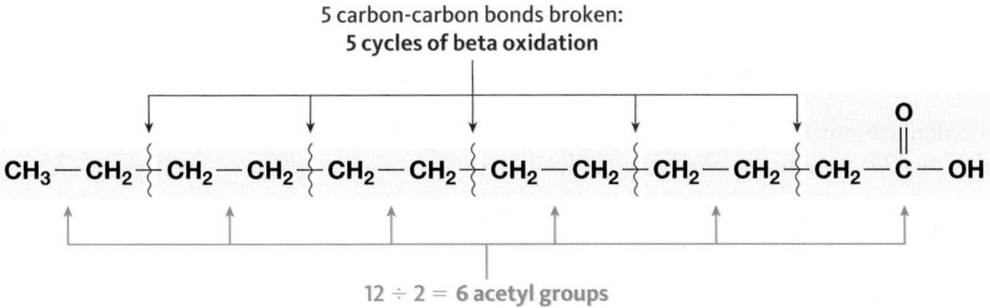

FIGURE 15.18 The breakdown of lauric acid into acetyl-CoA.

oxidation is that *we can use the new fatty acyl–CoA as the starting material for another cycle of beta oxidation.* If we repeat the cycle enough times, we will break down the entire fatty acid into acetyl-CoA. How many cycles of beta oxidation will this require? To answer this question, we simply count the number of bonds we must break in order to chop up the carbon skeleton into 2-carbon fragments. For example, lauric acid contains 12 carbon atoms. We must break five carbon–carbon bonds in order to chop a 12-carbon chain into 2-carbon fragments, so lauric acid requires five cycles of beta oxidation, as shown in Figure 15.18.

Sample Problem **15.7**

Calculating the number of beta oxidations for a fatty acid

How many cycles of beta oxidation are required to break down one molecule of palmitic acid, a saturated fatty acid that has the molecular formula $C_{16}H_{32}O_2$? How many molecules of acetyl-CoA will be formed?

SOLUTION

According to the molecular formula, palmitic acid contains a 16-carbon chain. We must break seven carbon–carbon bonds to chop this chain into 2-carbon fragments, so **seven**

continued

cycles of beta oxidation are required. This produces eight 2-carbon fragments, so we make **eight molecules of acetyl-CoA.**

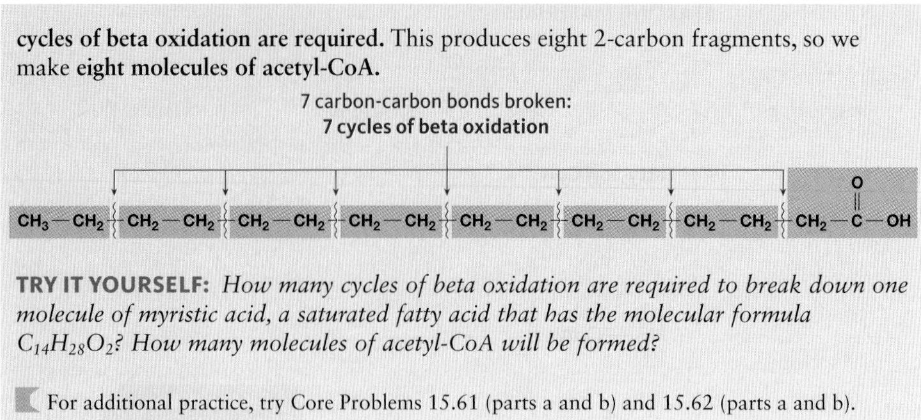

TRY IT YOURSELF: *How many cycles of beta oxidation are required to break down one molecule of myristic acid, a saturated fatty acid that has the molecular formula* $C_{14}H_{28}O_2$*? How many molecules of acetyl-CoA will be formed?*

For additional practice, try Core Problems 15.61 (parts a and b) and 15.62 (parts a and b).

We Can Calculate the ATP Yield from Any Saturated Fatty Acid

The end products of the beta oxidation of lauric acid are six molecules of acetyl-CoA. The enzymes of the citric acid cycle then break down the acetyl-CoA into CO_2. As we saw in Section 15.5, each turn of the citric acid cycle produces a molecule of ATP, three molecules of NADH, and a molecule of $FADH_2$. Using this information, we can calculate the total number of high-energy molecules that are formed and broken down when we oxidize a molecule of lauric acid, as shown in Table 15.5.

The mitochondria oxidize the NADH and $FADH_2$ and use the energy of these reactions to make more ATP. Remember that the mitochondria can make 2.5 molecules of ATP for each molecule of NADH, and they can make 1.5 molecules of ATP for each molecule of $FADH_2$.

$$23 \text{ NADH} \times 2.5 \text{ ATP per NADH} = 57.5 \text{ ATP}$$
$$11 \text{ FADH}_2 \times 1.5 \text{ ATP per FADH}_2 = 16.5 \text{ ATP}$$

To calculate our overall ATP yield, we must remember that we broke down two molecules of ATP to activate the fatty acid.

	6 ATP	(formed during the citric acid cycle)
+	57.5 ATP	(from the oxidation of NADH)
+	16.5 ATP	(from the oxidation of $FADH_2$)
−	2 ATP	(broken down at the beginning to activate the lauric acid)
	78 ATP	(overall yield)

Our bodies make 78 molecules of ATP when we oxidize one molecule of lauric acid.

TABLE 15.5 The Complete Oxidation of Lauric Acid, a Saturated Fatty Acid

Pathway	Function	High-Energy Molecules Formed or Consumed*	Number of Occurrences When Lauric Acid Is Oxidized	Total High-Energy Molecules Formed or Consumed*
Activation	Converts lauric acid into lauryl-CoA	2 ATP broken down	1	2 ATP broken down
Beta oxidation	Breaks down lauryl-CoA into 6 molecules of acetyl-CoA	1 NADH 1 $FADH_2$	5	5 NADH 5 $FADH_2$
Citric acid cycle	Oxidizes the acetyl group of acetyl-CoA into CO_2	1 ATP 3 NADH 1 $FADH_2$	6	6 ATP 18 NADH 6 $FADH_2$
Overall oxidation of lauric acid	**Oxidizes lauric acid into CO_2**			**2 ATP broken down** **6 ATP formed** **23 NADH** **11 $FADH_2$**

*Consumed molecules are in red.

Sample Problem 15.8

Calculating the ATP yield for a saturated fatty acid

What is the overall yield of ATP when one molecule of palmitic acid (a 16-carbon saturated fatty acid) is oxidized to CO_2 in our bodies?

SOLUTION

In Sample Problem 15.7, we found that palmitic acid undergoes seven cycles of beta oxidation, forming eight molecules of acetyl-CoA. Each cycle of beta oxidation produces one molecule of NADH and one molecule of $FADH_2$, so seven cycles produce seven molecules of NADH and seven molecules of $FADH_2$.

$$\text{beta oxidation: } 7\ \text{NADH} \quad + \quad 7\ \text{FADH}_2$$

Each molecule of acetyl-CoA is oxidized by the citric acid cycle, which produces one molecule of ATP, three molecules of NADH, and one molecule of $FADH_2$. We have eight molecules of acetyl-CoA, so we must multiply these numbers by eight.

$$\text{citric acid cycle: } 8\ \text{ATP} + 24\ \text{NADH} + 8\ \text{FADH}_2$$

Now we add up all of our energy molecules.

$$7 + 24 = 31\ \text{NADH}$$
$$7 + 8 = 15\ \text{FADH}_2$$
$$8\ \text{ATP}$$

Oxidative phosphorylation uses the energy stored in NADH and $FADH_2$ to make ATP.

$$31\ \text{NADH} \times 2.5\ \text{ATP per NADH} = 77.5\ \text{ATP}$$
$$15\ \text{FADH}_2 \times 1.5\ \text{ATP per FADH}_2 = 22.5\ \text{ATP}$$

Finally, we total up all of the ATP we made.

	8 ATP	(formed during the citric acid cycle)
+	77.5 ATP	(from the oxidation of NADH)
+	22.5 ATP	(from the oxidation of $FADH_2$)
−	2 ATP	(broken down at the beginning to activate the palmitic acid)
	106 ATP	(overall yield from one molecule of palmitic acid)

TRY IT YOURSELF: *What is the overall yield of ATP when one molecule of myristic acid (a 14-carbon saturated fatty acid) is oxidized to CO_2 in our bodies?*

For additional practice, try Core Problems 15.61 (part c) and 15.62 (part c).

So far, we have only considered saturated fatty acids. Unsaturated fatty acids undergo essentially the same sequence of reactions, but we form one fewer molecule of $FADH_2$ for each double bond in the hydrocarbon chain. This should seem reasonable, because the $FADH_2$ is formed in a dehydrogenation reaction. When the carbon chain already contains a double bond, this reaction is not needed. Sample Problem 15.9 shows how we can calculate the ATP yield for an unsaturated fatty acid.

Sample Problem 15.9

Calculating the ATP yield for an unsaturated fatty acid

In Sample Problem 15.8, we found that our bodies make 106 molecules of ATP when we oxidize a molecule of palmitic acid. How many molecules of ATP do we make when we oxidize a molecule of palmitoleic acid, which contains the same number of carbon atoms as palmitic acid but is a monounsaturated fatty acid?

continued

SOLUTION

Palmitoleic acid contains one carbon–carbon double bond. For each C=C bond in the chain, we make one fewer molecule of $FADH_2$, which is equivalent to 1.5 molecules of ATP. Therefore, we obtain $106 - 1.5 = 104.5$ molecules of ATP from one molecule of palmitoleic acid.

TRY IT YOURSELF: *Our bodies make 120 molecules of ATP when we oxidize a molecule of stearic acid, a saturated fatty acid that contains 18 carbon atoms. How many molecules of ATP do we make when we oxidize a molecule of linoleic acid, which contains 18 carbon atoms and has two carbon–carbon double bonds?*

For additional practice, try Core Problems 15.63 and 15.64.

Fatty Acids Produce Similar Amounts of ATP on a Mass Basis

We have seen that our bodies obtain 78 molecules of ATP from a molecule of lauric acid and 106 molecules of ATP from a molecule of palmitic acid. Does this mean that palmitic acid is a better source of energy? Not necessarily, because a molecule of palmitic acid also weighs more than a molecule of lauric acid. Let us compare the amounts of ATP that we obtain when we consume equal amounts of these two fatty acids. We can choose any amount we like, so we take 100 g of each.

We know that we make 78 molecules of ATP when we burn one molecule of lauric acid. Since molecule ratios are always equal to mole ratios, we make 78 mol of ATP when we burn 1 mol of lauric acid. The formula weight of lauric acid ($C_{12}H_{24}O_2$) is 200.3 g per mole. Therefore, *we make 78 mol of ATP when we break down 200.3 g (1 mol) of lauric acid.* We can use this relationship as a conversion factor to find the number of moles of ATP our bodies make from 100 g of lauric acid.

$$100 \text{ g } \cancel{\text{lauric acid}} \times \frac{78 \text{ mol ATP}}{200.3 \text{ g } \cancel{\text{lauric acid}}} = 38.9 \text{ mol ATP}$$

Now let us do the same calculation with palmitic acid, which has the molecular formula $C_{16}H_{32}O_2$ and a formula weight of 256.4 g/mol. One mole (256.4 g) of palmitic acid produces 106 mol of ATP. We can use this relationship as a conversion factor.

$$100 \text{ g } \cancel{\text{palmitic acid}} \times \frac{106 \text{ mol ATP}}{256.4 \text{ g } \cancel{\text{palmitic acid}}} = 41.3 \text{ mol ATP}$$

What do these numbers tell us? We are comparing the amount of ATP we get from equal masses of the two fatty acids. When we burn 100 g of lauric acid, we make 38.9 mol of ATP; when we burn 100 g of palmitic acid, we make 41.3 mol of ATP. These numbers are quite similar. In general, our bodies make about 40 moles of ATP when we burn 100 g of a fatty acid, regardless of the length of the chain.

Sample Problem 15.10

Calculating an ATP yield per 100 g of nutrient

Our bodies can use ethanol as a source of energy. We make 13 molecules of ATP when we oxidize one molecule of ethanol to CO_2. Calculate the number of moles of ATP that we make when we burn 100 g of ethanol.

SOLUTION

• This is another example of the unit conversion method you learned in Chapter 1.

The molecular formula of ethanol is C_2H_6O and its formula weight is 46.068 amu. Therefore, we make 13 mol of ATP when we burn 46.068 g (1 mol) of ethanol. Using this relationship, we can work out the ATP yield for 100 g of ethanol.

$$100 \text{ g } \cancel{\text{ethanol}} \times \frac{13 \text{ mol ATP}}{46.068 \text{ g } \cancel{\text{ethanol}}} = 28.2 \text{ mol ATP}$$

Our bodies make 28.2 mol of ATP when we burn 100 g of ethanol.

continued

TRY IT YOURSELF: *Our bodies make 18 molecules of ATP when we burn one molecule of glycerol ($C_3H_8O_3$). Calculate the number of moles of ATP that we make when we burn 100 g of glycerol.*

For additional practice, try Core Problems 15.61 (part d) and 15.62 (part d).

The ATP yield per 100 g of nutrient is useful when we compare two types of nutrients. For example, in Section 15.5 we found that our bodies make 32 molecules of ATP when we oxidize one molecule of glucose, and in Sample Problem 15.10 we saw that we make 13 molecules of ATP when we oxidize a molecule of ethanol. Again, this does not mean that glucose is a better energy source than ethanol, because a molecule of glucose is also much heavier than a molecule of ethanol. To compare these two nutrients, we need to calculate the ATP yield per 100 g of glucose. The molecular formula of glucose is $C_6H_{12}O_6$ and its formula weight is 180.156 amu, so 1 mol of glucose weighs 180.156 g.

$$100 \text{ g glucose} \times \frac{32 \text{ mol ATP}}{180.156 \text{ g glucose}} = 17.8 \text{ mol ATP}$$

In Sample Problem 15.10, we calculated that our bodies make 28.2 mol of ATP when we oxidize 100 g of ethanol. Therefore, we obtain substantially more energy from ethanol than we do from an equal weight of glucose.

Health Note: Because ethanol is a good source of energy, alcoholic beverages have a high Calorie content. However, they contain few other nutrients, so chronic alcoholics frequently suffer from a variety of dietary deficiencies. In addition, excessive consumption of ethanol damages the liver and produces many other health effects.

CORE PROBLEMS

15.55 Stearic acid has the chemical formula $C_{18}H_{36}O_2$. Write a balanced equation showing how stearic acid can be broken down into CO_2 and hydrogen atoms. Use [H] to represent hydrogen atoms that are removed by NAD^+ and FAD.

15.56 Palmitoleic acid has the chemical formula $C_{16}H_{30}O_2$. Write a balanced equation showing how palmitoleic acid can be broken down into CO_2 and hydrogen atoms. Use [H] to represent hydrogen atoms that are removed by NAD^+ and FAD.

15.57 What reaction must occur before any fatty acid can be oxidized?

15.58 How many molecules of ATP must be broken down to activate a fatty acid molecule?

15.59 Write chemical equations for the reactions in one cycle of beta oxidation, starting with the fatty acyl–CoA shown here:

$$CH_3{-}(CH_2)_{10}{-}CH_2{-}CH_2{-}\overset{\overset{\displaystyle O}{\|}}{C}{-}S{-}CoA$$

15.60 Write chemical equations for the reactions in one cycle of beta oxidation, starting with the fatty acyl–CoA shown here:

$$CH_3{-}(CH_2)_7{-}CH{=}CH{-}(CH_2)_5{-}CH_2{-}CH_2{-}\overset{\overset{\displaystyle O}{\|}}{C}{-}S{-}CoA$$

15.61 a) How many cycles of beta oxidation are required to break down one molecule of stearic acid?
b) How many molecules of acetyl-CoA will be formed when one molecule of stearic acid is broken down?
c) What is the overall ATP yield when one molecule of stearic acid is broken down to CO_2?
d) Calculate the number of moles of ATP your body will form when it burns 100 g of stearic acid. The molecular formula of stearic acid is $C_{18}H_{36}O_2$.

15.62 a) How many cycles of beta oxidation are required to break down one molecule of myristic acid?
b) How many molecules of acetyl-CoA will be formed when one molecule of myristic acid is broken down?
c) What is the overall ATP yield when one molecule of myristic acid is broken down to CO_2?
d) Calculate the number of moles of ATP your body will form when it burns 100 g of myristic acid. The molecular formula of myristic acid is $C_{14}H_{28}O_2$.

15.63 Linolenic acid contains the same number of carbon atoms as stearic acid (18), but it contains three double bonds. How many molecules of ATP can our bodies form when we oxidize one molecule of linolenic acid?

15.64 Myristoleic acid contains the same number of carbon atoms as myristic acid (14), but it contains one double bond. How many molecules of ATP can our bodies form when we oxidize one molecule of myristoleic acid?

15.7 Catabolism of Amino Acids

OBJECTIVES: *Describe how our bodies remove and excrete nitrogen from amino acids, and explain how amino acid catabolism is related to other catabolic pathways.*

Our bodies prefer to burn carbohydrates and fats to obtain energy, but some cells can also burn amino acids. Amino acids are a particularly important energy source during a fast, since they can be converted into glucose for the brain, while fatty acids cannot. In this section, we will examine how our bodies use amino acids as a source of energy.

Transamination and Oxidative Deamination Remove the Amino Group from Many Amino Acids

The most conspicuous difference between amino acids and the other fuels we have considered is that amino acids contain nitrogen. Our bodies cannot oxidize nitrogen-containing compounds, so we must remove the nitrogen atoms before we can use amino acids as an energy source. The primary reactions that remove nitrogen from amino acids are transamination and oxidative deamination. In a transamination reaction, the amino group is simply moved to a different organic molecule, while oxidative deamination converts the amino group into an ammonium ion.

The general scheme for a **transamination reaction** is shown in Figure 15.19. The reactants are an amino acid and an α-keto acid (a carboxylic acid that also has a ketone group on carbon 2). Although in principle any α-keto acid will work, in practice our bodies normally use α-ketoglutaric acid, which is one of the intermediates in the citric acid cycle (see Figure 15.16). The reaction interchanges the ketone group and the amino group, producing a new α-keto acid and glutamate ion (the physiological form of glutamic acid, one of the 20 amino acids). Of the 20 amino acids, 12 undergo at least one transamination reaction.

Health Note: In addition to its role as one of the building blocks of proteins, glutamate ion is one of the two principal chemicals responsible for transmitting pain impulses from one nerve cell to the next. In particular, glutamate makes the nerve cells more sensitive after an initial painful stimulus. As a result, even a light touch on an injured site may feel painful, helping prevent further injury.

Although at first glance this reaction does not seem very productive, since it simply exchanges one amino acid for another, it reduces the number of amino-containing compounds that our bodies must deal with. Instead of needing to remove the amino group from many different molecules, we need only remove the amino group from glutamate. This reduces the number of enzymes that our bodies must make.

Sample Problem 15.11

Drawing the product of a transamination reaction

When our bodies break down the amino acid tyrosine, the first reaction is a transamination. Draw the structure of the product that is formed when tyrosine undergoes transamination. (The structure of tyrosine is shown in Table 13.1.)

SOLUTION

Transamination replaces the amino group of tyrosine with a ketone group:

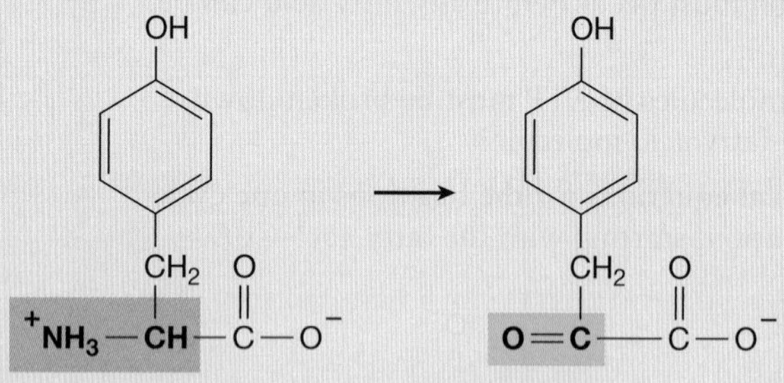

OH–C₆H₄–CH₂ on $^{+}NH_3$—CH—C(=O)—O^- → OH–C₆H₄–CH₂ on O=C—C(=O)—O^-

Tyrosine → The product: an α-keto acid

TRY IT YOURSELF: *The first step in the breakdown of leucine is also a transamination. Draw the structure of the product that is formed when leucine undergoes transamination. (The structure of leucine is shown in Table 13.1.)*

For additional practice, try Core Problems 15.67 and 15.68.

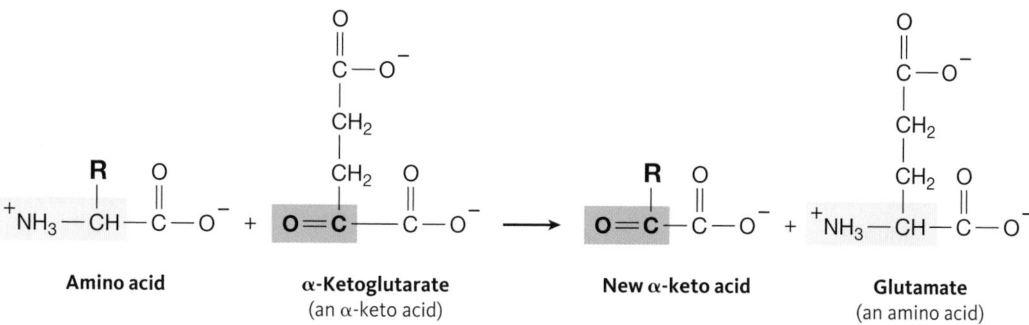

FIGURE 15.19 The transamination reaction.

The amino group of glutamate is not transferred to yet another molecule. Instead, our bodies remove the amino group in an **oxidative deamination reaction**, which replaces the amino group with a ketone group. This reaction regenerates the α-ketoglutarate we used in the transamination step. The oxygen for the ketone group comes from a water molecule, and the two hydrogen atoms from the water molecule are removed by NAD^+.

$$\underset{\text{Glutamate}}{{}^{+}NH_3-CH(CH_2CH_2COO^-)-COO^-} + H_2O + NAD^+ \longrightarrow \underset{\alpha\text{-Ketoglutarate}}{O=C(CH_2CH_2COO^-)-COO^-} + NH_4^+ + \mathbf{NADH}$$

Since the α-ketoglutarate is regenerated, the net effect of transamination and oxidative deamination is to replace the amino group of our original amino acid with a ketone group. The other products are ammonium ion and NADH.

Our bodies deal with the amino group of the other eight amino acids, as well as the side-chain nitrogen atoms of histidine, arginine, lysine, glutamine, and asparagine, using reactions that do not involve transamination. The specific reactions can be quite complex, and we will not examine them in this book. However, all of these pathways have one feature in common: they convert the nitrogen atoms into NH_4^+ ions. Since the transamination–oxidative deamination sequence also produces NH_4^+, we can make a general statement about nitrogen metabolism: *When our bodies break down amino acids, we convert virtually all of the nitrogen atoms into ammonium ions.*

The Urea Cycle Consumes ATP to Convert Ammonium Ions into Urea

Ammonium ions are very toxic, so our bodies must not allow them to reach significant concentrations in our body fluids. We can recycle ammonium ions to supply the nitrogen for building new amino acids, but we normally make more ammonium ions than we can use. Therefore, we must remove NH_4^+ ions by excreting them. Aquatic animals can excrete ammonium ions continuously into the surrounding water, but humans and other terrestrial animals store their waste products for a while before excreting, so we must convert the ammonium ions into a less toxic substitute. Humans (and all other mammals) combine ammonium ions with bicarbonate ions to

Fish excrete ammonium ions into their surroundings, where they are consumed by bacteria before they reach toxic levels.

TABLE 15.6 Fuel Sources for Selected Organs and Tissues

Organ	Fuels (In Approximate Order of Importance)
Liver	Fatty acids, amino acids, glucose
Kidney	Fatty acids, glucose, amino acids
Muscle	Fatty acids, glucose (resting) Glucose, fatty acids (working)
Adipose tissue (fat)	Glucose, fatty acids
Brain	Glucose

make urea, using a sequence of reactions called the **urea cycle**. The overall reaction of the urea cycle is

$$2\ NH_4^+ + HCO_3^- \longrightarrow H_2N{-}\overset{\overset{\displaystyle O}{\|}}{C}{-}NH_2 + 2\ H_2O + H^+$$

Urea

Health Note: The concentration of urea in blood (blood urea nitrogen, or BUN) can help in diagnosis of kidney failure. The kidneys normally remove urea from the blood efficiently, keeping the blood concentration between 7 and 20 mg/dL. Kidney damage would be suspected if the urea concentration rose above this level.

The urea cycle takes place in the liver, the organ that is generally responsible for dealing with toxic substances. The liver absorbs ammonium ions from the blood, converts them into urea, and releases the urea into the bloodstream, which carries it to the kidneys for disposal.

The urea cycle requires a substantial amount of energy, which must be supplied by ATP. Our bodies must break down four molecules of ATP for every molecule of urea we make. Since we make urea from two ammonium ions, *the urea cycle consumes two molecules of ATP to dispose of one ammonium ion.* This is the price our bodies pay for safely disposing of the nitrogen atoms from amino acids.

The Remainder of Any Amino Acid Can Be Burned to Produce Energy

Once our bodies have removed the nitrogen atoms from the amino acids, we can burn the remaining organic compounds to obtain energy. Each amino acid has its own pathway, but all of these merge with the main carbohydrate pathway. For example, when alanine is transaminated, the product is pyruvic acid, the end product of glycolysis. Thus, only one reaction in the catabolism of alanine is unique to alanine. All subsequent reactions are part of the carbohydrate pathway.

$$\overset{+}{N}H_3{-}\overset{\overset{\displaystyle CH_3}{|}}{CH}{-}\overset{\overset{\displaystyle O}{\|}}{C}{-}O^- \xrightarrow{\text{transamination}} O{=}\overset{\overset{\displaystyle CH_3}{|}}{C}{-}\overset{\overset{\displaystyle O}{\|}}{C}{-}O^- \longrightarrow \text{Acetyl-CoA} \xrightarrow{\text{citric acid cycle}} CO_2$$

Alanine **Pyruvate** **Part of the carbohydrate pathway**

Health Note: Amino acids that can be converted either to pyruvate or to oxaloacetate are called *glucogenic,* because the body can use pyruvate and oxaloacetate to make glucose. Of the 20 common amino acids, 18 are glucogenic. When the body is deprived of food for prolonged periods, glucose derived from glucogenic amino acids becomes an important energy source for the brain, which cannot use either fatty acids or amino acids directly.

In our bodies, only the liver and the kidneys make the enzymes needed to obtain energy directly from amino acids. However, amino acids can serve indirectly as an energy source for other body tissues, because the liver can convert the carbon skeletons of most of the amino acids into glucose. The liver then releases the glucose into the blood, which transports it to other tissues for use as a fuel. Table 15.6 shows the fuel sources for some major organs and tissues in the human body.

In Sections 15.5 and 15.6, we calculated the ATP yields for glucose and fatty acids. We can also calculate ATP yields for amino acids if we know the specific reactions involved in their catabolic pathways. However, each amino acid has a unique catabolic pathway, and some of these pathways are very complex. You do not need to learn specific pathways for amino acids, but you should be able to calculate ATP yields if you are given the number of high-energy molecules and intermediates of carbohydrate metabolism such as acetyl-CoA and pyruvate.

Sample Problem 15.12

Calculating the ATP yield for an amino acid

When our bodies oxidize the amino acid lysine to produce energy, we form one molecule of $FADH_2$, five molecules of NADH, two NH_4^+ ions, and two molecules of acetyl-CoA. The acetyl-CoA is then oxidized by the citric acid cycle. Calculate the total ATP yield from one molecule of lysine.

SOLUTION

In Section 15.4, we saw that the citric acid cycle produces one ATP, three NADH, and one $FADH_2$ when it oxidizes a molecule of acetyl-CoA. The pathway for lysine makes two molecules of acetyl-CoA, so we must double these numbers: we get two ATP, six NADH, and two $FADH_2$ from the citric acid cycle. Now we need to add up the total numbers of NADH and $FADH_2$.

	6 NADH	(from the citric acid cycle)
+	5 NADH	(from the initial breakdown of lysine)
	11 NADH	(total)

	2 $FADH_2$	(from the citric acid cycle)
+	1 $FADH_2$	(from the initial breakdown of lysine)
	3 $FADH_2$	(total)

The mitochondria oxidize the NADH and $FADH_2$, making additional ATP.

$$11 \text{ NADH} \times 2.5 \text{ ATP per NADH} = 27.5 \text{ ATP}$$
$$3 \text{ FADH}_2 \times 1.5 \text{ ATP per FADH}_2 = 4.5 \text{ ATP}$$

Our bodies must also break down some ATP to convert the NH_4^+ ions into urea. As we saw on page 666, we break down two molecules of ATP for each ammonium ion.

$$2 \text{ NH}_4^+ \times 2 \text{ ATP per NH}_4^+ = 4 \text{ ATP broken down in the urea cycle}$$

The overall yield is

	2 ATP	(from the initial breakdown of lysine)
+	27.5 ATP	(from the oxidation of NADH)
+	4.5 ATP	(from the oxidation of $FADH_2$)
−	4 ATP	(broken down in the urea cycle)
	30 ATP	(overall yield from one molecule of lysine)

TRY IT YOURSELF: *When our bodies burn the amino acid leucine to produce energy, we form two molecules of $FADH_2$, five molecules of NADH, two molecules of acetyl-CoA, and one ammonium ion, and we must break down one molecule of ATP. We then oxidize the acetyl-CoA in the citric acid cycle. Calculate the total ATP yield from one molecule of leucine.*

For additional practice, try Core Problems 15.73 and 15.74.

It is interesting to compare the ATP yields for amino acids to those from carbohydrates and fats. Table 15.7 shows the ATP yields for all 20 amino acids, and Table 15.8 shows ATP yields from several other types of nutrients. The ATP yields are shown in two ways: the number of molecules of ATP per each molecule of fuel and the number of moles of ATP per 100 g of fuel. ATP yields for amino acids range from 9.6 to 29.6 mol of ATP per 100 g of protein, but the average ATP yield for all amino acids is 17.9 mol of ATP per 100 g of protein. This is similar to the ATP yield for typical carbohydrates, and it is less than half of the values for fatty acids and triglycerides. Again, we see that gram for gram, fats are our most efficient source of energy.

We have now completed our look at catabolism in humans. Figure 15.20 summarizes the catabolic pathways we have encountered.

TABLE 15.7 ATP Yields for Amino Acids

Amino Acid	ATP Yield Per Molecule	Moles of ATP Per 100 g of Protein*	Amino Acid	ATP Yield Per Molecule	Moles of ATP Per 100 g of Protein*
Alanine	13	18.3	Leucine	32.5	28.8
Arginine	23.5	15.0	Lysine	30	23.4
Asparagine	11	9.6	Methionine	21.5	16.4
Aspartic acid	13	11.3	Phenylalanine	32	21.8
Cysteine	10.5	10.2	Proline	23	23.7
Glutamic acid	20.5	15.9	Serine	10.5	12.1
Glutamine	18.5	14.5	Threonine	18	17.8
Glycine	5.5	9.6	Tryptophan	35	18.8
Histidine	19	13.9	Tyrosine	34.5	21.2
Isoleucine	33.5	29.6	Valine	26	26.2

*Humans normally obtain all of their dietary amino acids in the form of proteins. Since amino acids lose water when they combine to form a protein, we must subtract 18.02 (the formula weight of water) from the formula weight of the amino acid when we calculate the ATP yield per 100 g of protein. For example, the formula weight of alanine is 89.10 amu, but the effective formula weight of alanine in a protein is 89.10 − 18.02 = 71.08 amu.

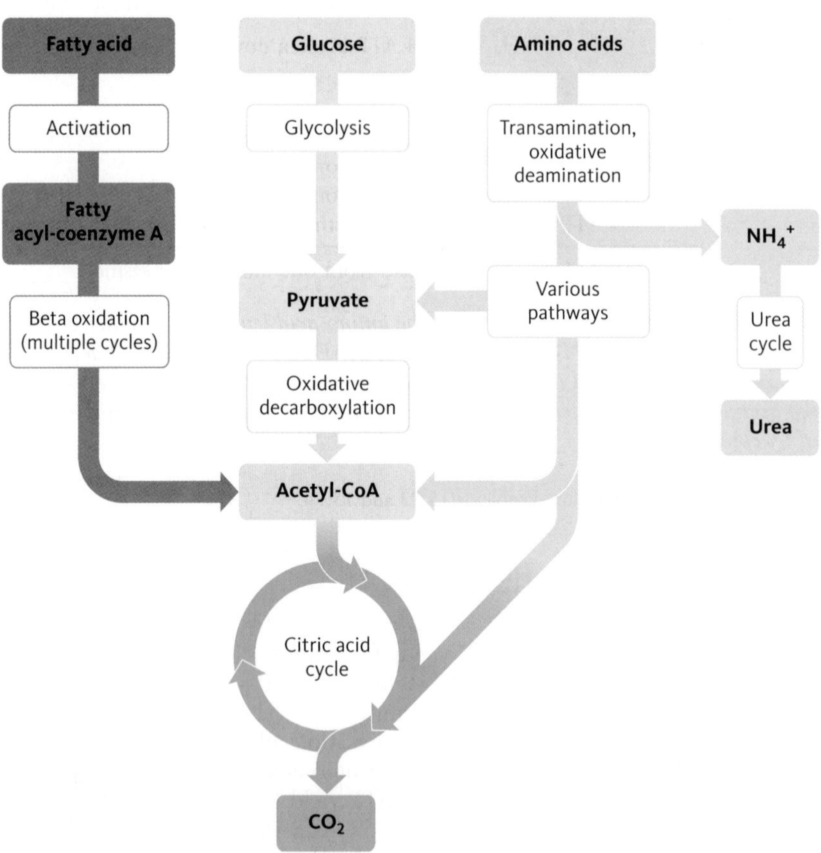

FIGURE 15.20 A summary of catabolic pathways in humans.

TABLE 15.8 ATP Yields for Several Common Nutrients

Fuel Molecule	Type of Nutrient	ATP Yield Per Molecule	Moles of ATP Per 100 g
Glucose and fructose	Carbohydrate	32	17.8
Sucrose and lactose		64	18.7
Starch and glycogen		Depends on the size of the molecule	19.8
Glycerol		18	19.6
Lauric acid (a 12-carbon saturated fatty acid)	Fatty acid	78	39.0
Stearic acid (an 18-carbon saturated fatty acid)		122	43.0
Trilaurin (a saturated fat made from three molecules of lauric acid)	Triglyceride	252	39.4
Tristearin (a saturated fat made from three molecules of stearic acid)		384	43.1

CORE PROBLEMS

15.65 What is a transamination reaction?

15.66 What is an oxidative deamination reaction?

15.67 The first reaction in the breakdown of the amino acid isoleucine is a transamination. Draw the structure of the product that is formed when isoleucine is transaminated. (The structure of isoleucine is shown in Table 13.1.)

15.68 The first reaction in the breakdown of the amino acid valine is a transamination. Draw the structure of the product that is formed when valine is transaminated. (The structure of valine is shown in Table 13.1.)

15.69 Most nitrogen atoms are removed from amino acids in the form of a specific ion. What is that ion?

15.70 Humans excrete nitrogen atoms by incorporating them into a specific compound. What is that compound?

15.71 How many molecules of ATP must your body break down to dispose of one ammonium ion?

15.72 How many molecules of ATP must your body break down to build one molecule of urea?

15.73 When your body breaks down a molecule of proline, it produces eight molecules of NADH, two molecules of $FADH_2$, two molecules of ATP, five molecules of CO_2, and one NH_4^+ ion. Calculate the overall yield of ATP from the breakdown of a molecule of proline. Be sure to consider the urea cycle.

15.74 When your body breaks down a molecule of asparagine, it produces five molecules of NADH, one molecule of $FADH_2$, one molecule of ATP, two NH_4^+ ions, and four molecules of CO_2. Calculate the overall ATP yield from one molecule of asparagine. Be sure to consider the urea cycle.

15.8 Anabolic Pathways and the Control of Metabolism

OBJECTIVES: *Describe the main anabolic pathways and how they are related to catabolic pathways, explain the role of activated molecules in anabolism, and describe how our bodies regulate anabolism and catabolism to avoid futile cycles.*

So far, we have devoted all of our attention to catabolic processes. However, catabolism is only half of the story, because cells must build molecules as well as break them down. In this section, we will take a brief look at anabolism, and we will examine the ways in which organisms control their metabolic pathways.

Anabolism can be divided into two parts: making the building blocks (monosaccharides, fatty acids, and amino acids) and putting these together to form macromolecules

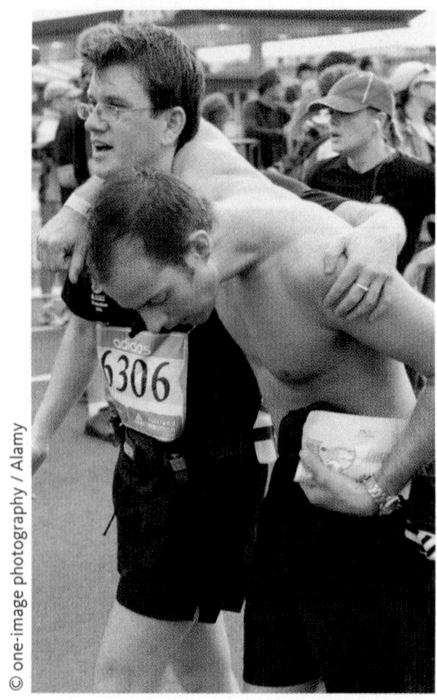

After a race, this runner relies on gluconeogenesis to convert excess lactic acid in his muscles back into glucose.

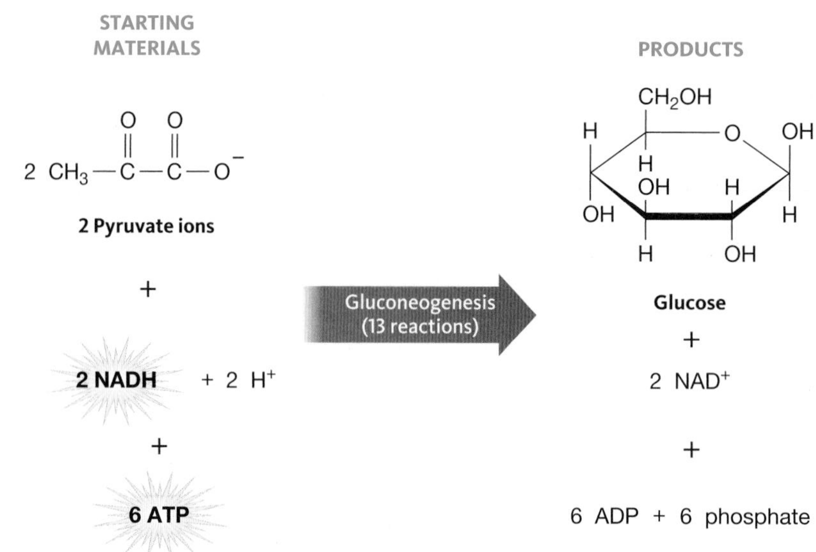

FIGURE 15.21 An overview of gluconeogenesis.

Health Note: Metformin (trade name Glucophage) is a drug that interferes with gluconeogenesis, reducing the amount of glucose that the liver makes. It also increases the amount of glucose that is absorbed by other cells by increasing their sensitivity to insulin. As a result, metformin is widely used to treat Type 2 diabetes, which occurs when muscle and fat cells do not respond adequately to insulin.

$$CH_3-N(CH_3)-C(=NH)-NH-C(=NH)-NH_2$$

Metformin

Health Note: Many Americans eat more food than they need. Their bodies convert excess carbohydrate and protein into fatty acids, which are stored in adipose tissues (fat deposits).

(polysaccharides, fats, and proteins). Our bodies can build all of the macromolecules we need, but we cannot make all of the building blocks. As we have seen in earlier chapters, we need a dietary source of polyunsaturated fatty acids and roughly half of the amino acids, so we rely on other organisms to make these molecules for us. Let us examine how we synthesize the other building blocks.

Gluconeogenesis Is the Formation of Glucose from Pyruvate

Our bodies can build glucose from a variety of substances, including lactate and 18 of the 20 amino acids, but not from fatty acids. Only our liver makes the needed enzymes, so lactate and amino acids must be brought to the liver by our blood. The liver converts most of these molecules into pyruvate, the end product of glycolysis. It then carries out a sequence of 13 reactions, called **gluconeogenesis**, that converts two pyruvate ions into a molecule of glucose. This pathway consumes energy in the form of six molecules of ATP and two molecules of NADH. Figure 15.21 shows a summary of gluconeogenesis.

Recall that we make two molecules of ATP (and two molecules of NADH) when our bodies break down glucose into pyruvate. Therefore, we break down more ATP in gluconeogenesis than we make in glycolysis. In general, *anabolic pathways consume more ATP than is made in the corresponding catabolic pathway.* Because gluconeogenesis consumes more energy than glycolysis returns, our bodies build glucose only under certain conditions:

- *To replenish the glycogen stored in the liver.* The liver can store enough glycogen to supply our energy needs for up to a day. Between meals, the liver is constantly breaking glycogen down to make glucose, which it releases into the blood to supply the needs of other tissues (particularly the brain, which can only use glucose as a fuel). After a meal, the liver converts excess amino acids into glucose, which it uses to help rebuild its glycogen stores.
- *To eliminate lactate from the blood during heavy exercise.* As we saw in Section 15.4, working muscles break down glucose into lactate. The liver rebuilds lactate into glucose and returns it to the blood to fuel additional muscular effort.
- *To maintain blood glucose levels during a prolonged fast.* The brain normally obtains all of its energy from glucose, which it continuously extracts from the blood. As a result, the blood glucose concentration must be maintained at or above 80 mg/dL. The liver normally breaks down its own glycogen to make the needed glucose, but it builds glucose from other compounds when its glycogen stores are exhausted.

Building Other Biomolecules Requires ATP

Our bodies build fatty acids from acetyl-CoA, using a sequence of reactions that is similar to the beta oxidation pathway for the breakdown of fatty acids. However, as was the case with glucose, it takes more energy to build a fatty acid than we get from breaking the same fatty acid down to acetyl-CoA. For example, it takes roughly 44 molecules of ATP to make one molecule of palmitic acid from acetyl-CoA, but the breakdown of palmitic acid into acetyl-CoA produces only 26 molecules of ATP. As a result, our bodies build fatty acids only when we eat more food than we need to supply our energy requirements.

The synthesis of amino acids plays a minor role in human metabolism, because a diet that contains enough of the essential amino acids normally contains sufficient amounts of the nonessential amino acids as well. Amino acid anabolism occurs primarily in plants and microorganisms. However, it is worth noting that it takes more energy to make an amino acid than we get by breaking it down. For example, a plant requires the energy equivalent of around 23 molecules of ATP to build a molecule of alanine from CO_2 and NH_4^+, but the same molecule of alanine produces only 15 molecules of ATP when we break it down into CO_2 and NH_4^+.

• Because we must convert the ammonium ion into urea, our bodies obtain only 13 molecules of ATP per molecule of alanine.

Building a protein, polysaccharide, or triglyceride from its components also requires energy in the form of ATP. As a rule, the building blocks (amino acids, monosaccharides, fatty acids, and glycerol) must be activated before they can be put together, and as we have seen, activation reactions require energy. However, we get none of this energy back in the form of ATP when we break down the protein, polysaccharide, or fat into its building blocks. This is quite different from the synthesis of glucose, fatty acids, or amino acids, all of which can be broken down to make ATP.

Our Bodies Activate the Building Blocks of Large Biomolecules

The triglycerides are a good example of how our bodies use activated molecules. We cannot make a triglyceride directly from glycerol and fatty acids. Instead, we convert glycerol into glycerol-1-phosphate in a reaction that consumes 2.2 kcal of energy for each mole of glycerol. A molecule of ATP supplies the energy for this reaction.

$$\begin{matrix} CH_2-OH \\ | \\ CH-OH \\ | \\ CH_2-OH \end{matrix} + \textbf{ATP} \longrightarrow \begin{matrix} CH_2-OH & & \\ | & & \\ CH-OH & & O \\ | & & \| \\ CH_2 & -O- & P-O^- \\ & & | \\ & & OH \end{matrix} + ADP$$

Glycerol **Glycerol-1-phosphate**

We activate fatty acids by converting them into fatty acyl–CoA, just as we do when we break them down to obtain energy. As we saw in Section 15.6, this reaction requires the breakdown of two molecules of ATP per fatty acid. Since a triglyceride contains three fatty acids in addition to the glycerol, it takes a total of seven molecules of ATP to make one molecule of triglyceride: six to activate the fatty acids and one to activate the glycerol.

Polysaccharides and polypeptides require ATP as well. For every molecule of glucose that is added to a polysaccharide, our bodies must break down two molecules of ATP. Protein synthesis is even more expensive, requiring four molecules of ATP for each amino acid that we add to the polypeptide. Protein synthesis also requires energy to make compounds called nucleic acids, which control the order of the amino acids in the protein. We will examine protein synthesis in detail in Chapter 16.

Sample Problem 15.13

Calculating the amount of ATP in an anabolic process

How many molecules of ATP must a plant break down when it adds 200 additional molecules of glucose to a molecule of starch?

SOLUTION

Since it takes two molecules of ATP for each molecule of glucose that is added to a polysaccharide, a plant needs to break down $200 \times 2 = 400$ molecules of ATP.

TRY IT YOURSELF: *How many molecules of ATP are needed to add 200 amino acids to a polypeptide?*

For additional practice, try Core Problems 15.81 and 15.82.

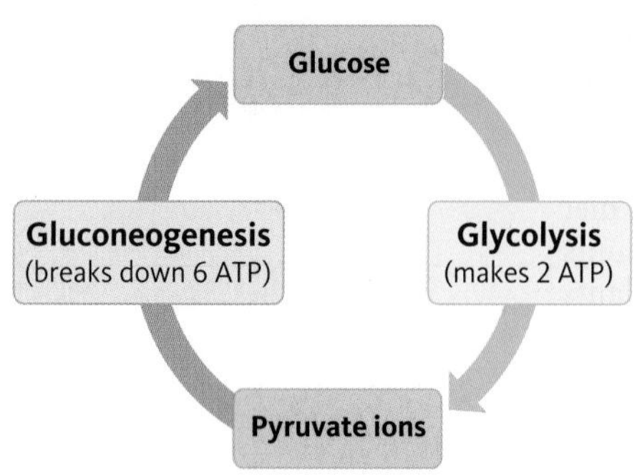

FIGURE 15.22 A futile cycle.

Health Note: Another way your body can produce extra heat is by shivering. In shivering, your muscles alternately contract and relax. With each contraction, muscle cells break down glucose and fatty acids to make ATP and then hydrolyze the ATP, producing energy in the form of heat.

Cells Must Control the Rates of Anabolic and Catabolic Pathways

Some cells, particularly liver cells, are able to both make and break down a range of molecules. If they do both at the same time, they carry out a **futile cycle**, which accomplishes nothing but the breakdown of ATP. Figure 15.22 illustrates a futile cycle involving glycolysis and gluconeogenesis.

Breaking down ATP releases energy, so futile cycles can be used to produce heat. However, in general, cells that can carry out both a catabolic and an anabolic pathway do not do so simultaneously. These cells prevent futile cycles by using *different enzymes* for the two pathways and by carrying out the pathways in *different locations* in the cell.

For example, cells in your liver are able to carry out both glycolysis and gluconeogenesis. These two pathways are quite similar and involve many of the same reactions and enzymes. However, the cells avoid a futile cycle by using different enzymes for certain key reactions. For example, the third reaction of glycolysis converts fructose-6-phosphate into fructose-1,6-*bis*phosphate. This reaction is catalyzed by an enzyme called phosphofructokinase (PFK).

$$\text{fructose-6-phosphate} + \text{ATP} \xrightarrow{\text{PFK}} \text{fructose-1,6-}bis\text{phosphate} + \text{ADP}$$

PFK is most active when the concentration of citrate ions is low and the concentration of adenosine monophosphate (AMP) is high. Citrate and AMP are effectors, controlling the rate at which PFK catalyzes its reaction.

In gluconeogenesis, fructose-1,6-*bis*phosphate must be converted back into fructose-6-phosphate. This reaction, though, does not involve ATP or ADP, and it is catalyzed by an entirely different enzyme called fructose-1,6-*bis*phosphatase (FBP). FBP uses the same effectors as PFK, but FBP is most active when the concentration of citrate ions is high and the concentration of AMP is low.

$$\text{fructose-1,6-}bis\text{phosphate} + H_2O \xrightarrow{\text{FBP}} \text{fructose-6-phosphate} + \text{phosphate}$$

Note that both citrate and AMP affect these two enzymes in opposite ways: each stimulates one enzyme while inhibiting the other. As a result, only one of the two enzymes is normally active at any given instant, preventing a futile cycle. The effects of citrate and AMP on these enzymes are shown in Figure 15.23.

The building and breaking down of fatty acids illustrates a different strategy for avoiding futile cycles. Cells in your liver and adipose tissues can carry out both pathways, but the two pathways do not occur in the same location. Cells break down fatty acids in the mitochondria, but they build fatty acids in the cytosol. The acetyl-CoA that is formed during beta oxidation cannot pass through the mitochondrial membrane, so the cell cannot use it to build new fatty acids. However, citrate can pass through the membrane via a specific transport protein, and the cytosol contains an enzyme that breaks down citrate into acetyl-CoA and oxaloacetic acid. When the cell contains more fuel than it needs, it diverts some of the citrate from the citric acid cycle, moving it out of the mitochondrion and using it as the source of acetyl-CoA for fatty acid synthesis. This process is illustrated in Figure 15.24.

Our bodies can control the rate of every metabolic pathway. If they could not, enzymes would run unchecked, breaking down critical building blocks and making others when they are not needed. Over the span of a billion years, evolution has produced a marvelously intricate array of control mechanisms. There are four general ways in which cells regulate metabolic pathways:

- *During cell development.* Although each cell carries the genetic instructions to build the enzymes for every metabolic pathway, many cells never make the enzymes for a particular pathway. The capability of each type of cell to make enzymes appears to be determined early during embryonic development.
- *During protein synthesis.* Most cells make some of their enzymes only when particular compounds are present (or absent). For example, liver cells only make the enzymes needed to break down amino acids when excess dietary protein is available.
- *Using hormones as messengers.* Some enzymes are normally inactive, but they become activated when the cell binds to a hormone. The hormone triggers a sequence of reactions that converts the inactive enzyme into its active form.

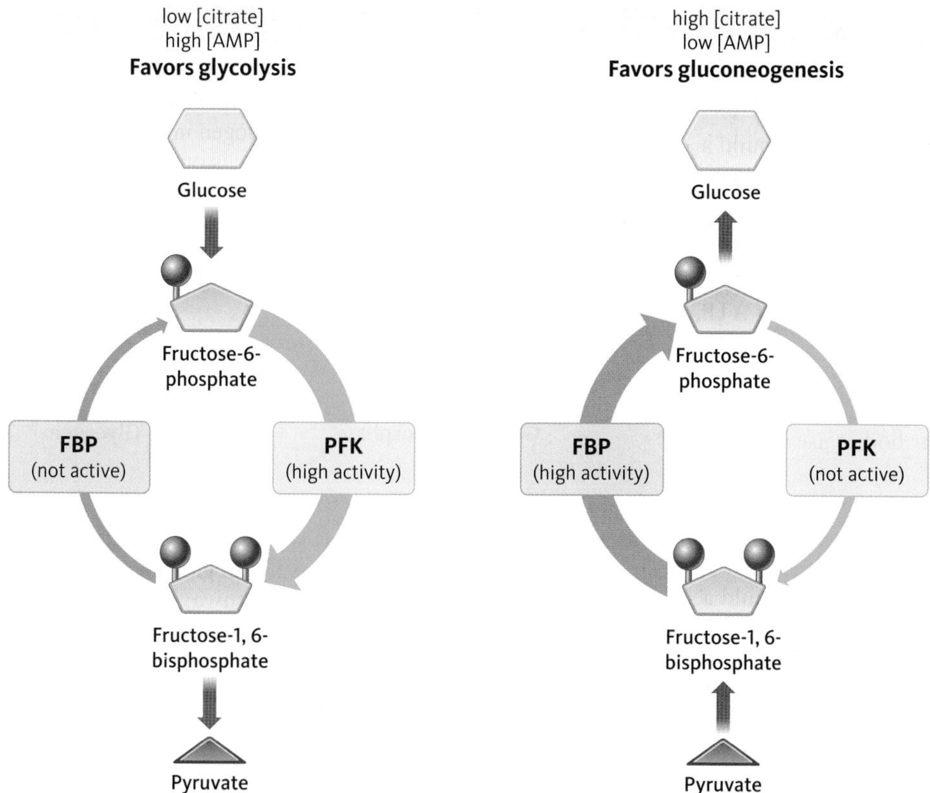

FIGURE 15.23 The regulation of glycolysis and gluconeogenesis.

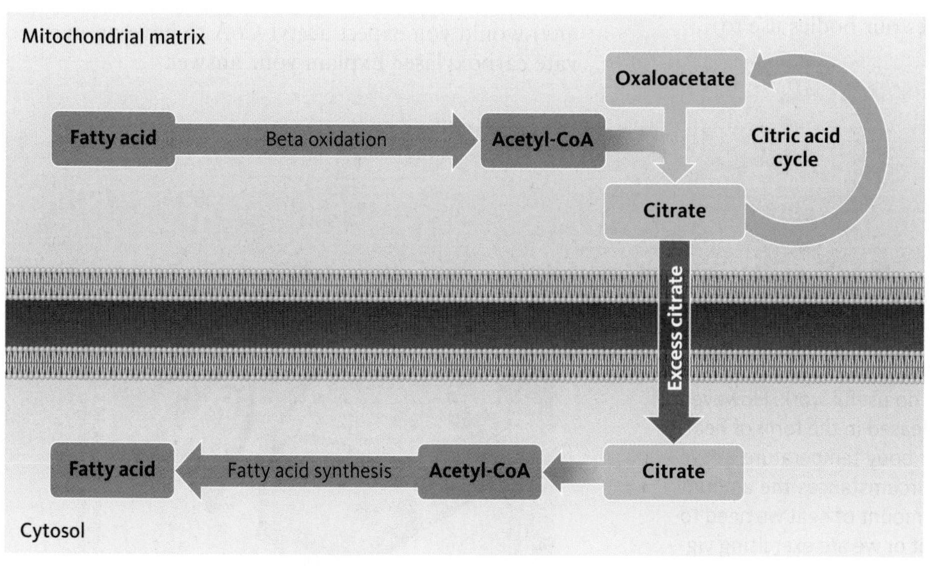

FIGURE 15.24 The regulation of fatty acid synthesis.

- *Using effectors.* Most pathways contain a key enzyme that is only active when a particular compound is present or absent, as described in Section 13.5.

A living organism is a collection of chemical compounds (a very large collection, to be sure), each of which undergoes certain chemical reactions. These compounds in turn are built from only 20 or so elements, and all of them obey the same fundamental laws of matter that govern the inanimate world. In a real sense, though, a living organism is more than the sum of its parts. The study of metabolism is endlessly fascinating, and much of it remains mysterious to this day. Scientists who explore the chemistry of life use words like *beautiful* and *elegant* to describe what they find. Perhaps now you will, too.

CORE PROBLEMS

15.75 What monosaccharide is formed in gluconeogenesis, and what organic molecules are used to build it?

15.76 What high-energy compounds are required to build a molecule of glucose, and how many molecules of each are needed?

15.77 Which involves a larger number of molecules of ATP, glycolysis or gluconeogenesis?

15.78 Which involves a larger number of molecules of ATP, building a fatty acid from acetyl-CoA or breaking down the same fatty acid into acetyl-CoA?

15.79 a) How many molecules of ATP are required to activate a fatty acid when our bodies use it to build a triglyceride?
b) What compound is formed when we activate a fatty acid?

15.80 a) How many molecules of ATP are required to activate glycerol when our bodies use it to build a triglyceride?
b) What compound is formed when we activate glycerol?

15.81 How many molecules of ATP are needed to add one molecule of glucose to glycogen?

15.82 How many molecules of ATP are needed to add one amino acid to a polypeptide?

15.83 What is a futile cycle?

15.84 What are the two main strategies our bodies use to avoid futile cycles?

15.85 The liver can both build and break down glycogen, using the following paired reactions. Glycogen phosphorylase breaks down glycogen into glucose-1-phosphate, and glycogen synthase is one of the two enzymes that build glycogen from glucose-1-phosphate. The activity of glycogen phosphorylase increases when AMP is present. What effect (if any) would you expect AMP to have on glycogen synthase? Explain your answer.

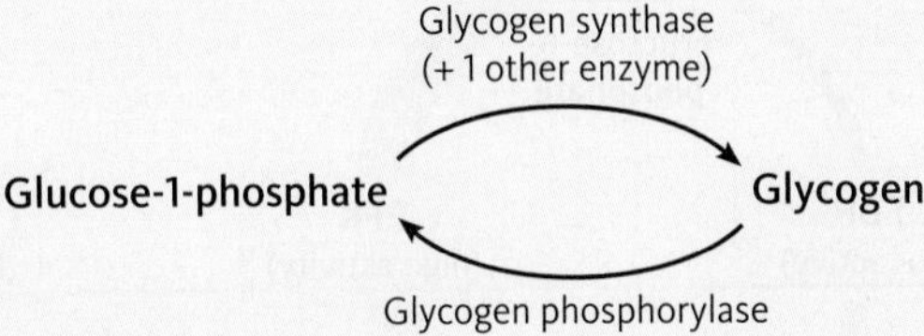

15.86 The last step in glycolysis is the conversion of phosphoenolpyruvate into pyruvate. In gluconeogenesis, this step is reversed. The two pathways use different enzymes, as shown here:

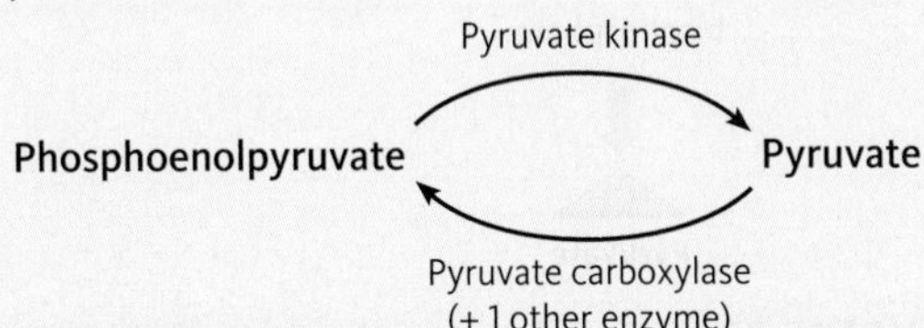

The activity of pyruvate kinase decreases when the concentration of acetyl-CoA is high. What effect (if any) would you expect acetyl-CoA to have on pyruvate carboxylase? Explain your answer.

CONNECTIONS

Brown Adipose Tissue and Uncouplers

One of the key features of any living organism is the ability to harness the energy of chemical reactions to do useful work. However, some of the reaction energy is always released in the form of heat. Our bodies use this heat to maintain our body temperature above the ambient temperature, but in some circumstances the amount of heat we generate does not equal the amount of heat we need to keep ourselves warm. If the weather is hot or we are exercising vigorously, our bodies produce more heat than we need. In response, we perspire, and the perspiration carries off the excess heat as it evaporates. In cold weather, we shiver, burning extra fuel to produce more heat. Shivering itself does not keep us warm—it is the extra heat that our muscles generate as a by-product of catabolism that warms us up.

A newborn baby is highly vulnerable to hypothermia, because a baby's body has a large surface area by comparison with its weight and babies' heads are disproportionately large, both of which allow rapid heat loss. In addition, babies are relatively inactive and cannot shiver, so they cannot use muscular activity to generate extra heat. However, infants have a special type of body fat, called *brown adipose tissue* or "brown fat," that allows them to generate extra heat. In brown fat, the mitochondria contain a special protein called *thermogenin* that allows hydrogen ions to pass through the inner membrane. Thermogenin is normally inactive, but when the baby's

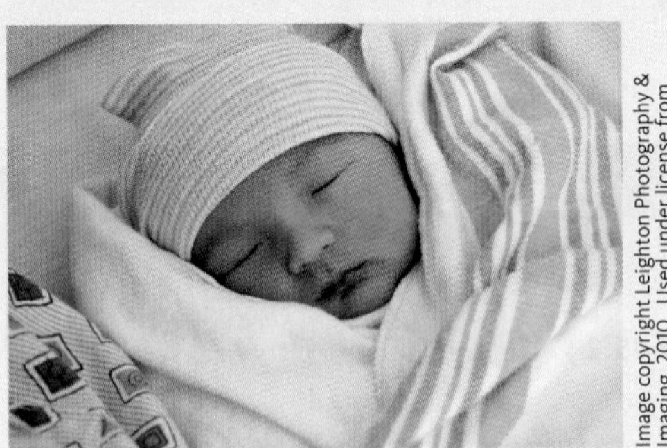

Babies rely on brown fat to maintain their body temperature.

continued

body temperature starts to drop, the cells activate the thermogenin, allowing hydrogen ions to bypass ATP synthase as they return to the matrix. Since the hydrogen ions do not pass through ATP synthase, the energy that would normally be used to make ATP is released as heat instead. This process is called *nonshivering thermogenesis.*

All newborn mammals contain substantial amounts of brown fat. However, the bodies of most adult mammals, including humans, contain little brown fat. Normal body fat, called "white fat," contains no thermogenin, so adults and older children rely primarily on shivering to generate extra heat. However, mammals such as bears that hibernate during the winter retain brown fat, which they use to keep warm during their long period of inactivity.

Thermogenin is an example of an *uncoupler,* a compound that breaks the link between oxidation and ATP formation in the mitochondria. The first known uncoupler, 2,4-dinitrophenol (DNP), was discovered by accident in the early 1920s when doctors noticed that ammunition workers who handled the highly explosive picric acid tended to lose weight. Soon afterward, it was recognized that the weight loss was due to DNP, which is a by-product of picric acid production. This chemical bonds to protons and carries them through the mitochondrial membrane, bypassing ATP synthase. DNP causes weight loss because the body must burn more fuel to make up for its lowered ability to make ATP. However, in the process, the body generates more heat, and overdoses of DNP can produce fatal hyperthermia (high body temperature). In the 1930s, DNP was widely prescribed as a diet pill, but increasing recognition of its dangers caused it to be banned in the United States in 1938. No uncoupler has been approved for weight loss since then, but interest in uncouplers as weight loss agents was renewed with the discovery of thermogenin in 1979. Since 1997, several additional uncoupling proteins have been discovered in humans, and genetic defects in one of these proteins have been linked to severe obesity. The exact role of these natural uncouplers is an area of active research.

OH, NO_2, NO_2

2,4-Dinitrophenol
(DNP)

OH, O_2N, NO_2, NO_2

Picric acid

Key Terms

activation reaction – 15.1
alcoholic fermentation – 15.4
anabolism – 15.1
anaerobic pathway – 15.4
ATP cycle – 15.1
beta oxidation – 15.6
catabolism – 15.1
charge gradient – 15.3
citric acid cycle (Krebs cycle) – 15.5
electron transport chain – 15.3
fermentation – 15.4
futile cycle – 15.8
gluconeogenesis – 15.8
glycolysis – 15.4
high-energy molecule – 15.1
lactic acid fermentation – 15.4
metabolism – 15.1
oxidative deamination reaction – 15.7
oxidative phosphorylation – 15.3
substrate-level phosphorylation – 15.4
transamination reaction – 15.7
urea cycle – 15.7

SUMMARY OF OBJECTIVES

Now that you have read the chapter, test yourself on your knowledge of the objectives, using this summary as a guide.

Section 15.1: Describe how the ATP cycle links catabolic and anabolic pathways.

- Catabolism breaks down molecules to produce energy, and anabolism uses energy to build large molecules from smaller ones.
- In the ATP cycle, ATP is broken down into and rebuilt from ADP and phosphate ion.
- The ATP cycle stores the energy from catabolism, and it makes the energy available for all cellular processes that require it.

Section 15.2: Describe the general strategy our bodies use to obtain energy from organic compounds, and write a chemical equation to summarize the breakdown of a typical nutrient.

- Our bodies use a three-part strategy to obtain energy from organic molecules.
- In the first part, we break down the molecule into CO_2, transferring the hydrogen atoms to NAD^+ and FAD.
- In the second part, we oxidize NADH and $FADH_2$, and we store the energy of these reactions in the form of a concentration gradient.
- In the third part, we use the energy of the gradient to make ATP.

continued

Section 15.3: Describe the mechanism by which the mitochondria harness the oxidation of NADH and $FADH_2$ to make ATP.

- Most catabolic pathways occur in the mitochondria, which are small compartments within each cell.
- The inner membrane of a mitochondrion contains the enzymes of the electron transport chain, which oxidize NADH and $FADH_2$ and pass the electrons to oxygen.
- The electron transport enzymes pump hydrogen ions through the inner membrane, creating a concentration gradient and a charge gradient across the membrane.
- ATP synthase allows hydrogen ions to return to the mitochondrial matrix, using the energy of the gradient to make ATP.
- Oxidation of NADH and $FADH_2$ supplies enough energy to make 2.5 and 1.5 molecules of ATP, respectively.

Section 15.4: Describe the overall chemical transformation that occurs during glycolysis, and understand the role of fermentation in obtaining energy from carbohydrates.

- Glycolysis is a sequence of 10 reactions that breaks glucose into two pyruvate ions, and it is the only catabolic pathway that does not occur in the mitochondria.
- Our bodies obtain two molecules of ATP and two molecules of NADH during glycolysis.
- Pyruvate can be converted into lactate, using the NADH that is formed during glycolysis.
- The overall pathway from glucose to lactate requires no net oxidation and is called lactic acid fermentation.
- Some organisms carry out alcoholic fermentation, breaking down glucose into ethanol and CO_2.

Section 15.5: Describe the overall chemical transformation that occurs in the citric acid cycle, and calculate the ATP yield for a typical carbohydrate.

- When our bodies oxidize pyruvate, we first convert it to acetyl-CoA. One molecule of NADH is formed in this reaction.
- The citric acid cycle is a series of eight reactions that oxidizes acetyl-CoA to CO_2, producing one ATP, three NADH, and one $FADH_2$.
- The first reaction of the citric acid cycle combines acetyl-CoA with oxaloacetate, and the last reaction regenerates oxaloacetate.
- Each reaction of the citric acid cycle has a specific function, with some reactions having more than one role.
- The complete oxidation of a molecule of glucose by glycolysis and the citric acid cycle produces up to 32 molecules of ATP.

Section 15.6: Write the reactions that occur during the oxidation of a fatty acid, calculate the ATP yield for a fatty acid, and convert ATP yields to a gram basis for comparison.

- Fatty acids are converted into fatty acyl–CoA before they are broken down. This activation reaction consumes two molecules of ATP.
- Beta oxidation removes two carbon atoms (in the form of acetyl-CoA) from a fatty acyl–CoA, producing a new fatty acyl–CoA that is two carbons shorter than the original.
- One cycle of beta oxidation produces a molecule of NADH and a molecule of $FADH_2$.
- Repeated cycles of beta oxidation break down the entire carbon skeleton of a fatty acid into acetyl-CoA, which is oxidized by the citric acid cycle.
- The ATP yield for a fatty acid is calculated by adding the high-energy molecules from beta oxidation and the citric acid cycle and then subtracting the two ATP that were broken down in the activation step.
- ATP yields for different nutrients can be compared based on 100 g of each nutrient. This calculation requires the formula weight of each nutrient and the mole ratio between ATP and the nutrient.

Section 15.7: Describe how our bodies remove and excrete nitrogen from amino acids, and explain how amino acid catabolism is related to other catabolic pathways.

- The liver and the kidneys can break down amino acids by removing the nitrogen atoms and burning the rest of the molecule to obtain energy.
- The amino group of most amino acids is removed using transamination and oxidative deamination. This sequence forms NH_4^+ and replaces the amino group with a ketone group.
- The liver converts ammonium ions into urea for excretion using the urea cycle, which breaks down two ATP per ammonium ion.
- All metabolic pathways for amino acids converge with the main pathway for glucose metabolism.

continued

Section 15.8: Describe the main anabolic pathways and how they are related to catabolic pathways, explain the role of activated molecules in anabolism, and describe how our bodies regulate anabolism and catabolism to avoid futile cycles.

- The two categories of anabolism are the formation of building blocks and the construction of macromolecules from the building blocks.
- Gluconeogenesis is a sequence of 13 reactions that converts pyruvate into glucose. This pathway consumes six molecules of ATP and two molecules of NADH.
- Since gluconeogenesis consumes more ATP that we obtain from glycolysis, the liver only makes glucose under specific conditions.
- Building amino acids and fatty acids also consumes more ATP that we obtain by burning these nutrients.
- Monosaccharides, amino acids, glycerol, and fatty acids must be activated before they can be incorporated into polysaccharides, proteins, and triglycerides.
- Cells that can carry out both anabolic and catabolic pathways can regulate the rate of each pathway, either by using different enzymes for one or more steps or by carrying out the pathways in different locations in the cell.

Concept Questions

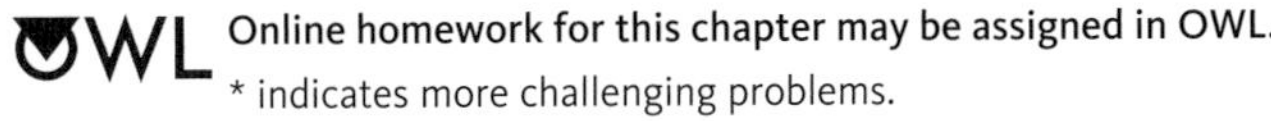

OWL
Online homework for this chapter may be assigned in OWL.
* indicates more challenging problems.

15.87 Describe the role of the ATP cycle in metabolism.

15.88 Describe the role of FAD and NAD^+ in obtaining energy from nutrients.

15.89 Explain why each of the following is considered to be a high-energy molecule:

a) ATP
b) NADH
c) acetyl-CoA

15.90 When our bodies oxidize an organic compound to obtain energy, what happens to the carbon atoms in the organic molecule? What happens to the hydrogen atoms?

15.91 Describe how the mitochondria use a concentration gradient to link the oxidation of NADH and $FADH_2$ to the formation of ATP.

15.92 ATP synthase requires only three hydrogen ions to make a molecule of ATP. Why is the ratio of H^+ to ATP given as 4 to 1, rather than 3 to 1?

15.93 What metabolic pathways are required to oxidize a molecule of glucose to CO_2? In what parts of a cell do these pathways occur?

15.94 What are the reactants and products in glycolysis? How do the reactants and products change in lactic acid fermentation?

15.95 During glycolysis, four separate molecules of ADP are converted into ATP. However, the ATP yield from glycolysis is always given as two molecules of ATP instead of four. Explain.

15.96 What are the reactants and products in the citric acid cycle?

15.97 What metabolic pathways are required to oxidize a fatty acid to CO_2? In what parts of a cell do these pathways occur?

15.98 What are the reactants and products in one cycle of beta oxidation?

15.99 Explain why your body obtains more ATP from a saturated fatty acid than it does from an unsaturated fatty acid with the same number of carbon atoms.

15.100 What two reactions remove the amino group from the majority of amino acids? What nitrogen-containing product do these reactions form?

15.101 What is the function of the urea cycle, and why is it important in the metabolism of amino acids?

15.102 Most cells in your body cannot oxidize amino acids to obtain energy. How does your liver make the energy from the oxidation of amino acids available to cells that cannot oxidize amino acids?

15.103 When your body oxidizes the amino acid valine to obtain energy, it converts valine into succinyl-CoA. Explain how this pathway allows your body to reduce the number of enzymes it must make. (Hint: Review the reactions of the citric acid cycle.)

15.104 What are the reactants and products in gluconeogenesis?

15.105 Why is it important that cells not carry out both a catabolic pathway and the corresponding anabolic pathway at the same time?

15.106 What are the two main strategies that cells use to prevent futile cycles?

15.107 Under what circumstances does your liver carry out gluconeogenesis at a significant rate?

15.108 Cells cannot build proteins, polysaccharides, and triglycerides directly from their building blocks (amino acids, monosaccharides, fatty acids, and glycerol). What must the cell do first?

Summary and Challenge Problems

15.109 Your body can make cholesterol, using acetyl groups from acetyl-CoA.

a) Is this an anabolic pathway, or is it a catabolic pathway?
b) Does this pathway make ATP, or does it consume ATP?
c) Does this pathway make ADP, or does it consume ADP?
d) What are some possible sources of the acetyl-CoA for this pathway?

15.110 ADP and AMP have similar structures to ATP, but they contain two and one phosphate groups, respectively. Your body can remove a phosphate ion from either of these molecules, as shown here. For each of these reactions, tell whether it should produce more energy than the breakdown of ATP, less energy, or a similar amount of energy. Explain your answers.

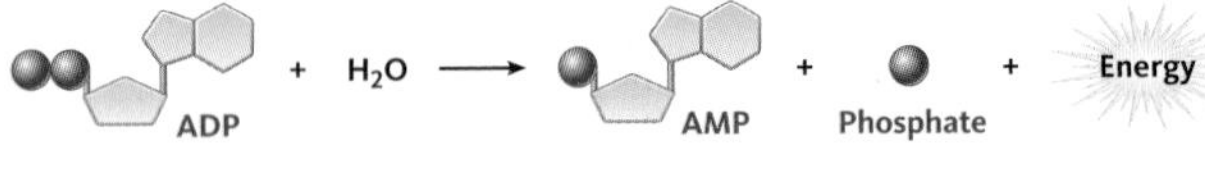

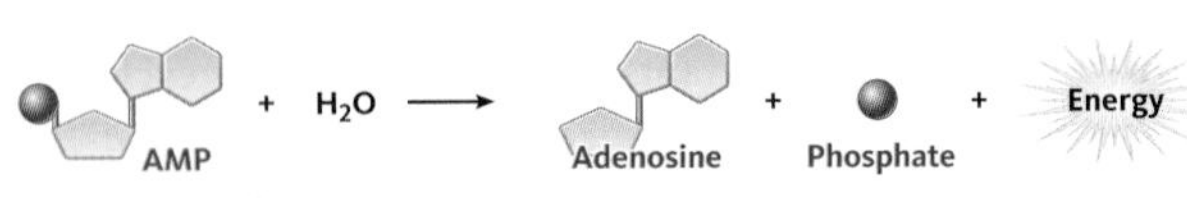

15.111 Your body can interconvert the amino acids glutamine and glutamate (the pH 7 form of glutamic acid), using the two reactions shown here. One of these reactions is always combined with the hydrolysis of ATP. Which one is it, and how can you tell?

glutamate + NH_4^+ + 3.4 kcal → glutamine + H_2O

glutamine + H_2O → glutamate + NH_4^+ + 3.4 kcal

15.112 Acetyl-CoA is a high-energy thioester that can be made from acetate ion and coenzyme A. The chemical equation for this reaction is

acetate + coenzyme A + ATP → acetyl-CoA + ADP + P_i

Is this an activation reaction? Explain why or why not.

15.113 Each of the following nutrients can be oxidized to produce energy in the form of ATP:

glucose lactose
stearic acid (a fatty acid) isoleucine (an amino acid)

For each of the following pathways, tell which of these four nutrients requires this pathway in its catabolism:

a) glycolysis
b) transamination
c) the citric acid cycle
d) oxidative deamination
e) beta oxidation
f) the urea cycle
g) oxidative phosphorylation

15.114 Which of the following metabolic pathways produces energy that is used to make ATP?

a) the breakdown of glycogen into glucose
b) the breakdown of glucose into pyruvate ions
c) the conversion of pyruvate ions into acetyl-CoA and carbon dioxide
d) the breakdown of acetyl-CoA into carbon dioxide
e) the breakdown of a triglyceride into fatty acids and glycerol
f) the conversion of a fatty acid into a fatty acyl–CoA
g) the breakdown of a fatty acyl–CoA into acetyl-CoA

15.115 Several amino acids are converted into succinic acid ($H_2C_4H_4O_4$) when they are broken down. The succinic acid is then oxidized to CO_2. Write balanced equations for each of the following reactions:

a) the combustion of succinic acid
b) the oxidation of succinic acid to CO_2 and hydrogen atoms (you may represent the hydrogen atoms as [H])
c) the reaction of succinic acid with NAD^+ and FAD to form CO_2, NADH, and $FADH_2$ (this reaction requires one molecule of FAD and more than one molecule of NAD^+)

15.116 When your body oxidizes citric acid to obtain energy, you produce six molecules of NADH and two molecules of $FADH_2$. You also make two molecules of ATP by substrate-level phosphorylation reactions.

a) Calculate the total ATP yield when you oxidize one molecule of citric acid.
b) Calculate the ATP yield per 100 g of citric acid. The molecular formula of citric acid is $H_3C_6H_5O_7$.

15.117 List all of the starting materials and products in glycolysis, including redox coenzymes.

15.118 What metabolic pathway is involved when a mixture of wheat starch and water is used to make beer? What chemical compound is responsible for the "fizz" in the beer?

15.119 What metabolic pathway is involved when milk spoils? What chemical compound is responsible for the unpleasant flavor of the spoiled milk?

15.120 When your body burns a molecule of glucose, it forms 32 molecules of ATP. What percentage of the ATP is formed by substrate-level phosphorylations, and what percentage is formed by oxidative phosphorylation?

15.121 Some organisms can convert ethanol into acetyl-CoA using the following sequence of reactions:

ethanol + NAD^+ → acetaldehyde + NADH + H^+

acetaldehyde + NAD^+ + CoA → acetyl-CoA + NADH + H^+

The acetyl-CoA is then broken down to CO_2 by the citric acid cycle. What is the total ATP yield when one molecule of ethanol is oxidized to CO_2?

15.122 *Your body can burn ribose (a five-carbon sugar) to make ATP. The ribose is first broken down into pyruvate ions.

$$3\ \text{ribose} + 5\ NAD^+ + 5\ ADP + 5\ \text{phosphate} \rightarrow 5\ \text{pyruvate} + 5\ NADH + 5\ H^+ + 5\ ATP + 5\ H_2O$$

Your body then breaks down the pyruvate ions into CO_2 in the normal way.

a) Calculate the total ATP yield when three molecules of ribose are oxidized to CO_2. (Remember that you must break down five pyruvate ions for every three molecules of ribose.)
b) Use your answer to part a to calculate the ATP yield for a single molecule of ribose.
c) Calculate the ATP yield per 100 g of ribose.

15.123 Capric acid is a 10-carbon saturated fatty acid.

a) Calculate the ATP yield when one molecule of capric acid is broken down into CO_2.
b) How many of the ATP molecules are a result of beta oxidation? Include ATP that is formed when NADH and $FADH_2$ that are produced during beta oxidation are oxidized.
c) How many of the ATP molecules are formed by substrate-level phosphorylations?

15.124 *A particular triglyceride contains two molecules of stearic acid and one molecule of oleic acid. Calculate the ATP yield when a molecule of this triglyceride is broken down into CO_2. Note that the hydrolysis of a triglyceride does not involve any high-energy molecules. The ATP yield for glycerol is given in Table 15.8.

15.125 Triolein is an unsaturated fat with the molecular formula $C_{57}H_{104}O_6$. Our bodies obtain 379.5 molecules of ATP when we burn one molecule of triolein. Calculate the ATP yield per 100 g of this triglyceride.

15.126 *Write a balanced equation for the breakdown of valine into carbon dioxide, hydrogen atoms (represent these using [H]), and an ammonium ion. The molecular formula of valine is $C_5H_{11}NO_2$. (Hint: You will need one H^+ ion on the reactant side.)

15.127 When the amino acid lysine is broken down, it undergoes a transamination reaction involving the amino group in the side chain. Draw the structure of the product of this reaction. (The structure of lysine is shown in Table 13.1.)

15.128 When your body breaks down a molecule of serine, it produces four molecules of NADH, one molecule of $FADH_2$, one molecule of ATP, one NH_4^+ ion, and three molecules of CO_2. Calculate the overall ATP yield from one molecule of serine. Be sure to consider the urea cycle.

15.129 Glutamic acid and glutamine have the same carbon skeleton. However, your body obtains 20.5 ATP from one molecule of glutamic acid, while it only obtains 18.5 ATP from a molecule of glutamine.

a) Why is this?
b) What would you expect the ATP yield to be for a molecule of glucosamine, given that the ATP yield for glucose is 32 ATP? (Glucosamine is identical to glucose except for having an amino group on carbon 2 instead of a hydroxyl group.)

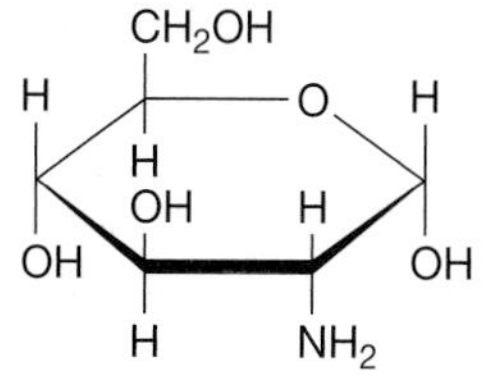

Glucosamine

15.130 When your body breaks down leucine, it first breaks leucine down into acetyl-CoA and CO_2. The overall reaction for this pathway is

$$\text{leucine} + NAD^+ + FAD + ATP + 3\ CoA \rightarrow 3\ \text{acetyl-CoA} + CO_2 + NH_4^+ + NADH + FADH_2 + ADP + \text{phosphate}$$

The acetyl-CoA is then broken down by the citric acid cycle. Calculate the total ATP yield from one molecule of leucine.

15.131 When your body breaks down alanine, it first converts alanine into pyruvate by the following reaction:

$$\text{alanine} + NAD^+ \rightarrow \text{pyruvate} + NH_4^+ + NADH$$

The pyruvate ion is then broken down in the normal way. Calculate the overall ATP yield from one molecule of alanine.

15.132 Your body obtains 26 molecules of ATP when it burns one molecule of valine. Calculate the ATP yield per 100 g of valine, using the following:

a) the formula weight of free valine
b) the formula weight of valine in a polypeptide

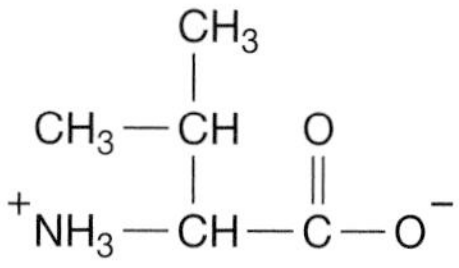

Free valine

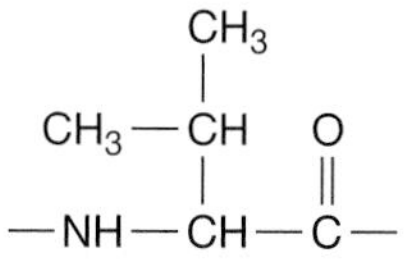

Valine within a polypeptide

15.133 When your body breaks down alanine, it first converts the alanine into pyruvate. Based on this, can your body use alanine to make glucose? If so, how?

15.134 Which of the following building blocks can your body use to make glucose?

a) fatty acids
b) amino acids
c) lactic acid

15.135 *It takes 44 molecules of ATP to make a molecule of palmitic acid from eight molecules of acetyl-CoA. How many molecules of ATP will be wasted in the following futile cycle?

$$\text{palmitic acid} \rightarrow 8\ \text{acetyl-CoA} \rightarrow \text{palmitic acid}$$

15.136 Describe the role of each of the following in the regulation of glycolysis and gluconeogenesis:

a) citrate ions
b) AMP

15.137 *The concentration of AMP in a cell is normally quite low, but it increases when the concentration of ATP drops. Use this fact to explain why it makes sense for AMP to be a positive effector of PFK, rather than a negative effector.

15.138 A patient eats a high-protein meal and then fasts for 48 hours. The following graph shows the rate of gluconeogenesis in this patient during this period:

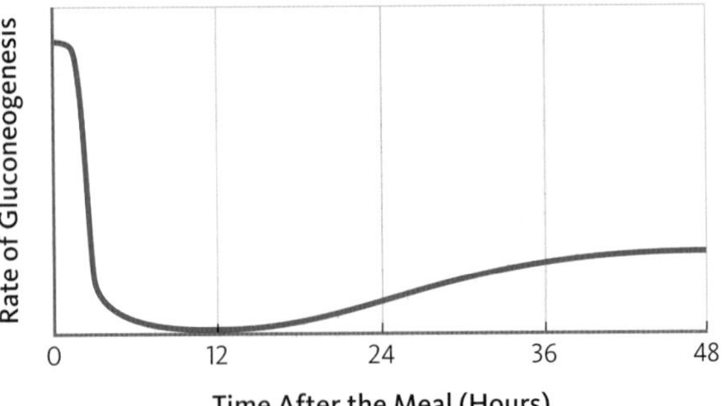

a) Explain why the rate is high immediately after the meal.
b) Explain why the rate decreases to a low level within 2 hours of the meal.
c) Explain why the rate increases starting about 12 hours after the meal.

15.139 The following graph shows the rate of gluconeogenesis for a person who is engaging in an exercise session:

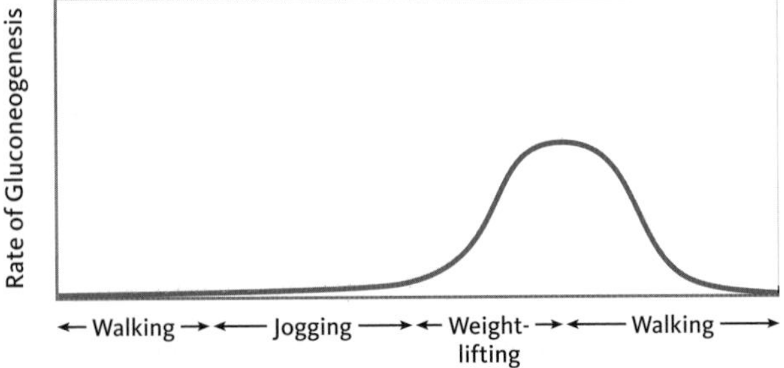

a) Why does the rate of gluconeogenesis increase sharply during the weight-lifting portion of the session?
b) Why does the rate remain high for a few minutes after the weight-lifting session is completed?

15.140 *750 mL of grape juice contains roughly 120 g of sugar. When the grape juice is turned into wine, essentially all of the sugar is converted into ethanol by alcoholic fermentation.

a) What mass of ethanol is formed? (You may assume that all of the sugar is glucose.)
b) What mass of carbon dioxide is formed?
c) A mole of any gas has a volume of 24 L at room temperature and 760 torr of pressure. What will be the volume of the carbon dioxide that is produced in part b?

15.141 *The main protein in cow's milk is called casein. The amino acid composition of casein is shown in the following table.

Amino acid	Number	Amino Acid	Number
Alanine	9	Leucine	17
Arginine	6	Lysine	14
Asparagine	8	Methionine	5
Aspartic acid	7	Phenylalanine	8
Cysteine	0	Proline	17
Glutamic acid	25	Serine	16
Glutamine	14	Threonine	5
Glycine	9	Tryptophan	2
Histidine	5	Tyrosine	10
Isoleucine	11	Valine	11

a) Using this information and the ATP values in Table 15.7, calculate the overall ATP yield from one molecule of casein.
b) Calculate the average ATP yield per amino acid in this protein (divide the overall ATP yield by the number of amino acids in the protein).
c) The formula weight of this protein is 22,950 amu. Calculate the ATP yield per 100 g for this protein.
d) How does the ATP yield you obtained in part c compare with the values for starch and triglycerides in Table 15.8?

15.142 *The overall reaction for lactic acid fermentation (excluding ATP) is

$$\underset{\text{glucose}}{C_6H_{12}O_6} \longrightarrow \underset{\text{lactate}}{2\ C_3H_5O_3^-} + 2\ H^+ + 47\text{ kcal}$$

a) How much of this energy is stored in the form of ATP? (Hint: How many molecules of ATP are formed during lactic acid fermentation?)
b) What percentage of the energy of this reaction is stored in the form of ATP?
c) If your body converts 10.0 g of glucose into lactate, how many kcal of energy will be produced, and how much of this energy will be stored in the form of ATP?

15.143 *The following reaction is at equilibrium in red blood cells:

$$\text{pyruvate} + \text{NADH} + H^+ \rightleftharpoons \text{lactate} + \text{NAD}^+$$

a) If some of the lactate ions pass out of the cell, what will happen to the concentration of pyruvate ions? Explain your answer.
b) If the concentration of NADH in the cell increases due to some other reaction, what will happen to the concentration of pyruvate ions? Explain your answer.
c) If the pH of the cell goes up, what will happen to the concentration of lactate ions in the cell? Explain your answer.

15.144 *One of the reactions of the citric acid cycle is the hydration of fumaric acid. This enzyme is catalyzed by an enzyme called fumarase. Does fumarase need to select one of two possible products of this hydration reaction? Explain why or why not.

15.145 *Which (if any) of the carbon atoms in each of the following ions are chiral?

a) lactate
b) pyruvate
c) citrate
d) isocitrate

15.146 *One of the reactions of the citric acid cycle is the dehydrogenation of succinate ion.

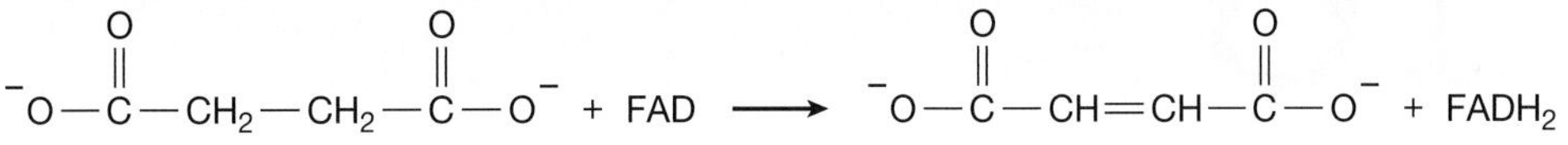

$$^{-}O-\overset{\displaystyle O}{\overset{\|}{C}}-CH_2-CH_2-\overset{\displaystyle O}{\overset{\|}{C}}-O^{-} + \text{FAD} \longrightarrow {}^{-}O-\overset{\displaystyle O}{\overset{\|}{C}}-CH{=}CH-\overset{\displaystyle O}{\overset{\|}{C}}-O^{-} + \text{FADH}_2$$

Succinate **Fumarate**

The activity of the enzyme that catalyzes this reaction decreases dramatically if malonate ions are added to the reaction mixture. Why do malonate ions have this effect on the enzyme?

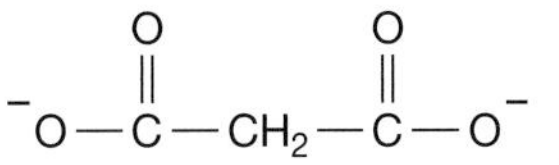

$$^{-}O-\overset{\displaystyle O}{\overset{\|}{C}}-CH_2-\overset{\displaystyle O}{\overset{\|}{C}}-O^{-} \qquad \textbf{Malonate}$$

15.147 *Your body breaks down the amino acid valine using a lengthy sequence of reactions. The first six reactions of this pathway are shown here. For each step, tell what type of reaction it is (hydration, oxidation, hydrolysis, etc.) and list any additional reactants and products (NAD^+, coenzyme A, ATP, etc.)

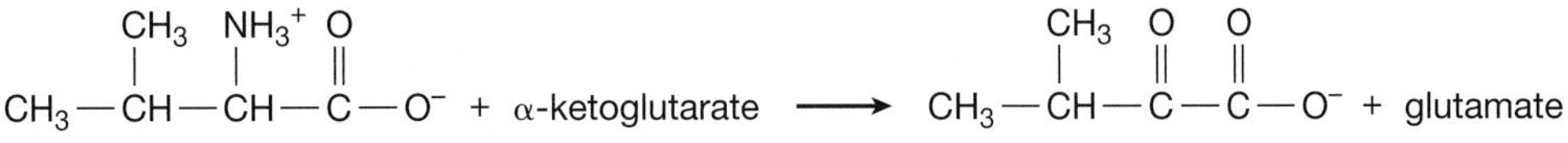

$$CH_3-\overset{\displaystyle CH_3}{\overset{|}{C}H}-\overset{\displaystyle NH_3^+}{\overset{|}{C}H}-\overset{\displaystyle O}{\overset{\|}{C}}-O^{-} + \alpha\text{-ketoglutarate} \longrightarrow CH_3-\overset{\displaystyle CH_3}{\overset{|}{C}H}-\overset{\displaystyle O}{\overset{\|}{C}}-\overset{\displaystyle O}{\overset{\|}{C}}-O^{-} + \text{glutamate}$$

Valine

$$CH_3-\overset{\displaystyle CH_3}{\overset{|}{C}H}-\overset{\displaystyle O}{\overset{\|}{C}}-\overset{\displaystyle O}{\overset{\|}{C}}-O^{-} \longrightarrow CH_3-\overset{\displaystyle CH_3}{\overset{|}{C}H}-\overset{\displaystyle O}{\overset{\|}{C}}-S-\text{CoA}$$

$$CH_3-\overset{\displaystyle CH_3}{\overset{|}{C}H}-\overset{\displaystyle O}{\overset{\|}{C}}-S-\text{CoA} \longrightarrow CH_2{=}\overset{\displaystyle CH_3}{\overset{|}{C}}-\overset{\displaystyle O}{\overset{\|}{C}}-S-\text{CoA}$$

$$CH_2{=}\overset{\displaystyle CH_3}{\overset{|}{C}}-\overset{\displaystyle O}{\overset{\|}{C}}-S-\text{CoA} \longrightarrow \overset{\displaystyle OH}{\overset{|}{C}H_2}-\overset{\displaystyle CH_3}{\overset{|}{C}H}-\overset{\displaystyle O}{\overset{\|}{C}}-S-\text{CoA}$$

$$\overset{\displaystyle OH}{\overset{|}{C}H_2}-\overset{\displaystyle CH_3}{\overset{|}{C}H}-\overset{\displaystyle O}{\overset{\|}{C}}-S-\text{CoA} \longrightarrow \overset{\displaystyle OH}{\overset{|}{C}H_2}-\overset{\displaystyle CH_3}{\overset{|}{C}H}-\overset{\displaystyle O}{\overset{\|}{C}}-O^{-}$$

$$\overset{\displaystyle OH}{\overset{|}{C}H_2}-\overset{\displaystyle CH_3}{\overset{|}{C}H}-\overset{\displaystyle O}{\overset{\|}{C}}-O^{-} \longrightarrow H-\overset{\displaystyle O}{\overset{\|}{C}}-\overset{\displaystyle CH_3}{\overset{|}{C}H}-\overset{\displaystyle O}{\overset{\|}{C}}-O^{-}$$

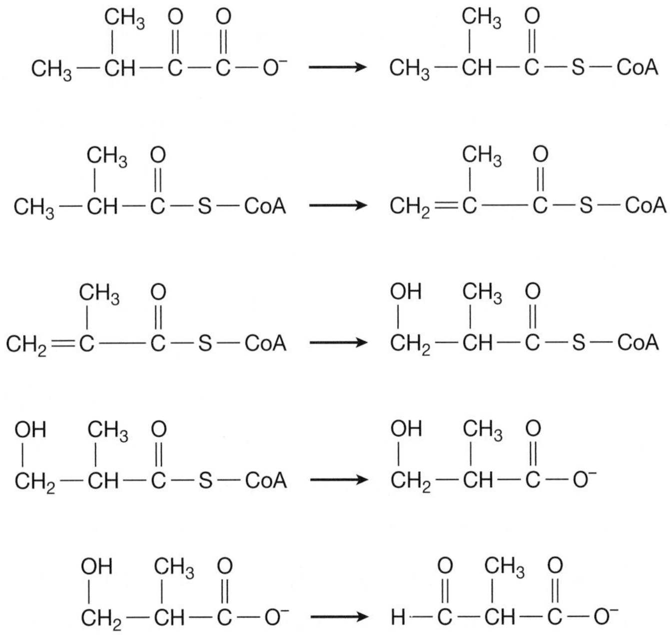

15.148 *The concentration of ATP in a red blood cell is around 7.5 mEq/L. How many grams of ATP are there in 1 L o f intracellular fluid? The molecular formula of ATP at pH 7 is $C_{10}H_{12}N_5O_{13}P_3^{4-}$.

16

Nuclear Chemistry

Two months ago, Flora started feeling vaguely ill and running a bit of a temperature. She assumed that she had just caught some sort of virus, but over the next few weeks, the fevers continue, accompanied by occasional chills. Flora also notices that she hasn't been eating well and has lost some weight. Finally, she calls her doctor, who asks her to come in for a physical exam. After running some lab tests and discussing Flora's general health history, the doctor refers Flora to an oncologist (a cancer specialist) for further testing. The oncologist orders a positron emission tomography (PET) scan, a procedure in which Flora is given a small dose of a radioactive compound called ^{18}F-fluorodeoxyglucose (^{18}F-FDG). This compound collects in parts of the body that are burning glucose at a high rate, and it produces radiation that can be detected outside the body. Because cancerous cells divide more rapidly than the surrounding tissues, they require a great deal of fuel, so they absorb ^{18}F-FDG and can be detected on a PET scan.

Radioactive elements are widely used in modern medicine, both to detect illness and to treat it. In a radioactive element, the nucleus of the atom is unstable and changes into a different element. ^{18}F-FDG contains radioactive fluorine-18, which produces a particle called a positron as it breaks down. The positron in turn collides with an electron and the two particles vanish, producing a burst of energy called gamma radiation that passes through body tissues and can be detected as it leaves the body. By measuring the gamma radiation over time, PET can construct an image of the body that shows where ^{18}F-FDG is concentrated.

Based on the results of the PET scan and other tests, the oncologist determines that Flora has Hodgkin's lymphoma, a cancer of the lymph system. Fortunately, the cancer is still confined to a small area in her body, and the oncologist assures Flora that more than 90% of people with her type of cancer can be treated successfully.

OUTLINE

16.1 **Nuclear symbols**
16.2 **Writing nuclear equations**
16.3 **Energy and nuclear reactions**
16.4 **Measuring radiation**
16.5 **Radiation sources and shielding**
16.6 **Nuclear decay and half-life**
16.7 **Medical applications of nuclear radiation**
16.8 **Nuclear fission and fusion**

NUCLEAR MEDICINE

GENERAL
☐ Bone Scan ☐ w/SPECT
☐ Lung V/Q
☐ Hepatobiliary (HIDA)
☐ Gastric Emptying
☐ Octreoscan
☐ MIBG
☐ Thyroid Scan
☐ I131 Uptake
☐ Leukocyte/Infection
☐ Dynamic Renal
☐ Lymphoscintigraphy
☐ DEXA-Bone Densitometr

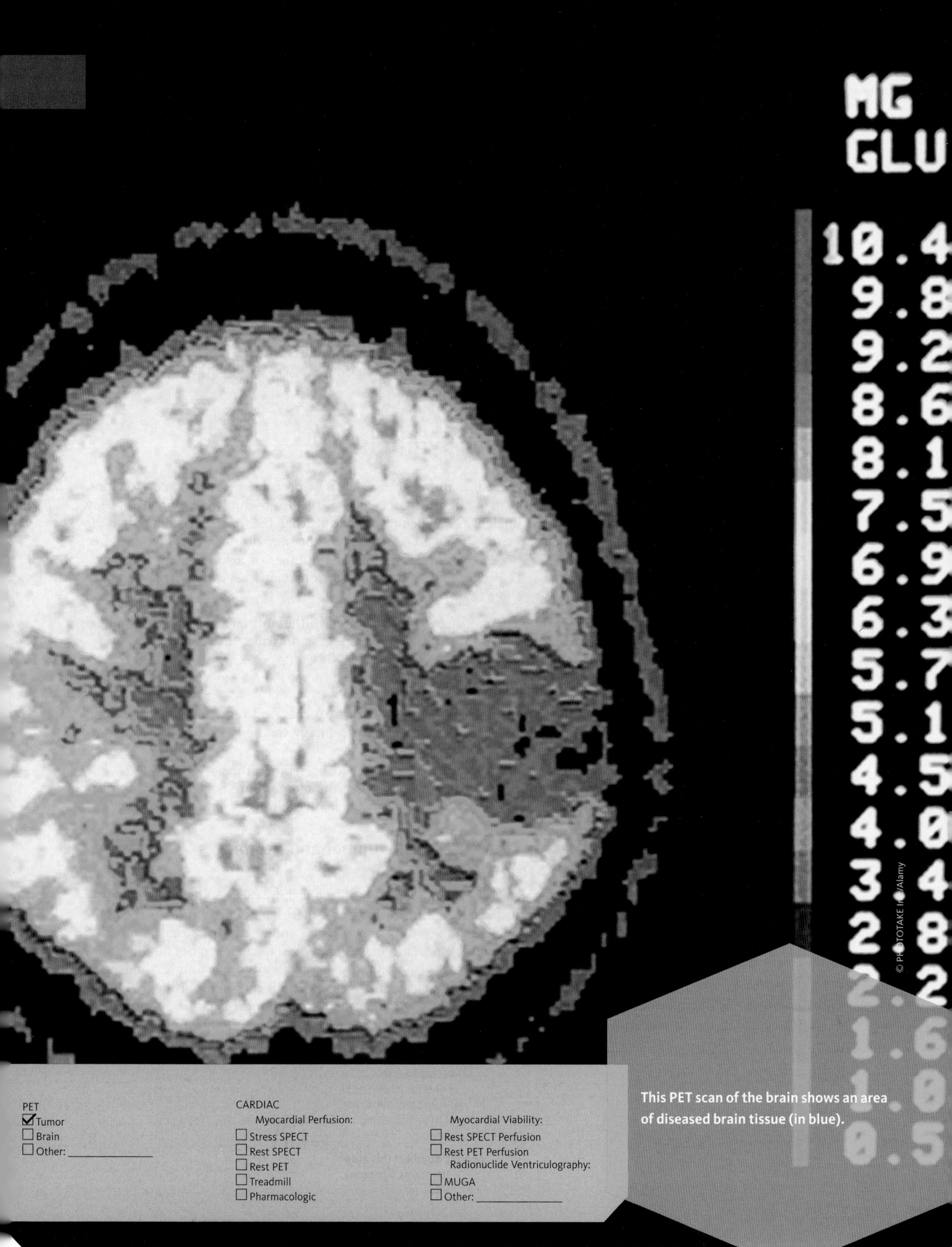

PET
- [x] Tumor
- [ ] Brain
- [ ] Other: ______________

CARDIAC

Myocardial Perfusion:
- [ ] Stress SPECT
- [ ] Rest SPECT
- [ ] Rest PET
- [ ] Treadmill
- [ ] Pharmacologic

Myocardial Viability:
- [ ] Rest SPECT Perfusion
- [ ] Rest PET Perfusion

Radionuclide Ventriculography:
- [ ] MUGA
- [ ] Other: ______________

This PET scan of the brain shows an area of diseased brain tissue (in blue).

OWL Online homework for this chapter may be assigned in OWL.

How can we see what is happening inside the human body? For thousands of years, the only way to answer this question was surgery, which is both hazardous and painful. Today, doctors can visualize the interior of the human body in detail, monitor the metabolic rates of different tissues, and destroy diseased tissues without surgery. Doctors can also measure concentrations of hormones and other solutes in blood at levels that were undetectable just a few years ago. All of these advances in medicine rely on a special class of reactions that involve the nucleus of the atom. These reactions form the basis of a branch of chemistry called nuclear chemistry.

The importance of nuclear chemistry reaches far beyond medicine. The sunlight that allows life to exist on Earth is produced by reactions that involve the nuclei of hydrogen atoms. Other nuclear reactions are harnessed to produce electricity, supplying a substantial fraction of the energy needs of many countries. We use nuclear chemistry to protect us from fire, to preserve food, to control insect pests, and to determine the age of ancient civilizations and cultures.

However, nuclear chemistry has its dark side. The same processes that allow doctors to diagnose and treat illness can cause cancer and birth defects. Nuclear chemistry lies behind one of the greatest industrial disasters of modern times, and it supplies the destructive power of nuclear weapons. In this chapter, we will explore the fascinating and often contradictory world of nuclear chemistry.

OBJECTIVES: *Distinguish nuclear reactions from chemical reactions, and write nuclear symbols for atoms and subatomic particles.*

16.1 Nuclear Symbols

In Chapter 2, you learned that atoms are made up of protons, neutrons, and electrons. The protons and neutrons make up the nucleus of the atom, and the electrons occupy the space around the nucleus. The chemical reactions that you have encountered so far change the way atoms are bonded to one another, but they do not affect the nuclei of the atoms. However, some reactions do change the number or arrangement of the particles in the nucleus. These are called **nuclear reactions**, and they differ from ordinary chemical reactions in three important ways:

Health Note: Only 0.01% of potassium atoms are capable of turning into calcium, and they react extremely slowly, so this nuclear reaction poses no health risk.

- Nuclear reactions do not need to be balanced in the normal sense. For example, a nuclear reaction that occurs in the body changes potassium into calcium.

$$K \rightarrow Ca$$

  This is clearly not a balanced equation.
- Nuclear reactions involve far more energy than chemical reactions. The preceding reaction produces over 100,000 times more energy than any chemical reaction involving potassium.
- Nuclear reactions are not generally affected by temperature or by catalysts. For example, chemical reactions speed up when the temperature is increased, but temperature changes have no effect on most nuclear reactions.

Nuclear Symbols Show the Mass Number and Atomic Number of an Atom

To describe a nuclear reaction, we must use symbols that show the atomic number and the mass number of each nucleus. Recall from Chapter 2 that the atomic number is the number of protons in the nucleus of an atom, and the mass number is the total number of protons and neutrons. Using this information, we can write a **nuclear symbol** for any atom. The nuclear symbol identifies the element, and it shows the atomic number and mass number of a particular atom of that element. For instance, all carbon atoms have six protons, and most have six neutrons as well. The nuclear symbol for a carbon atom that contains six neutrons and six protons is $^{12}_{6}C$. Note that we write the mass number above and to the left of the symbol, and we place the atomic number below the mass number.

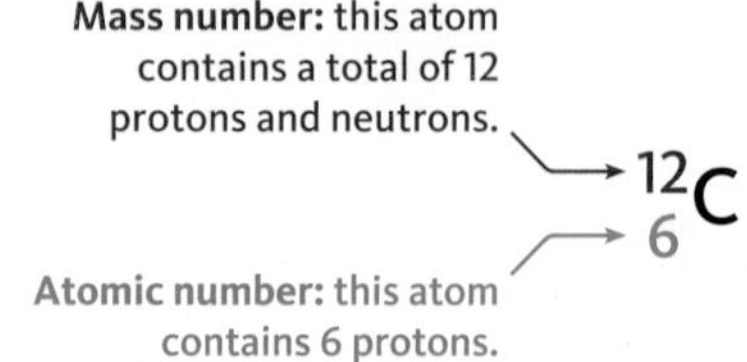
Mass number: this atom contains a total of 12 protons and neutrons.
12C
6
Atomic number: this atom contains 6 protons.

Sample Problem **16.1**

Writing a nuclear symbol

Write the nuclear symbol for an atom that contains 12 protons and 14 neutrons.

SOLUTION

The atomic number of this atom is 12, because the atom contains 12 protons. Looking on the periodic table, we see that element number 12 is magnesium (Mg). The mass number of the atom is the sum of the numbers of protons and neutrons, which is 26. The symbol for this atom is ${}^{26}_{12}Mg$.

TRY IT YOURSELF: *Write the nuclear symbol for an atom that contains 24 protons and 27 neutrons.*

For additional practice, try Core Problems 16.7 and 16.8.

Chemists sometimes omit the atomic number, because it is given on the periodic table and is the same for all atoms of a given element. For example, we can write ${}^{12}C$ rather than ${}^{12}_{6}C$. However, we must always include the mass number of each atom when we are describing a nuclear reaction. As we saw in Chapter 2, an element can have several isotopes, atoms that have the same number of protons but different numbers of neutrons. For instance, all carbon atoms have six protons, but some carbon atoms have six neutrons, while others have seven, and still others have eight. Here are the nuclear symbols for the three naturally occurring isotopes of carbon:

${}^{12}_{6}C$	${}^{13}_{6}C$	${}^{14}_{6}C$
Carbon-12	**Carbon-13**	**Carbon-14**
6 protons	6 protons	6 protons
6 neutrons	7 neutrons	8 neutrons
mass number = 12	mass number = 13	mass number = 14

• The periodic table lists atomic weights, which are the average mass of all atoms of an element on Earth.

Some Isotopes Are Stable, while Others Are Radioactive

The nuclei of most naturally occurring isotopes remain unchanged indefinitely. We say that these are **stable nuclei**. However, some nuclei are unstable and eventually break into two or more pieces. An atom whose nucleus is unstable is said to be **radioactive**, and such an atom is called a **radioisotope**. In the case of carbon, carbon-12 and carbon-13 are stable, but carbon-14 is radioactive. All of the carbon-14 atoms on Earth will eventually change into nitrogen atoms. We will examine how radioisotopes break down in the next section.

Most elements that occur on Earth have at least one stable isotope, and many elements have several. A sample of any element contains a mixture of all of its stable isotopes. For example, any sample of carbon contains 99.9% carbon-12 and 0.1% carbon-13. In addition, some elements have naturally occurring radioisotopes. Carbon samples normally contain a tiny amount of radioactive carbon-14 mixed with the two stable isotopes. Table 16.1 shows the natural isotope mixture for three other common elements. Note that all naturally occurring isotopes of fluorine and calcium are stable, but potassium has one radioactive isotope.

TABLE 16.1 Naturally Occurring Isotopes of Three Common Elements

Element	Naturally Occurring Isotope	Type of Isotope	Number of Protons	Number of Neutrons	Percentage of Each Isotope
Fluorine	^{19}F	Stable	9	10	100%
Potassium	^{39}K	Stable	19	20	93.26%
	^{40}K	**Radioactive**	19	21	0.01%
	^{41}K	Stable	19	22	6.73%
Calcium	^{40}Ca	Stable	20	20	96.94%
	^{42}Ca	Stable	20	22	0.65%
	^{43}Ca	Stable	20	23	0.13%
	^{44}Ca	Stable	20	24	2.09%
	^{46}Ca	Stable	20	26	Less than 0.01%
	^{48}Ca	Stable	20	28	0.19%

CORE PROBLEMS

All Core Problems are paired and the answers to the blue odd-numbered problems appear in the back of the book.

16.1 What do we mean when we say that an isotope is stable?

16.2 What do we mean when we say that an isotope is radioactive?

16.3 Which of the following is a nuclear reaction, and which is a chemical reaction?
a) $CuBr_2 \rightarrow Cu + Br_2$ b) $Ra \rightarrow Rn + He$

16.4 Which of the following is a nuclear reaction, and which is a chemical reaction?
a) $I \rightarrow Xe$ b) $2\,I \rightarrow I_2$

16.5 How many protons and neutrons are there in each of the following atoms?
a) an atom of $^{81}_{34}Se$ b) an atom of copper-67

16.6 How many protons and neutrons are there in each of the following atoms?
a) an atom of $^{58}_{26}Fe$ b) an atom of sulfur-33

16.7 Write the nuclear symbol for each of the following atoms:
a) an atom that has an atomic number of 17 and a mass number of 37
b) an atom that has 26 protons and 28 neutrons
c) an atom of cobalt-60

16.8 Write the nuclear symbol for each of the following atoms:
a) an atom that has an atomic number of 82 and a mass number of 206
b) an atom that has 35 protons and 44 neutrons
c) an atom of fluorine-18

OBJECTIVE: *Write balanced nuclear equations for common nuclear reactions.*

16.2 Writing Nuclear Equations

As we saw in Section 16.1, nuclear reactions can convert one element into another. Therefore, we cannot write a balanced equation for a nuclear reaction the way we did for chemical reactions. However, any nuclear reaction can be represented by a **nuclear equation**, which shows the symbols of all of the reactants and products in the reaction. Nuclear equations are balanced differently from chemical equations. In this section, we will examine the most common types of nuclear reactions and learn how to write their equations.

Most Nuclear Reactions Produce a Small Particle

Nuclear reactions form a variety of products. In most cases, though, the original nucleus gives off a small particle such as an electron or a helium nucleus. These particles are

TABLE 16.2 Names and Symbols of Particles Produced in Nuclear Reactions

Type of Radiation	Mass Number	Atomic Number (Charge)	Symbol
Alpha particle (helium-4 nucleus)	4	+2	$^{4}_{2}He$ or α
Proton (hydrogen-1 nucleus)	1	+1	$^{1}_{1}p$ or $^{1}_{1}H$
Neutron	1	0	$^{1}_{0}n$
Beta particle (electron)	0	−1	$^{0}_{-1}e$ or β
Positron	0	+1	$^{0}_{+1}e$ or β^{+}

ejected at a very high speed, giving them a great deal of energy. In many cases, the atom also emits a burst of pure energy called gamma radiation. These high-energy products are called **nuclear radiation.**

Table 16.2 lists the names and nuclear symbols of the most important particles that are formed in nuclear reactions. Three of these are the familiar building blocks of all atoms: protons, neutrons, and electrons. Note that when electrons are produced in a nuclear reaction, they are called **beta particles.** The fourth type of radiation is a combination of two protons and two neutrons, called an **alpha particle.** This combination is actually a helium-4 nucleus, and it is usually written $^{4}_{2}He$. The fifth particle, the **positron,** has the same mass as an electron but a +1 charge.

When we write an equation for a nuclear reaction, we must include symbols for any subatomic particles that are formed. The mass number is 1 for protons and neutrons, and it is zero for electrons and positrons. When we write the atomic number, we use the fact that the atomic number of an atom is the charge on the nucleus. Therefore, we use the charge on each subatomic particle in place of the atomic number. For protons and positrons, the charge is +1, and for electrons it is −1. It is customary to write a plus sign when we write the charge of a positron, to distinguish positrons from electrons.

$$^{1}_{1}p \quad \text{or} \quad ^{1}_{1}H \qquad ^{1}_{0}n \qquad ^{0}_{-1}e \qquad ^{0}_{+1}e$$

Proton (hydrogen nucleus) — **Neutron** — **Electron** — **Positron**

Atomic Numbers and Mass Numbers Must Be Balanced in a Nuclear Equation

Let us now look at how we write a nuclear equation, using radon (Rn) as an example. Radon is an inert gas and does not normally participate in chemical reactions, but all isotopes of radon are radioactive and undergo nuclear reactions. As a result, radon atoms break down rather rapidly, but radon is produced in other nuclear reactions, so there is always a small amount of this element in the atmosphere near Earth's surface. The most common isotope of radon is radon-222, which decays into an alpha particle (a helium-4 nucleus) and one other atom. We can represent this reaction using nuclear symbols.

$$^{222}_{86}Rn \rightarrow ? + ^{4}_{2}He$$

What is the missing atom? To identify it, we use two principles that govern all nuclear reactions:

1. *The sums of the mass numbers of the products and reactants must be equal.*
2. *The sums of the atomic numbers of the products and reactants must be equal.*

In this reaction, the mass number of the original radon atom is 222, so the mass numbers of the products must add up to 222.

$$222 = ? + 4$$

Therefore, the mass number of our missing product is 218. Likewise, the atomic numbers of the products must add up to 86, the atomic number of radon.

$$86 = ? + 2$$

The atomic number of our missing product is 84.

Health Note: When we inhale air that contains radon, some of the radon atoms break down into polonium. Polonium is also radioactive and is a solid, so it remains in the lungs and can cause cancer. Radon monitoring is discussed in Section 16.5.

To complete our nuclear equation, we need to identify the missing element. We have already found its atomic number, so we simply locate element 84 on the periodic table. The missing element is polonium (Po), so the symbol of the missing atom must be ${}^{218}_{84}\text{Po}$. We can now write a balanced nuclear equation for the breakdown of radon-222.

$${}^{222}_{86}\text{Rn} \rightarrow {}^{218}_{84}\text{Po} + {}^{4}_{2}\text{He}$$

In Alpha Decay, a Nucleus Loses Two Protons and Two Neutrons

The breakdown of radon-222 is an example of a common type of nuclear reaction called **alpha decay**. In alpha decay, a heavy atom breaks apart into an alpha particle and a different atom, which is a little lighter than the original atom, as shown in Figure 16.1. The alpha particle is ejected at a very high speed (around 16,000 km per second for radon-222, or around 36 million miles per hour).

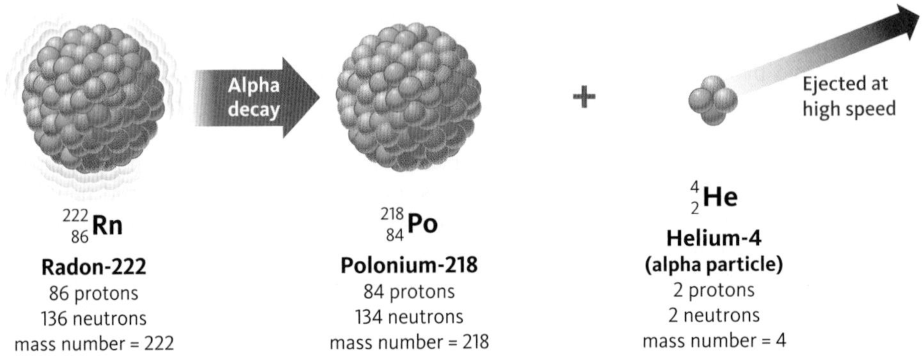

FIGURE 16.1 The alpha decay of radon-222.

Sample Problem 16.2

Writing the nuclear equation for an alpha decay reaction

Write a nuclear equation for the alpha decay of thorium-232.

SOLUTION

The symbol for thorium is Th (atomic number 90), and the nuclear symbol for thorium-232 is ${}^{232}_{90}\text{Th}$. In alpha decay, an atom loses a helium-4 nucleus, so we can write a partial equation as follows:

$${}^{232}_{90}\text{Th} \rightarrow ? + {}^{4}_{2}\text{He}$$

The mass numbers of the products must add up to 232, so the mass number of the missing atom is 232 − 4 = 228. Likewise, the atomic numbers of the products must add up to 90, so the atomic number of the missing atom is 90 − 2 = 88. Element 88 is radium (Ra), so the complete nuclear equation is

$${}^{232}_{90}\text{Th} \rightarrow {}^{228}_{88}\text{Ra} + {}^{4}_{2}\text{He}$$

TRY IT YOURSELF: *Write a nuclear equation for the alpha decay of uranium-238. (The symbol for uranium is U.)*

For additional practice, try Core Problems 16.13 (part a) and 16.14 (part b).

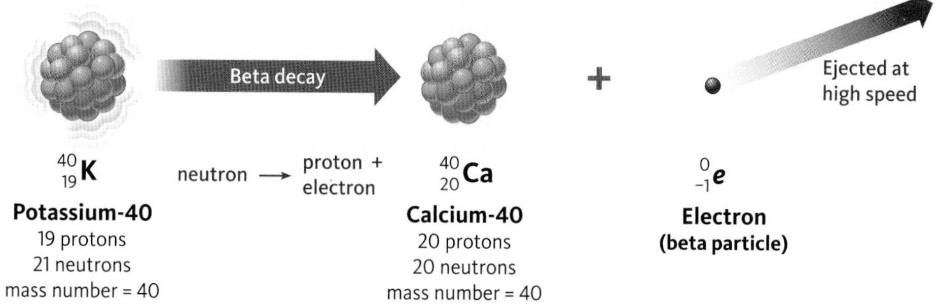

FIGURE 16.2 The beta decay of potassium-40.

In Beta Decay, a Nucleus Emits an Electron

Only very heavy atoms undergo alpha decay. For lighter radioisotopes, the most common type of nuclear reaction is **beta decay**, in which a neutron breaks apart into a proton and an electron. The proton remains in the nucleus, while the electron is ejected. Electrons that are produced in beta decay are called beta particles, but they are no different from other electrons. They are, however, moving at extremely high speeds, even faster than alpha particles.

We can write a balanced nuclear equation for beta decay using the nuclear symbol for the electron. For example, here is the nuclear equation for the beta decay of potassium-40, a naturally occurring radioactive isotope of potassium:

$$^{40}_{19}K \rightarrow ^{40}_{20}Ca + ^{0}_{-1}e$$

As always, both the mass numbers and the atomic numbers are balanced. Note that since the atomic number of the electron is −1, the atomic number of the product atom (calcium) is larger than that of the reactant (potassium). *Beta decay always increases the number of protons while leaving the mass unchanged.* Figure 16.2 shows the beta decay of potassium-40.

Sample Problem 16.3

Writing the nuclear equation for a beta decay reaction

Write a nuclear equation for the beta decay of iodine-131.

SOLUTION

The nuclear symbol for iodine-131 is $^{131}_{53}I$. In beta decay, an atom loses an electron, so we can write a partial equation as follows:

$$^{131}_{53}I \rightarrow ? + ^{0}_{-1}e$$

The mass number of the missing product is 131, because the mass number of an electron is 0. The atomic number of the missing product must be 54, because 53 = 54 + −1. (Remember that beta decay changes a neutron into a proton, so the number of protons increases.) Atomic number 54 corresponds to the element xenon (Xe), so the complete nuclear equation is

$$^{131}_{53}I \rightarrow ^{131}_{54}Xe + ^{0}_{-1}e$$

TRY IT YOURSELF: *Write a nuclear equation for the beta decay of cobalt-60.*

For additional practice, try Core Problems 16.13 (part b) and 16.14 (part c).

Virtually all naturally occurring radioisotopes undergo either alpha or beta decay. However, in the early twentieth century, researchers discovered that when they bombarded certain elements with high-velocity particles (protons, neutrons, and small nuclei) some of the atoms absorbed the particles and became new, previously unknown isotopes.

© VIEW Pictures Ltd / Alamy

Many radioactive isotopes are made in particle accelerators.

This process has since been used to make a number of elements that do not occur in nature, as well as many previously unknown isotopes of naturally occurring elements. Many of these radioisotopes undergo alpha or beta decay, but some can break down in other ways. For example, some artificially produced isotopes undergo **positron emission**, in which a proton breaks down into a neutron and a positron. Recall that positrons have the same mass as an electron but a +1 charge. The most commonly used positron emitter in medicine is fluorine-18, which undergoes the following reaction:

$$^{18}_{9}\text{F} \longrightarrow ^{18}_{8}\text{O} + \boxed{^{0}_{+1}e}$$

A positron

Positron emitters are used in a type of diagnostic imaging called PET, which we will examine in Section 16.7.

New Isotopes Can Be Made by Bombarding an Atom with Small Particles

Chemists use three techniques to make isotopes that do not occur in nature.

Health Note: Several nuclear reactors in North America and Europe have been closed over the past few years, reducing the supply of some radioisotopes for medical procedures.

1. *Neutron bombardment.* The most common method is to bombard a stable isotope with neutrons, which are produced by a nuclear reactor. (You will learn about nuclear reactors in Section 16.8.) Some of the atoms absorb a neutron, turning into a heavier isotope of the same element. For example, bombarding naturally occurring cobalt-59 with neutrons converts it into radioactive cobalt-60. Cobalt-60 has been used for decades in cancer treatment, and it is still used to sterilize medical supplies and to retard fruit spoiling.

$$^{59}_{27}\text{Co} + ^{1}_{0}\text{n} \rightarrow ^{60}_{27}\text{Co}$$

2. *Proton bombardment.* The second method is to bombard a stable isotope with protons. Protons are produced in a particle accelerator, a device that removes the electrons from an atom and accelerates the nucleus to very high speeds. For instance, proton bombardment is used to make fluorine-18 for PET. When oxygen-18 (a naturally occurring isotope of oxygen) collides with a proton, it absorbs the proton and expels a neutron to form fluorine-18.

$$^{18}_{8}\text{O} + ^{1}_{1}\text{p} \rightarrow ^{18}_{9}\text{F} + ^{1}_{0}\text{n}$$

Health Note: Samarium-153 is used to relieve the pain of bone cancer, and it may reduce the size of bone tumors. Most ^{153}Sm is produced by neutron bombardment using naturally occurring samarium-152.

If the protons are traveling at extremely high velocities, they can knock several particles out of the nucleus. For example, chemists can make samarium-153 by bombarding gadolinium with protons. In this reaction, three protons and three neutrons are knocked out of a gadolinium-158 atom.

$$^{158}_{64}\text{Gd} + ^{1}_{1}\text{p} \rightarrow ^{153}_{62}\text{Sm} + 3\ ^{1}_{1}\text{p} + 3\ ^{1}_{0}\text{n}$$

3. *Light atom bombardment.* The third method is to force a heavy atom to collide with the nucleus of a lighter atom. Chemists use this method to make many of the elements beyond uranium (atomic number 92). These transuranium elements do not exist on Earth, and all known isotopes of them are radioactive. For example, chemists can make nobelium (element 102) by bombarding curium-246 (itself a transuranium element) with carbon-12 nuclei. This reaction also produces four neutrons.

$$^{246}_{96}\text{Cm} + ^{12}_{6}\text{C} \rightarrow ^{254}_{102}\text{No} + 4\ ^{1}_{0}\text{n}$$

Sample Problem 16.4

Completing a nuclear equation

In 1982, physicists used the following reaction to make the first known atoms of an extremely heavy element. Complete the nuclear equation and identify the element.

$$^{209}_{83}\text{Bi} + ^{58}_{26}\text{Fe} \rightarrow ? + ^{1}_{0}\text{n}$$

continued

SOLUTION

The mass numbers of the reactants add up to 267, and the atomic numbers add up to 109. The mass numbers and atomic numbers of the products must also add up to these numbers, so the mass number of the missing product is 267 − 1 = 266 and the atomic number of the missing product is 109. Element 109 is meitnerium (Mt), so the complete nuclear equation is

$$^{209}_{83}\text{Bi} + ^{58}_{26}\text{Fe} \rightarrow ^{266}_{109}\text{Mt} + ^{1}_{0}\text{n}$$

TRY IT YOURSELF: *In 1974, physicists used the following reaction to make the first known atoms of another extremely heavy element. Complete the nuclear equation and identify the element.*

$$^{249}_{98}\text{Cf} + ^{18}_{8}\text{O} \rightarrow ? + 4\ ^{1}_{0}\text{n}$$

For additional practice, try Core Problems 16.15 and 16.16.

CORE PROBLEMS

16.9 Write the nuclear symbol for each of the following particles:
a) proton b) electron

16.10 Write the nuclear symbol for each of the following particles:
a) neutron b) positron

16.11 Classify each of the following nuclear reactions as an alpha decay, a beta decay, or a positron emission:
a) $^{200}_{83}\text{Bi} \rightarrow ^{200}_{82}\text{Pb} + ^{0}_{+1}e$
b) $^{209}_{83}\text{Bi} \rightarrow ^{205}_{81}\text{Tl} + ^{4}_{2}\text{He}$
c) $^{214}_{83}\text{Bi} \rightarrow ^{214}_{84}\text{Po} + ^{0}_{-1}e$

16.12 Classify each of the following nuclear reactions as an alpha decay, a beta decay, or a positron emission:
a) $^{210}_{84}\text{Po} \rightarrow ^{206}_{82}\text{Pb} + ^{4}_{2}\text{He}$
b) $^{207}_{84}\text{Po} \rightarrow ^{207}_{83}\text{Bi} + ^{0}_{+1}e$
c) $^{217}_{84}\text{Po} \rightarrow ^{217}_{85}\text{At} + ^{0}_{-1}e$

16.13 Write the nuclear equation for each of the following reactions:
a) the alpha decay of $^{209}_{84}\text{Po}$
b) the beta decay of oxygen-18
c) the positron emission of oxygen-15

16.14 Write the nuclear equation for each of the following reactions:
a) the positron emission of $^{99}_{45}\text{Rh}$
b) the alpha decay of uranium-234
c) the beta decay of silver-110

16.15 The following nuclear reaction is used to make one of the transuranium elements. Complete this nuclear equation.

$$^{209}_{98}\text{Cf} + ^{15}_{7}\text{N} \rightarrow ? + 4\ ^{1}_{0}\text{n}$$

16.16 The following nuclear reaction is used to make one of the transuranium elements. Complete this nuclear equation.

$$^{249}_{97}\text{Bk} + ^{22}_{10}\text{Ne} \rightarrow ? + 4\ ^{1}_{0}\text{n}$$

16.17 Iodine-131 is an important radioisotope in medicine. It is produced from naturally occurring tellurium-130 by the following sequence of reactions:

$$^{130}_{52}\text{Te} + ^{1}_{0}\text{n} \rightarrow ^{131}_{52}\text{Te}$$

$$^{131}_{52}\text{Te} \rightarrow ^{131}_{53}\text{I} + ^{0}_{-1}e$$

Is iodine-131 made in a nuclear reactor, or is it made in a particle accelerator? Explain your reasoning.

16.18 Indium-111 can be used to diagnose certain types of infections. It is produced from tin by the following nuclear reaction:

$$^{120}_{50}\text{Sn} + ^{1}_{1}\text{H} \rightarrow ^{111}_{49}\text{In} + 2\ ^{1}_{1}\text{H} + 8\ ^{1}_{0}\text{n}$$

Is indium-111 made in a nuclear reactor, or is it made in a particle accelerator? Explain your reasoning.

16.3 Energy and Nuclear Reactions

OBJECTIVES: *Explain how nuclear reactions produce energy, and describe the various types of electromagnetic radiation.*

Nuclear reactions produce a great deal of energy. As a result, people have harnessed nuclear reactions in a variety of ways, from generating electricity for our homes to supplying power for a spacecraft. However, the energy of a nuclear reaction poses a significant health hazard to us, because it is produced in a form that can damage vital molecules such as proteins and DNA. In this section, we will look at the source of the energy in a nuclear reaction and at the forms that this energy takes.

Nuclear Reactions Convert Matter into Energy

One of the most conspicuous differences between nuclear and chemical reactions is the amount of energy that each type produces. For example, here are two reactions involving carbon. The first is a chemical reaction, while the second is a nuclear reaction.

$$C + O_2 \rightarrow CO_2 + 94\text{ kcal} \qquad \text{chemical reaction}$$

$$^{14}_{6}C \rightarrow {}^{14}_{7}N + {}^{0}_{-1}e + 3{,}590{,}000\text{ kcal} \qquad \text{nuclear reaction}$$

The nuclear reaction produces more than 30,000 times as much energy as the chemical reaction. In general, *nuclear reactions produce far more energy than any chemical reaction.*

As we saw in Section 6.4, chemical reactions convert potential energy (which depends on the bonds between the atoms) into thermal energy (which we feel as heat). The numbers and kinds of atoms do not change in a chemical reaction, so the products and reactants have exactly the same mass. On the other hand, *nuclear reactions convert mass into energy.* In the preceding nuclear reaction, 1 mol of carbon-14 weighs 14.003241 g, while the products weigh only 14.003074 g. The difference between these two masses is very small (only 0.000167 g). However, a tiny amount of mass becomes an enormous amount of energy in a nuclear reaction. The relationship between mass and energy is based on Einstein's famous formula:

$$E = mc^2$$

In this formula, m is the mass that vanishes during the reaction, E is the resulting energy, and c is the speed of light, which is a very large number. The relationship between mass and energy in a nuclear reaction is

$$1\text{ g of mass lost} = 21{,}500{,}000{,}000\text{ kcal of energy}$$
$$= 2.15 \times 10^{10}\text{ kcal}$$

Using this relationship between mass and energy, we find that when our reaction destroys 0.000167 g of carbon-14, it produces 3,590,000 kcal of energy.

Sample Problem 16.5

Relating mass to energy in a nuclear reaction

Iodine-131 is a radioisotope of iodine that is used extensively to diagnose and treat thyroid disorders. When 131 g of iodine-131 undergoes beta decay, 1.04 mg of mass is converted into energy. How much energy is produced in this reaction?

SOLUTION

STEP 1: Identify the original measurement and the final unit.

Let us start by understanding the question. We are using 131 g of iodine-131, but only 1.04 mg of this is changing into energy. Therefore, we do not need to use the total mass of the iodine-131 to solve the problem. All we need to do is convert 1.04 mg of mass into the corresponding amount of energy. Our answer should be a number of kilocalories.

We know that we get 2.15×10^{10} kcal for every gram of mass that we convert into energy. However, our mass is given in milligrams, so our first step is to convert 1.04 mg into grams. To do this conversion, we move the decimal point three places to the left.

$$0001.04\text{ mg} = 0.00104\text{ g}$$

STEP 2: Write conversion factors that relate the two units.

Now we can translate this mass into energy. The conversion factors that relate mass to energy in a nuclear reaction are

$$\frac{2.15\times10^{10}\text{ kcal}}{1\text{ g}} \quad \text{and} \quad \frac{1\text{ g}}{2.15\times10^{10}\text{ kcal}}$$

STEP 3: Choose the conversion factor that allows you to cancel units.

The first of these two conversion factors allows us to cancel units correctly.

$$0.00104\,\text{g} \times \frac{2.15\times10^{10}\text{ kcal}}{1\,\text{g}} = 2.236\times10^{7}\text{ kcal} \quad \text{calculator answer}$$

continued

Finally, we round our answer to three significant figures. This reaction produces 2.24×10^7 kcal (22,400,000 kcal) of energy.

TRY IT YOURSELF: *Thallium-201 is used to detect and evaluate coronary artery disease. This isotope undergoes a type of nuclear decay called electron capture.*

$$^{201}_{81}Tl + {}^{0}_{-1}e \rightarrow {}^{201}_{80}Hg$$

When 201 g of ^{201}Tl decays, 0.517 mg of mass is converted into energy. How much energy is produced in this reaction?

For additional practice, try Core Problems 16.21 and 16.22.

The Energy of a Nuclear Reaction Can Appear in Two Forms

The energy of nuclear reactions is released in two forms. The first of these is the kinetic energy of the small particle (alpha or beta) that is released. As we saw in Section 4.1, any moving object has kinetic energy, because a moving object can do work when it hits something. The small particles that are emitted in a nuclear reaction are traveling extremely fast, so they have a great deal of kinetic energy.

The second type of energy that is formed by nuclear reactions is **electromagnetic radiation.** Although you may not have realized it, you have already encountered many types of electromagnetic radiation in your everyday life, including visible light, radio waves, microwaves, and X-rays. All forms of electromagnetic radiation come in tiny packets of energy called **photons**, which travel at 186,000 miles per second (the speed of light). Each type of radiation corresponds to a different amount of energy in these photons. Figure 16.3 shows the common types of electromagnetic radiation and their photon energies. Because the energy of one photon is extremely small, photon energies are expressed in kilocalories per mole. All types of electromagnetic radiation are fundamentally similar to light, but most types of electromagnetic radiation are invisible to humans, because our eyes only respond to radiation that has photon energies between 40 and 70 kcal/mol.

When a nuclear reaction produces electromagnetic radiation, it does so in the form of **gamma radiation**. Photons of gamma radiation have extremely high energies, typically more than 10 million kcal/mol. As we will see, these high energies make gamma radiation a significant health hazard.

Only a few nuclear reactions produce gamma radiation alone. One example is the nuclear decay of technetium-99. The protons and neutrons in this nucleus can arrange themselves in two ways, one of which (called the metastable state) is less stable than the other. Metastable technetium-99 changes into the more stable form by giving off gamma radiation. The nuclear symbol for gamma radiation is γ.

$$^{99m}_{43}Tc \rightarrow {}^{99}_{43}Tc + \gamma$$

Technetium-99m is widely used in diagnostic imaging, because gamma radiation (unlike alpha or beta particles) passes through body tissues easily, allowing it to be measured by a detector outside the body.

Health Note: Sunlight contains a significant amount of ultraviolet radiation, which has enough energy to break chemical bonds and remove electrons from molecules. As a result, ultraviolet radiation causes tissue damage and can produce cancer. Sunscreen blocks UV radiation or converts it to harmless heat.

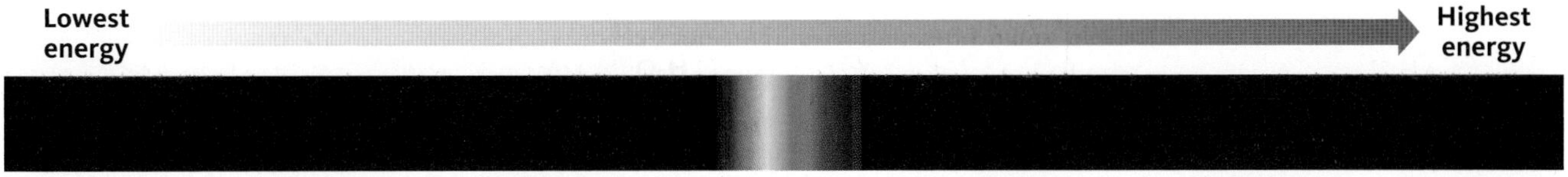

FIGURE 16.3 The main types of electromagnetic radiation.

Many nuclear reactions produce both a small particle (alpha, beta, or positron) and the gamma radiation. In these reactions, part of the reaction energy is carried off by the particle in the form of kinetic energy, while the rest appears as gamma radiation. For example, when 1 mol of cobalt-60 undergoes beta decay, it releases 65 million kcal of energy. About 7 million kcal are carried off by the beta particles, while the remaining 58 million kcal are released as gamma radiation. When we write the nuclear equation for this kind of reaction, we can include the gamma symbol, but this is not necessary.

$$^{60}_{24}\text{Co} \rightarrow\ ^{60}_{25}\text{Ni} +\ ^{0}_{-1}\text{e} + \gamma$$
or
$$^{60}_{24}\text{Co} \rightarrow\ ^{60}_{25}\text{Ni} +\ ^{0}_{-1}\text{e}$$

Note the difference between a reaction that produces a particle and one that produces only gamma radiation. When a nuclear reaction produces alpha particles, beta particles, or positrons, the product is a different element. By contrast, gamma emission produces a more stable nucleus of the same element.

Nuclear Reactions Produce Ionizing Radiation

The high energies of nuclear reactions make them hazardous to living organisms, because it only takes 200 to 300 kcal/mol of energy to remove an electron from a molecule or atom. Any type of radiation that has more energy than this can knock an electron out of a molecule, turning the molecule into a positively charged ion. Gamma radiation, X-rays, and high-energy ultraviolet light fall into this category, as do alpha or beta particles that are produced in nuclear reactions. These types of radiation are called **ionizing radiation**. Alpha, beta, and gamma radiation contain so much energy that they can ionize many molecules in materials that absorb them.

When any type of ionizing radiation (particle or photon) hits a molecule, the molecule loses an electron, as shown in Figure 16.4. The resulting ion has an odd number of electrons and cannot satisfy the octet rule. Molecules or ions that have an odd number of electrons are called **radicals**. Most radicals are not stable and immediately attack neighboring molecules, removing electrons to fill the empty spaces in their valence shells. These reactions break bonds in the neighboring molecules and create new radicals. As a result, ionizing radiation can be devastating to a living cell, because the radicals it forms can damage or destroy vital molecules in the cell. We will examine the biological effects of nuclear radiation in the next section.

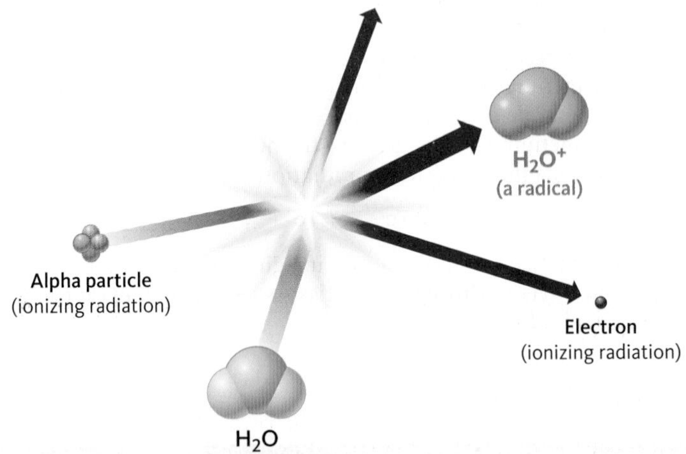

FIGURE 16.4 The formation of a radical.

CORE PROBLEMS

16.19 Classify each of the following as particles or electromagnetic radiation:
a) X-rays
b) alpha radiation
c) visible light

16.20 Classify each of the following as particles or electromagnetic radiation:
a) radio waves
b) gamma radiation
c) beta radiation

continued

16.21 In the following nuclear reaction, the products weigh 0.46 mg less than the reactant. How much energy does this reaction produce when 133 g of xenon-133 reacts?

$$^{133}_{54}\text{Xe} \rightarrow {}^{133}_{55}\text{Cs} + {}^{0}_{-1}e$$

16.22 In the following nuclear reaction, the products weigh 5.9 mg less than the reactant. How much energy does this reaction produce when 24 g of sodium-24 reacts?

$$^{24}_{11}\text{Na} \rightarrow {}^{24}_{12}\text{Mg} + {}^{0}_{-1}e$$

16.23 In the reaction in Problem 16.21, the energy of the beta particles is 8,000,000 kcal.

a) What other type of radiation must this reaction produce? (Hint: Compare the energy of the beta particles to your answer to Problem 16.21.)
b) What is the energy of the radiation you identified in part a?

16.24 In the reaction in Problem 16.22, the energy of the beta particles is 32,000,000 kcal.

a) What other type of radiation must this reaction produce? (Hint: Compare the energy of the beta particles to your answer to Problem 16.22.)
b) What is the energy of the radiation you identified in part a?

16.25 Metastable krypton-81 decays by emitting gamma radiation.

$$^{81m}_{36}\text{Kr} \rightarrow {}^{81}_{36}\text{Kr} + 4{,}400{,}000 \text{ kcal}$$

a) How much mass is converted into energy in this reaction?
b) The exact mass of 1 mol of ^{81}Kr is 80.916590 g. How much does 1 mol of ^{81m}Kr weigh?

16.26 Metastable cobalt-60 decays by emitting gamma radiation.

$$^{60m}_{27}\text{Co} \rightarrow {}^{60}_{27}\text{Co} + 1{,}361{,}000 \text{ kcal}$$

a) How much mass is converted into energy in this reaction?
b) The exact mass of 1 mol of ^{60}Co is 59.9338222 g. How much does 1 mol of ^{60m}Co weigh?

16.27 Which of the following are examples of ionizing radiation?

a) gamma radiation
b) infrared radiation
c) alpha particles

16.28 Which of the following are examples of ionizing radiation?

a) microwaves b) beta radiation c) X-rays

16.29 How does ionizing radiation produce radicals?

16.30 If one electron is removed from a molecule of NH_3, will the product be a radical? Why or why not?

16.4 Measuring Radiation

OBJECTIVE: *Describe the tools that are used to measure ionizing radiation and the units used to express amounts of radiation.*

Our bodies are exposed to ionizing radiation from a variety of sources, including naturally occurring radioactive elements and medical procedures such as X-rays. As we saw in Section 16.3, ionizing radiation has a great deal of energy and can be harmful to living tissues. Therefore, it is important to be able to measure both the amount of radiation a person is exposed to and the effect of the radiation on the human body. In this section, we will look at the ways that ionizing radiation is detected and measured, and in the next section, we will examine sources of radiation in our lives and how we can decrease our exposure to hazardous radiation.

There Are Several Ways to Detect Ionizing Radiation

We cannot see or feel ionizing radiation, but we can detect it in several ways. The simplest detection method uses a piece of photographic film covered by a cardboard barrier. The cardboard blocks visible light, but it does not block gamma radiation and X-rays, and it only partially blocks beta radiation. If the film absorbs a significant amount of ionizing radiation, it darkens, just as it would if it were exposed to light. People who work with radiation sources often wear radiation badges that contain film. These badges are collected and developed regularly. If a badge is darkened, the worker who wore that badge was exposed to excess radiation.

Film badges do not measure the amount of radiation. A common method for measuring beta or gamma radiation is the **Geiger counter**. In a Geiger counter, ionizing radiation passes through a tube filled with argon, one of the inert gases. When a particle or photon of ionizing radiation enters the tube, it ionizes an argon atom.

$$\text{Ar} + \text{radiation} \rightarrow \text{Ar}^+ + e^-$$

Charles D. Winters

A Geiger counter.

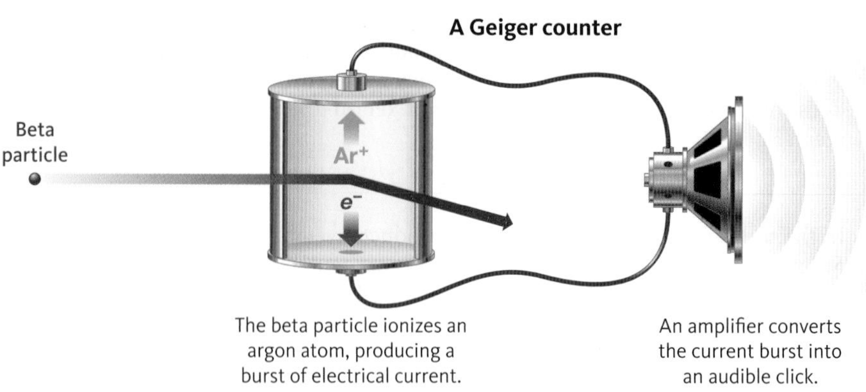
A Geiger counter
Beta particle
Ar+
e−
The beta particle ionizes an argon atom, producing a burst of electrical current.
An amplifier converts the current burst into an audible click.

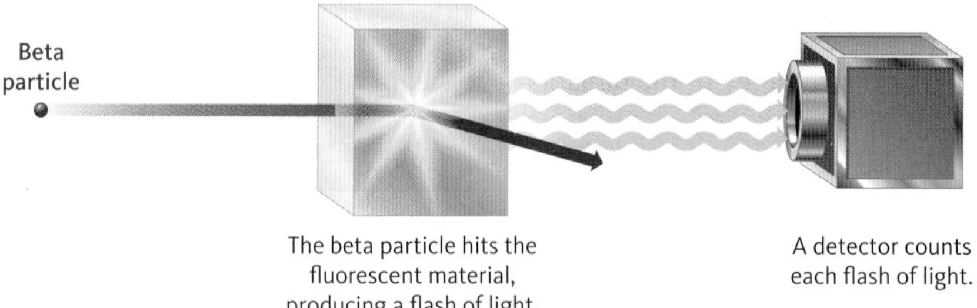
A scintillation counter
Beta particle
The beta particle hits the fluorescent material, producing a flash of light.
A detector counts each flash of light.

FIGURE 16.5 Two types of radiation detectors.

The argon ion collides with other atoms and ionizes them, producing a tiny burst of electrical current, which is amplified by the counter to an audible "click" and a reading on a meter.

A second method for measuring ionizing radiation is the **scintillation counter**, which uses a fluorescent material to detect ionizing radiation. When the material absorbs a particle or photon of ionizing radiation, it produces a brief flash of light, which can be detected and counted. Geiger counters are inexpensive and portable, but they are much less sensitive than scintillation counters. Figure 16.5 shows a simplified drawing of each of these two types of radiation detectors.

TABLE 16.3 Radiation Weighting Factors for Ionizing Radiation

Type of Radiation	Radiation Weighting Factor (W_R)
X-rays	1
Gamma radiation	1
Beta particles (electrons)	1
Positrons	1
Protons	2 to 5, depending on energy
Neutrons	5 to 20, depending on energy
Alpha particles	20

Equivalent Dose Measures the Effect of Radiation on Living Tissues

Scientists use several units to measure ionizing radiation. In medicine, we are most concerned with the effect of ionizing radiation on the living tissues in our bodies. The amount of tissue damage that is produced by an exposure to ionizing radiation is called the **equivalent radiation dose.** The most commonly used unit of equivalent dose is the *rem*. One rem is a significant amount of radiation, roughly the same as 200 chest X-rays or a single abdominal CT scan, so equivalent doses are often expressed in millirems (mrem).

When our bodies are exposed to ionizing radiation, the equivalent dose depends on two factors. The first of these is the amount of energy that we absorb as the radiation passes through our bodies. One rem corresponds to the effect of 0.01 J (0.0024 cal) of X-ray radiation. Therefore, if we absorb twice as much energy (0.02 J), the equivalent dose is 2 rem. The second factor is the type of radiation. For example, our bodies sustain 20 times as much damage from alpha radiation as they do from an equal amount of X-rays. As we will see in Section 16.5, X-rays only affect a small fraction of the cells that they pass through. As a result, tissues do not sustain much damage from exposure to X-rays, and the body can repair or replace the few cells that are damaged with no lasting ill effects. In contrast, alpha particles can produce many ions within a very small region of tissue, overwhelming the body's repair mechanisms and producing permanent tissue damage.

The relative effect of each type of radiation compared to X-rays is called the **radiation weighting factor (W_R)**. For instance, alpha particles produce 20 times as much damage as do X-rays, so the W_R for alpha radiation is 20. Table 16.3 lists several types of radiation and their weighting factors. Note that the older terms *quality factor (Q)* and *relative biological effectiveness (RBE)* are also widely used for the W_R.

Sample Problem 16.6

Relating radiation dose to equivalent dose

If you absorb 0.03 J of energy from exposure to X-rays, your equivalent dose is 3 rem. What is the equivalent dose if you absorb 0.03 J of energy from protons that have a W_R of 4?

SOLUTION

To calculate the equivalent dose for protons, we multiply the equivalent dose for X-rays (3 rem) by the W_R.

$$3 \text{ rem} \times 4 = 12 \text{ rem}$$

The equivalent dose is 12 rem.

TRY IT YOURSELF: *If you absorb 0.02 J of energy from exposure to X-rays, your equivalent dose is 2 rem. What is the equivalent dose if you absorb 0.02 J of energy from neutrons that have a W_R of 15?*

For additional practice, try Core Problems 16.39 and 16.40.

Activity Measures the Number of Atoms That Break Down in a Second

Devices such as Geiger counters and scintillation counters do not measure the biological effect of radiation. Instead, they measure the number of decay products (alpha particles, beta particles, or gamma photons) that are produced by a sample of radioactive material. The number of decay products that a radioactive sample produces per second is called the **activity** of the sample, and it is the same as the number of atoms that break down (disintegrate) in one second.

The traditional unit of activity is the *curie (Ci)*, which equals 37 billion disintegrations per second. This number was chosen because it is the activity of 1 g of the element radium. However, this is an inconveniently large unit for describing activities of radioisotopes in medicine. As a result, the activities of most samples in clinical work are measured in millicuries (mCi) or microcuries (μCi). A curie equals 1000 mCi or 1 million μCi.

Table 16.4 shows the activity of a 1-microgram sample of some important radioisotopes. The substances in this table have an enormous range of activities, because they break down at vastly different rates. For example, 99.99% of the ^{18}F atoms in a sample break down in one day, compared to only 0.00003% of the ^{14}C atoms. As a result, the activity of fluorine-18 is much greater than the activity of an equal amount of carbon-14.

TABLE 16.4 Radioisotope Activity

Isotope	Medical Significance	Activity of a 1-μg Sample
Carbon-14	Estimating the age of archeological specimens	0.0045 mCi (4.5 μCi)
Cobalt-60	Cancer treatment and sterilization of medical supplies	1.14 mCi
Iodine-131	Diagnosis and treatment of thyroid disorders	126 mCi
Technetium-99m	Diagnostic imaging	5300 mCi
Fluorine-18	Diagnostic imaging (PET scans)	96,000 mCi (96 Ci)

Sample Problem **16.7**

Relating activity to mass

A patient is given a dose of technetium-99m to evaluate his liver function. The activity of the dose is 7.0 mCi. What is the mass of technetium-99m in this sample?

SOLUTION

From Table 16.4, we see that 1 μg of ^{99m}Tc has an activity of 5300 mCi. We can use this relationship as a conversion factor.

$$7\ \cancel{\text{mCi}} \times \frac{1\ \mu\text{g}}{5300\ \cancel{\text{mCi}}} = 0.001320755\ \mu\text{g} \quad \text{calculator answer}$$

Finally, we round our answer to two significant figures. The mass of technetium-99m in the sample is 0.0013 μg.

TRY IT YOURSELF: *A patient is given a dose of iodine-131 to treat thyroid cancer. The activity of the dose is 200 mCi. What is the mass of iodine-131 in this sample?*

In clinical work, radiologists measure nuclear radiation by placing a detector close to the radioactive material and counting the number of ionizing particles or photons that enter the detector. Since the detector does not measure every atom that breaks down, these measurements are normally expressed in *counts per minute (cpm)*. A larger number of counts per minute indicates a higher activity for the radioactive sample.

Many Other Units Are Used in Nuclear Medicine

Health care professionals and other people who work with radioactive materials use a variety of units to measure radiation. For example, both activity and equivalent dose can be expressed using newer units that are part of the SI system. The SI unit of equivalent dose is the *sievert (Sv)*, and the SI unit of activity is the *becquerel (Bq)*. The relationships between the traditional and SI units are

$$1\ \text{Ci} = 37{,}000{,}000{,}000\ \text{Bq}\ (3.7 \times 10^{10}\ \text{Bq})$$

$$1\ \text{rem} = 0.01\ \text{Sv}$$

The becquerel is a very small unit, equal to just one disintegration per second. Therefore, activities of clinical samples are usually expressed in megabecquerels (MBq), where 1 MBq equals 1 million Bq. A convenient relationship between the traditional and SI units of activity that are used in clinical settings is

$$1\ \text{mCi} = 37\ \text{MBq}$$

Radiation doses can also be expressed in *rads*. A rad is similar to a rem, but it does not account for the differences between types of radiation. One rad equals 0.01 J of energy, regardless of the type of radiation. As a result, the number of rems is related to the number of rads as follows:

$$\text{rads} \times W_R = \text{rems}$$

Table 16.5 summarizes the base units used to measure radiation. Bear in mind that the base units are often inconveniently large or small, so health care workers often use derived units such as millirems, microcuries, and megabecquerels instead of the base units. Table 16.6 shows some of the metric prefixes that are used in nuclear medicine.

TABLE 16.5 Common Units Used to Measure Radiation

Base Unit	Type of Unit	Measurement	Useful Relationships
Rem	Traditional	Equivalent dose (amount of tissue damage produced by ionizing radiation)	100 rem = 1 Sv
Sievert (Sv)	Metric (SI)		
Curie (Ci)	Traditional	Activity of a radioactive sample (number of atoms that break down per second)	1 Ci = 3.7×10^{10} Bq (1 mCi = 37 MBq)
Becquerel (Bq)	Metric (SI)		
Rad	Traditional	Amount of energy absorbed by matter exposed to ionizing radiation	100 rad = 1 Gy
Gray (Gy)	Metric (SI)		

TABLE 16.6 Metric Prefixes Used in Nuclear Medicine

Prefix (Abbreviation)	Meaning	Example
Giga- (G)	1,000,000,000 base units	Gigabecquerel (GBq) 1 GBq = 1,000,000,000 Bq (1 GBq = 10^9 Bq)
Mega- (M)	1,000,000 base units	Megabecquerel (MBq) 1 MBq = 1,000,000 Bq (1 MBq = 10^6 Bq)
Milli- (m)	$\frac{1}{1000}$ of the base unit	Millirem (mrem) 1000 mrem = 1 rem (10^3 mrem = 1 rem)
Micro- (μ)	$\frac{1}{1,000,000}$ of the base unit	Microcurie (μCi) 1,000,000 μCi = 1 Ci (10^6 μCi = 1 Ci)
Nano- (n)	$\frac{1}{1,000,000,000}$ of the base unit	Nanocurie (nCi) 1,000,000,000 nCi = 1 Ci (10^9 nCi = 1 Ci)
Pico- (p)	$\frac{1}{1,000,000,000,000}$ of the base unit	Picocurie (pCi) 1,000,000,000,000 pCi = 1 Ci (10^{12} Ci = 1 Ci)

Sample Problem **16.8**

Converting traditional units into SI units

The activity of an ^{131}I sample is 26.4 mCi. Convert this activity into gigabecquerels.

SOLUTION

From Table 16.5, we see that 1 mCi equals 37 MBq. This relationship allows us to convert the activity into megabecquerels.

$$26.4\ \cancel{\text{mCi}} \times \frac{37\ \text{MBq}}{1\ \cancel{\text{mCi}}} = 976.8\ \text{MBq}$$

continued

• These metric prefixes appear on the extended metric railroad (Figure 1.12).

A gigabecquerel is 1 billion Bq, and a megabecquerel is 1 million Bq. Therefore, 1 GBq equals 1000 MBq. We can use this relationship to convert megabecquerels into gigabecquerels.

$$976.8 \cancel{\text{MBq}} \times \frac{1 \text{ GBq}}{1000 \cancel{\text{MBq}}} = 0.9768 \text{ GBq}$$

Finally, we round our answer to three significant figures. The activity of the sample is 0.977 GBq. (The relationship 37 MBq = 1 mCi is an exact number, so it does not affect the number of significant figures in the answer.)

TRY IT YOURSELF: *A sample of ^{32}P has an activity of 16 μCi. Convert this activity into megabecquerels.*

For additional practice, try Core Problems 16.35 and 16.36.

CORE PROBLEMS

16.31 Why do people who work with sources of ionizing radiation often wear a badge that contains a piece of photographic film?

16.32 List two instruments that are used to measure radiation.

16.33 Which of the following traditional units is used to measure the effect of ionizing radiation on the human body?
a) curie b) rad c) rem

16.34 Which of the units in Problem 16.33 is used to measure the number of atoms that disintegrate per second?

16.35 The activity of 1 μg of ^{32}P is 41 mCi. Convert this activity into each of the following units:
a) Ci b) μCi c) MBq d) Bq e) GBq

16.36 The activity of 1 μg of ^{103}Pd is 2.8 MBq. Convert this activity into each of the following units:
a) Bq b) GBq c) μCi d) mCi e) Ci

16.37 A patient absorbs 30 mrem during radiation therapy. Express this equivalent dose in each of the following units:
a) rem b) Sv c) mSv

16.38 A patient absorbs 4.2 mSv during radiation therapy. Express this equivalent dose in each the following units:
a) Sv b) rem c) mrem

16.39 Two patients absorbed equal amounts of energy from nuclear radiation. Patient 1 was exposed to gamma radiation and received a dose of 15 mrem. Patient 2 was exposed to a proton beam with a W_R of 3. What equivalent dose did patient 2 receive?

16.40 Two nuclear workers absorbed equal amounts of energy from nuclear radiation. Worker 1 was exposed to neutrons with a W_R of 12 and received a dose of 80 mrem. Worker 2 was exposed to beta radiation. What equivalent dose did worker 2 receive?

OBJECTIVES: *Identify common sources of radiation, compare the biological effect and penetrating ability of common types of nuclear radiation, and describe methods to protect the human body from exposure to nuclear radiation.*

16.5 Radiation Sources and Shielding

In our lives, we are constantly exposed to ionizing radiation. Some of this exposure is unavoidable. For example, the potassium in our bodies includes a small amount of potassium-40, a radioactive isotope that undergoes beta decay. Potassium is a necessary nutrient, and the ^{40}K cannot be separated from the nonradioactive isotopes of potassium, so we are always exposed to a small amount of beta radiation. We are also exposed to ionizing radiation as a result of human activities, such as X-rays and radioisotopes used in medical procedures. In this section, we will look at some of the sources of ionizing radiation and at the ways that people can limit their exposure to radiation.

Our Bodies Are Exposed to Many Sources of Radiation

Our bodies are constantly exposed to **background radiation**, ionizing radiation that is produced by naturally occurring materials. The sources of background radiation include radioisotopes in the atmosphere, food, and minerals and cosmic radiation from deep space, as shown in Table 16.7. The effective dose is typically around 300 mrem per year.

TABLE 16.7 Background Radiation Sources and Effective Dosages

Radiation Source	Typical Effective Dosage
Radon (an element that occurs in trace amounts in the atmosphere)	200 mrem per year (variable, depends on location)
Other inhaled and ingested sources (naturally occurring radioisotopes in dust, food, and water)	40 mrem per year
Mineral sources (radioactive elements in wood, stone, and various building materials)	20 to 100 mrem per year
Cosmic radiation (high-energy protons and alpha particles produced by the sun and other stars)	30 mrem at sea level, more at higher elevations
Total background radiation from natural sources	300 mrem per year (U.S. average)

The atmosphere absorbs cosmic radiation, so living or traveling at high elevations (where the atmosphere is thinner) increases your background radiation exposure.

Background radiation has been present since the formation of Earth, and living organisms have evolved to be able to repair the damage that it produces. As a result, our bodies normally suffer no discernible ill effects from a lifetime of exposure to background radiation.

By far the largest source of background radiation is radon, a colorless, odorless gaseous element. Radon is formed when the radioactive element uranium breaks down, and much of the radon escapes into the atmosphere before it too decays into lighter elements. Many kinds of rocks and minerals contain small amounts of uranium, as do most types of soil. As a result, radon is constantly diffusing from the ground into the air. The amount of radon produced by soil depends on the specific minerals in the soil, with some areas naturally containing more uranium than others.

Although all air contains some radon, the element tends to concentrate in indoor air, and it poses a particular problem in buildings that contain basements or ground floors that have poor ventilation. In such buildings, the radon concentration can be many times that in outdoor air, especially if the building is in an area that naturally produces more radon. In such areas, the background dose from radon can be higher than 500 mrem per year. Because radon is a naturally occurring element and cannot be removed from the air, radon exposure cannot be avoided completely. However, the U.S. Environmental Protection Agency recommends that homes with high levels of radon be modified to reduce the likelihood that radon will accumulate in the interior air. Figure 16.6 shows how the typical radon concentration in indoor air varies in the United States.

A variety of activities also expose people to ionizing radiation, the most significant of which is smoking. Tobacco smoke contains small amounts of lead-210 and polonium-210, both of which are radioactive and are deposited in the lungs of the smoker. Polonium-210 is an alpha emitter, so the lung tissue absorbs a high dose of radiation. The overall effective dose is around 300 mrem per year, but the actual effective dose to the lung tissue is estimated to be more than 10,000 mrem per year for a heavy smoker. Table 16.8 lists some other sources of radiation from human activities.

The radicals that are produced by ionizing radiation damage individual cells, but the long-term impact of low doses of radiation is not known. Cells that are severely damaged by ionizing radiation die, but the death of a small number of individual cells in otherwise healthy tissue normally has no observable impact on health. However, higher doses of radiation are known to cause cancer, because they can produce genetic mutations. Therefore, the U.S. government has set a limit of 5000 mrem per year for workers who are exposed to ionizing radiation.

Very high doses of radiation produce *radiation sickness,* in which enough cells are killed in vital organs to produce acute symptoms such as nausea, diarrhea, and lowered white blood cell counts. Symptoms of radiation sickness generally occur when a person has been exposed to 100 rem, and a whole-body dose between 400 and 500 rem is fatal to about 50% of people.

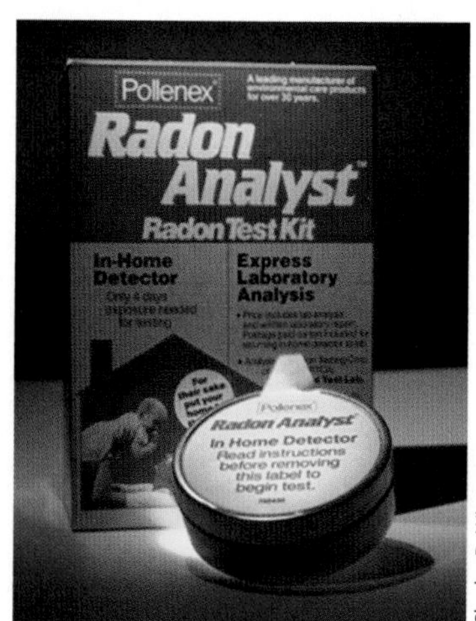

Charles D. Winters

Detectors like this one are recommended in areas that have increased levels of radon.

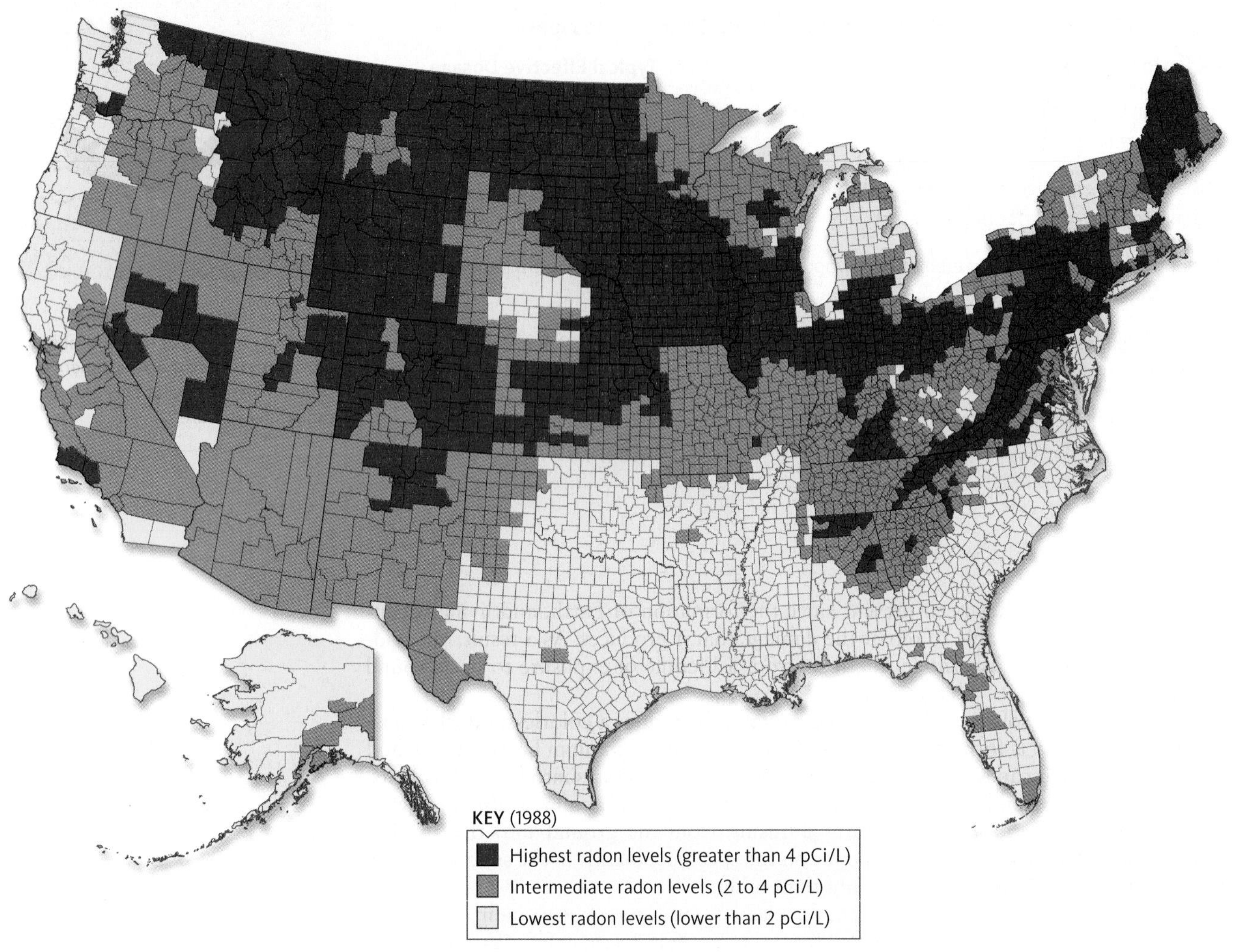

FIGURE 16.6 Radon in indoor air in the United States.

TABLE 16.8 Human Activities That Involve Radiation Exposure

Activity	Source of Exposure	Typical Effective Dose
Smoking	^{210}Pb and ^{210}Po in cigarette smoke	300 mrem per year (greater than 10,000 mrem per year to lung tissue)
Working in a nuclear power plant	Various radioisotopes	200 mrem per year
Radiologist or X-ray technician	X-rays	100 mrem per year
Medical procedures (patient exposure)	Primarily X-rays	40 mrem per year
Cooking using natural gas	Radon-222	7 mrem per year
Watching television	X-rays emitted by the television screen	1 mrem per year (assuming two hours of television per day)
Air travel	Cosmic radiation	0.6 mrem per hour of travel time
Living 5 miles from a nuclear power plant	Various radioisotopes	0.03 mrem per year

The Common Types of Ionizing Radiation Have Different Penetrating Abilities

The photons of X-rays and gamma radiation tend to pass through most types of matter rather easily without interacting with the atoms that they encounter. Only rather dense materials absorb significant amounts of X-ray and gamma radiation. As we will see in Section 16.7, the ability of X-rays to pass through soft tissues without being absorbed makes them useful in diagnostic imaging. By contrast, alpha and beta particles cannot normally penetrate far into any sort of material before they collide with an atom or molecule. Alpha particles in particular have limited penetrating ability. As a result, alpha emitters are extremely hazardous if ingested or inhaled, because the alpha particles produce extensive damage to nearby tissues. Recall from Section 16.4 that alpha particles have the highest W_R of all types of ionizing radiation. Figure 16.7 illustrates the different penetrating abilities of alpha, beta, and gamma radiation in living tissues.

Health care workers who are exposed to X-rays or radioactive materials must limit their exposure to ionizing radiation. One important way to limit exposure is by blocking the radiation with some sort of shielding material. The choice of material depends on the type of radiation. For example, alpha radiation has so little penetrating ability that it can be completely blocked by a piece of paper or a few centimeters of air. Even if an alpha source is held against the skin, most of the alpha particles will be absorbed by the layer of dead cells on the surface of the skin. As a result, alpha sources normally pose negligible risks to the people who must work with them. In contrast, only very dense materials such as a concrete wall or a sheet of lead can block gamma radiation and X-rays. Even these materials cannot block gamma radiation completely, so the goal is to keep the effective dose at a safe level.

Beta radiation poses a more complex problem. The beta particles themselves can be blocked by a variety of light materials such as cloth, plastic, and wood, as well as heavier materials like lead and concrete. However, when a beta particle hits an atom, the atom sometimes converts part of the energy of the beta particle into an X-ray photon. Heavy atoms are more prone to producing X-rays than are light atoms, so the preferred shielding for beta emitters is a piece of Plexiglas, a clear, durable plastic that is made from the light elements carbon, hydrogen, and oxygen. A thin sheet of lead is sometimes added outside the Plexiglas to block any X-rays that are produced. Figure 16.8 illustrates the types of materials that are used to shield people who must work with ionizing radiation.

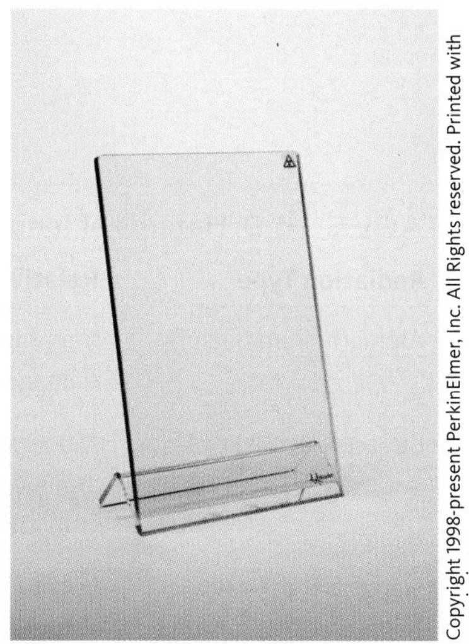

A lead-lined Plexiglas window for blocking beta radiation.

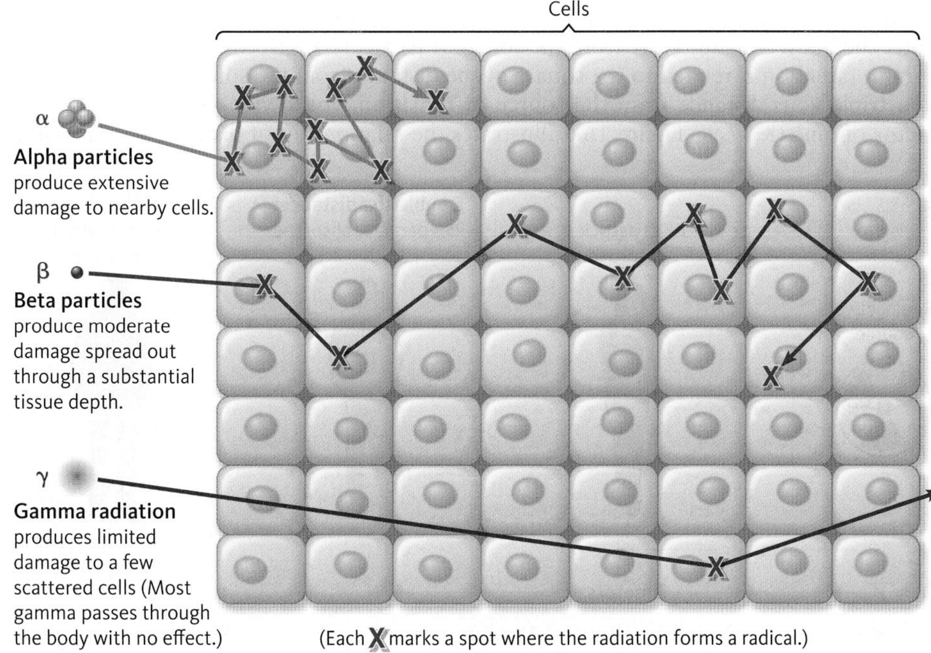

FIGURE 16.7 The penetrating ability of nuclear radiation in living tissues.

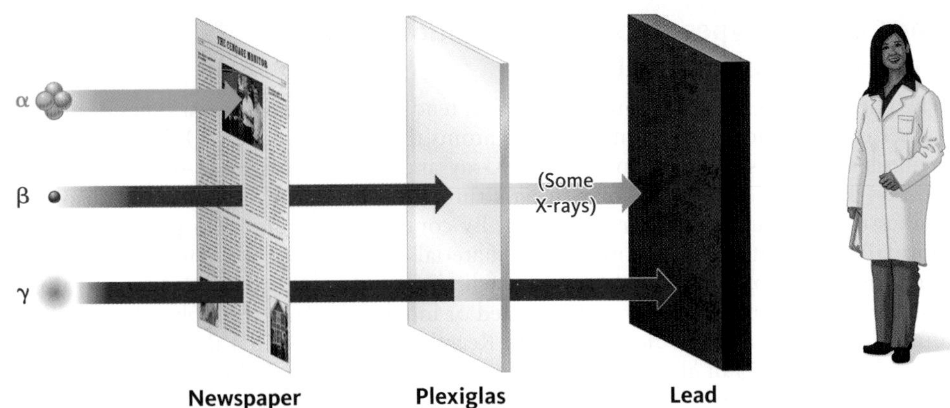

FIGURE 16.8 Shielding workers from ionizing radiation.

Table 16.9 summarizes the relative hazards of the common types of ionizing radiation.

TABLE 16.9 Hazards of Ionizing Radiation

Radiation Type	Relative Hazard if Taken Internally	Relative Hazard if from an External Source
Alpha (helium nuclei)	Very high: Alpha particles cause extensive damage to nearby cells.	Low: Alpha particles do not penetrate most materials and are blocked by a few centimeters of air.
Beta (electrons)	Moderate to high: Beta particles are lighter than alpha particles and penetrate farther, so individual cells suffer less damage than with alpha radiation.	Moderate: Beta particles can be blocked by wood, plastic, thick cloth, etc. Light materials are preferred to avoid production of X-rays.
Gamma and X-rays (high-energy photons)	Low to moderate: Most of the radiation passes through body tissues without doing damage.	High: Thick concrete or lead barriers are needed to block these types of radiation.

The Effects of Radiation Depend on Distance and Time

People can also decrease their exposure to ionizing radiation by moving away from the source of the radiation and by minimizing the amount of time that they are in the vicinity of the source. Both of these methods decrease the number of particles or photons that enter the body. Moving away from the source is particularly effective, because the exposure to radiation is related to the square of the distance from the source. For example, if you triple your distance from the source of radiation, you divide your exposure by a factor of nine ($3^2 = 9$). Figure 16.9 illustrates the relationship of distance to exposure.

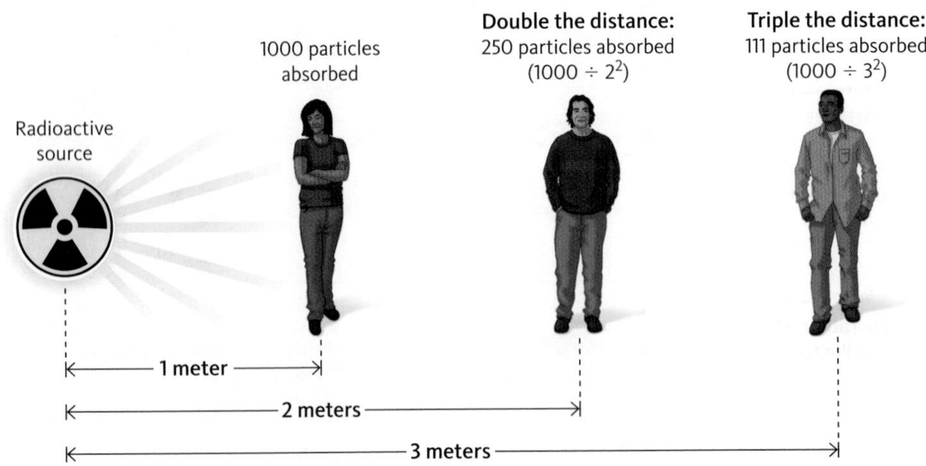

FIGURE 16.9 The relationship between distance and radiation absorption.

Sample Problem 16.9

Relating radiation exposure to distance

A worker standing 1 m from a radioactive source absorbs 2000 particles. How many particles would a worker standing 4 m from the source absorb during the same amount of time? Assume that none of the particles are blocked by air.

SOLUTION

The second worker is four times farther from the source than the first worker, so this worker absorbs 16 times fewer particles ($4^2 = 16$).

$$2000 \div 16 = 125 \text{ particles}$$

In practice, the second worker would probably absorb fewer than 125 particles, because 4 m of air blocks most alpha radiation and a significant fraction of beta radiation.

TRY IT YOURSELF: *How many particles would a worker absorb if he were standing 5 m from this source during the same amount of time, assuming that none of the particles are blocked by air?*

For additional practice, try Core Problems 16.49 and 16.50.

CORE PROBLEMS

16.41 What is background radiation?

16.42 List three sources of background radiation.

16.43 In areas that have high concentrations of uranium in the soil, homeowners are told that they should seal their basement floors with a piece of nonporous plastic. Why is this?

16.44 Some houses are built on top of wooden poles that are embedded in the ground. The lower story of these houses does not rest directly on the ground. Explain why people who live in such houses have lower-than-normal exposure to background radiation.

16.45 Which will produce a higher equivalent dose of radiation if it is taken internally: 10 μCi of ^{14}C (a beta emitter) or 10 μCi of ^{123}I (a gamma emitter)? Explain your answer.

16.46 Which of the radioisotopes in Problem 16.45 probably poses the lowest hazard to someone who is standing close to it? Explain your answer.

16.47 What would be an appropriate type of shielding for a sample of each of the following radioisotopes?
a) phosphorus-32 (a beta emitter)
b) technetium-99m (a gamma emitter)

16.48 What would be an appropriate type of shielding for a sample of each of the following radioisotopes?
a) bismuth-213 (an alpha emitter)
b) fluorine-18 (a positron emitter)

16.49 A worker standing 10 cm away from a gamma emitter received 50 mrem of radiation in one hour. How much radiation would this worker have absorbed if he had stood 1 m away from the radioisotope?

16.50 A scintillation counter measures 500 cpm of radiation when it is held 1 cm from a beta emitter. If the counter is 1 m away from the emitter, how much radiation will it measure? (Assume that the beta radiation can penetrate 1 m of air.)

16.6 Nuclear Decay and Half-Life

OBJECTIVES: *Use the half-life to relate the age of a radioactive sample to its activity, and describe how radioactive isotopes are used to estimate the age of various materials.*

Radioisotopes do not remain radioactive forever. Eventually, all of the atoms of any radioactive element break down into stable isotopes. Since radioisotopes can pose a significant health hazard, it is useful to know how long they will take to decay to nonradioactive elements. Unfortunately, there is no simple answer to this question, because nuclear reactions do not occur at a constant rate. Instead, nuclear reactions undergo **exponential decay**, in which a constant percentage breaks down in any given time. In this section, we will see how we can describe the decay of a sample of a radioisotope.

Half-Life Is the Time It Takes for Half of a Radioactive Sample to Decay

All radioisotopes have a **half-life**, which is the time required for half of a sample to break down. The half-life depends on the specific isotope, but it does not depend on the number of atoms in the sample. For example, the half-life of potassium-42 (a radioactive isotope of potassium that is used to study ion exchange in the heart) is 12 hours. Suppose that a sample of ^{42}K has an activity of 80 μCi at 6:00 a.m. By 6:00 p.m. (12 hours later), half of the atoms will have broken down, so the activity of our sample will be only 40 μCi. By 6:00 a.m. the next day, half of our remaining sample will decay, leaving us with only 20 μCi. Figure 16.10 shows how the activity of our potassium-42 sample decreases over time.

The curve in Figure 16.10 shows the activity of potassium-42 over a period of 60 hours. Note that the activity drops rapidly at first, but increasingly slowly as time goes on. We cannot calculate when all of the atoms of our sample will be broken down, but we can estimate the amount of time it will take for the sample to become small enough to pose no significant hazard.

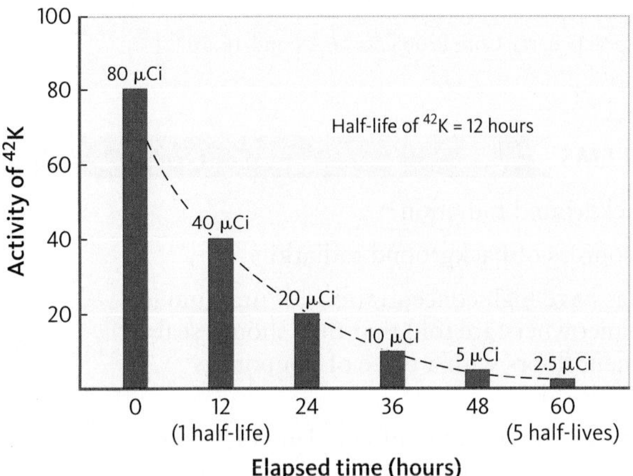

FIGURE 16.10 The decay of potassium-42.

Sample Problem 16.10

Relating half-life to activity

The half-life of nitrogen-13 is 10 minutes. A particle accelerator produces a sample of ^{13}N that has an activity of 28 μCi. How long will it take for the activity of this sample to drop to 2 μCi?

SOLUTION

Every 10 minutes the activity of our sample is cut in half. We can set up a table to follow the activity of the sample over time.

Elapsed Time	Number of Half-Lives	Activity of Sample
0 minutes	0	28 μCi
10 minutes	1	14 μCi
20 minutes	2	7 μCi
30 minutes	3	3.5 μCi
40 minutes	4	1.75 μCi

It will take between 30 and 40 minutes for the activity of the sample to drop to 2 μCi.

TRY IT YOURSELF: *The half-life of oxygen-15 is 2 minutes. How many minutes will it take for the activity of a sample of ^{15}O to decrease from 100 μCi to 20 μCi?*

For additional practice, try Core Problems 16.57 and 16.58.

TABLE 16.10 Half-Lives of Some Important Radioisotopes

Isotope	Uses and Source	Half-Life
Potassium-40	Estimating the age of mineral samples; naturally occurring	1.3 billion years
Carbon-14	Estimating the age of wood and fabric samples; naturally occurring	5730 years
Cobalt-60	Source of gamma radiation in nuclear medicine; artificial	5.27 years
Iodine-131	Diagnosing and treating thyroid conditions; artificial	8 days
Technetium-99m	Diagnostic imaging (most commonly used isotope); artificial	6 hours
Fluorine-18	Diagnostic imaging (PET); artificial	110 minutes

Half-lives vary enormously from one element to another. The shortest known half-lives are less than a microsecond, while ^{128}Te has the longest known half-life at 7.2×10^{24} years. Table 16.10 lists half-lives for some important radioisotopes. Note the inverse relationship between these half-lives and the activities of these radioisotopes (see Table 16.4). If the sample sizes are equal, *the radioisotope with the shorter half-life has the higher activity*. However, activity also depends on the size of the sample, while half-life does not.

Chemists Use Radioisotopes to Measure the Age of Minerals and Biological Materials

Scientists use several naturally occurring radioisotopes to estimate the age of various materials. For instance, potassium-40 can be used to estimate the age of a rock. This isotope is normally a beta emitter, but roughly 11% of the ^{40}K atoms in any sample absorb an electron and become argon-40. The two possible reactions of ^{40}K are shown here:

$$^{40}_{19}K \rightarrow {}^{40}_{20}Ca + {}^{0}_{-1}e \qquad \text{beta decay: 89\% of } ^{40}K \text{ atoms}$$

$$^{40}_{19}K + {}^{0}_{-1}e \rightarrow {}^{40}_{18}Ar \qquad \text{electron capture: 11\% of } ^{40}K \text{ atoms}$$

Argon is a gas and does not normally occur in mineral samples. However, the argon that is produced in the second reaction is trapped in the rock. As long as the rock is not melted, the argon remains within the mineral, so a high concentration of argon means that the rock is very old.

Carbon-14 occurs in any carbon-containing substance. This isotope is produced in the upper atmosphere when neutrons from solar radiation collide with nitrogen atoms.

$$^{14}_{7}N + {}^{1}_{0}n \rightarrow {}^{14}_{6}C + {}^{1}_{1}H$$

The atmosphere contains a constant concentration of carbon-14, because this isotope breaks down as fast as it is formed. Plants absorb carbon-14 in the form of CO_2, incorporating the carbon into organic compounds. Animals then eat the plants and absorb carbon-14 themselves. As a result, the tissues of all living organisms contain ^{14}C. However, once the organism dies, it no longer absorbs ^{14}C, so the concentration of this isotope slowly decreases as the atoms break down. The concentration of carbon-14 in a sample of organic matter is related to the number of years that have elapsed since the organism died. Sample Problem 16.11 shows how we can estimate the age of a wood sample from its carbon-14 activity.

This fragment of ancient manuscript was found to be 2100 years old by carbon-14 dating.

Sample Problem 16.11

Using carbon dating to estimate the age of an object

In a living organism, the organic material contains 0.22 Bq of ^{14}C per gram of carbon. A sample of wood from a dead tree contains 0.11 Bq of ^{14}C per gram of carbon. Approximately how long ago did the tree die?

SOLUTION

The activity of the wood sample is half of the normal ^{14}C activity, so one half-life has elapsed since the tree died. Table 16.10 tells us that the half-life of carbon-14 is 5730 years, so the tree died roughly 5700 years ago.

TRY IT YOURSELF: *A sample of charcoal from a campfire contains 0.055 Bq of ^{14}C per gram of carbon. How long ago was this campfire in use?*

For additional practice, try Core Problems 16.59 and 16.60.

CORE PROBLEMS

16.51 The half-life of phosphorus-32 is 14 days. If the activity of a sample of phosphorus-32 is 300 MBq on July 1, what will the activity of the sample be on August 12?

16.52 Strontium-90 is a radioactive isotope that is formed in nuclear explosions. The half-life of strontium-90 is 28 years. If a soil sample contains 36 pCi of strontium-90 in 2000, what will be the activity of the ^{90}Sr in this soil sample in 2084?

16.53 The half-life of ^{18}F is 110 minutes. A nuclear medicine clinic receives a 20-μCi sample of a compound containing ^{18}F at 1:00 p.m. If the ^{18}F was produced at 9:20 a.m., what was its activity when it was produced?

16.54 The half-life of ^{103}Pd is 17 days. A nuclear medicine clinic receives a set of ^{103}Pd seeds for prostate therapy on June 12, and the clinicians find that the activity of each seed is 18.6 μCi. If the ^{103}Pd was produced on May 9, what was the activity of each seed when it was produced?

16.55 A sample of radioactive ^{13}N has an activity of 40 μCi at 10:00 a.m. By 10:30 a.m., the activity of the sample has decreased to 5 μCi. What is the half-life of ^{13}N?

16.56 A sample of radioactive ^{11}C has an activity of 160 nCi at 2:00 p.m. By 3:20 p.m., the activity of the sample has decreased to 10 nCi. What is the half-life of ^{11}C?

16.57 A sample of iodine-131 (half-life = 8 days) has an activity of 10 mCi. Approximately how many days will it take for the activity of this sample to drop to 0.1 mCi?

16.58 A sample of technetium-99m (half-life = 6 hours) has an activity of 28 MBq. Approximately how many hours will it take for the activity of this sample to drop to 5 MBq?

16.59 Two samples of wood are taken from an archeological site. Sample A has a ^{14}C activity of 0.19 Bq per gram of carbon, while sample B has a ^{14}C activity of 0.17 Bq per gram of carbon.

a) Which of these samples is older? Explain your answer.

b) Could either of these samples be 6000 years old, given that the activity of live wood is 0.22 Bq per gram of carbon? Why or why not?

16.60 An archeologist measures the activity of the carbon in two ancient Egyptian baskets. Here are the results of the analysis:

Basket A: 12.1 cpm   Basket B: 11.4 cpm

a) Which basket is older? Explain your answer.

b) Carbon samples from modern baskets have an activity of 14.2 cpm. Based on this, is it likely that either of the ancient baskets was made at the same time that the Great Pyramid was built (around 2600 BC)? Why or why not?

OBJECTIVE: *Describe some of the ways in which ionizing radiation and nuclear reactions are used in medicine.*

16.7 Medical Applications of Nuclear Radiation

Over the past half century, nuclear medicine has become established as one of the most useful and versatile branches of medicine. Nuclear medicine can be divided into two broad categories: diagnostic procedures and therapeutic procedures. Diagnostic procedures attempt to identify a disorder and to determine its extent and its severity, while therapeutic procedures attempt to treat the disorder. More than 10 million diagnostic tests involving radioisotopes are performed every year in the United States, and roughly 1 million therapeutic procedures use radioisotopes. In this section, we will look at some of the uses of radioisotopes in medicine, and we will examine some other imaging methods that are related to nuclear medicine.

Diagnostic Imaging Uses X-Rays or Gamma Rays to Observe the Interior of the Body

The most familiar type of diagnostic procedure uses radiation to take a picture of the interior of the human body. This process, called **diagnostic imaging**, requires radiation that passes through body tissues. By far the most common type of diagnostic imaging technique is the X-ray image. Although X-rays are not produced in nuclear reactions, they are similar to gamma rays in that they have high energies and can penetrate body tissues. The ability of X-rays to pass through tissues is related to the density of the tissue, with very dense tissues like bones and teeth absorbing significant amounts of X-rays, while soft tissues allow most of the radiation to pass through them. X-rays are routinely used to detect disorders ranging from broken bones to lung tumors. A closely related technique is the CT scan, in which X-rays are aimed at the body from many directions and the results are fed into a computer, which generates a cross-sectional image of the body.

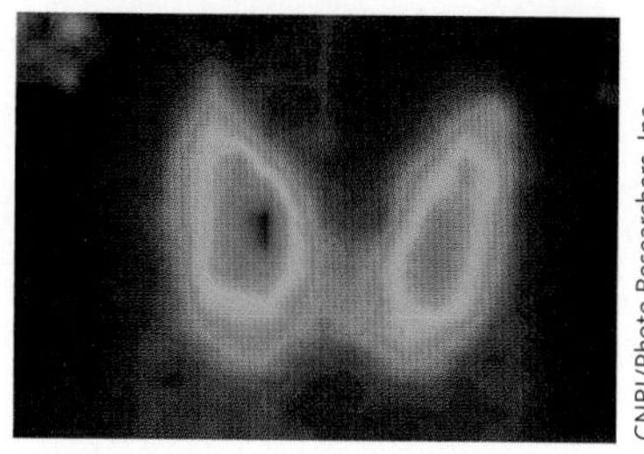

An image of the thyroid gland taken using radioactive iodine.

X-rays have significant limitations, because they cannot distinguish tissues of similar densities and they cannot distinguish functional tissues from malfunctioning regions. As a result, researchers have used radioisotopes to develop a range of procedures that allow physicians to get a clearer picture of the internal workings of the human body. A typical diagnostic procedure involves giving the patient a small dose of a radioisotope, allowing the isotope to collect in a particular region of the body, and then measuring the radiation emitted as the isotope decays. For example, a patient with a suspected thyroid disorder may be given a small dose of iodine-131 in the form of a sodium iodide tablet. The iodide ions pass into the bloodstream and are absorbed by the patient's thyroid gland, which uses iodide ions to make the hormone thyroxine. After 24 hours, a type of scintillation counter called a gamma camera is used to measure the amount of gamma radiation coming from the thyroid area. If the gamma level is higher than normal, the patient typically has a hyperactive thyroid gland. A lower-than-normal gamma level usually means that the thyroid contains some sort of abnormal growth, and it can be an indicator of thyroid cancer. Figure 16.11 illustrates this common diagnostic procedure.

Health Note: Iodine-131 increases the risk of thyroid cancer, so ^{131}I scans are only used when the benefit outweighs the risk to the patient.

Body tissues absorb alpha and beta particles, so isotopes that emit only alpha or beta particles are useless for diagnostic imaging. However, isotopes that produce gamma radiation can be used for imaging, because most of the gamma photons escape from our bodies and can be observed by an appropriate detector. In practice, the most common radioisotope in diagnostic imaging is technetium-99m, which emits gamma radiation without also producing alpha or beta particles. Chemists have found ways to link ^{99m}Tc to a range of molecules, allowing specific organs and tissues to be observed. For example, ^{99m}Tc bonds to a compound called methylene diphosphonate (MDP), which is absorbed strongly by bone tissue. The MDP delivers the radioactive technetium to the bones, where it can be used to detect fractures, tumors, and other bone abnormalities. Table 16.11 lists some other forms in which technetium-99m can be administered.

Health Note: Technetium-99m decays to technetium-99, which is also radioactive. However, ^{99}Tc decays very slowly (its half-life is more than 200,000 years) and our bodies eliminate it rapidly, so it poses no significant health risk.

PET Uses Positron Emitters to Produce an Image

Although alpha and beta sources cannot normally be used in diagnostic procedures, isotopes that produce positrons play an important role in diagnostic imaging. Positrons cannot coexist with normal matter, because they react with electrons to produce gamma radiation. The

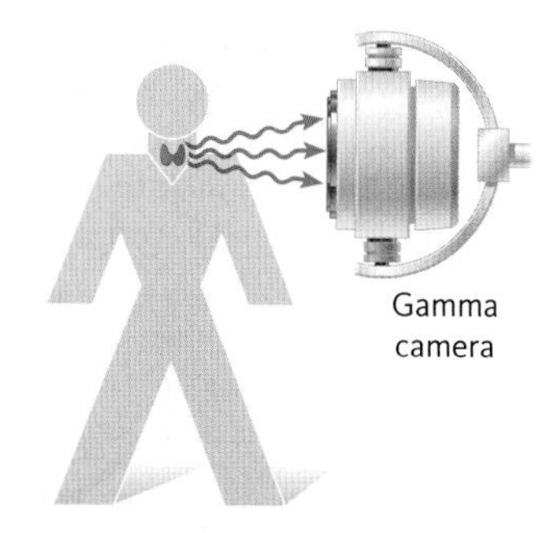

FIGURE 16.11 A thyroid scan using iodine-131.

TABLE 16.11 Chemicals Used in Technetium-99m Scans

Compound That Binds to ^{99m}Tc	Diagnostic Use
Phytate	Liver imaging
Mebrofenin	Monitoring of bile production
2-Methoxyisobutyl isonitrile (MIBI)	Monitoring cardiac blood flow
Diethylenetriamine pentaacetate (DTPA)	Monitoring kidney function
Ethyl cysteinate dimer (ECD)	Brain scans
Sulfur colloid	Spleen scans
Antibodies	Malignant tumors

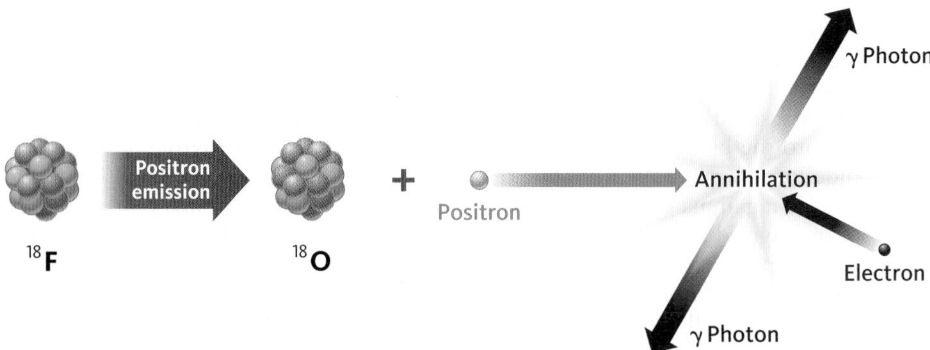

FIGURE 16.12 Positron emission and particle annihilation.

positron and the electron vanish altogether, a process called **particle annihilation** that converts all of the mass of the two particles into energy, as shown in Figure 16.12.

$$^{0}_{-1}e + ^{0}_{+1}e \rightarrow 2\gamma$$

The two gamma photons can be detected once they leave the body. Since the photons move in opposite directions, it is possible to determine the original location of the atom that emitted the positron. Over time, a computer can construct an image of the tissue that contains the radioactive material. This technique is called positron emission tomography (PET).

Positron emitters tend to have very short half-lives, so they do not occur in nature and they must be made immediately before they are to be used. The most commonly used radioisotope in PET is fluorine-18, which has a half-life of 110 minutes. Fluorine-18 does not exist in nature, but it can be made by bombarding naturally occurring ^{18}O with high-energy protons, according to the following nuclear equation:

$$^{18}_{8}O + ^{1}_{1}H \rightarrow ^{18}_{9}F + ^{1}_{0}n$$

Chemists then incorporate the ^{18}F into compounds that are similar to important biomolecules. For example, chemists can replace one of the hydroxyl groups in glucose with ^{18}F to produce ^{18}F-fluorodeoxyglucose (^{18}F-FDG). This molecule is absorbed into cells like glucose, but it cannot be metabolized, so the fluorine-18 remains in the cells until it decays into oxygen-18 and a positron.

CH$_2$OH, H, O, OH, H, OH, H, OH, H, H, F

Fluorodeoxyglucose (FDG)

Cancer cells have a high metabolic rate because they are dividing rapidly, so they absorb more ^{18}F-FDG than surrounding tissues. As a result, cancerous tumors appear as areas of particularly high gamma emission in a PET scan. The brain also absorbs a disproportionately high amount of glucose, so PET can be used to diagnose and study brain disorders such as Parkinson's disease, epilepsy, and Alzheimer's disease.

Radiation Therapy Uses Ionizing Radiation to Kill Diseased Cells

All of the procedures we have examined so far are used to diagnose illnesses. However, nuclear radiation is also used in **radiation therapy**, which uses large amounts of ionizing radiation to treat certain ailments, particularly cancers. These radiation doses, which are much higher than those used in diagnostic procedures, damage DNA so extensively that the affected cells cannot survive. Cancerous cells, which grow and divide rapidly, are particularly susceptible to the effects of radiation. However, ionizing radiation also damages healthy cells, so the dose must be carefully controlled and must be directed at the diseased tissue as much as possible. A great deal of research has been done to find ways to deliver doses of radiation to specific tissues.

Many types of radiation therapy use radiation sources that can be placed inside the body, either by surgery or by using a radioactive substance that collects in the target organ. For example, prostate cancer can be treated by implanting pellets containing radioactive palladium-103 into the prostate gland. This isotope decays fairly quickly, with a half-life of 17 days, and it delivers a large amount of ionizing radiation to the surrounding tissues. Thyroid cancers and thyroid hyperactivity can be treated with high doses of radioactive iodine-131, which is absorbed exclusively by the thyroid gland. Strontium-89 is absorbed by bone tissue and is used to relieve the pain associated with cancers that have spread to the bones.

Doses in Nuclear Procedures are Carefully Controlled

All medical procedures that involve ionizing radiation produce some damage to healthy tissues. Because of this, doctors use the lowest effective doses of radiation in both diagnostic and therapeutic procedures. In addition, they use radioisotopes with half-lives that are as short as possible, so the body is exposed to radiation for a limited time. Table 16.12 lists radiation doses for some diagnostic and therapeutic procedures. These are typical values and assume that the effect of the radiation is distributed throughout the body. Since dose is related to the amount of energy absorbed per kilogram of tissue, the effective dose for an individual organ is much higher than the whole-body dose. For example, a mammogram involves a whole-body dose of 10 to 20 mrem, but the radiation dose to the breast is several hundred millirems.

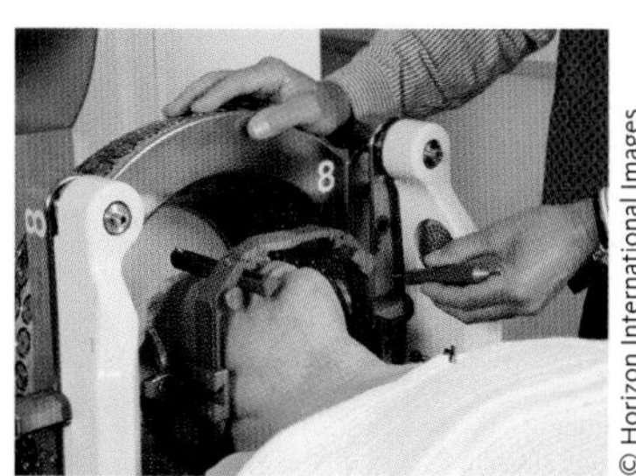

Gamma radiation can be delivered very precisely using modern radiation sources.

TABLE 16.12 Radiation Doses from Common Medical Procedures

Procedure	Type of Procedure	Equivalent Radiation Dose
Dental X-ray (one bitewing)	Diagnostic	0.4 mrem
Chest X-ray	Diagnostic	5 mrem
Mammogram	Diagnostic	15 mrem
^{131}I thyroid scan	Diagnostic	35 mrem
CT scan of head	Diagnostic	200 mrem
^{99m}Tc bone scan	Diagnostic	400 mrem
PET head scan (^{18}F-FDG)	Diagnostic	500 mrem
Lower gastrointestinal X-ray series	Diagnostic	700 mrem
CT scan of abdomen	Diagnostic	1000 mrem
X-ray radiation therapy (Hodgkin's lymphoma)	Therapeutic	2500 mrem
^{103}Pd prostate implants	Therapeutic	3000 mrem
X-ray radiation therapy (breast cancer)	Therapeutic	5000 mrem
^{131}I thyroid treatment	Therapeutic	7000 mrem

Sample Problem 16.12

Choosing a radioisotope for a medical application

Iodine-129 and iodine-131 are both beta emitters. ^{129}I has a half-life of 17 million years, while the half-life of ^{131}I is eight days. Which of these isotopes would be a better choice for the treatment of thyroid disorders, and why?

SOLUTION

Iodine-131 is the better choice. The half-life of iodine-129 is long, so this radioisotope breaks down slowly. We would need a large amount of ^{129}I to produce significant amounts of beta radiation. In addition, ^{129}I remains radioactive for an extremely long time, so the patient's body will be exposed to beta radiation for an extended period. By contrast, iodine-131 decays quickly, so the radiation exposure becomes negligible within a couple of months.

TRY IT YOURSELF: *Iodine-136 is also a beta emitter, with a half-life of 84 seconds. Why isn't this isotope used to treat thyroid disorders, rather than iodine-131?*

For additional practice, try Core Problems 16.63 and 16.64.

In recent years, a number of companies have started offering diagnostic CT scans to anyone willing to pay the fee. These scans are touted as a way to detect a variety of conditions, including heart disease and a variety of cancers, before any symptoms become apparent. However, as is evident from Table 16.12, CT scans involve exposure to a significant amount of radiation, comparable to radiation therapy. There is significant concern that the risks of widespread CT scanning may outweigh the benefits.

CORE PROBLEMS

16.61 Why aren't alpha and beta radiation used in diagnostic imaging?

16.62 Diagnostic procedures always use gamma emitters, while therapeutic procedures often use beta emitters. Why?

16.63 Radioactive strontium (Sr) is a beta emitter and is used to relieve the pain of bone cancer, because it is absorbed by bone tissue and kills the nerve cells around the bone. Both ^{89}Sr and ^{90}Sr produce beta radiation. The half-lives of these two radioisotopes are 51 days and 29 years, respectively. Which isotope is a better choice for radiation therapy, and why?

16.64 Oxygen-15 is a positron emitter, so glucose that contains ^{15}O can be used in place of ^{18}F-FDG in PET. The half-life of oxygen-15 is 2 minutes, and the half-life of fluorine-18 is 110 minutes. Why is the compound that contains ^{18}F generally preferred over the ^{15}O compound in PET?

16.65 Explain why FDG that contains ^{18}F is useful for detecting cancer tissues.

16.66 Explain why FDG that contains ^{18}F is useful for diagnosing brain disorders.

16.67 Patient A has a brain scan using ^{99m}Tc and receives 700 mrem of radiation. Patient B is given radiotherapy for a brain tumor and receives 5000 mrem of radiation. Why is patient B given a much larger radiation dose than patient A?

16.68 Two patients are given radioactive ^{131}I. Patient X is given a 35 mrem dose, while patient B is given a 6000 mrem dose. What is the most likely reason for this difference?

16.69 Iodine-131 is a beta emitter and is used to treat thyroid disorders. Why is radioactive iodine used rather than a radioactive isotope of some other element?

16.70 Compounds that contain ^{99m}Tc bound to phytate are particularly useful for diagnosing liver disorders. Why is this?

16.8 Nuclear Fission and Fusion

OBJECTIVES: *Compare fission and fusion reactions as sources of energy, and describe the role of each in modern society.*

As we have seen, nuclear reactions produce vast amounts of energy. Since the 1940s, people have searched for ways to harness the energy of nuclear reactions. These efforts have focused on two special types of nuclear reactions: fission and fusion. In this section, we will examine these two reaction types and how they can be used to produce energy for modern society.

Fission Reactions Break a Large Atom into Smaller Pieces

In most naturally occurring nuclear reactions, a nucleus emits a small particle. By contrast, in a **fission** reaction a large nucleus splits into two similarly sized pieces. The only naturally occurring radioisotope that undergoes fission is uranium-235, which makes up around 0.7% of the uranium on Earth. Uranium-235 is normally an alpha emitter and decays very slowly, with a half-life of 700 million years. However, when a neutron strikes a ^{235}U nucleus, the nucleus immediately breaks apart into two smaller nuclei and two or three neutrons. The reaction is capable of producing a range of products. Here are two typical examples:

$$^{235}_{92}U + ^{1}_{0}n \rightarrow ^{139}_{52}Te + ^{94}_{40}Zr + 3\ ^{1}_{0}n$$

$$^{235}_{92}U + ^{1}_{0}n \rightarrow ^{144}_{56}Ba + ^{90}_{36}Kr + 2\ ^{1}_{0}n$$

Sample Problem 16.13

Completing a nuclear equation for a fission reaction

Complete the following nuclear equation for the fission of ^{235}U:

$$^{235}_{92}U + ^{1}_{0}n \rightarrow ^{112}_{44}Ru + ? + 2\ ^{1}_{0}n$$

SOLUTION

The mass numbers of the reactants add up to 236, so the mass numbers of the products must also add up to 236. To get the mass of the missing atom, we need to subtract the masses of all of the other products from 236.

$$236 - 112 - 2 = 122$$ **(Mass number of the missing product)**

The reaction makes two neutrons.

The atomic numbers of the reactants must add up to 92. The atomic number of a neutron is zero, so the atomic number of the missing product must be 92 − 44 = 48. Element 48 is cadmium (Cd), so the complete nuclear equation is

$$^{235}_{92}U + ^{1}_{0}n \rightarrow ^{112}_{44}Ru + ^{122}_{48}Cd + 2\ ^{1}_{0}n$$

TRY IT YOURSELF: *Complete the following nuclear equation for the fission of* ^{235}U:

$$^{235}_{92}U + ^{1}_{0}n \rightarrow ^{127}_{51}Sb + ? + 3\ ^{1}_{0}n$$

For additional practice, try Core Problems 16.73 and 16.74.

All fission reactions produce more neutrons than they consume. These neutrons can cause other ^{235}U atoms to break down, releasing still more neutrons. The result is a **chain reaction**, in which an ever-increasing number of atoms undergo fission. Figure 16.13 shows a diagram of a chain reaction.

An uncontrolled chain reaction produces an enormous amount of energy in a very short time, and it can produce a violent explosion. However, naturally occurring uranium does not explode, because most of the atoms are ^{238}U, which does not undergo fission. Small samples of ^{235}U do not explode either, because most of the neutrons escape without hitting other uranium atoms.

TABLE 16.13 Nuclear Power Production in Some Countries

Country	Percentage of Electricity Generated by Nuclear Reactors (2004)
France	75%
Ukraine	49%
Japan	29%
Germany	26%
United States	20%
Russia	18%
Canada	15%
Argentina	7%
South Africa	5%
Mexico	5%
India	2%
China	2%

Data from World Nuclear Association, 2009.

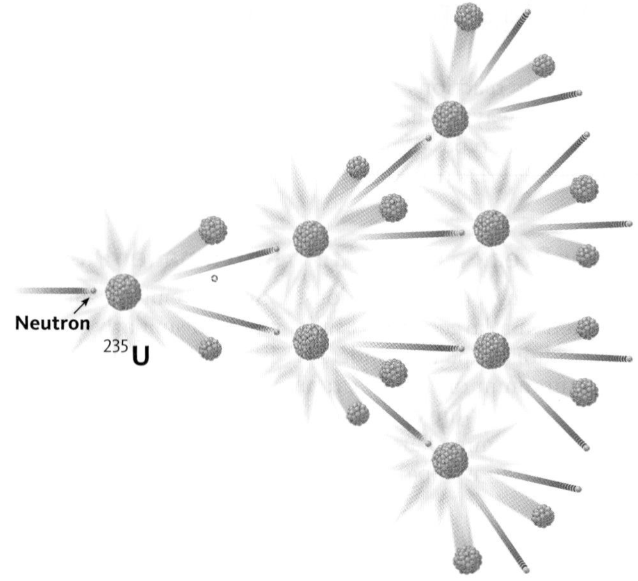

FIGURE 16.13 A fission chain reaction.

Fission Is Used to Produce Electrical Power

Fission reactions provide the energy for nuclear reactors. In a nuclear reactor, the concentration of ^{235}U atoms is adjusted so that the number of neutrons that produce fissions remains constant. The other materials in the reactor absorb the excess neutrons that would otherwise cause a runaway chain reaction. Nuclear reactors are important energy sources in many countries, because they produce a great deal of energy using relatively small amounts of uranium fuel. Table 16.13 shows the percentage of overall electrical production that comes from nuclear power in several countries.

Nuclear reactors are attractive sources of electrical energy primarily because they do not use fossil fuels. Much of the electrical power that is generated in the United States uses the energy from the combustion of coal or natural gas. The carbon dioxide that is produced in combustion reactions becomes part of the atmosphere. It is generally accepted that increasing levels of CO_2 in the atmosphere raise the average air temperature on Earth, because CO_2 absorbs energy that would otherwise escape into space in the form of infrared radiation. In addition, fossil fuel combustion produces by-products such as SO_2 and NO_2. These two gases are toxic and are major components of smog. They also dissolve in rainwater to form acids (acid rain), which are harmful to plants and wildlife.

However, nuclear reactors have some significant drawbacks. Reactors produce large amounts of radioactive by-products, some of which have very long half-lives. Since there is no way to prevent radioisotopes from breaking down, the waste material from nuclear power plants must be stored away from people for thousands of years. Although several countries, including the United States, have investigated locations where nuclear waste could be stored, no country has been able to choose a permanent site for waste disposal. Used nuclear fuel is currently stored at the reactors, and it is kept underwater because it generates a great deal of heat and lethal amounts of radiation.

An additional concern is the potential for a catastrophic accident that releases radioactive materials. This concern became a grim reality in 1986, when one of the four reactors at the Chernobyl power plant in the former Soviet Union (now in Ukraine) exploded during a test procedure, scattering a variety of radioisotopes over much of the globe. More than 200,000 people were evacuated from a 1000-square-mile area surrounding the plant because of high levels of radioactive elements, and thyroid cancer rates in Ukraine and neighboring Belarus have increased dramatically since the explosion, a result of the large amount of iodine-131 that contaminated portions of these countries.

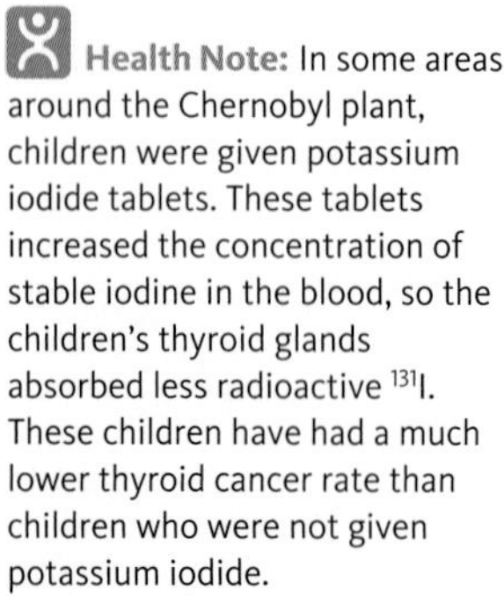

Health Note: In some areas around the Chernobyl plant, children were given potassium iodide tablets. These tablets increased the concentration of stable iodine in the blood, so the children's thyroid glands absorbed less radioactive ^{131}I. These children have had a much lower thyroid cancer rate than children who were not given potassium iodide.

Because of the concerns about waste disposal and safety, nuclear power generation has been controversial for decades. In the United States, no new construction of a nuclear power plant has begun since 1971, and the most recent plant to begin producing electricity was completed in 1996. Other countries also cut back or halted construction of new nuclear reactors in the last two decades of the twentieth century. However, with the increasing cost of fossil fuels and growing concern about global climate change, as well as growing demand for electricity, nuclear power is gaining renewed acceptance as an alternative to electrical generation using fossil fuels.

Nuclear reactors are important in medicine, because they are the source of a variety of radioactive isotopes that do not occur in nature. Many of the radioisotopes we have already encountered in this chapter are made by exposing stable isotopes to the neutrons that are produced during fission reactions. Some common examples are ^{131}I, ^{32}P, ^{99}Mo (which decays into ^{99m}Tc), and ^{103}Pd.

One of the two reactors at the Three Mile Island nuclear power plant in Pennsylvania was severely damaged in a 1979 accident. Cleanup and removal of the radioactive material took 14 years.

Fusion Reactions Combine Light Nuclei to Form a Heavier Atom

Nuclear **fusion** is the opposite of fission. In a fusion reaction, two or more small nuclei collide and stick together to make a larger nucleus. Fusion reactions produce energy if the product is an element no heavier than iron. For example, an atom of hydrogen-2 and an atom of hydrogen-3 can combine to make an atom of helium-4 and a neutron:

$$^{2}_{1}H + ^{3}_{1}H \rightarrow ^{4}_{2}He + ^{1}_{0}n + 400{,}000{,}000 \text{ kcal}$$

Gram for gram, fusion reactions produce substantially more energy than fission reactions, and they produce fewer radioactive by-products. In addition, fusion uses light elements such as hydrogen, which are abundant on Earth. As a result, fusion would seem to be an ideal energy source. Unfortunately, fusion reactions can only occur at extremely high temperatures, because the nuclei must collide violently in order to fuse. No one has yet succeeded in building a reactor that can produce such high temperatures. However, fusion reactions are the source of the energy that is produced by the sun and all other stars. In the interior of the sun, the temperature is more than 10 million degrees Celsius, hot enough to force hydrogen-1 nuclei (protons) to form helium. This process occurs in several steps, but the overall reaction is

$$4\ ^{1}_{1}H \rightarrow ^{4}_{2}He + 2\ ^{0}_{+1}e + \text{energy}$$

Figure 16.14 illustrates this reaction.

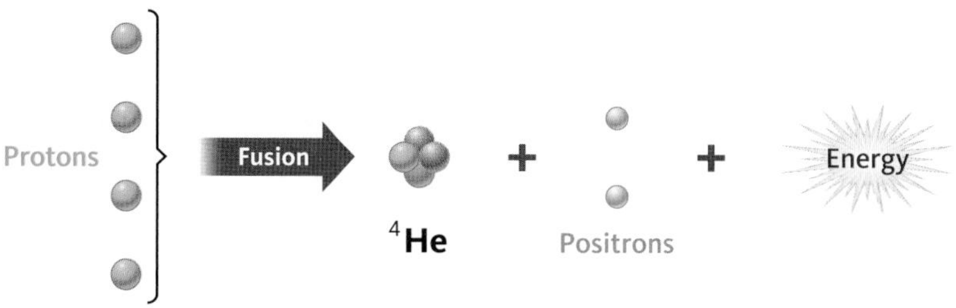

FIGURE 16.14 The fusion reaction of hydrogen-1.

Fusion reactions in the sun are the ultimate source of the energy required by all living organisms.

CORE PROBLEMS

16.71 What is a fission reaction?

16.72 What is a fusion reaction?

16.73 Balance the following fission reaction:

$$^{239}_{94}Pu + ^{1}_{0}n \rightarrow ^{104}_{42}Mo + ? \rightarrow 2\ ^{1}_{0}n$$

16.74 Balance the following fission reaction:

$$^{235}_{92}U + ^{1}_{0}n \rightarrow ^{93}_{37}Rb + ? + 2\ ^{1}_{0}n$$

16.75 A large piece of pure uranium-235 can explode extremely violently. Why is this?

16.76 Why don't small pieces of uranium-235 explode?

16.77 Uranium can burn, reacting with oxygen to produce several chemical compounds. Which will produce more energy, the combustion of 1 kg of uranium or the nuclear decay of 1 kg of uranium? Why?

16.78 Which will produce more energy, the fusion reaction of 1 g of hydrogen or the fission reaction of 1 g of uranium? Why?

16.79 In very old stars, carbon-12 atoms fuse to form magnesium-24. Write a balanced nuclear equation for this fusion reaction.

16.80 In very old stars, a carbon-12 atom can combine with a helium-4 atom. Write a balanced nuclear equation for this fusion reaction.

16.81 What are the advantages of fusion reactions over fission reactions as a source of energy?

16.82 Why aren't there any electrical power plants that use fusion reactions?

CONNECTIONS

Radioisotope Imaging

Most people's experience with diagnostic imaging is restricted to standard X-rays when they have a dental exam or a possible broken bone. However, modern medicine has a wider variety of techniques that allow the doctor to monitor the patient. While any exposure to radiation does carry some risk, if the benefit of using radioisotopes outweighs the risks, then doctors will recommend their use. As an example, let us look at how doctors use radioisotopes to tell whether a person has a blocked gall bladder duct.

Problems that affect the digestive system are notoriously difficult to diagnose, because there are so many possible causes of stomach and intestinal pain. Abdominal pain can be the result of acid indigestion, excess gas, food that causes an allergic reaction or that is not digested efficiently, pathogenic bacteria (food poisoning), intestinal parasites, an ulcer, appendicitis, and a variety of other disorders, one of which is a blocked gall bladder. The gall bladder is a small organ whose job is to collect bile produced in the liver and send it to the small intestine when the person has eaten a meal with fatty foods. The bile helps dissolve the fats so that they can be processed. When the gall bladder cannot secrete the bile into the small intestine, any attempt to do so causes intense pain.

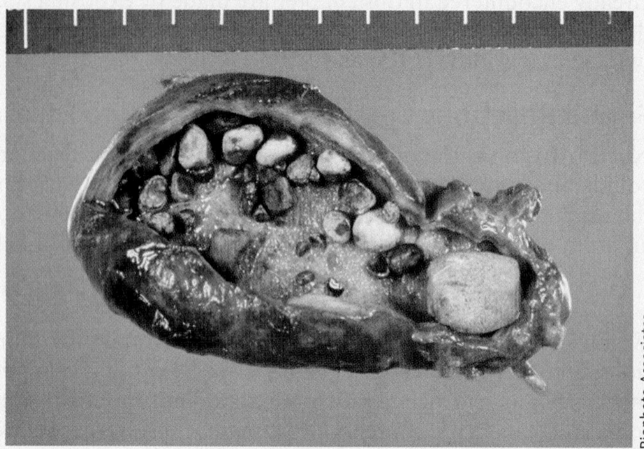
Biophoto Associates

This gall bladder is almost completely blocked by gallstones.

The most common cause of gall bladder blockage is gallstones, rocklike lumps containing cholesterol and other compounds that can grow large enough to interfere with gall bladder function or block the ducts that lead from the gall bladder to the intestine. Gallstones in the gall bladder can be detected using X-rays or *ultrasound,* extremely high-pitched sound waves (much higher than the ear can detect) that bounce off tissues and can be used to produce an image similar to an X-ray. However, neither of these imaging methods can detect gallstones that have moved into the bile ducts. Therefore, many hospitals are now diagnosing gall bladder problems using a technique based on a radioisotope. This technique is more sensitive than X-rays or ultrasound and can detect a greater range of problems with the gall bladder and bile production in general.

In the radioisotope test, the doctor starts by injecting the patient with a solution containing ^{99m}Tc bound to an organic compound called mebrofenin. The patient's abdomen is then observed using a gamma camera connected to a television monitor to detect the gamma radiation from the ^{99m}Tc. Mebrofenin is rapidly absorbed by the liver and excreted into the bile for removal from the body, so the liver almost immediately appears on the monitor as a glowing image. In the next 15 minutes, most of the radiation moves to the gall bladder, which glows brightly on the monitor. At this point, the patient is given an injection of a chemical that stimulates the gall bladder to contract and force the bile into the intestine. If the gall bladder duct is open, the glow will move from the gall bladder into the intestine, but if it is blocked, the gall bladder will continue to glow (and the patient will complain of pain). This method allows the health care practitioner to make a rapid and virtually certain diagnosis of gall bladder dysfunction.

Mebrofenin

Key Terms

activity – 16.4
alpha decay – 16.2
alpha particle – 16.2
background radiation –16.5
beta decay – 16.2
beta particle – 16.2
chain reaction – 16.8
diagnostic imaging – 16.7
electromagnetic radiation – 16.3
equivalent radiation dose – 16.4
exponential decay – 16.6
fission – 16.8
fusion – 16.8
gamma radiation – 16.3
Geiger counter – 16.4
half-life – 16.6
ionizing radiation – 16.3
nuclear equation – 16.2
nuclear radiation – 16.2
nuclear reaction – 16.1
nuclear symbol – 16.1
particle annihilation – 16.7
photon – 16.3
positron – 16.1
positron emission – 16.2
radiation therapy – 16.7
radical – 16.3
radiation weighting factor (W_R) – 16.4
radioactive – 16.1
radioisotope – 16.1
scintillation counter – 16.4
stable nucleus – 16.1

SUMMARY OF OBJECTIVES

Now that you have read the chapter, test yourself on your knowledge of the objectives, using this summary as a guide.

Section 16.1: Distinguish nuclear reactions from chemical reactions, and write nuclear symbols for atoms and subatomic particles.

- Nuclear reactions change the numbers of arrangement of particles in a nucleus, and they differ in many ways from chemical reactions.
- Nuclear symbols show the mass number and atomic number of a particle or nucleus.
- Isotopes are atoms of the same element that have different mass numbers.
- Radioactive isotopes break down into other atoms, while stable isotopes do not.

Section 16.2: Write balanced nuclear equations for common nuclear reactions.

- Atomic numbers and mass numbers must be balanced in any nuclear equation.
- In alpha decay, a heavy nucleus breaks down into a smaller nucleus and an alpha particle, which contains two protons and two electrons.
- In beta decay, a neutron in the nucleus breaks down into a proton and an electron, which is expelled from the atom. Beta decay increases the atomic number without changing the mass number.
- In positron emission, a proton in the nucleus breaks down into a neutron and a positron, which is expelled from the atom. Positron decay decreases the atomic number without changing the mass number.
- New isotopes and elements are made by bombarding atoms with neutrons, protons, or small nuclei.

Section 16.3: Explain how nuclear reactions produce energy, and describe the various types of electromagnetic radiation.

- Nuclear reactions convert mass directly into energy, producing 2.15×10^{10} kcal of energy for every gram of matter that is destroyed.
- The energy of a nuclear reaction can appear as kinetic energy, gamma radiation, or a combination of the two.
- Electromagnetic radiation exists as packets of energy called photons. The type of radiation depends on the amount of energy in each photon, with gamma radiation having the highest photon energies.
- Nuclear reactions produce ionizing radiation, which damages critical biomolecules by knocking electrons out of them.

Section 16.4: Describe the tools that are used to measure ionizing radiation and the units used to express amounts of radiation.

- Ionizing radiation can be measured using photographic film, a Geiger counter, or a scintillation counter.
- Equivalent dose measures the effect of radiation on the human body, and it is normally measured in rems.
- W_R is used to compare the biological effects of different types of radiation.
- Activity is the number of atoms that break down per second in a radioactive sample, and is normally measured in curies.
- Many other units are used to measure radiation.
- Symptoms of radiation sickness appear after doses of 100 rem or more, and doses of 400 rem or more can be lethal.

Section 16.5: Identify common sources of radiation, compare the biological effect and penetrating ability of common types of nuclear radiation, and describe methods to protect the body from exposure to nuclear radiation.

- Background radiation is the radiation produced by natural sources, primarily radon in the atmosphere.
- Many human activities involve exposure to ionizing radiation.
- Alpha particles cause the most damage to cells, but they have little penetrating ability and are blocked by a layer of any material.
- Beta particles cause substantial cell damage and have greater penetrating ability than alpha particles. They are normally blocked by a Plexiglas sheet, which may be supplemented with a thin sheet of lead to block X-rays.

continued

- Gamma radiation causes the least cell damage, but it has the highest penetrating ability and can only be blocked by very dense materials.
- Radiation exposure can be minimized by decreasing the time of exposure and increasing the distance from the source of the radiation.
- The amount of radiation absorbed is inversely related to the square of the person's distance from the source.

Section 16.6: Use the half-life to relate the age of a radioactive sample to its activity, and describe how radioactive isotopes are used to estimate the age of various materials.
- Half-life is the time required for half of a sample of a radioisotope to break down.
- The half-life of an isotope does not depend on the size of the sample or any other property.
- Potassium-40 and carbon-14 can be used to estimate the ages of rocks and organic materials.

Section 16.7: Describe some of the ways in which ionizing radiation and nuclear reactions are used in medicine.
- Diagnostic imaging procedures use X-rays or gamma radiation to observe the interior of the body.
- Radioisotopes that emit gamma radiation are used to produce an image of a particular organ or tissue type.
- PET uses the annihilation reaction of positrons and electrons to produce a gamma ray image.
- Radiation therapy uses ionizing radiation to kill diseased cells.

Section 16.8: Compare fission and fusion reactions as sources of energy, and describe the role of each in modern society.
- In a fission reaction, a neutron hits a heavy nucleus and breaks it apart into two smaller nuclei.
- Fission reactions produce more neutrons than they consume.
- A chain reaction occurs when the number of atoms that undergo fission increase over time.
- Fission can be harnessed as a useful source of power, but it raises significant health and environmental concerns.
- In a fusion reaction, two small nuclei become a single larger nucleus.
- Fusion reactions produce the energy in stars, but they are not yet practical energy sources for human society.

Concept Questions

OWL Online homework for this chapter may be assigned in OWL.
* indicates more challenging problems.

16.83 What are the two rules for balancing a nuclear equation?

16.84 Why does beta decay always increase the atomic number of an atom?

16.85 Why don't chemists write the mass numbers of the atoms when they write balanced equations for ordinary chemical reactions?

16.86 Nuclear reactions produce a great deal of energy. Where does this energy come from?

16.87 Nuclear reactions can produce radiation in the form of particles or electromagnetic radiation. How do these differ from each other?

16.88 Why is ionizing radiation dangerous to living organisms?

16.89 A friend is concerned about using her microwave oven, because she has heard people refer to microwave cooking as "nuking your food" and she is afraid that some sort of nuclear radiation is involved. How would you respond to your friend's concerns?

16.90 List two machines that are used to measure ionizing radiation.

16.91 What is an equivalent dose, and what units are used to express it?

16.92 Why do alpha particles have a much higher W_R than beta particles or gamma rays?

16.93 The half-life of cobalt-60 is around 5 years, and the half-life of cobalt-61 is 1 hour and 40 minutes. Which would have a higher activity, 10 mg of ^{60}Co or 10 mg of ^{59}Co? Explain your answer.

16.94 Alpha emitters are dangerous if they are ingested or inhaled. However, they are virtually harmless outside the body, even if they are held close to the skin. Why is this?

16.95 A sheet of Plexiglas blocks all beta particles. Why is a thin sheet of lead sometimes added to the Plexiglas when shielding a worker from beta radiation?

16.96 The walls in X-ray clinics are usually built of concrete rather than wood. Why is this?

16.97 It takes 8 days for half of a 1 g sample of iodine-131 to decay.

a) How long does it take for half of a 10 g sample of iodine-131 to decay? Explain.
b) Does it take 8 days for the other half of the 1 g sample of ^{131}I to decay? Why or why not?

16.98 Why is the concentration of argon higher in very old rocks than it is in rocks that were formed recently?

16.99 Positrons do not have much penetrating power, so they cannot be detected outside the body if they are produced internally. Why then are positron emitters useful in nuclear medicine?

16.100 Gamma radiation and X-rays are used in similar ways in medicine. Why?

16.101 Explain why technetium-99m is never used in radiation therapy.

16.102 An experimental cancer treatment uses radioactive ^{213}Bi, which breaks down as follows:

$$^{213}_{83}\text{Bi} \rightarrow\ ^{209}_{81}\text{Tl} +\ ^{4}_{2}\text{He}$$

The bismuth-213 is chemically bonded to a molecule that binds to cancer cells.

a) Why might this be an effective way to kill cancer cells?
b) Would this be more effective if bismuth-213 were a beta emitter instead of an alpha emitter? Why or why not?

16.103 A technique called magnetic resonance imaging (MRI) uses radio waves to produce an image of soft tissues. Explain why MRI poses less of a health hazard to a patient than X-rays or CT scans.

16.104 What are the economic and environmental advantages of electrical production using nuclear fission, as compared to using fossil fuel combustion? What are the disadvantages?

16.105 Life on Earth would not exist were it not for a fusion reaction. Explain.

16.106 Why are nuclear reactors important in medicine?

Summary and Challenge Problems

16.107 Use the periodic table to answer the following questions:

a) How many neutrons are there in an atom of cobalt-58?
b) How many protons are there in an atom of indium-111?
c) Write the nuclear symbol for an atom that contains 30 protons and 36 neutrons.

16.108 There are two naturally occurring isotopes of chlorine.

a) Do these two isotopes have the same atomic number? Explain why or why not.
b) Do these two isotopes have the same mass number? Explain why or why not.
c) One of these isotopes can combine with cerium to form $CeCl_3$. If the other isotope combines with cerium, what will be the chemical formula of the product?

16.109 Chemists will often omit the atomic number when they write the symbol for a particular isotope. (For example, they may write ^{14}C rather than $^{14}_{6}$C.) Why is this acceptable?

16.110 Write balanced nuclear equations for each of the following reactions:

a) ^{230}Th undergoes alpha decay.
b) ^{231}Th undergoes beta decay.
c) ^{191}Hg undergoes positron emission.

16.111 Radon-221 can undergo two types of radioactive decay. In a typical sample of radon-221 atoms, 22% decay to francium-221, while the other 78% decay to polonium-217. Classify each of these two reactions as an alpha decay, a beta decay, or a positron emission.

16.112 Thallium-207 can be formed by both alpha decay and beta decay.

a) What is the reactant in the alpha decay reaction that makes ^{207}Tl?
b) What is the reactant in the beta decay reaction that makes ^{207}Tl?

16.113 The following sequence of reactions is used to make isotopes of two transuranium elements. Complete the nuclear equations for these reactions.

$$^{240}_{94}\text{Pu} +\ ^{1}_{0}\text{n} \rightarrow \text{atom 1}$$

$$\text{atom 1} \rightarrow \text{atom 2} +\ ^{0}_{-1}\text{e}$$

$$\text{atom 2} \rightarrow \text{atom 3} +\ ^{4}_{2}\text{He}$$

16.114 Uranium-238 is a naturally occurring radioisotope. Atoms of ^{238}U undergo a sequence of 14 nuclear reactions, eventually forming a stable atom. The individual nuclear reactions are listed here. Identify the product of each reaction. (Each step uses the product of the preceding step. For example, the product of step 1 undergoes beta decay in step 2.)

Step 1: alpha decay	Step 2: beta decay
Step 3: beta decay	Step 4: alpha decay
Step 5: alpha decay	Step 6: alpha decay
Step 7: alpha decay	Step 8: alpha decay
Step 9: alpha decay	Step 10: beta decay
Step 11: beta decay	Step 12: alpha decay
Step 13: beta decay	Step 14: beta decay

16.115 *Use the nuclear equation given here to answer the following questions:

$$^{67}_{31}\text{Ga} +\ ^{0}_{-1}\text{e} \rightarrow\ ^{67}_{30}\text{Zn} + 23{,}000{,}000\ \text{kcal}$$

a) How much energy is produced when 1.00 g of ^{67}Ga turns into ^{67}Zn?
b) How much mass is lost when 1.00 g of ^{67}Ga turns into ^{67}Zn?

16.116 Calculate the energy that is produced in the nuclear reaction shown here, using the following exact formula weights of the reactants and products:

^{238}U: 238.050784 ^{234}Th: 234.0453593
^{4}He: 4.00260

$$^{238}_{92}\text{U} \rightarrow\ ^{234}_{90}\text{Th} +\ ^{4}_{2}\text{He}$$

16.117 Janice works in a nuclear medicine clinic and must handle small amounts of radioactive material. List three ways in which Janice can reduce her exposure to ionizing radiation (without looking for a different line of work).

16.118 *An airline pilot typically spends about 20 hours per week in the air. Assuming that a person is exposed to 0.6 mrem per hour spent flying, how much extra radiation does the pilot absorb in one year? Is this a significant exposure?

16.119 Cobalt-60 emits both beta and gamma radiation. Many disposable medical supplies, such as wound dressings and disposable syringes, are exposed to cobalt-60 after they are packaged. Explain why this is done.

16.120 Why do X-ray technicians always walk out of the examination room before taking an X-ray?

16.121 Sodium-24 emits both beta and gamma radiation. What would be appropriate shielding for a radiologist who is using this isotope to study electrolyte transport?

16.122 When a nuclear medicine clinic uses iodine-131, it orders the radioisotope from a separate manufacturer, which is usually many miles away from the clinic. However, fluorine-18 must be made at the clinic or close nearby. Explain this difference. (Hint: Look at Table 16.10.)

16.123 Technetium-99m and antimony-129 both produce gamma radiation, and they have similar half-lives (6 hours versus 4.4 hours). Why is ^{99m}Tc preferred for diagnostic imaging? The nuclear reaction for each isotope is shown here:

$$^{99m}_{43}\text{Tc} \rightarrow {}^{99}_{43}\text{Tc} + \gamma$$

$$^{129}_{51}\text{Sb} \rightarrow {}^{129}_{52}\text{Te} + {}^{0}_{-1}\text{e} + \gamma$$

16.124 All of the following radioisotopes are absorbed by bone tissue and tend to remain in the human body for a long time. Which of these isomers is probably the most hazardous to human health if it is taken internally, and which is the least hazardous? Explain your answer.

a) plutonium-239 (an alpha emitter)
b) strontium-90 (a beta emitter)
c) metastable barium-135 (a gamma emitter)

16.125 *Calcium in the diet is rapidly absorbed by bone tissues and remains in the body for extended periods, while the potassium in your diet is normally excreted within a few weeks. Based on this, explain why radioactive isotopes of strontium (Sr) are considered to be much more dangerous than radioactive isotopes of rubidium (Rb). (Hint: Find these four elements on the periodic table.)

16.126 *Children of people who were exposed to large doses of nuclear radiation have an unusually high rate of birth defects. What is a reasonable explanation for this?

16.127 *Earth is estimated to be around 5 billion years old. When Earth was formed, it contained both ^{238}U (half-life = 4.5 billion years) and ^{237}Np (half-life = 2.1 million years). The planet still contains a substantial amount of ^{238}U, but it does not contain any detectable ^{237}Np. Explain this difference.

16.128 *The uranium on Earth currently contains 99.3% ^{238}U (half-life = 4.5 billion years) and 0.7% ^{235}U (half-life = 700 million years).

a) During the next billion years, would you expect the percentage of ^{235}U to increase, decrease, or remain the same? Explain your answer.
b) When Earth was formed, was the percentage of ^{235}U greater, less than, or equal to its current percentage? Explain your answer.

16.129 You have 1 mg samples of ^{131}I and ^{123}I. The activity of the ^{131}I is 73 Ci, while the activity of the ^{123}I is 1090 Ci. Which isotope has the longer half-life? Explain your answer.

16.130 A geologist analyzes two rock samples to determine the amount of argon in each. Here are the results of the analysis:

Sample 1: 2.1 ppm of Ar   Sample 2: 0.7 ppm of Ar

Which sample is older? Explain your answer.

16.131 Earth is approximately 5 billion years old. Using this fact, explain why rocks on Earth contain potassium-40 (half-life = 1.3 billion years) but no potassium-42 (half-life = 12 hours).

16.132 *A patient is given 30 mL of an intravenous solution that contains 0.80 mCi of ^{99m}Tc per mL of solution. What is the total activity of the ^{99m}Tc in this solution?

16.133 *A patient is given an injection of a solution that contains 600 MBq of ^{99m}Tc. The volume of the solution is 15 mL.

a) What is the concentration of ^{99m}Tc in this solution in MBq/mL?
b) If 2.5 mL of this solution is mixed with 12.5 mL of water, what will be the concentration of ^{99m}Tc in the new solution in MBq/mL?

16.134 Fill in the missing numbers and symbols in the following nuclear equation for the fission of plutonium-239:

$$^{239}_{?}Pu + ^{?}_{?}n \rightarrow ^{?}_{58}? + ^{90}_{?}? + 3\ ^{?}_{?}n$$

16.135 How many neutrons are produced when uranium-235 absorbs a neutron and fissions into bromine-85 and lanthanum-148?

16.136 *In stars that have consumed most of their hydrogen, helium-4 atoms combine to make carbon-12.

a) Write a balanced nuclear equation for this fusion reaction.
b) The atomic weights of these two isotopes are 4.00260 g/mol and 12.00000 g/mol, respectively. Use this information to calculate the amount of energy that is produced when 1.00 mol of helium-4 is converted into carbon-12.

Essential Mathematics for Chemistry

OUTLINE

A.1 Decimal Notation and Place Value

In science and medicine, we represent parts of a unit with a decimal number, rather than a fraction. For example, if something weighs half a kilogram, we write 0.5 kg rather than $^1/_2$ kg. Therefore, you should familiarize yourself with the place values in decimal numbers. In a decimal number, the first decimal place represents tenths, the second decimal represents hundredths, and so forth. The following number represents two ten-thousandths ($^2/_{10,000}$):

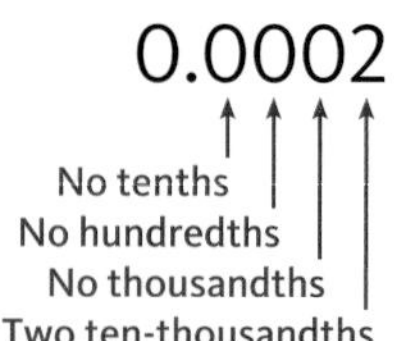

The following number can be thought of as representing $^{305}/_{1000}$ or three tenths plus five thousandths:

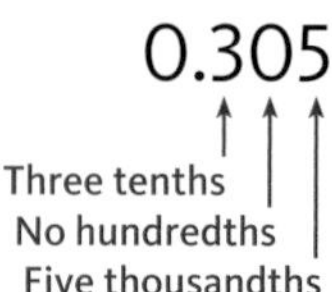

When we compare two decimal numbers, we must pay close attention to place value. For example, 0.1 is a smaller number than 0.9, but 0.1 is a larger number than 0.09, because one tenth is larger than nine hundredths.

Sample Problem A.1

Comparing decimal numbers

Which is the larger number, 0.0203 or 0.00799?

SOLUTION

0.0203 is the larger number, because it has a 2 in the hundredths place while 0.00799 has a 0 in the hundredths place. The 7 in 0.00799 is in the thousandths place, which is smaller than the hundredths place.

TRY IT YOURSELF: *Which is the larger number, 0.00503 or 0.0075?*

When you do calculations that involve decimal numbers, you normally use a calculator. However, be aware that when you add or subtract decimal numbers, you must match up the corresponding decimal places. This is no different from what you do when you add or subtract whole numbers. For instance, suppose you want to add 0.245 and 0.51. You must line up the tenths places first, as shown here:

tenths line up		tenths don't line up	
↓		↓	
0.245	Correct	0.245	Incorrect
+ 0.51		+ 0.51	
0.755		~~0.296~~	

There are two great advantages to using decimal numbers rather than fractions. First, it is easier to compare the sizes of decimal numbers. For instance, it is hard to tell whether $^3/_{17}$ or $^5/_{28}$ is larger. However, if we change these into decimal numbers, we get 0.1764 and 0.1786, respectively (rounded to four decimal places). Using the decimal forms, we can immediately see that 0.1786 ($^5/_{28}$) is the larger number. Second, all calculators can handle and display decimal numbers, but most calculators do not handle fractions. Since you will carry out most of the arithmetic in your chemistry course using a calculator, decimal numbers are more convenient than fractions.

Problems

A.1 Arrange the following numbers from largest to smallest:

0.00817 0.034 0.006512 0.0008999

A.2 Write the number $^{44}/_{1000}$ as a decimal number.

A.2 Interpreting and Using Fractions in Calculations

The most common way to convert a measurement from one unit into another involves multiplying the original measurement by one or more conversion factors, as described in Section 1.4. In this section, we will look at how to do the needed arithmetic. For example, if someone's arm is 27 inches long and we want to express this measurement in meters, we need to do the following calculation:

$$27 \times \frac{1}{39.37} = ?$$

To do this type of calculation, we must recognize that *a fraction is another way to express division*. For instance, $^2/_3$ is an alternate way of expressing 2 ÷ 3. Using this fact, we can rewrite our original problem as

$$27 \times (1 \div 39.37) = ?$$

To do the arithmetic on a calculator, we simply enter the numbers and operations in the order we see them, as shown in the following example. The parentheses do not change the final answer, so we can ignore them.

What you do:	**What you see:**
Enter the number 27:	27
Press the "×" key:	27
Enter the number 1:	1
Press the "÷" key: (the calculator does the multiplication: 27 × 1 = 27)	27
Enter the number 39.37:	39.37
Press the "=" key: (the calculator now does the division)	0.68580137

This answer tells us that the person's arm is 0.68580137 meters long. (Normally we would round this off to 0.69 meters. The rules for rounding calculated numbers are covered in Section A.5.)

If we have more than one fraction, we treat each fraction in the same way. For instance, the calculation

$$3.25 \times \frac{1}{2.54} \times \frac{100}{1} = ?$$

is the same as the calculation

$$3.25 \times (1 \div 2.54) \times (100 \div 1) = ?$$

Again, we can ignore the parentheses. The answer is 127.952756. (Try it on your calculator.)

Sample Problem **A.2**

Carrying out a calculation that involves fractions

Do the following calculation using your calculator:

$$66.9 \times \frac{39.37}{1} \times \frac{1}{12} = ?$$

SOLUTION

The correct answer is 219.48775. The key sequence you should use is

$$66.9 \times 39.37 \div 1 \times 1 \div 12 =$$

TRY IT YOURSELF: *Do the following calculation using your calculator:*

$$5.644 \times \frac{1}{2.54} \times \frac{10}{1} = ?$$

Problems

A.3 Carry out the following calculations:

a) $2.8 \times \frac{454}{1} = ?$

b) $0.0757 \times \frac{1}{2.2} = ?$

c) $75 \times \frac{13.6}{1} \times \frac{1}{454} = ?$

d) $10.58 \times \frac{1}{42} \times \frac{1}{3.785} = ?$

A.3 Averages

When you do laboratory work, you may need to repeat an experiment several times. If the numerical results of your trials are different, you will probably calculate an average. To calculate an average, you do two steps:

1. Add up all of the numbers you measured.
2. Divide the answer from step 1 by the number of trials you did.

For example, suppose a laboratory measures a patient's blood sugar level. To ensure a reliable result, the lab carries out the test three times and obtains the following results:

Trial 1: 85 mg/dL Trial 2: 88 mg/dL Trial 3: 84 mg/dL

The three results do not agree with one another, although they are quite close. This is normal in medical tests. To calculate the average, we first add up the three numbers.

$$85 + 88 + 84 = 257$$

Then we divide by 3, because there are three trials.

$$257 \div 3 = 85.66666667 \quad \text{the average}$$

Finally, we attach the unit and round off. The average always has the same unit as the individual trials, so the unit is milligrams per deciliter. To round off, a helpful guideline is that the average should have the same number of decimal places as the individual trials. Since our trials were reported to the nearest whole number, the average should be rounded to a whole number. The lab should report the result as 86 mg/dL. (Sections A.4 and A.5 discuss the rules for rounding off numbers.)

In general, the average of several trials is more likely to be close to the actual value than a single trial would be, as long as the experiment is accurate. When we carry out an experiment several times, the results tend to be scattered around the correct value, with some trials being too low and some being too high. When we take the average, these small errors cancel one another, leaving the average close to the correct value.

Sample Problem **A.3**

Calculating an average

A hospital laboratory tests a blood sample to determine the concentration of platelets in the blood. The lab obtains the following results (expressed in millions of platelets per milliliter of blood):

Trial 1: 385 Trial 2: 392 Trial 3: 401 Trial 4: 389

Calculate the average concentration of platelets in this patient's blood.

SOLUTION

First, we add up the four trials.

$$385 + 392 + 401 + 389 = 1567$$

Then we divide by four, because the lab carried out four trials.

$$1567 \div 4 = 391.75$$

Finally, we round to a whole number and attach the unit. This patient's average platelet concentration is 392 million platelets per milliliter of blood.

TRY IT YOURSELF: *A food manufacturer tests the vitamin C content of fruit punch and obtains the following results:*

0.38 mg/mL 0.43 mg/mL 0.39 mg/mL

Calculate the average vitamin C content in the fruit punch.

Problems

A.4 Calculate the average of the following experimental results:
Trial 1: 8.45 L Trial 2: 8.67 L Trial 3: 8.81 L

A.5 Calculate the average of the following experimental results:
Trial 1: 8.515 g/mL Trial 2: 8.487 g/mL
Trial 3: 8.496 g/mL Trial 4: 8.502 g/mL

A.4 Basic Concepts of Rounding

Often, a calculation will give a result that contains meaningless digits. For example, suppose that a map tells us that it is 55 km from your hometown to the nearest large city. If we convert this distance into miles using a calculator, we get

$$55 \text{ km} \times \frac{1 \text{ mile}}{1.609 \text{ km}} = 34.18272219 \text{ miles}$$

Although the calculator has given an answer with eight decimal places, we do not know the distance this precisely. Road maps round off distances to the nearest kilometer, so the distance is *approximately* 55 km. Therefore, when we translate this distance into an English unit, the best we can say is that the distance is *approximately* 34 miles. The digits beyond the decimal point are meaningless.

The process of removing meaningless digits in a number is called **rounding off**. When we round off a number, we must do three steps:

1. Decide where to round off the number.
2. Decide whether the last digit we keep will be rounded up.
3. Write the rounded number.

In this section, we look at the last two steps. Section A.5 covers the rules that govern where to round off a number.

When we decide whether or not to round up the last digit we will keep, *we only need to look at the first digit we will discard.* If this digit is 5 or greater, we round up; if it is 4 or less, we do not. Here are two examples:

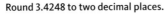

Round 3.4248 to two decimal places.

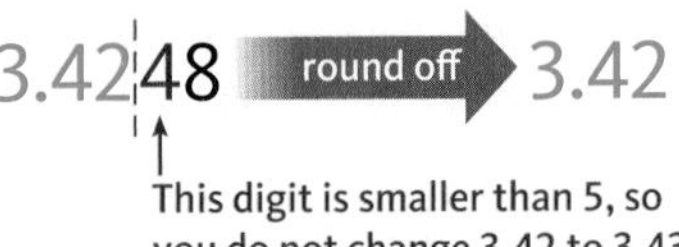

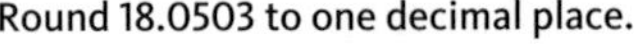

This digit is smaller than 5, so you do not change 3.42 to 3.43.

Round 18.0503 to one decimal place.

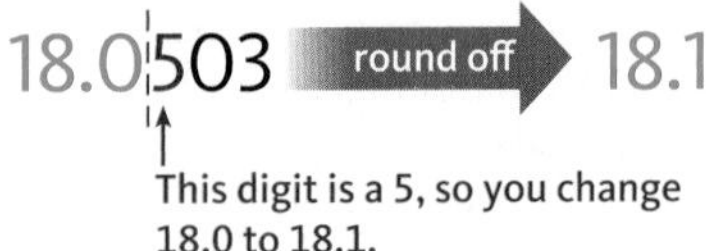

18.1
This digit is a 5, so you change 18.0 to 18.1.

If we need to round a 9 up, this will affect the digit before it, since the next number is 10. The following two examples illustrate what happens when the last digit we keep is a 9 and we need to round up:

Round 49.7621 to the nearest whole number.

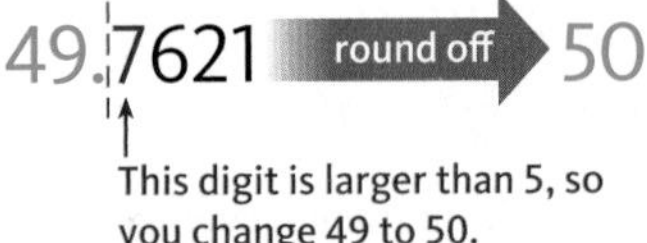

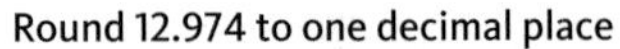

Round 12.974 to one decimal place

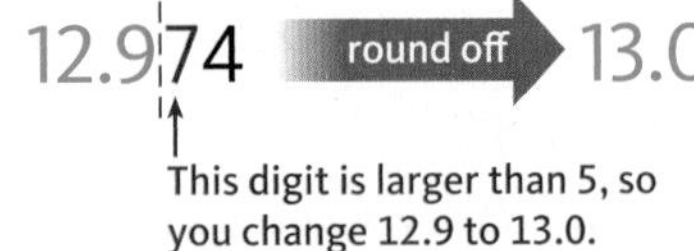

12.9|74

This digit is larger than 5, so you change 12.9 to 13.0.

In the last example, note that we did not drop the 0 in the number 13.0. When we need to round to a specific number of decimal places, the answer must have a digit in each of those places, even when one or more of those digits are zeros. The following example is an extreme case:

Round 19.999973 to four decimal places.

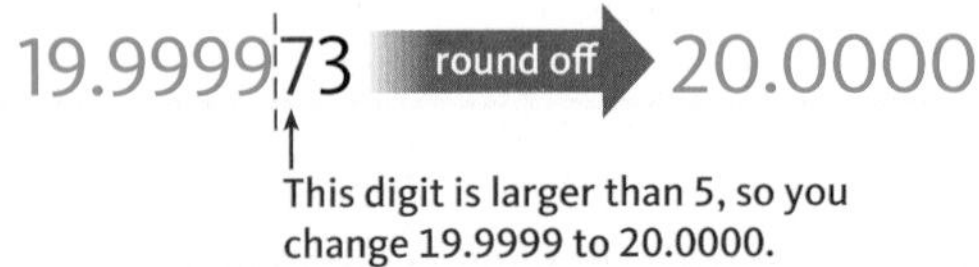

20.0000
This digit is larger than 5, so you change 19.9999 to 20.0000.

Sample Problem A.4

Rounding a number

Round the following numbers to two decimal places:

a) 64.004979

b) 13.6851

SOLUTION

a) **64.00** b) **13.69**

TRY IT YOURSELF: *Round the following numbers to one decimal place:*

This digit is larger than 5, so you change 49 to 50.

a) 315.552 b) 59.9823

Problems

A.6 Round off the number 13.7298 to the following numbers of decimal places:

a) none b) one c) two d) three

A.5 Rounding Off Calculated Values: Significant Figures

Whenever scientists do calculations, they must decide how many digits to report in the final answer. In general, the rule for rounding calculated values is the same as the rule for reporting measurements: write down all of the digits that are certain plus one uncertain digit. In this section, we will look at how to decide where to round a calculated value.

Additions and subtractions are rounded based on decimal places

When we add or subtract two numbers, the rule is that *the answer must have the same number of decimal places as the measurement with the fewest decimal places.* For example, suppose we weigh a large sample of salt on a balance that reports only one decimal place and find that it weighs 561.3 g. Now we take a bit more salt and weigh it on a more precise balance, which tells us that the extra salt weighs 1.237 g. If we put these two salt samples together, what is the total mass? Simply adding the two numbers gives us 562.537 g, but this is not an acceptable answer. In the first mass (561.3 g), we had no idea what the hundredths and thousandths places were, because the first balance was not precise enough to measure them. Therefore, we have no idea what the hundredths and thousandths places are in our final answer, as shown here. Since we only know the total mass to the tenths place, we report it as 562.5 g.

561.3?? g	We don't know the second and third decimal places in this mass . . .
+ 1.237 g	
562.5?? g	. . . so we do not know them in our final answer.

In general, it is easiest to do additions and subtractions on a calculator and then round off to the correct number of decimal places. For instance, suppose we start with 561.3 g of salt and then remove 1.237 g. As before, we must round our answer to one decimal place, but in this case we round up.

561.3 g	
− 1.237 g	
560.063 g	calculator answer
560.1 g	final answer, rounded to one decimal place

Calculators do not normally display zeros at the end of a decimal number, so we may need to add these to the end of the calculator answer. Here is an example that involves adding three masses. All three masses have three decimal places, so our answer must have three decimal places as well.

4.097 g	
3.276 g	
+ 2.227 g	
9.6 g	calculator answer
9.600 g	final answer: we add the two zeros that the calculator does not display

In this example, the calculator dropped the zeros in the hundredths and thousandths places, so we needed to add them to our final answer.

Sample Problem A.5

Rounding off after an addition

A beaker contains 5.23 g of salt. We add an additional 0.270 g of salt to the beaker. What is the total mass of salt in the beaker?

SOLUTION

To get the total mass of salt, we need to add the individual masses:

$$\begin{array}{r} 5.23\ \text{g} \\ +\ 0.270\ \text{g} \\ \hline 5.5\ \text{g} \end{array} \quad \text{calculator answer}$$

The calculator displays one decimal place, but we must report our answer to two decimal places. Therefore, we write 0 in the hundredths place. The total mass of salt is 5.50 g.

TRY IT YOURSELF: *A container holds 375 mL of water. If you remove 0.25 mL of water with a medicine dropper, what volume of water will remain in the container?*

Multiplications and divisions are rounded based on significant figures

For multiplication and division, we do not count decimal places. Instead, we round off based on **significant figures**. A significant figure is any digit in a measurement that is not simply present as a placeholder. Significant figures are digits that we actually measure.

To apply the rule for rounding off the results of multiplication and division, we must first be able to identify significant figures in a number. *Under normal circumstances, all of the digits starting from the first nonzero digit are significant.* Here are some examples:

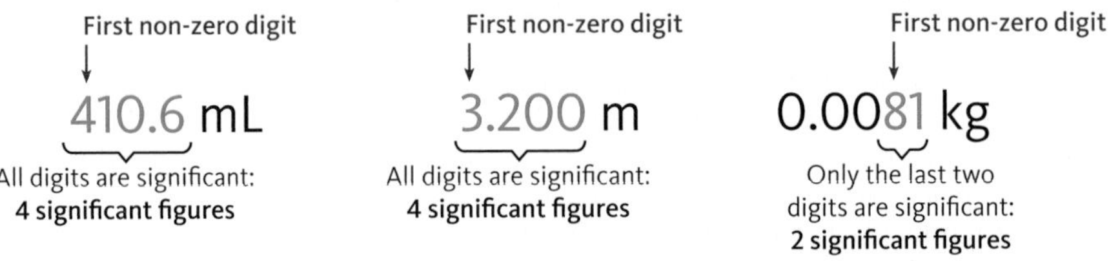

Sample Problem A.6

Determining the number of significant figures in a measurement

A bottle contains 0.803 L of saline solution. How many significant figures are there in this measurement?

SOLUTION

All of the digits except the initial zero are significant. Therefore, there are three significant figures in this measurement.

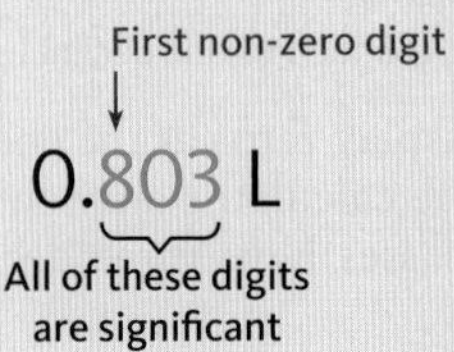

TRY IT YOURSELF: *A typical E. coli (a common type of bacterium) averages 0.0020 mm long. How many significant figures are there in this measurement?*

When we carry out multiplication or division, we must work out how many significant figures there are in each of the numbers we multiplied or divided. The rule for rounding our answer is that *the measurement with the fewest significant figures deter-*

mines the number of significant figures in the answer. For instance, suppose we need to multiply the following three numbers:

$$0.4576 \times 32.060 \times 4.18 = ?$$

The calculator answer to this multiplication problem is 61.32334208. (Your calculator may display one or two digits more or less than this, depending on the size of your display.)

How do we report this number? First, we determine the number of significant figures in each of the numbers we multiplied. The significant figures are shown in green.

0.4576 × 32.060 × 4.18

4 significant figures — 5 significant figures — 3 significant figures

The smallest number of significant figures is three, so our answer must be rounded to three significant figures. We start counting from the first nonzero digit, so the correct answer is 61.3.

Sample Problem A.7

Rounding a calculated value to the correct number of significant figures

The area of a rectangle is its length times its width. If a rectangle is 0.213 m long and 0.027 m wide, what is its area? Report the answer to the correct number of significant figures. (Ignore the units.)

SOLUTION

When we use a calculator to do the multiplication, we get

$$0.213 \times 0.027 = 0.005751$$

To determine where we should round off our answer, we begin by counting significant figures in the length and width. Remember to start with the first nonzero digit.

0.213 × 0.027

3 significant figures — 2 significant figures

The smallest number of significant figures is two, so we must round our answer to two significant figures. The three zeros at the start of our calculator answer are not significant, but we must keep them as placeholders so that we do not change the actual size of the number. Therefore, we round off after the 7 (the fourth decimal place). Since the next digit is a 5, we round the 7 up to 8. The area of the rectangle is 0.0058.

• The unit is square meters.

TRY IT YOURSELF: *If a rectangle has a height of 61.00 cm and a height of 3.27 cm, what is its area? Round off your answer to the correct number of significant figures.*

When you need to carry out more than two multiplication or division steps in solving a problem, it is best to round off only the final answer. You should keep at least one more digit than you need during the immediate steps, but it is easier to keep every digit in the calculator display than to keep rounding off after each step.

Ignore exact numbers when applying the significant figure rule

Three types of numbers should be ignored when applying the significant figure rules. These are called **exact numbers**, because they have no uncertainty.

1. *The number 1 in any conversion factor is an exact number.* For example, in the following unit conversion, we ignore the 1 in the conversion factor:

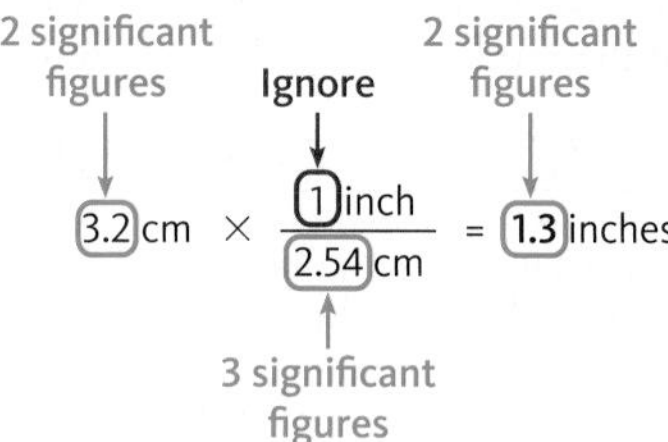

2. *Any equivalence that relates two units in the same measuring system (metric to metric or English to English) is an exact number.* Here are some examples:

1 foot	=	12 inches	(both are English units of distance)
1 pound	=	16 ounces	(both are English units of weight)
1 m	=	100 cm	(both are metric units of distance)
1 L	=	1000 mL	(both are metric units of volume)

We ignore these because they are not measurements; they are definitions, and as such they have no uncertainty. A foot is not *approximately* 12 inches (somewhere between 11 and 13 inches, for instance); it is *exactly* 12 inches. This is the definition of a foot in the English system. For example, if we convert 3.25 feet into inches, we ignore the 12 (and the 1) in the conversion factor, as shown here:

3 significant figures → 3.25 feet; Ignore → 12; 3 significant figures → 39.0 inches; Ignore → 1

$$3.25 \text{ feet} \times \frac{12 \text{ inches}}{1 \text{ foot}} = 39.0 \text{ inches}$$

On the other hand, we do not ignore conversion factors that relate English to metric units, because these are usually not exact numbers. For instance, if we convert 639.7 g into pounds using the relationship 1 pound = 454 g, our answer is limited to three significant figures, because 454 is an approximate number. (The exact relationship is 1 pound = 453.59237 g.)

4 significant figures → 639.7 g; Ignore → 1; 3 significant figures → 1.41 pounds; 3 significant figures → 454

$$639.7 \text{ g} \times \frac{1 \text{ pound}}{454 \text{ g}} = 1.41 \text{ pounds}$$

Sample Problem A.8

Applying the significant rules to a unit conversion

A student uses the following setup to convert 13.83 ounces into kilograms. Carry out the calculation and report the answer to the correct number of significant figures.

$$13.83 \text{ ounces} \times \frac{1 \text{ pound}}{16 \text{ ounces}} \times \frac{1 \text{ kg}}{2.20 \text{ pounds}} = ?$$

continued

SOLUTION

The calculator answer is 0.39289773 kg, which we must round off to an appropriate number of significant figures. In the setup, the relationship between pounds and ounces is exact, because it involves only English units, so we ignore the 16 when we apply the significant figure rules. However, the relationship between kilograms and pounds is not exact, so we must include the number 2.20. Therefore, the smallest number of significant figures is three, and we round off our answer to three significant figures.

$$\underset{\text{4 significant figures}}{13.83 \text{ ounces}} \times \frac{\overset{\text{Ignore}}{1} \text{ pound}}{\underset{\text{Ignore}}{16} \text{ ounces}} \times \frac{\overset{\text{Ignore}}{1} \text{ kg}}{\underset{\text{3 significant figures}}{2.20} \text{ pounds}} = \underset{\text{3 significant figures}}{0.393} \text{ kg}$$

TRY IT YOURSELF: *A student uses the following setup to convert 3.815 L into quarts. Carry out the calculation and report the answer to the correct number of significant figures.*

$$3.815 \text{ L} \times \frac{1 \text{ gallon}}{3.79 \text{ L}} \times \frac{4 \text{ quarts}}{1 \text{ gallon}} = ?$$

3. *Counting numbers are exact numbers, unless they are estimates.* Here are some examples:

"There are 132 people in the room."

"There are 7 eggs left in the refrigerator."

"I own 22 books about Elvis Presley."

These are exact numbers, obtained by counting whole objects. We cannot have half of a person, five-eighths of an egg, or 0.0334258 books, so there is no uncertainty about these numbers, and we ignore them when we apply the significant figure rules.

For example, suppose that we have a package that contains 25 tablets, each of which contains 0.0600 g of a decongestant. To calculate the total mass of decongestant in the package, we multiply 0.0600 g by 25, which gives us 1.5 g. However, we must report our answer to three significant figures, because the mass of decongestant has three significant figures and the number 25 is exact. The correct mass is 1.50 g.

$$\underset{\text{3 significant figures}}{0.0600} \text{ g} \times \underset{\text{Ignore}}{25} = \underset{\text{3 significant figures}}{1.50} \text{ g}$$

Trailing zeros in approximate numbers are not significant

Occasionally, you will encounter very large numbers that have been rounded off. Here are a few examples:

The distance between the sun and Venus is 108,000,000 km.

The population of Brazil is 161,000,000.

A human contains 3,000,000,000,000 cells.

These sorts of numbers are approximations. For example, the population of Brazil is not *exactly* 161,000,000; no one knows the exact number of people living in Brazil (and of course the number changes constantly). The intent of such a number is to give the reader a sense of size when the precise value is not known. Since the zeros at the end of such numbers are not actually measured, these zeros are not significant.

108,000,000	161,000,000	3,000,000,000,000
three significant figure	three significant figure	one significant figure

When we use such numbers in a calculation, we often need to round off a very large answer. For instance, suppose we want to convert the distance between the sun and Venus from kilometers into miles. The conversion factor setup is

$$108{,}000{,}000 \text{ km} \times \frac{1 \text{ mile}}{1.609 \text{ km}} = 67{,}122{,}436.3 \text{ miles} \quad \text{calculator answer}$$

The number 108,000,000 has three significant figures, and 1.609 has four, so we must round our answer to three significant figures. To do so, we keep the first three digits of our calculator answer and change all of the other digits to zeros. The correct answer is 67,100,000 miles.

Summary of significant figures

1. In *any multiplication or division,* the number with the fewest significant figures determines the number of significant figures in the answer. (For additions and subtractions, we count decimal places, not significant figures.)
2. In *measured numbers that have a decimal point,* all digits starting from the first nonzero digit are significant.

503.0 m	Four significant figures
80.000 L	Five significant figures
0.00032 g	Two significant figures
0.2003 km	Four significant figures

3. Significant figure rules do not apply to *conversion factors within a measuring system,* and they do not apply to the 1 in any conversion factor. (These are exact numbers.)

$\frac{39.37 \text{ inches}}{1 \text{ m}}$	Ignore the 1 when applying the significant figure rules. (However, do not ignore the 39.37, because the meter is a metric unit and the inch is an English unit. Metric-to-English conversions are usually approximate.)
$\frac{100 \text{ cm}}{1 \text{ m}}$	Ignore both numbers when applying the significant figure rules, because meters and centimeters are both metric units.

4. Significant figure rules do not apply to *counting numbers,* as long as the counting number is exact.

518 people	Significant figure rules do not apply (since people are counted in whole numbers).
88 shirts	Significant figure rules do not apply (since shirts are counted in whole numbers).

5. In *large, approximate numbers,* the final zeros are not significant, but all other digits are significant.

2,080,000 people	Three significant figures
200,000,000 kg	One significant figure

Problems

A.7 Carry out each of the following additions and subtractions, and round your answers to the appropriate number of digits:

a) 6.375 g + 8.216 g = ? b) 14.26 g − 13.91 g = ?

c) 105.6 g + 1.273 g = ? d) 18.51 cm + 6.22 cm + 1.27 cm = ?

A.8 How many significant figures are there in each of the following measurements?

a) 6.05 g b) 31 mg c) 0.082 L d) 520,000 pounds

A.9 Carry out each of the following calculations, and round your answer to the correct number of significant figures:

a) $3.815 \text{ L} \times \frac{1 \text{ gallon}}{3.79 \text{ L}} \times \frac{4 \text{ quarts}}{1 \text{ gallon}} = ?$

b) $0.008 \text{ m} \times \frac{39.37 \text{ inches}}{1 \text{ m}} = ?$

c) $3.50 \text{ feet} \times \frac{1 \text{ m}}{3.281 \text{ feet}} = ?$

A.10 Each of the following calculations involves an exact number. Carry out each calculation, and round your answers to the correct number of significant figures.

a) $27.5 \text{ mm} \times \frac{1 \text{ cm}}{10 \text{ mm}} = ?$ b) $28.5 \text{ feet} \times \frac{1 \text{ yard}}{3 \text{ feet}} = ?$

c) $18 \text{ tablets} \times \frac{2.50 \text{ mg}}{1 \text{ tablet}} = ?$

A.11 Carry out each of the following calculations to the correct number of significant figures:

a) $53.7 \text{ fluid ounces} \times \frac{1 \text{ pint}}{16 \text{ fluid ounces}} \times \frac{1 \text{ gallon}}{8 \text{ pints}} = ?$

b) $840.0 \text{ kg} \times \frac{2.2 \text{ pounds}}{1 \text{ kg}} \times \frac{1 \text{ ton}}{2000 \text{ pounds}} = ?$

c) $0.018 \text{ km} \times \frac{1000 \text{ m}}{1 \text{ km}} \times \frac{3.281 \text{ feet}}{1 \text{ m}} = ?$

A.12 The answer to each of the following calculations is a very large number. Carry out each calculation, and give the appropriate number of significant figures in your answers.

a) $350{,}000 \text{ kg} \times \frac{2.205 \text{ pounds}}{1 \text{ kg}} = ?$ b) $60{,}000 \text{ miles} \times \frac{5280 \text{ feet}}{1 \text{ mile}} = ?$

A.6 Exponents and Scientific Notation

Scientists often express very large numbers using *exponents*. An exponent (also called a *power*) is a way to show repeated multiplication, as in the following examples:

10^3 means $10 \times 10 \times 10$ (which equals 1000)

10^8 means $10 \times 10 \times 10 \times 10 \times 10 \times 10 \times 10 \times 10$ (which equals 100,000,000)

In the expression 10^3, the 3 is the exponent (or power), and we read it "10 to the third power." We can use exponents with numbers other than 10 (for instance, 2^3 is $2 \times 2 \times 2$, which equals 8), but this is rarely done in science.

TABLE A.1 Expressing Numbers as Powers of 10

Power of 10	Meaning	Equivalent Number
10^4	$10 \times 10 \times 10 \times 10$	10,000
10^3	$10 \times 10 \times 10$	1000
10^2	10×10	100
10^1	10	10
10^0	1	1
10^{-1}	$\frac{1}{10}$	0.1
10^{-2}	$\frac{1}{10 \times 10}$	0.01
10^{-3}	$\frac{1}{10 \times 10 \times 10}$	0.001
10^{-4}	$\frac{1}{10 \times 10 \times 10 \times 10}$	0.0001

• A reciprocal of a number is one divided by the number. For instance, the reciprocal of 3 is $^1/_3$.

We can also use exponents to express very small numbers. To do so, we use a negative exponent. Putting a minus sign in front of an exponent means to take the reciprocal of the number.

10^{-3} means $^1/_{10^3}$ (which is another way to write $^1/_{1000}$)

Finally, 10^0 equals 1 (not 0).

Table A.1 shows some of the powers of 10. Note that increasing or decreasing a power of 10 is equivalent to adding or removing a zero (for large numbers) or to moving the decimal point (for small numbers).

We can write numbers like 10,000,000 and 0.00000000001 as powers of 10, but we cannot write numbers like 2,300,000,000 and 0.00000000000045 in this way. Scientists express such numbers using *scientific notation.* To write a large number in scientific notation, we write it as a *small number* (between 1 and 10) *times a power of 10.* For example, 3000 is written 3×10^3 in scientific notation. Compare how we can write 1000 and 3000 using powers of 10.

1000	is the same as	1×1000	is the same as	1×10^3 *(scientific notation)*
3000	is the same as	3×1000	is the same as	3×10^3 *(scientific notation)*

To write a number like 3200, we must use a decimal number before the power of 10.

3200 is the same as 3.2×1000 is the same as 3.2×10^3 *(scientific notation)*

For small numbers, we use the same system, but we use a negative power of 10.

0.001	is the same as	1×0.001	is the same as	1×10^{-3} *(scientific notation)*
0.003	is the same as	3×0.001	is the same as	3×10^{-3} *(scientific notation)*
0.0032	is the same as	3.2×0.001	is the same as	3.2×10^{-3} *(scientific notation)*

If we need to convert a number into scientific notation, a useful trick is to move the decimal point over until we are left with a number between 1 and 10. The number of places we moved the decimal equals the size of the exponent. If we start with a small number (less than one), the exponent must be negative. If we start with a large number (larger than 10), the exponent must be positive. For example, suppose we need to express the number 0.00000407 in scientific notation. We begin by moving the decimal point to the right until we have a number between 1 and 10.

This tells us that 0.00000407 will be written as 4.07 times 10 to some power. To work out the exponent, we start by recognizing that 0.00000407 is a small number, so the exponent must be negative. Since we moved the decimal point six places, the numerical value of the exponent is −6. Therefore, in scientific notation, 0.00000407 is written 4.07×10^{-6}.

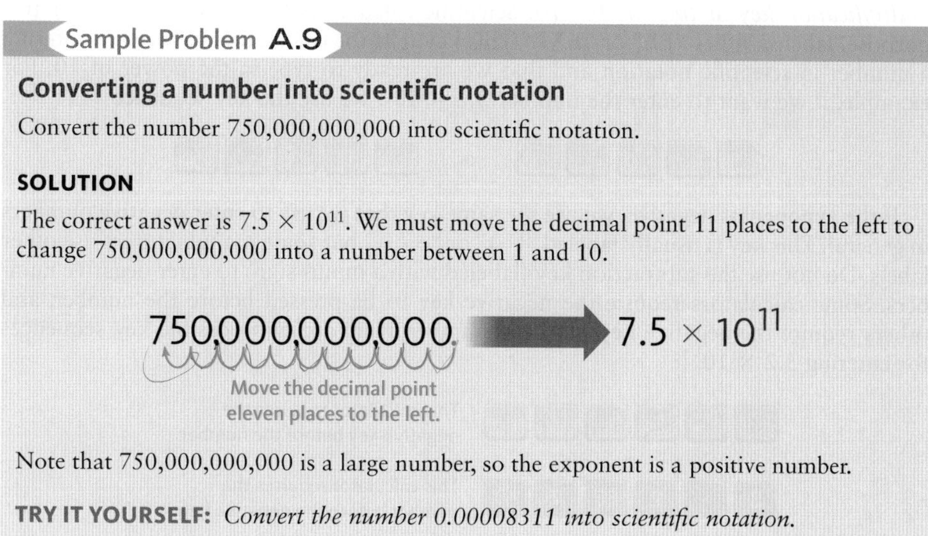

Sample Problem **A.9**

Converting a number into scientific notation

Convert the number 750,000,000,000 into scientific notation.

SOLUTION

The correct answer is 7.5×10^{11}. We must move the decimal point 11 places to the left to change 750,000,000,000 into a number between 1 and 10.

Note that 750,000,000,000 is a large number, so the exponent is a positive number.

TRY IT YOURSELF: *Convert the number 0.00008311 into scientific notation.*

If your teacher wants you to do calculations using scientific notation, you should be sure to purchase a calculator that can handle this format. Any *scientific calculator* can display and use scientific notation. Calculators display numbers in scientific notation in three ways, depending on the manufacturer. Some calculators display the entire number, using a smaller size for the number 10. Most calculators, however, do not display the 10 (or the multiplication sign). Here are the three common ways in which calculators display the number 4.07×10^{-6}:

Regardless of whether your calculator shows the 10, you must remember that when you see a number like the preceding ones, your calculator is displaying the number in scientific notation.

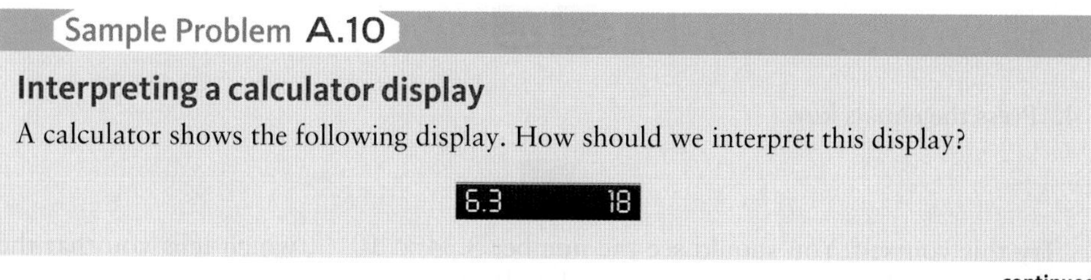

Sample Problem **A.10**

Interpreting a calculator display

A calculator shows the following display. How should we interpret this display?

continued

SOLUTION

This is the calculator's way of representing the number 6.3×10^{18}. The left side of the display shows the number that comes before the power of 10, and the right side shows the power of 10.

TRY IT YOURSELF: *Your calculator shows the following display. How should you interpret this display?*

When we type a number in scientific notation using a calculator, we *do not use the multiplication key or the number 10.* Scientific calculators have a special key for this purpose, labeled either "EE" or "EXP." This key tells the calculator that we are entering a number in scientific notation and that we are ready to type in the power of 10. For example, if we want to enter the number 3.2×10^7, we use the key sequence

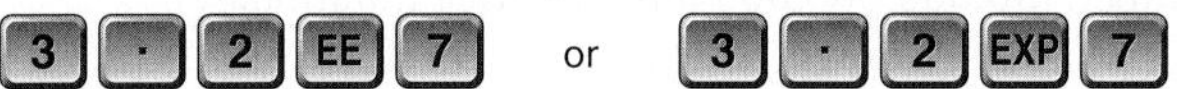

If the exponent is negative, we use the same key that we use to enter negative numbers in general. This key is usually labeled "(−)" or "+/−," but some manufacturers use other labels. Do not use the subtraction key (labeled with a minus sign) to enter negative numbers. Some calculators require the negative key to be pressed before the number, and others require the negative key after the number. Here are two possible key sequences for entering 3.2×10^{-7}:

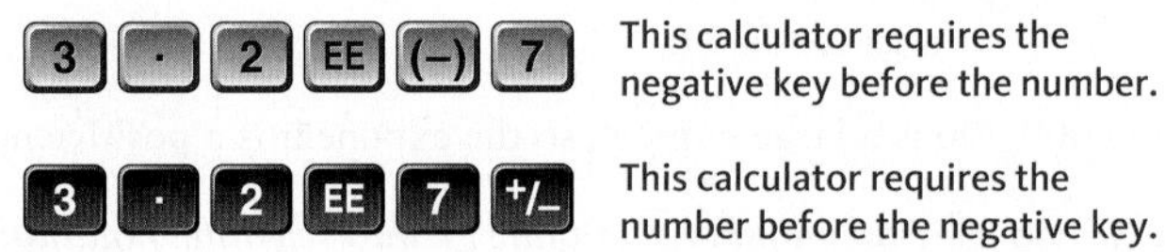

3 · 2 EE (−) 7
This calculator requires the negative key before the number.
3 · 2 EE 7 +/−
This calculator requires the number before the negative key.

We can use scientific notation to do any kind of arithmetical calculations. For example, a typical hydrogen atom weighs 1.67×10^{-24} g. Suppose that we wanted to know the weight of 20 hydrogen atoms. To calculate the weight of 20 atoms, we need to multiply the weight of one atom by 20. Here is how we might multiply 1.67×10^{-24} by 20 on a calculator:

1. Enter the number 1.67×10^{-24}.

Remember that your calculator may have an EXP key instead of EE, and you may need to press the negative key after the 24.

2. Press the multiplication key.

3. Enter the number 20.

4. Press the equals key.

Try this yourself. You should see the number 3.34×10^{-23}, which tells you that the total weight of the hydrogen atoms is 3.34×10^{-23} g.

Sample Problem A.11

Using scientific notation in a calculation

Do the following calculation using a calculator:

$$4.52 \times 10^{-16} \; - \; 8.16 \times 10^{-17} \; = \; ?$$

SOLUTION

The answer is 3.704×10^{-16}. Here is a typical key sequence:

1. Enter the number 4.52×10^{-16}.

2. Press the subtraction key.

3. Enter the number 8.16×10^{-17}.

4. Press the equals key.

TRY IT YOURSELF: *Do the following calculation using a calculator:*

$$(6.123 \times 10^{-18}) \; \times \; (3.55 \times 10^{4}) \; =$$

When a number is written in scientific notation, *all of the digits before the power of 10 are significant.* This rule allows us to use scientific notation to show the number of significant figures in a very large number. For example, in there were 20,000,000 people living in the state of California in 1970. The population was known to the nearest 100,000. If we simply wrote "20,000,000," a reader would assume that only the first digit was significant and that the population was somewhere between 10,000,000 and 30,000,000. However, by using scientific notation we can make it clear that the population is known to three significant figures, as shown here:

We need to show that all three of these digits are significant.

20,000,000 people → 2.00×10^{7} people

In this form, we would assume that the number has **1 significant figure.**

Scientific notation makes it clear that this number has **3 significant figures.**

Sample Problem A.12

Using scientific notation to show significant figures

A pharmaceutical company purchases 66 pounds of a medication. If it intends to make tablets that contain 15 mg of the medication, how many tablets can the company make? The conversion factor setup is

$$66 \text{ pounds} \times \frac{454 \text{ g}}{1 \text{ pound}} \times \frac{1000 \text{ mg}}{1 \text{ g}} \times \frac{1 \text{ tablet}}{15 \text{ mg}} = ?$$

SOLUTION

When we do the arithmetic on a calculator, we get 1,997,600 tablets. We need to round this number to two significant figures, based on the significant figure rule for multiplica-

continued

tion and division. However, rounding to two significant figures gives us 2,000,000, which looks like a number with only one significant figure.

1,997,600 → round off → 2,000,000

The third digit is a 9 . . . . . . so we round the first two digits up from 19 to 20.

To make it clear that our answer has two significant figures, we must write in it scientific notation and include two digits before the power of 10. The correct answer is 2.0×10^6 tablets.

TRY IT YOURSELF: *A patient's blood contains 5,000,000,000 red blood cells per milliliter. This value is known to two significant figures. Write this measurement in scientific notation to show the actual precision of the number.*

When we do a calculation using scientific notation, many calculators convert the answer into decimal notation automatically, as long as it is not too large or too small for the display. For instance, if we multiply 2.5×10^3 by 2, many calculators display the answer as 5000 rather than 5×10^3. In general, this does not pose a problem, but in some cases the calculator introduces a significant rounding error. For instance, when we multiply 5.0×10^{-5} by 4.8×10^{-5}, the correct answer is 2.4×10^{-9}. If the calculator automatically changes answers to decimal notation, however, it will display the number 0.000000002, which is the same as 2×10^{-9}. There is a significant difference between 2 and 2.4, so the calculator has created a large rounding error. To avoid this problem, be sure that you display extremely small numbers like this in scientific notation. All scientific calculators have a key that tells the calculator to display numbers in scientific notation, as well as a key that returns the calculator to a decimal display. Your owner's manual will tell you which keys these are (they may be the same key) and how to use them.

Problems

A.13 Express each of the following numbers using scientific notation:

a) 12,000,000,000 b) 0.000000752 c) 30

A.14 Express each of the following numbers as a decimal number or a whole number:

a) 6×10^4 b) 3.1×10^{-6} c) 5.33×10^1

A.15 Carry out each of the following calculations and write the answer in scientific notation. You do not need to round off your answers.

a) $5.1 \times 10^{18} + 3.2 \times 10^{19} = ?$

b) $3 \times 10^{-9} \times 1.8 \times 10^{-6} = ?$

c) $8.92 \times 10^6 - 9.18 \times 10^5 = ?$

d) $3.02 \times 10^{22} \div 4.55 \times 10^{22} = ?$

A.16 The bridge over the Flaxton River is estimated to weigh 62,000,000 kg. Using scientific notation, rewrite this number to show the following numbers of significant figures:

a) two significant figures b) four significant figures

A.17 The Earth is estimated to weigh 5.98×10^{24} kg. Convert this mass to pounds, using the fact that 1 kg = 2.205 pounds.

A.18 Distances between stars are often expressed in light years, where one light year equals 9.46×10^{12} km. If the distance between two galaxies is 280,000,000 light years, what is this distance in kilometers?

Key Terms

exact number – A.5
rounding off – A.4
significant figure – A.5

The Quantitative Behavior of Gases

OUTLINE

B.1 The Kelvin Temperature Scale

In this appendix, we will explore calculations involving the pressure, volume, and temperature of a gas sample, as well as the number of moles of the gas. To do these calculations, we must use the Kelvin scale. To calculate a Kelvin temperature, we add 273.15 to the Celsius temperature.

$$\text{Kelvin temperature} = \text{Celsius temperature} + 273.15$$

For example, the boiling point of water is 100.00°C, so the corresponding Kelvin temperature is 373.15 K. To convert a Kelvin temperature to Celsius, subtract 273.15. Note that the symbol for Kelvin temperatures is written without a degree sign.

The Kelvin scale is also called the *absolute* temperature scale, because a temperature of zero in the Kelvin scale is the lowest possible temperature. Recall that the temperature of a substance is related to how rapidly the atoms in the substance are moving. At 0 K, the atoms are not moving. It is impossible to slow the atoms further, so it is impossible to lower the temperature beyond 0 K. As a result, there are no negative temperatures in the Kelvin scale.

Sample Problem B.1

Interconverting Celsius and Kelvin temperatures

a) Mercury freezes at −39°C. Convert this to a Kelvin temperature.

b) Nitrogen changes from a gas to a liquid at 77.36 K. Convert this to a Celsius temperature.

SOLUTION

a) To convert a Celsius temperature to a Kelvin temperature, add 273.15.

$$-39°\text{C} + 273.15 = 234.15\text{ K} \quad \text{calculator answer}$$

Since the original temperature is given to the nearest whole number, the Kelvin temperature should be rounded to a whole number. The freezing point of mercury is 234 K.

b) To convert a Kelvin temperature to a Celsius temperature, subtract 273.15.

$$77.36\text{ K} - 273.15 = -195.79°\text{C}$$

In this case, the original temperature was given to two decimal places, so the answer is correct to two decimals as well. Nitrogen condenses to a liquid at −195.79°C.

TRY IT YOURSELF: *Acetone boils at 56.5°C. Convert this to a Kelvin temperature.*

Problems

B.1 The boiling point of isopropyl alcohol is 82.5°C. Convert this to a Kelvin temperature.

B.2 The freezing point of propane is 85.4 K. Convert this to a Celsius temperature.

B.2 The Combined Gas Law

In Section 4.3, we saw that the pressure that a gas exerts is related to its volume and temperature. Increasing the volume of a gas makes the pressure lower, and increasing its temperature makes the pressure higher. In addition, if we keep the pressure constant, increasing the temperature increases the volume of a gas.

The relationships among pressure, temperature, and volume of a gas sample can be expressed in a mathematical formula, called the **combined gas law**. This law allows us to predict how any of these three properties of a gas will change if we change one or both of the other two. For example, if we change the temperature of the gas inside a rigid steel cylinder, we can predict how the pressure of the gas will change. The mathematical form of the combined gas law is

$$\frac{P_1 \times V_1}{T_1} = \frac{P_2 \times V_2}{T_2} \qquad \text{the combined gas law}$$

In this formula, P stands for pressure, V stands for volume, and T stands for temperature. The subscript 1 means the *original* conditions, and the subscript 2 means the *final* conditions. The pressure and the volume can be in any units, metric or nonmetric, as long as we use the same units on both sides of the formula. However, *all temperatures must be Kelvin temperatures.*

For example, suppose we take a bicycle tire pump, seal the hose to prevent air from getting in or out, and then measure the properties of the air in the pump. We find that the pump contains 500 mL of air at a pressure of 760 torr and a temperature of 295 K (22°C). These are our initial conditions, so we can insert them into the left side of the combined gas law:

$$\frac{760 \text{ torr} \times 500 \text{ mL}}{295 \text{ K}} = \frac{P_2 \times V_2}{T_2}$$

Now let us push down on the handle until the volume of the air becomes 250 mL, as shown in Figure B.1. We don't heat or cool the pump, so the temperature of the air is still 295 K. What pressure does the air in the pump exert now? Since the pressure and volume of a gas sample are inversely related, we know that the pressure must have

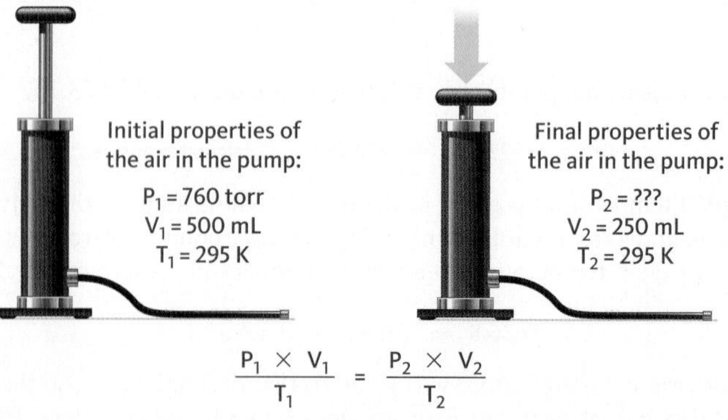

FIGURE B.1 Applying the combined gas law to the air in a bicycle pump.

increased as the volume decreased. We can use the combined gas law to calculate the new pressure, but we must first insert the final temperature and volume into our formula:

$$\frac{760 \text{ torr} \times 500 \text{ mL}}{295 \text{ K}} = \frac{P_2 \times 250 \text{ mL}}{295 \text{ K}}$$

To calculate P_2, we must divide both sides of our equation by 250 mL, and we then must multiply both sides by 295 K. This allows us to cancel all of the numbers and units on the right side of the equation, leaving us with P_2. It is easier to see what's going on if we combine all of the measurements on each side into one fraction, as shown here:

$$\frac{760 \text{ torr} \times 500 \text{ mL}}{295 \text{ K}} \times \frac{295 \text{ K}}{250 \text{ mL}} = \frac{P_2 \times 250 \text{ mL}}{295 \text{ K}} \times \frac{295 \text{ K}}{250 \text{ mL}} \quad \text{multiplying both sides by } \frac{295 \text{ K}}{250 \text{ mL}}$$

$$\frac{760 \text{ torr} \times 500 \text{ mL} \times 295 \text{ K}}{295 \text{ K} \times 250 \text{ mL}} = \frac{P_2 \times 250 \text{ mL} \times 295 \text{ K}}{295 \text{ K} \times 250 \text{ mL}} \quad \text{combining each side into a single fraction}$$

Next, we cancel as many numbers and units as we can. We can cancel 295 K on both sides of the equation, and we can cancel 250 mL on the right side of the equation. In addition, we can cancel the volume unit (milliliters) on the left side.

$$\frac{760 \text{ torr} \times 500 \cancel{\text{mL}} \times \cancel{295 \text{ K}}}{\cancel{295 \text{ K}} \times 250 \cancel{\text{mL}}} = \frac{P_2 \times \cancel{250 \text{ mL}} \times \cancel{295 \text{ K}}}{\cancel{295 \text{ K}} \times \cancel{250 \text{ mL}}}$$

After we cancel everything, we are left with

$$\frac{760 \text{ torr} \times 500}{250} = P_2$$

The final pressure in the bicycle pump is $760 \times 500 \div 250 = 1520$ torr. This is larger than the initial pressure (760 torr), as we expected.

Problems

B.3 A car tire holds 41.3 L of air at a pressure of 28.5 psi and a temperature of 22.5°C. After one half hour of driving on a hot day, the temperature of the air has increased to 41.9°C and the volume has expanded to 41.9 L.

a) Set up the combined gas law expression that you would need to solve in order to calculate the new pressure of the air.

b) Calculate the pressure of the air.

B.4 A hiker carries an empty plastic water bottle from the top of a mountain to the bottom. At the top of the mountain, the bottle contains 495 mL of air at 6°C and a pressure of 633 torr. At the bottom of the mountain, the air in the bottle is at 29°C and exerts a pressure of 681 torr.

a) Set up the combined gas law expression that you would need to solve in order to calculate the volume of the air at the end of the hike.

b) Calculate the volume of the air.

B.3 Relationships Derived from the Combined Gas Law

Whenever one of the three gas properties does not change, we can omit that property from the combined gas law. For instance, in our previous example the temperature did not change, so we can omit T_1 and T_2 from the combined gas law, giving us

$$P_1 \times V_1 = P_2 \times V_2$$

Omitting one of the three properties simplifies the problem-solving process a bit, as illustrated in Sample Problem B.2.

Sample Problem B.2

Using the combined gas law

A steel cylinder contains 8.5 L of oxygen at a pressure of 170 atm and a temperature of 10°C. If the cylinder and oxygen are heated to 50°C, what will be the pressure of the oxygen?

SOLUTION

We can begin by recognizing that a steel cylinder does not expand or contract, so the volume of the oxygen in the cylinder does not change. Therefore, we can omit the volume from the combined gas law. Doing so gives us a relationship between pressure and temperature.

$$\frac{P_1 \times \cancel{V_1}}{T_1} = \frac{P_2 \times \cancel{V_2}}{T_2} \longrightarrow \frac{P_1}{T_1} = \frac{P_2}{T_2}$$

Our simplified formula relates pressures and temperatures. We can keep the pressures in units of atmospheres, but we must convert the temperatures into Kelvin.

$$T_1 = 10 + 273.15 = 283.15 \text{ K}$$
$$T_2 = 50 + 273.15 = 323.15 \text{ K}$$

Now we can insert the measurements we know into our simplified gas law.

$$\frac{170 \text{ atm}}{283.15 \text{ K}} = \frac{P_2}{323.15 \text{ K}}$$

We solve this equation by multiplying both sides by 323.15 K.

$$\frac{170 \text{ atm}}{283.15 \text{ K}} \times 323.15 \text{ K} = \frac{P_2}{323.15 \text{ K}} \times 323.15 \text{ K}$$

Next, we write both sides as single fractions, and we then cancel as many numbers and units as we can.

$$\frac{170 \text{ atm} \times 323.15 \cancel{\text{K}}}{283.15 \cancel{\text{K}}} = \frac{P_2 \times \cancel{323.15 \text{ K}}}{\cancel{323.15 \text{ K}}}$$

$$\frac{170 \text{ atm} \times 323.15}{283.15} = P_2$$

Finally, we do the arithmetic.

$$170 \times 323.15 \div 283.15 = 194.0155395 \quad \text{calculator answer}$$

The final pressure of the oxygen in the tank is 194 atm.

TRY IT YOURSELF: *A balloon is inflated with 6.45 L of air at a temperature of 21°C. The balloon is then taken outdoors, where the temperature is −6°C. What will be the volume of the air in the balloon when it reaches −6°C? (Assume that the pressure of the air remains the same.)*

The name "combined gas law" comes from the fact that this law combines three separate relationships involving gas properties. Each of these relationships has its own name, which commemorates the person who discovered the relationship. However, it is easiest to derive each of these three specialized relationships from the combined gas law, as shown here:

1. If the temperature does not change, canceling the temperatures gives us a relationship between pressure and volume, called *Boyle's law.*

$$\frac{P_1 \times V_1}{\cancel{T_1}} = \frac{P_2 \times V_2}{\cancel{T_2}} \longrightarrow \boxed{P_1 \times V_1 = P_2 \times V_2} \longleftarrow \text{Boyle's Law}$$

2. If the volume does not change, canceling the volumes gives us a relationship between pressure and temperature, called *Charles's law.* We used Charles's law to solve Sample Problem B.2.

$$\frac{P_1 \times \cancel{V_1}}{T_1} = \frac{P_2 \times \cancel{V_2}}{T_2} \longrightarrow \boxed{\frac{P_1}{T_1} = \frac{P_2}{T_2}} \longleftarrow \text{Charles' Law}$$

3. If the pressure of the gas does not change, canceling the pressures gives us a relationship between temperature and volume, called *Gay-Lussac's law.*

$$\frac{\cancel{P_1} \times V_1}{T_1} = \frac{\cancel{P_2} \times V_2}{T_2} \longrightarrow \boxed{\frac{V_1}{T_1} = \frac{V_2}{T_2}} \longleftarrow \text{Gay-Lussac's Law}$$

Problems

B.5 Natasha has a balloon that contains 3.9 L of air at a pressure of 0.96 atm. She takes the balloon to the bottom of a swimming pool, where the pressure is 1.21 atm. The temperature of the air in the balloon does not change.

a) Which of the three gas laws in this section could you use to calculate the volume of the air in the balloon when it is at the bottom of the pool?

b) Write the gas law expression that you would need to solve in order to calculate the volume of the air in the balloon. (You do not need to do any calculations.)

B.6 LeRoy is transporting a steel tank filled with compressed oxygen to the respiratory clinic. The pressure of the oxygen in the tank is 525 psi at a temperature of 31°C. LeRoy has to leave the tank in his car on a cold winter evening, and the pressure of the oxygen drops to 440 psi.

a) Which of the three gas laws in this section could you use to calculate the temperature of the oxygen in the tank in LeRoy's car?

b) Write the gas law expression that you would need to solve in order to calculate the temperature of the oxygen in the tank. (You do not need to do any calculations.)

B.4 Manipulating and Solving the Combined Gas Law

Before we leave the combined gas law, let us look at how we handle the mathematics in two circumstances. First, we may face a situation in which we need to calculate a temperature. For example, suppose we have a rigid container filled with air at 100°C (373.15 K) and a pressure of 900 torr. We can lower the pressure by cooling the air. If we want to reduce the pressure to 850 torr, to what temperature must we cool the air? Applying Charles's law gives us

$$\frac{900\text{ torr}}{373.15\text{ K}} = \frac{850\text{ torr}}{T_2}$$

We need to solve this equation to find the final temperature, but T_2 is in the denominator of the fraction. *Whenever the unknown is in the denominator, we can turn both fractions upside down to move the unknown into the numerator.* In this case, we get

$$\frac{373.15\text{ K}}{900\text{ torr}} \times \frac{T_2}{850\text{ torr}}$$

Now we can solve for T_2 in the normal way, multiplying both sides by 850 torr and doing the needed arithmetic. Try this yourself: you should get 352 K, which equals 79°C.

The second situation we may encounter is when all three properties change. For example, at the beginning of this section, we squeezed the air in a bicycle pump while keeping the temperature constant. What if we also heat the air to 315 K (42°C)? The combined gas law expression will look like this:

$$\frac{760\text{ torr} \times 500\text{ mL}}{295\text{ K}} = \frac{P_2 \times 250\text{ mL}}{315\text{ K}}$$

We multiply both sides by 315 K and divide both sides by 250 mL, and then we combine each side into a single fraction.

$$\frac{760\text{ torr} \times 500\text{ mL}}{295\text{ K}} \times \frac{315\text{ K}}{250\text{ mL}} = \frac{P_2 \times 250\text{ mL}}{315\text{ K}} \times \frac{315\text{ K}}{250\text{ mL}}$$

$$\frac{760\text{ torr} \times 500\text{ mL} \times 315\text{ K}}{295\text{ K} \times 250\text{ mL}} = \frac{P_2 \times 250\text{ mL} \times 315\text{ K}}{315\text{ K} \times 250\text{ mL}}$$

We can cancel the temperatures and volumes in the right-hand fraction, just as we did before. However, none of the numbers on the left side cancel. All we can do with the left side is cancel the units.

$$\frac{760\text{ torr} \times 500\,\cancel{\text{mL}} \times 315\,\cancel{\text{K}}}{295\,\cancel{\text{K}} \times 250\,\cancel{\text{mL}}} = \frac{P_2 \times \cancel{250\text{ mL}} \times \cancel{315\text{ K}}}{\cancel{315\text{ K}} \times \cancel{250\text{ mL}}}$$

$$\frac{760\text{ torr} \times 500 \times 315}{295 \times 250} = P_2$$

There are two ways to deal with the remaining fraction on the left side. One is to recognize that it tells us to divide (760 × 500 × 315) by (295 × 250).

$$(760\text{ torr} \times 500 \times 315) \div (295 \times 250) = P_2$$

Since 760 × 500 × 315 equals 119,700,000 and 295 × 250 equals 73,750, our pressure calculation becomes

$$119{,}700{,}000 \div 73{,}750 = P_2$$

Doing this division gives us 1623 torr as the final pressure.

The second option is to recognize that we are dividing the top of our fraction by both 295 and 250. This option is simpler, because we can do the entire calculation in a single sequence. The arithmetic becomes

$$760\text{ torr} \times 500 \times 315 \div 295 \div 250 = P_2$$

As before, we get 1623 torr as our final pressure.

Problems

B.7 A researcher fills a weather balloon with 831 L of helium at 23°C and a pressure of 762 torr. The researcher then releases the balloon, which rises into the air. If the balloon reaches an altitude where the temperature is −22°C and the pressure is 422 torr, what will be the volume of the balloon?

B.8 A steel cylinder contains 4.15 L of nitrous oxide at 18°C and a pressure of 225 psi. If the nitrous oxide is cooled to 5°C, what will its pressure be? (Nitrous oxide is a gas under these conditions.)

B.9 A balloon contains 870 mL of air at 23°C. If you put the balloon into your freezer, where the temperature is −27°C, what will be the volume of the balloon? (The pressure of the gas inside a balloon is the same as the pressure outside the balloon.)

B.10 A car tire is filled with 425 L of air at 17°C and a pressure of 39.3 psi. The car is then driven for several miles during a hot summer day. Afterward, the volume of the tire has increased to 433 L and the pressure has increased to 43.2 psi. What is the temperature of the air in the tire?

B.5 Moles and the Ideal Gas Law

As we saw in Section 4.3, the pressure exerted by a gas depends on the number of molecules of the gas, as well as on the temperature and the volume. However, the pressure does not depend on what gas we use. Hydrogen, helium, oxygen, and carbon dioxide all exert the same pressure, as long as we have the same number of individual molecules of each gas (or individual atoms, if the atoms do not form chemical bonds with one another).

Chemists normally describe the number of molecules of a substance by giving a number of *moles*. A mole (abbreviated *mol*) is a specific number of molecules or atoms, just as a dozen is a specific number of objects (12). However, a mole is a very large number:

$$1 \text{ mol} = 602{,}000{,}000{,}000{,}000{,}000{,}000{,}000 \text{ molecules } (6.02 \times 10^{23} \text{ molecules})$$

This number is called *Avogadro's number*, in honor of the Italian chemist who discovered the relationship between gas properties and numbers of molecules. It is extremely large because molecules are extremely small. For example, the total mass of 6.02×10^{23} water molecules (one mole of water) is only 18 grams, roughly the same as three medium-sized cherries. Section 5.2 looks at the relationship between mass and number of moles.

The pressure exerted by a gas depends only on the temperature of the gas, the volume of the gas, and the number of moles of gas (remember that each mole is 6.02×10^{23} molecules). The relationship between these four gas properties is called the **ideal gas law**.

$$P \times V = n \times R \times T \quad \text{the ideal gas law}$$

In this formula, P, V, and T stand for pressure, volume, and temperature, respectively, and n stands for the number of moles. R represents a fundamental constant of nature called the *ideal gas constant*. In the ideal gas law, the temperature must be in the Kelvin scale, but we can choose a variety of possible units for P and V. The numerical value of R depends on the units we choose for P and V. Table B.1 lists some common combinations and the corresponding values of R. The first two values of R are the most commonly used.

We can use the ideal gas law to calculate any one of the four gas properties if we know the other three. The ideal gas law is particularly useful for calculating the number of moles of a gas, because this is difficult to measure directly.

TABLE B.1 Values of the Ideal Gas Constant in Various Units

Pressure Unit	Volume Unit	*R* Value
Atmospheres (atm)	Liters (L)	0.0821 L·atm/mol·K
Millimeters of mercury (mm Hg or torr)	Liters (L)	62.4 L·torr/mol·K
Atmospheres (atm)	Milliliters (mL)	82.1 mL·atm/mol·K
Millimeters of mercury (mm Hg or torr)	Milliliters (mL)	62,400 mL·torr/mol·K
Pounds per square inch (psi)	Liters (L)	1.21 L·psi/mol·K

Sample Problem B. 3

Using the ideal gas law to calculate a number of moles

A balloon holds 3.6 L of helium at 21°C and a pressure of 751 torr. How many moles of helium are in the balloon? How many helium atoms are in the balloon?

SOLUTION

The question tells us the pressure, volume, and temperature of the helium, and we can get the corresponding value of the gas constant *R* from Table B.1. However, the temperature must be in the Kelvin scale.

$$T = 21°\text{C} + 273.15 = 294.15\ \text{K}$$

The pressure is given in torr and the volume is given in liters, so the corresponding value of *R* is 62.4 L·torr/mol·K. Now we can insert all of these numbers into the ideal gas law.

$$751\ \text{torr} \times 3.6\ \text{L} = n \times 62.4\ \text{L·torr/mol·K} \times 294.15\ \text{K}$$

It is easiest to eliminate the unit labels before we do the arithmetic, to avoid excessive clutter. We already know that *n* represents the number of moles.

$$751 \times 3.6 = n \times 62.4 \times 294.15$$

To calculate *n*, we need to divide both sides by 62.4 and by 294.15.

$$\frac{751 \times 3.6}{62.4 \times 294.15} = \frac{n \times 62.4 \times 294.15}{62.4 \times 294.15}$$

All of the numbers in the right-hand fraction cancel, leaving us with *n*.

$$\frac{751 \times 3.6}{62.4 \times 294.15} = n$$

Finally, we do the arithmetic. The calculator answer is 0.14729534. Rounding this number to two significant figures gives us our final answer: there are **0.15 mol of helium** in the balloon. We know that 1 mol of helium contains 6.02×10^{23} helium atoms (not molecules, because helium atoms cannot form chemical bonds). Therefore, we can also say that the balloon contains **8.9×10^{22} helium atoms.**

$$0.14729534\ \text{mol} \times (6.02 \times 10^{23}) = 8.867179 \times 10^{22}\ \text{atoms}$$
$$= 8.9 \times 10^{22}\ \text{atoms (to two significant figures)}$$

TRY IT YOURSELF: *An oxygen tank contains 8500 mL of gaseous oxygen (O_2) at 17°C and a pressure of 23.4 atm. How many moles of oxygen are in the tank? How many O_2 molecules are in the tank?*

Problems

B.11 A steel cylinder is filled with 5.75 mol of nitrogen at 22°C. The volume of the cylinder is 18.4 L. Calculate the pressure inside the cylinder.

B.12 A balloon is filled with 0.388 mol of helium at 16.3°C. The pressure of the helium is 0.988 atm. Calculate the volume of the helium.

B.13 An aerosol can contains 525 mL of gaseous propane (C_3H_8) at a pressure of 1.22 atm and a temperature of 5°C.

a) How many moles of propane are in the can?

b) How many molecules of propane are in the can?

c) What is the mass of the propane? (Do this part only if you have covered Section 5.2.)

Key Terms

combined gas law – B.2
ideal gas law – B.5

Summary of Organic Functional Groups

This appendix summarizes the types of organic molecules that are covered in this textbook and their chemical reactions. For more details, refer to the sections listed by each functional group and reaction type.

Classes of Organic Molecules

Type of compound	Examples
Alkanes and cycloalkanes *(Sections 8.2–8.4)* Alkanes and cycloalkanes are made from carbon and hydrogen linked entirely by single bonds, and they do not contain functional groups.	$CH_3-CH_2-CH_2-CH_2-CH_3$ **Pentane** $CH_3-CH(CH_3)-CH_2-CH_2-CH_3$ **2-Methylpentane** [cyclopentane ring] **Cyclopentane**
Alkenes *(Sections 8.6 and 8.7)* contain $\mathrm{C{=}C}$ (with two bonds on each carbon). Alkenes may have *cis* and *trans* isomers.	$CH_2{=}CH-CH_2-CH_2-CH_3$ **1-Pentene** $CH_3(H)C{=}C(H)CH_2-CH_3$ (CH_3 and H on first C; H and CH_2-CH_3 on second C, trans) ***Trans*-2-pentene** [cyclopentene ring] **Cyclopentene**

continued

Classes of Organic Molecules—*continued*

Type of compound	Examples
Alkynes *(Sections 8.6 and 8.7)* contain $-C{\equiv}C-$	$HC{\equiv}C-CH_2-CH_2-CH_3$ **1-Pentyne** $CH_3-C{\equiv}C-CH_2-CH_3$ **2-Pentyne**
Aromatics *(Section 8.8)* contain  (benzene ring)	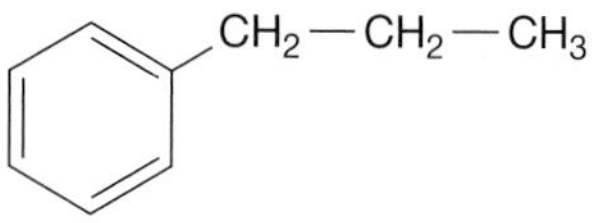 (benzene ring)$-CH_2-CH_2-CH_3$ **Propylbenzene**
Alcohols *(Sections 9.3 and 9.4)* contain $-\overset{|}{\underset{|}{C}}(OH)-$ Alcohols are classified as primary, secondary, or tertiary based on the number of carbon atoms surrounding the functional group carbon.	$CH_3-CH(OH)-CH_2-CH_2-CH_3$ **2-Pentanol** 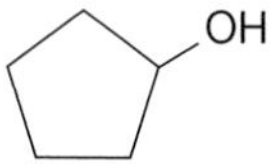 (cyclopentane ring)$-OH$ **Cyclopentanol**
Phenols *(Section 9.7)* contain 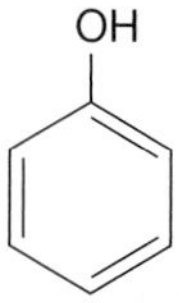 (benzene ring)$-OH$	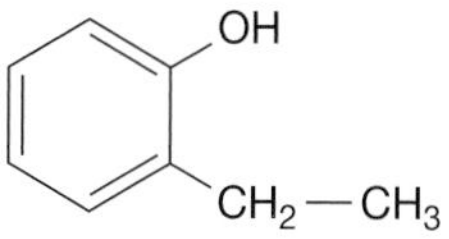 (benzene ring with OH and CH_2-CH_3 on adjacent carbons) (Names of compounds containing the phenol group are not covered in this book.)
Thiols *(Section 9.7)* contain $-\overset{|}{\underset{|}{C}}(SH)-$	$CH_3-CH(SH)-CH_2-CH_2-CH_3$ (Names of compounds containing the thiol group are not covered in this book.)
Ethers *(Section 12.1)* contain $-\overset{|}{\underset{|}{C}}-O-\overset{|}{\underset{|}{C}}-$	$CH_3-CH_2-O-CH_2-CH_2-CH_3$ **Ethyl propyl ether** (This book only covers trivial names of ethers.)

continued

Classes of Organic Molecules—*continued*

Type of compound	Examples
Aldehydes *(Section 10.3)* contain $-\overset{\overset{O}{\|}}{C}-H$	$CH_3-CH_2-CH_2-CH_2-\overset{\overset{O}{\|}}{C}-H$ **Pentanal**
Ketones *(Section 10.3)* contain $-\underset{\|}{\overset{\|}{C}}-\overset{\overset{O}{\|}}{C}-\underset{\|}{\overset{\|}{C}}-$	$CH_3-\overset{\overset{O}{\|}}{C}-CH_2-CH_2-CH_3$ **2-Pentanone** **Cyclopentanone**
Carboxylic acids *(Section 10.5)* contain $-\overset{\overset{O}{\|}}{C}-OH$	$CH_3-CH_2-CH_2-CH_2-\overset{\overset{O}{\|}}{C}-OH$ **Pentanoic acid**
Esters *(Section 12.2)* contain $-\overset{\overset{O}{\|}}{C}-O-\underset{\|}{\overset{\|}{C}}-$	$CH_3-\overset{\overset{O}{\|}}{C}-O-CH_2-CH_2-CH_3$ (Names of compounds containing the ester group are not covered in this book.)
Amines *(Section 11.3)* Amines contain a nitrogen atom bonded to at least one carbon atom. Amines are classified as primary, secondary, or tertiary based on the number of carbon atoms attached to the nitrogen atom.	$NH_2-CH_2-CH_2-CH_2-CH_2-CH_3$ **Pentylamine** $CH_3-CH_2-\underset{\underset{CH_3}{\|}}{N}-CH_3$ **Ethyldimethylamine** (This book only covers trivial names of amines.)
Amides *(Section 12.2)* contain $-\overset{\overset{O}{\|}}{C}-\underset{\|}{N}-$	$CH_3-CH_2-\overset{\overset{O}{\|}}{C}-NH-CH_3$ (Names of compounds containing the amide group are not covered in this book.)

Summary of Organic Reactions

Hydration of alkenes *(Section 9.1)*

$$\text{alkene} + H_2O \longrightarrow \text{alcohol}$$

$$CH_2{=}CH_2 + H_2O \longrightarrow CH_3{-}\underset{}{\overset{OH}{\overset{|}{C}H_2}}$$

Dehydration of alcohols *(Section 9.6)*

$$\text{alcohol} \longrightarrow \text{alkene} + H_2O$$

$$CH_3{-}\overset{OH}{\overset{|}{C}H_2} \longrightarrow CH_2{=}CH_2 + H_2O$$

Dehydrogenation *(Section 10.1)*

$$\text{alkane} \longrightarrow \text{alkene} + 2\,[H]$$

(This reaction only occurs in certain biochemical reactions, and it requires FAD.)

$$CH_3{-}CH_2{-}CH_2{-}\overset{O}{\overset{\|}{C}}{-}OH + FAD \longrightarrow CH_3{-}CH{=}CH{-}\overset{O}{\overset{\|}{C}}{-}OH + FADH_2$$

Hydrogenation *(Section 10.1)*

$$\text{alkene} + 2\,[H] \longrightarrow \text{alkane}$$

(In a living organism, this reaction normally requires NADPH; in a laboratory, other sources of hydrogen can be used.)

$$CH_3{-}CH{=}CH{-}\overset{O}{\overset{\|}{C}}{-}OH + NADPH + H^+ \longrightarrow CH_3{-}CH_2{-}CH_2{-}\overset{O}{\overset{\|}{C}}{-}OH + NADP^+$$

$$CH_3{-}CH{=}CH{-}CH_3 + H_2 \longrightarrow CH_3{-}CH_2{-}CH_2{-}CH_3$$

Oxidation of alcohols *(Section 10.2)*

$$\text{primary alcohol} \longrightarrow \text{aldehyde} + 2\,[H]$$

$$\text{secondary alcohol} \longrightarrow \text{ketone} + 2\,[H]$$

(In a living organism, these reactions normally require NAD$^+$; in a laboratory, other chemicals can be used to remove the hydrogen atoms.)

$$CH_3{-}CH_2{-}CH_2{-}\overset{OH}{\overset{|}{C}H_2} + NAD^+ \longrightarrow CH_3{-}CH_2{-}CH_2{-}\overset{O}{\overset{\|}{C}}{-}H + NADH + H^+$$

$$CH_3{-}CH_2{-}\overset{OH}{\overset{|}{C}H}{-}CH_3 + NAD^+ \longrightarrow CH_3{-}CH_2{-}\overset{O}{\overset{\|}{C}}{-}CH_3 + NADH + H^+$$

continued

Oxidation of aldehydes *(Section 10.4)*

$$\text{aldehyde} + H_2O \longrightarrow \text{carboxylic acid} + 2\,[H]$$

(In a living organism, this reaction normally requires NAD$^+$; in a laboratory, other chemicals can be used to remove the hydrogen atoms from water.)

$$CH_3-CH_2-CH_2-\overset{\overset{\displaystyle O}{\|}}{C}-H + H_2O + NAD^+ \longrightarrow CH_3-CH_2-CH_2-\overset{\overset{\displaystyle O}{\|}}{C}-OH + NADH + H^+$$

Oxidation of thiols *(Section 10.4)*

$$2\ \text{thiols} \longrightarrow \text{disulfide} + 2\,[H]$$

(In a living organism, this reaction normally requires NAD$^+$.)

$$2\ CH_3-CH_2-SH + NAD^+ \longrightarrow CH_3-CH_2-S-S-CH_2-CH_3 + NADH + H^+$$

Reduction of aldehydes and ketones *(Section 10.2)*

$$\text{aldehyde} + 2\,[H] \longrightarrow \text{primary alcohol}$$

$$\text{ketone} + 2\,[H] \longrightarrow \text{secondary alcohol}$$

(In a living organism, these reactions normally require NADPH; in a laboratory, other sources of hydrogen can be used.)

$$CH_3-CH_2-CH_2-\overset{\overset{\displaystyle O}{\|}}{C}-H + NADPH + H^+ \longrightarrow CH_3-CH_2-CH_2-\overset{\overset{\displaystyle OH}{|}}{CH_2} + NADP^+$$

$$CH_3-CH_2-\overset{\overset{\displaystyle O}{\|}}{C}-CH_3 + H_2 \longrightarrow CH_3-CH_2-\overset{\overset{\displaystyle OH}{|}}{CH}-CH_3$$

Decarboxylation of carboxylic acids *(Section 11.2)*

$$\text{carboxylic acid} \longrightarrow \text{smaller molecule} + CO_2$$

(This reaction normally requires an acid with a ketone group on the β-carbon atom.)

$$CH_3-\overset{\overset{\displaystyle O}{\|}}{C}-CH_2-\overset{\overset{\displaystyle O}{\|}}{C}-OH \longrightarrow CH_3-\overset{\overset{\displaystyle O}{\|}}{C}-CH_3 + CO_2$$

Oxidative decarboxylation *(Section 11.2)*

$$\text{carboxylic acid} + \text{thiol} \longrightarrow \text{thioester} + CO_2 + 2\,[H]$$

(This reaction normally requires an acid with a ketone group on the α-carbon atom, and it uses NAD$^+$ to remove the hydrogen atoms.)

$$CH_3-\overset{\overset{\displaystyle O}{\|}}{C}-\overset{\overset{\displaystyle O}{\|}}{C}-OH + HS-CoA + NAD^+ \longrightarrow CH_3-\overset{\overset{\displaystyle O}{\|}}{C}-S-CoA + CO_2 + NADH + H^+$$

continued

Condensation of alcohols *(Section 12.1)*

$$\text{2 alcohols} \longrightarrow \text{ether} + H_2O$$

$$2\,CH_3-CH_2-OH \longrightarrow CH_3-CH_2-O-CH_2-CH_3 + H_2O$$

Esterification *(Section 12.2)*

$$\text{carboxylic acid} + \text{alcohol} \longrightarrow \text{ester} + H_2O$$

$$CH_3-\overset{\overset{\displaystyle O}{\|}}{C}-OH + HO-CH_2-CH_3 \longrightarrow CH_3-\overset{\overset{\displaystyle O}{\|}}{C}-O-CH_2-CH_3 + H_2O$$

Amidation *(Section 12.2)*

$$\text{carboxylic acid} + \text{amine} \longrightarrow \text{amide} + H_2O$$

$$CH_3-\overset{\overset{\displaystyle O}{\|}}{C}-OH + H_2N-CH_2-CH_3 \longrightarrow CH_3-\overset{\overset{\displaystyle O}{\|}}{C}-NH-CH_2-CH_3 + H_2O$$

Phosphorylation *(Section 12.2)*

$$\text{alcohol} + \text{phosphate} \longrightarrow \text{phosphoester} + H_2O$$

$$CH_3-CH_2-OH + HO-\underset{\underset{\displaystyle O^-}{|}}{\overset{\overset{\displaystyle O}{\|}}{P}}-O^- \longrightarrow CH_3-CH_2-O-\underset{\underset{\displaystyle O^-}{|}}{\overset{\overset{\displaystyle O}{\|}}{P}}-O^- + H_2O$$

Hydrolysis of ethers *(Section 12.4)*

$$\text{ether} + H_2O \longrightarrow \text{2 alcohols}$$

$$CH_3-CH_2-O-CH_2-CH_2-CH_3 + H_2O \longrightarrow CH_3-CH_2-OH + HO-CH_2-CH_2-CH_3$$

Hydrolysis of esters *(Section 12.4)*

$$\text{ester} + H_2O \longrightarrow \text{carboxylic acid} + \text{alcohol}$$

$$CH_3-\overset{\overset{\displaystyle O}{\|}}{C}-O-CH_2-CH_3 + H_2O \longrightarrow CH_3-\overset{\overset{\displaystyle O}{\|}}{C}-OH + HO-CH_2-CH_3$$

Saponification of esters *(Section 12.5)*

$$\text{ester} + \text{strong base} \longrightarrow \text{carboxylate salt} + \text{alcohol}$$

$$CH_3-\overset{\overset{\displaystyle O}{\|}}{C}-O-CH_2-CH_3 + NaOH \longrightarrow CH_3-\overset{\overset{\displaystyle O}{\|}}{C}-O^-\ Na^+ + HO-CH_2-CH_3$$

continued

Summary of Organic Reactions—*continued*

Hydrolysis of amides *(Section 12.4)*

amide + H_2O ⟶ carboxylic acid + amine

(The products are normally formed as their conjugates.)

$$CH_3-\overset{\overset{\displaystyle O}{\|}}{C}-NH-CH_2-CH_3 + H_2O \longrightarrow CH_3-\overset{\overset{\displaystyle O}{\|}}{C}-O^- + \overset{+}{H_3N}-CH_2-CH_3$$

Hydrolysis of phosphoesters *(Section 12.4)*

phosphoester + H_2O ⟶ alcohol + phosphate

$$CH_3-CH_2-O-\underset{\underset{\displaystyle O^-}{|}}{\overset{\overset{\displaystyle O}{\|}}{P}}-O^- + H_2O \longrightarrow CH_3-CH_2-OH + HO-\underset{\underset{\displaystyle O^-}{|}}{\overset{\overset{\displaystyle O}{\|}}{P}}-O^-$$

Answers to Selected Problems

CHAPTER 1

Try It Yourself Exercises

1.1 5 m

1.2 73 mm

1.3 4 mL

1.4 15 mg

1.5 9 (the tenths place)

1.6 approximately 42.6 mL (42.5 and 42.7 mL are also reasonable answers)

1.7 balance 3

1.8 method 1

1.9 1 kilowatt = 1000 watts

1.10 0.245 mL

1.11 1 cm = 10,000 μm

1.12 $\frac{39.37 \text{ inches}}{1 \text{ m}}$ and $\frac{1 \text{ m}}{39.37 \text{ inches}}$

1.13 8.320 pounds

1.14 $11.3 \text{ cm} \times \frac{10 \text{ mm}}{1 \text{ cm}} = 113 \text{ mm}$

1.15 $17{,}000 \text{ L} \times \frac{1 \text{ gallon}}{3.785 \text{ L}} \times \frac{1 \text{ barrel}}{42 \text{ gallons}} = 107 \text{ barrels}$

1.16 $\frac{6 \text{ L}}{1 \text{ minute}}$ and $\frac{1 \text{ minute}}{6 \text{ L}}$

1.17 4.81 gallons

1.18 2 mL

1.19 2.5 mL

1.20 The density is 15.6 g/mL (ignoring significant figures), so the ring is made of 14-carat gold.

1.21 62 g

1.22 12°C

1.23 347°F

Section 1.1 Core Problems

1.1 a) mass b) volume c) distance

1.3 a) L b) cm c) mg d) μL

1.5 a) meter b) deciliter c) kilogram
d) micrometer

1.7 a) height b) mass c) volume

1.9 a) kilograms b) milliliters c) centimeters

1.11 measurements b, d, and f

Section 1.2 Core Problems

1.13 9 (the hundredths place)

1.15 about 6.8 cm (6.7 cm and 6.9 cm are also reasonable answers)

1.17 approximately 16.2 mL

1.19 a) balance 1, because the three masses are closer together
b) balance 2, because the three masses are closer to the true mass of the piece of metal

Section 1.3 Core Problems

1.21 a) three, right b) two, left
c) one, right d) nine, right

1.23 a) 0.272 m b) 272 mm c) 2.72×10^5 μm

1.25 a) 1 L = 10 dL b) 1 km = 1000 m
c) 1 g = 1,000,000 μg d) 1 cm = 10 mm

Section 1.4 Core Problems

1.27 a) $\frac{1.609 \text{ km}}{1 \text{ mile}}$ and $\frac{1 \text{ mile}}{1.609 \text{ km}}$
b) $\frac{2.205 \text{ pounds}}{1 \text{ kg}}$ and $\frac{1 \text{ kg}}{2.205 \text{ pounds}}$
c) $\frac{100 \text{ mL}}{1 \text{ dL}}$ and $\frac{1 \text{ dL}}{100 \text{ mL}}$

1.29 a) The conversion factor is incorrect, because 100 m is not the same as 1 cm. The correct conversion factor is $\frac{1 \text{ m}}{100 \text{ cm}}$.
b) The units do not cancel correctly, because *cm* must be in the denominator of the conversion factor. The correct conversion factor is $\frac{1 \text{ m}}{100 \text{ cm}}$.

1.31 a) 0.616 quarts b) 138 g c) 1.04 cups
d) 59.8 inches e) 3.5×10^{-4} inches

Section 1.5 Core Problems

1.33 First convert the weight from ounces to pounds, and then convert it from pounds to tons.

1.35 a) 771 feet b) 2.70 grains
c) 4.2 fluid ounces d) 5.6×10^4 tons

1.37 1.06 quaterns

Section 1.6 Core Problems

1.39 a) $\frac{22 \text{ cents}}{1 \text{ pound}}$ and $\frac{1 \text{ pound}}{22 \text{ cents}}$

b) $\frac{0.8 \text{ mg}}{1 \text{ teaspoon}}$ and $\frac{1 \text{ teaspoon}}{0.8 \text{ mg}}$

c) $\frac{65 \text{ mL}}{1 \text{ hour}}$ and $\frac{1 \text{ hour}}{65 \text{ mL}}$

d) $\frac{11.3 \text{ g}}{1 \text{ mL}}$ and $\frac{1 \text{ mL}}{11.3 \text{ g}}$

1.41 a) 1667 mL (should be rounded to 1670 mL or 1700 mL)
b) 497 mg

1.43 a) 254 miles (should be rounded to 250 miles)
b) 6.0 gallons

1.45 two tablets

1.47 7.5 mL

1.49 3.70 hours

1.51 0.79 mL

1.53 a) 0.238 g/mL b) 0.238

1.55 a) 658 g (should be rounded to 660 g)
b) 571 mL (should be rounded to 570 mL)

Section 1.7 Core Problems

1.57 a) 135°C b) 180°F c) 355.6 K

1.59 0°C, 32°F

CHAPTER 2

Try It Yourself Exercises

2.1 intensive property

2.2 mixture, because its composition can change

2.3 Si or Ge

2.4 Ba

2.5 Cl

2.6 anion, which contains 9 protons and 10 electrons

2.7 The mass number is 56, and the charge is +2.

2.8 30 protons and 36 neutrons

2.9 19 carbon atoms, 19 hydrogen atoms, 7 nitrogen atoms, and 6 oxygen atoms

2.10 shell 1: 2 electrons shell 2: 8 electrons
shell 3: 7 electrons

2.11 Al_2S_3

2.12 yes, because both elements have four valence electrons

2.13 ·$\dot{\underset{\cdot}{\text{Si}}}$·

2.14 seven valence electrons, which are in shell 5

2.15 Be, Mg, Ca, Sr, Ba, and Ra

2.16 one valence electron, group 1A, Cs

Section 2.1 Core Problems

2.1 a) homogeneous mixture
b) heterogeneous mixture

2.3 Some reasonable examples are alcohol, baking soda, soap, and vinegar.

2.5 a) intensive b) extensive
c) extensive d) intensive

2.7 a) Chalk is a compound, because it is made up of more than one substance and has a fixed composition
b) You cannot tell, because the problem does not give any information about the composition or behavior of quicklime.

2.9 mixture, because they can be combined in a variety of proportions

2.11 The combination is probably a compound, because its physiological properties differ from those of the original substances.

Section 2.2 Core Problems

2.13 a) carbon b) nitrogen c) chlorine
d) magnesium e) cobalt f) selenium

2.15 a) Fe b) Na c) Ag d) Pb

2.17 a) O, S, or Se
b) Sn or Pb
c) Ge or As
d) any metal; examples are Na, Mg, Al, Ca, Fe, Cu, and Ag
e) Cl f) Be, Mg, Ca, Sr, Ba, or Ra

2.19 metal

Section 2.3 Core Problems

2.21 statement d

2.23 statement c

2.25 five types of atoms, corresponding to the five elements

Section 2.4 Core Problems

2.27 a) electrons b) protons, neutrons
c) protons d) protons, electrons

2.29 a) S b) 33 c) 16 d) −2 e) 33 amu

2.31 a) 47 b) 60 c) 47 d) 46

2.33 This is the mass number of the oxygen atom.

Section 2.5 Core Problems

2.35 choice a

2.37 choice c

2.39 choice d

Section 2.6 Core Problems

2.41 $C_{12}H_{22}O_{11}$

2.43 a) one sodium atom, five carbon atoms, eight hydrogen atoms, one nitrogen atom, and four oxygen atoms
b) 15 carbon atoms

Section 2.7 Core Problems

2.45 choice c

2.47 a) shell 1: 2 electrons shell 2: 5 electrons
b) shell 1: 2 electrons shell 2: 8 electrons shell 3: 2 electrons

2.49 Ar

Section 2.8 Core Problems

2.51 a) Mg_3N_2 b) Be_3P_2

2.53 a) six b) :Ṡe:

2.55 ·Ċ·

2.57 carbon

Section 2.9 Core Problems

2.59 six valence electrons, shell 4

2.61 a) one valence electron b) Group 1A
c) Period 5

2.63 a) K· b) ·Ṗb· c) :B̈r:

2.65 a) Bi
b) Cs, Ba, Tl, Pb, Bi, Po, At, or Rn
c) Sc, Ti, V, Cr, Mn, Fe, Co, Ni, Cu, or Zn
d) S, Se, Te, or Po

CHAPTER 3

Try It Yourself Exercises

3.1 :C̈l:G̈: (:Cl:I: with lone pairs)

3.2 H:C̈l:

3.3 :F̈:S̈e:F̈:

3.4 :F̈: / :F̈:P̈:F̈: (P bonded to three F)

3.5 The central atom is nitrogen, and the Lewis structure is :C̈l: / H:N̈:H

3.6 S̈: / :C̈l:C:C̈l: (C double-bonded to S)

3.7 H—C≡C—C(=Ö:)—H

3.8 chlorine atom

3.9 The carbon atom is positively charged, and the nitrogen atom is negatively charged.

3.10 a) phosphorus pentafluoride
b) disulfur dichloride

3.11 SF_6

3.12 The selenium atom can gain two electrons. These electrons go into shell 4, giving the atom eight valence electrons. The atom becomes an ion with a −2 charge.

3.13 First, the two valence electrons on the calcium atom move to the sulfur atom, giving each atom an octet and turning the atoms into ions. Then the two ions attract each other to form a compound.

Ca: ·S̈: ⟶ Ca^{2+} :S̈:$^{2-}$ ⟶ Ca^{2+}:S̈:$^{2-}$

3.14 The charge on the ion is −2, and the symbol for the ion is Se^{2-}.

3.15 The formula is Li_3N.

3 Li· + ·N̈· ⟶ 3 Li^+ + :N̈:$^{3-}$ ⟶ Li^+:N̈:$^{3-}$ with three Li^+

3.16 Na_2S

3.17 Mg_3N_2

3.18 Cu_2S and CuS

3.19 sodium oxide

3.20 K_2O and Al_2S_3

3.21 chromium(II) chloride or chromous chloride

3.22 CoF_3

3.23 $Fe(OH)_3$

3.24 $CuSO_4$

3.25 magnesium phosphate

3.26 a) We expect $HgCl_2$ to be ionic, because it contains a metal and a nonmetal. *($HgCl_2$ is actually molecular, but you could not predict this from the formula.)*
b) molecular

3.27 Fe_2O_3 is called iron(III) oxide or ferric oxide, and N_2O_3 is called dinitrogen trioxide.

Section 3.1 Core Problems

3.1 Kr

3.3 three covalent bonds

3.5 oxygen (or any other element in Group 6A)

3.7 a) H:B̈r: b) :C̈l: / :C̈l:Si:C̈l: / :C̈l: c) H / H:P̈:H d) H:S̈:H

3.9 The Si atom is at the center, and the Lewis structure is :B̈r: / H:Si:H / :G̈: (:I:)

Section 3.2 Core Problems

3.11 fluorine, because fluorine atoms have only one open space in their valence shell and can share only one pair of electrons with another atom

3.13 choice c, because nitrogen forms more bonds than oxygen or bromine, so we expect the nitrogen atom to be in the center of the molecule

3.15 a) :C̈l:N̈::Ö: or :C̈l—N̈=Ö:

b) :F̈:C:F̈: (with :Ö: above C) or :F̈—C—F̈: (with :Ö: double-bonded above C)

c) H:C:::C:H or H—C≡C—H

3.17 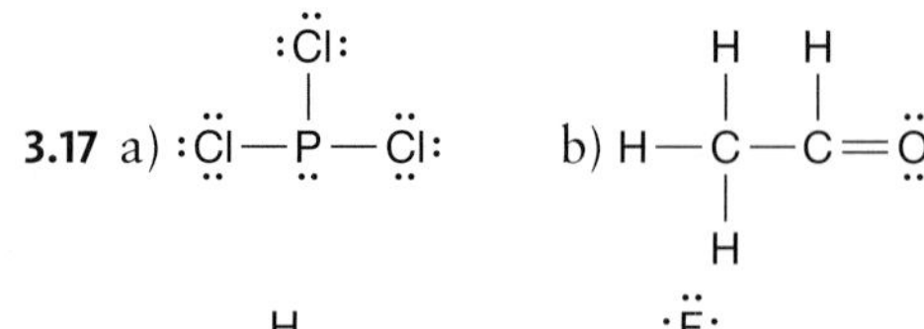

3.19 a) H—N̈—H (with H above N) b) :F̈—Si—F̈: (with :F̈: above and below Si) c) H—C—H (with :O: double-bonded above C)

Section 3.3 Core Problems

3.21 nitrogen

3.23 a) nitrogen b) hydrogen
c) neither atom has a positive charge

3.25 a) carbon b) nitrogen
c) neither atom has a positive charge

Section 3.4 Core Problems

3.27 a) chlorine trifluoride b) dinitrogen tetrafluoride
c) carbon monoxide

3.29 a) CF_4 b) SO_2

3.31 a) water b) nitric oxide

Section 3.5 Core Problems

3.33 The electron arrangement of aluminum is as follows:

shell 1: 2 electrons shell 2: 8 electrons
shell 3: 3 electrons

If the atom loses three electrons, its arrangement becomes the following:

shell 1: 2 electrons shell 2: 8 electrons

The outermost occupied shell (shell 2) contains 8 electrons, so the atom satisfies the octet rule.

3.35 a) An electrically neutral chlorine atom has seven valence electrons. If the atom gains one electron to form a −1 ion, it will have eight valence electrons, satisfying the octet rule.

·C̈l: ⟶ :C̈l:$^-$

b) An electrically neutral magnesium atom has two valence electrons. If the atom loses two electrons to form a +2 ion, the original valence shell will be empty, leaving the ion with eight electrons in the next shell.

Mg: ⟶ Mg^{2+}

3.37 a) +2 b) −1 c) −2 d) +1

3.39 −1

3.41 Be, Mg, Ca, Sr, Ba, or Ra

3.43 a) potassium, one electron
b) sulfur, two electrons
c) The potassium atoms have a +1 charge, and the sulfur atom has a −2 charge.
d) K_2S

Section 3.6 Core Problems

3.45 Sodium ions have a +1 charge and oxide ions have a −2 charge. These charges do not add up to zero, so the compound cannot contain a 1:1 ratio of sodium and oxide ions.

3.47 a) FeO b) Na_2Se c) SrF_2
d) CrI_3 e) Mg_3N_2

3.49 a) KBr b) $ZnCl_2$
c) Al_2S_3 d) $CoCl_2$ and $CoCl_3$

Section 3.7 Core Problems

3.51 a) potassium oxide
b) magnesium sulfide
c) aluminum chloride
d) copper(II) chloride or cupric chloride
e) chromium(III) oxide or chromic oxide
f) manganese(II) sulfide or manganous sulfide

3.53 a) NaF b) CaI_2 c) CrS
d) $FeCl_3$ e) ZnO

3.55 Calcium can only have a +2 charge in an ionic compound, but copper can be either +1 or +2. The name must tell which ion is present, so the correct name is copper(II) chloride (or cuprous chloride).

Section 3.8 Core Problems

3.57 a) NO_3^- b) ammonium
c) HCO_3^- d) phosphate

3.59 a) $Zn(OH)_2$ b) Ag_2SO_4
c) K_3PO_4 d) NH_4Br

3.61 a) $CaCO_3$ b) $Mg_3(PO_4)_2$
c) $Cr(OH)_3$ d) $Co(NO_3)_2$

3.63 a) potassium hydrogen carbonate or potassium bicarbonate
b) copper(II) phosphate or cupric phosphate
c) ammonium sulfate

Section 3.9 Core Problems

3.65 In IBr, the two atoms share a pair of electrons. In NaBr, the two atoms are ions and do not share electrons.

:Ï—B̈r: Na^+ :B̈r:$^-$

3.67 a) ionic b) molecular c) ionic d) molecular e) ionic f) molecular

3.69 a) sulfur dichloride b) magnesium chloride

CHAPTER 4

Try It Yourself Exercises

4.1 the cup of hot tea

4.2 997 cal

4.3 83,500 J, 20,000 cal, 20.0 kcal

4.4 The water molecule vibrates about a fixed position, but it does not move around.

4.5 0.018 millibars

4.6 5 g of oxygen in a 10 L container

4.7 less than 32 psi

4.8 liquid

4.9 3240 cal

4.10 approximately 360°C

4.11 The boiling point of HF is 20°C, and the boiling point of LiF is 1681°C. HF is a molecular compound while LiF is ionic, so HF has a much lower melting point than LiF.

4.12 CF_4 is a gas, CCl_4 is a liquid, and CBr_4 is a solid. The compound with the smallest halogen atoms has the weakest attractive forces and the lowest boiling and melting points, while the compound with the largest halogen atoms has the highest boiling and melting points.

4.13 The atoms in NH_3 can participate in hydrogen bonds, while the atoms in PH_3 cannot. Therefore, NH_3 molecules are attracted to each other more strongly than PH_3 molecules are to each other, giving NH_3 a higher boiling point.

4.14 The boiling point of compound 3 is closer to that of compound 1. Both molecules contain hydrogen atoms that can participate in hydrogen bonds.

4.15

```
      H
      |    ..              ..
  H — C — N — H - - - - - - - - :O — H
      |   |                     |
      H   H                     H
```

4.16 The oxygen atom in tetrahydrofuran can participate in hydrogen bonds, so it is attracted to the hydrogen atoms in water.

4.17 Ethylmethylamine dissolves well in water, because the nitrogen atom and the hydrogen that is attached to it can participate in hydrogen bonds. None of the atoms in ethyl methyl phosphine can participate in hydrogen bonds.

4.18 Calcium nitrate dissociates into Ca^{2+} and NO_3^- ions, which are solvated by water molecules.

4.19 Na_2CO_3 or K_2CO_3

4.20 Sodium bicarbonate is soluble in water. Since 0.09 kg is the same as 90 g, the solubility is 90 g/L.

4.21 You should cool the water: 20°C is above the boiling point of H_2S, so H_2S is a gas at this temperature. The solubilities of gases increase as the temperature goes down.

4.22 Carbon disulfide becomes more soluble as the pressure increases, because it is a gas at 75°C.

4.23

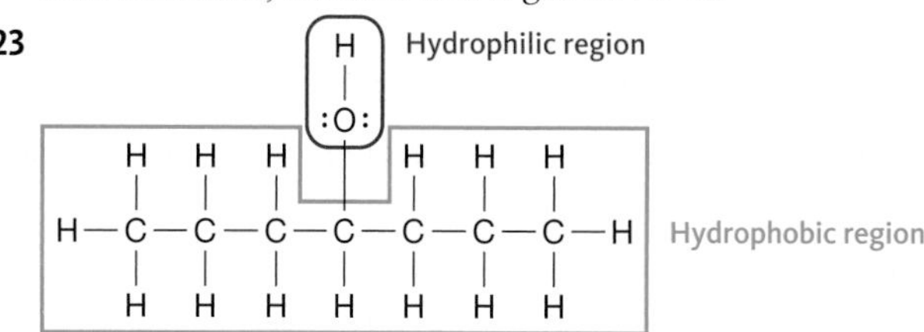

4.24 1,6-diaminohexane, because it contains two hydrophilic regions (one at each side of the molecule), while 1-aminoheptane has only one

Section 4.1 Core Problems

4.1 potential energy increases, kinetic energy decreases (because the ball slows down as it rises)

4.3 a) potential b) kinetic c) kinetic

4.5 a) the car moving 40 mph
b) the car
c) the atoms in 80°C water
d) The two batteries have the same amount of kinetic energy.

4.7 a) the airplane at 30,000 feet
b) the new battery
c) The two pieces of bread have the same amount of potential energy.
d) the large stone

4.9 a) slow down
b) decreases

4.11 a) 560 cal
b) 2300 J, 0.56 kcal (to two significant figures)

Section 4.2 Core Problems

4.13 a) gas b) liquid c) solid

4.15 choices a and c

4.17 The helium atom moves around randomly within the balloon, bouncing off other atoms and the walls of the balloon.

4.19 −100°C

4.21 In liquid nitrogen, the nitrogen molecules are in contact with one another, leaving little empty space between them. In gaseous nitrogen, the molecules are far apart, allowing for a great deal of empty space.

Section 4.3 Core Problems

4.23 a) The pressure decreases.
b) The pressure decreases.
c) The pressure increases.

4.25 Heating the can increases the pressure of the gas inside the can. If the pressure increases enough, the can will burst.

4.27 The atmospheric pressure is higher at the bottom of the mountain than it is at the top. The higher pressure crushes the water bottle.

4.29 a) 4100 torr b) 5.5 bar

4.31 5.64 atm

Section 4.4 Core Problems

4.33 a) evaporation b) freezing c) condensation

4.35 a) solid b) liquid

4.37 801°C

4.39 The boiling point is lower than 25°C because for a substance to be a gas, its temperature must be higher than the boiling point.

4.41 "At 20°C, water is normally a liquid, but it can also be a gas."

4.43 3975 cal (ignoring significant figures)

4.45 Isopropyl alcohol freezes at −89°C. The temperature cannot drop further until all of the isopropyl alcohol has turned to a solid.

4.47 a) approximately 5°C
b) gas
c) The benzene will initially be a liquid, and it will freeze to a solid as it cools.

Section 4.5 Core Problems

4.49 NF_3 is a molecular compound, and the attractive forces between individual NF_3 molecules are weak, so you do not need to add much thermal energy to overcome the attraction and turn the compound into a gas. CrF_3 is an ionic compound, and the attractive forces between the Cr^{3+} and the F^- ions are strong, so CrF_3 must be heated to a very high temperature to overcome the attraction.

4.51 a) methyl iodide, because iodine is a larger atom than chlorine or bromine
b) methyl iodide, because the compound with the strongest attractive forces between molecules has the highest boiling point
c) methyl chloride, because it has the weakest dispersion forces and therefore the lowest boiling point

4.53 a) C–Cl in isopropyl chloride, C=O in acetone
b) acetone
c) acetone

4.55

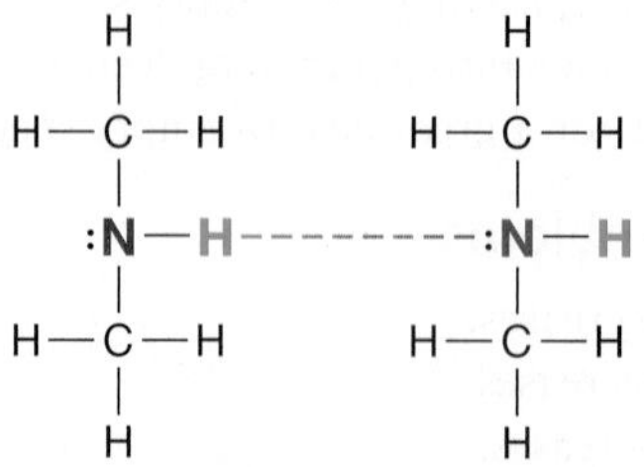

```
    H                  H
    |                  |
 H—C—H             H—C—H
    |                  |
  :N—H--------:N—H
    |                  |
 H—C—H             H—C—H
    |                  |
    H                  H
```

4.57 Compound 1 boils at 95°C, and compound 2 boils at 49°C. Compound 1 contains a hydrogen atom that can participate in hydrogen bonding, while compound 2 does not.

4.59 Butane cannot form hydrogen bonds, so the attraction between butane molecules is weak. 1-Propanol contains two atoms that can participate in hydrogen bonds, giving it a higher boiling point. Ethylene glycol contains four atoms that can participate in hydrogen bonds, giving it the highest boiling point.

4.61 The hydrogen atoms that can participate in hydrogen bonds are circled.

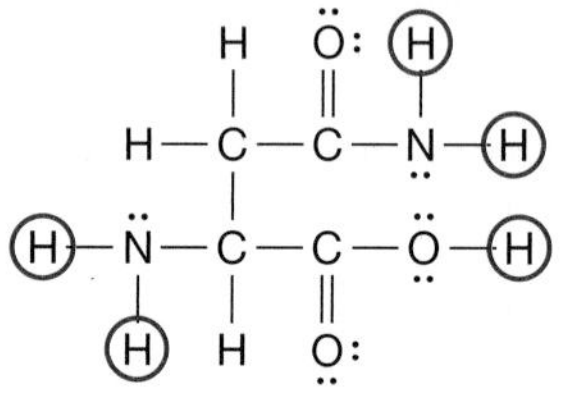

```
          H   Ö: (H)
          |   ||   |
       H—C—C—N—(H)
          |
 (H)—N—C—C—Ö—(H)
      |   |   ||
     (H)  H   O:
```

4.63 a) covalent bonds
b) dispersion forces and hydrogen bonds
c) dispersion forces and hydrogen bonds

Section 4.6 Core Problems

4.65 The mixture is a solution; NaOH is the solute and water is the solvent.

4.67 Pass a bright light through the mixture. If the beam is clearly visible, the mixture is a colloid.

4.69 You produce a suspension, because flour does not dissolve in water; it remains visible and settles to the bottom once you stop stirring.

4.71 compounds b and c

4.73 In the following drawing, water is the donor and N_2H_4 is the acceptor:

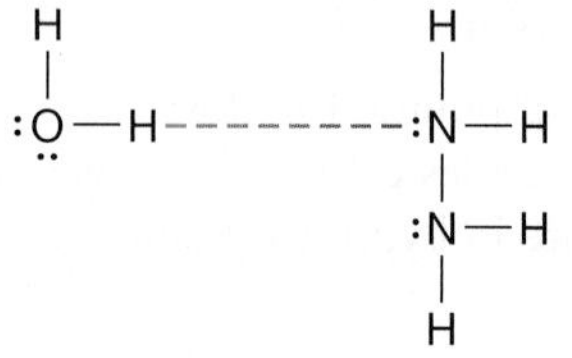

```
 H                 H
 |                 |
:O—H--------:N—H
                   |
                  :N—H
                   |
                   H
```

In the following drawing, water is the acceptor and N_2H_4 is the donor:

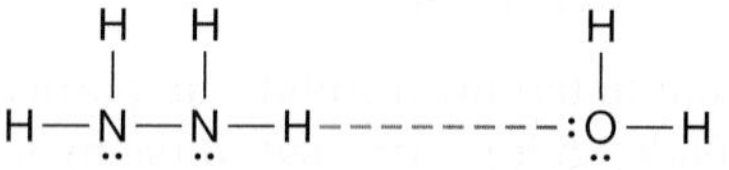

```
    H   H              H
    |   |              |
 H—N—N—H--------:O—H
```

4.75 Compound 3 can function as both a donor and an acceptor. Compounds 1 and 2 can function only as acceptors.

Section 4.7 Core Problems

4.77 $CaCl_2$ and $KC_2H_3O_2$

4.79 Magnesium chloride dissociates into Mg^{2+} and Cl^- ions. Each ion is solvated by water molecules. The oxygen atoms of the water molecules face the magnesium ions, and the hydrogen atoms of the water molecules face the chloride ions.

4.81 a) K^+ and S^{2-} b) Fe^{2+} and SO_4^{2-}
c) NH_4^+ and CO_3^{2-}

4.83

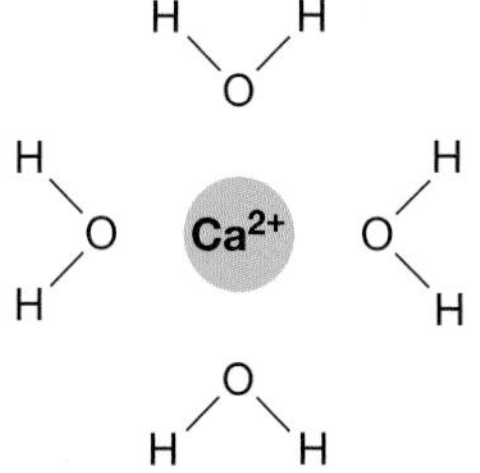

4.85 Na_2MoO_4 or K_2MoO_4

Section 4.8 Core Problems

4.87 no, it means that the solubility of vitamin A is very low, but a small amount can be dissolved in water

4.89 yes, you will produce an unsaturated solution

4.91 a) around 53°C
b) around 0.046 g/L

4.93 a) increase
b) remain the same

Section 4.9 Core Problems

4.95

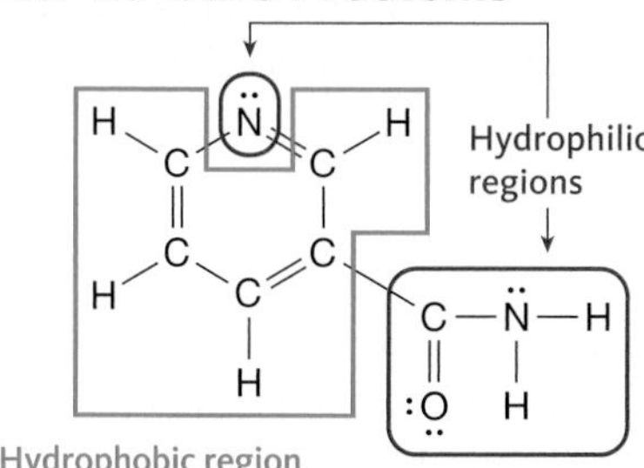

4.97 a) the second molecule
b) the second molecule
c) the second molecule

CHAPTER 5

Try It Yourself Exercises

5.1 4.2% (w/v), weight per volume

5.2 30 g

5.3 0.05 mg/dL, 0.5 ppm

5.4 2600 μg, or 2.6 mg (two significant figures; the calculator answer is 2552 μg)

5.5 14.01 g

5.6 132.144 g/mol

5.7 3.91 g

5.8 0.411 mol

5.9 1.2 M

5.10 4.2 g

5.11 Osmosis occurs; water flows from solution C into solution D.

5.12 0.28 M

5.13 a) Glucose moves from solution A to solution B, and sucrose moves from solution B to solution A.
b) Osmosis does not occur.

5.14 0.038 mol

5.15 2.99 g

5.16 806 mEq/L

5.17 2.5 g

5.18 0.83% (v/v)

5.19 300 mL

5.20 You need 0.03 L (30 mL) of the original solution, and you must add 0.97 L (970 mL) of water.

Section 5.1 Core Problems

5.1 a) $\frac{0.15 \text{ mL acetic acid}}{100 \text{ mL solution}}$

b) $\frac{50\ \mu\text{g Br}^-}{1 \text{ mL solution}}$

c) $\frac{3 \text{ mg fructose}}{1 \text{ dL solution}}$

d) $\frac{6.5 \text{ g MgSO}_4}{100 \text{ mL solution}}$

e) $\frac{20 \text{ ng Pb}^{2+}}{1 \text{ mL solution}}$

5.3 a) 9.24% (w/v) b) 72.8% (v/v) c) 8.46% (w/v)

5.5 a) 3.7 g of $CaCl_2$ b) 93.7 mL of ethylene glycol
c) 3.12 g of vitamin C

5.7 a) 45.8 mg/dL b) 45,800 μg/dL
c) 458 ppm d) 458,000 ppb

5.9 a) 62 μg of fluoride ions b) 23 mg of glucose
c) 770 ng of lead ions

Section 5.2 Core Problems

5.11 a) 32.06 amu b) 32.06 g c) 44.02 amu
d) 44.02 g e) 149.096 amu f) 149.096 g

5.13 a) 1400 g (to two significant figures; the calculator answer is 1396.25 g)
b) 6.89 g

5.15 a) 0.250 mol b) 0.09903 mol c) 7.20 mol

Section 5.3 Core Problems

5.17 a) 1.40 M b) 0.730 M c) 0.081 M

5.19 a) 0.207 M b) 0.0364 M c) 0.0939 M

5.21 a) 10.0 g b) 4.78 g
c) 140 g (to two significant figures)

Section 5.4 Core Problems

5.23 Water flows from solution A into solution B.

5.25 a) 0.250 M b) 0.66 M c) 0.54 M

5.27 a) hypotonic b) isotonic c) hypertonic

5.29 a) The cell will expand and burst.
b) The cell will not be affected.
c) The cell will crenate (shrivel up).

5.31 8.4 g

5.33 a) 0.33 M b) The solution is hypertonic.

5.35 a) Water flows from solution B into solution A.
b) Na^+ moves from solution A into solution B.
c) Glucose moves from solution B into solution A.

Section 5.5 Core Problems

5.37 0.4 Eq

5.39 a) 0.075 mol b) 1.8 g

5.41 a) 0.312 Eq, 312 mEq b) 0.470 Eq, 470 mEq

5.43 a) 4.04 g, 4040 mg (to three significant figures)
b) 1.0 g, 1000 mg (to two significant figures; the calculator answer is 1.02017 g)

5.45 Both are 500 mEq/L.

5.47 a) 0.0177 Eq/L b) 17.7 mEq/L

5.49 0.15 g

Section 5.6 Core Problems

5.51 a) 0.067 M b) 0.558% (w/v)

5.53 a) 0.19% (w/v) b) 0.086 M

5.55 The final volume must be 291 mL, so you must add 191 mL of water.

5.57 Use 18 mL of the original solution, and add 82 mL of water.

CHAPTER 6

Try It Yourself Exercises

6.1 a) chemical reaction b) physical change

6.2 $3\ Na + P \rightarrow Na_3P$

6.3 This expression represents six atoms of copper and three atoms of oxygen.

6.4 no, because there are four oxygen atoms on the left side of the arrow and only three on the right side

6.5 $2\ Al + 6\ HCl \rightarrow 2\ AlCl_3 + 3\ H_2$

6.6 $Mg(s) + 2\ HCl(aq) \rightarrow MgCl_2(aq) + H_2(g)$

6.7 53.96 amu of Al reacts with 212.7 amu of Cl_2
53.96 g of Al reacts with 212.7 g of Cl_2

6.8 1.12 g

6.9 When the reaction produces 109.71 g of $Ni(OH)_3$, it absorbs 252 kcal of heat. ΔH is a positive number (ΔH = 252 kcal).

6.10 4.44 g

6.11 200 Cal, or 200 kcal (the calculator answer is 204 Cal)

6.12 $C_4H_{10}O + 6\ O_2 \rightarrow 4\ CO_2 + 5\ H_2O$

6.13 the second reaction

6.14 $Fe^{2+}(aq) + 2\ OH^-(aq) \rightarrow Fe(OH)_2(s)$

6.15 the first reaction

6.16

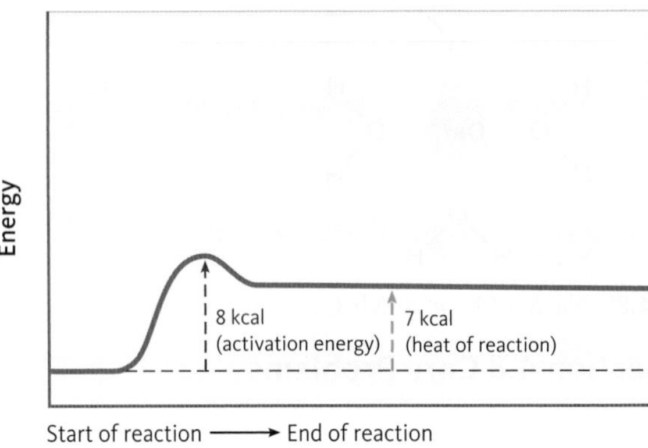

6.17 forward

6.18 forward

Section 6.1 Core Problems

6.1 a) physical change b) chemical reaction
c) chemical reaction d) physical change

6.3 a) chemical property b) physical property
c) chemical property d) physical property

6.5 5.00 g

6.7 chemical change

Section 6.2 Core Problems

6.9 This is not a reasonable answer because the student has changed the chemical formula of the product.

6.11 $PCl_3(s) + 3\ H_2O(l) \rightarrow H_3PO_3(aq) + 3\ HCl(aq)$

6.13 a) not balanced: there are two Cl atoms on the left and four on the right
b) balanced
c) not balanced: there are 17 O atoms on the left and 16 on the right

6.15 a) $S + 2\ Cl_2 \rightarrow SCl_4$
b) $2\ Ag + S \rightarrow Ag_2S$
c) $2\ K + Cl_2 \rightarrow 2\ KCl$

6.17 a) $CaO + 2\ HCl \rightarrow CaCl_2 + H_2O$
b) $4\ Fe + 3\ O_2 \rightarrow 2\ Fe_2O_3$
c) $CH_4 + 2\ O_2 \rightarrow CO_2 + 2\ H_2O$

6.19 a) $2\ C_4H_{10} + 13\ O_2 \rightarrow 8\ CO_2 + 10\ H_2O$
b) $2\ AlCl_3 + 3\ H_2O \rightarrow Al_2O_3 + 6\ HCl$
c) $2\ AgNO_3 + MgI_2 \rightarrow 2\ AgI + Mg(NO_3)_2$

6.21 a) $2\ Al(OH)_3 + 3\ H_2SO_4 \rightarrow Al_2(SO_4)_3 + 6\ H_2O$
b) $4\ C_5H_{11}NO_2 + 27\ O_2 \rightarrow 20\ CO_2 + 22\ H_2O + 2\ N_2$

Section 6.3 Core Problems

6.23 16.042 g of CH_4 reacts to produce 36.032 g of H_2O

6.25 a) 3.50 g b) 1.73 g c) 2.05 g

Section 6.4 Core Problems

6.27 a) cooler
b) endothermic
c) positive
d) When 106.984 g of NH_4Cl reacts with $Ba(OH)_2$, the reaction absorbs 5.5 kcal of heat.

6.29 a) hotter
b) product
c) $2\ Mg(s) + O_2(g) \rightarrow 2\ MgO(s) + 287$ kcal

6.31 43.2 kcal

6.33 a) 0.0905 kcal (90.5 cal)
b) 55.3 g

6.35 230 Cal (the calculator answer is 226 Cal)

6.37 5 g

Section 6.5 Core Problems

6.39 a) $C_7H_8 + 9\ O_2 \rightarrow 7\ CO_2 + 4\ H_2O$
b) $2\ C_4H_{10} + 13\ O_2 \rightarrow 8\ CO_2 + 10\ H_2O$
c) $C_4H_{10}O + 6\ O_2 \rightarrow 4\ CO_2 + 5\ H_2O$

6.41 a) combustion b) neither
c) neither d) precipitation

6.43 a) $Ag^+(aq) + Br^-(aq) \rightarrow AgBr(s)$
b) $3\ Mg^{2+}(aq) + 2\ PO_4^{3-}(aq) \rightarrow Mg_3(PO_4)_2(s)$
c) $Pb^{2+}(aq) + 2\ I^-(aq) \rightarrow PbI_2(s)$

Section 6.6 Core Problems

6.45 a) increase b) decrease
c) increase d) increase

6.47 All reactions slow down at lower temperatures, including reactions that are caused by bacterial action, because fewer molecules have the needed activation energy.

6.49 the first reaction

6.51

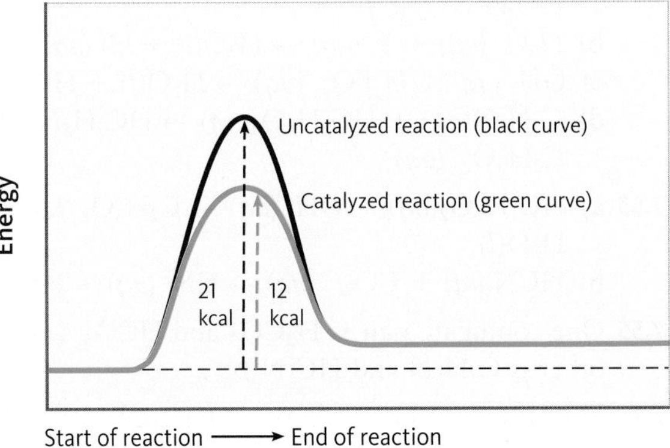

6.53 The activation energy is around 40 kcal, and the heat of reaction is around −20 kcal. This is an exothermic reaction.

Section 6.7 Core Problems

6.55 a stable mixture of the reactants and the products of a chemical reaction

6.57 statement c

6.59 a) This reaction is reversible, so the product is constantly breaking down into the reactants.
b) Some of the C_2H_6O will break down into C_2H_4 and H_2O, forming an equilibrium mixture.

6.61 a) forward
b) backward
c) forward

6.63 choices a and d

CHAPTER 7

Try It Yourself Exercises

7.1 2.9×10^{-12} M

7.2 2

7.3 Product 3 is acidic and products 1 and 2 are basic. The order of the solutions is as follows:

Solution 3 (*most acidic*) → Solution 2 → Solution 1 (*most basic*)

7.4 11.92

7.5 $[H_3O^+] = 1.3 \times 10^{-6}$ M, $[OH^-] = 7.8 \times 10^{-9}$ M

7.6 $HC_3H_5O_3(aq) + H_2O(l) \rightleftharpoons H_3O^+(aq) + C_3H_5O_3^-(aq)$

7.7 2×10^{-5} M sorbic acid

7.8 0.25 M hydrofluoric acid

7.9 ascorbic acid

7.10 Only two of the hydrogen atoms are attached to oxygen and have a second oxygen atom nearby, so it is reasonable that malonic acid can only lose two hydrogen atoms. The two atoms that can be removed are circled here:

```
       :Ö   H   Ö:
        ‖   |   ‖
(H)—Ö—C—C—C—Ö—(H)
            |
            H
```

7.11 Na_3PO_4 or K_3PO_4

7.12 a) HSO_4^- b) $HC_3H_7NO_2^+$

7.13 $C_3H_5O_3^-(aq) + H_2O(l) \rightleftharpoons HC_3H_5O_3(aq) + OH^-(aq)$

7.14 CN^-

7.15 0.25 M NH_3

7.16 The chemical equation is $NH_4^+(aq) + F^-(aq) \rightarrow NH_3(aq) + HF(aq)$. NH_4^+ and NH_3 are one conjugate pair, and HF and F^- are the other conjugate pair.

7.17 First reaction: $H_2SO_3(aq) + OH^-(aq) \rightarrow HSO_3^-(aq) + H_2O(l)$

Second reaction: $HSO_3^-(aq) + OH^-(aq) \rightarrow SO_3^{2-}(aq) + H_2O(l)$

7.18 a) $HPO_4^{2-}(aq) + HF(aq) \rightarrow H_2PO_4^-(aq) + F^-(aq)$
b) $HPO_4^{2-}(aq) + NH_3(aq) \rightarrow PO_4^{3-}(aq) + NH_4^+(aq)$

7.19 $HCHO_2$

7.20 3.76

7.21 Neutralizing H_3O^+: $NH_3(aq) + H_3O^+(aq) \rightarrow NH_4^+(aq) + H_2O(l)$

Neutralizing OH^-: $NH_4^+(aq) + OH^-(aq) \rightarrow NH_3(aq) + H_2O(l)$

7.22 more acidic

Section 7.1 Core Problems

7.1 $2\ H_2O(l) \rightleftharpoons H_3O^+(aq) + OH^-(aq)$

7.3 Hydrogen ions cannot exist on their own; they must always be bonded to some other molecule or ion. In the self-ionization of water, a hydrogen ion moves from one water molecule to a second water molecule.

7.5 a) 10^{-3} M b) 10^{-9} M c) 10^{-11} M

7.7 a) 0.024 M (or 2.4×10^{-2} M) b) 1.3×10^{-12} M

7.9 The HCl molecules break apart into H^+ and Cl^- ions, and each H^+ ion bonds to a water molecule to form H_3O^+.

Section 7.2 Core Problems

7.11 a) acidic b) basic c) neutral

7.13 0.1 M $NaHSO_4$ is the most acidic solution, and 0.1 M NH_4Cl is the least acidic solution.

7.15 a) 5 b) 11 c) 4 d) 9

7.17 a) 3.2×10^{-6} M b) 8.51

7.19 $[H_3O^+] = 7.4 \times 10^{-6}$ M, $[OH^-] = 1.3 \times 10^{-9}$ M

Section 7.3 Core Problems

7.21 a) $HNO_3(aq) + H_2O(l) \rightarrow H_3O^+(aq) + NO_3^-(aq)$
b) $HC_3H_5O_3(aq) + H_2O(l) \rightleftharpoons H_3O^+(aq) + C_3H_5O_3^-(aq)$
c) $H_2C_4H_4O_4(aq) + H_2O(l) \rightleftharpoons H_3O^+(aq) + HC_4H_4O_4^-(aq)$

7.23 0.01 M formic acid

7.25 weak acid, because only a small fraction of the 0.1 mol of formic acid ionizes in water

7.27 cyanoacetic acid, because it produces a more acidic solution

7.29 a) nitric acid b) nitrous acid c) nitrous acid

7.31 Only one of the two hydrogen atoms in formic acid can be removed (in the form of H^+), whereas both hydrogen atoms in carbonic acid can be removed.

7.33 a) Methylphosphoric acid can lose two hydrogen ions (the two hydrogen atoms that are attached to oxygen atoms).
b) $H_2CH_3PO_3$ (or any similar formula that lists two hydrogen atoms first, such as $H_2CH_3O_3P$)

7.35 the concentration of HCO_3^- ions

Section 7.4 Core Problems

7.37

```
    H  H            H                H  H
    |  |            |                |  |+             - ..
H — C — N — H + :O — H  ——>   H — C — N — H  +  :O — H
    |   ..          ..               |  |              ..
    H                                H  H
```

7.39 a) NH_3 b) NO_3^- c) $HC_{10}H_{14}N_2^+$
d) HSO_3^- e) $H_3C_6H_5O_7$ f) $HC_6H_5O_7^{2-}$

7.41 a) $OCH_3^-(aq) + H_2O(l) \rightarrow HOCH_3(aq) + OH^-(aq)$
b) $ClO^-(aq) + H_2O(l) \rightleftharpoons HClO(aq) + OH^-(aq)$
c) $C_3H_4N_2(aq) + H_2O(l) \rightleftharpoons HC_3H_4N_2^+(aq) + OH^-(aq)$
d) $SO_3^{2-}(aq) + H_2O(l) \rightleftharpoons HSO_3^-(aq) + OH^-(aq)$

7.43 NaF dissociates into Na^+ and F^- ions. F^- is a base and is attracted to H^+, so it can remove H^+ from water, forming HF and OH^-. The OH^- ions make the solution basic.

7.45 CN^- is the stronger base, since the solution that contains CN^- is more basic (has a higher pH) than the solution that contains F^-.

7.47 a) piperidine b) piperidine c) piperazine

Section 7.5 Core Problems

7.49

```
                        H                                    H
     ..     ..          |            - ..    ..              +|
H — O — N = O  +  H — N — H  ——>   :O — N = O  +  H — N — H
     ..     ..          ..              ..    ..              |
                                                              H
```

7.51 a) $HNO_2(aq) + C_2H_7NO(aq) \rightarrow NO_2^-(aq) + HC_2H_7NO^+(aq)$
b) $H_3O^+(aq) + F^-(aq) \rightarrow H_2O(l) + HF(aq)$
c) $OH^-(aq) + H_2PO_4^-(aq) \rightarrow H_2O(l) + HPO_4^{2-}(aq)$
d) $C_5H_5N(aq) + HC_2H_3O_2(aq) \rightarrow HC_5H_5N^+(aq) + C_2H_3O_2^-(aq)$

7.53 a) $HC_2H_3O_2(aq) + OH^-(aq) \rightarrow C_2H_3O_2^-(aq) + H_2O(l)$
b) $HCN(aq) + CO_3^{2-}(aq) \rightarrow CN^-(aq) + HCO_3^-(aq)$

7.55 One conjugate pair is H_2CO_3 and HCO_3^-, and the other is C_5H_5N and $HC_5N_5N^+$.

7.57 First reaction: $H_2CO_3(aq) + OH^-(aq) \rightarrow HCO_3^-(aq) + H_2O(l)$

Second reaction: $HCO_3^-(aq) + OH^-(aq) \rightarrow CO_3^{2-}(aq) + H_2O(l)$

Section 7.6 Core Problems

7.59 a) $HSO_3^-(aq) + OH^-(aq) \rightarrow SO_3^{2-}(aq) + H_2O(l)$, with HSO_3^- functioning as an acid
b) $HSO_3^-(aq) + H_3O^+(aq) \rightarrow H_2SO_3(aq) + H_2O(l)$, with HSO_3^- functioning as a base

7.61 a) $HC_3H_6NO_2(aq) + OH^-(aq) \rightarrow C_3H_6NO_2^-(aq) + H_2O(l)$
b) $HC_3H_6NO_2(aq) + H_3O^+(aq) \rightarrow H_2C_3H_6NO_2^+(aq) + H_2O(l)$

7.63 a) the hydrogen attached to oxygen (on the right side of the molecule)
b) H^+ bonds to the nitrogen atom (converting the nonbonding electron pair into a bonding pair).

Section 7.7 Core Problems

7.65

	Acidic component	Basic component
Buffer 1	$HCHO_2$	CHO_2^-
Buffer 2	$HC_3H_5O_3$	$C_3H_5O_3^-$
Buffer 3	$HC_2O_4^-$	$C_2O_4^{2-}$
Buffer 4	$H_2C_2O_4$	$HC_2O_4^-$
Buffer 5	H_2SO_3	HSO_3^-

7.67 $Na_2C_4H_4O_4$ or $K_2C_4H_4O_4$

7.69 mixtures a and c

7.71 a) 3.8
b) between 3.8 and 4.8
c) $C_8H_7O_3^-$ ion: $C_8H_7O_3^-(aq) + H_3O^+(aq) \rightarrow HC_8H_7O_3(aq) + H_2O(l)$
d) $HC_8H_7O_3$: $HC_8H_7O_3(aq) + OH^-(aq) \rightarrow C_8H_7O_3^-(aq) + H_2O(l)$

7.73 a) The concentration of $H_2PO_4^-$ must be higher than the concentration of HPO_4^{2-}. A pH of 6.9 is lower (more acidic) than 7.21, so the buffer must contain a higher concentration of the conjugate acid.
b) HPO_4^{2-}
c) $H_2PO_4^-(aq) + OH^-(aq) \rightarrow HPO_4^{2-}(aq) + H_2O(l)$

7.75 8.5 (choice e)

Section 7.8 Core Problems

7.77 the phosphate buffer and the protein buffer

7.79 a) $H_2PO_4^-$ and HPO_4^{2-}
b) HPO_4^{2-}
c) $H_2PO_4^-$

7.81 The pK_a of histidine is reasonably close to 7, so a mixture of histidine and its conjugate has a pH near 7 and functions as a buffer.

7.83 down, because some of the dissolved CO_2 combines with water to form carbonic acid (H_2CO_3), which makes the solution more acidic

7.85 When you breathe rapidly, you remove CO_2 from your blood more rapidly than your body makes it. The concentration of CO_2 drops, which in turn makes the concentration of H_2CO_3 decrease. As your blood loses H_2CO_3 (an acid), it becomes more basic.

7.87 Your kidneys excrete the excess bicarbonate ions.

7.89 The pH of the plasma goes down. HCO_3^- functions as a base in the plasma, so removing HCO_3^- makes the blood less basic (more acidic).

CHAPTER 8

Try It Yourself Exercises

8.1

```
    H   H   H   H   H
    |   |   |   |   |
H — C = C —(C)— C =(C)— H
                    |
                    H
```

8.2

```
    H   H   H   H   H   H
    |   |   |   |   |   |
H — C — C — C — C — C — C — H
    |   |   |   |   |   |
    H   H   H   H   H   H
```

8.3 $CH_3–CH_2–CH_2–CH_2–CH_2–CH_3$

8.4 (zigzag line structure)

8.5 molecule b

8.6 cycloheptane

8.7 4-propyloctane

8.8 4,4-diethyl-3-methylheptane

8.9

```
                   CH3
                    |
             CH3   CH2
              |     |
CH3 — CH2 — CH — CH — CH2 — CH2 — CH2 — CH3
```

8.10 propanoic acid

8.11

```
F       F
 \     /
  C = C
 /     \
F       F
```

8.12 2-heptene

8.13

```
    H   H           H   H
    |   |           |   |
H — C — C — C ≡ C — C — C — H        C
    |   |           |   |
    H   H           H   H

CH3 — CH2 — C ≡ C — CH2 — CH3
```

8.14 cyclooctene

8.15 yes

8.16 *cis*-2-nonene

8.17

```
CH3 — CH2       CH2 — CH2 — CH3
         \     /
          C = C
         /     \
        H       H
```

8.18 constitutional isomers

8.19 the second molecule

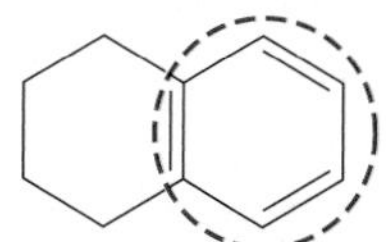

8.20

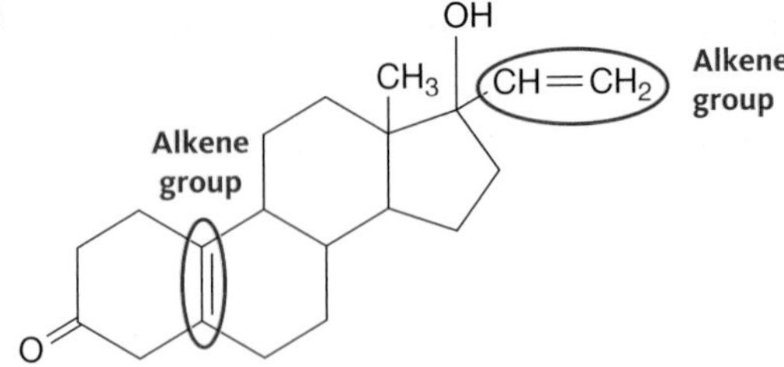

8.21 gas

8.22 cyclohexane

8.23 $2\ C_3H_6 + 9\ O_2 \rightarrow 6\ CO_2 + 6\ H_2O$

Section 8.1 Core Problems

8.1 Carbon atoms have four valence electrons, so they need four more electrons from other atoms to satisfy the octet rule. Each covalent bond adds one electron to the valence shell of carbon, so carbon must form four covalent bonds.

8.3 A tetrahedral arrangement is a triangular pyramid of atoms surrounding a central atom. CH_4 has this arrangement.

8.5
```
     H                  H   H
     |                  |   |
 H—C—H    and    H—C—C—H
     |                  |   |
     H                  H   H
```
(the first and third molecules)

8.7 Carbon atoms must form four bonds to satisfy the octet rule. In this structure, carbon only forms three bonds, so this is not a stable molecule.

8.9
```
   H   H   H   H   H
   |   |   |   |   |
H—C=C—(C)—C=C—H

   H   H   H
   |   |   |
H—(C)=(C)—C—H
   |   |   |
   H   H   H

   H
   |
H—C—(H)—H
   |
   H
```

Section 8.2 Core Problems

8.11
```
   H   H
   |   |
H—C—C—H
   |   |
   H   H
```
(the first molecule)

8.13 a) $CH_3–CH_2–CH_2–CH_2–CH_2–CH_3$

b)
```
   H   H   H   H
   |   |   |   |
H—C—C—C—C—H
   |   |   |   |
   H   H   H   H
```

8.15 a) [zigzag skeletal structure] b) [zigzag skeletal structure]

8.17 a)
```
   H   H   H   H   H   H   H   H
   |   |   |   |   |   |   |   |
H—C—C—C—C—C—C—C—C—H,
   |   |   |   |   |   |   |   |
   H   H   H   H   H   H   H   H
```
$CH_3–CH_2–CH_2–CH_2–CH_2–CH_2–CH_2–CH_3$

b)
```
   H   H   H
   |   |   |
H—C—C—C—H
   |   |   |
   H   H   H
```
$CH_3–CH_2–CH_3$

8.19 a)
```
   H   H   H   H   H   H   H
   |   |   |   |   |   |   |
H—C—C—C—C—C—C—C—H,
   |   |   |   |   |   |   |
   H   H   H   H   H   H   H
```
$CH_3–CH_2–CH_2–CH_2–CH_2–CH_2–CH_3$

b) C_7H_{16} c) heptane

Section 8.3 Core Problems

8.21 a) linear alkane b) branched alkane c) linear alkane d) cycloalkane

8.23 a)
```
       CH3        CH3
       |          |
CH3—CH—CH2—CH—CH3
```

b)
```
          H
          |
        H—C—H
          |
        H—C—H
   H   H  |    H   H
   |   |  |    |   |
H—C—C———C———C—C—H
   |   |  |    |   |
   H   H  H    H   H
```

8.25 a) [skeletal structure] b) [skeletal structure]

8.27 a)
```
       CH3        CH3
       |          |
CH3—CH—CH2—C—CH3
                  |
                  CH3
```

b)
```
      CH2
   CH2    CH—CH2—CH2—CH3
    \     /
    CH2-CH2
```

8.29 The carbon atom at the branch point is bonded to five other atoms (three carbon atoms and two hydrogen atoms). Carbon can only form four bonds, not five.
```
              CH3
              |
CH3—CH2—(CH2)—CH2—CH2—CH3
```

8.31 a) isomers

b) not isomers; these are two ways to draw the same molecule, pentane

c) not isomers, because they have different numbers of hydrogen atoms (the first molecule has 14 hydrogen atoms, the second has only 12)

Section 8.4 Core Problems

8.33 propyl

8.35 a) 3-methylpentane
b) 4-isopropyloctane
c) 4-ethyl-2-methylheptane
d) 2,3-dimethylhexane
e) 2,2,3-trimethylpentane
f) 5,5-diethyl-2-methylheptane
g) cyclohexane
h) methylcyclopentane

8.37 a) 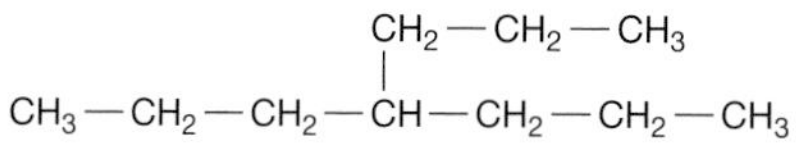
$CH_2—CH_2—CH_3$ (on C-4)
$CH_3—CH_2—CH_2—CH—CH_2—CH_2—CH_3$

b)
CH_3
$CH_3—C—CH_2—CH_2—CH_3$
CH_3

c)
$CH_3—CH_2$ $CH_2—CH_2—CH_3$
$CH_3—CH_2—CH—CH—CH_2—CH_2—CH_2—CH_2—CH_3$

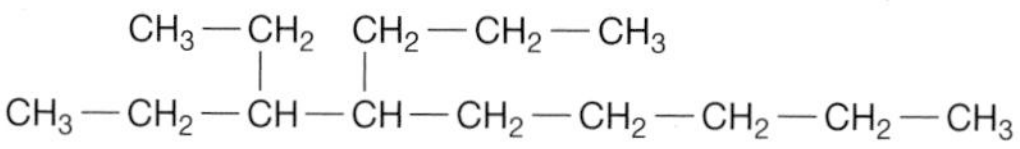

d) 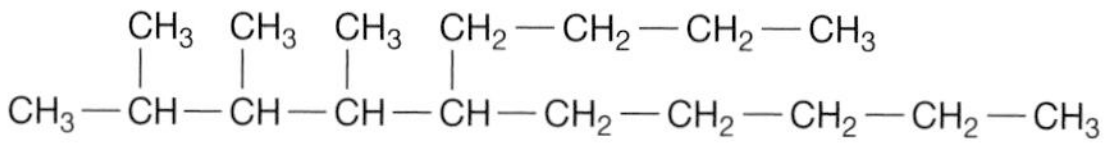
CH_3 CH_3 CH_3 $CH_2—CH_2—CH_2—CH_3$
$CH_3—CH—CH—CH—CH—CH_2—CH_2—CH_2—CH_2—CH_3$

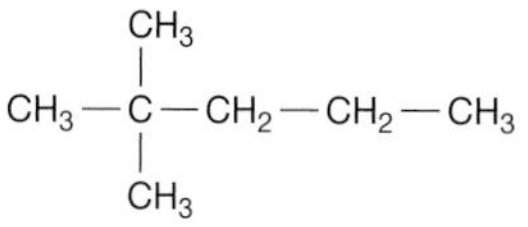

e) 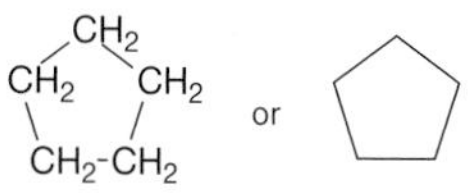 cyclopentane ring of five CH_2 groups (CH_2, CH_2, CH_2, CH_2-CH_2) or pentagon

f) 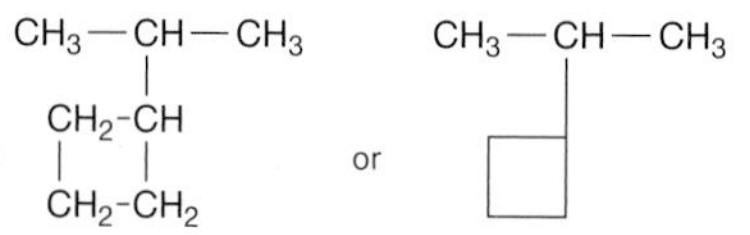
$CH_3—CH—CH_3$
CH_2-CH
CH_2-CH_2
or isopropyl on a square (cyclobutane) ring; $CH_3—CH—CH_3$

8.39 yes, because they have the same molecular formula (C_7H_{16}) but different structures

Section 8.5 Core Problems

8.41 $CH_3—CH(OH)—CH_3$ (OH circled) $CH_3—C(=CH_2)—CH_3$ (C=CH_2 circled)

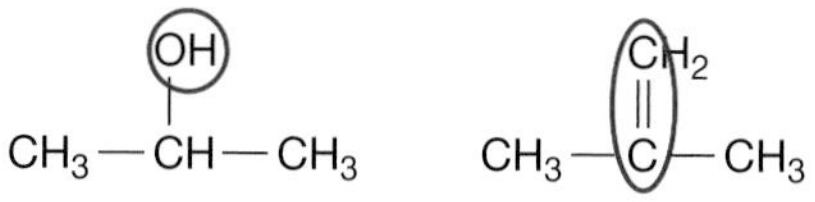

8.43 compounds c and d

Section 8.6 Core Problems

8.45 a double bond connecting two carbon atoms

8.47 a) alkane   b) alkyne   c) alkene

8.49 $Cl_2C=CCl_2$
Cl Cl
C=C
Cl Cl

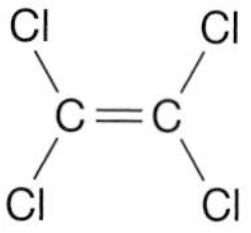

8.51 a) 1-hexene   b) cyclohexene   c) 2-heptyne
d) propyne   e) 6-methyl-3-heptene
f) 3-ethyl-2-methyl-2-pentene

8.53 a) 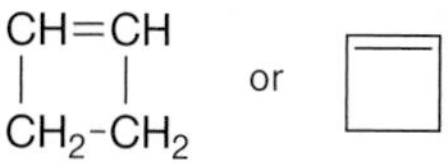
$CH=CH$
CH_2-CH_2
or square with one double bond

b) $CH_3–CH_2–CH=CH–CH_2–CH_2–CH_2–CH_3$

c) $HC≡C–CH_2–CH_2–CH_2–CH_3$

d) $HC≡CH$

e) 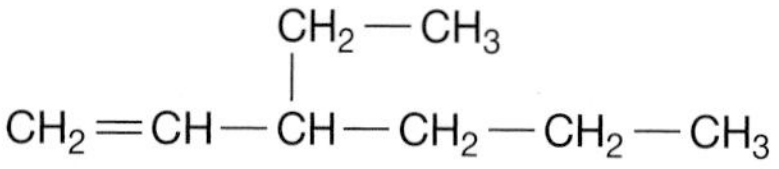
$CH_2—CH_3$
$CH_2=CH—CH—CH_2—CH_2—CH_3$

f) 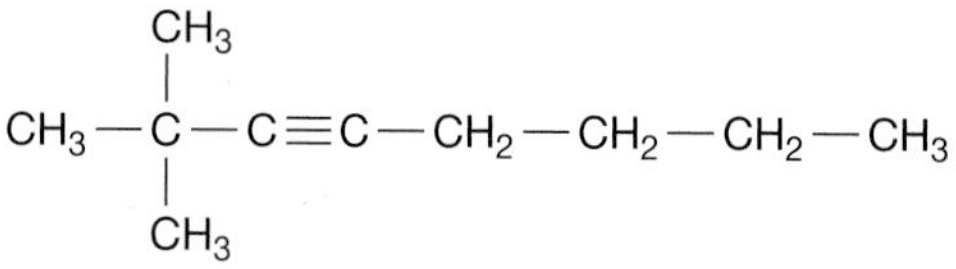
CH_3
$CH_3—C—C≡C—CH_2—CH_2—CH_2—CH_3$
CH_3

8.55 (bond-line structure)

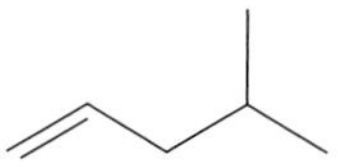

8.57
CH_3 CH_3
$CH_3—C=CH—CH—CH_2—CH_2—CH_3$

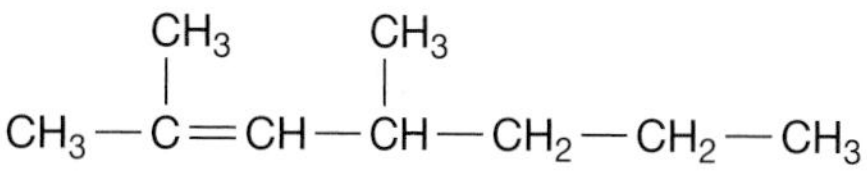

8.59 The circled carbon atom has five bonds:
CH_3
$CH_3—$(CH)$=CH—CH_3$

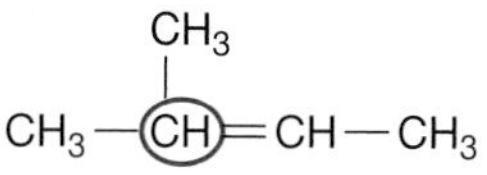

Section 8.7 Core Problems

8.61 3-hexene (choice c)

8.63 a) *trans*-3-heptene   b) *cis*-4-octene

8.65 a) 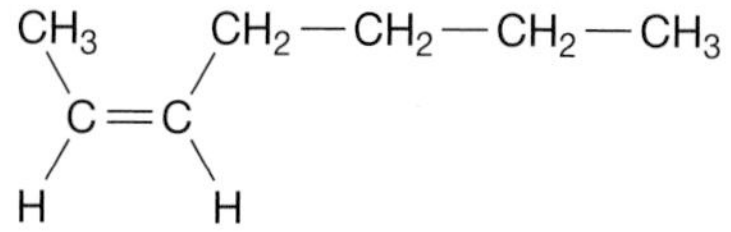
CH_3 $CH_2—CH_2—CH_2—CH_3$
C=C
H   H

b) 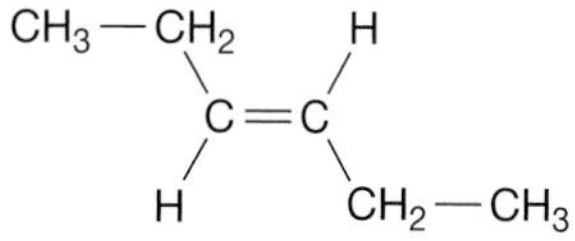
$CH_3—CH_2$ H
C=C
H $CH_2—CH_3$

8.67 a) stereoisomers   b) constitutional isomers
c) constitutional isomers   d) not isomers

Section 8.8 Core Problems

8.69 the second molecule

8.71 a) 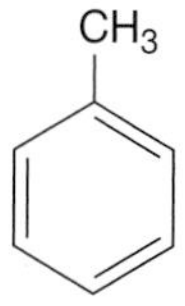 benzene ring with CH_3 b) 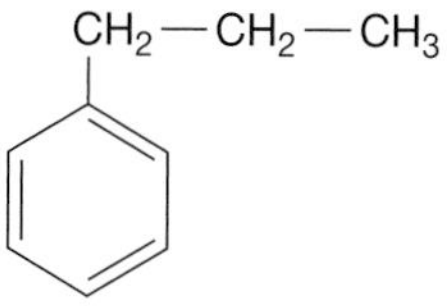 benzene ring with $CH_2—CH_2—CH_3$

8.73 ethylbenzene

8.75
Alkene group
Alkyne group
$CH=CH$ $C≡CH$
Alkene group
Aromatic ring

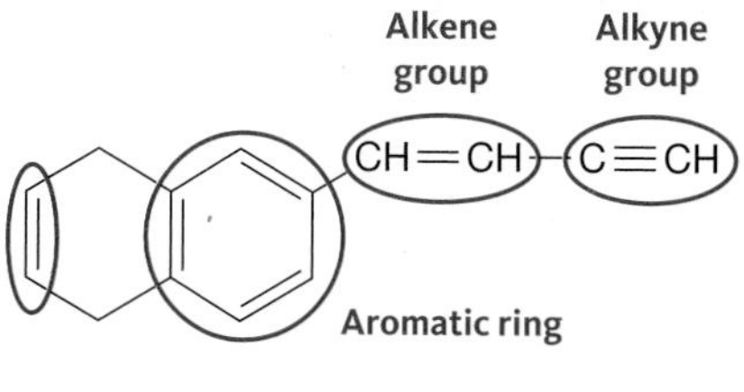

Section 8.9 Core Problems

8.77 Benzene is a liquid, and naphthalene is a solid. Benzene is a smaller molecule, so the dispersion forces that attract benzene molecules to one another are weaker than the dispersion forces among naphthalene molecules.

8.79 Pentane, like all hydrocarbons, cannot participate in hydrogen bonds. Water molecules are more strongly attracted to one another than they are to pentane molecules, so water molecules cluster together and force the pentane molecules into a separate area.

8.81 $2\ C_2H_2 + 5\ O_2 \rightarrow 4\ CO_2 + 2\ H_2O$

8.83 similar; they are roughly the same size and shape, so the dispersion forces that attract molecules to one another have similar strengths for both compounds

8.85 butane → 2-methylbutane and pentane → 2,2-dimethylbutane

8.87 Combustion reactions supply most of the energy for modern society.

CHAPTER 9

Try It Yourself Exercises

9.1 $CH_3-CH(CH_3)-CH(OH)-CH_3$ and $CH_3-CH(CH_3)-CH_2-CH_2-OH$

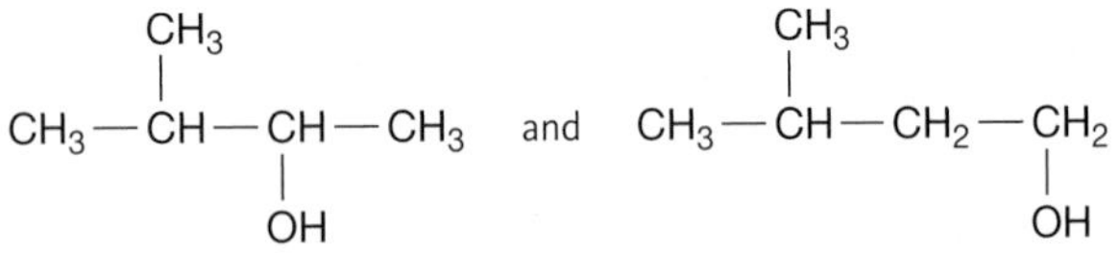

9.2 a) one product b) two different products

9.3 2-butanol

9.4

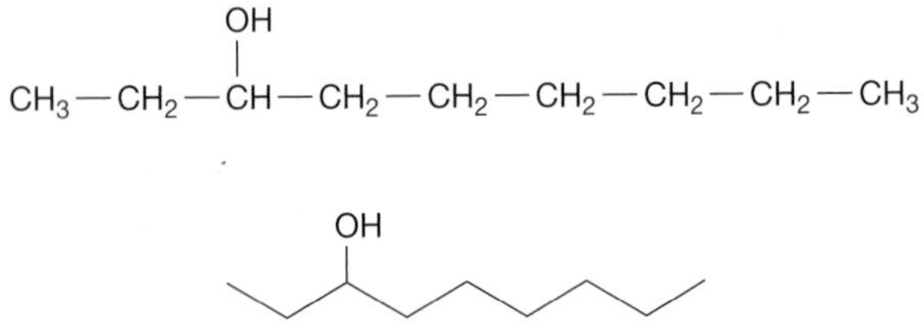

$CH_3-CH_2-CH(OH)-CH_2-CH_2-CH_2-CH_2-CH_2-CH_3$

OH

9.5 cyclohexanol

9.6 3-pentanol

9.7 compound X (least soluble) → compound Y → compound Z (most soluble)

9.8 no

9.9

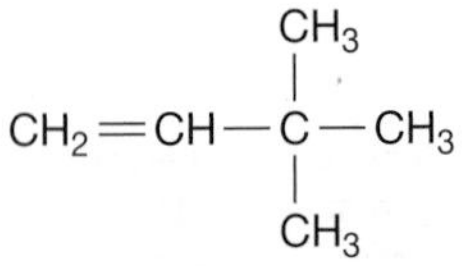

$CH_2=CH-C(CH_3)_2-CH_3$

9.10

$CH_3-CH_2-C(CH_3)=CH-CH_3$ and

$CH_3-CH_2-CH(CH_3)-CH=CH_2$

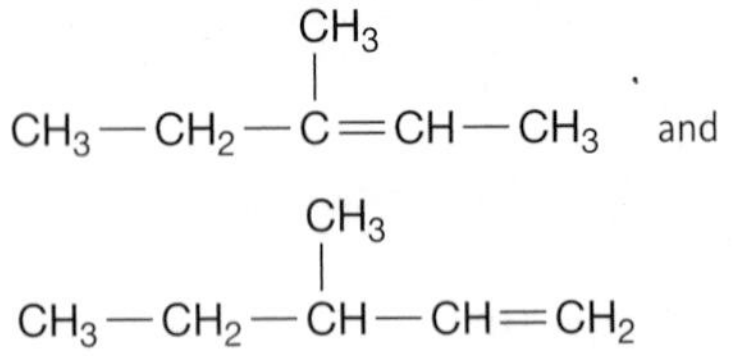

9.11 no

9.12 compound Y (least soluble) → compound X → compound Z (most soluble)

Section 9.1 Core Problems

9.1

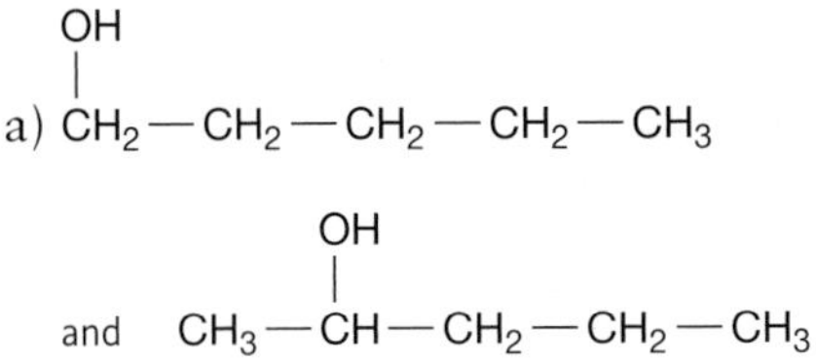

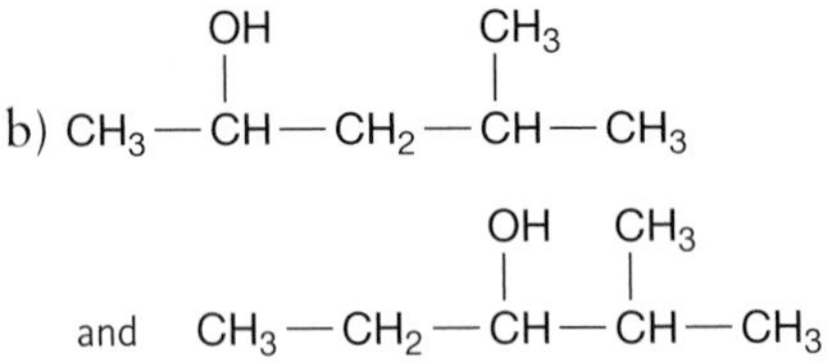

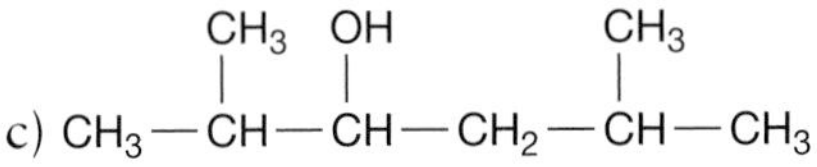

a) $CH_2(OH)-CH_2-CH_2-CH_2-CH_3$

and $CH_3-CH(OH)-CH_2-CH_2-CH_3$

b) $CH_3-CH(OH)-CH_2-CH(CH_3)-CH_3$

and $CH_3-CH_2-CH(OH)-CH(CH_3)-CH_3$

c) $CH_3-CH(CH_3)-CH(OH)-CH_2-CH(CH_3)-CH_3$
(only one product)

d) 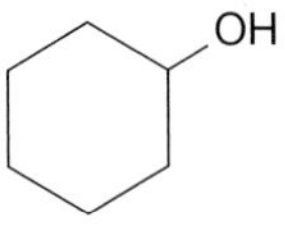 OH (only one product)

e) 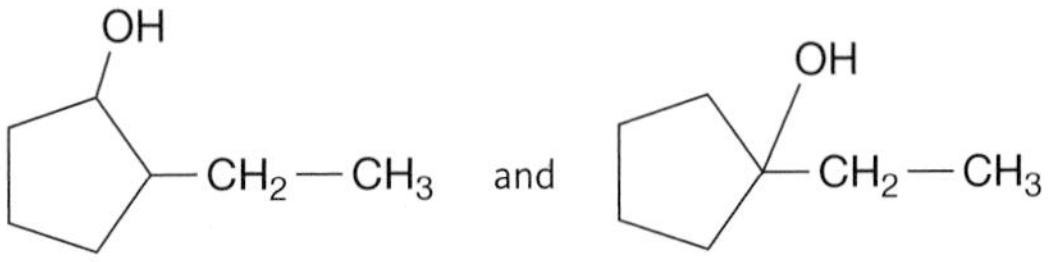 OH $-CH_2-CH_3$ and OH $-CH_2-CH_3$

f) 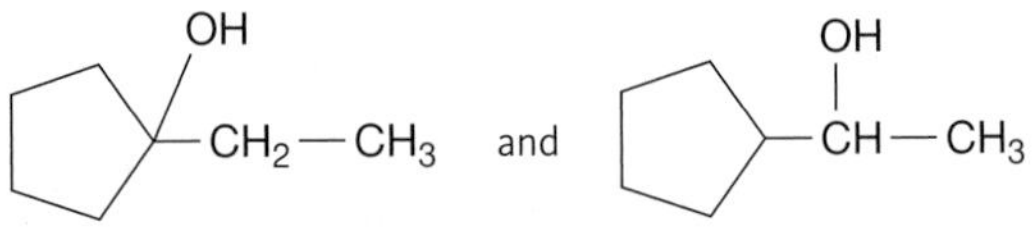 OH $-CH_2-CH_3$ and OH $-CH(OH)-CH_3$

g) 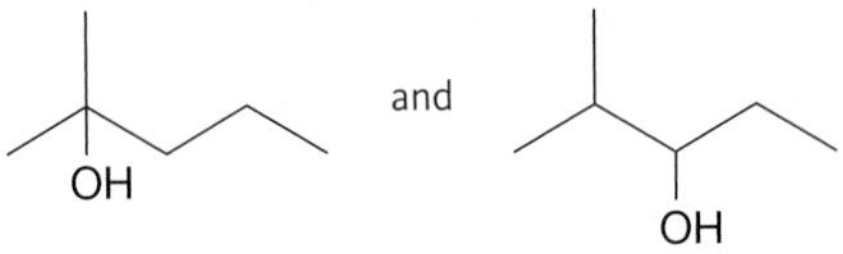 OH and OH

9.3 $CH_3-CH(CH_3)-CH(OH)-CH_3$

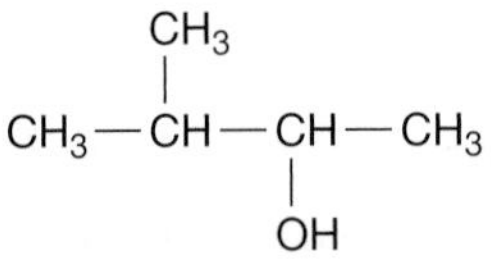

9.5 choices b and e

Section 9.2 Core Problems

9.7 An enzyme is a protein that catalyzes a reaction in a living organism.

9.9 yes; the alternate product is

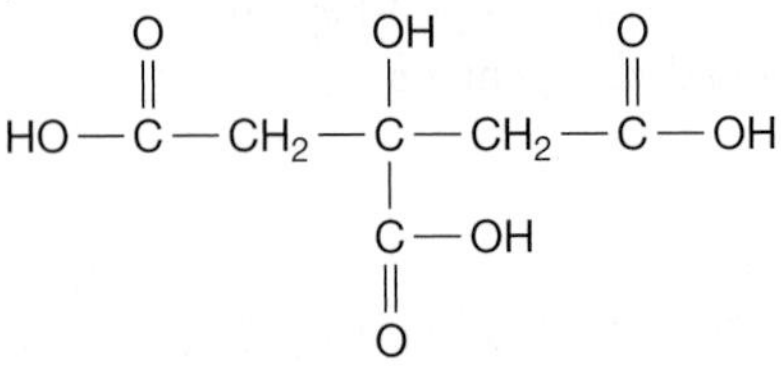

$HO-C(=O)-CH_2-C(OH)(C(=O)-OH)-CH_2-C(=O)-OH$

Section 9.3 Core Problems

9.11 a) 1-butanol b) cyclohexanol
c) 4-octanol d) 1-pentanol

9.13 a) 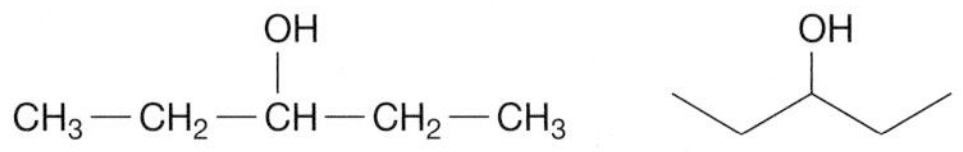 $CH_3—CH_2—CH(OH)—CH_2—CH_3$ OH

b) 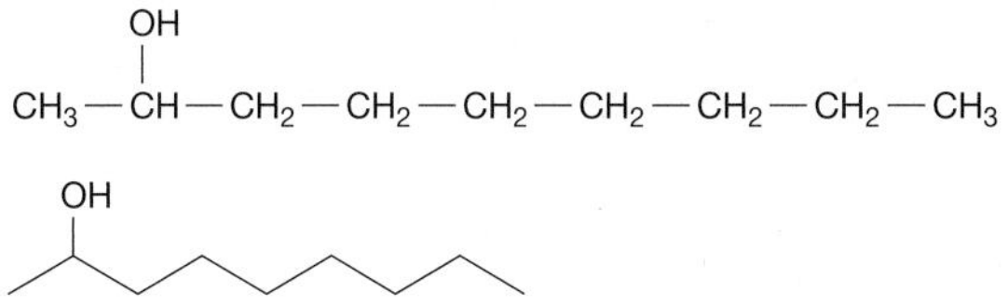 $CH_3—CH(OH)—CH_2—CH_2—CH_2—CH_2—CH_2—CH_2—CH_3$

OH

c) 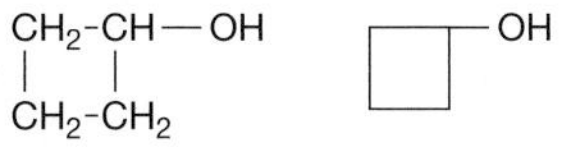 $CH_2\text{-}CH—OH$, $CH_2\text{-}CH_2$ (ring) OH

9.15 $CH_3–OH$ methanol

9.17 pentanol and 4-pentanol (choices a and d)

Section 9.4 Core Problems

9.19 $O(H)—H\text{- - - - - - - -}O(H)(CH_3)$ and $O(CH_3)—H\text{- - - - - - - -}O(H)(H)$

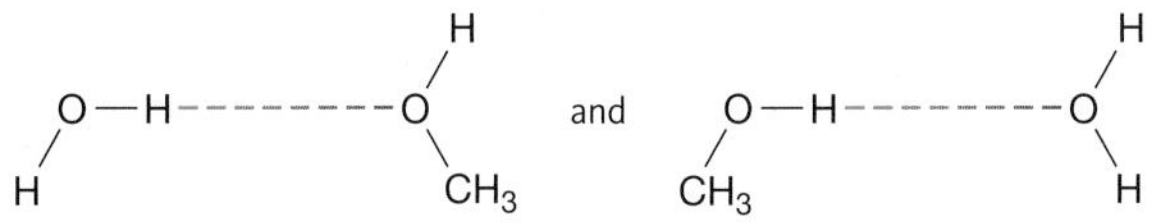

9.21 a) 3-pentanol b) 2-heptanol
c) 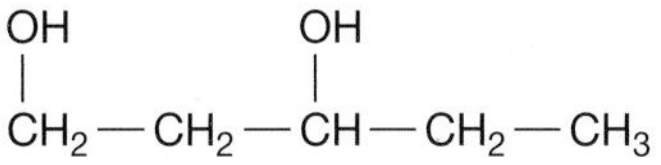 $CH_2(OH)—CH_2—CH(OH)—CH_2—CH_3$

9.23 a) 2-butanol b) 2-butanol c) ethanol

9.25 a) basic b) neutral

9.27 compound c

Section 9.5 Core Problems

9.29 a) chiral b) not chiral
c) not chiral d) not chiral

9.31 a) None are chiral.

b) 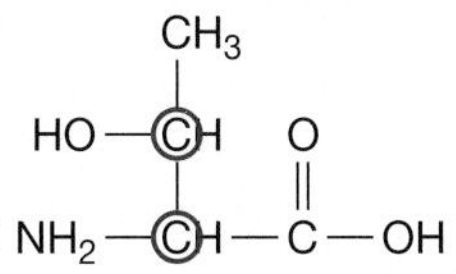 $CH_3—CH(OH)—$ (circled C) 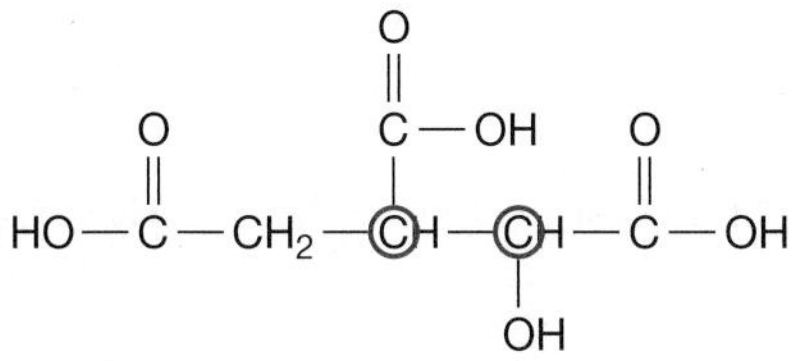 ; $NH_2—CH—C(=O)—OH$ (circled C)

c) $HO—C(=O)—CH_2—CH(C(=O)—OH)—CH(OH)—C(=O)—OH$ (circled C atoms)

9.33 3-methylheptane, because it is the only molecule that contains a chiral carbon atom (carbon 3).

9.35 Many biological molecules are chiral, and our bodies can only use one of the two enantiomers. Enzymes must be able to bind to the correct enantiomer. Only chiral molecules can distinguish other chiral molecules, so enzymes must be chiral.

Section 9.6 Core Problems

9.37 a) $CH_2{=}CH_2$
b) $CH_2{=}CH–CH_2–CH_2–CH_3$ and
$CH_3–CH{=}CH–CH_2–CH_3$

c) 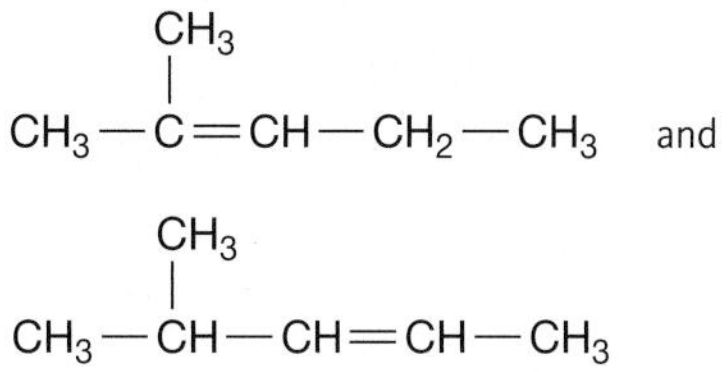 $CH_3—C(CH_3){=}CH—CH_2—CH_3$ and

$CH_3—CH(CH_3)—CH{=}CH—CH_3$

d) 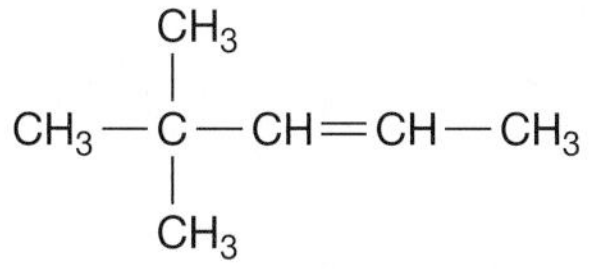 $CH_3—C(CH_3)_2—CH{=}CH—CH_3$

e) 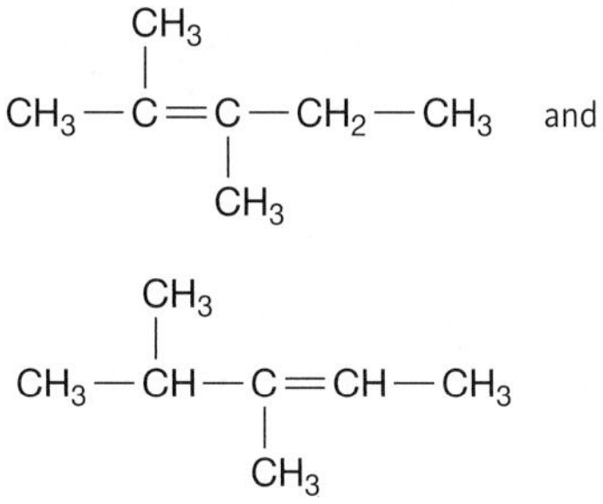 $CH_3—C(CH_3){=}C(CH_3)—CH_2—CH_3$ and

$CH_3—CH(CH_3)—C(CH_3){=}CH—CH_3$

f) 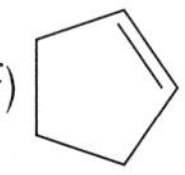 (cyclopentene)

9.39 The carbon atom that is adjacent to the alcohol group does not have a hydrogen atom attached to it.

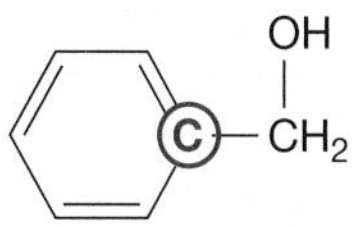

(benzene ring, circled C)$—CH_2—OH$

Section 9.7 Core Problems

9.41 SH OH OH CH_3 OH

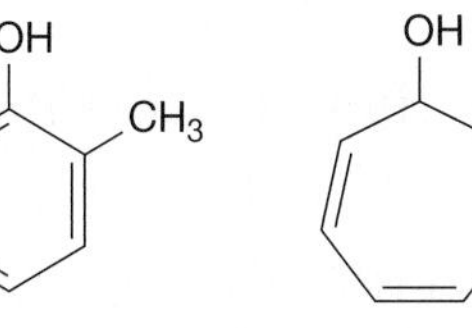

Thiol Alcohol Phenol Alcohol

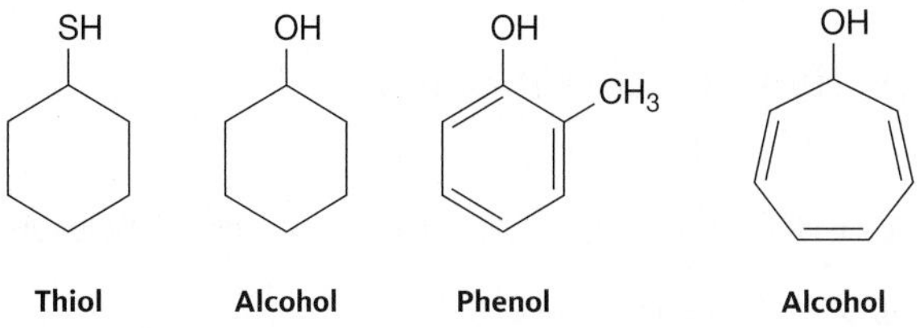

9.43 a) phenol b) $CH_3–CH_2–CH_2–OH$

9.45 $CH_3–CH_2–CH_2–OH$

CHAPTER 10

Try It Yourself Exercises

10.1 $\text{CH}_3\text{—(CH}_2)_7\text{—CH=CH—(CH}_2)_7\text{—C(=O)—OH}$

10.2 $\text{CH}_3\text{—CH(CH}_3)\text{—CH}_2\text{—CH}_2\text{—CH}_2\text{—CH}_3$

10.3 $\text{CH}_2\text{=CH—C(=O)—CH}_3$

10.4 a) secondary b) primary

10.5 $\text{C}_6\text{H}_5\text{—CH(OH)—CH}_3$

10.6 heptanal

10.7 $\text{CH}_3\text{—CH}_2\text{—CH}_2\text{—CH}_2\text{—CH}_2\text{—CH}_2\text{—CH}_2\text{—C(=O)—H}$

10.8 2-hexanone

10.9 cyclohexane (lowest) → cyclohexanone → cyclohexanol (highest)

10.10 nonanal (lowest) → heptanal → pentanal (highest)

10.11 $\text{C}_6\text{H}_{11}\text{—CH}_2\text{—S—S—CH}_2\text{—C}_6\text{H}_{11}$

10.12 Two molecules of $\text{CH}_3\text{—CH}_2\text{—CH(CH}_3)\text{—SH}$

10.13 reduction

10.14 $\text{HO—C(=O)—CH}_2\text{—C}_6\text{H}_5$

10.15 a) adipic acid
b) adipic acid

10.16 $\text{HO—C(=O)—CH(OH)—CH}_2\text{—C(=O)—OH} + \text{NAD}^+ \longrightarrow \text{HO—C(=O)—C(=O)—CH}_2\text{—C(=O)—OH} + \text{NADH} + \text{H}^+$

10.17 FAD

Section 10.1 Core Problems

10.1 $\text{HO—C(=O)—CH}_2\text{—CH=CH—C(=O)—}$rest of molecule

10.3 a) $\text{CH}_3\text{–CH}_2\text{–CH}_2\text{–CH}_2\text{–CH}_3$
b) $\text{CH}_3\text{—CH}_2\text{—CH(CH}_3)\text{—CH}_3$

10.5 This reaction removes two hydrogen atoms from the reactant, so it is an oxidation.

Section 10.2 Core Problems

10.7 a) $\text{CH}_3\text{—CH}_2\text{—C(=O)H}$
b) $\text{CH}_3\text{—C(=O)—CH(CH}_3)\text{—CH}_3$
c) no reaction
d) (cyclohexanone ring)=O

10.9 a) primary b) secondary
c) tertiary d) secondary

10.11 a) $\text{CH}_3\text{—CH(OH)—CH}_2\text{—CH}_2\text{—CH}_3$
b) $\text{CH}_3\text{—CH(OH)—CH}_2\text{—CH(CH}_3)\text{—CH}_3$
c) (cyclopentane ring)—OH
d) $\text{C}_6\text{H}_5\text{—CH(OH)—C}_6\text{H}_5$

10.13 2-Pentanone produces a chiral alcohol, 2-pentanol. The second carbon atom in this molecule is bonded to four different groups, making it a chiral carbon atom. On the other hand, 3-pentanone produces 3-pentanol, which has no chiral carbon atoms and therefore is not a chiral molecule.

Section 10.3 Core Problems

10.15 a) 2-hexanone b) propanal c) pentanal
d) cyclopentanone e) 3-heptanone

10.17 acetone

10.19 a) $\text{CH}_3\text{—CH}_2\text{—C(=O)—CH}_2\text{—CH}_3$
b) $\text{CH}_3\text{—CH}_2\text{—CH}_2\text{—CH}_2\text{—CH}_2\text{—CH}_2\text{—CH}_2\text{—C(=O)—H}$
c) H—C(=O)—H
d) (cyclobutanone ring)=O

10.21 butanal = 75°C   1-butanol = 99°C
pentane = 36°C

10.23 pentane = 0.1 g/L   pentanal = 12 g/L
heptanal = 1.2 g/L

Section 10.4 Core Problems

10.25 $CH_3-CH_2-CH_2-CH(CH_3)-S-S-CH(CH_3)-CH_2-CH_2-CH_3$

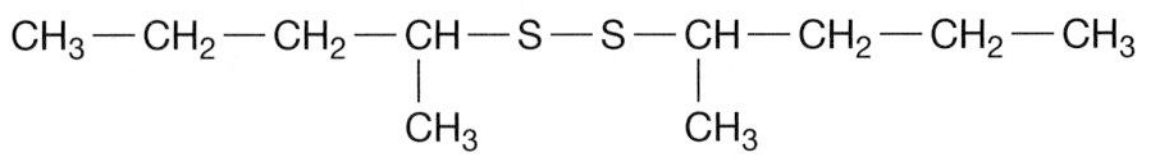

10.27 Two molecules of $CH_3–CH_2–SH$

10.29 oxidation, because the ascorbic acid molecule loses two hydrogen atoms (on the OH groups below the ring)

Section 10.5 Core Problems

10.31 a) 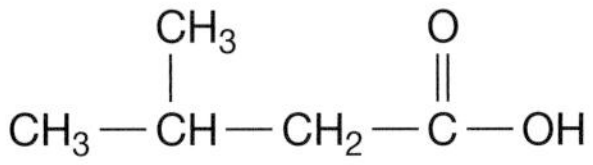 $CH_3-CH(CH_3)-CH_2-C(=O)-OH$

b) 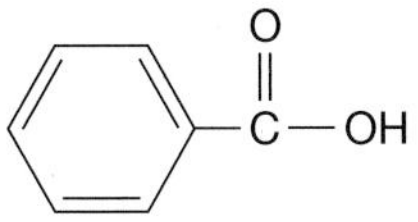 $C_6H_5-C(=O)-OH$

10.33 a) propanoic acid   b) heptanoic acid
c) hexanoic acid

10.35 a) 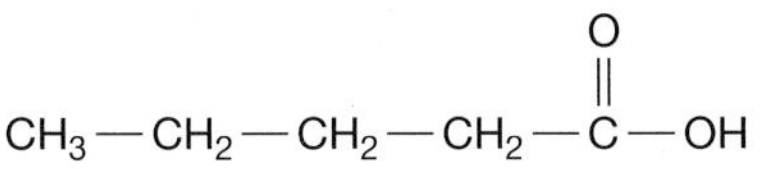 $CH_3-CH_2-CH_2-CH_2-C(=O)-OH$

b) 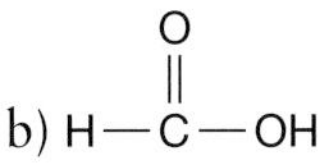 $H-C(=O)-OH$

10.37 pimelic acid

10.39 Pimelic acid is a solid and heptanoic acid is a liquid. Pimelic acid has twice as many groups that can participate in hydrogen bonds, so molecules of pimelic acid are more strongly attracted to one another than molecules of heptanoic acid are.

Section 10.6 Core Problems

10.41 NADPH

10.43 a) NAD^+

b) 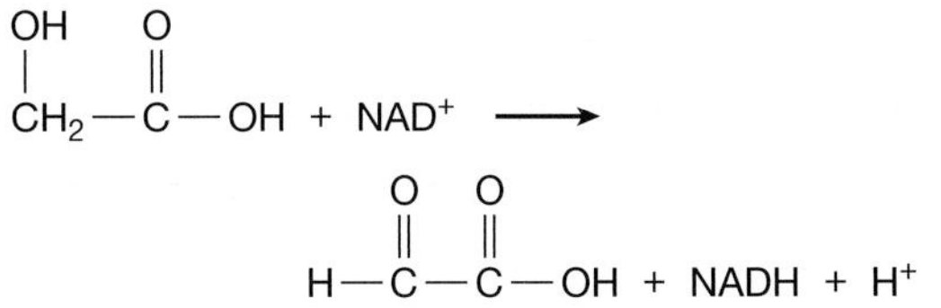 $CH_2(OH)-C(=O)-OH + NAD^+ \longrightarrow H-C(=O)-C(=O)-OH + NADH + H^+$

10.45 The second hydrogen atom loses its electron and becomes a hydrogen ion, H^+.

Section 10.7 Core Problems

10.47 Yes, because each successive reaction uses the product of the previous reaction. The starting material for this pathway is glucose, and the final product is starch.

10.49 Reaction 1: oxidation

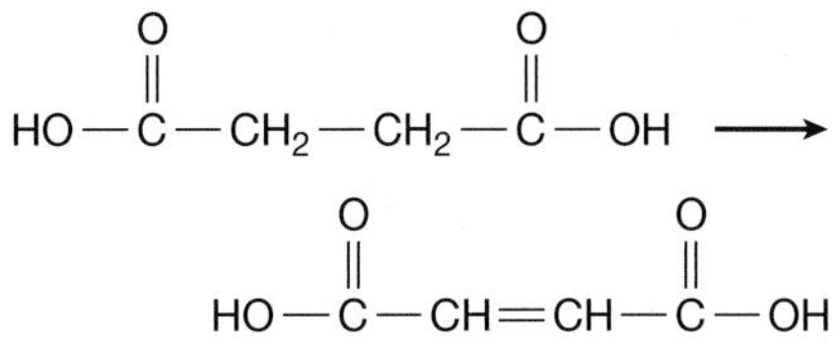

$HO-C(=O)-CH_2-CH_2-C(=O)-OH \longrightarrow HO-C(=O)-CH{=}CH-C(=O)-OH$

Reaction 2: hydration

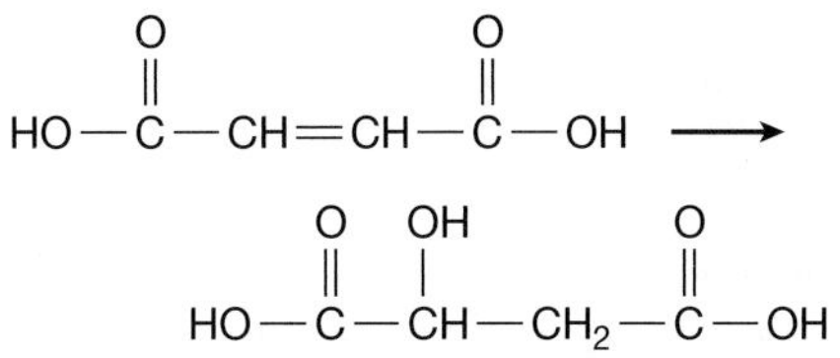

$HO-C(=O)-CH{=}CH-C(=O)-OH \longrightarrow HO-C(=O)-CH(OH)-CH_2-C(=O)-OH$

Reaction 3: oxidation

$HO-C(=O)-CH(OH)-CH_2-C(=O)-OH \longrightarrow HO-C(=O)-C(=O)-CH_2-C(=O)-OH$

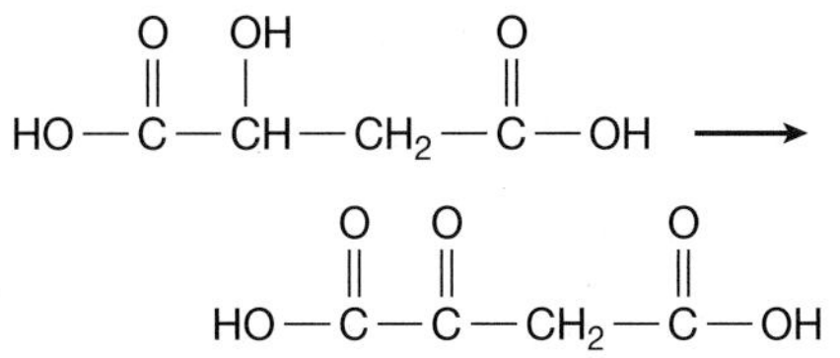

CHAPTER 11

Try It Yourself Exercises

11.1 $CH_3–CH_2–CH_2–CO_2H + H_2O \rightarrow$
$CH_3–CH_2–CH_2–CO_2^- + H_3O^+$

11.2 a) $C_3H_5O_2^-$ b) $Mg(C_3H_5O_2)_2$

11.3 a) insoluble   b) soluble

11.4 $CH_3–SH + OH^- \rightarrow CH_3–S^- + H_2O$

11.5 B (lowest pH) → A → C (highest pH)

11.6 $CH_3-C(=O)-CH_2(-CH_3)$ which can also be drawn as

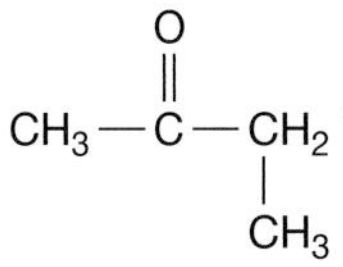

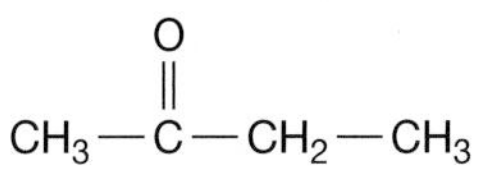

$CH_3-C(=O)-CH_2-CH_3$

11.7 $CH_3-CH(CH_3)-CH_2-C(=O)-S-CoA$

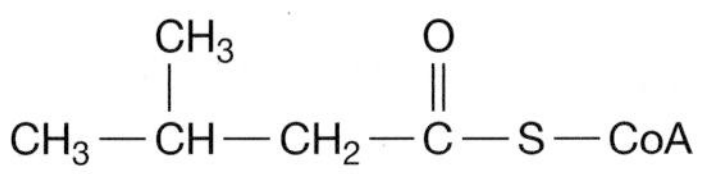

11.8 a) secondary   b) primary

11.9 $CH_3–CH_2–NH–CH_2–CH_2–CH_2–CH_2–CH_3$

11.10 cyclopentylamine

11.11 Trimethylamine has no hydrogen atom attached to the nitrogen atom, so it can only be a hydrogen bond receptor.

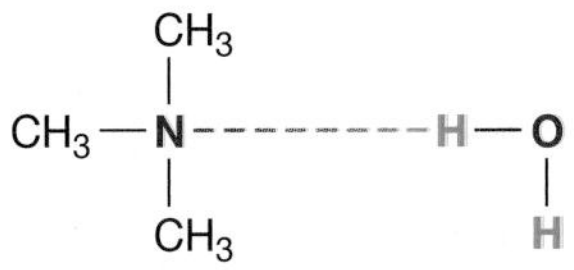

$(CH_3)_3N \cdots H-O-H$

11.12 (piperidine ring)N—H + $H—\overset{O}{\overset{\|}{C}}—OH$ ⟶

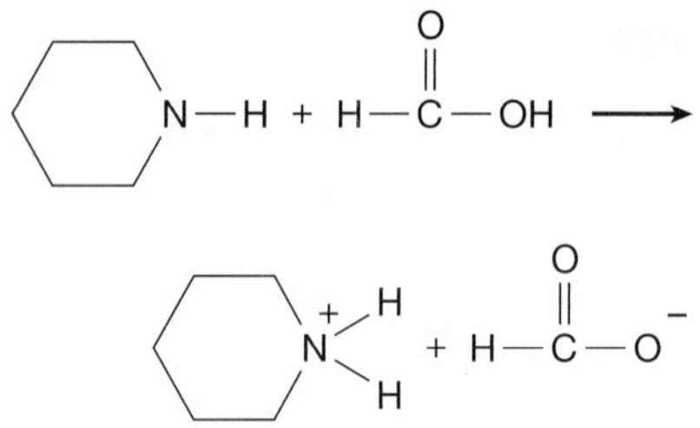

(piperidine ring)$N^{+}H_2$ + $H—\overset{O}{\overset{\|}{C}}—O^{-}$

11.13 $CH_3—CH_2—\overset{+}{N}H_2—CH_3$ F^{-}

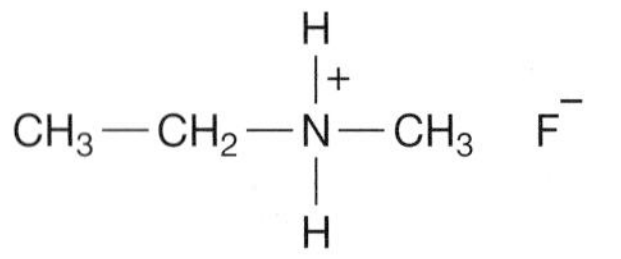

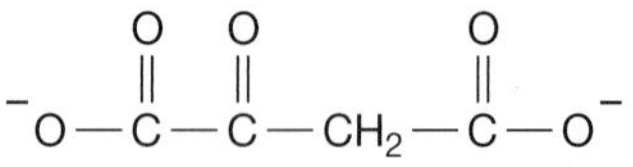

11.14 phenethylamine

11.15 $C_6H_5—\overset{OH}{CH}—\overset{CH_3}{CH}—\overset{+}{N}H_2—CH_3$ Cl^{-}

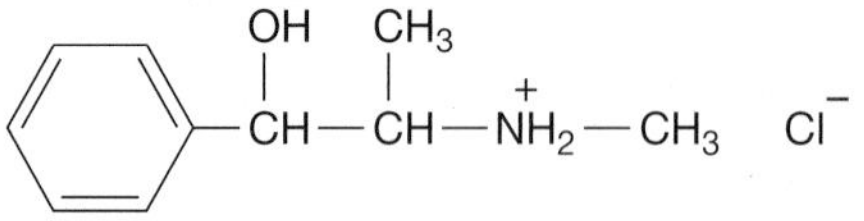

11.16 $^{-}O—\overset{O}{\overset{\|}{C}}—\overset{O}{\overset{\|}{C}}—CH_2—\overset{O}{\overset{\|}{C}}—O^{-}$

11.17 (pyridine ring)$—CH_2—CH_2—NH_3^{+}$

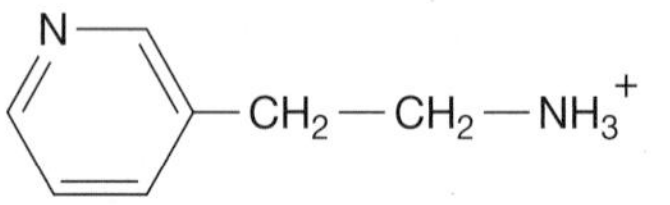

11.18 Dihydroxyacetone phosphate forms a mixture of the following two molecules:

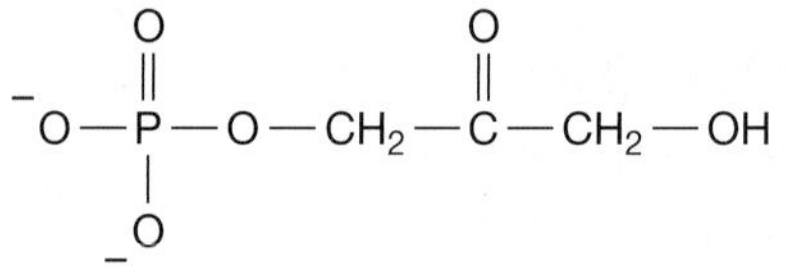

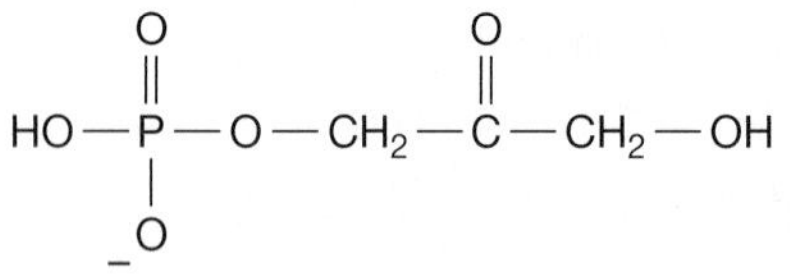

$^{-}O—\overset{O}{\overset{\|}{P}}(O^{-})—O—CH_2—\overset{O}{\overset{\|}{C}}—CH_2—OH$

$HO—\overset{O}{\overset{\|}{P}}(O^{-})—O—CH_2—\overset{O}{\overset{\|}{C}}—CH_2—OH$

Section 11.1 Core Problems

11.1 a) 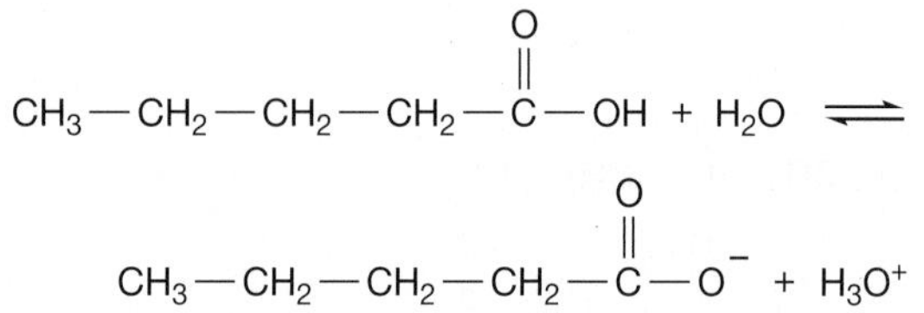 $CH_3—CH_2—CH_2—CH_2—\overset{O}{\overset{\|}{C}}—OH + H_2O \rightleftharpoons$

$CH_3—CH_2—CH_2—CH_2—\overset{O}{\overset{\|}{C}}—O^{-} + H_3O^{+}$

b) 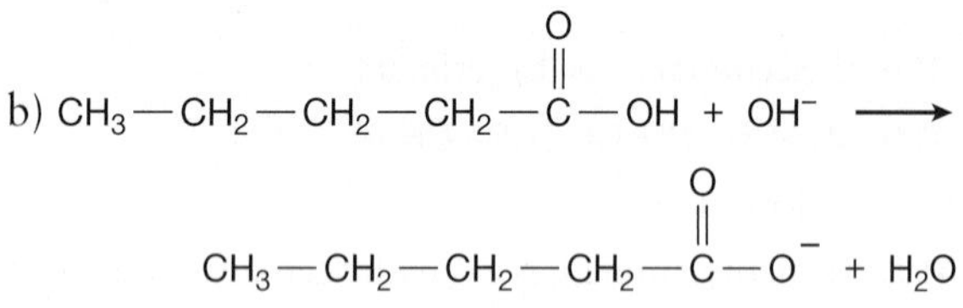 $CH_3—CH_2—CH_2—CH_2—\overset{O}{\overset{\|}{C}}—OH + OH^{-} \longrightarrow$

$CH_3—CH_2—CH_2—CH_2—\overset{O}{\overset{\|}{C}}—O^{-} + H_2O$

11.3 a) 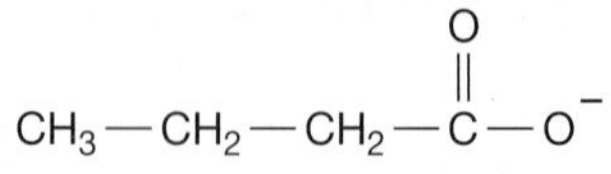 $CH_3—CH_2—CH_2—\overset{O}{\overset{\|}{C}}—O^{-}$

b) 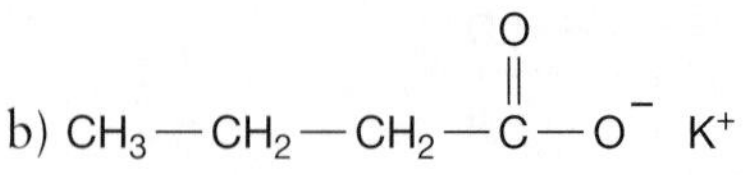 $CH_3—CH_2—CH_2—\overset{O}{\overset{\|}{C}}—O^{-}$ K^{+}

11.5 $Ca(C_4H_7O_2)_2$

11.7 a) acetate ion or ethanoate ion

b) magnesium acetate or magnesium ethanoate

11.9 Sodium hexanoate has the higher solubility. In general, sodium salts of carboxylic acids are more soluble than the acids themselves.

11.11 a) $CH_3–CH_2–CH_2–SH + H_2O \rightarrow CH_3–CH_2–CH_2–S^{-} + H_3O^{+}$

b) 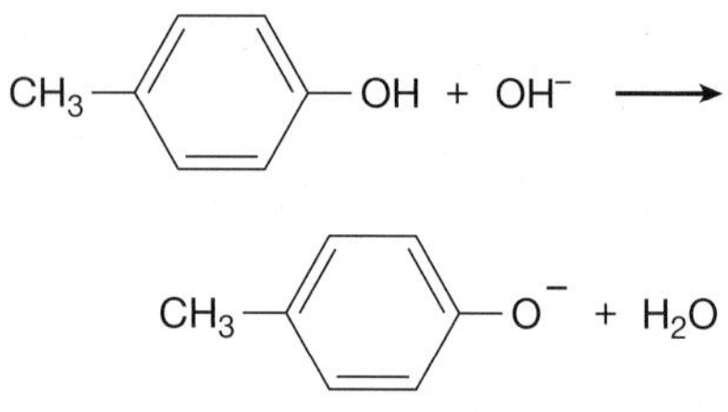 $CH_3—C_6H_4—OH + OH^{-} \longrightarrow$

$CH_3—C_6H_4—O^{-} + H_2O$

Section 11.2 Core Problems

11.13 CO_2

11.15 a) 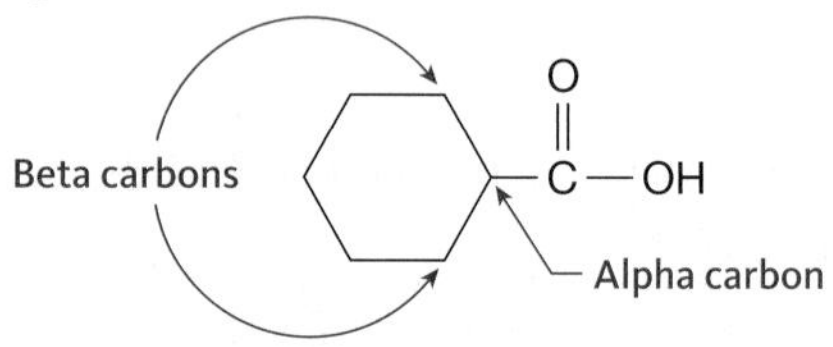 Beta carbons (cyclohexane ring)$—\overset{O}{\overset{\|}{C}}—OH$ Alpha carbon

b) no, because the molecule does not have a carbonyl group at the α or the β position

11.17 a) 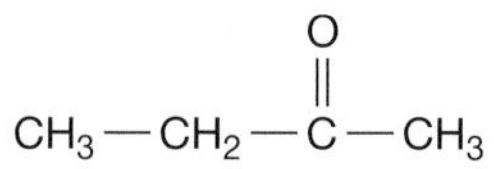 $CH_3—CH_2—\overset{O}{\overset{\|}{C}}—CH_3$ b) 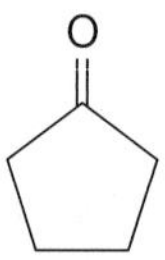 (cyclopentanone)

11.19 a) 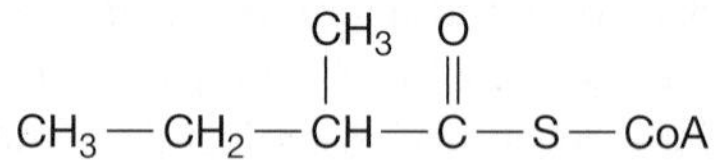 $CH_3—CH_2—\overset{CH_3}{CH}—\overset{O}{\overset{\|}{C}}—S—CoA$

b) 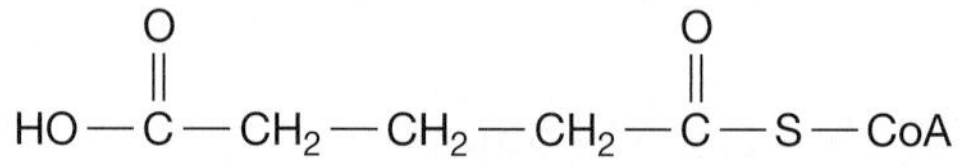 $HO—\overset{O}{\overset{\|}{C}}—CH_2—CH_2—CH_2—\overset{O}{\overset{\|}{C}}—S—CoA$

Section 11.3 Core Problems

11.21 a) secondary b) primary c) tertiary

11.23 the second molecule

11.25 a) $CH_3–CH_2–CH_2–CH_2–CH_2–NH_2$

b) $CH_3–CH_2–CH_2–NH–CH_2–CH_2–CH_3$

c) 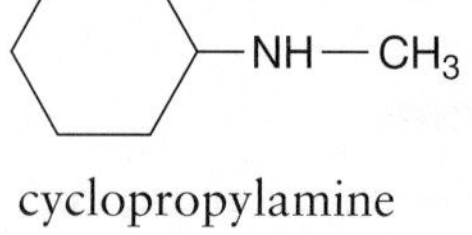 (cyclohexane ring)$—NH—CH_3$

11.27 a) cyclopropylamine b) butylethylamine

c) trimethylamine

11.29

a) 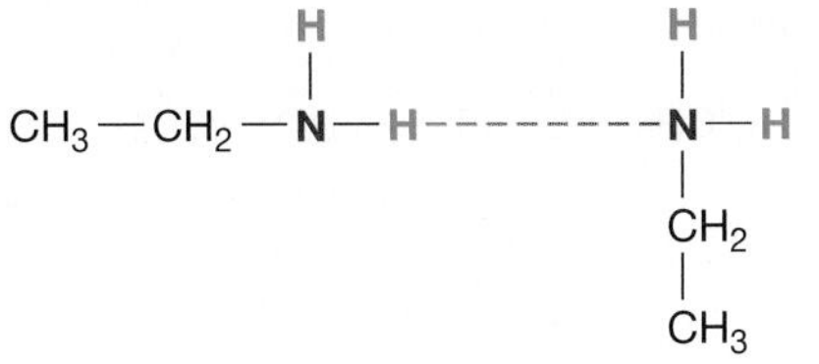 $CH_3—CH_2—N(H)—H$ - - - - - - - - $N(H)(H)—CH_2—CH_3$

b) 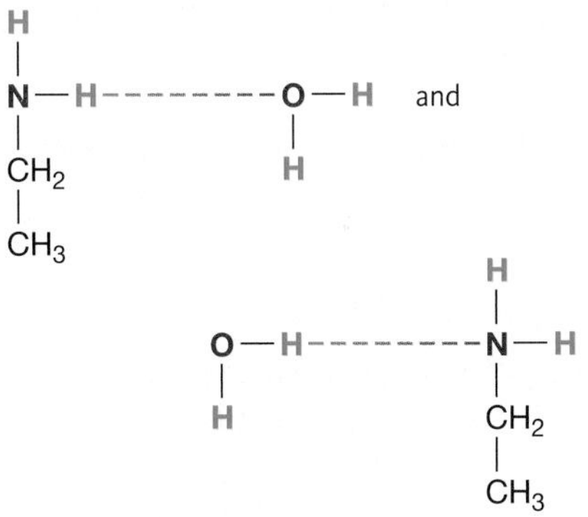 $CH_3—CH_2—N(H)—H$ - - - - - - - - $O(H)—H$ and

$H—O—H$ - - - - - - - - $N(H)(H)—CH_2—CH_3$

11.31 4-Methylpyridine boils at 145°C, and aniline boils at 185°C. Aniline has two hydrogen atoms attached to the nitrogen atom, so aniline molecules can be both hydrogen bond donors and acceptors, allowing them to form hydrogen bonds to each other. 4-Methylpyridine does not have a hydrogen atom attached to the nitrogen atom, so it cannot be a hydrogen bond donor; 4-methylpyridine molecules cannot form hydrogen bonds to each other.

11.33 ethylamine, because it has a smaller hydrophobic region than hexylamine

Section 11.4 Core Problems

11.35 a) 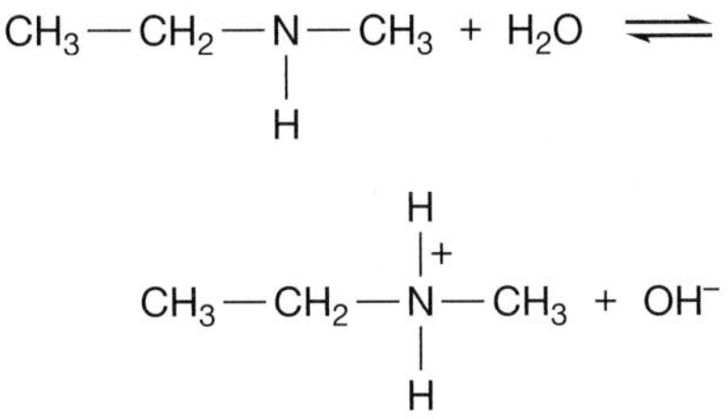 $CH_3—CH_2—N(H)—CH_3 + H_2O \rightleftharpoons CH_3—CH_2—N^{+}(H)(H)—CH_3 + OH^-$

b) 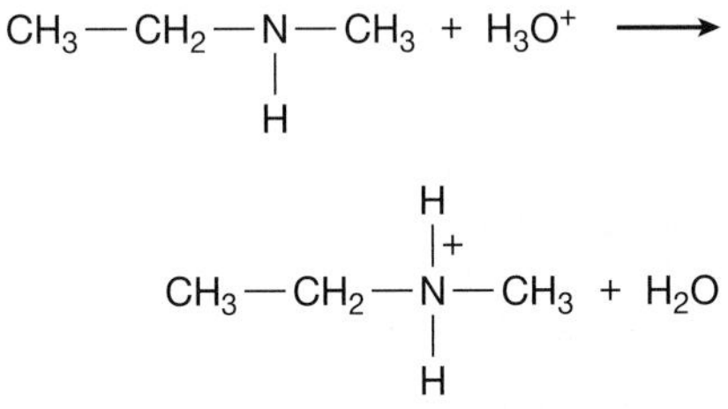 $CH_3—CH_2—N(H)—CH_3 + H_3O^+ \longrightarrow CH_3—CH_2—N^{+}(H)(H)—CH_3 + H_2O$

c) 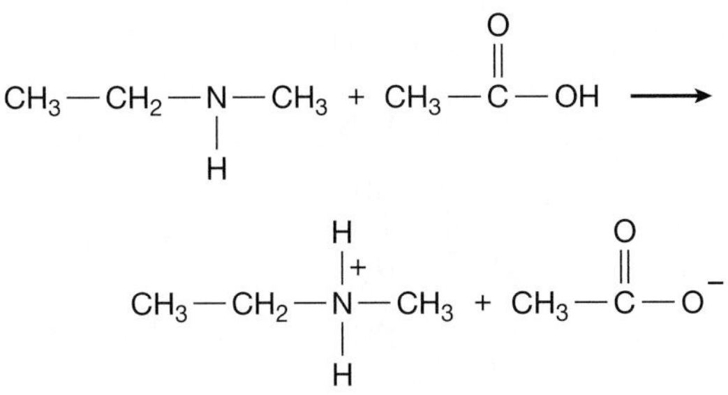 $CH_3—CH_2—N(H)—CH_3 + CH_3—C(=O)—OH \longrightarrow CH_3—CH_2—N^{+}(H)(H)—CH_3 + CH_3—C(=O)—O^-$

11.37 $^{+}H_3N—CH(CH_2—CH_2—S—CH_3)—C(=O)—O^-$

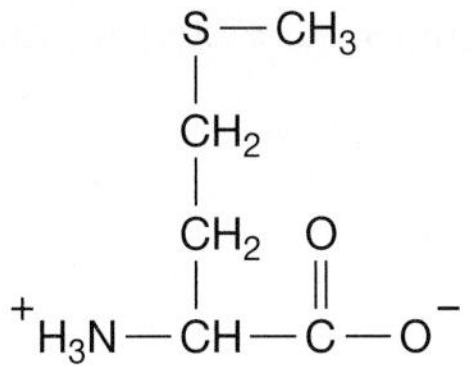

11.39 a) $CH_3–CH_2–CH_2–NH_3^+$

b) $CH_3–CH_2–CH_2–CH_2–NH_3^+ \ Br^-$

c) $CH_3—CH_2—CH_2—CH_2—CH_2—CH_2—\overset{+}{N}H_2—CH_3$ $H—C(=O)—O^-$

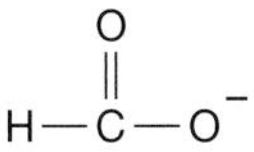

Section 11.5 Core Problems

11.41 Pseudoephedrine and fenfluramine are related to phenethylamine, and psilocybin is related to tryptamine.

11.43 a) 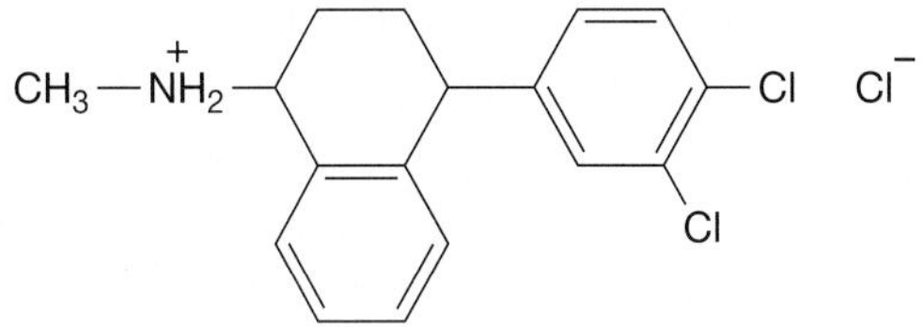 $CH_3—\overset{+}{N}H_2$–(tetrahydronaphthalene ring)–(dichlorophenyl ring: Cl, Cl) Cl^-

b) Sertraline hydrochloride is more soluble in water than sertraline is.

11.45 no, because it does not contain an amine group

Section 11.6 Core Problems

11.47 a) 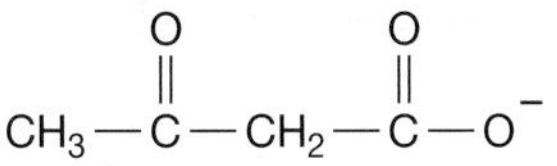 $CH_3—C(=O)—CH_2—C(=O)—O^-$

b) $CH_3—\overset{+}{N}H(CH_3)—CH_2—CH_3$

c) (benzene ring with $CH_2—CH_3$ and OH)

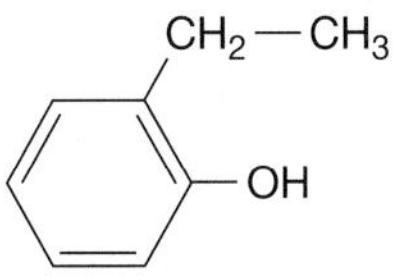

d) 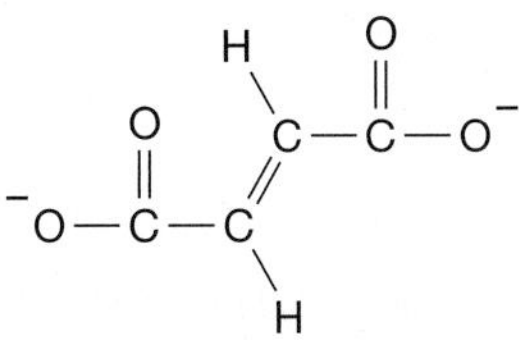 $^{-}O—C(=O)—C(H)=C(H)—C(=O)—O^-$

e) 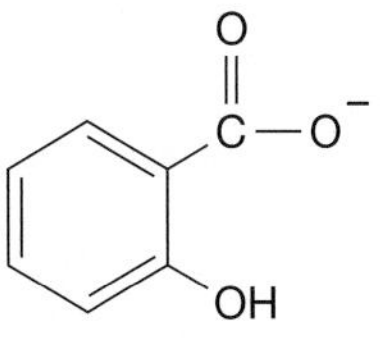 (benzene ring with $C(=O)—O^-$ and OH)

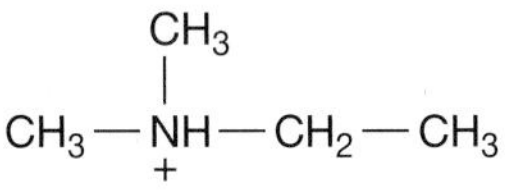

f) $^{+}NH_3–CH_2–CH_2–CH_2–CH_2–CH_2–NH_3^+$

11.49 Glyceraldehyde-3-phosphate forms a mixture of the following two molecules:

$$^{-}O-P(=O)(O^{-})-O-CH_2-CH(OH)-C(=O)-H$$

$$HO-P(=O)(O^{-})-O-CH_2-CH(OH)-C(=O)-H$$

CHAPTER 12

Try It Yourself Exercises

12.1 $CH_3-CH_2-CH_2-O-CH_2-CH_2-CH_3$

12.2 $CH_3-CH_2-CH_2-CH_2-O-CH_2-CH_2-CH_2-CH_3$

12.3 $CH_3-CH_2-C(=O)-O-C_6H_5$ (phenyl ring)

12.4 $CH_3-CH_2-CH_2-CH_2-C(=O)-NH_2$

12.5 $^{-}O-P(=O)(O^{-})-O-CH_3$

12.6 $HO-CH_2-CH_2-O-CH_2-CH_2-O-CH_2-CH_2-OH$

12.7 $H-N(H)-CH(CH_3)-C(=O)-N(H)-CH(CH_2-C(=O)-NH_2)-C(=O)-N(H)-CH((CH_2)_4-NH_2)-C(=O)-OH$

12.8 $HO-C_6H_4-C(CH_3)_2-C_6H_4-O-C(=O)-O-C_6H_4-C(CH_3)_2-C_6H_4-O-C(=O)-OH$

12.9 $C_6H_5-OH + HO-CH_2-CH_2-CH(CH_3)-CH_3$

12.10 $CH_3-C(CH_3)_2-CH_2-C(=O)-OH + HO-CH_3$

12.11 $NH_3 + HO-C(=O)-CH_2-CH_2-CH_2-CH_3$

12.12 $CH_3-C(CH_3)_2-CH_2-C(=O)-O^{-} + HO-CH_3$

12.13 $CH_3-CH_2-NH_3^{+} + {}^{-}O-C(=O)-CH_3$

12.14 $CH_3-C(=O)-O^{-}\ K^{+} + HO-C_6H_{10}-CH_3$ (cyclohexane ring)

Section 12.1 Core Problems

12.1 a) $CH_3-CH_2-O-CH_2-CH_2-CH_2-CH_3$

b) $CH_3-CH_2-CH_2-O-CH_2-CH_2-CH_3$

c) $CH_3-CH_2-O-CH(CH_3)-CH_2-CH_2-CH_3$

12.3 a) ethyl pentyl ether b) dimethyl ether

Section 12.2 Core Problems

12.5 a) $CH_3-C(=O)-O-C_6H_5$ (phenyl ring)

b) $CH_3-CH_2-C(=O)-O-CH(CH_3)-CH_3$

12.7 a) $CH_3-CH_2-N(CH_3)-C(=O)-H$

b) $C_6H_5-C(=O)-N(CH_2-CH_3)-CH_2-CH_3$ (phenyl ring)

12.9 the first molecule

12.11 a) 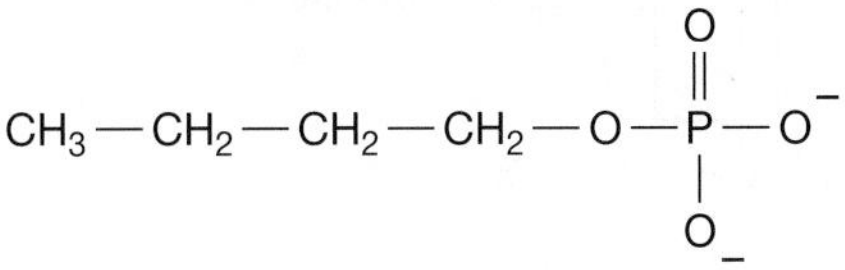 $CH_3{-}CH_2{-}CH_2{-}CH_2{-}O{-}P(=O)(O^-){-}O^-$

b) 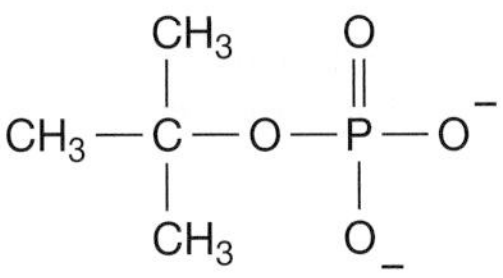 $CH_3{-}C(CH_3)_2{-}O{-}P(=O)(O^-){-}O^-$

Section 12.3 Core Problems

12.13 $HO{-}C_6H_4{-}O{-}C_6H_4{-}O{-}C_6H_4{-}OH$

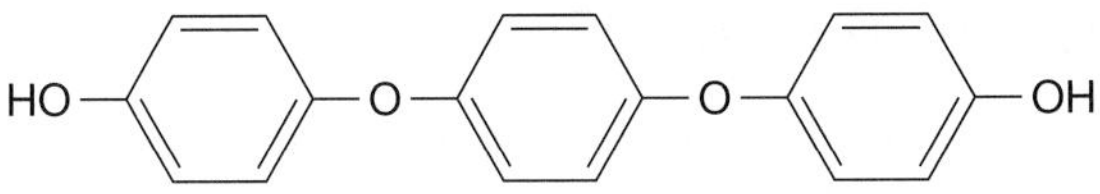

12.15 $HO{-}CH(CH_3){-}C(=O){-}O{-}CH(CH_3){-}C(=O){-}O{-}CH(CH_3){-}C(=O){-}OH$

12.17 $NH_2{-}CH[CH(CH_3){-}CH_2{-}CH_3]{-}C(=O){-}NH{-}CH[CH(CH_3){-}CH_2{-}CH_3]{-}C(=O){-}NH{-}CH[CH(CH_3){-}CH_2{-}CH_3]{-}C(=O){-}OH$

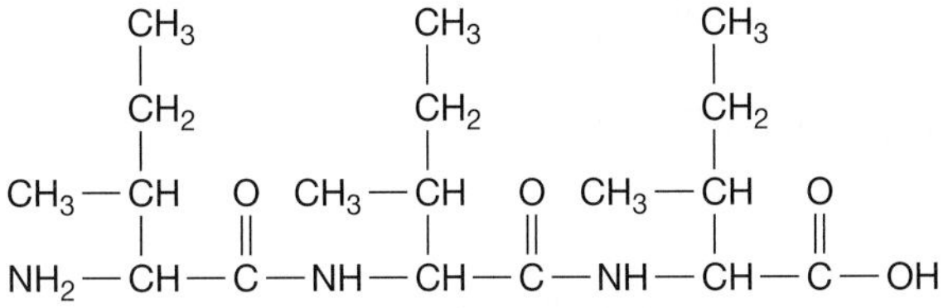

12.19

$NH_2{-}CH_2{-}CH_2{-}NH{-}C(=O){-}C(=O){-}NH{-}CH_2{-}CH_2{-}NH{-}C(=O){-}C(=O){-}OH$

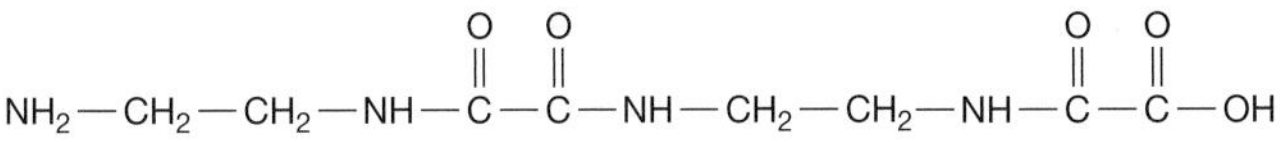

Section 12.4 Core Problems

12.21 a) 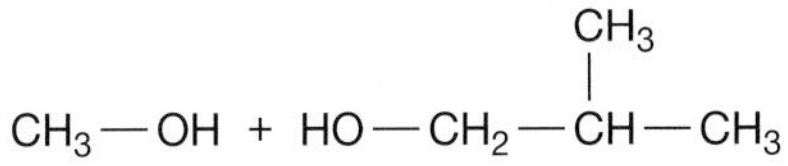 $CH_3{-}OH + HO{-}CH_2{-}CH(CH_3){-}CH_3$

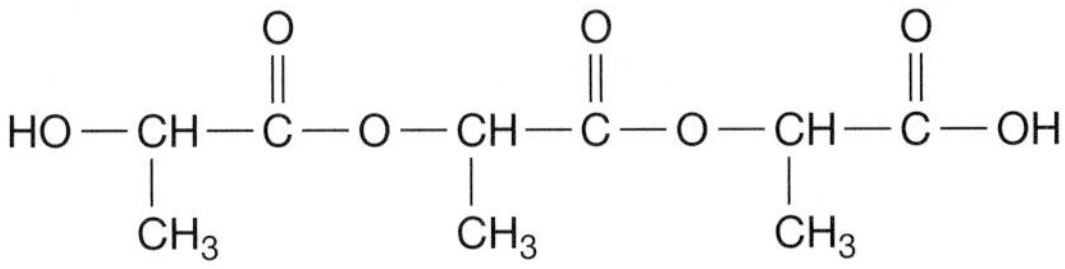

b) 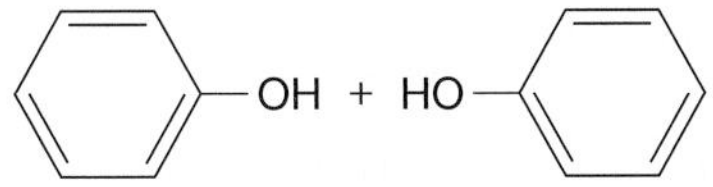 $C_6H_5{-}OH + HO{-}C_6H_5$

12.23 a) 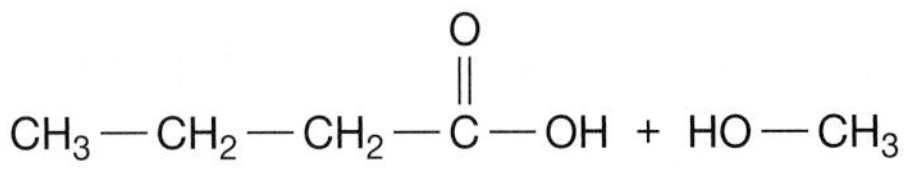 $CH_3{-}CH_2{-}CH_2{-}C(=O){-}OH + HO{-}CH_3$

b) $C_5H_9{-}OH + HO{-}C(=O){-}H$ (cyclopentyl)

c) $CH_3{-}CH_2{-}C(=O){-}OH + HO{-}CH(CH_3){-}CH_3$

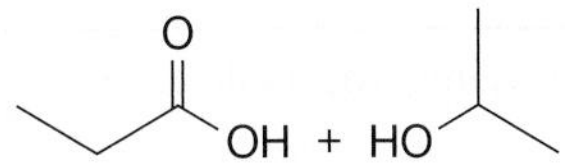

12.25 a) 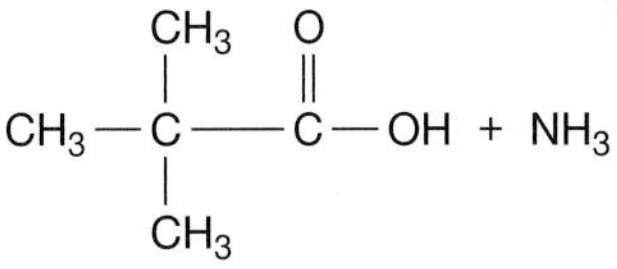 $CH_3{-}C(CH_3)_2{-}C(=O){-}OH + NH_3$

b) $CH_3{-}N(CH_3){-}H + HO{-}C(=O){-}CH_2{-}CH_2{-}CH_2{-}CH_2{-}CH_3$

c) pyrrolidine $N{-}H + HO{-}C(=O){-}CH(CH_3){-}CH_2{-}CH_2{-}CH_3$

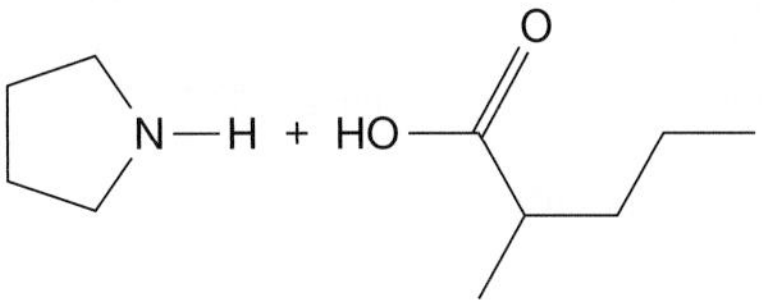

12.27 a) 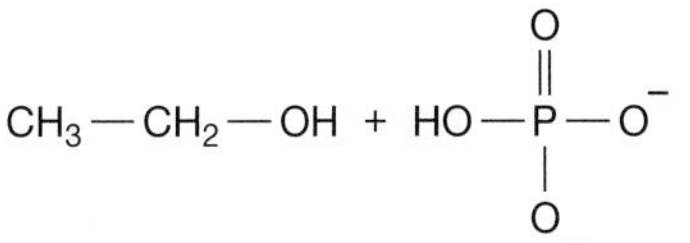 $CH_3{-}CH_2{-}OH + HO{-}P(=O)(O^-){-}O^-$

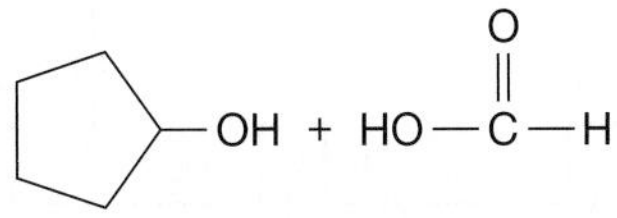

b) 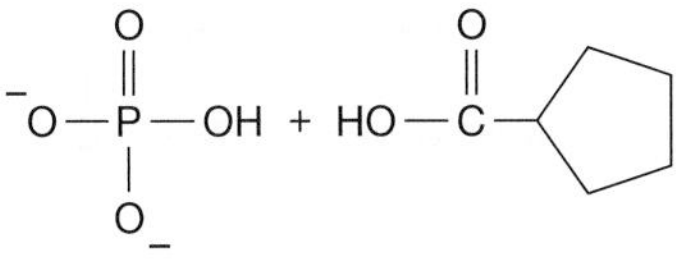 $^-O{-}P(=O)(O^-){-}OH + HO{-}C(=O){-}C_5H_9$ (cyclopentyl)

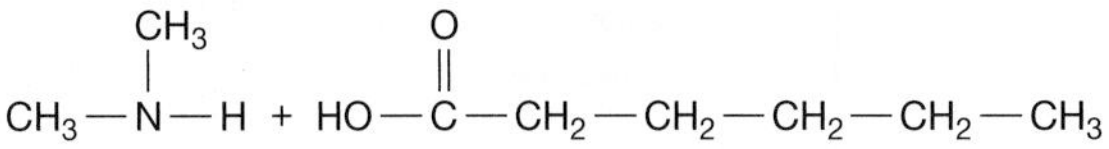

c) $CH_3{-}C(=O){-}OH + HS{-}CH_2{-}CH_3$

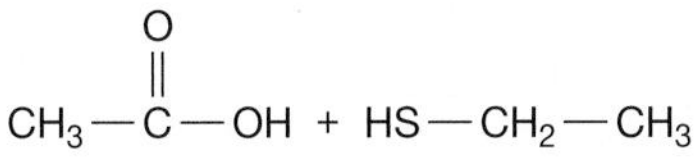

d) 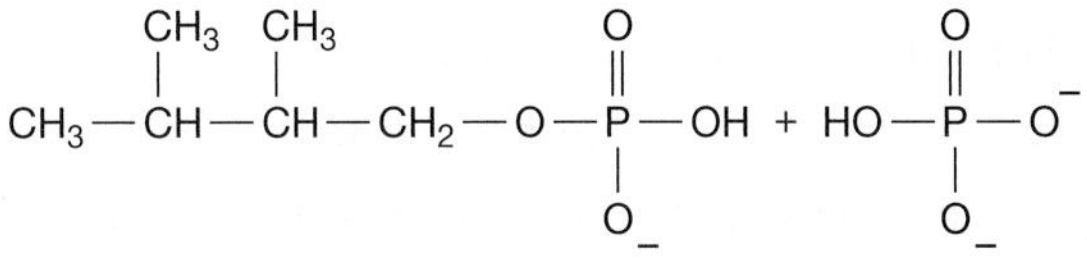 $CH_3{-}CH(CH_3){-}CH(CH_3){-}CH_2{-}O{-}P(=O)(O^-){-}OH + HO{-}P(=O)(O^-){-}O^-$

Section 12.5 Core Problems

12.29 a) 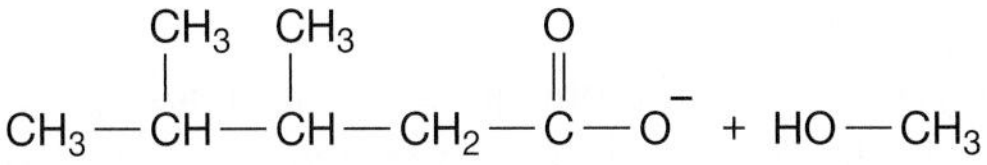 $CH_3{-}CH(CH_3){-}CH(CH_3){-}CH_2{-}C(=O){-}O^- + HO{-}CH_3$

b) 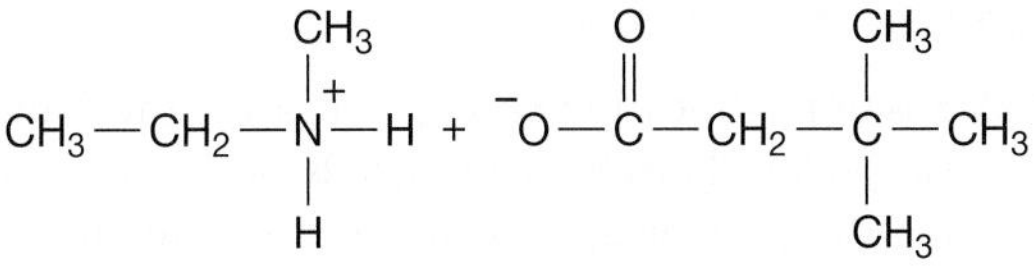 $CH_3{-}CH_2{-}N^+H(CH_3){-}H + {}^-O{-}C(=O){-}CH_2{-}C(CH_3)_2{-}CH_3$

12.31 a) 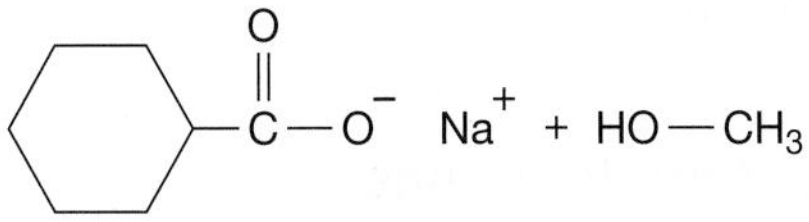 $C_6H_{11}{-}C(=O){-}O^-\ Na^+ + HO{-}CH_3$ (cyclohexyl)

b) 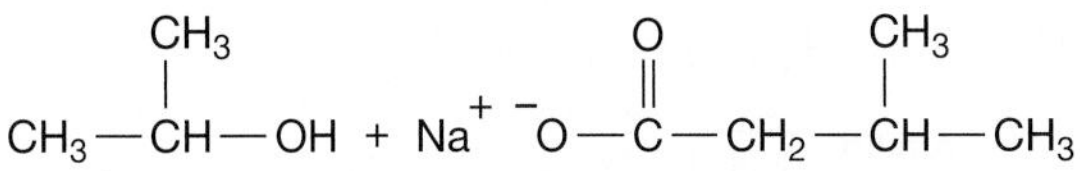 $CH_3{-}CH(CH_3){-}OH + Na^+\ {}^-O{-}C(=O){-}CH_2{-}CH(CH_3){-}CH_3$

12.33 $CH_3{-}(CH_2)_7{-}CH{=}CH{-}(CH_2)_7{-}C(=O){-}O^-\ K^+$

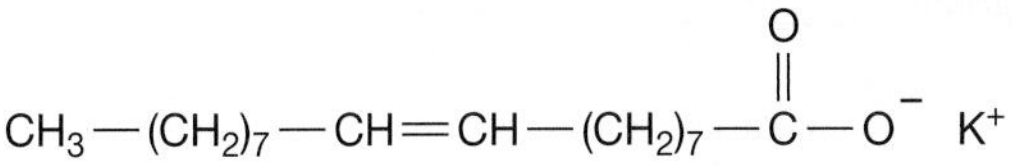

CHAPTER 13

Try It Yourself Exercises

13.1

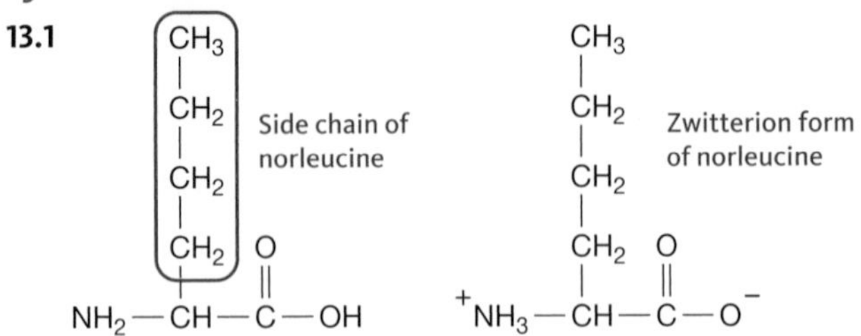

13.2 hydrophilic and acidic

13.3

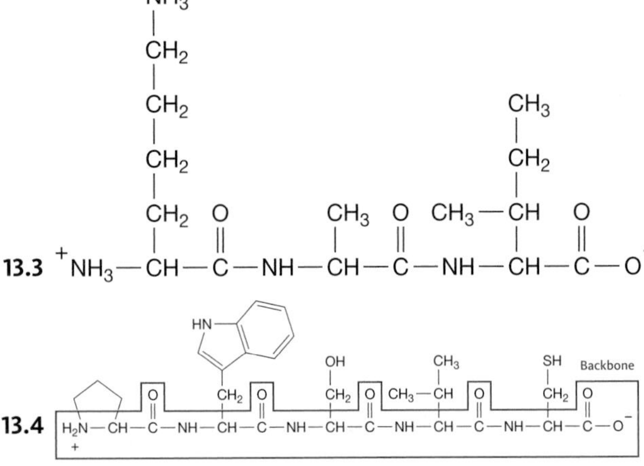

13.4

Pro–Trp–Ser–Val–Cys

13.5 aspartic acid and arginine

13.6 a) The two thiol groups form a disulfide bridge.

b) The side chains form a hydrogen bond.

13.7 At pH 7, lysine side chains are positively charged, so they repel each other strongly. At pH 12, each side chain loses H^+ and becomes an uncharged amino group. The amino groups no longer repel each other and can now form a hydrogen bond, so they are attracted to each other.

13.8 yes, because the phosphate group could potentially condense with either of the two carboxyl groups in aspartic acid, giving two different products

13.9 a positive effector

13.10 Susan is not eating enough carbohydrates and fat to supply her body's energy needs, so her body is burning the protein she eats instead of using it to make body proteins.

Section 13.1 Core Problems

13.1

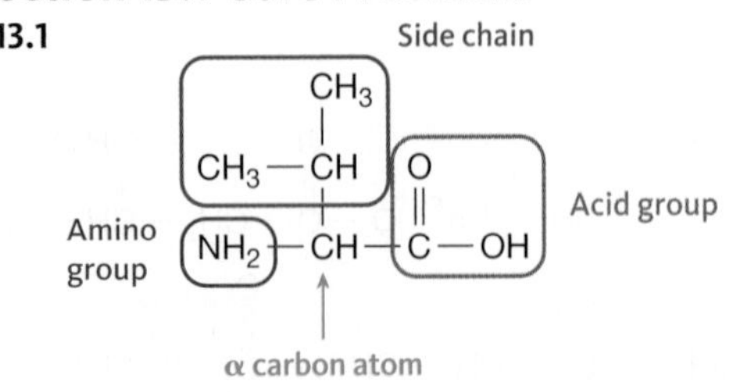

13.3 a) $NH_2—CH(CH_2—CH_2—OH)—C(=O)—OH$ (Side chain of homoserine)

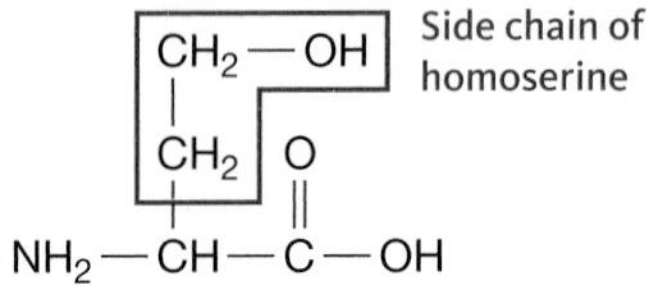

b) $^+NH_3—CH(CH_2—CH_2—OH)—C(=O)—O^-$ (Zwitterion form of homoserine)

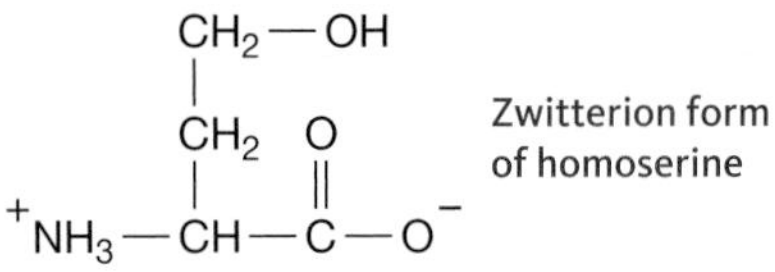

c) hydrophilic and neutral

13.5 $^+NH_3—CH(CH_2—CH_2—CH_2—NH—C(=O)—NH_2)—C(=O)—O^-$

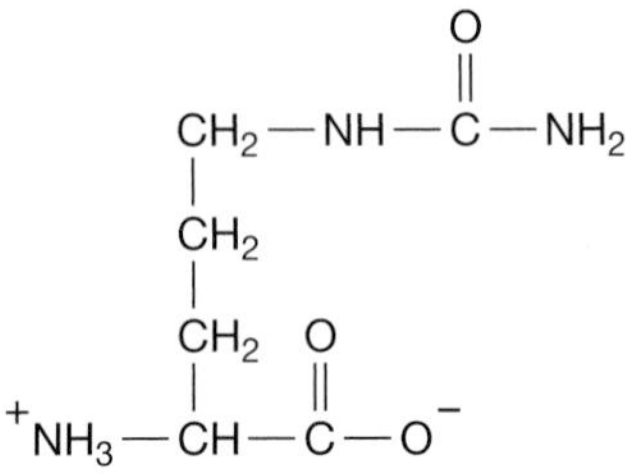

13.7 Amino acids are classified based on the unionized form of their side chains. The unionized form of lysine contains an amine group, which is a base, so lysine is classified as a basic amino acid.

13.9 $^+NH_3—CH(CH(OH)—CH_3)—C(=O)—O^-$

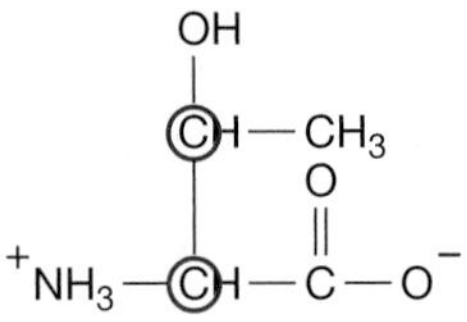

Section 13.2 Core Problems

13.11 a) $^+NH_3—CH(CH_2—CH_2—S—CH_3)—C(=O)—NH—CH(CH_2—CH_2—S—CH_3)—C(=O)—O^-$

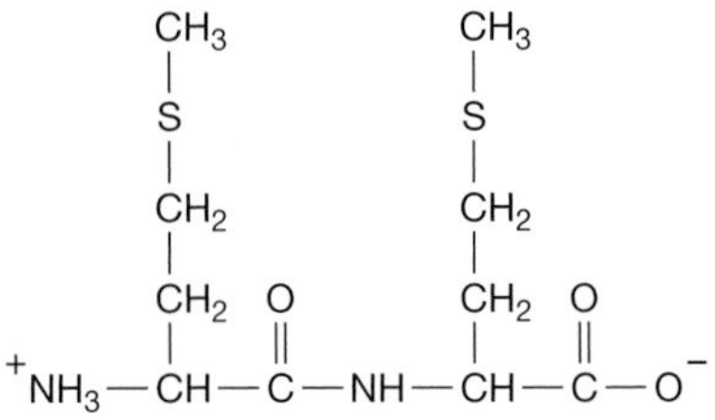

b) $^+NH_3—CH(CH_3)—C(=O)—NH—CH(CH_2—CH_2—CH_2—NH—C(=NH_2^+)—NH_2)—C(=O)—NH—CH_2—C(=O)—O^-$

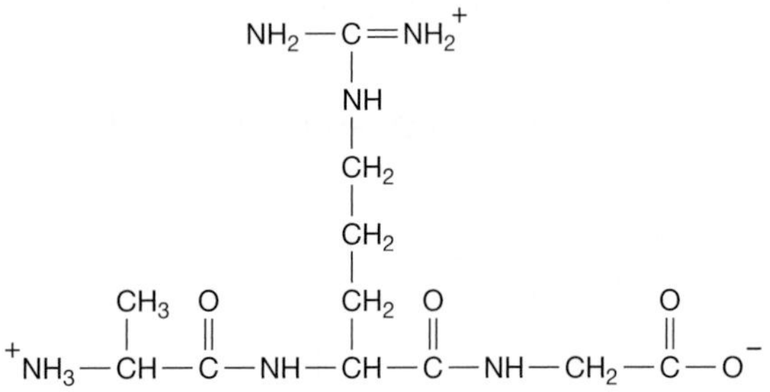

13.13 a) $^+NH_3—CH(CH_2C_6H_5)—C(=O)—NH—CH(CH_2—SH)—C(=O)—NH—CH(CH(CH_3)—CH_2—CH_3)—C(=O)—O^-$ (Backbone)

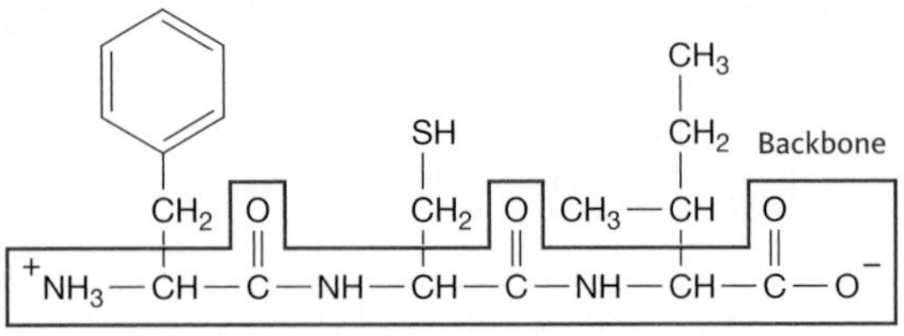

b) phenylalanine, cysteine, and isoleucine

c) phenylalanine

13.15 the sequence of amino acids that makes up the protein

13.17 In an α-helix, the backbone is twisted into a coil (a helix) and the side chains project outward from the coil.

13.19 the hydrogen atom and the oxygen atom

13.21 A β-turn is an abrupt turn in the polypeptide backbone. Proline is often found at a β-turn because its five-membered ring does not allow it to form one of the normal secondary structures and its nitrogen atom does not have a hydrogen atom attached to it, so it cannot participate in a hydrogen bond.

Section 13.3 Core Problems

13.23 The polypeptide chain folds up into a compact shape, like a ball but uneven and lumpy.

13.25 phenylalanine; glycine is also often found in the interior

13.27

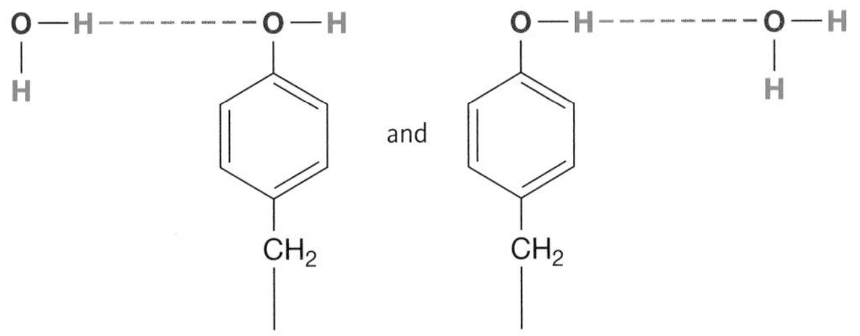

O—H--------O—H (water H–O–H hydrogen bonded to the O—H of a tyrosine side chain: ring—CH_2—) and O—H--------O—H (tyrosine side chain O—H hydrogen bonded to water O, with H)

13.29

O—H--------O (serine side chain CH_2—O—H hydrogen bonded to the C=O of an asparagine side chain CH_2—C(=O)—NH_2) and asparagine side chain CH_2—C(=O)—N(H)—H------O—H (hydrogen bonded to the O of a serine side chain CH_2—O—H)

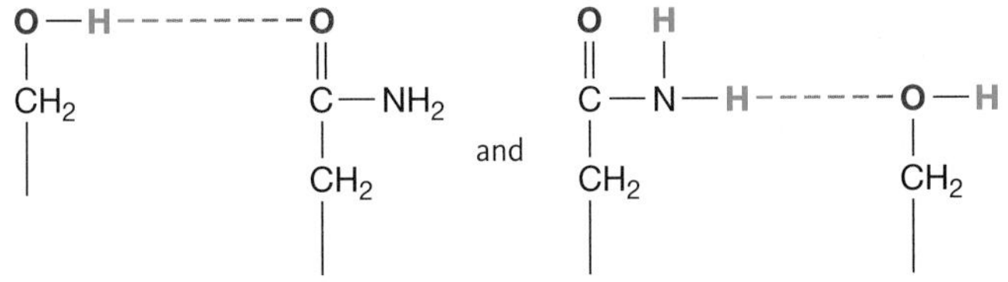

13.31 aspartic acid

13.33 a) The amide group of asparagine and the hydroxyl group of threonine form a hydrogen bond.
b) The side chains cluster together due to the hydrophobic interaction.
c) The side chain of threonine forms a hydrogen bond with the water molecule.

13.35 a) quaternary structure b) tertiary structure
c) secondary structure d) tertiary structure

Section 13.4 Core Problems

13.37 The way the backbone is folded and coiled changes, so the shape of the entire protein changes as well.

13.39 a) Adding HCl lowers the pH of the solution, converting the negatively charged carboxyl groups of aspartic acid and glutamic acid into unionized carboxylic acid groups and disrupting the ion–ion attraction within the polypeptide.
b) Hg^{2+} breaks the disulfide bridges in the polypeptide.
c) Agitating the protein solution disrupts many of the weak interactions between amino acid side chains.

Section 13.5 Core Problems

13.41 a protein that catalyzes a chemical reaction

13.43 The substrates are sucrose and water, the products are glucose and fructose, and the enzyme is sucrase.

13.45 a) the location on the surface of an enzyme where the substrate binds and the chemical reaction occurs
b) a combination of the enzyme and the substrate that forms when the substrate binds to the active site of the enzyme

13.47 Magnesium ions are positively charged, and phosphate ions are negatively charged. The phosphate is attracted to the magnesium, pulling it into the active site and holding it in place.

13.49 Enzymes decrease the activation energy of the reaction that they catalyze.

13.51 Papain shows its highest activity around pH 6, and catalase shows its highest activity around pH 8.

13.53 increase, because increasing the temperature raises the number of molecules that have enough energy to react (the activation energy)

13.55 a) a competitive inhibitor b) a positive effector

13.57 a negative effector

Section 13.6 Core Problems

13.59 A cofactor is any substance that an enzyme requires to be active. A coenzyme is an organic molecule that an enzyme requires to be active.

13.61 yes, because enzymes that use FAD require it to be active

13.63 from our diet

13.65 niacin

Section 13.7 Core Problems

13.67 The enzyme would be broken down into amino acids in the digestive system.

13.69 Our bodies can make some of the amino acids from other nutrients, so these amino acids are considered nonessential.

13.71 A person must eat enough protein to supply all of the essential amino acids and to supply enough nitrogen to make the nonessential amino acids (if they are not already present in the dietary protein).

13.73 An undernourished person burns amino acids to supply energy, leaving insufficient amounts of amino acids to build body proteins.

13.75 plants and most bacteria

13.77 Nitrogen fixation is the set of chemical reactions that certain bacteria use to convert nitrogen in the atmosphere (N_2) into ammonium ions. These organisms make nitrogen available to all other living organisms to build amino acids and other nitrogen-containing molecules.

13.79 urea

CHAPTER 14

Try It Yourself Exercises

14.1 H, H, O, CH_2OH, H, OH, OH, Ⓒ, OH, OH, H, H, hexose

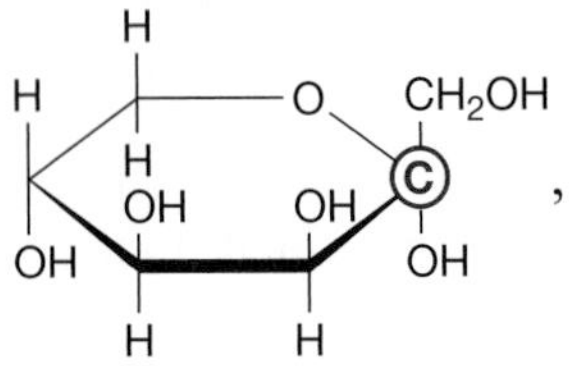

14.2 the β anomer

14.3 CH_2OH, HO, O, H, OH, H, H, H, OH, O, CH_2OH, O, OH, H, H, OH, H, H, H, OH

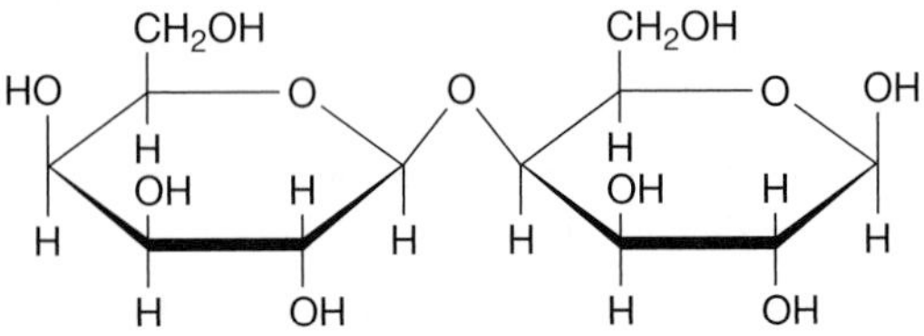

14.4
$CH_3-(CH_2)_7-CH=CH-(CH_2)_7-C(=O)-O-CH_2$
$CH_3-(CH_2)_7-CH=CH-(CH_2)_7-C(=O)-O-CH$
$CH_3-(CH_2)_7-CH=CH-(CH_2)_7-C(=O)-O-CH_2$

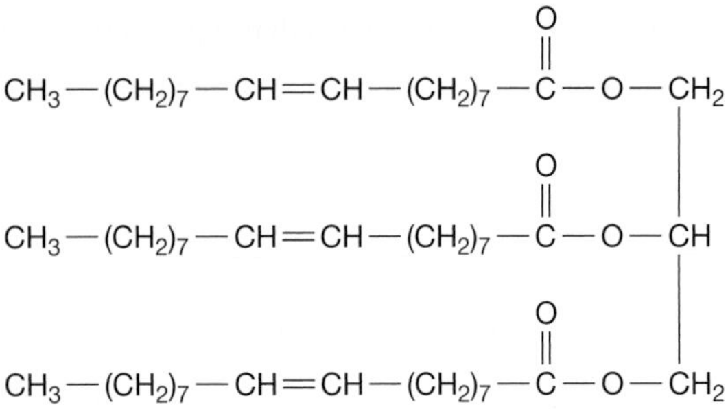

14.5 an omega-7 fatty acid

14.6 Triglyceride 3 has a higher melting point than tryglycerides 1 and 2.

14.7
$CH_3-(CH_2)_{10}-C(=O)-O-CH_2$
$CH_3-(CH_2)_{16}-C(=O)-O-CH$
$CH_3-(CH_2)_{14}-C(=O)-O-CH_2$

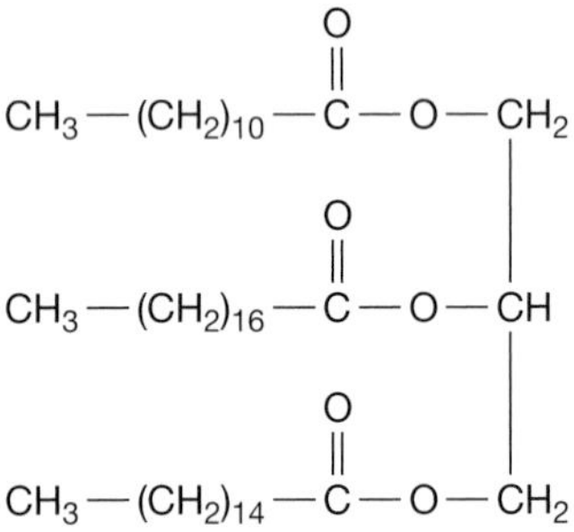

14.8 a)
$CH_3-(CH_2)_7-CH=CH-(CH_2)_7-C(=O)-O^-\ K^+$ $\quad$ $HO-CH_2$
$CH_3-(CH_2)_7-CH=CH-(CH_2)_7-C(=O)-O^-\ K^+$ $\quad + \quad$ $HO-CH$
$CH_3-(CH_2)_{14}-C(=O)-O^-\ K^+$ $\quad$ $HO-CH_2$

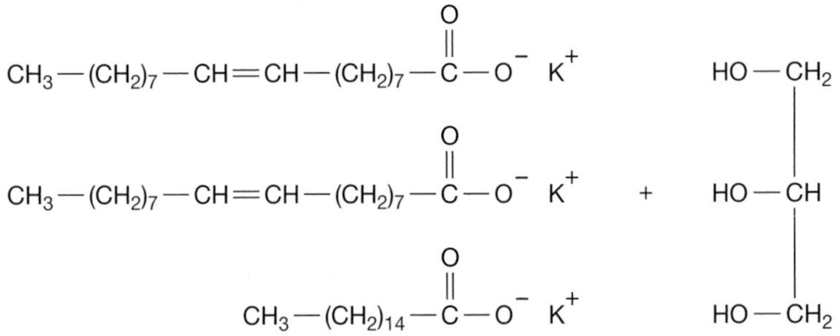

b)
$CH_3-(CH_2)_7-CH=CH-(CH_2)_7-C(=O)-OH$ $\quad$ $HO-CH_2$
$CH_3-(CH_2)_7-CH=CH-(CH_2)_7-C(=O)-OH$ $\quad + \quad$ $HO-CH$
$CH_3-(CH_2)_{14}-C(=O)-OH$ $\quad$ $HO-CH_2$

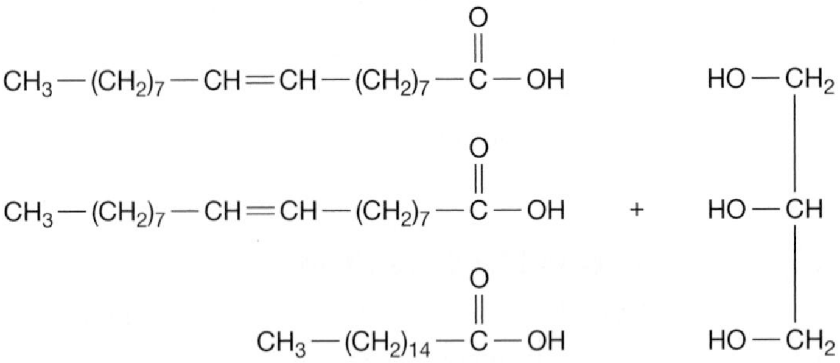

14.9
$CH_3-(CH_2)_{16}-C(=O)-O-CH_2$
$CH_3-(CH_2)_4-CH=CH-CH_2-CH=CH-(CH_2)_7-C(=O)-O-CH$
$CH_2-O-P(=O)(O^-)-O-CH_2-CH(C(=O)-O^-)-NH_3^+$

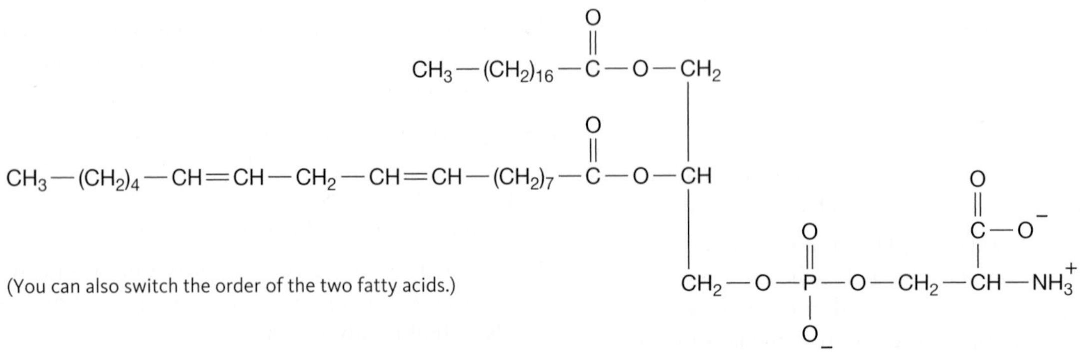

(You can also switch the order of the two fatty acids.)

14.10 passive transport

Section 14.1 Core Problems

14.1 $C_6H_{12}O_6$

14.3 a) hexose b) tetrose

14.5 a)

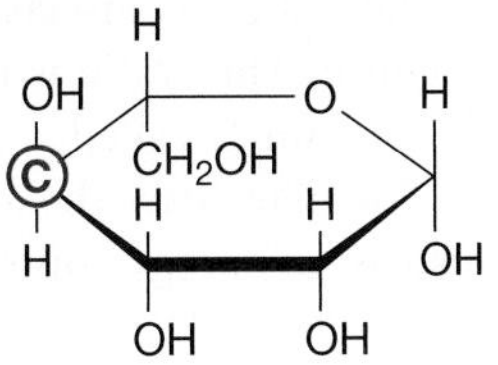

b)

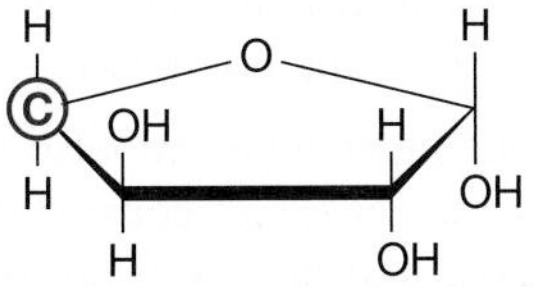

14.7 glucose, mannose, and galactose

14.9 glucose, because it contains several hydrophilic groups, while cyclohexane is entirely hydrophobic

Section 14.2 Core Problems

14.11

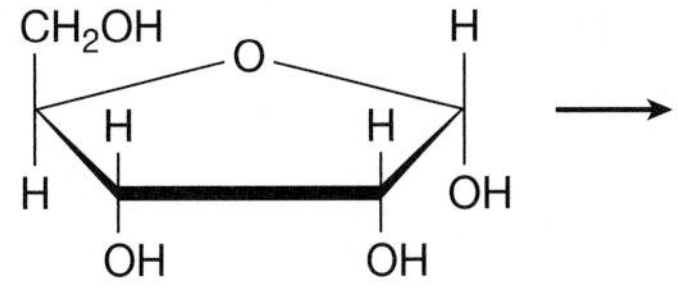

Ribose
(ring form)

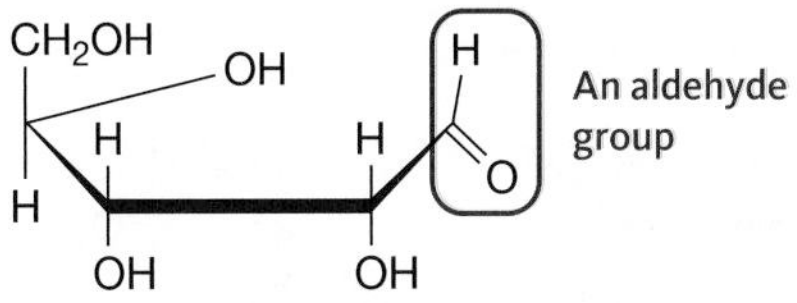

An aldehyde group

Ribose
(open-chain form)

14.13 a) yes, because it contains a hemiacetal group (outlined in red)

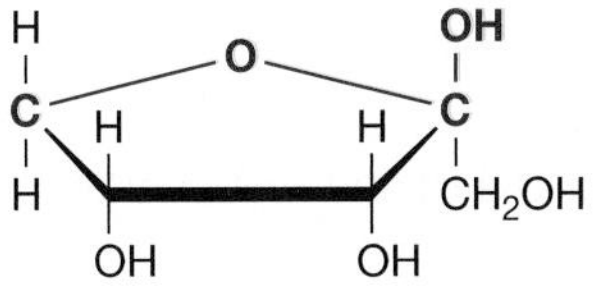

b) a ketose

14.15 a)

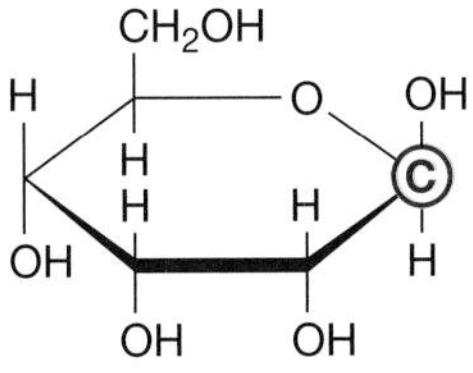

b) β-D-allose

14.17

α-D-allose

β-D-allose

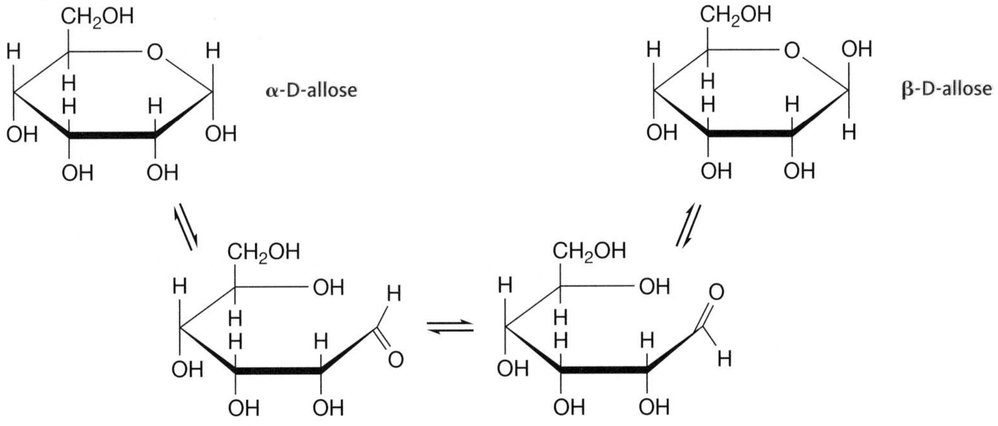

14.19 α-L-fructose

Section 14.3 Core Problems

14.21 α(1→4), because the oxygen atom links carbon 1 of the left-hand ring to carbon 4 of the right-hand ring, and the oxygen is below carbon 1 of the left-hand ring (the α position)

14.23 [Structures: two disaccharide ring structures shown, linked "or"]

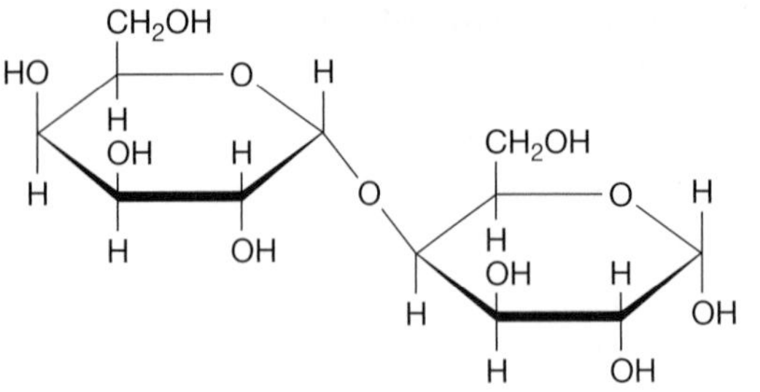

Section 14.4 Core Problems

14.25 a) β-maltose
b) yes, because the right-hand ring contains a hemiacetal group

14.27 glucose and fructose

14.29 a) sucrose has only one form, because the glycosidic bond uses the hydroxyl groups on the anomeric carbon atoms of both rings, so there are no hemiacetal groups available to open and rotate
b) no, because it does not have a hemiacetal group

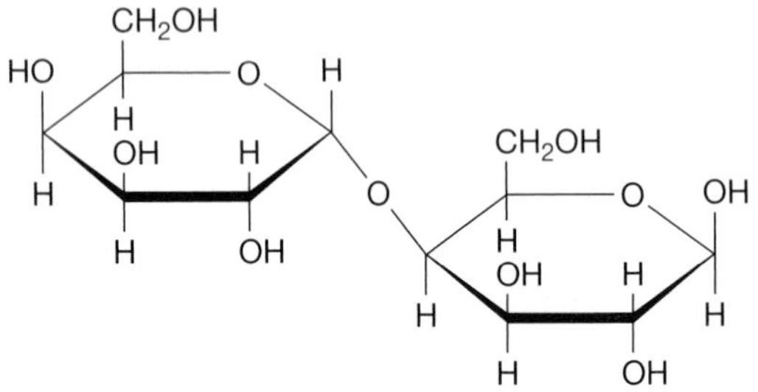

14.31 Many people lose the ability to make lactase as they age, so they cannot break lactose down into monosaccharides.

14.33 a) Animals with jointed shells such as insects, spiders, and crabs make chitin. The chitin is the main structural material of the animal's shell.
b) Plants make amylose. The plant uses the amylose to store glucose for use as an energy source.

14.35 glucose

14.37 Chitin contains β(1→4) glycosidic bonds, and amylose contains α(1→4) glycosidic bonds.

14.39 amylase and a debranching enzyme (we also need maltase, because these two enzymes convert starch into a mixture of glucose and maltose); our digestive tracts make these enzymes

Section 14.5 Core Problems

14.41 a) saturated b) polyunsaturated

14.43 a) The melting point of the first fatty acid is higher than room temperature, and the melting point of the second fatty acid is lower than room temperature.
b) The first fatty acid is a solid, and the second fatty acid is a liquid.

14.45

a) 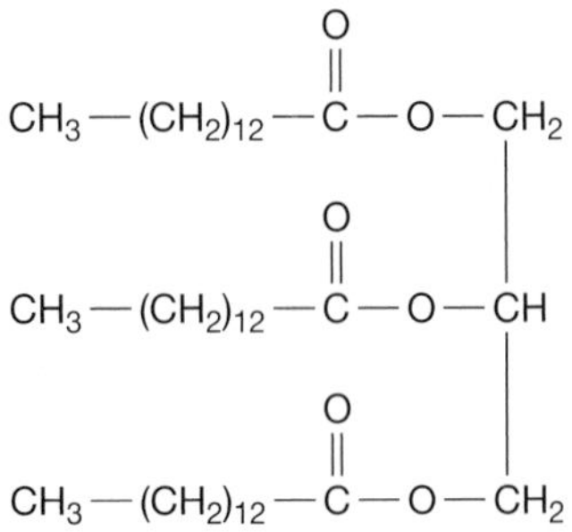 $CH_3-(CH_2)_{12}-C(=O)-O-CH_2$
$CH_3-(CH_2)_{12}-C(=O)-O-CH$
$CH_3-(CH_2)_{12}-C(=O)-O-CH_2$

b) 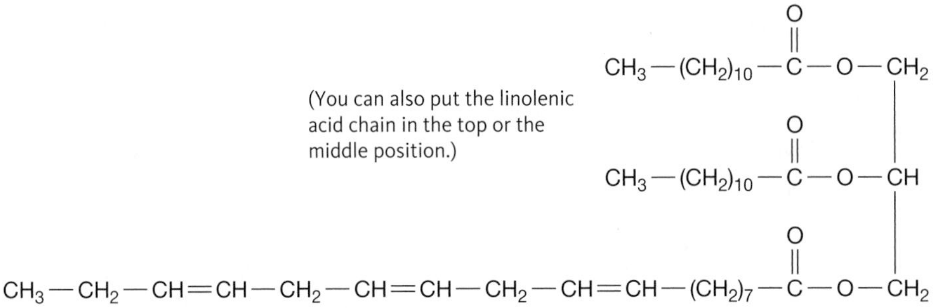 $CH_3-(CH_2)_{10}-C(=O)-O-CH_2$
$CH_3-(CH_2)_{10}-C(=O)-O-CH$
$CH_3-CH_2-CH=CH-CH_2-CH=CH-CH_2-CH=CH-(CH_2)_7-C(=O)-O-CH_2$

(You can also put the linolenic acid chain in the top or the middle position.)

14.47 triglyceride 1 (highest m.p.) → triglyceride 3 → triglyceride 2 (lowest m.p.)

14.49 an omega-6 fatty acid

Section 14.6 Core Problems

14.51 a)

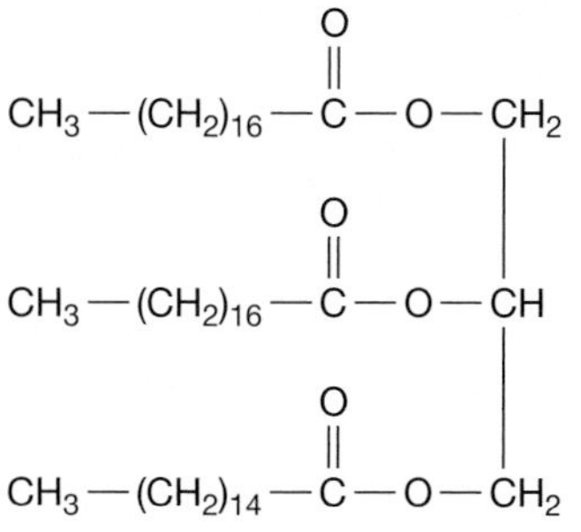

$$
\begin{array}{l}
CH_3-(CH_2)_{16}-\overset{O}{\overset{\|}{C}}-O-CH_2 \\
\qquad\qquad\qquad\qquad\qquad\quad | \\
CH_3-(CH_2)_{16}-\overset{O}{\overset{\|}{C}}-O-CH \\
\qquad\qquad\qquad\qquad\qquad\quad | \\
CH_3-(CH_2)_{14}-\overset{O}{\overset{\|}{C}}-O-CH_2
\end{array}
$$

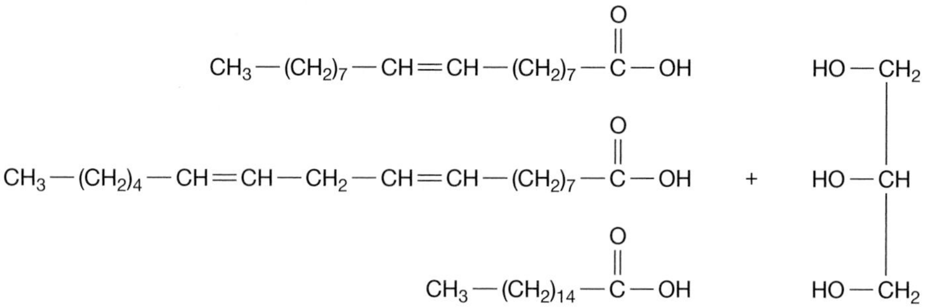

b)

$$
\begin{array}{rcl}
CH_3-(CH_2)_7-CH{=}CH-(CH_2)_7-\overset{O}{\overset{\|}{C}}-OH & & HO-CH_2 \\
CH_3-(CH_2)_4-CH{=}CH-CH_2-CH{=}CH-(CH_2)_7-\overset{O}{\overset{\|}{C}}-OH & + & HO-CH \\
CH_3-(CH_2)_{14}-\overset{O}{\overset{\|}{C}}-OH & & HO-CH_2
\end{array}
$$

c)

$$
\begin{array}{rcl}
CH_3-(CH_2)_7-CH{=}CH-(CH_2)_7-\overset{O}{\overset{\|}{C}}-O^-\ Na^+ & & HO-CH_2 \\
CH_3-(CH_2)_4-CH{=}CH-CH_2-CH{=}CH-(CH_2)_7-\overset{O}{\overset{\|}{C}}-O^-\ Na^+ & + & HO-CH \\
CH_3-(CH_2)_{14}-\overset{O}{\overset{\|}{C}}-O^-\ Na^+ & & HO-CH_2
\end{array}
$$

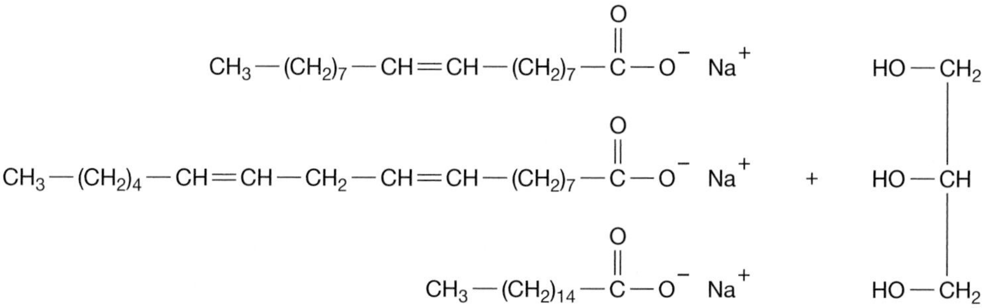

d) the three sodium salts in the answer to part c

14.53 oleic acid, linoleic acid, and palmitic acid

14.55 A *trans* fatty acid is a fatty acid that contains a *trans* double bond. *Trans* fatty acids are formed when fats are partially hydrogenated.

14.57 two fatty acids (in their ionized form) and a monoglyceride (a compound made from glycerol and one fatty acid)

14.59 Bile salts break up droplets of fats and allow them to mix with water, increasing the number of fat molecules that are in contact with the digestive juices.

Section 14.7 Core Problems

14.61 the phosphate group and the amino alcohol (or other polar molecule) that is linked to the phosphate group

14.63

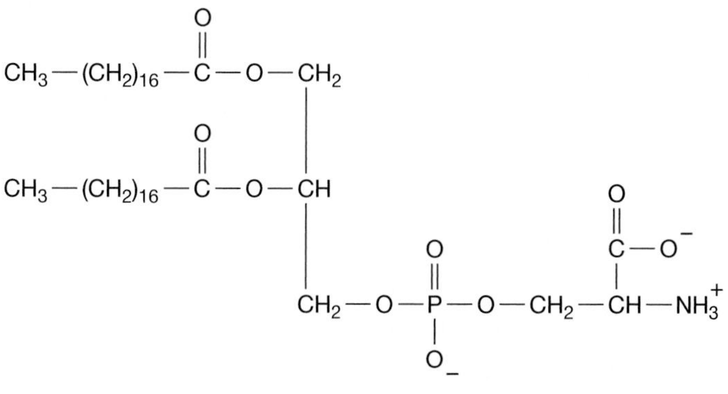

$$
\begin{array}{l}
CH_3-(CH_2)_{16}-\overset{O}{\overset{\|}{C}}-O-CH_2 \\
\qquad\qquad\qquad\qquad\qquad\quad | \\
CH_3-(CH_2)_{16}-\overset{O}{\overset{\|}{C}}-O-CH \\
\qquad\qquad\qquad\qquad\qquad\quad | \\
\qquad\qquad\qquad\qquad\qquad\quad CH_2-O-\underset{O^-}{\underset{|}{\overset{O}{\overset{\|}{P}}}}-O-CH_2-\underset{}{\overset{\overset{O}{\overset{\|}{C}}-O^-}{\overset{|}{CH}}}-\overset{+}{N}H_3
\end{array}
$$

14.65 the phosphate group and the polar molecule that is bonded to it, because they are attracted to the water molecules adjacent to the bilayer

14.67 CO_2 is a small molecule and is not highly charged, so it can leave the water around the lipid bilayer and enter the hydrophobic interior of the lipid bilayer. HCO_3^- is an ion and is strongly attracted to water, so it does not leave the water layer.

14.69 Transport proteins carry ions and very polar molecules across a membrane. Cells need transport proteins because they require certain ions and polar substances as nutrients, and they would not be able to obtain these substances without the transport proteins.

14.71 a) active transport
b) yes
c) yes

14.73 Concentration gradients are a source of potential energy that cells can use to power other energy-requiring activities.

Section 14.8 Core Problems

14.75 Cholesterol is a component of cell membranes. Its function is to ensure that the membrane is the correct consistency, neither too stiff nor too flexible.

14.77 a) mineralocorticoid b) estrogen

14.79 a significant impact, because the effect of a steroid hormone depends on its exact structure

14.81 Steroids have very low solubilities in water, so they do not dissolve in blood. Therefore, the body needs other molecules to carry the steroids through the bloodstream.

14.83 The two main cholesterol carriers in the blood are HDL and LDL. HDL carries cholesterol to the liver so that it can be broken down and excreted. LDL carries cholesterol to other body tissues for storage.

Section 14.9 Core Problems

14.85 We can eat foods that contain carbohydrates or build the glucose from amino acids and other nutrients.

14.87 a) polyunsaturated fatty acids, because our bodies cannot make them from other nutrients (including saturated and monounsaturated fatty acids)
b) from our diet

14.89 a) The starting materials for photosynthesis are carbon dioxide and water, and the products are glucose and oxygen.
b) Sunlight provides the energy that plants need to carry out photosynthesis.

CHAPTER 15

Try It Yourself Exercises

15.1 The first reaction forms an equilibrium mixture, and the second reaction goes to completion.

15.2 glycerol + ATP $\rightarrow$ glycerol-3-phosphate + ADP. This is an activation reaction.

15.3 $C_2H_6O + 3\ H_2O \rightarrow 2\ CO_2 + 12\ [H]$

15.4 $C_2H_6O + 5\ NAD^+ + FAD + 3\ H_2O \rightarrow 2\ CO_2 + 5\ NADH + 5\ H^+ + FADH_2$

15.5 The two solutions contain the same total concentration of ions, so there is no overall concentration gradient. There is, however, a concentration gradient for each individual ion, because the concentrations of Na^+ and Cl^- are different on each side of the membrane. Solution X contains more negative ions than positive ions, while solution Y contains more positive ions than negative ions, so there is also a charge gradient across the membrane.

15.6 34.5 molecules

15.7 six cycles of beta oxidation, seven molecules of acetyl-CoA

15.8 92 molecules

15.9 117 molecules

15.10 19.5 mol

15.11

```
          CH3
          |
    CH3 — CH
          |
          CH2    O
          |      ||
      O = C ———— C — O⁻
```

15.12 32.5 molecules

15.13 800 molecules

Section 15.1 Core Problems

15.1 ribose, adenine, and three phosphate groups

15.3 ADP + P_i + energy $\rightarrow$ ATP + H_2O

15.5 an anabolic process

15.7 the first reaction, because it supplies more than 7.3 kcal of energy

15.9 The first reaction goes nearly to completion, because it requires less than 7.3 kcal of energy. The second reaction, which requires more than 7.3 kcal, forms an equilibrium mixture that contains only a small amount of product.

15.11 a) break down ATP, because this produces energy that we can use for the endothermic reaction in this problem
b) fructose + ATP $\rightarrow$ fructose-1-phosphate + ADP
c) yes, because it uses the energy of ATP to build an organic phosphate

Section 15.2 Core Problems

15.13 NAD^+ and FAD

15.15 water molecules

15.17 $C_4H_8O_3 + 5\ H_2O \rightarrow 4\ CO_2 + 18\ [H]$

15.19 $C_4H_8O_3 + 7\ NAD^+ + 2\ FAD + 5\ H_2O \rightarrow 4\ CO_2 + 7\ NADH + 7\ H^+ + 2\ FADH_2$

Section 15.3 Core Problems

15.21 Mitochondria oxidize organic nutrients and use the energy to make ATP. In effect, they carry out most of the catabolism in the cell.

15.23 The electron transport chain oxidizes NADH and $FADH_2$ back to NAD^+ and FAD, uses the electrons produced by this reaction to combine H^+ with oxygen to form water, and uses the energy of this reaction to create an H^+ gradient across the inner membrane.

15.25 The enzymes of the electron transport chain pass electrons from NADH and $FADH_2$ to oxygen. This process produces energy, and the enzymes use this energy to push hydrogen ions from the matrix to the intermembrane space.

15.27 a) NAD^+, H^+, and two electrons
b) 10 electrons
c) 2.5 molecules
d) 50 molecules

15.29 a) yes, because the overall concentration of solution A is lower than the overall concentration of solution B; in addition, the concentration of each ion is different, so there is a concentration gradient for each ion
b) yes, because solution A contains an excess of positive ions and solution B contains an excess of negative ions

15.31 The electron transport chain moves H^+ ions from the matrix to the intermembrane space, but it does not move H^+ ions in the other direction. As a result, there is a higher concentration of H^+ ions in the intermembrane space than in the matrix.

15.33 8 molecules

Section 15.4 Core Problems

15.35 In an activation reaction, an enzyme breaks down ATP and uses the energy to make a high-energy molecule.

15.37 Glucose is broken down into two molecules of pyruvate during glycolysis.

15.39 Lactic acid fermentation does not produce NADH or $FADH_2$ (the NADH that is produced in the earlier steps is converted back into NAD^+ in the final step). Therefore, this pathway does not involve the electron transport chain, which in turn means that lactic acid fermentation does not require oxygen.

15.41 The NADH is this reaction was formed during glycolysis, while glucose was being converted into pyruvate.

Section 15.5 Core Problems

15.43 Two of the three carbon atoms end up in the acetyl group of acetyl-CoA, and the third carbon atom ends up in a molecule of CO_2.

15.45 acetyl-CoA

15.47 There are two decarboxylation reactions. This is reasonable because the acetyl group of acetyl-CoA contains two carbon atoms, and each carbon atom must eventually be incorporated into a molecule of CO_2.

15.49 The alcohol group in citrate is a tertiary alcohol and cannot be oxidized, but the alcohol group in isocitrate is a secondary alcohol and can be oxidized.

15.51 10 molecules of ATP

15.53 28

Section 15.6 Core Problems

15.55 $C_{18}H_{36}O_2 + 34\ H_2O \rightarrow 18\ CO_2 + 104\ [H]$

15.57 The fatty acid must be combined with a molecule of coenzyme A to form a fatty acyl–CoA.

15.59

$$CH_3{-}(CH_2)_{10}{-}CH_2{-}CH_2{-}\overset{O}{\overset{\|}{C}}{-}S{-}CoA + FAD \longrightarrow CH_3{-}(CH_2)_{10}{-}CH{=}CH{-}\overset{O}{\overset{\|}{C}}{-}S{-}CoA + FADH_2$$

$$CH_3{-}(CH_2)_{10}{-}CH{=}CH{-}\overset{O}{\overset{\|}{C}}{-}S{-}CoA + H_2O \longrightarrow CH_3{-}(CH_2)_{10}{-}\overset{OH}{\overset{|}{C}H}{-}CH_2{-}\overset{O}{\overset{\|}{C}}{-}S{-}CoA$$

$$CH_3{-}(CH_2)_{10}{-}\overset{OH}{\overset{|}{C}H}{-}CH_2{-}\overset{O}{\overset{\|}{C}}{-}S{-}CoA + NAD^+ \longrightarrow CH_3{-}(CH_2)_{10}{-}\overset{O}{\overset{\|}{C}}{-}CH_2{-}\overset{O}{\overset{\|}{C}}{-}S{-}CoA + NADH + H^+$$

$$CH_3{-}(CH_2)_{10}{-}\overset{O}{\overset{\|}{C}}{-}CH_2{-}\overset{O}{\overset{\|}{C}}{-}S{-}CoA + HS{-}CoA \longrightarrow CH_3{-}(CH_2)_{10}{-}\overset{O}{\overset{\|}{C}}{-}S{-}CoA + CH_3{-}\overset{O}{\overset{\|}{C}}{-}S{-}CoA$$

15.61 a) 8 cycles
b) 9 molecules
c) 120 molecules
d) 42.2 mol

15.63 115.5 molecules

Section 15.7 Core Problems

15.65 In a transamination reaction, the amino group from an amino acid is moved to an α-keto acid (usually α-ketoglutaric acid). The original amino acid becomes an α-keto acid, and the α-ketoglutaric acid becomes a molecule of glutamic acid. In effect, two molecules exchange an amino group and a ketone group.

15.67 $CH_3-CH(CH_2CH_3)-C(=O)-COO^-$

15.69 ammonium ion (NH_4^+)

15.71 two molecules

15.73 23 molecules

Section 15.8 Core Problems

15.75 Gluconeogenesis makes a molecule of glucose from two molecules of pyruvate.

15.77 gluconeogenesis

15.79 a) two molecules
b) fatty acyl–CoA

15.81 two molecules

15.83 a pair of metabolic pathways, normally a catabolic pathway and an anabolic pathway, that undo each other and consume ATP in the process

15.85 AMP should decrease the activity of glycogen synthase to prevent a futile cycle.

CHAPTER 16

Try It Yourself Exercises

16.1 $^{51}_{24}Cr$

16.2 $^{238}_{92}U \longrightarrow ^{234}_{90}Th + ^{4}_{2}He$

16.3 $^{60}_{27}Co \longrightarrow ^{60}_{28}Ni + ^{0}_{-1}e$

16.4 $^{249}_{98}Cf + ^{18}_{8}O \longrightarrow ^{263}_{106}Sg + 4\,^{1}_{0}n$, seaborgium

16.5 1.11×10^7 kcal

16.6 30 rem

16.7 1.59 μg

16.8 0.59 MBq

16.9 80 particles

16.10 between 4 and 6 minutes

16.11 roughly 11,000 years ago

16.12 The half-life of ^{136}I is so short that almost the entire sample of ^{136}I will break down before it can be brought to the clinic and used.

16.13 $^{235}_{92}U + ^{1}_{0}n \longrightarrow ^{127}_{51}Sb + ^{106}_{41}Nb + 3\,^{1}_{0}n$

Section 16.1 Core Problems

16.1 Stable isotopes are not radioactive, so their atoms do not break down.

16.3 a) chemical reaction b) nuclear reaction

16.5 a) 34 protons and 47 neutrons
b) 29 protons and 38 neutrons

16.7 a) $^{37}_{17}Cl$ b) $^{54}_{26}Fe$ c) $^{60}_{27}Co$

Section 16.2 Core Problems

16.9 a) $^{1}_{1}p$ or $^{1}_{1}H$ b) $^{0}_{-1}e$

16.11 a) positron emission b) alpha decay
c) beta decay

16.13 a) $^{209}_{84}Po \longrightarrow ^{205}_{82}Pb + ^{4}_{2}He$

b) $^{18}_{8}O \longrightarrow ^{18}_{9}F + ^{0}_{-1}e$

c) $^{15}_{8}O \longrightarrow ^{15}_{7}N + ^{0}_{-1}e$

16.15 $^{209}_{98}Cf + ^{15}_{7}N \longrightarrow ^{220}_{105}Db + 4\,^{1}_{0}n$

16.17 a nuclear reactor, because the first step requires a neutron and nuclear reactors supply the neutrons for this type of reaction

Section 16.3 Core Problems

16.19 a) electromagnetic radiation b) particles
c) electromagnetic radiation

16.21 9.9×10^6 kcal (9,900,000 kcal)

16.23 a) gamma radiation
b) 1.9×10^6 kcal (1,900,000 kcal)

16.25 a) 0.00020 g (0.20 mg)
b) 80.91679 g

16.27 choices a and c

16.29 Ionizing radiation knocks electrons out of atoms and molecules, producing ions with an odd number of electrons.

Section 16.4 Core Problems

16.31 Ionizing radiation exposes the film, so the film badge is used to determine whether the worker has been exposed to ionizing radiation.

16.33 the rem

16.35 a) 0.041 Ci b) 41,000 μCi c) 1500 MBq
d) 1.5×10^9 Bq (1,500,000,000 Bq) e) 1.5 GBq

16.37 a) 0.030 rem b) 0.00030 Sv c) 0.30 mSv

16.39 45 mrem

Section 16.5 Core Problems

16.41 all types of ionizing radiation that we are exposed to as a result of natural processes

16.43 Uranium breaks down into radon, which seeps up through the concrete into the basement. Sealing the basement floor prevents the radon from entering the house, lowering the background exposure for the people who live in the house.

16.45 ^{14}C, because most of the beta radiation is absorbed by body tissues while most of the gamma radiation from the ^{123}I passes harmlessly out of the body

16.47 a) a sheet of Plexiglass, preferably coated with lead to stop X-rays
b) a thick concrete wall or a sheet of lead

16.49 0.5 mrem

Section 16.6 Core Problems

16.51 37.5 MBq

16.53 80 μCi

16.55 10 minutes

16.57 between 48 and 56 days

16.59 a) sample B, because it has a lower activity; the older sample has fewer atoms of ^{14}C remaining in it
b) Neither sample is 6000 years old. The half-life of ^{14}C is 5700 years, which means that in 5700 years, the activity of the sample drops to 0.11 Bq. A 6000-year-old sample would have an even lower activity. The activity of both of these samples is higher than 0.11 Bq, so they must be less than 5700 years old.

Section 16.7 Core Problems

16.61 Alpha and beta radiation do not pass through body tissues effectively. Virtually all alpha particles and most beta particles are absorbed by the body.

16.63 ^{89}Sr, because it decays relatively rapidly, limiting the body's exposure to radiation

16.65 Cancer cells require a lot of glucose and absorb glucose rapidly from the blood. The structure of FDG is similar to that of glucose, so the cancer cells also absorb FDG more rapidly than other tissues do. The ^{18}F in the FDG produces radiation that can be detected and used to find the location of cancerous tissues.

16.67 For patient A, the radiation is being used to diagnose a medical condition, so patient A receives as small a dose as possible to minimize tissue damage. For patient B, the radiation is intended to kill the cells in the brain tumor, and this requires a higher radiation dose.

16.69 The thyroid gland rapidly absorbs iodine, so the ^{131}I collects in the thyroid and can be used to observe the gland. Other radioactive elements are not so specific and can be found in a variety of tissues.

Section 16.8 Core Problems

16.71 a nuclear reaction in which a heavy nucleus splits into two fairly large pieces

16.73 $^{239}_{94}Pu + ^{1}_{0}n \longrightarrow ^{104}_{42}Mo + ^{134}_{52}Te + 2\,^{1}_{0}n$

16.75 Uranium-235 can undergo a chain reaction, in which the fission of one atom produces two or more neutrons that cause other atoms to fission. The result is an ever-increasing sequence of fission reactions, each of which produces a great deal of energy. In a large piece of uranium-235, the rapid increase in the number of atoms that break down produces energy all at once, resulting in an explosion.

16.77 nuclear decay, because nuclear reactions always produce more energy than chemical reactions involving the same materials

16.79 $2\,^{12}_{6}C \longrightarrow ^{24}_{12}Mg$

16.81 Fusion reactions use hydrogen, which is abundant and inexpensive, and they do not produce radioactive byproducts. Fission reactions require very heavy elements that are harder to obtain, and they produce large amounts of radioactive material.

CHAPTER 17

Try It Yourself Exercises

17.1

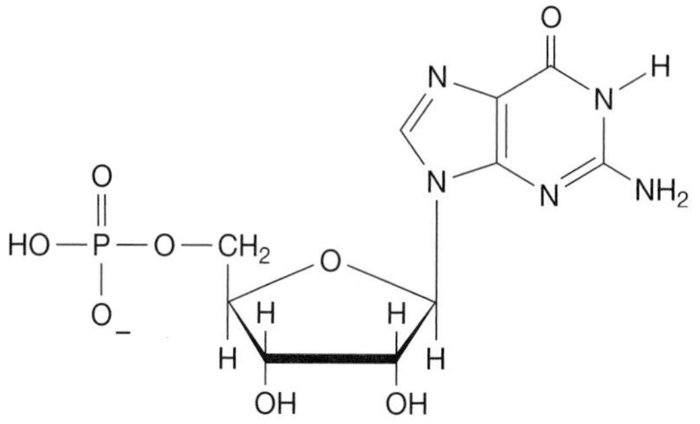

17.2 TTTGCAAA

17.3 ACAAUGG

17.4 Gly–Arg–Pro

17.5 Ser–Ala

17.6 This is a nonsense mutation, because it converts a normal codon into a stop codon. This mutation will produce a protein that is too short and that probably will not function.

17.7 The mutated protein has the amino acid sequence Ile–Ile–Thr. This mutation does not produce a frameshift, because it effectively removes an entire codon (three bases) from the DNA. The resulting protein is missing one amino acid, but it is otherwise normal.

Section 17.1 Core Problems

17.1 a five-carbon sugar, a phosphate group, and an organic base

17.3 carbon 1

17.5 thymine

17.7 ribose

17.9 GMP

17.11 a)

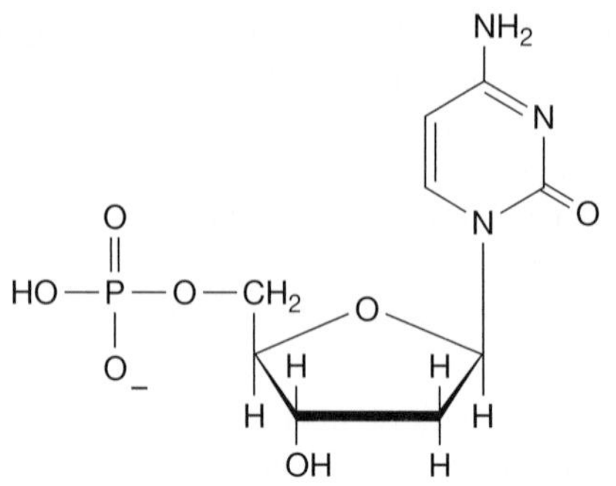

b) CMP has a hydroxyl group on carbon 2 of the sugar instead of a hydrogen atom.

c) dCTP has a chain of three phosphate groups instead of just one phosphate group.

Section 17.2 Core Problems

17.13 It connects two sugars to each other.

17.15

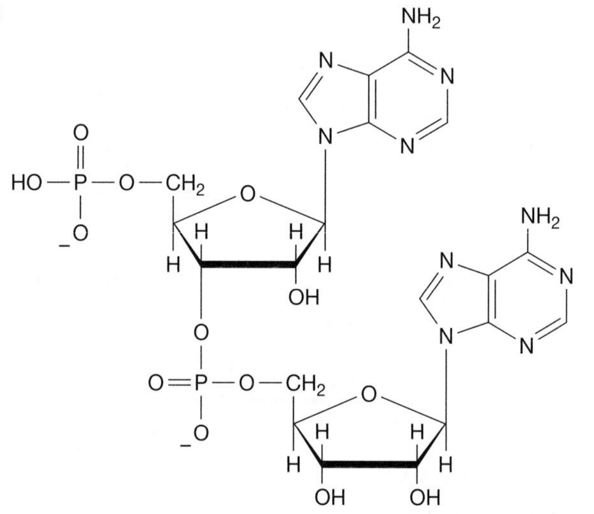

17.17 a) C b) T

17.19 a) A b) G c) GCCACT

17.21 a) a protein that binds to DNA
b) positively charged

17.23 in the nucleus of the cell

Section 17.3 Core Problems

17.25 DNA contains the genetic instructions to build the organism.

17.27 a) 46 chromosomes b) 44 chromosomes

17.29 a nucleotide that contains a chain of three phosphate groups rather than just one, such as ATP

17.31 a) start the process of DNA replication by making a short strand of RNA (a primer) using a DNA strand as a template

b) complete replication by replacing the RNA nucleotides of the primers with DNA nucleotides and sealing the gaps between the pieces of the new DNA strand

17.33 remove mismatched nucleotides during replication and replace them with the correct complementary nucleotides

Section 17.4 Core Problems

17.35 choice a

17.37 choice d

17.39 the template strand

17.41 AACCUUG

17.43 The initial transcript is cut apart, and extra nucleotides are removed.

17.45 An intron is a section of mRNA that is in the initial transcript but does not code for a protein. Introns are removed and broken down into nucleotides during mRNA processing.

17.47 The 5′ cap is a guanine nucleotide and an extra phosphate group that are added to the 5′ end of an mRNA molecule. This cap allows the cell to recognize the RNA as being mRNA.

Section 17.5 Core Problems

17.49 mRNA

17.51 three bases

17.53 A stop codon tells the ribosome that is has reached the end of the protein and translation is complete.

17.55 Asn–Arg–Leu

17.57 a) two codons b) methionine or tryptophan

17.59 Met–Leu–Ala–Tyr

17.61 Gln–Arg–Asp

17.63 a) ACAUCGUUC b) Thr–Ser–Phe

Section 17.6 Core Problems

17.65 a) tRNA b) mRNA c) rRNA

17.67 Ribosomes build polypeptides, using the code in an mRNA molecule.

17.69 a sequence of three bases in a tRNA molecule that can bind to a codon in mRNA

17.71 two codons

17.73 two molecules

17.75 The single tRNA has an anticodon that can bind to all four threonine codons. This allows the cell to make just one type of tRNA for threonine, rather than four.

Section 17.7 Core Problems

17.77 a) One base in a DNA strand is replaced by a different base.
b) One or more bases are removed from a DNA strand.

17.79 Adding one base pair changes the division points for all subsequent codons, as shown here:
Original: ABC–DEF–GHI–JKL
Mutated (adding X): AXB–CDE–FGH–IJK–L

17.81 a) missense b) silent c) nonsense

17.83 addition of one base pair within a DNA molecule, because it produces a frameshift that causes all subsequent codons to be read incorrectly

17.85 The ACA → CCA mutation is most likely to be harmful, because it replaces a hydrophilic amino acid (threonine) with a hydrophobic amino acid (proline). The ACA → TCA mutation should be less harmful because it replaces threonine with serine, which is similar to threonine (both are hydrophilic and neutral). The ACA → ACG mutation will be the least harmful, because it does not produce a change in the amino acid sequence of the corresponding protein.

17.87 a) Lys–His–Lys–Leu b) Lys–Arg–Lys–Leu c) Lys–His

17.89 A mutagen is a chemical that can cause DNA mutations.

17.91 A cell in a developing embryo will give rise to many cells in the mature adult. If the mutation kills the cell, the embryo may not develop correctly, producing a birth defect or killing the embryo outright. A mutation in one cell in an adult may kill that cell, but the body has many other cells that can take up the function of that cell.

17.93 Cancer is the result of a defect in DNA that allows cells to continue to divide and grow when they should not. Mutagens produce DNA mutations, including mutations that cause cancer.

17.95 An autosomal genetic disorder is a genetic defect that occurs in one of the autosomal chromosomes. All of the autosomal chromosomes occur in pairs, and a person normally needs only one functioning copy of each gene to be healthy, so a person only suffers from an autosomal genetic disorder if he or she inherits defective copies of the chromosome from both parents.

17.97 Women have two X chromosomes. As long as one of the X chromosomes is normal, the woman will be able to produce all of the proteins that she needs and will not show any signs of a genetic disorder.

APPENDIX A

Try It Yourself Exercises

A.1 0.0075

A.2 22.22047244

A.3 0.40 mg/mL

A.4 a) 315.6 b) 60.0

A.5 375 mL

A.6 two

A.7 199 square centimeters

A.8 4.03 quarts

A.9 8.311×10^{-5}

A.10 5×10^{-3}

A.11 2.17×10^{-13}

A.12 5.0×10^{9} cells per milliliter

Section A.1 Problems

A.1 0.0008999 (smallest) → 0.006512 → 0.00817 → 0.034 (largest)

A.2 0.044

Section A.2 Problems

A.3 a) 1271.2 b) 0.03440909 c) 2.24669604 d) 0.06655344

Section A.3 Problems

A.4 8.64 L

A.5 8.500 g/mL

Section A.4 Problems

A.6 a) 14 b) 13.7 c) 13.73 d) 13.730

Section A.5 Problems

A.7 a) 14.591 g b) 0.35 g c) 106.9 g d) 26.00 cm

A.8 a) three b) two c) two d) two

A.9 a) 7.7 dL b) 0.3 inches c) 1.07 m

A.10 a) 2.75 cm b) 9.50 yards c) 45.0 mg

A.11 a) 0.420 gallons b) 0.92 tons c) 59 feet

A.12 a) 770,000 pounds b) 300,000,000 feet

Section A.6 Problems

A.13 a) 1.2×10^{10} b) 7.52×10^{-7} c) 3×10^{1}

A.14 a) 60,000 b) 0.0000031 c) 53.3

A.15 a) 3.71×10^{19} b) 5.4×10^{-15} c) 8.002×10^{6} d) 6.637363×10^{-1}

A.16 a) 6.2×10^{7} kg b) 6.200×10^{7} kg

A.17 1.32×10^{25} pounds

A.18 2.6×10^{21} km

APPENDIX B

Try It Yourself Exercises

B.1 329.7 K

B.2 5.86 L

B.3 8.3 mol, 5.0×10^{24} molecules

Section B.1 Problems

B.1 355.6 K

Section B.2 Problems

B.3 a) $\frac{28.5 \text{ psi} \times 41.3 \text{ L}}{295.65 \text{ K}} = \frac{P_2 \times 41.9 \text{ L}}{315.05 \text{ K}}$

b) 29.9 psi

Section B.3 Problems

B.5 a) Boyle's law
b) $0.96 \text{ atm} \times 3.9 \text{ L} = P_2 \times 1.21 \text{ atm}$

Section B.4 Problems

B.7 1270 L

B.9 723 mL

Section B.5 Problems

B.11 7.57 atm

B.13 a) 0.0280 mol b) 1.69×10^{22} molecules
c) 1.24 g

INDEX

Italicized page numbers indicate pages containing figures, and those followed by "t" indicate tables.

B vitamins, 166, *560–561*, 561t
Backbone The chain of peptide groups and carbon atoms in a polypeptide, 537–*538*
Backbone of nucleic acid, 729, *730, 731,* 732
Background radiation All of the naturally occurring sources of ionizing radiation that humans are exposed to, 700–701, 701t
Balance, *10*
Balanced chemical equation, 222, 223–226
 for combustion reaction, 237–238
 heat of reaction and, 231, 233t
Bar, 129, 129t
Base A molecule or ion that can bond to a hydrogen ion, 261, 276–281. *See also* Acid-base reactions; pH
 amine as, 458–459
 amphiprotic, 286–*287*
 in nucleic acids, 724, 725t, *726, 729–732*
Base unit One of the fundamental units in the metric system, such as gram or liter, to which prefixes can be added to name other metric units, 5, 6, 6t
Basic (alkaline) Having a concentration of hydroxide ions that is larger than 10^{-7} M, 264, *265*
Basic amino acids, 532, 534, 544–545, *549*
Becquerel (Bq), 698, 699–700, 699t
Benedict's test, *580–581*, 588
Benzene, *344*
 compared to phenol, 388t
 solubility in water, 349
Benzoic acid, 444
Beta decay A nuclear reaction in which an atom emits an electron (beta particle), which is formed when a neutron breaks down into a proton and an electron, *689*–690, 694
Beta oxidation A metabolic pathway that breaks down fatty acids into acetyl-CoA, 657–660, *659*, 660t, 672, *673*
Beta particle An electron that is emitted during a nuclear reaction, 687, 687t, *689*, 694
 penetrating ability of, *703, 704,* 704t
 weighting factor for, 696t
Beta (β) sheet A protein structure in which the polypeptide backbone folds into a set of parallel strands, *539–541*, 542
Beta-lactamase, 513
β-turn, *541*
Bicarbonate ion
 acidosis and, 299
 as amphiprotic ion, 286–287
 as physiological buffer, *295*, 296–298, 297t, 467
 in urea cycle, 665–666
Bile salts, 603, *604*, 612, 615
Bilirubin, 216
Binary compound A compound made from two elements, 94
 covalent, 94–96, 94t, 95t, 96t
Blood, specific gravity of, *35*
Blood group molecules, 546
Blood plasma
 concentrations of ions in, 203, 203t, 205t
 molarities of solutes in, 196, 196t
 pH of, *295, 296–298,* 297t, 299
Blood urea nitrogen (BUN), 78, 666
Boiling, *134, 137,* 138
Boiling point The temperature at which a liquid boils; the highest temperature at which the liquid state can exist, *135*
 attractive forces affecting, 147t
 dipole–dipole attraction and, *143*
 elevation and, *135,* 168
 heating curve and, *137,* 138
 hydrogen bonds and, 145, 146–147, 147t
 of ionic vs. molecular substances, 140, 141t
 molecular size and, 141, 142t
 for some elements, 136, 136t
Bond. *See* Covalent bond; Hydrogen bond; Ionic bond
Bonding electron pair A pair of valence electrons that is shared by two atoms and that holds the atoms close to each other, *81*, 83–84
Boyle's Law, A-21
Branched alkane An alkane in which the carbon atoms do not form a single continuous chain, *316–319*, 317t, 318t
 naming, 323–328, 323t
Breathing, and plasma pH, 258, *296–297*, 299
Bronsted-Lowry concept A model of acid–base reactions in which acids donate and bases accept hydrogen ions, 276
Brown adipose tissue, 674–675
Buffer A solution that resists pH changes when acids or bases are added to it. Buffers normally contain a weak acid and its conjugate base, 288–293, 289t, *290, 292*
 in human physiology, 294–298, *295,* 467, 469, 470–471
 hydrolysis of ester and, 512
 summary of, 293
Burning. *See* Combustion reaction
Butane, 313t, *316*, 317t, 348t
Butene, 334
Butyl group, 323t

Cadaverine, 431
Caffeine, *465*
Calcium
 as cofactor, 560
 isotopes of, 686t
Calculator
 fractions, A-1–A-2
 rounding answers, A-3–A-10
 scientific notation, A-13–A-16
Calorie (cal), 122–124, 123t
Cancer
 mutations leading to, 756
 nuclear medicine and, 682, 711, 711t
Capping of mRNA, 740, *741, 743*
Carbohydrate An organic compound with a 1:2:1 ratio of carbon, hydrogen, and oxygen atoms, or a large molecule built from compounds that have this ratio. Carbohydrates are a major class of biological molecule and a source of energy for most organisms, 574. *See also* Disaccharide; Monosaccharide; Polysaccharide
 ATP yield for, 669t
 as blood group determinants, 546
 dietary sources of, 616–617, 617t
Carbon
 bonding properties of, 306–308, 307t
 chiral atom of, 378–380
 in human body, *73–74*
 isotopes of, *685*, 697t, 707–708, 707t
Carbon-14, 685, 697t, 707–708, 707t
Carbon cycle The series of chemical and biogenic sources of carbon (primarily CO_2 and ionic carbonates) into organic molecules, and vice versa, *618*
Carbon dioxide
 in blood, *198,* 248, 258, *295–297*
 catabolic production of, *635–636*
 decarboxylation and, 447–451
 in photosynthesis, *618*
 sublimation of, *134–135*
 transport from cells to lungs, *295*
Carbonate ion, 278t, 279t
Carbonic acid, 269, 269t, 272t
Carbonic acid buffer system, *295–298, 296,* 297t
 dopamine and, 469
Carbonic anhydrase, 295, 553, *559*
Carbonyl group A functional group that contains a carbon atom and an oxygen atom linked by a double bond, 404. *See also* Aldehyde; Ketone
 decarboxylation and, 448, 449, 450t
 reduction to alcohol group, 407–408
 water solubility and, 414–415
Carboxylate ion An anion that is formed when a carboxylic acid loses a hydrogen ion, 443–445
Carboxylate salts, 443–445
 from hydrolysis of ester, 514, A-31
 soap as, 473–474, 514–515
Carboxylic acid An organic compound that contains a carbonyl group bonded to a hydroxyl group, 330t, 420–422, A-28. *See also* Acetic acid; Citric acid cycle; Fatty acid
 acid–base reactions of, 442–443, 459
 condensation with alcohol, *491*–492, A-31
 condensation with amine, *493–495*, A-31
 conjugate base of, 443, 443t
 decarboxylation of, 447–451, 450t, A-30
 from hydrolysis of amides, *508–509*, 513–514, A-32
 from hydrolysis of esters, 506–508, *507,* 512–513, 514–515, A-31
 in metabolic pathways, 447
 physical properties of, 421–422
 physiological pH and, 467–468, 472t, 512
Catabolism The metabolic pathways that break down large molecules into smaller ones and that release energy, 628, 628t
 of amino acids, 664–667, *665,* 668t
 ATP synthase in, *642–643, 645*
 citric acid cycle in, *651–654, 652, 655*t, 660, 660t
 complete oxidation of glucose in, 633, 654–656, 655t
 electron transport chain in, 640–642, *641,* 643, *645*
 of fatty acids, 656–663, *659,* 660t, 672, *673*
 glycolysis in, 646–650, *648,* 654, 655–656, 655t, *672, 673*
 overview of, 634–637, *635,* 644, *645*
 regulation of, *672–673*
 summary of pathways in, *668*
Catalase, *246–247, 553*

Catalyst A substance that speeds up a chemical reaction but is not consumed by the reaction, 242–243, 243t, *246–247*. *See also* Enzyme
Cation A positively charged ion, 58–59
transition metal, 104–105, 104t, 108t
Cell, *639*, 639t. *See also* Intracellular fluid; Mitochondria
Cell membranes, 605, 606, 607–611, *608*
permeability of, 607–608, 608t
Cellobiose, *585*, 587
Cellulose, 591–*592*, 593t
Celsius temperature scale, 36–38, *37*
Chain reaction A process in which a fission reaction produces neutrons that cause other atoms to undergo fission at an ever-increasing rate, 713, *714*
Chair conformation, of cyclohexane, *321*
Changes of state, *134*–138, *135*. *See also* Boiling point; Melting point
Charge. *See* Electrical charge
Charge gradient Two solutions that are separated by a membrane and have unequal charges, 641–643, *642*
Charles's Law, A-21, A-22
Chemical behavior, 66–68, *67*, 68t, 70
Chemical bond An attractive force that holds atoms together in a chemical compound, *81*. *See also* Covalent bond; Ionic bond
Chemical change. *See* Chemical reaction
Chemical energy, 231, 232, 233t
Chemical equation A way to represent a chemical reaction that uses chemical formulas and coefficients to show types and numbers of each substance involved in the reaction, 220–226
abbreviations for states of matter in, 226, 226t
for dissociation of ionic compound, 156, 157
Chemical equilibrium A stable mixture of products and reactants in which the rates of the forward reaction and reverse reaction are equal, 248–251, *249*, *250*, *251*, 252t
Chemical formula A way to represent the numbers and types of atoms in a chemical compound, *63*
molecular, 314, 315t
Chemical property The ability of a substance to undergo a chemical reaction, 218
Chemical reaction (chemical change) A process that involves changes in the chemical formulas of the substances involved, *218–219*, 219t
combustion, 237–238, 349–350
equation for, 220–226, 226t
mass relationships in, *227–230*, *228*
organic, summary of, A-29–A-32
precipitation, *239*–240, 241t
rate of, 241–244, *242*, *243*
Chemical substance A substance that has a fixed composition, including elements and compounds, 48–49
Chiral Not superimposable on its mirror image, *376–380*
amino acids and, *534*
enzymes and, 380, *583*
monosaccharides and, *583*
proteins and, 540
reduction reactions and, 408
Chitin, *591*, *592*, *593*t
Chloroalkanes, 329, *330*, 330t
Cholesterol, 304–*305*, 612
in lipoproteins, 615–616, 615t
as trivial name, 337
Choline, 605, *606*
Chromosome A molecule of DNA and its associated proteins, 732, *734–735*
genetic disorders and, *756–757*
recombinations of, *754–755*
Chymotrypsin, *554*
Cinnamaldehyde, 410, 431
Ciprofloxacin, 346, 735
Cis isomers
of alkenes, *339–343*
of fatty acids, 601
Citric acid cycle (Krebs cycle) A catabolic pathway that breaks down the acetyl group of acetyl-CoA into CO_2, producing energy in the form of ATP, NADH, and $FADH_2$, *651–654*, *652*, 655t
fatty acid oxidation and, 660, 660t
Cobalt-60, 690, 694, 697t, 707t
Coding strand The strand in a DNA molecule that is not used as a template for RNA transcription, 738, *739*, *744*
Codon A set of three consecutive bases in an mRNA molecule that codes for a single amino acid, 742, 743t
Coefficient A number in a balanced chemical equation that shows how many molecules of a particular substance are required, 221–222, 223–226
Coenzyme An organic molecule that is required by an enzyme, 559–561, *560*, 561t. *See also* Redox coenzyme
Coenzyme A, 449–451, *651*
in fatty acid metabolism, 657–660, *659*, 660t, 670–671, 672, *673*
in glucose metabolism, *651–653*, 654, 655t
nucleotide structure in, 727
pantothenic acid and, 561t
Cofactor Any substance that is required by an enzyme, including coenzymes and metal ions, *559–561*, 561t
Collagen, *541–542*
Colloid A mixture containing large molecules or clusters of molecules with a solvent that exhibits the Tyndall effect and that can be separated by membranes but not filters, *150*
Combined gas law The mathematical relationship that relates changes in pressures, volumes, and temperatures of a gas sample to each other, A-18–A-22
Combustion reaction A reaction type in which a compound reacts with O_2 to form oxides of the elements, 237–238
of hydrocarbons, 349–350
Competitive inhibitor A molecule that fits into the active site of an enzyme and prevents the normal substrate from entering, *556*
Complementary base pair A pair of hydrogen-bonded bases in a DNA molecule, 730, *731*, *732*
Complex carbohydrate. *See* Polysaccharide
Compound A substance that is made from two or more elements in a fixed ratio, *48*, 49, 50t. *See also* Ionic compound; Molecular compound; Naming compounds
Compound unit A unit of measurement that is built from other units, typically as a ratio (such as miles per hour or grams per milliliter), 29–35, 30t
in medicine, 31–33, 31t
Concentration The strength of a solution; the ratio of the amount of solute to the amount of solution, *176*
comparing to normal clinical range, 182
dilution and, 206–210, *207*
mass per volume, 179–182, *180*, 180t
milliequivalents per liter, 202–205, 203t
molarity, *188*–190
parts per million or billion, 180–181
percent, 176–179, *177*
reaction rate and, *242*
relationships between common units, 205t
total molarity of solute particles, 194–*195*
Concentration gradient Two solutions that are separated by a membrane and have unequal concentrations of a solute, *610*–611, 610t
in mitochondria, 641–643, *642*
Condensation The conversion of a substance from a gas into a liquid, *134*
Condensation reaction A reaction in which two molecules combine to make a larger molecule and a molecule of water, *486*–491, 491t, 497
of alcohols, 487, 488–489, A-31
of carboxylic acid and alcohol, *491–492*
of carboxylic acid and amine, *493–495*
of phosphoric acid and alcohol, *495–497*
polymers formed by, 498–504
Condensed state The liquid or the solid state of a substance, 128
Condensed structural formula A way to represent an organic molecule that lists the number of hydrogen atoms beside the atom to which they are bonded, such as $CH_3–CH_3$, *312*, 313t, 314, 315t
Conjugate acid The acidic member of a conjugate pair; the member of a conjugate pair that has one extra hydrogen ion, 278–279, 282–283
Conjugate base The basic member of a conjugate pair; the member of a conjugate pair that has one fewer hydrogen ion, 278–279, 282–283
of carboxylic acid, 443, 443t
Conjugate pair Two substances whose formulas differ by one hydrogen ion, such as H_2CO_3 and HCO_3^-, 278–279, *282–283*. *See also* Buffer
Constitutional isomers Molecules that have the same chemical formula but differ in the order in which the atoms are connected to one another, 317–319, 317t, 318t
compared to stereoisomers, 341–*342*
Conversion factor A fraction that contains the numerical relationship between two units and that is used to convert a measurement from one unit to another, 21–25

Electron transport chain A group of enzymes that oxidize NADH and $FADH_2$, using the energy of these reactions to transport hydrogen ions through the inner mitochondrial membrane, 640–642, *641*, 643, *645*
Electronegativity A measure of the attraction of an element for electrons, 92–94, *93*
Electrophoresis, 566
Element A substance that cannot be broken down into other substances, 49, 50t. *See also* Isotope; Periodic table
broad categories of, 51–52, 52t
constant number of atoms of, 219
electron arrangement in, 65, 66t, 67–68, 68t, 71–72
existing as molecules, 81, *82*
in human body, 73–74
medically important, 54t
Elevation
atmospheric pressure and, 128, *129*
boiling point and, *135*
Enantiomers Mirror image forms of a compound that are not superimposable, 377–378, 378t
of amino acids, 534, 540
enzyme activity and, 380
of monosaccharides, *583*
reduction reactions and, 408
Endorphins, 536
Endothermic reaction A chemical reaction that absorbs energy from its surroundings, normally in the form of heat, *232*, 233t, 245, 245t
Energy The ability to do work, 120–124. *See also* Catabolism; Thermal energy
of activation, 243–247, *244, 245,* 245t, *246, 555*
chemical, 231, 232, 233t
conservation of, 121
dietary sources of, 235–236, 236t, 616–617, 617t
fuels for selected organs and tissues, 666, 666t
measurement of, 122–124, 123t
metabolic pathways and, 400, 428–429, 451
of nuclear reactions, 691–694, 714–715
nutritional requirements for, 253
from photosynthesis, *618*
primary fuels for human body, 572, 574, 619, 646
Energy diagram A graph that shows how the energy of the chemical changes during a chemical reaction, *244–247*
Energy level The energy of the electrons in a shell, 64
English system of units, 5, 5t, 6, 9
pressure in, 128
relationship to metric units, 7t, 8t, 9t
unit conversions with, 21–24, 26–28
Enzyme A protein that catalyzes a chemical reaction, *365–366, 552–558*
as chiral molecule, 380, *583*
for dehydration reactions, 385
digestive, 243, 243t, *555*, 562, 603, *604*
regulation of, *672–673*
specificity of, *552–553*
Enzyme assays, *565–566*
Enzyme–product complex The combination of an enzyme and the products of the reaction it catalyzes while the products remain in the active site, *554, 555*
Enzyme–substrate complex The combination of an enzyme and the reactants of the reaction it catalyzes. The reactant molecules are bound to the active site, 553–*554, 555*
EPA (eicosapentaenoic acid), 617
Epinephrine, 462–463
Equation. *See* Chemical equation; Nuclear equation
Equilibrium mixture A stable mixture of products and reactants that is formed by a reversible reaction, *249–251*, 252t
Equivalent (Eq) A unit that measures the amount of charge in a solution that contains dissolved ions, *199–205*, 203t
Equivalent radiation dose A measure of the amount of tissue damage caused by exposure to ionizing radiation, 696–697, 698, 699t
Essential amino acid An amino acid that humans cannot make from other nutrients and that must be present in the diet, 562, 562t
Essential fatty acid A fatty acid that humans cannot make from other nutrients and that must be present in the diet, 617
Ester An organic compound that contains an oxygen atom bonded to both a carbonyl group and an alkyl group, *491–492*, A-28. *See also* Triglycerides
fruit-scented, 431
hydrolysis of, 506–508, *507*, 512–513, 514–515, A-31
saponification of, A-31
Esterification reaction A reaction that combines an alcohol and a carboxylic acid to make an ester, *491–492*, A-31
Ethane, 311, 312, 313t, *314*, 348t
Ethanol
acetic acid reaction with, 491
ATP yield from, 663
Breathalyzer test for, *368*
dehydration reaction of, 487
denatured, 367, 390
ether formation from, 487
ether hydrolysis yielding, 505
fermentation to, 390, 649–*650*
hydrogen bonding in, *144, 145*
hydrogen bonding with water, *151*
liver function and, 358
naming of, 367, 370
oxidation of, 405, *420*, 424
protein denaturation by, *549*, 551
uses of, 390
Ethanolamine, 605
Ether An organic compound that contains an oxygen atom bonded to two alkyl groups, 489–490, A-27
hydrolysis of, *505*–506, A-31
Ethyl chloride, 329
Ethyl group, 323t
Ethylene, 332, 337
Ethylene glycol, 391
polymerization of, 498–499, 502–503
toxicity of, 499
Ethyne. *See* Acetylene
Eukaryotes, 639, 639t, 732, 733, 735
Evaporation, *134*, 135
Exact number A number that has no uncertainty, normally a counting number or a defined conversion factor, A-8–A-9
Exon A region of an RNA molecule that is not removed during posttranscriptional processing; also, the corresponding region of a DNA molecule, *741, 743*
Exothermic reaction A chemical reaction that gives off energy to its surroundings, normally in the form of heat, *232*, 233t, 245, 245t
Exponent, A-11–A-16
Exponential decay A process in which the number of particles decreases by a factor of two in a constant amount of time, 705–708, *706*, 707t
Extensive property A property whose numerical value depends on the amount of substance, such as mass or volume, 47

FAD (flavin adenine dinucleotide), 426, 427t, 429, 638
ATP molecules formed with, 643–644, 654–656
citric acid cycle and, 651, 654
as cofactor, *559, 560*
complete oxidation of glucose and, 654–656, 655t
electron transport chain and, 640, 642, *645*
fatty acid oxidation and, 656–661, *659*, 660t
nucleotide structure in, 727
overview of catabolism and, 634–637, *635*, *645*
Fahrenheit temperature scale, 36–38, *37*
Fats. *See also* Triglyceride
dietary, 617, 617t
as esters, 492
fatty acid composition of, 599, 599t
hydrogenation of, 403
ketone bodies derived from, 299, 398, *399*, 448, 619
physical properties of, 599t
saponification of, 473, 515
Fat-soluble vitamin An organic compound that is a dietary requirement in small amounts and that dissolves in nonpolar liquids but not in water, 166
Fatty acid An unbranched, long-chain carboxylic acid that is used by living organisms to make fats, 594–599, 596t
ATP yield for, 660–663, 669t
classification of, *596*, 597
as muscle energy source, 619
oxidation of, 656–663, *659*, 660t, 672, *673*
physical properties of, 597–598, 599t
synthesis of, 670–671, 672, *673*
Fermentation A catabolic pathway that breaks down carbohydrates using the reactions of glycolysis, but it does not require oxygen and does not produce NADH or $FADH_2$, 648
alcoholic, 390, 649–*650*
lactic acid, 428, *429*, 619, 633, 648–649
by microorganisms, *649–650*

Melatonin, *532*
Melting, *134, 137,* 138
Melting point (freezing point) The temperature at which a solid melts and the corresponding liquid freezes, 134, *135*
attractive forces affecting, 147t
heating curve and, *137,* 138
of ionic vs. molecular substances, 140, 141t
molecular size and, 141, 142t
for some elements, 136, 136t
Membrane protein A protein that is normally found embedded in a cell membrane, 542, *543, 546*
Meniscus The surface of a liquid in a container, *9, 12*
Menthol, *374*
Mercury toxicity, 551, 617
Mescaline, 463, *464*
Messenger RNA (mRNA) An RNA molecule that contains the genetic code for a polypeptide, 738
energy required for, 749–750
processing of, 740–*741*
translation of, 742–745, *743, 744, 746,* 747, *748–749, 750*
Metabolic acidosis, 299, 467
Metabolic alkalosis, 299
Metabolic pathway A sequence of reactions in a living organism that converts one key molecule into another, 428–430, *429. See also* Anabolism; Catabolism
carboxylic acids in, 447
effectors and, *557*
regulation of, *672–673*
Metabolism All of the reactions that occur in a living organism, 628
Metal An element or mixture of elements characterized by shiny appearance, ability to be hammered into different shapes without shattering, and ability to conduct heat and electricity, 51, *52–53,* 52t
Metallic cofactors, *559, 560*
Metalloid An element whose physical and chemical properties are intermediate between metals and nonmetals, 51–52, 52t, *53*
Meter, 5, 6t, 7t
Metformin, 670
Methamphetamine, 463, *464*
Methane, 84, *308,* 310, 313t, 349
Methanol, 367, 370
as achiral compound, *377*
toxicity of, 367, 375, 390
uses of, 390
Methionine, 532, 742
Methyl group, *323,* 323t
Metric railroad, *18, 20*
Metric system A widely used set of units based on powers of 10, 5–10
base units in, 5, 6, 6t
conversion between different units in, 24–25
conversion between English units and, 23–24, 26–28
distance in, 6–8, *7,* 7t
mass in, 9–10, 9t
modern (SI) version of, 10
prefixes in, 5, 6t, 20, 20t
prefixes in nuclear medicine, 699t
relationships between units in, 16–*20, 17, 18*
resistance to, 39
temperature scales and, 37, 38, A-17
volume in, *8–9,* 8t
Millibar, 129, 129t, 130
Millicurie (mCi), 697, 698
Milliequivalents, 199, 200–201
Milliequivalents per liter, 202–205, 203t
Millimeter of mercury (mm Hg), 129t
Millirem (mrem), 696
Mineral acids, 269, 269t
Minimal change syndrome, 528
Missense mutation A substitution mutation that results in the substitution of one amino acid for another in the resulting polypeptide, 750–751, 751t, 752, 752t
Mitochondria, 639–*640*
ATP synthase in, 642–*643, 645*
in brown fat, 674–675
citric acid cycle in, *651*–654, *652,* 655t
electron transport chain in, 640–642, *641,* 643, *645*
Mixture A combination of two or more substances in which the relative amounts of the substances can be varied, *48*–49, 50t. *See also* Solution
colloid, *150*
suspension, *150*
Molar mass The mass of one mole of a substance, *185*–187
Molarity (molar concentration) The number of moles of solute per liter of solution, *188*–190
total, of solute particles, 194–*195*
Mole (mol) An amount of a substance equal to its formula weight expressed in grams; also 6.022×10^{23} formula units of a substance, 183–187, *184, 185*
equivalents and, *199*–200
of a gas, A-23–A-24
of ions after dissociation, 194–*195*
Molecular compound (covalent compound) A compound whose atoms are held together solely by covalent bonds
naming, 94–96, 94t, 95t, 96t
as nonelectrolyte, *158,* 158t
physical properties of, 140, 141, 141t
recognizing, 112–113, 112t, 113t
solubility trends for, 164, 165t, 166
Molecular equation A chemical equation for a reaction that occurs in a solution and that represents all reactants and products as undissociated molecules, 284–285
Molecular formula, 314, 315t. *See also* Chemical formula
Molecular weight. *See* Formula weight
Molecule An electrically neutral group of atoms held together by covalent bonds, 81–*82*
Monatomic ion An ion that consists of a single charged atom, 108
naming, 105, 106t, 108t, 111t
Monoamine oxidase inhibitors (MAOIs), 463, 469
Monoamine oxidases, 463
Monoglyceride A biomolecule that is made from glycerol and one fatty acid; one of the products of the digestion of fats, 603, *604*
Monoprotic acid An acid that contains one ionizable hydrogen atom, 274
Monosaccharide (simple sugar) The simplest type of carbohydrate, 574–578. *See also* Fructose; Glucose; Ribose
aldoses and ketoses, 580–*581*
dietary, 617
hemiacetal group of, 579–580, *581*
isomeric forms of, 579–583, *581, 582, 583, 588*
main classes of, 574, 574t
naturally occurring forms of, 578
in nucleotides, 724, 725t, *726*
numbering carbon atoms in, 576–*577,* 724, *726*
physical properties of, 578, 578t
structures of, *575–576, 578*
Monounsaturated fatty acids, 596, 596t, 599t, 600, 617
Morphine, *465, 536*
mRNA. *See* Messenger RNA (mRNA)
MTBE (methyl tertiary butyl ether), 489
Muscle, fuels for, 619, 666t
Muscle fatigue, 648
Mutagen A chemical that can cause changes in the base sequence of a DNA molecule, 755, 755t
Mutarotation The interconversion of the anomers of a mono- or disaccharide, *582,* 588
Mutation A change in the base sequence of a DNA molecule, 750–757
causes of, *755,* 755t
effects on entire organism, 756–*757*
evolution and, 757
frameshifts, 753–754
recombinations, *754–755*
substitutions, 750–752, 751t, 752t

NAD^+ (nicotinamide adenine dinucleotide), 424–425, 427t, 429, 638
in amino acid catabolism, 665, 667
ATP molecules formed with, 643–644, 654–656
citric acid cycle and, 651, 653–654
as cofactor, *560,* 561t
complete oxidation of glucose and, 654–656, 655
electron transport chain and, 640, 642, *645*
fatty acid oxidation and, 656–661, *659,* 660t
in gluconeogenesis, *670*
in glycolysis, 646, 647–*648,* 654, 655–656, 655t
nucleotide structure in, 727
overview of catabolism and, 634–637, *635, 645*
in oxidative decarboxylation, 449, 450t, 651
NADPH (nicotinamide adenine dinucleotide phosphate), 426–427, 427t
Naming compounds. *See also* IUPAC rules
alcohols, 337, 367–370
aldehydes, 410, 411
alkenes and alkynes, 334–335, 336–337
amines, 453–454
aromatic, 345
branched alkanes, 323–328, 323t

ALPHABETICAL LIST OF THE CHEMICAL ELEMENTS

Name	Symbol	Atomic Number	Atomic Weight*	Name	Symbol	Atomic Number	Atomic Weight*
Actinium	Ac	89	(227)	Holmium	Ho	67	164.9
Aluminum	Al	13	26.98	Hydrogen	H	1	1.008
Americium	Am	95	(243)	Indium	In	49	114.8
Antimony	Sb	51	121.8	Iodine	I	53	126.9
Argon	Ar	18	39.95	Iridium	Ir	77	192.2
Arsenic	As	33	74.92	Iron	Fe	26	55.85
Astatine	At	85	(210)	Krypton	Kr	36	83.80
Barium	Ba	56	137.3	Lanthanum	La	57	138.9
Berkelium	Bk	97	(247)	Lawrencium	Lr	103	(262)
Beryllium	Be	4	9.012	Lead	Pb	82	207.2
Bismuth	Bi	83	209.0	Lithium	Li	3	6.941
Bohrium	Bh	107	(267)	Lutetium	Lu	71	175.0
Boron	B	5	10.81	Magnesium	Mg	12	24.31
Bromine	Br	35	79.90	Manganese	Mn	25	54.94
Cadmium	Cd	48	112.4	Meitnerium	Mt	109	(276)
Calcium	Ca	20	40.08	Mendelevium	Md	101	(258)
Californium	Cf	98	(251)	Mercury	Hg	80	200.6
Carbon	C	6	12.01	Molybdenum	Mo	42	95.96
Cerium	Ce	58	140.1	Neodymium	Nd	60	144.2
Cesium	Cs	55	132.9	Neon	Ne	10	20.18
Chlorine	Cl	17	35.45	Neptunium	Np	93	(237)
Chromium	Cr	24	52.00	Nickel	Ni	28	58.69
Cobalt	Co	27	58.93	Niobium	Nb	41	92.91
Copernicium	Cn	112	(285)	Nitrogen	N	7	14.01
Copper	Cu	29	63.55	Nobelium	No	102	(259)
Curium	Cm	96	(247)	Osmium	Os	76	190.2
Darmstadtium	Ds	110	(281)	Oxygen	O	8	16.00
Dubnium	Db	105	(268)	Palladium	Pd	46	106.4
Dysprosium	Dy	66	162.5	Phosphorus	P	15	30.97
Einsteinium	Es	99	(252)	Platinum	Pt	78	195.1
Erbium	Er	68	167.3	Plutonium	Pu	94	(244)
Europium	Eu	63	152.0	Polonium	Po	84	(209)
Fermium	Fm	100	(257)	Potassium	K	19	39.10
Fluorine	F	9	19.00	Praseodymium	Pr	59	140.9
Francium	Fr	87	(223)	Promethium	Pm	61	(145)
Gadolinium	Gd	64	157.3	Protactinium	Pa	91	231.0
Gallium	Ga	31	69.72	Radium	Ra	88	(226)
Germanium	Ge	32	72.64	Radon	Rn	86	(222)
Gold	Au	79	197.0	Rhenium	Re	75	186.2
Hafnium	Hf	72	178.5	Rhodium	Rh	45	102.9
Hassium	Hs	108	(269)	Roentgenium	Rg	111	(280)
Helium	He	2	4.003	Rubidium	Rb	37	85.47

*Numbers in parentheses are the mass numbers of the most stable isotopes

Continued